MORE ABOUT PRONUNCIATION

\ This slant line is placed at both the beginning and the end of all pronunciations in this book: *finish* \\'fin-ish\\.

' ˌ Some words have only one part when spoken: *pen* \\pen\\. Some words have two parts: *penman* \\pen-mən\\. Some words have three parts: *penmanship* \\pen-mən-ship\\. And so on. Each such part is called a syllable. When there is more than one syllable in a word, the syllables are separated, in the pronunciation as printed, by a
\- hyphen (the mark -). When such a word is spoken, however, a listener often cannot hear any kind of break or pause at the point where the printed hyphen occurs unless a t sound is shown in the printed pronunciation just before or just after the hyphen. *Amid* is shown as \\ə-'mid\\ but may just as easily be heard as \\əm-'id\\. On the other hand, *nitrate* is not likely to be heard as \\'nīt-ˌrāt\\ instead of \\'nī-ˌtrāt\\. Some syllables are spoken with greater force (stress) than others; thus in \\pen-mən-ship\\ the syllable \\pen\\ has strong stress, \\mən\\ has weak stress, and \\ship\\ has an amount that is in between, or medium. Before a syllable with strong stress we place a small straight-up-and-down mark at the top of the line and call it a "high mark", as in \\'pen\\; before a syllable with medium stress we place the same mark at the bottom of the line and call it a "low mark", as in \\ˌship\\; before a syllable with weak stress we do not place any stress mark at all, as in \\mən\\. Thus our complete pronunciation of *penmanship*, with the syllables separated by hyphens and with stress marks in front of the syllables that need them, is \\'pen-mən-ˌship\\.

For some words we give more than one pronunciation. Sometimes we do this by spelling out all or part of another pronunciation in symbols after a comma, as: *dol-*
( ) *drums* \\'däl-drəmz, 'dōl-\\. Sometimes we do it by placing curves around a symbol to mean that what the symbol stands for may be in the spoken word or may not be, as: *salary* \\'sal-r(-)ē\\, meaning \\'sal-r-ē, 'sal-rē\\. Some persons will not always regard all our variant pronunciations as equally good, although all of them may be heard from persons of excellent education. Thus some think that not pronouncing the first *c* in *arctic* is bad, although none or few of those who so think pronounce the *c* in *indict*. You will have to choose for yourself in cases like *arctic*, and may want to follow the example or recommendation of older persons you know whose speech as a whole seems good to you. In other cases, a variant pronunciation may be rare in some parts of the country (for instance, the pronunciation of *tomato* that more or less rhymes with *motto*), and you will be guided by the usage in your community.

Symbol Names. In naming symbols we use the terms *bar*, *one-dot*, and *two-dot;* thus **ā** is "bar a", **t͟h** is "bar t-h", **ȯ** is "one-dot o", **ü** is "two-dot u". Symbols having no modifier we call *plain*, to distinguish them from the same letter or letters modified; thus **a** is "plain a", **th** is "plain t-h". Call **i** "plain i" because the dot is not a modifier. **ə** is usually called *schwa* \\'shwä\\.

WEBSTER'S NEW PRACTICAL SCHOOL DICTIONARY

A NEW DICTIONARY FOR BOYS AND GIRLS

AMERICAN BOOK COMPANY

New York Cincinnati Atlanta Dallas Millbrae

Registered User of the Trademarks in Canada

CONTENTS

MADE IN THE U.S.A.

9 11 13 15 J 16 14 12 10 8

PREFACE

Webster's New Practical School Dictionary is based on a special study of school needs. One of the Merriam-Webster series, this dictionary may be used either as the middle dictionary in those schools that prefer a three-dictionary progression or as the first dictionary for schools preferring a two-dictionary progression. When a three-dictionary progression is preferred, *Webster's New Practical School Dictionary* may be preceded by *Webster's Elementary Dictionary* and followed by *Webster's New Students Dictionary.* When a two-dictionary progression is preferred, this dictionary may precede *Webster's New Students Dictionary.*

The choice of words and senses has been based on their occurrence in over ninety percent of all the textbooks now in use in the schools of the United States in the grades for which this dictionary has been prepared. In addition to this study of the words actually used in school textbooks, a number of word lists compiled by boards of education, city school systems, and testing bureaus have been carefully checked. Such reading and such checking have brought into this dictionary a remarkable increase of terms needed today by pupils in the study of science and mathematics. To this end especially, as well as to the general advance in all other subjects, we have gathered evidence for writing clear, simple, and accurate definitions.

An editorial staff trained in methods that have been developed for over a century of good dictionary making has brought to this book its experience as well as a fresh approach, and all the facilities that have produced other dictionaries in the Merriam-Webster series have been available and drawn upon for this one. Also in the background of these definitions lies a great deal of consultation with schoolteachers and principals (from whom we have received much generous advice) and of practical classroom experience in testing the definitions on pupils for whom they have been written.

The number of vocabulary entries in this dictionary is large enough to cover usefully all the recurring school needs of pupils for whom the dictionary has been prepared. In addition to the defined terms derivatives whose meaning is clear from a preceding definition are printed in boldface type as undefined run-ons. These are entered to show not only related use of basic meaning in a different function but also spelling and pronunciation. All the long-established prefixes and suffixes frequently used in English are entered at their alphabetical places in the vocabulary, explained, and exemplified. With a knowledge of these elements every user of this dictionary can extend his working vocabulary almost without limit.

The definitions are accompanied by many black-and-white line drawings. These have been kept simple to serve their main purpose at a glance. Besides these pictorial illustrations we have included many verbal illustrations of words as they combine with other words in phrases and sentences.

Preface

This dictionary includes examples of some of the features of more advanced Merriam-Webster dictionaries. Simple etymologies, given in brackets, introduce pupils to the fascinating study of word origins. The chosen etymologies represent most of the ways by which words have come into English from other languages and show also the backgrounds of certain groups of related words, like days of the week and months of the year. Synonym paragraphs, given at the end of definitions, illustrate a method of discriminating between words of similar meaning (as *error*, *mistake*, and *blunder*). Usage labels in italics (as *archaic* at *afeard*, *slang* at *ash can*, *Scottish* at *brae*) show how a dictionary informs users that some words are not standard or not used everywhere or on all occasions. Similarly usage notes, separated from the definition proper by brackets, a dash, or a fist, emphasize some interesting fact about syntax or grammar.

A section on the use of this dictionary comes right after this preface. It contains a large number of questions to be answered from information in the dictionary, and several sets of checkups and exercises so that the use of the dictionary can be thoroughly mastered. This matter lends itself to a variety of oral or written classroom lessons that can be assigned by a teacher to fit the needs of any class. It was designed to help the user of this dictionary to understand what is in it and to learn how to use it.

The back matter after the definitions contains in columns the names of the presidents and vice-presidents of the United States, the names of all the states and state capitals of the United States, the names of the nations of the world, and the names of all the cities of the world having a population of over 150,000 inhabitants. A pronunciation is given for each of these names.

The plans for this dictionary were jointly agreed upon by American Book Company and G. & C. Merriam Company. The reading and checking, the defining and editing, the proofreading and similar operations have been carried out by the permanent Merriam-Webster editorial staff. The front matter in "Using Your Dictionary" has been prepared chiefly by the editorial staff of American Book Company.

G. & C. MERRIAM COMPANY

USING YOUR DICTIONARY

WHAT IS A DICTIONARY?

If a younger brother or sister should ask you what a dictionary is, what would you say? Would you be able to tell all the different ways in which a dictionary can help you? Try writing your own definition. Then turn to the word *dictionary* in this book and see what further information you can find there. After that, you should be ready to answer the questions which follow. They will help you discover just what a dictionary is.

DISCOVERING WHAT A DICTIONARY IS

An alphabetical listing of words

1. How did the fact that a dictionary is "an alphabetically arranged book" help you find the word *dictionary* quickly?
2. Once you had found the *d*'s, how did the guide words at the top of the pages help you?
3. What is the left-hand guide word on page 225?
4. What is the right-hand guide word on that page?
5. Why does the second guide word consist of two separate words?
6. Do the guide words on page 225 tell you (a) all the words that are listed on that page, (b) the most important words, or (c) the first and last boldface words (words in heavy type) on that page?

A source for correct spelling

1. Suppose you need to know how to spell the word *dictionary*. Suppose you have forgotten whether it ends with *ary* or *ery*. Would you get the correct spelling from (a) the boldface entry word, (b) the pronunciation within the slant lines, or (c) the numbered definitions?
2. Suppose you need to know how to spell the plural of *dictionary*. (a) What abbreviation leads you to it? (b) How is the plural of *dictionary* spelled? (c) How does the type in which it is printed compare in size with the entry word?

A guide for word division when writing

1. Suppose you need to know where the word *dictionary* may be divided at the end of a line. How many centered dots do you find in the boldface type?
2. Say *dictionary* to yourself. How many syllables, or parts, do you hear?
3. This may be the first dictionary you have used which shows how to divide a word at the end of a line. You may already know that a syllable of one letter should not be carried to the next line. Why isn't the last syllable of *dic·tio·nary* separated from the preceding syllable by a centered dot as the last syllable of *dic·tio·nar·ies* is?
4. At how many points may you divide the word *dictionary* at the end of a line?

A guide for pronunciation

1. Suppose you need to know how to pronounce *dictionary*. Look at the respelling within the slant lines. The letters stand for sounds, and the hyphens divide the spoken syllables. How many spoken syllables does *dictionary* have?
2. Suppose you need to know which syllable or syllables of *dictionary* are spoken with more force or stress. Find the vertical stress marks. Are they in the boldface type or in the respelling? Why?
3. Say *dictionary* again. Upon which syllable do you place the strongest (primary) stress?
4. Is the stress mark for this syllable placed high or low?
5. To which syllable do you give a medium (secondary) stress?
6. Is the stress mark for this syllable placed high or low?
7. How does your dictionary show which syllables have the weakest stress?
8. Does a stress mark, either high or low, precede the stressed syllable, or does it follow the stressed syllable?

A guide to parts of speech

1. Suppose you need to know how *dictionary* may be used in a sentence. What abbreviation tells you that this word is defined as a noun?
2. How can you tell whether *dictionary* can be used as a verb or not?

A treasury of meanings

1. Suppose you need to know the meaning or meanings of the word *dictionary*. How many numbered meanings are given?
2. Which of the meanings fits this book the best?
3. How well does the definition fit this dictionary? Your judgment will depend on whether you can answer "yes" to the six questions below.

   a. Is this book alphabetically arranged?
   b. Does it list some of the words of our language?

c. Does it give the meanings of the words it lists?
d. Does it give spelling variations of some words? Look at *dietitian.*
e. Does this book give pronunciations?
f. Does it give the etymology of some words? If *etymology* is an unfamiliar word, look it up now. After you have done that, you may be interested in some examples of etymologies, such as those of *Diesel engine, abject, bedlam, dandelion, GI, radar.*

Now you should know the answer to question 3 above.

A carefully selected list of words

1. Since this desk dictionary is especially made to meet your needs, it does not list all the words in the English language. The less common words can be found in a large unabridged dictionary. What disadvantages would there be in listing thousands of uncommon words in this dictionary?
2. Suppose you need to know the meaning of the word *lexicon.* See if it is listed in this dictionary. What does it mean?
3. What does *lexicography* mean?
4. What is a *lexicographer?*
5. Why is *lexicography* listed, while *lexicology* is not?
6. Where would you go to find the meaning of *lexicology?*

HOW THIS DICTIONARY WILL HELP

From the preceding questions you should have become aware of some important features of this dictionary. You now know that it is a carefully selected, alphabetically arranged list of the most common words in our language. It has been made to help you in these ways:

1. To spell words
2. To divide words at the ends of lines
3. To pronounce words
4. To know their parts of speech
5. To know their meanings

Hundreds of thousands of dictionaries, exactly like this one, are in the hands of hundreds of thousands of students who are far from being exactly alike. How helpful this dictionary will become to you depends upon how well you become acquainted with its features. The sections that follow have been prepared to help you become better acquainted with this dictionary and to provide you with practice in using it.

CHECKUP

1. Look up the word *amoeba.* How may it be spelled?
2. What plurals does it have?
3. How many syllables does it have when you say it?
4. Why is the first syllable not separated by a dot in the boldface type?
5. Why is the first syllable separated by a hyphen in the respelling?
6. Which syllable is stressed the most?
7. If the etymology of *amoeba* were given, where would it be?
8. What is the etymology of *among?* Of *ampere?*

WHAT DO YOU KNOW ABOUT THIS DICTIONARY?

Which of the following statements describe this dictionary? What is wrong with the other statements?

1. This dictionary contains all the words in our language.
2. The words are arranged alphabetically.
3. The words at the top of each page are a guide to the words defined on that page.
4. Each boldface word has dots that always indicate how many spoken syllables the word has.
5. These dots show how to divide the word at the end of a line.
6. Only one spelling is given for each word.
7. The respelling shows the pronunciation of the word.
8. Each word has one more spoken syllable than it has hyphens in the respelling.
9. Stress marks are shown in the boldface words.
10. A stress mark comes after the stressed syllable.
11. When a syllable has no stress mark, it has the weakest stress.
12. A high stress mark is used for medium stress.
13. Parts of speech are indicated by their abbreviations.
14. The most commonly used meanings of the words are given.
15. This dictionary gives the etymology of each word.
16. When the plural is shown, it follows the abbreviation *pl.*

FINDING A WORD QUICKLY

Whether you want to know the spelling of a word, its pronunciation, or its meaning, you should first know how to find that word quickly. How quickly you can find a word in an alphabetical list depends upon your skill in the use of alphabetical order.

Opening the dictionary. Experts can open a dictionary surprisingly close to the right spot. If *vagabond* is the word they seek, they do not waste time by flipping pages from the front of the dictionary toward the back. They open it near the section where all words beginning with *v* are located. An expert dictionary user will not miss *vagabond* by more than twenty pages on his first try.

You may have noticed that the words of a dictionary are not evenly distributed among the twenty-six letters of the alphabet. There are more pages of words beginning with *s* than of words beginning with the ten letters *j*, *k*, *n*, *o*, *q*, *u*, *v*, *x*, *y*, and *z* combined. If you divide the total number of pages in this dictionary by two, you will find that the middle page is near the beginning of the *l*'s, rather than at the beginning of the *n*'s, as you might expect.

Through practice, you can train your thumbs to a degree of expertness that will save you many a precious minute.

CHECKUP

1. Try to open your dictionary the first time to some point within each of these letters, keeping a record of your score:

   s c p u b z l v r j

2. Now see if you can beat your own record on these letters:

   d x g i y q h n e t

3. Next try to open the dictionary within twenty pages of each of these words, keeping your score:

axis	forum	kayak	ellipse	indict
waif	oxide	soccer	trestle	vague

Using guide words. Once you have acquired a skillful thumb, you need a skillful eye to pick up guide words. These guide words are found at the top of every dictionary page except page 1. They name the boldface words that are alphabetically the first and last on the page (provided they do not overlap the guide words before or after them).

If the word you are seeking is *charlatan*, and if your skillful thumb has opened the dictionary to page 121, where the guide words are *cavernous* and *cellar*, do you turn toward the front or toward the back of your dictionary? The student who is sure of alphabetical order knows the answer. He has seen more than the first letter of the guide words. He knows that he must turn past this page of *ca* and *ce* words to a page having words beginning with *ch*.

Would you make the turn one page at a time or two or three pages at a time? If an expert user thinks he is only five or six pages away from the word he wants, he will quickly flip one page at a time to avoid the risk of overrunning his mark. If he thinks he is farther away, he will turn a few pages at a time.

What does a student with a skillful eye look at as he approaches his target? He looks at guide words only, paying no attention to the list of words below them. If the word he seeks is *charlatan,* he looks for the first guide word he can find which begins with *cha*.

When he comes to page 124, where the guide words are *certificate* and *challenging*, he knows he is close to *charlatan*. He sees that *challenging* is the last boldface word on this page and knows that *charlatan* must be on a later page. A glance at the next pair of guide words, *challie* and *channel* on page 125, tells him that words beginning with *char* are not to be found there. When he sees on page 127 the guide words *charge* and *chase*, he knows that he has found the right page.

Up to this point he has wasted not a fraction of a second looking at the words below the guide words. Since he can see that the *g* in *charge* alphabetically precedes the *l* in *charlatan* and that the *s* in *chase* alphabetically follows the *r* in *charlatan,* he is certain that the word he seeks is either on this page or not in this dictionary at all (unless it is a run-on that is alphabetically out of order). Now, and not until now, he glances at the top of both columns, just below the guide words, and his skillful eye instantly falls on the word he seeks. If it had not been at the top, his eye would have skimmed down the column to find it within a second.

That is the way an expert user of a dictionary skillfully finds the word he seeks — quickly, efficiently. His skill depends on his being absolutely sure of alphabetical order, even to the tenth letter or beyond.

CHECKUP

1. Put the following words in alphabetical order:

equip	equinox	equivocate
equal	equally	equinoctial
equity	equatorial	equipment
equator	equalize	equivocation

2. Check your order with the dictionary.

Practicing alphabetical order. If you made a perfect score on the checkup above, it is doubtless because you have been using and practicing alphabetical order for some time. If you did not make a good score, you need much practice. The following checkup will provide you with the kind of practice you need.

CHECKUP

1. On fifty small cards or slips of paper copy both guide words on twenty-five consecutive pages of this dictionary.
2. Shuffle these cards thoroughly and then put them back in alphabetical order without any help.
3. Check your order with the dictionary. If you made any mistakes, shuffle the cards and try again until you get a perfect score.
4. If you had to try more than once, you need more practice. Copy fifty other consecutive guide words, and repeat the activity.

Practice in locating words. All of this practice in alphabetizing words is good preparation for the next checkup, which tests your ability to find words. Remember to open your dictionary as close as you can to the word you are seeking, and to look only at the guide words until you find the right page.

CHECKUP

1. Time yourself in locating the twelve words below. See if you can find them all in two or three minutes.

nasal	cavort	optional	auxiliary
turban	sodium	blemish	vacillate
quill	episode	geology	imminent

2. Now try to cut your time in half, using the same list again.
3. See if you can beat your own record on this list:

yucca	fathom	winnow	quagmire
negate	density	utilize	judicious
potash	affable	kumquat	miniature

4. If by now you cannot find twelve words in two minutes, make up your own lists and time yourself until you can.
5. Every time you look up a word, see how fast you can find it.

What kind of dictionary user are you? Now that you have discovered how important it is to be a skillful dictionary user, try answering these questions:

1. Am I a person with skillful thumbs, who consistently opens the dictionary close to the right spot?

2. Am I a person with skillful eyes, who depends upon guide words to find exactly the right page?

3. Am I a person who has practiced putting words in alphabetical order, not only by the first and second letters, but also by the tenth or twelfth letters and beyond?

4. Am I a person who takes pride in the

degree to which I have acquired the skills of word finding?

You can be the kind of person who profits most from the use of a dictionary. For such a person a minute with the dictionary is a minute devoted to the word he has looked up, not to a back-and-forth search for the word itself.

There are efficient dictionary users, and there are clumsy ones. You do not doubt which you would like to be, do you? The choice is yours, and both choices have their price. The price of efficiency is a few hours of practice. The price of clumsiness is a lifetime of fumbling dissatisfaction.

CHECKUP

1. Which of these words would be on a dictionary page with the guide words *per capita* and *perfectionist?* Put these five words in alphabetical order.

per	percentage	perfectly
per cent	perfectible	perfection
people	per annum	percussion

2. Check your alphabetical list with your dictionary. Are they all on page 600?

ARE YOU AN EFFICIENT DICTIONARY USER?

1. Try to open your dictionary within twenty pages of each of the words below. Compare your score with the one you made in the checkup on page 5a.

homograph	idiom	schwa	variant	fistnote
synonym	prefix	dialect	archaic	consonant

2. Alphabetize the ten words below that would be on a dictionary page with the guide words *main* and *make*. Then check with your dictionary.

Maj.	major	malice	mailbox	make-believe
maim	mainly	majestic	maintop	maintenance
maize	maker	majority	mainland	major general

3. See if you can locate the twelve words below in two minutes. Try to beat your previous record for twelve words.

soapstone	bullfinch	fascism	turquoise
doleful	omnibus	atomic age	gimlet
unerring	whippet	invalidate	quizzical

A GUIDE TO CORRECT SPELLING

Three marks of a good speller are these: (1) He knows when he is sure that a word is spelled right; (2) he knows when he is not sure; and (3) he turns to his dictionary for help when he needs it. A good speller likes to have a dictionary beside him as he writes. A poor speller is on his way to becoming a good speller if he checks with his dictionary every time he writes.

Before dictionaries were published, people had to remember how to spell, or put down some combination of letters that seemed right. Written language attempts to represent by letters the sounds which make up our spoken words. The spelling of these words would be easy if each letter of the alph[illegible] represented a single sound, but th[illegible] the case. So our language has m[illegible] words like *hair* and *hare*, [illegible] differently but pronounced alike, and words such as *cough*, *rough*, *bough*, *through*, and *though*, which look alike but have several different sounds.

English spelling is difficult. A writer is therefore dependent upon a reliable and up-to-date dictionary.

Variations in spelling. Using the skills you have learned, find the word *catalog* as quickly as you can. You will see that you are given a choice of spellings, *catalog* or *catalogue*. Where two or more spellings are given for a word, all are correct. The spelling listed first is not better than the others, but usually it is the spelling most often found by the editors of this dictionary, who have counted the spelling preferences of many writers. When different spellings occur with almost equal frequency, the editors have used their judgment as to which should be placed first. The "*catalog* or *catalogue*" entry shows that the newer, shorter form has at last caught up with the older, longer form in frequency of use.

For a new spelling to become acceptable, it must first appear many times in writing that is careful in such matters as spelling. Widespread use of a new spelling by educated writers usually brings about general acceptance of the change in spelling. An accidental misspelling seldom does.

CHECKUP

According to this dictionary, which of the following spellings are correct?

abridgment	abridgement	abrijment
accommodate	acommodate	accomodate
advertize	advertise	addvertise
advizor	advisor	adviser
airline	air line	air-line
anesthetic	anaesthetic	aenesthetic
athletic	athaletic	atheletic

Irregular plurals. A dictionary is also a useful guide to the spelling of plurals. In this dictionary, the plural form of a noun is usually shown only when the plural is irregular (formed other than by the addition of *-s* or *-es* to an unchanged singular). A regular plural is shown, however, when there might be some doubt about its spelling, as in *piano* and *valley*.

CHECKUP

What, if any, are the plurals of the following words, according to this dictionary? Beside each plural indicate whether or not the plural form is shown and why. For which of these words is the plural the same as the singular?

a	aeronautics	arch
ability	algebra	arena
abscissa	alumnus	armful
acoustics	antithesis	arroyo

Two possible plurals. When two plural forms are given in this dictionary, as for *abscissa*, both are correct. Whether one or the other is to be preferred often depends upon circumstances. A fisherman, for example, may pull in his net full of *shrimp*. You may have *shrimps* for supper. You may call a handful of mushrooms you have just gathered *funguses*. In science class your teacher may expect you to call them *fungi*.

CHECKUP

What, according to this dictionary, are the two possible plurals for each of these words?

zero	banjo	wharf	stadium
tuna	trout	Eskimo	antelope
bass	cargo	brother	medium

Irregular principal parts. In addition to showing the spelling of irregular plurals, a dictionary also shows the spelling of the principal parts of verbs when these are irregular (formed other than by the addition of *-ed* and *-ing* to an unchanged entry word). The principal parts are also shown when there are two possible forms or when there might be some doubt about the spelling, as in *veto* and *journey*.

CHECKUP

In what way or ways, according to this dictionary, are the principal parts of the following verbs spelled? In each case indicate whether or not the forms are shown and why.

arc	atrophy	canoe	look
arise	bat	control	obey
arouse	bite	level	picnic

HOW DOES YOUR DICTIONARY HELP YOU WITH SPELLING?

1. Which of these statements are true and which are false? Explain what is wrong with each false statement.

   a. When two or more spellings are given, the first is usually more common.
   b. The spelling *catalog* is at least as common as *catalogue.*
   c. There are two acceptable spellings for *accommodate.*
   d. Plurals of nouns are shown only when they are formed in some other way than by adding *-s* or *-es.*
   e. Some nouns are spelled the same in the plural as in the singular.
   f. Some nouns have no plural form.
   g. When two plurals are given, both are always acceptable under all circumstances.
   h. If a verb is changed before *-ed* or *-ing* is added (as *y* is changed to *i* in *deny*), the principal parts are shown.
   i. Principal parts are shown only when they are irregular.
   j. A good speller checks spelling with his dictionary only when he is unsure.

2. Use your dictionary if you need to in answering these questions:

   a. Which spelling is preferred — *judgment* or *judgement*?
   b. How else may *gaiety* and *gaily* be spelled?
   c. What are two possible plurals for *attorney general?*
   d. What is the plural of *sister-in-law?*
   e. Why is it shown in the dictionary?
   f. Why is the plural of *journey* shown?
   g. What is the plural of *mathematics?* Of *athletics?*
   h. Which is better — *traveled* or *travelled?*
   i. What are the principal parts of *rebel, fly,* and *deny?*
   j. Why are they shown in each case?

RULES FOR SPELLING

Your dictionary is always the final authority on the spelling of words. Whenever you write, keep your dictionary handy so that you may verify the spelling of words which give you trouble.

You will also want to familiarize yourself with the most useful spelling rules — those which apply to many words. The rules which follow will be helpful in developing spelling skill. Since they apply to the whole vocabulary of English they are sometimes illustrated by words or word forms (for example, certain proper nouns and adjectives, various compounds and alternative spellings) not considered necessary or suitable for this dictionary.

1. Words ending in -x are unchanged before any suffix:

coax coaxed coaxing
fix fixable fixer
six sixteen sixty

2. Words ending in -c remain unchanged before *a*, *o*, *u*, or a consonant:

tropic tropical zinc zincoid
sac saclike frolic frolicsome

Before *e* or *i* they usually add *k* if the pronunciation of the *c* remains hard:

picnic picnicked picnicking

but add nothing if the pronunciation of the *c* becomes soft:

critic criticism criticize
magic magician

3. Words ending in consonant plus -c usually remain unchanged before any suffix:

disc disced discing

4. Words ending in a single consonant except x or c immediately preceded by two or more vowels in the same syllable remain unchanged before any suffix:

air aired airing airy
brief briefed briefer briefly
cloud clouded cloudless cloudy
suit suitable suited suitor

5. Words ending in a single consonant immediately preceded by a single vowel bearing primary stress double the consonant before a suffix beginning with a vowel:

abet abetted abetting abettor
bag baggage bagged bagging
clan clannish

They do not double the consonant before a suffix beginning with a consonant:

drop droplet fit fitness
glad gladly win winsome

EXCEPTIONS (among others):

chagrin chagrined chagrining
prefer preferable preference

6. Words ending in a single consonant immediately preceded by a single vowel bearing secondary stress vary greatly in their derivatives:

a. Some always double the consonant:

handicap handicapped handicapping

b. Some have a single consonant only:

chaperon chaperoned chaperoning

c. Some have both forms:

kidnap kidnapped *or* kidnaped
kidnapping *or* kidnaping

7. Words ending in a single consonant immediately preceded by one or more vowels without stress remain unchanged before any suffix:

credit credited crediting creditor
solid solider solidest solidify

EXCEPTIONS: A large group of words doubles a final consonant; in British use such doubling is the regular practice; in U.S. use it is usually an accepted alternative:

travel — traveled *or* travelled; traveling *or* travelling

8. Words ending in a single consonant that is silent remain unchanged before any suffix:

hurrah — hurrahed — hurrahing

9. Words ending in two or more consonants the last of which is not c remain unchanged before any suffix:

attach	attached	attachment	
condemn	condemnatory	condemned	condemning
length	lengthen	lengthy	

EXCEPTIONS: Words ending in *-ll:*

a. One *l* is often dropped:

dull — dulness — skill — skilful

b. The second *l* of final *-ll* always disappears before a suffix beginning with *l:*

dull — dully — full — fully

c. The second *l* of final *-ll* may disappear before *-less*, but hyphened forms retaining all three *l*'s are more frequent:

hull — hull-less — skill — skill-less

d. The hyphened form retaining all three *l*'s is usually used with *-like:*

bell — bell-like — scroll — scroll-like

10. Words ending in silent -e drop the vowel before a suffix beginning with a vowel:

bone	boned	boning	
curve	curvature	curved	curving
imagine	imaginable	imagining	

They remain unchanged before a suffix beginning with a consonant:

bone — boneless — curve — curvesome

EXCEPTIONS: The final *-e* is retained in some instances.

a. Proper names ending in single *-e* preceded by one or more consonants usually keep the *-e* before the suffix *-an:*

Europe — European — Shakespeare — Shakespearean

b. mile — mileage

c. Words ending in *-le* usually drop the *-le* before the suffix *-ly:*

gentle — gently — subtle — subtly

d. Some words ending in *-re* retain the *-e* before a suffix beginning with a vowel:

acre — acreage

e. Words ending in *-ce* or *-ge* usually retain the *-e* before any suffix beginning with a vowel other than *e, i,* or *y*, thus preserving the softness of the *c* or *g:*

change — changeable
peace — peaceable

A *d* preceding *g* may in a few cases act as a preserver of the soft sound and permit the dropping of the *-e:*

judge — judgment

f. Although final *-e* regularly drops before the suffix *-able*, some adjectives in *-able* have alternatives retaining the *-e:*

like — likable *or* likeable
love — lovable *or* loveable

g. Usage varies greatly with regard to dropping or retaining final *-e* before the suffix *-y*.

Many words have both the *-ey* and the *-y:*

home — homey *or* homy — stone — stony *or* stoney

Some words have only one form in common usage:

rose — rosy — shade — shady

h. In some present participles the silent *-e* remains to distinguish them from the corresponding forms of other verbs:

dye — dyeing (*in contrast to* dying)
singe — singeing (*in contrast to* singing)

11. Words ending in -e preceded by a vowel drop the final *-e* before *-a-* or *-e-* in the suffix:

argue arguable argued
blue blued bluer bluest
lie liar

EXCEPTIONS: The ending is sometimes unchanged:

a. Words ending in *-ee* usually retain both *e*'s before *-a-* and always before *-i-* in the suffix:

agree agreeable agreeing

b. In an accented syllable *-ie* becomes *-y* before *-i-* in the suffix:

die dying

c. In an unaccented syllable *-ie* remains unchanged before *-i-* in the suffix:

stymie stymieing

d. Final *-oe* remains unchanged before *-i-* in the suffix:

canoe canoeing hoe hoeing

e. Final *-ue* usually drops *-e* before *-i-* in the suffix:

argue arguing true truism

f. Final *-ye* alternatively keeps or drops *-e* before *-i-* in the suffix:

eye eyeing *or* eying

g. Adjectives with the suffix *-y* retain *-e:*

glue gluey

h. A double vowel usually remains unchanged before a suffix beginning with a consonant:

agree agreement blue blueness
woe woeful *or* woful

12. Verbs derived from the French and ending in -é usually form their past and past participle in *-éd* or less often in *-éed:*

visé viséd *or* viséed

They form their present participle in *-éing:*

appliqué appliquéing

13. Words ending in -y preceded by a consonant usually change the *-y* to *-i-* before any letter in the suffix except *i* and the possessive sign *'s:*

beauty beautiful beautify
defy defiant defying
fancy fanciful fancying
everybody everybody's

EXCEPTIONS: The *-y* is not always changed to *-i-:*

a. One-syllable words usually retain *-y* before *-ly* and *-ness:*

dry dryly dryness

b. Comparatives and superlatives of one-syllable adjectives alternatively retain *-y* or replace it with *-i-:*

dry drier *or* dryer driest *or* dryest

c. Before *-er* alternative uses of *-y* and *-i-* occur:

fly flier *or* flyer

d. Before *-like* and *-ship* and in derivatives of *baby* the *-y* remains unchanged:

lady ladylike ladyship
baby babyhood

e. When separated by one or more syllables from the primary stress of the base word, the *-y* may be lost completely before *-i-* in a suffix:

accompany accompanist
military militarist militarize

14. Words ending in -y preceded by a vowel usually remain unchanged before any suffix:

alloy alloys attorney attorneys
play played playing player playful

EXCEPTIONS: The *-y* is sometimes changed to *-i-:*

a. A few words ending in *-ay* change *-y* to *-i-:*

day	daily	lay	laid
say	saith	slay	slain

b. A few words alternatively retain *-y* or replace it with *-i-:*

gay	gaiety *or* gayety	gaily *or* gayly
stay	stayed *or* staid	

c. Comparatives and superlatives of adjectives ending in *-ey* replace these two letters with *-i-:*

gluey	gluier	gluiest
phoney	phonier	phoniest

d. Adjectives ending in *-wy* change the *-y* to *-i-* before any suffix:

showy showier showiest showily showiness

15. Verbs ending in a vowel except e or y, when adding a suffix beginning with a vowel, remain unchanged before their inflectional suffixes:

alibi	alibied	alibiing	
radio	radioed	radioing	
ski	skied	skiing	skier

EXCEPTIONS: Verbs ending in single *-o* usually insert *e* before adding *-s* for the third person singular:

echo	echoes	lasso	lassoes

16. Nouns ending in a vowel when adding one of the suffixes -esque, -ism, -ist usually remain unchanged especially if the base word is short and the final vowel is essential to its recognition:

solo	soloist	Zola	Zolaesque

17. Geographical and personal names ending in -a regularly drop the *-a* before the suffix *-an* or *-ian:*

America	American	Canada	Canadian

18. Some geographical names ending in -o drop the *-o* before *-an* or *-ian:*

Mexico	Mexican	San Diego	San Diegan

19. Scientific terms of Greek or Latin origin ending in -a regularly drop the *-a* before a suffix beginning with a vowel:

pleura	pleural	urea	urease	ureic

20. Words ending in -o insert *e* before the suffix *-y:*

goo	gooey	mosquito	mosquitoey

21. Geographical and personal names ending in -o or a combination of vowels pronounced \ō often insert *n* or *v* before *-an* or *-ian:*

Buffalo	Buffalonian	Marlow	Marlovian

22. When a prefix is added that forms a new word, a base word usually remains unchanged:

act	enact	call	recall
change	exchange	prove	disprove

23. Two or more words joining to form a compound usually retain the full spelling of both component words:

billfold makeup sidestep widespread

CHECKUP

Use the rules for spelling to write the past of:

beg	gain	attack
box	fancy	benefit
dye	delay	imagine
ski	frolic	handicap

WHAT HAVE YOU LEARNED ABOUT SPELLING RULES?

1. Add *-ed* and *-ing* to each of these words, using your dictionary if necessary:

fix	air	relay	gallop
bat	cry	hurry	revolt
lie	pay	corral	employ
hoe	skate	picnic	bargain

2. To the following words add the suffixes given in parentheses. Check with the dictionary if you are not sure.

hand(-y)	radio(-ed)	courage(-ous)	care(-ful, -ing)
stone(-y)	music(-al)	state(-ment)	defy(-ant, -ing)
lie(-ing)	lady(-like)	decorate(-ive)	encourage(-ing)
dye(-ing)	home(-like)	sun(-y)	carry(-age, -ing)
drop(-ed)	grace(-ful)	play(-ed, -ful)	arrive(-al, -ing)
true(-ly)	baby(-hood)	fit(-ing, -ly)	enjoy(-ing, -ment)
begin(-er)	elevate(-or)	credit(-ed, -or)	glad(-en, -est, -ly)
boat(-ing)	frolic(-some)	journey(-s, -ed)	kindly(-er, -est, -ness)

A GUIDE TO PRONUNCIATION

Your dictionary provides you with four kinds of help in the respelling of words to show their pronunciation:

1. Division into syllables. Many words have more than one of the units of pronunciation called syllables. In the respelling of such words the syllables are separated by hyphens. The respelling is what you find in this dictionary between two slant lines: \'fin-ish\.

When a word of more than one syllable is spoken, a listener often cannot hear any kind of break or pause at the point where the printed hyphen occurs unless a *t* sound is shown in the respelling just before or just after the hyphen. *Amid* is shown as \ə-'mid\ but may just as easily be heard as \əm-'id\. On the other hand, *nitrate* is not likely to be heard as \'nīt-ˌrāt\ instead of \'nī-ˌtrāt\.

The spelling of a word with more than one spoken syllable is also composed of syllables. The dots that you find in the boldface spellings are not there for the same reason as the hyphens in the respellings. The dots show the most desirable places to interrupt a word when it must be divided at the end of a line of writing or print.

Many pronunciation syllables consist of only one sound, and many spelling syllables consist of only one letter. This is true of the first syllable of the pronunciation \ə-'flōt\ and of its spelling *a·float*. It is true of the last syllable of the pronunciation \'shō-ē\ and of its spelling *show·y*. But careful writers, typists, and printers would never put *a-* at the end of a line and *float* at the beginning of the next. They would never put *show-* at the end of a line and *y* at the beginning of the next. Therefore this dictionary does not show any dot in the spelling of *afloat* or *showy*.

Do not, then, expect in all cases to find the same number of dots in the spelling as there are hyphens in the respelling. The hyphen is the proper guide to the syllables of the spoken word.

CHECKUP

1. How are written syllables shown in the boldface entry words?
2. How are spoken syllables shown in the respellings?
3. Which division should be used at the end of a line?
4. Why doesn't the boldface word always show all the spoken syllables?

2. Stress marks. Some syllables are spoken with greater force or emphasis than others. This emphasis, sometimes called accent and sometimes called stress, is shown in this dictionary by the vertical marks which precede an accented syllable. Primary, or the strongest, accent is shown by a high mark in front of a syllable, as in the second syllable of *debate* \dē-ˈbāt\ and in the first syllable of *penmanship* \ˈpen-mən-ˌship\. Secondary, or medium, accent is shown by a low mark in front of a syllable, as in the last syllable of *penmanship*. The weakest accent is shown by no mark at all, as in the middle syllable of *penmanship*.

CHECKUP

Which syllables have the strongest stress (primary), medium stress (secondary), and the weakest stress in these respelled words?

\ˈrat-l-ˌsnāk\	\ˈkēp\	\ˈbī-ˌsik-l\
\ˌmak-r-ˈō-nē\	\ˈrē-ˈlōd\	\ˈrāl-ˌrōd\
\ˈred-ē-ˈmād\	\rē-ˈbel\	\ˈlȯng-ˈlīvd\

3. Pronunciation symbols. Some syllables consist of a single sound, but most syllables consist of more than one sound. To represent sounds, this dictionary uses the thirty-nine symbols that appear on the inside front and back covers of this book and also on page 21a. The symbols are shown more briefly in the pronunciation key lines at the foot of the vocabulary pages. Suppose you did not know whether *seine* rhymes with *mean, main, mine,* or *men.* The letters *ei* cannot tell you, since they spell the sound of \ē\ in *seize,* of \ā\ in *vein,* of \ī\ in *height,* and of \e\ in *heifer.* To learn the sound represented by *ei* in *seine* you either need to hear the word spoken by someone who knows how to pronounce it, or you need to turn to your dictionary, which shows that the pronunciation is \ˈsān\.

The dictionary can help you to learn the pronunciation of a word only if you are familiar with the symbols used to indicate pronunciations. If you know that the pronunciation symbol \ā\, called bar a, represents the sound of the vowel in *age* and *vein,* you then know that the same symbol in \ˈsān\ represents the same vowel sound. The word *seine* therefore rhymes with *main* \ˈmān\.

CHECKUP

Does each of these words rhyme with *man, main, men, mean, mine, moan,* or *moon?* Use your dictionary.

fen	roan	feign	prone	deign
tine	dune	preen	skein	ravine
scan	ken	hewn	wane	opine
lien	align	inane	serene	cuisine

4. Variant pronunciations. Your dictionary provides you with information about variations in the pronunciation of some words. The word *abdomen,* for example, is pronounced either \ˈab-də-mən\ or \ab-ˈdō mən\. If you pronounce this word in either of these ways, there is no reason for you to change your pronunciation just because someone else pronounces it the other way. It is always a good idea to check with your dictionary before you jump to the conclusion that your own or somebody else's pronunciation is not acceptable.

Many words have more than one acceptable pronunciation. The one shown first in this dictionary is not necessarily better. The fact that it is first sometimes means that it is the pronunciation most frequently used by educated speakers. On the other hand, in many cases usage is evenly divided, and the placing of a pronunciation first may mean only that it is at least as frequently used as any that follows it. Your pronunciation of *tomato* is likely to be the pronunciation you heard most often on first becoming acquainted with the word. Whether it is listed first, second, or third, it is a standard, acceptable pronunciation, and there is no reason for you to change it to something that sounds strange to you.

Some people will not regard all the pronunciations as equally good, though all of them may be heard from persons of excellent education. Thus some people think that not pronouncing the first *c* in *arctic* is bad, although few of them pronounce the *c* in *indict*. You will have to choose for yourself in cases like *arctic*, and you may want to follow the example of educated persons whose speech seems good to you. In other cases, a variant pronunciation may be rare in some parts of the country, and you will do well to be guided by the usage in your community.

As this dictionary emphasizes American rather than British pronunciations, such typically British pronunciations as \'diksh-n-rē\ for *dictionary* and \'bēn\ for *been* are not included.

CHECKUP

Choose the best ending for this sentence:

When variant pronunciations are given in this dictionary,

1. the first is always preferred.
2. the last is the one used by the poorest speakers.
3. all of them are acceptable.

HOW MUCH DO YOU KNOW ABOUT RESPELLINGS?

1. Why is the syllable division in the respelling apt to be different from the division in the boldface entry word? Give at least two reasons.
2. Why is it often difficult to know just where to place the hyphens in respellings?
3. What is meant by primary stress and how is it shown?
4. What is secondary accent and how is it marked?
5. How is the weakest stress indicated?
6. Do most syllables have just one sound or more than one sound?
7. Why are pronunciation symbols necessary?
8. Where may they be found in this dictionary?
9. What is the symbol for the vowel sound in *pain* and *eight*, and what is it called in this dictionary?
10. Why are two or more pronunciations often given for a word?

11. If one pronunciation is more common in this country than another pronunciation, which is placed first?
12. Under what circumstances should you change your pronunciation of a word?

WRITTEN AND SPOKEN SYLLABLES

How effective your dictionary is in helping you with the four elements of pronunciation — syllabication, stress, sounds represented by letters, and acceptable variations in pronunciation — depends upon how well you know the symbols used to indicate these elements. This section and the ones that follow will help you become familiar with all of them.

You know now that this dictionary shows two kinds of syllables — written syllables in the boldface spellings and spoken syllables in the respellings or pronunciations.

Find the entry *ab•bre•vi•a•tion* as quickly as you can. The four hyphens in the respelling mean that the word has five syllables when it is spoken. The four dots in the boldface entry mean that the word can be divided at any one of four places at the end of a line.

Now find the entry *idea*. The hyphens show that the spoken word usually has three syllables. The absence of dots in the entry word *idea* means that the word should not be divided at the end of a line. Neither possibility (*i-* and *dea*, or *ide-* and *a*) is considered good by careful writers because they would not put a one-letter syllable by itself.

Pay close attention to the syllables between the slant lines when you are trying to find out the pronunciation of a word. But pay no attention to these syllables when you are dividing a word at the end of a line. For one thing, if you were led by \ī-'dē-ə\ to divide this word between the *i* and the *d* or between the *e* and the *a* you would be using an undesirable division. For another, the two kinds of division often do not match each other. This is the case, for instance, with *pre•cious* \'presh-əs\. When *e* is pronounced as it is in this word, it is commonly followed by one or more other sounds in the same syllable, in both the respelling and the spelling, as in *ven•om* \'ven-əm\. But if *c* or *ci* were placed in the same syllable with *e* in *precious*, the resulting *prec•ious* or *preci•ous* would suggest a pronunciation \'pres-ē-əs\, which does not occur.

CHECKUP

The hyphens and stress marks have been omitted from the respellings below. Without any help, copy the respellings, inserting the hyphens. Then check with your dictionary to see how good a syllabic sense you have.

miser \mīzr\	magnet \magnət\
muzzle \məzl\	magnetic \magnetik\
matter \matr\	mutual \myüchəwəl\
meadow \medō\	munition \myünishn\
measles \mēzlz\	magnetism \magnətizm\

The syllables of spoken English. From the preceding activity you should have observed that most but not all syllables contain a vowel sound. Syllables which do not contain a vowel sound contain one of the consonants *l*, *m*, *n*, or *r*, called syllabic consonants. These syllabic consonants are found only in unstressed syllables (syllables with the weakest stress). For example, *chauffeur* has a syllabic *r* in the pronunciation \'shōf-r\ but not in \shō-'fər\. A syllabic consonant may be the only sound in a syllable, or there may be other consonants in the syllable: \'kat-l\, \'mēz-lz\.

Specialists in the subject of pronunciation

often hear a pronunciation in the same way but disagree in their respelling of it. One respelling is often as good as the other. There is a great deal of such disagreement in the indication of syllable boundaries in respellings, and in the matter of whether to use a syllabic consonant or a vowel plus a consonant in many unstressed syllables.

Both of these types of disagreement can be illustrated by a large number of words — *tribal*, for instance. An examination of many dictionaries shows a variety of respellings for this word. Here are four: (1) with \b\ at the end of the first syllable and with no vowel in the second syllable; (2) with \b\ at the end of the first syllable and with a vowel in the second syllable; (3) with \b\ at the beginning of the second syllable and with no vowel after it; (4) with \b\ at the beginning of the second syllable and with a vowel after it. If A saw \'trīb-l\ in a book, B saw \'trīb-əl\, C saw \'trī-bl\, and D saw \'trī-bəl\, and each was asked to pronounce the respelling in his book, the pronunciations of all four would sound identical to a listener. In other words, there is frequently more than one good way of reaching the same goal, and a difference of practice in these matters does not necessarily mean that one way is right and another is wrong.

On the other hand, you should not conclude that it is safe for *you* to take liberties with the respelling divisions in your dictionary. The sound \t\, for instance, behaves in a very troublesome way, and if you ignored \ə-'täm-ik\ for *atomic* and decided that \ət-'äm-ik\ would do just as well, you would produce a pronunciation that would sound very strange. The \t\ and the \r\ of words like *citric* and *metric* are further examples of the troublesome behavior of \t\. There is a widely held belief that a "short" vowel must have at least one consonant after it in the same syllable if that syllable is stressed, and many books put the \t\ of words like *citric* and *metric* at the end of the first syllable. However, the \t\ and the \r\ of such words sound more like the \t\ and \r\ of *trick* than of *fat robin*, and this book therefore pronounces these words \'si-trik\ and \'me-trik\, with \t\ and \r\ in the same syllable.

CHECKUP

1. How many spoken syllables does each word have? Some of these words may be syllabicated in more than one way. Write your answers and then check each word with your dictionary.

alien	athlete
giant	adenoids
patio	forecastle
ratio	American

2. Where must you look to find the spoken syllables of a word — at the spelling or at the respelling?

DO YOU UNDERSTAND SYLLABICATION?

1. Supply the word that is missing in each of these sentences:

   a. Spoken syllables are separated by — in this dictionary.
   b. Written syllables are separated by —.
   c. These two kinds of syllabic division often do not — each other.
   d. A one-letter — should never be separated at the end of a line.
   e. Most but not all syllables contain a — sound.

f. Syllabic consonants are found only in syllables having the — stress.
g. There may be other — in the same syllable with a syllabic consonant.
h. Specialists may hear a pronunciation in the same way but disagree in their — of it.
i. The \t\ and \r\ in *citrịc* and *metric* belong in the same spoken —.
j. The correct — of a word doesn't always reveal the number of spoken syllables it has.

2. Match the numbers 1–12 with the letters at the right. You will need to use one letter twice.

(1) It shows five spoken syllables.
(2) It shows five written syllables.
(3) A three-syllable word that may not be divided at the end of a line.
(4) A misleading entry division.
(5) A misleading respelling division.
(6) A respelling containing syllabic *r*.
(7) It has a syllabic consonant and another consonant in the same syllable.
(8) An example of syllabic *m*.
(9) It shows a syllabic *n*.
(10) One of four possible respellings for a word.
(11) It may have either two or three spoken syllables.
(12) It has two possible pronunciations, one with a syllabic consonant.

(a) idea
(b) ratio
(c) \'trīb-l\
(d) \'mīz-r\
(e) \'mēz-lz\
(f) \'sit-rik\
(g) preci·ous
(h) chauffeur
(i) \'mag-nə-ˌtiz-m\
(j) ab·bre·vi·a·tion
(k) \ə-ˌbrē-vē-'āsh-n\

THE THREE DEGREES OF STRESS

When you read poetry aloud, you can usually notice that the sounds of the words fall into a regular pattern of emphasized and unemphasized syllables. If you have written poetry, you are probably even more aware of this rhythm, and you know how dissatisfied you are with a line in which emphasis is unnaturally forced upon a syllable.

"Oh come with me",
She said with glee,
"And you will be
Very happy!"

That last line is about as bad as verse can get because the rhythmic beat of the preceding lines forces an unnatural stress upon the second and fourth syllables. The point is, of course, that spoken words, in or out of verse, have a rhythm of their own. Rhythm is produced by a combination of strongly stressed, moderately stressed, and weakly stressed syllables. If this rhythm is preserved, the words sound right when heard by another person. If this rhythm is changed, the words sound wrong. Stress, or accent, is therefore a very important element of pronunciation.

The three degrees of stress — strongest, medium, and weakest — are found in the word *indicate* \'in-də-ˌkāt\, in which the first syllable is given the strongest stress (by the high mark '), the last syllable is given medium stress (by the low mark ˌ), and the middle syllable is given the weakest stress (by the absence of any stress mark). The strongest stress is also called primary stress; medium stress is also called secondary stress; and a syllable with the weakest stress is often said to be without stress or to be unstressed. Remember that the stress mark is at the beginning of the stressed syllable.

Some words, such as *indicate* and *davenport,* contain all three degrees of stress. Some, such as *dangerous* and *physician*, contain only primary and the weakest stress. Some words, such as *doorstep* and *knighthood*, contain only primary and secondary stress. Most words of one syllable, such as *glue*, have primary stress; others, such as *a*, usually have the weakest stress. The word *a* has the weakest stress in "I'll give you a dollar", and primary stress in "I'll give you *a* dollar, not two dollars".

Stress is extremely important in the difference between the acceptable and unacceptable pronunciation of many words.

DO YOU UNDERSTAND STRESS?

1. Copy the following respellings, adding the missing stress marks. Then check your marks with this dictionary.

celebrate \sel-ə-brāt\	circulate \sərk-yə-lāt\	countryseat \kən-trē-sēt\
celebration \sel-ə-brāsh-n\	circulation \sərk-yə-lāsh-n\	countryside \kən-trē-sīd\
celebrity \sə-leb-rət-ē\	convict (*verb*) \kən-vikt\	derivation \der-ə-vāsh-n\
chameleon \kə-mēl-yən\	convict (*noun*) \kän-vikt\	derivative \dē-riv-ət-iv\
chamois \sham-ē\	cottony \kät-n-ē\	derive \dē-rīv\
champion \champ-ē-ən\	counterpane \kau̇nt-r-pān\	design \dē-zīn\
chaperon \shap-r-ōn\	country \kən-trē\	designate \dez-ig-nāt\
chauffeur \shōf-r, shō-fər\	countryman \kən-trē-mən\	designation \dez-ig-nāsh-n\

2. When *chaperon* is spelled *chaperone*, which syllables receive the primary and secondary stress?
3. When *chaperon* is used as a verb, what is its respelling?
4. What is the difference in stress between the verb *convict* and the noun *convict?*
5. Why is the respelling \'shōf-r\ placed before \shō-'fər\?
6. Some people pronounce *champion* in two syllables, stressing the second more than the first: \ˌcham-'pēn\. How many pronunciations for the word are recognized by this dictionary?
7. Which syllable receives the primary stress in each of these related words: *celebrate, celebration, celebrity?*
8. Which two of these words have syllables with secondary stress?
9. Which word has three unstressed syllables, or syllables with the weakest stress?
10. What conclusion can you draw concerning the stress in such related words?

THE PRONUNCIATION SYMBOLS

a ....**mat**, **map**

ā ....**age**, **vein**

ä ....**cot**, **bother**; most speakers have this vowel also in **cart** and **father**

ȧ ....**cart**, **father** when a speaker makes the *a* in these words different from the *o* in **cot** and **bother**

aü ....**sound**, **now**

b ....**buy**, **rib**

ch ....**chin**, **itch** [actually, this sound is t + sh]

d ....**day**, **odd**, **ladder**

e ....**bet**, **bed**

ē ....**evenly**, **beat**, **sleepy** [pronounce ē very lightly when it is in a syllable that does not have a stress mark before it — for example, the second ē in \'slēp-ē\]

f ....**fig**, **cuff**

g ....**go**, **big**

h ....**hum**, **ahead**

i ....**tip**, **invent**

ī ....**side**, **buy** [actually, this sound is ä + i, or ȧ + i]

j ....**job**, **edge** [actually, this sound is d + zh]

k ....**kin**, **cook**, **ache**

l ....**lip**, **pill**, **vessels** \'ves-lz\

m ....**me**, **dim**, **atoms** \'at-mz\

n ....**no**, **own**, **vacant** \'vāk-nt\

ng ....**sing**, **singer** \'sing-r\, **finger** \'fing-gr\, **ink** \'ingk\ [actually, this is a single sound, not two]

ō ....**bone**, **snow**

ȯ ....**corn**, **saw**, **all**

ȯi ....**coin**, **boy**

p ....**pay**, **lip**

r ....**rid**, **tar**, **lizard** \'liz-rd\

s ....**so**, **less**

sh ....**shy**, **dish** [actually, this is a single sound, not two]

t ....**tie**, **bet**, **latter**

th ....**thin**, **ether** [actually, this is a single sound, not two]

t͟h ....**then**, **either** [actually, this is a single sound, not two]

ü ....**rule**, **fool**, **few** \'fyü\, **union** \'yün-yən\

u̇ ....**pull**, **wood**

v ....**vote**, **give**

w ....**we**, **away**

y ....**yard**, **cue** \'kyü\, **union** \'yün-yən\

z ....**zone**, **raise**

zh ....**vision** \'vizh-n\ [actually, this is a single sound, not two]

ə					
banana	**silent**	**capital**	**collect**	**suppose**	**perplex**
bun	**cut**	**putty**	**color**	**supper**	**pup**
burn	**curt**	**pert**	**curl**	**serpent**	**purple**

In the words in the first line **ə** is spoken with very weak force. In the words in the second and third lines **ə** is spoken with stronger force.

The pronunciation symbols on the preceding page are also listed for your convenience on the inside front and back covers of this dictionary and (in part) in the key lines at the foot of the vocabulary pages.

The difference between symbols and letters. Most of these symbols look like familiar letters of the alphabet. True, they have the shape of letters, but they are not letters.

The symbol \a\, for example, is the symbol of a single sound, the sound of the vowel in *mat*, *map*, and *add*.

The letter *a*, on the other hand, represents not only the sound of the vowel in *map*, but also the very different vowel sounds found in *made*, *father*, and *sofa*.

Whereas many of the letters of the alphabet may be used to represent any of several sounds, each pronunciation symbol represents only one sound.

No one seeing the word *colonel* for the first time would be likely to guess that its pronunciation is identical with that of *kernel*. Look up both words in this dictionary to see how their pronunciation is indicated. Are you convinced that the letters of the alphabet are not a reliable guide to the pronunciation of a word? Are you convinced that, for a guide to pronunciation, we need a set of symbols, each of which is limited to a single sound?

The value of pronunciation symbols. If the sign $ makes you think of nothing but a capital S with two lines drawn through it, you do not recognize it as a symbol. But if $ immediately makes you think of dollars, you have learned to use this sign as a symbol.

So it is with all the pronunciation symbols. If you look at \ə\ and think, "That's the letter *e* upside down", \ə\ has no value for you as a symbol of pronunciation. But if you think instantaneously of the schwa sound, the most frequently used vowel sound in our language, then \ə\ has meaning for you as a symbol.

The letter *s* is pronounced in several different ways, and in some words is not pronounced at all. For instance, in each of the words *sun*, *easy*, *sure*, and *vision*, the letter *s* has a different pronunciation, and in *island* it has no sound at all. The pronunciation symbol \s\ and the letter *s* have the same form. If the symbol makes you think only of the letter, it does not have value for you as a symbol. But if the symbol \s\ makes you think immediately of the sound of the *s* in *school* \'skül\, of the *sc* in *science* \'sī-ən(t)s\, of the *c* in *cell* \'sel\ and *rice* \'rīs\, and of the last sound in *tax* \'taks\ and *quartz* \'kwȯrts\, then \s\ does have value for you — a single value — as a pronunciation symbol.

The thirty-nine pronunciation symbols include twenty-four symbols representing consonant sounds and fifteen symbols representing vowel sounds. These symbols will be useful to you only to the degree that you become familiar with them.

After you have used this dictionary for a while, you should not have to glance at the key lines or turn to the front or back of your book to see what a symbol stands for. You should become so familiar with each symbol that you instantly think of the sound it represents.

The sections which follow, entitled "The Consonant Symbols" and "The Vowel Symbols", provide activities to help you become familiar with all thirty-nine symbols of pronunciation.

WHAT DO YOU KNOW ABOUT THE PRONUNCIATION SYMBOLS?

1. How many different sounds does a pronunciation symbol have — one or several?
2. How many different sounds may a letter have — one or several?
3. Why are symbols necessary to show the pronunciation of English words?
4. What is the difference between the letter *s* and the symbol \s\?
5. How is the letter *c* respelled in *dance* and in *scale?*
6. How is the letter *q* respelled in *queer?*
7. How is *x* respelled in *ax* and in *exact?*
8. Why are *c*, *q*, and *x* not needed as symbols?
9. Among the fifteen words illustrating the schwa \ə\ in the list of symbols, what five different letters represent the \ə\ sound?
10. Why must there be thirty-nine pronunciation symbols to represent the sounds of twenty-six letters of the alphabet?

THE CONSONANT SYMBOLS

\b The sound represented by the symbol \b\ is spelled with the letter *b* as in *boy*, *cab*, and *able*, or with *bb* as in *robber*. In the spelling of certain words, such as *climb*, *comb*, *doubt*, and *debt*, the *b* is silent.

CHECKUP

Write these respellings correctly, omitting the question marks and inserting \b\ wherever there is a \b\ sound. Then check with your dictionary.

blurb \ˈ?lər?\	subtle \ˈsə?t-l\
bomb \ˈ?äm?\	cupboard \ˈkə?-?rd\
debit \ˈde?-ət\	subpoena \sə?-ˈpē-nə\

\ch This is really a \t\ sound quickly followed by an \sh\ sound. The \ch\ sound may be spelled by several letters and letter combinations: *ch* as in *church*, *tch* as in *watch*, *ti* as in *question*, *t* as in *situation*, or *si* as in *pension*.

CHECKUP

Respell these words correctly, substituting \ch\, \sh\, or \k\ for the question marks:

ache \ˈā?\	chaperon \ˈ?ap-r-ˌōn\
match \ˈma?\	merchant \ˈmər?-nt\
machine \mə-ˈ?ēn\	natural \ˈna?-r(-)əl\
pasture \ˈpas-?ər\	tachometer \tə-ˈ?äm-ət-r\

\d The sound represented by the symbol \d\ is spelled with the letter *d* as in *dad* or with *dd* as in *daddy*.

CHECKUP

Copy these respellings correctly, inserting \d\, \j\, or \t\ where they are needed:

bed \ˈbe?\	soldier \ˈsōl?-r\
damp \ˈ?amp\	dropped \ˈdräp?\
judge \ˈjə?j\	bedridden \ˈbe?-ˌri?-n\
stirred \ˈstər?\	handsome \ˈhan?s-m\

\f This sound may be spelled with the letter *f* as in *fan*, with *ff* as in *offer*, with *ph* as in *telephone*, or with *gh* as in *cough.*

CHECKUP

Respell the following words correctly:

fat \\'?at\\	sofa \\'sō-?ə\\
off \\'ȯ?\\	enough \\ə-'nə?\\
of \\(')ə?\\	photograph \\'?ōt-ə-ˌgra?\\

\g The sound represented by \g\\ may be spelled with the letter *g* as in *go*, with *gg* as in *egg*, with *gh* as in *ghost*, or with *gu* as in *guard;* and \g\\ is the first of the two sounds \gz\\ spelled with *x* as in *exact.*

CHECKUP

Write these respellings correctly, inserting \g\\, \f\\, \j\\, or \zh\\ where they are needed:

rage \\'rā?\\	ragged \\'ra?-əd\\
sign \\'sī?n\\	ghastly \\'?ast-lē\\
cough \\'kȯ?\\	garage \\?ə-'rä?\\
gnat \\'?nat\\	signal \\'si?-nəl\\

\h This sound is spelled with the letter *h* as in *hat*. The sound occurs only at the beginning of syllables, even when the spelling is *wh*, as in *whale* \\'hwāl\\.

CHECKUP

Respell these words correctly:

hen \\'?en\\	whole \\'?ōl\\
sigh \\'sī?\\	whittle \\'?wit-l\\
hole \\'?ōl\\	telephone \\'tel-ə-ˌ?ōn\\

\j This is really a \d\\ sound quickly followed by a \zh\\ sound. The sound \j\\ may be spelled with the letter *j* as in *jam* and *project*, with *g* as in *gem* and *page*, with *dg* as in *judgment*, with *di* as in *soldier*, or with *d* as in *graduation.*

CHECKUP

Copy the respellings below, inserting \j\\, \g\\, or \zh\\:

jail \\'?āl\\	grudge \\'grə?\\
rouge \\'rü?\\	subject \\'səb-?ikt\\
gilt \\'?ilt\\	submerge \\səb-'mər?\\
fringe \\'frin?\\	suggest \\sə(g)-'?est\\

\k This sound may be spelled with the letter *k* as in *kite*, with *c* as in *cat*, with *ck* as in *pick*, with *ch* as in *ache*, with *q* as in *quite*, or with *qu* as in *conquer;* and \k\\ is the first of the two sounds \ks\\ spelled with *x* as in *tax.*

CHECKUP

Respell the following words correctly:

stick \\'sti?\\	crank \\'?rang?\\
chic \\'?ē?\\	liquid \\'li?-wəd\\
chaos \\'?ā-ˌäs\\	accident \\'a?s-ə-dənt\\
exact \\i?-'za?t\\	excellent \\'e?s-l(-)ənt\\

\l The sound represented by the symbol \l\\ is spelled with the letter *l* as in *lap* and *pal*, or with *ll* as in *pull.* This sound may occur in a syllable that contains a vowel sound, or it may occur as a syllabic consonant in a syllable that lacks a vowel sound. Examples of its occurrence as a syllabic consonant are *brittle* \\'brit-l\\, *measles* \\'mēz-lz\\, and *catalog* \\'kat-l-ˌȯg\\.

CHECKUP

Write these respellings correctly:

call \'kȯ?\	clam \'k?am\
calf \'ka?f\	metal \'met-?\
balk \'bȯ?k\	epilogue \'ep-?-ˌȯg\
calm \'kä?m\	mythical \'mith-ik-?\

\m\

The sound represented by the symbol \m\ may be spelled with the letter *m* as in *made*, *dismay*, and *him*, with *mm* as in *accommodate* and *trimmer*, with *lm* as in *calm*, with *mn* as in *autumn* and *column*, or with *mb* as in *bomb* and *climb*. It may occur in a syllable that contains a vowel sound, or it may occur as a syllabic consonant in a syllable that lacks a vowel sound. Examples of its occurrence as a syllabic consonant are *chasm* \'kaz-m\, *anachronism* \ə-'nak-rə-ˌniz-m\, and *maximum* \'maks-m-əm\.

CHECKUP

Copy the following respellings correctly:

may \'?ā\	hymn \'hi?\
ham \'ha?\	glimmer \'gli?-r\
palm \'pä?\	rhythm \'rith-?\
comb \'kō?\	diaphragm \'dī-ə-ˌfra?\

\n\

The sound represented by \n\ may be spelled with the letter *n* as in *net* and *ten*, with *nn* as in *winner*, or with *kn* as in *knight*. This sound may occur as a syllabic consonant, as in *prison* \'priz-n\, *didn't* \'did-nt\, and *mechanize* \'mek-n-ˌīz\.

CHECKUP

Respell the following words correctly:

gun \'gə?\	autumn \'ȯt-m?\
knee \'?ē\	listening \'lis-?(-)ing\
runner \'rə?-r\	lightning \'līt-?ing\
season \'sēz-?\	lightening \'līt-?(-)ing\

\ng\

The sound \ng\ may be spelled with the letters *ng* as in *sing* and *singer*, and in both syllables of *ringing*, or with *n* as in *finger*, *longer*, *rink*, *lynx*, *anchor*, *uncle*, and *conquer*. Many speakers have trouble with words in which the letters *ng* are followed by an unstressed vowel. In some such words the *ng* is pronounced as in *singer*, in others as in *finger*, with a \g\ sound. Some speakers (especially those with parents or grandparents to whom English was not a native language) are apt to pronounce either word either way, a practice that most educated listeners find distressing. In this dictionary the pronunciation of *singer* is shown as \'sing-r\, while the pronunciation of *finger* is shown as \'fing-gr\. That is, words of the second class have a second \g\ in them. One of the main reasons for all this difficulty is the fact that the sound represented by \ng\ in our set of symbols and by the *ng* in *ring* is a single sound, not two sounds.

CHECKUP

Write the correct respellings for these words:

singing \'si?-i?\	anchor \'a?k-r\
singeing \'si?-?i?\	dangle \'da?-gl\
congress \'kä?-grəs\	anxiety \a?-'zī-ət-ē\

congratulate \kə?-'grach-l-ˌāt\

\p The sound represented by the symbol \p\ is spelled with the letter *p* as in *pan* and *nap* or with *pp* as in *happen.*

CHECKUP

Copy the following respellings correctly:

peep \\'?ē?\\	hiccough \\'hik-ˌə?\\
sphere \\'s?ir\\	diphthong \\'di?-thȯng\\
happy \\'ha?-ē\\	pneumonia \\?nü-'mōn-yə\\

\r The sound \r\ is spelled with the letter *r* as in *rat, brass, parade,* and *deer*, or with *rr* as in *merry.* This sound may occur before a vowel as in *rat,* may follow a vowel as in *deer*, may occur between vowels as in *parade* and *merry,* or may occur as a syllabic consonant as in *baker* \\'bāk-r\\, *leopard* \\'lep-rd\\, and *tolerate* \\'täl-r-ˌāt\\.

Most Americans and Canadians have as many \r\ sounds in their pronunciation of a word as there are letters *r* or letter groups *rr* in the spelling. Such speakers may be called *r*-retainers. But speakers who are natives of southeastern United States, of eastern New England, of New York City, and of southern England frequently do not have \r\ sounds before consonants or pauses. Such speakers are called *r*-droppers. The pronunciations used by *r*-droppers are as correct as those used by *r*-retainers, but are not given in the vocabulary of this book simply because giving them would have made the book too big.

R-droppers do one of several things: (1) they use \ə\ instead of \r\; (2) they simply omit the \r\ sounds; (3) they omit the \r\ sound but make the preceding vowel very long; or (4) they use instead of vowel plus \r\ a single vowel different in quality from the vowel of the *r*-retainers. Examples of *r*-droppers' pronunciation: \\'ban-ə\\ instead of \\'ban-r\\ for *banner*, \\'lep-əd\\ instead of \\'lep-rd\\ for *leopard,* \\'fȯm-yə-lə\\ instead of \\'fȯrm-yə-lə\\ for *formula.* Additions to our list of symbols would be necessary to show some of the kinds of *r*-dropping mentioned.

Even *r*-retainers sometimes drop an *r* when a word contains one or more other *r*'s. They often drop an *r*, for instance, from the first syllable of *surprise* and from the first syllable of *thermometer.* An *r* that even an *r*-retainer may drop is shown in parentheses.

CHECKUP

Respell these words, inserting \r\ only if it is natural to your own speech. If it is not, then insert a \ə\.

tire \\'tī?\\	dollar \\'däl-?\\
rhyme \\'?īm\\	anchor \\'angk-?\\
store \\'stō?\\	thinker \\'thingk-?\\
story \\'stō?-ē\\	macaroni \\ˌmak-?-'ō-nē\\

\s This sound may be spelled with the letter *s* as in *say,* with *ss* as in *miss,* with *sc* as in *scene,* with *ps* as in *psychology,* with *c* as in *cent,* or with *z* as in *quartz;* and it is the second of the two sounds \ks\ spelled with *x* as in *tax.*

The letter *s* is used to spell four different sounds: \s\ as in *yes,* \z\ as in *days,* \sh\ as in *sure,* and \zh\ as in *vision;* it may also be silent as in *isle;* and *si* after *n* often spells the sound \ch\ as in *pension* and *dimension.*

CHECKUP

Write the following respellings correctly:

lots \\'lät?\\	sugar \\'?u̇g-r\\
pods \\'päd?\\	island \\'ī?-lənd\\
scent \\'?ent\\	practice \\'prak-tə?\\
psalm \\'?äm\\	churches \\'chərch-ə?\\

\sh The sound represented by \sh\ may be spelled with the letters *sh* as in *fish*, with *s* as in *sure*, with *ss* as in *issue*, with *ci* as in *special*, with *ti* as in *nation*, with *xi* as in *anxious*, or with *ch* as in *machine*. This sound is not a combination of \s\ and \h\, but a single sound, different from both \s\ and \h\.

CHECKUP

Copy these respellings correctly:

shape \'?āp\	mission \'mi?-n\
sugar \'?u̇g-r\	mansion \'man?-n\
ocean \'ō?-n\	chivalry \'?iv-l-rē\
action \'ak?-n\	musician \myü-'zi?-n\

\t The sound \t\ may be spelled with the letter *t* as in *sat* and *tap*, with *tt* as in *attack*, or with *ed* as in *walked*.

CHECKUP

Write the correct respellings for these words:

try \'?rī\	letter \'le?-r\
apt \'ap?\	listen \'lis?-n\
fried \'frī?\	stopped \'stäp?\

\th\ \\<u>th</u> The sound represented by \th\, called plain t-h, is the sound spelled with the letters *th* in *thing* and *breath*. The sound represented by \\<u>th</u>\\, called bar t-h, is the sound spelled with the letters *th* in *these* and *breathe*. Both the \th\ and \\<u>th</u>\\ sounds are single sounds, quite different from either the \t\ or the \h\ sound. The difference between \th\ and \\<u>th</u>\\ is that \\<u>th</u>\\ is voiced (uttered with the vocal cords close together and vibrating) whereas \th\ is voiceless (uttered with the vocal cords wide apart and not vibrating). This difference will be extremely clear if you will press your opened hands tightly over your ears and say each sound in turn. The \\<u>th</u>\\ sound will cause a loud buzzing; the \th\ sound will not.

CHECKUP

Copy the following respellings, inserting \th\ when the missing sound is voiceless and \\<u>th</u>\\ when the missing sound is voiced.

bath \'ba?\	this \'?is\
bathe \'bā?\	thistle \'?is-l\
cloth \'klȯ?\	wreath \'rē?\
clothe \'klō?\	nothing \'nə?-ing\

\v The sound represented by the symbol \v\ is spelled with the letter *v* as in *very*, *save*, and *never*.

CHECKUP

Write the correct respellings for the words below:

of \'ə?\	even \'ē?-n\	knives \'nī?z\
off \'ȯ?\	prove \'prü?\	valor \'?al-r\

\w The consonant sound \w\ may be spelled with the letter *w* as in *wait* and *twist*, with *u* as in *queer* and *persuade*, or with *o* as in *choir*. This sound occurs only before vowels. The letter *w* is often silent, as in *who* and *sword*. But in many words beginning with *wh* the \w\ and \h\ sounds are reversed, as in *white* \'hwīt\. In some words a \w\ sound is inserted to make the word easier to pronounce, as in *January* \'jan-yə-ˌwer-ē\ and *mutual* \'myü-chə-wəl\.

CHECKUP

Respell these words correctly:

why \'h?ī\	liquid \'lik-?əd\
whole \'h?ōl\	memoir \'mem-ˌ?är\
suave \'s?äv\	actual \'ak-chə-?əl\
sword \'s?ōrd\	masquerade \ˌmask-?r-'ād\

\y The consonant sound \y\ may be spelled with the letter *y* as in *yes*, with *i* as in *onion*, or with *e* as in *feud*. Often the single letter *u* represents the two sounds \y\ plus \ü\, or \y\ plus \u̇\, or \y\ plus \ə\, as in *puny* \'pyü-nē\, *fury* \'fyu̇r-ē\, and *January* \'jan-yə-ˌwer-ē\. The verb *use* is pronounced exactly like *yews* \'yüz\.

CHECKUP

Write the correct respellings for these words:

unite \?ü-'nīt\	million \'mil-?ən\
futile \'f?üt-l\	beyond \bē-'?änd\
player \'plā-?ər\	European \ˌ?u̇r-ə-'pē-ən\
lawyer \'lȯ-?ər\	hallelujah \ˌhal-ə-'lü-?ə\

\z The sound \z\ may be spelled with the letter *z* as in *zone*, *wizard*, and *whiz*, with *zz* as in *buzz*, or with *s* as in *wise* and *busy*.

CHECKUP

Respell the following words correctly:

zipper \'?ip-r\	house (*noun*) \'hau̇?\
haze \'hā?\	houses \'hau̇-?ə?\
knows \'nō?\	analysis \ə-'nal-ə-?ə?\
dizzy \'di?-ē\	analyses \ə-'nal-ə-ˌ?ē?\

\zh The sound \zh\ may be spelled with the letter *z* as in *azure*, with *s* as in *leisure*, with *si* as in *vision*, or with *g* as in *rouge*. The \zh\ sound is a single sound, different from either \z\ or \h\.

CHECKUP

Write the correct respellings:

treasure \'tre?-r\	camouflage \'kam-ə-ˌflä?\
version \'vər?-n\	explosion \iks-'plō?-n\
brazier \'brā?-r\	expulsion \iks-'pəl?-n\

CAN YOU RECOGNIZE THE TWENTY-FOUR CONSONANT SOUNDS?

Each line below contains a consonant symbol followed by four words which may or may not contain the sound represented by the symbol. Say each sound and word to yourself. Write the symbols and the words in each line that contain the sound. Then check with your dictionary.

\b\	dumb	possible	cupboard	subtlety
\ch\	nature	mansion	chaperon	question
\d\	stopped	handsome	declared	handkerchief
\f\	of	laugh	phone	conference
\g\	gnaw	guide	raged	exactly
\h\	wholly	honest	Utah	elephant
\j\	judge	soldier	adjective	gesture

\k\	quick	headache	exist	exercise
\l\	half	you'll	palm	article
\m\	bomb	hymn	stomach	criticism
\n\	gnat	autumn	autumnal	knowledge
\ng\	uncle	conquer	singe	congratulate
\p\	spirit	hiccough	spherical	pneumonia
\r\	parade	ferry	tolerant	granite
\s\	island	relax	ranches	psychology
\sh\	action	pension	unsure	television
\t\	listen	rapped	rotten	dodged
\th\	thin	then	wreath	wreathed
\<u>th</u>\	cloth	clothing	whether	weather
\v\	off	various	evening	recover
\w\	sword	whole	quiet	January
\y\	billion	united	feudal	employer
\z\	rise	quartz	lockers	business
\zh\	rogue	erasure	erosion	measure

THE VOWEL SYMBOLS

\ə One of the most frequent sounds in English is the schwa sound, represented by the symbol \ə\. When stressed, this sound may be spelled with the letter *u* as in *cut* and *hurt*, with *e* as in *herd*, with *i* as in *bird*, or with *o* as in *front* and *word*. When unstressed, the schwa sound may be spelled with any of the vowel letters, as in *about* \ə-'bau̇t\, *silent* \'sī-lənt\, *capital* \'kap-ət-l\, *collect* \kə-'lekt\, and *suppose* \sə-'pōz\.

CHECKUP

Which of the following words contain boldface vowels having the schwa sound?

magn**e**t or magn**e**tic	fi**e**rce or f**i**rst
exh**i**bit or exh**i**bition	**a**nt or defi**a**nt
algebr**a** or algebr**a**ic	sw**o**rd or w**o**rd
abandon or **a**bsence	st**u**mp or st**u**pid
m**ea**nt or merrim**e**nt	c**o**ntrol or c**o**nsul

\a\ \ā\ \ä\ \ȧ The four "a" symbols are: \a\, called plain a, which represents the sound of the *a* in *fat* and *carry;* \ā\, called bar a, which represents the sound of the *a* in *age*, the *ai* in *main*, the *ei* in *vein*, the *ea* in *break*, the *ay* in *day*, the *ey* in *prey*, and the *au* in *gauge;* \ä\, called two-dot a, which represents the sound of the *o* in *cot* and *bother*, and also the sound used by most American speakers for the *a* in *cart* and *father;* and \ȧ\, called one-dot a, which represents the vowel sound used by some speakers in *aunt* and *cart* and in the first syllable of *father*. Most Americans do not have the \ȧ\ sound in their speech. If you are one of them, you may ignore this symbol, which is included in this dictionary for the benefit of many Americans who, though not a majority, do have this sound.

In words like *vary, harem* (stress on the penult, single *r* in the spelling) and like *various* (stress on antepenult, two consecutive vowel sounds following the *r* sound) the stressed vowel may be like that of *marry* or like that of *merry*.

CHECKUP

Copy these words, writing the symbol for the sound of the boldface letter or letters in each:

stop	plaid	heart	marry
they	bathe	hobby	gather
calm	fancy	weigh	solemn
bomb	great	camel	sergeant

\e\ \ē The symbol \e\, called plain e, represents the vowel sound in *met, said, says, death, friend,* and *care.*

The symbol \ē\, called bar e, stands for the vowel sound in *he, feed, seat, field, key,* and *eve,* in the stressed syllable of *people, deceive,* and *machine,* and in the unstressed syllable of *emerge* and *city.*

Many words which contain the letter *e* do not contain either the \e\ sound or the \ē\ sound. In such words as *excite* and *examine,* the sound of the initial vowel is usually \i\. In such words as *magnet, perplex,* and *element,* the sound of the unaccented vowel is the \ə\.

CHECKUP

Copy these words and write the symbols for the sounds of the boldface letters:

any	merry	conceit
head	mercy	careful
steak	extent	meander
heard	people	subpoena
carpet	receipt	machinery

\i\ \ī The symbol \i\, called plain i, represents the vowel sound in *sit, build, hymn, deer, fear,* and *sieve,* and in the stressed syllable of *busy, women,* and *England.* The first vowel in *excite, exaggerate,* and *encourage* is usually pronounced \i\.

The symbol \ī\, called bar i, stands for the vowel sound in *light, height, try, buy, bite, fire,* and *aisle.*

Many words that contain the letter *i* do not contain either the \i\ sound or the \ī\ sound. In such words as *possible, vanity, policy,* and *animal* the letter *i* is pronounced \ə\.

CHECKUP

Write the words below and the symbols for the sounds of the boldface letters:

pity	cheer	concise
bird	cereal	famine
here	except	machine
choir	sleight	gymnasium

\ō\ \ȯ The symbol \ō\, called bar o, represents the sound of the vowel letter or letters in *go, coat, though,* and *beau,* of the *o* in *cone,* of the *ew* in *sew,* and of the *ow* in *bowl.* (In the last two words, the *w* is a vowel letter.)

The symbol \ȯ\, called one-dot o, stands for the vowel sound in *soft, corn, saw, all, caught, fought,* and *broad.* Speakers in some parts of the country make no consistent distinction between \ȯ\ and \ä\, and this lack of distinction may be correct for your speech.

Many words that contain the letter *o* do not contain either the \ō\ sound or the \ȯ\ sound. In such words as *cot, lock,* and *rod* the vowel sound is \ä\. In such words as *color* and *comfort* the vowel sound in the stressed syllable is the \ə\. In such words as *confirm* and *baron,* the vowel sound in the unstressed syllable is the \ə\.

CHECKUP

Write each word and the symbol for the sound of the boldface letter or letters:

l**aw**	curi**o**	c**ou**ple	c**a**lling
cr**ow**	n**o**vel	sh**o**vel	curi**ou**s
el**o**pe	cr**o**ss	c**o**nnect	curi**o**sity
sh**or**t	d**o**llar	c**o**ngress	trouss**eau**

\ü\

\u̇\

The two "u" symbols are: \ü\, called two-dot u, which stands for the vowel sound in *flu*, *school*, *blue*, *youth*, *rule*, and *crew;* and \u̇\, called one-dot u, which represents the vowel sound in *pull*, *wood*, *poor*, and *sugar*. In a word such as *few*, the \ü\ sound is preceded by the consonant sound \y\: \'fyü\. (The *w* in words such as *crew* and *few* is a vowel.)

The treatment of words like *due*, *tube*, and *new* (in which one of the sounds \d\, \t\, \n\ precedes the vowel or vowels) is not uniform in the United States. With some speakers the beginnings of these three words are as in *doing*, *too*, and *noose* (\'dü\, \'tü\, \'nü\) but with other speakers a \y\ sound is present before the \ü\ (\'dyü\, \'tyüb\, \'nyü\). The pronunciation with \y\ is especially common in the southern states.

Many words that contain the letter *u* do not have either of these sounds. The vowel sound in *cut*, for example, is \ə\. The letter *u* in an unstressed syllable frequently has the \ə\ sound, as in *cactus* \'kak-təs\.

Is your pronunciation of *roof* the only pronunciation recognized by the dictionary?

CHECKUP

Write the words below and the sound symbols for the boldface letters:

c**ue**	r**oo**f	ch**u**te	w**o**man
c**u**re	s**u**re	sh**oo**t	cany**o**n
sh**oe**	f**eu**d	**u**nion	**u**nhappy
p**u**sh	d**o**ne	h**u**man	Jan**u**ary
sh**u**t	h**u**rt	b**eau**ty	n**ew** (2 ways)

\au̇\

\ȯi\

In the word *out* \'au̇t\ two vowel sounds occur in succession as part of a single syllable. Such a succession of two vowel sounds is called a diphthong.

This dictionary uses two diphthong symbols: \au̇\, representing the vowel sounds of *cow* and *sound* and of both *au's* in *sauerkraut;* and \ȯi\, representing the vowel sounds of *join* and *boy*. (In *cow* and *boy* the *w* and *y* are vowels.) When the \ȯi\ sequence of sounds is immediately followed by the \ng\ sound the sequence is usually regarded as belonging to two separate syllables, as in the pronunciation of present participles like *sawing* \'sȯ-ing\.

The sound of the words *eye* and *I* (represented by \ī\ in this dictionary because the letter *i* is so often its spelling) is really a diphthong, too, consisting of \ä\ and \i\ or of \ȧ\ and \i\.

CHECKUP

Copy the following words and write the sound symbols for the boldface letters:

c**oi**n	p**oi**nt	b**ou**gh	mem**oi**r
s**ou**l	r**oy**al	l**aw**yer	cham**oi**s
c**ow**l	r**ou**gh	th**ou**gh	c**oi**ncide
b**ow**l	r**ou**nd	th**ou**ght	c**oi**ncidence

ARE YOU SURE OF THE FIFTEEN VOWEL SOUNDS?

Each line below contains a vowel symbol followed by four words which may or may not contain the sound represented by the symbol. Say each sound and word to yourself. Write the symbols and the words in each line that contain the sound. Then check with your dictionary.

\a\	grab	grapple	behave	barrier
\ā\	there	gauze	taped	restrain
\ä\	sober	spotted	father	farther
\ȧ\	fast	mark	palm	married
\au̇\	mower	bound	vowel	ought
\e\	chair	fearless	person	weather
\ē\	queer	every	report	fatigue
\i\	expire	merely	rhyme	rhythm
\ī\	entire	height	ravine	divine
\ō\	scowl	bureau	sewing	thought
\ȯ\	scorn	recall	worthy	taught
\ȯi\	coinage	coincide	lawyer	employee
\ü\	you're	gradual	reunion	costume
\u̇\	fooling	woolen	insure	February
\ə\	sir	density	supple	confide

CAN YOU READ THE PRONUNCIATION SYMBOLS?

The following quotations have been respelled to provide you with practice in reading the symbols of this dictionary. Write the quotations in sentence form.

\'if ət 'fərst yü 'dōnt sək-'sēd, 'trī, 'trī ə-'gen\

\'ər-lē tə 'bed n 'ər-lē tə 'rīz 'māks ə man 'hel-thē, 'wel-thē, ən 'wīz\

\'dü 'ən-tü 'əth-rz əz 'yü wəd hav 'them dü 'ən-tə 'yü\

\'gäd 'helps 'thōz hü 'help thəm-'selvz\

\ə 'pen-ē 'sāvd iz ə 'pen-ē 'ərnd\

\ən 'au̇n(t)s əv prē-'vench-n iz 'wərth ə 'pau̇nd əv 'kyu̇r\

\'tōl 'ōks frəm 'lit-l 'ā-ˌkȯrnz 'grō\

\'wāst nät, 'wänt nät\

\'tü 'rȯngz dōnt 'māk ə 'rīt\

\'hē thət 'fōlz in 'ləv with im-'self wil 'hav nō 'rīv-lz\

\'līvz əv 'grāt 'men 'ȯl rē-'mīnd əs 'wē kən 'māk 'au̇r 'līvz sə-'blīm,
'an, dē-'pärt-ing, 'lēv bē-'hīnd əs 'fu̇t-ˌprin(t)s än thə 'san(d)z əv 'tīm\

\'this ə-bəv 'ȯl, tü thīn 'ōn 'self bē 'trü, and it məst 'fäl-ō, əz thə 'nīt thə 'dā,
thau̇ 'kan(t)st nät 'then bē 'fȯls tü 'en-ē 'man\

\hü 'stēlz mī 'pərs stēlz 'trash; tiz 'səm(p)-thing, 'nəth-ing; twəz 'mīn, tiz 'hiz, ənd haz bin 'slāv tə 'thaủz-n(d)z; bət 'hē <u>th</u>ət 'filch-əz 'frəm mē 'mī gủd 'nām 'räbz mē əv '<u>th</u>at hwich 'nät in-'rich-əz 'him, ən 'māks 'mē pủr in-'dēd\

\wē 'hōld '<u>th</u>ēz 'trü<u>th</u>z tə bē 'self-'ev-ə-dənt: <u>th</u>ət 'ȯl 'men ər krē-'āt-əd 'ēk-wəl; <u>th</u>ət <u>th</u>ā ər in-'daủd bī <u>th</u>ar krē-'āt-r wi<u>th</u> 'sərt-n ˌən-'āl-yə-nəb-l 'rīts; <u>th</u>ət ə-məng '<u>th</u>ēz ər 'līf, 'lib-rt-ē, ənd <u>th</u>ə pər-'süt əv 'hap-ē-nəs\

\'wē, <u>th</u>ə 'pēp-l əv <u>th</u>ə yü-'nīt-əd 'stāts, in 'ȯrd-r tə 'fȯrm ə mōr 'pər-fikt 'yün-yən, ə-'stab-lish 'jəs-təs, in-'shủr də-'mes-tik tran(g)-'kwil-ət-ē, prə-'vīd fər <u>th</u>ə 'käm-ən dē-'fen(t)s, prə-'mōt <u>th</u>ə 'jen-r(-)əl 'wel-ˌfar, an sē-'kyủr <u>th</u>ə 'bles-ingz əv 'lib-rt-ē tü aủr-'selvz n aủr päs-'ter-ət-ē, dü ȯr-'dān ən(d) ə-'stab-lish <u>th</u>is ˌkän(t)s-tə-'tüsh-n fər <u>th</u>ə yü-'nīt-əd 'stāts əv ə-'mer-ə-kə\

VARIANT PRONUNCIATIONS

Many words, as you know, have more than one correct pronunciation. Variations are shown in this dictionary in three different ways:

1. Respelling the whole word again. Sometimes when this dictionary gives a second pronunciation, it is written out in full, as in these entries:

sloth \'slȯth, 'slōth\
ha·rass \hə-'ras, 'har-əs\

2. Respelling part of the word again. Often it is not necessary to write out a second pronunciation in full. In a long word the difference between two pronunciations may be confined to only a part of the word. For such words the second pronunciation may be indicated for only the part of the word where the difference is. The rest of the second pronunciation is the same as for the first pronunciation, as in these entries:

en·dure \in-'dủr, -'dyủr\
goose·ber·ry \'güs-ˌber-ē, 'güz-\
per·sist·ent \pər-'sis-tənt, -'zis-\

The full second pronunciations for these words are:

\in-'dyủr\ \'güz-ˌber-ē\ \pər-'zis-tənt\

In such partial second pronunciations only whole syllables are recorded and there is always at least one hyphen. A hyphen at the beginning of a partial pronunciation means that the first part is missing and is to be supplied from the pronunciation that precedes within the same slant lines. The hyphen before \-'dyủr\ means that there is something that goes ahead of it: \in-\. Other examples are:

mer·can·tile \'mərk-n-ˌtēl, -ˌtīl\
par·a·dise \'par-ə-ˌdīs, -ˌdīz\

A hyphen at both the beginning and the end of a partial pronunciation means that both the first and the last parts of the pronunciation are missing. The missing parts are to be supplied from a pronunciation that precedes within the same slant lines. The hyphens with \-'zis-\ after *per·sist·ent* tell you that something goes ahead of this syllable and something comes after it.

In addition to hyphens, stress marks and sound symbols will help you to figure out in what part of the word the difference lies.

For instance, in *op·por·tu·ni·ty* \ˌäp-r-ˈtü-nət-ē, -ˈtyü-\ there is only one primary stress in the first pronunciation; it is on the third syllable. The partial pronunciation consists of only one syllable, and that syllable has a high mark. The primary stress should be an instant signal to you that the third syllable is the part of the word that may be pronounced in either of two ways.

In *ex·traor·di·nary* \iks-ˈtrȯrd-n-ˌer-ē, ˌeks-trə-ˈȯrd-\ the group of sound symbols \-ȯrd-\ that you see in the second pronunciation occurs at only one place in the first pronunciation — just before the last three syllables. This should tell you that to complete the second pronunciation you have to add to it the last three syllables of the first pronunciation.

When one syllable of a word can be pronounced two ways and another syllable can also be pronounced two ways, the total number of possible pronunciations is four. Thus the respelling \ˈȯr-inj, ˈär-, -ənj\ for *or·ange* adds up to \ˈȯr-inj, ˈär-inj, ˈȯr-ənj, ˈär-ənj\.

3. Putting an optional symbol in parentheses. If a sound symbol, stress mark, or hyphen may be written or omitted in the respelling, depending on the pronunciation, that symbol is enclosed in parentheses. Since *dense* may be pronounced either \ˈdens\ or \ˈdents\, the word is respelled as \ˈden(t)s\. Since the word *me* may have either primary stress or the weakest stress, depending on its use in the sentence, it is respelled \(ˈ)mē\. And since *awfully* may have either two syllables \ˈȯf-lē\ or three syllables \ˈȯf-l-ē\, the optional hyphen is put in parentheses: \ˈȯf-l(-)ē\. Here are three other examples:

ad·vi·so·ry \əd-ˈvīz-r(-)ē\
al·ways \ˈȯl-wēz, -(ˌ)wāz, -wəz\
thou·sand \ˈthaůz-n(d)\

DO YOU UNDERSTAND VARIANT PRONUNCIATIONS?

Write out in full all the respellings given for each word below, just as the four pronunciations of *orange* were written out in full. The number in parentheses shows how many pronunciations are given.

always (4)	usually (3)	inglorious (4)
oasis (2)	granary (4)	wherefrom (8)
ratio (2)	transact (3)	presentation (3)
they're (4)	naturally (3)	rudimentary (2)

A GUIDE TO MEANINGS

A dictionary helps you to extend your knowledge of the meanings of familiar words and introduces you to the meanings of unfamiliar words. If the word *accelerator* makes you think only of a pedal on the floor of an automobile, you have a limited understanding of its meaning. If, however, the word *accelerator* makes you think of a pedal by which the driver makes the car go faster, you have a wider understanding of the word's meaning. If your thoughts about *accelerator* spread out beyond an automobile pedal, you are capable of still wider understanding of the word. For example, there are *accelerator* nerves and muscles in the body. There are fuels called *accelerators* which are used to speed up the burning of charcoal. There are fluids called *accelerators* which are used to speed up the drying time of varnish. If a dictionary of the size of this one attempted to define all the possible meanings of *accelerator*, it would contain fewer entries in the same space.

CHECKUP

Look up the definition of *back*, a word which you have spoken, heard, written, and read thousands of times.

1. As what parts of speech is it used?
2. How many different meanings are given altogether?
3. Count the number of times *back* is in italics to see how many examples of its use are given. Are there more examples or meanings?
4. Write a sentence using *back* as each of the four parts of speech. Number each sentence with the number of its corresponding meaning in the dictionary.

Part-of-speech labels. In most of the entries in this dictionary, immediately after the pronunciation, you will find one of the following abbreviations in italics: *n.*, *v.*, *adj.*, *adv.*, *pron.*, *prep.*, *conj.*, *interj.* These stand for the eight parts of speech: noun, verb, adjective, adverb, pronoun, preposition, conjunction, interjection.

One of these abbreviations used in this way is called a "part-of-speech label". Such labels are used in this dictionary in three different situations: (1) Usually the label immediately follows a defined entry word and its respelling. (2) If within a group of definitions the part of speech changes, another label is used. (3) Sometimes at the end of the definitions a label is used after a word that is formed from the entry word, usually by the addition of a suffix. Such a word is "run on" without a respelling or a definition because the pronunciation and meaning can be figured out from a study of the entry word.

These examples show the use of part-of-speech labels after the respelling of the main entries and after run-on entries:

de·scribe \dē-'skrīb\ *v.;* **de·scribed**; **de·scrib·ing. 1** To write or tell about; to give an account of; as, to *describe* a sunset; to *describe* a football game. **2** To draw the outline of; as, to *describe* a circle with compasses. — **de·scrib·a·ble**, *adj.* — **de·scrib·er**, *n.*

de·scrip·tion \dē-'skripsh-n\ *n.* **1** An account of something; especially. an account that presents a picture to a person who reads or hears it; as, a vivid *description* of last night's game. **2** Kind; sort; as, people of every *description.*

de·scrip·tive \dē-'skrip-tiv\ *adj.* Serving to describe. "Blue" is a *descriptive* word. — **de·scrip·tive·ly**, *adv.*

When a main entry refers you to another entry word, no part-of-speech label or definition is necessary.

analyse. Variant of *analyze.*
begun. Past part. of *begin.*
children. Pl. of *child.*

Many words are used as more than one part of speech. The word *blot* can be a noun meaning "a spot or stain" or a verb meaning "to make a spot or stain". When *alien* is used as an adjective, it means "belonging to another country"; when it is used as a noun, it means "a person not a citizen of the country in which he lives".

Sometimes, when one definition can be used for two parts of speech, the entry word is given a double part-of-speech label, as in these examples:

along·side \ə-'lȯng-ˌsīd\ *adv.* or *prep.* Along or beside; side by side with.

abreast \ə-'brest\ *adj.* or *adv.* **1** Side by side; in an even line; as, to walk four *abreast.* **2** Up to a certain level or line; as, to keep *abreast* of the times.

However, the wording of a definition will usually fit only one part of speech. If the same entry word is labeled again as another part of speech, a separate definition must be given. In this dictionary a heavy dash (—), followed by a new part-of-speech label, separates the definitions for the different parts of speech, as in this entry for *coast:*

coast \'kōst\ *n.* **1** The seashore or the land near it. **2** A slope suited to sliding downhill, as on a sled. **3** A slide down such a slope. — *v.* **1** To steam or sail along a coast; to follow the coast of. **2** To slide over snow or ice, as on a sled. **3** To ride or glide without applying power, as on a bicycle when not pedaling.

The heavy dash takes the place of the entry word. It tells you that the next definition explains the meaning of *coast* when it is put to a new use. The part-of-speech label (*v.*) tells what the new use is.

CHECKUP

As what parts of speech may each of these words be used?

off	after	short	neither
one	bodily	brown	chemical
quiz	asleep	accent	well (2 entries)

Different pronunciations for different parts of speech. When a word changes its pronunciation in changing its part of speech, the new pronunciation is given between the heavy dash and the part-of-speech label, as in this entry for *absent:*

ab·sent \ab-'sent\ *v.* To keep (oneself) away; to withdraw (oneself); as, to *absent* oneself from a meeting. — \'ab-sənt\ *adj.* **1** Not present; away; missing; lacking; as, to be *absent* from home. **2** Absent-minded; as, to have an *absent* look on one's face. — **ab·sent·ly** \'ab-sənt-lē\ *adv.*

CHECKUP

After reading each sentence below, give the part of speech of the italicized word and tell which syllable should be stressed. Then check with the dictionary.

1. The principal will *conduct* the band.
2. Jim won a medal for good *conduct.*
3. The *content* of the speech was difficult.
4. The dog is *content* to lie in the shade.
5. This *contract* was written by a lawyer.
6. Cold causes steel to *contract.*
7. We all *object* to undeserved criticism.
8. A transitive verb requires an *object.*
9. His *progress* in arithmetic is slow.
10. He doesn't *progress* very rapidly.

Open compounds. Most of the main entries in the dictionary are single words. Sometimes, however, two or more words together have a special meaning and so must be entered in the dictionary. You may know what *post* means and what *road* means, but you may have to look in the dictionary to find out what a *post road* is. You will find the two words entered in the dictionary as a two-word compound in the alphabetical position they would have if written *postroad* without a space. But you will notice that in this dictionary "open compounds" are not given part-of-speech labels. Some compounds occur regularly in both open and closed forms. These are shown as follows:

air·lin·er \'ar-ˌlīn-r, 'er-\ *n.*, or **air liner.** A large commercial passenger aircraft operating over an airline.

CHECKUP

1. Try guessing what each of these compounds means, judging by the two separate words. Then look up the compounds and write their meanings.

dead heat	warm front
sour gum	night letter
pitch pipe	Adam's apple
booby trap	vicious circle
fool's gold	hasty pudding
baker's dozen	Arabic numerals

2. Which of these open compounds, if any, have part-of-speech labels?

Noun plurals. Plurals made by the simple addition of *-s* or *-es* to an unchanged entry word (*antlers, books, annexes, churches*) are considered regular and are not usually given. They *are* given, however, with the label *pl.*, when there might be some doubt about the spelling or pronunciation. In the following entries the plurals are shown because there might be doubt about their spelling:

at·tor·ney \ə-'tər-nē\ *n.; pl.* **at·tor·neys.** **1** A person who is legally appointed by another person to transact any business for him. **2** A lawyer.

can·to \'kan-ˌtō\ *n.; pl.* **can·tos.** One of the chief divisions of a long poem.

to·ma·to \tə-'māt-ō, -'mȧt-, -'mät-\ *n.; pl.* **to·ma·toes.** **1** A plant of the same family as the potato, with hairy stem and leaves and yellow flowers. **2** The red or yellow edible fruit of this plant.

Irregular plurals are always given, as in the entry below.

child \'chīld\ *n.; pl.* **chil·dren** \'child-r(ə)n\. **1** A baby; an infant. **2** A boy or girl; as, books written especially for *children.* **3** Any person as innocent and trusting as a child. **4** A son or daughter; as, to be an only *child.*

CHECKUP

List the plurals of these nouns in four columns: *Regular; Same as singular; Irregular; Two plurals.* Use your dictionary.

fox	loaf	larva	series	scarf
bus	lynx	horse	dozen	index
gas	calf	quail	brush	mouse
fish	man	torch	lasso	moose
echo	piano	sheep	hobby	valley

Special meanings of plurals. The plural of a noun usually means simply more than one of whatever is named by the singular. Sometimes, however, a noun has a sense in which it is always or generally used in the plural and which differs from any of its meanings as a singular. In each of the entries below, a note in brackets points out a special meaning of the plural.

lodg·ing \'läj-ing\ *n.* **1** A dwelling; especially, a temporary dwelling or sleeping place. **2** [in the plural] A room or rooms in the house of another person, rented as a dwelling place.

gro·cery \'grōs-r(-)ē\ *n.; pl.* **gro·cer·ies.** **1** A retail grocer's store. **2** The trade or business of a grocer. **3** [in the plural] The foodstuffs sold by grocers.

CHECKUP

What special meaning does each of these plural nouns have?

dues	honors	notions	securities
greens	glasses	heavens	instructions

Principal parts of verbs. When the past tense and past participle of a verb are formed by the simple addition of *-ed* to an unchanged entry word (as in *acted*), these forms are not usually given in the dictionary.

When the past tense and the past participle are made in any other way, as by doubling the final consonant before adding *-ed* (as in *admitted*), by dropping silent *e* (as in *cared*), or by changing the final *y* to *i* (as in *cried*), these forms are given. They are also given when the past tense and past participle are different from the present tense in other ways (as in *go, went, gone*).

In the following entry, *admitted* is given for both the past tense and the past participle, and *admitting* is given as the present participle:

ad·mit \əd-'mit\ *v.;* **ad·mit·ted**; **ad·mit·ting.** **1** To let in; to give the right to enter; to accept; as, to *admit* a statement as evidence. Each ticket *admits* one person. **2** To have room for; as, a dock that *admits* two boats. **3** To allow; to permit; as, a rule that *admits* no exceptions.

This entry shows that the past tense *arose* is not the same as the past participle *arisen*. The present participle *arising* is also given.

arise \ə-'rīz\ *v.;* **arose** \ə-'rōz\; **aris·en** \ə-'riz-n\; **aris·ing** \ə-'rī-zing\. **1** To move upward; to ascend. Mist *arose* from the valley. **2** To get up from sleep or after lying down. **3** To spring up; to come into existence; to occur. A dispute *arose* between the leaders.

The verb *shrink* has variant forms for the past tense (*shrank* or *shrunk*) and for the past participle (*shrunk* or *shrunken*). The present participle is *shrinking*.

shrink \'shringk\ *v.;* **shrank** \'shrangk\ or **shrunk** \'shrəngk\; **shrunk** \'shrəngk\ or **shrunk·en** \'shrəngk-n\; **shrink·ing.** **1** To withdraw or move away, as in fear or pain; to cower. **2** To make or become smaller. The sweater *shrank* when it was washed. **3** To refuse to take action, as from fear or disgust; as, to *shrink* from a quarrel. **4** To cause to shrink, as cloth.

CHECKUP

What are the principal parts of these verbs? In each case, why are they given or not given in your dictionary?

fly	look	speak	forsake
dot	float	hurry	journey
find	lasso	freeze	harmonize

Comparison of adjectives and adverbs. Comparatives and superlatives of adjectives and adverbs are sometimes given in this dictionary and sometimes not given. The rules that follow are general. Many times there will be little to choose between comparing with *-er* and *-est* and *more* and *most:*

1. They are not usually given when they are made by the simple addition of *-er* and *-est* to an unchanged entry word (as in *slow, slower, slowest*) or when *more* and *most* are placed before the entry word, or positive degree (as in *beautiful, more beautiful, most beautiful*).

2. They *are* given (provided they are in common use) when they are formed by doubling the final consonant of the positive and adding *-er* and *-est* (as in *big, bigger, biggest*), by dropping final *e* and adding *-er* and *-est* (as in *noble, nobler, noblest*), or by changing final *y* to *i* and adding *-er* and *-est* (as in *pretty, prettier, prettiest*).

3. They *are* given when they are entirely different words from the positive (as in *good, better, best*).

CHECKUP

Give the comparative and superlative of each word below. In each case, why are these forms listed or not listed in your dictionary?

ill	dark	thin	much	lively
fat	nice	short	many	loudly
bad	blue	early	little	rapid

Homographs (different words with the same spelling). Have you noticed that some words are entered more than once in your dictionary? Find *bay* as quickly as you can. How many different words are spelled b-a-y? You will see that a bay may be a body of water, a part of a building, a tree, the sound of an animal, or a color. You can understand how important it is to find the right homograph. If you are not looking at the right word, you cannot find the right meaning.

CHECKUP

1. How many entry words in this dictionary are spelled like each word below?

box	lock	scale	bound
egg	seal	chase	sorrel
row	hold	brake	capital
pelt	down	pupil	scuttle

2. For the spelling above that has four homographs, write a sentence to illustrate one meaning under each.
3. What do the six italic words mean in the paragraph below? Be sure to look at the right entry words.

A *tar* had been sent forward to see how *grave* the damage was. He reported that the *bark* was *fast* on a *shoal* with a hole in her *bow*.

Words with more than one meaning. You know that some of the words in this dictionary have only one meaning given, while others have several meanings given. Look once more at the five words spelled b-a-y. How many meanings are given for the first *bay?* For the second? For the third? For the fourth? Count carefully here and you will see that there are six meanings — three for the verb and three for the noun.

How many meanings are given altogether for *cover?* For *foul?* For *shoot?*

CHECKUP

Look up the italic word in each of the sentences below. Read all the definitions, from beginning to end. Then write the meaning which best fits the word as it is used in the sentence.

1. A large *body* of children marched in the parade.
2. Father is reading in his *den*.
3. We went for a *tramp* in the woods.
4. Broken bones *knit* slowly.
5. Most dogs *bolt* their food.
6. Screens *admit* air but not insects.
7. One word is printed in slanting *type*.
8. We found a good *spot* for our picnic.
9. I heard the *report* of a distant gun.
10. The cellar has been flooded by a broken *pipe*.

Now think up ten new sentences using each of these ten words with a different meaning.

Fitting the definition to the context. While *infinitesimal* can be used to describe something very small, and while a dwarf is a very small person, we would not think of describing a dwarf as an infinitesimal person. While a *hoax* is a kind of trick, we do not teach a dog to perform a hoax.

Since many words have various meanings, we must know which meaning of a word fits the context in which it is used. If someone asks you, \hwät iz t͟hə 'mē-ning əv 'kar-ət\, you cannot tell from the sound of the last word whether he means *carat*, *carrot*, or *caret*. If he asks you, "What is the meaning of c-a-r-a-t?" you still cannot tell him, because *carat* has two quite different meanings. If, however, he asks, "What is 14-carat gold?" or "What is a two-carat diamond?" he has given you sufficient context to pinpoint the definition of *carat*. In relation to diamonds a carat is "a unit of weight". In relation to gold a carat is "a twenty-fourth part". These two meanings are numbered 1 and 2 in the definition of *carat* to set them clearly apart.

CHECKUP

Look up the italicized words in the following sentences. Which numbered meaning fits the context? Give the part of speech of each word and the number of its definition.

1. I am *anxious* to see you.
2. I am *anxious* because I haven't seen him lately.
3. He lives three *blocks* from here.
4. She is not likely to *break* her promise.
5. I need a new *cartridge* for my pen.
6. The miner staked out his *claim*.
7. Oxygen combines more easily with some *elements* than with others.
8. The license will be granted after you have filled out this *form*.

HOW DOES YOUR DICTIONARY HELP YOU WITH MEANINGS?

Look up the word *fine* as quickly as possible and answer the following questions:

1. Why are there two entries spelled f-i-n-e?
2. What do we call different words having the same spelling?
3. As what four parts of speech may *fine* be used?
4. How many meanings are given altogether for these four parts of speech?
5. What do the heavy dashes (—) mean?
6. How many examples of the use of *fine* are there?
7. Why are the comparative and superlative forms of the adjective given?
8. Why are the principal parts of the verb included?
9. Why are there only two principal parts instead of three?
10. Why is the plural of the noun *fine* not included?
11. What is the part of speech of *fine* and of *fined* in the sentence below?
    He had a *fine* trip except that he was *fined* for speeding.
12. Why is *fine art* listed as a separate entry?
13. Why is the plural of *fine art* not given?
14. What are the comparative and superlative forms of the adverb *finely?*
15. Why is the plural of *finery* given?
16. What is the part of speech of *fining* (listed on the next page)?
17. What special meaning does the plural of *finance* have?
18. What part of speech is *financial?*

19. What part of speech is its run-on entry?
20. On the opposite page, why is the plural of *Filipino* given?

Now find the word *subject* and answer these questions:

1. As what three parts of speech may *subject* be used?
2. How many meanings are included altogether?
3. How many examples of the use of *subject* are given?
4. Why is there a respelling after the second heavy dash but not after the first heavy dash?
5. On which syllable does the accent fall in the italicized words below? The king's *subjects* were often *subjected* to severe punishment.
6. What is the part of speech and definition number of *subjects* and of *subjected* above?
7. What are the comparative and superlative forms of the adjective *subject?* Either one may be used in this sentence: Which boy is — to colds?
8. Why are these forms not given?
9. Why is the plural of the noun not included?
10. Why are the principal parts of the verb omitted?

SPECIAL HELPS WITH MEANING

Prefixes and suffixes. In such words as *reappear*, *recapture*, *rediscover*, and *reload* you find the same prefix (*re-*) applied to different root words, all with similar effect. These words mean "appear again", "capture again", "discover again", and "load again". The prefix *re-* usually means "again" or "back".

In such words as *comfortable*, *marketable*, *pleasurable*, and *readable* you find the same suffix (*-able*) applied to different root words, all with similar effect. These words mean "capable of giving comfort", "capable of being marketed", "capable of giving pleasure", and "capable of being read". The suffix *-able* may mean "capable of giving or being", "fit or worthy to be", "able or liable to", or "tending to".

Our language is greatly enriched by means of its many prefixes and suffixes, which change the meanings of the words to which they are attached. A word such as *immeasurable*, for example, containing a prefix (*im-*) meaning "not" and a suffix (*-able*) meaning "capable of being", takes the place in our language of a whole phrase, "not capable of being measured".

A familiarity with the meanings of the most common prefixes and suffixes is essential to the development of an adequate vocabulary for listening and speaking, as well as for reading and writing. You don't have time to look up the prefixes, the root words, and the suffixes when a radio commentator announces that there are "*unmistakable* signs of *uneasiness* in the *nondemocratic* nations". He expects you to understand him instantly. How well you understand him depends upon how well you understand his use of prefixes and suffixes, as well as the root words to which he applies them.

This dictionary defines prefixes such as *un-* and suffixes such as *-ness*. You will find them alphabetically arranged among the entry words.

CHECKUP

Look up the twenty-three prefixes and suffixes used in the following words and write the meanings they have in these particular words. Remember that a word can have more than one suffix.

heroic	antitoxin	impersonal
pianist	inactively	interaction
reliant	poisonous	subdivision
rapidity	friendship	unreasonable
falsehood	dishonesty	childishness

Etymologies of words. Sometimes a knowledge of the history of a word, or even of its source from another language, adds significantly to the meanings provided by the definitions. A reference to the history or source of a word, called an etymology, is given in brackets for some words (*aardvark* and *abrupt*, for example).

CHECKUP

1. What is the Italian meaning of *a cappella?*
2. Is the origin of the word *acre* English or foreign?
3. What is the literal meaning, in French, of *adieu?*
4. What is the origin and the original meaning of *alias?*
5. What is the etymology of *ampere?*
6. What is the meaning of the Greek and Latin words from which *asterisk* has been derived?
7. What was the original Latin meaning of *doctor?*
8. What was the literal meaning of the Dutch word from which *etch* was derived?

Historical order of definitions. "The people crowded into the car". What picture formed in your mind when you saw that word *car?* For some people it would be a picture of an automobile; for others, a picture of a railroad coach or a streetcar. If you were standing in a tall building, you might think of an elevator. It is most unlikely that you would think of an ancient Roman war chariot, and yet "war chariot" is the first thing specifically referred to under the definition of *car* in this dictionary.

The definitions in this dictionary are generally listed in historical order. The meaning first used, in the history of the English language, is very likely to be the one that appears first in the definition. And the most recent meaning to be applied to the word will probably be the one that appears last in the definition.

CHECKUP

1. What meaning of *body* was first used?
2. What connection is there between this meaning and meaning number 6?
3. How is the third meaning of *bazaar* more general than the original meaning?
4. Read the definitions of *awful.* How is the original meaning stronger than the latest one?
5. Which meaning of *awful* applies to disasters? Which applies to clothes?
6. When you say you will be there *soon,* do you mean without delay, or before long?
7. What is the original meaning of *soon?*
8. Which numbered definition fits its use in the sentence, "I would just as *soon* stay home"?

Synonyms. Sometimes a definition may include one or more synonyms, or words that mean about the same as the entry word. When we look up *broad*, we find the synonyms *wide*, *spacious*, *open*, *clear*, *plain*, *obvious*, *coarse*, *indelicate*, *large*, and *extended*. These words are not necessarily synonyms of each other. A joke, for example, may be *broad*, *coarse*, or *indelicate*, but not *spacious*. A river may be *broad* or *wide*, and still *hidden* instead of *obvious*, and *short* rather than *extended*.

After some definitions, comparisons of synonyms are provided, following a light dash. The verb *abandon*, for example, is compared with *desert* and *forsake*. Cross-references to this paragraph are given at *desert* and *forsake* for the benefit of the person who looks up one of these words instead of *abandon*.

CHECKUP

1. At what entry will you find a discussion of synonyms for *divert?* For *condemn?* For *argue?*
2. Which is the strongest word of these three: *captivate, charm, or fascinate?* Where did you find the comparison?
3. When you teach a dog a trick, do your give him *education* or *training?* What is the difference?
4. When you have done something wrong, is an *apology* or an *excuse* expected of you? At which entry are the two words compared?
5. Where are synonyms for the verb *excuse* discussed?
6. What is the difference between a *fretful* person and a *cross* person? Where did you have to look to find out?

Usage notes. If someone yelled, "Avast!" or "Belay!" would you know what to do? What kind of person would use these words to mean "stop"? In the definition of each of these words you will find a note, preceded by a light dash, explaining this special usage. Such explanations are called usage notes.

CHECKUP

1. What is the special meaning of *delicatessen* when it is used as a plural? What is the word for two or more delicatessen stores?
2. If you had a pleasant time at a party, would you say, "I had a *clement* time"? In what sense is *clement* used to mean "pleasant"?
3. Would you use *cuneiform* to describe a wedge-shaped piece of cheese? In what sense does *cuneiform* mean "wedge-shaped"?
4. Do we speak of Americans in the plural as *the American*, as we speak of *the British* or *the French?* Write sentences using *English* and *Irish* in this sense.
5. If you defined the adjective *lucrative* in an examination as "bringing in lucre" would you expect to receive full credit? If not, why not?

Usage labels. What is the meaning of *archaic* as defined in this dictionary? Look up the word *affright* to see how it is labeled. What do *dialect* and *slang* mean? What is the British meaning of *davenport?* The American meaning?

When *archaic*, *dial.* (for *dialect*), *slang*, *British*, or *Scottish* is printed in italics before a definition, it is called a usage label. It tells how the word defined is limited in its use.

CHECKUP

What is the usage label and the meaning (in that particular use) of each of these words?

sooth	corker	afeard	erstwhile
petrol	corking	allergy	aerodrome
lift	pottage	methinks	bust (v., n.)
ken (v.)	burn (n.)	barrister	galligaskins

Fistnotes. Interesting, helpful notes regarding the uses or meanings of a word are sometimes preceded by the hand-shaped symbol ☞. Such notes are called fistnotes.

CHECKUP

1. Does the fistnote under *ain't* define this contraction or explain its use?
2. How does the fistnote under *bear* clarify the use of *born* and *borne?*
3. Is *brethren* the correct plural of *brother* in such a sentence as, "My sister and my two brethren are helping my parents"? How may *brethren* be used?
4. What is the meaning of *and* in "Let's go out and play"?

Idioms and phrases. You have learned that many open compounds of two or more words, such as *cream of tartar*, are listed as main entries in this dictionary. But there are numerous other phrases and expressions, such as *on the fence*, that cannot be listed alphabetically as main entries. These expressions are often called idioms. Each language has its own idioms.

Look up the word *idiom* and decide which definition fits the expression *on the fence.* Does this expression mean literally "on top of the fence"? Look under the most important word, *fence*, and you will find the meaning after the noun definitions, following a light dash. How do you suppose *on the fence* came to mean "undecided"? Could you have guessed its meaning if you had never heard it used or seen it in print?

Many verbs, such as *take*, have special meanings when followed by words like *in*, *out*, *to*, *from*, *up*, *down*, *off*, *on*, and *back*. How many idioms are defined under the verb *take?* Under the verb *go?* Under the verb *put?*

CHECKUP

Write sentences correctly using the idioms that are listed under the entries below. The number of idioms under each word is shown in parentheses.

pull (2)	short (1)	course (1)
step (6)	prick (1)	feather (2)
mark (2)	degree (2)	account (3)

HOW USEFUL ARE THE SPECIAL HELPS TO YOU?

1. What does each prefix and suffix in the following words mean?

actor	nonstop	foretell	starvation	recall	midday
freedom	prepayment	golden	hopeful	westward	hopelessness

2. Give the etymology of each word below.

i.e.	Sunday	manual	gladiolus	N.B.	August
gingham	postscript	circus	good-by	farewell	trench mouth

3. For each of these words, give the usage label and the meaning in that particular sense:

aye	lief	gaol	croft	throw	quickie	eld	kirk	mere
loony	quick	quality	nay	toil	leech	belike	kirtle	egghead

4. Name two synonyms for each of these words and use all three in sentences that show the difference:

lazy victory heroism refuse (v). thrifty business fling (v.) alert (adj.)

5. Write sentences using all the idioms given under each of these entries:

pay (3) come (4) break (5)

HOW SKILLFUL ARE YOU NOW IN USING THIS DICTIONARY?

1. Time yourself in locating the twelve words below, remembering to look only at the guide words till you find the right page. See if you can beat your own record.

infinite	alluvial	magistrate	zoological	volcanic	leniency
saltpeter	galvanize	criterion	tinderbox	jubilation	uproarious

2. Which of the following spellings are correct?

boxes, boxxes	buses, busses	skimed, skimmed	indices, indexes
fish, fishes	finded, found	allied, allyed	drought, drouth
draft, draught	dwelled, dwelt	potatos, potatoes	picnicer, picnicker
defying, defiing	fining, finning	canoeing, canoing	destroied, destroyed
prettiest, prettyest	repeated, repeatted	traveler, traveller	top-notch, topnotch
travelogue, travelog	analyses, analysises	pianoes, pianos	

3. Write each of these words, indicating all the points at which it may be divided at the end of a line. After each word put the number of *spoken* syllables it has.

area	usual	ebony	anybody	dressed	naughty
oral	arena	utopia	athletic	dressing	watched
idea	usurp	utensil	business	obituary	wretched

4. Respell each of these words without looking at your dictionary. Be careful to include the hyphens and stress marks, as well as the correct vowel and consonant symbols. Then check with your dictionary.

   ouch glider German dictionary using smooth oilcloth photograph

5. Write out in full all the respellings given for each of these words. The numbers indicate how many pronunciations are given.

   where (5) sentence (3) histamine (2) scenery (2) dangerous (2) elasticity (2)

6. For each italicized word in the sentences below give the respelling, part of speech, number of the corresponding definition, plural or plurals (if any), principal parts (if any), and comparative and superlative (if any).

   a. The boys caught several *bass* in the ocean.
   b. Is your father a *bass* or a tenor?
   c. Pearl Harbor is a naval *base.*
   d. Betraying a friend is a *base* thing to do.
   e. How long does it take to *digest* a big dinner?
   f. Here is a *digest* of that article.
   g. Jane and Mary have *separate* rooms.
   h. Does the Mississippi *separate* the two cities?
   i. Many young people like to chew *gum.*
   j. Jim's *gum* is sore where the tooth was pulled out.

THE HISTORY OF YOUR DICTIONARY

NOAH WEBSTER AND HIS DICTIONARIES

This dictionary, which bears the distinguished label *A Merriam-Webster*, has a proud history that goes back well over a hundred years. The first of its line appeared at a time when the United States was a young nation, rejoicing in the success of the American Revolution.

This dictionary which you are now using developed from the work of America's first lexicographer, Noah Webster. A zealous patriot, Webster felt that the people of the United States needed a dictionary of their language — not a dictionary of English as it was spoken or spelled in Great Britain. In patriotic fervor Webster argued against continuing dependence upon Great Britain: "We have thrown off the shackles of her government, why not her language also?"

With devoted singleness of purpose Webster spent most of his life making two dictionaries. His goal was the recording of American language for Americans. He had no assistants to lighten his laborious task and no assurance of financial reward for years of hard work.

Noah Webster was born in West Hartford, Connecticut, October 16, 1758. Although he attended the village school, tutored privately, and graduated from Yale, Webster was largely a self-taught man. He studied all his

life, devoting his energies to language — its origins, its spelling, its sounds, its meanings.

As a young man Noah Webster lived through the exciting days of the Revolution. He even went with the militia toward Saratoga but turned back when word came that the fighting was over. Perhaps more than others of his day Webster was carried away with enthusiasm for America and all things American. He disliked the British then and, in a sense, continued to fight them and their language all his life.

During the few years that he taught school, Webster found that the textbooks were not adequate for young American scholars. Since nearly all books were shipped from England, the content of the texts centered around British life with references to the king, parliament, and other objectionable or inappropriate subjects. Then, too, books were hard to obtain, for trade with England diminished greatly just after the Revolution.

Webster recognized the need for American schoolbooks and set about to fill that need. In 1783 he found a publisher for a spelling book — later called the *Blue-Backed Speller*. This little book treated the letters and their sounds as used by Americans and emphasized patriotic and moral virtues. So famous did this speller become that every peddler carried it in his pack, every store stocked it along with food staples, and every family bought it for their simple home library. The *Blue-Backed Speller* is still sold today.

In the years immediately following the publication of his speller, Noah Webster pursued many interests. He fought for uniform copyright laws. He began a career as lecturer — something he enjoyed doing all his life. He published pamphlets which revealed a vast knowledge of government and statesmanship. He continued in law, the profession for which he had studied, and he even served as an editor of several newspapers in New York. His interest in science produced a two-volume work remarkable for its time: *A Brief History of Epidemic and Pestilential Diseases*.

During a prolonged stay in Philadelphia Webster frequently talked with Benjamin Franklin, who was also interested in the language as spoken and written by Americans. The two men agreed that a reform in English spelling was highly desirable.

Noah Webster was well equipped to write the first dictionary of the American language. He always took notes on words he met in his reading and failed to find in English dictionaries. He traveled through the colonies by stage, by boat, and on horseback, listening to people talk and noting the words they used, how they used them, and how they said them.

In 1806 Webster's first dictionary, a work of some 400 pages, was published. It bore the awesome title *A Compendious Dictionary of the English Language*. Noteworthy because it was the first dictionary in the United States, it still was only a start toward the great publication that was to come.

After publishing a grammar in 1807, Webster began the task that was to consume his time and efforts for the next twenty years — the making of his *American Dictionary of the English Language*, 1828. Noah Webster worked diligently to make his *American Dictionary* more useful to Americans than the most authoritative work of English origin: Dr. Samuel Johnson's dictionary published in 1755.

Webster observed that the language was constantly changing and believed that those changes should be recorded. He states: "The process of a living language is like the motion of a broad river, which flows with a slow, silent, irresistible current". He also argued that "a living language must keep pace with improvements in knowledge and with the multiplication of ideas".

Webster prepared his dictionary for the

plain reader. He considered it to be a vast schoolbook. His goal was to write a book that would make all other books of its class unnecessary. Above everything else Webster made good the title of the dictionary by eliminating many references applicable only in Great Britain and by constantly emphasizing American usage.

The *American Dictionary* was widely acclaimed on its publication. It was America's first work of impressive scholarship. It became a chief factor in unifying the language of a new nation.

Noah Webster read the final proofs of his great dictionary at the age of 70. During these years he had supported himself and his family largely on royalties from the sale of the *Blue-Backed Speller*. He lived to be 84, continuing his literary and lexicographical interests to the very end.

CHECKUP

1. How does Noah Webster's life reflect his patriotism?
2. Why is the adjective *versatile* frequently used to describe Noah Webster?
3. What contributions did Noah Webster make toward the education of young people?
4. How did Noah Webster collect evidence for his dictionary entries?

NOAH WEBSTER AND AMERICAN ENGLISH

Noah Webster influenced for all time the English language as used by Americans. He brought order to spelling and usage in the early days of the United States. He contributed much to the homogeneous quality of American English today — an English that is fairly uniform and not broken up into many provincial dialects.

The changes in spelling and usage which Webster effected in his *American Dictionary* are interesting to observe:

1. The letter *k* was dropped from such words as *public* and *music* (not *publick, musick*).
2. The letter *u* was omitted from such words as *honor* and *favor* (not *honour, favour*).
3. The letters *er* were substituted for letters *re* in such words as *center* and *sepulcher* (not *centre, sepulchre*).
4. The final consonant of verbs having the accent on the first syllable or on a syllable preceding the last was not doubled before endings: *travel, traveler, traveling* (not *traveller, travelling*).
5. New words which had appeared in American English were included: *applesauce, moccasin, scow, skunk,* and many others. None of these words had previously been entered in Dr. Johnson's English dictionary.

In addition to the Americanization of many entries Noah Webster made two other great contributions to lexicography. Perhaps his greatest distinction lies in the completeness and accuracy of his definitions. His strength is said to derive from the fact that he was "a born definer".

Another contribution to lexicography was Webster's inclusion of detailed etymologies — the histories of words. Webster claimed to have "mastered twenty languages" in order to substantiate his etymologies. Be that as it may, he surrounded himself with dictionaries in various languages and attempted for the first time to write scholarly etymologies.

As for the new words which Webster added to his dictionary, he himself enumerates the words under five heads:

1. Words of common use, formerly omitted from Dr. Johnson's literature-centered dictionary

2. Participles of verbs
3. Terms of frequent occurrence in historical works
4. Legal terms
5. Terms in the arts and sciences

In summary, then, Noah Webster may be credited with the following contributions which made his *American Dictionary* superior to the highly regarded English dictionary of Dr. Johnson:

more words
American spelling and pronunciation
American usage
more exact definitions
fuller etymologies

CHECKUP

1. In what way are users of American English indebted to Noah Webster?
2. Name three spelling changes that appeared in the *American Dictionary*.
3. What were Noah Webster's greatest contributions to lexicography?
4. What kinds of new words appeared in the *American Dictionary?*

THE MERRIAM-WEBSTER DICTIONARIES

The name *Webster* is immortalized by the man's scholarly efforts to produce a dictionary for American usage. The name *Merriam* became associated with the name *Webster* in 1843. In that year the Merriam brothers, George and Charles, owners of a printing office and bookstore in Springfield, Massachusetts, arranged to revise and print the 1841 edition of the *American Dictionary*. After acquiring all rights from Webster's heirs and an Amherst company, G. & C. Merriam Company gathered together a well-trained staff of editors and produced their first product: *An American Dictionary of the English Language*, 1847.

Today as in those early days G. & C. Merriam Company insists upon scholarship. It states decisively the function of dictionary makers: To record the language as it is used by the majority of its users, not to create it or legislate concerning it.

In place of one dedicated man, Noah Webster, who jotted down what he saw and heard, a large staff reads widely in all areas of written communication and listens to all forms of oral communication.

This Merriam-Webster editorial staff is comprised of scholars from every part of the United States, representing many different universities and cultural backgrounds. Former college professors now contribute their scholarship to dictionary making. Included on the staff are specialists in varied fields: linguistics, pronunciation, dialect, etymology, sports, science, religion, music, and so on.

The vast amount of information acquired by the editorial staff is recorded on cards which make up a unique "citation file" insured for over a million dollars. A citation is the quotation of a passage *exactly* as it was written or spoken, with source and date.

General readers and specialists read everything available printed in the English language: fiction and nonfiction, journals, magazines, reviews, reports, mail-order catalogs, menus, schoolbooks, word lists supplied by school systems and testing bureaus. The staff draws upon its own editorial library, university libraries, and public libraries including the Springfield (Massachusetts) City Library.

Similarly, pronunciation editors listen attentively to the words spoken by educated people. They record radio, television, and live speeches for evidence in the citation files.

Each word entered in this very dictionary has traveled a long, arduous route. First, it was marked in various contexts by readers who wanted to determine (1) what kinds of matter included the word; (2) how the word was used; (3) by whom the word was used; and (4) when the word was used. Next, the word in the marked material was sent to assistants for photographing or typing on citation slips. File clerks then sorted the citation slips and filed them for future analysis. Such accumulated evidence helps the editors decide which words ought to be included in the dictionary and how they should be defined.

Then came the time for an editor to define the word. He first drew the citation slips from the files and studied the word to determine many things: scope of meaning, currency of use, level of use, etymology, pronunciation, variant spellings, usage, part of speech. Then the editor assembled the complete entry. His work passed on to a reviewing editor, to a supervisory editor, to a copyreader, and finally to a printer.

The editors recognize, as did Noah Webster, that the vocabulary is constantly changing in meaning and acquiring new senses. The scholarly editing of the Merriam-Webster staff keeps the dictionary up to date by:

1. Inclusion of new words in the language
2. Recording of shifts of meaning in established words
3. Indication of transference of application from one subject to another, as certain senses now used in both radio and television

From this brief account of dictionary making today, you can readily see how the goals toward which Noah Webster aspired have been realized. Today, Merriam-Webster dictionaries are used in law courts, international councils, universities, and schools everywhere.

CHECKUP

1. Why is the name *Merriam* associated with the name *Webster?*
2. How was evidence for each word in your dictionary collected?
3. How do staff lexicographers use the citation files at G. & C. Merriam?
4. How is your dictionary kept up to date?
5. What significance lies in the label *A Merriam-Webster?*

A DICTIONARY OF THE ENGLISH LANGUAGE

a \'ā\ *n.; pl.* **a's** \'āz\. The first letter of the alphabet.

a \ə, (')ā\ *adj.* or *indefinite article.* **1** One. Suddenly *a* man ran by. **2** In each; for every; as, twice *a* week; a dollar *a* dozen. **3** One kind of; some kind of. Copper is *a* metal. **4** Any; each; as, too much for *a* man to bear.

☞ *a* is used (instead of *an*) before words beginning with a consonant sound.

A or **a.** Abbreviation for *acre.*

aard·vark \'ärd-ˌvärk, 'ȧrd-ˌvȧrk\ *n.* [From Afrikaans, meaning "earth pig".] A mammal of Africa that burrows in the ground and lives on ants that it catches with its long, slimy tongue.

ab- or **abs-.** A prefix that can mean: from, away, off, away from, as in *abduct* or *abstain.*

aback \ə-'bak\ *adv. Archaic.* Back; backward. — **taken aback.** Checked suddenly, as in motion, action, or hopes; surprised and upset; disconcerted; as, *taken aback* by his unexpected disapproval.

ab·a·cus \'ab-ə-kəs\ *n.; pl.* **ab·a·cus·es** \-kə-səz\. A frame on which beads are moved along rods or wires in counting.

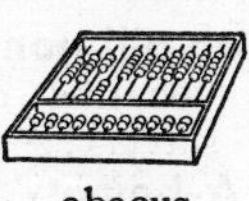
abacus

abaft \ə-'baft\ *prep.* Toward the stern from; to the rear of; behind; as, standing *abaft* the bridge. — *adv.* Toward or at the stern; aft.

ab·a·lo·ne \ˌab-l-'ō-nē\ *n.* A mollusk with a slightly spiral shell perforated along the edge and lined with mother-of-pearl.

aban·don \ə-'ban-dən\ *v.* **1** To give up completely; to forsake; to desert; as, to *abandon* a sinking ship. **2** To give (oneself) up without attempt at self-control; as, to *abandon* oneself to grief.

— The words *desert* and *forsake* are synonyms of *abandon: abandon* may suggest the complete giving up of something, often to the mercy of someone else; *desert* often implies the abandonment of something to which one has certain obligations; *forsake* generally suggests the breaking off of association with something familiar or dear.

— *n.* A yielding completely to one's natural impulses; a throwing off of customary or expected restraint; careless freedom or ease. — **aban·don·ment,** *n.*

aban·doned \ə-'ban-dənd\ *adj.* **1** Deserted; forsaken; as, an *abandoned* house. **2** Wholly given up to wickedness or vice; as, an *abandoned* criminal.

abase \ə-'bās\ *v.;* **abased; abas·ing.** To lower in rank or position; to humble; to degrade; as, to refuse to *abase* oneself by begging for mercy. — **abase·ment,** *n.*

abash \ə-'bash\ *v.* To embarrass, confuse, or shame; to disconcert; as, a child *abashed* by harsh words. — For synonyms see *embarrass.* — **abash·ment,** *n.*

abate \ə-'bāt\ *v.;* **abat·ed; abat·ing.** To make or to become less, as in amount, number, or force; to reduce; to decrease; as, to *abate* the severity of a punishment. The storm *abated.* — **abate·ment,** *n.*

ab·at·toir \'ab-ə-ˌtwär, -ˌtwȧr\ *n.* A slaughterhouse.

ab·bey \'ab-ē\ *n.; pl.* **ab·beys. 1** A monastery governed by a man called an **ab·bot** \'ab-ət\. **2** A convent for women governed by a woman called an **ab·bess** \'ab-əs\. **3** A church that once belonged to an abbey; as, Westminster *Abbey.*

abbr. or **abbrev.** Abbreviation for *abbreviation.*

ab·bre·vi·ate \ə-'brē-vē-ˌāt\ *v.;* **ab·bre·vi·at·ed; ab·bre·vi·at·ing.** To put in a shorter form or to make briefer; as, to *abbreviate* "year" to "yr."

ab·bre·vi·a·tion \ə-ˌbrē-vē-'āsh-n\ *n.* **1** A making shorter. **2** A shortened form of a word or phrase, such as *in.* for *inch,* and *U.S.A.* for *United States of America.*

ab·di·cate \'ab-də-ˌkāt\ *v.;* **ab·di·cat·ed; ab·di·cat·ing. 1** To give up or to resign a position of power or trust; to renounce. **2** To give up a throne.

ab·di·ca·tion \ˌab-də-'kāsh-n\ *n.* The giving up of a position of power or authority; especially, a king's giving up his throne.

ab·do·men \'ab-də-mən, ab-'dō-mən\ *n.* **1** The lower part of the vertebrate trunk, containing the stomach and other digestive organs; the belly. **2** The back or hind section of the body of an insect.

ab·dom·i·nal \ab-'däm-ən-l\ *adj.* Relating to or located in the abdomen; as, *abdominal* organs; an *abdominal* operation. — **ab·dom·i·nal·ly** \-l-ē\ *adv.*

ab·duct \ab-'dəkt\ *v.* To take a person away unlawfully and, usually, by force. — **ab·duc·tion** \-'dəksh-n\ *n.* — **ab·duc·tor** \-'dəkt-r\ *n.*

abeam \ə-'bēm\ *adv.* Off to one side of a ship at right angles to her keel.

abed \ə-'bed\ *adv.* In bed.

ab·er·ra·tion \ˌab-r-'āsh-n\ *n.* **1** The action of wandering away or going astray, especially from something expected; as, an *aberration* from the truth. **2** A wandering or disorder of the mind; as, a mind showing symptoms of *aberration.*

abet \ə-'bet\ *v.;* **abet·ted; abet·ting.** To encourage or aid, especially in doing wrong; as, to *abet* a person in committing a crime. — **abet·tor** or **abet·ter** \ə-'bet-r\ *n.*

abey·ance \ə-'bā-ən(t)s\ *n.* A condition of suspended action, progress, or development; temporary inactivity. For the time being, the plan was held in *abeyance.*

ab·hor \ab-'hȯr\ *v.;* **ab·horred; ab·hor·ring.** To shrink from with disgust; to hate; to detest; as, to *abhor* the thought of murder. — **ab·hor·rence** \-'hȯr-ən(t)s, -'här-\ *n.*

ab·hor·rent \ab-'hȯr-ənt, -'här-\ *adj.* Detestable; repulsive; as, an act *abhorrent* to any decent person.

abide \ə-'bīd\ *v.;* **abode** \ə-'bōd\ or **abid·ed; abid·ing. 1** To remain; to stay; as, to *abide* in the city. **2** To last; to endure; as, love that *abides* forever. **3** To wait for; as, to *abide* the coming of summer. **4** To bear patiently; to put up with; as, unable to *abide* bad manners. — **abide by.** To be faithful to; to accept the terms of; as, to *abide by* one's promise; to *abide by* the law.

abid·ing \ə-'bīd-ing\ *adj.* Lasting; permanent; as, an *abiding* friendship.

abil·i·ty \ə-'bil-ət-ē\ *n.; pl.* **abil·i·ties. 1** The condition of being able; power to do or to accomplish; as, the *ability* of a magnet to attract iron. **2** Skill in doing; as, a workman of great *ability.* **3** A natural talent, not learned by study or practice; a gift; as, a child of promising artistic *abilities.*

— The words *aptitude* and *talent* are synonyms of *ability: ability* generally suggests a natural power to perform certain tasks; *aptitude* usually refers to a quickness to learn and natural liking for certain fields; *talent* usually suggests great ability, especially in a creative field, which can be improved by study or practice.

ab·ject \'ab-ˌjekt, ab-'jekt\ *adj.* [From Latin *abjectus* originally meaning "thrown away".] Very low in spirit or hope; wretched; cringing; as, *abject* misery; an *abject* coward. — **ab·ject·ly,** *adv.*

ab·jure \ab-'ju̇r\ *v.;* **ab·jured; ab·jur·ing.** To promise solemnly to give up; to swear to give up; to repudiate; as, to *abjure* the use of force in settling disputes.

ablaze \ə-'blāz\ *adj.* **1** On fire; as, a log *ablaze* in the fireplace. **2** As if on fire; brilliant; as, autumn trees *ablaze* with color.

able \'āb-l\ *adj.;* **abler** \'āb-l(-)ər\; **ablest** \'āb-l(-)əst\. **1** Having enough power, skill, or resources to do something; as, *able* to swim; not *able* to buy new clothes. **2** Competent; skillful; as, an *able* musician.

-a·ble \əb-l\. A suffix that can mean: **1** Capable of being, or fit or worthy to be, as in *readable* or *eatable.* **2** Tending or given to, as in *peaceable.* **3** Able or liable to, as in *perishable.*

able-bod·ied \'āb-l-'bäd-ēd\ *adj.* Having a sound, strong body; physically fit.

ab·lu·tion \ab-'lüsh-n\ *n.* A washing or cleansing, as of the hands in a religious ceremony.

ably \'āb-lē\ *adv.* In an able manner; with ability.

ab·ne·ga·tion \ˌab-nē-'gāsh-n\ *n.* A denial; a renouncing; self-denial; as, the *abnegation* of luxuries.

ab·nor·mal \ab-'nȯrm-l\ *adj.* **1** Different from most persons or things of the same kind or group; clearly above or below the usual level; as, an *abnormal* child. **2** Unusual; extraordinary; strangely irregular; as, *abnormal* weather. — **ab·nor·mal·ly** \-'nȯrm-l-ē\ *adv.*

ab·nor·mal·i·ty \ˌab-ˌnȯr-'mal-ət-ē\ *n.; pl.* **ab·nor·mal·i·ties. 1** The state of being abnormal. **2** An abnormal thing or happening.

aboard \ə-'bōrd, ə-'bȯrd\ *adv.* or *prep.* On board; in or on a boat, train, bus, or airplane.

abode \ə-'bōd\. A past tense and past part. of *abide.* — *n.* The place where one stays or lives; a dwelling; residence; as, one's *abode* in town.

abol·ish \ə-'bäl-ish\ *v.* To do away with; to put an end to; as, to *abolish* an unjust law. — **abol·ish·ment,** *n.*

ab·o·li·tion \ˌab-l-'ish-n\ *n.* The act of abolishing; a complete destroying or doing away with; as, the *abolition* of slavery — sometimes used alone to mean "abolition of Negro slavery".

ab·o·li·tion·ist \ˌab-l-'ish-n-əst\ *n.* A person advocating or favoring abolition, especially of slavery. — **ab·o·li·tion·ism** \-n-ˌiz-m\ *n.*

A-bomb \'ā-ˌbäm\ *n.* An atomic bomb.

abom·i·na·ble \ə-'bäm-ə-nəb-l\ *adj.* **1** Hateful; disgusting; as, *abominable* cruelties. **2** Extremely disagreeable; as, *abominable* weather. — **abom·i·na·bly** \-nə-blē\ *adv.*

abom·i·nate \ə-'bäm-ə-ˌnāt\ *v.;* **abom·i·nat·ed; abom·i·nat·ing.** To feel great dislike for; to loathe, detest, or abhor.

abom·i·na·tion \ə-ˌbäm-ə-'nāsh-n\ *n.* **1** A feeling of disgust and loathing. **2** Something disgusting and hateful. Lack of respect for the rights of others is an *abomination* to decent people.

ab·o·rig·i·nal \ˌab-r-'ij-n(-)əl\ *adj.* **1** First; original; native; as, the *aboriginal* tribes of America. **2** Of or relating to aborigines; as, *aboriginal* languages. — For synonyms see *native.* — **ab·o·rig·i·nal·ly** \-n(-)ə-lē\ *adv.*

ab·o·rig·i·nes \ˌab-r-ˈij-n-(ˌ)ēz\ *n. pl.; sing.* **ab·o·rig·i·ne** \-n-(ˌ)ē\. The earliest known inhabitants of a country.

abor·tion \ə-ˈbȯrsh-n\ *n.* **1** A premature birth. **2** Any project or action that fails to reach full development; a complete failure.

abor·tive \ə-ˈbȯrt-iv\ *adj.* **1** Failing to achieve a desired end; unsuccessful; as, an *abortive* attempt. **2** Imperfectly formed or developed; rudimentary.

abound \ə-ˈbau̇nd\ *v.* **1** To be plentiful. Opportunities to go swimming *abound* during summer vacation. **2** To be well supplied. These books *abound* with pictures.

about \ə-ˈbau̇t\ *adv.* **1** On all sides; here and there; as, to wander *about.* **2** Approximately; as, in *about* three years. **3** Almost; as, *about* ready to go. **4** Half around; as, to face *about.* **5** In rotation. Turn *about* is fair play. — *prep.* **1** On every side of; as, to look *about* you. **2** By or on one's person; as, to keep your wits *about* you. **3** Here and there in; as, to roam *about* the world. **4** On the verge of; in the act of; as, *about* to leap. **5** Of; concerning; as, to hear *about* it. **6** In connection with; as, something peculiar *about* him.

about-face \ə-ˈbau̇t-ˈfās\ *n.* The act of turning round and facing in the opposite direction; a reversal of position or attitude. — *v.;* **about-faced**; **about-fac·ing**. To perform an about-face.

above \ə-ˈbəv\ *adv.* **1** At a higher point; overhead; as, planes flying high *above.* **2** In a preceding place, as of a book. **3** In a position of superior rank or power; as, to appeal to the court *above.* — *prep.* **1** In or to a higher place than; higher than; over; as, *above* the earth. **2** Farther up or along than; beyond; as, the house just *above* the school. **3** Superior to. A captain is *above* a lieutenant. **4** Too great or good to stoop to or be subject to; as, to be *above* taking unfair advantage; a man *above* criticism. **5** Greater than in number or amount; as, to make a score well *above* the average.

above·board \ə-ˈbəv-ˌbōrd, -ˌbȯrd\ *adj.* or *adv.* Honest; straightforward.

ab·ra·ca·dab·ra \ˌab-rə-kə-ˈdab-rə\ *n.* **1** A word said to have magic power, as in preventing disease. **2** Rapid, confused talk; gibberish.

abrade \ə-ˈbrād\ *v.;* **abrad·ed**; **abrad·ing**. To rub off or scrape off; to wear away by friction.

abra·sion \ə-ˈbrāzh-n\ *n.* **1** A rubbing or wearing away; as, a coin worn down by *abrasion.* **2** A place where the surface has been rubbed or scraped off; as, an *abrasion* on one's knee.

abra·sive \ə-ˈbrā-siv, -ziv\ *adj.* Having the effect of abrading; producing abrasion. — *n.* A substance, as emery, for grinding and polishing.

abreast \ə-ˈbrest\ *adj.* or *adv.* **1** Side by side; in an even line; as, to walk four abreast. **2** Up to a certain level or line; as, to keep *abreast* of the times.

abridge \ə-ˈbrij\ *v.;* **abridged**; **abridg·ing**. **1** To diminish; to make less; as, laws that *abridge* persons' liberties. **2** To shorten in length of time; as, to *abridge* one's stay at the seashore. **3** To shorten by omitting words; as, to *abridge* a report; an *abridged* dictionary.

abridg·ment or **abridge·ment** \ə-ˈbrij-mənt\ *n.* **1** The action of abridging. **2** A shortened form, as of a written work.

abroad \ə-ˈbrȯd\ *adv.* **1** In or to a foreign country; as, to travel *abroad.* **2** Over a wide space or area; out of doors. The animals that escaped from the circus roamed *abroad* all night. **3** Widely known. The report was *abroad* that the game had been postponed. **4** Widely; broadly; as, a tree spreading its branches *abroad.*

ab·ro·gate \ˈab-rə-ˌgāt\ *v.;* **ab·ro·gat·ed**; **ab·ro·gat·ing**. To abolish by authority; to repeal; to put an end to; as, to *abrogate* a law. — **ab·ro·ga·tion** \ˌab-rə-ˈgāsh-n\ *n.*

abrupt \ə-ˈbrəpt\ *adj.* [From Latin *abruptus* originally meaning "broken off".] **1** Steep. An *abrupt* cliff rose at the edge of the plain. **2** Sudden; as, an *abrupt* change in the weather. **3** So quick as to seem rude; curt; as, offended by the *abrupt* remark. — **abrupt·ly**, *adv.*

abs-. Variant of *ab-*.

ab·scess \ˈab-ˌses\ *n.* A collection of pus at some point in the body. — **ab·scessed** \-ˌsest\ *adj.*

ab·scis·sa \ab-ˈsis-ə\ *n.; pl.* **ab·scis·sas** \-əz\ or **ab·scis·sae** \-(ˌ)ē\. **1** The distance of a point on a graph to the right or to the left of the ordinate. **2** The horizontal reference line of a graph.

ab·scond \ab-ˈskänd\ *v.* To go away hurriedly and secretly; to steal off and hide; to sneak off; as, to *abscond* with money left in one's care.

ab·sence \ˈab-sən(t)s\ *n.* **1** A being away; as, an *absence* from school. **2** A lack; a want. The *absence* of sunlight made it difficult to take good pictures.

ab·sent \ab-ˈsent\ *v.* To keep (oneself) away; to withdraw (oneself); as, to *absent* oneself from a meeting. — \ˈab-sənt\ *adj.* **1** Not present; away; missing; lacking; as, to be *absent* from home. **2** Absent-minded; as, to have an *absent* look on one's face. — **ab·sent·ly** \ˈab-sənt-lē\ *adv.*

ab·sen·tee \ˌab-sən-ˈtē\ *n.* A person who is absent.

ab·sent-mind·ed \ˈab-sənt-ˈmīn-dəd\ *adj.* Lost in thought and not paying attention to what is going on or to what one is doing. — **ab·sent-mind·ed·ly**, *adv.*

ab·so·lute \ˈab-sə-ˌlüt\ *adj.* **1** Complete; perfect; whole; as, the *absolute* truth. **2** Not limited in power; as, an *absolute* king. **3** Not mixed with anything else; pure; as, *absolute* alcohol. **4** Positive; certain. The police found *absolute* proof that the watch had been stolen.

ab·so·lute·ly \ˈab-sə-ˌlüt-lē, ˌab-sə-ˈlüt-lē\ *adv.* **1** Wholly; as, to be *absolutely* absorbed in a book. **2** Most certainly or positively; as, *absolutely* not.

absolute value. The number of units by which a number differs from zero.

ab·so·lu·tion \ˌab-sə-ˈlüsh-n\ *n.* A setting free, as from guilt, sin, or penalty; forgiveness.

ab·solve \əb-ˈsälv, -ˈzälv\ *v.;* **ab·solved**; **ab·solv·ing**. To set free; to pronounce free, as from a responsibility, a promise, or the consequences of guilt. The accused man was *absolved* from all blame.

ab·sorb \əb-'sȯrb, -'zȯrb\ *v.* **1** To cause to disappear as if by swallowing. The new corporation *absorbed* three small companies. **2** To suck up or drink in. A blotter *absorbs* ink. **3** To take up without giving back. Heavy curtains *absorb* sound. **4** To hold all one's interest; to occupy fully; as, a book that *absorbed* everyone who read it.

ab·sorbed \əb-'sȯrbd, -'zȯrbd\ *adj.* Deeply interested; wholly engaged in some thought or activity; as, too *absorbed* to hear surrounding noises.

ab·sorb·ent \əb-'sȯrb-nt, -'zȯrb-\ *adj.* Able to suck up or to take in; as, *absorbent* cotton. — *n.* An absorbent substance.

ab·sorb·ing \əb-'sȯr-bing, -'zȯr-\ *adj.* Highly interesting; as, an *absorbing* tale of the sea. — **ab·sorb·ing·ly**, *adv.*

ab·sorp·tion \əb-'sȯrpsh-n, -'zȯrpsh-n\ *n.* **1** An absorbing; a sucking up or taking in; as, the *absorption* of water by the earth; the *absorption* of sound by thick curtains. **2** A being absorbed; s, an *absorption* in sports. **3** The taking in of food in a liquid state by living cells or tissues. **4** The passing of digested food through the walls of the alimentary canal into the blood or lymph.

ab·stain \əb-'stān\ *v.* To check or restrain oneself; to refrain; as, to *abstain* from eating between meals.

ab·ste·mi·ous \ab-'stē-mē-əs\ *adj.* **1** Moderate, especially in one's eating and drinking; temperate; as, a man of *abstemious* habits. **2** Sparingly used or indulged in; as, an *abstemious* diet.

ab·sten·tion \əb-'stench-n\ *n.* An abstaining; abstinence; as, *abstention* from intoxicating drink.

ab·sti·nence \'ab-stə-nən(t)s\ *n.* A restraining of oneself from satisfying one's appetite or from eating certain foods; especially, an abstaining from drinking alcoholic liquors.

ab·stract \'ab-ˌstrakt, ab-'strakt\ *adj.* **1** Expressing a quality without reference to an actual person or thing that possesses it. The word "honesty" is an *abstract* word. **2** So general in meaning that it is difficult to understand; as, a book too *abstract* for children. — \'ab-ˌstrakt\ *n.* A brief statement of the main points, as of a book; a summary. — *v.* **1** \ab-'strakt\ To take away; to remove by drawing out, often secretly or dishonestly. **2** To separate or distinguish in one's mind, as a quality of an object from the object itself; as, to *abstract* the idea of roundness from a baseball. **3** \'ab-ˌstrakt\ To put into a shorter form; to summarize; as, to *abstract* a written report. — **ab·stract·ly** \'ab-ˌstrakt-lē, ab-'strakt-\ *adv.*

ab·stract·ed \ab-'strak-təd\ *adj.* Not paying attention to near-by persons or things; absent-minded; as, to gaze with an *abstracted* look. — **ab·stract·ed·ly**, *adv.*

ab·strac·tion \ab-'straksh-n\ *n.* **1** The action of taking away or of taking or drawing out, especially secretly or dishonestly; withdrawal; removal. **2** An abstract idea or term, as *honesty*, *bravery*, *whiteness*, *softness*. **3** The process by which an abstract idea is arrived at; the distinguishing in one's mind between a quality of an object and the object itself. **4** Something theoretical; a purely imaginary idea; as, the fleeting *abstractions* in a dream. **5** A state of not paying attention to near-by persons or things; absent-mindedness; as, to arouse a daydreamer from his *abstraction*. **6** An artistic composition or creation, especially in the art of painting or sculpture, characterized by designs not recognizably representing objects in actual existence (**pure abstraction**) or by designs not precisely representing concrete objects or figures but with recognizable elements (**near abstraction**).

ab·struse \ab-'strüs\ *adj.* Hard to understand; obscure; difficult; as, an *abstruse* question. — **ab·struse·ly**, *adv.*

ab·surd \əb-'sərd, -'zərd\ *adj.* Highly unreasonable or untrue; silly; as, an *absurd* excuse; the *absurd* antics of a clown. — **ab·surd·ly**, *adv.*

ab·surd·i·ty \əb-'sərd-ət-ē, -'zərd-\ *n.; pl.* **ab·surd·i·ties.** **1** The state of being absurd; foolishness; as, the *absurdity* of believing that toads cause warts. **2** Something, especially an idea, that is absurd.

abun·dance \ə-'bən-dən(t)s\ *n.* A large quantity; a great plenty.

abun·dant \ə-'bən-dənt\ *adj.* More than enough; existing in great plenty; as, *abundant* harvests. — **abun·dant·ly**, *adv.*

abuse \ə-'byüz\ *v.;* **abused**; **abus·ing.** **1** To use wrongly or badly; to misuse; as, to *abuse* privileges. **2** To treat badly or cruelly; to mistreat; as, to *abuse* a dog. **3** To put too heavy a strain on; as, to *abuse* one's health. **4** To blame or scold rudely. — \ə-'byüs\ *n.* **1** Wrong, improper, or unfair treatment; misuse; as, *abuse* of an animal; *abuse* of one's health. **2** Corrupt practice; crime; fault; as, *abuses* in public office. **3** Insulting, harsh words. No one likes to listen to *abuse*.

abu·sive \ə-'byü-siv, -ziv\ *adj.* **1** Using abuse. There is no excuse for being *abusive*. **2** Consisting of or containing abuse; as, *abusive* language. — **abu·sive·ly**, *adv.*

abut \ə-'bət\ *v.;* **abut·ted**; **abut·ting**. To touch or border on, as portions of land that lie next to each other; as, a farm *abutting* on the road.

abut·ment \ə-'bət-mənt\ *n.* **1** An abutting. **2** Something against which another thing rests its weight or pushes with force; as, *abutments* that support a bridge.

abys·mal \ə-'biz-məl\ *adj.* Like an abyss; of unbelievable depth; as, *abysmal* ignorance. — **abys·mal·ly** \-mə-lē\ *adv.*

abyss \ə-'bis\ *n.* **1** A huge, deep hole or opening in the earth's surface. **2** Any immeasurable depth or extent; as, an *abyss* of ignorance.

Ab·ys·sin·i·an \ˌab-ə-'sin-ē-ən, -'sin-yən\ *adj.* or *n.* Ethiopian.

A.C. \ˈā-ˈsē\. Abbreviation for *alternating current.*

aca·cia \ə-ˈkāsh-ə\ *n.* **1** A bush or a small tree, often with fernlike leaves and thorny stems. **2** The North American locust tree.

acacia, 1: leaf and flowers

ac·a·dem·ic \ˌak-ə-ˈdem-ik\ *adj.* **1** Having to do with schools or colleges; as, the *academic* year. **2** Not expected to produce a practical result; theoretical; as, an *academic* discussion. — **ac·a·dem·i·cal·ly** \-ik-l(-)ē\ *adv.*

acad·e·my \ə-ˈkad-m-ē\ *n.; pl.* **acad·e·mies. 1** A school or college; especially, a private school of high-school grade. **2** A place of training in special subjects; as, an *academy* of music; a military *academy.* **3** A society of scholars formed for the advancement of art or science.

a cap·pel·la \ˌäk-ə-ˈpel-ə, ˌák-\. [An Italian phrase meaning "in chapel style".] Without instrumental accompaniment; as, to sing *a cappella.*

ac·cede \ak-ˈsēd\ *v.;* **ac·ced·ed; ac·ced·ing. 1** To succeed to an office or a position of dignity; as, to *accede* to a throne. **2** To agree or assent; as, to *accede* to a proposed plan.

ac·cel·er·ate \ik-ˈsel-r-ˌāt, ak-\ *v.;* **ac·cel·er·at·ed; ac·cel·er·at·ing. 1** To cause to move, act, or proceed faster; to hasten; as, to *accelerate* an automobile; to *accelerate* an educational program. **2** To move with constantly increasing speed. This automobile *accelerates* easily.

ac·cel·er·a·tion \ik-ˌsel-r-ˈāsh-n, ak-\ *n.* **1** The action of accelerating. **2** An increase in speed or progress.

ac·cel·er·a·tor \ik-ˈsel-r-ˌāt-r, ak-\ *n.* **1** One that accelerates. **2** On an automobile or other machine, a pedal or lever used in increasing and decreasing the speed of the motor.

ac·cent \ˈak-ˌsent\ *n.* **1** Increased force or emphasis given to a syllable of a word in speaking or to a beat in music. "Abandon" is pronounced with an *accent* on the second syllable. **2** A way of speaking found in a part of a country. **3** A combining of certain pronunciations and tones of one language with those of another; as, to speak English with a French *accent.* **4** [in the plural] Words; speech; as, to reply in *accents* of scorn. — **accent mark.** A mark (as ˈ or ˌ) used in writing to show the place of increased force or emphasis on a syllable, as ˈkid-ˌnap. — \ak-ˈsent, ˈak-ˌsent\ *v.* **1** To give increased force or emphasis to; to stress; as, to *accent* a syllable of a word in speaking or a note in singing. **2** To place an accent mark (as ˈ or ˌ) so as to indicate an emphasized syllable.

ac·cen·tu·ate \ak-ˈsench-ə-ˌwāt\ *v.;* **ac·cen·tu·at·ed; ac·cen·tu·at·ing. 1** To pronounce or mark with an accent; as, to *accentuate* every third syllable. **2** To bring out distinctly; to emphasize; as, to *accentuate* the importance of good manners. — **ac·cen·tu·a·tion** \(ˌ)ak-ˌsench-ə-ˈwāsh-n\ *n.*

ac·cept \ik-ˈsept, ak-\ *v.* **1** To receive with consent or favor; as, to *accept* an offer; to be *accepted* as a member of the club. **2** To agree or assent to; as, to *accept* an excuse. **3** To recognize and receive as true or significant; as, unwilling to *accept* new ideas. **4** To acknowledge as binding and promise to pay; as, to *accept* a grocer's bill. — For synonyms see *take.*

ac·cept·a·ble \ik-ˈsep-təb-l, ak-\ *adj.* **1** Worthy of being accepted; as, an *acceptable* excuse. **2** Satisfactory; capable; as, to play an *acceptable* game of tennis. — **ac·cept·a·bil·i·ty** \ik-ˌsep-tə-ˈbil-ət-ē, (ˌ)ak-\ *n.* — **ac·cept·a·bly** \ik-ˈsep-tə-blē, ak-\ *adv.*

ac·cept·ance \ik-ˈsep-tən(t)s, ak-\ *n.* **1** The act of accepting, especially with approval; as, the *acceptance* of a gift. **2** The state or condition of being accepted or acceptable; as, a plan assured of *acceptance.*

ac·cep·ta·tion \ˌak-ˌsep-ˈtāsh-n\ *n.* The meaning in which a word or expression is generally understood.

ac·cess \ˈak-ˌses\ *n.* **1** Approach; entrance; admittance; as, to have *access* to a playground; to have *access* to the city officials. **2** A means or way of approach. The only *access* to the cave is by water.

ac·ces·si·ble \ak-ˈses-əb-l, ik-\ *adj.* **1** Easy to approach; as, a summer resort *accessible* by train, car, and airplane. **2** Obtainable; as, to get all *accessible* information. — **ac·ces·si·bil·i·ty** \(ˌ)ak-ˌses-ə-ˈbil-ət-ē, ik-\ *n.*

ac·ces·sion \ak-ˈsesh-n\ *n.* **1** The act of coming to or near, as to a throne or an office; as, the *accession* of a new king. **2** An increase by addition; as, an *accession* of wealth. **3** The thing added; as, *accessions* to a library.

ac·ces·so·ry \ak-ˈses-r(-)ē, ik-\ *adj.* Helping a more important person or thing; useful but not absolutely necessary; as, an automobile with all the latest *accessory* equipment. — *n.; pl.* **ac·ces·so·ries. 1** Something not absolutely necessary that adds to the convenience or usefulness of something else; as, automobile *accessories.* **2** A person who helps another in wrongdoing or who aids an offender in an attempt to escape justice.

ac·ci·dent \ˈaks-ə-dənt, -ˌdent\ *n.* **1** Something that happens unexpectedly; something done but not intended; especially, an unexpected event having unfortunate consequences; a mishap; as, an automobile *accident.* **2** Chance; as, to break a dish by *accident.*

ac·ci·den·tal \ˌaks-ə-ˈdent-l\ *adj.* **1** Happening by chance or unexpectedly; as, an *accidental* discovery of oil. **2** Not intended; as, to be the cause of an *accidental* injury to a teammate. — *n.* Any sharp, flat, or natural occurring in a piece of music after the key signature.

ac·ci·den·tal·ly \ˌaks-ə-ˈdent-l(-)ē\ *adv.* By accident; by chance; unintentionally.

ac·claim \ə-ˈklām\ *v.* **1** To welcome with applause; as, to *acclaim* the winner of a race. **2** To declare or proclaim by shouting approval. The crowd *ac-*

claimed the speaker their leader. — *n.* Applause; as, greeted with loud *acclaim.*

ac·cla·ma·tion \ˌak-lə-ˈmāsh-n\ *n.* **1** Applause; warm praise or approval; a shout of approval. **2** Mass or group voting done orally; as, elected by *acclamation.*

ac·cli·mate \ə-ˈklī-mət, ˈak-lə-ˌmāt\ *v.;* **ac·cli·mat·ed; ac·cli·mat·ing.** Acclimatize.

ac·cli·ma·tize \ə-ˈklī-mə-ˌtīz\ *v.;* **ac·cli·ma·tized; ac·cli·ma·tiz·ing.** To accustom to a new climate or to new surroundings; to adapt to new conditions.

ac·co·lade \ˈak-l-ˌād\ *n.* **1** A ceremony or salute marking the conferring of knighthood on a person, consisting usually of a tap on the shoulder with the blade of a sword. **2** A recognition, as of merit or success; an award.

ac·com·mo·date \ə-ˈkäm-ə-ˌdāt\ *v.;* **ac·com·mo·dat·ed; ac·com·mo·dat·ing.** **1** To adapt; as, to *accommodate* oneself to the inconveniences of travel. **2** To oblige. My neighbor *accommodated* me with a ride downtown. **3** To provide with lodgings; to have room for. The hotel can *accommodate* 300 guests.

ac·com·mo·dat·ing \ə-ˈkäm-ə-ˌdāt-ing\ *adj.* Ready to help; obliging. Our next-door neighbors are very *accommodating* people.

ac·com·mo·da·tion \ə-ˌkäm-ə-ˈdāsh-n\ *n.* **1** The act of accommodating or adjusting; adaptation. **2** Something that supplies what is needed. A ride home is a real *accommodation.* **3** [in the plural] Lodgings; sometimes, lodgings and food; as, hotel *accommodations* for five. **4** A loan. **5** The automatic adjustment of the eye for seeing at different distances.

ac·com·pa·ni·ment \ə-ˈkəmp-n(-)ē-mənt\ *n.* Something that goes with another thing; especially, music played along with a solo part.

ac·com·pa·nist \ə-ˈkəmp-n(-)əst\ *n.* A musician who plays an accompaniment.

ac·com·pa·ny \ə-ˈkəmp-n(-)ē\ *v.;* **ac·com·pa·nied; ac·com·pa·ny·ing.** **1** To go along with, especially as a companion. Some dogs *accompany* their masters everywhere. **2** To occur at the same time as; to be found along with. Lightning often *accompanies* thunder. **3** To play a musical accompaniment for a soloist.

— The words *attend* and *escort* are synonyms of *accompany: accompany* generally indicates going with someone for companionship or association; *attend* usually implies waiting upon someone, as by a servant or helper; *escort* may suggest attendance for protection, courtesy, or honor.

ac·com·plice \ə-ˈkäm-pləs\ *n.* A partner or associate in wrongdoing.

ac·com·plish \ə-ˈkäm-plish, -ˈkəm-\ *v.* To bring to a successful finish; to perform; to carry out; as, to *accomplish* a task; to *accomplish* all one set out to do.

— The words *achieve* and *effect* are synonyms of *accomplish: accomplish* may refer to any successful completion; *achieve* usually suggests accomplishment of more important tasks; *effect* may suggest accomplishment in spite of resistance or obstacles.

ac·com·plished \ə-ˈkäm-plisht, -ˈkəm-\ *adj.* **1** Completed; done; as, an *accomplished* fact, beyond change. **2** Having the skill, learning, or training necessary to do something very well; skilled; expert; as, an *accomplished* pianist. **3** Having many accomplishments; as, a very *accomplished* person.

ac·com·plish·ment \ə-ˈkäm-plish-mənt, -ˈkəm-\ *n.* **1** A completing; as, to look forward to the *accomplishment* of a task. **2** Something accomplished; as, a day without a single *accomplishment.* **3** A special skill or ability gained by study or training; as, a man of many *accomplishments.*

ac·cord \ə-ˈkȯrd\ *v.* **1** To grant as suitable or proper; to concede; as, to *accord* due praise to the winner. **2** To agree; to be in harmony. Father's plans usually *accord* with Mother's. — *n.* **1** Agreement; harmony. All the boys were in *accord* with the camp leaders. **2** Voluntary action; willingness. Everyone went of his own *accord.* — **with one accord.** With complete agreement; unanimously.

ac·cord·ance \ə-ˈkȯrd-n(t)s\ *n.* Agreement; harmony; as, to act in *accordance* with the rules.

ac·cord·ing as \ə-ˈkȯrd-ing\. **1** In accord with the way in which. **2** Depending on how or whether.

ac·cord·ing·ly \ə-ˈkȯrd-ing-lē\ *adv.* **1** In accordance; fittingly. Everyone knew the instructions and conducted himself *accordingly.* **2** Therefore; consequently. It was lunch time; *accordingly,* the men stopped work.

according to. **1** In agreement with; in the order of. The students were seated *according to* age. **2** As stated by; as, *according to* the latest report.

ac·cor·di·on \ə-ˈkȯrd-ē-ən\ *n.* A musical instrument with a bellows, a keyboard at one side, and metal reeds. — *adj.* Creased so as to fold like an accordion. Some skirts have *accordion* pleats.

accordion

ac·cost \ə-ˈkȯst\ *v.* To speak first to; to address; as, to be *accosted* in the street by a stranger.

ac·count \ə-ˈkau̇nt\ *v.* **1** To make a report or a statement of money received and money paid out. **2** To give a reason or explanation. **3** To be the cause. Illness *accounts* for many absences. **4** To consider; to think. His friends *account* him generous. — *n.* **1** A record of money received and money paid out. **2** A record of the things a customer has bought and of the money he owes for them; a bill; as, the grocer's *account* for last month. **3** A bank's record of money deposited and of money taken out by a person. **4** A statement of reasons that explain; as, to give an *account* of one's actions. **5** A statement of facts; a report; a story; as, to write an *account* of a baseball game. **6** Worth; value; importance; as, to throw something away as being of no *account.* — For synonyms see *narrative.* — **on account of.** For the sake of; by reason of; because of. — **on no account.** Under no circumstances. — **on one's own account.** For one's own interest; by oneself.

ac·count·a·ble \ə-ˈkau̇nt-əb-l\ *adj.* **1** Responsible for giving an account of one's acts. Leaders in the government are *accountable* to the people. **2** Capable of being accounted for; able to be explained; as, a fear of water easily *accountable* by a childhood experience. — **ac·count·a·bil·i·ty** \ə-ˌkau̇nt-ə-ˈbil-ət-ē\ *n.* — **ac·count·a·bly** \ə-ˈkau̇nt-ə-blē\ *adv.*

ac·count·ant \ə-ˈkau̇nt-nt\ *n.* A person skilled in making and examining records of money received and money paid out.

ac·count·ing \ə-ˈkau̇nt-ing\ *n.* The skill or system of recording money transactions of a person or business.

ac·cou·ter or **ac·cou·tre** \ə-ˈküt-r\ *v.;* **ac·cou·tered** or **ac·cou·tred**; **ac·cou·ter·ing** or **ac·cou·tring** \ə-ˈküt-r-ing, ə-ˈkü-tring\. To furnish with equipment, especially for military service; to equip; as, to *accouter* troops for a winter campaign.

ac·cou·ter·ment or **ac·cou·tre·ment** \ə-ˈküt-r-mənt, ə-ˈkü-trə-mənt\ *n.* **1** [in the plural] Equipment; especially, a soldier's outfit other than clothes and weapons. **2** The action of equipping.

ac·cred·it \ə-ˈkred-ət\ *v.* **1** To give official power to a person as a representative; to send with credentials and authority to act; as, our ambassador *accredited* to France. **2** To certify as up to a certain standard; as, an *accredited* school. **3** To believe; to credit; as, to *accredit* a statement as reliable.

ac·cru·al \ə-ˈkrü-əl\ *n.* **1** The process of accruing. **2** Something that accrues.

ac·crue \ə-ˈkrü\ *v.;* **ac·crued**; **ac·cru·ing. 1** To come as an addition or advantage; as, benefits that have *accrued* to society from free education. **2** To be added by increase or growth over a period of time. Interest *accrues* to money in a savings bank.

acct. Abbreviation for *account.*

ac·cu·mu·late \ə-ˈkyüm-yə-ˌlāt\ *v.;* **ac·cu·mu·lat·ed**; **ac·cu·mu·lat·ing.** [From Latin *accumulatus,* past participle of *accumulare* meaning "to heap up".] To heap up in a mass; to gather; to collect; as, to let rubbish *accumulate;* to *accumulate* a fortune.

ac·cu·mu·la·tion \ə-ˌkyüm-yə-ˈlāsh-n\ *n.* **1** A heaping up; a collecting; as, to devote one's life to the *accumulation* of wealth. **2** A collection; a heap; as, an *accumulation* of souvenirs; an *accumulation* of rubbish.

ac·cu·ra·cy \ˈak-yər-ə-sē\ *n.; pl.* **ac·cu·ra·cies.** Freedom from mistakes; correctness; exactness. Answers will be marked for *accuracy* and neatness.

ac·cu·rate \ˈak-yər-ət\ *adj.* [From Latin *accuratus,* past participle of *accurare* meaning "to do carefully".] Free from mistakes; exact; precise; as, an *accurate* answer; an *accurate* watch. — For synonyms see *correct.* — **ac·cu·rate·ly** \-yər-ət-lē, -yərt-lē\ *adv.*

ac·cursed \ə-ˈkər-səd, ə-ˈkərst\ or **ac·curst** \ə-ˈkərst\ *adj.* **1** Under a curse. **2** Bad enough to be cursed; as, vile, *accursed* weather.

ac·cu·sa·tion \ˌak-yə-ˈzāsh-n\ *n.* A statement that a person has done something wrong or criminal; a charge against a person; as, called to face an *accusation* of cheating.

ac·cu·sa·tive \ə-ˈkyü-zət-iv\ *n.* or **ac·cu·sa·tive case.** The case of a noun or pronoun when it is the direct object of a verb or the object of a preposition, or, in some languages, of some prepositions but not others — usually called in English grammar *objective* or *objective case.*

ac·cuse \ə-ˈkyüz\ *v.;* **ac·cused**; **ac·cus·ing.** To declare that a person has done something wrong or criminal; to charge; to blame; as, unfairly *accused* of cowardice. — **ac·cus·er,** *n.*

ac·cus·tom \ə-ˈkəst-m\ *v.* To make used to; as, to *accustom* oneself to getting up early.

ac·cus·tomed \ə-ˈkəst-md\ *adj.* Usual; regular; customary; as, to go for one's *accustomed* morning walk.

ace \ˈās\ *n.* **1** A card or a die marked with a single spot. **2** A very small amount or degree; a particle; a jot; as, to come within an *ace* of falling over the cliff. **3** An aviator who has brought down five or more enemy planes. **4** A person who has great ability in anything; as, a baseball *ace.* — *adj.* Of the highest ability, quality, or rank; as, an *ace* pilot.

ac·e·tate \ˈas-ə-ˌtāt\ *n.* A salt derived from acetic acid.

ace·tic \ə-ˈsēt-ik\ *adj.* Having to do with, or producing, vinegar.

acetic acid. A colorless chemical compound that is used in medicine and industry and that gives the sour taste to vinegar.

acet·y·lene \ə-ˈset-l-ən, -l-ˌēn\ *n.* A colorless gas that burns with a brilliant white light, used in welding metals and, sometimes, for illumination.

ache \ˈāk\ *v.;* **ached**; **ach·ing. 1** To suffer continuous pain; to throb painfully. **2** To wish earnestly; to long. Thoughts of their mother made the boys *ache* to go home. — *n.* A continuous pain.

achieve \ə-ˈchēv\ *v.;* **achieved**; **achiev·ing. 1** To bring to a successful end; to accomplish; as, to *achieve* a task. **2** To get as a result of effort; to gain; to win; as, to *achieve* honors in school. — For synonyms see *accomplish.* — **achiev·a·ble,** *adj.*

achieve·ment \ə-ˈchēv-mənt\ *n.* **1** The act of achieving. **2** Something achieved; especially, something accomplished by bravery or by great effort; as, heroic *achievements* by the early settlers.

ac·id \ˈas-əd\ *adj.* **1** Sour, sharp, or biting to the taste; like vinegar in taste. **2** Sour in temper; cross; as, to make *acid* remarks. **3** Of an acid; having to do with an acid. — *n.* **1** A sour substance. **2** A chemical compound that is sour to the taste, dissolves in water, and turns litmus paper red. — **ac·id·ly,** *adv.*

acid·i·fy \ə-ˈsid-ə-ˌfī\ *v.;* **acid·i·fied**; **acid·i·fy·ing. 1** To make or become acid. **2** To change into an acid; as, to *acidify* sugar.

acid·i·ty \ə-ˈsid-ət-ē\ *n.; pl.* **acid·i·ties.** Acid or sour quality; as, the *acidity* of lemon juice.

ac·knowl·edge \ik-ˈnäl-ij, ak-\ *v.;* **ac·knowl·edged; ac·knowl·edg·ing. 1** To admit; to recognize as true; as, to *acknowledge* a mistake. **2** To allow a claim; to recognize; as, to *acknowledge* the rights of others. **3** To say or show that something has been received or noticed; as, to *acknowledge* a letter.

— The words *admit* and *confess* are synonyms of *acknowledge: acknowledge* generally suggests the making public of one's knowledge of something that has or might have remained undisclosed; *admit* usually refers to the granting of a fact as true; *confess* may suggest the acknowledgment of some wrong that one has committed.

ac·knowl·edg·ment or **ac·knowl·edge·ment** \ik-ˈnäl-ij-mənt, ak-\ *n.* **1** An acknowledging. **2** A thing done or given in return for something, such as a favor or a service, that one has received.

ac·me \ˈak-mē\ *n.* The top or highest point; as, to reach the very *acme* of one's ambition.

ac·ne \ˈak-nē\ *n.* An abnormal condition of the skin caused by inflammation of certain small glands and marked by pimples, especially on the face.

ac·o·lyte \ˈak-l-ˌīt\ *n.* **1** A man or boy who assists a priest at the altar. **2** An assistant or attendant; a follower.

ac·o·nite \ˈak-n-ˌīt\ *n.* **1** A poisonous plant about five feet tall with spikes of hooded bluish flowers. **2** A drug obtained from this plant.

acorn \ˈā-ˌkȯrn, ˈāk-rn\ *n.* The nut of the oak tree.

acous·tic \ə-ˈküs-tik\ or **acous·ti·cal** \-tik-l\ *adj.* Of or relating to acoustics or to the sense or organs of hearing. — **acous·ti·cal·ly** \-tik-l(-)ē\ *adv.*

acorns

acous·tics \ə-ˈküs-tiks\ *n. sing. and pl.* **1** The science dealing with sound. **2** Those qualities in a room or hall that make it easy or hard for a person in it to hear distinctly. The *acoustics* of the hall permitted the faintest sound to be heard.

ac·quaint \ə-ˈkwānt\ *v.* To make familiar; to give personal knowledge of; as, to *acquaint* a person with the facts. — **acquainted with.** Having personal knowledge of; as, a man *acquainted with* all parts of the city.

ac·quaint·ance \ə-ˈkwānt-n(t)s\ *n.* **1** Knowledge gained by personal observation, contact, or experience. **2** A person one knows slightly. — **ac·quaint·ance·ship** \-n-ˌship, -n(t)s-ˌship\ *n.*

ac·qui·esce \ˌak-wē-ˈes\ *v.;* **ac·qui·esced; ac·qui·esc·ing.** To accept or agree by keeping silent or by not raising objections; as, to *acquiesce* in a plan of which one does not fully approve.

ac·qui·es·cence \ˌak-wē-ˈes-n(t)s\ *n.* An acquiescing; consent or acceptance without expressed objection. — **ac·qui·es·cent** \-nt\ *adj.*

ac·quire \ə-ˈkwīr\ *v.;* **ac·quired; ac·quir·ing.** To gain or get for one's own, usually by one's own efforts; as, to *acquire* a fortune by hard work. — For synonyms see *obtain.*

ac·quire·ment \ə-ˈkwīr-mənt\ *n.* **1** The act of acquiring. **2** Something acquired, especially through an effort of mind; an attainment; an accomplishment. Mastery of a musical instrument is an *acquirement* well worth striving for.

ac·qui·si·tion \ˌak-wə-ˈzish-n\ *n.* **1** A gaining or acquiring; as, the *acquisition* of knowledge through reading. **2** Something gained or acquired. Our most recent *acquisition* at home is a puppy.

ac·quis·i·tive \ə-ˈkwiz-ət-iv\ *adj.* Fond of acquiring things; grasping; greedy.

ac·quit \ə-ˈkwit\ *v.;* **ac·quit·ted; ac·quit·ting. 1** To free from a charge of wrongdoing. The prisoner was *acquitted* by the jury. **2** To behave (oneself); to do one's part. Each player on the team *acquitted* himself well.

ac·quit·tal \ə-ˈkwit-l\ *n.* The act of acquitting, especially the freeing of a person from an accusation, as by the verdict of a jury.

acre \ˈāk-r\ *n.* [From Old English *aecer* meaning "field".] A measure of land equal to 160 square rods, or 4,840 square yards, or 43,560 square feet.

acre·age \ˈāk-r(-)ij\ *n.* Acres; land measured in acres.

ac·rid \ˈak-rəd\ *adj.* **1** Bitter or harsh to the taste; sharp; biting; as, an *acrid* flavor. **2** Irritating to the feelings; sharp in manner; as, an *acrid* remark. — **ac·rid·ly,** *adv.*

ac·ri·mo·ni·ous \ˌak-rə-ˈmō-nē-əs\ *adj.* Showing a sharp or bitter temper; as, an *acrimonious* reply. — **ac·ri·mo·ni·ous·ly,** *adv.*

ac·ri·mo·ny \ˈak-rə-ˌmō-nē\ *n.; pl.* **ac·ri·mo·nies.** Harsh or biting sharpness, as in speech or manner; as, a dispute marked by great *acrimony.*

ac·ro·bat \ˈak-rə-ˌbat\ *n.* [From Greek *akrobatēs* meaning "tightrope walker".] A person who performs gymnastic or tumbling exercises or similar exercises requiring skillful control of the body.

ac·ro·bat·ic \ˌak-rə-ˈbat-ik\ *adj.* Having to do with acrobats or with acrobatics.

ac·ro·bat·ics \ˌak-rə-ˈbat-iks\ *n. sing. and pl.* **1** The performances of an acrobat. **2** Skilled stunts like those of an acrobat; as, airplane *acrobatics.*

acrop·o·lis \ə-ˈkräp-l-əs\ *n.* **1** The upper fortified part of an ancient Greek city. **2** [with a capital] The acropolis at Athens.

across \ə-ˈkrȯs\ *adv.* or *prep.* **1** From side to side of something; crosswise or crosswise of; as, with arms folded *across* one's chest; a river more than a mile *across.* **2** On or to the opposite side; as, the house directly *across* the street; to hurry to get *across* before the lights change.

act \ˈakt\ *n.* **1** Something that is done; a deed; as, an *act* of kindness. **2** The doing of something; as, caught in the *act* of stealing. **3** A law made by a governing body; a decree; an edict; as, an *Act* of Congress. **4** One of the main parts of a play; an item on a program, as of a television show; as, a comedy in three *acts.* — *v.* **1** To do something; to make an effort; to move; as, to *act* quickly in an emergency. **2** To do what is required. The brakes failed to *act.* **3** To behave; as, to *act* like a coward. **4** To perform on the stage or in motion pictures. **5** To play the part of; as, to *act* the hero in a play. **6** To have an effect. The medicine *acts* on the heart.

act·ing \'ak-ting\ *adj.* Serving for a short time only; serving in place of someone else; as, an *acting* manager.

ac·tion \'aksh-n\ *n.* **1** The doing of something; performance; activity; as, a man of *action.* **2** The working of one thing on another so as to produce a change. The *action* of the water wore away the rocks. **3** The way of working; as, the *action* of a typewriter. **4** A deed; an act; [in the plural] behavior; conduct. The guests' *actions* at the party were rude. **5** The events forming the subject matter, as of a play. **6** Combat; battle; as, a soldier killed in *action.* **7** A legal proceeding by which one demands or enforces one's right in a court of law; as, to bring an *action* to recover property.

ac·ti·vate \'ak-tə-ˌvāt\ *v.;* **ac·ti·vat·ed; ac·ti·vat·ing. 1** To make capable of reacting chemically or of promoting reaction. **2** To make radioactive. **3** To place on active status, as a body of soldiers. — **ac·ti·va·tion** \ˌak-tə-'vāsh-n\ *n.*

ac·tive \'ak-tiv\ *adj.* **1** Quick in movement; lively; as, an *active* child. **2** In action or operation; functioning; as, an *active* organization; an *active* volcano. **3** Energetic; busy; as, an *active* mind. **4** Requiring or involving action; as, on *active* duty. **5** In grammar, representing the subject as the doer or agent of the action expressed by the verb; as, a verb in the *active* voice. — **ac·tive·ly,** *adv.*

ac·tiv·i·ty \ak-'tiv-ət-ē\ *n.; pl.* **ac·tiv·i·ties. 1** A state of being active; motion or action; vigorous action; liveliness. Holidays are times of much *activity.* **2** A recreation, especially one that is a regular part of school life but is not a part of the course of study. **3** Any educational procedure that assists one in learning.

ac·tor \'akt-r\ *n.* One who acts, as in a play or a motion picture.

ac·tress \'ak-trəs\ *n.* A female actor.

ac·tu·al \'ak-chə-wəl, 'ak-chəl\ *adj.* Really existing or happening; not imaginary; real; as, the *actual* state of affairs.

ac·tu·al·i·ty \ˌak-chə-'wal-ət-ē\ *n.; pl.* **ac·tu·al·i·ties. 1** The state of being actual; as, to question the *actuality* of ghosts. **2** An actual thing or condition; as, to face the *actualities* of the situation.

ac·tu·al·ly \'ak-chə-lē, 'ak-chə-wə-lē, 'aksh-l(-)ē\ *adv.* In fact; really; in truth.

ac·tu·ate \'ak-chə-ˌwāt\ *v.;* **ac·tu·at·ed; ac·tu·at·ing. 1** To put into action. The windmill *actuates* the pump. **2** To move to action; to stir or arouse to activity.

acu·men \ə-'kyü-mən\ *n.* Keenness of mind; shrewdness; as, business *acumen.*

acute \ə-'kyüt\ *adj.;* **acut·er; acut·est. 1** Pointed; not blunt. **2** Keen; shrewd; as, *acute* eyesight; an *acute* judge of men. **3** Sharp; severe; as, an *acute* pain. **4** High; shrill; as, an *acute* sound. **5** At or near a turning point; critical; as, an *acute* situation that may lead to war. — For synonyms see *sharp.* — **acute·ly,** *adv.*

acute accent. A mark [′] on certain letters in some words borrowed from a foreign language, as *éclair* or *café.*

acute angle. An angle that is less than a right angle.

acute angle

ad \'ad\ *n.* An advertisement.

A.D. \'ā-'dē\. [Abbreviated from Latin *anno Domini* meaning "in the year of our Lord".] In a particular year after the birth of Christ; as, *A.D.* 1918.

ad-. A prefix that can mean: to, toward, in addition to, as in *administer, advert,* or *admixture.*

ad·age \'ad-ij\ *n.* A saying that has gained value or force by long use; a proverb.

ada·gio \ə-'däj-(ˌ)ō, -'dåj-, ə-'däzh-(ˌ)ō, -'dåzh-\ *adj.* or *adv.* Done or played in an easy or graceful manner; slow; slowly. — *n.; pl.* **ada·gios. 1** A musical composition in adagio tempo. **2** A ballet dance done by two persons, characterized by difficult feats of balancing.

ad·a·mant \'ad-m-ənt, -ˌant\ *n.* **1** An imaginary stone of extreme hardness. **2** Hardness that cannot be softened or pierced; as, a heart of *adamant.* — *adj.* Adamantine.

ad·a·man·tine \ˌad-m-'an-ˌtēn, -ˌtīn\ *adj.* Made of, or having the qualities of, adamant; unbending; unyielding; as, *adamantine* courage; an *adamantine* refusal.

Ad·am's apple \'ad-mz\. The projection in the front of a person's neck formed by a cartilage of the larynx.

adapt \ə-'dapt\ *v.* **1** To make suitable or fit; especially, to change so as to fit new uses. The boys *adapted* an old automobile for a tractor. **2** To cause to fit in, as to new surroundings; to adjust; as, to *adapt* oneself to life in a new school.

adapt·a·ble \ə-'dap-təb-l\ *adj.* Able to be adapted; able easily to adapt oneself; as, holiday plans *adaptable* to rain or shine. — **adapt·a·bil·i·ty** \ə-ˌdap-tə-'bil-ət-ē\ *n.*

ad·ap·ta·tion \ˌad-ˌap-'tāsh-n\ *n.* **1** A making suitable or fit; an adjustment; as, the *adaptation* of the eye to a strong light. **2** A modification of a plant or an animal that fits it better for the conditions under which it lives. **3** Something adapted from something else. This movie is an *adaptation* of a novel.

adapt·ed \ə-'dap-təd\ *adj.* Suited by nature, character, or design to a particular use or purpose; as, soil well *adapted* to the growing of grapes.

A.D.C. Abbreviation for *Aide-de-camp.*

add \'ad\ *v.* **1** In arithmetic, to put together two or more numbers so as to get a total or sum; as, to *add* 3 and 4 and get 7. **2** To join one thing to another so as to increase the number of things or so as to make them into one thing; as, to *add* a few more desks in a schoolroom. **3** To say further.

ad·dend \'ad-ˌend\ *n.* A number that is to be added to another number.

ad·den·dum \ə-'dend-m\ *n.; pl.* **ad·den·da** \-'den-də\. **1** A thing added. **2** A supplement to a book.

ad·der \'ad-r\ *n.* [From earlier English *naddre, a naddre* being understood as *an addre.*] **1** A poisonous snake of Europe. **2** One of several harmless snakes of North America.

ad·dict \'ad-(ˌ)ikt\ *n.* A person who has given himself up to a habit, especially a harmful habit.

ad·dict·ed \ə-'dik-təd\ *adj.* Given up to a habit or practice; given over to; as, *addicted* to smoking.

ad·dic·tion \ə-'diksh-n\ *n.* The state of being addicted, especially to a habit-forming drug.

ad·di·tion \ə-'dish-n\ *n.* **1** The adding together of two or more numbers in order to find their sum. **2** The act of adding one thing to another; as, to sweeten lemonade by the *addition* of sugar. **3** Anything added to something else; as, to build an *addition* to a house. — **in addition to.** Besides; as well as; as, candy *in addition to* ice cream.

```
  867
   59
 +905
-----
1,831
```

addition, 1

ad·di·tion·al \ə-'dish-n(-)əl\ *adj.* Added; extra; as, an *additional* charge for delivery. — **ad·di·tion·al·ly** \-n(-)ə-lē\ *adv.*

ad·di·tive \'ad-ət-iv\ *n.* A substance that, when combined with a second substance, adds desirable qualities to it or improves those already in it; as, a gasoline *additive* to give more power. — *adj.* Relating to or produced by addition.

ad·dle \'ad-l\ *adj.* **1** Rotten; putrid; as, an *addle* egg. **2** Confused; muddled; as, *addle* brains. — *v.;* **ad·dled**; **ad·dling** \'ad-l(-)ing\. To make or become addle; to confuse.

ad·dress \ə-'dres\ *v.* **1** To apply (oneself); as, to *address* oneself to the day's lessons. **2** To direct a message of any kind; to write or speak to a person or persons; as, to *address* an audience; to *address* a petition to the president. **3** To write mailing directions on a letter or parcel. — \ə-'dres, 'ad-ˌres\ *n.* **1** A written or spoken message; a speech; as, an *address* of welcome. **2** Mailing directions written on a letter or parcel. **3** The place where a person can usually be reached; as, a business *address.* Write your *address* plainly. **4** A manner of talking with people; as, a man of pleasing *address.*

ad·dress·ee \ˌad-ˌres-'ē, ə-ˌdres-'ē\ *n.* A person to whom mail is addressed.

ad·duce \ə-'düs, ə-'dyüs\ *v.;* **ad·duced**; **ad·duc·ing.** To offer as an argument, reason, or proof; as, to *adduce* facts to support a statement.

ad·e·noids \'ad-n-ˌȯidz, 'ad-ˌnȯidz\ *n. pl.* Fleshy growths behind the back openings of a person's nostrils. — **ad·e·noi·dal** \ˌad-n-'ȯid-l\ *adj.*

adept \ə-'dept\ *adj.* Skilled; expert; as, to be *adept* at swimming. — **adept·ly**, *adv.*

ad·e·qua·cy \'ad-ə-kwə-sē\ *n.* The state of being adequate; sufficiency.

ad·e·quate \'ad-ə-kwət\ *adj.* Enough to meet some need; enough to satisfy requirements; as, to spend *adequate* time in preparing one's lessons. — **ad·e·quate·ly**, *adv.*

ad·here \ad-'hir\ *v.;* **ad·hered**; **ad·her·ing.** **1** To stick fast as glue does; to hold fast. **2** To cling; to remain attached or devoted; as, to *adhere* to a belief.

ad·her·ence \ad-'hir-ən(t)s\ *n.* The quality or action of adhering; a firm attachment; loyalty; as, *adherence* to a cause.

ad·her·ent \ad-'hir-ənt\ *adj.* Sticking; clinging; adhering. — *n.* One who clings to a belief, to a leader, or to an organization; a follower.

ad·he·sion \ad-'hēzh-n\ *n.* **1** The sticking together of substances touching each other; as, the *adhesion* of glue to wood. **2** Adherence. **3** The abnormal union of surfaces normally separate, as after a surgical operation.

ad·he·sive \ad-'hē-siv, -ziv\ *adj.* **1** Sticky; holding tightly as if glued. **2** Prepared for sticking or holding fast; as, *adhesive* tape. — *n.* An adhesive material.

adieu \ə-'dü, ə-'dyü\ *interj.* [From French, meaning literally "to God".] Good-by; farewell. — *n.; pl.* **adieus** or **adieux** \-'düz, -'dyüz\. The act of taking one's leave; a farewell; as, to say one's *adieus* before leaving.

ad·i·os \ˌad-ē-'ōs, ˌäd-, ˌȧd-\ *interj.* [Spanish.] Adieu.

ad·i·pose \'ad-ə-ˌpōs\ *adj.* Of or relating to animal fat; fatty; as, *adipose* tissue.

adj. Abbreviation for *adjective.*

Adj. or **Adjt**. Abbreviation for *Adjutant.*

ad·ja·cent \ə-'jās-nt\ *adj.* Lying next or near; bordering on; as, a field *adjacent* to the road.

ad·jec·ti·val \ˌaj-ik-'tīv-l\ *adj.* Of an adjective; playing the part of an adjective; as, an *adjectival* phrase; an *adjectival* clause. — **ad·jec·ti·val·ly** \-'tīv-l-ē\ *adv.*

ad·jec·tive \'aj-ik-tiv\ *n.* In grammar, a word used to modify a noun or pronoun by limiting (as *three* in "three weeks"), by describing (as *blue* in "blue sky"), by pointing out (as *this* in "this man"), or by showing possession (as *your* in "your book"). — *adj.* Of an adjective; playing the part of an adjective; as, words with *adjective* endings; an *adjective* phrase. — **ad·jec·tive·ly**, *adv.*

ad·join \ə-'jȯin\ *v.* To be next to; to touch; to be situated next. The garage *adjoins* the house.

ad·journ \ə-'jərn\ *v.* To bring or to come to a close for the day or for the time being; as, to *adjourn* a meeting. The court *adjourned* for the day.

ad·journ·ment \ə-'jərn-mənt\ *n.* **1** The action of adjourning or the state of being adjourned. **2** The period of time during which a group is adjourned.

ad·judge \ə-'jəj\ *v.;* **ad·judged**; **ad·judg·ing.** **1** To decide judicially; to judge; as, to *adjudge* a case. **2** *Archaic.* To sentence; to condemn. **3** To regard; to declare to be; to consider; as, to be *adjudged* worthy. **4** To award judicially.

ad·ju·di·cate \ə-ˈjüd-i-ˌkāt\ *v.;* **ad·ju·di·cat·ed**; **ad·ju·di·cat·ing**. To hear and settle judicially. — **ad·ju·di·ca·tion** \-ˌjüd-i-ˈkāsh-n\ *n.*

ad·junct \ˈaj-ˌəng(k)t\ *n.* Something joined or added to another thing but not an essential part of it. A radio is a common *adjunct* to an automobile.

ad·jure \ə-ˈju̇r\ *v.;* **ad·jured**; **ad·jur·ing**. To charge or command solemnly as if under oath; to entreat earnestly; as, to *adjure* a person to speak the truth. — **ad·ju·ra·tion** \ˌaj-r-ˈāsh-n\ *n.*

ad·just \ə-ˈjəst\ *v.* **1** To settle or arrange; to bring to a satisfactory state; to set right; as, to *adjust* a quarrel; to *adjust* a bill. **2** To fit; to adapt; to accommodate; as, to *adjust* oneself to a new school. **3** To move the parts of an instrument or a piece of machinery until they fit together in the best working order; to regulate; as, to *adjust* a watch; to *adjust* the brakes on an automobile. — **ad·just·a·ble**, *adj.*

ad·just·er or **ad·jus·tor** \ə-ˈjəst-r\ *n.* One that adjusts; especially, a person who adjusts claims.

ad·just·ment \ə-ˈjəs(t)-mənt\ *n.* **1** The bringing of a thing or things into exact or proper position or relation; arrangement; settlement; as, motor trouble caused by faulty *adjustment* of the carburetor. **2** A satisfactory relationship with one's surroundings. **3** A means of adjusting one part, as in a machine, to another; as, an *adjustment* for focusing a microscope.

ad·ju·tant \ˈaj-ə-tənt\ *n.* **1** An assistant. **2** An army officer who assists a commanding officer by handling correspondence, keeping records, and preparing and distributing orders. **3** A stork, six or seven feet high, common in India.

ad-lib \ˈad-ˈlib\ *v.;* **ad-libbed**; **ad-lib·bing**. Also **ad lib**. [Abbreviated from Latin *ad libitum* meaning "at pleasure", "as one wishes".] To improvise; to express something without previous preparation or rehearsal; as, to *ad-lib* remarks not in one's prepared speech. — *n.* Something that is adlibbed. The whole speech was an *ad-lib.* — *adj.* Spoken or composed without preparation or rehearsal; as, an *ad-lib* answer. — *adv.* Without restraint or limit; freely.

Adm. Abbreviation for *Admiral.*

ad·min·is·ter \əd-ˈmin-əst-r\ *v.;* **ad·min·is·tered**; **ad·min·is·ter·ing** \-əst-r(-)ing\. **1** To manage; to direct the affairs of; as, to *administer* an athletic program. **2** To serve out; to dispense; as, to *administer* justice. **3** To apply, as a remedy; as, to *administer* a drug; to *administer* first aid. **4** To bring aid or relief; as, to *administer* to the sick. **5** To give as a punishment; as, to *administer* a beating. **6** To settle, as an estate.

ad·min·is·tra·tion \əd-ˌmin-əs-ˈtrāsh-n, ˌad-ˌmin-\ *n.* **1** The act of managing or directing; as, the *administration* of a government. The *administration* of justice is the business of the courts. **2** The persons who direct affairs, as of a nation, a city, or a school.

ad·min·is·tra·tive \əd-ˈmin-əs-ˌtrāt-iv\ *adj.* Of or relating to administration, especially to management; executive; as, an *administrative* position.

ad·min·is·tra·tor \əd-ˈmin-əs-ˌtrāt-r\ *n.* A person who manages or directs; especially, a person appointed by law to manage someone's estate.

ad·mi·ra·ble \ˈad-mər-əb-l, ˈad-mrəb-l\ *adj.* Deserving to be admired; excellent; as, an *admirable* piece of work. — **ad·mi·ra·bly** \-mər-ə-blē, -mrə-blē\ *adv.*

ad·mi·ral \ˈad-mər-əl, ˈad-mrəl\ *n.* **1** The officer who commands a country's navy or a fleet. **2** A naval officer of the highest rank. **3** Any of several butterflies.

ad·mi·ral·ty \ˈad-mər-əl-tē, ˈad-mrəl-tē\ *n.; pl.* **ad·mi·ral·ties**. **1** The office or rank of admiral. **2** The extent of authority of an admiral. **3** The department of a government that has authority over naval affairs. **4** The court that has the authority to deal with nautical questions and offenses.

ad·mi·ra·tion \ˌad-mər-ˈāsh-n\ *n.* **1** Delighted and respectful approval; as, *admiration* for a war hero. **2** Someone or something that arouses such approval; as, a brave deed that is the *admiration* of the world.

ad·mire \əd-ˈmīr\ *v.;* **ad·mired**; **ad·mir·ing**. **1** To look at, think about, or speak about with pleasure and approval; as, to *admire* the scenery. **2** To regard highly; as, to *admire* a man's courage. — **ad·mir·er** \-ˈmīr-r\ *n.* — **ad·mir·ing·ly**, *adv.*

ad·mis·si·ble \əd-ˈmis-əb-l\ *adj.* Deserving to be admitted or allowed; allowable; as, an *admissible* excuse. — **ad·mis·si·bly** \-ə-blē\ *adv.*

ad·mis·sion \əd-ˈmish-n\ *n.* **1** The act of admitting. **2** The right or permission to enter; admittance; as, high standards of *admission* to a school. **3** The price of entrance. No *admission* will be charged. **4** A granting of something that has not been fully proved; as, an *admission* of guilt. — For synonyms see *admittance.*

ad·mit \əd-ˈmit\ *v.;* **ad·mit·ted**; **ad·mit·ting**. **1** To let in; to give the right to enter; to accept; as, to *admit* a statement as evidence. Each ticket *admits* one person. **2** To have room for; as, a dock that *admits* two boats. **3** To allow; to permit; as, a rule that *admits* no exceptions. **4** To agree to as true; to confess to; to acknowledge; as, to *admit* a mistake. — For synonyms see *acknowledge.*

ad·mit·tance \əd-ˈmit-n(t)s\ *n.* Entrance; admission to a place.

— The word *admission* is a synonym of *admittance: admittance* usually indicates allowance to enter a building or other place; *admission* may refer to the granting of rights, privileges, or membership, as in an organization or state.

ad·mit·ted \əd-ˈmit-əd\ *adj.* Confessed; granted; acknowledged. An *admitted* weakness of this plan is its high cost.

ad·mit·ted·ly \əd-ˈmit-əd-lē\ *adv.* Without disagreement; by general admission; undeniably; as, an *admittedly* bad mistake.

ad·mix·ture \ad-'miks-chər\ *n.* **1** A mixing; as, made by *admixture* of chemicals. **2** Something formed by mixing; a mixture. **3** Something added to another thing in mixing.

ad·mon·ish \əd-'män-ish\ *v.* **1** To warn of a fault; to reprove gently but seriously; as, to *admonish* a pupil for talking. **2** To urge with a warning; as, to *admonish* silence in the room. — For synonyms see *rebuke.* — **ad·mon·ish·ment,** *n.*

ad·mo·ni·tion \ˌad-mə-'nish-n\ *n.* A friendly warning; a gentle reproof.

ad·mon·i·to·ry \ad-'män-ə-ˌtōr-ē, -ˌtȯr-ē\ *adj.* Warning; reproving; as, an *admonitory* look.

ado \ə-'dü\ *n.* Fuss; excitement; trouble; as, much *ado* about nothing.

ado·be \ə-'dō-bē\ *n.* [From Spanish, there borrowed from Arabic *at-tub* meaning "the brick".] **1** Brick made of earth or clay dried in the sun. **2** A house built of adobe. — *adj.* Made of adobe; as, an *adobe* wall.

ad·o·les·cence \ˌad-l-'es-n(t)s\ *n.* The process of growth from childhood to maturity or the period during which such growth takes place.

ad·o·les·cent \ˌad-l-'es-nt\ *adj.* **1** Growing from childhood to maturity. **2** Characteristic of adolescence; youthful. — *n.* One that is in the state of adolescence.

adopt \ə-'däpt\ *v.* **1** To take legally a child of other parents and treat it as one's own; as, to *adopt* an orphan. **2** To take for one's own; as, to *adopt* someone else's idea. **3** To accept and approve; as, to *adopt* a plan at a meeting.

adop·tion \ə-'däpsh-n\ *n.* **1** An adopting or a being adopted; as, a son by *adoption.* **2** Acceptance or approval, as of a plan or policy.

ador·a·ble \ə-'dōr-əb-l, -'dȯr-\ *adj.* **1** Deserving to be adored. **2** Charming; lovely; as, an *adorable* child. — **ador·a·bly** \-ə-blē\ *adv.*

ad·o·ra·tion \ˌad-r-'āsh-n\ *n.* Worship; deep love.

adore \ə-'dōr, ə-'dȯr\ *v.;* **adored; ador·ing.** To worship; to have deep love and admiration for; as, to *adore* one's mother. — **ador·er** \-'dōr-r, -'dȯr-r\ *n.*

adorn \ə-'dȯrn\ *v.* To decorate with ornaments; to ornament; to beautify; as, to *adorn* oneself with jewelry.

adorn·ment \ə-'dȯrn-mənt\ *n.* **1** An adorning; decoration. **2** Something that adorns or is used for adorning.

ad·re·nal \ə-'drēn-l\ *adj.* Relating to, produced in, or derived from the adrenal glands.

adrenal gland. One of two ductless glands, located near the kidneys, in which the hormone **ad·ren·al·ine** \ə-'dren-l-ən\ is produced.

adrift \ə-'drift\ *adj.* or *adv.* **1** Drifting, without being tied or anchored; as, a damaged ship *adrift* in the storm. **2** Moving without aim or purpose; wandering.

adroit \ə-'drȯit\ *adj.* Skillful and ready with one's body or mind; clever; as, to be *adroit* at arithmetic; to make an *adroit* reply. — **adroit·ly,** *adv.*

ad·sorb \ad-'sȯrb, -'zȯrb\ *v.* To condense and hold without absorbing.

ad·sorp·tion \ad-'sȯrpsh-n, -'zȯrpsh-n\ *n.* The sticking of the molecules of gases, of dissolved substances, or of liquids to the surfaces of solid bodies with which the molecules are in contact.

ad·u·la·tion \ˌaj-l-'āsh-n\ *n.* Excessive praise; slavish flattery or worship. — **ad·u·la·to·ry** \'aj-l-ə-ˌtōr-ē, -ˌtȯr-ē\ *adj.*

adult \ə-'dəlt, 'ad-ˌəlt\ *adj.* Grown to full size and strength. — *n.* A fully grown person, animal, or plant.

adul·ter·ant \ə-'dəlt-r-ənt\ *n.* Something used to adulterate another thing.

adul·ter·ate \ə-'dəlt-r-ˌāt\ *v.;* **adul·ter·at·ed; adul·ter·at·ing.** To make impure or weaker by adding some other thing; as, to *adulterate* milk with water.

adul·ter·a·tion \ə-ˌdəlt-r-'āsh-n\ *n.* **1** The process of adulterating. **2** An adulterated product.

adul·ter·er \ə-'dəlt-r-r\ *n.* A person, especially a man, who commits adultery.

adul·ter·ess \ə-'dəlt-r-əs, ə-'dəl-trəs\ *n.* A woman who commits adultery.

adul·ter·ous \ə-'dəlt-r-əs, ə-'dəl-trəs\ *adj.* **1** Guilty of adultery. **2** Relating to adultery.

adul·tery \ə-'dəlt-r-ē\ *n.;* *pl.* **adul·ter·ies.** Sexual unfaithfulness on the part of a married person.

adv. Abbreviation for: **1** *adverb.* **2** *adverbial.* **3** *advertisement.*

ad·vance \əd-'van(t)s\ *v.;* **ad·vanced; ad·vanc·ing.** **1** To move forward; as, to *advance* a few yards. **2** To help forward; to help along; as, to *advance* a road-building job by hiring more laborers. **3** To promote or to be promoted; as, to be *advanced* from clerk to assistant manager. **4** To raise, or to rise, in rate or price. Gasoline has *advanced* another two cents. **5** To furnish, as money, before it is due; to furnish beforehand. **6** To bring forward; to propose; as, to *advance* a new plan. — *n.* **1** Movement forward; improvement; promotion; as, a new *advance* in medical science. **2** A rise in price; as, an *advance* in the cost of food. **3** A first step toward accomplishing a purpose, as toward making an acquaintance or patching up a quarrel. **4** Money supplied beforehand for some purpose; as, to ask for an *advance* on one's salary. — **in advance.** In front; ahead; before; beforehand.

ad·vanced \əd-'van(t)st\ *adj.* **1** In advance; in front; forward. **2** Ahead of others; above an elementary level; as, to have *advanced* ideas; to study *advanced* science. **3** Far along in years or progress; as, a man of *advanced* age; a disease in an *advanced* stage.

ad·vance·ment \əd-'van(t)s-mənt\ *n.* Movement forward; improvement; promotion; as, rapid *advancement* in school.

ad·van·tage \əd-'vant-ij\ *n.* Something that can be of help; a benefit; as, the *advantage* of a college education. — **take advantage of.** To make use of and profit from a favorable circumstance; as, to take *advantage* of an opportunity.

ad·van·ta·geous \ˌad-vən-'tā-jəs, ˌad-ˌvan-\ *adj.* Of advantage; favorable; useful; helpful; as, an *advantageous* position. — For synonyms see *beneficial.* — **ad·van·ta·geous·ly**, *adv.*

ad·vent \'ad-ˌvent\ *n.* **1** A coming; arrival; as, the *advent* of spring. **2** [with a capital] The period including the four Sundays before Christmas.

ad·ven·ti·tious \ˌad-vən-'tish-əs\ *adj.* **1** Added externally and not becoming a main part; additional; accidental. **2** Appearing out of the usual or normal place; as, *adventitious* buds. — **ad·ven·ti·tious·ly**, *adv.*

ad·ven·ture \əd-'vench-r\ *n.* **1** A bold undertaking in which risks are to be run and chances taken; as, the *adventures* of the pioneers. **2** The encountering of risks; as, a life free from *adventure.* **3** An unusual experience.

ad·ven·tur·er \əd-'vench-r-r\ *n.* **1** A person who seeks out adventures, or new and risky experiences. **2** A person who tries to gain profit for himself by tricking others.

ad·ven·ture·some \əd-'vench-rs-m\ *adj.* Inclined to take risks; daring.

ad·ven·tur·ous \əd-'vench-r(-)əs\ *adj.* **1** Daring; bold; as, an *adventurous* explorer. **2** Dangerous; risky; as, an *adventurous* trip. — **ad·ven·tur·ous·ly**, *adv.*

ad·verb \'ad-ˌvərb\ *n.* In grammar, a word used to modify a verb, adjective, or another adverb and often used to show degree (as *unusually* in "unusually tall"), manner (as *slowly* in "walk slowly"), place (as *here* in "sit here"), or time (as *soon* in "return soon").

ad·ver·bi·al \ad-'vər-bē-əl\ *adj.* Of an adverb; playing the part of an adverb; as, an *adverbial* phrase; an *adverbial* clause. — **ad·ver·bi·al·ly** \-ə-lē\ *adv.*

ad·ver·sary \'ad-vər-ˌser-ē\ *n.; pl.* **ad·ver·sar·ies.** An opponent; an enemy.

ad·verse \ad-'vərs, 'ad-ˌvərs\ *adj.* **1** Directed against a person or thing; opposing; as, *adverse* winds; *adverse* criticism. **2** Unfavorable to a person's interests or to the success of something; as, *adverse* circumstances. — **ad·verse·ly**, *adv.*

ad·ver·si·ty \ad-'vər-sət-ē\ *n.; pl.* **ad·ver·si·ties.** Misfortune; suffering; trouble. — For synonyms see *misfortune.*

ad·vert \ad-'vərt\ *v.* To turn one's attention, especially in the course of speaking or writing; refer; allude; as, to *advert* to a remark made by a previous speaker.

ad·ver·tise \'ad-vər-ˌtīz\ *v.;* **ad·ver·tised; ad·ver·tis·ing. 1** To announce publicly, as in print, over the radio, or on television; as, to *advertise* a sale. **2** To call to public attention, especially by stressing desirable qualities, in order to arouse a desire to purchase; as, to *advertise* a breakfast food. **3** To issue a notice or request; as, to *advertise* for a lost dog. — **ad·ver·tis·er** \-ˌtīz-r\ *n.*

ad·ver·tise·ment \ˌad-vər-'tīz-mənt, əd-'vərt-əz-mənt\ *n.* A notice advertising something.

ad·vice \əd-'vīs\ *n.* **1** A recommendation about what to do or say; as, to ask a friend's *advice* about buying a bicycle. **2** [usually in the plural] Information; news; as, the latest *advices* from Europe.

ad·vis·a·ble \əd-'vī-zəb-l\ *adj.* Reasonable or proper under the circumstances; wise. It is not *advisable* to swim just after a meal. — **ad·vis·a·bil·i·ty** \-ˌvī-zə-'bil-ət-ē\ *n.* — **ad·vis·a·bly** \-'vī-zə-blē\ *adv.*

ad·vise \əd-'vīz\ *v.;* **ad·vised; ad·vis·ing. 1** To give advice to; to recommend what is to be done; as, to *advise* a sick friend to see a doctor. **2** To inform; to notify. The travelers were *advised* of danger ahead.

ad·vised \əd-'vīzd\ *adj.* Thought out; considered; as, badly *advised* conduct. — **ad·vis·ed·ly** \-'vī-zəd-lē\ *adv.*

ad·vise·ment \əd-'vīz-mənt\ *n.* Careful consideration; as, to take a matter under *advisement.*

ad·vis·er or **ad·vi·sor** \əd-'vīz-r\ *n.* A person who gives advice, especially one appointed to advise students, as in their choice of studies.

ad·vi·so·ry \əd-'vīz-r(-)ē\ *adj.* **1** Having the power or right to advise; as, an *advisory* committee. **2** Giving or containing advice; as, an *advisory* opinion.

ad·vo·ca·cy \'ad-və-kə-sē\ *n.* An advocating; support. The majority gave strong *advocacy* to the proposal.

ad·vo·cate \'ad-və-kət, -ˌkāt\ *n.* **1** A person who takes up and supports, or argues for, any cause or policy; as, an *advocate* of free education. **2** A lawyer. — \-ˌkāt\ *v.;* **ad·vo·cat·ed; ad·vo·cat·ing.** To declare oneself in favor of; to recommend, or speak in favor of, publicly; as, to *advocate* higher wages and shorter working hours.

advt. Abbreviation for *advertisement.*

adz or **adze** \'adz\ *n.* A cutting tool with a thin curving blade set at right angles to the handle, used to trim off the surface of a piece of wood.

adz

aë·des \ā-'ēd-ēz\ *n. sing. and pl.* The mosquito that carries yellow fever from one person to another.

ae·gis \'ē-jəs\ *n.* **1** A shield or protection. **2** Sponsorship; patronage; as, a community drive waged under the *aegis* of the city council.

ae·on or **eon** \'ē-ən, 'ē-ˌän\ *n.* A vast period of time; an age.

aer·ate \'ā-ər-ˌāt, 'ar-ˌāt, 'er-ˌāt\ *v.;* **aer·at·ed; aer·at·ing. 1** To force gas into water or some other liquid. **2** To expose to air in order to purify or to freshen. — **aer·a·tion** \ˌā-ər-'āsh-n, ar-, er-\ *n.*

aer·i·al \'ar-ē-əl, 'er-ē-əl, *and, rarely for the noun,* ā-'ir-ē-əl\ *adj.* **1** Of the air; living in, produced by, done in, or used in, the air; as, an *aerial* circus; *aerial* warfare. **2** Resembling air; light and thin as air; as, *aerial* shapes like those in a dream. **3** Operating or operated high overhead upon or by means of elevated cables or rails; as, an *aerial* railroad. — *n.* A radio or television antenna.

aer·ie or **aery** \'ar-ē, 'er-ē, 'ir-ē, 'ā-rē\ *n.; pl.* **aer·ies.** A bird's nest, especially an eagle's, high on a rock.

aero-. A prefix meaning: air, aerial, as in *aeroplane.*

aer·o·bat·ics \ˌar-ə-'bat-iks, ˌer-\ *n. sing. and pl.* Performance of acrobatic stunts with an airplane, as for training or exhibition; air acrobatics.

aer·o·bic \ar-'ō-bik, er-\ *adj.* **1** Living or active only in the presence of oxygen. **2** Relating to or caused by aerobic bacteria.

aer·o·drome \'ar-ə-ˌdrōm, 'er-ə-\ *n. Chiefly British.* An airport.

aer·o·dy·nam·ics \ˌar-ō-dī-'nam-iks, ˌer-\ *n.* The science that deals with air and other gaseous substances under the action of force, and with their mechanical effects.

aer·ol·o·gy \ar-'äl-ə-jē, er-\ *n.* The branch of physics that treats of the atmosphere. — **aer·o·log·i·cal** \ˌar-ə-'läj-ik-l, ˌer-\ *adj.* — **aer·ol·o·gist** \ar-'äl-ə-jəst, er-\ *n.*

aer·o·naut \'ar-ə-ˌnȯt, 'er-\ *n.* A person who operates or travels in an airship or a balloon.

aer·o·nau·tics \ˌar-ə-'nȯt-iks, ˌer-\ *n.* The science that deals with the operation of aircraft. — **aer·o·nau·ti·cal** \-ik-l\ *adj.*

aer·o·pause \'ar-ə-ˌpȯz, 'er-\ *n.* The level above the earth's surface just above the altitude at which planes are (now or at any given time) able to fly.

aer·o·plane \'ar-ə-ˌplān, 'er-\ *n.* An airplane.

aer·o·sol bomb \'ar-ə-ˌsȯl, 'er-\. A small container from which an insecticide can be released in the form of a mist or a fine spray.

aer·o·space \'ar-ō-ˌspās, 'er-\ *n.* The earth's atmosphere and the space beyond.

aes·thet·ic or **es·thet·ic** \es-'thet-ik\ *adj.* **1** Having to do with beauty or with what is beautiful, especially as distinguished from what is useful; as, an *aesthetic* interest in antique furniture. **2** Sensitive to what is beautiful.

aes·thet·ics or **es·thet·ics** \es-'thet-iks\ *n.* The branch of philosophy that studies and explains the principles and forms of beauty, especially in art and literature.

afar \ə-'fär, ə-'får\ *adv.* At, to, or from a great distance; as, to see a man *afar* off; to travel *afar.*

afeard or **afeared** \ə-'fird\ *adj. Dialect.* Afraid.

af·fa·ble \'af-əb-l\ *adj.* Easy to speak to; courteous and friendly in conversation. — **af·fa·bil·i·ty** \ˌaf-ə-'bil-ət-ē\ *n.* — **af·fa·bly** \'af-ə-blē\ *adv.*

af·fair \ə-'far, ə-'fer\ *n.* **1** Something done or to be done; business of any kind; matter; concern; as, government *affairs;* a difficult *affair* to manage. **2** An event; a happening. **3** A brief romantic relationship.

af·fect \ə-'fekt\ *v.* **1** To attack or act on as a disease does. It used to be thought that night air *affected* the lungs. **2** To influence; to have an effect upon. The coach's criticism *affected* the players strongly. — For synonyms see *concern.*

af·fect \ə-'fekt\ *v.* **1** To be fond of using or wearing; as, to *affect* bright colors. **2** To pretend; to sham; as, to *affect* ignorance about something.

af·fec·ta·tion \ˌaf-ˌek-'tāsh-n\ *n.* An unnatural way of acting, intended to impress others.

af·fect·ed \ə-'fek-təd\ *adj.* Not natural or genuine; pretended; as, an *affected* interest in music; a man with *affected* manners. — **af·fect·ed·ly,** *adv.*

af·fect·ing \ə-'fek-ting\ *adj.* Arousing pity, sympathy, or sorrow; as, an *affecting* story.

af·fec·tion \ə-'feksh-n\ *n.* A feeling of love; a great fondness; as, *affection* for one's parents.

af·fec·tion \ə-'feksh-n\ *n.* A sickness; disease; as, an *affection* of the brain.

af·fec·tion·ate \ə-'feksh-n(-)ət\ *adj.* Feeling or showing a great liking for a person or thing; loving; tender. — **af·fec·tion·ate·ly,** *adv.*

af·fer·ent \'af-r-ənt\ *adj.* Conducting inward to a part or an organ; as, *afferent* nerves.

af·fi·ance \ə-'fī-ən(t)s\ *v.;* **af·fi·anced; af·fi·anc·ing.** To engage to marry; to betroth; as, his *affianced* bride.

af·fi·da·vit \ˌaf-ə-'dā-vət\ *n.* A sworn written statement, especially one made under oath before an authorized official.

af·fil·i·ate \ə-'fil-ē-ˌāt\ *v.;* **af·fil·i·at·ed; af·fil·i·at·ing.** To unite or associate in a close relationship; as, to *affiliate* oneself with a newly organized political party. Several stores *affiliated* to form a citywide chain. — \-ē-ət, -ē-ˌāt\ *n.* **1** A person who has affiliated himself. **2** A branch organization.

af·fil·i·a·tion \ə-ˌfil-ē-'āsh-n\ *n.* **1** The action of affiliating or the state of being affiliated. **2** An affiliated group.

af·fin·i·ty \ə-'fin-ət-ē\ *n.; pl.* **af·fin·i·ties. 1** A close relationship or connection; kinship; as, an *affinity* between two languages. **2** A special attraction supposed to exist between some persons. **3** A person who has a special attraction for another person.

af·firm \ə-'fərm\ *v.* To state with confidence; to declare positively; to assert; as, to *affirm* one's innocence of any wrongdoing.

af·fir·ma·tion \ˌaf-r-'māsh-n\ *n.* An assertion or declaration, as of the truth of something; a positive statement.

af·firm·a·tive \ə-'fər-mət-iv\ *adj.* Answering "yes" to a question; as, an *affirmative* reply. — *n.* **1** A word or phrase expressing agreement. **2** The affirmative side of a question or debate. — **af·firm·a·tive·ly,** *adv.*

af·fix \ə-'fiks\ *v.* **1** To fasten; to attach; as, to *affix* a stamp to a letter. **2** To add at the end; as, to *affix* one's signature to a document. — \'af-ˌiks\ *n.* Something affixed; especially, a prefix or a suffix.

af·flict \ə-'flikt\ *v.* To cause some great hurt or trouble to; to make miserable; as, a city *afflicted* by an epidemic; a child *afflicted* with boils.

af·flic·tion \ə-'fliksh-n\ *n.* **1** A condition of pain, distress, or grief; great sorrow or suffering. **2** Anything that causes pain or distress. Boils are an *affliction.*

af·flu·ence \'af-ˌlü-ən(t)s\ *n.* **1** Great wealth or property; riches; as, a man of *affluence.* **2** Great prosperity; as, a period of *affluence.*

af·flu·ent \'af-ˌlü-ənt\ *adj.* **1** Abundant; plentifully supplied. **2** Well supplied with material possessions; wealthy; rich. — *n.* A stream flowing into a larger stream or into a lake; a tributary.

af·ford \ə-'fōrd, ə-'fȯrd\ *v.* **1** To have money enough to buy; as, to be unable to *afford* a new car. **2** To be able to do or to bear without serious harm. No one can *afford* to waste his strength. **3** To give; to furnish. Playing tennis *affords* healthful exercise.

af·fray \ə-'frā\ *n.* A noisy quarrel or fight; a brawl.

af·fright \ə-'frīt\ *v. Archaic.* To frighten.

af·front \ə-'frənt\ *v.* To offend by showing disrespect; to insult. — *n.* A deliberately offensive act or word; an insult.

Af·ghan \'af-gən\ *adj.* Of or relating to Afghanistan. — *n.* **1** A native of Afghanistan. **2** The chief language of Afghanistan. **3** [with a small letter] A blanket or shawl of knitted or crocheted colored wool.

afield \ə-'fēld\ *adv.* **1** To, in, or on, the field. **2** Away from home. **3** Out of one's regular path or course.

afire \ə-'fīr\ *adj.* On fire; burning.

aflame \ə-'flām\ *adj.* **1** In flames; flaming. **2** Glowing; as, a face *aflame* with blushes.

afloat \ə-'flōt\ *adj.* **1** Floating. **2** On board a ship; at sea; as, sailors eager to be *afloat.* **3** Covered with water; flooded; as, a ship with decks *afloat.* **4** Circulating; as, a rumor that was *afloat* in the town.

aflut·ter \ə-'flət-r\ *adj.* In a flutter; fluttering; as, hearts *aflutter* with excitement.

afoot \ə-'fu̇t\ *adv.* or *adj.* **1** On foot; as, to go the whole way *afoot.* **2** In motion; stirring; as, trouble *afoot.*

afore \ə-'fōr, -'fȯr\ *adv., prep.,* or *conj. Archaic* or *dial.* Before.

afore·men·tioned or **afore–men·tioned** \ə-'fōr-'mench-nd, -'fȯr-\ *adj.* Mentioned previously.

afore·said \ə-'fōr-ˌsed, -'fȯr-\ *adj.* Said, named, or stated before; as, the *aforesaid* persons.

afore·thought \ə-'fōr-ˌthȯt, -'fȯr-\ *adj.* Thought of, planned, or designed beforehand; premeditated; as, malice *aforethought.*

afoul \ə-'fau̇l\ *adv.* or *adj.* In collision; in a tangle. — **run afoul of.** To get into trouble with.

afraid \ə-'frād; *in the South, also* ə-'fred\ *adj.* **1** Filled with fear; frightened. **2** Filled with concern, regret, or reluctance.

afresh \ə-'fresh\ *adv.* Freshly; again; once more; as, to forget past failures and start *afresh.*

Af·ri·can \'af-rik-n\ *adj.* Of or relating to Africa. — *n.* A native or inhabitant of Africa.

African violet. A perennial plant that is a popular house plant, with soft hairy clustered leaves that are often purplish beneath and with showy violetlike flowers that are usually violet-colored but in some varieties are white, pink, or blue.

aft \'aft\ *adv.* Near or toward the stern of a boat.

af·ter \'aft-r\ *adv.* Later; afterward. The storm broke shortly *after.* — *prep.* **1** Behind in place; as, in line one *after* another. **2** Later in time than; as, *after* dinner. **3** Below in rank or order. A colonel comes *after* a general. **4** In search of. What is he *after?* **5** In imitation of; for; as, to be named *after* one's father. **6** According to; as, *after* an old custom. **7** In view of; considering. *After* our objections, you should not have gone. — *adj.* **1** Later; as, in *after* years. **2** Rear; especially, nearer the stern of a ship; as, the *after* lifeboats. — *conj.* Later than the time when. The sun came out *after* the storm ceased.

af·ter·burn·er \'aft-r-ˌbərn-r\ *n.* An auxiliary burner attached to the tail pipe of a turbojet engine, used for forcing fuel into the hot exhaust gases and burning it to provide additional thrust; a tail-pipe burner.

af·ter·deck \'aft-r-ˌdek\ *n.* The rear half of the deck of a boat.

af·ter·ef·fect \'aft-r-ə-ˌfekt\ *n.* **1** An effect that follows its cause after some time has passed. **2** A secondary effect coming on after the first or immediate effect has subsided; as, a medicine with no noticeable *aftereffects.*

af·ter·glow \'aft-r-ˌglō\ *n.* A glow remaining where a light has disappeared, as in the sky after sunset.

af·ter·math \'aft-r-ˌmath\ *n.* **1** A second mowing; a second-growth crop, as of hay. **2** Consequences, or a consequence; as, the *aftermath* of war.

af·ter·noon \ˌaft-r-'nün\ *n.* The time of day between noon and evening.

af·ter·thought \'aft-r-ˌthȯt\ *n.* A later thought about something one has done or said.

af·ter·ward \'aft-r-wərd\ or **af·ter·wards** \-wərdz\ *adv.* At a later time.

again \ə-'gen\ *adv.* **1** In return. Bring us word *again.* **2** Another time; anew; as, to visit *again* the scenes of one's childhood. **3** In addition; as, half as much *again.* **4** On the other hand. **5** Further; moreover. *Again,* there is another matter to consider.

against \ə-'gen(t)st\ *prep.* **1** In an opposite direction to; in opposition to; contrary to; as, to swim *against* the current. **2** So as to hit, strike, or touch; as, to lean *against* the wall. **3** In preparation for; as, to store food *against* the winter.

agape \ə-'gāp, ə-'gap\ *adj.* Having the mouth open in wonder or surprise; gaping; as, a crowd *agape* at the speaker.

agar or **agar-agar** \'ä-ˌgär-'ä-ˌgär, 'å-ˌgår-'å-ˌgår\ *n.* **1** A jellylike substance obtained from certain seaweeds, used especially in nutritive material for raising bacteria and fungi. **2** A culture medium containing agar.

ag·ate \'ag-ət\ *n.* **1** A stone with colors formed in strips or cloudy masses. **2** A child's marble of agate or of agate-colored glass.

aga·ve \ə-'gä-vē, -'gå-\ *n.* A plant of the amaryllis family, having spiny-edged leaves, and flowers on a long upright stem; especially, the century plant.

agave

age \'āj\ *n.* **1** The time from birth or beginning to a certain date; as, a boy six years of *age.* **2** The time of life when a person receives full legal rights; as, to come of *age.* **3** The later part of life; as, a mind as active in *age* as in youth. **4** Normal lifetime. The *age* of dogs is about twelve years. **5** A period of history; as, the machine *age.* **6** A long period of time. It happened *ages* ago. — *v.;* **aged** \'ājd\; **ag·ing** or **age·ing.** To make old; to become old; as, to be *aged* by long years of hard work.

-age \ij\. A suffix that can mean: **1** The act or process of, as in *passage* or *marriage.* **2** The result of, as in *shrinkage* or *breakage.* **3** State, condition, or rank, as in *baronage* or *peerage.* **4** The total number or amount of, as in *mileage* or *leverage.* **5** The fee charged for or for the use of, as in *postage* or *towage.* **6** The home of, as in *parsonage* or *orphanage.*

aged *adj.* **1** \'ā-jəd\ Very old; as, an *aged* man; an *aged* oak. **2** \'ājd\ Of age; as, a boy *aged* ten.

age·less \'āj-ləs\ *adj.* Timeless; seeming to be young or new or fresh forever; as, an *ageless* story.

agen·cy \'āj-n-sē\ *n.; pl.* **agen·cies. 1** Action; active influence; as, a quarrel settled through the *agency* of neighbors. **2** The business or the place of business of a person or company that acts for someone else; as, an automobile *agency.*

agen·da \ə-'jen-də\ *n. pl.; sing.* **agen·dum** \-'jend-m\. A list, outline, or plan of things to be done; the items of business to be considered, as at a meeting.

agent \'āj-nt\ *n.* **1** A person trusted to do business for someone else; as, a local *agent* for an insurance company. **2** Anything that will produce a certain effect. Sunlight and water are *agents* that help to make plants grow.

age-old \'ā-ˌjōld\ *adj.* Having existed for ages; ancient; as, an *age-old* problem.

ag·glu·ti·nate \ə-'glüt-n-ˌāt\ *v.;* **ag·glu·ti·nat·ed; ag·glu·ti·nat·ing.** To unite or fasten together as if with glue; to cause to adhere; to clump together. — **ag·glu·ti·na·tion** \ə-ˌglüt-n-'āsh-n\ *n.*

ag·gran·dize \ə-'gran-ˌdīz, 'ag-rən-ˌdīz\ *v.;* **ag·gran·dized; ag·gran·diz·ing. 1** To increase; to make great or greater, as in power, rank, or resources. **2** To make appear great or greater; to exaggerate. — **ag·gran·dize·ment** \ə-'gran-dəz-mənt, -ˌdīz-, ˌag-rən-'dīz-mənt\ *n.*

ag·gra·vate \'ag-rə-ˌvāt\ *v.;* **ag·gra·vat·ed; ag·gra·vat·ing. 1** To make worse or more severe; as, rising flood waters *aggravated* by rain. **2** To irritate; to annoy; to provoke; as, to be *aggravated* by an unfriendly remark.

ag·gra·va·tion \ˌag-rə-'vāsh-n\ *n.* **1** The act of making something worse or more severe; an increase in severity. The treatment caused an *aggravation* of the pain. **2** Something that makes a thing worse or more severe. The cold winter was an *aggravation* of their misery. **3** Irritation; annoyance.

ag·gre·gate \'ag-rig-ət, -rə-ˌgāt\ *adj.* Formed by the collection of individual items or units into one mass or sum; total; combined; as, the *aggregate* expenses for a trip. — *n.* A collection or sum of individual items or units. — \-rə-ˌgāt\ *v.;* **ag·gre·gat·ed; ag·gre·gat·ing. 1** To collect or unite into one mass or sum. **2** To amount to as a whole; as, daily expenses *aggregating* ten dollars.

ag·gre·ga·tion \ˌag-rə-'gāsh-n\ *n.* **1** The collection or gathering of units into one mass or sum. **2** A number of separate units, especially persons or objects, brought together to form a whole.

ag·gres·sion \ə-'gresh-n\ *n.* An attack; especially, a first attack by one country on territory belonging to another country.

ag·gres·sive \ə-'gres-iv\ *adj.* **1** Showing a readiness to attack others; as, an *aggressive* dog; an *aggressive* nation. **2** Energetic; forceful; as, an *aggressive* salesman; an *aggressive* campaign to raise money for a new library. — **ag·gres·sive·ly,** *adv.*

ag·gres·sor \ə-'gres-r\ *n.* A person or a country that makes a first attack or begins a quarrel.

ag·grieved \ə-'grēvd\ *adj.* Having a grievance; feeling that one has been unjustly treated; distressed.

aghast \ə-'gast\ *adj.* Showing signs of terror or horror; struck with amazement or surprise.

ag·ile \'aj-l\ *adj.* **1** Able to move quickly and easily; quick and active; nimble. **2** Mentally quick; as, an *agile* thinker. — **ag·ile·ly** \'aj-l-(l)ē\ *adv.*

agil·i·ty \ə-'jil-ət-ē\ *n.* The quality or state of being agile in body or mind; ability to move quickly and easily; nimbleness; as, the grace and *agility* of a born gymnast.

aging. A pres. part. of *age.*

ag·i·tate \'aj-ə-ˌtāt\ *v.;* **ag·i·tat·ed; ag·i·tat·ing. 1** To shake jerkily; to set in violent or irregular motion; as, water *agitated* by wind. **2** To stir up; to excite; to disturb; as, to be *agitated* by bad news. **3** To arouse public interest in something, especially by discussion or appeals; as, to *agitate* for better schools.

ag·i·ta·tion \ˌaj-ə-'tāsh-n\ *n.* **1** The action of agitating or the state of being agitated; violent, especially irregular, movement. **2** Disturbance of mind or feelings; as, *agitation* over a child's illness. **3** The arousing of public feeling, as through discussion or appeals; as, *agitation* against any increase in taxes.

ag·i·ta·tor \'aj-ə-ˌtāt-r\ *n.* A person or thing that agitates; especially, a person who tries to arouse public feeling about something.

agleam \ə-'glēm\ *adj.* Gleaming.

aglit·ter \ə-'glit-r\ *adj.* Glittering.

aglow \ə-'glō\ *adj.* Glowing.

ag·nos·tic \ag-'näs-tik\ *n.* A person who does not deny the possible existence of God but holds that this existence, and the origin of the universe, are not known and probably cannot be known. — **ag·nos·ti·cism** \-tə-ˌsiz-m\ *n.*

ago \ə-'gō\ *adj.* or *adv.* Past; gone by; in the past; as, a week *ago;* long *ago.*

agog \ə-'gäg\ *adj.* Eager; stirred up. The whole school was *agog* with excitement.

ag·o·nize \'ag-n-ˌīz\ *v.;* **ag·o·nized; ag·o·niz·ing. 1** To suffer, or to cause to suffer, extreme pain or anguish of body or mind. **2** To strive desperately; to struggle. — **ag·o·niz·ing·ly** \-ˌī-zing-lē\ *adv.*

ag·o·ny \'ag-n-ē\ *n.; pl.* **ag·o·nies. 1** Extreme suffering of mind or body; great pain. **2** A sudden apparently uncontrollable display of feeling or emotion. **3** The last sufferings of a dying person or animal.

ag·o·ra \'ag-r-ə\ *n.; pl.* **ag·o·ras** \-r-əz\ or **ag·o·rae** \-r-ˌē\. An assembly or a place of assembly; especially, the market place in an ancient Greek city.

agrar·i·an \ə-'grer-ē-ən\ *adj.* **1** Having to do with the land or with its ownership; as, *agrarian* reforms. **2** Organized or designed to aid farmers and farming interests; as, an *agrarian* political party.

agree \ə-'grē\ *v.;* **agreed; agree·ing. 1** To give one's approval; to consent; as, to *agree* to a plan. **2** To admit. The driver *agreed* that he had been going too fast. **3** To be alike. The two statements *agree* in every detail. **4** To get on well together. The two children now *agree* better than they did. **5** To come to an understanding; as, to *agree* on a price. **6** To go well. Too much rich food will not *agree* with you. **7** In grammar, to be alike or correspond in gender, number, case, or person.

agree·a·ble \ə-'grē-əb-l\ *adj.* **1** Pleasing; pleasant; as, food *agreeable* to the taste; an *agreeable* speaking voice. **2** Willing to agree; as, to be *agreeable* to a friend's suggestion. — **agree·a·bly** \-ə-blē\ *adv.*

agreed \ə-'grēd\ *adj.* Settled by agreement; agreed upon; as, to buy a bicycle at a previously *agreed* price.

agree·ment \ə-'grē-mənt\ *n.* **1** An agreeing; harmony of opinion or action. **2** An exchange of promises; a mutual understanding or arrangement; as, a trade *agreement* between two countries. **3** A written record of a mutual understanding. **4** In grammar, correspondence with respect to gender, number, case, or person.

— The words *bargain* and *contract* are synonyms of *agreement: agreement* generally suggests a mutual arrangement between two persons or two groups; *bargain* may refer to an informal agreement, especially one concerning purchases and sales; *contract* usually applies to a formal legal agreement, often written.

ag·ri·cul·tur·al \ˌag-rə-'kəlch-r(-)əl\ *adj.* Having to do with farming; as, *agricultural* areas; *agricultural* machinery.

ag·ri·cul·ture \'ag-rə-ˌkəlch-r\ *n.* The science or practice of producing crops and raising livestock; farming.

ag·ri·cul·tur·ist \ˌag-rə-'kəlch-r(-)əst\ or **ag·ri·cul·tur·al·ist** \-'kəlch-r(-)ə-ləst\ *n.* **1** A farmer. **2** An expert in agriculture.

agron·o·my \ə-'grän-ə-mē\ *n.* The branch of agriculture that deals with the raising of crops and the treatment of the soil. — **agron·o·mist** \-ə-məst\ *n.*

aground \ə-'graůnd\ *adv.* or *adj.* On the ground; ashore; stranded; as, a ship *aground* on a reef.

agt. Abbreviation for *agent.*

ague \'ā-ˌgyü\ *n.* **1** A disease in which chills, fever, and sweating occur at regular intervals. **2** A state of shaking, as with cold; a chill.

ah \'ä, 'å\ *interj.* An exclamation expressing various feelings, such as regret, scorn, or delight.

aha \ä-'hä, å-'hå\ *interj.* An exclamation expressing various feelings, such as triumph or scorn.

ahead \ə-'hed\ *adv.* **1** At the front; in front; as, to follow the man *ahead* of one. **2** Toward the front; forward; as, to walk straight *ahead.* **3** In advance; as, *ahead* of one's class in arithmetic. **4** In a position of advantage; as, to be ten dollars *ahead.*

ahoy \ə-'hȯi\ *interj.* A word used by sailors in hailing or attracting attention; as, ship *ahoy!*

aid \'ād\ *v.* To help; to assist. — *n.* **1** Help; assistance; as, to need *aid* in lifting a heavy box. **2** A person who aids; an assistant; a helper. **3** Something that is of help or assistance; as, a sale of household *aids* and appliances.

aide \'ād\ *n.* **1** A military or naval officer acting as assistant to a superior. **2** Any assistant.

aide-de-camp or **aid-de-camp** \'ād-də-'kamp\ *n.; pl.* **aides-de-camp** or **aids-de-camp** \'ādz-də-\. An officer who is in attendance upon a general or a chief official, as a governor, whom he serves as a special assistant.

ai·grette \ā-'gret, 'ā-ˌgret\ *n.* A plume or decorative tuft for the head.

ail \'āl\ *v.* **1** To be ill or uncomfortable. Persons who are *ailing* should report to the doctor. **2** To trouble; to make miserable; to be the matter with. The doctor soon discovered what *ailed* his patient.

ai·ler·on \'āl-r-ˌän\ *n.* A hinged flap on an airplane, usually part of the outer rear surface of a wing.

aileron

ail·ment \'āl-mənt\ *n.* A sickness.

aim \'ām\ *v.* **1** To point or direct, as a weapon or a blow, toward something one wishes to hit; as, to *aim* carefully before firing. **2** To direct one's effort towards achieving a purpose; as, to *aim* at becoming a doctor. **3** To have for one's purpose; to intend; to attempt; as, to *aim* to please; to *aim* to succeed. — *n.* **1** An aiming; the directing of a weapon or missile at a target; as, to take good *aim.* **2** Purpose; goal; as, to decide what will be one's chief *aim* in life.

aim·less \'ām-ləs\ *adj.* Without purpose or aim; as, *aimless* wandering around the city; an *aimless* life. — **aim·less·ly**, *adv.*

ain't \(')ānt\. A contraction of *are not,* used also for *am not, is not, has not,* and *have not.*

☞ Though many people disapprove of the use of *ain't,* the word is heard in all parts of the United States and among all kinds of people. It is, however, heard more commonly among less well-educated people and it is seldom seen in print except as part of the dialogue in stories and plays.

air \'ar, 'er\ *n.* **1** The invisible mixture of odorless, tasteless gases that surrounds the earth. **2** Air in motion; a light breeze. Not a breath of *air* was stirring. **3** Outward appearance; apparent nature; as, a small boy with the *air* of an old man. The old house had an *air* of mystery. **4** [in the plural] Unnatural manners put on in order to impress other people; as, to give oneself *airs* at a party. **5** A tune; a melody; as, to whistle the *air* of an old song. **6** The substance through which radio waves are regarded as being transmitted; as, to go on the *air.* — *v.* **1** To place in the air for the purpose of cooling, refreshing, or cleansing; as, to *air* blankets. **2** To make known in public; as, to *air* one's opinion. — *adj.* **1** Holding, conducting, or supplying air; as, an *air* bladder; an *air* passage. **2** Worked or driven by air or, especially, by compressed air; as, an *air* hammer; an *air* rifle. **3** Of or having to do with aircraft or the navigation of the air; as, an *air* attack; an *air* lane.

air base. A base of operations for aircraft, especially military aircraft.

air brake. **1** A brake operated by a piston driven by compressed air, as on a railroad car or motor truck. **2** A surface that may be projected into the air stream for increasing the resistance and lowering the speed of an airplane, as in gliding or landing.

air-con·di·tion \ˌark-n-'dish-n, ˌerk-\ *v.* To treat by a process (**air conditioning**) in which the air is cleaned and provided with the proper amount of moisture, and sometimes with a desired temperature, before it enters a room or a building; as, to *air-condition* a store.

air·craft \'ar-ˌkraft, 'er-\ *n. sing. and pl.* Any machine that can rise in the air and move through it, as an airplane, a balloon, or a dirigible.

aircraft carrier. A ship designed to carry aircraft and so designed that aircraft can be launched from it and landed on it.

air·drome \'ar-ˌdrōm, 'er-\ *n.* An airport.

air·drop \'ar-ˌdräp, 'er-\ *n.* A parachuting of food, ammunition, or other supplies or equipment from an airplane, especially to isolated personnel. — *v.;* **air·dropped**; **air·drop·ping.** To drop, as supplies, from an airplane.

air·field \'ar-ˌfēld, 'er-\ *n.* A field where aircraft may take off or land.

air·foil \'ar-ˌfȯil, 'er-\ *n.* Any surface of an aircraft, as a wing or rudder, designed to produce reaction from the air through which it moves.

air force. The military organization of a nation for air warfare.

airier. Comparative of *airy.*

airiest. Superlative of *airy.*

air·i·ly \'ar-ə-lē, 'er-\ *adv.* In an airy manner; lightly.

air·ing \'ar-ing, 'er-\ *n.* **1** Exposure to air for freshening or drying. **2** A walk, run, or ride in the open air.

air letter. **1** An airmail letter. **2** A sheet of paper designed for folding and sealing, with a message written on the inside, so as to form an envelope, sometimes bearing a stamp, for airmail delivery.

air·lift \'ar-ˌlift, 'er-\ *n.* A supply line operated by aircraft. — *v.* To transport by aircraft.

air·line \'ar-ˌlīn, 'er-\ *n.*, or **air line**. **1** A system of transportation by aircraft. **2** A company operating such a system. **3** A regular route followed by such a system.

air·lin·er \'ar-ˌlīn-r, 'er-\ *n.*, or **air liner**. A large commercial passenger aircraft operating over an airline.

airliner

air·mail \'ar-'māl, 'er-\ *n.* **1** The system of transporting mail by aircraft. **2** Mail transported by aircraft. — *v.* To send by airmail.

air·man \'ar-mən, 'er-\ *n.; pl.* **air·men** \-mən\. **1** A man who flies in an aircraft, especially as its pilot or as a member of its crew; an aviator. **2** An enlisted man or woman of the United States Air Force.

air mass. A vast body of air extending hundreds or, sometimes, thousands of miles and having approximately the same temperature and humidity at any given level throughout its whole extent.

air-mind·ed \'ar-'mīn-dəd, 'er-\ *adj.* Interested in aviation or in air travel. We live in an increasingly *air-minded* age.

air·plane \'ar-ˌplān, 'er-\ *n.* An aircraft that is heavier than air and is driven through the air by a propeller or a rearward jet.

air pocket. Any condition of the air that causes an airplane to drop suddenly.

air·port \'ar-ˌpōrt, 'er-, -ˌpȯrt\ *n.* A place either on land or on water where aircraft may land to receive or discharge passengers or cargo, or to take on fuel or make repairs.

air pump. A pump for removing air from, or compressing air in, a closed space.

air raid. A raid by aircraft, especially for dropping bombs on a town or city.

air·ship \'ar-ˌship, 'er-\ *n.* An aircraft that is lifted and kept in the air by gas, and that has a propeller and rudder; a dirigible balloon.

air·sick \'ar-ˌsik, 'er-\ *adj.* Sick at the stomach from the rapid change of altitude, high speed, or rolling and pitching of an aircraft.

air·strip \'ar-ˌstrip, 'er-\ *n.* A long, narrow, hard-surfaced runway on which aircraft can take off and land.

air·tight \'ar-'tīt, 'er-\ *adj.* **1** So tightly sealed that no air can get in or out. **2** Leaving no opening for attack; as, *airtight* defenses; an *airtight* argument.

air·way \'ar-ˌwā, 'er-\ *n.* **1** A passage for a current of air. **2** A regular route for aircraft.

air·wor·thy \'ar-ˌwər-t͟hē, 'er-\ *adj.* Fit or safe for operation in the air; as, a new plane that had not yet proved itself *airworthy.*

airy \'ar-ē, 'er-ē\ *adj.;* **air·i·er** \-ē-ər\; **air·i·est** \-ē-əst\. **1** Of or belonging to the air; aerial; as, *airy* spirits. **2** Open to the air; breezy; as, an *airy* room. **3** Like air in lightness; delicate; graceful; as, *airy* music. **4** Without sound or solid basis; as, a speech made up of *airy* nothings.

aisle \'īl\ *n.* A passageway into which rows of seats open, as in a church or a theater.

ajar \ə-'jär, ə-'jȧr\ *adj.* Slightly open, as a door or a gate.

ajar \ə-'jär, ə-'jȧr\ *adj.* Out of harmony.

akim·bo \ə-'kim-ˌbō\ *adj.* or *adv.* With the hand on the hip and the elbow turned outward.

man with arms akimbo

akin \ə-'kin\ *adj.* **1** Related by blood. **2** Of the same or similar kind; alike. Pity is *akin* to love.

-al \əl, l\. A suffix that can mean: **1** Belonging to, of or relating to, appropriate to, or having the character of, as in *autumnal, natural, architectural, continental.* **2** The action of, as in *arrival, acquittal, disposal, rehearsal.*

al·a·bas·ter \'al-ə-ˌbast-r\ *n.* A stone of fine texture, usually white. — *adj.* Of or resembling the color and texture of alabaster.

à la carte \ˌal-ə-'kärt, -'kȧrt\. By the bill of fare; dish by dish from the menu, with a stated price for each; as, to order a meal *à la carte.*

alack \ə-'lak\ *interj.* An exclamation expressing sorrow or regret.

alac·ri·ty \ə-'lak-rət-ē\ *n.* A cheerful readiness to do something; briskness; liveliness.

ala·mode \ˌal-ə-'mōd\ *adj.* [From French phrase *à la mode* meaning "according to the fashion".] **1** Fashionable; in style. **2** Served topped by a mound of ice cream; as, pie *alamode.*

alarm \ə-'lärm, ə-'lȧrm\ *n.* [From French *alarme,* there borrowed from Italian *all' arme* meaning "to arms".] **1** A warning of danger. **2** A bell or other device to wake or warn people. **3** Sudden surprise and fear; as, the campers' *alarm* at the rising water. — For synonyms see *fear.* — *v.* To fill with sudden surprise and fear; as, to be *alarmed* by an explosion.

alarm clock. A clock that can be set to sound an alarm at any desired time.

alarm·ist \ə-'lär-məst, -'lȧr-\ *n.* A person easily alarmed or fond of alarming others, especially needlessly.

alar·um \ə-'lar-əm\. Variant of *alarm.*

alas \ə-'las\ *interj.* An exclamation expressing sorrow, regret, pity, or fear of evil.

Alas·kan \ə-'lask-n\ *adj.* Of or relating to Alaska. — *n.* A native or inhabitant of Alaska.

alb \'alb\ *n.* A full-length white linen garment worn by priests of some churches when celebrating Mass.

alb

Al·ba·ni·an \al-'bā-nē-ən, ȯl-\ *adj.* Of or relating to Albania. — *n.* **1** A native of Albania. **2** The language of the Albanians.

al·ba·tross \'al-bə-ˌtrȯs, -ˌträs\ *n.* A very large web-footed sea bird, often seen at great distances from land.

al·be·it \ȯl-'bē-ət, al-\ *conj.* Even though; although.

al·bi·no \al-'bī-ˌnō\ *n.; pl.* **al·bi·nos.** **1** A human being or lower animal lacking normal coloring matter in skin, hair, and eyes. **2** A plant that lacks coloring matter. — **al·bi·nism** \'alb-n-ˌiz-m\ *n.*

al·bum \'al-bəm\ *n.* **1** A book with blank pages, in which to put a collection, as of photographs or stamps. **2** A published collection, as of piano music or reproductions of paintings, in book form. **3** A container in the form of an envelope, a book, or a box, for holding one or more phonograph records.

al·bu·men \al-'byü-mən\ *n.* **1** The white of an egg. **2** Albumin.

al·bu·min \al-'byü-mən\ *n.* A protein found in blood serum and in milk and muscle, and also in many vegetable tissues and fluids.

al·che·mist \'alk-m-əst\ *n.* One studying or practicing alchemy.

al·che·my \'alk-m-ē\ *n.* A medieval chemistry aiming to change base metals into gold and to find a single cure for all diseases.

al·co·hol \'al-kə-ˌhȯl\ *n.* **1** A colorless flammable liquid that is made chiefly from molasses and grain, is the intoxicating substance in fermented and distilled liquors, and is used especially as a solvent. **2** Any liquor containing alcohol, as beer, wine, or gin; such liquors in general.

al·co·hol·ic \ˌal-kə-'hȯl-ik, -'häl-\ *adj.* Of or containing alcohol; as, an *alcoholic* drink. — *n.* A person that is affected with alcoholism.

al·co·hol·ism \'al-kə-ˌhȯl-ˌiz-m\ *n.* Continued excessive and usually uncontrollable use of alcoholic drinks or the sickness associated with this practice.

al·cove \'al-ˌkōv\ *n.* **1** A section of a room set back from the main part; a recess. **2** A small room opening into and forming part of a larger room.

Ald. or **Aldm.** Abbreviation for *Alderman.*

al·der \'ȯld-r\ *n.* Any one of a number of trees and shrubs related to the birches.

al·der·man \'ȯld-r-mən\ *n.; pl.* **al·der·men** \-mən\. A member of the governing or legislative body of certain cities, towns, or boroughs. — **al·der·man·ic** \ˌȯld-r-'man-ik\ *adj.*

ale \'āl\ *n.* **1** An alcoholic drink made, like beer, from malt and flavored with hops but in some countries differing from beer in color and taste. **2** A nonalcoholic drink made from roots or from other parts of plants; as, ginger *ale.*

alee \ə-'lē\ *adv.* or *adj.* On or toward the side of a ship away from the wind.

alert \ə-'lərt\ *adj.* [From Italian *all' erta* meaning "on the watch".] **1** Watchful; wide-awake; as, an *alert* guard. **2** Nimble; active; brisk; as, *alert* movements. — For synonyms see *vigilant.* — *n.* **1** An alarm warning of coming danger, as from enemy aircraft. **2** The period of time during which such an alarm lasts. — *v.* To make alert; as, to *alert* a city for an air raid. — **on the alert.** Watchful, especially against attack or surprise. — **alert·ly,** *adv.*

al·fal·fa \al-'fal-fə\ *n.* A plant with cloverlike leaves and purple flowers, used as a food for horses and cattle.

alfalfa

al·ga \'al-gə\ *n.; pl.* **al·gae** \'al-(ˌ)jē\. Any plant of a group that forms the lowest division of the vegetable kingdom and that includes seaweeds and related forms growing in fresh water or on land. — **al·gal** \'alg-l\ *adj.*

al·ge·bra \'al-jə-brə\ *n.* The branch of mathematics that uses a system of letters and other symbols in calculating and that deals with negative and imaginary numbers as well as with the positive and real numbers of arithmetic.

al·ge·bra·ic \ˌal-jə-'brā-ik\ *adj.* Of, relating to, or used in algebra; as, an *algebraic* equation. — **al·ge·bra·i·cal·ly** \-ik-l(-)ē\ *adv.*

ali·as \'ā-lē-əs, 'āl-yəs\ *adv.* [From Latin, meaning "otherwise".] Otherwise; otherwise called; as, John Doe *alias* Richard Roe. — *n.; pl.* **ali·as·es.** Another name; a false name; as, to go about under an *alias.*

al·i·bi \'al-ə-ˌbī\ *n.; pl.* **al·i·bis** \-ˌbīz\. **1** The plea made by a person accused of a crime that, when the crime occurred, he was somewhere else. **2** An excuse. — *v.;* **al·i·bied** \-ˌbīd\; **al·i·bi·ing** \-ˌbī-ing\. To give an alibi for. The accused man was able to *alibi* the presence of stolen goods in his car.

alien \'āl-yən\ *adj.* **1** Belonging to another country; foreign; as, *alien* lands. **2** Wholly different in nature; out of harmony; as, behavior *alien* to one's usual ways. — *n.* A person not a citizen of the country in which he lives; a foreigner.

alien·ate \'āl-yə-ˌnāt\ *v.;* **alien·at·ed; alien·at·ing. 1** To transfer to another person, as property. **2** To cause a loss of love, loyalty, or friendship; as, to *alienate* a friend; to *alienate* a child from its parents. — **alien·a·tion** \ˌāl-yə-'nāsh-n\ *n.*

alien·ist \'āl-yə-nəst\ *n.* A doctor specializing in mental diseases.

alight \ə-'līt\ *v.;* **alight·ed** \ə-'līt-əd\, sometimes **alit** \ə-'lit\; **alight·ing. 1** To get down; to get off; to dismount; as, to *alight* from a train. **2** To light; to settle or stop. A bird *alighted* on the bush.

alight \ə-'līt\ *adj.* Lighted; aflame.

align or **aline** \ə-'līn\ *v.;* **aligned** or **alined; align·ing** or **alin·ing.** To arrange in line; to get or bring into line; as, to *align* a body of troops; to *align* the wheels of an automobile.

align·ment or **aline·ment** \ə-'līn-mənt\ *n.* **1** The action of aligning or the state of being aligned; formation in line. **2** The line formed by the action of aligning.

alike \ə-'līk\ *adj.* Similar; as, two persons whose ways are *alike.* — *adv.* In the same manner; similarly; as, two persons who walk *alike.*

al·i·ment \'al-ə-mənt\ *n.* Food; nourishment.

al·i·men·ta·ry \ˌal-ə-'ment-r-ē, -'men-trē\ *adj.* Having to do with food and nourishment.

alimentary canal. The long tube that takes food through the body; the digestive tube of an animal.

al·i·mo·ny \'al-ə-ˌmō-nē\ *n.* An allowance of money made by a man to a woman during or after her divorce or legal separation from him.

aline. Variant of *align.*

alinement. Variant of *alignment.*

alit. A past tense and past part. of *alight.*

alive \ə-'līv\ *adj.* **1** Living. **2** In action or operation; active; going; as, to keep a fire *alive.* **3** Swarming; as, blossoms *alive* with bees.

al·ka·li \'alk-l-ˌī\ *n.; pl.* **al·ka·lies** or **al·ka·lis** \-ˌīz\. **1** Any of a number of substances, such as caustic soda and potash, that have a bitter taste and neutralize acids. **2** A salt or a mixture of salts sometimes found in large amounts in the soil of dry regions.

al·ka·line \'alk-l-ˌīn, -ən\ *adj.* Of, relating to, or having the properties of, an alkali. — **al·ka·lin·i·ty** \ˌalk-l-'in-ət-ē\ *n.*

al·ka·loid \'alk-l-ˌȯid\ *n.* An organic substance having alkaline properties; especially, any of certain plant substances, such as nicotine, morphine, strychnine, and cocaine, used as a drug.

all \'ȯl\ *adj.* **1** The whole of; as, *all* the time. **2** Every one of. *All* men must die. **3** The greatest possible; as, with *all* speed. — *adv.* **1** Wholly; entirely; as, *all* alone. **2** Apiece. The score was two games *all.* — *pron.* All people; everyone. The news was known to *all.* — *n.* Everything; especially, everything that a person owns or values; as, to lose one's *all.*

all-around \'ȯl-ə-ˌrau̇nd\ *adj.* All-round.

al·lay \ə-'lā\ *v.;* **al·layed; al·lay·ing.** To quiet; to calm; to make less severe; as, to *allay* a person's fears; to *allay* pain.

al·le·ga·tion \ˌal-ə-ˈgāsh-n\ *n.* **1** The action of alleging; the assertion of something as being so, or true. **2** That which is alleged; an assertion, especially one that is not backed up by proof or evidence.

al·lege \ə-ˈlej\ *v.;* **al·leged; al·leg·ing. 1** To state positively but without proof; to declare; as, to *allege* a person's guilt. **2** To offer as a reason or an excuse; as, to *allege* illness in order to avoid work. — **al·leg·ed·ly** \ə-ˈlej-əd-lē\ *adv.*

al·le·giance \ə-ˈlēj-n(t)s\ *n.* **1** Loyalty and service owed to one's country and government. **2** Loyalty and service given to a person or thing; as, *allegiance* to one's school. — For synonyms see *loyalty.*

al·le·gor·i·cal \ˌal-ə-ˈgȯr-ik-l, -ˈgär-\ *adj.* Consisting of or containing allegory; having the characteristics of allegory; as, *allegorical* figures; an *allegorical* tale. — **al·le·gor·i·cal·ly** \-ik-l(-)ē\ *adv.*

al·le·go·ry \ˈal-ə-ˌgōr-ē, -ˌgȯr-ē\ *n.; pl.* **al·le·go·ries.** A story in which the characters and events are symbols expressing truths or generalizations about human life.

al·le·gret·to \ˌal-ə-ˈgret-ˌō\ *adj.* or *adv.* In music, faster than andante but slower than allegro.

al·le·gro \ə-ˈlā-ˌgrō, -ˈleg-ˌrō\ *adj.* or *adv.* In music, in quick time; lively and fast. — *n.; pl.* **al·le·gros.** A quick movement or section in a musical composition such as a symphony or a sonata.

al·le·lu·ia \ˌal-ə-ˈlü-yə\. Variant of *hallelujah.*

al·ler·gic \ə-ˈlər-jik\ *adj.* **1** Of or having to do with allergy; as, an *allergic* reaction. **2** Possessing allergy; disagreeably sensitive; as, to be *allergic* to strawberries.

al·ler·gy \ˈal-r-jē\ *n.; pl.* **al·ler·gies. 1** Extreme sensitiveness to certain things, as germs, pollen, food, hair, or cloth, that are harmless to most people. **2** *Slang.* A feeling of dislike.

al·le·vi·ate \ə-ˈlē-vē-ˌāt\ *v.;* **al·le·vi·at·ed; al·le·vi·at·ing.** To make easier to be endured; to relieve; to lessen or lighten; as, to *alleviate* pain. — **al·le·vi·a·tion** \ə-ˌlē-vē-ˈāsh-n\ *n.*

al·ley \ˈal-ē\ *n.; pl.* **al·leys.** A superior white or colored marble used in games of marbles.

al·ley \ˈal-ē\ *n.; pl.* **al·leys. 1** A garden path bordered by trees or bushes. **2** A narrow passageway, especially between buildings in a city or town and usually giving access to the rear of the building. **3** A very narrow back street. **4** A place for playing certain games in which balls are rolled; as, a bowling *alley.*

al·ley·way \ˈal-ē-ˌwā\ *n.* An alley, especially between buildings.

All Fools' Day. The first day of April, a day on which mischievous tricks are widely played.

all fours. All four legs of a four-legged animal; the arms and legs, hands and feet, or hands and knees of a person; as, to go down on *all fours* to search for a needle.

All·hal·lows \ȯl-ˈhal-ōz\ *n.* All Saints' Day.

al·li·ance \ə-ˈlī-ən(t)s\ *n.* **1** A union between two or more persons, families, or nations; as, an *alliance* between England and France. **2** A treaty or agreement establishing such a union. **3** The persons or nations that make such a treaty.

al·lied \ə-ˈlīd, ˈal-ˌīd\. Past tense and past part. of *ally.* — *adj.* **1** United by an agreement; as, *allied* nations. **2** Connected; related; as, chemistry and *allied* subjects.

allies. Pl. of *ally.*

al·li·ga·tor \ˈal-ə-ˌgāt-r\ *n.* [From Spanish *el lagarto* meaning "the lizard".] A large crawling reptile resembling a crocodile but having a shorter and broader snout. **2** Leather made from an alligator's hide. **3** A machine with a strong movable jaw like an alligator's.

alligator pear. An avocado.

al·lit·er·a·tion \ə-ˌlit-r-ˈāsh-n\ *n.* The beginning of two or more words with the same letter; as, the *alliteration* of *s* in "In a summer season when soft was the sun". — **al·lit·er·a·tive** \ə-ˈlit-r-ˌāt-iv\ *adj.* — **al·lit·er·a·tive·ly,** *adv.*

al·lo·cate \ˈal-ə-ˌkāt\ *v.;* **al·lo·cat·ed; al·lo·cat·ing.** To assign; to allot; especially, to allot something limited in supply, usually as a governmental control measure. — **al·lo·ca·tion** \ˌal-ə-ˈkāsh-n\ *n.*

al·lot \ə-ˈlät\ *v.;* **al·lot·ted; al·lot·ting.** To give out in parts to each one of several persons or groups; to distribute; to assign; as, to *allot* rooms in a dormitory; to *allot* tasks to all the campers.

al·lot·ment \ə-ˈlät-mənt\ *n.* **1** An allotting. **2** Something allotted; a portion.

all-out \ˈȯl-ˈau̇t\ *adj.* Thoroughgoing; complete; as, to make an *all-out* effort to win.

all·o·ver \ˈȯl-ˌōv-r\ *adj.* Covering a whole surface; as, an *allover* design on cloth.

al·low \ə-ˈlau̇\ *v.* **1** To permit; as, to *allow* smoking. **2** To admit or acknowledge; as, to *allow* a claim. **3** To assign an amount, as of time or money, for some purpose; as, to *allow* an hour for lunch. **4** To assign as a share or reward; as, to *allow* a boy pocket money. **5** To grant as a deduction or an addition; as, to *allow* an extra inch of cloth for shrinkage; to *allow* ten per cent off a bill for cash. — **allow for.** To take into consideration; as, a good game, *allowing for* the inexperience of the team.

al·low·a·ble \ə-ˈlau̇-əb-l\ *adj.* Permissible; not forbidden.

al·low·ance \ə-ˈlau̇-ən(t)s\ *n.* **1** An amount, as of money, given to a person for some purpose; as, a schoolboy's weekly *allowance.* **2** An amount put on or taken off; as, an *allowance* for cash; an *allowance* for waste. — **make allowances.** To take into consideration things that may partly excuse an offence or a mistake; as, to *make allowances* for a person's inexperience.

al·loy \ˈal-ˌȯi, ə-ˈlȯi\ *n.* **1** A substance made of two or more metals melted together. Brass is an *alloy* of copper and zinc. **2** A metal mixed with a more valuable metal to add hardness or wearing quality.

Copper is used as an *alloy* in gold coins. — \ə-'lȯi, 'al-ˌȯi\ *v.* **1** To reduce the purity of by mixing with a less valuable metal. **2** To mix so as to form an alloy. **3** To reduce or weaken by mixing; as, pleasure *alloyed* with sadness.

all right. **1** Agreeable; as, to feel *all right* about the matter. **2** Correct; correctly; satisfactorily; as, a temporary repair job that served *all right.* The teacher checked the arithmetic and found it *all right.* **3** Safe; well; as, to feel *all right* again after being sick. **4** Yes; agreed. *All right,* I see what you mean.

all-round \'ȯl-ˌraủnd\ *adj.* Having knowledge or ability in many branches; useful in many ways; as, an *all-round* athlete; an *all-round* tool.

All Saints' Day. The first of November, a church festival.

all·spice \'ȯl-ˌspīs\ *n.* The berry of the West Indian pimento tree or a spice prepared from this berry.

al·lude \ə-'lüd\ *v.;* **al·lud·ed**; **al·lud·ing.** To talk about indirectly without actually saying what is meant; to refer by suggestion; as, to be uncertain just what a speaker is *alluding* to.

— The word *refer* is a synonym of *allude: allude* usually indicates speaking of something indirectly without actually mentioning it; *refer* may indicate definite mention by name.

al·lure \ə-'lủr\ *v.;* **al·lured**; **al·lur·ing.** To tempt by an offer of something attractive; to entice. — *n.* Allurement.

al·lure·ment \ə-'lủr-mənt\ *n.* **1** The action of alluring; fascination. **2** Something that allures; an attraction; as, the *allurements* offered by a big city.

al·lu·sion \ə-'lüzh-n\ *n.* **1** An implied reference; a hint. **2** An indirect reference or passing mention, as in a book, to something supposed to be generally familiar; as, a book containing many literary *allusions.*

al·lu·sive \ə-'lü-siv, -ziv\ *adj.* Making or containing an allusion; referring indirectly. — **al·lu·sive·ly**, *adv.*

al·lu·vi·al \ə-'lü-vē-əl\ *adj.* Relating to or composed of **al·lu·vi·um** \-vē-əm\, material such as soil, sand, and gravel deposited by flowing water; as, *alluvial* deposits; *alluvial* soil.

al·ly \ə-'lī, 'al-ˌī\ *v.;* **al·lied**; **al·ly·ing.** To form a union or a connection; to unite; to join. The two nations *allied* themselves for protection against their enemies. — \'al-ˌī, ə-'lī\ *n.; pl.* **al·lies.** **1** A person or a state united to another for some common purpose; especially, a nation that helps another according to the terms of a treaty. **2** A plant or animal linked to another by genetic or evolutionary relationship; as, the mosses and their *allies.* **3** An assistant or helper.

al·ma ma·ter \'al-mə 'mät-r, 'måt-r\. [From Latin, meaning "fostering mother".] A person's school, college, or university.

al·ma·nac \'ȯl-mə-ˌnak, 'al-\ *n.* A book containing a calendar of days, weeks, and months, often with facts about the rising and setting of sun and moon, changes in the tides, and sometimes with weather predictions and other information.

al·mighty \ȯl-'mīt-ē\ *adj.* All-powerful; not limited in power. — **the Almighty.** God.

al·mond \'äm-ənd, 'am-ənd, 'al-mənd, 'åm-ənd\ *n.* **1** A small tree having flowers like those of a peach tree. **2** The nutlike kernel of the fruit of the almond tree.

almond: leaves and fruit

al·mon·er \'al-mən-r, 'äm-ən-, 'åm-ən-\ *n.* A person who distributes alms for someone else; as, the king's *almoner.*

al·most \'ȯl-ˌmōst, ȯl-'mōst\ *adv.* Nearly.

alms \'ämz, 'åmz\ *n. sing. and pl.* Anything, especially money, given freely to help the poor; charity.

alms·house \'ämz-ˌhaủs, 'åmz-\ *n.; pl.* **alms·hous·es** \-ˌhaủ-zəz\. A building or an institution where the very poor may be cared for free of charge.

al·oe \'al-ˌō\ *n.; pl.* **al·oes.** **1** A South African plant of the lily family, with spikelike, often showy flowers. **2** A bitter-tasting medicine made from the dried juice of the leaves of the aloe.

aloft \ə-'lȯft\ *adv.* **1** High in the air; as, to fly *aloft.* **2** In the upper rigging of a ship; to the top of the mast.

alo·ha \ä-'lō-ˌhä, ə-'lō-ə, å-'lō-ˌhå\ *interj.* [Hawaiian.] **1** Greetings. **2** Farewell.

alone \ə-'lōn\ *adj.* or *adv.* **1** Apart from others; all by oneself or itself; as, to be *alone* in the house. **2** Without anyone or anything else; only. The food *alone* cost ten dollars.

along \ə-'lȯng\ *prep.* Lengthwise of; parallel to the length of; as, to run *along* the beach; to arrange the chairs *along* the wall. — *adv.* **1** Onward; as, to hurry *along.* **2** In company; together; as, to go *along* with a friend.

along·side \ə-'lȯng-ˌsīd\ *adv.* or *prep.* Along or beside; side by side with.

aloof \ə-'lüf\ *adv.* or *adj.* Apart in distance, or in interest or feeling; as, to stand *aloof;* a person with a shy, *aloof* manner.

aloud \ə-'laủd\ *adv.* **1** So as to be heard; out loud; as, to read *aloud.* **2** Loudly; as, to cry *aloud.*

alp \'alp\ *n.* A high mountain.

al·paca \al-'pak-ə\ *n.* **1** A sheeplike animal of South America with fine long woolly hair. **2** The wool of this animal. **3** A thin cloth woven from this wool, often with a mixture of silk or cotton.

al·pen·stock \'alp-n-ˌstäk\ *n.* A long iron-pointed staff used in mountain climbing.

al·pha \'al-fə\ *n.* **1** The first letter of the Greek alphabet, often used to indicate something that is first in position or importance. **2** The first; the beginning. — **alpha and omega** \ō-'meg-ə, -'mē-gə\. The beginning and end.

al·pha·bet \'al-fə-ˌbet, -bət\ *n.* [From Greek *alpha* and *beta*, the first two letters of the Greek alphabet.] The letters of a language arranged in their customary order.

al·pha·bet·ic \ˌal-fə-'bet-ik\ or **al·pha·bet·i·cal** \-ik-l\ *adj*. Arranged according to the order of the letters of the alphabet. — **al·pha·bet·i·cal·ly** \-ik-l(-)ē\ *adv.*

al·pha·bet·ize \'al-fə-bə-ˌtīz\ *v.;* **al·pha·bet·ized; al·pha·bet·iz·ing.** To arrange in alphabetical order. — **al·pha·bet·i·za·tion** \ˌal-fə-ˌbet-ə-'zāsh-n\ *n.*

Al·pine \'al-ˌpīn\ *adj.* **1** Of or relating to the Alps. **2** [with a small letter] Of, like, or relating to high mountains; as, *alpine* scenery.

al·ready \ȯl-'red-ē, 'ȯl-ˌred-ē\ *adv.* Before a stated time; by this time; previously; as, to be given a book one has *already* read. When the firemen arrived the fire, which was small, was *already* out.

al·so \'ȯl-ˌsō\ *adv.* In addition; too.

al·so-ran \'ȯl-ˌsō-ˌran\ *n.* **1** A horse that finishes a race behind the money-winning horses. **2** Any contestant that fails to win a prize or points.

alt. Abbreviation for: **1** *alternate.* **2** *altitude.*

al·tar \'ȯlt-r\ *n.* **1** Any raised place on which sacrifices are offered in religious worship. **2** A table or tablelike structure at which principal acts of worship are performed by clergymen in religious services.

al·ter \'ȯlt-r\ *v.* To change partly but not completely; to make or become different in some details; as, to *alter* a dress. My opinion on that question has never *altered.* — **al·ter·a·ble** \-əb-l\ *adj.*

al·ter·a·tion \ˌȯlt-r-'āsh-n\ *n.* An altering; a change; as, a plan adopted without *alteration.* Some stores make free *alterations* on new clothing.

al·ter·ca·tion \ˌȯlt-r-'kāsh-n\ *n.* A noisy or angry dispute; a wrangle.

al·ter·nate \'ȯlt-r-nət, 'alt-\ *adj.* **1** Occurring by turns; changing back and forth by turns; as, *alternate* rain and sunshine. **2** Every other from a complete list; as, the *alternate* numbers 1, 3, 5, 7. — *n.* A substitute; a person named to take the place of another whenever necessary. — \-ˌnāt\ *v.;* **al·ter·nat·ed; al·ter·nat·ing.** To do, happen, or act in turns; to change back and forth. The land *alternates* between sandy hills and rocky plains. — **al·ter·nate·ly** \-nət-lē\ *adv.*

alternating current. An electric current that reverses its direction at regular intervals.

al·ter·na·tion \ˌȯlt-r-'nāsh-n, ˌalt-\ *n.* **1** An alternating; alternate position or occurrence; as, a disease marked by chills and fever in *alternation.* **2** In biology, a method of reproduction in which descendants are unlike their immediate parents and organisms of a given type are produced only with every second, or alternate, generation.

al·ter·na·tive \ȯl-'tər-nət-iv, al-\ *n.* **1** A chance to choose between two things; as, the *alternative* of going by train or by automobile. **2** One of the two things between which a choice is to be made. — *adj.* Offering a choice of two or more things, or offering something else as a choice; as, *alternative* plans. — **al·ter·na·tive·ly,** *adv.*

alt·horn \'alt-ˌhȯrn, 'al-ˌtȯrn\ *n.* or **al·to horn** \'al-ˌtō ˌhȯrn\. A brass horn often used in bands in place of the French horn.

al·though or **al·tho** \ȯl-'t͟hō\ *conj.* Even if; though; supposing that; in spite of the fact that.

al·tim·e·ter \al-'tim-ət-r, 'al-tə-ˌmēt-r\ *n.* An instrument for measuring altitude; especially, one used in an aircraft to show the height at which it is flying.

altimeter

al·ti·tude \'al-tə-ˌtüd, -ˌtyüd\ *n.* **1** Height above a given level, especially above sea level; as, the *altitude* of a mountain. **2** A high position or region; as, mountain *altitudes.* — For synonyms see *height.*

al·to \'al-ˌtō\ *n.; pl.* **al·tos.** **1** The part in music usually sung by the lowest female voice. **2** A voice, a singer, or an instrument that sings or plays such a part.

al·to·geth·er \ˌȯl-tə-'get͟h-r\ *adv.* **1** Wholly; entirely; as, to be not *altogether* displeased. **2** On the whole; taking everything into consideration. *Altogether,* it had been a pretty good day.

al·tru·ism \'al-ˌtrü-ˌiz-m\ *n.* Unselfish interest in the welfare of others. — **al·tru·ist** \'al-trə-wəst\ *n.* — **al·tru·is·tic** \ˌal-ˌtrü-'is-tik\ *adj.* — **al·tru·is·ti·cal·ly** \-'is-tik-l(-)ē\ *adv.*

al·um \'al-əm\ *n.* **1** A colorless crystalline chemical compound used in medicine for many purposes, as to cause vomiting and to stop bleeding. **2** A colorless salt used in baking powders, for purifying water, and for other purposes.

alu·mi·nize \ə-'lü-mə-ˌnīz\ *v.;* **alu·mi·nized; alu·mi·niz·ing.** To treat or coat with aluminum.

alu·mi·num \ə-'lü-mə-nəm\ *n.* A silver-white metal, one of the chemical elements, very light in weight, with many uses in manufacturing.

alum·na \ə-'ləm-nə\ *n.; pl.* **alum·nae** \-(ˌ)nē\. A girl or woman alumnus.

alum·nus \ə-'ləm-nəs\ *n.; pl.* **alum·ni** \-ˌnī\. A graduate or, sometimes, a former pupil of a school, college, or university.

al·ve·o·lus \al-'vē-ə-ləs\ *n.; pl.* **al·ve·o·li** \-ˌlī\. A small pit or cavity, as an air sac of the lung, a cell in a honeycomb, or the socket of a tooth.

al·ways \'ȯl-wēz, -(ˌ)wāz, -wəz\ *adv.* At all times.

am \əm, (')am\. The form of the verb *be* that is used with *I* to show present time.

A.M. or **a.m.** \'ā-'em\. [Abbreviated from Latin *ante meridiem* meaning "before midday".] In the morning; between midnight and the following noon; as, at 9 *A.M.*

amain \ə-'mān\ *adv.* **1** With might or full force. **2** At full speed; in great haste.

amal·gam \ə-'malg-m\ *n.* **1** An alloy of mercury with some other metal or metals, used in making dental cement or in silvering mirrors. **2** A mixture or union of different things.

amal·gam·ate \ə-ˈmalg-m-ˌāt\ *v.;* **amal·gam·at·ed**; **amal·gam·at·ing.** **1** To unite in an amalgam. **2** To combine into a single body, as two or more business organizations or two races of people.

amal·gam·a·tion \ə-ˌmalg-m-ˈāsh-n\ *n.* **1** The act or process of amalgamating; as, made by the *amalgamation* of mercury with silver. **2** The result of amalgamating.

aman·u·en·sis \ə-ˌman-yə-ˈwen(t)s-əs\ *n.; pl.* **aman·u·en·ses** \-ˈwen-ˌsēz\. A person employed to write from dictation or to copy what another has written.

am·a·ranth \ˈam-r-ˌan(t)th\ *n.* **1** An imaginary unfading flower. **2** Any of various plants of a family of herbs and low shrubs, some of which are weeds and some of which are cultivated for their green, purple, or crimson flowers.

am·a·ran·thine \ˌam-r-ˈan(t)th-n, -ˈan-ˌthīn\ *adj.* **1** Of or relating to amaranth. **2** Unfading; undying.

am·a·ryl·lis \ˌam-r-ˈil-əs\ *n.* Any plant, or its flower, of a family related to the lily family, and including the narcissus; especially, the **bel·la·don·na lily** \ˈbel-ə-ˌdän-ə ˈlil-ē\, a South African plant with rose-colored flowers.

amass \ə-ˈmas\ *v.* To collect into a mass or heap; to pile up; to accumulate; as, to *amass* a fortune.

am·a·teur \ˈam-ə-ˌtər, -ət-r, -ə-ˌtu̇r, -ə-ˌtyu̇r, -ə-ˌchu̇r, -əch-r\ *n.* **1** A person who takes part in sports or occupations for pleasure only, not for money. High-school athletes are *amateurs.* **2** A person who engages in something about which he does not have thorough knowledge; as, an essay containing mistakes that show it was written by an *amateur.* — *adj.* Being an amateur; performed by amateurs; as, an *amateur* athlete; *amateur* plays. — **am·a·teur·ish** \ˌam-ə-ˈtər-ish, -ˈtu̇r-ish, -ˈtyu̇r-\ *adj.* — **am·a·teur·ish·ly**, *adv.*

am·a·to·ry \ˈam-ə-ˌtōr-ē, -ˌtȯr-ē\ *adj.* Relating to, causing, or expressing love; amorous; as, an *amatory* look.

amaze \ə-ˈmāz\ *v.;* **amazed**; **amaz·ing.** To surprise or astonish greatly; to fill with wonder; as, to be *amazed* at the speed of the newest airplanes. — **amaz·ed·ly** \ə-ˈmā-zəd-lē\ *adv.*

amaze·ment \ə-ˈmāz-mənt\ *n.* Great surprise or astonishment; as, to be filled with *amazement* at the tricks of a magician.

amaz·ing \ə-ˈmā-zing\ *adj.* Astonishing; surprising; wonderful. — **amaz·ing·ly**, *adv.*

Am·a·zon \ˈam-ə-ˌzän, -əz-n\ *n.* **1** In mythology, a member of a race or nation of female warriors with whom the Greeks repeatedly warred. **2** [with a small letter] A tall, strong, masculine woman.

Am·a·zo·ni·an \ˌam-ə-ˈzō-nē-ən\ *adj.* **1** Of or like an Amazon; warlike. **2** Of or belonging to the Amazon river or its valley.

am·bas·sa·dor \am-ˈbas-əd-r\ *n.* **1** A person sent to the government of a foreign country as the chief official representative of his own government or ruler. **2** A government representative appointed for a special and often temporary assignment. **3** An authorized or appointed representative or messenger.

am·ber \ˈam-br\ *n.* **1** A yellowish substance that is a fossil tree resin and is used mostly for jewelry. **2** The color of this substance, a light orange-yellow. — *adj.* **1** Made of amber; like amber. **2** Of the color of amber.

am·ber·gris \ˈam-br-ˌgris, -ˌgrēs, -ˌgrē\ *n.* A waxy substance obtained from the sperm whale, used in the manufacture of perfumes.

am·bi·dex·trous \ˌam-bə-ˈdeks-trəs\ *adj.* Using both hands with equal ease; as, an *ambidextrous* tennis player. — **am·bi·dex·trous·ly**, *adv.*

am·bi·ent \ˈam-bē-ənt\ *adj.* Surrounding on all sides; encompassing; as, the *ambient* air.

am·bi·gu·i·ty \ˌam-bə-ˈgyü-ət-ē\ *n.; pl.* **am·bi·gu·i·ties.** **1** Uncertainty or confusion of meaning, as of a word or phrase. **2** An ambiguous word or passage.

am·big·u·ous \am-ˈbig-yə-wəs\ *adj.* Not clear in meaning; able to be understood in more than one way; as, an *ambiguous* question. — **am·big·u·ous·ly**, *adv.*

am·bi·tion \am-ˈbish-n\ *n.* **1** An eager desire to improve oneself or one's position in life; as, to be full of *ambition.* **2** The aim or object for which one strives. The *ambition* of many boys is to be a jet pilot.

am·bi·tious \am-ˈbish-əs\ *adj.* **1** Stirred by or possessing ambition; as, *ambitious* to be captain of the team **2** Showing ambition; as, an *ambitious* plan to build a space ship. — **am·bi·tious·ly**, *adv.*

am·ble \ˈam-bl\ *n.* **1** An easy gait of a horse in which the legs on the same side of the body move together. **2** Any gentle, easy gait. — *v.;* **am·bled**; **am·bling** \-bl(-)ing\. To go at an amble; as, to *amble* down the road.

am·bro·sia \am-ˈbrō-zhə, -zhē-ə\ *n.* **1** In ancient legend, the food of the gods. **2** Anything extremely pleasant in taste or smell. — **am·bro·sial** \-ˈbrōzh-l, -ˈbrō-zhē-əl\ *adj.*

am·bu·lance \ˈam-byə-lən(t)s\ *n.* [From French, originally meaning "field hospital", "traveling hospital", from *ambulant* meaning "traveling".] A special vehicle for carrying sick or injured persons.

am·bu·la·to·ry \ˈam-byə-lə-ˌtōr-ē, -ˌtȯr-ē\ *adj.* **1** Having to do with walking. **2** Able to walk about; as, the *ambulatory* patients in a hospital.

am·bus·cade \ˈam-bəs-ˌkād\ *n.* An ambush. — *v.;* **am·bus·cad·ed**; **am·bus·cad·ing.** To ambush. Our troops were *ambuscaded* in the mountains.

am·bush \ˈam-ˌbu̇sh\ *n.* **1** A trap by which troops are concealed in a place for the purpose of attacking the enemy by surprise. **2** The place in which troops are concealed for a surprise attack. **3** The body of troops concealed for a surprise attack. — *v.* **1** To station in an ambush. **2** To attack from ambush; as, to *ambush* an enemy.

ameba. Variant of *amoeba.*

amebic. Variant of *amoebic*.

amel·io·rate \ə-ˈmēl-yər-ˌāt\ *v.;* **amel·io·rat·ed**; **amel·io·rat·ing**. To make better; to grow better; to improve; as, to *ameliorate* living conditions. — **amel·io·ra·tion** \ə-ˌmēl-yər-ˈāsh-n\ *n.* — **amel·io·ra·tive** \ə-ˈmēl-yər-ˌāt-iv\ *adj.*

amen \ˈā-ˈmen, ˈä-, ˈȧ-; *in singing,* ˈä- *or* ˈȧ- *only*\ *interj.* or *n.* A word meaning "So be it", used at the end of a prayer or a blessing.

ame·na·ble \ə-ˈmē-nəb-l, ə-ˈmen-əb-l\ *adj.* **1** Liable to be called to account; as, to be *amenable* to the law. **2** Easily influenced or managed; responsive; as, *amenable* to discipline. — **ame·na·bil·i·ty** \ə-ˌmē-nə-ˈbil-ət-ē, ə-ˌmen-ə-\ *n.* — **ame·na·bly** \ə-ˈmē-nə-blē, ə-ˈmen-ə-\ *adv.*

amend \ə-ˈmend\ *v.* **1** To change; to alter; as, to *amend* the constitution of a state. **2** To change for the better; to improve; as, to promise to *amend* one's conduct.

amend·ment \ə-ˈmen(d)-mənt\ *n.* **1** An altering, especially for the better; a correction; an improvement. **2** An addition to or a change in a law, rule, or constitution.

amends \ə-ˈmen(d)z\ *n. sing. and pl.* Something done or given by a person to make up for a loss or injury he has caused someone else; as, to try hard to make *amends* for an unkindness.

amen·i·ty \ə-ˈmen-ət-ē\ *n.; pl.* **amen·i·ties. 1** Pleasantness; agreeableness. **2** [usually in the plural] Anything that makes life pleasant and agreeable; as, plays and concerts and other *amenities* of city life. In warfare there is little time or place for the social *amenities*.

am·ent \ˈam-ənt, ˈā-mənt\ *n.* A spikelike flower cluster in which the flowers have no petals but grow in close circular rows on a slender stalk, as in the alder, willow, birch, and poplar; a catkin.

Amer·i·can \ə-ˈmer-ək-n\ *adj.* Of, belonging to, or living or growing in, America, especially the United States of America. — *n.* Any native or inhabitant of America; especially, a citizen of the United States of America.

Amer·i·can·ism \ə-ˈmer-ək-n-ˌiz-m\ *n.* **1** Loyalty or attachment to the United States of America, its traditions, ideals, and interests. **2** An American custom or characteristic. **3** A word or phrase or a pronunciation peculiar to or originating in the United States.

Amer·i·can·i·za·tion \ə-ˌmer-ək-n-ə-ˈzāsh-n\ *n.* **1** The act of making American or the process of becoming American. **2** The instruction of immigrants in subjects designed to help them adjust themselves to life in the United States.

Amer·i·can·ize \ə-ˈmer-ək-n-ˌīz\ *v.;* **Amer·i·can·ized**; **Amer·i·can·iz·ing**. To make or become American, as in ways or methods, habits or speech.

American plan. In hotels, a plan by which guests pay for room and board in one inclusive charge.

am·er·i·ci·um \ˌam-r-ˈish-ē-əm\ *n.* A metallic chemical element artificially produced in the cyclotron.

am·e·thyst \ˈam-ə-thəst\ *n.* A precious stone, clear purple or bluish-violet in color.

ami·a·ble \ˈā-mē-əb-l\ *adj.* Good-natured; agreeable; friendly. — **ami·a·bil·i·ty** \ˌā-mē-ə-ˈbil-ət-ē\ *n.* — **ami·a·bly** \ˈā-mē-ə-blē\ *adv.*

am·i·ca·ble \ˈam-ə-kəb-l\ *adj.* Showing a friendly attitude; friendly; peaceable; as, an *amicable* solution to an international problem. — **am·i·ca·bil·i·ty** \ˌam-ə-kə-ˈbil-ət-ē\ *n.* — **am·i·ca·bly** \ˈam-ə-kə-blē\ *adv.*

am·ice \ˈam-əs\ *n.* A white linen cloth worn over the shoulders under other vestments by a priest at Mass.

amid \ə-ˈmid\ *prep.* In the midst of.

amid·ships \ə-ˈmid-ˌships\ *adv.* In or near the middle of a ship.

amidst \ə-ˈmidst\ *prep.* In or into the midst of; among.

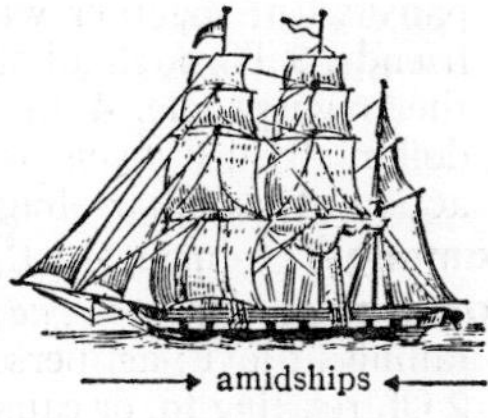
amidships

ami·no acid \ə-ˈmē-nō, ˈam-ə-ˌnō\. Any acid of a group occurring combined in protein, some of which are needed in the human diet for health or growth.

amiss \ə-ˈmis\ *adv.* In the wrong way; improperly; as, to act *amiss.* — *adj.* Incorrect; wrong; out of order. Something seems to be *amiss* here.

am·i·ty \ˈam-ət-ē\ *n.; pl.* **am·i·ties.** Friendship; friendly relations, especially between or among nations.

am·me·ter \ˈam-ˌēt-r\ *n.* An instrument for measuring electric current.

am·mo·nia \ə-ˈmōn-yə\ *n.* **1** A colorless gas with a very sharp smell and taste, easily liquefied and much used in artificial fertilizers and cleaning fluids, and in the manufacture of ice. **2** Also **ammonia water.** A solution of this gas in water. — **am·mo·ni·ac** \ə-ˈmō-nē-ˌak\ *adj.*

ammeter

am·mo·nite \ˈam-ə-ˌnīt\ *n.* Any of numerous fossil shells having the form of a flat spiral similar to that of the nautilus.

am·mo·ni·um \ə-ˈmō-nē-əm\ *n.* A chemical radical consisting of nitrogen and hydrogen and occurring in salts such as **ammonium chlo·ride** \ˈklōr-ˌīd, ˈklȯr-\, used as a source of ammonia, and **ammonium sul·fate** \ˈsəl-ˌfāt\, used as a fertilizer.

am·mu·ni·tion \ˌam-yə-ˈnish-n\ *n.* **1** Anything that can be hurled at a target, especially anything propelled by or containing explosives, as bullets, shells, grenades, and bombs. **2** Any material that may be used in attack or defense.

am·ne·sia \am-ˈnē-zhə\ *n.* Loss of memory due to brain injury, illness, shock, or similar cause.

am·nes·ty \ˈam-nəs-tē\ *n.; pl.* **am·nes·ties.** A general pardon granted by a ruler or government for offenses that have been committed, especially against the state.

amoe·ba or **ame·ba** \ə-ˈmē-bə\ *n.; pl.* **amoe·bas** \-bəz\ or **amoe·bae** \-(ˌ)bē\ or **ame·bas** \-bəz\. A very minute animal that is constantly changing its shape, is found commonly in stagnant fresh water, and is one of the simplest forms of animal life.

amoeba

amoe·bic or **ame·bic** \ə-ˈmē-bik\ *adj.* **1** Relating to or resembling an amoeba. **2** Caused by amoebas; as, *amoebic* dysentery.

amok \ə-ˈmək, -ˈmäk\ *adv.* **1** In a wild, raging, or murderous manner; as, to run *amok.*

among \ə-ˈməng\ *prep.* [From Old English *on gemonge* meaning "in the crowd".] **1** In the midst of; as, to disappear *among* the crowd. **2** In company with; together with; as, to be *among* one's friends. **3** Through all of; as, dissatisfaction *among* the townspeople. **4** In shares to each of; as, ten dollars divided *among* four persons. **5** By common action of; as, quarreling *among* themselves.

amongst \ə-ˈməng(k)st\ *prep.* Among.

am·o·rous \ˈam-r-əs\ *adj.* **1** Inclined to love; easily falling in love; as, persons of an *amorous* nature. **2** Of, relating to, or caused by love; as, an *amorous* look. — **am·o·rous·ly,** *adv.*

amor·phous \ə-ˈmór-fəs\ *adj.* Without definite shape or form; as, *amorphous* cloud masses.

amount \ə-ˈmau̇nt\ *v.* **1** To reach, or come to, as a total or whole. The bill *amounted* to ten dollars. **2** To be equal or to extend in effect, meaning, or importance; as, admiration *amounting* almost to worship. — *n.* **1** The total of two or more sums added together; as, to pay the whole *amount* at one time. **2** A quantity; as, a surprising *amount* of patience.

amour \ə-ˈmu̇r\ *n.* A love affair; especially, a secret love affair.

amp. Abbreviation for *ampere.*

am·per·age \ˈamp-r-ij\ *n.* The strength of a current of electricity measured in amperes.

am·pere \ˈam-ˌpir\ *n.* [Named in honor of André M. *Ampère,* a French physicist who died in 1836.] A unit for measuring the strength of an electric current.

am·per·sand \ˈamp-r-ˌsand\ *n.* The character & or &, read "and", as in *tea & coffee.*

am·phib·i·an \am-ˈfib-ē-ən\ *n.* **1** An animal, such as a frog or toad, belonging to the zoological class between the fishes and the reptiles. **2** Any animal having the ability to live both on land and in water. **3** An airplane so built as to be able to rise from, and alight on, land or water. **4** A military vehicle that can be operated on land or in water, used principally for landing troops and equipment. — *adj.* Amphibious.

am·phib·i·ous \am-ˈfib-ē-əs\ *adj.* **1** Able to live both on land and in water. A crocodile is an *amphibious* animal. **2** Adapted for both land and water; as, *amphibious* aircraft.

am·phi·the·a·ter \ˈam(p)-fə-ˌthē-ət-r\ *n.* **1** A round or oval building with seats rising in curved rows around an open space on which games and plays take place. **2** Anything resembling an amphitheater, such as a piece of level ground surrounded by hills. **3** An operating room with a gallery from which medical students may look on.

am·ple \ˈamp-l\ *adj.;* **am·pler** \-lər\; **am·plest** \-ləst\. **1** Of large size; roomy; as, an *ample* fireplace. **2** Enough to satisfy; abundant; as, an *ample* supply of food.

am·pli·fi·ca·tion \ˌamp-lə-fə-ˈkāsh-n\ *n.* **1** An amplifying; enlargement. **2** Matter which enlarges a statement; an amplified statement.

am·pli·fi·er \ˈamp-lə-ˌfīr\ *n.* One that amplifies; especially, a device for magnifying electric impulses, as in a radio set.

am·pli·fy \ˈamp-lə-ˌfī\ *v.;* **am·pli·fied** \-ˌfīd\; **am·pli·fy·ing.** **1** To increase in size; to enlarge, as by adding details; as, to *amplify* a story. **2** To increase, as current of radio frequency, by means of electron tubes. **3** To make louder; as, to *amplify* the voice by using a megaphone.

am·pli·tude \ˈamp-lə-ˌtüd, -ˌtyüd\ *n.* **1** Ample extent or amount, especially of surface or of space; size. **2** Abundance. **3** The up-and-down extent of the vibration of an electric wave.

am·ply \ˈamp-lē\ *adv.* Fully; sufficiently; abundantly.

am·pu·tate \ˈamp-yə-ˌtāt\ *v.;* **am·pu·tat·ed; am·pu·tat·ing.** To cut off, especially a limb or other projecting part of a person or animal. — **am·pu·ta·tion** \ˌamp-yə-ˈtāsh-n\ *n.*

amt. Abbreviation for *amount.*

amuck \ə-ˈmək\. Variant of *amok.*

am·u·let \ˈam-yə-lət\ *n.* A small object, often inscribed with a magic incantation or symbol, worn as a charm against evil.

amuse \ə-ˈmyüz\ *v.;* **amused; amus·ing.** **1** To entertain with something pleasant; to divert; as, to *amuse* a child with a toy. **2** To please or delight the sense of humor of. His story *amused* everyone.

— The words *divert* and *entertain* are synonyms of *amuse: amuse* generally refers to occupation with pleasant subjects or with things that appeal to one's sense of humor; *divert* may suggest the turning of thoughts from everyday events to other interests; *entertain* usually refers to more elaborate or formal amusement, often involving activity by someone else.

amuse·ment \ə-ˈmyüz-mənt\ *n.* **1** The condition of being amused; pleasant entertainment; as, to watch with *amusement* a puppy chasing its tail. Skating provides *amusement* for young and old. **2** A means of amusement; something that amuses or entertains. Most of the *amusements* at the beach were free.

amus·ing \ə-ˈmyü-zing\ *adj.* Giving amusement; entertaining. — **amus·ing·ly,** *adv.*

am·y·lop·sin \ˈam-l-ˌäps-n\ *n.* An enzyme present in the pancreatic juice.

an \ən, (ˈ)an\ *adj.* or *indefinite article.* **1** One. **2** In each; for every. **3** One kind of; some kind of. **4** Any; each.

☞ *An* is used (instead of *a*) before words beginning with a vowel sound; as, *an* oak; *an* hour.

-an \(ə)n\. A suffix that has the general sense of belonging to, as a country, a place, or a zoological group, forming adjectives and nouns, as in *European, sylvan,* or *crustacean.*

anab·o·lism \ə-'nab-l-ˌiz-m\ *n.* The part of the process of metabolism in which the building up of the substance of plants and animals takes place. — **an·a·bol·ic** \ˌan-ə-'bäl-ik\ *adj.*

anach·ro·nism \ə-'nak-rə-ˌniz-m\ *n.* **1** The error of placing a person or thing in a period to which it does not belong; as, the *anachronism* of describing Napoleon as riding in an automobile. **2** A person or thing thus misplaced. — **anach·ro·nis·tic** \ə-ˌnak-rə-'nis-tik\ *adj.*

an·a·con·da \ˌan-ə-'kän-də\ *n.* **1** Any large snake that crushes its prey. **2** A large South American snake of the boa family.

anaemia. Variant of *anemia.*

an·aer·o·bic \ˌan-r-'ō-bik\ *adj.* Living or active in the absence of free oxygen; as, *anaerobic* bacteria.

anaesthesia. Variant of *anesthesia.*

anaesthetic. Variant of *anesthetic.*

anaesthetist. Variant of *anesthetist.*

anaesthetize. Variant of *anesthetize.*

an·a·gram \'an-ə-ˌgram\ *n.* **1** A word or phrase made out of another by changing the order of the letters. "Read" is an *anagram* of "dear". **2** [in the plural] A game in which players compete in forming words from letters drawn from a stock of cards or blocks each bearing one letter.

anal \'ān-l\ *adj.* Of or near the anus.

an·al·ge·sia \ˌan-l-'jē-zhə\ *n.* Insensibility to pain. — **an·al·ge·sic** \-zik, -sik\ *adj.* or *n.*

anal·o·gous \ə-'nal-ə-gəs\ *adj.* Similar in one or more important ways; having some resemblances in spite of great differences; comparable. The wings of an airplane are *analogous* to those of a bird. — **anal·o·gous·ly,** *adv.*

an·a·logue \'an-l-ˌȯg\ *n.* **1** Something analogous to some other thing. **2** An organ similar in function to an organ of another animal or plant but differing in structure and origin. The gill of a fish is the *analogue* of the lung in a quadruped.

anal·o·gy \ə-'nal-ə-jē\ *n.; pl.* **anal·o·gies.** A similarity of one or more characteristics in two different things; as, to point out an *analogy* between a village and a hive.

analyse. Variant of *analyze.*

anal·y·sis \ə-'nal-ə-səs\ *n.; pl.* **anal·y·ses** \-ˌsēz\. [From Greek, originally meaning "loosening", "dissolving".] The separation of something into its parts; an examination of anything to find out of what it is made up; as, the *analysis* of a sentence into its subject, predicate, and modifiers; the *analysis* of soil.

an·a·lyst \'an-l-əst\ *n.* A person who makes analyses.

an·a·lyt·ic \ˌan-l-'it-ik\ or **an·a·lyt·i·cal** \-ik-l\ *adj.* Having to do with analysis; as, an *analytic* experiment; an *analytical* mind. — **an·a·lyt·i·cal·ly** \-ik-l(-)ē\ *adv.*

an·a·lyze \'an-l-ˌīz\ *v.;* **an·a·lyzed; an·a·lyz·ing.** To separate a thing into its parts; to find the elements that make up a thing; as, to *analyze* a sentence; to *analyze* drinking water.

an·a·paest or **an·a·pest** \'an-ə-ˌpest\ *n.* A metrical foot consisting of two unaccented syllables followed by an accented syllable, as in *to de'part.* — **an·a·paes·tic** or **an·a·pes·tic** \ˌan-ə-'pes-tik\ *adj.*

an·arch·ist \'an-rk-əst\ *n.* A person who favors anarchy or believes in the theory that all government is harmful to man's best interests. — **an·arch·ism** \'an-r-ˌkiz-m\ *n.* — **an·ar·chis·tic** \ˌan-r-'kis-tik\ *adj.*

an·archy \'an-rk-ē\ *n.; pl.* **an·arch·ies. 1** The condition of society where there is no government or law and order. **2** A state of lawlessness; confusion or disorder.

anath·e·ma \ə-'nath-m-ə\ *n.* **1** A solemn curse or ban, especially when pronounced by the authorities of a church. **2** Any person or thing that has been cursed. **3** Any object of intense dislike or of loathing. Modern jazz is *anathema* to some people.

anath·e·ma·tize \ə-'nath-m-ə-ˌtīz\ *v.;* **anath·e·ma·tized; anath·e·ma·tiz·ing.** To pronounce an anathema against; to curse.

an·a·tom·ic \ˌan-ə-'täm-ik\ or **an·a·tom·i·cal** \-ik-l\ *adj.* Of or relating to anatomy. — **an·a·tom·i·cal·ly** \-ik-l(-)ē\ *adv.*

anat·o·mist \ə-'nat-m-əst\ *n.* A person who is skilled in anatomy.

anat·o·mize \ə-'nat-m-ˌīz\ *v.;* **anat·o·mized; anat·o·miz·ing. 1** To dissect so as to show or to examine the structure and use of the parts. **2** To analyze.

anat·o·my \ə-'nat-m-ē\ *n.; pl.* **anat·o·mies. 1** A cutting up of an animal or a plant in order to learn the arrangement of its parts. **2** The science that studies and explains the structure of the body and the way its parts fit together. **3** The structure, or make-up, of the body.

-ance \(ə)n(t)s\ or **-an·cy** \(ə)n-sē\ or **-ence** \(ə)n(t)s\ or **-en·cy** \(ə)n-sē\. A suffix that can mean: **1** The act, process, or fact of, as in *assistance* or *resistance.* **2** Condition of being or of doing habitually, as in *violence, compliancy, sufficiency,* or *elegance.* **3** A concrete fact or thing, as in *eminence* or *dependency.*

an·ces·tor \'an-ˌsest-r\ *n.* **1** A person from whom another person is descended; a person far back in one's family, as a great-grandfather; a forefather. **2** Something from which something else descends; as, the *ancestors* of the modern airplane.

an·ces·tral \an-'sest-rəl\ *adj.* Having to do with ancestors; inherited from, or owned by, ancestors; as, *ancestral* portraits; an *ancestral* home.

an·ces·try \'an-ˌsest-rē\ *n.; pl.* **an·ces·tries. 1** Ancestral line; descent; as, to be proud of one's *ancestry.* **2** A series of ancestors.

an·chor \'angk-r\ *n.* **1** A heavy iron or steel device attached to a ship by a cable or chain, and so made that, when thrown overboard, it digs into the earth and holds the ship in place. **2** Anything that secures or steadies or that gives a feeling of stability; as, the *anchor* of a bridge. — *v.;* **an·chored; an·chor·ing** \-r(-)ing\. **1** To hold in place by means of an anchor; as, to *anchor* a ship. **2** To fasten securely to a firm foundation; as, to *anchor* the cables of a bridge. **3** To drop anchor; to become anchored. The ship *anchored* in the harbor.

anchor

an·chor·age \'angk-r(-)ij\ *n.* **1** A place where boats may be anchored. **2** A secure hold to resist a strong pull. **3** A means of security; reliance.

an·cho·rite \'angk-r-,īt\ *n.* A person who gives up worldly things and lives in solitude, usually for religious reasons.

an·cho·vy \an-'chō-vē, 'an-,chō-\ *n.; pl.* **an·cho·vies.** A small fish resembling a herring; especially, a Mediterranean variety used for sauces and relishes.

an·cient \'ān-chənt, 'ān-shənt, 'āngk-shənt\ *adj.* **1** Existing from times long past; as, *ancient* customs. **2** Belonging to times long past, especially to the period preceding the fall of Rome; as, *ancient* books; *ancient* customs. **3** Of or relating to the people of times long past; as, *ancient* history. **4** Very old, as in style or condition; as, an *ancient* pair of shoes. — *n.* **1** An aged person. **2** A person who lived in ancient times. — **the ancients.** The civilized people who lived in ancient times.

an·cient·ly \-lē\ *adv.* In ancient times.

-ancy. Variant of *-ance.*

and \ən(d), (')an(d), n, m, ng\ *conj.* Added to; as well as. Two *and* two make four. This boy is outstanding in sports *and* in studies.
☞ In certain expressions, the meaning of *and* is like the meaning of *to* used in expressing purpose, as in "try and stop me" or "come and see me".

an·dan·te \än-'dän-tē, an-'dan-, ån-'dån-\ *adj.* or *adv.* In music, moderately slow.

and·i·ron \'an-,dīrn\ *n.* One of a pair of metal supports for firewood in a fireplace.

An·dor·ran \an-'dȯr-ən, -'där-\ *adj.* Of or relating to Andorra. — *n.* A native or an inhabitant of Andorra.

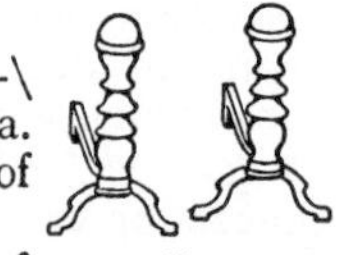
andirons

an·ec·dote \'an-ik-,dōt\ *n.* A brief story of some interesting happening; as, *anecdotes* about George Washington.

ane·mia or **anae·mia** \ə-'nē-mē-ə\ *n.* A condition in which the red corpuscles in the blood are reduced in number or deficient in hemoglobin, causing paleness of the skin, shortness of breath, and irregular heart action. — **ane·mic** or **anae·mic** \ə-'nē-mik\ *adj.*

an·e·mom·e·ter \,an-ə-'mäm-ət-r\ *n.* An instrument for measuring the force or velocity of the wind.

anem·o·ne \ə-'nem-ə-(,)nē\ *n.* **1** A spring-flowering plant with white or bright-colored flowers. **2** The sea anemone.

an·er·oid barometer \'an-r-,ȯid\. An instrument in which the atmospheric pressure in bending a metallic surface, as of a box from which part of the air has been removed, is made to move a pointer.

an·es·the·sia or **an·aes·the·sia** \,an-əs-'thē-zhə\ *n.* The loss of feeling or sensation, as caused by disease or an anesthetic.

an·es·thet·ic or **an·aes·thet·ic** \,an-əs-'thet-ik\ *n.* A substance, as a gas or a drug, that produces anesthesia, either by causing numbness in one part of the body (**local anesthesia**) or by bringing about a complete loss of consciousness (**general anesthesia**). — *adj.* **1** Capable of producing anesthesia; as, an *anesthetic* drug. **2** Connected with anesthesia. The drug produced an *anesthetic* effect.

an·es·the·tist or **an·aes·the·tist** \ə-'nes-thə-təst\ *n.* A person who administers anesthetics.

an·es·the·tize or **an·aes·the·tize** \ə-'nes-thə-,tīz\ *v.;* **an·es·the·tized** or **an·aes·the·tized; an·es·the·tiz·ing** or **an·aes·the·tiz·ing.** To make insensible to pain, especially by the use of an anesthetic.

anew \ə-'nü, ə-'nyü\ *adv.* **1** Over again; as if a new start were being made; afresh; as, to begin *anew.* **2** In a new or different form.

an·gel \'ānj-l\ *n.* [From Latin *angelus*, there borrowed from Greek *angelos* meaning "messenger".] **1** A messenger of God; a heavenly being. **2** A person as lovely or as good as an angel. **3** An accompanying spirit; as, one's good *angel.* **4** A messenger; a harbinger. — **an·gel·ic** \an-'jel-ik\ or **an·gel·i·cal** \-ik-l\ *adj.*

an·gel·fish \'ānj-l-,fish\ *n.; pl.* **an·gel·fish** or **an·gel·fish·es.** **1** A shark with fins that spread like wings. **2** Any of several tropical fishes, especially one from the Amazon River, barred with silver and black.

an·ger \'ang-gr\ *n.* A strong feeling of displeasure and usually of antagonism; a fit of bad temper; rage. — *v.;* **an·gered; an·ger·ing** \-gr(-)ing\. To make or become angry.

an·gi·o·sperm \'an-jē-ō-,spərm\ *n.* Any plant having the seeds in a closed ovary. — **an·gi·o·sper·mous** \,an-jē-ō-'spər-məs\ *adj.*

an·gle \'ang-gl\ *v.;* **an·gled; an·gling** \-gl(-)ing\. **1** To fish with hook and line. **2** To use sly or tricky means of getting what one wants; as, to *angle* for a compliment.

an·gle \'ang-gl\ *n.* **1** The figure formed by two lines meeting at a point; the space between two such lines. **2** A measure of the amount of turning that would be required to bring one of such lines over to meet the other at all points. **3** A sharp projecting corner. **4** A point of view; an aspect; as, to consider a problem from a new *angle.*

right angle

— For synonyms see *corner*. — *v.;* **an·gled**; **an·gling** \-gl(-)ing\. **1** To turn, bend, or move at an angle. **2** To present a news story, article, or speech from a particular point of view or so as to stress the interests of a particular group.

an·gler \'ang-glər\ *n.* **1** A fisherman, especially one who fishes for sport. **2** A sea fish having a large flat head with projections that draw other fish within reach of its broad mouth.

an·gle·worm \'ang-gl-ˌwərm\ *n.* An earthworm.

an·gli·cize \'ang-glə-ˌsīz\ *v.;* **an·gli·cized**; **an·gli·ciz·ing.** [often with a capital] To make or become English, as in habits, speech, or character.

an·gling \'ang-gl(-)ing\ *n.* Fishing with hook and line, especially for sport.

An·glo–Sax·on \'ang-(ˌ)glō-'saks-n\ *adj.* Of or relating to Anglo-Saxons or their language, or to a nation or people largely descended from Anglo-Saxons. — *n.* **1** A member of the German tribes that invaded England in the 5th and 6th centuries. **2** A person of the mixed stock that forms the English nation. **3** The Old English language.

An·go·ra \an(g)-'gōr-ə, -'gȯr-ə\ *n.* **1** A cat, goat, or rabbit with long silky hair. **2** Yarn or cloth made from the hair of the Angora goat or the Angora rabbit.

an·gry \'ang-grē\ *adj.;* **an·gri·er**; **an·gri·est.** **1** Inflamed; as, an *angry* sore. **2** Stirred by anger; enraged; wrathful; as, to become *angry* at the slightest provocation. The storekeeper was *angry* with the boys for breaking his window. **3** Showing or arising from anger; threatening as if in anger; as, *angry* words; an *angry* sky. — **an·gri·ly** \-grə-lē\ *adv.*

an·guish \'ang-gwish\ *n.* Great pain or suffering of body or mind. The mother's *anguish* touched all hearts.

an·guished \'ang-gwisht\ *adj.* Full of anguish; tormented; as, an *anguished* call for help.

an·gu·lar \'ang-gyəl-r\ *adj.* **1** Having one or more angles; sharp-cornered; pointed; as, the *angular* outline of a mountain. **2** Measured by an angle. **3** Lean and bony; as, the *angular* figure of Abraham Lincoln. — **an·gu·lar·i·ty** \ˌang-gyə-'lar-ət-ē\ *n.*

an·i·line \'an-l-ən\ *n.* A colorless, oily, poisonous fluid used in making dyes and medicines. — *adj.* Relating to aniline; made from or with the use of aniline; as, *aniline* dyes.

an·i·mad·ver·sion \ˌan-ə-ˌmad-'vərzh-n\ *n.* **1** A critical remark or comment. **2** Hostile criticism; blame.

an·i·mad·vert \ˌan-ə-ˌmad-'vərt\ *v.* To remark by way of criticism; to comment unfavorably; as, to *animadvert* on a display of bad manners at a party.

an·i·mal \'an-əm-l\ *n.* **1** A living being that is capable of moving and feeling, especially one that can move itself from place to place at will, as men, lions, birds, and fish. **2** Any of the animals, such as apes, dogs, or horses, that are below man in the animal world but above birds, snakes, and fish. — *adj.* **1** Of, relating to, resembling, or characteristic of, animals; as, *animal* diseases. **2** Of the body, as distinguished from the mind; sensuous; as, man's *animal* appetites.

an·i·mal·cule \ˌan-ə-'mal-ˌkyül\ *n.* A very small animal, invisible or nearly invisible to the naked eye.

an·i·mate \'an-ə-ˌmāt\ *v.;* **an·i·mat·ed**; **an·i·mat·ing.** **1** To give life to; to make alive; as, belief that the soul *animates* the body. **2** To give spirit and vigor to; to enliven. The speaker's arguments *animated* the discussion. **3** To give the appearance of life to; to put in motion or operation; as, to *animate* a cartoon. — \-mət\ *adj.* Living; having life. Animals and plants are *animate* things.

an·i·mat·ed \'an-ə-ˌmāt-əd\ *adj.* **1** Full of life and spirit; lively; as, an *animated* discussion. **2** Alive, or seeming to be alive; as, *animated* cartoons. — **an·i·mat·ed·ly**, *adv.*

an·i·ma·tion \ˌan-ə-'māsh-n\ *n.* **1** Spirit; liveliness. The topic was discussed with increasing *animation*. **2** The preparation of animated cartoons or drawings.

an·i·mos·i·ty \ˌan-ə-'mäs-ət-ē\ *n.; pl.* **an·i·mos·i·ties.** Bitter hatred or ill will.

an·i·mus \'an-ə-məs\ *n.* **1** Animating spirit; will; intention. **2** Feeling of hostility or hatred; animosity.

an·ise \'an-əs\ *n.* **1** An herb of the carrot family, having sweet-smelling seeds. **2** The seed of this plant, from which an oil (**anise oil**), used in flavoring, is made.

an·kle \'angk-l\ *n.* **1** The joint between the foot and the leg of a person or an animal. **2** The part of the lower leg around this joint.

an·klet \'angk-lət\ *n.* **1** Something worn around the ankle, such as an ornamental ring or chain. **2** A sock reaching slightly above the ankle.

an·nal·ist \'an-l-əst\ *n.* A writer of annals.

an·nals \'an-lz\ *n. pl.; sing.* **an·nal.** **1** A written record of events, with those of each year placed in one section. **2** A history; historical records.

an·neal \ə-'nēl\ *v.* To bring into contact with high heat followed by cooling so as to soften thoroughly and make less brittle; to temper or toughen; as, to *anneal* metal.

an·ne·lid \'an-l-əd\ *n.* Any animal belonging to a group that includes the earthworms and leeches, whose bodies are composed of ringlike divisions or segments.

an·nex \ə-'neks, 'an-ˌeks\ *v.* To join a smaller thing to a larger, and to make both into one. The United States *annexed* Texas in 1845. — \'an-ˌeks\ *n.* Something annexed; especially, a building added to or situated near a larger building.

an·nex·a·tion \ˌan-ˌeks-'āsh-n\ *n.* **1** An annexing, especially of new territory. **2** Something annexed.

an·ni·hi·late \ə-'nī-ə-ˌlāt\ *v.;* **an·ni·hi·lat·ed**; **an·ni·hi·lat·ing.** To destroy entirely; to put completely out of existence; as, to *annihilate* an entire army. — **an·ni·hi·la·tion** \ə-ˌnī-ə-ˈlāsh-n\ *n.*

an·ni·ver·sa·ry \ˌan-ə-ˈvərs-r(-)ē\ *n.; pl.* **an·ni·ver·sa·ries.** **1** The return each year of the date on which something took place; as, a wedding *anniversary.* April 19 is the *anniversary* of the battle of Lexington. **2** A celebration of such a day. — *adj.* Returning with the year; celebrated on the same date each year; having to do with an anniversary; as, an *anniversary* feast.

an·no·tate \ˈan-ə-ˌtāt\ *v.;* **an·no·tat·ed; an·no·tat·ing.** **1** To furnish with notes, usually critical or explanatory; as, to *annotate* a play for study in school. **2** To make critical or explanatory notes.

an·no·ta·tion \ˌan-ə-ˈtāsh-n\ *n.* **1** An annotating, as of a text. **2** A critical or explanatory note, as one relating to a text.

an·nounce \ə-ˈnau̇n(t)s\ *v.;* **an·nounced; an·nounc·ing.** **1** To give public notice of; to proclaim, as by word of mouth, over the radio, on television, or by printed notices; as, to *announce* the next item on a program; to *announce* a sale. **2** To give notice of the arrival or presence of; as, to *announce* a visitor.

an·nounce·ment \ə-ˈnau̇n(t)s-mənt\ *n.* **1** The act of announcing. **2** A public notice announcing something.

an·nounc·er \ə-ˈnau̇n(t)s-r\ *n.* One that announces; especially, a person who makes announcements on radio or television.

an·noy \ə-ˈnȯi\ *v.* To disturb by bothering; to vex by small, disagreeable acts; to pester; to irritate. The interruptions *annoyed* the speaker.

an·noy·ance \ə-ˈnȯi-ən(t)s\ *n.* **1** The act of annoying. **2** The feeling of being annoyed; vexation. **3** Anyone or anything that annoys; a nuisance. The roar of the trains was a constant *annoyance.*

an·nu·al \ˈan-yə-wəl, ˈan-yəl\ *adj.* **1** Once a year; yearly; as, the *annual* Halloween party. **2** Computed by the year; as, an *annual* salary. **3** Made during a year; as, the *annual* revolution of the earth around the sun. **4** Lasting for only one year or one season; as, an *annual* plant. **5** Marking one year's growth; as, the *annual* rings in the stems of trees and shrubs. — *n.* **1** A book or magazine that comes out once a year; as, the school *annual.* **2** A plant that completes its growth in a single year.

an·nu·al·ly \ˈan-yə-lē, ˈan-yə-wə-lē\ *adv.* Yearly; every year; year by year.

an·nu·i·ty \ə-ˈnü-ət-ē, -ˈnyü-\ *n.; pl.* **an·nu·i·ties.** **1** A sum of money paid every year; a yearly allowance or income. **2** The right to receive such yearly payments; as, to buy an *annuity* from an insurance company.

an·nul \ə-ˈnəl\ *v.;* **an·nulled; an·nul·ling.** To do away with; to cancel; especially, to make no longer legally binding; as, to *annul* a company's charter; to *annul* a marriage. — **an·nul·ment,** *n.*

an·nu·lar \ˈan-yəl-r\ *adj.* Forming a ring; shaped like a ring, as an **annular eclipse,** in which a thin ring of sunlight shows around the dark moon.

an·nun·ci·ate \ə-ˈnən(t)s-ē-ˌāt\ *v.;* **an·nun·ci·at·ed; an·nun·ci·at·ing.** To announce.

an·nun·ci·a·tion \ə-ˌnən(t)s-ē-ˈāsh-n\ *n.* **1** The act of announcing; announcement. **2** [usually with a capital] The announcement by the angel Gabriel to the Virgin Mary that she was to be the mother of Christ. **3** [with a capital] The church festival held on March 25 in memory of this event.

an·ode \ˈan-ˌōd\ *n.* A positive electrode.

anoint \ə-ˈnȯint\ *v.* **1** To rub or cover with oil or grease. **2** In certain religious ceremonies, to touch a person with oil or to pour oil on his head. — **anoint·ment,** *n.*

anom·a·lous \ə-ˈnäm-l-əs\ *adj.* Departing from a general rule or method; abnormal; irregular; as, an *anomalous* procedure. — **anom·a·lous·ly,** *adv.*

anom·a·ly \ə-ˈnäm-l-ē\ *n.; pl.* **anom·a·lies.** **1** A departing from the common rule; an irregularity. **2** Anything not following the usual rule or standard. A bird that cannot fly is an *anomaly.*

anon \ə-ˈnän\ *adv.* Soon; again.

anon. Abbreviation for *anonymous.*

anon·y·mous \ə-ˈnän-ə-məs\ *adj.* Without the name of the writer or sender; unknown by name; as, an *anonymous* author. — **an·o·nym·i·ty** \ˌan-ə-ˈnim-ət-ē\ *n.* — **anon·y·mous·ly** \ə-ˈnän-ə-məs-lē\ *adv.*

anoph·e·les \ə-ˈnäf-l-ˌēz\ *n. sing. and pl.* The mosquito that, after biting a person infected with malaria, transmits the disease to other persons.

an·oth·er \ə-ˈnət͟h-r\ *pron.* One more; an additional one; a different one; as, to discuss one plan after *another.* — *adj.* A different; one more or an additional; as, to eat *another* potato; to change to *another* pair of shoes.

an·ox·ia \(ˈ)an-ˈäks-ē-ə\ *n.* The condition of being deprived of sufficient oxygen, as in flying at high altitudes.

ans. Abbreviation for *answer.*

an·swer \ˈan(t)s-r\ *n.* **1** Something said or written in reply; as, an *answer* to a letter. **2** Any action of the nature of a reply. The enemy's *answer* was a volley of shells. **3** The solution of a problem, as in mathematics. — *v.;* **an·swered; an·swer·ing** \-r(-)ing\. **1** To make an answer; to reply to; as, to *answer* a question; to refuse to *answer.* **2** To respond; to act in response to. The ship *answers* her helm. **3** To be accountable; to take responsibility; as, to *answer* for one's actions; to *answer* for the children's safety on the trip. **4** To be sufficient; to serve the purpose; to satisfy; as, an arrangement that *answers* everyone's needs. **5** To correspond to; to suit; as, a garment tailored to *answer* specifications.

an·swer·a·ble \ˈan(t)s-r(-)əb-l\ *adj.* **1** Obliged to answer; liable to be called to account; responsible; as, to be *answerable* for one's actions; *answerable* for a debt. **2** Capable of being answered; capable of being proved wrong; as, an *answerable* argument.

ant \ˈant\ *n.* Any of a family of small insects

closely related to the bees and wasps, living in communities and notable for their industrious habits.

ant. Abbreviation for *antonym.*

-ant \(ə)nt\. A suffix that can mean: **1** Having the quality, manner, or condition of a person or thing that, as in *observant* or *defiant.* **2** A person or thing that, as in *defendant* or *servant.*

an·tag·o·nism \an-'tag-n-ˌiz-m\ *n.* Active opposition or resistance.

an·tag·o·nist \an-'tag-n-əst\ *n.* A person who opposes another person, especially in a contest or combat; an opponent.

an·tag·o·nis·tic \(ˌ)an-ˌtag-n-'is-tik\ *adj.* Showing antagonism; hostile. — **an·tag·o·nis·ti·cal·ly** \-tik-l(-)ē\ *adv.*

an·tag·o·nize \an-'tag-n-ˌīz\ *v.;* **an·tag·o·nized**; **an·tag·o·niz·ing.** To cause someone else to be opposed or unfriendly to oneself; to arouse dislike; as, to *antagonize* one's friends by boasting.

ant·arc·tic \(')ant-'är(k)t-ik, -'ȧr(k)t-\ *adj.* Of or having to do with the South Pole or the region near it. — *n.* The antarctic region.

Antarctic Circle. An imaginary circle of the earth parallel to the equator about 23 degrees from the South Pole.

ant bear. A large, maned anteater of South America having shaggy gray fur with a black band on the breast.

ant cow. Any aphid from which an ant obtains honeydew.

ante-. A prefix that can mean: **1** Before in time, as in *antedate.* **2** Before in place, as in *anteroom.*

ant·eat·er \'ant-ˌēt-r\ *n.* One of several animals that have long snouts and long sticky tongues and that feed chiefly on ants and termites.

an·te·ced·ent \ˌant-ə-'sēd-nt\ *adj.* Coming or taking place earlier than something else; as, the period *antecedent* to the war. — *n.* **1** Someone or something that is earlier in time. One's ancestors are called one's *antecedents.* **2** In grammar, the word or group of words for which a pronoun stands. In "the house that Jack built", the word "house" is the *antecedent* of the pronoun "that".

an·te·cham·ber \'ant-ē-ˌchām-br\ *n.* An outer room leading to a usually more important room.

an·te·date \'ant-ē-ˌdāt\ *v.;* **an·te·dat·ed**; **an·te·dat·ing.** **1** To put a date on, as a paper or check, as of an earlier day than that on which it was actually written or signed. **2** To come before in time. Automobiles *antedate* airplanes.

an·te·di·lu·vi·an \ˌant-ē-də-'lü-vē-ən, -ˌdī-'lü-\ *adj.* Of or relating to the period before the great flood of the days of Noah; antiquated; extremely old or old-fashioned; as, an *antediluvian* car; a cranky old codger with *antediluvian* ideas.

an·te·lope \'ant-l-ˌōp\ *n.; pl.* **an·te·lope** or **an·te·lopes.** One of a group of cud-chewing animals that are allied to the goats and oxen but are distinguished from them by a more graceful build and by horns that extend upward and backward.

an·ten·na \an-'ten-ə\ *n.* **1** *pl.* **an·ten·nae** \-'ten-(ˌ)ē\. One of two or four threadlike movable feelers on the heads of insects, spiders, lobsters, and crabs. **2** *pl.* **an·ten·nas** \-'ten-əz\. A wire or a set of wires on a radio or television set, which receives electric waves from the air; a set of wires used to send such waves from a radio station.

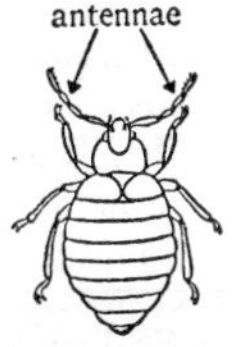

antenna, 1

an·ten·nule \an-'ten-ˌyül\ *n.* A small antenna, as in the crayfish.

an·te·pe·nult \ˌant-ē-'pē-ˌnəlt\ *n.* The second from the last syllable of a word, as *ti* in *an·ti·sep·tic.* — **an·te·pe·nul·ti·mate** \-pə-'nəlt-m-ət\ *adj.* or *n.*

an·te·ri·or \an-'tir-ē-ər\ *adj.* **1** Toward the front or the head; as, the *anterior* part of an insect's body. **2** Before in place or time.

an·te·room \'ant-ē-ˌrüm, -ˌru̇m\ *n.* A room used as an entrance to another; a waiting room.

an·them \'an(t)th-m\ *n.* **1** A sacred choral composition with words taken usually from the Scriptures. **2** A song of praise or gladness.

an·ther \'an(t)th-r\ *n.* One of the small balls or heads containing pollen that grow on threadlike stems, or filaments, in the center of a flower.

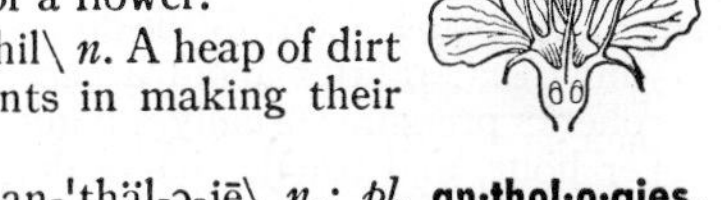

ant·hill \'ant-ˌhil\ *n.* A heap of dirt built up by ants in making their nest.

an·thol·o·gy \an-'thäl-ə-jē\ *n.; pl.* **an·thol·o·gies.** A collection of poems or other literary selections chosen from the works of various authors.

an·thra·cite \'an-thrə-ˌsīt\ *n.* A hard, glossy coal that burns without much smoke or flame.

an·thrax \'an-ˌthraks\ *n.* An infectious, usually fatal, bacterial disease of animals, especially cattle and sheep.

an·thro·poid \'an-thrə-ˌpȯid\ *adj.* Resembling man; as, the *anthropoid* apes. — *n.* An anthropoid ape.

an·thro·pol·o·gist \ˌan-thrə-'päl-ə-jəst\ *n.* A specialist in anthropology.

an·thro·pol·o·gy \ˌan-thrə-'päl-ə-jē\ *n.* The science that collects and studies the facts about man, especially those about his physical characteristics, the origin and distribution of races, human environment and social relations, and culture. — **an·thro·po·log·i·cal** \-pə-'läj-ik-l\ *adj.*

anti-. A prefix that can mean: **1** Against, opposed to, or contrary to, as in *anti-American* or *anti-slavery.* **2** Used to fight against or to destroy, as in *antiaircraft.*

an·ti·air·craft \ˌant-ē-'ar-ˌkraft, -'er-\ *adj.* Designed or used for defense against aircraft; as, an *antiaircraft* gun.

an·ti·bi·ot·ic \ˌant-ē-ˌbī-'ät-ik, ˌant-ə-, 'an-ˌtī-, -bē-\ *n.* A substance produced by living things, especially bacteria and fungi, used to kill or prevent the growth of harmful bacteria. Penicillin is an *antibiotic.*

an·ti·body \'ant-ə-ˌbäd-ē\ *n.; pl.* **an·ti·bod·ies.** A substance, usually in the blood, that serves to counteract the effects of disease-producing bacteria or their poisons.

an·tic \'ant-ik\ *adj.* Fantastic; queer; grotesque, as in appearance or behavior. — *n.* **1** An amusing trick; a playful movement or act; as, the *antics* of a clown. **2** A clown; a buffoon.

an·tic·i·pate \an-'tis-ə-ˌpāt\ *v.;* **an·tic·i·pat·ed; an·tic·i·pat·ing. 1** To take up, use, or introduce ahead of time; as, to *anticipate* an opponent's argument. **2** To be before in doing or acting; to forestall. **3** To foresee and do beforehand; as, to *anticipate* a person's wishes. **4** To experience beforehand; to expect; as, to *anticipate* the pleasure of a year of travel.

an·tic·i·pa·tion \(ˌ)an-ˌtis-ə-'pāsh-n\ *n.* **1** A looking forward to; expectation. The *anticipation* of Uncle's visit made everyone happy. **2** A seeing beforehand; a providing for. — **an·tic·i·pa·to·ry** \an-'tis-ə-pə-ˌtōr-ē, -ˌtȯr-ē\ *adj.*

an·ti·cli·max \ˌant-ə-'klī-ˌmaks\ *n.* **1** A sentence or passage in which the ideas fall off in dignity or importance at the close. **2** Any event, especially the last in a series, that is strikingly less important than the preceding. — **an·ti·cli·mac·tic** \-klī-'mak-tik\ *adj.*

an·ti·cy·clone \ˌant-ē-'sīk-ˌlōn\ *n.* A system of winds that rotates about a center of high atmospheric pressure, usually advances 20 to 30 miles per hour, and usually has a diameter of 1500 to 2500 miles. — **an·ti·cy·clon·ic** \-sī-'klän-ik\ *adj.*

an·ti·dote \'ant-ə-ˌdōt\ *n.* **1** A remedy that works against the effects of poison. **2** Anything that tends to counteract evil produced by something else; as, an *antidote* for juvenile delinquency. — **an·ti·dot·al** \'ant-ə-ˌdōt-l\ *adj.*

an·ti·freeze \'ant-ē-ˌfrēz\ *n.* A substance added to the liquid in an automobile radiator to prevent its freezing.

an·ti·gen \'ant-ij-n\ *n.* A substance, as a toxin or an enzyme, that, when introduced into the body, stimulates the production of an antibody.

an·ti·his·ta·mine \ˌant-ē-'hist-m-ˌēn, -m-ən\ *n.* One of various drugs used for treating allergic reactions and cold symptoms.

an·ti·knock \ˌant-ē-'näk\ *n.* A substance that, when added to the fuel of an internal-combustion engine, helps to prevent knocking.

an·ti·mo·ny \'ant-ə-ˌmō-nē\ *n.* A brittle metallic substance, tin-white in color, used chiefly in alloys to give hardness to soft metals.

an·tip·a·thy \an-'tip-ə-thē\ *n.; pl.* **an·tip·a·thies. 1** Strong and deep-seated dislike or distaste. **2** A person or thing that arouses strong dislike.

an·tip·o·des \an-'tip-ə-ˌdēz\ *n. pl.* Regions on the opposite sides of the earth. Americans say that Australians live in the *antipodes.* — **an·tip·o·de·an** \(ˌ)an-ˌtip-ə-'dē-ən\ *adj.*

an·ti·quar·i·an \ˌant-ə-'kwer-ē-ən\ *adj.* Relating to antiquaries or antiquities. — *n.* An antiquary.

an·ti·quary \'ant-ə-ˌkwer-ē\ *n.; pl.* **an·ti·quar·ies** A person who collects and studies antiquities.

an·ti·quat·ed \'ant-ə-ˌkwāt-əd\ *adj.* Old-fashioned; out-of-date; as, an *antiquated* car; *antiquated* ideas.

an·tique \an-'tēk\ *adj.* Belonging to a time very long ago; extremely old; old-fashioned; as, *antique* statues; *antique* furniture. — *n.* Something that is extremely old. The first automobiles made are now *antiques.*

an·tiq·ui·ty \an-'tik-wət-ē\ *n.; pl.* **an·tiq·ui·ties. 1** Ancient times; former ages, especially those before A.D. 476. **2** Very great age; as, a castle of great *antiquity.* **3** [usually in the plural] Something, as a building, a work of art, or a coin, that has come down from ancient times; something that has to do with the life of ancient times.

an·ti·sep·tic \ˌant-ə-'sep-tik\ *adj.* **1** Killing or making harmless the germs that cause decay or infection. Iodine is *antiseptic.* **2** Like, relating to, or using antiseptics; as, *antiseptic* surgery. — *n.* An antiseptic substance. — **an·ti·sep·ti·cal·ly** \-tik-l(-)ē\ *adv.*

an·ti·slav·ery \ˌant-ē-'slāv-r(-)ē, 'an-ˌtī-\ *adj.* Opposed to slavery; as, *antislavery* laws.

an·ti·so·cial \ˌant-ē-'sōsh-l\ *adj.* **1** Hostile to the well-being of society. Crime is *antisocial.* **2** Disliking the society of others; misanthropic.

an·tith·e·sis \an-'tith-ə-səs\ *n.; pl.* **an·tith·e·ses** \-ə-ˌsēz\. **1** An opposition or contrast of ideas, especially one emphasized by the position of the contrasting words, as in *Beauty and the Beast.* **2** The direct opposite; the contrary. White is the *antithesis* of black.

an·ti·tox·in \ˌant-ē-'täks-n\ *n.* A substance that is formed in the blood of a person who is ill with a germ disease, such as diphtheria, and that helps in overcoming the disease. A similar substance in the blood of animals is used in treating human beings.

ant·ler \'ant-lər\ *n.* The solid bony usually branched horn of a deer or related animal.

ant·lered \'ant-lərd\ *adj.* **1** Having antlers. **2** Decorated with antlers.

ant lion. A four-winged insect that, when a larva, digs a cone-shaped hole in which it catches insects, especially ants.

an·to·nym \'an-tə-ˌnim, 'ant-n-ˌim\ *n.* A word that is opposite in meaning to another word. "Dull" is an *antonym* of "sharp". — **an·ton·y·mous** \an-'tän-ə-məs\ *adj.*

anus \'ā-nəs\ *n.* The posterior opening of the alimentary canal.

an·vil \'an-vəl\ *n.* [From Old English *anfilt* originally meaning "something to beat on".] **1** An iron block on which pieces of metal are hammered into shape. **2** Anything resembling an anvil; especially, the middle one of the chain of three small bones in the ear of mammals.

anvil, 1

anx·i·e·ty \ang-'zī-ət-ē\ *n.; pl.* **anx·i·e·ties. 1** Painful uneasiness of mind; especially, fear that something unpleasant or unfortunate will happen; as, to be filled with *anxiety* about one's health. **2** Earnest desire; as, an *anxiety* to make friends.

anx·ious \'ang(k)-shəs\ *adj.* **1** Fearful of what may happen; worried; as, a mother *anxious* about her son's health. It is natural for us to feel *anxious* at times. **2** Desiring earnestly; eager; as, a boy *anxious* to make good. — **anx·ious·ly**, *adv.*

any \'en-ē\ *adj.* **1** One or some, but no matter which; as, willing to take *any* job that comes along. **2** Every; as, a poem that *any* schoolboy knows. — *pron.* **1** Any person or persons. **2** Any thing or things. **3** Any part or quantity. — *adv.* Even a little; a bit; as, to rest before going *any* farther.

an·y·body \'en-ē-ˌbäd-ē\ *pron.* Anyone.

an·y·how \'en-ē-ˌhau̇\ *adv.* **1** In any way, manner, or order. **2** At any rate; in any case.

an·y·one \'en-ē-(ˌ)wən\ *pron.* Any person; anybody.

an·y·thing \'en-ē-ˌthing\ *pron.* Any object or fact.

an·y·way \'en-ē-ˌwā\ *adv.* Anyhow.

an·y·where \'en-ē-ˌhwer\ *adv.* In, at, or to any place.

an·y·wise \'en-ē-ˌwīz\ *adv.* In any way; at all.

A1 \'ā-'wən\. In first-class condition; first rate.

aor·ta \ā-'ȯrt-ə\ *n.; pl.* **aor·tas** \ā-'ȯrt-əz\ or **aor·tae** \ā-'ȯr-ˌtē\. The large artery that carries blood from the heart to be distributed by branch arteries. — **aor·tic** \ā-'ȯrt-ik\ *adj.*

aou·dad \'au̇-ˌdad\ *n.* A wild sheep of North Africa.

apace \ə-'pās\ *adv.* At a quick pace; fast.

apanage. Variant of *appanage.*

apart \ə-'pärt, ə-'pȧrt\ *adv.* **1** Not together in time or place; as, towns many miles *apart.* **2** Aside; as, joking *apart.* **3** Into two or more parts; to pieces; as, to tear a book *apart.*

apart·ment \ə-'pärt-mənt, -'pȧrt-\ *n.* **1** A set of two or more rooms, as in a house or hotel, that are used together, especially to live in; as, a building with 25 *apartments.* **2** A single room, especially one equipped for light housekeeping.

apartment house. A building divided into apartments to live in.

ap·a·thet·ic \ˌap-ə-'thet-ik\ *adj.* Not feeling deep emotion; unemotional; indifferent. Some illnesses leave one *apathetic* for a time. — **ap·a·thet·i·cal·ly** \-ik-l(-)ē\ *adv.*

ap·a·thy \'ap-ə-thē\ *n.* **1** Lack of feeling; lack of emotion or excitement. **2** Indifference to what appeals to the feelings or interest.

ape \'āp\ *n.* **1** A monkey; especially, a large tailless monkey. **2** A person who mimics; an imitator. — *v.;* **aped**; **ap·ing**. To imitate; to mimic; as, children *aping* the manners of their elders.

ape·ri·ent \ə-'pir-ē-ənt\ *n.* A food or medicine that gently moves the bowels; a laxative. — *adj.* Having a laxative effect.

ap·er·ture \'ap-r-ˌchu̇r, -rch-r\ *n.* An opening; a hole; as, the *apertures* in a blockhouse. Pores are tiny *apertures* in the skin.

apex \'ā-ˌpeks\ *n.; pl.* **apex·es** \'ā-ˌpeks-əz\ or **ap·i·ces** \'ap-ə-ˌsēz, 'āp-ə-\. The tip, point, or top of anything; as, the *apex* of a pyramid.

aphid \'ā-fəd, 'af-əd\ *n.* A plant louse that lives on plants and sucks their juices.

aphis \'ā-fəs, 'af-əs\ *n.; pl.* **aph·i·des** \'af-ə-ˌdēz, 'ā-fə-\. An aphid.

aph·o·rism \'af-r-ˌiz-m\ *n.* A short sentence stating some general philosophical or practical observation. "There never was a good war or a bad peace" is an *aphorism.*

api·ary \'āp-ē-ˌer-ē\ *n.; pl.* **api·ar·ies.** A place where bees are kept; a collection of beehives.

apices. A pl. of *apex.*

apiece \ə-'pēs\ *adv.* For each one; each; as, melons for sale at fifty cents *apiece.*

ap·ish \'āp-ish\ *adj.* Like an ape; mimicking.

aplen·ty \ə-'plent-ē\ *adj.* or *adv.* Enough; in plenty.

aplomb \ə-'pläm, -'pləm\ *n.* Self-assurance; self-possession; poise.

ap·o·gee \'ap-ə-(ˌ)jē\ *n.* The point in the orbit of a satellite of the earth at the greatest distance from the earth.

apol·o·get·ic \ə-ˌpäl-ə-'jet-ik\ *adj.* Said, written, or done by way of apology; making an apology. — **apol·o·get·i·cal·ly** \-ik-l(-)ē\ *adv.*

apol·o·gist \ə-'päl-ə-jəst\ *n.* A person who argues in defense, as of a cause or policy.

apol·o·gize \ə-'päl-ə-ˌjīz\ *v.;* **apol·o·gized**; **apol·o·giz·ing.** To make an apology; to express regret for something one has done.

apol·o·gy \ə-'päl-ə-jē\ *n.; pl.* **apol·o·gies.** **1** An expression of regret for something that one has done; as, to make an *apology* for being late. **2** A poor substitute; a makeshift. This pole is an *apology* for a fishing rod.

— The word *excuse* is a synonym of *apology: apology* usually suggests that one has been in the wrong, and offers an explanation, acknowledges error, or expresses regret; *excuse* may indicate that one is trying to remove or avoid blame.

ap·o·plec·tic \ˌap-ə-'plek-tik\ *adj.* **1** Caused by apoplexy; as, an *apoplectic* stroke. **2** Affected with or inclined to apoplexy. **3** Having or giving the appearance of one possibly inclined to apoplexy; red-faced and hot-tempered.

ap·o·plexy \'ap-ə-ˌpleks-ē\ *n.* A sudden loss of consciousness, or of power to feel and move, caused by the breaking of a blood vessel in the brain or by the cutting off of the supply of blood to the brain by a clot in a blood vessel.

aport \ə-'pōrt, -'pȯrt\ *adv.* On or toward the port side of a ship.

apos·ta·sy \ə-'päs-tə-sē\ *n.; pl.* **apos·ta·sies.** A complete giving up or renouncing of something formerly believed in or professed, as religious faith, loyalty to a party, or devotion to a cause.

apos·tate \ə-ˈpäs-ˌtāt, -tət\ *n.* A person who abandons his religion, his faith, or the principles in which he has believed.

apos·tle \ə-ˈpäs-l\ *n.* **1** One of the twelve close followers of Christ whom he sent out to teach the gospel. **2** The first Christian missionary in any region. **3** The first advocate or the beginner, as of a reform.

ap·os·tol·ic \ˌap-əs-ˈtäl-ik\ *adj.* **1** Of or relating to an apostle or apostles, especially the twelve apostles, their times, or their teachings. **2** Coming from or having to do with the pope; papal; as, an *apostolic* delegate.

apos·tro·phe \ə-ˈpäs-trə-(ˌ)fē\ *n.* The addressing of an absent person as if present or of an abstract idea or inanimate object as if capable of understanding, as in "O grave, where is thy victory?"

apos·tro·phe \ə-ˈpäs-trə-(ˌ)fē\ *n.* A mark ['] used in printing and writing to show various things, such as: the dropping of one or more letters or figures, as in *can't* (for *cannot*) or '76 (for 1776); ownership or possession, as in *child's* (for *of a child*), *doctors'* (for *of doctors*), *James's* (for *of James*), or *Moses'* (for *of Moses*); the plural of letters or figures. Dot your *i's* and cross your *t's*. Six 7*'s* make 42.

apoth·e·cary \ə-ˈpäth-ə-ˌker-ē\ *n.; pl.* **apoth·e·car·ies.** A druggist.

ap·pall or **ap·pal** \ə-ˈpȯl\ *v.;* **ap·palled; ap·pall·ing.** To fill with terror or horror. The onlookers were *appalled* to see the cars crash together.

ap·pall·ing \ə-ˈpȯl-ing\ *adj.* Such as to appall; shocking; as, an *appalling* accident. — **ap·pall·ing·ly,** *adv.*

ap·pa·nage or **ap·a·nage** \ˈap-n-ij\ *n.* **1** The provision, as a grant of land, made by a ruler for the younger members of his family. **2** A person's share of property. **3** Something that belongs to a person by custom or right.

ap·pa·rat·us \ˌap-r-ˈat-əs, -ˈāt-əs\ *n.; pl.* **ap·pa·rat·us** \-əs\ or **ap·pa·rat·us·es** \-ə-səz\. **1** The equipment, such as tools or machinery, used to do a particular kind of work; as, gymnasium or laboratory *apparatus;* an *apparatus* for washing cars. **2** Any complex instrument, appliance, or piece of machinery.

ap·par·el \ə-ˈpar-əl\ *n.* Clothing; outer garments or undergarments; as, a store noted for its men's *apparel.* — *v.;* **ap·par·eled** or **ap·par·elled; ap·par·el·ing** or **ap·par·el·ling.** To clothe; to dress. The marchers were *appareled* in white uniforms.

ap·par·ent \ə-ˈpar-ənt, -ˈper-\ *adj.* **1** Easily seen; easily understood; as, a night in which many stars are *apparent.* After his long day's work, the boy's reason for going to bed early is *apparent.* **2** As it appears to the eye rather than as it really is. The *apparent* size of the moon is much smaller than its actual size.

ap·par·ent·ly \-ənt-lē\ *adv.* **1** Clearly; plainly. **2** As far as one can judge; seemingly.

ap·pa·ri·tion \ˌap-r-ˈish-n\ *n.* Something unusual or startling that comes into sight; a ghost or ghostlike figure.

ap·peal \ə-ˈpēl\ *v.* **1** To take the proper steps to have a decision made in a lower law court reviewed in a higher court. **2** To make an earnest request, as for aid, support, or sympathy; as, to *appeal* to the public for money for flood relief. The lost boy *appealed* to the policeman for help. **3** To call upon some authority, as for a decision; as, to *appeal* to the referee. **4** To please; to interest; to attract; as, a program that *appeals* to almost everybody. — *n.* **1** A proceeding by which a case in law is brought to a superior court for re-examination. **2** An earnest request, as for help or money; a plea; as, the annual *appeal* for the community chest; an *appeal* to reason. **3** An address intended to arouse a sympathetic response. **4** Power to interest or attract; as, music that has a great *appeal* for children.

ap·pear \ə-ˈpir\ *v.* **1** To come into sight; to become clear or plain; to show. Stars *appeared* in the sky. **2** To present oneself, as to answer a charge or to plead a cause; as, to *appear* in court. **3** To become clear to the mind; to reveal itself; to be obvious. **4** To come out in printed form; as, a book that is to *appear* next month. **5** To come before the public on stage or screen. This actor *appears* on television. **6** To seem; to look; as, to *appear* to be tired.

ap·pear·ance \ə-ˈpir-ən(t)s\ *n.* **1** The act of appearing; as, the *appearance* of the sun over the horizon. Motion picture actors sometimes make personal *appearances* in local theaters. **2** The look of a person or thing. Green decorations give a room a cool *appearance.* **3** Outward show; semblance; pretense; as, to give the *appearance* of working; to keep up *appearances.* **4** A sense impression of a thing as different from the true nature of that thing. The blades of a rapidly moving electric fan often have the *appearance* of a solid object.

ap·pease \ə-ˈpēz\ *v.;* **ap·peased; ap·peas·ing.** To pacify, especially by satisfying; to quiet, calm, or soothe; as, to *appease* a person's curiosity; to *appease* hunger. — For synonyms see *pacify.* — **ap·pease·ment,** *n.*

ap·pel·lant \ə-ˈpel-ənt\ *adj.* Appealing; relating to an appeal. — *n.* One who appeals, as from a decision of a court of law.

ap·pel·late \ə-ˈpel-ət\ *adj.* Relating to appeals; especially, having the power to review the decisions of a lower court; as, an *appellate* court.

ap·pel·la·tion \ˌap-l-ˈāsh-n\ *n.* **1** The act of calling by a name. **2** A name or title, especially a descriptive name or title, given to a person or thing. George Washington is often referred to by the *appellation* "Father of his country".

ap·pend \ə-ˈpend\ *v.* To add as an extra or as a less important part; as, to *append* a postscript to a letter.

ap·pend·age \ə-ˈpen-dij\ *n.* **1** Something attached to a larger or more important thing. **2** In biology, a subordinate part; especially, an external limb or organ.

ap·pen·dec·to·my \ˌap-n-'dekt-m-ē\ *n.; pl.* **ap·pen·dec·to·mies.** Surgical removal of the human appendix.

ap·pen·di·ci·tis \ə-ˌpen-də-'sīt-əs\ *n.* Inflammation of the appendix.

ap·pen·dix \ə-'pen-diks\ *n.; pl.* **ap·pen·dix·es** \-dik-səz\ or **ap·pen·di·ces** \-də-ˌsēz\. **1** A part of a book giving additional information, such as notes or tables. **2** A small tubelike outgrowth from the intestine.

ap·per·tain \ˌap-r-'tān\ *v.* To belong or be connected with as a possession, a part, or a right; to pertain; as, the duties that *appertain* to the office of magistrate.

ap·pe·tite \'ap-ə-ˌtīt\ *n.* **1** A desire for food or drink. **2** Eager desire; as, to have an *appetite* for adventure.

ap·pe·tiz·er \'ap-ə-ˌtīz-r\ *n.* A food or a drink that gives one an appetite; especially, a tasty bit of food served before or at the beginning of a dinner.

ap·pe·tiz·ing \'ap-ə-ˌtī-zing\ *adj.* Giving an appetite; tempting the appetite; as, an *appetizing* smell from the kitchen. — **ap·pe·tiz·ing·ly,** *adv.*

ap·plaud \ə-'plȯd\ *v.* **1** To show enjoyment or approval by clapping one's hands or by cheering; as, to *applaud* the actors at the end of a play. **2** To praise; to approve; as, to *applaud* a person's courage.

ap·plause \ə-'plȯz\ *n.* Approval publicly expressed, as by clapping the hands.

ap·ple \'ap-l\ *n.* **1** A round or oval fruit with a red, yellow, or green skin, firm white flesh, a seed core, and, usually, a tart taste. **2** The tree that bears this fruit.

ap·pli·ance \ə-'plī-ən(t)s\ *n.* A useful article, especially a small one, that can be worked by hand or by mechanical or electrical means. Electric fans, washing machines, and irons are *appliances.*

ap·pli·ca·ble \'ap-lə-kəb-l, ə-'plik-əb-l\ *adj.* Capable of being put to use or put into practice; fit; suitable; as, a method of solution *applicable* to any problem. — **ap·pli·ca·bil·i·ty** \ˌap-lə-kə-'bil-ət-ē, ə-ˌplik-ə-\ *n.*

ap·pli·cant \'ap-lə-kənt\ *n.* A person who applies for something; as, an *applicant* for work; *applicants* for admission to a school.

ap·pli·ca·tion \ˌap-lə-'kāsh-n\ *n.* **1** The act of applying; as, the *application* of paint to a house. **2** Something put or spread on a surface; as, hot *applications* on a sprained ankle. **3** The act of putting something to a practical use; a use; as, new *applications* of electricity; the *application* of a law. **4** Ability to fix one's attention on one's work; as, a man who has no power of *application.* **5** A petition; as, an *application* for aid. **6** A request made personally or in writing; as, an *application* for a job.

ap·pli·ca·tor \'ap-lə-ˌkāt-r\ *n.* Any device, such as a cotton-tipped stick or a glass rod, for applying medicine, as to the nose or throat.

ap·plied \ə-'plīd\ *adj.* Put to practical use; especially, applying general principles to solve definite problems; as, the *applied* sciences.

ap·ply \ə-'plī\ *v.;* **ap·plied** \-'plīd\; **ap·ply·ing. 1** To put on; to place in contact; as, to *apply* a coat of paint; to *apply* heat. **2** To put to use; as, to *apply* knowledge. **3** To give one's full attention; to devote (oneself). The children *applied* themselves to the task. **4** To have connection. This law *applies* to everyone. **5** To ask personally or by letter; as, to *apply* for a job.

ap·point \ə-'pȯint\ *v.* **1** To fix or set officially; to agree upon; as, to *appoint* a day for a meeting. **2** To name officially to an office or position. The president *appoints* the members of his cabinet.

ap·point·ed \ə-'pȯint-əd\ *adj.* Furnished; equipped; as, a well-*appointed* house.

ap·poin·tee \ə-ˌpȯin-'tē, ˌa-\ *n.* A person appointed to a position or an office.

ap·poin·tive \ə-'pȯint-iv\ *adj.* Filled by appointment and not by election; as, an *appointive* office.

ap·point·ment \ə-'pȯint-mənt\ *n.* **1** An agreement to meet at a fixed time; as, a two-o'clock *appointment* with the dentist. **2** A position or office to which a person is named but not elected; as, a man who received an *appointment* from the president. **3** Selection by a superior official; as, a man who holds his office by *appointment.* **4** [usually in the plural] Equipment; furniture; as, the *appointments* of a room.

ap·por·tion \ə-'pōrsh-n, -'pȯrsh-n\ *v.;* **ap·por·tioned; ap·por·tion·ing** \-n(-)ing\. To portion out; to allot; as, to *apportion* one's time among various duties. — **ap·por·tion·ment** \-n-mənt\ *n.*

ap·po·si·tion \ˌap-ə-'zish-n\ *n.* **1** The placing of two things next to one another. **2** The relationship between a noun and some other similar word or group of words that is placed right after the noun and that explains it. In the sentence "The visitor, an old friend, stayed to dinner", "an old friend" is in *apposition* with "visitor".

ap·pos·i·tive \ə-'päz-ət-iv\ *adj.* Standing in apposition; as, an *appositive* phrase. — *n.* A word or a group of words that explains some other word, as *an expert swimmer* in "Our neighbor, an expert swimmer, rescued the child".

ap·prais·al \ə-'prāz-l\ *n.* **1** The action of appraising. **2** The value fixed by appraisers.

ap·praise \ə-'prāz\ *v.;* **ap·praised; ap·prais·ing.** To set a value on; especially, to determine the money value of; as, a house *appraised* at $9,000.

ap·prais·er \ə-'prāz-r\ *n.* A person who appraises; especially, an official having this duty, as in setting a value on real estate.

ap·pre·cia·ble \ə-'prē-shəb-l\ *adj.* Large enough to be recognized and measured, or to be felt; as, an *appreciable* difference in temperature.

ap·pre·cia·bly \-shə-blē\ *adv.* To an appreciable

degree. Within one hour the weather turned *appreciably* cooler.

ap·pre·ci·ate \ə-'prē-shē-ˌāt\ *v.;* **ap·pre·ci·at·ed; ap·pre·ci·at·ing. 1** To see the worth of; to set a just value on; as, to *appreciate* one's friends. **2** To enjoy intelligently; as, to *appreciate* good music. **3** To be grateful for; as, to *appreciate* a kindness. **4** To be fully aware of; to recognize; as, to *appreciate* the necessity of working hard. **5** To rise in value; as, a neighborhood in which real estate has steadily *appreciated.*

ap·pre·ci·a·tion \ə-ˌprē-shē-'āsh-n\ *n.* **1** The act of appreciating. **2** Awareness or understanding of worth or value; as, a deep *appreciation* of music. **3** A rise in value.

ap·pre·cia·tive \ə-'prē-shət-iv, -shē-ˌāt-iv\ *adj.* Having or showing appreciation; as, to speak before an *appreciative* audience. — **ap·pre·cia·tive·ly,** *adv.*

ap·pre·hend \ˌap-rē-'hend\ *v.* **1** To seize; to arrest; as, to *apprehend* a burglar. **2** To seize with the mind; to have understanding of; as, to *apprehend* the difference between right and wrong. **3** To feel that something dreadful is going to happen; to foresee with fear; as, to *apprehend* danger.

ap·pre·hen·sion \ˌap-rē-'hench-n\ *n.* **1** Capture; arrest; as, the *apprehension* of a burglar. **2** Understanding; as, a man of slow *apprehension.* **3** Fear of what may be coming; dread of the future.

ap·pre·hen·sive \ˌap-rē-'hen(t)s-iv\ *adj.* Fearful of what may be coming. — **ap·pre·hen·sive·ly,** *adv.*

ap·pren·tice \ə-'prent-əs\ *n.* **1** A person learning a trade or a craft by practical experience under a skilled worker. **2** An inexperienced person; a novice. — *v.;* **ap·pren·ticed; ap·pren·tic·ing.** To send into service as an apprentice. The father *apprenticed* his son to a printer.

ap·pren·tice·ship \ə-'prent-əsh-ˌship, -əs-ˌship\ *n.* **1** Service as an apprentice. **2** The period during which a person serves as an apprentice.

ap·prise \ə-'prīz\ *v.;* **ap·prised; ap·pris·ing.** Also **ap·prize.** To give notice; to inform; as, to be *apprised* by the secretary of a meeting to be held.

ap·proach \ə-'prōch\ *v.* **1** To come near, as in space, time, or quality; to go near; to draw close. **2** To approximate; as, a price *approaching* what one can afford. — *n.* **1** The act of drawing near; as, the gradual *approach* of the sun to the horizon; the *approach* of winter. **2** A step or means taken toward accomplishing something; as, to make friendly *approaches* toward one's new neighbors. **3** A way or passage, such as a path or a road, by which one comes up to something; a means of access. The *approach* to the house was by a narrow lane.

ap·proach·a·ble \ə-'prō-chəb-l\ *adj.* **1** Accessible. **2** Easily approached, especially in speech; as, a very *approachable* man.

ap·pro·ba·tion \ˌap-rə-'bāsh-n\ *n.* Approval; commendation.

ap·pro·pri·ate \ə-'prō-prē-ət\ *adj.* Specially fitting or suitable; as, to wear clothes *appropriate* to the weather. — For synonyms see *fit.* — \-ˌāt\ *v.;* **ap·pro·pri·at·ed; ap·pro·pri·at·ing. 1** To set apart for a special use or purpose. Congress *appropriates* money for the armed services. **2** To take for one's own use; as, to *appropriate* the most comfortable chair in the room. — **ap·pro·pri·ate·ly** \-ət-lē\ *adv.*

ap·pro·pri·a·tion \ə-ˌprō-prē-'āsh-n\ *n.* **1** The act of appropriating, as for oneself or for a particular use. **2** A thing or an amount appropriated, especially for some special purpose.

ap·prov·al \ə-'prüv-l\ *n.* **1** A favorable decision; an opinion that someone or something is good; as, a plan that had the *approval* of the whole class. **2** Examination to determine suitability, without obligation to accept; as, goods sent on *approval.*

ap·prove \ə-'prüv\ *v.;* **ap·proved; ap·prov·ing. 1** To have or to express a favorable opinion; to think well of a person or thing; as, a boy of whom all who knew him *approved.* **2** To accept officially as satisfactory. The school board *approved* the plan for a new gymnasium. — **ap·prov·ing·ly,** *adv.*

ap·prox·i·mate \ə-'präks-m-ət\ *adj.* Nearly correct; not exact but nearly so. The *approximate* cost will be five dollars. — \-ˌāt\ *v.;* **ap·prox·i·mat·ed; ap·prox·i·mat·ing.** To come close to; to be nearly the same as; as, colors that *approximate* each other but are not a perfect match.

ap·prox·i·mate·ly \ə-'präks-m-ət-lē\ *adv.* Nearly; about; as, at *approximately* three o'clock.

ap·prox·i·ma·tion \ə-ˌpräks-m-'āsh-n\ *n.* An approximating; nearness, as to the correct or exact amount or size; a nearly exact estimate or figure.

ap·pur·te·nance \ə-'pərt-n(-)ən(t)s\ *n.* Something that belongs to or goes along with some other usually larger and more important thing; as, a house for sale with its furniture and all other *appurtenances.*

Apr. Abbreviation for *April.*

apri·cot \'āp-rə-ˌkät, 'ap-\ *n.* A fruit like a plum in shape and size, like a yellow peach in skin, flesh, and color, and like both plum and peach in flavor.

April \'āp-rəl\ *n.* [From Latin *Aprilis,* the second month of the old Roman year.] The fourth month of the year, having 30 days.

April fool. One who is tricked on the first day of April, All Fools' Day.

apron \'āp-rən, -rn\ *n.* [From earlier English *napron, a napron* being understood as *an apron.*] **1** A garment worn on the front of the body to protect the clothing. **2** Something resembling such a garment in shape, position, or use.

ap·ro·pos \ˌap-rə-'pō\ *adj.* Suiting the occasion or the subject; as, an *apropos* remark. — *adv.* At the right time; fittingly; opportunely; as, to speak absolutely *apropos.* — **apropos of.** With respect to; concerning.

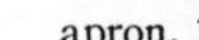
apron. 1

apse \'aps\ *n.* A projecting part of a building, especially of a church, usually semicircular in shape.

apt \'apt\ *adj.* **1** Fitting; suitable; as, an *apt* quotation. **2** Likely; inclined; as, a person *apt* to become angry over nothing. **3** Quick to learn; as, a pupil *apt* in arithmetic. — **apt·ly**, *adv.*

ap·ti·tude \'ap-tə-ˌtüd, -ˌtyüd\ *n.* **1** Quickness in learning; aptness. **2** Natural ability; talent; as, an *aptitude* for mathematics. — For synonyms see *ability.*

aq·ua·cade \'ak-wə-ˌkād, 'äk-\ *n.* An elaborate water spectacle consisting of exhibitions of swimming, diving, and acrobatics, accompanied by music.

aq·ua·lung \'ak-wə-ˌləng, 'äk-\ *n.* An underwater breathing device consisting of one or more cylinders of compressed air and a watertight face mask.

aq·ua·ma·rine \ˌak-wə-mə-'rēn, ˌäk-\ *n.* **1** A transparent semiprecious bluish or greenish stone. **2** A pale blue-green color with a tinge of gray.

aq·ua·plane \'ak-wə-ˌplān, 'äk-\ *n.* A wide board to be towed behind a speeding motorboat and ridden by a person who stands on it. — *v.;* **aq·ua·planed; aq·ua·plan·ing.** To ride on an aquaplane; to engage in the sport of aquaplaning.

aquaplane

aquar·ist \ə-'kwer-əst\ *n.* A person who keeps an aquarium.

aquar·i·um \ə-'kwer-ē-əm\ *n.; pl.* **aquar·i·ums** \-ē-əmz\ or **aquar·ia** \-ē-ə\. **1** A container, such as a tank or a bowl, in which living fish or other water animals or water plants are kept. **2** A building in which water animals or water plants are kept and shown.

aquat·ic \ə-'kwat-ik, -'kwät-\ *adj.* **1** Growing or living in water; as, *aquatic* animals. **2** Practiced in or on the water; as, *aquatic* sports. — *n.* An aquatic animal or plant.

aq·ua·tint \'ak-wə-ˌtint\ *n.* An etching in which spaces are eaten in with nitric acid (**aq·ua for·tis** \'ak-wə 'fȯrt-əs\), producing an effect resembling a drawing in water colors or India ink.

aq·ue·duct \'ak-wə-ˌdəkt\ *n.* An artificial channel for carrying flowing water from place to place; especially, a bridgelike structure that carries the water of a canal across a river or hollow.

aque·ous \'ā-kwē-əs, 'ak-wē-\ *adj.* **1** Consisting of water; like water; watery. **2** Made of, by, or with water; as, an *aqueous* solution.

aqueous humor. A clear fluid between the lens and the cornea of the eye.

aq·ui·line \'ak-wə-ˌlīn, -lən\ *adj.* **1** Of or like an eagle. **2** Curved like an eagle's beak; as, an *aquiline* nose.

ar. Abbreviation for: **1** *arrive.* **2** *arrives.*

Ar·ab \'ar-əb\ *adj.* Of or relating to the Arabs. — *n.* A member of the Arabic race or a native of Arabia.

ar·a·besque \ˌar-ə-'besk\ *n.* A design or a form of decoration consisting of interlacing lines and figures, usually of flowers and leaves but sometimes of geometric figures. — *adj.* Relating to or like arabesque.

arabesque

Ara·bi·an \ə-'rā-bē-ən\ *adj.* Of or relating to Arabia or the Arabs. — *n.* A native or inhabitant of Arabia.

Ar·a·bic \'ar-ə-bik\ *adj.* Arabian. — *n.* The language of the Arabs.

Arabic numerals. The nine figures 1, 2, 3, 4, 5, 6, 7, 8, 9, and the cipher 0.

ar·a·ble \'ar-əb-l\ *adj.* Fit for or cultivated by plowing; suitable for producing crops; as, *arable* land.

arach·nid \ə-'rak-nəd\ *n.* Any of a class of invertebrate animals, including the spiders and scorpions, mites and ticks, having eight legs and a body divided into two distinct parts.

ar·bi·ter \'är-bət-r, 'år-\ *n.* **1** A person chosen to settle a dispute; a judge; an arbitrator. **2** Any person having absolute authority to judge and decide what is right or proper.

ar·bit·ra·ment \är-'bi-trə-mənt\ *n.* **1** The settling of a dispute by an arbiter; arbitration. **2** A decision or an award made by an arbiter.

ar·bi·trary \'är-bə-ˌtrer-ē, 'år-\ *adj.* **1** Decided or done without considering the wishes or opinions of other people or without considering all the facts in the case; as, an *arbitrary* decision. **2** Guided by no law except one's own will or judgment; despotic; as, an *arbitrary* ruler. — **ar·bi·trar·i·ly** \ˌär-bə-'trer-ə-lē, ˌår-\ *adv.*

ar·bi·trate \'är-bə-ˌtrāt, 'år-\ *v.;* **ar·bi·trat·ed; ar·bi·trat·ing. 1** To settle a dispute after hearing and considering the arguments of both sides; to hear and decide as an arbiter; as, a committee appointed to *arbitrate* between the company and the striking workmen. **2** To refer a dispute to others for settlement; to submit to arbitration. The two groups agreed to *arbitrate* their differences.

ar·bi·tra·tion \ˌär-bə-'trāsh-n, ˌår-\ *n.* A method of settling a dispute in which both sides present their arguments to a third person or group for decision.

ar·bi·tra·tor \'är-bə-ˌtrāt-r, 'år-\ *n.* A person chosen to settle the differences between other persons or groups having a controversy.

ar·bor \'ärb-r, 'årb-r\ *n.* **1** A lattice or trellis for vines. **2** A shady spot covered by vines or branches.

Arbor Day. A day appointed for planting trees.

ar·bo·re·al \är-'bōr-ē-əl, år-, -'bȯr-\ *adj.* **1** Of or relating to trees; like trees. **2** Living in trees; as, *arboreal* animals.

ar·bor·vi·tae \ˌärb-r-'vīt-ē, ˌårb-\ *n.; pl.* **ar·bor·vi·taes.** A cone-shaped evergreen tree whose spreading branches bear smaller branches in fan-shaped, flat sprays.

ar·bu·tus \är-ˈbyüt-əs, ȧr-\ *n.* **1** Any of several trees or shrubs of the heath family, bearing white flowers and scarlet berries. **2** A trailing spring-blossoming plant that bears clusters of small fragrant flowers with five white or pink petals.

arbutus, 2

arc \ˈärk, ˈȧrk\ *n.* **1** A part or section of a curved line; as, an *arc* of a circle. **2** A luminous discharge of electricity through the air or through a gas, as the glowing light formed between the ends of a broken conductor. — *v.;* **arced** \ˈärkt, ˈȧrkt\; **arc·ing** \ˈärk-ing, ˈȧrk-\. To make an arc, especially an electric arc.

ar·cade \är-ˈkād, ar-\ *n.* **1** A row of arches with the columns that support them. **2** An arched or covered passageway, especially one lined with shops.

arch \ˈärch, ˈȧrch\ *n.* **1** A structure, usually curved and made up of separate wedge-shaped pieces, used to span an opening and capable of supporting weight from above; as, the *arches* of a bridge. **2** Any place covered by an arch. **3** Something resembling an arch; as, the *arch* of the foot. — *v.* **1** To cover with or as if with an arch or arches; as, shade trees *arching* the street. **2** To form or shape into an arch; as, to *arch* one's eyebrows.

arches

arch \ˈärch, ˈȧrch\ *adj.* **1** Chief; principal — often used as a prefix, as in *archbishop.* **2** Slyly mischievous; as, an *arch* look.

ar·chae·ol·o·gist or **ar·che·ol·o·gist** \ˌärk-ē-ˈäl-ə-jəst, ˌȧrk-\ *n.* A specialist in archaeology.

ar·chae·ol·o·gy or **ar·che·ol·o·gy** \ˌärk-ē-ˈäl-ə-jē, ˌȧrk-\ *n.* The science which deals with past human life and activities as shown by the monuments and relics left by ancient peoples. — **ar·chae·o·log·i·cal** or **ar·che·o·log·i·cal** \-ə-ˈläj-ik-l\ *adj.*

ar·cha·ic \är-ˈkā-ik, ȧr-\ *adj.* Belonging to an earlier time; no longer in general use; old-fashioned. "Affright", "sooth", and "erstwhile" are all *archaic* words.

ar·cha·ism \ˈärk-ē-ˌiz-m, ˈȧrk-, -ˌā-ˌiz-m\ *n.* **1** The use of archaic words. **2** An archaic word or expression.

arch·an·gel \ˈärk-ˌānj-l, ˈȧrk-\ *n.* A chief angel.

arch·bish·op \ˈärch-ˈbish-əp, ˈȧrch-\ *n.* The bishop of highest rank in a group of dioceses.

arch·dea·con \ˈärch-ˈdēk-n, ˈȧrch-\ *n.* A chief deacon, ranking next below a bishop.

arch·du·cal \ˈärch-ˈdük-l, ˈȧrch-, -ˈdyük-l\ *adj.* Of or relating to an archduke or an archduchy.

arch·duch·ess \ˈärch-ˈdəch-əs, ˈȧrch-\ *n.* **1** The wife or widow of an archduke. **2** A princess of the imperial family of Austria.

arch·duchy \ˈärch-ˈdəch-ē, ˈȧrch-\ *n.; pl.* **arch·duch·ies**. The territory of an archduke or archduchess.

arch·duke \ˈärch-ˈdük, ˈȧrch-, -ˈdyük\ *n.* A prince of the imperial family of Austria.

arch·duke·dom \-dəm\ *n.* **1** An archduchy. **2** The rank or title of an archduke.

arched \ˈärcht, ˈȧrcht\ *adj.* Made or formed as or with an arch; having or forming an arch or arches.

arch·en·e·my \ˈärch-ˈen-ə-mē, ˈȧrch-\ *n.; pl.* **arch·en·e·mies**. Chief enemy.

archeological. Variant of *archaeological.*

archeologist. Variant of *archaeologist.*

archeology. Variant of *archaeology.*

ar·cher \ˈärch-r, ˈȧrch-r\ *n.* A person who shoots with a bow and arrow; a bowman.

ar·chery \ˈärch-r(-)ē, ˈȧrch-\ *n.* **1** Shooting with bows and arrows. **2** Archers; as, an attack on the castle by the *archery.*

archer

ar·che·type \ˈärk-ə-ˌtīp, ˈȧrk-\ *n.* The original pattern or model of a work or the model from which a thing is made or formed. — **ar·che·typ·al** \-ˌtīp-l\ or **ar·che·typ·i·cal** \ˌärk-ə-ˈtip-ik-l, ˌȧrk-\ *adj.*

ar·chi·epis·co·pal \ˌärk-ē-ə-ˈpis-kəp-l, ˌȧrk-\ *adj.* Of or relating to an archbishop.

ar·chi·pel·a·go \ˌärk-ə-ˈpel-ə-ˌgō, ˌärch-, ˌȧrk-, ˌȧrch-\ *n.; pl.* **ar·chi·pel·a·goes** or **ar·chi·pel·a·gos**. **1** A sea that is dotted with islands. **2** The group of islands in such a sea.

ar·chi·tect \ˈärk-ə-ˌtekt, ˈȧrk-\ *n.* A person who designs buildings and oversees their construction.

ar·chi·tec·tur·al \ˌärk-ə-ˈtek-chər-əl, ˌȧrk-, -ˈteksh-r(-)əl\ *adj.* Of or relating to architecture. — **ar·chi·tec·tur·al·ly** \-ə-lē\ *adv.*

ar·chi·tec·ture \ˈärk-ə-ˌtek-chər, ˈȧrk-\ *n.* **1** The art of making plans for buildings; the work of an architect. **2** The style or styles of building that architects produce or imitate; as, a church of modern *architecture.* **3** Architectural work; buildings.

ar·chi·trave \ˈärk-ə-ˌtrāv, ˈȧrk-\ *n.* The line or course of stone just above the columns in an ancient Greek or Roman building.

ar·chives \ˈär-ˌkīvz, ˈȧr-\ *n. pl.* **1** A place for keeping public records. **2** Public records and documents. **3** Other historical records; as, family *archives.*

ar·chi·vist \ˈär-kə-vəst, ˈȧr-, -ˌkī-\ *n.* A keeper of archives or records.

arch·ly \ˈärch-lē, ˈȧrch-\ *adv.* In an arch manner; roguishly; mischievously.

arch·way \ˈärch-ˌwā, ˈȧrch-\ *n.* A passage under an arch; an arched gateway.

arcked. A past tense and past part. of *arc.*

arcking. A pres. part. of *arc.*

arc lamp or **arc light**. A lamp whose light is produced when an electric current passes between two electrodes surrounded by gas.

arc·tic \'är(k)t-ik, 'ȧr(k)t-\ *adj.* Of or having to do with the North Pole or the region near it. — *n.* **1** The arctic region. **2** A waterproof overshoe, usually covering the ankle.

Arctic Circle. An imaginary circle of the earth parallel to the equator about 23 degrees from the North Pole.

ar·dent \'ärd-nt, 'ȧrd-\ *adj.* **1** Fiery; hot. **2** Eager; zealous; as, an *ardent* worker for the cause of freedom. — **ar·dent·ly**, *adv.*

ar·dor \'ärd-r, 'ȧrd-r\ *n.* Warmth of feeling; eagerness; zeal.

ar·du·ous \'är-jə-wəs, 'ȧr-\ *adj.* Extremely difficult; laborious; as, the *arduous* climb up the mountain; *arduous* tasks.

are \ər, (')är, (')ȧr\. The form of the verb *be* that is used with *you* (singular or plural), or with any plural, as *we, they, birds,* or *men,* to show present time.

ar·ea \'ar-ē-ə, 'er-, 'ā-rē-ə\ *n.* **1** Any flat surface, as of the ground; as, a parking lot covering a large *area.* **2** The size of such a space; surface extent; as, an *area* of 2000 square feet. **3** A region; as, the farming *areas* of the country.

ar·e·a·way \-ˌwā\ *n.* A space, often below street level, leading to and giving air and light to a cellar or basement.

are·na \ə-'rē-nə\ *n.* **1** Any place where public contests or spectacles are staged; as, a boxing *arena.* **2** Any place of contest; as, the political *arena.*

aren't \'ärnt, 'är-ənt, 'ȧrnt, 'ȧr-ənt\. A contraction of *are not.*

ar·gent \'ärj-nt, 'ȧrj-\ *adj.* Of silver; silvery white.

Ar·gen·tine \'ärj-n-ˌtēn, 'ȧrj-, -ˌtīn\ *adj.* Of or relating to Argentina. — *n.* A citizen or a native of Argentina.

Ar·gen·tin·e·an \ˌärj-n-'tin-ē-ən, ˌȧrj-\ *n.* An Argentine.

Ar·gen·tin·i·an \ˌärj-n-'tin-ē-ən, ˌȧrj-\ *adj.* Argentine.

ar·gon \'är-ˌgän, 'ȧr-\ *n.* A colorless, odorless, gaseous chemical element found in the air, in volcanic gases, and elsewhere.

ar·go·sy \'är-gə-sē, 'ȧr-\ *n.; pl.* **ar·go·sies. 1** A large merchant ship. **2** A fleet of ships, especially merchant ships.

ar·gue \'ärg-yü, 'ȧrg-\ *v.;* **ar·gued; ar·gu·ing** \-yə-wing\. **1** To give reasons for or against; as, to *argue* in favor of going to the beach instead of to the park. **2** To debate or discuss some matter; to dispute; as, to *argue* about politics; to *argue* a question. **3** To persuade by giving reasons. The boy could not *argue* his father into getting a new car. **4** To indicate. The boy's manner *argued* his guilt. — For synonyms see *discuss.*

ar·gu·ment \'ärg-yə-mənt, 'ȧrg-\ *n.* **1** A reason for or against a thing. **2** A discussion in which reasons for and against a thing are given; a dispute or debate. **3** Subject matter or topic, as of a book, or a summary of such subject matter.

ar·gu·men·ta·tion \ˌärg-yə-ˌmen-'tāsh-n, ˌȧrg-\ *n.* **1** The act or process of forming reasons and drawing conclusions and applying them to a case in discussion. **2** Debate; discussion.

ar·gu·men·ta·tive \ˌärg-yə-'ment-ət-iv, ˌȧrg-\ *adj.* Fond of arguing; quarrelsome.

aria \'är-ē-ə, 'ȧr-\ *n.* A melody sung by one voice with an instrumental accompaniment, as in an opera.

ar·id \'ar-əd\ *adj.* Dry; barren; having little rain or moisture. — **arid·i·ty** \a-'rid-ət-ē\ *n.*

aright \ə-'rīt\ *adv.* Rightly; correctly.

arise \ə-'rīz\ *v.;* **arose** \ə-'rōz\; **aris·en** \ə-'riz-n\; **aris·ing** \ə-'rī-zing\. **1** To move upward; to ascend. Mist *arose* from the valley. **2** To get up from sleep or after lying down. **3** To spring up; to come into existence; to occur. A dispute *arose* between the leaders.

ar·is·toc·ra·cy \ˌar-əs-'täk-rə-sē\ *n.; pl.* **ar·is·toc·ra·cies. 1** A government that is in the hands of a noble or privileged class. **2** The noble or privileged class thus governing. **3** A state having such a government. **4** Persons thought of as superior to the rest of the community in rank, wealth, culture, or intelligence.

aris·to·crat \ə-'ris-tə-ˌkrat\ *n.* **1** A member of an aristocracy. **2** A person who has the point of view and habits of a ruling class, or of a class considered superior in a community.

aris·to·crat·ic \ə-ˌris-tə-'krat-ik\ *adj.* **1** Having to do with an aristocracy. **2** Belonging to or having qualities of a ruling or privileged class. **3** Having a manner supposedly that of an aristocrat; socially exclusive; proud; snobbish. — **aris·to·crat·i·cal·ly** \-ik-l(-)ē\ *adv.*

arith·me·tic \ə-'rith-mə-ˌtik\ *n.* The art or science of adding, subtracting, multiplying, and dividing by the use of figures.

ar·ith·met·i·cal \ˌar-(ˌ)ith-'met-ik-l\ *adj.* **1** Of or relating to arithmetic. **2** According to the rules and methods of arithmetic; as, an *arithmetical* calculation. — **ar·ith·met·i·cal·ly** \-ik-l(-)ē\ *adv.*

arith·me·ti·cian \ə-ˌrith-mə-'tish-n, ˌar-(ˌ)ith-\ *n.* A person skilled in arithmetic.

ark \'ärk, 'ȧrk\ *n.* **1** Also **ark of the covenant.** In Jewish history, a chest kept in the holiest part of the temple and containing the two stone tables inscribed with the Ten Commandments; a similar chest in a modern synagogue. **2** The vessel in which Noah was saved from the great flood of Biblical times.

arm \'ärm, 'ȧrm\ *n.* **1** One of the two upper limbs of a person or of a monkey, especially the part between the shoulder and the wrist. **2** Something that is like an arm in appearance or use; as, the *arm* of a chair; an *arm* of the sea. **3** Power; might; as, the *arm* of the law.

arm \'ärm, 'ȧrm\ *n.* **1** Any weapon of offense or defense. **2** A branch of the army, as the infantry. — *v.* **1** To provide with weapons; as, to *arm* and equip a new regiment. **2** To provide with some means of defense; as, to *arm* oneself with facts.

3 To provide oneself with arms and armament. The country *armed* for war.

ar·ma·da \är-ˈmäd-ə, ȧr-ˈmȧd-ə, -ˈmād-ə\ *n.* **1** A large fleet of armed ships — [with a capital] usually, the fleet sent by Spain against England in 1588. **2** A fleet of military or naval aircraft.

ar·ma·dil·lo \ˌär-mə-ˈdil-ō, ˌȧr-\ *n.; pl.* **ar·ma·dil·los.** A small burrowing animal of South America and Central America and some parts of southern North America, whose head and body are protected by hard bony armorlike plates.

ar·ma·ment \ˈär-mə-mənt, ˈȧr-\ *n.* **1** The whole war equipment of a nation. **2** The total supply of weapons, ammunition, and related equipment of a ship, a fort, or any system of defense.

ar·ma·ture \ˈär-məch-r, ˈȧr-, -mə-ˌchủr\ *n.* **1** Armor or a protective covering resembling armor. **2** A piece of soft iron or steel used to connect the poles of a magnet. **3** The part of an electric generator, consisting of coils of wire around an iron core, that induces an electric current when it is rotated in a magnetic field. **4** The part of an electric motor, consisting of coils of wire around an iron core, that is caused to rotate in a magnetic field when an electric current is passed through the coils.

arm·chair \ˈärm-ˌcher, ˈȧrm-\ *n.* A chair with arms.

armed forces \ˈärmd, ˈȧrmd\. All of the military, naval, and air forces of a country.

arm·ful \ˈärm-ˌfủl, ˈȧrm-\ *n.; pl.* **arm·fuls.** As much as a person's arm or arms can hold.

arm·hole \ˈärm-ˌhōl, ˈȧrm-\ *n.* A hole for the arm in a garment.

armies. Pl. of *army.*

ar·mi·stice \ˈär-mə-stəs, ˈȧr-\ *n.* A pause in a war, brought about by agreement between the two sides; a truce.

arm·let \ˈärm-lət, ˈȧrm-\ *n.* A bracelet or band for the upper arm.

ar·mor \ˈärm-r, ˈȧrm-r\ *n.* **1** A covering, as of metal or leather, to protect the body in battle. **2** A protective covering of any kind, such as steel plates on battleships. **3** Armored forces and equipment, such as tanks and artillery, taken together. — *v.* To equip with armor.

armor, 1

ar·mored \ˈärm-rd, ˈȧrm-\ *adj.* **1** Protected by armor; as, an *armored* car. **2** Supplied with armored equipment; as, an *armored* force.

ar·mor·er \ˈärm-r-r, ˈȧrm-\ *n.* **1** A man who makes or repairs armor and arms. **2** A person who has charge of arms and armor, as on a warship.

ar·mo·ri·al \är-ˈmōr-ē-əl, ȧr-, -ˈmȯr-\ *adj.* Relating to coats of arms.

ar·mory \ˈärm-r(-)ē, ˈȧrm-\ *n.; pl.* **ar·mor·ies.** **1** A place where arms are manufactured. **2** A place where arms are stored, and where, usually, military drill may be held.

arm·pit \ˈärm-ˌpit, ˈȧrm-\ *n.* The hollow, or pit, under a person's arm, where the arm joins the shoulder.

arms \ˈärmz, ˈȧrmz\ *n. pl.* **1** Weapons; instruments of warfare; as, *arms* and ammunition. **2** Deeds of war; warfare; as, bravery in *arms.* **3** Military service. The president sent out a call to *arms.* **4** Pictures of animal figures or other objects, or other signs or designs, often on a shield or banner, used as a mark of honor or distinction; as, the *arms* of a noble family; the coat of *arms* of the United States.

arms, 4

ar·my \ˈär-mē, ˈȧr-\ *n.; pl.* **ar·mies.** **1** A large organized group of men and women trained for war. **2** [usually with a capital] The complete organization of a country for land warfare; as, *Army,* Navy, and Air Force. **3** A large organized group of persons working for a common cause. **4** A great number; as, an *army* of children running down the street.

ar·ni·ca \ˈär-nik-ə, ˈȧr-\ *n.* A medicinal liquid made from the roots of a mountain herb of the aster family, used as a remedy for sprains and bruises.

aro·ma \ə-ˈrō-mə\ *n.* A pleasant smell; fragrance; as, the *aroma* of coffee.

ar·o·mat·ic \ˌar-ə-ˈmat-ik\ *adj.* Fragrant; spicy. — For synonyms see *fragrant.*

arose. Past tense of *arise.*

around \ə-ˈraủnd\ *adv.* **1** In circumference; as, a tree five feet *around.* **2** On all sides; here and there on every side. **3** Near by. **4** In an opposite direction. — *prep.* **1** In a circle or circuit along the outside boundary of; as, to run all the way *around* the house. **2** On every side of; here and there in; as, the fields *around* the city. **3** Near to, in number or amount; as, costing *around* five dollars.

arouse \ə-ˈraủz\ *v.;* **aroused; arous·ing.** **1** To cause to move or act; to stir; to excite; as, to *arouse* a wild beast to anger. **2** To awaken.

ar·peg·gio \är-ˈpej-ˌō, ȧr-, -ē-ˌō\ *n.; pl.* **ar·peg·gios.** **1** The playing of the tones of a chord in rapid succession instead of at the same moment. **2** A chord played in this manner.

ar·que·bus \ˈär-kwē-bəs, ˈȧr-\. Variant of *harquebus.*

ar·raign \ə-ˈrān\ *v.* **1** To call before a court to answer to an accusation. **2** To accuse; to denounce. — **ar·raign·ment,** *n.*

ar·range \ə-ˈrānj\ *v.;* **ar·ranged; ar·rang·ing.** **1** To put in order; especially, to put in a certain order; as, to *arrange* books on shelves. **2** To make plans for; to prepare; as, to *arrange* a meeting; to *arrange* a program. **3** To adjust; to settle; as, to *arrange* one's affairs so as to have the weekend free. **4** To adapt a musical composition for voices or instruments for which it was not originally written; as, to *arrange* piano music for the violin.

ar·range·ment \ə-ˈrānj-mənt\ *n.* **1** A putting in

order or the order in which things are put; as, to change the *arrangement* of furniture in a room. **2** Preparation; plan; as, to make *arrangements* for a trip. **3** Something made by arranging; as, a flower *arrangement*. This kite is an *arrangement* of paper and wood. **4** An adaptation; especially, an adaptation of a piece of music to voices or instruments for which it was not originally written.

ar·rang·er \ə-ˈrānj-r\ *n.* One that arranges; especially, a person whose occupation is making arrangements of music.

ar·rant \ˈar-ənt\ *adj.* Out-and-out; thoroughgoing; as, an *arrant* coward.

ar·ras \ˈar-əs\ *n.* **1** A tapestry, originally one woven in Arras, France. **2** A wall hanging or screen of tapestry.

ar·ray \ə-ˈrā\ *n.* **1** Regular order or arrangement; as, soldiers in battle *array*. **2** A large group of persons drawn up in regular order; as, an *array* of troops. **3** Rich or beautiful clothing; as, a bride in her wedding *array*. **4** A large or fine display; as, an *array* of jewels. **5** A group of mathematical elements, as numbers or letters, arranged in rows and columns. — *v.* **1** To draw up in regular order; as, soldiers *arrayed* for review. **2** To dress in rich or beautiful clothing; as, *arrayed* in silks and satins.

ar·rears \ə-ˈrirz\ *n. pl.* Something that is due but not yet paid; as, *arrears* of wages. — **in arrears.** Behind; in debt; not yet paid; as, rent that has been *in arrears* for three months.

ar·rest \ə-ˈrest\ *v.* **1** To stop the progress or movement of; to hold back; to check; as, an *arrested* motion picture. Some diseases that cannot now be cured can be *arrested*. **2** To seize and hold as a policeman does; as, to *arrest* a man on suspicion of robbery. **3** To attract and hold; as, bright colors that *arrest* the eye. — *n.* **1** A stopping from motion; a check. **2** The act of seizing and holding a person for breaking the law.

ar·riv·al \ə-ˈrīv-l\ *n.* **1** A coming or arriving; as, to await the *arrival* of guests. **2** The person or thing that has arrived; as, late *arrivals* at a concert.

ar·rive \ə-ˈrīv\ *v.*; **ar·rived**; **ar·riv·ing.** **1** To reach a certain place, especially one's destination; as, to *arrive* home at six o'clock. **2** To gain an end or object; as, to *arrive* at success; to *arrive* at a decision. **3** To come. At last, vacation time *arrived*.

ar·ro·gance \ˈar-ə-gən(t)s\ *n.* A sense of one's own importance that shows itself in an offensively proud manner; haughtiness.

ar·ro·gant \ˈar-ə-gənt\ *adj.* Thinking too well of oneself or of one's own opinions; conceited; as, an *arrogant* person; *arrogant* remarks. — **ar·ro·gant·ly,** *adv.*

ar·ro·gate \ˈar-ə-ˌgāt\ *v.*; **ar·ro·gat·ed**; **ar·ro·gat·ing.** **1** To take or claim for one's own either without right or in a haughty manner. The dictator *arrogated* to himself the powers of parliament. **2** To ascribe or attribute to another, especially unduly or without right; as, to *arrogate* to a rival intentions he had never given evidence of. — **ar·ro·ga·tion** \ˌar-ə-ˈgāsh-n\ *n.*

ar·row \ˈar-ō\ *n.* **1** A weapon or missile made to be shot from a bow, and usually in the form of a straight, slender stick of wood with a sharp point at one end and with feathers fastened at the other. **2** A sign or mark like an arrow, used to show direction, as on a map or a road sign.

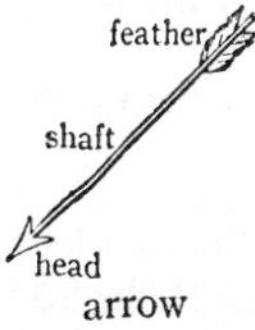

arrow

ar·row·head \ˈar-ō-ˌhed\ *n.* The pointed end of an arrow; a tip for an arrow.

ar·row·root \ˈar-ō-ˌrüt, -ˌrůt, ˈar-r-ˌüt, -ˌůt\ *n.* A starch obtained from the potatolike roots of a tropical plant.

ar·royo \ə-ˈrȯi-ˌō\ *n.*; *pl.* **ar·roy·os.** **1** A watercourse, as a creek or similar stream. **2** A small, often dry, gully or channel.

ar·se·nal \ˈärs-n(-)əl, ˈȧrs-\ *n.* A place where military equipment, especially arms, is made and stored.

ar·se·nic \ˈärs-n(-)ik, ˈȧrs-\ *n.* **1** A brittle, grayish, very poisonous chemical element. **2** A highly poisonous white or transparent compound of this element, used in industry and medicine.

ar·son \ˈärs-n, ˈȧrs-n\ *n.* The deliberate, spiteful burning of a person's dwelling house or other building. — **ar·son·ist** \-n(-)əst\ *n.*

art \ˈärt, ˈȧrt\ *n.* **1** The power of doing something easily and skillfully; skill in performance; knack; as, the *art* of making friends. **2** Any occupation that requires a natural skill in addition to training and practice; as, the *art* of cookery. **3** The rules or ideas that a person must know in order to follow a certain profession or craft; as, the *art* of medicine; the *art* of war. **4** A branch of learning; especially, one of the nonscientific branches of learning, as history, philosophy, or literature — usually used in the plural; as, to get a bachelor's degree in *arts*. **5** The study of drawing, painting, and sculpture. **6** The works produced by artists, such as painters, sculptors, or writers.

art \ərt, (ˈ)ärt, (ˈ)ȧrt\. An archaic form of *are*, used chiefly with *thou*.

art. Abbreviation for *article*.

ar·te·ri·al \är-ˈtir-ē-əl, ȧr-\ *adj.* Of or relating to an artery or to arteries.

ar·te·ri·ole \är-ˈtir-ē-ˌōl, ȧr-\ *n.* A very small artery connecting a larger artery with capillaries.

ar·te·ri·o·scle·ro·sis \är-ˈtir-ē-(ˌ)ō-sklə-ˈrō-səs, ȧr-\ *n.* A hardening and thickening of the walls of the arteries.

ar·tery \ˈärt-r-ē, ˈȧrt-\ *n.*; *pl.* **ar·ter·ies.** **1** One of the branching tubes that carry blood from the heart to all parts of the body. **2** Any road or channel of communication. Broadway is one of the main *arteries* of New York City.

ar·te·sian well \är-ˈtēzh-n, ȧr-\. A bored well from which water flows up like a fountain.

art·ful \ˈärt-fəl, ˈȧrt-\ *adj.* **1** Skillful; skillfully done or designed; as, *artful* workmanship. **2** Artificial; imitative. **3** Sly; cunning; as, *artful* tricks. — **art·ful·ly** \-fə-lē\ *adv.*

ar·thri·tis \är-'thrīt-əs, ȧr-\ *n.* Inflammation of the joints.

ar·thro·pod \'är-thrə-ˌpäd, 'ȧr-\ *n.* Any member of a large group of invertebrate animals such as insects, spiders, centipedes, and lobsters, with jointed legs and a body in segments.

ar·ti·choke \'ärt-ə-ˌchōk, 'ȧrt-\ *n.* A tall thistlelike plant of the aster family, or its flower head, cooked and eaten as a vegetable.

artichokes

ar·ti·cle \'ärt-ik-l, 'ȧrt-\ *n.* **1** A distinct part of a document such as a constitution, contract, or treaty, dealing with a single subject. **2** A piece or section in a newspaper, a magazine, or a book such as an encyclopedia, dealing with a single subject; as, an *article* on winter sports. **3** A thing of some particular kind; as, *articles* of trade; useful *articles.* **4** In grammar, one of the words *a, an,* or *the,* used before nouns to limit their application.

ar·tic·u·late \är-'tik-yə-lət, ȧr-\ *adj.* **1** Jointed; segmented, as the legs of many insects. **2** Expressed clearly and logically; as, an *articulate* argument. **3** Divided clearly into words and syllables; as, *articulate* speech. **4** Able to speak; especially, able to speak easily and effectively. — \-ˌlāt\ *v.;* **ar·tic·u·lat·ed; ar·tic·u·lat·ing. 1** To unite in a joint or joints or by means of a joint or joints. **2** To make articulate sounds. Of all animals only man can *articulate.* **3** To speak in distinct syllables or words; to express clearly and distinctly; as, a speaker who *articulates* well; a man who could *articulate* every shade of meaning. — **ar·tic·u·late·ly** \-lət-lē\ *adv.*

ar·tic·u·la·tion \är-ˌtik-yə-'lāsh-n, ȧr-\ *n.* **1** The making of articulate sounds, as in pronunciation. The speaker's *articulation* was remarkable for its distinctness. **2** A joint or juncture between bones or cartilages in an animal.

ar·ti·fact \'ärt-ə-ˌfakt, 'ȧrt-\ *n.* A product of human workmanship, especially of simple, primitive workmanship; as, *artifacts* of the Stone Age.

ar·ti·fice \'ärt-ə-fəs, 'ȧrt-\ *n.* **1** Skill; ingenuity. **2** A clever or, especially, a crafty device; a cunning trick; as, to escape from jail by an *artifice.*

ar·tif·i·cer \är-'tif-əs-r, ȧr-\ *n.* A skilled or artistic workman; a craftsman.

ar·ti·fi·cial \ˌärt-ə-'fish-l, ˌȧrt-\ *adj.* **1** Not natural; as, an *artificial* lake. **2** Made or changed to resemble something natural; as, *artificial* flowers. **3** Not genuine or sincere; forced; as, *artificial* laughter. — **ar·ti·fi·ci·al·i·ty** \-ˌfish-ē-'al-ət-ē\ *n.* — **ar·ti·fi·cial·ly** \-'fish-l-ē\ *adv.*

artificial respiration. The forcing of air into and out of the lungs of a person whose breathing has stopped.

ar·til·ler·ist \är-'til-r-əst, ȧr-\ *n.* An artilleryman.

ar·til·lery \är-'til-r(-)ē, ȧr-\ *n.* **1** Heavy guns, in distinction from such small arms as rifles and revolvers; cannon. **2** The branch of an army that uses heavy guns. — **ar·til·ler·y·man** \-mən\ *n.*

ar·ti·san \'ärt-əz-n, 'ȧrt-\ *n.* A person who works at a trade requiring skill with the hands, as a bricklayer or a carpenter.

art·ist \'ärt-əst, 'ȧrt-\ *n.* **1** A person skilled in one of the arts, such as painting, sculpture, music, or writing; especially, a painter. **2** A person showing unusual ability in any occupation requiring skill.

ar·tis·tic \är-'tis-tik, ȧr-\ *adj.* **1** Having to do with art or artists. **2** Having or showing taste and skill. — **ar·tis·ti·cal·ly** \-tik-l(-)ē\ *adv.*

art·ist·ry \'ärt-əs-trē, 'ȧrt-\ *n.* **1** Artistic quality of workmanship or of appearance. **2** Artistic ability.

art·less \'ärt-ləs, 'ȧrt-\ *adj.* **1** Lacking art; unskilled; as, *artless* savage tribes. **2** Natural; simple and sincere; free from deceit; as, the *artless* behavior of a child. — **art·less·ly,** *adv.*

ar·um \'ar-əm, 'er-\ *n.* Any of a family of plants having heart-shaped or sword-shaped leaves and a flower consisting of a fleshy spike enclosed in a leafy sheath, as the jack-in-the-pulpit or the skunk cabbage.

-ary. A suffix that can mean: **1** Belonging to or connected with, as in *revolutionary.* **2** One that belongs to or is connected with, as in *aviary.*

as \əz, (')az\ *adv.* **1** To the same extent; equally. My hands were *as* cold as ice. **2** For example; as, science courses, *as* chemistry and biology. — *conj.* **1** To the extent or degree that; as, slippery *as* an eel. **2** In the same manner in which; according to the way that; as, to do *as* the rest do. **3** While; when. Some others came just *as* we left. **4** Though. The soldiers marched on, tired *as* they were. **5** Because; since. I was unable to accept, *as* I already had an engagement. — *prep.* **1** In a manner like that of. The audience rose *as* one man. **2** In the character or position of; as, to act *as* chairman.

a's. Pl. of *a.*

as·a·fet·i·da or **as·a·foet·i·da** \ˌas-ə-'fet-əd-ə, as-'fid-əd-ē\ *n.* A hard gum with a disagreeable smell and a taste like garlic, used in medicine.

as·bes·tos \as-'bes-təs, az-\ *n.* A nonburning and heat-resistant grayish mineral substance found in rock and used in making various fireproof materials and articles.

as·cend \ə-'send\ *v.* To go upward; to climb; to rise; as, to *ascend* a hill. Smoke *ascends.* — **as·cend·a·ble** or **as·cend·i·ble** \-əb-l\ *adj.*

— The words *mount* and *climb* are synonyms of *ascend: ascend* may indicate any progress upward; generally *mount* indicates getting up on something raised or high; *climb* usually suggests ascending by a series of steps, often slow or difficult.

as·cend·an·cy or **as·cend·en·cy** \ə-'sen-dən-sē\ *n.* A controlling influence; control; as, to gain *ascendancy* over a bad habit.

as·cend·ant or **as·cend·ent** \ə-'sen-dənt\ *n.* The place of power or influence or the condition of

having dominant power or influence; as, to be in the *ascendant.* — *adj.* **1** Moving or directed upward; rising. **2** Above or greater in power or influence; controlling; dominant.

as·cen·sion \ə-'sench-n\ *n.* **1** A rising; an ascending. **2** [with a capital] The ascending of Christ to heaven on the fortieth day after his resurrection.

as·cent \ə-'sent\ *n.* **1** The act of going or climbing upward; as, an *ascent* in a balloon. **2** Upward slope; rise; as, the steep *ascent* of a hill.

as·cer·tain \ˌas-r-'tān\ *v.* To find out, especially for a certainty; to make sure of; as, to *ascertain* when the train will arrive. — **as·cer·tain·a·ble** \-əb-l\ *adj.*

as·cet·ic \ə-'set-ik\ *adj.* **1** Given to self-denial, especially for religious reasons; as, an *ascetic* life. **2** Marked by a deliberate absence of material comforts; as, to live in *ascetic* surroundings. — *n.* A person who leads an ascetic life. — **as·cet·i·cism** \-'set-ə-ˌsiz-m\ *n.*

ascor·bic acid \ə-'skȯr-bik\. A white crystalline substance, prepared commercially from glucose, that has the property of preventing scurvy — called also *vitamin C.*

as·cribe \ə-'skrīb\ *v.;* **as·cribed; as·crib·ing. 1** To think or say that a thing is the result of another thing; as, to *ascribe* one's success to hard work. **2** To regard as belonging; as, to *ascribe* good intentions to a person. — **as·crip·tion** \-'skripsh-n\ *n.*

asep·tic \(')ā-'sep-tik\ *adj.* Free or made free from harmful organisms, as bacteria that cause disease.

asex·u·al \(')ā-'sek-shə-wəl, -'seksh-l\ *adj.* Having no sex; without sexual action; as, *asexual* reproduction. — **asex·u·al·ly** \-'seksh-l(-)ē, -'sek-shə-wə-lē\ *adv.*

ash \'ash\ *n.* A common shade tree or timber tree with furrowed bark and winged seeds.

ash: leaf and fruit

ash \'ash\ *n.; sing.* of **ashes. 1** The solid stuff left when material is thoroughly burned; as, burned to an *ash.* **2** The color of wood ashes.

ashamed \ə-'shāmd\ *adj.* **1** Feeling shame; as, *ashamed* of a mean action. **2** Kept by pride from doing something; as, *ashamed* to beg.

ash can. 1 A metal container for ashes and trash. **2** *Slang.* A depth charge.

ash·en \'ash-n\ *adj.* Of or relating to the ash tree or its wood; made of ash.

ash·en \'ash-n\ *adj.* Of the color of ashes.

ash·es \'ash-əz\ *n. pl.; sing.* **ash. 1** A collection of ash left after something has been burned; as, the *ashes* of a wood fire. **2** The remains of the dead human body, especially after cremation. **3** Ruins or last traces, as of a bygone civilization.

ashore \ə-'shōr, ə-'shȯr\ *adv.* or *adj.* On or to the shore; on land.

ash·tray \'ash-ˌtrā\ *n.* A receptacle, usually shallow, for tobacco ashes.

Ash Wednesday. The first day of Lent.

ashy \'ash-ē\ *adj.;* **ash·i·er; ash·i·est. 1** Covered with ashes. **2** Pale; ashen.

Asian \'āzh-n\ *adj.* Of or relating to Asia. — *n.* A native of Asia or a member of any Asian people.

Asi·at·ic \ˌā-zhē-'at-ik\ *adj.* or *n.* Asian.

aside \ə-'sīd\ *adv.* **1** To one side; as, to step *aside.* **2** Apart; away; as, to lay *aside* money for a rainy day. — *n.* Something spoken aside, as a remark made by an actor supposedly not heard by others on the stage.

as·i·nine \'as-n-ˌīn\ *adj.* Like or suited to an ass; stupid; extremely silly; as, an *asinine* remark; *asinine* behavior.

ask \'ask\ *v.;* **asked** \'as(k)t\; **ask·ing** \'as-king\. **1** To question; to inquire. Those who do not understand should *ask.* **2** To make a request; as, to *ask* for help. **3** To demand; to expect; as, to *ask* twenty dollars for a bicycle. **4** To invite; as, to be *asked* to a party.

— The words *request* and *beg* are synonyms of *ask: ask* is a general word lacking suggestion about the attitude of the speaker; *request* may suggest asking in a formal manner; *beg* usually indicates formality and especial politeness; as, to *beg* one's pardon.

askance \ə-'skan(t)s\ *adv.* **1** Sideways; with a side glance. **2** With distrust, suspicion, or disapproval; as, to look *askance* at a stranger.

askew \ə-'skyü\ *adv.* or *adj.* Twisted or turned to one side; awry; crooked or crookedly; as, to get one's hat knocked *askew* in the crowd.

aslant \ə-'slant\ *adj.* or *adv.* In a slanting direction. — *prep.* In a slanting direction over; athwart.

asleep \ə-'slēp\ *adj.* or *adv.* **1** In or into a state of sleep; sleeping; as, to fall *asleep;* sound *asleep.* **2** Numb and tingling. My foot is *asleep.*

asp \'asp\ *n.* **1** A small poisonous snake of Egypt. **2** Any of a number of other poisonous snakes, as the common European viper.

as·par·a·gus \ə-'spar-ə-gəs\ *n.* **1** The thick young edible stalks of a plant related to the lily of the valley. **2** The plant that bears these stalks.

as·pect \'as-ˌpekt\ *n.* **1** Position facing or fronting in a particular direction; as, the northern *aspect* of a house. **2** Look; appearance. The broken windows and uncut lawn gave the old place a forlorn and deserted *aspect.* **3** The appearance of something to the eye or to the mind when looked at from a particular point of view; as, to study every *aspect* of a question before giving an answer.

as·pen \'asp-n\ *n.* A poplar tree whose leaves flutter in the lightest breeze.

as·per·i·ty \as-'per-ət-ē\ *n.; pl.* **as·per·i·ties. 1** Harshness; severity; as, to speak with *asperity.* **2** Something harsh or severe; as, the *asperities* of winter weather.

leaves of the aspen

as·perse \ə-'spərs\ *v.;* **as·persed; as·pers·ing.** To say mean, damaging, or false things about a person; to slander.

as·per·sion \ə-'spərzh-n\ *n.* A mean, damaging, or

untrue statement; a slanderous remark; as, to cast *aspersions* on a person.

as·phalt \'as-ˌfölt\ *n.* **1** A dark-colored substance obtained from natural beds or from certain petroleums and tars. **2** Any of various compositions of asphalt, having many uses, as in paving streets, roofing houses, and tiling floors. — *v.* To cover with asphalt. — **as·phalt·ic** \as-'föl-tik\ *adj.*

as·pho·del \'as-fə-ˌdel\ *n.* **1** A lilylike plant with spikes of white or yellow flowers. **2** One of several related plants; especially, in former times, the daffodil or the narcissus.

as·phyx·ia \as-'fiks-ē-ə\ *n.* A lack of oxygen or excess of carbon dioxide in the body usually caused by interruption of breathing and resulting in unconsciousness.

as·phyx·i·ate \as-'fiks-ē-ˌāt\ *v.;* **as·phyx·i·at·ed**; **as·phyx·i·at·ing**. To cause asphyxia of, usually by cutting off the supply of air or interfering with the action of breathing. — **as·phyx·i·a·tion** \(ˌ)as-ˌfiks-ē-'āsh-n\ *n.*

as·pic \'as-pik\ *n.* A jelly made from fish or meat stock thickened with gelatin, usually used to make a mold with meat, fish, or vegetables and served cold.

as·pi·rant \'asp-r-ənt, ə-'spīr-ənt\ *n.* A person who aspires; an ambitious person.

as·pi·rate \'asp-r-ət\ *n.* The sound of *h.* — *adj.* Pronounced with an *h* sound. — \-r-ˌāt\ *v.;* **as·pi·rat·ed**; **as·pi·rat·ing**. To pronounce with an *h* sound ahead of or at the beginning of; as, to *aspirate* the "e" in "herb". We do not *aspirate* the word "hour".

as·pi·ra·tion \ˌasp-r-'āsh-n\ *n.* **1** The act of breathing; a breath. **2** Strong desire to attain something high or great; noble ambition. **3** An aspirating; the act of pronouncing with an *h* sound before or at the beginning.

as·pire \ə-'spīr\ *v.;* **as·pired**; **as·pir·ing.** To desire eagerly; to seek to attain something high or great; as, to *aspire* to the presidency.

as·pi·rin \'asp-r(-)ən\ *n.* A white crystalline drug used as a remedy for pain and fever.

ass \'as\ *n.* **1** An animal like a horse but smaller, with a shorter mane, shorter hair on the tail, and longer ears; a donkey. **2** A dull, stupid, or silly person.

assafetida or **assafoetida**. Variant of *asafetida.*

as·sa·gai or **as·se·gai** \'as-ə-ˌgī\ *n.* A slender wooden spear, usually having an iron tip, used by some South African tribes.

point of an assagai

as·sail \ə-'sāl\ *v.* To attack suddenly with violence. — **as·sail·a·ble**, *adj.*

as·sail·ant \ə-'sā-lənt\ *n.* A person who assails; an attacker.

as·sas·sin \ə-'sas-n\ *n.* A person who kills another person by a surprise or secret attack; especially, a hired murderer.

as·sas·si·nate \ə-'sas-n-ˌāt\ *v.;* **as·sas·si·nat·ed**; **as·sas·si·nat·ing**. To murder by a surprise or secret attack, especially for pay. — **as·sas·si·na·tion** \-ˌsas-n-'āsh-n\ *n.*

as·sault \ə-'sölt\ *n.* A violent or sudden attack; as, an *assault* on an innocent bystander; an *assault* on a fortress. — *v.* To attack violently.

as·say \'as-ˌā, a-'sā\ *n.* Examination or analysis, as of an ore, a metal, or a drug, for the purpose of determining composition, measure, or quality. — \a-'sā, 'as-ˌā\ *v.;* **as·sayed**; **as·say·ing.** **1** To test or analyze an ore, a metal, or a drug to determine its weight, amount, quality, or value. **2** To try; to attempt. — **as·say·er**, *n.*

as·sem·blage \ə-'sem-blij\ *n.* **1** A collection of persons or things; a gathering; an assembly. **2** The fitting together of parts and pieces, as of machinery.

as·sem·ble \ə-'sem-bl\ *v.;* **as·sem·bled**; **as·sem·bling** \-bl(-)ing\. **1** To gather into one place; to collect into a body; to meet; as, to *assemble* at nine o'clock at the bus station. **2** To collect and fit together the parts of; as, to *assemble* an automobile.

as·sem·bly \ə-'sem-blē\ *n.; pl.* **as·sem·blies.** **1** A gathering of persons for a certain purpose; as, a school *assembly.* **2** [with a capital] In some states of the United States, the lawmaking body, especially the lower branch of such a body. **3** A signal, as by a drum or bugle, for troops to assemble. **4** The act of assembling or of putting together the parts of a thing; as, the *assembly* of an automobile. **5** A collection of parts that go to make up a complete unit; as, the tail *assembly* of an airplane.

assembly line. A grouping of machines, other equipment, and workers so arranged that work passes from one to another in direct line until the finished product has been assembled.

as·sent \ə-'sent\ *v.* To agree; to consent; as, to *assent* to a proposed plan. — *n.* Agreement; consent; as, to give a nod of *assent.*

as·sert \ə-'sərt\ *v.* **1** To state clearly and strongly; to declare positively; as, to *assert* an opinion in a loud voice. **2** To maintain or defend; as, to *assert* one's rights. — **assert oneself.** To demand and insist that others recognize one's rights.

as·ser·tion \ə-'sərsh-n\ *n.* **1** The act of asserting. **2** A positive statement.

as·sert·ive \ə-'sərt-iv\ *adj.*. Positive or plain-spoken; aggressive.

as·sess \ə-'ses\ *v.* **1** To set a value on, especially on property for purposes of taxation; as, a house *assessed* at $6300. **2** To lay a tax, or a forced contribution of money, on a person or a piece of property. The city government *assessed* all car owners five dollars for additional traffic lights. — **as·sess·a·ble**, *adj.*

as·sess·ment \ə-'ses-mənt\ *n.* **1** An assessing. **2** The amount or value assessed.

as·ses·sor \ə-'ses-r\ *n.* An official who assesses property for purposes of taxation.

as·set \'as-ˌet\ *n.* **1** Anything of value that is owned by or belongs to a person or to a business

or other organization. Good health is one of the greatest *assets* a person can have. **2** [in the plural] The entire property, as of a person or a business organization, that may be used to pay debts.

as·sev·er·ate \ə-'sev-r-ˌāt\ *v.;* **as·sev·er·at·ed; as·sev·er·at·ing.** To state positively or earnestly; to aver; as, to *asseverate* that one has been completely innocent of any wrongdoing.

as·sev·er·a·tion \ə-ˌsev-r-'āsh-n\ *n.* **1** The act of asseverating. **2** That which is asseverated; a positive or earnest statement; a solemn declaration.

as·si·du·i·ty \ˌas-ə-'dü-ət-ē, -'dyü-\ *n.* Close and careful attention, as to one's work; diligence.

as·sid·u·ous \ə-'sij-ə-wəs\ *adj.* Attentive and persevering; diligent; as, an *assiduous* student; *assiduous* efforts. — **as·sid·u·ous·ly,** *adv.*

as·sign \ə-'sīn\ *v.* **1** To appoint to a place, a position, or a duty; as, to *assign* the new pupil to his room. **2** To fix; to select; to name; as, to *assign* a day for the test. **3** To give out; to allot; as, to *assign* a lesson. **4** To transfer, as property, to another, especially for the benefit of creditors. — **as·sign·a·ble** \-əb-l\ *adj.* — **as·sign·er** \ə-'sīn-r\ or **as·sign·or** \ə-ˌsī-'nȯr, ˌas-n-'ȯr\ *n.*

as·sign·ee \ə-ˌsī-'nē, ˌas-n-'ē\ *n.* A person to whom an assignment is made.

as·sign·ment \ə-'sīn-mənt\ *n.* **1** The act of assigning; as, to finish the *assignment* of seats. **2** Something assigned; an assigned task.

as·sim·i·late \ə-'sim-l-ˌāt\ *v.;* **as·sim·i·lat·ed; as·sim·i·lat·ing.** To take something in and make it part of the thing it has joined or make it like the thing it has joined; to absorb; as, to *assimilate* the food we eat. The United States has *assimilated* people from all parts of the world. — **as·sim·i·la·ble** \-əb-l\ *adj.*

as·sim·i·la·tion \ə-ˌsim-l-'āsh-n\ *n.* The act or process of assimilating; especially, the process by which digested food is converted into the fluid or solid substance of the living body. Good health depends upon the proper *assimilation* of food. — **as·sim·i·la·tive** \-'sim-l-ˌāt-iv\ *adj.*

as·sist \ə-'sist\ *v.* To aid; to help. — *n.* An assisting; aid; as, to give an *assist.*

as·sist·ance \ə-'sis-tən(t)s\ *n.* Aid; help; support.

as·sist·ant \ə-'sis-tənt\ *adj.* Helping; acting under another person whom one is assisting; as, an *assistant* manager of a store. — *n.* A person who assists or is subordinate to another; an aid.

as·siz·es \ə-'sī-zəz\ *n. pl.* Sessions of court held periodically in every county of England.

assn. Abbreviation for *association.*

as·so·ci·ate \ə-'sō-s(h)ē-ˌāt\ *v.;* **as·so·ci·at·ed; as·so·ci·at·ing.** **1** To join as a friend, partner, companion, or assistant; as, to *associate* with children of one's own age; to *associate* oneself with a newly formed business firm. **2** To connect in thought; as, to *associate* clowns with circuses. — \ə-'sō-s(h)ē-ət, -ˌāt, ə-'sō-shət\ *adj.* **1** Closely joined with another person, as in position, responsibility, or duties; as, an *associate* judge. **2** Admitted to some, but not to all, rights and privileges; as, an *associate* member of a club. — *n.* **1** A person joined with another person or persons, as in a company; a partner; as, business *associates.* **2** A companion; as, a boy and his *associates.*

as·so·ci·a·tion \ə-ˌsō-s(h)ē-'āsh-n\ *n.* **1** An associating or a state of being associated; the joining or connecting of one thing with another; as, to enjoy one's *association* with one's schoolmates. **2** An organization of persons having a common purpose or common interests; as, an athletic *association.* **3** A feeling, memory, or thought connected with some person, place, or thing; as, a city that has many pleasant *associations* in one's mind.

as·so·ci·a·tive \ə-'sō-s(h)ē-ˌāt-iv\ *adj.* **1** Of or relating to association. **2** Combining elements in such a way that the result is independent of their grouping. Addition is an *associative* operation.

as·sort \ə-'sȯrt\ *v.* To sort out; to distribute into classes; to classify; as, *assorted* by size.

as·sort·ed \ə-'sȯrt-əd\ *adj.* **1** Sorted into classes. **2** Of various kinds; as, *assorted* chocolates.

as·sort·ment \ə-'sȯrt-mənt\ *n.* **1** Arrangement in classes. **2** A collection of things of different sorts or kinds; as, an *assortment* of tools.

asst. Abbreviation for *assistant.*

as·suage \ə-'swāj\ *v.;* **as·suaged; as·suag·ing.** To ease or lessen; to soothe; to quench or satisfy; as, to *assuage* sorrow by comforting words; to *assuage* thirst with cool water. — **as·suage·ment,** *n.*

as·sume \ə-'süm\ *v.;* **as·sumed; as·sum·ing.** **1** To take upon oneself; to take on; as, to *assume* new duties. **2** To put on; as, to *assume* a disguise. **3** To pretend to have; to put on in appearance only; as, to wonder whether someone's manner is real or *assumed.* **4** To take for granted; to accept as a fact; to suppose to be true; as, to *assume* that tomorrow will be a good day.

as·sum·ing \ə-'sü-ming\ *adj.* Arrogant; pretentious.

as·sump·tion \ə-'səm(p)sh-n\ *n.* **1** The act of assuming; as, the *assumption* of power by a new administration. **2** Something taken for granted; as, the *assumption* that a man will do as he says; an unproved *assumption.*

as·sur·ance \ə-'shu̇r-ən(t)s\ *n.* **1** A statement intended to give a feeling of comfort or trust; a pledge; a guarantee; as, to receive *assurances* of help from a friend. **2** *Chiefly British.* Insurance. **3** Certainty; confidence; as, to undertake a job with no *assurance* of success. **4** Faith in one's ability; self-confidence.

as·sure \ə-'shu̇r\ *v.;* **as·sured; as·sur·ing.** **1** To make sure or certain; as, to take steps to *assure* the safety of all present. Good care will *assure* the patient's quick recovery. **2** To make safe against risks; to insure. **3** To state confidently to; to inform positively. The doctor *assured* us that the injury was not serious.

as·sured \ə-'shu̇rd\ *adj.* **1** Made sure or certain; sure; as, to feel that victory is *assured.* **2** Confident; as, a very *assured* young man. — *n.* A person whose life or property is insured.

as·sur·ed·ly \ə-'shu̇r-əd-lē\ *adv.* Certainly; surely; undoubtedly.

astar·board \ə-'stärb-rd -'stårb-\ *adv.* On or toward the starboard side of a ship.

as·ta·tine \'as-tə-ˌtēn\ *n.* A chemical element artificially produced in the cyclotron.

as·ter \'ast-r\ *n.* A fall-blooming, leafy-stemmed plant, growing from one to five feet high and having white, pink, purple, or yellow flowers.

aster

as·ter·isk \'ast-r-ˌisk\ *n.* [From Latin *asteriscus*, there borrowed from Greek *asteriskos* meaning "small star".] A star-shaped sign [*] often used in printing and writing to refer the reader to a note given somewhere else, as at the bottom of a page, or to mark an omission.

astern \ə-'stərn\ *adv.* **1** Behind a ship; in the rear; as, to leave the harbor lights *astern.* **2** Backward; to the rear; as, full speed *astern.*

as·ter·oid \'ast-r-ˌȯid\ *n.* A starlike body; especially, one of many small planets, estimated to number 30,000 or more, between Mars and Jupiter.

asth·ma \'az-mə\ *n.* A disease that causes difficulty in breathing, a feeling of tightness in the chest, and coughing.

asth·mat·ic \az-'mat-ik\ *adj.* **1** Relating to asthma; affected with or caused by asthma; as, an *asthmatic* cough; an *asthmatic* child. **2** Wheezy; as, an *asthmatic* old automobile. — *n.* A person suffering from asthma. — **asth·mat·i·cal·ly** \-ik-l(-)ē\ *adv.*

astig·ma·tism \ə-'stig-mə-ˌtiz-m\ *n.* A defect of the eye, or of a lens, that prevents it from being properly focused and thus results in blurred images or indistinct vision. — **as·tig·mat·ic** \ˌas-tig-'mat-ik\ *adj.*

astir \ə-'stər\ *adj.* In a state of activity or motion; stirring; out of bed; as, a late hour to be still *astir;* a house *astir* with holiday excitement.

as·ton·ish \ə-'stän-ish\ *v.* To surprise greatly; to amaze.

as·ton·ish·ing \ə-'stän-ish-ing\ *adj.* Amazing; surprising. — **as·ton·ish·ing·ly,** *adv.*

as·ton·ish·ment \ə-'stän-ish-mənt\ *n.* **1** Amazed wonder; great surprise. **2** Something that causes wonder or surprise; as, the many *astonishments* of a great fair.

as·tound \ə-'stau̇nd\ *v.* To astonish; to amaze.

astrad·dle \ə-'strad-l\ *adj.* Straddling; astride.

as·tra·khan \'as-trək-n\ *n.* **1** The curly fur of a young lamb of a karakul sheep, formerly obtained from the Astrakhan region of southeastern Russia. **2** A lustrous cloth of wool or of cotton and wool made with a surface of curled loops, sometimes cut, in imitation of astrakhan fur.

astray \ə-'strā\ *adv.* Out of the right way; as, a letter that went *astray;* to be led *astray.* — *adj.* Straying; wrong; as, figures that are all *astray.*

astride \ə-'strīd\ *adj.* With one leg on each side, as a man on horseback; astraddle. — *prep.* Straddling; as, to sit *astride* a chair.

as·trin·gent \ə-'strinj-nt\ *adj.* **1** Shrinking tissues and driving the blood from them; contracting. **2** Stern; austere; severe; as, an *astringent* manner. — *n.* An astringent substance. — **as·trin·gen·cy** \-n-sē\ *n.*

astro-. A prefix that can mean: of the stars, relating to the stars.

as·tro·gate \'as-trə-ˌgāt\ *v.;* **as·tro·gat·ed; as·tro·gat·ing.** To guide a spaceship or a rocket in flight; to navigate in space. — **as·tro·ga·tion** \ˌas-trə-'gāsh-n\ *n.* — **as·tro·ga·tor** \'as-trə-ˌgāt-r\ *n.*

as·tro·labe \'as-trə-ˌlāb\ *n.* An instrument, now superseded by the sextant, for observing the positions of the heavenly bodies, as stars, planets, and comets.

as·trol·o·ger \ə-'sträl-əj-r\ *n.* A person who practices astrology.

as·trol·o·gy \ə-'sträl-ə-jē\ *n.* The so-called science that treats of the influence of the stars upon human events; the telling of fortunes by the stars. — **as·tro·log·ic** \ˌas-trə-'läj-ik\ or **as·tro·log·i·cal** \-ik-l\ *adj.* — **as·tro·log·i·cal·ly** \-ik-l(-)ē\ *adv.*

as·tro·naut \'as-trə-ˌnȯt\ *n.* A traveler in a spacecraft.

as·tro·nau·tics \ˌas-trə-'nȯt-iks\ *n.* **1** The science of the construction and operation of spacecraft. **2** The navigation of spacecraft.

as·tron·o·mer \ə-'strän-əm-r\ *n.* A person who has a knowledge of astronomy.

as·tro·nom·ic \ˌas-trə-'näm-ik\ or **as·tro·nom·i·cal** \-ik-l\ *adj.* **1** Having to do with astronomy. **2** Extremely or unbelievably large; as, an *astronomical* amount of money. — **as·tro·nom·i·cal·ly** \-ik-l(-)ē\ *adv.*

as·tron·o·my \ə-'strän-ə-mē\ *n.* The science that collects, studies, and explains facts about the heavenly bodies, including their sizes, positions, movements, and composition.

as·tute \ə-'stüt\ *adj.* Shrewd and wise; crafty; as, an *astute* businessman; *astute* reasoning. — **as·tute·ly,** *adv.*

asun·der \ə-'sənd-r\ *adv.* or *adj.* In or into two or more parts; into different pieces; apart.

asy·lum \ə-'sī-ləm\ *n.* **1** A shelter; a place of safety. **2** A place for the care of persons who are unable to care for themselves, as orphans or blind persons; especially, a place for the care of insane persons.

at \ət, (')at\ *prep.* A word that indicates: **1** Relationship in place or time; as, to live *at* home; to return *at* four o'clock. **2** Direction toward; as, to fire *at* the target. **3** Position, condition, or occupation of a person or thing; as, caught *at* a disadvantage; hard *at* work. **4** Cause or reason; as, to laugh *at* a joke.

at. Abbreviation for *atomic.*

ate \'āt\. Past tense of *eat.*

a tem·po \ä 'tem-ˌpō, å\. In time — used in music as a direction to return to the regular tempo.

athe·ism \'ā-thē-ˌiz-m\ *n.* The belief that there is no God; denial of the existence of a supreme being.

athe·ist \'ā-thē-əst\ *n.* A person who believes there is no God. — **athe·is·tic** \ˌā-thē-'is-tik\ *adj.*

athirst \ə-'thərst\ *adj.* **1** Thirsty. **2** Eager; longing; as, boys *athirst* for adventure.

ath·lete \'ath-ˌlēt\ *n.* A person who is good at games and exercises that require physical skill, endurance, and strength.

athlete's foot. A disease of the foot, caused by a fungus and often acquired in locker rooms.

ath·let·ic \ath-'let-ik\ *adj.* **1** Of or relating to athletes or athletics. **2** Like an athlete; strong and active; robust. — **ath·let·i·cal·ly** \-ik-l(-)ē\ *adv.*

ath·let·ics \ath-'let-iks\ *n. sing. and pl.* Games, sports, and exercises requiring strength and skill.

athwart \ə-'thwȯrt\ *adv.* Across. — *prep.* **1** Across; from side to side of. **2** Across the length, direction, or course of, as of a ship. **3** In opposition to; so as to thwart.

-a·tion \'āsh-n\. A suffix that can mean: **1** The act of doing or the state of being, as in *observation* or *starvation*. **2** The thing that, as in *decorations* or *discoloration*.

-a·tive \ət-iv, ˌāt-iv\. A suffix that can mean: **1** Tending to or given to, as in *talkative*. **2** Of the nature of or relating to, as in *administrative*.

At·lan·tic \ət-'lant-ik\ *adj.* Relating to or bordering upon the ocean that lies between Europe and Africa on the east and America on the west.

at·las \'at-ləs\ *n.* A book of maps.

at·mo·sphere \'at-mə-ˌsfir\ *n.* **1** The whole mass of air surrounding the earth. **2** The air in a particular place; as, the stuffy *atmosphere* of this room. **3** Any surrounding influence or set of conditions; as, a holiday *atmosphere;* a child's home *atmosphere*. **4** The pressure of the air at sea level (about 14.7 pounds to the square inch), used as a unit of measurement in physics.

at·mo·spher·ic \ˌat-mə-'sfir-ik, -'sfer-ik\ *adj.* Of or relating to the atmosphere; as, static caused by *atmospheric* conditions; *atmospheric* pressure. — **at·mo·spher·i·cal·ly** \-ik-l(-)ē\ *adv.*

atoll \'a-ˌtäl, 'a-ˌtȯl, ə-'täl, ə-'tȯl\ *n.* A ring-shaped coral island or string of islands consisting of a coral reef surrounding a lagoon.

at·om \'at-m\ *n.* **1** The smallest particle of anything. **2** One of the tiny particles that make up an element; as, an *atom* of iron; an *atom* of hydrogen.

atom·ic \ə-'täm-ik\ *adj.* **1** Of atoms; concerning or related to atoms; as, *atomic* power. **2** Extremely small; tiny.

atomic age. The period of history characterized by the use of atomic energy.

atomic bomb or **atom bomb**. A bomb whose great power is due to the sudden release of the energy in the central portion of the atom.

atomic energy. Power stored inside atoms, some of which can be made to give up part of this power, producing heat either slowly, as for running engines, or rapidly, as for exploding atomic bombs.

atomic fission. The splitting or breaking apart of the nucleus of an atom into two or more parts and the consequent release of enormous energy.

atomic pile. An apparatus for producing and controlling an atomic chain reaction.

atomic weight. The relative weight of an atom of a chemical element in comparison with that of an oxygen atom, taken as a standard.

at·om·ize \'at-m-ˌīz\ *v.;* **at·om·ized; at·om·iz·ing.** To divide into atoms, or into a very fine spray.

at·om·iz·er \'at-m-ˌīz-r\ *n.* A device for spraying a liquid, as for the nose and throat.

atomizer

atone \ə-'tōn\ *v.;* **atoned; aton·ing.** To do something to make up for a wrong that has been done; to make amends. We should try to *atone* for our unkind acts.

atone·ment \ə-'tōn-mənt\ *n.* **1** The act of atoning; something done to atone. **2** [with a capital] The redeeming of men by Christ through his suffering and death.

atop \ə-'täp\ *adj.* or *adv.* At or to the top. — *prep.* On top of.

atrem·ble \ə-'trem-bl\ *adj.* Trembling.

atro·cious \ə-'trō-shəs\ *adj.* Savage and brutal; extremely cruel or wicked; as, an *atrocious* crime. — **atro·cious·ly**, *adv.*

atroc·i·ty \ə-'träs-ət-ē\ *n.; pl.* **atroc·i·ties.** **1** Savage brutality; as, the unbelievable *atrocity* of the attack. **2** A savage and brutal deed; as, the *atrocities* of war.

at·ro·phy \'a-trə-fē\ *n.* A wasting away of a bodily part or tissue, as from disuse or disease. — *v.;* **at·ro·phied** \-fēd\; **at·ro·phy·ing.** To undergo, or cause to undergo, atrophy.

at·tach \ə-'tach\ *v.* **1** To take money or property by legal authority, as a means of forcing payment of a debt; as, to *attach* a man's salary. **2** To fasten or join one thing to another; to bind; to tie; as, to *attach* a bell to a bicycle. **3** To tie or bind by feelings of affection. The boy was *attached* to his dog. **4** To assign by authority; to appoint; as, to *attach* an officer to a headquarters company. **5** To think of as belonging to something; to attribute; as, to *attach* no importance to a remark. **6** To be associated or connected; as, the interest that naturally *attaches* to a statement by the president. — **at·tach·a·ble**, *adj.*

at·ta·ché \ˌat-ə-'shā, ˌa-ˌta-'shā, ə-ˌta-'shā\ *n.* A member of the diplomatic staff of an ambassador or minister to a foreign country.

at·taché case \ə-'tash-ē-\. A small suitcase used especially for carrying papers.

at·tach·ment \ə-'tach-mənt\ *n.* **1** The act of attaching or the state of being attached. **2** A seizing, especially of property, by legal procedures. **3** Strong affection; fondness. **4** That by which one thing is attached to another; a connection. **5** Something that is or may be fastened to something else; as, *attachments* for a vacuum cleaner.

at·tack \ə-'tak\ *v.;* **at·tacked** \ə-'takt, *not* ə-'taktəd\; **at·tack·ing. 1** To use force against, intending to hurt; as, to *attack* a snake with a stick; to *attack* enemy troops. **2** To use unfriendly words against; as, to *attack* the mayor over the radio. **3** To set to work upon; as, to *attack* a problem. **4** To begin to act upon harmfully. The camp was *attacked* by fever. **5** To make an attack upon; as, to *attack* in full force. — *n.* **1** The act of attacking. The *attack* upon the enemy began at dawn. **2** Unfriendly speech or writing intended to hurt; as, to broadcast an *attack* on the mayor. **3** A harmful, unpleasant condition or action of any kind; as, an *attack* of illness.

at·tain \ə-'tān\ *v.* **1** To gain; to achieve; as, to *attain* an ambition. **2** To arrive at; to reach; as, to *attain* the top of a mountain. — For synonyms see *obtain.* — **at·tain·a·bil·i·ty** \ə-ˌtā-nə-'bil-ət-ē\ *n.* — **at·tain·a·ble** \ə-'tā-nəb-l\ *adj.*

at·tain·der \ə-'tānd-r\ *n.* The taking away of a person's civil rights when he has been declared an outlaw or sentenced to death.

at·tain·ment \ə-'tān-mənt\ *n.* **1** An attaining; as, the *attainment* of a wish. **2** Something attained; an accomplishment; as, a man of great *attainments* in science.

at·tar \'at-r, 'a-ˌtär, 'a-ˌtȧr\ *n.* A perfume obtained from flowers; especially, a sweet-smelling oil (**attar of roses**) obtained from rose petals.

at·tempt \ə-'tem(p)t\ *v.* **1** To try to do or perform; to make an effort to accomplish; as, to *attempt* an experiment. **2** To try to take by force; to attack; as, to *attempt* a man's life. **3** To endeavor; to try; as, to *attempt* to get away; *attempted* to solve the problem. — *n.* **1** An effort; especially, an unsuccessful effort. **2** An attack.

at·tend \ə-'tend\ *v.* **1** To care for; to look after; to take charge of; as, to *attend* to taking out the rubbish. **2** To serve; to wait on. Nurses *attend* the sick. **3** To go with or stay with as a servant or companion; as, a king *attended* by his court. **4** To be present at; as, to *attend* a party. **5** To be present with; to accompany; to be found along with; as, an illness *attended* by high fever and muscular weakness. **6** To pay attention; as, to *attend* to what the teacher is saying. — For synonyms see *accompany.*

at·tend·ance \ə-'ten-dən(t)s\ *n.* **1** The action of attending; as, a prize for perfect *attendance.* **2** The number of persons present at a particular time or place. The *attendance* at the play was larger than had been expected.

at·tend·ant \ə-'ten-dənt\ *adj.* Accompanying or following, especially as a result; as, war and its *attendant* evils. — *n.* **1** A person who attends another person, especially as a companion or a servant; as, a bride and her *attendants.* **2** A person who is in attendance, as at a hotel, a public institution, or a place of business, to perform general or special services for customers or patrons; as, hospital *attendants;* an *attendant* at a gasoline station.

at·ten·tion \ə-'tench-n\ *n.* **1** The act or the power of fixing one's mind closely upon something; careful listening or watching; as, to give *attention* to a speaker. **2** Careful consideration of something with a view to taking action on it; as, a matter requiring the *attention* of the president. **3** [usually in the plural] A thoughtful act of kindness, care, or courtesy; as, the little *attentions* that brighten life for a sick person. **4** A military position of readiness to act on the next command.

at·ten·tive \ə-'tent-iv\ *adj.* **1** Paying attention; as, an *attentive* listener. **2** Thoughtful and courteous; as, a boy *attentive* to his mother. — **at·ten·tive·ly,** *adv.*

at·ten·u·ate \ə-'ten-yə-ˌwāt\ *v.;* **at·ten·u·at·ed; at·ten·u·at·ing. 1** To make or become thin or slender. **2** To lessen in amount, force, or value; to weaken. — **at·ten·u·a·tion** \ə-ˌten-yə-'wāsh-n\ *n.*

at·test \ə-'test\ *v.* To give proof of; to testify to; to certify; as, to *attest* the truth of a statement; an *attested* document.

at·tic \'at-ik\ *n.* A room or a space just under the roof of a building; a garret.

at·tire \ə-'tīr\ *v.;* **at·tired; at·tir·ing.** To dress; especially, to dress richly and splendidly. — *n.* Clothes; dress; especially, fine clothes.

at·ti·tude \'at-ə-ˌtüd, -ˌtyüd\ *n.* **1** A person's position or bearing as showing his feeling or purpose; as, a threatening *attitude.* **2** Feeling or mood; frame of mind. What is your *attitude* toward cheating?

at·tor·ney \ə-'tər-nē\ *n.; pl.* **at·tor·neys. 1** A person who is legally appointed by another person to transact any business for him. **2** A lawyer.

attorney general; *pl.* **attorneys general** or **attorney generals.** The chief law officer of a nation or state, having the power to act for the government in all legal matters.

at·tract \ə-'trakt\ *v.* **1** To draw to or towards oneself or itself; to cause to approach or adhere; to draw by the force of attraction. A magnet *attracts* iron. **2** To draw by appealing to interest or feeling; as, to *attract* attention.

at·trac·tion \ə-'traksh-n\ *n.* **1** The act or power of attracting; especially, personal charm or appeal. **2** Something that attracts. The circus is an *attraction* for children. **3** A force acting both ways between particles of matter and tending to draw them together.

at·trac·tive \ə-'trak-tiv\ *adj.* Having the power or quality of attracting; charming; pleasing; as, an *attractive* smile. — **at·trac·tive·ly,** *adv.*

at·trib·ute \ə-'trib-yət\ *v.;* **at·trib·ut·ed; at·trib·ut·ing. 1** To say or think that a quality belongs to a person or thing; as, to *attribute* good intentions to a person. **2** To say or think that one thing is the result of another. The president of the company *attributed* his success to hard work.

at·tri·bute \'a-trə-ˌbyüt\ *n.* **1** A quality thought

of as belonging to a particular person or thing. Honesty is an *attribute* of every good citizen. **2** A symbol thought of as fitting a person or thing. A scepter and crown are *attributes* of a king. — **at·trib·ut·a·ble** \ə-'trib-yət-əb-l\ *adj.* — **at·tri·bu·tion** \ˌa-trə-'byüsh-n\ *n.*

at·tune \ə-'tün, ə-'tyün\ *v.;* **at·tuned; at·tun·ing.** To bring into harmony; to tune; as, ears *attuned* to the sounds of the forest.

atty. Abbreviation for *attorney.*

atyp·i·cal \(')ā-'tip-ik-l\ *adj.* Unlike the type; not normal; irregular.

au·burn \'ȯb-rn\ *adj.* Reddish-brown.

auc·tion \'ȯksh-n\ *n.* [From Latin *auctio* originally meaning "increase".] A public sale in which things are sold to the person who offers the most money for them. — *v.;* **auc·tioned; auc·tion·ing** \-n(-)ing\. To sell at auction.

auc·tion·eer \ˌȯksh-n-'ir\ *n.* A person who is in charge of an auction or one who makes a business of running auctions. — *v.* To auction.

au·da·cious \ȯ-'dā-shəs\ *adj.* **1** Daring; bold. **2** Impudent. — **au·da·cious·ly,** *adv.*

au·dac·i·ty \ȯ-'das-ət-ē\ *n.; pl.* **au·dac·i·ties. 1** Boldness; daring. **2** Impudence.

au·di·ble \'ȯd-əb-l\ *adj.* Loud enough to be heard. The sound was barely *audible.* — **au·di·bil·i·ty** \ˌȯd-ə-'bil-ət-ē\ *n.* — **au·di·bly** \'ȯd-ə-blē\ *adv.*

au·di·ence \'ȯd-ē-ən(t)s\ *n.* **1** An assembled group that listens or watches, as at a play, a concert, or a sports event. **2** An opportunity of being heard; especially, a formal interview with a person of very high rank. **3** Those of the general public who give attention to something said, done, or written; as, the radio *audience;* a writer who of recent years has lost a large part of his *audience.*

au·dio \'ȯd-ē-ˌō\ *adj.* **1** Of or relating to electric currents or frequencies corresponding to normally audible sound waves. **2** Relating to or used in the transmission or reception of sound in telecasting; as, to lose the *audio* part of a television show while the video portion remains clear.

au·di·om·e·ter \ˌȯd-ē-'äm-ət-r\ *n.* An instrument for measuring the power of hearing in the individual ear.

au·dit \'ȯd-ət\ *n.* **1** A searching examination of accounts and account books, as of a business or a charitable organization. **2** The final report of such an examination. — *v.* To make an audit of.

au·di·tion \ȯ-'dish-n\ *n.* **1** The sense of hearing; ability to hear. **2** A hearing, especially one to try out a speaker or a musical performer. — *v.;* **au·di·tioned; au·di·tion·ing** \-n(-)ing\. To try out, as for an engagement as a singer, in an audition.

au·di·tor \'ȯd-ət-r\ *n.* **1** A hearer; a listener. **2** A person who examines business accounts.

au·di·to·ri·um \ˌȯd-ə-'tōr-ē-əm, -'tȯr-\ *n.* **1** The part of a church, theater, or other building where an audience sits. **2** A room, hall, or building suitable for entertainments such as concerts and plays.

au·di·to·ry \'ȯd-ə-ˌtōr-ē, -ˌtȯr-ē\ *adj.* Of or relating to hearing or to the sense or organs of hearing; as, the *auditory* nerve; the *auditory* canal.

auditory nerve. The nerve connecting the inner ear with the brain and transmitting impulses concerned with hearing and with balance.

Aug. Abbreviation for *August.*

au·ger \'ȯg-r\ *n.* A carpenter's tool used for boring holes larger than those bored by a gimlet.

auger

aught \'ȯt, 'ät\ *pron. Archaic.* Anything. — *n.* In arithmetic, a zero; a naught.

aug·ment \ȯg-'ment\ *v.* To increase or enlarge, as in size or amount; to add to; as, to *augment* one's bank account by weekly deposits. — **aug·ment·a·ble,** *adj.*

aug·men·ta·tion \ˌȯg-mən-'tāsh-n\ *n.* An augmenting or that which augments; enlargement; increase.

au·gur \'ȯg-r\ *n.* A person who foretells events by studying signs and omens. — *v.;* **au·gured; au·gur·ing** \-r(-)ing\. **1** To predict or foretell, as from signs or omens. **2** To indicate; to serve as a sign. Today's report *augurs* well for our success.

au·gu·ry \'ȯg-yər-ē, 'ȯg-r-ē\ *n.; pl.* **au·gu·ries. 1** The art or practice of foretelling the future by signs or omens. **2** An indication of the future; a sign; an omen.

au·gust \ȯ-'gəst\ *adj.* Stately and noble; majestic; as, the *august* presence of the king. — **au·gust·ly,** *adv.*

Au·gust \'ȯg-əst\ *n.* [From Latin *Augustus,* the sixth month of the old Roman year, named in honor of *Augustus* Caesar, the first Roman emperor.] The eighth month of the year, having 31 days.

auk \'ȯk\ *n.* A diving sea bird of the cold regions of the Northern Hemisphere, having a heavy, thickset body and very short wings and tail.

aunt \'ant, 'ȧnt\ *n.* **1** A sister of one's father or mother. **2** The wife of one's uncle.

au·ra \'ȯr-ə\ *n.; pl.* **au·ras** \-əz\ or **au·rae** \'ȯ-ˌrē\. Something very delicate and invisible supposed to radiate from and surround certain persons and things.

au·re·ole \'ȯr-ē-ˌōl\ *n.* **1** A halo, especially one around the head of a saint or other holy person. **2** The bright space surrounding the sun, as when seen through a mist.

au·re·o·my·cin \ˌȯr-ē-ˌō-'mīs-n\ *n.* An antibiotic used against typhoid fever and certain other diseases.

au re·voir \ˌōr-əv-'wär, -'wȧr\ [From French, meaning literally "to the seeing again".] Till we meet again; good-by.

au·ri·cle \'ȯr-ik-l\ *n.* **1** The external part of the ear. **2** Either of the two chambers of the heart that receive the blood from the veins.

au·ric·u·lar \ȯ-'rik-yəl-r\ *adj.* **1** Of or relating to the ear or the sense of hearing. **2** Told in the ear; private; intimate; as, an *auricular* confession. **3** Known through the sense of hearing; as, *auricular* evidence. **4** Relating to an auricle.

au·rochs \'ȯr-ˌäks\ *n. sing. and pl.* The European bison.

au·ro·ra \ə-'rōr-ə, ȯ-, -'rȯr-\ *n.* **1** The rising light of morning; dawn. **2** The aurora borealis or the aurora australis. — **au·ro·ral** \-əl\ *adj.*

aurora aus·tra·lis \ȯs-'trā-ləs, -'tral-əs\. A display of light in the Southern Hemisphere corresponding to the aurora borealis.

aurora bo·re·al·is \ˌbōr-ē-'al-əs, ˌbȯr-, -'ā-ləs\. Streamers of light sometimes seen in the northern sky at night; northern lights.

aus·pice \'ȯs-pəs\ *n.; pl.* **aus·pic·es** \-pə-səz\. **1** A sign, as the flight of birds, used in augury. **2** An omen, especially a favorable omen, as to the future. **3** [usually in the plural] Protection and support; as, a concert given under the *auspices* of the school.

aus·pi·cious \ȯs-'pish-əs\ *adj.* **1** Promising success; favorable; as, an *auspicious* beginning. **2** Prosperous; fortunate; as, an *auspicious* year. — **aus·pi·cious·ly**, *adv.*

aus·tere \ȯs-'tir\ *adj.* **1** Stern; severe; strict; as, an *austere* man. **2** Very simple and plain; as, an *austere* room. — **aus·tere·ly**, *adv.*

aus·ter·i·ty \ȯs-'ter-ət-ē\ *n.; pl.* **aus·ter·i·ties. 1** The quality or state of being austere; sternness; severity. **2** [usually in the plural] An austere practice. **3** Extreme economy and self-denial.

Aus·tra·lian \ȯs-'trāl-yən, äs-\ *adj.* Of or relating to Australia. — *n.* A native or an inhabitant of Australia.

Aus·tri·an \'ȯs-trē-ən, 'äs-\ *adj.* Of or relating to Austria. — *n.* A native or an inhabitant of Austria.

au·then·tic \ȯ-'thent-ik, ə-\ *adj.* **1** Being really what it seems to be; genuine; as, an *authentic* signature of George Washington. **2** True; correct; as, a report *authentic* in every detail. — **au·then·ti·cal·ly** \-ik-l(-)ē\ *adv.*

au·then·ti·cate \ȯ-'thent-ə-ˌkāt, ə-\ *v.;* **au·then·ti·cat·ed; au·then·ti·cat·ing.** To prove, or to give assurance, that something is genuine or real; to establish the authenticity of; as, to *authenticate* a signature.

au·then·tic·i·ty \ˌȯ-ˌthen-'tis-ət-ē, ˌȯth-n-'tis-\ *n.* Genuineness; as, to establish the *authenticity* of a document.

au·thor \'ȯth-r\ *n.* **1** A person who writes something, as a book or a play; a writer. **2** The beginner of anything; the creator; as, the *author* of a plan.

au·thor·i·tar·i·an \ə-ˌthȯr-ə-'ter-ē-ən, -ˌthär-\ *adj.* Favoring the principle of obedience to authority as opposed to individual liberty. All dictators are *authoritarian* rulers.

au·thor·i·ta·tive \ə-'thȯr-ə-ˌtāt-iv, -'thär-\ *adj.* **1** Having authority; coming from or based on authority; entitled to obedience or acceptance; as, an *authoritative* order; *authoritative* teachings. **2** Having an air of authority; positive; as, an *authoritative* manner; *authoritative* tones. — **au·thor·i·ta·tive·ly**, *adv.*

au·thor·i·ty \ə-'thȯr-ət-ē, -'thär-\ *n.; pl.* **au·thor·i·ties. 1** The right to command or to act; power to force obedience; as, the *authority* of parents. **2** [usually in the plural] The persons who have the powers of government; as, to report a crime to the *authorities.* **3** A person who is consulted about a subject because he knows more about it than most persons do; as, an *authority* on stamps. **4** A written source of trustworthy information.

au·tho·rize \'ȯth-r-ˌīz\ *v.;* **au·tho·rized; au·tho·riz·ing. 1** To give authority to; to give the right to do certain things; to empower; as, an *authorized* agent; to *authorize* a son to act for his father. **2** To give legal or official approval to something; as, to *authorize* a loan. **3** To establish by authority or as if by authority; to approve; to sanction; as, customs *authorized* by time; the so-called *authorized* pronunciation of a word. — **au·tho·ri·za·tion** \ˌȯth-r(-)ə-'zāsh-n\ *n.*

au·thor·ship \'ȯth-r-ˌship\ *n.* **1** The work of being an author; the profession of writing. **2** Origin, as of a book, with reference to the author or creator; origination; as, a novel of unknown *authorship.*

au·to \'ȯt-ˌō, 'ät-ˌō\ *n.; pl.* **au·tos.** An automobile.

au·to·bi·o·graph·ic \ˌȯt-ə-ˌbī-ə-'graf-ik\ or **au·to·bi·o·graph·i·cal** \-ik-l\ *adj.* Dealing with one's own life history. — **au·to·bi·o·graph·i·cal·ly** \-ik-l(-)ē\ *adv.*

au·to·bi·og·ra·phy \ˌȯt-ə-bī-'äg-rə-fē\ *n.; pl.* **au·to·bi·og·ra·phies.** A history of a person's life written by himself.

au·toc·ra·cy \ȯ-'täk-rə-sē\ *n.; pl.* **au·toc·ra·cies. 1** Absolute power or rule. **2** Government by one person who has complete power.

au·to·crat \'ȯt-ə-ˌkrat\ *n.* A person, especially a ruler, who has, or acts as if he had, complete power; an absolute ruler.

au·to·crat·ic \ˌȯt-ə-'krat-ik\ *adj.* Of, relating to, or like autocracy or an autocrat; despotic. — **au·to·crat·i·cal·ly** \-ik-l(-)ē\ *adv.*

au·to·graph \'ȯt-ə-ˌgraf\ *n.* Something that is written by a person's own hand; especially, a person's own signature. — *v.* To write one's own signature in or on something; as, to *autograph* a baseball.

au·to·mat \'ȯt-m-ˌat\ *n.* A restaurant in which orders are delivered to customers mechanically through a bank of slots.

au·to·mat·ic \ˌȯt-m-'at-ik\ *adj.* **1** Moving or acting without being controlled by a person's will, as movements of the heart or stomach. **2** Made so that certain parts act in a desired manner at the proper time; self-acting or self-regulating; as, an *automatic* machine; an *automatic* pistol. — *n.* An automatic machine; especially, an automatic firearm. — **au·to·mat·i·cal·ly** \-ik-l(-)ē\ *adv.*

au·to·ma·tion \ˌȯt-m-'āsh-n\ *n.* **1** Control of machines or of sets or systems of machines by other machines instead of directly by human operators. **2** The replacement of human beings by machines in a manufacturing or other process.

au·tom·a·ton \ȯ-'täm-ə-tən, -ˌtän\ *n.; pl.* **au·tom·a·tons** \-tənz, -ˌtänz\ or **au·tom·a·ta** \-tə, -ˌtä, -ˌtȧ\. **1** A machine that can move by itself, especially one made to imitate the motions of a man or an animal. **2** A person who acts in a mechanical fashion.

au·to·mo·bile \'ȯt-m-ō-ˌbēl, -'bēl, ˌȯt-m-'ō-ˌbēl\ *adj.* Self-moving; self-propelling. — *n.* A self-moving vehicle intended for use on streets and highways; a motorcar.

au·to·mo·tive \ˌȯt-m-'ōt-iv\ *adj.* **1** Self-moving; as, *automotive* vehicles. **2** Concerned with self-moving vehicles or machines; as, *automotive* engineering; *automotive* supplies.

au·to·nom·ic \ˌȯt-ə-'näm-ik\ *adj.* **1** Autonomous; self-governing. **2** Of or relating to that part of the nervous system which regulates reactions, as those of glands or involuntary muscles, not controlled by the will. — **au·to·nom·i·cal·ly** \-ik-l(-)ē\ *adv.*

au·ton·o·mous \ȯ-'tän-ə-məs\ *adj.* Independent of all outside control; self-governing. — **au·ton·o·mous·ly**, *adv.*

au·ton·o·my \ȯ-'tän-ə-mē\ *n.; pl.* **au·ton·o·mies**. The power or right of self-government.

au·top·sy \'ȯ-ˌtäp-sē, 'ȯt-əp-\ *n.; pl.* **au·top·sies**. The examination and partial dissection of a dead body to learn the cause of death or the effects of an injury or disease.

au·tumn \'ȯt-m, 'ät-m\ *n.* The season between summer and winter; fall.

au·tum·nal \ȯ-'təm-nəl\ *adj.* Of or characteristic of autumn; coming in or having to do with autumn; as, *autumnal* weather.

aux·il·ia·ry \ȯg-'zil-yər-ē\ *adj.* Assisting; aiding; as, an *auxiliary* engine. — *n.; pl.* **aux·il·ia·ries**. **1** A person or a thing that assists. **2** An auxiliary verb.

auxiliary verb. A verb (such as *have, be, may, do, shall, will, can, must*) that is used with another verb to help in forming tense, voice, or mood; a helping verb.

av. Abbreviation for: **1** *avoirdupois*. **2** *average*.

avail \ə-'vāl\ *v.* To be of use or advantage; to have enough strength or force to accomplish a purpose; to benefit; to help. Our best efforts *availed* us nothing. — *n.* Help; usefulness; value; benefit. The team did its best to win, but to no *avail*.

avail·a·bil·i·ty \ə-ˌvā-lə-'bil-ət-ē\ *n.; pl.* **avail·a·bil·i·ties**. **1** The state of being available. **2** An available person or thing; as, to consider all the *availabilities* before making a choice.

avail·a·ble \ə-'vā-ləb-l\ *adj.* Usable; accessible; obtainable; handy; as, to use every *available* means to gain one's purpose. There are few popular books that are not *available* at the library.

av·a·lanche \'av-l-ˌanch\ *n.* **1** A large mass of snow and ice, or of earth and rock, sliding down a mountainside or over a steep cliff. **2** A sudden overwhelming quantity of something seeming to descend like an avalanche; as, an *avalanche* of greeting cards; an *avalanche* of words.

av·a·rice \'av-r(-)əs\ *n.* Too strong a desire for wealth or for possessions; greed.

av·a·ri·cious \ˌav-r-'ish-əs\ *adj.* Greedy, especially for money; grasping. — **av·a·ri·cious·ly**, *adv.*

avast \ə-'vast\ *interj.* Stop! Cease! — used as a command in sailors' language.

avaunt \ə-'vȯnt, -'vänt\ *interj. Archaic.* Begone! Go away! Get out!

avdp. Abbreviation for *avoirdupois*.

Ave. Abbreviation for *Avenue*.

avenge \ə-'venj\ *v.;* **avenged**; **aveng·ing**. To give just punishment for a crime or for a wrong done to a person; as, to *avenge* an insult. — **aveng·er**, *n.*

av·e·nue \'av-n-ˌü, -n-ˌyü\ *n.* **1** A way or road by which one can approach or leave. All *avenues* of escape were blocked. **2** A street; especially, a broad street bordered with trees.

aver \ə-'vər\ *v.;* **averred**; **aver·ring**. To state with confidence; to declare as true; as, to *aver* one's innocence.

av·er·age \'av-r(-)ij\ *n.* **1** The answer got by dividing the sum of two or more figures by the number of these figures. The *average* of 3, 5, 7, and 9 is 6. **2** The kind most usually seen or known; as, skill above the *average*. — *adj.* **1** Figured out by finding the average. The *average* age of this class is 10 years. **2** Usual; ordinary. The *average* man eats three meals a day. — *v.;* **av·er·aged**; **av·er·ag·ing**. **1** To figure the average of. **2** To amount to on the average; to be usually. These children *average* four feet in height.

averse \ə-'vərs\ *adj.* Feeling dislike and a desire to turn away; opposed; unwilling; as, to be *averse* to taking part in a dishonest scheme.

aver·sion \ə-'vərzh-n\ *n.* **1** A feeling of repugnance toward something with a desire to turn away from it; strong dislike. Some people have an *aversion* to snakes. **2** Someone or something that is strongly disliked.

avert \ə-'vərt\ *v.* **1** To turn away; as, to *avert* one's eyes. **2** To prevent from happening. The driver narrowly *averted* an accident.

avg. Abbreviation for *average*.

avi·ary \'ā-vē-ˌer-ē\ *n.; pl.* **avi·ar·ies**. A place, as a large cage or a building, where many live birds are kept, especially for exhibition purposes.

avi·a·tion \ˌā-vē-'āsh-n, ˌav-ē-\ *n.* The art or practice of operating airplanes.

avi·a·tor \'ā-vē-ˌāt-r, 'av-ē-\ *n.* The operator or pilot of an airplane.

av·id \'av-əd\ *adj.* Very eager; greedy; as, *avid* for praise; *avid* for knowledge. — **av·id·ly**, *adv.*

avid·i·ty \ə-'vid-ət-ē\ *n.* Extreme eagerness; greediness; as, to eat with *avidity*.

av·o·ca·do \ˌav-ə-'käd-ō, -'kȧd-\ *n.; pl.* **av·o·ca·dos**. The green, pulpy, pear-shaped or egg-shaped fruit of a tropical American tree; an alligator pear.

av·o·ca·tion \ˌav-ə-'kāsh-n\ *n.* **1** An occupation

or interest that a person has that is less important than his main business or profession; a hobby. **2** A person's customary employment; a vocation. — **av·o·ca·tion·al** \-n(-)əl\ *adj.*

avoid \ə-'vȯid\ *v.* **1** To make void; to annul. **2** To keep away from; to try not to meet; as, to *avoid* trouble. — **avoid·a·ble**, *adj.*

avoid·ance \ə-'vȯid-n(t)s\ *n.* **1** The act of annulling. **2** The act of keeping away from or clear of.

av·oir·du·pois \ˌav-r-də-'pȯiz\ *n.* **1** Avoirdupois weight. **2** Weight; heaviness.

avoirdupois weight. The system in common use in English-speaking countries for weighing everything except precious stones, precious metals, and drugs.

avouch \ə-'vau̇ch\ *v.* **1** To declare positively; to affirm. **2** To vouch for; to guarantee.

avow \ə-'vau̇\ *v.* To declare or acknowledge openly and frankly; as, to *avow* one's fault and ask for pardon.

avow·al \ə-'vau̇-əl\ *n.* An open declaration; a frank confession or acknowledgment; as, an *avowal* of principles and beliefs.

avowed \ə-'vau̇d\ *adj.* Openly acknowledged, confessed, or declared; admitted. — **avow·ed·ly** \-'vau̇-əd-lē\ *adv.*

awag \ə-'wag\ *adj.* Wagging; as, a dog with tail *awag.*

await \ə-'wāt\ *v.* **1** To wait for; to stay for; to expect; as, to *await* a train. **2** To be ready or waiting for. A reward *awaits* each pupil who has a perfect attendance record.

awake \ə-'wāk\ *adj.* Not asleep; alert; as, *awake* at seven o'clock; *awake* to a danger. — *v.;* **awoke** \ə-'wōk\ or **awaked**; **awak·ing**. To wake up, as from sleep or from doing nothing; to arouse; to awaken; to stir up.

awak·en \ə-'wāk-n\ *v.;* **awak·ened**; **awak·en·ing** \-n(-)ing\. To awake.

awak·en·ing \ə-'wāk-n(-)ing\ *n.* A rousing from sleep or from lack of concern about something; as, a sudden *awakening* to the danger of a situation.

award \ə-'wȯrd\ *v.* **1** To give by judicial decision, as after a lawsuit; as, to *award* damages. **2** To give or grant as a reward to one among a number of contestants or competitors; as, to *award* a prize to the best speaker. — *n.* Something awarded, as a prize or an honor; as, to win *awards* in both running and jumping. The winner was given a gold medal and a cash *award.*

aware \ə-'war, ə-'wer\ *adj.* Knowing; conscious; informed; as, to become suddenly *aware* of the lateness of the hour; to be *aware* that one is wrong.

aware·ness \ə-'war-nəs, -'wer-\ *n.* The state of being aware; consciousness; as, to show a keen *awareness* of world problems.

awash \ə-'wȯsh, -'wäsh\ *adj.* or *adv.* **1** Washed by waves or tide; as, rocks that were *awash* at high tide. **2** Floating in water. At the height of the flood almost everything that would float was *awash.* **3** Overflowed by water; as, streets *awash* from the sudden downpour.

away \ə-'wā\ *adv.* **1** From a place; in another direction. The birds flew *away.* **2** Far. The squirrel ran *away* up on the roof. **3** Out of one's possession; as, to give free samples *away.* **4** On and on; continuously; as, to work *away* until the job is done. — *adj.* **1** Absent; gone; as, to be *away* from home. **2** Distant; as, a lake ten miles *away.*

awe \'ȯ\ *n.* Mingled fear, respect, and wonder; as, to have a feeling of *awe* in a storm at sea. — *v.;* **awed**; **aw·ing**. **1** To fill with awe. **2** To control by filling with awe; as, a sight that *awed* everyone into silence.

awea·ry \ə-'wir-ē\ *adj.* Wearied.

awe·some \'ȯs-m\ *adj.* **1** Causing awe; as, an *awesome* sight. **2** Expressing awe; as, an *awesome* glance.

awe-strick·en \'ȯ-ˌstrik-n\ or **awe-struck** \-ˌstrək\ *adj.* Filled with awe; greatly moved by awe.

aw·ful \'ȯf-l\ *adj.* **1** Filling with awe; frightful; as, an *awful* storm; an *awful* disaster. **2** Shocking; as, an *awful* thing to say of anyone. Their behavior at the party was *awful.* **3** Very bad; extreme; as, an *awful* cold in the head; an *awful* hat.

aw·ful·ly \'ȯf-l(-)ē\ *adv.* **1** Terribly; dreadfully. **2** Very; extremely; as, to try *awfully* hard to win.

awhile \ə-'hwīl\ *adv.* For a while; for a short time; as, to sit down and rest *awhile.*

awhirl \ə-'hwərl\ *adj.* or *adv.* In a whirl; whirling; as, a dance that set everyone's head *awhirl.*

awk·ward \'ȯk-wərd\ *adj.* **1** Clumsy; not graceful; as, an *awkward* basketball player. **2** Not convenient or comfortable; as, an *awkward* bundle to carry. **3** Difficult to manage; as, an *awkward* street to cross in heavy traffic. **4** Embarrassing; as, an *awkward* question. — **awk·ward·ly**, *adv.*

awl \'ȯl\ *n.* A pointed tool for making small holes, as in leather or wood.

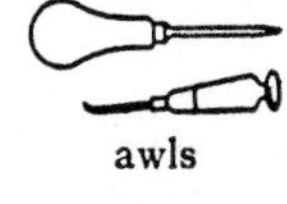
awls

aw·ning \'ȯn-ing\ *n.* A rooflike cover, especially of canvas, extended over or in front of something to serve as a shade or a shelter; as, window *awnings.*

awoke. A past tense and past part. of *awake.*

A.W.O.L. \'ā-ˌwȯl, *or as four letters*\. Abbreviation for *absent without leave.*

awry \ə-'rī\ *adv.* or *adj.* Turned or twisted to one side; out of the right course; wrong; as, a woman with hat *awry;* plans gone *awry.*

ax or **axe** \'aks\ *n.; pl.* **ax·es** \'aks-əz\. A tool consisting of an edged head fitted to a handle, for chopping or splitting wood.

axes

ax·es \'ak-ˌsēz\. Pl. of *axis.*

ax·i·al \'aks-ē-əl\ *adj.* Of or relating to an axis; in the direction of or along an axis. — **ax·i·al·ly** \-ə-lē\ *adv.*

ax·il \'aks-l\ *n.* In botany, the angle between a

branch or leaf and the stem from which it arises.

ax·il·lary \'aks-l-ˌer-ē\ *adj.* **1** Of or relating to the armpit. **2** Situated in or growing from an axil.

ax·i·om \'aks-ē-əm\ *n.* A truth or principle that is generally accepted without proof. It is an *axiom* that the whole is greater than any of its parts.

ax·i·o·mat·ic \ˌaks-ē-ə-'mat-ik\ *adj.* Of or relating to an axiom; having the nature of an axiom; self-evident. — **ax·i·o·mat·i·cal·ly** \-ik-l(-)ē\ *adv.*

ax·is \'aks-əs\ *n.; pl.* **ax·es** \'ak-ˌsēz\. **1** A straight line, real or imaginary, which passes through a body and on which the body turns or is supposed to turn; as, the earth's *axis.* **2** Any lengthwise central line around which parts of a body are arranged in a symmetrical way, as the stem on which leaves and flowers grow on plants. **3** An alliance between two or more major powers; as, the Rome-Berlin *axis* of the second World War.

ax·le \'aks-l\ *n.* The pin or rod on which a wheel turns, or which turns with a wheel.

ax·on \'ak-ˌsän\ *n.* The threadlike branching part of a nerve cell, which conducts impulses away from the body of the cell.

aye or **ay** \'ā\ *adv. Archaic.* Always; ever; as, forever and *aye.*

aye or **ay** \'ī\ *adv.* Yes; yea. — *n.; pl.* **ayes.** A vote or a voter that answers "yes" to a question.

aza·lea \ə-'zāl-yə\ *n.* A bush with fragrant, funnel-shaped, usually pink or white flowers.

az·i·muth \'az-m-əth\ *n.* Horizontal direction usually measured in degrees from north.

azure \'azh-r\ *n.* The blue color of the clear sky. — *adj.* **1** Like the blue of the sky. **2** Cloudless.

b \'bē\ *n.; pl.* **b's** \'bēz\. The second letter of the alphabet.

b *b* B b 𝕭

baa \'ba, 'bä, 'bȧ\ *n.; pl.* **baas** \'baz, 'bäz, 'bȧz\. The cry of a sheep; a bleat. — *v.;* **baaed** \'bad, 'bäd, 'bȧd\; **baa·ing.** To bleat.

Bab·bitt metal \'bab-ət\. An alloy used for lining bearings, as of an automobile.

bab·ble \'bab-l\ *v.;* **bab·bled; bab·bling** \-l(-)ing\. **1** To utter words indistinctly. The child *babbled* at his play. **2** To chatter; to talk without sense or purpose. **3** To reveal or make known in prattling; as, to *babble* secrets. **4** To murmur, as a brook. — *n.* **1** Indistinct talk; senseless chatter. **2** A murmuring, as that of a brook.

babe \'bāb\ *n.* A baby; an infant.

ba·bel \'bāb-l, 'bab-l\ *n.* [often with a capital] A place or scene of noise and confusion; a confusion of sounds; as, a *babel* of voices.

ba·boon \ba-'bün\ *n.* A large monkey of Africa and Asia, with a doglike muzzle and short tail.

ba·bush·ka \bə-'büsh-kə\ *n.* [From Russian, meaning "grandmother".] A kerchief for the head, usually folded triangularly.

ba·by \'bā-bē\ *n.; pl.* **ba·bies.** **1** An infant; a child too young to talk or walk. **2** A childish person. **3** The youngest of a family or group; as, the *baby* of the class. — *v.;* **ba·bied; ba·by·ing.** To treat as a baby; to fondle; as, to *baby* a kitten. We all *babied* Dad while he was sick. — *adj.* **1** Used by or for a baby; as, *baby* clothes. **2** Small or young; as, a *baby* deer.

ba·by·hood \'bā-bē-ˌhu̇d\ *n.* The time or condition of being a baby.

ba·by·ish \'bā-bē-ish\ *adj.* Like a baby; childish; simple.

ba·by-sit \'bā-bē-ˌsit\ *v.;* **ba·by-sat** \-ˌsat\; **ba·by-sit·ting.** To act as a baby sitter.

baby sitter. A person who takes care of a child during the temporary absence of the parents or usual guardians.

bac·ca·lau·re·ate \ˌbak-l-'ȯr-ē-ət, -'är-\ *n.* **1** The degree of bachelor, as of arts or science, granted by colleges and universities. **2** Also **baccalaureate sermon.** A sermon delivered to a graduating class at commencement.

bach·e·lor \'bach-l(-)ər\ *n.* **1** A man who has not married. **2** A person who has obtained the first degree given by a college or a university.

bach·e·lor's-but·ton \'bach-l(-)ərz-'bət-n\ *n.* A plant one to two feet tall with narrow, almost grasslike leaves and blue, purple, pink, or white daisylike flowers; the cornflower.

ba·cil·lus \bə-'sil-əs\ *n.; pl.* **ba·cil·li** \-'sil-ˌī\. A tiny rod-shaped living body. Bacilli are known also as germs or bacteria.

back \'bak\ *n.* **1** The rear part of the human body from the neck to the end of the spine; the upper part of the body of an animal. **2** The part of anything that is opposite or away from the front or lower part; as, the *back* of the hand; the *back* of a house. **3** Something placed at or on the back, as for a support or a lining; as, the *back* of a chair. **4** In certain games, as football or hockey, a position behind the front line of players or a player stationed in such a position. — *v.* **1** To help; to support; as, to *back* a friend. **2** To move, to go, or to drive backward; as, to *back* an automobile out of a garage; to *back* away from a fire. **3** To make or form a back for; as, to *back* a wall with bricks. — *adj.* **1** Located at the back or rear; as, the *back* door of a house. **2** Unpaid; overdue; as, *back* rent. **3** No longer current; as, the *back* numbers of a magazine. — *adv.* **1** At, to, or toward the rear; backward. The crowd moved *back.* **2** In or to a former time, condition, or place; as, some years *back;* to go *back* home. **3** In return or repayment; as, to give *back* a borrowed book. **4** In reserve; as, to keep *back* bad news. **5** In answer; as a retort; as, to talk *back.* **6** As if not said, made, or given; as, to take *back* a promise.

back·bite \'bak-ˌbīt\ *v.;* **back·bit** \-ˌbit\; **back·bit·ten** \-ˌbit-n\; **back·bit·ing** \-ˌbīt-ing\. To blame or speak evil of one who is absent.

back·bone \'bak-'bōn\ *n.* **1** The column of bones in the back; the spine. **2** Anything resembling a backbone; the main part; as, the *backbone* of the matter. **3** Firmness; determination; as, to have enough *backbone* to stand up for one's rights.

back·drop \'bak-ˌdräp\ *n.* A curtain that can be raised and lowered, as at the back of a theatrical stage.

back·er \'bak-r\ *n.* A person who supports someone or something, as a candidate for office or a business undertaking.

back·field \'bak-ˌfēld\ *n.* In football, the backs when considered as a group.

back·fire \'bak-ˌfīr\ *n.* **1** A fire that is set to check the spread of a forest fire or a grass fire by burning off a strip of land ahead of it. **2** In a gas engine, an explosion of gas at a wrong time or in a wrong place. — *v.;* **back·fired**; **back·fir·ing. 1** To set or to use a backfire. **2** To have a backfire; as, the sound of a car *backfiring.* **3** To have an effect that is the reverse of the one intended. The attempt to put the blame on someone else *backfired.*

back·gam·mon \'bak-ˌgam-ən\ *n.* A game played by two persons on a double board with 12 spaces on each side, each player having 15 men the movements of which are determined by throwing dice.

back·ground \'bak-ˌgraůnd\ *n.* **1** The scenery, ground, or surface that is, or appears to be, behind a main figure or object; as, material with flowers on a gray *background.* **2** A place or position that attracts little attention; as, to keep in the *background* at a party. **3** Whatever is logically or historically behind some argument or event; as, the *background* of a revolution. **4** The total of a person's experience, knowledge, and education. Travel broadens one's *background.*

back·hand \'bak-ˌhand\ *adj.* Made or done with the back of the hand or arm turned in the direction in which the hand is moving. — *n.* **1** A backhand stroke, as in tennis. **2** Handwriting in which the letters slant to the left.

backhand, 1

back·hand·ed \'bak-'han-dəd\ *adj.* **1** Backhand; as, a *backhanded* blow. **2** Written in backhand. **3** Not sincere; sarcastic; as, *backhanded* praise.

back·ing \'bak-ing\ *n.* **1** Support or aid; as, to give a project all the *backing* one can. **2** Backers considered as a group. **3** Whatever forms the back of anything and gives it strength; as, the *backing* of a wall.

back·log \'bak-ˌlȯg, -ˌläg\ *n.* **1** The large log at the back of a hearth fire. **2** A reserve, as of surplus funds or unfilled orders.

back·side \'bak-'sīd\ *n.* The hind part of a person or animal; the rump.

back·slide \'bak-ˌslīd\ *v.;* **back·slid** \-ˌslid\; **back·slid·den** \-ˌslid-n\ or **back·slid**; **back·slid·ing** \-ˌslīd-ing\. To lose ground morally; especially, to abandon the faith and practice of a religion previously followed. — **back·slid·er** \-ˌslīd-r\ *n.*

back·stage \'bak-'stāj\ *adv.* **1** Toward the rear of a stage. **2** In the dressing rooms or on the stage behind the curtain; as, to go *backstage* to talk with the actors. — *adj.* Taking place or located backstage.

back·stop \'bak-ˌstäp\ *n.* A screen or fence used in some games to keep a ball from going too far.

back·stroke \'bak-ˌstrōk\ *n.* A stroke, especially a racing stroke, used by a swimmer lying on his back.

back·ward \'bak-wərd\ *adv.* **1** Toward the back or rear; as, to look *backward.* **2** With the back first; as, to ride *backward.* **3** On the back or with the back downward; as, to fall over *backward.* **4** Contrary to or in reverse of the usual way; as, to count *backward.* **5** From one condition to a worse one; as, to seem to go *backward* in one's studies. — *adj.* **1** Directed or turned back; as, a *backward* glance. **2** Slow in learning, development, or progress; as, a *backward* country; a *backward* child. **3** Shy; bashful; as, *backward* about asking favors.

back·wards \'bak-wərdz\ *adv.* Backward.

back·wash \'bak-ˌwȯsh, -ˌwäsh\ *n.* **1** Water or waves washed or thrown back, as by the oars of a boat. **2** A disturbance or agitation resulting from some action or occurrence; as, the *backwash* of hard times.

back·wa·ter \'bak-ˌwȯt-r, -ˌwät-r\ *n.* **1** Water held, pushed, or turned back from its course. **2** A backward, stagnant place or condition; as, a *backwater* of civilization.

back·woods \'bak-'wůdz\ *n. pl.* Forests or partly cleared regions away from cities or towns.

back·woods·man \'bak-'wůdz-mən\ *n.; pl.* **back·woods·men** \-mən\. A man from the backwoods.

ba·con \'bāk-n\ *n.* **1** Salted and smoked meat from the sides and sometimes the back of a pig. **2** A reward; a prize; as, to bring home the *bacon.*

bac·te·ria \bak-'tir-ē-ə\ *n. pl.; sing.* **bac·te·ri·um** \-ē-əm\. Tiny living plants, so small that they can be seen only with the aid of a microscope. Some of them are harmless, some are useful, and others cause disease or cause food to spoil. — **bac·te·ri·al** \-ē-əl\ *adj.*

bac·te·ri·ol·o·gist \(ˌ)bak-ˌtir-ē-'äl-ə-jəst\ *n.* A specialist in bacteriology.

bac·te·ri·ol·o·gy \(ˌ)bak-ˌtir-ē-'äl-ə-jē\ *n.* The science that studies bacteria. — **bac·te·ri·o·log·i·cal** \-ē-ə-'läj-ik-l\ *adj.*

bad \'bad\ *adj.;* **worse** \'wərs\; **worst** \'wərst\. **1** Not good; evil; as, a *bad* man. **2** Wrong; faulty. He spoke *bad* English. **3** Unfavorable; as, *bad* news. **4** Disagreeable; as, a *bad* taste. **5** Injurious; harmful; as, *bad* for the health. **6** Severe; as, a *bad* cold. **7** Spoiled; as, a *bad* egg. **8** Unfit; inadequate; as, a *bad* light. **9** Sick; not well. His sore throat made him feel *bad.* **10** Sorry; distressed; as, to feel *bad* about a mistake.

bade. A past tense of *bid.*

badge \'baj\ *n.* **1** A mark, sign, or emblem worn to show that a person belongs to a certain group, class, or rank; as, a policeman's *badge.* **2** An outward sign; as, a man who seems to have the *badge* of nobility.

badg·er \'baj-r\ *n.* **1** A furry, burrowing animal with short, thick legs and long claws on the front feet. **2** The fur of this animal. — *v.* To tease or annoy persistently; to pester.

bad·lands \'bad-ˌlan(d)z\ *n. pl.* A region where erosion has made the soft rocks into unusual shapes and where plant life is scarce.

bad·ly \'bad-lē\ *adv.* **1** In a bad manner; poorly; disagreeably. **2** Very much; as, to be *badly* in need of rest.

bad·min·ton \'bad-ˌmint-n\ *n.* A game played on a court with a shuttlecock and a lightweight bat similar to a tennis racket.

baf·fle \'baf-l\ *v.;* **baf·fled**; **baf·fling** \-l(-)ing\. **1** To prevent a person from understanding or accomplishing something by being confusing or difficult; to puzzle; to defeat; as, a problem in arithmetic that *baffled* everybody in the class. **2** To check, turn, or disperse in its course; as, plates used to *baffle* the flow of water in a radiator. — *n.* A plate, wall, or screen for regulating flow, as of a liquid or gas.

bag \'bag\ *n.* **1** A sack or pouch for holding things; as, a paper *bag.* **2** A purse or handbag. **3** A suitcase or traveling bag. **4** The amount of game or fish killed or caught. **5** Something that hangs or swells out like a bag or pouch; as the *bag* of a cow; the *bag* of a sail. **6** [usually in the plural] Hanging, flabby skin, especially beneath the eyes. **7** A base in baseball. — *v.;* **bagged**; **bag·ging**. **1** To bulge or swell out like a full bag. The trousers *bagged* at the knee. **2** To cause to swell or bulge. **3** To put into or cover with a bag; as, to *bag* potatoes. **4** To kill or capture in hunting; as, to *bag* a rabbit. **5** To seize; to capture; to get possession of; as, to *bag* an army.

bag·gage \'bag-ij\ *n.* **1** The trunks, suitcases, bags, and boxes that one takes on a trip; luggage. **2** The clothes, tents, utensils, guns and other equipment of an army.

bag·gy \'bag-ē\ *adj.;* **bag·gi·er**; **bag·gi·est**. Like a bag; bulging; hanging loosely; as, *baggy* trousers.

bag·pipe \'bag-ˌpīp\ *n.* A musical wind instrument, consisting of a bag that supplies air steadily to a melody pipe like an oboe and several drone pipes.

bagpipe

bag·pip·er \'bag-ˌpīp-r\ *n.* A person who plays the bagpipe.

bail \'bāl\ *v.* To dip and throw out; to dip and throw out water from; as, to *bail* a boat. The water in the boat became so deep it had to be *bailed.* — **bail out**. To jump with a parachute from an aircraft in flight.

bail \'bāl\ *n.* **1** Security given to guarantee the appearance of a prisoner when legally required and to obtain his release from prison in the meanwhile. **2** The person or persons who give such security or the release thus secured. — *v.* To let out on bail; to obtain the release of by providing bail.

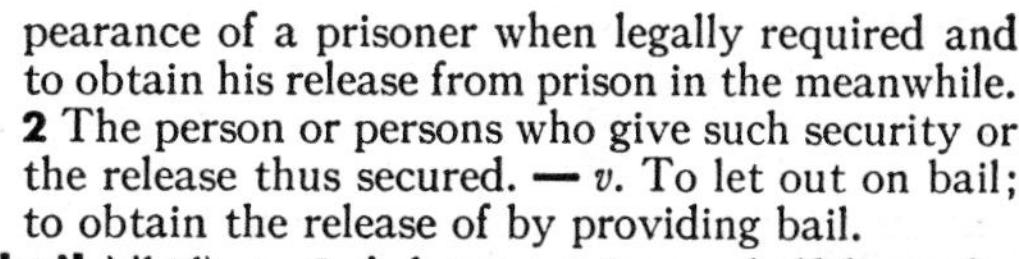

bail \'bāl\ *n.* **1** A hoop or ring; a half hoop for holding up something, as the cover of a wagon. **2** The curved handle of a kettle or a pail.

bail

bai·liff \'bā-ləf\ *n.* **1** In England, an official who represented a lord, or especially the king, in a district and who was responsible for the collection of revenues and for the administration of justice. **2** In England, the title of the chief magistrates of various towns. **3** A sheriff's deputy. **4** An agent who is in charge of property for another person; a steward in charge of an estate of land.

bairn \'barn, 'bern\ *n. Scottish.* A child.

bait \'bāt\ *n.* **1** Anything, especially food, used to attract or tempt fish or other animals so that they may be caught on a hook, or in a trap or a net. **2** A temptation; a lure. — *v.* **1** To worry with dogs for sport; to attack and worry by biting and tearing as dogs attack bears. **2** To persecute by repeated attacks. **3** To feed, especially along a journey; as, to *bait* one's horses. **4** To allure; to entice. **5** To furnish with bait, as a hook or trap.

baize \'bāz\ *n.* A coarse cloth, usually of wool and dyed in plain colors, as used for covering tables.

bake \'bāk\ *v.;* **baked**; **bak·ing**. **1** To cook, or to be cooked, in a dry heat, especially in an oven; as, to *bake* a pie. **2** To dry or harden by heat; as, to *bake* bricks; earth *baked* by the summer sun. **3** To prepare baked foods. Mother is *baking* today. **4** To become dry and hard when subjected to heat.

bak·er \'bāk-r\ *n.* A person who bakes and sells bread, cakes, or pastry.

bak·er's doz·en \'bāk-rz 'dəz-n\. Thirteen.

bak·ery \'bāk-r(-)ē\ *n.;* *pl.* **bak·er·ies**. A place where bread, cakes, and pastry are made; a shop where these are sold.

bake·shop \'bāk-ˌshäp\ *n.* A bakery.

bak·ing \'bāk-ing\ *n.* **1** The action or work of a baker. **2** The amount baked at one time.

baking powder. A powder consisting of baking soda, an acid such as cream of tartar, and a starch, used in baking cakes and biscuits to make the dough rise and become light.

baking soda. Bicarbonate of soda.

bal. Abbreviation for *balance.*

bal·ance \'bal-ən(t)s\ *n.* **1** An instrument for weighing, especially one consisting of a bar supported at the middle and having a pan or scale hung from each end. **2** Any weight, force, or influence that counteracts the effect of another. **3** Any condition in which weights, opposing forces, or influences exactly offset each other; a steady posi-

balance, 1

tion. The tightrope walker kept her *balance* with the aid of a parasol. **4** In bookkeeping, equal total sums on the two sides of an account. **5** In bookkeeping, the amount by which one side of an account is greater than the other; as, a *balance* of 10 dollars on the credit side. **6** The remainder; the rest; as, to spend part of one's allowance for clothes and the *balance* for entertainment. **7** A vibrating wheel that operates with a hairspring to regulate the movement of a timepiece. — *v.;* **bal·anced; bal·anc·ing. 1** To weigh in a balance. **2** To weigh one thing against another; to compare; as, to *balance* the chances of the two teams. **3** To make two things come to a balance or equality of weight; to offset; as, to make gains *balance* the losses. **4** To keep an object steady so that it does not fall or tip over; to poise; as, to *balance* a plate on one's finger. **5** To be or to make proportionate to. Recreation should *balance* work. **6** To make the parts proportionate to each other; as, a *balanced* diet. **7** In bookkeeping, to figure the difference, if any exists, between the credit and debit sides. **8** In bookkeeping, to arrange so that the sum of the debits equals the sum of the credits; as, to *balance* a set of books. **9** To be equally weighted. The scales *balance*. **10** To be equal in value or amount; especially, to be equal in credits and debits, as a financial statement. **11** To waver; to hesitate; to fluctuate. The basketball *balanced* on the edge of the basket before going in. **12** In dancing, to move toward and then back from; as, to *balance* partners.

ba·la·ta \bə-'lät-ə, -'låt-ə\ *n.* A South American tree yielding a milky juice that when dried forms an elastic gum (**balata gum**) used for insulating cables and making golf balls.

bal·co·ny \'balk-n-ē\ *n.; pl.* **bal·co·nies. 1** A platform, enclosed by a low wall or a railing, built out from the side of a building. **2** A gallery inside a building, as in a theater.

bald \'bȯld\ *adj.* **1** Having no hair on the head. **2** Not having the natural covering, such as trees, feathers, or leaves; as, a *bald* mountaintop. **3** Bare; simple and plain; as, the *bald* truth. — **bald·ly,** *adv.*

bald eagle. The common North American eagle, which, when a few years old, has white head and neck feathers.

bal·dric \'bȯl-drik\ *n.* A belt worn over the shoulder and across the body, as to hold a sword or bugle.

bale \'bāl\ *n.* A large bundle or package of goods or other material, for storing or shipping; as, a *bale* of cotton. — *v.;* **baled; bal·ing.** To put up in a bale.

bale·ful \'bālf-l\ *adj.* Harmful or deadly in influence. — **bale·ful·ly** \-l-ē\ *adv.*

balk \'bȯk\ *v.* **1** To hinder or check. A thunderstorm *balked* our plans for a hike. **2** To stop and refuse to go. The horse *balked* at the steep hill. — *n.* **1** A hindrance; a disappointment. **2** In baseball, failure to complete a pitch once begun.

balky \'bȯk-ē\ *adj.;* **balk·i·er; balk·i·est.** Apt to balk; balking.

ball \'bȯl\ *n.* **1** Any round body; as, a *ball* of twine. The earth is a *ball*. **2** A round or egg-shaped object used in playing games, as in *football* or *basketball*. **3** A game in which a ball is thrown, kicked, or hit; especially, baseball. **4** A solid shot, usually round, for a firearm; as, a cannon *ball*. **5** In baseball, a pitched ball, not struck at by the batter, that does not cross the home plate below the batter's shoulders and above his knees. **6** The rounded bulge at the base of the thumb or great toe; as, the *ball* of the foot. — *v.* To form into a ball

ball \'bȯl\ *n.* A large, usually formal, party for dancing.

bal·lad \'bal-əd\ *n.* **1** A simple song, especially one that tells a story. **2** A popular narrative poem, usually in stanzas of two or four lines, especially one of unknown authorship that passes orally from generation to generation.

ball-and-sock·et joint \'bȯl-ən-'säk-ət\. A joint, as in the hip, in which a rounded part moves within a socket, allowing movements in many directions.

bal·last \'bal-əst\ *n.* **1** Anything heavy carried in a ship to steady it. **2** Anything heavy put into the car of a balloon to steady it or to control its ascent. **3** Gravel, cinders, or crushed stone used in making a roadbed, as of a railroad. — *v.* To provide with ballast.

ball bearing. 1 A bearing in which the revolving part turns on steel balls that roll easily in a groove. **2** One of the balls in a ball bearing.

bal·le·ri·na \ˌbal-r-'ē-nə\ *n.* A professional female dancer, especially a ballet dancer.

bal·let \'bal-ˌā, bal-'ā\ *n.* **1** Dancing consisting of conventional poses and light flowing movements. **2** A stage dance that tells a story in movement and pantomime and is performed by a group of persons. **3** The persons who perform a ballet.

bal·lis·tic \bə-'lis-tik\ *adj.* Relating to ballistics.

ballistic missile. A device that contains an explosive, has its own means of propulsion, as a rocket engine, and can be guided while it is going up but descends as a freely falling body.

bal·lis·tics \bə-'lis-tiks\ *n.* **1** The science that deals with the motion of bullets and other projectiles. **2** The firing characteristics of a firearm or cartridge.

bal·loon \bə-'lün\ *n.* **1** An airtight bag filled with heated air or with a gas lighter than air so as to rise and float above the ground. **2** A toy consisting of a baglike rubber case that can be blown up with air or gas. — *v.* **1** To swell or puff out like a balloon. **2** To go up or travel in a balloon. — *adj.* Puffed out like a balloon; as, *balloon* sleeves. — **bal·loon·ist,** *n.*

bal·lot \'bal-ət\ *n.* **1** An object, especially a printed sheet of paper, used in voting. **2** The act or system of voting. **3** The total number of votes cast at an election. — *v.* To vote or decide by ballot.

ball park. A park or enclosed ground in which ball, especially baseball, is played.

ball-point \'bȯl-ˌpȯint\ *adj.* Having as a writing point a tiny metal ball that rotates against an inner inking part; as, a *ball-point* pen.

ball·room \'bȯl-ˌrüm, -ˌru̇m\ *n.* A large room for balls or dancing.

bal·ly·hoo \'bal-ē-ˌhü\ *n.* **1** Noisy demonstration to attract attention, interest, or favor. **2** Sensational writing or propaganda. — *v.* **1** To direct ballyhoo at. The barker *ballyhooed* the crowd. **2** To stir up interest in; to publicize; as, to *ballyhoo* a new product placed on the market.

balm \'bäm, 'bȧm\ *n.* **1** Any fragrant ointment used for healing or soothing. **2** Anything that comforts or refreshes. Sleep is *balm* to a tired body. **3** A fragrant herb grown in gardens.

balmy \'bäm-ē, 'bȧm-ē\ *adj.;* **balm·i·er**; **balm·i·est.** Gently soothing; mild; refreshing; as, a *balmy* breeze.

bal·sa \'bȯl-sə\ *n.* **1** A tropical tree or its strong wood, so light in weight that it is often called *corkwood.* **2** A raft made of bundles of grass or reeds lashed together. **3** A life raft made of two cylinders of metal or wood joined by a framework, often used for landing through surf.

bal·sam \'bȯls-m\ *n.* **1** A fragrant substance coming from certain plants or trees. **2** Any plant or tree that yields balsam, as the **balsam fir. 3** A preparation smelling like balsam, used as a medicine.

bal·us·ter \'bal-əst-r\ *n.* **1** A short columnlike support with a vaselike outline, as one of the supports of a balustrade rail. **2** A banister post in a stair rail.

baluster, 1

bal·us·trade \'bal-ə-ˌstrād\ *n.* **1** A row of balusters topped by a rail to serve as an open barrier, as along the edge of a terrace or a balcony. **2** A stair rail, especially a wide rail having heavy supports.

bam·boo \(')bam-'bü\ *n.; pl.* **bam·boos. 1** A tall, treelike tropical grass with a hard, jointed stem. **2** The wood of this plant; as, a fishpole of *bamboo.*

ban \'ban\ *n.* **1** A public or official order prohibiting something. A *ban* was placed on riding bicycles on the sidewalk. **2** A curse, especially one declared by the church. — *v.;* **banned**; **ban·ning.** To forbid or prohibit by official order; as, to *ban* campfires during a drought.

ba·nana \bə-'nan-ə\ *n.* **1** A large, treelike tropical plant with large leaves and flower clusters that develop into a bunch of finger-shaped fruit that becomes yellow or red when ripe. **2** The fruit of this plant.

band \'band\ *n.* **1** Anything that binds, ties, or goes around something; as, a rubber *band.* **2** A stripe; a strip of material around something, as in *hatband.* **3** A group of people united for a common purpose; as, a *band* of robbers. **4** A group of performers on various musical instruments, especially wind instruments and drums. **5** A range of frequencies or wave lengths. — *v.* **1** To bind, to tie, or to mark with a band. **2** To unite in a group. The settlers *banded* together for protection.

ban·dage \'ban-dij\ *n.* A strip of cloth or other material used in binding up wounds or other injuries. — *v.;* **ban·daged**; **ban·dag·ing.** To bind or cover with a bandage.

bandage

ban·dan·na or **ban·dana** \(')ban-'dan-ə\ *n.* A large colored handkerchief; a kerchief.

band·box \'ban(d)-ˌbäks\ *n.* A light box, often of pasteboard, as for hats.

ban·dit \'ban-dət\ *n.; pl.* **ban·dits** \'ban-dəts\ or **ban·dit·ti** \(')ban-'dit-ē\. An outlaw; a robber, especially a highwayman. — **ban·dit·ry** \'ban-də-trē\ *n.*

band·mas·ter \'ban(d)-ˌmast-r\ *n.* The leader of a musical band.

ban·do·lier or **ban·do·leer** \ˌband-l-'ir\ *n.* A belt slung over the shoulder and across the breast and used to carry heavy articles, as ammunition, or as a part of ceremonial dress.

band·stand \'ban(d)-ˌstand\ *n.* An outdoor platform used for band concerts.

ban·dy \'ban-dē\ *v.;* **ban·died** \-dēd\; **ban·dy·ing. 1** To toss back and forth, as a ball. **2** To exchange, especially in rapid succession; as, to *bandy* blows. **3** To pass about as a subject of gossip; as, a story that is *bandied* around town. — *adj.* Curved; especially, curved outward; as, *bandy* legs.

ban·dy-legged \'ban-dē-'legd, -'leg-əd\ *adj.* Having bandy legs.

bane \'bān\ *n.* **1** Anything that destroys life; especially, deadly poison. **2** Any destructive influence; a source of injury, harm, ruin, or woe. Cold and hunger were the *bane* of the early settlers. — **bane·ful** \-fəl\ *adj.*

bang \'bang\ *v.* To beat, strike, thump, or shut with a loud noise. — *n.* **1** A sudden loud noise; as, to shut the door with a *bang.* **2** A violent blow; a thump; as, to receive a *bang* on the head. **3** A sudden emotional pleasure; a thrill; as, to get a *bang* out of winning.

bang \'bang\ *n.* Hair cut short and even, and worn hanging over the forehead. — *v.* To cut short and squarely across.

bang·le \'bang-gl\ *n.* An ornamental bracelet or anklet.

bang-up \'bang-ˌəp\ *adj. Slang.* First-rate; excellent; as, to have a *bang-up* time.

banian. Variant of *banyan.*

ban·ish \'ban-ish\ *v.* **1** To compel to leave a country. The king *banished* the traitors. **2** To drive out from a home or as if from a home; to expel; to dismiss; as, to *banish* fears.

ban·ish·ment \'ban-ish-mənt\ *n.* A banishing; exile from a country.

ban·is·ter \'ban-əst-r\ *n.* **1** One of the slender posts used to support the handrail of a staircase. **2** [often in the plural] A stair rail and its supporting posts. **3** The handrail of a staircase.

ban·jo \'ban-ˌjō\ *n.; pl.* **ban·jos** or **ban·joes.** A musical instrument having a long neck, a body shaped like a tambourine, and, usually, five strings.

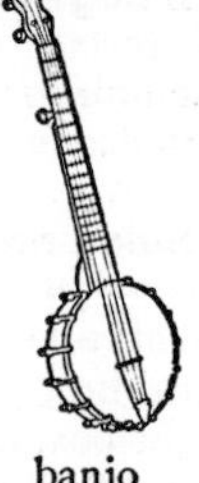
banjo

bank \'bangk\ *n.* **1** A mound or a ridge of earth. **2** A steep slope, as of a hill. **3** Anything shaped like a mound; as, a *bank* of clouds; a *bank* of snow. **4** Rising ground bordering a stream or forming the edge of a hollow; as, a river *bank*. **5** A shoal or shallow on the sea bottom; as, the *banks* of Newfoundland. **6** The sideways slope of an airplane, as when it rounds a curve. — For synonyms see *shore.* — *v.* **1** To make a bank of earth, especially around something; as, a cabin *banked* with earth. **2** To heap up or pile up; to rise in or form a bank. The wind *banked* the snow against the doorstep. **3** To build up in a slope; as, a *banked* curve. **4** To cover with fuel or ashes to reduce the speed of burning; as, to *bank* a fire. **5** To incline sideways when turning; as, to *bank* an airplane. The birds wheeled and *banked* over the trees.

bank \'bangk\ *n.* A group or series of objects arranged in rows or tiers; as, a *bank* of seats; an organ with two *banks* of keys.

bank \'bangk\ *n.* [From Italian *banca* originally meaning "bench", "counter", where the money changers sat.] **1** A place of business that lends, issues, exchanges, and takes care of money, extends credit, and provides ways of sending money and credit quickly from place to place. **2** A small, closed container into which coins may be dropped for savings, as a **pig·gy bank** \'pig-ē ˌbangk\, called that from its shape. **3** A storage place for any reserve supply, as of human blood. — *v.* **1** To conduct the business of a bank. **2** To put in a bank; to deposit money in a bank; as, to *bank* ten dollars every week. **3** To have money in a bank. **4** To rely; as, to *bank* on a person's honesty.

bank·er \'bangk-r\ *n.* A person who has to do with managing the business of a bank.

bank·ing \'bangk-ing\ *n.* The business of a bank or banker.

bank note. A promissory note issued by a bank, payable to the bearer on demand but without interest and circulating as money.

bank·rupt \'bangk-(ˌ)rəpt\ *n.* A person who becomes unable to pay his debts; especially, one whose property by court order is divided among his creditors. — *adj.* **1** Unable to pay one's debts; as, a *bankrupt* merchant. **2** Having to do with a bankrupt; as, a *bankrupt* sale. — *v.* To make bankrupt; to make very poor.

bank·rupt·cy \'bangk-(ˌ)rəp(t)-sē\ *n.; pl.* **bank·rupt·cies.** The condition of one who is bankrupt.

ban·ner \'ban-r\ *n.* **1** A flag. **2** A piece of cloth with a design, a picture, or some writing on it. — *adj.* Foremost; leading; as, a *banner* crop of wheat.

banns \'banz\ *n. pl.* A public announcement, especially in church, of a proposed marriage.

ban·quet \'ban(g)-kwət, -ˌkwet\ *n.* **1** A feast. **2** A formal dinner at which speeches are made. — *v.* To entertain or be entertained at a banquet; as, to *banquet* twelve guests.

ban·shee or **ban·shie** \'ban-(ˌ)shē\ *n.* In Irish and Scottish folklore, a female spirit whose wailing is regarded as a warning of approaching death.

ban·tam \'bant-m\ *n.* A small fowl of any one of many dwarf breeds.

ban·ter \'bant-r\ *n.* Good-humored joking. — *v.* To talk in a joking way; to ridicule lightly.

ban·yan or **ban·ian** \'ban-yən\ *n.* A large East Indian tree from whose branches aerial roots grow downward into the ground and form new supporting trunks.

bao·bab \'baù-ˌbab, 'bā-ə-ˌbab\ *n.* A broad-trunked African timber tree that bears a gourdlike fruit.

bap·tism \'bap-ˌtiz-m\ *n.* **1** The act of baptizing; the religious ceremony of admitting a person into the Christian church by dipping him in water or sprinkling water on him. **2** Any act or experience that purifies or initiates. — **bap·tis·mal** \bap-'tiz-məl\ *adj.*

bap·tist·ery \'bap-təs-trē, bap-'tist-r-ē\ or **bap·tist·ry** \'bap-təs-trē\ *n.; pl.* **bap·tist·er·ies** or **bap·tist·ries.** A place used for baptisms; especially, a part of a church in which persons are baptized.

bap·tize \(')bap-'tīz\ *v.;* **bap·tized; bap·tiz·ing. 1** To dip in water, or to sprinkle water on, as a part of the ceremony of receiving a person into the Christian church. **2** To cleanse or to purify, as if by baptism. **3** To give a name to a person, as in the ceremony of baptism; to christen.

bar \'bär, 'bȧr\ *n.* **1** A slender, rigid piece of wood, metal, or other material, especially one used for a lever or for fastening something; as, the *bar* of a door. **2** A bar-shaped piece of something; as, a *bar* of soap. **3** A band or stripe; as, a *bar* of color. **4** In music, a vertical line across the staff marking equal measures of time; a measure. **5** Anything that hinders or is in the way; as, a *bar* to success. **6** A bank of sand or a reef, as at the mouth of a river or a harbor. **7** In a court of justice, the railing at which prisoners are stationed and where judicial business is carried on. **8** A court or system of courts; the legal profession. **9** A counter at which food or liquor is served or a place having such a counter. **10** The solid mouthpiece of a horse's bit. — *v.;* **barred; bar·ring. 1** To fasten, surround, confine, or obstruct by a bar or bars; as, to *bar* a door. **2** To mark with bars; to stripe. **3** To block up; to obstruct; as, to *bar* the way. **4** To shut out; to exclude; as, to *bar* someone from attending a meeting.

bar, 4

bar \'bär, 'bȧr\ *prep.* With the exception of; as, the best speaker, *bar* none.

barb \'bärb, 'bȧrb\ *n.* A sharp point that extends out or backward, as from the tip of an arrow or a fishhook. — *v.* To furnish with a barb or barbs; as, to *barb* an arrowhead.

bar·bar·i·an \bär-'ber-ē-ən, bȧr-\ *n.* **1** An uncivilized person. **2** A civilized person who lacks an appreciation of or feeling for culture. — *adj.* Of or characteristic of barbarians; as, *barbarian* customs.

bar·bar·ic \bär-'bar-ik, bȧr-'bar-ik\ *adj.* **1** Of early or low civilization and culture; primitive; as, *barbaric* empires. **2** Of or characteristic of uncivilized people. **3** Of rude or primitive style or taste; as, *barbaric* splendor.

bar·ba·rism \'bärb-r-ˌiz-m, 'bȧrb-\ *n.* **1** The use in speaking or writing of an expression not accepted as standard English. **2** A stage of social development between savagery and civilization. **3** Barbaric culture or manners.

bar·bar·i·ty \bär-'bar-ət-ē, bȧr-'bar-\ *n.; pl.* **bar·bar·i·ties. 1** Cruelty. **2** A cruel or brutal act. **3** Barbaric taste or style.

bar·ba·rous \'bärb-r(-)əs, 'bȧrb-\ *adj.* **1** Filled with barbarisms; uncivilized; as, *barbarous* speech. **2** Living in or characterized by an early or low civilization and culture. **3** Cruel; brutal; as, the *barbarous* treatment of prisoners.

bar·be·cue \'bär-bə-ˌkyü, 'bȧr-\ *n.* **1** A gathering or a feast, especially out of doors, at which animals are cooked whole. **2** A hog, ox, or other animal roasted whole. **3** A stove or fireplace for outdoor cooking. — *v.;* **bar·be·cued; bar·be·cu·ing. 1** To cook whole. **2** To cook meat or fish in a highly seasoned sauce. **3** To roast in large pieces before an open fire.

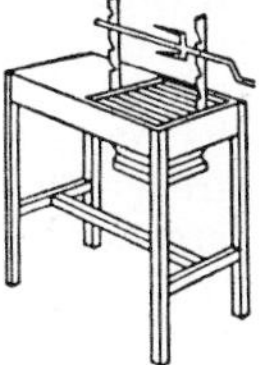
barbecue, 3

barbed \'bärbd, 'bȧrbd\ *adj.* Having a barb or barbs; as, a *barbed*-wire fence.

bar·ber \'bärb-r, 'bȧrb-r\ *n.* A person whose business it is to cut hair and to shave or trim beards. — *v.;* **bar·bered; bar·ber·ing** \-r(-)ing\. To shave; to cut the hair or trim the beard of.

bar·ber·ry \'bär-ˌber-ē\ *n.; pl.* **bar·ber·ries. 1** An ornamental shrub of eastern Asiatic origin, having spines, yellow flowers, and oblong red berries. **2** The berry of this shrub.

bar·ber·shop \'bärb-r-ˌshäp, 'bȧrb-\ *n.* A place where a barber conducts his business.

bar·ca·role or **bar·ca·rolle** \'bärk-r-ˌōl, 'bȧrk-\ *n.* A popular song sung by Venetian gondoliers or music imitating such a song.

bard \'bärd, 'bȧrd\ *n.* **1** In olden times, a person who composed and sang songs about heroes. **2** A poet.

bare \'bar, 'ber\ *adj.;* **bar·er; bar·est. 1** Naked; without covering; as, *bare* hands. The trees were *bare* of leaves. **2** Exposed; open to view. The man's guilt was laid *bare.* **3** Empty; not furnished with the usual contents. The cupboard was *bare.* **4** Plain; simple; as, the *bare* facts of the case. **5** Mere; just enough and with nothing to spare; as, elected by a *bare* majority. — *v.;* **bared; bar·ing.** To make bare; to show. The wolf *bared* his fangs.

bare·back \'bar-ˌbak, 'ber-\ *adv.* or *adj.* On a horse's bare back; without a saddle; as, to ride *bareback.*

bare·faced \'bar-ˌfāst, 'ber-\ *adj.* Without concealment; shameless; bold; as, a *barefaced* lie.

bare·foot \'bar-ˌfu̇t, 'ber-\ *adj.* or *adv.* With the feet bare. — **bare·foot·ed** \-əd\ *adj.*

bare·hand·ed \'bar-'han-dəd, 'ber-\ *adj.* or *adv.* **1** With the hands bare; without gloves or mittens. **2** With a bare hand. The pitcher made a *barehanded* catch of the ball.

bare·head·ed \'bar-'hed-əd, 'ber-\ *adj.* or *adv.* With the head bare; without a hat.

bare·leg·ged \'bar-'leg-əd, 'ber-, -'legd\ *adj.* With the legs bare.

bare·ly \'bar-lē, 'ber-\ *adv.* **1** Insufficiently; poorly; as, a *barely* furnished room. **2** Without concealment or disguise. **3** Scarcely; hardly; as, *barely* enough to eat.

barer. Comparative of *bare.*

barest. Superlative of *bare.*

bar·gain \'bärg-n, 'bȧrg-n\ *n.* **1** An agreement between persons settling what each shall give and receive; as, to make a *bargain* to mow a neighbor's lawn for $2.00 a week. **2** Something bought or offered for sale at a desirable price. This bicycle was a great *bargain.* — For synonyms see *agreement.* — *v.* **1** To make a bargain; to trade. **2** To talk over or to argue about the terms of a business deal. In some countries you must *bargain* for everything you buy. — **bargain for.** To expect; to plan for; as, more trouble than one *bargained for.*

barge \'bärj, 'bȧrj\ *n.* **1** A broad flat-bottomed boat used chiefly in harbors and on rivers and canals; as, a coal *barge.* **2** A houseboat. — *v.;* **barged; barg·ing. 1** To carry by barge. **2** To lurch or lumber along; to thrust oneself rudely; as, to *barge* in late and disturb everyone.

bar·i·tone or **bar·y·tone** \'bar-ə-ˌtōn\ *n.* **1** A male voice between bass and tenor or a person who has such a voice. **2** A wind instrument of the tuba family. — *adj.* Having the range and quality of a baritone voice.

bar·i·um \'bar-ē-əm, 'ber-\ *n.* A chemical metallic element that is obtained as a silver-white malleable substance.

bark \'bärk, 'bȧrk\ *n.* The outside covering of the trunk, branches, and roots of a tree. — *v.* **1** To remove the bark from. **2** To rub or scrape the skin off; as, to *bark* one's shins.

bark \'bärk, 'bȧrk\ *n.* The short, loud noise uttered by a dog; any sound resembling this noise, such as a cough. — *v.* **1** To utter a bark; to make a similar noise. The guns *barked* a salute. **2** To shout or to speak sharply; as, to *bark* out a command.

bark or **barque** \'bärk, 'ȧrk\ *n.* **1** Any boat with sails. **2** A specially rigged three-masted ship.

bark·er \'bärk-r, 'ȧrk-r\ *n.* A person who stands at the entrance to a show or a store and tries to attract customers to it; as, a sideshow *barker.*

bar·ley \'bär-lē, 'bȧr-lē\ *n.* **1** A widely grown cereal grass. **2** The seed or grain of this plant, used for food and in making malt.

barley

bar·ley·corn \'bär-lē-ˌkȯrn, 'bȧr-\ *n.* **1** A grain of barley. **2** One third of an inch, a measure equal to the average length of a grain of barley, used in measuring the length of shoes. — **John Barleycorn** \'jän\. A personification of barley as the source of malt liquor or whiskey.

barn \'bärn, 'bȧrn\ *n.* A building used for storing grain and hay, and for housing farm animals such as cows and horses.

bar·na·cle \'bär-nik-l, 'bȧr-\ *n.* A small salt-water shellfish that fastens itself on rocks or on wharves and ship bottoms.

barn·storm \'bärn-ˌstȯrm, 'bȧrn-\ *v.* **1** To make a trip through rural districts for the purpose of presenting plays in barns or makeshift theaters, usually in one-night stands. **2** To make speeches, as on politics, in small towns or in the country. **3** To pilot one's own airplane, for a living, in irregular sightseeing flights with passengers or in exhibition flying, especially in rural districts.

barn·yard \'bärn-ˌyärd, 'bȧrn-ˌyȧrd\ *n.* The yard around a barn.

ba·rom·e·ter \bə-'räm-ət-r\ *n.* **1** An instrument that measures air pressure and shows changes of the weather. **2** Something that registers changes, as in public opinion. — **bar·o·met·ric** \ˌbar-ə-'me-trik\ or **bar·o·met·ri·cal** \-trik-l\ *adj.*

barometer

bar·on \'bar-ən\ *n.* **1** A nobleman of the lowest rank, just below a viscount. **2** In English history, a nobleman who held his lands and rights directly from the king or from a feudal superior.

bar·on·age \'bar-ə-nij\ *n.* **1** The whole body of barons. **2** The dignity or rank of a baron.

bar·on·ess \'bar-ə-nəs\ *n.* **1** The wife or widow of a baron. **2** A woman who has in her own right a rank equal to that of a baron.

bar·on·et \'bar-ə-nət\ *n.* A man holding a rank of honor below a baron but above a knight and, like a knight, having the title *Sir,* as in *Sir* John Doe.

ba·ro·ni·al \bə-'rō-nē-əl\ *adj.* Belonging to or suitable for a baron or the baronage; as, a *baronial* castle.

bar·ony \'bar-ə-nē\ *n.; pl.* **bar·on·ies.** The lands, rank, or title of a baron.

ba·roque \bə-'rōk, ba-'räk\ *adj.* Irregular in form; unusual; grotesque.

ba·rouche \bə-'rüsh\ *n.* A four-wheeled carriage with the driver's seat in front, two double seats inside facing one another, and a folding top.

barque. Variant of *bark* (the vessel).

bar·racks \'bar-əks, -iks\ *n. pl.* **1** A building or group of buildings in which soldiers live. **2** A plain, large building.

bar·ra·cu·da \ˌbar-ə-'küd-ə\ *n.; pl.* **bar·ra·cu·da** or **bar·ra·cu·das.** Any of several ferocious and gluttonous fishes resembling the pike, as the **great barracuda** of the West Indies.

bar·rage \bə-'räzh, -'rȧzh\ *n.* A barrier formed by continuous artillery or machine-gun fire directed upon a narrow strip of ground.

barred \'bärd, 'bȧrd\. Past tense and past part. of *bar.* — *adj.* Marked by bars; striped.

bar·rel \'bar-əl\ *n.* **1** A round, bulging container, longer than it is wide and having flat ends. **2** The amount contained in a full barrel. **3** A cylindrical or tubelike part; as, a gun *barrel;* the *barrel* of a pump. — *v.;* **bar·reled** or **bar·relled**; **bar·rel·ing** or **bar·rel·ling.** To put or pack in a barrel.

bar·ren \'bar-ən\ *adj.* **1** Not capable of bearing seed, fruit, or young; as, *barren* plants, trees, or animals. **2** Not producing useful plants; bare; as, the *barren* lands of northern Canada. **3** Without interest, information, or charm; as, *barren* writing. **4** Unprofitable; as, a *barren* scheme. — *n.* An area of barren land.

bar·rette \bə-'ret\ *n.* A clasp used by women and girls for holding the hair in place.

bar·ri·cade \'bar-ə-ˌkād\ *n.* A hastily made barrier for protection against attack or for blocking the way. The police put a *barricade* of cars across the road. — *v.;* **bar·ri·cad·ed**; **bar·ri·cad·ing.** To strengthen or to block with a barricade; as, to *barricade* a door with a chair.

bar·ri·er \'bar-ē-ər\ *n.* **1** Something, as a fence or railing or a natural obstacle, that blocks the way; as, a mountain *barrier.* **2** Something that keeps apart or that makes progress difficult; as, language *barriers* between nations. Envy is a *barrier* to true friendship. **3** An extension of the antarctic continental ice sheet into the sea, resting partly on the bottom.

bar·ring \'bär-ing, 'bȧr-\. Pres. part. of *bar.* — *prep.* Excepting; as, *barring* none.

bar·ris·ter \'bar-əst-r\ *n. British.* A lawyer who is permitted to plead cases in court.

bar·row \'bar-ō\ *n.* A large burial mound of earth or stones.

bar·row \'bar-ō\ *n.* **1** A framework having handles, and sometimes a wheel or wheels, used for carrying things. **2** A cart with a shallow box body, two wheels and shafts for pushing it; a pushcart.

bar·ter \'bärt-r, 'bȧrt-\ *v.* To trade one thing for another without the use of money; as, to *barter* skins for beads. — For synonyms see *sell.* — *n.* The exchange of goods without the use of money.

barytone. Variant of *baritone.*

bas·al \'bās-l\ *adj.* Relating to, placed at, or forming a base; as, a *basal* plan.

basal metabolism. The metabolism of a living organism in the fasting and resting state as measured by the heat given off when the organism is using just enough energy to maintain the cell activity, respiration, and circulation necessary to life.

ba·salt \bə-'sȯlt\ *n.* A hard, dark-colored, usually fine-grained rock.

base \'bās\ *n.; pl.* **bas·es** \'bā-səz\. **1** A thing or a part on which anything rests; bottom; foundation; as, the *base* of a statue; the *base* of a triangle. **2** The chief or necessary part of a thing; a basis; as, a paint with an oil *base*. **3** A goal or station in various games. The runner slid into third *base*. **4** In chemistry, a compound capable of reacting with acids to form salts. **5** A place where an army, navy, or similar force keeps its supplies, or from which it starts its operations; as, air *bases*. — *v.;* **based**; **bas·ing**. To put on a base; to establish; as, an opinion *based* on facts.

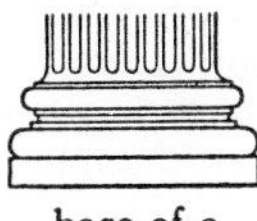
base of a column

base \'bās\ *adj.;* **bas·er**; **bas·est**. **1** *Archaic.* Of humble birth; lowly; as, a person of *base* parentage. **2** Inferior; of comparatively little value; as, precious metals and *base* metals. **3** Morally low; mean; cowardly; as, *base* conduct.

base·ball \'bās-ˌbȯl\ *n.* **1** A game played with a bat and a ball by two teams of nine players each, on a field with four bases that mark the course a runner must take to score. **2** The ball used in this game.

base·board \'bās-ˌbōrd, -ˌbȯrd\ *n.* A line of boards or molding extending around the walls of a room and touching the floor.

base·born \'bās-'bȯrn\ *adj.* **1** Of lowly parentage; mean; low. **2** Of illegitimate birth.

base·less \'bās-ləs\ *adj.* Without basis or reason; groundless; as, a *baseless* accusation.

base·line \'bās-ˌlīn\ *n.* **1** A line used as a base. **2** In baseball, a line connecting two bases.

base·man \'bās-mən\ *n.; pl.* **base·men** \-mən\. In baseball, a player stationed at a base; as, the first *baseman*.

base·ment \'bās-mənt\ *n.* The floor or story in a building next below the main floor and partly or wholly below ground level.

bases. **1** \'bā-ˌsēz\ Pl. of *basis*. **2** \'bā-səz\ Pl. of *base*.

base word. A word to which a prefix or a suffix can be added to form a new word; a root word.

bash \'bash\ *v.* **1** To strike violently; to smash by a blow; as, to *bash* someone on the head with a club. A tree *bashed* in the roof. **2** To crash. The car *bashed* into a tree.

bash·ful \'bash-fəl\ *adj.* Shy; timid in the presence of others; very modest. — For synonyms see *shy*. — **bash·ful·ly** \-fə-lē\ *adv.*

ba·sic \'bā-sik\ *adj.* Having to do with the base or foundation of a thing; fundamental; essential; as, the *basic* facts. — **ba·si·cal·ly** \-sik-l(-)ē\ *adv.*

bas·il \'baz-l, 'bās-, 'bāz-\ *n.* A tropical sweet-smelling plant of the mint family, especially the common **sweet basil**, the leaves of which are used in cooking.

ba·sil·i·ca \bə-'sil-ik-ə\ *n.* **1** An oblong public hall with columns along the sides and with a semicircular projection at one end. **2** An early Christian church building of simple oblong type.

bas·i·lisk \'bas-ə-ˌlisk, 'baz-\ *n.* **1** A mythical serpent, lizard, or dragon with a deadly breath or look. **2** A small tropical American lizard that has on its head a bag made of membrane that it can fill with air.

ba·sin \'bās-n\ *n.* **1** A wide, shallow dish or bowl, usually round, for holding water or other liquids. **2** The amount that a basin holds. **3** A hollow area or enclosed place containing water, such as a dock for ships; as, a yacht *basin*. **4** The land drained by a river and its branches, called in full a **river basin**.

basing. Pres. part. of *base*.

ba·sis \'bā-səs\ *n.; pl.* **ba·ses** \'bā-ˌsēz\. Foundation; base; groundwork; as, a story with a *basis* in fact.

bask \'bask\ *v.* To lie in warmth, as in the sunshine or before an open fire.

bas·ket \'bas-kət\ *n.* **1** A container made by weaving together twigs, straw, cane, strips of wood, or similar material. **2** The contents of a basket; as, berries for sale at forty cents a *basket*. **3** Anything that resembles a basket in shape or use; as, the *basket* of a balloon. **4** In basketball, a goal.

basket, 1

bas·ket·ball \'bas-kət-ˌbȯl\ *n.* or **basket ball**. **1** A game, usually played indoors, in which each of two teams tries to toss a round, air-filled leather ball through a raised basketlike goal. **2** The ball used in this game.

bas·ket·ry \'bas-kə-trē\ *n.* **1** The making of baskets. **2** Work made of interwoven twigs or reeds.

bas-re·lief \'bä-rē-'lēf, 'bá-\ *n.* A sculpture in relief in which the design is raised very slightly from the background.

bass \'bas\ *n.; pl.* **bass** or **bass·es**. **1** Any of a number of edible spiny-finned freshwater fishes of eastern North America, especially the **black bass**, a food and game fish, and the **rock bass**. **2** Any of several salt-water fishes resembling the perch, as the **sea bass** of Southern Europe and the **black sea bass**, a food fish of the Atlantic coast of the United States.

bass \'bās\ *n.; pl.* **bass·es**. **1** A low, or deep, sound or tone. **2** The lowest part in a harmony or a male voice that sings this part. **3** A singer or an instrument having a bass voice or part. — *adj.* Low or deep in tone.

bass drum \'bās\. The largest kind of drum, having two heads and giving forth a deep sound.

bass horn \'bās\. A tuba.

bas·si·net \ˌbas-n-'et\ *n.* A basket, usually of

wickerwork and often with a covering over one end, used as a bed for babies.

bas·soon \ba-'sün, bə-\ *n.* A musical instrument in the form of a doubled wooden tube with holes and keys, played by blowing into a long, curved mouthpiece at the side.

bassoon

bass vi·ol \'bās 'vī-əl, 'vīl\. A stringed musical instrument like a violin and larger than a cello, used for playing a bass part.

bass·wood \'bas-ˌwu̇d\ *n.* The linden tree or its wood.

bast \'bast\ *n.* The tough fiber from the inner bark of some trees, as used for making ropes or matting.

baste \'bāst\ *v.;* **bast·ed**; **bast·ing.** To moisten roasting meat with melted butter or fat.

baste \'bāst\ *v.;* **bast·ed**; **bast·ing.** To sew loosely, or with long stitches, so as to hold the work temporarily in place.

bast·ing \'bās-ting\ *n.* **1** The act of one that stitches loosely. **2** A thread used in loose stitching.

bas·tion \'bas-chən\ *n.* A part of a fortification that projects outward from the main enclosure.

bat \'bat\ *n.* **1** A stout, solid stick; a club, especially one with one end thicker or broader than the other; as, a baseball *bat.* **2** A turn at batting. **3** A sharp blow or slap; as, to receive a *bat* on the jaw. **4** A spree; as, to go on a *bat.* — *v.;* **bat·ted**; **bat·ting.** To strike or hit with or as with a bat; to hit.

bat \'bat\ *n.* A small furry animal that has a mouselike body and long front limbs covered with skin so as to form wings.

bat \'bat\ *v.;* **bat·ted**; **bat·ting.** To wink; to flutter. The prisoner did not *bat* an eye when accused of murder.

bat boy. In baseball, a boy employed to look after the bats of a team during the game.

batch \'bach\ *n.* **1** A quantity of bread baked at one time. **2** A quantity of any material for use at one time or produced at one operation; as, a *batch* of dough; a *batch* of cement. **3** A group of persons or things of the same kind; as, a *batch* of letters.

bate \'bāt\ *v.;* **bat·ed**; **bat·ing.** To lessen; to lower; to reduce; to moderate; as, to listen with *bated* breath.

bath \'bath\ *n.; pl.* **baths** \'ba<u>th</u>z\. **1** A washing of the body; an exposure of the body, as to air or sun, for purposes of health or comfort. **2** Water for bathing; as, to draw a *bath.* **3** A place, a room, or a building where persons may bathe. **4** A large container holding water for bathing. **5** Any liquid in which objects are placed so that it can act upon them; the container holding such a liquid.

bathe \'bā<u>th</u>\ *v.;* **bathed**; **bath·ing.** **1** To take a bath. **2** To go swimming. **3** To give a bath to; as, to *bathe* a baby. **4** To go into the sea or into some other body of water, as a river or lake, for pleasure. **5** To apply water or other liquid to; as, to *bathe* the eyes. **6** To wash against; to wet. The sea *bathes* the islands. **7** To surround or cover as water does; as, fields *bathed* in sunlight.

bath·er \'bā<u>th</u>-r\ *n.* One that bathes: especially, one that bathes in the sea.

bath·house \'bath-ˌhau̇s\ *n.; pl.* **bath·hous·es** \-ˌhau̇-zəz\. **1** A building, sometimes public, where baths can be taken. **2** A building, as at a beach or a lake, with dressing rooms for bathers.

bath·robe \'bath-ˌrōb\ *n.* A long loose garment worn to or from a bath or while dressing.

bath·room \'bath-ˌrüm -ˌru̇m\ *n.* A room with facilities for taking a bath or shower and usually with a plumbing device for disposing of waste matter.

bath·tub \'bath-ˌtəb\ *n.* A tub in which to bathe.

bath·y·sphere \'bath-ə-ˌsfir\ *n.* A round diving device used in deep-sea observation.

ba·tiste \bə-'tēst\ *n.* A fine cotton fabric.

ba·ton \ba-'tän, bə-\ *n.* **1** A staff or a stick carried as a symbol of office or authority. **2** In music, the stick with which a leader beats time, as for an orchestra or a band.

bats·man \'bats-mən\ *n.; pl.* **bats·men** \-mən\. A batter in baseball or cricket.

bat·tal·ion \bə-'tal-yən\ *n.* **1** Any large part of an army; [in the plural] military forces. **2** Any large body of persons organized to act together; as, labor *battalions.*

bat·ten \'bat-n\ *n.* **1** A strip of sawed timber, as used for flooring. **2** A narrow strip of wood for nailing across two other pieces, as to cover a crack. **3** A bar, now usually of iron, used on shipboard to hold one side of a canvas hatch cover in place. — *v.;* **bat·tened**; **bat·ten·ing** \-n(-)ing\. To furnish or fasten with battens; as, to *batten* down the hatches of a ship.

bat·ter \'bat-r\ *v.* **1** To beat with repeated blows; to beat violently. The waves *battered* the shore. **2** To wear down or injure by hard use; as, a *battered* hat. — *n.* A thin mixture made by beating together flour, liquid, and other ingredients, used in making certain cakes and biscuits.

bat·ter \'bat-r\ *n.* A person who bats or whose turn it is to bat, as in baseball.

bat·ter·ing ram \'bat-r-ing\. **1** An ancient military machine consisting of a heavy iron-tipped beam mounted in a frame in such a way that it could be swung back and forth and used to batter down walls. **2** Any beam or bar used in a similar way, as by firemen.

battering ram, 1

bat·tery \'bat-r-ē, 'ba-trē\ *n.; pl.* **bat·ter·ies.** **1** A battering or beating; especially, the unlawful beating of another person; as, assault and *battery.* **2** A number of machines or devices grouped together or forming a unit; as, a *battery* of lights or of cameras. **3** A group of two or more electric cells connected together for furnishing electric current; as, a storage *battery.* **4** In baseball, the pitcher and catcher together. **5** Two or more big guns, especially if forming a unit, under a single command.

bat·ting \'bat-ing\ *n.* **1** The act of a person who bats; the use of a bat. **2** Cotton or wool in sheets, for use in quilts and linings.

bat·tle \'bat-l\ *n.* **1** A fight, especially one between armies, warships, or airplanes. **2** Any fight or struggle; as, a *battle* of wits. **3** Fighting; warfare. — *v.;* **bat·tled**; **bat·tling** \-l(-)ing\. **1** To contend or fight in battle or as if in battle; as, to *battle* for a city; to *battle* for one's beliefs. **2** To fight; to contend against; as, to *battle* a storm.

bat·tle-ax or **bat·tle-axe** \'bat-l-ˌaks\ *n.* An ax with a broad blade, formerly used as a weapon.

bat·tle·cry \'bat-l-ˌkrī\ *n.; pl.* **bat·tle·cries.** **1** A war cry of persons battling. **2** A slogan, as used in any public contest or in propaganda.

bat·tle·dore \'bat-l-ˌdōr, -ˌdȯr\ *n.* A light flat bat or racket with which a shuttlecock is hit in playing a game called **battledore and shut·tle·cock** \'shət-l-ˌkäk\.

bat·tle·field \'bat-l-ˌfēld\ *n.* A place where a battle is fought or was once fought; as, to visit historic *battlefields.*

bat·tle·front \'bat-l-ˌfrənt\ *n.* A line of battle; the most advanced part of a field of battle.

bat·tle·ground \'bat-l-ˌgraůnd\ *n.* **1** A battlefield. **2** A field or ground of conflict; as, the *battleground* of life.

bat·tle·ment \'bat-l-mənt\ *n.* A low wall with open spaces in it, formerly built at the top of fortified buildings.

bat·tle·ship \'bat-l-ˌship\ *n.* A large warship, having heavy armor and carrying large guns.

bau·ble \'bȯb-l\ *n.* A trifling piece of finery; a showy but useless thing; as, to waste one's money on *baubles* and gimcracks.

baux·ite \'bȯks-ˌīt\ *n.* A clayey substance consisting of several minerals, used in the preparation of aluminum.

bawdy \'bȯd-ē\ *adj.;* **bawd·i·er**; **bawd·i·est.** Obscene; lewd. — **bawd·i·ly** \'bȯd-l-ē\ *adv.*

bawl \'bȯl\ *v.* **1** To shout or cry loudly; as, to *bawl* a command. **2** To cry noisily, as with pain; to howl. — *n.* A loud cry.

bay \'bā\ *n.* A part of a sea or other large body of water, like a gulf but smaller.

bay \'bā\ *n.* **1** A section of a building, set off from other parts, as by pillars or beams. **2** A compartment in a barn for storing hay or other fodder. **3** A bay window.

bay \'bā\ *n.* **1** The laurel tree. **2** [usually in the plural] A wreath woven from sprigs of laurel, given as a prize for excellence.

bay \'bā\ *v.* **1** To bark with long deep tones, like a dog in hunting. **2** To bay at; as, a dog *baying* the moon. **3** To utter with bays; as, to *bay* a welcome. — *n.* **1** The baying of a dog; a deep bark. **2** The position of an animal or a person obliged to face pursuers when it is impossible to escape; as, brought to *bay.* **3** The position of pursuers who are held off. The stag kept the hounds at *bay.*

bay \'bā\ *n.* **1** A dull dark reddish-brown color. **2** A bay-colored horse or other animal.

bay·ber·ry \'bā-ˌber-ē\ *n.; pl.* **bay·ber·ries.** **1** A West Indian tree of the myrtle family yielding an aromatic oil used in bay rum. **2** The fruit of the wax myrtle, used in making candles.

bay·o·net \'bā-ə-nət, 'bā-ə-ˌnet, ˌbā-ə-'net\ *n.* A weapon, like a knife or dagger in form, made to fit on the end of a rifle. — *v.;* **bay·o·net·ed** or **bay·o·net·ted**; **bay·o·net·ing** or **bay·o·net·ting.** To stab with a bayonet.

bayonets

bay·ou \'bī-ˌō, -ˌü\ *n.* An outlet of a lake, a creek, or a branch stream that has a slow current and connects at both ends with other bodies of water.

bay rum \'bā 'rəm\. A fragrant medicinal and cosmetic liquid chiefly prepared from volatile oils, alcohol, and water.

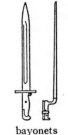

bay window \'bā\. A window or a set of windows in a compartment that projects outwards from the wall of a building.

ba·zaar or **ba·zar** \bə-'zär, -'zȧr\ *n.* **1** In Oriental countries, a market place or a group of shops. **2** A large hall where many kinds of goods are sold. **3** A fair for the sale of fancy goods.

ba·zoo·ka \bə-'zük-ə\ *n.* A portable rocket gun, consisting of a tube open at both ends, that shoots an explosive rocket able to pierce armor.

bbl. Abbreviation for *barrel.*

B.C. \'bē-'sē\. Abbreviation for *before Christ.*

bdl. Abbreviation for *bundle.*

be \(')bē\ *v.;* **was** \(')wəz, 'wäz\; **been** \(')bin\; **be·ing** \'bē-ing\. **1** To have the same meaning or identity as; to equal. That man *is* my father. **2** To serve as a sign for; to represent; as, to let "x" *be* ten. **3** To come under the name or description of; to belong to the class of; as, the boy who *was* sick. Collies *are* dogs. **4** To exist or have reality; to live. I think; therefore I *am.* **5** To keep a position or condition; to remain; as, to *be* at ease.

☞ The forms of *be* (*am, are, is, was, were*) are commonly used as helping or auxiliary verbs with other verbs. The books *were* returned yesterday. We *are* going to town. It *is* getting cold.

be- \bē, bə\. A prefix that can mean: **1** About, over, all over, as in *bedaub* or *besmear.* **2** To make or cause to be, as in *bedim* or *benumb.* **3** To provide with or cover with, as in *bejewel* or *begem.*

beach \'bēch\ *n.* The shore of the sea or of a lake, especially the sandy or pebbly part. — For synonyms see *shore.* — *v.* To run or drive something upon a beach; as, to *beach* a boat.

beach·head \'bēch-ˌhed\ *n.* An area on an enemy-held shore occupied by an advance attacking force to protect the later landing of troops or supplies.

beach plum. **1** A shrub with showy white flowers

that grows wild along the Atlantic shores of the northern United States and Canada. **2** The dark-purple fruit of this shrub.

beach wagon. A station wagon.

bea·con \'bēk-n\ *n.* **1** A signal to guide or to warn of danger, especially a light or a fire on a pole, building, or other high place. **2** A structure bearing a light to guide sailors or aviators. **3** A **radio beacon,** or radio station that sends out signals to guide aviators. — *v.* To provide with a beacon; to shine as a beacon for.

bead \'bēd\ *n.* **1** A tiny ball, or a piece of glass or other material, with a hole through it, to be strung on a thread; [in the plural] a string of beads. **2** Any small round body, such as a drop of sweat or of dew. **3** A small knob on a gun near the front end, used in taking aim. — *v.* To put beads on; to form beads. — **to draw a bead on.** To aim at.

bead·ing \'bēd-ing\ *n.* **1** Material, or a part or piece of material, consisting of a bead or beads. **2** A beaded molding, as of wood. **3** An openwork trimming. **4** Beadwork.

bead·work \'bēd-ˌwərk\ *n.* Ornamental work done with beads.

beady \'bēd-ē\ *adj.;* **bead·i·er; bead·i·est. 1** Like a bead; small, round, and glistening; as, *beady* eyes. **2** Decorated with or as if with beads.

bea·gle \'bēg-l\ *n.* A small short-legged hound with a smooth coat.

beak \'bēk\ *n.* **1** The bill of a bird or of some other animal, as a turtle; especially, a strong, hooked bill, as that of an eagle or a hawk. **2** A beaklike part or projection.

beak, 1

beaked \'bēkt\ *adj.* Having a beak; like a beak; beak-shaped.

bea·ker \'bēk-r\ *n.* A deep, wide-mouthed cup or glass, often with a lip for pouring.

beam \'bēm\ *n.* **1** Any long heavy piece of timber or metal prepared for use, especially one used as a main horizontal support of a building or a ship. **2** The part of a plow by which it is drawn. **3** A bar; especially, the bar of a balance, from which the scales hang. **4** The breadth of a ship at its widest part. **5** A ray or gleam of light; as, a sun*beam.* **6** In full, **radio beam.** A constant invisible radio signal sent out to guide airplane pilots along a particular course. — *v.* **1** To send forth light; to shine. **2** To look or smile with joy.

bean \'bēn\ *n.* **1** The smooth, edible seed borne in long pods by certain plants. **2** A plant or a pod bearing these seeds. **3** A seed or fruit like a bean; as, a coffee *bean.*

bean·bag \'bēn-ˌbag\ *n.* **1** A cloth bag partly filled, usually with dried beans, and used in many games. **2** A game played with one or more beanbags.

bean·stalk \'bēn-ˌstȯk\ *n.* The stem of a bean plant.

bear \'bar, 'ber\ *v.;* **bore** \'bōr, 'bȯr\; **borne** \'bōrn, 'bȯrn\ or **born** \'bȯrn\; **bear·ing. 1** To support and move; to carry; to sustain; as, a bridge not strong enough to *bear* the weight of heavy trucks. **2** To have in one's mind or emotions for; as, the love the son *bore* his mother. **3** To carry as a communication and usually to tell; as, a person who makes a practice of *bearing* tales about his friends. **4** To behave (oneself); to conduct. The soldier *bore* himself well in battle. **5** To be equipped or marked with; to possess or have; as, to *bear* arms. The man *bears* a good name. **6** To grow or produce; as, the land that *bears* the best crops. **7** To give birth to; to bring forth. **8** To endure; to suffer; to tolerate; as, to *bear* pain or grief. **9** To press; to drive; as, to *bear* down on a crayon. The waves *bore* the boat against the rocks. **10** To hold in the mind; as, to *bear* a grudge. **11** To move, turn, or incline. The road *bears* to the left. **12** To relate to; to refer to. What you say may be true, but it does not *bear* on the problem we are trying to solve **13** To have influence or force; as, to bring pressure to *bear* on someone. — **bear out.** To make more certain; to confirm. — **bear up.** To keep up one's courage. — **bear with.** To endure. — **bear down on.** To press toward with force or determination; to try to reach; as, a fleet *bearing down on* the enemy. The pursued man suddenly saw the police *bearing down on* him in the crowd.

☞ For all senses of *bear* except no. 7 above the past participle is *borne.* When the meaning intended is "the action or process of giving birth", the passive participle commonly used is *borne* followed by the preposition *by,* as in "children *borne* by the same mother", and the active participle is usually *borne* without the preposition, as in "the woman had already *borne* several children". When the meaning intended is "the fact of having been given birth", the passive participle used is usually *born* without the preposition, as in "persons *born* in the city", or "the child was *born* yesterday".

bear \'bar, 'ber\ *n.* **1** A large, heavy mammal that has long shaggy hair and a rudimentary tail and walks on the soles of its feet with the heels touching the ground. **2** A gruff or sullen person. **3** A person who sells stocks or commodities on an exchange with the intention of buying them back later at a lower price. — *adj.* Falling; as, a *bear* market.

bear·a·ble \'bar-əb-l, 'ber-\ *adj.* Capable of being borne or endured. Visitors made the days in bed *bearable.*

beard \'bird\ *n.* **1** The hair on the chin, lips, and sides of the face of a man. **2** Anything like a beard, as the tuft of hairs on a goat's chin. **3** Bristlelike or barbed hairs; as, the *beard* of rye. — *v.* To pull the beard of; to defy.

beard·ed \'bird-əd\ *adj.* Having a beard.

beard·less \'bird-ləs\ *adj.* Without a beard; lacking a beard; as, a *beardless* boy.

bear·er \'bar-r, 'ber-r\ *n.* **1** A person or thing that bears, supports, or carries. **2** A messenger. **3** A person who presents a check or a note for payment.

bear·ing \'bar-ing, 'ber-\ *n.* **1** The manner in which a person carries or conducts himself; behavior; as, to have the *bearing* of a soldier. **2** An object, surface, or point that supports something. **3** Direction; way; position; as, to lose one's *bearings*. **4** Effect; relationship; connection. The weather had no *bearing* on our decision to postpone the trip. **5** In a machine, a part in which another part turns.

beast \'bēst\ *n.* **1** Any four-footed animal; especially, one of the larger animals. A **beast of burden** is an animal used for carrying burdens. **2** A person thought of as like a beast; a brutal, vile person.

beast·ly \'bēst-lē\ *adj.;* **beast·li·er**; **beast·li·est.** **1** Of, relating to, or like a beast; bestial. **2** Disgusting; abominable; disagreeable; as, *beastly* weather; a *beastly* headache. — *adv.* Very; as, *beastly* cold.

beat \'bēt\ *v.;* **beat**; **beat·en** \-n\; **beat·ing.** **1** To strike again and again; as, to *beat* a mule; to *beat* a drum. **2** To compress underfoot by continual use. Animals had *beaten* a path to the water hole. **3** To defeat or to overcome. The team was *beaten* in the ninth inning. **4** To go through, striking bushes, thickets, and grass to rouse game; to seek game by beating a wood or field. **5** To throb or to pulsate. The heart *beats*. **6** To mix by stirring; as, to *beat* eggs. **7** To sound, as by beating a drum; as, to *beat* an alarm. **8** To dash or strike against repeatedly or with force; as, rain *beating* on the roof. The sun *beat* down from a cloudless sky. **9** To flap; as, with wings *beating* the air. **10** To measure or to mark off by strokes; as, to *beat* time. **11** To cheat or defraud; as, to *beat* a person out of his hard-earned savings. **12** To sound when beaten; as, with drums *beating*. **13** In a boat, to make progress against the wind, as by tacking. — **beat about the bush** or **beat around the bush.** To approach a matter in a roundabout manner. — *n.* **1** A blow or a stroke made again and again; as, the *beat* of drums; hoof *beats*. **2** A throb or a pulsation; as, the *beat* of the heart. **3** A measurement of time or accent in music. **4** A course or round made regularly; as, a policeman's *beat*. **5** A person or thing that excels or surpasses. I have never seen the *beat* of that.

beat·en \'bēt-n\ *adj.* **1** Made smooth by treading; as, a *beaten* path. **2** Shaped by beating or hammering; as, *beaten* silver. **3** Defeated; overcome; exhausted; as, a discouraged and *beaten* team. **4** Whipped or mixed by beating; as, *beaten* eggs.

beat·er \'bēt-r\ *n.* **1** A person or thing that beats. **2** A device for beating. **3** A person who beats for game.

be·a·tif·ic \ˌbē-ə-'tif-ik\ *adj.* Giving great joy or bliss.

be·at·i·fy \bē-'at-ə-ˌfī\ *v.;* **be·at·i·fied** \-ˌfīd\; **be·at·i·fy·ing.** **1** To make happy or blessed. **2** In the Roman Catholic Church, to declare officially that a dead person is one of the blessed in heaven. — **be·at·i·fi·ca·tion** \bē-ˌat-ə-fə-'kāsh-n\ *n.*

beat·ing \'bēt-ing\ *n.* **1** A whipping; a thrashing; as, barely to escape a *beating* by the mob. **2** A defeat. The team suffered a *beating* over the weekend.

beau \'bō\ *n.; pl.* **beaux** \'bōz\ or **beaus** \'bōz\. **1** A man who dresses very carefully in the latest fashion; a dandy. **2** A man who is courting; a lover; an admirer; an escort.

beau·te·ous \'byüt-ē-əs\ *adj.* Beautiful.

beau·ti·ful \'byüt-əf-l\ *adj.* Pleasing to the senses, especially to the eye or the ear; full of beauty; lovely; as, a *beautiful* woman; *beautiful* music. — **beau·ti·ful·ly** \-əf-l(-)ē\ *adv.*

beau·ti·fy \'byüt-ə-ˌfī\ *v.;* **beau·ti·fied** \-ˌfīd\; **beau·ti·fy·ing.** To make beautiful; to adorn; as, to *beautify* the school grounds by planting a flower garden.

beau·ty \'byüt-ē\ *n.; pl.* **beau·ties.** **1** The qualities of a person or a thing that give pleasure to the senses; loveliness; as, the *beauty* of a face; the *beauty* of a piece of music. **2** A lovely person or thing; especially, a lovely woman.

beauty parlor or **beauty shop.** A place of business for the care of women's hair, skin, and nails.

beaux. A pl. of *beau.*

bea·ver \'bēv-r\ *n.* **1** A fur-bearing animal, having webbed hind feet and a broad flat tail, and noted for damming streams and building underwater houses of mud and branches. **2** The fur of this animal. **3** A hat made of beaver fur or of a fabric imitating it. **4** A heavy fabric of felted wool or of cotton with a nap on both sides.

bea·ver \'bēv-r\ *n.* In a helmet, the piece of armor protecting the lower part of the face.

be·calm \bē-'käm, -'kȧm\ *v.* **1** To make calm or quiet. **2** To bring to a stop because of lack of wind. Sailing ships were sometimes *becalmed* for several days.

became. Past tense of *become.*

be·cause \bə-'kȯz, bə-(')kəz\ *conj.* For the reason that; since. The children stayed inside *because* it was raining. — **because of.** On account of; by reason of. The children stayed inside *because of* the rain.

beck \'bek\ *n.* A silent signal or call, as by a nod or motion of the finger; a bidding; as, to be at someone's *beck* and call.

beck·et \'bek-ət\ *n.* A device for holding something in place, as a ring, a bracket, a pocket, a handle of rope, or a hook.

beck·on \'bek-n\ *v.;* **beck·oned**; **beck·on·ing** \-n(-)ing\. To signal to, or to call, a person by a nod or by a motion of the hand. — *n.* A beckoning gesture. — **beck·on·ing·ly,** *adv.*

be·cloud \bē-'klaủd\ *v.* To overcast with clouds; to darken; to make obscure; as, to *becloud* a question with arguments over unimportant details.

be·come \bē-'kəm\ *v.;* **be·came** \-'kām\; **become**; **be·com·ing.** **1** To come or grow to be. A tadpole *becomes* a frog. The days *become* shorter as summer ends. **2** To suit; to be suitable. Her dress *becomes* her. — **become of.** To happen to; to be the state of; as, to wonder what has *become of* an old friend.

be·com·ing \bē-'kəm-ing\ *adj.* Suitable; fitting; as, a *becoming* dress. — **be·com·ing·ly,** *adv.*

bed \'bed\ *n.* **1** A piece of furniture on which to sleep or rest. **2** Anything or any place on which to sleep or rest; as, to make a *bed* in the grass. **3** A level piece of ground prepared for growing plants or flowers. **4** The bottom or base of anything; as, the *bed* of a river. **5** A layer; as, a *bed* of sandstone. — *v.;* **bed·ded; bed·ding. 1** To go to bed; to put to bed or provide with a bed; as, to *bed* down animals. **2** To plant or arrange in beds. **3** To fix in a foundation; to embed; as, *bedded* on rock.

be·daub \bē-'dȯb, -'däb\ *v.* To daub over; to smear or soil with anything dirty or sticky.

be·daz·zle \bē-'daz-l\ *v.;* **be·daz·zled; be·daz·zling** \-l(-)ing\. To dazzle or confuse thoroughly; as, a driver *bedazzled* by the lights of oncoming cars. — **be·daz·zle·ment** \-l-mənt\ *n.*

bed·bug \'bed-ˌbəg\ *n.* A small wingless, blood-sucking insect, sometimes found in houses and especially in beds.

bedbug

bed·clothes \'bed-ˌklō(th)z\ *n. pl.* Coverings for a bed, as sheets, blankets, and pillowcases.

bed·ding \'bed-ing\ *n.* **1** Bedclothes. **2** Material for a bed. Straw is good *bedding* for cows.

be·deck \bē-'dek\ *v.* To decorate; to adorn; as, a room *bedecked* with flowers.

be·dew \bē-'dü, -'dyü\ *v.* To wet with dew or as if with dew.

bed·fast \'bed-ˌfast\ *adj.* Confined to bed; bedridden.

bed·fel·low \'bed-ˌfel-ō\ *n.* One who shares a bed with another.

be·dight \bē-'dīt\ *adj.* Adorned; decorated.

be·dim \bē-'dim\ *v.;* **be·dimmed; be·dim·ming.** To make dim; to cloud or obscure; as, eyes *bedimmed* with tears; a mind *bedimmed* by advancing age.

be·di·zen \bē-'dīz-n, -'diz-n\ *v.;* **be·di·zened; be·di·zen·ing** \-n(-)ing\. To dress or adorn in a showy way, especially with gaudy finery.

bed·lam \'bed-ləm\ *n.* [Named after the Hospital of St. Mary of *Bedlam* (or Bethlehem), a famous insane asylum of 16th century England.] **1** An asylum for the insane. **2** Any place or scene of uproar and confusion.

bed·lam·ite \'bed-lə-ˌmīt\ *n.* A madman.

bed·pan \'bed-ˌpan\ *n.* **1** A pan for warming beds. **2** A shallow pan for use as a toilet by a person confined to bed by illness.

be·drag·gle \bē-'drag-l\ *v.;* **be·drag·gled; be·drag·gling** \-l(-)ing\. To soil and make limp, as by dragging through rain or mud; as, a tired, *bedraggled* group of hikers.

bed·rid·den \'bed-ˌrid-n\ *adj.* Forced to stay in bed by sickness or weakness, especially for a long time.

bed·rock \'bed-'räk\ *n.* **1** The solid rock underlying the surface layers of the earth. **2** A solid foundation.

bed·roll \'bed-ˌrōl\ *n.* Bedding rolled up for carrying.

bed·room \'bed-ˌrüm, -ˌru̇m\ *n.* A room to sleep in.

bed·side \'bed-ˌsīd\ *n.* The side of a bed or the place beside a bed, especially of a sick or dying person.

bed·sore \'bed-ˌsōr, -ˌsȯr\ *n.* A sore caused by constant pressure against a bed, as in a prolonged illness.

bed·spread \'bed-ˌspred\ *n.* A top covering, usually decorative, for a bed.

bed·stead \'bed-ˌsted\ *n.* The framework of a bed, usually including head, foot, and side rails.

bed·time \'bed-ˌtīm\ *n.* Time for going to bed; as, already an hour past *bedtime.*

bee \'bē\ *n.* **1** Any of various small four-winged pollen-gathering insects living mostly in colonies and differing from the closely related wasps in their heavier, hairy bodies and sucking as well as biting mouth parts. **2** A gathering of people for the purpose of doing something together; as, a quilting *bee;* a spelling *bee.*

bee·bread \'bē-ˌbred\ *n.* A bitter yellowish-brown substance, consisting of pollen stored up by bees in honeycomb cells and used, mixed with honey, as food for young bees.

beech \'bēch\ *n.* **1** A tree with smooth gray bark, deep-green leaves, and small, triangular, edible nuts. **2** The wood of the beech. — **beech** \'bēch\ or **beech·en** \-n\ *adj.*

beech·nut \'bēch-ˌnət\ *n.* The nut of the beech.

beech: leaves and fruit

beef \'bēf\ *n.* **1** The flesh of a steer, cow, or bull used for food. **2** *pl.* **beeves** \'bēvz\ or **beefs** \'bēfs\. A cow, an ox, or a bull; especially, a steer fattened for food.

beef·steak \'bēf-ˌstāk\ *n.* A slice of beef suitable for broiling or frying.

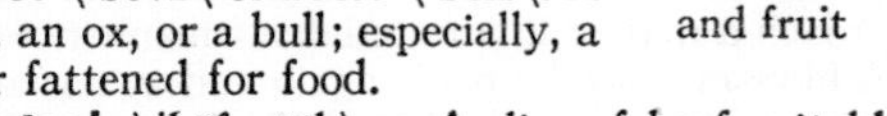

beefy \'bē-fē\ *adj.;* **beef·i·er; beef·i·est.** Large and fleshy, like a cow fattened for food.

bee·hive \'bē-ˌhīv\ *n.* A hive for bees. — *adj.* Shaped like a dome-shaped or conical beehive; as, a *beehive* coke oven.

old-fashioned beehive

bee·line \'bē-ˌlīn\ *n.* The shortest line to a place, like the line taken by a bee to its hive.

been. Past part. of *be.*

beer \'bir\ *n.* **1** An alcoholic drink made from malt and flavored with hops. **2** A nonalcoholic drink made from roots or from other parts of plants; as, root *beer;* ginger *beer.*

bees·tings \'bēs-tingz\ *n. pl.* The first milk given by a cow after giving birth to a calf.

bees·wax \'bēz-ˌwaks\ *n.* Wax made by bees and used by them in building honeycomb. — *v.* To wax with beeswax.

beet \'bēt\ *n.* **1** A leafy plant with a thick, juicy root that is used as a vegetable or as a source of sugar. **2** The root of the beet.

bee·tle \'bēt-l\ *n.* A heavy tool, usually with a wooden head, for hammering.

bee·tle \'bēt-l\ *n.* **1** Any of a group of insects with four wings, the outer pair being stiff cases which cover the others when folded. **2** Any insect or bug resembling a beetle.

bee·tle \'bēt-l\ *v.;* **bee·tled; bee·tling** \-l(-)ing\. To jut out; to overhang; as, a *beetling* cliff; *beetling* eyebrows.

beeves. A pl. of *beef.*

be·fall \bē-'fȯl\ *v.;* **be·fell** \-'fel\; **be·fall·en** \-'fȯl-ən\; **be·fall·ing.** To come to pass; to happen; to happen to; as, to be prepared for whatever may *befall.*

be·fit \bē-'fit\ *v.;* **be·fit·ted; be·fit·ting.** To be suitable to; to be right or proper for; as, clothes *befitting* the occasion. — **be·fit·ting·ly,** *adv.*

be·fog \bē-'fȯg, -'fäg\ *v.;* **be·fogged; be·fog·ging.** **1** To make foggy; to obscure. **2** To confuse.

be·fool \bē-'fül\ *v.* To deceive.

be·fore \bə-'fōr, -'fȯr\ *adv.* **1** In front; ahead; as, to go on *before.* **2** In the past; previously; as, to visit a city where one has not been *before.* **3** Earlier; sooner; as, to leave at six o'clock, not *before.* — *prep.* **1** In advance of; as, to think carefully *before* answering. **2** In front of; as, to stand *before* a mirror. **3** In the presence of; as, to make a statement *before* witnesses. — *conj.* **1** Earlier than the time when. Look both ways *before* you cross a street. **2** Sooner than; rather than; as, a man who would starve *before* he would steal.

be·fore·hand \bə-'fōr-ˌhand, -'fȯr-\ *adv.* In advance; ahead of time; as, to think out *beforehand* what you are going to say.

be·foul \bē-'fau̇l\ *v.* To make dirty; to soil.

be·friend \bē-'frend\ *v.* To act as a friend to; to aid in a friendly way; as, to *befriend* those in need; to *befriend* a new student.

be·fud·dle \bē-'fəd-l\ *v.;* **be·fud·dled; be·fud·dling** \-l(-)ing\. **1** To dull, as the senses or mental powers; as, a mind *befuddled* by weariness. **2** To confuse; to perplex; as, a problem that *befuddled* even the experts. — **be·fud·dle·ment** \-l-mənt\ *n.*

beg \'beg\ *v.;* **begged; beg·ging.** **1** To ask for money, food, or help as a charity; as, to *beg* in the streets. **2** To ask earnestly or politely, as for a favor; as, to *beg* to be taken to the circus; to *beg* pardon. — **beg the question.** To assume as true or take for granted the thing that is the subject of argument. — For synonyms see *ask.*

began. Past tense of *begin.*

be·gem \bē-'jem\ *v.;* **be·gemmed; be·gem·ming.** To adorn with gems or as if with gems.

be·get \bē-'get\ *v.;* **be·got** \-'gät\ formerly **be·gat** \-'gat\; **be·got** \-'gät\ or **be·got·ten** \-n\; **be·get·ting.** **1** To become the father of; to father. **2** To produce as an effect; to cause. Poverty *begets* crime. — **be·get·ter** \-r\ *n.*

beg·gar \'beg-r\ *n.* A person who begs, especially one who lives by asking for charity. — *v.* **1** To reduce to poverty; as, a family *beggared* by extravagance. **2** To cause to seem poor or inadequate; as, a scene that *beggared* description.

beg·gar·ly \'beg-r-lē\ *adj.* Like or fit for a beggar; poor; mean.

beg·gar's-lice \'beg-rz-ˌlīs\ or **beg·gar-lice** \-r-ˌlīs\ *n. sing. and pl.* The prickly fruits of any of a number of plants, which cling to clothing.

beg·gar-ticks \'beg-r-ˌtiks\ or **beg·gar's-ticks** \-rz-ˌtiks\ *n. sing. and pl.* **1** The barbed seeds of any bur marigold or the plant itself. **2** Beggar's-lice.

beg·gary \'beg-r-ē\ *n.* Extreme poverty or want.

be·gin \bē-'gin\ *v.;* **be·gan** \-'gan\; **be·gun** \-'gən\; **be·gin·ning.** **1** To start; to do the first part of some action. *Begin* your spelling now. **2** To come into existence; to originate; as, since the world *began.* **3** To be or do in the least degree. This does not *being* to fill our needs.

be·gin·ner \bē-'gin-r\ *n.* A person who is beginning something or doing something for the first time; any inexperienced person; as, a *beginner's* class in dancing.

be·gin·ning \bē-'gin-ing\ *n.* **1** The action of starting. **2** The point in time or space at which something begins. From the very *beginning* there was no doubt about the outcome of the game. **3** The first part or earliest stage; as, a story with a dull *beginning;* the *beginnings* of American history. **4** Source or origin; first cause.

be·gone \bē-'gȯn\ *v.* Go away; depart — used chiefly as a command.

be·go·nia \bē-'gōn-yə\ *n.* A juicy-stemmed plant with ornamental leaves and small waxy flowers, usually red or pink in color.

begot. Past tense and past part. of *beget.*

begotten. A past part. of *beget.*

be·grime \bē-'grīm\ *v.;* **be·grimed; be·grim·ing.** To soil with grime or dirt.

be·grudge \bē-'grəj\ *v.;* **be·grudged; be·grudg·ing.** **1** To grumble at or be annoyed by; to do reluctantly. **2** To envy a person possession or enjoyment of something; to grudge. — **be·grudg·ing·ly,** *adv.*

be·guile \bē-'gīl\ *v.;* **be·guiled; be·guil·ing.** **1** To deceive by means of flattery, or by a trick or a lie. **2** To draw notice or interest by the use of wiles or charm; as, a *beguiling* manner. **3** To cause time to pass pleasantly; to while away; as, to *beguile* the time by telling stories. — **be·guile·ment** \-mənt\ *n.* — **be·guil·er** \-r\ *n.*

begun. Past part. of *begin.*

be·half \bē-'haf, -'håf\ *n.* Support; defense; interest; as, to speak in *behalf* of a friend; to act on one's own *behalf.*

be·have \bē-'hāv\ *v.;* **be·haved; be·hav·ing.** **1** To conduct oneself or itself; to act. The children *behaved* well at the party. **2** To conduct oneself properly. Small children cannot be expected to *behave* all the time. **3** To act under the conditions of use; to react; to work; as, a car that *behaves* well in heavy traffic.

be·hav·ior \bē-ˈhāv-yər\ *n.* **1** The way in which a person conducts himself; deportment; as, the *behavior* of a child at a party. **2** The way in which a thing, as a machine or a substance, acts, especially in response to some outside influence; as, the *behavior* of a ship in a storm; the *behavior* of steel under heavy strain.

be·head \bē-ˈhed\ *v.* To cut off the head of.

beheld. Past tense and past part. of *behold.*

be·he·moth \bē-ˈhē-məth, ˈbē-ə-ˌmȯth\ *n.* An animal, possibly a hippopotamus, described in the Bible; any very large or strong animal.

be·hest \bē-ˈhest\ *n.* A command; an order.

be·hind \bē-ˈhīnd\ *adv.* **1** Back in time, place, or direction; as, to stay *behind.* **2** Backward in progress; as, to be *behind* in school. — *prep.* **1** On or at the back side of; as *behind* the door. **2** Inferior to; not up to the level of; as, to be *behind* one's class. — *adj.* In a position in the rear; following; as, to recognize a friend in the car *behind.*

be·hind·hand \bē-ˈhīnd-ˌhand\ *adv.* or *adj.* Not keeping up; late; backward; behind; as, *behindhand* with the rent.

be·hold \bē-ˈhōld\ *v.;* **be·held** \-ˈheld\; **be·hold·ing.** To see; to gaze upon. — **be·hold·er** \-r\ *n.*

be·hold·en \bē-ˈhōl-dən\ *adj.* Under obligation; indebted; as, to be *beholden* to a neighbor for many kindnesses.

be·hoof \bē-ˈhüf\ *n.* Profit; advantage; benefit; as, an action taken solely for one's own *behoof.*

be·hoove \bē-ˈhüv\ or **be·hove** \bē-ˈhōv\ *v.;* **be·hooved** or **be·hoved; be·hoov·ing** or **be·hov·ing.** To be necessary for as a matter of duty or obligation; to be fitting or proper for; as, an example which it would *behoove* any ambitious boy to follow. It *behooves* a soldier to obey orders.

beige \ˈbāzh\ *n.* The color of unbleached cloth; light brown.

be·ing \ˈbē-ing\. Pres. part. of *be.* — *n.* **1** Existence; life; as, to come into *being.* **2** Anything that exists; especially, a living thing; as, a human *being.*

be·la·bor \bē-ˈlāb-r\ *v.;* **be·la·bored; be·la·bor·ing** \-r(-)ing\. To beat hard; to hit with all one's strength, especially over and over again.

be·lat·ed \bē-ˈlāt-əd\ *adj.* Delayed beyond the usual or expected time; too late; as, a *belated* arrival. — **be·lat·ed·ly,** *adv.*

be·lay \bē-ˈlā\ *v.;* **be·layed; be·lay·ing. 1** To make secure, as a rope or cable, by winding or turning around a pin (**belaying pin**) or cleat. **2** To stop; to quit; to hold back on — used chiefly by sailors as a command.

belch \ˈbelch\ *v.* **1** To throw up wind or gas from the stomach through the mouth. **2** To throw out; to burst forth. The volcano *belched* smoke and fire. — *n.* A belching.

bel·dam or **bel·dame** \ˈbeld-m\ *n.* An old woman, especially one that is ugly or loathsome; a hag.

be·lea·guer \bē-ˈlēg-r\ *v.* To blockade by surrounding with an army; to besiege; as, a *beleaguered* city.

bel·fry \ˈbel-frē\ *n.; pl.* **bel·fries.** A tower, or a room in a tower, for a bell or bells.

Bel·gian \ˈbelj-n\ *adj.* Of or relating to Belgium. — *n.* A native or inhabitant of Belgium.

be·lie \bē-ˈlī\ *v.;* **be·lied; be·ly·ing** \-ˈlī-ing\. **1** To misrepresent; as, words that *belie* one's feelings. **2** To be false or unfaithful to; as, to *belie* one's principles. **3** To show to be false. The man's actions *belie* his promise.

be·lief \bə-ˈlēf\ *n.* **1** Confidence that a person or thing exists, or is true or trustworthy; faith; trust; as, a child's *belief* in his parents; a *belief* in the democratic way of government. **2** Religious faith; especially, a creed. **3** The thing that is believed; a conviction; opinion; as, political *beliefs.* In spite of the clerk's statement, the customer remained of the same *belief.*

— The words *faith* and *conviction* are synonyms of *belief: belief* may suggest something one accepts as true on the basis of evidence or reason; *faith* often implies acceptance without actual proof or evidence, and may also suggest trust and confidence; *conviction* generally refers to a strongly fixed belief.

be·liev·a·ble \bə-ˈlē-vəb-l\ *adj.* Capable of being believed.

be·lieve \bə-ˈlēv\ *v.;* **be·lieved; be·liev·ing. 1** To accept as true; as, to *believe* a story. **2** To accept the word of; as, to *believe* a person. **3** To have faith or confidence, as in the existence or truth of something; as, to *believe* in ghosts. **4** To have faith in the truths of religion. **5** To think; to have an opinion; as, to *believe* that it is going to rain. — **be·liev·er** \-r\ *n.*

be·like \bē-ˈlīk\ *adv. Archaic.* Perhaps.

be·lit·tle \bē-ˈlit-l\ *v.;* **be·lit·tled; be·lit·tling** \-l(-)ing\. To make a person or a thing seem little or unimportant; to speak of in a slighting way; as, to *belittle* the success of a rival.

bell \ˈbel\ *n.* **1** A hollow, usually cup-shaped metallic device that makes a ringing sound when struck; as, a dinner *bell;* church *bells.* **2** The stroke or sound of a bell that tells the hour, especially on shipboard. **3** The time indicated by the stroke of a bell; on shipboard, a half hour. **4** Something shaped like a bell, as a flower or the flaring mouth of a trumpet. — *v.* **1** To put a bell upon; as, to *bell* an animal. **2** To make flaring at the mouth like a bell; as, to *bell* a tube. **3** To take the form of a bell. The blossom *belled* out as it opened.

electric bell and hand bell

bel·la·don·na \ˌbel-ə-ˈdän-ə\ *n.* **1** A European poisonous perennial herb of the potato family, having reddish bell-shaped flowers and shining black berries. **2** A drug obtained from this plant.

bell·bird \ˈbel-ˌbərd\ *n.* Any of several birds whose notes suggest the sound of a bell, as the wood thrush in the United States.

bell·boy \'bel-ˌbȯi\ *n.* A hotel or club employee who escorts guests to their rooms, assists them with their luggage, and is available for running errands.

belle \'bel\ *n.* A beautiful girl or woman; especially, one much admired for her charm.

bell·flow·er \'bel-ˌflau̇r\ *n.* A campanula with bell-shaped flowers.

bell·hop \'bel-ˌhäp\ *n.* A bellboy.

bel·li·cose \'bel-ə-ˌkōs\ *adj.* Inclined to quarrel or fight; warlike.

bellied. Past tense and past part. of *belly.*

bellies. Pl. of *belly.*

bel·lig·er·ence \bə-'lij-r-ən(t)s\ *n.* **1** Belligerent attitude or nature; willingness or inclination to fight. **2** The action of waging war; warlike activity.

bel·lig·er·en·cy \bə-'lij-r-ən-sē\ *n.* **1** The status of a nation that is at war. **2** Warfare, as between nations.

bel·lig·er·ent \bə-'lij-r-ənt\ *adj.* **1** Carrying on war; at war; as, *belligerent* nations. **2** Warlike; showing a willingness to fight; as, a *belligerent* manner. **3** Relating to war or to parties or nations at war; as, *belligerent* rights. — *n.* A nation or a person that is at war. — **bel·lig·er·ent·ly,** *adv.*

bell jar. A glass vessel resembling a bell in being open at the bottom and closed at the top.

bell·man \'bel-mən\ *n.; pl.* **bell·men** \-mən\. A man who rings a bell, as a town crier or a night watchman.

bel·low \'bel-ō\ *v.* To give a loud deep roar like that of a bull; to shout or bawl; to roar. The captain *bellowed* orders through the storm. — *n.* A loud, deep roar.

bel·lows \'bel-ōz, -əs\ *n. sing. and pl.* **1** A device whose two sides can be spread apart and then pressed together to force air through a tube at one end. **2** A bellowslike part of some cameras.

bellows, 1

bell·pull \'bel-ˌpu̇l\ *n.* A cord or wire, or the handle attached to such a cord or wire, by which one rings a bell.

bell·weth·er \'bel-'weth-r\ *n.* A sheep that leads a flock, wearing a bell on its neck.

bel·ly \'bel-ē\ *n.; pl.* **bel·lies.** **1** The lower part of the human body containing the stomach and other digestive organs; the abdomen. **2** The under part of an animal's body. **3** The stomach; as, an empty *belly.* **4** The internal cavity of a person's or an animal's body. **5** A bulging or a hollow middle part; as, the *belly* of an airplane. — *v.;* **bel·lied; bel·ly·ing.** To swell out; to bulge; as, sails *bellying* in the breeze.

bel·ly·ache \'bel-ē-ˌāk\ *n.* Pain in the abdomen, especially in the bowels; colic. — *v.;* **bel·ly·ached; bel·ly·ach·ing.** *Slang.* To complain, especially in a whining or peevish way.

bel·ly·land \'bel-ē-ˌland\ *v.* To land an airplane without use of landing gear, on the underside of the fuselage.

be·long \bə-'lȯng\ *v.* **1** To be a part of; to be connected with or to go with; as, parts *belonging* to a watch. This book *belongs* on the top shelf. **2** To be the property of; to be owned by. This book *belongs* to me. **3** To be the business or concern of. Fighting *belongs* to soldiers. **4** To be attached to or connected with by some relation, as of birth or residence; as, to guess from a person's accent where he *belongs.* **5** To be a member of a group, as a club. **6** To be properly classed. Whales *belong* among the mammals.

be·long·ings \bə-'lȯng-ingz\ *n. pl.* The things that belong to a person; possessions.

be·lov·ed \bə-'ləv-əd, -'ləvd\ *adj.* Greatly loved; very dear or cherished. — *n.* A person who is much loved.

be·low \bə-'lō\ *adv.* In or to a lower place; beneath; as, a view of the city lying *below.* — *prep.* Lower than, as in place, position, rank, or value; beneath; as, to hang one picture *below* another; temperatures *below* zero.

belt \'belt\ *n.* **1** A strip of leather, cloth, or other flexible material, worn around a person's body for holding in or supporting clothing or weapons, or for ornament. **2** Anything resembling a belt; a band; a circle; as, a *belt* of trees. **3** In machinery, a flexible, endless band running around wheels or pulleys and used for moving or carrying something; as, a fan *belt* on an automobile. **4** A region suited to or characterized by certain products or activities; as, the cotton *belt.* — **below the belt.** Below the waistline; unfairly. — *v.* **1** To put a belt on or around. **2** To strike with a belt; to strike hard. The batter *belted* a home run.

belying. Pres. part. of *belie.*

bench \'bench\ *n.* **1** A long seat for two or more persons. **2** A long table for holding work and tools, as those of a carpenter or a shoemaker. **3** The seat where the judges sit in a court of law. **4** The position or rank of a judge. **5** A person sitting as a judge or the persons who sit as judges taken together. **6** A seat where the members of a team wait for an opportunity to play. — *v.* **1** To provide with a bench or benches. **2** To seat on a bench, especially in the position of judge. **3** In sports, to keep on the bench or to recall to the bench; as, a player who was *benched* for the first three games of the season.

bench, 1

bend \'bend\ *v.;* **bent** \'bent\ or **bend·ed; bend·ing.** **1** To pull taut or tense, as a bow. **2** To curve or cause a change of shape of any kind; as, to *bend* a wire into a circle and then *bend* it straight again. **3** To turn in a certain direction; to direct. The hiker *bent* his steps toward town. **4** To force to yield. The father *bent* all his family to his will. **5** To apply closely; to direct; as, to *bend* all one's energy to the task. **6** To be bent out of line; to curve; to crook. The road *bends* to the left. **7** To curve downward; to stoop; as, to *bend* over to pick up something. **8** To bow; to yield; to submit; as, to refuse to *bend* beneath the oppressor's yoke. **9** To apply oneself closely or vigorously; as, to *bend* to one's work. — *n.* **1** A bending; a turn from a straight line or direction; a curve. The river made a sharp *bend* to the south. **2** A bent thing, or a bent part of anything; a curve; a crook; as, a *bend* in a wire. **3** [in the plural] A sickness resulting from rapid decompression, marked by intense pain in muscles and joints due to formation of gas bubbles in the tissues.

be·neath \bə-ˈnēth\ *adv.* In a lower place; below; directly below; as, rain falling on the earth *beneath.* — *prep.* **1** Lower than, as in place, rank, or excellence; under; as, the ground *beneath* one's feet. **2** Unworthy of; as, to feel that a remark is *beneath* one's notice.

ben·e·dic·tion \ˌben-ə-ˈdiksh-n\ *n.* The act of blessing; a blessing, especially one spoken by a clergyman at the end of a religious meeting.

ben·e·fac·tion \ˈben-ə-ˌfaksh-n\ *n.* **1** The action of benefiting. **2** A benefit conferred; especially, a charitable donation.

ben·e·fac·tor \ˈben-ə-ˌfakt-r\ *n.* One who confers a benefit on another; especially, one who makes charitable gifts.

ben·e·fice \ˈben-ə-fəs\ *n.* Any post held by a clergyman that gives him the right to use certain property and to receive income from stated sources.

be·nef·i·cence \bə-ˈnef-ə-sən(t)s\ *n.* **1** Goodness or kindness as shown in one's actions. **2** A benefaction.

be·nef·i·cent \bə-ˈnef-ə-sənt\ *adj.* Characterized by beneficence; doing good; productive of good.

ben·e·fi·cial \ˌben-ə-ˈfish-l\ *adj.* Producing good results; being of benefit or help; as, *beneficial* advice.

— The words *advantageous* and *profitable* are synonyms of *beneficial: beneficial* usually refers to something that produces general good; *advantageous* may imply something leading to success or personal advancement; *profitable* usually describes something leading to useful or productive ends, or to increase of wealth.

ben·e·fi·ci·ary \ˌben-ə-ˈfish-ē-ˌer-ē, -ˈfish-r-ē\ *n.; pl.* **ben·e·fi·ci·ar·ies.** A person who benefits or who receives a gift, benefit, or advantage; as, the *beneficiary* of an insurance policy.

ben·e·fit \ˈben-ə-ˌfit\ *n.* **1** An act of kindness; a favor. **2** Something that does good to a person or thing; a help; as, the *benefits* of sunshine. **3** Money or other assistance paid or given in time of death, sickness, or unemployment, or in old age, as by an insurance company or a public agency. **4** A performance the proceeds of which are given to a particular person or for a specific purpose. — *v.;* **ben·e·fit·ed; ben·e·fit·ing.** **1** To do good to; to help. **2** To receive advantage or aid; as, to *benefit* from an education.

be·nev·o·lence \bə-ˈnev-l(-)ən(t)s\ *n.* **1** Generous nature or disposition; goodwill. **2** An act of kindness; a generous gift, as to a charity.

be·nev·o·lent \bə-ˈnev-l(-)ənt\ *adj.* **1** Having or showing good will to others; kindly; as, a *benevolent* smile. **2** Freely or generously giving to charity or to institutions for human welfare; as, *benevolent* millionaires. **3** Existing or operated for the purpose of doing good to others and not for profit; as, orphanages and other *benevolent* institutions. — **be·nev·o·lent·ly,** *adv.*

be·night·ed \bē-ˈnīt-əd\ *adj.* **1** Overtaken by night or darkness; as, *benighted* travelers. **2** Ignorant; as, *benighted* heathen.

be·nign \bē-ˈnīn\ *adj.* **1** Kindly, gracious, and gentle; as, a *benign* countenance. **2** Not threatening or harmful; as, *benign* influences. **3** In medicine, not malignant; as, a *benign* tumor. — **be·nign·ly,** *adv.*

be·nig·nant \bē-ˈnig-nənt\ *adj.* Benign; gracious, as to one's subjects or dependents; as, a *benignant* king. — **be·nig·nant·ly,** *adv.*

be·nig·ni·ty \bē-ˈnig-nət-ē\ *n.; pl.* **be·nig·ni·ties.** **1** Benign or kindly nature; gentleness. **2** A kind deed.

ben·i·son \ˈben-əs-n, -əz-n\ *n.* A blessing; a benediction.

bent \ˈbent\. A past tense and a past part. of *bend.* — *adj.* **1** Changed by bending; no longer straight; crooked; as, a *bent* old man. **2** Determined; strongly inclined; as, *bent* on going his own way; a group of youngsters *bent* on mischief.

bent \ˈbent\ *n.* An inclination; a natural liking or fondness; as, a child with a *bent* for music.

be·numb \bē-ˈnəm\ *v.* To make numb, as by cold; as, fingers *benumbed* by the wind.

ben·zene \ˈben-ˌzēn\ *n.* A colorless, flammable liquid that smells like ether, obtained chiefly by distilling coal and used in making gas for lighting purposes and in the manufacture of dyes and chemicals.

ben·zine \ˈben-ˌzēn\ *n.* A flammable liquid obtained from petroleum and used in cleaning, dyeing, and painting and as a motor fuel.

be·queath \bē-ˈkwēth, -ˈkwēth\ *v.* **1** To give or leave by means of a will; as, to be *bequeathed* some money by an aunt. **2** To hand down; to leave behind; as, knowledge *bequeathed* to later times. — **be·queath·al** \-l\ *n.*

be·quest \bē-ˈkwest\ *n.* **1** The act of bequeathing. **2** Something which has been given or left by a person in his will.

be·rate \bē-ˈrāt\ *v.;* **be·rat·ed; be·rat·ing.** To scold violently.

be·reave \bə-ˈrēv\ *v.;* **be·reaved** \-ˈrēvd\ or **be·reft** \-ˈreft\; **be·reav·ing.** To deprive of some cherished person or thing, especially by death; as, a woman recently *bereaved* of her husband; to be almost *bereft* of one's senses by fright.

be·reave·ment \bə-ˈrēv-mənt\ *n.* The condition or the fact of being bereaved; especially, the loss of a loved one by death.

be·ret \bə-'rā\ *n.* A round, flat, visorless cap of wool or similar soft material.

berg \'bərg\ *n.* An iceberg.

ber·i·beri \ˌber-ē-'ber-ē\ *n.* A deficiency disease, common in Oriental countries, in which nerves, digestive organs, and heart become inflamed or degenerated and which results from lack of vitamin B in the diet.

beret

berke·li·um \'bərk-lē-əm\ *n.* An artificially prepared radioactive chemical element.

ber·ry \'ber-ē\ *n.; pl.* **ber·ries.** **1** Any small pulpy fruit like the strawberry, the raspberry, or the blueberry. **2** The dry seed or kernel of certain plants; as, the coffee *berry.* — *v.;* **ber·ried; ber·ry·ing.** **1** To produce berries. **2** To gather or look for berries; as, to go *berrying.*

ber·serk \bər-'sərk, bər-'zərk, 'bər-ˌsərk\ *n.* A berserker. — *adj.* Frenzied; as, a *berserk* lunatic. — *adv.* In frenzied rage; as, to run *berserk* through the streets.

ber·serk·er \-r\ *n.* One of a class of warriors in Norse folklore who in the frenzy of battle foamed at the mouth and bit their shields, howled like wolves or growled like bears, and who it was believed could not be conquered.

berth \'bərth\ *n.* **1** A bed on a ship, a train, or an airplane; a bunk. **2** A position; a job; an appointment; as, to win a *berth* on the football team. **3** A place where a ship lies when at anchor or at a wharf. — *v.* To bring or come to a berth, as a ship.

ber·yl \'ber-əl\ *n.* A very hard green or greenish-blue mineral of which the emerald and the aquamarine are transparent varieties.

be·ryl·li·um \bə-'ril-ē-əm\ *n.* A rare metallic chemical element that occurs always in combination.

be·seech \bə-'sēch\ *v.;* **be·sought** \-'sȯt\; **be·seech·ing.** To ask earnestly; to beg; to implore. — **be·seech·ing·ly,** *adv.*

be·seem \bē-'sēm\ *v.* To be proper or fitting for; to become. It does not *beseem* a child to correct his elders.

be·set \bē-'set\ *v.;* **be·set; be·set·ting.** **1** To attack from all sides. **2** To hem in or surround; as, a task *beset* with difficulties.

be·set·ting \bē-'set-ing\ *adj.* Persistently attacking; constantly present; as, a *besetting* danger. Undernourishment is a *besetting* problem in many parts of the world.

be·shrew \bē-'shrü\ *v. Archaic.* To call down evil upon; to curse.

be·side \bə-'sīd\ *adv.* Besides. — *prep.* **1** At or by the side of; near by; as, a house *beside* the river. **2** Compared with. The cost of repairing the house would be small *beside* that of building a new one. **3** In addition to; besides. **4** Away from; to the side of; as, *beside* the point; *beside* the question. — **beside oneself.** Out of one's wits or senses; crazy; as, to be *beside oneself* with worry.

be·sides \bə-'sīdz\ *adv.* In addition; also; as, to have ice cream and cake at the party, and candy *besides.* — *prep.* In addition to; other than. Many *besides* children like fairy tales.

be·siege \bē-'sēj\ *v.* **1** To surround with armed forces for the purpose of capturing; to lay siege to. **2** To crowd around; as, to *besiege* a baseball hero for his autograph. — **be·sieg·er** \-r\ *n.*

be·smear \bē-'smir\ *v.* To smear over.

be·smirch \bē-'smərch\ *v.* To smirch; to soil.

be·som \'bēz-m\ *n.* A broom made of twigs.

besought. Past tense and past part. of *beseech.*

be·spat·ter \bē-'spat-r\ *v.* To soil by spattering; to spatter; as, all *bespattered* with muddy water.

be·speak \bē-'spēk\ *v.;* **be·spoke** \-'spōk\ or *archaic* **be·spake** \-'spāk\; **be·spo·ken** \-'spōk-n\ or **bespoke; be·speak·ing.** **1** To speak for beforehand; to arrange for ahead of time; as, to *bespeak* a seat for a concert. **2** To indicate by appearances; to show; as, manners that *bespeak* good training.

best \'best\ *adj.* Superlative of *good.* **1** Good or useful in the highest degree; most excellent. **2** Most; largest; as, the *best* part of a week. — *adv.* Superlative of *well.* **1** In the most excellent way; as, the girl who sang *best.* **2** Most; to the fullest extent. The boy *best* able to do the work will be given first chance. — *n.* **1** A person or a thing that is best. Even the *best* of us make mistakes. **2** The greatest effort; the utmost; as, to do one's *best.* — *v.* To get the better of; to overcome; to defeat; as, to be able to *best* all one's schoolmates at swimming.

be·stead \bē-'sted\ *adj. Archaic.* Placed; situated; especially, put in peril; beset.

bes·tial \'bes-chəl\ *adj.* **1** Of or belonging to beasts. **2** Like a beast; brutish; beastly; as, *bestial* manners.

be·stir \bē-'stər\ *v.;* **be·stirred; be·stir·ring.** To stir up; to rouse to action; as, to *bestir* oneself early in the morning.

be·stow \bē-'stō\ *v.* To give; to grant; as, to *bestow* money on a beggar; sunshine and rain and other benefits *bestowed* by nature. — **be·stow·al** \-əl\ *n.*

be·strew \bē-'strü\ *v.;* **be·strewed** \-'strüd\; **be·strewed** \-'strüd\ or **be·strewn** \-'strün\; **be·strew·ing.** To strew or scatter over; to lie scattered over. Leaves *bestrewed* the path.

be·stride \bē-'strīd\ *v.;* **be·strode** \-'strōd\; **be·strid·den** \-'strid-n\; **be·strid·ing** \-'strīd-ing\. **1** To ride, sit, or stand astride of; as, to *bestride* a horse. The victor *bestrode* his foe. **2** To stride over or across; as, to *bestride* a threshold.

bet \'bet\ *n.* **1** An agreement requiring the person whose guess proves wrong about the result of a contest or the outcome of some other event to give something to the person whose guess proves right. **2** The making of such an agreement; a wager. **3** The money or thing risked; as, a *bet* of ten cents. — *v.;* **bet** or **bet·ted; bet·ting.** **1** To risk upon the outcome of some contest or event. **2** To be certain enough to bet. I *bet* it will rain tonight.

be·take \bē-'tāk\ *v.;* **be·took** \-'tu̇k\; **be·tak·en** \-'tāk-n\; **be·tak·ing.** To go — used with a reflexive pronoun; as, to *betake* oneself to a restaurant for dinner.

be·tel \'bēt-l\ *n.* A climbing species of pepper, the leaves of which, wrapped about the orange-colored fruit (**betel nut**) of an Asiatic palm, are chewed in Eastern countries.

beth·el \'beth-l\ *n.* [From Hebrew *beth'el* meaning "house of God".] A place of worship, especially for seamen.

be·think \bē-'thingk\ *v.;* **be·thought** \-'tho̅t\; **be·think·ing.** To remember; to call to mind; to remind (oneself); to reflect; as, to *bethink* oneself of a good excuse.

be·tide \bē-'tīd\ *v.;* **be·tid·ed; be·tid·ing.** To happen; to happen to; to befall. Woe *betide* the one who breaks the rule!

be·times \bē-'tīmz\ *adv.* In good time; early.

be·to·ken \bē-'tōk-n\ *v.* To be a sign of; to indicate. Those black clouds *betoken* a storm.

betook. Past tense of *betake.*

be·tray \bē-'trā\ *v.* **1** To give over to an enemy by treachery or fraud; as, to *betray* a fort. **2** To be unfaithful or treacherous to; to fail; as, to *betray* one's trust. **3** To lead into error, sin, or danger; to deceive; to seduce; as, a person *betrayed* by the company he keeps. **4** To show or reveal, especially unintentionally; as, to *betray* one's ignorance. **5** To tell in violation of a trust; as, to *betray* a secret. — **be·tray·al** \-əl\ *n.* — **be·tray·er** \-ər\ *n.*

be·troth \bē-'tro̅th, -'trōth\ *v.* To promise to marry; to engage to marry; as, a man and woman who are *betrothed.*

be·troth·al \bē-'tro̅th-l, -'trōth-l\ *n.* **1** An engagement to be married. **2** The act or ceremony of becoming engaged to be married.

be·trothed \bē-'tro̅tht, -'trōthd\ *n.* **1** A person engaged to be married. **2** The person to whom one is engaged.

bet·ter \'bet-r\ *adj.* Comparative of *good.* **1** Preferable to something else; more satisfactory; superior. **2** Greater; larger; as, the *better* part of a week. **3** Improved in health; as, to feel *better* after being sick. — *adv.* Comparative of *well.* **1** In a superior or more excellent way. My brother swims *better* than I do. **2** In a higher or greater degree; more. No man could have been *better* loved. — *n.* **1** A person or a thing that is preferable to something else; as, the *better* of two bicycles; a change for the *better.* **2** An advantage or superiority. My brother got the *better* of me in the fight. — *v.* **1** To improve. The firm tried to *better* working conditions. **2** To surpass; to excel. This *betters* our expectations. — **had better.** Should; ought to. The boys *had better* go immediately after school.

bet·ter·ment \'bet-r-mənt\ *n.* Improvement.

bet·tor or **bet·ter** \'bet-r\ *n.* A person who bets.

be·tween \bə-'twēn\ *prep.* **1** In the space, time, or amount that separates one thing from another; as, a house *between* two trees; to go *between* nine and ten o'clock. The bill will be *between* four and five dollars. **2** Separating from each other; as, the difference *between* soccer and football. **3** From one to another of. A bus runs *between* the town and the beach. **4** Connecting; joining; as, a bond *between* friends. **5** In common to; by joint action of. *Between* them, the two children ate all of the sandwiches. **6** Involving the mutual or opposite action of; as, rivalry *between* two persons. **7** Out of; as, to choose *between* two things. — *adv.* In a position between others.

be·twixt \bə-'twikst\ *prep.* or *adv.* Between. — **betwixt and between.** In a midway position; neither one thing nor the other; as, to leave the matter *betwixt and between.*

bev·el \'bev-l\ *n.* A slant or slope of one surface or line against another. — *v.;* **bev·eled** or **bev·elled; bev·el·ing** or **bev·el·ling** \-l(-)ing\. **1** To cut or shape an edge or surface so as to be slanting or sloping against another; as, to *bevel* the edge of a board. **2** To incline; to slant; as, a surface that *bevels.* — *adj.* Slanting; oblique; as, a *bevel* edge.

bev·er·age \'bev-r(-)ij\ *n.* Any liquid that is drunk for food or for pleasure; drink.

bevy \'bev-ē\ *n.* A group or cluster; as, a *bevy* of girls.

be·wail \bē-'wāl\ *v.* To express deep sorrow for; to lament; to wail over; as, to *bewail* the loss of a pet.

be·ware \bē-'war, -'wer\ *v.* To be on one's guard; to be cautious or careful — used chiefly either as a command or in the infinitive form. *Beware* of the dog! We were warned to *beware* of the icy pavements. Woodsmen must *beware* that they do not become lost.

be·wil·der \bē-'wild-r\ *v.;* **be·wil·dered; be·wil·der·ing** \-r(-)ing\. To confuse; to fill with uncertainty; as, a child *bewildered* by the unfamiliar streets of a strange city. — For synonyms see *puzzle.*

be·wil·der·ment \bē-'wild-r-mənt\ *n.* The condition of being bewildered; confusion; uncertainty.

be·witch \bē-'wich\ *v.* **1** To gain an influence over by means of magic or witchcraft; to put under a spell; as, to act as if one were *bewitched.* We no longer believe that one person can be *bewitched* by another. **2** To charm; to fascinate.

be·witch·ing \bē-'wich-ing\ *adj.* Charming; fascinating; captivating; as, a *bewitching* smile. — **be·witch·ing·ly,** *adv.*

be·wray \bē-'rā\ *v. Archaic.* To betray; to reveal; to disclose.

be·yond \bē-'änd\ *adv.* At a distance; yonder; as, to travel on to places lying *beyond.* — *prep.* **1** Farther away than. *Beyond* the school was the athletic field. **2** Out of reach of; as, to be *beyond* help. **3** In a greater degree or amount than. The sunset was lovely *beyond* description. — *n.* That which is at a distance, or yonder.

Bhu·tan·ese \ˌbüt-n-'ēz, -'ēs\ *adj.* Of or relating to

Bhutan. — *n.* **1** *sing. and pl.* A native of Bhutan. **2** One of the languages of Bhutan.

bi- \bī\. A prefix that can mean: two, twice, or doubly, as in *biannual, biennial, bilateral, bisect.*

bi·an·nu·al \(')bī-'an-yə-wəl, -'an-yəl\ *adj.* Occurring twice a year. — **bi·an·nu·al·ly** \-yə-lē, -yə-wə-lē\ *adv.*

bi·as \'bī-əs\ *n.* **1** A seam, cut, or stitching running in a slant across cloth. **2** An inclination to feel or act in a certain way; tendency; prejudice; as, to show a *bias* against those of different background from one's own. — *v.;* **bi·ased** or **bi·assed** \'bī-əst\; **bi·as·ing** or **bi·as·sing.** To give a bias to; to prejudice; as, to be *biased* by ignorance.

bib \'bib\ *n.* **1** A cloth tied under a child's chin to protect the clothes. **2** The upper part of an apron.

Bi·ble \'bīb-l\ *n.* [From Latin *biblia,* there borrowed from Greek *biblia* originally meaning "books".] **1** The book made up of the writings accepted by Christians as inspired by God. **2** A book containing the sacred writings of any religion.

Bib·li·cal \'bib-lik-l\ *adj.* Relating to, drawn from, or found in, the Bible — often written with a small letter.

bib·li·og·ra·pher \ˌbib-lē-'äg-rəf-r\ *n.* **1** A writer of a bibliography or bibliographies. **2** An expert in bibliography.

bib·li·og·ra·phy \ˌbib-lē-'äg-rə-fē\ *n.; pl.* **bib·li·og·ra·phies.** **1** A list of writings about an author or a subject. **2** The study of books and manuscripts with respect to the dates and circumstances of their composition or publication and their later history. — **bib·li·o·graph·ic** \ˌbib-lē-ə-'graf-ik\ or **bib·li·o·graph·i·cal** \-ik-l\ *adj.*

bib·u·lous \'bib-yə-ləs\ *adj.* **1** Absorbent, as a sponge. **2** Fond of alcoholic drinks.

bi·cam·er·al \(')bī-'kam-r(-)əl\ *adj.* Consisting of two chambers, or legislative branches; as, a *bicameral* legislature. The Congress of the United States is *bicameral.*

bi·car·bon·ate of soda \bī-'kärb-n-ət, -'kärb-\. A white crystalline salt used in making baking powders, in cooking, and in medicine.

bi·cen·ten·ni·al \ˌbī-ˌsen-'ten-ē-əl, ˌbīs-n-'ten-\ *adj.* Relating to or marking a two-hundredth anniversary. — *n.* A two-hundredth anniversary or its celebration.

bi·ceps \'bī-ˌseps\ *n.; pl.* **bi·ceps·es** \-ˌsep-səz\. The large muscle of the front of the upper arm.

bick·er \'bik-r\ *v.;* **bick·ered; bick·er·ing** \-r(-)ing\. To quarrel peevishly; to wrangle. — *n.* Peevish quarreling; a wrangle.

bi·cus·pid \(')bī-'kəs-pəd\ *n.* Either of the two double-pointed teeth between the canines and the molars on each side of each jaw of a person. — *adj.* Also **bi·cus·pi·date** \-pə-ˌdāt\. Having or ending in two points, as a tooth or a leaf.

bi·cy·cle \'bī-ˌsik-l\ *n.* A light vehicle having two wheels, one behind the other, a handlebar for steering, and pedals by which it is propelled. — *v.;* **bi·cy·cled; bi·cy·cling** \-l(-)ing\. To ride a bicycle. — **bi·cy·cler** \-lər\ *n.*

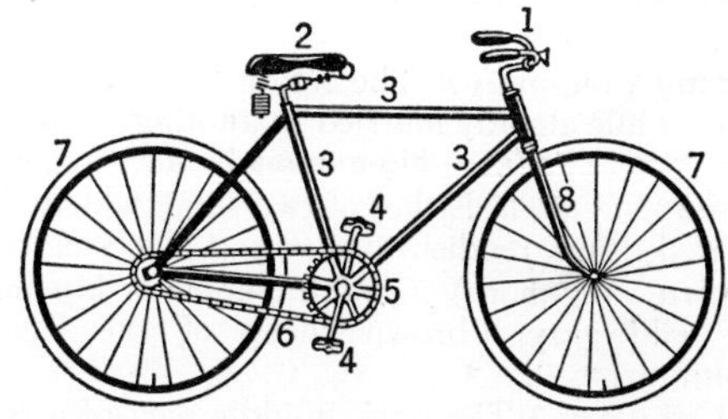

bicycle: *1* handlebar, *2* saddle, *3, 3, 3* frame, *4, 4* pedals, *5* sprocket wheel, *6* chain, *7, 7* tires, *8* fork

bi·cy·clist \'bī-ˌsik-ləst\ *n.* One who rides a bicycle; a bicycler.

bid \'bid\ *v.;* **bade** \'bad, 'bād\ or **bid; bid·den** \'bid-n\ or **bid; bid·ding.** **1** To order; to command. A soldier is expected to do as he is *bidden.* **2** To express a greeting, a welcome, or a farewell. Mother *bade* her guests good-by. **3** To make an offer for something; especially, to offer a certain price at an auction; as, to *bid* three dollars for a chair — in this sense and sense 5 below, past tense and past part. *bid.* **4** To invite; to request to come; as, to *bid* a person to a feast. **5** In card games, to state what one proposes to undertake, such as the winning of a certain number of tricks. — **bid fair.** To seem likely. The weather *bids fair* to be good tomorrow. — **bid up.** At an auction, to raise the price of by bids; as, an antique that was *bid up* to 100 dollars. — *n.* **1** A bidding; an offer of a price, as at an auction. **2** In card games, a statement by a player of what he proposes to undertake, such as the winning of a certain number of tricks. **3** A person's turn at bidding. It is your *bid.* **4** An invitation; as, to receive a *bid* to a party. **5** An effort to win, achieve, or attract. The team made a strong *bid* for the championship.

bid·der \'bid-r\ *n.* One who bids.

bide \'bīd\ *v.;* **bode** \'bōd\ or **bid·ed** \'bīd-əd\; **bid·ed; bid·ing.** To wait or wait for. — **bide one's time.** To wait for a favorable opportunity.

bi·en·ni·al \bī-'en-ē-əl\ *adj.* **1** Taking place once in two years; as, a *biennial* election. **2** Lasting two years, producing only leaves the first year and storing up food in the roots or other organs to be used the following year in the development of fruit and seed; as, a *biennial* plant. — *n.* **1** Something that takes place once in two years. **2** A biennial plant.

bier \'bir\ *n.* A frame on which a coffin is placed or on which it is carried to the grave.

bi·fo·cal \(')bī-'fōk-l\ *adj.* Having two focuses, as an eyeglass lens having one part for seeing near objects and another part for seeing at distances.

big \'big\ *adj.;* **big·ger; big·gest.** **1** Large, as in size, bulk, or extent; as, a *big* load; a *big* city. **2** Full and loud; as, a man with a *big* voice. **3** Important; imposing; as, a *big* man in the town government. A birthday is a *big* day in a child's life.

big·a·mist \'big-m-əst\ *n.* One that practices bigamy.

big·a·my \'big-m-ē\ *n.* The action of marrying one person while already married to another. — **big·a·mous** \-m-əs\ *adj.* — **big·a·mous·ly**, *adv.*

big·eye \'big-ˌī\ *n.* Either of two small widely distributed fishes, reddish to silvery, valued as food.

big·horn \'big-ˌhórn\ *n.; pl.* **big·horns** or **big·horn.** The wild grayish-brown sheep of the Rocky Mountains.

bight \'bīt\ *n.* **1** The slack, middle part of a rope when it is fastened at both ends; a loop or double part of a bent rope. **2** A bend or curve, as in a river. **3** A bend in a coast or the bay it forms.

big·ot \'big-ət\ *n.* A person who obstinately and unreasonably believes in his own ideas and opinions.

big·ot·ed \'big-ət-əd\ *adj.* Obstinately and blindly attached to a belief, opinion, or practice; lacking tolerance for the ideas and opinions of others.

big·ot·ry \'big-ə-trē\ *n.; pl.* **big·ot·ries. 1** The point of view or attitude of a bigot; obstinate or unreasoning attachment to one's own beliefs and opinions. **2** Acts or beliefs due to such an attitude or attachment.

big top. The main tent of a circus; the circus as a whole.

big wheel. *Slang.* A person of importance; one in authority.

big·wig \'big-ˌwig\ *n.* An important person.

bike \'bīk\ *n.* A bicycle. — *v.;* **biked**; **bik·ing.** To bicycle.

bi·lat·er·al \(')bī-'lat-r-əl, -'la-trəl\ *adj.* **1** Having two sides, especially two corresponding sides. **2** Having to do with two sides or parties; as, a *bilateral* treaty. — **bi·lat·er·al·ly** \-'lat-r-ə-lē, -'la-trə-lē\ *adv.*

bile \'bīl\ *n.* **1** A thick, bitter, yellow or greenish fluid supplied by the liver to aid in digestion. **2** Anger; ill-humor.

bilge \'bilj\ *n.* **1** The bulging part of a cask or barrel. **2** The part of a ship's hull that is between the bottom and the point where the sides go straight up. **3** Bilge water. — *v.;* **bilged**; **bilg·ing. 1** To burst or to make a hole in the bilge of a ship. **2** To leak in the bilge.

bilge water. The water that collects in the bottom of a ship.

bil·i·ary \'bil-ē-ˌer-ē, 'bil-yər-ē\ *adj.* Relating to or conveying bile; as, a *biliary* duct.

bi·lin·gual \(')bī-'ling-gwəl\ *adj.* Of, expressed in, or using two languages; as, a *bilingual* dictionary. Children of first-generation immigrants are often *bilingual.*

bil·ious \'bil-yəs\ *adj.* **1** Of or relating to the bile. **2** Suffering from or resulting from a disordered functioning of the liver. **3** Irritable; ill-natured; as, a person with a *bilious* disposition. — **bil·ious·ly**, *adv.*

bill \'bil\ *n.* **1** The beak of a bird, consisting of the jaws and their horny covering. **2** A similar beak in other animals, as in a turtle. — *v.* To touch beaks, as doves; to show affection. — **bill and coo** \'kü\. To exchange caresses.

bills, 1

bill \'bil\ *n.* **1** A draft of a law presented to a legislature for consideration; a proposed law; as, to introduce a *bill* in Congress. **2** A written or printed paper advertising something; a placard; a poster; a handbill. **3** A program of a theatrical entertainment or the entertainment itself. **4** A record of goods sold, services performed, or work done, with the price or charge; as, a grocery *bill.* **5** A promissory note; especially, a piece of paper money, as a bank note or a treasury note. **6** In law, a written statement of some wrong that one person has suffered from another or of some breach of law by a person. — *v.* **1** To make a bill or list of; as, to *bill* the day's sales. **2** To send a bill to; as, to *bill* a customer for his purchases. **3** To advertise by bills or posters; as, to *bill* goods that are on sale.

bill·board \'bil-ˌbōrd, -ˌbórd\ *n.* A board or a flat surface on which notices or advertisements are posted.

bil·let \'bil-ət\ *n.* **1** A written order, especially one by a military officer, directing a person to provide lodging for a soldier. **2** The lodging provided in accordance with such an order. **3** An appointment; a position. — *v.* To assign a billet to; to lodge.

bil·let \'bil-ət\ *n.* **1** A small stick of wood, as for firewood. **2** A bar of metal, especially of iron or steel.

bil·let-doux \ˌbil-ˌā-'dü\ *n.; pl.* **bil·lets-doux** \-ˌā-'düz\. A love letter or note.

bill·fold \'bil-ˌfōld\ *n.* A folding pocketbook for paper money.

bil·liards \'bil-yərdz\ *n.* A game played with solid balls (**billiard balls**) and a cue on a large oblong table (**billiard table**).

bil·lion \'bil-yən\ *n.* In American and French numbering, a thousand millions (1,000,000,000); in English and German numbering, a million millions (1,000,000,000,000).

bill of fare. A list of dishes in a restaurant that may be ordered at a meal.

bill of rights. 1 A statement of the rights and privileges claimed by a people. **2** [with capitals] The first ten amendments to the Constitution of the United States.

bil·low \'bil-ō\ *n.* **1** A great wave. **2** A mass, as of smoke or flame, surging or rolling like a great wave. — *v.* **1** To roll in great waves; as, the *billowing* ocean. **2** To bulge or swell out; as, sails that *billow* in the breeze.

bil·lowy \'bil-ə-wē\ *adj.;* **bil·low·i·er**; **bil·low·i·est.** Full of or resembling billows; rolling or swelling in or like waves.

bil·ly \'bil-ē\ *n.; pl.* **bil·lies.** A club, especially one carried by a policeman.

bi·man·u·al \(')bī-'man-yə-wəl, -'man-yəl\ *adj.* Done with or requiring the use of both hands. — **bi·man·u·al·ly** \-yə-lē, -yə-wə-lē\ *adv.*

bi·month·ly \(')bī-'mən(t)th-lē\ *adj.* **1** Occurring, coming, or done, once in two months. **2** Occurring, coming, or done twice a month. — *n.; pl.* **bi·month·lies.** A bimonthly magazine or other publication. — *adv.* **1** Once in two months. **2** Twice a month.

bin \'bin\ *n.* A box or an enclosed place used for storage; as, a coal *bin.*

bind \'bīnd\ *v.;* **bound** \'baund\; **bind·ing. 1** To tie up or fasten together, as with a cord or band; as, to *bind* wheat. **2** To hold, confine, or restrain by force of any kind; as, a river *bound* by ice; to be *bound* to another by ties of friendship and gratitude. **3** To stick together in a mass; as, to *bind* a road surface with tar. **4** To bandage; as, to *bind* a wound. **5** To protect or decorate by a band of material; as, to *bind* the edge of a dress. **6** To fasten together and enclose in a cover; as, to *bind* a book. **7** To place under an obligation to do something; as, to *bind* oneself by a vow. **8** To place under legal obligation to serve another person; as, to be *bound* as an apprentice.

bind·er \'bīnd-r\ *n.* **1** A person who performs an operation of binding something, as books. **2** A band or cord used for binding. **3** A substance that binds, as tar or cement. **4** A mechanical device or machine used for binding; especially, a harvesting machine that cuts grain and binds it into bundles. **5** A cover for holding together loose sheets of paper.

bind·ery \'bīnd-r(-)ē\ *n.; pl.* **bind·er·ies.** A place where books are bound.

bind·ing \'bīn-ding\ *n.* **1** The act of one that binds. **2** The material used to bind, such as braid for the edge of a coat. **3** The cover and the fastenings for the pages of a book. **4** A substance, as tar, used to bind a mixture.

bind·weed \'bīn-ˌdwēd\ *n.* A climbing plant with arrowhead-shaped leaves and slender stems that twine themselves around other plants.

bin·na·cle \'bin-ik-l\ *n.* A box or a stand containing a ship's compass and a lamp for use at night.

bin·oc·u·lar \bə-'näk-yəl-r, bī-\ *adj.* **1** Having to do with or using both eyes; as, *binocular* vision. **2** Made for the use of both eyes at once; as, a *binocular* microscope. — *n.* A binocular instrument; [in the plural] field glasses.

binoculars

bi·no·mi·al \(')bī-'nō-mē-əl\ *n.* **1** In algebra, an expression consisting of two terms connected by the sign plus (+) or minus (−). **2** In biology, a species name consisting of two terms, as *Quercus alba* (an American species of white oak). — *adj.* Consisting of or relating to binomials.

bi·og·ra·pher \bī-'äg-rəf-r\ *n.* A person who writes a biography.

bi·o·graph·i·cal \ˌbī-ə-'graf-ik-l\ *adj.* **1** Of or relating to biography; as, a *biographical* dictionary; *biographical* literature. **2** Of a kind suitable for or used in biography; of or relating to a person's life; as, *biographical* information required on an application form. — **bi·o·graph·i·cal·ly** \-ik-l(-)ē\ *adv.*

bi·og·ra·phy \bī-'äg-rə-fē\ *n.; pl.* **bi·og·ra·phies. 1** A written history of a person's life. **2** The literature that consists of biographical writings.

bi·o·log·i·cal \ˌbī-ə-'läj-ik-l\ *adj.* **1** Of or relating to life and living processes; as, *biological* forces. **2** Of or relating to the science of biology; as, *biological* supplies. — **bi·o·log·i·cal·ly** \-ik-l(-)ē\ *adv.*

biological warfare. Warfare in which disease germs are used against the enemy or chemicals are used to harm plant life in the enemy's country.

bi·ol·o·gist \bī-'äl-ə-jəst\ *n.* A person skilled in biology.

bi·ol·o·gy \bī-'äl-ə-jē\ *n.* The science which collects, studies, and explains facts about animals and plants.

bi·o·tin \'bī-ə-tən\ *n.* A substance in the vitamin-B complex that promotes growth, found especially in liver, yeast, and egg yolk.

bi·par·ti·san \(')bī-'pärt-əz-n, -əs-n, -'pårt-\ *adj.* Representing or made up of members of two parties; as, a *bipartisan* committee; a *bipartisan* foreign policy.

bi·par·tite \(')bī-'pär-ˌtīt, -'pår-\ *adj.* Having two parts, especially two corresponding parts.

bi·ped \'bī-ˌped\ *n.* A two-footed animal. Men and birds are *bipeds.*

bi·plane \'bī-ˌplān\ *n.* An airplane with two wings on each side of the body, one above the other.

birch \'bərch\ *n.* **1** A tree with hard wood and a smooth bark that can be peeled off in thin layers. **2** A birch stick or a bundle of birch twigs used as a whip. — *v.* To whip or flog with a birch. — **birch** \'bərch\ or **birch·en** \-n\ *adj.*

birch·bark \'bərch-ˌbärk, -ˌbårk\ *n.* The bark of any birch tree, used in making baskets and canoes.

bird \'bərd\ *n.* Any member of a class of warm-blooded, egg-laying animals that have wings and bodies covered with feathers. — *v.* To identify or observe wild birds in their natural environment; as, to go *birding.* — **bird·er** \-r\ *n.*

bird·bath \'bərd-ˌbath\ *n.* An artificial bath, usually in a garden, for birds to bathe in.

bird·house \'bərd-ˌhaus\ *n.; pl.* **bird·hous·es** \-ˌhau-zəz\. **1** A small house or box for birds to nest in. **2** A building where birds are exhibited.

bird·lime \'bərd-ˌlīm\ *n.* A sticky substance smeared on twigs to catch and hold small birds.

bird·man \'bərd-mən\ *n.; pl.* **bird·men** \-mən\. **1** One who deals with birds, as an ornithologist. **2** An aviator.

bird of paradise. A brilliantly colored plumed bird related to the crow, found in New Guinea and the adjacent islands.

bird of passage. A bird that migrates from one climate to another.

bird of prey. Any of a number of flesh-eating birds such as hawks, eagles, and owls.

bird·seed \'bərd-ˌsēd\ *n.* A mixture of small seeds, as those of hemp, millet, and certain grasses, used chiefly for feeding caged birds.

bird's-eye \'bərd-ˌzī\ *adj.* **1** Seen from above, as if by a flying bird; seen at a glance; not detailed; as, to get a *bird's-eye* view of a subject before studying it in detail. **2** Having spots resembling birds' eyes; as, *bird's-eye* maple.

bi·ret·ta \bə-'ret-ə\ *n.* A square cap having a crown divided into three, or sometimes four, projecting sections, worn by Roman Catholic clergy in one of four colors, white, scarlet, purple, and black, that signify rank in the church.

birth \'bərth\ *n.* **1** The act or fact of coming into life, or of being born; the act of bringing into life. **2** Beginning; origin; as, the *birth* of a nation. **3** A person's descent; as, a man of noble *birth.*

birth·day \'bərth-ˌdā\ *n.* **1** The day on which a person is born. **2** A day of origin or beginning. **3** The return each year of the date on which a person was born or something began; as, to have a party on one's tenth *birthday.*

birth·mark \'bərth-ˌmärk, -ˌmȧrk\ *n.* Any unusual spot or mark present on the skin at birth. — **birth·marked** \-ˌmärkt, -ˌmȧrkt\ *adj.*

birth·place \'bərth-ˌplās\ *n.* A place where a person was born or where something began.

birth·rate \'bərth-ˌrāt\ *n.* The number of births for every hundred or every thousand persons in a given area or group, during a given time.

birth·right \'bərth-ˌrīt\ *n.* Any right belonging to a person because of his birth.

birth·stone \'bərth-ˌstōn\ *n.* A precious stone associated with a certain month and considered to be specially appropriate to be worn by a person born in that month.

bis·cuit \'bis-kət\ *n.; pl.* **bis·cuits** or **bis·cuit. 1** A small cake of raised dough baked in an oven. **2** A crisp flat cake; a cracker.

bi·sect \'bī-ˌsekt, bī-'sekt\ *v.* **1** To divide or cut into two parts, especially into two equal parts. **2** To fork, as a road.

bi·sec·tor \'bī-ˌsekt-r, bī-'sekt-r\ *n.* One that bisects; especially, a line that bisects something, as an angle.

bish·op \'bish-əp\ *n.* **1** A clergyman of high rank who is the head of a church district. **2** One of the pieces in the game of chess.

bish·op·ric \'bish-əp-(ˌ)rik\ *n.* **1** The church district over which a bishop has charge; a diocese. **2** The office or rank of a bishop.

bis·muth \'biz-məth\ *n.* A brittle, grayish-white metallic chemical element with a reddish tinge, used chiefly in alloys and in medicine.

bi·son \'bīs-n, 'bīz-n\ *n.* A large, shaggy-maned ox-like animal with short horns and heavy, humped forequarters; a buffalo.

bit \'bit\ *n.* **1** A part of a bridle that is put in the horse's mouth. **2** A tool with a cutting end or edge used for drilling or boring.

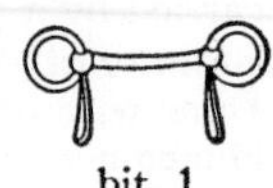

bit, 1

bit \'bit\ *n.* **1** A small piece or quantity of anything; a little; as, a *bit* of food. **2** Somewhat; as, a *bit* of a fool. **3** A short time; as, to rest a *bit.*

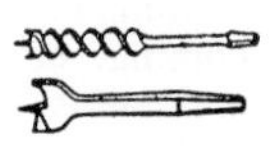

bits, 2

bitch \'bich\ *n.* A female dog.

bite \'bīt\ *v.;* **bit** \'bit\; **bit·ten** \'bit-n\ or **bit** \'bit\; **bit·ing** \'bīt-ing\. **1** To seize, grip, or cut into with the teeth or as if with teeth; as, to *bite* an apple. A steam shovel *bites* into the earth. **2** To wound or sting with any part of the mouth, as the fangs of a poisonous snake. **3** To cut or pierce, as with a sharp-edged instrument or weapon. The sword *bit* into the flesh. **4** To cause to smart; to sting. Pepper *bites* the mouth. **5** To take a bait, as fish; to respond to a lure. **6** To grip so as to hold. The anchor *bit* into the bottom. — *n.* **1** A seizing of something with the teeth or the mouth. **2** A wound made by biting; a sting; as, a mosquito *bite.* **3** The amount taken by the teeth or mouth at one time; as, a *bite* of food. **4** The grip by which something is seized or pierced. The turtle would not release its *bite.* **5** A sharp or biting sensation; as, the *bite* of the cold wind.

bit·ing \'bīt-ing\ *adj.* Sharp; cutting; sarcastic; as, *biting* remarks.

bitten. A past part. of *bite.*

bit·ter \'bit-r\ *adj.* **1** Sharp, biting, and unpleasant to the taste. **2** Disagreeable; hard to bear; painful; as, a *bitter* insult; a *bitter* disappointment. **3** Arising from anger, distress, or sorrow; as, *bitter* tears. **4** Piercingly harsh; stinging; as, a *bitter* wind. — **bit·ter·ly**, *adv.*

bit·tern \'bit-rn\ *n.* A small heron that has soft streaked plumage and that nests on the ground, noted for its booming cry.

bit·ter·sweet \'bit-r-ˌswēt\ *n.* **1** A poisonous vine with purple flowers and red berries. **2** A woody climbing plant with orange seedcases that open and show the red-coated seeds. — *adj.* Sweet and bitter at the same time.

bi·tu·men \bə-'tü-mən, bī-, -'tyü-\ *n.* Any of a number of flammable mineral substances, such as asphalt, naphtha, and petroleum.

bi·tu·mi·nous \bə-'tü-mə-nəs, bī-, -'tyü-\ *adj.* Like or containing bitumen. — **bituminous coal**. A soft coal that gives off much smoke when burned.

bi·valve \'bī-ˌvalv\ *n.* An animal with a shell composed of two separate parts that open and shut, usually on a hinge, as a clam or an oyster.

biv·ouac \'biv-ˌwak\ *n.* An encampment for a short stay, as for a single night, usually without tents or other shelter. — *v.;* **biv·ouacked**; **biv·ouack·ing**. To encamp for a short stay without tents or housing.

bi·week·ly \(')bī-'wēk-lē\ *adj.* **1** Occurring, coming, or done once in two weeks; fortnightly. **2** Occurring, coming, or done twice a week; semiweekly. — *n.; pl.* **bi·week·lies.** A biweekly publication. — *adv.* **1** Every two weeks. **2** Twice a week.

bi·year·ly \(')bī-'yir-lē\ *adj.* **1** Occurring twice a year; biannual. **2** Occurring once in two years; biennial.

bi·zarre \bə-'zär, -'zȧr\ *adj.* Strikingly unusual or odd in appearance, especially in fashion, design, or color; as, the *bizarre* costumes of gypsies.

blab \'blab\ *v.;* **blabbed; blab·bing.** To talk too much; to tell secrets; to tattle. — *n.* A person who blabs; a tattletale.

black \'blak\ *adj.* **1** Of the color of soot or coal. **2** Without light; very dark; as, a *black* night. **3** Having dark skin, hair, and eyes; as, the *black* races of mankind. **4** Soiled; dirty. **5** Dismal; gloomy; as, *black* despair. **6** Threatening; sullen; as, *black* looks. **7** Evil; wicked; as, *black* deeds; *black* magic. — *n.* **1** The color of coal; the opposite of white; the darkest color. **2** Black clothes; as, dressed in *black*. **3** A Negro; a person of any dark-skinned race. — *v.* **1** To make black; to soil; to dirty. **2** To polish with blacking; as, to *black* a pair of shoes. — **black out. 1** To make dark, especially by putting out all lights as a protection against air raids in wartime. **2** To lose consciousness, or to lose the ability to see, for a short period.

black·a·moor \'blak-m-,ůr\ *n.* A black person; especially, a Negro.

black-and-blue \'blak-n-'blü\ *adj.* Darkly discolored, as from a bruise.

black art. The art of magic as practiced by conjurers and witches.

black·ball \'blak-,bȯl\ *n.* **1** A black object used to cast a negative vote. **2** Any secret negative vote. — *v.* To vote against; especially, to vote to exclude a person, as from membership in a club.

black·ber·ry \'blak-,ber-ē\ *n.; pl.* **black·ber·ries. 1** The small pulpy fruit of any of several kinds of bushes, which becomes black or purple when ripe. **2** Any bush that bears these berries.

black·bird \'blak-,bərd\ *n.* **1** Any of a number of North American birds so called because the males are largely black, as the grackle or the swamp-breeding **red-winged blackbird** \-,wingd\, which has a patch of bright scarlet on the shoulders. **2** A common thrush of England.

black·board \'blak-,bōrd, -,bȯrd\ *n.* Any dark, smooth surface, such as one of slate, used for writing or drawing on with chalk or crayons.

black book. A book containing a blacklist. — **in one's black books.** Out of one's favor; in disgrace with a person.

black·cap \'blak-,kap\ *n.* **1** Any of various black-crowned birds, as the chickadee. **2** A black-fruited raspberry of eastern North America.

black·en \'blak-n\ *v.* **1** To make or become black; to darken. **2** To soil; to dirty. **3** To injure the reputation of; to defame; as, to *blacken* a person's character.

black-eyed Su·san \'blak-,īd 'süz-n\. A daisy with deep-yellow or orange petals and a dark center.

black-eyed Susan

black·fish \'blak-,fish\ *n.; pl.* **black·fish** or **black·fish·es. 1** Any of several small, toothed whales. **2** Any of various dark-colored fishes, as the black sea bass.

black flag. The flag of a pirate, often bearing a skull and crossbones.

black·guard \'blag-rd, -,ärd, -,ȧrd\ *n.* A vicious scoundrel. — *v.* To abuse with bad language; to revile. — **black·guard·ly,** *adj.* or *adv.*

black·head \'blak-,hed\ *n.* A small, black-topped lump of fatty matter in a pore of the skin, especially on the face.

black·ing \'blak-ing\ *n.* A preparation that makes things black, as a paste for blacking shoes or stoves.

black·ish \'blak-ish\ *adj.* Somewhat black.

black·jack \'blak-,jak\ *n.* **1** A small, leather-covered club with a flexible handle. **2** A common oak of the eastern United States, with a black bark. — *v.* To hit with a blackjack.

black lead \'led\. Graphite.

black·list \'blak-,list\ *n.* A list of persons regarded as suspicious or undesirable in some way. — *v.* To put on a blacklist.

black·ly \'blak-lē\ *adv.* In a black manner; darkly; gloomily; threateningly.

black·mail \'blak-,māl\ *n.* **1** A payment of money forced from a person by a threat to reveal some secret information that will bring trouble and disgrace upon him. **2** The getting of money, or an attempt to get money, by the use of trouble-making threats. — *v.* To force, or attempt to force, to pay blackmail. — **black·mail·er** \-r\ *n.*

black mark. A mark placed beside a person's name to record failure, bad conduct, or other fault.

black market. Trade in violation of government controls, as price controls or official currency exchange rates, or illegal trade in government property. — **black mar·ket·er** \'märk-ət-r, 'mȧrk-\ or **black mar·ke·teer** \,märk-ə-'tir, ,mȧrk-\.

black·out \'blak-,aůt\ *n.* **1** A period of darkness enforced as a precaution against air raids in wartime. **2** A period of unconsciousness, as one sometimes experienced by an airplane pilot during violent changes of speed or direction.

black·smith \'blak-,smith\ *n.* A workman who shapes iron by heating it and then hammering it on an iron block.

black·snake \'blak-,snāk\ *n.* or **black snake. 1** Either of two dark-colored, harmless snakes common in the United States. **2** A long braided whip of rawhide.

black·thorn \'blak-,thȯrn\ *n.* A European thorny tree of the same family as the peach and plum, bearing small yellow or reddish plumlike fruits and having a very hard wood that is often used for walking sticks.

black·top \'blak-ˌtäp\ *n.* A blackish road surface used for highways, parking lots, and play areas. — *v.;* **black·topped; black·top·ping.** To cover with blacktop; as, a *blacktopped* playground.

black widow. The female of a poisonous American spider, so named because of its shining black body and its habit of eating its mate.

blad·der \'blad-r\ *n.* **1** In persons and animals, a bag or sac into which the urine passes from the kidneys. **2** Something like a bladder; especially, a bag or container that can be filled with air or gas; as, the *bladder* of a football.

blad·der·wort \'blad-r-ˌwərt, -ˌwȯrt\ *n.* A slender plant growing in water or on wet shores, with insect-catching bladders on the stem, scalelike leaves, and irregular yellow or purple flowers.

blade \'blād\ *n.* **1** A leaf of a plant, especially of a grass. **2** The broadened part of a leaf. **3** Anything that widens out like the blade of a leaf; as, the *blade* of an oar; a shoulder *blade.* **4** The cutting part of an instrument, a tool, or a machine; as, the *blade* of a knife or of a sword. **5** A sword. **6** A smart or dashing fellow; as, a gay *blade.*

blam·a·ble \'blā-məb-l\ *adj.* Deserving blame; faulty. — **blam·a·bly** \-mə-blē\ *adv.*

blame \'blām\ *v.;* **blamed; blam·ing. 1** To find fault with; to express disapproval of. **2** To hold responsible. The wrong boy was *blamed* for the broken window. — For synonyms see *censure.* — *n.* **1** Expression of disapproval; as, to receive both *blame* and praise. **2** Responsibility for something that fails; fault; as, to take the *blame* for the defeat.

blame·less \'blām-ləs\ *adj.* Free from blame or fault. The jury found the driver of the car *blameless* for the accident. — **blame·less·ly,** *adv.*

blame·wor·thy \'blām-ˌwər-t͟hē\ *adj.* Deserving blame.

blanch \'blanch\ *v.* **1** To take the color out of and make white; to bleach; as, to *blanch* cloth. **2** To whiten by scalding the skin off; as, to *blanch* almonds. **3** To whiten by keeping the light from; as, to *blanch* celery. **4** To make pale; to become pale; as, to *blanch* with fear.

bland \'bland\ *adj.* **1** Smooth and soothing in manner; gentle; as, a *bland* smile. **2** Having soft and soothing qualities; not irritating; as, a *bland* oil; a *bland* diet. — **bland·ly,** *adv.*

blan·dish \'blan-dish\ *v.* To flatter; to coax; to wheedle.

blan·dish·ment \'blan-dish-mənt\ *n.* Speech or action that flatters or coaxes; [in the plural] soft words and artful caresses.

blank \'blangk\ *adj.* **1** Without writing, printing, or marks; as, a *blank* sheet of paper. **2** Having empty spaces to be filled in; as, a *blank* form. **3** Appearing dazed or confused; expressionless; as, a *blank* look. **4** Empty; fruitless; as, a *blank* day. **5** Lacking variety; lacking lively expression of interest; as, a *blank* face. **6** Absolute; downright; as, a *blank* refusal. **7** Not shaped into finished form; as, a *blank* key. — *n.* **1** An empty space, as in a paper, or a period of time in which nothing happens. There was nothing but a *blank* where the advertisement should have been. **2** A sheet, card, or document with empty spaces to be filled in. **3** A piece of material partly shaped, to be finished into something by further labor. — *v.* In games, to prevent from scoring. The team was *blanked* twice in succession. — **blank·ly,** *adv.*

blan·ket \'blangk-ət\ *n.* **1** A heavy, woven covering, often of wool, used for beds. **2** A covering of any kind; as, a horse *blanket;* a *blanket* of snow. — *v.* To cover with or as if with a blanket. — *adj.* Covering all individuals or instances of a class or group; as, a *blanket* approval.

blank verse. Poetry in lines that do not rhyme; especially, lines of poetry in the form of unrhymed iambic pentameter.

blare \'blar, 'bler\ *v.;* **blared; blar·ing. 1** To sound loud and harsh, as a trumpet. **2** To utter or proclaim in a harsh, noisy manner; as, loudspeakers *blaring* advertisements. — *n.* A harsh, loud noise; as, the *blare* of a horn.

blar·ney \'blär-nē, 'blȧr-\ *n.* Flattering, coaxing talk. — *v.;* **blar·neyed; blar·ney·ing.** To influence by blarney; to wheedle.

blas·pheme \blas-'fēm, 'blas-ˌfēm\ *v.;* **blas·phemed; blas·phem·ing.** To speak very disrespectfully of sacred things; to curse and swear; to utter blasphemy about.

blas·phe·mous \'blas-fə-məs\ *adj.* Speaking blasphemy; profane; as, *blasphemous* language. — **blas·phe·mous·ly,** *adv.*

blas·phe·my \'blas-fə-mē\ *n.; pl.* **blas·phe·mies.** Great disrespect or irreverence shown to God or sacred things, especially in words or writings.

blast \'blast\ *n.* **1** A strong gust of wind; as, the icy *blasts* of winter. **2** A current of air or gas forced through an opening, as in an organ or furnace. **3** The blowing which a charge of ore or metal receives in a blast furnace. **4** The sound made by a wind instrument such as a horn, or by a whistle. **5** An explosion, as of dynamite used to break rock or earth; the dynamite so used. **6** A sudden, harmful effect, as from a hot wind; blight, as of plants. — *v.* **1** To shatter by an explosion, especially one caused by dynamite. **2** To injure plants and trees by strong winds; to blight; to shrivel up; as, plants that *blast* easily. — **blast off.** Of a rocket or space ship, to take off or begin to travel.

blast-off \'blas-ˌtȯf\ *n.* A blasting off, as of a rocket.

blast furnace. A furnace used in making steel, in which air is forced on the fuel in order to melt the ore or metal.

blas·tu·la \'blas-chə-lə\ *n.; pl.* **blas·tu·las** \-ləz\ or **blas·tu·lae** \-ˌlē\. In embryos, a form in the early development, typically consisting of a single layer of cells arranged around a central closed cavity.

blat \'blat\ *v.;* **blat·ted; blat·ting.** To cry, as a calf or sheep; to bleat.

bla·tant \'blāt-nt\ *adj.* Noisy; loudmouthed; clamorous.

blaze \'blāz\ *n.* **1** A bright flame; a fire. **2** Intense brightness accompanied with heat; as, the *blaze* of the sun. **3** An outburst; as, a *blaze* of anger. **4** A bright or shining display; as, a *blaze* of color. — *v.;* **blazed; blaz·ing. 1** To burn with a bright flame; as, logs *blazing* on the hearth. **2** To shine with intense brightness and heat. The sun *blazed* overhead. **3** To shine as if on fire; to shine brilliantly; as, eyes *blazing* with anger.

blaze \'blāz\ *n.* **1** A white mark, especially a stripe running lengthwise, on the face of an animal. **2** A mark made on a tree by chipping off a piece of the bark. — *v.;* **blazed; blaz·ing. 1** To make a blaze on a tree. **2** To mark by blazed trees; as, to *blaze* a trail.

blaze \'blāz\ *v.;* **blazed; blaz·ing.** To make public far and wide; as, to *blaze* the news abroad.

blaz·er \'blāz-r\ *n.* A lightweight, usually bright-colored jacket.

bldg. Abbreviation for *building.*

bleach \'blēch\ *v.* To make a thing white by removing the color or stains; to become white; to blanch; as, cloth *bleached* by the sun. — *n.* A chemical used for bleaching.

bleach·ers \'blēch-rz\ *n. pl.* Seats or a stand, usually uncovered, for spectators at sports or games.

bleak \'blēk\ *adj.* **1** Exposed to wind or weather; as, a *bleak* coast. **2** Dreary; cheerless; as, a *bleak* outlook. **3** Cold and cutting; as, a *bleak* wind. — **bleak·ly,** *adv.*

blear \'blir\ *v.* To make sore or watery, as the eyes; to dim. — *adj.* **1** Dimmed by tears or by a watery discharge; as, *blear* eyes. **2** Causing or caused by dimness of sight; as, *blear* vision. — **bleary** \'blir-ē\ *adj.*

bleat \'blēt\ *n.* The cry of a sheep, goat, or calf or a sound like it. — *v.* To make or utter with a bleat.

bleed \'blēd\ *v.;* **bled** \'bled\; **bleed·ing. 1** To lose or shed blood. A cut finger *bleeds.* **2** To be wounded; as, to *bleed* for one's country. **3** To feel pain or deep sympathy. My heart *bleeds* for him. **4** To run out from a wounded surface, as sap from an injured tree. **5** To draw blood, sap, or other liquid from; as, to *bleed* a patient; to *bleed* a carburetor. **6** To draw or extort money from.

bleeding heart. A garden plant with deep-pink drooping heart-shaped flowers, related to Dutchman's-breeches.

blem·ish \'blem-ish\ *n.* Any mark that makes something imperfect; a flaw; a defect.

— The words *defect* and *flaw* are synonyms of *blemish: blemish* usually refers to something on the outside of an object marring its appearance; *defect* may imply a lack (which does not always appear on the outside) of something essential to completeness or perfection; *flaw* generally suggests a nick, crack, or break in smoothness, or the weakness or imperfection that causes these.

— *v.* To mar; to injure.

blench \'blench\ *v.* To shrink back; to flinch.

blench \'blench\ *v.* To grow or make pale; to blanch.

blend \'blend\ *v.* **1** To mix, especially so thoroughly that the separate things mixed cannot be distinguished. **2** To shade into each other, as colors; to merge; to harmonize; as, furniture that *blends* with the draperies. — For synonyms see *mingle.* — *n.* **1** A thorough mixture of things, as colors. **2** A product prepared by blending; as, a *blend* of coffee.

bless \'bles\ *v.;* **blessed** \'blest\ or **blest** \'blest\; **bless·ing.** [From Old English *blētsian* or *bloedsian* originally meaning "to sprinkle with the blood of a sacrificed animal".] **1** To make holy; to declare to be holy; to hallow; as, to *bless* an altar. **2** To ask God's favor for; as, to *bless* a congregation in church. **3** To confer happiness or good fortune on; to make happy; as, to be *blessed* with good health. **4** To make the sign of the cross on or over; as, to *bless* oneself. **5** To guard; to protect. God *bless* us. **6** To praise; to honor; as, to *bless* the Lord.

bless·ed \'bles-əd, 'blest\ *adj.* **1** Holy; hallowed. **2** Favored with blessings; happy; fortunate. — **bless·ed·ly** \'bles-əd-lē\ *adv.*

bless·ing \'bles-ing\ *n.* **1** The act of one who blesses; a prayer asking God's favor; a benediction. **2** Something that makes one happy or comfortable; as, the *blessings* of democracy.

blest \'blest\. A past tense and past part. of *bless.* — *adj.* Blessed.

blew. Past tense of *blow.*

blight \'blīt\ *n.* **1** Any disease of plants that causes withering or decay. **2** Anything that destroys or ruins. — *v.* To injure or destroy by a blight; to wither; to blast; to ruin.

blimp \'blimp\ *n.* A small balloonlike airship.

blind \'blīnd\ *adj.* **1** Sightless; unable to see. **2** Lacking in judgment or understanding; as, *blind* trust. **3** Closed at one end; as, a *blind* street. **4** Having no opening; as, a *blind* wall. **5** Made or done without the aid of sight; as, *blind* flying. — *v.* **1** To make blind or sightless. **2** To dazzle; to make it impossible to see well; as, *blinded* by the lights of an approaching car. **3** To make it impossible to judge well. Love may *blind* parents to the faults of their children. — *n.* **1** Something to hinder sight or to keep out light, as a window shade. **2** A place or means of hiding, especially one used by hunters; as, a duck *blind.* — **blind·ly,** *adv.*

blind alley. 1 An alley closed at one end. **2** Something, as a position or a situation, that offers no hope of progress or improvement.

blind·er \'blīnd-r\ *n.* A flap on a horse's bridle to prevent sight of objects at the side.

blind flying. The flying of an aircraft solely from readings of the various instruments within the aircraft.

blind·fold \'blīn(d)-ˌfōld\ *v.* To cover the eyes of, as with a bandage. — *adj.* With the eyes covered. — *n.* A bandage over the eyes.

blind·man's buff \'blīn(d)-ˌmanz 'bəf\. A game of tag in which the player who is "it" is blindfolded.

blind·ness \'blīn(d)-nəs\ *n.* The quality or state of being blind; especially, inability to see.

blind spot. **1** A tiny area of the retina insensitive to light. **2** Any weak part of a larger field, as a spot where radio reception is poor.

blind·worm \'blīn-ˌdwərm\ *n.* A small, burrowing, snakelike lizard with very tiny eyes.

blink \'blingk\ *v.* **1** To look with half-shut, winking eyes. **2** To wink quickly; as, to *blink* back tears. **3** To twinkle, as a star. **4** To shine with a light that goes, or seems to go, on and off; as, street lights *blinking* through rain. **5** To shut one's eyes to; to ignore; as, to *blink* the facts. — *n.* **1** A glimmer; a sparkle; as, a *blink* of light beneath a drawn blind. **2** A winking; a wink; as, a *blink* of the eye.

blink·er \'blingk-r\ *n.* **1** A person or thing that blinks; especially, a blinking light used as a warning signal. **2** A blinder.

blip \'blip\ *n.* A spot on a radar screen indicating the return of radar waves reflected from an object.

bliss \'blis\ *n.* Great happiness; joy.

bliss·ful \'blis-fəl\ *adj.* Filled with or causing bliss; supremely happy; joyful. — **bliss·ful·ly** \-fə-lē\ *adv.*

blis·ter \'blist-r\ *n.* **1** A small raised area of the skin filled with a watery liquid, as that caused by a burn. **2** Any swelling resembling this, as an air bubble in paint. **3** A gunner's or observer's compartment swelling out from the fuselage of an aircraft and often covered by a transparent dome. — *v.;* **blis·tered; blis·ter·ing** \-r(-)ing\. **1** To cause blisters. New shoes may *blister* one's feet. **2** To rise in blisters. The paint *blistered* under the hot sun. — **blis·tery** \-r(-)ē\ *adj.*

blithe \'blīth, 'blīth\ *adj.;* **blith·er; blith·est.** Gay; cheerful. — **blithe·ly,** *adv.*

blithe·some \'blīths-m, 'blīth-səm\ *adj.* Cheery; gay; merry. — **blithe·some·ly,** *adv.*

blitz. Short for *blitzkrieg.*

blitz·krieg \'blits-ˌkrēg\ *n.* [From German, there meaning literally "lightning war".] **1** A violent lightninglike military offensive. **2** Any sudden overpowering attack. — *v.* To attack or overpower with a blitzkrieg.

bliz·zard \'bliz-rd\ *n.* A driving storm of wind and snow; a long and severe snowstorm.

bloat \'blōt\ *v.* To swell by filling with water or air; to puff up or puff out.

blob \'bläb\ *n.* A small lump or drop of something not solid but thick, as of paste or paint.

bloc \'bläk\ *n.* A combination of countries, of political groups, or of individuals, working for some common cause or purpose; especially, in the United States, a combination of members of different political parties; as, the farm *bloc* in Congress.

block \'bläk\ *n.* **1** A solid piece of some material such as stone or wood, usually with one or more flat sides; as, building *blocks.* **2** A piece of wood on which condemned persons are beheaded. **3** A stand for something to be sold at auction. **4** A mold or form on which something is shaped; as, a hat *block.* **5** A grooved pulley in a frame. **6** A number of things thought of as forming a group or unit; as, a *block* of seats. **7** A large building divided into separate houses or shops, or a number of houses or shops joined together; as, an apartment *block;* a business *block.* **8** A space, especially in a city, enclosed by streets; a city square. **9** The length of one of the sides of a city square; as, three *blocks* south. **10** A section of railroad track controlled by block signals. **11** Something that stops or hinders passage or progress; an obstruction; as, a traffic *block.* — *v.* **1** To stop or hinder passage by closing up or closing off; to prevent progress; to obstruct; as, to *block* a doorway with a bicycle. **2** To shape on a block, or form; as, to *block* a hat. **3** To support with blocks; as, to *block* up a car. **4** To mark the chief lines of; as, to *block* out a plan; to *block* in a drawing. **5** To arrange writing, as in a letter or an address, in a shape suggesting a block, with none of the lines indented.

blocks, 5

block·ade \blä-'kād\ *n.* **1** The shutting up of a place by troops or warships to prevent coming in or going out. **2** The troops or warships thus used. **3** Any measures taken to prevent communication or cut off commerce with an enemy. — *v.;* **block·ad·ed; block·ad·ing.** To close to traffic or commerce by means of a blockade.

block·ade-run·ner \-ˌrən-r\ *n.* A vessel or a person that gets through or attempts to get through a blockade. — **block·ade-run·ning,** *n.*

block and tackle. A set of pulley blocks and ropes for hoisting or hauling.

block·bust·er \'bläk-ˌbəst-r\ *n.* A huge bomb, usually several tons in weight, designed to be dropped from an airplane.

block·head \'bläk-ˌhed\ *n.* A stupid person.

block·house \'bläk-ˌhau̇s\ *n.; pl.* **block·hous·es** \-ˌhau̇-zəz\. A building, often made of heavy logs, built with holes in its sides through which persons inside may fire out at an enemy.

blockhouse

block system. A system by which a railroad track is divided into short sections, or blocks, and trains are so run by signals (**block signals**) that no train enters a block until the preceding train has left it.

bloke \'blōk\ *n. Chiefly British slang.* A man; a fellow.

blond or **blonde** \'bländ\ *adj.* **1** Fair in color; light-colored. **2** Having yellowish-brown or light-colored hair, blue or gray eyes, and pale or rosy-white skin. — **blond·ness** or **blonde·ness** \'blän(d)-nəs\ *n.*

blond \'bländ\ *n.* A blond man or boy.

blonde \'bländ\ *n.* A blond woman or girl.

blood \'bləd\ *n.* **1** The fluid, usually red, which circulates in the heart, arteries, and veins of animals, carrying nourishment to all parts of the body and bringing away waste products. **2** Lineage; descent; birth; especially, honorable birth; as, a man of noble *blood. Blood* will tell. **3** Relationship by descent from a common ancestor; as, ties of *blood.* **4** Temper; anger; as, to stir up bad *blood.* The boy's *blood* was up. **5** A man of fire and spirit; as, the young *bloods* of the town.

blood bank. A reserve supply of blood or plasma or the place where it is stored.

blood cell. Any of the cells that float in the blood, being of two main kinds, a red cell that carries oxygen and a white cell that fights infection.

blood count. A counting of the number of red and white blood cells in a certain volume of blood, as to learn something about a person's health.

blood·cur·dling \'bləd-ˌkərd-ling\ *adj.* Seeming to have the effect of congealing the blood through fear or horror; terrifying; horrible; as, *bloodcurdling* screams.

blood·ed \'bləd-əd\ *adj.* Of pure blood or approved breed; of the best stock; as, *blooded* horses.

blood group. One of several types into which blood may be classified on the basis of its ability to blend with the blood of other individuals without harmful effects.

blood·hound \'bləd-ˌhaủnd\ *n.* A hound with long, drooping ears, a wrinkled face, and a keen sense of smell, often used in searching for missing persons.

bloodied. Past tense and past part. of *bloody.*

bloodier. Comparative of *bloody.*

bloodiest. Superlative of *bloody.*

blood·less \'bləd-ləs\ *adj.* **1** Without or seeming to be without blood; as, *bloodless* cheeks. **2** Done or accomplished without shedding blood; as, *bloodless* surgery; a *bloodless* revolution. **3** Cold of heart; unfeeling. — **blood·less·ly**, *adv.*

blood·let·ting \'bləd-ˌlet-ing\ *n.* The act or practice of opening a vein for the purpose of drawing blood.

blood·mo·bile \'bləd-mō-ˌbēl\ *n.* An automobile staffed and equipped for the purpose of collecting blood from donors.

blood poisoning. A diseased condition of the blood caused by poisonous matter in it.

blood pressure. The pressure of the blood on the walls of the blood vessels, varying in amount according to age and physical condition.

blood·root \'bləd-ˌrüt, -ˌrủt\ *n.* A plant of the poppy family with a red root, red sap, and a white flower.

blood·shed \'bləd-ˌshed\ *n.* The shedding of blood, especially human blood; slaughter.

blood·shot \'bləd-ˌshät\ *adj.* Tinged with blood; red and inflamed; as, *bloodshot* eyes.

blood·stone \'bləd-ˌstōn\ *n.* A green variety of quartz sprinkled with red spots.

blood stream. The blood moving through the blood vessels.

blood·sucker \'bləd-ˌsək-r\ *n.* An animal that sucks blood, as a leech.

blood·thirsty \'bləd-ˌthərs-tē\ *adj.* Eager to shed blood; cruel. — **blood·thirst·i·ly**, *adv.*

blood vessel. A tube or canal in the body through which the blood flows; an artery, vein, or capillary.

bloody \'bləd-ē\ *adj.;* **blood·i·er**; **blood·i·est**. **1** Smeared or stained with blood; as, a *bloody* nose. **2** Causing or accompanied by bloodshed; as, a *bloody* battle. **3** Bloodthirsty; murderous. — *v.;* **blood·ied** \-ēd\; **blood·y·ing**. To make bloody; to stain or smear with blood.

bloom \'blüm\ *n.* **1** A blossom; a flower. **2** A condition or time of flowering; as, roses in full *bloom.* **3** A condition or time of beauty, freshness, and vigor; as, the *bloom* of youth. **4** The rosy color of the cheek; a flush. **5** The delicate powdery coating on some fruits or leaves or a surface coating resembling this, as on newly minted coins. — *v.* **1** To blossom; to flower. **2** To be in a state of youthful beauty and freshness. **3** To glow with rosy color.

bloo·mers \'blüm-rz\ *n. pl.* [Named after Mrs. Amelia *Bloomer*, an American editor and advocate of dress reform for women (1818–1894).] **1** Short loose trousers gathered at the knees and worn by women in athletics. **2** An undergarment of similar design worn by women and girls.

bloom·ing \'blü-ming\ *adj.* **1** Blossoming; flowering. **2** Thriving in health, beauty, and vigor.

blos·som \'bläs-m\ *n.* **1** The flower or a flower of a seed plant; a bloom. **2** The condition of a plant when it has flowers; as, apple trees in *blossom.* **3** The time when something blooms or develops. — *v.* **1** To flower; to bloom. **2** To flourish and prosper.

blot \'blät\ *n.* **1** A spot or stain, as of ink. **2** A wiping out or erasing of something written or printed. **3** A blemish; a disgrace; as, a *blot* on one's reputation. — *v.;* **blot·ted**; **blot·ting**. **1** To spot; to stain; to make blots on; as, a pen that *blots* the paper. **2** To dry or absorb, as ink, with a blotter. **3** To disgrace; as, a man's whole career *blotted* by one bad mistake. **4** To obscure; to dim; to conceal completely; as, fog so thick that it *blotted* out the traffic lights. **5** To take a blot; to become blotted; as, paper that *blots* easily.

blotch \'bläch\ *n.* **1** A blot or a spot, as of ink or color. **2** A breaking out of the skin; a blemish. — *v.* To cover with blotches; to break out in blotches.

blot·ter \'blät-r\ *n.* **1** A card or a paper used for absorbing excess ink. **2** A book in which occurrences are noted down as they take place or are reported, and from which they are later transferred to permanent records; as, a police *blotter*.

blot·ting paper \'blät-ing\. A spongy paper for drying or absorbing wet ink.

blouse \'blaůs\ *n.; pl.* **blous·es** \'blaů-səz, -zəz\. **1** A loose overgarment like a smock, extending to the hip or to the calf of the leg, as worn by workmen or artists. **2** The upper garment of a uniform. **3** A garment, usually loose-fitting and covering the body from the neck to the waist, made either with or without a collar, sleeves, and belt.

blow \'blō\ *n.* **1** A hard stroke with the fist, hand, or some object. **2** A sudden act, as in an attack. **3** Something that causes suffering or loss, especially when sudden. The death of a pet can be a severe *blow* to anyone.
— The word *stroke* is a synonym of *blow: blow* generally suggests violent or forceful impact; *stroke* may indicate sweep or precision of movement.

blow \'blō\ *v.;* **blew** \'blü\; **blown** \'blōn\; **blow·ing. 1** To move or to be moved, as air or gas, especially rapidly or with power; as, wind *blowing* from the north at six miles an hour. **2** To send forth a strong current of air, as from the mouth or from a bellows; as, to *blow* on one's hands. **3** To drive by a current of air; as, a tree *blown* down in a storm. Several small boats were *blown* ashore. **4** To make a sound by blowing, as a whistle; to cause to sound, as a trumpet. **5** To pant or puff, as from exertion. **6** To swell by forcing air into; as, to *blow* glass; to *blow* bubbles. **7** To clear by forcing air through; as, to *blow* one's nose. **8** To shatter or destroy by an explosion; as, to *blow* up a bridge. — **blow hot and cold.** To favor a thing and then turn against it. — **blow over.** To cease; to cease to matter; to pass. — **blow up. 1** To explode. **2** To increase in intensity. A storm was *blowing up.* **3** To scold. The manager *blew up* his assistant. **4** To enlarge, as a photograph. — *n.* **1** A blowing; especially, a violent blowing of the wind; a gale. **2** A forcing of air from the mouth or nose, or through some instrument.

blow \'blō\ *v.;* **blew** \'blü\; **blown** \'blōn\; **blow·ing.** To blossom; to flower; as, a full-*blown* rose.

blow·er \'blōr, 'blō-ər\ *n.* **1** One that blows; as, a glass *blower.* **2** Any device that produces a current, as of air; as, a snow *blower.*

blow·fly \'blō-ˌflī\ *n.; pl.* **blow·flies** \-ˌflīz\. Any of various flies, as the bluebottle, that deposit eggs or larvae on meat or in wounds.

blow·gun \'blō-ˌgən\ *n.* A tube from which an arrow or a dart may be shot by the force of the breath.

blow·hole \'blō-ˌhōl\ *n.* **1** A hole for the escape of air or gas. **2** A nostril in the top of the head of whales and some other sea mammals. **3** A hole in the ice to which whales or seals come to breathe.

blown \'blōn\. Past part. of *blow.* — *adj.* **1** Swollen or puffed up, as cattle when they have eaten too much green food. **2** Out of breath; winded. Our horses were *blown.*

blow·out \'blō-ˌaůt\ *n.* **1** A sudden escape of air, gas, or steam from a container in which it was held under pressure. **2** The bursting of an automobile tire. **3** *Slang.* A feast; a big social affair.

blow·pipe \'blō-ˌpīp\ *n.* **1** A small, round tube for blowing air or gas into a flame so as to increase its heat. **2** A blowgun.

blow·torch \'blō-ˌtȯrch\ *n.* A lamp or torch that burns liquid fuel and shoots out a very hot flame, used to melt metal or to soften paint.

blowtorch

blow·up \'blō-ˌəp\ *n.* **1** An explosion. **2** An outburst, as of temper. **3** An enlargement, as of a photograph.

blowy \'blō-ē\ *adj.;* **blow·i·er; blow·i·est.** Windy.

blub·ber \'bləb-r\ *n.* **1** The fat of whales and other large sea mammals, from which oil is obtained. **2** A noisy crying, or blubbering. — *v.;* **blub·bered; blub·ber·ing** \-r(-)ing\. To weep noisily and childishly, or so as to swell or disfigure one's face.

bludg·eon \'bləj-n\ *n.* A short club with one end thicker and heavier than the other; any clublike weapon. — *v.* To hit or beat with a bludgeon.

blue \'blü\ *adj.;* **blu·er** \'blü-ər\; **blu·est** \-əst\. **1** Of the color blue. **2** Of a color resembling blue; as, hands *blue* with cold. **3** Low in spirits; sad; discouraged; as, to feel *blue.* — *n.* **1** The color in the rainbow between green and violet; the color of the clear sky. **2** Something blue in color, especially the sea or the sky; as, birds soaring in the *blue.* — *v.;* **blued; blu·ing** or **blue·ing.** To make or turn blue; as, to *blue* clothes.

blue·bell \'blü-ˌbel\ *n.* A plant with blue, bell-shaped flowers.

blue·ber·ry \'blü-ˌber-ē\ *n.; pl.* **blue·ber·ries. 1** The edible blue berry of a bush having urn-shaped flowers, differing from the huckleberry in having many tiny seeds instead of ten small nutlike seeds. **2** The shrub itself, tall in some species, low in others.

bluebell flowers

blue·bird \'blü-ˌbərd\ *n.* Any of several small North American songbirds more or less blue above, related to the robin.

blue·bot·tle \'blü-ˌbät-l\ *n.* Any of several true flies, especially a large hairy-bodied blowfly with steel-blue abdomen.

blue·fish \'blü-ˌfish\ *n.; pl.* **blue·fish** or **blue·fish·es.** A very active and greedy salt-water food and game fish related to the mackerel, bluish above and silvery below.

blue flag. 1 The common iris of the eastern United States. **2** Any blue iris.

blue·grass \'blü-ˌgras\ *n.* A meadow or pasture grass with bluish-green stems.

blue gum. A variety of eucalyptus.

blueing. Variant of *bluing.*

blue·jack·et \'blü-ˌjak-ət\ *n.* An enlisted man in the navy.

blue·jay \'blü-ˌjā\ *n.* or **blue jay**. A crested bird of eastern North America with bright-blue plumage.

blue plate. A plate with a blue design; especially, one divided into several compartments for serving several kinds of food as a single item on a bill of fare.

blue·print \'blü-ˌprint\ *n.* **1** A photographic print, white on a blue background, used for copying maps and building plans. **2** A detailed outline of something to be accomplished; a plan. **—** *v.* **1** To make a blueprint of. **2** To outline in detail; to plan.

blue racer. A bluish variety of the black snake, found from Ohio to Texas.

blue ribbon. The highest honor or award; first prize.

blues \'blüz\ *n. pl.* **1** Low spirits; melancholy. **2** A jazz song in a style originating among American Negroes, of melancholy character, and usually in a slow, dragging tempo. **3** The blue uniform of the United States Navy.

bluff \'bləf\ *n.* A high steep bank; a cliff. **—** *adj.* **1** Rising steeply with a broad front, as from a plain or shore; as, a *bluff* coastline. **2** Frank and outspoken in a rough but good-natured manner; as, a *bluff* remark.
— The words *blunt* and *curt* are synonyms of *bluff: bluff* generally suggests hearty and good-natured roughness; *blunt* may imply directness of speech not softened by tact; *curt* usually indicates rude or disconcerting shortness of speech.

bluff \'bləf\ *v.* To deceive or frighten by pretending to have strength or confidence that one does not really have. **—** *n.* **1** The act of bluffing. **2** A person who bluffs. — **bluff·er**, *n.*

blu·ing or **blue·ing** \'blü-ing\ *n.* A preparation, as of indigo, used in laundering.

blu·ish \'blü-ish\ *adj.* Somewhat blue.

blun·der \'blənd-r\ *n.* A bad or a stupid mistake. — For synonyms see *error.* **—** *v.;* **blun·dered**; **blun·der·ing** \-r(-)ing\. **1** To make a blunder. **2** To move clumsily; to stumble; as, to *blunder* along in the darkness. **3** To utter stupidly or in confusion; as, to *blunder* out an excuse. **4** To bungle. — **blun·der·ing·ly**, *adv.*

blun·der·buss \'blənd-r-ˌbəs\ *n.* **1** A short gun, no longer used, for shooting at close range without taking exact aim. **2** A stupid, blundering person.

blunt \'blənt\ *adj.* **1** Having a thick edge or point; dull; as, a *blunt* knife. **2** Abrupt or outspoken in speech or manners. *Blunt* criticism is not always welcome. — For synonyms see *bluff.* **—** *v.* To take the edge off; to make blunt; to dull. — **blunt·ly**, *adv.*

blunderbuss

blur \'blər\ *v.;* **blurred**; **blur·ring**. **1** To obscure; to smear; as, to *blur* a paper with ink. **2** To make indistinct or confused; to cloud; as, vision *blurred* by tears. Fog *blurred* the lights of the city. **3** To become blurred or indistinct; as, a television picture that *blurs.*

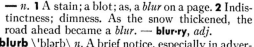

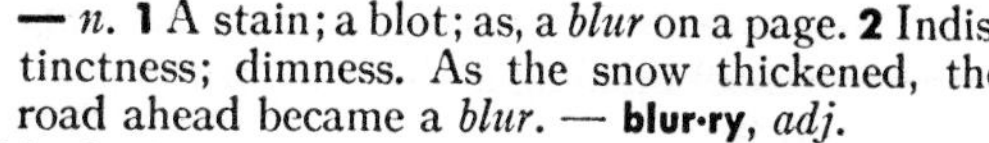

— *n.* **1** A stain; a blot; as, a *blur* on a page. **2** Indistinctness; dimness. As the snow thickened, the road ahead became a *blur.* — **blur·ry**, *adj.*

blurb \'blərb\ *n.* A brief notice, especially in advertising, praising a product extravagantly.

blurt \'blərt\ *v.* To utter suddenly and without thinking; as, to *blurt* out a secret.

blush \'bləsh\ *v.* **1** To become red, especially in the face, from shame or confusion; to flush. **2** To feel shame; as, to *blush* at a mistake one has made. **—** *n.* **1** A reddening of the cheeks from shame or confusion; a flush. **2** A red or rosy color. — **at first blush**. At first glance; offhand. — **blush·ing·ly**, *adv.*

blus·ter \'bləst-r\ *v.;* **blus·tered**; **blus·ter·ing** \-r(-)ing\. **1** To blow violently and noisily, as the wind. **2** To talk or act in a noisy, boastful way; to swagger; to storm; to rage. **—** *n.* **1** Noise and violence; as, the *bluster* of the storm. **2** Noisy, boastful language. — **blus·ter·ing·ly**, *adv.* — **blus·tery** \-r(-)ē\ *adj.*

blvd. Abbreviation for *boulevard.*

boa \'bō-ə\ *n.* **1** Any large snake that crushes its prey by winding itself around it, such as the **boa con·stric·tor** \kən-'strikt-r\ of tropical America. **2** A long fluffy snakelike scarf of fur, feathers, or delicate fabric.

boar \'bōr, 'bȯr\ *n.* **1** A male pig. **2** A wild pig.

board \'bōrd, 'bȯrd\ *n.* **1** A thin sawed piece of lumber, comparatively broad and long. **2** A piece of wood or other material used for some special purpose; as, a diving *board;* a drawing *board.* **3** Pasteboard; as, a book bound in *boards.* **4** A table, especially for food. **5** [in the plural] The stage in a theater; as, the old actor's last appearance on the *boards.* **6** Meals furnished regularly for pay; as, to work for one's *board.* **7** A number of persons authorized to manage or direct something; as, a school *board.* **—** *v.* **1** To cover with boards. The windows of the old house were *boarded* up. **2** To provide or to be provided with regular meals or with regular meals and lodging; as, to *board* workers on a construction job; to *board* at a hotel.

board \'bōrd, 'bȯrd\ *n.* **1** The border, side, or edge of anything, as in *seaboard.* **2** The side of a ship, as in *overboard.* — **on board**. Aboard; on or in, as a ship, train, or airplane. **—** *v.* To go on board of; to get on or into; as, to *board* a bus.

board·er \'bōrd-r, 'bȯrd-r\ *n.* A person who pays for meals, or for meals and lodging, at another's house.

board·ing·house \'bōrd-ing-ˌhau̇s, 'bȯrd-\ *n.; pl.* **board·ing·hous·es** \-ˌhau̇-zəz\. A house where meals, or meals and lodging, are furnished for pay.

board·ing school. A school at which some or all of the pupils live during the school term.

board·walk \'bōrd-ˌwȯk, 'bȯrd-\ *n.* A walk made of boards, especially one built along a beach.

boast \'bōst\ *v.* **1** To praise one's own possessions or accomplishments; to brag; as, to *boast* of one's strength. **2** To have and be proud of having; as, a school that *boasts* a winning team. **—** *n.* **1** A boasting; a bragging. **2** A cause of boasting or pride. The new school building is the *boast* of the town. — **boast·er**, *n.*

boast·ful \'bōst-fəl\ *adj.* Inclined to boast or marked by boasting; as, a *boastful* person; *boastful* talk. — **boast·ful·ly** \-fə-lē\ *adv.*

boat \'bōt\ *n.* **1** A small open vessel moved by oars or paddles, or by sail or power, as a rowboat or a sailboat. **2** A ship; any vessel for traveling on the water. **3** A table dish, as for gravy. — *v.* **1** To place, carry, or cross in a boat. All our supplies will have to be *boated* to the camp. **2** To row, sail, or travel in a boat.

boat hook. A metal hook, often with a point or a knob on the back, fixed to the end of a pole and used for pulling or pushing a boat into place.

boat·house \'bōt-ˌhau̇s\ *n.; pl.* **boat·hous·es** \-ˌhau̇-zəz\. A house or shelter for boats.

boat·ing \'bōt-ing\ *n.* The use of a boat, especially a rowboat, for pleasure; as, a happy summer divided between tennis and *boating.*

boat·man \'bōt-mən\ *n.; pl.* **boat·men** \-mən\. A man who manages, works on, or deals in, boats.

boat·swain \'bōs-n\ *n.* An officer on a warship or a seaman on a merchant ship who has charge of the anchors, cables, and rigging — sometimes written *bos'n.*

bob \'bäb\ *n.* **1** A short, jerky motion; as, a *bob* of the head. **2** A woman's or child's short haircut. **3** A ball or weight hanging from a rod or line. **4** A cork or float on a fishing line. **5** A bobsled. — *v.;* **bobbed**; **bob·bing**. **1** To move or to cause to move with a short jerky motion; as, to *bob* up and down. **2** To cut short, as hair.

bob·bin \'bäb-n\ *n.* A spool or reel, as in a sewing machine.

bob·ble \'bäb-l\ *v.;* **bob·bled**; **bob·bling** \-l(-)ing\. **1** To move up and down or back and forth in a short jerky manner. The old lady laughed so hard that her little black hat *bobbled.* **2** To make an error or mistake; to fumble. — *n.* A mistake; a fumble.

bob·by \'bäb-ē\ *n.; pl.* **bob·bies.** [From a nickname for Sir *Robert* Peel, who was helpful in organizing the London police.] *British.* A policeman.

bob·by pin \'bäb-ē ˌpin\. A flat metal hairpin shaped so as to clasp the hair tightly and hold it in place.

bobby socks or **bobby sox** \ˌsäks\. Socks reaching well above the ankle, especially for wear by girls in the early teens.

bob·by-sox·er \-ˌsäks-r\ or **bob·by-sock·er** \-ˌsäk-r\ or **bob·by-socks·er** \-ˌsäks-r\ *n.* An adolescent girl, especially in the early teens.

bob·cat \'bäb-ˌkat\ *n.* A wildcat; a lynx.

bob·o·link \'bäb-l-ˌingk\ *n.* An American songbird of the same family as the blackbirds and the meadow larks, noted for its song.

bob·sled \'bäb-ˌsled\ or **bob·sleigh** \-ˌslā\ *n.* **1** A short sled, usually one of a pair joined by a coupling. **2** A sled made by joining two short sleds together. — *v.;* **bob·sled·ded**; **bob·sled·ding.** To coast or ride on a bobsled. — **bob·sled·der** \-ˌsled-r\ *n.*

bob·tail \'bäb-ˌtāl\ *n.* **1** A short tail; a tail cut short. **2** An animal with a short tail. — **bob·tailed** \-ˌtāld\ *adj.*

bob·white \'bäb-'hwīt\ *n.* An American quail with gray, white, and reddish coloring, named from its call.

bode \'bōd\ *v.;* **bod·ed**; **bod·ing.** To indicate beforehand by signs or portents; to foreshadow; to portend. The rumble of thunder *boded* ill for the picnic.

bode. A past tense of *bide.*

bod·ice \'bäd-əs\ *n.* **1** The close-fitting top of a dress. **2** A woman's tight-fitting outer garment, usually laced up the front, reaching from the waist to the breast.

bodice, 2

bod·i·less \'bäd-ē-ləs, -l-əs\ *adj.* Having no body; not being in material form.

bod·i·ly \'bäd-l-ē\ *adj.* **1** Having a body or physical form; physical; as, to suffer *bodily* harm. **2** Having to do with the body; as, *bodily* ills. — *adv.* In one body or mass; all together; completely; as, to be carried *bodily* upstairs; an audience coming *bodily* to its feet.

bod·kin \'bäd-kən\ *n.* **1** A dagger. **2** A daggerlike tool, especially one for punching holes in cloth. **3** A blunt needle with a blunt eye, for drawing tape or ribbon through a loop or hem.

body \'bäd-ē\ *n.; pl.* **bod·ies.** **1** The physical whole of a person or an animal, living or dead. **2** The trunk, or main part, of a person, animal, or plant. **3** The main or central part of anything; as, the *body* of a letter. **4** The part of a garment that covers the trunk of a person; as, the *body* of a dress. **5** A group of persons or things united for some purpose; as, a *body* of troops. **6** A mass or portion of matter distinct from other masses; as, a *body* of water; a *body* of cold air. **7** A person. **8** Consistency; substance; as, paint with a good *body.* **9** Richness of flavor; strength, as of wine.

bod·y·guard \'bäd-ē-ˌgärd, -ˌgȧrd\ *n.* A man or a number of men whose duty it is to protect a person.

bog \'bäg, 'bȯg\ *n.* Wet, spongy ground; a marsh; a swamp. — *v.;* **bogged**; **bog·ging.** To sink or to stick fast in a bog or as if in a bog. — **bog·gy** \'bäg-ē, 'bȯg-ē\ *adj.*

bo·gey or **bo·gy** or **bo·gie** \'bu̇g-ē, 'bō-gē, 'bü-gē\ *n.; pl.* **bo·geys** or **bo·gies.** **1** A goblin; a specter; a phantom. **2** Something that one dreads, fears, or loathes; as, faced with the *bogey* of starvation. **3** Something that annoys, disturbs, or worries a person; as, the *bogey* of doing homework every night.

bo·gus \'bō-gəs\ *adj.* Not genuine; sham; as, *bogus* money.

Bo·he·mi·an \bō-'hē-mē-ən\ *n.* **1** A native of Bohemia. **2** The language of the people of Czechoslovakia. **3** A person, especially one of artistic tastes, who does not conform to the usual social conventions and manner of living. **4** A gypsy. — *adj.* **1** Of or relating to Bohemia, its people, or their language. **2** Unconventional in social relations and manner of life.

boil \'bȯil\ *v.* **1** Of a liquid, to heat or to be heated to the point (**boil·ing point**) at which bubbles rise and break at the surface; as, to *boil* water. When water *boils* it becomes steam. **2** To be in seething motion like the surface of boiling water; to seethe; as, the *boiling* waters of the flood. **3** To cook or to be cooked in boiling water; as, to *boil* eggs. **4** To be excited, as with anger; to rage. **5** To be in boiling liquid, as for cooking. The potatoes are *boiling.* **6** To treat by boiling or by an evaporation process requiring boiling; as, to *boil* maple sap to make syrup. — *n.* The condition of something that is boiling; as, to bring water to a *boil.*

boil \'bȯil\ *n.* A hard, inflamed, painful lump or swelling in a person's skin, caused by infection.

boil·er \'bȯil-r\ *n.* **1** A container in which something is boiled. **2** A tank holding hot water. **3** A strong metal container used in making steam for heating buildings or for driving engines.

bois·ter·ous \'bȯist-r(-)əs\ *adj.* **1** Violent; stormy; as, *boisterous* winds. **2** Rough and noisy; as, *boisterous* play. — **bois·ter·ous·ly**, *adv.*

bo·la \'bō-lə\ *n.* A device consisting of metal or stone weights on the end of a long cord, used by South American cowboys, who throw it at animals in such a way as to entangle their legs.

bold \'bōld\ *adj.* **1** Willing to meet danger or take risks; brave; daring. **2** Too forward; rude; impudent; as, two brothers, one bashful and one *bold.* **3** Showing or requiring courage or daring; as, a *bold* plan. **4** Steep; abrupt; as, a *bold* cliff. **5** Standing out clearly or sharply; as, a dress with *bold* stripes. — **bold·ly**, *adv.*

bold·face \'bōl(d)-ˌfās\ *n.* A heavy-faced type or printing done in this type. The entry words in this dictionary are printed in *boldface.*

bole \'bōl\ *n.* The trunk of a tree.

bo·le·ro \bə-'ler-ˌō\ *n.; pl.* **bo·le·ros**. **1** A Spanish dance in ¾ time or the music for it. **2** A loose, short jacket, with or without sleeves, extending no lower than the waist.

Bo·liv·i·an \bə-'liv-ē-ən\ *adj.* Of or relating to Bolivia. — *n.* A native or inhabitant of Bolivia.

boll \'bōl\ *n.* The seed pod of a plant, especially of cotton or flax.

boll wee·vil \'wēv-l\. A grayish weevil, the larvae of which live in and feed on the buds and bolls of the cotton plant.

bo·lo \'bō-ˌlō\ *n.; pl.* **bo·los**. A large, heavy single-edged knife used in the Philippines.

bo·lo·gna \bə-'lō-nē, -nə\ *n.* A large sausage made of beef, veal, and pork, enclosed in a casing, smoked, and cooked.

Bol·she·vik \'bōl-shə-ˌvik, 'bȯl-, 'bäl-, -ˌvēk\ *n.; pl.* **Bol·she·viks** \-ˌviks, -ˌvēks\ or **Bol·she·vi·ki** \-ˌvik-ē, -ˌvēk-ē\. [often with a small letter] **1** A member or supporter of a radical party that came into power in Russia in 1917. **2** An extreme radical, especially one who favors the overthrow of capitalism by force. — **Bol·she·vism** \-ˌviz-m\ *n.* — **Bol·she·vist** \-vəst\ *n.* or *adj.* — **Bol·she·vis·tic** \ˌbōl-shə-'vis-tik, ˌbȯl-, ˌbäl-\ *adj.*

bol·ster \'bōlst-r\ *n.* **1** A long pillow or cushion, especially one extending from side to side of a bed. **2** A pad; a support. — *v.;* **bol·stered**; **bol·ster·ing** \-r(-)ing\. **1** To support with a bolster. **2** To support in any way; as, to *bolster* up a person's courage; to try to *bolster* a weak argument.

bolt \'bōlt\ *v.* To sift or separate, as bran from flour, by means of a sieve. — **bolt·er**, *n.*

bolt \'bōlt\ *n.* **1** A short blunt-headed arrow for a crossbow. **2** A sliding bar used to fasten a door. **3** The part of a lock worked by a key. **4** A pin or a rod, usually with a head at one end and a screw thread at the other, used to hold something in place. **5** Lightning; a thunderbolt. **6** A sudden surprise; as, a *bolt* from the blue. **7** A package or roll, as of cloth or wallpaper. **8** The act of bolting; as, to swallow one's breakfast at one *bolt.* — *v.* **1** To swallow hurriedly or without chewing. **2** To fasten with a bolt. **3** To start or dart forth like an arrow; to come or to go suddenly; to run away; as, to *bolt* out of a room. **4** To refuse to support the candidate or policy of a group one has previously backed; as, to *bolt* a political party. — **bolt·er**, *n.*

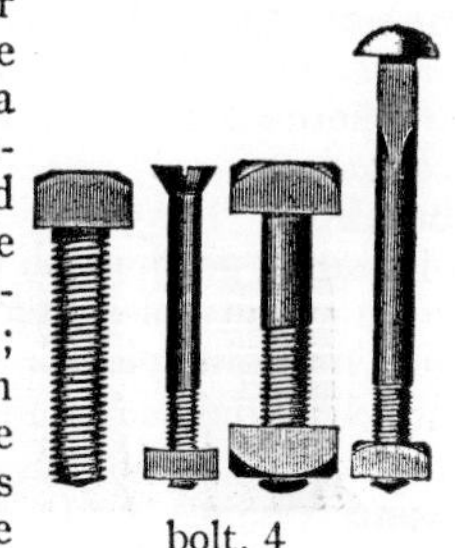

bolt, 4

bo·lus \'bō-ləs\ *n.* A rounded mass of medicine larger than an ordinary pill; especially, a large pill for a horse.

bomb \'bäm\ *n.* **1** A hollow case or shell containing explosive material and variously made to be dropped from an airplane, thrown by hand, or set off by a fuse. **2** A container, often having some resemblance to a bomb, for a substance such as an insecticide, which is stored under pressure and released in the form of a fine spray; as, a mosquito *bomb.* — *v.* To attack with bombs; to drop bombs on.

bom·bard \bäm-'bärd, bəm-, -'bȧrd\ *v.* **1** To attack with heavy fire from big guns; to shell; as, to *bombard* a fort. **2** To attack repeatedly; as, to *bombard* a person with questions. — **bom·bard·ment**, *n.*

bom·bar·dier \ˌbäm-bə(r)-'dir\ *n.* A member of a bomber crew who is responsible for releasing the bombs.

bom·bast \'bäm-ˌbast\ *n.* Language too pompous or high-flown for the occasion; as, a speech in which there was more *bombast* than good sense.

bom·bas·tic \bäm-'bas-tik\ *adj.* [From Old French *bombace* meaning "cotton", "padding".] Marked by or given to bombast; high-sounding;

as, *bombastic* language; a *bombastic* speaker. — **bom·bas·ti·cal·ly** \-tik-l(-)ē\ *adv.*

bomb bay \'bäm ˌbā\. A compartment in the underside of an airplane, with doors swinging down and out through which bombs can be dropped.

bomb·er \'bäm-r\ *n.* One that bombs; especially, an aircraft used for dropping bombs.

bomb·proof \'bäm-'prüf\ *adj.* Safe against the explosive force of bombs; as, an underground *bombproof* shelter.

bomb·shell \'bäm-ˌshel\ *n.* A bomb.

bo·na fi·de \'bō-nə ˌfīd-ē, 'bän-ə, ˌfīd, ˌfīd-ə\ [From Latin phrase, meaning "in or with good faith".] Without fraud or deceit; genuine; as, a *bona fide* transaction; a *bona fide* offer for a house.

bo·nan·za \bə-'nan-zə\ *n.* **1** A rich mass of ore in a mine. **2** Anything that brings a rich return. Sometimes a small investment proves to be a *bonanza.*

bon·bon \'bän-ˌbän\ *n.* [From French, meaning literally "good, good".] A small candy having any of a variety of centers and a coating of fondant, often bright-colored.

bond \'bänd\ *adj.* In serfdom or slavery; not free; as, a *bond* servant.

bond \'bänd\ *n.* **1** Anything that binds or confines; a band. **2** [in the plural] Chains; fetters; imprisonment. **3** A force or influence that unites; as, a *bond* of friendship. **4** A binding or connection made by overlapping parts of a structure, as in laying brick. **5** A legal agreement in which a person binds himself to meet certain stated requirements and, usually, to pay a certain sum of money if he fails to do so. **6** A certificate promising payment of a certain sum on or before a stated day, issued by a government or business corporation as an evidence of debt. — *v.* **1** To place under a bond to do something in the future. **2** To connect or bind by or as if by bonds, as bricks by overlapping them.

bond·age \'bän-dij\ *n.* Slavery; captivity.

bond·hold·er \'bänd-ˌhōld-r\ *n.* A person who holds or owns a bond or bonds, especially of a government or corporation.

bond·man \'bän(d)-mən\ *n.; pl.* **bond·men** \-mən\. A male slave.

bonds·man \'bän(d)z-mən\ *n.; pl.* **bonds·men** \-mən\. **1** A bondman. **2** A person who assumes responsibility for someone else by giving a bond.

bone \'bōn\ *n.* **1** The hard material of which the skeleton of most animals is formed. **2** One of the hard pieces of the framework of the body; as, to break a *bone.* **3** A bone with meat on it; as, a soup *bone.* **4** A similar hard animal substance, as whalebone or ivory. **5** [in the plural] Something usually or originally made from bone, as dice or clappers. **6** [in the plural] One of the end men in a minstrel show. — *v.;* **boned; bon·ing. 1** To take the bones from; as, to *bone* a fish. **2** *Slang.* To study hard; as, to *bone* up on science.

bone·head \'bōn-ˌhed\ *n. Slang.* A stupid person; a blockhead.

bone meal. Bone crushed or ground, used chiefly as a fertilizer but also in the feed of farm animals.

bon·er \'bōn-r\ *n. Slang.* A stupid or ridiculous mistake.

bone·set \'bōn-ˌset\ *n.* A rough, hairy plant of the aster family, with pointed leaves and white flowers.

bon·fire \'bän-ˌfīr\ *n.* [From earlier *bonefire,* a fire for burning bones or corpses.] A large fire built in the open air.

bon·net \'bän-ət\ *n.* **1** A covering for the head, usually tied under the chin by ribbons or strings, now worn chiefly by children. **2** A soft woolen cap worn by men in Scotland. **3** The headdress of an Indian.

bon·ny or **bon·nie** \'bän-ē\ *adj.* **1** Handsome; beautiful; pretty. **2** Healthy; healthy-looking.

bo·nus \'bō-nəs\ *n.* Something given to a person in addition to what is usual or what is strictly due him; especially, money given in addition to an agreed salary or wages.

bon voy·age \'bän vwä-'yäzh, vwȧ-'yȧzh\ [French.] A good journey or trip — used as a phrase of farewell.

bony \'bō-nē\ *adj.;* **bon·i·er; bon·i·est. 1** Of or having to do with bones; as, the *bony* structure of the body. **2** Full of bones; as, a *bony* fish. **3** Like bone or bones; as, a *bony* substance. **4** Having large or prominent bones; as, a rugged *bony* face. **5** Skinny; scrawny; as, *bony* underfed children.

boo \'bü\ *interj.* or *n.; pl.* **boos. 1** An exclamation used to startle, especially children. **2** A cry expressing dislike or disapproval. — *v.;* **booed; boo·ing. 1** To cry "boo". **2** To attack with cries of "boo". The unfriendly audience *booed* the speaker.

boo·by \'bü-bē\ *n.; pl.* **boo·bies. 1** A dunce; a stupid fellow. **2** In some games, the player whose score is poorest. **3** A large, heavy sea bird.

booby trap. 1 A concealed explosive device attached to some harmless-looking object. **2** Any trap set to catch a careless or unthinking person.

book \'bu̇k\ *n.* **1** A collection of sheets of paper bound or strung together; a bound volume. **2** A literary composition of some length; as, to write a *book.* **3** A subdivision of a literary work; as, the *books* of the Bible. — **the Book.** The Bible. — *v.* To enter or register one's name in a book or list so as to engage service or accommodation; as, to *book* passage on a boat. — *adj.* **1** That is shown by bookkeeping records; as, *book* value. **2** Bookish; as, *book* learning.

book·case \'bu̇k-ˌkās\ *n.* A case for books; especially, a piece of furniture consisting of shelves to hold books.

book·end \'bu̇k-ˌend\ *n.* A support placed at the end of a row of books to hold them up.

book·ish \'bu̇k-ish\ *adj.* **1** Fond of books; acquainted with books rather than with people. **2** Giving careful attention to literary form. **3** Formal; including too much book learning; depending too much on book learning; as, a *bookish* speech.

book·keep·er \'bu̇k-ˌkēp-r\ *n.* A person who keeps accounts, as for a business.

book·keep·ing \'bu̇k-ˌkēp-ing\ *n.* The work of keeping business accounts.

book·let \'bu̇k-lət\ *n.* A little book, especially one having paper covers and only a few pages.

book·lore \'bu̇k-ˌlōr, -ˌlȯr\ *n.* Book learning.

book·mark \'bu̇k-ˌmärk, -ˌmȧrk\ *n.* Something placed in a book to mark a place.

book·mo·bile \'bu̇k-mō-ˌbēl\ *n.* A truck, with shelves of books, serving as a library or bookstore, especially for rural areas or towns that have no libraries.

book·plate \'bu̇k-ˌplāt\ *n.* A label placed on or in a book, showing who owns it or where it belongs in a library.

book·shop \'bu̇k-ˌshäp\ *n.* A bookstore.

book·store \'bu̇k-ˌstōr, -ˌstȯr\ *n.* A store in which books are the main item offered for sale.

book·worm \'bu̇k-ˌwərm\ *n.* **1** The larva of any insect that injures books, feeding on the binding and paste and often piercing the leaves. **2** A person who is unusually devoted to reading or studying books.

boom \'büm\ *n.* **1** A long pole used especially to stretch the bottom of a sail. **2** A long beam projecting from the mast of a derrick to support or guide the thing that is being lifted. **3** A line of connected floating timbers to hold logs together, as in a river.

boom

boom \'büm\ *v.* **1** To make a deep, hollow rumbling sound, like that made by waves or cannon. **2** To move along, making a booming noise, as a boat under full sail. **3** To increase or develop rapidly. Most kinds of business *boomed* during the war. — *n.* **1** A hollow roar or cry. **2** A rapid increase, as in value or in amount of business.

boom·er·ang \'büm-r-ˌang\ *n.* **1** A curved club or stick, used by Australian natives as a weapon. Some *boomerangs* can be thrown so as to return to the thrower. **2** Anything that reacts with harm to its maker or doer. The lie proved a *boomerang.* — *v.* To bring back unexpectedly upon a person or persons effects often intended for someone else and usually damaging to the originator.

boom·town \'büm-ˌtau̇n\ *n.* A town that has undergone sudden growth as the result of a boom.

boon \'bün\ *n.* **1** *Archaic.* Something asked or granted as a favor; a gift. **2** A thing to be thankful for; a blessing; a benefit. The steady rain came as a *boon* to the farmers.

boon \'bün\ *adj.* **1** Bounteous; kind. **2** Merry; jovial; intimate; as, a *boon* companion.

boor \'bu̇r\ *n.* **1** A peasant; especially, a rough clownish countryman. **2** A rude, ill-bred, or clownish person.

boor·ish \'bu̇r-ish\ *adj.* Like a boor; rude; unmannerly. — **boor·ish·ly,** *adv.*

boost \'büst\ *v.* **1** To raise or push up. My brother *boosted* me into the window. **2** To assist over obstacles; to advance; as, to *boost* a candidate for office. **3** To increase in force, power, or amount; as, to *boost* aircraft production; to *boost* prices. — *n.* A helping push or shove. — **boost·er,** *n.*

boost·er \'büst-r\ *n.* **1** An injection given to maintain or revive the effects of a previously established immunization. **2** A device for strengthening radio or television signals in areas where reception is weak.

boot \'büt\ *n.* Something to equalize an exchange. — **to boot.** In addition; besides; as, to win a race and a prize *to boot.* — *v.* To be of use; to profit; to be of advantage. It will *boot* him little to complain.

boot \'büt\ *n.* **1** A covering for the foot and part of the leg, as of rubber or leather. **2** A high shoe. **3** A storage space, as at the rear of a vehicle. **4** A kick. — *v.* **1** To put boots on. **2** To kick; as, to *boot* a football.

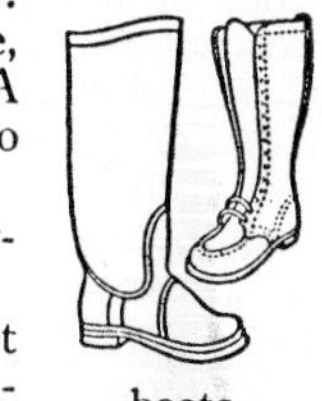
boots

boot·black \'büt-ˌblak\ *n.* A person who shines boots and shoes.

boo·tee \'bü-ˌtē, bü-'tē\ *n.* A boot with a short leg; especially, an infant's boot of knitted wool.

booth \'büth\ *n.; pl.* **booths** \'bü<u>th</u>z\. **1** A covered stall or stand for selling or displaying goods, as at a fair, market, or exhibition. **2** A small enclosed, or partly enclosed, stall or compartment; as, a telephone *booth;* a *booth* in a restaurant.

boot·jack \'büt-ˌjak\ *n.* A V-shaped device for use in pulling off one's boots.

boot·leg \'büt-ˌleg\ *n.* **1** The upper part of a boot. **2** Anything, especially liquor, that is made, transported, sold, or distributed without legal right. — *v.;* **boot·legged**; **boot·leg·ging.** **1** To make, transport, distribute, or sell illegally, as liquor. **2** To bootleg liquor or other goods. — *adj.* **1** Bootlegged; as, *bootleg* liquor. **2** Of or dealing with bootlegging. — **boot·leg·ger,** *n.*

boot·less \'büt-ləs\ *adj.* Useless; unprofitable; to no advantage.

boot tree. A device put into a boot or shoe to preserve its shape.

boo·ty \'büt-ē\ *n.* **1** Goods seized from the enemy in war; plunder. **2** Any rich gain.

bo·rax \'bōr-ˌaks, -əks, 'bȯr-\ *n.* A saltlike substance, colorless or white when pure, used as a cleansing agent and antiseptic.

bor·der \'bȯrd-r\ *n.* **1** The outer part or edge of anything; as, the *border* of a lake. **2** A boundary or frontier. **3** A strip or stripe on or near the edge, as of a garment or a rug.

— The words *margin* and *edge* are synonyms of *border: edge* usually refers to a sharply defined boundary line or to the place where two planes meet; as, the *edge* of a table; *border* may indicate the part of a surface on or just within the boundary line; *margin* generally suggests a border of definite width, often clearly distinguished from the remaining surface. — For other synonyms see *boundary.*

— *v.;* **bor·dered; bor·der·ing** \-r(-)ing\. **1** To make a border for; as, to *border* a garden with flowers. **2** To touch at the edge or boundary; to bound; to adjoin. The United States *borders* on Canada. **3** To come near to; to verge; as, a remark that *bordered* on insult.

bor·der·land \'bȯrd-r-ˌland\ *n.* **1** Land next to or forming a border, frontier, or boundary. **2** Something not clearly pictured but thought of as a region lying close to something else; as, the *borderland* of dreams; the *borderland* between sleeping and waking.

bor·der·line \'bȯrd-r-ˌlīn\ *adj.* **1** Situated at or near a border or boundary. **2** Having characteristics of a certain state or condition without clearly being in it; uncertain; as, a *borderline* case of mental illness. **3** Having characteristics of two states or conditions without clearly belonging to either; in between; as, *borderline* organisms, not clearly plants or animals.

bore. Past tense of *bear.*

bore \'bōr, 'bȯr\ *v.;* **bored; bor·ing. 1** To make a hole in, especially with a tool that turns round; to pierce; as, to *bore* a piece of wood. **2** To make by piercing or drilling; as, to *bore* a hole; to *bore* a well. **3** To weary by being dull; to tire. The book *bored* me with its long descriptions. — *n.* **1** A hole made by boring. **2** The tube which forms the inside of a gun barrel or of a pipe. **3** The diameter of a hole; especially, the inside diameter of a gun barrel. **4** A tiresome person or thing.

bore \'bōr, 'bȯr\ *n.* A tidal flood with high, abrupt front, usually due to a rapidly narrowing inlet.

bore·dom \'bōrd-m, 'bȯrd-m\ *n.* The condition of being bored, or wearied by dullness.

bor·er \'bōr-r, 'bȯr-r\ *n.* One that bores, as a tool or any of certain insects or larvae that bore into plants.

bo·ric acid \'bōr-ik, 'bȯr-\. A white acid mixture used as an antiseptic and preservative.

born \'bȯrn\. A past part. of *bear* meaning "brought into life". — *adj.* Having certain natural abilities or character from birth; as, a *born* leader.

borne \'bōrn, 'bȯrn\. A past part. of *bear.*

bo·ron \'bōr-ˌän, 'bȯr-\ *n.* A nonmetallic chemical element occurring only in combination, as in borax and boric acid.

bor·ough \'bər-ō, 'bə-rō\ *n.* **1** In England, a town having the right to send a member or members to parliament or a town having by charter the right of self-government in local affairs. **2** In some states of the United States, a self-governing town or village. **3** One of the five political divisions of New York City.

bor·row \'bär-ō\ *v.* **1** To take or receive something with the promise or intention of returning it. **2** To take for one's own use; to copy or imitate; to adopt; as, to *borrow* an idea. — **bor·row·er** \-ə-wər\ *n.*

bos'n \'bōs-n\ *n.* A boatswain.

bos·om \'bu̇z-m\ *n.* **1** The breast of a human being. **2** Anything thought of as like the breast; as, the *bosom* of the earth or of the sea. **3** The place of secret thoughts or feelings; as, to keep a secret locked in one's *bosom.* **4** The part of a garment, as a shirt or a dress, that is worn over the breast. — *adj.* Close; intimate; as, a *bosom* friend.

boss \'bȯs, 'bäs\ *n.* A rounded projecting part; especially, a knoblike ornament, as on a shield or a ceiling; a stud. — *v.* To decorate with bosses; to stud.

boss \'bȯs\ *n.* **1** A person who directs or supervises workers; an employer, manager, or foreman. **2** Anyone who directs, controls, or has authority. **3** A political leader who controls a large number of votes. — *v.* To be boss over; to direct; to superintend; as, to *boss* a job.

bossy \'bȯs-ē, 'bäs-ē\ *adj.* Ornamented with bosses; studded.

bossy \'bȯs-ē\ *adj.;* **boss·i·er; boss·i·est.** Inclined to act like a boss.

bo·tan·i·cal \bə-'tan-ik-l\ or **bo·tan·ic** \-ik\ *adj.* Having to do with botany.

bot·a·nist \'bät-n-əst\ *n.* A specialist in botany; a person who studies or experiments with plants.

bot·a·ny \'bät-n-ē\ *n.* The science treating of the structure, life processes, classification, and breeding of plants.

botch \'bäch\ *v.* **1** To repair; to mend; especially, to patch clumsily. **2** To bungle; as, to *botch* a job. — *n.* Bungling work; a bungle. — **botchy** \'bäch-ē\ *adj.*

both \'bōth\ *adj.* or *pron.* The one and the other; the two. *Both* dresses were red. *Both* of us were born in February. — *conj.* As well; not only; equally; as, *both* the good and the bad.

both·er \'bäth-r\ *v.;* **both·ered; both·er·ing** \-r(-)ing\. **1** To annoy; to trouble; as, to be *bothered* by flies. **2** To take trouble; to feel care or anxiety; to worry. If I had known I would see you today, I would not have *bothered* to write. — *n.* **1** Trouble, or a source of trouble; especially, petty annoyance. What a *bother* a cold can be! **2** Fuss; disturbance. What is all the *bother* about?

both·er·some \'bäth-rs-m\ *adj.* Causing bother; as, a *bothersome* problem.

bot·tle \'bät-l\ *n.* **1** A hollow glass or earthenware container, usually with a narrow neck or mouth and without handles. **2** The contents of a bottle; as, to drink a *bottle* of milk. — *v.;* **bot·tled; bot·tling** \-l(-)ing\. **1** To put into bottles; as, to *bottle* milk. **2** To enclose, as if in a bottle; to keep shut up; as, to *bottle* up one's anger. The fleet was *bottled* up in the harbor.

bot·tle·neck \'bät-l-ˌnek\ *n.* **1** A narrow passageway. **2** A place, a condition, or a point in a process where progress is held up. A narrow bridge can be a bad *bottleneck* on a heavily traveled road.

bot·tom \'bät-m\ *n.* **1** The lowest part of anything; the base. **2** The part of a thing that is under and that supports the contents or bulk; as, the *bottom* of a chair. **3** The bed of a body of water. **4** Low land along a river; as, the Mississippi River *bottoms.* **5** The part of a boat that is usually under water; the boat itself. Shipments must be delayed because of the lack of *bottoms.* — *adj.* **1** Having to do with the bottom. **2** Lowest; as, *bottom* prices.

bot·tom·less \'bät-m-ləs\ *adj.* **1** Without a bottom. **2** Very deep; as, a *bottomless* pit.

bot·u·lism \'bäch-l-ˌiz-m\ *n.* Poisoning by a substance produced by certain bacteria that may infect preserved food.

bou·doir \'bu̇d-ˌwär, 'büd-\ *n.* A small room furnished for use by a woman as a private sitting room or dressing room and often adjoining a bedroom.

bough \'bau̇\ *n.* An arm or a branch of a tree, especially a main branch.

bought. Past tense and past part. of *buy.*

bouil·lon \'bü-ˌyän, 'bu̇l-yən\ *n.* A clear soup of beef or other meat; broth.

boul·der or **bowl·der** \'bōld-r\ *n.* A large rounded or worn stone.

bou·le·vard \'bu̇l-ə-ˌvärd, 'bül-, -ˌvȧrd\ *n.* A broad avenue or thoroughfare.

bounce \'bau̇n(t)s\ *v.;* **bounced; bounc·ing. 1** To throw something against a surface so that it will spring back; as, to *bounce* a ball. **2** To spring backward after striking. The ball *bounced* over the fence. **3** To throw violently; to discharge; as, to *bounce* a person out of a restaurant; to be *bounced* from one's job. **4** To leap or spring suddenly; as, to *bounce* out of a chair. — *n.* **1** A sudden leap or bound; a spring; a rebound; as, to catch a ball on the first *bounce.* **2** The quality of resilience or quick recovery, as from discouragement; a lively spirit or temper; as, to lack one's customary *bounce.*

bounc·er \'bau̇n(t)s-r\ *n.* **1** A person or thing that bounces. **2** A man employed in a public place to remove disorderly persons.

bounc·ing \'bau̇n(t)s-ing\ *adj.* Big and lively; as, a *bouncing* baby.

bouncing Bet \'bet\ or **bouncing Bess** \'bes\. A narrow-leaved, smooth-stemmed plant about two feet tall, bearing pinkish-white clusters of flowers with notched petals.

bound \'bau̇nd\ *adj.* Going; on the way; headed; as, homeward *bound;* hundreds of cars, all *bound* for the city.

bound \'bau̇nd\ *n.* **1** A boundary line, as of a piece of property. **2** A limit; a point or a line beyond which a person or thing cannot go; as, out of *bounds.* — *v.* **1** To form the limit or boundary of. A river *bounded* the farm on one side, forests on the others. **2** To name the boundaries of; as, to *bound* the United States. **3** To adjoin. — **boundless,** *adj.* — **bound·less·ly,** *adv.*

bound \'bau̇nd\ *n.* **1** A leap; a spring; as, to cover a distance in three *bounds.* **2** A bounce, as of a ball. — *v.* **1** To move with bounds; to spring; to leap. The dog *bounded* over the fence. **2** To spring back, as a rubber ball; to bounce. **3** To cause to rebound; to bounce; as, to *bound* a ball on the floor.

bound \'bau̇nd\. Past tense and past part. of *bind.* — *adj.* **1** Fastened; tied; as, a package *bound* with string. **2** Held or tied down; restrained. **3** Morally or legally obliged; as, a man *bound* over to keep the peace. **4** Covered with binding; as, a *bound* book. **5** Certain; sure; as, a plan that is *bound* to succeed. **6** Resolved; determined; as, a person who is *bound* to have his own way.

bound·a·ry \'bau̇nd-r(-)ē\ *n.; pl.* **bound·a·ries.** Something that marks or shows a limit or end, as of a region or a piece of land; a dividing line.
— The words *border* and *frontier* are synonyms of *boundary* when they refer to geographical limits: *boundary* usually indicates a definitely established dividing line, as between countries or states; *border* may suggest an indefinite section of territory adjoining a boundary; *frontier* may refer to the farthest extent of territory that has been settled.

bound·en \'bau̇n-dən\ *adj.* Placed upon a person as a duty; binding; as, our *bounden* duty.

boun·te·ous \'bau̇nt-ē-əs\ *adj.* **1** Generous. **2** Given plentifully; as, *bounteous* gifts. — **boun·te·ous·ly,** *adv.*

boun·ti·ful \'bau̇nt-əf-l\ *adj.* **1** Generous; giving in abundance; as, a *bountiful* host. **2** Plentiful; abundant; as, a *bountiful* supply. — **boun·ti·ful·ly** \-əf-l(-)ē\ *adv.*

boun·ty \'bau̇nt-ē\ *n.; pl.* **boun·ties. 1** Generosity; generous gifts. The old servant depends on the *bounty* of his master. **2** Money given as a reward or inducement. The state gives a *bounty* for every wolf killed.

bou·quet \bō-'kā, bü-\ *n.* **1** A bunch of flowers. **2** Fragrance.

bour·geois \'bu̇rzh-ˌwä, -ˌwȧ\ *n. sing. and pl.* A person of the middle class of society. — *adj.* Characteristic of the middle class; as, a *bourgeois* point of view.

bour·geoi·sie \ˌbu̇rzh-ˌwä-'zē, -ˌwȧ-\ *n.* The middle class of society.

bourn or **bourne** \'bōrn, 'bȯrn, 'bu̇rn\ *n.* A brook.

bourn or **bourne** \'bōrn, 'bȯrn, 'bu̇rn\ *n.* **1** A boundary. **2** A goal; a destination.

bour·rée \bü-'rā\ *n.* A lively old French dance.

bout \'bau̇t\ *n.* **1** As much of an action as is done at one time; a turn, spell, or period; as, a *bout* of work. **2** A contest; a trial of skill or strength; as, a wrestling *bout.*

bou·ton·niere \ˌbüt-n-'ir, ˌbü-tən-'yer\ *n.* A flower or bouquet worn in the buttonhole.

bo·vine \'bō-ˌvīn, -ˌvēn\ *adj.* **1** Of or like the cow or ox. **2** Slow, dull, and patient. — *n.* A bovine animal.

bow \'bau̇\ *v.* **1** To bend the head, body, or knee in greeting, reverence, respect, or submission; as, to *bow* to a friend; to *bow* down before an altar. **2** To submit or yield; as, to *bow* to authority. **3** To bend; as, a man *bowed* with age; to *bow* the head in prayer. The trees *bowed* their branches before the wind. **4** To express by bowing; as, to *bow* one's thanks. — *n.* A bend of the head or body to express courtesy, reverence, or submission.

bow \ˈbō\ *n.* **1** A rainbow. **2** A weapon for shooting arrows that is made of a strip of wood or other elastic material bent by a cord connecting the two ends. **3** Anything shaped in a curve like a bow; a bend. **4** A wooden rod with horsehairs stretched from end to end, used for playing a violin or a similar instrument. **5** A knot, especially a slipknot, formed by doubling a ribbon or string into one or two loops. — *adj.* Bent like a bow; bowed; curved. — *v.* **1** To bend like a bow; to curve. The wall *bows* inward. **2** In music, to use a bow or play with a bow.

bow

bow \ˈbau̇\ *n.* The forward part of a boat, ship, or aircraft.

bow·el \ˈbau̇-əl, ˈbau̇l\ *n.* **1** [usually in the plural] The tubelike organ, consisting of an upper, narrower, part (**small bowel**) and a lower, broader, part (**large bowel**), through which food passes after it has left the stomach; an intestine. **2** [in the plural] The innermost parts; as, the *bowels* of the earth.

bow·er \ˈbau̇r\ *n.* **1** A shelter in a garden, made of boughs of trees or vines; an arbor. **2** A place where one may go to rest; a retreat.

bow·ie knife \ˈbü-ē, ˈbō-ē\. [Named after Colonel James *Bowie*, American soldier and frontiersman, said to be its inventor.] A straight, heavy, single-edged hunting knife found especially handy and effective in self-defense.

bowl \ˈbōl\ *n.* **1** A rounded, hollowed dish, generally deeper than a basin and larger than a cup. **2** The contents of a bowl; as, to eat a *bowl* of cereal for breakfast. **3** The bowl-shaped part of anything; as, the *bowl* of a spoon; the *bowl* of a tobacco pipe. **4** A bowl-shaped amphitheater.

bowl, 1

bowl \ˈbōl\ *n.* **1** A round ball for rolling on a level surface in certain games. **2** The rolling of a bowl. — *v.* **1** To roll a ball, as in bowling. **2** In cricket, to throw the ball to the batsman with a smooth movement of the arm. **3** To move rapidly and smoothly, as if rolling. The car *bowled* along the turnpike. **4** To hit, as if with something rolled. The waves *bowled* the bathers over.

bowlder. Variant of *boulder*.

bow·leg \ˈbō-ˈleg\ *n.* A crooked leg, especially one bowed outward.

bow·leg·ged \ˈbō-ˈleg-əd, -ˈlegd\ *adj.* Having bowlegs.

bowl·er \ˈbōl-r\ *n.* **1** A person who plays at bowls or bowling. **2** A cricket player who bowls.

bow·ler \ˈbōl-r\ *n.* A derby hat.

bowl game. A football game played after the regular season between specially invited teams.

bow·line \ˈbō-lən, -ˌlīn\ *n.* **1** A rope used to keep the weather, or windward, edge of a square sail pulled forward. **2** Also **bowline knot**. A knot used for making a loop that will not slip.

bowline

bowl·ing \ˈbō-ling\ *n.* **1** A game played by rolling balls so as to knock down wooden pins that are set up at the far end of an alley; ninepins or tenpins. **2** Bowls.

bowls \ˈbōlz\ *n.* **1** A game played on a level lawn by rolling specially shaped balls towards a smaller stationary ball called a *jack*. **2** Ninepins or tenpins.

bow·man \ˈbō-mən\ *n.; pl.* **bow·men** \-mən\. An archer.

bow·shot \ˈbō-ˌshät\ *n.* The distance that an arrow can be shot from a bow.

bow·sprit \ˈbau̇-ˌsprit, ˈbō-\ *n.* A strong spar or boom projecting forward from the bow of a vessel.

bow·string \ˈbō-ˌstring\ *n.* The cord connecting the two ends of a bow.

bow window \ˈbō\. A bay window, especially a curved one.

box \ˈbäks\ *n.* A blow with the hand; a slap. — *v.* **1** To strike with the open hand or with the fist. **2** To fight with the fists for sport or for money; as, to *box* the champion.

box \ˈbäks\ *n.* An evergreen shrub or small tree used for hedges.

box \ˈbäks\ *n.* **1** A receptacle, usually with four sides, a bottom, and a cover. **2** The amount held by such a receptacle; as, to eat a *box* of popcorn. **3** A small compartment for a group of spectators in a theater. **4** A stall for a horse. **5** The driver's seat on a carriage. **6** A shed that protects; as, a sentry *box*. **7** In baseball, the place where the pitcher stands or the place where the batter stands. — *v.* To inclose in a box or as if in a box.

box·car \ˈbäks-ˌkär, -ˌkȧr\ *n.* A roofed freight car, usually with sliding doors in the sides.

box elder \ˈeld-r\. An American maple with compound leaves like the ash, used as a shade tree.

box·er \ˈbäks-r\ *n.* **1** A person who boxes with his fists. **2** A person who packs things.

box·er \ˈbäks-r\ *n.* A sturdy, medium-sized dog, related to the bulldog, with a short, smooth, brown coat.

box·ing \ˈbäks-ing\ *n.* Fighting with the fists as a sport, usually with padded gloves.

box office. In theaters, stadiums, and other public places, the office where admission tickets are sold.

box score. In baseball, the complete score of a game arranged in the form of a table giving the names and positions of the players and a complete record of every play.

box·wood \ˈbäks-ˌwu̇d\ *n.* **1** The hard, tough wood of the box tree. **2** The box tree.

boy \ˈbȯi\ *n.* **1** A male child from birth to young

manhood. **2** A male servant; especially, as in the Far East, a native manservant.

boy·cott \'bȯi-ˌkät\ *v.* [Named after Captain Charles C. *Boycott*, an Irish land agent who was so treated by the Irish Land League in 1880.] To refrain from having any dealings with, as a person, business firm, or nation. — *n.* The action or an instance of boycotting.

boy·hood \'bȯi-ˌhu̇d\ *n.* The time or condition of being a boy.

boy·ish \'bȯi-ish\ *adj.* Like a boy; relating to boys or boyhood; as, *boyish* pranks. — **boy·ish·ly**, *adv.*

boy scout. A boy who is a member of one of various organizations called "**Boy Scouts**", whose purpose is to develop healthy, active boys trained in good citizenship.

boy·sen·ber·ry \'bȯiz-n-ˌber-ē, 'bȯis-\ *n.; pl.* **boy·sen·ber·ries.** A large berry shaped like a blackberry and resembling a raspberry in flavor, valued for canning.

bra \'brä, 'bra̍\ *n.* **1** A brassiere. **2** A piece of clothing resembling a brassiere, as the top of a two-piece bathing suit.

brace \'brās\ *n.* A curved handle for turning bits or small tools used for boring.

brace \'brās\ *v.;* **braced**; **brac·ing.** **1** To bind; to fasten. **2** To set so as to resist pressure; as, to *brace* oneself against the wind. **3** To give strength to; to stimulate. Sight of the goal *braced* the runner. **4** To furnish or support with braces; as, to *brace* a wall with poles. **5** To rouse one's energies or courage; as, to *brace* up before the big test. — *n.* **1** Anything that connects or fastens, as a clamp. **2** A cord or rod for producing or maintaining tightness. **3** A support, as for the legs or shoulders. **4** [often in the plural] Metal wire fastened to teeth by dentists to correct irregularities in their growth or position. **5** [in the plural] Suspenders. **6** A pair; a couple; as, a *brace* of ducks. **7** In building, a piece of material used to carry, turn aside, or resist weight or pressure. **8** A character [{] connecting two or more words or lines or staffs of music that are to be taken together.

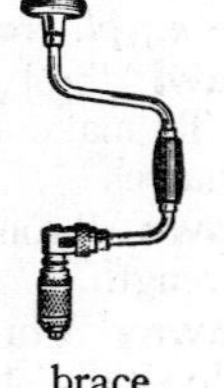
brace

brace·let \'brās-lət\ *n.* An ornamental band or chain for the wrist or arm.

brac·ing \'brā-sing\ *adj.* Strengthening; refreshing; invigorating; as, *bracing* weather.

brack·en \'brak-n\ *n.* A large, coarse, branching fern or a growth of such ferns.

brack·et \'brak-ət\ *n.* **1** A support for a shelf or other weight, usually attached to a wall. **2** A shelf or a set of shelves held up by such a support. **3** A fixture or holder, as for an electric light, projecting from a wall. **4** Either of two written or printed marks ([ ]) used to enclose something not a part of a sentence. **5** A class of taxpayers graded according to income. — *v.* **1** To furnish with a bracket or brackets; to place within or connect by brackets. **2** To group together as being of the same kind.

brack·ish \'brak-ish\ *adj.* Somewhat salty, as water in marshes near the sea.

bract \'brakt\ *n.* **1** A leaf out of which a flower grows. **2** A leaf that grows on a flower-bearing stem.

brad \'brad\ *n.* A thin small nail.

brae \'brā\ *n. Scottish.* A hillside; a slope; a bank.

brag \'brag\ *v.;* **bragged**; **brag·ging.** To boast. — *n.* **1** A boast; boasting; bragging. **2** The thing that is bragged about. **3** A boaster; a braggart.

brag·ga·do·cio \ˌbrag-ə-'dō-shē-ˌō, -'dō-ˌshō\ *n.; pl.* **brag·ga·do·ci·os.** **1** A braggart. **2** Empty boasting; brag.

brag·gart \'brag-rt\ *n.* A person who brags.

braid \'brād\ *v.* **1** To weave together three or more strands, as of hair or cloth; to plait. **2** To trim or bind with braid. — *n.* **1** Something that is braided; especially, a plait of hair. My sister wears her hair in *braids*. **2** A band, ribbon, or cordlike fabric used for trimming or binding cloth or garments.

braille \'brāl\ *n.* [Named after Louis *Braille*, a French teacher of the blind, who invented it.] [often with a capital] A system of printing for the blind in which the letters are represented by raised dots on the paper.

brain \'brān\ *n.* **1** The mass of grayish matter consisting of nerve tissue that is enclosed in the skull of a person or animal and forms the main organ of the nervous system. **2** [usually in the plural] A good mind; intelligence; understanding. That child has *brains*. **3** *Slang.* An exceptionally intelligent or intellectual person. — *v.* To beat out or knock out the brains of a person or animal.

brain·less \'brān-ləs\ *adj.* Without brains; lacking intelligence or understanding; stupid; silly; thoughtless. — **brain·less·ly**, *adv.*

brain·storm \'brān-ˌstȯrm\ *n.* **1** A temporary but violent mental upset or disturbance. **2** A sudden burst of inspiration; a startling idea.

brainy \'brā-nē\ *adj.;* **brain·i·er**; **brain·i·est.** Having or showing brains; intelligent; clever; as, a *brainy* student; a *brainy* idea.

braise \'brāz\ *v.;* **braised**; **brais·ing.** To cook by first browning quickly in fat and then simmering in a covered dish in a small amount of moisture.

brake \'brāk\ *n.* A coarse fern often growing several feet high.

brake \'brāk\ *n.* A thick growth of shrubs, small trees, or canes; a thicket.

brake \'brāk\ *n.* A device for slowing up or stopping motion, as of a car wheel, especially by friction. — *v.;* **braked**; **brak·ing.** To slow up or stop by using a brake.

brake

brake·man \'brāk-mən\ *n.; pl.* **brake·men** \-mən\. A man employed or assigned to operate brakes, as on a railroad train.

bram·ble \'bram-bl\ *n.* A prickly shrub, such as a blackberry or a raspberry bush; especially, the common English blackberry, used as a hedge plant.

bran \'bran\ *n.* The broken coat or covering of the seed of wheat, rye, or other cereal grain, left after the grain has been ground and the flour or meal sifted out.

branch \'branch\ *n.* **1** A part of a tree that grows out from the trunk or from a large bough. **2** Anything extending from a main line or body like a branch of a tree; as, a *branch* of an antler; a *branch* of a river. **3** A part; a division. The infantry is a *branch* of the army. **4** A subordinate office or part of a central system, as of a bank or a library. — *v.* To send forth a branch; to spread or divide into branches; as, a tree *branching* widely close to the ground. The river *branches* north of the town. — **branch out.** To extend one's activities; to do something on a larger scale.

brand \'brand\ *n.* **1** A charred or burning piece of wood. **2** A mark put on criminals with a hot iron; any mark of disgrace. **3** A mark made by burning, as on cattle, to show ownership. **4** A similar mark made by stamping or printing, as on manufactured goods, to show maker or quality; a label or trademark. **5** A kind or quality of goods as known by the label; as, a good *brand* of flour. **6** An iron stamp used for branding. — *v.* **1** To mark with a brand or with a label; as, to *brand* a calf. **2** To show up or reveal as clearly as if marked with a brand; especially, to reveal or to point out as in some way bad; as, an action so wicked as to *brand* a man for the rest of his life.

bran·dish \'bran-dish\ *v.* To wave or shake, usually in a threatening manner; as, to *brandish* a stick at a growling dog.

— The word *flourish* is a synonym of *brandish*: *brandish* may suggest threatening movement; *flourish* generally indicates showy or triumphant movement.

brand-new or **bran-new** \'bran-'nü, -'nyü\ *adj.* Quite new; noticeably new.

bran·dy \'bran-dē\ *n.; pl.* **bran·dies.** An alcoholic liquor distilled from wine; a similar liquor made from fruit juices. — *v.;* **bran·died** \-dēd\; **bran·dy·ing.** To flavor or treat with brandy; as, *brandied* peaches.

brant \'brant\ *n.; pl.* **brant** or **brants.** A dark wild goose that breeds in arctic regions, the smallest of wild geese.

brash \'brash\ *adj.* **1** Hasty or rash; as, a *brash* decision. **2** Saucy; impudent; as, a *brash* remark.

brass \'bras\ *n.* **1** An alloy made by combining copper and zinc. **2** The reddish-yellow color of this alloy. **3** The officers of high rank or position; especially, military and naval officers in top commands. **4** Impudence; brazen actions; extreme boldness; as, to lack the *brass* to press the matter any further. **5** A brass utensil, fixture, or fitting. **6** Also **brass·es.** The brass wind instruments of an orchestra.

brass band. A band of musicians who play upon brass wind instruments.

bras·siere \brə-'zir; ˌbräs-ē-'er, ˌbrȧs-\ *n.* A woman's undergarment worn to support or shape the breasts.

brassy \'bras-ē\ *adj.;* **brass·i·er; brass·i·est.** **1** Of brass; decorated with brass. **2** Impudent; bold; as, a person noted for his *brassy* ways. **3** Like or sounding like brass.

brat \'brat\ *n.* A child; an annoying child.

bra·va·do \brə-'väd-ˌō, -'vȧd-\ *n.; pl.* **bra·va·does** or **bra·va·dos.** A show or pretense of bravery.

brave \'brāv\ *adj.;* **brav·er; brav·est.** **1** Fearless; courageous; as, a *brave* man. **2** Making a fine show or display. — *n.* An Indian warrior. — *v.;* **braved; brav·ing.** To meet or face with courage; to defy; to dare; as, to *brave* the fire of the enemy; to *brave* a storm. — **brave·ly,** *adv.*

brav·ery \'brāv-r(-)ē\ *n.* **1** Courage; fearlessness. **2** Showy display; fine dress. — For synonyms see *courage.*

bra·vo \'brä-ˌvō, 'brȧ-\ *n.; pl.* **bra·voes** or **bra·vos.** A desperate villain; especially, a hired assassin.

bra·vo \'brä-ˌvō, brä-'vō, (')brȧ-\ *interj.* An exclamation used to express applause or approval. — *n.; pl.* **bra·vos.** A cry of *bravo.*

brawl \'brȯl\ *v.* **1** To quarrel noisily and roughly. **2** To make a loud, confused noise. — *n.* A noisy quarrel.

brawn \'brȯn\ *n.* Large, strong muscles; muscular strength.

brawny \'brȯn-ē\ *adj.;* **brawn·i·er; brawn·i·est.** Physically strong; muscular.

bray \'brā\ *n.* The loud, harsh cry of a donkey or an ass, or a sound like it. — *v.* To make a bray.

braze \'brāz\ *v.;* **brazed; braz·ing.** To solder with a hard solder, as with brass.

bra·zen \'brāz-n\ *adj.* **1** Made of brass or bronze; like brass, as in strength or color. **2** Sounding harsh and loud; as, *brazen* voices. **3** Impudent; shameless; as, a *brazen* girl. — *v.* To face impudently or shamelessly; as, to *brazen* out one's guilt.

bra·zier \'brāzh-r\ *n.* A pan for holding burning coals.

Bra·zil·ian \brə-'zil-yən\ *adj.* Of or relating to Brazil. — *n.* A native or inhabitant of Brazil.

Bra·zil nut \brə-'zil\. One of the three-sided oily nuts, 18 to 24 in number, packed inside the round fruit of a large Brazilian tree.

nut
husk
Brazil nuts

breach \'brēch\ *n.* **1** A break or a being broken; an opening made by breaking through; as, a *breach* in a wall. **2** A breaking by not obeying; a violation; as, a *breach* of the law. **3** A gap made by breaking or battering, as in a wall. **4** A breaking up of friendly relations, as between persons. — *v.* To make a break in; as, to *breach* a wall.

bread \'bred\ *n.* **1** A baked food made from flour or meal. **2** Food; as, our daily *bread.* — *v.* To cover with bread crumbs before cooking; as, to *bread* a veal chop.

bread·bas·ket \'bred-ˌbas-kət\ *n.* Any region important for its agricultural products, especially one producing cereal grains.

bread·fruit \'bred-ˌfrüt\ *n.* The large round fruit of a tropical tree of the mulberry family, which when baked resembles bread.

bread·stuff \'bred-ˌstəf\ *n.* **1** Grain or flour. **2** Bread.

breadth \'bredth\ *n.* Distance measured from side to side; width.

break \'brāk\ *v.;* **broke** \'brōk\; **bro·ken** \'brōk-n\; **break·ing.** **1** To separate suddenly or forcibly into two or more parts; to smash, burst, split, or crack; as, to *break* a dish, a wire, or a bone. Glass *breaks* easily. **2** To open up the surface of, as land in plowing. **3** To destroy the arrangement or firmness of. The troops *broke* ranks. **4** To defeat; as, to *break* a strike. **5** To crush the strength or spirit of; as, a man *broken* by bad news. **6** To tame; as, to *break* a colt. **7** To degrade or bring down in rank or dignity; to dismiss; as, a soldier *broken* from sergeant to private. **8** To lay or force open and pass in or out; to penetrate; as, to *break* prison. **9** To violate; as, to *break* the law; to *break* one's promise. **10** To make known; to reveal; to disclose; as, to *break* the news. **11** To open; as, to *break* an electric circuit. **12** To turn aside the force of. The branches of a tree *broke* the paratrooper's fall. **13** To discontinue; to end; as, to *break* the silence. **14** To go beyond; to exceed; as, to *break* a record. **15** To burst forth violently, as a storm. **16** To give way; to yield ground. The troops *broke* under fire. **17** To be crushed with grief; as, a person whose heart is *breaking.* **18** To lose health or strength; as, to *break* under the strain. **19** To end friendly relations, as two countries. **20** To fail in musical quality. The singer's voice *broke* on some of the high notes. **21** To change from one register to another, as the voice. **22** To appear suddenly; to come into sight or notice. Day *breaks* in the east. — **break down.** **1** To come down by breaking; to collapse. The wagon *broke down.* **2** To give way to emotion, especially by weeping; as, to *break down* and confess. — **break in.** **1** To force in, as a door. **2** To train; to accustom; to adjust; as, to *break in* a new man for the job. **3** To enter forcibly. **4** To interrupt; as, to *break in* with a question. — **break off.** To part or become separated; to discontinue relationship; as, to *break off* with an old friend. — **break out.** **1** To burst forth; to appear suddenly, as a fire or an epidemic. **2** To show itself in eruptions on the skin; to have a rash or eruption on the skin; as, a person whose face is *broken out.* — **break up.** **1** To separate into parts by breaking; as, to *break up* the candy into small pieces. **2** To bring to an end; to prevent the continuance of; to end. The meeting *broke up* soon afterwards. **3** To upset; to disturb deeply; as, to be all *broken up* over something. **4** To stop the progress of; to cure; as, to *break up* a cold. **5** To become separated into parts or fragments. The ice in the river will *break up.* — *n.* **1** A breaking; as, to make a *break* for freedom; the *break* of day. **2** Something made or produced by breaking, such as a crack or hole; as, a bad *break* of the leg; a *break* in a dam. **3** An awkward blunder. **4** A chance, either good or bad; as, to get a lucky *break.* **5** An opening in an electric circuit, interrupting the flow of current. — **break·a·ble** *adj.*

break·age \'brāk-ij\ *n.* **1** A breaking. **2** Articles broken. **3** The cost of replacing or repairing broken things.

break·down \'brāk-ˌdau̇n\ *n.* **1** The act or the result of breaking down; especially, a collapse or failure, as of machinery or health, or a giving way to emotion. **2** Chemical decomposition. **3** The division into categories or smaller units; analysis; classification; as, to make a *breakdown* of the time spent on a job.

break·er \'brāk-r\ *n.* **1** A person or thing that breaks. **2** A wave that breaks into foam on the shore.

break·fast \'brek-fəst\ *n.* The first meal of the day. — *v.* To eat breakfast.

break·neck \'brāk-ˌnek\ *adj.* Involving risk of a broken neck; as, to travel at *breakneck* speed.

break·up \'brāk-ˌəp\ *n.* The action of breaking up or of bringing to an end; a disruption; a dissolution.

break·wa·ter \'brāk-ˌwȯt-r, -ˌwät-r\ *n.* A wall or other structure built to protect a beach or a harbor from the force of waves.

bream \'brim\ *n.; pl.* **bream** or **breams.** Any of several spiny-finned sunfishes.

breast \'brest\ *n.* **1** The front part of the body between the neck and the abdomen. **2** A gland that gives milk. **3** The place of the emotions and inner thoughts; as, to keep a secret locked in one's *breast.* **4** Anything thought of as like the human breast or bosom; as, the *breast* of a hill. **5** The part of a piece of clothing that covers the chest. — *v.* To meet, breast forward; to face or oppose bravely; as, to *breast* a storm.

breast·bone \'brest-'bōn\ *n.* The bony framework connecting the ribs at the front and in the center of the chest; the sternum.

breast·plate \'brest-ˌplāt\ *n.* A piece of armor for covering the breast.

breastplate

breast stroke. A swimming stroke made by extending the arms in front of the head while lying flat on the breast, then turning the palms out and sweeping the arms back like a pair of oars.

breast·work \'brest-ˌwərk\ *n.* A hastily built wall high enough to serve as a defense in battle.

breath \'breth\ *n.* **1** Air taken in or sent out by the lungs. **2** A single effort of breathing; an instant. It all happened in a *breath.* **3** A slight breeze; as, not a *breath* of air. **4** Fragrant aroma; air filled with fragrance; as, the *breath* of roses; the *breath* of spring. **5** Power of breathing naturally; as, to be out of *breath.* **6** Something produced by breathing, as a film of vapor. It was cold enough to see one's *breath.* — **under one's breath.** In low tones; in a whisper.

breathe \\'brēth\\ *v.;* **breathed**; **breath·ing** \\'brēth-ing\\. **1** To draw air into the lungs and send it out again; to inhale and exhale. **2** To continue to breathe; to live; to exist. **3** To pass like a breath or to blow gently. **4** To send forth, as fragrance. **5** To force into, with, or as if with a breath; as, to *breathe* new life into an organization. **6** To utter softly; to whisper; as, to *breathe* a secret. **7** To permit to draw breath; to allow to rest; as, to *breathe* a horse after a gallop.

breath·er \\'brēth-r\\ *n.* **1** One who breathes. **2** A pause to draw one's breath.

breath·less \\'breth-ləs\\ *adj.* **1** Not breathing; dead. **2** Out of breath; panting. **3** Holding one's breath, as from excitement or fear; as, a tale of adventure that leaves one *breathless.* — **breath·less·ly**, *adv.*

breath·tak·ing \\'breth-ˌtāk-ing\\ *adj.* **1** Causing one to be out of breath; as, a *breathtaking* climb. **2** Causing one to hold one's breath; thrilling; as, the *breathtaking* scenery of the mountains. — **breath·tak·ing·ly**, *adv.*

bred. Past tense and past part. of *breed.*

breech \\'brēch, 'brich\\ *n.* **1** The buttocks. **2** The back part of a cannon or gun, behind the bore. — *v.* **1** To provide with a breech, as a rifle. **2** \\'brich, 'brēch\\ To put into breeches; to clothe with breeches.

breech·es \\'brich-əz\\ *n. pl.* **1** Short trousers fastening below the knee; as, riding *breeches.* **2** Trousers.

breech·es buoy \\'brē-chəz\\. A canvas sling in the form of a pair of short-legged breeches hung from a life buoy which runs along a cable stretched from ship to shore or from one ship to another, used to take persons off a ship, especially in rescue operations.

breed \\'brēd\\ *v.;* **bred** \\'bred\\; **breed·ing. 1** To give birth to, as by hatching. **2** To raise, as horses or flowers, for sale or to develop improved forms. **3** To bring up; to train. The boy's manners showed that he had been well *bred.* **4** To provide favorable conditions for breeding; produce. Standing water *breeds* mosquitoes. **5** To produce offspring; as, to *breed* like flies. Some animals *breed* very fast. **6** To be produced; to originate. Crime *breeds* in poverty. — *n.* A kind or variety of animals or plants related by descent and similar in most respects; race; stock; as, dogs of many different *breeds.* — **breed·er**, *n.*

breed·ing \\'brēd-ing\\ *n.* **1** The act of one that breeds. **2** The raising of animals to improve their quality. **3** The production of new forms of plants and flowers by crossing existing forms. **4** Training, especially in manners. Good manners show good *breeding.*

breeze \\'brēz\\ *n.* A gentle wind.

breeze·way \\'brēz-ˌwā\\ *n.* A covered passage, often open at the sides, connecting a building with an accessory building such as a garage.

breezy \\'brē-zē\\ *adj.;* **breez·i·er**; **breez·i·est. 1** Windy; swept by breezes. **2** Full of life; brisk; lively; as, a *breezy* manner.

brethren. A pl. of *brother.*

breve \\'brēv\\ *n.* A mark [˘] used in some books over *a, e, i, o, u* to show that they are pronounced as in *bat, bet, bit, not, nut.*

bre·via·ry \\'brēv-r-ē, -yər-ē, 'brē-vē-ˌer-ē\\ *n.; pl.* **bre·via·ries**. A prayer book made up of psalms, other Bible readings, and selections from other religious writings, a section of which is recited each day, as by priests and monks.

brev·i·ty \\'brev-ət-ē\\ *n.* Shortness of duration; briefness of time.

brew \\'brü\\ *v.* **1** To prepare by steeping, boiling, and fermenting, as beer from malt and hops, or by steeping only, as tea from tea leaves. **2** To plot or plan; as, to *brew* mischief. **3** To be mixing, forming, or gathering. A storm is *brewing.* — *n.* A brewed beverage; as, a strong *brew.*

brew·er \\'brü-ər, 'brůr\\ *n.* One that brews; especially, a person whose business or occupation is the brewing of beer and ale.

brew·ery \\'brü-ər-ē, 'brůr-ē\\ *n.; pl.* **brew·er·ies**. A place where malt liquors, as beer and ale, are brewed.

briar. Variant of *brier.*

briary. Variant of *briery.*

bribe \\'brīb\\ *n.* [From Old French *bribe* meaning "scrap of bread given to a beggar".] Something given or promised to a person, especially one in a position of trust, in order to influence dishonestly his decision or action. — *v.;* **bribed**; **brib·ing**. To give or promise a bribe; to influence by a bribe. — **brib·a·ble**, *adj.* — **brib·er**, *n.*

brib·ery \\'brīb-r(-)ē\\ *n.; pl.* **brib·er·ies**. The act or practice of giving or taking a bribe.

bric-a-brac \\'brik-ə-ˌbrak\\ *n.* Small ornamental articles; knickknacks; curios.

brick \\'brik\\ *n.* **1** A building or paving material made from clay molded into blocks and baked. **2** One of these blocks. **3** A brick-shaped mass; as, a *brick* of ice cream. — *adj.* **1** Made of brick; as, a *brick* house. **2** Of the reddish color of some kinds of brick. — *v.* To cover or pave with bricks; to close with bricks; as, to *brick* up a window.

brick·bat \\'brik-ˌbat\\ *n.* A piece of a broken brick, especially of one broken so as to leave one end whole.

brick·lay·er \\'brik-ˌlā-ər, -ˌler\\ *n.* A person who builds or paves with bricks. — **brick·lay·ing** \\-ˌlā-ing\\ *n.*

brid·al \\'brīd-l\\ *adj.* Of or relating to a bride or a wedding; as, a *bridal* gown; a *bridal* feast. — *n.* A wedding.

bride \\'brīd\\ *n.* A woman just married or about to be married.

bride·groom \'brīd-ˌgrüm, -ˌgru̇m\ *n.* A man just married or about to be married.

brides·maid \'brīdz-ˌmād\ *n.* An unmarried woman who attends a bride at her wedding.

bridge \'brij\ *n.* **1** Something built over a depression or an obstacle, as a river or a railroad, for use as a passageway. **2** A platform above and across the deck of a ship for the captain or officer in charge. **3** Something like a bridge in use or form, as the upper bony part of the nose or the small arch on a violin that raises the strings. **4** A card game. **5** A device for replacing missing teeth by fastening artificial teeth to natural teeth. — *v.;* **bridged**; **bridg·ing.** To build or make a bridge or bridges on or over; as, to *bridge* a river.

bridge·head \'brij-ˌhed\ *n.* **1** The head, or end, of a bridge. **2** A fortified position protecting a bridge. **3** An advanced position seized in enemy territory and defended as a foothold for invasion forces or for further advance.

bri·dle \'brīd-l\ *n.* **1** The part of a horse's harness that fits over the head and is used to control the animal. **2** A restraint; a curb; a check. — *v.;* **bri·dled**; **bri·dling** \-l(-)ing\. **1** To put a bridle on; as, to *bridle* a horse. **2** To restrain or check with or as if with a bridle; as, to *bridle* one's tongue. **3** To hold the head high and draw in the chin as an expression of pride or anger; as, to *bridle* at a criticism.

bridle

bridle path. A path suitable for, or open only to, horseback riders.

brief \'brēf\ *adj.* **1** Short, especially in time; as, a *brief* visit. **2** Concise; not wordy; as, a *brief* answer to a question. — *v.* **1** To give someone a short explanation or summary of information about something. **2** To give exact final instructions, as to the crew of a bombing plane before a mission. — **brief·ly**, *adv.*

brief·case \'brēf-ˌkās\ *n.* A flat, flexible case, usually of leather, for carrying papers.

bri·er or **bri·ar** \'brīr\ *n.* Any plant with a thorny or prickly woody stem, as the blackberry or the wild rose. — **bri·ery** or **bri·ary**, *adj.*

bri·er or **bri·ar** \'brīr\ *n.* A southern European tree whose woody root is used for making tobacco pipes.

brig \'brig\ *n.* A two-masted square-rigged sailing ship.

brig \'brig\ *n.* The place of confinement for offenders on a ship of the United States Navy.

Brig. Abbreviation for: **1** *Brigade.* **2** *Brigadier.*

bri·gade \bri-'gād\ *n.* **1** A body of soldiers consisting of two or more regiments. **2** Any group of persons organized for acting together; as, a fire *brigade.*

brig

brig·a·dier \ˌbrig-ə-'dir\ *n.* A brigadier general.

brigadier general; *pl.* **brigadier generals.** A commissioned officer ranking above a colonel and below a major general.

brig·and \'brig-nd\ *n.* A lawless person who lives by plundering, usually a member of a band; a bandit.

brig·an·tine \'brig-n-ˌtēn\ *n.* A two-masted square-rigged boat differing from a brig in not carrying a square mainsail.

bright \'brīt\ *adj.* **1** Shedding much light; shining; glowing; as, a *bright* fire; a *bright* day. **2** Very clear or vivid in color; as, a *bright* red. **3** Clever; as, a *bright* boy. **4** Lively. **5** Cheerful; happy; as, a *bright* future.

— The words *shining* and *brilliant* are synonyms of *bright: bright* usually applies to objects that radiate or reflect light; *shining* may indicate steady or constant brightness; *brilliant* may describe something that gleams or flashes conspicuously.

bright·en \'brīt-n\ *v.;* **bright·ened**; **bright·en·ing** \-n(-)ing\. To make or to become bright or brighter.

bright·ly \'brīt-lē\ *adv.* **1** In a way that sheds much light; as, a fire burning *brightly.* **2** Cleverly; intelligently; as, to reply *brightly.*

bril·liance \'bril-yən(t)s\ or **bril·lian·cy** \-yən-sē\ *n.* Great brightness; splendor.

bril·liant \'bril-yənt\ *adj.* **1** Flashing with light; sparkling; very bright; as, *brilliant* jewels. **2** Very clever or successful; distinguished by qualities that arouse admiration; splendid; as, a *brilliant* student; a *brilliant* career. — For synonyms see *bright.* — *n.* A diamond or other gem cut with many facets so as to sparkle. — **bril·liant·ly**, *adv.*

brim \'brim\ *n.* **1** The edge or rim of something, especially of something hollow; as, a cup filled to the *brim.* **2** The part of a hat that projects from the lower edge of the crown. — *v.;* **brimmed**; **brim·ming.** To come to or overflow the brim. Tears *brimmed* in her eyes.

brim·ful \'brim-'fu̇l\ *adj.* Full to the brim.

brim·stone \'brim-ˌstōn\ *n.* Sulfur.

brin·dle \'brind-l\ *n.* **1** A brindled color. **2** A brindled animal.

brin·dled \'brind-ld\ *adj.* Having dark streaks or spots on a gray or brownish background.

brine \'brīn\ *n.* **1** Water containing a great deal of salt. **2** The ocean; the water of an ocean, sea, or salt lake.

bring \'bring\ *v.;* **brought** \'bro̊t\; **bring·ing** \'bring-ing\. **1** To cause to come with oneself, as by carrying or leading. We were told to *bring* our lunches. **2** To cause to arrive or come about. The storm *brought* heavy losses. **3** To persuade; to induce; as, to *bring* a person to agree. **4** In law, to present, as a charge or an action; as, to *bring* suit against someone. **5** To sell for. The apple crop *brought* a good price. — **bring about.** To cause to take place; to accomplish. — **bring around** or **bring round. 1** To win over, especially gradually; as, a hard person to *bring around* to your way of thinking. **2** To restore to health or consciousness. — **bring forth.** To bear, as fruit or young; to give birth to. — **bring on.** To cause to come into action or existence; as, to *bring on* a fit of coughing. — **bring over.** To win over; as, a person *brought over* to a new point of view. — **bring to.** To restore to consciousness. — **bring up. 1** To rear; to train; to educate; as, to *bring up* a family. **2** To vomit.

brink \'bringk\ *n.* The edge at the top of a steep place.

briny \'brī-nē\ *adj.;* **brin·i·er; brin·i·est.** Of or like brine; salty.

brisk \'brisk\ *adj.* **1** Very active; lively; as, a *brisk* walk. **2** Invigorating; refreshing; as, *brisk* autumn weather. — **brisk·ly,** *adv.*

bris·ket \'bris-kət\ *n.* The breast or lower part of the chest of four-footed animals used as food.

bris·tle \'bris-l\ *n.* **1** A short, stiff, coarse hair, as on the back of a hog. **2** One of the stiff hairs, or something like a hair, in a brush. — *v.;* **bris·tled; bris·tling** \-l(-)ing\. **1** To stand up like the bristles of a hog. **2** To show signs of anger or defiance. The boy *bristled* when he was criticized. **3** To appear as if covered with bristles; as, a harbor *bristling* with the masts of ships. — **bris·tly** \-l(-)ē\ *adj.*

britch·es \'brich-əz\ *n. pl.* Breeches.

Brit·ish \'brit-ish\ *adj.* **1** Relating to the original inhabitants of Britain. **2** Of or relating to Great Britain, or its people, government, or empire. — *n.* The people of Great Britain or of the British Empire — used as a plural with *the.*

Brit·on \'brit-n\ *n.* **1** A member of one of the Celtic peoples inhabiting Great Britain before the Anglo-Saxon invasions. **2** A native or subject of Great Britain; especially, an Englishman.

brit·tle \'brit-l\ *adj.* Hard but not tough; easily broken; as, *brittle* glass.

broach \'brōch\ *n.* A small, long, round, pointed tool, especially one used for rounding out irregularly shaped holes in metal. — *v.* **1** To pierce; to tap, as a barrel, in order to draw off liquor. **2** To introduce as a topic of conversation; as, to *broach* a subject.

broad \'brȯd\ *adj.* **1** Wide; not narrow; as, a *broad* highway. **2** Extending far and wide; spacious; as, *broad* prairies. **3** Open; clear; as, *broad* daylight. **4** Plain; obvious; as, a *broad* hint. **5** Coarse; indelicate; as, a *broad* joke. **6** Liberal in thought; as, a *broad* man. **7** Large, not limited; extended, as in range or amount; as, a *broad* choice of subjects for a story; education in its *broadest* sense. **8** Main and essential; as, the *broad* outlines of a problem. **9** Of the vowel *a,* sounded as in *father,* as contrasted with the *a* in *man.*

broad·ax or **broad·axe** \'brȯd-ˌaks\ *n.; pl.* **broad·ax·es.** A broad-bladed ax.

broad·cast \'brȯd-ˌkast\ *adj.* **1** Cast in all directions, as seed in sowing. **2** In radio and television, transmitted by broadcasting. — *adv.* So as to scatter; so as to spread far and wide; as, to sow seeds *broadcast.* — *v.;* **broad·cast** or **broad·cast·ed; broad·cast·ing. 1** To scatter or sow broadcast. **2** To send out by radio or television from a transmitting station; as, to *broadcast* a speech. — *n.* **1** A broadcasting. **2** The material broadcast by radio or television; a single program of such material. — **broad·cast·er,** *n.*

broad·cloth \'brȯd-ˌklȯth\ *n.* **1** A fine woolen or worsted fabric made compact and glossy in finishing. **2** A fine cloth, usually of cotton, silk, or rayon, made in plain and ribbed weaves.

broad·en \'brȯd-n\ *v.;* **broad·ened; broad·en·ing** \-n(-)ing\. To make or to become broad or broader; to widen; as, to *broaden* one's interests.

broad-mind·ed \'brȯd-'mīn-dəd\ *adj.* Free from prejudice; not stubbornly attached to one's own beliefs or opinions; tolerant.

broad·side \'brȯd-ˌsīd\ *n.* **1** The part of a ship's side above the water line. **2** All of the guns of a ship that can be fired from the same side of the ship. **3** A discharge of all these guns together; as, to fire a *broadside.* **4** A storm of abuse; a strongly worded attack; as, to deliver a *broadside* against a political opponent. **5** A sheet of paper printed on one side, as for advertising. — *adv.* With the broadside turned toward a given object or point; as, a ship drifting *broadside* downstream.

broad·sword \'brȯd-ˌsōrd, -ˌsȯrd\ *n.* A broad-bladed sword.

bro·cade \brō-'kād\ *n.* A cloth with a raised design woven into it, often of silk or of gold or silver thread. — **bro·cad·ed** \-'kād-əd\ *adj.*

broc·co·li \'bräk-l(-)ē\ *n.* An open, branching form of cauliflower whose green stalks and tops are cooked as a vegetable.

bro·chure \brō-'shu̇r\ *n.* A pamphlet.

bro·gan \'brōg-n, brō-'gan\ *n.* A heavy, coarse shoe, often with a hobnailed sole.

brogue \'brōg\ *n.* **1** A brogan. **2** A strong low shoe for ordinary wear, with decorative perforations along the overlapping seams of the upper leather.

brogue \'brōg\ *n.* A strongly marked dialectal pronunciation, as the Irish pronunciation of English.

broil \'brȯil\ *v.* **1** To cook, or to be cooked, by direct exposure to fire or flame. **2** To make, or to be, extremely hot; as, a *broiling* sun.

broil \'brȯil\ *n.* A brawl. — *v.* To brawl; to fight.

broil·er \'brȯil-r\ *n.* **1** A rack and pan, or an oven equipped with a rack and pan, for broiling meats. **2** A young chicken suitable for broiling.

broke. Past tense of *break.*

bro·ken \'brōk-n\. Past part. of *break.* — *adj.* **1** Shattered or in pieces; as, *broken* glass. **2** Rough; uneven; having gaps or breaks; as, a *broken* line. **3** Not kept; as, a *broken* promise. **4** Subdued; crushed; as, *broken* spirit. **5** Imperfectly spoken; as, *broken* English.

bro·ken·heart·ed \'brōk-n-'härt-əd, -'hȧrt-\ *adj.* Crushed by sorrow; heartbroken. — **bro·ken·heart·ed·ly,** *adv.*

bro·ker \'brōk-r\ *n.* [From Old Norman French *brokeor* meaning "wine-seller", literally "keg-tapper".] A person who acts as an agent for others in the purchase and sale of property.

bro·ker·age \'brōk-r(-)ij\ *n.* **1** The business of a broker. **2** The fee or commission charged by a broker.

bro·mine \'brō-ˌmēn\ *n.* A chemical element that is normally a dark red caustic fluid giving off an irritating reddish-brown vapor.

bronc \'brängk\ *n.* A bronco.

bronchi. Pl. of *bronchus*.

bron·chi·al \'brängk-ē-əl\ *adj.* Of or relating to the bronchi and their branches (**bronchial tubes** and **bron·chi·oles** \-ē-ˌōlz\).

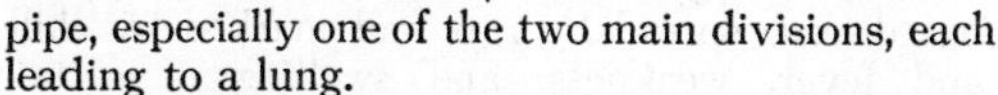

bronchial tubes

bron·chi·tis \brän(g)-'kīt-əs\ *n.* An inflammation of the bronchial tubes.

bron·chus \'brängk-əs\ *n.; pl.* **bron·chi** \'bräng-ˌkī\. One of the divisions of the trachea, or windpipe, especially one of the two main divisions, each leading to a lung.

bron·co or **bron·cho** \'bräng-ˌkō\ *n.; pl.* **bron·cos** or **bron·chos**. A small, half-wild horse of western North America, used chiefly as a saddle horse or a pack horse.

bron·co·bust·er or **bron·cho·bust·er** \'bräng-ˌkō-ˌbəst-r\ *n. Slang.* One who breaks broncos to the saddle; a cowboy.

bron·to·sau·rus \ˌbrän-tə-'sȯr-əs\ *n.; pl.* **bron·to·sau·rus·es** \-'sȯr-ə-səz\ or **bron·to·sau·ri** \-'sȯr-ˌī\. An extinct American plant-eating reptile sometimes 65 feet long and 12 feet high, with long neck and tail, small head, and five-toed limbs.

bronze \'bränz\ *n.* **1** A metallic substance that is a hard alloy of copper and tin, sometimes with other elements, as zinc. **2** A work of art, as a statue, bust, or medallion, made of bronze. **3** A brown color of a yellowish-orange shade. — *v.;* **bronzed**; **bronz·ing**. To make like bronze, as in color; as, a face *bronzed* by the sun and wind.

Bronze Age. A period of man's cultural development following the Stone Age and marked by the use of bronze weapons, tools, and utensils.

brooch \'brōch, 'brüch\ *n.* An ornament to be worn at or near the neck of a dress, held by a hinged pin and catch.

brood \'brüd\ *n.* **1** The young of birds, hatched or cared for at the same time; as, a *brood* of chicks. **2** A group of young children or animals having the same mother; offspring. — *v.* **1** To sit on eggs to hatch them; as, *brooding* hens. **2** To think long and anxiously over something; as, to *brood* over a mistake. — *adj.* Kept for breeding purposes; as, a *brood* mare.

brood·er \'brüd-r\ *n.* **1** A person or an animal that broods. **2** A building or a compartment that can be heated, used for raising chicks and other young fowl.

broody \'brüd-ē\ *adj.;* **brood·i·er**; **brood·i·est**. Brooding; inclined to brood.

brook \'bru̇k\ *n.* A stream smaller than a river or a creek.

brook \'bru̇k\ *v.* To put up with; to bear; to tolerate; as, an insult that could not be *brooked*.

brook·let \'bru̇k-lət\ *n.* A little brook.

broom \'brüm, 'bru̇m\ *n.* **1** A plant of the pea family with long slender branches along which grow many drooping yellow flowers. **2** A long-handled brush used for sweeping, originally made from twigs of broom.

broom·stick \'brüm-ˌstik, 'bru̇m-\ *n.* The handle of a broom.

broth \'brȯth\ *n.* The liquid in which any meat, fish, or vegetable has been boiled.

broth·er \'brət͟h-r\ *n.; pl.* **broth·ers** \-rz\ or **breth·ren** \'bret͟h-r(-)ən, -rn\. **1** A boy or man related to another person by having the same parents. **2** One of the same family, country, or race with another; a fellow man. All men are *brothers.* **3** A fellow member of some profession, union, or association. **4** A fellow Christian; a member of the same religion or of the same religious order.

☞ The plural *brethren* is often used in referring to male members of religious or professional organizations.

broth·er·hood \'brət͟h-r-ˌhu̇d\ *n.* **1** The state of being brothers or a brother; as, united in *brotherhood;* the *brotherhood* of man. **2** An association of men for any purpose, as a society of monks or a labor union; a fraternity. **3** All of those who are engaged in the same business or profession; as, the legal *brotherhood.*

broth·er-in-law \'brət͟h-r-ən-ˌlȯ\ *n.; pl.* **broth·ers-in-law**. **1** The brother of one's husband or wife. **2** The husband of one's sister.

broth·er·ly \'brət͟h-r-lē\ *adj.* Of or relating to brothers; kindly; affectionate; as, *brotherly* advice.

brougham \'brüm, 'brü-əm\ *n.* A vehicle with a closed part for the passengers and an outside seat for the driver.

brought. Past tense and past part. of *bring.*

brow \'brau̇\ *n.* **1** The eyebrow. **2** The forehead. **3** The edge or projecting upper part of a steep slope; as, the *brow* of a hill.

brow·beat \'brau̇-ˌbēt\ *v.;* **brow·beat**; **brow·beat·en** \-ˌbēt-n\; **brow·beat·ing**. To frighten, as by threats; to bully; to abuse.

brown \'brau̇n\ *adj.* **1** Of the color brown. **2** Having skin of that color; as, the *brown* races of mankind. **3** Sunburned or tanned. — *n.* **1** Any of a group of darkish colors with a tinge of reddish yellow. **2** A pigment or dye that colors brown. — *v.* To make or become brown; as, to *brown* meat; to lie *browning* in the sun.

brown·ie \'brau̇-nē\ *n.* **1** A cheerful goblin supposed to perform helpful services by night. **2** A member of a junior division of the Girl Scouts. **3** A chocolate nut cookie or small cake.

brown·ish \'brau̇-nish\ *adj.* Somewhat brown.

brown·stone \'brau̇n-ˌstōn\ *n.* A reddish-brown sandstone used for building.

brown study. A condition of being absorbed in thought; reverie.

browse \'braůz\ *v.;* **browsed**; **brows·ing**. **1** To nibble young shoots and foliage; to graze; as, *browsing* cattle. **2** To read here and there in a book or in a library.

bru·in \'brü-ən\ *n.* A bear.

bruise \'brüz\ *v.;* **bruised**; **bruis·ing**. **1** To injure the flesh, as by a blow, without breaking the skin. **2** To wound the feelings of; to hurt. **3** To become bruised or to show the effects of bruises; as, to *bruise* easily. **4** To crush or pound, as in a mortar; as, to *bruise* mint leaves. — *n.* A black-and-blue spot on the body, caused by a blow, bump, or fall.

bruit \'brüt\ *n. Archaic.* Report; rumor. — *v.* To make widely known; to report. The news was *bruited* abroad.

brunch \'brənch\ *n.* [From a combination of the *br-* in *breakfast* and the *-unch* in *lunch.*] A meal eaten late in the morning and taking the place of both breakfast and lunch.

bru·net or **bru·nette** \brü-'net\ *adj.* Having hair and eyes that are dark-brown or black. — *n.* A person with dark hair and eyes.

brunt \'brənt\ *n.* The main force of a blow or an attack; the heaviest damage, stress, or strain. The island town bore the *brunt* of the storm.

brush \'brəsh\ *n.* **1** A device made of bristles, wire, or other material set in a back or a handle and used for cleaning, smoothing, or painting. **2** A brushing; as, to give one's hair a *brush.* **3** A light stroke; as, a *brush* of the hand. **4** A short fight; as, a *brush* with the enemy. **5** The bushy tail of an animal, as of a fox or squirrel, or of certain dogs and cats. **6** A conductor for an electric current between a moving and a non-moving part of an electric motor or generator. — *v.* **1** To clean, scrub, or paint with a brush. **2** To touch lightly; to pass lightly against. A falling branch *brushed* his cheek.

brush \'brəsh\ *n.* **1** Branches and twigs cut from trees. **2** A heavy growth of small trees and bushes.

brush-off or **brush·off** \'brəsh-ˌȯf\ *n.* A rudely abrupt or offhand dismissal; as, to give an applicant the *brush-off.*

brush·wood \'brəsh-ˌwu̇d\ *n.* **1** The wood of small branches cut from trees. **2** A thicket.

brushy \'brəsh-ē\ *adj.;* **brush·i·er**; **brush·i·est**. Resembling a brush; rough; shaggy.

brushy \'brəsh-ē\ *adj.;* **brush·i·er**; **brush·i·est**. Covered with brush or brushwood.

brusque \'brəsk\ *adj.* Rough and short in manner or speech; blunt; as, a *brusque* reply. — **brusque·ly**, *adv.*

Brus·sels sprouts \'brəs-lz\. Tiny green cabbage-like heads, growing thickly on the stem of a plant of the cabbage family, and cooked and eaten as a vegetable.

bru·tal \'brüt-l\ *adj.* Cruel and inhuman; savage; as, a *brutal* crime. — **bru·tal·ly** \-l-ē\ *adv.*

bru·tal·i·ty \brü-'tal-ət-ē\ *n.; pl.* **bru·tal·i·ties.** **1** Brutal conduct; savageness. **2** A brutal act.

brute \'brüt\ *n.* **1** A beast; especially, a wild beast. **2** A brutal person. — *adj.* **1** Not having human reasoning power; as, a *brute* beast. **2** Savage; brutal; as, to use *brute* force to get one's way.

brut·ish \'brüt-ish\ *adj.* Of or like a brute; stupid, coarse, and savage; as, *brutish* behavior.

bry·o·phyte \'brī-ə-ˌfīt\ *n.* Any of the mosses or liverworts.

b's. Pl. of *b.*

bu. Abbreviation for *bushel.*

bub·ble \'bəb-l\ *n.* **1** A tiny round body of air or gas in a liquid; as, *bubbles* in boiling water. **2** A round body of air within a solid; as, a *bubble* in glass. **3** A thin film of liquid filled with air or gas; as, soap *bubbles.* — *v.;* **bub·bled**; **bub·bling** \-l(-)ing\. **1** To rise in bubbles; to form bubbles. The ginger ale *bubbled* over the glass. **2** To flow or pour out with a gurgle; as, a *bubbling* brook. **3** To make a sound like water bubbling. — **bub·bly** \-l(-)ē\ *adj.*

bu·bon·ic plague \byü-'bän-ik\. A very dangerous disease spread by rats and marked by chills and fever, weakness, and swelling of certain glands, especially in the groin.

buc·ca·neer \ˌbək-n-'ir\ *n.* A pirate.

buck \'bək\ *n.* **1** The male of deer or antelopes, or of goats, hares, rabbits, or rats. **2** A dashing young man; a dandy. **3** The plunge of a bucking horse. — *v.* **1** To spring or plunge upward, as a horse or mule, with head bent downward and back arched. **2** To push or charge against something as if butting. **3** To start or move with jerks; as, a wagon *bucking* over the ruts. **4** To throw by bucking; as, a bronco that *bucked* off its rider. **5** To oppose; to resist; as, an organization that is hard to *buck.*

buck·board \'bək-ˌbōrd, -ˌbȯrd\ *n.* A lightweight four-wheeled carriage with a seat supported by a springy platform.

buck·et \'bək-ət\ *n.* **1** A pail for drawing up water from a well. **2** Any pail or paillike container in which something is collected, or scooped, and carried; as, a coal *bucket.* **3** The amount that a bucket can hold; as, to feed a horse a *bucket* of oats.

buck·et·ful \'bək-ət-ˌfu̇l\ *n.; pl.* **buck·et·fuls**. The amount held by a bucket.

bucket seat. A low, separate, single seat with rounded back, often hinged for tipping or folding forward, chiefly used in automobiles and airplanes.

buck·eye \'bək-ˌī\ *n.* A shrub or tree related to and resembling the horse chestnut but with yellowish-green flowers and egg-shaped spineless fruit.

buck·le \'bək-l\ *n.* **1** A fastening through which the loose end of a strap or a belt is passed and held. **2** A similar ornamental device, as worn on shoes. — *v.;* **buck·led**; **buck·ling** \-l(-)ing\. **1** To fasten with a buckle. **2** To apply oneself with vigor; as, to *buckle* down to work.

buck·le \'bək-l\ *v.;* **buck·led**; **buck·ling** \-l(-)ing\. To become bent; to bend or crumple up. The steel girders *buckled* in the heat of the flames. — *n.* A bend, bulge, or twist, as of a metal beam or a pipe.

buck·ler \'bək-lər\ *n.* A small shield worn on the arm.

buck·ram \'bək-rəm\ *n.* A coarse cloth, as of linen or cotton, stiffened with sizing and used in making hat frames and in binding books.

buck·saw \'bək-ˌsȯ\ *n.* A saw, set in a deep frame shaped like an H, used for sawing wood on a sawhorse.

buck·shot \'bək-ˌshät\ *n.* A coarse lead shot used in shotguns.

buck·skin \'bək-ˌskin\ *n.* **1** The skin of a buck. **2** [in the plural] Breeches made of such skin. **3** A soft yellowish or grayish leather used for gloves and other articles of clothing.

buck·tooth \'bək-ˌtüth, -'tüth\ *n.; pl.* **buck·teeth** \-ˌtēth, -'tēth\. A tooth that juts out.

buck·wheat \'bək-ˌhwēt\ *n.* **1** A plant growing about two feet tall, with pinkish-white flowers and triangular seeds. **2** The seeds of buckwheat from which a flour is ground.

buckwheat

bu·col·ic \byü-'käl-ik\ *adj.* Pastoral; rural. — *n.* A pastoral poem.

bud \'bəd\ *n.* **1** A small growth, at the tip or on the side of a stem, that later develops into a flower, a leaf, or a new stem or branch. **2** A flower that has not fully opened. **3** A part that grows out from the body of an organism and develops into a new organism; as, the *buds* or eyes of a potato; the *buds* of a coral. **4** The stage of development when something puts forth buds; an early stage or condition; as, trees in *bud;* a plan still in the *bud.* — *v.;* **bud·ded; bud·ding. 1** To put forth buds; to develop as a bud. **2** To be like a bud in freshness and promise of growth; as, a *budding* diplomat. **3** To insert a bud from one plant into an opening specially cut in a stem or branch of another plant in order to have the bud grow on the stem or branch.

Bud·dhist \'büd-əst, 'bu̇d-\ *n.* A person who believes in the teachings of Gautama Buddha. — *adj.* Having to do with Gautama Buddha or his teachings.

bud·dy \'bəd-ē\ *n.; pl.* **bud·dies.** A companion; a pal.

budge \'bəj\ *v.;* **budged; budg·ing.** To move or to cause to move from one position to another; to stir; as, a box so heavy that two men could not *budge* it. The dog would not *budge* from his master's side.

budg·er·i·gar \'bəj-r(-)ē-ˌgär, -ˌgȧr\ *n.* A small Australian parrot of various colors, used as a pet and for show.

budg·et \'bəj-ət\ *n.* [From Old French *bougette* meaning "bag", "wallet", then "contents of a bag", "financial statement".] **1** A stock or store; a collection; as, a *budget* of stories. **2** A statement of estimated income and probable expenses for a certain period of time; a plan for using money; as, a government *budget;* a family *budget* for each week. — *v.* To put or to allow for in a budget; to plan for taking care of expenses by making a budget. — **budg·et·ary** \-ə-ˌter-ē\ *adj.*

budg·ie \'bəj-ē\ *n.* A budgerigar.

buff \'bəf\ *n.* **1** A high-grade leather made from the skin of the ox, elk, or buffalo. **2** A polishing stick or wheel covered with fine leather. **3** The color of buff, a dull yellowish orange, lighter than tan. — *adj.* Of or like buff; of the color of buff. — *v.* To polish with a buff. — **buff·er,** *n.*

buf·fa·lo \'bəf-l-ˌō\ *n.; pl.* **buf·fa·loes** or **buf·fa·los.** Any of various kinds of wild ox, such as the **water buffalo** of India and China, the **Cape buffalo** of South Africa, and the American bison.

buf·fer \'bəf-r\ *n.* Anything that lessens or softens a shock, as of a collision between two opposing forces.

buffer state. A small independent state lying between two larger, usually rival, states.

buf·fet \'bəf-ət\ *n.* A blow with the hand; a slap; any blow. — *v.* **1** To strike with the hand or with the fist; to knock about; as, to be *buffeted* by a crowd. **2** To pound repeatedly; to struggle against; as, a swimmer *buffeting* the waves. Waves *buffet* the rocks.

buf·fet \(ˌ)bə-'fā, bü-\ *n.* **1** A set of shelves or drawers for holding dishes, silverware, and table linen; a sideboard. **2** *Chiefly British.* A counter at which refreshments are served primarily as a public convenience, as in a railway station. — *adj.* Set out on tables so that guests may serve themselves; as, a *buffet* lunch.

buf·foon \(ˌ)bə-'fün\ *n.* A person who amuses others by tricks, jokes, and antics; a clown.

buf·foon·ery \(ˌ)bə-'fün-r(-)ē\ *n.; pl.* **buf·foon·er·ies.** The art or the conduct of a buffoon; especially, coarse jokes or vulgar actions.

bug \'bəg\ *n.* **1** An insect or other small creeping or crawling creature. **2** Any of a large group of insects with hard outer wings and young that are nymphs. **3** A disease-producing germ.

bug·a·boo \'bəg-ə-ˌbü\ *n.* An imaginary object of which one is afraid; a bogy.

bug·bear \'bəg-ˌbar, -ˌber\ *n.* **1** A bugaboo. **2** Something of which one is afraid without reason; any object of dread.

bug·gy \'bəg-ē\ *adj.;* **bug·gi·er; bug·gi·est.** Infested with bugs.

bug·gy \'bəg-ē\ *n.; pl.* **bug·gies.** A light single-seated carriage, usually drawn by one horse.

bu·gle \'byüg-l\ *n.* [Short for earlier *bugle-horn* meaning "musical instrument made from the horn of a wild ox", from *bugle* meaning "wild ox", from Latin *buculus.*] A musical instrument like a trumpet but shorter, used chiefly for sounding calls. — *v.;* **bu·gled; bu·gling** \-l(-)ing\. **1** To sound a bugle. **2** To summon by a bugle call.

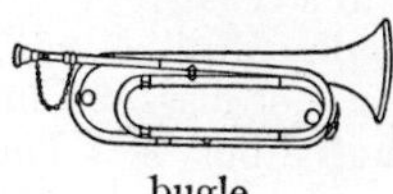
bugle

bu·gler \'byüg-lər\ *n.* A person who plays a bugle.

build \'bild\ *v.;* **built** \'bilt\ or *archaic* **build·ed**

\'bil-dəd\; **build·ing.** **1** To make by putting together parts or materials; to construct; as, to *build* a house; to *build* a bridge. **2** To produce or create gradually by effort; as, to *build* a winning team; to *build* a reputation. — *n.* Form or kind of construction; general figure; shape; as, a man of strong *build.*

build·er \'bild-r\ *n.* One that builds; especially, a person whose business is the building of houses and similar structures.

build·ing \'bil-ding\ *n.* **1** The act of one that builds; as, birds busy at nest *building.* **2** Any structure such as a house, barn, church, school, or factory; as, an office *building;* a five-story *building.* **3** The art, work, or business of erecting houses and similar structures.

built. Past tense and past part. of *build.*

built-in \'bilt-'in\ *adj.* Belonging to or fitted into the structure, as of a house; not movable or detachable; as, a *built-in* bookcase; a *built-in* radio.

bulb \'bəlb\ *n.* **1** A large bud, usually underground, sending out roots from below and bearing overlapping, scalelike leaves, as in the lily, onion, or tulip. **2** A short fleshy plant stem resembling a bulb; as, a dahlia *bulb.* **3** Any bulb-shaped object or part; as, an electric-light *bulb.*

hyacinth bulb

bulb·ous \'bəl-bəs\ *adj.* **1** Having a bulb or bulbs; growing from or bearing bulbs. **2** Having a bulblike form; round; swollen.

Bul·gar·i·an \ˌbəl-'gar-ē-ən, ˌbu̇l-, -'ger-\ *adj.* Of or relating to Bulgaria. — *n.* Also **Bul·gar** \'bəl-ˌgär, 'bu̇l-, -ˌgår\. **1** A native or inhabitant of Bulgaria. **2** The language of Bulgaria.

bulge \'bəlj\ *n.* A swelling part; a part that has an outward bend; as, a *bulge* in a line. — *v.;* **bulged; bulg·ing.** To swell or bend outward; as, *bulging* muscles. The bag *bulged* with groceries.

bulk \'bəlk\ *n.* **1** Greatness of size or mass; as, hard to handle not because of its weight but because of its *bulk.* **2** The largest or chief part; the main mass. The *bulk* of the population lived on farms. — **in bulk. 1** Not already packaged. **2** In large quantities. — *v.* **1** To form a bulk; to swell or expand. **2** To have a bulky appearance; to be, or seem to be, of great size or importance.

bulk·head \'bəlk-ˌhed, 'bəl-ˌked\ *n.* **1** Any of the upright partitions separating sections in a ship. **2** A framework with a sloping door, as one enclosing a set of steps leading from outside ground level to a cellar.

bulky \'bəl-kē\ *adj.;* **bulk·i·er; bulk·i·est. 1** Large in size or mass. **2** Clumsy; not easily handled.

bull \'bu̇l\ *n.* **1** The male of any animal of the ox and cow family, and of certain other large animals, as the elephant, the moose, and the whale. **2** One like a bull, as in size, strength, or loud roaring. **3** A person who buys something with the intention of selling it later at a higher price or of helping to raise market prices. — *adj.* **1** Male. **2** Rising; as, a *bull* market.

bull·dog \'bu̇l-ˌdȯg\ *n.* A short-haired, thick-set, powerful dog noted for its courage. — *adj.* Of or like a bulldog; stubborn; as, *bulldog* courage. — *v.;* **bull·dogged; bull·dog·ging.** To throw a steer by seizing its horns and twisting its neck.

bull·doze \'bu̇l-ˌdōz\ *v.;* **bull·dozed; bull·doz·ing. 1** To move earth with a bulldozer. **2** To restrain or force by use of threats or violence; as, to *bulldoze* someone into signing an agreement.

bull·doz·er \'bu̇l-ˌdōz-r\ *n.* A powerful tractorlike machine equipped with a broad blade for moving earth, used in building roads and in other construction work.

bulldozer

bul·let \'bu̇l-ət\ *n.* A shaped piece of metal made to be shot from a firearm.

bul·le·tin \'bu̇l-ət-n\ *n.* **1** A short statement of news for the public, especially one issued by an official source; as, a weather *bulletin;* a special *bulletin* on a train wreck. **2** A publication appearing at regular intervals, especially a record of proceedings, as of a society.

bulletin board. A board for posting bulletins and other announcements.

bul·let·proof \'bu̇l-ət-'prüf\ *adj.* So made as to prevent the passing through of bullets; as, *bulletproof* glass.

bull·fight \'bu̇l-ˌfīt\ *n.* A public entertainment in which men excite and fight with a bull in an arena (**bull ring**).

bull·finch \'bu̇l-ˌfinch\ *n.* A thick-billed, red-breasted European songbird often kept as a cage bird.

bull·frog \'bu̇l-ˌfrȯg, -ˌfräg\ *n.* A large, heavy frog that makes a booming or bellowing sound.

bull·head \'bu̇l-ˌhed\ *n.* Any of various fishes that have a large head.

bull·head·ed \'bu̇l-'hed-əd\ *adj.* Headstrong; obstinate.

bul·lion \'bu̇l-yən\ *n.* Gold or silver, especially in bars or blocks.

bul·lock \'bu̇l-ək\ *n.* An ox or steer.

bull's-eye \'bu̇l-ˌzī\ *n.* **1** The center of a target. **2** A shot that hits the center of a target. **3** Any striking success; as, to score a *bull's-eye* on a mathematics test. **4** A lens used in a small lantern (**bull's-eye lantern**) that concentrates the rays of light it throws out.

bul·ly \'bu̇l-ē\ *n.; pl.* **bul·lies.** A person who constantly teases, hurts, or threatens smaller or weaker persons. — *adj.* Fine; first-rate; as, a *bully* day. — *v.;* **bul·lied** \-ēd\; **bul·ly·ing.** To act like a bully; to frighten or hurt persons smaller or weaker than oneself. An older brother *bullied* him for years.

bul·rush \'bu̇l-ˌrəsh\ *n.* Any of several large rushes or rushlike plants that grow in water or in wet land.

bul·wark \'bu̇l-(ˌ)wərk, -ˌwȯrk; 'bəl-(ˌ)wərk\ *n.* **1** A solid, wall-like structure built for defense against an enemy. **2** Anything that defends or protects. Freedom of speech is one of the *bulwarks* of democracy. **3** The side of a ship above the deck.

bum \ˈbəm\ *v.;* **bummed; bum·ming.** *Slang.* **1** To lead an idle life; to loaf; as, to spend a summer *bumming* about the country. **2** To get for nothing; to beg; as, to *bum* a ride. — *n. Slang.* **1** A loafer or vagrant, especially one that drinks heavily. **2** A hobo; a tramp. — *adj. Slang.* Of poor quality or in poor condition; not good.

bum·ble·bee \ˈbəm-bl-ˌbē\ *n.* A large bee that makes a loud humming sound.

bump \ˈbəmp\ *v.* **1** To strike or knock against anything; as, to *bump* into a door. **2** To move along unevenly; to jolt; as, *bumping* along a rough road. — *n.* **1** A heavy blow or thump, as from a collision; a jolt. **2** A swelling, as from a blow or a sting.

bump·er \ˈbəmp-r\ *n.* A cup or glass filled to the brim. — *adj.* Very large or fine; as, a *bumper* crop of wheat.

bump·er \ˈbəmp-r\ *n.* A bar across the front or back of an automobile, intended to lessen the shock or damage from a collision.

bump·kin \ˈbəm(p)-kən\ *n.* An awkward country fellow.

bumpy \ˈbəmp-ē\ *adj.;* **bump·i·er; bump·i·est.** Marked by bumps or bumping; as, a *bumpy* ride. — **bump·i·ly** \-l-ē\ *adv.*

bun \ˈbən\ *n.* A slightly sweetened, raised biscuit or roll.

bunch \ˈbənch\ *n.* **1** A cluster; a tuft; as, a *bunch* of grapes; a *bunch* of grass. **2** A number of things of the same kind; a group; a collection; as, a *bunch* of cattle; a *bunch* of keys. — *v.* To form or to gather in a bunch or bunches.

bun·dle \ˈbənd-l\ *n.* A number of things tied or wrapped together; a package; a parcel; as, a *bundle* of old clothes. — *v.;* **bun·dled; bun·dling** \-l(-)ing\. **1** To wrap up or tie up in a bundle. **2** To hurry off; to hasten. Mother *bundled* us off to school.

bung \ˈbəng\ *n.* **1** A stopper for the hole in the side of a cask. **2** Also **bung·hole** \-ˌhōl\. The hole stopped by a bung. — *v.* **1** To close with a bung. **2** *Slang.* To bruise badly.

bun·ga·low \ˈbəng-gl-ˌō\ *n.* A dwelling house, usually of one story, with low sweeping lines and a wide veranda.

bun·gle \ˈbəng-gl\ *v.;* **bun·gled; bun·gling** \-gl(-)ing\. To act, do, make, or work in a clumsy manner. — *n.* Something that has been bungled. — **bun·gler** \-gl(-)ər\ *n.*

bun·ion \ˈbən-yən\ *n.* An inflamed swelling on the first joint of the big toe.

bunk \ˈbəngk\ *n.* **1** A bed attached to a wall, as on a ship. **2** Any bed or sleeping place. — *v.* **1** To go to bed in a bunk. **2** To occupy or share a bed or a room; as, to *bunk* with a friend overnight.

bunk \ˈbəngk\ *n. Slang.* Nonsense.

bun·ker \ˈbəngk-r\ *n.* **1** A large bin, as for coal on a ship. **2** Any obstacle, especially a mound of earth, on a golf course.

bunk·house \ˈbəngk-ˌhau̇s\ *n.; pl.* **bunk·hous·es** \-ˌhau̇-zəz\. A rough, simple building providing sleeping quarters, as for construction workers.

bun·ny \ˈbən-ē\ *n.; pl.* **bun·nies.** A rabbit — a pet name.

Bun·sen burner \ˈbən(t)s-n\. [Named after Robert Wilhelm *Bunsen*, German chemist, who invented it.] A gas burner consisting typically of a tube with small holes at the bottom, where air enters and mixes with the gas to produce a very hot blue flame.

bunt \ˈbənt\ *v.* **1** To strike or push with the horns or head; to butt. **2** In baseball, to tap the ball lightly by meeting it with a loosely held bat and no swing. — *n.* **1** A butt, shove, or push. **2** In baseball, a bunted ball or a hit made by bunting.

bun·ting \ˈbənt-ing\ *n.* Any of various stout-billed birds of the size and habits of a sparrow, such as the **indigo bunting**, a small finch of the eastern United States, and the **snow bunting**, a finch of northern regions that often appears during snowstorms.

bun·ting \ˈbənt-ing\ *n.* **1** A thin cloth used chiefly for making flags and patriotic decorations. **2** Flags or decorations made of bunting.

buoy \ˈbȯi, ˈbü-ē\ *n.* **1** A floating object anchored in a body of water so as to mark a channel or to warn of danger. **2** A life buoy. — *v.* **1** To keep from sinking; to keep afloat. **2** To keep up or raise, as one's courage or spirits; as, *buoyed* up by the hope of success. **3** To mark by or as if by a buoy or buoys.

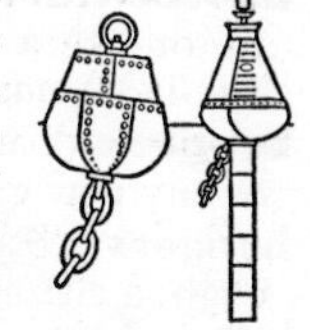
buoys

buoy·an·cy \ˈbȯi-ən-sē, ˈbü-yən-\ *n.* **1** The power of rising and floating, as on water or in air; as, the *buoyancy* of cork. **2** The power of a liquid to hold up a floating body; as, the *buoyancy* of sea water. **3** Lightheartedness; natural lightness of spirit.

buoy·ant \ˈbȯi-ənt, ˈbü-yənt\ *adj.* **1** Able to rise and float in the air or on the surface of a liquid. Cork is *buoyant.* **2** Able to keep a body afloat, as a liquid; buoying up. **3** Lighthearted; cheerful; lively. — **buoy·ant·ly,** *adv.*

bu·pres·tid beetle \byü-ˈpres-təd\. Any of a number of usually small blue or bronze beetles with short heads and large eyes and long legless larvae some of which are destructive borers in the wood of fruit trees and other trees.

bur or **burr** \ˈbər\ *n.* **1** Any rough or prickly covering or shell of a fruit. **2** Anything that clings or sticks like a bur. — *v.;* **burred; bur·ring.** To remove burs from, as from wool in cleaning.

bur·ble \ˈbərb-l\ *v.;* **bur·bled; bur·bling** \-l(-)ing\. **1** To bubble or to make a bubbling noise. **2** To jabber. — *n.* A burbling noise; as, the *burble* of a brook.

bur·den \ˈbərd-n\ *n.* **1** Something carried; a load.

2 Anything that is hard to bear; as, a heavy *burden* of sorrow. **3** The carrying of loads; as, a beast of *burden.* **4** The capacity of a ship for carrying cargo; as, a vessel of a hundred tons *burden.* — *v.;* **bur·dened**; **bur·den·ing** \-n(-)ing\. To put a burden on; to overload; to oppress.

bur·den \'bərd-n\ *n.* **1** The refrain or chorus of a song. **2** Main theme or central idea; gist; as, to remember the *burden* of a person's remarks but not the details.

bur·den·some \'bərd-ns-m\ *adj.* So heavy or hard to bear as to be a burden; oppressive.

bur·dock \'bər-ˌdäk\ *n.* A tall, coarse plant of the aster family with purple burlike flower heads.

bu·reau \'byu̇r-ˌō\ *n.; pl.* **bu·reaus** or **bu·reaux** \-ˌōz\. **1** A chest of drawers for a bedroom, usually low and with a mirror. **2** A business office of various kinds; as, a travel *bureau;* an employment *bureau.* **3** A government department or office; as, the Weather *Bureau.*

bu·reauc·ra·cy \byü-'räk-rə-sē\ *n.; pl.* **bu·reauc·ra·cies.** **1** A system of carrying on the business of government through departments, especially in a formal, routine way. **2** Government officials taken as a whole.

bu·reau·crat \'byu̇r-ə-ˌkrat\ *n.* An official of a government department, especially one who carries out his duties in a narrow, routine way.

bu·reau·crat·ic \ˌbyu̇r-ə-'krat-ik\ *adj.* Of, relating to, or like a bureaucracy. — **bu·reau·crat·i·cal·ly** \-ik-l(-)ē\ *adv.*

bur·geon \'bərj-n\ *v.* To send forth buds, branches, or any new growth; to sprout.

bur·gess \'bər-jəs\ *n.* **1** An inhabitant of a borough; a citizen. **2** A member of the lower house of the legislature of colonial Virginia.

burgh \'bər-ō, 'bə-rō, 'bərg\ *n.* A borough; especially, a Scottish town with certain local law-making rights.

burgh·er \'bərg-r\ *n.* **1** A citizen of a burgh, or borough. **2** Any inhabitant of a borough or of a town.

bur·glar \'bərg-lər\ *n.* A person who is guilty of burglary; a thief.

bur·gla·ry \'bərg-lər-ē\ *n.; pl.* **bur·gla·ries.** The breaking into a house or other building, especially during the night, with the intention of stealing or committing some other crime.

bur·go·mas·ter \'bər-gə-ˌmast-r\ *n.* The official head of a city or town in some parts of Europe, as Germany, Austria, and the Netherlands.

bur·i·al \'ber-ē-əl\ *n.* The act of burying; the placing of a dead body in a grave or a tomb.

buried. Past tense and past part. of *bury.*

bur·lap \'bər-ˌlap\ *n.* A coarse fabric made usually from jute or hemp, and used for bags and wrappings, and also for curtains and couch covers.

bur·lesque \(ˌ)bər-'lesk\ *n.* A literary, dramatic, or other imitation intended to make ridiculous the person or thing imitated. — *adj.* Characterized by burlesque; imitating in a comic way. — *v.;* **bur·lesqued**; **bur·lesqu·ing.** To mock or ridicule through burlesque; to imitate in such a way as to make ridiculous.

bur·ly \'bər-lē\ *adj.;* **bur·li·er**; **bur·li·est.** Large and strong; as, a *burly* football center. — For synonyms see *stout.*

bur marigold. Any of a number of coarse herbs of the aster family, whose burs adhere to clothing.

Bur·mese \(')bər-'mēz, -'mēs\ *adj.* Of or relating to Burma. — *n.* **1** *sing. and pl.* A native of Burma. **2** The language of Burma.

burn \'bərn\ *v.;* **burned** \'bərnd\ or **burnt** \'bərnt\; **burn·ing.** **1** To be on fire or to set on fire. **2** To destroy or to be destroyed by fire or heat; as, to *burn* trash. The house *burned* to the ground. **3** To make or produce by fire or heat; as, to *burn* a hole in a coat. **4** To give light or to cause to give light; as, to leave a light *burning* all night. **5** To injure or affect, or to be injured or affected, by fire or heat or by something that acts in a similar way; as, to *burn* one's finger. Some acids *burn* the skin. **6** To affect in a way suggesting heat. Pepper *burns* the mouth. **7** To feel, or to cause to feel, as if on fire; as, to *burn* with anger; to *burn* with thirst. — *n.* An injury or an effect caused by burning or by being burned; as, a cigarette *burn* on a table. *Burns* are very painful. — **burn·a·ble**, *adj.*

burn \'bərn\ *n. British.* A brook; a small stream.

burn·er \'bərn-r\ *n* **1** A person who burns something. **2** The part of a stove or furnace, or of an oil or gas lamp, where the flame or heat is produced.

burning glass. A convex lens for producing an intense heat by focusing the rays of the sun through it.

bur·nish \'bər-nish\ *v.* To make shiny, especially by rubbing; to polish. — *n.* The effect of burnishing; gloss; shine.

bur·noose or **bur·nous** \(ˌ)bər-'nüs\ *n.* A one-piece cloaklike garment and hood worn by Arabs and Moors.

burnt. A past tense and past part. of *burn.*

burp \'bərp\ *n.* A belch. — *v.* **1** To belch. **2** To help a baby to expel gas from the stomach, especially by patting or rubbing the back.

burr \'bər\ *n.* **1** Variant of *bur.* **2** Any rounded growth or knot on a tree. **3** A roughness left on the edge of something made by cutting or drilling. **4** A whir; a rough humming sound. **5** A rough-sounding trilled pronunciation of *r;* as, a Scottish *burr.* **6** Also **bur**. A small drill used by dentists. — *v.* **1** Variant of *bur.* **2** To speak or pronounce with a burr. **3** To whir. **4** To form into a burr, or rough edge. **5** To smooth burrs from.

burred. Past tense and past part. of *bur* or *burr.*

burring. Pres. part. of *bur* or *burr.*

bur·ro \'bər-ō, 'bə-rō, 'bu̇r-ō\ *n.; pl.* **bur·ros.** A donkey, especially a small one used as a pack animal.

bur·row \'bər-ō, 'bə-rō\ *n.* A hole in the ground made by certain animals, such as rabbits and foxes, for shelter or protection. — *v.* **1** To make a burrow. **2** To live in a burrow. — **bur·row·er**, *n.*

bur·sar \ˈbərs-r; ˈbər-ˌsär, -ˌsȧr\ *n.* A treasurer, especially of a college.

burst \ˈbərst\ *v.;* **burst**; **burst·ing. 1** To fly apart or to break all to pieces from a blow or from pressure from within; as, buds ready to *burst* open; bombs *bursting* in the air. **2** To cause to break apart or into pieces; as, to *burst* a paper bag. **3** To come or go suddenly and unexpectedly; as, to *burst* into a room. **4** To be filled to the breaking point; as, barns *bursting* with grain. — *n.* **1** A bursting; an outbreak; as, a *burst* of applause. **2** The result of bursting; a break; as, a *burst* in the dam. **3** A short, violent effort; a spurt; as, a *burst* of speed. **4** A brief, sharp firing of rifles or artillery. **5** A series of shots fired by one pressure on the trigger.

bur·then \ˈbərt͟h-n\. Archaic variant of *burden.*

bury \ˈber-ē\ *v.;* **bur·ied** \-ēd\; **bur·y·ing. 1** To cover a dead body out of sight, as in a grave or tomb or in the sea. **2** To conceal; to hide; to cover up; as, to *bury* the face in the hands; a car *buried* in a snowdrift. **3** To remove from the world of action; as, to *bury* oneself in a book.

bus \ˈbəs\ *n.; pl.* **bus·es** or **bus·ses** \ˈbəs-əz\. A large passenger vehicle; a motor coach.

bus boy \ˈbəs ˌbȯi\. A man or boy employed to help a waiter in a restaurant, as by removing soiled dishes and cleaning and resetting tables after use.

bush \ˈbu̇sh\ *n.* **1** A plant that is smaller than a tree and that has dense, low-growing branches; a shrub. **2** A stretch or a region of uncleared country.

bush·el \ˈbu̇sh-l\ *n.* **1** A dry measure containing 4 pecks, or 32 quarts. **2** A container holding a bushel.

bush·ing \ˈbu̇sh-ing\ *n.* A detachable metal lining, used especially as a bearing, as for an axle or a shaft.

bush·man \ˈbu̇sh-mən\ *n.; pl.* **bush·men** \-mən\. **1** A person skilled at living in the bush or forest; a woodsman. **2** A person living as a settler in the Australian bush.

bush·mas·ter \ˈbu̇sh-ˌmast-r\ *n.* A large venomous snake of the tropical parts of America.

bush pilot. A pilot who flies a small plane over or between points in uncleared or sparsely settled country.

bushy \ˈbu̇sh-ē\ *adj.;* **bush·i·er**; **bush·i·est. 1** Overgrown with bushes. **2** Thick and spreading; as, *bushy* whiskers.

busied. Past tense and past part. of *busy.*

busier. Comparative of *busy.*

busiest. Superlative of *busy.*

bus·i·ly \ˈbiz-l-ē\ *adv.* In a busy manner; actively; as, *busily* engaged with household tasks.

busi·ness \ˈbiz-nəs, -nəz\ *n.* **1** Something that takes a person's time, attention, or effort, especially as a regular occupation. **2** An affair; a matter; as, a sad *business;* to be told to mind one's own *business.* **3** A commercial or industrial enterprise of any kind; as, to own one's own *business.* **4** The making, buying, and selling of goods; as, a record-breaking year for *business.* — For synonyms see *trade.*

busi·ness·like \ˈbiz-nəs-ˌlīk, -nəz-\ *adj.* Having or showing qualities desirable in business; efficient; practical.

busi·ness·man \ˈbiz-nəs-ˌman, -nəz-\ *n.; pl.* **busi·ness·men** \-ˌmen\. A man who is in business, especially on his own account; a man who understands and uses business methods.

busses. A pl. of *bus.*

bust \ˈbəst\ *n.* A piece of sculpture representing the upper part of the human figure, including the head and neck.

bust \ˈbəst\ *v.;* **bust·ed**; **bust·ing.** *Dial.* or *Slang.* **1** To burst. **2** To break. **3** To make or become bankrupt. **4** To hit, as with the fist. **5** To lower in rank, as a soldier; to demote. — *n. Dial.* or *Slang.* **1** A burst or break. **2** A spree. **3** A complete failure.

bust

bus·tle \ˈbəs-l\ *v.;* **bus·tled**; **bus·tling** \-l(-)ing\. To move about with fussy or noisy activity. — *n.* Fussy activity; stir; commotion; as, the *bustle* of the holiday crowds.

bus·tle \ˈbəs-l\ *n.* A pad or a light frame formerly worn by women just below the back waistline to give fullness to the skirt.

busy \ˈbiz-ē\ *adj.;* **bus·i·er**; **bus·i·est. 1** Actively at work; not idle; as, to be *busy* with one's homework; too *busy* to eat. **2** Crowded with business or activity; as, a *busy* street; a *busy* day.

— The words *industrious* and *diligent* are synonyms of *busy: busy* usually suggests active occupation absorbing all of one's time or attention; *industrious* may indicate constant or habitual devotion to work; *diligent* may imply serious application to a particular pursuit.

— *v.;* **bus·ied** \-ēd\; **bus·y·ing.** To keep or make busy; to be busy; as, to *busy* oneself with household tasks.

bus·y·body \ˈbiz-ē-ˌbäd-ē\ *n.; pl.* **bus·y·bod·ies.** A person who meddles in the affairs of others.

but \(ˈ)bət\ *prep.* **1** With the exception of. Everyone was on time *but* me. **2** Other than. Nothing will satisfy him *but* that I go with him. — *conj.* **1** On the contrary; despite that fact. The sky darkened *but* no rain fell. **2** Unless; except that. It never rains *but* it pours. **3** That — after negatives. There is no doubt *but* he will succeed. — *adv.* Only; merely. We are young *but* once.

butch·er \ˈbu̇ch-r\ *n.* [From Old French *bochier* or *bouchier* originally meaning "goat butcher".] **1** A person whose business is killing animals for sale as food. **2** A person who cuts and sells meat. **3** A person who kills in large numbers or brutally. **4** A vendor, as on a train or at a sporting event; as, a candy *butcher.* — *v.* **1** To slaughter as a butcher does. **2** To mangle; to botch; to bungle.

butch·er·bird \ˈbu̇ch-r-ˌbərd\ *n.* Any of certain shrikes that impale their prey upon thorns.

butch·ery \ˈbu̇ch-r(-)ē\ *n.; pl.* **butch·er·ies.** **1** A slaughterhouse. **2** The business of a butcher. **3** Brutal murder; great slaughter.

but·ler \ˈbət-lər\ *n.* A male servant, usually the head servant, in a household.

butt \ˈbət\ *n.* A large cask, especially one for wine or beer.

butt \ˈbət\ *n.* **1** The thicker or bottom end of something; as, the *butt* of a rifle; the *butt* of a tree. **2** A person who is a target for jokes or ridicule; as, the *butt* of many pranks. **3** A mound, as of earth, for catching missiles fired in target practice. **4** [in the plural] A range for target shooting. **5** A push, thrust, or sudden blow, as one given by the head of a goat. — *v.* To push or shove, as with the head.

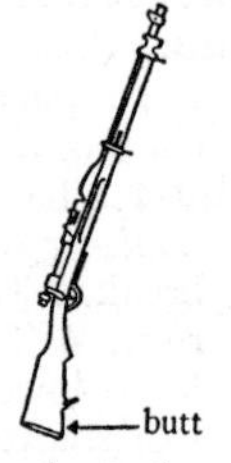

butt, 1

butte \ˈbyüt\ *n.* A steep hill standing alone.

but·ter \ˈbət-r\ *n.* **1** The solid yellowish fat obtained from cream or milk, usually by churning. **2** A substance resembling butter in appearance, texture, or use, such as **apple butter** or **peanut butter.** — *v.* To cover or spread with butter.

but·ter·cup \ˈbət-r-ˌkəp\ *n.* A common wild flower having bright-yellow cup-shaped blossoms.

buttercup

but·ter·fat \ˈbət-r-ˌfat\ *n.* The natural fatty substance in milk.

but·ter·fish \ˈbət-r-ˌfish\ *n.; pl.* **but·ter·fish** or **but·ter·fish·es.** Any of several fishes with a slippery coating of mucus.

but·ter·fly \ˈbət-r-ˌflī\ *n.; pl.* **but·ter·flies.** **1** Any of various slender-bodied insects, with four large, broad wings, often brightly colored. **2** A person suggesting a butterfly, as in gay appearance, lightness, or frivolous manner.

but·ter·milk \ˈbət-r-ˌmilk\ *n.* The liquid that is left after the butterfat has been churned from milk or cream.

but·ter·nut \ˈbət-r-ˌnət\ *n.* **1** The edible, oily nut of an American tree of the walnut family. **2** The tree that bears this nut.

but·ter·scotch \ˈbət-r-ˌskäch\ *n.* A candy made chiefly of brown sugar and butter. — *adj.* Having the same flavor or composed of the same ingredients as butterscotch.

but·tery \ˈbət-r-ē\ *n.; pl.* **but·ter·ies.** A storeroom for provisions; a pantry.

but·tock \ˈbət-ək\ *n.* The back of the hip, which forms one of the fleshy parts on which a person sits; [in the plural] the rump.

but·ton \ˈbət-n\ *n.* **1** A small knob or disk of any material used for holding parts of a garment together or as an ornament. **2** Any buttonlike part or object; as, an electric push *button.* — *v.;* **but·toned; but·ton·ing** \-n(-)ing\. To fasten with buttons.

but·ton·hole \ˈbət-n-ˌhōl\ *n.* The slit or loop for a button on a garment. — *v.;* **but·ton·holed; but·ton·hol·ing.** **1** To hold in close conversation, as if by holding on to a button or buttonhole. **2** To make buttonholes in.

but·ton·hook \ˈbət-n-ˌhu̇k\ *n.* A hook for drawing buttons through buttonholes.

but·ton·wood \ˈbət-n-ˌwu̇d\ *n.* A tall North American plane tree having round buttonlike fruits; the American sycamore.

but·tress \ˈbə-trəs\ *n.* **1** A structure built out against a wall or building to give support and strength. **2** Anything that supports, props, or strengthens. — *v.* To furnish or support with a buttress; to prop; to brace.

buttress, 1

bux·om \ˈbəks-m\ *adj.* Healthy, vigorous, and jolly; plump and rosy.

buy \ˈbī\ *v.;* **bought** \ˈbȯt\; **buy·ing.** To get by paying for; to purchase. — *n.* Something bought or to be bought, especially to the profit or advantage of the buyer; a bargain.

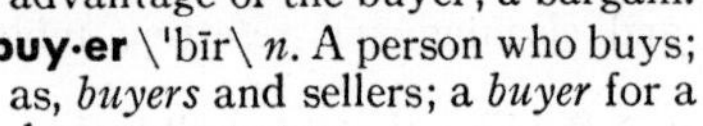

buy·er \ˈbīr\ *n.* A person who buys; as, *buyers* and sellers; a *buyer* for a department store.

buzz \ˈbəz\ *v.* **1** To make a low, humming sound such as bees make. **2** To be filled with a low hum or murmur. The room *buzzed* with excitement. **3** To fly an airplane low over; as, to *buzz* an airfield. — *n.* **1** A continuous humming sound, as of bees in flight or of a power-driven saw. **2** A confused murmur or hum; as, the *buzz* of conversation in the next room.

buz·zard \ˈbəz-rd\ *n.* **1** Any of numerous heavy, short-winged hawks that are rather slow in flight. **2** Any of various other birds of prey, especially the **turkey buzzard**, a vulture that feeds on the flesh of dead animals.

buzz·er \ˈbəz-r\ *n.* An electric signaling device that makes a buzzing sound.

bx. Abbreviation for *box.*

by \(ˈ)bī; *before some words, also* bə\ *prep.* **1** Near; close to; as, *by* the side of the road. **2** Along, over, or through; as, to travel *by* air. **3** To the amount of; as, to win *by* two points. **4** According to; as, for sale *by* the quart; to call *by* another name. **5** With respect to; as, a doctor *by* profession. **6** Through the means or agency of; as, to lead *by* the hand; a house lighted *by* electricity. **7** Past; as, to walk *by* the post office every day. **8** In; during; as, to travel *by* night. **9** Not later than. We were to be there *by* ten o'clock. — *adv.* **1** Near at hand; as, to stand *by.* **2** Past; as, in days gone *by.* **3** Aside; apart, away; as, to put something *by* for a rainy day. — *adj.* Apart from the main or common. — **by and by** \ˈbī ən ˈbī\. After a while; presently. — **by and large.** In general; on the whole. — **by the way.** **1** Incidentally. **2** In addition; also.

by-and-by \'bī-ən-'bī\ *n.* A future time.

by·gone \'bī-ˌgȯn\ *adj.* Past; gone by; as, *bygone* days. — *n.* Something gone by or past. Let *bygones* be *bygones.*

by·law \'bī-ˌlȯ\ *n.* A law or rule made by the directors of a business, by a city council, or by the members of some other organized body, as an association or club, for the management of its internal affairs.

by-line \'bī-ˌlīn\ *n.* A line under the title or heading of an article, especially in a newspaper, telling by whom it was written.

by·pass \'bī-ˌpas\ *n.* A passage to one side, as a road to turn traffic around a place. — *v.* To make a detour or circuit round; as, to *bypass* a city.

by·path \'bī-ˌpath\ *n.; pl.* **by·paths** \-ˌpat͟hz\. A side path or road.

by-prod·uct \'bī-ˌpräd-(ˌ)əkt\ *n.* **1** Something that is left over or produced in addition to the main product in manufacturing, especially when having a market value of its own. **2** A secondary result, often not intended or expected. Famine and epidemics are *by-products* of war.

by·road \'bī-ˌrōd\ *n.* A side road, especially one that is little traveled.

by·stand·er \'bī-ˌstand-r\ *n.* A person standing near but taking no part.

by·street \'bī-ˌstrēt\ *n.* A side street; a quiet street off the main thoroughfare.

by·way \'bī-ˌwā\ *n.* A way or road off the main highway; a byroad or bypath; as, highways and *byways.*

by·word \'bī-ˌwərd\ *n.* **1** A proverbial saying. **2** A person or thing that has come to be considered as typical, especially of some bad class or quality; an object of scorn or contempt; as, a man whose meanness made him a *byword* in the town.

Byz·an·tine \'biz-n-ˌtēn, bə-'zan-ˌtēn\ *adj.* **1** Of or having to do with Byzantium (later Constantinople, now Istanbul) or the Byzantine Empire. **2** Of or like a style of architecture developed in the Byzantine Empire in the 5th and 6th centuries, characterized by a central dome over a square space and by much use of mosaics. — *n.* A native or inhabitant of Byzantium.

c \'sē\ *n.; pl.* **c's** \'sēz\. **1** The third letter of the alphabet. **2** As a Roman numeral, 100.

c *c* C *c* *C*

C. Abbreviation for *centigrade.*

c. Abbreviation for: **1** *cent.* **2** *centimeter.* **3** *century.* **4** *chapter.* **5** *cubic.*

cab \'kab\ *n.* **1** A horse-drawn carriage, usually one for hire. **2** A taxicab. **3** The covered compartment for the engineer and fireman of a locomotive or for the driver of a truck.

ca·bal \kə-'bal\ *n.* A small group of persons working together to promote their own plans or interests, especially by secret scheming.

ca·bana \kə-'ban-(y)ə\ *n.* A beach shelter resembling a cabin, usually with an open side facing the sea.

cab·a·ret \ˌkab-r-'ā\ *n.* A restaurant where entertainment is provided by hired performers, as dancers and singers, usually with a central space for dancing by patrons.

cab·bage \'kab-ij\ *n.* A vegetable with thick overlapping leaves in a dense round head.

cab·by \'kab-ē\ *n.; pl.* **cab·bies.** A cab driver.

cab·in \'kab-n\ *n.* **1** A small, roughly built house. **2** A small room on a ship for officers or passengers. **3** The part of an airplane or airship where the pilot and passengers are seated.

cab·i·net \'kab-n-ət\ *n.* **1** A case, a set of drawers, or a cupboard, usually of wood or metal and either movable or built-in, for keeping or displaying various articles; as, a filing *cabinet;* a kitchen *cabinet.* **2** The group of persons who serve as advisers to the political head of a country.

cab·i·net·mak·er \'kab-n-ət-ˌmāk-r\ *n.* A person whose business is the making of fine woodwork, as cabinets, furniture, and the interior fittings of houses.

ca·ble \'kāb-l\ *n.* **1** A strong rope of ten or more inches in circumference; any heavy, very strong rope, wire, or chain. **2** A bundle of wires bound together inside a waterproof covering and used to carry electric current. **3** A cablegram. — *v.;* **ca·bled; ca·bling** \-l(-)ing\. **1** To provide with, or fasten with, cables. **2** To send a message by submarine cable.

cable car. A car moved along rails (**cable railway**) by an endless cable operated by a stationary engine.

ca·ble·gram \'kāb-l-ˌgram\ *n.* A message sent by submarine cable.

ca·boose \kə-'büs\ *n.* A car on a freight or a construction train for workmen or the train crew.

ca·cao \kə-'kā-ˌō\ *n.; pl.* **ca·ca·os. 1** A South American tree with small yellowish flowers followed by fleshy yellow pods with many seeds. **2** The seeds of this tree from which cocoa and chocolate are made.

cache \'kash\ *n.* **1** A place for hiding, storing, or safeguarding treasure, food, or other supplies which it is inconvenient to carry. **2** The material thus hidden or stored. — *v.;* **cached; cach·ing.** To hide or store in a cache.

cack·le \'kak-l\ *v.;* **cack·led; cack·ling** \-l(-)ing\. **1** To make the sharp broken noise or cry of a hen or goose. **2** To laugh or chatter noisily. — *n.* A cackling sound, as that of harsh laughter or noisy chatter.

cac·tus \'kak-təs\ *n.; pl.* **cac·tus·es** \-tə-səz\ or **cac·ti** \-ˌtī\. Any plant of a large group of plants able to live in dry regions and having fleshy stems and branches that bear scales or prickles instead of leaves.

cad \'kad\ *n.* A person who behaves, especially deliberately, in an ungentlemanly way.

ca·dav·er \kə-'dav-r\ *n.* A dead body, especially of a human being; a corpse.

ca·dav·er·ous \kə-'dav-r(-)əs\ *adj.* Of, relating to, or having the look of a cadaver; pale and ghastly; thin and haggard.

cad·die or **cad·dy** \'kad-ē\ *n.; pl.* **cad·dies.** [From a Scottish variant of *cadet,* meaning also "boy", "golf attendant".] A person who carries a golfer's clubs. — *v.;* **cad·died** \-ēd\; **cad·dy·ing.** To serve as a caddie.

cad·dis fly \'kad-əs\. A four-winged insect whose larvae (**caddis worms**) are found in streams and ponds, living in a silklike case covered with hard bits of shell and gravel.

cad·dish \'kad-ish\ *adj.* Having or showing the behavior of a cad; ungentlemanly; ill-bred. — **cad·dish·ly,** *adv.*

cad·dy \'kad-ē\ *n.; pl.* **cad·dies.** A small box, can, or chest, often used for holding tea.

ca·dence \'kād-n(t)s\ *n.* **1** The measure or beat of any rhythmical motion or sound; rhythm; as, the *cadence* of a dance. **2** The close or conclusion of a section of a musical composition. — **ca·denced,** *adj.*

ca·den·za \kə-'den-zə\ *n.* A brilliant, showy passage in a musical composition, as in an aria or a concerto, usually just before the end.

ca·det \kə-'det\ *n.* [From French, meaning "younger son", "army officer".] **1** A younger son or brother. **2** A young man in training to become an officer in the armed forces. **3** A student at a military school.

cad·mi·um \'kad-mē-əm\ *n.* A white metallic chemical element used especially as a coating on steel to prevent rust.

cae·cum \'sēk-m\ *n.; pl.* **cae·ca** \'sēk-ə\. The pouch in which the large intestine begins and into which the small intestine opens.

cae·su·ra \sē-'z(h)u̇r-ə\ *n.* A break in the rhythm of a line of poetry, usually occurring about the middle.

ca·fe or **ca·fé** \kə-'fā, ka-\ *n.* A restaurant.

caf·e·te·ria \ˌkaf-ə-'tir-ē-ə\ *n.* A restaurant in which the customers serve themselves, or are served, at a counter but take the food to tables to eat.

caf·feine \(')ka-'fēn\ *n.* A stimulating substance in coffee and tea.

cage \'kāj\ *n.* **1** An openwork box or enclosure for birds or other animals. **2** Anything like a cage in shape or purpose. — *v.;* **caged; cag·ing.** To shut up in a cage or as if in a cage; as, a *caged* lion; to be *caged* in the house during bad weather.

cage·ling \'kāj-ling\ *n.* A caged bird.

ca·gey \'kā-jē\ *adj.;* **ca·gi·er; ca·gi·est.** Wary of being trapped or deceived; shrewd; cautious. — **ca·gi·ly** \'kāj-l-ē\ *adv.*

cairn \'karn, 'kern\ *n.* A heap of stones piled up as a landmark or as a memorial.

cais·son \'kā-ˌsän, 'kās-n\ *n.* **1** A chest for ammunition, usually mounted on two wheels. **2** A watertight box or chamber used for carrying on building or construction work under water.

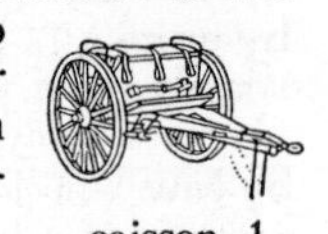
caisson, 1

cai·tiff \'kāt-əf\ *n.* A mean and wicked man. — *adj.* Wicked and mean; base and contemptible.

ca·jole \kə-'jōl\ *v.;* **ca·joled; ca·jol·ing.** To coax or persuade, especially by flattery or false promises; to wheedle.

ca·jol·ery \kə-'jōl-r(-)ē\ *n.; pl.* **ca·jol·er·ies.** The act of cajoling; coaxing or wheedling language or behavior.

cake \'kāk\ *n.* **1** A small mass of dough or batter, or of other food, as meat or fish, cooked on both sides; as, fish *cakes;* griddle *cakes.* **2** A baked food made from a mixture of flour, sugar, eggs, and other ingredients; as, a layer *cake;* ice cream and *cake.* **3** A substance hardened or molded into a solid mass; as, a *cake* of soap. — *v.;* **caked; cak·ing.** To form, shape, or harden into a cake; as, shoes *caked* with mud.

cal·a·bash \'kal-ə-ˌbash\ *n.* A gourd; especially, the large hard-shelled fruit of a tropical American tree (**calabash tree**) used for making utensils.

ca·lam·i·tous \kə-'lam-ət-əs\ *adj.* Causing calamity; accompanied by calamity; disastrous; as, a *calamitous* journey. — **ca·lam·i·tous·ly,** *adv.*

ca·lam·i·ty \kə-'lam-ət-ē\ *n.; pl.* **ca·lam·i·ties.** **1** Great distress or misfortune. **2** An event that causes great harm or destruction; a disaster.

cal·ci·fy \'kal-sə-ˌfī\ *v.;* **cal·ci·fied** \-ˌfīd\; **cal·ci·fy·ing.** To make or become stony or like calcite by the deposit or secretion of lime salts.

cal·ci·mine \'kals-m-ˌīn\ *n.* A white or colored thin paint for a ceiling or other plastering. — *v.;* **cal·ci·mined; cal·ci·min·ing.** To paint with calcimine.

cal·cine \kal-'sīn\ *v.;* **cal·cined; cal·cin·ing.** **1** To make or become powdery by heat. **2** To oxidize as by heat.

cal·cite \'kal-ˌsīt\ *n.* A crystalline mineral substance composed of calcium carbonate and found in a number of forms, including limestone, chalk, and marble.

cal·ci·um \'kal-sē-əm\ *n.* A silver-white soft metal that is found only in combination with other chemical elements and that is one of the essential parts of the bodies of most plants and animals.

calcium carbonate. A solid substance found in nature as limestone and marble and also in plant ashes, bones, and shells.

cal·cu·late \'kalk-yə-ˌlāt\ *v.;* **cal·cu·lat·ed; cal·cu·lat·ing.** **1** To find out by adding, subtracting, multiplying, or dividing; to compute; as, to *calculate* the cost of heating a building. **2** To plan by careful thought; as, a plan *calculated* to succeed. **3** To rely; to depend; as, to be able to *calculate* on being paid every week.

cal·cu·lat·ing \'kalk-yə-ˌlāt-ing\ *adj.* Scheming;

coldly analytical; as, a person with a *calculating* disposition. — **cal·cu·lat·ing·ly,** *adv.*

cal·cu·la·tion \ˌkalk-yə-ˈlāsh-n\ *n.* **1** The act or process of calculating. **2** The result obtained by calculating; as, a correct *calculation* of costs. **3** Discretion; caution.

cal·cu·la·tor \ˈkalk-yə-ˌlāt-r\ *n.* **1** One that calculates. **2** A machine that solves mathematical problems.

cal·cu·lus \ˈkalk-yə-ləs\ *n.; pl.* **cal·cu·li** \-ˌlī\ or **cal·cu·lus·es** \-lə-səz\. [From Latin, meaning "act of calculating", literally "pebble" (such as those used in calculating).] **1** A solid mass formed in the body, as a gallstone. **2** A branch of higher mathematics.

cal·dron or **caul·dron** \ˈkȯld-rən\ *n.* A large kettle or boiler.

cal·en·dar \ˈkal-ənd-r\ *n.* **1** An arrangement of time into days, weeks, months, and years. **2** A sheet, folder, or book containing a record of such an arrangement for a certain period, as a year. **3** An orderly list or schedule of coming events; as, a church *calendar.* **4** A list of cases to be tried in court. — *v.* To enter in a calendar.

cal·en·der \ˈkal-ənd-r\ *n.* A machine for calendering cloth or paper. — *v.* To press, as cloth or paper, between rollers so as to produce a glossy or a watered finish.

calf \ˈkaf, ˈkȧf\ *n.; pl.* **calves** \ˈkavz, ˈkȧvz\. **1** The young of the cow. **2** The young of the elephant, moose, rhinoceros, or whale, and of certain other large animals. **3** Leather made from the skin of a calf. **4** An awkward or silly young person, especially a boy.

calf \ˈkaf, ˈkȧf\ *n.; pl.* **calves** \ˈkavz, ˈkȧvz\. The fleshy back part of the leg below the knee.

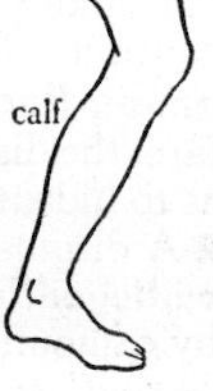

calf·skin \ˈkaf-ˌskin, ˈkȧf-\ *n.* The skin of a calf or the fine leather made from this skin.

cal·i·ber or **cal·i·bre** \ˈkal-əb-r\ *n.* **1** The diameter of a projectile. **2** The diameter of the bore of a gun. **3** Mental ability; measure of excellence; quality; as, a man of high *caliber.*

cal·i·brate \ˈkal-ə-ˌbrāt\ *v.;* **cal·i·brat·ed; cal·i·brat·ing. 1** To determine, mark, or correct the measuring marks on, as a thermometer tube. **2** To make agree with a standard; as, to *calibrate* a weighing scale. — **cal·i·bra·tion** \ˌkal-ə-ˈbrāsh-n\ *n.*

cal·i·co \ˈkal-ə-ˌkō\ *n.; pl.* **cal·i·coes** or **cal·i·cos.** Cotton cloth; especially, cotton cloth with a colored pattern printed on one side. — *adj.* **1** Made of calico. **2** Looking like calico; spotted; as, a *calico* cat.

cal·i·for·ni·um \ˌkal-ə-ˈfȯr-nē-əm\ *n.* An artificially prepared radioactive chemical element.

cal·i·pers or **cal·li·pers** \ˈkal-əp-rz\ *n. pl.* An instrument with two legs, usually curved and fastened together at one end, used in measuring the thickness of objects or the distances between objects.

ca·liph or **ca·lif** \ˈkā-ləf\ *n.* A title used by rulers of Mohammedan countries.

cal·is·then·ics \ˌkal-əs-ˈthen-iks\ *n. sing. and pl.* **1** The science or practice of bodily exercise, without apparatus, to develop strength and grace. **2** The exercises used for this purpose. — **cal·is·then·ic** \-ik\ *adj.*

calk or **caulk** \ˈkȯk\ *v.* To fill up a crack, a seam, or a joint so as to make it watertight.

calk \ˈkȯk\ *n.* **1** A pointed metal piece fixed on the shoe of a horse or an ox to prevent slipping. **2** A similar device worn on the sole of a shoe. — *v.* **1** To furnish with calks. **2** To wound with a calk. The horse *calked* itself while struggling in the deep mud.

call \ˈkȯl\ *v.* **1** To speak in a loud distinct voice so as to be heard at a distance; to cry; to shout. We *called* again and again but no help came. **2** To utter in a loud clear voice; as, to *call* a roll; to *call* out a command. **3** To announce with authority; to proclaim; as, to *call* a halt. **4** To summon with a shout; as, to *call* someone to dinner. **5** To bring into action or discussion; as, to *call* up reserves; to *call* a case in court. **6** To appeal to; to invoke; as, to *call* on a person's sense of decency. **7** To get into touch with by telephone; to make a telephone call. **8** To summon; as, to *call* a special meeting. **9** To make a brief visit. **10** To give a name to; to address by name. **11** To regard as being of a certain kind. A whale is *called* a mammal. **12** To estimate as being; as, to *call* the distance ten miles. — *n.* **1** A loud shout or cry; as, a *call* for help. **2** A reading aloud of a list of names; as, a roll *call.* **3** A summons; an invitation. **4** A signal to summon a person, as to a telephone. **5** A short social visit; as, to pay a *call* on a friend. **6** The cry of a bird or other animal.

call·er \ˈkȯl-r\ *n.* **1** One that calls, as the arrival or departure of trains. **2** A person who makes a brief visit.

call·ing \ˈkȯl-ing\ *n.* **1** The act of one that calls. **2** A person's usual occupation or business; as, to follow the *calling* of a doctor.

cal·li·o·pe \kə-ˈlī-ə-(ˌ)pē\ *n.* [Named after *Calliope,* the Muse that presides over poetry in Greek and Roman mythology, from Greek *Kalliopē* meaning literally "the one with a beautiful voice".] A musical instrument consisting of a series of whistles, played by keys arranged as in an organ.

callipers. Variant of *calipers.*

cal·lous \ˈkal-əs\ *adj.* **1** Having a callus; hardened; as, a person *callous* to ridicule. **2** Lacking in sympathy or sensitivity; unfeeling; hardhearted; as, a *callous* person. — *v.* To make callous; to become callous; as, hands *calloused* by years of hard work. — **cal·lous·ly,** *adv.*

cal·low \ˈkal-ō\ *adj.* **1** Not having the feathers needed for flying, as a young bird; not fledged.

2 Immature; without experience of life; as, a *callow* youth.

cal·lus \'kal-əs\ *n.* **1** A hard thickened place on the skin or on the bark of a plant. **2** A substance that encloses fragments of a broken bone, aiding in repairs by being finally converted into bone. — *v.* To form a callus.

calm \'käm, 'kȧm\ *n.* Freedom from motion or disturbance, as of winds or waves; quiet; peacefulness. — *adj.* **1** Not stormy; quiet; serene; as, a *calm* night. **2** Not excited; quiet in action or in words; as, a *calm* tone of voice. — *v.* To make or to become calm or quiet; as, to *calm* an excited child. — **calm·ly,** *adv.*

cal·o·mel \'kal-əm-l, -ə-ˌmel\ *n.* A tasteless, white or yellowish powder used as a medicine.

cal·o·rie or **cal·o·ry** \'kal-r(-)ē\ *n.; pl.* **cal·o·ries.** A unit for measuring heat, especially for measuring the value of foods for producing heat and energy in the human body.

cal·o·rim·e·ter \ˌkal-r-'im-ət-r\ *n.* An apparatus for measuring quantities of heat, as those developed by combustion.

ca·lum·ni·ate \kə-'ləm-nē-ˌāt\ *v.;* **ca·lum·ni·at·ed; ca·lum·ni·at·ing.** To accuse falsely and maliciously; to slander. — **ca·lum·ni·a·tor** \-ˌāt-r\ *n.*

cal·um·ny \'kal-əm-nē\ *n.; pl.* **cal·um·nies.** A false accusation made to injure another person's character. — **ca·lum·ni·ous** \kə-'ləm-nē-əs\ *adj.* — **ca·lum·ni·ous·ly,** *adv.*

calve \'kav, 'kaf, 'kȧv, 'kȧf\ *v.;* **calved; calv·ing.** To give birth to a calf.

calves. Pl. of *calf.*

ca·lyp·so \kə-'lip-ˌsō\ *n.; pl.* **ca·lyp·sos.** A ballad of the British West Indies made up on a current topic or as a parody and sung in English with an African rhythm.

ca·lyx \'kā-liks\ *n.; pl.* **ca·lyx·es** \-liks-əz\ or **ca·ly·ces** \-lə-ˌsēz\. The part of a flower, usually green, leaflike, and cup-shaped, that grows at the base of the flower, outside the colored petal part.

calyx

cam \'kam\ *n.* A rotating or sliding piece or projection, as on the wheel of a machine, for giving or receiving motion.

ca·ma·ra·de·rie \ˌkam-r-'ad-r-ē, ˌkäm-r-'äd-, ˌkȧm-r-'ȧd-\ *n.* The good feeling existing between comrades.

cam·bi·um \'kam-bē-əm\ *n.* The soft tissue, in such trees as the maple and the elm, from which new wood and bark develop.

Cam·bo·di·an \kam-'bōd-ē-ən\ *adj.* Of or relating to Cambodia. — *n.* A native of Cambodia.

cam·bric \'kām-brik\ *n.* A fine white linen cloth or a similar closely woven cotton fabric.

came. Past tense of *come.*

cam·el \'kam-l\ *n.* A large, hoofed, cud-chewing animal used in the desert regions of Asia and Africa for carrying burdens and for riding, the **A·ra·bi·an camel** \ə-'rā-bē-ən\, called also *dromedary,* having one large hump on its back and the central Asian **Bac·tri·an camel** \'bak-trē-ən\ having two humps.

ca·mel·lia \kə-'mēl-yə\ *n.* [Named after Georg Josef *Kamel* (also called *Camellus*), a 17th century missionary who is said to have brought it to Europe from Asia.] A greenhouse shrub with glossy evergreen leaves and red or white double roselike flowers.

cam·el's hair \'kam-lz\. A fabric made of the hair of camels or of a mixture of this hair with another fiber, usually wool.

cam·eo \'kam-ē-ˌō\ *n.; pl.* **cam·e·os.** A gem carved in such a way that the design is higher than its background.

cam·era \'kam-r(-)ə\ *n.* [From Late Latin *camera* meaning "chamber", "room".] **1** A light-tight box fitted with a lens through the opening of which the image of an object is recorded on a material that is sensitive to light. **2** The part of a television transmitting apparatus in which the image to be televised is formed for change into electrical impulses. — **in camera.** In the judge's chamber; in private.

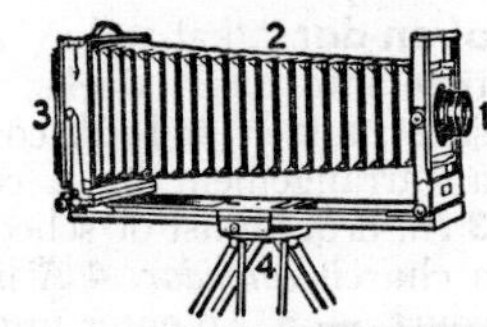

camera, 1: *1* lens, *2* bellows, *3* back and film or plate-holder, *4* tripod

cam·er·a·man \'kam-r(-)ə-ˌman, -mən\ *n.; pl.* **cam·er·a·men** \-ˌmen, -mən\. A man whose occupation is taking pictures, especially one who operates a motion-picture or television camera.

cam·i·sole \'kam-ə-ˌsōl\ *n.* A short and usually sleeveless undergarment for women.

cam·o·mile or **cham·o·mile** \'kam-ə-ˌmīl\ *n.* A daisylike plant of the aster family whose flowers contain a bitter substance used in medicine.

cam·ou·flage \'kam-ə-ˌfläzh, -ˌflȧzh\ *n.* **1** In warfare, the disguising of a camp, a ship, or a weapon so as to hide it or make it difficult for an enemy to see. **2** A disguise; a deceptive appearance. — *v.;* **cam·ou·flaged; cam·ou·flag·ing.** To protect or disguise by camouflage; as, to *camouflage* a fortification; to *camouflage* one's real intentions by flattering words.

camp \'kamp\ *n.* **1** A group of tents, huts, or other shelters; the place where these are located; as, an army *camp;* a summer *camp.* **2** A single tent or other shelter, especially one used on a vacation or outing. **3** The people who occupy a camp. — *v.* **1** To stay or live temporarily in a camp. **2** To make a camp; as, to *camp* for the night; to *camp* on the shore of a lake. — **camp·er,** *n.*

cam·paign \(')kam-'pān\ *n.* **1** A series of military operations which together form one stage of a war. **2** A connected series of activities to bring about a desired result; as, the governor's *campaign* for re-election; an advertising *campaign.* — *v.* To take part in a campaign; to go on a campaign. — **cam·paign·er,** *n.*

cam·pa·ni·le \ˌkamp-n-ˈē-lē\ *n.* A bell tower, especially one built separate from another building.

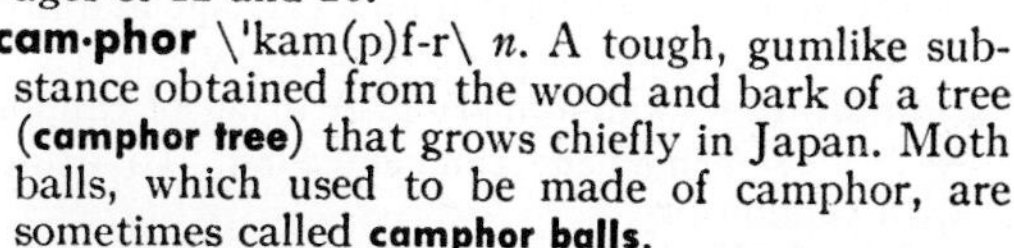
campanile

cam·pan·u·la \kam-ˈpan-yə-lə\ *n.* A garden plant with usually blue or white bell-shaped flowers and a bitter juice.

camp·fire \ˈkamp-ˌfīr\ *n.* **1** A fire in a camp, especially when considered as the center of a social gathering in the evening. **2** A gathering held around a campfire.

campfire girl. A member of "The Camp Fire Girls of America", an organization of girls between the ages of 12 and 20.

cam·phor \ˈkam(p)f-r\ *n.* A tough, gumlike substance obtained from the wood and bark of a tree (**camphor tree**) that grows chiefly in Japan. Moth balls, which used to be made of camphor, are sometimes called **camphor balls**.

cam·po·ree \ˌkamp-r-ˈē\ *n.* A gathering of Boy Scouts representing a section of a country, not a whole nation.

camp stool. A folding stool.

cam·pus \ˈkamp-əs\ *n.* [From Latin, meaning "plain", "field".] The grounds of a college or of a school.

can \kən, ˈkan\ *v.; past tense* **could** \kəd, ˈku̇d\. **1** Know or knows how to. I *can* swim. **2** Am, is, or are able to. A camel *can* live for days without drinking. **3** Has or have the power or right to. Only the teacher *can* give us permission to go. **4** May. Everyone *can* have a second helping.

can \ˈkan\ *n.* **1** A container of metal in any of various sizes and shapes; as, a milk *can;* an oil *can.* **2** The contents of a can; as, a *can* of tomatoes. — *v.;* **canned**; **can·ning**. To put in a can or in cans; especially, to preserve foods by putting them in sealed cans or jars; as, to *can* peaches.

Can·a·da goose \ˈkan-əd-ə\. The common wild goose of North America, chiefly gray and brownish in color, with black head and neck.

Ca·na·di·an \kə-ˈnād-ē-ən\ *adj.* Of or relating to Canada. — *n.* A native or inhabitant of Canada.

ca·nal \kə-ˈnal\ *n.* **1** An artificial waterway used for passage of boats or for irrigation of land. **2** A tubelike passage in the body; a duct; as, the alimentary *canal.*

ca·nary \kə-ˈner-ē\ *n.; pl.* **ca·nar·ies**. **1** A wine made in the Canary Islands. **2** Also **canary bird**. A small yellow songbird now reared in captivity as the best-known of cage birds. **3** Usually **canary yellow**. A light-yellow color with a tinge of orange.

ca·nas·ta \kə-ˈnas-tə\ *n.* A variety of rummy.

can·cel \ˈkan(t)s-l\ *v.;* **can·celed** or **can·celled**; **can·cel·ing** or **can·cel·ling** \-l(-)ing\. **1** To cross out or strike out with a line or lines; as, to *cancel* what one has written. **2** To mark a postage stamp or a check to show that it has been used. **3** To wipe out; to do away with; to take back or withdraw; as, to *cancel* an order; to *cancel* an appointment. **4** To divide by the same number, as the numerator and denominator of a fraction; to remove equivalents on opposite sides, as of an equation. **5** To oppose with something of equal force or value; to balance. A bad action often *cancels* a good one. — For synonyms see *erase.*

can·cel·la·tion \ˌkan(t)s-l-ˈāsh-n\ *n.* **1** An act of canceling; as, to reduce a fraction by *cancellation;* the *cancellation* of a game because of bad weather. **2** A mark or marks made to cancel something; as, a *cancellation* on a postage stamp.

can·cer \ˈkan(t)s-r\ *n.* **1** A malignant growth of tissue, usually ulcerating and tending to spread, causing ill health and wasting away. **2** A dangerous evil that eats away slowly but fatally. — **can·cer·ous** \ˈkan(t)s-r(-)əs\ *adj.*

can·de·la·brum \ˌkand-l-ˈäb-rəm, -ˈab-, -ˈāb-, -ˈȧb-\ *n.; pl.* **can·de·la·bra** \-rə\ or **can·de·la·brums** \-rəmz\. A candlestick that has several branches, for holding more than one candle. ☞ Sometimes *candelabra* is used as a singular, with a plural *candelabras.*

candelabrum

can·did \ˈkan-dəd\ *adj.* **1** Not prejudiced; fair; just; as, to try to form a *candid* opinion. **2** Frank; straightforward; sincere; as, to give a *candid* reply to an unwelcome question. — **can·did·ly**, *adv.*

can·di·da·cy \ˈkan-də-də-sē\ *n.* The state of being a candidate; as, to announce one's *candidacy* for the office of state senator.

can·di·date \ˈkan-də-ˌdāt, -dət\ *n.* [From Latin *candidatus* meaning literally "clothed in white"; so named because office seekers in ancient Rome wore white togas.] A person who offers himself or is proposed by another as a suitable person for an office or honor; as, to be a *candidate* for governor.

can·di·da·ture \ˈkan-də-də-ˌchu̇r\ *n.* Candidacy.

can·died \ˈkan-dēd\. Past tense and past part. of *candy.* — *adj.* **1** Preserved in, or coated with, sugar; as, *candied* apples. **2** Changed into sugar crystals; as, *candied* syrup. **3** Like candy; sweet; flattering; as, *candied* words.

candies. Pl. of *candy.*

can·dle \ˈkand-l\ *n.* **1** A stick of tallow or wax shaped, usually by molding, around a wick and burned to give light. **2** A unit of measurement for the intensity of light, based formerly on the light given by a candle regarded as standard, now (**international candle**) on the light given off by a specified surface of platinum heated to a certain temperature. — *v.;* **can·dled**; **can·dling** \-l(-)ing\. To inspect, especially eggs, by holding before a light. — **can·dler** \-l(-)ər\ *n.*

can·dle·light \ˈkand-l-ˌlīt\ *n.* **1** The light of a candle or candles; artificial illumination. **2** The time when candles are lighted; nightfall; twilight.

can·dle·lit \ˈkand-l-ˌlit\ *adj.* Illuminated by candlelight; as, a *candlelit* ballroom.

candle power. The intensity of light or the power of giving light, as of a lamp, expressed in international candles.

can·dle·stick \'kand-l-ˌstik\ *n.* A holder for a candle, often in the form of a saucer with a socket at the center.

can·dor \'kand-r\ *n.* **1** Freedom from prejudice; impartiality. **2** Frankness; outspokenness.

can·dy \'kan-dē\ *n.; pl.* **can·dies. 1** Sugar crystals or a solid mass formed by boiling or evaporating sugar or syrup. **2** A sugary food made by boiling a syrup and other ingredients. **3** A piece of such candy, sometimes coated, as with chocolate. — *v.;* **can·died** \-dēd\; **can·dy·ing. 1** To preserve by boiling with sugar; to coat with sugar. **2** To turn into sugar or candy.

can·dy·tuft \'kan-dē-ˌtəft\ *n.* Any of a number of plants of the mustard family cultivated for their clusters of white, pink, or purple flowers.

cane \'kān\ *n.* **1** Any jointed plant stem, usually slender and more or less flexible. **2** Sugar cane. **3** A stick made from a piece of cane of a length and weight suitable for use in walking; any walking stick. — *v.;* **caned**; **can·ing. 1** To beat or switch with a cane. **2** To make or to repair with cane; as, to *cane* the seat of a chair.

cane·brake \'kān-ˌbrāk\ *n.* A thicket of tall bamboolike grass.

ca·nine \'kā-ˌnīn\ *adj.* **1** Having to do with dogs or with animals that are related to the dog, including wolves, jackals, and foxes. **2** Relating to the canine tooth. — *n.* **1** The pointed tooth next to the incisors of a person, or a tooth of similar shape. **2** A dog.

can·is·ter \'kan-əst-r\ *n.* **1** A small box or can, such as one for holding tea, coffee, flour, or sugar. **2** A shell for close-range artillery fire, consisting of a number of bullets enclosed in a lightweight case which is burst by the firing charge.

can·ker \'kangk-r\ *n.* **1** A spreading sore that eats into the flesh, especially one about the mouth. **2** Anything that corrupts or destroys. — *v.;* **cankered**; **can·ker·ing** \-r(-)ing\. To eat or be eaten away by canker. — **can·ker·ous** \-r(-)əs\ *adj.*

can·ker·worm \'kangk-r-ˌwərm\ *n.* A caterpillar, especially a measuring worm, that injures fruit and shade trees.

can·na \'kan-ə\ *n.* A tall plant with a stout unbranched stem, large leaves, and bright-colored flower clusters that grow at the end of the stem.

canned \'kand\. Past tense and past part. of *can.* — *adj.* Preserved in sealed cans or jars; as, *canned* tomatoes; *canned* apple juice.

can·ner \'kan-r\ *n.* A person whose business or occupation is canning food.

can·nery \'kan-r-ē\ *n.; pl.* **can·ner·ies.** A factory where foodstuffs are canned.

can·ni·bal \'kan-əb-l\ *n.* [From Spanish *caníbal*, there borrowed from an American Indian word recorded by Columbus in Cuba, meaning "Carib Indians", literally "strong men" or "brave men".] **1** A human being who eats human flesh. **2** An animal that eats other animals of its own kind.

can·ni·bal·ism \'kan-əb-l-ˌiz-m\ *n.* The eating of human flesh by human beings or the flesh of an animal by another animal of the same kind. — **can·ni·bal·is·tic** \ˌkan-əb-l-'is-tik\ *adj.*

can·ni·bal·ize \'kan-əb-l-ˌīz\ *v.;* **can·ni·bal·ized**; **can·ni·bal·iz·ing.** To dismantle a machine for parts to be used as replacements in other machines of the same make.

cannier. Comparative of *canny.*

canniest. Superlative of *canny.*

can·ning \'kan-ing\ *n.* The process or business of preserving foodstuffs in sealed cans or jars.

can·non \'kan-ən\ *n.; pl.* **can·nons** or **can·non.** A heavy gun that is mounted on a carriage and fired from that position; a piece of artillery.

can·non·ade \ˌkan-ə-'nād\ *n.* A firing of cannon. — *v.;* **can·non·ad·ed**; **can·non·ad·ing.** To attack with cannon fire.

cannon ball. A missile, especially a solid round missile, designed to be shot from a cannon.

can·non·eer \ˌkan-ə-'nir\ *n.* An artilleryman who tends and fires cannon; a gunner.

can·not \'kan-ˌät; kə-'nät, ka-; 'kan-ət\. The compound form of *can not.*

can·ny \'kan-ē\ *adj.;* **can·ni·er**; **can·ni·est.** Cautious or shrewd; watchful of one's own interests; as, a *canny* man where money is concerned. — **can·ni·ly** \'kan-l-ē\ *adv.*

ca·noe \kə-'nü\ *n.* A small, light, narrow boat, sharp at both ends, usually propelled by one or more paddles. — *v.;* **ca·noed**; **ca·noe·ing.** To paddle, sail, or travel in a canoe. — **ca·noe·ist** \-'nü-əst\ *n.*

can·on \'kan-ən\ *n.* **1** A rule or law of a church. **2** An established and accepted rule or principle; as, the *canons* of good taste. **3** An official or authoritative list, as of the saints or of the books of the Bible accepted as genuine. **4** A musical composition for two or more voices, in which one voice begins a melody and is imitated by others beginning later.

can·on \'kan-ən\ *n.* A clergyman on the staff of a cathedral.

ca·ñon \'kan-yən\. Variant of *canyon.*

ca·non·i·cal \kə-'nän-ik-l\ *adj.* **1** Set as prescribed by a canon, or by church law. **2** Belonging to a canon; as, the *canonical* books of the Bible. — **ca·non·i·cal·ly** \-l(-)ē\ *adv.*

can·on·ize \'kan-ə-ˌnīz\ *v.;* **can·on·ized**; **can·on·iz·ing.** To declare a deceased person officially a saint in a public ceremony; to put into the canon of recognized saints. — **can·on·i·za·tion** \ˌkan-ə-nə-'zāsh-n\ *n.*

can·o·py \'kan-ə-pē\ *n.; pl.* **can·o·pies. 1** A covering fixed over a bed, throne, or shrine, or carried on poles over a person of high rank or over some sacred object. **2** Any overhanging shade or shelter. — *v.;* **can·o·pied** \-pēd\; **can·o·py·ing.** To cover with or as if with a canopy.

canst \kən(t)st, 'kan(t)st\. An archaic form of the verb *can*, used chiefly with *thou.*

cant \'kant\ *n.* **1** A slanting surface, as of a buttress or bank of earth. **2** A tilt; a slope; an incline; as, the steep *cant* of the road.

cant \'kant\ *n.* **1** A secret jargon or language, as of thieves or tramps. **2** The special vocabulary and expressions of a trade or profession. **3** Insincere speech; especially, pious words or statements.

can't \'kant, 'kȧnt; *in the South, often* 'kānt\. A contraction of *cannot* or of *can not.*

can·ta·loupe or **can·ta·loup** \'kant-l-ˌōp\ *n.* A muskmelon with a hard, thick skin and firm, juicy flesh, which is eaten raw.

can·tan·ker·ous \(')kan-'tangk-r(-)əs\ *adj.* Ill-natured; quarrelsome; as, a *cantankerous* child. — **can·tan·ker·ous·ly**, *adv.*

can·ta·ta \kən-'tät-ə, -'tȧt-ə\ *n.* A poem, a story, or a play set to music to be sung by a chorus and soloists.

can·teen \(')kan-'tēn\ *n.* **1** A store in which food, drinks, and small supplies are sold, as in a camp or a factory. **2** A place of recreation and entertainment for soldiers and sailors. **3** A small container used for carrying drinking water or other liquid.

can·ter \'kant-r\ *n.* A horse's gait, like the gallop but less rapid. — *v.* To move in, or as if in, a canter.

cant hook \'kant\. A wooden lever with an adjustable metal hook near one end, used for handling logs.

can·ti·cle \'kant-ik-l\ *n.* A little song; a hymn of praise used in a church service.

can·ti·le·ver \'kant-l-ˌēv-r\ *n.* **1** A projecting beam or similar structure fastened only at one end, as by being built into a wall or pier. **2** Either of two beams or structures that project from piers toward each other and when joined form a span in a **cantilever bridge.**

cantilever bridge

can·tle \'kant-l\ *n.* The rear part of a saddle.

can·to \'kan-ˌtō\ *n.; pl.* **can·tos.** One of the chief divisions of a long poem.

can·ton \'kant-n, 'kan-ˌtän\ *n.* A small division of a country; a district; especially, one of the states of the Swiss confederation.

can·ton·ment \kan-'tän-mənt, -'tōn-\ *n.* A group of temporary buildings for housing troops.

can·tor \'kant-r\ *n.* **1** A singer. **2** A soloist in charge of music in a synagogue.

can·vas \'kan-vəs\ *n.* **1** A strong cloth of hemp, flax, or cotton, used for making tents and sails, and as the material on which oil paintings are made. **2** Something made of canvas or on canvas; especially, an oil painting.

can·vas·back \'kan-vəs-ˌbak\ *n.* A North American wild duck with reddish head and grayish back.

can·vass \'kan-vəs\ *v.* **1** To examine carefully; to discuss; as, to *canvass* a question. **2** To go through a district or to go to individual persons in seeking orders, contributions, or votes; as, to *canvass* for a political candidate. **3** To ask for orders, contributions, or votes. — *n.* **1** A careful examination, as of votes cast in an election. **2** A canvassing for orders, contributions, or votes.

can·yon or **ca·ñon** \'kan-yən\ *n.* A deep valley with high, steep slopes, often with a stream flowing through it.

caou·tchouc \'kau̇-ˌchük\ *n.* Rubber; especially, pure rubber.

cap \'kap\ *n.* **1** A covering, especially one without a brim, for a person's head. **2** Something that is like a cap in appearance, position, or use; as, a bottle *cap;* the *cap* of a fountain pen. **3** A small explosive charge, as for a toy pistol. — *v.;* **capped**; **cap·ping. 1** To cover with a cap or other covering; to cover the end or top of something; as, to *cap* a bottle. **2** To match with something equal or better; as, to *cap* one story with another.

cap. Abbreviation for *capital.*

ca·pa·bil·i·ty \ˌkāp-ə-'bil-ət-ē\ *n.; pl.* **ca·pa·bil·i·ties. 1** The quality of being capable; capacity; ability; especially, mental ability. **2** Capacity of receiving or undergoing certain use or treatment.

ca·pa·ble \'kāp-əb-l\ *adj.* **1** Having ability, capacity, or power to do something; as, a room *capable* of holding fifty people; to be *capable* of doing better work. **2** Of such a nature as to permit; susceptible; as, work that is *capable* of improvement; a remark *capable* of being misunderstood. **3** Efficient; competent; as, a *capable* salesman. — **ca·pa·bly** \-ə-blē\ *adv.*

ca·pa·cious \kə-'pā-shəs\ *adj.* Able to contain much; larger than ordinary; spacious; roomy; as, *capacious* pockets.

ca·pac·i·tor \kə-'pas-ət-r\ *n.* A device for holding or storing an electric charge; a condenser.

ca·pac·i·ty \kə-'pas-ət-ē\ *n.; pl.* **ca·pac·i·ties. 1** Power to receive or contain something; as, the seating *capacity* of a room. **2** Extent of room or space; content; as, a jug with a *capacity* of one gallon. **3** Ability to do or learn. **4** Position; as, to serve in the *capacity* of chairman.

ca·par·i·son \kə-'par-əs-n, -əz-n\ *n.* **1** An ornamental covering for a horse. **2** The clothing and ornaments worn by a person. — *v.* To adorn with rich and beautiful clothing.

cape \'kāp\ *n.* A sleeveless garment, or part of a garment, worn hanging from a person's neck over the shoulders, arms, and back.

cape \'kāp\ *n.* A point of land that juts out into the sea or into a lake.

ca·per \'kāp-r\ *n.* **1** Any of a family of low prickly shrubs of the Mediterranean region related to the mustard family. **2** [in the plural] The greenish flower buds and young berries of the caper, pickled and used in sauces.

ca·per \'kāp-r\ *v.;* **ca·pered**; **ca·per·ing** \-r(-)ing\.

To jump about or leap about in a lively manner; to prance; to frisk. The excited dog *capered* about its master. — *n.* **1** A prancing movement; a skip. **2** A prank; a trick.

cap·il·lar·i·ty \ˌkap-l-ˈar-ət-ē\ *n.* The action by which the surface of a liquid where it is in contact with a solid, as in a slender tube, is raised or lowered.

cap·il·lary \ˈkap-l-ˌer-ē\ *adj.* **1** Resembling a hair; very slender; as, a *capillary* tube. **2** Relating to very slender tubes or vessels, or to capillarity, as in **capillary attraction**, the apparent attraction between a solid and a liquid as seen in capillarity. — *n.; pl.* **cap·il·lar·ies.** **1** A capillary tube or vessel. **2** One of the slender hairlike tubes in the network connecting the arteries and veins.

cap·i·tal \ˈkap-ət-l\ *adj.* **1** Punishable by death; having to do with punishment by death; as, a *capital* crime. **2** First in importance or position; chief, as through being the seat of government; as, the *capital* city of a country. **3** First-rate; excellent; as, a *capital* story. — *n.* **1** A capital letter. **2** A capital city. **3** An amount of accumulated wealth; especially, such an amount of wealth used in running a business.

cap·i·tal \ˈkap-ət-l\ *n.* The top part or piece of an architectural column.

capital

cap·i·tal·ism \ˈkap-ət-l-ˌiz-m\ *n.* An economic system under which the ownership of natural resources and the means of production and distribution of goods are for the most part in the hands of private individuals or private business and industrial organizations working under competitive conditions.

cap·i·tal·ist \ˈkap-ət-l-əst\ *n.* **1** A person who has capital; especially, one who has or controls a great amount of wealth used in business. **2** A person who believes in capitalism.

cap·i·tal·is·tic \ˌkap-ət-l-ˈis-tik\ *adj.* **1** Of or relating to capitalism or capitalists; as, a *capitalistic* economic system. **2** In favor of capitalism; as, to be *capitalistic* in one's thinking. — **cap·i·tal·is·ti·cal·ly** \-tik-l(-)ē\ *adv.*

cap·i·tal·i·za·tion \ˌkap-ət-l-ə-ˈzāsh-n\ *n.* **1** The act or process of capitalizing. **2** The amount of money used as capital in a business.

cap·i·tal·ize \ˈkap-ət-l-ˌīz\ *v.;* **cap·i·tal·ized**; **cap·i·tal·iz·ing.** **1** To write with a capital letter or in capital letters. **2** To use as capital, as in a business; to furnish capital for a business. **3** To turn something to one's own advantage; as, to *capitalize* on another's mistakes.

capital letter. A letter larger in size than the corresponding small letter and often different in form, used to begin the name of a person or place, or to begin the first word of a sentence.

cap·i·tal·ly \ˈkap-ət-l-ē\ *adv.* In a capital manner; excellently; as, to get along *capitally* in school.

Cap·i·tol \ˈkap-ət-l\ *n.* **1** The building in Washington in which the United States Congress meets. **2** [often with a small letter] The building in which a state legislature meets; a statehouse.

ca·pit·u·late \kə-ˈpich-l-ˌāt\ *v.;* **ca·pit·u·lat·ed**; **ca·pit·u·lat·ing.** To surrender, usually on certain terms agreed upon in advance.

ca·pit·u·la·tion \kə-ˌpich-l-ˈāsh-n\ *n.* **1** A summary of the main points of a subject. **2** A surrender, especially when made in accordance with terms agreed upon.

ca·pon \ˈkā-ˌpän\ *n.* A castrated rooster specially fattened for eating.

capped. Past tense and past part. of *cap.*

capping. Pres. part. of *cap.*

ca·price \kə-ˈprēs\ *n.* **1** A sudden change in feeling, opinion, or action that occurs without an apparent cause, reason, or motive; a whim; a fancy. **2** A musical composition written in a free and irregular style.

ca·pri·cious \kə-ˈprish-əs, -ˈprē-shəs\ *adj.* Moved or controlled by caprice; apt to change suddenly; fickle; changeable; as, a *capricious* child; *capricious* weather. — **ca·pri·cious·ly**, *adv.*

cap·size \kap-ˈsīz, ˈkap-ˌsīz\ *v.;* **cap·sized**; **cap·siz·ing.** To upset; to overturn; as, to *capsize* a small boat by rocking it. Canoes *capsize* easily.

cap·stan \ˈkap-stən\ *n.* A mechanical device consisting of an upright revolving drum or cylinder to which a rope is fastened, much used on ships for moving or raising weights and for exerting pulling force.

capstan

cap·sule \ˈkaps-l, ˈkap-ˌsül\ *n.* **1** A case enclosing the seeds of some plants. **2** A small container, usually of gelatin, holding a dose of medicine so that it may be easily swallowed. **3** A small sealed compartment for an astronaut. — *adj.* Of a small type or in a condensed form; as, a *capsule* review of a new book.

Capt. Abbreviation for *Captain.*

cap·tain \ˈkap-tən\ *n.* **1** A chief or leader of a group; as, the *captain* of a band of gypsies; the *captain* of a team. **2** An army officer ranking above a first lieutenant and below a major. **3** A naval officer ranking below a rear admiral and above a commander. **4** The master, or commanding officer, of a ship. — *v.* To act as captain or chief of something; to lead; as, to *captain* a team.

cap·tain·cy \ˈkap-tən-sē\ *n.; pl.* **cap·tain·cies.** The rank or position of captain.

cap·tion \ˈkapsh-n\ *n.* **1** The heading of a chapter, a section, a page, or an article. **2** The title or brief description printed beneath an illustration or picture in a book or newspaper.

cap·tious \ˈkap-shəs\ *adj.* Quick to find fault, especially over trifles. — **cap·tious·ly**, *adv.*

cap·ti·vate \ˈkap-tə-ˌvāt\ *v.;* **cap·ti·vat·ed**; **cap·ti·vat·ing.** To attract and win over; to charm; to fascinate; as, music that *captivated* everybody who heard it.

— The words *charm* and *fascinate* are synonyms of

captivate: captivate may apply to arousing pleasurable attention and overcoming doubt and reserve, though often only temporarily; *charm* usually indicates compelling attention or interest, often by, or seemingly by magic; *fascinate* may imply so strong an appeal that resistance to it is useless.

cap·ti·va·tion \ˌkap-tə-ˈvāsh-n\ *n.* **1** The act of captivating. **2** Something that captivates or charms; an irresistible attraction.

cap·tive \ˈkap-tiv\ *n.* A prisoner; especially, a prisoner of war. — *adj.* **1** Made or held prisoner; kept in confinement; as, a *captive* soldier. **2** Fastened so as to prevent escape; as, a *captive* balloon.

cap·tiv·i·ty \kap-ˈtiv-ət-ē\ *n.; pl.* **cap·tiv·i·ties. 1** The state of being a prisoner, especially of war; as, prisoners released after five years of *captivity.* **2** The state of being held in confinement; as, the first gorilla born in *captivity.*

cap·tor \ˈkapt-r\ *n.* One that captures; a person who takes or holds another person captive.

cap·ture \ˈkap-chər\ *v.;* **cap·tured; cap·tur·ing. 1** To seize or to take by force, surprise, or greater skill; as, to *capture* a robber; to *capture* a city in war. **2** To attract and hold; as, to *capture* the attention of an audience. — *n.* **1** The act of capturing something. With the *capture* of the city, the war ended. **2** Any person or thing that has been captured.

car \ˈkär, ˈkȧr\ *n.* **1** A vehicle moved on wheels, as a war chariot, a pleasure carriage, a railroad coach, or an automobile. **2** The cage of an elevator. **3** The part of a balloon or an airship in which passengers or equipment can be carried.

car·a·bao \ˌkar-ə-ˈbau̇\ *n.; pl.* **car·a·baos.** The water buffalo of the Philippines.

car·a·bi·neer or **car·a·bi·nier** \ˌkar-ə-bə-ˈnir\ *n.* A soldier, usually mounted, armed with a carbine.

car·a·cul \ˈkar-ək-l\ *n.* **1** The tightly curled, glossy, black coat of newborn Karakul lambs. **2** The sheep that produce these lambs.

ca·rafe \kə-ˈraf\ *n.* A bottle, usually made of glass and having a wide base and flaring lip, for holding water, as at the table or in a hotel room.

car·a·mel \ˈkar-əm-l, ˈkärm-l, ˈkȧrm-l\ *n.* **1** A firm candy that can be chewed. **2** Burnt sugar, used for coloring and flavoring.

car·a·pace \ˈkar-ə-ˌpās\ *n.* A bony or horny case covering the back of an animal, as the upper shell of a turtle.

car·at \ˈkar-ət\ *n.* **1** A unit of weight for precious stones, such as diamonds. **2** A twenty-fourth part — used in stating the fineness of gold; thus, gold 14 carats fine, often called *14-carat gold,* consists of 14 parts gold and 10 parts alloy.

car·a·van \ˈkar-ə-ˌvan\ *n.* **1** A group of travelers, such as merchants or pilgrims, traveling together on a long journey through a desert or through dangerous country; as, a camel *caravan.* **2** A covered vehicle of various kinds; a van.

car·a·van·sa·ry \ˌkar-ə-ˈvan(t)s-r-ē\ *n.; pl.* **car·a·van·sa·ries.** An inn where caravans rest at night, as in Turkey and Arabia; any large inn or hotel.

car·a·vel \ˈkar-əv-l\ *n.* A small sailing vessel of the 15th and 16th centuries with a broad bow and a high stern and three or four masts; as, the *caravels* Nina, Pinta, and Santa Maria.

caravel

car·a·way \ˈkar-ə-ˌwā\ *n.* A plant with flattish white flower heads and seeds (**caraway seeds**) that are used in cooking and in medicine.

car·bine \ˈkär-ˌbīn, -ˌbēn, ˈkȧr-\ *n.* A short light rifle.

car·bo·hy·drate \ˌkär-bō-ˈhī-ˌdrāt, ˌkȧr-\ *n.* A chemical compound composed of carbon, hydrogen, and oxygen. Sugars and starches are *carbohydrates.*

car·bol·ic acid \ˈkär-ˌbäl-ik, ˈkȧr-\. A poisonous acid derived from coal tar and used in diluted form as an antiseptic.

car·bon \ˈkärb-n, ˈkȧrb-n\ *n.* [From French *carbone,* there borrowed from Latin *carbo* meaning "coal".] **1** A chemical element that is found in nature as diamonds and as graphite and that is one of the elements in coal and petroleum and in plant and animal bodies. **2** A piece or stick of carbon. **3** A piece of carbon paper or a copy made with carbon paper.

car·bon·ate \ˈkärb-n-ˌāt, ˈkȧrb-, -ət\ *n.* A salt or an ester derived from carbonic acid. — \-ˌāt\ *v.;* **car·bon·at·ed; car·bon·at·ing. 1** To burn to carbon. **2** To charge with carbonic acid or carbon dioxide; as, *carbonated* water. — **car·bon·a·tion** \ˌkärb-n-ˈāsh-n, ˌkȧrb-\ *n.*

carbon di·ox·ide \dī-ˈäk-ˌsīd\. A heavy, colorless gas formed by the burning of fuels and by the decay of living matter, and forming the simple raw material from which plants build up more complex compounds for their nourishment and development.

car·bon·ic \kär-ˈbän-ik, kȧr-\ *adj.* Of, relating to, or obtained from carbon, as **carbonic acid,** an acid existing only in solution and reacting with bases to form carbonates.

car·bon·if·er·ous \ˌkärb-n-ˈif-r(-)əs, ˌkȧrb-\ *adj.* Producing or containing carbon or coal.

car·bon·ize \ˈkärb-n-ˌīz, ˈkȧrb-\ *v.;* **car·bon·ized; car·bon·iz·ing. 1** To turn into carbon; to char. **2** To coat or become coated with carbon. — **car·bon·i·za·tion** \ˌkärb-n-ə-ˈzāsh-n, ˌkȧrb-\ *n.*

carbon mon·ox·ide \mə-ˈnäk-ˌsīd\. A colorless, odorless, very poisonous gas, formed by the incomplete burning of carbon.

carbon paper. Thin paper coated on one side with lampblack and used for making copies of something written or typed.

car·bun·cle \ˈkär-ˌbəngk-l, ˈkȧr-\ *n.* **1** A precious stone, as the garnet or ruby. **2** A severe inflamed spot like a boil with several heads that occurs especially on the back of the neck.

car·bu·ret·or \ˈkärb-r-ˌāt-r, ˈkärb-yər-, ˈkȧrb-\ *n.* The part of a motor or an engine in which liquid fuel, such as gasoline, is mixed with air to make it explosive.

car·cass or **car·case** \'kär-kəs, 'kȧr-\ *n.* The dead body of an animal; especially, the body of an animal slaughtered and dressed for food.

card \'kärd, 'kȧrd\ *n.* An instrument for combing wool, cotton, or other fibers. — *v.* To comb with a card; to cleanse and untangle wool, cotton, or other fibers before spinning.

card \'kärd, 'kȧrd\ *n.* **1** A playing card. **2** [in the plural] A game played with playing cards; the playing of cards. **3** A strange or amusing person; as, someone noted for being quite a *card.* **4** A flat, stiff, usually rectangular piece of paper or pasteboard; as, a visiting *card;* a birthday *card.*

card·board \'kärd-ˌbōrd, 'kȧrd-, -ˌbȯrd\ *n.* Stiff pasteboard used for making cards and paper boxes.

card·er \'kärd-r, 'kȧrd-r\ *n.* A person or machine that cards wool or other fiber.

car·di·ac \'kärd-ē-ˌak, 'kȧrd-\ or **car·di·a·cal** \kär-'dī-ək-l, kȧr-\ *adj.* **1** Of or relating to the heart; situated near the heart; as, a *cardiac* disease. **2** Of, relating to, or denoting the part of the stomach into which the esophagus opens or the whole stomach except the narrow end.

car·di·gan \'kärd-ig-n, 'kȧrd-\ *n.* A knitted collarless sweater of the jacket type.

car·di·nal \'kärd-n(-)əl, 'kȧrd-\ *adj.* **1** Chief; principal; of first importance; as, *cardinal* principles. **2** Of or relating to a cardinal. **3** Of the color cardinal red. — *n.* **1** A high official of the Roman Catholic Church, appointed by the pope. **2** Usually **cardinal red.** A bright red. **3** The cardinal bird.

cardinal bird or **cardinal grosbeak.** A bright-red, crested songbird with a loud whistling warble.

cardinal flower. The brilliant red flower of a North American herb of the lobelia family.

cardinal number. One of the numbers used in simple counting or in reply to the question *how many?*

cardinal points. The four principal points of the compass: north, south, east, west.

car·di·o·gram \'kärd-ē-ə-ˌgram, 'kȧrd-\ *n.* The tracing made by a cardiograph.

car·di·o·graph \'kärd-ē-ə-ˌgraf, 'kȧrd-\ *n.* An instrument that traces lines that record the duration and character of the movements of the heart.

care \'ker\ *n.* **1** A heavy sense of responsibility; worry; anxiety; concern; as, weighed down by many *cares.* **2** Serious attention; heed; watchfulness; as, to take *care* in crossing streets. **3** Protection; supervision; as, to be under a doctor's *care.* **4** A person or thing that is an object of one's watchful attention. The child was the mother's constant *care.* — *v.; **cared**; **car·ing**.* **1** To feel interest or concern; to be troubled or anxious; as, not to *care* what happens. **2** To wish; to be willing; as, not to *care* to attend the party. **3** To feel a liking for a person or thing; as, to *care* deeply for one's parents. — **care for.** To watch over; to guard; to provide for.

ca·reen \kə-'rēn\ *v.* **1** To cause to lean or tilt over on one side, as a boat. **2** To lean over, as a ship under a strong wind or a car rounding a curve at high speed; to tilt.

ca·reer \kə-'rir\ *n.* **1** A running or other course of progress, especially at high speed; as, a horse in full *career.* **2** A course of action or events, as of a person's life; especially, the progress of a person in his chosen occupation; as, to have a distinguished *career* as a lawyer. **3** An occupation or profession followed as a life's work. — *v.* To move or run rapidly.

care·free \'ker-ˌfrē\ *adj.* Free from care or worry; happy; lighthearted; as, *carefree* childhood.

care·ful \'kerf-l\ *adj.* **1** Using care; taking care; watchful; cautious; as, a *careful* driver. **2** Made, done, or said with care; as, a *careful* examination. — The words *cautious* and *wary* are synonyms of *careful: careful* generally suggests watchfulness and alertness in one's actions to prevent mistakes or mishaps; *cautious* may indicate prudence in guarding against possible future dangers; *wary* usually implies suspicion and fear of dangers, or cunning in escaping them.

care·ful·ly \'kerf-l(-)e\ *adv.* In a careful manner.

care·less \'ker-ləs\ *adj.* **1** Free from care or worry; as, a *careless,* happy child. **2** Not taking proper care; heedless; as, *careless* of danger. **3** Done, made, or said without due care; as, a *careless* mistake; *careless* work. — **care·less·ly,** *adv.*

ca·ress \kə-'res\ *n.* A tender or loving touch or embrace. — *v.* To touch or stroke tenderly or lovingly.

car·et \'kar-ət\ *n.* A mark [∧] used by writers and proofreaders to show where additional material is to be inserted.

care·tak·er \'ker-ˌtāk-r\ *n.* A person who takes care of a place, thing, or person.

care·worn \'ker-ˌwōrn, -ˌwȯrn\ *adj.* Showing effects of worry.

car·fare \'kär-ˌfar, 'kȧr-, -ˌfer\ *n.* The fare charged for carrying a passenger on a car, as a streetcar.

car·go \'kär-ˌgō, 'kȧr-\ *n.; pl.* **car·goes** or **car·gos.** The goods carried in a ship or an airplane; freight; as, a *cargo* of lumber; a ship carrying both passengers and *cargo.*

car·i·bou \'kar-ə-ˌbü\ *n. sing. and pl.* A reindeer of Greenland and the northern parts of North America.

car·i·ca·ture \'kar-ək-ə-ˌchu̇r\ *n.* **1** The exaggerating or distorting of parts or features in order to produce a ridiculous effect, as in a cartoon. **2** A picture or description with features ridiculously exaggerated or twisted. — *v.;* **car·i·ca·tured**; **car·i·ca·tur·ing.** To make a caricature of.

car·ies \'kar-ēz, 'ker-\ *n.* **1** Decay of animal tissues, especially of bone. **2** Tooth decay. — **car·i·ous** \-ē-əs\ *adj.*

car·il·lon \'kar-ə-ˌlän, -ə-lən\ *n.* **1** A set of bells played by machinery or from a keyboard. **2** A tune for use on a carillon.

car·load \'kär-'lōd, 'kȧr-\ *n.* A load that fills a car.

car·mine \'kär-mən, 'kȧr-, -ˌmīn\ *n.* **1** A rich crimson coloring matter, as used in foods, drugs, and cosmetics. **2** The vivid red color of carmine. — *v.;* **car·mined**; **car·min·ing.** To make carmine in color; to add or apply carmine to.

car·nage \'kär-nij, 'kȧr-\ *n.* Great destruction of life, as in battle; slaughter.

car·nal \'kärn-l, 'kȧrn-l\ *adj.* **1** Of the body; fleshly; not spiritual. **2** Sensual. — **car·nal·ly** \-l-ē\ *adv.*

car·na·tion \kär-'nāsh-n, kȧr-\ *n.* **1** A red color, nearly scarlet. **2** A cultivated, usually double-flowered plant with narrow leaves, and reddish, yellow, or white flowers about two inches across. **3** The flower of this plant.

carnation, 3

car·ne·lian \kär-'nēl-yən, kȧr-\ *n.* A hard, tough stone, reddish in color, used as a gem.

car·ni·val \'kär-nəv-l, 'kȧr-\ *n.* **1** The season or festival of merrymaking before Lent. **2** Any noisy merrymaking. **3** A group of small businesses, such as sideshows, lunch counters, games, and amusement rides, that commonly are run independently but that travel together. **4** A program or entertainment; as, a church's annual fair and *carnival;* a winter sports *carnival.*

car·ni·vore \'kär-nə-ˌvōr, 'kȧr-, -ˌvȯr\ *n.* **1** A flesh-eating animal; especially, any of an order of mammals, mostly flesh-eating, including the dogs, cats, and many others. **2** An insect-eating plant. — **car·niv·o·ral** \kär-'niv-r-əl, kȧr-\ *adj.*

car·niv·o·rous \kär-'niv-r(-)əs, kȧr-\ *adj.* **1** Feeding on the flesh of animals; meat-eating. **2** Of or belonging to a large order of mammals, mostly flesh eaters, including the dogs, cats, bears, and seals.

car·ol \'kar-əl\ *n.* A song of joy, praise, or devotion; as, a Christmas *carol.* — *v.;* **car·oled** or **car·olled**; **car·ol·ing** or **car·ol·ling.** To sing; especially, to sing joyfully; as, birds *caroling* in the trees. — **car·ol·er** or **car·ol·ler,** *n.*

car·om \'kar-əm\ *n.* **1** In billiards, a shot in which the cue ball strikes each of two object balls. **2** A striking and rebounding. — *v.* To make a carom.

car·o·tene \'kar-ə-ˌtēn\ *n.* A substance, found in many yellow or orange-colored fruits and vegetables, from which the body makes vitamin A.

ca·rous·al \kə-'raůz-l\ *n.* A drunken revel; a carouse.

ca·rouse \kə-'raůz\ *n.* A drinking bout; a drunken revel. — *v.;* **ca·roused**; **ca·rous·ing.** To drink freely; to take part in a carouse.

carousel. Variant of *carrousel.*

carp \'kärp, 'kȧrp\ *v.* To complain; to find fault.

carp \'kärp, 'kȧrp\ *n.* A soft-finned freshwater fish that has a single dorsal fin and that sometimes lives to a great age, weighing as much as forty pounds.

car·pal \'kärp-l, 'kȧrp-l\ *adj.* Of or relating to the wrist. — *n.* A wristbone.

car·pel \'kärp-l, 'kȧrp-l\ *n.* In the flower of a seed plant, a part of the pistil, shaped like a folded leaf, that holds the seeds.

car·pen·ter \'kärp-n-tər, 'kȧrp-\ *n.* A workman who repairs or builds wooden structures, as houses or ships. — *v.* To work or make as a carpenter. — **car·pen·ter·ing** \-tə-ring, -tring\ *n.*

car·pen·try \'kärp-n-trē, 'kȧrp-\ *n.* The work or trade of a carpenter.

car·pet \'kärp-ət, 'kȧrp-\ *n.* **1** A heavy woven fabric, used especially as a floor covering. **2** A floor covering made of this fabric. **3** Any carpetlike covering; as, a *carpet* of grass. — *v.* To cover with a carpet.

car·pet·bag \-ˌbag\ *n.* A traveling bag made of carpeting.

car·pet·bag·ger \-ˌbag-r\ *n.* **1** A person who travels with his belongings in a carpetbag. **2** A Northerner who went to the South after the Civil War to make money by taking advantage of the unsettled conditions or through corrupt political practices.

car·pet·ing \'kärp-ət-ing, 'kȧrp-\ *n.* Material for carpets; carpets.

car·port \'kär-ˌpōrt, 'kȧr-, -ˌpȯrt\ *n.* An open-sided roofed automobile shelter, usually made by extending the roof from the side of a building.

car·pus \'kärp-əs, 'kȧrp-\ *n.; pl.* **car·pi** \-ˌī\. The wrist; the wristbones.

car·riage \'kar-ij\ *n.* **1** A carrying of goods; as, a box damaged in *carriage.* **2** Cost of such carrying of goods; as, *carriage* prepaid. **3** Manner of holding or carrying one's body or oneself; bearing; as, a man of proud *carriage.* **4** A wheeled vehicle for carrying persons; as, to drive a horse and *carriage;* a baby *carriage.* **5** A wheeled support for carrying any load; as, a gun *carriage.* **6** In a machine, a moving part that carries or supports some other moving part.

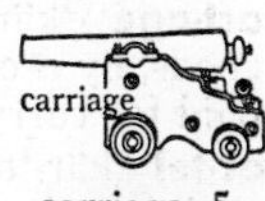

carriage, 5

car·ri·er \'kar-ē-ər\ *n.* **1** A person or thing that carries; as, a mail *carrier;* an aircraft *carrier.* **2** A company in the transportation business. **3** A bearer and transmitter of disease germs; especially, a person who carries in his system germs of a disease, as typhoid fever, to which he is immune. **4** The wave, current, or frequency transmitted in electrical communication.

car·ri·on \'kar-ē-ən\ *n.* The dead and decaying body or flesh of an animal. Vultures feed on *carrion.* — *adj.* Of or like carrion; feeding on carrion.

car·rot \'kar-ət\ *n.* The long, tapering, edible root of a common garden plant, eaten as a vegetable.

car·rou·sel or **car·ou·sel** \ˌkar-ə-'sel, 'kar-ə-ˌsel\ *n.* A merry-go-round.

car·ry \'kar-ē\ *v.;* **car·ried** \-ēd\; **car·ry·ing.** **1** To bear; to transport; to transfer from one place to another; as, to *carry* a package; to *carry* a number in addition. **2** To support; to hold up; as, pillars that *carry* the weight. **3** To extend; as, to *carry* a line to the edge of the page. **4** To lead or bring along in thought or feeling; as, *carried* away by enthusiasm. The speaker *carried* his audience with him. **5** To maintain successfully, as in a contest; as, to *carry* one's point. **6** To continue; to pursue; as, to *carry* on one's work. **7** To win; to succeed in; as, to *carry* an election. **8** To hold or bear the body or some part of it; as, to *carry* one's head high. **9** In business, to stand the expense of keeping in stock or on one's books; to hold over for future sale or settlement; as, to *carry* fireworks as a side-line; to *carry* an account for three months. **10** To go for a distance; to cover a distance; as, a voice that *carries* well. The bullet *carried* half a mile. — **carry on.** To carry farther; to continue; to keep up; to conduct; as, to *carry on* a business, or a correspondence. — **carry out.** To put into action or effect; to continue to the end; as, to *carry out* an assignment. — *n.; pl.* **carries. 1** The range, as of a gun. **2** A carrying of boats or goods overland between navigable waters or the distance thus covered.

carrying charge. 1 Expense resulting from owning or using property, as taxes or interest. **2** A charge added to the price of merchandise sold on the installment plan.

cart \'kärt, 'kȧrt\ *n.* **1** A two-wheeled farm wagon. **2** A light vehicle, usually two-wheeled; any small wheeled vehicle; as, a pony *cart.* — *v.* To carry in or as if in a cart; as, to *cart* groceries home; to have some rubbish *carted* away. — **cart·er,** *n.*

cart·age \'kärt-ij, 'kȧrt-\ *n.* **1** The carrying, as of goods, by a cart or carts. **2** The price charged or paid for carrying by cart.

car·tel \kär-'tel, kȧr-\ *n.* **1** A letter of defiance or challenge, as to a duel. **2** A written agreement between opposing nations. **3** A combination of business firms to control world markets and to fix prices.

car·ti·lage \'kärt-l-ij, 'kȧrt-\ *n.* **1** An elastic substance that makes up most of the skeleton of young children and young animals, and some of which develops into bone; gristle. **2** A part or structure composed of cartilage.

car·ti·lag·i·nous \ˌkärt-l-'aj-n-əs, ˌkȧrt-\ *adj.* **1** Of, relating to, or like cartilage. **2** Having the skeleton composed mostly of cartilage, as certain fishes.

car·tog·ra·phy \kär-'täg-rə-fē, kȧr-\ *n.* The drawing or making of maps or charts. — **car·tog·ra·pher,** *n.* — **car·to·graph·ic** \ˌkärt-ə-'graf-ik, ˌkȧrt-\ *adj.*

car·ton \'kärt-n, 'kȧrt-n\ *n.* **1** A pasteboard box; a container; as, a milk *carton.* **2** The contents of such a box; as, a *carton* of cigarettes.

car·toon \(')kär-'tün, (')kȧr-\ *n.* **1** A drawing or sketch, as in a newspaper, making persons or objects amusing or absurd. **2** A full-size sketch or design made by an artist, to be transferred or copied, as in fresco painting. **3** A comic strip.

car·toon·ist \kär-'tü-nəst, kȧr-\ *n.* A person who draws cartoons, especially as an occupation.

car·tridge \'kär-trij, 'kȧr-\ *n.* **1** A case or shell filled with an explosive for use in blasting. **2** A case or shell containing gunpowder and a bullet or shot, for use in a firearm. **3** A container shaped somewhat like a cartridge, as one used for a roll of film for a camera.

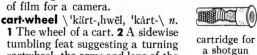

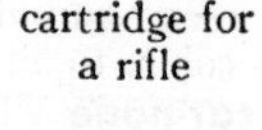
cartridge for a rifle

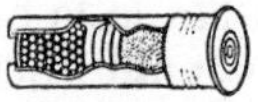
cartridge for a shotgun

cart·wheel \'kärt-ˌhwēl, 'kȧrt-\ *n.* **1** The wheel of a cart. **2** A sidewise tumbling feat suggesting a turning cartwheel, the arms and legs of the tumbler representing the spokes.

carve \'kärv, 'kȧrv\ *v.;* **carved; carv·ing. 1** To cut in an artistic manner; to shape by cutting; as, to *carve* ivory; to *carve* the legs of a table. **2** To cut up or slice, as meat for serving at table.

carv·en \'kärv-n, 'kȧrv-n\ *adj.* Made by carving; as, a *carven* image.

carv·er \'kärv-r, 'kȧrv-r\ *n.* **1** A person who carves. **2** A large knife for carving meat.

carv·ing \'kär-ving, 'kȧr-\ *n.* **1** The act or the art of one who carves. **2** Carved work; as, wood *carvings.*

car·y·at·id \ˌkar-ē-'at-əd\ *n.; pl.* **car·y·at·ids** \-ədz\ or **car·y·at·i·des** \-ə-ˌdēz\. A sculptured figure of a woman in flowing robes, used as an architectural column.

ca·sa·ba \kə-'sä-bə, -'sȧ-\ *n.* Also **casaba melon.** Any of several winter melons having sweet green or whitish flesh and a yellow rind.

cas·cade \(')kas-'kād\ *n.* A steep, usually small, waterfall, often one of a series. — *v.;* **cas·cad·ed; cas·cad·ing.** To fall in a cascade; as, a stream *cascading* down a canyon.

cas·cara \(')kas-'kar-ə\ *n.* The dried bark of a tree that grows along the Pacific coast of the United States, used as a laxative.

case \'kās\ *n.* **1** A particular instance; a special situation or event; as, a *case* of injustice. **2** The existing situation; actual condition; as, such being the *case.* **3** An instance of sickness or injury; as, ten *cases* of chicken pox in the neighborhood. **4** A patient. **5** A person or family under observation or treatment, as by a social-service organization. **6** A question to be settled in a court of law. **7** A particular form of a noun or pronoun, and in some languages of an adjective, that shows its sense relation, as that of subject, object, or possessor, to another word or group of words. The word "him" in "I saw him" is in the accusative, or objective, *case.* **8** The sense relation of a noun, pronoun, or adjective to another word or group of words, even when not shown by the use of a particular form. The subject of a verb is in the nominative *case.*

case \'kās\ *n.* **1** A covering; especially, a protective covering; as, a watch with a gold *case;* to carry one's glasses in a leather *case.* **2** A box; as, a packing *case;* a jewel *case.* **3** The contents of, or quantity in, a box; as, a *case* of books; to buy soda water by the *case.* **4** An enclosing frame; as, a window *case.*

ca·sein \'kā-ˌsēn, 'kā-sē-ən\ *n.* **1** A white protein substance occurring in milk, seen especially in the curd in sour milk. **2** A protein that is produced when milk is curdled by rennet and that is one of the chief constituents of cheese.

case knife. **1** A knife kept or carried in a case; a sheath knife. **2** A table knife.

case·ment \'kās-mənt\ *n.* **1** A window sash opening on hinges like a door. **2** A window with such a sash.

casement window

cash \'kash\ *n.* **1** Money, especially ready money; currency. **2** Money or its equivalent, as a check, paid for goods at the time of purchase or delivery. — *v.* To get or give cash for; as, to *cash* a check. — **cash in on.** To turn to one's profit or advantage.

cash·ew \'kash-ˌü\ *n.* A tropical American tree of the sumac family that yields gum and a kidney-shaped fruit (**cashew nut**) that is edible when roasted.

cash·ier \(')ka-'shir\ *n.* **1** One of the chief officers of a bank, responsible for all money received and paid out. **2** An employee of a store or a restaurant who receives and records payments made by customers.

cash·ier \(')ka-'shir\ *v.* To discharge; especially, to discharge in disgrace from a position of responsibility or trust.

cashier's check. A check drawn by a bank upon its own funds and signed by the cashier.

cash·mere \'kash-ˌmir, 'kazh-\ *n.* [From *Cashmere*, an old form of *Kashmir*, a state in northern India where fine wool and cloth are produced.] **1** A fine soft wool found beneath the hair of goats of Kashmir and the Himalayas. **2** A soft fabric for shawls and scarves, originally made from this wool. **3** A dress fabric made in imitation of the original cashmere.

cas·ing \'kā-sing\ *n.* **1** A case or covering or material for a case or covering. **2** An enclosing framework, especially of a door or window. **3** The part of a pneumatic tire that, when mounted on a wheel, encloses the inner, air-filled tube.

ca·si·no \kə-'sē-ˌnō\ *n.; pl.* **ca·si·nos.** A building or a large room for social amusements, as for dancing or, especially in European countries, for gambling.

cask \'kask\ *n.* **1** A barrel-shaped container, usually for liquids. **2** The amount contained in a cask.

cas·ket \'kas-kət\ *n.* **1** A small box or chest, as for jewels. **2** A coffin.

casque \'kask\ *n.* A piece of armor for the head; a helmet.

cas·sa·va \kə-'sä-və, -'sȧ-\ *n.* **1** A tropical plant with a fleshy root often eaten as a vegetable and yielding a nutritious starch. **2** The starch obtained from the root of the cassava, from which tapioca is made.

cas·se·role \'kas-r-ˌōl\ *n.* **1** A covered dish in which food can be baked and served. **2** The food cooked and served in a casserole.

cas·sia \'kash-ə\ *n.* **1** Any of several herbs, shrubs, and trees whose leaves yield the drug senna and whose sweet pulp is a mild laxative. **2** Any coarse variety of cinnamon, originally one (**cassia bark**) from China.

cas·sock \'kas-ək\ *n.* A long close-fitting garment reaching to the feet, worn by the clergy of certain churches.

cas·so·wary \'kas-ə-ˌwer-ē\ *n.; pl.* **cas·so·war·ies.** A large swift-running bird native to Australia and New Guinea, somewhat like the ostrich but smaller.

cast \'kast\ *v.;* **cast; cast·ing.** **1** To throw; to fling; to toss; to throw off or away; as, to *cast* a stone or a fishing line. Snakes *cast* their skins. **2** To give a special form to liquid material by pouring it into a mold and letting it harden; as, to *cast* a statue in bronze. **3** To assign actors to parts or parts to actors for a play; as, to be *cast* as Tom Sawyer. **4** To deposit, as a ballot; to give, as one's vote. **5** To direct; as, to *cast* a glance. **6** To throw a fishing line. — **cast about.** **1** To turn about; to look about; as, to *cast about* for a good place to camp. **2** To consider; to lay plans. — **cast down.** **1** To throw down; to demolish; to destroy. The columns of the building were *cast down* by an earthquake. **2** To put into a mood of discouragement or sadness; to make dejected or depressed in spirits. — *n.* **1** A throw; a fling. **2** The distance to which a thing is or can be thrown; as, to make a good *cast* in fishing. **3** A glance of the eye. **4** Anything that has been cast into a mold; as, a bronze *cast* of George Washington. **5** A stiff surgical bandage of plaster hardened around a part of the body; as, to have a *cast* on one's leg. **6** A tinge of color; a hue; as, a reddish *cast.* **7** Appearance; look; as, to notice the sad *cast* of a person's face. **8** Something that is thrown out or off, shed, or ejected, as the skin of an insect or the excrement of an earthworm. **9** The group of actors to whom parts in a play are assigned.

cas·ta·net \ˌkas-tə-'net\ *n.* [usually in the plural] An instrument consisting of two small ivory or wooden shells that are held in the hand and clicked together in accompaniment to dancing and music.

castanets

cast·away \'kas-tə-ˌwā\ *adj.* **1** Thrown away; cast off. **2** Shipwrecked. — *n.* **1** A person or thing cast off. **2** A shipwrecked person.

caste \'kast\ *n.* **1** One of the classes into which the people of India have been divided from the earliest times. **2** A similar division or class of society in any place. **3** The social position or rank held by a person by reason of his birth.

cas·tel·lan \'kas-tə-lən\ *n.* The governor or warden of a castle or fort.

cas·tel·lat·ed \'kas-tə-ˌlāt-əd\ *adj.* Having battlements, like a castle.

cast·er \'kast-r\ *n.* **1** A person or a thing that casts. **2** Also **cas·tor** \'kast-r\. A small container to hold seasoning, as salt and pepper, at the table. **3** A small tray for a set of such containers. **4** A small free-turning wheel used for supporting furniture.

caster, 4

cas·ti·gate \'kas-tə-ˌgāt\ *v.;* **cas·ti·gat·ed**; **cas·ti·gat·ing.** To punish or correct, as with words or blows; to reprove. — **cas·ti·ga·tion** \ˌkas-tə-'gāsh-n\ *n.*

cast·ing \'kas-ting\ *n.* **1** The act of a person or a thing that casts. **2** Something that is cast in a mold; as, a bronze *casting.* **3** Something that is cast up or off, as skin, feathers, or waste matter; as, earthworm *castings.*

casting vote or **casting voice.** The deciding vote cast by a presiding officer in case of a tied vote.

cast iron. A hard and brittle iron shaped by pouring it into molds while it is molten, and allowing it to harden.

cas·tle \'kas-l\ *n.* **1** A large fortified building or group of buildings usually having high walls with towers and a surrounding moat. **2** Any building thought of as like a castle, especially one used as a residence. **3** A piece in the game of chess; a rook. **—** *v.;* **cas·tled**; **cas·tling** \-l(-)ing\. To put in or as if in a castle.

cast·off \'kas-ˌtȯf\ *adj.* Thrown away as no longer wanted; discarded; as, a *castoff* suit. **—** *n.* A castoff person or thing.

castor. Variant of *caster.*

cas·tor oil \'kast-r\. A thick yellowish liquid extracted from the seeds (**castor beans**) of a tropical herb and used as a lubricant, in soap, and as a cathartic.

cas·trate \'kas-ˌtrāt\ *v.;* **cas·trat·ed**; **cas·trat·ing.** To remove the testicles from.

ca·su·al \'kazh-ə-wəl, 'kazh-l\ *adj.* **1** Happening unexpectedly or by chance; not planned or foreseen; as, a *casual* meeting. **2** Coming irregularly; occasional. **3** Unconcerned; offhand; as, a *casual* remark. **4** Seeming to be unplanned; as, *casual* manners. — **ca·su·al·ly** \'kazh-l-ē, -ə-wə-lē\ *adv.*

ca·su·al·ty \'kazh-l-tē, 'kazh-ə-wəl-tē\ *n.; pl.* **ca·su·al·ties.** **1** Chance; accident. **2** An unfortunate occurrence; a mishap. **3** A person in military service who, because of sickness, wounds, or death, is not available for duty. **4** [usually in the plural] Losses in war, especially those caused by death, wounds, and capture; as, a battle in which both sides had heavy *casualties.* **5** Injury or death from accident; a person injured or killed by an accident. The plane was badly damaged but there was only one *casualty.*

ca·su·ist \'kazh-ə-wəst\ *n.* A person skilled in or devoted to casuistry. — **ca·su·is·tic** \ˌkazh-ə-'wis-tik\ or **ca·su·is·ti·cal** \-tik-l\ *adj.*

ca·su·ist·ry \'kazh-ə-wəs-trē\ *n.; pl.* **ca·su·ist·ries.** **1** The science of dealing with questions of right and wrong in conduct. **2** False reasoning or application of principles, especially with regard to morals.

cat \'kat\ *n.* **1** A common domestic flesh-eating mammal kept as a pet or for catching mice and rats. **2** Any animal of the cat family, as the lion or the tiger. **3** A person, as a spiteful woman. **4** Short for *cat-o'-nine-tails.*

ca·tab·o·lism \kə-'tab-l-ˌiz-m\ *n.* The part of the process of metabolism in which the destruction of the substance of plants and animals takes place.

cat·a·clysm \'kat-ə-ˌkliz-m\ *n.* **1** A great flood. **2** Any violent and destructive upheaval of nature, such as an earthquake. **3** Any great social or political upheaval or change.

cat·a·comb \'kat-ə-ˌkōm\ *n.* An underground place of burial, especially one that has passages with hollowed places in the sides for tombs; as, the *catacombs* of ancient Rome.

cat·a·lep·sy \'kat-l-ˌep-sē\ or **cat·a·lep·sis** \ˌkat-l-'ep-səs\ *n.* A nervous condition in which the muscles become rigid and the body and limbs stay in any position in which they are placed. — **cat·a·lep·tic** \ˌkat-l-'ep-tik\ *adj.*

cat·a·log or **cat·a·logue** \'kat-l-ˌȯg\ *n.* **1** A list of names, titles, or articles arranged according to a system. **2** A book or a file containing such a list. **—** *v.;* **cat·a·loged** or **cat·a·logued** \-ˌȯgd\; **ca·ta·log·ing** or **cat·a·logu·ing** \-ˌȯg-ing\. To make a list or catalog of; to put in a catalog; as, to *catalog* books.

ca·tal·pa \kə-'tal-pə\ *n.* An ornamental tree of America and Asia, with broad oval leaves, flowers brightly striped inside and spotted outside, and long narrow pods.

cat·a·lyst \'kat-l-əst\ *n.* A substance that speeds up a chemical reaction but remains unchanged at the end of the process.

cat·a·mount \'kat-ə-ˌmau̇nt\ *n.* A wildcat, usually the cougar or a lynx.

cat·a·pult \'kat-ə-ˌpəlt, -ˌpu̇lt\ *n.* **1** A military machine used in ancient times to throw stones, arrows, or spears. **2** A device for launching an airplane from the deck of a ship. **3** A slingshot. **—** *v.* To throw from or as if from a catapult.

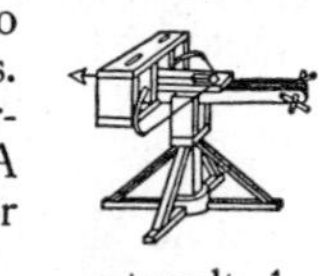
catapult, 1

cat·a·ract \'kat-r-ˌakt\ *n.* **1** A large waterfall. **2** A downpour, as of a rain; a deluge; a flood. **3** A cloudiness of the crystalline lens of the eye, or of the saclike structure that encloses it, obstructing vision.

ca·tarrh \kə-'tär, -'tȧr\ *n.* An inflamed condition of the membrane of the nose or air passages. — **ca·tarrh·al** \-əl\ *adj.*

ca·tas·tro·phe \kə-'tas-trə-(ˌ)fē\ *n.* A sudden calamity; a great disaster or misfortune; as, earthquakes, floods, and other *catastrophes.* — **cat·a·stroph·ic** \ˌkat-ə-'sträf-ik\ *adj.*

cat·bird \'kat-ˌbərd\ *n.* An American songbird allied to the mockingbird, dark gray in color with a black cap, with one call like a cat's mewing.

cat·boat \'kat-ˌbōt\ *n.* A sailboat with a single mast set far forward and a single large sail extended by a long boom.

catboat

cat·call \'kat-ˌkȯl\ *n.* A sound like the cry of a cat, or any loud noise, expressing disapproval.

catch \'kach, 'kech\ *v.;* **caught** \'kȯt\; **catch·ing. 1** To seize; to capture; to take; as, to *catch* a thief; to *catch* fish. **2** To overtake; to reach in time; as, to *catch* up with a person; to *catch* a train. **3** To come upon by surprise; to detect; as, to *catch* a person stealing. **4** To be seized or affected by; to get; as, to *catch* a cold. The curtain *caught* fire. **5** To grasp and hold something in motion; to lay hold of; as, to *catch* a ball. My friend *caught* me when I tripped. **6** To get entangled; as, to *catch* one's foot. **7** To take or get suddenly or temporarily; as, to *catch* a glimpse; to *catch* a nap. **8** To reach or snatch, as if to seize something; as, to *catch* at a straw. **9** To take and keep hold. This lock does not *catch*. — *n.* **1** The act of catching, especially a ball. **2** That which is caught or taken; as, a *catch* of fish. **3** Something that catches, as a device for fastening; as, a *catch* on a door. **4** A slight stoppage or hesitation; as, a *catch* in the voice. **5** A game consisting of throwing and catching a ball. **6** A musical round, usually jolly or humorous.

catch·all \'kach-ˌȯl, 'kech-\ *n.* A receptacle for all kinds of objects.

catch·er \'kach-r, 'kech-r\ *n.* One that catches; especially, a baseball player who stands behind the batter to catch the ball when it is pitched.

catch·ing \'kach-ing, 'kech-\ *adj.* **1** Spreading from one person to another by contact or exposure; contagious. Scarlet fever is *catching*. **2** Alluring; captivating; as, *catching* ways.

catchup. Variant of *catsup*.

catchy \'kach-ē, 'kech-ē\ *adj.;* **catch·i·er; catch·i·est. 1** Likely to attract; as, *catchy* music. **2** Tricky; apt to entangle one; as, a *catchy* question.

cat·e·chism \'kat-ə-ˌkiz-m\ *n.* **1** A book of questions and answers to be used in giving instruction, especially religious instruction. **2** A series of formal questions.

cat·e·chize or **cat·e·chise** \'kat-ə-ˌkīz\ *v.;* **cat·e·chized** or **cat·e·chised; cat·e·chiz·ing** or **cat·e·chis·ing. 1** To instruct or to examine by putting one question after another. **2** To question at length or closely. — **cat·e·chiz·er** \-ˌkīz-r\ or **cat·e·chist** \-kəst\ *n.*

cat·e·gor·i·cal \ˌkat-ə-'gȯr-ik-l, -'gär-\ *adj.* **1** Direct; absolute; positive; as, to make a *categorical* denial. **2** Of, relating to, or in the form of a category. — **cat·e·gor·i·cal·ly** \-ik-l(-)ē\ *adv.*

cat·e·go·ry \'kat-ə-ˌgōr-ē, -ˌgȯr-ē\ *n.; pl.* **cat·e·go·ries. 1** One of the divisions or groupings used in any system of classification. "Species" and "genus" are botanical and zoological *categories*. **2** A class; a variety; a kind.

ca·ter \'kāt-r\ *v.* **1** To provide a supply of food; as, to *cater* for parties of all kinds. **2** To supply what is wanted or needed; as, a sporting-goods store *catering* especially to fishermen.

cat·er–cor·ner or **cat·ty–cor·ner** \'kat-ē-'kȯrn-r, 'kat-ə-\ *adj.* or *adv.* Cater-cornered.

cat·er–cor·nered or **cat·ty–cor·nered** \-'kȯrn-rd\ *adj.* Set crosswise; diagonally placed. — *adv.* Diagonally; crosswise.

ca·ter·er \'kāt-r-r\ *n.* A person who provides food and service, usually to special order and away from his own place of business.

cat·er·pil·lar \'kat-r-ˌpil-r, 'kat-ə-\ *n.* [From Old French *catepelose* meaning literally "hairy cat".] **1** The long, wormlike larva of a butterfly or moth, with strong biting jaws for eating the juicy parts of plants. **2** Any of the similar larvae of certain other insects, as the sawflies.

cat·fish \'kat-ˌfish\ *n.; pl.* **cat·fish** or **cat·fish·es.** Any of various fishes with catlike teeth or with feelers about the mouth resembling the whiskers of a cat; especially, a stout-bodied scaleless fish with large head and long whiskerlike feelers.

cat·gut \'kat-ˌgət\ *n.* A tough cord made from intestines of animals, used for strings of musical instruments and rackets, and for sewing in surgery.

ca·thar·tic \kə-'thärt-ik, -'thårt-\ *n.* A medicine that causes a bowel movement; a strong laxative.

ca·the·dral \kə-'thēd-rəl\ *n.* The principal church of a district over which a bishop presides.

cath·ode \'kath-ˌōd\ *n.* A negative electrode.

Cath·o·lic \'kath-l(-)ik\ *n.* **1** A member of a Christian church tracing its history back to the apostles. **2** Also **Roman Catholic**. A member of the church of which the pope, the bishop of Rome, is the head. — *adj.* **1** Of or relating to Catholics. **2** [with a small letter] General in scope; universal; including or affecting all men; as, to be *catholic* in one's interests.

cat·kin \'kat-kən\ *n.* A flower cluster in which the flowers grow in close circular rows along a slender stalk, as in the willow and birch.

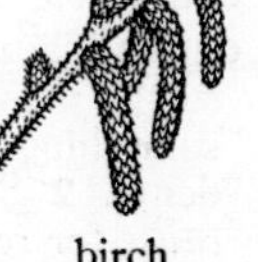
birch catkins

cat·like \'kat-ˌlīk\ *adj.* Like a cat; stealthy; as, a *catlike* tread.

cat nap. A very short light sleep; a short nap.

cat·nip \'kat-ˌnip\ *n.* A common strong-scented plant of the mint family of which cats are especially fond.

cat–o'–nine–tails \ˌkat-ə-'nīn-ˌtālz\ *n. sing. and pl.* A whip used in flogging, consisting of nine knotted cords fastened to a handle.

cat's cradle. A game played, especially by children, with a string looped on the fingers in such a way as to resemble a small cradle.

cat's–eye \'kats-ˌī\ *n.* Either of two gems with a

changeable luster suggestive of reflections from the eye of a cat.

cat's–paw \'kats-ˌpȯ\ *n.* **1** A light breeze that ruffles the surface of the water in patches. **2** A person used by another person for his own ends.

cat·sup or **catch·up** or **ketch·up** \'kech-əp, 'kach-, 'kats-\ *n.* A sauce, especially a tomato sauce, for use on meat, fish, and similar foods.

cat·tail \'kat-ˌtāl\ *n.* A tall marsh plant with long, flat, sword-shaped leaves and brown, furry spikes made up of very tiny flowers.

cat·tle \'kat-l\ *n.* Livestock, especially domesticated cows, bulls, and steers, raised for some use; as, dairy *cattle;* beef *cattle.*

cat·tle·man \'kat-l-mən\ *n.; pl.* **cat·tle·men** \-mən\. A man who tends or raises cattle.

cat·ty \'kat-ē\ *adj.;* **cat·ti·er**; **cat·ti·est.** **1** Of or like a cat. **2** Slyly spiteful; malicious; mean. — **cat·ti·ly** \'kat-l-ē\ *adv.*

catty–corner. Variant of *cater-corner.*

catty–cornered. Variant of *cater-cornered.*

cat·walk \'kat-ˌwȯk\ *n.* Any narrow walk or way, as along a bridge, or over or around a large machine or tank.

Cau·ca·sian \kȯ-'kāzh-n, -'kazh-n\ *adj.* **1** Of or relating to the Caucasus, the mountain range lying between the Black and Caspian seas. **2** Relating to or belonging to the division of mankind, or race, that includes the chief peoples of Europe, northern Africa, and southwestern Asia and was so named in the belief that the people of the Caucasus were typical of this race. — *n.* **1** A member of one of the native peoples of the Caucasus. **2** A member of the Caucasian race; a white person.

cau·cus \'kȯk-əs\ *n.* A meeting of the members or leaders of a political party to make plans for future action or to decide on the candidates to be supported. — *v.* To hold, or meet in, a caucus.

cau·dal \'kȯd-l\ *adj.* **1** Of or like a tail. **2** At or near the tail or the hind end of the body.

caught. Past tense and past part. of *catch.*

cauldron. Variant of *caldron.*

cau·li·flow·er \'kȯl-ə-ˌflau̇r\ *n.* A cabbage in which the head is made up of a thick cluster of flowers.

caulk. Variant of *calk.*

cause \'kȯz\ *n.* **1** That which brings about a result; a person or a thing that brings about or does something. Carelessness is the *cause* of many accidents. **2** Sufficient reason; good ground; as, a *cause* for rejoicing. There is no *cause* for anxiety. **3** The side of a question supported by a person or a group; as, a worthy *cause;* to work for the *cause* of freedom. **4** A ground for a suit or action in a court of law; a case.

— The words *motive* and *reason* are synonyms of *cause: motive* may suggest an emotion or desire that makes a person act in a certain way; *cause* may apply to any condition or circumstance, whether involving a person or not, that brings about a certain effect or result; *reason* usually indicates something thought out as an explanation or justification of a result.

— *v.;* **caused**; **caus·ing.** To be the cause of; to bring about. The heavy rain *caused* the rivers to rise.

cause·less \'kȯz-ləs\ *adj.* Without cause; especially, without good or sufficient reason; as, a victim of *causeless* fears. — **cause·less·ly**, *adv.*

cause·way \'kȯz-ˌwā\ *n.* A raised road or way, especially across wet ground or water.

caus·tic \'kȯs-tik\ *adj.* **1** Capable of destroying or eating away by chemical action; burning. **2** Biting; stinging; sarcastic; as, a *caustic* remark. — *n.* A caustic substance. — **caus·ti·cal·ly** \-tik-l(-)ē\ *adv.*

caustic soda. A white, brittle, strongly alkaline substance that is a compound of sodium, used in making soap and paper, and in bleaching.

cau·ter·ize \'kȯt-r-ˌīz\ *v.;* **cau·ter·ized**; **cau·ter·iz·ing.** To burn with a hot iron or a caustic substance, usually for the purpose of destroying infected tissue; as, to *cauterize* a wound. — **cau·ter·i·za·tion** \ˌkȯt-r-ə-'zāsh-n\ *n.*

cau·tion \'kȯsh-n\ *n.* **1** A warning against something; a word or act that warns. **2** Carefulness in regard to danger; cautiousness; as, to drive with *caution.* — *v.;* **cau·tioned**; **cau·tion·ing** \-n(-)ing\. To notify of danger; to warn.

cau·tion·ary \'kȯsh-n-ˌer-ē\ *adj.* Containing or conveying a warning; as, to speak a few *cautionary* words; a *cautionary* wave of the hand.

cau·tious \'kȯsh-əs\ *adj.* Careful in trying to avoid danger or mistakes; prudent; wary. — For synonyms see *careful.* — **cau·tious·ly**, *adv.*

cav·al·cade \ˌkav-l-'kād\ *n.* **1** A procession of persons on horseback. **2** A procession of any sort, as of automobiles. **3** A procession or series of scenes or events; a pageant; as, a *cavalcade* of American history.

cav·a·lier \ˌkav-l-'ir\ *n.* **1** A mounted soldier; a knight. **2** A man who in his manners and conduct is like the knights of old; a gay and courtly gentleman. **3** A man acting as escort for a woman, as at a party; as, the ladies and their *cavaliers.* — *adj.* **1** Gay and easy in manner. **2** Haughty; disdainful. — **cav·a·lier·ly**, *adv.*

cav·al·ry \'kav-l-rē\ *n.; pl.* **cav·al·ries.** The part of a military force that serves on horseback; mounted soldiers. — **cav·al·ry·man** \-mən\ *n.*

cave \'kāv\ *n.* A hollowed-out place in the earth or in the side of a hill or cliff; especially, a large natural underground cavity with an opening to the surface; a cavern. — *v.;* **caved**; **cav·ing.** To collapse; to fall down; as, the *caving* walls. — **cave in.** To collapse; to give way, as a tunnel or mine.

cave–in \'kā-ˌvin\ *n.* A caving in or a part that has caved in.

cave man \'kāv ˌman\. **1** Also **cave dweller.** One who lives in a cave; especially, a man of the Stone Age. **2** A man who acts in a rough, rude way, especially towards women.

cav·ern \'kav-rn\ *n.* An underground hollow or chamber; a cave, especially a large or deep cave.

cav·ern·ous \'kav-r-nəs\ *adj.* **1** Full of caverns; filled with cavities or cells. **2** Of, belonging to, or like a cavern; as, a *cavernous* cellar; *cavernous* gloom. — **cav·ern·ous·ly,** *adv.*

cav·i·ar or **cav·i·are** \'kav-ē-ˌär, -ˌår\ *n.* The salted roe, or eggs, of the sturgeon or of certain other large fish, used as an appetizer or relish.

cav·il \'kav-l\ *v.;* **cav·iled** or **cav·illed; cav·il·ing** or **cav·il·ling** \-l(-)ing\. To raise unimportant objections; to find fault without good reason. — *n.* A trifling and unreasonable objection.

cav·i·ty \'kav-ət-ē\ *n.; pl.* **cav·i·ties.** A hollow place; a hollow; a hole; as, a *cavity* in a tooth.

ca·vort \kə-'vȯrt\ *v.* To prance about, as a horse; to caper.

caw \'kȯ\ *n.* The cry of a crow or a raven. — *v.* To utter a caw.

cay·enne \kī-'en, kā-\ *n.* Also **cayenne pepper** \'kī-ˌen, 'kā-\. A very hot, sharp-tasting powder made by drying and grinding the seeds or fruits of certain plants, as chilies; red pepper.

cay·use \'kī-ˌyüs\ *n.* In the western United States, an Indian pony.

cc \'sē-'sē\. Abbreviation for *cubic centimeter.*

cd. Abbreviation for *cord.*

Cdr. Abbreviation for *Commander.*

cease \'sēs\ *v.;* **ceased; ceas·ing.** To come or bring to an end; to leave off; to stop; as, a storm that *ceased* as abruptly as it began; to order a body of soldiers to *cease* firing.

cease·less \'sēs-ləs\ *adj.* Without pause or stop; continuous; unceasing. — **cease·less·ly,** *adv.*

Ce·cro·pi·a moth \sə-'krōp-ē-ə\. A very large silkworm moth of the eastern United States.

ce·cum \'sēk-m\. Variant of *caecum.*

ce·dar \'sēd-r\ *n.* **1** A cone-bearing tree of the pine family, having evergreen leaves, erect cones, and fragrant, durable wood. **2** A juniper, especially the common **red cedar,** the wood of which is used for lead pencils. **3** The tallest of the arborvitaes, a valuable timber tree of western North America.

cedar: leaves and cones

ce·dar·bird \'sēd-r-ˌbərd\ *n.* The cedar waxwing.

cede \'sēd\ *v.;* **ced·ed; ced·ing.** To surrender; to yield; to give up; as, territory *ceded* by one country to another.

ce·dil·la \sə-'dil-ə\ *n.* A mark [̧] sometimes used under the letter *c* in certain words from French when the *c* precedes *a, o,* or *u* and is pronounced like *s.* Thus *facade,* which is pronounced \fə-'säd\ or \fə-'såd\ is sometimes written *façade.*

ceil·ing \'sē-ling\ *n.* **1** The overhead inside lining or finish of a room. **2** Any overhanging surface seen from below. **3** The greatest height to which an airplane can rise under certain conditions or at which it can fly and still have a clear view of the earth. **4** The highest amount that may legally be charged for rent, goods, or services; any figure set as an upper limit. **5** The height above the ground of the base of a layer of clouds.

cel·an·dine \'sel-ən-ˌdīn, -ˌdēn\ *n.* A plant having yellow flowers in clusters, related to the poppy.

cel·e·brant \'sel-ə-brənt\ *n.* A person who celebrates; especially, the officiating priest at the Mass.

cel·e·brate \'sel-ə-ˌbrāt\ *v.;* **cel·e·brat·ed; cel·e·brat·ing. 1** To perform publicly and according to a certain rule or form; to officiate at; as, to *celebrate* Mass; to *celebrate* a marriage. **2** To observe in some special way, as by merrymaking or by staying away from business; as, to *celebrate* one's birthday with a party; to *celebrate* Christmas quietly at home. **3** To praise; to make known publicly. **4** To observe a holiday, anniversary, or other special day or event with festivities. — **cel·e·bra·tor** \-ˌbrāt-r\ *n.*

cel·e·brat·ed \'sel-ə-ˌbrāt-əd\ *adj.* Famous; distinguished; renowned; as, a *celebrated* violinist.

cel·e·bra·tion \ˌsel-ə-'brāsh-n\ *n.* **1** The act of celebrating. **2** The activities or ceremonies for celebrating a special occasion, as a birthday or holiday.

ce·leb·ri·ty \sə-'leb-rət-ē\ *n.; pl.* **ce·leb·ri·ties. 1** The state of being celebrated, or widely known; renown; fame. **2** A famous person.

ce·ler·i·ty \sə-'ler-ət-ē\ *n.* Rapidity of motion; swiftness; speed.

cel·ery \'sel-r(-)ē\ *n.* A plant of the carrot family, with thick stalks that are bleached during growth and eaten either raw or cooked.

ce·les·ta \sə-'les-tə\ *n.* A keyboard instrument with a range of four octaves and a pianolike action, but giving its tones from steel plates struck by hammers.

ce·les·tial \sə-'les-chəl\ *adj.* **1** Of or relating to the sky or heavens. A star is a *celestial* body. **2** Of or relating to the spiritual heaven; heavenly; seeming to be heavenly; as, *celestial* happiness. — **ce·les·tial·ly** \-chə-lē\ *adv.*

cel·i·ba·cy \'sel-ə-bə-sē\ *n.* The state of being unmarried; single life, especially that of a person bound by vows not to marry.

cel·i·bate \'sel-ə-bət\ *adj.* Unmarried, especially because of a religious vow. — *n.* A celibate person.

cell \'sel\ *n.* **1** A very small room or compartment, as in a prison or a monastery. **2** A small enclosed part or division, as in a honeycomb. **3** A jar or other container enclosing electrodes and a substance specially prepared for generating electricity by chemical action. **4** One of the very small, usually microscopic, units of which all plants and animals are composed, each consisting of a tiny mass of protoplasm that includes a smaller and denser body, or nucleus, and is surrounded by a membrane (**cell membrane**) and in most plants and some animals by an additional outer covering, the **cell wall.**

cel·lar \'sel-r\ *n.* A room, or a set of rooms, below ground level and generally under a building.

cel·list or **'cel·list** \'chel-əst\ *n.* A person who plays the cello; a violoncellist.

cel·lo or **'cel·lo** \'chel-,ō\ *n.; pl.* **cel·los** or **'cel·los.** A stringed instrument like the violin but larger and with a deeper tone; a iolоncello.

cel·lo·phane \'sel-ə-,fān\ *n.* A thin, transparent, usually waterproof material made from cellulose, used especially as a wrapping.

cel·lu·lar \'sel-yəl-r\ *adj.* Relating to or consisting of a cell or cells.

cel·lu·loid \'sel-yə-,lȯid, 'sel-ə-\ *n.* [From *Celluloid*, a trademark.] A very flammable substance made from cellulose and camphor, used in the manufacture of various articles, as toilet articles and photographic film.

cel·lu·lose \'sel-yə-,lōs\ *n.* A substance that is the chief part of the solid framework or cell walls of plants and of products of plant origin, as wood, linen, paper, and rayon.

Celt \'selt, 'kelt\ *n.* **1** A member of any Celtic-speaking people. **2** A member of a tall blond people living in central and western Europe in ancient times.

Celt·ic \'sel-tik, 'kel-\ *adj.* Of or relating to the Celts or their language. — *n.* A group of languages now found only in the Scottish Highlands, Wales, and Ireland, and in the part of northern France called Brittany.

cel·tuce \'sel-təs\ *n.* A celerylike vegetable, closely related to lettuce, with stalks that combine the flavor of celery and lettuce.

ce·ment \sə-'ment\ *n.* **1** Any substance that, by hardening, sticks objects together firmly. **2** A building material; especially, a mixture, as of lime, cement, sand, and water, used in masonry. **3** Mortar made with such a substance. **4** In dentistry, a material for filling cavities in teeth. — *v.* **1** To join together with cement. **2** To cover with cement; as, to *cement* a road. **3** To become cemented.

ce·men·tum \sə-'ment-m\ *n.* A bonelike substance that forms a layer covering the root and neck, and sometimes parts of the crown, of the teeth of mammals.

cem·e·tery \'sem-ə-,ter-ē\ *n.; pl.* **cem·e·ter·ies.** A place set apart for burial of the dead; a graveyard.

cen·o·taph \'sen-ə-,taf\ *n.* An empty tomb or a monument made for a person who is buried elsewhere.

cen·ser \'sen(t)s-r\ *n.* A container in which incense is burned.

cen·sor \'sen(t)s-r\ *n.* **1** In ancient Rome, one of two magistrates who took the census, handled the public finances, and acted as inspectors of morals and conduct. **2** An official who has the authority to examine written or printed matter or motion pictures in order to prevent the publication or distribution of anything considered harmful. **3** A faultfinder. — *v.;* **cen·sored; cen·sor·ing** \-r(-)ing\. To examine for the purpose of removing anything thought harmful.

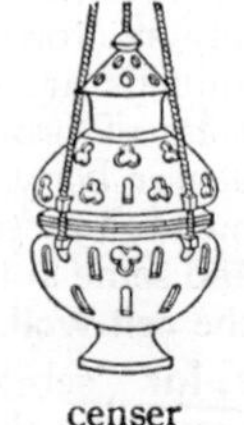
censer

cen·sor·ship \'sen(t)s-r-,ship\ *n.* **1** The office or authority of a censor. **2** The action of a censor, especially in stopping the transmission or publication of forbidden or objectionable matter.

cen·sure \'sench-r\ *n.* The act of finding fault with or blaming; unfriendly criticism. — *v.;* **cen·sured; cen·sur·ing** \-r(-)ing\. To find fault with; as, to *censure* a public official for his conduct in office. — The words *blame* and *condemn* are synonyms of *censure: censure* may refer to strong criticism, often public or official, from a person in authority; *blame* generally refers to the placing of responsibility for some error or wrong; *condemn* may indicate a final and completely unfavorable judgment.

cen·sus \'sen(t)s-əs\ *n.* An official count of the population of a country, city, or town, often with statistics of economic, educational, and social conditions.

cent \'sent\ *n.* **1** A hundredth part of the unit of the money system in a number of different countries. In the United States 100 *cents* equal one dollar. **2** A coin of this value.

cen·taur \'sen-,tȯr\ *n.* In Greek mythology, a creature that was half man and half horse.

cen·te·nar·i·an \,sent-n-'er-ē-ən\ *adj.* Of or relating to 100 years. — *n.* A person 100 years old.

cen·ten·a·ry \sen-'ten-r-ē, 'sent-n-,er-ē\ *adj.* Centennial. — *n.; pl.* **cen·ten·a·ries.** A centennial celebration.

cen·ten·ni·al \sen-'ten-ē-əl\ *adj.* **1** Relating to a period of 100 years or its completion. **2** Lasting one hundred years. — *n.* A hundredth anniversary or a celebration of this event.

cen·ter or **cen·tre** \'sent-r\ *n.* **1** The middle point of a circle or a sphere, equally distant from every point of the circumference. **2** The middle point or part of anything; as, the *center* of a city; the *center* of a room. **3** A point at which things meet or from which they proceed; a place of great activity; as, a railroad *center;* a shopping *center.* **4** A group of nerve cells having a common function; as, the visual *center.* **5** In some sports, a player occupying a central position on a team or in a line; as, a football *center.* — *v.;* **cen·tered** or **cen·tred; cen·ter·ing** or **cen·tring** \'sent-r-ing, 'sen-tring\. **1** To place or fix at the center. **2** To collect at or around one point; as, to *center* attention on one fact. **3** To furnish or mark with a center.

cen·ter·board or **cen·tre·board** \'sent-r-,bōrd, -,bȯrd\ *n.* In a sailboat, a slab of board or metal pivoted so that it can be lowered to decrease sideways movement of the boat.

cen·ter·piece \'sent-r-,pēs\ *n.* A piece put in the center of anything; especially, an ornament for the center of a table.

cen·ti·grade \'sent-ə-,grād\ *adj.* Consisting of 100

degrees or divisions. In a **centigrade thermometer** the distance between the freezing point and the boiling point of water is divided into 100 equal parts or degrees, zero degrees centigrade corresponding to 32 degrees Fahrenheit.

cen·ti·gram or **cen·ti·gramme** \ˈsent-ə-ˌgram\ *n.* A weight of one hundredth of a gram.

cen·ti·me·ter or **cen·ti·me·tre** \ˈsent-m-ˌēt-r\ *n.* A measure of length equal to one hundredth of a meter.

cen·ti·pede \ˈsent-ə-ˌpēd\ *n.* A small animal with long flattened body of many segments, each with a pair of jointed legs, the foremost pair being modified into poison fangs.

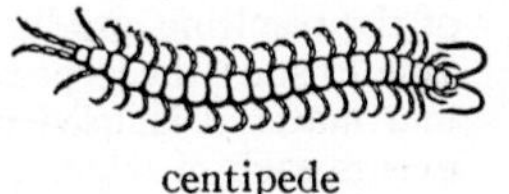
centipede

cen·tral \ˈsen-trəl\ *adj.* **1** Having to do with the center; equally distant from certain points; lying in or near the center; containing or constituting the center. **2** Chief; leading; as, the *central* person in a story. — *n.* A telephone exchange or a telephone operator at an exchange. — **cen·tral·ly** \-trə-lē\ *adv.*

cen·tral·ize \ˈsen-trə-ˌlīz\ *v.;* **cen·tral·ized; cen·tral·iz·ing.** To bring to a central point; to bring under a single control; as, a *centralized* school system. — **cen·tral·i·za·tion** \ˌsen-trə-lə-ˈzāsh-n\ *n.*

central nervous system. In vertebrates, the brain and spinal cord.

centre. Variant of *center.*

centreboard. Variant of *centerboard.*

cen·trif·u·gal \sen-ˈtrif-yəg-l, -ˈtrif-ig-l\ *adj.* **1** Going from the center outward; developing outward; as, *centrifugal* force. **2** Using or acting by centrifugal force; as, a *centrifugal* pump. — **cen·trif·u·gal·ly** \-l-ē\ *adv.*

cen·trip·e·tal \sen-ˈtrip-ət-l\ *adj.* **1** Going or directed toward the center; as, *centripetal* force. **2** Using or acting by centripetal force. — **cen·trip·e·tal·ly** \-l-ē\ *adv.*

cen·tu·ry \ˈsench-r(-)ē\ *n.; pl.* **cen·tu·ries. 1** A group of 100. **2** A period of 100 years. — **cen·tu·ri·al** \sen-ˈtyu̇r-ē-əl\ *adj.*

century plant. A Mexican fleshy-leaved agave that flowers only once and then dies.

ceph·a·lo·pod \ˈsef-l-ə-ˌpäd\ *n.* A mollusk of the class containing the squids, cuttlefishes, and octopuses, having sucker-bearing arms growing out of the head and able to throw out an inklike fluid.

ceph·a·lo·tho·rax \ˌsef-l-ə-ˈthōr-ˌaks, -ˈthȯr-\ *n.; pl.* **ceph·a·lo·tho·rax·es** \-ˌaks-əz\ or **ceph·a·lo·tho·ra·ces** \-thə-ˈrā-ˌsēz\. The united head and thorax in spiders, scorpions, and crustaceans.

ce·ram·ic \sə-ˈram-ik\ *adj.* Of or relating to pottery.

ce·ram·ics \sə-ˈram-iks\ *n.* The art of making things of baked clay, such as pottery or tiles.

ce·re·al \ˈsir-ē-əl\ *adj.* Having to do with grain or with the grasses that produce it; as, *cereal* products. — *n.* **1** Any grass yielding grain used for food, such as wheat, rice, or oats. **2** The grain, or a foodstuff prepared from it.

cer·e·bel·lum \ˌser-ə-ˈbel-əm\ *n.; pl.* **cer·e·bel·lums** \-əmz\ or **cer·e·bel·la** \-ə\. A large projecting portion of the rear part of the brain.

ce·re·bral \sə-ˈrē-brəl, ˈser-ə-\ *adj.* Having to do with the brain of a person, or with the cerebrum.

cerebral palsy. A disability due to damage of centers of the brain before or during birth, resulting in imperfect control of the muscles, paralysis, and speech disturbances.

ce·re·bro·spi·nal \sə-ˌrē-brō-ˈspīn-l, ˌser-ə-(ˌ)brō-\ *adj.* Of or relating to the brain or spinal cord.

ce·re·brum \sə-ˈrē-brəm, ˈser-ə-\ *n.; pl.* **ce·re·brums** \-brəmz\ or **ce·re·bra** \-brə\. In man, the two similar rounded parts (**cerebral hemispheres**) of the foremost part of the brain, which fill the upper part of the skull.

cere·cloth \ˈsir-ˌklȯth\ *n.* A cloth treated with melted wax and used especially for wrapping a corpse.

cere·ment \ˈser-ə-mənt, ˈsir-mənt\ *n.* [usually in the plural] A cerecloth or any shroud for the dead.

cer·e·mo·ni·al \ˌser-ə-ˈmō-nē-əl\ *adj.* Having to do with or of the nature of ceremony or ceremonies; as, the *ceremonial* dances of Indian tribes. — *n.* A system of rules and ceremonies, brought about by law or custom; as, the *ceremonial* of a church service.

cer·e·mo·ni·ous \ˌser-ə-ˈmō-nē-əs\ *adj.* **1** Ceremonial. **2** Careful to observe forms and ceremonies; formal. **3** In agreement with established forms and ceremonies. — **cer·e·mo·ni·ous·ly,** *adv.*

cer·e·mo·ny \ˈser-ə-ˌmō-nē\ *n.; pl.* **cer·e·mo·nies. 1** An act or series of acts performed in some regular order, as required by law or settled by custom; as, a marriage *ceremony;* graduation *ceremonies.* **2** A mere outward form, still often observed but not rigidly required. **3** Social behavior according to strict rules and customs; formality; as, a family that lives with very little *ceremony.*

— The words *form* and *rite* are synonyms of *ceremony: form* is a general term, usually suggesting any method of procedure fixed by custom or tradition; *ceremony* may apply to a solemn, elaborate, or dignified form, and is used especially of religious services; *rite* usually suggests the words and actions prescribed, as by a church or other organization, for a ceremony.

ce·rise \sə-ˈrēs\ *n.* A very bright deep-red color, like that of a ripe cherry. — *adj.* Of the color cerise.

cer·tain \ˈsərt-n\ *adj.* **1** One or some; as, a *certain* town in Ohio. *Certain* rivers have waterfalls. **2** Sure; reliable; as, a *certain* cure. **3** Having no doubts; not to be questioned; as, to be *certain* of something. **4** Destined; as, something that is *certain* to happen.

cer·tain·ly \ˈsərt-n-lē\ *adv.* **1** In a manner that is certain, sure, or fixed. **2** Without doubt.

cer·tain·ty \ˈsərt-n-tē\ *n.; pl.* **cer·tain·ties. 1** The state of being sure or certain; as, to answer with *certainty.* **2** Something that is certain.

cer·tif·i·cate \sər-'tif-ik-ət\ *n.* **1** A written or printed statement testifying to the truth of a fact; as, a vaccination *certificate.* **2** A document testifying that a student has fulfilled the requirements of a school or college.

cer·ti·fi·ca·tion \ˌsərt-ə-fə-'kāsh-n\ *n.* **1** A certifying or a being certified. **2** A certificate; as, to present one's *certification* of citizenship.

cer·ti·fy \'sərt-ə-ˌfī\ *v.;* **cer·ti·fied** \-ˌfīd\; **cer·ti·fy·ing.** **1** To give sure information about; to verify; as, to *certify* a student for admission to a college; to *certify* a signature on a check. **2** To guarantee the quality or fitness of; as, *certified* milk. **3** To guarantee a bank check as good by a statement stamped on its face and signed by an officer of the bank on which it is drawn.

cer·ti·tude \'sərt-ə-ˌtüd, -ˌtyüd\ *n.* Certainty.

ce·ru·le·an \sə-'rü-lē-ən\ *adj.* or *n.* Azure.

cer·vi·cal \'sər-vik-l\ *adj.* Of or relating to the neck.

ces·sa·tion \se-'sāsh-n\ *n.* A ceasing of an action; a stop; as, to bring about a *cessation* of the pain.

ces·sion \'sesh-n\ *n.* The action of giving something over; as, the *cession* of California to the United States.

cess·pool \'ses-ˌpül\ *n.* A pit or tank in a sewer, to collect waste matter.

ce·ta·cean \sē-'tāsh-n\ *adj.* Of or relating to a group of aquatic mammals that includes the whales, porpoises, and dolphins. — *n.* A cetacean animal. — **ce·ta·ceous** \-'tā-shəs\ *adj.*

Cey·lon·ese \ˌsē-lə-'nēz, -ˌlä-, -'nēs\ *adj.* Of or relating to Ceylon. — *n. sing. and pl.* A native of Ceylon.

cf. \kəm-'par, -'per\. Abbreviation for *confer,* a Latin word meaning "compare".

ch. Abbreviation for: **1** *chapter.* **2** *church.*

chafe \'chāf\ *v.;* **chafed; chaf·ing.** **1** To rub in order to make warm; as, to *chafe* one's hands. **2** To rub so as to wear away or to make sore; as, to *chafe* a rope; clothing that *chafes* the skin. **3** To cause anger in; to annoy. The repeated interruptions *chafed* the speaker. **4** To be irritated or annoyed; to fret; as, to *chafe* over a delay.

chaff \'chaf\ *n.* **1** The husks of grains and grasses separated from the seed, as by threshing. **2** Anything light and worthless.

chaff \'chaf\ *n.* Light, jesting talk. — *v.* To make fun of in a good-natured way; to tease.

chaf·fer \'chaf-r\ *v.;* **chaf·fered; chaf·fer·ing** \-r(-)ing\. To bargain; to dispute about a price.

chaf·finch \'chaf-ˌinch\ *n.* A common European finch with a cheerful song, often kept as a cage bird.

chaf·ing dish \'chā-fing\. A utensil for cooking or warming food at the table.

cha·grin \shə-'grin\ *n.* A feeling of annoyance caused by failure or disappointment. — *v.* To cause to feel chagrin.

chain \'chān\ *n.* **1** A series of connected links or rings, usually of metal. **2** Something that confines or binds; a bond; as, the *chains* of habit. **3** A series of things joined together as if by links; as, a *chain* of mountains or of lakes; a *chain* of events. **4** A chainlike measuring instrument. — *v.* **1** To fasten or secure by a chain; as, to *chain* a dog. **2** To bind; to restrain.

chains, 1

chain reaction. **1** In chemistry and physics, a process that is able to continue itself because one of the resulting products of the reaction is always able to start the process over again until the original material is used up. **2** Any series of similar events each of which causes the next.

chain store. One of a number of retail stores under the same ownership and general management, and selling the same lines of goods.

chair \'cher\ *n.* **1** A movable single seat with a back. **2** An official seat; a seat of authority or dignity; as, to take the *chair* at a meeting. **3** The office or position of authority or dignity; especially, the position of a professor or judge. **4** A sedan chair. **5** A chairman; as, to address the *chair.*

chair·man \'cher-mən\ *n.; pl.* **chair·men** \-mən\. A person who occupies a chair of authority; especially, an official who presides at a meeting. — **chair·man·ship** \-ˌship\ *n.*

chaise \'shāz\ *n.* **1** A two-wheeled horse-drawn carriage with a folding top. **2** Any light horse-drawn carriage.

chaise longue \(')shāz 'lȯng, 'laủnj\. A couch that resembles an easy chair with a long seat.

cha·let \sha-'lā\ *n.* **1** A herdsman's cabin, or small wooden cottage, of the Swiss mountains. **2** A cottage built in the style of the Swiss chalets.

chal·ice \'chal-əs\ *n.* **1** A drinking cup or goblet. **2** The cup that holds the wine in a Communion service. **3** A flower cup.

chalk \'chȯk\ *n.* **1** A soft white, gray, or buff limestone composed chiefly of very small sea shells. **2** Any material like chalk, especially material used in crayons for writing on a blackboard. **3** A piece of such material. — *v.* **1** To write or mark with chalk. **2** To record an account with chalk; to charge. — **chalk·y** \-ē\ *adj.*

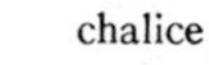
chalice

chal·lenge \'chal-ənj\ *n.* **1** An invitation to engage in a contest; a summons to fight, as a duel. **2** An exception taken to something as not being true, accurate, or justified; as, a *challenge* to one's claim. **3** In law, an objection to a juror summoned for trying a case. **4** The action of a sentry in questioning, examining, or demanding the countersign of a person appearing near his post. — *v.;* **chal·lenged; chal·leng·ing.** **1** To claim as due or deserved; as, an act that *challenged* everyone's admiration. **2** To take exception to; to dispute; as, to *challenge* a person's right to speak. **3** To summon defiantly to a contest, as a duel. **4** In law, to object to; to take formal exception to, as to a juror. **5** To question and demand the countersign from. — **chal·leng·er** \-ənj-r\ *n.*

chal·lis or **chal·lie** \'shal-ē\ *n.* A lightweight, usually printed fabric, as of wool or cotton and wool.

cham·ber \'chām-br\ *n.* [From French *chambre,* there derived from Late Latin *camera.*] **1** A room in a house; especially, a bedroom. **2** A hall where the members of an assembly or other government body meet. **3** A group of people organized into a lawmaking body; as, the lower *chamber* of a congress. **4** A group of persons who make up a council for some business purpose; as, a *chamber* of commerce. **5** An enclosed space or compartment; as, the *chamber* of a gun. **6** A room in which a judge transacts official business that can be dealt with out of court. — *v.* To put or reside in a chamber. — **cham·bered** \-brd\ *adj.*

cham·ber·lain \'chām-br-lən\ *n.* **1** In Europe, one of the high officers of a court. **2** A steward, as in a nobleman's household. **3** A treasurer or receiver of public money; as, city *chamberlain.*

cham·ber·maid \'chām-br-ˌmād\ *n.* A maidservant who takes care of bedrooms.

chamber music. Music suitable for performance in a small hall or private residence.

cham·bray \'sham-ˌbrā, -brē, (')sham-'brā\ *n.* A gingham fabric woven of colored and white threads.

cha·me·leon \kə-'mēl-yən\ *n.* A lizard that has the ability to vary the color of its skin.

cham·ois \'sham-ē\ *n. sing. and pl.* **1** A small goatlike antelope living on the highest mountains of Europe and Asia. **2** A soft, yellowish leather made from the skin of this animal, or from that of sheep or goats.

champ \'champ\ *v.* To bite and chew noisily; as, a horse *champing* his bit.

champ \'champ\ *n. Slang.* A champion.

cham·pagne \(')sham-'pān\ *n.* A white sparkling wine.

cham·pi·on \'champ-ē-ən\ *n.* **1** A person who fights or speaks in behalf of another person or in behalf of a cause; a defender. **2** A person formally acknowledged as better than all others in a sport or in a game of skill. **3** A person or a thing winning first place in a competition. — *v.* To defend as champion; to protect; as, to *champion* the cause of freedom.

cham·pi·on·ship \'champ-ē-ən-ˌship\ *n.* **1** The act of defending as a champion; championing; as, a senator known for his *championship* of states' rights. **2** The position of being champion; as, to win the national skating *championship.*

chance \'chan(t)s\ *n.* **1** The way in which things take place; the happening of events; fortune. It occurred by *chance.* **2** An opportunity; as, to have a *chance* to travel. **3** A risk or gamble; as, to take *chances.* **4** A possibility or likelihood of anything happening; probability. The *chances* of success are good. **5** Luck; as, the goddess of *chance.* — *v.;* **chanced; chanc·ing. 1** To happen; to come without plan; as, to *chance* upon an old friend. **2** To risk; as, to *chance* a fall. — *adj.* Happening by chance; casual; as, a *chance* meeting.

chan·cel \'chan(t)s-l\ *n.* The part of a church reserved for the clergy and officials, often separated from the rest of the church by a railing.

chan·cel·lery \'chan(t)s-l(-)ər-ē\ *n.; pl.* **chan·cel·ler·ies. 1** The position or office of a chancellor. **2** The building or room containing the chancellor's office.

chan·cel·lor \'chan(t)s-l(-)ər\ *n.* **1** A secretary; especially, an official secretary of a nobleman, prince, or king. **2** In some countries, a high official of state. **3** The head of some universities.

chan·cery \'chan(t)s-r(-)ē\ *n.; pl.* **chan·cer·ies. 1** A court of equity. **2** A court whose proceedings are recorded; an office of public records. **3** A chancellery.

chan·de·lier \ˌshand-l-'ir\ *n.* A candlestick, or a gas or electric-light fixture, with several branches, especially one hanging from the ceiling.

change \'chānj\ *v.;* **changed; chang·ing. 1** To alter by putting one thing for another or by giving up one thing for something else; as, to *change* one's clothes; to *change* a five-dollar bill. **2** To be altered; to vary. Leaves *change* in the fall. **3** To change the clothes or covering of; as, to *change* a bed. **4** To exchange; as, to *change* places with another. **5** To make different; as, to *change* the looks of a room. **6** To change one's clothes; as, to *change* before dinner. — *n.* **1** A changing; putting one thing in place of another; as, a *change* of seasons. **2** Any variation or alteration; as, a *change* of habits. **3** A fresh set of clothes to replace those being worn. **4** Money given in place of other money of a higher denomination; as, *change* for $1.00. **5** The money returned when payment is made by coin or note greater than the sum due; as, to wait for one's *change.* — **chang·er** \'chānj-r\ *n.*

change·a·ble \'chān-jəb-l\ *adj.* **1** Capable of change; variable; as, *changeable* weather. **2** Appearing different, as in color, from different points of view; as, *changeable* silk. — **change·a·bil·i·ty** \ˌchān-jə-'bil-ət-ē\ *n.* — **change·a·bly** \'chān-jə-blē\ *adv.*

change·ful \'chānj-fəl\ *adj.* Full of change; uncertain.

change·less \'chānj-ləs\ *adj.* Unchanging; constant.

change·ling \'chānj-ling\ *n.* A child secretly exchanged for another in infancy, supposedly by fairies or elves.

chan·nel \'chan-l\ *n.* **1** The bed of a stream. **2** The deeper part of any waterway, as a river or harbor. **3** A strait, or narrow sea; as, the English *Channel.* **4** A closed course, such as a tube, through which anything flows; a passageway; as, the *channels* of trade. **5** A long gutter, groove, or furrow. **6** A means by which something is passed or carried. The same news was reported through several different *channels.* **7** In radio or television, a range of frequencies of sufficient width for transmission. — *v.;* **chan·neled** or **chan·nelled**; **chan·nel·ing** or **chan·nel·ling. 1** To form a channel in; to groove. **2** To direct into or through a channel.

chant \'chant\ *n.* **1** A melody in which several words or syllables are sung on one tone. **2** Song; singing. — *v.* To sing, especially in the way a chant is sung; to speak in the manner of a chant.

chan·tey or **chan·ty** \'shant-ē, 'chant-ē\ *n.; pl.* **chan·teys** or **chan·ties.** A song sung by sailors in rhythm with their work.

chan·ti·cleer \'chant-ə-ˌklir, -'klir\ *n.* A rooster.

cha·os \'kā-ˌäs\ *n.* Complete confusion and disorder.

cha·ot·ic \kā-'ät-ik\ *adj.* In a state of chaos; completely confused. — **cha·ot·i·cal·ly** \-ik-l(-)ē\ *adv.*

chap \'chap\ *v.;* **chapped** or **chapt**; **chap·ping.** To open in slits; to crack; to make or to become rough; as, skin *chapped* from the cold.

chap \'chap\ *n.* A man or boy; a fellow.

chap. Abbreviation for *chapter.*

chap·el \'chap-l\ *n.* [From Middle Latin *cappella* meaning literally "small cloak"; named from the shrine in which St. Martin's cloak was kept as a holy relic.] **1** A place of worship smaller or less important than a church. **2** In a large church, a room or recess with an altar. **3** A building or room, as in an institution, for religious services.

chap·er·on or **chap·er·one** \'shap-r-ˌōn\ *n.* A person, especially a married woman, who accompanies and is responsible for a young woman or a group of young people, as at a dance or a house party. — *v.;* **chap·er·oned**; **chap·er·on·ing.** To act as a chaperon.

chap·lain \'chap-lən\ *n.* **1** A clergyman who conducts services in the chapel of an institution, as a school, hospital, or prison. **2** A clergyman officially serving in the army, navy, or air force or attached to some other group, as a legislature.

chap·let \'chap-lət\ *n.* **1** A wreath for the head. **2** A string of beads, especially beads used in counting prayers.

chapped. A past tense and past part. of *chap.*

chaps \'shaps\ *n. pl.* [A shortened form of Mexican Spanish *chaparreras,* from *chaparro* meaning "scrub oak" or "thorny bush", against which they afford protection.] Leather trousers or overalls worn, especially by cowboys, as protection against thorns.

chaps

chapt. A past tense and past part. of *chap.*

chap·ter \'chapt-r\ *n.* **1** A main division of a book or of a long story. **2** An organized branch of a society, having its own officers and holding its own meetings.

char \'chär, 'chȧr\ *v.;* **charred**; **char·ring. 1** To change to charcoal or carbon by burning. **2** To burn slightly; to scorch. **3** To burn to a cinder. — For synonyms see *scorch.*

char·ac·ter \'kar-ikt-r\ *n.* **1** A mark, a sign, or a symbol, especially one written or printed, as a letter or figure. **2** A feature, especially a distinguishing feature of a person or thing, as the color of a flower or the shape of a leaf; a characteristic. **3** The total sum of the distinguishing qualities of a person or of a national or racial group; nature. **4** Moral strength; as, to be a man of *character.* **5** A person in a story or a play. **6** A person having notable traits or characteristics; often, an odd or peculiar person.

char·ac·ter·is·tic \ˌkar-ikt-r-'is-tik\ *adj.* Having to do with or showing the character, or the distinguishing qualities or features, of an individual, group, or type; typical; as, behavior *characteristic* of children of that age; the *characteristic* sound of a contented cat. — *n.* A special trait or quality that makes one individual, group, or type different from others; distinctive feature; as, the outstanding *characteristics* of a good soldier.

— The words *trait* and *feature* are synonyms of *characteristic: characteristic* usually suggests some mark or quality that distinguishes one person or thing from others of the same kind; *trait* may refer to a sharply defined characteristic; *feature* may apply to a quite conspicuous detail.

char·ac·ter·is·ti·cal·ly \-tik-l(-)ē\ *adv.* In a characteristic way or a way that characterizes; typically; as, a *characteristically* straightforward reply. Elms are *characteristically* tall spreading trees.

char·ac·ter·i·za·tion \ˌkar-ikt-r-ə-'zāsh-n\ *n.* **1** The act of characterizing; description by a statement of characteristics. **2** The creation of characters in fiction or drama; the artistic representation of a fictitious person or persons; as, a story in which the *characterization* was more interesting than the plot.

char·ac·ter·ize \'kar-ikt-r-ˌīz\ *v.;* **char·ac·ter·ized**; **char·ac·ter·iz·ing. 1** To indicate the character or characteristics of a person or thing; to describe; as, a strange sound, hard to *characterize;* to *characterize* someone as stupid. **2** To be characteristic of; to mark as a characteristic. Good nature *characterizes* all his actions.

character sketch. A piece of writing, usually short, dealing with a character or characters of strongly marked individuality.

cha·rade \shə-'rād\ *n.* A game in which each syllable of a word to be guessed is acted out by some of the persons playing the game while the others try to guess the word.

char·coal \'chär-ˌkōl, 'chȧr-\ *n.* **1** A black or dark porous form of carbon made by charring, or partly burning, wood or other vegetable or animal substances in a kiln from which air is excluded. **2** A piece of fine charcoal used for drawing. **3** A drawing made with charcoal.

chard \'chärd, 'chȧrd\ *n.* A variety of the common

beet having juicy leaves and stalks that are cooked and eaten as a vegetable.

charge \'chärj, 'chȧrj\ *v.;* **charged**; **charg·ing.** **1** To load; to fill; as, to *charge* a gun; a wire *charged* with electricity. **2** To give a task, duty, or responsibility to a person. The janitor is *charged* with looking after the building. **3** To accuse; to lay blame on; as, to be *charged* with speeding. **4** To instruct. It is the duty of a judge to *charge* a jury before it gives its verdict. **5** To demand as payment; to ask or set a price for something. This store *charges* too much for everything. **6** To make a record of something to be paid for later or of something borrowed; to debit. It is convenient to be able to have one's purchases *charged.* **7** To attack with a rush. **8** To restore the active materials in a battery by passing a direct current through it in the opposite direction to that of discharge when the battery is furnishing current. — *n.* **1** The quantity, as of ammunition or fuel, required to load or fill something; as, a *charge* of powder for a gun; a *charge* of electricity in a battery. **2** A task, duty, or order given to a person. **3** Someone or something given to a person to look after. A nursemaid's *charges* are the children she takes care of. **4** Care; custody; responsibility. The arrangements are in the teacher's *charge.* **5** An accusation. **6** A statement about a case under trial, made by the judge to the jury before it considers its verdict. **7** Cost; expense; the price asked for anything; as, storage *charges.* **8** A rushing attack. — For synonyms see *price.* — **in charge.** Having the charge or care of something; as, to be *in charge* of selling tickets. — **charge·a·ble,** *adj.*

char·ger \'chärj-r, 'chȧrj-r\ *n. Archaic.* A large flat dish or platter for carrying meat.

charg·er \'chärj-r, 'chȧrj-r\ *n.* **1** A horse trained to charge; a war horse, for battle or parade. **2** A device for charging storage batteries.

charier. Comparative of *chary.*

chariest. Superlative of *chary.*

char·i·ly \'char-ə-lē, 'cher-\ *adv.* In a chary manner; carefully; cautiously; frugally.

char·i·ness \'char-ē-nəs, 'cher-\ *n.* The quality of being chary; care; caution; frugality.

char·i·ot \'char-ē-ət\ *n.* A two-wheeled vehicle of ancient times, pulled by horses and used in war and racing and in processions.

char·i·o·teer \ˌchar-ē-ə-'tir\ *n.* A driver of a chariot.

chariot

char·i·ta·ble \'char-ət-əb-l\ *adj.* **1** Liberal with money or help for poor and needy persons; generous. **2** Given for the needy; of service to the needy; as, *charitable* funds; a *charitable* institution. **3** Generous and kindly in judging other people; forgiving; lenient; as, a *charitable* attitude towards the failings of others. — **char·i·ta·bly** \-ə-blē\ *adv.*

char·i·ty \'char-ət-ē\ *n.; pl.* **char·i·ties.** **1** Love for one's fellowmen. **2** Kindliness in judging others. **3** The giving of aid to the poor and suffering. **4** Public aid for the poor. **5** Any institution or fund for aiding the needy.

char·la·tan \'shär-lə-tən, 'shȧr-, -lət-n\ *n.* A person who pretends to have knowledge and ability he does not have; a quack.

char·ley–horse \'chär-lē-ˌhȯrs, 'chȧr-\ *n.* Stiffness in an arm or leg from muscular strain, as from overuse or injury.

char·lotte russe \'shär-lət 'rüs, 'shȧr-\. A pudding made in a mold with strips of cake around a center of whipped cream or custard.

charm \'chärm, 'chȧrm\ *n.* **1** Any word, action, or thing believed to have magic powers. **2** Something worn or carried to keep away evil and bring good luck. **3** A small decorative object worn on a chain or bracelet. **4** A quality that attracts and pleases, as if by some magical power. — *v.* **1** To affect or influence by magic or as if by magic; as, to *charm* a snake. **2** To attract strongly; to fascinate; to give great delight to; to enchant; as, sounds that *charm* the ear. **3** To protect as if by magic; as, a soldier who seemed to bear a *charmed* life. — For synonyms see *captivate.* — **charm·er,** *n.*

charm·ing \'chär-ming, 'chȧr-\ *adj.* Pleasing the mind or senses in a high degree; delightful; fascinating. — **charm·ing·ly,** *adv.*

char·nel house \'chärn-l, 'chȧrn-l\. A place for dead bodies or for the bones of the dead.

charred. Past tense and past part. of *char.*

charring. Pres. part. of *char.*

chart \'chärt, 'chȧrt\ *n.* **1** A map; especially, a map of a part of the sea for the use of sailors, showing coasts, reefs, currents, and depths of water. **2** An outline map, as one showing temperature variations in different places at a given time. **3** A sheet giving information in the form of a table or of lists, or by means of diagrams or graphs. — *v.* **1** To make a map of; as, to *chart* the arctic regions. **2** To show on paper in tables or diagrams; as, to *chart* the rise and fall in the price of butter.

char·ter \'chärt-r, 'chȧrt-r\ *n.* An official document granting rights or privileges from a ruler or a governing body; as, the *charter* of a colony; the *charter* of a college. — *v.* **1** To grant a charter to. **2** To hire for one's own use, as a ship or a bus.

char·wom·an \'chär-ˌwu̇m-ən, 'chȧr-\ *n.; pl.* **char·wom·en** \-ˌwim-ən\. [From *char* (another form of *chore*) and *woman.*] A woman hired, usually by the day, to do scrubbing and cleaning and other odd jobs of household work.

chary \'char-ē, 'cher-ē\ *adj.;* **char·i·er; char·i·est.** **1** Cautiously sparing or frugal; as, to be *chary* of giving praise; a man very *chary* of speech. **2** Cautiously watchful, especially in preserving something; as, to be *chary* of one's reputation.

chase \'chās\ *v.;* **chased; chas·ing.** **1** To follow in order to capture or to overtake; as, to *chase* a thief; to *chase* a bus to the next stop. **2** To hunt; as, to *chase* the fox. **3** To drive away; as, to *chase* a strange dog off the lawn. The sun *chased* the clouds from the sky. — For synonyms see *follow.* — *n.*

1 A chasing; pursuit; as, to join in the *chase* after a thief. **2** The hunting of game; as, the pleasures of the *chase.* **3** That which is chased; especially, an animal being hunted.

chase \'chās\ *v.;* **chased; chas·ing.** To ornament a metal surface by embossing or engraving; as, *chased* bronze.

chasm \'kaz-m\ *n.* A deep opening or gap, such as a great split in the earth.

chas·sis \'shas-ē, 'chas-ē\ *n.; pl.* **chas·sis** \-ēz\. A supporting framework, as that bearing the body of an automobile or airplane, or the parts of a radio or television receiving set.

chaste \'chāst\ *adj.* **1** Unmarried; celibate. **2** Pure in thought and act; modest; virtuous. **3** Pure and simple in design and expression; not ornate. — **chaste·ly,** *adv.*

chas·ten \'chās-n\ *v.;* **chas·tened; chas·ten·ing** \-n(-)ing\. **1** To correct by punishment; to discipline; to chastise. **2** To purify or refine by freeing from faults or excesses; to keep from being too great or too strong; to subdue; as, ambition *chastened* and restrained by common sense.

chas·tise \(')chas-'tīz\ *v.;* **chas·tised; chas·tis·ing.** To punish; especially, to punish bodily, as by whipping. — **chas·tise·ment** \(')chas-'tīz-mənt, 'chas-təz-mənt\ *n.*

chas·ti·ty \'chas-tət-ē\ *n.* The state or quality of being chaste; especially, personal purity and modesty.

chas·u·ble \'chaz(h)-əb-l, 'chas-\ *n.* A sleeveless outer vestment worn by the officiating priest at Mass.

chat \'chat\ *v.;* **chat·ted; chat·ting.** To talk in a light and easy manner; as, to *chat* with a friend about trifles. — *n.* **1** Light, familiar conversation; an informal talk. **2** Any of several birds so named from the sound of their call, including in America the **yellow-breasted chat** and the **long-tailed chat.**

cha·teau \(')sha-'tō\ *n.; pl.* **cha·teaux** \-'tōz\. [From French, there derived from Latin *castellum* meaning "castle", "fort", from which English *castle* is also derived.] **1** A French castle or fortress. **2** A large country house, especially in France.

chat·e·laine \'shat-l-ˌān\ *n.* **1** The mistress of a chateau. **2** An ornamental clasp or pin worn by a woman, usually at the waist, and having a chain or chains attached for such things as keys, purse, or watch.

chat·tel \'chat-l\ *n.* **1** A slave; a bondman. **2** Any piece of property other than real estate, as furniture, money, goods, or jewelry.

chat·ter \'chat-r\ *v.* **1** To utter quick speechlike but meaningless sounds; as, monkeys *chattering* in the trees. **2** To speak rapidly, thoughtlessly, or indistinctly. **3** To make a series of noises by rapid and repeated striking together; as, teeth *chattering* from the cold. — *n.* Chattering sounds or talk; as, the *chatter* of children at play. The *chatter* of the monkeys was almost human. — **chat·ter·er** \-r-r\ *n.*

chat·ter·box \'chat-r-ˌbäks\ *n.* A person who talks unceasingly; a constant chatterer.

chat·ty \'chat-ē\ *adj.;* **chat·ti·er; chat·ti·est. 1** Fond of chatting; talkative; as, a girl who is *chatty* but not silly. **2** Having the style and manner of light, familiar conversation; as, a *chatty* letter. — **chat·ti·ly** \'chat-l-ē\ *adv.*

chauf·feur \'shōf-r, shō-'fər\ *n.* [From French, meaning originally "stoker", "fireman" (on a locomotive).] A person who drives an automobile as an occupation.

cheap \'chēp\ *adj.* **1** Of low cost or price; as, a *cheap* watch. **2** Worth little; of inferior quality. *Cheap* material wears out quickly. **3** Gained with little effort; not worth gaining; as, *cheap* applause. **4** Lowered in one's own opinion; abashed; as, to feel *cheap.* **5** Dealing in low prices or inferior goods; as, a *cheap* store. — *adv.* At low cost; as, an opportunity to buy cloth *cheap* in large quantities. — **cheap·ly,** *adv.*

cheap·en \'chēp-n\ *v.;* **cheap·ened; cheap·en·ing** \-n(-)ing\. To make or to become cheap or cheaper; to lessen the value of.

cheat \'chēt\ *n.* **1** Something unfair or deceitful. **2** A person who does something unfair or dishonest in order to gain something for himself. — *v.* To be unfair; to deceive or to trick; as, to *cheat* a person out of his earnings.

check \'chek\ *n.* **1** In chess, the position of the king when the square he occupies is attacked by an opposing piece. **2** A sudden stopping of advance or progress; a stop, pause, or interruption; as, to hold something in *check;* to go along without *check.* **3** Something that causes a delay or stop. **4** The action of going over something to be sure it is in place and correct; supervision or examination to determine accuracy or progress; as, to keep *check* of employees. **5** A standard or guide for testing accuracy or progress. **6** A mark on written or printed matter to show that something has been specially noted. **7** A ticket or token that shows that a person has a claim to something; as, a baggage *check.* **8** A written order directing a bank to pay out a sum of money according to instructions on the order; as, to pay a bill by *check.* **9** A slip of paper showing a price or charge; as, a dinner *check.* **10** A crack, as in wood or steel. **11** A pattern made of squares like a checkerboard; a square or a fabric in such a pattern. — *v.* **1** In chess, to put the king in check. **2** To bring to a sudden pause; to stop. **3** To restrain; to curb; as, to *check* a horse. **4** To make sure of the correctness of; to mark printing or writing with a check to show that something has been specially noted. **5** To mark with squares or checks; to checker; as, a *checked* suit. **6** To leave something for a short time for safekeeping, receiving a check with which to reclaim it; as, to *check* one's baggage. **7** To correspond item for item, usually with some original or standard; as, to see whether the money *checks* with the figures. **8** To crack in small openings, as wood or steel. — *adj.* Serving to check; as, a *check* list. — **check·er,** *n.*

check·book \'chek-ˌbu̇k\ *n.* A book of blank bank checks.

check·er \'chek-r\ *n.* **1** A square or a spot resembling the squares of a checkerboard or a pattern of such squares. **2** A piece, or man, in checkers or backgammon. — *v.;* **check·ered**; **check·er·ing** \-r(-)ing\. **1** To mark with checkers, or with spots of different colors; as, a *checkered* tablecloth. **2** To subject to frequent changes, as of fortune; as, a *checkered* career.

check·er·board \'chek-r-ˌbōrd, -ˌbȯrd\ *n.* A board used in playing checkers, marked in two colors into 64 squares with every other square of the same color.

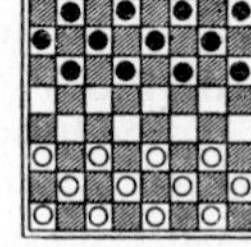
checkerboard

check·ers \'chek-rz\ *n.* A game played on a checkerboard by two persons, each having 12 pieces or men.

check·ing account \'chek-ing\. An account in a bank from which the depositor can draw money by writing checks.

check·mate \'chek-ˌmāt\ *n.* **1** In chess, a checkmating or the position of a king when checkmated. **2** A complete check; a defeat. — *v.;* **check·mat·ed**; **check·mat·ing.** **1** In chess, to check an opponent's king so that escape is impossible. **2** To defeat; to frustrate.

check·rein \'chek-ˌrān\ *n.* A short rein fastened so that it prevents a horse from lowering its head.

check·up or **check–up** \'chek-ˌəp\ *n.* **1** An examination of something to be sure that it is in order. **2** A test, as of progress or development. **3** A physical examination.

cheek \'chēk\ *n.* **1** The side of the face below the eye and above and beside the mouth. **2** Saucy speech or behavior; impudence.

cheek·bone \'chēk-'bōn\ *n.* The bone or the bony projection below the eye.

cheeky \'chēk-ē\ *adj.;* **cheek·i·er**; **cheek·i·est.** Saucy; impudent; as, a *cheeky* reply.

cheep \'chēp\ *v.* To make a peeping sound, like a young bird. — *n.* A peep; a chirp.

cheer \'chir\ *n.* **1** The state of a person's feelings; as, to be of good *cheer.* **2** Gaiety; mirth; as, full of *cheer.* **3** Something that cheers or gladdens; as, words of *cheer.* **4** Provision for feasting; especially, food and drink. **5** A shout of joy, applause, or approval; as, to give three *cheers* for the team. — *v.* **1** To comfort, give hope to, or make happier; as, to *cheer* a sick person. **2** To urge on, especially with shouts or cheers; as, to *cheer* one's team to victory. **3** To shout with joy, approval, or enthusiasm.

cheer·ful \'chirf-l\ *adj.* Full of cheer; gay; pleasant and bright; as, a *cheerful* smile; a *cheerful* room. — **cheer·ful·ly** \-l(-)ē\ *adv.*

cheer·lead·er \'chir-ˌlēd-r\ *n.* A person who directs organized cheering.

cheer·less \'chir-ləs\ *adj.* Without cheer; joyless; gloomy; as, a cold, *cheerless* morning.

cheery \'chir-ē\ *adj.;* **cheer·i·er**; **cheer·i·est.** Cheerful; lively; bright; as, a *cheery* log fire; a *cheery* greeting. — **cheer·i·ly** \'chir-ə-lē\ *adv.*

cheese \'chēz\ *n.* The curd of milk, pressed and used as food.

cheese·cloth \'chēz-ˌklȯth\ *n.* A thin, loose-woven cotton cloth.

chee·tah \'chēt-ə\ *n.* A long-legged Asiatic and African leopardlike animal of the cat family, the fastest of all four-footed animals, often trained to hunt deer.

chef \'shef\ *n.* A cook; especially, a head cook.

che·la \'kē-lə\ *n.; pl.* **che·lae** \-ˌlē\ or **che·las** \-ləz\. The pincerlike claw on certain limbs of crustaceans and arachnids, as lobsters and scorpions.

chem·i·cal \'kem-ik-l\ *n.* **1** A substance formed when two or more other substances act upon one another to cause a permanent change. **2** A substance that acts upon something else to cause a permanent change; as, a *chemical* that turns starch blue. — *adj.* **1** Of or relating to the forces and processes of chemistry. **2** Acting, operating, or performed by the use of chemicals. — **chem·i·cal·ly** \-ik-l(-)ē\ *adv.*

che·mise \shə-'mēz\ *n.* A woman's shirtlike undergarment.

chem·ist \'kem-əst\ *n.* A person who knows or works at chemistry.

chem·is·try \'kem-əs-trē\ *n.* **1** The science that collects, studies, and explains facts about substances, what they are made up of, and what changes they undergo. **2** Chemical composition, properties, or processes.

che·nille \shə-'nēl\ *n.* A fabric with a deep, fuzzy, more or less widely spaced pile, used for such articles as bedspreads and rugs.

cheque \'chek\ *n. British.* A bank check.

cher·ish \'cher-ish\ *v.* **1** To treat with care and affection; to hold dear; as, to *cherish* a friend. **2** To keep in mind; to cling to; as, to *cherish* a hope.

cher·ry \'cher-ē\ *n.; pl.* **cher·ries.** **1** The round red or reddish fruit of a common tree with shiny reddish-brown bark, pointed leaves, and clusters of white flowers. **2** This tree, or its wood. **3** Also **cherry red.** A bright red color.

cher·ub \'cher-əb\ *n.; pl.* **cher·u·bim** \-ə-ˌbim\ or **cher·ubs** \-əbz\. **1** Plural *cherubim.* An angel. **2** Plural *cherubs.* A painting or drawing of a beautiful child, usually with wings. **3** Plural *cherubs.* A chubby, rosy child. — **che·ru·bic** \chə-'rü-bik\ *adj.*

chess \'ches\ *n.* A game for two persons, played on a board (**chess·board** \-ˌbōrd ,-ˌbȯrd\) like a checkerboard, each player having 16 pieces called **chessmen** \-mən\.

chest \'chest\ *n.* **1** A box with a lid, especially for the safekeeping of one's possessions. **2** Also **chest of drawers.** A frame holding drawers, as for clothing. **3** The treasury of a public institution or the funds in the treasury. **4** The part of the body enclosed by the ribs and breastbone; the thorax. **5** A boxlike receptacle, as for steam or gas.

chest·nut \'ches-(ˌ)nət\ *n.* **1** An eatable nut from certain trees of the beech family. **2** Any of these trees or the wood from any of them. **3** Also **chestnut brown.** A dull dark-brown color with a tinge of orange.

chestnut burs

chev·a·lier \ˌshev-l-'ir\ *n.* **1** *Archaic.* A knight. **2** A member of certain orders of knighthood or of merit, as the Legion of Honor in France.

chev·i·ot \'shev-ē-ət\ *n.* **1** A heavy rough woolen fabric, used for coats and suits. **2** A heavy cotton fabric, as used for shirts.

chev·ron \'shev-rən\ *n.* A device consisting usually of bars meeting at an angle, worn on the coat sleeve to indicate rank or service.

chew \'chü\ *v.* To bite and grind with the teeth. — *n.* A chewing or the thing chewed.

chew·ing gum \'chü-ing\. Gum prepared for chewing, usually sweetened and flavored chicle.

che·wink \chə-'wingk\ *n.* A finch of eastern North America related to the sparrow.

chgd. Abbreviation for *charged.*

chic \'shēk\ *n.* Stylishness. — *adj.* Stylish; smart.

chi·ca·nery \shi-'kān-r(-)ē\ *n.; pl.* **chi·ca·ner·ies.** Trickery; deceit.

chick \'chik\ *n.* **1** A young chicken; a young bird. **2** A child.

chick·a·dee \'chik-ə-(ˌ)dē\ *n.* A small bird with fluffy grayish feathers and, usually, a black cap.

chick·en \'chik-n\ *n.* **1** A young cock or hen. **2** A barnyard fowl or its flesh used as food. **3** The young of various other birds.

chick·en·heart·ed \'chik-n-'härt-əd, -'hȧrt-\ *adj.* Cowardly; timid.

chicken pox \ˌpäks\. A contagious disease, chiefly of children, in which the skin breaks out in a rash or in small watery blisters.

chick·weed \'chik-ˌwēd\ *n.* A weed with small pointed leaves and whitish flowers.

chi·cle \'chik-l\ *n.* A gum obtained from the sap of certain trees and used in making chewing gum.

chic·o·ry \'chik-r(-)ē\ *n.; pl.* **chic·o·ries.** **1** A hairy-stemmed plant with small leaves and stalkless blue flowers growing along the stem. **2** The roasted root of this plant, sometimes mixed with coffee.

chide \'chīd\ *v.;* **chid** \'chid\ or **chid·ed** \'chīd-əd\; **chid** \'chid\ or **chid·den** \'chid-n\ or **chid·ed; chid·ing** \'chīd-ing\. To scold; to rebuke; to find fault with; as, to *chide* a student for being late.

chief \'chēf\ *n.* [From Old French *chief* or *chef,* there derived from Latin *caput* meaning "head".] A person at the head; a leader; as, an Indian *chief;* the *chief* of police. — *adj.* Highest in office or rank; most important; main; as, the *chief* officials of a town.

chief·ly \'chēf-lē\ *adv.* **1** Above all; principally; as, cloth used *chiefly* for women's dresses. We went to the circus *chiefly* to see the animals. **2** For the most part; mostly. The guests were *chiefly* children.

chief·tain \'chēf-tən\ *n.* A chief, especially of a tribe or a clan. — **chief·tain·cy** \-sē\ *n.*

chif·fon \shi-'fän, 'shif-ˌän\ *n.* A sheer silk fabric.

chif·fo·nier \ˌshif-n-'ir\ *n.* A high narrow chest of drawers, often with a mirror.

chig·ger \'chig-r\ *n.* **1** A chigoe. **2** The six-legged larva of certain mites, which clings to the skin and causes itching.

chig·oe \'chig-ˌō, 'chig-ə\ *n.* **1** A common tropical flea the female of which burrows under the skin of man and animals. **2** A chigger.

chil·blain \'chil-ˌblān\ *n.* An itchy sore or swelling on the hands or feet, caused by cold.

child \'chīld\ *n.; pl.* **chil·dren** \'child-r(ə)n\. **1** A baby; an infant. **2** A boy or girl; as, books written especially for *children.* **3** Any person as innocent and trusting as a child. **4** A son or daughter; as, to be an only *child.*

child·bear·ing \'chīl(d)-ˌbar-ing, -ˌber-\ *n.* The producing of or giving birth to children.

child·birth \'chīl(d)-ˌbərth\ *n.* The giving birth to a child.

child·hood \'chīld-ˌhu̇d\ *n.* The condition of being a child; the period of life between infancy and youth.

child·ish \'chīl-dish\ *adj.* **1** Of, like, or suitable to a child or children. **2** Foolish; silly. — For synonyms see *childlike.*

child·ish·ness \'chīl-dish-nəs\ *n.* Childish nature or behavior.

child·like \'chīl-ˌdlīk\ *adj.* Of a child; characteristic of or suitable to a child; innocent; trustful. — The words *childish* and *infantile* are synonyms of *childlike,* but all three may be used of adults as well as children: *childlike* usually refers to such likable qualities of childhood as innocence, simplicity, or trust; *childish* may suggest the less admirable qualities of childhood, as helplessness or immaturity; *infantile* is often used contemptuously to describe extremely childish behavior.

children. Pl. of *child.*

Chil·e·an \'chil-ē-ən\ *adj.* Of or relating to Chile. — *n.* A native or inhabitant of Chile.

chili or **chil·li** \'chil-ē\ *n.; pl.* **chil·ies** or **chil·lies** \-ēz\. **1** A tropical plant, or its fruit, from which red pepper is made. **2** A sauce seasoned with chilies. **3** Also **chili con car·ne** \-ē (ˌ)kän 'kär-nē, -ēk-n 'kär-, 'kȧr\. A dish made of red peppers and meat.

chill \'chil\ *n.* **1** A feeling of coldness, with shivering; as, to have a *chill.* **2** Moderate but disagreeable coldness; as, a *chill* in the air. — *adj.* **1** Fairly cold; as, a *chill* wind. **2** Unfriendly; not cordial; as, a *chill* greeting. — *v.* **1** To make or become cool or cold; as, to *chill* a dessert. **2** To harden the surface, as of cast iron, by sudden cooling.

chilly \'chil-ē\ *adj.;* **chill·i·er; chill·i·est.** **1** Making cold, shivery, or depressed; chilling; as, a *chilly* night; a *chilly* greeting. **2** Disagreeably cold; chilled; as, to feel *chilly.*

chime \'chīm\ *n.* **1** A set of bells which are in tune with each other. **2** [in the plural] The music from such a set of bells. **3** Any musical bell-like sound; as, the *chime* of distant laughter. — *v.* **1** To ring chimes; to make bell-like sounds. The clock *chimed* softly. **2** To indicate, as an hour of the day, with chimes. **3** To agree; to be in harmony; as, a suggestion that *chimed* perfectly with the general plan. — **chime in.** To join in, or break into, a conversation.

chi·me·ra \kī-'mir-ə\ *n.* **1** [with a capital] A she-monster of Greek mythology, represented as vomiting flames and, usually, as having a lion's head, goat's body, and dragon's tail. **2** Any frightful creation of the imagination. **3** Any wild or foolish fancy.

chi·mer·i·cal \kī-'mer-ik-l, -'mir-\ *adj.* **1** Existing only in the imagination; fanciful; fantastic. **2** Inclined to favor fantastic ideas or schemes.

chim·ney \'chim-nē\ *n.; pl.* **chim·neys.** **1** A passage for smoke; especially, an upright structure of brick or stone, extending above the roof of a building. **2** A glass tube around a lamp flame.

chimney pot. A pipe or tube at the top of a chimney, used to increase draft and carry off smoke.

chimney sweep \ˌswēp\. A person who cleans soot from chimneys.

chimney swift \ˌswift\. A small sooty-gray bird with long, narrow wings, noted for attaching its nest to the inside of a chimney.

chimp \'chimp, 'shimp\. Short for *chimpanzee.*

chim·pan·zee \ˌchim-ˌpan-'zē, ˌshim-, -pən-; chim-'pan-zē, shim-\ *n.* An African manlike ape, smaller and less savage than the gorilla.

chin \'chin\ *n.* The part of the face below the mouth; the point of the lower jaw. — *v.;* **chinned; chin·ning.** **1** To raise oneself when hanging by the hands until the chin is level with the hands. **2** *Slang.* To talk or converse.

chi·na \'chī-nə\ *n.* **1** Porcelain or porcelain ware, as dishes, cups, and vases, originally that from the Far East. **2** Crockery in general.

chi·na·ber·ry \'chī-nə-ˌber-ē\ *n.; pl.* **chi·na·ber·ries.** **1** A soapberry of the southern United States and Mexico. **2** A China tree.

China tree. A handsome purple-flowered Asiatic tree of the mahogany family, planted in America as a shade tree; a chinaberry.

chi·na·ware \'chī-nə-ˌwar, -ˌwer\ *n.* Articles, especially dishes, made of china.

chinch \'chinch\ *n.* **1** Also **chintz** \'chin(t)s\. A bedbug. **2** A chinch bug.

chinch bug. A small insect, black and white in color when adult, that does great damage to grass and grain, especially in dry weather.

chin·chil·la \(')chin-'chil-ə\ *n.* **1** A squirrellike South American animal having soft pearl-gray fur. **2** The fur of the chinchilla. **3** A heavy woolen cloth with a tufted surface, used for coats.

Chi·nese \(')chī-'nēz, -'nēs\ *adj.* Of or relating to China. — *n.* **1** *sing. and pl.* A native of China or a person descended from a native of China. **2** The language of China.

Chinese lantern. A collapsible lantern of thin colored paper.

Chinese puzzle. Something hard to solve, like the complicated puzzles of the Chinese.

Chinese white. Zinc white, especially in a dense form.

chink \'chingk\ *n.* A narrow slit or crack, as in a wall. — *v.* **1** To crack. **2** To fill up the cracks of; as, to *chink* the walls of a log cabin with clay.

chink \'chingk\ *n.* A short, sharp sound as of glass or metal lightly struck. — *v.* To make, or cause to make, a chink.

chinned. Past tense and past part. of *chin.*

chinning. Pres. part. of *chin.*

chintz \'chin(t)s\ *n.* A printed cotton cloth, usually having a flowery design and often a glossy finish, used for furniture covers, curtains, and clothing.

chintz. Variant of *chinch.*

chip \'chip\ *n.* **1** A small piece, as of wood, stone, or glass, broken off by a sharp blow; a flake. **2** The place where such a piece has been broken or cut out; as, a *chip* in the rim of a cup. **3** A thin, crisp piece of food; as, potato *chips.* **4** A flat counter used in poker and various other games. — *v.;* **chipped; chip·ping.** **1** To cut or break chips from; to break away a little at a time; as, to *chip* ice off a sidewalk. **2** To break off in small pieces at the edges. Fine china *chips* easily.

chip·munk \'chip-ˌməngk\ *n.* A gnawing animal like a squirrel but smaller than the squirrel and striped.

chipped beef \'chip(t) 'bēf\. Smoked beef cut into very thin slices.

chip·per \'chip-r\ *adj.* Lively and cheerful in spirits or manner.

chip·ping sparrow \'chip-ing\. A small sparrow whose song is a weak monotonous trill, one of the most familiar North American birds, which often builds its nest near a dwelling.

chi·rop·o·dy \kə-'räp-əd-ē\ *n.* The treatment of minor ailments of the feet, as corns and bunions. — **chi·rop·o·dist** \-əst\ *n.*

chi·ro·prac·tic \'kī-rə-ˌprak-tik\ *n.* The treatment of bodily ailments through the manipulation, or adjustment by hand, of the joints, especially of the spine. — **chi·ro·prac·tor** \-ˌprakt-r\ *n.*

chirp \'chərp\ *n.* The short, quick sound made by crickets and some small birds. — *v.* To make a chirp.

chir·rup \'chir-əp\ *v.* To chirp, especially over and over, in the manner of a cricket. — *n.* A repeated chirp.

chi·rur·geon \kī-'rərj-n\ *n.* *Archaic.* A surgeon.

chis·el \'chiz-l\ *n.* A metal tool with a cutting edge at the end of a blade, used to shape or chip away stone or wood. — *v.;* **chis·eled** or **chis·elled**; **chis·el·ing** or **chis·el·ling** \-l(-)ing\. To chip or to shape with or as if with a chisel.

chisels

chis·eled or **chis·elled** \'chiz-ld\ *adj.* **1** Cut or shaped with a chisel. **2** Appearing as if shaped with a chisel; finely or sharply cut; as, *chiseled* features.

chi·tin \'kīt-n\ *n.* A horny substance forming the harder part of the outer body wall of insects and crustaceans. — **chi·tin·ous** \-n-əs\ *adj.*

chit·ter \'chit-r\ *v.* To twitter, as a bird; to chirp or chatter.

chi·val·ric \shi-'val-rik\ *adj.* Of or relating to chivalry; chivalrous.

chiv·al·rous \'shiv-l-rəs\ *adj.* **1** Of or relating to chivalry. **2** Of, relating to, or having the qualities of an ideal knight of the age of chivalry; brave, honorable, generous, and courteous. **3** Courteously attentive; gentlemanly. — **chiv·al·rous·ly,** *adv.*

chiv·al·ry \'shiv-l-rē\ *n.* **1** A body of knights; an assembly of gallant warriors or brave gentlemen. **2** The system, spirit, ways, or customs of medieval knighthood. **3** The qualifications of an ideal knight such as bravery, honor, protection of the weak, and generous treatment of foes.

chive \'chīv\ *n.* An herb related to the onion, used for flavoring — usually used in the plural.

chlo·ral \'klōr-əl, 'klòr-\ *n.* A white crystalline drug used to bring sleep.

chlor·dane \'klōr-ˌdān, 'klòr-\ or **chlor·dan** \-ˌdan\ *n.* An odorless liquid insecticide, especially effective against grasshoppers.

chlo·ride \'klōr-ˌīd, 'klòr-\ *n.* A chemical compound of chlorine with another element or radical.

chloride of lime. A whitish powdery substance made by passing chlorine gas over slaked lime and used as a bleaching agent, disinfectant, and deodorant.

chlo·rin·ate \'klōr-ə-ˌnāt, 'klòr-\ *v.;* **chlo·rin·at·ed**; **chlo·rin·at·ing.** To treat with chlorine in order to purify, as water or sewage. — **chlo·rin·a·tion** \ˌklōr-ə-'nāsh-n, ˌklòr-\ *n.*

chlo·rin·a·tor \'klōr-ə-ˌnāt-r, 'klòr-\ *n.* An apparatus for passing chlorine gas into water to be disinfected.

chlo·rine \'klōr-ˌēn, -ən, 'klòr-\ *n.* A chemical element that is a poisonous greenish-yellow gas with a disagreeable, suffocating odor.

chlo·ro·form \'klōr-ə-ˌfòrm, 'klòr-\ *n.* A colorless, sweetish-tasting liquid smelling like ether and used as an anesthetic. — *v.* **1** To make unconscious with chloroform. **2** To kill with chloroform; as, to have an injured dog *chloroformed.*

chlo·ro·phyll or **chlo·ro·phyl** \'klōr-ə-ˌfil, 'klòr-, -əf-l\ *n.* The green coloring matter in plants, necessary in the manufacture of plant food mainly starch, from carbon dioxide and water.

chlo·ro·plast \'klōr-ə-ˌplast, 'klòr-\ *n.* A tiny body within a plant cell, containing chlorophyll.

chm. or **chmn.** Abbreviation for *chairman.*

chock \'chäk\ *n.* A wedge or block to fill in a space or to prevent something, as a wheel or a barrel, from moving. — *v.* To fasten or wedge with chocks.

chock-full \'chäk-'fu̇l\ or **chuck-full** \'chək-\ *adj.* Full to the limit.

choc·o·late \'chäk-l(-)ət, 'chòk-\ *n.* **1** A food substance formed from ground and roasted cacao beans. **2** A drink made by cooking or mixing some of this with milk or water. **3** A candy made of chocolate or coated with chocolate. — **chocolate brown.** The dark-brown color of chocolate.

choice \'chòis\ *n.* **1** The act of choosing or of selecting one person or thing from two or more persons or things. **2** The power or opportunity of choosing; as, to have one's *choice* of going or staying home. **3** A person or thing that is chosen. My brother was the *choice* of his teammates for captain. **4** A variety or number of things to choose from; as, a wide *choice* of toys. — *adj.;* **choic·er**; **choic·est.** Very fine; better than most; as, a supply of *choice* fruits.

choir \'kwīr\ *n.* **1** An organized group of singers, especially in a church. **2** The part of a church reserved for these singers.

choir·boy \'kwīr-ˌbòi\ *n.* A boy member of a choir.

choir·mas·ter \'kwīr-ˌmast-r\ *n.* A director or leader of a choir.

choke \'chōk\ *v.;* **choked**; **chok·ing.** **1** To hinder from breathing; to kill by cutting off the supply of air. The thick smoke *choked* the firemen. **2** To have the windpipe stopped, entirely or partly; to be strangled; as, to *choke* on a bone. **3** To check the growth or action of; to suppress; to smother; as, to *choke* a fire; to *choke* back the tears. **4** To clog; to close or to make very narrow. Leaves *choked* the sewer. **5** To fill to the limit. The store was *choked* with customers. **6** To decrease or shut off the air intake of the carburetor of a gasoline engine in order to make the fuel mixture richer. — *n.* **1** Something that chokes, or the act or sound of choking. **2** A narrowing in size, such as the narrowing toward the muzzle in the bore of a gun. **3** A device to prevent too great a flow of something. An automobile *choke* is a valve to regulate the supply of air to the carburetor.

choke·cher·ry \'chōk-ˌcher-ē, -'cher-ē\ *n.; pl.* **choke·cher·ries.** A tall bush or small tree with pointed leaves, long clusters of white flowers, and fruit that is nearly black when ripe.

chokecherry: leaves and fruit

choky or **chok·ey** \'chōk-ē\ *adj.;* **chok·i·er**; **chok·i·est.** **1** Having the power to choke; as, a *choky* gas. **2** Inclined to choke; having a tendency to choke; as, to grow *choky* with fear.

chol·era \'käl-r-ə\ *n.* Any of certain diseases marked by vomiting, increased looseness of the bowels, and extreme weakness; especially, an epidemic disease originating in Asia, which is often fatal.

chol·er·ic \'käl-r-ik, kə-'ler-ik\ *adj.* Hot-tempered; apt to have fits of anger; irritable; as, a *choleric* old man.

choose \'chüz\ *v.;* **chose** \'chōz\; **cho·sen** \'chōz-n\; **choos·ing** \'chü-zing\. **1** To select; to make choice of; as, to *choose* a leader. **2** To see fit; to think proper; to please. Anyone may go who *chooses* to do so.

chop \'chäp\ *v.;* **chopped**; **chop·ping. 1** To cut by striking, especially by striking more than once with something sharp; as, to *chop* down a tree. **2** To cut into small pieces; to mince; as, to *chop* meat. — *n.* **1** A sudden stroke, as with an ax. **2** A small cut of meat; especially, a slice from the ribs or loin of lamb, veal, or pork. **3** A short, quick movement, as of a wave.

chop \'chäp\ *v.;* **chopped**; **chop·ping.** To shift suddenly, as the wind; to veer.

chop \'chäp\ *n.* A jaw; [in the plural] the jaws and their covering of flesh. The dog licked his *chops.*

chop·py \'chäp-ē\ *adj.;* **chop·pi·er**; **chop·pi·est. 1** Rough with small waves; as, a *choppy* sea. **2** Full of abrupt transitions.

chop·py \'chäp-ē\ *adj.;* **chop·pi·er**; **chop·pi·est.** Constantly shifting; changeable; as, a *choppy* wind.

chop·stick \'chäp-ˌstik\ *n.* One of two small sticks used to eat with, chiefly by the Chinese.

chopsticks

cho·ral \'kōr-əl, 'kȯr-\ *adj.* Sung or recited, or intended to be sung or recited, by a chorus or choir. — **cho·ral·ly** \-ə-lē\ *adv.*

cho·ral or **cho·rale** \kə-'ral, -'räl, -'rȧl\ *n.* A hymn or a hymn tune, sung in unison.

chord \'kȯrd\ *n.* **1** A string of a musical instrument, as a harp. **2** A special feeling; as, to strike a familiar *chord.* **3** A string or cord or something like it; as, the *chord* of the tongue. **4** A straight line joining two points on a curve or circle.

chord \'kȯrd\ *n.* In music, a combination of tones that blend harmoniously when sounded together. — *v.* To harmonize together.

chor·date \'kȯr-ˌdāt\ *n.* One of a group of animals that at some stage of their development have an elastic rod of cells forming a support along the back, a central nervous system situated in the back, and gill clefts.

chore \'chōr, 'chȯr\ *n.* **1** A small task or odd job. **2** [in the plural] The regular light work about a house or farm.

cho·re·og·ra·phy \ˌkōr-ē-'äg-rə-fē, ˌkȯr-, ˌkär-\ or **cho·reg·ra·phy** \kə-'reg-rə-fē\ *n.* The art of dancing or of arranging dances, especially ballets. — **cho·re·og·ra·pher** or **cho·reg·ra·pher** \-rəf-r\ *n.*

cho·ris·ter \'kōr-əst-r, 'kȯr-, 'kär-\ *n.* **1** A choir singer. **2** A choir leader.

cho·roid \'kōr-ˌoid, 'kȯr-\ or **cho·ri·oid** \-ē-ˌȯid\ *adj.* Relating to the membrane (called **choroid coat**) between the sclerotic and the retina of the eye. — *n.* The choroid coat.

chor·tle \'chȯrt-l\ *v.;* **chor·tled**; **chor·tling** \-l(-)ing\. To make a sound like chuckling or snorting; to laugh with such a sound.

cho·rus \'kōr-əs, 'kȯr-\ *n.; pl.* **cho·rus·es. 1** A company of singers; a choir. **2** A group of dancers and usually singers trained to perform special numbers. **3** The part performed by such a group. **4** Any song intended to be sung by a group. **5** A part of a song that is repeated at intervals, as at the end of each stanza. **6** Group singing or utterance. **7** Any sounds uttered by a number of people together; as, a *chorus* of approving shouts. — *v.* To speak, sing, or sound at the same time or together. The birds *chorused* a song. — **cho·ric** \'kōr-ik, 'kȯr-, 'kär-\ *adj.*

chose. Past tense of *choose.*

chosen. Past part. of *choose.*

chow \'chaů\ *n.* **1** A thick-coated, straight-legged, muscular dog with a blue-black tongue and a short tail curled close to the back. **2** *Slang.* Food.

chow·der \'chaůd-r\ *n.* A soup or stew made of fish, clams, or a vegetable, usually stewed in milk.

chris·ten \'kris-n\ *v.;* **chris·tened**; **chris·ten·ing** \-n(-)ing\. **1** To baptize. **2** To give a name to at baptism; as, to *christen* a baby Mary. **3** To name, as a ship, at a ceremony thought of as like baptism.

Chris·ten·dom \'kris-n-dəm\ *n.* **1** The entire body of Christians. **2** All the countries or peoples that are predominantly Christian.

chris·ten·ing \'kris-n(-)ing\ *n.* Baptism; the act or ceremony of giving a name.

Chris·tian \'kris-chən\ *adj.* **1** Of or relating to Jesus Christ or the religion based on his teachings. **2** Consisting chiefly of Christians; as, a *Christian* nation. **3** Characteristic of Christians; kind; gentle; as, an act of simple *Christian* kindness. — *n.* **1** A person who believes in Jesus Christ and follows his teachings. **2** A member of any Christian church.

Chris·ti·an·i·ty \ˌkris-chē-'an-ət-ē\ *n.* **1** The whole body of Christian believers. **2** The religion of Christians. **3** The state or fact of being a Christian; Christian character.

Chris·tian·ize \'kris-chə-ˌnīz\ *v.;* **Chris·tian·ized**; **Chris·tian·iz·ing.** To make Christian; to convert to Christianity.

Christian name. The name given to a person in baptism; first name; given name.

Christ·mas \'kris-məs\ *n.* [From Old English *Cristes maesse* meaning "Christ's mass".] **1** A church festival kept on December 25 (**Christmas Day**) in memory of the birth of Christ. **2** Christmas Day, generally celebrated by special gifts and greetings.

Christmas Eve. The evening before Christmas Day.

Christ·mas·tide \'kris-məs-ˌtīd\ *n.* The season of Christmas.

Christmas tree. A tree, especially an evergreen, decorated as part of the Christmas celebration.

chro·mat·ic \krō-'mat-ik\ *adj.* **1** Of or relating to color or colors. **2** In music, including or using tones that do not belong to a given key. **3** Proceeding by half steps of the musical scale; progressing by semitones. — *n.* In full, **chromatic sign.** An accidental. — **chro·mat·i·cal·ly** \-ik-l(-)ē\ *adv.*

chromatic scale. A musical scale that consists wholly of half steps.

chro·ma·tin \'krō-mə-tən\ *n.* A substance that occurs in the nucleus of a plant or animal cell and enters into the formation of chromosomes.

chrome \'krōm\ *n.* Chromium.

chro·mi·um \'krō-mē-əm\ *n.* A grayish-white metallic chemical element much used in making alloys, as a lustrous rust-resisting plating, and, in its compounds, in dyes and paints.

chro·mo·some \'krō-mə-ˌsōm\ *n.* Any of the bodies in the nucleus of a cell that contain chromatin and genes, are the carriers of heredity, and appear as rodlike structures in cells about to divide.

chron·ic \'krän-ik\ *adj.* **1** Continuing for a long time; as, a *chronic* disease. **2** Having had a disease, or a habit, for a long time; as, a *chronic* invalid. — **chron·i·cal·ly** \-ik-l(-)ē\ *adv.*

chron·i·cle \'krän-ik-l\ *n.* An account or history of events in the order of their occurrence; a history. — *v.;* **chron·i·cled; chron·i·cling** \-l(-)ing\. To record in or as if in a chronicle; to record; to tell the story of.

chron·i·cler \'krän-ik-lər\ *n.* A writer or compiler of a chronicle; a recorder of events; a historian.

chron·o·log·i·cal \ˌkrän-ə-'läj-ik-l\ *adj.* Arranged in or according to the order of time; as, *chronological* tables of American history; *chronological* order. — **chron·o·log·i·cal·ly** \-ik-l(-)ē\ *adv.*

chro·nol·o·gy \krə-'näl-ə-jē\ *n.; pl.* **chro·nol·o·gies. 1** The science that deals with measuring time and dating events. **2** A table or list of events arranged in the order of their occurrence. **3** Arrangement, as of events, in the order of occurrence. — **chro·nol·o·gist** \-jəst\ *n.*

chro·nom·e·ter \krə-'näm-ət-r\ *n.* An instrument for measuring time, especially one intended to keep time with great accuracy, as for use in navigation or astronomy.

chrys·a·lis \'kris-l-əs\ *n.; pl.* **chrys·a·lis·es** \-ə-səz\ or **chry·sal·i·des** \kri-'sal-ə-ˌdēz\. **1** An insect, like a butterfly or a moth, in the stage in which it is enclosed in a cocoon, or case, and is changing into its winged form. **2** A cocoon or protective case.

chrysalis, 2

chry·san·the·mum \kri-'san(t)th-m-əm\ *n.* **1** A plant of the aster family with toothed or divided leaves, and white, pinkish, or yellowish flowers. **2** The flower of this plant.

chrys·o·lite \'kris-l-ˌīt\ *n.* A mineral, usually greenish-yellow, sometimes used as a gem.

chub·by \'chəb-ē\ *adj.;* **chub·bi·er; chub·bi·est.** Plump and round; as, a *chubby* child.

chuck \'chək\ *v.* **1** To give a pat or a tap; as, to *chuck* a person under the chin. **2** To throw easily or carelessly; to toss; as, to *chuck* a ball back and forth. — *n.* **1** A light pat under the chin. **2** A toss or jerk.

chuck \'chək\ *n.* **1** A portion of a side of dressed beef including most of the neck and the parts about the shoulder blade and the first three ribs. **2** Any of various devices for holding work or a tool in a machine, especially in a lathe.

chuck-full. Variant of *chock-full.*

chuck·hole \'chək-ˌhōl\ *n.* A hole or rut in a road; a mudhole; especially, a deep hole in a wagon rut.

chuck·le \'chək-l\ *v.;* **chuck·led; chuck·ling** \-l(-)ing\. To laugh quietly, as to oneself. — *n.* A low, quiet laugh.

chuck·le·head \'chək-l-ˌhed\ *n.* A blockhead. — **chuck·le·head·ed** \-'hed-əd\ *adj.*

chuck wag·on \'chək ˌwag-n\. A wagon carrying a stove and provisions for cooking, as on a ranch or in a lumber camp.

chuck·wal·la \'chək-ˌwäl-ə\ *n.* A large but harmless lizard of the desert regions of the southwestern United States.

chug \'chəg\ *n.* A dull explosive sound; as, the *chug* of a tugboat. — *v.;* **chugged; chug·ging.** To move or go with chugs; as, a locomotive *chugging* along.

chum \'chəm\ *n.* A steady companion; a close friend. — *v.;* **chummed; chum·ming.** To go about with; to be on terms of close friendship.

chum·my \'chəm-ē\ *adj.;* **chum·mi·er; chum·mi·est.** Like a chum; intimate; sociable.

chunk \'chəngk\ *n.* A short thick piece or lump, as of wood or coal; a hunk.

chunky \'chəngk-ē\ *adj.;* **chunk·i·er; chunk·i·est. 1** Short and thick; thickset; as, a boy of *chunky* build. **2** Lumpy.

church \'chərch\ *n.* [From Old English *cirice,* there borrowed from Greek *kyriakon* meaning "the Lord's house".] **1** A building for public worship, especially Christian worship. **2** A religious service held in such a building. **3** [often with a capital] An organized body of Christians; a branch of the Christian religion. — **church·ly,** *adj.*

church·man \'chərch-mən\ *n.; pl.* **church·men** \-mən\. **1** A clergyman; a priest. **2** A devoted member of a church.

church·ward·en \'chərch-'wȯrd-n\ *n.* **1** A church officer, not a clergyman, whose duties relate chiefly to the management of church business and property. **2** A tobacco pipe, often of clay, with a long, slightly curved stem.

church·yard \'chərch-ˌyärd, -ˌyȧrd\ *n.* The ground around a church, part of which is often used as a burial ground.

churl \'chərl\ *n.* **1** A man of the lowest station in life in early English society; a peasant. **2** A rough, ill-bred man; a surly fellow.

churl·ish \'chər-lish\ *adj.* Surly; rude; ill-mannered. — **churl·ish·ly,** *adv.*

churn \'chərn\ *n.* A container in which milk or cream is violently stirred or beaten until its fat, or butter, is separated from the other parts. — *v.* **1** To stir in a churn. **2** To stir or shake violently. The wind *churned* the waves into foam.

churn

chute \'shüt\ *n.* **1** A quick drop, as of water in a river; a rapid. **2** A trough or tube for dropping or sliding things down to a lower level; as, a coal *chute;* a mail *chute.* **3** A parachute.

chyle \'kīl\ *n.* A milky fluid containing bits of fat, found in vessels surrounding the small intestine and serving to carry the digested fat to the blood.

chyme \'kīm\ *n.* The semifluid mass into which food is converted in the stomach and in which it passes into the small intestine.

ci·ca·da \sə-'kād-ə, -'käd-ə\ *n.* A stout-bodied insect with wide blunt head and large transparent wings, the male of which produces shrill notes by vibrating membranes on the underside of the abdomen.

ci·der \'sīd-r\ *n.* The juice pressed out of apples, used as a drink and in making vinegar.

ci·gar \si-'gär, -'gȧr\ *n.* A small tight roll of tobacco leaf, usually tapered at the ends or at one end, for smoking.

cig·a·rette \ˌsig-r-'et, 'sig-r-ˌet\ *n.* A small roll of cut tobacco, wrapped in paper for smoking.

cil·ia \'sil-ē-ə\ *n. pl.; sing.* **cil·i·um** \-ē-əm\. **1** The eyelashes. **2** Very small hairlike projections found on many cells, as in the nasal cavity and the windpipe.

cil·i·ary \'sil-ē-ˌer-ē\ *adj.* **1** Of or relating to cilia. **2** Relating to certain structures of the eye.

cinch \'sinch\ *n.* **1** A strong band or strap for holding a saddle or a pack on a horse or other animal. **2** A tight grip. **3** *Slang.* A sure or easy thing. It will be a *cinch* to make the trip in one day. — *v.* **1** To put a cinch upon; to tighten a cinch. **2** To get a sure hold on; to make sure of.

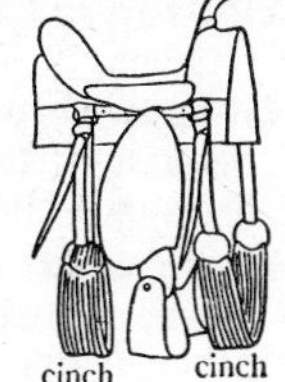

cinch

cin·cho·na \sin(g)-'kō-nə\ *n.* A South American or East Indian tree whose bark yields quinine and other related drugs.

cinc·ture \'singk-chər\ *n.* A belt; a girdle.

cin·der \'sind-r\ *n.* **1** Waste matter from the smelting of metal ores; slag. **2** A piece of partly burned coal or wood that will burn further but will not flame. **3** [in the plural] Ashes; especially, clinkers left after burning soft coal.

cinder block. A building block made of concrete and coal cinders.

cin·e·ma \'sin-ə-mə\ *n.* **1** A motion picture. **2** A motion-picture theater.

cin·na·mon \'sin-ə-mən\ *n.* **1** The bark of any of several trees, used as a spice. **2** An Asiatic tree with thick, ribbed leaves and bark that may be used as a spice. — *adj.* **1** Of the color of cinnamon; reddish-brown; as, a *cinnamon* bear. **2** Spiced with cinnamon; as, *cinnamon* toast.

ci·on \'sī-ən\ *n.* A detached shoot or part of a plant containing buds; especially, a shoot prepared for grafting; a scion.

ci·pher \'sīf-r\ *n.* **1** A symbol [0] indicating the absence of all magnitude or quantity; a naught; a zero. **2** A person of no worth or influence. **3** A method of secret writing or the alphabet or characters used in such writing. **4** A document written according to this method. **5** An interweaving of letters or initials, as in a monogram. — *v.;* **ci·phered; ci·pher·ing** \-r(-)ing\. **1** To use figures in mathematical work; to figure. **2** To encipher.

cir·cle \'sərk-l\ *n.* **1** A closed curve every point of which is equally distant from a point within it, called the center. **2** The space inside such a closed curve. **3** A ring. The children sat in a *circle* around the storyteller. **4** Anything resembling a circle or part of a circle, as a group of tiers of seats in a theater. **5** A series of things thought of as joined into one round whole; a cycle; as, a *circle* of pleasures. **6** A group of people bound together by common interests; as, a family *circle;* musical *circles.* — *v.;* **cir·cled; cir·cling** \-l(-)ing\. **1** To move in a circle. An eagle *circled* overhead. **2** To surround by a circle or as if by a circle; to enclose; to move around; as, to *circle* the earth in three months; an island *circled* by a blue sea.

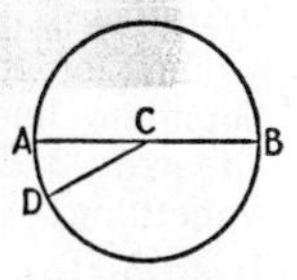

center C, diameter AB, and radius CD of circle

cir·cuit \'sərk-ət\ *n.* **1** A boundary around an enclosed space. **2** An enclosed space; a region; an area. **3** A moving around, as in a circle or orbit; a circling; as, the *circuit* of the earth around the sun. **4** A regular traveling from place to place in the course of one's duties, as required of certain judges. **5** The course or route regularly traveled. **6** A chain of theaters at which productions are shown in turn. **7** The complete path of an electric current, or any part of this path. **8** In radio and television, a hookup.

cir·cu·i·tous \(ˌ)sər-'kyü-ət-əs\ *adj.* Roundabout; indirect; as, a *circuitous* road. — **cir·cu·i·tous·ly,** *adv.*

cir·cu·lar \'sərk-yəl-r\ *adj.* **1** In the form of a circle; bounded by a circle; round; as, a *circular* saw. **2** Passing or going around in a circle; as, *circular* motion. **3** Circuitous; roundabout; as, a *circular* explanation. **4** Sent around to a number of persons, to interest them in something; as, a *circular* letter. — *n.* A circular letter or paper, often an advertisement. — **cir·cu·lar·ly**, *adv.*

cir·cu·lar·ize \'sərk-yəl-r-ˌīz\ *v.;* **cir·cu·lar·ized**; **cir·cu·lar·iz·ing.** To send circulars to.

cir·cu·late \'sərk-yə-ˌlāt\ *v.;* **cir·cu·lat·ed**; **cir·cu·lat·ing.** **1** To move around in a regular course, as the blood in the body. **2** To go, pass, or send about from place to place, or from person to person. Money *circulates.* **3** To cause to circulate; as, to *circulate* a report. — **cir·cu·la·tor** \-ˌlāt-r\ *n.*

cir·cu·la·tion \ˌsərk-yə-'lāsh-n\ *n.* **1** A circulating. **2** A passing from place to place or from person to person; especially, the average number of copies of a publication, as a newspaper, sold each issue, or of books loaned from a public library each year. **3** The movement of the blood in the vessels caused by pulsations of the heart.

cir·cu·la·to·ry \'sərk-yə-lə-ˌtōr-ē, -ˌtȯr-ē\ *adj.* Having to do with circulation, as of the blood; as, the *circulatory* system.

cir·cum·cise \'sərk-m-ˌsīz\ *v.;* **cir·cum·cised**; **cir·cum·cis·ing.** To cut off the foreskin of. — **cir·cum·ci·sion** \ˌsərk-m-'sizh-n\ *n.*

cir·cum·fer·ence \sər-'kəm(p)-fərn(t)s, -fər-ən(t)s, -frən(t)s\ *n.* **1** The line that goes around, or encloses, a circle. **2** A boundary line or circuit enclosing an area. **3** The distance around something.

cir·cum·flex accent \'sərk-m-ˌfleks\. A mark [^] sometimes used over certain letters in some words borrowed from a foreign language. Thus *chateau* is often written *château.*

cir·cum·lo·cu·tion \ˌsərk-m-lō-'kyüsh-n\ *n.* The use of many words to express an idea that might be briefly expressed.

cir·cum·nav·i·gate \ˌsərk-m-'nav-ə-ˌgāt\ *v.;* **cir·cum·nav·i·gat·ed**; **cir·cum·nav·i·gat·ing.** To sail round; as, to *circumnavigate* the earth. — **cir·cum·nav·i·ga·tion** \-ˌnav-ə-'gāsh-n\ *n.*

cir·cum·scribe \ˌsərk-m-'skrīb\ *v.;* **cir·cum·scribed**; **cir·cum·scrib·ing.** **1** To draw a line around; to encircle. **2** To limit, especially narrowly; as, to *circumscribe* a person's activities. — **cir·cum·scrip·tion** \-'skripsh-n\ *n.*

cir·cum·spect \'sərk-m-ˌspekt\ *adj.* Careful to consider all the circumstances and consequences; cautious; prudent; wary. — **cir·cum·spect·ly** \-ˌspekt-lē, -'spekt-\ *adv.*

cir·cum·spec·tion \ˌsərk-m-'speksh-n\ *n.* Prudent or watchful action or behavior; care.

cir·cum·stance \'sərk-m-ˌstan(t)s\ *n.* **1** Any fact or event that must be considered along with another fact or event. **2** [in the plural] Surrounding conditions; as, impossible under the *circumstances.* **3** [in the plural] Condition or situation with respect to wealth; as, to be in easy *circumstances.* **4** The formality accompanying an event; ceremony; as, with pomp and *circumstance.* **5** A detail, incident, or fact in a chain of events; as, to tell every *circumstance* of what happened.

cir·cum·stan·tial \ˌsərk-m-'stanch-l\ *adj.* **1** Consisting of or relating to circumstances; dependent on circumstances; as, *circumstantial* evidence. **2** Relating to a matter but not essential to it; incidental. **3** Containing full details; as, a *circumstantial* account of what happened.

cir·cum·vent \ˌsərk-m-'vent\ *v.* To gain an advantage over by trickery or deception. — **cir·cum·ven·tion** \-'vench-n\ *n.*

cir·cus \'sərk-əs\ *n.; pl.* **cir·cus·es.** [From Latin, meaning literally "circle", "ring".] **1** In ancient Rome, a level oblong space with tiers of seats on three sides and a course for chariot races, games, and public shows. **2** An enclosure, often covered by a tent, used for entertaining spectators by a variety of exhibitions including riding, acrobatic feats, wild animal displays, and the performances of jugglers and clowns. **3** The exhibition or performances given in such an enclosure. **4** The performers and equipment of such an exhibition.

cir·rus \'sir-əs\ *n.; pl.* **cir·ri** \-ˌī\. A white filmy cloud, usually formed at altitudes of 20,000 to 40,000 feet, generally consisting of ice crystals.

cis·tern \'sist-rn\ *n.* An artificial reservoir or tank, often underground, for storing water, especially rain water.

cit·a·del \'sit-əd-l, -ə-ˌdel\ *n.* A fortress, especially one that overlooks a city.

ci·ta·tion \sī-'tāsh-n\ *n.* **1** An official order to a person to appear, as before a court. **2** The act of citing or quoting a passage exactly as it was written or spoken. **3** The words or the passage quoted. **4** Mention, especially of a soldier's name in a military report; as, to receive a *citation* for bravery.

cite \'sīt\ *v.;* **cit·ed**; **cit·ing.** **1** To summon officially to appear, as before a court. **2** To quote a passage from a book or article; as, to *cite* the Bible. **3** To bring forward as proof or as an example; as, to *cite* facts; to *cite* an instance from one's own experience. **4** In a military organization, to mention in orders or dispatches.

cit·i·zen \'sit-əz-n, -əs-n\ *n.* **1** A person who, by birth or by naturalization, owes allegiance to a government and is entitled to protection by it. **2** An inhabitant of a city or town. **3** A civilian, as opposed to a soldier or a policeman.

cit·i·zen·ry \'sit-əz-n-rē, -əs-\ *n.* The whole body of citizens.

cit·i·zen·ship \'sit-əz-n-ˌship, -əs-\ *n.* The state of being a citizen; possession of the rights and privileges of a citizen.

cit·ric acid \'si-trik\. A pleasantly sour-tasting substance extracted from lemons, currants, and other fruits and used in making artificial lemonade.

cit·ron \'si-trən\ *n.* **1** The oval, lemonlike fruit of an Asiatic citrus tree. **2** The preserved rind of this fruit, used in fruitcake and puddings.

cit·ron·el·la \ˌsi-trə-'nel-ə\ *n.* A fragrant grass of

southern Asia which yields an oil (**citronella oil**) used in perfumes and for driving away insects.

cit·rus \'si-trəs\ *adj.* Of or relating to a group of trees or shrubs, often thorny, that bear such fruits as the citron, orange, lemon, lime, and grapefruit.

city \'sit-ē\ *n.; pl.* **cit·ies.** **1** A large or important town, especially one that manages its own affairs. **2** In the United States, a legal body holding a charter from the state in which it is located and serving as a unit of local government. **3** The inhabitants of a city, considered as a group.

city-state \'sit-ē-ˌstāt, -'stāt\ *n.* An independent city governing itself and the territory surrounding it, as ancient Athens.

civ·et \'siv-ət\ *n.* A strong-smelling yellowish substance obtained from a catlike wild animal of Africa (**civet cat**) and used in making perfume.

civ·ic \'siv-ik\ *adj.* Of or relating to a citizen, a city, or citizenship; as, *civic* pride; *civic* duty.

civ·ics \'siv-iks\ *n.* The study that deals with the rights and duties of citizens.

civ·il \'siv-l\ *adj.* **1** Of or relating to citizens; as, *civil* liberties. **2** Of or relating to the state as an organized political body; as, *civil* institutions; *civil* strife. **3** Of or relating to ordinary or civic affairs, as distinguished from military or church affairs; as, a *civil* marriage. **4** Courteous; polite; as, to give a *civil* answer. **5** Relating to legal proceedings in connection with private, not public or political, rights and obligations; as, a *civil* suit; a *civil*, not a criminal case.

civil defense. Protective measures and emergency relief activities carried on by civilians under civilian authority in order to reduce casualties and property damage and to maintain essential services in case of enemy attack.

civil engineering. The designing and construction of public works, such as roads, harbors, and bridges. — **civil engineer**.

ci·vil·ian \sə-'vil-yən\ *n.* A person not serving in the armed forces. — *adj.* Of or relating to civilians; as, *civilian* clothes.

ci·vil·i·ty \sə-'vil-ət-ē\ *n.; pl.* **ci·vil·i·ties.** **1** Politeness; courtesy. **2** A polite act or expression.

civ·i·li·za·tion \ˌsiv-l-ə-'zāsh-n\ *n.* **1** The process of civilizing or of becoming civilized; advancement in social culture. **2** An advanced or relatively advanced stage in social development, as in art, science, and government. **3** The special culture of a people or a period; as, Greek *civilization;* 18th century *civilization.*

civ·i·lize \'siv-l-ˌīz\ *v.;* **civ·i·lized; civ·i·liz·ing.** To bring up from a savage or barbarous state to a more advanced form of social culture; to instruct in the customs of civilization; to educate; to refine.

civ·il·ly \'siv-l-(l)ē\ *adv.* In a civil manner; especially, politely; as, to answer *civilly.*

civil rights. The nonpolitical rights of a citizen; especially, the rights of personal liberty guaranteed to citizens of the United States by the 13th and 14th amendments to the Constitution and by certain other bills passed by Congress.

civil service. All of the branches of the public service of a country that are not military, naval, legislative, or judicial.

civil war. A war between different sections or parties of the same nation.

clack \'klak\ *n.* **1** Chatter; prattle; as, the *clack* of voices. **2** A sharp sudden sound made by the striking together of objects; as, the *clack* of a typewriter. — *v.* **1** To make a clack. **2** To chatter.

clad. A past tense and past part. of *clothe.*

claim \'klām\ *v.* **1** To ask for something as rightfully belonging to oneself; as, to *claim* an inheritance; to *claim* a lost umbrella. **2** To state as a right or a fact that ought to be acknowledged by others; as, to *claim* the championship. **3** To require; to call for; to demand. This matter *claims* our attention. — *n.* **1** A demand for something that is due or supposed to be due. The man put in a *claim* for the reward. **2** A right or title to a thing; as, to have a *claim* to an inheritance. **3** A thing that is claimed; especially, an area claimed and marked out by a settler or prospector.

claim·ant \'klā-mənt\ *n.* A person who claims or asserts his right to something.

clam \'klam\ *n.* A shellfish somewhat like an oyster, with a soft body and a hinged double shell, especially one whose flesh is edible. — *v.;* **clammed; clam·ming.** To dig or to gather clams.

clam·bake \'klam-ˌbāk\ *n.* **1** The baking or steaming of clams, especially on heated stones with a covering of seaweed, often with other food. **2** A gathering at which clams are thus cooked.

clam·ber \'klam-br\ *v.* To climb with difficulty, as by crawling up or over; as, to *clamber* over steep rocks.

clam·my \'klam-ē\ *adj.;* **clam·mi·er; clam·mi·est.** Damp, soft, and sticky and usually cool.

clam·or \'klam-r\ *n.* **1** A great outcry or loud shouting. **2** A continued violent expression of discontent. **3** Any loud and continued noise, as of animals or a storm. — *v.;* **clam·ored; clam·or·ing** \-r(-)ing\. **1** To make a clamor. **2** To make a loud, noisy demand; as, to *clamor* for higher wages.

clam·or·ous \'klam-r(-)əs\ *adj.* Full of clamor; noisy; as, a *clamorous* mob. — **clam·or·ous·ly,** *adv.*

clamp \'klamp\ *n.* Any of various devices that hold things securely together. — *v.* **1** To fasten with a clamp. **2** To place in a clamp.

clamp

clan \'klan\ *n.* **1** A group made up of households whose heads claim descent from a common ancestor. **2** Any group of persons united by some common interest; as, the whole *clan* of actors.

clan·des·tine \klan-'des-tən\ *adj.* Managed with planned secrecy; underhand; as, a *clandestine* meeting. — **clan·des·tine·ly,** *adv.*

clang \'klang\ *n.* A loud, ringing sound, like that made by pieces of metal striking each other; as, the *clang* of a fire alarm. — *v.* To make, or to cause to make, a clang; as, *clanging* bells.

clang·or \'klang-r, 'klang-gr\ *n.* A clang. — **clang·or·ous** \-əs\ *adj.*

clank \'klangk\ *n.* A sharp, short, ringing sound, duller than a clang. — *v.* To sound or to move with a clank; as, a *clanking* chain.

clan·nish \'klan-ish\ *adj.* Of or belonging to a clan; inclined to associate only with one's clique or select group. — **clan·nish·ly**, *adv.*

clans·man \'klanz-mən\ *n.; pl.* **clans·men** \-mən\. A member of a clan.

clap \'klap\ *v.;* **clapped** or **clapt**; **clap·ping. 1** To strike or to bring together so as to make a noise; to bang; to slam; as, to *clap* a door shut. **2** To strike with the open hand; as, to *clap* a friend on the shoulder. **3** To strike the hands together in applause; to applaud. **4** To put or place vigorously; as, to *clap* a hat on one's head; to *clap* a man into jail. — *n.* **1** A loud noisy crash such as is made by the striking together of two hard surfaces; as, a *clap* of thunder. **2** A hard slap; as, a *clap* on the shoulder. **3** The sound made by clapping the hands together; applause.

clap·board \'klab-rd, -ˌōrd, -ˌȯrd; 'klap-ˌbōrd, -ˌbȯrd\ *n.* A narrow board, thicker at one edge than at the other, used, usually horizontally, for covering the outside of wooden buildings. — *v.* To cover with clapboards.

clap·per \'klap-r\ *n.* **1** The tongue of a bell. **2** [usually in the plural] Pieces of wood held between the fingers and clapped in rhythm with music or song. **3** A person who claps or applauds.

clar·et \'klar-ət\ *n.* **1** A red wine. **2** Also **claret red.** A dark, purplish red.

clar·i·fi·ca·tion \ˌklar-ə-fə-'kāsh-n\ *n.* **1** The act or process of clarifying. **2** An explanation intended to clear up or prevent misunderstanding.

clar·i·fy \'klar-ə-ˌfī\ *v.;* **clar·i·fied** \-ˌfīd\; **clar·i·fy·ing. 1** To make or to become pure or clear; as, to *clarify* a liquid. **2** To make or become more readily understandable; as, to *clarify* one's meaning.

clar·i·net \ˌklar-ə-'net, 'klar-ə-nət\ *n.* A musical instrument in the form of a long tube, typically of wood or plastics, bell-shaped at one end and with holes and keys along its side.

clarinet

clar·i·net·ist or **clar·i·net·tist** \ˌklar-ə-'net-əst\ *n.* A person who plays a clarinet.

clar·i·on \'klar-ē-ən\ *n.* A trumpet having very clear and shrill tones. — *adj.* Loud and clear; as, a *clarion* call to action.

clar·i·ty \'klar-ət-ē\ *n.* Clearness.

clash \'klash\ *n.* **1** A loud, sharp, usually metallic sound; as, the *clash* of swords and rattle of guns. **2** Collision or conflict; as, a *clash* between two armies; a *clash* of opinion. — *v.* **1** To make a clash; as, *clashing* cymbals. **2** To collide; to come into conflict. The rebels *clashed* with the police. **3** To be sharply out of harmony; to produce a jarring effect. Some colors *clash* when placed side by side.

clasp \'klasp\ *n.* **1** Any of a number of devices for holding together two objects or two parts of anything; as, a belt *clasp;* the *clasp* of a necklace. **2** An embrace. **3** A grasp with the hand. — *v.;* **clasped** or **claspt**; **clasp·ing. 1** To fasten with a clasp. **2** To embrace. **3** To grasp with or in the hand.

clasp knife. A jackknife with a blade folding into the handle; especially, one having a clasp for holding the blade open.

class \'klas\ *n.* **1** A group of persons or things ranked together as of the same general kind or position. **2** A group or rank of society; as, the poorer *classes.* **3** A group of pupils meeting regularly for study or instruction; as, a *class* in arithmetic. **4** A meeting of such a body of students. **5** A body of students who are due to graduate at the same time; as, the *class* of 1960. **6** A grouping of goods or services based on grade or quality; as, first-*class* mail; to travel by second *class.* **7** In botany and zoology, a group of plants or animals ranking above an order and below a phylum. — *v.* To place in a class; to classify.

clas·sic \'klas-ik\ *adj.* **1** Of or relating to the highest class or rank; serving as a standard of excellence for its own kind; as, a *classic* example of true courage. **2** Of or relating to the ancient Greeks and Romans or their culture; classical. — *n.* **1** A work, especially of literature or art, considered to be of the highest degree of excellence; as, one of the *classics* of English literature. **2** The author or creator of such a work. **3** [in the plural] The noted works and authors of Greek and Latin literature. **4** A sporting event of great importance, usually having a long history; as, a football *classic.*

clas·si·cal \'klas-ik-l\ *adj.* **1** Of the highest class or degree of excellence; standard; classic. **2** Of or relating to the classics of literature or art. **3** Of or relating to the ancient Greek and Roman classics; as, *classical* studies; a fine *classical* scholar. **4** Concerned with a general study of the arts and sciences; not specializing in technical studies; as, a *classical* high school. **5** Composed in accordance with a long-established musical form; appealing to a highly developed musical taste.

clas·si·cal·ly \'klas-ik-l(-)ē\ *adv.* In a classic or classical manner.

clas·si·fi·ca·tion \ˌklas-ə-fə-'kāsh-n\ *n.* **1** The act of classifying, or arranging in classes. **2** Orderly or systematic arrangement in classes, as of animals and plants by natural relationships into phyla, classes, orders, families, genera, species, and varieties.

clas·si·fy \'klas-ə-ˌfī\ *v.;* **clas·si·fied** \-ˌfīd\; **clas·si·fy·ing.** To group or arrange persons or things in classes; as, to *classify* books according to their subjects.

class·mate \'klas-ˌmāt\ *n.* A person in the same class with another in school or college.

class·room \'klas-ˌrüm, -ˌrům\ *n.* A room in a school or college in which classes meet.

clat·ter \'klat-r\ *n.* **1** A confused rattling noise made by hard bodies striking together; as, the *clatter* of pots and pans. **2** Commotion; disturbance. — *v.* To make a clatter; to move with a clatter; as, to *clatter* down the stairs.

clause \'klȯz\ *n.* **1** A separate, distinct part of a written or printed article or document; as, a *clause* in a will. **2** A group of words having its own subject and predicate but forming only part of a compound or complex sentence, as "when it rained" or "they went inside" in the sentence "When it rained, they went inside."

clav·i·chord \'klav-ə-ˌkȯrd\ *n.* A stringed instrument with a keyboard, in use before the piano.

clav·i·cle \'klav-ik-l\ *n.* A bone of the shoulder, joined to the breastbone and the shoulder blade; the collarbone.

claw \'klȯ\ *n.* **1** A sharp nail on the finger or toe of an animal, especially a nail that is slender and curved, as that of a cat or bird. **2** One of the pincerlike growths on the end of certain limbs of some animals, such as crabs or lobsters. **3** Anything that resembles a claw in shape or use, as the forked end of a type of hammer (**claw hammer**). — *v.* To scratch, dig, or tear with claws.

clay \'klā\ *n.* **1** An earthy material that is sticky and easily molded when wet, and hard and brittle when baked. **2** Earth, especially when moist; mud; mire.

clay·ey \'klā-ē\ *adj.;* **clay·i·er**; **clay·i·est.** Like clay or containing much clay; as, a *clayey* soil.

clean \'klēn\ *adj.* **1** Free from dirt; not soiled; as, *clean* clothes. **2** Morally pure; as, a *clean* heart. **3** Leaving no obstructions; complete; as, a *clean* sweep. **4** Shapely; trim; as, a ship with *clean* lines. **5** Done skillfully; smart; as, a *clean* hit. **6** Cleanly in habits. Cats are *clean* animals. — *adv.* Skillfully; fully; completely. The horse jumped *clean* over the fence. — *v.* **1** To make clean; to purify; to cleanse; as, to *clean* one's shoes. **2** To do the work of making something clean; as, to *clean* up before dinner.

clean-cut \'klēn-'kət\ *adj.* **1** Cut so that the surface or edge is smooth and even. **2** Sharply defined or outlined; well-formed; as, *clean-cut* features. **3** Giving an effect of wholesomeness; as, a *clean-cut* youth.

clean·er \'klēn-r\ *n.* **1** A person who cleans things; as, a window *cleaner.* **2** A device for cleaning; as, a vacuum *cleaner.* **3** A preparation for use in cleaning.

clean·li·ness \'klen-lē-nəs\ *n.* The condition of being clean; the habit of keeping clean.

clean·ly \'klen-lē\ *adj.;* **clean·li·er**; **clean·li·est.** **1** Careful to keep clean; as, a *cleanly* animal. **2** Habitually kept clean; as, *cleanly* surroundings.

clean·ly \'klēn-lē\ *adv.* In a clean manner; as, to hit a ball *cleanly.*

cleanse \'klenz\ *v.;* **cleansed**; **cleans·ing.** To make clean; to clean.

cleans·er \'klenz-r\ *n.* A cleaner; especially, a preparation used for cleaning.

clear \'klir\ *adj.* **1** Bright; light; not stormy; as, *clear* sunlight; *clear* weather. **2** Clean; not dirty; as, *clear* water. **3** Pure in color; as, a *clear* blue. **4** Fresh and blooming; as, a *clear* complexion. **5** Easily heard; distinct; as, a *clear* voice. **6** Plain; not confusing; as, a *clear* statement. **7** Able to see or to understand distinctly; keen; as, *clear* vision. **8** Free from anything that covers or hides; open; as, a *clear* view. **9** Free from doubt; sure. The speaker was very *clear* on each point he made. **10** Free from guilt; innocent; as, to be *clear* of any misbehavior. **11** Without debt; as, property that is free and *clear.* **12** Free from charges or deductions; as, *clear* profit. — *adv.* **1** In a clear manner. **2** Wholly; quite; as, to cut a branch *clear* off. — *v.* **1** To make clear; to free from dirt, cloudiness, or obstruction. **2** To become clear. The sky is *clearing.* **3** To make clear mentally; to enlighten; as, to *clear* a person up on certain points. **4** To free, as from guilt or blame; as, to be *cleared* of any connection with a crime. **5** To open, as for passage, action, or use; as, to *clear* land. **6** To disentangle; as, to *clear* a cable. **7** To take and move away; as, to *clear* snow from the walk. **8** To leap; to pass by, over, or around; as, to *clear* a hedge. **9** To make as a profit after all deductions; as, to *clear* 10 dollars. **10** In banking, to pass a check or claim through a clearinghouse; to get the cash for. **11** To conform to port regulations regarding a ship, as by paying duties, in order to obtain permission to leave port or to discharge cargo. — *n.* A clear space. — **in the clear.** Free from guilt or suspicion; free from obligation, as debt; as, to be *in the clear* with the police. — **clear·ly**, *adv.*

clear·ance \'klir-ən(t)s\ *n.* **1** The act or process of clearing. **2** The distance by which one object avoids hitting or touching another, or the clear space between them. **3** In banking, passage of checks and claims through a clearinghouse.

clear-cut \'klir-'kət\ *adj.* Having a sharp, distinct outline; sharply defined; as, a *clear-cut* argument.

clear·ing \'klir-ing\ *n.* **1** A making or a becoming clear; as, rain followed by *clearing.* **2** A tract of land cleared of wood.

clear·ing·house \'klir-ing-ˌhau̇s\ *n.; pl.* **clear·ing·hous·es** \-ˌhau̇-zəz\. In banking, an institution established and maintained by banks for making an exchange of checks and claims held by each bank against other banks.

cleat \'klēt\ *n.* **1** A wedge-shaped piece fastened to something and used as a support or check, as for a rope on the spar of a ship. **2** A wooden or metal device used to fasten a rope. **3** A strip fastened on or across something to give strength, to provide a grip, or to prevent slipping; as, the *cleats* on football shoes. — *v.* To fasten by a cleat; to fasten to a cleat.

cleat, 2

cleav·age \'klē-vij\ *n.* **1** A cleaving; a splitting.

2 In biology, the dividing of cells, especially any of the series of divisions by which the egg becomes the embryo composed of many cells.

cleave \'klēv\ *v.;* **cleaved; cleav·ing.** To cling to a person or thing closely; to stick.

cleave \'klēv\ *v.;* **cleft** \'kleft\ or **cleaved** \'klēvd\ or **clove** \'klōv\; **cleft** or **cleaved** or **clo·ven** \'klōv-n\; **cleav·ing.** To separate or pierce by force, as with a cutting blow; to split; to cut; as, to *cleave* a block of wood.

cleav·er \'klēv-r\ *n.* A person or a thing that cleaves; especially, a heavy knife used by butchers for cutting up meat.

meat cleaver

clef \'klef\ *n.* A sign placed on the staff in writing music, to show what pitch is represented by each line and each space.

cleft \'kleft\. A past tense and past part. of *cleave* (to cut). — *adj.* **1** Split; divided; as, a *cleft* stick. **2** Seeming to be split or divided; as, a *cleft* chin.

cleft \'kleft\ *n.* **1** A space or opening made by splitting or cracking; a crevice; as, a *cleft* in the rock. **2** Any opening like a crack or a hollow; as, a *cleft* in one's chin.

clem·a·tis \'klem-ət-əs, klə-'mat-əs\ *n.* A bush or a vine with pointed leaves and sweet-smelling flowers, often in clusters.

clem·en·cy \'klem-ən-sē\ *n.* **1** Mercy; kindness. **2** Mildness, as of the weather. — For synonyms see *mercy.*

clem·ent \'klem-ənt\ *adj.* **1** Inclined to be merciful; lenient; as, a *clement* judge. **2** Mild; pleasant — used of weather.

clench \'klench\ *v.* **1** To close tightly or set firmly together; as, to *clench* one's fist or one's jaws. **2** To grasp firmly; as, to *clench* a club. **3** To clinch; as, to *clench* an argument. — *n.* A clenching.

cler·gy \'klər-jē\ *n.* The body of religious officials especially prepared to conduct religious services, as priests, ministers, and rabbis.

cler·gy·man \'klər-jē-mən, -jə-\ *n.; pl.* **cler·gy·men** \-mən\. A member of the clergy.

cler·ic \'kler-ik\ *n.* A clergyman.

cler·i·cal \'kler-ik-l\ *adj.* **1** Of or relating to the clergy or a clergyman. **2** Of or relating to a clerk, or office worker; as, the *clerical* force.

clerk \'klərk\ *n.* **1** A person employed to keep records or accounts, sometimes having the authority to transact important business for an employer; as, a bank *clerk;* a town *clerk.* **2** A salesman or saleswoman in a store. — *v.* To act or work as a clerk.

clev·er \'klev-r\ *adj.* **1** Quick in learning; as, a *clever* child; to be *clever* at one's lessons. **2** Skillful; expert; as, a *clever* workman. **3** Showing skill; as, a *clever* trick. — **clev·er·ly,** *adv.*

clew or **clue** \'klü\ *n.* **1** A ball of thread, yarn, or cord. **2** Usually *clue.* Anything that guides one in solving something difficult or perplexing. Fingerprints were a *clue* in solving the murder. **3** A metal loop attached to the lower corner of a sail to hold ropes for hauling the sail up or down. — *v.* To haul a sail up or down by ropes through the clews.

cli·ché \(')klē-'shā, 'klē-ˌshā\ *n.* A phrase that has been used so many times that it has become trite or dulled in meaning.

click \'klik\ *n.* A slight sharp noise, like the sound made by latching a door. — *v.* To make or to cause something to make a click; as, to *click* one's tongue; to *click* the heels together.

cli·ent \'klī-ənt\ *n.* **1** A person who consults or employs the services of a professional man, as a lawyer or a doctor. **2** A customer of any business or store.

cli·en·tele \ˌklī-ən-'tel, ˌklē-\ *n.* **1** A group or body of clients. **2** A group of patrons or customers.

cliff \'klif\ *n.* A high steep face of rock.

cli·mac·tic \klī-'mak-tik\ *adj.* Of or relating to a climax.

cli·mate \'klī-mət\ *n.* The average weather conditions of a particular place or region over a period of years. — **cli·mat·ic** \klī-'mat-ik\ *adj.*

cli·ma·tol·o·gy \ˌklī-mə-'täl-ə-jē\ *n.* The science that deals with climates. — **cli·ma·tol·o·gist** \-jəst\ *n.*

cli·max \'klī-ˌmaks\ *n.* **1** A series of ideas or statements so arranged that they increase in force and power from the first to the last. **2** The highest or most forceful one in such a series. **3** The highest point; the culmination. The storm had reached its *climax.*

climb \'klīm\ *v.* **1** To go up or down by grasping or clinging with hands and feet; as, to *climb* a flagpole; to *climb* down a ladder. **2** To rise gradually to a higher point; as, smoke *climbing* in the still air; to *climb* from poverty to wealth. **3** To slope upward, as a road. — *n.* **1** The act of climbing. The *climb* up the mountain took several hours. **2** A place where climbing is necessary; as, a steep *climb.* — For synonyms see *ascend.*

clime \'klīm\ *n.* Climate; a region with reference to its climate; as, to travel to warmer *climes.*

clinch \'klinch\ *v.* **1** To fasten securely, as by driving a nail through boards and bending its point over. **2** To confirm; to establish as certain or true. The testimony of the last witness *clinched* the case. **3** To seize or grasp one another, as in boxing; to grapple. — *n.* **1** A clinching, as of a nail. **2** The clinched part of a nail or bolt. **3** A position in which two boxers hold each other around the body with one or both arms.

clinch·er \'klinch-r\ *n.* **1** One that clinches, as a tool for clinching nails. **2** A decisive statement or argument.

cling \'kling\ *v.;* **clung** \'kləng\; **cling·ing. 1** To stick together in a stiff mass, as liquid in freezing. **2** To hold fast or stick closely to a surface, as ivy to a wall or wet clothing to the body. **3** To hold fast by grasping or twining around; as, to *cling* to the top of a ladder; a man in the water *clinging* to a life preserver. **4** To remain close; to stay attached to; as, to *cling* to one's family; to *cling* to an idea.

cling·stone \'kling-ˌstōn\ *n.* A peach or plum having a stone that clings to the flesh.

clin·ic \'klin-ik\ *n.* **1** The instruction of a class of medical students by treatment of patients in their presence. **2** An institution, usually connected with a hospital or medical school, for treatment of outpatients. **3** An organization, often connected with a school or with a social settlement, in which special problems are studied by concrete examples and expert advice or treatment is given.

clin·i·cal \'klin-ik-l\ *adj.* **1** Of or relating to a clinic. **2** Concerned with investigation of disease in the living patient by observation. — **clin·i·cal·ly** \-l(-)ē\ *adv.*

clinical thermometer. A thermometer especially designed for measuring body temperature.

clink \'klingk\ *n.* A slight tinkling sound, as of glasses struck together. — *v.* To make or to cause to make a clink.

clink·er \'klingk-r\ *n.* A mass of stony matter fused together by fire, as in a furnace from impurities in the coal.

clip \'klip\ *n.* A device for holding tightly together two things or two parts of a thing; especially, a clasp or holder for papers. — *v.;* **clipped** or **clipt**; **clip·ping.** To fasten with a clip.

paper clips

clip \'klip\ *v.;* **clipped** or **clipt**; **clip·ping. 1** To cut or snip off, as with shears or scissors; as, to *clip* a hedge; to *clip* an item from a newspaper. **2** To cut off or trim the hair or wool of; as, to *clip* a sheep; to have a dog *clipped.* **3** To strike with a sharp blow. **4** To make clippings. — *n.* **1** Something that is clipped off; especially, a sheep's fleece when sheared or a season's crop of wool. **2** A clipping or shearing. **3** A sharp blow. **4** A rapid rate of speed; as, moving along at a good *clip.*

clip·board \'klip-ˌbōrd, -ˌbȯrd\ *n.* A small writing board with a clip at the top for holding papers.

clip·per \'klip-r\ *n.* **1** One that clips. **2** [usually in the plural] A device used for clipping; as, hair *clippers;* wire *clippers.* **3** A fast sailing vessel with an overhanging bow, tall masts, and a large sail area.

clip·ping \'klip-ing\ *n.* **1** A cutting or shearing. **2** A piece clipped or cut out or off of something; as, a newspaper *clipping;* hedge *clippings.*

clipt. A past tense and past part. of *clip.*

clique \'klēk, 'klik\ *n.* A small and exclusive group or set of people; a coterie.

clo·a·ca \klō-'āk-ə\ *n.; pl.* **clo·a·cas** \-'āk-əz\ or **clo·a·cae** \-'ā-ˌsē\. **1** A sewer. **2** A water closet. **3** A cavity or chamber in the body of birds, reptiles, amphibians, and many fishes, into which the intestinal, urinary, and generative canals all discharge. — **clo·a·cal** \-'āk-l\ *adj.*

cloak \'klōk\ *n.* **1** A loose outer garment, usually longer than a cape. **2** Something that conceals or covers; as, under the *cloak* of darkness; a *cloak* of secrecy. — *v.* **1** To cover with a cloak. **2** To hide or conceal; as, to *cloak* one's anger under a smile.

cloak, 1

cloak·room \'klōk-ˌrüm, -ˌru̇m\ *n.* A room where coats and hats may be left for a time, as in a school.

clob·ber \'kläb-r\ *v.;* **clob·bered**; **clob·ber·ing** \-r(-)ing\. *Slang.* **1** To beat mercilessly; to pound. **2** To defeat overwhelmingly.

clock \'kläk\ *n.* **1** A device for measuring or telling the time, especially one not intended to be worn or carried about by a person. **2** A dial or other registering device attached to something, as a machine, to measure or record its performance. — *v.* To time a person or thing; to register with a mechanical recording device; as, to *clock* a swimmer.

clock \'kläk\ *n.* An ornamental design extending up the side of a stocking.

clock·wise \'kläk-ˌwīz\ *adv.* or *adj.* In the direction in which the hands of a clock turn; as, to go *clockwise;* a *clockwise* motion.

clock·work \'kläk-ˌwərk\ *n.* **1** The wheels and springs that make a clock go. **2** Similar machinery in other devices, as in mechanical toys. **3** Anything that is regular and precise in action.

clod \'kläd\ *n.* **1** A lump or mass, especially of earth or clay. **2** A dull or stupid fellow.

clod·hop·per \'kläd-ˌhäp-r\ *n.* **1** A plowman; any rustic person. **2** [in the plural] Heavy shoes such as are worn by plowmen.

clog \'kläg\ *n.* **1** A block or weight attached to a person or an animal to hinder motion. **2** Anything that hinders or restrains. **3** A wooden-soled shoe. **4** A leather shoe, usually with a heavy sole, for use in clog dancing. — *v.;* **clogged**; **clog·ging. 1** To hinder or restrain in any way. Traffic became *clogged* when the signals failed. **2** To prevent or obstruct passage through; to choke up; as, rain gutters *clogged* with leaves. Snow *clogged* the roads. **3** To perform a clog dance.

clog dance. A dance in which the performer wears clogs and beats out a clattering rhythm on the floor. — **clog dancing.**

clois·ter \'klȯist-r\ *n.* **1** A monastery or convent. **2** A covered passageway, usually arched and vaulted, along the walls of a court or a building. — *v.;* **clois·tered**; **clois·ter·ing** \-r(-)ing\. **1** To confine in or as if in a cloister; to seclude or shut away from the world; as, to lead a *cloistered* life. **2** To surround with a cloister; as, *cloistered* gardens.

close \'klōs\ *adj.;* **clos·er**; **clos·est. 1** Shut in with little space; confined; as, *close* quarters. **2** Stifling; as, a hot *close* day. **3** Stingy; as, to be *close* with one's money. **4** Near in time, place, or relationship; as, *close* neighbors; *close* relatives. **5** Careful;

accurate; as, a *close* observer. **6** Nearly equal or even; as, a *close* race. **7** Short; as, a *close* haircut. — *adv.* In a close position or manner.

close \'klōz\ *v.;* **closed**; **clos·ing. 1** To stop up; to fill up; to stop access to; as, to *close* a gap; to *close* a road. **2** To shut; as, to *close* one's eyes. A properly fitted door *closes* easily. **3** To bring or come to an end; to end; to complete; as, to *close* a meeting. **4** To come near; to engage at close quarters; to grapple; as, to *close* with the enemy. **5** To bring together; to unite; as, to *close* ranks. — **close down.** To stop or suspend, permanently or temporarily, as work in a factory; to shut completely. — **close in.** To come in upon from all sides; to come nearer; as, fog *closing in* from the sea. — **close out.** To get rid of, as a line of goods; to sell off. — *n.* Conclusion; end.

close \'klōs\ *n.* An enclosed place, as the land around a cathedral.

close call \'klōs\. A narrow escape.

closed \'klōzd\ *adj.* **1** Shut. **2** Ended. **3** Enclosed; as, a *closed* car.

closed season \'klōzd\ or **close season** \'klōs\. A period during which it is against the law to kill or catch certain game or fish; as, a *closed season* on deer.

closed shop. A business or industrial establishment in which the employer by agreement with a labor union hires only union members or, in some cases, workmen who apply for union membership before beginning work.

close-fist·ed \'klōs-'fis-təd\ *adj.* Stingy. — **close-fist·ed·ly,** *adv.*

close·ly \'klōs-lē\ *adv.* **1** In narrow space or under strict watch; as, a *closely* confined prisoner. **2** Tightly; compactly; as, a *closely* packed box. **3** With careful attention; as, to watch a magician *closely.* **4** Very nearly; almost completely; as, *closely* alike.

close·ness \'klōs-nəs\ *n.* The state of being close.

clos·et \'kläz-ət\ *n.* **1** A small private room. **2** A small room, or a recess in a room, usually with a door, for clothing or household supplies; as, a clothes *closet;* a linen *closet.* **3** A water closet. — *v.* **1** To shut up, as if in a closet. **2** To take into a private room for a private interview. The ambassador was *closeted* with the president for an hour.

close-up \'klō-ˌsəp\ *n.* **1** A picture taken with the camera at close range. **2** A close view or examination of something.

clo·sure \'klōzh-r\ *n.* **1** The action of closing or shutting. **2** Something that serves to close or fasten.

clot \'klät\ *n.* A mass or lump made by a liquid substance thickening and sticking together; as, a *clot* of blood; a *clot* of cream. — *v.;* **clot·ted**; **clot·ting.** To become, or thicken into, a clot.

cloth \'klȯth\ *n.; pl.* **cloths** \'klȯthz, 'klȯths\. **1** A woven or knitted fabric, especially one made of natural fiber, as cotton, wool, linen, silk, or of synthetic fiber alone or in combination with natural fiber. **2** A piece of such material used for a particular purpose; as, a polishing *cloth.* **3** The special clothing worn by members of a particular profession, especially the clergy. — **the cloth.** The clergy. — *adj.* Made of cloth.

clothe \'klōth\ *v.;* **clothed** \'klōthd\ or **clad** \'klad\; **cloth·ing** \'klō-thing\. **1** To put clothes on; to dress. **2** To provide clothing for; as, to feed and *clothe* a family. **3** To cover as if with a garment; as, hills *clothed* with snow; to *clothe* one's thoughts in suitable words.

clothes \'klō(th)z\ *n. pl.* **1** Coverings for the body; dress; apparel. **2** Coverings, as sheets and blankets, for a bed; bedclothes.

clothes·horse \'klō(th)z-ˌhȯrs\ *n.* A frame on which to hang clothes for drying or airing.

clothes·line \'klō(th)z-ˌlīn\ *n.* A rope or other line on which clothes can be hung for drying or airing.

clothes moth. Any of several small moths whose larvae eat woolen goods, furs, and feathers.

clothes·pin \'klō(th)z-ˌpin\ *n.* Any device, as a forked piece of wood or a small clamp, for holding clothes in place on a line.

clothespins

clothes pole. A stick used to support a clothesline.

clothes·press \'klō(th)z-ˌpres\ *n.* A chest, wardrobe, or closet in which to keep clothes.

clothes tree. A stand with hooks or pegs at the top, on which to hang clothes.

cloth·ier \'klōth-yər, -ē-ər\ *n.* **1** *Archaic.* A person who makes cloth. **2** A person who is in the business of selling clothes; as, a men's *clothier* and outfitter.

cloth·ing \'klō-thing\ *n.* **1** Garments in general; clothes. **2** A covering.

cloud \'klau̇d\ *n.* [From Old English *clud* meaning "rock", "hill", "lump", so named from the lumpy appearance of cumulus clouds.] **1** A visible mass of tiny bits of water or ice hanging in the air, usually high above the earth, ranging in color from white to almost black. **2** Any visible mass of small particles in the air; as, a *cloud* of dust; *clouds* of smoke. **3** A vast multitude massed together; as, a *cloud* of mosquitoes. **4** Anything that is suggestive of a dark or threatening appearance; as, *clouds* of war. **5** A dark vein or spot, as in marble. — *v.* **1** To make or to become cloudy. The sky *clouded* over. **2** To darken or to conceal as if by a cloud; as, eyes *clouded* by weariness.

cloud·burst \'klau̇d-ˌbərst\ *n.* A sudden heavy rainfall, as if from the bursting of a cloud.

cloud·less \'klau̇d-ləs\ *adj.* Without a cloud; clear; bright. — **cloud·less·ly,** *adv.*

cloud·let \'klau̇d-lət\ *n.* A little cloud.

cloudy \'klau̇d-ē\ *adj.;* **cloud·i·er**; **cloud·i·est. 1** Overspread with clouds; clouded; as, a *cloudy* sky. **2** Clouded by gloom, anxiety, or ill-temper. **3** Confused; as, a *cloudy* situation. **4** Having visible material in suspension; murky; as, a *cloudy* liquid. **5** Marked with veins or spots, as marble. — **cloud·i·ly** \'klaud-l-ē\ *adv.*

clout \'klaut\ *n.* **1** *Archaic and dial.* A cloth; a rag. **2** A blow, as with the hand; a hard hit. — *v.* To hit; to strike; as, to *clout* a ball over the fence.

clove \'klōv\ *n.* The dried flower bud of a tropical myrtle tree, used as a spice and yielding an oil used in perfumery and medicine.

clove. A past tense of *cleave.*

clo·ven \'klōv-n\. A past part. of *cleave.* — *adj.* Split; divided; as, a *cloven* hoof.

clo·ven-foot·ed \'klōv-n-'fut-əd\ *adj.* Having the foot divided into two or more parts, as the ox.

clo·ven-hoofed \'klōv-n-'hu̇ft, -'hüft\ *adj.* Cloven-footed.

clo·ver \'klōv-r\ *n.* A low-growing plant of the pea family with leaves consisting of three leaflets and with dense rounded flower heads of red, white, yellow, or purple.

clover

clo·ver-leaf \'klōv-r-,lēf\ *n.* A road plan having a resemblance to a four-leaf clover, for passing one highway over another and routing traffic for turns by way of connecting turnoffs, each branching only to the right and leading around to enter the other highway from the right, thus merging traffic without left-hand turns or direct crossings.

clown \'klaun\ *n.* **1** A person who amuses others by tricks and jokes, especially one who makes this his business or profession. **2** A rude, ill-bred fellow. — *v.* To act like a clown.

clown·ish \'klaun-ish\ *adj.* Like or characteristic of a clown. — **clown·ish·ly**, *adv.*

cloy \'klȯi\ *v.* To become distasteful, as food, through overabundance or excessive sweetness or richness.

club \'kləb\ *n.* **1** A heavy wooden stick, usually thicker at one end, used as a weapon. **2** The stick, bat, or mallet used in striking a ball in various games; as, a golf *club.* **3** A playing card belonging to the suit (**clubs**) marked with black figures resembling clover leaves. **4** A group of people associated for a common purpose; as, an athletic *club;* a social *club.* **5** The rooms or building used by such a group. — *v.;* **clubbed**; **club·bing. 1** To beat with a club or as if with a club. **2** To unite for some common purpose; as, to *club* together to buy a boat.

club·foot \'kləb-,fut\ *n.* **1** *pl.* **club·feet** \-,fēt\. A short, misshapen foot. **2** The deformity, usually present from birth, shown by such a foot. — **club-foot·ed** \'kləb-'fut-əd\ *adj.*

club moss. Any of a number of low, often trailing evergreen plants, as the ground pine, having branching stems covered with small mosslike leaves and reproducing by spores that are usually formed within club-shaped cones.

cluck \'klək\ *n.* The call of a hen to her chickens, or a sound like this. — *v.* To make a cluck; to call together with a cluck.

clue. Variant of *clew.*

clump \'kləmp\ *n.* **1** An unshaped mass, as of wood or earth; a lump. **2** A cluster; a group, as of trees or bushes. **3** A heavy tramping sound. — *v.* **1** To tread clumsily and noisily; as, to *clump* down the stairs. **2** To arrange in a clump or cluster.

clum·sy \'kləm-zē\ *adj.;* **clum·si·er**; **clum·si·est. 1** Lacking skill or grace; awkward; as, *clumsy* fingers; a *clumsy* dancer. **2** Badly shaped, made, or done; as, a *clumsy* drawing. — **clum·si·ly** \'kləmz-l-ē\ *adv.*

clung. Past tense and past part. of *cling.*

clus·ter \'kləst-r\ *n.* A number of things of the same kind, or of similar kinds, growing, collected, or lying together; as, a *cluster* of houses; flower *clusters.* — *v.;* **clus·tered**; **clus·ter·ing** \-r(-)ing\. To grow, gather, or unite in a cluster or clusters.

clutch \'kləch\ *v.* **1** To grip with the hands or with the claws; to grasp. **2** To reach out as if to seize; to snatch; as, to *clutch* at a swinging rope. — *n.* **1** A grasp or grip, as with fingers or claws; as, a mouse in the *clutches* of a cat. **2** Any device for gripping an object; especially, a coupling for connecting two working parts in machinery, permitting one to be thrown into or out of gear with the other by moving a lever. **3** A critical moment; a pinch; as, a pitcher who can be depended on in the *clutch.*

clut·ter \'klət-r\ *v.;* **clut·tered**; **clut·ter·ing** \-r-ing\. To throw into disorder; to disarrange; as, to *clutter* up a room. — *n.* A confused collection of things; disorder.

Co. Abbreviation for: **1** *Company.* **2** *County.*

co-. A prefix that can mean: **1** Together, with others, jointly, as in *co-operate* or *coexist.* **2** Joint, in common, as in *coeducation* or *coheir.* **3** Fellow, associate, as in *coauthor* or *coadjutor.* **4** To the same degree or extent, in the same amount, as in *coextensive* or *coequal.*

☞ Words beginning with the prefix *co* followed by *op* or *or* may be written with a hyphen between the o's, as one unbroken word, or as one unbroken word with a diaresis over the second *o.* Thus: *co-operate, cooperate,* or *coöperate.*

coach \'kōch\ *n.* **1** A large, four-wheeled, horse-drawn carriage, with a raised seat outside in front for the driver. **2** A railroad passenger car, as distinguished from a sleeping car. **3** A closed two-door automobile for four or five passengers. **4** A teacher who tutors students, especially for examinations. **5** An instructor in athletics, debating, or dramatics. — *v.* **1** To prepare a person for an examination; as, to be *coached* in arithmetic. **2** In baseball, to direct the movements of a player, especially a base runner. **3** To teach, train, and direct a group of persons in athletics, debating, or dramatics; as, to *coach* a football team.

coach·man \'kōch-mən\ *n.;* *pl.* **coach·men** \-mən\. A man whose business is driving a coach or carriage.

co·ad·ju·tor \ˌkō-ə-ˈjüt-r, kō-ˈaj-ət-r\ *n.* An assistant; especially, a bishop who assists the bishop in charge of a diocese.

co·ag·u·late \kō-ˈag-yə-ˌlāt\ *v.;* **co·ag·u·lat·ed; co·ag·u·lat·ing.** To gather into a thickened, compact mass; to clot. — **co·ag·u·la·tion** \kō-ˌag-yə-ˈlāsh-n\ *n.*

coal \ˈkōl\ *n.* **1** A piece of glowing or charred wood; an ember. **2** A black, solid mineral that is formed by the partial decay of vegetable matter under pressure within the earth and is mined for use as a fuel. — *v.* **1** To take on a supply of coal, as a ship. **2** To supply with coal.

co·a·lesce \ˌkō-ə-ˈles\ *v.;* **co·a·lesced; co·a·lesc·ing.** **1** To grow together; to unite by growth into one body. The ends of the broken bones *coalesced.* **2** To unite into one mass or body. The gases *coalesced.* **3** To come together into one community or body. The two political parties *coalesced.*

coal gas. Gas from coal; especially, gas made by distilling bituminous coal, as used for heating.

co·a·li·tion \ˌkō-ə-ˈlish-n\ *n.* A union; especially, a temporary union of persons, parties, or countries for a common purpose.

coal oil. Petroleum, or oil refined from it; especially, kerosene.

coal tar. Tar obtained by distilling bituminous coal and used in making dyes and explosives.

coarse \ˈkōrs, ˈkȯrs\ *adj.;* **coars·er; coars·est.** **1** Of poor quality or appearance; common; unrefined, as metal. **2** Made up of large parts or particles; not fine; as, *coarse* bread; *coarse* sand. **3** Harsh; rough; not delicate or dainty; as, *coarse* surroundings; *coarse* fare. **4** Rude; vulgar; unpolished; as, *coarse* manners; *coarse* language. — **coarse·ly,** *adv.*

coars·en \ˈkōrs-n, ˈkȯrs-n\ *v.;* **coars·ened; coars·en·ing** \-n(-)ing\. To make or become coarse.

coast \ˈkōst\ *n.* **1** The seashore or the land near it. **2** A slope suited to sliding downhill, as on a sled. **3** A slide down such a slope. — *v.* **1** To steam or sail along a coast; to follow the coast of. **2** To slide over snow or ice, as on a sled. **3** To ride or glide without applying power, as on a bicycle when not pedaling.

coast·al \ˈkōst-l\ *adj.* Having to do with a coast; on, near, or along a coast; as, *coastal* trade.

coast·er \ˈkōst-r\ *n.* **1** One that coasts; especially, a ship that trades from port to port along a coast. **2** A round low tray, often on wheels. **3** A shallow container or a plate or mat to protect a surface, especially of a table. **4** A sled used in coasting.

coast guard. **1** Any force of men who guard or patrol a coast. **2** A member of such a force.

coast·line \ˈkōst-ˌlīn\ *n.* Also **coast line.** The outline or shape of a coast.

coast·wise \ˈkōst-ˌwīz\ or **coast·ways** \ˈkōst-ˌwāz\ *adv.* or *adj.* By way of or along the coast; as, *coastwise* shipping.

coat \ˈkōt\ *n.* **1** An outer garment fitting the upper part of a person's body. **2** The fur, skin, wool, hair, or feathers of an animal, thought of as like an outer garment. **3** A layer of anything that covers something else; as, a *coat* of paint. — *v.* To cover with a coat; as, sidewalks *coated* with ice; to *coat* a cake with frosting.

co·a·ti \kə-ˈwät-ē\ or **co·a·ti·mun·di** \kə-ˌwät-ē-ˈmən-dē\ *n.* A tropical American mammal related to the raccoon but with a longer body and tail and a long flexible snout.

coat·ing \ˈkōt-ing\ *n.* **1** A coat or covering; as, a thin *coating* of ice on the surface of a pond. **2** Cloth for coats.

coat of arms. The arms or emblems that a person wears or displays, as on a shield.

coat of mail. A garment of metal scales or rings, worn as armor.

coat of mail

co·au·thor \ˈkō-ˈȯth-r\ *n.* A joint or associate author.

coax \ˈkōks\ *v.* **1** To persuade, or to try to persuade, by gentle but constant asking; to wheedle. **2** To move, persuade, or induce toward a desired end by persistent, gentle measures; as, to *coax* a fire to burn; to *coax* a horse to jump a fence.

co·ax·i·al cable \kō-ˈaks-ē-əl\. An insulated cable used to transmit telegraph, telephone, and television signals.

cob \ˈkäb\ *n.* **1** A male swan. **2** A strong, short-legged horse, especially one used for riding or for drawing light carriages. **3** A corncob.

co·balt \ˈkō-ˌbȯlt\ *n.* A tough, shiny, silver-white metal found with iron and nickel.

cob·ble \ˈkäb-l\ *n.* A cobblestone. — *v.;* **cob·bled; cob·bling** \-l(-)ing\. To pave with cobblestones.

cob·ble \ˈkäb-l\ *v.;* **cob·bled; cob·bling** \-l(-)ing\. To make or mend roughly, especially shoes.

cob·bler \ˈkäb-lər\ *n.* **1** A person who mends shoes. **2** A clumsy workman. **3** A drink made of wine, sugar, and fruit juice, with cracked ice. **4** A deep-dish fruit pie with a thick upper crust.

cob·ble·stone \ˈkäb-l-ˌstōn\ *n.* A naturally rounded stone, especially one from six inches to a foot in diameter.

co·bra \ˈkōb-rə\ *n.* A very poisonous snake of Asia and Africa that puffs out the skin around its neck into a broad hood when it is excited.

cob·web \ˈkäb-ˌweb\ *n.* **1** The fine network spread by a spider to catch small insects. **2** Something resembling or suggesting a spider's web, as being flimsy or entangling. — **cob·webbed,** *adj.* — **cob·web·by** \-ˌweb-ē\ *adj.*

co·caine \kō-ˈkān\ *n.* A drug obtained from the leaves of a South American shrub (**co·ca** \ˈkōk-ə\) used as a medicine to deaden pain and to cause sleep.

coc·cyx \ˈkäk-siks\ *n.; pl.* **coc·cy·ges** \käk-ˈsī-ˌjēz\. The bone at the lower end of the spinal column.

coch·i·neal \ˈkäch-n-ˌēl\ *n.* A dyestuff, often scarlet, made from the dried bodies of the female of an insect native to Mexico and Central America.

coch·lea \'käk-lē-ə\ *n.; pl.* **coch·le·ae** \-lē-ˌē\. The part of the inner ear, shaped like a snail's shell, that includes the actual organ of hearing.

cock \'käk\ *n.* **1** A male bird; a rooster. **2** A faucet or valve for regulating the flow of a liquid or a gas. **3** A cocked position of the hammer of a gun; as, a rifle at half *cock.* **4** A turning or tipping upward, as of the chin. — *v.* **1** To turn or tip upward or to one side; as, to *cock* one's hat. **2** To draw back the hammer of; as, to *cock* a pistol.

cock \'käk\ *n.* A small cone-shaped pile, as of hay. — *v.* To make into cocks; as, to *cock* hay.

cock·ade \kä-'kād\ *n.* A rosette, knot, or similar device worn upon the hat as a badge.

cock·a·too \'käk-ə-ˌtü\ *n.; pl.* **cock·a·toos.** Any one of several parrots, many of them crested and with brilliant plumage, found chiefly in Australia.

cock·crow \'käk-ˌkrō\ *n.* The time of day at which cocks first crow; early morning.

cock·er·el \'käk-r(-)əl\ *n.* A young cock.

cock·er spaniel \'käk-r\. A small hunting dog of a short-legged breed, with a silky coat.

cock·eyed \'käk-ˌīd\ *adj.* **1** Having a squinting eye. **2** *Slang.* Slanted or twisted in a wrong direction; as, a *cockeyed* idea. **3** *Slang.* Intoxicated.

cock·le \'käk-l, 'kək-l\ *n.* Any of several weeds growing in fields of grain, as the **corn cockle,** a white-hairy weed with bright-red flowers.

cock·le \'käk-l\ *n.* **1** An edible shellfish with a heart-shaped double shell. **2** A cockleshell. **3** A small, shallow boat.

cock·le·shell \'käk-l-ˌshel\ *n.* **1** One of the shells of a cockle. **2** A small, light, and often flimsy boat.

cockleshell, 1

cock·les of the heart \'käk-lz\. The depths of the heart.

cock·ney \'käk-nē\ *n.; pl.* **cock·neys.** **1** A native of London, especially of the East End of London, speaking with a characteristic twang. **2** The cockney dialect. — *adj.* Of or relating to a cockney; like a cockney.

cock·pit \'käk-ˌpit\ *n.* **1** A sheltered space, lower than the rest of the deck, in yachts and small vessels. **2** The space in an airplane for pilot and passengers.

cock·roach \'käk-ˌrōch\ *n.* A swift-running insect with long feelers and leathery body wall, found in houses and ships, and active chiefly at night.

cocks·comb \'käks-ˌkōm\ *n.* **1** A cock's comb or crest. **2** A coxcomb. **3** A garden plant of the same family as the amaranth, with showy, wavy-crested flower clusters.

cock·sure \'käk-'shu̇r\ *adj.* **1** Wholly sure; certain. **2** More certain than the facts justify; overconfident.

cockswain. Variant of *coxswain.*

cock·tail \'käk-ˌtāl\ *n.* **1** An iced drink of alcoholic liquor or liquors mixed with flavoring ingredients. **2** An appetizer, as of oysters with a peppery tomato sauce or of chilled fruit or tomato juice.

cocky \'käk-ē\ *adj.;* **cock·i·er; cock·i·est.** Pert; conceited; as, a *cocky* manner.

co·co or **co·coa** \'kōk-ˌō\ *n.; pl.* **co·cos** or **co·coas.** **1** The coconut palm. **2** A coconut.

co·coa \'kōk-ˌō\ *n.* **1** Cacao. **2** Chocolate ground to a powder after some of its fat is removed. **3** A drink made from this powder.

co·co·nut or **co·coa·nut** \'kōk-ə-(ˌ)nət\ *n.* [From Spanish and Portuguese *coco* meaning literally "bogey" and English *nut;* so named from the resemblance of a coconut to a grotesque head.] The egg-shaped, husk-covered nutlike fruit of the **coconut palm,** or **coconut tree,** a tall palm of tropical regions.

co·coon \kə-'kün, ku̇-'kün\ *n.* The silky covering which caterpillars make around themselves and in which they are protected while changing into butterflies or moths.

cod \'käd\ *n.; pl.* **cod** or sometimes **cods.** A large deep-water food fish with soft fins found in the colder parts of the North Atlantic Ocean.

C.O.D. \'sē-ˌō-'dē\. Abbreviation for: **1** *cash on delivery.* **2** *collect on delivery.*

co·da \'kōd-ə\ *n.* A closing passage in a piece of music.

cod·dle \'käd-l\ *v.;* **cod·dled; cod·dling** \-l(-)ing\. **1** To cook slowly in water below the boiling point; as, to *coddle* eggs. **2** To treat as a little child or a pet; to pamper.

code \'kōd\ *n.* **1** Any collection of laws systematically arranged. **2** Any system of rules or principles that govern the conduct of people in certain classes and under certain conditions; as, the *code* of a gentleman. **3** A system of signals for communicating; as, the Morse *code.* **4** A system of letters or symbols used with special meanings, as in secret communications. — *v.;* **cod·ed; cod·ing.** To put in the form of a code.

co·deine \'kō-ˌdēn\ *n.* A drug obtained from opium, feebler than morphine.

co·dex \'kō-ˌdeks\ *n.; pl.* **co·di·ces** \'kōd-ə-ˌsēz, 'käd-\. A manuscript book, as of the Scriptures.

cod·fish \'käd-ˌfish\ *n.; pl.* **cod·fish** or **cod·fish·es.** The cod.

codg·er \'käj-r\ *n.* An odd or cranky fellow.

cod·i·fy \'käd-ə-ˌfī\ *v.;* **cod·i·fied** \-ˌfīd\; **cod·i·fy·ing.** To arrange in a systematic form, as a collection of laws.

cod·ling \'käd-ling\ *n.* **1** A small immature apple. **2** One of various apples that normally have a long, tapering form.

cod·ling moth \'käd-ling\. A small stout-bodied moth with lightly fringed wings, the larva of which lives in apples, pears, and quinces.

cod-liver oil. An oil obtained from the liver of the cod and closely related fishes, used as a medicine to remedy improper nutrition.

co·ed or **co–ed** \'kō-ˌed\ *n.* A female student at a coeducational school or college.

co·ed·u·ca·tion \ˌkō-ˌej-ə-'kāsh-n\ *n.* The education of male and female students at the same school or college. — **co·ed·u·ca·tion·al** \-n(-)əl\ *adj.*

co·ef·fi·cient \ˌkō-ə-'fish-nt\ *n.* Any number or symbol placed before another symbol or combination of symbols as a multiplier, as *3* in the expression *3x*.

coe·len·ter·ate \sē-'lent-r-ət\ *n.* Any of a group of salt-water animals having a hollow saclike body with an internal digestive cavity and one central mouth but no system of blood vessels, including the sea anemones, corals and hydroids, and jellyfishes.

co·e·qual \(')kō-'ēk-wəl\ *adj.* Equal, as in rank, age, or extent. — **co·e·qual·ly** \-wə-lē\ *adv.*

co·erce \kō-'ərs\ *v.;* **co·erced**; **co·erc·ing.** **1** To restrain by force; to repress. **2** To compel; as, to *coerce* obedience.

co·er·cion \kō-'ərsh-n, -'ərzh-n\ *n.* **1** A restraining by force. **2** The action of compelling; a being compelled; as, a confession signed under *coercion.* — **co·er·cive** \-'ər-siv\ *adj.*

co·e·val \kō-'ēv-l\ *adj.* Of the same period or age; contemporary; as, extinct animals that were *coeval.*

co·ex·ist \ˌkō-ig-'zist\ *v.* To exist together; to exist at the same time. — **co·ex·ist·ence** \-'zis-tən(t)s\ *n.* — **co·ex·ist·ent** \-tənt\ *adj.*

co·ex·tend \ˌkō-iks-'tend\ *v.* To extend through the same space or time with another; as, two tunnels that *coextend* under a river. — **co·ex·ten·sion** \-'tench-n\ *n.* — **co·ex·ten·sive** \-'ten(t)s-iv\ *adj.*

cof·fee \'kȯf-ē\ *n.* **1** A drink made from the roasted and ground seeds of a tropical plant. **2** The seeds (**coffee beans**) of this plant.

cof·fer \'kȯf-r\ *n.* **1** A casket, chest, or trunk, especially for holding valuables. **2** [usually in the plural] Treasure; funds.

cof·fin \'kȯf-n\ *n.* [From Old French *cofin* meaning "basket".] A box or case to hold a dead body.

cog \'käg\ *n.* A tooth on the rim of a wheel, adjusted to fit the notches in a receiving wheel or bar and to give or receive motion.

co·gent \'kōj-nt\ *adj.* Forceful; compelling; convincing; especially, appealing forcefully to the mind; as, *cogent* reasoning. — **co·gen·cy** \-n-sē\ *n.* — **co·gent·ly**, *adv.*

cog·i·tate \'käj-ə-ˌtāt\ *v.;* **cog·i·tat·ed**; **cog·i·tat·ing.** To think over; to ponder; to plan. — **cog·i·ta·tion** \ˌkäj-ə-'tāsh-n\ *n.*

co·gnac \'kōn-ˌyak, 'kȯn-\ *n.* [From *Cognac,* a district in France where it is made.] A French brandy.

cog·ni·tion \käg-'nish-n\ *n.* **1** The power or process by which the mind comes to know anything. **2** Anything that one knows or comes to know; as, the first *cognitions* of an infant.

cog·ni·zance \'käg-nə-zən(t)s\ *n.* **1** Knowledge; as, to have a wide *cognizance* of the habits of animals. **2** Notice; heed; as, to take *cognizance* of what is happening.

cog·ni·zant \'käg-nə-zənt\ *adj.* Having cognizance; aware; as, *cognizant* of the danger in an undertaking.

cog·no·men \käg-'nō-mən\ *n.* **1** A family name; a surname. **2** A name; a nickname.

cog·wheel \'käg-ˌhwēl\ *n.* A wheel with cogs or teeth.

co·hab·it \kō-'hab-ət\ *v.* To live together as man and wife. — **co·hab·i·ta·tion** \(ˌ)kō-ˌhab-ə-'tāsh-n\ *n.*

co·heir \'kō-'ar, -'er\ *n.* A joint heir.

cogwheel

co·here \kō-'hir\ *v.;* **co·hered**; **co·her·ing.** **1** To stick together, as parts of the same mass. **2** To be joined by a common principle, relationship, or interest. The parts of the argument do not logically *cohere.* — **co·her·ence** \kō-'hir-ən(t)s\ *n.*

co·her·ent \kō-'hir-ənt\ *adj.* **1** Sticking together, as parts of the same mass. **2** Logically clear and well connected; as, a *coherent* plan. — **co·her·ent·ly**, *adv.*

co·he·sion \kō-'hēzh-n\ *n.* The action of sticking together tightly; a close union of parts or of particles; as, the *cohesion* of glue and wood. — **co·he·sive** \-'hē-siv\ *adj.*

co·hort \'kō-ˌhȯrt\ *n.* **1** One of the ten divisions of a Roman legion. **2** A band of warriors or followers; a troop.

coif \'kȯif\ *n.* A small close-fitting cap. — *v.* To provide with a coif or with a similar covering for the head.

coif·fure \kwä-'fyu̇r\ *n.* A headdress or a way of arranging the hair.

coil \'kȯil\ *v.* To wind in a circle or in circles; as, to *coil* a rope. The snake *coiled* and struck. — *n.* **1** A series of rings, a spiral, or a single ring, as of rope or cable. **2** A series of connected pipes arranged in rows, layers, or windings, as in water-heating apparatus. **3** A spiral of wire or an electrical instrument composed of such a spiral and its accessories.

coin \'kȯin\ *n.* [From French *coin* meaning "wedge" and also "die for stamping money".] **1** A piece of metal money. **2** Metal money; as, to change bills for *coin.* — *v.* **1** To make gold, silver, or other metal into coins; to make coins by stamping pieces of metal. A mint is a place where money is *coined.* **2** To make or invent, as a new word or phrase.

coin·age \'kȯi-nij\ *n.* **1** The act of coining, as money or a new word. **2** That which is coined. **3** Coins; especially, the various coins of a country considered together; as, the *coinage* of the United States.

co·in·cide \ˌkō-ən-'sīd, 'kō-ən-ˌsīd\ *v.;* **co·in·cid·ed**; **co·in·cid·ing.** **1** To happen at the same time; to occupy the same period of time. The unlucky girl's birthday *coincided* with Christmas. **2** To occupy the same place in space; to be the same shape and cover the same area. The soles of the suspect's shoes *coincided* with the footprints in the garden. **3** To correspond or agree exactly; as, to read in the newspaper an opinion that *coincides* with one's own.

co·in·ci·dence \kō-'in(t)s-ə-dən(t)s\ *n.* **1** The act or condition of coinciding, as in space, time, or opinion. **2** Two things that happen at the same time by accident but seem to have some connection. **3** Either one of these happenings.

co·in·ci·dent \kō-'in(t)s-ə-dənt\ *adj.* Coinciding; as, *coincident* events; a theory *coincident* with the facts. — **co·in·ci·dent·ly**, *adv.*

co·in·ci·den·tal \(ˌ)kō-ˌin(t)s-ə-'dent-l\ *adj.* Happening, acting, or done by coincidence; having the nature of a coincidence. — **co·in·ci·den·tal·ly** \-'dent-l(-)ē\ *adv.*

coke \'kōk\ *n.* Gray porous lumps of fuel made by heating soft coal in a closed chamber (**coke oven**) until some of its gases have passed off.

Col. Abbreviation for *Colonel.*

col-. A form of *com-* used before *l.*

col·an·der \'kəl-ənd-r, 'käl-\ *n.* A bowl-shaped kitchen utensil with holes in its sides and bottom, used as a strainer.

cold \'kōld\ *adj.* **1** Having a low temperature or one decidedly below normal; as, a *cold* day; a *cold* drink. **2** Without warmth of feeling; unfriendly; as, a *cold* welcome. **3** Suffering from lack of warmth; as, to feel *cold.* — *n.* **1** A condition of low temperature; cold weather; chilliness; as, to go out into the *cold.* **2** An inflammation of the nose and throat resulting in sneezing and coughing; as, to catch *cold;* to have a *cold.*

cold-blood·ed \'kōl(d)-'bləd-əd\ *adj.* **1** Having cold blood; especially, having a body temperature that changes to approximate variations in the temperature of the surroundings. Fish are *cold-blooded* creatures. **2** Sensitive to cold. **3** Lacking, or showing a lack of, natural human feelings; not moved by sympathy; as, a *cold-blooded* criminal. — **cold-blood·ed·ly**, *adv.*

cold chisel. A strong steel chisel for chipping and cutting cold metal.

cold cream. A creamy preparation for cleansing, softening, and soothing the skin.

cold frame. A glass-covered frame without artificial heat, used to protect plants and seedlings.

cold front. The boundary between an advancing mass of cold or cool air and a mass of warmer air.

cold·ly \'kōl-(d)lē\ *adv.* **1** In a calm manner; without emotion; as, to consider a question *coldly.* **2** In an unkind or unfriendly manner; as, to be *coldly* polite; to stare *coldly.*

cold sore. A blisterlike patch that sometimes appears about the mouth during the course of a cold or a fever.

cold war. A struggle or a state of strife between two nations or groups of nations carried on by means of propaganda, economic pressure, formation of political alliances, and, sometimes, threatening military maneuvers, but without resort to true acts of war and usually without breaking off diplomatic relations.

cole \'kōl\ *n.* Any plant of the same genus as the cabbage.

cole·slaw \'kōl-ˌslȯ\ *n.* A salad made of sliced or chopped raw cabbage.

col·ic \'käl-ik\ *n.* Sharp, sudden pain in the bowels. — **col·icky** \-ik-ē\ *adj.*

col·i·se·um \ˌkäl-ə-'sē-əm\ *n.* [From a Medieval Latin word derived from Latin *Colosseum,* a huge amphitheater in ancient Rome.] A large building, amphitheater, or stadium in which athletic contests and other public entertainments may be held.

col·lab·o·rate \kə-'lab-r-ˌāt\ *v.;* **col·lab·o·rat·ed; col·lab·o·rat·ing. 1** To work or act in association with another person or persons, as in writing a book. **2** To co-operate with, or willingly assist, enemy soldiers or civil authorities occupying one's country. — **col·lab·o·ra·tion** \kə-ˌlab-r-'āsh-n\ *n.* — **col·lab·o·ra·tor** \-'lab-r-ˌāt-r\ *n.*

col·lab·o·ra·tion·ist \kə-ˌlab-r-'āsh-n-əst\ *n.* A person who collaborates with an enemy occupying his country.

col·lapse \kə-'laps\ *v.;* **col·lapsed; col·laps·ing. 1** To fall down; to fall in; to give way suddenly or without warning. **2** To fold together; as, to *collapse* a card table. **3** To be made so that the parts fold or snap down into a compact form, as for storage or transportation. **4** To break down completely; to fail. Plans for a picnic *collapsed* when it began to rain. **5** To suffer a physical breakdown. — *n.* A collapsing; breakdown.

col·laps·i·ble \kə-'lap-səb-l\ *adj.* Capable of collapsing or of being collapsed; especially, capable of being folded together; as, a *collapsible* chair.

col·lar \'käl-r\ *n.* **1** The part of a dress, shirt, or coat worn at or around the neck. **2** A band or a chain for the neck; as, a dog's *collar.* **3** A part of the harness of draft animals, fitting over the shoulders. **4** A ring or piece around an object to hold it in place or to limit motion. — *v.* **1** To put a collar on. **2** To seize by the collar; to catch.

collar, 4

col·lar·bone \'käl-r-'bōn, -ˌbōn\ *n.* A bone of the shoulder, joined to the breastbone and the shoulder blade; the clavicle.

col·lat·er·al \kə-'lat-r-əl, -'la-trəl\ *adj.* **1** Associated but of secondary importance; as, the main question and certain *collateral* questions. **2** Descended from the same ancestors but not in the same line. Cousins are *collateral* relatives. — *n.* Property such as stocks, bonds, and insurance policies handed over as security for the repayment of a loan.

col·league \'käl-ˌēg\ *n.* An associate in a profession; a fellow worker.

col·lect \'käl-ikt, -ˌekt\ *n.* An opening prayer said in the Communion service or the Mass.

col·lect \kə-'lekt\ *v.* **1** To gather together at one place; to assemble; as, to *collect* wood for a campfire. A crowd *collected.* **2** To make a collection of specimens for study or exhibition; as, to *collect* butterflies or postage stamps. **3** To get money that is owed; as, to *collect* a bill. **4** To regain control of (oneself); as, to break down for a moment but soon *collect* oneself. — For synonyms see *gather.* — *adj.* or *adv.* Payable by the person who receives it; as, a *collect* telegram. — **col·lect·i·ble** or **col·lect·a·ble** \-'lek-təb-l\ *adj.*

col·lect·ed \kə-'lek-təd\ *adj.* Calm; self-possessed. — **col·lect·ed·ly**, *adv.*

col·lec·tion \kə-'leksh-n\ *n.* **1** An assembling; a gathering together; as, two *collections* of mail daily. **2** A group of persons or things assembled together; especially, a group of specimens gathered in order to be studied or exhibited; as, a large *collection* of sea shells. **3** A gathering of money, as for charitable purposes; as, to take up a *collection* in church.

col·lec·tive \kə-'lek-tiv\ *adj.* **1** Formed by collecting or being collected; as, the *collective* experience of mankind. **2** Done or shared by a number of persons working together; as, *collective* farming. **3** Relating to a group of individuals; as, the *collective* needs of a community. **4** Treating a number of individuals as a unit; as, the word "man" used in a *collective* sense, to include all men. — *n.* **1** A collective noun. **2** A body of individuals gathered together, as for a joint undertaking. **3** A collective farm.

collective bargaining. Bargaining, as over wages, between an employer or employers and an organized group of employees.

collective farm. In communist countries, a farm made up of the lands held by many individuals and worked co-operatively with modern machinery collectively owned, under partial or complete state control.

col·lec·tive·ly \kə-'lek-tiv-lē\ *adv.* **1** In a collective manner. **2** In a collective sense.

collective noun. A noun naming a collection or group of individuals by a singular form, as *assembly, army, jury,* and taking a singular verb when the group is thought of as a unit, a plural verb when the individuals making up the group are in mind.

collective security. Security of all members of an association of nations from aggression by any other nation or nations.

col·lec·tor \kə-'lekt-r\ *n.* **1** A person who collects; as, a stamp *collector;* a ticket *collector.* **2** A person whose business it is to collect or receive money due another person, a firm, or a government; as, a tax *collector;* a bill *collector.*

col·leen \kä-'lēn\ *n. Irish.* A girl.

col·lege \'käl-ij\ *n.* **1** A body of persons having certain common rights or duties; as, the *college* of cardinals. **2** An educational institution higher than a high school or an academy; a university or one of its schools. **3** The building or buildings and grounds used by a university or by one of its schools.

col·le·gian \kə-'lēj-n, -'lē-jē-ən\ *n.* A member of a college; a college student.

col·le·giate \kə-'lē-jət, -jē-ət\ *adj.* **1** Of or relating to a college; as, *collegiate* studies. **2** Of, relating to, or characteristic of college students; as, the latest *collegiate* styles.

col·lide \kə-'līd\ *v.;* **col·lid·ed**; **col·lid·ing**. To come together with full force; to strike against each other; to clash. The two cars *collided.*

col·lie \'käl-ē\ *n.* [Probably from the English dialect word *colly* meaning "coal-black".] A large heavy-coated dog of a Scottish breed long used in tending sheep.

col·lier \'käl-yər\ *n.* **1** A coal miner. **2** A ship for carrying coal.

col·liery \'käl-yər-ē\ *n.; pl.* **col·lier·ies.** A coal mine and the buildings connected with it.

col·li·sion \kə-'lizh-n\ *n.* The action of colliding or coming together with force; a clash; as, a *collision* between two automobiles; a *collision* of interests between two nations.

col·lo·ca·tion \ˌkäl-ə-'kāsh-n\ *n.* A placing together; especially, arrangement of words in a definite order.

col·lo·di·on \kə-'lōd-ē-ən\ *n.* A thick sticky substance that hardens in the air, used for forming a skinlike covering over wounds and for coating photographic films.

col·lo·qui·al \kə-'lōk-wē-əl\ *adj.* Used in conversation; acceptable in ordinary conversation, friendly letters, and informal speeches as distinguished from formal speech or writing. — **col·lo·qui·al·ly** \-wē-ə-lē\ *adv.*

col·lo·qui·al·ism \kə-'lōk-wē-ə-ˌliz-m\ *n.* **1** A colloquial style of speaking or writing. **2** A colloquial expression.

col·lo·quy \'käl-ə-kwē\ *n.; pl.* **col·lo·quies.** A conversation, especially a formal conversation or conference.

col·lu·sion \kə-'lüzh-n\ *n.* Secret agreement and co-operation for a wrongful purpose, especially in a fraudulent scheme. — **col·lu·sive** \-'lü-siv\ *adj.*

co·logne \kə-'lōn\ *n.* [From *Cologne,* a city in Germany where it was first manufactured.] A perfumed toilet water composed of alcohol and certain aromatic oils.

Co·lom·bi·an \kə-'ləm-bē-ən, -'läm-\ *adj.* Of or relating to Colombia. — *n.* A native or inhabitant of Colombia.

co·lon \'kō-lən\ *n.* That part of the large intestine which extends from the caecum to the rectum.

co·lon \'kō-lən\ *n.* A mark of punctuation [:] that is used: **1** After the salutation of a business letter or the written form of a speech. **2** Before a long quotation forming an important part of a sentence. **3** After words that introduce a series of statements or of details. **4** To separate hours, minutes, and seconds.

co·lo·nel \'kərn-l\ *n.* A military officer ranking next below a brigadier general and usually commanding a regiment in the army or a group in the air force.

co·lo·nel·cy \'kərn-l-sē\ *n.; pl.* **co·lo·nel·cies.** The rank or position of colonel.

co·lo·ni·al \kə-'lō-nē-əl, -'lōn-yəl\ *adj.* **1** Of or relating to a colony or colonies; as, a *colonial* government. **2** Of or relating to the 13 colonies that formed the United States of America; as, *colonial* history; *colonial* architecture. — *n.* A citizen or inhabitant of a colony.

col·o·nist \'käl-ə-nəst\ *n.* **1** An inhabitant of a colony. **2** A person who takes part in founding a colony.

col·o·ni·za·tion \ˌkäl-ə-nə-'zāsh-n\ *n.* The settlement of a country or a region by colonists.

col·o·nize \'käl-ə-ˌnīz\ *v.;* **col·o·nized**; **col·o·niz·ing. 1** To establish a colony or colonies in. England *colonized* Australia. **2** To settle in a distant country; to establish a colony. — **col·o·niz·er** \-ˌnīz-r\ *n.*

col·on·nade \ˌkäl-ə-'nād\ *n.* A row of columns set at regular intervals along one or more sides of a building and usually supporting the base of the roof structure. — **col·on·nad·ed** \-'nād-əd\ *adj.*

col·o·ny \'käl-ə-nē\ *n.; pl.* **col·o·nies. 1** A group of persons who move from their native land to found a settlement elsewhere but who remain subjects of their mother country. **2** A group of persons so situated as to resemble a colony; as, the American *colony* in Paris. **3** The place or country settled or occupied by any such group. **4** Any distant territory belonging to a nation; as, the British *colonies* in America. **5** A group of animals or plants of the same kind living in close association; as, a *colony* of ants.

col·or \'kəl-r\ *n.* **1** The appearance of a thing, apart from size and shape, when light strikes it. Red is the *color* of blood. **2** A hue; a tint; as, to dress in bright *colors.* **3** Complexion; a healthy complexion; as, to regain one's *color* after being ill. **4** A blush. The words of praise tinged the girl's cheeks with *color.* **5** The complexion of persons not classed as white. **6** [in the plural] A national flag or an ensign flown from a ship or borne by soldiers. **7** [in the plural] A party or side that one favors; as, to stick to one's *colors.* **8** Outward appearance; as, a story that has the *color* of truth. **9** Vividness; picturesqueness; as, a writer whose style is noted for its *color.* **10** The harmony of hues and tints combined in painting. That painter is a master of *color.* — *v.;* **col·ored**; **col·or·ing** \-r(-)ing\. **1** To change the color of; to dye, tint, paint, or stain. **2** To give color to. A blush *colored* the girl's cheeks. **3** To misrepresent; to falsify. The accused man *colored* his story to conceal his guilt. **4** To take on or change color. Leaves *color* in the fall.

col·or·a·tion \ˌkəl-r-'āsh-n\ *n.* Combination of different colors or shades; coloring; as, to study the *coloration* of a flower.

col·or-blind \'kəl-r-ˌblīnd\ *adj.* Affected with **color blindness**, a total or partial lack of ability to distinguish colors.

col·or·cast \'kəl-r-ˌkast\ *n.* A television broadcast in color. — **col·or·cast·ing**, *n.*

col·ored \'kəl-rd\ *adj.* **1** Having color; neither black nor white; as, *colored* pictures. **2** Of some other race than the white; especially, Negro.

col·or·fast \'kəl-r-ˌfast\ *adj.* Not liable to fade; having fast color; as, *colorfast* cloth.

col·or·ful \'kəl-rf-l\ *adj.* **1** Full of color; especially, abounding in contrasts and variety. **2** Clear; lively; having the qualities of a good picture; as, a *colorful* story of life in the jungle.

col·or·ing \'kəl-r(-)ing\ *n.* **1** The action of a person or thing that colors. **2** Anything that produces color. **3** A change of appearance, as by use of color. The *coloring* of the water was due to rust. **4** The effect of the use of color, as in art. **5** Complexion; as, a person of delicate *coloring.*

col·or·less \'kəl-r-ləs\ *adj.* **1** Without color; as, a *colorless* face. **2** Clear and transparent; as, a *colorless* liquid.

co·los·sal \kə-'läs-l\ *adj.* Of very great size; huge; gigantic; as, a *colossal* statue, more than three times life size. — For synonyms see *monstrous.*

co·los·sus \kə-'läs-əs\ *n.; pl.* **co·los·si** \-'läs-ˌī\ or **co·los·sus·es** \-'läs-ə-səz\. **1** A huge statue. **2** A huge person or thing.

colt \'kōlt\ *n.* A young horse, donkey, or zebra.

col·um·bine \'käl-əm-ˌbīn\ *n.* **1** A slender branching plant about two feet tall, with drooping flowers and light-green leaves divided into three parts. **2** The flower of this plant, which has five tubelike petals, each topped with a small knob.

col·umn \'käl-əm\ *n.* **1** A pillar supporting a roof or a gallery. **2** Anything resembling such a column in shape, position, or use; as, the spinal *column*, or backbone, of a person; a *column* of smoke. **3** A long straight row; as, a *column* of soldiers. **4** One of two or more vertical divisions of a printed page separated by a line or by a blank space; as, a two-*column* page. **5** A special department in a newspaper, often one column wide and usually run by one person, that deals with a particular subject; as, a sports *column;* a gossip *column.*

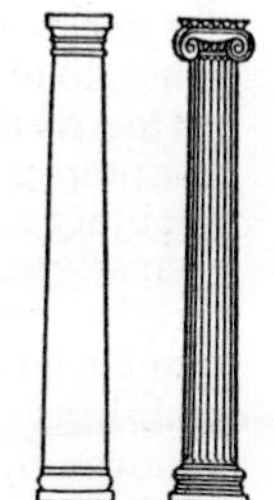
two types of column

col·um·nist \'käl-əm-(n)əst, 'käl-yəm-\ *n.* A person who conducts a special, signed column, as in a newspaper.

com-. A prefix, used before *b, m, p,* and sometimes *f,* that can mean: with, together, as in *commingle, compassion, compress.*

co·ma \'kō-mə\ *n.* A sleeplike state of unconsciousness caused by disease, injury, or poison.

comb \ˈkōm\ *n.* **1** A toothed implement used to smooth and arrange the hair, or worn in the hair to hold it in place. **2** Any of various toothed instruments used for separating fibers, as of wool or flax. **3** A fleshy crest with toothlike points on the head of a fowl and of certain related birds. **4** A honeycomb. — *v.* **1** To smooth, arrange, or untangle with a comb; as, to *comb* one's hair; to *comb* wool. **2** To go over or through carefully in search of something; to search thoroughly; as, to *comb* an area a mile square.

comb, 3

com·bat \kəm-ˈbat, ˈkäm-ˌbat\ *v.;* **com·bat·ed** or **com·bat·ted**; **com·bat·ing** or **com·bat·ting.** To fight or struggle, as with an enemy; to fight against something; to oppose; as, to *combat* disease. — \ˈkäm-ˌbat\ *n.* **1** A fight; a struggle; a contest; as, a naval *combat.* **2** Fighting; battle; as, soldiers experienced in *combat.*

com·bat·ant \kəm-ˈbat-nt, ˈkäm-bə-tənt\ *adj.* Engaged, or prepared to engage, in active fighting. — *n.* A person who takes part in a fight or a battle.

com·bat·ive \kəm-ˈbat-iv\ *adj.* Eager to fight; pugnacious. — **com·bat·ive·ly,** *adv.*

comb·er \ˈkōm-r\ *n.* **1** A workman or a machine that combs fibers, as of wool or flax. **2** A long curling wave rolling in from the ocean.

com·bi·na·tion \ˌkäm-bə-ˈnāsh-n\ *n.* **1** The action of combining or the state of being combined. **2** A whole thing made by combining a number of different things. A cake is a *combination* of many ingredients. **3** A union of persons or of groups of persons for a set purpose; as, a political *combination.* **4** A series of letters or numbers which when indicated in succession by a disk attached to a lock (**combination lock**) will open the lock. **5** The action or process by which two or more elements unite to form a chemical compound.

com·bine \kəm-ˈbīn\ *v.;* **com·bined**; **com·bin·ing.** To join together so as to make, or to seem, one thing; to unite; to mix; as, cloth made of wool and cotton *combined.* — \ˈkäm-ˌbīn\ *n.* **1** A combination; especially, a combination of persons formed to obtain some business or political advantage for themselves. **2** A machine that harvests and threshes grain while moving over the field. — **com·bin·a·ble** \kəm-ˈbī-nəb-l\ *adj.*

comb·ings \ˈkō-mingz\ *n. pl.* Loose hairs or fibers removed by a comb.

com·bus·ti·ble \kəm-ˈbəs-təb-l\ *adj.* **1** Capable of being burned. **2** Catching fire or burning easily. — *n.* A combustible substance.

com·bus·tion \kəm-ˈbəs-chən\ *n.* **1** The process of burning. **2** A chemical process in which substances combine with oxygen, as when food is used by the animal body to produce growth, energy, and heat.

come \(ˈ)kəm\ *v.;* **came** \ˈkām\; **come**; **com·ing** \ˈkəm-ing\. **1** To approach; to move toward. **2** To appear or arrive, as on a scene of action; as, to *come* home. The police *came* to our rescue. **3** To reach the point of being or becoming; to amount; as, the rope that *came* untied. The bill *came* to 10 dollars. **4** To take place; to result; to follow; to have its place, as in a series or calendar; as, the holiday that *came* on Thursday. Accidents often *come* from carelessness. **5** To spring from as a source; as, to *come* from a good family. **6** To be obtainable; to be obtained; as, an article that *comes* in three sizes. **7** To be attainable; to be attained. Success *came* to the writer after years of work. **8** To extend; to reach; as, a coat that *comes* to the knees. — **come about. 1** To come to pass; to occur; as, to explain how it all *came about.* **2** To change the course of a sailing boat that is sailing into the wind so as to bring the wind on the opposite side of the bow. — **come out. 1** To emerge; to be seen or known. **2** To be presented in society. **3** To be issued or published. The book *came out* last year. — **come round** or **come around. 1** To regain consciousness, as after fainting. **2** To change; as, to *come around* to the opinion of the majority. — **come to.** To recover, as from a state of unconsciousness. — **com·er** \ˈkəm-r\ *n.*

come·back \ˈkəm-ˌbak\ *n.* A coming back or return to a former position or condition, as of health, power, popularity, or prosperity.

co·me·di·an \kə-ˈmēd-ē-ən\ *n.* **1** An actor of comic parts. **2** An amusing person.

com·e·dy \ˈkäm-əd-ē\ *n.; pl.* **com·e·dies. 1** A light, amusing play. **2** A play with a happy ending.

come·ly \ˈkəm-lē\ *adj.;* **come·li·er**; **come·li·est.** Pleasing to the sight; good-looking; as, a *comely* girl.

com·et \ˈkäm-ət\ *n.* [From Latin *cometa,* there borrowed from Greek *komētēs* meaning literally "long-haired".] A bright heavenly body traveling around the sun and usually having a long cloudy tail.

com·fit \ˈkəm(p)-fət, ˈkäm(p)-\ *n.* A dry sweetmeat; any kind of fruit, root, or seed preserved with sugar and dried.

com·fort \ˈkəm(p)-fərt\ *v.* To give hope and strength to; to quiet the grief and trouble of; to cheer. — *n.* **1** Acts or words that comfort. **2** The feeling of the one that is comforted; as, to find *comfort* in a mother's love. **3** Something that makes a person comfortable; as, the *comforts* of home life.

com·fort·a·ble \ˈkəm(p)f-təb-l, ˈkəm(p)-fərt-əb-l, ˈkəm(p)-təb-l\ *adj.* **1** Giving comfort; as, a *comfortable* chair. **2** Enjoying comfort; at ease; as, to feel quite *comfortable* in spite of the heat. **3** Adequate; more than just enough; as, to win an election by a *comfortable* majority. — *n.* A stuffed or quilted cover for a bed. — **com·fort·a·bly** \-lē\ *adv.*

com·fort·er \ˈkəm(p)-fə(r)t-r\ *n.* **1** A person who comforts. **2** A comfortable. **3** A long woolen scarf or muffler.

com·fort·less \ˈkəm(p)-fərt-ləs\ *adj.* Having or giving no comfort.

com·ic \ˈkäm-ik\ *adj.* **1** Relating to comedy. **2** Funny; laughable; comical. — *n.* **1** A comic actor; a comedian. **2** [in the plural] Comic strips. **3** A comic book.

com·i·cal \'käm-ik-l\ *adj.* Causing mirth or laughter as being humorous, witty, or queer; funny; amusing.
— The words *ridiculous* and *droll* are synonyms of *comical: comical* generally applies to anything that calls forth lighthearted, spontaneous laughter; *droll* may apply especially to oddity or quaintness; *ridiculous* usually describes something that arouses derisive laughter because of its absurdity or foolishness.

com·i·cal·ly \'käm-ik-l(-)ē\ *adv.* In a comical manner.

comic book. A paper-bound book or magazine made up of a series of comic strips, usually related.

comic strip. A strip of drawings in black and white or in color, sometimes carrying a situation through several stages to an outcome that is ludicrous or fantastic, and sometimes relating an episode in a continuing story, often of adventure, and ranging in treatment from humorous to moralistic.

com·ing \'kəm-ing\ *adj.* **1** Approaching; drawing near; as, this *coming* week. **2** Gaining success or fame; as, a *coming* man in the political world. — *n.* Approach; arrival; as, the *coming* of spring.

com·i·ty \'käm-ət-ē\ *n.; pl.* **com·i·ties.** Courtesy; civility. — **comity of nations. 1** The friendly code of behavior by which nations get along together. **2** The group of nations observing such a code.

com·ma \'käm-ə\ *n.* A mark of punctuation [,] used to show separation of words or phrases from the rest of a sentence.

com·mand \kə-'mand\ *v.* **1** To order or direct with authority. The general *commanded* the troops to advance. **2** To have power or control over; to govern. The admiral *commands* the fleet. **3** To secure as right or due; as, the goods that *command* the best prices. **4** To dominate or overlook, as from a higher position. The hill *commands* the town. — *n.* **1** A commanding; an ordering. **2** An order given; as, to obey a *command.* **3** The power or right to command; control. The captain is in *command* of his men. **4** A force, such as a body of troops, under a commander. **5** A position, as a military post, in which one is directing operations.

com·man·dant \'käm-ən-ˌdant, -ˌdänt, -ˌdȧnt\ *n.* A commanding officer; a commander.

com·man·deer \ˌkäm-ən-'dir\ *v.* To take by force; to seize for military or other uses; as, to *commandeer* food for the army.

com·mand·er \kə-'mand-r\ *n.* **1** A person who commands. **2** The chief officer commanding an army or a subdivision of an army. **3** A naval officer ranking next below a captain.

commander in chief; *pl.* **commanders in chief. 1** The person in supreme command of the armed forces of a nation. **2** The highest commanding officer in an area or of a detached force.

com·mand·ment \kə-'man(d)-mənt\ *n.* Something given as an order or command; especially, one of the ten commandments said in the Bible to have been given by God to Moses on Mount Sinai.

com·man·do \kə-'man-ˌdō\ *n.; pl.* **com·man·dos** or **com·man·does. 1** A band or unit of troops trained for making surprise raids into enemy territory, as for obtaining information or capturing prisoners. **2** A soldier of such a raiding group.

com·mem·o·rate \kə-'mem-r-ˌāt\ *v.;* **com·mem·o·rat·ed; com·mem·o·rat·ing.** To call or recall to mind; to serve as a memorial of; as, a monument *commemorating* a battle.

com·mem·o·ra·tion \kə-ˌmem-r-'āsh-n\ *n.* A commemorating; a memorial celebration; as, a statue in *commemoration* of Abraham Lincoln.

com·mem·o·ra·tive \kə-'mem-r-ˌāt-iv, -ət-iv\ *adj.* Tending or intended to commemorate some event; as, a *commemorative* postage stamp.

com·mence \kə-'men(t)s\ *v.;* **com·menced; com·menc·ing.** To begin; to start.

com·mence·ment \kə-'men(t)s-mənt\ *n.* **1** The action or the time of commencing; a beginning. **2** The day on which degrees or diplomas are conferred in a school or college. **3** The ceremonies at which such degrees or diplomas are conferred.

com·mend \kə-'mend\ *v.* **1** To give into another's care; to entrust; as, to *commend* oneself to God. **2** To praise; to speak of someone or something with approval. The teacher *commended* the pupils for their fine work. — **com·mend·a·ble** \-'men-dəb-l\ *adj.* — **com·mend·a·bly** \-də-blē\ *adv.*

com·men·da·tion \ˌkäm-ən-'dāsh-n\ *n.* A commending; praise; approval.

com·mend·a·to·ry \kə-'men-də-ˌtōr-ē, -ˌtȯr-ē\ *adj.* Commending; giving praise; as, a *commendatory* speech.

com·men·sal·ism \kə-'men(t)s-l-ˌiz-m\ *n.* The relation existing between two kinds of plants or animals in which one secures food, protection, or other benefits without damaging or benefiting the other in, with, or on which it lives.

com·men·su·rate \kə-'men(t)s-r-ət, -'mench-r-ət\ *adj.* **1** Equal in measure or extent. **2** Corresponding; proportionate; as, an income *commensurate* with one's needs. — **com·men·su·rate·ly**, *adv.*

com·ment \'käm-ˌent\ *n.* **1** An expression of opinion, either in speech or writing; as, to listen without making any *comment.* **2** A remark or criticism. — For synonyms see *remark.* — *v.* To make a comment; to remark; as, to *comment* on the large number of absences.

com·men·tary \'käm-ən-ˌter-ē\ *n.; pl.* **com·men·tar·ies. 1** A series of comments or notes. **2** A book composed of such material; as, a *commentary* on the Bible.

com·men·ta·tor \'käm-ən-ˌtāt-r\ *n.* A person who makes comments on something; especially, a person employed to give talks on news events over radio and television.

com·merce \'käm-rs, -ˌərs\ *n.* The buying and selling of goods, especially in a large way and between different places; trade.

com·mer·cial \kə-'mərsh-l\ *adj.* **1** Having to do with commerce or business; as, a *commercial* firm. **2** Having financial profit as the chief aim; as, a *commercial* drama. — *n.* An advertising message on a radio or television program. — **com·mer·cial·ly** \-mərsh-l-ē\ *adv.*

com·mer·cial·ism \kə-'mərsh-l-ˌiz-m\ *n.* A spirit, method, or practice characteristic of business.

com·mer·cial·ize \kə-'mərsh-l-ˌīz\ *v.;* **com·mer·cial·ized**; **com·mer·cial·iz·ing.** To manage something with the idea of making a profit out of it; to put on a business basis; as, to *commercialize* a hobby.

com·min·gle \kə-'ming-gl\ *v.;* **com·min·gled**; **com·min·gling** \-'ming-gl(-)ing\. To mix; to mingle; as, to *commingle* two liquids.

com·mis·er·ate \kə-'miz-r-ˌāt\ *v.;* **com·mis·er·at·ed**; **com·mis·er·at·ing.** To feel or express sorrow or pity for; as, to *commiserate* a friend on his misfortune. — **com·mis·er·a·tion** \kə-ˌmiz-r-'āsh-n\ *n.*

com·mis·sar \'käm-ə-ˌsär, -ˌsȧr\ *n.* The head of a government department in Soviet Russia.

com·mis·sar·i·at \ˌkäm-ə-'ser-ē-ət\ *n.* The persons and agencies in an army that provide food and other daily necessities.

com·mis·sary \'käm-ə-ˌser-ē\ *n.; pl.* **com·mis·sar·ies. 1** A person to whom a duty or office is entrusted by a superior. **2** A department or store supplying provisions, as in a lumber camp. **3** An officer responsible for supplying food and daily necessities to troops.

com·mis·sion \kə-'mish-n\ *n.* **1** An order or instruction giving a person certain rights or duties to perform; the right or duty thus authorized. The teacher gave some of her students the *commission* of going to the library for her. **2** Anything done or to be done by one person as agent for another. **3** A certificate that gives rank and authority to military or naval officers. **4** A group of persons given orders and authority to perform certain duties; as, a park *commission.* **5** A sum of money received by a person who sells something as an agent. **6** A committing; as, to be charged with the *commission* of a burglary. — *v.* **1** To give a commission to. **2** To put a ship into service. — **in commission.** In or into use; fit for service; as, to put a ship *in commission.* — **out of commission.** Out of service; not fit for use or service.

com·mis·sion·er \kə-'mish-n(-)ər\ *n.* **1** A member of a commission. **2** An official in charge of a government department; as, the *Commissioner* of Public Safety.

com·mit \kə-'mit\ *v.;* **com·mit·ted**; **com·mit·ting. 1** To entrust to; to give over for care or safekeeping; to consign; as, to *commit* a thief to prison; to *commit* a poem to memory. **2** To put in the charge of a jailer; to imprison; as, a person *committed* for robbery. **3** To do something wrong; as, to *commit* a crime. **4** To pledge or bind; as, to *commit* oneself to a certain course of action.

com·mit·ment \kə-'mit-mənt\ *n.* **1** The action of committing or the state of being committed, as to jail. **2** The action of doing or performing something; as, the *commitment* of a crime. **3** A promise or a pledge to do something; as, a *commitment* to follow a certain course of action.

com·mit·tee \kə-'mit-ē\ *n.* A group of persons appointed or elected to consider some particular matter or to perform some duty; as, the *committee* in charge of decorations. — **com·mit·tee·man** \-mən, -ˌman\ *n.*

com·mode \kə-'mōd\ *n.* **1** A chest of drawers. **2** A movable washstand with a cupboard underneath.

com·mo·di·ous \kə-'mōd-ē-əs\ *adj.* Roomy; not crowded or cramped for space; as, *commodious* living quarters.

com·mod·i·ty \kə-'mäd-ət-ē\ *n.; pl.* **com·mod·i·ties.** Any article of trade or commerce, including raw material, manufactured goods, and the produce of land, as cotton, wool, flax, wheat, and corn; goods; wares.

com·mo·dore \'käm-ə-ˌdōr, -ˌdȯr\ *n.* **1** A naval officer ranking next above a captain and below a rear admiral. **2** The president or chief officer of a yacht club. **3** The senior captain of a line of merchant ships.

com·mon \'käm-ən\ *adj.* **1** Having to do with, belonging to, or used by everybody; public; as, to work for the *common* good. Railroads are *common* carriers. **2** Belonging to or shared by two or more individuals, especially the members of a family or group; as, a *common* ancestor. **3** Widely or generally known, met, or seen; as, facts of *common* knowledge. **4** Frequent; familiar; as, a *common* sight. **5** Ordinary; not above the average in rank, merit, or social position; as, a *common* soldier; the *common* people. **6** Plain and practical; as, *common* sense. **7** Coarse; vulgar. — *n.* **1** Land owned by a community, especially a park; as, a New England village *common.* **2** One that is common, general, or usual; as, a man above the *common;* out of the *common.*

common denominator. A common multiple, usually the least, of the denominators of two or more fractions.

common divisor. A number that divides two or more numbers without remainder.

com·mon·er \'käm-ən-r\ *n.* A person who is not a nobleman; one of the common people.

com·mon·ly \'käm-ən-lē\ *adv.* Usually; ordinarily; generally; as, a word that is not *commonly* used.

common multiple. A multiple of each of two or more numbers.

common noun. A noun that names a class of persons or things or any individual of a class, as *chair* or *fear.*

com·mon·place \'käm-ən-ˌplās\ *adj.* Very common or ordinary; uninteresting; as, a *commonplace* remark. — *n.* Anything that is commonplace.

com·mons \'käm-ənz\ *n. pl.* **1** The mass of the people as distinguished from the nobility. **2** Provisions for a common table, as in colleges; rations.

3 Quarters, usually a dining hall, especially in a college.

common school. A public elementary school.

com·mon·weal *n.* or **common weal** \'käm-ən-ˌwēl, ˌkäm-ən-'wēl\. **1** The general welfare. **2** *Archaic.* A commonwealth.

com·mon·wealth \'käm-ən-ˌwelth, ˌkäm-ən-'welth\ *n.* **1** A state or nation, or the whole body of people living in it. **2** Any of the individual states of the United States.

com·mo·tion \kə-'mōsh-n\ *n.* **1** Disturbed or violent motion; agitation; as, a *commotion* of the water. **2** A disturbance; excitement and confusion.

com·mu·nal \kə-'myün-l, 'käm-yən-l\ *adj.* **1** Of or relating to a commune or to people organized in communes. **2** Of or belonging to the people in general.

com·mune \kə-'myün\ *v.;* **com·muned; com·mun·ing. 1** To talk together intimately. **2** To receive Communion.

com·mune \'käm-ˌyün, kə-'myün\ *n.* **1** The smallest administrative district in France and in certain other countries, as Belgium. **2** The inhabitants or the government of such a district.

com·mu·ni·ca·ble \kə-'myü-nə-kəb-l\ *adj.* Capable of being communicated or carried from one person or thing to another, as a disease.

com·mu·ni·cant \kə-'myü-nə-kənt\ *n.* **1** A person who partakes or is entitled to partake of Communion; a church member. **2** A person who imparts or transmits, as information.

com·mu·ni·cate \kə-'myü-nə-ˌkāt\ *v.;* **com·mu·ni·cat·ed; com·mu·ni·cat·ing. 1** To make known; as, to *communicate* news. **2** To spread; to transfer; to impart; as, to *communicate* a disease. **3** To converse; to have communication, as by telephone, telegraph, or letter. **4** To be connected; to join; as, rooms that *communicate.*

com·mu·ni·ca·tion \kə-ˌmyü-nə-'kāsh-n\ *n.* **1** A communicating; a transmission; as, the *communication* of news; the *communication* of yellow fever by mosquitoes. **2** The exchange of thought between persons, as by speech or letter. **3** A verbal or written message; as, a *communication* from one's family. **4** The means of passing from place to place, or the means of carrying things back and forth; as, lines of *communication* in time of war. **5** [in the plural] A system of speaking or sending messages, as by telephone, telegraph, or radio.

com·mu·ni·ca·tive \kə-'myü-nə-ˌkāt-iv, -kət-iv\ *adj.* **1** Inclined to communicate; talkative. **2** Of or relating to communication.

com·mun·ion \kə-'myün-yən\ *n.* **1** The act of communing; a sharing with others, especially of intimate thoughts and opinions. **2** A body of Christians or of Christian churches having a common faith or organization; a religious denomination. **3** [with a capital] The sacrament commemorating with bread and wine the last supper of Jesus Christ. **4** The religious service which includes this sacrament.

com·mu·ni·qué or **com·mu·ni·que** \kə-ˌmyü-nə-'kā\ *n.* An official communication, such as one giving a report of military or naval operations.

com·mu·nism \'käm-yə-ˌniz-m\ *n.* **1** A system of social organization in which property and goods are held in common. **2** Any theory of social organization that advocates common ownership of the means of production and an approach to an equal distribution of the products of industry. — **com·mu·nis·tic** \ˌkäm-yə-'nis-tik\ *adj.*

com·mu·nist \'käm-yə-nəst\ *n.* **1** A person who believes in communism. **2** [with a capital] A member of the communist party in any country. — *adj.* Of or relating to communism or communists.

com·mu·ni·ty \kə-'myü-nət-ē\ *n.; pl.* **com·mu·ni·ties. 1** The people living in a particular place, such as a village or city. **2** A group of persons living together in order to lead a particular kind of life; as, a *community* of monks. **3** The public, or people in general; as, for the good of the *community.* **4** Joint ownership or participation; as, a *community* of goods. **5** Common character; likeness; as, a *community* of ideas.

community chest. A general fund made up of individual subscriptions in a community to provide public aid.

com·mu·ta·tion \ˌkäm-yə-'tāsh-n\ *n.* **1** A substitution, as of a lesser thing for a greater. **2** Regular travel on a **commutation ticket**, a railroad ticket issued at a reduced rate for a certain number of trips or for daily trips between stated places. **3** In law, the change of a greater to a lesser penalty.

com·mu·ta·tive \'käm-yə-ˌtāt-iv\ *adj.* Combining elements in such a way that the result is independent of the order in which they are taken. Addition is *commutative.*

com·mu·ta·tor \'käm-yə-ˌtāt-r\ *n.* A device for reversing the direction of an electric current.

com·mute \kə-'myüt\ *v.;* **com·mut·ed; com·mut·ing. 1** To exchange; to substitute; especially, to substitute a less severe penalty for a greater one; as, to *commute* a death sentence to life imprisonment. **2** To travel by use of a commutation ticket. **3** To travel daily or frequently to and from a city. — **com·mut·er** \kə-'myüt-r\ *n.*

com·pact \kəm-'pakt, 'käm-ˌpakt\ *adj.* **1** Closely united or packed; solid; firm. **2** Arranged so as to save space; as, a *compact* house. **3** Brief; not wordy; as, a *compact* statement. — \'käm-ˌpakt\ *n.* A small case containing face powder and often rouge. — \kəm-'pakt\ *v.* **1** To join firmly; to unite closely. **2** To form by connecting closely; to compose; as, a wall *compacted* of stone and mortar. — **com·pact·ly** \kəm-'pakt-lē, 'käm-ˌpakt-\ *adv.*

com·pact \'käm-ˌpakt\ *n.* An agreement or contract.

com·pan·ion \kəm-'pan-yən\ *n.* [From Old French *compagnon*, there derived from Latin *companio* meaning literally "one who breaks bread with another".] **1** A person or thing that accompanies another; an associate; a comrade.

2 One of a pair or set of like things; a mate. — **com·pan·ion·less** \-ləs\ *adj.*

com·pan·ion·a·ble \kəm-ˈpan-yə-nəb-l\ *adj.* Fitted to be a companion; agreeable. — **com·pan·ion·a·bly** \-nə-blē\ *adv.*

com·pan·ion·ship \kəm-ˈpan-yən-ˌship\ *n.* Fellowship; association; company; as, a close *companionship* lasting many years.

com·pan·ion·way \kəm-ˈpan-yən-ˌwā\ *n.* A set of steps leading below from the deck of a ship; the space occupied by these steps.

com·pa·ny \ˈkəmp-n(-)ē\ *n.; pl.* **com·pa·nies. 1** Fellowship; companionship; society; as, to enjoy someone's *company.* **2** Companions; associates; as, to be known by the *company* one keeps. **3** A band or group of people; especially, a social gathering; a party. **4** The members of a partnership whose names do not appear in the name of the firm; as, John Doe and *company.* **5** A band of musical or dramatic performers. **6** Guests; visitors; as, to have *company.* **7** An association of persons for a joint purpose, such as a firm for carrying on business, or a band of performers. **8** A body of soldiers, normally commanded by a captain. **9** The crew of a boat, including its officers.

com·pa·ra·ble \ˈkämp-r(-)əb-l\ *adj.* **1** Capable of being compared. **2** Worthy of being compared; as, cloth of a quality *comparable* to the best. — **com·pa·ra·bly** \-r(-)ə-blē\ *adv.*

com·par·a·tive \kəm-ˈpar-ət-iv\ *adj.* **1** Having to do with comparison; measured or estimated by making comparisons; as, to live in *comparative* comfort. The *comparative* lightness of gasoline brings it to the surface of water. **2** Studied systematically by making comparisons; as, *comparative* literature. **3** Expressing the degree of an adjective or an adverb that is greater or less than its positive degree. "Taller" is the *comparative* degree of "tall". — *n.* The comparative degree, or a word or phrase expressing it. "More slowly" and "less slowly" are *comparatives* of "slowly". — **com·par·a·tive·ly,** *adv.*

com·pare \kəm-ˈpar, -ˈper\ *v.;* **com·pared; com·par·ing. 1** To represent as similar; to liken; as, to *compare* an anthill to a town. **2** To examine in order to discover likenesses or differences; as, to *compare* two bicycles. **3** To be worthy of comparison; to be like. Most people think roller skating does not *compare* with ice skating. **4** To state the positive, comparative, and superlative forms of an adjective or an adverb. — *n.* Comparison; as, beauty beyond *compare.*

com·par·i·son \kəm-ˈpar-əs-n\ *n.* **1** The act of comparing or the condition of being compared. **2** An examination of two or more objects to find the likenesses and differences between them. **3** Change in form and meaning of an adjective or an adverb, as by adding *-er* or *-est* or by prefixing *more* or *most,* to show degree or amount.

com·part·ment \kəm-ˈpärt-mənt, -ˈpȧrt-\ *n.* One of the parts into which an enclosed space is divided; a separate division or section of anything; as, the *compartments* of a cabinet; a *compartment* on a train.

com·pass \ˈkəmp-əs, ˈkämp-\ *n.* **1** The enclosing limit or boundary of any area. **2** An enclosed space; extent. **3** The range of tones that a voice or a musical instrument can produce. **4** [usually in the plural] An instrument for drawing circles or marking measurements, consisting of two pointed legs joined at the top by a pivot. **5** A device for determining directions on the earth's surface by means of a magnetic needle that points toward the north. — *v.* **1** To bring about; as, to *compass* an enemy's defeat. **2** To make the circuit of; to enclose; to surround; as, to *compass* a city.

compass, 5

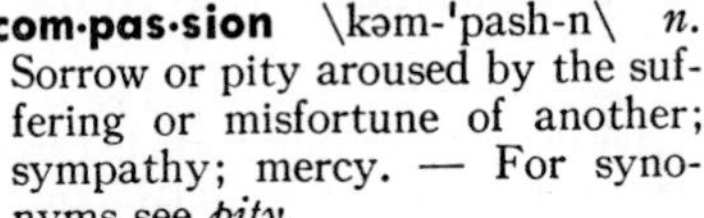

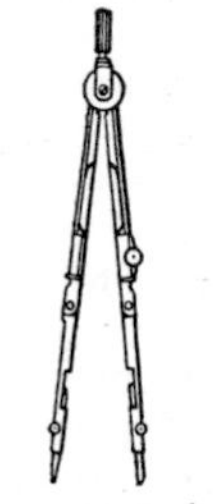

compass, 4

com·pas·sion \kəm-ˈpash-n\ *n.* Sorrow or pity aroused by the suffering or misfortune of another; sympathy; mercy. — For synonyms see *pity.*

com·pas·sion·ate \kəm-ˈpash-n-ət\ *adj.* Having or showing compassion; sympathetic. — **com·pas·sion·ate·ly,** *adv.*

com·pat·i·bil·i·ty \kəm-ˌpat-ə-ˈbil-ət-ē\ *n.* The quality of being compatible; the capability of existing together without clashing.

com·pat·i·ble \kəm-ˈpat-əb-l\ *adj.* **1** Capable of existing together in harmony; not antagonistic; as, *compatible* colors; two friends whose tastes were *compatible* in everything except music. **2** Relating to a system of television broadcasting in which colorcasts may be received in black and white on receivers not equipped for color reception. — **com·pat·i·bly** \-ə-blē\ *adv.*

com·pa·tri·ot \kəm-ˈpā-trē-ət, käm-\ *n.* A fellow countryman; a person living in or belonging to the same country as another.

com·peer \ˈkäm-ˌpir, kəm-ˈpir\ *n.* **1** An equal; a peer. **2** A companion.

com·pel \kəm-ˈpel\ *v.;* **com·pelled; com·pel·ling.** To force; to oblige; as, *compelled* by illness to spend several days in bed. Governments have the power to *compel* their citizens to pay taxes.

com·pen·sate \ˈkämp-n-ˌsāt, ˈkäm-ˌpen-\ *v.;* **com·pen·sat·ed; com·pen·sat·ing. 1** To be equivalent to in value or effect; to counterbalance; to make up for. **2** To make amends. Nothing can *compensate* for the loss of reputation. **3** To make equal return to; to remunerate; to pay; as, to *compensate* a workman for his labor. — For synonyms see *pay.*

com·pen·sa·tion \ˌkämp-n-ˈsāsh-n, ˌkäm-ˌpen-\ *n.* **1** The act of compensating. **2** Something given to make up, or regarded as making up, for something else; especially, money given to make amends for a loss or injury suffered. **3** Salary or wages; pay.

com·pete \kəm-ˈpēt\ *v.;* **com·pet·ed; com·pet·ing.** To strive for the same thing, as a prize or a reward, for which another is striving; to contend in rivalry; to contest. Five teams will *compete* for the state championship.

com·pe·tence \'kämp-ə-tən(t)s\ *n.* **1** Financial means sufficient for the necessaries of life. **2** The quality of being competent; fitness; ability; as, to demonstrate one's *competence* to hold a position.

com·pe·ten·cy \'kämp-ə-tən-sē\ *n.* Competence.

com·pe·tent \'kämp-ə-tənt\ *adj.* Capable; qualified; fit; as, a *competent* teacher; a man *competent* to lead others. — **com·pe·tent·ly,** *adv.*

com·pe·ti·tion \ˌkämp-ə-'tish-n\ *n.* **1** The act of competing. **2** A contest between two or more persons for the same thing. **3** The effort of two or more persons or firms, acting independently, to secure business by offering the most favorable terms.

com·pet·i·tive \kəm-'pet-ət-iv\ *adj.* Having to do with competition; based on, used in, or resulting from competition; as, a *competitive* sport; a *competitive* examination. — **com·pet·i·tive·ly,** *adv.*

com·pet·i·tor \kəm-'pet-ət-r\ *n.* A person who competes, as in a contest or in business; a rival.

com·pi·la·tion \ˌkämp-l-'āsh-n\ *n.* **1** The action or process of compiling; gathering. **2** That which is compiled; especially, a book of materials gathered from other books.

com·pile \kəm-'pīl\ *v.*; **com·piled**; **com·pil·ing. 1** To collect into a volume. **2** To put together in a new form out of materials already existing in books or documents; as, to *compile* a history of baseball. — **com·pil·er,** *n.*

com·pla·cence \kəm-'plās-n(t)s\ *n.* Complacency.

com·pla·cen·cy \kəm-'plās-n-sē\ *n.* Contentment; satisfaction; especially, self-satisfaction.

com·pla·cent \kəm-'plās-nt\ *adj.* Satisfied; especially, self-satisfied; as, a *complacent* smile. — **com·pla·cent·ly,** *adv.*

com·plain \kəm-'plān\ *v.* **1** To express grief, pain, or discontent; to find fault; as, to *complain* of a headache; to *complain* about the weather. **2** To make an accusation; as, to *complain* to the police.

com·plain·ant \kəm-'plā-nənt\ *n.* A person who makes a complaint, as in a legal action or proceeding.

com·plaint \kəm-'plānt\ *n.* **1** Expression of grief, pain, or discomfort; as, sounds of *complaint.* **2** A cause or reason for complaining. **3** An ailment or disease; sickness; as, the common *complaints* of old age. **4** A formal charge against a person.

com·plai·sance \kəm-'plās-n(t)s, -'plāz-; ˌkämp-lə-'zan(t)s\ *n.* Disposition or desire to please or oblige.

com·plai·sant \kəm-'plās-nt, -'plāz-; ˌkämp-lə-'zant\ *adj.* Having or showing a disposition or a desire to please; obliging; as, to find a person more *complaisant* than one had expected.

com·ple·ment \'kämp-lə-mənt\ *n.* **1** Something that fills up, completes, or makes perfect, as a quantity necessary to make a thing complete or one of two parts necessary to make a complete whole. A shoe is of little use without its *complement.* **2** Full quantity, number, or amount; full allowance; as, a ship's *complement* of officers and men. The troop had its *complement* of scouts and no more could be admitted. **3** An added word or group of words by which the predicate of a sentence is made complete in sense or in grammar, as *president* in "they elected him president" or *with milk* in "he filled the glass with milk". — \-ˌment\ *v.* To supply a lack; to supplement and make complete.

com·ple·men·ta·ry \ˌkämp-lə-'ment-r-ē, -'men-trē\ *adj.* Forming or serving as a complement; completing.

complementary angles. Two angles whose sum is a right angle.

complementary colors. A pair of contrasting colors that when mixed in proper proportions give a neutral color, or gray.

com·plete \kəm-'plēt\ *adj.* **1** With no part lacking; filled up; as, a *complete* set of books. **2** Finished; concluded; as, when one's work is *complete.* **3** Thorough; entire; absolute; as, *complete* freedom; a *complete* failure. — *v.*; **com·plet·ed**; **com·plet·ing.** To make complete; to accomplish; to fulfill; to finish; as, to *complete* an assignment.

com·plete·ly \kəm-'plēt-lē\ *adv.* Entirely; wholly; thoroughly; as, to be *completely* finished with something; a *completely* satisfactory explanation.

com·ple·tion \kəm-'plēsh-n\ *n.* The act of completing or the condition of being complete; the finishing of something; as, a job near *completion.*

com·plex \(')käm-'pleks, kəm-\ *adj.* **1** Made up of parts, especially of many parts; not simple; as, a *complex* machine. **2** Complicated; intricate; as, a *complex* problem. — \'käm-ˌpleks\ *n.* **1** A whole made up of complicated or interrelated parts. **2** A controlling mental attitude that leads a person to regard someone or something with an exaggerated feeling of concern, as of love, fear, or hostility. — **com·plex·ly** \(')käm-'pleks-lē, kəm-\ *adv.*

complex fraction. A fraction having a fraction or a mixed number in the numerator or denominator or in each.

com·plex·ion \kəm-'pleksh-n\ *n.* **1** The color or the general appearance of the skin, especially of the face; as, a dark *complexion;* a clear *complexion.* **2** General appearance; aspect; character; as, to receive information that changes the whole *complexion* of a situation. — **com·plex·ioned** \-'pleksh-nd\ *adj.*

com·plex·i·ty \kəm-'pleks-ət-ē, käm-\ *n.*; *pl.* **com·plex·i·ties. 1** The condition of being complex in nature or structure; as, the *complexity* of a problem; an organization of great *complexity.* **2** Something complex; a complication; as, the occasional *complexities* of daily life.

complex sentence. A sentence having one principal clause and one or more subordinate clauses.

com·pli·ance \kəm-'plī-ən(t)s\ *n.* **1** The act of complying; a yielding; submission to the wish or the command of another person. **2** A readiness or tendency to yield to others. — **in compliance with.** In accordance with; in obedience to; as, *in compliance with* your request for further information.

com·pli·an·cy \kəm-'plī-ən-sē\ *n.* Compliance; especially, compliant quality.

com·pli·ant \kəm-'plī-ənt\ *adj.* Complying or having a disposition to comply; inclined to yield to the wishes of others; submissive. — **com·pli·ant·ly,** *adv.*

com·pli·cate \'kämp-lə-ˌkāt\ *v.;* **com·pli·cat·ed; com·pli·cat·ing.** To make complex; to make more difficult to understand or deal with. The uncertainty of the weather *complicated* the planning of the picnic.

com·pli·cat·ed \'kämp-lə-ˌkāt-əd\ *adj.* **1** Made up of parts intricatel combined; complex. **2** Difficult to understand or explain. — **com·pli·cat·ed·ly,** *adv.*

com·pli·ca·tion \ˌkämp-lə-'kāsh-n\ *n.* **1** The act of complicating or the state of being complicated. **2** A confused situation; a mixed-up matter. **3** Anything that makes a situation more complicated or difficult. **4** A disease existing at the same time as, and affecting the course or severity of, another disease.

com·plic·i·ty \kəm-'plis-ət-ē\ *n.; pl.* **com·plic·i·ties.** The state of being an accomplice; a sharing in the guilt for some wrongful act.

com·pli·ment \'kämp-lə-mənt\ *n.* **1** An act or expression of praise, approval, or admiration; a flattering speech or attention. **2** [in the plural] A formal greeting; as, to send one's *compliments;* with the *compliments* of the season.

— The word *flattery* is a synonym of *compliment: compliment* usually suggests sincerity, but may refer to a conventional expression of approval; *flattery* may suggest insincerity and an appeal to vanity, often for selfish or deceitful purposes.

— \-ˌment\ *v.* To pay a compliment to.

com·pli·men·ta·ry \ˌkämp-lə-'ment-r-ē, -'mentrē\ *adj.* **1** Expressing or containing a compliment; as, a *complimentary* remark. **2** Given free as a compliment or ccurtesy; as, a *complimentary* ticket.

com·ply \kəm-'plī\ *v.;* **com·plied** \-'plīd\; **com·ply·ing.** To yield to the wish of another; to consent; to act in accordance or obedience; as, to *comply* with a request; to *comply* with all regulations.

com·po·nent \kəm-'pō-nənt, käm-; 'käm-ˌpō-\ *adj.* Being or forming a part; helping to form or constitute; composing; constituent; as, the *component* parts of a machine. — *n.* A component part or element.

com·port \kəm-'pōrt, -'pȯrt\ *v.* **1** To bear or conduct (oneself); to behave; as, to *comport* oneself with dignity. **2** To be in harmony; to accord; to agree; as, a display of cowardice that *comported* badly with the boy's brave talk.

com·port·ment \kəm-'pōrt-mənt, -'pȯrt-\ *n.* Behavior; bearing; demeanor.

com·pose \kəm-'pōz\ *v.;* **com·posed; com·pos·ing.** **1** To form by putting together; to construct; as, to *compose* a sentence; to *compose* a song. **2** To constitute; to make up; as, a cake *composed* of many ingredients. **3** To arrange type in order for printing; to set. **4** To put in order; to settle; to arrange; as, to *compose* oneself in an armchair. **5** To quiet; to calm; as, to try to *compose* one's feelings.

com·posed \kəm-'pōzd\ *adj.* Calm; serene; self-possessed. — **com·pos·ed·ly** \-'pō-zəd-lē\ *adv.*

com·pos·er \kəm-'pōz-r\ *n.* A person who composes; especially, a writer of music.

com·pos·ite \kəm-'päz-ət, (')käm-\ *adj.* **1** Made up of various distinct parts or elements; compounded; as, a *composite* photograph. **2** In botany, of, belonging to, or having the form typical of the largest family of flowering plants; especially, bearing small flowers closely united into compact heads surrounded by bracts and resembling single flowers, as in the daisy, dandelion, and aster. — *n.* **1** Something that is composite, or made up of different parts; a compound. **2** A plant of the family characterized by composite flowers.

composite number. A product of two or more whole numbers each greater than 1.

com·po·si·tion \ˌkämp-ə-'zish-n\ *n.* **1** A composing; especially, a putting words together to make sentences; writing; the art of writing. **2** The manner in which the parts of a thing are put together, especially as forming a harmonious whole; as, a picture famous for its beautiful *composition.* **3** A literary, musical, or artistic production. **4** A short piece of writing done as an educational exercise; as, to write one *composition* each week. **5** The make-up, or substance, of something; as, the *composition* of rubber. **6** A combination; as, a *composition* made of several different metals.

com·pos·i·tor \kəm-'päz-ət-r\ *n.* A person who sets type.

com·post \'käm-ˌpōst\ *n.* A mixture for fertilizing land, especially one containing rotted plant material.

com·po·sure \kəm-'pōzh-r\ *n.* Calmness; self-possession; repose.

com·pote \'käm-ˌpōt\ *n.* **1** A dish of fruits cooked in syrup. **2** A bowl-shaped dish, usually with a base and stem and sometimes a cover, for serving compotes, and for candy or nuts.

com·pound \'käm-ˌpaund\ *n.* [From Malay *kampung, kampong* meaning "group", "gathering", "cluster of buildings".] In the Far East, an enclosure containing a house or houses and other buildings; especially, such an enclosure occupied by foreigners.

com·pound \kəm-'paund, käm-; 'käm-ˌpaund\ *v.* [From Old French *compondre,* there derived from Latin *componere* meaning "to put together".] **1** To mix or unite together into a whole; to form by putting together; to combine; as, to *compound* a medicine. **2** To settle peaceably; as, to *compound* a dispute. **3** To increase by an amount that will itself be increased; as, to *compound* interest quarterly. — \'käm-ˌpaund\ *n.* **1** Anything that is formed by combining two or more parts, ingredients, or elements. **2** A substance formed by the union of two or more chemical elements in definite proportions by weight. **3** A combination of two or more distinct words into a solid or hyphened form, as in *steamboat* or *passer-by*, or of a word with a prefix or suffix, as in *supernatural* or *goodness*, or of two or more words into a phrase (**open compound**) serving as a single word, as in *post office* or *all right*. — \'käm-ˌpau̇nd, kəm-'pau̇nd\ *adj.* Made of or by the union of two or more parts or elements; as, a *compound* substance.

compound–complex sentence. A compound sentence having one or more subordinate clauses.

compound flower. A composite flower.

compound fraction. A complex fraction.

compound fracture. The breaking of a bone in such a way as to produce an open wound through which the broken bone often sticks out.

compound interest. Interest paid or to be paid both on the original capital of a loan and on accumulated unpaid interest.

compound leaf. A leaf in which the blade, or body, is divided to the central vein forming two or more distinct leaflets on a common stem.

compound sentence. A sentence made up of two or more independent clauses.

com·pre·hend \ˌkämp-rē-'hend\ *v.* **1** To grasp the meaning of; to understand fully. **2** To take in; to include; to contain; as, the states *comprehended* in the United States. — **com·pre·hend·i·ble**, *adj.*

com·pre·hen·si·ble \ˌkämp-rē-'hen(t)s-əb-l\ *adj.* Capable of being comprehended; understandable. — **com·pre·hen·si·bil·i·ty** \-ˌhen(t)s-ə-'bil-ət-ē\ *n.* — **com·pre·hen·si·bly** \-'hen(t)s-ə-blē\ *adv.*

com·pre·hen·sion \ˌkämp-rē-'hench-n\ *n.* Power or ability to understand. This subject is beyond my *comprehension*.

com·pre·hen·sive \ˌkämp-rē-'hen(t)s-iv\ *adj.* **1** Including much; full; inclusive; as, a *comprehensive* description. **2** Having the power to understand many things; of wide mental grasp; as, a *comprehensive* mind.

com·press \kəm-'pres\ *v.* To press or squeeze together; to reduce in volume by pressure; to condense. — \'käm-ˌpres\ *n.* **1** A folded cloth or pad applied to some part of the body, especially with a bandage, to reduce inflammation; as, a cold *compress*. **2** A press, as for compressing cotton into bales. — **com·press·i·ble** \kəm-'pres-əb-l\ *adj.*

com·pres·sion \kəm-'presh-n\ *n.* The act of compressing or the state of being compressed; pressure.

com·pres·sor \kəm-'pres-r\ *n.* One that compresses; especially, an instrument or machine for compressing something; as, an air *compressor*.

com·prise \kəm-'prīz\ *v.;* **com·prised; com·pris·ing.** To include; to consist of or be made up of; as, a family that *comprises* five sons.

com·pro·mise \'kämp-rə-ˌmīz\ *n.* **1** A settlement of a dispute, reached by each party giving up part of his demands. **2** A giving up to something objectionable or dangerous; a surrender; as, a *compromise* of one's principles. **3** The thing agreed upon as a result of concessions. — *v.;* **com·pro·mised; com·pro·mis·ing. 1** To settle by means of a compromise. **2** To put in danger; to expose to suspicion; as, to *compromise* one's reputation by keeping bad company.

comp·trol·ler \kən-'trōl-r, käm(p)-; 'käm(p)-ˌtrōl-r\ *n.* A public officer who examines and certifies accounts; a controller.

com·pul·sion \kəm-'pəlsh-n\ *n.* The action of compelling; the state of being compelled; force. If persuasion fails, *compulsion* may be necessary.

com·pul·so·ry \kəm-'pəls-r(-)ē\ *adj.* **1** Enforced; required; as, *compulsory* education. **2** Having the power of compelling.

com·punc·tion \kəm-'pəng(k)sh-n\ *n.* **1** Sharp uneasiness caused by a sense of guilt; remorse. **2** A little, passing feeling of regret for some slight wrong; a qualm.

com·pu·ta·tion \ˌkämp-yə-'tāsh-n\ *n.* **1** A computing; a reckoning; calculation. **2** Result obtained by computing.

com·pute \kəm-'pyüt\ *v.;* **com·put·ed; com·put·ing.** To reckon or count; to determine by calculation; as, to *compute* the area of a playground; to *compute* the cost of an outing. — **com·put·a·ble**, *adj.* — **com·put·er**, *n.*

com·rade \'käm-ˌrad, -rəd\ *n.* [From Old French *camarade*, there borrowed from Old Spanish *camarada* meaning "group of soldiers sleeping in one room", "roommate".] A companion; an associate or fellow worker.

con \'kän\ *v.;* **conned; con·ning.** [From Old English, a variant of *can*, which in Old English meant "know" as well as "be able".] To study carefully; to commit to memory; as, to *con* a lesson.

con \'kän\ *adv.* [A shortened form of Latin *contra* meaning "opposite", "against".] Against; in opposition; on the negative side; as, to argue pro and *con*. — *n.* One that opposes, as an argument, a voter, or a vote. The debate was won by the *cons*.

con-. A form of *com-* used before any consonant except *b, h, l, m, p, r*, and *w*.

con·cave \(')kän-'kāv, 'kän-ˌkāv\ *adj.* Hollow and curved or rounded like the inside of a bowl or circle; curving in, as the bowl of a spoon. — **con·cav·i·ty** \kän-'kav-ət-ē\ *n.*

concave

con·ceal \kən-'sēl\ *v.* To hide from sight; to keep secret; as, to carry a *concealed* weapon; to *conceal* a fact.

con·ceal·ment \kən-'sēl-mənt\ *n.* **1** The act of hiding or the state of being hidden. **2** A hiding place.

con·cede \kən-'sēd\ *v.;* **con·ced·ed; con·ced·ing. 1** To admit to be true; to acknowledge; to yield; as, to *concede* that a statement is correct; to *concede* defeat. **2** To grant, as a right or a privilege. The law *concedes* everyone the right to a fair trial. — For synonyms see *grant*.

con·ceit \kən-'sēt\ *n.* **1** Excessive pride in oneself or one's ability; personal vanity. **2** A curious or fanciful idea; a witty thought or way of saying something. — For synonyms see *pride*.

con·ceit·ed \kən-'sēt-əd\ *adj.* Having too high an opinion of oneself; vain. — **con·ceit·ed·ly**, *adv.*

con·ceiv·a·ble \kən-'sē-vəb-l\ *adj.* Capable of being conceived, imagined, or understood; as, to consider every *conceivable* way of earning some money. — **con·ceiv·a·bly** \-və-blē\ *adv.*

con·ceive \kən-'sēv\ *v.;* **con·ceived; con·ceiv·ing. 1** To come to be with young; to become pregnant with. **2** To imagine; to form an idea of; as, unable to *conceive* how it could happen. **3** To have an idea or opinion; to think; as, to *conceive* of a person as a genius.

con·cen·trate \'kän(t)s-n-ˌtrāt\ *v.;* **con·cen·trat·ed; con·cen·trat·ing. 1** To bring or come to, or to direct toward, a common center; to gather into one body, mass, or force; as, to *concentrate* one's attention. Population tends to *concentrate* in cities. **2** To increase in strength by reducing the bulk; to condense; as, *concentrated* orange juice. **3** To fix all one's attention on one thing; as, to *concentrate* upon a problem.

con·cen·tra·tion \ˌkän(t)s-n-'trāsh-n\ *n.* **1** The act of concentrating or a state of being concentrated. **2** Close mental attention fixed on a subject; as, a problem calling for close *concentration.* **3** The relative amount of a substance dissolved in a solution; strength.

concentration camp. 1 A military camp in which troops are temporarily concentrated. **2** A detention camp, as one for confining prisoners of war, interned foreign civilians, political prisoners, or refugees.

con·cen·tric \kən-'sen-trik, kän-\ *adj.* Having the same center, as one circle inside another.

con·cept \'kän-ˌsept\ *n.* **1** A mental impression; an idea; a conception; as, changing *concepts* of the rights and duties of a citizen; to have a clear *concept* of one's aim in life. **2** A general idea of a class of things formed by selecting and combining the characteristics common to all things called by the same name. By studying hundreds of flowers of different kinds, forms, and colors, we can form a *concept* of "flower".

con·cep·tion \kən-'sepsh-n\ *n.* **1** The act of conceiving; a beginning. **2** The power of the mind to form ideas or to work out plans or designs; as, aircraft flying at a speed almost beyond *conception;* an artist whose powers of *conception* were greater than his skill. **3** That which is conceived; an idea, plan, or design formed in the mind; a general idea; a notion.

con·cern \kən-'sərn\ *v.* **1** To relate to; to belong to; to be of interest or of importance to; to affect. This problem *concerns* everyone. **2** To engage the interest or attention of; to interest; as, to *concern* oneself in the affairs of one's neighbors. **3** To be or to make anxious or worried. Don't *concern* yourself about me.

The word *affect* is a synonym of *concern: concern* may refer to the bearing or influence of one thing upon another; *affect* usually implies direct action on something, as in changing or altering it.

— *n.* 1 A business organization; as, a banking *concern.* **2** Something that relates or belongs to a person; business; affair; as, a day taken up with the usual *concerns.* **3** Interest; anxiety; as, a mother's *concern* about her child.

con·cerned \kən-'sərnd\ *adj.* Disturbed; anxious; worried; as, to be *concerned* about one's health.

con·cern·ing \kən-'sər-ning\ *prep.* Regarding; relating to; about; as, news *concerning* friends.

con·cert \'kän(t)s-rt, 'kän-ˌsərt\ *n.* [From French, there borrowed from Italian *concerto* originally meaning "a musical composition".] **1** A musical performance by several voices or instruments or by both; a public musical entertainment. **2** Agreement; harmony; as, to work in *concert.* **—** \kən-'sərt\ *v.* **1** To plan together; to settle by agreement. **2** To plan; to devise.

con·cert·ed \kən-'sərt-əd\ *adj.* **1** Arranged or contrived by agreement; planned by two or more persons or groups; agreed on; as, *concerted* schemes; *concerted* action. **2** Arranged in parts for several voices or instruments. — **con·cert·ed·ly**, *adv.*

con·cer·ti·na \ˌkän(t)s-r-'tē-nə\ *n.* A small musical wind instrument played much like an accordion.

con·cert·mas·ter \'kän(t)s-rt-ˌmast-r\ *n.* The first violinist or leader of the strings in an orchestra.

con·cer·to \kən-'chert-ˌō\ *n.; pl.* **con·cer·tos** \-ˌōz\ or **con·cer·ti** \-(ˌ)ē\. A musical composition, usually in three movements, in which one or more solo instruments stand out sharply against an orchestra.

con·ces·sion \kən-'sesh-n\ *n.* **1** The act of conceding or yielding. **2** A thing conceded; an acknowledgment. **3** A grant or lease of a part of a piece of property, or of a right of entry, for some special purpose; as, to have a *concession* for a lunch counter at a fair.

con·ces·sion·aire \kən-ˌsesh-n-'ar, -'er\ *n.* A person to whom a concession, as at an amusement park or a stadium, has been granted.

conch \'kängk, 'känch\ *n.; pl.* **conchs** \'kängks\ or **conch·es** \'kän-chəz\. A large spiral sea shell.

con·cil·i·ate \kən-'sil-ē-ˌāt\ *v.;* **con·cil·i·at·ed; con·cil·i·at·ing.** To gain the good will of; to make friendly; to reconcile; as, to try to *conciliate* an enemy. — **con·cil·i·a·tor** \-ˌāt-r\ *n.* — **con·cil·i·a·to·ry** \-ə-ˌtōr-ē, -ˌtȯr-ē\ *adj.*

con·cil·i·a·tion \kən-ˌsil-ē-'āsh-n\ *n.* A conciliating or a being conciliated. The disagreement between employer and workers was settled by *conciliation.*

con·cise \kən-'sīs\ *adj.* Expressing much in few words; condensed; brief; as, a *concise* account of an experience. — **con·cise·ly**, *adv.*

con·clave \'kän-ˌklāv\ *n.* A private meeting; a secret assembly; as, a *conclave* of boy scouts.

con·clude \kən-'klüd\ *v.;* **con·clud·ed; con·clud·ing. 1** To bring to an end; to come to an end; to finish;

as, to *conclude* a speech; to *conclude* with a word of warning. **2** To form an opinion; to decide by reasoning; as, to *conclude* that a statement is true. **3** To bring about as a result; to arrange; as, to *conclude* an agreement.

con·clu·sion \kən-ˈklüzh-n\ *n.* **1** Final decision, especially one reached by reasoning; as, to form *conclusions* from experience. **2** The last part of anything; end; result; as, at the *conclusion* of the contest. **3** A concluding; settlement or arrangement, as of a treaty or a bargain.

con·clu·sive \kən-ˈklü-siv, -ziv\ *adj.* Decisive; convincing; final; as, a *conclusive* argument. — **con·clu·sive·ly,** *adv.*

con·coct \kən-ˈkäkt, (ˈ)kän-\ *v.* [From Latin *concoctus,* past participle of *concoquere* meaning "to boil together".] **1** To prepare, as food, by combining ingredients; as, to *concoct* a stew. **2** To invent; to make up; as, to *concoct* a plan.

con·coc·tion \kən-ˈkäksh-n, kän-\ *n.* **1** A concocting. **2** Anything that is concocted.

con·com·i·tant \kän-ˈkäm-ət-ənt, kən-\ *adj.* Going along with; accompanying; as, *concomitant* circumstances. — *n.* Something that accompanies; an accompaniment.

con·cord \ˈkän(g)-ˌkȯrd\ *n.* Agreement; harmony; as, peace and *concord* among nations.

con·cord·ance \kən-ˈkȯrd-n(t)s\ *n.* **1** Agreement; accordance; harmony. **2** An alphabetical index of the words in a book, showing the passages in which they occur.

con·cord·ant \kən-ˈkȯrd-nt\ *adj.* Agreeing; correspondent; harmonious; as, *concordant* opinions. — **con·cord·ant·ly,** *adv.*

con·course \ˈkän-ˌkōrs, -ˌkȯrs\ *n.* **1** A flocking together, as of people. **2** Any flowing or running together; as, the *concourse* of two rivers. **3** An assemblage; a gathering. **4** An open space where several roads or paths meet, as in a park or plaza; an open space or hall where crowds may gather.

con·crete \(ˈ)kän-ˈkrēt, ˈkän-ˌkrēt\ *adj.* **1** Naming a thing or class of things, not a quality or characteristic possessed by things. "Goodness" is an abstract word, whereas "man" is a *concrete* word. **2** Actual; particular; specific; not general; as, a *concrete* example. **3** Made of concrete. — \ˈkän-ˌkrēt\ *n.* A mixture, especially when hardened, of cement and sand with gravel or broken stone, used for sidewalks and in building. — \ˈkän-ˌkrēt\ *v.;* **con·cret·ed; con·cret·ing.** To cover with concrete; to form of concrete.

con·cu·bine \ˈkän(g)-kyə-ˌbīn\ *n.* Among some peoples a woman who, though not legally a wife, lives with a man and has a recognized position in his household.

con·cur \kən-ˈkər, kän-\ *v.;* **con·curred; con·cur·ring.** **1** To happen together; to coincide, as two events. **2** To act together; to combine. Unforeseen troubles *concurred* to make the whole trip unpleasant. **3** To be in agreement; to accord. Each member of the committee *concurred* with the proposal.

con·cur·rence \kən-ˈkər-ən(t)s, kän-, -ˈkə-rən(t)s\ *n.* **1** A meeting or a coming together; as, at the *concurrence* of the highways. **2** Agreement in action or opinion. The committee reached a *concurrence* about the action that should be taken. **3** In geometry, a point of meeting common to three or more lines.

con·cur·rent \kən-ˈkər-ənt, kän-, -ˈkə-rənt\ *adj.* **1** Running together; happening or existing at the same time; as, *concurrent* expeditions to the North Pole. **2** Meeting in or directed to the same point; as, *concurrent* lines. **3** Co-operating; as, *concurrent* efforts. — **con·cur·rent·ly,** *adv.*

con·cus·sion \kən-ˈkəsh-n\ *n.* **1** A shaking or agitation. **2** An abnormal condition of lowered activity without any visible change in structure produced in an organ of the body by a shock, as a blow; as, *concussion* of the brain.

con·demn \kən-ˈdem\ *v.* **1** To declare to be wrong; to disapprove of; as, to *condemn* a person's actions. **2** To pronounce guilty; to convict of guilt. **3** To sentence; as, to *condemn* a criminal to death. **4** To declare to be unfit for use; as, to *condemn* a bridge. **5** To declare to be forfeited or taken for public use. — For synonyms see *censure.*

con·dem·na·ble \kən-ˈdem-(n)əb-l\ *adj.* Capable of being condemned.

con·dem·na·tion \ˌkän-ˌdem-ˈnāsh-n, -dəm-\ *n.* **1** A condemning or a being condemned. **2** Blame; censure; as, bitter *condemnation* of the opposition. **3** The state of being condemned. — **con·dem·na·to·ry** \kən-ˈdem-nə-ˌtōr-ē, -ˌtȯr-ē\ *adj.*

con·den·sa·tion \ˌkän-ˌden-ˈsāsh-n, -dən-\ *n.* **1** A condensing or a being condensed; as, the *condensation* of a book into one third its original length. **2** Something that has been condensed. **3** A reduction from one form to a form that is denser; as, the *condensation* of steam into water.

con·dense \kən-ˈden(t)s\ *v.;* **con·densed; con·dens·ing.** **1** To make or to become more close, compact, concise, or dense; to concentrate; to compress; as, to *condense* a paragraph into a sentence; to *condense* milk. **2** To change from a less dense to a denser form. When steam *condenses,* it becomes water.

con·dens·er \kən-ˈden(t)s-r\ *n.* One that condenses; especially, a device for holding or storing an electric charge.

con·de·scend \ˌkän-də-ˈsend\ *v.* **1** To stoop to a level considered less dignified or lower than one's own. **2** To grant favors with a superior air. — **con·de·scend·ing·ly** \-ing-lē\ *adv.*

con·de·scen·sion \ˌkän-də-ˈsench-n\ *n.* A condescending; a stooping from one's rank or dignity to meet an inferior in a courteous way.

con·di·ment \ˈkänd-m-ənt\ *n.* Something used to give an appetizing taste to food; especially, a seasoning such as pepper or mustard.

con·di·tion \kən-ˈdish-n\ *n.* **1** Something agreed upon or required as necessary if some other thing is to be or to take place; a provision. The bicycle was to be his on the *condition* that he got good marks in school. **2** State of affairs; circumstances; as, living *conditions.* **3** A state of existence or being; as, a gaseous *condition.* **4** Rank; station in life; as, men of humble *condition.* **5** State of health; fitness; as, to be in good *condition.* — *v.* To put into proper condition or into a desired condition; as, to *condition* a horse for a race; to *condition* air.

con·di·tion·al \kən-ˈdish-n(-)əl\ *adj.* Expressing, containing, or depending on a condition or conditions; made or granted on certain terms; as, a *conditional* promise; a *conditional* clause. — **con·di·tion·al·ly** \-n(-)ə-lē\ *adv.*

con·di·tioned \kən-ˈdish-nd\ *adj.* Arising because of special conditions, experience, or training; especially, caused by establishment of an unusual relation between a stimulus, as a flashing light, and a bodily reaction, as secretion of saliva; as, a *conditioned* response; a *conditioned* reflex.

con·dole \kən-ˈdōl\ *v.;* **con·doled; con·dol·ing.** To grieve in sympathy with another person; to express sympathetic sorrow; as, to *condole* with a widow in her misfortune.

con·do·lence \kən-ˈdō-lən(t)s, ˈkän-də-\ *n.* The expression of sympathy with another in sorrow or grief.

con·done \kən-ˈdōn\ *v.;* **con·doned; con·don·ing.** To pardon; to overlook; as, to *condone* a fault in a friend. — **con·do·na·tion** \ˌkän-də-ˈnāsh-n\ *n.*

con·dor \ˈkänd-r, ˈkän-ˌdȯr\ *n.* A very large American vulture, having a bare head and neck, and a white neck ruff.

con·duce \kən-ˈdüs, -ˈdyüs\ *v.;* **con·duced; con·duc·ing.** To lead or tend, especially to a favorable result; contribute. Careful investigation of the facts *conduced* to the success of the experiment.

con·du·cive \kən-ˈdü-siv, -ˈdyü-\ *adj.* Tending to promote, advance, or aid; contributing; as, action *conducive* to success.

con·duct \ˈkän-(ˌ)dəkt\ *n.* **1** Personal behavior; as, to be punished for bad *conduct.* **2** The act or manner of carrying on, as a business management. — \kən-ˈdəkt\ *v.* **1** To lead; to guide; as, to *conduct* visitors through the school building. **2** To manage or carry on; to control; as, to *conduct* a business or an orchestra. **3** To behave (oneself); as, to *conduct* oneself well at a party. **4** To act as conductor; to direct the performing of, as an orchestra. **5** To serve as a channel or a medium through which or along which something passes. Wires *conduct* electricity. — **con·duct·i·bil·i·ty** \kən-ˌdək-tə-ˈbil-ət-ē\ *n.* — **con·duct·i·ble** \kən-ˈdək-təb-l\ *adj.*

con·duct·ance \kən-ˈdək-tən(t)s\ *n.* The capacity or power of conducting or transmitting, as electricity.

con·duc·tion \kən-ˈdəksh-n\ *n.* **1** Conveyance, as of water through a pipe. **2** Transmission through a conductor, as electricity.

con·duc·tive \kən-ˈdək-tiv\ *adj.* Having the power to conduct or transmit, as heat or electricity.

con·duc·tiv·i·ty \ˌkän-ˌdək-ˈtiv-ət-ē\ *n.* The quality or power of conducting, as electricity or heat.

con·duc·tor \kən-ˈdəkt-r\ *n.* **1** A person in charge of a public conveyance, such as a bus, streetcar, or railroad train. **2** A person or thing that directs, leads, or conveys; as, a *conductor* of an orchestra; a *conductor* for rain water. **3** A substance or body capable of transmitting heat, electricity, or sound.

con·du·it \ˈkän-ˌdü-ət, -ˌdwit, -də-wət, -dət\ *n.* **1** A pipe or similar passage for carrying a fluid, as water. **2** A tube or trough for protecting electric wires or cables, as for telephones.

cone \ˈkōn\ *n.* **1** In trees of the pine family, a mass of overlapping woody scales mounted on an axis, bearing the seeds between them. **2** A solid body tapering evenly to a point from a circular base. **3** Anything having a similar shape; as, an ice-cream *cone.*

cone, 1

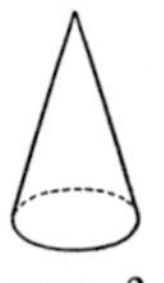

cone, 2

Con·es·to·ga wagon \ˈkän-ə-ˌstō-gə\. A covered wagon having broad-rimmed wheels, used for traveling in soft soil and over the prairie.

coney. Variant of *cony.*

con·fec·tion \kən-ˈfeksh-n\ *n.* Any sweet concoction intended to be eaten, as a fancy dessert, jam, ice cream, or a piece of candy.

con·fec·tion·er \kən-ˈfeksh-n-ər\ *n.* A person who makes or sells confections, especially ice cream and candy.

con·fec·tion·ery \kən-ˈfeksh-n-ˌer-ē\ *n.; pl.* **con·fec·tion·er·ies.** **1** Confections in general; especially, candy. **2** A confectioner's shop; a candy store. **3** The business of a confectioner.

con·fed·er·a·cy \kən-ˈfed-r(-)ə-sē\ *n.; pl.* **con·fed·er·a·cies.** **1** A league of persons, parties, or states; an alliance; a confederation. **2** [with a capital] The Confederate States of America, the eleven southern states that seceded from the United States in 1860 and 1861.

con·fed·er·ate \kən-ˈfed-r(-)ət\ *adj.* **1** United in a league; allied. **2** [with a capital] Of or belonging to the Confederacy; as, the *Confederate* flag. — *n.* **1** A member of a confederacy; an ally; an accomplice. **2** [with a capital] A soldier of the Confederacy or a person who sided with the Confederacy. — \kən-ˈfed-r-ˌāt\ *v.;* **con·fed·er·at·ed; con·fed·er·at·ing.** To unite in a league or alliance.

con·fed·er·a·tion \kən-ˌfed-r-ˈāsh-n\ *n.* **1** The action of confederating, or joining in a league; federation. **2** A league; an alliance; a confederacy; a federation.

con·fer \kən-ˈfər\ *v.;* **con·ferred; con·fer·ring.** **1** To grant; to give; to bestow; as, to *confer* an honor on someone. **2** To consult; to discuss; to compare views; as, to *confer* with other members of a committee.

con·fer·ee or **con·fer·ree** \ˌkän-fə-ˈrē\ *n.* A person taking part in a conference.

con·fer·ence \ˈkän-fərn(t)s, -fər-ən(t)s, -frən(t)s\

n. **1** A meeting for discussion or exchange of opinions. **2** The discussion itself. **3** A meeting of committees of two branches of a legislature to adjust differences, as with respect to laws in process of adoption. **4** An association of athletic teams representing educational institutions.

con·fess \kən-'fes\ *v.* **1** To admit as true; to acknowledge, as a fault or crime; to own up. **2** To make known one's sins, especially in privacy and to a priest. **3** To act as confessor for; to hear the confession of a penitent. — For synonyms see *acknowledge.*

con·fess·ed·ly \kən-'fes-əd-lē\ *adv.* By confession; admittedly.

con·fes·sion \kən-'fesh-n\ *n.* **1** The act of confessing; acknowledgment, as of one's faults or sins; especially, a disclosing of one's sins to a priest. **2** A statement of what is confessed. The robber signed a *confession.* **3** Also **confession of faith.** A formal statement of beliefs, as of a church; a creed.

con·fes·sion·al \kən-'fesh-n(-)əl\ *n.* **1** The enclosed place in which a priest sits and hears confessions. **2** The practice of confessing to a priest.

con·fes·sor \kən-'fes-r\ *n.* **1** A person who confesses. **2** A priest who has the authority to hear confessions.

con·fet·ti \kən-'fet-ē\ *n. pl.* [From Italian, plural of *confetto,* originally meaning "candy", then "paper and plaster imitations of candy", "paper strips".] Small bits of colored paper, made to be easily thrown broadcast, as at weddings and festivals.

con·fi·dant \'kän-fə-ˌdant\ *n.* A person to whom secrets are confided; a confidential or bosom friend.

con·fi·dante \'kän-fə-ˌdant\ *n.* A girl or woman confidant. My sister's special *confidante* is the girl next door.

con·fide \kən-'fīd\ *v.;* **con·fid·ed; con·fid·ing. 1** To put or have faith in; to have trust or confidence; as, a man in whose integrity you can *confide* absolutely. **2** To show trust or confidence by telling something secret; as, to *confide* in a friend. **3** To give in charge; to commit; as, to *confide* one's safety to the police.

con·fi·dence \'kän-fə-dən(t)s, -ˌden(t)s\ *n.* **1** Trust; belief; as, to have *confidence* in a person. **2** Boldness; assurance; as, to speak with *confidence;* to be full of *confidence.* **3** Reliance upon another person's secrecy or loyalty; as, to tell something in *confidence.* **4** Something told in confidence; a secret; as, to exchange *confidences.*

confidence game. Any swindle in which the swindler (**confidence man**) takes advantage of the trust he has persuaded the victim to place in him.

con·fi·dent \'kän-fə-dənt, -ˌdent\ *adj.* Having or showing confidence; sure; certain; as, to be *confident* of winning; to have a *confident* manner. —*n.* A confidant or confidante. — **con·fi·dent·ly,** *adv.*

con·fi·den·tial \ˌkän-fə-'dench-l\ *adj.* **1** Secret; private; as, *confidential* information. **2** Intimate; familiar; as, a *confidential* tone of voice; to be on *confidential* terms with someone. **3** Trusted with secret matters; as, a *confidential* secretary. — **con·fi·den·tial·ly** \-'dench-l(-)ē\ *adv.*

con·fid·ing \kən-'fīd-ing\ *adj.* Trustful; trusting; as, a very *confiding* child. — **con·fid·ing·ly,** *adv.*

con·fig·u·ra·tion \kən-ˌfig-yər-'āsh-n\ *n.* Shape; form; especially, shape or form as produced by an arrangement of parts.

con·fine \'kän-ˌfīn\ *n.* A boundary; a limit; as, the *confines* of a city. — \kən-'fīn\ *v.;* **con·fined; con·fin·ing. 1** To keep or hold within limits; to restrict; as, to *confine* oneself to a brief statement of the facts of the case. **2** To shut up; to imprison; as, to *confine* a bird in a cage or a man in a prison. **3** To keep indoors, especially on account of sickness; as, to be *confined* for several days with a cold. — **con·fine·ment** \kən-'fīn-mənt\ *n.*

con·firm \kən-'fərm\ *v.* **1** To make firm or firmer; to strengthen, as in a habit, in faith, or in intention. **2** To make sure of the truth of; to verify; as, to *confirm* a suspicion by careful investigation. Early reports of the disaster have not been *confirmed.* **3** To approve; to ratify; as, to *confirm* a treaty. Some appointments to office must be *confirmed* by the legislature. **4** To admit a baptized person to full church privileges.

con·fir·ma·tion \ˌkän-fər-'māsh-n\ *n.* **1** The act of confirming. **2** Something that confirms; proof. **3** The ceremony of admitting a baptized person to full church privileges.

con·firmed \kən-'fərmd\ *adj.* **1** Established; settled; as, a man with a *confirmed* distrust of everything new. **2** Habitual; as, a *confirmed* idler. **3** Chronic; as, a *confirmed* invalid.

con·fis·cate \'kän-fəs-ˌkāt\ *v.;* **con·fis·cat·ed; con·fis·cat·ing.** To seize by public authority for public use or as a penalty. Smuggled goods may be *confiscated* and the smugglers fined or imprisoned. — **con·fis·ca·tion** \ˌkän-fəs-'kāsh-n, -ˌfis-\ *n.*

con·fla·gra·tion \ˌkän-flə-'grāsh-n\ *n.* A large and destructive fire.

con·flict \'kän-ˌflikt\ *n.* **1** A fight; a battle; a struggle; especially, a prolonged struggle. **2** A clashing or a sharp disagreement, as between ideas, interests, or purposes. — \kən-'flikt, 'kän-ˌflikt\ *v.* To clash; to be in opposition; as, *conflicting* opinions. Duty and desire often *conflict.*

con·flu·ence \'kän-ˌflü-ən(t)s\ *n.* **1** A flowing or coming together, especially of two or more streams. **2** A flocking or crowding together in one place. **3** A place where two or more streams meet.

con·flu·ent \'kän-ˌflü-ənt\ *adj.* Coming together to form one stream or body, as two or more rivers.

con·form \kən-'fȯrm\ *v.* **1** To make or be like; as, a dress that *conforms* exactly to the pattern. **2** To be or act in obedience, as to established rules or laws, or in agreement and harmony, as with accepted ideas or standards. All pupils are required to *conform* to the rules. — **con·form·er,** *n.*

con·form·a·ble \kən-'fȯr-məb-l\ *adj.* **1** Being like; being in agreement or harmony. **2** Obedient; submissive. — **con·form·a·bly** \-mə-blē\ *adv.*

con·for·ma·tion \ˌkän-(ˌ)fȯr-'māsh-n, -fər-\ *n.* **1** The act of conforming, or bringing into agreement or harmony. **2** A shaping or putting into form. **3** Formation resulting from arrangement of parts; structure; form; shape.

con·form·ist \kən-'fȯr-məst\ *n.* **1** A person who conforms, especially one who practices conformity in religion. **2** One who shows a marked tendency towards conformity in general.

con·form·i·ty \kən-'fȯr-mət-ē, (')kän-\ *n.; pl.* **con·form·i·ties. 1** Harmony; agreement; as, measures taken in *conformity* with the plan agreed upon. **2** A point of similarity or agreement; correspondence; likeness. **3** The act or behavior of a person who brings his thought or conduct into agreement with generally accepted standards or practices. **4** Acceptance of a religion established by law or generally favored throughout a country.

con·found \kən-'faund, (')kän-\ *v.* **1** *Archaic.* To destroy. **2** To throw into confusion or disorder; to mix up; to confuse. **3** To damn — used chiefly to express displeasure or annoyance; as, a *confounded* nuisance. *Confound* it!

con·found·ed·ly \(')kän-'faun-dəd-lē, kən-\ *adv.* Detestably; damnably; extremely; as, a *confoundedly* hot day.

con·front \kən-'frənt\ *v.* **1** To face, especially hostilely or defiantly; to oppose; as, to *confront* an enemy. **2** To bring face to face; to cause to face or meet; as, to *confront* a person with his accuser; to be *confronted* with difficulties.

Con·fu·cian \kən-'fyüsh-n\ *adj.* Of or relating to the Chinese philosopher Confucius, his philosophical and moral teachings, or his followers. — *n.* A follower of Confucius or his teachings.

Con·fu·cian·ist \kən-'fyüsh-n-əst\ *n.* or *adj.* Confucian.

con·fuse \kən-'fyüz\ *v.;* **con·fused; con·fus·ing. 1** To disturb in mind; to make uncertain; to throw into disorder; to disconcert. The unruly audience *confused* the speaker. **2** To mistake one person or thing for another; to mix up; as, to *confuse* "m" and "n". It is easy to *confuse* twin brothers. — **con·fus·ed·ly** \-'fyü-zəd-lē\ *adv.*

con·fu·sion \kən-'fyüzh-n\ *n.* **1** The state of being thrown into disorder; turmoil. At the scene of the accident all was *confusion.* **2** The state of being disconcerted; loss of self-possession; embarrassment; as, to be unable to conceal one's *confusion.* **3** The act of confusing; especially, the mistaking of one thing for another.

con·fute \kən-'fyüt\ *v.;* **con·fut·ed; con·fut·ing. 1** To prove to be false or wrong; as, to *confute* an argument. **2** To overwhelm by argument; to silence; as, to *confute* one's opponent in a debate. — **con·fu·ta·tion** \ˌkän-(ˌ)fyü-'tāsh-n\ *n.*

con·ga \'käng-gə\ *n.* **1** A Cuban dance of African origin, performed by couples or in single file following a leader. **2** A bass drum beaten with the hands, used to provide rhythm for the conga.

con·geal \kən-'jēl\ *v.* **1** To change from a fluid to a solid state by cold; to freeze. **2** To make or become hard, stiff, or thick, from cold or other causes; as, *congealed* blood. — **con·geal·a·ble,** *adj.*

con·gen·ial \kən-'jēn-yəl\ *adj.* **1** Alike or sympathetic in spirit, tastes, and interests; as, a group of *congenial* people. **2** Suited to one's taste or nature; agreeable; as, a *congenial* climate; *congenial* work. — **con·gen·ial·ly** \-yə-lē\ *adv.*

con·ge·ni·al·i·ty \kən-ˌjē-nē-'al-ət-ē, -ˌjēn-'yal-\ *n.* The quality or state of being congenial.

con·gen·i·tal \kən-'jen-ət-l, kän-\ *adj.* Existing at or dating from birth; born with one; inborn; as, *congenital* disease; a *congenital* defect. — **con·gen·i·tal·ly** \-ət-l-ē\ *adv.*

con·ger eel \'käng-gr\. A scaleless salt-water eel that sometimes grows to a length of eight feet and is an important food fish of Europe.

con·gest \kən-'jest\ *v.* To make too full; to block, obstruct, or affect by an abnormally great accumulation of anything or by overcrowding; as, highways *congested* with holiday traffic; *congested* blood vessels.

con·ges·tion \kən-'jes-chən\ *n.* **1** The condition of being too crowded or too full. **2** An unusual increase in the amount of blood in the blood vessels of some part of the body, caused sometimes by an increased flow of blood to the affected part, sometimes by obstruction in the vessels leading away from it.

con·glom·er·ate \kən-'gläm-r(-)ət\ *adj.* **1** Gathered into a ball, mass, or cluster. **2** Made up of parts gathered from various sources. — *n.* **1** A mass formed of fragments from various sources. **2** A rock composed of rounded fragments, varying in size from pebbles to boulders, held together by a cementing material, as of hardened clay. — \kən-'gläm-r-ˌāt\ *v.;* **con·glom·er·at·ed; con·glom·er·at·ing.** To gather or form into a compact mass.

con·glom·er·a·tion \kən-ˌgläm-r-'āsh-n\ *n.* **1** The action or process of conglomerating or the state of being conglomerated. **2** A mass of things from various sources mixed up together.

con·go snake or **congo eel** \'käng-ˌgō\. Either of two eellike amphibians of the southeastern United States, bluish-black in color and having two pairs of very short limbs.

con·grat·u·late \kən-'grach-l-ˌāt\ *v.;* **con·grat·u·lat·ed; con·grat·u·lat·ing.** To express to a person pleasure over his happiness, success, or good fortune; to wish joy to; as, to *congratulate* the winner of a race; to *congratulate* a friend on his birthday.

con·grat·u·la·tion \kən-ˌgrach-l-'āsh-n\ *n.* **1** The act of congratulating. **2** [usually in the plural] An expression of joy or pleasure at another's success, happiness, or good fortune.

con·grat·u·la·to·ry \kən-'grach-l-ə-ˌtōr-ē, -ˌtȯr-ē\ *adj.* Expressing congratulations; as, a few *congratulatory* remarks.

con·gre·gate \'käng-grə-ˌgāt\ *v.;* **con·gre·gat·ed; con·gre·gat·ing.** To collect or gather into a crowd or mass; to assemble.

con·gre·ga·tion \ˌkäng-grə-'gāsh-n\ *n.* **1** The action of congregating or the state of being congregated. **2** A collection of separate things. **3** An assembly of persons, especially one meeting for religious worship.

con·gre·ga·tion·al \ˌkäng-grə-'gāsh-n(-)əl\ *adj.* Of or belonging to a congregation or to congregationalism.

con·gre·ga·tion·al·ism \ˌkäng-grə-'gāsh-n(-)ə-ˌliz-m\ *n.* A form of church organization in which each congregation governs itself.

con·gress \'käng-grəs\ *n.* **1** A gathering or assembly, especially of representatives; a conference. **2** [usually with a capital] The body of senators and representatives of a nation, especially of a republic, forming its chief lawmaking body; as, the *Congress* of the United States.

con·gres·sion·al \kən-'gresh-n(-)əl, kän-\ *adj.* Having to do with a congress; as, a *congressional* election.

con·gress·man \'käng-grəs-mən\ *n.; pl.* **con·gress·men** \-mən\. A member of the United States Congress, especially of the House of Representatives.

con·gress·wom·an \'käng-grəs-ˌwu̇m-ən\ *n.; pl.* **con·gress·wom·en** \-ˌwim-ən\. A female member of the United States Congress, especially of the House of Representatives.

con·gru·ent \kən-'grü-ənt, 'käng-ˌgrü-\ *adj.* **1** Suitable; agreeing; corresponding. The report proved to be *congruent* with the facts. **2** In geometry, capable of being placed over another figure so that all points of the one correspond to all points of the other. — **con·gru·ence** \-ən(t)s\ or **con·gru·en·cy** \-ən-sē\ *n.* — **con·gru·ent·ly,** *adv.*

con·gru·i·ty \kən-'grü-ət-ē, kän-\ *n.* **1** Agreement or correspondence between things; as, the *congruity* of two reports; the *congruity* of two triangles. **2** A point of agreement or harmony, as in an argument.

con·gru·ous \'käng-grü-əs\ *adj.* **1** Suitable in nature or qualities; in harmony; fitting. The proposed plan was not *congruous* to the needs of the community. **2** In geometry, congruent.

con·ic \'kän-ik\ or **con·i·cal** \-ik-l\ *adj.* Shaped like a cone; as, a *conic* figure; a *conical* tower. — **con·i·cal·ly** \-ik-l(-)ē\ *adv.*

co·ni·fer \'kō-nəf-r, 'kän-əf-r\ *n.* Any cone-bearing tree or shrub, such as a pine or a spruce. — **co·nif·er·ous** \kō-'nif-r(-)əs\ *adj.*

conj. Abbreviation for *conjunction.*

con·jec·tur·al \kən-'jek-chər-əl\ *adj.* Of, relating to, or of the nature of a conjecture or guess. Reasons for the explosion in the airplane are only *conjectural.*

con·jec·ture \kən-'jek-chər\ *n.* **1** A guessing; a surmising. **2** A conclusion based on inadequate evidence; a surmise. — *v.;* **con·jec·tured; con·jec·tur·ing.** To guess; to surmise.

con·join \kən-'jȯin, kän-\ *v.* To join together, as in action or purpose; to unite.

con·joint \kən-'jȯint, kän-\ *adj.* **1** United; conjoined. **2** Made up of or carried on by two or more in combination; joint. — **con·joint·ly,** *adv.*

con·ju·gal \'kän-jəg-l, kən-'jüg-l\ *adj.* Of or relating to marriage; matrimonial; as, *conjugal* happiness. — **con·ju·gal·ly** \-l-ē\ *adv.*

con·ju·gate \'kän-jə-gət, -ˌgāt\ *adj.* United, especially in pairs; coupled. — \-ˌgāt\ *v.;* **con·ju·gat·ed; con·ju·gat·ing.** **1** To unite; to couple. **2** To give the various forms of a verb in their proper order.

con·ju·ga·tion \ˌkän-jə-'gāsh-n\ *n.* **1** The action of joining together. **2** In grammar, the act of giving the various forms of a verb in their proper order. **3** A class of verbs having the same general kind of inflectional forms; as, the strong *conjugation.*

con·junc·tion \kən-'jəng(k)sh-n\ *n.* **1** A joining together; a combination; as, to act in *conjunction* with others. **2** A word, such as *and, but, when,* or *because,* used to connect other words, phrases, or clauses.

con·junc·ti·va \ˌkän-ˌjəng(k)-'tī-və\ *n.; pl.* **con·junc·ti·vas** \-vəz\ or **con·junc·ti·vae** \-ˌvē\. The membrane lining the eyelid and covering part of the eyeball.

con·junc·tive \kən-'jəng(k)-tiv\ *adj.* **1** Connective. **2** Done or existing in conjunction. **3** Of the nature of a conjunction; as, a *conjunctive* adverb. — *n.* A conjunctive word; a conjunction.

con·jure \'kənj-r, 'känj-r; *sense 5 is* kən-'ju̇r\ *v.;* **con·jured; con·jur·ing.** **1** To use magic, as in summoning a spirit. **2** To summon by conjuring. **3** To make come or go as if by magic; as, to *conjure* up a scene of horror in one's imagination. **4** To perform the tricks of a magician, as for entertainment. **5** To entreat; to implore; to beseech. — **con·jur·er** or **con·jur·or,** *n.*

conk \'käŋk, 'kȯŋk\ *v.* To stall, fail, or break down, as an engine or motor.

con·nect \kə-'nekt\ *v.* **1** To join or link together, directly or by something coming between; as, to *connect* two wires. The towns were *connected* by a railroad. **2** To attach by personal relationship or association; as, *connected* by marriage; to be *connected* with a business organization. **3** To associate in the mind; as, to *connect* two ideas. **4** To meet, as two trains, at a time and place suitable for transferring passengers or freight. — **con·nec·tor** or **con·nect·er,** *n.*

con·nect·ed·ly \kə-'nek-təd-lē\ *adv.* In a connected manner; coherently.

con·nec·tion \kə-'neksh-n\ *n.* **1** The act of connecting. **2** The fact or condition of being connected; relationship; as, the close *connection* between dirt and disease; to see the *connection* between two ideas. **3** A thing that connects; any means by which two things are connected; a bond or link; as, a loose *connection* in a radio; to be unable to get a *connection* on the telephone. **4** Personal relationship or a person connected with others in such a relationship; as, a *connection* by marriage; business *connections.* **5** The act or the means of continuing a journey by transferring, as to another train, ship, or airplane; as, to make a *connection* for San Francisco at Chicago.

con·nec·tive \kə-'nek-tiv\ *n.* Something that connects; especially, a word that connects other words, as a conjunction or a relative pronoun. — *adj.* Connecting.

connective tissue. A tissue which supports and binds together the other tissues in nearly all parts of the body, forming a framework for the organs and making up the tendons and ligaments.

conn·ing tower \'kän-ing\. **1** An armored pilot-house, as on a battleship. **2** A raised structure on the deck of a submarine, used as an observation post and as an entrance to the boat.

con·niv·ance \kə-'nīv-n(t)s\ *n.* The act of conniving; pretended ignorance of wrongdoing or secret co-operation with wrongdoers.

con·nive \kə-'nīv\ *v.;* **con·nived; con·niv·ing. 1** To pretend not to see something that is going on and that one ought to oppose or stop; as, officials *conniving* at the acts of known criminals. **2** To co-operate secretly; to have a secret understanding.

con·nois·seur \ˌkän-ə-'sər, -'sür\ *n.* A person competent to act as a judge in matters involving taste and appreciation; an expert; as, a *connoisseur* of rare books; a *connoisseur* of French painting.

con·no·ta·tion \ˌkän-ə-'tāsh-n, ˌkän-(ˌ)ō-\ *n.* A meaning or significance suggested by a word or an expression apart from and in addition to its primary or central meaning, or denotation; as, the word "home" with all its heart-warming *connotations.*

con·note \kə-'nōt\ *v.;* **con·not·ed; con·not·ing.** To suggest or mean along with or in addition to the exact meaning; to have the additional meaning of. The word "cell" means a small compartment but it may *connote* imprisonment.

con·nu·bi·al \kə-'nü-bē-əl, -'nyü-\ *adj.* Of or relating to marriage; matrimonial. — **con·nu·bi·al·ly** \-ə-lē\ *adv.*

co·noid \'kō-ˌnȯid\ *adj.* Cone-shaped.

con·quer \'kängk-r\ *v.;* **con·quered; con·quer·ing** \-r(-)ing\. **1** To get or gain by force; to win by fighting. The army *conquered* the whole country. **2** To overcome; to subdue; as, to *conquer* a bad habit. **3** To be victorious.

con·quer·or \'kängk-r-r\ *n.* One who conquers; a victor.

con·quest \'kän(g)-ˌkwest\ *n.* **1** The act or process of conquering; a gaining of victory; as, the Spanish *conquest* of Mexico. **2** That which is conquered, as territory won in war and retained by the conqueror. **3** A person whose affections have been won. — For synonyms see *victory.*

con·quis·ta·dor \kȯng-'kēs-tə-ˌdȯr\ *n.; pl.* **con·quis·ta·dors** \-ˌdȯrz\ or **con·quis·ta·do·res** \(ˌ)kȯng-ˌkēs-tə-'dȯr-ēz, -'dōr-ēz, -ās\. [From Spanish, meaning "conqueror".] A conqueror; especially, one of the 16th-century Spanish leaders in the conquest of America.

con·san·guin·i·ty \ˌkän-ˌsan(g)-'gwin-ət-ē\ *n.* Relationship by blood; descent from a common ancestor; kinship.

con·science \'känch-n(t)s\ *n.* A sense or consciousness of right and wrong; sensitiveness to the rightness or wrongness of one's own acts and motives; a feeling that one ought to do what is right and to avoid what is wrong. The boy's *conscience* told him that he had done wrong.

con·sci·en·tious \ˌkänch-ē-'ench-əs\ *adj.* Directed by or in accordance with one's conscience; guided by a proper sense of right and wrong; as, a *conscientious* workman. — **con·sci·en·tious·ly,** *adv.*

conscientious objector. A person who, acting in accordance with his conscience, objects to warfare or to military service.

con·scious \'känch-əs\ *adj.* **1** Aware of facts or feelings; as, to be *conscious* of what is going on. **2** Mentally awake or active; as, to become *conscious* again after a faint. **3** Known or felt by one's inner self; as, *conscious* guilt. **4** Intentional; planned; as, a *conscious* smile. — **con·scious·ly,** *adv.*

con·scious·ness \'känch-əs-nəs\ *n.* **1** The state that distinguishes beings that have feelings and powers of thought from beings that are lacking in these. **2** The normal condition of conscious life as distinguished from sleep or insensibility; as, to lose *consciousness* from a blow on the head. **3** Mind; thoughts. Gradually the sound of the bell penetrated the dozing man's *consciousness.*

con·script \'kän-ˌskript\ *adj.* Enrolled for military or naval service or for other work by order of a government; formed by compulsory enrollment; conscripted; as, a *conscript* army; *conscript* labor. — *n.* A conscripted person, especially one serving in the armed forces. — \kən-'skript\ *v.* To compel to enroll for military, naval, or other service; to draft.

con·scrip·tion \kən-'skripsh-n\ *n.* **1** A compulsory enrollment of persons, especially for military or naval service; a draft. **2** A forced contribution, as of money, imposed by a government in time of war or other emergency.

con·se·crate \'kän(t)s-ə-ˌkrāt\ *v.;* **con·se·crat·ed; con·se·crat·ing. 1** To declare to be sacred or holy; to set apart or devote to the service of God; as, to *consecrate* a church or a cemetery. **2** To dedicate or devote to some particular purpose; as, a life *consecrated* to helping the needy. — **con·se·cra·tor,** *n.*

con·se·cra·tion \ˌkän(t)s-ə-'krāsh-n\ *n.* **1** A consecrating or a being consecrated. **2** A ceremony used in consecrating; a dedication.

con·sec·u·tive \kən-'sek-(y)ət-iv\ *adj.* Following one another in regular order and without gaps; successive; as, fifty *consecutive* years. — **con·sec·u·tive·ly,** *adv.*

con·sen·sus \kən-ˈsen(t)s-əs\ *n.* Agreement, as in opinion or testimony; accord; the trend of opinion; as, the *consensus* of opinion.

con·sent \kən-ˈsent\ *v.* To agree; to give one's approval; as, to *consent* to a request; to *consent* to make a speech. — *n.* Approval of what is done or proposed by another person; as, to give one's *consent;* to need the *consent* of one's parents.

con·se·quence \ˈkän(t)s-ə-ˌkwen(t)s, -kwən(t)s\ *n.* **1** A result; as, to face the *consequences* of one's acts. The fire was a *consequence* of carelessness. **2** Importance; distinction; as, a man of *consequence* in his city; a matter of no *consequence.*

con·se·quent \ˈkän(t)s-ə-ˌkwent, -kwənt\ *adj.* Following as a result or effect; resulting; as, the sinking of a ship and the *consequent* loss of life.

con·se·quen·tial \ˌkän(t)s-ə-ˈkwench-l\ *adj.* **1** Of the nature of a consequence or result; following as a consequence. **2** Showing self-importance; as, a person with a *consequential* manner.

con·se·quent·ly \ˈkän(t)s-ə-ˌkwent-lē, -kwənt-lē\ *adv.* As a result; accordingly.

con·ser·va·tion \ˌkän(t)s-r-ˈvāsh-n\ *n.* **1** A planned protecting, preserving, or supervising of something, as a natural resource. **2** A field of knowledge concerned with the preservation and wise use of natural resources.

con·serv·a·tism \kən-ˈsər-və-ˌtiz-m\ *n.* The disposition or tendency to keep to the old familiar ways of doing things; opposition to change.

con·serv·a·tive \kən-ˈsər-vət-iv\ *adj.* **1** Tending to conserve or to preserve. **2** Favoring a policy of keeping things as they are; opposed to change; as, the *conservative* citizens of a community. **3** Indicating, relating to, or characteristic of a political party that usually favors existing forms and methods of government. **4** Safe; not risky; as, a *conservative* investment. — *n.* **1** A preservative. **2** A person who holds conservative views. — **con·serv·a·tive·ly**, *adv.*

con·serv·a·to·ry \kən-ˈsər-və-ˌtōr-ē, -ˌtȯr-ē\ *n.; pl.* **con·serv·a·to·ries.** **1** A greenhouse, especially a small one attached to a house. **2** A public place of instruction in some special study; as, a *conservatory* of music.

con·serve \ˈkän-ˌsərv\ *n.* **1** A candy, or candied fruit. **2** [in the plural] Preserved fruit; preserves. — \kən-ˈsərv; *sense 2 is also* ˈkän-ˌsərv\ *v.;* **conserved**; **con·serv·ing.** **1** To keep in a safe or sound condition; to save; as, to *conserve* a country's resources. **2** To make into conserves; to preserve.

con·sid·er \kən-ˈsid-r\ *v.;* **con·sid·ered**; **con·sid·er·ing** \-r(-)ing\. **1** To think over carefully; to ponder; to reflect; as, to *consider* a problem from every angle. **2** To regard highly; to esteem; as, a man well *considered* by those who know him. **3** To think of in a certain way; to regard; as, to *consider* the price too high. **4** To think about with the idea of buying or accepting; as, to *consider* an offer.

con·sid·er·a·ble \kən-ˈsid-rb-l, -r(-)əb-l\ *adj.* **1** Important; highly regarded; as, a *considerable* man among the bankers in town. **2** Large in extent; large in amount or quantity; as, a *considerable* area; a *considerable* number. — **con·sid·er·a·bly** \-r-blē, -r(-)ə-blē\ *adv.*

con·sid·er·ate \kən-ˈsid-r-ət\ *adj.* **1** Noted for or given to careful thought. **2** Thoughtful of the rights and feelings of other persons; showing thoughtful kindness; as, a *considerate* person; a *considerate* act. — **con·sid·er·ate·ly**, *adv.*

con·sid·er·a·tion \kən-ˌsid-r-ˈāsh-n\ *n.* **1** Careful thought; deliberation. The plan received due *consideration.* **2** Thoughtfulness for other people; as, to show *consideration* for the rights of others. **3** Motive; reason; as, the *considerations* that move one to do something. **4** Respect; regard; as, a writer held in high *consideration.* **5** A payment made in return for something; a compensation.

con·sid·er·ing \kən-ˈsid-r(-)ing\ *prep.* Taking into account; in view of. *Considering* the difficulties, the job was done quite well.

con·sign \kən-ˈsīn\ *v.* **1** To give, send, or deliver formally to another person; as, a child *consigned* to the care of its grandmother. **2** To put in a prepared place; as, to *consign* a body to the grave. **3** To send to an agent for handling or selling; as, to *consign* goods. — **con·sign·a·ble** \-ˈsī-nəb-l\ *adj.*

con·sign·ee \ˌkän-ˌsī-ˈnē, ˌkän(t)s-n-ˈē\ *n.* A person to whom goods are consigned.

con·sign·ment \kən-ˈsīn-mənt\ *n.* **1** The action of a person who consigns something. **2** Anything, such as a shipment of goods, delivered to an agent for handling.

con·sist \kən-ˈsist\ *v.* **1** To have as a cause, basis, or essential part; to lie or reside; to be contained. Bravery *consists* partly in knowing when to fight and when to run. **2** To be made up; to be composed. Our breakfast *consisted* of cereal, milk, and fruit.

con·sist·ence \kən-ˈsis-tən(t)s\ *n.* Consistency.

con·sist·en·cy \kən-ˈsis-tən-sē\ *n.; pl.* **con·sist·en·cies.** **1** The condition of sticking together; thickness; firmness. This mud has the *consistency* of glue. **2** Agreement; harmony; congruity; as, action that is in *consistency* with one's character. **3** A being consistent; uniformity, as of practice; as, behavior marked by *consistency* at all times.

con·sist·ent \kən-ˈsis-tənt\ *adj.* **1** Having firmness; having the quality of sticking together; as, a *consistent* substance. **2** Agreeing; harmonious; as, separate but *consistent* accounts of an accident; to keep one's conduct *consistent* with one's beliefs. — **con·sist·ent·ly**, *adv.*

con·so·la·tion \ˌkän(t)s-l-ˈāsh-n\ *n.* **1** The act of consoling or the state of being consoled. **2** Comfort offered to lessen a person's misery or grief. **3** Any person or thing that brings comfort or that lessens disappointment.

con·sol·a·to·ry \kən-ˈsäl-ə-ˌtōr-ē, -ˌtȯr-ē, -ˈsō-lə-\ *adj.* Giving consolation; consoling; comforting.

con·sole \kən-ˈsōl\ *v.;* **con·soled**; **con·sol·ing.** To comfort in times of grief or distress; to lessen the suffering and raise the spirits of. It is not easy to *console* a child who has lost a pet. — **con·sol·a·ble** \-'sō-ləb-l\ *adj.*

con·sole \'kän-ˌsōl\ *n.* **1** A wall bracket, usually ornamental, as a bracketlike projection from a wall. **2** Also **console table.** A table, usually placed against a wall, having its top supported by brackets or bracketlike legs. **3** The desklike part of an organ, which contains the keyboard, stops, and pedals, and at which the organist sits. **4** A radio, phonograph, or television cabinet that stands on the floor.

console, 4

con·sol·i·date \kən-'säl-ə-ˌdāt\ *v.;* **con·sol·i·dat·ed; con·sol·i·dat·ing. 1** To unite; to combine. Two of the largest banks in the city have recently *consolidated.* **2** To make firm or firmer; to strengthen; as, to *consolidate* one's position in the community. The army ceased its advance while it *consolidated* its position.

consolidated school. A school attended by pupils from several school districts.

con·sol·i·da·tion \kən-ˌsäl-ə-'dāsh-n\ *n.* **1** The act or process of consolidating or the state of being consolidated. **2** In business, the combination of two or more companies into one.

con·som·mé \ˌkän(t)s-m-'ā\ *n.* [French, from the past participle of *consommer* meaning "to boil down".] A clear soup, usually made from a combination of veal, beef, and chicken.

con·so·nance \'kän(t)s-n-ən(t)s\ *n.* Agreement; harmony; especially, harmony of sounds.

con·so·nant \'kän(t)s-n(-)ənt\ *adj.* **1** In agreement; according; consistent; as, behavior *consonant* with the boy's nature. **2** Consonantal. — *n.* **1** A speech sound produced when the outgoing breath is squeezed or stopped somewhere between the throat and the lips. **2** Any letter of the alphabet that stands for such a sound (in general, any letter except *a, e, i, o, u,* which are called *vowels,* except that *y* is sometimes a vowel and sometimes a consonant).

con·so·nan·tal \ˌkän(t)s-n-'ant-l\ *adj.* Of or relating to a consonant.

con·sort \'kän-ˌsȯrt\ *n.* **1** A wife or a husband; a mate. **2** A ship sailing in company with another ship. — \kən-'sȯrt\ *v.* **1** To associate; as, to *consort* with all sorts of people. **2** To come into or be in accord; to harmonize; to be suited to; as, a house that *consorted* well with its surroundings.

con·spic·u·ous \kən-'spik-yə-wəs\ *adj.* **1** Plainly visible; easily seen. Many scars become less *conspicuous* as time passes. **2** Attracting attention; prominent; striking; as, a soldier *conspicuous* for his bravery. A man seven feet tall would be *conspicuous* in any crowd. — For synonyms see *prominent.* — **con·spic·u·ous·ly,** *adv.*

con·spir·a·cy \kən-'spir-ə-sē\ *n.; pl.* **con·spir·a·cies. 1** The act of conspiring or plotting. **2** Any combination of persons for an evil purpose.

con·spir·a·tor \kən-'spir-ət-r\ *n.* A person who takes part in a conspiracy; a plotter.

con·spir·a·to·ri·al \kən-ˌspir-ə-'tōr-ē-əl, -'tȯr-\ *adj.* Of, relating to, or characteristic of conspiracy or conspirators; as, *conspiratorial* activities; a *conspiratorial* silence. — **con·spir·a·to·ri·al·ly** \-ē-ə-lē\ *adv.*

con·spire \kən-'spīr\ *v.;* **con·spired; con·spir·ing. 1** To make an agreement, especially in secret, to do some unlawful act; to plot together; as, to *conspire* to overthrow a government. **2** To act in harmony; to work with other things towards one end. Everything, including the weather, *conspired* to make the outing a success.

con·sta·ble \'kän(t)s-təb-l, 'kən(t)s-\ *n.* [From Old French *conestable,* there borrowed from Late Latin *comes stabuli* originally meaning "officer of the stable".] **1** A high court official of medieval times. **2** The warden or keeper of a royal castle or fortress. **3** A policeman.

con·stab·u·lary \kən-'stab-yə-ˌler-ē\ *n.; pl.* **con·stab·u·lar·ies. 1** The whole body of police officers, or constables, of any place. **2** A fully armed civil police force organized on military lines; as, a state *constabulary.*

con·stan·cy \'kän(t)s-tən-sē\ *n.* **1** Firmness in one's beliefs; steadfastness. **2** Firmness and loyalty in one's personal relationships; faithfulness.

con·stant \'kän(t)s-tənt\ *adj.* **1** Firm; steadfast; faithful; loyal; as, to be *constant* to one's friends; *constant* in one's beliefs. **2** Unchanging; regular; invariable; as, a *constant* reader of a newspaper. The boy's dog was his *constant* companion. **3** Occurring over and over again; continual; persistent; as, the *constant* ringing of a bell. — *n.* **1** Anything that is fixed or unchanging. **2** A quantity in mathematics whose value does not change during a certain discussion or problem.

con·stant·ly \'kän(t)s-tənt-lē\ *adv.* In a constant manner; especially, invariably or continually; over and over again.

con·stel·la·tion \ˌkän(t)s-tə-'lāsh-n\ *n.* Any one of about 90 recognized groups of fixed stars, as the Big Dipper, or a division of the heavens including such a group.

con·ster·na·tion \ˌkän(t)st-r-'nāsh-n\ *n.* A mingled feeling of amazement and dismay so great that one is unable to think of a way to avoid the danger that threatens; a state of confused and distressing excitement; as, to read with *consternation* the news of the outbreak of war.

con·sti·pate \'kän(t)s-tə-ˌpāt\ *v.;* **con·sti·pat·ed; con·sti·pat·ing.** To cause constipation in.

con·sti·pa·tion \ˌkän(t)s-tə-'pāsh-n\ *n.* A condition of the bowels in which movements are infrequent and difficult.

con·stit·u·en·cy \kən-'stich-ə-wən-sē\ *n.; pl.* **con·stit·u·en·cies. 1** A body of voters or residents in a district electing a representative to a lawmaking body. **2** The election district itself.

con·stit·u·ent \kən-'stich-ə-wənt\ *adj.* **1** Forming

part of a whole; serving to make up; as, the *constituent* elements of a substance. **2** Having power to elect or appoint, or to make or revise a constitution; as, a *constituent* assembly. — *n.* **1** One of the parts of which a thing is made up; an element; an ingredient. Flour is the chief *constituent* of bread. **2** A resident in an election district; a voter; an elector; as, a congressman's *constituents.*

con·sti·tute \ˈkän(t)s-tə-ˌtüt, -ˌtyüt\ *v.;* **con·sti·tut·ed; con·sti·tut·ing. 1** To appoint to an office or duty; as, a duly *constituted* representative of the group. **2** To set up; to establish; to fix. A fund was *constituted* to help needy students. **3** To make up; to form. Twelve months *constitute* a year.

con·sti·tu·tion \ˌkän(t)s-tə-ˈtüsh-n, -ˈtyüsh-n\ *n.* **1** The act or process of constituting. **2** The physical make-up of a person; as, a man of strong *constitution.* **3** The natural structure of any animal or thing; as, the *constitution* of the earth. **4** The basic law or rules of government of a nation, a state, or any organized body, drawn up in written documents or established by long custom. **5** A written document containing such basic law.

con·sti·tu·tion·al \ˌkän(t)s-tə-ˈtüsh-n(-)əl, -ˈtyüsh-\ *adj.* **1** Of or relating to a person's physical make-up; as, a *constitutional* weakness. **2** Of, relating to, or in accordance with the constitution of a nation or state; as, a *constitutional* amendment; a person's *constitutional* rights. — *n.* A walk or other exercise taken for one's health. — **con·sti·tu·tion·al·ly** \-n(-)ə-lē\ *adv.*

con·sti·tu·tion·al·i·ty \ˌkän(t)s-tə-ˌtüsh-n-ˈal-ət-ē, -ˌtyüsh-\ *n.* The state of being in accordance with the constitution of an organized body, especially a nation or a state. The Supreme Court has authority to rule on the *constitutionality* of laws enacted by Congress.

con·strain \kən-ˈstrān\ *v.* **1** To force; to compel; to oblige; as, *constrained* by poverty to go to work at an early age. **2** To hold back by force; to restrain.

con·strained \kən-ˈstrānd\ *adj.* Marked by constraint; forced; unnatural; as, a *constrained* manner; a *constrained* smile. — **con·strain·ed·ly** \-ˈstrā-nəd-lē\ *adv.*

con·straint \kən-ˈstrānt\ *n.* **1** The act of constraining or the state of being constrained; force, acting either to compel or to restrain; as, to act under *constraint.* **2** A keeping back of one's natural feelings; unnaturalness in speech and behavior; embarrassment; as, to show *constraint* among strangers.

con·strict \kən-ˈstrikt\ *v.* To make narrower or smaller by drawing together; to squeeze or tighten; to cramp; as, to live in *constricted* quarters. — **con·stric·tive** \-ˈstrik-tiv\ *adj.*

con·stric·tion \kən-ˈstriksh-n\ *n.* **1** A constricting or a being constricted; tightness; as, the *constriction* of a snake's coils. **2** Anything that constricts or a part that is constricted.

con·stric·tor \kən-ˈstrikt-r\ *n.* **1** One that constricts. **2** A snake that kills its prey by crushing it with its coils.

con·struct \kən-ˈstrəkt\ *v.* To put together the parts of a thing; to build; to make; as, to *construct* a house. — **con·struct·er** or **con·struc·tor,** *n.*

con·struc·tion \kən-ˈstrəksh-n\ *n.* **1** The building or making of something; as, to work on the *construction* of a dollhouse. **2** An interpretation or explanation of a statement or a fact; as, to put the wrong *construction* on a remark. **3** Something built or put together; a structure; as, a flimsy *construction.* **4** The way in which a thing is constructed; arrangement; as, a chair of peculiar *construction.* **5** The arrangement and connection of words in a sentence; the relationship between words in a sentence.

con·struc·tive \kən-ˈstrək-tiv\ *adj.* **1** Fitted for or given to constructing. Edison was a great *constructive* genius. **2** Helping to construct or build up something; not destructive; as, *constructive* suggestions.

con·strue \kən-ˈstrü\ *v.;* **con·strued; con·stru·ing. 1** To explain the grammatical relationships of the words in a sentence, clause, or phrase. **2** To explain the sense or intention of; to interpret the meaning of; as, to *construe* the remark as an insult.

con·sul \ˈkän(t)s-l\ *n.* **1** Either of the two officials at the head of the government of ancient republican Rome. **2** An official appointed by a government to live in a foreign country in order to look after the interests of his own country. — **con·sul·ar** \ˈkän(t)s-l-ər\ *adj.*

con·sul·ate \ˈkän(t)s-l-ət\ *n.* **1** Government by consuls. **2** The position or the term of office of a consul. **3** The residence or the official premises of a consul.

con·sul·ship \ˈkän(t)s-l-ˌship\ *n.* The office or term of office of a consul.

con·sult \kən-ˈsəlt\ *v.* **1** To seek the opinion or advice of; to confer or advise; as, to *consult* a doctor or a lawyer; to *consult* with friends. **2** To seek information from; as, to *consult* an encyclopedia. **3** To consider; to have regard to; as, to *consult* one's best interests before acting.

con·sult·ant \kən-ˈsəlt-nt\ *n.* **1** A person who consults or confers with another. **2** A person who gives professional advice or services, as a doctor.

con·sul·ta·tion \ˌkän(t)s-l-ˈtāsh-n\ *n.* **1** The action of consulting or conferring. **2** A conference to consider a special case; as, a *consultation* of physicians.

con·sume \kən-ˈsüm\ *v.;* **con·sumed; con·sum·ing. 1** To destroy by fire or as if by fire. The flames *consumed* the building; *consumed* by disease. **2** To use up; to spend; as, to *consume* hours in reading. **3** To eat or drink up; as, to *consume* enough food for three. **4** To take up one's attention; to engage one's interest; as, to be *consumed* with curiosity. — **con·sum·a·ble,** *adj.*

con·sum·er \kən-ˈsüm-r\ *n.* A person or thing that consumes; especially, a person who buys and uses up goods of any kind.

con·sum·mate \kən-ˈsəm-ət, ˈkän(t)s-m-ət\ *adj.*

Of the highest degree or quality; complete; perfect; as, a man of *consummate* skill. — \'kän(t)s-m-ˌāt\ *v.;* **con·sum·mat·ed; con·sum·mat·ing.** To bring to completion; to complete; to achieve; as, to *consummate* the purpose of a trip. — **con·sum·ma·tion** \ˌkän(t)s-m-'āsh-n\ *n.*

con·sump·tion \kən-'səm(p)sh-n\ *n.* **1** Destruction, as by fire, waste, or decay. **2** The using up of anything, such as food, coal, or time; as, the weekly *consumption* of food by a family of three. **3** A wasting away of the body, especially from tuberculosis of the lungs; this kind of tuberculosis.

con·sump·tive \kən-'səm(p)-tiv\ *adj.* **1** Destructive; wasteful. **2** Relating to consumption or tuberculosis of the lungs. **3** Affected with consumption; inclined to consumption. — *n.* A person affected with consumption.

con·tact \'kän-ˌtakt\ *n.* **1** A meeting or touching of persons or things. A storekeeper comes into *contact* with all kinds of people. **2** A coming in touch or a being in touch, physically or mentally; as, to maintain *contact* with the enemy. **3** The connection of two conductors through which an electric current passes. **4** A special part made for such a connection. **5** A social or business connection; as, a salesman with *contacts* in all parts of the country. — \'kän-ˌtakt, kən-'takt\ *v.* To come into contact with; to get in touch with; as, to *contact* a person by telephone.

con·ta·gion \kən-'tāj-n\ *n.* **1** The passing of a disease from one person to another as a result of some contact between them. **2** A contagious disease. **3** Transmission of any influence to the mind of others; as, the *contagion* of enthusiasm.

con·ta·gious \kən-'tā-jəs\ *adj.* **1** Capable of being passed from one person to another by contact; catching; as, *contagious* diseases. **2** Spreading from person to person; as, *contagious* enthusiasm.

con·tain \kən-'tān\ *v.* **1** To hold within itself; to enclose. The room *contained* fifty people. **2** To be able to hold; to be equivalent to. A bushel *contains* four pecks. **3** To hold back; to restrain; to check; as, unable to *contain* one's anger. **4** In mathematics, to be a multiple of or to be divisible by, usually without a remainder. — **con·tain·a·ble,** *adj.*

con·tain·er \kən-'tān-r\ *n.* A receptacle for holding things.

con·tam·i·nate \kən-'tam-ə-ˌnāt\ *v.;* **con·tam·i·nat·ed; con·tam·i·nat·ing.** To soil or spoil by contact; to make impure or unfit for use; as, drinking water *contaminated* by disease germs.

con·tam·i·na·tion \kən-ˌtam-ə-'nāsh-n\ *n.* A contaminating or a being contaminated; pollution.

con·temn \kən-'tem\ *v.;* **con·temned** \-'temd\; **con·temn·ing** \-'tem-ing\. To view or treat with contempt.

con·tem·plate \'kän-təm-ˌplāt, -ˌtem-\ *v.;* **con·tem·plat·ed; con·tem·plat·ing.** **1** To consider carefully and for a long time; to meditate; as, to *contemplate* a suggestion. **2** To look forward to; to have in mind; to intend. The carpenters *contemplate* finishing the job today.

con·tem·pla·tion \ˌkän-təm-'plāsh-n, -ˌtem-\ *n.* **1** Attention fixed for some time upon a subject; meditation, as on spiritual matters; a musing. **2** The act of looking at something or thinking about something steadily; as, *contemplation* of a landscape; the child's unwinking *contemplation* of the stranger. **3** Expectation; intention; as, preparations made in *contemplation* of the coming of winter.

con·tem·pla·tive \kən-'temp-lət-iv, 'kän-təm-ˌplāt-, 'kän-ˌtem-ˌplāt-\ *adj.* Thoughtful; meditative; especially, devoted to prayer and meditation on spiritual things.

con·tem·po·ra·ne·ous \kən-ˌtemp-r-'ā-nē-əs, (ˌ)kän-\ *adj.* Contemporary.

con·tem·po·rary \kən-'temp-r-ˌer-ē\ *adj.* **1** Living or occurring at the same period of time; contemporaneous; as, *contemporary* events in different countries. **2** Of the same age. **3** Of the present time; living; modern; as, our *contemporary* writers. — *n.; pl.* **con·tem·po·rar·ies.** One who lives at the same time or is of about the same age as another person.

con·tempt \kən-'tem(p)t\ *n.* **1** The feeling with which one regards something considered mean, vile, or worthless; scorn. **2** The condition of being despised; disgrace. **3** Disobedience to or disrespect of a court of justice or a legislative body.

con·tempt·i·ble \kən-'tem(p)-təb-l\ *adj.* Deserving contempt; as, a *contemptible* lie. — **con·tempt·i·bly** \-tə-blē\ *adv.*

con·temp·tu·ous \kən-'tem(p)-chə-wəs\ *adj.* Feeling or showing contempt; scornful; as, a *contemptuous* sneer.

— The words *scornful* and *disdainful* are synonyms of *contemptuous: contemptuous* usually suggests a lofty attitude of disgust or aversion; *scornful* may imply proud, angry, and often mocking contempt; *disdainful* often indicates haughty or insolent disregard, as of something considered unworthy of notice.

con·temp·tu·ous·ly \kən-'tem(p)-chə-wəs-lē\ *adv.* In a contemptuous manner.

con·tend \kən-'tend\ *v.* **1** To compete with another or others in opposition or in rivalry. Five swimmers *contended* for the championship. **2** To strive; to struggle; as, to *contend* against difficulties. In winter there were severe storms to *contend* with. **3** To argue; to maintain; as, to *contend* that one's opinion is right. — **con·tend·er,** *n.*

con·tent \'kän-ˌtent, kən-'tent\ *n.* **1** [usually in the plural] The thing or things held in a container or enclosed in a certain space; as, the *contents* of a room; the *contents* of a bottle. **2** [in the plural] The subject matter or topics treated, as in a book; as, a table of *contents.* **3** The significant part, as of a book or a speech; the essential meaning; as, to enjoy a poem for its musical quality without fully understanding its *content.* **4** Capacity; as, a jug with a *content* of one gallon.

con·tent \kən-'tent\ *adj.* **1** Satisfied; as, *content* with one's job. Some people are *content* with very little. **2** Agreeable; willing; as, to be *content* to follow another's lead. — *v.* To make content; to satisfy; as, a child who was easily *contented;* to *content* oneself with a book during a journey. — *n.* The condition of being satisfied; contentment.

con·tent·ed \kən-'tent-əd\ *adj.* Easy in mind; satisfied, as with one's situation at the moment or with one's lot in life. — **con·tent·ed·ly**, *adv.*

con·ten·tion \kən-'tench-n\ *n.* **1** The action of contending in words; dispute; especially, controversy or quarreling; as, a meeting marked by a great deal of *contention.* **2** An idea or point for which a person argues or to which he holds in spite of opposition. — **bone of contention.** A cause or subject of contention or dispute.

con·ten·tious \kən-'tench-əs\ *adj.* Inclined to find or seek reasons for contention, often over unimportant matters; quarrelsome. — **con·ten·tious·ly**, *adv.*

con·tent·ment \kən-'tent-mənt\ *n.* The state of being contented; peaceful satisfaction; absence of worry or restlessness.

con·test \kən-'test, 'kän-ˌtest\ *v.* **1** To dispute or argue over something; to oppose; as, to *contest* an election; to *contest* a decision. **2** To struggle to get or to hold. The troops *contested* every yard of ground. — \'kän-ˌtest\ *n.* **1** A competition; a struggle for victory or superiority, as in a test of strength, skill, or knowledge; as, a boxing *contest;* a *contest* for a prize. **2** Opposition; rivalry; as, to meet in friendly *contest.*

con·test·ant \kən-'tes-tənt, 'kän-ˌtes-\ *n.* One who contests; one who takes part in a contest; as, a *contestant* on a quiz program.

con·text \'kän-ˌtekst\ *n.* The parts of a written or spoken passage that are near a certain word or group of words and that help to explain its meaning.

con·ti·gu·i·ty \ˌkän-tə-'gyü-ət-ē\ *n.* The state of adjoining or being very near; nearness.

con·tig·u·ous \kən-'tig-yə-wəs\ *adj.* **1** In contact; touching; as, *contiguous* bands of color. **2** Very near though not in actual contact; neighboring. — **con·tig·u·ous·ly**, *adv.*

con·ti·nence \'känt-n-ən(t)s, 'kän-tə-nən(t)s\ *n.* Self-restraint in the face of temptation.

con·ti·nent \'känt-n-ənt, 'kän-tə-nənt\ *adj.* [From Old French, there borrowed from Latin *continent-*, *continens* meaning literally "repressing", "holding together", "containing".] Having control over one's actions; exercising self-restraint in giving in to desires.

con·ti·nent \'känt-n-ənt, 'kän-tə-nənt, 'känt-nənt\ *n.* [Latin *continent-*, *continens* meaning "continuous mass of land", literally, "something held together".] One of the great divisions of land on the globe: North America, South America, Europe, Asia, Africa, Australia, and often, Antarctica. — **the Continent.** The mainland of Europe.

con·ti·nen·tal \ˌkänt-n-'ent-l, ˌkän-tə-'nent-l\ *adj.* **1** Of or relating to a continent or [usually with a capital] to the Continent. **2** [with a capital] Of or relating to the loosely allied American colonies at the time of the Revolutionary War; as, the *Continental* army. — *n.* [with a capital] **1** A person belonging to one of the countries of the continent of Europe. **2** A soldier in the Continental army; as, Washington's ragged *Continentals.*

continental shelf. A submarine plain bordering nearly every continent and terminating in a sharp slope (**continental slope**) descending to the depths of the ocean.

con·tin·gen·cy \kən-'tinj-n-sē\ *n.; pl.* **con·tin·gen·cies.** **1** The state of being contingent; possibility of happening. **2** A chance happening or event. **3** A possible event, or one foreseen as possible but dependent upon the occurrence of another event. Arctic explorers must be prepared for every *contingency* of the long polar winter.

con·tin·gent \kən-'tinj-nt\ *adj.* **1** Liable to happen but not certain; possible. **2** Happening by chance; not planned or foreseen; as, the *contingent* results of war. **3** Dependent; conditional. All our plans must be *contingent* upon the weather. — *n.* **1** A chance occurrence; a contingency. **2** A number of persons representing or drawn from a larger number, as a quota of troops or a group of delegates or other representatives; as, the junior high *contingent* at the all-school track meet; a *contingent* of soldiers for foreign service. — **con·tin·gent·ly**, *adv.*

con·tin·u·al \kən-'tin-yə-wəl, -yəl\ *adj.* **1** Going on without interruption; continuous; as, three days of *continual* rain. **2** Occurring in rapid succession; repeated again and again; frequent; as, *continual* interruptions. — **con·tin·u·al·ly** \-yə-lē, -yə-wə-lē\ *adv.*

con·tin·u·ance \kən-'tin-yə-wən(t)s\ *n.* **1** The act of continuing; a persisting, as in a course or condition, or a remaining, as in a place or position; as, during the *continuance* of the illness. **2** Unbroken succession; continuation. **3** Postponement of proceedings in a court of law to a specified day. The lawyers for the defense asked for a *continuance* of the case.

con·tin·u·a·tion \kən-ˌtin-yə-'wāsh-n\ *n.* **1** A going on or carrying on; continuance. **2** A going on or carrying on after an interruption; resumption; as, the *continuation* of a meeting after a short recess. **3** A thing or part by which something is continued; as, a garage built as a *continuation* of a house. Today's paper contains a *continuation* of yesterday's story.

con·tin·ue \kən-'tin-yü\ *v.;* **con·tin·ued; con·tin·u·ing.** **1** To remain in a place or a condition; to stay; as, to *continue* in one's present position. **2** To endure; to last. The cold weather *continued* throughout the week. **3** To go on or carry forward in some course; as, to *continue* to study hard; to *continue* the study of French. **4** To go on or to carry on after an interruption; to resume. The play *continued* after the intermission. **5** To postpone, as a legal case, to a later date. **6** To allow or to cause to re-

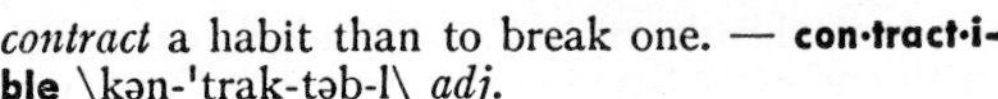

main, especially in a position. All the town officials but one were *continued* in office.

con·ti·nu·i·ty \ˌkän-tən-ˈü-ət-ē, ˌkänt-n-, -ˈyü-\ *n.; pl.* **con·ti·nu·i·ties. 1** The quality or state of being continuous; duration without interruption. **2** An uninterrupted succession, as of actions or thoughts. **3** A motion-picture scenario. **4** The script for a radio or television program or commercial.

con·tin·u·ous \kən-ˈtin-yə-wəs\ *adj.* Without a break or an interruption; continued; unbroken; as, a *continuous* line; a *continuous* showing of a moving picture. — **con·tin·u·ous·ly,** *adv.*

con·tort \kən-ˈtȯrt\ *v.* To twist into an unusual appearance or unnatural shape; to distort. A scowl *contorted* the angry boy's face.

con·tor·tion \kən-ˈtȯrsh-n\ *n.* A contorting or a being contorted; a contorted shape or thing; as, the *contortions* of an acrobat.

con·tor·tion·ist \kən-ˈtȯrsh-n(-)əst\ *n.* A person who contorts; especially, an acrobat who puts himself into unusual postures.

con·tour \ˈkän-ˌtu̇r\ *n.* The outline of a figure or body; a line or a drawing representing such an outline; as, the *contours* of a coast or of a mountain. — *adj.* Following the lines (**contour lines**) that connect points of equal elevation, as in plowing around, instead of up and down, a hillside to prevent soil erosion; as, *contour* farming.

contra-. A prefix that can mean: against, in opposition, as in *contradiction.*

con·tra·band \ˈkän-trə-ˌband\ *n.* [From Italian *contrabbando* meaning literally "against a statute or proclamation".] **1** Goods whose importing and exporting is forbidden by law. Opium is a *contraband* in many countries. **2** Smuggled goods; as, a shipload of *contraband.* — **contraband of war.** Any goods that, under international law, cannot be supplied to a country at war except at the risk of seizure by the country warring against it.

con·tra·bass \ˈkän-trə-ˌbās\ *n.* **1** An instrument or a voice with a range an octave lower than the normal bass; double bass. **2** A stringed musical instrument larger than a cello and having a very deep bass tone; a double bass.

contrabass, 2

con·tract \ˈkän-ˌtrakt\ *n.* **1** A legal agreement between two or more persons to do or not to do something. **2** The written paper containing such an agreement. — For synonyms see *agreement.* — \kən-ˈtrakt; *sense 2 is often* ˈkän-ˌtrakt\ *v.* **1** To enter into by contract; to make a contract; as, to *contract* marriage. **2** To undertake by contract; as to *contract* to build a bridge. **3** To draw together; to draw up; as, to *contract* the brows; to *contract* a muscle. **4** To shorten; to shrink; to narrow; as, to *contract* "does not" into "doesn't". Metal *contracts* in cold weather, expands in hot. **5** To get; to catch; to form; as, to *contract* a cold. It is easier to *contract* a habit than to break one. — **con·tract·i·ble** \kən-ˈtrak-təb-l\ *adj.*

con·trac·tile \kən-ˈtrakt-l\ *adj.* Having the power or quality of contracting; contractive.

con·trac·tion \kən-ˈtraksh-n\ *n.* **1** The act or process of contracting; the state of being contracted; as, the *contraction* of a metal in cold weather. **2** The shortening of a word or words, as by leaving out some letters; the form of a word thus shortened. "Don't" is a *contraction* for "do not". — **con·trac·tive** \-ˈtrak-tiv\ *adj.*

con·trac·tor \ˈkän-ˌtrakt-r, kən-ˈtrakt-r\ *n.* A person who enters into a contract; especially, one who agrees to perform certain work or to provide certain articles at a given price or within a given time.

con·trac·tu·al \kən-ˈtrak-chə-wəl, ˈkän-ˌtrak-\ *adj.* Of, relating to, or of the nature of a contract; as, a *contractual* agreement.

con·tra·dict \ˌkän-trə-ˈdikt\ *v.* **1** To deny the truth of a statement; to say the opposite of what someone else has said. **2** To be contrary or opposed to; as, two reports that *contradict* each other.

con·tra·dic·tion \ˌkän-trə-ˈdiksh-n\ *n.* **1** A statement that contradicts another; denial of the truth of something said. **2** Opposition existing between things; as, a *contradiction* in facts.

con·tra·dic·to·ry \ˌkän-trə-ˈdikt-r(-)ē\ *adj.* Tending to contradict; involving contradiction; opposed; as, *contradictory* statements.

con·tra·dis·tinc·tion \ˈkän-trə-dis-ˈting(k)sh-n\ *n.* Distinction by contrast. The difficulty of the second voyage was in sharp *contradistinction* to the ease of the first.

con·tral·to \kən-ˈtral-ˌtō\ *n.; pl.* **con·tral·tos. 1** The part in music usually sung by the lowest female voice; alto. **2** A voice or a singer that sings such a part.

con·trap·tion \kən-ˈtrapsh-n\ *n.* A device; a contrivance; a gadget; as, the early *contraptions* in which men tried to fly.

con·trary \ˈkän-ˌtrer-ē; *sense 4 is also* kən-ˈtrer-ē\ *adj.* **1** Exactly opposite; wholly different; as, *contrary* opinions. **2** Opposed; as, an act *contrary* to law. **3** Unfavorable; as, a *contrary* wind. **4** Inclined to oppose or resist; wayward; as, a *contrary* child. — *n.; pl.* **con·trar·ies.** Something opposite or contrary; especially, one of two contrary terms or statements.

con·trast \kən-ˈtrast, ˈkän-ˌtrast\ *v.* **1** To show noticeable differences; as, two colors that *contrast* sharply. **2** To compare two persons or things so as to show the differences between them; as, to *contrast* winter and summer. — \ˈkän-ˌtrast\ *n.* **1** Difference or unlikeness between things as shown when they are compared; as, the *contrast* between winter and summer. **2** A person or thing that shows such unlikeness.

con·trib·ute \kən-ˈtrib-yət\ *v.;* **con·trib·ut·ed; con·trib·ut·ing. 1** To give along with others; as, to *contribute* annually to the Red Cross. **2** To have a share in something; as, factors *contributing* to the high cost of living. Every member of the class *contributed* to the success of the exhibit. **3** To supply for publication, as an article in a newspaper or a poem in a magazine.

con·tri·bu·tion \ˌkän-trə-ˈbyüsh-n\ *n.* **1** The act of contributing; as, to encourage *contribution* to the athletic fund. **2** The sum or thing contributed. One *contribution* to the rummage sale was an old chair. **3** A writing submitted for publication.

con·trib·u·tor \kən-ˈtrib-yət-r\ *n.* A person or a thing that contributes; especially, one who contributes articles for publication, as in a magazine or a newspaper.

con·trib·u·to·ry \kən-ˈtrib-yə-ˌtōr-ē, -ˌtȯr-ē\ *adj.* Contributing; especially, helping to accomplish a result. Safety precautions taken by school children are *contributory* to the prevention of traffic accidents.

con·trite \ˈkän-ˌtrīt, kən-ˈtrīt\ *adj.* **1** Sorrowful for some wrong that one has done; deeply repentant; as, a *contrite* heart. **2** Caused by repentance; as, *contrite* tears. — **con·trite·ly**, *adv.*

con·tri·tion \kən-ˈtrish-n\ *n.* Sincere repentance.

con·triv·ance \kən-ˈtrīv-n(t)s\ *n.* **1** The action or power of contriving. **2** The way in which something is contrived; inventive ability. **3** Something that is contrived; an invention; especially, a mechanical device or appliance.

con·trive \kən-ˈtrīv\ *v.;* **con·trived; con·triv·ing. 1** To plan; to plot; to scheme; as, to *contrive* a way to escape. **2** To form or make in some skillful or ingenious way; to invent; as, to *contrive* a new type of model plane. **3** To bring about; to manage. An ambitious boy can always *contrive* to find a summer job.

con·trol \kən-ˈtrōl\ *v.;* **con·trolled; con·trol·ling. 1** To exercise restraint over, as a person, animal, or thing; to hold in check; to curb; as, to *control* one's temper. **2** To regulate; to have power over; to govern; as, to *control* a machine; to *control* a country. — *n.* **1** The power or authority to control or command; as, a child under his parents' *control.* **2** Restraint; ability to control; as, anger that is out of *control;* to lose *control* of an automobile. **3** Regulation; as, traffic *control;* price *controls.* **4** A device or apparatus used to regulate a machine; as, the *controls* of an airplane. **5** Anything used in an experiment or a study to provide a basis for comparing results or for checking their accuracy. — **con·trol·la·ble**, *adj.*

con·trol·ler \kən-ˈtrōl-r\ *n.* **1** An official whose duty it is to check expenditures; a comptroller; as, a city *controller.* **2** Any regulating or controlling device, as one for governing the speed of a machine.

con·tro·ver·sial \ˌkän-trə-ˈvərsh-l, -ˈvər-sē-əl\ *adj.* **1** Of or relating to controversy. **2** Open to or likely to cause controversy; as, a *controversial* question. Politics is likely to be a *controversial* subject. **3** Fond of controversy; argumentative; as, an unpleasantly *controversial* manner. — **con·tro·ver·sial·ly** \-ˈvərsh-l-ē, -ˈvər-sē-ə-lē\ *adv.*

con·tro·ver·sy \ˈkän-trə-ˌvər-sē\ *n.; pl.* **con·tro·ver·sies.** A discussion about a question over which there is strong disagreement; a dispute; a quarrel.

con·tro·vert \ˈkän-trə-ˌvərt\ *v.* To oppose by argument; to deny; to contradict; as, a theory *controverted* by obvious facts.

con·tu·ma·cious \ˌkän-t(y)ə-ˈmā-shəs\ *adj.* Stubbornly disobedient or rebellious. — **con·tu·ma·cious·ly**, *adv.*

con·tu·ma·cy \kən-ˈtü-mə-sē, kən-ˈtyü-, ˈkän-t(y)ə-\ *n.; pl.* **con·tu·ma·cies.** Stubborn opposition to authority; defiance.

con·tu·me·ly \kən-ˈtüm-l-ē, kən-ˈtyüm-; ˈkän-tə-ˌmē-lē\ *n.; pl.* **con·tu·me·lies. 1** Contemptuous or insolent treatment. **2** An insult.

con·tuse \kən-ˈtüz, -ˈtyüz\ *v.;* **con·tused; con·tus·ing.** To bruise.

con·tu·sion \kən-ˈtüzh-n, -ˈtyüzh-n\ *n.* A bruise.

co·nun·drum \kə-ˈnən-drəm\ *n.* **1** A riddle. **2** Any puzzling question.

con·va·lesce \ˌkän-və-ˈles\ *v.;* **con·va·lesced; con·va·lesc·ing.** To gather strength after sickness; to recover health gradually; as, to be *convalescing* after an operation.

con·va·les·cence \ˌkän-və-ˈles-n(t)s\ *n.* The process or period of convalescing.

con·va·les·cent \ˌkän-və-ˈles-nt\ *adj.* Recovering gradually from sickness; partly well again after an illness. — *n.* A person who is partly recovered from an illness.

con·vec·tion \kən-ˈveksh-n\ *n.* The transference of heat by moving masses of matter, as, in gases and liquids, by currents caused by differences in density, the warmer portions rising and the colder, denser portions sinking.

con·vene \kən-ˈvēn\ *v.;* **con·vened; con·ven·ing. 1** To assemble; to meet. The legislature *convened* on Tuesday. **2** To cause to assemble; to call together. The chairman *convened* the committee for a special meeting.

con·ve·nience \kən-ˈvēn-yən(t)s\ *n.* **1** The quality of being convenient; fitness; suitability; as, to rent a house because of the *convenience* of its location. **2** Personal comfort; freedom from trouble; as, to think only of one's own *convenience.* **3** A suitable or convenient time; opportunity. Come at your earliest *convenience.* **4** Anything that gives comfort or advantage; as, a house with modern *conveniences.*

con·ve·nient \kən-ˈvēn-yənt\ *adj.* **1** Suited to a person's comfort or ease; as, a *convenient* time; a *convenient* house. **2** Prepared or suited for a person's use; as, *convenient* tools. **3** Easy to reach; near at hand. Our school is quite *convenient* for almost all of us. — **con·ve·nient·ly**, *adv.*

con·vent \ˈkän-ˌvent, -vənt\ *n.* **1** A group of nuns living together and devoting themselves to a religious life under a superior. **2** A house or a set of buildings occupied by a community of nuns; a nunnery.

con·ven·tion \kən-ˈvench-n\ *n.* **1** An assembly of

persons gathered together for some common purpose; as, a teachers' *convention;* the national *convention* of a political party. **2** An agreement; as, an international *convention* for the treatment of prisoners of war. **3** A general way of acting or doing things established by custom; as, to behave according to *convention.* **4** Any practice or form permitted or required by general social custom; as, the *conventions* of middle class society.

con·ven·tion·al \kən-'vench-n(-)əl\ *adj.* **1** Behaving according to convention; as, a very *conventional* man. **2** Settled by or depending on convention; customary; as, *conventional* dress. **3** Commonplace; ordinary; as, *conventional* remarks about the weather. **4** According to established rules or traditions; not showing originality; as, curtains of a *conventional* floral design; the *conventional* way of beginning a letter. — **con·ven·tion·al·ly** \-n(-)ə-lē\ *adv.*

con·ven·tion·al·i·ty \kən-ˌvench-n-'al-ət-ē\ *n.; pl.* **con·ven·tion·al·i·ties.** **1** The quality or state of being conventional; formality, especially in social customs and practices. **2** Any conventional practice, custom, or rule; a convention.

con·verge \kən-'vərj\ *v.;* **con·verged; con·verg·ing.** **1** To tend to draw together at one point; to approach or cause to approach one common center; as, crowds of people *converging* on the city square. The spokes of a wheel *converge* toward the hub. **2** To develop like characteristics, as separate organisms.

con·ver·gence \kən-'vərj-n(t)s\ *n.* **1** The act or state of converging. **2** The degree to which things converge or the point at which converging things meet. **3** Tendency to grow alike; development of similarities, as in habits or tastes.

con·ver·gent \kən-'vərj-nt\ *adj.* Converging.

con·ver·sant \kən-'vərs-nt\ *adj.* Well acquainted; familiar; as, to be *conversant* with several foreign languages; *conversant* with all the facts of a case.

con·ver·sa·tion \ˌkän-vər-'sāsh-n\ *n.* Informal and, usually, friendly exchange of views and opinions through speech; talk; a talk.

con·ver·sa·tion·al \ˌkän-vər-'sāsh-n(-)əl\ *adj.* **1** Of, relating to, or suitable for informal friendly talk. **2** Fond of talking; talkative. — **con·ver·sa·tion·al·ly** \-n(-)ə-lē\ *adv.*

con·ver·sa·tion·al·ist \ˌkän-vər-'sāsh-n(-)ə-ləst\ *n.* A person who is fond of or good at conversation; one who talks easily and interestingly in conversation.

con·verse \kən-'vərs\ *v.;* **con·versed; con·vers·ing.** To exchange thoughts and opinions in speech; to talk. — \'kän-ˌvərs\ *n.* Talk; conversation.

con·verse \'kän-ˌvərs, (')kän-'vərs\ *adj.* Turned about; opposite; contrary. — \'kän-ˌvərs\ *n.* Something that is the opposite of something else; reverse. "Good" is the *converse* of "bad". — **con·verse·ly** \(')kän-'vərs-lē, kən-; 'kän-ˌvərs-\ *adv.*

con·ver·sion \kən-'vərzh-n\ *n.* **1** The act of converting or the state of being converted. **2** A change in the nature or form of a thing; as, the *conversion* of water into steam by boiling. **3** A spiritual change in a person, as from a bad to a good life, associated with a change of beliefs with respect to religion or with the definite adoption of religion.

con·vert \kən-'vərt\ *v.* **1** To change from one form to another; to change; to turn; as, to *convert* water into ice. **2** To turn one thing into another by an exchange; as, to *convert* goods into money. **3** To cause to change in one's beliefs or in one's way of living; especially, to turn from one faith to another. — \'kän-ˌvərt\ *n.* A converted person.

con·vert·er or **con·ver·tor** \kən-'vərt-r\ *n.* **1** A person who converts. **2** An apparatus for converting, as a device for changing electric current from alternating to direct.

con·vert·i·ble \kən-'vərt-əb-l\ *adj.* Capable of being converted into something else; as, a sofa that is *convertible* into a bed. — *n.* Anything that is convertible; especially, an automobile having a top that can be raised or lowered. — **con·vert·i·bil·i·ty** \kən-ˌvərt-ə-'bil-ət-ē\ *n.*

con·vex \(')kän-'veks, 'kän-ˌveks\ *adj.* Rounded like the outside of any part of a globe or ball; curving outward. — **con·vex·i·ty** \kän-'veks-ət-ē, kən-\ *n.* — **con·vex·ly,** *adv.* — **con·vex·ness,** *n.*

←convex

con·vey \kən-'vā\ *v.* **1** To carry from one place to another; to transport; as, to *convey* passengers to an airfield by bus. **2** To serve as a means of transferring or transmitting. Pipes *convey* water. **3** To serve as a means of imparting or communicating; as, to choose words that clearly *convey* one's meaning. A flashing red light *conveys* a warning of danger ahead. **4** To transfer to another, especially real estate by a legal document duly signed and sealed.

con·vey·ance \kən-'vā-ən(t)s\ *n.* **1** The act of conveying. **2** Something used to transport goods or passengers; especially, a vehicle; as, taxicabs and other public *conveyances.* **3** A legally drawn paper transferring the ownership of property.

con·vey·anc·ing \kən-'vā-ən(t)s-ing\ *n.* The procedure or the business of drawing up legal papers for transferring property from one owner to another. — **con·vey·anc·er** \-ən(t)s-r\ *n.*

con·vey·er or **con·vey·or** \kən-'vā-ər\ *n.* One that conveys; especially, a mechanical apparatus for carrying packages or bulk material from one place to another, as by means of an endless belt or chain.

con·vict \kən-'vikt\ *v.* To prove or find guilty of an offense. — \'kän-ˌvikt\ *n.* **1** A person convicted of a crime. **2** A person serving a prison sentence, usually for a long term.

con·vic·tion \kən-'viksh-n\ *n.* **1** The act of convicting or the state of being convicted; the decision that a person is guilty of a crime or offense. The trial ended with the thief's *conviction.* **2** The state of mind of a person who is convinced that what he believes or says is true; certainty; as, to speak with *conviction.* **3** A strong belief or opinion on some matter; as, a man with *convictions.* — For synonyms see *belief.*

con·vince \kən-'vin(t)s\ *v.;* **con·vinced; con·vinc·ing.** To argue so as to make another person agree or believe; to persuade firmly; to satisfy by proof or evidence; to overcome the disbelief or objections of; as, to be *convinced* of an accused man's complete innocence. I cannot *convince* my father that I need a larger allowance.

con·vinc·ing \kən-'vin(t)s-ing\ *adj.* Having the power or the effect of overcoming objection or disbelief; strongly persuasive; as, a *convincing* argument; a very *convincing* speaker. — **con·vinc·ing·ly,** *adv.*

con·viv·i·al \kən-'viv-ē-əl\ *adj.* Fond of or given over to companionship and the pleasures of eating and drinking; festive; jovial; as, a man of *convivial* habits; a *convivial* gathering. — **con·viv·i·al·ly** \-ē-ə-lē\ *adv.*

con·viv·i·al·i·ty \kən-ˌviv-ē-'al-ət-ē\ *n.; pl.* **con·viv·i·al·i·ties.** Convivial spirit; festivity.

con·vo·ca·tion \ˌkän-və-'kāsh-n\ *n.* **1** The act of convoking; a summons to a meeting. **2** An assembly; a meeting.

con·voke \kən-'vōk\ *v.;* **con·voked; con·vok·ing.** To call together; to summon to meet.

con·vo·lute \'kän-və-ˌlüt\ *v.;* **con·vo·lut·ed; con·vo·lut·ing.** To twist around; to roll together; to coil. — *adj.* Rolled or wound together, one part upon another, as leaves in a bud, or many shells. — **con·vo·lute·ly,** *adv.*

con·vo·lu·tion \ˌkän-və-'lüsh-n\ *n.* **1** A rolling or coiling together; a twisted formation. **2** One of the folds or coils in a convolute body, as one of the ridges on the surface of the brain.

con·vol·vu·lus \kən-'välv-yə-ləs\ *n.; pl.* **con·vol·vu·lus·es** \-lə-səz\ or **con·vol·vu·li** \-ˌlī\. A trailing or twining plant of the morning-glory family, with showy funnel-shaped flowers.

con·voy \'kän-ˌvȯi\ *v.* To go along with someone or something in order to protect or guide; to accompany as an escort. A fleet of cruisers *convoyed* the troopships. — *n.* **1** The act of convoying or the state of being convoyed; as, ships traveling in *convoy.* **2** A person or a thing that convoys; especially, an armed escort, as a warship. **3** Something that is accompanied by an armed escort; as, a *convoy* of merchant ships.

con·vulse \kən-'vəls\ *v.;* **con·vulsed; con·vuls·ing.** To shake or agitate violently; especially, to shake with or as if with irregular spasms, as in uncontrollable laughter or in grief or pain; as, land *convulsed* by an earthquake; a face *convulsed* with rage.

con·vul·sion \kən-'vəlsh-n\ *n.* **1** [usually in the plural] A violent and involuntary contraction or series of contractions of the muscles; a spasm. **2** Any violent disturbance; an upheaval; as, a *convulsion* of nature.

con·vul·sive \kən-'vəl-siv\ *adj.* **1** Like a convulsion; as, *convulsive* movements. **2** Producing or accompanied by convulsions. — **con·vul·sive·ly,** *adv.*

co·ny or **co·ney** \'kō-nē\ *n.; pl.* **co·nies** or **co·neys.** **1** A rabbit. **2** Rabbit fur or skin.

coo \'kü\ *v.;* **cooed** \'küd\; **coo·ing.** To make the soft low sound made by doves and pigeons, or a sound like this. — *n.* The sound made in cooing.

cook \'ku̇k\ *v.* **1** To prepare food for eating by the use of heat, as by boiling, baking, or broiling. **2** To do the work of a cook. **3** To undergo the process of cooking; as, food left to *cook* for hours. **4** To invent; to devise; as, to *cook* up a story. — *n.* A person who cooks.

cook·book \'ku̇k-ˌbu̇k\ *n.* A book of directions and recipes for cooking.

cook·er \'ku̇k-r\ *n.* One that cooks something: especially, an apparatus in which food is cooked.

cook·ery \'ku̇k-r(-)ē\ *n.* The art or practice of cooking.

cook·out \'ku̇k-ˌau̇t\ *n.* **1** An outing at which a meal is cooked and served in the open. **2** The meal cooked at such an outing.

cook·stove \'ku̇k-ˌstōv\ *n.* A stove for cooking; especially, a cast-iron stove for wood or coal, often with a reservoir at the rear or side for heating water.

cooky or **cook·ie** \'ku̇k-ē\ *n.; pl.* **cook·ies.** A small cake, usually thin and flat.

cool \'kül\ *adj.* **1** Somewhat cold; without warmth; as, a *cool* day; a *cool* room. **2** Protecting a person from heat; not admitting or retaining heat; as, *cool* clothes. **3** Not excited; calm; as, to keep *cool* in time of danger. **4** Not affectionate or interested; indifferent; as, a *cool* greeting. — *n.* Cool air; a cool time or place; as, in the *cool* of the morning. — *v.* **1** To make or become cool. **2** To calm; to quiet; as, to *cool* down an angry person. — **cool·ish** \'kü-lish\ *adj.* — **cool·ly** \'kül-lē\ *adv.*

cool·er \'kül-r\ *n.* **1** A vessel or device used to cool liquids. **2** A refrigerator. **3** A substance used for refrigerating. **4** *Slang.* A prison.

coo·lie or **coo·ly** \'kü-lē\ *n.; pl.* **coo·lies.** **1** In China, India, and Japan, a native unskilled laborer who does odd jobs. **2** A cheap laborer transported from the Orient.

coon \'kün\ *n.* A raccoon.

coon·skin \'kün-ˌskin\ *n.* The skin of the raccoon, used as a material, as for caps.

coop \'küp, 'ku̇p\ *n.* [From Old English *cupe* meaning "basket".] A small enclosure for chickens; a house or cage for small animals. — *v.* To shut up or keep in a coop, or in a small place; as, a family living *cooped* up in one room.

co-op or **co·op** \kō-'äp, 'kō-ˌäp, 'küp\ *n.* A cooperative.

coop·er \'küp-r, 'ku̇p-r\ *n.* A person who makes or repairs barrels and casks.

coop·er·age \'küp-r(-)ij, 'ku̇p-\ *n.* **1** Work done by a cooper. **2** The pay for a cooper's work. **3** A place for cooper's work.

co-op·er·ate \kō-'äp-r-ˌāt\ *v.;* **co-op·er·at·ed; co-**

op·er·at·ing. To join others in doing something; to work together. All of the pupils *co-operated* in keeping the classroom neat.

co-op·er·a·tion \(ˌ)kō-ˌäp-r-'āsh-n\ *n.* A co-operating; joint action.

co-op·er·a·tive \kō-'äp-r(-)ət-iv, -r-ˌāt-iv\ *adj.* **1** Co-operating; showing willingness to work with others; as, to show a *co-operative* spirit. **2** Having to do with an association formed to enable its members to buy or sell to better advantage; as, a *co-operative* store. — *n.* A co-operative store, business, or association. — **co-op·er·a·tive·ly**, *adv.*

co-or·di·nate \kō-'ȯrd-n(-)ət\ *adj.* **1** Equal in rank or order. **2** Of like rank in a compound sentence; as, *co-ordinate* clauses. **3** Also **co-or·di·nat·ing** \kō-'ȯrd-n-ˌāt-ing\. Joining words or word groups of the same grammatical rank. The word "and" is a *co-ordinate* conjunction. — \kō-'ȯrd-n-ˌāt\ *v.;* **co-or·di·nat·ed**; **co-or·di·nat·ing**. **1** To make or become co-ordinate; as, to *co-ordinate* two ideas. **2** To cause to work together or to act smoothly or harmoniously; to adjust; as, to *co-ordinate* the duties of various committees; a well-*co-ordinated* athlete. — \kō-'ȯrd-n(-)ət\ *n.* **1** One that is co-ordinate. **2** Any one of the numbers, as on a graph, that determine the position of a line or body in space. — **co-or·di·nate·ly** \-n(-)ət-lē\ *adv.* — **co-or·di·na·tor** \-n-ˌāt-r\ *n.*

co-or·di·na·tion \(ˌ)kō-ˌȯrd-n-'āsh-n\ *n.* **1** A making co-ordinate; a being co-ordinate; as, *co-ordination* of the branches of government. **2** Harmonious working together, as of parts; as, muscular *co-ordination.* — **co-or·di·na·tive** \kō-'ȯrd-n(-)ət-iv, -n-ˌāt-iv\ *adj.*

coot \'küt\ *n.* **1** A ducklike bird of the rail family. **2** Any North American scoter.

cop \'käp\ *n.* A policeman; as, to play *cops* and robbers.

cope \'kōp\ *n.* **1** A long capelike garment worn by priests and bishops in certain services. **2** A vault or canopy; especially, the vault of heaven; the sky.

cope \'kōp\ *v.;* **coped**; **cop·ing**. To struggle or contend, especially with some success; as, a situation too difficult to *cope* with.

copied. Past tense and past part. of *copy.*

cop·i·er \'käp-ē-ər\ *n.* One who copies.

copies. Pl. of *copy.*

co-pi·lot \'kō-ˌpī-lət\ *n.* An assistant pilot in an aircraft.

cop·ing \'kōp-ing\ *n.* The top or covering layer of a wall, often with a sloping surface.

co·pi·ous \'kōp-ē-əs\ *adj.* Very plentiful; abundant; as, a *copious* supply. — **co·pi·ous·ly**, *adv.*

cop·per \'käp-r\ *n.* **1** A tough reddish metal that can be hammered thin or drawn into fine wire and that is one of the best conductors of heat and electricity. **2** A copper or bronze coin; especially, a cent. **3** A large boiler. **4** The color of copper, orange brown with a reddish tinge.

cop·per·as \'käp-r(-)əs\ *n.* A green saltlike substance used in making inks and in dyeing.

cop·per·head \'käp-r-ˌhed\ *n.* **1** A brown poisonous snake of the eastern United States, related to the rattlesnake but without rattles. **2** [with a capital] A person in the northern states who sympathized with the South during the Civil War.

cop·per·smith \'käp-r-ˌsmith\ *n.* A worker in copper.

cop·pery \'käp-r(-)ē\ *adj.* Mixed with copper; like copper.

cop·pice \'käp-əs\ *n.* A thick growth of small trees or young trees; a thicket.

co·pra \'kōp-rə\ *n.* The dried meat of coconuts, from which coconut oil is obtained.

copse \'käps\ *n.* A coppice.

copy \'käp-ē\ *n.; pl.* **cop·ies**. **1** An exact likeness or imitation of something; as, a *copy* of a letter; a *copy* of a painting. **2** One of the entire number of books, magazines, or papers made at the same printing; as, two *copies* of today's newspaper. **3** Something set up for imitation; especially, a model for those learning to write. **4** Written or printed matter to be set up in print. — *v.;* **cop·ied** \'käp-ēd\; **cop·y·ing**. **1** To make a copy or copies of something; to reproduce. **2** To imitate; to ape. Children *copy* the manners and expressions of their parents.

cop·y·book \'käp-ē-ˌbu̇k\ *n.* A book containing copies, especially of penmanship, for learners to imitate.

copy boy. One that carries copy and runs errands, as in a newspaper office or publishing house.

cop·y·ist \'käp-ē-əst\ *n.* **1** One employed to make copies. **2** An imitator.

cop·y·read·er \'käp-ē-ˌrēd-r\ *n.* One that revises newspaper copy and adds headlines before the copy is sent to the composing room.

cop·y·right \'käp-ē-ˌrīt\ *n.* The sole right to reproduce, publish, and sell the contents and form of a literary or artistic work. — *v.* To secure a copyright on. Books are usually *copyrighted.*

co·quet·ry \'kōk-ə-trē\ *n.; pl.* **co·quet·ries**. The conduct or art of a coquette.

co·quette \kō-'ket\ *n.* A flirt. — **co·quet·tish** \-'ket-ish\ *adj.* — **co·quet·tish·ly**, *adv.*

co·qui·na \kō-'kē-nə\ *n.* A soft, whitish natural limestone of broken shells and corals cemented together, used in the southern United States for building.

cor-. A form of *com-* used before *r.*

cor·a·cle \'kȯr-ək-l, 'kär-\ *n.* A boat made of hoops covered with horsehide or tarpaulin.

cor·al \'kȯr-əl, 'kär-\ *n.* **1** A stony substance composed of the combined skeletons of tiny sea creatures, found in several colors and much used in making jewelry. **2** The sea creature whose skeleton becomes coral. **3** The color of red coral, an orange red. — *adj.* **1** Made of coral; as, a *coral* reef. **2** Of the color of coral; coral red; as, *coral* lips.

coral branch

coral snake. Any of a number of snakes most of which are poisonous and all of which have red in their markings.

cord \ˈkȯrd\ *n.* [From French *corde*, there derived from Latin *chorda* meaning "catgut", "string".] **1** A string or small rope. **2** Such string as a material; as, a hammock made of *cord*. **3** A tendon or other cordlike structure. **4** A certain quantity of wood cut for fuel. A *cord* of closely piled wood is 8 feet long, 4 feet high, and 4 feet wide. **5** A cordlike rib or ridge on cloth; a ribbed cloth, such as corduroy. **6** A small insulated cable with fittings used to connect a lamp or an electrical appliance with a socket. — *v.* **1** To furnish, bind, or connect with a cord or cords. **2** To pile up in cords; as, to *cord* wood.

cord·age \ˈkȯrd-ij\ *n.* **1** Cords or ropes; especially, the ropes in the rigging of a ship. **2** The number of cords, as of wood, on a given area.

cord·ed \ˈkȯrd-əd\ *adj.* **1** Bound with cords. **2** Having ridges or ribs; twilled; as, *corded* cloth. **3** Made of cords. **4** Piled in cords, as wood.

cor·dial \ˈkȯrj-l\ *adj.* **1** Tending to revive or cheer; as, a *cordial* medicine. **2** Warm and friendly; sincere; hearty; as, to greet a friend with a *cordial* handshake. — *n.* **1** Any stimulating preparation, as a medicine. **2** An aromatic, sweetened alcoholic drink. — **cor·dial·ly** \ˈkȯrj-l-ē\ *adv.*

cor·dial·i·ty \ˌkȯr-jē-ˈal-ət-ē, kȯr-ˈjal-\ *n.; pl.* **cor·dial·i·ties**. Cordial quality; warmth of regard.

cor·don \ˈkȯrd-n, ˈkȯr-ˌdän\ *n.* **1** An ornamental cord, used especially on costumes. **2** A line of persons or things around any person or place; as, a *cordon* of police; a *cordon* of forts. **3** A cord or ribbon worn as a badge or decoration.

cor·du·roy \ˈkȯrd-r-ˌȯi\ *n.* **1** A heavy corded or ribbed fabric, usually of cotton, woven like velvet. **2** [in the plural] Trousers made of this cloth. — *adj.* **1** Made of corduroy; as, *corduroy* trousers. **2** Made of logs laid side by side, as across a swampy place; as, a *corduroy* road.

cord·wood \ˈkȯrd-ˌwu̇d\ *n.* Wood cut for fuel and sold by the cord.

core \ˈkōr, ˈkȯr\ *n.* **1** The central part of some fruits, such as apples or pears. **2** The inmost part of anything; the center; as, the *core* of a boil. **3** A bar of iron or a bundle of wires used to intensify an induced magnetic field, as in a transformer or an armature. — *v.;* **cored**; **cor·ing**. To cut out the core of a fruit; as, to *core* an apple.

cor·er \ˈkōr-r, ˈkȯr-r\ *n.* An instrument or device for coring fruit.

Co·rin·thi·an \kə-ˈrin(t)th-ē-ən\ *adj.* **1** Relating to Corinth, an ancient city of central Greece. **2** Belonging to a style of Greek architecture whose chief feature was a bell-shaped capital surrounded with figures of leaves. — *n.* An inhabitant of Corinth.

1 Doric capital, *2* Ionic capital, *3* Corinthian capital

cork \ˈkȯrk\ *n.* [From Arabic *qurq*, there borrowed from Latin *cortex* meaning "bark", "cork".] **1** A tissue in the stems of most woody plants, making up the greater part of the bark. **2** This tissue in the tough elastic form in which it occurs in the outer layer of bark of a tree (**cork oak**) of southern Europe and northern Africa. **3** A bottle stopper, especially one made of cork. **4** A float or bob used in fishing. — *v.* **1** To stop with a cork; to seal; as, to *cork* a bottle. **2** To hold in with a cork, or as if with a cork; to restrain; as, to *cork* up one's laughter. **3** To blacken with burnt cork; as, to *cork* one's face.

cork·er \ˈkȯrk-r\ *n.* **1** A person or a machine that corks. **2** *Slang.* Something, as an argument or a retort, that puts an end to a discussion. **3** *Slang.* A person or thing that is outstanding, as in quality or ability; as, an exhibition of high diving that was a *corker*.

cork·ing \ˈkȯrk-ing\ *adj. Slang.* First-class; excellent; fine; as, a *corking* adventure story.

cork·screw \ˈkȯrk-ˌskrü\ *n.* An instrument for drawing corks from bottles. — *adj.* Like a corkscrew; spiral; as, a *corkscrew* curl.

corkscrew

cork tree. **1** A cork oak. **2** Any of several trees having corky bark.

cork·wood \ˈkȯrk-ˌwu̇d\ *n.* Any of several trees having light or corky wood, as the balsa.

corky \ˈkȯrk-ē\ *adj.;* **cork·i·er**; **cork·i·est**. Having the dry, porous, buoyant quality of cork; corklike; as, *corky* wood.

corm \ˈkȯrm\ *n.* A solid bulblike underground stem, usually with a few thin scales, as in the crocus and gladiolus.

cor·mo·rant \ˈkȯrm-r(-)ənt, -r-ˌant\ *n.* [From Old French *cormaran*, there borrowed from Latin *corvus marinus* meaning "raven of the sea".] A large black web-footed sea bird related to the pelican, having a long neck with a bare patch of skin at the upper throat and a slender hooked beak.

corn \ˈkȯrn\ *n.* [From Old English *corn* meaning "grain".] **1** The seeds or kernels of various cereal plants such as wheat, oats, and barley, or any of the plants that bear these seeds; grain. **2** The large seeds or kernels produced on a hard woody core, or corncob, by a tall cereal plant with broad grasslike leaves, or the plant that bears these seeds; Indian corn; maize. **3** A single grain of any of various cereal plants. **4** Granular snow. **5** Corny playing or acting; corny humor. — *v.* To preserve by packing with salt, originally in grains, or by soaking in salty water; as, *corned* beef.

☞In England the name *corn* usually means wheat; in Scotland and Ireland it usually means oats; in North America and Australia it usually means Indian corn, or maize.

corn \ˈkȯrn\ *n.* [From Old French, there derived from Latin *cornu* meaning "horn".] A hardening and thickening of the skin, as on a person's toe, at a point where there has been pressure or rubbing.

corn bread. Bread made of the meal of Indian corn baked in a shallow pan.

corn·cob \ˈkȯrn-ˌkäb\ *n.* **1** The woody core on which the kernels of Indian corn grow in rows. **2** A tobacco pipe with a bowl made by hollowing out a piece of corncob.

corn·crib \ˈkȯrn-ˌkrib\ *n.* A crib or ventilated bin for holding or storing unshelled Indian corn.

cor·nea \ˈkȯr-nē-ə\ *n.* The transparent part of the coating of the eyeball, which covers the iris and the pupil and admits light.

cor·ner \ˈkȯrn-r\ *n.* **1** The point or angle formed by the meeting of two edges or sides of a thing; the place near this point; as, the *corners* of a table or a box; to sit in the *corner* of a room. **2** The place where two streets come together; as, to live just around the *corner* from a friend. **3** An out-of-the-way place; as, an old house with all sorts of odd *corners;* a quiet *corner* of a great city. **4** An edge or end; the part farthest from the center; as, the four *corners* of the earth. **5** A difficult place, or one from which there is no escape; as, to be driven into a *corner*. **6** A piece designed to form, protect, or ornament an outward angle of something; as, a book bound in cloth with leather back and *corners*. **7** The situation which results when speculators buy up the whole available supply of something; as, to make a *corner* in wheat.

— The word *angle* is a synonym of *corner: corner* is likely to refer to the point where two or three sides of a material structure come together; *angle*, usually more technical, is likely to suggest the meeting of two lines or planes or the number of degrees formed by their meeting.

— *v.* **1** To drive into a corner; to put in a difficult position; as, to *corner* a rat; to *corner* a person in an argument. **2** To bring about a corner in a market for goods or securities; as, to *corner* the wheat market. **—** *adj.* **1** Situated at a corner; as, a *corner* store. **2** Fitted for use in a corner; as, a *corner* table.

cor·ner·stone \ˈkȯrn-r-ˌstōn\ *n.* **1** A stone forming part of a corner in a wall; especially, such a stone laid at the formal beginning of the erection of a building. **2** Something of basic importance; as, a *cornerstone* of this country's foreign policy. Thrift is a *cornerstone* of success.

cor·net \(ˈ)kȯr-ˈnet, ˈkȯr-ˌnet\ *n.* **1** A musical instrument, usually of brass, shaped and played like a trumpet. **2** Something shaped like a horn, as a piece of paper twisted into the form of a cone.

cor·net·tist or **cor·net·ist** \kȯr-ˈnet-əst\ *n.* A person who plays the cornet.

corn·field \ˈkȯrn-ˌfēld\ *n.* **1** A field in which Indian corn is grown. **2** *British.* A field of wheat, rye, barley, or oats.

corn·flow·er \ˈkȯrn-ˌflau̇r\ *n.* A bachelor's-button.

corn·husk \ˈkȯrn-ˌhəsk\ *n.* The husk of an ear of Indian corn.

cor·nice \ˈkȯr-nəs\ *n.* **1** The ornamental projecting piece that forms the top edge of the front of a building or of a pillar. **2** An ornamental molding placed where the walls meet the ceiling of a room.

cornice

corn·meal \ˈkȯrn-ˈmēl\ *n.* Ground corn.

corn pone \ˈpōn, ˌpōn\. Corn bread, often without milk or eggs, shaped into irregular ovals by hand and baked or fried on a griddle.

corn·stalk \ˈkȯrn-ˌstȯk\ *n.* A stalk of corn, especially of Indian corn.

corn·starch \ˈkȯrn-ˌstärch, -ˌstȧrch\ *n.* A fine starch or starchy flour made from corn and used in cooking.

cor·nu·co·pia \ˌkȯr-nə-ˈkōp-ē-ə, ˌkȯrn-yə-\ *n.* **1** A horn-shaped container overflowing with fruits and flowers, used as a symbol of abundance; the horn of plenty. **2** Any container shaped like a horn or a cone, such as a paper cone for holding candy.

cornucopia, 1

corny \ˈkȯr-nē\ *adj.;* **corn·i·er; corn·i·est.** Old-fashioned or countrified; tiresomely simple or sentimental; outworn; as, *corny* music; *corny* jokes.

co·rol·la \kə-ˈräl-ə\ *n.* The part of a flower that is formed by the petals. A buttercup has a yellow *corolla.*

cor·ol·lary \ˈkȯr-ə-ˌler-ē, ˈkär-\ *n.; pl.* **cor·ol·lar·ies. 1** A deduction or additional inference from a proposition that has been proved true. **2** Something that naturally follows; a result.

co·ro·na \kə-ˈrō-nə\ *n.; pl.* **co·ro·nas** \-nəz\ or **co·ro·nae** \-(ˌ)nē\. **1** A circle often seen around a luminous body; especially, a shining ring around the sun, seen during a total eclipse. **2** A crownlike part on the inner side of the corolla of a flower, as in the jonquil. **3** The discharge of electricity often seen as a glow around a conductor. — **co·ro·nal** \kə-ˈrōn-l; ˈkȯr-ən-l, ˈkär-\ *adj.*

cor·o·nal \ˈkȯr-ən-l, ˈkär-\ *n.* **1** An ornamental band for the head. **2** A crown or coronet.

cor·o·nary \ˈkȯr-ə-ˌner-ē, ˈkär-\ *adj.* Of or relating to either of two arteries that lead from the aorta and supply blood to the tissues of the heart itself.

cor·o·na·tion \ˌkȯr-ə-ˈnāsh-n, ˌkär-\ *n.* The act or the ceremony of crowning a king or queen.

cor·o·ner \ˈkȯr-ən-r, ˈkär-\ *n.* A public official whose chief duty is to discover the reasons for the death of any person who dies suddenly and not as a result of known illness.

cor·o·net \ˌkȯr-ə-ˈnet, ˌkär-\ *n.* **1** A small crown worn by a person of high rank but not of royal rank; as, a duke's *coronet.* **2** An ornamental wreath or band worn around the head; as, a *coronet* of flowers.

coronet, 1

cor·po·ral \ˈkȯrp-r(-)əl\ *adj.* Of the body; bodily;

as, whipping and other forms of *corporal* punishment. — **cor·po·ral·ly** \'-r(-)ə-lē\ *adv.*

cor·po·ral \'kȯrp-r(-)əl\ *n.* In army rank, the lowest noncommissioned officer.

cor·po·rate \'kȯrp-r(-)ət\ *adj.* **1** Combined into one body; especially, united legally and given the rights and liabilities of a person; as, a *corporate* company; a *corporate* town. **2** Belonging to a corporation; as, *corporate* property.

cor·po·ra·tion \ˌkȯrp-r-'āsh-n\ *n.* A group of persons who are organized to carry on a business or a particular kind of work and who are authorized by law to act as a single person.

cor·po·re·al \kȯr-'pōr-ē-əl, -'pȯr-\ *adj.* **1** Physical; material; not spiritual or immaterial. **2** Of or relating to the body; bodily.

corps \'kōr, 'kȯr\ *n.; pl.* **corps** \'kōrz, 'kȯrz\. A group of persons acting under a leader; especially, a section of an army.

corpse \'kȯrps\ *n.* A dead body.

cor·pu·lent \'kȯrp-yə-lənt\ *adj.* Very stout and heavy; extremely fat. — **cor·pu·lence** \-lən(t)s\ *n.*

cor·pus·cle \'kȯr-(ˌ)pəs-l\ *n.* **1** A minute particle. **2** A free-floating cell, as any of those found in blood, lymph, or pus; especially, a blood cell. — **cor·pus·cu·lar** \kȯr-'pəs-kyəl-r\ *adj.*

cor·ral \kə-'ral\ *n.* [From Spanish, meaning "stockyard".] **1** An enclosure for keeping or capturing animals. **2** An enclosure, as of wagons drawn into a circle, set up for defense. — *v.;* **cor·ralled**; **cor·ral·ling.** **1** To confine in or as if in a corral; to coop or pen up. **2** To surround; to capture. **3** To arrange, as wagons, so as to form a corral.

cor·rect \kə-'rekt\ *v.* **1** To make right; to free from mistakes or faults; as, to *correct* a misspelled word. **2** To show how a thing can be improved or made right. The teacher *corrects* our compositions. **3** To scold or punish for a fault or mistake. **4** To counteract by means of opposite qualities or tendencies; to neutralize, as a faulty physical condition. **5** To adjust so as to bring into conformity with a standard; as, a barometer *corrected* for an altitude of 500 feet. — *adj.* Agreeing with an accepted standard or with fact or truth; without fault or mistake; right; true; proper; as, a *correct* answer; the *correct* time.

— The words *accurate* and *exact* are synonyms of *correct: correct* may suggest either freedom from error, or compliance with convention; *accurate* usually implies conformity to truth or fact through the use of great care to avoid error; *exact* may indicate strict agreement to fact.

cor·rec·tion \kə-'reksh-n\ *n.* **1** The act of correcting; a making or setting right. **2** Reproof or punishment intended to correct faults of character or behavior; as, a house of *correction.* Most children are now and then in need of *correction.* **3** A change which corrects something. Teachers often write their *corrections* in red ink.

cor·rec·tive \kə-'rek-tiv\ *adj.* Serving to correct; having the power of making right, normal, or regular; as, *corrective* exercises. — *n.* Something that serves to correct.

cor·rect·ly \kə-'rekt-lē\ *adv.* In a correct manner; without fault or error; as, to do all the examples *correctly;* to behave *correctly* at a party.

cor·re·late \'kȯr-ə-ˌlāt, 'kär-\ *v.;* **cor·re·lat·ed**; **cor·re·lat·ing.** To connect things or parts of things in an orderly, systematic way; to put things in their proper relations with each other; as, to *correlate* the study of literature and history in school.

cor·re·la·tion \ˌkȯr-ə-'lāsh-n, ˌkär-\ *n.* **1** The act or process of correlating. **2** The state of being correlated; especially, a mutual relation discovered to exist between things; as, the apparent *correlation* between the degree of poverty in a society and the crime rate.

cor·rel·a·tive \kə-'rel-ət-iv\ *adj.* **1** Mutually related. **2** In grammar, having a mutual relation and regularly used together. "Either" and "or" are *correlative* conjunctions. — *n.* Either of two correlative things, especially words or expressions. — **cor·rel·a·tive·ly**, *adv.*

cor·re·spond \ˌkȯr-ə-'spänd, ˌkär-\ *v.* **1** To be like or equal to something else, as in use, position, or amount. The forefeet of a dog *correspond* to the hands of a man. **2** To suit, fit, or agree; as, a house that *corresponded* with the needs and desires of its owners. **3** To communicate by means of letters; to exchange letters. My father *corresponds* with many people. — **cor·re·spond·ing·ly** \-ing-lē\ *adv.*

cor·re·spond·ence \ˌkȯr-ə-'spän-dən(t)s, ˌkär-\ *n.* **1** A likeness; agreement; harmony; the adaptation of one thing to another; as, *correspondence* between words and deeds. **2** Communication by means of letters or the letters exchanged; as, to answer the day's *correspondence.*

cor·re·spond·ent \ˌkȯr-ə-'spän-dənt, ˌkär-\ *adj.* Answering to something in fitness or adaptation; suitable; congruous; as, a result that is *correspondent* to one's expectation. — *n.* **1** Something that corresponds or conforms to something else. **2** A person with whom one communicates by letter. **3** A person employed to contribute news regularly from a particular place; as, the London *correspondent* of a newspaper. **4** One who keeps up regular business relations with another, especially with a firm at a distance.

cor·ri·dor \'kȯr-əd-r, 'kär-, -ə-ˌdȯr\ *n.* **1** A passageway into which rooms open, especially a long passageway or one in a large building, as a school, hotel, or office building; a long hallway. **2** [often with a capital] A narrow strip of land across territory previously wholly foreign, joining a country to a seaport.

cor·rob·o·rate \kə-'räb-r-ˌāt\ *v.;* **cor·rob·o·rat·ed**; **cor·rob·o·rat·ing.** To make more certain or more convincing; to confirm; as, to *corroborate* another person's account of an accident; a fine theory but without evidence to *corroborate* it. — **cor·rob·o·ra·tor**, *n.*

cor·rob·o·ra·tion \kə-ˌräb-r-'āsh-n\ *n.* The act of corroborating or something that corroborates; confirmation. The boy's explanation of his absence could not be accepted without *corroboration.*

cor·rob·o·ra·tive \kə-'räb-r-ˌāt-iv, -r(-)ət-iv\ *adj.* Corroborating; confirming; as, *corroborative* evidence. — **cor·rob·o·ra·tive·ly**, *adv.*

cor·rode \kə-'rōd\ *v.;* **cor·rod·ed**; **cor·rod·ing.** To eat away, or to be eaten away, gradually, as by rust or by an acid. Salt *corrodes* silver.

cor·ro·sion \kə-'rōzh-n\ *n.* The action or effect of something that corrodes.

cor·ro·sive \kə-'rō-siv\ *adj.* Corroding or likely to corrode. — *n.* A substance that corrodes other substances. — **cor·ro·sive·ly**, *adv.*

cor·ru·gate \'kȯr-ə-ˌgāt, -yə-ˌgāt, 'kär-\ *v.;* **cor·ru·gat·ed**; **cor·ru·gat·ing.** To make wrinkled; to make with wavelike folds; as, to *corrugate* paper; a shack roofed with *corrugated* iron.

cor·ru·ga·tion \ˌkȯr-ə-'gāsh-n, -yə-'gāsh-n, ˌkär-\ *n.* **1** A corrugating. **2** A wrinkle or a groove of a corrugated surface.

cor·rupt \kə-'rəpt\ *adj.* Changed from a good to a bad state; no longer sound or honest; depraved; as, a *corrupt* government. — *v.* **1** To make or become putrid; to taint. **2** To make corrupt; to change from good to bad. Children's manners may be *corrupted* by poor example. **3** To draw aside from what is right and proper; to pervert; as, an official whom no one could *corrupt.* **4** To falsify, as a painting or a text. **5** To become debased. — **cor·rupt·ly**, *adv.* — **cor·rupt·er**, *n.*

cor·rupt·i·ble \kə-'rəp-təb-l\ *adj.* Capable of being corrupted. — **cor·rupt·i·bil·i·ty** \kə-ˌrəp-tə-'bil-ət-ē\ *n.*

cor·rup·tion \kə-'rəpsh-n\ *n.* **1** Physical decay or rotting. **2** Lack of honesty. **3** The causing of other persons to do something wrong, as by giving bribes; a corrupting.

cor·sage \kȯr-'säzh, -'säj, -'sȧzh, -'sȧj\ *n.* [From French, meaning "upper part of the body", "bodice", from Old French *cors* meaning "body".] **1** The waist or bodice of a woman's dress. **2** A bouquet of flowers to be worn by a woman.

cor·sair \'kȯr-ˌsar, -ˌser\ *n.* **1** A privateer. **2** A pirate. **3** The boat of a corsair.

corse \'kȯrs\ *n. Archaic.* A corpse.

corse·let, *n.* **1** \'kȯrs-lət\. Also **cors·let.** The body armor worn by a knight, especially the pieces worn on the upper part of the body. **2** \ˌkȯrs-l-'et\. A woman's corsetlike undergarment.

cor·set \'kȯr-sət\ *n.* A tight-fitting, stiffened undergarment worn by women to support or to give shape to waist and hips. — *v.* To dress in or fit with a corset.

cor·tege or **cor·tège** \kȯr-'tezh, 'kȯr-ˌtezh\ *n.* **1** A train of attendants; a retinue. **2** A procession.

cor·tex \'kȯr-ˌteks\ *n.; pl.* **cor·tex·es** \-ˌteks-əz\ or **cor·ti·ces** \'kȯrt-ə-ˌsēz\. **1** The bark of a tree. **2** The outer part of an organ, as the kidney; especially, the outer layer of gray matter of the brain.

cor·ti·cal \'kȯrt-ik-l\ *adj.* Of, relating to, or consisting of cortex. — **cor·ti·cal·ly** \-ik-l(-)ē\ *adv.*

cor·ti·sone \'kȯrt-ə-ˌsōn, -ˌzōn\ *n.* A compound found in a part of the adrenal gland and also produced synthetically, used in treating arthritis and certain allergies.

cor·vette \kȯr-'vet\ *n.* [From French, there probably borrowed from Dutch *corf* meaning "basket", then "a kind of ship shaped like a basket".] **1** A warship of old navies, ranking below a frigate and usually having only one tier of guns. **2** A highly maneuverable warship smaller than a destroyer, used to escort and protect other boats.

cos. Abbreviation for *cosine.*

cosier. Variant of *cozier.*

cosies. Variant of *cozies.*

cosiest. Variant of *coziest.*

cosily. Variant of *cozily.*

co·sine \'kō-ˌsīn\ *n.* With reference to an acute angle in a right triangle, the ratio of the side adjacent to that angle to the hypotenuse.

cos·met·ic \käz-'met-ik\ *adj.* Beautifying; as, *cosmetic* preparations. — *n.* Any preparation, as a cream, lotion, or powder, intended to beautify the skin or the hair.

cos·mic \'käz-mik\ *adj.* Of or relating to the whole universe or something similarly vast and systematic; grand; mighty; as, a topic of *cosmic* proportions.

cosmic ray. A stream of atomic nuclei of high frequency and great penetrating power that enter the earth's atmosphere from outer space at great speed.

cos·mo·naut \'käz-mə-ˌnȯt\ *n.* An astronaut.

cos·mo·pol·i·tan \ˌkäz-mə-'päl-ət-n\ *adj.* **1** Belonging to or having to do with the world as a whole; not limited to any particular countries, nations, or races; as, a *cosmopolitan* point of view. **2** At home in all lands; not narrow in interests or sympathies; as, a *cosmopolitan* person. — *n.* One who is cosmopolitan.

cos·mos \'käz-məs; *senses 1 and 2 are also* -ˌmäs *or* -ˌmōs\ *n.* **1** The universe, thought of as an ordered whole. **2** Any system having order and harmony among its parts. **3** A tall garden plant with white, pinkish, or rose-colored flowers.

cosmos

Cos·sack \'käs-ˌak, 'käs-ək\ *n.* [From Russian *kazak*, there borrowed from Turkish *kazak* meaning "adventurer", "vagabond".] One of a warlike pastoral people of the Russian steppes, formerly used as cavalry.

cost \'kȯst\ *n.* **1** The amount paid or asked in return for a thing; charge; price. The *cost* of the book is three dollars. **2** Anything required to be used or spent in getting something; as, to spare no *cost* in gaining one's ends. The greatest *cost* of war is in human lives. **3** [in the plural] The expenses of a lawsuit. — *v.;* **cost**; **cost·ing.** **1** To have as its price. Each ticket *costs* one dollar. **2** To cause one to pay, spend, or lose. Selfishness can *cost* us many friends.

cos·tal \'käst-l\ *adj.* Relating to the ribs or the sides of the body.

Cos·ta Ri·can \ˌkäs-tə 'rēk-n, ˌkȯs-, ˌkōs-\ *adj.* Of or relating to Costa Rica. — *n.* A native or inhabitant of Costa Rica.

cos·ter. Short for *costermonger*.

cos·ter·mon·ger \'käst-r-ˌməng-gr\ *n.* *Chiefly British.* A person who sells fruit or vegetables in the street, from a stand or cart.

cos·tive \'käs-tiv\ *adj.* Constipated.

cost·ly \'kȯst-lē\ *adj.;* **cost·li·er**; **cost·li·est.** Costing a great deal; expensive; dear; as, *costly* jewels; a *costly* victory. — **cost·li·ness**, *n.*

cost·mary \'kȯst-ˌmer-ē\ *n.; pl.* **cost·mar·ies.** A scented herb of the aster family, used as a potherb.

cos·tume \'käs-ˌtüm, -ˌtyüm\ *n.* **1** Clothes; a suit or dress. **2** Dress in general, including ornaments and style of wearing the hair. **3** The distinctive dress of a people, class, region, or period, especially as worn on the stage or at a masquerade party. — *v.;* **cos·tumed**; **cos·tum·ing.** To provide with a costume; to dress in a costume.

cos·tum·er \'käs-ˌtüm-r, -ˌtyüm-r\ *n.* **1** A person who makes or deals in costumes, as for theatrical shows and masquerade parties. **2** A clothes tree.

cosy. Variant of *cozy*.

cot \'kät\ *n.* **1** A cottage; a hut. **2** A cote.

cot \'kät\ *n.* A narrow bed, often consisting of a sheet of canvas or interwoven strips of webbing stretched on a collapsible frame.

cote \'kōt, 'kät\ *n.* A shed or coop for small domestic animals, as sheep or doves.

co·te·rie \'kōt-r-(ˌ)ē, ˌkōt-r-'ē\ *n.* A group of persons who are in the habit of associating together on familiar terms, especially for social purposes.

co·til·lion \kō-'til-yən\ *n.* **1** An aborate and complicated dance performed as part of a formal ball, led by one couple but marked by frequent changing of partners. **2** A formal ball, as one at which debutantes are presented to society for social purposes or in pursuit of some common interest.

cot·tage \'kät-ij\ *n.* **1** A small house; any simple, detached, one-family house. **2** A house at a vacation resort.

cottage cheese. The drained, seasoned curd of sour milk.

cottage pudding. A pudding consisting of a piece of plain cake covered with a sweet sauce.

cot·tag·er \'kät-ij-r\ *n.* A person living in a cottage; especially, in the United States, one occupying a private house at a vacation resort.

cot·ter or **cot·tar** \'kät-r\ *n.* A peasant occupying a small holding of land in Scotland.

cot·ter \'kät-r\ *n.* **1** A wedge-shaped piece of wood or metal used to fasten parts together. **2** Also **cotter pin**. A split metal pin, the ends of which are bent back after insertion through a slot or hole.

cot·ton \'kät-n\ *n.* **1** A soft, whitish, fibrous substance composed of twisted hairs covering the seeds of an erect branching plant (**cotton plant**) having yellowish flowers that become red the second day and bearing the seeds in a capsule, or boll. **2** The cotton plant. **3** Thread spun from cotton or a fabric woven from such thread. — *adj.* Made of cotton. — *v.;* **cot·toned**; **cot·ton·ing** \-n(-)ing\. To take a liking; as, to *cotton* to a new acquaintance at first meeting.

cotton: leaves and flowers

cotton gin. A machine for separating the seeds from cotton.

cot·ton·mouth \'kät-n-ˌmau̇th\ *n.; pl.* **cot·ton·mouths** \-ˌmau̇t͟hz, -ˌmau̇ths\. A poisonous snake of the moccasin family; a water moccasin.

cot·ton·seed \'kät-n-ˌsēd\ *n.* The seed of the cotton plant, yielding an oil (**cottonseed oil**) used in cooking and in the manufacture of soap, and a meal (**cottonseed meal**) used as a feed and fertilizer.

cot·ton·tail \'kät-n-ˌtāl\ *n.* Any of several small brownish-gray rabbits with white-tufted tail.

cot·ton·wood \'kät-n-ˌwu̇d\ *n.* **1** A tree of the poplar family, having rough, light-colored bark, shiny leaves, and seeds covered with a cottony substance. **2** The wood of this tree or of various other poplars.

cottonwood leaves

cot·tony \'kät-n-ē\ *adj.* **1** Covered with hairs like cotton; downy; woolly. **2** Of or relating to cotton. **3** Soft and fluffy like cotton.

cot·y·le·don \ˌkät-l-'ēd-n\ *n.* The first leaf, or one of the first pair of leaves, that develops in a seed plant, usually folded within the seed until germination, and serving as a storehouse for food.

couch \'kau̇ch\ *n.* A bed; especially, an upholstered bed or lounge. — *v.* **1** To place or lay on a couch. **2** To bring down; to lower; as, knights charging with *couched* lances. **3** To put in words; to express; as, a proposal carefully thought out and well *couched*.

couch·ant \'kau̇ch-nt\ *adj.* Lying down; especially, in heraldry, lying down with the head raised; as, a coat of arms bearing a lion *couchant*.

cou·gar \'küg-r, 'kü-ˌgär, -ˌgȧr\ *n.* A large tawny-brown unspotted animal of the cat family, longer limbed and less bulky than the jaguar — called also *puma*, *panther*, and *mountain lion*.

cough \'kȯf\ *v.* **1** To force air from the lungs with a sharp, short noise or series of noises. **2** To get rid of by coughing; as, to *cough* up phlegm. — *n.* **1** The act or sound of coughing. **2** The habit of coughing often; coughing as a sign of a disease; as, to have a bad *cough*.

could \kəd, (')ku̇d\. Past tense of *can*. **1** Knew how to. My sister *could* read at the age of five. **2** Was or were able to. My brother *could* lift heavy weights. **3** Should or would be able to. I *could* learn to play the piano if I practiced. **4** Had the power or right to. Only the governor *could* free him.

couldn't \'ku̇d-nt\. A contraction of *could not.*

couldst \kədst, (')ku̇dst\. An archaic form of *could,* used chiefly with *thou.*

cou·lee \'kü-lē\ *n.* **1** A solidified stream or sheet of lava. **2** A steep-sided trenchlike valley.

coun·cil \'kau̇n(t)s-l\ *n.* **1** A group of persons called together to give advice or to make decisions. **2** An official body of advisers or lawmakers, either elected or appointed, as in a city.

coun·cil·man \'kau̇n(t)s-l-mən\ *n.; pl.* **coun·cil·men** \-mən\. A member of a council, especially in a city government.

coun·ci·lor or **coun·cil·lor** \'kau̇n(t)s-l(-)ər\ *n.* A member of a council, as of a governor's council.

coun·sel \'kau̇n(t)s-l\ *n.* **1** Advice given; as, a father's *counsel* to his son. **2** The discussion of reasons for or against a thing; an exchange of opinions; as, to take *counsel* with friends. **3** A person who gives advice, especially in legal matters; the lawyer or lawyers employed to manage a case. — *v.;* **coun·seled** or **coun·selled**; **coun·sel·ing** or **coun·sel·ling** \-l(-)ing\. **1** To give counsel; to advise; as, to *counsel* a student on a choice of studies. **2** To recommend, as an act or course; as, to *counsel* more careful thought before taking action. **3** To take counsel; as, to *counsel* with friends.

coun·se·lor or **coun·sel·lor** \'kau̇n(t)s-l(-)ər\ *n.* **1** An adviser. **2** A lawyer. **3** A group leader and supervisor of activities at a summer camp, especially one for children.

count \'kau̇nt\ *v.* **1** To name or tell one by one in order to find the whole number of units in a collection; to reckon; as, to *count* the apples in a box. **2** To name the numerals in regular order up to a particular point; as, to *count* ten; to *count* up to one hundred by fives. **3** To include in a reckoning or counting; to take into account; as, a period of 40 days, not *counting* Sundays. Each contestant is allowed two practice jumps which are not *counted.* **4** To depend upon someone or something; to rely. We *count* upon you for help. **5** To consider; to judge; as, to *count* oneself lucky. **6** To have value, force, or influence; to be of account; to be taken into consideration. Every vote *counts.* — *n.* **1** An act of counting; as, to make a *count.* **2** The number found by counting; as, a *count* of ten.

count \'kau̇nt\ *n.* A European nobleman having a rank about the same as that of an English earl.

count·down \'kau̇nt-ˌdau̇n\ *n.* An audible backward counting off, in fixed units from an arbitrary starting number, of the time remaining before the final execution of an operation, as in the launching of a rocket.

coun·te·nance \'kau̇nt-n-ən(t)s, 'kau̇n-tə-nən(t)s, 'kau̇nt-nən(t)s\ *n.* **1** The face; as, a kind *countenance.* **2** The expression of the face; especially, facial expression as showing calmness of mind; as, to keep one's *countenance* in spite of a strong desire to laugh; to be put out of *countenance* by the laughter of the crowd. **3** Encouragement or approval; as, to give *countenance* to a plan. — *v.;* **coun·te·nanced**; **coun·te·nanc·ing.** To favor by approving or encouraging. The boy's father does not *countenance* his rude behavior.

count·er \'kau̇nt-r\ *n.* **1** A person or a thing that counts; a computer. **2** A piece, usually round, of wood, metal, or other material used for keeping and counting a score in a game. **3** A table or board on which money is counted and over which business is transacted; a long narrow table or board on which goods are handled or food is served, as in a store or a restaurant.

coun·ter \'kau̇nt-r\ *adv.* In another or a contrary direction; against; as, to go *counter* to advice. — *adj.* Moving or acting in an opposite way; contrary; opposing; as, a *counter* offer. — *n.* **1** The act of going counter; something that goes counter. **2** A stiff piece of leather or fiber used to give shape to the upper of a shoe around the heel. — *v.* **1** To go, act, move, or speak counter to; to oppose. **2** To give a blow in return for one received. The boxer *countered* with his left.

counter-. A prefix that can mean: **1** Against or in the opposite direction, as in *countercurrent* or *countermarch.* **2** In return or retaliation, as in *counterattack* or *counterrevolution.* **3** So as to undo, as in *counteract* or *countermand.* **4** Matching, as in *counterfoil* or *counterpart.*

coun·ter·act \ˌkau̇nt-r-'akt\ *v.* To act so as to prevent something from acting in its own way; to neutralize; as, a drug that *counteracts* the effect of a poison. — **coun·ter·ac·tion** \-'aksh-n\ *n.* — **coun·ter·ac·tive** \-'ak-tiv\ *adj.*

coun·ter·at·tack \'kau̇nt-r-ə-ˌtak\ *n.* An attack made in return for an enemy attack. — *v.* To make a counterattack; to attack in return.

coun·ter·bal·ance \'kau̇nt-r-ˌbal-ən(t)s\ *n.* **1** A weight that balances another; a counterpoise. **2** Any force or influence that offsets or compensates for the effects of a contrary force or influence. The girl's good sense served as a *counterbalance* for her sudden enthusiasms. — \ˌkau̇nt-r-'bal-ən(t)s\ *v.;* **coun·ter·bal·anced**; **coun·ter·bal·anc·ing.** To act as a counterbalance to; to counteract.

coun·ter·check \'kau̇nt-r-ˌchek\ *n.* **1** Something intended to restrain or control; a check. **2** A check upon one already existing; a double check. — *v.* **1** To place a check on, in order to restrain or control. **2** To check a second time, to control or verify; to recheck.

counter check. A blank check obtainable at a bank, especially one that must be cashed at the bank by the person who draws it.

coun·ter·claim \'kau̇nt-r-ˌklām\ *n.* A claim made in opposition to another claim. — *v.* To present as a counterclaim. — **coun·ter·claim·ant** \ˌkau̇nt-r-'klā-mənt\ *n.*

coun·ter·clock·wise \'kau̇nt-r-'kläk-ˌwīz\ *adj.* or *adv.* Rotating in a direction opposite to that in which the hands of a clock rotate.

coun·ter·cur·rent \ˈkau̇nt-r-ˌkər-ənt, -ˌkə-rənt\ *n.* A current flowing against a main current, as in an eddy.

coun·ter·feit \ˈkau̇nt-r-ˌfit\ *adj.* Made in exact imitation of something genuine and intended to be passed off as genuine; as, *counterfeit* money. — *n.* Something made to imitate another thing, with the desire to deceive; as, a poor *counterfeit* of the original. — *v.* **1** To imitate, especially in order to deceive; to make counterfeits; as, to *counterfeit* money. **2** To pretend; as, astonishment so well *counterfeited* that it seemed real. — **coun·ter·feit·er**, *n.*

coun·ter·foil \ˈkau̇nt-r-ˌfȯil\ *n.* The stub of a bank check or a corresponding part of a receipt or money order.

coun·ter·in·tel·li·gence \ˈkau̇nt-r-in-ˈtel-ə-jən(t)s\ *n.* Organized activities of an intelligence service intended to counter the activities of an enemy's intelligence service by blocking its sources of information and to deceive the enemy through ruses and misinformation.

coun·ter·mand \ˌkau̇nt-r-ˈmand\ *v.* **1** To cancel by withdrawing or replacing, as an order or a command; to revoke. **2** To recall by a later contrary order; as, to *countermand* additional supplies.

coun·ter·march \ˈkau̇nt-r-ˌmärch, -ˌmȧrch\ *n.* **1** A marching back. **2** A movement of troops by which they reverse their direction. — *v.* To march back; to perform a countermarch or to cause to countermarch.

coun·ter·pane \ˈkau̇nt-r-ˌpān\ *n.* An outer covering for a bed; a bedspread.

coun·ter·part \ˈkau̇nt-r-ˌpärt, -ˌpȧrt\ *n.* **1** A part or thing corresponding to another, as in appearance, position, or use. The left arm is the *counterpart* of the right arm. **2** Something that serves to complete something else; a complement. **3** A person closely resembling another person. The twins were *counterparts* of each other.

coun·ter·plot \ˈkau̇nt-r-ˌplät\ *n.* A plot made to defeat another plot. — *v.*; **coun·ter·plot·ted**; **coun·ter·plot·ting.** To lay a counterplot.

coun·ter·point \ˈkau̇nt-r-ˌpȯint\ *n.* **1** A melody added to another melody as an accompaniment. **2** The art of composing music in which one melody moves on with the accompaniment of one or more other independent melodies, all woven into one harmonious whole; the art of combining melodies.

coun·ter·poise \ˈkau̇nt-r-ˌpȯiz\ *n.* **1** A counterbalance. **2** A state of balance; equilibrium. — *v.*; **coun·ter·poised**; **coun·ter·pois·ing.** To counterbalance.

coun·ter·rev·o·lu·tion \ˈkau̇nt-r-ˌrev-l-ˈüsh-n\ *n.* A revolution intended to counteract an earlier revolution. — **coun·ter·rev·o·lu·tion·ary** \-ˈüsh-n-ˌer-ē\ *adj.* — **coun·ter·rev·o·lu·tion·ist** \-n-əst\ *n.*

coun·ter·sign \ˈkau̇nt-r-ˌsīn\ *n.* A sign used in reply to another sign; especially, a secret signal that must be given by a person wishing to pass a guard or a sentry; a password. — *v.* To sign something, as a document, already signed by someone else in order to confirm its genuineness.

coun·ter·sink \ˈkau̇nt-r-ˌsingk\ *v.*; **coun·ter·sunk** \-ˌsəngk\; **coun·ter·sink·ing.** **1** To form a hollowed-out place around the top of a hole in wood or metal into which a screw or bolt is to be placed. **2** To sink the head, as of a screw, bolt, or nail, even with or below the surface. — *n.* **1** A countersunk hole. **2** A tool for countersinking a hole.

coun·ter·ten·or \ˈkau̇nt-r-ˈten-r\ *n.* **1** One of the middle parts in music, between the tenor and the soprano. **2** A man's falsetto voice singing such a part; a male alto.

coun·ter·weight \ˈkau̇nt-r-ˌwāt\ *n.* A counterpoise.

count·ess \ˈkau̇nt-əs\ *n.* **1** The wife or widow of a count or, in England, of an earl. **2** A woman who has in her own right a rank equal to that of a count or an earl.

count·ing·house \ˈkau̇nt-ing-ˌhau̇s\ *n.*; *pl.* **count·ing·hous·es** \-ˌhau̇-zəz\. A building, room, or office used for keeping accounts and transacting business.

count·less \ˈkau̇nt-ləs\ *adj.* More than can be counted or seeming to be more than can be counted; innumerable; as, *countless* grains of sand; *countless* thousands of years.

coun·tri·fied or **coun·try·fied** \ˈkən-trē-ˌfīd\ *adj.* Looking or acting like a person from the country; rustic.

coun·try \ˈkən-trē\ *n.*; *pl.* **coun·tries.** **1** A region or district; as, good farming *country.* **2** The territory of a nation; a land inhabited by a people with a common government. How many *countries* can you find on a map of South America? **3** A person's native or adopted land. We all owe allegiance to our *country.* **4** The people of a nation. The whole *country* was up in arms. **5** Rural regions; districts away from thickly settled areas; as, to spend the summer in the *country.* — *adj.* **1** Rural; rustic; as, a *country* road; *country* music. **2** Rude; without refinement; as, *country* manners.

coun·try·man \ˈkən-trē-mən\ *n.*; *pl.* **coun·try·men** \-mən\. **1** An inhabitant of a certain country; a person born in the same country as another; a fellow citizen. **2** A person who lives and works in the country; a rustic.

coun·try·seat \ˈkən-trē-ˈsēt\ *n.* A dwelling or estate in the country.

coun·try·side \ˈkən-trē-ˌsīd\ *n.* A rural district or its people.

coun·try·wom·an \ˈkən-trē-ˌwu̇m-ən\ *n.*; *pl.* **coun·try·wom·en** \-ˌwim-ən\. **1** A woman of the country; a rustic woman. **2** A woman who is an inhabitant of a certain country or of the same country as another person.

coun·ty \ˈkau̇nt-ē\ *n.*; *pl.* **coun·ties.** **1** The domain of a count or earl. **2** A division of a state or of a country for purposes of local government.

county agent. An official appointed to promote agricultural improvement in a certain county.

county seat. A town or city that is the seat of county government.

coup \'kü\ *n.; pl.* **coups** \'küz\. A brilliant, sudden, or unexpected stroke or stratagem.

coup d'é·tat \ˌküd-ˌā-'tä, -'tȧ\. [From French, meaning "stroke of state".] A sudden political move overthrowing an existing government.

cou·pé \kü-'pā\ or **coupe** \kü-'pā: *sense 2 is also* 'küp\ *n.* [From French *coupé*, shortened from *carosse coupé* meaning literally "cut-off coach".] **1** A four-wheeled horse-drawn carriage with an enclosed body seating two persons, and with an outside seat for the driver. **2** A two-door automobile with an enclosed body.

coupé, 1

coupé, 2

cou·ple \'kəp-l\ *n.* **1** Two things of the same kind that are connected or that are thought of together; a pair. **2** Two persons who are closely associated, such as partners in a dance or a husband and wife.
— The word *pair* is a synonym of *couple: couple* usually applies to two things of the same sort, regarded as associated; *pair* may apply to two things which belong together or are used together, or to a single object composed of two parts.
— *v.;* **cou·pled; cou·pling** \'kəp-l(-)ing\. **1** To join, link, or tie together; as, to *couple* freight cars. **2** To join in pairs.

cou·plet \'kəp-lət\ *n.* A pair of verses; especially, two successive rhyming lines of poetry, usually of the same length.

cou·pling \'kəp-ling\ *n.* **1** A joining; a connecting. **2** Connection between two electric circuits by means of a part in common. **3** The connecting part between two electric circuits, as a capacitor. **4** Something that joins or connects two parts or things; as, a car *coupling;* a pipe *coupling.*

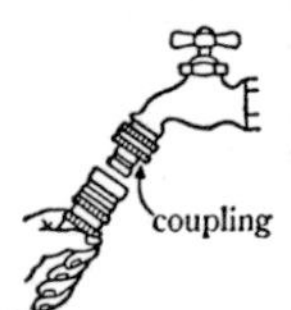

cou·pon \'kyü-ˌpän, 'kü-\ *n.* **1** A ticket or certificate or a detachable part of a ticket or certificate that shows the right of the holder to receive some service, payment, or discount. **2** A section of a ticket kept by the holder to show his claim, as to a seat or a service. **3** A certificate given to a purchaser of goods and redeemable in merchandise or cash. **4** A part of a printed advertisement designed to be cut out, as for ordering or for requesting a free sample.

cour·age \'kər-ij, 'kə-rij\ *n.* The quality of mind that enables one to meet danger and difficulties with firmness; bravery; fearlessness; valor.
— The words *bravery* and *heroism* are synonyms of *courage: courage* usually suggests fearlessness or the overcoming of fear in the face of danger; *bravery* may imply bold and daring defiance of danger; *heroism* is likely to suggest boldness and bravery springing from a noble and self-sacrificing devotion.

cou·ra·geous \kə-'rā-jəs\ *adj.* Having or showing courage; bold; brave; daring; as, a *courageous* boy; a *courageous* act. — **cou·ra·geous·ly,** *adv.*

cour·i·er \'kər-ē-ər, 'ku̇r-\ *n.* **1** A messenger; especially, a messenger whose duty it is to deliver important government papers with speed. **2** A person who attends travelers and makes hotel and other arrangements for them.

course \'kōrs, 'kȯrs\ *n.* **1** Motion from one place to another; progress in space; passage; as, the stars in their *course* through the sky. **2** Progress in time; as, during the *course* of a year. **3** The ground or space gone over, as in certain sports; as, a golf *course.* **4** A natural channel for water. We followed the river's *course* for several miles. **5** Direction of motion or progress; as, the *course* of a ship. **6** A part of a meal served at one time; as, the meat *course.* **7** A series of acts or proceedings arranged in regular order; as, a *course* of lectures. **8** A method of procedure; conduct; behavior. The people disapproved of the *course* the president chose. **9** A continuous level range of brick or masonry throughout the face or faces of a building. **10** A series of studies leading to a diploma or a degree or one of these studies as customarily taken for a school term or a college year; as, a four-year *course* in medicine; to take four *courses* each term. — **of course.** As was to be expected; naturally; certainly. **—** *v.;* **coursed; cours·ing.** **1** To run through or over; as, when buffaloes *coursed* the plain. **2** To move rapidly; to race; as, blood *coursing* through the veins.

cours·er \'kōrs-r, 'kȯrs-r\ *n.* A swift or spirited horse.

court \'kōrt, 'kȯrt\ *n.* **1** An open space wholly or partly surrounded by buildings. **2** A short street or lane. **3** A space arranged for playing one of various games with a ball; as, a tennis *court.* **4** The residence of a king or other sovereign; a palace. **5** The people in attendance upon a sovereign; any formal assembling of a sovereign and his followers. **6** A ruler and his officials considered as a political body. **7** Attention given to a person in power; especially, the attention given to a woman by a man who wishes to gain her affections. **8** A place where justice is administered. **9** The persons assembled to administer justice; the judge or judges meeting for the trial of law cases. **10** A session held by a judge or judges. **—** *v.* **1** To try to gain the favor of by attention or flattery; as, to *court* a mighty prince. **2** To try to gain the affection of; to make love to; to woo. **3** To try to get; to ask for; to seem to be asking for; as, to *court* disaster; to *court* danger. **—** *adj.* Suitable to a princely court; as, *court* etiquette.

cour·te·ous \'kərt-ē-əs\ *adj.* Of courtlike manners; civil; polite. — **cour·te·ous·ly,** *adv.*

cour·te·sy \'kərt-ə-sē\ *n.; pl.* **cour·te·sies.** **1** Courtly politeness; as, old-world *courtesy.* **2** A favor courteously performed. **3** A favor as distinguished from a right; as, a title by *courtesy* only; to give a former governor his old title by *courtesy.*

court·house \'kōrt-ˌhau̇s, 'kȯrt-\ *n.; pl.* **court-**

hous·es \-ˌhau̇-zəz\. A building in which courts meet for the trial of cases.

cour·ti·er \'kōrt-ē-ər, 'kōrt-yər, 'kȯrt-\ *n.* **1** A person who is in attendance at the court of a ruler. **2** A person who practices courtly flattery.

court·ly \'kōrt-lē, 'kȯrt-\ *adj.* **1** Suitable to a sovereign's court; elegant; as, *courtly* manners. **2** Insincerely flattering.

court-mar·tial \'kōrt-'märsh-l, 'kȯrt-, -'märsh-l\ *n.; pl.* **courts-mar·tial.** A military or naval court or a trial in such a court. — *v.;* **court-mar·tialed** or **court-mar·tialled**; **court-mar·tial·ing** or **court-mar·tial·ling** \-l(-)ing\. To try a person in a court-martial.

court plaster. Silk or other fabric coated with a mixture of isinglass and glycerin, formerly used for cosmetic or medical purposes.

court·room \'kōrt-ˌrüm, 'kȯrt-, -ˌru̇m\ *n.* A room in which a court of law is held.

court·ship \'kōrt-ˌship, 'kȯrt-\ *n.* A courting or wooing.

court·yard \'kōrt-ˌyärd, 'kȯrt-, -ˌyärd\ *n.* A court or enclosure attached to a house, castle, or palace.

cous·in \'kəz-n\ *n.* [From Old French, there derived from Latin *consobrinus* meaning "child of a mother's sister".] **1** A son or daughter of one's uncle or aunt. **2** A person considered as belonging to the same group as another; as, our Canadian *cousins.*

cove \'kōv\ *n.* **1** A small sheltered inlet or bay. **2** A sheltered nook in hills or woods.

cov·e·nant \'kəv-n-ənt\ *n.* An agreement between persons or groups of persons; especially, a formal agreement solemnly promising mutual help or common effort. — *v.* To enter into a formal agreement; to engage; to contract.

cov·er \'kəv-r\ *v.;* **cov·ered**; **cov·er·ing** \-r(-)ing\. **1** To place or spread something over or upon; to overspread; as, to *cover* a typewriter when not in use. Darkness *covered* the earth. **2** To conceal; to shelter; as, to be unable to *cover* one's confusion; to try to *cover* up a mistake. **3** To extend or pass over; as, to *cover* three miles in an hour. **4** Include; as, a review *covering* three weeks' work; a loss fully *covered* by insurance. **5** To bring or hold within range, as of a gun. **6** To be sufficient for; to embrace. The answer *covers* the question. **7** To have as one's field; as, to *cover* a certain territory. **8** To report the news of an event, as for a newspaper; as, to *cover* a robbery. — *n.* **1** Anything placed over another thing, as a blanket for a bed or a lid for a box. **2** A binding or protecting case, as for a book or a magazine. **3** Anything that hides, shelters, or protects; as, under the *cover* of darkness. Thick brush is good *cover* for wild animals. **4** A table setting for one person. **5** An envelope or wrapper, especially one that has passed through the mail and bears postal markings.

cov·er·age \'kəv-r(-)ij\ *n.* The act or fact of covering or including; the condition or degree of being covered; the number of items covered; as, the *coverage* of an insurance policy; the *coverage* given to a political convention by radio and television.

cov·er·all \'kəv-r-ˌȯl\ *n.* A loose-fitting work garment combining trousers and shirt or jacket.

coverall

cover charge. A charge made by a restaurant for service, in addition to the charge made for food.

cover crop. A growing crop, such as rye or clover, planted in orchards or harvested fields to enrich the soil and prevent erosion, especially over the winter.

covered wagon. Any large long wagon with an arched cover, as a Conestoga wagon or prairie schooner.

cov·er·ing \'kəv-r(-)ing\ *n.* Anything that covers or conceals, as a roof, a hat or garment, a wrapper or envelope, or a blanket.

cov·er·let \'kəv-r-lət\ *n.* An outer covering for a bed; bedspread; counterpane.

cov·ert \'kəv-rt, 'kōv-rt, 'kō-ˌvərt\ *adj.* **1** Sheltered; as, a *covert* nook. **2** Secret; hidden; partly hidden; as, a *covert* glance. — *n.* **1** A shelter or sheltered place. **2** A thicket or underbrush which gives shelter to wild birds and animals. **3** Also **covert cloth.** A firm durable cloth woven from yarns in mixed colors, usually of wool or silk and wool but also of cotton or rayon. — **cov·ert·ly,** *adv.*

cov·et \'kəv-ət\ *v.* To long for, especially something belonging to another person.

cov·et·ous \'kəv-ət-əs\ *adj.* Too eager to get or to own something, especially something belonging to another person. — **cov·et·ous·ly,** *adv.*

cov·et·ous·ness \'kəv-ət-əs-nəs\ *n.* Excessive desire for gain or possession, especially for things belonging to others; greed; avarice.

cov·ey \'kəv-ē\ *n.; pl.* **cov·eys.** **1** A brood of birds; a small flock, as of partridge or quail. **2** A company; a bevy.

cow \'kau̇\ *n.* **1** The full-grown female of any bovine, or oxlike, animal or of certain other animals the male of which is called *bull,* as the elephant, the moose, and the whale. **2** A domestic bovine animal without regard to age or sex; as, farmhouses and barns and *cows* in every pasture.

cow \'kau̇\ *v.* To subdue the spirits or courage of; to make afraid; as, to be *cowed* by threats.

cow·ard \'kau̇rd\ *adj.* Lacking or showing a lack of courage; cowardly; as, a *coward* act. — *n.* A person who has no courage.

cow·ard·ice \'kau̇rd-əs\ *n.* Lack of courage to face danger; shameful fear.

cow·ard·ly \'kau̇rd-lē\ *adj.* **1** Lacking courage; disgracefully timid; not brave. **2** Characteristic of a coward; as, a *cowardly* act. — **cow·ard·li·ness** \-lē-nəs\ *n.*

cow·bell \'kau̇-ˌbel\ *n.* A bell hung about the neck of a cow to indicate its whereabouts.

cow·bird \'kau̇-ˌbərd\ *n.* Also **cow blackbird.** The

smallest of the North American blackbirds, which is often found near or around cattle.

cow·boy \'kaů-ˌbòi\ *n.* **1** A boy who has charge of cows. **2** A cattle herder, especially one working on a ranch, much of the time on horseback.

cow·catch·er \'kaů-ˌkach-r, -ˌkech-r\ *n.* A strong frame on the front of a railroad engine for throwing off obstructions.

cowcatcher

cow·er \'kaůr\ *v*, To crouch down, as from fear or cold. A beaten dog will *cower* at the sight of a whip.

cow·girl \'kaů-ˌgərl\ *n.* A female cattle herder, working on a ranch or at a rodeo.

cow·hand \'kaů-ˌhand\ *n.* A person working on a cattle ranch; a cowboy.

cow·herd \'kaů-ˌhərd\ *n.* One who tends cows.

cow·hide \'kaů-ˌhīd\ *n.* **1** The hide of a cow or leather made from it. **2** A coarse whip of rawhide or braided leather. **— *v.;* cow·hid·ed; cow·hid·ing.** To whip with a cowhide.

cowl \'kaůl\ *n.* **1** A monk's hood, usually attached to a gown. **2** The top of that part of an automobile body which is just forward of the doors and to which the windshield and dashboard are attached. **3** A cowling. — **cowled** \'kaůld\ *adj.*

cowl

cow·lick \'kaů-ˌlik\ *n.* A turned-up tuft of hair, usually at the forehead, that cannot be controlled by brushing.

cowl·ing \'kaůl-ing\ *n.* A removable metal covering over the engine, and sometimes over part of the fuselage, of an airplane.

co–work·er \'kō-'wərk-r\ *n.* One who works with another; a fellow worker.

cow·pea \'kaů-ˌpē\ *n.* **1** A vine of the pea family used as forage and as green manure. **2** The seed of this plant, often used for food.

cow·poke \'kaů-ˌpōk\ *n.* A cowboy.

cow pony. A horse used in herding cattle.

cow·pox \'kaů-ˌpäks\ *n.* A disease of the cow, which, when communicated to man, as by vaccination, protects from smallpox.

cow·punch·er \'kaů-ˌpənch-r\ *n.* A cowboy.

cow·rie or **cow·ry** \'kaů-rē\ *n.; pl.* **cow·ries**. A shell shaped like a coffee bean, often used as money in parts of Africa and Asia.

cow·slip \'kaů-ˌslip\ *n.* **1** The marsh marigold, a yellow-flowered swamp plant. **2** In England, a yellow-flowered primrose blooming in early spring.

cox \'käks\. Short for *coxswain*.

cox·comb \'käks-ˌkōm\ *n.* **1** A strip of notched red cloth worn by court jesters on their caps. **2** A cap with such a strip on it. **3** A conceited, silly man. **4** A cockscomb.

cox·swain or **cock·swain** \'käks-n\ *n.* [From the older English *cockswain*, from *cock* meaning "a kind of boat" and *swain* meaning "servant".] The person who steers a boat, especially a ship's boat or a racing shell.

coy \'kòi\ *adj.* **1** Bashful; shy. **2** Affectedly shy. — **coy·ly**, *adv.*

coy·ote \'kī-ˌōt, kī-'ōt-ē\ *n.* A small wolf of the plains of western North America; a prairie wolf.

coz·en \'kəz-n\ *v.;* **coz·ened**; **coz·en·ing** \-n(-)ing\. To cheat.

co·zy or **co·sy** \'kō-zē\ *adj.;* **co·zi·er** or **co·si·er**; **co·zi·est** or **co·si·est**. Snug; comfortable. **— *n.; pl.* co·zies** or **co·sies**. A padded cover that fits over a teapot to keep the contents hot. — **co·zi·ly** or **co·si·ly** \'kōz-l-ē\ *adv.*

Cpl. Abbreviation for *Corporal*.

crab \'krab\ *n.* **1** A crustacean distinguished by a short, broad, and usually flattened bony shell, small abdomen that is curled up beneath the body, and short feelers. **2** Any of various machines for lifting heavy weights, originally having clawlike parts to grip the objects lifted. — **to catch a crab.** To upset or unseat oneself when making a stroke in rowing a boat. **— *v.;* crabbed; crab·bing.** To hunt for or catch crabs.

crab \'krab\ *n.* **1** A crab apple. **2** A sour, ill-tempered person.

crab \'krab\ *v.;* **crabbed**; **crab·bing**. To find fault; as, a person who *crabs* about everything.

crab apple \'krab\. **1** A small, wild, sour apple. **2** A cultivated apple, small and tart in flavor.

crab·bed \'krab-əd\ *adj.* **1** Showing a peevish or sour temper; cross. **2** Obscure; difficult; as, a *crabbed* writer. **3** Cramped; irregular; as, *crabbed* handwriting. — **crab·bed·ly**, *adv.*

crab·by \'krab-ē\ *adj.;* **crab·bi·er**; **crab·bi·est**. Cross; ill-tempered; crabbed; as, a *crabby* reply.

crab grass \'krab\. A grass with stalk topped with fingerlike spikes growing from a creeping stem that roots easily at the joints.

crack \'krak\ *v.* **1** To break or to cause to break with a sudden, sharp sound; to snap. **2** To make such a sound, as if breaking; as, to *crack* a whip. **3** To break, with or without quite separating into parts. The ice *cracked* in several places. **4** To tell, especially in a clever or witty way; as, to *crack* jokes. **5** To praise; to extol; as, to *crack* a person up to be a genius. **6** To subject petroleum to cracking. **7** *Slang*. To break into. The thieves *cracked* the safe with dynamite. **8** To fail; to break down; as, to *crack* under a strain. **9** Of a voice, to break or become harsh. **10** To strike or to receive a sharp blow; as, to fall and *crack* one's head. — **crack down.** To take strong action, especially to bring about obedience. — **crack up. 1** To collapse or crash from strain, collision, or faulty landing, as an airplane; to cause to crash or collapse. **2** To experience a breakdown or collapse, as in mind or body. **— *n.*** **1** A sharp, sudden sound, as of something breaking; a snap. **2** A shot, as with a rifle. **3** A sharp, resounding blow; as, to receive a *crack* on the head. **4** *Slang*. An attempt; a try. Give me a *crack* at it. **5** A clever, sarcastic remark; as, a *crack* that made everyone laugh. **6** A chink; a crevice; a fissure. **7** The breaking or broken tone of the voice, as when it is changing. — *adj.* Of superior quality; as, *crack* troops.

crack·brain \'krak-ˌbrān\ *n.* A crackbrained or crazy person.

crack·brained \'krak-ˌbrānd\ *adj.* Crazy; reasonless.

crack·down \'krak-ˌdau̇n\ *n.* The action of cracking down or an instance of such action.

cracked \'krakt\ *adj.* **1** Broken; especially, broken into coarse particles; as, *cracked* wheat. **2** *Slang.* Crazy. **3** Having harsh or breaking sounds; as, a *cracked* voice.

crack·er \'krak-r\ *n.* **1** One that cracks. **2** A firecracker. **3** The snapping part at the end of a whiplash. **4** A dry, thin, crisp biscuit.

crack·ing \'krak-ing\ *n.* A process in which the substances composing petroleum and similar oils are changed by heat and pressure into simpler substances.

crack·le \'krak-l\ *v.;* **crack·led; crack·ling** \-l(-)ing\. To make small, sharp, sudden, and repeated noises. — *n.* A crackling, as of burning wood.

crack·ling \'krak-ling; *senses 2 and 3 are often* 'krak-lən\ *n.* **1** A series of small, sharp, cracking sounds. **2** The well-browned, crisp rind of roasted pork. **3** [usually in the plural] *Dial.* The crisp fat, especially of hogs, left after the lard has been removed.

crack-up \'krak-ˌəp\ *n.* A crashing, as of an airplane.

cra·dle \'krād-l\ *n.* **1** A baby's bed or cot, usually on rockers. **2** Place of beginning or origin; as, the *cradle* of civilization; a *cradle* of liberty. **3** Something resembling a baby's cradle in appearance or use, as a rockerlike device for washing earth and sand in the search for gold. **4** An attachment of fingerlike rods for a scythe or a scythe with such an attachment. **5** A strong framework built to support heavy weights, as ships in dry dock. — *v.;* **cra·dled; cra·dling** \-l(-)ing\. **1** To place or rock in a cradle or as if in a cradle; as, to *cradle* a frightened puppy in one's arms. **2** To nurse or train in infancy. **3** To wash earth or sand in a cradle. **4** To mow with a cradle.

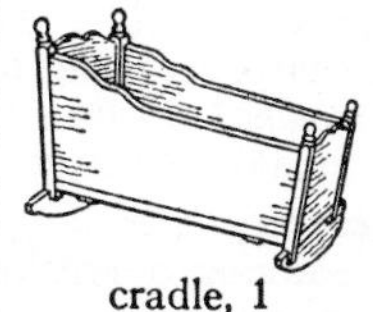

cradle, 1

craft \'kraft\ *n.* **1** Art or skill, especially in some manual work. **2** An occupation that requires manual skill; a trade. Carpentry is a *craft.* **3** The association of persons engaged in any trade; a guild. **4** Cunning; skill used for a bad purpose. **5** *pl.* usually **craft.** A vessel; boats of any kind; as, fishing *craft.* **6** *pl.* usually **craft.** Aircraft. — For synonyms see *trade.*

craft·i·ly \'kraf-tə-lē\ *adv.* In a crafty, cunning, or wily manner.

crafts·man \'kraf(t)s-mən\ *n.; pl.* **crafts·men** \-mən\. A person who works at a trade or manual occupation.

crafty \'kraf-tē\ *adj.;* **craft·i·er; craft·i·est.** Skillful at deceiving others. — For synonyms see *cunning.*

crag \'krag\ *n.* **1** A steep, rugged rock. **2** A rough, broken cliff or projecting point of rock. — **crag·gy** \'krag-ē\ *adj.*

cram \'kram\ *v.;* **crammed; cram·ming. 1** To stuff or crowd in; as, to *cram* clothes into a bag. **2** To fill full; as, barns *crammed* with hay. **3** To study hastily in preparation for an examination. **4** To eat greedily; to stuff.

cramp \'kramp\ *n.* **1** A device, usually of iron bent at both ends, as used to hold together blocks of stone or timbers. **2** A sudden and painful involuntary contraction of a muscle or muscles. **3** A paralysis of certain muscles due to too much use; as, writer's *cramp.* **4** [usually in the plural] Sharp pains in the abdomen. — *v.* **1** To cause to have a cramp; as, to be *cramped* by sitting too long in one position. **2** To keep from having free action; to confine; to contract; to hamper; as, a mind *cramped* by too much knowledge. **3** To fasten or hold with a cramp.

cram·pon \'kram-ˌpän\ *n.* A steel frame with spikes to be attached to boots or shoes, as for climbing or walking on ice.

cran·ber·ry \'kran-ˌber-ē, -bər-ē\ *n.; pl.* **cran·ber·ries. 1** The sour, bright-red berry of a trailing evergreen shrub, grown in a low, periodically flooded area (**cranberry bog**). **2** The shrub that bears this berry.

crane \'krān\ *n.* **1** A tall wading bird with long neck and bill, related to the rails. **2** The great blue heron. **3** A machine with a projecting, swinging arm for lifting and carrying heavy weights. **4** Any mechanical arm that swings freely from a center and is used to support or carry a weight, such as an iron arm for supporting a kettle over a fire. — *v.;* **craned; cran·ing.** To stretch out one's neck, as a crane does.

cra·ni·al \'krā-nē-əl\ *adj.* Of or relating to the skull.

cranial nerve. Any of the paired nerves that arise from the lower surface of the brain and pass through openings in the skull.

cra·ni·um \'krā-nē-əm\ *n.* The skull; especially, that part of the skull that encloses the brain.

crank \'krangk\ *n.* **1** In a machine, a part or arm that is or can be attached at right angles to the end of a shaft and turned to start or operate the machinery. **2** A person who has a peculiar mental twist or one who is very enthusiastic about a particular subject or hobby; as, a *crank* on collecting old coins. **3** An ill-tempered, irritable person; a grouch. — *v.* To start or operate by turning a crank.

crank·case \'krang(k)-ˌkās\ *n.* The covering of the crankshaft of an engine, as in an automobile.

crank·shaft \'krangk-ˌshaft\ *n.* A shaft turning or driven by a crank.

cranky \'krangk-ē\ *adj.;* **crank·i·er; crank·i·est. 1** Irritable; difficult to please. **2** Odd; queer. **3** Not in good working order; shaky; unsteady. — **crank·i·ly** \'krangk-l-ē\ *adv.*

cran·ny \'kran-ē\ *n.; pl.* **cran·nies.** A small, narrow opening; a chink or crevice. — **crannied** \'kran-ēd\ *adj.*

crape \'krāp\ *n.* Crepe; especially, a piece of heavy black crepe used as a sign of mourning.

craps \'kraps\ *n. sing.* A gambling game played with two dice.

crap·shoot·er \'krap-ˌshüt-r\ *n.* A person who plays craps. — **crap·shoot·ing** \-ˌshüt-ing\ *n.*

crash \'krash\ *n.* A coarse, rough cloth of linen, cotton, or rayon, used for towels, draperies, and tablecloths, and in a smooth-finished form for clothing.

crash \'krash\ *v.* **1** To break or dash in pieces violently and noisily; to smash. **2** To clash or collide violently. **3** To force one's way noisily; as, to *crash* through the forest. **4** *Slang.* To attend, as a party, although not invited; as, to *crash* a dance. **5** To bring an airplane down in such a way that it is smashed or damaged in landing. — *n.* **1** A loud, sudden, confused sound, as of many things falling and breaking at once. **2** A collision or the shock of a collision; as, to be injured in a *crash.* **3** The crashing of an airplane. **4** A sudden failure or collapse, as of a business.

crash-land \'krash-'land\ *v.* To land an airplane in trouble in such a way as to damage it.

crass \'kras\ *adj.* Stupid; crude; gross; as, *crass* ignorance. — **crass·ly,** *adv.*

crate \'krāt\ *n.* **1** A box, usually made of wooden slats, for packing fruit or vegetables. **2** An enclosing framework for protecting furniture in shipment. **3** A large wicker basket, as one for packing china. — *v.;* **crat·ed; crat·ing.** To pack in a crate; as, to *crate* furniture for shipping.

crate, 2

cra·ter \'krāt-r\ *n.* **1** The bowl-shaped depression around the opening of a volcano or a geyser. **2** The hole formed by the explosion of a shell, bomb, or mine.

cra·vat \krə-'vat\ *n.* A necktie.

crave \'krāv\ *v.;* **craved; crav·ing. 1** To ask earnestly; to beg; to entreat; as, to *crave* someone's aid. **2** To long for; as, to *crave* rest. **3** To require; to need. The stomach *craves* food.

cra·ven \'krāv-n\ *adj.* Cowardly. — *n.* A coward. — **cra·ven·ly,** *adv.*

crav·ing \'krā-ving\ *n.* A great desire or longing for something; especially, an abnormal desire, as for a habit-forming drug.

craw \'krȯ\ *n.* **1** The crop of a bird or insect. **2** The stomach of an animal.

craw·fish \'krȯ-ˌfish\ *n.; pl.* **craw·fish** or **craw·fish·es.** A crayfish.

crawl \'krȯl\ *v.* **1** To move slowly by drawing the body along the ground. **2** To go on hands and knees. **3** To go very slowly or carefully; as, to *crawl* along an icy road in a car. **4** To swarm or be alive with crawling things. The floor was *crawling* with ants. **5** To feel as if insects were crawling over the body. My flesh *crawled* with horror. — *n.* **1** The act or motion of crawling; slow motion, like that of a creeping animal. **2** A racing stroke in which a swimmer, lying flat in the water with face submerged except for breathing intervals, propels himself by overarm strokes and a thrashing movement of the legs.

cray·fish \'krā-ˌfish\ *n.; pl.* **cray·fish** or **cray·fish·es. 1** A freshwater shellfish resembling the lobster but much smaller. **2** A salt-water shellfish resembling the lobster but not having huge claws.

cray·on \'krā-ˌän, -ən, 'kran\ *n.* **1** A small rounded stick, usually of chalk, clay, lead, or wax, used in writing or drawing. **2** A drawing made with crayons. — *v.* To draw or color with crayons.

craze \'krāz\ *v.;* **crazed; craz·ing. 1** To make or to become insane; as, *crazed* by grief. **2** To produce tiny cracks on the surface or glaze of a piece of pottery. — *n.* **1** A strong but temporary interest in something or the object of such an interest; as, the latest *craze* among schoolgirls. **2** A tiny crack in glaze or enamel.

cra·zy \'krā-zē\ *adj.;* **cra·zi·er; cra·zi·est.** [From an earlier meaning "cracked", "broken".] **1** Insane; mad; unsound; as, a *crazy* man. **2** Wildly excited; eager; as, to be *crazy* about swimming. — **cra·zi·ly** \'krāz-l-ē\ *adv.*

crazy bone. The funny bone.

crazy quilt. A quilt with a covering made of pieces of cloth of various sizes, shapes, and colors sewed together; a patchwork quilt.

creak \'krēk\ *v.* To make, or cause to make, a long, sharp, grating or squeaking sound. The door *creaked* on its rusty hinges. — *n.* The sound of creaking; a squeak.

creaky \'krēk-ē\ *adj.;* **creak·i·er; creak·i·est. 1** Making a creaking sound. **2** Apt to creak; as, *creaky* stairs. — **creak·i·ly** \'krēk-l-ē\ *adv.*

cream \'krēm\ *n.* **1** The rich, oily, yellowish part of milk. **2** Something like cream in color, consistency, or oiliness, as a candy, a sauce, or a cosmetic. **3** The best part of anything; as, the *cream* of society. **4** The color of fresh cream, a pale yellow. — *v.* **1** To form cream. **2** To skim the cream from; as, to *cream* a pan of milk. **3** To put cream into; as, to *cream* and sugar coffee. **4** To rub, stir, or beat butter, or butter and sugar, until it becomes creamy.

cream cheese. An unripened soft white cheese made from whole milk enriched with cream.

cream·cups \'krēm-ˌkəps\ *n. sing. and pl.* A California annual plant of the poppy family, having cream-colored flowers.

cream·er \'krēm-r\ *n.* **1** A small pitcher for holding cream. **2** A device for separating cream from milk.

cream·ery \'krēm-r(-)ē\ *n.; pl.* **cream·er·ies.** A place where butter and cheese are made or where milk and cream are sold or prepared for the market.

cream of tartar. Purified tartar, a white crystalline acid-tasting substance used in medicine and in baking powder.

creamy \'krē-mē\ *adj.;* **cream·i·er; cream·i·est.** **1** Containing cream. **2** Resembling cream. — **cream·i·ly** \'krēm-l-ē\ *adv.*

crease \'krēs\ *n.* **1** A line or mark made by folding, as paper or cloth. **2** Any similar line or mark, as one in the ground or in the flesh of an animal. — *v.;* **creased; creas·ing.** **1** To make a crease or creases in; to wrinkle. **2** To become wrinkled; as, cloth that does not *crease* easily. **3** To wound slightly, as with a bullet that barely furrows the flesh.

cre·ate \krē-'āt, 'krē-ˌāt\ *v.;* **cre·at·ed; cre·at·ing.** To cause to exist; to bring into existence; to produce; to make.

cre·a·tion \krē-'āsh-n\ *n.* **1** The act of creating or fact of being created; especially, the bringing of the world into existence out of nothing. **2** Something created; as, an artistic *creation;* a *creation* of silks and satins. **3** All created things; the world; as, the whole *creation;* to think of oneself as lord of *creation.*

cre·a·tive \krē-'āt-iv\ *adj.* Able to create; especially, having or showing the power to produce original work, as in literature; as, a great *creative* genius. — **cre·a·tive·ly,** *adv.*

cre·a·tor \krē-'āt-r, -'ā-ˌtȯr\ *n.* One that creates or produces. — **the Creator.** God.

crea·ture \'krēch-r\ *n.* **1** A living created being; an animal or a human being. **2** A person who is completely dependent upon and obedient to another, whom he serves as a tool; a servile dependent.

cre·dence \'krēd-n(t)s\ *n.* Belief; credit; as, to give *credence* to a rumor.

cre·den·tials \krē-'dench-lz\ *n. pl.* Documents, such as letters given by a government to its ambassador, showing that a person has official authority or is to be treated with confidence.

cred·i·ble \'kred-ə-bl\ *adj.* Capable of being credited or believed; deserving to be believed; trustworthy; as, a *credible* witness; a *credible* story. — **cred·i·bil·i·ty** \ˌkred-ə-'bil-ət-ē\ *n.* — **cred·i·bly** \'kred-ə-blē\ *adv.*

cred·it \'kred-ət\ *n.* **1** Reliance on the truth or reality of something; trust; belief; as, a story that deserves little *credit.* **2** Trustworthiness; reputation; good name; as, a man of *credit* in the community. **3** Something that adds to a person's reputation or honor; as, to give a person *credit* for a discovery. **4** A source of honor; as, a *credit* to one's school. **5** The balance in a person's favor, as in a bank account. **6** Time given for payment for goods purchased; as, thirty days' *credit.* **7** An acknowledgment of a payment received, made by entering on an account the amount of the payment. **8** Any item in, or the total of the items in, the right hand side of an account. **9** In schools and colleges, official certification of the completion of a course of study. **10** A unit of academic work for which such acknowledgment is made. **11** Trust given to a customer for future payment for goods purchased; as, a man whose *credit* is good for any amount. — *v.* **1** To believe; as, to *credit* a statement. **2** To give a person credit or honor; as, to *credit* Columbus with the discovery of America. **3** To place in a person's favor on a financial record; as, to *credit* an account with ten dollars. **4** In schools and colleges, to give a credit or credits to; as, to be *credited* with elementary algebra.

cred·it·a·ble \'kred-ət-əb-l\ *adj.* Deserving credit or praise; as, a *creditable* attempt, even though it failed. — **cred·it·a·bly** \-ə-blē\ *adv.*

cred·i·tor \'kred-ət-r\ *n.* A person to whom a debt is owed; a person to whom money or goods are due.

cre·do \'krēd-ˌō, 'krād-\ *n.; pl.* **cre·dos.** A creed; a set of declared opinions.

cre·du·li·ty \krē-'dü-lət-ē, -'dyü-\ *n.* A willingness to believe statements, especially with little or no evidence.

cred·u·lous \'krej-l-əs\ *adj.* Quick to believe things, especially without sufficient grounds; easily deceived. — **cred·u·lous·ly,** *adv.*

creed \'krēd\ *n.* [From Old English *creda,* there borrowed from Latin *credo* meaning "I believe".] **1** A statement of the essential beliefs of a religious faith. **2** Any set of guiding principles or beliefs; as, to act according to one's *creed.*

creek \'krēk, 'krik\ *n.* **1** A small stream of water, usually larger than a brook and smaller than a river. **2** A narrow bay or inlet extending some distance into the land. **3** A small river emptying into a bay or inlet.

creel \'krēl\ *n.* A wickerwork basket for carrying fish.

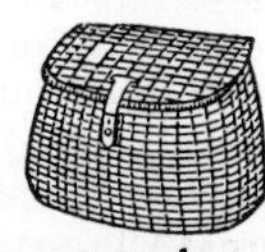
creel

creep \'krēp\ *v.;* **crept** \'krept\; **creep·ing.** **1** To move along with the body close to the ground or floor; to crawl; as, *creeping* along on hands and knees. **2** To grow or spread along the ground or along a surface; as, ivy *creeping* up a wall. **3** To advance slowly, timidly, or stealthily. The tide *crept* up the beach. **4** To feel as though insects were crawling on the body. The shriek made my flesh *creep.* **5** To slip or become slightly displaced. Varnish sometimes *creeps* as it dries. — *n.* **1** The act of creeping. **2** [in the plural] A sensation as of insects crawling over the body; a feeling of horror; as, a tale that gives one the *creeps.*

creep·er \'krēp-r\ *n.* **1** A person or thing that creeps. **2** A small bird that creeps about trees and bushes, especially the American **brown creeper.** **3** A creeping or climbing plant; as, the Virginia *creeper.* **4** A spiked device for a shoe to prevent slipping, as in climbing a pole.

creepy \'krēp-ē\ *adj.;* **creep·i·er; creep·i·est.** Having or causing a sensation as if insects were creeping on the skin, or a feeling of nervous fear; as, a *creepy* story.

cre·mate \'krē-ˌmāt, krē-'māt\ *v.;* **cre·mat·ed; cre·mat·ing.** To reduce to ashes by means of fire or great heat, as the body of a dead person. — **cre·ma·tion** \krē-'māsh-n\ *n.*

cre·ma·to·ri·um \ˌkrē-mə-'tōr-ē-əm, ˌkrem-ə-, -'tȯr-ē-əm\ *n.; pl.* **cre·ma·to·ri·ums** \-ē-əmz\ or **cre·ma·to·ria** \-ē-ə\. A crematory.

cre·ma·to·ry \'krē-mə-ˌtōr-ē, 'krem-ə-, -ˌtȯr-ē\ *n.; pl.* **cre·ma·to·ries.** A furnace for cremating or a structure containing such a furnace. — *adj.* Of, relating to, or used in cremation.

cre·o·sol \'krē-ə-ˌsȯl, -ˌsōl\ *n.* A colorless fragrant liquid resembling carbolic acid, obtained chiefly from beech tar.

cre·o·sote \'krē-ə-ˌsōt\ *n.* **1** An oily antiseptic liquid obtained by distilling wood tar, used in preserving wood and meat. **2** A similar substance made from coal tar.

crepe or **crêpe** \'krāp\ *n.* A thin crinkled fabric of silk, wool, cotton, or other fiber.

crepe paper. A crinkled paper made to resemble crepe.

crept. Past tense and past part. of *creep.*

cre·scen·do \krə-'shen-ˌdō\ *adj.* or *adv.* In music, gradually increasing in fullness or loudness. — *n.; pl.* **cre·scen·dos.** A gradual increase in loudness or force.

cres·cent \'kres-nt\ *n.* **1** The new moon, or the moon in its first quarter, as it starts to grow fuller. **2** The figure formed by the new moon. **3** Anything having this shape. — *adj.* **1** Shaped like the new moon. **2** Growing; increasing.

crescent

cre·sol \'krē-ˌsȯl, -ˌsōl\ *n.* A colorless substance like carbolic acid, obtained from coal tar and wood tar and used as a disinfectant.

cress \'kres\ *n.* Any of numerous plants of the mustard family, whose leaves are used in salads.

crest \'krest\ *n.* **1** A tuft on the head of a bird or an animal, such as the comb of a rooster. **2** Anything resembling such a tuft, especially as marking the top of something; as, the *crest* of a hill; the *crest* of a wave. **3** The plume worn on a helmet, as by a knight, or the helmet itself. **4** An ornamental design or picture found on a coat of arms, and also used as a decoration or marking, as on table silver or letter paper.

crest, 4

crest·ed \'kres-təd\ *adj.* Having a crest; as, a *crested* flycatcher.

crest·fal·len \'krest-ˌfȯl-ən\ *adj.* With drooping crest or hanging head; depressed; disheartened; sad; dejected; as, to be *crestfallen* over a defeat.

cre·tin \'krēt-n\ *n.* One afflicted with cretinism; often, an idiot.

cre·tin·ism \'krēt-n-ˌiz-m\ *n.* An unhealthy condition caused by inadequate secretion of the thyroid gland and characterized by stunted growth, deformity, goiter, and, commonly, by idiocy.

cre·tonne \'krē-ˌtän\ *n.* [From French, derived from *Creton*, the name of a village in Normandy where it was made.] A strong printed cotton or linen cloth used especially for furniture coverings and for curtains.

cre·vasse \krə-'vas\ *n.* **1** A deep crack or crevice, as in a glacier. **2** A break in a levee.

crev·ice \'krev-əs\ *n.* A narrow opening that results from a split or crack; a fissure; a cleft; as, a *crevice* in a rock.

crew. A past tense of *crow.*

crew \'krü\ *n.* **1** Any group or gathering of persons; as, a happy *crew* on a picnic. **2** A group of persons associated in some joint work; as, a train *crew;* a gun *crew.* **3** The group of seamen who man a ship. **4** The oarsmen and steersman of a rowboat or racing shell; as, to row on a college *crew.*

crew haircut or **crew cut.** A short haircut that leaves the hair standing up on the crown of the head and more or less level on top.

crib \'krib\ *n.* **1** A manger for feeding animals. **2** A box, bin, or building for storing grain or corn. **3** A small bedstead with high sides, for a child. **4** Any of various devices of cratelike or open construction, as a framework of beams used in building. **5** A translation, key, or notes to aid a student, sometimes in violation of rules, as in reciting lessons. **6** The action or an instance of cribbing. — *v.;* **cribbed; crib·bing. 1** To copy, as an idea or passage, and use it as if it were one's own; to plagiarize. **2** To make use of a translation or notes in a forbidden or dishonest way.

crib, 3

crib·bage \'krib-ij\ *n.* A game of cards in which the chief object is to form counting combinations, the dealer having an extra set of players' discards called the **crib** \'krib\, and the score being kept by moving pegs on a special board (**cribbage board**).

crick·et \'krik-ət\ *n.* A small, leaping insect with leatherlike forewings and thin hind wings, noted for the chirping notes made by the males.

crick·et \'krik-ət\ *n.* An outdoor game played with bats, ball, and wickets, usually between sides of eleven players each. — **crick·et·er,** *n.*

crick·et \'krik-ət\ *n.* A low wooden footstool.

cried. Past tense and past part. of *cry.*

cri·er \'krīr\ *n.* A person who cries; especially, one who calls out announcements; as, a town *crier.*

crime \'krīm\ *n.* **1** The doing of something that one is forbidden by law to do, or the failure to do something that one is required by law to do; especially, a serious offense against the law. **2** Sinful conduct; any evil act.

crim·i·nal \'krim-ən-l, 'krim-nəl\ *adj.* **1** Of the nature of a crime; as, a *criminal* act. **2** Having to do with crime or with the punishment of crime; as, *criminal* law; a *criminal* court. — *n.* A person who has committed a crime. — **crim·i·nal·i·ty** \ˌkrim-ə-ˈnal-ət-ē\ *n.* — **crim·i·nal·ly** \ˈkrim-ən-l-ē, ˈkrim-nə-lē\ *adv.*

crim·i·nol·o·gist \ˌkrim-ə-ˈnäl-ə-jəst\ *n.* A person who specializes in criminology.

crim·i·nol·o·gy \ˌkrim-ə-ˈnäl-ə-jē\ *n.* The scientific study of crime, or criminals, and of the punishment or corrective treatment of criminals.

crimp \ˈkrimp\ *v.* To fold or press, as paper or cloth, into small, regular ridges or waves; to give a wavy appearance to; as, festoons of *crimped* paper. — *n.* **1** The act of crimping. **2** A small fold or wave resulting from pressing or pleating, or a series of such folds or waves. **3** A device for crimping. **4** *Slang.* Something that interferes, hinders, or cramps. The unexpected bad weather put a *crimp* in our plans. — **crimp·er,** *n.*

crimpy \ˈkrimp-ē\ *adj.;* **crimp·i·er; crimp·i·est.** Having a crimped appearance; frizzly.

crim·son \ˈkrimz-n\ *n.* The color of blood; a deep or vivid red color. — *adj.* Of the color crimson. — *v.* To make or become crimson; as, to *crimson* with embarrassment.

cringe \ˈkrinj\ *v.;* **cringed; cring·ing. 1** To shrink; to wince; to cower in fear; as, a dog *cringing* at the sight of a whip. **2** To bend or crouch in complete abandonment of self-respect; to behave towards another with excessive humility; to fawn; as, *cringing* beggars.

crin·kle \ˈkringk-l\ *v.;* **crin·kled; crin·kling** \-l(-)ing\. **1** To form little waves or wrinkles on the surface; to wrinkle, to ripple. The lake *crinkled* in the light breeze. **2** To rustle, as stiff cloth; as, *crinkling* silk. — *n.* **1** A small wave; a ripple. **2** A crinkling sound; a rustle.

crin·kly \ˈkringk-lē\ *adj.;* **crin·kli·er; crin·kli·est. 1** Wavy; wrinkled. **2** Rustling.

crin·o·line \ˈkrin-l-ən\ *n.* **1** A cloth, originally made of horsehair and linen thread, used for stiffening and lining, as of very full skirts. **2** A very full and stiff skirt, especially one lined with this material. **3** A hoop skirt.

crip·ple \ˈkrip-l\ *n.* A person who has lost, or has never had, the use of a limb or limbs; a lame person. — *v.;* **crip·pled; crip·pling** \-l(-)ing\. **1** To deprive of the use of a limb, especially of a leg; to lame; as, *crippled* in an accident; to be *crippled* by rheumatism. **2** To disable; to weaken; to deprive of activity or capability; as, a *crippling* blow to a boxer's jaw. Telephone service was *crippled* by the blizzard.

cri·sis \ˈkrī-səs\ *n.; pl.* **cri·ses** \-ˌsēz\. **1** That change in a sickness which shows whether the result is to be recovery or death. **2** The decisive moment in any course of action; turning point. **3** A state of things in which some decisive change seems likely to take place; an anxious or trying time.

crisp \ˈkrisp\ *adj.* **1** Curly; wavy; as, *crisp* hair. **2** Brittle; as, *crisp* snow. **3** Easily crumbled; short; flaky; as, *crisp* pastry. **4** Clear; sharp; distinct; as, *crisp* outlines; *crisp* speech. **5** Firm and fresh; as, *crisp* lettuce. **6** Brisk; bracing; as, *crisp* weather. — *n.* Something, as a confection, that is crisp or brittle. — *v.* To make or become crisp. — **crisp·ly,** *adv.*

crispy \ˈkris-pē\ *adj.;* **crisp·i·er; crisp·i·est. 1** Formed into short, close ringlets; curly; as, *crispy* hair. **2** Short; flaky; as, *crispy* pastry.

criss·cross \ˈkris-ˌkrȯs\ *n.* A pattern formed by crossed lines. — *adj.* Marked by crossed lines; as, a *crisscross* design. — *adv.* In a way to cross something else; in opposite directions. — *v.* **1** To mark or cover with crossed lines. **2** To go or pass crosswise.

cri·te·ri·on \krī-ˈtir-ē-ən\ *n.; pl.* **cri·te·ria** \-ē-ə\ or **cri·te·ri·ons** \-ē-ənz\. A standard of judgment; a rule or test by which something is tried in forming a judgment about it.

crit·ic \ˈkrit-ik\ *n.* **1** A person who gives his judgment of the value, worth, beauty, or excellence of anything; especially, a person whose profession is to write articles expressing trained judgment on work in art, music, drama, or literature. **2** A faultfinder.

crit·i·cal \ˈkrit-ik-l\ *adj.* **1** Inclined to criticize, especially unfavorably; tending to find fault. **2** Using or requiring careful judgment; as, a *critical* examination of a patient. **3** Attended by risk; uncertain; causing anxiety; as, a *critical* situation. **4** Relating to a crisis; as, the *critical* stage of a fever. **5** Belonging or relating to criticism or critics; as, a *critical* review of an opera. — **crit·i·cal·ly** \-ik-l(-)ē\ *adv.*

crit·i·cism \ˈkrit-ə-ˌsiz-m\ *n.* **1** The act of criticizing; especially, faultfinding. **2** A critical remark or observation. **3** A careful judgment or review, especially by a critic. **4** The art of judging expertly the merits and faults of works of art or literature.

crit·i·cize \ˈkrit-ə-ˌsīz\ *v.;* **crit·i·cized; crit·i·ciz·ing. 1** To examine and judge as a critic. **2** To express criticism, especially of an unfavorable kind. Children who are always *criticizing* are not likely to be very popular. **3** To find fault with. Some people are quick to *criticize* others.

crit·ter \ˈkrit-r\ *n. Dial.* A creature; especially, a domestic animal, as a horse or a cow.

croak \ˈkrōk\ *v.* **1** To make a low hoarse noise in the throat, like a frog or a crow. **2** To grumble or complain; to predict misfortune. **3** *Slang.* To die. **4** *Slang.* To kill. — *n.* A low harsh cry, as of a frog. — **croaky,** *adj.*

croak·er \ˈkrōk-r\ *n.* **1** An animal that croaks, as a frog. **2** Any of various fishes that produce croaking or grunting noises. **3** A person who grumbles or who prophesies evil.

cro·chet \krō-ˈshā\ *v.;* **cro·cheted** \-ˈshād\; **cro·chet·ing** \-ˈshā-ing\. To knit with a single long, hooked needle (**crochet hook**). — *n.* Crocheted work. — **cro·chet·er** \-ˈshā-ər\ *n.*

crock \ˈkräk\ *n.* **1** Any pot, jar, or pitcher made of baked clay; an earthenware vessel. **2** A broken piece of earthenware, as one used to cover the hole in a flowerpot.

crock·ery \'kräk-r(-)ē\ *n.* Earthenware; crocks and dishes collectively.

croc·o·dile \'kräk-ə-ˌdīl\ *n.* A thick-skinned, long-tailed reptile reaching 14 feet in length, found in tropical rivers and marshes of Africa, Asia, Australia, and America.

crocodile tears. [From the fiction that crocodiles weep in sympathy for their prey.] False or pretended tears; insincere sorrow.

cro·cus \'krōk-əs\ *n.* **1** A dwarf plant of the iris family that grows from a bulb, has narrow grasslike leaves, and blooms very early in the spring, having purple, white, or yellow funnel-shaped flowers. **2** The bulb or flower of this plant.

crocus

croft \krȯft\ *n. British.* **1** A small enclosed field. **2** A small farm worked by a tenant (**croft·er**).

Cro-Ma·gnon \(')krō-'man-yən\ *adj.* Belonging or relating to a race of tall, erect men, remains of whom have been found in the Cro-Magnon cave in southwestern France, and who are regarded as belonging to the same species as modern man.

crone \'krōn\ *n.* A withered old woman.

cro·ny \'krō-nē\ *n.; pl.* **cro·nies.** A close companion; a chum.

crook \'kru̇k\ *n.* **1** An implement having a bent or hooked form; as, a shepherd's *crook.* **2** A bishop's staff; a crosier. **3** A turn, bend, or curve out of a straight line; any curved or hooked part of a thing; as, the *crook* of an umbrella handle; the *crook* of one's arm. **4** A thief; a swindler. — *v.;* **crooked** \'kru̇kt\; **crook·ing.** To bend; to curve; as, to *crook* a finger.

crook·ed \'kru̇k-əd\ *adj.* **1** Not straight; bent. **2** Dishonest; wicked. — **crook·ed·ly,** *adv.*

crook·neck \'kru̇k-ˌnek\ *n.* A squash with a tapering, curved neck.

crook·necked \'kru̇k-ˌnekt\ *adj.* Having a crooked, bent, or curved neck; as, a *crooknecked* flask.

croon \'krün\ *v.* [From Middle English *croynen* meaning "to bellow", there borrowed from medieval Dutch *cronen.*] **1** To hum or sing in a low voice; as, to *croon* a lullaby. **2** To sing popular songs in an exaggerated sentimental style. — **croon·er,** *n.*

crop \'kräp\ *n.* **1** A pouchlike place in the throat of many birds, for receiving food and preparing it for digestion. **2** The handle or stock of a whip; especially, a short riding whip with a loop on the end for opening gates. **3** The amount of grain or fruit, whether already gathered or still growing, in a single field, of a single kind, or in a single season; as, a *crop* of apples; a poor wheat *crop.* **4** Any product or yield. The investigation brought forth nothing but a *crop* of lies. **5** The act or a result of cropping; especially, hair cut short or close to the head. — *v.;* **cropped; crop·ping. 1** To cut or bite off the tops or tips of growing grass or bushes. Sheep *crop* more closely than cattle. **2** To trim or cut; to snip off; as, to *crop* a horse's tail; a dog with *cropped* ears. **3** To yield a crop or crops. — **crop out.** To come to the surface, as rock. — **crop up.** To come or appear unexpectedly.

crop·per \'kräp-r\ *n.* **1** One that crops. **2** A person who raises a crop; especially, one who cultivates land belonging to another, receiving as pay a share of the crop raised.

crop·per \'kräp-r\ *n.* A severe fall, as from a horse ridden at full speed. — **come a cropper.** To fall heavily; to fail badly; to meet with disaster.

cro·quet \krō-'kā\ *n.* [From French, meaning "hockey stick", and originally meaning "shepherd's crook".] A game in which the players use mallets to drive wooden balls through a series of hoops set in the ground.

cro·quette \krō-'ket\ *n.* A roll or ball of hashed meat, or of fish, or sometimes of chopped vegetables, fried in deep fat.

cro·sier or **cro·zier** \'krōzh-r\ *n.* The staff of a bishop, abbot, or abbess, shaped like a shepherd's crook and carried as a symbol of office.

cross \'krȯs\ *n.* **1** A structure consisting in its simple forms of a straight bar and a crossbar, used in ancient times for executing criminals. **2** [with a capital] The structure on which Jesus Christ was crucified; a representation of this structure as the symbol of Christianity and of the Christian religion; a crucifix. **3** Any figure or mark formed by the crossing of two straight lines, especially one made as a mark of signature; an object shaped like a cross. **4** Sorrow or suffering as a test of Christian patience or virtue; trial; trouble. **5** A mixing of breeds, races, or kinds or the product of such a mixing; as, a *cross* between a bulldog and a terrier. — *v.* **1** To make the sign of the cross upon or over a person or thing, especially as a religious symbol or act. **2** To cancel by marking crosses on or by drawing a line through; as, to *cross* out a word. **3** To put or lay across; to lie or pass across; to intersect; as, to *cross* the legs. **4** To move across or past; to traverse; as, to *cross* the river. **5** To meet and pass; as, letters that *cross* in the mail. **6** To obstruct; to oppose; to thwart; as, a man who is dangerous if he is *crossed.* **7** To draw a line across; as, to *cross* one's t's. **8** To interbreed or to cause to interbreed; as, to *cross* a lion and a tiger. — *adj.* **1** Lying, falling, or passing across; as, a *cross* street. **2** Contrary; opposed; as, at *cross* purposes. **3** Ill-natured; fretful; peevish. — For synonyms see *peevish.*

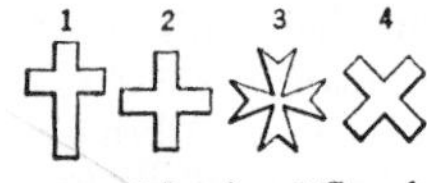

cross: *1* Latin; *2* Greek; *3* Maltese; *4* Saint Andrew's

cross·bar \'krȯs-ˌbär, -ˌbȧr\ *n.* A bar, piece, or stripe placed crosswise or across.

cross·bill \'krȯs-ˌbil\ *n.* A large finch having the

upper and lower parts of the bill strongly curved and crossing each other.

cross·bones \\'krȯs-ˌbōnz\\ *n. pl.* Two leg bones or arm bones pictured as lying across each other; as, a skull and *crossbones.*

cross·bow \\'krȯs-ˌbō\\ *n.* An old weapon for shooting stones and short square-headed arrows.

cross·breed \\'krȯs-'brēd\\ *v.;* **cross·bred** \\-'bred\\; **cross·breed·ing.** To breed by intermixing two varieties or breeds of the same species. — \\'krȯs-ˌbrēd\\ *n.* A breed or an individual produced by crossbreeding.

cross-coun·try \\'krȯs-ˌkən-trē\\ *adj.* Across the country or fields; not by roads; as, a *cross-country* race.

cross·cut \\'krȯs-ˌkət\\ *adj.* **1** Made or used for crosscutting; as, a *crosscut* saw. **2** Cut crosswise, especially across the grain. — *n.* A direct path cutting across the main road. — *v.;* **cross·cut; cross·cut·ting.** To cut or saw crosswise, especially across the grain of wood.

cross-ex·am·ine \\'krȯs-ig-'zam-ən\\ *v.;* **cross-ex·am·ined; cross-ex·am·in·ing.** To examine or question, especially as a check to a previous examination. — **cross-ex·am·i·na·tion** \\-ig-ˌzam-ə-'nāsh-n\\ *n.* — **cross-ex·am·in·er** \\-ig-'zam-ən-r\\ *n.*

cross-eyed \\'krȯs-'īd\\ *adj.* Having one or both eyes turned toward the nose.

cross-fer·ti·li·za·tion \\'krȯs-ˌfərt-l-ə-'zāsh-n\\ *n.* **1** Fertilization by cross-pollination. **2** The fertilizing of the eggs of an animal that has both male and female reproductive organs with the spermatozoa of another individual. — **cross-fer·ti·lize** \\-'fərt-l-ˌīz\\ *v.*

cross-grained \\'krȯs-'grānd\\ *adj.* **1** Having the grain running crosswise or irregularly, as a board. **2** Hard to manage; contrary; perverse; as, a person with a *cross-grained* disposition.

cross·ing \\'krȯs-ing\\ *n.* **1** The action of one that crosses. **2** A point where two lines, tracks, or streets cross each other. **3** A place provided for going across a street or railroad tracks. **4** A voyage across a large body of water, as a sea or a lake; as, to have a rough *crossing.*

cross-leg·ged \\'krȯs-'leg-əd, -'legd\\ *adj.* **1** Having the legs crossed with the knees spread wide. **2** Having one leg extending across the other.

cross·ly \\'krȯs-lē\\ *adv.* In a cross or peevish manner.

cross·ness \\'krȯs-nəs\\ *n.* Bad temper; peevishness.

cross·piece \\'krȯs-ˌpēs\\ *n.* A piece of any structure placed crosswise of another or others.

cross-pol·li·na·tion \\'krȯs-ˌpäl-ə-'nāsh-n\\ *n.* The depositing of pollen from one flower on the stigma of another, as by wind or insects.

cross-pur·pose \\'krȯs-'pərp-əs\\ *n.* An opposing purpose. — **at cross-pur·pos·es.** Acting contrary to another without meaning to do so.

cross-ques·tion \\'krȯs-'kwes-chən\\ *v.* To cross-examine.

cross-reference \\'krȯs-'ref-rn(t)s, -r(-)ən(t)s\\ *n.* A reference made from one place to another place, as in a book.

cross·road \\'krȯs-ˌrōd, -'rōd\\ *n.* **1** A road that crosses a main road, or runs across country between main roads and connects them. **2** [often in the plural] A place where two or more roads meet; as, a village of a dozen buildings at a *crossroads.*

cross section. 1 A section cut across anything, as across a log or an apple. **2** A number of persons or things selected from a group to represent or show the general nature of the whole; as, a *cross section* of society; a *cross section* of the news.

cross·tie \\'krȯs-ˌtī\\ *n.* A tie placed across something for support; especially, the ties under a railroad track.

cross·town \\'krȯs-ˌtau̇n\\ *adj.* **1** Situated at opposite points of a town; as, *crosstown* neighbors. **2** Extending across a town; as, a *crosstown* route. **3** Running across a town, especially to main routes; as, a *crosstown* bus. — \\-ˌtau̇n, -'tau̇n\\ *adv.* In a direction extending or running across town; as, a bus that runs *crosstown.*

cross·trees \\'krȯs-ˌtrēz\\ *n. pl.* Two crosspieces near the top of a mast on a ship to spread apart the upper ropes that support the mast.

cross·walk \\'krȯs-ˌwȯk\\ *n.* A specially marked or paved path crossing a street or road, for persons on foot.

cross·way \\'krȯs-ˌwā\\ *n.* A crossroad.

cross·ways \\'krȯs-ˌwāz\\ *adv.* Crosswise.

cross·wise \\'krȯs-ˌwīz\\ *adv.* **1** In the form of a cross. **2** So as to cross something; across; as, logs placed *crosswise* in a fireplace.

cross·word puzzle \\'krȯs-ˌwərd\\. A word-guessing puzzle in which the words, when correctly filled in, cross one another in such a way that most letters appear in two words.

crotch \\'kräch\\ *n.* The angle formed by the parting or spreading apart of two legs or branches, or of a limb from its trunk; a fork; as, the *crotch* of a tree; the *crotch* of a pair of trousers.

crotch·et \\'kräch-ət\\ *n.* An odd notion; a curious fancy; a whim. — **crotch·ety,** *adj.*

crouch \\'krau̇ch\\ *v.* **1** To stoop or bend low to the ground, as an animal waiting to spring. **2** To bend or shrink down in fear; to cower; to cringe. — *n.* **1** The action of crouching. **2** The position of crouching.

croup \\'krüp\\ *n.* The rear part of a four-footed animal's back, especially a horse's back, over the hind legs; rump.

croup \\'krüp\\ *n.* A disease of the throat and windpipe, marked by a hoarse, ringing cough and difficult breathing. — **croupy,** *adj.*

crou·ton \\'krü-ˌtän, krü-'tän\\ *n.* A small piece, usually a small cube, of bread toasted or fried crisp, used in soups and in garnishes.

crow \\'krō\\ *v.;* **crowed** or, in sense 1 only, **crew**

\'krü\; **crowed**; **crow·ing. 1** To make the loud shrill sound that a rooster makes. **2** To make sounds of happiness or delight. **3** To boast; to brag. The team *crowed* about winning. **—** *n.* **1** The cry of a rooster. **2** A sound of joy or pleasure. The baby reached for the ball with a *crow* of delight.

crow \'krō\ *n.* **1** A large glossy-black perching bird with a harsh cry or caw, in America living in flocks and, except the fish-eating **fish crow** of the southern United States, feeding chiefly on grains. **2** Any bird of a large family of which the common crow is typical, including the ravens, rooks, magpies, and jays. **3** A crowbar.

crow·bar \'krō-ˌbär, -ˌbȧr\ *n.* A bar of iron or steel, usually wedge-shaped at one end, used as a lever.

crowd \'kraůd\ *n.* **1** A large number of persons together; a throng. The accident drew a *crowd.* **2** The masses of the people; the populace. A demagogue appeals to the *crowd.* **3** A special group of people; a set; as, my sister's *crowd.* — For synonyms see *multitude.* **—** *v.* **1** To press forward; to push one's way; as, to *crowd* into an elevator. **2** To collect in numbers; to press together; to throng; as, to *crowd* around a speaker. **3** To press or squeeze, as into a smaller space; as, to *crowd* one's neighbor; to *crowd* clothes into a bag. **4** To fill, or to cause to fill, with persons or things; as, a street *crowded* with shoppers; to *crowd* a room.

crow·foot \'krō-ˌfůt\ *n.; pl.* **crow·foots. 1** An herb, called also *buttercup,* having five-petaled yellow flowers and in most species lobed leaves suggestive of a crow's foot. **2** Any plant of a large family of which the crowfoot is typical, including the anemone, larkspur, and peony.

crown \'kraůn\ *n.* **1** A wreath or band for the head, especially as a mark of victory or honor; a reward; as, a *crown* of laurel. **2** A royal headdress. **3** [often with a capital] Royal power or authority; the sovereign. **4** The top of the head or the head itself; the top part of a hat. **5** Any of several coins; especially, a British silver coin worth five shillings. **6** Anything resembling a crown in shape or position; as, the *crown* of a hill; the *crown* of a tooth. **7** A crownlike part within the corolla, as in the jonquil. **—** *v.* **1** To place a crown on; to make sovereign; to enthrone. **2** To honor; to reward; as, heroes *crowned* with glory. **3** To top; to cap; as, a hill *crowned* with a grove of trees. **4** To complete, to perfect. The victory *crowned* the general's career. **5** To round upward; as, to *crown* the surface of a road. **6** To put an artificial top on; as, to *crown* a tooth.

crown prince. The heir apparent to a crown or throne.

crown princess. 1 The wife of a crown prince. **2** A female heir apparent.

crow's-foot \'krōz-ˌfůt\ *n.; pl.* **crow's-feet** \-ˌfēt\. **1** [usually plural] One of the small wrinkles at the outer corners of the eyes. **2** A device of two pieces fastened crosswise to prop up a post. **3** Crowfoot.

crow's-nest \'krōz-ˌnest\ *n.* A partly enclosed platform high on the mast of a ship for a lookout; any similar lookout.

crozier. Variant of *crosier.*

cruces. A pl. of *crux.*

cru·cial \'krüsh-l\ *adj.* **1** Having the form of a cross. **2** Having to do with a final or very important test or decision; decisive; as, a *crucial* battle; the *crucial* moment. **3** Difficult; trying; severe; as, to go through a *crucial* period. — **cru·cial·ly** \'krüsh-l-ē\ *adv.*

cru·ci·ble \'krü-səb-l\ *n.* **1** A pot or similar vessel made of some substance that resists fire, used for holding metals or ores that are treated under great heat in the process of manufacture. **2** A severe trial or test.

cru·ci·fix \'krü-sə-ˌfiks\ *n.* **1** A Christian symbol consisting of a cross bearing the image of the crucified Jesus Christ. **2** The cross as a Christian emblem.

cru·ci·fix·ion \ˌkrü-sə-'fiksh-n\ *n.* **1** The action of crucifying. **2** [with a capital] The crucifying of Christ on the cross. **3** A painting or statue representing this.

cru·ci·form \'krü-sə-ˌfȯrm\ *adj.* Cross-shaped.

cru·ci·fy \'krü-sə-ˌfī\ *v.;* **cru·ci·fied** \-ˌfīd\; **cru·ci·fy·ing. 1** To put a person to death by nailing his hands and feet to a cross. **2** To treat cruelly; to torture.

crude \'krüd\ *adj.;* **crud·er**; **crud·est. 1** In a natural condition; not prepared for use by any process; especially, not refined; as, *crude* oil. **2** Lacking grace, tact, or taste; rude and unpolished; as, *crude* manners. **3** Bald; bare; as, the *crude* facts. — **crude·ly,** *adv.* — **cru·di·ty** \'krüd-ət-ē\ *n.*

cru·el \'krü-əl\ *adj.* **1** Ready to hurt others; savage; merciless. **2** Showing savageness; causing suffering; as, a *cruel* joke; *cruel* treatment of animals. — **cru·el·ly** \-ə-lē\ *adv.*

cru·el·ty \'krü-əl-tē\ *n.; pl.* **cru·el·ties. 1** An inclination to inflict needless pain. **2** A cruel act; cruel treatment; as, *cruelty* to animals.

cru·et \'krü-ət\ *n.* A small glass bottle for holding vinegar, oil, or sauce for the table.

cruet

cruise \'krüz\ *v.;* **cruised**; **cruis·ing.** [From Dutch *kruisen* meaning literally "to make a cross", "to move crosswise", from *kruis* meaning "cross".] **1** To travel by ship with no set destination; to sail about touching at a series of ports and not going directly to one port only; as, to *cruise* along the coast. **2** To make a similar trip on or over land, as in an airplane. **3** To travel at the most efficient operating speed, as an aircraft or automobile. **—** *n.* A trip made by a ship or an airplane that is cruising.

cruis·er \'krüz-r\ *n.* **1** A warship with less armor and armament than a battleship. **2** A police automobile equipped with radio for communicating with headquarters; a squad car. **3** A powerboat with cabin and equipment suitable for short cruises.

crul·ler \'krəl-r\ *n.* [From Dutch *krulle* meaning "a twisted cake", from *krul* meaning "curly".] A friedcake made of rich egg batter, usually cut in strips or twists, and fried brown in deep fat.

crumb \'krəm\ *n.* **1** A small piece, especially of bread, broken or rubbed off. **2** A little bit; as, a *crumb* of hope. — *v.* **1** To break into crumbs; to crumble; as, to *crumb* bread. **2** To cover or dress with crumbs, as in frying or baking certain foods. **3** To remove the crumbs from; as, to *crumb* a table after a meal.

crum·ble \'krəm-bl\ *v.;* **crum·bled; crum·bling** \-bl(-)ing\. **1** To break into small pieces; as, to *crumble* bread with one's fingers. **2** To fall to pieces; to break apart; to fall into decay or ruin; as, a *crumbling* wall. The enemy's forces *crumbled* under our attack.

crum·bly \'krəm-blē\ *adj.;* **crum·bli·er; crum·bli·est.** Easily crumbled.

crum·pet \'krəmp-ət\ *n.* A flat, soft, unsweetened cake cooked on a griddle or in a frying pan and usually toasted and eaten hot.

crum·ple \'krəmp-l\ *v.;* **crum·pled; crum·pling** \-l(-)ing\. **1** To wrinkle; to rumple; to crush together; as, to *crumple* paper. **2** To become creased or wrinkled. This cloth *crumples* easily. **3** To collapse, as if crumpled; as, to *crumple* into a heap.

crunch \'krənch\ *v.* **1** To chew with a crushing or grinding noise; as, to *crunch* a piece of stale toast. **2** To press or grind with a similar noise; as, to *crunch* through snow. **3** To make a sound as of something being noisily crushed or ground; as, snow *crunching* under the feet of passers-by. — *n.* **1** The act of crunching. **2** A sound made by crunching.

crup·per \'krəp-r\ *n.* **1** A leather loop passing under a horse's tail and buckled to the harness. **2** The rump of a horse; a croup.

cru·sade \krü-'sād\ *n.* **1** [often with a capital] Any one of the military expeditions undertaken by Christian countries in the 11th, 12th, and 13th centuries to recover the Holy Land from the Moslems. **2** Any campaign or expedition of war undertaken in the name of religion and with the support of the church. **3** Any campaign with a noble purpose, as one for the improvement of conditions in a city or country, which is undertaken with zeal and enthusiasm; as, a *crusade* against gambling. — *v.;* **cru·sad·ed; cru·sad·ing.** To take part in a crusade.

cru·sad·er \krü-'sād-r\ *n.* A person who takes part in a crusade.

cruse \'krüz\ *n.* A jar, pot, or cup for holding a liquid, as water or oil.

crush \'krəsh\ *v.* **1** To squeeze together so as to break or bruise or so as to destroy the natural shape or condition; as, to *crush* one's hat by sitting on it; to *crush* grapes. **2** To break into fine pieces by pounding or grinding; as, to *crush* stone. **3** To ruin; to subdue; to overwhelm; as, to *crush* an enemy. **4** To be or become crushed; as, to pack fruit so that it will not *crush* when shipped. — *n.* **1** A crushing or a squeezing together. **2** A tightly packed crowd. — **crush·er,** *n.*

crust \'krəst\ *n.* **1** The hardened outside surface of bread; a piece of this, or any hard dry piece of bread. **2** The cover or case of a pie. **3** A hard outer covering or surface layer, as of earth or snow. **4** The outer part of the earth. — *v.* To cover or become covered with a crust. Ice *crusted* the river.

crus·ta·cean \ˌkrəs-'tāsh-n\ *n.* Any of a large class of water-breathing animals with jointed body or limbs, usually living in or near the water and having a firm crustlike shell, as lobsters, crabs, and shrimps. — *adj.* Of or belonging to the crustaceans.

crusty \'krəs-tē\ *adj.;* **crust·i·er; crust·i·est.** **1** Having a crust. **2** Abrupt or rough in manner; ill-natured. — **crust·i·ly** \'krəs-tə-lē\ *adv.*

crutch \'krəch\ *n.* **1** A staff with a crosspiece at the top to fit under the armpit, used to support lame persons in walking. **2** Anything like a crutch in shape or use.

crux \'krəks\ *n.; pl.* **crux·es** \'krəks-əz\ or **cru·ces** \'krü-ˌsēz\. **1** A cross. **2** Anything very puzzling or difficult to explain. **3** A crucial or critical point.

cry \'krī\ *v.;* **cried** \'krīd\; **cry·ing.** **1** To make a loud call or cry; to shout; to exclaim. **2** To shed tears; to weep; to cause by weeping; as, to *cry* oneself to sleep. **3** Of an animal or a bird, to utter its characteristic sound or call. **4** To beg; to implore; as, to *cry* mercy. **5** To advertise by calling out; as, to *cry* one's wares in the street. — **cry down.** To belittle; to disparage. — *n.; pl.* **cries.** **1** A loud call or shout expressing strong emotion, as of pain, fear, or joy. **2** An appeal; as, the *cries* of the poor. **3** A fit of weeping. **4** The characteristic sound uttered by a bird or an animal. **5** A watchword, as of a party. — **a far cry.** A great distance; a great change.

cry·ba·by \'krī-ˌbā-bē\ *n.; pl.* **cry·ba·bies.** One who cries as easily or often as a baby.

cry·ing \'krī-ing\ *adj.* Calling out to be noticed; calling for attention and correction; as, a *crying* evil; a *crying* shame.

crypt \'kript\ *n.* An underground vault or room, especially one under the floor of a church, used as a burial place.

cryp·tic \'krip-tik\ *adj.* **1** Hidden; secret; as, nature's *cryptic* ways. **2** Having or seeming to have a hidden meaning; as, a *cryptic* remark. — **cryp·ti·cal·ly** \-tik-l(-)ē\ *adv.*

cryp·to·gam \'krip-tə-ˌgam\ *n.* A plant that does not produce flowers or seeds, as ferns, mosses, and algae. — **cryp·to·gam·ic** \ˌkrip-tə-'gam-ik\ or **cryp·tog·a·mous** \krip-'täg-m-əs\ *adj.*

cryp·to·gram \'krip-tə-ˌgram\ *n.* A writing in cipher or secret arrangement of letters or words.

cryp·to·graph \'krip-tə-ˌgraf\ *n.* A cryptogram.

cryp·tog·ra·pher \krip-'täg-rəf-r\ *n.* A person

who solves or deciphers cryptograms or decodes any secret writing. — **cryp·tog·ra·phy** \-rə-fē\ *n.*

crys·tal \'krist-l\ *n.* **1** Quartz that is colorless and transparent or nearly so or a piece of such quartz. **2** Anything resembling this quartz, especially in transparency. **3** A body formed by a substance solidifying so that it has flat surfaces in regular even arrangement; as, snow or ice *crystals.* **4** Glass of great brilliancy, used in making table articles, or glassware made of this glass. **5** The glass over a watch dial. — *adj.* Consisting of or like crystal; clear; transparent.

snow crystals

crys·tal·line \'kris-tə-lən\ *adj.* **1** Consisting or made of crystal. **2** Like crystal; clear; transparent. **3** Of, or of the nature of, a crystal or crystals; as, a *crystalline* salt; *crystalline* form.

crystalline lens. The lens of the eye in vertebrates.

crys·tal·lize \'kris-tə-ˌlīz\ *v.;* **crys·tal·lized; crys·tal·liz·ing. 1** To form, or to cause to form, crystals or grains; to become crystalline in structure. **2** To become, or to cause to become, settled and fixed in form. The boy's ambition to become a pilot soon *crystallized* into a determination that nothing could shake. **3** To coat with crystals, as of sugar; as, *crystallized* ginger. — **crys·tal·li·za·tion** \ˌkris-tə-lə-'zāsh-n\ *n.*

crys·tal·log·ra·phy \ˌkris-tə-'läg-rə-fē\ *n.* The science that deals with crystals, their form and structure. — **crys·tal·log·ra·pher** \-rəf-r\ *n.*

c's. Pl. of *c.*

CST. Abbreviation for *Central Standard Time.*

ct. Abbreviation for: **1** *cent.* **2** *court.*

cu. Abbreviation for *cubic.*

cub \'kəb\ *n.* **1** The young of various animals, such as the bear, wolf, and lion, and sometimes of the whale or shark. **2** A young person, especially an awkward or ill-mannered boy. **3** A light airplane with high wings and low horsepower; a grasshopper. — *adj.* Serving as an apprentice; undergoing learning or training; as, a *cub* pilot; a *cub* newspaper reporter.

Cu·ban \'kyüb-n\ *adj.* Of or relating to Cuba or its people. — *n.* A native or inhabitant of Cuba.

cub·by·hole \'kəb-ē-ˌhōl\ *n.* A snug or confined place, as one to hide or play in, or to store things in.

cube \'kyüb\ *n.* **1** A solid body having six equal square sides or faces. **2** In mathematics, the third power of a number; the product obtained by taking a number or quantity three times as a factor; as, $2 \times 2 \times 2$, the *cube* of 2. — *v.;* **cubed; cub·ing. 1** To raise to the third power; to form the cube of. **2** To form or cut into a cube or cubes; as, to *cube* carrots for cooking.

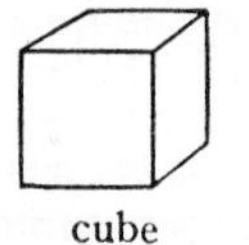
cube

cube root. In mathematics, a number or quantity obtained by dividing a number or quantity into its three equal factors. The *cube root* of 27 is 3.

cu·bic \'kyü-bik\ *adj.* **1** Having the form of a cube. **2** Having the three dimensions, length, height, and width. **3** In mathematics, of the third degree, order, or power. — **cu·bi·cal** \-bik-l\ *adj.* — **cu·bi·cal·ly** \-bik-l(-)ē\ *adv.*

cubic centimeter. A volume equal to the volume of a cube each of whose sides is one centimeter long — commonly used as a unit of measurement for serums and vaccines injected by hypodermic needle.

cubic foot. A volume equal to the volume of a cube each of whose sides is one foot long.

cubic inch. A volume equal to the volume of a cube each of whose sides is one inch long.

cu·bi·cle \'kyü-bik-l\ *n.* **1** A sleeping place, especially one partitioned off from a dormitory. **2** Any small partitioned space.

cubic yard. A volume equal to the volume of a cube each of whose sides is one yard long.

cu·bit \'kyü-bət\ *n.* A measure of length, originally the length from the elbow to the end of the middle finger; in English measure, eighteen inches.

cub scout. A member of the Cub Scout Program, a junior division of the Boy Scouts.

cuck·oo \'kü-ˌkü, 'ku̇k-ˌü\ *n.; pl.* **cuck·oos. 1** A European bird that has a two-syllabled whistle and lays its eggs in the nests of other birds for them to hatch. **2** In America, either of two related birds, one black-billed and the other yellow-billed, that hatch their own eggs. **3** The call or whistle of the cuckoo.

cu·cum·ber \'kyü-ˌkəm-br\ *n.* **1** A long, fleshy, many-seeded vegetable, used in salads and in making pickles. **2** The vine that bears this vegetable.

cud \'kəd, 'ku̇d\ *n.* A portion of food brought up into the mouth from the first stomach of some animals, to be chewed again; as, a cow chewing its *cud.*

cud·dle \'kəd-l\ *v.;* **cud·dled; cud·dling** \-l(-)ing\. **1** To hold closely and tenderly; to caress. **2** To lie snug; to nestle. — *n.* An embrace; a nestling for comfort or affection.

cudg·el \'kəj-l\ *n.* A short heavy stick or club used as a weapon. — *v.;* **cudg·eled** or **cudg·elled; cudg·el·ing** or **cudg·el·ling** \-l(-)ing\. To beat with a cudgel. — **cudgel one's brains.** To force oneself to think hard.

cue \'kyü\ *n.* **1** In a play, a word of a speech or an action on the stage indicating that it is time for the next actor to speak or act. **2** A word or other signal for beginning any action; a hint; a suggestion. When her husband began to yawn she took her *cue* and began to say goodby to their hosts.

cue \'kyü\ *n.* **1** A tight braid of hair hanging down the back; a pigtail. **2** A straight tapering stick used in playing billiards or pool.

cue ball. The ball that a player strikes with his cue in billiards and pool.

cuff \'kəf\ *n.* **1** A band or turned-over piece at the end of a sleeve. **2** The turned-up part at the bottom of the legs of some long trousers. — *v.* To furnish with a cuff or cuffs; as, *cuffed* trousers.

cuff \'kəf\ *v.* To strike with or as if with the palm or flat of the hand; to slap. — *n.* A slap.

cui·rass \kwē-'ras\ *n.* A piece of armor covering the body from the neck to the waist, or the breastplate of such armor.

cuir·as·sier \ˌkwir-ə-'sir\ *n.* A mounted soldier wearing a cuirass.

cui·sine \kwi-'zēn\ *n.* Manner or style of cooking or preparing food; quality of meals served; as, a hotel with excellent *cuisine.*

cul·i·nary \'kəl-ə-ˌner-ē, 'kyü-lə-\ *adj.* Having to do with cooking or with the kitchen.

cull \'kəl\ *v.* **1** To select; to pick out; to choose and gather; as, to *cull* flowers. **2** To make selections from; as, to *cull* a garden. — *n.* Something sorted out as being poor or worthless; as, the *culls* from a herd of cattle.

cul·mi·nate \'kəl-mə-ˌnāt\ *v.;* **cul·mi·nat·ed**; **cul·mi·nat·ing.** To reach the highest point, as of power, rank, or development; to come to a climax. The meeting *culminated* in the election of officers for the coming year.

cul·mi·na·tion \ˌkəl-mə-'nāsh-n\ *n.* **1** The action of culminating. **2** The highest point or position reached; the summit; as, at the *culmination* of a long and successful career.

cul·pa·ble \'kəl-pəb-l\ *adj.* Deserving blame; guilty; as, to punish only those who are *culpable.* — **cul·pa·bil·i·ty** \ˌkəl-pə-'bil-ət-ē\ *n.* — **cul·pa·bly** \'kəl-pə-blē\ *adv.*

cul·prit \'kəl-prət\ *n.* [From Old French *cul prist* meaning "the guilt is ready to be tried".] **1** A person who is guilty of a crime or a fault. **2** A person who is accused of a crime, as in a court.

cult \'kəlt\ *n.* **1** Worship, especially according to a particular system of ceremonies; as, the *cult* of Apollo. **2** A system of ceremonies used in worship; religious rites. **3** Enthusiastic devotion to a person, idea, or thing, especially for only a short time. **4** A group of persons showing such devotion.

cul·ti·va·ble \'kəl-tə-vəb-l\ or **cul·ti·vat·a·ble** \-ˌvāt-əb-l\ *adj.* Capable of being cultivated.

cul·ti·vate \'kəl-tə-ˌvāt\ *v.;* **cul·ti·vat·ed**; **cul·ti·vat·ing.** **1** To prepare land for the raising of crops; to till. **2** To loosen soil about the roots of plants, as for killing weeds. **3** To raise crops or assist their growth by tilling or by labor and care. **4** To improve or develop by careful attention, training, or study; as, to *cultivate* one's mind. **5** To devote time and thought to; as, to *cultivate* a hobby. **6** To seek the society and friendship of.

cul·ti·vat·ed \'kəl-tə-ˌvāt-əd\ *adj.* **1** Under cultivation; used for growing crops; as, *cultivated* land. **2** Grown with human care; not wild; as, *cultivated* varieties of violets. **3** Refined in manners, taste, and thought; cultured.

cul·ti·va·tion \ˌkəl-tə-'vāsh-n\ *n.* **1** The process or the art of cultivating the soil and its products; agriculture; farming. **2** The state of being cultivated, or tilled; as, to have 50 acres under *cultivation.* **3** The process of cultivating the mind or taste. **4** Culture; refinement; as, a man of great *cultivation.*

cul·ti·va·tor \'kəl-tə-ˌvāt-r\ *n.* One that cultivates something, as the soil, an art, or the mind; especially, an implement or machine used to loosen the soil around growing plants.

garden cultivator

cul·tur·al \'kəlch-r(-)əl\ *adj.* **1** Having to do with culture; producing or designed to produce culture; as, people of different *cultural* backgrounds; *cultural* studies. **2** Produced by selective breeding; as, *cultural* varieties of grapes. — **cul·tur·al·ly** \-r(-)ə-lē\ *adv.*

cul·ture \'kəlch-r\ *n.* **1** The cultivation of the land. **2** The process of improving or developing by careful attention; as, bee *culture;* physical *culture.* **3** The result of the improvement of the mind, tastes, and manners through careful training; refinement. **4** A particular form of civilization or stage of advancement; as, ancient Greek *culture.* **5** Cultivation of small organisms, as bacteria or fungi, or of bodily tissue, in specially prepared substances (**culture mediums**). **6** A growth, as of bacteria, cultivated or produced in this way. — *v.;* **cul·tured**; **cul·tur·ing** \-r(-)ing\. **1** To cultivate. **2** To grow, as organisms or tissue, in a prepared medium.

cul·tured \'kəlch-rd\ *adj.* **1** Under cultivation, as land or crops. **2** Having refined tastes, manners, and speech; having culture. **3** Grown or produced under artificial conditions; as, *cultured* pearls; *cultured* bacteria.

cul·vert \'kəlv-rt\ *n.* A drain crossing under a road, railroad, or canal; an arched drain or sewer.

cum·ber \'kəm-br\ *v.;* **cum·bered**; **cum·ber·ing** \-br(-)ing\. **1** To hinder or hamper by being in the way; as, to be *cumbered* in walking by heavy winter clothing. **2** To weigh down; to burden; as, *cumbered* with cares and responsibilities.

cum·ber·some \'kəm-brs-m\ *adj.* **1** Clumsy; as, heavy, *cumbersome* field equipment. **2** Burdensome; troublesome; as, *cumbersome* requirements; the *cumbersome* details of arranging a trip. — **cum·ber·some·ly**, *adv.*

cum·brous \'kəm-brəs\ *adj.* Making action or motion difficult; cumbersome. The heavy knapsack proved *cumbrous* during the climb.

cum·mer·bund \'kəm-r-ˌbənd\ *n.* A sash or band worn round the waist.

cu·mu·la·tive \'kyüm-yə-lət-iv, -ˌlāt-\ *adj.* Increasing, as in force, strength, or amount, by successive additions, one on another; as, *cumulative* evidence of crime; *cumulative* effects. — **cu·mu·la·tive·ly**, *adv.*

cu·mu·lus \'kyüm-yə-ləs\ *n.;* *pl.* **cu·mu·li** \-ˌlī\. **1** A heap; a mound. **2** A cloud with a flat base and rounded masses often piled up like a mountain.

cu·ne·i·form \kyü-ˈnē-ə-ˌfȯrm, ˈkyü-nē-\ *adj.* Wedge-shaped — used especially of the wedge-shaped characters of certain ancient writing, as that of ancient Persia and Assyria. — *n.* Cuneiform characters as writing.

cuneiform writing

cun·ning \ˈkən-ing\ *adj.* **1** Cleverly deceitful; sly; tricky; artful; as, a *cunning* thief. **2** Skillful; clever; as, the *cunning* hands of an artist. **3** Prettily pleasing or attractive; as, a *cunning* baby; a *cunning* little house.

— The words *sly* and *crafty* are synonyms of *cunning: sly* may suggest secret and furtive deception; *cunning* may apply to animal cleverness or skill in escaping difficulty or danger or in evading obstacles; *crafty* usually indicates a highly developed and artful ability to deceive by secret devices and schemes.

— *n.* **1** *Archaic.* Skill; dexterity. **2** Cleverness in gaining one's ends, especially through deceit or what seems like deceit; craftiness; as, to have the *cunning* of a fox. — **cun·ning·ly**, *adv.*

cup \ˈkəp\ *n.* **1** A small open container or vessel, usually with a handle, used chiefly to drink from; as, a *cup* and saucer. **2** The contents of a cup; a cupful; as, to drink a *cup* of tea. **3** Anything like a cup in shape or use. **4** A larger vessel having a cup-shaped body, often with two handles, given as a prize in a contest, especially in games or racing. — **in one's cups.** Drunk. — *v.;* **cupped; cup·ping. 1** To receive, take, or scoop up in a cup; as, to *cup* water from a bucket. **2** To place in a cup or as if in a cup; as, to *cup* one's chin in one's hand. **3** To make a cup of; as, to *cup* one's hands.

cup·bear·er \ˈkəp-ˌbar-r, -ˌber-r\ *n.* A person who has the duty of filling and handing cups of drink, as at a feast.

cup·board \ˈkəb-rd\ *n.* A closet with shelves for dishes or food; any small closet.

cup·cake \ˈkəp-ˌkāk\ *n.* A small cake baked in a cup-shaped mold.

cup·ful \ˈkəp-ˌfu̇l\ *n.; pl.* **cup·fuls.** As much as a cup will hold; in cooking, a half pint.

cu·pid \ˈkyüp-əd\ *n.* A painting or other representation of Cupid, the Roman god of love, as a naked, winged child with a bow (**Cupid's bow**) and arrow.

cu·pid·i·ty \kyü-ˈpid-ət-ē\ *n.* Excessive desire or longing, especially for wealth; greed; as, a cranky old man well known for his meanness and *cupidity.*

cu·po·la \ˈkyüp-l-ə, -l-ˌō\ *n.* **1** A rounded roof or ceiling; a dome. **2** A small structure built on top of a roof or building.

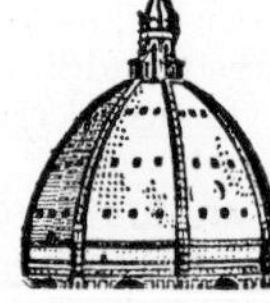
cupola, 1

cur \ˈkər\ *n.* **1** A mongrel or inferior dog. **2** A low, contemptible fellow.

cur·a·ble \ˈkyu̇r-əb-l\ *adj.* Capable of being cured.

cu·rate \ˈkyu̇r-ət\ *n.* A clergyman who assists the rector or vicar of a church.

cur·a·tive \ˈkyu̇r-ət-iv\ *adj.* Relating to or used in the cure or treatment of diseases.

cu·ra·tor \kyu̇-ˈrāt-r, ˈkyu̇r-ˌāt-r\ *n.* A person having the care of anything; especially, a person in charge of a museum or an art collection.

curb \ˈkərb\ *n.* **1** A chain or strap attached to a horse's bit, used to check the horse by drawing against the lower jaw. **2** Anything that restrains, checks, or controls; as, to place a *curb* on spending. **3** A frame or a raised edge or margin, as a wall or casing, as at the top of a well. **4** Also **curb·stone** \ˈkərb-ˌstōn\. A border, as of upright stone, along the outer edge of a street or sidewalk. — *v.* **1** To check, restrain, or control as if with a curb; as, to *curb* one's temper. **2** To provide with a curb, as a sidewalk.

curb·ing \ˈkər-bing\ *n.* Material forming a curb.

curd \ˈkərd\ *n.* The thickened or solid part of milk. — *v.* To clot or thicken; to curdle; to separate into curds and whey.

cur·dle \ˈkərd-l\ *v.;* **cur·dled; cur·dling** \-l(-)ing\. To change into curd; to clot or thicken; as, *curdled* milk.

cure \ˈkyu̇r\ *n.* **1** The office or duties of a rector, pastor, or curate, or the parish of which he is in charge. **2** A method or period of medical or healing treatment; as, a rest *cure.* **3** An act of healing or the condition of being healed; as, a doctor famous for his *cures.* **4** A remedy; as, a *cure* for colds. — *v.;* **cured; cur·ing. 1** To heal; to restore to health or soundness. **2** To preserve in good condition, as by drying or salting; as, to *cure* bacon. **3** To be or become cured; as, hay *curing* in the sun.

cu·ré \kyu̇-ˈrā\ *n.* A parish priest.

cure-all \ˈkyu̇r-ˌȯl\ *n.* A remedy for all ills.

cur·few \ˈkər-ˌfyü\ *n.* [From Old French *covrefeu,* originally a signal to put out the fires for the night, meaning literally "cover the fire".] **1** A signal such as the ringing of a bell, given in the evening to warn children or other unauthorized persons to leave the streets. **2** The time when a curfew is sounded. **3** An order or regulation requiring certain persons, as children, or sometimes during emergencies, all unauthorized persons, to be off the streets at a specified time.

cu·rio \ˈkyu̇r-ē-ˌō\ *n.; pl.* **cu·ri·os.** A rare or unusual article; a curiosity.

cu·ri·os·i·ty \ˌkyu̇r-ē-ˈäs-ət-ē\ *n.; pl.* **cu·ri·os·i·ties. 1** An eager desire to learn, especially to learn something that does not concern one; inquisitiveness. **2** Something strange or unusual; especially, an object or article valued because of its strangeness or rarity.

cu·ri·ous \ˈkyu̇r-ē-əs\ *adj.* **1** Eager to learn; as, a *curious* scholar. **2** Inquisitive; prying; as, too *curious* about the affairs of others. **3** Strange; rare; unusual; as, a *curious* insect. **4** Odd; eccentric. The old man had many *curious* ideas. — **cu·ri·ous·ly**, *adv.*

cu·ri·um \'kyůr-ē-əm\ *n.* A metallic chemical element artificially produced in the cyclotron.

curl \'kərl\ *v.* **1** To twist or form into ringlets, as the hair. **2** To curve; to coil; as, to *curl* a rope; to *curl* up in a chair. — *n.* **1** A ringlet of hair. **2** A spiral or winding form; a coil; as, a *curl* of smoke. **3** The state of being curled; as, to keep the hair in *curl*.

curl·er \'kərl-r\ *n.* **1** One that curls, as a device for putting a curl into hair. **2** A player in the game of curling.

cur·lew \'kər-ˌlü\ *n.* A shore bird related to the woodcocks, with long legs and a long, slender, downward-curving bill.

curl·i·cue \'kər-lə-ˌkyü, 'kər-lē-\ *n.* Something curled in a fanciful manner, as the final stroke of a letter in handwriting.

curl·ing \'kər-ling\ *n.* A game in which specially made stones (**curling stones**) are slid along ice toward a mark.

curly \'kər-lē\ *adj.*; **curl·i·er**; **curl·i·est.** **1** Curling or tending to curl; as, *curly* hair. **2** Having curls; as, a *curly* head.

cur·rant \'kər-ənt, 'kə-rənt\ *n.* [From Old French *raisin de Corauntz* meaning "raisin of Corinth", a city and region of Greece.] **1** A small seedless raisin, much used in baking and cooking. **2** A thin-skinned tart berry, usually red or black, that grows in clusters on a shrub of the same family as the gooseberry. **3** The shrub that bears these berries.

currant: leaves and fruit

cur·ren·cy \'kər-ən-sē, 'kə-rən-\ *n.*; *pl.* **cur·ren·cies.** **1** That which is used for money, including coin and paper money. **2** The state of being current or in general use; circulation; general acceptance; as, a belief that had wide *currency*.

cur·rent \'kər-ənt, 'kə-rənt\ *adj.* **1** Now passing; as, the *current* month. **2** Belonging to the present time; as, *current* events. **3** In general use; commonly accepted; as, the *current* meaning of a word. **4** Passing from person to person; circulating; as, a *current* rumor; *current* coin. — *n.* **1** A body of fluid or air moving in a certain direction; a stream, especially its swiftest part. **2** A similar movement or flow of electricity or the rate of such movement. **3** The general course or movement of anything; tendency; as, the *current* of events. — **cur·rent·ly,** *adv.*

cur·ri·cle \'kər-ik-l, 'kə-rik-l\ *n.* A two-wheeled carriage drawn by two horses abreast.

cur·ric·u·lum \kə-'rik-yə-ləm\ *n.*; *pl.* **cur·ric·u·lums** \-ləmz\ or **cur·ric·u·la** \-lə\. A course of study; especially, the whole body of courses offered in a school or college or in one of its departments. — **cur·ric·u·lar** \-lər\ *adj.*

cur·ri·er \'kər-ē-ər, 'kə-rē-\ *n.* A person who curries leather after it is tanned.

cur·ry \'kər-ē, 'kə-rē\ *v.*; **cur·ried**; **cur·ry·ing.** **1** To rub and clean the coat of, as a horse; to dress with a currycomb. **2** To prepare leather after tanning, by scraping, cleansing, smoothing, and coloring. — **curry favor.** To try to gain favor, as by flattery.

cur·ry \'kər-ē, 'kə-rē\ *n.*; *pl.* **cur·ries.** **1** A highly spiced yellowish powder used in cooking, or a sauce made with this powder. **2** A dish prepared with curry powder or eaten with curry sauce; as, a chicken *curry*. — *v.*; **cur·ried** \'kər-ēd, 'kə-rēd\; **cur·ry·ing.** To cook or flavor with curry; as, to *curry* chicken.

cur·ry·comb \'kər-ē-ˌkōm, 'kə-rē-\ *n.* A metal-toothed comb for grooming horses. — *v.* To groom with a currycomb.

curse \'kərs\ *v.*; **cursed** \'kərst\ or **curst**; **curs·ing.** **1** To call upon some power considered to be supernatural to send harm or evil upon. **2** To use profane language or words regarded as bad; to swear; to swear at. **3** To bring unhappiness or evil upon; to afflict; to torment; as, a country *cursed* for centuries with floods; to be *cursed* with a bad temper. — *n.* **1** A prayer that harm or injury may come upon someone. **2** A word or an expression used in cursing or swearing. **3** Evil or misfortune that comes as if in answer to a curse; a cause of great harm or evil. Floods are the *curse* of this region.

cursed \'kər-səd, 'kərst\ *adj.* **1** Being under a curse; damned. **2** Deserving to be cursed.

cur·sive \'kər-siv\ *adj.* Written or formed with the strokes of the letters joined together and the angles rounded; as, *cursive* handwriting.

cur·so·ry \'kərs-r(-)ē\ *adj.* Hastily done or given; passing hurriedly over something; as, a *cursory* glance; a *cursory* inspection. — **cur·so·ri·ly** \-r(-)ə-lē\ *adv.*

curt \'kərt\ *adj.* Short in language; rudely abrupt; brief; as, a *curt* reply. — For synonyms see *bluff*. — **curt·ly,** *adv.*

cur·tail \(ˌ)kər-'tāl\ *v.* To shorten, as by cutting off the end or any part of; to lessen; to reduce; as, to *curtail* expenses. — **cur·tail·ment,** *n.*

cur·tain \'kərt-n\ *n.* **1** A hanging screen, usually one that can be drawn up or back; especially, a piece of cloth or other material intended to darken, conceal, or divide, or merely to decorate; as, window *curtains;* an asbestos theater *curtain.* **2** Something that covers, conceals, or separates like a curtain; as, a *curtain* of fire or smoke; an iron *curtain.* — *v.*; **cur·tained**; **cur·tain·ing** \-n(-)ing\. To furnish with curtains.

curt·sy or **curt·sey** \'kərt-sē\ *n.*; *pl.* **curt·sies** or **curt·seys.** A bow, made especially by women, consisting of a slight lowering of the body, with bending of the knees. — *v.*; **curt·sied** or **curt·seyed** \-sēd\; **curt·sy·ing** or **curt·sey·ing.** To make a curtsy.

cur·va·ture \'kər-və-ˌchůr, -vəch-r\ *n.* **1** A curving or bending; the condition of being curved; as, the *curvature* of the earth's surface. **2** An abnormal curving; as, *curvature* of the spine.

curve \'kərv\ *n.* **1** A bending or turning without angles; a bend; as, a *curve* in the road. **2** A curved outline, form, or part. **3** In baseball, a ball so thrown that its course is a curve different from that ordinarily caused by the force of gravity. — *v.;* **curved; curv·ing. 1** To bend; to turn from a straight direction; as, a road that *curved* to the right. **2** To cause to move in a curve; as, to *curve* a baseball.

cur·vet \ˌkər-ˈvət\ *n.* A leap made by a horse in which it raises both front legs together and then, as they are falling, raises its hind legs. — *v.;* **cur·vet·ted** or **cur·vet·ed; cur·vet·ting** or **cur·vet·ing. 1** To make a curvet; to leap; to bound. **2** To frisk; to frolic.

cur·vi·lin·e·ar \ˌkər-və-ˈlin-ē-ər\ *adj.* Consisting of or bounded by curved lines.

cush·ion \ˈku̇sh-n\ *n.* **1** A soft pillow or pad to rest on or against. **2** Something resembling a cushion in shape, use, or softness. **3** The elastic lining along the inner rim of a billiard table. **4** An elastic medium, as of air or steam, for lessening shock in machinery. — *v.;* **cush·ioned; cush·ion·ing** \-n(-)ing\. **1** To place on a cushion. **2** To furnish with cushions. **3** To check gradually so as to lessen shock.

cusp \ˈkəsp\ *n.* **1** A point, especially one on the crown of a tooth. **2** Either of the two pointed ends of a crescent moon.

cusp
cusp
cusp, 2

cus·pid \ˈkəs-pəd\ *n.* One of the sharp-pointed teeth next to the front biting teeth; a canine tooth.

cus·pi·dor \ˈkəs-pə-ˌdȯr\ *n.* A spittoon.

cus·tard \ˈkəst-rd\ *n.* A cooked, sweetened mixture of milk and eggs.

custard apple. 1 A brown heart-shaped fruit with reddish-yellow custardlike pulp, borne by a tree native to tropical America. **2** The North American papaw.

cus·to·di·an \(ˌ)kəs-ˈtōd-ē-ən\ *n.* A person who has the care or custody of something; especially the keeper or caretaker of a public building.

cus·to·dy \ˈkəs-təd-ē\ *n.* **1** The act of keeping or guarding or the state of being guarded or watched. **2** Care; charge; as, to have the *custody* of the town's records. **3** Arrest; confinement; keeping; imprisonment. The thief was taken into *custody.*

cus·tom \ˈkəst-m\ *n.* **1** The usual way of doing things; that which is usually done; as, the *custom* of shaking hands; European *customs.* **2** [in the plural] Duties or taxes imposed by law on goods imported into a country, or, rarely, on goods exported from a country. **3** Support given to a business by its customers. — *adj.* **1** Made or done to order; as, *custom* clothes. **2** Manufacturing or dealing in things made to order; as, a *custom* tailor.

cus·tom·ary \ˈkəst-m-ˌer-ē\ *adj.* According to custom; usual. — For synonyms see *usual.* — **cus·tom·ar·i·ly** \ˌkəst-m-ˈer-ə-lē\ *adv.*

cus·tom·er \ˈkəst-m-ər\ *n.* **1** A person who buys; especially, one who buys regularly from the same store. **2** A person; a fellow; as, a queer *customer.*

cus·tom·house \ˈkəst-m-ˌhau̇s\ *n.; pl.* **cus·tom·hous·es** \-ˌhau̇-zəz\. The building where customs are paid and where vessels are entered and cleared at a port.

cus·tom-made \ˈkəst-m-ˈ(m)ād\ *adj.* Made to order.

cut \ˈkət\ *v.;* **cut; cut·ting. 1** To divide, slash, or wound with something sharp; to cleave; to gash; as, to *cut* a finger; to *cut* a cake. **2** To make or form by cutting; as, to *cut* a diamond; to *cut* a tunnel through rock. **3** To make less; to reduce; to shorten; to dilute; as, to *cut* prices; to *cut* a motion picture film. **4** To pass through or across; as, lines that *cut* each other. **5** To go quickly, or by a short or direct route; as, to *cut* corners; to *cut* across a field. **6** To strike sharply, as with a whip; to hurt the feelings; to sting; as, a wind that *cuts* the face; to be *cut* by a remark. **7** To refuse to recognize an acquaintance; as, to *cut* an old friend. **8** To absent oneself from; as, to *cut* a class. **9** To perform; to make; as, to *cut* capers. **10** To divide a deck of cards. **11** To strike a ball so as to turn its course or give it a certain spin. **12** To be able to be divided or cleaved. Cheese *cuts* easily. **13** To make a stroke. The trainer *cut* at the lion with his whip. — **cut a tooth** or **cut one's teeth.** To have a tooth or teeth cut the way through the gum. — **cut off. 1** To put to an untimely end; to put an end to; as, a person *cut off* in his prime. **2** To interrupt; to intercept; as, to *cut off* communication. **3** To disinherit. The angry father threatened to *cut off* his son without a cent. — **cut out. 1** To fit; to intend; as, a person who is not *cut out* for acting. **2** To eliminate; as, to *cut out* unnecessary waste of material. **3** To stop doing or using; to cease; to omit. The policeman told the boys to *cut out* making so much noise. — *adj.* **1** Severed; slashed; divided; separated; pierced; as, a *cut* finger; *cut* flowers. **2** Shaped or ornamented, as by cutting or grinding; as, a *cut* diamond. **3** Reduced; as, attracted by *cut* prices. — *n.* **1** An opening made with something sharp; a gash; a wound. **2** A notch, passage, or channel made by excavating or worn by natural action, as of water. The road follows a *cut* through the hills. **3** The action or result of cutting; an injury; a wound; especially, a stroke or blow, as with a knife or whip. **4** A part cut off; as, a *cut* of pie; a *cut* of meat. **5** A reduction in amount or extent; as, a *cut* in pay. **6** The way in which a thing is cut or formed; style; shape; as, the *cut* of a coat. **7** A straight or easy passage. The old woods road provided a convenient *cut* through the forest. **8** An absence, as from class. **9** An engraved block or plate for printing or the picture printed from it; as, a book with fine *cuts.* **10** An action or expression that hurts the feelings; especially, a slight.

cu·ta·ne·ous \kyü-ˈtā-nē-əs\ *adj.* Of or relating to the skin; existing on or affecting the skin; as, a *cutaneous* infection.

cut·a·way \ˈkət-ə-ˌwā\ *n.* or **cutaway coat.** A

man's coat with skirts tapering from the front waistline to the tails.

cute \'kyüt\ *adj.;* **cut·er**; **cut·est**. [A shortened form of *acute.*] **1** Clever; shrewd; sharp. **2** Attractive, especially in a dainty or pretty way, as a child or a small animal.

cu·ti·cle \'kyüt-ik-l\ *n.* **1** A skin or membrane. **2** In animals having a backbone, the epidermis. **3** Dead skin, like that at the base and sides of a fingernail. **4** A thin detachable skin covering a plant.

cut·lass \'kət-ləs\ *n.; pl.* **cut·lass·es**. A short, heavy, curved sword, used especially by sailors.

cut·ler \'kət-lər\ *n.* One who makes, deals in, or repairs cutlery.

cut·lery \'kət-lər-ē\ *n.* **1** The business of a cutler. **2** Edged or cutting instruments, as knives and scissors. **3** Implements used in cutting, serving, and eating food.

cut·let \'kət-lət\ *n.* **1** A small piece of meat, cut usually from the leg or ribs of an animal, for broiling or frying. **2** A piece of fish or other food shaped like a cutlet.

cut·off \'kət-ˌȯf\ *n.* A passage or road that provides a short cut.

cut·out \'kət-ˌau̇t\ *n.* **1** Something cut out or prepared for cutting out from something else, such as a picture, shape, or design on paper or cardboard; as, a page of animal *cutouts.* **2** An electrical device, as a switch or circuit breaker, for interrupting or closing a connection.

cut·ter \'kət-r\ *n.* **1** A person or a thing that cuts; as, a diamond *cutter;* a cooky *cutter.* **2** A small sleigh. **3** A boat used by warships for carrying passengers and stores to and from the shore. **4** A small one-masted sailing vessel. **5** A small, armed vessel in the coast guard.

cut·throat \'kət-ˌthrōt\ *n.* A murderer. — *adj.* Murderous; cruel; destructive; ruinous; as, *cutthroat* competition.

cut·ting \'kət-ing\ *n.* **1** The act or process of a person or thing that cuts. **2** Something cut, cut off, or cut out; as a piece of stem, leaf, or root cut from a plant and used to produce new roots and a new plant. — *adj.* **1** That cuts or is suited to cut; as, the *cutting* edge of a knife. **2** Piercing; sharp; severe; as, a *cutting* wind; a *cutting* reply.

cut·tle·fish \'kət-l-ˌfish\ *n.; pl.* **cut·tle·fish** or **cut·tle·fish·es**. A ten-armed shellfish that sends out an inky fluid when pursued and that differs from the squid in having a hard inner shell (**cut·tle·bone** \'kət-l-ˌbōn\), which is used for polishing powder and bird food.

cut·worm \'kət-ˌwərm\ *n.* The night-feeding caterpillar of certain brown or gray stout-bodied moths, which eats off young plants, as cabbage and corn.

cy·a·nide \'sī-ə-ˌnīd\ *n.* Either of two highly poisonous compounds, **potassium cyanide** and **sodium cyanide**, used in exterminating vermin.

cy·cad \'sī-ˌkad, -kəd\ *n.* A fernlike tropical evergreen plant often grown in greenhouses.

cy·cle \'sīk-l\ *n.* **1** A period of time taken up by a series of events or actions that repeat themselves regularly and in the same order; as, the *cycle* of the seasons. **2** A complete course or series of events or operations, returning to the original state; circle; round; as, the *cycle* of the blood from the heart, through the blood vessels, and back to the heart again. **3** A long period of time; an age. **4** A bicycle or a motorcycle. **5** A complete set of two movements of an alternating electric current, one movement being opposite in direction to the other and following it in time. — *v.;* **cy·cled**; **cy·cling** \-l(-)ing\. To ride a cycle.

cy·clic \'sīk-lik, 'sik-\ *adj.* **1** Of or relating to a cycle. **2** Moving or repeating in cycles; as, the *cyclic* action of the heart. — **cy·cli·cal** \-lik-l\ *adj.*

cy·clist \'sīk-l(-)əst\ *n.* A person who rides a cycle, especially a bicycle.

cy·clone \'sīk-ˌlōn\ *n.* **1** A wind blowing circularly, especially in a storm. **2** A tornado. **3** A storm with rain and winds that rotate at 90 to 130 miles an hour in a counterclockwise direction in the Northern Hemisphere, around a calm central area of low atmospheric pressure; a hurricane; a typhoon. — **cy·clon·ic** \sī-'klän-ik\ or **cy·clon·i·cal** \-ik-l\ *adj.*

cy·clo·pe·dia or **cy·clo·pae·dia** \ˌsīk-lə-'pēd-ē-ə\ *n.* An encyclopedia.

cy·clo·tron \'sīk-lə-ˌträn\ *n.* A device for giving high speeds to charged particles by means of the combined action of a large magnetic force and a rapidly oscillating electric force.

cyg·net \'sig-nət\ *n.* A young swan.

cyl·in·der \'sil-ənd-r\ *n.* **1** A long round body, either hollow or solid. **2** Any body having the form of a cylinder, as the piston chamber in an engine, the barrel of a pump, or the part of a revolver which turns and into which the cartridges fit. — **cy·lin·dri·cal** \sə-'lin-drik-l\ or **cy·lin·dric** \-drik\ *adj.* — **cy·lin·dri·cal·ly** \-drik-l(-)ē\ *adv.*

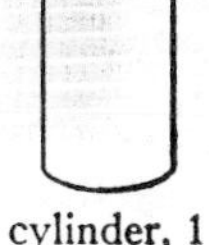
cylinder, 1

cym·bal \'sim-bl\ *n.* In music, one of a pair of brass concave plates that are clashed together to make a sharp, ringing sound.

cymbals

cyn·ic \'sin-ik\ *n.* A person who hates or distrusts others; especially, one who believes that human actions are prompted chiefly by self-interest.

cyn·i·cal \'sin-ik-l\ *adj.* Having the qualities or views of a cynic; especially, having or showing scornful distrust of men's goodness. — **cyn·i·cal·ly** \-ik-l(-)ē\ *adv.*

cyn·i·cism \'sin-ə-ˌsiz-m\ *n.* **1** A cynical temper or quality; the attitude of a cynic. **2** An instance or expression of such a quality or attitude; as, to reply with a *cynicism.*

cy·no·sure \'sī-nə-ˌshu̇r, 'sin-ə-\ *n.* **1** [with a capital] The constellation known as the Little Dipper.

2 A center of attraction or attention; as, the *cynosure* of all eyes.

cy·press \'sīp-rəs\ *n.* **1** A fragrant evergreen tree of the pine family, with small overlapping scalelike leaves and globe-shaped cones. **2** The similar related **bald cypress** of the southern United States. **3** The wood of any cypress.

cyst \'sist\ *n.* **1** A closed pouch or sac of fluid that develops in the body in some diseased conditions. **2** A cystlike covering such as that developed around bacteria in a resting stage.

cy·to·plasm \'sīt-ə-ˌplaz-m\ *n.* The protoplasm of a plant or animal cell exclusive of the nucleus.

czar \'zär, 'zȧr\ *n.* The title of the former emperors of Russia.

czar·i·na \zä-'rē-nə, zȧ-\ *n.* The title of the former empresses of Russia.

Czech \'chek\ *n.* **1** An individual of the most westerly branch of the Slavs. **2** The Czechoslovak language; especially, the language of the Czechs.

Czecho·slo·vak or **Czecho-Slo·vak** \ˌchek-ə-'slō-ˌväk, -ˌvak, -ˌvȧk\ *adj.* Of or relating to Czechoslovakia. — *n.* **1** A citizen or a native of Czechoslovakia. **2** The Slavic language of the Czechoslovaks. — **Czecho·slo·vak·i·an** or **Czecho-Slo·vak·i·an** \-slō-'väk-ē-ən, -'vak-, -'vȧk-\ *adj.* or *n.*

d \'dē\ *n.; pl.* **d's** \'dēz\. **1** The fourth letter of the alphabet. **2** As a Roman numeral, 500.

d. Abbreviation for: **1** *penny.* **2** *pence.*

dab \'dab\ *v.;* **dabbed; dab·bing. 1** To strike or hit with a sudden motion; to peck; as, hens *dabbing* at scattered grain. **2** To strike or touch gently, as with something soft; to tap or pat; as, to *dab* one's eyes with a handkerchief. — *n.* **1** A sharp or sudden jab, poke, or slap. **2** A gentle blow or pat. **3** A small, flattish mass of anything soft or moist; as, a *dab* of paint.

dab \'dab\ *n.* A flatfish; especially, any of several flounders.

dab·ble \'dab-l\ *v.;* **dab·bled; dab·bling** \-l(-)ing\. **1** To wet by splashing; to spatter. **2** To paddle in the water, as with the hands. **3** To work at something in a light or careless manner, without serious effort; as, to *dabble* in politics; to *dabble* at painting. — **dab·bler** \-l(-)ər\ *n.*

dace \'dās\ *n.; pl.* **dace** or **dac·es.** Any of several small North American freshwater fishes of the carp family.

dachs·hund \'däks-ˌhu̇nt, 'dȧks-, -ˌhu̇nd\ *n.* A small short-legged and long-bodied dog of a German breed developed for hunting badgers.

dac·tyl \'dakt-l\ *n.* A metrical foot consisting of one accented syllable followed by two unaccented syllables, as in *'kissable* or *'fashioned it.* — **dac·tyl·ic** \dak-'til-ik\ *adj.*

dad \'dad\ *n.* Father.

dad·dy \'dad-ē\ *n.; pl.* **dad·dies.** Father.

daddy long·legs \'lȯng-ˌlegz\. A spiderlike insect with a small rounded body and long slender legs.

da·do \'dād-ˌō\ *n.; pl.* **da·does. 1** The flat face of a pedestal between the base and top moldings. **2** The lower part of the wall of a room when specially set off, as by moldings.

dae·mon \'dē-mən\ *n.* **1** A guardian or attendant spirit. **2** A demon. — **dae·mon·ic** \dē-'män-ik\ *adj.*

daf·fo·dil \'daf-ə-ˌdil\ *n.* [From Dutch *de affodil* meaning "the asphodel".] A plant with blade-shaped leaves and showy yellow, white, or pinkish trumpet-shaped flowers having a scalloped edge and surrounded by leaflike segments at the base.

daf·fy \'daf-ē\ *adj.;* **daf·fi·er; daf·fi·est.** Foolish; crazy; daft.

daft \'daft\ *adj.* **1** Foolish; silly. **2** Crazy; insane.

dag·ger \'dag-r\ *n.* **1** A short knifelike weapon used for stabbing. **2** A mark [†] often used in printed matter to refer the reader to a note given somewhere else or to indicate the date of a person's death.

da·guerre·o·type \də-'ger-ə-ˌtīp, -ē-ə-ˌtīp\ *n.* An early form of photograph, produced on a silver plate or on a copper plate covered with silver.

dahl·ia \'dal-yə\ *n.* [Named after Anders *Dahl,* Swedish botanist, who died in 1789.] **1** A usually tall plant of the aster family with a root consisting of a potatolike tuber and with large, many-petaled flowers of bright red and other colors. **2** The flower or the root of the dahlia.

dai·ly \'dā-lē\ *adj.* Happening, done, or issued every day; as, a *daily* swim; a *daily* newspaper. — *adv.* Every day; day by day; as, to exercise *daily.* — *n.; pl.* **dai·lies.** A daily newspaper.

dain·ty \'dānt-ē\ *adj.;* **dain·ti·er; dain·ti·est. 1** Pleasing to the taste; delicious. **2** Delicately pretty; having soft, pleasing colors or a frail form; as, a *dainty* flower. **3** Having or showing delicate taste; fastidious; as, a *dainty* eater. — *n.; pl.* **dain·ties.** Something pleasing to the taste; a delicacy. — **dain·ti·ly** \'dānt-l-ē\ *adv.*

dairy \'der-ē\ *n.; pl.* **dair·ies. 1** A place where milk is stored or is made into butter and cheese. **2** Also **dairy farm.** A farm that produces and sells milk, butter, and cheese. **3** A company or a store that sells milk, butter, and cheese.

dairy cattle. Cattle raised especially to produce milk.

dair·y·ing \'der-ē-ing\ *n.* The business of operating a dairy.

dair·y·maid \'der-ē-ˌmād\ *n.* A woman or girl who works in a dairy.

dair·y·man \'der-ē-mən\ *n.; pl.* **dair·y·men** \-mən\. **1** A man who keeps or works in a dairy. **2** A man who sells dairy products.

da·is \'dā-əs, 'dī-\ *n.* A raised platform in a hall or in a large room.

dai·sy \'dā-zē\ *n.; pl.* **dai·sies.** [From Old English *daegeseage* meaning literally "day's eye".] **1** A low-growing European plant of the aster family, bearing solitary flower heads with yellow centers and small white or pink rays — in the United States called **English daisy. 2** A tall leafy-stemmed plant of the same family, the common American field daisy (**ox·eye daisy** \'äk-ˌsī\), with sharply notched leaves and larger flower heads with yellow center and long white rays.

daisies, 2

dale \'dāl\ *n.* A valley; a vale.

dalles \'dalz\ *n. pl.* The nearly vertical walls of a canyon or gorge or rapids between such walls.

dal·li·ance \'dal-ē-ən(t)s, 'dal-yən(t)s\ *n.* A dallying or trifling.

dal·ly \'dal-ē\ *v.;* **dal·lied** \-ēd\; **dal·ly·ing. 1** To play or toy with something; to sport; to trifle; as, to *dally* with an idea. **2** To waste time; to idle; as, to *dally* at one's work. **3** To linger; to delay; as, to *dally* on the way home.

dam \'dam\ *n.* **1** A wall or barrier to hold back a flow of water. **2** The water held back by a dam. **—** *v.;* **dammed; dam·ming.** To provide with a dam; to check the flow of; as, to *dam* a stream.

dam \'dam\ *n.* A female parent — used especially of four-footed animals.

dam·age \'dam-ij\ *n.* **1** Loss due to injury. **2** Injury to a person, or to property or reputation; harm; hurt. The storm did great *damage* to the trees. **3** [in the plural] Money demanded or paid for injuries to a person or for harm done to property; as, to collect *damages* from an automobile accident. **—** *v.;* **dam·aged; dam·ag·ing. 1** To cause damage to; to injure; as, a book *damaged* by careless handling. **2** To become damaged; as, goods that *damage* easily.

dam·ask \'dam-əsk\ *n.* **1** A cloth, commonly of silk or linen, having a woven satin pattern and a plain ground on one side and the reverse on the other, used for tablecloths and draperies. **2** A tough steel (**damask steel**) decorated with wavy lines. **3** A deep rose color. **—** *adj.* **1** Relating to or coming from the city of Damascus. **2** Made of damask. **3** Made of or resembling damask steel. **4** Of the color damask.

dame \'dām\ *n.* **1** A woman of position and authority, as, formerly, the mistress of a household. **2** [with a capital] A title sometimes used in place [illegible] *Lady, Madam, Mistress,* or *Miss,* as in ad[illegible]sing or referring to the widow of a knight or [illegible]t, the mistress of a household, or any elder[illegible] widow. **3** [with a capital] The title of [illegible] equal to that of knight.

damn[illegible] **damned** \'damd\; **damn·ing** [illegible] doom to everlasting punish[illegible] as bad or as a failure; to [illegible] To curse; to swear or swear at, using "damn" — often used to express mere annoyance or displeasure. **—** *n.* A curse.

dam·na·ble \'dam-nəb-l\ *adj.* **1** Deserving to be condemned; detestable; as, *damnable* conduct. **2** Very bad; very annoying; as, *damnable* weather; a *damnable* cold in the head. — **dam·na·bly** \-nə-blē\ *adv.*

dam·na·tion \dam-'nāsh-n\ *n.* The act of damning or the state of being damned; everlasting punishment — often used as an interjection expressing anger, annoyance, or disappointment.

damp \'damp\ *n.* **1** A harmful gas or mixture of gases occurring in coal mines. **2** Moisture; humidity. **—** *adj.* Moist; slightly wet; humid; as, *damp* night air. — For synonyms see *moist.* **—** *v.* **1** To make damp or moist. **2** To deaden; to dull; to check; as, to *damp* a fire; ambition *damped* by many failures. **3** To check the vibration of, as a piano string.

damp·en \'damp-n\ *v.;* **damp·ened; damp·en·ing** \-n(-)ing\. **1** To make or become moist; to wet slightly; as, to *dampen* a cloth. During the cool night the ground *dampened* slightly. **2** To dull; to deaden; as, news that *dampened* everyone's spirits. In spite of discouragements, our enthusiasm did not *dampen.*

damp·er \'damp-r\ *n.* **1** One that checks, discourages, or deadens; as, to be a *damper* at a party. **2** A valve or a movable plate that regulates the draft in the flue of a stove or a fireplace. **3** A device, as one of the felt-covered pieces of wood in a piano, used to deaden vibrations.

dam·sel \'damz-l\ *n.* A girl; a maiden.

dance \'dan(t)s\ *v.;* **danced; danc·ing. 1** To glide, step, or move through a rhythmic series of movements, usually in time to music; as, to learn to *dance.* **2** To move or seem to move about quickly and lightly; as, to *dance* with joy. The lights of the city *danced* in the rippling water of the lake. **3** To perform or take part in as a dancer; as, to *dance* a waltz **4** To dandle; as, to *dance* a baby on one's knee. **—** *n.* **1** A leaping, stepping, or gliding in a rhythmic series of movements, usually performed in time to music. **2** A turn at dancing; as, to plan to go home after the next *dance.* **3** A party at which dancing is the means of entertainment. **4** A piece of music for dancing.

danc·er \'dan(t)s-r\ *n.* One who dances; especially, one who dances professionally.

dan·de·li·on \'dand-l-ˌī-ən\ *n.* [From 16th century French *dent de lion* meaning literally "lion's tooth", and so called from the shape of the leaves.] **1** A weed of the chicory family, with deeply toothed stemless leaves and yellow flowers on hollow stems. **2** A flower of this weed.

dandelion

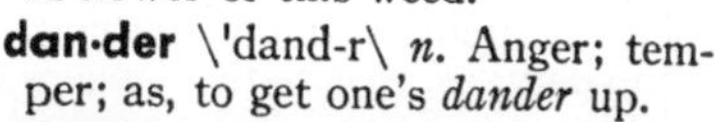

dan·der \'dand-r\ *n.* Anger; temper; as, to get one's *dander* up.

dan·dle \'dand-l\ *v.;* **dan·dled; dan·dling** \-l(-)ing\. **1** To move up and down on one's knee or in one's arms in affectionate play; as, to *dandle* a baby. **2** To fondle; to pamper.

dan·druff \'dan-drəf\ *n.* A thin, whitish crust that forms chiefly on hairy skin surfaces, especially the scalp, and comes off in small flakes. — **dan·druffy,** *adj.*

dan·dy \'dan-dē\ *n.; pl.* **dan·dies.** **1** A man who pays a great deal of attention to his clothing. **2** Something that is very good. This jackknife is a *dandy.* — *adj.;* **dan·di·er**; **dan·di·est.** Very good; first-class; as, a *dandy* bicycle. Everybody had a *dandy* time.

Dane \'dān\ *n.* A native or inhabitant of Denmark or a person of Danish descent.

dan·ger \'dānj-r\ *n.* **1** Exposure or liability to injury, harm, or other evil; peril. **2** Something that may cause injury or harm; a case of danger; as, storms and other *dangers* of the sea.

— The words *peril* and *risk* are synonyms of *danger: danger* may suggest some evil, as harm or injury, that is constantly in prospect; *peril* is likely to suggest an immediate and fearful danger or threat hanging over one; *risk* usually implies a voluntarily undertaken chance which places one in dangerous or doubtful circumstances.

dan·ger·ous \'dānj-r(-)əs\ *adj.* Full of danger; causing danger; risky; not safe; as, a *dangerous* crossing; a *dangerous* illness. — **dan·ger·ous·ly,** *adv.*

dan·gle \'dang-gl\ *v.;* **dan·gled**; **dan·gling** \-gl(-)ing\. **1** To hang loosely with a swinging or jerking motion; as, keys *dangling* from a chain. **2** To be left without proper grammatical connection; as, a *dangling* participle. **3** To be a hanger-on or a dependent; as, fortune hunters *dangling* after an heiress. **4** To cause to dangle; as, to sit on a bank and *dangle* one's feet in the water.

Dan·ish \'dā-nish\ *adj.* Of or relating to Denmark. — *n.* **1** The Danish people. **2** The language of Denmark.

dank \'dangk\ *adj.* Damp; wet; especially, disagreeably wet. — For synonyms see *moist.* — **dank·ly,** *adv.*

daph·nia \'daf-nē-ə\ *n.* A small water flea.

dap·per \'dap-r\ *adj.* **1** Neat in dress or appearance; trim. **2** Small and active.

dap·ple \'dap-l\ *n.* **1** A dappled state or appearance; a spotting; as, the *dapple* on a horse's sides. **2** A dappled animal, as a horse. — *v.;* **dap·pled**; **dap·pling** \-l(-)ing\. To mark with different-colored spots or patches. — *adj.* Dappled. The horse was a *dapple* gray.

dap·pled \'dap-ld\ *adj.* Marked with spots, especially with gray spots; as, a *dappled* horse.

dare \'dar, 'der\ *v.;* **dared** \'dard, 'derd\ or **durst** \'dərst\; **dared**; **dar·ing.** **1** To have courage enough for some purpose; to be unafraid; to be bold; to venture; as, to *dare* to undertake the journey. **2** To meet boldly; to defy; as, to *dare* the dangers of the sea. **3** To challenge to some action as proof of skill, strength, or courage; as, to *dare* a person to climb a tree. — *n.* A challenge; as, to swim across the river on a *dare.*

dare·dev·il \'dar-ˌdev-l, 'der-\ *n.* A recklessly bold person. — *adj.* Reckless; as, *daredevil* stunts.

dar·ing \'dar-ing, 'der-\ *n.* Fearless boldness; as, a boy with *daring* enough to do anything. — *adj.* Bold; as, a *daring* test pilot. — **dar·ing·ly,** *adv.*

dark \'därk, 'dȧrk\ *adj.* **1** Without light or without much light; as, a *dark* day. In winter it gets *dark* early. **2** Not light in color; more like black than white; as, a *dark* suit; *dark* blue. **3** Gloomy; not bright and cheerful; as, to look on the *dark* side of things. **4** Without knowledge and culture; ignorant; as, the *Dark* Ages. **5** Silent; secretive; as, to keep *dark* about the matter. — *n.* **1** Darkness; a dark place or time; night; nightfall; as, to get home just before *dark.* **2** A dark color, shade, or part, as in a painting. **3** The condition of being secret or obscure; underhand secrecy; ignorance; as, to be left in the *dark* about something. — **dark of the moon.** The time between a full moon and the next new moon, especially the few days when no moon is visible. — **dark·ly,** *adv.*

Dark Ages. Usually, the earlier part of the Middle Ages, the period from 476 A.D. to about 1400 A.D., characterized by its lack of learning and culture; sometimes, the whole period.

dark·en \'därk-n, 'dȧrk-n\ *v.;* **dark·ened**; **dark·en·ing** \-n(-)ing\. **1** To make or to grow dark or darker. Clouds *darkened* the sky. **2** To make or become gloomy; as, a life *darkened* by misfortune.

dark horse. **1** In racing, a horse whose chances of winning are not known, or a little-known horse that unexpectedly wins. **2** In politics, a candidate who is unexpectedly nominated for an office.

dark·ish \'därk-ish, 'dȧrk-\ *adj.* Somewhat dark; dusky.

dark lantern. A lantern with a single opening that may be closed to conceal the light.

dark·ling \'därk-l(-)ing, 'dȧrk-\ *adv.* In the dark. — *adj.* Being or occurring in darkness; dark.

dark·ness \'därk-nəs, 'dȧrk-\ *n.* The condition of being dark; absence of light; as, to leave a room in *darkness.*

dark·room \'därk-ˌrüm, 'dȧrk-, -ˌrům\ *n.* In photography, a room protected from rays of light harmful in the process of developing sensitive plates and film.

dark·some \'därks-m, 'dȧrks-m\ *adj.* Dark; darkish.

dar·ling \'där-ling, 'dȧr-\ *n.* A person whom one loves dearly. — *adj.* Dearly loved.

darn \'därn, 'dȧrn\ *v.* To mend, as a hole in cloth with interlacing stitches; as, to *darn* socks. — The action or result of darning; a place tha been darned; as, a *darn* that could hardly b

dar·nel \'därn-l, 'dȧrn-l\ *n.* A a weed from one small bristly clusters of greenish flo

darning needle. **1** A long, strong darning. **2** A dragonfly.

dart \ˈdärt, ˈdȧrt\ *n.* **1** A pointed missile to be thrown by the hand. **2** Any sharp-pointed missile, as one shot from a bow or blown from a blowgun. **3** A quick, sudden movement. **4** A short tapering seam made in fitting a garment to the figure. — *v.* **1** To throw with a sudden effort, as a weapon. **2** To shoot out suddenly. The toad *darted* its tongue at a fly. **3** To move like a dart; to shoot along rapidly; as, fish *darting* here and there in a pool.

dart, 1

dash \ˈdash\ *v.* **1** To smash; to shatter; as, to *dash* a glass on the floor. **2** To knock; to throw; to thrust; as, to *dash* away one's tears. **3** To splash; to spatter; as, to *dash* water on a person. **4** To write, sketch, or paint rapidly or carelessly; as, to *dash* off a letter. **5** To rush; to advance violently. The horse *dashed* wildly away. **6** To ruin; to frustrate; to depress; as, to *dash* a person's hopes. — *n.* **1** A blow or stroke; as, to destroy with a *dash* of the hand. **2** A mark [—] used in writing or printing to show a break in thought in a sentence, or to set off one part of a sentence from the rest. **3** The violent striking of a liquid or the sound of this; as, the *dash* of waves. **4** In signaling by telegraph, a long click that stands for a letter or part of a letter. **5** A small amount; a bit; as, a *dash* of salt. **6** Energy in manner or action; as, a man of *dash* and vigor. **7** A short, rapid movement; a rush; as, a *dash* for the goal. **8** A dashboard, as of a buggy. **9** A short race that can be run very fast; as, a 50-yard *dash*.

dash·board \ˈdash-ˌbōrd, -ˌbȯrd\ *n.* **1** A screen on the forepart of a vehicle to keep out water, mud, or snow. **2** In automobiles, a partition at the front of the body below the windshield.

dash·er \ˈdash-r\ *n.* Something that dashes, as a device that agitates the contents of a churn.

dash·ing \ˈdash-ing\ *adj.* **1** Full of dash or energy; spirited; as, a football team's *dashing* attack. **2** Showy; stylish; as, to make a *dashing* appearance in the Easter parade. — **dash·ing·ly**, *adv.*

das·tard \ˈdast-rd\ *n.* A coward; one that sneakingly does mean and spiteful things.

das·tard·ly \-lē\ *adj.* Mean and cowardly.

da·ta \ˈdāt-ə, ˈdat-ə, ˈdät-ə, ˈdȧt-ə\ *n. pl.; sing.* **da·tum** \-m\. Facts and information about something; as, to gather *data* for a study.

date \ˈdāt\ *n.* The edible brownish, pulpy fruit of a certain palm tree (**date palm**).

date \ˈdāt\ *n.* **1** A statement that gives the time and often the place of making or issuing something, as a book or a coin. **2** The day, month, or year on or in which something takes place; as, the *date* of a person's birth. **3** The period of time to which something belongs; as, airplanes of an early *date*. **4** An appointment to meet a person at a certain time; as, a *date* to go skating. **5** A person, especially one of the opposite sex, with whom one has a social appointment. — **out of date**. Behind the times; no longer in fashion. — **up to date**. **1** Up to the present time. **2** Up to modern standard or style. — *v.;* **dat·ed**; **dat·ing**. **1** To write a date on; as, to *date* a letter. **2** To give or assign a date to. **3** To belong to a certain period; as, styles *dating* from the 1920's. **4** To have or make a social appointment with a person of the opposite sex.

date·less \ˈdāt-ləs\ *adj.* **1** Without a date; undated. **2** Too old to be assigned a date. **3** Having no fixed term; endless. **4** Of lasting interest; never losing its appeal.

da·tive \ˈdāt-iv\ *n.* or **dative case**. The case of a noun or pronoun when it is the indirect object of a verb or, in some languages, the object of some prepositions, in English grammar distinguished from the accusative only by position or meaning.

datum. Sing. of *data*.

daub \ˈdȯb, ˈdäb\ *v.* **1** To cover with something soft and sticky; to smear; to plaster; as, to be *daubed* with mud. **2** To paint unskillfully. — *n.* **1** A daubed spot; a smear. **2** A badly painted picture. — **daub·er**, *n.*

daugh·ter \ˈdȯt-r\ *n.* **1** A girl or woman thought of in relation to her father or mother. **2** A woman or girl thought of as standing in relation to something, as a country, race, or religion, as child to parent; as, sons and *daughters* of America.

daughter cell. One of the cells resulting from the primary division of another cell, as in the process of growth.

daugh·ter-in-law \ˈdȯt-r-ən-ˌlȯ\ *n.; pl.* **daugh·ters-in-law**. The wife of one's son.

daugh·ter·ly \ˈdȯt-r-lē\ *adj.* Suited to or befitting a daughter; as, *daughterly* affection.

daunt \ˈdȯnt, ˈdänt\ *v.* To make afraid; to discourage.

daunt·less \ˈdȯnt-ləs, ˈdänt-\ *adj.* Not to be daunted; fearless; as, *dauntless* courage; a *dauntless* fighter. — **daunt·less·ly**, *adv.*

dau·phin \ˈdȯf-n\ *n.* The title of the eldest son of the kings of France.

dav·en·port \ˈdav-n-ˌpōrt, -ˌpȯrt\ *n.* **1** *Chiefly British.* A small writing desk. **2** A large upholstered sofa.

da·vit \ˈdā-vət, ˈdav-ət\ *n.* One of a pair of posts having curved arms and fitted with ropes and pulleys, used especially on ships for raising and lowering small boats.

davit davit

Da·vy Jones's locker \ˈdā-vē ˌjōnz(-əz)\. The bottom of the ocean; the grave of persons drowned at sea.

daw \ˈdȯ\ *n.* A jackdaw.

daw·dle \ˈdȯd-l\ *v.;* **daw·dled**; **daw·dling** \-l(-)ing\. To linger idly; to loiter; to waste time; as, to *dawdle* over breakfast; to *dawdle* on the way home. — **daw·dler** \-l(-)ər\ *n.*

dawn \ˈdȯn, ˈdän\ *v.* **1** To begin to grow light in the morning; as, to wait for the day to *dawn*. **2** To begin to appear or develop. A new age *dawned* with the invention of the steam engine. **3** To begin to make an impression. It *dawned* on me that I had been fooled. — *n.* **1** The break of day; the first light of morning. **2** First appearance; beginning; as, the *dawn* of travel by air.

day \'dā\ *n.* **1** The time of light between sunrise and sunset; daylight; as, to walk out of the house into the bright *day.* **2** The time the earth takes to make one turn on its axis. **3** A set period used in reckoning time, usually 24 hours, starting at midnight. **4** A contest or conflict taking place on some particular day; as, to win the *day.* **5** An age; time; as, a man well known in his *day.* **6** The time during a day set apart by custom or law for work; as, an eight-hour *day.*

day·break \'dā-ˌbrāk\ *n.* The dawn or the time at which dawn comes; as, to get up at *daybreak.*

day coach. An ordinary or standard railroad passenger car.

day·dream \'dā-ˌdrēm\ *n.* Dreamy thinking, usually of pleasant things. — *v.* To have daydreams. — **day·dream·er,** *n.*

day laborer. One who works by the day or for daily wages, especially as an unskilled laborer.

day·light \'dā-ˌlīt\ *n.* **1** The light of day; as, to play out of doors while *daylight* lasts. **2** Dawn; as, to work from *daylight* to dark.

daylight saving. The practice of making possible the fullest use of the hours of daylight by setting timepieces ahead, usually by one hour, in the early spring and setting them back to standard time in the fall.

day·star \'dā-ˌstär, -ˌstȧr\ *n.* The morning star.

day·time \'dā-ˌtīm\ *n.* The period of daylight.

daze \'dāz\ *v.;* **dazed; daz·ing.** To dazzle, stun, or confuse, as by too much light or by a sudden blow, or with fear or grief. — *n.* The confused state of mind of a person who is dazed. — **daz·ed·ly** \'dā-zəd-lē\ *adv.*

daz·zle \'daz-l\ *v.;* **daz·zled; daz·zling** \-l(-)ing\. **1** To confuse or to be confused by too much light or by moving lights; as, to be *dazzled* by the sunlight of the desert. **2** To bewilder, surprise, or excite admiration by a display of any kind; as, to be *dazzled* by a performance of acrobats. — *n.* A dazzling; anything that dazzles; as, a *dazzle* of lights. — **daz·zling·ly,** *adv.*

D.C. \'dē-'sē\. Abbreviation for *direct current.*

DDT \'dē-ˌdē-'tē\. A colorless, odorless substance used, usually in mixtures, to kill insects.

de-. A prefix that can mean: **1** Down, as in *depress.* **2** Away, off, or out of, as in *dethrone, detrain.* **3** Reversing, undoing, or taking away, as in *decentralize, deforest, deform.*

dea·con \'dēk-n\ *n.* **1** A clergyman or a layman who assists a priest or a minister. **2** A clergyman just below a priest in rank.

dead \'ded\ *adj.* **1** Lifeless; not living. **2** Without sensation or consciousness; deathlike; as, a *dead* faint. **3** Without motion; without activity, energy, or power; as, to come to a *dead* stop. **4** No longer in use; as, a *dead* custom; a *dead* language. **5** Lacking fire, glow, brightness, color, or sharp flavor. **6** Certain; never-failing; as, to be a *dead* shot with a rifle. **7** Complete; as, a *dead* loss. **8** In some games, out of play; as, a *dead* ball. — *n.* **1** A dead person; dead persons; as, to honor both the living and the *dead.* **2** The most quiet or deathlike time; as, the *dead* of night; the *dead* of winter. — *adv.* **1** Absolutely; entirely; as, apples that are *dead* ripe. **2** With sudden stopping of motion. The motor stopped *dead.* **3** Directly; exactly. The lights of the airport appeared *dead* ahead.

dead-beat \'ded-'bēt\ *adj.* Completely tired out.

dead·beat \'ded-ˌbēt\ *n.* A person who habitually fails to pay his debts, or to pay his way when in company with others.

dead·en \'ded-n\ *v.;* **dead·ened; dead·en·ing** \-n(-)ing\. To make dull or less strong; as, to *deaden* pain with drugs; to *deaden* sound with heavy curtains.

dead end \'ded 'end\. **1** An end, as of a street or other passage, having no opening. **2** A street or other passage having a dead end; a blind alley.

dead-end \'ded-ˌend\ *adj.* Having a dead end; as, a *dead-end* street.

dead·eye \'ded-ˌī\ *n.* A round flat wooden block pierced with holes, used on board ships for fastening the ropes that help to support the masts.

deadeye

dead heat. A heat, race, or other trial of skill in which the contestants reach the goal at the same time, so that there is no victor.

dead letter. **1** A letter that cannot be delivered, as because of an incorrect address or lack of postage, and is sent after a fixed time to a department of the general post office (**dead-letter office**) to be opened and then returned to the sender or destroyed. **2** A law or regulation that has lost its force but has not been officially abolished.

dead·line \'ded-ˌlīn\ *n.* The time set as a limit for doing or completing something; especially, the time after which no more copy can be accepted for publication, as in an edition of a newspaper.

dead·lock \'ded-ˌläk\ *n.* Stoppage of all action because one side in a struggle is as strong as the other side and neither will give in. — *v.* To bring or to come to a deadlock; as, a *deadlocked* meeting.

dead·ly \'ded-lē\ *adj.;* **dead·li·er; dead·li·est.** **1** Causing, or capable of causing, death; as, a *deadly* weapon; a *deadly* poison. **2** Fatal to spiritual progress; as, a *deadly* sin. **3** Aiming to destroy; willing to destroy; as, *deadly* enemies. **4** Like death; deathly; as, a *deadly* paleness. — *adv.* **1** Like death; as, *deadly* pale. **2** Extremely; excessively; as, *deadly* dull.

deadly nightshade. The belladonna plant.

dead march. A funeral march.

dead reckoning. A method of reckoning the position of a ship by figuring the distances it has covered and the direction it has traveled, without

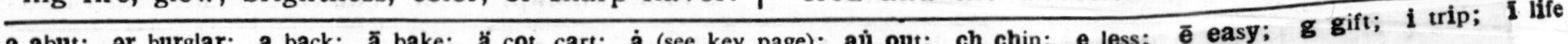

taking observations of celestial bodies, as the sun or stars.

dead weight. **1** The full weight of any inert or lifeless body. **2** A heavy or oppressive burden.

dead·wood \'ded-ˌwu̇d\ *n.* **1** Wood dead on the tree; dead branches. **2** Any useless or unsatisfactory material.

deaf \'def\ *adj.* **1** Wholly or partly unable to hear. **2** Unwilling to hear; as, *deaf* to all suggestions.

deaf·en \'def-n\ *v.* **1** To make deaf; as, to be *deafened* in childhood by an illness. **2** To stun with noise. The roar of the low-flying airplanes was *deafening.* — **deaf·en·ing·ly** \-n(-)ing-lē\ *adv.*

deaf-mute \'def-'myüt, -ˌmyüt\ *n.* A deaf person who cannot speak or has not been taught to speak; a deaf and dumb person.

deaf·ness \'def-nəs\ *n.* The condition or the degree of being deaf.

deal \'dēl\ *n.* **1** A part or portion; a share; an amount; as, to deserve a great *deal* of praise. **2** A considerable amount.

deal \'dēl\ *v.;* **dealt** \'delt\; **deal·ing** \'dē-ling\. **1** To give out in portions or shares; to distribute; as, to *deal* cards; to *deal* out sandwiches. **2** To give or deliver; as, to *deal* someone a blow. **3** To have to do with; as, a book that *deals* with airplanes. **4** To treat, act, or do; as, to *deal* harshly with anyone who breaks the rules. **5** To buy and sell; to trade; to handle in business; as, to *deal* in used cars. — *n.* **1** The action of dealing. **2** The distributing of the cards to the players in a card game; a player's turn to distribute the cards; a hand. **3** A business transaction; a bargain; as, to make a *deal* for a used car. **4** The treatment a person receives in business or other relations; as, to get a good *deal* on a new suit; to promise voters a fair *deal.* **5** A secret arrangement, as in political bargains.

deal·er \'dēl-r\ *n.* **1** A person who makes a business of buying and selling; as, an automobile *dealer.* **2** A person who deals the cards in a card game.

deal·ing \'dē-ling\ *n.* **1** [usually in the plural] Business transactions; as, to have *dealings* with an automobile agency. **2** A way of acting or of doing business; as, a man who is known to be fair in his *dealing.*

dealt. Past tense and past part. of *deal.*

dean \'dēn\ *n.* **1** In a cathedral church, the head of a body of canons or clergy. **2** A college official, under the president, supervising a school, a faculty, or students. **3** The senior member of a group; as, the *dean* of a diplomatic corps.

dear \'dir\ *adj.* **1** Highly valued; loved; precious; as, a *dear* friend. **2** In letters, an expression of politeness; as, *Dear* Sir. **3** High-priced; costly; expensive. That coat is too *dear* for my pocketbook. **4** Sincere; earnest. The boy's *dearest* wish is to see his mother. — *n.* A person that one loves. — *adv.* At a high price; as, to buy cheap and sell *dear.*

dear·ly \'dir-lē\ *adv.* **1** Fondly; very much; as, to love someone *dearly.* **2** At a high price or cost; as, to pay *dearly* for a mistake.

dearth \'dərth\ *n.* Scarcity; lack; as, a *dearth* of food.

death \'deth\ *n.* **1** The end of life in an animal or a plant; the act of dying; as, a painless *death.* **2** The cause of loss of life. Carelessness has been the *death* of many swimmers. **3** Anything so dreadful as to seem like death. **4** [with a capital] The destroyer of life, usually represented as a skeleton with a scythe. **5** The state of being dead; as, eyes closed in *death.* **6** A total loss; end; as, the *death* of all hope.

death·bed \'deth-'bed, -ˌbed\ *n.* **1** The bed in which a person dies. **2** The last hours of a person's life.

death·blow \'deth-'blō, -ˌblō\ *n.* A fatal or crushing blow.

death·less \'deth-ləs\ *adj.* Not subject to death; immortal; as, *deathless* fame.

death·like \'deth-ˌlīk\ *adj.* Like death; deathly; as, a *deathlike* paleness.

death·ly \'deth-lē\ *adj.* **1** Deadly; fatal. **2** Like death; as, a *deathly* silence. — *adv.* Deadly; as, *deathly* white; *deathly* sick.

death's-head \'deths-ˌhed\ *n.* A human skull thought of as standing for death.

de·bark \dē-'bärk, -'bȧrk\ *v.* To disembark. — **de·bar·ka·tion** \ˌdē-ˌbär-'kāsa-n, -ˌbȧr-\ *n.*

de·base \dē-'bās\ *v.;* **de·based; de·bas·ing.** To lower, as in value, purity, quality, or dignity; to degrade; as, to *debase* gold by mixing an alloy with it; to *debase* oneself by cheating. — **de·base·ment,** *n.*

de·bat·a·ble \dē-'bāt-əb-l\ *adj.* Able to be debated or disputed; open to question or dispute; as, a *debatable* question; a decision of *debatable* wisdom.

de·bate \dē-'bāt\ *v.;* **de·bat·ed; de·bat·ing.** **1** To discuss or examine a question by presenting and considering arguments on both sides. **2** To take part in a debate. **3** To present or consider the reasons for and against; to discuss; to consider. — For synonyms see *discuss.* — *n.* **1** A discussion; a controversy; an argument. **2** A formal discussion of a question between two sides, often as a test of speaking and reasoning ability.

de·bat·er \dē-'bāt-r\ *n.* One who debates; especially, a person who takes part in a formal debate.

de·bauch \dē-'bȯch, -'bäch\ *v.* To lead away from virtue or morality; to corrupt. — *n.* A period of indulgence in immoral or sensual pleasures; a time of debauchery.

de·bauch·ery \dē-'bȯch-r(-)ē, -'bäch-\ *n.; pl.* **de·bauch·er·ies.** Excessive indulgence of one's sensual desires; intemperance; sensuality.

de·bil·i·tate \dē-'bil-ə-ˌtāt\ *v.;* **de·bil·i·tat·ed; de·bil·i·tat·ing.** To make feeble; to weaken; as, to find oneself somewhat *debilitated* after a long series of colds; a climate of cold, bracing winters and hot, *debilitating* summers.

de·bil·i·ty \dē-'bil-ət-ē\ *n.; pl.* **de·bil·i·ties.** A weakened condition, especially of the body; feebleness.

deb·it \'deb-ət\ *n.* **1** Something, usually a sum of

money, entered in an account as a debt. **2** Any entry, or the sum of all entries on the side of an account that shows the amounts owed to a person or business. **3** The left-hand side of an account, where such entries are made. — *v.* To enter as a debit; to charge with, or as, a debt.

deb·o·nair or **deb·o·naire** \ˌdeb-n-ˈar, -ˈer\ *adj.* Courteous, graceful, and lighthearted; as, a *debonair* young man; a *debonair* manner. — **deb·o·nair·ly,** *adv.*

de·bris or **dé·bris** \də-ˈbrē, dā-\ *n.* **1** Rubbish, especially such as is left by the breaking down of something; ruins; litter. **2** In geology, any accumulation of fragments of rock.

debt \ˈdet\ *n.* **1** Something owed to another; the thing or the amount owed; as, to pay a *debt* of ten dollars. **2** The condition of owing money, especially in amounts greater than one can pay; as, to be hopelessly in *debt.*

debt·or \ˈdet-r\ *n.* One that owes a debt.

de·bunk \(ˈ)dē-ˈbəngk\ *v.* To remove the bunk from; especially, to show to be false or purely legendary long-held or widely accepted beliefs, as about a national hero.

de·but \ˈdā-ˌbyü; dā-ˈbyü, də-\ *n.* **1** The beginning of or entering upon a career; especially, the first public appearance, as of an actor or musician. **2** The formal entrance of a young woman into society.

deb·u·tante \ˈdeb-yə-ˌtänt, ˌdeb-yə-ˈtänt\ *n.* A young woman making her formal entrance into society.

Dec. Abbreviation for *December.*

dec·ade \ˈdek-ˌād, de-ˈkād, ˈdek-əd\ *n.* A group of ten; especially, a period of ten years.

dec·a·dence \ˈdek-ə-dən(t)s, dē-ˈkād-n(t)s\ *n.* A falling off to a lower level, as in morals, culture, or art; decline; decay.

dec·a·dent \ˈdek-ə-dənt, dē-ˈkād-nt\ *adj.* Showing decadence, as an art, a society, or a period of time. — *n.* One that is decadent.

de·cal \dē-ˈkal, ˈdē-ˌkal\ or **de·cal·co·ma·nia** \dē-ˌkal-kə-ˈmā-nē-ə\ *n.* **1** A picture or design so made that it can be permanently transferred to some object, as china or glass. **2** A process of transferring such pictures or designs from specially prepared paper.

dec·a·logue or **dec·a·log** \ˈdek-l-ˌȯg\ *n.* **1** [usually with a capital] The Ten Commandments, the laws given to Moses, in the Biblical account, by God on Mt. Sinai. **2** Any basic set of rules of action or behavior considered of the highest authority; as, a *decalogue* for diplomats.

de·camp \dē-ˈkamp\ *v.* **1** To move away from a camp, usually secretly or at night. **2** To leave suddenly; to run away; as, to *decamp* with money belonging to one's employer.

de·cant \dē-ˈkant\ *v.* **1** To pour off gently, as wine or a solution, so as not to disturb any sediment in the container. **2** To pour from one container into another.

de·cant·er \dē-ˈkant-r\ *n.* **1** A vessel for decanting liquids or receiving decanted liquids. **2** An ornamental glass bottle, usually fitted with a glass stopper, into which wine may be decanted; any ornamental wine or liquor bottle.

decanter

de·cap·i·tate \dē-ˈkap-ə-ˌtāt\ *v.;* **de·cap·i·tat·ed; de·cap·i·tat·ing.** To cut off the head of; to behead.

de·cath·lon \dē-ˈkath-lən, -ˌlän\ *n.* An athletic contest in which each competitor must participate in each of a series of ten track and field events.

de·cay \dē-ˈkā\ *v.* **1** To pass gradually from a healthy or prosperous condition to one that is unsound or imperfect; to fail; to waste away. **2** To decompose; to rot; to spoil; as, apples that *decayed* in storage. **3** To cause to undergo decay. — *n.* **1** Gradual failure, as of strength, health, or prosperity; as, the *decay* of a person's mind; the *decay* of a business. **2** Rot or rotting. Fruit picked and left in the hot sun is quickly affected by *decay.*

de·cease \dē-ˈsēs\ *n.* Death. — *v.;* **de·ceased; de·ceas·ing.** To die.

de·ceased \dē-ˈsēst\ *adj.* Dead; recently dead. — **the deceased.** The dead person.

de·ceit \dē-ˈsēt\ *n.* **1** An attempt to deceive; a statement or an act that misleads a person or causes him to believe what is false; a trick. **2** A leaning toward deceiving people; deceitfulness; as, to live a life free from *deceit.*

de·ceit·ful \dē-ˈsēt-fəl\ *adj.* **1** Practicing or tending to practice deceit. *Deceitful* people cannot expect to be trusted. **2** Showing or containing deceit or fraud; misleading; tricky; as, a *deceitful* answer. — **de·ceit·ful·ly** \-fə-lē\ *adv.*

de·ceive \dē-ˈsēv\ *v.;* **de·ceived; de·ceiv·ing. 1** To cause to believe what is untrue; to mislead; as, to *deceive* a person about one's real intentions. **2** To impose upon; to deal with dishonestly; to cheat. **3** To use or practice deceit. — **de·ceiv·er,** *n.*

de·cel·er·ate \dē-ˈsel-r-ˌāt\ *v.;* **de·cel·er·at·ed; de·cel·er·at·ing.** To slow down; to move with decreasing speed. — **de·cel·er·a·tion** \(ˌ)dē-ˌsel-r-ˈāsh-n\ *n.*

De·cem·ber \dē-ˈsem-br\ *n.* [From Latin, the tenth month of the ancient Roman year, derived from *decem* meaning "ten".] The twelfth and last month of the year, having 31 days.

de·cen·cy \ˈdēs-n-sē\ *n.; pl.* **de·cen·cies. 1** The quality or state of being decent or proper; modest or proper behavior or words; as, to keep one's language within the bounds of *decency.* Ordinary *decency* demanded that we help the injured man. **2** [usually in the plural] That which is proper; as, to be brought up to pay attention to the *decencies* of everyday life.

de·cen·ni·al \dē-ˈsen-ē-əl\ *adj.* Consisting of or happening every ten years; as, a *decennial* census. — *n.* A tenth anniversary. — **de·cen·ni·al·ly** \-ē-ə-lē\ *adv.*

de·cent \'dēs-nt\ *adj.* **1** Up to an accepted standard, as of speech, dress, or behavior; respectable; as, to keep oneself looking *decent.* **2** Modest; not obscene; as, to keep one's language *decent* at all times. **3** Fairly good; as, to earn quite a *decent* living; to try to get *decent* marks in school. — **de·cent·ly**, *adv.*

de·cen·tral·ize \dē-'sen-trə-ˌlīz\ *v.;* **de·cen·tral·ized; de·cen·tral·iz·ing. 1** To divide, as the administration of public affairs, and distribute among local governments. **2** To remove or disperse, as population or industry, from centers of concentration and resettle in outlying districts. — **de·cen·tral·i·za·tion** \(ˌ)dē-ˌsen-trə-lə-'zāsh-n\ *n.*

de·cep·tion \dē-'sepsh-n\ *n.* **1** The act of deceiving or the state or fact of being deceived. **2** Something that deceives or is meant to deceive; a trick.

de·cep·tive \dē-'sep-tiv\ *adj.* Deceiving; false; misleading; as, a *deceptive* appearance of strength. — **de·cep·tive·ly**, *adv.*

dec·i·bel \'des-ə-ˌbel, 'des-əb-l\ *n.* A unit for measuring the loudness of sounds.

de·cide \dē-'sīd\ *v.;* **de·cid·ed; de·cid·ing. 1** To determine; to settle; to choose; as, to *decide* a law case in favor of the defendant; to let a series of three games *decide* which is the better team. **2** To come to a conclusion; to make up one's mind; as, to *decide* where to spend the holidays; to *decide* to study medicine.

de·cid·ed \dē-'sīd-əd\ *adj.* **1** Clear; unmistakable; as, a *decided* smell of gas in the cellar. **2** Firm; determined; as, to speak in a *decided* tone of voice.

de·cid·ed·ly \dē-'sīd-əd-lē\ *adv.* Definitely; clearly; unmistakably; as, *decidedly* the better of the two.

de·cid·u·ous \dē-'sij-ə-wəs\ *adj.* **1** Falling off or shed at maturity or at certain seasons, as the leaves of some trees or the antlers of deer. **2** Having leaves that fall at certain seasons; as, *deciduous* trees.

dec·i·mal \'des-m-əl\ *adj.* Based on the number 10; numbered or counting by 10's, each unit being 10 times the next smaller unit; as, a *decimal* system of weights and measures. — *n.* A fraction (**decimal fraction**) in which the denominator is 10 or some multiple of 10, usually written with a point or dot (**decimal point**) at its left, as in .2 for $\frac{2}{10}$ or .02 for $\frac{2}{100}$. — **dec·i·mal·ly** \-ə-lē\ *adv.*

dec·i·mate \'des-m-ˌāt\ *v.;* **dec·i·mat·ed; dec·i·mat·ing. 1** To take or destroy the tenth part of. **2** To destroy a large part of; as, a population *decimated* by an epidemic. — **dec·i·ma·tion** \ˌdes-m-'āsh-n\ *n.*

de·ci·pher \(')dē-'sīf-r\ *v.* **1** To find out the meaning of; to translate from code or other secret writing; to decode; as, to *decipher* a message. **2** To make out; to read; as, to *decipher* writing that has been partly erased.

de·ci·sion \dē-'sizh-n\ *n.* **1** The act or the result of deciding; as, to await the *decision* of the judges. **2** Promptness and firmness in deciding; determination; as, a man of courage and *decision.*

de·ci·sive \dē-'sī-siv\ *adj.* **1** Having the power to decide a question or argument; as, to have the *decisive* vote in a meeting. **2** Of such nature as to settle a question or dispute; as, a *decisive* victory; *decisive* proof. **3** Marked by or showing decision; as, to speak in a *decisive* manner. — **de·ci·sive·ly**, *adv.*

deck \'dek\ *v.* **1** To clothe richly; to adorn; as, to *deck* oneself with jewels; all *decked* out in her Sunday best. **2** To furnish with a deck; as, to *deck* a ship. — *n.* **1** A floorlike platform that extends from side to side of a ship. **2** A flat space resembling a ship's deck, as a flat surface on an airplane. **3** A pack of playing cards.

deck·hand \'dek-ˌhand\ *n.* or **deck hand**. A sailor that works on the deck of a ship; a common seaman.

de·claim \dē-'klām\ *v.* To speak or deliver in the manner of a formal oration. — **de·claim·er**, *n.*

dec·la·ma·tion \ˌdek-lə-'māsh-n\ *n.* **1** The delivery of a formal speech in public; especially, the recitation of selected speeches as a school exercise. **2** Something suitable for declaiming.

de·clam·a·to·ry \dē-'klam-ə-ˌtōr-ē, -ˌtȯr-ē\ *adj.* **1** Relating to or of the nature of declamation. **2** Loud and impressive; as, a *declamatory* voice.

dec·la·ra·tion \ˌdek-lə-'rāsh-n\ *n.* **1** A declaring; a statement; an announcement; as, to make a *declaration* of one's purpose. **2** Something that is declared, or a document containing it; as, the *Declaration* of Independence.

de·clar·a·tive \dē-'klar-ət-iv\ *adj.* Making a declaration or statement; as, a *declarative* sentence. — **de·clar·a·to·ry** \-ə-ˌtōr-ē, -ˌtȯr-ē\ *adj.*

de·clare \dē-'klar, -'kler\ *v.;* **de·clared; de·clar·ing. 1** To make known clearly to other persons; to announce; to proclaim; as, to *declare* one's intentions; to *declare* war. **2** To state positively; to affirm. The prisoner *declared* that he was innocent. **3** To mention or list taxable articles in one's possession, especially those being brought or sent into one's own country from abroad; as, to *declare* a camera bought in Switzerland and three bottles of French perfume.

de·clen·sion \dē-'klench-n\ *n.* **1** A sloping downward; a descent; as, the *declension* of the land toward the sea. **2** In grammar, changes in the case of a noun, pronoun, or adjective to show the relationship of any of these words to other words in a sentence. **3** A regular or schematic arrangement of the case forms of a noun, a pronoun, or an adjective.

dec·li·na·tion \ˌdek-lə-'nāsh-n\ *n.* **1** A bending downward; an inclining. **2** A courteous refusal. **3** The angle that the magnetic needle makes with a true north and south line.

de·cline \dē-'klīn\ *v.;* **de·clined; de·clin·ing. 1** To bend or slope downward; to depress. The hill *declined* toward the road. **2** To draw toward a close, decay, or downfall; to become weaker. The power of the dictator *declined* as his armies were defeated. **3** To refuse; to reject; as, to *decline* an invitation. **4** To give in order the changes in case of a noun, pronoun, or adjective.

— The words *refuse* and *reject* are synonyms of *decline: decline* may suggest courtesy, and is used especially in connection with invitations or offers of help; *refuse* may be more positive, and may imply decisiveness or ungraciousness; *reject* usually indicates a complete throwing aside or a refusal to have anything to do with a person or thing.

— *n.* **1** The action or time of declining; a diminishing or decay; the period when something nears its end; as, the *decline* of day. **2** A downward incline, as in price; a downward slope; as, a slight *decline* in the road.

de·cliv·i·ty \dē-'kliv-ət-ē\ *n.; pl.* **de·cliv·i·ties. 1** A slope downward; a descent. The lawn has a graded *declivity* toward the street. **2** A descending slope, as of a hill.

de·code \(')dē-'kōd\ *v.;* **de·cod·ed**; **de·cod·ing.** To change from code to ordinary language; as, to *decode* a secret message.

de·com·mis·sion \ˌdēk-m-'ish-n\ *v.* To put out of commission; as, a *decommissioned* battleship.

de·com·pose \ˌdēk-m-'pōz\ *v.;* **de·com·posed**; **de·com·pos·ing. 1** To separate a thing into its parts or into simpler compounds. **2** To rot; to decay.

de·com·po·si·tion \(ˌ)dē-ˌkämp-ə-'zish-n\ *n.* The act or process of decomposing; decay.

de·com·press \ˌdēk-m-'prēs\ *v.* To release from pressure or compression, as a diver. — **de·com·pres·sion** \-'presh-n\ *n.*

dec·o·rate \'dek-r-ˌāt\ *v.;* **dec·o·rat·ed**; **dec·o·rat·ing. 1** To make a thing more attractive by adding something beautiful or becoming; to adorn; as, to *decorate* a room. **2** To award a decoration of honor to; as, to *decorate* a soldier for bravery.

dec·o·ra·tion \ˌdek-r-'āsh-n\ *n.* **1** The act of decorating; an ornamenting. **2** Something that adorns or beautifies; an ornament; as, Christmas tree *decorations.* **3** A mark of honor, as a medal, cross, or ribbon to be worn on a person's breast.

Decoration Day. Memorial Day.

dec·o·ra·tive \'dek-r(-)ət-iv, 'dek-r-ˌāt-\ *adj.* Ornamental.

dec·o·ra·tor \'dek-r-ˌāt-r\ *n.* A person who decorates; especially, one who makes a business of decorating the interiors of houses.

dec·o·rous \'dek-r-əs, dē-'kōr-əs, dē-'kȯr-\ *adj.* Proper; seemly; suitable to the time, place, or occasion; as, *decorous* behavior. — **dec·o·rous·ly**, *adv.*

de·co·rum \dē-'kōr-əm, -'kȯr-\ *n.* **1** Conformity to accepted standards of conduct; proper behavior; as, social *decorum.* **2** Orderliness; propriety; as, to disturb the *decorum* of the meeting.

de·coy \'dē-ˌkȯi, dē-'kȯi\ *n.* [From Dutch *de kooi* meaning literally "the cage".] **1** Something used to lead a person or creature into a snare; a bait. **2** A duck, or an imitation of one, used to attract other ducks within range of the hunter. **3** A person employed to lure another person into a position where he may be robbed or trapped. — \dē-'kȯi\ *v.* To lure or be lured by a decoy.

de·crease \dē-'krēs\ *v.;* **de·creased**; **de·creas·ing.** To grow less; to cause to grow less; to diminish; as, to *decrease* the speed of a car. The number of college students *decreased* during the war. — \'dē-ˌkrēs, dē-'krēs\ *n.* **1** A diminishing; a lessening. Safety experts are working for a *decrease* in automobile accidents. **2** The amount by which a thing decreases; a reduction; as, a *decrease* of three dollars a week in wages.

de·cree \dē-'krē\ *n.* An order or decision given by a person or group that has authority; a law. The general's *decree* ordered that the streets be cleared by nine o'clock. — *v.;* **de·creed**; **de·cree·ing.** To issue a decree; to order.

de·crep·it \dē-'krep-ət\ *adj.* Broken down with age; worn out.

de·crep·i·tude \dē-'krep-ə-ˌtüd, -ˌtyüd\ *n.* Weakness, as from old age; infirmity; as, the pitiful *decrepitude* of the old soldier.

de·cre·scen·do \ˌdā-krə-'shen-ˌdō\ *adj.* or *adv.* In music, gradually decreasing in fullness or loudness. — *n.; pl.* **de·cre·scen·dos.** A gradual decrease in loudness.

de·cry \dē-'krī\ *v.;* **de·cried** \-'krīd\; **de·cry·ing. 1** To speak slightingly of; to belittle publicly; as, to *decry* a hero's deeds. **2** To find fault with; to condemn. The president *decried* the waste of our country's natural resources.

ded·i·cate \'ded-ə-ˌkāt\ *v.;* **ded·i·cat·ed**; **ded·i·cat·ing. 1** To set apart for a certain purpose, especially a sacred or serious purpose; to devote; as, to *dedicate* a church; to *dedicate* one's life to helping others. **2** To address or inscribe as a compliment. The novelist *dedicated* his first book to his mother. — **ded·i·ca·tor** \-ˌkāt-r\ *n.*

ded·i·ca·tion \ˌded-ə-'kāsh-n\ *n.* **1** A dedicating to a sacred use; a setting aside of something for a special purpose. **2** The rites used in dedicating. **3** A name or a message in the front of a book or article, expressing admiration for a friend or a cause. — **ded·i·ca·tive** \'ded-ə-ˌkāt-iv\ or **ded·i·ca·to·ry** \-kə-ˌtōr-ē, -ˌtȯr-ē\ *adj.*

de·duce \dē-'düs, -'dyüs\ *v.;* **de·duced**; **de·duc·ing. 1** To trace the course of; as, to *deduce* one's descent. **2** To reach a conclusion by deduction; to derive by reasoning. — **de·duc·i·ble** \-'dü-səb-l, -'dyü-\ *adj.*

de·duct \dē-'dəkt\ *v.* To take away an amount of something; to subtract; as, to *deduct* one's expenses. — **de·duct·i·ble** \-'dək-təb-l\ *adj.*

de·duc·tion \dē-'dəksh-n\ *n.* **1** A deducting or taking away; subtraction; as, a weekly *deduction* from one's wages. **2** The amount deducted. **3** A reaching of a conclusion by reasoning or the conclusion reached. **4** The method of reasoning by which one argues that something that is true of all instances must be true of individual instances; reasoning from the general to the particular.

de·duc·tive \dē-'dək-tiv\ *adj.* Of deduction; using

deduction; as, *deductive* reasoning. — **de·duc·tive·ly**, *adv.*

deed \'dēd\ *n.* **1** Something that is done; an act; an action; as, a brave *deed;* to judge a person by his *deeds.* **2** A legal document that contains the record of a transfer of property, of a bargain, or of a contract. — **in deed.** In fact; in truth. — *v.* To transfer by deed; as, to *deed* a house.

deem \'dēm\ *v.* To think; to have an opinion; to judge; to suppose; as, to *deem* it wise.

deep \'dēp\ *adj.* **1** Reaching down far below the surface; as, *deep* roots; *deep* snow. **2** Reaching far back from the front or outer part; remote; hidden away; as, a *deep* forest; *deep* in seclusion. **3** Coming from or reaching to a place far down, back, or within; as, a *deep* sigh. **4** Hard to understand; as, a *deep* book. **5** Dark and rich in color. Ruby is a *deep* red. **6** Extremely busy with something; completely occupied; as, to be *deep* in study. **7** Heavy; heartfelt; as, *deep* sleep; *deep* sorrow. **8** Low or full in tone; as, a *deep* voice. — *n.* **1** An extremely deep place, especially the ocean; as, the briny *deep.* **2** The middle or most intense part; as, the *deep* of winter. — *adv.* **1** To a great depth; deeply; as, to drink *deep.* **2** Far along; as, *deep* in the night. — **deep·ly**, *adv.*

deep·en \'dēp-n\ *v.;* **deep·ened**; **deep·en·ing** \-n(-)ing\. To make or to become deep or deeper; to increase in depth or strength; as, to *deepen* a well.

deep-root·ed \'dēp-'rüt-əd, -'růt-\ *adj.* Having deep roots; deeply embedded or implanted; as, a *deep-rooted* tree; *deep-rooted* ideas.

deep-sea \'dēp-'sē\ *adj.* Of or relating to the deeper parts of the sea; as, *deep-sea* fishing.

deep-seat·ed \'dēp-'sēt-əd\ *adj.* Settled deeply within; not easily removed; as, a *deep-seated* dislike.

deep-set \'dēp-'set\ *adj.* Set far in; sunken; as, *deep-set* eyes.

deer \'dir\ *n. sing. and pl.* [From Old English *deor* meaning "animal".] A cud-chewing animal the male of which has long branching horns that are shed and renewed annually; especially, in Europe and Asia, the red deer, or common stag, the smaller fallow deer, or the still smaller roe deer, and, in America, the white-tailed Virginia deer of the eastern United States or the long-eared mule deer of western North America.

deer·skin \'dir-ˌskin\ *n.* **1** The skin of a deer or leather made from it. **2** A garment made of such leather.

def. Abbreviation for *definition.*

de·face \dē-'fās\ *v.;* **de·faced**; **de·fac·ing**. To mar the face or appearance of; to disfigure; as, to *deface* a picture. — **de·face·ment**, *n.*

de·fal·ca·tion \ˌdē-ˌfal-'kāsh-n, -ˌfȯl-\ *n.* **1** A misuse or theft of money by a person who holds it in trust for someone else. **2** The sum misused or stolen.

def·a·ma·tion \ˌdef-ə-'māsh-n\ *n.* The act of defaming; injury to the good name of another; slander; libel.

de·fam·a·to·ry \dē-'fam-ə-ˌtōr-ē, -ˌtȯr-ē\ *adj.* Intended to defame or having the effect of defaming; harmful to another's reputation.

de·fame \dē-'fām\ *v.;* **de·famed**; **de·fam·ing**. To injure or destroy the good name of; to speak evil of; to slander; to libel.

de·fault \dē-'fȯlt\ *n.* Failure to do something required by law or duty, as to pay a debt, to appear for the trial of a case in which one is either plaintiff or defendant, or to engage in or finish a contest in which one has declared oneself a contestant. — *v.* To fail to carry out a contract, obligation, or duty; to fail to perform or to pay.

de·feat \dē-'fēt\ *v.* **1** To cause to fail or to prevent the success of; to bring to nothing; to frustrate; as, to have all one's plans *defeated.* **2** To overcome; to vanquish; as, to *defeat* an enemy in battle. — *n.* **1** A thwarting or frustrating; prevention of success; as, the *defeat* of one's hopes. **2** An overthrow; loss of a contest; as, to meet *defeat* in a basketball game.

de·feat·ism \dē-'fēt-ˌiz-m\ *n.* An attitude of expecting the defeat of one's own cause or undertaking or of accepting or wishing for such defeat on the ground that further effort would be useless or unwise. — **de·feat·ist** \-'fēt-əst\ *n.* or *adj.*

de·fect \'dē-ˌfekt, dē-'fekt\ *n.* A lack of something necessary for completeness or perfection; a fault; a flaw; an imperfection; as, a *defect* in vision. Goods are often reduced in price because of having small *defects.* — For synonyms see *blemish.*

de·fec·tion \dē-'feksh-n\ *n.* The act of abandoning or deserting a person, party, or cause to which one is bound by ties of duty or allegiance.

de·fec·tive \dē-'fek-tiv\ *adj.* Imperfect; faulty; as, *defective* electric wiring; *defective* hearing. — *n.* One that is defective, as a person lacking normal intelligence. — **de·fec·tive·ly**, *adv.*

de·fend \dē-'fend\ *v.* **1** To protect from danger or harm; to guard against attack; to protect; as, to *defend* oneself against enemies. **2** To uphold; to maintain against opposition; as, to *defend* an idea in an argument. **3** To act on behalf of, as a lawyer for an accused person. **4** To oppose the claim of another, as in a lawsuit; to contest. — **de·fend·er**, *n.*

de·fend·ant \dē-'fen-dənt\ *n.* A person required to make answer in a legal action or suit.

de·fense or, chiefly British, **de·fence** \dē-'fen(t)s\ *n.* **1** The act of defending; resistance against attack; as, to take part in the *defense* of a city. **2** Something that defends or protects; as, the *defenses* of the city. Vaccination is the best *defense* against smallpox. **3** The answer made by the defendant in a legal action or suit. **4** In games, the guarding of oneself or one's goal from attack, or the player or players whose primary duty is to protect the goal. — **de·fense·less** or **de·fence·less**, *adj.*

de·fen·si·ble \dē-'fen(t)s-əb-l\ *adj.* Capable of

being defended. — **de·fen·si·bil·i·ty** \dē-ˌfen(t)s-ə-'bil-ət-ē\ *n.* — **de·fen·si·bly** \dē-'fen(t)s-ə-blē\ *adv.*

de·fen·sive \dē-'fen(t)s-iv\ *adj.* Serving or intended to defend or protect; as, a *defensive* war; a *defensive* alliance. — *n.* A defensive position, attitude, or course of action; as, to be put on the *defensive* by the unexpected attack. — **de·fen·sive·ly**, *adv.*

de·fer \dē-'fər\ *v.;* **de·ferred; de·fer·ring.** To put off to a future time; to postpone; to delay; as, to *defer* making a difficult decision as long as possible. Many things can be bought on credit, with payment *deferred* until later.

de·fer \dē-'fər\ *v.;* **de·ferred; de·fer·ring.** To yield to the opinion or wishes of another or to authority. It is polite for young people to *defer* to their elders.

def·er·ence \'def-rn(t)s, -r(-)ən(t)s\ *n.* The act of deferring to another; courteous regard for the wishes of another; respect; as, to treat one's parents with *deference.* Very old people have a right to expect *deference* from the young.

def·er·en·tial \ˌdef-r-'ench-l\ *adj.* Showing deference; courteously respectful; as, a *deferential* manner. — **def·er·en·tial·ly** \-'ench-l-ē\ *adv.*

de·fer·ment \dē-'fər-mənt\ *n.* The act of deferring or delaying; a postponement; especially, an official postponement of compulsory service in the armed forces.

de·fer·ra·ble or **de·fer·a·ble** \dē-'fər-əb-l\ *adj.* Subject to or eligible for deferment, especially from compulsory service in the armed forces. — *n.* One that is eligible for deferment.

de·fi·ance \dē-'fī-ən(t)s\ *n.* **1** The act of defying; a challenge; as, a shout of *defiance.* **2** A willingness to resist; contempt of opposition or authority; as, to cross the street in *defiance* of traffic rules; to show *defiance* toward those in authority.

de·fi·ant \dē-'fī-ənt\ *adj.* Showing defiance; bold; insolent. — **de·fi·ant·ly**, *adv.*

de·fi·cien·cy \dē-'fish-n-sē\ *n.; pl.* **de·fi·cien·cies.** **1** The quality or state of being deficient; a lack of something necessary for completeness; as, a vitamin *deficiency.* **2** A shortage, as of money; a deficit; as, a *deficiency* of 15 dollars in the class treasury.

deficiency disease. A disease, as scurvy or beriberi, caused by a diet lacking in certain elements, usually vitamins or minerals.

de·fi·cient \dē-'fish-nt\ *adj.* Lacking something necessary for completeness; not up to a given or normal standard; defective; as, a diet *deficient* in proteins; to be *deficient* in arithmetic on one's first report. — *n.* One that is deficient; especially, a person who is mentally deficient.

def·i·cit \'def-ə-sət\ *n.* A deficiency in amount; a shortage, especially of money; as, a large *deficit* in the finances of the city government.

de·file \dē-'fīl\ *v.;* **de·filed; de·fil·ing.** **1** To make filthy; to corrupt; to foul. **2** To make unfit or unclean for ceremonial use by disrespectful treatment; to desecrate; as, to *defile* a church; to *defile* a shrine. **3** To bring dishonor upon; as, to *defile* a person's reputation.

de·file \dē-'fīl, 'dē-ˌfīl\ *n.* A narrow pass or gorge.

de·file \dē-'fīl\ *v.;* **de·filed; de·fil·ing.** To march off in a single line, one file after another.

de·file·ment \dē-'fīl-mənt\ *n.* **1** The act of defiling or state of being defiled; a dirtying or making foul. **2** Something that defiles.

de·fine \dē-'fīn\ *v.;* **de·fined; de·fin·ing.** **1** To establish or state clearly and with authority; as, to *define* the duties and powers of an official. **2** To mark the limits of; as, to *define* the area of a playground. **3** To make distinct and clear in outline; as, a tree sharply *defined* against the sky. **4** To describe or explain; to determine and state the meaning of, as a word. — **de·fin·a·ble**, *adj.*

def·i·nite \'def-n(-)ət\ *adj.* **1** Having certain or distinct limits; fixed; as, a *definite* amount of money; a *definite* period of time. **2** Clear in meaning; exact; explicit; as, a *definite* answer.

definite article. The word *the* used before a noun to show that the noun refers to one or more particular persons or things.

def·i·nite·ly \'def-n(-)ət-lē\ *adv.* Clearly; unquestionably; without doubt.

def·i·ni·tion \ˌdef-n-'ish-n\ *n.* **1** An explanation of the meaning or meanings of a word or a term; as, to look up a *definition* in a dictionary. **2** The act or power of making definite and clear or of bringing into sharp outline; as, the *definition* of a pair of binoculars. **3** Clearness of outline or detail, as in a photograph. **4** The degree of precision with which a radio or television receiver reproduces sounds or images.

de·fin·i·tive \dē-'fin-ət-iv\ *adj.* Serving to define or settle something finally; conclusive; positive; as, a *definitive* answer. — **de·fin·i·tive·ly**, *adv.*

de·flate \(')dē-'flāt\ *v.;* **de·flat·ed; de·flat·ing.** **1** To let the air or gas out of something that has been blown up; as, to *deflate* a balloon; a *deflated* tire. **2** To reduce, as a currency, from a state of inflation.

de·fla·tion \dē-'flāsh-n\ *n.* **1** The act of deflating or the state of being deflated. **2** A reduction in the amount of currency or credit available for use in relation to the amount of goods available for purchase, usually causing a fall in prices.

de·flect \dē-'flekt\ *v.* To turn or cause to turn aside, as from a course or direction; as, a stream *deflected* from its course by a large rock; a bullet *deflected* by striking a wall. — **de·flec·tion** \dē-'fleksh-n\ *n.*

de·for·est \(')dē-'fȯr-əst, -'fär-\ *v.* To clear of forests; to remove trees from in large numbers. Fires and woodcutters had *deforested* the hills. — **de·for·est·a·tion** \(ˌ)dē-ˌfȯr-əs-'tāsh-n, -ˌfär-\ *n.*

de·form \dē-'fȯrm\ *v.* To spoil the form or the natural appearance of; to disfigure; as, a leg *deformed* by an injury; a face *deformed* by grief. — **de·for·ma·tion** \ˌdē-ˌfȯr-'māsh-n, ˌdef-r-\ *n.*

de·formed \dē-'fȯrmd\ *adj.* Distorted in form; especially, misshapen in body or limbs.

de·form·i·ty \dē-'fȯr-mət-ē\ *n.; pl.* **de·form·i·ties.** **1** The condition of being deformed; an irregular or wrong formation of some part of the body; as, a *deformity* of the foot. **2** The result of departing from what is right or beautiful; as, *deformity* of character.

de·fraud \dē-'frȯd\ *v.* To deprive of some right, interest, or property by deceiving; to cheat; as, to *defraud* a person of his savings.

de·fray \dē-'frā\ *v.* To pay; to provide money for. Each child's parents were expected to *defray* his expenses on the trip. — **de·fray·al,** *n.*

de·frost \(')dē-'frȯst\ *v.* **1** To free from frost or ice; as, to *defrost* a refrigerator; to *defrost* a windshield. **2** To thaw out, as frozen foods, for cooking or serving.

de·frost·er \(')dē-'frȯst-r\ *n.* A device for freeing or keeping free from frost or ice, especially one for a windshield.

deft \'deft\ *adj.* Quick and neat in action, especially in using the hands; skillful; dexterous; as, *deft* fingers; a *deft* workman. — **deft·ly,** *adv.*

de·funct \dē-'fəngkt\ *adj.* Having finished the course of its existence; dead; deceased; extinct; as, a *defunct* organization.

de·fy \dē-'fī\ *v.;* **de·fied** \-'fīd\; **de·fy·ing.** **1** To challenge a person to do something considered impossible; to dare. The magician *defied* his audience to explain the trick. **2** To treat as of no account; to refuse boldly to obey or to yield to; to disregard; as, to *defy* public opinion; to *defy* the law. **3** To resist attempts at; to withstand; to baffle; as, a scene that *defies* description. — \dē-'fī, 'dē-ˌfī\ *n.; pl.* **de·fies.** *Slang.* A challenge.

de·gen·er·a·cy \dē-'jen-r(-)ə-sē\ *n.* A degenerate condition; degeneration.

de·gen·er·ate \dē-'jen-r(-)ət\ *adj.* Having sunk to a condition below that which is normal to a type; having declined, as in nature or character, from one's ancestors or from what one formerly was; degraded. — *n.* A person who has a degraded nature, especially by birth. — \dē-'jen-r-ˌāt\ *v.;* **de·gen·er·at·ed; de·gen·er·at·ing.** **1** To pass from a higher to a lower type or condition; to become depraved. **2** In biology, to sink or return to a less highly organized type in the evolution of a group of animals or plants.

de·gen·er·a·tion \(ˌ)dē-ˌjen-r-'āsh-n\ *n.* **1** A growing or becoming worse; a degenerating. **2** A change in a tissue or an organ resulting in diminished activity or usefulness; as, *degeneration* of the kidneys resulting from old age.

deg·ra·da·tion \ˌdeg-rə-'dāsh-n\ *n.* **1** A reduction in rank, dignity, or standing. **2** Disgrace; humiliation. **3** Degeneration; deterioration.

de·grade \dē-'grād\ *v.;* **de·grad·ed; de·grad·ing.** **1** To reduce from a higher to a lower rank or degree; to deprive of an office or position; as, to *degrade* an officer for disobedience. **2** To lower the character of; to debase; as, a man *degraded* by crime.

de·gree \dē-'grē\ *n.* **1** A step in a series; a point of advancement or withdrawal; as, to advance by *degrees.* **2** Station in life; rank; as, a person of high *degree.* **3** A grade or rank to which scholars are admitted by a college or university as a recognition of their attainments; as, the *degree* of Master of Arts. **4** A mark or grade, as on a thermometer or barometer, that shows the amount of something, as heat or cold. The thermometer registered 70 *degrees.* **5** A position or space on the earth or in the heavens as measured by degrees (sense 9) of latitude or longitude. **6** A division, space, or interval marked on an instrument, as on a thermometer. **7** The symbol [°], as in 32° F. **8** In algebra, rank as defined by the sum of exponents of the factors. **9** A 360th part of the circumference of a circle. **10** One of the three forms an adjective or an adverb may have when it is compared. **11** A line or space of the staff in music or the interval between two adjacent notes. **12** In law, the relative grade of guiltiness; as, murder in the first *degree.* — **by degrees.** Step by step; gradually. — **to a degree.** To a considerable extent; somewhat; as, a statement that is true *to a degree.*

degree, 9

de·hy·drate \(')dē-'hī-ˌdrāt\ *v.;* **de·hy·drat·ed; de·hy·drat·ing.** To take water from; to lose water; to become free of water; as, *dehydrated* dog food. — **de·hy·dra·tion** \(ˌ)dē-ˌhī-'drāsh-n\ *n.*

de·ice \(')dē-'īs\ *v.;* **de·iced; de·ic·ing.** To rid or keep free of ice, as by applying an antifreeze or by alternately inflating and deflating air-filled bags overlying wing and tail surfaces of an aircraft. — **de·ic·er,** *n.*

de·i·fy \'dē-ə-ˌfī\ *v.;* **de·i·fied** \-ˌfīd\; **de·i·fy·ing.** **1** To make a god of; to enroll among the deities. **2** To treat as an object of supreme regard; as, to *deify* money. — **de·i·fi·ca·tion** \ˌdē-ə-fə-'kāsh-n\ *n.*

deign \'dān\ *v.* To think fit or in keeping with one's dignity; to condescend; as, not to *deign* to reply to a rude remark. The girl had not dreamed that the prince would *deign* to notice her.

de·i·ty \'dē-ət-ē\ *n.; pl.* **de·i·ties.** **1** A god or goddess; as, one of the Roman *deities.* **2** [with a capital and *the*] God.

de·ject·ed \dē-'jek-təd\ *adj.* Low-spirited; sad; as, to feel *dejected* over a failure. — **de·ject·ed·ly,** *adv.*

de·jec·tion \dē-'jeksh-n\ *n.* Lowness of spirits; sadness; depression. — For synonyms see *melancholy.*

de·lay \dē-[illegible]\ *v.;* **de·layed; de·lay·ing.** **1** To put off; to po[illegible]e; as, to *delay* one's departure for a day. **2** [illegible]tain or hinder for a time; as, to be *delaye*[illegible] accident. **3** To move slowly; to sto[illegible]e; as, to *delay* until the others can c[illegible]

[illegible] *detain* and *retard* are synonyms of [illegible]y imply a holding back, especially by interference, from completion or arrival at a set time; *detain* may suggest a holding or being held beyond an appointed time, whether deliberate or merely accidental; *retard* is likely to suggest a reduction of speed or of rate of movement or development.

— *n.* A putting off or a postponing of something; a being delayed; as, a *delay* of five hours owing to a blizzard.

de·lec·ta·ble \dē-'lek-təb-l\ *adj.* Highly pleasing; delightful. — **de·lec·ta·bly** \-tə-blē\ *adv.*

de·lec·ta·tion \ˌdē-lek-'tāsh-n\ *n.* Great pleasure; delight; diversion. The speaker told several funny stories, to the *delectation* of his audience.

del·e·gate \'del-ig-ət, -ə-ˌgāt\ *n.* A person sent with power to act for another. — \'del-ə-ˌgāt\ *v.;* **del·e·gat·ed**; **del·e·gat·ing. 1** To send as one's representative. The club members *delegated* their president to talk with the principal of the school. **2** To entrust to the care or management of another; as, to *delegate* some of one's duties to an assistant.

del·e·ga·tion \ˌdel-ə-'gāsh-n\ *n.* **1** The act of delegating. **2** One or more persons authorized to represent others; a group of delegates.

de·lete \dē-'lēt\ *v.;* **de·let·ed**; **de·let·ing.** To erase; to strike out; as, to *delete* several sentences from a composition.

del·e·te·ri·ous \ˌdel-ə-'tir-ē-əs\ *adj.* Hurtful; harmful; as, *deleterious* drugs.

de·le·tion \dē-'lēsh-n\ *n.* **1** The action of deleting. **2** A deleted passage.

delft·ware \'delft-ˌwar, -ˌwer\ *n.* A kind of pottery made in Delft, Holland, or pottery resembling this.

de·lib·er·ate \dē-'lib-r(-)ət\ *adj.* **1** Decided upon as a result of careful thought; carefully considered; as, a *deliberate* judgment. **2** Weighing facts and arguments; careful and slow in deciding; as, a *deliberate* man. **3** Slow in action; not hurried; as, *deliberate* movements. — For synonyms see *voluntary.* — \dē-'lib-r-ˌāt\ *v.;* **de·lib·er·at·ed**; **de·lib·er·at·ing.** To weigh the reasons for and against a thing; to reflect upon; to consider; as, to *deliberate* a question; to *deliberate* for several minutes before answering.

de·lib·er·ate·ly \dē-'lib-r(-)ət-lē, -rt-lē\ *adv.* **1** With careful consideration; slowly; as, to speak *deliberately.* **2** Purposely; not accidentally.

de·lib·er·a·tion \dē-ˌlib-r-'āsh-n\ *n.* **1** Careful c[illegible]sideration; discussion of reasons for and against; as, to give an important question the *deliberation* it deserves. **2** Slowness, as of action or decision; as, to speak with extreme *deliberation.*

del·i·ca·cy \'del-ə-kə-sē\ *n.; pl.* **del·i·[illegible]cies. 1** A luxury; a dainty; as, candy and othe[illegible]*licacies.* **2** Fineness of quality or workmanship,[illegible]lace of great *delicacy.* **3** Nicety of touch, as in [illegible] or music. **4** Weakness; frailty. **5** A state [illegible]rs that requires very tactful handling; as, th[illegible] of a situation. **6** Sensitiveness; refinemen[illegible]ing, thought, taste, or conduct; as, to show *delicacy* in doing a kindness.

del·i·cate \'del-ik-ət\ *adj.* **1** Satisfying or pleasing because of its fineness; refined; as, a *delicate* color. **2** Exquisite, as in workmanship or structure; fragile; frail; as, *delicate* lace; a *delicate* child. **3** Capable of sensing slight differences; highly sensitive; showing slight changes; as, a *delicate* ear for music; a *delicate* thermometer. **4** Requiring fine skill or expert knowledge; as, a *delicate* operation by a surgeon. — **del·i·cate·ly**, *adv.*

del·i·ca·tes·sen \ˌdel-ə-kə-'tes-n\ *n.* [From German *delikatessen*, plural of *delikatesse* meaning "delicacy", there borrowed from French *délicatesse.*] **1** Prepared foods such as cooked meats, salads, and relishes — used as a plural. **2** A store where such foods are sold.

de·li·cious \dē-'lish-əs\ *adj.* Delightful; pleasing; especially, very pleasing to the taste. — **de·li·cious·ly**, *adv.*

de·light \dē-'līt\ *n.* **1** Great satisfaction; joy. The child's face glowed with *delight.* **2** Anything that gives great pleasure. On hot days our swimming pool is a real *delight.* — *v.* **1** To give joy or satisfaction to; to please highly. The play *delighted* the audience. **2** To be greatly pleased; as, to *delight* in helping others.

de·light·ed \dē-'līt-əd\ *adj.* Highly pleased; joyous; gratified; as, *delighted* with the gift. — **de·light·ed·ly**, *adv.*

de·light·ful \dē-'līt-fəl\ *adj.* Highly pleasing; giving delight; as, a *delightful* child; a *delightful* vacation. — **de·light·ful·ly** \-fə-lē\ *adv.*

de·lim·it \(')dē-'lim-ət\ *v.* To fix the boundaries of something; to bound; as, to *delimit* the territory that troops will occupy. — **de·lim·i·ta·tion** \(ˌ)dē-ˌlim-ə-'tāsh-n\ *n.*

de·lin·e·ate \dē-'lin-ē-ˌāt\ *v.;* **de·lin·e·at·ed**; **de·lin·e·at·ing. 1** To indicate by lines; to sketch. **2** To picture in words; to describe; as, to *delineate* the characters in a story. — **de·lin·e·a·tion** \dē-ˌlin-ē-'āsh-n\ *n.*

de·lin·quen·cy \dē-'lin(g)-kwən-sē\ *n.; pl.* **de·lin·quen·cies.** A failure to do what one ought to do; a violation of duty; a fault; as, *delinquency* in paying one's debts.

de·lin·quent \dē-'lin(g)-kwənt\ *adj.* Guilty of delinquency; offending by neglect or violation of duty or law. — *n.* A delinquent person.

del·i·ques·cent \ˌdel-ə-'kwes-nt\ *adj.* **1** Liquefying by absorbing moisture from the air. **2** Dividing into many branches. Certain trees are *deliquescent.*

de·lir·i·ous \dē-'lir-ē-əs\ *adj.* **1** In a delirium. **2** Wildly excited, as with enthusiasm, interest, or anticipation; as, *delirious* with joy.

de·lir·i·um \dē-'lir-ē-əm\ *n.* **1** A disordered condition of the mind, usually temporary. **2** Strong or wild excitement; as, a *delirium* of joy.

de·liv·er \dē-'liv-r\ *v.;* **de·liv·ered**; **de·liv·er·ing** \-r(-)ing\. **1** To set free; to save. *Deliver* us from evil. **2** To give or transfer; to hand over; as, to *deliver* a letter. **3** To yield or surrender, as a prisoner. **4** To give birth to — used in the passive voice. The woman was *delivered* of a child. **5** To aid a woman in the process of childbirth. **6** To utter; to communicate; as, to *deliver* a speech. **7** To give; to send forth; as, to *deliver* a blow or a kick. — **de·liv·er·er** \-'liv-r-r\ *n.*

de·liv·er·ance \dē-'liv-r(-)ən(t)s\ *n.* **1** A delivering or a being delivered; liberation; as, *deliverance* from the hands of the enemy. **2** Anything delivered or communicated, as a publicly expressed opinion.

de·liv·ery \dē-'liv-r(-)ē\ *n.; pl.* **de·liv·er·ies. 1** A delivering; a rescue; a release; as, to pray for *delivery* from danger. **2** Speaking, or the manner of speaking; as, the *delivery* of a speech; to have a pleasing *delivery.* **3** A surrender; the transfer of a thing from one place or person to another; as, the special *delivery* of a letter. **4** The act of giving birth to a child. **5** The act or manner of sending forth or throwing; as, a baseball pitcher's *delivery.* **6** Something that is delivered.

dell \'del\ *n.* A small secluded valley.

del·ta \'del-tə\ *n.* The triangular or fan-shaped piece of land made by deposits of mud and sand at the mouths of some rivers.

de·lude \dē-'lüd\ *v.;* **de·lud·ed; de·lud·ing.** To lead into error; to mislead purposely; to deceive; to trick; as, *deluded* by false promises.

del·uge \'del-ˌyüj\ *n.* **1** An overflowing of the land by water; a flood. **2** An overwhelming number of things that come in a great rush; as, a *deluge* of mail at Christmas time. — **the Deluge.** The flood in the days of Noah. — *v.;* **del·uged; del·ug·ing. 1** To overflow; to flood. **2** To overwhelm as if with a deluge; as, to be *deluged* with inquiries.

de·lu·sion \dē-'lüzh-n\ *n.* **1** A deluding; deception. **2** A false or mistaken belief; especially, a belief in the truth or reality of something false or nonexistent.

de·lu·sive \dē-'lü-siv\ *adj.* Deluding; deceiving; as, *delusive* ideas.

de·lu·so·ry \dē-'lüs-r-ē\ *adj.* Delusive.

de luxe \də 'lu̇ks, 'ləks, 'lüks\. Specially elegant; as, a *de luxe* edition of a book.

delve \'delv\ *v.;* **delved; delv·ing. 1** To dig, as with a spade. **2** To work hard looking for information in books or other written records.

de·mag·net·ize \(')dē-'mag-nə-ˌtīz\ *v.;* **de·mag·net·ized; de·mag·net·iz·ing.** To deprive of magnetic qualities. — **de·mag·net·i·za·tion** \(ˌ)dē-ˌmag-nət-ə-'zāsh-n\ *n.*

dem·a·gog·ic \ˌdem-ə-'gäj-ik, -'gäg-\ or **dem·a·gog·i·cal** \-ik-l\ *adj.* Of, relating to, or like a demagogue; encouraging popular discontent.

dem·a·gogue or **dem·a·gog** \'dem-ə-ˌgäg\ *n.* A person who appeals to the emotions and prejudices of people to arouse discontent and to advance his own political ends.

de·mand \dē-'mand\ *v.* **1** To ask or call for with authority; to claim as one's right; as, to *demand* payment of a debt; to *demand* an apology. **2** To ask earnestly or in the manner of a command. The sentry *demanded* the password. **3** To call for; to require; to need; as, an illness that *demands* constant care. — *n.* **1** The act of demanding; the act of claiming something as due. This bill is to be paid on *demand.* **2** Something that is demanded, especially by right; a claim; as, to give a person his full *demand.* **3** A seeking; the condition of being sought after. Linen is in great *demand.* **4** An expressed desire to own or use something. The *demand* for new cars was greater than the supply. **5** The desire to purchase goods on the part of those who have the money to pay for them. **6** The quantity of an article that is wanted at a stated price. — **on demand.** Upon request for payment. — **de·mand·er,** *n.*

de·mar·ca·tion \ˌdē-ˌmär-'kāsh-n, -ˌmȧr-\ *n.* The marking of the boundaries or limits of a region; a separation; a distinction; as, to draw a sharp line of *demarcation* between passing grades and failing grades.

de·mean \dē-'mēn\ *v.* To debase; to degrade; as, to refuse to *demean* oneself by dishonesty.

de·mean \dē-'mēn\ *v.* To behave or conduct (oneself); as, to *demean* oneself as a true hero.

de·mean·or \dē-'mēn-r\ *n.* Behavior; conduct; bearing; as, a professional *demeanor.*

de·ment·ed \dē-'ment-əd\ *adj.* Insane; mad.

de·men·tia \dē-'mench-ə\ *n.* Insanity.

de·mer·it \dē-'mer-ət\ *n.* **1** Anything that deserves blame; a fault. **2** A mark against a person's record for some fault.

de·mesne \dē-'mān, -'mēn\ *n.* [From Old French *demesne, demeine,* there derived from Latin *dominium* meaning "property of a master".] **1** Possession of land as one's own. **2** A lord's manor place; an estate. **3** A region. **4** A realm, especially of interests or activities; as, a writer whose *demesne* is chiefly history.

dem·i·god \'dem-ē-ˌgäd\ *n.* A divine or semidivine being of less power and lower rank than a god.

dem·i·john \'dem-ē-ˌjän\ *n.* A large bottle of glass or earthenware, usually enclosed in wicker.

demijohn

de·mise \dē-'mīz\ *n.* Death.

dem·i·tasse \'dem-ē-ˌtas, -ˌtäs, -ˌtȧs\ *n.* **1** A small cup for black coffee. **2** A small cup of black coffee.

de·mo·bi·lize \(')dē-'mōb-l-ˌīz\ *v.;* **de·mo·bi·lized; de·mo·bi·liz·ing.** To dismiss soldiers from military service; to change from a state of war to a state of peace; as, to allow time for the country to *demobilize.*

de·moc·ra·cy \dē-'mäk-rə-sē\ *n.; pl.* **de·moc·ra·cies.** [From Greek *demokratia* meaning "rule of the people", from *demos* "people" and *-kratia* "rule".] **1** Government by the people; government in which the highest power is held by the people, as in a republic. **2** Any state or city governed by the people themselves. **3** Belief in, or practice of, the idea that all people are socially equal; as, a man noted for his *democracy*.

dem·o·crat \'dem-ə-ˌkrat\ *n.* **1** A person who believes in or practices democracy. **2** [with a capital] A member of the Democratic Party.

dem·o·crat·ic \ˌdem-ə-'krat-ik\ *adj.* **1** Relating to or based on the principles of democracy; as, a *democratic* system of government. **2** Characteristic or representative of the common people; as, *democratic* art. **3** Believing in or practicing the idea that people are equal; disregarding social distinctions; not snobbish. **4** Of or relating to the Democratic Party. — **dem·o·crat·i·cal·ly** \-ik-l(-)ē\ *adv.*

de·moc·ra·tize \dē-'mäk-rə-ˌtīz\ *v.;* **de·moc·ra·tized; de·moc·ra·tiz·ing.** To make democratic.

de·mol·ish \dē-'mäl-ish\ *v.* To throw or pull down; to tear down; to destroy; as, to *demolish* an old building.

dem·o·li·tion \ˌdem-l-'ish-n, ˌdēm-\ *n.* The action of demolishing; destruction.

de·mon \'dē-mən\ *n.* **1** An attendant spirit; a daemon. **2** An evil spirit; a devil. **3** An extremely cruel person. **4** A person of great energy or skill; as, a *demon* for work; a *demon* in spelling.

de·mo·ni·ac \dē-'mō-nē-ˌak\ or **de·mo·ni·a·cal** \ˌdē-mə-'nī-ək-l\ *adj.* **1** Influenced or caused, or seemingly influenced or caused, by a demon; as, *demoniac* energy; *demoniac* rage. **2** Devilish; fiendish; as, *demoniac* cruelty. — **de·mo·ni·a·cal·ly** \ˌdē-mə-'nī-ək-l(-)ē\ *adv.*

de·mo·ni·ac \dē-'mō-nē-ˌak\ *n.* A person supposed to be possessed by an evil spirit.

de·mon·stra·ble \dē-'män-strəb-l, 'dem-ən-\ *adj.* Capable of being demonstrated or proved. — **de·mon·stra·bil·i·ty** \dē-ˌmän-strə-'bil-ət-ē, ˌdem-ən-\ *n.*

dem·on·strate \'dem-ən-ˌstrāt\ *v.;* **dem·on·strat·ed; dem·on·strat·ing.** **1** To make clear; to prove by reasoning; to establish as true; as, to *demonstrate* that a plan cannot succeed. **2** To explain, as in teaching, by use of examples or other illustrative material; as, to *demonstrate* the movement of the earth. **3** To show publicly the good qualities of an article or a product; as, to *demonstrate* a new car. **4** To make a public display, as of feelings or military force. Thousands of citizens *demonstrated* in the streets in opposition to the proposed alliance.

dem·on·stra·tion \ˌdem-ən-'strāsh-n\ *n.* **1** An outward expression; as, a *demonstration* of joy. **2** A public display by a group of persons of sympathy for or opposition to some person, party, or cause; as, a *demonstration* against the government in the public square. **3** The action, process, or means of demonstrating the truth of something; proof. The accused man's lawyer offered a convincing *demonstration* of his innocence. **4** A showing or trial of an article for sale to point out its merits; as, to ask for a *demonstration* of a new vacuum cleaner. **5** In mathematics, a course of reasoning intended to prove that a certain result or conclusion must follow when certain conditions are accepted as a starting point. **6** A movement of ships or troops as if in readiness to attack, made either to show preparedness for war or to conceal the real place of an intended attack.

de·mon·stra·tive \dē-'män-strət-iv\ *adj.* **1** Showing feeling or sentiment without restraint; effusive; gushing; as, a *demonstrative* child; a *demonstrative* farewell. **2** In grammar, serving to point out the person or thing referred to, distinguishing it from others; as, the *demonstrative* pronouns "this" and "that"; the *demonstrative* adjective "that" in "that boy over there". — *n.* A demonstrative word; especially, a demonstrative pronoun. — **de·mon·stra·tive·ly,** *adv.*

dem·on·stra·tor \'dem-ən-ˌstrāt-r\ *n.* **1** A person who makes or takes part in a demonstration. **2** A manufactured article or product, as an automobile or washing machine, used for purposes of demonstration.

de·mor·al·ize \(')dē-'mȯr-ə-ˌlīz, -'mär-\ *v.;* **de·mor·al·ized; de·mor·al·iz·ing.** **1** To corrupt in morals; to make bad. **2** To destroy the morale of; to weaken in discipline or spirit; to disorganize; as, *demoralized* by fear. The unexpected attack *demoralized* the army. — **de·mor·al·i·za·tion** \(ˌ)dē-ˌmȯr-ə-lə-'zāsh-n, -ˌmär-\ *n.*

de·mote \(')dē-'mōt\ *v.;* **de·mot·ed; de·mot·ing.** To reduce to a lower grade or rank, as in a school or in the armed forces.

de·mount \(')dē-'mau̇nt\ *v.* To remove from a mounted position, as a tire from a rim. — **de·mount·a·ble,** *adj.*

de·mur \dē-'mər\ *v.;* **de·murred; de·mur·ring.** To object; to hesitate; to express reluctance or unwillingness; as, to *demur* at accepting new responsibilities. — *n.* An objection; as, to agree to a suggestion without *demur.*

de·mure \dē-'myu̇r\ *adj.;* **de·mur·er; de·mur·est.** **1** Sober or serious in manner. **2** Affectedly modest or prim; coy. — **de·mure·ly,** *adv.*

den \'den\ *n.* **1** The shelter or resting place of a wild beast. **2** A hiding place, as for thieves. **3** Any dirty, wretched place in which people live or gather; as, *dens* of misery. **4** A quiet, snug private room, especially one set apart for reading and relaxation.

de·na·ture \(')dē-'nāch-r\ *v.;* **de·na·tured; de·na·tur·ing** \-r(-)ing\. To change the nature of; especially, to make unfit for eating or drinking without harming for other purposes; as, *denatured* alcohol.

den·drite \'den-ˌdrīt\ *n.* Any of the branching extensions of a nerve cell, over which impulses travel toward the body of the cell.

de·ni·al \dē-'nī-əl, -'nīl\ *n.* **1** A refusal to grant something asked for. Our request met with a *denial.* **2** A refusal to admit the truth of a statement; a contradiction; as, a flat *denial* of the charges. **3** A refusal to acknowledge something; especially, a statement of disbelief or rejection; a disowning; as, to make a public *denial* of political beliefs once held. **4** A cutting down or limiting; as, a *denial* of one's appetite.

den·im \'den-əm\ *n.* [From French (*serge*) *de Nîmes* meaning "serge of Nîmes", from Nîmes, France, where it was made.] **1** A firm, often coarse, cotton cloth used especially for overalls and play clothes. **2** [in the plural] Overalls or trousers designed for work or other rough use.

den·i·zen \'den-əz-n\ *n.* [From medieval French *denzein* meaning "one living within a city or country".] An inhabitant; especially, a person, animal or plant found or naturalized in a certain region or among certain surroundings; as, the *denizens* of the forest; a *denizen* of the underworld.

de·nom·i·nate \dē-'näm-ə-ˌnāt\ *v.;* **de·nom·i·nat·ed**; **de·nom·i·nat·ing**. To give a name to; to call; to name.

de·nom·i·nate number \dē-'näm-ə-nət\. A number, as 7 in 7 *feet,* that specifies a quantity in terms of a unit of measurement.

de·nom·i·na·tion \dē-ˌnäm-ə-'nāsh-n\ *n.* **1** The act of denominating; a naming. **2** A name or title; especially, a general name for a class of things. Baseball, tennis, and skiing come under the *denomination* of sports. **3** One of the large religious organizations uniting in a single administrative body a number of local congregations; as, the various Protestant *denominations.* **4** One of a series of related values each of which is called by a special name. A one-dollar bill and a ten-dollar bill represent two *denominations* of United States money.

de·nom·i·na·tion·al \dē-ˌnäm-ə-'nāsh-n(-)əl\ *adj.* Of or relating to a denomination, especially a religious denomination; as, a *denominational* college.

de·nom·i·na·tor \dē-'näm-ə-ˌnāt-r\ *n.* In arithmetic and algebra, the part of a fraction below the line, in simple fractions stating into how many equal parts the unit is supposed to be divided.

de·no·ta·tion \ˌdē-nō-'tāsh-n\ *n.* **1** The marking out of something; an indicating. **2** A sign, name, or designation by which something is marked out. **3** The meaning of a word or expression, especially its precise, literal meaning, as distinguished from its connotation.

de·note \dē-'nōt\ *v.;* **de·not·ed**; **de·not·ing.** **1** To mark out plainly; to indicate; to point out. The hands of a clock *denote* the time. **2** To make known; to show. A dog wags his tail to *denote* pleasure. **3** To have the meaning of; to mean. In the United States the word "corn" *denotes* Indian corn.

de·noue·ment \ˌdā-ˌnü-'män, dā-'nü-ˌmän\ *n.* **1** The final solution or untangling of the conflicts or difficulties that make up a plot, as in a play. **2** A solution or working out, especially of a complex or difficult situation. The case had an unexpected *denouement* when the star witness confessed that he was the murderer.

de·nounce \dē-'nau̇n(t)s\ *v.;* **de·nounced**; **de·nounc·ing.** **1** To point out a person or thing as deserving of blame or punishment; as, to *denounce* dishonest officials. **2** To inform against; to accuse; as, to *denounce* a traitor. **3** To give notice of intention to terminate or cease to abide by, as a treaty. — **de·nounce·ment,** *n.*

dense \'den(t)s\ *adj.* **1** Having its parts packed closely together; thick; compact; as, a *dense* forest; a *dense* fog. **2** Stupid; as, a person too *dense* to learn anything. — **dense·ly,** *adv.*

den·si·ty \'den(t)s-ət-ē\ *n.; pl.* **den·si·ties.** **1** The state of being dense; closeness; compactness. **2** The quantity of anything in each specified unit of volume or area; especially, in physics, the quantity of matter, energy, or electricity per unit volume, in substances, as iron, water, or oxygen, measured by weight. The *density* of iron is 491 pounds per cubic foot. **3** Stupidity; thickness of mind or head. — **density of population.** The average number of persons living in a definite area, usually a square mile.

dent \'dent\ *n.* A small notch or hollow, like that made by a blow on a smooth surface. — *v.* To make a dent upon; to become marked by a dent. Some kinds of wood *dent* easily.

den·tal \'dent-l\ *adj.* Of or relating to the teeth, dentistry, or dentists; as, a *dental* appointment; a *dental* school.

den·ti·frice \'dent-ə-frəs\ *n.* [From medieval French, there borrowed from Latin *dentifricium* meaning literally "something for rubbing the teeth".] A powder, paste, or liquid used in cleaning the teeth.

den·tin \'dent-n\ or **den·tine** \'den-ˌtēn\ *n.* A hard, bony material composing the main part of a tooth.

dentine

section of tooth

den·tist \'dent-əst\ *n.* A person whose profession is the care, treatment, and repair of the teeth and the fitting of artificial teeth.

den·tist·ry \'dent-əs-trē\ *n.* The profession or practice of a dentist.

den·ti·tion \den-'tish-n\ *n.* **1** The development of teeth. **2** The teeth of a person or animal.

den·ture \'dench-r\ *n.* A set of teeth; especially, a set, complete or partial, of artificial teeth.

de·nude \(')dē-'nüd, -'nyüd\ *v.;* **de·nud·ed**; **de·nud·ing.** **1** To strip of all covering; as, to *denude* the land of trees. **2** To lay bare; as, boulders *denuded* of all soil by erosion. — **de·nu·da·tion** \ˌdē-ˌn(y)ü-'dāsh-n, ˌden-yə-\ *n.*

de·nun·ci·a·tion \dē-ˌnən(t)s-ē-'āsh-n\ *n.* **1** The act of denouncing. **2** A public accusation; as, to publish a *denunciation* of a city official.

de·ny \dē-'nī\ *v.;* **de·nied** \-'nīd\; **de·ny·ing.** **1** To declare not to be true; to contradict; as, to *deny* a report. **2** To refuse to grant; to refuse; as, to *deny* a request. **3** To refuse to acknowledge; to disown; as, to *deny* one's faith. **4** To reject as false; as, to *deny* the theory of evolution.

de·o·dor·ant \dē-'ōd-r-ənt\ *adj.* Destroying or masking offensive odors; as, a *deodorant* liquid. — *n.* Anything that deodorizes.

de·o·dor·ize \dē-'ōd-r-ˌīz\ *v.;* **de·o·dor·ized; de·o·dor·iz·ing.** To deprive of odor, especially of offensive odor. — **de·o·dor·i·za·tion** \dē-ˌōd-r-ə-'zāsh-n\ *n.* — **de·o·dor·iz·er** \(ˌ)dē-'ōd-r-ˌīz-r\ *n.*

de·part \dē-'pärt, -'pärt\ *v.* **1** To go away; to leave. The guests *departed* at 10 o'clock. **2** To turn aside; as, to *depart* from one's usual methods. **3** To pass away; to die.

de·part·ment \dē-'pärt-mənt, -'pȧrt \ *n.* A distinct part or division of something, as of a government, a business, or a college.

department store. A store keeping a great variety of goods arranged in departments.

de·par·ture \dē-'pärch-r, -'pȧrch-r\ *n.* **1** A departing or going away; as, to make an early *departure.* **2** A setting out or beginning; a change of plan or method; as, a new *departure* in business.

de·pend \dē-'pend\ *v.* **1** To hang down; as, a vine *depending* from a tree. **2** To rely for support. Children *depend* on their parents. **3** To be determined by or based on some action or condition. The success of the picnic will *depend* on the weather. **4** To trust; to rely; as, a man you can *depend* on.

de·pend·a·ble \dē-'pen-dəb-l\ *adj.* Trustworthy; reliable. — **de·pend·a·bil·i·ty** \dē-ˌpen-də-'bil-ət-ē\ *n.* — **de·pend·a·bly** \dē-'pen-də-blē\ *adv.*

de·pend·ence \dē-'pen-dən(t)s\ *n.* **1** A being dependent; the condition of being influenced and determined by something else; as, plans made uncertain by their *dependence* on the weather. **2** Inability to help or provide for oneself; as, to live in a state of *dependence.* **3** Reliance; trust; as, a man one can put full *dependence* upon. **4** Something on which a person depends or relies, as for assistance or comfort.

de·pend·en·cy \dē-'pen-dən-sē\ *n.; pl.* **de·pend·en·cies. 1** The condition of being dependent; dependence. **2** A country or territory subject to the control of another country. Puerto Rico is a *dependency* of the United States.

de·pend·ent \dē-'pen-dənt\ *adj.* **1** Hanging down. **2** Relying on something else for support; as, a *dependent* relative. **3** Of a clause, playing the part of a noun, adjective, or adverb and having full meaning only in relation to a main clause to which it is attached; subordinate. — *n.* Also **de·pend·ant** \-dənt\. **1** *Archaic.* Something that depends; a dependency. **2** A person who is dependent on another for support.

de·pict \dē-'pikt\ *v.* **1** To represent by a picture; as, historical scenes *depicted* on the walls of a post office. **2** To describe in words; as, a newspaper story *depicting* the scene of an accident. — **de·pic·tion** \-'piksh-n\ *n.*

de·plete \dē-'plēt\ *v.;* **de·plet·ed; de·plet·ing.** To reduce in amount by using up; to exhaust, as of strength or resources; as, a soil *depleted* of minerals. The new government faced a *depleted* treasury.

de·ple·tion \dē-'plēsh-n\ *n.* The action or process of depleting or the state of being depleted; as, oil resources in danger of *depletion.*

de·plor·a·ble \dē-'plōr-əb-l, -'plȯr-\ *adj.* **1** Deserving to be deplored; sad; regrettable; as, a *deplorable* accident. **2** Wretched; very bad; as, to leave one's room in a *deplorable* condition. — **de·plor·a·bly** \-ə-blē\ *adv.*

de·plore \dē-'plōr, -'plȯr\ *v.;* **de·plored; de·plor·ing.** To feel or express deep grief for; to regret deeply; as, to *deplore* the necessity of punishing a child.

de·ploy \dē-'plȯi\ *v.* To spread out, as troops or ships in order for battle.

de·po·nent \dē-'pō-nənt\ *n.* A person who gives evidence, especially in writing.

de·pop·u·late \(')dē-'päp-yə-ˌlāt\ *v.;* **de·pop·u·lat·ed; de·pop·u·lat·ing.** To reduce greatly the population of, as a city or a region, by destroying or driving away the inhabitants; as, a city *depopulated* by an epidemic of plague. — **de·pop·u·la·tion** \(ˌ)dē-ˌpäp-yə-'lāsh-n\ *n.*

de·port \dē-'pōrt, -'pȯrt\ *v.* **1** To behave or conduct (oneself). **2** To force to leave a country, as an alien who has entered it illegally; to send away, as into banishment or exile.

de·por·ta·tion \ˌdē-ˌpōr-'tāsh-n, -ˌpȯr-\ *n.* The act of deporting; banishment; especially, the expulsion from a country of an alien who has entered illegally or whose presence is considered harmful to the public welfare.

de·port·ment \dē-'pōrt-mənt, -'pȯrt-\ *n.* Manner of conducting oneself; behavior.

de·pose \dē-'pōz\ *v.;* **de·posed; de·pos·ing. 1** To remove from office, especially from a throne or other high station. The unpopular king was *deposed* and allowed to go into exile. **2** To make a statement under oath; to testify, especially in writing. The witness *deposed* that he had seen the accused with the weapon in his hand.

de·pos·it \dē-'päz-ət\ *v.* **1** To place for safekeeping; especially, to put money in a bank. **2** To put down or give as a pledge that a purchase will be made or a service used; as, to *deposit* ten dollars on a new bicycle. **3** To lay down; to place; to put; as, to *deposit* a parcel on a table. **4** To let fall or sink; as, sand and silt *deposited* by a flood. — *n.* **1** The state of being deposited; as, money on *deposit.* **2** Something entrusted to another's care; as, to have a large *deposit* of money in a bank. **3** Anything given as a pledge or security; as, to make a *deposit* of ten dollars on a new bicycle. **4** Something laid or thrown down; as, a *deposit* of silt left by the flood. **5** An accumulation of mineral matter, as iron ore, oil, or gas, in nature.

dep·o·si·tion \ˌdep-ə-'zish-n, ˌdēp-\ *n.* **1** The act of deposing, as a sovereign; removal of a person from high office; as, a revolution ending in the *deposition* of the king. **2** A statement, especially one in writing, made under oath; testimony. **3** The action or process of depositing; as, the *deposition* of silt by a stream. **4** That which is deposited.

de·pos·i·tor \dē-'päz-ət-r\ *n.* A person who makes a deposit, especially of money in a bank.

de·pos·i·to·ry \dē-'päz-ə-ˌtōr-ē, -ˌtȯr-ē\ *n.; pl.* **de·pos·i·to·ries.** A place in which things are deposited or stored for safekeeping.

de·pot \'dē-ˌpō; *sense 3 is usually* 'dep-ˌō\ *n.* **1** A place of deposit for goods; a storehouse. **2** A railroad station. **3** A place where military supplies are kept or where troops are assembled and trained.

de·prave \dē-'prāv\ *v.;* **de·praved; de·prav·ing.** To make bad; to corrupt the morals of.

de·praved \dē-'prāvd\ *adj.* Morally bad; immoral; corrupt; vile.

de·prav·i·ty \dē-'prav-ət-ē\ *n.; pl.* **de·prav·i·ties.** **1** The state of being depraved; corruption; vileness. **2** A depraved act or practice.

dep·re·cate \'dep-rə-ˌkāt\ *v.;* **dep·re·cat·ed; dep·re·cat·ing.** To express disapproval of, especially with expressions of regret; as, to *deprecate* the bad manners shown by a friend. — **dep·re·ca·tion** \ˌdep-rə-'kāsh-n\ *n.* — **dep·re·cat·ing·ly** \'dep-rə-ˌkāt-ing-lē\ *adv.*

dep·re·ca·to·ry \'dep-rə-kə-ˌtōr-ē, -ˌtȯr-ē\ *adj.* **1** Serving to deprecate; as, a *deprecatory* comment. **2** Apologetic; as, to confess to a mistake with a *deprecatory* smile. — **dep·re·ca·to·ri·ly** \ˌdep-rə-kə-'tōr-ə-lē, -'tȯr-\ *adv.*

de·pre·ci·ate \dē-'prē-shē-ˌāt\ *v.;* **de·pre·ci·at·ed; de·pre·ci·at·ing.** **1** To lessen in price or in estimated value or worth; as, a neighborhood which is slowly *depreciating.* Perishable goods *depreciate* rapidly. **2** To undervalue; to belittle; to disparage.

de·pre·ci·a·tion \dē-ˌprē-shē-'āsh-n\ *n.* **1** A reduction in the purchasing power or exchange value of money; as, a ten per cent *depreciation* of the dollar in six months. **2** The act of belittling; disparagement. The boy's constant *depreciation* of his friends became very tiresome. **3** A decline in the sale, resale, or trade-in value of an article, as from age or wear and tear.

dep·re·da·tion \ˌdep-rə-'dāsh-n\ *n.* The action or an act of plundering or laying waste; a ravaging or pillaging; robbery; as, a people facing *depredation* by an invading army; the *depredations* of a gang of thieves.

de·press \dē-'pres\ *v.* **1** To press down; to lower; as, to *depress* the keys of a typewriter. **2** To lessen the activity or force of. Merchants report that the bad weather has *depressed* sales. **3** To lower the pitch of, as the voice. **4** To lessen in price or value; to depreciate. **5** To sadden; to make low in spirits; as, to be *depressed* by news of a friend's illness.

de·pres·sant \dē-'pres-nt\ *adj.* Lowering the normal activity of an organ, as in causing the heart to beat more slowly. — *n.* A depressant drug or other agent.

de·pres·sion \dē-'presh-n\ *n.* **1** The act of depressing or a being depressed. **2** A depressed or hollowed place or part; a hollow; as, a *depression* in a road. **3** Sadness; gloominess; as, to be unable to throw off a feeling of *depression.* **4** A reduction or lowering of activity or force, as in business. **5** A period during which a severe reduction of business activity continues, especially when accompanied by a scarcity of goods and money, low prices, and mass unemployment.

de·pres·sor \dē-'pres-r\ *n.* One that depresses, as a muscle that draws down a part, or an implement or device used for depressing something; as, a tongue *depressor.*

dep·ri·va·tion \ˌdep-rə-'vāsh-n\ *n.* The act of depriving or the state of being deprived of something; loss; want; privation.

de·prive \dē-'prīv\ *v.;* **de·prived; de·priv·ing.** **1** To take away from; as, to *deprive* a king of his power. **2** To stop from having; as, to be *deprived* of sleep by street noises.

dept. Abbreviation for *department.*

depth \'depth\ *n.; pl.* **depths** \'dep(th)s\. **1** Something that is deep; especially, the deep part of a body of water, as a sea or a lake. **2** An abyss. **3** Measurement from top to bottom or from front to back; distance down or through; deepness; as, the *depth* of a well; the *depth* of a cupboard. **4** [often in the plural] The innermost part of anything; the middle, as of a period of darkness or of cold; as, the *depths* of the jungle; the *depth* of winter. **5** Profoundness; abundance; completeness; as, a man with great *depth* of knowledge. **6** Degree of intensity; as, the *depth* of a color. **7** Lowness of pitch; as, *depth* of sound.

depth charge. A bomb set to go off under water, used especially against submarines.

dep·u·ta·tion \ˌdep-yə-'tāsh-n\ *n.* **1** The act of designating another to act for or in place of oneself; a delegation, as of duty or power. **2** A group of persons appointed to act for others, usually for a much larger body.

de·pute \dē-'pyüt\ *v.;* **de·put·ed; de·put·ing.** **1** To appoint as a substitute or representative, especially for oneself; to deputize. **2** To hand over to another to do; to assign to a deputy. The gym teacher *deputed* the supervision of the annual exhibition to his assistant.

dep·u·tize \'dep-yə-ˌtīz\ *v.;* **dep·u·tized; dep·u·tiz·ing.** **1** To appoint as a deputy; as, to *deputize* one's assistant to act in one's place. The sheriff *deputized* four of the town's citizens to serve during the emergency. **2** To act as deputy. One of the duties of a vice-president may be to *deputize* for his chief.

dep·u·ty \'dep-yət-ē\ *n.; pl.* **dep·u·ties.** A person appointed to act for or in place of someone else; a substitute in office or an assistant empowered to act as a substitute. — *adj.* Serving as deputy; as, a *deputy* sheriff; the *deputy* director.

de·rail \dē-'rāl\ *v.* To cause to run off the rails; as, a train *derailed* by heavy snow. — **de·rail·ment,** *n.*

de·range \dē-'rānj\ *v.;* **de·ranged; de·rang·ing.** **1** To put out of order; to disarrange; to upset; as, to have the household routine completely *deranged* by a power failure. **2** To make insane; as, a mind *deranged* by grief.

de·ranged \dē-'rānjd\ *adj.* Insane.

de·range·ment \dē-'rānj-mənt\ *n.* The act of deranging or the state of being deranged; especially, the state of being mentally deranged; madness; insanity.

der·by \'dər-bē\ *n.* [Named after the twelfth Earl of *Derby*, who in 1780 instituted the race.] **1** [with a capital] A race for three-year-old horses run each year at Epsom, England. **2** [often with a capital] A race or contest of similar importance in its own field; as, the Kentucky *Derby;* an automobile *derby.* **3** [Short for *Derby hat,* probably named after the English Derby.] A stiff dome-shaped hat for men.

derby, 3

der·e·lict \'der-ə-ˌlikt\ *adj.* **1** Abandoned by the owner; as, a *derelict* ship. **2** Neglectful; negligent; as, to be *derelict* in one's duty. — *n.* **1** A ship that has been abandoned on the high seas and is a danger to navigation. **2** In law, anything voluntarily abandoned. **3** A person who has sunk below the level of respectable society.

der·e·lic·tion \ˌder-ə-'liksh-n\ *n.* **1** The act of abandoning or the state of being abandoned; as, the *dereliction* of a cause by one of its most trusted leaders. **2** A failure in duty; a shortcoming. One must expect to be held responsible for one's *derelictions.*

de·ride \dē-'rīd\ *v.;* **de·rid·ed**; **de·rid·ing.** To laugh at scornfully; to make fun of.

de·ri·sion \dē-'rizh-n\ *n.* **1** Scornful or contemptuous ridicule. **2** An object of ridicule.

de·ri·sive \dē-'rī-siv\ *adj.* Expressing derision; mocking; as, a *derisive* laugh. — **de·ri·sive·ly**, *adv.*

de·ri·so·ry \dē-'rīs-r-ē\ *adj.* Derisive.

de·riv·a·ble \dē-'rī-vəb-l\ *adj.* Capable of being derived.

der·i·va·tion \ˌder-ə-'vāsh-n\ *n.* **1** The act or process of deriving; a drawing or obtaining from a source. **2** The source from which something is derived; origin. **3** The formation or development of a word from its original elements; as, the *derivation* of the word "detrain" from the root word "train" and the prefix "de-".

de·riv·a·tive \dē-'riv-ət-iv\ *adj.* Derived from something else; not original; not fundamental. — *n.* A thing that is derived from another thing; especially, a word that has developed from another word by any process of development, as by the addition of a prefix or suffix, or by internal change. — **de·riv·a·tive·ly**, *adv.*

de·rive \dē-'rīv\ *v.;* **de·rived**; **de·riv·ing.** **1** To receive or obtain from a source; as, to *derive* new ideas from reading; to *derive* benefit from exercise. **2** To trace the origin, descent, or derivation of. **3** To come from a certain source. The word "cafe" *derives* from French.

der·ma \'dər-mə\ *n.* The dermis.

der·mis \'dər-məs\ *n.* The layer of skin directly under the epidermis, or outer skin. — **der·mal** \'dərm-l\ *adj.*

de·rog·a·to·ry \dē-'räg-ə-ˌtōr-ē, -ˌtȯr-ē\ *adj.* Intended to lower the reputation of a person or thing; expressing a low opinion; disparaging; as, *derogatory* remarks. — **de·rog·a·to·ri·ly** \dē-ˌräg-ə-'tōr-ə-lē, -'tȯr-\ *adv.*

der·rick \'der-ik\ *n.* [From an old name for a gallows, derived from *Derrick,* the name of a famous 17th century English hangman.] **1** Any of various machines for moving or hoisting heavy weights by means of a long beam fitted with pulleys and ropes. **2** A framework or tower built over an oil well, for supporting machinery, as that used in drilling the well.

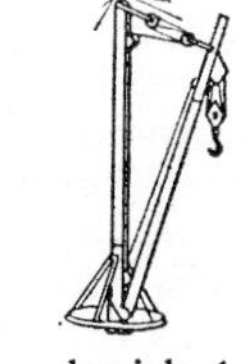
derrick, 1

der·vish \'dər-vish\ *n.* A member of any of various Moslem religious societies living under strict rules and vows of poverty.

derrick, 2

des·cant \'des-ˌkant\ *n.* **1** Originally, a melody sung above a principal melody. **2** The art of composing or singing part music or a piece of music so composed. **3** A song; a strain of melody. **4** A discourse or comment on a subject. — \des-'kant, 'des-ˌkant\ *v.* **1** To sing or play a descant. **2** To sing. **3** To discourse at length; as, to *descant* on the shortcomings of the government.

de·scend \dē-'send\ *v.* **1** To come down or go down from a higher place, position, or rank to a lower one; as, to *descend* a hill. The rain *descended* in sheets of water. **2** To come down upon violently; to attack. The enemy *descended* upon the city. **3** To come down from an earlier time; as, a custom *descended* from ancient times. **4** To come from; as, a person *descended* from a noble family. **5** To be handed down to an heir. The property will *descend* to the son. **6** To come down in the social, mental, or moral scale; to stoop; as, to *descend* to thievery.

de·scend·ant \dē-'sen-dənt\ *adj.* Descendent. — *n.* One that descends, as from an ancestor; as, a *descendant* of a colonial sea captain.

de·scend·ent \dē-'sen-dənt\ *adj.* **1** Descending. **2** Proceeding from an ancestor or source.

de·scent \dē-'sent\ *n.* **1** A coming down or going down; change from a higher to a lower place or rank. **2** A downward slope, as a stairway or a hill; as, a steep *descent.* **3** A sudden attack; as, the *descent* of an army upon a city. **4** Birth; ancestry; as, a person of English *descent.*

de·scribe \dē-'skrīb\ *v.;* **de·scribed**; **de·scrib·ing.** **1** To write or tell about; to give an account of; as, to *describe* a sunset; to *describe* a football game.

2 To draw the outline of; as, to *describe* a circle with compasses. — **de·scrib·a·ble,** *adj.* — **de·scrib·er,** *n.*

de·scrip·tion \dē-ˈskripsh-n\ *n.* **1** An account of something; especially, an account that presents a picture to a person who reads or hears it; as, a vivid *description* of last night's game. **2** Kind; sort; as, people of every *description.*

de·scrip·tive \dē-ˈskrip-tiv\ *adj.* Serving to describe. "Blue" is a *descriptive* word. — **de·scrip·tive·ly,** *adv.*

de·scry \dē-ˈskrī\ *v.;* **de·scried** \-ˈskrīd\; **de·scry·ing. 1** To catch sight of; to spy out or discover by the eye; as, to *descry* a person in the distance. **2** To discover or detect by observation or investigation; as, to *descry* a flaw in the argument.

des·e·crate \ˈdes-ə-ˌkrāt\ *v.;* **des·e·crat·ed; des·e·crat·ing.** To treat something sacred in a wrong or disrespectful manner; to profane; as, to *desecrate* a Christian church by the worship of idols. — **des·e·crat·er** or **des·e·cra·tor** \-ˌkrāt-r\ *n.* — **des·e·cra·tion** \ˌdes-ə-ˈkrāsh-n\ *n.*

de·seg·re·gate \(ˈ)dē-ˈseg-rə-ˌgāt\ *v.;* **de·seg·re·gat·ed; de·seg·re·gat·ing.** To free of any law, provision, or practice requiring isolation of the members of a particular race in separate units, especially in military service or in education. — **de·seg·re·ga·tion** \(ˌ)dē-ˌseg-rə-ˈgāsh-n\ *n.*

de·sert \dē-ˈzərt\ *n.* **1** Worthiness of reward or punishment. Each was rewarded according to his *deserts.* **2** A just reward or punishment. The thief got his *deserts.*

des·ert \ˈdez-rt\ *n.* **1** A region left unoccupied. **2** A dry region where only a few specialized plants grow; a waste region. — *adj.* Like a desert; barren; without life; as, a *desert* island.

de·sert \dē-ˈzərt\ *v.* **1** To leave a person or a thing that one should stay with; to abandon or forsake a person or thing; as, to *desert* one's family. **2** To fail one in need. The leader's courage *deserted* him. **3** In the armed forces, to leave without permission and with the intention of not returning. — For synonyms see *abandon.*

de·sert·er \dē-ˈzərt-r\ *n.* **1** One who deserts a duty, a cause, or a person to whom he owes service. **2** One in the armed forces who abandons the service without leave.

de·ser·tion \dē-ˈzərsh-n\ *n.* **1** A deserting; abandonment. **2** A leaving without being authorized to do so, as from one of the armed services. **3** The state of being deserted; desolation.

de·serve \dē-ˈzərv\ *v.;* **de·served; de·serv·ing.** To be worthy of; to merit; as, conduct *deserving* praise. The punishment was greater than the boy *deserved.*

de·serv·ed·ly \dē-ˈzər-vəd-lē\ *adv.* According to merit; justly; as, a prize *deservedly* awarded.

de·serv·ing \dē-ˈzər-ving\ *adj.* **1** Worthy; as, *deserving* of praise. **2** Meriting assistance. All *deserving* families were given help. — **de·serv·ing·ly,** *adv.*

des·ic·cate \ˈdes-ə-ˌkāt\ *v.;* **des·ic·cat·ed; des·ic·cat·ing.** To dry; to preserve by drying, as fish, fruit, and eggs.

de·sid·er·a·tum \dē-ˌsid-r-ˈāt-m, -ˌzid-, -ˈät-, -ˈåt-\ *n.; pl.* **de·sid·er·a·ta** \-ˈāt-ə, -ˈät-, -ˈåt-\. Anything desired as essential or needed.

de·sign \dē-ˈzīn\ *v.* **1** To intend; to set apart, as for a special purpose; as, to *design* something for one's own use; a lesson *designed* for reviewing. **2** To plan mentally; to outline; to scheme. **3** To make a pattern or sketch of something; as, to *design* an airplane; to *design* a dress. — *n.* **1** A purpose; a plan; as, to fulfill one's *design* of saving money. **2** A purpose in view; an aim. **3** A secret scheme; a plot; as, *designs* against the government. **4** A plan or sketch of something; as, the *design* for an airplane. **5** A decorative pattern; the arrangement of details in a work of art; as, a prize for the best cover *design;* a bracelet of fine *design.*

des·ig·nate \ˈdez-ig-ˌnāt\ *v.;* **des·ig·nat·ed; des·ig·nat·ing. 1** To mark out; to point out; to indicate; to show; as, a detour clearly *designated* by signs. **2** To name; to appoint or choose for a special purpose; as, to *designate* someone to clean the blackboards. **3** To call by a name or title. Dogs, cats, and horses are all *designated* as animals.

des·ig·na·tion \ˌdez-ig-ˈnāsh-n\ *n.* **1** A designating; an indication; as, *designation* of a route by white markers. **2** A selection for a purpose; as, the *designation* of the members of a committee. **3** Anything that designates; a distinguishing mark or title. "Thanksgiving" is the *designation* of a holiday.

de·sign·ed·ly \dē-ˈzī-nəd-lē\ *adv.* Purposely; as, to be late *designedly.*

de·sign·er \dē-ˈzīn-r\ *n.* A person who designs; especially, one whose business it is to design certain things, as dresses or machines.

de·sign·ing \dē-ˈzī-ning\ *n.* The act or art of making designs, plans, or sketches. — *adj.* Planning; plotting; scheming; as, a *designing* woman.

de·sir·a·ble \dē-ˈzīr-əb-l\ *adj.* Such as to arouse desire; to be desired; pleasing; agreeable; as, a house in a *desirable* part of the town. — **de·sir·a·bil·i·ty** \dē-ˌzīr-ə-ˈbil-ət-ē\ *n.* — **de·sir·a·bly** \dē-ˈzīr-ə-blē\ *adv.*

de·sire \dē-ˈzīr\ *v.;* **de·sired; de·sir·ing. 1** To long for; to wish earnestly for; as, to *desire* wealth; to *desire* peace. **2** To express a wish for; to request. The librarian *desires* us to return all overdue books. — *n.* **1** A strong wish; a longing; as, a *desire* for knowledge. **2** A request. **3** The thing that is wished; as, to get one's *desire.*

de·sir·ous \dē-ˈzīr-əs\ *adj.* Desiring; eagerly wishing for; as, *desirous* of an invitation to the party.

de·sist \dē-ˈzist, -ˈsist\ *v.* To cease to act; to stop; as, to be unable to *desist* from laughing at a clown.

desk \ˈdesk\ *n.* A piece of furniture with a flat or sloping surface to be used by writers or readers.

des·o·late \ˈdes-l-ət, ˈdez-\ *adj.* **1** Lacking inhabitants; deserted; gloomy; as, a *desolate* countryside; a *desolate* mood. **2** In a neglected condition; in ruins; as, a *desolate* farmhouse. **3** Left alone; lonely; miserable; as, a *desolate* life on a small island. — \-ˌāt\ *v.;* **des·o·lat·ed; des·o·lat·ing. 1** To cause to be ruined or deserted; as, a village *desolated* by fire. **2** To deprive of inhabitants. **3** To make unhappy or miserable; as, to be *desolated* by bad news. — **des·o·late·ly** \-ət-lē\ *adv.*

des·o·la·tion \ˌdes-l-ˈāsh-n, ˌdez-\ *n.* **1** A state of being desolate; waste; ruin; gloominess. The abandoned house was the picture of *desolation* and neglect. **2** A desolate region. **3** Grief; woe; sadness. **4** Loneliness.

de·spair \dē-ˈspar, -ˈsper\ *v.* To give up hope; as, to *despair* of finishing a job on time. — *n.* **1** Loss of hope; feeling of complete hopelessness; as, to be in *despair* about one's health. **2** A cause of despair. A lazy, ill-behaved child can be the *despair* of his parents.

de·spair·ing \dē-ˈspar-ing, -ˈsper-\ *adj.* Feeling or expressing despair; as, a *despairing* cry. — **de·spair·ing·ly,** *adv.*

des·patch \dis-ˈpach\ *v.* or *n.* Dispatch.

des·per·a·do \ˌdesp-r-ˈād-ˌō, -ˈäd-, -ˈȧd-\ *n.; pl.* **des·per·a·does** or **des·per·a·dos.** [From Old Spanish *desperado,* past participle of *desperar* meaning "to despair".] A bold and reckless criminal.

des·per·ate \ˈdesp-r(-)ət\ *adj.* **1** Beyond, or almost beyond, hope; causing despair; as, a *desperate* illness. **2** Reckless because of despair; rash; as, a *desperate* attempt to escape from prison. — **des·per·ate·ly** \ˈdesp-r(-)ət-lē, ˈdes-pərt-\ *adv.*

des·per·a·tion \ˌdesp-r-ˈāsh-n\ *n.* A state of despair or hopelessness leading to a reckless act; as, driven to *desperation* by hunger.

de·spic·a·ble \də-ˈspik-əb-l, ˈdes-pək-əb-l\ *adj.* Deserving to be despised; contemptible; as, *despicable* manners. — **de·spic·a·bly** \-ə-blē\ *adv.*

de·spise \dē-ˈspīz\ *v.;* **de·spised; de·spis·ing.** To look down on; to have a scornful dislike for; as, to *despise* liars; to *despise* cruelty.

de·spite \dē-ˈspīt\ *n.* An insulting, malicious, or defiant act; outrageous treatment. — **in despite of.** In defiance of; in spite of. — *prep.* In spite of; as, to play out of doors *despite* the cold weather.

de·spite·ful \dē-ˈspīt-fəl\ *adj.* Full of despite; insulting. — **de·spite·ful·ly** \-fə-lē\ *adv.*

de·spoil \dē-ˈspȯil\ *v.* To rob a person or thing; to plunder.

de·spo·li·a·tion \dē-ˌspō-lē-ˈāsh-n\ *n.* A stripping or plundering; pillage. Police were on duty to prevent *despoliation* of the burned-out buildings.

de·spond \dē-ˈspänd\ *v.* To become discouraged or disheartened.

de·spond·ence \dē-ˈspän-dən(t)s\ *n.* Despondency.

de·spond·en·cy \dē-ˈspän-dən-sē\ *n.* The state of being despondent; the loss of hope; discouragement. *Despondency* in a young person is seldom of long duration.

de·spond·ent \dē-ˈspän-dənt\ *adj.* In low spirits; very discouraged; as, a person *despondent* over his poor health. — **de·spond·ent·ly,** *adv.*

des·pot \ˈdes-pət, -ˌpät\ *n.* A person, especially a ruler, who has unlimited power; a tyrant. — **des·pot·ic** \des-ˈpät-ik\ *adj.* — **des·pot·i·cal·ly** \-ik-l(-)ē\ *adv.*

des·pot·ism \ˈdes-pə-ˌtiz-m\ *n.* **1** The power or principles of a despot; the attitude of a despot; tyranny. **2** A government that is directed by a despot.

des·sert \də-ˈzərt\ *n.* The last course at a meal, usually some sweet food or fruit.

des·ti·na·tion \ˌdes-tə-ˈnāsh-n\ *n.* The place set for the end of a journey; the place to which something is sent; the goal. Our *destination* on our trip was San Francisco.

des·tine \ˈdes-tən\ *v.;* **des·tined; des·tin·ing. 1** To settle in advance; as, a plan *destined* to fail. **2** To design. The father *destined* his son for the study of law. **3** To be bound or directed; as, a ship *destined* for New York.

des·ti·ny \ˈdes-tə-nē\ *n.; pl.* **des·ti·nies. 1** The fate or lot of a person or thing; doom. **2** The course of events, considered as something arranged by a power greater than man's.

— The words *fate* and *doom* are synonyms of *destiny: destiny* may indicate either a future course of events determined by some higher agency, or a good, fitting, or natural fulfillment; *fate* is likely to imply an unchangeable course, sometimes more or less unfortunate or unjust; *doom* usually suggests a grim and completely disastrous judgment or end.

des·ti·tute \ˈdes-tə-ˌtüt, -ˌtyüt\ *adj.* **1** Lacking something needed or desirable; as, an official *destitute* of the power to take action; a family *destitute* of the barest necessities of life. **2** Extremely poor; in great want; as, a *destitute* family.

des·ti·tu·tion \ˌdes-tə-ˈtüsh-n, -ˈtyüsh-n\ *n.* The state of being destitute; extreme poverty.

de·stroy \dē-ˈstrȯi\ *v.* **1** To put an end to; to do away with; to ruin; as, to *destroy* trash by burning it; a city almost *destroyed* by an earthquake. **2** To kill; as, to have a hopelessly sick animal *destroyed.* In medieval times plague *destroyed* men by the thousands.

de·stroy·er \dē-ˈstrȯi-ər\ *n.* A person or thing that destroys; especially, a small fast warship carrying guns, torpedoes, and usually depth charges for fighting submarines.

destroyer escort. A warship used chiefly against submarines, smaller than a destroyer and carrying depth charges as its principal weapon.

de·struct·i·ble \dē-ˈstrək-təb-l\ *adj.* Liable to destruction; capable of being destroyed; as, toys not *destructible* under normal conditions. — **de·struct·i·bil·i·ty** \dē-ˌstrək-tə-ˈbil-ət-ē\ *n.*

de·struc·tion \dē-ˈstrəksh-n\ *n.* **1** The action or process of destroying; as, to watch the *destruction* of a building by a wrecking crew. An automobile is not supposed to be an instrument of *destruction.* **2** The condition or fact of being destroyed; ruin;

widespread damage; as, carefully laid plans brought to *destruction* by one unwise move; the *destruction* caused by a flood.

de·struc·tive \dē-ˈstrək-tiv\ *adj.* **1** Causing destruction; ruinous; as, a *destructive* four-alarm fire; pests *destructive* to fruit trees. **2** Designed or tending to tear down and destroy rather than build up or support; not constructive; as, *destructive* criticism. — **de·struc·tive·ly**, *adv.*

de·struc·tor \dē-ˈstrəkt-r\ *n.* One that destroys; especially, a furnace or oven for burning refuse or the solid parts of sewage.

des·ul·to·ry \ˈdes-l-ˌtōr-ē, -ˌtȯr-ē\ *adj.* Passing from one thing or subject to another aimlessly; disconnected; as, *desultory* reading.

de·tach \dē-ˈtach\ *v.* To separate a person or a thing from something, especially for a particular purpose; to unfasten; as, to *detach* a key from a ring; to *detach* two boys from the group to look for a camp site. — **de·tach·a·ble**, *adj.*

de·tached \dē-ˈtacht\ *adj.* **1** Not joined or connected; separate; as, a *detached* house. **2** Aloof; unconcerned; impartial; as, a *detached* attitude.

de·tach·ment \dē-ˈtach-mənt\ *n.* **1** The action or process of detaching; separation; as, erosion of soft rock through *detachment* of particles. **2** A body of troops or ships sent on special duty away from the main body. **3** The state of being detached; a keeping away or apart; as, to live a life of *detachment* from affairs of the world. **4** Impartiality; freedom from bias or prejudice; as, the *detachment* of a trained scientific observer.

de·tail \dē-ˈtāl, ˈdē-ˌtāl\ *n.* **1** A dealing with something item by item; as, to go into *detail* about an adventure. **2** A small part; an item; as, the *details* of a story; a dress finished except for such *details* as buttons and trimming. **3** Selection, as of a soldier or group of soldiers, for some special service; as, to be on *detail* at headquarters. **4** A soldier or group of soldiers appointed for some special duty; as, a scouting *detail* of ten men. — **in detail.** Item by item, omitting nothing; fully; thoroughly; as, to explain *in detail*. — *v.* **1** To give the details of. **2** To appoint for some special duty; as, to *detail* three boys to chop wood.

de·tailed \ˈdē-ˌtāld, dē-ˈtāld\ *adj.* Including many details; as, a *detailed* drawing; a *detailed* knowledge of American history.

de·tain \dē-ˈtān\ *v.* **1** To hold or keep in custody or as if in custody; as, to be *detained* by the police as a suspicious character. The teacher *detained* the boys after school. **2** To delay; to hold back; as, to be *detained* by unexpected business. — For synonyms see *delay*. — **de·tain·ment**, *n.*

de·tect \dē-ˈtekt\ *v.* To discover the existence, presence, or fact of; to find out; to make out; as, to *detect* smoke. Radar *detects* the approach of an airplane long before it can be seen or heard.

de·tec·tion \dē-ˈteksh-n\ *n.* The act or process of detecting or the state or fact of being detected; as, the *detection* of crime. The thief escaped *detection* for several months.

de·tec·tive \dē-ˈtek-tiv\ *adj.* **1** Fitted for or used in detecting something; as, a *detective* device for coal gas. **2** Of or relating to detectives or their work; as, a *detective* agency; a *detective* story. — *n.* A policeman or other person whose business is to find out how crimes were committed, to capture criminals, and to watch suspicious persons.

de·tec·tor \dē-ˈtekt-r\ *n.* **1** One that detects or that gives warning; as, a fire *detector.* **2** A device in a radio receiving set for converting the high-frequency current of radio waves into current that with proper amplification can vibrate a loudspeaker, reproducing the original sound.

de·ten·tion \dē-ˈtench-n\ *n.* The act of detaining or the state of being detained; confinement or forced delay; as, to be punished by *detention* after school. We were late because of our *detention* by a breakdown on the road.

de·ter \dē-ˈtər\ *v.;* **de·terred**; **de·ter·ring.** To turn aside or discourage; to prevent from doing something, as through fear of consequences or of difficulties involved; as, to refuse to be *deterred* from trying by the failure of others.

de·ter·gent \dē-ˈtərj-nt\ *adj.* Cleansing; as, a *detergent* oil for automobile engines. — *n.* A cleansing agent, as water or soap; especially, a soluble or liquid chemical preparation that is like soap in its ability to cleanse things of dirt.

de·te·ri·o·rate \dē-ˈtir-ē-ə-ˌrāt\ *v.;* **de·te·ri·o·rat·ed**; **de·te·ri·o·rat·ing.** To make or become worse or of less value; to degenerate; as, a neighborhood that *deteriorated* almost to the point of becoming a slum. Relations between the allies temporarily *deteriorated* as a result of the disagreement. — **de·te·ri·o·ra·tion** \dē-ˌtir-ē-ə-ˈrāsh-n\ *n.*

de·ter·mi·nant \dē-ˈtər-mə-nənt\ *n.* Something that serves to determine, fix, or settle.

de·ter·mi·nate \dē-ˈtər-mə-nət\ *adj.* **1** Having fixed limits; definite. **2** Definitely settled, as by authority; as, arranged in a *determinate* order. — **de·ter·mi·nate·ly**, *adv.*

de·ter·mi·na·tion \dē-ˌtər-mə-ˈnāsh-n\ *n.* **1** The act of coming to a decision or the decision or conclusion reached. **2** The act of fixing the extent, position, or character of something; as, the *determination* of the position of a ship at sea. **3** Accurate measurement, as of length or volume. *Determination* of the size of a room requires only an ordinary tape measure. **4** Firmness; firm or fixed purpose; as, a man of great *determination;* to fail for lack of *determination.*

de·ter·mine \dē-ˈtər-mən\ *v.;* **de·ter·mined**; **de·ter·min·ing.** **1** To settle or decide on something; to make up one's mind; as, to *determine* to learn to spell; to *determine* what friends to invite to a party. **2** To find out for oneself, as by measuring, observing, or thinking; as, to *determine* the size of a room; to *determine* the direction of the wind. **3** To be the cause of or reason for; to decide. The quality of a pupil's work *determines* his mark.

de·ter·mined \dē-ˈtər-mənd\ *adj.* **1** Decided; resolved; as, to be *determined* to go even though the weather is bad. **2** Firm; resolute; fixed; as, a man with a *determined* look on his face. — **de·ter·mined·ly** \-mənd-lē, -mə-nəd-lē\ *adv.*

de·ter·rent \dē-'tər-ənt, -'ter-\ *adj.* Having the effect of deterring or stopping. — *n.* Something that deters. Fear of punishment may serve as a *deterrent* from crime.

de·test \dē-'test\ *v.* To hate intensely; to loathe. — For synonyms see *hate.*

de·test·a·ble \dē-'tes-təb-l\ *adj.* Deserving to be detested; arousing strong dislike; as, *detestable* vice.

de·throne \(')dē-'thrōn\ *v.;* **de·throned**; **de·thron·ing**. To remove from a throne or as if from a throne; to displace; as, to *dethrone* a champion. — **de·throne·ment,** *n.*

det·o·nate \'det-ən-ˌāt\ *v.;* **det·o·nat·ed**; **det·o·nat·ing**. To explode with sudden violence; as, to *detonate* a charge of dynamite. — **det·o·na·tion** \ˌdet-ən-'āsh-n\ *n.* — **det·o·na·tor** \'det-ən-ˌāt-r\ *n.*

de·tour \'dē-ˌtu̇r, dē-'tu̇r\ *n.* A turning from a direct course; especially, a roundabout way temporarily used instead of a regular road. — *v.* To go by a detour.

de·tract \dē-'trakt\ *v.* **1** To take away; to withdraw; to subtract; as, to *detract* from a person's reputation. **2** To distract; as, to *detract* attention. — **de·trac·tor** \-'trakt-r\ *n.*

de·trac·tion \dē-'traksh-n\ *n.* A taking away of a part of the reputation or good name of a person, especially by slander.

de·train \(')dē-'trān\ *v.* To leave or to cause to leave a railroad train.

det·ri·ment \'de-trə-mənt\ *n.* Injury or damage, or something that causes it. Getting too little sleep is a *detriment* to one's health.

det·ri·men·tal \ˌde-trə-'ment-l\ *adj.* Causing detriment or injury; harmful; as, the *detrimental* effect of getting too little sleep.

de·tri·tus \dē-'trīt-əs\ *n.* Any loose material that results directly from the natural breaking up of rocks, as by the action of frost.

deuce \'düs, 'dyüs\ *n.* [From medieval French *deus* meaning "two", there derived from Latin *duos,* the accusative case of *duo* meaning "two".] **1** The side of a die marked with two spots. **2** A cast of dice in which two aces turn up. **3** A playing card with two spots. **4** A tied score at three points for each side in a game of tennis. **5** Bad luck; the devil — used as an oath.

deu·te·ri·um \dü-'tir-ē-əm, dyü-\ *n.* A form of hydrogen that is twice as heavy as ordinary hydrogen.

dev·as·tate \'dev-əs-ˌtāt\ *v.;* **dev·as·tat·ed**; **dev·as·tat·ing**. To lay waste; to ruin; as, a country *devastated* by invading armies. — **dev·as·tat·ing·ly** \-ˌtāt-ing-lē\ *adv.* — **dev·as·ta·tor** \-ˌtāt-r\ *n.*

dev·as·ta·tion \ˌdev-əs-'tāsh-n\ *n.* The action of devastating; the state of being devastated; a laying waste; as, the *devastation* caused by a hurricane.

de·vel·op \dē-'vel-əp\ *v.* **1** To unfold gradually or in detail; to reveal; as, to *develop* a plan. **2** To change from one state into another; to make or to grow more advanced or more nearly perfect; as, to *develop* the mind by study. Buds *develop* into flowers. **3** To make more usable; as, to *develop* our natural resources. **4** To apply chemicals to a photographic negative in order to bring out the picture.

de·vel·op·er \dē-'vel-əp-r\ *n.* One that develops; especially, a chemical agent used in developing photographic film and prints.

de·vel·op·ment \dē-'vel-əp-mənt\ *n.* A developing or state of being developed; an unfolding, growth, or progress; as, *development* of a flower from a bud.

de·vi·ate \'dē-vē-ˌāt\ *v.;* **de·vi·at·ed**; **de·vi·at·ing.** To turn aside from a course; to stray, as from a topic or a standard. — **de·vi·a·tion** \ˌdē-vē-'āsh-n\ *n.*

de·vice \dē-'vīs\ *n.* **1** Something made or thought up to bring about a desired result; an invention; a scheme; as, a *device* for holding doors shut. **2** [in the plural] Desire; will; inclination. When left to their own *devices,* most children find things to do. **3** A design, badge, or emblem; a motto.

dev·il \'dev-l\ *n.* [From Old English *diofol, deofol,* there borrowed from Late Latin *diabolus,* from Greek *diabolos* meaning literally "slanderer".] **1** [often with a capital] The evil spirit; Satan. **2** Any evil spirit; a demon or fiend. **3** A wicked, cruel person; a fiend. **4** A wretched person; as, a poor *devil* begging in the streets. — *v.;* **dev·iled** or **dev·illed**; **dev·il·ing** or **dev·il·ling** \-l(-)ing\. **1** To tease; to annoy. **2** To season highly; as, to *devil* eggs.

dev·iled or **dev·illed** \'dev-ld\ *adj.* Chopped fine and highly seasoned, usually after being cooked; as, *deviled* ham.

dev·il·fish \'dev-l-ˌfish\ *n.; pl.* **dev·il·fish** or **dev·il·fish·es**. **1** A large ray of the Gulf of Mexico. **2** An octopus.

dev·il·ish \'dev-l(-)ish\ *adj.* Like or relating to the Devil. — *adv.* Extremely; excessively; as, *devilish* hot. — **dev·il·ish·ly,** *adv.*

dev·il·ment \'dev-l-mənt, -ˌment\ *n.* Reckless mischief.

dev·il·try \'dev-l-trē\ *n.; pl.* **dev·il·tries**. Wickedness; mischief; as, up to some *deviltry.*

de·vi·ous \'dē-vē-əs\ *adj.* **1** Out of the straight or usual path or line; winding; as, a *devious* route. **2** Going astray; not straightforward; as, to get money by *devious* means. — **de·vi·ous·ly,** *adv.*

de·vise \dē-'vīz\ *v.;* **de·vised**; **de·vis·ing. 1** To think up; to plan; to contrive; as, to *devise* a way to escape. **2** To bequeath; to leave by will.

de·vi·tal·ize \(')dē-'vīt-l-ˌīz\ *v.;* **de·vi·tal·ized**; **de·vi·tal·iz·ing**. To deprive of life or vitality; to make weak; as, *devitalized* by a long illness. — **de·vi·tal·i·za·tion** \ˌdē-ˌvīt-l-ə-'zāsh-n\ *n.*

de·void \dē-'vȯid\ *adj.* Entirely lacking; as, a book *devoid* of interest for children.

de·vote \dē-ˈvōt\ *v.;* **de·vot·ed; de·vot·ing. 1** To set apart for a special purpose, often by a vow; to dedicate; as, to *devote* an hour to worship. **2** To give up to wholly; as, to *devote* oneself to one's friends; to *devote* too much attention to sports.

de·vot·ed \dē-ˈvōt-əd\ *adj.* **1** Sincerely given over to a purpose; zealous; devout; as, *devoted* admirers; *devoted* labors. **2** Affectionate; fond; loving; as, a *devoted* mother. — **de·vot·ed·ly,** *adv.*

dev·o·tee \ˌdev-ə-ˈtē, -ˈtā\ *n.* One who is extremely devout or devoted to something.

de·vo·tion \dē-ˈvōsh-n\ *n.* **1** Strong love or affection. **2** [in the plural] Prayers, especially for private worship; as, a woman kneeling at her *devotions.* **3** The act of devoting oneself to something; as, a lifelong *devotion* to music. — **de·vo·tion·al** \-ˈvōsh-n(-)əl\ *adj.* — **de·vo·tion·al·ly** \-ə-lē\ *adv.*

de·vour \dē-ˈvaůr\ *v.* **1** To swallow or eat up greedily. The dog *devoured* his food. **2** To consume; to lay waste; as, buildings *devoured* by the flames. **3** To enjoy deeply; to take in eagerly by the eyes or mind; as, to *devour* a book.

de·vout \dē-ˈvaůt\ *adj.* **1** Devoted to religion; as, a child of *devout* parents. **2** Sincere; earnest; as, to extend *devout* wishes for a safe journey. — **de·vout·ly,** *adv.*

dew \ˈdü, ˈdyü\ *n.* **1** Moisture, often in small drops, formed on the surfaces of cool objects at night. **2** Anything that falls or comes lightly and in a refreshing manner; as, the *dew* of sleep. — **dewy,** *adj.*

dew·ber·ry \ˈdü-ˌber-ē, ˈdyü-\ *n.; pl.* **dew·ber·ries. 1** A creeping blackberry with trailing stems that root at the joints or tip. **2** The fruit of this plant, a small purplish berry.

dew·drop \ˈdü-ˌdräp, ˈdyü-\ *n.* A drop of dew.

dew·lap \ˈdü-ˌlap, ˈdyü-\ *n.* The hanging fold of skin under the neck of various animals, as cows and deer.

dewlap

dew point. The temperature at which a vapor, as the moisture in the air, begins to be deposited as a liquid.

dex·ter·i·ty \deks-ˈter-ət-ē\ *n.* **1** Quickness, skill, and ease in physical activity, especially in using the hands; as, *dexterity* in painting. **2** Mental skill or quickness; as, *dexterity* in argument.

dex·ter·ous \ˈdeks-tər-əs, -trəs\ *adj.* **1** Skillful in thinking or acting; quick; ready; as, a *dexterous* mind. **2** Skillfully done; as, *dexterous* tricks. — **dex·ter·ous·ly,** *adv.*

dex·trose \ˈdeks-ˌtrōs\ *n.* Naturally occurring glucose.

dex·trous \ˈdeks-trəs\ *adj.* Dexterous.

di·a·be·tes \ˌdī-ə-ˈbēt-ēz, -əs\ *n.* A disease marked by excessive thirst, hunger, loss of flesh, and the discharge of abnormal amounts of urine. — **sugar diabetes.** A serious form of diabetes in which insulin is lacking and sugar passes out in the urine.

di·a·bet·ic \ˌdī-ə-ˈbet-ik, -ˈbēt-\ *adj.* Of or relating to diabetes. — *n.* A person having diabetes.

di·a·bol·ic \ˌdī-ə-ˈbäl-ik\ or **di·a·bol·i·cal** \-ik-l\ *adj.* **1** Of or relating to the Devil or devils. **2** Devilish; fiendish. — **di·a·bol·i·cal·ly** \-ik-l(-)ē\ *adv.*

di·a·crit·ic \ˌdī-ə-ˈkrit-ik\ *adj.* Diacritical. — *n.* A diacritical mark.

di·a·crit·i·cal \ˌdī-ə-ˈkrit-ik-l\ *adj.* Serving to separate or distinguish. — **diacritical mark.** A mark, point, or sign written with a letter to distinguish it from another letter with a different mark or from a letter without a mark.

di·a·dem \ˈdī-ə-ˌdem\ *n.* **1** A crown. **2** An ornamental band for the head, worn by some monarchs.

diadem, 2

di·aer·e·sis or **di·er·e·sis** \dī-ˈer-ə-səs\ *n.; pl.* **di·aer·e·ses** or **di·er·e·ses** \-ˌsēz\. A mark [¨] placed over a vowel to show that it is pronounced separately from the preceding letter, as in *naïve.*

di·ag·nose \ˈdī-əg-ˌnōs, -ˌnōz\ *v.;* **di·ag·nosed; di·ag·nos·ing.** To recognize by its symptoms, as a disease; to make a diagnosis. The child's illness was soon *diagnosed* as measles.

di·ag·no·sis \ˌdī-əg-ˈnō-səs\ *n.; pl.* **di·ag·no·ses** \-ˌsēz\. **1** The recognizing or naming of a disease from its symptoms. **2** A careful, critical study of something, as to determine its nature or importance; as, an official *diagnosis* of traffic problems. **3** The conclusion reached after such a study. — **di·ag·nos·tic** \-ˈnäs-tik\ *adj.*

di·ag·o·nal \dī-ˈag-n-əl\ *adj.* **1** Running from one corner to the opposite corner of a four-sided figure. **2** Running in a slanting direction; as, *diagonal* stripes in cloth. — *n.* A diagonal line, marking, part, or weave. — **di·ag·o·nal·ly** \-ˈag-n(-)ə-lē\ *adv.*

diagonal

di·a·gram \ˈdī-ə-ˌgram\ *n.* Any drawing, sketch, plan, or chart that makes something clearer or easier to understand. — *v.;* **di·a·gramed** or **di·a·grammed** \-ˌgramd\; **di·a·gram·ing** or **di·a·gram·ming** \-ˌgram-ing\. To put in the form of a diagram. — **di·a·gram·mat·ic** \ˌdī-ə-grə-ˈmat-ik\ or **di·a·gram·mat·i·cal** \-ik-l\ *adj.* — **di·a·gram·mat·i·cal·ly** \-ik-l(-)ē\ *adv.*

di·al \ˈdī-əl, ˈdīl\ *n.* **1** A sundial. **2** The face of a clock or watch. **3** A plate or face with a pointer that indicates something, as pressure in a boiler. **4** A lettered or numbered plate for making connections, as by radio or telephone. — *v.;* **di·aled** or **di·alled; di·al·ing** or **di·al·ling.** To make connections with, by use of a dial; to use a dial; as, to *dial* a telephone number.

clock dial

dial. Abbreviation for: **1** dialect **2** dialectal.

di·a·lect \ˈdī-ə-ˌlekt\ *n.* **1** A form of a language that belongs to a certain region; as, rural *dialect.* **2** The words or manner of speech belonging to a particular trade, profession, or class; as, the *dialect* of baseball.

di·a·lect \ˈdī-ə-ˌlekt\ or **di·a·lec·tal** \ˌdī-ə-ˈlekt-l\ *adj.* **1** Belonging to a dialect; being a part of a dialect. **2** Characteristic of a dialect. — **di·a·lec·tal·ly** \ˌdī-ə-ˈlek-tə-lē\ *adv.*

di·a·logue or **di·a·log** \ˈdī-ə-ˌlȯg\ *n.* **1** A conversation between two or more persons. **2** Conversation parts, as in a book or play.

di·am·e·ter \dī-ˈam-ət-r\ *n.* **1** A straight line that passes through the center of a figure or body, as a circle, sphere, or cube. **2** The distance through the center of a thing from one side to the other; thickness; as, the *diameter* of a tree trunk.

di·a·met·ric \ˌdī-ə-ˈme-trik\ or **di·a·met·ri·cal** \trik-l\ *adj.* **1** Of or relating to a diameter. **2** As distant as possible, as if at opposite ends of a diameter; directly opposed; as, two brothers who were *diametric* opposites in temperament.

di·a·met·ri·cal·ly \ˌdī-ə-ˈme-trik-l(-)ē\ *adv.* **1** Along a diameter or with diametrical directness; as, to measure *diametrically;* an avenue running almost *diametrically* through the city. **2** As if at the end of a diameter; as, *diametrically* opposed.

di·a·mond \ˈdī-mənd, -ə-mənd\ *n.* **1** A valuable, very hard stone consisting of crystallized carbon. **2** A piece of this stone cut, polished, and used as a gem. **3** A flat figure [◇] that resembles one of the surfaces of certain cut diamonds, formed by four equal straight lines bounding two acute and two obtuse angles. **4** In baseball, the space inside the lines connecting the four bases; the infield. **5** A playing card belonging to the suit **(diamonds)** marked with red diamond-shaped figures.

di·a·per \ˈdī-əp-r, ˈdīp-r\ *n.* **1** A fabric, usually of white linen or cotton, woven in a pattern (**diaper pattern**) formed by the repetition of a simple, usually geometric design. **2** A piece of cloth used as an article of underclothing for a baby. — *v.;* **di·a·pered; di·a·per·ing** \-r(-)ing\. **1** To furnish with a diaper pattern; as, *diapered* cloth. **2** To put a diaper on; as, to *diaper* a baby.

di·a·phragm \ˈdī-ə-ˌfram\ *n.* **1** A partition made of muscles and sinews; especially, the fleshy, muscular wall that separates the chest cavity from the abdominal cavity. **2** In various devices, such as a telephone or a hearing aid, a thin circular plate that vibrates rapidly when a sound is made at the mouthpiece. **3** A device to regulate the size of an opening, as to control the amount of light passing through the lens of a camera. — **di·a·phrag·mat·ic** \ˌdī-ə-ˌfrag-ˈmat-ik\ *adj.*

di·ar·rhea or **di·ar·rhoea** \ˌdī-ə-ˈrē-ə\ *n.* An abnormally large or frequent discharge of loose or fluid material from the bowels.

di·a·ry \ˈdīr-ē\ *n.; pl.* **di·a·ries. 1** A daily record, especially of personal experiences, observations, and thoughts. **2** A book for keeping such private notes and records.

di·as·to·le \dī-ˈas-tə-(ˌ)lē\ *n.* The expansion or dilation of the heart as it beats, in the course of which its cavities fill with blood. — **di·as·tol·ic** \ˌdī-ə-ˈstäl-ik\ *adj.*

di·a·tom \ˈdī-ə-ˌtäm, -ət-m\ *n.* Any of a number of microscopic algae having a hard, flinty cell wall that remains as a skeleton after death and occurring abundantly in fresh and salt water and in soil.

di·a·tom·ic \ˌdī-ə-ˈtäm-ik\ *adj.* Consisting of two atoms; having two atoms in the molecule.

di·a·ton·ic \ˌdī-ə-ˈtän-ik\ *adj.* Relating or referring to a standard major or minor scale of eight tones to the octave.

di·a·tribe \ˈdī-ə-ˌtrīb\ *n.* A bitter or violent attack upon a person or thing in words; an angry criticism or denunciation.

dib·ble \ˈdib-l\ *n.* A small gardening tool for making holes in the ground, as for planting seeds.

dice \ˈdīs\ *n.; pl.* of *die.* **1** Small cubes marked with from one to six spots in each side, used in playing a number of games. **2** Gambling with dice; a game played with dice. — *v.;* **diced; dic·ing. 1** To play games with dice; to gamble. **2** To cut into small cubes resembling dice; as, to *dice* potatoes. — **dic·er,** *n.*

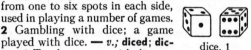

dice, 1

dick·ens \ˈdik-nz\ *n.* The devil; the deuce; as, a *dickens* of a hard time; to tell someone to go to the *dickens.*

dick·er \ˈdik-r\ *v.;* **dick·ered; dick·er·ing** \-r(-)ing\. To trade or barter by bargaining, especially on a small scale; to haggle. The two boys were *dickering* over a jackknife. — *n.* **1** A petty trade or bargain. **2** A deal, as between politicians.

dick·ey or **dicky** \ˈdik-ē\ *n.; pl.* **dick·eys** or **dick·ies. 1** Any of various articles of clothing, as a false shirt front, a woman's partial blouse, consisting of a front and sometimes a back panel, for wear with a suit, or a child's bib or pinafore. **2** One of various animals, as a small bird or a donkey. **3** A seat for the driver in certain carriages. **4** A seat at the rear of a vehicle, especially behind the enclosure of the body; a rumble seat.

Dick test \ˈdik\. A test to determine whether a person can contract scarlet fever, made by injecting scarlet fever toxin into the skin.

di·cot \ˈdī-ˌkät\ *n.* A dicotyledon.

di·cot·y·le·don \ˌdī-ˌkät-l-ˈēd-n\ *n.* A plant having two cotyledons, or seed leaves, as most deciduous trees and most herbs and shrubs.

di·cot·y·le·don·ous \ˌdī-ˌkät-l-ˈēd-n-əs, -ˈed-n-əs\ *adj.* Having two cotyledons.

dicta. A pl. of *dictum.*

dic·tate \ˈdik-ˌtāt\ *v.;* **dic·tat·ed; dic·tat·ing. 1** To tell or speak for someone else to write down; as, to *dictate* a letter to a secretary; to *dictate* a list of words to be spelled. **2** To say or state with authority; to command or order someone to do a certain thing; as, to *dictate* the terms of surrender to a defeated army. Few people enjoy being *dictated* to. — *n.* A direction delivered with the force of authority; an order or command; a rule or principle; as, the *dictates* of conscience; the *dictates* of good taste.

dic·ta·tion \dik-'tāsh-n\ *n.* **1** The dictating of words; as, to write from *dictation;* an exercise in *dictation.* **2** That which is dictated or is taken down as dictated; as, to take *dictation;* to have no mistakes in one's *dictation.* **3** The act or practice of arbitrarily dictating the behavior of others. **4** A being dictated to, or told what to do; as, to listen willingly to advice but object to *dictation.*

dic·ta·tor \'dik-ˌtāt-r, dik-'tāt-r\ *n.* **1** A person who dictates. **2** A ruler, often self-appointed, who is not a king or a queen but has the power of an absolute monarch.

dic·ta·to·ri·al \ˌdik-tə-'tōr-ē-əl, -'tȯr-\ *adj.* Relating to or suited to a dictator or a dictatorship; autocratic; arbitrary; as, a *dictatorial* regime; a *dictatorial* manner. — **dic·ta·to·ri·al·ly** \-ē-ə-lē\ *adv.*

dic·ta·tor·ship \dik-'tāt-r-ˌship, 'dik-ˌtāt-r-\ *n.* **1** The office or the term of office of a dictator. **2** Absolute power or authority.

dic·tion \'diksh-n\ *n.* **1** The way anything is expressed in words; the choice and use of words for expressing ideas; as, poetic *diction.* **2** The art or manner of speaking or singing, especially in public; vocal expression; enunciation. The singer's voice was better than his *diction.*

dic·tio·nary \'diksh-n-ˌer-ē\ *n.; pl.* **dic·tio·nar·ies.** **1** An alphabetically arranged book listing the words of a language or of some part of it, usually with their meanings, spelling variations, and pronunciations, and sometimes with their etymology; an alphabetized vocabulary with definitions. **2** An alphabetical reference book in which words and phrases found in a particular field of knowledge are explained or identified; as, a medical *dictionary*; a biographical *dictionary.* **3** An alphabetized book listing a vocabulary in one language and definitions in another; as, a French-English *dictionary.*

dic·tum \'dikt-m\ *n.; pl.* **dic·tums** \'dikt-mz\ or **dic·ta** \'dik-tə\. **1** An authoritative statement. **2** A current saying; as, a mere *dictum* of the moment.

did. Past tense of *do.*

di·dac·tic \dī-'dak-tik\ *adj.* **1** Intended primarily to instruct rather than to entertain; especially, intended to teach a moral lesson; as, *didactic* literature. **2** Having or showing a tendency to instruct or lecture others; as, a *didactic* manner. — **di·dac·ti·cal·ly** \-tik-l(-)ē\ *adv.*

didn't \'did-nt\. A contraction of *did not.*

didst \(')didst\. An archaic form of *did* used chiefly with *thou.*

die \'dī\ *v.;* **died** \'dīd\; **dy·ing** \'dī-ing\. **1** To stop living. **2** To cease; to disappear; to pass away; as, a *dying* race of people; beauty that *dies.* **3** To long; to desire greatly; as, to be *dying* to hear a secret.

die \'dī\ *n.* **1** *pl.* **dice** \'dīs\. One of the small cubes used in a game of chance. **2** *pl.* **dies** \'dīz\. One of a pair of metal blocks so shaped as to give a desired form to any object that is pressed between them; as, a *die* for coining money.

dieresis. Variant of *diaeresis.*

Die·sel \'dēz-l, 'dēs-l\ *n.* **1** A Diesel engine. **2** Something, as a truck or a train, driven by a Diesel engine.

Diesel engine or **Diesel motor**. [Named after Rudolf *Diesel* (1858–1913), German mechanical engineer who invented it.] An internal-combustion engine that burns a mixture of air and crude oil that is ignited by the heat generated when it is compressed in the cylinder.

di·et \'dī-ət\ *n.* **1** The food and drink that a person or animal usually takes; customary nourishment. **2** The kind and amount of food selected for a person or animal for a special reason, as ill health or overweight; as, a high-protein *diet.* — *v.* To eat or cause to eat smaller amounts of food than one has been accustomed to or only certain prescribed foods. It is usually unwise to *diet* without the approval of a doctor.

di·et \'dī-ət\ *n.* **1** A congress. **2** [with a capital] The name of various national and local assemblies; as, the Japanese *Diet.*

di·e·tary \'dī-ə-ˌter-ē\ *adj.* Relating to diet or to certain rules of diet; as, the *dietary* laws of the Jewish people.

di·e·tet·ic \ˌdī-ə-'tet-ik\ *adj.* Of or relating to diet. — **di·e·tet·i·cal·ly** \-ik-l(-)ē\ *adv.*

di·e·tet·ics \ˌdī-ə-'tet-iks\ *n.* The science of feeding individuals or groups in accordance with the principles of nutrition.

di·e·ti·tian or **di·e·ti·cian** \ˌdī-ə-'tish-n\ *n.* A person who has studied what kinds and amounts of food people or animals should eat in order to be healthy, and who gives advice about these things; a specialist in dietetics; especially, a person who plans meals or diets, as in a hospital.

dif·fer \'dif-r\ *v.;* **dif·fered; dif·fer·ing** \-r(-)ing\. **1** To be not the same; to be unlike; as, brothers that *differ* in looks. **2** To disagree; as, to *differ* about what should be done.

dif·fer·ence \'dif-rn(t)s, -r(-)ən(t)s\ *n.* **1** Unlikeness between two or more persons or things; as, the striking *difference* in the sisters' looks. **2** The amount by which one quantity differs from another of the same kind; the number that is obtained by subtracting one number from another. The *difference* between 4 and 6 is 2. **3** A disagreement in opinion; a dispute; as, persons unable to settle their *differences.*

dif·fer·ent \'dif-rnt, -r(-)ənt\ *adj.* **1** Not of the same kind; unlike another person or thing in every way or in some ways. This apple is *different* from the others in size and color. **2** Not the same; other; separate; as, to see the same person at *different* times and places. — **dif·fer·ent·ly,** *adv.*

dif·fer·en·tial \ˌdif-r-'ench-l\ *adj.* Relating to or showing a difference or differences; as, *differential* freight rates. — *n.* Also **differential gear.** An arrangement of gears in an automobile that allows one of the wheels giving motion, usually a rear one, to turn faster than the other, as in going around curves or corners.

dif·fer·en·ti·ate \ˌdif-r-ˈench-ē-ˌāt\ *v.;* **dif·fer·en·ti·at·ed; dif·fer·en·ti·at·ing. 1** To make a person or a thing different in some way. The color of their eyes *differentiates* the twins. **2** To recognize or state the difference or differences; as, to *differentiate* between two plants. — **dif·fer·en·ti·a·tion** \ˌdif-r-ˌench-ē-ˈāsh-n\ *n.*

dif·fi·cult \ˈdif-ə-ˌkəlt, -ək-lt\ *adj.* **1** Hard to do, make, or understand; as, a *difficult* job; a *difficult* lesson. **2** Hard to please or to manage; trying; as, a *difficult* person.

dif·fi·cul·ty \ˈdif-ə-ˌkəl-tē, -ək-l-tē\ *n.; pl.* **dif·fi·cul·ties. 1** Difficult nature; as, to be slowed up by the *difficulty* of a task. **2** Great effort; as, to accomplish a task only with *difficulty.* **3** Anything that is hard to do; an obstacle; as, to overcome *difficulties.* **4** A difficult or trying situation; trouble; as, to be in financial *difficulties.* **5** Disagreement. The two partners finally ironed out their *difficulties.*

dif·fi·dence \ˈdif-ə-dən(t)s, -ˌden(t)s\ *n.* A modest or timid nature; bashfulness.

dif·fi·dent \ˈdif-ə-dənt, -ˌdent\ *adj.* Lacking self-confidence; bashful. — For synonyms see *shy.*

dif·fuse \di-ˈfyüs\ *adj.* **1** Poured out; spread out; as, *diffuse* evidence that primitive tribes once inhabited the island. **2** Wordy in style; as, a *diffuse* writer. — \di-ˈfyüz\ *v.;* **dif·fused; dif·fus·ing. 1** To pour out and cause to spread, as liquid; as, tar *diffused* over the surface of a road. **2** To scatter or spread. The candles *diffused* a soft light. **3** To intermingle or to cause to intermingle, as one liquid with another.

dif·fu·sion \di-ˈfyüzh-n\ *n.* **1** A diffusing or a being diffused. **2** The intermingling of the particles of gases or of liquids. **3** The reflection of light from a rough surface or the transmission of light through a partly transparent material, as frosted glass.

dig \ˈdig\ *v.;* **dug** \ˈdəg\ or **digged** \ˈdigd\; **digging. 1** To turn up the soil, as with a spade or hoe; to hollow out or form by removing earth; as, to *dig* a hole; to *dig* a cellar. **2** To uncover or to seek by turning up earth; as, to *dig* potatoes; to *dig* for gold. **3** To bring to light; to discover; as, to *dig* up information. **4** To poke; to prod; to thrust; as, to *dig* a person in the ribs. **5** To work hard; as, to *dig* at one's lessons. — *n.* **1** A poke or a thrust. **2** A cutting remark; a gibe; as, to give a person a *dig* about his love of money.

di·gest \ˈdī-ˌjest\ *n.* A body of information, often in condensed or shortened form, classified and arranged for easy use; as, a *digest* of laws. — \dī-ˈjest, də-\ *v.* **1** To change food that has been eaten into some form in which it can be used in the body. **2** To be or become usable by the body. Eggs *digest* easily. **3** To think over and arrange in the mind; as, to read and *digest* a lesson.

di·gest·i·ble \də-ˈjes-təb-l, dī-\ *adj.* Capable of being digested. — **di·gest·i·bil·i·ty** \də-ˌjes-tə-ˈbil-ət-ē, dī-\ *n.*

di·ges·tion \də-ˈjes-chən, dī-\ *n.* The process or power of digesting, especially food.

di·ges·tive \də-ˈjes-tiv, dī-\ *adj.* Having to do with digestion; having the power to cause or aid digestion; as, the *digestive* system of the body.

dig·ger \ˈdig-r\ *n.* A person or thing that digs.

dig·gings \ˈdig-ingz\ *n. pl.* **1** A place where ore, metals, or precious stones are dug. **2** Lodgings.

dig·it \ˈdij-ət\ *n.* **1** A finger or toe. **2** Any of the figures 1 through 9 and usually the symbol 0.

dig·i·tal·is \ˌdij-ə-ˈtal-əs\ *n.* A drug made of the dried leaves of the foxglove.

dig·ni·fied \ˈdig-nə-ˌfīd\ *adj.* Stately; marked by self-respect or pride; as, a *dignified* man.

dig·ni·fy \ˈdig-nə-ˌfī\ *v.;* **dig·ni·fied** \-ˌfīd\; **dig·ni·fy·ing.** To give dignity or distinction to; to honor.

dig·ni·tary \ˈdig-nə-ˌter-ē\ *n.; pl.* **dig·ni·tar·ies.** A person of high position; as, *dignitaries* of the church.

dig·ni·ty \ˈdig-nət-ē\ *n.; pl.* **dig·ni·ties. 1** The quality of being worthy or honorable; true worth; as, a working man with more *dignity* than many a prince. **2** The quality of being dignified, or having a stately manner; as, to walk with *dignity.* **3** A high position or rank; as, to be raised to the *dignity* of president. **4** Importance, rank, or honor; as, to consider something beneath one's *dignity.*

di·gress \dī-ˈgres, də-\ *v.* To turn aside; to deviate, especially from the main subject in speaking or writing. — **di·gres·sion** \-ˈgresh-n\ *n.*

di·gres·sive \dī-ˈgres-iv, də-\ *adj.* Inclined to digress; turning aside from the main topic. — **di·gres·sive·ly,** *adv.*

dike \ˈdīk\ *n.* **1** A ditch. **2** A bank of earth thrown up from a ditch. **3** A bank of earth forming a barrier or boundary; especially, a levee; a river embankment. — *v.;* **diked; dik·ing. 1** To surround or protect with a dike. **2** To drain by a dike or ditch.

di·lap·i·dat·ed \də-ˈlap-ə-ˌdāt-əd\ *adj.* Partly ruined or decayed; as, a *dilapidated* old house.

di·lap·i·da·tion \də-ˌlap-ə-ˈdāsh-n\ *n.* A dilapidated condition; partial ruin, as from neglect.

di·late \dī-ˈlāt, ˈdī-ˌlāt\ *v.;* **di·lat·ed; di·lat·ing.** To make or to grow larger or wider; to swell; to distend; as, eyes *dilated* with fear; lungs *dilated* with air. — **di·lat·a·ble,** *adj.*

di·la·tion \dī-ˈlāsh-n\ *n.* A dilating or a being dilated; expansion; as, *dilation* of the eyes.

dil·a·to·ry \ˈdil-ə-ˌtōr-ē, -ˌtȯr-ē\ *adj.* **1** Planned to cause delay; as, a *dilatory* policy. **2** Tardy; slow; not prompt; as, a *dilatory* answer.

di·lem·ma \də-ˈlem-ə\ *n.* A choice or a situation in which a person has to choose between two or more things, ways, or plans no one of which seems really desirable; any difficult choice.

dil·et·tante \ˌdil-ə-ˈtant(-ē), -ˈtänt(-ē), -ˈtȧnt(-ē)\ *n.; pl.* **dil·et·tan·ti** \-nt-ē\ or **dil·et·tantes.** [From Italian, meaning "lover of music or painting", from *dilettare* meaning "to take delight in".] A lover of the fine arts; especially, one who practices one of these arts for pleasure only; an amateur.

dil·i·gence \'dil-ə-jən(t)s\ *n.* A stagecoach.

dil·i·gence \'dil-ə-jən(t)s\ *n.* Careful and continued work; conscientious effort; industry.

dil·i·gent \'dil-ə-jənt\ *adj.* Taking pains with one's work; steady and earnest; industrious; as, a *diligent* pupil. — For synonyms see *busy.* — **dil·i·gent·ly**, *adv.*

dill \'dil\ *n.* A European herb whose seeds and leaves are used in cookery, as for flavoring pickles.

dil·ly·dal·ly \'dil-ē-ˌdal-ē\ *v.;* **dil·ly·dal·lied** \-ēd\; **dil·ly·dal·ly·ing.** To waste time; to dawdle; to loiter or trifle.

di·lute \dī-'lüt, də-\ *v.;* **di·lut·ed**; **di·lut·ing.** To make thinner or more liquid by mixing with something else, especially with water. — *adj.* Diluted; weak; thin; as, *dilute* wine.

dim \'dim\ *adj.;* **dim·mer**; **dim·mest.** **1** Not bright or distinct; obscure; faint; as, a *dim* light. **2** Dull; without luster. The colors of the old painting had grown *dim.* **3** Not seeing clearly; not understanding clearly; as, eyes *dim* with tears; a mind *dim* from weariness. — *v.;* **dimmed**; **dim·ming.** **1** To make less bright; to obscure; as, to *dim* automobile headlights; a memory *dimmed* by time. **2** To lose or deprive of clear vision or understanding. Age had not *dimmed* the old sailor's eyes.

dime \'dīm\ *n.* A United States silver coin worth ten cents.

di·men·sion \də-'mench-n, dī-\ *n.* **1** The measure of a thing along a straight line, as along the line of length or width. **2** [in the plural] The measure of a thing in length, breadth, and thickness. **3** Magnitude; scope; importance; as, an undertaking of vast *dimensions.* — **di·men·sion·al** \-'mench-n(-)əl\ *adj.*

di·min·ish \də-'min-ish\ *v.* To make less or become less, as in amount, size, or importance; to lessen; to decrease; as, a weather forecast of clear skies and *diminishing* winds.

di·min·u·en·do \də-ˌmin-yə-'wen-ˌdō\ *adj.* or *adv.* In music, gradually decreasing in fullness or loudness. — *n.; pl.* **di·min·u·en·dos.** A gradual decrease in loudness.

dim·i·nu·tion \ˌdim-ə-'nüsh-n, -'nyüsh-n\ *n.* A lessening or reduction in size, quantity, or degree; as, to vote for a *diminution* of the tax rate.

di·min·u·tive \də-'min-yət-iv\ *adj.* **1** Indicating that something is small or young; as, a *diminutive* suffix. **2** Extremely small; tiny; as, a *diminutive* tree only a foot high. — *n.* **1** A word that is formed from another word, as by adding the suffix *-ette, -ie, -kin,* or *-let,* and that indicates something small or young, as *gosling* or *ringlet.* **2** A very small object, form, or variety of something.

dim·i·ty \'dim-ət-ē\ *n.; pl.* **dim·i·ties.** **1** A cotton fabric with raised stripes or cords used for hangings and furniture coverings. **2** A fine thin corded cotton fabric, white or colored and often figured, used for dresses.

dim·ly \'dim-lē\ *adv.* In a dim or obscure manner.

dim·mer \'dim-r\. Comparative of *dim.* — *n.* A device used to dim a light.

dimmest. Superlative of *dim.*

dim·ple \'dimp-l\ *n.* A slight hollow spot or dent, especially in the cheek or chin. — *v.;* **dim·pled**; **dim·pling** \-l(-)ing\. To form or to mark with dimples. The child's cheeks *dimpled* as he smiled.

din \'din\ *n.* Loud, confused, or clanging noise; deafening uproar; hubbub. The dishes fell with a *din.* — *v.;* **dinned**; **din·ning.** **1** To make a din. The noise of the machines *dinned* in our ears. **2** To impress by repeating; as, to *din* orders into a person.

dine \'dīn\ *v.;* **dined**; **din·ing.** **1** To eat dinner; as, to *dine* out; to *dine* at six. **2** To give a dinner to; as, to *dine* a group of friends.

din·er \'dīn-r\ *n.* **1** A person eating dinner. **2** A railroad dining car or any restaurant resembling this.

di·nette \dī-'net\ *n.* **1** An alcove used for a dining room, as in a small apartment. **2** A small diner.

ding \'ding\ *v.;* **dinged** \'dingd\; **ding·ing** \'ding-ing\. **1** To sound; to ring; as, to hear the bell *dinging.* **2** To talk or urge vehemently; to din; as, to *ding* on a topic until everyone is tired of it.

ding·dong \'ding-ˌdäng, -ˌdȯng\ *n.* [An imitation of the sound.] The sound of repeated strokes on a bell or a similar sound. — *adj.* Vigorously contested; as, a *dingdong* race.

din·ghy \'ding-ē, 'dingk-ē\ *n.; pl.* **din·ghies.** **1** A small, light boat; especially, a small boat used as a tender for a large boat. **2** A sailboat or yacht used in racing. **3** An inflatable rubber life raft used by fliers forced to parachute into the sea.

dinghy, 2

din·gle \'ding-gl\ *n.* A small, narrow, wooded valley.

din·go \'ding-ˌgō\ *n.; pl.* **din·goes.** A wild dog with a wolflike face and bushy tail, found in Australia.

din·gy \'din-jē\ *adj.;* **din·gi·er**; **din·gi·est.** Dark; dull; not fresh, bright, or light; grimy; as, *dingy* wallpaper. — **din·gi·ly** \'dinj-l-ē\ *adv.*

din·ing car \'dī-ning\. **1** A railroad car, containing tables, in which meals are served. **2** A diner.

dining hall. A dining room of an institution, as a college, or a building containing such a room.

dining room. A room where dinner and other meals are eaten.

dink·ey \'dingk-ē\ *n.; pl.* **dink·eys.** A small locomotive used in logging and in handling freight and shunting cars.

dinky \'dingk-ē\ *adj.;* **dink·i·er**; **dink·i·est.** Small; insignificant; as, a *dinky* little parade.

dinned. Past tense and past part. of *din.*

din·ner \'din-r\ *n.* **1** The main meal of the day.

2 A formal banquet; as, a *dinner* in honor of the president.

dinning. Pres. part. of *din*.

di·no·saur \'dī-nə-ˌsȯr\ *n.* [From Greek *deinos* meaning "fearful", "terrible", and *saura* meaning "lizard".] Any of a group of extinct reptiles varying in length from two to 90 feet, having limbs adapted for walking, and a long tail.

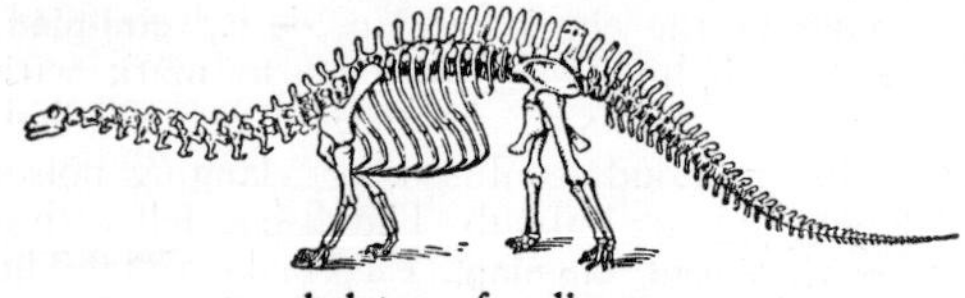

skeleton of a dinosaur

dint \'dint\ *n.* **1** A blow; a stroke. **2** Force; power; as, to succeed by *dint* of hard work. **3** The mark left by a blow; a dent. — *v.* To mark with a dint; to dent.

di·oc·e·san \dī-'äs-əs-n\ *adj.* Of or relating to a diocese; as, a *diocesan* high school. — *n.* The bishop of a diocese.

di·o·cese \'dī-ə-səs, -ˌsēs, -ˌsēz\ *n.* The district over which a bishop has authority.

di·oe·cious \dī-'ē-shəs\ *adj.* Having the male reproductive organs in one individual and the female in another, as the willow, which in some individual plants produces flowers bearing only stamens and in other plants flowers bearing only pistils.

di·o·rama \ˌdī-ə-'ram-ə, -'räm-ə, -'ram-ə\ *n.* A scenic representation in which a partly transparent painting is viewed from a distance through an opening or in which lifelike sculptured figures and surrounding details are realistically illuminated against a painted background.

di·ox·ide \dī-'äk-ˌsīd\ *n.* An oxide having two atoms of oxygen in the molecule; as, carbon *dioxide*.

dip \'dip\ *v.;* **dipped** or **dipt**; **dip·ping. 1** To sink or thrust for a short time into something liquid; as, to *dip* one's fingers into water. **2** To take out with a ladle or as if with a ladle; as, to *dip* water from a pail. **3** To lower and quickly raise again; to drop or sink down and quickly rise again; to sink out of sight; as, to *dip* a flag or the wing of an airplane. The moon *dipped* behind a cloud. **4** To slope or incline downward, as a road. **5** To make by repeatedly plunging a wick into wax or fat; as, the candle-*dipping* process. **6** To enter slightly into something; to read superficially; as, to *dip* into a book. — *n.* **1** The action of dipping; a plunge, as into water. **2** A sudden drop. **3** A downward slope. **4** A thing made by dipping, as a candle. **5** A portion dipped; as, a *dip* of ice cream. **6** Any liquid into which objects may be dipped, as for cleaning or coloring.

diph·the·ria \dif-'thir-ē-ə, dip-\ *n.* An infectious and contagious bacterial disease, with fever, in which the air passages become coated with a soft weblike layer, or membrane, that often obstructs breathing. — **diph·the·ri·al** \-ē-əl\ or **diph·the·rit·ic** \ˌdifth-r-'it-ik\ *adj.*

diph·thong \'dif-ˌthȯng, 'dip-\ *n.* Two vowel sounds pronounced one after the other but without making two syllables, as *ou* in *out* or *oy* in *boy*.

di·plo·ma \də-'plō-mə\ *n.* A document conferring a privilege, honor, or power; especially, an official paper showing graduation from a school or college.

di·plo·ma·cy \də-'plō-mə-sē\ *n.; pl.* **di·plo·ma·cies. 1** The business of carrying on negotiations and other communications between nations. **2** Skill in conducting affairs with other people without arousing irritation or hard feelings; tact.

dip·lo·mat \'dip-lə-ˌmat\ *n.* **1** A person engaged in or skilled in conducting official business between nations. **2** A person skilled in dealing with others without offending them; a tactful person.

dip·lo·mat·ic \ˌdip-lə-'mat-ik\ *adj.* **1** Having to do with diplomats and their work. **2** Tactful; as, a *diplomatic* way of saying something. — **dip·lo·mat·i·cal·ly** \-ik-l(-)ē\ *adv.*

di·plo·ma·tist \də-'plō-mət-əst\ *n.* A diplomat.

dip·lo·pod \'dip-lə-ˌpäd\ *n.* Any of various small wormlike animals having round segmented bodies with a hard outer covering and two pairs of legs on most segments.

dipped. A past tense and past part. of *dip*.

dip·per \'dip-r\ *n.* **1** One that dips; especially, a ladle or scoop for dipping. **2** [written with a capital letter] Either of two groups of seven stars of the Northern Hemisphere arranged in the shape of a ladle with a handle. One group is called the **Big Dipper**; the other, the **Little Dipper**.

dipper, 1

dipping. Pres. part. of *dip*.

dipt. A past tense and past part. of *dip*.

dip·ter·ous \'dipt-r-əs\ *adj.* Two-winged; especially, belonging to the zoological group of insects that includes the true or winged flies, the mosquitoes, and the gnats.

dire \'dīr\ *adj.;* **dir·er**; **dir·est. 1** Very dreadful or terrible; horrible; as, earthquakes and other *dire* events. **2** Extreme; as, to be in *dire* need.

di·rect \də-'rekt, dī-\ *adj.* **1** Straight; going from one point to another without turn or stop; as, the *direct* road to town. **2** Straightforward; plain; frank; as, a *direct* reply to a question. **3** Immediate; personal; as, to take *direct* charge of a job. **4** In the straight line of descent from an ancestor; as, a *direct* descendant of a hero of the Revolutionary War. **5** Quoted in the exact words of the original speaker; as, *direct* discourse. — *adv.* Without turn or stop; as, to go *direct* to school. — *v.* **1** To put an address on; as, to *direct* a letter. **2** To aim or point; as, to *direct* one's energies to something useful. **3** To cause to move in or follow a certain direction or course; as, to *direct* all traffic around the scene of a fire. **4** To show or point out the right way to; as, to *direct* a stranger to a hotel. **5** To control; to guide the performance of; as, to *direct* plays; to *direct* an orchestra. **6** To order or instruct; to command. A judge sometimes *directs* a jury to bring in a certain verdict.

direct current. Electric current that flows in only one direction.

di·rec·tion \də-'reksh-n, dī-\ *n.* **1** The act of directing; management; guidance; as, to work under the teacher's *direction.* **2** An order or instruction to be followed; as, to ask for *directions* to the beach; to follow the *directions* on a bottle of medicine. **3** The address on a letter or parcel. **4** The course along which anything moves, lies, or points; as, to travel in an easterly *direction;* paper blown in every *direction* by the wind.

di·rec·tion·al \də-'reksh-n(-)əl, dī-\ *adj.* Of or relating to direction in space; as, the *directional* signals on an automobile; a *directional* television antenna.

di·rec·tive \də-'rek-tiv, dī-\ *n.* A general instruction as to procedure; as, to receive a new *directive* from the head office.

di·rect·ly \də-'rek(t)-lē, dī-\ *adv.* **1** In a direct manner or line; without anything or anyone intervening; straight; as, to aim *directly* at a target; to deal *directly* with the owner of a house for sale. **2** Completely; wholly; as, two *directly* opposed ideas. **3** At once; without delay. **4** Almost at once; very soon.

direct object. A word that names the person or thing that receives the action of a verb, as *ball* in "The pitcher threw the ball".

di·rec·tor \də-'rekt-r, dī-\ *n.* **1** A person who directs or manages; a manager. **2** One of a group of persons chosen to direct the affairs of a company.

di·rec·tor·ship \də-'rekt-r-ˌship, dī-\ *n.* The office or the term of office of a director.

di·rec·to·ry \də-'rekt-r(-)ē\ *n.; pl.* **di·rec·to·ries.** A book containing the names and addresses of the inhabitants of a place, or of a certain class of the inhabitants; as, a telephone *directory.*

dire·ful \'dīrf-l\ *adj.* Dire; terrible. — **dire·ful·ly** \'dīrf-l-ē\ *adv.*

dire·ly \'dīr-lē\ *adv.* In a dire manner; in the worst way possible; to an extreme degree; as, *direly* in need of help.

dirge \'dərj\ *n.* A piece of music, especially a song of mourning, to accompany funeral or memorial services.

dir·i·gi·ble \'dir-ə-jəb-l, də-'rij-əb-l\ *adj.* Capable of being controlled by steering; as, a *dirigible* balloon. — *n.* An engine-driven lighter-than-air aircraft; an airship. — **dir·i·gi·bil·i·ty** \ˌdir-ə-jə-'bil-ət-ē, də-ˌrij-ə-\ *n.*

dirk \'dərk\ *n.* A dagger. — *v.* To stab with a dirk.

dirt \'dərt\ *n.* **1** Any filthy substance, or any substance, as mud, grime, soot, or dust that by adhering to something else makes it unclean. **2** Loose or packed earth; soil; as, to cover seeds with *dirt;* to fill a flowerpot with good, clean *dirt* from the garden. **3** Uncleanness in action, thought, or speech.

dirty \'dərt-ē\ *adj.;* **dirt·i·er; dirt·i·est. 1** Not clean; filthy; soiled; as, *dirty* clothes. **2** Base; low; unfair; as, a *dirty* trick. **3** Indecent; smutty; as, *dirty* talk. **4** Foggy; stormy; muddy; as, *dirty* weather. **5** Not clear in color; dull; as, a *dirty* red. — *v.;* **dirt·ied** \-ēd\; **dirt·y·ing.** To make or become dirty.

dis-. A prefix that can mean: **1** Not, as in *dishonest* or *dislike.* **2** A destroying of, lack of, as in *disagreement* or *disunion.* **3** To take away, remove, as in *disarm* or *dismast.* **4** To make not, undo, reverse, as in *disable* or *disconnect.*

dis·a·bil·i·ty \ˌdis-ə-'bil-ət-ē\ *n.; pl.* **dis·a·bil·i·ties. 1** The condition of being disabled; lack of ability, power, or fitness to do something. **2** Something that disables, as a physical injury. **3** In law, something that prevents a person from serving or acting in a certain capacity; a legal disqualification.

dis·a·ble \dis-'āb-l, diz-\ *v.;* **dis·a·bled; dis·a·bling** \-l(-)ing\. **1** To make unable or incapable; to deprive of force, strength, or power of action; to cripple; as, a *disabling* illness; a soldier *disabled* in war. **2** In law, to disqualify. — **dis·a·ble·ment,** *n.*

dis·a·buse \ˌdis-ə-'byüz\ *v.;* **dis·a·bused; dis·a·bus·ing.** To set free from mistakes in reasoning or belief; to set right; to undeceive; as, to *disabuse* a person's mind of a false idea.

dis·ad·van·tage \ˌdis-əd-'vant-ij\ *n.* **1** Something that hinders success; an unfavorable condition; handicap; as, to work under *disadvantages.* Short stature is a *disadvantage* in basketball. **2** Loss; injury; damage; as, to hear something to the *disadvantage* of a friend; a business venture which turned out to one's *disadvantage.*

dis·ad·van·ta·geous \'dis-ˌad-vən-'tā-jəs, -ˌad-ˌvan-\ *adj.* Unfavorable to success. — **dis·ad·van·ta·geous·ly,** *adv.*

dis·af·fect·ed \ˌdis-ə-'fek-təd\ *adj.* Not wholly loyal, as to a government, party, or cause; inclined to rebel; discontented.

dis·af·fec·tion \ˌdis-ə-'feksh-n\ *n.* The state of being disaffected; disloyalty; discontent; ill will.

dis·a·gree \ˌdis-ə-'grē\ *v.;* **dis·a·greed; dis·a·gree·ing. 1** To fail to agree; to be unlike; to differ; as, statements that *disagree* with the known facts. **2** To differ in opinion; as, to *disagree* over the price. **3** To quarrel. **4** To be unsuitable or injurious, as food or climate.

dis·a·gree·a·ble \ˌdis-ə-'grē-əb-l\ *adj.* **1** Displeasing; offensive; as, a *disagreeable* taste. **2** Ill-tempered; irritable; cross. Loss of sleep often makes people *disagreeable* the next morning. **3** Uncomfortable; as, to be in a *disagreeable* situation. — **dis·a·gree·a·bly** \-ə-blē\ *adv.*

dis·a·gree·ment \ˌdis-ə-'grē-mənt\ *n.* **1** The act or fact of disagreeing; difference of opinion; as, a look that clearly showed *disagreement;* to be in *disagreement* over the best way to proceed. **2** A quarrel; a dispute; as, a *disagreement* over a game of checkers. **3** The condition of being different; unlikeness; as, a *disagreement* between two accounts of a happening.

dis·al·low \ˌdis-ə-ˈlaủ\ *v.* To refuse to admit or recognize, as a claim; to reject.

dis·ap·pear \ˌdis-ə-ˈpir\ *v.* **1** To cease to be visible; to pass out of sight; to vanish; as, to watch a friend *disappear* around the corner. Smoke soon *disappears* in a well-ventilated room. **2** To cease to be. The dinosaur *disappeared* thousands of years ago. **3** To be lost. The boy's dog *disappeared* but was found the next day.

dis·ap·pear·ance \ˌdis-ə-ˈpir-ən(t)s\ *n.* The act or fact of disappearing; a passing out of sight or of existence; vanishing; as, to wait impatiently for the *disappearance* of the marks of chicken pox. The child's *disappearance* was not discovered for several hours.

dis·ap·point \ˌdis-ə-ˈpȯint\ *v.* **1** To defeat or fail to fulfil the hope or expectation of; as, to *disappoint* one's parents by doing badly in school; to be *disappointed* by a new book. **2** To fail to keep an engagement with or a promise to; as, to have to *disappoint* someone because of illness.

dis·ap·point·ed \ˌdis-ə-ˈpȯint-əd\ *adj.* Unhappy by reason of failure or defeat of one's hopes or expectations; as, a lonely, *disappointed* old man. — **dis·ap·point·ed·ly,** *adv.*

dis·ap·point·ment \ˌdis-ə-ˈpȯint-mənt\ *n.* **1** Failure of a hope or expectation. The boy suffered a severe *disappointment* when he was not accepted for the team. **2** The condition or feeling of being disappointed; as, to be unable to conceal one's *disappointment.* **3** A person or thing that disappoints. The show proved to be a *disappointment* to everybody.

dis·ap·pro·ba·tion \ˌdis-ˌap-rə-ˈbāsh-n\ *n.* Disapproval.

dis·ap·prov·al \ˌdis-ə-ˈprüv-l\ *n.* **1** The act of disapproving; as, to frown in *disapproval.* **2** Unfavorable opinion or judgment; failure to approve. The plan met with the *disapproval* of the principal.

dis·ap·prove \ˌdis-ə-ˈprüv\ *v.;* **dis·ap·proved; dis·ap·prov·ing. 1** To consider unfavorably or pass unfavorable judgment on; to feel or express disapproval; as, to *disapprove* of children staying up late. **2** To refuse to approve; to reject; as, to *disapprove* a proposed budget for class activities. — **dis·ap·prov·ing·ly,** *adv.*

dis·arm \dis-ˈärm, diz-, -ˈȧrm\ *v.* **1** To deprive of arms; to take arms or weapons from; as, to *disarm* a prisoner. **2** To disband or, especially, to reduce the size and strength of the armed forces of a country, as at the close of a war or in agreement with other countries. The nation is *disarming.* **3** To make harmless, peaceable, or friendly; to remove dislike or suspicion; as, a *disarming* smile.

dis·ar·ma·ment \-ˈär-mə-mənt, -ˈȧr-\ *n.* A disarming; especially, reduction of military and naval strength to a level determined in advance, as bv agreement among several nations.

dis·ar·range \ˌdis-r-ˈānj\ *v.;* **dis·ar·ranged; dis·ar·rang·ing.** To disturb the arrangement of; to disorder. — **dis·ar·range·ment,** *n.*

dis·ar·ray \ˌdis-r-ˈā\ *v.* **1** To throw into disorder. **2** To undress. — *n.* **1** Disorder; confusion. **2** Disorder of dress; incomplete attire. The fire alarm sent the hotel guests hurrying to the street in all stages of *disarray.*

di·sas·ter \di-ˈzast-r, -ˈsast-r\ *n.* A sudden great misfortune, especially one bringing with it destruction of life or property or causing complete ruin, as to a career; a calamity; as, a *disaster* at sea. Floods, fires, and earthquakes are among the most terrible *disasters* of times of peace.

di·sas·trous \di-ˈzast-rəs, -ˈsast-\ *adj.* Accompanied by, or resulting in, disaster, great suffering, or misery; as, a *disastrous* fire. — **di·sas·trous·ly,** *adv.*

dis·a·vow \ˌdis-ə-ˈvaủ\ *v.* To refuse to own or acknowledge; to refuse responsibility for or approval of; to disclaim; to disown.

dis·band \dis-ˈband\ *v.* To break up the organization of; to scatter; as, to *disband* an army. — **dis·band·ment** \-ˈban(d)-mənt\ *n.*

dis·bar \dis-ˈbär, -ˈbȧr\ *v.;* **dis·barred; dis·bar·ring.** To take away from a lawyer his rights and privileges as a member of the legal profession. — **dis·bar·ment,** *n.*

dis·be·lief \ˌdis-bə-ˈlēf\ *n.* A disbelieving; belief that something, as a statement, is not true. — For synonyms see *unbelief.*

dis·be·lieve \ˌdis-bə-ˈlēv\ *v.;* **dis·be·lieved; dis·be·liev·ing.** To hold not to be true; to refuse to believe; as, to *disbelieve* a rumor. — **dis·be·liev·er,** *n.*

dis·bur·den \dis-ˈbərd-n\ *v.;* **dis·bur·dened; dis·bur·den·ing** \-n(-)ing\. To rid of a burden; to relieve of something oppressive; as, to *disburden* one's conscience.

dis·burse \dis-ˈbərs\ *v.;* **dis·bursed; dis·burs·ing.** To pay out; to expend; as, to *disburse* money.

dis·burse·ment \dis-ˈbərs-mənt\ *n.* **1** A paying out of money, as to meet expenses. **2** Money expended.

disc. Variant of *disk.*

dis·card \dis-ˈkärd, -ˈkȧrd; ˈdis-ˌkärd, -ˌkȧrd\ *v.* **1** In card games, to put aside a card or cards from the hand. **2** To cast off as useless or not required; to throw or lay aside; as, to *discard* old clothing. — \ˈdis-ˌkärd, -ˌkȧrd\ *n.* A discarding; something cast off or discarded, as a card or cards in certain card games.

dis·cern \di-ˈsərn, -ˈzərn\ *v.* To make out with the eye or by the mind; to see or distinguish; as, to *discern* an airplane in the clouds. — **dis·cern·i·ble** \-əb-l\ *adj.* — **dis·cern·i·bly** \-ə-blē\ *adv.*

dis·cern·ing \di-ˈsər-ning, -ˈzər-\ *adj.* Having or showing discernment; as, a *discerning* critic. — **dis·cern·ing·ly,** *adv.*

dis·cern·ment \di-ˈsərn-mənt, -ˈzərn-\ *n.* The power of discerning; especially, mental quickness and accuracy in detecting or discriminating; keen insight.

dis·charge \dis-ˈchärj, -ˈchȧrj; ˈdis-ˌchärj, -ˌchȧrj\

v.; **dis·charged; dis·charg·ing. 1** To relieve of a load or a burden; to unload, as a ship. **2** To shoot or to fire; as, to *discharge* a gun. **3** To set free, as a prisoner. **4** To dismiss from service; as, to *discharge* an employee or a soldier. **5** To get rid of. This train stops only to *discharge* passengers. **6** To give forth fluid or other contents. This river *discharges* into the ocean. **7** To get rid of by paying or doing; as, to *discharge* a debt or a duty. — \'dis-ˌchärj, -ˌchȧrj; dis-'chärj, -'chȧrj\ *n.* **1** The act of discharging, unloading, releasing, or firing off; as, the *discharge* of a ship's cargo; the *discharge* of artillery. **2** That which discharges; especially, a certificate of dismissal; as, a soldier's *discharge.* **3** A firing, as of guns or bullets. **4** Something discharged; as, the *discharge* from a wound. **5** A flow of electricity, as in lightning, along a wire.

disci. A pl. of *discus.*

dis·ci·ple \də-'sīp-l\ *n.* A pupil or follower who accepts and helps to spread his master's teachings; as, the *disciples* of Jesus.

dis·ci·pli·nar·i·an \ˌdis-ə-plə-'ner-ē-ən\ *n.* A person who maintains discipline and order.

dis·ci·pli·nary \'dis-ə-plə-ˌner-ē\ *adj.* Of or relating to discipline; corrective; as, *disciplinary* problems; to take *disciplinary* action.

dis·ci·pline \'dis-ə-plən, -(ˌ)plin\ *n.* **1** Strict training that corrects or strengthens; as, natural ability improved by *discipline.* **2** Control gained through obedience or strict training; orderly conduct. The children showed excellent *discipline* in the parade. **3** Punishment. — *v.;* **dis·ci·plined; dis·ci·plin·ing. 1** To train in self-control or obedience; as, a person *disciplined* by misfortune and suffering. **2** To bring under control; to govern strictly; as, to *discipline* an army. **3** To punish; as, to *discipline* a child for running away.

disc jockey or **disk jockey** \'disk\. One who conducts and announces a radio program of musical recordings, often with comments that are not related to music.

dis·claim \dis-'klām\ *v.* To deny having any connection with or responsibility for; to disown. The prisoner *disclaimed* any part in the crime.

dis·close \dis-'klōz\ *v.;* **dis·closed; dis·clos·ing. 1** To uncover. **2** To expose to view; to reveal; to make known; as, to *disclose* secrets. The open door *disclosed* a large room.

dis·clo·sure \dis-'klōzh-r\ *n.* **1** A disclosing. **2** Something that is disclosed, made known, or revealed.

dis·col·or \dis-'kəl-r\ *v.;* **dis·col·ored; dis·col·or·ing** \-r(-)ing\. To change in color, especially for the worse; to stain; as, wallpaper *discolored* by smoke. — **dis·col·or·a·tion** \(ˌ)dis-ˌkəl-r-'āsh-n\ *n.*

dis·com·fit \dis-'kəm(p)-fət; *in the South, also* ˌdisk-m-'fit\ *v.* To throw into confusion; to upset; to frustrate; as, to *discomfit* one's enemies. — **dis·com·fi·ture** \dis-'kəm(p)-fə-ˌchůr, -fəch-r\ *n.*

dis·com·fort \dis-'kəm(p)-fərt\ *v.* To make uneasy or uncomfortable; to trouble. Fear that an earthquake would occur *discomforted* the city. — *n.* **1** Lack of comfort; pain; distress. Winter was a period of great *discomfort* to the early settlers. **2** Something that causes distress or inconvenience. The worst *discomfort* was having no food for two days.

dis·com·mode \ˌdisk-m-'ōd\ *v.;* **dis·com·mod·ed; dis·com·mod·ing.** To disturb; to trouble.

dis·com·pose \ˌdisk-m-'pōz\ *v.;* **dis·com·posed; dis·com·pos·ing. 1** To disturb the calmness or peace of; to agitate; to upset; as, not visibly *discomposed* by the bad news. **2** To disarrange; as, hair *discomposed* by the wind.

dis·com·po·sure \ˌdisk-m-'pōzh-r\ *n.* Agitation; disturbance.

dis·con·cert \ˌdisk-n-'sərt\ *v.* **1** To throw into confusion; to unsettle; to disturb; as, measures to *disconcert* and baffle the enemy. **2** To disturb or destroy the composure of; to fluster; to embarrass; as, *disconcerted* by the unexpected praise.

dis·con·nect \ˌdisk-n-'ekt\ *v.* To undo or to break the connection of; as, to *disconnect* two pipes. — **dis·con·nec·tion** \-'eksh-n\ *n.*

dis·con·nect·ed \ˌdisk-n-'ek-təd\ *adj.* **1** Not connected; separated. **2** Rambling; incoherent; as, *disconnected* speech. — **dis·con·nect·ed·ly,** *adv.*

dis·con·so·late \dis-'kän(t)s-l-ət\ *adj.* Lacking consolation or comfort; sad; dejected; as, *disconsolate* over the death of a friend. — **dis·con·so·late·ly,** *adv.*

dis·con·tent \ˌdisk-n-'tent\ *n.* Lack of contentment; uneasiness; dissatisfaction. — *v.* To dissatisfy; to displease. Decreased rations of food *discontented* the soldiers. — **dis·con·tent·ment,** *n.*

dis·con·tent·ed \ˌdisk-n-'tent-əd\ *adj.* Dissatisfied; uneasy. — **dis·con·tent·ed·ly,** *adv.*

dis·con·tin·u·ance \ˌdisk-n-'tin-yə-wən(t)s\ *n.* A discontinuing; interruption; abandonment; as, the *discontinuance* of delivery service.

dis·con·tin·u·a·tion \ˌdisk-n-ˌtin-yə-'wāsh-n\ *n.* Discontinuance.

dis·con·tin·ue \ˌdisk-n-'tin-yü\ *v.;* **dis·con·tin·ued; dis·con·tin·u·ing.** To leave off; to break off; to stop; to give up; as, to *discontinue* taking a newspaper; to *discontinue* work.

dis·con·tin·u·ous \ˌdisk-n-'tin-yə-wəs\ *adj.* Not continuous; having interruptions; broken off; as, a *discontinuous* flight. — **dis·con·ti·nu·i·ty** \ˌdis-ˌkän-tən-'ü-ət-ē, -ˌkänt-n-, -'yü-\ *n.* — **dis·con·tin·u·ous·ly** \ˌdisk-n-'tin-yə-wəs-lē\ *adv.*

dis·cord \'dis-ˌkȯrd\ *n.* **1** Lack of agreement or harmony; strike; conflict. The vote showed that the committee were in *discord.* **2** In music, a harsh and unpleasant combination of sounds. **3** A harsh uproar; din.

dis·cord·ance \dis-'kȯrd-n(t)s\ or **dis·cord·an·cy** \-n-sē\ *n.; pl.* **dis·cord·anc·es** or **dis·cord·an·cies. 1** Disagreement; as, a *discordance* of opinion. **2** A discord of sounds.

dis·cord·ant \dis-'kȯrd-nt\ *adj.* **1** Disagreeing; quarrelsome; as, *discordant* views on a subject.

2 Without harmony; jarring; as, *discordant* sounds. — **dis·cord·ant·ly,** *adv.*

dis·count \'dis-ˌkau̇nt\ *v.* **1** To reduce or deduct from the amount of a bill, debt, or charge. Merchants sometimes *discount* a certain percentage of a bill for cash payment. **2** To make allowance for exaggeration in; as, to *discount* a friend's tale of his adventures. **3** To reduce the importance of something by taking into account its significance or probable effects before it actually happens. The business world had already *discounted* the effects of the presidential election. — *n.* The amount by which a bill, debt, or charge is discounted; as, a *discount* of ten per cent for cash. — **dis·count·a·ble,** *adj.*

dis·coun·te·nance \(')dis-'kau̇nt-n-ən(t)s, -'kau̇n-tə-nən(t)s, -'kau̇nt-nən(t)s\ *v.;* **dis·coun·te·nanced; dis·coun·te·nanc·ing. 1** To put to shame; to embarrass; to abash. **2** To look with disfavor upon; to disapprove.

dis·cour·age \dis-'kər-ij, -'kə-rij\ *v.;* **dis·cour·aged; dis·cour·ag·ing. 1** To lessen the courage or confidence of; to dishearten; as, to be unreasonably *discouraged* by a single failure. **2** To check or deter through fear of consequences; to try to check by an expression of disapproval; as, laws that *discourage* speeding. — **dis·cour·ag·ing·ly,** *adv.*

dis·cour·age·ment \dis-'kər-ij-mənt, -'kə-rij-\ *n.* **1** The act of discouraging; as, a plan for the *discouragement* of slovenly dressing. **2** The condition of being discouraged. Sick people often have to go through long periods of *discouragement.* **3** Something that discourages.

dis·course \'dis-ˌkōrs, -ˌkȯrs; dis-'kōrs, -'kȯrs\ *n.* **1** Conversation; talk. **2** Orderly communication of thought in speech or writing. **3** A long spoken or written treatment of a subject, as a sermon or a lecture. — *v.* To talk, especially at some length; to give a discourse.

dis·cour·te·ous \(')dis-'kərt-ē-əs\ *adj.* Rude; impolite. — **dis·cour·te·ous·ly,** *adv.*

dis·cour·te·sy \(')dis-'kərt-ə-sē\ *n.; pl.* **dis·cour·te·sies. 1** Rudeness; bad manners. **2** A rude or impolite act.

dis·cov·er \dis-'kəv-r\ *v.;* **dis·cov·ered; dis·cov·er·ing** \-r(-)ing\. **1** *Archaic.* To disclose or make known, especially unintentionally through one's actions. **2** To find out, see, or learn of the first time in one's own experience or that of mankind; especially, to obtain the first sight or knowledge of something already existing but not previously found or known; as, to *discover* a new star; to look out the window and *discover* that snow is falling. — **dis·cov·er·a·ble** \-r(-)əb-l\ *adj.* — **dis·cov·er·er** \-r-r\ *n.*

dis·cov·ery \dis-'kəv-r(-)ē\ *n.; pl.* **dis·cov·er·ies. 1** The act or fact of discovering; as, the importance of the *discovery* of the circulation of the blood. **2** Something found out or seen for the first time; as, the island *discoveries* of the Portuguese navigators.

dis·cred·it \(')dis-'kred-ət\ *v.* **1** To refuse to accept as true; to disbelieve; as, to *discredit* a rumor. **2** To destroy confidence or trust in. Sharp questioning by the lawyers for the defense soon *discredited* the witness. **3** To destroy the reputation of; to disgrace; as, a leader *discredited* among his followers by his cowardly behavior. — *n.* **1** Doubt or disbelief; as, to bring a story into *discredit* by proving some of its details to be false. **2** Loss of reputation; disgrace; as, to bring *discredit* on one's family. **3** A person or thing that brings about loss of reputation; as, to be a *discredit* to one's family.

dis·cred·it·a·ble \(')dis-'kred-ət-əb-l\ *adj.* Causing discredit; disreputable; disgraceful. — **dis·cred·it·a·bly** \-ə-blē\ *adv.*

dis·creet \dis-'krēt\ *adj.* Having or showing good judgment in conduct and especially in speech; careful; prudent; as, to be *discreet* in choosing one's companions. Only a very *discreet* person can be trusted with secrets. — **dis·creet·ly,** *adv.*

dis·crep·an·cy \dis-'krep-n-sē\ *n.; pl.* **dis·crep·an·cies. 1** Difference or disagreement, as between two records or accounts of the same event or between an actual and a stated amount of money. **2** An instance of such difference.

dis·crep·ant \dis-'krep-nt\ *adj.* Showing discrepancy.

dis·cre·tion \dis-'kresh-n\ *n.* **1** The power or right of free decision; free choice; individual judgment; as, to leave a course of action to the president's *discretion.* **2** Careful judgment in action and especially in speech; caution; prudence; as, a man of great *discretion,* who could be trusted not to do anything foolish.

dis·cre·tion·ary \dis-'kresh-n-ˌer-ē\ *adj.* Left to discretion, or individual judgment; as, an ambassador with *discretionary* powers.

dis·crim·i·nate \dis-'krim-ə-ˌnāt\ *v.;* **dis·crim·i·nat·ed; dis·crim·i·nat·ing. 1** To see and note the differences between two things; to distinguish accurately between one thing and another; as, to *discriminate* between blue and purple. One purpose of education is to train the pupil to *discriminate* between the worthless and the good. **2** To make a distinction in favor of or against one person or thing as compared with others; as, to make up one's mind never to *discriminate* against anyone because his race or religion is different from one's own.

dis·crim·i·na·tion \dis-ˌkrim-ə-'nāsh-n\ *n.* **1** The act of discriminating or the state of being discriminated. **2** Ability to discriminate, or make fine distinctions between things; as, a man of taste and *discrimination.* **3** A distinction, especially an unjust distinction, made in favor of one person or group over another, or the practice of making such distinctions.

dis·crim·i·na·to·ry \dis-'krim-ə-nə-ˌtōr-ē, -ˌtȯr-ē\ *adj.* Showing favoritism.

dis·cur·sive \dis-'kər-siv\ *adj.* Passing from one subject or topic to another, especially without apparent plan. — **dis·cur·sive·ly,** *adv.*

dis·cus \'dis-kəs\ *n.; pl.* **dis·cus·es** \-kə-səz\ or

dis·ci \'dis-ˌī\. [From Latin *discus* meaning "quoit", "dish", "discus", there borrowed from Greek *diskos* — see *dish* and *disk.*] A heavy round plate to be hurled as a trial of strength and skill.

dis·cuss \dis-'kəs\ *v.* **1** To argue or consider carefully by presenting the various sides, as of a question or a proposal; to debate fully and openly. **2** To talk about; as, to *discuss* the weather for a moment; to *discuss* one friend with another.

— The words *argue* and *debate* are synonyms of *discuss: discuss* may suggest examining various considerations and exchanging opinions; *argue* is likely to indicate the presenting of evidence in support of a conviction in order to convince someone else of its truth; *debate* usually indicates a formal public argument between opposing sides, often according to a fixed procedure.

dis·cus·sion \dis-'kəsh-n\ *n.* Conversation or debate for the purpose of understanding various sides of a question.

dis·dain \dis-'dān\ *v.* To look down upon; to scorn; to reject as not worth notice; as, to *disdain* to ask for help; to *disdain* a small contribution. **— *n.*** A feeling of contempt for something considered beneath one; scorn; as, to have nothing but *disdain* for the proposal.

dis·dain·ful \dis-'dān-fəl\ *adj.* Full of or expressing disdain; scornful. — For synonyms see *contemptuous.* — **dis·dain·ful·ly** \-fə-lē\ *adv.*

dis·ease \di-'zēz\ *n.* **1** Any condition in which the health is weakened or damaged; illness; sickness. **2** Any ailment that causes such a condition.

dis·eased \di-'zēzd\ *adj.* Afflicted with or as if with a disease; as, *diseased* tonsils; a *diseased* imagination.

dis·em·bark \ˌdis-m-'bärk, -'bárk\ *v.* To remove to shore from on board a boat; to land; as, to *disembark* troops.

dis·em·body \ˌdis-m-'bäd-ē\ *v.;* **dis·em·bod·ied** \-ēd\; **dis·em·bod·y·ing**. To deprive of bodily existence; as, *disembodied* spirits.

dis·en·chant \ˌdis-n-'chant\ *v.* To free from enchantment. — **dis·en·chant·ment**, *n.*

dis·en·cum·ber \ˌdis-n-'kəm-br\ *v.;* **dis·en·cum·bered**; **dis·en·cum·ber·ing** \-br(-)ing\. To free from anything that clogs or obstructs.

dis·en·gage \ˌdis-n-'gāj\ *v.;* **dis·en·gaged**; **dis·en·gag·ing**. To free or release from an engagement, an entanglement, or an incumbrance; to extricate; to disentangle; as, to *disengage* oneself from a business partnership; to *disengage* the clutch of an automobile.

dis·en·tan·gle \ˌdis-n-'tang-gl\ *v.;* **dis·en·tan·gled**; **dis·en·tan·gling** \-gl(-)ing\. To free from any tangle or confusion; to straighten out; as, to *disentangle* string. — **dis·en·tan·gle·ment**, *n.*

dis·es·teem \ˌdis-ə-'stēm\ *n.* Lack of esteem; disfavor; disrepute.

dis·fa·vor \(')dis-'fāv-r\ *n.* **1** Disapproval; dislike; as, to look with *disfavor* on a plan. **2** The condition of being regarded with dislike or displeasure; as, to be in *disfavor* at school because of misbehaving. **— *v.;*** **dis·fa·vored**; **dis·fa·vor·ing** \-r(-)ing\. To regard with disfavor; as, to *disfavor* the proposed plan.

dis·fig·ure \dis-'fig-yər\ *v.;* **dis·fig·ured**; **dis·fig·ur·ing**. To mar or spoil the looks of; to deface; as, to *disfigure* the landscape with billboards. — **dis·fig·ure·ment**, *n.*

dis·fran·chise \(')dis-'fran-ˌchīz\ *v.;* **dis·fran·chised**; **dis·fran·chis·ing**. To deprive of a franchise; especially, to deprive of the rights of a citizen, as the right to vote or to hold office.

dis·gorge \dis-'gȯrj\ *v.;* **dis·gorged**; **dis·gorg·ing**. **1** To vomit. **2** To discharge or give up violently, confusedly, or as a result of force; as, a thief forced to *disgorge* his plunder. The volcano *disgorges* lava.

dis·grace \dis-'grās\ *n.* **1** The condition of being out of favor; loss of respect; as, to be in *disgrace* with one's schoolmates. **2** Shame; dishonor; as, to fear the *disgrace* of being a coward. **3** A cause of shame; as, to be a *disgrace* to one's school. **— *v.;*** **dis·graced**; **dis·grac·ing**. To dishonor; to bring reproach or shame to; as, to *disgrace* one's family.

dis·grace·ful \dis-'grās-fəl\ *adj.* Bringing or deserving disgrace; shameful. — **dis·grace·ful·ly** \-fə-lē\ *adv.*

dis·grun·tle \dis-'grənt-l\ *v.;* **dis·grun·tled**; **dis·grun·tling**. To put in bad humor; to make peevish or dissatisfied.

dis·guise \dis-'gīz\ *v.;* **dis·guised**; **dis·guis·ing**. **1** To change the dress or looks of, so as to conceal who one is, or so as to resemble someone else; as, to *disguise* oneself with a wig and false beard. **2** To hide; to conceal; to alter; as, to *disguise* one's true feelings; to *disguise* one's voice. **— *n.* 1** Clothing put on to conceal one's identity; especially, an actor's costume. **2** Anything that hides or changes the true character or looks of a person or thing; as, blessings that come in *disguise.*

dis·gust \dis-'gəst\ *v.* **1** To sicken the stomach of; to nauseate. **2** To offend the taste or feelings of. The children's bad table manners *disgusted* everyone. **— *n.*** Strong dislike; distaste; loathing.

dis·gust·ed \dis-'gəs-təd\ *adj.* Having a feeling of disgust or loathing; disturbed by something offensive; as, *disgusted* by the children's lack of good manners. — **dis·gust·ed·ly**, *adv.*

dis·gust·ing \dis-'gəs-ting\ *adj.* Causing disgust; revolting. — **dis·gust·ing·ly**, *adv.*

dish \'dish\ *n.* [From Old English *disc,* there borrowed from Latin *discus* — see *disk* and *discus.*] **1** A bowl, cup, plate, platter, or something similar, for serving food at table. **2** Food served in a dish; as, a *dish* fit for a king. **3** The amount of food that a dish holds; as, to eat a *dish* of ice cream. **— *v.* 1** To put into a dish or dishes; as, to *dish* up the dinner. **2** To make concave like a dish. The right front wheel of the car was *dished* in the accident.

dis·heart·en \dis-'härt-n, -'hárt-n\ *v.;* **dis·heart·ened**; **dis·heart·en·ing** \-n(-)ing\. To discourage; to deject. — **dis·heart·en·ing·ly**, *adv.*

di·shev·el \di-'shev-l\ *v.*; **di·shev·eled** or **di·shev·elled**; **di·shev·el·ing** or **di·shev·el·ling** \-l(-)ing\. To let one's hair fall in disorder; to disarrange, as hair or clothing. The man's long, stringy hair and rumpled clothing created a *disheveled* appearance.

dis·hon·est \(')dis-'än-əst\ *adj.* **1** Not honest; untrustworthy; as, a *dishonest* man. **2** Marked by fraud; deceitful; corrupt; as, *dishonest* dealings. — **dis·hon·est·ly**, *adv.*

dis·hon·es·ty \(')dis-'än-əs-tē\ *n.* **1** Lack of honesty; lack of uprightness. **2** A dishonest act; a fraud.

dis·hon·or \(')dis-'än-r\ *n.* **1** Disgrace; shame; loss of honor or reputation. **2** A cause of disgrace; a dishonorable action, person, or condition; as, a man who is a *dishonor* to his country. — *v.*; **dis·hon·ored**; **dis·hon·or·ing** \-r(-)ing\. **1** To disgrace; to bring shame upon. **2** To refuse to accept or pay, as a check or draft.

dis·hon·or·a·ble \(')dis-'än-r(-)əb-l, -rb-l\ *adj.* Not honorable; disgraceful; shameful. — **dis·hon·or·a·bly** \-r(-)ə-blē, -r-blē\ *adv.*

dish·wash·er \'dish-ˌwȯsh-r, -ˌwäsh-r\ *n.* A person or a machine that washes dishes.

dis·il·lu·sion \ˌdis-l-'üzh-n\ *v.* To free from illusion. — **dis·il·lu·sion·ment**, *n.*

dis·in·cli·na·tion \ˌdis-ˌin-klə-'nāsh-n\ *n.* An unwillingness to do something; a dislike or distaste.

dis·in·cline \ˌdis-n-'klīn\ *v.*; **dis·in·clined**; **dis·in·clin·ing.** To make unwilling; to be unwilling; as, *disinclined* to accept the offer.

dis·in·fect \ˌdis-n-'fekt\ *v.* To cleanse of germs which might cause disease; as, to *disinfect* a room. — **dis·in·fec·tion** \-'feksh-n\ *n.* — **dis·in·fec·tor** \-'fekt-r\ *n.*

dis·in·fect·ant \ˌdis-n-'fek-tənt\ *adj.* Disinfecting; as, a solution containing a *disinfectant* chemical. — *n.* Something that disinfects or destroys germs.

dis·in·her·it \ˌdis-n-'her-ət\ *v.* To prevent a person from inheriting property that would naturally be passed on to him.

dis·in·te·grate \(')dis-'in-tə-ˌgrāt\ *v.*; **dis·in·te·grat·ed**; **dis·in·te·grat·ing.** **1** To separate or break up into small pieces or into powder; to fall into small pieces. The old house *disintegrated* under the force of the storm. **2** To destroy the wholeness or identity of something. Repeated attacks *disintegrated* the army of the enemy as a fighting unit. — **dis·in·te·gra·tion** \(ˌ)dis-ˌin-tə-'grāsh-n\ *n.* — **dis·in·te·gra·tor** \(')dis-'in-tə-ˌgrāt-r\ *n.*

dis·in·ter \ˌdis-n-'tər, ˌdis-in-\ *v.*; **dis·in·terred**; **dis·in·ter·ring.** To take out of the grave or tomb; to dig up.

dis·in·ter·est·ed \(')dis-'in-trəs-təd, -'int-r-ˌes-, -'int-rs-, -'in-ˌtres-, -'int-r-əs-\ *adj.* Free from selfish interest; not prejudiced; as, to give a *disinterested* report of an automobile accident.

dis·join \(')dis-'jȯin\ *v.* To undo the joining of; to disunite; to separate; to detach. The house and garage, originally built as one structure, were now *disjoined.*

dis·joint \(')dis-'jȯint\ *v.* **1** To break up into parts; to disconnect; to disunite. **2** To separate joint from joint; to take in pieces at the joints; as, to *disjoint* a chicken in carving.

dis·joint·ed \(')dis-'jȯint-əd\ *adj.* Disconnected; not clear and orderly; as, *disjointed* speech.

disk or **disc** \'disk\ *n.* [From Latin *discus* meaning "quoit", "dish", "discus" — see *dish* and *discus.*] **1** A flat round plate or platelike object. **2** A round flat surface. **3** Usually *disc.* In biology, any of various flat roundish parts or structures. **4** Usually *disc.* A phonograph record.

disk harrow. A harrow with round cutting plates for cultivating the soil.

disk jockey. Variant of *disc jockey.*

disk harrow

dis·like \(')dis-'līk\ *n.* A feeling of not liking; distaste. — *v.*; **dis·liked**; **dis·lik·ing.** To regard with dislike; to disapprove.

dis·lo·cate \'dis-lō-ˌkāt, (')dis-'lō-ˌkāt\ *v.*; **dis·lo·cat·ed**; **dis·lo·cat·ing.** **1** To put out of its proper place; to displace; especially, to disconnect a bone from its proper connection with another bone of the body; as, to *dislocate* one's shoulder. **2** To cause confusion in; to disarrange, as plans. — **dis·lo·ca·tion** \ˌdis-lō-'kāsh-n\ *n.*

dis·lodge \(')dis-'läj\ *v.*; **dis·lodged**; **dis·lodg·ing.** To force out of a resting place; to drive out of a place of hiding or defense; as, to *dislodge* a rock from a hillside.

dis·loy·al \(')dis-'lȯi-əl, -'lȯil\ *adj.* Not loyal; false; faithless. — **dis·loy·al·ly** \-'lȯi-ə-lē\ *adv.*

dis·loy·al·ty \(')dis-'lȯi-əl-tē, -'lȯil-tē\ *n.* **1** Lack of loyalty; unfaithfulness. **2** A disloyal act.

dis·mal \'diz-məl\ *adj.* **1** Gloomy to the eye or ear; dreary; depressing; as, a *dismal* sight; *dismal* news. **2** Cheerless; depressed. — **dis·mal·ly** \-mə-lē\ *adv.*

dis·man·tle \(')dis-'mant-l\ *v.*; **dis·man·tled**; **dis·man·tling** \-l(-)ing\. **1** To strip of furniture or equipment, as a house, a fort, or a ship. **2** To tear down; to destroy; as, to *dismantle* the remains of a building ruined by fire. **3** To take to pieces temporarily, as for repairs or for moving or shipping.

dis·mast \(')dis-'mast\ *v.* To remove, carry away, or break off the mast or masts of; as, a ship *dismasted* in a storm.

dis·may \dis-'mā, diz-\ *v.* To disable or dishearten with fear or alarm; to lower the spirits or courage of; to daunt; as, dangers great enough to *dismay* the bravest man. — *n.* Loss of spirit and courage through fear or apprehension; a sudden and complete feeling of inability or inadequacy, as in the face of a disturbing prospect or of alarming news.

dis·mem·ber \(')dis-'mem-br\ *v.*; **dis·mem·bered**; **dis·mem·ber·ing** \-br(-)ing\. **1** To tear limb from limb; to remove the limbs or members of; as, a *dismembered* corpse. **2** To divide or break up, as if by tearing apart; as, a defeated nation *dismembered* by its conquerors. — **dis·mem·ber·ment**, *n.*

dis·miss \dis-'mis\ *v.* **1** To send away; to cause or allow to go; as, to *dismiss* a messenger; to *dismiss* a class. **2** To discharge from office or service; as, to *dismiss* a workman with two weeks' notice. **3** To put aside or out of mind; as, to *dismiss* an unjust thought. **4** In law, to refuse to hear or consider further, as a complaint or a plea. After a preliminary hearing the magistrate *dismissed* the charge.

dis·miss·al \dis-'mis-l\ *n.* The act of dismissing or the state or fact of being dismissed; as, to receive a *dismissal* from one's job. The defendant's lawyer asked for a *dismissal* of the charges.

dis·mount \(')dis-'maủnt\ *v.* **1** To get down from something, as a horse or bicycle. **2** To throw down from a horse; to unhorse; as, a steeplechase rider *dismounted* at the first jump. **3** To take from its carriage or mountings, as a cannon. **4** To take apart, as a machine; to dismantle.

dis·o·be·di·ence \ˌdis-ə-'bēd-ē-ən(t)s\ *n.* Lack of obedience; neglect or refusal to obey.

dis·o·be·di·ent \ˌdis-ə-'bēd-ē-ənt\ *adj.* Neglecting or refusing to obey. — **dis·o·be·di·ent·ly**, *adv.*

dis·o·bey \ˌdis-ə-'bā\ *v.* To refuse or neglect to obey.

dis·o·blige \ˌdis-ə-'blīj\ *v.;* **dis·o·bliged**; **dis·o·blig·ing.** To refuse to oblige; to be unaccommodating to. Courteous people do not willingly *disoblige* others. — **dis·o·blig·ing·ly**, *adv.*

dis·or·der \(')dis-'ȯrd-r\ *n.* **1** Lack of order or of orderly arrangement; confusion; as, papers and books left in *disorder* on a desk. **2** Disturbance of the peace; riot; tumult; as, scenes of *disorder* in the streets of the besieged city. **3** A sickness; an ailment; as, a mental *disorder;* a *disorder* of the blood. — *v.;* **dis·or·dered**; **dis·or·der·ing** \-r(-)ing\. **1** To disturb the order of; to disarrange. The unruly children completely *disordered* the room. **2** To upset the regular or proper functioning of; as, a *disordered* stomach. Excessive worry and brooding may *disorder* the mind.

dis·or·der·ly \(')dis-'ȯrd-r-lē\ *adj.* **1** Not in an orderly condition; disarranged; as, a *disorderly* mass of papers. **2** Not observing the rules of law and order; unruly; as, *disorderly* conduct; a *disorderly* meeting.

dis·or·gan·ize \(')dis-'ȯrg-n-ˌīz\ *v.;* **dis·or·gan·ized**; **dis·or·gan·iz·ing.** To break up the regular arrangement or system of; to upset the proper working of; to throw into disorder; as, an office *disorganized* by an outbreak of illness among the employees. One of the effects of a flood is to *disorganize* transportation systems. — **dis·or·gan·i·za·tion** \(')dis-ˌȯrg-n-ə-'zāsh-n\ *n.*

dis·own \(')dis-'ōn\ *v.* To refuse to acknowledge as belonging to oneself; to repudiate; to renounce; as, a son *disowned* by his father; to *disown* one's allegiance to one's country.

dis·par·age \dis-'par-ij\ *v.;* **dis·par·aged**; **dis·par·ag·ing.** [From Medieval French *desparagier* meaning originally "to marry beneath oneself", "to cause someone to marry beneath himself".] **1** To lessen in honor or esteem; to lower in opinion; to bring discredit on; as, a discourtesy more *disparaging* to the doer than to its object. **2** To speak slightingly of; to belittle; as, to *disparage* the accomplishments of a rival. — **dis·par·ag·ing·ly**, *adv.*

dis·par·age·ment \dis-'par-ij-mənt\ *n.* **1** A lowering of standing or honor or something that causes such a lowering; disgrace; discredit. There is no *disparagement* in honest failure. **2** The act of disparaging; a belittling; as, a smile of *disparagement.*

dis·par·i·ty \dis-'par-ət-ē\ *n.; pl.* **dis·par·i·ties.** Inequality or difference, as in age, rank, character, or kind. The two children were fast friends in spite of the *disparity* in their ages.

dis·pas·sion·ate \dis-'pash-n(-)ət\ *adj.* Not influenced by feeling or emotion; calm; impartial. It is hard to get a *dispassionate* account of a quarrel from those who have taken part in it. — **dis·pas·sion·ate·ly**, *adv.*

dis·patch \dis-'pach\ *v.* **1** To send away promptly or rapidly to a particular place or for a particular purpose; as, to *dispatch* a messenger; to *dispatch* a train. **2** To attend to rapidly; to dispose of speedily; to get rid of; as, to *dispatch* some business. **3** To put to death. Civilized nations no longer *dispatch* prisoners of war. — *n.* **1** The sending of a message or messenger. **2** A message; especially, an important official message. **3** An item of news sent in by a reporter or correspondent to a newspaper; as, a *dispatch* from London. **4** Promptness in attending to a task; speed; haste; as, to manage an affair with great *dispatch.* **5** The act of putting to death; killing; as, to arrange for a merciful *dispatch* of a wounded animal.

dis·patch·er \dis-'pach-r\ *n.* A person who dispatches, as trains or aircraft.

dis·pel \dis-'pel\ *v.;* **dis·pelled**; **dis·pel·ling.** To drive away by scattering; to clear away. The morning sunshine *dispelled* the fog.

dis·pen·sa·ry \dis-'pen(t)s-r(-)ē\ *n.; pl.* **dis·pen·sa·ries.** A place where medicines are prepared and given out, especially free or at very low cost to the poor.

dis·pen·sa·tion \ˌdisp-n-'sāsh-n, ˌdis-ˌpen-\ *n.* **1** The act of dispensing, or dealing out; distribution. **2** That which is dispensed. **3** A certain definite or seemingly definite arrangement or provision. By a happy *dispensation* of nature man has two eyes and two ears. **4** A dispensing with, or doing without; especially, a permit from church authorities to do something ordinarily not allowed. **5** A system of rules and principles for managing affairs, especially religious affairs; as, the Christian *dispensation.*

dis·pense \dis-'pen(t)s\ *v.;* **dis·pensed**; **dis·pens·ing.** **1** To deal out in portions; to distribute; as, to *dispense* charity. **2** To apply or administer, as laws or justice. **3** To put up or prepare medicine in a form ready for use. — **dispense with.** To give up; to do or get along without. — **dis·pens·a·ble**, *adj.*

dis·pens·er \dis-'pen(t)s-r\ *n.* **1** A person who dispenses; especially, a druggist who prepares medicines from prescriptions. **2** A container, as a bottle or package, so made as to release part of its contents without being fully opened; as, a squeeze-bottle *dispenser* for nose drops.

dis·per·sal \dis-'pərs-l\ *n.* The act or the result of dispersing or scattering; dispersion; distribution.

dis·perse \dis-'pərs\ *v.;* **dis·persed; dis·pers·ing. 1** To break up and scatter; to send or go in different directions; as, crowds *dispersing* after a football game. The police soon *dispersed* the mob. **2** To spread; to distribute; as, to *disperse* one's money in a variety of investments. It is the function of a newspaper to *disperse* the news as widely as possible. **3** To dispel, as a cloud or a vapor.

dis·per·sion \dis-'pərzh-n, -'pərsh-n\ *n.* **1** The act of dispersing or the state of being dispersed; a breaking up and scattering of parts. **2** The separation of light, as by a prism, into its different colored rays.

dis·pir·it \(')dis-'pir-ət\ *v.* To discourage; to depress; to dishearten; as, a man *dispirited* by many failures; a tired, *dispirited* group of captured soldiers.

dis·place \(')dis-'plās\ *v.;* **dis·placed; dis·plac·ing. 1** To remove from the usual or proper place; to put out of place; as, furniture *displaced* by romping children. Many persons were *displaced* from their homes by the war. **2** To take the place of; to replace. In many places, electric lights have largely *displaced* other kinds. **3** To remove from office; to discharge; to depose.

— The words *misplace* and *mislay* are synonyms of *displace: displace* may imply putting something out of the usual or proper place, often by putting something else in it; *misplace* generally indicates putting something in a wrong or unworthy place; *mislay* is likely to suggest putting something in a place that one cannot recall.

dis·placed person \'dis-ˌplāst, dis-'plāst\. A person driven from his country by war or by other conditions threatening his liberty or safety, as persecution because of politics, race, or religion.

dis·place·ment \(')dis-'plās-mənt\ *n.* **1** The act of displacing or the state of being displaced. **2** The volume or weight of a fluid, as water, displaced by a floating body, as a ship, the weight of the displaced fluid being equal to that of the displacing body; as, a ship of 3000 tons *displacement.*

dis·play \dis-'plā\ *v.* **1** To unfold; to spread out; as, to *display* the flag on national holidays. **2** To spread purposely so as to be in the view of others; to exhibit; as, to *display* the latest women's fashions. **3** To permit to be seen; to reveal; as, to *display* one's ignorance. — *n.* **1** An exhibition; a showing; as, a *display* of goods in a store window. **2** An exhibition given for effect; an exaggerated showing; as, to make a *display* of one's grief.

dis·please \(')dis-'plēz\ *v.;* **dis·pleased; dis·pleas·ing.** To arouse feelings of disapproval and dislike; to give displeasure to; to offend.

dis·plea·sure \(')dis-'plezh-r, -'plāzh-r\ *n.* A feeling of annoyance and dislike accompanying disapproval; dissatisfaction; as, to incur the *displeasure* of one's teacher by talking in class. Only a slight frown showed the girl's *displeasure.*

dis·port \dis-'pōrt, -'port\ *v.* To amuse; to play; to frolic; as, children *disporting* themselves on the beach.

dis·pos·al \dis-'pōz-l\ *n.* **1** A disposing; an arrangement; an orderly distribution; as, the general's *disposal* of his troops for battle. **2** A getting rid of; a putting out of the way; as, *disposal* of trash. **3** Management; administration. **4** The transfer or placing of anything into new hands; as, a *disposal* of property. **5** The power to dispose of control; command; as, to have only limited funds at one's *disposal.*

dis·pose \dis-'pōz\ *v.;* **dis·posed; dis·pos·ing. 1** To distribute and put in place; to arrange; as, to *dispose* troops for combat. **2** To give a tendency to; to incline in mind; to incline; as, to be *disposed* to refuse a request. — **dispose of. 1** To settle or determine the fate, condition, or use of; as, the right to *dispose of* one's possessions. **2** To get rid of; to put out of the way; to finish with; as, to *dispose of* rubbish; to *dispose of* the morning's mail. **3** To transfer to the control of someone else; to part with; as, to *dispose of* some old clothes. — **dis·pos·a·ble,** *adj.*

dis·po·si·tion \ˌdis-pə-'zish-n\ *n.* **1** The act or power of disposing or managing; disposal; as, to have plenty of money at one's *disposition.* **2** The giving up or transferring of anything; as, the *disposition* of real estate. **3** Arrangement; as, the *disposition* of furniture in a room. **4** Tendency; inclination; as, a person's natural *disposition* to avoid pain. **5** Natural attitude toward things; as, a man of cheerful *disposition.*

dis·pos·sess \ˌdis-pə-'zes\ *v.* To deprive of the occupancy of land or houses; to put off; to put out. The landlord *dispossessed* the tenants for not paying their rent.

dis·proof \(')dis-'prüf\ *n.* **1** A proving that something is not as believed or stated. **2** Evidence that disproves.

dis·pro·por·tion \ˌdis-prə-'pōrsh-n, -'porsh-n\ *n.* A lack of proper proportion between things; a lack of symmetry; as, a drawing showing a figure with one arm in *disproportion* to the body. — *v.* To make out of proportion. — **dis·pro·por·tion·al** \-n(-)əl\ *adj.* — **dis·pro·por·tion·al·ly** \-n(-)ə-lē\ *adv.*

dis·pro·por·tion·ate \ˌdis-prə-'pōrsh-n(-)ət, -'porsh-\ *adj.* Not in proper proportion; out of proper relations to other things or parts; not symmetrical; as, a store in which prices are *disproportionate* to the quality of the goods. — **dis·pro·por·tion·ate·ly,** *adv.*

dis·prove \(')dis-'prüv\ *v.;* **dis·proved; dis·prov·ing.** To show to be false; as, to *disprove* a statement.

dis·put·a·ble \dis-'pyüt-əb-l, 'dis-pyət-\ *adj.* Liable to be disputed, debated, or contested; debatable. — **dis·put·a·bly** \-ə-blē\ *adv.*

dis·pu·tant \'dis-pyət-ənt, dis-'pyüt-nt\ *n.* A person who takes part in a dispute.

dis·pu·ta·tion \ˌdis-(ˌ)pyü-ˈtāsh-n\ *n.* A disputing; a controversy.

dis·pu·ta·tious \ˌdis-(ˌ)pyü-ˈtā-shəs\ *adj.* Inclined to dispute; argumentative.

dis·pute \dis-ˈpyüt\ *v.;* **dis·put·ed; dis·put·ing. 1** To argue against some person or thing; to argue irritably; to wrangle. **2** To deny the truth or rightness of; to oppose; as, to *dispute* a statement or a claim. **3** To fight about; to contest; as, to *dispute* every foot of the enemy's advance. **—** *n.* An argument; a debate; a quarrel.

— The word *quarrel* is a synonym of *dispute: dispute* usually suggests a heated verbal contention; *quarrel* may indicate an angry or violent argument that results in broken or strained relations.

dis·qual·i·fy \(ˈ)dis-ˈkwäl-ə-ˌfī\ *v.;* **dis·qual·i·fied** \-ˌfīd\; **dis·qual·i·fy·ing. 1** To make or declare unfit; as, to *disqualify* all voters who cannot read and write. **2** To deprive of the qualifications necessary for fulfilling a purpose; to unfit; as, a man *disqualified* for military service by poor vision. — **dis·qual·i·fi·ca·tion** \(ˈ)dis-ˌkwäl-ə-fə-ˈkāsh-n\ *n.*

dis·qui·et \(ˈ)dis-ˈkwī-ət\ *v.* To make uneasy or restless; to disturb; as, to receive *disquieting* news. **—** *n.* Uneasiness; anxiety. The rumor that war was about to be declared caused *disquiet* throughout the nation.

dis·qui·e·tude \(ˈ)dis-ˈkwī-ə-ˌtüd, -ˌtyüd\ *n.* Disquiet.

dis·qui·si·tion \ˌdis-kwə-ˈzish-n\ *n.* A formal inquiry or discussion; an elaborate essay.

dis·re·gard \ˌdis-rē-ˈgärd, -ˈgȧrd\ *v.* To fail to regard, notice, or observe; to pay no heed or attention to; as, to *disregard* traffic signals. — For synonyms see *neglect.* **—** *n.* A disregarding; a being disregarded; neglect. — **dis·re·gard·ful** \-fəl\ *adj.*

dis·rel·ish \(ˈ)dis-ˈrel-ish\ *n.* Lack of relish; distaste; as, a *disrelish* for some kinds of food.

dis·re·pair \ˌdis-rē-ˈpar, -ˈper\ *n.* A condition of being in need of repair.

dis·rep·u·ta·ble \(ˈ)dis-ˈrep-yət-əb-l\ *adj.* Not reputable; discreditable or disgraceful; of bad reputation; as, a *disreputable* character; a *disreputable* act. — **dis·rep·u·ta·bly** \-ə-blē\ *adv.*

dis·re·pute \ˌdis-rē-ˈpyüt\ *n.* Loss or lack of good name; bad character; dishonor; as, a man who has fallen into *disrepute.*

dis·re·spect \ˌdis-rē-ˈspekt\ *n.* Lack of respect; discourtesy. — **dis·re·spect·ful** \-fəl\ *adj.* — **dis·re·spect·ful·ly** \-fə-lē\ *adv.*

dis·robe \(ˈ)dis-ˈrōb\ *v.;* **dis·robed; dis·rob·ing.** To undress.

dis·rupt \dis-ˈrəpt\ *v.* To break apart; to break up; as, *disrupted* plans. — **dis·rup·tion** \-ˈrəpsh-n\ *n.* — **dis·rup·tive** \-ˈrəp-tiv\ *adj.*

dis·sat·is·fac·tion \ˌdi(s)-ˌsat-əs-ˈfaksh-n\ *n.* The state of being dissatisfied; discontent.

dis·sat·is·fac·to·ry \(ˌ)di(s)-ˌsat-əs-ˈfakt-r(-)ē\ *adj.* Causing dissatisfaction.

dis·sat·is·fy \(ˈ)di(s)-ˈsat-əs-ˌfī\ *v.;* **dis·sat·is·fied** \-ˌfīd\; **dis·sat·is·fy·ing.** To make unsatisfied; to make displeased by lack of something; as, to be *dissatisfied* with one's station in life.

dis·sect \di-ˈsekt\ *v.* **1** To divide into separate parts for examination, as an animal or a plant. **2** To analyze; as, to *dissect* a proposed plan. — **dis·sec·tion** \-ˈseksh-n\ *n.*

dis·sem·ble \di-ˈsem-bl\ *v.;* **dis·sem·bled; dis·sem·bling** \-bl(-)ing\. **1** To disguise; as, to *dissemble* one's fear. **2** To pretend; to feign; as, to *dissemble* sleep. **3** To ignore; as, to *dissemble* the wrongs done to one.

dis·sem·i·nate \di-ˈsem-ə-ˌnāt\ *v.;* **dis·sem·i·nat·ed; dis·sem·i·nat·ing. 1** To sow broadcast; to scatter; as, to *disseminate* seed. **2** To spread abroad; to circulate; as, to *disseminate* news. — **dis·sem·i·na·tion** \di-ˌsem-ə-ˈnāsh-n\ *n.*

dis·sen·sion \di-ˈsench-n\ *n.* Disagreement in opinion; discord; a quarreling; as, *dissension* between juniors and seniors.

dis·sent \di-ˈsent\ *v.* **1** To differ in opinion; to disagree. **2** To differ in doctrines, rites, or church government from an established church. **—** *n.* **1** Difference of opinion; disagreement; as, to shake one's head in *dissent.* **2** Separation from an established church, especially that of England; nonconformity.

dis·sent·er \di-ˈsent-r\ *n.* **1** A person who dissents. **2** One who separates from an established church. **3** [with a capital] In England, a nonconformist.

dis·ser·ta·tion \ˌdis-r-ˈtāsh-n\ *n.* A long treatment of a subject, especially in writing.

dis·serv·ice \(ˈ)di(s)-ˈsər-vəs\ *n.* Ill service; harm; an injury.

dis·sev·er \di-ˈsev-r\ *v.;* **dis·sev·ered; dis·sev·er·ing** \-r(-)ing\. To sever thoroughly; to separate; to disunite.

dis·sim·i·lar \(ˈ)di(s)-ˈsim-l-ər\ *adj.* Not similar; unlike.

dis·sim·i·lar·i·ty \(ˌ)di(s)-ˌsim-l-ˈar-ət-ē\ *n.; pl.* **dis·sim·i·lar·i·ties.** Difference in appearance or in nature. The *dissimilarities* in dogs of various breeds is greater than that in cats.

dis·sim·u·late \(ˈ)di(s)-ˈsim-yə-ˌlāt\ *v.;* **dis·sim·u·lat·ed; dis·sim·u·lat·ing.** To hide under a false appearance; to pretend with intent to deceive; to feign. The boy's nervous manner suggested that he was not telling the truth, but *dissimulating.* — **dis·sim·u·la·tion** \ˌdi(s)-ˌsim-yə-ˈlāsh-n\ *n.*

dis·si·pate \ˈdis-ə-ˌpāt\ *v.;* **dis·si·pat·ed; dis·si·pat·ing. 1** To break up and drive off or to break up into small parts and disappear; to dispel; to disperse. The breeze *dissipated* the fog. **2** To scatter aimlessly or foolishly; as, to *dissipate* one's energies. **3** To squander, as money; to be wasteful. **4** To be wasteful or uncontrolled in the pursuit of pleasure; especially, to drink to excess.

dis·si·pat·ed \ˈdis-ə-ˌpāt-əd\ *adj.* Habitually indulging to excess in pleasures considered foolish or harmful; dissolute.

dis·si·pa·tion \ˌdis-ə-ˈpāsh-n\ *n.* **1** The action of dissipating or the state of being dissipated; a scattering; dispersion. **2** Wasteful spending. **3** Wasteful or foolish pleasure or amusement. **4** Dissolute behavior; a dissipated way of living.

dis·so·ci·ate \(ˈ)di-ˈsō-s(h)ē-ˌāt\ *v.;* **dis·so·ci·at·ed; dis·so·ci·at·ing.** To separate from union or association; as, to *dissociate* oneself from a group one has belonged to. — **dis·so·ci·a·tion** \ˌdi-ˌsō-s(h)ē-ˈāsh-n\ *n.*

dis·sol·u·ble \di-ˈsäl-yəb-l\ *adj.* Capable of being dissolved. — **dis·sol·u·bil·i·ty** \di-ˌsäl-yə-ˈbil-ət-ē\ *n.*

dis·so·lute \ˈdis-l-ˌüt\ *adj.* Evil in morals and conduct; vicious. — **dis·so·lute·ly,** *adv.*

dis·so·lu·tion \ˌdis-l-ˈüsh-n\ *n.* **1** The action or process of dissolving or breaking up; separation into parts; disintegration; decomposition. **2** Destruction; ruin. **3** The breaking up of an assembly by ending its sessions; as, the *dissolution* of parliament. **4** The breaking up of a partnership in business.

dis·solve \di-ˈzälv\ *v.;* **dis·solved; dis·solv·ing. 1** To break up into component parts. **2** To pass or cause to pass into solution; to melt; to liquefy. Sugar *dissolves* in water. **3** To bring to an end; as, to *dissolve* a partnership. **4** To bring to an end by dispersing; as, to *dissolve* parliament. **5** To waste or fade away, as if by breaking up or by melting. The boy's courage *dissolved* in the face of the horrible sight. **6** In moving pictures and television, to appear or fade out gradually, so that one scene is replaced by another.

dis·so·nance \ˈdis-n-ən(t)s\ *n.* **1** A mingling of discordant sounds. **2** Discord; disagreement.

dis·so·nant \ˈdis-n-ənt\ *adj.* **1** Marked by dissonance in sound; discordant. **2** Disagreeing; not harmonious; as, *dissonant* views of the best course of action. — **dis·so·nant·ly,** *adv.*

dis·suade \di-ˈswād\ *v.;* **dis·suad·ed; dis·suad·ing.** To advise against a course of action; to persuade or try to persuade not to do something. — **dis·sua·sion** \-ˈswāzh-n\ *n.*

dis·taff \ˈdis-ˌtaf\ *n.* The staff for holding the flax, tow, or wool in spinning. — **distaff side.** The female branch or side of a family.

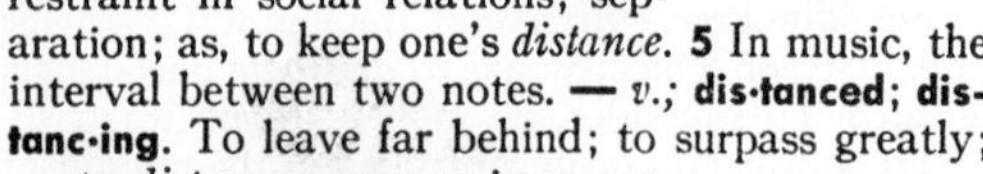

dis·tance \ˈdis-tən(t)s\ *n.* **1** The space between two objects; the measure of separation in space. **2** Length or interval of time. **3** A distant point or region; as, lights seen in the *distance.* **4** Reserve or restraint in social relations; separation; as, to keep one's *distance.* **5** In music, the interval between two notes. — *v.;* **dis·tanced; dis·tanc·ing.** To leave far behind; to surpass greatly; as, to *distance* everyone in a race.

dis·tant \ˈdis-tənt\ *adj.* **1** Separated in space or time; as, two objects *distant* from each other by one inch. **2** Far separated; not near in time, space, or other scale; remote; as, a *distant* city; a *distant* cousin. **3** Reserved; somewhat haughty; not cordial; as, a person with a *distant* manner. — **dis·tant·ly,** *adv.*

dis·taste \(ˈ)dis-ˈtāst\ *n.* **1** Dislike, as for certain foods. **2** Any dislike; aversion.

dis·taste·ful \(ˈ)dis-ˈtāst-fəl\ *adj.* **1** Unpleasant to the taste. **2** Disagreeable; as, the *distasteful* job of washing the dishes. — **dis·taste·ful·ly** \-fə-lē\ *adv.*

dis·tem·per \dis-ˈtemp-r\ *n.* **1** An unhealthy state of the bodily system; illness; ailment. **2** An infectious, often fatal, disease of some animals, especially young dogs.

dis·tend \dis-ˈtend\ *v.* To stretch out or extend in all directions; to expand; to swell; as, a balloon *distended* to its full capacity; the *distended* cheeks of a horn player. — **dis·ten·tion** \-ˈtench-n\ *n.*

dis·till or **dis·til** \dis-ˈtil\ *v.;* **dis·tilled; dis·till·ing. 1** To fall or let fall in drops; to trickle. **2** To obtain or extract by distillation; as, to *distill* brandy from wine. **3** To purify by distillation; as, *distilled* water.

dis·til·la·tion \ˌdis-tə-ˈlāsh-n\ *n.* **1** The process of heating a liquid or other substance until it sends off a gas or vapor, and then cooling the gas or vapor until it returns to liquid or solid form. **2** Something obtained by or as if by a process of distilling; an abstract or essence.

dis·till·er \dis-ˈtil-r\ *n.* One that distills; especially, a person whose occupation or business is distilling alcoholic liquors.

dis·till·ery \dis-ˈtil-r(-)ē\ *n.; pl.* **dis·till·er·ies.** A place where distilling, especially of alcoholic liquors, is carried on.

dis·tinct \dis-ˈting(k)t\ *adj.* **1** Distinguished from others; separate; different; as, a man guilty of three *distinct* crimes. **2** Clearly seen, heard, or understood; plain; unmistakable; as, a *distinct* sound; *distinct* handwriting.

dis·tinc·tion \dis-ˈting(k)sh-n\ *n.* **1** The act of distinguishing a difference; that which makes a difference; as, a clear *distinction* between right and wrong. **2** A distinguishing quality or mark. A forked tail is a chief *distinction* of most swallows. **3** A special recognition; as, to have the *distinction* of being the first man to climb the mountain. **4** A mark or sign of such recognition, as a medal. **5** Honor; as, to serve with *distinction.*

dis·tinc·tive \dis-ˈting(k)-tiv\ *adj.* Clearly marking a person or a thing as different from others; characteristic; as, a *distinctive* way of speaking. — **dis·tinc·tive·ly,** *adv.*

dis·tinct·ly \dis-ˈting(k)t-lē\ *adv.* Clearly; plainly; as, *distinctly* American.

dis·tin·guish \dis-ˈting-gwish\ *v.* **1** To recognize one thing among others by some mark or characteristic; as, to *distinguish* the sound of a piano in an orchestra. **2** To hear or see clearly; to make out; as, to *distinguish* a light in the distance. **3** To make distinctions; as, to *distinguish* between right and wrong. **4** To set apart; to mark as different. The long body and short legs of the dachshund *distinguish* it from other dogs. **5** To separate from others by a mark of honor; to make outstanding; as, to *distinguish* oneself in athletics. — **dis·tin·guish·a·ble** \-əb-l\ *adj.* — **dis·tin·guish·a·bly** \-ə-blē\ *adv.*

dis·tin·guished \dis-'ting-gwisht\ *adj.* Famous; notable; as, a *distinguished* writer.

dis·tort \dis-'tȯrt\ *v.* **1** To twist out of natural or regular shape; as, a face *distorted* with pain. **2** To turn from the true meaning; to misrepresent; as, to *distort* an account of a quarrel so as to conceal the facts.

dis·tor·tion \dis-'tȯrsh-n\ *n.* A distorting or a condition of being distorted; as, a *distortion* of the truth.

dis·tract \dis-'trakt\ *v.* **1** To draw the mind or attention to something else; to turn aside. The sound of fire engines *distracted* the attention of the class. **2** To agitate or trouble in mind to a point of complete confusion sometimes seemingly close to madness; to unsettle in mind.

dis·trac·tion \dis-'traksh-n\ *n.* **1** A distracting or a being distracted; confusion; disorder. There was so much *distraction* that no one could hear the speaker. **2** Confusion of mind; madness; despair; as, to be driven to *distraction* by worry. **3** Something that diverts attention; a diversion; as, a welcome *distraction* from the day's work. — **dis·trac·tive** \-'trak-tiv\ *adj.*

dis·traught \dis-'trȯt\ *adj.* Distracted; perplexed; crazed; as, *distraught* with fear.

dis·tress \dis-'tres\ *n.* **1** Great suffering of body or mind; pain; worry, anguish; as, to suffer *distress* from loss of a friend. **2** That which causes suffering; misfortune; trouble; sorrow. All the shipwrecked passengers were brothers in *distress.* **3** A condition of danger; desperate need; as, a ship in *distress.* — *v.* To cause distress; to pain. — **dis·tress·ful** \-fəl\ *adj.* — **dis·tress·ful·ly** \-fə-lē\ *adv.*

dis·trib·ute \dis-'trib-yət\ *v.;* **dis·trib·ut·ed; dis·trib·ut·ing. 1** To divide among a number; to deal out; as, to *distribute* presents at a Christmas party. **2** To spread out so as to cover; as, to *distribute* grass seed over a lawn. **3** To separate or divide, as into classes; to classify; to sort. — **dis·trib·ut·a·ble,** *adj.* — **dis·trib·ut·er,** *n.*

dis·tri·bu·tion \ˌdis-trə-'byüsh-n\ *n.* **1** The act of distributing. **2** The manner in which things are distributed; division and arrangement; as, a map showing the *distribution* of rainfall in the United States. **3** Something that is distributed.

dis·trib·u·tive \dis-'trib-yət-iv\ *adj.* **1** Serving to divide or distribute in portions. **2** Producing the same element when operating on a whole as when operating on each part and collecting the results. — **dis·trib·u·tive·ly,** *adv.*

dis·trib·u·tor \dis-'trib-yət-r\ *n.* **1** One that distributes; a distributer. **2** An agent or agency for marketing goods. **3** A device for distributing electric current to the spark plugs, as of an automobile engine.

dis·trict \'dis-(ˌ)trikt\ *n.* **1** A fixed part of a state or city, as for administrative or electoral purposes. **2** Any portion of territory; a region. — *v.* To divide into districts.

district attorney. The prosecuting attorney of a particular district, as a county.

dis·trust \(')dis-'trəst\ *v.* To have no trust or confidence in; to mistrust; as, to *distrust* strangers. — *n.* Lack of confidence; suspicion. — For synonyms see *doubt.* — **dis·trust·ful** \-fəl\ *adj.* — **dis·trust·ful·ly** \-fə-lē\ *adv.*

dis·turb \dis-'tərb\ *v.* **1** To throw into disorder or confusion; as, to *disturb* a meeting; to *disturb* the peace. **2** To interrupt; to interfere with; as, to *disturb* a person's rest. **3** To trouble the mind of; to upset; to make uneasy; as, to be *disturbed* by failure to hear from a friend. **4** To move from its place; as, to try to move a piano without *disturbing* other things. **5** To put to inconvenience. Please do not *disturb* yourself about the matter.

dis·turb·ance \dis-'tərb-n(t)s\ *n.* **1** A disturbing, as of peace or quiet. **2** Mental confusion; upset; as, an emotional *disturbance.* **3** Public turmoil.

dis·un·ion \(')dis(h)-'yün-yən\ *n.* Separation; lack of union or agreement.

dis·u·nite \ˌdis(h)-yü-'nīt\ *v.;* **dis·u·nit·ed; dis·u·nit·ing.** To separate; to divide; to destroy the unity of.

dis·use \(')dis(h)-'yüs\ *n.* The state of not being used; lack of use or a stopping of use; as, muscles grown weak from *disuse;* a pleasant custom long since fallen into *disuse.*

dis·used \(')dis(h)-'yüzd\ *adj.* Not used; especially, no longer used.

ditch \'dich\ *n.* A narrow channel or groove dug in the earth. — *v.* **1** To dig a ditch or ditches in or around, as for drainage. **2** To run into a ditch, as an automobile. **3** *Slang.* To get rid of; to abandon; to discard. **4** To land any plane not a seaplane on water, especially as an emergency measure.

dith·er \'di<u>th</u>-r\ *n.* A highly nervous and overexcited state; as, to be in a *dither* over speaking at the school assembly.

dit·to \'dit-ˌō\ *n.; pl.* **dit·tos.** [From Italian *ditto* or *detto* meaning literally "said", the past participle of *dire* meaning "to say".] The same or another or more of the same. Lost: one shirt (white); *ditto* (blue); one tennis racket (new); *ditto* (used). *Ditto* is often abbreviated to *do.* or represented, in columns, by two small marks ["] called **ditto marks.**

dit·ty \'dit-ē\ *n.; pl.* **dit·ties.** A song; especially, a short, simple song or poem intended to be sung.

di·ur·nal \dī-'ərn-l\ *adj.* **1** Daily; occurring every day. **2** Relating to the daytime. — **di·ur·nal·ly** \-'ərn-l-ē\ *adv.*

di·van \'dī-ˌvan\ *n.* **1** A low couch with no back or arms. **2** Any piece of furniture similar to a couch or sofa.

dive \'dīv\ *v.;* **dived** \'dīvd\ or **dove** \'dōv\; **dived; div·ing. 1** To plunge into water, especially headfirst. **2** To thrust suddenly into something, as with the body or hand. **3** To plunge deeply into any subject. **4** In aviation, to plunge downward at a steep angle. The airplane *dived* in flames. — *n.* **1** The act of one that dives. **2** In aviation, a steep descent at high speed. **3** *Slang.* A cheap, disreputable place of amusement.

dive bomber. A bombing plane that descends in a steep dive toward its target before releasing the bomb.

div·er \'dīv-r\ *n.* One that dives; especially, a person who works under water, often having air supplied from the surface.

di·verge \dī-'vərj, də-\ *v.;* **di·verged; di·verg·ing.** **1** To extend from a common point in two or more directions; as, spokes *diverging* from the hub of a wheel. **2** To turn aside, as from a set or given course; as, a path *diverging* from the road. **3** To differ or vary, as from a typical or normal form or after a period of agreement; as, boyhood chums whose interests began to *diverge* as they grew older; a cowboy picture with an ending *diverging* from the usual one.

di·ver·gence \dī-'vərj-n(t)s, də-\ *n.* **1** An extension, as of two or more lines or courses, in different directions from a common center. **2** Difference; variation from a standard; disagreement; as, a sharp *divergence* of opinion.

di·ver·gent \dī-'vərj-nt, də-\ *adj.* Diverging; moving or having moved away or apart. — **di·ver·gent·ly,** *adv.*

di·vers \'dīv-rz, 'dī-ˌvərz\ *adj.* Several; various; as to ask a question of *divers* persons; a choice made for *divers* reasons.

di·verse \dī-'vərs, də-; 'dī-ˌvərs\ *adj.* Different; unlike; separate. — **di·verse·ly,** *adv.*

di·ver·si·fy \də-'vər-sə-ˌfī, dī-\ *v.;* **di·ver·si·fied** \-ˌfīd\; **di·ver·si·fy·ing.** To make diverse, or various, in form or quality; to give variety to; as, to *diversify* a new neighborhood by building houses in various styles; to *diversify* the school day by studying several subjects. — **di·ver·si·fi·ca·tion** \-ˌvər-sə-fə-'kāsh-n\ *n.*

di·ver·sion \də-'vərzh-n, dī-\ *n.* **1** The act of diverting, or turning from a course; as, the *diversion* of water from a river into a canal. **2** Anything that relaxes or amuses; entertainment; recreation. **3** A military attack intended to draw the attention of the enemy away from the scene of the principal operation.

di·ver·si·ty \də-'vər-sət-ē, dī-\ *n.; pl.* **di·ver·si·ties.** **1** A condition or a point of difference; unlikeness; variation. The *diversity* between the two girls was so great it was hard to believe they were sisters. **2** Variety; as, great *diversity* of opinion.

di·vert \də-'vərt, dī-\ *v.* **1** To turn aside; as, to *divert* river water into a canal. The driver found the scenery *diverting* his attention from the road. **2** To amuse; to entertain. There are few children or adults who are not *diverted* by a circus. — For synonyms see *amuse.*

di·vest \də-'vest, dī-\ *v.* **1** To strip, as of clothes or arms. The aged man had trouble *divesting* himself of his overcoat. **2** To deprive, as of a right. Under the dictator the people were *divested* of their right of free speech.

di·vide \də-'vīd\ *v.;* **di·vid·ed; di·vid·ing.** **1** To separate into two or more parts or pieces; as, to *divide* an orange. The road *divides* at a fork just above the bridge. **2** To separate into equal parts by division; as, to *divide* 18 by 2. **3** To cause to be separate; to keep apart, as by a partition. A wall *divides* the two houses. **4** To distribute among a number; to give out in shares; to share with another or others; as, to *divide* profits; a boy who was never willing to *divide* his candy. **5** To differ, or to cause to differ, in opinion or interest. The committee *divided* on the question of the best way to raise the money. — *n.* A ridge or section of high ground between two areas of drainage; a watershed.

div·i·dend \'div-ə-ˌdend, -dənd\ *n.* **1** A number or quantity to be divided by another number or quantity. **2** A sum or amount to be divided and distributed, such as profits to be divided among shareholders; the share of such a sum that each person receives.

di·vid·er \də-'vīd-r\ *n.* **1** A person or thing that divides. **2** [usually in the plural] An instrument for dividing lines; a pair of compasses.

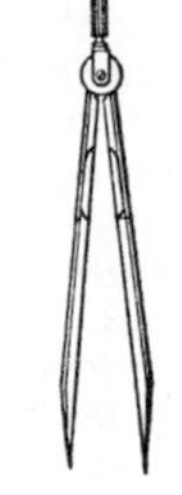
divider, 2

div·i·na·tion \ˌdiv-n-'āsh-n\ *n.* **1** The act or the practice of foreseeing the future or of discovering hidden knowledge by mystical or magical means, as by the study of omens or the use of supposedly magical implements. **2** A prophecy or prediction seemingly impossible without supernatural knowledge; any acute prediction of the future.

di·vine \də-'vīn\ *adj.* **1** Of or relating to God or a god; as, the *divine* will. **2** God-given; as, the *divine* right of kings. **3** In praise of God; religious; holy; as, *divine* service. **4** Godlike; heavenly; excellent in the highest degree; as, *divine* music. — *n.* A priest; a clergyman. — *v.;* **di·vined; di·vin·ing.** **1** To perceive through intuition or sympathy; to feel; to detect; to guess; as, to *divine* that a person is unhappy. **2** To foretell; to prophesy; as, to try to *divine* the future. **3** To foretell by divination. — **di·vine·ly,** *adv.*

di·vin·er \də-'vīn-r\ *n.* One that divines; especially, a person who practices divination; a prophet.

div·ing bell \'dī-ving\. A hollow inverted vessel, sometimes bell-shaped, in which men may work under water, air for breathing being supplied from a supply of compressed air in the vessel or through a tube leading to the surface.

di·vin·i·ty \də-'vin-ət-ē\ *n.; pl.* **di·vin·i·ties.** **1** The condition or quality of being divine. **2** A deity; a god. **3** A celestial being inferior to God but superior to man. **4** The study of religion; theology. — **the Divinity.** God.

di·vis·i·ble \də-'viz-əb-l\ *adj.* Capable of being

divided or separated. — **di·vis·i·bil·i·ty** \-ˌviz-ə-ˈbil-ət-ē\ *n.*

di·vi·sion \də-ˈvizh-n\ *n.* **1** The act or process of dividing or the state of being divided; separation; distribution. **2** Anything that divides or keeps apart; a partition; a dividing line. **3** A part or portion; a section; as, a *division* of a government. **4** A large section of an army, usually commanded by a major general. **5** The process of finding out how many times one number or quantity is contained in another. **6** Difference in opinion or feeling; as, a sharp *division* between the president and his advisers.

$$6\overline{)876}\ \text{quotient } 146 \qquad \frac{9.89}{4.3}=2.3 \qquad 28\div10=2.8$$

division, 5

di·vi·sion·al \də-ˈvizh-n(-)əl\ *adj.* **1** Of or relating to a division, or section, as of an army; as, *divisional* artillery; *divisional* orders. **2** Making a division, or separation; dividing.

division mark or **division sign.** A sign [÷] placed between numerical expressions to indicate that the preceding quantity is to be divided by the following quantity, as in 12 ÷ 3.

di·vi·sor \də-ˈvīz-r\ *n.* The number by which another number, the dividend, is divided.

di·vorce \də-ˈvōrs, -ˈvȯrs\ *n.* **1** A complete legal breaking up of a marriage. **2** Complete separation; as, to believe in the *divorce* of religion and politics. — *v.;* **di·vorced; di·vorc·ing. 1** To break up a marriage or separate the partners to a marriage by granting or obtaining a divorce. **2** To separate; as, two questions completely *divorced* from each other. — **di·vorce·ment,** *n.*

di·vulge \də-ˈvəlj, dī-\ *v.;* **di·vulged; di·vulg·ing.** To make public; to disclose; to reveal; as, to *divulge* a secret. Plans had been completed, but not yet *divulged,* for mass evacuation of cities.

diz·zi·ness \ˈdiz-ē-nəs\ *n.* The state of being dizzy; especially, a whirling sensation; vertigo.

diz·zy \ˈdiz-ē\ *adj.;* **diz·zi·er; diz·zi·est.** [From Old English *dysig* meaning "foolish", "ignorant".] **1** Having a sensation of whirling; giddy. **2** Confused or unsteady in mind. **3** Causing a feeling of being dizzy or giddy; as, a *dizzy* height. — *v.;* **diz·zied** \ˈdiz-ēd\; **diz·zy·ing.** To make dizzy; to cause dizziness. — **diz·zi·ly** \-l-ē\ *adv.*

DNA \ˌdē-ˌen-ˈā\. An organic substance in cells important in heredity and synthesis.

do \(ˈ)dü, də\ *v.;* **did** \(ˈ)did, dəd\; **done** \ˈdən\; **do·ing** \ˈdü-ing\. **1** To bring about; to make; to render; to pay; as, to *do* the man justice. **2** To perform; to transact; as, to *do* business; to *do* one's duty. **3** To bring to an end; to finish; as, to have *done* all one's homework. **4** To put forth; to exert; as, to *do* one's best. **5** To work at; as, to *do* odd jobs for a living; to wonder what one's new neighbor *does.* **6** To treat or deal with; to prepare or arrange; as, to *do* a room; to *do* one's hair. **7** To cover; as, to *do* 400 miles in a day. **8** To serve; to suit. That will *do.* **9** To fare; to be. How do you *do?* — **do away with. 1** To get rid of. **2** To kill; to destroy. — **do for.** To put an end to; to ruin; to kill. — **do up.** To wrap up, as in a bundle or parcel. ☞ *Do* is often used to add emphasis, as in "*Do* help me". It is often used in place of some other verb, to save repetition, as in "This man thinks as we *do*", and also in negative statements, inverted constructions, and interrogative sentences, as in "I *do* not care", "Little *do* you care", and "*Do* you see?"

do \ˈdō\ *n.* A syllable used in music to name the first note of the scale.

do. Abbreviation for *ditto.*

do·a·ble \ˈdü-əb-l\ *adj.* Capable of being done.

dob·bin \ˈdäb-n\ *n.* [From *Dobbin,* a favorite name for horses, probably a nickname for *Robert.*] A farm horse; a gentle horse for family use.

doc·ile \ˈdäs-l\ *adj.* Easily taught, led, or managed; as, a *docile* child. — **doc·ile·ly** \ˈdäs-l-(l)ē\ *adv.* — **do·cil·i·ty** \dä-ˈsil-ət-ē, dō-\ *n.*

dock \ˈdäk\ *n.* Any of several herbs of the buckwheat family, as the broad-leaved **yellow dock** with bitter rootstock, and the **curled dock** with wavy-margined leaves.

dock \ˈdäk\ *n.* The solid part of an animal's tail. — *v.* **1** To cut off the end of; to cut short. **2** To cut off a part from; to deduct from; as, to *dock* a man's wages.

dock \ˈdäk\ *n.* **1** An artificial basin to receive vessels, with gates to keep the water in or out. **2** A slip or waterway, usually between two piers, to receive ships. **3** A wharf. — *v.* To haul or guide into a dock; to come or go into dock.

dock \ˈdäk\ *n.* The place in court where a prisoner stands or sits.

dock·et \ˈdäk-ət\ *n.* **1** The record containing the list of cases to be tried in a court of law. **2** A list of business matters to be acted on in an assembly. **3** A label attached to goods and containing directions, as for handling. — *v.* **1** To inscribe or endorse a letter or bill with a docket. **2** To mark with a ticket. **3** In law, to enter a case in a docket book or list.

dock·yard \ˈdäk-ˌyärd, -ˌyȧrd\ *n.* A place where ships are built or repaired, or where naval supplies or shipbuilding materials are stored.

doc·tor \ˈdäkt-r\ *n.* [From Medieval French *doctour,* there borrowed from Latin *doctor* meaning "teacher".] **1** An advanced academic title or degree from a university or college. **2** A person holding this degree; as, a *doctor* of philosophy. **3** A person licensed to practice medicine; a physician; a surgeon. — *v.;* **doc·tored; doc·tor·ing** \-r(-)ing\. **1** To treat as a physician does; to apply remedies to; as, to *doctor* a cold. **2** To tamper with and arrange to suit one's own purposes; as, to *doctor* up an old speech for a new occasion. **3** To practice medicine; as, a man who has been *doctoring* for 30 years.

doc·tor·ate \ˈdäkt-r(-)ət\ *n.* The degree, title, or rank of doctor.

doc·trine \ˈdäk-trən\ *n.* **1** Something that is taught; the principle or principles taught in any branch of knowledge. **2** A teaching or the teachings of a church; a dogma. — **doc·tri·nal** \'däk-trən-l\ *adj.*

doc·u·ment \'däk-yə-mənt\ *n.* A written or printed paper furnishing information or used as proof of something else. — \-ˌment\ *v.* To furnish evidence of something by means of a document or documents. — **doc·u·men·tal** \ˌdäk-yə-'ment-l\ *adj.*

doc·u·men·ta·ry \ˌdäk-yə-'ment-r-ē, -'men-trē\ *adj.* **1** Consisting of documents; of the nature of documents; contained or certified in writing; as, *documentary* proof. **2** Giving a factual presentation in artistic form; as, a *documentary* film.

doc·u·men·ta·tion \ˌdäk-yə-mən-'tāsh-n, -ˌmen-\ *n.* **1** The providing or the using of documents in proof of something. **2** Evidence in the form of a document or documents.

dod·der \'däd-r\ *v.;* **dod·dered**; **dod·der·ing** \-r(-)ing\. To shake; to tremble; to totter, as with age.

dod·der·ing \'däd-r(-)ing\ *adj.* Foolish; senile; as, a *doddering* old man.

dodge \'däj\ *v.;* **dodged**; **dodg·ing**. **1** To move suddenly aside; to avoid by moving quickly aside; as, to *dodge* a batted ball. **2** To avoid, as a duty, by trickery. — *n.* **1** A sudden movement to one side. **2** A trick by which to evade, deceive, or cheat; as, to avoid paying a bill by a clever *dodge.*

dodg·er \'däj-r\ *n.* **1** A person who dodges or uses tricky ways. **2** A small handbill. **3** A cake made of Indian meal.

do·do \'dōd-ˌō\ *n.; pl.* **do·does** or **do·dos**. [From Portuguese *doudo* meaning literally "fool".] A large, heavy bird, unable to fly, that formerly lived on some of the islands of the Indian Ocean.

doe \'dō\ *n.* The female of any kind of deer, antelope, hare, or other animal the male of which is called a *buck.*

do·er \'dü-ər\ *n.* A person who does or acts; an agent.

does \(')dəz\. A form of the verb *do* showing present time, and used with *he, she,* or *it* or with words for which these stand.

doe·skin \'dō-ˌskin\ *n.* **1** The skin of the doe, or a leather made from it. **2** A soft, firm woolen cloth.

doesn't \'dəz-nt\. A contraction of *does not.*

doff \'däf, 'dȯf\ *v.* [A contraction of *do off.*] To take off, as one's clothes; to remove or lift; as, to *doff* one's hat.

dog \'dȯg\ *n.* **1** A flesh-eating domestic animal related to the wolves and foxes. **2** A male dog, as distinguished from the female. **3** A showy style or a pretended dignity; as, to put on the *dog.* **4** A device for holding, gripping, or fastening something, as one made of a metal bar with a hook at the end. — *v.;* **dogged**; **dog·ging**. To hunt or track like a dog; to worry as if by dogs; as, to be *dogged* by bad luck.

dogs, 4

dog·cart \'dȯg-ˌkärt, -ˌkȧrt\ *n.* **1** A cart drawn by dogs. **2** A light one-horse carriage with two seats, usually back to back.

dog days. The hot, close part of summer, from July to September.

doge \'dōj\ *n.* The chief magistrate in the former republics of Venice and Genoa.

dog-ear \'dȯg-ˌir\ *n.* A turned down corner of a leaf in a book. — **dog-eared** \-ˌird\ *adj.*

dog·fight \'dȯg-ˌfīt\ *n.* A fight at close quarters between aircraft.

dog·fish \'dȯg-ˌfish\ *n.; pl.* **dog·fish** or **dog·fish·es**. Any of various small sharks that hunt in packs.

dog·ged \'dȯg-əd\ *adj.* Obstinate and determined; as, *dogged* persistence. — **dog·ged·ly**, *adv.*

dog·ger·el \'dȯg-r(-)əl, 'däg-\ *adj.* Loosely styled and irregular in measure; as, *doggerel* rhymes. — *n.* Doggerel rhymes or verse.

dog·house \'dȯg-ˌhau̇s\ *n.; pl.* **dog·hous·es** \-ˌhau̇-zəz\. **1** A shelter for a dog; a kennel. **2** A state of being temporarily in disfavor; as, to be in the *doghouse* for coming home late.

do·gie \'dō-gē\ *n.* A cowboy's name for a motherless calf in a range herd.

dog·ma \'dȯg-mə, 'däg-\ *n.* **1** An established opinion or principle held as true. **2** A doctrine laid down by a church.

dog·mat·ic \dȯg-'mat-ik, däg-\ or **dog·mat·i·cal** \-ik-l\ *adj.* **1** Having to do with dogma. **2** Positive in manner or utterance. Very *dogmatic* people are likely to be annoying to others. **3** Stated directly and positively; as, a *dogmatic* declaration. — **dog·mat·i·cal·ly** \-ik-l(-)ē\ *adv.*

dog·ma·tism \'dȯg-mə-ˌtiz-m, 'däg-\ *n.* **1** Positiveness in stating matters of opinion. **2** Such positiveness when not justified or when accompanied by arrogance.

dog·ma·tize \'dȯg-mə-ˌtīz, 'däg-\ *v.;* **dog·ma·tized**; **dog·ma·tiz·ing**. To speak or write dogmatically.

Dog Star. The star Sirius; sometimes, the star Procyon.

dog·trot \'dȯg-ˌträt\ *n.* A gentle trot.

dog watch. A watch of two hours on shipboard, from 4 to 6 P.M. or from 6 to 8 P.M.

dog·wood \'dȯg-ˌwu̇d\ *n.* Any of a family of shrubs and trees having small flowers often surrounded by four broad petallike leaves, berrylike stone fruits, and in some varieties branches and twigs that are bright red-purple in color.

doi·ly \'dȯi-lē\ *n.; pl.* **doi·lies**. A small napkin or ornamental piece, as of linen or lace, used on a table.

doing. Pres. part. of *do.*

do·ings \'dü-ingz\ *n. pl.* **1** Deeds; actions. **2** A social gathering; entertainment; as, to attend the *doings* in the town hall.

doily

dol·drums \'däl-drəmz, 'dōl-\ *n. pl.* **1** Low spirits; dullness; depression. **2** A part of the ocean near the equator, noted for its calms.

dole \'dōl\ *n.* **1** A giving out, especially of gifts of charity. **2** That which is given out as charity; especially, alms. **3** Any government grant to the unemployed. — *v.;* **doled**; **dol·ing**. **1** To deal out in small portions. The leader *doled* out the dwindling supply of food to the members of the expedition. **2** To distribute in the form of a dole; as, to *dole* out charity.

dole·ful \'dōlf-l\ *adj.* Full of grief; sad. — **dole·ful·ly** \'dōlf-l-ē\ *adv.*

doll \'däl, 'dȯl\ *n.* **1** A small figure of a baby or other person, used as a plaything. **2** A pretty but empty-headed woman.

dol·lar \'däl-r\ *n.* [From Dutch *daler*, there borrowed from German *taler*, a short form of *Joachimstaler* meaning "a coin made in Sankt Joachimstal in Bohemia".] **1** The unit of money of the United States, equal in value to 100 cents. **2** A United States silver coin, or a piece of paper money, representing this unit and having the same legal value. **3** A corresponding unit, coin, or piece of paper money in certain other countries, as Canada. **4** Any of various coins regarded as in some way equivalent to the United States dollar, as the Mexican peso. — **dollar mark** or **dollar sign**. A symbol [$] placed before a number to mean dollar or dollars, as in $300.

dolly \'däl-ē\ *n.; pl.* **doll·ies**. **1** A child's name for a doll. **2** Any of various mechanical devices, as a small wheeled truck for moving heavy beams or a wheeled platform on which a moving picture camera is mounted for movement about a set.

dol·man \'dōl-mən, 'dȯl-, 'däl-\ *n.* A woman's cloak with a capelike piece instead of sleeves.

dol·o·mite \'däl-ə-ˌmīt, 'dō-lə-\ *n.* A mineral that includes much of the common white marble.

do·lor \'dōl-r, 'däl-\ *n.* Sorrow; grief; anguish.

dol·or·ous \'däl-r-əs, 'dōl-\ *adj.* **1** Causing anguish; painful; grievous; as, a knight struck down with a *dolorous* wound; a *dolorous* sight. **2** Sorrowful; sad; mournful; as, a weak, *dolorous* smile. — **dol·or·ous·ly**, *adv.*

dol·phin \'dälf-n, 'dȯlf-\ *n.* **1** Any of various long-nosed sea mammals like a small [illegible]hale, some of which, including the common [illegible]rican **bot·tle-nosed dolphin** \-ˌnōzd\, ar[illegible]d porpoises. **2** Either of two spiny-finned [illegible]es noted for their brilliant coloring w[illegible] out of the water and dying.

dolt \'dōlt\ *n.* A stupid [illegible]ckhead; a dunce.

-dom \d(ə)m\. A suffix [illegible] **1** The office, realm, or territory [illegible] or *dukedom*. **2** The state of bei[illegible] *wisdom*. **3** Those who have a[illegible]n office, occupation, or charac[illegible].

do·main \dō-'mān\ [illegible]der rule or control, as of a ki[illegible]y other powerful authority.[illegible]ion or thought; scope; rang[illegible]*ain* of science; a problem [illegible]f the law.

dome \'dōm\ *n.* **1** A large roof shaped like a hemisphere; a cupola; as, the *dome* of a capitol. **2** Something shaped like a dome. — *v.;* **domed**; **dom·ing**. **1** To cover with or as if with a dome; as, a *domed* building. **2** To shape or to swell out like a dome; as, a massive *domed* forehead.

dome, 1

do·mes·tic \də-'mes-tik\ *adj.* **1** Of or relating to a household, family, or home; as, *domestic* life; *domestic* duties. **2** Of, relating to, or produced in one's own country; native; not foreign; as, *domestic* trade; *domestic* wines. **3** Of animals, living with or in association with people; not wild; tame. **4** Often remaining at home; devoted to home; as, a man of very *domestic* habits. — *n.* A house servant. — **do·mes·ti·cal·ly** \-tik-l(-)ē\ *adv.*

do·mes·ti·cate \də-'mes-tə-ˌkāt\ *v.;* **do·mes·ti·cat·ed**; **do·mes·ti·cat·ing**. To make or become domestic; to reclaim from a wild state; to tame for use in or around the home; to bring under cultivation; as, a recently *domesticated* variety of the sweet potato. Dogs, cats, and horses are *domesticated* animals. — **do·mes·ti·ca·tion** \də-ˌmes-tə-'kāsh-n\ *n.*

do·mes·tic·i·ty \ˌdō-ˌmes-'tis-ət-ē\ *n.; pl.* **do·mes·tic·i·ties**. **1** The condition of being domestic or domesticated; domestic character; domestic life. **2** [in the plural] Domestic affairs.

domestic science. The study that deals with the care and management of a household, including the arts of cooking and sewing.

dom·i·cile \'däm-ə-ˌsīl, -əs-l; 'dō-mə-ˌsīl\ *n.* A dwelling place; a place of residence; a home. — *v.;* **dom·i·ciled**; **dom·i·cil·ing**. To establish or settle in; to have one's place of residence in; as, Europeans *domiciled* in India for many generations.

dom·i·nance \'däm-ə-nən(t)s\ *n.* The state or fact of being dominant; authority; predominance.

dom·i·nant \'däm-ə-nənt\ *adj.* **1** Having or exercising ruling or controlling influence or power; as, the rise of a new *dominant* figure in a political party. **2** Predominant; most outstanding; as, the *dominant* features of a landscape. **3** In biology, reappearing in a larger number of offspring than a contrasting characteristic. **4** In music, based upon, related to, or in the key of the dominant. — *n.* **1** A dominant characteristic. **2** A plant or animal with dominant characteristics. **3** The fifth note of a musical scale.

dom·i·nate \'däm-ə-ˌnāt\ *v.;* **dom·i·nat·ed**; **dom·i·nat·ing**. **1** To rule; to control; as, to refuse to be *dominated* by one's friends. In primitive societies the strong *dominate* over the weak. **2** To have a commanding position or controlling power over. The rock of Gibraltar *dominates* the straits below. **3** To rise high above in a position suggesting power to dominate. The mountain range was *dominated* by a single snow-capped peak.

dom·i·na·tion \ˌdäm-ə-'nāsh-n\ *n.* **1** The act of dominating; especially, the exercise of authority or power in ruling others; control; rule. **2** Insolent or arbitrary rule.

dom·i·neer \ˌdäm-ə-'nir\ *v.* To rule in an arrogant manner; to be overbearing.

dom·i·neer·ing \ˌdäm-ə-'nir-ing\ *adj.* Inclined to domineer.

doming. Pres. part. of *dome.*

Do·min·i·can \də-'min-ik-n\ *adj.* **1** Of or relating to St. Dominic or the religious communities named after him. **2** Of or relating to the Dominican Republic. **—** *n.* **1** A friar or a nun belonging to one of the religious orders founded by St. Dominic. **2** A native or inhabitant of the Dominican Republic.

do·mi·nie *n.* **1** \'däm-ə-nē\ A schoolmaster. **2** \'dō-mə-\ A clergyman; a minister.

do·min·ion \də-'min-yən\ *n.* **1** Highest authority; the power of governing and controlling; rule. **2** A territory governed; as, the *dominions* of a king. **3** [usually with a capital] One of certain self-governing overseas territories included in the British Commonwealth of Nations; as, the *Dominion* of Canada.

dom·i·no \'däm-ə-ˌnō\ *n.; pl.* **dom·i·noes** or **dom·i·nos. 1** A masquerade costume consisting of a robe with a hood, and a half mask. **2** [in the plural] A game played with flat, oblong, dotted pieces, or men. **3** One of the pieces used in playing dominoes.

dominoes, 3

don \'dän\ *n.* **1** A Spanish nobleman or gentleman — used also as a title of address. **2** A head of a college or a tutor at Oxford or Cambridge University.

don \'dän\ *v.;* **donned; don·ning.** To put on; to dress in; as, to *don* an apron for washing dishes.

do·nate \'dō-ˌnāt, dō-'nāt\ *v.;* **do·nat·ed; do·nat·ing.** To make a gift of; to bestow; to present or contribute; as, to *donate* money to charity; to *donate* blood to a blood bank.

do·na·tion \dō-'nāsh-n\ *n.* **1** The act of giving. **2** A grant; a gift; a contribution. — For synonyms see *present.*

done. Past part. of *do.*

don·jon \'dänj-n, 'dənj-n\ *n.* The inner tower, large and massive in construction, of an ancient castle.

donjon

don·key \'däng-kē, 'dəngk-, 'dȯngk-\ *n.; pl.* **don·keys. 1** An ass. **2** A stupid or obstinate person.

donkey engine. A small steam engine used in hauling and lifting, as on a ship for loading and unloading carg

don·key·man \'däng-kē-mən, 'dəngk-, *n.; pl.* **don·key·men** \-mən\. A man w a donkey engine.

do·nor \'dōn-r, 'dō-ˌnȯr\ *n.* A person as, a blood *donor;* the *donor* of a sch

don't \'dōnt\. A contraction of *do n*

doo·dle \'düd-l\ *v.;* **doo·dled; doo·d** To draw or scribble aimlessly an

scious effort while occupied with something else, as with answering a telephone. **—** *n.* Something produced by doodling.

doo·dle·bug \'düd-l-ˌbəg\ *n.* The larva of the ant lion.

doom \'düm\ *n.* **1** A judgment or sentence. **2** A determining of what is just; judgment; as, the day of *doom.* **3** Destiny or fate, especially of an unhappy kind; ruin; death; as, a man who met his untimely *doom* in an accident. — For synonyms see *destiny.* **—** *v.* **1** To pronounce judgment or sentence on; to condemn; as, a man *doomed* to death for treason. **2** To decide the fate of.

dooms·day \'dümz-ˌdā\ *n.* **1** The day of the Last Judgment. **2** A day of judgment.

door \'dōr, 'dȯr\ *n.* **1** The movable frame or barrier of boards or other material by which an entrance, as into a house or a room, is closed and opened. **2** A doorway. **3** A passage; a means of entering; as, the *door* to success.

door·keep·er \'dōr-ˌkēp-r, 'dȯr-\ *n.* One who guards a door or entrance, as of a home, hotel, or theater.

door·knob \'dōr-ˌnäb, 'dȯr-\ *n.* A knob that, when turned, releases a door latch.

door·man \'dōr-ˌman, 'dȯr-, -mən\ *n.; pl.* **door·men** \-ˌmen, -mən\. **1** A doorkeeper. **2** An employee, as of a hotel or a department store, who attends upon automobiles and taxicabs for patrons.

door·plate \'dōr-ˌplāt, 'dȯr-\ *n.* A plate on the door of a house or apartment, giving the name of the occupant.

door·step \'dōr-ˌstep, 'dȯr-\ *n.* A step or steps before an outer door.

door·way \'dōr-ˌwā, 'dȯr-\ *n.* The opening or passageway that a door closes; an entrance into a house or room.

door·yard \'dōr-ˌyärd, 'dȯr-, -ˌyärd\ *n.* A yard outside the door of a house.

dope \'dōp\ *n.* **1** Any thick liquid or pasty preparation. **2** An opiate. **3** *Slang.* Information; especially, confidential information; as, to get the *dope* on who cted. **—** *v.;* **doped; dop·ing. 1** To tr *Slang.* To guess the result of; to as by means of special infor horse race; to *dope* out which

j. Belonging to the oldest

Doric capital
Ionic capital
Corinthian capital

ome animals lie *dor*nyms see *latent.*

dor·mer \'dórm-r\ *n.* **1** A window, often called **dormer window**, upright in a sloping roof. **2** The built-out part that contains such a window.

dormer

dor·mi·to·ry \'dór-mə-ˌtōr-ē, -ˌtór-ē\ *n.; pl.* **dor·mi·to·ries.** **1** A sleeping room, especially one containing a number of beds. **2** A building containing a number of sleeping rooms; as, a college *dormitory.*

dor·mouse \'dór-ˌmau̇s\ *n.; pl.* **dor·mice** \-ˌmīs\. A small European squirrellike animal that lives in trees and feeds on nuts and acorns.

dor·sal \'dórs-l\ *adj.* Having to do with the back; near or on the back; as, the *dorsal* fins of a fish.

do·ry \'dōr-ē, 'dór-ē\ *n.; pl.* **do·ries.** [From American Indian *dori, duri* meaning "dugout".] A flat-bottomed boat, with high sides that curve upward and outward, and a sharp bow.

dos·age \'dō-sij\ *n.* **1** The giving of medicine in doses. **2** The amount of a medicine in a single dose.

dose \'dōs\ *n.* The measured amount of a medicine to be taken at one time. — *v.;* **dosed**; **dos·ing.** To give medicine to; as, to *dose* a puppy for worms.

dost \(')dəst\. An archaic form of *do* used chiefly with *thou.*

dot \'dät\ *n.* **1** A small point, mark, or spot. **2** A precise point in time; as, to arrive right on the *dot.* **3** A click forming part of a letter in telegraphy. **4** A point placed after a musical note or rest to indicate that its length is to be increased by one half. **5** A point placed over a note to indicate staccato. — *v.;* **dot·ted**; **dot·ting.** To mark with or as if with a dot or dots; as, to *dot* one's i's and cross one's t's; a lake *dotted* with boats.

dot·age \'dōt-ij\ *n.* Feebleness or childishness of mind caused by or accompanying old age; senility; as, an old man in his *dotage.*

do·tard \'dōt-rd\ *n.* A foolish or weak-minded person, especially one in his old age.

dote \'dōt\ *v.;* **dot·ed**; **dot·ing.** **1** To be weak-minded, as from old age. **2** To be foolishly fond; as, a mother that *dotes* on her child.

doth \(')dəth\. An archaic form of *does.*

dot·ing \'dōt-ing\ *adj.* Foolishly or excessively fond or loving. — **dot·ing·ly**, *adv.*

dot·tle \'dät-l\ *n.* Half-burned tobacco forming a small mass in the bottom of a pipe.

dou·ble \'dəb-l\ *adj.* **1** Twofold; multiplied by two; being twice as great, as large, as much, as many, as strong, or as valuable; as, a *double* helping of ice cream; to receive *double* pay for working on a holiday. **2** Being in pairs; coupled; as, *double* doors; a gun with a *double* barrel. **3** Combining two things or qualities, usually unlike; as, a word of *double* meaning. **4** Having the petals increased beyond the usual number, usually by cultivation; as, a *double* carnation. — *n.* **1** Twice as much, as in number, amount, or value. Twelve is the *double* of six. **2** A person or thing that closely resembles another; a duplicate. This boy is his brother's *double.* **3** A fold, as in a sheet of paper. **4** A substitute or understudy, as for an actor. **5** [in the plural] In some games, as tennis, a game between two pairs of players. — *v.;* **dou·bled**; **dou·bling** \-l(-)ing\. **1** To make twice as great; to multiply by two; as, to *double* a number. **2** To duplicate; to be the double of; to play as a double for. **3** To make of two thicknesses by bending together; to fold; to clench; as, to *double* a blanket; to *double* one's fist. **4** To turn sharply and go back over the same ground; as, to *double* on one's tracks. **5** To pass or sail around; as, to *double* the cape. — *adv.* Doubly; in a pair; two together; as, to ride *double* on a bicycle.

double bass \'bās\. Contrabass.

double cross. A betraying or cheating of an associate. — **dou·ble-cross** \'dəb-l-'krós\ *v.* — **dou·ble-cross·er** \-r\ *n.*

dou·ble-deal·ing \'dəb-l-'dē-ling\ *n.* Insincere or deceitful conduct; duplicity. — **dou·ble-deal·er** \-'dēl-r\ *n.*

dou·ble-deck·er \'dəb-l-'dek-r\ *n.* **1** Something having two decks, as a ship, bus, or bed. **2** A sandwich having two layers or tiers.

dou·ble-head·er \'dəb-l-'hed-r\ *n.* **1** A train with two engines at the front. **2** Two games, as of baseball, usually one right after the other, between the same teams on the same day.

dou·ble-joint·ed \'dəb-l-'jöint-əd\ *adj.* Having joints that permit parts of the body, as the back, arms, or legs, to be bent freely to unusual angles.

dou·ble-quick \'dəb-l-'kwik\ *adj.* In marching, performed in the fastest time or step next to a run. — *n.* Double-quick time or a double-quick step or march. — *v.* To march in double-quick time.

double star. Two stars very near to each other and generally seen as separate only by means of a telescope.

dou·blet \'dəb-lət\ *n.* **1** A close-fitting jacket worn by men of western Europe, chiefly in the 16th century. **2** One of a pair. **3** One of two words or more in a language derived by different courses from the same original, as *dish* and *disk*, or *yard* and *garden.*

doublet, 1

double talk. Talk or writing that appears to be sensible but is actually a mixture of sense and nonsense intended to mislead or deceive.

double time. The quickest step in marching next to a run, in the United States Army 180 steps of 36 inches each to the minute; double-quick.

doubling. Pres. part. of *double.*

dou·bloon \ˌdəb-'lün\ *n.* A Spanish gold coin originally equal to 16 silver dollars but later much reduced in value, now no longer issued.

dou·bly \'dəb-lē\ *adv.* In twice the amount; to twice the degree; as, to be *doubly* repaid for one's efforts; *doubly* welcome.

doubt \'daůt\ *v.* **1** To be undecided in opinion or belief; to be inclined not to believe; to distrust. **2** To be fearful of; to suspect; as, to *doubt* the future. — *n.* **1** Hesitation of mind; uncertainty; as, to be in *doubt* about what to do. **2** The condition of being unsettled, or an unsettled point or question; as, to have several *doubts* in one's mind as to the best plan to follow.

— The words *distrust* and *suspicion* are synonyms of *doubt: doubt* may imply uncertainty about the truth or reality of something, often leaving one unable to make a decision; *distrust* usually implies a lack of confidence in a person; *suspicion* usually suggests vague doubt, especially of someone's goodness or honesty, and often with only slight evidence to support one's doubt.

doubt·ful \'daůt-fəl\ *adj.* **1** Not clear or certain as to fact; as, a *doubtful* claim. **2** Of questionable character; as, *doubtful* intentions. **3** Not settled in opinion; undecided; as, to be *doubtful* about what to do. **4** Not certain in outcome; as, a *doubtful* battle. — **doubt·ful·ly** \-fə-lē\ *adv.*

doubt·less \'daůt-ləs\ *adj.* Free from doubt. — *adv.* **1** Undoubtedly; certainly. **2** Presumably; probably.

dough \'dō\ *n.* **1** A soft mass of moistened flour or meal, thick enough to knead or roll. **2** Any similar soft, pasty mass.

dough·boy \'dō-ˌbȯi\ *n.* An infantryman in the United States Army.

dough·nut \'dō-(ˌ)nət\ *n.* A small cake made usually in the form of a ring or twist and fried in deep fat.

dough·ty \'daůt-ē\ *adj.;* **dough·ti·er; dough·ti·est.** Strong and valiant; bold; as, a *doughty* knight; *doughty* deeds. — **dough·ti·ly** \'daůt-l-ē\ *adv.*

doughy \'dō-ē\ *adj.;* **dough·i·er; dough·i·est.** Like dough; pasty.

dour *in Scotland,* 'dür; *in the U.S.*, 'daůr *or* 'důr\ *adj.* **1** *Chiefly Scottish.* Stern; severe. **2** Sour or sullen in looks.

douse \'daůs, 'daůz\ *v.;* **doused; dous·ing. 1** To extinguish; to put out; as, to *douse* a light. **2** To plunge into liquid. **3** To throw water over. **4** To lower hastily, as a sail.

dove \'dəv\ *n.* Any of various pigeons, especially of a small-sized species.

dove \'dōv\. A past tense of *dive.*

dove·cot \'dəv-ˌkät\ or **dove·cote** \-ˌkōt, -ˌkät\ *n.* A small house or box for domestic pigeons, raised off the ground and usually divided into compartments.

dove·tail \'dəv-ˌtāl\ *n.* Something shaped like a dove's tail; especially, a tongue or a groove cut in the end of a board. — *v.* **1** To fit or fasten together by means of dovetails; as, to *dovetail* two boards. **2** To fit together closely or neatly; as, to *dovetail* the several stages of a complex job; to make one's vacation plans *dovetail* with those of a friend.

dow·a·ger \'daů-əj-r\ *n.* **1** A widow who has the continued use of certain property, especially a title, coming from her husband. **2** A dignified elderly woman.

dowdy \'daůd-ē\ *adj.;* **dowd·i·er; dowd·i·est.** Not neatly or becomingly dressed; shabby; untidy. — *n.; pl.* **dowd·ies.** An untidily or badly dressed woman.

dow·el \'daů-əl, 'daůl\ *n.* A pin or peg projecting from one of two parts or surfaces, as of wood, to be fastened together, and fitting into a hole prepared in the other part. — *v.;* **dow·eled** or **dow·elled; dow·el·ing** or **dow·el·ling.** To fasten by dowels; to furnish with dowels.

dow·er \'daůr\ *n.* **1** That part of or interest in the real estate of her dead husband which the law gives for life to a widow. **2** A dowry. **3** A quality with which a person is endowed by nature; as, the priceless *dower* of an alert mind. — *v.* To provide with a dower; to endow.

down \'daůn\ *n.* **1** A hill, especially a little hill, of sand piled up by the wind on or near the shore; a dune. **2** [usually in the plural] A tract or stretch of open, rolling, usually grassy upland.

down \'daůn\ *n.* **1** Soft, fluffy feathers, as on young birds or under the ordinary feathers of grown birds. **2** Any soft, hairy growth.

down \'daůn\ *adv.* **1** Toward a lower position or level, as the ground or floor; in a direction opposite to up; as, to fall *down;* to set a burden *down.* **2** Away from upright; as, to bend *down.* **3** Actively; seriously; as, to settle *down* to work. **4** From a past time; as, handed *down* to the present. **5** To a lesser amount or bulk; as, to boil *down* a syrup. **6** In cash; as, paid *down.* — *adj.* **1** Occupying or returned to a low or lower position. The shades are *down.* **2** Moving or extending down; as, a *down* pipe. **3** Downcast; depressed. **4** Made at the time of purchase; as, a *down* payment. **5** In games, behind; as, one game *down.* — *prep.* **1** In a descending direction along; as, to go *down* a hill. **2** Along, through, or over, in a direction considered the opposite of up. — *n.* Misfortune; defeat; as, to have one's ups and *downs.* — *v.* To bring or pass down; to cause to go down; as, to *down* a dose of medicine.

down·beat \'daůn-ˌbēt\ *n.* The downward stroke of a conductor's baton, marking the principally accented note of a measure of music.

down·cast \'daůn-ˌkast, -'kast\ *adj.* **1** Discouraged; dejected; as, a *downcast* manner. **2** Directed down; as, a *downcast* glance.

down·fall \'daůn-ˌfȯl\ *n.* **1** A fall, especially a sudden or heavy fall, as of rain. **2** A sudden coming down or descent, as from a high position or rank or from a state of prosperity; ruin; as, the *downfall* of a government; a man whose *downfall* surprised no one. — **down·fall·en** \-ˌfȯl-ən\ *adj.*

down·grade \'daůn-ˌgrād\ *n.* **1** A downward grade or slope. **2** A decline toward a worse condition; as, a neighborhood that is on the *downgrade.* — *v.;* **down·grad·ed; down·grad·ing.** To lower in grade, rank, position, or status. — \-'grād\ *adv.* Downhill.

down·heart·ed \'daůn-'härt-əd, -'hårt-\ *adj.* Dejected; discouraged; depressed.

down·hill \'daůn-'hil\ *adv.* Toward the bottom of a hill; downward. — \-ˌhil\ *adj.* Sloping downward.

down·pour \'daůn-ˌpōr, -ˌpór\ *n.* A heavy rain.

down·right \'daůn-ˌrīt\ *adv.* Thoroughly; as, *downright* mean. — *adj.* **1** Plain; blunt; outspoken; as, a very *downright* man. **2** Absolute; complete; as, a *downright* lie; *downright* nonsense.

down·stairs \'daůn-'starz, -'sterz\ *adv.* Down the stairs; on or to a lower floor; as, to go *downstairs;* the family that lives *downstairs.* — *adj.* On a lower floor; especially, on the first floor; as, a *downstairs* room. — *n.* The lower floor or floors of a house; as, to give the *downstairs* a cleaning.

down·stream \'daůn-'strēm\ *adv.* Down the stream; with the current; as, to float *downstream* and then row up. — *adj.* In the direction of the flow of a stream; as, the *downstream* face of a dam.

down·town \'daůn-'taůn\ *adv.* To, toward, or in the business center of a town. — *adj.* Located downtown; having to do with the business center of a city; as, *downtown* merchants; *downtown* traffic.

down·trod·den \'daůn-'träd-n\ *adj.* Trampled down; crushed by superior power; oppressed; as, the revolt of a *downtrodden* people.

down·ward \'daůn-wərd\ or **down·wards** \-wərdz\ *adv.* **1** From a higher place or condition to a lower; as, a road running *downward* in a dangerous grade. For some days the sick child's condition seemed to go steadily *downward.* **2** From an earlier time; as, from the time of the Romans *downward* to today.

down·ward \'daůn-wərd\ *adj.* Moving or extending downward; as, a *downward* slope; to find one's business taking a *downward* turn.

downy \'daů-nē\ *adj.;* **down·i·er**; **down·i·est.** **1** Made of down; like down; soft; fluffy. **2** Covered with down.

dow·ry \'daůr-ē\ *n.; pl.* **dow·ries.** The property that a woman brings to her husband in marriage.

dox·ol·o·gy \däk-'säl-ə-jē\ *n.; pl.* **dox·ol·o·gies.** One of certain hymns or chants of praise to God used in religious services, as the one beginning "Praise God from whom all blessings flow!"

doz. Abbreviation for *dozen.*

doze \'dōz\ *v.;* **dozed**; **doz·ing.** To sleep lightly. — *n.* A light sleep.

doz·en \'dəz-n\ *n.; pl.* **doz·en** or **doz·ens.** A group, set, or collection of twelve.

doz·enth \'dəz-n(t)th\ *adj.* Twelfth.

DP or **D.P.** \'dē-'pē\ *n.; pl.* **DPs**, **DP's**, or **D.P.'s** \-'pēz\. A displaced person.

dpt. Abbreviation for *department.*

Dr. Abbreviation for: **1** *Doctor.* **2** *debtor.* **3** *Drive.*

drab \'drab\ *n.* A dull grayish-brown color. — *adj.;* **drab·ber**; **drab·best.** **1** Of the color drab. **2** Dull; monotonous; as, a *drab* life with nothing but work.

draft or **draught** \'draft\ *n.* **1** The action of drawing or hauling. **2** The thing or amount that is hauled. **3** A representing of something by words or lines; a drawing, map, or plan; as, a final *draft* of a speech. **4** [usually *draught*] The action of drawing a net. **5** The quantity of fish caught in a net. **6** [usually *draught*] A drinking or the liquid drunk; a drink; as, a long *draught* of water. **7** [usually *draught*] A drawing from a keg on order; as, beer on *draught.* **8** A current, especially of air; as, a *draft* from an open window. **9** A device to regulate the air supply, as of a stove or furnace. **10** An order from one person or party to another, directing the payment of money; a check. **11** A heavy demand; a strain; as, a *draft* upon a person's strength. **12** The selecting of persons for compulsory armed service or the body of persons thus selected. **13** [usually *draught*] The depth of water a ship requires to float, especially when loaded. — *v.* **1** To make a draft of; to draw up; to sketch; to outline; as, to *draft* a speech; to *draft* a plan for a house. **2** To draw by selection for a particular purpose, as men for service. — *adj.* **1** Used for or adapted to drawing loads; as, a *draft* horse. **2** [usually *draught*] On draught; drawn, as from a keg; as, *draught* beer.

draft·ee \draf-'tē\ *n.* A person who is drafted, as for service in the armed forces.

draft·ing board \'draf-ting\. A drawing board.

drafts·man or **draughts·man** \'draf(t)s-mən\ *n.; pl.* **drafts·men** or **draughts·men** \-mən\. A person who draws plans and sketches, as of machinery or buildings.

drafty or **draughty** \'draf-tē\ *adj.;* **draft·i·er** or **draught·i·er**; **draft·i·est** or **draught·i·est.** Exposed to a draft or current of air; as, a *drafty* room.

drag \'drag\ *v.;* **dragged**; **drag·ging.** **1** To draw along; to haul slowly or heavily; as, to *drag* a box across a room. **2** To search or fish with a drag; as, to *drag* a pond for a drowned man. **3** To move, pass, or continue slowly; to be tiresomely drawn out; as, to *drag* out one's life in prison. The hot afternoon *dragged* slowly on. **4** To be drawn along on the ground; to trail. Several tin cans *dragged* noisily behind the car of the newly married couple. — *n.* **1** A device for dragging under water to catch something. **2** A sledge for carrying heavy material, as stone. **3** A harrow for breaking up soil. **4** A heavy horse-drawn coach with seats on top. **5** Anything that slows up movement or retards, as a skid under a carriage wheel. **6** Influence that secures special privilege; as, to have *drag* with one's employer.

drag·gle \'drag-l\ *v.;* **drag·gled**; **drag·gling** \-l(-)ing\. **1** To wet and soil by dragging, as over wet ground. **2** To follow slowly; to straggle in the rear.

drag·net \'drag-ˌnet\ *n.* **1** A net to be drawn along the bottom of the water or along the surface of land in order to catch something. **2** A network of planned actions for pursuing and catching; as, a police *dragnet.*

drag·on \'drag-n\ *n.* An imaginary animal, usually pictured as a huge, winged, scaly serpent.

drag·on·fly \'drag-n-ˌflī\ *n.; pl.* **drag·on·flies.** A large four-winged insect with movable head, large eyes, and a long, slender body.

dra·goon \drə-'gün, dra-\ *n.* A heavily armed cavalry soldier. — *v.* To compel submission or obedience by violent measures, as if by the use of dragoons; to force.

dragoon

drain \'drān\ *v.* **1** To draw off or flow off gradually, as water from a tank. **2** To make or become gradually dry or empty; as, to *drain* a swamp; to let the dishes *drain.* **3** To exhaust of wealth, strength, or resources. The long war *drained* the country of its best manpower. **4** To empty its waters; as, a river that *drains* into the ocean. — *n.* **1** A gradual using up or withdrawal; as, a *drain* on one's strength or one's funds. **2** A means of draining, as a trench or a pipe.

drain·age \'drā-nij\ *n.* **1** A draining or a method of draining. **2** A drain or a system of drains. **3** Anything that is drained off; as, *drainage* from a swamp.

drain·pipe \'drān-ˌpīp\ *n.* A pipe that serves as a drain.

drake \'drāk\ *n.* A male duck.

dram \'dram\ *n.* **1** A weight; in apothecaries' weight, one eighth of an ounce; in avoirdupois weight, one sixteenth of an ounce. **2** A small drink, especially of alcoholic liquor.

dra·ma \'dräm-ə, 'dram-ə, 'dråm-ə\ *n.* **1** A play to be acted on a stage. **2** The art of writing plays; plays in general; as, to study American *drama.* **3** A series of events in real life like a play in interest or excitement; as, the *drama* of a college football game.

dra·mat·ic \drə-'mat-ik\ *adj.* **1** Having to do with the drama. **2** Like a drama; expressed with or as if with action; stirring; vivid. — **dra·mat·i·cal·ly** \-ik-l(-)ē\ *adv.*

dra·mat·ics \drə-'mat-iks\ *n. sing. and pl.* Dramatic writings or performances, especially of amateurs.

dram·a·tis per·so·nae \'dram-ət-əs pər-'sō-ˌnē\. [Latin.] The characters or actors in a drama.

dram·a·tist \'dram-ət-əst, 'dräm-, 'dråm-\ *n.* A person who writes plays; a playwright.

dram·a·ti·za·tion \ˌdram-ət-ə-'zāsh-n, ˌdräm-, ˌdråm-\ *n.* **1** The action of dramatizing. **2** A dramatized version of something.

dram·a·tize \'dram-ə-ˌtīz, 'dräm-, 'dråm-\ *v.;* **dram·a·tized; dram·a·tiz·ing. 1** To make into a drama; as, to *dramatize* a novel. **2** To make dramatic; as, a person who *dramatizes* everything that happens to him.

drank. Past tense of *drink.*

drape \'drāp\ *v.;* **draped; drap·ing. 1** To decorate or cover with drapery or as if with drapery; as, to *drape* the speakers' platform with bunting. **2** To arrange or hang in folds; as, to *drape* a gown. — *n.* A hanging; a curtain.

drap·er \'drāp-r\ *n.* A dealer in cloths or dry goods.

dra·pery \'drāp-r(-)ē\ *n.; pl.* **dra·per·ies. 1** A fabric used for decoration, especially when hung loosely and in folds. **2** Hangings, as of a room or bed; especially, decorative curtains hung across or at the sides of a window. **3** The draping or arrangement of textile-fabric hangings or coverings. — **dra·per·ied** \-r(-)ēd\ *adj.*

dras·tic \'dras-tik\ *adj.* Acting rapidly and violently; extreme in effect; as, a *drastic* remedy. — **dras·ti·cal·ly** \-tik-l(-)ē\ *adv.*

draught. Variant of *draft.*

draughtsman. Variant of *draftsman.*

draughty. Variant of *drafty.*

draw \'drȯ\ *v.;* **drew** \'drü\; **drawn** \'drȯn\; **drawing. 1** To pull; to haul; to drag; to carry; to bring; to bring to the surface; as, to *draw* a sled; to *draw* blood. **2** To move; to come or go; as, to *draw* near. **3** To attract; as, to *draw* a crowd. **4** To inhale; as, to *draw* a long breath. **5** To utter as if by drawing in one's breath; as, to *draw* a sigh. **6** To require a certain depth of water in which to float. The ship *draws* 20 feet. **7** To accumulate or gain; as, money that *draws* interest. **8** To cause to come out; to let run; as, to *draw* water for a bath. **9** To bring forth; to bring out; as, words that *drew* no reply. **10** To extract the contents or essence of something, as by sucking, by pulling out the insides, or by steeping; as, to *draw* a chicken; to let a pot of tea *draw.* **11** To leave a contest undecided; to come out even, as two teams. **12** To change the shape of something by pulling or as if by pulling; as, a face *drawn* with sorrow. **13** To sketch or trace; as, to *draw* a map or a picture. **14** To take out; to withdraw; as, to *draw* money from the bank. **15** To write; as, to *draw* a check; to *draw* up a will. **16** To select; as, to *draw* a card from a pack. **17** To attract patrons. The play still *draws.* **18** To take out a weapon; as, to *draw* a sword; to be quick to *draw.* **19** To stretch; to lengthen; as, to *draw* a rope tight. **20** To make a draft or written demand for payment of money deposited or due; as, to *draw* on one's account at the bank. **21** To make a demand; to serve as a drain; as, to *draw* on one's reserve strength. **22** To produce or make use of a draft or current of air; as, a furnace that will not *draw.* — *n.* **1** The action of drawing or the state of being drawn. **2** A tie; as, a game that ended in a *draw.* **3** A lot or chance drawn; as, to win the lucky number at the first *draw.* **4** The movable part of a drawbridge. **5** A gully.

draw·back \'drȯ-ˌbak\ *n.* A disadvantage; a hindrance.

draw·bridge \'drȯ-ˌbrij\ *n.* A bridge made in such a way that all or part of it can be drawn up, down, or aside to permit or hinder passage.

draw·er \'drȯr\ *n.* **1** A person or thing that draws. **2** A sliding, boxlike compartment, as in a table or desk. **3** [in the plural] An undergarment worn on the legs and lower part of the body.

draw·ing \'drȯ-ing\ *n.* **1** The action of a person who draws. **2** A picture or sketch. **3** The art of making such a picture or sketch.

drawing board. A board on which paper to be drawn on is fastened.

drawing room. A room for receiving company.

drawl \'drȯl\ *v.* To speak in a slow, long-drawn-out way. — *n.* A drawling manner of talking.

drawn. Past part. of *draw.*

drawn butter \'drȯn\. Butter melted for use as a sauce.

dray \'drā\ *n.* A strong, low, usually two-wheeled cart for heavy loads.

dray

dray·man \'drā-mən\ *n.; pl.* **dray-men** \-mən\. One who drives a dray.

dread \'dred\ *v.* To fear greatly. — *n.* Great fear, especially of some harm to come. — *adj.* **1** Causing great fear; frightful. **2** Inspiring awe; as, a *dread* sovereign.

dread·ful \'dred-fəl\ *adj.* **1** Inspiring great dread; fearful; as, a *dreadful* storm. **2** Arousing pity or sympathy; distressing; as, a *dreadful* automobile accident. **3** Very disagreeable; very bad; as, a *dreadful* cough. — **dread·ful·ly** \-fə-lē\ *adv.*

dread·nought or **dread·naught** \'dred-ˌnȯt, -ˌnät\ *n.* A very large battleship armed with big guns.

dream \'drēm\ *n.* **1** A series of thoughts, images, or feelings that come to a person during sleep. **2** A state of mind in which a person is lost in fancies or reveries. **3** Any dreamlike vision or experience. — *v.;* **dreamed** \'drēmd\ or **dreamt** \'drem(p)t\; **dream·ing** \'drē-ming\. **1** To have dreams; as, to sleep through the night without *dreaming.* **2** To indulge in reveries or in fanciful, unreal thinking. That girl spends too much time *dreaming.* **3** To think of as something that might happen; to consider as possible or probable; as, to *dream* of becoming a great explorer.

dream·er \'drēm-r\ *n.* **1** A person who dreams. **2** A person who lives in a world of fancy and imagination; especially, one who has wild, impractical ideas and schemes; a visionary.

dream·i·ly \'drēm-l-ē\ *adv.* In a dreamy manner; as, to sit looking *dreamily* out over the water.

dream·land \'drēm-ˌland\ *n.* An unreal, delightful country such as is sometimes pictured in dreams, sleeping or waking.

dreamt. A past tense and a past part. of *dream.*

dreamy \'drē-mē\ *adj.;* **dream·i·er**; **dream·i·est.** **1** Having many dreams; causing dreams; as, a *dreamy* sleep. **2** Given to daydreaming; impractical. **3** Like a dream; soothing; as, *dreamy* music.

drear \'drir\ *adj.* Dreary.

dreary \'drir-ē\ *adj.;* **drear·i·er**; **drear·i·est.** **1** *Archaic.* Sad; doleful. **2** Causing feelings of cheerlessness; dismal; gloomy; as, a *dreary* landscape; a *dreary* day. — **drear·i·ly** \'drir-ə-lē\ *adv.*

dredge \'drej\ *n.* **1** A machine for scooping up or removing earth, as in deepening a river or digging ditches. **2** A heavy iron frame, with a net attached, to be dragged over the sea bottom, as for gathering oysters. — *v.;* **dredged**; **dredg·ing.** To dig or gather with a dredge or as if with a dredge; as, to *dredge* a channel; to try to *dredge* up something from one's memory.

dredge \'drej\ *v.;* **dredged**; **dredg·ing.** To scatter or sprinkle, as flour over meat or meat with flour.

dredg·er \'drej-r\ *n.* One that gathers or digs by dredging; especially, a boat with a dredge on it.

dredg·er \'drej-r\ *n.* One that scatters or sprinkles; especially, a box or can with holes in the top for sprinkling flour or sugar.

dregs \'dregz\ *n. pl.* **1** The part of certain liquids that settles to the bottom in small particles; grounds; sediment; as, the *dregs* of coffee. **2** The worthless part of anything; as, the *dregs* of humanity.

drench \'drench\ *v.* To wet thoroughly; to soak; as, to be caught in a downpour and *drenched.*

dress \'dres\ *v.;* **dressed** or **drest**; **dress·ing.** **1** To scold; to rebuke; as, to *dress* down a lazy boy. **2** To prepare for display; as, to *dress* a store window. **3** To prepare for use; as, to *dress* a chicken. **4** To smooth or finish; as, to *dress* leather. **5** To put on clothes; to clothe; as, to *dress* for a party; to *dress* oneself in a hurry. **6** To treat with remedies and bind with bandages; as, to *dress* a wound. **7** To do up; to arrange; as, to *dress* hair. **8** To make or set straight, as a line of soldiers on parade. — *n.* **1** Clothes; as, evening *dress;* to pay a great deal of attention to one's *dress.* **2** A woman's or girl's outer garment; a frock: a gown. — *adj.* **1** Used for a dress or dresses; as, a piece of *dress* goods. **2** Suitable for wear on formal occasions, especially at night; as, *dress* clothes for men.

dress·er \'dres-r\ *n.* One that dresses; as, to work as *dresser* for a famous actress; a window *dresser.*

dress·er \'dres-r\ *n.* **1** A bench on which meat and other things are dressed. **2** A cupboard for dishes. **3** A piece of bedroom furniture, such as a bureau, with a mirror.

dress·ing \'dres-ing\ *n.* **1** The act of one that dresses. **2** Material used to dress a wound. **3** A sauce added to certain foods, especially salads. **4** Stuffing, as for a turkey. — **dressing down.** A scolding.

dressing gown. A loose robe for wear while partly dressed or while lounging.

dressing room. A room in which to dress, as one adjoining a bedroom or one backstage in a theater.

dressing table. **1** A low table or stand with a mirror, for use by a person while dressing. **2** A table on which something is dressed.

dress·mak·ing \'dres-ˌmāk-ing\ *n.* The art, process, or occupation of making dresses. — **dress-mak·er** \-ˌmāk-r\ *n.*

dress rehearsal. A rehearsal, usually the last rehearsal, of a play in the costumes to be worn and with all the stage properties to be used in the actual performance.

dressy \'dres-ē\ *adj.;* **dress·i·er; dress·i·est.** Showy in dress; stylish; smart.

drest. A past tense and past part. of *dress.*

drew. Past tense of *draw.*

drib·ble \'drib-l\ *v.;* **drib·bled; drib·bling** \-l(-)ing\. **1** To fall or let fall in a series of small drops; to trickle. **2** To slobber. **3** To move along by tapping or kicking; as, to *dribble* a basketball. — *n.* **1** A small trickling stream. **2** A drizzling shower. **3** The action of dribbling a ball. — **drib·bler** \-l(-)ər\ *n.*

drib·let or **drib·blet** \'drib-lət\ *n.* A small piece; a small amount; a falling drop.

dried. Past tense and past part. of *dry.*

drier. Comparative of *dry.*

dri·er or **dry·er** \'drīr\ *n.* **1** A person or thing that dries, as a device for drying by heat or air. **2** A substance put into paints and varnishes to make them dry more quickly.

driest. Superlative of *dry.*

drift \'drift\ *n.* **1** The motion or course of something drifting. The *drift* of the raft was toward shore. **2** General intention; meaning; as, the *drift* of a person's remarks. **3** A mass, as of snow or sand, piled in a heap by the wind. **4** Earth, gravel, or rock deposited by water or ice. — *v.* **1** To float or to be driven along by winds, waves, or ocean currents. **2** To move along with little effort; as, to *drift* through life. **3** To pile up in heaps under the force of the wind. Snow *drifted* near the fence.

drift·wood \'drift-ˌwu̇d\ *n.* Wood that is drifting on water or has been washed ashore.

drill \'dril\ *n.* [From Dutch *drillen* originally meaning "to make round".] **1** A tool for making holes in hard substances. **2** The training of soldiers, as in marching and in handling weapons. **3** Regular, strict training and instruction in any subject; as, *drills* in arithmetic; athletic *drill.* — *v.* **1** To pierce or bore with or as if with a drill; as, to *drill* a hole; to *drill* a tooth. **2** To train and instruct; as, to *drill* students in arithmetic; to *drill* soldiers.

drill, 1

drill \'dril\ *n.* A machine for making holes or furrows and dropping seed into them. — *v.* To sow seeds by use of a drill.

drill \'dril\ or **drill·ing** \'dril-ing\ *n.* [A shortened form of German *drillich,* there borrowed from medieval Latin *trilix* meaning literally "three-threaded".] A heavy linen or cotton fabric with a diagonal weave.

drill·er \'dril-r\ *n.* One that drills.

drill·mas·ter \'dril-ˌmast-r\ *n.* A person who drills, especially one who drills soldiers in marching.

drily. Variant of *dryly.*

drink \'dringk\ *v.;* **drank** \'drangk\; **drunk** \'drəngk\; **drink·ing. 1** To swallow liquid. **2** To absorb a liquid. The plant *drinks* up water. **3** To take in through the senses. The children *drank* in the exciting story. **4** To drink a toast: as, to *drink* to the president. **5** To drink alcoholic liquor, especially to excess. — *n.* **1** Liquid for drinking; a beverage. **2** Intoxicating liquor. — **drink·a·ble,** *adj.*

drink·er \'dringk-r\ *n.* One who drinks; especially, one who drinks intoxicating liquors to excess.

drip \'drip\ *v.;* **dripped** or **dript; drip·ping. 1** To let fall in drops. The man's clothes were *dripping* rain. **2** To let fall drops of moisture or liquid; as, a *dripping* faucet. **3** To fall drop by drop; as, rain *dripping* from the eaves. — *n.* **1** A falling in drops; as, the *drip* of rain from the trees. **2** Anything that drips; as, the *drip* from a leaky faucet.

drip·pings \'drip-ingz\ *n. pl.* Fat and juice that have dripped from roasting meat.

drive \'drīv\ *v.;* **drove** \'drōv\; **driv·en** \'driv-n\; **driv·ing** \'drī-ving\. **1** To urge, push, or force onward. **2** To direct the movement or course of, as a vehicle, or animals drawing a vehicle; to transport in a vehicle under one's own direction; as, to *drive* an automobile; to *drive* into town. **3** To carry along or keep in motion; as, to *drive* machinery by electricity. **4** To carry through strongly; as, to *drive* a bargain. **5** To force or compel; to bring into some condition; as, noise enough to *drive* a person crazy. Rain *drove* us into the house. **6** To force a passage through, as by drilling; as, to *drive* a well. **7** To rush and press with violence. The police *drove* into the mob. — *n.* **1** A driving; especially, a trip in an automobile or a carriage. **2** A road for driving. **3** A driving together of animals, as for capture, killing, or branding. **4** The mass of animals thus collected. **5** An organized effort to carry out some purpose; as, a *drive* to raise funds. **6** In logging, a mass of logs floated down a river. **7** In automobiles, the apparatus by means of which the movement of the car is directed; as, a left-hand *drive.* **8** In machinery, the means for giving motion to a machine or part of a machine; as. a chain *drive.* **9** In games, the act or the manner of driving the ball; the stroke or blow for this purpose; as, a backhand *drive* in tennis.

drive-in \'drī-ˌvin\ *adj.* Arranged and equipped so as to allow patrons to watch a performance or to be served while remaining in their automobiles. — *n.* A drive-in theater, refreshment stand, or bank.

driv·el \'driv-l\ *v.;* **driv·eled** or **driv·elled; driv·el·ing** or **driv·el·ling** \-l(-)ing\. **1** To let saliva drip from one's mouth; to slobber. **2** To be silly in manner of speech; as, a *driveling* idiot. — *n.* **1** Saliva drooling from the mouth. **2** Foolish talk; twaddle. — **driv·el·er** or **driv·el·ler** \-l(-)ər\ *n.*

driven. Past part. of *drive.*

driv·er \'drīv-r\ *n.* A person or a thing that drives; especially, a person that drives animals, or that controls the movements of an automobile.

drive·way \'drīv-ˌwā\ *n.* **1** A short road leading from the street to a house or garage. **2** Any road or way along which vehicles or animals may be driven.

driz·zle \'driz-l\ *v.;* **driz·zled; driz·zling** \-l(-)ing\. To rain in very small drops. — *n.* A fine mistlike rain. — **driz·zly** \-l(-)ē\ *adj.*

droll \'drōl\ *adj.* Odd and amusing; queer and laughable; as, the *droll* expression of a clown. — For synonyms see *comical.*

droll·ery \'drōl-r-ē\ *n.; pl.* **droll·er·ies.** **1** Something droll. **2** Jesting; comical gestures or manners. **3** The quality of being droll; humor.

drom·e·dary \'dräm-ə-ˌder-ē, 'drəm-\ *n.; pl.* **drom·e·dar·ies.** A light, swift camel trained for riding, especially the Arabian or one-humped camel.

drone \'drōn\ *n.* **1** The male of bees, especially of the honeybee, which has no sting and gathers no honey. **2** A lazy person; one who lives on the labor of others. **3** A pilotless airplane controlled by radio, from the ground or from another airplane.

drone \'drōn\ *v.;* **droned; dron·ing.** To make or speak with a low, dull, monotonous, humming sound; as, to *drone* through a long speech. — *n.* **1** A humming sound; as, the *drone* of bees; the *drone* of airplanes overhead. **2** One of the pipes of a bagpipe, sounding a continuous bass tone.

drool \'drül\ *v.* **1** To drivel; to slobber. **2** To talk foolishly.

droop \'drüp\ *v.* **1** To sink, bend, or hang down, as an animal or plant from weakness, weariness, or hunger; as, flowers *drooping* in the hot sun. **2** To be or grow weak with grief or disappointment; to be depressed in spirits. News from home revived the soldier's *drooping* spirits. — *n.* A drooping.

droopy \'drüp-ē\ *adj.;* **droop·i·er; droop·i·est.** Drooping or tending to droop; dejected.

drop \'dräp\ *n.* **1** A small amount of liquid such as will fall naturally in one rounded mass. **2** Something that looks or hangs like a small mass of liquid about to fall, as an earring or a lump of candy. **3** A small quantity, especially of a liquid; as, a *drop* of whiskey. **4** [in the plural] Any medicine, as one for the eyes or nose, measured in drops. **5** A sudden fall or descent; as, an unexpected *drop* in temperature. **6** The distance through which one falls or may fall. There was a *drop* of thirty feet from the roof to the ground. **7** A slot into which something is to be dropped; as, a letter *drop.* **8** Something arranged to drop, hang, or fall, as a trap door. — *v.;* **dropped** or **dropt; drop·ping.** **1** To fall or let fall in drops. **2** To let fall; as, to *drop* a book. The ship *dropped* anchor in the harbor. **3** To send; as, to *drop* someone a letter. **4** To let go; to dismiss; as, to *drop* the subject; to *drop* several workmen. **5** To knock down; to cause to fall; as, to *drop* an opponent in a fight. **6** To lower; as, to *drop* a curtain; to *drop* one's voice. **7** To go lower. Prices *dropped.* **8** To come or go unexpectedly or informally. Friends *dropped* in to call. **9** To pass from one state into another considered less active; as, to *drop* asleep. **10** To move downward, or with a current; as, a boat *dropping* down a stream.

drop·let \'dräp-lət\ *n.* A very small drop.

drop·per \'dräp-r\ *n.* One that drops; especially, a glass tube fitted at one end with a rubber bulb, used for measuring out medicine in drops.

drop·sy \'dräp-sē\ *n.* An illness in which an unusual amount of thick fluid collects in cavities and tissues of the body. — **drop·si·cal** \-sik-l\ *adj.*

dropt. A past tense and past part. of *drop.*

dross \'dräs, 'drȯs\ *n.* **1** The scum formed on molten ore or metal. **2** Waste matter; refuse.

drought or **drouth** \'draủth, 'draủt\ *n.* **1** Lack of rain or of water; dryness. **2** A long period of dry weather. **3** *Dial.* Thirst. — **droughty** or **drouthy,** *adj.*

drove \'drōv\ *n.* **1** A number of cattle being driven together, or gathered to be driven. **2** Any collection of animals moving forward. **3** A crowd of people moving along together in one direction.

drove. Past tense of *drive.*

dro·ver \'drōv-r\ *n.* **1** A person that drives animals, as cattle, sheep, and pigs, to market. **2** A dealer in cattle.

drown \'draủn\ *v.;* **drowned** \'draủnd, *not* 'draủn-dəd\; **drown·ing.** **1** To sink and die in water. **2** To kill by holding under water. **3** To be suffocated in water or other liquid. **4** To overpower; to overcome; as, a single dissenting vote *drowned* in the roar of approval. — **drown out.** **1** To drive out, as from one's home or place of shelter, by a flood or downpour. **2** To keep from being heard because of greater loudness. The noise of passing trucks *drowned out* our words.

drowse \'draủz\ *v.;* **drowsed; drows·ing.** To sleep lightly or be half asleep; to doze. — *n.* A doze.

drow·sy \'draủ-zē\ *adj.;* **drow·si·er; drow·si·est.** **1** Sleepy; half asleep. **2** Making one sleepy; lulling; as, a *drowsy* summer afternoon; the *drowsy* hum of bees in the garden. — **drow·si·ly** \'draủz-l-ē\ *adv.*

drub \'drəb\ *v.;* **drubbed; drub·bing.** **1** To beat with a stick; to cudgel. **2** To drive out; to expel; as, to *drub* those ideas out of his head. — **drub·bing,** *n.*

drudge \'drəj\ *v.;* **drudged; drudg·ing.** To work hard at a tiresome task. — *n.* A person who drudges.

drudg·ery \'drəj-r(-)ē\ *n.; pl.* **drudg·er·ies.** Hard, tiresome, or uninteresting work.

drug \'drəg\ *n.* **1** Any substance used as a medicine or in making medicines. **2** Any article for which there is no demand; as, a *drug* on the market. **3** Medicine used to deaden pain or to bring sleep or rest. — *v.;* **drugged; drug·ging.** **1** To dose with drugs or medicines in an effort to cure. **2** To dull a person's senses with drugs.

drug·gist \'drəg-əst\ *n.* A person who sells drugs; a pharmacist.

drug·store \'drəg-ˌstōr, -ˌstȯr\ *n.* A retail store where drugs and various small articles are sold; a pharmacy.

dru·id \'drü-əd\ *n.* A member of a religious order in ancient Gaul, Britain, and Ireland — often with a capital.

drum \'drəm\ *n.* **1** A musical instrument, usually a

metal or wooden cylinder with flat ends covered by tightly drawn skin (called the **drum·head** \'drəm-ˌhed\). **2** The sound of a drum or any similar sound. **3** Any drum-shaped object, as a metal barrel for holding oil or a cylindrical device upon which brake bands exert pressure in the braking of an automobile. — *v.;* **drummed**; **drum·ming. 1** To beat or play on a drum. **2** To gather together by or as if by beating a drum; as, to *drum* up recruits; to *drum* up customers. **3** To beat with rapid strokes; as, to *drum* on the table with one's fingers. **4** To throb, beat, or sound like a drum. **5** To drive or force by repeated efforts; as, to *drum* a lesson into someone's head.

drum·lin \'drəm-lən\ *n.* A long or oval hill of material left by a glacier.

drum ma·jor \'māj-r\. The marching leader of a band or drum corps.

drum ma·jor·ette \ˌmāj-r-'et\. A female drum major.

drum·mer \'drəm-r\ *n.* **1** A person who beats or plays a drum. **2** A person who travels about soliciting business for a wholesale dealer.

drum·stick \'drəm-ˌstik\ *n.* **1** A stick for beating a drum. **2** A leg of a fowl, as a chicken or turkey.

drunk \'drəngk\. Past part. of *drink.* — *adj.* **1** So much under the influence of alcohol that normal thinking and acting become difficult or impossible; intoxicated. **2** In a mental or emotional state leading to behavior suggestive of intoxication with strong drink; as, *drunk* with power. — *n.* **1** A person who is drunk. **2** A drunkard. **3** A period of excessive drinking; a spree.

drunk·ard \'drəngk-rd\ *n.* A person who is often drunk.

drunk·en \'drəngk-n\ *adj.* **1** Drunk; as, a loud dispute between two *drunken* men. **2** Caused by, characterized by, or showing the effect of excessive drinking; as, a *drunken* brawl; a *drunken* sleep. **3** Unsteady or uneven, as if reeling from being drunk. — **drunk·en·ly,** *adv.*

drupe \'drüp\ *n.* A fleshy fruit with one seed enclosed in a stone or pit, as in the plum, cherry, apricot, and peach.

dry \'drī\ *adj.;* **dri·er** \'drīr\; **dri·est** \'drī-əst\. **1** Free from moisture; not wet or moist. **2** Not in or under water; as, *dry* land. **3** Empty of water or other liquid; as, a *dry* creek; a *dry* fountain pen. **4** Not giving milk; as, a *dry* cow. **5** Thirsty. **6** Not shedding tears; as, to bear grief with *dry* eyes. **7** Served or used without butter; as, *dry* toast. **8** Sharp; shrewd; as, a *dry* wit. **9** Uninteresting; dull; as, a *dry* speech. **10** Harsh; as, a *dry* cough. **11** Not sweet; as, a *dry* wine. **12** Forbidding the sale of alcoholic drinks; as, *dry* laws; a *dry* state. — *v.;* **dried** \'drīd\; **dry·ing.** To make or become dry. — *n.; pl.* **drys.** A person who opposes the sale or use of alcoholic drinks.

dry·ad \'drī-əd, -ˌad\ *n.; pl.* **dry·ads** \'drī-ədz, -ˌadz\ or **dry·a·des** \'drī-ə-ˌdēz\. In Greek mythology, a tree-dwelling nymph; a wood nymph.

dry cell \ˌsel\. A cell that contains electricity-producing chemicals and something, as sawdust, to keep the chemicals from spilling.

dry-clean \'drī-'klēn\ *v.* To subject to dry cleaning.

dry cleaning. The cleaning of cloth with liquids other than water, as with benzine. — **dry cleaner.**

dry dock \ˌdäk\. A dock from which the water may be removed, used in building and repairing ships.

dryer. Variant of *drier.*

dry farming. Farming without irrigation in regions of little rainfall, using methods of cultivation that save the moisture in the soil and growing drought-resisting crops. — **dry-farm** \'drī-'färm, -'fårm\ *v.* — **dry farmer.**

dry goods \'drī ˌgu̇dz\. Cloth goods as distinguished from such articles as hardware, jewelry, and groceries.

dry·ly or **dri·ly** \'drī-lē\ *adv.* In a dry manner.

dry measure. A system of measures of volume for dry things such as grain, fruit, and vegetables; especially, the system in which two pints make one quart, eight quarts one peck, and four pecks one bushel.

dry·ness \'drī-nəs\ *n.* The condition or quality of being dry.

dry-shod \'drī-'shäd\ *adj.* Having dry shoes; not getting one's shoes wet.

d's. Pl. of *d.*

DST. Abbreviation for *Daylight Saving Time.*

du·al \'dü-əl, 'dyü-\ *adj.* **1** Composed of two parts; twofold; double; as, to have a *dual* responsibility towards a child as uncle and legal guardian. **2** To be shared by two; as, an airplane with *dual* controls; *dual* ownership.

dub \'dəb\ *v.;* **dubbed**; **dub·bing. 1** To confer knighthood upon. **2** To call; to name; as, a boy *dubbed* "Speedy" because he was so slow. **3** To rub or dress smooth, as timber.

du·bi·ous \'dü-bē-əs, 'dyü-\ *adj.* **1** Doubtful; uncertain; as, a *dubious* answer; a *dubious* battle. **2** Of questionable character; as, to win a victory by *dubious* means. — **du·bi·ous·ly,** *adv.*

du·cal \'dük-l, 'dyük-l\ *adj.* Of or relating to a duke or a dukedom; as, a *ducal* title; *ducal* lands.

duc·at \'dək-ət\ *n.* **1** Any of various gold coins once used in European countries. **2** *Slang.* A ticket, as for a theater or a sports event.

duch·ess \'dəch-əs\ *n.* **1** The wife or widow of a duke. **2** A woman who has in her own right a rank equal to that of a duke or is the ruler of a duchy.

duchy \'dəch-ē\ *n.; pl.* **duch·ies.** The territory of a duke or duchess.

duck \'dək\ *n.* **1** A canvaslike linen or cotton fabric made in several weights. **2** [in the plural] Clothes, especially trousers, made of this fabric.

duck \'dək\ *n.* Any of various swimming birds of a family with heavy body, stout wings and legs, webbed feet, and a bill with a hard plate at the tip and hard biting edges.

duck \ˈdək\ *v.* **1** To push or pull under water for a moment. **2** To bow; to bob; to dodge; as, to *duck* a blow; to *duck* one's head. — *n.* **1** The act of ducking; a sudden lowering of the head; a dodging. **2** A dip or quick plunge; as, to take a *duck* in the lake.

duck \ˈdək\ *n.* A truck equipped with a propeller and capable of locomotion on land and water.

duck·bill \ˈdək-ˌbil\ *n.* A small, web-footed, egg-laying animal of Australia, with a bill like that of a duck.

duckbill

duck·ling \ˈdək-ling\ *n.* A young duck.

duck·weed \ˈdək-ˌwēd\ *n.* A very small free-floating stemless water plant found on ponds and other bodies of still water.

duct \ˈdəkt\ *n.* **1** Any tube, pipe, or canal for conveying a fluid. **2** In the body, a tube or vessel; as, a tear *duct.* — **duct·less** \-ləs\ *adj.*

duc·tile \ˈdəkt-l, ˈdək-ˌtīl\ *adj.* **1** Capable of being permanently drawn out, as into wire, or hammered thin — used especially of metals, as gold. **2** Easily led, taught, or influenced; docile; as, a *ductile* mind. — **duc·til·i·ty** \dək-ˈtil-ət-ē\ *n.*

duct·less gland \ˈdəkt-ləs\. Any of certain glands that, having no duct to take away their secretion, pour it into the lymph or into blood circulating through them.

dud \ˈdəd\ *n.* **1** A garment; [usually in the plural] clothes. **2** [in the plural] Belongings; things in general. **3** A bomb or shell that fails to explode. **4** A person or thing that proves to be a complete failure.

dude \ˈdüd, ˈdyüd\ *n.* **1** A person who gives extreme attention to dress; a silly, conceited person. **2** An Easterner or city-bred person. — **dud·ish** \ˈdüd-ish, ˈdyüd-\ *adj.*

dude ranch. A ranch run for entertainment of outsiders on vacation.

dudg·eon \ˈdəj-n\ *n.* Angry feeling; bad humor.

due \ˈdü, ˈdyü\ *adj.* **1** Owed or owing as a debt; payable; as, to pay all that is *due* on the bill. **2** Fit; suitable; as, to show *due* respect. **3** Sufficient; as, to arrive in *due* time. **4** Regular; lawful; as, *due* process of law. **5** Owing. The accident was *due* to carelessness. **6** Scheduled; appointed or scheduled to arrive; as, a train *due* in five minutes. — *n.* **1** Something that is owed; a debt; as, to pay a man his *due.* **2** [in the plural] A regular or legal charge or fee, as for club membership. — *adv.* Directly; as, a town *due* east of here.

du·el \ˈdü-əl, ˈdyü-\ *n.* **1** A combat between two persons, fought with deadly weapons by agreement, usually before witnesses called *seconds.* **2** Any combat or contest between two opponents. — *v.;* **du·eled** or **du·elled**; **du·el·ing** or **du·el·ling.** To fight or kill in a duel; to engage in a hard-fought contest. — **du·el·er** or **du·el·ler,** *n.*

du·el·ist or **du·el·list** \ˈdü-ə-ləst, ˈdyü-\ *n.* One who fights duels.

du·en·na \dü-ˈen-ə, dyü-\ *n.* **1** An elderly lady in charge of the younger ladies in a Spanish or Portuguese family. **2** A governess; a chaperon.

du·et \dü-ˈet, dyü-\ *n.* A musical composition for two voices or two instruments.

duf·fel \ˈdəf-l\ *n.* An outfit of supplies, as for camping; a kit. — *adj.* Carrying or made to carry duffel; as, a *duffel* bag.

dug. A past tense and past part. of *dig.*

du·gong \ˈdü-ˌgäng, -ˌgȯng\ *n.* A large mammal of tropical seas, with a fishlike body, paddle-shaped forelimbs, and whalelike tail.

dug·out \ˈdəg-ˌau̇t\ *n.* **1** A canoe or boat made by hollowing out a large log. **2** A shelter, such as one dug in a hillside or in the side of a trench.

duke \ˈdük, ˈdyük\ *n.* **1** A nobleman of the highest rank after that of prince. **2** The ruler of a territory known as a duchy.

duke·dom \ˈdük-dəm, ˈdyük-\ *n.* **1** A duchy. **2** The title or rank of a duke.

dul·cet \ˈdəl-sət\ *adj.* Sweet to the ear; melodious; agreeable; as, *dulcet* tones.

dul·ci·mer \ˈdəls-m-ər\ *n.* A musical instrument having metallic strings played with two light hammers.

dull \ˈdəl\ *adj.* **1** Not sharp in edge or point; blunt; as, a *dull* knife. **2** Stupid; slow to sense or to understand; as, a *dull* pupil. **3** Slow in action; sluggish. Business was *dull* today. **4** Dim; cloudy; as, a *dull* glow from the fire; a *dull* day. **5** Uninteresting; tedious; as, a *dull* story. **6** Not clear and ringing; as, a *dull* sound. **7** Grayish in color; not vivid; as, *dull* paint. — *v.* To make or become dull. Smoke *dulled* the newly-painted walls.

dull·ard \ˈdəl-rd\ *n.* A stupid person.

dul·ly \ˈdəl-(l)ē\ *adv.* In a dull manner.

du·ly \ˈdü-lē, ˈdyü-\ *adv.* In a due or fit manner, time, or degree; properly; as, a bill received and *duly* paid.

dumb \ˈdəm\ *adj.* **1** Lacking the natural power of speech; as, deaf and *dumb* persons. **2** Naturally unable to speak; as, *dumb* animals. **3** Not willing to speak; silent; mute; as, to remain *dumb* in spite of the repeated questions. **4** Dull; stupid; as, to have a *dumb* look on one's face.

— The words *mute* and *speechless* are synonyms of *dumb: dumb* usually suggests inability to speak due to lack of the proper organs, or it may suggest loss of speech; *mute* may describe someone who has never learned to speak, as many deaf persons, or one who deliberately refrains from speaking; *speechless* usually implies temporary loss of speech, as from astonishment or fear.

dumb·bell \ˈdəm-ˌbel\ *n.* **1** A weight, consisting of two rounded ends joined by a short bar as a handle, generally used in pairs for physical exercise. **2** A stupid person.

dumbbell, 1

dumb·ly \ˈdəm-lē\ *adv.* In a dumb manner.

dumb-wait·er \ˈdəm-ˈwāt-r\ *n.* **1** A portable serving table. **2** A small elevator on which things are passed from one room or story of a house to another.

dum·dum \'dəm-ˌdəm\ *n.* or **dumdum bullet**. A bullet with a soft end that expands as it strikes.

dum·found or **dumb·found** \'dəm-'faủnd\ *v.* [A compound formed from *dumb* and the *-found* of *confound.*] To strike dumb, as with astonishment; to amaze; as, to be *dumfounded* at the discovery.

dum·my \'dəm-ē\ *n.; pl.* **dum·mies.** **1** A person who lacks or seems to lack the power of speech. **2** One who seems to be acting for himself but is really acting for another. The bank teller who was on duty at the time of the burglary was really a *dummy* for the robbers. **3** A stupid person. **4** An imitation of something, to be used as a substitute; as, the *dummies* in the window of a clothing store. **5** In certain card games, an exposed hand played by one of the players in addition to his own hand. **6** A card player who lays his cards face up on the table to be played by his partner. — *adj.* Having the appearance of a thing but lacking the capacity to function; fictitious; sham; as, *dummy* windows painted on a doll's house.

dump \'dəmp\ *v.* To let fall in a mass; to unload, as coal from a cart by tilting it. — *n.* **1** A place for dumping anything, especially trash. **2** A place for temporary storage, as of army supplies.

dump·ling \'dəmp-ling\ *n.* **1** A light ball of dough boiled in meat broth. **2** A ball of dough with a fruit center, either steamed or baked.

dumps \'dəmps\ *n. pl.* Low spirits; a dull, gloomy state of mind.

dumpy \'dəmp-ē\ *adj.;* **dump·i·er**; **dump·i·est.** Short and thick in build.

dun \'dən\ *v.;* **dunned**; **dun·ning**. To ask over and over again for payment of a debt. — *n.* **1** A person who duns another. **2** An urgent and repeated request or demand for payment.

dun \'dən\ *adj.* Dull or dingy yellow or grayish brown in color.

dunce \'dən(t)s\ *n.* [Named after John *Duns* Scotus (1265–1308), a Scottish theologian whose writings were ridiculed.] **1** A person slow in learning from books. **2** A stupid person.

dune \'dün, 'dyün\ *n.* A hill or ridge of sand piled up by the wind.

dung \'dəng\ *n.* Waste matter from animals; manure.

dun·ga·ree \ˌdəng-gr-'ē, 'dəng-gr-ˌē\ *n.* **1** A coarse cotton fabric. **2** [in the plural] Trousers or working clothes of this fabric.

dung beetle. Any of numerous beetles, as the tumblebug, that breed in and feed on dung.

dun·geon \'dənj-n\ *n.* **1** A donjon. **2** A close, dark prison, commonly underground.

dung·hill \'dəng-ˌhil\ *n.* A heap of dung; a manure pile.

dunk \'dəngk\ *v.* To dip, as bread into coffee, tea, or some other drink while eating.

dun·nage \'dən-ij\ *n.* **1** Loose material placed around or between pieces of a ship's cargo to prevent damage. **2** Baggage or personal effects, especially of a sailor.

duo \'dü-ˌō, 'dyü-\ *n.; pl.* **du·os**. A duet, especially an instrumental duet.

du·o·de·num \ˌdü-ə-'dē-nəm, ˌdyü-\ *n.* The first part of the small intestine, leading from the stomach. — **du·o·de·nal** \ˌdü-ə-'dēn-l, ˌdyü-; dü-'äd-n-əl, dyü-\ *adj.*

dupe \'düp, 'dyüp\ *n.* A person that has been or is easily deceived or cheated; as, to become the *dupe* of a confidence man. — *v.;* **duped**; **dup·ing**. To make a dupe of; to deceive; to trick.

du·ple \'düp-l, 'dyüp-l\ *adj.* **1** Twofold; taken by twos. **2** In music, having two beats or a multiple of two beats to the measure; as, *duple* time.

du·plex \'dü-ˌpleks, 'dyü-\ *adj.* Double; twofold. — *n.* A duplex house or apartment.

duplex apartment. An apartment having rooms on two floors and an inner stairway.

duplex house. A two-family house.

du·pli·cate \'düp-lik-ət, 'dyüp-\ *adj.* **1** Double; twofold. **2** Corresponding exactly to something else; as, *duplicate* keys. — *n.* A thing that exactly resembles or corresponds to something else; a copy; as, to make a *duplicate* of a key. A carbon copy of a letter is a *duplicate* of the original letter. — \-lə-ˌkāt\ *v.;* **du·pli·cat·ed**; **du·pli·cat·ing**. **1** To double; to fold. **2** To make a duplicate or a copy of. **3** To repeat exactly; as, to *duplicate* one's elder brother's fine record in a school. — **in duplicate**. **1** With a copy accompanying each original. **2** In pairs.

du·pli·ca·tion \ˌdüp-lə-'kāsh-n, ˌdyüp-\ *n.* **1** The act of duplicating or the state of being duplicated; a doubling, copying, or repetition. **2** A duplicate; a copy or counterpart.

du·pli·ca·tor \'düp-lə-ˌkāt-r, 'dyüp-\ *n.* One that duplicates; especially, a machine for making exact copies of a typewritten page.

du·plic·i·ty \dü-'plis-ət-ē, dyü-\ *n.; pl.* **du·plic·i·ties**. Deception by pretending to feel one way while acting another; double-dealing; deceitfulness.

du·ra·bil·i·ty \ˌdủr-ə-'bil-ət-ē, ˌdyủr-\ *n.* The quality or state of being durable; ability to last or to stand continued use or wear.

du·ra·ble \'dủr-əb-l, 'dyủr-\ *adj.* Not wearing out or decaying quickly; enduring; lasting; as, *durable* cloth. — For synonyms see *lasting*. — **du·ra·bly** \-ə-blē\ *adv.*

dur·ance \'dủr-ən(t)s, 'dyủr-\ *n.* Imprisonment.

du·ra·tion \dủ-'rāsh-n, dyủ-, də-\ *n.* The time during which anything lasts; as, a storm of short *duration*. Taxes were increased for the *duration* of the war.

du·ress \dü-'res, dyü-, də-\ *n.* **1** Imprisonment. **2** Compulsion by force or by threat of force; as, a false confession made under *duress*.

dur·ing \'dủr-ing, 'dyủr-\ *prep.* [From the present participle of *dure*, an obsolete verb meaning "to last", from French *durer,* there derived from Latin *durare,* which is also the source of the English words *durable, duration, endure, endurance.*] In the time of; within the period of; throughout the course of; as, to have three vacations and several single holidays *during* the school year; to go swimming daily *during* the summer.

durst. A past tense of *dare.*

dusk \'dəsk\ *n.* **1** The darker part of twilight or of dawn. **2** Partial darkness; gloom. — *adj.* Moderately dark; dusky.

dusky \'dəs-kē\ *adj.;* **dusk·i·er; dusk·i·est.** Somewhat dark; grayish or blackish; as, a *dusky* cave; *dusky* clouds. — **dusk·i·ly** \'dəsk-l-ē\ *adv.*

dust \'dəst\ *n.* **1** Fine, dry, powdery particles of earth; any fine powder. **2** The earthy remains of bodies once alive; especially, the human corpse. **3** The earth; the surface of the ground. **4** Something worthless. — *v.* **1** To sprinkle with dust or powder; as, to *dust* plants with insecticide. **2** To free from dust; to brush or wipe away dust; as, to *dust* furniture.

dust bowl. A region that suffers from long droughts and dust storms; especially, [often with a capital] the region along the western border of the Great Plains.

dust·er \'dəst-r\ *n.* **1** A person or thing that dusts. **2** A light overgarment to protect clothing from dust.

dust jacket. A paper cover for a book, usually illustrated and often containing one or more blurbs.

dust storm. A violent dust-bearing wind moving across a dry region.

dusty \'dəs-tē\ *adj.;* **dust·i·er; dust·i·est. 1** Filled or covered with dust; as, a *dusty* desk. **2** Like dust; powdery; as, a *dusty* white. — **dust·i·ly** \'dəs-tə-lē\ *adv.*

Dutch \'dəch\ *adj.* **1** German. **2** Of or relating to the Netherlands or its inhabitants. — *n.* **1** The language of the Dutch. **2** The people of the Netherlands — used as a plural with *the.*

Dutch·man \'dəch-mən\ *n.; pl.* **Dutch·men** \-mən\. **1** A native of the Netherlands. **2** A German.

Dutch·man's-breech·es \'dəch-mənz-'brich-əz\ *n. sing. and pl.* A delicate woods herb allied to the bleeding heart, having finely divided leaves and cream-white double-spurred flowers.

Dutch treat. A treat in which each person treats himself or pays his own way.

du·te·ous \'düt-ē-əs, 'dyüt-\ *adj.* Fulfilling one's duty; dutiful. — **du·te·ous·ly,** *adv.*

du·ti·a·ble \'düt ē-əb-l, 'dyüt-\ *adj.* Subject to a duty, as imported goods.

du·ti·ful \'düt-ēf-l, 'dyüt-, -əf-l\ *adj.* **1** Respectful; obedient; as, a *dutiful* servant. **2** Controlled by a sense of duty; coming from a sense of duty; as, *dutiful* affection. — **du·ti·ful·ly** \-l(-)ē\ *adv.*

du·ty \'düt-ē, 'dyüt-ē\ *n.; pl.* **du·ties. 1** The way a person ought to act or behave toward his superiors; as, to know one's *duty* to one's parents. **2** The service that is required by one's position or occupation; as, the *duties* of a policeman. The lifeguards are on *duty* all day. **3** Something that a person is morally bound to do or not to do. **4** A tax, especially one on goods imported into a country.

dwarf \'dwȯrf\ *n.; pl.* **dwarfs** \'dwȯrfs, 'dwȯrvz\. **1** A person, animal, or plant much below the normal size of its species or kind. **2** In stories, a small, deformed, manlike being, often skillful in metalwork. — *v.* **1** To hinder from growing to natural size; to stunt; as, to *dwarf* a tree. **2** To cause to look smaller than usual. — *adj.* Of less than the usual size; stunted. — **dwarf·ish** \'dwȯr-fish\ *adj.*

dwell \'dwel\ *v.;* **dwelt** \'dwelt\; **dwell·ing. 1** To remain; to linger; to stay for a while; as, a scene that *dwells* in one's memory. **2** To live in a place; to reside; as, to be forced to *dwell* apart. **3** To keep attention or emphasis on something; to make much of; as, to *dwell* on a sore point.

dwell·er \'dwel-r\ *n.* One that dwells; especially, an inhabitant; a resident; as, a city *dweller;* a cave *dweller.*

dwell·ing \'dwel-ing\ *n.* A house; residence.

dwelling place. A place of residence.

dwelt. Past tense of *dwell.*

dwin·dle \'dwind-l\ *v.;* **dwin·dled; dwin·dling** \-l(-)ing\. To become less; to diminish; to waste away; as, a *dwindling* supply of coal.

dye \'dī\ *v.;* **dyed; dye·ing.** To stain; to color; to make a color permanent in a fabric. — *n.* **1** A color produced by dyeing. **2** A material used for dyeing. — **dy·er** \'dīr\ *n.*

dye·ing \'dī-ing\ *n.* The action of fixing coloring matters in fibers, as of wool or cotton.

dye·stuff \'dī-ˌstəf\ *n.* Material used for dyeing; dye.

dy·ing \'dī-ing\. Pres. part. of *die.* — *adj.* **1** In the act of dying; perishable; as, the dried leaves of *dying* plants. **2** Of or relating to dying or death; as, to insist until one's *dying* day.

dyke \'dīk\ *n.* A dike. — *v.;* **dyked; dyk·ing.** To surround, protect, or drain by a dike.

dy·nam·ic \dī-'nam-ik\ *adj.* **1** Of or relating to physical forces or energy. **2** Of or relating to dynamics; active. **3** Forceful; full of energy; as, a *dynamic* personality. — **dy·nam·i·cal·ly** \-ik-l(-)ē\ *adv.*

dy·nam·ics \dī-'nam-iks\ *n.* **1** The science of the motion of bodies and the action of forces in producing or changing their motion. **2** Moral or physical forces, or the laws relating to them.

dy·na·mite \'dī-nə-ˌmīt\ *n.* [A compound formed from Greek *dynamis* meaning "force", "power" and the English suffix *-ite.*] An explosive made of nitroglycerin absorbed in a porous material, much used in blasting. — *v.;* **dy·na·mit·ed; dy·na·mit·ing.** To blow up with dynamite.

dy·na·mo \'dī-nə-ˌmō\ *n.; pl.* **dy·na·mos.** A machine for producing electric current; a generator.

dy·nas·ty \'dī-nəs-tē, 'dī-ˌnas-\ *n.; pl.* **dy·nas·ties. 1** A series of kings of the same line or family. **2** The continued rule of such a series of kings. — **dy·nas·tic** \dī-ˈnas-tik\ *adj.*

dys·en·tery \ˈdis-n-ˌter-ē\ *n.* A painful intestinal disease in which mucus and blood are discharged from the bowels. — **dys·en·ter·ic** \ˌdis-n-ˈter-ik\ *adj.*

dys·pep·sia \dis-ˈpep-shə, -sē-ə\ *n.* Indigestion.

dys·pep·tic \dis-ˈpep-tik\ *adj.* Relating to or having dyspepsia. — *n.* A person who has dyspepsia. — **dys·pep·ti·cal·ly** \-tik-l(-)ē\ *adv.*

dz. Abbreviation for *dozen.*

e \ˈē\ *n.; pl.* **e's** \ˈēz\. The fifth letter of the alphabet.

e-. A form of the prefix *ex-*.

E. Abbreviation for: **1** *east.* **2** *eastern.*

each \ˈēch\ *adj.* Every one (of two or more) considered individually. The teacher soon knew *each* child by name. — *pron.* Each one; as, *each* of the players had a turn. — *adv.* To or for each; apiece; as, two helpings *each.*

ea·ger \ˈēg-r\ *adj.* Desiring very much; very anxious; as, *eager* to go for a walk; *eager* for knowledge. — **ea·ger·ly**, *adv.*

ea·gle \ˈēg-l\ *n.* **1** Any of several large birds of prey of the same family as the hawks, noted for keenness of vision and powers of flight. **2** The seal or standard of any nation, as the United States, having an eagle as its emblem. **3** A gold coin formerly circulating in the United States, worth ten dollars.

ea·glet \ˈēg-lət\ *n.* A young eagle.

ear \ˈir\ *n.* **1** The organ of hearing. **2** The external part of this organ. The boy's *ears* stood out from his head. **3** The sense of hearing; as, a good *ear* for music. **4** Attention; as, to give *ear* to a request. **5** Anything resembling an ear in shape or position. — **eared** \ˈird\ *adj.*

ear \ˈir\ *n.* The seed-bearing spike of a grain such as wheat, rice, or Indian corn, including the kernels or grains; as, an *ear* of corn. — *v.* To put forth ears.

ear of corn

ear·ache \ˈir-ˌāk\ *n.* An ache or pain in the ear.

ear·drum \ˈir-ˌdrəm\ *n.* The thin membrane that stretches across the cavity of the middle part of the ear and that vibrates when sound waves strike it, the vibrations being transmitted to the nerves of hearing.

earl \ˈərl\ *n.* A nobleman ranking below a marquis and above a viscount.

earl·dom \ˈərl-dəm\ *n.* The position, title, or territorial possessions of an earl.

ear·ly \ˈər-lē\ *adv.;* **ear·li·er; ear·li·est. 1** At or near the beginning of a period or a series; as, to get up *early* every day. **2** Before the usual or expected time. The postman came *early.* — *adj.* Coming near the beginning; coming or occurring early in time; as, to plan on making an *early* start.

ear·mark \ˈir-ˌmärk, -ˌmȧrk\ *n.* **1** A mark of identification on the ear, as of a horse or cow. **2** Any mark of identification. — *v.* **1** To place an earmark on; to mark in any distinctive way. **2** To set aside for a special purpose. Ten per cent of all the money collected was *earmarked* for the building fund.

ear·muff \ˈir-ˌməf\ *n.* One of a pair of coverings of cloth or fur used to protect the ears in cold weather.

earn \ˈərn\ *v.* **1** To deserve as a result of labor or service; as, to *earn* every cent one is paid. **2** To get for services given; as, to *earn* a good salary.

ear·nest \ˈər-nəst\ *adj.* Not light or playful; serious; as, to speak in an *earnest* tone; an *earnest* student. — **in earnest.** Serious; determined; as, to be *in earnest* about saving up for a bicycle. — **ear·nest·ly**, *adv.*

ear·nest \ˈər-nəst\ *n.* **1** Something of value given by a buyer to a seller to bind a bargain. **2** Something given as a pledge that certain things will be done.

earn·ings \ˈər-ningz\ *n. pl.* Money earned; especially, wages.

ear·phone \ˈir-ˌfōn\ *n.* A receiver held over the ear by a band passing over the head, used to listen to telephone, telegraph, or radio messages.

ear·ring \ˈir-ˌring, ˈir-ˌing\ *n.* An ornament worn on or hanging from the lobe of the ear.

ear·shot \ˈir-ˌshät\ *n.* The distance within which an unaided human voice can be heard; the range of a person's hearing.

earphone

ear·split·ting \ˈir-ˌsplit-ing\ *adj.* Distressingly loud or shrill; deafening; as, an *earsplitting* clap of thunder.

earth \ˈərth\ *n.* **1** Soil or dirt, as distinguished from rock. **2** The world as the home of man, as distinguished from heaven and hell. **3** Land, as distinguished from sea and air. **4** The planet on which we live. **5** The burrow of an animal, as a fox. **6** Any of several metallic oxides formerly classified as chemical elements.

earth·en \ˈərth-n, ˈərt͟h-\ *adj.* Made of earth or of baked clay; as, an *earthen* floor; *earthen* dishes.

earth·en·ware \ˈərth-n-ˌwar, ˈərt͟h-, -ˌwer\ *n.* Articles, as utensils or ornaments, made of baked clay, especially the coarser kinds.

earth·ly \ˈərth-lē\ *adj.;* **earth·li·er; earth·li·est. 1** Of, relating to, or belonging to the earth; not heavenly or spiritual; as, *earthly* joys; to lose all one's *earthly* possessions in a fire. **2** Possible; imaginable; as, a tool that is of no *earthly* use.

earth·quake \ˈərth-ˌkwāk\ *n.* A shaking or trembling of a portion of the earth, caused by movement of rock masses or by volcanic shocks.

earth·work \'ərth-ˌwərk\ *n.* An embankment or other construction of earth, especially one made as a fortification.

earth·worm \'ərth-ˌwərm\ *n.* A long slender worm with segmented body that lives in damp earth; an angleworm.

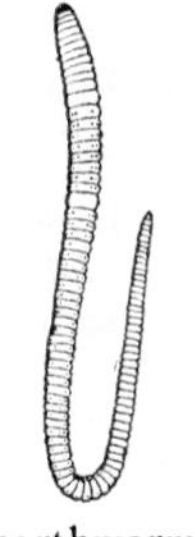
earthworm

earthy \'ər-thē\ *adj.;* **earth·i·er**; **earth·i·est.** **1** Consisting of, or like, earth. **2** Of or relating to the earth; worldly; not spiritual. **3** Not refined; coarse; as, *earthy* humor.

ear·wax \'ir-ˌwaks\ *n.* A yellow waxlike substance produced by the glands of the external ear.

ear·wig \'ir-ˌwig\ *n.* [From Old English *earwicga*, from *eare* meaning "ear" and *wicga* meaning "insect", literally, "something that wiggles"; so called from the belief that the insect crawled into the ear.] **1** A harmless insect having slender many-jointed antennae and a pair of forcepslike appendages at the end of its body. **2** A small centipede.

ease \'ēz\ *n.* **1** Freedom from pain or trouble; comfort of body or mind; as, a life of *ease.* **2** Freedom from any sense or feeling of difficulty or embarrassment; naturalness; as, to speak or write with *ease.* — *v.;* **eased**; **eas·ing.** **1** To free from discomfort or worry; to give relief; as, to *ease* a pain; to *ease* a person's mind. **2** To make or become easier. The pain *eased* after hot applications. **3** To make less tight; to loosen; as, to *ease* a rope in pulling. **4** To move very carefully; as, to *ease* a table through a door.

ea·sel \'ēz-l\ *n.* [From Dutch *ezel* meaning literally "donkey", there borrowed from Latin *asinus*, the source of English *ass.* Compare the use of *horse* in *clotheshorse* and *sawhorse.*] A frame for holding a flat surface, as a picture or a blackboard, upright.

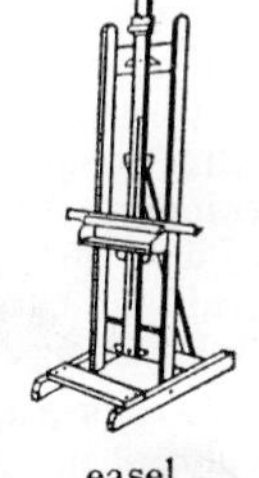
easel

eas·i·ly \'ēz-l(-)ē\ *adv.* **1** In an easy manner; without difficulty; as, to win *easily.* **2** Without doubt or question; as, a player who is *easily* the best on the team.

east \'ēst\ *n.* **1** One of the four main points of the compass; the direction of the sunrise. **2** [with a capital] Regions or countries east of Europe; Asiatic countries; as, the religions of the *East.* **3** [with a capital] New England and the Atlantic states; the territory east of the Mississippi River, especially the part north of Maryland and the Ohio River. — *adj.* **1** Toward or at the east; as, a city on the *east* coast. **2** From the east; as, an *east* wind. — *adv.* Eastward; as, to travel *east.*

East·er \'ēst-r\ *n.* [From Old English *Eastre*, originally a pagan spring festival in honor of the ancient Germanic goddess of spring and light.] A Christian festival observed in memory of the resurrection of Christ; the day on which this festival is celebrated, a Sunday between March 21 and April 26.

east·er·ly \'ēst-r-lē\ *adj.* **1** Situated, directed, or moving toward the east; as, to set out in an *easterly* direction. **2** From the east; as, an *easterly* wind. — *adv.* Toward the east.

east·ern \'ēst-rn\ *adj.* **1** Of or relating to the east. **2** At, in, or toward the east. **3** From the east. **4** [with a capital] Of or relating to the East.

east·ern·er \'ēst-rn-r\ *n.* A person native to or living in the east, especially [with a capital] the eastern part of the United States.

east·ern·most \'ēst-rn-ˌmōst\ *adj.* Most eastern.

east·ward \'ēst-wərd\ *adv.* Toward the east. — *adj.* Going or facing eastward. — *n.* An eastward direction or part. — **east·ward·ly**, *adj.* or *adv.*

east·wards \'ēst-wərdz\ *adv.* Eastward.

easy \'ē-zē\ *adj.;* **eas·i·er**; **eas·i·est.** **1** Not hard to do or get; not difficult; as, an *easy* lesson. **2** Not hard to please; as, an *easy* teacher. **3** Comfortable; as, an *easy* chair. **4** Natural; showing ease; unaffected; as, an *easy* manner. **5** Free from pain, trouble, or worry; as, to feel *easy* in one's mind. **6** Unhurried; leisurely; as, to go along at an *easy* pace.

eas·y·go·ing \'ē-zē-'gō-ing\ *adj.* Taking life easily; carefree.

eat \'ēt\ *v.;* **ate** \'āt\; **eat·en** \'ēt-n\; **eat·ing.** **1** To take into the mouth and swallow food. **2** To chew and swallow; as, to *eat* and drink. **3** To take a meal or meals; as, to *eat* at home; to *eat* at six o'clock. **4** To destroy as if by eating; to wear away; as, rocks *eaten* away by waves. Rust *eats* away metal.

eat·a·ble \'ēt-əb-l\ *adj.* Safe or fit to eat; edible. — *n.* **1** Something that can be eaten. **2** [in the plural] Things to eat.

eaten. Past part. of *eat.*

eat·er \'ēt-r\ *n.* One that eats; as, a poor *eater* for such a big boy. Cats are greedy fish *eaters.*

eaves \'ēvz\ *n. pl.* The overhanging lower edge of a roof projecting beyond the wall of a building; as, icicles hanging from the *eaves.*

eaves

eaves·drop \'ēvz-ˌdräp\ *v.;* **eaves·dropped**; **eaves·drop·ping.** To listen secretly to what is being said in private. — **eaves·drop·per**, *n.*

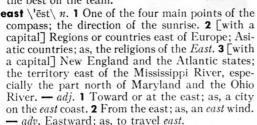

ebb \'eb\ *n.* **1** The flowing back from the shore of water brought in by the tide; as, the *ebb* and flow of the sea. **2** A passing from a high to a low point; a decline or a time of decline; as, a person whose fortunes are at an *ebb.* — *v.* **1** To recede from its flood state, as the tide toward the ocean. **2** To decline; to weaken; as, *ebbing* daylight; the *ebbing* strength of a dying soldier.

ebb tide. **1** The tide while ebbing. **2** A period or state of decline.

eb·on \'eb-n\ *adj.* Ebony.

eb·ony \'eb-n-ē\ *n.* **1** A hard, heavy, durable wood obtained from certain tropical trees. **2** A tree yielding this wood. — *adj.* **1** Made of ebony. **2** Like ebony in color; black.

ec·cen·tric \ik-'sen-trik, ek-\ *adj.* **1** Not having the same center; not concentric; as, *eccentric* circles. **2** Not following the line of a circle; elliptic; as, *eccentric* motion. **3** Acting or thinking in a strange way; behaving queerly; as, an *eccentric* person. **4** Queer; unusual; as, *eccentric* actions. — *n.* **1** An eccentric person. **2** A disklike device that turns around a point not at its center, used in machinery for changing circular motion into back-and-forth motion. — **ec·cen·tri·cal·ly** \-trik-l(-)ē\ *adv.*

ec·cen·tric·i·ty \ˌek-ˌsen-'tris-ət-ē, ˌeks-n-\ *n.; pl.* **ec·cen·tric·i·ties.** The condition of being eccentric; especially, peculiarity of thought or manner; oddity; queerness.

ec·cle·si·as·tic \ə-ˌklē-zē-'as-tik\ *adj.* Ecclesiastical. — *n.* A clergyman.

ec·cle·si·as·ti·cal \ə-ˌklē-zē-'as-tik-l\ *adj.* Of or relating to the church or its organization or government; as, *ecclesiastical* history; *ecclesiastical* affairs.

ech·e·lon \'esh-l-ˌän\ *n.* A subdivision of any arrangement consisting of or resembling a series of steps, as one of the levels of command or authority in a military or other organization, or one of the subdivisions of a military force arranged in order from front to rear; as, the forward *echelons* of an attacking army; the higher *echelons* of business and industry.

echid·na \ē-'kid-nə\ *n.* A toothless burrowing egg-laying mammal of Australia, somewhat like a hedgehog but with a tapering snout for eating ants.

echi·no·derm \ē-'kī-nə-ˌdərm\ *n.* Any of a group of sea animals with radially arranged body parts and often stony outer skeletons that move by hollow water-filled processes, as the starfishes or the sea urchins.

echo \'ek-ˌō\ *n.; pl.* **ech·oes.** **1** The repetition of a sound or of sounds already heard, caused by the reflection of the sound waves. **2** Any repetition, as of the style or opinions of another person or of a past event. **3** A person who echoes another. — *v.;* **ech·oed; ech·o·ing.** **1** To send back or repeat a sound. **2** To be repeated or heard again. The thunder of the cannonade *echoed* among the distant hills. **3** To repeat or imitate another person.

éclair \ā-'klar, -'kler; 'ā-ˌklar, -ˌkler\ *n.* A frosted oblong pastry shell filled with custard or whipped cream.

éclat \ā-'klä, -'klȧ\ *n.* **1** Brilliance, as of performance or achievement. **2** Conspicuous success. **3** Acclaim; applause.

eclipse \ē-'klips\ *n.* **1** A complete or partial darkening of the sun or the moon caused, when the sun is eclipsed, by the moon's passing between the sun and the earth, or, when the moon is eclipsed, by the moon's entering the shadow of the earth. **2** A dimming, darkening, or obscuring, especially when temporary; as, a statesman suffering an *eclipse* of his popularity. — *v.;* **eclipsed; eclips·ing.** **1** To cause an eclipse of. **2** To make appear less bright; to outshine; to surpass greatly; as, to *eclipse* all one's classmates in arithmetic.

eclip·tic \ē-'klip-tik\ *n.* The great circle that is the apparent path of the sun or of the earth considered as seen from the sun.

ecol·o·gy \ē-'käl-ə-jē\ *n.* Biology dealing with the interrelations between living things and their surroundings. — **ec·o·log·ic** \ˌek-l-'äj-ik, ˌēk-\ or **ec·o·log·i·cal** \-ik-l\ *adj.* — **ec·o·log·i·cal·ly** \-ik-l(-)ē\ *adv.* — **ecol·o·gist** \ē-'käl-ə-jəst\ *n.*

ec·o·nom·ic \ˌek-n-'äm-ik, ˌēk-\ *adj.* **1** Of or relating to the sources of wealth and its use; as, the *economic* condition of a country. **2** Of or relating to the science of economics; as, *economic* studies; *economic* theory. **3** Of or relating to the satisfaction of man's needs; as, *economic* botany.

ec·o·nom·i·cal \ˌek-n-'äm-ik-l, ˌēk-\ *adj.* **1** Economic. **2** Managing or managed without waste; careful in the use of money or goods; thrifty. — For synonyms see *frugal.*

ec·o·nom·i·cal·ly \ˌek-n-'äm-ik-l(-)ē, ˌēk-\ *adv.* **1** With respect to any economy or to economics; as, an *economically* sound foreign-trade policy. **2** In an economical way; without waste; as, to manage to spend a year abroad by living very *economically.*

ec·o·nom·ics \ˌek-n-'äm-iks, ˌēk-\ *n.* The science which studies and explains facts about wealth, its production, its distribution, and its use.

econ·o·mist \ē-'kän-ə-məst\ *n.* **1** One who economizes, especially skillfully; a thrifty manager. **2** A specialist in the science of economics.

econ·o·mize \ē-'kän-ə-ˌmīz\ *v.;* **econ·o·mized; econ·o·miz·ing.** **1** To be economical; to be thrifty. **2** To reduce expenses.

econ·o·my \ē-'kän-ə-mē\ *n.; pl.* **econ·o·mies.** **1** The management of affairs, as of a nation, a community, or a business, so as to keep down expenses while keeping up values, productiveness, and income; as, a national *economy* adapted to the needs of war. **2** Thrifty and frugal management in general; the careful use of money and goods; thrift. **3** Anything done to keep down expenses.

ec·ru \'ek-ˌrü, 'ā-ˌkrü\ *n.* The pale brown natural color of undyed wool; beige.

ec·sta·sy \'eks-tə-sē\ *n.; pl.* **ec·sta·sies.** **1** The condition of being beyond all reason and control, as from emotion. **2** A condition of great emotion, especially of joy or bliss.

ec·stat·ic \ek-'stat-ik\ *adj.* **1** In a state of ecstasy; full of joy and rapture. **2** Causing ecstasy. — **ec·stat·i·cal·ly** \-ik-l(-)ē\ *adv.*

ec·to·derm \'ek-tə-ˌdərm\ *n.* The outer layer of cells of an animal in the embryonic stage, from which develop the skin, nerves, and certain other structures.

ec·to·plasm \'ek-tə-ˌplaz-m\ *n.* In biology, an outer modified layer of the cytoplasm.

Ec·ua·dor·i·an \ˌek-wə-ˈdȯr-ē-ən\ *adj.* Of or relating to Ecuador. — *n.* A native or inhabitant of Ecuador.

ec·ze·ma \ig-ˈzē-mə, ˈeks-m-ə, ˈegz-m-ə\ *n.* A disease of the skin marked by redness, itching, and a breaking out of small blisters.

-ed *pronounced* d *when added to verbs ending in a vowel sound or in one of the sounds* b, g, j, l, m, n, ng, r, th, v, z, zh; *pronounced* t *when added to verbs ending in one of the sounds* ch, f, k, p, s, sh, th; *pronounced* əd *when added to verbs ending in one of the sounds* t, d; *also pronounced* əd *in certain other cases, as sometimes in poetry to make the meter right, or in some -ed words that are used like adjectives (examples: "a beloved son", "such accursed luck"), or often when -ly is added after -ed to make an adverb (example: "advisedly")*\. A suffix that can mean: **1** Possessed of, provided or furnished with, characterized by, as in *cultured* or *moneyed.* **2** Having the characteristics of, as in *bigoted* or *wretched.* ☞ The suffix *-ed* is used in forming the past tense and past participle of regular or weak verbs, as in "mended", "talked", "hedged", or "cried".

ed·dy \ˈed-ē\ *n.; pl.* **ed·dies.** A current of air or water running contrary to the main current; especially, a current moving in a circle, like a whirlpool. The leaves whirled around in *eddies* of the wind. — *v.;* **ed·died** \ˈed-ēd\; **ed·dy·ing.** To move in an eddy or so as to form an eddy. The stream *eddied* about a large rock.

eden·tate \ē-ˈden-ˌtāt\ *adj.* Without teeth. — *n.* Any of a group of mammals with the teeth lacking or imperfect, including the sloths, armadillos, and anteaters.

edge \ˈej\ *n.* [From Old English *ecg* meaning originally the edge or point of a sword, knife, or spear.] **1** The cutting side of a blade. **2** The outer side; the rim; the boundary line; the margin; as, the *edge* of a city; the *edge* of a wood. **3** Sharpness; keenness; as, the biting *edge* of sarcasm. **4** Any sharp terminating border; a line where something ceases to be; as, the *edge* of a page; the *edge* of a dish. — **on edge.** Eager; impatient; anxious. — For synonyms see *border.* — *v.;* **edged; edg·ing. 1** To give an edge to; as, to *edge* a knife; to *edge* a sleeve with lace. **2** To move along slowly and little by little. The boys *edged* their chairs closer.

edge·ways \ˈej-ˌwāz\ or **edge·wise** \-ˌwīz\ *adv.* **1** With the edge foremost; on, along, by, or with, the edge; sideways; as, to saw a board *edgeways.* **2** Barely; as if by an edge; as, unable to get a word in *edgeways.*

edg·ing \ˈej-ing\ *n.* A border; an edge, as of lace.

edgy \ˈej-ē\ *adj.;* **edg·i·er; edg·i·est. 1** Sharp; angular; disagreeably sharp in line; as, an *edgy* statue. **2** Being on edge; snappish; as, *edgy* nerves.

ed·i·ble \ˈed-əb-l\ *adj.* Fit or safe to eat; eatable.

edict \ˈē-(ˌ)dikt\ *n.* A command or law given or made by a ruler; a public notice or order issued by official authority; a decree.

ed·i·fice \ˈed-ə-fəs\ *n.* A building, especially a large, impressive building such as a church.

ed·i·fy \ˈed-ə-ˌfī\ *v.;* **ed·i·fied** \-ˌfīd\; **ed·i·fy·ing.** To instruct and improve, especially by good example; to benefit morally or spiritually; as, plays that *edify* the audience. — **ed·i·fi·ca·tion** \ˌed-ə-fə-ˈkāsh-n\ *n.*

ed·it \ˈed-ət\ *v.* **1** To correct, revise, and prepare for publication; to collect and arrange material to be printed; as, to *edit* a book of poems. **2** To be in charge of the publication of something, as an encyclopedia or a newspaper, that is the work of many writers. **3** To assemble and arrange for use or presentation, as a film or a tape recording.

edi·tion \ə-ˈdish-n, ē-\ *n.* **1** The whole number of copies of a book, magazine, or newspaper printed at one time; as, a first, second, or third *edition.* **2** The form in which a book is published; as, an illustrated *edition;* a pocket *edition.*

ed·i·tor \ˈed-ət-r\ *n.* **1** A person who edits, as a book or magazine. **2** A person who writes editorials. — **ed·i·tor·ship** \-ˌship\ *n.*

ed·i·to·ri·al \ˌed-ə-ˈtōr-ē-əl, -ˈtȯr-\ *adj.* Having to do with editors; as, an *editorial* staff. — *n.* A newspaper or magazine article giving the opinions of its editors or publishers. — **ed·i·to·ri·al·ly** \-ē-ə-lē\ *adv.*

editor in chief. An editor serving as the head of the entire editorial staff of a publication or a publishing house.

ed·u·ca·ble \ˈej-ə-kəb-l\ *adj.* Capable of being educated.

ed·u·cate \ˈej-ə-ˌkāt\ *v.;* **ed·u·cat·ed; ed·u·cat·ing. 1** To bring up, as young persons, by teaching or training; to instruct; to train. **2** To provide means and opportunity for education. — **ed·u·ca·tor** \-ˌkāt-r\ *n.*

ed·u·ca·tion \ˌej-ə-ˈkāsh-n\ *n.* **1** The act or process of educating; schooling; training through study or instruction. **2** Knowledge, skill, and development gained from study or training. **3** The study or science of the methods and problems of teaching.

— The word *training* is a synonym of *education: education* is a general term for schooling of any kind, but is applied especially to development of the mind in an institution of learning; *training* generally indicates exercise or practice in order to gain skill, endurance, or facility.

ed·u·ca·tion·al \ˌej-ə-ˈkāsh-n(-)əl\ *adj.* **1** Having to do with education. **2** Offering information or something of value in learning; as, an *educational* moving picture.

ed·u·ca·tive \ˈej-ə-ˌkāt-iv, -kət-iv\ *adj.* Tending to educate.

educe \ē-ˈdüs, -ˈdyüs\ *v.;* **educed; educ·ing.** To draw out; to bring out; to elicit. The questioning *educed* some surprising answers.

-ee \ˈē, ˌē\. A suffix that can mean: the one to whom an act is done, the one on whom a right is conferred, as in *payee.*

eel \ˈēl\ *n.; pl.* **eels** or **eel.** A snakelike fish having a smooth slimy skin, often without scales, and no pelvic fins.

eel·grass \'ēl-ˌgras\ *n.* A plant that grows underwater and has long ribbonlike leaves.

eel·pout \'ēl-ˌpau̇t\ *n.; pl.* **eel·pout** or **eel·pouts.** **1** Any of various elongated sea fishes having a pointed tail and a fin continuing down the back, around the tail, and up the under surface nearly to the middle of the body. **2** A freshwater fish closely related to the true codfish.

e'en \'ēn\ *adv.* A contraction of *even.*

-eer \'ir\. A suffix that can mean: one concerned with, one who conducts or produces professionally, as in *auctioneer* or *engineer.*

e'er \'er\ *adv.* A contraction of *ever.*

ee·rie or **ee·ry** \'ir-ē\ *adj.* Arousing fear, especially fear of ghosts; weird; uncanny. The swaying lantern cast *eerie* shadows on the wall. — **ee·ri·ly** \-ə-lē\ *adv.*

ef-. A form of the prefix *ex-* used before *f.*

ef·face \ə-'fās\ *v.;* **ef·faced; ef·fac·ing.** To erase or blot out completely; to destroy as if by rubbing out; as, to *efface* an inscription; to *efface* unpleasant memories. — For synonyms see *erase.* — **ef·face·ment** \-mənt\ *n.*

ef·fect \ə-'fekt\ *n.* **1** An event, condition, or state of affairs that is produced by a cause; the result of something that has been done or has happened; outcome. The victory was the *effect* of good team play. **2** Fulfillment; execution; performance. The law went into *effect* today. **3** Reality; fact; as, an excuse that was in *effect* a plain refusal. **4** The act of making a particular impression; as, to talk for *effect.* **5** Influence; as, the *effect* of climate on growth. **6** [in the plural] Goods; possessions; as, household *effects.* — *v.* To bring about; to accomplish; as, to *effect* one's purpose. — For synonyms see *accomplish.* — **ef·fect·er,** *n.*

ef·fec·tive \ə-'fek-tiv\ *adj.* **1** Producing an effect; likely to bring about a desired result; as, *effective* measures to reduce traffic accidents. **2** Impressive; striking; as, an *effective* speech; an *effective* speaker. **3** Put into actual operation; in force. The new law will not become *effective* for two months. **4** Ready for service or action, as troops or warships. — *n.* One trained, equipped, and ready for service, as in war. — **ef·fec·tive·ly,** *adv.*

ef·fec·tor \ə-'fekt-r\ *n.* One that effects; an effecter; especially, an organ, as a muscle or a gland, that responds to a nerve impulse.

ef·fec·tu·al \ə-'fek-chə-wəl, -chəl\ *adj.* Producing or able to produce a desired effect; as, an *effectual* remedy; an *effectual* plan for traffic control. — **ef·fec·tu·al·ly** \-chə-lē, -chə-wə-lē\ *adv.*

ef·fem·i·nate \ə-'fem-ə-nət\ *adj.* Having unsuitable womanlike qualities; lacking in manliness; especially, marked by weakness and love of ease. — **ef·fem·i·na·cy** \-nə-sē\ *n.*

ef·fer·ent \'ef-r-ənt\ *adj.* Bearing or leading out or away from a part or an organ; as, *efferent* nerves.

ef·fer·vesce \ˌef-r-'ves\ *v.;* **ef·fer·vesced; ef·fer·vesc·ing.** **1** To bubble, hiss, and foam, as ginger ale. **2** To show liveliness and happy excitement; to be gay and boisterous. — **ef·fer·ves·cence** \-'ves-n(t)s\ *n.* — **ef·fer·ves·cent** \-nt\ *adj.*

ef·fete \e-'fēt, ə-\ *adj.* No longer productive; worn out; exhausted; as, an *effete* civilization; a once mighty empire now become *effete.*

ef·fi·ca·cious \ˌef-ə-'kā-shəs\ *adj.* Having efficacy; producing or able to produce a desired result; as, a new medicine which proved to be less *efficacious* than was expected. — **ef·fi·ca·cious·ly,** *adv.*

ef·fi·ca·cy \'ef-ə-kə-sē\ *n.; pl.* **ef·fi·ca·cies.** Power to produce effects; efficient action; as, a medicine of well-tested *efficacy.*

ef·fi·cien·cy \ə-'fish-n-sē\ *n.; pl.* **ef·fi·cien·cies.** The quality or the degree of being efficient; the ability to do things well, capably, and with the least possible waste of time and effort. *Efficiency* is valuable in men and machines.

ef·fi·cient \ə-'fish-nt\ *adj.* Fully capable of accomplishing what is undertaken; effective in operation; competent; capable; as, an *efficient* machine; workers who are both *efficient* and industrious. — **ef·fi·cient·ly,** *adv.*

ef·fi·gy \'ef-ə-jē\ *n.; pl.* **ef·fi·gies.** **1** An image or other likeness of a person, especially one sculptured on a tomb or a monument. **2** A figure understood to be a representation of a person, usually one disliked or hated; as, a cruel landlord hanged in *effigy* by his tenants.

ef·fort \'ef-rt, -ˌȯrt\ *n.* **1** Hard work of mind or body. Success is seldom won without *effort.* **2** An attempt; a try; an endeavor; a product of exertion; as, a literary *effort.* After several *efforts* to reach the mountaintop, the climbers succeeded.

ef·fort·less \'ef-rt-ləs\ *adj.* Showing little or no effort; easy; smooth. — **ef·fort·less·ly,** *adv.*

ef·fron·tery \ə-'frənt-r-ē\ *n.; pl.* **ef·fron·ter·ies.** Shameless impudence; insulting boldness. The thieves had the *effrontery* to deny their guilt.

ef·ful·gent \e-'fəlj-nt\ *adj.* Shining forth brilliantly; radiant; as, the *effulgent* light of the sun. — **ef·ful·gence** \-n(t)s\ *n.*

ef·fu·sion \ə-'fyüzh-n\ *n.* A pouring out; a gushing forth, as of escaping liquid; especially, an unrestrained flow of words.

ef·fu·sive \ə-'fyü-siv, -ziv\ *adj.* **1** Pouring out freely, as water. **2** Demonstrative beyond what is called for or expected; gushing; as, to be embarrassed by a stranger's *effusive* thanks for a trifling favor. — **ef·fu·sive·ly,** *adv.*

eft \'eft\ *n.* A lizard.

eft·soons \eft-'sünz\ or **eft·soon** \-'sün\ *adv. Archaic.* **1** Again; also; soon afterward. **2** Often.

e.g. \'ē-'jē *or* fər ig-'zamp-l\. [Abbreviated from Latin *exempli gratia* meaning "for the sake of example".] For example.

egg \'eg\ *v.* [From medieval English *eggen,* there borrowed from Old Norse *eggja* meaning literally "to sharpen", derived from *egg* "edge of a sword", a word akin to Old English *ecg* — see *edge.*] To urge; to encourage; to incite; as, to *egg* the boys on to fight.

egg \'eg\ *n.* [From medieval English *egge*, there borrowed from Old Norse *egg*.] **1** An oval or rounded body enclosed in a shell or tough membrane, which is laid by birds and some reptiles and from which, after a time, the young hatches out. **2** A corresponding body, often without an enclosing membrane, produced by lower animals, as fishes, lobsters, crabs, and insects. **3** Also **egg cell.** A female germ cell. **4** Something like an egg, as in shape.

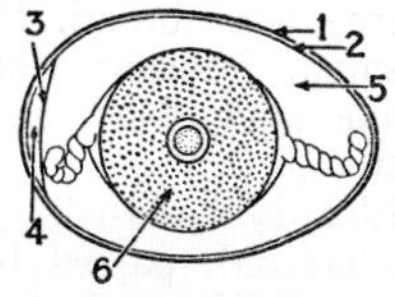

diagram of hen's egg, showing: *1* shell; *2, 3* membrane enclosing air space, *4; 5* albumen or white; *6* yolk

egg·head \'eg-ˌhed\ *n. Slang.* A highbrow.

egg·nog \'eg-ˌnäg\ *n.* A drink made of eggs beaten with sugar, milk, and, often, an alcoholic liquor.

egg·plant \'eg-ˌplant\ *n.* **1** An egg-shaped vegetable with a glossy purplish surface and a white inside. **2** The plant, of the potato family, that bears this vegetable.

egg·shell \'eg-ˌshel\ *n.* The shell of an egg. — *adj.* **1** Having the thin and fragile quality of an eggshell; as, *eggshell* china. **2** Having the slightly glossy appearance of an eggshell; as, *eggshell* enamel.

eg·lan·tine \'eg-lən-ˌtīn, 'eg-lən-ˌtēn\ *n.* The sweetbrier.

ego \'ē-ˌgō, 'eg-ˌō\ *n.; pl.* **egos. 1** One's self; oneself as a person. **2** A deep interest in oneself; conceit.

ego·ism \'ē-gə-ˌwiz-m, 'eg-ə-\ *n.* **1** Excessive interest in oneself; a self-centered attitude. **2** Egotism.

ego·ist \'ē-gə-wəst, 'eg-ə-\ *n.* A person whose chief interest is himself; a self-centered person. — **ego·is·tic** \ˌē-gə-'wis-tik, ˌeg-ə-\ *adj.* — **ego·is·ti·cal·ly** \-tik-l(-)ē\ *adv.*

ego·tism \'ē-gə-ˌtiz-m, 'eg-ə-\ *n.* **1** Too frequent reference to oneself, especially by use of the word *I;* conceit. **2** Egoism.

ego·tist \'ē-gə-təst, 'eg-ə-\ *n.* A conceited person. — **ego·tis·tic** \ˌē-gə-'tis-tik, ˌeg-ə-\ or **ego·tis·ti·cal** \-tik-l\ *adj.*

egre·gious \ē-'grē-jəs, -jē-əs\ *adj.* [From Latin *egregius* meaning "distinguished", "eminent", literally "apart from the herd".] Remarkable for bad quality; shocking; gross; as, *egregious* errors.

egress \'ē-ˌgres\ *n.* **1** A going out; a leaving; as, to forbid *egress* from the room before the examination is finished. **2** A way out; an exit; as, an entanglement from which there was no *egress.*

egret \'ē-grət, ē-'gret, 'ē-ˌgret, 'eg-rət\ *n.* Any of various herons which, during the breeding season, have long plumes that are commercially called *aigrettes.*

Egyp·tian \ē-'jipsh-n\ *adj.* Of or relating to Egypt or the Egyptians. — *n.* **1** A native of Egypt. **2** The language of the ancient Egyptians. **3** A gypsy.

ei·der \'īd-r\ *n.* **1** A large northern sea duck, mostly white above and black below, with very soft down — called also **eider duck. 2** Eiderdown.

ei·der·down \'īd-r-ˌdau̇n\ *n.* **1** The down of the eider, used for filling quilts and pillows. **2** A quilt padded with down.

eight \'āt\ *adj.* One more than seven; as, *eight* years. — *n.* **1** The sum of seven and one; two times four; eight units or objects. **2** The figure standing for eight units, as 8 or VIII.

eight·een \'ā(t)-'tēn\ *adj.* Eight and ten; one more than seventeen. — *n.* **1** The sum of ten and eight; eighteen units or objects. **2** The figure standing for eighteen units, as 18 or XVIII.

eight·eenth \'ā(t)-'tēn(t)th\ *adj.* Next after the seventeenth. — *n.; pl.* **eight·eenths** \-'tēn(t)s, -'tēn(t)ths\. One of eighteen equal parts.

eighth \'ātth\ *adj.* Next after the seventh. — *n.; pl.* **eighths** \'āt(th)s\. One of eight equal parts.

eight·i·eth \'āt-ē-əth\ *adj.* Next after the seventy-ninth. — *n.* One of eighty equal parts.

eighty \'āt-ē\ *adj.* Eight times ten; one more than seventy-nine. — *n.; pl.* **eight·ies. 1** The sum of eight tens; eighty units or objects. **2** The figure standing for eighty units, as 80 or LXXX.

ei·kon \'ī-ˌkän\ *n.* An icon.

ei·ther \'ēth-r, 'īth-r\ *adj.* **1** Each of two; one and the other; as, kissed on *either* cheek. **2** One or the other. The lake can be reached by *either* road. — *pron.* The one or the other. The boy looked at two footballs in the store but didn't buy *either.* — *conj.* According to one choice or possibility. The statement is *either* true or false — used as a connecting word before two words or groups of words that offer a choice. — *adv.* Any more truly; as, not wise or handsome *either.*

ejac·u·late \ē-'jak-yə-ˌlāt\ *v.;* **ejac·u·lat·ed; ejac·u·lat·ing.** To throw forth, as an exclamation; to say or speak with startling suddenness; to exclaim.

ejac·u·la·tion \ē-ˌjak-yə-'lāsh-n\ *n.* An ejaculated utterance, as a short, sudden exclamation.

eject \ē-'jekt\ *v.* **1** To throw forth or out. A blowtorch *ejects* a hot flame from a nozzle. **2** To drive or cast out; to expel; as, to *eject* a disorderly person from a meeting; to have a tenant *ejected* for nonpayment of rent.

ejec·tion \ē-'jeksh-n\ *n.* **1** The act of ejecting or the state of being ejected. **2** Ejected matter, as from a volcano.

eke \'ēk\ *v.;* **eked; ek·ing.** [used with *out*] **1** To piece out or add to bit by bit. The woman *eked* out her small income by sewing for neighbors. **2** To provide by scanty means; as, to be barely able to *eke* out a living.

elab·o·rate \i-'lab-r(-)ət\ *adj.* Worked out with great care or with much detail; as, to make *elaborate* preparations for a party; a piece of satin with a very *elaborate* design. — \-r-ˌāt\ *v.;* **elab·o·rat·ed; elab·o·rat·ing. 1** To work out in careful detail; to develop fully; as, to *elaborate* a preliminary sketch of a house into a fully developed building plan. **2** To work, write, or speak in great or in additional detail; as, to *elaborate* upon a story every time one tells it. — **elab·o·rate·ly** \-r(-)ət-lē\ *adv.* — **elab·o·ra·tor** \-r-ˌāt-r\ *n.*

elab·o·ra·tion \i-ˌlab-r-'āsh-n\ *n.* **1** The action or process of elaborating; as, to approve a plan in principle but send it back for further *elaboration.* **2** The state of being elaborated or elaborate; elaborateness. **3** Something that is added; a detail that elaborates or is the product of elaborating; as, to accept an architect's basic plan but reject certain *elaborations.*

eland \'ē-lənd, -ˌland\ *n.* Either of two large African oxlike antelopes with short horns twisted into spirals.

elapse \i-'laps\ *v.;* **elapsed**; **elaps·ing**. To slip or glide away; to go by; to pass. Ten days *elapsed* before another message came.

elas·mo·branch \i-'laz-mə-ˌbrangk\ *adj.* Of or belonging to a class of fishes, including the sharks and rays, having the skeleton wholly composed of cartilage and having thin platelike gills. — *n.* An elasmobranch fish.

elas·tic \i-'las-tik\ *adj.* **1** Capable of returning to its original shape or size after being stretched, pressed, or squeezed together; springy. Rubber is *elastic.* **2** Able to recover quickly, as from depression or fatigue; as, to be blessed with *elastic* spirits. **3** Flexible; adaptable; as, a plan *elastic* enough to be changed at any time. — *n.* **1** Fabric made elastic by rubber woven into it; a piece of such fabric. **2** A rubber band.

elas·tic·i·ty \i-ˌlas-'tis-ət-ē, ˌē-\ *n.* The quality or condition of being elastic. Old rubber loses its *elasticity.*

elate \i-'lāt\ *v.;* **elat·ed**; **elat·ing**. To fill with joy and pride; as, to be *elated* by news of a victory.

elat·ed \i-'lāt-əd\ *adj.* In high spirits. — **elat·ed·ly,** *adv.*

ela·tion \i-'lāsh-n\ *n.* A feeling of joy and satisfaction or of buoyant cheer brought about by success or by the confidence of success; high spirits; as, the natural *elation* of a victor.

el·bow \'el-ˌbō\ *n.* **1** The joint of the arm; the outer curve of a bent arm. **2** A corresponding joint in the front limb of an animal. **3** A turn or bend like that of an elbow; as, an *elbow* in a pipe. — *v.* To push with or as if with the elbows; to force a passage by such pushing; to jostle; as, to *elbow* one's way through a crowd of onlookers.

elbow

el·bow·room \'el-ˌbō-ˌrüm, -ˌrům\ *n.* Room to extend the elbows on each side; enough room for motion or action.

eld \'eld\ *n.* **1** *Dial.* Old age. **2** *Archaic.* Old times; days long gone by; antiquity.

eld·er \'eld-r\ *adj.* Older; as, an *elder* brother. — *n.* **1** A person who is older; a senior. **2** A person who because of his age occupies a position of dignity or authority; as, the village *elders.* **3** An official in certain churches chosen for special duties in keeping with his age and experience.

el·der·ber·ry \'eld-r-ˌber-ē\ *n.; pl.* **el·der·ber·ries.** **1** Also **el·der** \'eld-r\. A bush or tree with broad, flat clusters of small, fragrant white flowers. **2** The juicy black or red fruit of this tree or bush.

elderberries

eld·er·ly \'eld-r-lē\ *adj.* **1** Somewhat old; passed beyond middle age. **2** Of or relating to later life; as, *elderly* pursuits. — For synonyms see *old.*

eld·est \'el-dəst\ *adj.* Oldest; as, the *eldest* son.

elect \i-'lekt\ *v.* **1** To choose; to decide by choosing; as, to *elect* to spend one's vacation in the mountains; to *elect* French as a foreign-language course rather than German or Spanish. **2** To select by voting; as, to *elect* a class president. — *adj.* Chosen; elected but not yet holding office; as, the president-*elect.*

elec·tion \i-'leksh-n\ *n.* An electing; especially, the process of voting to choose a person to hold some office.

elec·tion·eer \i-ˌleksh-n-'ir\ *v.* To work in the interest of a candidate or party in an election.

elec·tive \i-'lek-tiv\ *adj.* **1** Chosen by election; as, an *elective* official. **2** Filled by a person who is elected, not appointed. The presidency is an *elective* office. **3** Followed or taken by choice; not specifically required; as, to study three required subjects and one *elective* subject. — *n.* A subject or course which a student may choose for study.

elec·tor \i-'lekt-r\ *n.* **1** A person who has the right to vote in an election. **2** One of the persons chosen by the vote of the people to an electoral college.

elec·tor·al \i-'lekt-r(-)əl\ *adj.* Of or relating to an election or electors.

electoral college. A body of electors chosen by vote of the people whose function is to elect, formally and officially, the president and vice-president of the United States.

elec·tor·ate \i-'lekt-r(-)ət\ *n.* The whole body of persons having the right to vote in an election.

elec·tric \i-'lek-trik\ or **elec·tri·cal** \-trik-l\ *adj.* [From scientific Latin *electricus,* derived from Latin *electrum* meaning "amber" there borrowed from Greek *elektron;* so called from the fact that the phenomenon of static electricity was first observed in amber, which was thought to be its source.] **1** Of electricity; having to do with electricity or its use; as, an *electric* current; *electrical* engineering. **2** Heated, moved, or operated by electricity; as, an *electric* iron; an *electric* locomotive; *electrical* appliances. **3** Produced by electricity; as, *electric* light; an *electric* shock. **4** Having an effect like that of an electric shock; thrilling. The speaker addressed the audience with an *electric* eloquence. — **elec·tri·cal·ly** \-trik-l(-)ē\ *adv.*

electric charge. A quantity of electricity.

electric eel. A South American eel-shaped fish capable of giving severe electric shocks.

elec·tri·cian \i-ˌlek-'trish-n\ *n.* A

up or looks after electric systems or who makes or repairs electric instruments and machinery.

elec·tric·i·ty \i-ˌlek-'tris-ət-ē\ *n.* An important source of energy that is found in nature but can be artificially produced by rubbing together two unlike things such as glass and silk, by chemical action, or by means of a generator.

elec·tri·fy \i-'lek-trə-ˌfī\ *v.;* **elec·tri·fied** \-ˌfīd\; **elec·tri·fy·ing.** **1** To charge with electricity. **2** To equip for use of electric power; as, to *electrify* a railroad. **3** To excite suddenly; to thrill. The announcement *electrified* the audience. — **elec·tri·fi·ca·tion** \i-ˌlek-trə-fə-'kāsh-n\ *n.*

electro-. A prefix meaning: electric, electricity.

elec·tro·car·di·o·gram \i-'lek-trō-'kärd-ē-ə-ˌgram, -'kȧrd-\ *n.* A photographic record of the heart's action, made by an electrocardiograph.

elec·tro·car·di·o·graph \i-'lek-trō-'kärd-ē-ə-ˌgraf, -'kȧrd-\ *n.* An instrument for recording electrical changes occurring during the heartbeat.

elec·tro·cute \i-'lek-trə-ˌkyüt\ *v.;* **elec·tro·cut·ed**; **elec·tro·cut·ing.** To kill by electric shock. — **elec·tro·cu·tion** \i-ˌlek-trə-'kyüsh-n\ *n.*

elec·trode \i-'lek-ˌtrōd\ *n.* Either terminal of an electric source; especially, either conductor by which the current enters or leaves an electrolyte.

elec·trol·y·sis \i-ˌlek-'träl-ə-səs\ *n.* **1** Production of chemical changes by passage of electric current through an electrolyte with ions carrying current to the electrodes where they may form new substances deposited as metals or freed as gases. **2** Destruction of hair roots by electric current.

elec·tro·lyte \i-'lek-trō-ˌlīt\ *n.* A liquid conductor containing charged particles, called *ions,* through which an electric current can be passed with a resulting liberation of matter at the electrodes either in the form of a gas or a solid.

elec·tro·lyt·ic \i-ˌlek-trō-'lit-ik\ or **elec·tro·lyt·i·cal** \-ik-l\ *adj.* Relating to electrolysis or an electrolyte.

elec·tro·mag·net \i-'lek-trō-'mag-nət\ *n.* A core of magnetic material, as soft iron, surrounded by a coil of wire through which an electric current is passed to magnetize the core.

electromagnetic wave. A wave, as a radio wave or wave of light, that consists of an associated electrical and magnetic effect and travels at the speed of light.

elec·tro·mag·net·ism \i-'lek-trō-'mag-nə-ˌtiz-m\ *n.* Magnetism developed by a current of electricity. — **elec·tro·mag·net·ic** \-ˌmag-'net-ik\ *adj.*

elec·tro·mo·tive \i-ˌlek-trō-'mōt-iv\ *adj.* Relating to motion of electricity; produced by electricity; producing an electric current or effect.

elec·tron \i-'lek-ˌträn\ *n.* A very small charge of negative electricity forming one part of an atom.

electron gun. A vacuum tube that contains a heated filament for giving off electrons, as well as agents for increasing their speed and guiding them into a narrow stream.

elec·tron·ics \i-ˌlek-'trän-iks\ *n.* The science that deals with such things as vacuum tubes, radar, radio, and television; the branch of physics that is concerned with electrons. — **elec·tron·ic** \-ik\ *adj.* — **elec·tron·i·cal·ly** \-ik-l(-)ē\ *adv.*

electron microscope. An instrument in which a beam of electrons is used to produce an enlarged image of a minute object in a way similar to that in which light is used to form the image in an ordinary microscope.

electron tube. A device in which a current of electrons is used to amplify electrical energy, to convert alternating current to direct current or vice versa, or for other electrical purposes.

elec·tro·plate \i-'lek-trō-ˌplāt\ *v.;* **elec·tro·plat·ed**; **elec·tro·plat·ing.** To cover with a coating, as of metal or rubber, by means of electrolysis.

elec·tro·type \i-'lek-trō-ˌtīp\ *n.* **1** A plate for use in printing, made by making a mold of the matter to be printed, covering this mold with a thin shell of metal by electrolysis, and putting on a backing of heavy metal. **2** A print made from such a plate.

el·e·gance \'el-ə-gən(t)s\ *n.* Tasteful richness; great refinement; as, *elegance* in dress.

el·e·gant \'el-ə-gənt\ *adj.* **1** Showing good taste, as in dress or manners; marked by beauty and refinement; as, a room with *elegant* furnishings. **2** Very good; excellent. — **el·e·gant·ly,** *adv.*

el·e·gy \'el-ə-jē\ *n.; pl.* **el·e·gies.** **1** A poem expressing sorrow for the dead; a funeral poem. **2** Any poem that is sad and mournful in spirit. — **el·e·gi·ac** \ˌel-ə-'jī-ək, i-'lē-jē-ˌak\ or **el·e·gi·a·cal** \ˌel-ə-'jī-ək-l\ *adj.*

el·e·ment \'el-ə-mənt\ *n.* **1** One of the substances or principles, fire, air, water, and earth, formerly believed to make up the physical universe. **2** One of the constituent parts of which something is made up; as, a story in which there was not a single *element* of truth. Protein and fat are *elements* of milk. **3** A substance that cannot be separated by ordinary chemical means into simpler substances. Gold and silver are chemical *elements.* **4** One of the simplest principles of a study; something that must be learned before one can advance; as, the *elements* of arithmetic. **5** [in the plural] The forces of nature; especially, wind and bad weather; as, a ship battling the *elements.* **6** [in the plural] The bread and wine used in the sacrament of Communion. **7** Also **heat·ing element.** The active or heating part of an electrical device, as of an electric iron or stove.

el·e·men·tal \ˌel-ə-'ment-l\ *adj.* **1** Of or relating to the four elements of the ancients, fire, air, water, and earth, or one of them. **2** Of or relating to the forces of nature in general. **3** In chemistry, uncombined; simple. **4** Elementary; fundamental. **5** Forming a constituent part; being an element of or in.

el·e·men·ta·ry \ˌel-ə-'ment-r-ē, -'men-trē\ *adj.* Relating to, or treating of, the beginnings or first stages or principles of anything; as, an *elementary* school; *elementary* arithmetic.

el·e·phant \'el-ə-fənt\ *n.* A huge, thickset, nearly hairless animal having a very long snout, or trunk, and two incisors in the upper jaw developed into long outward-curving pointed tusks, which furnish ivory.

elephant

el·e·phan·tine \ˌel-ə-'fan-ˌtīn, -ˌtēn\ *adj.* Of, like, or suited to the elephant; huge; ponderous; ungainly; as, an *elephantine* walk; a man of *elephantine* build.

el·e·vate \'el-ə-ˌvāt\ *v.;* **el·e·vat·ed; el·e·vat·ing. 1** To lift up; to raise. **2** To raise in rank or station; as, *elevated* to the presidency by the vote of the people. **3** To raise in loudness or pitch; as, to *elevate* one's voice almost to a shout. **4** To raise in moral or intellectual level; as, books that *elevate* the mind. — For synonyms see *raise.*

el·e·vat·ed \'el-ə-ˌvāt-əd\ *adj.* **1** Lifted up; raised. **2** On a high moral or intellectual plane. — *n.* An elevated railroad.

elevated railroad or **elevated railway.** A railroad supported by a structure of trestles and girders high enough to permit movement of traffic underneath, usually electrically operated and forming part of the transportation system of a city.

el·e·va·tion \ˌel-ə-'vāsh-n\ *n.* **1** The act of elevating or the condition of being elevated. **2** A height; a raised place, as a hill. **3** Height above sea level. The *elevation* of the hill was 1500 feet. **4** Height above the earth's surface; altitude. **5** A drawing, as of a building, that shows the vertical or upright parts; as, a sketch of the front *elevation* of a house. — For synonyms see *height.*

el·e·va·tor \'el-ə-ˌvāt-r\ *n.* **1** A cage or platform, as in a building or a mine, which can be raised or lowered for carrying persons or goods from one level to another. **2** An endless belt or chain conveyer for raising material. **3** A building for storing grain. **4** A device on an airplane for producing motion up or down, as in climbing and diving.

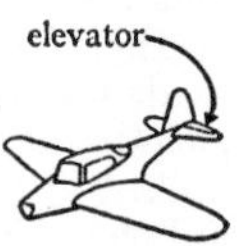

elev·en \ə-'lev-n\ *adj.* One more than ten. — *n.* **1** The sum of ten and one; eleven units or objects. **2** The figure standing for eleven units, as 11 or XI.

elev·enth \ə-'lev-n(t)th\ *adj.* Next after the tenth. — *n.; pl.* **elev·enths** \-n(t)s, -n(t)ths\. One of eleven equal parts.

elf \'elf\ *n.; pl.* **elves** \'elvz\. A tiny, often mischievous, fairy or sprite.

elf·in \'elf-n\ *adj.* **1** Of or relating to elves. **2** Resembling elves or an elf; especially, having a strange beauty or charm; as, *elfin* music.

elf·ish \'el-fish\ *adj.* **1** Elflike; elfin. **2** Mischievous; impish; as, an *elfish* prank. — **elf·ish·ly,** *adv.*

elic·it \ē-'lis-ət, i-\ *v.* To draw forth or bring out something not yet known or told, as by skillful questioning or discussion; as, to *elicit* the truth from an unwilling witness.

el·i·gi·bil·i·ty \ˌel-ə-jə-'bil-ət-ē\ *n.* The quality or state of being eligible; fitness; qualification.

el·i·gi·ble \'el-ə-jəb-l\ *adj.* Fitted or qualified to be chosen; satisfying all requirements. Only a native-born citizen is *eligible* to be president of the United States. — *n.* One who is eligible. — **el·i·gi·bly** \-jə-blē\ *adv.*

elim·i·nate \i-'lim-ə-ˌnāt\ *v.;* **elim·i·nat·ed; elim·i·nat·ing. 1** To get rid of; to remove; to do away with; as, to *eliminate* the causes of an epidemic disease; to recopy a composition in order to *eliminate* all mistakes in spelling. **2** To expel from the system; to excrete; as, to *eliminate* waste from the body.

elim·i·na·tion \i-ˌlim-ə-'nāsh-n\ *n.* **1** The act or process of eliminating. **2** The discharging or excreting of waste matter from the body.

elite \ā-'lēt\ *n.* The choice or select part of any body of persons; especially, a group of people considered to be socially superior.

elix·ir \i-'liks-r\ *n.* **1** A magic substance believed by the alchemists to have the power of changing common metals into gold. **2** A magic substance once believed to have the power of prolonging life indefinitely; any marvelous remedy. **3** A preparation, as a medicine, containing various substances held in solution in alcohol. **4** The refined spirit of something; an essence.

elk \'elk\ *n.* **1** A large deer of Europe and Asia with broad spreading antlers like those of a moose. **2** A large North American deer with curved antlers having many branches.

ell \'el\ *n.* An old measure of length, 45 inches in England and 37 inches in Scotland, used chiefly for cloth.

ell \'el\ *n.* An extension or addition to a house built at right angles to the main part.

el·lipse \i-'lips\ *n.; pl.* **el·lips·es** \-'lip-səz\. A closed curve of an oval shape.

el·lip·sis \i-'lip-səs\ *n.; pl.* **el·lip·ses** \-ˌsēz\. The omission from an expression of a word or words clearly understood in sense, as of an understood *am* from the expression "older than I".

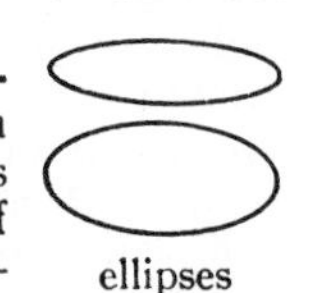
ellipses

el·lip·tic \i-'lip-tik\ or **el·lip·ti·cal** \-tik-l\ *adj.* **1** Of or like an ellipse; oval. **2** Relating to ellipsis; having a part omitted. — **el·lip·ti·cal·ly** \-tik-l(-)ē\ *adv.*

elm \'elm\ *n.* **1** A tall shade tree with a broad rather flat top and spreading branches, toothed leaves, and nearly circular one-seeded winged fruits. **2** The hard, tough wood of this tree.

American elm leaves

el·o·cu·tion \ˌel-ə-'kyüsh-n\ *n.* **1** A style or manner of speaking or reading in public. **2** The art of reading or speaking effectively, especially in public. — **el·o·cu·tion·ary** \-ˌer-ē\ *adj.*

el·o·cu·tion·ist \ˌel-ə-ˈkyüsh-n(-)əst\ *n.* One who is skilled in elocution.

elon·gate \i-ˈlȯng-ˌgāt\ *v.;* **elon·gat·ed; elon·gat·ing.** To lengthen; to extend; as, to *elongate* a line; an *elongated* tooth.

elon·ga·tion \ˌē-ˌlȯng-ˈgāsh-n\ *n.* **1** A lengthening; an extending. **2** Something that lengthens out; a continuation, as of a line.

elope \i-ˈlōp\ *v.;* **eloped; elop·ing. 1** To run away from husband, wife, or home with a lover. **2** To depart secretly; to slip away. — **elope·ment** \-mənt\ *n.*

el·o·quence \ˈel-ə-kwən(t)s\ *n.* **1** Speaking or writing that has force and ease. **2** The art or power of using such a manner of speaking or writing; as, a man of great *eloquence.*

el·o·quent \ˈel-ə-kwənt\ *adj.* **1** Expressing oneself, or expressed, with ease and force; as, an *eloquent* speaker or speech. **2** Movingly expressive or revealing; as, an *eloquent* look. — **el·o·quent·ly,** *adv.*

else \ˈels\ *adj.* Other and in addition; other and different; as, to have something *else* to say; to ask somebody else. — *adv.* At or to what other place; at what other time; in a different manner or respect. When or where *else* but here and now? How *else* could it have been done? — *conj.* If not; otherwise.

else·where \ˈels-ˌhwer\ *adv.* In or to another place.

elu·ci·date \i-ˈlü-sə-ˌdāt\ *v.;* **elu·ci·dat·ed; elu·ci·dat·ing.** To make clear or plain; to explain; as, to *elucidate* a theory. — **elu·ci·da·tion** \i-ˌlü-sə-ˈdāsh-n\ *n.*

elude \ē-ˈlüd\ *v.;* **elud·ed; elud·ing.** To avoid or escape by being quick, skillful, or tricky; to evade; as, to *elude* a blow; to *elude* the police.

elu·sive \ē-ˈlü-siv, -ziv\ *adj.* **1** Tending to elude; evasive; especially, eluding mental grasp; as, an *elusive* reply. **2** Hard to comprehend or to define; as, an *elusive* idea. — **elu·sive·ly,** *adv.*

elu·so·ry \ē-ˈlüs-r-ē\ *adj.* Elusive.

elves. Pl. of *elf.*

elv·ish \ˈel-vish\ *adj.* Elfish; mischievous.

Ely·si·um \ē-ˈliz(h)-ē-əm\ *n.* [From *Elysium* (Greek *Elysion*), in Greek mythology a paradise for certain favored souls after death, originally depicted as fields or islands at the ends of the earth.] Any place or condition of ideal happiness; paradise. — **Ely·sian** \ē-ˈlizh-n\ *adj.*

em-. A form of *en-* used before *b, p,* or *m,* as in *embroil.*

ema·ci·ate \ē-ˈmā-shē-ˌāt\ *v.;* **ema·ci·at·ed; ema·ci·at·ing.** To cause to lose flesh so as to become thin; as, *emaciated* by illness. — **ema·ci·a·tion** \ē-ˌmā-s(h)ē-ˈāsh-n\ *n.*

em·a·nate \ˈem-ə-ˌnāt\ *v.;* **em·a·nat·ed; em·a·nat·ing.** To come out from a source; to flow; to arise; to send forth; as, the fragrance *emanating* from flowers.

em·a·na·tion \ˌem-ə-ˈnāsh-n\ *n.* **1** A flowing out. **2** Something that goes out from a source, as heat.

eman·ci·pate \ē-ˈman(t)s-ə-ˌpāt\ *v.;* **eman·ci·pat·ed; eman·ci·pat·ing.** To set free from control or restraint; especially, to free from bondage; to liberate; as, to *emancipate* slaves. — **eman·ci·pa·tor** \-ˌpāt-r\ *n.*

eman·ci·pa·tion \ē-ˌman(t)s-ə-ˈpāsh-n\ *n.* A setting free; liberation.

emas·cu·late \ē-ˈmas-kyə-ˌlāt\ *v.;* **emas·cu·lat·ed; emas·cu·lat·ing. 1** To castrate. **2** To deprive of masculine vigor or spirit; to weaken. — **emas·cu·la·tion** \ē-ˌmas-kyə-ˈlāsh-n\ *n.*

em·balm \im-ˈbäm, -ˈbȧm\ *v.* **1** To treat a dead body with special preparations to preserve it from decay. **2** To perfume. Flowers *embalmed* the air. **3** To preserve in one's memory. — **em·balm·er,** *n.*

em·bank \im-ˈbangk\ *v.* To protect or keep within limits by constructing a bank, as of earth.

em·bank·ment \im-ˈbangk-mənt\ *n.* **1** The action of embanking. **2** A raised bank or wall, usually of earth or stone, used to carry a roadway, to prevent floods, or to hold back water in a reservoir.

em·bar·go \im-ˈbär-ˌgō, -ˈbȧr-\ *n.; pl.* **em·bar·goes.** [From Spanish, derived from *embargar* originally meaning "to obstruct", literally "to put up a barrier".] **1** An order of a government forbidding the coming in or going out of ships of commerce at any of its ports. **2** A similar order, as to railroads, forbidding transportation of freight between certain places. **3** A stoppage; a hindrance. — *v.* To put an embargo on, as ships or commerce.

em·bark \im-ˈbärk, -ˈbȧrk\ *v.* **1** To go on or put on board ship for a voyage; as, to *embark* for England. **2** To go into some enterprise or undertaking; to begin activities; as, to *embark* on a business career. — **em·bar·ka·tion** \ˌem-ˌbär-ˈkāsh-n, -ˌbȧr-\ *n.*

em·bar·rass \im-ˈbar-əs\ *v.* **1** To hinder from liberty of movement; to impede. Heavy packs *embarrassed* the troops' movements during the attack. **2** To make confused or upset in mind; to cause a feeling of uneasiness in; to bewilder; to disconcert. The unexpected laughter *embarrassed* the speaker. **3** To involve in financial difficulties; as, *embarrassed* for cash to pay his workmen with.

— The word *abash* is a synonym of *embarrass: embarrass* usually implies an uneasiness and confusion of mind brought about by a sudden hampering of choice or action; *abash* may indicate the sudden calling up of feelings of shyness, unworthiness, or shame.

em·bar·rass·ment \im-ˈbar-əs-mənt\ *n.* **1** The state of being embarrassed; confusion or uneasiness of mind; difficulty arising from the want of money to pay debts. **2** Something that embarrasses; as, the *embarrassment* to commerce as a result of the embargo on transportation.

em·bas·sy \ˈem-bə-sē\ *n.; pl.* **em·bas·sies. 1** The function or position of an ambassador. **2** The business entrusted to an ambassador. **3** The person or group of persons sent as ambassadors. **4** The residence or office of an ambassador.

em·bat·tled \im-ˈbat-ld\ *adj.* **1** Arranged in battle order; prepared for battle; as, *embattled* troops. **2** Fortified; protected by forts.

em·bed \im-'bed\ *v.;* **em·bed·ded; em·bed·ding.** To set solidly as if in a bed; to lay firmly in surrounding matter; as, stones *embedded* in soil.

em·bel·lish \im-'bel-ish\ *v.* **1** To make attractive by ornamental additions; to adorn; to decorate; as, to *embellish* a book with pictures and maps. **2** To enlarge or heighten the interest of, as a story, by adding fanciful details. — **em·bel·lish·ment** \-mənt\ *n.*

em·ber \'em-br\ *n.* **1** A glowing piece of coal or wood from a fire; especially, such a piece smoldering in ashes. **2** [in the plural] Smoldering remains of a fire.

em·bez·zle \im-'bez-l\ *v.;* **em·bez·zled; em·bez·zling** \-l(-)ing\. To take dishonestly for one's own use money or other property entrusted to one's care. — **em·bez·zler** \-l(-)ər\ *n.*

em·bez·zle·ment \im-'bez-l-mənt\ *n.* The act of embezzling; dishonest taking over by a person for his own use of property entrusted to his care, as of an employer's money by his clerk or of public funds by the official in charge.

em·bit·ter \im-'bit-r\ *v.* To make bitter or more bitter; especially, to arouse bitter feeling in; as, to refuse to let misfortune *embitter* one. — **em·bit·ter·ment** \-mənt\ *n.*

em·bla·zon \im-'blāz-n\ *v.;* **em·bla·zoned; em·bla·zon·ing** \-n(-)ing\. **1** To inscribe or ornament with markings or emblems used in heraldry; as, a knight bearing a shield with a lion *emblazoned* on it. **2** To decorate richly; to make bright with color. **3** To celebrate; to glorify; as, deeds of heroism *emblazoned* in a thousand poems.

em·blem \'em-bləm\ *n.* **1** An object, or a likeness of an object, that is used to suggest a thing that cannot be pictured; a symbol. The flag is the *emblem* of one's country. **2** Any device, symbol, design, or figure used as an identifying mark.

— The words *symbol* and *token* are synonyms of *emblem: symbol* may apply to anything serving as an outward sign of something else, usually spiritual or abstract; *emblem* usually indicates a pictorial device, as on a banner or flag, representing a nation, family, or organization; *token* may suggest something, as an action or object, which gives evidence of the existence of another thing, or acts as a reminder of it.

em·blem·at·ic \ˌem-blə-'mat-ik\ or **em·blem·at·i·cal** \-ik-l\ *adj.* Relating to, containing, or being an emblem; symbolic. A crown is *emblematic* of royalty and a laurel wreath of victory. — **em·blem·at·i·cal·ly** \-ik-l(-)ē\ *adv.*

em·bod·i·ment \im-'bäd-ē-mənt\ *n.* **1** The act of embodying or the state of being embodied. **2** A person or thing in which something, as an idea, a principle, or a type, is or seems to be embodied; incarnation; as, a soldier so brave that he seemed the *embodiment* of courage.

em·body \im-'bäd-ē\ *v.;* **em·bod·ied** \-ēd\; **em·bod·y·ing.** **1** To bring together so as to form a body, or system. The Constitution *embodies* the fundamental laws of the United States. **2** To make a part of a body or system; as, to *embody* a new law in a state constitution. **3** To express in a concrete or definite form; as, to *embody* one's ideas in suitable words. **4** To represent in visible form; as, a man who *embodies* courage.

em·bold·en \im-'bōl-dən\ *v.* To make bold; as, to be *emboldened* to enter a contest by a friend's encouragement.

em·bo·lism \'em-bə-ˌliz-m\ *n.* The blocking of a blood vessel by an embolus.

em·bo·lus \'em-bə-ləs\ *n.; pl.* **em·bo·li** \-ˌlī\. Any foreign or abnormal particle circulating in the blood, as a bubble of air or a blood clot.

em·bos·om \im-'bu̇z-m\ *v.* **1** To embrace; to take to one's heart. **2** To enclose; to shelter; as, a house *embosomed* in a grove of trees.

em·boss \im-'bȯs, -'bäs\ *v.* To ornament with a pattern or design having a raised surface made by pressing or engraving, as a head on a coin or type on a letterhead; as, a belt of *embossed* leather. — **em·boss·ment,** *n.*

em·bossed book \im-'bȯst, -'bäst\. A book printed in raised type, as braille, for the blind.

em·bow·er \im-'bau̇r\ *v.* To shelter or enclose in or as if in a bower.

em·brace \im-'brās\ *v.;* **em·braced; em·brac·ing.** **1** To clasp in the arms; to hug. **2** To join in an embrace. **3** To encircle; to enclose. Low hills *embraced* the valley. **4** To include; to take in. The study of biology *embraces* all forms of animal and plant life. **5** To take up; to adopt; as, to *embrace* an opportunity; to *embrace* an idea. — *n.* A close encircling with the arms; a clasp; a hug. — **embrace·ment,** *n.*

em·bra·sure \im-'brāzh-r\ *n.* **1** A recess in a room made by setting a window or door farther forward than the line of the inner wall. **2** An opening with sides flaring outward, as in a wall of a fort, through which a cannon is fired.

em·bro·ca·tion \ˌem-brō-'kāsh-n\ *n.* A medicinal lotion or liniment.

em·broi·der \im-'brȯid-r\ *v.;* **em·broi·dered; em·broi·der·ing** \-r(-)ing\. **1** To make or fill in a design with needlework; as, to *embroider* a flower on a towel. **2** To ornament with needlework; as, to *embroider* a towel. **3** To add to the interest of, as a story, with details far beyond the truth; to exaggerate; to elaborate upon. It was quite an adventure, though as it was told it was plainly *embroidered.*

em·broi·dery \im-'brȯid-r(-)ē\ *n.; pl.* **em·broi·der·ies.** **1** The act or art of embroidering; as, to be taught *embroidery* in school. **2** Needlework done to decorate cloth. **3** Embroidered work. **4** Elaboration in details, as for the purpose of making an account of an actual happening more interesting.

em·broil \im-'brȯil\ *v.* **1** To throw into confusion or strife. The argument *embroiled* the neighborhood. **2** To bring into or cause to take part in a quarrel or dispute; to involve; as, to try not to become *embroiled* in the quarrels of one's friends. — **em·broil·ment,** *n.*

em·bryo \'em-brē-ˌō\ *n.; pl.* **em·bry·os. 1** Any living thing in the earliest stages of its development, as an animal before birth or before hatching from the egg or a young plant still contained within a seed. **2** A beginning or undeveloped stage; as, a plan still in *embryo.*

embryo

diagram of a hen's egg

em·bry·ol·o·gy \ˌem-brē-'äl-ə-jē\ *n.* The branch of biology that deals with the formation and development of the embryo. — **em·bry·o·log·ic** \-ə-'läj-ik\ or **em·bry·o·log·i·cal** \-ik-l\ *adj.* — **em·bry·ol·o·gist** \-'äl-ə-jəst\ *n.*

em·bry·on·ic \ˌem-brē-'än-ik\ *adj.* **1** Of or relating to an embryo. **2** Still in an early undeveloped stage; in embryo; as, an *embryonic* idea.

emend \ē-'mend\ *v.* To free from faults; to make corrections in; to improve.

emen·da·tion \ˌē-ˌmen-'dāsh-n\ *n.* **1** The act of emending; correction. **2** An alteration intended to correct a fault or make an improvement, as in something written; a correction.

em·er·ald \'em-r(-)əld\ *n.* **1** A precious stone, rich green in color. **2** The color of the emerald, green with a yellow tinge.

emerge \ē-'mərj\ *v.;* **emerged; emerg·ing. 1** To come out into view, as out of water or anything that covers; as, the blinding sight of the sun *emerging* from behind a cloud. **2** To come forth, as if into view, from an inferior condition; as, to *emerge* from poverty. **3** To become known, especially as a result of study or questioning. Some good ideas *emerged* from the conference.

emer·gence \ē-'mərj-n(t)s\ *n.* The act of emerging or an instance of emerging; a rising into view; as, the sudden *emergence* of a politician from obscurity to national fame.

emer·gen·cy \ē-'mərj-n-sē\ *n.; pl.* **emer·gen·cies. 1** An unexpected happening or condition calling for prompt action. A necessary quality of a good leader is an ability to deal with *emergencies.* **2** Urgent need; crisis; as, a plan of action ready for use in times of *emergency.*

emer·i·tus \ē-'mer-ət-əs\ *adj.* Retired from active duty without change or loss of rank, usually because of age or long service; as, a professor *emeritus.*

em·ery \'em-r(-)ē\ *n.* A dark mineral formed of very hard grains and used in a crushed or powdered form for polishing and grinding.

emet·ic \ē-'met-ik\ *adj.* Causing vomiting. — *n.* A medicine or other substance that causes vomiting, used chiefly when poison has been taken into the stomach.

em·i·grant \'em-ə-grənt\ *n.* A person who leaves his native country to settle elsewhere.

em·i·grate \'em-ə-ˌgrāt\ *v.;* **em·i·grat·ed; em·i·grat·ing.** To leave a country or region to settle somewhere else.

em·i·gra·tion \ˌem-ə-'grāsh-n\ *n.* **1** A going away from one region or country to live in another. **2** A body of emigrants; emigrants taken collectively.

em·i·nence \'em-ə-nən(t)s\ *n.* **1** The condition of being eminent; high rank or position. **2** A high ground or place; a height; an elevation. **3** [with a capital] A title used in addressing or referring to a cardinal.

em·i·nent \'em-ə-nənt\ *adj.* Standing above all others, as in rank, merit, or virtue; notable; as, *eminent* men; *eminent* deeds of heroism.

eminent domain. The dominion of the government over property within the state that authorizes it to take any property necessary for public use by making reasonable payment for it.

em·i·nent·ly \'em-ə-nənt-lē\ *adv.* In an eminent degree; notably; extraordinarily; as, a man *eminently* qualified for the office to which he was elected.

emir \ə-'mir\ *n.* **1** An Arabian military commander, chieftain, or ruler of a province. **2** A title given to descendants of Mohammed.

em·is·sary \'em-ə-ˌser-ē\ *n.; pl.* **em·is·sar·ies.** A person sent out as an agent, especially in secret, to further certain interests or to gain information.

emis·sion \ē-'mish-n\ *n.* The act of emitting or that which is emitted; a discharge.

emit \ē-'mit\ *v.;* **emit·ted; emit·ting.** To give out or off; to throw out or off; to send forth; as, to *emit* a whistle of surprise. Fire *emits* flame and smoke.

emol·li·ent \ē-'mäl-ē-ənt\ *adj.* Softening; soothing, as to the skin or to the mucous membranes. — *n.* A softening or soothing medicinal or cosmetic preparation.

emol·u·ment \ē-'mäl-yə-mənt\ *n.* Profit from one's employment or from an office held; salary, wages, or fees.

emo·tion \ē-'mōsh-n\ *n.* **1** Strong feeling; excitement; as, to speak with *emotion.* **2** Any one of the feelings, as anger, joy, hate, or fear.

emo·tion·al \ē-'mōsh-n(-)əl\ *adj.* **1** Of the emotions; as, an *emotional* upset. **2** Inclined to show or express emotion; easily moved; as, an *emotional* person. **3** Appealing to or arousing emotion; as, an *emotional* speech. — **emo·tion·al·ly** \-n(-)ə-lē\ *adv.*

em·per·or \'emp-r-r\ *n.* The ruler of an empire.

em·pha·sis \'em(p)-fə-səs\ *n.; pl.* **em·pha·ses** \-ˌsēz\. **1** In reading or speaking, a special force or impressiveness given to one or more words or syllables. **2** Special importance given to something, as an idea or statement; as, to place *emphasis* on accident prevention.

em·pha·size \'em(p)-fə-ˌsīz\ *v.;* **em·pha·sized; em·pha·siz·ing.** To give emphasis to; to place emphasis on; to stress; as, to *emphasize* the need for accuracy.

em·phat·ic \im-'fat-ik\ *adj.* **1** Spoken or done with emphasis; as, an *emphatic* gesture. **2** Using emphasis in speech or action; as, an *emphatic* person. **3** Attracting special attention; striking; as, an *emphatic* contrast. — **em·phat·i·cal·ly** \-ik-l(-)ē\ *adv.*

em·pire \'em-ˌpīr\ *n.* **1** A group of countries united under one ruler; as, the British *empire.* **2** A state that includes wide territories and a number of different peoples under one ruler. **3** A country whose ruler is called an emperor. **4** The power or rule of an emperor. **5** Rule; sovereignty.

em·pir·ic \em-'pir-ik\ *n.* A person, especially a physician, who depends on practical experience alone; a quack.

em·pir·i·cal \em-'pir-ik-l\ or **em·pir·ic** \-ik\ *adj.* **1** Depending on experience or observation alone rather than science or theory; as, *empirical* remedies. **2** Relating to or founded on scientific observation and experiment; as, *empirical* knowledge. — **em·pir·i·cal·ly** \-ik-l(-)ē\ *adv.*

em·pir·i·cism \em-'pir-ə-ˌsiz-m\ *n.* **1** The method of an empiric; quackery. **2** The seeking of knowledge through observation and experiment, as in scientific investigation.

em·place·ment \im-'plās-mənt\ *n.* **1** A putting in or an assignment to a definite place. **2** The space in a fortification occupied by a gun or a group of guns. **3** The base, platform, or protecting wall for a gun.

em·ploy \im-'plȯi\ *v.* **1** To make use of; to use; as, to *employ* bricks in building. **2** To use the services of; to hire; as, a factory that *employs* hundreds of workers. **3** To occupy; to devote; as, to *employ* time in study. — *n.* The condition of being employed; employment; as, to be in the *employ* of the same company for many years.

em·ploy·ee \im-'plȯi-(ˌ)ē, im-ˌplȯi-'ē, ˌem-ˌplȯi-'ē\ *n.* A person who works for pay in the service of an employer.

em·ploy·er \im-'plȯi-ər\ *n.* A person who employs others to work for him.

em·ploy·ment \im-'plȯi-mənt\ *n.* **1** The act of employing or the condition of being employed; as, to be out of *employment.* **2** An occupation, business, profession, or trade.

em·po·ri·um \em-'pōr-ē-əm, -'pȯr-\ *n.; pl.* **em·po·ri·ums** \-ē-əmz\ or **em·po·ria** \-ē-ə\. **1** A place of trade; a market place; especially, a commercial center. **2** A store carrying a wide variety of merchandise.

em·pow·er \im-'paůr\ *v.* **1** To give power or authority to; to authorize; as, to *empower* a person to act in one's place. **2** To give ability to; to enable.

em·press \'em-prəs\ *n.* **1** The wife of an emperor. **2** A woman who is the ruler of an empire in her own right.

emp·ty \'em(p)-tē\ *adj.;* **emp·ti·er**; **emp·ti·est.** **1** Containing nothing; as, an *empty* box. **2** Unoccupied; vacant; as, an *empty* house. **3** Without reality or substance; as, *empty* dreams. **4** Lacking in value, sense, effect, or sincerity; as, *empty* pleasures; *empty* threats. **5** Hungry; as, to feel *empty* before dinner.

— The word *vacant* is a synonym of *empty: empty* usually applies to something that has nothing at all in it; *vacant* may describe something, as a room, a chair, or a position, which is to be occupied or filled, but is temporarily unoccupied or unfilled.

— *v.;* **emp·tied** \-tēd\; **emp·ty·ing.** **1** To make empty; to remove the contents of; as, to *empty* a barrel. **2** To transfer by emptying; as, to *empty* the flour from a bag. **3** To become empty. Within five minutes after the alarm sounded the school building had *emptied.* **4** To give forth fluid or other contents; to discharge. The river *empties* into the ocean. — **emp·ti·ly** \-tə-lē\ *adv.*

em·pur·ple \im-'pərp-l\ *v.;* **em·pur·pled**; **em·pur·pling** \-l(-)ing\. To tinge or color purple; as, the *empurpled* hills in the distance.

em·py·re·al \ˌem-pə-'rē-əl\ *adj.* Of or relating to the empyrean; celestial; sublime.

em·py·re·an \ˌem-pə-'rē-ən\ *n.* **1** The highest heaven or heavenly sphere. **2** The heavens; the sky. — *adj.* Empyreal.

emu \'ē-ˌmyü\ *n.* A swift-running Australian bird with undeveloped wings, related to the ostrich but smaller.

em·u·late \'em-yə-ˌlāt\ *v.;* **em·u·lat·ed**; **em·u·lat·ing.** To strive to equal or excel; to rival; as, to *emulate* great men. — **em·u·la·tor** \-ˌlāt-r\ *n.*

em·u·la·tion \ˌem-yə-'lāsh-n\ *n.* Ambition or endeavor to equal or excel; rivalry. — **em·u·la·tive** \'em-yə-ˌlāt-iv\ *adj.*

em·u·lous \'em-yə-ləs\ *adj.* Eager or ambitious to equal or excel another; as, *emulous* competitors. — **em·u·lous·ly,** *adv.*

emul·si·fy \ē-'məl-sə-ˌfī\ *v.;* **emul·si·fied** \-ˌfīd\; **emul·si·fy·ing.** To make an emulsion of. — **emul·si·fi·ca·tion** \ē-ˌməl-sə-fə-'kāsh-n\ *n.*

emul·sion \ē-'məlsh-n\ *n.* A preparation consisting of droplets or particles of liquid or sometimes other matter dispersed in a second liquid; as, an *emulsion* of oil and water.

en-. A prefix that can mean: **1** Put into, put upon, cover or wrap with, as in *entomb* or *enthrone.* **2** Make, make into, make like, as in *enslave.* **3** In, as in *enfold* or *enclose.*

☞ In some words, *en-* intensifies the meaning of the root word, as in *enkindle.*

-en \-n, ən\. Either of two suffixes of Old English origin, one giving the meaning "made of", as in *wooden* or *oaken,* and the other giving the meaning "to make", as in *whiten* or *deaden.*

☞ A third suffix *-en* is used to form the past participle of many strong, or irregular, verbs, as in *broken* or *fallen.* Still another *-en* suffix is used to form the plurals *oxen* and *children* and formerly many others.

en·a·ble \i-'nāb-l\ *v.;* **en·a·bled**; **en·a·bling** \-l(-)ing\. **1** To give strength, power, or authority to; to make able. The microscope *enables* us to see things invisible to the naked eye. **2** To make possible or easy. Airplanes *enable* rapid transit.

en·act \i-'nakt\ *v.* **1** To make into law; as, a bill to control gambling *enacted* by the legislature. **2** To act, as in a play; to play; as, to *enact* the part of Julius Caesar.

en·act·ment \i-ˈnak(t)-mənt\ *n.* **1** The act of making into law, as a legislative bill. **2** A law or decree.

en·am·el \i-ˈnam-l\ *n.* **1** A glasslike substance, usually opaque, used for coating the surface of metal, glass, and pottery. **2** Any glossy surface resembling enamel. **3** The hard outer surface of the teeth. **4** A kind of paint that flows out smoothly when applied, and usually dries with a glossy appearance. **5** Enameled ware. — *v.;* **en·am·eled** or **en·am·elled**; **en·am·el·ing** or **en·am·el·ling** \-l(-)ing\. To coat or decorate with enamel.

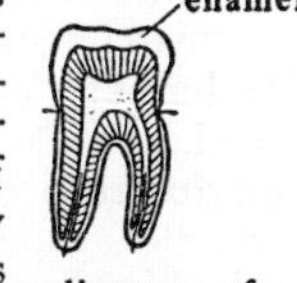

diagram of a tooth

en·am·ored \i-ˈnam-rd\ *adj.* Passionately in love; completely charmed or fascinated; as, to imagine oneself *enamored* of a famous actor.

en·camp \in-ˈkamp\ *v.* **1** To set up and occupy a camp; to camp. **2** To place or establish in a camp, as troops.

en·camp·ment \in-ˈkamp-mənt\ *n.* **1** The act of making camp or of placing in camp. **2** A camp.

en·case \in-ˈkās\ *v.;* **en·cased**; **en·cas·ing.** To incase.

-ence. Variant of *-ance.*

en·ceph·a·li·tis \(ˌ)en-ˌsef-l-ˈīt-əs\ *n.* Any of certain infectious or contagious diseases in which the substance of the brain is inflamed; especially, sleeping sickness.

en·chain \in-ˈchān\ *v.* **1** To fasten or restrain with or as if with chains. **2** To attract and hold fast, as the attention or interest. — **en·chain·ment** \-mənt\ *n.*

en·chant \in-ˈchant\ *v.* **1** To put under a spell, as by charms or magic. **2** To charm; to delight; as, to be *enchanted* with a new friend.

en·chant·er \in-ˈchant-r\ *n.* One that enchants; especially, a sorcerer.

en·chant·ing \in-ˈchant-ing\ *adj.* Charming; fascinating; giving great delight; as, *enchanting* music; an *enchanting* child. — **en·chant·ing·ly**, *adv.*

en·chant·ment \in-ˈchant-mənt\ *n.* **1** The act or art of enchanting or the state of being enchanted. **2** Something that enchants or charms; a spell or charm.

en·chant·ress \in-ˈchan-trəs\ *n.* **1** A woman who practices the art of enchantment; a witch or sorceress. **2** A woman of bewitching charm.

en·cir·cle \in-ˈsərk-l\ *v.;* **en·cir·cled**; **en·cir·cling** \-l(-)ing\. **1** To form a circle around; to surround. The soldiers *encircled* the enemy fortress. **2** To pass completely around; as, to *encircle* the earth by airplane. — **en·cir·cle·ment** \-mənt\ *n.*

en·close \in-ˈklōz\ *v.;* **en·closed**; **en·clos·ing.** **1** To close in all around; to shut in; as, to have a porch *enclosed* with glass. **2** To put in the same parcel or envelope with something else; as, to *enclose* a snapshot with a letter. **3** To surround; to fence in; as, a flower garden *enclosed* by a hedge.

en·clo·sure \in-ˈklōzh-r\ *n.* **1** The act of enclosing or the state of being enclosed. **2** An enclosed space. **3** Something that encloses, as a fence. **4** Something enclosed; as, a letter with two *enclosures.*

en·code \in-ˈkōd\ *v.;* **en·cod·ed**; **en·cod·ing.** To put in the form or symbols of a code; as, to *encode* a secret message.

en·co·mi·um \en-ˈkō-mē-əm\ *n.; pl.* **en·co·mi·ums** \-mē-əmz\ or **en·co·mia** \-mē-ə\. Warm or high praise, especially formally expressed; a eulogy.

en·com·pass \in-ˈkəmp-əs, -ˈkämp-\ *v.* **1** To encircle; to surround. **2** To enclose; to contain. — **en·com·pass·ment** \-mənt\ *n.*

en·core \ˈän(g)-ˌkōr, -ˌkȯr\ *interj.* Once more! Again! — *n.* **1** The demand, expressed by applause from an audience, for the repetition of an item on a program or for a further appearance by a performer. **2** A further appearance or performance given in response to such applause. — *v.;* **en·cored**; **en·cor·ing.** To call for a further performance or appearance; as, to *encore* a song. The great violinist was *encored* over and over again.

en·coun·ter \in-ˈkau̇nt-r\ *v.;* **en·coun·tered**; **en·coun·ter·ing** \-ˈkau̇nt-r-ing, -ˈkau̇n-tring\. **1** To meet in opposition; to fight. **2** To meet; to come face to face with; to come upon; as, to *encounter* stormy weather; to *encounter* a friend on the street. — *n.* **1** A battle; a combat; as, a bloody *encounter.* **2** A meeting face to face, especially a chance meeting.

en·cour·age \in-ˈkər-ij, -ˈkə-rij\ *v.;* **en·cour·aged**; **en·cour·ag·ing.** **1** To give courage, spirit, or hope to; to hearten; to cheer up or on. **2** To give help to; to aid; to foster or promote by help or approval; as, to *encourage* thrift; to *encourage* the planting of trees by providing free seedlings.

en·cour·age·ment \in-ˈkər-ij-mənt, -ˈkə-rij-\ *n.* **1** The act of encouraging or the state of being encouraged; as, to be in need of *encouragement.* **2** Something that encourages. The daily visits of his friends were a great *encouragement* to the sick boy.

en·cour·ag·ing \in-ˈkər-ə-jing, -ˈkə-rə-\ *adj.* Giving hope or reason for hope; favorable; as, *encouraging* news of the progress of a battle. — **en·cour·ag·ing·ly**, *adv.*

en·croach \in-ˈkrōch\ *v.* **1** To enter or force oneself gradually upon another's property or rights; to trespass; to intrude; as, to *encroach* upon a neighbor's land. One radio program is not permitted to *encroach* on time allotted to another. **2** To advance beyond the usual or proper limits; as, a cove formed by the gradually *encroaching* sea. — **en·croach·ment** \-mənt\ *n.*

en·crust \in-ˈkrəst\ *v.* To incrust. — **en·crus·ta·tion** \ˌen-ˌkrəs-ˈtāsh-n\ *n.*

en·cum·ber \in-ˈkəm-br\ *v.;* **en·cum·bered**; **en·cum·ber·ing** \-br(-)ing\. **1** To hinder the motion or action of something; to obstruct; as, to be *encumbered* in walking by two heavy suitcases. **2** To make clumsy or disagreeable by addition of unnecessary parts or features. **3** To burden; to weigh down; as, to be *encumbered* with debts.

en·cum·brance \in-'kəm-brən(t)s\ *n.* **1** Something that encumbers; a load or burden. **2** A dependent person, especially a child. **3** In law, a claim or obligation against property, as a mortgage.

-ency. Variant of *-ance.*

en·cyc·li·cal \en-'sik-lik-l\ *adj.* Sent to many places and persons; as, an *encyclical* letter. — *n.* An encyclical letter; especially, a letter from the pope addressed to his bishops all over the world.

en·cy·clo·pe·dia or **en·cy·clo·pae·dia** \in-ˌsīk-lə-'pēd-ē-ə\ *n.* [From Greek *enkyklopaideia, enkyklios paideia* meaning "general education", "general knowledge".] A book or series of books containing information from all branches of learning, usually in articles alphabetically arranged according to the subjects treated.

en·cy·clo·pe·dic or **en·cy·clo·pae·dic** \in-ˌsīk-lə-'pēd-ik\ *adj.* **1** Of or relating to an encyclopedia. **2** Covering a wide range of subjects; as, *encyclopedic* knowledge; an *encyclopedic* memory.

end \'end\ *n.* **1** A limit or boundary; as, to come to the *end* of a town; to go to the *ends* of the earth. **2** The last or final state of any event or series of events; the last part of anything; as, to leave before the *end;* the *end* of the year. **3** The last point or part of any material thing considered lengthwise; as, both *ends* of a stick; the front *end* of an automobile. **4** Death; destruction; as, to meet one's *end* bravely. **5** Something aimed at; purpose; as, an *end* in view; to gain one's *ends.* **6** Something left over; a remnant; as, odds and *ends.* **7** A player stationed at the end of a line or team, as in football. — *v.* **1** To come or bring to an end; to stop; to finish. The meeting *ended* abruptly. **2** To form or be at the end of. The letter "t" *ends* the word "cat".

en·dan·ger \in-'dānj-r\ *v.;* **en·dan·gered; en·dan·ger·ing** \-r(-)ing\. To bring into danger; as, to *endanger* one's life by reckless driving. Impure drinking water *endangers* the health of the community.

en·dear \in-'dir\ *v.* To cause to become dear or beloved; as, a smile that *endears* a person to everyone. — **en·dear·ing·ly** \-ing-lē\ *adv.*

en·dear·ment \in-'dir-mənt\ *n.* A word or act showing love or affection, as a caress.

en·deav·or \in-'dev-r\ *v.;* **en·deav·ored; en·deav·or·ing** \-r(-)ing\. To make an effort; to try; to work for a certain end; as, to *endeavor* to do better. — *n.* An effort made to do or get something; an attempt; as, a money-raising *endeavor.*

en·dem·ic \en-'dem-ik\ *adj.* Peculiar to a district or to a class of persons; as, an *endemic* disease. — *n.* An endemic disease.

end·ing \'en-ding\ *n.* **1** An end; a conclusion; as, a novel with a happy *ending.* **2** One or more letters or sounds added to a root word, as *ed* in *laughed, like* in *catlike,* or *ing* in *going;* a suffix.

en·dive \'en-ˌdīv\ *n.* Either of two chicories, one with finely divided, curled leaves or one with broad, fleshy leaves, both of which are used in salads.

end·less \'en-(d)ləs\ *adj.* **1** Without end, or seeming to be without end; as, *endless* time; the *endless* prairie. **2** Joined at the ends; continuous; as, an *endless* belt. — **end·less·ly,** *adv.*

end man. The last man in a row; especially, the man at either end of the line of performers in a minstrel show.

end·most \'end-ˌmōst\ *adj.* Farthest; at the very end.

en·do·crine \'en-dō-krən, -ˌkrīn\ *adj.* Relating to ductless glands whose secretions pass directly into the blood or lymph. — *n.* An endocrine gland or its secretion.

en·do·plasm \'en-dō-ˌplaz-m\ *n.* The inner portion of the cytoplasm.

en·dorse \in-'dȯrs\ *v.;* **en·dorsed; en·dors·ing. 1** To sign one's name on the back of a paper for some special purpose; as, to *endorse* a check. **2** To give one's support to; to approve; as, to *endorse* a plan or a candidate. — **en·dors·er,** *n.*

en·dorse·ment \in-'dȯrs-mənt\ *n.* **1** An endorsing, as of a check. **2** A writing and a signature endorsing a check or note. **3** Approval; as, to give one's *endorsement* to a plan.

en·do·skel·e·ton \ˌen-dō-'skel-ət-n\ *n.* An internal skeleton or supporting framework in an animal.

en·do·sperm \'en-dō-ˌspərm\ *n.* The nutritive tissue formed within the embryo sac in seed plants.

en·dow \in-'daů\ *v.* **1** To furnish with money for support or maintenance; as, to *endow* a hospital. **2** To furnish with anything of the nature of a gift. Man is *endowed* with reason.

en·dow·ment \in-'daů-mənt\ *n.* **1** The providing of a permanent fund for support or the fund provided; as, a college with a large *endowment.* **2** A gift of nature; a person's abilities or talents; as, a person fitted for the job by his natural *endowments.*

en·due \in-'dü, -'dyü\ *v.;* **en·dued; en·du·ing.** To provide with a quality or power; as, *endued* with grace.

en·dur·ance \in-'důr-ən(t)s, -'dyůr-\ *n.* **1** The ability to endure, or to last; as, a person possessed of great *endurance.* **2** An act or instance of suffering; a continuing under pain, hardship, or distress without being overcome; as, a situation that is beyond *endurance.*

en·dure \in-'důr, -'dyůr\ *v.;* **en·dured; en·dur·ing. 1** To last; to continue in existence; as, a civilization that has *endured* for centuries. **2** To bear patiently; to stand, as pain or misfortune. — **en·dur·a·ble,** *adj.*

en·dur·ing \in-'důr-ing, -'dyůr-\ *adj.* Lasting; durable; long-suffering; as, an *enduring* faith. — **en·dur·ing·ly,** *adv.*

end·ways \'en-ˌdwāz\ or **end·wise** \'en-ˌdwīz\ *adv.* **1** On end. **2** With the end forward. **3** Lengthwise.

en·e·ma \'en-ə-mə\ *n.* A liquid injected into the rectum, usually to clear the bowels.

en·e·my \'en-ə-mē\ *n.; pl.* **en·e·mies. 1** A person

who hates another; one who attacks or tries to harm another; a foe. **2** An opponent, as of something considered bad. **3** Anything that harms. **4** A nation with which one's own country is at war or a military force, a ship, or a person belonging to such a nation.

en·er·get·ic \ˌen-r-ˈjet-ik\ *adj.* Having or showing energy; vigorous; active; forceful; as, an *energetic* salesman; to lead an *energetic* life. — **en·er·get·i·cal·ly** \-ik-l(-)ē\ *adv.*

en·er·gize \ˈen-r-ˌjīz\ *v.; **en·er·gized**; **en·er·giz·ing.*** **1** To give or impart energy to; to make vigorous; to invigorate. **2** To put forth energy; to act.

en·er·gy \ˈen-r-jē\ *n.; pl.* **en·er·gies. 1** Power or capacity to be active; strength of body or mind to do things or to work; as, a man of great *energy.* **2** Natural power vigorously exerted; vigorous action; as, to work with *energy.* **3** The capacity for performing work, such as exists in heat, light, electricity, and running water. — For synonyms see *power.*

en·er·vate \ˈen-r-ˌvāt\ *v.;* **en·er·vat·ed**; **en·er·vat·ing.** To cause to grow less in strength or vigor; to weaken; as, an *enervating* climate.

en·fee·ble \in-ˈfēb-l\ *v.;* **en·fee·bled**; **en·fee·bling** \-l(-)ing\. To make feeble; as, *enfeebled* by old age. — **en·fee·ble·ment** \-mənt\ *n.*

en·fold \in-ˈfōld\ *v.* **1** To wrap up or cover with folds, as of cloth. **2** To embrace; to clasp; as, to *enfold* a child in one's arms.

en·force \in-ˈfōrs, -ˈfȯrs\ *v.;* **en·forced**; **en·forc·ing. 1** To force; to compel; as, to *enforce* obedience to a law. **2** To put into force; to carry out effectively; as, to *enforce* a law. — **en·force·a·ble**, *adj.*

en·force·ment \in-ˈfōrs-mənt, -ˈfȯrs-\ *n.* The act or process of enforcing; especially, the putting into force of laws or regulations.

en·fran·chise \in-ˈfran-ˌchīz\ *v.;* **en·fran·chised**; **en·fran·chis·ing. 1** To set free from slavery. **2** To give the right to vote; to admit to citizenship. — **en·fran·chise·ment** \-ˌchīz-mənt, -chəz-\ *n.*

en·gage \in-ˈgāj\ *v.;* **en·gaged**; **en·gag·ing. 1** To pledge; to bind oneself; to undertake; as, to *engage* to assist with the decorations. **2** To hold the attention of a person; to occupy; as, to have a hobby that *engages* all one's spare time. **3** To take part in something; to occupy or busy oneself; as, to *engage* in sports. **4** To hire; to employ; to arrange for the use or services of; as, to *engage* a carpenter; to *engage* a room in a hotel. **5** To promise in marriage; as, to become *engaged.* **6** To enter into conflict or battle with; as, to *engage* the enemy. **7** To mesh, as cogwheels; to interlock.

en·gaged \in-ˈgājd\ *adj.* **1** Occupied; employed; busy; as, *engaged* in conversation. **2** Pledged to be married; as, an *engaged* couple.

en·gage·ment \in-ˈgāj-mənt\ *n.* **1** The act or action of engaging. **2** The state of being engaged; especially, the state of being engaged to be married. **3** A pledge; an obligation; as, a man with many financial *engagements* to fulfill. **4** Employment, especially for a stated time. The singer had a week's *engagement* at the local theater. **5** A battle. **6** An appointment or arrangement to meet someone or do something at a certain time; as, an *engagement* to go to the movies.

en·gag·ing \in-ˈgā-jing\ *adj.* Attractive; pleasing; as, an *engaging* manner. — **en·gag·ing·ly**, *adv.*

en·gen·der \in-ˈjend-r\ *v.;* **en·gen·dered**; **en·gen·der·ing** \-r(-)ing\. To bring forth; to produce; to create. Angry words *engender* quarrels.

en·gine \ˈenj-n\ *n.* **1** Any machine or mechanical device; as, tanks, planes, and other *engines* of war; a fire *engine.* **2** Any machine by which physical power is applied to produce a physical effect; especially, a machine powered by steam, gasoline, or oil and used for running, driving, moving, or operating something else. **3** A railroad locomotive.

en·gi·neer \ˌenj-n-ˈir\ *n.* **1** A person who designs or makes engines. **2** A person who operates an engine, as a steam engine or locomotive. **3** A person trained in engineering; as, a mining *engineer.* **4** In the army or navy, a member of the corps that carries out engineering duties and takes care of machinery. — *v.* **1** To plan, build, or manage as an engineer. **2** To guide the course of; to manage; as, to *engineer* a fund-raising campaign.

en·gi·neer·ing \ˌenj-n-ˈir-ing\ *n.* The art, science, or profession of developing and using nature's power and resources in ways that are useful to man, as in the planning and building of roads, bridges, and tunnels, the designing and building of engines and machines, and the creation and improvement of manufactured products.

En·glish \ˈing-glish\ *adj.* [From Old English *englisc*, derived from *Engle* meaning "Angles", one of the Germanic peoples which settled in England in the 5th century A.D.] **1** Of or relating to England. **2** Of or relating to the English language. — *n.* **1** The English people — used as a plural with *the.* **2** The language of England, the United States, and most of the British dominions and colonies.

English horn. A musical instrument like an oboe but with tones lower in pitch.

En·glish·man \ˈing-glish-mən\ *n.; pl.* **En·glish·men** \-mən\. A native or a citizen of England. — **En·glish·wom·an** \-ˌwu̇m-ən\ *n.*

English sparrow. The house sparrow.

en·graft \in-ˈgraft\ *v.* To graft, as a shoot from one plant onto another.

English horn

en·grave \in-ˈgrāv\ *v.;* **en·graved**; **en·grav·ing. 1** To cut or carve letters, figures, or designs on a hard surface; as, to *engrave* a name on a brass plate; to *engrave* a tombstone. **2** To cut wood, metal, or stone in preparation for printing; as, to *engrave* a plate for a new bank note. **3** To print from a surface so cut; as, an invitation *engraved* on white cards. **4** To impress deeply; as, an incident that *engraved* itself on the child's mind. — **en·grav·er**, *n.*

en·grav·ing \in-ˈgrā-ving\ *n.* **1** The art of cutting letters, pictures, or patterns in wood, stone, or metal. **2** A print made from an engraved surface.

en·gross \in-ˈgrōs\ *v.* **1** To copy or write in a large hand, as a formal document. **2** To take up the whole interest of; to absorb; to occupy fully; as, to be *engrossed* in a puzzle; an *engrossing* story. — **en·gross·ment**, *n.*

en·gulf \in-ˈgəlf\ *v.* To swallow up as if in a gulf; as, to be suddenly *engulfed* in darkness.

en·hance \in-ˈhan(t)s\ *v.;* **en·hanced**; **en·hanc·ing.** To make or become greater, as in value or desirability; to increase. A well-kept garden *enhances* the appearance of a house. — **en·hance·ment** \-mənt\ *n.*

enig·ma \ē-ˈnig-mə\ *n.* Something hard to understand or explain; a riddle; a puzzle. Where the money went was an *enigma.* — **en·ig·mat·ic** \ˌen-ig-ˈmat-ik, ˌē-nig-\ or **en·ig·mat·i·cal** \-ik-l\ *adj.* — **en·ig·mat·i·cal·ly** \-ik-l(-)ē\ *adv.*

en·join \in-ˈjȯin\ *v.* **1** To command; to direct. The police *enjoined* the students to observe the rules for use of bicycles. **2** To forbid; to prohibit; as, a person *enjoined* from leaving the country.

en·joy \in-ˈjȯi\ *v.* **1** To take pleasure in; as, to *enjoy* camping. **2** To have and use with satisfaction; to have the benefit of; as, to *enjoy* good health.

en·joy·a·ble \in-ˈjȯi-əb-l\ *adj.* Giving pleasure; as, an *enjoyable* day at the beach. — **en·joy·a·bly** \-ə-blē\ *adv.*

en·joy·ment \in-ˈjȯi-mənt\ *n.* **1** The condition of enjoying something; the possession and use of something with satisfaction; as, the *enjoyment* of good health. **2** Pleasure; satisfaction: as, to find great *enjoyment* in ice skating; to read for *enjoyment.* **3** Something that gives pleasure; as, the *enjoyments* of old age.

en·kin·dle \en-ˈkind-l\ *v.;* **en·kin·dled**; **en·kin·dling** \-l(-)ing\. To kindle.

en·large \in-ˈlärj, -ˈlȧrj\ *v.;* **en·larged**; **en·larg·ing.** **1** To make or grow larger; to increase; to expand; as, to *enlarge* a house; to *enlarge* a picture. **2** To elaborate; as, to *enlarge* on a story.

en·large·ment \in-ˈlärj-mənt, -ˈlȧrj-\ *n.* **1** An enlarging or a being enlarged. **2** Something that is enlarged, as a photographic print made larger than the negative. **3** Something that adds to something else. The box requires an *enlargement* of one inch in length.

en·larg·er \in-ˈlärj-r, -ˈlȧrj-r\ *n.* One that enlarges; especially, a camera used to produce an enlargement.

en·light·en \in-ˈlīt-n\ *v.;* **en·light·ened**; **en·light·en·ing** \-n(-)ing\. To give knowledge to; to free from ignorance; to inform; to instruct. — **en·light·en·ment** \-mənt\ *n.*

en·list \in-ˈlist\ *v.* **1** To enroll for military or naval service; especially, to join one of the armed services voluntarily. **2** To obtain the help or support of; as, to *enlist* the aid of one's friends. — **en·list·ment** \-ˈlis(t)-mənt\ *n.*

enlisted man. A soldier, seaman, airman, or member of the coast guard below the grade of commissioned officer, warrant officer, cadet, or midshipman.

en·liv·en \in-ˈlīv-n\ *v.;* **en·liv·ened**; **en·liv·en·ing** \-n(-)ing\. To put life or spirit into; to make active, cheerful, bright, gay. The children's laughter *enlivened* the gloomy old house.

en masse \än ˈmas\. In mass; in a body. All the students in the school marched *en masse* in the parade.

en·mesh \en-ˈmesh\ *v.* To tangle in or as if in meshes; as, to become *enmeshed* in crime.

en·mi·ty \ˈen-mət-ē\ *n.; pl.* **en·mi·ties.** Ill will; hatred; especially, mutual hatred or ill will.

en·no·ble \i-ˈnōb-l\ *v.;* **en·no·bled**; **en·no·bling** \-l(-)ing\. **1** To make noble; to elevate. **2** To raise to the rank of nobility.

en·nui \(ˈ)än-ˈwē\ *n.* A feeling of weariness and dissatisfaction; boredom.

enor·mi·ty \ē-ˈnȯr-mət-ē\ *n.; pl.* **enor·mi·ties.** **1** Huge size. **2** Great wickedness; outrageousness; as, the *enormity* of the offense. **3** An outrageous act or offense.

enor·mous \ē-ˈnȯr-məs\ *adj.* [From Latin *enormis* meaning literally "unusual", "out of the norm", derived from *e, ex* meaning "out of" and *norma* meaning "rule", "norm".] **1** Huge; immense; much beyond the usual in size. **2** Monstrous; outrageous; as, an *enormous* crime. — **enor·mous·ly,** *adv.*

enough \ə-ˈnəf, i-, ē-; *after some sounds,* n-ˈəf\ *adj.* Equal to the needs or demands; sufficient; as, to lack *enough* food. — *adv.* **1** In sufficient amount or degree; sufficiently; as, to fail to run fast *enough.* **2** Fully; quite; as, ready *enough* to admit the truth. **3** Tolerably. Although she lacked experience, the soprano sang well *enough.* — *n.* A sufficient amount.

enow \ē-ˈnau̇\ *adj.* or *adv. Archaic.* Enough.

en·quire \in-ˈkwīr\ *v.;* **en·quired**; **en·quir·ing.** To inquire.

en·quiry \in-ˈkwīr-ē, ˈin-ˌkwīr-ē, ˈin(g)-kwər-ē\ *n.; pl.* **en·quir·ies.** An inquiry.

en·rage \in-ˈrāj\ *v.;* **en·raged**; **en·rag·ing.** To fill with rage; to madden.

en·rap·ture \in-ˈrap-chər\ *v.;* **en·rap·tured**; **en·rap·tur·ing.** To delight greatly; as, *enraptured* at the sight.

en·rich \in-ˈrich\ *v.* **1** To make rich. **2** To ornament; to adorn; as, a ceiling *enriched* with paintings. **3** To increase the knowledge or capacity of; as, to *enrich* the mind. **4** To improve the nourishment in food by adding vitamins and minerals. **5** To make more fertile, as soil. — **en·rich·ment** \-mənt\ *n.*

en·roll or **en·rol** \in-ˈrōl\ *v.;* **en·rolled**; **en·roll·ing.** **1** To enter on a roll or a list; to register; as, to *enroll* new pupils; to *enroll* at a new school. **2** To record; to enlist (oneself) for armed service; as, to *enroll* in the navy.

en·roll·ment or **en·rol·ment** \in-'rōl-mənt\ *n.* **1** An enrolling or a being enrolled; registration. **2** The number of persons enrolled.

en route \än 'rüt, en, in\. On or along the way.

Ens. Abbreviation for *Ensign.*

en·sconce \in-'skän(t)s\ *v.;* **en·sconced; en·sconc·ing. 1** To place or hide securely; to conceal; as, to *ensconce* oneself behind a tree. **2** To establish comfortably; to settle snugly; as, a child safely *ensconced* between his father and mother.

en·sem·ble \än-'säm-bl\ *n.* **1** A whole; all the parts taken together. **2** The combined performance of a group of musicians, as a quartet. **3** The group of musicians giving such a performance. **4** A costume composed of matching or harmonizing garments or pieces, as a suit and coat.

en·shrine \in-'shrīn\ *v.;* **en·shrined; en·shrin·ing. 1** To enclose in a shrine or as if in a shrine. **2** To cherish as something sacred; as, a memory *enshrined* in one's thoughts.

en·shroud \in-'shraủd\ *v.* To shroud.

en·sign \'en(t)s-n; *sense 1 is also* 'en-ˌsīn\ *n.* **1** A flag; a banner; especially, a national flag. **2** A badge of office, rank, or power. **3** A naval officer equal in rank to a second lieutenant in the army.

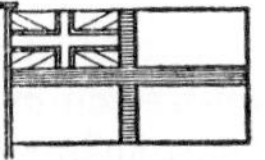
ensign of Great Britain

en·sign·cy \'en(t)s-n-sē\ *n.; pl.* **en·sign·cies.** The rank or office of an ensign.

en·si·lage \'en(t)s-l-ij\ *n.* Silage.

en·slave \in-'slāv\ *v.;* **en·slaved; en·slav·ing.** To make a slave or slaves of.

en·snare \in-'snar, -'sner\ *v.;* **en·snared; en·snar·ing. 1** To catch in a snare. **2** To take by tricks or wiles; to involve in difficulties or a complex situation; as, *ensnared* in legal technicalities.

en·sue \in-'sü\ *v.;* **en·sued; en·su·ing.** To come after in time or as a result; to follow; as, the *ensuing* year; *ensuing* effects.

en·sure \in-'shủr\ *v.;* **en·sured; en·sur·ing.** To make sure, certain, or safe; to insure; to guarantee; as, to *ensure* food and shelter for everyone.

-ent \(ə)nt\. A suffix that can mean: **1** Having the quality, manner, or condition of a person or thing that, as in *excellent* or *adherent.* **2** A person or thing that, as in *superintendent* or *correspondent.*

en·tail \in-'tāl\ *v.* **1** To leave property to a person and his descendants or to a certain line of descendants with the legal provision that no others may inherit it. **2** To require or include as a necessary result; as, work that *entails* great expense. — *n.* **1** An entailing or an entailed estate. **2** The rule by which descent is fixed. — **en·tail·ment** \-mənt\ *n.*

en·tan·gle \in-'tang-gl\ *v.;* **en·tan·gled; en·tan·gling** \-gl(-)ing\. **1** To tangle. **2** To snare; to trap; as, to *entangle* birds in a net. **3** To involve; to perplex; to bewilder; as, *entangled* in endless argument. — **en·tan·gle·ment** \-mənt\ *n.*

en·ter \'ent-r\ *v.;* **en·tered; en·ter·ing** \'ent-r-ing, 'en-tring\. **1** To go or come into; to go or come in; as, to *enter* a room; to *enter* and leave by the back door. **2** To pierce; to penetrate. The arrow had *entered* the target just at the edge of the bull's-eye. **3** To cause to go into or be admitted to; as, to *enter* a child in kindergarten. **4** To join; to become a member of; as, to *enter* the hikers' club. **5** To begin; to start; as, to *enter* into business. **6** To take part or form a part; as, to *enter* into a discussion. Tin *enters* into the composition of pewter. **7** To take possession; as, to *enter* upon one's inheritance. **8** To take a friendly and active part in; as, to *enter* into the spirit of the party. **9** To list; to set down in a book or list; as, to *enter* words in a dictionary. Pupils' names are *entered* in the class register. **10** To place before a court or other legal authority; as, to *enter* a complaint.

en·ter·ic \en-'ter-ik\ *adj.* Of or relating to the alimentary canal; intestinal.

en·ter·i·tis \ˌent-r-'īt-əs\ *n.* Inflammation of the intestines.

en·ter·prise \'ent-r-ˌprīz\ *n.* **1** An undertaking, especially one calling for boldness and energy; a project; a venture; as, a man who had engaged successfully in a number of business *enterprises.* **2** Capacity and willingness to undertake projects calling for energy, boldness, and initiative; as, a man of ability and *enterprise.*

en·ter·pris·ing \'ent-r-ˌprī-zing\ *adj.* Having or showing enterprise; bold, active, and energetic. — **en·ter·pris·ing·ly**, *adv.*

en·ter·tain \ˌent-r-'tān\ *v.* **1** To receive and provide for, especially in one's home; to have as a guest; as, to *entertain* friends over the weekend. **2** To provide entertainment, especially for guests; as, a born hostess, who loved to *entertain.* **3** To have in mind; as, to *entertain* kind thoughts about someone; to *entertain* for a few days the idea of trying to go on the stage. **4** To amuse; to divert; as, a show that never ceased to *entertain* the spectators. — For synonyms see *amuse.*

en·ter·tain·er \ˌent-r-'tān-r\ *n.* One who entertains; especially, one who gives or takes part in public entertainments.

en·ter·tain·ing \ˌent-r-'tā-ning\ *adj.* Giving entertainment; amusing; interesting. — **en·ter·tain·ing·ly**, *adv.*

en·ter·tain·ment \ˌent-r-'tān-mənt\ *n.* **1** Provision for guests, especially in public places, as hotels and inns; as, a hotel that had furnished *entertainment* for travelers for more than a century. **2** Amusement; recreation; diversion; as, to play the piano only for one's own *entertainment.* **3** Something that entertains; a means of amusement or recreation; especially, a public performance such as a concert.

en·thrall or **en·thral** \in-'thrȯl\ *v.;* **en·thralled; en·thrall·ing. 1** To enslave. **2** To charm or captivate; to hold spellbound; as, to be *enthralled* by a tale of romantic adventure.

en·throne \in-'thrōn\ *v.;* **en·throned; en·thron·ing. 1** To seat on a throne in a formal ceremony, as a king or a bishop. **2** To raise to an exalted position; as, a baseball player securely *enthroned* among the great of all time. — **en·throne·ment** \-mənt\ *n.*

en·thuse \in-ˈthüz, -ˈthyüz\ *v.;* **en·thused; en·thus·ing. 1** To become enthusiastic; to show enthusiasm. **2** To make enthusiastic.

en·thu·si·asm \in-ˈthü-zē-ˌaz-m, -ˈthyü-\ *n.* [From Greek *enthousiasmos* meaning literally "inspiration from a god".] An intense and absorbing interest in or feeling for something, as a cause, a subject, or a pursuit; zeal; fervor.

en·thu·si·ast \in-ˈthü-zē-ˌast, -ˈthyü-, -əst\ *n.* A person filled with enthusiasm for something; as, a magazine for sports *enthusiasts.*

en·thu·si·as·tic \in-ˌthü-zē-ˈas-tik, -ˌthyü-\ *adj.* Filled with enthusiasm; eager; ardent. — **en·thu·si·as·ti·cal·ly** \-tik-l(-)ē\ *adv.*

en·tice \in-ˈtīs\ *v.;* **en·ticed; en·tic·ing.** To attract or draw on by arousing hope or desire; to tempt; to allure. — **en·tic·ing·ly,** *adv.*

en·tice·ment \in-ˈtīs-mənt\ *n.* **1** The act of enticing or the state of being enticed. **2** Something that entices; an allurement; as, farm boys drawn to the city by the *enticements* of good pay and short hours.

en·tire \in-ˈtīr, ˈen-ˌtīr\ *adj.* **1** Complete in all parts; whole; unbroken; undivided; as, an *entire* regiment of soldiers; to spend an *entire* hour in daydreaming. **2** Full; thorough; unqualified; as, to do something with the *entire* approval of one's parents. **3** In botany, having the edges free from notches or indentations, as a leaf.

en·tire·ly \in-ˈtīr-lē\ *adv.* Completely; wholly; fully; as, to be *entirely* recovered from an illness; a room decorated *entirely* in bright colors.

en·tire·ty \in-ˈtīr-ət-ē, -ˈtīrt-ē\ *n.; pl.* **en·tire·ties. 1** The state of being entire; completeness; wholeness. **2** That which is entire; the sum total.

en·ti·tle \in-ˈtīt-l\ *v.;* **en·ti·tled; en·ti·tling** \-l(-)ing\. **1** To give a right or claim to; as, a coupon that *entitles* one to a free sample; to be *entitled* to vote. **2** To give a title to; to call; to name; as, a book *entitled* "Favorite Fairy Tales".

en·ti·ty \ˈent-ət-ē\ *n.; pl.* **en·ti·ties.** Something that has a real existence either as a thing that can be known through the senses, as a chair or a building, or as a thing that can be understood through the mind, as a nation or a religion.

en·tomb \in-ˈtüm\ *v.* To place in a tomb; to bury. — **en·tomb·ment** \-ˈtüm-mənt\ *n.*

en·to·mol·o·gy \ˌent-m-ˈäl-ə-jē\ *n.* The branch of zoology that treats of insects. — **en·to·mo·log·ic** \-ə-ˈläj-ik\ or **en·to·mo·log·i·cal** \-ik-l\ *adj.* — **en·to·mol·o·gist** \-ˈäl-ə-jəst\ *n.*

en·trails \ˈen-ˌtrālz, -trəlz\ *n. pl.* The internal parts of animal bodies; especially, the intestines.

en·train \in-ˈtrān\ *v.* To put or go aboard a railroad train.

en·trance \ˈen-trən(t)s\ *n.* **1** The act of entering; as, to make a noisy *entrance* into a room. **2** A door, gate, or way for entering; as, to use the front *entrance.* **3** Permission to enter; admittance; as, to be refused *entrance* to a meeting.

en·trance \in-ˈtran(t)s\ *v.;* **en·tranced; en·tranc·ing. 1** To put into a trance. **2** To fill with delight and wonder; as, *entrancing* music. — **en·trance·ment** \-mənt\ *n.* — **en·tranc·ing·ly,** *adv.*

en·trant \ˈen-trənt\ *n.* A person who enters; as, an *entrant* in a contest.

en·trap \in-ˈtrap\ *v.;* **en·trapped; en·trap·ping.** To catch in or as if in a trap; to trap; to ensnare.

en·treat \in-ˈtrēt\ *v.* To ask earnestly; to beg; to beseech; as, to *entreat* help. The servant *entreated* his master not to dismiss him.

en·treaty \in-ˈtrēt-ē\ *n.; pl.* **en·treat·ies.** Earnest request; appeal; plea; as, the piteous *entreaties* of an aged beggar.

en·tree \ˈän-ˌtrā\ *n.* [French *entrée.*] **1** Entrance; as, to have *entree* into the best society. **2** A dish served between two chief courses in a meal or a dish, not a roast, served as a main course.

en·trench \in-ˈtrench\ *v.* **1** To encroach; to trespass; as, to *entrench* upon the land of one's neighbor. **2** To surround with a trench or trenches, as a position taken up by soldiers. **3** To establish firmly or in a strong position; as, to *entrench* oneself in the organization in which one works.

en·trench·ment \in-ˈtrench-mənt\ *n.* **1** The act of entrenching or the state of being entrenched. **2** An entrenched position. **3** Any defense or protection; especially, a defensive work consisting of a trench and a wall of earth.

en·trust \in-ˈtrəst\ *v.* **1** To give into the care of another, as for safekeeping or handling according to instructions; as, to *entrust* one's savings to a bank; to *entrust* a package to a messenger boy. **2** To give custody, care, or charge of something to another as a trust; as, to *entrust* a bank with one's savings.

en·try \ˈen-trē\ *n.; pl.* **en·tries. 1** The act of entering; entrance. **2** A place through which entrance is made; a hall; a vestibule; a passage. **3** The act of making a written record of something, as in a book or a list; the thing thus recorded. **4** A person or thing entered in a contest or race.

en·twine \in-ˈtwīn\ *v.;* **en·twined; en·twin·ing.** To twist or twine together or around; as, a tree trunk *entwined* with vines.

enu·mer·ate \ē-ˈnüm-r-ˌāt, -ˈnyüm-\ *v.;* **enu·mer·at·ed; enu·mer·at·ing.** To count over; to name over; as, to *enumerate* the days of the week. — **enu·mer·a·tion** \ē-ˌnüm-r-ˈāsh-n, -ˌnyüm-\ *n.* — **enu·mer·a·tive** \ē-ˈnüm-r-ˌāt-iv, -ˈnyüm-, -ət-iv\ *adj.* — **enu·mer·a·tor** \-ˌāt-r\ *n.*

enun·ci·ate \ē-ˈnən(t)s-ē-ˌāt\ *v.;* **enun·ci·at·ed; enun·ci·at·ing. 1** To state; to announce; to proclaim; as, to *enunciate* the plan to be followed. **2** To pronounce; to articulate; as, to *enunciate* clearly. — **enun·ci·a·tion** \ē-ˌnən(t)s-ē-ˈāsh-n\ *n.*

en·vel·op \in-ˈvel-əp\ *v.* To put a covering around; to wrap up or in. Fog *enveloped* the city. — **en·vel·op·ment** \-mənt\ *n.*

en·ve·lope \'en-və-ˌlōp, 'än-\ *n.* **1** A cover or wrapper; especially, a piece of folded gummed paper used for enclosing a letter for mailing. **2** In a balloon or airship, the bag that contains the gas. **3** In biology, any enclosing cover, as a membrane.

en·ven·om \in-'ven-əm\ *v.* **1** To taint or fill with venom or poison; as, a story in which a character is killed by putting on an *envenomed* robe. **2** To embitter. Thoughts of the abuses he had suffered *envenomed* the speaker's tongue.

en·vi·a·ble \'en-vē-əb-l\ *adj.* Worth envying; of a kind to arouse envy or a desire to have or be like; as, to achieve an *enviable* record. — **en·vi·a·bly** \-ə-blē\ *adv.*

en·vi·ous \'en-vē-əs\ *adj.* Feeling or showing envy; caused by envy; proceeding from envy; as, *envious* of a neighbor's wealth. — **en·vi·ous·ly,** *adv.*

en·vi·ron \in-'vī-rən\ *v.* To form a ring around; to surround. A wall *environs* the ancient city.

en·vi·ron·ment \in-'vī-rən-mənt\ *n.* **1** An environing; encirclement. **2** Surroundings; especially, the conditions or influences that affect the growth and development of a person, an animal, or a plant. Children from a city *environment* enjoy a vacation in the country. — **en·vi·ron·men·tal** \in-ˌvī-rən-'ment-l\ *adj.*

en·vi·rons \in-'vī-rənz, 'en-və-\ *n. pl.* The suburbs or districts round about a place; surroundings.

en·vis·age \in-'viz-ij\ *v.;* **en·vis·aged; en·vis·ag·ing.** To visualize; to picture in the mind; as, to *envisage* a world free from poverty and disease.

en·voy \'än-ˌvȯi, 'en-\ *n.* **1** A messenger. **2** A representative sent by one government to another government; a diplomatic agent ranking below an ambassador and above a minister.

en·vy \'en-vē\ *n.; pl.* **en·vies. 1** A feeling of discontent at the sight of another's good fortune, together with a desire to have the same good fortune oneself. The little boy was filled with *envy* when he saw his playmate's presents. **2** A person or a thing that is envied; as, to be the *envy* of all one's friends.
— The word *jealousy* is a synonym of *envy: envy* may imply a desire, sometimes accompanied by anger or chagrin, to have what another has or something equally valuable; *jealousy* is likely to suggest great envy accompanied by strong personal dislike or even hatred.
— *v.;* **en·vied** \-vēd\; **en·vy·ing. 1** To feel envy towards; as, to *envy* a friend because of his fine clothes. **2** To feel envy on account of; to begrudge; as, to *envy* a friend his fine clothes.

en·wrap \in-'rap\ *v.;* **en·wrapped; en·wrap·ping.** To enfold; to wrap.

en·zyme \'en-ˌzīm\ *n.* Any of a group of complex substances, as pepsin, that are produced by cells and speed up chemical changes in plants and animals, as in the digestion of foods.

eo·lith·ic \ˌē-ə-'lith-ik\ *adj.* Relating to the earliest stage (**Eolithic period**) of human culture marked by the use of stone implements.

eon. Variant of *aeon.*

ep·au·let or **ep·au·lette** \ˌep-l-'et\ *n.* A shoulder ornament on uniforms, especially of military and naval officers.

man wearing epaulets

ephem·er·al \i-'fem-r-əl\ *adj.* **1** Lasting one day only; as, an *ephemeral* flower. **2** Lasting a very short time; short-lived; as, *ephemeral* fashions.

ephem·er·id \i-'fem-r-əd\ *n.* A slender delicate insect with net-veined wings, having an adult life of only a few hours or a few days; a May fly.

ep·ic \'ep-ik\ *n.* A long poem telling the story of one or more heroes and their deeds. — *adj.* Like an epic; worthy of being told in an epic; as, an *epic* voyage.

ep·i·cen·ter \'ep-ə-ˌsent-r\ *n.* The earth's surface directly above the focus of an earthquake. — **ep·i·cen·tral** \ˌep-ə-'sen-trəl\ *adj.*

ep·i·cure \'ep-ə-ˌkyu̇r\ *n.* [Named after *Epicurus* (Greek *Epikouros*), a Greek philosopher of the 4th–3rd century B.C., who had a reputation for advocating a life of pleasure and ease.] A person having or professing to have great knowledge of, and a very refined taste in, food and drink.

ep·i·cu·re·an \ˌep-ə-kyu̇-'rē-ən, -'kyu̇r-ē-ən\ *adj.* **1** Given to the pursuit of refined but luxurious pleasures. **2** Suited to an epicure; as, an *epicurean* banquet. — *n.* A person of epicurean tastes.

ep·i·dem·ic \ˌep-ə-'dem-ik\ *adj.* Spreading widely and affecting large numbers of people at the same time; as, an *epidemic* disease. — *n.* **1** A rapidly spreading attack of disease. **2** Anything that spreads like an epidemic of disease; as, an *epidemic* of roller skating that comes with early spring. — **ep·i·dem·i·cal·ly** \-ik-l(-)ē\ *adv.*

ep·i·de·mi·ol·o·gy \ˌep-ə-ˌdē-mē-'äl-ə-jē, -ˌdem-ē-\ *n.* The branch of medical science that treats of epidemics. — **ep·i·de·mi·ol·o·gist** \-jəst\ *n.*

ep·i·der·mis \ˌep-ə-'dər-məs\ *n.* **1** The outer layer of an animal's skin. **2** The thin, outermost protective layer of cells in seed plants and ferns. **3** Any of various other covering layers, as the outer covering of the shells of many mollusks. — **ep·i·der·mal** \-'dərm-l\ *adj.*

ep·i·glot·tis \ˌep-ə-'glät-əs\ *n.* A thin plate of flexible cartilage in front of the glottis that folds back over and protects the glottis during swallowing.

ep·i·gram \'ep-ə-ˌgram\ *n.* A brief, clever saying or a short poem ending with a witty turn of expression.

ep·i·gram·mat·ic \ˌep-ə-grə-'mat-ik\ *adj.* **1** Like or containing epigrams; short and witty in expression. **2** Fond of making epigrams. — **ep·i·gram·mat·i·cal·ly** \-ik-l(-)ē\ *adv.*

ep·i·lep·sy \'ep-l-ˌep-sē\ *n.* A nervous disease characterized by convulsive fits and loss of consciousness.

ep·i·lep·tic \ˌep-l-'ep-tik\ *adj.* **1** Of or relating to epilepsy; as, an *epileptic* fit. **2** Having epilepsy; as, an *epileptic* patient. — *n.* A person who has epilepsy.

ep·i·logue or **ep·i·log** \'ep-l-ˌȯg\ *n.* **1** A speech or a poem spoken directly to the audience by an actor after the close of a play. **2** A concluding section, as of a novel, coming after the completion of the main events and rounding out the general plan.

ep·i·neph·rine \ˌep-ə-'nef-rən\ *n.* Adrenaline.

Epiph·a·ny \ē-'pif-n-ē\ *n.* A church festival on January 6th, celebrating the coming of the three wise men to Jesus at Bethlehem.

epis·co·pa·cy \ē-'pis-kə-pə-sē\ *n.; pl.* **epis·co·pa·cies.** **1** Government of the church by bishops. **2** The rank, office, or term of office of a bishop. **3** The whole body of bishops.

epis·co·pal \ē-'pis-kəp-l\ *adj.* **1** Of or relating to a bishop or bishops; as, *episcopal* vestments. **2** Governed by bishops; as, an *episcopal* church. **3** [with a capital] Of or relating to the Church of England or certain Protestant churches in the United States that are governed by bishops.

epis·co·pa·lian \ē-ˌpis-kə-'pāl-yən\ *adj.* Episcopal. — *n.* [with a capital] A person who belongs to an Episcopal church, especially the Protestant Episcopal Church in the United States.

epis·co·pate \ē-'pis-kə-pət\ *n.* **1** The rank, office, or term of office of a bishop. **2** The whole body of bishops.

ep·i·sode \'ep-ə-ˌsōd\ *n.* **1** Any incident or action introduced into a story to give greater variety and interest. **2** An event or a series of events that stands out clearly in one's life, in history, or in a story. — **ep·i·sod·ic** \ˌep-ə-'säd-ik\ *adj.*

epis·tle \ē-'pis-l\ *n.* A letter to a person; especially, a formal, carefully written letter.

epis·to·lary \ē-'pis-tə-ˌler-ē\ *adj.* Of, relating to, or suitable for letters.

ep·i·taph \'ep-ə-ˌtaf\ *n.* An inscription, as on a tombstone, in memory of a dead person.

ep·i·the·li·um \ˌep-ə-'thē-lē-əm\ *n.; pl.* **ep·i·the·li·ums** \-lē-əmz\ or **ep·i·the·lia** \-lē-ə\. Any membranelike tissue covering an external surface of the body, as the epidermis, or lining its cavities, as a mucous membrane.

ep·i·thet \'ep-ə-ˌthet, -thət\ *n.* A word or phrase that expresses some quality belonging to or associated with a person or thing, as *Lion-heart* in "Richard Lion-heart" or *fire-breathing* in "a fire-breathing warrior".

epit·o·me \ē-'pit-m-ˌē\ *n.* **1** A brief, condensed statement of the contents of a work; a summary; an abstract. **2** A part that is typical of a whole; something considered to represent or to embody the characteristics of something else larger or greater than itself; as, a remark that was the *epitome* of good common sense.

epit·o·mize \ē-'pit-m-ˌīz\ *v.;* **epit·o·mized; epit·o·miz·ing.** To make or serve as an epitome of; to summarize.

ep·och \'ep-ək, -ˌäk, 'ē-ˌpäk\ *n.* **1** Any event or time that is the starting point of a new period in history. The end of slavery marked an *epoch* in American history. **2** A period marked by unusual or important events; as, an *epoch* of almost incredible scientific discovery. — **ep·och·al** \'ep-ək-l, -ˌäk-l\ *adj.*

Ep·som salts or **Epsom salt** \'eps-m\. A bitter colorless or white crystalline salt commonly used as a cathartic.

eq·ua·ble \'ek-wəb-l, 'ēk-\ *adj.* Even; uniform; especially, free from extremes or sudden or harsh changes; as, an *equable* temper; an *equable* climate. — **eq·ua·bly** \-wə-blē\ *adv.*

equal \'ēk-wəl\ *adj.* **1** Exactly the same in number, amount, degree, rank, or quality; as, an *equal* number of apples and oranges; officers of *equal* rank. **2** Evenly balanced or proportioned; as, an *equal* contest; an *equal* mixture. **3** Having enough strength, ability, or means; adequate; as, to be *equal* to a difficult task. — For synonyms see *identical.* — *n.* A person or a thing that is equal to another, as in age, rank, or ability. — *v.;* **equaled** or **equalled; equal·ing** or **equal·ling.** To be or become equal to, as in quantity, value, degree, or rank; to match.

equal·i·ty \ē-'kwäl-ət-ē\ *n.; pl.* **equal·i·ties.** The condition of being equal; sameness in number, quantity, or degree; likeness in quality, rank, or position.

equal·ize \'ēk-wə-ˌlīz\ *v.;* **equal·ized; equal·iz·ing.** **1** To make equal; as, to *equalize* taxes. **2** To make uniform or constant; to distribute evenly; to balance; as, to *equalize* steam pressure in a heating system. — **equal·i·za·tion** \ˌēk-wə-lə-'zāsh-n\ *n.* — **equal·iz·er** \'ēk-wə-ˌlīz-r\ *n.*

equal·ly \'ēk-wə-lē\ *adv.* In an equal manner or degree; in equal shares; alike; evenly.

equa·nim·i·ty \ˌēk-wə-'nim-ət-ē, ˌek-\ *n.* Evenness of mind; calm temper; composure; as, to accept misfortunes with *equanimity.*

equate \ē-'kwāt\ *v.;* **equat·ed; equat·ing.** To make equal or to represent or express as equal or equivalent.

equa·tion \ē-'kwāzh-n, -'kwāsh-n\ *n.* **1** The act or process of equating, or making equal. **2** The state of being equal; equality. **3** In mathematics, an expression of equality between two quantities, the equality being shown by the sign = placed between them. **4** In chemistry, an expression representing a chemical reaction by means of chemical symbols.

equa·tor \ē-'kwāt-r, 'ē-ˌkwāt-r\ *n.* An imaginary great circle around the earth, everywhere equally distant from the North Pole and the South Pole, dividing the earth's surface into the northern and southern hemispheres.

equa·to·ri·al \ˌēk-wə-'tōr-ē-əl, ˌek-, -'tȯr-\ *adj.* **1** Of or relating to the equator; lying near the equator; as, *equatorial* Africa. **2** Resembling conditions at or near the equator, especially in climate; as, *equatorial* heat.

eq·uer·ry \'ek-wər-ē, ē-'kwer-ē\ *n.; pl.* **eq·uer·ries.**

1 An official in charge of the horses belonging to a prince or nobleman. 2 A personal attendant upon one of the members of the British royal household.

eques·tri·an \ē-'kwes-trē-ən\ *adj.* 1 Of or relating to horses, horsemen, or horsemanship. 2 Mounted on horseback; as, *equestrian* troops; an *equestrian* statue. — *n.* A horseback rider.

eques·tri·enne \ē-ˌkwes-trē-'en\ *n.* A woman horseback rider.

equi·an·gu·lar \ˌēk-wē-'ang-gyəl-r\ *adj.* Having all angles equal. A square is *equiangular.*

equi·dis·tant \ˌēk-wə-'dis-tənt\ *adj.* Equally distant.

equi·lat·er·al \ˌēk-wə-'lat-r-əl, -'la-trəl\ *adj.* Having all sides equal; as, an *equilateral* triangle. — *n.* A figure having equal sides. — **equi·lat·er·al·ly** \-'lat-r-ə-lē, -'la-trə-lē\ *adv.*

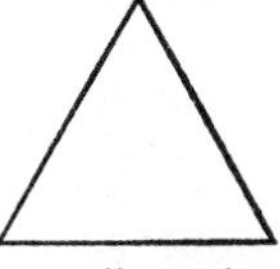
equilateral triangle

equi·lib·ri·um \ˌēk-wə-'lib-rē-əm, ˌek-\ *n.* A state of balance, as between weights, forces, or influences; physical or mental balance.

equine \'ē-ˌkwīn\ *adj.* [From Latin *equinus*, derived from *equus* meaning "horse".] Of, relating to, or like a horse. — *n.* A horse.

equi·noc·tial \ˌēk-wə-'näksh-l\ *adj.* 1 Relating to or occurring at the equinox; as, *equinoctial* storms. 2 Relating to the regions or climate of the equator; as, *equinoctial* heat. — *n.* An equinoctial storm.

equi·nox \'ēk-wə-ˌnäks\ *n.* Either of the two times during the year, about March 21 (**vernal equinox**) and September 23 (**autumnal equinox**), when the sun's center crosses the equator and day and night are everywhere of equal length.

equip \ē-'kwip\ *v.;* **equipped**; **equip·ping.** To furnish for some special purpose; to fit out; to supply with what is necessary for efficient action; as, to raise, train, and *equip* an army; a kitchen *equipped* with all modern laborsaving devices.

eq·ui·page \'ek-wə-pij\ *n.* 1 Equipment; furnishings. 2 A carriage. 3 A carriage with its horses, driver, and other attendants.

equip·ment \ē-'kwip-mənt\ *n.* 1 The act of equipping; a fitting out or supplying. 2 The state or manner of being equipped. 3 Supplies needed for a special purpose; as, fire-fighting *equipment;* office *equipment.* 4 The qualities and resources that equip a person for his life and work.

eq·ui·poise \'ek-wə-ˌpȯiz, 'ēk-\ *n.* 1 Equality of weight or force; a state of balance; equilibrium. 2 A weight that is or may be used to balance another weight.

eq·ui·ta·ble \'ek-wət-əb-l\ *adj.* Fair; just; impartial; reasonable; as, an *equitable* distribution of the world's goods. — **eq·ui·ta·bly** \-ə-blē\ *adv.*

eq·ui·ty \'ek-wət-ē\ *n.; pl.* **eq·ui·ties.** 1 Fairness or justice in dealings between persons. 2 A system or body of rules and principles of law which developed as a more flexible supplement to the fixed common and statute law. 3 The amount or value of a property above all amounts that may be owed on it.

equiv·a·lent \ē-'kwiv-l-ənt\ *adj.* Alike or equal in number, value, or meaning. — For synonyms see *identical.* — *n.* Something equivalent; as, five dollars or its *equivalent* in English money. — **equiv·a·lence** \-ən(t)s\ *n.*

equiv·o·cal \ē-'kwiv-ək-l\ *adj.* 1 Having two or more possible meanings; ambiguous; as, an *equivocal* answer. 2 Uncertain; doubtful; as, an *equivocal* result. 3 Suspicious; questionable; as, *equivocal* behavior. — **equiv·o·cal·ly** \-ək-l(-)ē\ *adv.*

equiv·o·cate \ē-'kwiv-ə-ˌkāt\ *v.;* **equiv·o·cat·ed**; **equiv·o·cat·ing.** 1 To use equivocal language, especially with intent to deceive. 2 To lie. — **equiv·o·ca·tor** \-ˌkāt-r\ *n.*

equiv·o·ca·tion \ē-ˌkwiv-ə-'kāsh-n\ *n.* 1 The use of expressions having more than one possible meaning, especially with the purpose of deceiving or misleading. 2 An equivocal expression.

-er \(ə)r\. A suffix that can mean: 1 One who has to do with, as by way of occupation, as in *potter* or *sawyer.* 2 One of a size, capacity, value, or date, as in *forty-niner* or *three-decker.* 3 A resident of, one living in, as in *islander* or *southerner.* 4 A person or thing that performs an action, as *maker* or *blotter.*

-er \(ə)r\. A suffix meaning "more", used to form the comparative degree of adjectives and adverbs, as in *warmer, later,* or *livelier.*

era \'ir-ə, 'er-ə, 'ē-rə\ *n.* 1 A period of time reckoned from some special date or event; as, the Christian *era.* 2 Any important period of history; as, the Revolutionary *era.* 3 One of the major divisions of geologic time.

erad·i·ca·ble \ē-'rad-ə-kəb-l\ *adj.* Capable of being eradicated.

erad·i·cate \ē-'rad-ə-ˌkāt\ *v.;* **erad·i·cat·ed**; **erad·i·cat·ing.** 1 To tear up by the roots. 2 To destroy completely; to get rid of entirely; to exterminate; as, to *eradicate* a disease. — **erad·i·ca·tion** \ē-ˌrad-ə-'kāsh-n\ *n.* — **erad·i·ca·tive** \ē-'rad-ə-ˌkāt-iv\ *adj.*

erad·i·ca·tor \ē-'rad-ə-ˌkāt-r\ *n.* One that eradicates, as a chemical preparation for removing ink.

erase \ē-'rās\ *v.;* **erased**; **eras·ing.** To rub out or scratch out, as something written or drawn.

— The words *cancel* and *efface* are synonyms of *erase: erase* may suggest removing something, especially writing or printing, by rubbing or scratching it off a surface; *cancel* often implies crossing something out, as by lines, thus removing its effectiveness or making it no longer usable; *efface* may indicate making something indistinct or illegible, or may suggest such a complete removal as to leave no trace.

eras·er \ē-'rās-r\ *n.* One that erases; especially, a sharp tool or a piece of rubber used for erasing marks.

era·sure \ē-ˈrāsh-r\ *n.* **1** An erasing; a rubbing or scratching out. **2** Something erased.

ere \ˈer, ˈar\ *prep.* or *conj.* Before; as, to waken *ere* the dawn; to go back *ere* it is too late.

erect \ē-ˈrekt\ *adj.* **1** Upright; straight up and down; as, a tall, *erect* pine tree. **2** Directed upward; raised. — *v.* **1** To raise, as a building; to build. Workmen *erected* booths for the fair on the village green. **2** To set upright; as, to *erect* a flagpole. **3** In geometry, to draw or construct a line or figure on a given base. **4** To put together in position for use; to set up; to assemble, as a machine. — **erect·ly,** *adv.* — **erect·er** or **erec·tor** \ē-ˈrekt-r\ *n.*

erec·tion \ē-ˈreksh-n\ *n.* **1** An erecting or a being erected; a raising, building, or constructing. **2** Something erected, as a building. **3** An assembling or connecting, as of the parts of a machine.

ere·long \ˈer-ˈlȯng, ˈar-\ *adv.* Before long; soon.

er·e·mite \ˈer-ə-ˌmīt\ *n.* A hermit.

er·go \ˈer-ˌgō, ˈər-\ *conj.* or *adv.* Therefore; hence.

er·mine \ˈər-mən\ *n.; pl.* **er·mine** or **er·mines. 1** A weasel of northern countries whose fur becomes pure white in winter, except for the black tip of the tail. **2** The white fur of this animal. **3** The office or function of a judge.

ermine

erode \ē-ˈrōd\ *v.;* **erod·ed; erod·ing.** To eat into; to wear away; to destroy by slowly wearing away. The sea is *eroding* the shore.

ero·sion \ē-ˈrōzh-n\ *n.* The action of eroding or the state of being eroded; a wearing away, as of land by wind and water.

ero·sive \ē-ˈrō-siv\ *adj.* Eating or wearing away; as, the *erosive* effect of water upon rock.

erot·ic \ē-ˈrät-ik\ *adj.* Of or relating to sexual love. — **erot·i·cal·ly** \-ik-l(-)ē\ *adv.*

err \ˈər, ˈer\ *v.* **1** To make a mistake; as, to *err* in judgment. **2** To do wrong; to sin.

er·rand \ˈer-ənd\ *n.* **1** A short trip taken to do some business; as, to go on an *errand* after school. **2** The business done on such a trip.

er·rant \ˈer-ənt\ *adj.* **1** Wandering in search of adventure; as, an *errant* knight. **2** Erring; wrong; mistaken; as, *errant* ideas.

er·rant·ry \ˈer-ən-trē\ *n.; pl.* **er·rant·ries.** Errant character; a deed characteristic of a knight-errant; a roving in search of adventure.

er·rat·ic \i-ˈrat-ik\ *adj.* **1** Having no certain course; wandering; as, a vacation consisting of unplanned, *erratic* trips to various points of interest. **2** Queer; odd; eccentric; as, *erratic* conduct. — **er·rat·i·cal·ly** \-ik-l(-)ē\ *adv.*

er·ra·tum \e-ˈrät-m, -ˈrāt-, -ˈrat-\ *n.; pl.* **er·ra·ta** \e-ˈrät-ə, -ˈrāt-, -ˈrat-\. An error in writing or printing.

er·ro·ne·ous \i-ˈrō-nē-əs\ *adj.* Mistaken; wrong; incorrect; as, an *erroneous* idea. — **er·ro·ne·ous·ly,** *adv.*

er·ror \ˈer-r\ *n.* **1** A belief in something that is not true. Honest *error* is no sin. **2** The state of holding such a belief; as, to be in *error.* **3** A mistake; an inaccuracy; as, an *error* in spelling. **4** In baseball, a fault by a player of the side in the field as a result of which a player of the side at bat gains an advantage.

— The words *mistake* and *blunder* are synonyms of *error: error* may indicate a deviation from correct or approved belief or procedure; *mistake* usually suggests a misunderstanding or an unintentionally wrong decision or action; *blunder* may imply ignorance or stupidity or blameworthy lack of care.

erst·while \ˈərst-ˌhwīl, -ˌwīl\ *adv. Archaic.* Formerly; heretofore. — *adj.* Former.

eruct \ē-ˈrəkt\ *v.* To belch. — **eruc·ta·tion** \ˌē-ˌrək-ˈtāsh-n\ *n.*

er·u·dite \ˈer-yə-ˌdīt, ˈer-ə-\ *adj.* Learned; scholarly; as, an *erudite* speech.

er·u·di·tion \ˌer-yə-ˈdish-n, ˌer-ə-\ *n.* Learning, especially in literature, history, or criticism; scholarship.

erupt \ē-ˈrəpt\ *v.* **1** To burst forth or cause to burst forth, as ashes or lava from a volcano. **2** To break through a surface, as teeth through the gums, or a rash through the skin.

erup·tion \ē-ˈrəpsh-n\ *n.* **1** A bursting forth, as of lava from a volcano. **2** The breaking out of a rash on the skin. **3** A rash. — **erup·tive** \ē-ˈrəp-tiv\ *adj.*

-ery \r-ē, rē, ər-ē\. A suffix that can mean: **1** Behavior, conduct, or character, as in *snobbery* or *foolery.* **2** Act, art, trade, occupation, or condition, as in *cookery* or *robbery.* **3** Place, as where something is done or kept or where something grows, or where a person is kept or lives, as in *bakery, piggery,* or *nunnery.* **4** Products or wares considered as a group or whole, as *pottery* or *machinery.*

er·y·sip·e·las \ˌer-ə-ˈsip-l(-)əs, ˌir-\ *n.* An acute disease caused by bacteria and marked by a fever and a reddish inflammation of the skin.

es·ca·la·tor \ˈesk-l-ˌāt-r\ *n.* A moving stairway or incline arranged like an endless belt.

es·cal·oped or **es·cal·loped** \ə-ˈskäl-əpt, -ˈskal-\ *adj.* Scalloped; especially, baked with bread crumbs, butter, and milk.

es·ca·pade \ˈes-kə-ˌpād\ *n.* A mischievous adventure; a prank.

es·cape \ə-ˈskāp\ *v.;* **es·caped; es·cap·ing. 1** To get away; to get free or clear; as, to *escape* from a burning building; a funny story about an elephant that *escaped* from a circus. **2** To keep free of; to avoid; as, to fall down the stairs but *escape* being hurt. **3** To leak out from some enclosed place; as, air *escaping* from a tire. **4** To remain outside the range of; to fail to be noticed by; as, a fact that *escaped* one's attention. **5** To come out from or be uttered by a person involuntarily. A sigh of weariness *escaped* him. — *n.* **1** The act of escaping; the fact of having escaped; as, to make a daring *escape;* to have a lucky *escape.* **2** The means of escaping; as, a fire *escape.* **3** Leakage; as, to hear the *escape* of steam.

es·cape·ment \ə-'skāp-mənt\ *n.* **1** In a timepiece, a device through which the energy of the weight or spring is transmitted to the pendulum or balance. **2** In a typewriter, the mechanism that controls movement of the carriage.

es·cap·ist \ə-'skāp-əst\ *n.* A person who makes a practice of directing his thoughts to purely imaginary things to escape from reality or routine. — **es·cap·ism** \-'skā-ˌpiz-m\ *n.*

es·carp·ment \ə-'skärp-mənt, -'skårp-\ *n.* **1** A long, steep face of rock; a cliff. **2** The ground around a fort, cut away steeply to prevent the approach of an enemy.

es·chew \es-'chü\ *v.* To shun or avoid something as wrong or distasteful; as, to *eschew* bad manners.

es·cort \'es-ˌkȯrt\ *n.* **1** A person or group of persons accompanying another for protection, or to show honor or courtesy; as, a girl's *escort* to a dance. A motorcycle *escort* rode ahead of the President's car. **2** An accompanying as a protection or honor. — \es-'kȯrt, 'es-ˌkȯrt\ *v.* To accompany as an escort. — For synonyms see *accompany.*

es·cort carrier \'es-ˌkȯrt\. A small auxiliary aircraft carrier of about 4000 tons or a cargo ship or a tanker rebuilt to carry airplanes.

es·cu·lent \'es-kyə-lənt\ *adj.* Eatable.

es·cutch·eon \ə-'skəch-n\ *n.* In heraldry, the surface on which a coat of arms is shown.

escutcheon

-ese \ēz, ēs\. A suffix, as in *Chinese* or *Japanese*, that can mean: **1** Of or relating to a certain country. **2** A person or persons belonging to, or the language of, a certain country.

Es·ki·mo \'esk-m-ˌō\ *n.; pl.* **Es·ki·mos** or **Es·ki·mo.** A member of a race living on the arctic coasts of America.

Eskimo dog. 1 A dog of a broad-chested powerful breed used by the Eskimos to draw sleds. **2** Any American sled dog.

Eskimo dog

esoph·a·gus \ē-'säf-ə-gəs\ *n.; pl.* **esoph·a·gi** \-ˌgī, -ˌjī\. The tube that leads from the throat to the stomach; the gullet.

es·o·ter·ic \ˌes-ə-'ter-ik\ *adj.* **1** Taught only to the initiated; understood only by the chosen few; secret; as, an *esoteric* ritual. **2** Of, relating to, or communicating esoteric doctrines; as, *esoteric* religions.

esp. Abbreviation for: **1** *especial.* **2** *especially.*

es·pe·cial \ə-'spesh-l\ *adj.* Special; particular; as, to pay *especial* attention to spelling when writing a letter.

es·pe·cial·ly \ə-'spesh-l(-)ē\ *adv.* Particularly. The children *especially* wanted to see the monkeys.

es·pi·o·nage \'es-pē-ə-ˌnäzh, -ˌnäj, -ˌnȧzh, -ˌnȧj, 'es-pē-ə-nij, es-'pē-ə-nij\ *n.* The practice of spying or the use of spies, especially to get information about the plans and activities of foreign governments.

es·pla·nade \'es-plə-ˌnäd, -ˌnād\ *n.* A clear level space, especially one along a shore used for public walks or drives.

es·pous·al \ə-'spaủz-l\ *n.* **1** The ceremony of becoming betrothed or married; a wedding. **2** The taking up of a cause or policy as a supporter.

es·pouse \ə-'spaủz, -'spaủs\ *v.;* **es·poused; es·pous·ing. 1** To marry. **2** To adopt a cause or theory as one's own; to support; to defend; as, to *espouse* the plan for a new school building.

es·prit \es-'prē\ *n.* [From French, meaning literally "spirit" and derived from Latin *spiritus,* the source of English *spirit.*] A lively wit and understanding.

es·prit de corps \'es-ˌprē də 'kōr, es-'prē, 'kȯr\. The common spirit existing in the members of a group and inspiring enthusiasm, devotion, and strong regard for the honor of the group.

es·py \es-'pī\ *v.;* **es·pied** \-'pīd\; **es·py·ing.** To catch sight of; to spy; as, to *espy* a small bird high in a tree.

Esq. Abbreviation for *Esquire.*

es·quire \'es-ˌkwīr, es-'kwīr\ *n.* **1** In the age of chivalry, a candidate for knighthood who served as an attendant on a knight. **2** A man of the English gentry next in rank and dignity below a knight. **3** [with a capital] A formal title of courtesy, now usually written in the abbreviated form "Esq." after a person's surname; as, John Smith, *Esq.*

-ess \əs, *sometimes* es\. A suffix that can mean: female, as in *authoress* or *lioness.*

es·say \e-'sā, 'es-ˌā\ *v.;* **es·sayed; es·say·ing.** To make an effort to do something; to attempt; to try. — *n.* **1** An attempt. **2** \'es-ˌā\ A piece of writing, usually short, on one subject; a composition.

es·say·ist \'es-ˌā-əst\ *n.* A writer of essays.

es·sence \'es-n(t)s\ *n.* **1** The basic nature of a thing; the quality or sum of qualities that make a thing what it is. The *essence* of love is unselfishness. **2** A substance distilled or otherwise extracted from another substance, usually a plant or drug, and having the special qualities of the original substance; as, *essence* of peppermint. **3** Perfume; scent.

es·sen·tial \ə-'sench-l\ *adj.* **1** Forming or belonging to the fundamental nature of a thing. Free speech is an *essential* right of citizenship. **2** Containing or having the character of an essence, or concentrated extraction; as, *essential* oils. **3** Important in the highest degree; necessary. Food is *essential* to life. — *n.* Something that is essential, necessary, or fundamental; as, to have the *essentials* for success in business.

es·sen·tial·ly \ə-'sench-l(-)ē\ *adv.* In essentials; basically; as, an *essentially* sound program; *essentially* a fine boy.

-est \əst\. A suffix meaning "most", used to form the superlative degree of adjectives and adverbs, as in *warmest, latest,* or *liveliest.*

EST. Abbreviation for *Eastern Standard Time.*

es·tab·lish \ə-'stab-lish\ *v.* **1** To fix firmly; to

settle; as, to *establish* a fact as true. **2** To enact, as laws or a constitution. **3** To found; as, to *establish* a colony; to *establish* a business. **4** To gain recognition of; to cause to be accepted; as, to *establish* a claim. **5** To set up or place (oneself), as in business.

es·tab·lished church \ə-'stab-lisht\. A church recognized by a government as the official church of the state.

es·tab·lish·ment \ə-'stab-lish-mənt\ *n.* **1** The act of establishing or the state or fact of being established. **2** Something that is established, as an organized force for carrying on public or private affairs; as, the military *establishment* of a country. **3** The place where one is settled, either for residence or business; such a place with its grounds, buildings, furnishings, and employees; as, to operate a dry-cleaning *establishment.*

es·tate \ə-'stāt\ *n.* **1** State or condition of being; as, to reach man's *estate.* **2** A social or political class or rank; as, the three *estates* (clergy, nobles, and commons) of feudal times. **3** The property of all kinds that a person leaves to be divided at his death. **4** A fine country house and lands.

es·teem \ə-'stēm\ *v.* **1** To regard; to consider; as, to *esteem* it a privilege to collect money for charity. **2** To think well of; to regard highly; to value; as, a man who is *esteemed* by all his neighbors. — *n.* Favorable opinion; high regard; as, to have the affection and *esteem* of one's neighbors.

es·ter \'est-r\ *n.* An organic salt.

esthetic. Variant of *aesthetic.*

esthetics. Variant of *aesthetics.*

es·ti·mate \'est-m-ˌāt\ *v.;* **es·ti·mat·ed; es·ti·mat·ing. 1** To give or form a general idea of the value, size, or cost of something; to calculate approximately; to judge; as, to *estimate* the cost of repairing a car; to *estimate* the length of a journey. **2** To form an opinion of; to judge; as, the difficulty of *estimating* the age in which one lives. — \-m-ət, -m-ˌāt\ *n.* **1** An opinion; a judgment. **2** A rough calculation, as of value, size, or cost; as, to get several *estimates* on painting the house. **3** A statement of the amount for which certain work will be done, made by the person who will do the work.

es·ti·ma·tion \ˌest-m-'āsh-n\ *n.* **1** The making of an estimate; a judgment; a reckoning. **2** An estimate. **3** Judgment; opinion. **4** Respect; honor; esteem; as, a person held in high *estimation* by his friends.

es·ti·vate \'es-tə-ˌvāt\ *v.;* **es·ti·vat·ed; es·ti·vat·ing. 1** To spend the summer. **2** To spend the summer in a temporarily inactive state. — **es·ti·va·tion** \ˌes-tə-'vāsh-n\ *n.*

Es·to·ni·an \es-'tō-nē-ən\ *adj.* Of or relating to Estonia. — *n.* **1** A member of a Caucasian people dwelling chiefly in Estonia. **2** The language of the Estonians.

es·trange \ə-'strānj\ *v.;* **es·tranged; es·trang·ing.** To cause to become separated, as by hard feelings; as, friends who had been *estranged* for many years by an unfortunate misunderstanding. — **es·trange·ment** \-mənt\ *n.*

es·tu·ary \'es-chə-ˌwer-ē\ *n.; pl.* **es·tu·ar·ies.** A passage where the tide meets the river current; especially, an arm of the sea at the lower end of a river.

etc. \ən 'sō ˌfōrth, ˌfȯrth; *or* et 'set-r-ə, 'se-trə\. Abbreviation for *et cetera.*

et cet·era \et 'set-r-ə, 'se-trə\. And others (of the same kind); and so forth; and so on.

etch \'ech\ *v.* [From Dutch *etsen,* borrowed from German *aetzen* meaning "to consume", "to corrode", literally "to cause to eat".] **1** To produce designs or figures on metal or glass by lines eaten into the substance by acid; as, to *etch* a copper plate. **2** To make etchings. — **etch·er,** *n.*

etch·ing \'ech-ing\ *n.* **1** The process of producing drawings or pictures by means of impressions taken from etched plates. **2** An impression taken in ink from an etched plate.

eter·nal \ē-'tərn-l\ *adj.* **1** Lasting forever; having no beginning and no end. **2** Continuing without interruption; unceasing. The dog's *eternal* barking annoyed everyone. — **eter·nal·ly** \-'tərn-l-ē\ *adv.*

eter·ni·ty \ē-'tər-nət-ē\ *n.; pl.* **eter·ni·ties. 1** Endless duration. **2** The state after death; immortality. **3** Seeming endlessness; as, an *eternity* of waiting.

ether \'ēth-r\ *n.* **1** The upper regions of space; the clear sky. **2** A strong-smelling flammable liquid that evaporates easily, much used as an anesthetic and for dissolving fats. **3** In physics, the invisible substance supposed to fill all space, including that occupied by fluids and solids, and to transmit waves, as of light and electricity.

ethe·re·al \ē-'thir-ē-əl\ *adj.* **1** Heavenly; as, *ethereal* spirits. **2** Light and airy; delicate; as, *ethereal* music. — **ethe·re·al·ly** \-ē-ə-lē\ *adv.*

eth·i·cal \'eth-ik-l\ *adj.* **1** Of or relating to ethics; having to do with morality; as, an *ethical* problem. **2** In accordance with professional standards or with other accepted rules of conduct. In some professions it is not *ethical* to advertise. — **eth·i·cal·ly** \-ik-l(-)ē\ *adv.*

eth·ics \'eth-iks\ *n.* **1** The branch of philosophy which treats of man's moral duties and obligations. **2** Moral principles; standards of conduct; as, the *ethics* of the medical profession.

Ethi·o·pi·an \ˌē-thē-'ōp-ē-ən\ *adj.* Of or relating to Ethiopia or the Ethiopian race. — *n.* **1** A native of Ethiopia, especially of the modern country. **2** A member of one of the five divisions into which mankind was formerly classified, the **Ethiopian race,** including the Negro peoples of Africa.

eth·nic \'eth-nik\ *adj.* Of or relating to races or groups of races classed according to common traits and customs; ethnological; as, two closely related *ethnic* groups; the *ethnic* divisions of mankind.

eth·nol·o·gy \eth-'näl-ə-jē\ *n.* The science that treats of the division of mankind into races, their origin, distribution, relations, and characteristics. — **eth·no·log·ic** \ˌeth-nə-ˈläj-ik\ or **eth·no·log·i·cal** \-ik-l\ *adj.* — **eth·nol·o·gist** \eth-ˈnäl-ə-jəst\ *n.*

et·i·quette \ˈet-ə-ˌket, ˈet-ik-ət\ *n.* The body of rules governing the way in which people behave in social or official life or the way in which a ceremony is conducted; as, flag *etiquette;* diplomatic *etiquette.*

-ette \ˈet, ˌet\. A suffix that can mean: **1** Small or little, as in *cigarette* or *kitchenette.* **2** Female, as in *farmerette.* **3** An imitation of or substitute for, as in *satinette.*

étude \ˈā-ˌtüd, -ˌtyüd\ *n.* [From French, derived from Old French *estudie,* the source of English *study.*] A piece of music intended to develop technical skill; a study.

et·y·mol·o·gy \ˌet-m-ˈäl-ə-jē\ *n.; pl.* **et·y·mol·o·gies. 1** The origin and history of a word as shown by a study of its elements or by reference to an earlier form of the word. **2** The branch of language study that has to do with the origin and history of words. — **et·y·mo·log·i·cal** \-ə-ˈläj-ik-l\ *adj.* — **et·y·mo·log·i·cal·ly** \-ik-l(-)ē\ *adv.* — **et·y·mol·o·gist** \-ˈäl-ə-jəst\ *n.*

eu·ca·lypt \ˈyük-l-ˌipt\ *n.* A eucalyptus.

eu·ca·lyp·tus \ˌyük-l-ˈip-təs\ *n.; pl.* **eu·ca·lyp·tus·es** \-tə-səz\ or **eu·ca·lyp·ti** \-ˌtī\. Any of a genus of trees of the myrtle family native to Australia but widely cultivated in certain other parts of the world and important for timber, gum, and oil.

Eu·cha·rist \ˈyük-r-əst\ *n.* **1** The sacrament of the Lord's Supper. **2** The consecrated bread and wine used in this sacrament.

eu·gen·ics \yü-ˈjen-iks\ *n.* The science that deals with the improvement of inborn or inherited qualities in future generations, especially of human beings.

eu·gle·na \yü-ˈglē-nə\ *n.* Any of numerous microscopic fresh water organisms that are green like plants and make their food by using the sun's energy but swim about like animals by means of a long whiplike projection of the body called a *flagellum.*

eu·lo·gis·tic \ˌyü-lə-ˈjis-tik\ *adj.* Of or relating to eulogy. Characterized by or containing eulogy; giving high praise; laudatory.

eu·lo·gize \ˈyü-lə-ˌjīz\ *v.;* **eu·lo·gized**; **eu·lo·giz·ing.** To speak or write in high praise of; to praise highly; to extol.

eu·lo·gy \ˈyü-lə-jē\ *n.; pl.* **eu·lo·gies. 1** A speech or a writing in praise of a person or thing; especially, a formal speech in praise of a deceased person. **2** High praise.

eu·nuch \ˈyü-nək\ *n.* A castrated man; especially, in some Eastern countries, such a man employed as a palace official or attendant or placed in charge of a harem.

eu·phe·mism \ˈyü-fə-ˌmiz-m\ *n.* **1** The substitution of an indirect or inoffensive expression for one that may offend or have unpleasant associations. **2** Any substitute expression used in this way. "Pass away" is a widely used *euphemism* for "die". — **eu·phe·mis·tic** \ˌyü-fə-ˈmis-tik\ *adj.* — **eu·phe·mis·ti·cal·ly** \-tik-l(-)ē\ *adv.*

eu·pho·ni·ous \yü-ˈfō-nē-əs\ *adj.* Pleasing to the ear; smooth-sounding. — **eu·pho·ni·ous·ly,** *adv.*

eu·pho·ni·um \yü-ˈfō-nē-əm\ *n.* A band instrument similar to the baritone but having a broader, mellower tone.

eu·pho·ny \ˈyüf-n-ē\ *n.; pl.* **eu·pho·nies.** Pleasing or sweet sound; the smooth-sounding effect of words combined in such a way as to please the ear.

Eur·a·sian \(ˈ)yu̇r-ˈāzh-n\ *adj.* Of or relating to Europe and Asia as a whole or to Eurasians. — *n.* A person of mixed European and Asiatic descent.

Eu·ro·pe·an \ˌyu̇r-ə-ˈpē-ən\ *adj.* Of or relating to Europe. — *n.* A native or inhabitant of Europe.

European plan. In hotels, a plan by which a fixed charge is made for lodging and service, with meals taken by guests at their option and separately charged.

Eu·sta·chian tube \yü-ˈstāsh-n, -ˈstāk-ē-ən\. A tube connecting the middle part of the ear with the throat and equalizing air pressure on both sides of the eardrum.

evac·u·ate \ē-ˈvak-yə-ˌwāt\ *v.;* **evac·u·at·ed**; **evac·u·at·ing. 1** To make empty; to empty of contents. **2** To discharge, as waste matter from the body. **3** To withdraw from; as, to *evacuate* a city threatened by enemy attack. **4** To remove people from a place of danger. All families in the flood area were *evacuated.*

evac·u·a·tion \ē-ˌvak-yə-ˈwāsh-n\ *n.* **1** Withdrawal or removal, as of troops from a fortress under attack or of a population from a city or area threatened by danger. **2** Discharge of waste matter by the natural passages of the body.

evac·u·ee \ē-ˌvak-yə-ˈwē\ *n.* A person removed by public authorities from home, town, or country, especially because of the danger from bombing or other military action.

evade \ē-ˈvād\ *v.;* **evad·ed**; **evad·ing. 1** To get away from or avoid by skill or trickery; as, to *evade* a question; to *evade* punishment. **2** To baffle; to foil; as, a problem that *evades* all efforts at solution.

eval·u·ate \ē-ˈval-yə-ˌwāt\ *v.;* **eval·u·at·ed**; **eval·u·at·ing. 1** To find or estimate the value, worth, or amount of; to appraise. **2** In mathematics, to express numerically, as by substituting numbers for algebraic terms. — **eval·u·a·tion** \ē-ˌval-yə-ˈwāsh-n\ *n.*

ev·a·nes·cent \ˌev-n-ˈes-nt\ *adj.* Tending to vanish like vapor; not lasting; quickly passing; as, *evanescent* pleasures.

evan·gel·i·cal \ˌē-ˌvan-ˈjel-ik-l, ˌev-n-\ or **evan·gel·ic** \-ˈjel-ik\ *adj.* **1** Of, relating to, or contained in the four Gospels or the New Testament. **2** Relating to those churches that stress salvation by faith in Jesus as read of in the New Testament more than they stress salvation by conformity to sacraments and church dogma. — **evan·gel·i·cal·ly** \-ik-l(-)ē\ *adv.*

evan·ge·lism \ē-'vanj-l-ˌiz-m\ *n.* The preaching of the gospel, especially in revival services.

evan·ge·list \ē-'vanj-l-əst\ *n.* A preacher of religion; especially, a person who goes about from place to place preaching and trying to awaken religious enthusiasm. — **evan·ge·lis·tic** \ē-ˌvanj-l-'is-tik\ *adj.*

evap·o·rate \ē-'vap-r-ˌāt\ *v.;* **evap·o·rat·ed**; **evap·o·rat·ing.** [From Latin *evaporatus*, past participle of *evaporare* meaning "to evaporate", from *e* meaning "out of" and *vapor* meaning "steam", "vapor".] **1** To change into vapor. Some liquids *evaporate* quickly when exposed to air. **2** To disappear, as a vapor; to vanish without being seen or used. Boldness sometimes *evaporates* in a moment of danger. **3** To remove some of the water from something, as by heating it; as, *evaporated* milk. — **evap·o·ra·tion** \ē-ˌvap-r-'āsh-n\ *n.*

evap·o·ra·tor \ē-'vap-r-ˌāt-r\ *n.* One that evaporates; especially, an apparatus for driving off or evaporating liquid, as in making maple syrup.

eva·sion \ē-'vāzh-n\ *n.* **1** An evading; especially, an evading of the truth or of something being considered. **2** A means of evading.

eva·sive \ē-'vā-siv, -ziv\ *adj.* Not straightforward; not frank; as, an *evasive* answer. — **eva·sive·ly**, *adv.*

eve \'ēv\ *n.* **1** Evening. **2** The evening or day before a saint's day or holiday; as, Christmas *Eve.* **3** The period just before an important event; as, the *eve* of an election.

even \'ēv-n\ *n. Archaic.* The evening.

even \'ēv-n\ *adj.* **1** Level; smooth; as, a house built on *even* ground. **2** Regular; steady; uniform; as, *even* breathing; an *even* temper. **3** On the same line or level; as, water *even* with the rim of a glass. **4** Equal in size, number, or amount; as, divided into *even* shares; bread cut in *even* slices. **5** With no advantage on either side; fair; as, an *even* trade. **6** Fully paid up; as, to be *even* with one's creditors. **7** Revenged; as, to get *even* with a person for an insult. **8** Not odd; capable of being divided by two without a remainder. Ten is an *even* number. **9** Exact; as, an *even* dozen. — *adv.* **1** At the very time; at the same moment; as, *even* as the clock struck. **2** Still; yet; as, to try to do *even* better next time. **3** Exactly; precisely. It is *even* so. **4** In a way or to a degree that is unexpected; as, a man honored *even* by his enemies. — *v.;* **evened**; **even·ing** \-n(-)ing\. **1** To make or become even, level, or smooth; as, to *even* the lawn with a roller. **2** To make equal; as, to *even* things up. — **even·er** \-n(-)ər\ *n.* — **even·ly** \-n-lē\ *adv.*

even·hand·ed \'ēv-n-'han-dəd\ *adj.* Fair; impartial; as, *evenhanded* justice.

eve·ning \'ēv-ning\ *n.* **1** The end of the day and early part of the night. **2** The latter part, as of life.

evening star. The bright planet seen in the western sky in the early evening.

even·song \'ēv-n-ˌsȯng\ *n.* [often with a capital] An evening service such as Vespers.

event \ē-'vent\ *n.* **1** The fact of taking place or happening. In the *event* of the visitors' coming, the class will go to the assembly hall. **2** Anything that happens, especially an important thing; as, to review the principal *events* of the past year. **3** A result or outcome; as, to await the *event* of an action. **4** Any one of the contests in a program of sports. The next *event* was the hundred-yard dash.

event·ful \ē-'vent-fəl\ *adj.* **1** Full of events; as, an *eventful* day. **2** Highly important; momentous. — **event·ful·ly** \-fə-lē\ *adv.*

even·tide \'ēv-n-ˌtīd\ *n.* Evening.

even·tu·al \ē-'vench-ə-wəl, -'vench-l\ *adj.* Final; ultimate. Hard work brought *eventual* success.

even·tu·al·i·ty \ē-ˌvench-ə-'wal-ət-ē\ *n.; pl.* **even·tu·al·i·ties.** An outcome or result; especially, a possible result; as, to be prepared for all *eventualities.*

even·tu·al·ly \ē-'vench-l(-)ē, -'vench-ə-wə-lē\ *adv.* Finally; at last; in the end.

ev·er \'ev-r\ *adv.* **1** At all times; always; as, *ever* faithful; a boy who was *ever* ready to help others. **2** At any time; as, a person who seemed to be seldom if *ever* home. Has this *ever* been done before? **3** In any case; at all. How *ever* did that book get there?

ev·er·glade \'ev-r-ˌglād\ *n.* A low-lying tract of swampy or marshy land.

ev·er·green \'ev-r-ˌgrēn\ *adj.* Bearing green foliage the year round, as pines and most other cone-bearing trees. — *n.* **1** An evergreen plant. **2** [in the plural] Branches and twigs of evergreen plants used as decorations.

ev·er·last·ing \ˌev-r-'las-ting\ *adj.* **1** Lasting forever; as, *everlasting* fame. **2** Going on for a long time or for too long a time; as, *everlasting* complaints. — *n.* **1** Eternity. **2** Any of several plants, chiefly of the thistle family, whose flowers may be dried without loss of form or color. — **ev·er·last·ing·ly**, *adv.*

ev·er·more \'ev-r-'mōr, -'mȯr\ *adv.* Always; forever. — *n.* Eternity — used especially in the phrase *for evermore.*

ev·ery \'ev-rē\ *adj.* **1** Each of a group or series, without leaving out any; each without exception. *Every* word he said was clearly heard. **2** Complete; entire; as, to have *every* confidence in the loyalty of a friend. — **every now and then** or **every once in a while.** Occasionally. — **every other.** Each second or alternate; as, *every other* day. — **every which way. 1** In every direction. **2** In a disorderly state.

ev·ery·body \'ev-rē-ˌbäd-ē, 'ev-rə-\ *pron.* Every person.

ev·ery·day \'ev-rē-ˌdā\ *adj.* **1** Used or suitable for every day or every ordinary day; as, *everyday* clothes. **2** Happening every day; usual; as, *everyday* matters; an *everyday* occurrence.

ev·ery·one \'ev-rē-(ˌ)wən\ *pron.* Everybody — written also as two words, especially with *of;* as, news of great interest to *every one* of those present.

ev·ery·thing \'ev-rē-ˌthing\ *pron.* **1** Every object, act, state, event, or fact whatever; all. **2** All that pertains to the subject under consideration. You have not told me *everything.* **3** The most important of all things. To some people money is *everything.*

ev·ery·where \'ev-rē-ˌhwer\ *adv.* In every place; in all places.

evict \ē-'vikt\ *v.* To put out, as a tenant from a house, by legal means. — **evic·tion** \-'viksh-n\ *n.*

ev·i·dence \'ev-ə-dən(t)s, -ˌden(t)s\ *n.* **1** An outward sign or indication; any form of proof; as, to find *evidence* of a robbery; to give *evidence* of one's friendship for someone by doing him a favor. **2** Material submitted, as to a judge or jury, to determine the truth of a charge or to prove or disprove a claim. — **in evidence.** In a position to be easily seen or noticed. — *v.;* **ev·i·denced; ev·i·denc·ing.** To make evident.

ev·i·dent \'ev-ə-dənt, -ˌdent\ *adj.* Clear to the sight and to the mind; plain; apparent. It was *evident* that the boy and girl were twins.

ev·i·dent·ly \'ev-ə-ˌdent-lē, -dənt-lē, ˌev-ə-'dent-lē\ *adv.* Clearly; plainly; obviously; apparently.

evil \'ēv-l\ *adj.* **1** Harmful; tending to injure; as, *evil* influences; the *evil* teeth of a shark. **2** Bad; morally wicked; as, an *evil* king; an *evil* deed. — *n.* **1** Anything that lessens or destroys happiness or welfare. Poverty and disease are *evils.* **2** Wrongdoing; moral wickedness; as, to choose between good and *evil;* to fight the *evil* in the world. — **evil·ly** \'ēv-l-ē\ *adv.*

evil·do·er \'ēv-l-'dü-ər\ *n.* A person who does evil; a wrongdoer. — **evil·do·ing** \-ing\ *n.*

evil-mind·ed \'ēv-l-'mīn-dəd\ *adj.* Having an evil character or intentions; bad.

evince \ē-'vin(t)s\ *v.;* **evinced; evinc·ing.** To show clearly; to display; as, to *evince* anger.

evis·cer·ate \ē-'vis-r-ˌāt\ *v.;* **evis·cer·at·ed; evis·cer·at·ing.** To remove the entrails from; as, to *eviscerate* a fowl.

evoke \ē-'vōk\ *v.;* **evoked; evok·ing.** To call forth; to summon; as, a remark that *evoked* an angry answer. — **evo·ca·tion** \ˌē-vō-'kāsh-n, ˌev-ə-\ *n.*

ev·o·lu·tion \ˌev-l-'üsh-n, ˌēv-l-\ *n.* **1** Any one of a series of related movements; as, the *evolutions* of a dancer. **2** In military or naval exercises, a movement by which a body of troops or a part of a fleet passes from one position to another. **3** Gradual growth by a series of steps, each developed out of the preceding; as, the *evolution* of the airplane. **4** The process by which simpler forms of plant and animal life are succeeded by more complex forms. **5** The theory that the various kinds of animals and plants now existing have developed from previously existing kinds and that all animals and plants are descended from simple forms. — **ev·o·lu·tion·ary** \-ˌer-ē\ *adj.*

ev·o·lu·tion·ist \ˌev-l-'üsh-n-əst, ˌēv-l-\ *n.* A person who holds a doctrine of evolution.

evolve \ē-'välv\ *v.;* **evolved; evolv·ing.** To produce by or pass through a process of evolution; to develop; as, the theory that complex forms of life have *evolved* from simpler forms; to *evolve* a plan.

ewe \'yü\ *n.* A female sheep.

ew·er \'yü-ər, 'yůr\ *n.* A wide-mouthed jug or pitcher.

ex- *in pronunciations below in which* ik *or* ig *are shown as the beginning sounds, it is to be understood that the sounds* ek *or* eg *are also heard but are less frequent*\. A prefix that can mean: **1** Out, as in *exhale, exclude,* or *expatriate.* **2** Beyond, as in *exceed* or *excel.* **3** Thoroughly, as in *exasperate* or *excruciating.* **4** Formerly but not now, as in *ex-president.*

☞ The prefix *ex-* appears as *e-* before *b, d, g, h, l, m, n, r,* and *v* and as *ef-* before *f.*

ex·act \ig-'zakt\ *adj.* **1** Accurate; precise; as, *exact* knowledge. **2** Agreeing with the truth or with some standard; correct; as, an *exact* copy. **3** Capable of great accuracy, as in measuring; as, *exact* instruments. — For synonyms see *correct.* — *v.* **1** To demand; to require; as, to *exact* vengeance. **2** To compel to furnish; to force the payment of; as, to *exact* a ransom.

ex·act·ing \ig-'zak-ting\ *adj.* Making many or difficult demands upon a person; trying; as, an *exacting* task; an *exacting* teacher. — **ex·act·ing·ly,** *adv.*

ex·ac·tion \ig-'zaksh-n\ *n.* **1** An exacting; extortion; as, the *exaction* of tribute. **2** Something that is exacted.

ex·act·i·tude \ig-'zak-tə-ˌtüd, -ˌtyüd\ *n.* Exactness.

ex·act·ly \ig-'zak(t)-lē\ *adv.* **1** In an exact manner; precisely; as, to copy *exactly;* at *exactly* three o'clock. **2** Quite so; just as you say — used to express agreement.

ex·act·ness \ig-'zak(t)-nəs\ *n.* The quality of being exact.

ex·ag·ger·ate \ig-'zaj-r-ˌāt\ *v.;* **ex·ag·ger·at·ed; ex·ag·ger·at·ing.** [From Latin *exaggeratus,* past participle of *exaggerare* meaning literally "to increase by piling up", from *ex* meaning "out of" and *aggerare* meaning "to pile up".] To enlarge a fact or statement beyond what is actual or true; to overstate; as, to *exaggerate* in telling about one's luck at fishing; to *exaggerate* difficulties. — **ex·ag·ger·at·ed·ly** \-ˌāt-əd-lē\ *adv.*

ex·ag·ger·a·tion \ig-ˌzaj-r-'āsh-n\ *n.* **1** An exaggerating or a being exaggerated; as, to be guilty of *exaggeration* in telling a story. **2** An exaggerated statement.

ex·alt \ig-'zólt\ *v.* **1** To raise, as in rank, dignity, wealth, or power; to promote; as, men *exalted* by their fellows to the highest offices in the land. **2** To worship or glorify; to praise highly. **3** To lift up with joy, pride, or a feeling of success; to elate.

ex·al·ta·tion \ˌeg-ˌzól-'tāsh-n\ *n.* **1** The act of exalting. **2** The state of being exalted; especially, a greatly heightened sense of personal well-being, power, or importance.

ex·alt·ed \ig-'zól-təd\ *adj.* **1** Very high or great;

as, the responsibilities that go with *exalted* rank. **2** In or showing a state of mental exaltation; as, an *exalted* mood; *exalted* thoughts. — **ex·alt·ed·ly**, *adv.*

ex·am \ig-'zam\ *n.* An examination.

ex·am·i·na·tion \ig-ˌzam-ə-'nāsh-n\ *n.* **1** The act of examining or the state of being examined; inspection; investigation; as, to make an *examination* of a strange flower; to go to the doctor for a physical *examination.* **2** Any test given to determine progress, fitness, or knowledge; as, an entrance *examination;* to take an *examination* in arithmetic.

— The words *inquiry* and *inspection* are synonyms of *examination: examination* generally suggests careful observation and investigation to determine the true nature, quality, or condition of something; *inspection* is likely to apply to an official examination to discover errors, flaws, or defects; *inquiry* may suggest a searching for truth, usually through questions, but sometimes through experimentation or observation.

ex·am·ine \ig-'zam-ən\ *v.;* **ex·am·ined**; **ex·am·in·ing.** **1** To look at or inspect closely; as, to *examine* rock specimens; to *examine* an old coat for moth holes. **2** To test the condition of; as, to have one's eyes *examined.* **3** To question closely in order to determine progress, fitness, or knowledge; as, to *examine* a class in arithmetic.

ex·am·in·er \ig-'zam-ən-r\ *n.* A person that examines, as one who gives or supervises an examination in a school or one whose work is to make examinations, as by inspecting manufactured articles for flaws.

ex·am·ple \ig-'zamp-l\ *n.* **1** A sample of anything taken to show what the whole is like; an instance; as, to show a new customer an *example* of one's work. **2** A problem to be solved in order to show how a rule works; as, an *example* in arithmetic. **3** Something to be imitated; a model; as, to set a good *example* for others. **4** Something that is a warning to others; as, punishment intended partly as an *example* to other wrongdoers.

ex·as·per·ate \ig-'zasp-r-ˌāt\ *v.;* **ex·as·per·at·ed**; **ex·as·per·at·ing.** To make angry; to irritate; as, to be *exasperated* by a needless delay. — For synonyms see *irritate.*

ex·as·per·a·tion \ig-ˌzasp-r-'āsh-n\ *n.* **1** The act of exasperating. **2** The state of being exasperated; extreme irritation or annoyance; anger; as, to be unable to conceal one's *exasperation.*

ex·ca·vate \'eks-kə-ˌvāt\ *v.;* **ex·ca·vat·ed**; **ex·ca·vat·ing.** **1** To hollow out; to form a hole in; as, to *excavate* the side of a hill. **2** To make by hollowing out; as, to *excavate* a tunnel. **3** To dig out and remove; as, to *excavate* sand. **4** To uncover by digging away covering earth; as, to *excavate* a long-buried city. — **ex·ca·va·tor** \-ˌvāt-r\ *n.*

ex·ca·va·tion \ˌeks-kə-'vāsh-n\ *n.* **1** The act or process of excavating. **2** A hollowed-out place formed by excavating.

ex·ceed \ik-'sēd\ *v.* **1** To go or to be beyond the limit of; as, to *exceed* one's authority; to *exceed* the speed limit. **2** To be greater than. This player's skill *exceeds* that of all his teammates.

ex·ceed·ing \ik-'sēd-ing\ *adj.* Much more than usual; extraordinary; as, a voice of *exceeding* richness. — *adv. Archaic.* Exceedingly.

ex·ceed·ing·ly \ik-'sēd-ing-lē\ *adv.* To an unusual degree; extraordinarily; very; as, *exceedingly* happy.

ex·cel \ik-'sel\ *v.;* **ex·celled**; **ex·cel·ling.** **1** To outdo others, as in good qualities or ability; to be better than others; as, a pupil that *excels* in arithmetic. **2** To outdo; to surpass; as, a jump *excelling* the previous record by two inches.

ex·cel·lence \'eks-l(-)ən(t)s\ *n.* **1** The quality of being excellent; high quality or merit. **2** An excellent quality; a virtue; a merit. Among the many *excellences* of this book two are especially outstanding.

ex·cel·len·cy \'eks-l(-)ən-sē\ *n.; pl.* **ex·cel·len·cies.** **1** Excellence. **2** [usually with a capital] A title of honor given to certain high officials, as governors and ambassadors.

ex·cel·lent \'eks-l(-)ənt\ *adj.* Extremely good of its kind; very fine; first-class. — **ex·cel·lent·ly**, *adv.*

ex·cel·si·or \ik-'sel-sē-ər\ *n.* Curled shreds of wood used for stuffing furniture and for packing.

ex·cept \ik-'sept, ek-\ *v.* To leave out from a number or a whole; to omit. The law applies to everybody; no one is *excepted.* — *conj. Archaic.* Unless. — *prep.* **1** Leaving out; with the exception of; as, everybody *except* John. **2** Other than; otherwise than; as, a place that cannot be reached *except* on foot.

ex·cept·ing \ik-'sep-ting, ek-\ *prep.* With the exception of; except.

ex·cep·tion \ik-'sepsh-n\ *n.* **1** An excepting or leaving out. **2** Anyone or anything that is excepted, omitted, or taken out from a whole class, group, or number. All but one of the drawings were in pencil, the *exception* being a charcoal sketch. **3** Objection; complaint; as, conduct that is beyond *exception.* — **take exception to.** To object to.

ex·cep·tion·a·ble \ik-'sepsh-n(-)əb-l\ *adj.* Liable to exception or objection; objectionable.

ex·cep·tion·al \ik-'sepsh-n(-)əl\ *adj.* **1** Forming an exception; unusual; as, an *exceptional* amount of rain. **2** Better than average; superior; as, a person of *exceptional* ability. — **ex·cep·tion·al·ly** \-n(-)ə-lē\ *adv.*

ex·cerpt \ek-'sərpt, 'ek-ˌsərpt, eg-'zərpt, 'eg-ˌzərpt\ *v.* To select; to extract, as a literary passage. — \'ek-ˌsərpt, 'eg-ˌzərpt\ *n.* A passage selected or copied, as from a book or record.

ex·cess \ik-'ses, 'ek-ˌses, ek-'ses\ *n.* **1** The fact of being more than enough; an exceeding of what is needed or allowed; as, to eat to *excess;* a region suffering from an *excess* of rain. **2** Intemperance; as, a person whose health suffered because of his *excesses.* **3** The amount by which one quantity exceeds another; the amount that exceeds what is needed or allowed. The difference between two numbers is the *excess* of one over the other. — \'ek-ˌses, ik-'ses\ *adj.* More than is usual or permitted; as, *excess* weight; *excess* baggage.

ex·ces·sive \ik-'ses-iv, ek-\ *adj.* Showing excess; going beyond what is usual or proper; as, a price that seems *excessive. Excessive* sunbathing can be harmful. — **ex·ces·sive·ly**, *adv.*

ex·change \iks-'chānj\ *n.* **1** A giving or taking of one thing in return for another thing; trade; barter; as, a fair *exchange.* **2** The act of giving and receiving between two groups; interchange; as, an *exchange* of students between two countries; an *exchange* of courtesies. **3** A place where trades are made; a market place; especially, a place where bankers, brokers, and merchants meet to do business; as, a produce *exchange;* the stock *exchange.* **4** A central office; as, a telephone *exchange.* **5** The interchange of money of different countries, with the adjustment for differences in value. — *v.;* **ex·changed**; **ex·chang·ing. 1** To give in exchange; to trade; to swap; as, to *exchange* a knife for a book. **2** To part with as a substitute; as, to be unwilling to *exchange* one's humble home for the palace of a king. — **ex·change·a·ble**, *adj.*

ex·cheq·uer \'eks-ˌchek-r, iks-'chek-r\ *n.* **1** A treasury; especially, a national treasury. **2** [with a capital] The department of the British government that has to do with national finances. **3** A person's own finances, or funds available for use; as, to find one's *exchequer* low at the end of the month.

ex·cise \'ek-ˌsīz, -ˌsīs\ *n.* A tax placed on certain goods within the country where they are manufactured or sold.

ex·cise \ek-'sīz\ *v.;* **ex·cised**; **ex·cis·ing.** To cut out; to remove by cutting out; as, to have a small growth *excised* by a doctor; to *excise* certain passages from a manuscript. — **ex·ci·sion** \-'sizh-n\ *n.*

ex·cit·a·ble \ik-'sīt-əb-l\ *adj.* **1** Capable of being excited. **2** Easily excited. — **ex·cit·a·bil·i·ty** \ik-ˌsīt-ə-'bil-ət-ē\ *n.*

ex·cite \ik-'sīt\ *v.;* **ex·cit·ed**; **ex·cit·ing.** To stir to activity in any way; to rouse to feeling; as, a deed that *excited* everybody's admiration; a crowd *excited* to anger by an injustice.

ex·cit·ed \ik-'sīt-əd\ *adj.* Having or showing strong feeling; stirred up; worked up; as, to talk in an *excited* whisper; to be too *excited* to sleep. — **ex·cit·ed·ly**, *adv.*

ex·cite·ment \ik-'sīt-mənt\ *n.* **1** The act of exciting. **2** The state of being excited; agitation; stir; as, eyes sparkling with *excitement;* an event that caused great *excitement* in the town. **3** Anything that excites, arouses, or stirs up.

ex·cit·ing \ik-'sīt-ing\ *adj.* Causing excitement; stirring; as, an *exciting* story of the sea; a letter containing *exciting* news. — **ex·cit·ing·ly**, *adv.*

ex·claim \iks-'klām\ *v.* To cry out or speak out suddenly or with strong feeling. "We've won!" the boys *exclaimed.*

ex·cla·ma·tion \ˌeks-klə-'māsh-n\ *n.* **1** A sharp or sudden cry expressing some strong feeling. **2** A word or group of words that shows strong feeling or excitement.

exclamation point or **exclamation mark.** A mark of punctuation [!] used to show forceful utterance or strong feeling.

ex·clam·a·to·ry \iks-'klam-ə-ˌtōr-ē, -ˌtȯr-ē\ *adj.* Containing or using exclamation; as, an *exclamatory* sentence; an *exclamatory* way of talking.

ex·clude \iks-'klüd, eks-\ *v.;* **ex·clud·ed**; **ex·clud·ing. 1** To shut out; to keep out; to keep from entering or taking part; as, to *exclude* the light from a sickroom; an organization that *excluded* children under twelve years of age. **2** To expel; to eject. — **ex·clud·a·ble**, *adj.*

ex·clu·sion \iks-'klüzh-n, eks-\ *n.* The act of excluding or the state of being excluded; a shutting out or keeping out.

ex·clu·sive \iks-'klü-siv, eks-, -ziv\ *adj.* **1** Excluding or inclined to exclude certain persons or certain classes, as from ownership, membership, or privileges; catering to a special class, especially a fashionable class; as, an *exclusive* neighborhood; an *exclusive* school. **2** Sole; single; as, to have *exclusive* use of a bathing beach. **3** Complete; undivided; as, to give something one's *exclusive* attention. **4** Not taking into account; not inclusive; as, for five days *exclusive* of today. — **ex·clu·sive·ly**, *adv.*

ex·com·mu·ni·cate \ˌeks-kə-'myü-nə-ˌkāt\ *v.;* **ex·com·mu·ni·cat·ed**; **ex·com·mu·ni·cat·ing.** To cut off or shut out officially from communion with or membership in the church; especially, to bar from receiving the sacraments. — **ex·com·mu·ni·ca·tor** \-ˌkāt-r\ *n.*

ex·com·mu·ni·ca·tion \ˌeks-kə-ˌmyü-nə-'kāsh-n\ *n.* **1** Exclusion from communion with or membership in the church. **2** An official pronouncement ordering such exclusion.

ex·cre·ment \'eks-krə-mənt\ *n.* Waste matter discharged from the body.

ex·cres·cence \eks-'kres-n(t)s\ *n.* An outgrowth; especially, an abnormal outgrowth on the body, as a wart.

ex·cre·ta \eks-'krēt-ə\ *n. pl.* Waste products excreted.

ex·crete \eks-'krēt\ *v.;* **ex·cret·ed**; **ex·cret·ing.** To separate from the blood and tissues and expel, as sweat, urine and similar waste products.

ex·cre·tion \eks-'krēsh-n\ *n.* **1** The act or process of excreting; discharge of wastes from the blood and tissues. **2** Excreted matter.

ex·cre·to·ry \'eks-krə-ˌtōr-ē, -ˌtȯr-ē\ *adj.* **1** Relating to excretion. **2** Serving to excrete; as, *excretory* organs.

ex·cru·ci·at·ing \iks-'krü-shē-ˌāt-ing\ *adj.* Extremely painful; causing intense suffering; agonizing; as, an *excruciating* toothache. — **ex·cru·ci·at·ing·ly**, *adv.*

ex·cul·pate \'eks-(ˌ)kəl-ˌpāt, eks-'kəl-\ *v.;* **ex·cul-**

pat·ed; **ex·cul·pat·ing.** To clear or free from a charge of fault or guilt; to prove to be guiltless.

ex·cul·pa·tion \ˌeks-(ˌ)kəl-ˈpāsh-n\ *n.* The act of freeing from a charge of fault or guilt; excuse.

ex·cur·sion \iks-ˈkərzh-n\ *n.* **1** A going forth; as, a brief *excursion* against the enemy. **2** A pleasure trip; especially, a day or weekend trip by train, bus, or boat at reduced rates. **3** A departure from a definite path or course, as a digression in a speech or a piece of writing.

ex·cur·sion·ist \iks-ˈkərzh-n-əst\ *n.* A person who goes on an excursion.

ex·cuse \iks-ˈkyüz\ *v.;* **ex·cused**; **ex·cus·ing.** **1** To make apology for; to offer excuse for; to try to remove blame from; as, to *excuse* oneself for being late; to try to *excuse* a mistake one has made. **2** To pardon; to forgive; as, to *excuse* another's mistake. **3** To free or let off from doing something; as, to *excuse* a pupil from reciting; to *excuse* a person from a debt. **4** To serve as an acceptable reason or explanation for something said or done; to free from blame; to justify. Nothing can *excuse* bad manners.

— The words *pardon* and *forgive* are synonyms of *excuse: excuse* usually indicates passing over a fault or error without further consideration or blame, generally in view of the reasons which prompted it, but may also refer to formal social or organization procedure; *pardon* may refer to the action of a superior in formally or legally removing punishment and returning to good standing; *forgive* may suggest a sincere change of feeling so that resentment is no longer felt.

— \iks-ˈkyüs\ *n.* **1** The act of excusing. **2** Anything that is said as a reason for being excused; an apology. **3** Anything that excuses or serves as a reason for excusing. — For synonyms see *apology.* — **ex·cus·a·ble** \-ˈkyü-zəb-l\ *adj.* — **ex·cus·a·bly** \-zə-blē\ *adv.*

ex·e·cra·ble \ˈeks-ə-krəb-l\ *adj.* Detestable; abominable. — **ex·e·cra·bly** \-krə-blē\ *adv.*

ex·e·crate \ˈeks-ə-ˌkrāt\ *v.;* **ex·e·crat·ed**; **ex·e·crat·ing.** **1** To call down evil upon; to curse. **2** To detest; to abhor. — **ex·e·cra·tion** \ˌeks-ə-ˈkrāsh-n\ *n.*

ex·e·cute \ˈeks-ə-ˌkyüt\ *v.;* **ex·e·cut·ed**; **ex·e·cut·ing.** **1** To carry out to completion; to perform; as, to *execute* a plan. The soldiers *executed* the captain's order. **2** To do what is required by; as, to *execute* a writ. **3** To put to death according to legal orders. **4** To produce by art in accordance with a design or plan; as, a statue *executed* in bronze. **5** To perform, as a piece of music. **6** To do what is necessary to give legal force to; as, to *execute* a will.

ex·e·cu·tion \ˌeks-ə-ˈkyüsh-n\ *n.* **1** The action or process of executing; a carrying through of anything to its finish. **2** A putting to death by legal orders. **3** The way in which a work of art is made or performed; as, a statue perfect in its *execution.* **4** A judicial writ authorizing an official to execute a judgment.

ex·e·cu·tion·er \ˌeks-ə-ˈkyüsh-n(-)ər\ *n.* A person who legally executes criminals.

ex·ec·u·tive \ig-ˈzek-(y)ət-iv\ *adj.* **1** Fitted for executing or carrying out things to completion; as, *executive* ability. **2** Having to do with or connected with managing; as, to hold an *executive* position. — *n.* **1** The branch of government that puts laws into action or the persons making up this branch. **2** Any person who manages or directs.

ex·ec·u·tor \ig-ˈzek-yət-r\ *n.* The person named in a will as the one to see that its provisions are carried out.

ex·ec·u·trix \ig-ˈzek-yə-ˌtriks\ *n.* A female executor.

ex·em·pla·ry \ig-ˈzem-plər-ē\ *adj.* **1** Serving as an example or pattern; deserving imitation; as, *exemplary* conduct. **2** Serving as a warning. The accident was an *exemplary* lesson on the dangers of fast driving.

ex·em·pli·fy \ig-ˈzem-plə-ˌfī\ *v.;* **ex·em·pli·fied** \-ˌfīd\; **ex·em·pli·fy·ing.** To show by example; to serve as an example of; as, stories that *exemplify* courage. — **ex·em·pli·fi·ca·tion** \ig-ˌzem-plə-fə-ˈkāsh-n\ *n.*

ex·empt \ig-ˈzem(p)t\ *adj.* Free or released from some requirement to which other persons are subject; as, to be *exempt* from military service. — *v.* To make exempt; to free; to excuse; as, to *exempt* certain pupils from taking a test. — **ex·emp·tion** \-ˈzem(p)sh-n\ *n.*

ex·er·cise \ˈeks-r-ˌsīz\ *n.* **1** The act of exercising; a putting into action, use, or practice; employment; as, the *exercise* of patience. **2** Bodily exertion for the sake of health. Walking is good *exercise.* **3** A school lesson or other task assigned for practice; practice work; drill; as, spelling *exercises.* **4** [usually in the plural] A program, as of songs, speeches, and recitations; as, graduation *exercises.* — *v.;* **ex·er·cised**; **ex·er·cis·ing.** **1** To put into use; to set in action; to use; as, to *exercise* authority. **2** To train; as, to *exercise* the fingers on the piano. **3** To exert oneself for the sake of health or training; as, to *exercise* every day. — **ex·er·cis·er**, *n.*

ex·ert \ig-ˈzərt\ *v.* To put forth or make use of such things as strength, ability, force, power; as, to *exert* one's best efforts to win.

ex·er·tion \ig-ˈzərsh-n\ *n.* **1** An exerting. With the *exertion* of a little more effort the game might have been won. **2** Effort; activity; use of strength or ability. Clearing land without power tools requires great *exertion.*

ex·e·unt \ˈeks-ē-(ˌ)ənt\ *n.* [From Latin, meaning "they go out", "they leave" — see *exit.*] A stage direction meaning "they go out" or "they leave the scene".

ex·ha·la·tion \ˌeks-(h)ə-ˈlāsh-n, ˌegz-ə-\ *n.* **1** An exhaling, as of steam or vapor; as, an *exhalation* of breath. **2** Something that is exhaled; as, *exhalations* of steam from a geyser.

ex·hale \eks-ˈhāl\ *v.;* **ex·haled**; **ex·hal·ing.** **1** To breathe out; as, to *exhale* breath. **2** To send forth; to emit; as, the fragrance that flowers *exhale*.

ex·haust \ig-'zȯst\ *v.* **1** To draw out or let out completely; as, to *exhaust* the air from a jar. **2** To use up completely; as, to *exhaust* one's strength or one's patience. **3** To tire out; to fatigue. The long race *exhausted* the runners. **4** To empty by drawing or letting out the contents; as, to *exhaust* a reservoir; to *exhaust* a treasury. — For synonyms see *tire*. — *n.* **1** The escape of used fuel or used steam from an engine; as, to hear the *exhaust* of an automobile. **2** The used fuel or used steam that escapes from an engine. — **ex·haust·i·bil·i·ty** \ig-ˌzȯs-tə-'bil-ət-ē\ *n.* — **ex·haust·i·ble** \ig-'zȯs-təb-l\ *adj.*

ex·haust·ed \ig-'zȯs-təd\ *adj.* **1** Used up; spent; consumed. All available funds have been *exhausted*. **2** Emptied; as, an *exhausted* well. **3** Tired out; worn out; as, *exhausted* by a day of hard work.

ex·haus·tion \ig-'zȯs-chən\ *n.* **1** An exhausting. **2** The condition of being exhausted; extreme weariness; fatigue.

ex·haus·tive \ig-'zȯs-tiv\ *adj.* **1** Serving or acting to exhaust. **2** Thorough; complete; as, an *exhaustive* discussion. — **ex·haus·tive·ly**, *adv.*

ex·hib·it \ig-'zib-ət\ *v.* **1** To show; to reveal; as, to *exhibit* an interest in music at an early age; to *exhibit* great courage in battle. **2** To put on display; as, to *exhibit* a collection of paintings. **3** To present in legal form to a court. — *n.* **1** Something that is exhibited; especially, an article or a collection of articles shown in an exhibition. **2** Anything produced and identified in court for use as evidence.

ex·hi·bi·tion \ˌeks-ə-'bish-n\ *n.* **1** The act of exhibiting; a showing. **2** That which is exhibited. **3** Any public display, as of works of art, products of industry, or feats of skill; as, an *exhibition* of paintings; an *exhibition* of horseback riding by a troop of soldiers.

ex·hib·i·tor or **ex·hib·it·er** \ig-'zib-ət-r\ *n.* One that exhibits something, especially in an exhibition; as, an art show with *exhibitors* from all over the country.

ex·hil·a·rate \ig-'zil-r-ˌāt\ *v.;* **ex·hil·a·rat·ed**; **ex·hil·a·rat·ing.** **1** To make cheerful or jolly; as, to be *exhilarated* by an unexpected football victory. **2** To fill with a lively sense of well-being; to invigorate; as, an *exhilarating* autumn day.

ex·hil·a·ra·tion \ig-ˌzil-r-'āsh-n\ *n.* **1** The action of exhilarating. **2** The state of being exhilarated; liveliness; high spirits.

ex·hort \ig-'zȯrt, eg-; ik-'sȯrt, ek-\ *v.* To arouse, as by words or advice; to urge strongly; to warn; as, to *exhort* one's countrymen to greater patriotism.

ex·hor·ta·tion \ˌeks-ˌ(h)ȯr-'tāsh-n, ˌeks-r-, ˌeg-ˌzȯr-\ *n.* **1** The act or an instance of exhorting. **2** A speech, especially a sermon, intended to exhort others; any earnestly spoken words of urgent advice or warning.

ex·hume \ig-'züm, ig-'zyüm, iks-'yüm, eks-'hyüm\ *v.;* **ex·humed**; **ex·hum·ing.** To dig out of the ground; especially, to uncover and take out of a place of burial. — **ex·hu·ma·tion** \ˌeks-ˌ(h)yü-'māsh-n\ *n.*

ex·i·gence \'eks-ə-jən(t)s\ *n.* Exigency.

ex·i·gen·cy \'eks-ə-jən-sē, ig-'zij-n-sē\ *n.; pl.* **ex·i·gen·cies.** A case or a state of affairs demanding immediate action or remedy; an emergency; urgent need; as, a man capable of dealing with the *exigencies* of any situation likely to arise.

ex·ile \'ek-ˌsīl, 'eg-ˌzīl\ *n.* **1** The sending or forcing of a person away from his own country or the situation of a person who is thus sent away; banishment; as, to live in *exile*; sent into *exile*. **2** A person who is expelled from his native country. — *v.;* **ex·iled**; **ex·il·ing.** To banish or expel from one's native country.

ex·ist \ig-'zist\ *v.* **1** To be; to have actual being; to be real; as, to wonder if other worlds than ours *exist*. **2** To live; to continue to live; as, to earn hardly enough to *exist* on. How long can a man *exist* without water? **3** To occur; to be found; as, a disease that once *existed* in America but has been wiped out; a fancy *existing* only in the mind.

ex·ist·ence \ig-'zis-tən(t)s\ *n.* **1** The fact or the condition of having being or of being real; as, to doubt the *existence* of dragons; the largest animal in *existence*. **2** Life; continuance in living or way of living; as, to owe one's *existence* to a doctor's skill; to lead a happy *existence*. **3** Actual occurrence; as, to recognize the *existence* of a state of war.

ex·ist·ent \ig-'zis-tənt\ *adj.* Having being; existing; as, under *existent* circumstances.

ex·it \'egz-ət, 'eks-\ *n.* [Partly from Latin *exit* meaning "(he or she) goes out", "leaves", from *exire* meaning "to go out", "leave", partly from Latin *exitus* meaning "departure", "outlet", from past participle of *exire*.] **1** The act of leaving a place. **2** The departure of an actor from the stage — commonly used as a stage direction. **3** A way of departure; a passage out; as, an *exit* to be used in case of fire.

ex·o·dus \'eks-əd-əs\ *n.* A going out or away, especially of a large number of people; as, the yearly *exodus* to the mountains and the seashore. — **the Exodus.** The departure of the ancient people of Israel from Egypt under the leadership of Moses.

ex of·fi·cio \ˌeks ə-'fish-ē-ˌō\. [Latin] Because of an office held. The president of the class was *ex officio* a member of all committees.

ex·on·er·ate \ig-'zän-r-ˌāt\ *v.;* **ex·on·er·at·ed**; **ex·on·er·at·ing.** To clear from an accusation or from blame; to declare innocent. — **ex·on·er·a·tion** \ig-ˌzän-r-'āsh-n\ *n.*

ex·or·bi·tant \ig-'zȯr-bə-tənt\ *adj.* Going beyond the limits of what is fair, reasonable, or expected; excessive; as, *exorbitant* prices; a task that requires an *exorbitant* amount of time. — **ex·or·bi·tance** \-tən(t)s\ *n.* — **ex·or·bi·tant·ly**, *adv.*

ex·or·cise \'ek-ˌsȯr-ˌsīz, 'eks-r-\ *v.;* **ex·or·cised**; **ex-**

or·cis·ing. **1** To drive off, as a devil or an evil spirit, by calling upon some holy name or by spells. **2** To free from an evil spirit. — **ex·or·cism** \-ˌsiz-m\ *n.* — **ex·or·cist** \-ˌsist, -səst\ *n.*

ex·o·skel·e·ton \ˌeks-ō-'skel-ət-n\ *n.* A hard supporting or protective structure developed on the outside of the body, as the shell of a crustacean.

ex·ot·ic \ig-'zät-ik\ *adj.* **1** Introduced from a foreign country; as, *exotic* plants. **2** Strikingly unusual, as in color or design; excitingly strange. — *n.* An exotic thing, as a plant.

ex·pand \iks-'pand\ *v.* **1** To open wide; to unfold; as, a bird with wings *expanded.* **2** To take up or to cause to take up more space; to enlarge; to swell. Metals *expand* under heat. **3** To develop more fully; to work out in greater detail; as, to *expand* an argument; to *expand* a sentence into a paragraph. **4** In mathematics, to state in enlarged form; to develop in a series; as, to *expand* an equation.

ex·panse \iks-'pan(t)s\ *n.* The extent to which something expands, or spreads out; a wide space, area, or stretch; as, the vast *expanse* of the ocean.

ex·pan·sion \iks-'panch-n\ *n.* **1** The act or process of expanding or the state of being expanded; enlargement. **2** Something expanded, or spread out; an expanded surface or part. **3** The extent by which something is expanded. **4** In mathematics, the developed result of an indicated operation. The *expansion* of $(a + b)^2$ is $a^2 + 2ab + b^2$.

ex·pan·sive \iks-'pan(t)s-iv\ *adj.* **1** Capable of expanding or tending to expand. **2** Wide-spreading; extensive. **3** Free in expressing one's feelings; unrestrained; demonstrative. — **ex·pan·sive·ly,** *adv.*

ex·pa·ti·ate \iks-'pā-shē-ˌāt\ *v.;* **ex·pa·ti·at·ed; ex·pa·ti·at·ing.** To talk or write at length; as, to *expatiate* upon the pleasures and benefits of outdoor life.

ex·pa·tri·ate \eks-'pā-trē-ət, -ˌāt\ *adj.* Exiled; expatriated. — *n.* **1** An exile. **2** A person who leaves his own country to live in another. — \-ˌāt\ *v.;* **ex·pa·tri·at·ed; ex·pa·tri·at·ing.** **1** To make an exile of; to banish. **2** To withdraw from one's own country and become a citizen of another country. — **ex·pa·tri·a·tion** \(ˌ)eks-ˌpā-trē-'āsh-n\ *n.*

ex·pect \iks-'pekt\ *v.* **1** To look for, or to look forward to, something that ought to or probably will happen; as, to *expect* rain. We *expect* to go into town tomorrow. **2** To consider as obliged; as, to *expect* a person to do as he promised. **3** To suppose. Judging from his appearance, I *expect* he may be a Scandinavian.

ex·pect·an·cy \iks-'pek-tən-sē\ *n.; pl.* **ex·pect·an·cies.** **1** Expectation. **2** Something that is or may reasonably be expected; as, the normal life *expectancy* of American children born in 1950.

ex·pect·ant \iks-'pek-tənt\ *adj.* Expecting; having or showing expectation; as, looking towards the door in an *expectant* manner. — **ex·pect·ant·ly,** *adv.*

ex·pec·ta·tion \ˌeks-ˌpek-'tāsh-n, iks-\ *n.* **1** The act or state of expecting; a looking forward to or waiting for something; as, to be in happy *expectation* of a friend's visit. **2** Prospect for good or bad fortune; as, to have great *expectations.* **3** Something expected or looked for; as, to have all one's *expectations* prove wrong.

ex·pec·to·rate \iks-'pekt-r-ˌāt\ *v.;* **ex·pec·to·rat·ed; ex·pec·to·rat·ing.** [From Latin *expectoratus,* past participle of *expectorare* meaning "to expel from the chest", from *ex* meaning "out of" and *pector-,* stem of *pectus* meaning "chest".] To discharge from the throat or lungs, as phlegm, by coughing and spitting; to spit. — **ex·pec·to·ra·tion** \iks-ˌpekt-r-'āsh-n\ *n.*

ex·pe·di·ence \iks-'pēd-ē-ən(t)s\ *n.* Expediency.

ex·pe·di·en·cy \iks-'pēd-ē-ən-sē\ *n.; pl.* **ex·pe·di·en·cies.** **1** The quality or state of being expedient; suitability or convenience, as of a thing for a purpose; as, to question the *expediency* of a proposal to have one-way traffic in school corridors. **2** The use of means and methods advantageous to oneself, or consideration of one's personal advantage, without regard to principles of fairness and rightness; as, to be guided in one's life solely by *expediency.*

ex·pe·di·ent \iks-'pēd-ē-ənt\ *adj.* Suitable for bringing about a desired result, sometimes without regard to fairness or rightness; as, the cheaper and more *expedient* of two methods; to do what seems *expedient* under the circumstances. — *n.* That which is expedient; a means to accomplish an end, often one used in place of something better but not available.

ex·pe·dite \'eks-pə-ˌdīt\ *v.;* **ex·pe·dit·ed; ex·pe·dit·ing.** **1** To hasten the process or progress of; to facilitate; as, to *expedite* the passage of a bill through a legislature; modern machinery that *expedites* the manufacture of goods. **2** To carry through rapidly; as, to *expedite* several items of business before lunch.

ex·pe·di·tion \ˌeks-pə-'dish-n\ *n.* **1** The act of expediting or the state of being expedited; efficiency and promptness; as, directions carried out with great *expedition.* **2** A sending or setting forth for some object or purpose; as, the sudden *expedition* of the fleet into foreign waters. **3** A journey or trip for a particular purpose, as for war or exploring. **4** The people making such a journey.

ex·pe·di·tion·ary \ˌeks-pə-'dish-n-ˌer-ē\ *adj.* Of, relating to, or forming an expedition; as, a military *expeditionary* force.

ex·pe·di·tious \ˌeks-pə-'dish-əs\ *adj.* Prompt and efficient; speedy. Perishable goods require *expeditious* handling and transportation. — **ex·pe·di·tious·ly,** *adv.*

ex·pel \iks-'pel\ *v.;* **ex·pelled; ex·pel·ling.** **1** To drive out; to force out; as, to *expel* air from the lungs. **2** To cut off from active membership in, as a school or a club; as, to *expel* a student from college for bad conduct.

ex·pend \iks-'pend\ *v.* To consume by use in any

way, as time, money, or strength; to use up; to spend.

ex·pend·a·ble \iks-'pen-dəb-l\ *adj.* That may be used up in an ordinary way or sacrificed to delay an enemy; as, *expendable* ammunition; *expendable* troops. — *n.* An item of equipment or a member or unit of one of the armed forces that is regarded as expendable. — **ex·pend·a·bil·i·ty** \-ˌpen-də-'bil-ət-ē\ *n.* — **ex·pend·a·bly** \-'pen-də-blē\ *adv.*

ex·pend·i·ture \iks-'pen-dəch-r, -də-ˌchůr, -də-ˌt(y)ůr\ *n.* **1** The act of expending; a laying out or spending, as of money, time, or energy. **2** That which is spent; as, this month's *expenditures.*

ex·pense \iks-'pen(t)s\ *n.* **1** Something spent, as money or time; outlay; cost; as, the *expenses* of a trip. The greatest *expense* of war is in human lives. **2** A cause for spending; as, to have one *expense* after another.

ex·pen·sive \iks-'pen(t)s-iv\ *adj.* Costly; high-priced; dear. — **ex·pen·sive·ly,** *adv.*

ex·pe·ri·ence \iks-'pir-ē-ən(t)s\ *n.* **1** The actual living through an event or events; as, to learn by *experience.* **2** The skill or knowledge gained by actually doing or feeling a thing; as, a job that requires men with *experience.* **3** The amount or kind of work a person or animal has done or the time during which work has been done; as, a man with five years' *experience.* **4** Something that one has actually done or lived through; as, a soldier's *experiences* in war. To travel round the world would be an interesting *experience.* — *v.;* **ex·pe·ri·enced; ex·pe·ri·enc·ing.** To learn by experience; to have experience of; to feel; to undergo; as, to *experience* what war is like; to *experience* pleasure.

ex·pe·ri·enced \iks-'pir-ē-ən(t)st\ *adj.* Having experience; skillful or wise as a result of experience; as, an *experienced* pilot; an *experienced* eye.

ex·per·i·ment \iks-'per-ə-mənt\ *n.* A trial or test to find out about something; as, *experiments* in chemistry; a discovery that was the result of *experiment.* — For synonyms see *trial.* — \-ˌment\ *v.* To make experiments. — **ex·per·i·men·ta·tion** \iks-ˌper-ə-ˌmen-'tāsh-n, -mən-\ *n.* — **ex·per·i·ment·er** \iks-'per-ə-ˌment-r\ *n.*

ex·per·i·men·tal \iks-ˌper-ə-'ment-l\ *adj.* **1** Relating to or based on experience, especially on personal experience as distinct from theory; as, *experimental* familiarity with city life; *experimental* religion. **2** Of the nature of experiment; based on or derived from experiment; as, *experimental* science. **3** Skilled in or devoted to experiment; as, an *experimental* scientist. **4** Used as a means of experimentation; as, an *experimental* school. — **ex·per·i·men·tal·ly** \-'ment-l-ē\ *adv.*

ex·pert \'eks-(ˌ)pərt; iks-'pərt, eks-\ *adj.* Skillful; clever; showing special skill or knowledge; as, an *expert* swimmer; an *expert* photographer. — For synonyms see *skillful.* — \'eks-(ˌ)pərt\ *n.* An expert or skilled person; especially, one who has special knowledge of a subject; a specialist; as, to learn to skate from an *expert.* — **ex·pert·ly** \'eks-(ˌ)pərt-lē; iks-'pərt-, eks-\ *adv.*

ex·pi·a·ble \'eks-pē-əb-l\ *adj.* Capable of being expiated or atoned for.

ex·pi·ate \'eks-pē-ˌāt\ *v.;* **ex·pi·at·ed; ex·pi·at·ing.** To do something to make up for a wrong; to atone for; as, to *expiate* a crime.

ex·pi·a·tion \ˌeks-pē-'āsh-n\ *n.* **1** An expiating; an atonement. **2** A means of atonement.

ex·pi·ra·tion \ˌeks-pə-'rāsh-n\ *n.* **1** The act of expiring, or breathing air out of the lungs; a breathing out. **2** A coming to a close; the end; as, the *expiration* date of a magazine subscription.

ex·pir·a·to·ry \eks-'pīr-ə-ˌtōr-ē, -ˌtòr-ē\ *adj.* Relating to the expiration of air from the lungs.

ex·pire \iks-'pīr\ *v.;* **ex·pired; ex·pir·ing. 1** To breathe out air from the lungs. **2** To die. The soldier *expired* on the battlefield. **3** To come to an end; to stop. Annual memberships usually *expire* on December 31st.

ex·plain \iks-'plān\ *v.* To make plain; to give the reasons for; as, to *explain* an absence; to *explain* the meaning of a word. — **ex·plain·a·ble,** *adj.*

ex·pla·na·tion \ˌeks-plə-'nāsh-n\ *n.* **1** The act or process of explaining; as, a problem that needs *explanation.* **2** Something that explains; a statement that makes clear. Illness was the *explanation* of the boy's long absence.

ex·plan·a·to·ry \iks-'plan-ə-ˌtōr-ē, -ˌtòr-ē\ *adj.* Giving explanation; helping to make clear.

ex·ple·tive \'eks-plət-iv\ *adj.* Normally or frequently used in a construction or idiom without contributing anything to the meaning. — *n.* **1** An expletive word, as *there* in "There is a storm coming" or *it* in "Make it clear what you mean". **2** An oath; an exclamation.

ex·plic·a·ble \eks-'plik-əb-l, 'eks-(ˌ)plik-əb-l\ *adj.* Capable of being explained.

ex·plic·it \iks-'plis-ət, eks-\ *adj.* So clear in statement that there is no doubt about the meaning; as, *explicit* instructions. — **ex·plic·it·ly,** *adv.*

ex·plode \iks-'plōd\ *v.;* **ex·plod·ed; ex·plod·ing. 1** To cause to be given up or rejected. Science has *exploded* many old ideas. **2** To burst or to cause to burst violently and noisily; as, to *explode* a bomb. **3** To burst forth, as with anger or laughter.

ex·ploit \'eks-ˌplòit\ *n.* A deed or act; especially, a heroic act. — \iks-'plòit, eks-; 'eks-ˌplòit\ *v.* **1** To get the value or use out of; as, to *exploit* a coal mine. **2** To make use of unfairly for one's own advantage; as, to *exploit* the kindness of one's friends. — **ex·ploit·a·ble** \-əb-l\ *adj.* — **ex·ploi·ta·tion** \ˌeks-ˌplòi-'tāsh-n\ *n.* — **ex·ploit·er** \iks-'plòit-r, eks-; 'eks-ˌplòit-r\ *n.*

ex·plo·ra·tion \ˌeks-plər-'āsh-n, -ˌplōr-, -ˌplòr-\ *n.* The act of exploring; exploring done for the purpose of making discoveries, especially in geography. — **ex·plor·a·tive** \iks-'plōr-ət-iv, -'plòr-\ or **ex·plor·a·to·ry** \-'plōr-ə-ˌtōr-ē, -'plòr-ə-ˌtòr-ē\ *adj.*

ex·plore \iks-'plōr, -'plòr\ *v.;* **ex·plored; ex·plor·ing. 1** To search through or travel in for purposes of discovery; as, to *explore* an uncharted body of water. **2** To examine closely; to consider carefully; as, to *explore* the matter further. **3** In medicine, to search carefully in; to probe; as, to *explore* a wound.

ex·plor·er \iks-'plōr-r, -'plȯr-\ *n.* One that explores; especially, a traveler seeking new scientific information.

ex·plo·sion \iks-'plōzh-n\ *n.* **1** The action of exploding; a sudden and noisy bursting, as of a firecracker. **2** A sudden outburst of feeling, as of anger.

ex·plo·sive \iks-'plō-siv, -ziv\ *adj.* **1** Relating to or characterized by explosion; able to cause explosion; as, the *explosive* power of gunpowder. **2** Likely to explode; as, an *explosive* temper. — *n.* An explosive substance. Dynamite is an *explosive.*

ex·po·nent \iks-'pō-nənt, eks-; 'eks-ˌpō-\ *n.* **1** In algebra, a figure or symbol written above and to the right of a second figure or symbol to show how many times the second is to be repeated as a factor. In $(a + b)^3$ the *exponent* is *3.* **2** A person who explains or interprets; as, an *exponent* of modern music. **3** One that serves as an example or representative; as, a man who is an *exponent* of democratic principles. — **ex·po·nen·tial** \ˌeks-pō-'nench-l\ *adj.*

ex·port \eks-'pōrt, -'pȯrt; 'eks-ˌpōrt, -ˌpȯrt\ *v.* To send or carry abroad, especially for sale in foreign countries. — \'eks-ˌpōrt, -ˌpȯrt\ *n.* **1** The action of exporting; as, to prohibit the *export* of gold. **2** Anything that is exported. — **ex·port·a·ble** \eks-'pōrt-əb-l, -'pȯrt-; 'eks-ˌpōrt-əb-l, -ˌpȯrt-\ *adj.*

ex·por·ta·tion \ˌeks-ˌpōr-'tāsh-n, -ˌpȯr-\ *n.* **1** The exporting of goods. **2** Something that is exported.

ex·port·er \eks-'pōrt-r, -'pȯrt-; 'eks-ˌpōrt-r, -ˌpȯrt-\ *n.* One who exports goods.

ex·pose \iks-'pōz\ *v.;* **ex·posed; ex·pos·ing. 1** To lay open, as to attack or danger; to leave without protection, shelter, or care; as, young plants *exposed* to all kinds of weather. The children were *exposed* to measles. **2** In photography, to let light strike the photographic film or plate. **3** To cast out; to abandon; as, to *expose* an infant to die. **4** To make known; to reveal; as, to *expose* a dishonest scheme. **5** To put where it can be seen; to display; as, to *expose* goods for sale.

ex·po·sé \ˌeks-pō-'zā\ *n.* An exposure of something discreditable.

ex·po·si·tion \ˌeks-pə-'zish-n\ *n.* **1** An explaining of the meaning or purpose of something, as a piece of writing or a device. **2** A composition that explains something. **3** A public exhibition or show. — **ex·pos·i·to·ry** \eks-'päz-ə-ˌtōr-ē, -ˌtȯr-ē\ *adj.*

ex·pos·i·tor \eks-'päz-ət-r\ *n.* One who expounds or explains.

ex·pos·tu·late \eks-'päs-chə-ˌlāt\ *v.;* **ex·pos·tu·lat·ed; ex·pos·tu·lat·ing.** To reason earnestly with a person against something he has done or intends to do; to remonstrate; as, to *expostulate* with a student regarding his frequent absences from school. — **ex·pos·tu·la·tion** \(ˌ)eks-ˌpäs-chə-'lāsh-n\ *n.* — **ex·pos·tu·la·to·ry** \eks-'päs-chə-lə-ˌtōr-ē, -ˌtȯr-ē\ *adj.*

ex·po·sure \iks-'pōzh-r\ *n.* **1** An exposing or laying open; as, the *exposure* of a spy. **2** A being exposed; as, to suffer from *exposure* to the cold. **3** The action of exposing or abandoning, as of unwanted infants. **4** Position with respect to direction; as, a room with a southern *exposure.* **5** A section of photographic film for an individual picture. **6** The act of letting light strike a photographic film or the time during which a film is exposed.

ex·pound \iks-'paůnd\ *v.* **1** To state; to set forth, as an idea or a theory. **2** To lay open the meaning of; to explain. — **ex·pound·er,** *n.*

ex-pres·i·dent \'eks-'prez-ə-dənt, -'prez-dənt, -ə-ˌdent\ *n.* One who was president but is so no longer.

ex·press \iks-'pres\ *adj.* **1** Clearly stated; as, an *express* reply. **2** Special; as, to go to town for an *express* purpose. **3** Sent with speed; rapid; as, an *express* package; an *express* train. **4** Adapted for travel at high speed; as, an *express* highway. **5** Of, relating to, or controlling a system for special transportation of goods; as, an *express* company. — *adv.* By express; as, to send the package *express.* — *n.* **1** A system for the special transportation of money or goods; as, to send a package by *express.* **2** The goods so carried. **3** A means of transportation, as a train or elevator, run at special speed with few stops. — *v.* **1** To press or squeeze out. **2** To make known the opinions or feelings of, as by words or actions; to show; as, to *express* approval; to *express* oneself well. **3** To mean. The + sign *expresses* addition. **4** To send by express; as, to *express* a package. — **ex·press·i·ble** \-əb-l\ *adj.*

ex·pres·sion \iks-'presh-n\ *n.* **1** The act or process of expressing, especially in words. **2** A word, phrase, or sign that expresses a thought, feeling, or quality; especially, a significant word or phrase; as, a common *expression.* **3** Way of speaking, or of singing or playing an instrument, so as to show mood or feeling; as, to read with *expression.* **4** A look; appearance; as, to wear a pleased *expression.* **5** In mathematics, a group of characters or signs representing a quantity or operation.

ex·pres·sive \iks-'pres-iv\ *adj.* **1** Of, relating to, or marked by expression. **2** Serving to represent; indicative; as, words *expressive* of one's feelings. **3** Full of expression; significant; as, *expressive* eyes. — **ex·pres·sive·ly,** *adv.*

ex·press·ly \iks-'pres-lē\ *adv.* **1** Clearly; plainly; as, to be told *expressly* to be home by four o'clock. **2** Purposely; especially; as, to visit a friend *expressly* to wish him a happy birthday.

ex·press·man \iks-'pres-ˌman, -mən\ *n.; pl.* **ex·press·men** \-ˌmen, -mən\. A person employed in the express business.

ex·press·way \iks-'pres-ˌwā\ *n.* A superhighway.

ex·pul·sion \iks-'pəlsh-n\ *n.* The act of expelling or the state of being expelled; as, to be punished by *expulsion* from school. — **ex·pul·sive** \-'pəl-siv\ *adj.*

ex·punge \iks-'pənj\ *v.;* **ex·punged; ex·pung·ing.** To blot out; to rub out; to erase; to cancel; as, to *expunge* the offensive words from a speech.

ex·pur·gate \'eks-pər-ˌgāt\ *v.;* **ex·pur·gat·ed; ex·pur·gat·ing.** To clear of anything wrong or objectionable; especially, to clear a book or other written matter of objectionable words or passages.

ex·quis·ite \eks-'kwiz-ət; 'eks-(ˌ)kwiz-ət, -kwə-zət\ *adj.* [From Latin *exquisitus* meaning literally "sought out", from past participle of *exquirere* meaning "to search out", "to look for".] **1** Carefully made; surpassing in quality; excellent; as, a cabinet that shows *exquisite* workmanship. **2** Keenly appreciative; discriminating; as, *exquisite* taste. **3** Beautiful; delicate; as, the *exquisite* petals of a flower. **4** Keen; intense; as, *exquisite* pleasure or pain. — **ex·quis·ite·ly,** *adv.*

ex·tant \'eks-tənt, -ˌtant; eks-'tant\ *adj.* In existence; not destroyed or lost; as, *extant* documents.

ex·tem·po·ra·ne·ous \(ˌ)eks-ˌtemp-r-'ā-nē-əs\ *adj.* Not planned beforehand; made up or given on the spur of the moment, as a speech; impromptu. — **ex·tem·po·ra·ne·ous·ly,** *adv.*

ex·tem·po·re \iks-'temp-r-(ˌ)ē\ *adv.* Without preparation; extemporaneously; as, a very clever speech made quite *extempore.* — *adj.* Extemporaneous; as, a few *extempore* remarks.

ex·tem·po·rize \iks-'temp-r-ˌīz\ *v.;* **ex·tem·po·rized; ex·tem·po·riz·ing.** To do, make, or utter extempore, or on the spur of the moment; to improvise. — **ex·tem·po·ri·za·tion** \iks-ˌtemp-r-ə-'zāsh-n\ *n.*

ex·tend \iks-'tend\ *v.* **1** To stretch out; to lengthen; as, to *extend* a road. The path *extends* along the river. **2** To lengthen in time; to prolong; as, to *extend* a visit at the urging of one's host. **3** To straighten out; to stretch forth, as the arm or leg. **4** To increase or widen; to expand; as, to *extend* one's interests; to *extend* the school district to include the next town. **5** To hold out; to offer; as, to *extend* friendship to a stranger.

ex·ten·si·ble \iks-'ten(t)s-əb-l\ *adj.* Capable of being extended. — **ex·ten·si·bil·i·ty** \iks-ˌten(t)s-ə-'bil-ət-ē\ *n.*

ex·ten·sion \iks-'tench-n\ *n.* **1** The act of extending or the state of being extended; a stretching out; an increase, as in length or time. **2** An addition; something serving to enlarge or lengthen; as, to build an *extension* on a house; a telephone with an *extension* on the second floor.

ex·ten·sive \iks-'ten(t)s-iv\ *adj.* Having wide extent; broad; widespread; far-reaching; thorough; as, a man whose travels had been *extensive;* an old house needing *extensive* repairs. — **ex·ten·sive·ly,** *adv.*

ex·ten·sor \iks-'ten(t)s-r\ *n.* A muscle serving to extend or straighten a limb or part.

ex·tent \iks-'tent\ *n.* **1** The space or amount to which anything is extended; space; size; length. **2** Degree or measure, as of greatness, largeness, smallness, or importance; as, the *extent* of a person's injuries; to agree to a certain *extent* but not fully.

ex·ten·u·ate \iks-'ten-yə-ˌwāt\ *v.;* **ex·ten·u·at·ed; ex·ten·u·at·ing.** To diminish; to underestimate; especially, to represent, as a crime, fault, or mistake, as of less importance than it really is or appears to be; to make excuses for; as, an offense that could not be *extenuated* by the offender's youth.

ex·ten·u·a·tion \iks-ˌten-yə-'wāsh-n\ *n.* **1** The act of extenuating or the state of being extenuated; as, to plead ignorance of the law in *extenuation* of an offense. **2** Something that extenuates; a partial excuse.

ex·te·ri·or \eks-'tir-ē-ər\ *adj.* **1** Outer; external; as, the *exterior* surface of a bottle. **2** On the outside; happening or coming from outside; as, *exterior* conditions; *exterior* influences. — *n.* The outside; as, the *exterior* of a house.

ex·ter·mi·nate \iks-'tər-mə-ˌnāt\ *v.;* **ex·ter·mi·nat·ed; ex·ter·mi·nat·ing.** To destroy utterly; to get rid of completely; as, to *exterminate* the termites infesting a house. — **ex·ter·mi·na·tion** \iks-ˌtər-mə-'nāsh-n\ *n.* — **ex·ter·mi·na·tor** \iks-'tər-mə-ˌnāt-r\ *n.*

ex·ter·nal \eks-'tərn-l\ *adj.* **1** Outside; exterior; coming from or having to do with the outside; as, *external* influences; a medicine for *external* use only. **2** Visible; physical, as distinguished from mental or moral. *External* appearances are often a poor guide to character. **3** Beyond the limits of a thing or place; as, the *external* affairs of a country. — *n.* [usually in the plural] An outside part; an appearance; as, to make the mistake of judging others by *externals.* — **ex·ter·nal·ly** \-'tərn-l-ē\ *adv.*

ex·tinct \iks-'ting(k)t, eks-\ *adj.* **1** No longer existing; as, an *extinct* nation; *extinct* animals. **2** No longer active; as, an *extinct* volcano.

ex·tinc·tion \iks-'ting(k)sh-n, eks-\ *n.* **1** The act of extinguishing or the state of being extinguished. **2** A wiping out or annihilation; destruction; extermination; as, the *extinction* of a whole village by an epidemic disease; wild animal life in danger of *extinction.*

ex·tin·guish \iks-'ting-gwish, eks-\ *v.* **1** To put out, as a fire or a light. **2** To cause to die out, as life or hope; to destroy.

ex·tin·guish·er \iks-'ting-gwish-r, eks-\ *n.* One that extinguishes; especially, a portable device, commonly consisting of a tank filled with chemicals, for extinguishing fires.

ex·tir·pate \'eks-tər-ˌpāt, eks-'tər-ˌpāt\ *v.;* **ex·tir·pat·ed; ex·tir·pat·ing.** To pull up by the roots; to eradicate or destroy wholly. — **ex·tir·pa·tion** \ˌeks-(ˌ)tər-'pāsh-n\ *n.*

ex·tol or **ex·toll** \iks-'tōl\ *v.;* **ex·tolled; ex·tol·ling.** To praise highly; to glorify. The general *extolled* the bravery of his troops.

ex·tort \iks-'tórt, eks-\ *v.* To use force or threats to get something from a person, as money or a confession; to wring from; to exact. — **ex·tort·er,** *n.*

ex·tor·tion \iks-'tórsh-n, eks-\ *n.* **1** An extorting. **2** Something that is extorted.

ex·tor·tion·ate \iks-'tórsh-n(-)ət, eks-\ *adj.* **1** Characterized by extortion. **2** Excessive; exorbitant; as, *extortionate* demands.

ex·tra \'eks-trə\ *adj.* Beyond or greater than what is usual, expected, or due; additional; as, *extra* quality; to need *extra* time to finish. — *n.* **1** Something in addition to what is usual; especially, an added charge or something for which an additional charge is made; as, to pay *extra* for installation of an appliance. **2** An edition of a newspaper published at other than the regular time; as, a sports *extra.* **3** An extra workman; as, to retain the regular workmen and hire *extras* during the busy season. — *adv.* Beyond the usual, as in size, amount, or degree; as, *extra*-large; *extra*-fine.

ex·tract \iks-'trakt, eks-\ *v.* **1** To pull out; to draw out; as, to *extract* a tooth. **2** To get out by pressing, distilling, or by some chemical process; as, to *extract* juice from apples. **3** To choose and take out; as, to *extract* a few lines from a poem. — \'eks-ˌtrakt\ *n.* **1** Something extracted; especially, a substance obtained from something else by pressing, distilling, or by a chemical process; as, vanilla *extract.* **2** A selection, as from a book or a speech. — **ex·tract·a·ble** or **ex·trac·ti·ble** \iks-'trak-təb-l, eks-\ *adj.*

ex·trac·tion \iks-'traksh-n, eks-\ *n.* **1** An extracting or pulling out; as, the *extraction* of a tooth. **2** The origin of a person; descent; as, a man of French *extraction.* **3** Something extracted; an extract.

ex·trac·tor \iks-'trakt-r, eks-\ *n.* One that extracts, as a device for withdrawing a cartridge from the chamber of a firearm.

ex·tra·cur·ric·u·lar \'eks-trə-kə-'rik-yəl-r\ *adj.* Not falling within the curriculum; especially, of or relating to those activities, as debating and athletics, that form part of the life of students but are not part of the courses of study.

ex·tra·dite \'eks-trə-ˌdīt\ *v.;* **ex·tra·dit·ed; ex·tra·dit·ing.** To cause to be delivered or given up to a different legal authority as an alleged criminal for trial. The prisoner was *extradited* from New York to New Jersey. — **ex·tra·dit·a·ble,** *adj.*

ex·tra·di·tion \ˌeks-trə-'dish-n\ *n.* The surrender or delivery of a criminal by one state or power to another.

ex·tra·ne·ous \eks-'trā-nē-əs\ *adj.* Not belonging to something; not essential; foreign; as, argument that is *extraneous* to the topic being considered. — **ex·tra·ne·ous·ly,** *adv.*

ex·traor·di·nary \iks-'tròrd-n-ˌer-ē, ˌeks-trə-'òrd-\ *adj.* **1** Unusual; uncommon; remarkable; as, a person with an *extraordinary* memory. **2** Employed on a special service; as, an ambassador *extraordinary.* — **ex·traor·di·nar·i·ly** \-'er-ə-lē\ *adv.*

ex·tra·ter·ri·to·ri·al \'eks-trə-ˌter-ə-'tōr-ē-əl, -'tór-ē-\ *adj.* Outside the territorial limits of an authority.

ex·tra·ter·ri·to·ri·al·i·ty \'eks-trə-ˌter-ə-ˌtōr-ē-'al-ət-ē, -ˌtór-ē-\ *n.* A being exempt from the jurisdiction of local courts, as in the case of diplomatic agents.

ex·trav·a·gance \iks-'trav-ə-gən(t)s\ *n.* **1** The quality of being extravagant, especially in spending money; unnecessary expenditure. **2** An extravagant action or thing. The girl's desire for jewelry carried her into *extravagances.*

ex·trav·a·gant \iks-'trav-ə-gənt\ *adj.* **1** Going beyond what is reasonable or suitable; excessive; as, to give *extravagant* praise. **2** Wasteful, as of money or food. **3** Too high; as, an *extravagant* price. — **ex·trav·a·gant·ly,** *adv.*

ex·trav·a·gan·za \iks-ˌtrav-ə-'gan-zə\ *n.* A wildly irregular musical or dramatic composition; especially, a spectacular theatrical presentation with elaborate setting.

ex·treme \iks-'trēm\ *adj.* **1** Farthest; utmost; as, the *extreme* tip of the peninsula. **2** Far out toward the end; as, at an *extreme* point on the peninsula. **3** Existing in or going to the greatest degree; greatest; as, to pay the *extreme* penalty. **4** Going beyond the usual limits; excessive; as, *extreme* fashion. — *n.* **1** The greatest possible degree; an excessive degree; as, to go to the *extreme* in being cautious. **2** [in the plural] Things that are very far apart or as different as possible from each other; as, the *extremes* of heat and cold. **3** An unusual measure, extent, or degree; as, to go to *extremes* to gain one's end. **4** In mathematics, the first or last term of a proportion or series.

ex·treme·ly \iks-'trēm-lē\ *adv.* Unusually; very; as, an *extremely* clever pupil; to be *extremely* careful in crossing streets.

ex·trem·ist \iks-'trē-məst\ *n.* A person who believes in extreme measures, especially in politics.

ex·trem·i·ty \iks-'trem-ət-ē\ *n.; pl.* **ex·trem·i·ties.** **1** The farthest limit, point, or part; as, the northern *extremity* of the island. **2** [usually in the plural] An arm, leg, hand, or foot. **3** The greatest degree; as, an *extremity* of happiness or misery. **4** The highest degree of pain, danger, or suffering; extreme need; as, a family reduced to *extremity.* **5** A very severe act; as, to go to *extremities* to gain one's ends.

ex·tri·cate \'eks-trə-ˌkāt\ *v.;* **ex·tri·cat·ed; ex·tri·cat·ing.** To free, as from danger or difficulty; as, to *extricate* oneself from the clinging mud of a swamp.

ex·trin·sic \eks-'trin-zik, -'trin(t)s-ik\ *adj.* Not essential, as to a subject being considered; as, *extrinsic* details that were interesting but unimportant. — **ex·trin·si·cal·ly** \-'trin-zik-l(-)ē, -'trin(t)s-ik-l(-)ē\ *adv.*

ex·tro·vert \'eks-trə-ˌvərt\ *n.* A person who is more interested in what he does and what goes on about him than in what he thinks or imagines; one who finds most of his interests and satisfactions in external things.

ex·trude \eks-'trüd\ *v.;* **ex·trud·ed; ex·trud·ing. 1** To force, press, or push out; to protrude. **2** To shape, as metal or plastic, by forcing through molds or dies by pressure. — **ex·tru·sion** \eks-'trüzh-n\ *n.*

ex·u·ber·ance \ig-'züb-r-ən(t)s\ *n.* **1** The state of being in great abundance; luxuriance; lavishness; as, *exuberance* of vegetation; an *exuberance* of feeling. **2** A state of being filled with life and high spirits. The children burst into the room in wild *exuberance.*

ex·u·ber·ant \ig-'züb-r-ənt\ *adj.* **1** Characterized by great abundance; plenteous; luxuriant; as, *exuberant* foliage. **2** Filled with life, vigor, and high spirits; as, *exuberant* children romping on a beach. **3** Carried to or experienced in an extreme degree; as, *exuberant* praise; *exuberant* joy. — **ex·u·ber·ant·ly,** *adv.*

ex·ude \ig-'züd\ *v.;* **ex·ud·ed; ex·ud·ing.** [From Latin *exsudare* meaning literally "to come out by sweating", "to sweat out", from *ex* meaning "out of" and *sudare* meaning "to sweat".] To discharge through pores or cuts; as, to *exude* sweat; sap *exuding* from a hole in a tree. — **ex·u·da·tion** \ˌeks-ə-'dāsh-n, ˌegz-\ *n.*

ex·ult \ig-'zəlt\ *v.* To be in high spirits; to rejoice, as in victory or success; to triumph.

ex·ult·ant \ig-'zəlt-nt\ *adj.* Exulting; joyful; triumphant; as, an *exultant* shout of victory.

ex·ul·ta·tion \ˌegz-l-'tāsh-n, ˌeks-; ˌeg-ˌzəl-, ˌek-ˌsəl-\ *n.* Great joy at success; great rejoicing.

-ey \ē\. A form of the suffix *-y* that can mean: containing, full of, or like — used especially after words ending in *y,* as in *clayey.*

eye \'ī\ *n.* **1** An organ of seeing; especially, the nearly round mass, the **eye·ball** \'ī-ˌbȯl\, in a cavity of the skull. **2** The ability to see; power to appreciate; as, to have a keen *eye* for a bargain. **3** A look or glance; close attention; watch; as, to keep an *eye* on a store for the owner. **4** The central or most important spot or location; as, to be in the *eye* of the news. **5** Opinion; judgment; as, to be guilty in the *eyes* of the law. **6** Something like or suggesting an eye, as the hole in a needle, a small loop or ring to receive a hook, or the calm center of a hurricane. — **have an eye to.** To pay particular attention to; to watch; as, to *have an eye to* expenses. — **make eyes at.** To look at amorously. — **see eye to eye.** To be in complete agreement; to have the same opinion. — *v.;* **eyed** \'īd\; **ey·ing** or **eye·ing.** To look at; especially, to watch sharply; as, to *eye* a stranger with suspicion.

eye, 6: hook and eye

eye·brow \'ī-ˌbrau̇\ *n.* **1** The arch or ridge over the eye. **2** The hair that grows on this ridge.

eye·ful \'ī-ˌfu̇l\ *n.; pl.* **eye·fuls. 1** A sight that is satisfying or convincing. Those who enjoy looking at tall buildings get an *eyeful* when they visit New York City. **2** One that has an unusual or striking appearance; especially, a young woman whose looks or dress excites unusual attention.

eye·glass \'ī-ˌglas\ *n.* **1** A glass lens used to improve faulty eyesight. **2** [in the plural] A pair of such lenses, used together. **3** An eyepiece, as of a telescope or microscope.

eyeglass

eye·hole \'ī-ˌhōl\ *n.* **1** The opening in the skull for the eye. **2** A hole to see through, as in a mask; a peephole. **3** A round opening, as for a rope; an eyelet.

eye·lash \'ī-ˌlash\ *n.* **1** The fringe of hair on an eyelid. **2** A single hair of this fringe; an eyewinker.

eye·let \'ī-lət\ *n.* **1** A small hole, as in cloth or leather, for a lacing or rope. **2** A metal ring to line such a hole, as in a shoe.

eye·lid \'ī-ˌlid\ *n.* The movable skin with which the eye can be covered or uncovered.

eye·piece \'ī-ˌpēs\ *n.* A lens or lenses at the eye end of an optical instrument, as a microscope.

eye·sight \'ī-ˌsīt\ *n.* **1** Sight; vision; as, keen *eyesight.* **2** *Archaic.* Observation.

eye·sore \'ī-ˌsōr, -ˌsȯr\ *n.* Something displeasing to the sight. That old building is an *eyesore.*

eye·strain \'ī-ˌstrān\ *n.* Weariness or strained condition of the eye, caused by faulty eyesight or excessive use of the eyes.

eye·tooth \'ī-'tüth\ *n.; pl.* **eye·teeth** \-'tēth\. The tooth between the last incisor and the first premolar on either side of the upper jaw; an upper canine.

eye·wink·er \'ī-ˌwingk-r\ *n.* An eyelash.

eye·wit·ness \'ī-'wit-nəs\ *n.* A person who from having seen an occurrence with his own eyes is able to give a reliable account of it; as, an *eyewitness* to an accident.

ey·rie or **ey·ry** \'īr-ē, 'ir-ē, 'ā-rē\ *n.* An aerie.

f \'ef\ *n.; pl.* **f's** \'efs\. The sixth letter of the alphabet.

F. Abbreviation for *Fahrenheit.*

fa \'fä, 'fȧ\ *n.* A syllable used in music to name the fourth note of the scale.

fa·ble \'fāb-l\ *n.* **1** A story that is not true. **2** A short story that teaches a lesson; especially, one in which animals talk and act like people.

fa·bled \'fāb-ld\ *adj.* **1** Told or told of in fable or in story; legendary; as, the *fabled* chameleon; the *fabled* cities of past civilizations. **2** Made up; fictitious.

fab·ric \'fab-rik\ *n.* **1** A cloth or other textile woven or knitted from natural or synthetic fibers; as, cotton *fabrics;* a nylon *fabric.* **2** A structure; framework; as, the *fabric* of society.

fab·ri·cate \'fab-rə-ˌkāt\ *v.;* **fab·ri·cat·ed; fab·ri·cat·ing. 1** To construct; to build or frame; to manufacture. **2** To make up; to invent; as, to *fabricate* a story; an excuse *fabricated* on the spur of the moment.

fab·ri·ca·tion \ˌfab-rə-'kāsh-n\ *n.* **1** The act of fabricating; construction or manufacture; invention, as of a story or legend. **2** Something fabricated; especially, a story falsely invented to deceive; a falsehood.

fab·u·lous \'fab-yə-ləs\ *adj.* **1** Told in fable or based on fable; as, *fabulous* animals. **2** Like a fable, especially in exaggeration; beyond belief; extraordinary; wonderful; as, the *fabulous* adventures of an explorer; a man of *fabulous* wealth. — **fab·u·lous·ly**, *adv.*

fa·cade or **fa·çade** \fə-'säd, -'såd\ *n.* **1** The face or front of a building. **2** Any face or front; outside appearance; as, a *facade* of wealth; a prisoner frightened behind his *facade* of composure.

facade, 1

face \'fās\ *n.* **1** The front part of the head. **2** A look; an expression; as, to wear a sad *face.* **3** A grimace; as, to make a *face.* **4** Impudence; boldness. We would never have believed she had the *face* to contradict the teacher. **5** Outward appearance; present appearance; as, a candidate elected on the *face* of the returns. **6** Dignity; reputation; prestige; as, to be anxious not to lose *face* with one's fellows. **7** Presence; sight; as, to be brave in the *face* of danger. **8** The surface of something, especially the front, upper, or outer part; as, the *face* of a building; the *face* of a cliff. **9** A side or surface that is marked or specially prepared; as, the *face* of a clock; the *face* of a playing card. — *v.;* **faced; fac·ing. 1** To have the face or front toward; as, a house that *faces* the east. **2** To turn bravely toward; to oppose; as, to *face* danger courageously; to *face* death. **3** To put an additional surface on; as, a house *faced* with brick. **4** To line near the edge, especially with a different material; as, to *face* a hem. **5** To turn the face and body; to front; as, to *face* to the right.

face card. A playing card marked with a representation of a human face; a king, queen, or jack.

fac·et \'fas-ət\ *n.* [From French *facette* meaning literally "little face".] **1** One of the surfaces on a gem that has been cut. **2** A phase or aspect, as of a topic or a situation. **3** The surface of one of the similar visual units making up a compound eye, as of an insect. — **fac·et·ed** \-ət-əd\ *adj.*

gem cut with facets

fa·ce·tious \fə-'sē-shəs\ *adj.* Humorous, especially in a sly or mischievous way; teasing; jocular; as, a *facetious* remark; a boy with a *facetious* turn of mind. — **fa·ce·tious·ly**, *adv.*

face value. 1 The value stated on the face, as of a bond. **2** Apparent value or significance; as, to take a person's words at their *face value* and not question his sincerity.

fa·cial \'fāsh-l\ *adj.* Of or relating to the face; as, *facial* expressions; a *facial* massage. — *n.* A facial treatment or massage.

fac·ile \'fas-l\ *adj.* **1** Easy to do; as, a *facile* task. **2** Easy and mild in nature; easily persuaded; yielding; as, a man of very *facile* disposition. **3** Doing or expressing something easily; quick; ready; expert; fluent; as, a *facile* speaker; made with a *facile* hand. — **fac·ile·ly** \'fas-l-(l)ē\ *adv.*

fa·cil·i·tate \fə-'sil-ə-ˌtāt\ *v.;* **fa·cil·i·tat·ed; fa·cil·i·tat·ing.** To make easy or easier; as, to *facilitate* a job by putting more men on it; machines that *facilitate* production.

fa·cil·i·ty \fə-'sil-ət-ē\ *n.; pl.* **fa·cil·i·ties. 1** Ease; freedom from difficulty; skill; as, to read with *facility.* **2** [usually in the plural] Something that facilitates, or makes any action, operation, or course of conduct easier; a help; an advantage; an opportunity; as, a kitchen with all the most modern *facilities;* a school with excellent *facilities* for the study of art.

fac·ing \'fā-sing\ *n.* **1** A covering in front, as for ornament or protection; as, the tile *facing* of a fireplace; a wooden house with brick *facing.* **2** A lining near the edge of a garment. **3** [in the plural] The collar, cuffs, and trimmings of a military coat; as, a scarlet tunic with blue *facings.* **4** Any material used for facing.

fac·sim·i·le \fak-'sim-l-(ˌ)ē\ *n.* **1** An exact copy; as, a *facsimile* of a letter. **2** The process of sending and reproducing printed matter and pictures by radio or telegraph.

fact \'fakt\ *n.* **1** Something that is done or happens; an event, occurrence, or circumstance; as, the *facts* of the case. The victory that everyone hoped for is now a *fact.* **2** The quality of being real or actual; the realness or truth of something; actuality; as, a matter of *fact* and not of opinion. **3** The statement of something that is done or exists; as, a book filled with *facts.* **4** A thing that exists; an actuality. Crime is a *fact* that must be faced.

fac·tion \'faksh-n\ *n.* A group or combination acting together within and usually against a larger body, as in a state, political party, or church; a clique. — For synonyms see *party.* — **fac·tion·al** \'faksh-n(-)əl\ *adj.*

fac·tious \'fak-shəs\ *adj.* **1** Inclined towards forming or joining factions, or towards causing discontent and dissension. **2** Caused by faction; connected with factions; as, a *factious* dispute.

fac·ti·tious \fak-'tish-əs\ *adj.* Not natural or genuine; artificial; as, a *factitious* display of grief. — **fac·ti·tious·ly**, *adv.*

fac·tor \'fakt-r\ *n.* **1** A person who does business for someone else; an agent. **2** Any circumstance or influence that helps to bring about a result. The weather was an important *factor* in the decision to postpone the picnic. **3** In mathematics, any of the elements, quantities, or symbols that form a given product when multiplied together. — *v.;* **factored; fac·tor·ing** \'fakt-r(-)ing\. To find the factors of a number; to separate into factors.

fac·to·ry \'fakt-r(-)ē\ *n.; pl.* **fac·to·ries.** **1** A trading station where factors, or agents, live and carry on business. **2** A building or group of buildings used for manufacturing goods.

fac·to·tum \fak-'tōt-m\ *n.* A person employed to do a great variety of tasks.

fac·tu·al \'fak-chə-wəl, -chəl\ *adj.* Relating to fact; containing facts; actual. — **fac·tu·al·ly** \'fak-chə-lē, 'fak-chə-wə-lē\ *adv.*

fac·ul·ty \'fak-l-tē\ *n.; pl.* **fac·ul·ties.** **1** Ability to do something; talent; knack; as, a great *faculty* for making friends. **2** One of the powers of the mind or body; as, the *faculty* of hearing. **3** The teachers in a school or college. **4** A department of learning in a university; as, the *faculty* of law.

fad \'fad\ *n.* A fashion, custom, or amusement followed for a time with exaggerated enthusiasm; a craze. — **fad·dist** \'fad-əst\ *n.*

fade \'fād\ *v.;* **fad·ed**; **fad·ing.** **1** To wither, as a flower. **2** To grow dim, pale, or faint; to disappear gradually; as, a color that *fades* easily. Toward morning the stars *fade.* **3** To cause to lose color or brightness. The sun *faded* the red curtains. **4** To change gradually in distinctness or loudness, as a picture on a screen or a sound effect.

fade-out \'fād-ˌau̇t\ *n.* A fading out or away; especially, the gradual disappearance of a picture on a moving-picture or television screen.

faery \'fā-ər-ē, 'far-ē, 'fer-ē\ *adj.* Fairy.

fag \'fag\ *v.;* **fagged**; **fag·ging.** **1** To work or make someone else work until exhausted; as, to be *fagged* out by the end of the day. **2** To act as a fag. — *n.* **1** In English schools, a boy who waits on another boy of a higher grade. **2** A drudge.

fag end \'fag 'end\. The last part or coarser end of a web of cloth or the untwisted end of a rope; any remnant; a poor, old, or worn-out end of anything.

fag·ot or **fag·got** \'fag-ət\ *n.* A bundle of sticks or twigs, as for fuel.

fag·ot·ing or **fag·got·ing** \'fag-ət-ing\ *n.* Ornamental stitching in which threads are tied in hourglass-shaped clusters.

Fahr·en·heit \'far-ən-ˌhīt\ *adj.* [Named after Gabriel Daniel *Fahrenheit* (1686–1736), German physicist who invented the Fahrenheit scale.] Denoting or according to the scale of measuring used on a **Fahrenheit thermometer**, on which the boiling point of water is at 212 degrees above the zero and the freezing point at 32 degrees above the zero.

fail \'fāl\ *v.* **1** To be insufficient, unsuccessful, or disappointing; as, an attempt that *failed.* Crops may *fail* if the weather is bad. **2** To become weaker; as, eyesight *failing* with age. **3** To be found wanting or lacking in some action or duty; to fall short of what is expected or desired; as, to *fail* to keep one's word; to *fail* in a test. **4** To disappoint; to neglect or desert; as, to *fail* a friend. **5** To become bankrupt. — *n.* Failure; failing; as, to promise to go without *fail.*

fail·ing \'fā-ling\ *n.* **1** A failure. **2** A fault; a weakness; a deficiency. The boy's chief *failing* was his lack of perseverance. — *prep.* Lacking; in the absence of. *Failing* help, the castaways could expect only death.

faille \'fīl\ *n.* A heavy ribbed silk fabric, commonly used in making dresses.

fail·ure \'fāl-yər\ *n.* **1** A falling short; a deficiency or lack; as, a *failure* of crops. **2** A failing to do; neglect to do what is expected; as, *failure* in one's duty. **3** Lack of success; as, a *failure* in a test. **4** A breaking down; a decline; a weakening; as, a *failure* of memory. **5** Bankruptcy. **6** A person or thing that fails. The girl was a *failure* as an actress.

fain \'fān\ *adj. Archaic.* **1** Well-pleased; glad; as, *fain* to see old friends. **2** Desirous; as, *fain* to lie down to rest. — *adv. Archaic.* With joy; gladly.

faint \'fānt\ *adj.* **1** Lacking courage or spirit; timid; cowardly. **2** Lacking strength; weak; inclined to swoon; as, to feel *faint* at the sight of blood. **3** Done weakly or feebly; slight; as, to make a *faint* attempt. **4** Lacking in distinctness; hardly able to be perceived; as, a *faint* sound; a *faint* similarity. — *v.* To lose consciousness because of a temporary decrease in the blood supply to the brain; to swoon. — *n.* The act or condition of fainting; as, to fall down in a *faint.* — **faint·ly,** *adv.*

faint·heart·ed \'fānt-'härt-əd, -'hȧrt-\ *adj.* Lacking in courage; fearful; timid; as, a *fainthearted* attempt.

fair \'far, 'fer\ *adj.* **1** Beautiful; as, this *fair* land of ours. **2** Light in color; blond; as, *fair* hair. **3** Frank; just; honest; according to the rules; as, *fair* play. **4** Distinct; easy to read; as, to write a *fair* hand. **5** Open to legitimate pursuit; as, a person who is *fair* game for ridicule. **6** Average; pretty good; as, to make a *fair* grade in arithmetic; to be in *fair* health. **7** Clean; without blemish; as, a *fair* name. **8** Clear; not cloudy or stormy; favorable; as, *fair* weather. **9** Likely; promising; as, to have a *fair* chance of winning. — *adv.* In a fair manner; as, to play *fair.* — **fair·ness,** *n.*

fair \'far, 'fer\ *n.* **1** A gathering of people at a stated time and place for the purpose of buying and selling. **2** A festival and sale of articles, usually for charity; as, a church *fair.* **3** An exhibition and sale of goods, animals, machinery, and farm products; as, a county *fair.*

fair ball. A batted ball that first strikes the ground beyond first or third base and within the foul lines, or that comes to rest before passing first or third base and within the foul lines, or that after striking the ground passes first or third base within the foul lines.

fair·ground \'far-ˌgrau̇nd, 'fer-\ *n.* An area set aside for the holding of fairs and similar gatherings.

fair·ly \'far-lē, 'fer-\ *adv.* **1** Favorably; as, to be *fairly* situated. **2** In a fair manner; justly; as, to treat each person *fairly.* **3** Rather; as, a *fairly* easy job. **4** Completely; as, to be *fairly* beside oneself.

fairy \'far-ē, 'fer-ē\ *n.; pl.* **fair·ies.** [From medieval English *fairie* originally meaning "enchantment", "fairyland", borrowed from Old French *faerie,* this in turn derived from Latin *Fata,* a goddess of fate — see *fay.*] An imaginary being who is supposed to look like a very tiny human being and to have magic powers. — *adj.* Of or like a fairy; having to do with fairies.

fair·y·land \'far-ē-ˌland, 'fer-\ *n.* **1** The home or country of the fairies. **2** Any delicately charming place.

fairy ring. A circle in a lawn or meadow consisting of certain mushroom fungi.

fairy tale or **fairy story. 1** A story about fairies. **2** Any story that is made up; a fib.

faith \'fāth\ *n.; pl.* **faiths** \'fāths, 'fāthz\. **1** Belief in God. **2** Belief without proof; as, blind *faith.* **3** Slight grounds for belief; the unsupported word of another person; as, to take a story on *faith.* **4** Something believed in; a particular religion. **5** Trust; confidence; as, to have *faith* in a friend. **6** A promise to be loyal; loyalty; as, to keep *faith* with one's friends. — For synonyms see *belief.* — *interj.* By my faith; truly.

faith·ful \'fāth-fəl\ *adj.* **1** Full of faith; believing, especially in God. **2** Steadfast in keeping promises or in fulfilling duties; as, a *faithful* worker. **3** True; loyal; as, a *faithful* friend. **4** True to the facts; accurate; as, a *faithful* account of something; a *faithful* copy. — **faith·ful·ly** \-fə-lē\ *adv.*

faith·less \'fāth-ləs\ *adj.* **1** Not believing, especially in God or in any organized religion. **2** False to promises or duty; not loyal.

fake \'fāk\ *v.;* **faked; fak·ing. 1** To treat so as to give a false quality or appearance to; to counterfeit; as, to *fake* a signature. **2** To pretend; as, to *fake* surprise. — *n.* Any person or thing that is not really what is pretended; a fraud. The picture is a *fake.* — *adj.* False; sham.

fak·er \'fāk-r\ *n.* One who fakes; a pretender; a fraud.

fa·kir \fə-'kir\ *n.* **1** A member of any of the Moslem religious orders; a dervish. **2** A wandering beggar of India who performs tricks.

fal·chion \'fȯlch-n, 'fȯlsh-n\ *n.* A broad-bladed, slightly curved sword used in the Middle Ages.

fal·con \'falk-n, 'fȯ(l)k-n\ *n.* **1** A hawk, bred and trained for pursuing game birds. **2** Any of the long-winged hawks having a notch and tooth on the upper jaw.

fal·con·er \'falk-n(-)ər, 'fȯ(l)k-\ *n.* **1** A breeder or trainer of hawks for hunting. **2** One who hunts with hawks.

fal·con·ry \'falk-n-rē, 'fȯ(l)k-\ *n.* **1** The art of training falcons to pursue game. **2** The sport of hunting with falcons.

fall \'fȯl\ *v.;* **fell** \'fel\; **fall·en** \'fȯl-ən\; **fall·ing. 1** To move or go to a lower place or level; to drop; to drop down from; as, to *fall* from a ladder. In autumn the leaves *fall.* **2** To hang or extend downward. The girl's hair *falls* loosely. **3** To take on a look of discouragement or dejection. The child's face *fell* at the rebuke. **4** To come upon, reach, or strike as if by dropping down. Darkness *fell* upon the earth. **5** To drop from an upright position; as, to trip and *fall.* The great tree *fell* in the storm. **6** To lose uprightness, station, or character; as, to *fall* into error. The king *fell* from power. **7** To be wounded or killed; as, to *fall* in battle. **8** To come; to occur. On what day does Christmas *fall* this year? **9** To pass from one condition of body or mind to another; as, to *fall* ill; to *fall* asleep. **10** To be divided; to be arranged; as, a story that *falls* into three parts. **11** To fell; to cut down, as a tree. — **fall back.** To go back; to retreat; to give way. — **fall back on.** To have recourse to, as a reserved fund; as, to have something to *fall back on* in an emergency. — **fall flat.** To produce no result; to fail of the intended effect. The speaker's attempt to be funny *fell flat.* — **fall in.** To take one's proper place in a military line. — **fall on** or **fall upon.** To assault; to attack; as, to *fall on* an enemy patrol. — **fall out. 1** To quarrel. **2** To leave one's place in a military line. — **fall through.** To fail; to come to nothing, as a plan. — **fall to. 1** To begin, to set about; as, to *fall to* quarreling. **2** To begin to eat. — **fall under.** To be classifiable under; as, items that do not *fall under* a general heading. — *n.* **1** The act of falling; as, a *fall* from a horse; to have a bad *fall.* **2** A thing that falls or has fallen; the amount that falls; the distance something falls; as, a heavy *fall* of snow; a *fall* of ten feet. **3** [usually in the plural] A waterfall. **4** Ruin; downfall; as, the *fall* of Rome. **5** Autumn. **6** A lowering; a sinking; a decrease; as, a *fall* in temperature; a *fall* in prices. **7** The act or method of throwing an opponent to the ground in wrestling; a bout at wrestling; as, to win two *falls* out of three.

fal·la·cious \fə-'lā-shəs\ *adj.* **1** Mistaken; incorrect; as, *fallacious* reasoning; a *fallacious* conclusion. **2** Misleading; as, a deliberately *fallacious* answer. — **fal·la·cious·ly,** *adv.*

fal·la·cy \'fal-ə-sē\ *n.; pl.* **fal·la·cies. 1** A false notion; a mistaken idea; as, the common *fallacy* that the rich are always happy. **2** False reasoning or an instance of false reasoning. Debaters try to detect and point out the *fallacies* in their opponents' arguments.

fall·en \'fȯl-ən\ *adj.* **1** Dropped; as, a *fallen* arch in the foot. **2** Dead; as, funeral services for a *fallen* hero. **3** Ruined; disgraced; degraded; as, a *fallen* leader of the people living wretchedly in exile.

fal·li·ble \'fal-əb-l\ *adj.* Capable of making mistakes or of being deceived. Even experts are *fallible* at times. — **fal·li·bil·i·ty** \ˌfal-ə-'bil-ət-ē\ *n.* — **fal·li·bly** \'fal-ə-blē\ *adv.*

fall·ing star \'fȯl-ing\. A meteor.

fall-out \'fȯl-ˌau̇t\ *n.* **1** The descent through the atmosphere of particles, often radioactive, resulting from or stirred up by a nuclear explosion. **2** These particles taken collectively.

fal·low \'fal-ō\ *n.* **1** Land for crops that lies idle during a growing season. **2** The plowing or tilling of land without sowing it for a season. — *adj.* Plowed but not tilled or seeded; uncultivated. — *v.* To cultivate land without seeding it.

fallow deer. A European deer smaller than the red deer, with broad, lobed antlers, and a pale-yellow coat that is white-spotted in summer.

false \'fȯls\ *adj.* **1** Not true; not correct; as, a *false* statement. **2** Not truthful; dishonest; as, a *false* witness. **3** Not faithful or loyal; deceitful; as, a *false* friend. **4** Not real or genuine; artificial; as, *false* teeth; *false* modesty. **5** Not well founded; as, a *false* claim; a *false* charge. **6** Out of tune; as, a *false* note. **7** Not essential; designed for appearance or for a purpose other than structural; as, a *false* ceiling. — *adv.* In a false manner; as, to play a person *false.* — **false·ly**, *adv.*

false·hood \'fȯls-ˌhu̇d\ *n.* **1** Falseness; falsity. **2** A lie. **3** Lying.

false·ness \'fȯls-nəs\ *n.* The state of being false; especially, deceitfulness or unfaithfulness.

fal·set·to \fȯl-'set-(ˌ)ō\ *n.; pl.* **fal·set·tos.** **1** A false or artificial voice; especially, a man's voice pitched higher than his natural voice. **2** A falsetto singer. — *adj.* Using falsetto or having the range and quality of falsetto. — *adv.* In falsetto; as, to sing *falsetto.*

fal·si·fy \'fȯl-sə-ˌfī\ *v.;* **fal·si·fied** \-ˌfīd\; **fal·si·fy·ing.** **1** To make false; to change so as to deceive; as, to *falsify* the financial accounts in one's charge. **2** To tell lies; to lie. **3** To prove to be false; to show to be untrue. — **fal·si·fi·ca·tion** \ˌfȯl-sə-fə-'kāsh-n\ *n.* — **fal·si·fi·er** \'fȯl-sə-ˌfīr\ *n.*

fal·si·ty \'fȯl-sət-ē\ *n.; pl.* **fal·si·ties.** **1** The state of being false, or untrue. **2** Something that is false; a lie.

fal·ter \'fȯlt-r\ *v.;* **fal·tered; fal·ter·ing** \'fȯlt-r-ing, 'fȯl-tring\. **1** To move unsteadily; to waver. **2** To hesitate in speech; to stammer; as, to *falter* out thanks. **3** To hesitate in purpose or action; as, courage that never *falters.* — *n.* A faltering sound or movement. — **fal·ter·ing·ly**, *adv.*

fame \'fām\ *n.* The fact or condition of being known to the public; reputation; renown; as, to win *fame* as an inventor; to care little for *fame.*

famed \'fāmd\ *adj.* Famous; well-known; renowned.

fa·mil·iar \fə-'mil-yər\ *adj.* **1** Closely acquainted; intimate; as, *familiar* friends. **2** Informal; easy; as, a *familiar* greeting; a *familiar* conversation. **3** Well-known; common; as, a *familiar* scene. **4** Having a good knowledge of; as, to be *familiar* with a subject. **5** Unduly intimate; bold; forward; as, to consider someone too *familiar.* — *n.* **1** An intimate friend. **2** Also **familiar spirit.** A supernatural being supposed to guard and serve an individual human being. — **fa·mil·iar·ly**, *adv.*

fa·mil·iar·i·ty \fə-ˌmil-'yar-ət-ē, fə-ˌmil-ē-'ar-\ *n.; pl.* **fa·mil·iar·i·ties.** **1** Close friendship; intimacy. **2** Close acquaintance with or knowledge of something; as, to acquire a *familiarity* with several languages. **3** Lack of formality; freedom and ease in personal relations with others. **4** [usually in the plural] Unduly bold or forward behavior or actions.

fa·mil·iar·ize \fə-'mil-yə-ˌrīz\ *v.;* **fa·mil·iar·ized; fa·mil·iar·iz·ing.** **1** To make familiar or thoroughly acquainted; to accustom; as, to *familiarize* oneself with a new job; a practice game intended mainly to *familiarize* newcomers with the rules. **2** To make well known. One purpose of advertising is to *familiarize* the name of a product.

fam·i·ly \'fam-l(-)ē\ *n.; pl.* **fam·i·lies.** **1** All of the people that live under one head and in one house. **2** All of the people that are descended from the same ancestor; as, a *family* that has ruled a kingdom for centuries. **3** A group of closely related persons; especially, a group formed of parents and their children. **4** A group of closely related things; as, a *family* of languages. **5** In biology, a group of related plants or animals ranking in classification below an order and above a genus; as, the plants of the mustard *family.* Lions, tigers, and leopards belong to the cat *family.*

fam·ine \'fam-ən\ *n.* **1** An extreme general lack of food. **2** Hunger; starvation. **3** Any serious lack or shortage; as, a coal *famine.*

fam·ish \'fam-ish\ *v.* **1** To starve. **2** To suffer or cause to suffer from extreme hunger.

fa·mous \'fā-məs\ *adj.* **1** Much talked about; very well known; famed; as, a *famous* explorer; a *famous* battle. **2** Deserving to be remembered; splendid; first-class; as, to have a *famous* time at a party.

fa·mous·ly \'fā-məs-lē\ *adv.* Splendidly; excellently. The boys got along *famously* from the day they met.

fan \'fan\ *n.* **1** A device that stirs the air by the motion of its broad surface, as a small hand device for waving to and fro or a mechanical device with rotating blades. **2** Something shaped like or suggesting this hand device. — *v.;* **fanned; fan·ning.** **1** To move air with or as if with a fan; to stir up; to set in motion. **2** To direct a current of air on something with or as if with a fan; as, to *fan* a fire with a newspaper; to *fan* oneself.

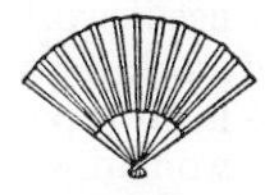
hand fan

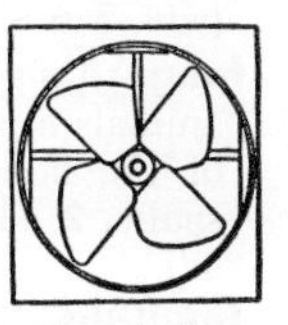
electric fan

fan \'fan\ *n.* **1** An enthusiastic follower of some sport or entertainment. **2** An enthusiastic admirer, as of an athlete or movie star.

fa·nat·ic \fə-'nat-ik\ *n.* A person who is excessively enthusiastic about something; especially, one who is unreasonable in his beliefs; as, to be a *fanatic* on the subject of proper diet; a religious *fanatic.* — *adj.* Also **fa·nat·i·cal** \-ik-l\. Unreasonable; too enthusiastic. — **fa·nat·i·cal·ly** \-ik-l(-)ē\ *adv.*

fa·nat·i·cism \fə-'nat-ə-ˌsiz-m\ *n.* Excessive, unreasoning enthusiasm in one's beliefs or behavior, especially in matters having to do with religion.

fan·ci·er \'fan(t)s-ē-ər\ *n.* A person who has a special liking for and interest in something, especially a class or variety of animals or plants; as, a dog *fancier;* an orchid *fancier.*

fan·ci·ful \'fan(t)s-ēf-l, -əf-l\ *adj.* **1** Full of fancy or guided by fancy; as, a *fanciful* and completely impractical person; a *fanciful* tale of an imaginary kingdom. **2** Coming from the fancy rather than from the reason; as, a *fanciful* scheme for getting rich. **3** Curiously made or shaped; as, the *fanciful* forms of ice on a windowpane. — **fan·ci·ful·ly** \-l-ē\ *adv.*

fan·cy \'fan(t)s-ē\ *n.; pl.* **fan·cies. 1** The power of the mind to think of things not present; imagination; as, a story that stirs one's *fancy.* **2** A liking; as, to take a *fancy* to a person at first sight. **3** A notion; a thought; an idea; as, a passing *fancy.* **4** Taste or judgment, as in matters of art, literature, or decoration; as, a whimsical tale likely to please the *fancy* of most readers. — *v.;* **fan·cied** \-ēd\; **fan·cy·ing. 1** To have a fancy for; as, to *fancy* some fruit. **2** To believe without being certain; to imagine; to suppose; as, to *fancy* that one hears a sound. — *adj.;* **fan·ci·er** \-ē-ər\; **fan·ci·est. 1** Not ordinary; intended to give special pleasure; as, a *fancy* dress; a *fancy* cake. **2** Above the real value; extravagant; as, a store that charges *fancy* prices. **3** Requiring unusual skill or grace; as, an exhibition of *fancy* diving. — **fan·ci·ly** \'fan(t)s-l-ē\ *adv.*

fancy dress. Dress chosen to suit the fancy of the wearer, as for a masquerade ball or party. — **fan·cy–dress** \'fan(t)s-ē-'dres\ *adj.*

fan·cy–free \'fan(t)s-ē-'frē\ *adj.* Not centering the attention on any one person or thing; especially, not in love.

fan·cy·work \'fan(t)s-ē-ˌwərk\ *n.* Ornamental needlework, as embroidery.

fan·dan·go \fan-'dang-ˌgō\ *n.; pl.* **fan·dan·gos.** A lively Spanish dance performed by a man or a woman with much use of castanets.

fan·fare \'fan-ˌfar, -ˌfer\ *n.* **1** A flourish of trumpets. **2** A showy display.

fang \'fang\ *n.* **1** A long sharp tooth by which animals seize and hold their prey; especially, one of the hollow or grooved teeth of a poisonous snake. **2** The root of a tooth. — **fanged** \'fangd\ *adj.*

fan·light \'fan-ˌlīt\ *n.* A semicircular window with the bars that divide the panes radiating like the sticks of a fan, placed over a door or another window.

fanned. Past tense and past part. of *fan.*

fanning. Pres. part. of *fan.*

fan·tail \'fan-ˌtāl\ *n.* **1** A tail or end in the shape of a fan. **2** A domestic pigeon having a broad rounded tail. **3** A goldfish of a fancy breed having its tail fins double.

fan·ta·sia \fan-'tā-zhə, ˌfant-ə-'zē-ə\ *n.* A musical composition free and fanciful in form.

fan·tas·tic \fan-'tas-tik, fən-\ or **fan·tas·ti·cal** \-tik-l\ *adj.* **1** Produced by the fancy or like something produced by the fancy; imaginary; unreal; strange; as, *fantastic* dreams; a *fantastic* design. **2** Going beyond belief; incredible or hardly credible. Airplanes now travel at *fantastic* speeds. — **fan·tas·ti·cal·ly** \-tik-l(-)ē\ *adv.*

fan·ta·sy or **phan·ta·sy** \'fant-ə-sē, -zē\ *n.; pl.* **fan·ta·sies** or **phan·ta·sies. 1** Imagination; fancy. **2** Something produced by a person's imagination; especially, an illusion. **3** A fantasia.

far \'fär, 'får\ *adv.* **1** At or to a great distance in space or time; as, to wander *far;* to sit reading *far* into the night. **2** By a great interval; greatly; as, to be not *far* wrong about something; in the *far* distant future. **3** To or at a certain distance, point, or degree; as, to walk only so *far.* — **by far.** By much; greatly; as, *by far* the better of the two. — **far and away.** Decidedly; greatly; by far. — **far and wide.** To a great distance in all directions. — *adj.;* **far·ther** \'fär<u>th</u>-r, 'får<u>th</u>-r\; **far·thest** \'fär<u>th</u>əst, 'får-\. [See *further* and *furthest.*] **1** Very different or distant in time, amount, or nature; as, stories of the *far* past; to dream of traveling to *far* countries. **2** Long; extending over a great space; as, a *far* journey. **3** The more distant of two; as, on the *far* side of the lake.

far·a·way \'fär-ə-ˌwā, 'får-\ *adj.* **1** Distant; as, to read about *faraway* lands. **2** Dreamy; abstracted; as, a *faraway* look.

farce \'färs, 'fårs\ *n.* **1** A play made up of ridiculous and absurd situations and happenings, intended to make people laugh. **2** Humor of the kind characteristic of such a play. **3** A ridiculous action, display, or pretense; as, a meeting that from the point of view of orderly democratic procedure was a *farce.*

far·ci·cal \'fär-sik-l, 'får-\ *adj.* Relating to farce; ridiculous; absurd.

far cry. A long way; a great contrast; as, to find summer camp a *far cry* from what one expected. It is a *far cry* from private to general.

fare \'far, 'fer\ *v.;* **fared; far·ing. 1** To go; especially, to journey; as, to *fare* forth on one's travels. **2** To be in any condition or pass through any experience; to have good or bad fortune; as, to *fare* well in business. **3** To happen or turn out. How did things *fare* with you today? — *n.* **1** The money a person pays to travel, as on a train, bus, or airplane. **2** A person paying a fare; a passenger. **3** Food; as, excellent hotel *fare;* party *fare.*

Far East. The countries of eastern Asia.

fare·well \(')far-'wel, (')fer-\ *interj.* [From medieval English, originally meaning "travel well!", "have a good trip!"] An exclamation used at parting to express good wishes; goodby. — *n.* **1** An expression of good wishes at parting. **2** A departure; as, a tearful *farewell.* — \'far-ˌwel, 'fer-\ *adj.* Last; final; as, a retiring president's *farewell* address; a *farewell* wave of the hand.

far·fetched \'fär-'fecht, 'får-\ *adj.* Not naturally introduced or closely related; out of place; forced; as, a *farfetched* argument; a *farfetched* joke.

far-flung \ˈfär-ˈfləng, ˈfȧr-\ *adj.* Covering great areas; having wide range; as, a *far-flung* empire.

fa·ri·na \fə-ˈrē-nə\ *n.* A fine meal made chiefly from cereal grains and used for puddings and as a breakfast cereal.

farm \ˈfärm, ˈfȧrm\ *n.* **1** A tract of land used for growing crops or raising livestock; as, a sixty-acre *farm;* a dairy *farm.* **2** A tract of water used for the cultivation of marine animals, especially varieties used as food; as, an oyster *farm.* — *v.* **1** To devote to agriculture; to cultivate; as, to *farm* sixty acres. **2** To manage a farm or work on a farm; to cultivate land; as, to *farm* for a living; to spend one's whole life *farming.* **3** To give, or to obtain, the control of something, as the collection of a tax, in return for a fixed payment.

farm·er \ˈfärm-r, ˈfȧrm-r\ *n.* A person who owns or works on a farm.

farm·er·ette \ˌfärm-r-ˈet, ˌfȧrm-\ *n.* A woman or girl who works on a farm, especially as an employee.

farm·house \ˈfärm-ˌhau̇s, ˈfȧrm-\ *n.; pl.* **farm·hous·es** \-ˌhau̇-zəz\. The dwelling house of a farm.

farm·ing \ˈfär-ming, ˈfȧr-\ *n.* The occupation or business of a person who farms; agriculture.

farm·stead \ˈfärm-ˌsted, ˈfȧrm-\ *n.* A farm.

farm·yard \ˈfärm-ˌyärd, ˈfȧrm-ˌyȧrd\ *n.* The yard around or enclosed by farm buildings.

far-off \ˈfär-ˌȯf, ˈfȧr-\ *adj.* Faraway; distant.

far-reach·ing \ˈfär-ˈrē-ching, ˈfȧr-\ *adj.* Having a wide range, influence, or effect; as, a *far-reaching* decision by a judge.

far·row \ˈfar-ō\ *n.* A litter of pigs. — *v.* To give birth to young — used of pigs.

far·see·ing \ˈfär-ˈsē-ing, ˈfȧr-\ *adj.* **1** Farsighted. **2** Having foresight; thinking of the future.

far·sight·ed \ˈfär-ˈsīt-əd, ˈfȧr-\ *adj.* **1** Seeing to a great distance. **2** Having or showing an ability to see how something will work out in the future; shrewd; of good judgment. **3** Able to see distant things more clearly than near ones. — **far·sight·ed·ness,** *n.*

far·ther \ˈfärt͟h-r, ˈfȧrt͟h-r\. Comparative of *far.* — *adj.* **1** More distant; as, the *farther* shore of the lake. **2** Beyond the present point; further. — *adv.* **1** At or to a greater distance or extent; as, to move *farther* away from the fire. **2** Moreover; in addition.

far·ther·most \ˈfärt͟h-r-ˌmōst, ˈfȧrt͟h-\ *adj.* Most distant.

far·thest \ˈfär-t͟həst, ˈfȧr-\. Superlative of *far.* — *adj.* **1** Most distant; as, the *farthest* star that can be seen. **2** Longest; as, the *farthest* journey. — *adv.* To or at the greatest distance; as, to see who can throw a ball *farthest.*

far·thing \ˈfär-t͟hing, ˈfȧr-\ *n.* **1** One fourth of an English penny. **2** A small bronze coin of this value.

fas·ci·nate \ˈfas-n-ˌāt\ *v.;* **fas·ci·nat·ed; fas·ci·nat·ing. 1** To grip the attention of, especially so as to take away the power to move, act, or think for oneself. Some serpents are said to *fascinate* their prey. **2** To allure and hold, especially by charming qualities; as, a child *fascinated* by his first Christmas tree. — For synonyms see *captivate.*

fas·ci·nat·ing \ˈfas-n-ˌāt-ing\ *adj.* Having an extraordinary power to attract; charming; as, a *fascinating* speaker. — **fas·ci·nat·ing·ly,** *adv.*

fas·ci·na·tion \ˌfas-n-ˈāsh-n\ *n.* **1** A fascinating or a being fascinated. **2** The power of fascinating; great charm.

fas·ci·na·tor \ˈfas-n-ˌāt-r\ *n.* **1** One that fascinates. **2** A crocheted head covering for women.

fas·cism \ˈfash-ˌiz-m\ *n.* Any political system with a dictatorial central government that has strong nationalistic policies and that rigidly controls industry, commerce, finance, and the press.

fas·cist \ˈfash-əst\ *n.* One who practices or advocates fascism. — *adj.* Of or relating to fascism or fascists; supporting fascism; as, the *fascist* press. — **fa·scis·tic** \fa-ˈshis-tik, fə-\ *adj.* — **fa·scis·ti·cal·ly** \-tik-l(-)ē\ *adv.*

fash·ion \ˈfash-n\ *n.* **1** The build, make, shape, or looks of something; as, a coat of an odd *fashion.* **2** Manner; way; as, to behave in a peculiar *fashion.* **3** The accepted style of a thing at a particular time or among certain people; as, *fashions* in women's hats; an idea that is out of *fashion.* — *v.;* **fash·ioned; fash·ion·ing** \-n(-)ing\. To make or build; to form; to shape; as, to *fashion* a dish out of clay. — **fash·ion·er** \ˈfash-n(-)ər\ *n.*

fash·ion·a·ble \ˈfash-n(-)əb-l\ *adj.* **1** Following the fashion or established style; stylish; as, *fashionable* clothes. **2** Dressing or behaving according to the fashion of the time; as, *fashionable* people. — **fash·ion·a·bly** \-n(-)ə-blē\ *adv.*

fast \ˈfast\ *v.* **1** To refrain from eating any food. **2** To eat sparingly or to abstain from certain kinds of food. — *n.* **1** A fasting. **2** A period for fasting.

fast \ˈfast\ *adj.* **1** Firmly fixed; not easily moved; as, a boat *fast* on a sandbar. **2** That will not fade; as, *fast* colors. **3** Faithful; as, a *fast* friend. **4** Swift; rapid; as, a *fast* train. **5** Giving speed to some object; as, a *fast* pitcher. **6** Of a nature to aid in attaining speed; as, a *fast* race track. **7** Ahead of the correct time; as, a clock that is *fast.* **8** Taking only a short time; quick; as, a *fast* trip. **9** Loose in morals or conduct; wild; as, a *fast* crowd. — *adv.* **1** In a fast or fixed manner; as, a wheel that is stuck *fast* in the mud. **2** Soundly; deeply; as, to be *fast* asleep. **3** Swiftly; as, to run *fast.* **4** In a dissipated manner; recklessly; as, to live too *fast.*

fas·ten \ˈfas-n\ *v.;* **fas·tened; fas·ten·ing** \-n(-)ing\. **1** To attach or join, as by or as if by pinning, tying, or nailing; as, to *fasten* clothes on a line; to *fasten* blame on someone. **2** To make fast, as something that is loose or free; to fix securely; as, to *fasten* a door; to *fasten* an idea in one's mind. **3** To fix or set steadily and intently; as, to *fasten* one's eyes on an object. **4** To be or become fixed or joined; as, a shoe that *fastens* with a buckle. — **fas·ten·er** \ˈfas-n(-)ər\ *n.*

fas·ten·ing \ˈfas-n(-)ing\ *n.* A thing that fastens, such as a lock, bolt, hook, or zipper.

fas·tid·i·ous \fas-'tid-ē-əs\ *adj.* Hard to please; very particular; as, a *fastidious* eater. — **fas·tid·i·ous·ly**, *adv.*

fast·ness \'fast-nəs\ *n.* **1** The condition of being fast. **2** A strongly defended or fortified place; a stronghold; as, a mountain *fastness*.

fat \'fat\ *adj.;* **fat·ter; fat·test. 1** Plump; fleshy; as, a *fat* person. **2** Oily; greasy; as, *fat* meat. **3** Well-filled or stocked; as, a *fat* purse. **4** Profitable; paying well; as, a *fat* job. — *n.* **1** Animal tissue containing much greasy or oily matter; the oily substance itself or a similar matter in plants, especially in certain seeds. **2** An oily or greasy substance used in cooking; as, to fry something in *fat*. **3** The best or richest part; as, the *fat* of the land. **4** In chemistry, a substance that is composed of carbon, hydrogen, and oxygen, that is soluble in ether but not in water, and that, as food, is an important source of energy. — *v.;* **fat·ted; fat·ting.** To make fat; to grow fat.

fa·tal \'fāt-l\ *adj.* **1** Causing death; mortal; disastrous; as, a *fatal* accident or injury. The team's lack of experienced players proved *fatal* in the play-off. **2** Fateful; as, a *fatal* day in one's life. — **fa·tal·ly** \'fāt-l-ē\ *adv.*

fa·tal·ism \'fāt-l-ˌiz-m\ *n.* **1** The belief that events are determined by powers beyond man's control. **2** The attitude of mind of a person holding this belief. — **fa·tal·ist** \-əst\ *n.* — **fa·tal·is·tic** \ˌfāt-l-'is-tik\ *adj.*

fa·tal·i·ty \fā-'tal-ət-ē, fə-\ *n.; pl.* **fa·tal·i·ties. 1** The quality or condition of being fated to disaster. **2** The quality of being fatal; deadliness; as, the *fatality* of certain diseases. **3** A disaster ending in death. **4** A death occurring in a disaster; as, a train wreck in which there were twenty *fatalities*.

fate \'fāt\ *n.* [From Latin *fatum* meaning "prophecy", "fate", and derived from Latin *fari* meaning "to speak".] **1** A power beyond men's control that is supposed to determine what happens; destiny; as, to blame something on *fate*. **2** Something that happens as though determined by such a power; fortune; as, one whose *fate* it was to become president; to accept one's *fate*. **3** The end; the outcome. Everyone awaited news of the *fate* of the polar expedition. **4** Ruin; disaster; death. — For synonyms see *destiny*.

fat·ed \'fāt-əd\ *adj.* Determined by fate; destined; as, to fear that one is *fated* to fail.

fate·ful \'fāt-fəl\ *adj.* **1** Having serious consequences; important; as, a *fateful* decision. **2** Ominous; prophetic; as, the *fateful* circling of the vultures overhead. **3** Determined by fate. **4** Deadly; destructive; as, to deliver the *fateful* blow.

fa·ther \'fäth-r, 'fȧth-r\ *n.* **1** A male parent. **2** [with a capital] God. **3** A forefather; an ancestor; as, the land of one's *fathers*. **4** The person or thing that gives rise to something else; the originator. The wish is sometimes *father* to the thought. **5** One who cares for as a father might; one deserving of the respect and love given to a father; as, the *father* of his country. **6** A priest. — *v.;* **fa·thered; fa·ther·ing** \-r(-)ing\. **1** To become the father of; as, to *father* a fine, healthy child. **2** To be the founder, originator, or author of; as, to *father* a plan; to *father* a lie. **3** To treat or care for as a father.

fa·ther·hood \'fäth-r-ˌhu̇d, 'fȧth-r-\ *n.* The condition of being a father.

fa·ther-in-law \'fäth-r-ən-ˌlȯ, 'fȧth-\ *n.; pl.* **fa·thers-in-law.** The father of one's husband or of one's wife.

fa·ther·land \'fäth-r-ˌland, 'fȧth-\ *n.* One's native land.

fa·ther·less \'fäth-r-ləs, 'fȧth-\ *adj.* **1** Having no living father. **2** Having no known father; lacking a father's care and protection.

fa·ther·ly \'fäth-r-lē, 'fȧth-\ *adj.* **1** Of or like a father; as, a *fatherly* old man. **2** Showing the affection or concern of a father; as, a *fatherly* kiss; *fatherly* advice. — **fa·ther·li·ness** \-lē-nəs\ *n.*

fath·om \'fath-m\ *n.* A measure of length equal to six feet, used chiefly in measuring lengths of ship's ropes and depths of water. — *v.* **1** To measure the depth of water in fathoms. **2** To get to the bottom of; to reach an understanding of; to penetrate; as, to *fathom* a mystery. — **fath·om·a·ble**, *adj.*

fath·om·less \'fath-m-ləs\ *adj.* Incapable of being fathomed.

fa·tigue \fə-'tēg\ *n.* **1** Weariness resulting from work or exertion. **2** Also **fatigue duty.** Work done by soldiers aside from strictly military duty, as cleaning grounds. **3** The condition of parts of the body, as muscles or glands, which as a result of excessive activity have lost power to respond to stimulation. — *v.;* **fa·tigued; fa·tigu·ing.** To tire; to make or become weary; as, to be easily *fatigued*. — For synonyms see *tire*.

fat·ness \'fat-nəs\ *n.* **1** Plumpness. **2** Oiliness; fattiness. **3** Richness, as of soil.

fatted. Past tense and past part. of *fat*.

fat·ten \'fat-n\ *v.;* **fat·tened; fat·ten·ing** \-n(-)ing\. **1** To make or become fat; as, to *fatten* pigs for market; cattle *fattening* on the range. **2** To make fertile, as land.

fatter. Comparative of *fat*.

fattest. Superlative of *fat*.

fatting. Pres. part. of *fat*.

fat·ty \'fat-ē\ *adj.;* **fat·ti·er; fat·ti·est.** Containing fat or having the qualities of fat; greasy; as, *fatty* meat. — **fat·ti·ness** \'fat-ē-nəs\ *n.*

fau·cet \'fȯs-ət, 'fäs-ət\ *n.* A fixture for drawing or for regulating the flow of water or other fluid from a pipe or tank; a tap.

faucet

fault \'fȯlt\ *n.* **1** A weakness in character; an imperfection; a flaw; a failing; as, to love someone in spite of his *faults*. **2** An act that deserves blame or correction; a mistake in conduct; a mistake in one's work. **3** Responsibility for something wrong; blame; as, nobody's *fault* but one's own. **4** A break in the earth's crust with a displacement of rock masses. — **at fault.** Wrong; as, to find one's recollections *at fault.* — **find fault.** To discover faults; to criticize unfavorably; to complain. — **to a fault.** Excessively; as, generous *to a fault.*

fault·find·er \'fȯlt-ˌfīnd-r\ *n.* A person who is inclined to find fault or to complain, especially unreasonably. — **fault·find·ing,** *n.* or *adj.*

fault·less \'fȯlt-ləs\ *adj.* Free from fault; without error or imperfection; perfect. — **fault·less·ly,** *adv.*

faulty \'fȯl-tē\ *adj.;* **fault·i·er; fault·i·est.** Weak; imperfect; having flaws; as, *faulty* brakes; *faulty* hearing.

faun \'fȯn, 'fän\ *n.* A Roman god of country life, part goat and part man.

faun

fau·na \'fȯn-ə, 'fän-ə\ *n.* The animals or animal life of a particular period, region, or environment; as, marine *fauna*; the flora and *fauna* of the western plains.

fa·vor \'fāv-r\ *n.* **1** Strong liking or approval; as, to look with *favor* on a plan. **2** A kind act; a kindness; as, to do a *favor* for a friend. **3** A privilege; help or assistance; as, to ask a *favor.* **4** A present; a gift; a souvenir; as, the *favors* distributed at a party. **5** Preference or sympathy for one side over another; as, to do one's job without fear or *favor.* — **in favor of. 1** Approving; endorsing; for. **2** Also **in one's favor.** To one's benefit or advantage. — *v.;* **fa·vored; fa·vor·ing** \-r(-)ing\. **1** To prefer; to support; as, to *favor* the first of two plans. **2** To oblige; as, to ask to be *favored* with an immediate reply. **3** To treat with special care; as, to *favor* a lame leg in walking. **4** To make possible or easy; to help to success. Darkness *favored* the attack. **5** To prefer unfairly; as, to *favor* one child over another. **6** To look like; to resemble; as, to *favor* one's father.

fa·vor·a·ble \'fāv-rb-l, -r(-)əb-l\ *adj.* **1** Showing favor; approving; as, a *favorable* opinion. **2** Helpful; promising; advantageous; as, *favorable* weather for a trip. — **fa·vor·a·bly** \'fāv-r-blē, -r(-)ə-blē\ *adv.*

fa·vor·ite \'fāv-r(-)ət\ *n.* **1** A person or a thing that is favored above others. The baby is the *favorite* of the family. **2** In sports, the contestant regarded as having the best chance to win. — *adj.* Favored; best-liked; as, a boy's *favorite* games.

fa·vor·it·ism \'fāv-r(-)ə-ˌtiz-m\ *n.* Unfairly favorable treatment of some to the neglect of others.

fawn \'fȯn, 'fän\ *n.* **1** A young deer; a buck or doe of the first year. **2** A light, yellowish brown, the color of a young deer.

fawn \'fȯn, 'fän\ *v.* **1** To show happiness or affection by crouching and wagging the tail — used especially of dogs. **2** To try to win favor by behavior that shows lack of self-respect.

fay \'fā\ *n.* [From French *fée,* this derived from Latin *Fata,* a goddess of fate, derived from Latin *fatum* meaning "fate" — see *fate.*] A fairy; an elf.

faze \'fāz\ *v.;* **fazed; faz·ing.** To disquiet or upset; to daunt. That boy had so much self-confidence that nothing could *faze* him.

fe·al·ty \'fē-əl-tē, 'fēl-tē\ *n.* **1** Loyalty of a feudal vassal to his lord. **2** Wholehearted loyalty; allegiance.

fear \'fir\ *n.* **1** A feeling of dread; fright; alarm; as, to have a *fear* of the dark or of high places. **2** Anxious concern; worry; as, a mother's *fear* for the safety of her child. **3** Awe; profound reverence, especially for God.

— The words *alarm* and *fright* are synonyms of *fear: fear* is a general term suggesting great dread of harm to oneself and a resulting loss of courage; *alarm* may describe intense disturbance of mind and body caused by unexpected danger; *fright* generally suggests the shock of sudden, startling, and often only brief fear.

— *v.* **1** To be afraid of; to have fear; as, to *fear* danger; to *fear* for one's life. **2** To have a feeling of awe of; as, to *fear* God. **3** To feel painful uncertainty; to doubt. Your lost money will be found, never *fear.*

fear·ful \'firf-l\ *adj.* **1** Causing fear; as, the *fearful* roar of a lion. **2** Filled with fear; as, to be *fearful* of danger. **3** Showing or caused by fear; as, a *fearful* glance. **4** Existing in the extreme; extremely bad, large, or intense; as, to catch a *fearful* cold.

fear·ful·ly \'firf-l(-)ē\ *adv.* **1** In a fearful manner. **2** Extremely; very; as, to be *fearfully* tired.

fear·less \'fir-ləs\ *adj.* Free from fear; feeling no fear; brave. — **fear·less·ly,** *adv.*

fear·some \'firs-m\ *adj.* **1** Frightful; causing fear; as, the *fearsome* sight of the approaching tornado. **2** Extremely timid.

fea·si·ble \'fē-zəb-l\ *adj.* Capable of being done or carried out; as, a *feasible* plan. — **fea·si·bil·i·ty** \ˌfē-zə-'bil-ət-ē\ *n.* — **fea·si·bly** \'fē-zə-blē\ *adv.*

feast \'fēst\ *n.* **1** A festival, especially a religious festival or holy day. **2** A plentiful or elaborate meal; as, a Thanksgiving *feast.* — *v.* **1** To eat plentifully; to entertain with rich and plentiful food. **2** To delight; as, to *feast* one's eyes on a beautiful scene.

feat \'fēt\ *n.* An act or deed; especially, one showing courage, strength, skill, or ingenuity; as, acrobatic *feats;* the *feat* of swimming the English Channel.

feath·er \'fe<u>th</u>-r\ *n.* **1** One of the light, horny outgrowths that together make up the outer covering of birds. **2** The same kind or sort; as, birds of a *feather.* — **a feather in one's cap.** An honor or mark of distinction. — *v.;* **feath·ered; feath·er·ing** \-r(-)ing\. **1** To furnish with a feather, as an arrow. **2** To line, cover, or furnish with feathers; as, to tar and *feather* a man. **3** In rowing, to turn an oar blade almost horizontal when lifting it from the water at the end of a stroke and to hold it thus until squaring it up for the beginning of the next stroke. **4** To grow or form feathers, as a bird. **5** In aeronautics, to turn the edges of a dead propeller blade toward the line of flight so as to decrease air resistance. — **feather one's nest.** To provide well for one's own comfort.

feath·er·bed \'fet͟h-r-ˌbed, -'bed\ *n.* A bed or mattress filled with feathers. — *v.;* **feath·er·bed·ded; feath·er·bed·ding.** To require unneeded workmen or the slowing up of work under a union rule. — **feath·er·bed·ding,** *n.*

feath·er·brain \'fet͟h-r-ˌbrān\ *n.* A weak-brained, foolish person. — **feath·er·brained** \-ˌbrānd\ *adj.*

feath·ered \'fet͟h-rd\ *adj.* Clothed, covered, or fitted with or as if with feathers or wings.

feath·er·edge \'fet͟h-r-ˌej, -'ej\ *n.* A very thin edge, easily broken or bent, as on a knife or chisel. — **feath·er·edged** \-ˌejd, -'ejd\ *adj.*

feath·er·weight \'fet͟h-r-ˌwāt\ *n.* **1** A very light weight. **2** A boxer weighing between 118 and 126 pounds.

feath·ery \'fet͟h-r(-)ē\ *adj.* **1** Like feathers; light; fluffy. **2** Covered with feathers.

fea·ture \'fēch-r\ *n.* **1** The shape or appearance of the face; as, a man stern of *feature.* **2** A single part of the face, as the nose or the mouth. **3** Something especially noticeable about a thing; a prominent detail; as, a plan with a number of good *features.* **4** The main attraction; any outstanding attraction, as an important item in a program, a special column or section in a newspaper or magazine; as, to enter a movie just as the *feature* is starting. — For synonyms see *characteristic.* — *v.;* **fea·tured; fea·tur·ing** \-r(-)ing\. **1** To mark or distinguish the face of; to be a feature of. **2** To give special prominence to; as, to *feature* a story in a newspaper; a sale of used cars *featuring* the latest models.

feaze \'fēz\ *v.;* **feazed; feaz·ing.** To faze.

Feb. Abbreviation for *February.*

Feb·ru·ary \'feb-(y)ə-ˌwer-ē, 'feb-rə-\ *n.; pl.* **Feb·ru·ar·ies.** [From medieval English, there borrowed from Latin *Februarius* the last month of the ancient Roman year, meaning literally "month of purification", derived from *Februa,* a feast of purification that took place on the 15th day.] The second month of the year, having 28 days in ordinary years and 29 days in leap years.

fe·ces \'fē-ˌsēz\ *n. pl.* **1** Sediment; dregs. **2** Waste matter discharged from the intestines; excrement.

fe·cund \'fēk-nd, 'fek-\ *adj.* **1** Fruitful in offspring or vegetation. **2** Rich in powers of invention; as, a *fecund* mind. — **fe·cun·di·ty** \fē-'kən-dət-ē\ *n.*

fed. Past tense and past part. of *feed.*

fed·er·al \'fed-r(-)əl\ *adj.* **1** Formed by compact or league, as between states that give up some or all of their supreme political authority to unite in a new state. The United States is a *federal* union. **2** Of or relating to a nation that is formed by the union of several smaller states or nations; as, the *federal* government. **3** [often with a capital] Of or relating to the government of the United States; as, a *Federal* court; a *Federal* tax. — *n.* [with a capital] A supporter of the government of the United States in the Civil War.

fed·er·al·ist \'fed-r(-)ə-ləst\ *n.* **1** One who believes in federal government. **2** [with a capital] In American history, a member of a group prominent in urging the adoption of the Constitution of the United States or, later, of a political party favoring the principle of a government with strong centralized power. — **fed·er·al·ism** \-ˌliz-m\ *n.*

fed·er·ate \'fed-r-ˌāt\ *v.;* **fed·er·at·ed; fed·er·at·ing.** To unite in a league or federation.

fed·er·a·tion \ˌfed-r-'āsh-n\ *n.* **1** The act of federating; formation of a league or union of states or societies. **2** A federal union, especially of states. **3** Any union of societies or organizations; a league; as, a *federation* of school athletic associations.

fee \'fē\ *n.* **1** Land held in ownership; especially, a **fee simple,** a landed estate that can be disposed of by the owner as he wishes. **2** A charge for professional services, as from a lawyer or doctor, or for one of certain privileges, as attendance at a school, admission to a museum, or use of a library. **3** A small sum of money given in return for a personal service; a tip. — *v.;* **feed** \'fēd\; **fee·ing.** To give a tip to.

fee·ble \'fēb-l\ *adj.;* **fee·bler** \'fēb-l(-)ər\; **fee·blest** \'fēb-l(-)əst\. **1** Weak; lacking in strength or endurance; as, a *feeble* old man. **2** Not vigorous or loud; ineffective; inadequate; as, a *feeble* cry for help; a *feeble* protest. — For synonyms see *weak.* — **fee·bly** \'fēb-lē\ *adv.*

fee·ble-mind·ed \'fēb-l-'mīn-dəd\ *adj.* Weak in mental ability; lacking normal intelligence. — **fee·ble-mind·ed·ness,** *n.*

feed \'fēd\ *v.;* **fed** \'fed\; **feed·ing. 1** To give food to; as, to *feed* a baby; to *feed* the animals in a zoo. **2** To take food; to eat. **3** To furnish with that which is necessary for something to go on; as, to *feed* a furnace with coal; to *feed* a machine. **4** To be nourished as if by food. Hate *feeds* on envy. — *n.* **1** Food; fodder. **2** A meal. **3** The mechanism for feeding material to a machine.

feed·er \'fēd-r\ *n.* **1** A device for holding or giving food or nourishment; as, a *feeder* for wild birds. **2** A person or an apparatus that feeds material into a machine or furnace. **3** A source of supply, as a branch stream. **4** An eater; as, a heavy *feeder*

feel \'fēl\ *v.;* **felt** \'felt\; **feel·ing. 1** To touch; to handle; to examine or search for with the fingers; to test by touching; as, to *feel* cloth; to *feel* in one's pocket. **2** To get knowledge of through the senses; as, to *feel* a blow; to *feel* cold. **3** To be hurt in one's feelings; as, to *feel* an insult deeply. **4** To appear or seem, especially to the sense of touch. The air *feels* cold. **5** To be conscious of something, especially an emotion; as, to *feel* pity; to *feel* friendly. **6** To know, or to be aware, without special reason; as, to *feel* that something is wrong. **7** To have sympathy; as, to *feel* for the poor. — *n.* **1** A feeling; awareness through the senses. **2** The sense of touch; as, soft to the *feel.* **3** A quality of a thing that can be learned through the touch; as, to recognize something by its *feel.*

feel·er \'fēl-r\ *n.* **1** One that feels; especially, a movable organ of touch, as one of the antennae of an insect. **2** A proposal or remark made to find out the views of other people.

feel·ing \'fē-ling\ *n.* **1** The act or condition of one that feels. **2** The sense by which a person knows whether things are hard or soft, hot or cold, heavy or light. **3** A sensation, as of temperature or pressure; as, a *feeling* of cold; a *feeling* of pain. **4** A state of mind; an emotion; as, a *feeling* of joy; a *feeling* of anger. **5** Sensitiveness; as, a man of deep *feeling*. **6** [in the plural] General emotional condition; outward signs of emotion; as, to show one's *feelings*. **7** The condition of being aware or conscious of something without knowing how; as, to have a *feeling* that something is going to happen. **8** Sympathy; as, to have *feeling* for others. **9** Opinion. What is the general *feeling* about this matter? — *adj.* Sensitive; as, a very *feeling* and sympathetic person. — **feel·ing·ly**, *adv.*

feet. Pl. of *foot.*

feign \'fān\ *v.* **1** To make up and tell as if true; as, to *feign* an excuse for absence. **2** To pretend; to sham; as, to *feign* illness. The girl's emotion appeared genuine but she might have been *feigning.*

feint \'fānt\ *n.* **1** A pretense; a trick. **2** A pretended attack at one point when another part is really intended to be struck, as in fencing, boxing, or war. — *v.* To make a feint, or pretended attack.

feist \'fīst\ or **fice** \'fīs\ *n. Dial.* A small dog.

feld·spar \'fel(d)-ˌspär, -ˌspär\ *n.* A glasslike mineral of white, reddish, or greenish color.

fe·lic·i·tate \fə-'lis-ə-ˌtāt\ *v.;* **fe·lic·i·tat·ed**; **fe·lic·i·tat·ing**. To wish joy to; to congratulate; as, to *felicitate* a student upon his graduation from high school. — **fe·lic·i·ta·tion** \fə-ˌlis-ə-'tāsh-n\ *n.*

fe·lic·i·tous \fə-'lis-ət-əs\ *adj.* **1** Suitably expressed; apt; as, to write a letter with *felicitous* wording. **2** Possessing a talent for apt expression; as, a *felicitous* speaker.

fe·lic·i·ty \fə-'lis-ət-ē\ *n.; pl.* **fe·lic·i·ties**. **1** Great happiness; bliss. **2** Something that promotes happiness; success. **3** A pleasing ability of expression, especially in language or art. **4** An apt expression.

fe·line \'fē-ˌlīn\ *adj.* [From Latin *felinus* meaning "of a cat", from *feles* meaning "cat".] **1** Belonging to the family of lithe-bodied, soft-furred, flesh-eating mammals including the cats, lions, tigers, leopards, pumas, and lynxes. **2** Of or like a cat; characteristic of cats; sly; stealthy. — *n.* An animal of the cat family. — **fe·line·ly**, *adv.*

fell \'fel\ *n.* The skin of an animal; a hide.

fell \'fel\ *v.* **1** To cut down; to knock down; as, to *fell* a tree; to *fell* one's opponent in a boxing match. **2** To finish a seam by hemming one edge down over the other. — *n.* **1** Timber cut during one season. **2** A seam formed by felling.

fell \'fel\ *adj.* Cruel; savage; deadly.

fell \'fel\. Past tense of *fall.*

fel·loe \'fel-ō\ *n.* A felly.

fel·low \'fel-ō\ *n.* **1** A companion; a comrade; as, *fellows* in arms. **2** A mate; a match; one of a pair. That shoe is too big to be the *fellow* to this one. **3** A person or thing of the same kind and with the same needs. All men are *fellows.* **4** A man; a person; as, a *fellow* who sells ice cream. **5** A student holding a fellowship. **6** A member of an incorporated scientific or literary society. — *adj.* Being a companion; sharing with another; as, *fellow* passengers.

fel·low·man \'fel-ō-'man\ *n.; pl.* **fel·low·men** \-'men\. A human being as a fellow creature.

fel·low·ship \'fel-ō-ˌship\ *n.* **1** The condition of friendly relationship existing among persons; companionship; as, good *fellowship* among shipmates. **2** A community of interest or feeling. **3** A group with similar interests; a membership, as of a church. **4** In colleges and universities, a fund whose income is given to a student; the income from such a fund.

fel·ly \'fel-ē\ *n.; pl.* **fel·lies**. The outside rim or part of the rim of a wheel, as of a farm wagon.

fel·on \'fel-ən\ *n.* A person who is guilty of a very serious crime; a criminal.

fel·on \'fel-ən\ *n.* An inflammation of the finger or toe, especially near the end or around the nail, usually with pus.

fel·o·ny \'fel-ə-nē\ *n.; pl.* **fel·o·nies**. A serious offense against the law; a crime punishable by a heavy sentence. — **fe·lo·ni·ous** \fə-'lō-nē-əs\ *adj.* — **fe·lo·ni·ous·ly**, *adv.*

felt \'felt\ *n.* **1** A heavy cloth or hat material made by rolling and pressing together fibers of wool, fur, or hair; any similar material. **2** An article, as a hat, made of these materials. — *adj.* Made of felt; as, a *felt* hat. — *v.* **1** To make into felt. **2** To cover with felt.

felt \'felt\. Past tense and past part. of *feel.*

felt·ing \'fel-ting\ *n.* **1** The material of which felt is made. **2** Felted cloth. **3** The process by which felted cloth is made.

fe·male \'fē-ˌmāl\ *n.* **1** A woman or girl. **2** An animal that belongs to the sex that brings forth young; the plant that produces fruit. — *adj.* **1** Of or relating to a female; being a female; as, a *female* animal. **2** Womanly; feminine; as, a *female* tenderness for children.

fem·i·nine \'fem-ə-nən\ *adj.* **1** Female; of the female sex. **2** Characteristic of women; belonging to women; as, a *feminine* concern with clothes. **3** In grammar, belonging to or having to do with the class of words that ordinarily includes most nouns referring to female persons or animals and also in many languages a considerable number of nouns referring to things that are really neither male nor female; as, a *feminine* noun; the *feminine* gender.

fe·mur \'fēm-r\ *n.; pl.* **fe·murs** \'fēm-rz\ or **fem·o·ra** \'fem-r-ə\. The thigh bone. — **fem·o·ral** \'fem-r-əl\ *adj.*

fen \'fen\ *n.* Low swampy land; a marsh.

fence \'fen(t)s\ *n.* **1** A barrier, as of stone, wood, or wire, set up about a place. **2** A person who receives stolen goods or a shop where stolen goods are disposed of. — **on the fence**. Undecided, as between two plans or policies. — *v.;* **fenced**; **fenc·ing.** **1** To enclose with a fence. **2** To practice fencing. **3** To dispute or argue in the manner of fencers' actions; to defend oneself against arguments by continually shifting ground.

fenc·er \'fen(t)s-r\ *n.* **1** One who is skilled in fencing with sword or foil. **2** One who builds or repairs fences.

fenc·ing \'fen(t)s-ing\ *n.* **1** The art or sport of attacking and defending with swords or foils. **2** Materials for making fences. **3** Fences.

fend \'fend\ *v.* **1** To ward off; as, to *fend* off a blow. **2** To try to get along without help; to shift; as, to have to *fend* for oneself.

fend·er \'fend-r\ *n.* **1** A thing that protects or that lessens shock, as a frame on the lower front of a locomotive or a trolley car to catch or throw off anything that is hit. **2** A guard over the wheel of an automobile. **3** A low metal frame set in front of a fireplace.

fen·nel \'fen-l\ *n.* A garden herb of the carrot family, with compound leaves and small yellow flowers in branching flat-topped clusters, grown for its fragrant seeds.

fer-de-lance \ˌfer-də-'lan(t)s\ *n.* A large poisonous snake of the same family as the rattlesnake and copperhead, found in South and Central America.

fer·ment \'fər-ˌment, fər-'ment\ *n.* **1** A substance that causes fermentation. Yeast is a *ferment.* **2** State of excitement; commotion. The crowd was in a *ferment.* — \fər-'ment\ *v.* **1** To cause or undergo fermentation. **2** To become or cause to become excited.

fer·men·ta·tion \ˌfər-mən-'tāsh-n, -ˌmen-\ *n.* **1** A breaking down of organic material into simpler substances, as alcohol or acids and usually carbon dioxide, by enzymes, as of yeasts. **2** Commotion; unrest.

fern \'fərn\ *n.* Any of an order of flowerless, seedless plants resembling seed plants in having root, stem, and leaves and a vascular system but reproducing by means of asexual spores. — **ferny** \'fər-nē\ *adj.*

fe·ro·cious \fə-'rō-shəs\ *adj.* Fierce; savage; cruel; threatening; as, a *ferocious* beast; a *ferocious* growl. — **fe·ro·cious·ly**, *adv.*

fe·roc·i·ty \fə-'räs-ət-ē\ *n.; pl.* **fe·roc·i·ties**. The quality of being ferocious; savage wildness; fierceness.

fer·ret \'fer-ət\ *n.* An animal of the weasel family pale yellow or white in color with red eyes, sometimes kept for hunting rabbits and killing rats. — *v.* To drive or hunt out of a hiding place; to find by keen searching or questioning; as, to *ferret* out the truth.

Fer·ris wheel \'fer-əs\. An amusement device consisting of a giant upright power driven steel wheel, carrying around its rim a succession of free-swinging small cars for riders.

fer·rous \'fer-əs\ *adj.* Of, relating to, or derived from iron; as, *ferrous* compounds.

fer·rule \'fer-əl\ *n.* A metal ring or cap placed around the end of a slender shaft of wood, as a walking stick or a section of a fishing rod or around a tool handle, to prevent splitting or to provide a strong well-fitting joint.

fer·ry \'fer-ē\ *v.;* **fer·ried** \-ēd\; **fer·ry·ing.** **1** To cross or convey in a boat over a body of water such as a river, a bay, or a strait; as, to *ferry* automobiles; to *ferry* a river. **2** To deliver a ship or an airplane under its own power. **3** To transport, as troops or supplies, by regular air service. — *n.; pl.* **fer·ries.** **1** A place where persons or things are ferried. **2** Also **fer·ry·boat** \-ˌbōt\. A boat designed for or used in ferrying. **3** An organized service and route for flying aircraft, especially across a sea or continent, for the regular transportation of troops or supplies.

fer·ry·man \'fer-ē-mən\ *n.; pl.* **fer·ry·men** \-mən\. One who operates or is employed in the operation of a ferryboat.

fer·tile \'fərt-l\ *adj.* **1** Producing vegetation or crops plentifully; fruitful; rich; as, *fertile* land. **2** Producing abundantly in any way; as, a *fertile* mind. **3** Capable of developing and growing; as, a *fertile* seed; a *fertile* egg. **4** Capable of producing fruit, as a flower.

— The word *fruitful* is a synonym of *fertile: fertile* usually suggests, when applied to soil or environment, the ability or readiness to advance new growth, or, when applied to persons or animals, the natural ability to produce offspring; *fruitful* may describe anything actually bearing fruit or offspring in great abundance or producing very profitable results.

fer·til·i·ty \(ˌ)fər-'til-ət-ē\ *n.* The condition of being fertile; fruitfulness; productive power; as, to improve the *fertility* of soil; *fertility* of imagination.

fer·ti·li·za·tion \ˌfərt-l-ə-'zāsh-n\ *n.* **1** The act or process of making fertile. **2** In biology, the union of a female and male germ cell to form a new individual.

fer·ti·lize \'fərt-l-ˌīz\ *v.;* **fer·ti·lized**; **fer·ti·liz·ing.** **1** To make fertile or more fertile; especially, to supply with nourishment for plants; as, to *fertilize* soil with manure. **2** In biology, to cause fertilization of.

fer·ti·liz·er \'fərt-l-ˌīz-r\ *n.* Any substance added to the soil to make it more productive of plant life.

fer·ule \'fer-əl, 'fer-ˌül\ *n.* A rod or ruler used in punishing children. — *v.;* **fer·uled**; **fer·ul·ing**. To punish with a ferule.

fer·ven·cy \'fərv-n-sē\ *n.* The state of being fervent; warmth of feeling; ardor; as, to pray with *fervency.*

fer·vent \'fərv-nt\ *adj.* **1** Hot; glowing; as, *fervent* coals. **2** Warm and earnest in feeling; ardent; as, a *fervent* wish; *fervent* prayer. — **fer·vent·ly**, *adv.*

fer·vid \'fər-vəd\ *adj.* **1** Very hot. **2** Filled with intense feeling; passionate; as, *fervid* language.

fer·vor \'fərv-r\ *n.* **1** Intense heat. **2** Intensity of feeling; fervid emotion or words; enthusiasm.

fes·tal \'fest-l\ *adj.* Of or relating to a feast or festival; festive; as, a *festal* day. — **fes·tal·ly** \'fest-l-ē\ *adv.*

fes·ter \'fest-r\ *v.*; **fes·tered**; **fes·ter·ing** \-r(-)ing\. **1** To generate pus or fill with pus; as, a cut that was neglected until it *festered.* **2** To become painful and inflamed. **3** To grow increasingly more acute and harder to bear, as an injury to the pride or feelings. The boy's feeling of resentment *festered* in his mind. — *n.* A small sore that fills with pus.

fes·ti·val \'fes-təv-l\ *adj.* Of, relating to, or set apart as a festival; as, a *festival* day. — *n.* **1** A time of feasting and celebration; a feast. Christmas is a church *festival.* **2** A series of entertainments of a special kind or the whole period occupied by such a series; as, a music *festival* lasting two weeks.

fes·tive \'fes-tiv\ *adj.* Relating to or suitable for a feast or festival; marked by festivity; joyous; gay; as, *festive* decorations; a *festive* gathering. — **fes·tive·ly**, *adv.*

fes·tiv·i·ty \fes-'tiv-ət-ē, fəs-\ *n.*; *pl.* **fes·tiv·i·ties.** **1** Joyousness; gaiety; as, a scene of *festivity.* **2** The events celebrating a happy occasion; festive activities; as, wedding *festivities.*

fes·toon \fes-'tün\ *n.* **1** A decorative rope, as of leaves or flowers, hung so as to fall in curves. **2** A carved or molded representation of such decoration, as on furniture or walls. — *v.* **1** To form in festoons. **2** To decorate with festoons.

festoon

fetch \'fech\ *v.* **1** To go, get, and bring back; as, to teach a dog to *fetch* a stick. **2** To cause to come; to bring out; as, a sight that *fetched* tears from the eyes. **3** *Dial.* To draw, as a breath, or heave, as a sigh. **4** To bring as a price; to sell for. How much do you suppose these old books would *fetch?* **5** To strike; as, to *fetch* someone a blow in the face. **6** To arrive. We *fetched* up at the wharf exactly on time.

fetch·ing \'fech-ing\ *adj.* Attractive; pleasing; fascinating; as, a *fetching* costume. — **fetch·ing·ly**, *adv.*

fete or **fête** \'fāt\ *n.* A festival; an entertainment, especially one held out of doors; as, a lawn *fete.* — *v.*; **fet·ed**; **fet·ing.** To honor with festivities; to entertain.

fet·id \'fet-əd, 'fēt-\ *adj.* Having an offensive smell; stinking.

fet·ish or **fet·ich** \'fet-ish, 'fēt-\ *n.* **1** An object, as an idol or an image, supposed to have supernatural or magical powers. **2** Anything that is made an object of unreasoning devotion or concern; as, to make a *fetish* of social position.

fet·lock \'fet-ˌläk\ *n.* **1** A projection with a tuft of hair on the back of a horse's leg above the hoof. **2** The tuft of hair growing out of this projection.

fet·ter \'fet-r\ *n.* **1** A chain or shackle for the feet. **2** Anything that keeps one down or hampers one's movement. — *v.* To chain down; to bind; to hamper.

fet·tle \'fet-l\ *n.* The state of being in readiness; condition; trim; as, to be in fine *fettle.*

fe·tus or **foe·tus** \'fēt-əs\ *n.* The young of an animal while in the body of its mother or in the egg, especially in the later stages of development.

feud \'fyüd\ *n.* **1** A long bitter conflict between families or clans, marked by acts of violence or revenge. **2** An extended quarrel or dispute; as, a *feud* between the mayor and the chief of police. — *v.* To carry on a feud.

feu·dal \'fyüd-l\ *adj.* Of or having to do with feudalism.

feu·dal·ism \'fyüd-l-ˌiz-m\ *n.* A system of government, existing in Europe in the Middle Ages, under which landowners held their property as a gift from the king or a lord and could keep it in their possession as long as they and their heirs served the king or lord faithfully. — **feu·dal·is·tic** \ˌfyüd-l-'is-tik\ *adj.*

feu·da·to·ry \'fyüd-ə-ˌtōr-ē, -ˌtȯr-ē\ *n.*; *pl.* **feu·da·to·ries.** **1** A person who holds lands by feudal law or usage. **2** A fief. — *adj.* Belonging to or being in the relation of a feudal vassal to his lord.

fe·ver \'fēv-r\ *n.* **1** An increase in the heat of the body above normal body temperature. **2** A diseased state marked by increased body heat, quickened pulse, and often other disturbances of body activities. **3** Excessive restlessness caused by strong feeling; as, to be in a *fever* of excitement.

fe·ver·ish \'fēv-r(-)ish\ *adj.* **1** Having a fever; as, to be *feverish.* **2** Showing or caused by fever; as, *feverish* symptoms. **3** Excited; restless; as, *feverish* activity. — **fe·ver·ish·ly**, *adv.*

fe·ver-rid·den \'fēv-r-ˌrid-n\ *adj.* Tormented by fever; harassed by repeated attacks of fever; as, to lie *fever-ridden* for many days.

few \'fyü\ *adj.* Not many; of small number; as, on a *few* occasions. — *pron.* Few persons or things. *Few* succeed.

fez \'fez\ *n.*; *pl.* **fez·zes.** A felt or cloth cap, usually red and having a tassel.

fi·an·cé \ˌfē-ˌän-'sā, fē-'än-ˌsā\ *n.* [From French, there derived from the masculine form of the past participle of *fiancer* meaning "to betroth".] A man engaged to be married.

fi·an·cée \ˌfē-ˌän-'sā, fē-'än-ˌsā\ *n.* [From French, there derived from the feminine form of the past participle of *fiancer.*] A woman or girl engaged to be married.

fi·as·co \fē-'as-ˌkō\ *n.*; *pl.* **fi·as·coes** or **fi·as·cos.** A crash; a complete or ridiculous failure. The senior play turned out to be a *fiasco* because no one knew his lines.

fi·at \'fī-ˌat, -ət\ *n.* An order; a decree.

fib \'fib\ *n.* A lie about some trivial matter. — *v.*; **fibbed**; **fib·bing.** To tell a fib; to lie. — **fib·ber**, *n.*

fi·ber or **fi·bre** \'fīb-r\ *n.* **1** A thread or threadlike structure or object. **2** A threadlike root, as that of a grass. **3** A tough substance or tissue made up of threadlike parts; especially, a substance like raw wool, cotton, or silk, the parts of which can be separated and spun into thread or yarn; as, hemp *fiber.* **4** Whatever gives texture or substance; character; as, a man of incorruptible *fiber.*

fi·brin \'fī-brən\ *n.* A white fibrous substance formed in the clotting of blood.

fi·brous \'fīb-rəs\ *adj.* Having fibers; like fiber or fibers; stringy; as, the *fibrous* husk of a coconut.

fib·u·la \'fib-yə-lə\ *n.; pl.* **fib·u·las** \-ləz\ or **fib·u·lae** \-ˌlē\. The outer, usually smaller, of the two bones in the lower leg of a human being, or a corresponding bone in the hind leg of other animals.

-fi·ca·tion \fə-'kāsh-n\. A suffix that can mean: the act or process of or the result of, as in *amplification* or *fortification.*

fice. Variant of *feist.*

fick·le \'fik-l\ *adj.* Changeable; not firm or steadfast in disposition or character; as, *fickle* friends; *fickle* weather.

fic·tion \'fiksh-n\ *n.* **1** Something told or written that is not fact; something made up. There is both fact and *fiction* in that newspaper story. **2** A made-up story about real or imaginary persons or events; such stories as a class; as, a writer of *fiction;* science *fiction.* — **fic·tion·al** \'fiksh-n(-)əl\ *adj.*

fic·tion·ize \'fiksh-n-ˌīz\ *v.;* **fic·tion·ized**; **fic·tion·iz·ing.** To make into fiction; to treat in the manner of fiction; as, a *fictionized* account of the Battle of Gettysburg.

fic·ti·tious \fik-'tish-əs\ *adj.* Not real; made-up; imaginary; as, a *fictitious* story without a grain of truth in it. An alias is a *fictitious* name. — **fic·ti·tious·ly,** *adv.*

fid·dle \'fid-l\ *n.* A violin. — *v.;* **fid·dled**; **fid·dling** \-l(-)ing\. **1** To play the violin. **2** To move the hands or fingers restlessly; as, to *fiddle* with one's pencil. **3** To trifle; to putter; as, to *fiddle* with painting.

fid·dler \'fid-l(-)ər\ *n.* One that fiddles; especially, a violinist.

fiddler crab. A small burrowing crab common on the salt marshes of the Atlantic coast.

fid·dle·stick \'fid-l-ˌstik\ *n.* **1** A violin bow. **2** A thing or matter of no importance; a mere nothing — used, chiefly in the plural, as an interjection equivalent to "Nonsense!"

fi·del·i·ty \fə-'del-ət-ē, fī-\ *n.; pl.* **fi·del·i·ties.** **1** Faithfulness, as to trust, duty, or obligation; loyalty. **2** Exactness or accuracy of reproduction; as, the *fidelity* of a translation; a record player of exceptionally high *fidelity.*

fidg·et \'fij-ət\ *v.* **1** To move one's body or hands about restlessly or nervously. **2** To make restless, nervous, or uneasy. — *n.* **1** A state of nervous restlessness; as, to be in a *fidget.* **2** [in the plural] Restlessness as shown by nervous movements; inability to sit still; as, to have the *fidgets.* **3** One who fidgets. — **fidg·ety,** *adj.*

fie \'fī\ *interj.* An exclamation expressing disgust or shocked disapproval and equivalent to "Shame!" or "For shame!"

fief \'fēf\ *n.* An estate granted to a vassal for his own use by a feudal lord.

field \'fēld\ *n.* **1** [usually in the plural] Open country. **2** A piece of open, cleared, or cultivated land. **3** A piece of land put to some special use or yielding some special product; as, an oil *field;* an athletic *field.* **4** A place where a battle is fought or the region in which military operations are carried on; as, a soldier with little experience in the *field.* **5** Any open space or expanse; as, a *field* of ice. **6** A sphere or range of activity or influence; as, to prepare for a career in the *field* of science. **7** A range of observation, as the area visible through the lens of a telescope. **8** A background on which something is drawn, painted, or mounted. The American flag has white stars on a blue *field.* **9** In physics, the region throughout which a force, as that exerted by a magnet or an electric current, can be detected. **10** An athletic or playing area; especially, the central part of such an area, often encircled by a running track, in which are held such events as jumping contests and other tests of strength or skill (**field events**). — *adj.* **1** Growing in or inhabiting the fields; as, a *field* mouse; *field* flowers. **2** Done or used in the field; as, military *field* equipment. **3** Performed on the field, as distinguished from the track. — *v.* **1** To catch, stop, or throw a ball as a fielder. **2** To put into the field for actual play; as, to *field* a strong team.

field day. **1** A day devoted to outdoor sports and athletic contests, especially on a large scale, as by representatives of all the schools of a city. **2** A time or opportunity for unusual activity, especially successful activity; as, caterpillars having a *field day* among the maples. The unexpected snowstorm provided a *field day* for ski enthusiasts.

field·er \'fēld-r\ *n.* A player stationed in the field, as in baseball, to catch or stop balls driven out by the team at bat; especially, in baseball, a member of the outfield.

field glasses. A small portable double telescope, such as is used by naturalists and army officers; binoculars.

field glasses

field hospital. A military organization of doctors and nurses with equipment for establishing a temporary hospital in the field.

field marshal. In some armies, an officer of the highest rank except that of commander in chief.

field·piece \'fēld-ˌpēs\ *n.* A cannon mounted on wheels for use in campaigns in the field.

fiend \'fēnd\ *n.* [From Old English *feond* meaning "enemy", "devil".] **1** A demon or devil. **2** An extremely wicked or cruel person. **3** A person devoted beyond the bounds of reason or self-control to a pursuit or practice; an addict; as, a golf *fiend;* a dope *fiend.*

fiend·ish \'fēn-dish\ *adj.* Like a fiend; cruel; devilish. — **fiend·ish·ly**, *adv.*

fierce \'firs\ *adj.;* **fierc·er**; **fierc·est**. Terrifyingly cruel, savage, or violent; as, a *fierce* animal; a *fierce* storm. — **fierce·ly**, *adv.*

fi·ery \'fīr-ē\ *adj.;* **fi·er·i·er**; **fi·er·i·est**. **1** On fire; flaming; as, a *fiery* furnace. **2** Hot or glowing as if on fire; as, a *fiery* sun; a *fiery* fever. **3** Easily aroused; as, a *fiery* temper. **4** Passionate; vehement; as, a *fiery* speech.

fi·es·ta \fē-'es-tə\ *n.* **1** A religious festival; a saint's day. **2** Any holiday or festivity.

fife \'fīf\ *n.* A small shrill musical instrument like a flute.

fif·teen \'fif-'tēn\ *adj.* Five and ten; one more than fourteen. — *n.* **1** The sum of ten and five; fifteen units or objects. **2** The figure standing for fifteen units, as 15 or XV.

fif·teenth \'fif-'tēn(t)th\ *adj.* Next after the fourteenth. — *n.; pl.* **fif·teenths** \-'tēn(t)s, -'tēn(t)ths\. One of fifteen equal parts.

fifth \'fif(t)th, 'fift\ *adj.* Next after the fourth. — *n.* One of five equal parts.

fif·ti·eth \'fif-tē-əth\ *adj.* Next after the forty-ninth. — *n.* One of fifty equal parts.

fif·ty \'fif-tē\ *adj.* Five times ten; forty-nine and one more. — *n.; pl.* **fif·ties**. **1** The sum of five tens; fifty units or objects. **2** The figure standing for fifty units, as 50 or L.

fig \'fig\ *n.* **1** The oblong or pear-shaped fruit of a fig tree, eaten raw, preserved, or dried in sugar. **2** Any of a genus of trees of the mulberry family distinguished by such fruit. **3** The value of a fig; a little bit; as, not to care a *fig* about skating.

fig. Abbreviation for *figure.*

fight \'fīt\ *n.* **1** A violent struggle with fists or weapons; a battle. **2** A verbal disagreement. **3** Strength for fighting; desire to fight; as, a person with no *fight* left in him. — *v.;* **fought** \'fȯt\; **fight·ing**. **1** To attempt to defeat, subdue, or destroy an enemy; to engage in contest; as, to accept the enemy's challenge to *fight.* **2** To act in opposition to anything; to struggle; to contend; as, to *fight* for the right. **3** To carry on or wage; as, to *fight* a battle. **4** To uphold, win, or gain by struggle; as, to *fight* a good fight. **5** To war against. The ships *fought* the enemy for three hours. **6** To oppose; as, to *fight* a crime wave; to *fight* a bad habit. — **fight shy of**. To avoid meeting fairly or at close quarters.

fight·er \'fīt-r\ *n.* **1** One that fights, as a soldier; especially, a person who is inclined to fight or one who is not easily intimidated. **2** A fighter plane.

fighter plane. A military airplane of high speed, high rate of climb, great maneuverability, and heavy firepower, used for overtaking and attacking enemy aircraft.

fig·ment \'fig-mənt\ *n.* Something imagined or made up; as, a *figment* of a child's mind.

fig·ur·a·tive \'fig-yər-ət-iv, 'fig-r(-)ət-\ *adj.* **1** Representing by a figure; emblematic; as, a statue *figurative* of American soldiers in the Revolutionary War. **2** Not literal; having a symbolic meaning; as, *figurative* language. **3** Having many figures of speech; flowery; as, a *figurative* description. — **fig·ur·a·tive·ly**, *adv.*

fig·ure \'fig-yər, 'fig-r\ *n.* **1** A written or printed character, such as 1, 2, or 3, that stands for a number. **2** [in the plural] The use of figures in reckoning; arithmetic; as, a person who is good at *figures.* **3** An object having shape or form; a body; as, to notice a dim *figure.* A triangle is a three-sided *figure.* **4** Shape; form; as, to have a slender *figure.* **5** A drawing or diagram; as, a *figure* illustrating each step in building a model ship. **6** A pattern or design, as in cloth. **7** An appearance or impression made, especially by a person; as, a sorry *figure.* **8** A personage; a character, as of history. **9** A set of movements in a dance; an outline traced by a series of movements, as with skates on ice. **10** Value or amount expressed in figures; price; as, to buy something at a high *figure.* — *v.;* **fig·ured**; **fig·ur·ing** \-yər-ing, -r(-)ing\. **1** To decorate with figures or designs, as a wall or ceiling. **2** To get by using arithmetic; to calculate; to compute; as, to *figure* the total cost. **3** To regard; to think; as, to *figure* oneself lucky. **4** To be distinguished or conspicuous; as, to *figure* in a crime. — **figure in**. To include in a reckoning; as, to *figure in* even the smallest expense. — **figure on**. **1** To take into consideration in planning; as, to *figure on* three guests for dinner. **2** To depend on; to rely on; as, a man you can always *figure on* for a helping hand. — **figure out**. To understand; to make out; as, unable to *figure out* what it all means.

fig·ured \'fig-yərd, 'fig-rd\ *adj.* Decorated with figures; as, *figured* silk.

fig·ure·head \'fig-yər-ˌhed, 'fig-r-\ *n.* **1** A figure, statue, or bust on the bow of a ship. **2** A person who has the title but not the powers of the head of something, as a business.

figure of speech. A form of expression, as a simile or metaphor, used to convey meaning or heighten effect, often by comparing or identifying one thing with another that has a special meaning or connotation familiar to the reader or listener.

fig·u·rine \ˌfig-yə-'rēn, ˌfig-r-'ēn\ *n.* A small carved or molded figure.

fig·wort \'fig-ˌwərt, -ˌwȯrt\ *n.* **1** An erect, coarse, strong-smelling herb with toothed leaves and small greenish-yellow or purple flowers in clusters. **2** Any of a family typified by this, including the foxglove and snapdragon.

fil·a·ment \'fil-ə-mənt\ *n.* **1** A thread or a slender threadlike object or part, such as the fine wire that becomes heated and gives light in an electric bulb. **2** The threadlike stalk of a stamen of a plant, bearing the anther. — **fil·a·men·ta·ry** \ˌfil-ə-'ment-r-ē, -'men-trē\ *adj.*

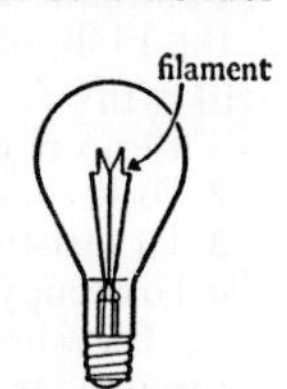

fil·bert \'filb-rt\ *n.* [From medieval

English, named after St. *Filbert* or *Philibert*, on whose name day (Aug. 22) filbert nuts were said to ripen.] **1** A European hazel with hairy and sticky twigs and foliage. **2** The thick-shelled edible nut of this shrub or small tree.

filch \'filch\ *v.* To steal, especially something of little value; as, to *filch* pennies from a child's bank. — **filch·er**, *n.*

file \'fīl\ *n.* **1** Any device, as a folder, a case, or a cabinet, by means of which papers or records may be kept in order. **2** The papers or records kept in such a device. **3** A row of persons, animals, or things arranged one behind the other; an orderly line; as, to walk in single *file;* a *file* of soldiers. — *v.;* **filed**; **fil·ing**. **1** To lay away in a file; to arrange in order; as, to *file* cards in alphabetical order. **2** To march in a file; as, to *file* out of a building. — **fil·er**, *n.*

file \'fīl\ *n.* A metal tool, usually steel, with sharp ridges or teeth on its surface for smoothing or rubbing down metal and other hard substances. — *v.;* **filed**; **fil·ing**. **1** To rub, smooth, or cut with a file. **2** To remove with a file; as, to *file* off a rough edge. — **fil·er**, *n.*

fi·let \fə-'lā, 'fil-ˌā, 'fil-ē\ *n.* **1** A piece of lean meat or fish without bone; a fillet. **2** A lace or net with a square mesh.

fil·i·al \'fil-ē-əl, 'fil-yəl\ *adj.* Of or befitting a son or a daughter; as, *filial* obedience. — **fil·i·al·ly** \-ē-ə-lē, -yə-lē\ *adv.*

fil·i·bus·ter \'fil-ə-ˌbəst-r\ *n.* **1** A person who organizes or joins a military expedition against a country with which his own country is at peace; a military adventurer. **2** A member of a lawmaking body who tries to prevent or delay action on a bill, usually by speaking merely to use up time. **3** An instance of filibustering or filibustering as a procedure designed to hinder legislative action. — \'fil-ə-ˌbəst-r, ˌfil-ə-'bəst-r\ *v.;* **fil·i·bus·tered**; **fil·i·bus·ter·ing** \-r(-)ing\. **1** To act as a military adventurer. **2** To delay or try to prevent action in a lawmaking body by using up time, as through long speeches. — **fil·i·bus·ter·er** \-r-r\ *n.*

fil·i·gree \'fil-ə-ˌgrē\ *n.* **1** Ornamental openwork, usually of fine wire, used in decorating gold and silver. **2** Any ornamental openwork of delicate and intricate design. **3** A pattern or design of a kind found in filigree.

fil·ing \'fī-ling\ *n.* **1** The act of one who files. **2** A small piece scraped off by a file; as, iron *filings.*

Fil·i·pi·no \ˌfil-ə-'pē-ˌnō\ *adj.* Of or relating to the Filipinos. — *n.; pl.* **Fil·i·pi·nos**. **1** A member of a native tribe, especially a Christian tribe, of the Philippine Islands. **2** A citizen of the Republic of the Philippines.

fill \'fil\ *v.* **1** To make full; to put or pour into until no more can be received; as, to *fill* a basket. **2** To become full; as, to wait for a bucket to *fill.* **3** To satisfy; as, to *fill* all requirements for a job. **4** To occupy fully; to take up whatever space there is. Bicycles *filled* the sidewalk. **5** To spread through, as air. Children's laughter *filled* the room. **6** To stop up; to plug, as crevices or holes; as, to *fill* a crack with putty; to *fill* a tooth. **7** To have and perform the duties of; to occupy or to put into a position; as, to *fill* the office of president. Several jobs remain to be *filled.* **8** To supply according to directions; as, to *fill* a prescription; to *fill* an order for groceries. — **fill in**. To insert or to complete by insertions; as, to *fill in* one's name and address; to *fill in* the blanks in an exercise. — **fill out**. **1** To make or grow larger, as in bulk; as, a tall skinny boy who had not begun to *fill out.* **2** To fill in; as, to *fill out* an application form. — *n.* **1** A full supply; as much as is wanted; as, to eat one's *fill.* **2** Material used for filling, especially a ditch or hollow in the ground.

fill·er \'fil-r\ *n.* One that fills, as a substance added to another substance to increase bulk or weight or a material used for filling cracks and pores in wood before painting.

fil·let \'fil-ət; *sense 3 is more often* fə-'lā, 'fil-ˌā, 'fil-ē\ *n.* **1** A little band, especially one to encircle the hair. **2** A thin, narrow ribbon or a part or ornament resembling a ribbon, as a border on a book cover. **3** A piece of lean, boneless meat or fish; a filet. — *v.* **1** To bind or decorate with a fillet, as of ribbon. **2** To cut into fillets, as a fish.

fill·ing \'fil-ing\ *n.* Material that is used to fill something; as, a gold *filling* for a tooth.

filling station. A place where gasoline and oil for automobiles are sold at retail.

fil·lip \'fil-əp\ *v.* **1** To tap with the finger by flicking the fingernail outward across the end of the thumb. **2** To arouse; to stimulate. — *n.* **1** A flick of the finger across the thumb; a smart blow or tap. **2** Something that serves to arouse or stimulate.

fil·ly \'fil-ē\ *n.; pl.* **fil·lies**. **1** A young female horse usually of less than four years. **2** A girl.

film \'film\ *n.* **1** A thin skin or membrane. **2** A thin coating or layer; as, a *film* of ice on a windshield. **3** A roll or strip of thin flexible material coated with a chemical substance sensitive to light and used in taking pictures. **4** A motion picture; as, a *film* about Mexico. — *v.* **1** To cover or become covered with film; as, eyes *filmed* with tears. **2** To photograph on a film; to make a motion picture of; as, a picture *filmed* in Europe; to *film* a battle scene.

film·strip \'film-ˌstrip\ *n.* A strip of film bearing still photographs, sketches, or diagrams, often with explanatory material, to be projected upon a screen as a teaching aid or to accompany a lecture.

filmy \'film-ē\ *adj.;* **film·i·er**; **film·i·est**. **1** Of or like film; very thin; as, *filmy* cobwebs. **2** Covered with or as if with film; cloudy; misty.

fil·ter \'filt-r\ *n.* **1** Any porous substance through which water or other fluid is passed to purify or clear it. **2** A device containing such a substance. **3** A material or a device, as a colored screen for the lens of a camera, that partly absorbs light rays, admitting only those desired for a special purpose. — *v.;* **fil·tered**; **fil·ter·ing** \'filt-r-ing, 'fil-tring\. **1** To purify, as a liquid, by means of a filter; to strain. **2** To pass through or as if through a filter. Moonlight *filtered* through the trees. **3** To remove from a fluid by a filter; as, to *filter* out impurities.

fil·ter·a·ble \'filt-r-əb-l, 'fil-trəb-l\ *adj.* Capable of being filtered or of passing through a filter.

filth \'filth\ *n.* **1** Disgusting dirt; foul matter. **2** Disgusting or nasty language or thoughts; obscenity.

filthy \'fil-thē\ *adj.;* **filth·i·er**; **filth·i·est**. Disgustingly dirty; foul; obscene; nasty. — **filth·i·ly** \'filth-l-ē\ *adv.*

fil·tra·ble \'fil-trəb-l\ *adj.* Filterable.

fil·trate \'fil-ˌtrāt\ *n.* The fluid that has passed through a filter.

fil·tra·tion \fil-'trāsh-n\ *n.* The act or process of filtering.

fin \'fin\ *n.* **1** One of the thin paddlelike parts on the bodies of fish and cetaceans, used in propelling, steering, and balancing the body. **2** A finlike part, as of an airplane.

fi·nal \'fīn-l\ *adj.* [From medieval English, there borrowed from French, where it was derived from Latin *finalis*, this in turn derived from *finis* meaning "end" — see *finale, finis.*] **1** Coming or happening at the end; last; closing; as, the *final* day of vacation. **2** Ending doubt or questioning; as, to give a *final* answer. — For synonyms see *last.* — *n.* **1** A final or deciding game. **2** A final examination in a course.

fi·na·le \fə-'näl-ē, -'nal-ē, -'nȧl-ē\ *n.* [From Italian, there derived from the adjective *finale* meaning "final", this in turn derived from Latin *finalis* — see *final.*] The close; the end; especially, in music, the last section.

fi·nal·ist \'fīn-l-əst\ *n.* Any of the contestants who meet in the final of an elimination contest.

fi·nal·i·ty \fī-'nal-ət-ē, fə-\ *n.; pl.* **fi·nal·i·ties**. **1** The condition of being final, settled, or complete; as, to speak with *finality.* **2** Something that is final.

fi·nal·ly \'fīn-l(-)ē\ *adv.* **1** At last; in the end. The speaker *finally* managed to get the attention of his audience. **2** In a final way; decisively; as, to rule *finally* on the matter.

fi·nance \'fī-ˌnan(t)s; fə-'nan(t)s, fī-\ *n.* **1** [usually in the plural] Funds; money on hand; resources; income. The city's *finances* are low. **2** The management of large sums of money; as, skilled in *finance.* — *v.;* **fi·nanced**; **fi·nanc·ing**. To provide money for; as, to *finance* a trip out of one's savings.

fi·nan·cial \fə-'nanch-l, fī-\ *adj.* Having to do with finance or with finances; as, to be in *financial* difficulties; the *financial* world. — **fi·nan·cial·ly** \-'nanch-l-ē\ *adv.*

fin·an·cier \ˌfin-ən-'sir, ˌfī-ˌnan-, fə-ˌnan-\ *n.* **1** A person skilled in managing large funds. **2** A person who carries on financial operations; especially, a person who has large sums of money to invest.

finch \'finch\ *n.* A small seed-eating songbird with short conical bill, such as the sparrow, linnet, bunting, or canary.

find \'fīnd\ *v.;* **found** \'fau̇nd\; **find·ing**. **1** To come upon; to meet with someone or something by chance; as, to *find* a kitten on the porch. **2** To come upon by searching, study, or effort; to discover; as, to *find* the answer to a problem in arithmetic. **3** To gain; as, unable to *find* time to do it. **4** To arrive at; to reach; as, to *find* one's place in the world. **5** To decide on; to decide and declare; as, to *find* a verdict. The judges *found* no contestant worthy of the prize. **6** To know by experience. People *found* the boy honest. **7** To gain or regain the use of. When she *found* her voice again, the girl told what had frightened her. **8** To provide; to supply; as, to *find* room for an unexpected guest. — **find fault**. To criticize unfavorably. — **find oneself**. To come to realize one's powers or capacities. — **find out**. To detect, as a thief; to discover, as a secret; to make sure; as, to *find out* for yourself. — *n.* A finding or something that is found. The old book in the attic proved to be a valuable *find.*

find·er \'fīnd-r\ *n.* A person or thing that finds as a small telescope attached to a larger one, for finding an object, or a lens on a camera that shows the view being photographed by the camera.

find·ing \'fīn-ding\ *n.* **1** The action of finding. **2** Something that is found. **3** In law, the result of a judicial examination or inquiry as shown in the verdict of a jury or court.

fine \'fīn\ *adj.;* **fin·er**; **fin·est**. **1** Refined; free from impurities, as metal. **2** Not coarse and heavy; not thick or clumsy; as, *fine* sand; *fine* thread. **3** Small; as, *fine* print. **4** Delicate; as, *fine* china. **5** Better than most in character, quality, or ability; excellent; as, a *fine* man; a *fine* book. — *adv.* Excellently; very well; finely.

fine \'fīn\ *n.* A sum of money required to be paid as a penalty for breaking a law or a rule. — *v.;* **fined**; **fin·ing**. To set a fine on; to punish by a fine; as, to be *fined* for speeding.

fine art. Any art concerned with the creation of things of beauty; especially, one of the group including painting, drawing, sculpture, and architecture.

fine·ly \'fīn-lē\ *adv.* In a fine manner; excellently.

fine·ness \'fīn-nəs\ *n.* **1** The quality or condition of being fine. **2** The proportion of pure silver or gold in an alloy, as in coins or jewelry. The *fineness* of United States coin is $\frac{9}{10}$.

fin·ery \'fīn-r(-)ē\ *n.; pl.* **fin·er·ies**. Ornaments; especially, fine or showy clothes or jewels.

fi·nesse \fə-'nes\ *n.* **1** Refinement or delicacy of skill in the doing or making of something; as, a painting executed with great *finesse.* **2** Skillful handling of any situation; cunning; subtlety; as, to accomplish by the use of *finesse* what could not have been done by force. — *v.;* **fi·nessed**; **fi·ness-**

ing. To use finesse, skill, or cunning in accomplishing a purpose.

fin·ger \'fing-gr\ *n.* **1** One of five divisions of the end of the hand; especially, one of the four divisions other than the thumb. **2** The breadth of a finger or a depth or amount of something, as a fluid, equivalent to this measurement. **3** A part of a glove that covers a finger. **4** Something that resembles or does the work of a finger. — *v.;* **fingered**; **fin·ger·ing** \-gr(-)ing\. **1** To touch with the fingers; to handle. **2** In music, to perform with the fingers or with a certain fingering. **3** To mark the notes of a piece of music to show what fingers are to be used.

fin·ger·ing \'fing-gr(-)ing\ *n.* **1** The act or process of handling or touching with the fingers. **2** The method of using the fingers in playing a musical instrument. **3** The marking on a piece of music of a scheme for the use of the fingers.

fin·ger·nail \'fing-gr-ˌnāl, -'nāl\ *n.* The hard covering on the upper part of the end of a finger.

finger painting. **1** A method of forming a picture or design by spreading jellylike pigments on wet paper with the fingers or hand. **2** A picture or design produced by this method.

fin·ger·print \'fing-gr-ˌprint\ *n.* The pattern of marks made by pressing the tip of a finger or thumb on any surface; especially, such a pattern taken for the purpose of identifying a person later. — *v.* To take fingerprints of.

fingerprint

fin·i·cal \'fin-ik-l\ *adj.* Having or showing exaggerated refinement in manners or tastes; too dainty or fussy. — **fin·i·cal·ly** \-ik-l(-)ē\ *adv.*

fin·ick·ing \'fin-ik-ing\ or **fin·icky** \'fin-ik-ē\ *adj.* Finical; unduly particular.

fining. Pres. part. of *fine*.

fin·is \'fin-is, 'fī-nis\ *n.* [From Latin — see *final, finale.*] An end or the end; conclusion — formerly often printed at the end of a book.

fin·ish \'fin-ish\ *v.* **1** To arrive at the end of or bring to an end; to complete; as, to *finish* a meal; to *finish* the day's work. **2** To come to an end. Amateur plays seldom *finish* on time. **3** To treat the surface of, as by polishing or painting. — *n.* **1** The end; conclusion; as, a close *finish* in a race; to fight to the *finish*. **2** The treatment given a surface, or the appearance given by finishing; as, the shiny *finish* on a new bicycle. **3** Cultivation in manners and speech; social polish. — **fin·ish·er**, *n.*

fin·ished \'fin-isht\ *adj.* **1** Ended; concluded. **2** Perfected; trained, developed, or polished to the highest degree of excellence; as, a *finished* performance by a great violinist.

fi·nite \'fī-ˌnīt\ *adj.* **1** Having certain definite limits. **2** Not infinite; restricted in power or scope. Man is a *finite* being. **3** Showing distinction of grammatical person, especially in agreement with a subject; as, a *finite* verb. — **fi·nite·ly**, *adv.*

Finn \'fin\ *n.* A native of Finland or a member of one of several related, Finnish-speaking peoples living in adjacent parts of Russia.

fin·nan had·die \'fin-ən 'had-ē\. A smoked haddock.

finned \'find\ *adj.* Having a fin or fins.

Finn·ish \'fin-ish\ *adj.* Of or relating to Finland or the Finns. — *n.* The language of the Finns.

fin·ny \'fin-ē\ *adj.* **1** Having fins. **2** Like a fin. **3** Of or relating to fish or abounding in fish; as, the *finny* tribe; the *finny* deep.

fiord or **fjord** \'fyȯrd\ *n.* A narrow inlet of the sea between high banks or rocks.

fir \'fər\ *n.* **1** A cone-shaped evergreen tree of the pine family having erect cones and foliage in flattened sprays. **2** The wood of any fir tree.

fire \'fīr\ *n.* **1** The light and heat, and especially the flame, produced by burning. **2** Fuel that is burning, as in a fireplace or stove. **3** The destructive burning of something, as a building or a forest. **4** Liveliness and warmth; enthusiasm; as, a person with *fire* in his eye. **5** The discharge of firearms; shooting; as, the sound of distant rifle *fire*. — **catch fire**. To begin to burn. — **on fire**. **1** Burning. **2** Ardent; eager. — **under fire**. **1** Exposed to the firing of an enemy's guns. **2** Under attack of any kind. — *v.;* **fired**; **fir·ing**. **1** To set on fire; to kindle; to ignite. **2** To stir; to enliven; as, a story that *fires* one's imagination. **3** To discharge; as, to *fire* a gun. **4** To subject to intense heat; as, to *fire* pottery. **5** To feed the fire of; as, to *fire* a furnace. **6** To take fire; to burst into flame; to glow or redden. **7** To dismiss, as from a position; as, to be *fired* for laziness. — **fire up**. **1** To start a fire, as in a furnace. **2** To grow angry; to show temper.

fire·arm \'fīr-ˌärm, -ˌȧrm\ *n.* Any weapon from which shot is discharged by an explosive; especially, a small weapon, as a rifle or a pistol.

fire·ball \'fīr-ˌbȯl\ *n.* **1** A ball of fire. **2** A glowing meteor. **3** A ball filled with combustible or explosive material, formerly thrown among enemy forces. **4** The luminous cloud of dust and vapor created by a nuclear explosion, as of an atomic bomb.

fire·brand \'fīr-ˌbrand\ *n.* **1** A piece of burning wood. **2** A person who stirs up strife and conflict by exciting others to anger.

fire·brick \'fīr-ˌbrik\ *n.* A brick capable of withstanding great heat.

fire·bug \'fīr-ˌbəg\ *n.* A person who deliberately sets destructive fires, as to buildings or forests.

fire·crack·er \'fīr-ˌkrak-r\ *n.* A paper tube containing an explosive to be fired in celebrations.

fire·damp \'fīr-ˌdamp\ *n.* A combustible gas that forms in coal mines or the explosive mixture formed by this gas with air.

fire·dog \'fīr-ˌdȯg\ *n.* One of a pair of supports for wood in a fireplace; an andiron.

fire engine. **1** An apparatus for throwing water on a fire to put it out. **2** A motor truck equipped with such an apparatus. **3** Any motor truck specially equipped for fighting fires.

fire escape. A stairway or ladder that provides a means of escape from a building in case of fire.

fire extinguisher. Something that is used to put out a fire; especially, a portable hand-operated metal contrivance for ejecting a stream or spray of fire-extinguishing chemicals.

fire·fly \'fīr-ˌflī\ *n.; pl.* **fire·flies.** A small soft-bodied beetle that produces a soft intermittent light from the lower abdomen.

fire·house \'fīr-ˌhau̇s\ *n.; pl.* **fire-hous·es** \-ˌhau̇-zəz\. A building housing fire engines and, usually, firemen.

fire extinguisher

fire irons. Implements for handling burning wood or coal in a fireplace, as tongs and a poker.

fire·light \'fīr-ˌlīt\ *n.* The light of a fire, especially one burning in a fireplace.

fire·man \'fīr-mən\ *n.; pl.* **fire·men** \-mən\. **1** A member of a body of men (**fire company**) organized to put out fires. **2** A man who tends or feeds a fire; a stoker; as, a *fireman* on a locomotive.

fire·place \'fīr-ˌplās\ *n.* A part of a chimney in which a fire can be made, usually an open recess in a wall; a hearth.

fire·plug \'fīr-ˌpləg\ *n.* A hydrant to which a large hose can be attached and water drawn from the main water pipes for extinguishing fires.

fire·proof \'fīr-'prüf\ *adj.* Not easily burned; made safe against fire. — *v.* To make fireproof; as, to *fireproof* the roof of a house.

fire·side \'fīr-ˌsīd\ *n.* **1** A place near the fire or hearth. **2** One's own hearth; home.

fire tower. 1 A tower from which a watch for fires is kept, as in a forest. **2** A fireproof compartment extending from top to bottom of a building and containing a stairway; an interior fire escape.

fire·trap \'fīr-ˌtrap\ *n.* **1** A building difficult to escape from in case of fire. **2** A place or building in which there exist many conditions favorable to the spread of fire.

fire·wa·ter \'fīr-ˌwȯt-r, -ˌwät-r\ *n.* Intoxicating liquor.

fire·wood \'fīr-ˌwu̇d\ *n.* Wood cut to be used for fuel.

fire·work \'fīr-ˌwərk\ *n.* [usually in the plural] A firecracker, skyrocket, or similar device designed to produce a striking display of illumination or noise.

fir·kin \'fərk-n\ *n.* **1** A small wooden cask. **2** A measure of capacity, usually one fourth of a barrel.

firm \'fərm\ *adj.* **1** Hard; solid; compact; as, *firm* flesh; *firm* ground. **2** Steady; not easily shaken; loyal; as, *firm* friends. **3** Decided; positive; determined; as, to speak in a *firm* voice. **4** Steady; not fluctuating; as, a *firm* market. The price of eggs remained *firm.* — **firm·ly,** *adv.*

firm \'fərm\ *n.* **1** The name under which a company does business. **2** A partnership of two or more persons in a business.

fir·ma·ment \'fər-mə-mənt\ *n.* The arch of the sky; the heavens.

first \'fərst\ *adj.* **1** Earliest; ahead of all others in time or place; as, the *first* day of school; to sit in the *first* row. **2** In music, higher in pitch; most prominent in carrying the melody; as, *first* soprano; *first* violin. — *adv.* **1** Before any other person or thing in time, space, or rank; as, to reach the goal line *first.* **2** For the first time; as, when the sailors *first* sighted land. **3** In preference to something else. Surrender? We will die *first.* — *n.* **1** Anything that is first; as, the *first* of June; to be the *first* to leave a party. **2** The finest grade of an article that is sold. This store sells only *firsts.* **3** In sports, the winning place in a contest; as, to take *first* in the cross-country race.

first aid. Care or treatment given to an ill or injured person before regular medical aid can be obtained. — **first-aid,** *adj.*

first-born \'fərst-'bȯrn\ *adj.* Born first; oldest. — *n.* A first-born child.

first class. The highest class of accommodations, as on a ship or aircraft.

first-class \'fərst-'klas\ *adj.* Of the best or highest class or quality. — *adv.* By a first-class means of transportation; as, to travel *first-class.*

first·hand \'fərst-'hand\ *adv.* Straight from the original source; as, to get information *firsthand.* — *adj.* Obtained firsthand; as, a *firsthand* account.

first·ling \'fərst-ling\ *n.* The first of a class or kind; the first produce, offspring, or result.

first·ly \'fərst-lē\ *adv.* In the first place; first.

first-rate \'fərst-'rāt\ *adj.* **1** First-class, as in size; as, a *first-rate* ship. **2** Of the highest efficiency; outstanding, as in quality or value; as, a problem of *first-rate* importance. **3** Extremely good; admirable. — *adv.* Very well; quite well.

firth \'fərth\ *n.* A narrow arm of the sea.

fis·cal \'fisk-l\ *adj.* **1** Of or relating to the public treasury. **2** Of or relating to financial matters generally.

fish \'fish\ *n.; pl.* **fish** or **fish·es. 1** A cold-blooded, water-inhabiting, water-breathing vertebrate animal with a typically long, scaly, tapering body, limbs developed as fins, and a vertical tail fin. **2** The flesh of fish, used as food. **3** A chap; a fellow; as, a queer *fish.* — *adj.* Of or relating to fish or to the catching or selling of fish. — *v.* **1** To attempt to catch fish. Many people like to *fish.* **2** To attempt to catch fish in; as, to *fish* a stream. **3** To search for something that is buried or hidden; as, to *fish* in a drawer for a pencil. **4** To try to find out something by shrewd questioning or trickery; as, to *fish* for information. **5** To draw forth; as, to *fish* out a jackknife from one's pocket.

fish·er \'fish-r\ *n.* **1** One that fishes; a fisherman. **2** A meat-eating arboreal mammal of the weasel family, found in eastern North America.

fish·er·man \'fish-r-mən\ *n.; pl.* **fish·er·men**

\-mən\. A person who fishes, especially one who makes his living by fishing.

fish·ery \'fish-r(-)ē\ *n.; pl.* **fish·er·ies.** **1** The occupation or business of catching fish. **2** A place for catching fish, especially as a business.

fish hawk. The osprey.

fish·hook \'fish-ˌhu̇k\ *n.* A hook used for catching fish.

fish·ing \'fish-ing\ *n.* The sport or business of catching fish.

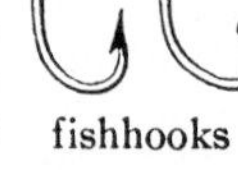
fishhooks

fish·mon·ger \'fish-ˌməng-gr\ *n.* A person who buys and sells fish.

fish·wife \'fish-ˌwīf\ *n.; pl.* **fish-wives** \-ˌwīvz\. **1** A woman who sells fish. **2** A woman who uses abusive language.

fishy \'fish-ē\ *adj.;* **fish·i·er; fish·i·est.** **1** Like a fish, as in appearance, taste, or smell. **2** Improbable; hard to believe; as, a *fishy* excuse. **3** Arousing suspicion; dubious; as, a person known as a *fishy* character.

fis·sion \'fish-n, 'fizh-\ *n.* **1** A splitting or breaking into parts. **2** The spontaneous division of the body or a cell into two or more parts each of which becomes a new living individual, as in bacteria. **3** The splitting of the nucleus of an atom resulting in the freeing of large amounts of energy.

fis·sion·a·ble \'fish-n(-)əb-l, 'fizh-\ *adj.* Capable of undergoing fission; as, *fissionable* material.

fission bomb. An atomic bomb.

fis·sure \'fish-r\ *n.* A narrow crack; a cleft; as, a *fissure* in a rock.

fist \'fist\ *n.* **1** The hand with the fingers doubled tight into the palm. **2** In printing, the index mark ☞.

fist·i·cuff \'fis-tə-ˌkəf\ *n.* **1** A blow with the fist. **2** [in the plural] A fight with fists.

fist·note \'fist-ˌnōt\ *n.* A written or printed comment or explanation preceded by the index mark ☞.

fis·tu·la \'fis-chə-lə\ *n.; pl.* **fis·tu·las** \-ləz\ or **fis·tu·lae** \-ˌlē\. **1** A reed; a pipe or tube. **2** An abnormal opening in an abscess or hollow organ.

fit \'fit\ *adj.;* **fit·ter; fit·test.** **1** Suitable to; proper for; as, food that is *fit* for a king. **2** Proper, right, or becoming; as, words that are not *fit* for a child to hear. **3** Prepared; ready; as, *fit* for service. **4** In good health; in good physical condition.

— The words *suitable* and *appropriate* are synonyms of *fit: fit* may describe something especially adaptable to a purpose or especially ready for use or action; *suitable* may describe something that meets the requirements of a particular occasion or use or in no way conflicts with them; *appropriate* generally describes something that perfectly and often pleasingly agrees with or suits the situation in which it is found.

— *v.;* **fit·ted; fit·ting.** [From medieval English *fitten* meaning "to array", there probably borrowed from Old Norse *fitja* meaning "to knit together".] **1** To be suitable to or proper for; as, to dress to *fit* an occasion. **2** To be of the right shape or size; as, a suit that *fits* perfectly. **3** To adjust something so as to make it the right shape or size; as, to have a new suit *fitted.* **4** To supply with what is suitable for a purpose; to outfit; as, to *fit* out a boat for an ocean voyage. — *n.* **1** A way of fitting or of being fitted; as, the *fit* of one's gloves. **2** Something that fits; as, a suit that is a good *fit.* — **fit·ly,** *adv.*

fit \'fit\ *n.* [From Old English *fitt* meaning "struggle", "contest", "fight".] **1** A sudden, violent attack of a disorder, especially epilepsy; a convulsion. **2** A sudden outburst, as of laughter.

fitch \'fich\ *n.* A fitchew or its fur.

fitch·et \'fich-ət\ *n.* A fitchew or its fur.

fitch·ew \'fich-ˌü\ *n.* The European polecat.

fit·ful \'fit-fəl\ *adj.* Not regular; restless; as, *fitful* sleep. — **fit·ful·ly** \-fə-lē\ *adv.*

fit·ter \'fit-r\ *n.* One that fits; especially, one who tries on and adjusts articles of dress, or one who fits, adjusts, or assembles parts, as of machinery.

fit·ting \'fit-ing\ *n.* **1** The action of one that fits. **2** [in the plural] Fixtures; parts; as, *fittings* for an engine. — *adj.* Suitable; proper; as, a *fitting* remark. — **fit·ting·ly,** *adv.*

five \'fīv\ *adj.* Four and one more. — *n.* **1** The sum of three and two; five units or objects. **2** The figure standing for five units, as 5 or V.

five·fold \'fīv-ˌfōld, -'fōld\ *adj.* or *adv.* Having five parts; five times as much or as many.

fix \'fiks\ *v.;* **fixed** or **fixt** \'fikst\; **fix·ing.** **1** To fasten; to make firm; as, to *fix* a machine in place; to *fix* one's attention on something. **2** To set definitely; to establish; as, to *fix* a price; to *fix* the rules of a contest. **3** To repair; as, to *fix* a clock. **4** To make permanent; as, a custom *fixed* by long practice. **5** To get into a desired position or condition by a wrongful act; to arrange the outcome of something dishonestly; as, to *fix* a horse race by bribing the jockey. **6** To arrange or put in order; to prepare; as, to *fix* one's hair; to *fix* dinner. — *n.* An unpleasant or difficult position; as, to get oneself into a *fix.* — **fix·a·ble** \'fiks-əb-l\ *adj.* — **fix·er** \'fiks-r\ *n.*

fix·ate \'fik-ˌsāt\ *v.;* **fix·at·ed; fix·at·ing.** To make or become fixed; especially, to direct upon an object; as, to *fixate* the eyes. — **fix·a·tion** \fik-'sāsh-n\ *n.*

fixed \'fikst\ *adj.* **1** Securely placed or fastened. **2** Settled; firm; intent; as, a *fixed* policy; a *fixed* gaze. — **fix·ed·ly** \'fiks-əd-lē\ *adv.*

fixed star. A star whose position in relation to surrounding stars seems not to change for long periods of time.

fix·ing \'fiks-ing\ *n.* **1** A putting in permanent form. **2** [in the plural] Arrangements; trimmings; decorations; as, a birthday party with all the *fixings.*

fix·ture \'fiks-chər\ *n.* **1** A fixing or a being fixed. **2** One firmly established in a place. During his many years of service the old man had become a *fixture* on the ranch. **3** Something attached to another thing as a permanent part of it; as, bathroom *fixtures*.

fizz or **fiz** \'fiz\ *v.;* **fizzed**; **fizz·ing**. To make a hissing or sputtering sound. — *n.; pl.* **fizz·es**. **1** A hissing sound. **2** Any bubbling drink; as, a glass of *fizz*. — **fizzy**, *adj.*

fiz·zle \'fiz-l\ *v.;* **fiz·zled**; **fiz·zling** \-l(-)ing\. **1** To fizz. **2** To fail after making a good start. The baseball season *fizzled* out badly. — *n.* **1** A hissing or sputtering sound. **2** A failure; as, a plan that turned out to be a *fizzle*.

fjord. Variant of *fiord*.

flab·ber·gast \'flab-r-ˌgast\ *v.* To astonish; to make helpless with amazement; to dumfound.

flab·by \'flab-ē\ *adj.;* **flab·bi·er**; **flab·bi·est**. Soft; not hard and firm; as, *flabby* muscles.

flag \'flag\ *n.* **1** Any of several irises with long sword-shaped leaves. **2** The leaf, or blade, of one of these plants.

flag \'flag\ *n.* **1** A piece of cloth or other material that has on it a symbol or symbols indicating nationality, party or other affiliation, rank, or office; a standard; a banner. **2** A piece of cloth or other material, with or without a symbol, used in giving information; as, signal *flags;* a red *flag* warning of danger. — *v.;* **flagged**; **flag·ging**. **1** To put a flag or flags on; as, buildings *flagged* for a holiday. **2** To signal with a flag or flags; to convey, as a message, by means of flags; as, to *flag* a train.

flag \'flag\ *n.* A flagstone; any hard stone suitable for paving. — *v.;* **flagged**; **flag·ging**. To pave with flags.

flag \'flag\ *v.;* **flagged**; **flag·ging**. To lose strength or energy; to droop; as, to find one's interest in a study *flagging*.

flag·el·late \'flaj-l-ˌāt\ *v.;* **flag·el·lat·ed**; **flag·el·lat·ing**. To whip; to lash. — \-ət, -ˌāt\ *adj.* Having flagella or like a flagellum. — **flag·el·la·tion** \ˌflaj-l-'āsh-n\ *n.*

fla·gel·lum \flə-'jel-əm\ *n.; pl.* **fla·gel·la** \-'jel-ə\ or **fla·gel·lums** \-əmz\. A whiplike appendage or process by which certain cells and one-celled organisms swim about.

flag·eo·let \ˌflaj-l-'et\ *n.* A small wood-wind instrument belonging to the flute class.

flag·ging \'flag-ing\ *n.* A pavement of flagstones.

flag·man \'flag-mən\ *n.; pl.* **flag·men** \-mən\. A person who carries a flag or signals with a flag, as on a railroad.

flag·on \'flag-n\ *n.* A container for liquids, usually having a handle, spout, and lid.

flag·pole \'flag-ˌpōl\ *n.* A flagstaff.

fla·gran·cy \'flāg-rən-sē\ *n.* Flagrant nature.

fla·grant \'flāg-rənt\ *adj.* Conspicuously bad; glaring; notorious; as, *flagrant* disobedience; a *flagrant* criminal. — **fla·grant·ly**, *adv.*

flag·ship \'flag-ˌship\ *n.* The ship carrying the commander of a fleet or squadron and flying his flag.

flag·staff \'flag-ˌstaf\ *n.; pl.* **flag·staffs** \-ˌstafs\ or **flag·staves** \-ˌstavz\. A staff on which to display a flag.

flag·stone \'flag-ˌstōn\ *n.* A flat stone used in paving.

flail \'flāl\ *n.* A tool for threshing grain by hand. — *v.* To beat with or as if with a flail; as, to *flail* the air with one's arms.

flail

flair \'flar, 'fler\ *n.* **1** Keenness of mind; sharp insight; as, a *flair* for detecting errors in reasoning. **2** Natural ability; taste; as, a *flair* for acting.

flak \'flak\ *n.* Antiaircraft guns or the bursting shells fired from them.

flake \'flāk\ *n.* A small fleecy or filmy mass or chip of anything; a scale; as, a *flake* of snow; a *flake* of dandruff. — *v.;* **flaked**; **flak·ing**. To form or separate into flakes; to make or become flaky. This paint *flakes* off.

flaky \'flāk-ē\ *adj.;* **flak·i·er**; **flak·i·est**. Consisting of flakes; separating into flakes; as, *flaky* piecrust. — **flak·i·ly** \-l-ē\ *adv.*

flam·beau \'flam-ˌbō\ *n.; pl.* **flam·beaux** \-ˌbōz\ or **flam·beaus** \-ˌbōz\. A flaming torch.

flam·boy·ant \flam-'bȯi-ənt\ *adj.* **1** Having waving or flamelike curves. **2** Highly decorated; florid; as, a *flamboyant* dress. **3** Gorgeous; showy. The autumn colors made a *flamboyant* picture. — **flam·boy·ance** \-ən(t)s\ or **flam·boy·an·cy** \-ən-sē\ *n.* — **flam·boy·ant·ly**, *adv.*

flame \'flām\ *n.* **1** The fire of burning material; as, the *flame* of a candle. **2** Any flamelike appearance; glow; brilliance; as, to show a sudden *flame* of anger. — *v.;* **flamed**; **flam·ing**. **1** To burn with a flame; to blaze. **2** To show strong emotion; to burst forth violently; as, resentment *flaming* into violent anger.

flam·ing \'flā-ming\ *adj.* **1** Blazing; afire. **2** Of the color of flame; brilliant; as, *flaming* autumn foliage. **3** Burning with eagerness; as, a *flaming* appeal to all patriotic citizens. — **flam·ing·ly**, *adv.*

fla·min·go \flə-'ming-ˌgō\ *n.; pl.* **fla·min·gos** or **fla·min·goes**. A very long-legged and long-necked water bird with scarlet wings and a broad bill bent downward at the end.

flam·ma·ble \'flam-əb-l\ *adj.* Likely to catch fire easily; inflammable.

flange \'flanj\ *n.* A rib or rim used for strength, for guiding, or for attachment to another object; as, the *flange* on a locomotive wheel.

flank \'flangk\ *n.* **1** The side of an animal between the ribs and the hip. **2** A cut of beef from this part. **3** The side of anything; as, the *flank* of a hill. **4** The right or left side of a body of troops or of a fleet; a wing. — *v.* **1** To threaten or attack the flank of. **2** To pass around the flank of; as, to *flank* an army. **3** To be situated at the flank of. — **flank·er**, *n.*

flan·nel \'flan-l\ *n.* **1** A soft cloth made of wool or cotton or one of these combined with other fibers, such as rayon. **2** [in the plural] Flannel clothing. — **flan·nel·ly** \ˈflan-l-ē\ *adj.*

flan·nel·ette or **flan·nel·et** \ˌflan-l-ˈet\ *n.* A soft flannellike fabric with a nap on one or both sides.

flap \ˈflap\ *n.* **1** A stroke with something broad; as, a *flap* of the hand. **2** Anything broad and limber or flat and thin that hangs loose; as, the *flap* of a pocket. **3** The motion or sound that is made by something hanging loose and moving back and forth; as, the *flap* of a windowshade. **4** A movable auxiliary airfoil attached to the trailing edge of an airplane wing, permitting a steeper gliding angle in landing. — *v.;* **flapped**; **flap·ping**. **1** To strike with a flap; as, a loose sole *flapping* against the pavement. **2** To move with a beating motion. The flag *flapped* in the wind.

flap·jack \ˈflap-ˌjak\ *n.* A griddlecake.

flap·per \ˈflap-r\ *n.* **1** One that flaps. **2** A young game bird, especially a duck not yet able to fly well. **3** A flippant, worldly young woman or girl who is extreme in manners, dress, and speech.

flare \ˈflar, ˈfler\ *v.;* **flared**; **flar·ing**. **1** To blaze with a sudden unsteady light; to flame up brightly. **2** To become suddenly excited or angry; as, to *flare* up at a remark. **3** To spread outward; as, a vase that *flares* at the rim; a skirt *flaring* at the bottom. — *n.* **1** An unsteady, glaring light or flame. **2** A blaze used to signal, to give light, or to attract attention, or the device or material that produces the blaze. **3** A sudden outburst, as of sound or feeling. **4** A spreading outward, or a part that spreads outward; as, the *flare* of a vase;. the *flare* of a trumpet.

flare-up \ˈflar-ˌəp, ˈfler-\ *n.* A flaring up in a sudden burst, as of flame or anger.

flash \ˈflash\ *v.* **1** To break forth in or like a sudden flame. Lightning *flashed.* **2** To send out in or as if in flashes; as, to *flash* a message. **3** To come or pass very suddenly. A car *flashed* by. **4** To make a sudden display, as of brilliance or feeling. The girl's eyes *flashed* with excitement. — *n.* **1** A sudden burst of light; as, a *flash* of lightning. **2** A sudden showing or display; as, a *flash* of wit. **3** The duration of a flash; an instant; a very short time; as, to add figures in a *flash.* **4** A movement of a light or flag in signaling; as, the *flash* of a beacon. **5** A flashlight. — *adj.* Arising suddenly and developing rapidly; as, a *flash* fire; a *flash* flood.

flash·bulb \ˈflash-ˌbəlb\ *n.* An electric bulb that gives a sudden bright light, used in photography.

flash card. A printed card held up briefly before a class by a teacher, especially as a visual aid in the learning of reading, spelling, arithmetic, and foreign languages.

flash·i·ly \ˈflash-l-ē\ *adv.* In a flashy, or showy, manner; as, *flashily* dressed.

flash·light \ˈflash-ˌlīt\ *n.* **1** A light that flashes, as a revolving light in a lighthouse. **2** A small portable electric light. **3** A sudden bright artificial light used in photography.

flashy \ˈflash-ē\ *adj.;* **flash·i·er**; **flash·i·est**. **1** Flashing; glaring. **2** Showy; gaudy; as, *flashy* clothes.

flask \ˈflask\ *n.* A narrow-necked bottle, especially one with a broad, flat body, used for carrying liquor.

flat \ˈflat\ *adj.;* **flat·ter**; **flat·test**. **1** Having a smooth, level, horizontal surface; as, a *flat* rock; *flat* ground. **2** Having a smooth, even surface; as, the *flat* face of a wall. **3** Spread out on or along a surface; as, to lie *flat* on the ground. **4** Having a broad, smooth surface and little thickness. A phonograph record is *flat.* **5** Downright; positive; as, a *flat* refusal. **6** Fixed; unchanging; as, to charge a *flat* rate for one's services. **7** Exact; as, to run a mile in a *flat* four minutes. **8** Dull; uninteresting; tasteless; as, a *flat* story; water that tastes *flat.* **9** With the air or gas let out; as, a *flat* tire. **10** In music, below the tone pitch; lower by a half step. — *adv.* **1** Exactly; as, to run a mile in four minutes *flat.* **2** In music, below the proper pitch; as, to sing *flat.* — *n.* **1** A level place; a plain; as, a river *flat.* **2** The flat part of something; as, the *flat* of one's hand. **3** A tire from which the air has escaped. **4** In music, a flat tone or note or a sign [♭] meaning that the pitch of a tone or note is to be made lower by a half step. — *v.;* **flat·ted**; **flat·ting**. **1** To make flat; to flatten. **2** In music, to lower in pitch, especially by a half step, or to sing or play below the true pitch.

flat \ˈflat\ *n.* A floor of a building or a number of rooms on one floor, used as a residence; an apartment.

flat·boat \ˈflat-ˌbōt\ *n.* A large, flat-bottomed boat with square ends, used for transporting heavy freight on rivers.

flat·bread \ˈflat-ˌbred\ *n.* A dry Norwegian bread baked on a special stove in thin flat cakes about three feet in diameter.

flat·car \ˈflat-ˌkär, -ˌkȧr\ *n.* A railroad car without sides or roof.

flat·fish \ˈflat-ˌfish\ *n.; pl.* **flat·fish** or **flat·fish·es**. Any of a large group of fishes, including the halibut, flounder, and sole, that swim on one side of a markedly flattened body and have both eyes on the upper side.

flat·iron \ˈflat-ˌīrn\ *n.* An iron for pressing clothes.

flat·ly \ˈflat-lē\ *adv.* In a flat manner; especially, bluntly or positively; as, to refuse *flatly;* to tell someone *flatly* one's opinion of his behavior.

flatted. Past tense and past part. of *flat.*

flat·ten \ˈflat-n\ *v.;* **flat·tened**; **flat·ten·ing** \-n(-)ing\. To make or become flat in surface or position. — **flatten out**. To level off, as an aircraft after a climb or a dive.

flat·ter \ˈflat-r\ *v.;* **flat·tered**; **flat·ter·ing** \ˈflat-r-ing, ˈfla-tring\. **1** To praise too much or without sincerity, in order to gain some advantage or benefit for oneself or to gratify another's vanity. **2** To represent too favorably; as, a picture that *flatters* a person. **3** To judge (oneself) favorably or too favorably, as in respect to an accomplishment or ability; as, a boy who *flattered* himself on his skill as a swimmer. — **flat·ter·er** \-r-r\ *n.*

flatter. Comparative of *flat.*

flat·tery \'flat-r-ē, 'fla-trē\ *n.; pl.* **flat·ter·ies. 1** The act of flattering. **2** Flattering speech or attentions; insincere or excessive praise. — For synonyms see *compliment.*

flattest. Superlative of *flat.*

flatting. Pres. part. of *flat.*

flat·tish \'flat-ish\ *adj.* Somewhat flat.

flat·top \'flat-ˌtäp\ *n. Slang.* An aircraft carrier.

flat·worm \'flat-ˌwərm\ *n.* Any of a large number of worms having a flat ribbon-shaped body, some living in water but most living as parasites in or on animals.

flattop

flaunt \'flȯnt, 'flänt\ *v.* **1** To wave or flutter showily, as a banner. **2** To make an impudent show of something; to parade; as, to *flaunt* one's wealth.

flau·tist \'flȯt-əst, 'flau̇t-\ *n.* A flutist.

fla·vor \'flāv-r\ *n.* **1** Taste; relish; savor; the quality of a thing that affects the taste; as, fruit with a delicious *flavor.* Salt and pepper bring out the natural *flavor* of potatoes. **2** A substance added to food to give it a certain taste; as, to add lemon *flavor.* — *v.;* **fla·vored**; **fla·vor·ing** \-r(-)ing\. To give flavor or relish to; as, to *flavor* a pudding with vanilla; meat too strongly *flavored* with garlic.

fla·vor·ing \'flāv-r(-)ing\ *n.* A substance, as an essence or extract, used to flavor food; as, natural and artificial *flavorings.*

flaw \'flȯ\ *n.* A crack; an imperfect part; a fault; a defect; as, a *flaw* in a plan; a *flaw* in a diamond. — For synonyms see *blemish.* — *v.* To make a flaw in; as, a gem *flawed* by inexpert cutting.

flaw·less \'flȯ-ləs\ *adj.* Without a flaw; perfect. — **flaw·less·ly**, *adv.*

flax \'flaks\ *n.* **1** A slender, erect, blue-flowered plant grown for its fiber and seeds. **2** The fiber of this plant prepared for spinning, to be made into linen.

flax·en \'flaks-n\ *adj.* Made of flax or like flax; especially, like flax in color; of light straw color.

flax·seed \'flak(s)-ˌsēd\ *n.* The seed of the flax, used in medicine and as the source of linseed oil.

flay \'flā\ *v.* **1** To strip off the skin or surface of. **2** To scold severely.

flea \'flē\ *n.* Any of certain small, hard-bodied, wingless, blood-sucking insects with extraordinary powers of leaping.

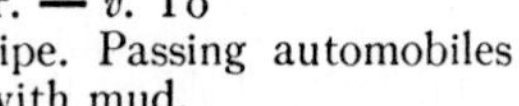

flea

fleck \'flek\ *n.* **1** A small spot, as a freckle; a speck. **2** A flake; as, *flecks* of snow in the air. — *v.* To spot; to streak; to stripe. Passing automobiles *flecked* the pedestrians with mud.

fled. Past tense and past part. of *flee.*

fledge \'flej\ *v.;* **fledged**; **fledg·ing. 1** To develop the feathers necessary for flying. **2** To furnish with feathers; as, to *fledge* an arrow.

fledg·ling or **fledge·ling** \'flej-ling\ *n.* **1** A young bird that has just grown the feathers necessary for flying. **2** A person who is not mature.

flee \'flē\ *v.;* **fled** \'fled\; **flee·ing. 1** To run away, as from danger; to run away from; as, to *flee* before it is too late; to *flee* one's enemies. **2** To pass away swiftly; to vanish. The mist *fled* before the rising sun.

fleece \'flēs\ *n.* The coat of wool that covers a sheep or similar animal. — *v.;* **fleeced**; **fleec·ing. 1** To shear, as a sheep. **2** To strip of money or property by dishonest means; to cheat.

fleecy \'flē-sē\ *adj.;* **fleec·i·er**; **fleec·i·est.** Like fleece; covered with fleece; made of fleece; as, *fleecy* sheep; *fleecy* clouds.

fleet \'flēt\ *adj.* **1** Swift; fast; as, a *fleet* runner. **2** Quickly passing; not enduring. — **fleet·ly**, *adv.*

fleet \'flēt\ *n.* **1** A group of war vessels under one command; a country's navy. **2** Any group of vessels or vehicles that move together or are operated under one management; as, a *fleet* of trucks.

fleet admiral. A naval officer with a grade next higher than that of admiral.

fleet·ing \'flēt-ing\ *adj.* Passing quickly; short-lived; as, *fleeting* hours.

flesh \'flesh\ *n.* **1** The soft parts of an animal's body, especially the muscular parts. **2** These parts used as food; meat. **3** The human body as distinguished from the soul. **4** Mankind; living beings as a group; as, a characteristic common to all *flesh.* **5** Human nature, especially with regard to physical pleasure; as, temptations of the *flesh.* **6** Kindred; stock; as, one of his own *flesh* and blood. **7** The pulp of fruit; the edible part of a fruit or vegetable. **8** The average color of a white person's skin. — *v.* **1** To remove flesh from; as, to *flesh* hides. **2** To put on flesh; to become fleshy; as, to *flesh* up again after discontinuing a rigid diet.

flesh·ly \'flesh-lē\ *adj.;* **flesh·li·er**; **flesh·li·est. 1** Of or relating to the flesh or the body; as, *fleshly* ills. **2** Sensuous; as, *fleshly* pleasures.

flesh·pot \'flesh-ˌpät\ *n.* **1** A pot in which flesh is cooked. **2** [in the plural] Plenty; luxury.

fleshy \'flesh-ē\ *adj.;* **flesh·i·er**; **flesh·i·est. 1** Having to do with flesh; like flesh. **2** Plump; fat; corpulent; as, a *fleshy* person. **3** Juicy or pulpy, like certain fruits.

fleur–de–lis \ˌflər-də-'lē\ *n.; pl.* **fleurs–de–lis** \ˌflər-də-'lēz, ˌflər(z)-də-'lē\. [From French, meaning literally "flower of the lily".] **1** The iris. **2** A design said to have been suggested by the iris flower.

flew. Past tense of *fly.*

flex \'fleks\ *v.* To bend; as, to *flex* the knee.

flex·i·ble \'fleks-əb-l\ *adj.* **1** Bending easily; capable of being bent; not stiff. **2** Easily changed; adaptable; as, *flexible* working hours; a *flexible* mind. — **flex·i·bil·i·ty** \ˌfleks-ə-'bil-ət-ē\ *n.* — **flex·i·bly** \'fleks-ə-blē\ *adv.*

flex·ion \'fleksh-n\ *n.* The action of flexing or bending, especially a muscle.

flex·or \'fleks-r\ *n.* A muscle that bends a part of the body, as the arm.

flex·ure \'fleksh-r\ *n.* **1** A flexing or a being flexed. **2** A turn; a bend; a fold.

flick \'flik\ *n.* **1** A light snapping stroke, as with the lash of a whip; a quick jerk; as, with a *flick* of the wrist. **2** A streak; a daub; as, a *flick* of mud on one's coat. — *v.* **1** To snap; to toss; to whip lightly; as, to *flick* a switch that turns on a light. **2** To dart; to flit. The toad *flicked* out its tongue to catch a fly.

flick·er \'flik-r\ *v.;* **flick·ered; flick·er·ing** \-r(-)ing\. **1** To flutter; to flap the wings without flying. **2** To waver, as a flame in the wind. — *n.* **1** A flickering; a brief interval of brightness; as, a *flicker* of light. **2** A flickering light. **3** A brief stirring; as, a *flicker* of the eyelids; a *flicker* of interest. — **flick·er·ing·ly**, *adv.* — **flick·ery**, *adj.*

flick·er \'flik-r\ *n.* A large insect-eating North American woodpecker with a black crescent on the breast, red on the back of the neck, and yellow shafts on tail feathers and wing feathers.

flied. A past tense and past part. of *fly.*

fli·er or **fly·er** \'flīr\ *n.* **1** A person or thing that flies. **2** An aviator. **3** Something that travels very fast, as an express train. **4** A speculative undertaking; especially, an attempt to gain large profits in a business venture by one who has little knowledge of the facts or who is inexperienced in such dealings. **5** A printed notice or message scattered or distributed in large numbers, as an advertising leaflet.

flies. Pl. of *fly.*

flight \'flīt\ *n.* **1** The act or manner of flying; as, a *flight* in a plane; the *flight* of birds. **2** The distance covered at one time in the air; as, a two-hour *flight.* **3** A number of things that fly through the air together; as, a *flight* of ducks; a *flight* of bombers. **4** A passing above or beyond ordinary limits; as, a *flight* of fancy. **5** A series of stairs from one floor of a building to the next, or from one landing to the next.

flight \'flīt\ *n.* The action of running away or fleeing, as from danger.

flighty \'flīt-ē\ *adj.;* **flight·i·er; flight·i·est.** **1** Subject to flights of fancy; inclined to sudden change of mind. **2** Slightly insane. — **flight·i·ly** \'flīt-l-ē\ *adv.*

flim·sy \'flim-zē\ *adj.;* **flim·si·er; flim·si·est.** Weak; feeble; limp; without strength or solidity; as, *flimsy* furniture; a *flimsy* argument. — **flim·si·ly** \'flimz-l-ē\ *adv.*

flinch \'flinch\ *v.* To draw or shrink back, as from pain or danger; to wince. — *n.* A flinching or wincing.

flin·der \'flind-r\ *n.* Piece; splinter; as, broken to *flinders.*

fling \'fling\ *v.;* **flung** \'fləng\; **fling·ing** \'fling-ing\. **1** To cast or throw from, or as if from, the hand; as, to *fling* stones into a lake. **2** To put or send forcibly; as, to *fling* a man into jail; to *fling* oneself upon a sofa. **3** To extend or toss suddenly; as, to *fling* back the head. **4** To rush hastily; as, to *fling* out of a room. — For synonyms see *throw.* — *n.* **1** A throwing, flinging, or hurling; as, to give a stone a *fling.* **2** A try; as, to have a *fling* at painting. **3** A time of freedom for pleasure; as, to feel that one deserves a little *fling.* **4** A lively dance of Scotland.

flint \'flint\ *n.* **1** A grayish or dark extremely hard quartz, which produces fire when struck with steel. **2** A piece of this quartz used for striking fire. **3** Anything hard and unyielding like this quartz; as, a heart of *flint.*

flint·lock \'flint-ˌläk\ *n.* **1** An old-fashioned firearm using a flint for striking a spark to fire the charge. **2** The lock of such a firearm.

flinty \'flint-ē\ *adj.;* **flint·i·er; flint·i·est.** Made of flint; like flint; stony; very hard; a person with a *flinty* heart; a *flinty* soil. — **flint·i·ly** \'flint-l-ē\ *adv.*

flip \'flip\ *v.;* **flipped; flip·ping.** **1** To turn by tossing; as, to *flip* a coin. **2** To turn quickly; as, to *flip* the pages of a book. **3** To flick; to jerk; as, to *flip* a light switch. — *n.* A toss; a flick.

flip \'flip\ *adj.* Flippant; pert; as, a *flip* reply.

flip·pan·cy \'flip-n-sē\ *n.; pl.* **flip·pan·cies.** The state or quality of being flippant; trifling gaiety.

flip·pant \'flip-nt\ *adj.* Treating lightly something serious or worthy of respect; lacking earnestness; saucy. — **flip·pant·ly**, *adv.*

flip·per \'flip-r\ *n.* **1** A broad, flat limb adapted for swimming, as in seals and whales. **2** *Slang.* The hand.

flirt \'flərt\ *v.* **1** To toss or move quickly about; as, to *flirt* a fan. **2** To play at lovemaking. **3** To dally; as, to *flirt* with an idea. — *n.* **1** The action of flirting; a quick throw or movement. **2** A person who flirts.

flir·ta·tion \flər-'tāsh-n\ *n.* **1** A playing at courtship. **2** A coquettish love affair. — **flir·ta·tious** \-'tā-shəs\ *adj.*

flit \'flit\ *v.;* **flit·ted; flit·ting.** To pass swiftly; to dart; to flutter. The bird *flits* from tree to tree. — *n.* The action or motion of flitting.

fliv·ver \'fliv-r\ *n.* Anything that is small and cheap; especially, a small low-priced automobile.

float \'flōt\ *n.* **1** Anything that rests on the top of a liquid, as a raft. **2** A hollow ball that controls the flow or level of the liquid it floats on, as in a tank or cistern. **3** A platform on wheels used to carry a display in a parade; this decorated vehicle and the display it carries. **4** A cork or other floating object on a fishing line to hold up the part of the line leading to the bait and to show when a fish is biting. — *v.* **1** To rest on or in a liquid or air. **2** To drift along on, or as if on, water; to move gently

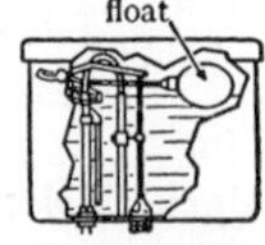

toilet tank cut away to show float

along. Dust *floats* through the air. **3** To cause to float; as, to *float* logs down the river.

flock \'fläk\ *n.* **1** A number of animals or birds of one kind living together or kept together; as, a *flock* of sheep; a *flock* of geese. **2** Any group over which someone watches; as, a minister's *flock.* — *v.* To gather or move in crowds. The whole town *flocked* to the circus.

floe \'flō\ *n.* A sheet or mass of floating ice.

flog \'fläg\ *v.;* **flogged; flog·ging.** To beat with a rod or whip; to whip severely.

flood \'fləd\ *n.* **1** A great flow of water that rises and spreads over the land. **2** The flowing in of the tide. **3** A great quantity of anything; a great stream or flow of any kind; as, a *flood* of letters or of light. — *v.* **1** To overflow with water; to cause to be covered with water; as, a river that *floods* every spring. Sometimes fields are *flooded* to help certain crops grow. **2** To fill as if with a flood; to supply abundantly or excessively; as, a room *flooded* with light. The teacher was *flooded* with papers to be graded.

flood·gate \'fləd-ˌgāt\ *n.* A gate used to keep out or let in a body of water or to regulate its flow, as in a canal.

flood·light \'fləd-ˌlīt\ *n.* **1** A bright, broad beam of light. **2** A lighting unit with a reflector for projecting a broad beam.

flood·plain \'fləd-ˌplān\ *n.* **1** Flat land that may be submerged by watercourses at flood stage. **2** A plain built up from deposits of earth by flood waters.

flood tide. **1** The tide while rising or at its greatest height. **2** A great stream or flow of any kind; as, a *flood tide* of troubles. **3** The highest point; as, a writer whose genius was at *flood tide.*

flood·wa·ter \'fləd-ˌwȯt-r, -ˌwät-r\ *n.* The water of a flood.

floor \'flōr, 'flȯr\ *n.* **1** The bottom of a room, on which one stands. **2** Any ground surface; as, the ocean *floor;* the *floor* of a forest. **3** A story of a building. The elevator goes to the tenth *floor.* **4** The main part of a hall as distinguished from the balcony. **5** The right to speak from one's place in the hall. The senator has the *floor.* — *v.* **1** To cover or provide with a floor; to pave; as, to *floor* a garage with cement. **2** To knock down or throw to the ground; as, a boxer *floored* in the first round. **3** To silence or defeat. The puzzle *floored* the boy.

floor·ing \'flōr-ing, 'flȯr-\ *n.* **1** A floor or floors. **2** Material for floors.

floor·walk·er \'flōr-ˌwȯk-r, 'flȯr-\ *n.* A man employed in a large retail store to oversee the sales force and to aid customers.

flop \'fläp\ *v.;* **flopped; flop·ping.** **1** To flap about; as, a fish *flopping* on the deck; the brim of a hat *flopping* in the wind. **2** To throw oneself heavily or awkwardly; as, to *flop* into a chair. **3** To fail. In spite of all efforts to make it a success, the play *flopped.* — *n.* **1** The act or sound of flopping. **2** A failure.

flo·ra \'flōr-ə, 'flȯr-ə\ *n.* The plants of a particular region or period.

flo·ral \'flōr-əl, 'flȯr-\ *adj.* Of or relating to flowers; like flowers; as, a *floral* pattern in wallpaper.

flo·ret \'flōr-ət, 'flȯr-\ *n.* A small flower; especially, one of the small flowers that make up the head in composite plants, as the daisy.

flor·id \'flȯr-əd, 'flär-\ *adj.* **1** Flowery; elaborately adorned; overdecorated; as, *florid* dress; *florid* writing. **2** Bright in color; flushed with red; as, a *florid* complexion.

flor·in \'flȯr-ən, 'flär-\ *n.* A European coin varying, with time and place used, in composition and value; especially, the British silver two-shilling piece.

flo·rist \'flōr-əst, 'flȯr-\ *n.* A person who raises or deals in flowers and other plants.

floss \'flȯs, 'fläs\ *n.* **1** Untwisted silk thread, used in embroidery. **2** Also **dental floss.** A waxed thread used to clean between the teeth. **3** A soft, fluffy, silky substance.

flo·ta·tion \flō-'tāsh-n\ *n.* The act or state of floating.

flo·til·la \flō-'til-ə\ *n.* A small fleet or a fleet of small vessels.

flot·sam \'fläts-m\ *n.* Rubbish or debris, especially that from the wreckage of a ship, found on or near the water.

flounce \'flau̇n(t)s\ *v.;* **flounced; flounc·ing.** **1** To move oneself about this way and that with a jerky motion; to flop. **2** To fling oneself suddenly, as in anger. — *n.* A flouncing movement.

flounce \'flau̇n(t)s\ *n.* A strip of fabric gathered or pleated and stitched to the edge of something, as a skirt. — *v.;* **flounced; flounc·ing.** To decorate with a flounce or flounces.

floun·der \'flau̇nd-r\ *n.; pl.* **floun·der** or **floun·ders.** A flatfish.

floun·der \'flau̇nd-r\ *v.;* **floun·dered; floun·der·ing** \-r(-)ing\. To struggle in a clumsy manner; to move or to progress in a clumsy, struggling fashion; as, a ship *floundering* through a stormy sea; to *flounder* through deep snow. — *n.* A floundering movement.

flour \'flau̇r\ *n.* [From medieval English, meaning literally "flower", that is "the flower or best part of the grain" — see *flower.*] The finely ground powdery meal of any grain, especially wheat. — *v.* To cover with flour; as, dough rolled on a *floured* board.

flour·ish \'flər-ish, 'flə-rish\ *v.* **1** To grow vigorously; to thrive; to prosper. Plants will *flourish* in this rich soil. **2** To make sweeping movements, as with a pen or sword. — For synonyms see *brandish.* — *n.* **1** A brilliant musical passage; a fanfare; as, a *flourish* of drums. **2** A sweeping movement; as, handwriting with many *flourishes.* The visitor removed his hat with a *flourish.*

floury \'flau̇r-ē\ *adj.;* **flour·i·er; flour·i·est.** **1** Of or relating to flour; like flour. **2** Covered with flour.

flout \'flau̇t\ *v.* **1** To mock, insult, or jeer at. **2** To treat with contemptuous disregard; as, to *flout* authority by openly disobeying the school's regulations.

flow \'flō\ *v.* **1** To move as water does; to run; to stream. **2** To glide along smoothly; to be easily and smoothly done or spoken. The speaker's words *flowed* on. **3** To rise, as the tide. **4** To hang loose and waving; as, a flag *flowing* in the breeze. **5** To pass in a way that seems like a stream. Heavy traffic *flowed* over the bridge. — *n.* **1** A flowing. **2** A smooth, even movement, as of thought or music. **3** A stream; a current; anything that seems to move like a stream; as, the *flow* of traffic. **4** The rising of the tide. **5** The amount that flows at any time; as, to measure the *flow* of water over a dam.

flow·er \'flau̇r\ *n.* [From medieval English *flour,* there borrowed from Old French, where it was derived from Latin *flor-*, stem of *flos* meaning "flower" — see *flour.*] **1** The part of a plant that normally bears the seed; a blossom; a bloom. **2** A plant grown chiefly for its blossoms. **3** The finest and best part or example of anything. A country's young people are sometimes called the *flower* of the nation. **4** The time when energies and abilities are at their best; a time of flowering; as, to be in the *flower* of youth. **5** In botany, any modified branch or shoot which produces seeds or spores, as the cone of scale leaves in the pine or the tassel and silk of corn. — *v.* **1** To blossom; to bloom; to produce flowers. **2** To come into the finest or best condition or period; to flourish. — *adj.* Of or relating to a flower; of or for flowers; as, a *flower* bed; a *flower* show.

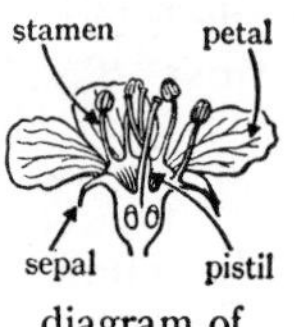

diagram of a flower

flow·ered \'flau̇rd\ *adj.* **1** Having or bearing flowers. **2** Decorated with flowers or flowerlike figures or patterns; as, *flowered* silk.

flow·er·et \'flau̇r-ət\ *n.* A small flower; a floret.

flow·er·ing \'flau̇r-ing\ *adj.* **1** In bloom; blossoming. **2** Having showy flowers; as, *flowering* dogwood.

flow·er·pot \'flau̇r-ˌpät\ *n.* A pot in which to grow plants.

flow·ery \'flau̇r-ē\ *adj.;* **flow·er·i·er**; **flow·er·i·est. 1** Full of flowers; covered with flowers. **2** Full of fine words or phrases; florid; as, *flowery* language.

flown. Past part. of *fly.*

flu \'flü\ *n.* Influenza.

fluc·tu·ate \'flək-chə-ˌwāt\ *v.;* **fluc·tu·at·ed**; **fluc·tu·at·ing. 1** To move up and down or back and forth like a wave. **2** To be constantly changing, as between two points, levels, or conditions; to rise and fall; to waver; as, *fluctuating* temperatures; to *fluctuate* in one's mind between hope and fear. — **fluc·tu·a·tion** \ˌflək-chə-'wāsh-n\ *n.*

flue \'flü\ *n.* An enclosed passage for smoke or air, as in a chimney.

flu·en·cy \'flü-ən-sē\ *n.* The quality of being fluent, especially in speech; easy flow; smoothness; as, to learn to speak a foreign language with *fluency.*

flu·ent \'flü-ənt\ *adj.* **1** Flowing or capable of flowing; liquid. **2** Smoothly and easily uttered; as, *fluent* speech; to speak *fluent* French. **3** Ready or easy in the use of words; as, a *fluent* speaker. — **flu·ent·ly**, *adv.*

fluff \'fləf\ *n.* **1** Down or nap, as from cotton or fur. **2** A light, soft mass, as of dust. — *v.* To make or become fluffy; to puff out into a soft, yielding mass; as, to *fluff* up a pillow.

fluffy \'fləf-ē\ *adj.;* **fluff·i·er**; **fluff·i·est.** Covered or filled with fluff; soft and downy like fluff; as, the *fluffy* fur of a kitten.

flu·id \'flü-əd\ *adj.* **1** Capable of flowing like a liquid or a gas; liquid or gaseous; as, to be in a *fluid* condition. **2** Flowing; smooth; as, the *fluid* movements of a dancer; *fluid* speech. — *n.* A substance that is capable of flowing, as water, steam, or air; a liquid or a gas.

flu·id·i·ty \flü-'id-ət-ē\ *n.* The quality or condition of being fluid; ability to flow.

fluke \'flük\ *n.* **1** A flatfish. **2** Any of various flattened parasitic worms.

fluke \'flük\ *n.* **1** The part of an anchor designed to catch in the ground. **2** A barb, as on a harpoon or lance. **3** Either of the two parts, or lobes, of a whale's tail.

fluke \'flük\ *n.* An accidental stroke of luck; any lucky stroke, shot, or hit; as, to win by a *fluke.* — **fluky** \'flük-ē\ *adj.*

flume \'flüm\ *n.* **1** A ravine or gorge with a stream running through it. **2** An inclined channel for carrying water from a distance, as for power or irrigation.

flung. Past tense and past part. of *fling.*

flunk \'fləngk\ *v.* To fail, especially in an examination or test. — **flunk out.** To dismiss or be dismissed from a school or college for failure. — *n.* A failure.

flunky or **flunk·ey** \'fləngk-ē\ *n.; pl.* **flunk·ies** or **flunk·eys. 1** A servant in livery; especially, a footman. **2** A person who fawns upon another; a toady.

flu·o·res·cence \flür-'es-n(t)s\ *n.* **1** The giving off by certain substances when exposed to ultraviolet rays, or in the case of some substances to X rays, of light of a color different from their own. **2** The light so produced. **3** The property of such substances to give off light in this way.

flu·o·res·cent \flür-'es-nt\ *adj.* Having or showing fluorescence.

fluorescent lamp. A tubular electric lamp in which light is produced on the fluorescent coating of the inner surface of the tube by the action of ultraviolet light.

flu·o·ri·date \'flür-ə-ˌdāt\ *v.;* **flu·o·ri·dat·ed**; **flu·o·ri·dat·ing.** To treat with a fluoride; as, to *fluoridate* drinking water for the purpose of retarding tooth decay. — **flu·o·ri·da·tion** \ˌflür-ə-'dāsh-n\ *n.*

flu·o·ride \'flür-ˌīd\ *n.* A compound of fluorine with another chemical element or radical.

flu·o·rine \ˈflu̇r-ˌēn, -ən\ *n.* A chemical element of the chlorine family, a strong-smelling greenish-yellow gas.

flu·o·ro·scope \ˈflu̇r-ə-ˌskōp\ *n.* An instrument for studying an object by observing light and shadows produced on a screen by the action of X rays passing through the object, useful in examining inner parts of the body, as the lungs.

flur·ry \ˈflər-ē, ˈflə-rē\ *n.; pl.* **flur·ries.** **1** A sudden, brief disturbance of the air, as a light gust of wind or a brief fall of snow accompanied by wind. **2** Nervous commotion; bustle; as, a *flurry* of excitement. — *v.;* **flur·ried** \ˈflər-ēd, ˈflə-rēd\; **flur·ry·ing.** To excite or agitate; to fluster.

flush \ˈfləsh\ *v.* **1** To become overspread suddenly, as with color; as, to *flush* with pleasure. **2** To blush. **3** To show red; to glow. **4** To pour water freely over or through something; to clean or wash out by a rush of liquid. **5** To make red or glowing; as, a face *flushed* with anger. A sunset *flushed* the sky. **6** To enliven; to stir; as, troops *flushed* with victory. — *n.* **1** A glow or tinge of red; a blush. **2** A sudden rush, as of water. **3** A sudden rush of feeling; as, a *flush* of triumph. **4** Vigor; as, in the *flush* of youth. **5** A fit of extreme heat, as in a fever.

flush \ˈfləsh\ *adj.* **1** Fully supplied with something, especially money. **2** Unbroken in surface or even with the surface that joins it; level; as, a *flush* door; a river *flush* with its banks. — *adv.* So as to be level; without break; straight.

flush \ˈfləsh\ *v.* To start up or cause to start up suddenly, as a game bird from the ground; as, to *flush* a partridge.

flus·ter \ˈfləst-r\ *v.;* **flus·tered; flus·ter·ing** \-r(-)ing\. To confuse; to make nervous and unsure; as, to be *flustered* by the unexpected laughter of some friends. — *n.* A state of nervous confusion.

flute \ˈflüt\ *n.* **1** A musical instrument in the form of a hollow slender tube open at only one end, played by blowing across a hole near the closed end. **2** A channel or groove, as in the surface of an architectural column. — *v.;* **flut·ed; flut·ing.** **1** To play on a flute. **2** To make a sound like that of a flute. **3** To form flutes, or grooves, in.

flute

flut·ed \ˈflüt-əd\ *adj.* **1** Flutelike; clear and mellow; as, *fluted* notes. **2** Decorated with flutes; grooved.

flut·ing \ˈflüt-ing\ *n.* **1** The act of one who flutes. **2** Decoration by means of flutes or grooves; as, the *fluting* of a carved table leg.

flut·ist \ˈflüt-əst\ *n.* A flute player.

flut·ter \ˈflət-r\ *v.* **1** To move the wings rapidly without flying at all or else flying in short flights. Butterflies *flutter.* **2** To move with a quick to-and-fro motion; to wave, shake, or vibrate rapidly back and forth. A flag *flutters* in the wind. **3** To move about with great bustle and show but without accomplishing much. **4** To agitate or confuse; to fluster. — *n.* **1** A fluttering; a quick waving back and forth; as, the *flutter* of a fan; a *flutter* of wings. **2** A state of agitation or confusion; as, to be in a *flutter* over nothing. — **flut·tery,** *adj.*

flux \ˈfləks\ *n.* **1** An excessive fluid discharge from the body, as from the bowels. **2** A continuous moving on or passing by, as of a flowing stream. **3** A series of changes or a state of continuous change. **4** A substance, as limestone, used to assist the fusing together of metals or minerals. — *v.* To melt or fuse with some other substance; to treat with a flux.

fly \ˈflī\ *v.;* **flew** \ˈflü\; **flown** \ˈflōn\; **fly·ing.** **1** To move in the air or to pass through it with wings, as a bird. **2** To operate or travel in an airplane. **3** To run away; to flee. **4** To move through the air or before the wind; as, paper *flying* in all directions. **5** To go or pass swiftly; as, to *fly* to the rescue. **6** To float or wave, or to cause to float or wave, in the air; as, flags *flying* in the breeze; to *fly* a kite. **7** To seem to pass rapidly. Time *flies.* **8** *Past tense and past part.* **flied** \ˈflīd\. In baseball, to hit a fly. **9** To journey over by flying; as, to *fly* the Atlantic. **10** To carry by air; as, to *fly* passengers. — *n.; pl.* **flies** \ˈflīz\. **1** A flap of material to cover a fastening in a garment. **2** The outer canvas of a tent that has a double roof. **3** The length of an extended flag from its staff or the outer end of a flag. **4** In baseball, a ball batted high in the air. **5** [in the plural] In theaters, the space over the stage.

fly \ˈflī\ *n.; pl.* **flies.** **1** A winged insect. **2** Any of a group of mostly two-winged insects including horseflies, houseflies, and mosquitoes; especially, a housefly. **3** A fishhook dressed to look like a fly.

fly, 3

fly·blown \ˈflī-ˌblōn\ *adj.* Infested with the eggs or larvae of the blowfly; tainted; spoiled.

fly·catch·er \ˈflī-ˌkach-r, -ˌkech-r\ *n.* A small bird that feeds on insects that it captures in the air.

flyer. Variant of *flier.*

fly·ing \ˈflī-ing\ *n.* The action of one that flies. — *adj.* **1** Passing through the air with or as if with wings; as, *flying* sparks from a fire. **2** Hasty; fast; temporary; as, to make a *flying* trip to the store before dinner.

flying boat. A seaplane with a hull built for floating.

flying buttress. A projecting arched structure to support a wall or building.

flying fish. A fish with large fins that enable it to jump from the water and move for some distance through the air.

flying machine. An apparatus for navigating the air; especially, an airplane.

flying saucer. Any of various unidentified moving objects repeatedly reported as seen in the air, usually said to be shaped like a saucer or a disk.

flying squirrel. A squirrel that has parachutelike

folds of skin connecting the fore and hind legs, enabling it to make long leaps.

fly·leaf \'flī-ˌlēf\ *n.; pl.* **fly·leaves** \-ˌlēvz\. A blank leaf at the beginning or end of a book.

fly·pa·per \'flī-ˌpäp-r\ *n.* Poisoned paper or paper coated with a sticky substance for killing or catching flies.

fly·speck \'flī-ˌspek\ *n.* **1** A spot left by a fly on a surface. **2** Any very small spot. — *v.* To soil with flyspecks.

fly·way \'flī-ˌwā\ *n.* An air route followed by birds that move regularly from one part of the country to another.

fly·wheel \'flī-ˌhwēl\ *n.* A heavy wheel that regulates the speed of certain machinery.

foal \'fōl\ *n.* The young of animals of the horse family. — *v.* To give birth to a foal.

foam \'fōm\ *n.* Whitish stuff, made of small bubbles, that sometimes forms on liquids, or in the mouths or on the skins of animals; froth. — *v.* To form foam; to froth; as, waves breaking and *foaming* on a beach.

foam rubber. A spongy substance made of real or artificial rubber with many tiny air bubbles spread throughout it, widely used in mattresses, pillows, and upholstery.

foamy \'fō-mē\ *adj.;* **foam·i·er**; **foam·i·est**. Full of or like foam; covered with foam; as, water *foamy* with soapsuds; a collar of *foamy* lace.

fob \'fäb\ *n.* **1** A watch chain or ribbon, especially one hanging from a small watch pocket near the waistband in trousers. **2** A small ornament worn on a watch chain.

F.O.B. \'ef-ˌō-'bē\. Abbreviation for *free on board.*

fo·cal \'fōk-l\ *adj.* Of or relating to a focus.

fo'c'sle \'fōks-l\. Short for *forecastle.*

fo·cus \'fōk-əs\ *n.; pl.* **fo·cus·es** \-ə-səz\ or **fo·ci** \'fō-ˌsī\. **1** A point at which rays, as of light, heat, or sound, meet after being reflected or bent, or from which they diverge or appear to diverge. **2** The point at which an optical image is formed. **3** The distance, as from a lens or mirror, to the point where the rays from it come together. **4** An adjustment, as of a person's eyes or glasses, that gives clear vision; as, to bring into *focus.* **5** A central point; the center, as of interest or activity; as, to be the *focus* of everybody's attention. **6** The place of origin of an earthquake. — *v.;* **fo·cused** or **fo·cussed**; **fo·cus·ing** or **fo·cus·sing**. **1** To bring to a focus; as, to *focus* light rays. **2** To adjust the focus, as of the eyes or a lens; as, to *focus* a telescope. **3** To center; to concentrate; as, to *focus* one's attention. **4** To come to a focus. All eyes *focused* on the plane overhead.

fod·der \'fäd-r\ *n.* Coarse food, as hay and cornstalks, for horses, cattle, and sheep.

foe \'fō\ *n.* An enemy; especially, an enemy in war.

foetus. Variant of *fetus.*

fog \'fóg, 'fäg\ *n.* **1** Fine particles of water suspended in the air at or near the ground; a cloud at ground level. **2** Any cloudiness in the air. **3** A bewildered state. — *v.;* **fogged**; **fog·ging**. **1** To cover or be covered with fog; to cloud. **2** To bewilder or confuse.

fog·gy \'fóg-ē, 'fäg-ē\ *adj.;* **fog·gi·er**; **fog·gi·est**. **1** Thick with fog; filled with fog; misty. **2** Not clear; muddled; confused; as, *foggy* ideas.

fog·horn \'fóg-ˌhórn, 'fäg-\ *n.* A horn sounded in foggy weather to warn ships.

fo·gy \'fō-gē\ *n.; pl.* **fo·gies**. A person who is behind the times; a dull person.

foi·ble \'fóib-l\ *n.* A minor failing or weak point in a person's character; as, a likable boy in spite of a few *foibles.*

foil \'fóil\ *v.* To get the better of; to outwit. The hero of a story is expected to *foil* the villain. — *n.* A long, thin, blunted sword used in fencing.

foil \'fóil\ *n.* **1** A very thin sheet of metal; as, tin or aluminum *foil.* **2** A thin leaf of polished and colored metal used in jewelry to give color and brilliancy to paste and inferior stones. **3** Something that contrasts sharply with another thing, usually setting it off either to advantage or to disadvantage. The light, gay passage served as a *foil* to the somber music which followed it.

foist \'fóist\ *v.* To pass off something false as genuine; as, to *foist* worthless goods on a buyer.

fold \'fōld\ *v.* **1** To double something over itself; as, to *fold* a blanket. **2** To clasp together; as, to *fold* one's hands. **3** To lay close to the body; as, birds *folding* their wings. **4** To enclose in or as if in a fold or folds; to wrap by folding into something; as, a letter with a circular *folded* in it. **5** To embrace; as, a small girl *folding* her doll in her arms. — *n.* A doubling of something over on itself; a part of something laid over on another part; as, the *folds* of a blanket.

fold \'fōld\ *n.* **1** A pen for sheep. **2** A flock of sheep. — *v.* To pen up in an enclosed piece of land; as, to *fold* sheep.

-fold \ˌfōld, 'fōld\. A suffix that can mean: having so many parts or multiplied so many times, as in *twofold* or *manifold.*

fold·er \'fōld-r\ *n.* **1** A person or thing that folds. **2** A small booklet of folded but unstitched sheets; as, a railroad *folder;* a *folder* on vacation trips. **3** A sheet of cardboard or heavy paper folded in half and used for holding loose papers.

fo·li·age \'fō-lē-ij, 'fō-lij, 'fōl-yij\ *n.* The leaves of a plant or tree; leafage. — **fo·li·aged** \-jd\ *adj.*

fo·lio \'fō-lē-ˌō, 'fōl-ˌyō\ *n.; pl.* **fo·li·os**. **1** A leaf of a book or a manuscript. **2** A book made of sheets each folded once, making two leaves or four pages; a book of the largest size. — *adj.* Formed of sheets each folded once; as, a *folio* edition.

folk \'fōk\ *n.; pl.* **folk** or **folks**. **1** A group of people forming a tribe or nation. **2** People in general; persons as a group; as, country *folk;* old *folks.* **3** The persons of one's own family; as, to visit one's *folks.* — *adj.* Of, relating to, or originating among the common people and handed down from age to age; as, *folk* dances; *folk* songs.

folk·lore \'fōk-ˌlōr, -ˌlȯr\ *n.* Customs, beliefs, stories, and sayings of a people handed down from generation to generation.

fol·li·cle \'fäl-ik-l\ *n.* **1** A dry one-celled fruit developing from a single ovary, which splits open by one seam only when ripe, as in the peony, larkspur, and milkweed. **2** In the body, a small cavity. A **hair follicle** is the depression from which a hair grows. — **fol·lic·u·lar** \fə-'lik-yəl-r\ *adj.*

fol·low \'fäl-ō\ *v.* **1** To go or come after. Night *follows* day. **2** To take as a leader; to obey; as, to *follow* one's conscience; to *follow* instructions. **3** To pursue; as, to *follow* a clue. **4** To proceed along; as, to *follow* a path. **5** To attend upon closely, as a business or profession; as, to *follow* the sea. **6** To come after in order, as of rank or natural sequence. Two *follows* one. **7** To keep one's eyes or attention fixed on something; as, to *follow* a speech; to *follow* a lesson. **8** To result from. Disaster *followed* the general's blunder.

— The words *pursue* and *chase* are synonyms of *follow: follow* is a general term for coming behind another in action or thought but suggests little about the manner or attitude of the follower; *pursue* usually describes an eager, persistent, or determined following in order to overtake or to attain some desired end; *chase* usually suggests a hostile following either to capture or to drive away.

fol·low·er \'fäl-ə-wər\ *n.* **1** One that follows, as a pursuer. **2** A supporter; as, a politician and his *followers.* **3** An attendant; as, the *followers* of the king.

fol·low·ing \'fäl-ə-wing\ *n.* The group of a person's followers, adherents, or attendants. — *adj.* Next; succeeding, as in order or time; as, the *following* day.

fol·ly \'fäl-ē\ *n.; pl.* **fol·lies. 1** The state of being foolish; lack of good sense. **2** A foolish act or idea; silly conduct; foolishness; as, the *follies* of one's youth. **3** An unprofitable undertaking; especially, a building left unfinished because of its cost.

fo·ment \fō-'ment\ *v.* **1** To bathe, as a wound or swelling, with warm water or a medicinal liquid. **2** To stir up; to rouse; as, to *foment* trouble; to *foment* a rebellion. — **fo·men·ta·tion** \ˌfō-mən-'tāsh-n, -ˌmen-\ *n.* — **fo·ment·er** \fō-'ment-r\ *n.*

fond \'fänd\ *adj.* **1** Greatly pleased; desirous; prizing highly; as, *fond* of praise. **2** Foolishly loving. **3** Affectionate; loving; tender; as, a *fond* mother; a *fond* embrace. **4** Cherished; doted on; as, *fond* hopes of success. — **be fond of.** To take pleasure in; to like greatly; to have an affection for. — **fond·ly,** *adv.*

fon·dant \'fän-dənt\ *n.* A creamy preparation of sugar commonly used as the basis of candy.

fon·dle \'fänd-l\ *v.;* **fon·dled; fon·dling** \-l(-)ing\. To touch or handle in a tender or loving manner; to caress; to pet; as, to *fondle* a kitten.

fond·ness \'fän(d)-nəs\ *n.* Affection; liking; as, to have a great *fondness* for animals.

font \'fänt\ *n.* In printing, an assortment of type of one size and style.

font \'fänt\ *n.* **1** A deep basin, commonly of stone, to hold water for baptizing. **2** A basin smaller than this, for holy water. **3** A fountain; a spring; a source; as, a *font* of knowledge.

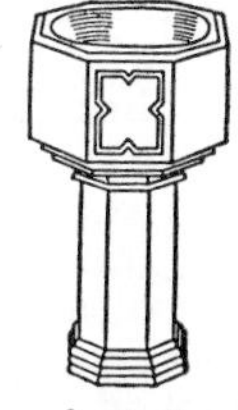
font, 1

food \'füd\ *n.* **1** Material containing carbohydrates, fats, proteins, and supplementary substances that is taken into the animal body to support growth and other life processes and to supply energy. **2** Inorganic material absorbed by plants. **3** Organic material produced by green plants and used like animal food. **4** Nourishment in a solid form, as contrasted with drink. **5** Anything that nourishes or sustains.

food·stuff \'füd-ˌstəf\ *n.* A substance with food value; a nutrient.

fool \'fül\ *n.* **1** A person who lacks sense or judgment; as, a risk that only a *fool* would take. **2** A person formerly kept, especially in royal courts, to amuse people with such devices as seemingly nonsensical remarks and actions; a jester. — *v.* **1** To act like a fool; to be silly. **2** To spend time idling; as, to *fool* around instead of working. **3** To tamper, especially by making unwanted changes; to tinker; as, to *fool* with an engine. **4** To deceive; to trick; as, to be *fooled* by flattery. — **fool away.** To spend idly or foolishly; as, to *fool away* time.

fool·ery \'fül-r(-)ē\ *n.; pl.* **fool·er·ies. 1** The habit of fooling; the behavior of a fool. School is no place for *foolery.* **2** A foolish act; horseplay.

fool·har·dy \'fül-ˌhärd-ē, -ˌhȧrd-ē\ *adj.;* **fool·har·di·er; fool·har·di·est.** Foolishly daring; rash. — **fool·har·di·ness** \-ē-nəs\ *n.*

fool·ish \'fü-lish\ *adj.* Showing or arising from folly or poor judgment; silly. — **fool·ish·ly,** *adv.*

fool·ish·ness \'fü-lish-nəs\ *n.* **1** The condition of being foolish. **2** Foolish behavior.

fool·proof \'fül-'prüf\ *adj.* So simple, plain, or reliable as to leave no opportunity for error, misuse, or failure; as, *foolproof* directions.

fools·cap \'fülz-ˌkap\ *n.* [Named after the watermark in the form of a dunce's cap once used on paper of this type.] Paper in sheets approximately 13 inches wide and 16 or 17 inches long.

fool's gold \'fülz\. Pyrites of iron or copper.

foot \'fu̇t\ *n.; pl.* **feet** \'fēt\. **1** The part of the leg below the ankle; that part of an animal on which it stands or moves. **2** A measure of length; one third of a yard, or 12 inches. **3** Something like a foot in position or use; bottom; as, the *foot* of a mountain; the *foot* of the class. **4** A group of syllables marked off as forming a unit in a line of poetry. **5** Foot soldiers; infantry; as, a regiment of *foot.* — *v.* **1** To run, walk, or dance; as, to *foot* it to town. **2** To add up the numbers in a column. **3** To pay; as, to *foot* the bill for the crowd.

foot·ball \'fu̇t-ˌbȯl\ *n.* **1** A ball usually made of a bladder or bag put in a leather covering and blown up tight, for use in certain games. **2** A game played with such a ball.

foot·board \'fu̇t-ˌbōrd, -ˌbȯrd\ *n.* **1** A board or narrow platform on which to stand or to brace the feet. **2** The upright section forming the foot of a bed.

foot·bridge \'fu̇t-ˌbrij\ *n.* A bridge for foot passengers.

foot-can·dle \'fu̇t-'kand-l\ *n.* In physics, a unit for measuring illumination, consisting of the illumination on a surface all parts of which are one foot from a light of one international candle.

foot·ed \'fu̇t-əd\ *adj.* **1** Having a foot or feet. **2** Having feet of the number or kind stated or described, as in *barefooted* or *four-footed.*

foot·fall \'fu̇t-ˌfȯl\ *n.* A footstep or its sound.

foot·hill \'fu̇t-ˌhil\ *n.* A hill near the bottom of higher hills.

foot·hold \'fu̇t-ˌhōld\ *n.* A place where a person may stand; a footing.

foot·ing \'fu̇t-ing\ *n.* **1** The placing of one's feet in a position to secure a firm or safe stand. **2** A place for the foot to rest on; a foothold; as, to gain a *footing.* **3** A basis for operation. **4** A moving on foot; a walk; a tread; a dance. **5** Material for making the feet, as of socks. **6** The action of putting a foot to anything. **7** The position that one person or group occupies with relation to another person or group; as, nations on a friendly *footing.* **8** The action of adding up a column of figures. **9** The total amount of such a column.

foot·lights \'fu̇t-ˌlīts\ *n. pl.* **1** A row of lights in front of the stage in a theater. **2** The stage; the theater, especially as a profession; as, the lure of the *footlights.*

foot-loose \'fu̇t-ˌlüs\ *adj.* Free; without ties; unrestrained.

foot·man \'fu̇t-mən\ *n.; pl.* **foot·men** \-mən\. A male servant with duties such as waiting on table and admitting visitors.

foot·note \'fu̇t-ˌnōt\ *n.* A note at the bottom of a page, as in a book.

foot·pad \'fu̇t-ˌpad\ *n.* A highwayman or robber on foot.

foot·path \'fu̇t-ˌpath\ *n.; pl.* **foot·paths** \-ˌpat͟hz\. A path for people on foot.

foot-pound \'fu̇t-'pau̇nd\ *n.* A unit of energy or work equal to the work done in raising one pound avoirdupois against gravity to the height of one foot.

foot·print \'fu̇t-ˌprint\ *n.* The print or impression of the foot.

foot·rest \'fu̇t-ˌrest\ *n.* A support for the feet.

foot soldier. An infantryman.

foot·sore \'fu̇t-ˌsōr, -ˌsȯr\ *adj.* Having sore or tender feet from much walking.

foot·step \'fu̇t-ˌstep\ *n.* **1** A step or tread of the foot; a footfall. **2** The distance covered in one step. **3** A footprint; a track. **4** A step on which to go up or down.

foot·stool \'fu̇t-ˌstül\ *n.* A low stool to support a person's feet.

foot·wear \'fu̇t-ˌwar, -ˌwer\ *n.* Anything to be worn on the feet; especially, shoes, slippers, and boots.

foot·work \'fu̇t-ˌwərk\ *n.* The management of the feet, as in boxing and tennis.

foo·zle \'füz-l\ *v.;* **foo·zled**; **foo·zling** \-l(-)ing\. To bungle; to manage or play unskillfully; as, to *foozle* a stroke in tennis. — *n.* A bungling action.

fop \'fäp\ *n.* A man who is vain about his dress or appearance; a dandy. — **fop·pish** \-ish\ *adj.*

fop·pery \'fäp-r(-)ē\ *n.; pl.* **fop·per·ies.** Anything characteristic of a fop, as behavior or dress.

for \fər, (')fȯr\ *prep.* **1** In preparation towards; as, to dress *for* dinner. **2** With the purpose of; as, money *for* study. **3** With the purpose of getting or saving; as, to strive *for* fame. **4** Intending to go to; as, to leave *for* the South. **5** Intended to help; as, treatment *for* a sprain. **6** In exchange as the equal of; as, an eye *for* an eye. **7** In hopes of getting; as, to run *for* office. **8** As being; as, to take *for* granted. **9** Because of; as, a person selected *for* his dramatic skill. **10** In aid of; as, to work *for* a cause. **11** In spite of; as, to succeed *for* all one's mistakes. **12** As regards; concerning. That will do *for* that subject. **13** Considering; as, tall *for* his age. **14** Throughout; as, *for* days and days. **15** Amounting to; as, a check *for* ten dollars. **16** Transferred to; passed on to; incumbent upon; as, to leave debts *for* someone else to pay. — *conj.* For this reason; because. The children must come home, *for* it is their bedtime. — **for·as·much as** \'fȯr-əz-ˌməch əz\. In consideration that; seeing that; since.

for·age \'fȯr-ij, 'fär-\ *n.* **1** Food for animals, especially for horses and cattle. **2** A search for food; the action of foraging. — *v.;* **for·aged**; **for·ag·ing. 1** To collect forage from; as, to *forage* a meadow. **2** To get by foraging. **3** To wander in search of provisions; to raid. The only means of securing food was by *foraging.* — **for·ag·er**, *n.*

for·ay \'fȯr-ˌā, fȯ-'rā\ *v.* To raid in search of plunder; to pillage; as, to *foray* the lands of one's enemies. — *n.* A sudden invasion or attack made for plunder; a raid.

for·bear \fȯr-'bar, fər-, -'ber\ *v.;* **for·bore** \-'bōr, -'bȯr\; **for·borne** \-'bōrn, -'bȯrn\; **for·bear·ing. 1** To do without; to hold back; to refrain; as, to *forbear* from striking back. **2** To control oneself when provoked.

for·bear·ance \fȯr-'bar-ən(t)s, fər-, -'ber-\ *n.* **1** The act of forbearing; continued patience or waiting. **2** Kindness or mildness toward an enemy. — For synonyms see *patience.*

for·bid \fər-'bid\ *v.;* **for·bade** \-'bad, -'bād\ or **for·bad** \-'bad\; **for·bid·den** \-'bid-n\; **for·bid·ding.** To order a person not to do something; to prohibit; as, to *forbid* a child to play in the street.

for·bid·ding \fər-'bid-ing\ *adj.* Discouraging or frightening; disagreeable. The forest looks *forbidding* at night. — **for·bid·ding·ly**, *adv.*

force \'fōrs, 'fȯrs\ *n.* **1** Strength or energy; active power; as, the *force* of a blow; *force* of character.

2 The power to persuade, bind, or convince; as, the *force* of an appeal. **3** Sharpness; clearness; impressiveness; as, writing that lacks *force.* **4** Any body of persons gathered together or trained for action; as, a police *force;* the armed *forces.* **5** Power or violence used on a person or thing; as, to open a door by *force.* **6** The cause that makes bodies move in a certain direction or at a certain speed; as, the *force* of gravity. — *v.;* **forced; forc·ing. 1** To compel by any means; as, to *force* men to work. **2** To drive or get by strength or violence; as, to *force* one's way through a crowd. **3** To break open by force; as, to *force* a door. **4** To hasten the growth or development of; as, to *force* bulbs or plants. **5** To press or urge; as, to *force* one's attentions on someone. **6** To produce by unnatural effort; as, to *force* a laugh.

forced \ˈfōrst, ˈfȯrst\ *adj.* **1** Compelled by force or by circumstances; as, a *forced* landing; *forced* labor. **2** Done or produced under special effort or difficulty; as, a *forced* laugh.

force·ful \ˈfōrs-fəl, ˈfȯrs-\ *adj.* Having much force; effective; as, a *forceful* man; a *forceful* argument. — **force·ful·ly** \-fə-lē\ *adv.*

for·ceps \ˈfȯr-səps\ *n. sing. and pl.* A pair of pincers or tongs, especially for precise or delicate work, as that of a watchmaker, surgeon, or dentist.

forceps

for·ci·ble \ˈfōr-səb-l, ˈfȯr-\ *adj.* **1** Got, made, or done by force or violence; as, a *forcible* entrance. **2** Showing force or energy; as, a *forcible* speech; a *forcible* effort. — **for·ci·bly** \-sə-blē\ *adv.*

ford \ˈfōrd, ˈfȯrd\ *n.* A place in a river or other stream where a person or an animal can wade across. — *v.* To cross by a ford. — **ford·a·ble,** *adj.*

fore \ˈfōr, ˈfȯr\ *adv.* In the front part; especially, in or toward the bow of a ship; as, to pace a deck *fore* and aft, back and forth, over and over again. — *adj.* Being or coming first in time, place, or order. — *n.* The front; the forefront. Crowded schools bring new educational problems to the *fore.*

fore \ˈfōr, ˈfȯr\ *interj.* A call used by golfers to warn persons in the probable line of flight of a ball.

fore-. A prefix that can mean: **1** Before or in front, as in *forearm* or *foreword.* **2** Beforehand or preceding in time, as in *forefather* or *foregoing.*

fore-and-aft \ˈfōr-ən-ˈaft, ˈfȯr-\ *adj.* In a line with the length of a ship; as, *fore-and-aft* sails.

fore·arm \ˈfōr-ˌärm, ˈfȯr-, -ˌȧrm\ *n.* The part of the arm between the elbow and the wrist.

fore·arm \(ˈ)fōr-ˈärm, (ˈ)fȯr-, -ˈȧrm\ *v.* To arm beforehand; to make ready in advance of a need.

fore·bear \ˈfȯr-ˌbar, ˈfōr-, -ˌber\ *n.* An ancestor; a forefather.

fore·bode \fōr-ˈbōd, fȯr-\ *v.;* **fore·bod·ed; fore·bod·ing. 1** To foretell; to be a sign or warning of. His father's frowning face *foreboded* no good to the disobedient boy. **2** To have a feeling of something about to happen, especially something evil or unfortunate.

fore·bod·ing \fōr-ˈbōd-ing, fȯr-\ *n.* A feeling that something bad is going to happen.

fore·cast \ˈfōr-ˌkast, ˈfȯr-\ *v.;* **fore·cast** or **fore·cast·ed; fore·cast·ing. 1** To predict; as, to *forecast* the weather for the coming week. **2** To serve as a sign warning of something that is to come; as, events that *forecast* war. — *n.* A prediction; as, a weather *forecast.* — **fore·cast·er,** *n.*

fore·cas·tle \ˈfōks-l; ˈfōr-ˌkas-l, ˈfȯr-\ *n.* **1** The part of the upper deck of a vessel in front of the foremast. **2** The forward compartment of a vessel, where the sailors live.

fore·close \fōr-ˈklōz, fȯr-\ *v.;* **fore·closed; fore·clos·ing. 1** To shut out. **2** To take legal measures to terminate a mortgage and take possession of the mortgaged property because the conditions of the mortgage have not been met.

fore·closure \fōr-ˈklōzh-r, fȯr-\ *n.* The act of foreclosing; especially, the legal procedure of foreclosing a mortgage.

fore·deck \ˈfōr-ˌdek, ˈfȯr-\ *n.* The forward part of the deck of a ship, especially of the main deck.

fore·fa·ther \ˈfōr-ˌfäth-r, ˈfȯr-, -ˌfȧth-r\ *n.* An ancestor.

fore·fin·ger \ˈfōr-ˌfing-gr, ˈfȯr-\ *n.* The finger next to the thumb.

forefinger

fore·foot \ˈfōr-ˌfu̇t, ˈfȯr-\ *n.; pl.* **fore·feet** \-ˌfēt\. One of the front feet of a four-footed animal.

fore·front \ˈfōr-ˌfrənt, ˈfȯr-\ *n.* The foremost part or place; the place of greatest activity or interest; as, an event in the *forefront* of the news.

foregather. Variant of *forgather.*

forego. Variant of *forgo.*

fore·go·ing \ˈfōr-ˌgō-ing, ˈfȯr-\ *adj.* Going before; preceding; as, a topic dealt with in a *foregoing* chapter.

foregoing. Variant of *forgoing.*

fore·gone \ˈfōr-ˌgȯn, ˈfȯr-\ *adj.* Determined or settled in advance. The boy's success seemed a *foregone* conclusion to everyone who knew his ability and persistence.

foregone. Variant of *forgone.*

fore·ground \ˈfōr-ˌgraůnd, ˈfȯr-\ *n.* The part of a picture or scene that is nearest to and in front of the person looking at it.

fore·hand \ˈfōr-ˌhand, ˈfȯr-\ *adj.* Made or done with the palm of the hand turned in the direction in which the hand is moving. — *n.* A forehand stroke, as in tennis.

fore·hand·ed \ˈfōr-ˈhan-dəd, ˈfȯr-\ *adj.* Mindful of the future; thrifty; prudent.

fore·head \ˈfȯr-əd, ˈfär-; ˈfōr-ˌhed, ˈfȯr-\ *n.* The part of the face above the eyes; the brow.

for·eign \ˈfȯr-ən, ˈfär-\ *adj.* [From medieval English *forene,* there borrowed from Old French *forain,* which in turn is derived from Late Latin *foranus* meaning "on the outside".] **1** Situated outside of a place or country, especially outside of one's own country; as, *foreign* nations. **2** Having to do with countries other than one's own; as, *foreign* trade; *foreign* affairs. **3** Not native; belonging to some other country; as, the *foreign* population of an American city. **4** Not related to what is being talked about or done; as, to introduce material that is *foreign* to the topic being discussed.

for·eign·er \'fȯr-ən-r, 'fär-\ *n.* A person who belongs to, or owes allegiance to, a foreign country; an alien.

fore·know \fōr-'nō, fȯr-\ *v.;* **fore·knew** \-'nü, -'nyü\; **fore·known** \-'nōn\; **fore·know·ing.** To know beforehand. — **fore·knowl·edge** \'fōr-ˌnäl-ij, 'fȯr-\ *n.*

fore·land \'fōr-lənd, 'fȯr-\ *n.* A headland; a promontory.

fore·leg \'fōr-ˌleg, 'fȯr-\ *n.* A front leg.

fore·lock \'fōr-ˌläk, 'fȯr-\ *n.* The lock of hair that grows from the front central part of the scalp.

fore·man \'fōr-mən, 'fȯr-\ *n.; pl.* **fore·men** \-mən\. A chief man in a group, as the spokesman of a jury or a head workman.

fore·mast \'fōr-ˌmast, 'fȯr-, -məst\ *n.* The mast nearest the bow of a boat.

fore·most \'fōr-ˌmōst, 'fȯr-\ *adj.* First in time, place, or order; most advanced; most important; as, the *foremost* writer of his time. — *adv.* First of all; in the first place.

fore·noon \'fōr-ˌnün, 'fȯr-\ *n.* The early part of the day, from sunrise to noon; the morning.

fo·ren·sic \fə-'ren(t)s-ik\ *adj.* Of, used in, or suitable to courts of justice or to public speaking and debate; as, *forensic* eloquence.

fore·or·dain \ˌfōr-ˌȯr-'dān, ˌfȯr-\ *v.* To ordain or decree beforehand. — **fore·or·di·na·tion** \-ˌȯrd-n-'āsh-n\ *n.*

fore·part \'fōr-ˌpärt, 'fȯr-, -ˌpärt\ *n.* The part most advanced or first in place or in time; as, in the *forepart* of April.

fore·paw \'fōr-ˌpȯ, 'fȯr-\ *n.* A front paw.

fore·quar·ter \'fōr-ˌkwȯrt-r, 'fȯr-\ *n.* A front quarter or part, as of beef or lamb.

fore·run·ner \'fōr-ˌrən-r, 'fȯr-\ *n.* **1** One that goes before another and indicates its approach. The dark clouds were *forerunners* of a storm. **2** A predecessor; an ancestor.

fore·sail \'fōr-ˌsāl, 'fȯr-; 'fōrs-l, 'fȯrs-l\ *n.* **1** The lowest sail on the foremast of a square-rigged boat. **2** The lower sail set toward the stern on the foremast of a schooner.

fore·see \fōr-'sē, fȯr-\ *v.;* **fore·saw** \-'sȯ\; **fore·seen** \-'sēn\; **fore·see·ing.** To see or have knowledge of beforehand; to expect; as, to *foresee* trouble.

fore·shad·ow \fōr-'shad-ō, fȯr-\ *v.* To give a hint or suggestion of something beforehand; to represent beforehand. Events *foreshadowed* a victory.

fore·short·en \fōr-'shȯrt-n, fȯr-\ *v.;* **fore·short·ened**; **fore·short·en·ing** \-n(-)ing\. To shorten a detail, as in a drawing or painting, so that it appears in its right relation with other details.

fore·sight \'fōr-ˌsīt, 'fȯr-\ *n.* **1** The act or power of foreseeing; knowledge of something before it happens. **2** The act of looking forward; a view forward. **3** Care or provision for the future; prudence. — **fore·sight·ed** \-ˌsīt-əd\ *adj.*

fore·skin \'fōr-ˌskin, 'fȯr-\ *n.* The fold of skin that covers the end of the male sex organ.

for·est \'fȯr-əst, 'fär-\ *n.* A dense growth of trees and underbrush covering a large area. — *adj.* **1** Of, in, or relating to a forest; as, *forest* trees. **2** Sylvan; as, *forest* glades. — *v.* To cover with trees or forests.

fore·stall \fōr-'stȯl, fȯr-\ *v.* To keep out, hinder, or prevent by measures taken in advance; as, to *forestall* unnecessary questions by giving careful directions; to *forestall* an opponent by clever planning.

for·est·a·tion \ˌfȯr-əs-'tāsh-n, ˌfär-\ *n.* The planting and care of a forest or of forests.

for·est·ed \'fȯr-əs-təd, 'fär-\ *adj.* Covered with trees or forests; wooded; as, *forested* slopes.

for·est·er \'fȯr-əst-r, 'fär-\ *n.* **1** A person trained in the care of forests. **2** A dweller in the forest.

forest ranger. An officer who patrols a forest and is responsible for guarding it against forest fires and for the enforcement of laws governing its use by the public.

for·est·ry \'fȯr-əs-trē, 'fär-\ *n.* The science and practice of caring for forests; the profession of a forester.

fore·taste \'fōr-ˌtāst, 'fȯr-\ *n.* A preliminary or partial experience of something that will not be fully experienced until later; an advance notion. Through field maneuvers a soldier gets a *foretaste* of real campaigning.

fore·tell \fōr-'tel, fȯr-\ *v.;* **fore·told** \-'tōld\; **fore·tell·ing.** To tell of a thing before it happens; to predict; to prophesy.

— The words *predict* and *prophesy* are synonyms of *foretell: foretell,* a general term, applies to a describing of future events but suggests little about the manner of discovering them; *predict* is generally used to indicate a foretelling that draws its conclusions from factual information or laws of nature; *prophesy* usually suggests mystical inspiration or supernatural knowledge.

fore·thought \'fōr-ˌthȯt, 'fȯr-\ *n.* Thought taken before something happens; care taken in advance; as, difficulties that might have been prevented by a little *forethought.*

fore·top \'fōr-ˌtäp, 'fȯr-\ *n.* The platform at the top of the foremast of a ship.

for·ev·er \fə-'rev-r\ *adv.* **1** For a limitless time; everlastingly. **2** At all times; always; constantly; as, a dog that was *forever* chasing cars.

for·ev·er·more \fə-ˌrev-r-'mōr, -'mȯr\ *adv.* Forever; eternally.

fore·warn \fōr-'wȯrn, fȯr-\ *v.* To warn beforehand;

to caution before something happens; as, to be *forewarned* of danger.

forewent. Variant of *forwent.*

fore·wing \'fōr-ˌwing, 'fȯr-\ *n.* One of the front pair of two pairs of wings, as in insects.

fore·word \'fōr-ˌwərd, 'fȯr-\ *n.* An introductory statement or passage appearing before the main body of a printed work; a preface.

for·feit \'fȯr-fət\ *n.* **1** Something lost by or taken away from a person because of an offense or error committed by him; a penalty; a fine; as, to pay for the crime of murder with the *forfeit* of one's own life. **2** [in the plural] A game in which the players redeem personal articles by paying amusing or embarrassing penalties. — *v.* To lose, or lose the right to, something through some fault, error, or neglect; as, to *forfeit* one's freedom; to *forfeit* a game.

for·fei·ture \'fȯr-fə-ˌchu̇r, -fəch-r\ *n.* **1** The act of forfeiting. **2** Something forfeited; a penalty; a fine.

for·gath·er or **fore·gath·er** \fȯr-'ga*th*-r, fōr-\ *v.;* **for·gath·ered** or **fore·gath·ered**; **for·gath·er·ing** or **fore·gath·er·ing** \-r(-)ing\. **1** To assemble; to come together; to meet. **2** To associate; to fraternize; to meet as friends.

forgave. Past tense of *forgive.*

forge \'fōrj, 'fȯrj\ *n.* [From medieval English, there borrowed from medieval French, where it was derived from Latin *fabrica* meaning "workshop".] **1** A furnace, or a place with a furnace, where metal is shaped and worked by heating and hammering; a smithy. **2** A workshop where wrought iron is produced directly from the ore or where iron is refined so that it can be worked. — *v.;* **forged**; **forg·ing.** **1** To shape and work metal by heating and hammering; as, to *forge* the links of a chain. **2** To form in any way; to produce; to make; as, pioneers *forging* the western states out of prairie and mountain. **3** To produce something that is not genuine; especially, to counterfeit a signature, as on a bank check.

forge \'fōrj, 'fȯrj\ *v.;* **forged**; **forg·ing.** To move forward steadily but gradually; as, to *forge* ahead in the voting for class president.

forg·er \'fōrj-r, 'fȯrj-r\ *n.* One that forges; especially, one guilty of forgery.

for·gery \'fōrj-r(-)ē, 'fȯrj-\ *n.; pl.* **for·ger·ies.** **1** The crime of falsely making or changing a written paper or signing someone else's name. **2** Something, as a signature, that has been forged.

for·get \fər-'get\ *v.;* **for·got** \-'gät\; **for·got·ten** \-'gät-n\ or **for·got**; **for·get·ting.** **1** To let go from the memory; to be unable to recall; as, to *forget* someone's address. **2** To neglect; to fail to think of; as, to *forget* one's hat; to *forget* to turn out a light.

for·get·ful \fər-'get-fəl\ *adj.* **1** Forgetting easily; having a bad memory. People often become *forgetful* as they grow old. **2** Careless; neglectful; heedless; as, to be *forgetful* of one's manners. — **for·get·ful·ly** \-fə-lē\ *adv.*

for·get·ful·ness \fər-'get-fəl-nəs\ *n.* The condition of failing to remember; a forgetting; as, the increasing *forgetfulness* that comes with old age.

for·get-me-not \fər-'get-mē-ˌnät\ *n.* A small low plant with one-sided clusters of small bright-blue or white flowers.

forget-me-not

forging. Pres. part. of *forge.*

for·give \fər-'giv\ *v.;* **for·gave** \-'gāv\; **for·giv·en** \-'giv-n\; **for·giv·ing.** **1** To pardon; to cease to feel anger or resentment against; as, to *forgive* one's enemies. **2** To give up resentment for an offense or wrong; to stop trying to exact; as, to *forgive* a debt. — For synonyms see *excuse.* — **for·giv·a·ble** \-'giv-əb-l\ *adj.* — **for·giv·er** \-r\ *n.*

for·give·ness \fər-'giv-nəs\ *n.* **1** The act of forgiving or the conditions of being forgiven; pardon. **2** Willingness to forgive.

for·giv·ing \fər-'giv-ing\ *adj.* Showing forgiveness; inclined or ready to forgive; as, a person with a *forgiving* nature.

for·go or **fore·go** \fȯr-'gō, fōr-\ *v.;* **for·went** or **fore·went** \-'went\; **for·gone** or **fore·gone** \-'gȯn\; **for·go·ing** or **fore·go·ing** \-'gō-ing\. To give up; to let pass; to go without; as, to *forgo* lunch; to *forgo* an opportunity.

forgot. Past tense and past part. of *forget.*

forgotten. A past part. of *forget.*

fork \'fȯrk\ *n.* **1** An implement having a handle and two or more prongs or tines, used for piercing, taking up, holding, or pitching; as, a salad *fork.* **2** Anything that resembles a fork in shape; as, a tuning *fork.* **3** The place where something divides or branches; one of the parts into which anything divides or branches; as, a *fork* in the road; to follow the *fork* of the road that leads to the right. — *v.* **1** To divide into branches; as, the place where the road *forks.* **2** To make fork-shaped. **3** To pitch or toss with a fork, as hay.

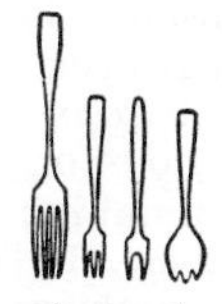
forks, 1

forked \'fȯrkt, 'fȯrk-əd\ *adj.* Fork-shaped; having a fork; as, *forked* lightning; a *forked* tongue.

for·lorn \fər-'lȯrn\ *adj.* Deserted or feeling deserted or neglected; wretched. — **for·lorn·ly,** *adv.*

form \'fȯrm\ *n.* **1** The shape or structure of anything. **2** A body, especially of a human being. Suddenly a *form* appeared in the doorway. **3** A set or fixed way of doing something; as, certain *forms* of worship; *forms* of behavior. **4** Empty ceremony; as, merely a matter of *form.* **5** The manner of doing something; as, to display good *form* in swimming. **6** A special manner of arrangement; as, the sonnet *form* in poetry. **7** A kind; a variety; as, a low *form* of animal life. **8** Something by which shape is given or determined; a mold; as, a *form* for laying concrete. **9** Physical and mental condition, as of an athlete; as, a runner who is at the top of his *form.* **10** A long seat or bench, especially in a schoolroom. **11** A class of students in a school; as, a boy in the fourth *form.* **12** A printed document with blank spaces for inserting required information; as, an income tax *form.* **13** In grammar, one of the different ways in which a word is changed to show differences in use; as, the singular and plural *forms* of a noun. — For synonyms see *ceremony.* — *v.* **1** To give form or shape to; to fashion; to make; as, to *form* a letter of the alphabet. **2** To train; to instruct. Education *forms* the mind. **3** To develop; to get; to contract; as, to *form* a habit. **4** To make up; to constitute; as, a compound *formed* of several elements. **5** To arrange in order; as, to *form* a battle line. **6** To take form; to arise. Fog *forms* in the valleys. **7** To take a definite form, shape, or arrangement; to draw up. Each column of soldiers marched away as soon as it was *formed.* — **form·er**, *n.*

for·mal \'fȯrm-l\ *adj.* **1** Of or relating to form; in accordance with fixed custom or convention; conventional; stiff; as, a *formal* dinner; a *formal* manner. **2** Regular; lawful; in due form; as, a *formal* contract. **3** Having the form or appearance without the content; as, *formal* worship. — **for·mal·ly** \'fȯrm-l-ē\ *adv.*

form·al·de·hyde \fȯr-'mal-də-ˌhīd\ *n.* A colorless gas with a sharp odor, used as a preservative and disinfectant.

for·mal·ism \'fȯrm-l-ˌiz-m\ *n.* The strict observance of forms or conventions, as in religion or art. — **for·mal·ist** \-əst\ *n.* — **for·mal·is·tic** \ˌfȯrm-l-'is-tik\ *adj.*

for·mal·i·ty \fȯr-'mal-ət-ē\ *n.; pl.* **for·mal·i·ties.** **1** A being formal. **2** A complying with fixed procedure or rules; ceremony. **3** A legal, social, religious, or customary requirement.

for·mal·ize \'fȯrm-l-ˌīz\ *v.;* **for·mal·ized**; **for·mal·iz·ing.** **1** To give a certain or definite form to something; to shape. **2** To make formal.

for·mat \'fȯr-ˌmat\ *n.* The shape, size, and general style and arrangement of a publication, as a book or a magazine.

for·ma·tion \fȯr-'māsh-n\ *n.* **1** A forming; as, the *formation* of good habits during childhood. **2** Something that is formed; as, new word *formations.* **3** The manner in which a thing is formed; structure; shape; as, an abnormal *formation* of the jaw. **4** An arrangement of troops, ships, or airplanes; as, battle *formation;* planes flying in *formation.*

form·a·tive \'fȯr-mət-iv\ *adj.* Giving or having the power of giving form; molding; as, the *formative* years of a person's life.

for·mer \'fȯrm-r\ *adj.* Coming before, as in time or position; past; earlier; as, a *former* president; in *former* days. — **the former**. The first mentioned of two persons or things.

for·mer·ly \'fȯrm-r-lē\ *adv.* In time past; of old; heretofore.

for·mi·da·ble \'fȯr-məd-əb-l\ *adj.* Arousing fear or dread; having qualities that discourage approach or attack; as, a *formidable* enemy; a *formidable* man to talk to. — **for·mi·da·bly** \-ə-blē\ *adv.*

form·less \'fȯrm-ləs\ *adj.* Lacking a definite or fixed form or shape. — **form·less·ly**, *adv.*

for·mu·la \'fȯrm-yə-lə\ *n.; pl.* **for·mu·las** \-ləz\ or **for·mu·lae** \-ˌlē, -ˌlī\. **1** A set form of words for use in any ceremony; as, a *formula* of faith. **2** A rule giving the ingredients, with proportions, for preparing a compound; a recipe. **3** A fixed or conventional method in which anything is to be done, arranged, or said; as, to try to make friends by *formula.* **4** In chemistry, an expression in symbols of the composition of a substance. The *formula* for water, which is composed of two parts of hydrogen to one of oxygen, is H_2O.

for·mu·late \'fȯrm-yə-ˌlāt\ *v.;* **for·mu·lat·ed**; **for·mu·lat·ing.** **1** To express in a formula. **2** To put in the form of a systematic statement; to state definitely and clearly; as, to *formulate* a plan. — **for·mu·la·tion** \ˌfȯrm-yə-'lāsh-n\ *n.* — **for·mu·la·tor** \'fȯrm-yə-ˌlāt-r\ *n.*

for·sake \fər-'sāk, fȯr-\ *v.;* **for·sook** \-'sůk\; **for·sak·en** \-'sāk-n\; **for·sak·ing.** To abandon; to give up; to desert; to leave; as, to *forsake* old friends for new ones. — For synonyms see *abandon.*

for·sooth \fər-'süth\ *adv.* Certainly; in truth; indeed.

for·swear \fȯr-'swar, -'swer\ *v.;* **for·swore** \-'swōr, -'swȯr\; **for·sworn** \-'swōrn, -'swȯrn\; **for·swear·ing.** **1** To swear falsely; to commit perjury. **2** To pledge oneself to give up; as, to *forswear* gambling.

for·syth·ia \fər-'sith-ē-ə\ *n.* A shrub of the olive family with yellow bell-shaped flowers that appear before the leaves in early spring.

forsythia

fort \'fōrt, 'fȯrt\ *n.* [From medieval French, there derived from the adjective *fort* meaning "strong", which is derived from Latin *fortis.*] A strong or fortified place; especially, a building or set of buildings surrounded with defenses and occupied by soldiers.

forte \'fōrt, 'fȯrt\ *n.* [From French, meaning "strong point" and derived from the adjective *fort* meaning "strong" — see *fort.*] Anything in which a person excels or shows special ability; a person's strong point. Baseball and not books was that boy's *forte.*

for·te \'fȯr-ˌtā, 'fȯrt-ē\ *adj.* or *adv.* In music, loud.

forth \'fōrth, 'fȯrth\ *adv.* **1** Forward; onward; as, from that time *forth;* and so *forth.* **2** Out; out into view; as, plants putting *forth* leaves.

forth·com·ing \(')fōrth-'kəm-ing, (')fȯrth-\ *adj.* **1** About to appear; approaching; as, a list of *forthcoming* events. **2** Coming forth; readily available; as, to be confident that all supplies needed for a project will be *forthcoming.* — *n.* A coming forth; approach; as, first signs of the *forthcoming* of spring.

forth·right \'fōrth-ˌrīt, 'fȯrth-\ *adj.* Straightforward; direct; as, a *forthright* answer. — **forth·right·ly** \-'rīt-lē\ *adv.*

forth·with \(')fōrth-'wi<u>th</u>, (')fȯrth-, -'with\ *adv.* Immediately; promptly; as, to expect an answer *forthwith.*

for·ti·eth \'fȯrt-ē-əth\ *adj.* Next after the thirty-ninth. — *n.* One of forty equal parts.

for·ti·fi·ca·tion \ˌfȯrt-ə-fə-'kāsh-n\ *n.* **1** The act of fortifying; especially, the building of military defenses for a place. **2** A construction built for the defense of a place; a fort. **3** A place defended by a fort or forts.

for·ti·fy \'fȯrt-ə-ˌfī\ *v.;* **for·ti·fied** \-ˌfīd\; **for·ti·fy·ing.** **1** To make strong; to strengthen physically or morally; as, to be *fortified* in time of trouble by the loyalty of friends. Good living habits *fortify* the body against many illnesses. **2** To strengthen by military defenses; as, to *fortify* a harbor. **3** To strengthen by adding alcohol, as wines. **4** To make more nutritious by adding vitamins and minerals.

for·tis·si·mo \fȯr-'tis-ə-ˌmō\ *adj.* or *adv.* In music, very loud.

for·ti·tude \'fȯrt-ə-ˌtüd, -ˌtyüd\ *n.* Firmness of mind, as in meeting and enduring danger, trouble, or pain; courage to endure without yielding.

fort·night \'fōrt-ˌnīt, 'fȯrt-\ *n.* A period of fourteen days; two weeks.

fort·night·ly \'fōrt-ˌnīt-lē, 'fȯrt-\ *adj.* Occurring or appearing once in a fortnight; as, a *fortnightly* magazine; to look forward to the regular *fortnightly* visit of a friend. — *adv.* Once in a fortnight.

for·tress \'fȯr-trəs\ *n.* A fortified place; especially, a large and permanent fortification, often including a town.

for·tu·i·tous \fȯr-'tü-ət-əs, fər-, -'tyü-\ *adj.* Happening by chance; chance; accidental; as, an entirely *fortuitous* meeting with an old friend. — **for·tu·i·tous·ly,** *adv.*

for·tu·nate \'fȯrch-n(-)ət\ *adj.* **1** Coming or happening by good luck; bringing a benefit or good that was not expected or was not foreseen as certain; as, a storm-tossed sailing ship saved by a *fortunate* change in the wind. **2** Receiving some unexpected good; lucky; as, a *fortunate* man; to consider oneself *fortunate* in having good health. — **for·tu·nate·ly,** *adv.*

for·tune \'fȯrch-n, 'fȯr-(ˌ)chün\ *n.* **1** The supposed cause of something that happens to one suddenly and unexpectedly; chance; luck. **2** That which happens to a person; good or bad luck; as, the *fortunes* of war; to have the good *fortune* to be elected class president. **3** A person's destiny or fate; as, to tell *fortunes* with cards. **4** Riches; wealth; a large sum of money; as, to inherit a *fortune;* to make a *fortune* out of oil.

for·tune·tell·er \'fȯrch-n-ˌtel-r, 'fȯr-(ˌ)chün-\ *n.* A person who professes to foretell future events. — **for·tune·tell·ing,** *n.*

for·ty \'fȯrt-ē\ *adj.* Four times ten; thirty-nine and one more. — *n.* **1** The sum of four tens; forty units or objects. **2** The figure standing for forty units, as 40 or XL.

for·ty-nin·er \'fȯrt-ē-'nīn-r\ *n.* A person who went to California in the gold rush of 1849.

fo·rum \'fōr-əm, 'fȯr-əm\ *n.; pl.* **fo·rums** \-əmz\ or **fo·ra** \-ə\. **1** The market place or public place of an ancient Roman city, serving as a center for public business and as a gathering place for the people. **2** A court; a tribunal. **3** An assembly or a series of assemblies for open discussion, usually of previously announced topics of widespread public interest.

for·ward \'fȯr-wərd; *in the South, also* 'fär-\ *adj.* **1** Near, at, or belonging to the front part. **2** Ahead of the ordinary; advanced; early. Spring was *forward* that year. **3** Onward; leading or moving to the front; as, a *forward* movement of troops; a *forward* pass resulting in a touchdown. **4** Eager; too eager; too bold; as, a *forward* child. — *adv.* Toward the front; as, to push *forward.* — *n.* In some games, a player at or near the front of his team whose chief duty is to carry on the offensive play. — *v.* **1** To help onward; as, to *forward* the cause of peace. **2** To send on or ahead; as, to *forward* a letter.

for·ward·er \-wərd-r\ *n.* One that forwards; especially, an agent who forwards goods; as, a freight *forwarder.* — **for·ward·ing,** *n.*

for·ward·ness \-nəs\ *n.* **1** An advanced stage of progress or development. **2** Boldness; impudence.

for·wards \-wərdz\ *adv.* Forward.

forwent. Past tense of *forgo.*

fos·sil \'fäs-l\ *n.* **1** Any trace, impression, or remains of a plant or animal of a past age preserved in the earth's crust. **2** A person whose ideas are out-of-date; a thing that is behind the times. — *adj.* Fossilized; of the nature of a fossil; as, *fossil* plants.

fos·sil·ize \'fäs-l-ˌīz\ *v.;* **fos·sil·ized; fos·sil·iz·ing.** **1** To change into a fossil; to become or cause to become like rock. **2** To become or cause to become out-of-date, as in ideas or opinions.

fos·ter \'fȯst-r, 'fäst-r\ *adj.* Giving, receiving, or sharing nourishment and care though not related by blood, as in **foster parent** (**foster mother** or **father**), one who acts as parent to the child of other parents, **foster brother** or **sister,** a person brought up as brother or sister to another person to whom he or she is not related by blood, **foster child,** one who has been brought up by a foster parent. — *v.;* **fos·tered; fos·ter·ing** \-r(-)ing\. **1** To feed; to nourish. **2** To promote the growth of; to encourage; as, to *foster* the spread of higher education; to *foster* ability wherever one finds it.

fought. Past tense and past part. of *fight.*

foul \'faul\ *adj.* **1** Disgusting; filthy; offensive in looks, taste, or smell; as, *foul* odors. **2** Clogged or covered with dirt; not clear or clean. **3** Obscene; indecent; abusive; as, *foul* language. **4** Hateful;

wicked; as, a *foul* crime. **5** Unfair; not according to the rules; as, a *foul* blow. **6** Rainy, rough, or stormy; as, *foul* weather. **7** In baseball, of or relating to a batted ball that is not a fair ball. — *n.* **1** In various games, a play that is not according to the rules. **2** In baseball, a foul ball. — *v.* **1** To make foul or filthy; as, to *foul* the air; to *foul* a stream. **2** To disgrace; to dishonor; as, to *foul* one's good name. **3** In certain games, to make a foul against an opponent; in baseball, to hit a foul ball. **4** To entangle or become entangled; as, to *foul* a rope. The anchor *fouled.* **5** To collide, as one boat with another; as, to *foul* a launch in moving away from the dock.

fou·lard \fü-ˈlärd, fə-, -ˈlȧrd\ *n.* A thin, soft silk or silk and cotton fabric with a satin finish, usually decorated with a printed pattern, much used in making scarves and ties.

foul ball. In baseball, a batted ball that is not a fair ball.

foul line. In baseball, either of two straight lines extending from the rear corner of the home plate through the outer corner of first and third base and continued to the boundary of the field.

foul·ly \ˈfau̇l-lē\ *adv.* In a foul manner; especially, offensively or shamefully; as, a story about a man who was *foully* murdered.

foul play. **1** Unfair play or dealing; dishonest conduct. **2** Violence; assault or murder. The police feared the man had been the victim of *foul play.*

found \ˈfau̇nd\. Past tense and past part. of *find.*

found \ˈfau̇nd\ *v.* **1** To place on something solid for support; to fix firmly; as, a house *founded* on a rock. **2** To take the first steps in building up; as, to *found* a colony; to *found* a family.

found \ˈfau̇nd\ *v.* To melt and pour into a mold or to form by this process; to cast.

foun·da·tion \fau̇n-ˈdāsh-n\ *n.* **1** The act of founding or the state of being founded. **2** A permanent fund set up to support one or more institutions or activities, usually charitable or educational. **3** An institution provided for through such a permanent fund. **4** The support upon which anything rests; a base; a supporting structure; as, the *foundation* of a building; suspicions having no *foundation* in fact.

found·er \ˈfau̇nd-r\ *n.* A person that founds or establishes; as, a society made up of descendants of the *founders* of the country.

found·er \ˈfau̇nd-r\ *n.* A person that founds, or casts, metals.

foun·der \ˈfau̇nd-r\ *v.*; **foun·dered**; **foun·der·ing** \-r(-)ing\. **1** To stumble and go lame, as a horse. **2** To fill with water and sink; as, a ship that *foundered* on a reef.

found·ling \ˈfau̇n-dling\ *n.* An infant found after its unknown parents have abandoned it.

found·ry \ˈfau̇n-drē\ *n.*; *pl.* **found·ries**. **1** The casting of metals. **2** A building or works where metals are cast.

fount \ˈfau̇nt\ *n.* A fountain; a source.

foun·tain \ˈfau̇nt-n\ *n.* **1** A spring of water. **2** A mechanically produced jet or spray of water or the ornamental structure in which it rises and flows. **3** Also **drinking fountain**. A basin equipped with a device for producing a jet of water that can be drunk without the use of a glass. **4** A container or series of containers, usually concealed within a service counter, holding a liquid or liquids to be drawn off as needed; as, a soda *fountain.* **5** Source; spring.

drinking fountain

foun·tain·head \ˈfau̇nt-n-ˌhed\ *n.* **1** A fountain or spring that is the source of a stream. **2** Source; especially, primary source; origin; as, the *fountainhead* of our liberties; a *fountainhead* of wisdom.

fountain pen. A pen with a reservoir in the holder which furnishes a supply of ink.

four \ˈfōr, ˈfȯr\ *adj.* One more than three; twice two. — *n.* **1** The sum of three and one; four units or objects. **2** The figure standing for four units, as 4 or IV.

four·fold \ˈfōr-ˌfōld, ˈfȯr-, -ˈfōld\ *adj.* or *adv.* Having four parts; four times as much or as many.

four-foot·ed \ˈfōr-ˈfu̇t-əd, ˈfȯr-\ *adj.* Having four feet; quadruped.

four-o'clock \ˈfōr-ə-ˌkläk, ˈfȯr-\ *n.* An American herb with fragrant solitary flowers that open late in the afternoon.

four-post·er \ˈfōr-ˈpōst-r, ˈfȯr-\ *n.* A large bedstead with tall posts at the corners, originally intended to support curtains or a canopy.

four·score \ˈfōr-ˌskōr, ˈfȯr-ˌskȯr\ *adj.* Four times twenty; eighty.

four·some \ˈfōrs-m, ˈfȯrs-\ *n.* **1** A party of four. **2** A match between four players, two on each side, as in golf.

four·square \ˈfōr-ˈskwar, ˈfȯr-, -ˈskwer\ *adj.* or *adv.* **1** Square; in a square form. **2** With unshakable firmness; as, a man who stood *foursquare* for equal justice for all.

four·teen \ˈfōr(t)-ˈtēn, ˈfȯr(t)-\ *adj.* Four and ten more; one more than thirteen. — *n.* **1** The sum of ten and four; fourteen units or objects. **2** The figure standing for fourteen units, as 14 or XIV.

four·teenth \ˈfōr(t)-ˈtēn(t)th, ˈfȯr(t)-\ *adj.* Next after the thirteenth. — *n.*; *pl.* **four·teenths** \-ˈtēn(t)s, -ˈtēn(t)ths\. One of fourteen equal parts.

fourth \ˈfōrth, ˈfȯrth\ *adj.* Next after the third. — *n.* One of four equal parts; a quarter.

fourth estate. The public press; the newspapers.

Fourth of July. Independence Day in the United States.

fowl \ˈfau̇l\ *n.*; *pl.* **fowl** or **fowls**. **1** A bird of any kind; as, wild *fowl.* **2** A domestic hen or rooster; a chicken; especially, a full-grown hen. **3** The meat of fowls used as food. — *v.* To hunt, catch, or kill wildfowl for game or food. — **fowl·er** \-r\ *n.*

fowl·ing piece \ˈfau̇-ling\. A light gun, especially for shooting birds.

fox \'fäks\ *n.* **1** A flesh-eating animal related to the dog and the wolf but smaller than the wolf and noted for craftiness, including among its varieties the common **red fox**, the **silver fox**, and the **gray fox. 2** A sly, cunning person. — *v.* To trick; to beguile; to outwit; to fool; as, to *fox* a person into revealing a secret.

fox·glove \'fäks-ˌgləv\ *n.* An erect herb that is the source of the drug digitalis, belonging to the figwort family and having spikes of dotted white or purple tube-shaped flowers suggestive of fingers of a glove.

fox·hole \'fäks-ˌhōl\ *n.* A small pit or trench for shelter from enemy fire, sometimes built with roof and sandbags.

fox·hound \'fäks-ˌhau̇nd\ *n.* A large swift hound of a breed trained to hunt foxes.

fox·tail \'fäks-ˌtāl\ *n.* **1** A fox's brush. **2** A meadow grass with brushlike leaves.

fox terrier. A small lively terrier of a breed formerly used to dig out foxes.

fox trot. 1 An easy gait, as of a horse in passing from a walk to a trot. **2** A ballroom dance in 4/4 time. — **fox-trot** \'fäks-ˌträt\ *v.*

foxy \'fäks-ē\ *adj.;* **fox·i·er**; **fox·i·est.** Crafty; like a fox in cunning. — **fox·i·ly** \-l-ē\ *adv.*

foy·er \'fȯi-(y)ər, 'fȯi-ˌ(y)ā\ *n.* **1** A lobby, especially in a theater or other public building. **2** An entrance hall.

fra·cas \'frāk-əs, 'frak-əs\ *n.* A noisy quarrel; a brawl; an uproar.

frac·tion \'fraksh-n\ *n.* **1** A piece broken off; a scrap; a fragment. **2** One or more parts of a whole or unit. The *fraction* ¾ (three fourths) plus the *fraction* ¼ (one fourth) equals 1.

frac·tion·al \'fraksh-n(-)əl\ *adj.* **1** Of or relating to fractions or a fraction. **2** Quite small; not important; as, not to get a *fractional* part of the assignment done. — **frac·tion·al·ly** \-n(-)ə-lē\ *adv.*

frac·ture \'frak-chər\ *n.* **1** A breaking or a being broken; especially, the breaking of a bone. **2** A crack made by breaking; a break. — *v.;* **frac·tured**; **frac·tur·ing.** To break; to crack; as, to *fracture* an arm. The bones of old people *fracture* easily.

frag·ile \'fraj-l, -ˌīl\ *adj.* Easily broken; delicate; as, the *fragile* stem of a flower; *fragile* china. — **fra·gil·i·ty** \frə-'jil-ət-ē\ *n.*

frag·ment \'frag-mənt\ *n.* **1** A part broken off; a small detached portion or an incomplete part of something; as, a dish broken into *fragments.* **2** A sentence fragment. — For synonyms see *part.*

frag·men·tary \'frag-mən-ˌter-ē\ *adj.* Consisting of fragments; disconnected; incomplete; as, *fragmentary* evidence; a *fragmentary* report.

fra·grance \'frāg-rən(t)s\ *n.* Sweetness of smell; a sweet smell.

fra·grant \'frāg-rənt\ *adj.* Sweet or agreeable in smell; as, *fragrant* flowers; *fragrant* spices.

— The words *odorous* and *aromatic* are synonyms of *fragrant: odorous* generally describes anything having a strong or distinctive smell; *fragrant* applies especially to sweet smells, as of flowers or fruit; *aromatic* usually suggests pungent or spicy smells, such as those of pine, cedar, lavender, and clove.

frail \'frāl\ *adj.* **1** Easily broken; fragile; physically weak; as, a *frail* antique chair; a *frail* old man. **2** Having a weak character; morally weak.

frail·ty \'frāl-tē, 'frā-əl-tē\ *n.; pl.* **frail·ties. 1** The condition of being frail; weakness. **2** A fault growing out of weakness of character.

frame \'frām\ *n.* **1** A structure composed of parts fitted or joined together, usually designed to give strength and shape to an object; as, the *frame* of a house or of a boat. **2** The bony structure of the body. **3** An open case or structure for holding or enclosing something; as, a window *frame;* a picture *frame.* **4** The shape or way in which anything is made or put together; structure; system; as, a *frame* of government. **5** A particular state or condition; as, a happy *frame* of mind. — *adj.* Having a frame of wood; as, a *frame* house. — *v.;* **framed**; **fram·ing. 1** To form; to construct; to plan; to compose; as, to *frame* a constitution. **2** To provide with a frame; as, to *frame* a picture. **3** To make up falsely, as a charge against a person; to charge falsely; to arrange secretly and unfairly the results of; as, to *frame* a person; to *frame* a race.

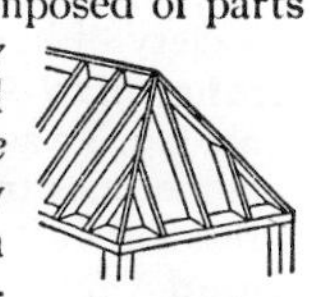
frame of a roof

frame-up \'frā-ˌməp\ *n.* **1** A plan or scheme to bring about a certain result, usually to the disadvantage of another person or group of persons; especially, a plot to cause a person to be accused falsely. **2** The action resulting from a frame-up.

frame·work \'frām-ˌwərk\ *n.* Frame; the structure of anything; as, the *framework* of a building; the *framework* of the United Nations.

franc \'frangk\ *n.* **1** A French coin varying with time in composition and value. **2** A corresponding coin of Switzerland, Belgium, and Luxembourg. **3** The unit of money in France, Switzerland, Belgium, and Luxembourg.

fran·chise \'fran-ˌchīz\ *n.* **1** A privilege granted by a sovereign or a government to a person or a company of persons; as, a *franchise* to operate a ferry. **2** The right to vote.

frank \'frangk\ *adj.* Free in expressing one's feelings and opinions; outspoken. — **frank·ly,** *adv.*

frank·furt·er \'frangk-fə(r)t-r, -ˌfərt-r\ *n.* [A shortened form of German *Frankfurter wuerstchen* meaning "Frankfurt sausage" and named after *Frankfurt,* a city in Germany.] A sausage made mostly of beef or of beef and pork.

frank·in·cense \'frangk-n-ˌsen(t)s\ *n.* A resin obtained from various African and Asiatic trees, and burned for its sweet odor.

fran·tic \'frant-ik\ *adj.* Frenzied; wildly excited; as, *frantic* cries for help; to be *frantic* with pain. — **fran·ti·cal·ly** \-ik-l(-)ē\ *adv.*

fra·ter·nal \frə-'tərn-l\ *adj.* **1** Having to do with brothers; belonging to brothers; brotherly; as, to have a *fraternal* interest in someone. **2** Composed of members banded together like brothers; as, a *fraternal* society.

fraternal twins. Twins developed from different fertilized egg cells and not necessarily of the same sex, appearance, or disposition; twins that are not identical.

fra·ter·ni·ty \frə-'tər-nət-ē\ *n.; pl.* **fra·ter·ni·ties.** **1** Brotherliness; brotherhood. **2** A social, honorary, or professional organization; especially, a club or society of boys or men, as in a college.

frat·er·nize \'frat-r-ˌnīz\ *v.;* **frat·er·nized; frat·er·niz·ing.** To associate closely, as brothers or friends. Sometimes troops are forbidden to *fraternize* with residents of occupied territories.

fraud \'frȯd\ *n.* **1** Deceit; trickery. **2** Something false passed off as genuine; a hoax; a trick. **3** A person who pretends to be what he is not.

fraud·u·lent \'frȯj-l-ənt\ *adj.* **1** Using fraud; deceiving; cheating; as, a *fraudulent* person. **2** Based on fraud; as, to gain one's ends by *fraudulent* methods. **3** Obtained or done by fraud; as, *fraudulent* elections; *fraudulent* gains.

fraught \'frȯt\ *adj.* Filled; laden; as, an undertaking *fraught* with danger.

fray \'frā\ *n.* A fight; a brawl; a commotion.

fray \'frā\ *v.* To wear or rub off in shreds; to wear down, as cloth, until the loose threads show; to ravel; as, a coat that is beginning to *fray* at the elbows.

fraz·zle \'fraz-l\ *v.;* **fraz·zled; fraz·zling** \-l(-)ing\. **1** To fray; to wear or pull into tatters; as, a *frazzled* end of a rope. **2** To tire; to weary; as, to feel *frazzled* out at the end of a long, hot day. — *n.* A frazzled or worn-out condition; as, to be worn to a *frazzle.*

freak \'frēk\ *n.* **1** A whim; a sudden fancy or change of mind. **2** A strange, abnormal, unusual person or thing; as, circus *freaks.* — *adj.* Having the nature of a freak; unusual; as, a *freak* storm; a *freak* accident. — **freak·ish** \-ish\ *adj.*

freck·le \'frek-l\ *n.* A small brownish spot on the skin, especially on the face, neck, or hands. — *v.;* **freck·led; freck·ling** \-l(-)ing\. To mark, or become marked, with freckles; as, a person who *freckles* easily.

free \'frē\ *adj.;* **fre·er** \'frē-ər\; **fre·est** \-əst\. **1** Having liberty; not being a slave; not controlled by others; independent; as, a *free* citizen; a *free* country. **2** Released from a duty, tax, or other charge; as, *free* goods; *free* trade. **3** Released or not suffering from something unpleasant or painful; as, *free* from worry; *free* from disease. **4** Given without charge; as, a *free* ticket; a *free* ride. **5** Not controlled or influenced by any power outside itself; as, a *free* press; *free* will. **6** Made voluntarily; as, a *free* offer. **7** Lavish; as, a *free* spender. **8** Plentiful; copious; as, a *free* supply. **9** Not held back by fear or distrust; open; frank; as, a *free* expression of opinion. **10** Not observing or made in accordance with conventional forms; as, *free* verse. **11** Not literal or exact; as, a *free* translation. **12** Not obstructed; clear; as, a road *free* of ice. **13** Performed, under the rules of a game, without interference from the opponents; as, a *free* kick. **14** Uncombined; as, *free* oxygen. — *adv.* Without charge; as, to be admitted *free.* — *v.;* **freed** \'frēd\; **free·ing** \'frē-ing\. To set free; to make free; as, to *free* the slaves.

free·board \'frē-ˌbōrd, -ˌbȯrd\ *n.* The side of a boat or the vertical distance between water line and deck.

free·boot·er \'frē-ˌbüt-r\ *n.* [From Dutch *vrijbuiter,* there derived from *vrij* meaning "free", *buit* meaning "booty", and the suffix *-er.*] A pirate; a buccaneer.

free·born \'frē-'bȯrn\ *adj.* **1** Born free; not born in slavery; as, a *freeborn* citizen. **2** Relating to or suitable to a free person; as, a citizen's *freeborn* rights.

freed·man \'frēd-mən\ *n.; pl.* **freed·men** \-mən\. A man who had been a slave and has been set free.

free·dom \'frēd-m\ *n.* **1** The condition of being free; liberty; independence. **2** Ease; facility; as, an arrangement of furniture to permit *freedom* of movement. **3** Frankness; outspokenness; as, to speak with too much *freedom.* **4** A being free from any burden, duty, or anxiety; as, *freedom* from worry. **5** Free and unrestricted use; as, to give someone the *freedom* of one's house. **6** The condition of being unmixed with anything else; as, *freedom* from dirt.

free·hand \'frē-ˌhand\ *adj.* Done by hand without the aid of instruments or measurements; as, a *freehand* drawing.

free·hand·ed \'frē-'han-dəd\ *adj.* Generous.

free lance. **1** A knight whose services could be bought by any ruler or state. **2** A person who acts as he chooses without regard to authority. **3** A person who writes, especially for periodicals, without being regularly employed. — **free-lance,** *adj.*

free·ly \'frē-lē\ *adv.* In a free manner; as, to move *freely* back and forth; to speak one's mind *freely.*

free·man \'frē-mən\ *n.; pl.* **free·men** \-mən\. **1** A free person, especially one who has civil or political liberty. **2** A citizen of a town, city, or state.

free on board. Delivered free of charge onto the means of transportation, as a train or boat.

freer. Comparative of *free.*

free-spo·ken \'frē-'spōk-n\ *adj.* Outspoken; frank.

freest. Superlative of *free.*

free·stone \'frē-ˌstōn\ *n.* **1** Any stone, especially sandstone or limestone, that may be cut freely without splitting. **2** A stone, as in certain peaches or cherries, that does not cling to the flesh of the fruit. **3** A fruit having such a stone.

free·think·er \'frē-'thingk-r\ *n.* A person who forms opinions independently; especially, a person who rejects the authority or teachings of the church. — **free·think·ing** \-ing\ *n.* or *adj.*

free trade. **1** Trade free from any tariffs or restrictions intended to change its natural course. **2** The system or policy of maintaining this condition of trade.

free verse. Verse or poetry without meter, rhyme, or regular division into stanzas; irregular but usually rhythmical verse.

free·way \'frē-ˌwā\ *n.* An express highway that bypasses towns and is mostly free of intersections; a superhighway.

free·will \'frē-ˌwil\ *adj.* Of one's own free will; voluntary; as, a *freewill* offering.

freeze \'frēz\ *v.;* **froze** \'frōz\; **fro·zen** \'frōz-n\; **freez·ing**. **1** To harden into ice or to be hardened by cold into ice; as, to *freeze* cream; to wait for the river to *freeze* over. **2** To chill with cold; especially, to injure or kill with cold; as, a night cold enough to *freeze* all the plants. **3** To become motionless; to cling or stick as if frozen; as, to *freeze* in one's tracks. The rusty muffler *froze* to the exhaust pipe. **4** To clog or to become clogged with ice, as a water pipe. — *n.* **1** A freezing or a being frozen. **2** A freezing condition; a period of freezing weather. — **freez·ing point** \'frē-zing\. The temperature at which a liquid solidifies, as indicated on a scale of measurement. The *freezing point* of water is 32 degrees Fahrenheit or zero degrees centigrade.

freez·er \'frēz-r\ *n.* **1** A person or thing that freezes; as, an ice cream *freezer*. **2** An insulated compartment or room equipped to freeze perishable foods rapidly. **3** A box equipped for both quick freezing and storage, especially for the use of one family.

freight \'frāt\ *n.* **1** The amount paid, as to a railroad or a steamship company, for carrying goods. **2** Goods or cargo carried by a ship, train, truck, or airplane; as, a ship that carries *freight* and passengers. **3** The carrying of goods from one place to another, as by train or truck; as, to ship something by *freight*. **4** A train that carries freight; as, a slow *freight*. — *v.* **1** To load with goods to be carried from one place to another; to load; as, a vessel *freighted* with miscellaneous cargo. **2** To send or carry by freight; as, to *freight* one's household goods across the country.

freight·er \'frāt-r\ *n.* **1** A person employed in receiving and forwarding freight. **2** A ship used mainly for carrying freight; a cargo vessel.

French \'french\ *adj.* Of or relating to France. — *n.* **1** The French people — used as a plural with *the*. **2** The language of France.

French horn. A musical instrument in the form of a long, bent, cone-shaped tube flaring at one end and having a funnel-shaped mouthpiece at the other.

French horn

French·man \'french-mən\ *n.; pl.* **French·men** \-mən\. A native or a citizen of France. — **French·wom·an** \-ˌwu̇m-ən\ *n.*

fre·net·ic \frə-'net-ik\ *adj.* Frantic; frenzied. — **fre·net·i·cal·ly** \-ik-l(-)ē\ *adv.*

fren·zied \'fren-zēd\ *adj.* Wildly excited and agitated; frantic.

fren·zy \'fren-zē\ *n.; pl.* **fren·zies**. Wild excitement; violent agitation almost like madness; as, to tear one's hair in a *frenzy* of rage.

fre·quence \'frēk-wən(t)s\ *n.* Frequency.

fre·quen·cy \'frēk-wən-sē\ *n.; pl.* **fre·quen·cies**. **1** The condition or fact of being frequent; repeated occurrence; as, to be concerned about the *frequency* of accidents. **2** Rate of occurrence. **3** In physics, the number of vibrations or cycles in a period of time, as the number of complete cycles of current produced by an alternating-current generator per second.

fre·quent \'frēk-wənt\ *adj.* Often repeated; occurring often; as, to make *frequent* trips to the city. — \frē-'kwent, 'frēk-wənt\ *v.* To visit often; to have the habit of going to; to be often found in; as, to cultivate a habit of *frequenting* the library; a restaurant much *frequented* by people of fashion. — **fre·quent·er** \frē-'kwent-r, 'frēk-wənt-r\ *n.*

fre·quent·ly \'frēk-wənt-lē\ *adv.* At frequent or short intervals; often.

fres·co \'fres-ˌkō\ *n.; pl.* **fres·cos**. **1** The art or method of painting on freshly spread plaster before it dries. **2** A picture painted by this method. — *v.;* **fres·coed**; **fres·co·ing**. To paint in fresco, as walls.

fresh \'fresh\ *adj.* **1** Newly produced, gathered, or made; not stored, preserved, or frozen; as, *fresh* vegetables. **2** Not salt; as, *fresh* water. **3** Pure; cool; as, *fresh* air. **4** Fairly strong; brisk; as, a *fresh* wind. **5** New; recent; as, *fresh* news. **6** Not stale, sour, or decayed; as, *fresh* bread; *fresh* meat. **7** Not tired; lively; as, a *fresh* horse; to get up feeling *fresh* and vigorous after a good night's sleep. **8** Inexperienced; as, to take on a *fresh* helper. **9** Impudent; bold; forward. — For synonyms see *new*.

fresh·en \'fresh-n\ *v.;* **fresh·ened**; **fresh·en·ing** \-n(-)ing\. **1** To make fresh; to refresh; to revive; as, to *freshen* oneself up with a quick wash. **2** To grow brisk or strong. The wind *freshened*. **3** To brighten in appearance; as, to *freshen* a room with new paper and paint.

fresh·et \'fresh-ət\ *n.* A sudden overflowing of a stream; as, spring *freshets*.

fresh·ly \'fresh-lē\ *adv.* In a fresh manner; especially, newly or recently; as, *freshly* baked rolls; a *freshly* papered and painted room.

fresh·man \'fresh-mən\ *n.; pl.* **fresh·men** \-mən\. A first year student, as in high school or college.

fresh·wa·ter \'fresh-ˌwȯt-r, -ˌwät-r\ *adj.* **1** Of or living in water that is not salt; as, *freshwater* fish. **2** Accustomed only to navigation on fresh water and not on the ocean; as, a *freshwater* sailor.

fret \'fret\ *v.;* **fret·ted**; **fret·ting**. **1** To wear out; to rub away or cause by rubbing away; as, to *fret* a hole in cloth. **2** To worry; to be irritated; as, to *fret* oneself sick; nothing to *fret* about. — *n.* An irritated or worried state; as, to be in a *fret*.

fret \'fret\ *n.* A decorative design, as for a wall molding, consisting of short lines or bars arranged in symmetrical patterns. — *v.;* **fret·ted**; **fret·ting.** To decorate with frets.

frets

fret \'fret\ *n.* A ridge, usually of metal or ivory, fixed across the long neck or finger board of a banjo, guitar, or similar instrument. — **fret·ted** \'fret-əd\ *adj.*

fret·ful \'fret-fəl\ *adj.* Ill-humored; irritable; peevish; as, a *fretful* child. — For synonyms see *peevish.* — **fret·ful·ly** \-fə-lē\ *adv.*

fret·work \'fret-ˌwərk\ *n.* Ornamental work adorned with frets; decorative openwork, carving, or molding in the form of frets or similar designs.

Fri. Abbreviation for *Friday.*

fri·a·ble \'frī-əb-l\ *adj.* Easily crumbled or reduced to powder; as, *friable* soil. — **fri·a·bil·i·ty** \ˌfrī-ə-'bil-ət-ē\ or **fri·a·ble·ness** \'frī-əb-l-nəs\ *n.*

fri·ar \'frīr\ *n.* A member of one of certain Roman Catholic religious orders for men in which monastic life is combined with preaching and other priestly duties.

fri·ary \'frīr-ē\ *n.; pl.* **fri·ar·ies.** A monastery; a brotherhood of friars.

fric·as·see \ˌfrik-ə-'sē, 'frik-ə-ˌsē\ *n.* A dish made of chicken, veal, or other meat cut into small pieces and stewed in a thickened gravy. — *v.;* **fric·as·seed**; **fric·as·see·ing.** To cook as a fricassee.

fric·tion \'friksh-n\ *n.* **1** The rubbing of one thing against another. **2** Clash in opinions between persons or groups; disagreement that prevents smooth or harmonious co-operation. **3** The resistance to motion between two surfaces that are touching each other, especially as caused by the roughness of the surfaces. The purpose of lubrication is to reduce *friction.*

fric·tion·al \'friksh-n(-)əl\ *adj.* Relating to friction; produced by friction; as, *frictional* electricity. — **fric·tion·al·ly** \-n(-)ə-lē\ *adv.*

Fri·day \'frīd-ē\ *n.* [From Old English *Frigedaeg,* meaning literally "day of Frig", and named after *Frig,* Germanic goddess of love.] The sixth day of the week.

fried. Past tense and past part. of *fry.*

fried·cake \'frīd-ˌkāk\ *n.* A cake in the form of a ring, twist, ball, or strip, fried in deep fat; a doughnut; a cruller.

friend \'frend\ *n.* **1** A person who has a real liking for and confidence in another person. **2** A person who is not an enemy. Who goes there? *Friend* or foe? **3** A person who aids, favors, or approves; as, a *friend* of modern music. **4** [with a capital] A member of a religious sect called the Society of Friends; a Quaker.

friend·less \'fren-(d)ləs\ *adj.* Having no friends.

friend·ly \'fren-(d)lē\ *adj.;* **friend·li·er**; **friend·li·est.** **1** Showing friendship; kind; as, an unusually *friendly* person; a *friendly* smile. **2** Not hostile; as, *friendly* nations.

friend·ship \'fren(d)-ˌship\ *n.* The state of being friends; friendly attachment between persons; friendly liking; friendliness; as, a lifelong *friendship;* to be unsure of someone's *friendship.*

frieze \'frēz, frē-'zā\ *n.* A woolen cloth with a shaggy surface.

frieze \'frēz\ *n.* A horizontal band or stripe, usually decorated, extending along a wall or around a building or room.

frig·ate \'frig-ət\ *n.* **1** A medium-sized three-masted, square-sailed warship of the late 18th and early 19th centuries. **2** An escort vessel of the British navy, smaller than a destroyer, for use against submarines.

frigate bird. A man-o'-war bird.

fright \'frīt\ *n.* **1** Great fear caused by sudden danger; sudden terror; alarm; as, to cry out in *fright.* **2** Something that frightens. **3** Something that is ugly or shocking. — For synonyms see *fear.*

fright·en \'frīt-n\ *v.;* **fright·ened**; **fright·en·ing** \-n(-)ing\. **1** To throw into a state of fright; to scare; to make afraid. **2** To drive or force by frightening; as, to *frighten* away a burglar.

fright·ened \'frīt-nd\ *adj.* Afraid; scared.

fright·ful \'frīt-fəl\ *adj.* **1** Causing fear or alarm; terrifying; as, a *frightful* sound; a *frightful* accident. **2** Very unpleasant or uncomfortable; shocking. — **fright·ful·ly** \-fə-lē\ *adv.*

frig·id \'frij-əd\ *adj.* **1** Freezing cold; intensely cold; as, a *frigid* climate. **2** Not friendly; as, a *frigid* glance; a *frigid* reply. — **fri·gid·i·ty** \fri-'jid-ət-ē\ *n.* — **frig·id·ly** \'frij-əd-lē\ *adv.*

frill \'fril\ *n.* **1** A gathered, pleated, or ruffled edging, as of lace. **2** Any merely ornamental addition. — *v.* To furnish or be furnished with a frill or frills. — **frilly** \'fril-ē\ *adj.*

fringe \'frinj\ *n.* **1** A border or trimming made of the loose ends of the cloth; an edging made to look like this. **2** Something like a fringe; as, the *fringe* of a forest. — *v.;* **fringed**; **fring·ing.** To decorate with a fringe; to serve as a fringe for.

frip·pery \'frip-r-ē\ *n.; pl.* **frip·per·ies.** **1** Cheap, showy finery. **2** Affected elegance; pretentious display.

frisk \'frisk\ *v.* To jump, skip, or dance in a lively or playful way; as, *frisking* like a puppy.

frisky \'fris-kē\ *adj.;* **frisk·i·er**; **frisk·i·est.** Playful; lively; as, to feel *frisky;* a *frisky* colt.

frit·ter \'frit-r\ *n.* A fried cake of batter to which fruit, corn, or some other ingredient may be added.

frit·ter \'frit-r\ *v.* To scatter; to waste; to spend on unimportant things; as, to *fritter* one's time away.

fri·vol·i·ty \fri-'väl-ət-ē\ *n.; pl.* **fri·vol·i·ties.** **1** Light-mindedness; giddiness; trifling. **2** A frivolous act or thing.

friv·o·lous \'friv-l(-)əs\ *adj.* **1** Of little importance; trivial; as, a *frivolous* matter. **2** Lacking in seriousness; light-minded; giddy; as, to have a *frivolous* attitude. — **friv·o·lous·ly,** *adv.*

friz or **frizz** \'friz\ *v.;* **frizzed**; **friz·zing.** To curl in small crisp curls. — *n.* Something frizzed or curled.

friz·zle \'friz-l\ *v.;* **friz·zled**; **friz·zling** \-l(-)ing\. To fry or broil with a sputtering, sizzling sound; to sizzle.

friz·zle \'friz-l\ *v.;* **friz·zled**; **friz·zling** \-l(-)ing\. To friz. — *n.* A friz. — **friz·zly** \'friz-l(-)ē\ *adj.*

friz·zy \'friz-ē\ *adj.;* **friz·zi·er**; **friz·zi·est.** Tightly curled.

fro \'frō\ *adv.* From a place; away. — **to and fro.** From one side to the other; this way and then that way; back and forth; as, a pendulum swinging *to and fro.*

frock \'fräk\ *n.* **1** A coarse gown worn by monks and friars. **2** A woman's or girl's dress.

frog \'fròg, 'fräg\ *n.* **1** A small tailless web-footed leaping animal that usually lives in water but is capable of living on land. **2** A soreness or swelling in the throat; hoarseness. **3** An ornamental fastening, usually a loop of braid or cord, as on a coat or dress.

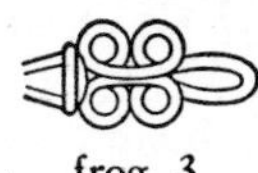

frog, 3

frog·man \'fròg-,man, 'fräg-, -mən\ *n.; pl.* **frog-men** \-,men, -mən\. A swimmer, especially a person in military service, with equipment, such as oxygen helmet and swim fins, permitting an extended stay under water for observation and other activities.

frol·ic \'fräl-ik\ *n.* **1** Lighthearted, merry play; gaiety. **2** A merrymaking. — *v.;* **frol·icked** \-ikt\; **frol·ick·ing** \-ik-ing\. To play pranks; to romp. — **frol·ick·er** \-ik-r\ *n.*

frol·ic·some \'fräl-iks-m\ *adj.* Playful; full of gaiety and mirth. — **frol·ic·some·ly,** *adv.*

from \(')frəm, (')främ\ *prep.* **1** Leaving behind; out of; as, released *from* prison. **2** Starting with; as, to measure *from* here to there. **3** Leaving out, as by avoidance; as, to refrain *from* laughter. **4** After; since; as, a song one has known *from* childhood. **5** Out of; as, to quote *from* a book. **6** By; with; as, a rap *from* his baton. **7** Short of; as, far *from* safe. **8** As a result of; as, to suffer *from* a cold. **9** Out of the control of; as, a child snatched *from* its mother.

frond \'fränd\ *n.* **1** A leaf of a fern. **2** A leaflike shoot or extension, as of a lichen.

front \'frənt\ *n.* **1** The expression of the face or the manner of carrying or behaving oneself; as, to put on a bold *front.* **2** The appearance of wealth or position; as, to put up a false *front.* **3** The forward part or surface of a thing; as, the *front* of a building. **4** A position before a person or thing; as, to stand in *front* of someone. **5** Land that faces something, as a body of water or a road; as, a cottage on the lake *front.* **6** Something worn in a forward position; as, a shirt *front.* **7** In war, the region in which there is active fighting; as, troops being sent to the *front.* **8** The forward boundary of a moving current of air; as, a cold *front.* — *adj.* Being of, on, at, or in the front; as, a *front* room. — *v.* **1** To oppose face to face; to confront. **2** To face; to look toward; as, a house that *fronts* the east. **3** To be in front of. A lawn *fronts* the house.

front·age \'frənt-ij\ *n.* **1** The front face of a building or the direction in which it faces. **2** The front boundary line of a lot abutting on a street. **3** The length of such a line.

fron·tal \'frənt-l\ *adj.* **1** Having to do with the front; on the front; as, a *frontal* attack; a *frontal* view of someone's head. **2** Of or forming the forehead; as, the *frontal* bone.

fron·tier \,frən-'tir, 'frən-, (')frän-\ *n.* **1** The part of a country that borders on another country; a border. **2** The edge of the settled part of a country. **3** A region, as of thought or feeling, not fully explored or developed; as, the *frontiers* of science. — For synonyms see *boundary.*

fron·tiers·man \,frən-'tirz-mən, frän-\ *n.; pl.* **fron·tiers·men** \-mən\. A person living on a frontier.

fron·tis·piece \'frənt-əs-,pēs\ *n.* An illustration facing the first page or the title page of a book.

front·let \'frənt-lət\ *n.* **1** A band for the forehead. **2** The forehead.

frost \'fròst\ *n.* **1** Temperature cold enough to cause freezing; temperature below the freezing point. **2** Frozen dew or vapor; as, trees white with *frost.* **3** A covering of ice crystals forming on a cold surface. — *v.* **1** To injure by frost; to freeze. **2** To make frostlike in appearance or surface; as, to *frost* a cake; to *frost* glass.

frost·bite \'fròst-,bīt\ *v.;* **frost·bit** \-,bit\; **frost-bit·ten** \-,bit-n\; **frost·bit·ing** \-,bīt-ing\. To blight or nip with frost, as a person's finger. — *n.* The freezing of a part of the body, or the effect of having a part frozen. — **frost·bit·ten** \-,bit-n\ *adj.*

frost·ed \'fròs-təd\ *adj.* **1** Covered with frost or with something like frost; as, *frosted* glass. **2** Ornamented with frosting; as, a *frosted* cake. **3** Quick-frozen to preserve and to make easier to ship; as, *frosted* foods.

frost·ing \'fròs-ting\ *n.* **1** A sweet topping for a cake; an icing. **2** A dull finish on glass. **3** A finely pulverized glass used with a mixture of varnish and glue, as in frosting paper shades.

frosty \'fròs-tē\ *adj.;* **frost·i·er**; **frost·i·est.** **1** Freezing; having or causing frost; as, a *frosty* night; *frosty* weather. **2** Not friendly; cold in manner or in feelings; as, to be met with a *frosty* silence. **3** Without warmth; not cordial; as, a *frosty* glance. — **frost·i·ly** \'fròs-tə-lē\ *adv.*

froth \'fròth\ *n.* **1** The bubbly foam caused in liquids by fermentation or stirring. **2** The foam produced by saliva in cases of certain diseases or nervous excitement. **3** Anything light, frivolous, or of little value; as, a speech full of *froth.*

frothy \'fròth-ē\ *adj.;* **froth·i·er**; **froth·i·est.** **1** Foamy; covered with froth; full of froth. **2** Light; of little value. — **froth·i·ly** \'fròth-l-ē\ *adv.*

fro·ward \'frō-(w)ərd\ *adj.* Unwilling to do what is necessary or reasonable; obstinate; willful.

frown \'fraůn\ *v.* **1** To wrinkle the forehead, as in anger, displeasure, or thought; to put on a stern look. **2** To look with disapproval; as, to *frown* upon rudeness. **3** To express with a frown; as, to *frown* one's disapproval. — *n.* A wrinkling of the brow, as in anger.

frowzy or **frowsy** \'frau̇-zē\ *adj.;* **frowz·i·er** or **frows·i·er; frowz·i·est** or **frows·i·est.** Dirty and disordered; slovenly and uncared for.

froze. Past tense of *freeze.*

fro·zen \'frōz-n\. Past part. of *freeze.* — *adj.* **1** Hardened by cold; as, *frozen* custard; *frozen* foods. **2** Having a frigid climate; as, the *frozen* north. **3** Injured or killed by frost or cold. **4** Clogged with ice; as, a *frozen* pipe. **5** Unfriendly; unfeeling; as, a *frozen* stare. **6** Fixed in form or character; unable to move; as, to be *frozen* in one's tracks because of fear.

fruc·tose \'frük-ˌtōs, 'frək-\ *n.* A sugar occurring naturally as levulose.

fru·gal \'früg-l\ *adj.* **1** Economical; thrifty; saving; not wasteful; as, a *frugal* wife. **2** In keeping with economy; involving little expense; as, a *frugal* meal.

— The words *thrifty* and *economical* are synonyms of *frugal: frugal* usually indicates severe simplicity, great moderation, and the absence of luxury; *thrifty* usually suggests industriousness and the habit of saving or of avoiding wastefulness; *economical* suggests not only thrifty use of resources but also careful and skillful use of things to their best advantage.

fru·gal·i·ty \frü-'gal-ət-ē\ *n.; pl.* **fru·gal·i·ties.** Thrift; frugal nature or quality.

fru·gal·ly \'früg-l-ē\ *adv.* In a frugal manner.

fruit \'früt\ *n.* **1** The edible pulpy or juicy part of a plant, tree, shrub, or vine containing the seeds, as an apple or strawberry. **2** The ripened seed vessel with or without its attached parts, as the pod of the pea, a nut, grain, or berry. **3** Any product of plant growth useful to man or animals; as, the *fruits* of the earth. **4** Any product or result, as of study or training; as, the *fruits* of labor.

fruit·age \'früt-ij\ *n.* **1** Fruit; a crop of fruit. **2** The process of bearing fruit.

fruit·cake \'früt-ˌkāk\ *n.* A rich cake usually containing raisins, citron, and currants, and often highly spiced.

fruit·er \'früt-r\ *n.* A ship for transporting fruit.

fruit·er·er \'früt-r-r\ *n.* A fruit dealer.

fruit·fly \'früt-ˌflī\ *n.; pl.* **fruit·flies.** A small two-winged fly whose larvae feed on fruit or decaying vegetable matter.

fruit·ful \'früt-fəl\ *adj.* **1** Producing fruit abundantly; as, a *fruitful* tree. **2** Bringing results; as, a *fruitful* idea. — For synonyms see *fertile.* — **fruit·ful·ly** \-fə-lē\ *adv.*

fru·i·tion \frü-'ish-n\ *n.* **1** The state of bearing fruit; fruitage. **2** Realization; fulfillment; as, the *fruition* of one's hopes.

fruit·less \'früt-ləs\ *adj.* **1** Not bearing fruit. **2** Having no results; unsuccessful; as, *fruitless* efforts. — **fruit·less·ly,** *adv.*

fruity \'früt-ē\ *adj.;* **fruit·i·er; fruit·i·est.** Of or like fruit, as in taste or smell.

frus·trate \'frəs-ˌtrāt\ *v.;* **frus·trat·ed; frus·trat·ing.** To prevent from carrying out a purpose; to defeat; to block; to bring to nothing; as, to have one's plans *frustrated* by an illness. — **frus·tra·tion** \(ˌ)frəs-'trāsh-n\ *n.*

fry \'frī\ *n. sing. and pl.* **1** The young of fishes; very small fishes that swim in schools. **2** A swarm or brood of young of any kind; a crowd of small persons or things; as, a holiday party for the small *fry.*

fry \'frī\ *v.;* **fried** \'frīd\; **fry·ing.** To cook or be cooked in a pan or on a griddle, especially by the use of fat or oil; to brown or sear in hot fat. — *n.; pl.* **fries** \'frīz\. A dish of something fried.

ft. Abbreviation for: **1** *foot.* **2** *feet.*

fuch·sia \'fyü-shə\ *n.* [From scientific Latin, named after Leonhard *Fuchs* (1501–1556), German botanist.] A decorative shrub with deep-pink, red, or purple nodding tube-shaped flowers with long stamens and styles.

fud·dle \'fəd-l\ *v.;* **fud·dled; fud·dling** \-l(-)ing\. To confuse or muddle, as with liquor.

fudge \'fəj\ *n.* **1** Nonsense; humbug. **2** A soft creamy candy, often containing chocolate and nuts.

fu·el \'fyü-əl\ *n.* **1** Any substance, such as coal, wood, or gasoline, that can be burned to produce heat or power. **2** Anything that increases emotional feeling, excitement, or disorder; as, to add *fuel* to the smoldering revolution. — *v.;* **fu·eled** or **fu·elled; fu·el·ing** or **fu·el·ling.** To supply with fuel; to take on fuel; as, to *fuel* an airplane.

fu·gi·tive \'fyü-jət-iv\ *adj.* **1** Fleeing; running away from danger; trying to escape a pursuer; as, a *fugitive* slave. **2** Liable to vanish suddenly; not fixed or lasting; as, *fugitive* thoughts. — *n.* A person who is running away; as, a *fugitive* from justice.

fugue \'fyüg\ *n.* A musical composition in which different parts repeat the theme one after the other.

-ful *in senses 1 and 2,* fəl *or* fl; *in sense 3,* ˌfu̇l\. A suffix that can mean: **1** Full of, abounding in, or characterized by, as in *painful, colorful, tactful.* **2** Tending to, able to, as in *mournful.* **3** Quantity that would fill, as in *cupful* or *mouthful.*

ful·crum \'fu̇lk-rəm, 'fəlk-\ *n.; pl.* **ful·crums** \-rəmz\ or **ful·cra** \-rə\. The support, as a wedge or hinge, about which a lever turns.

fulcrum

ful·fill or **ful·fil** \(')fu̇l-'fil\ *v.;* **ful·filled; ful·fill·ing.** To carry into effect, as a purpose; to bring to pass; as, to *fulfill* a promise; to have all one's greatest hopes *fulfilled.* — **ful·fill·ment** or **ful·fil·ment,** *n.*

full \'fu̇l\ *v.* To thicken by moistening, heating, and pressing, as newly-woven cloth.

full \'fu̇l\ *adj.* **1** Filled; able to hold or contain nothing more; as, a *full* glass. **2** Having an occupant; not vacant. The seats are all *full.* **3** Satisfied with food or drink; serving to satisfy; as, a *full* stomach; a *full* meal. **4** Complete, as in number, amount, or duration; as, a *full* orchestra; a *full* year. **5** Of maximum size or development; as, a *full* moon. **6** Having volume and depth; as, *full* tones. **7** That fills; as, a *full* cargo. **8** Filled or rounded out; as, a *full* face; *full* sails. **9** Abundantly supplied; as, a *full* purse. **10** Wholly taken up or occupied, as with a thought or plan; as, a person *full* of good intentions. **11** Hanging in folds or gathers; as, a *full* skirt. — *n.* Full measure, length, or size; fullness; as, filled to the *full.* — **full of the moon.** The time during which the moon is full. — *adv.* Entirely; completely; fully; as, to fill a bucket *full;* to look a person *full* in the eye. — *v.* To make or become full; especially, to gather or pucker, as cloth. — **full·ness** or **ful·ness,** *n.*

full·back \'fu̇l-ˌbak\ *n.* One of the backs on a football team, originally the one stationed farthest from the opponent's goal.

full-blown \'fu̇l-'blōn\ *adj.* **1** Fully expanded; fully developed; as, a *full-blown* rose. **2** Fully distended with wind, as a sail.

full dress. The style of clothes required by custom or fashion for ceremonial occasions; especially, the style of clothes required for formal evening wear.

full·er \'fu̇l-r\ *n.* A person whose occupation is to full cloth.

full·er's earth \'fu̇l-rz\. A claylike substance used in fulling cloth, in filtering, as oil, and as a catalyst.

full-fledged \'fu̇l-'flejd\ *adj.* **1** Having full plumage; as, a *full-fledged* robin. **2** Having reached the developed stage; as, a *full-fledged* lawyer.

full-rigged \'fu̇l-'rigd\ *adj.* Having three or more masts, each with its full set of square sails.

ful·ly \'fu̇l-(l)ē\ *adv.* Completely; wholly; abundantly; as, to be *fully* satisfied; to be *fully* aware of what one is doing.

ful·mi·nate \'fu̇l-mə-ˌnāt, 'fəl-\ *v.;* **ful·mi·nat·ed; ful·mi·nat·ing.** [From Latin *fulminatus,* past participle of *fulminare* meaning literally "to strike with lightning".] **1** To explode suddenly and violently. **2** To thunder out, as threats or orders; to denounce something violently. The speaker *fulminated* against the proposed law. — *n.* A fulminating powder. — **ful·mi·na·tion** \ˌfu̇l-mə-'nāsh-n, ˌfəl-\ *n.*

ful·some \'fu̇ls-m\ *adj.* Too flattering; offensive; disgusting; as, *fulsome* praise.

fum·ble \'fəm-bl\ *v.;* **fum·bled; fum·bling** \-bl(-)ing\. **1** To feel or grope about clumsily; as, to *fumble* in one's pocket for a key. **2** To handle or manage something clumsily; to fail to grasp firmly; especially, in certain games, as baseball and football, to fail to hold, catch, or handle the ball properly. — *n.* The action of fumbling. — **fum·bling·ly** \-bl(-)ing-lē\ *adv.* — **fum·bler** \-blər\ *n.*

fume \'fyüm\ *n.* [usually in the plural] **1** Smoke having a strong smell, as from tobacco or incense. **2** A heavy disagreeable odor; as, the *fumes* of coal gas. — *v.;* **fumed; fum·ing. 1** To give off fumes; as, a *fuming* volcano. **2** To show bad temper; to give expression to annoyance or irritation; as, to *fume* over a delay.

fu·mi·gant \'fyü-mə-gənt\ *n.* Any substance used for fumigation.

fu·mi·gate \'fyü-mə-ˌgāt\ *v.;* **fu·mi·gat·ed; fu·mi·gat·ing.** To expose to smoke, vapor, or gas, especially in order to disinfect of germs of disease or to destroy insect pests; as, to *fumigate* a room; to *fumigate* the clothing of persons exposed to a disease. — **fu·mi·ga·tion** \ˌfyü-mə-'gāsh-n\ *n.* — **fu·mi·ga·tor** \'fyü-mə-ˌgāt-r\ *n.*

fumy \'fyü-mē\ *adj.;* **fum·i·er; fum·i·est.** Producing fumes; fumelike.

fun \'fən\ *n.* Sport; merriment; amusement. — **make fun of.** To laugh at; to hold up to ridicule. — *v.;* **funned; fun·ning.** To act in fun; to make fun; to joke; as, a rude thing to say even if one were only *funning.*

func·tion \'fəng(k)sh-n\ *n.* **1** The particular purpose for which a thing exists; the natural or proper action or work of anything; as, the *function* of the heart. The *function* of a knife is cutting. **2** An impressive ceremony or social affair. **3** In mathematics, a quantity so related to another quantity that any change in the value of one is associated with a corresponding change in the other. — *v.;* **func·tioned; func·tion·ing** \-n(-)ing\. To perform its function or the function of; to act; to operate; to work; as, an engine that does not *function* well in cold weather; a shortstop who could also *function* as a pitcher.

func·tion·al \'fəng(k)sh-n(-)əl\ *adj.* **1** Of or relating to a function or functions. **2** Serving a function or purpose; especially, designed and developed in all details to serve a special, useful purpose; as, the purely *functional* construction of a modern office building; *functional* styles in furniture. **3** In medicine, affecting functioning but not structure, as of an organ; as, a *functional* disease of the heart. — **func·tion·al·ly** \-n(-)ə-lē\ *adv.*

func·tion·ary \'fəng(k)sh-n-ˌer-ē\ *n.; pl.* **func·tion·ar·ies.** A person charged with the performance of a certain function; especially, an official.

fund \'fənd\ *n.* **1** A stock; a supply; as, an old soldier with a *fund* of exciting stories. **2** A sum of money, especially one the income from which is to be used for a special purpose; as, a *fund* for library books. **3** [in the plural] Money in one's possession; as, to be out of *funds.* — *v.* To convert, as current or short-term financial obligations, into long-term debt bearing interest; as, the *funded* debt of a corporation.

fun·da·men·tal \ˌfənd-m-'ent-l\ *adj.* Of or relating to the foundation; basic; essential; as, a *fundamental* principle of arithmetic. The right to trial by jury is *fundamental* in our legal system. — *n.* A principle or law that serves as the groundwork of a system; essential part; as, to teach the *funda-*

mentals of arithmetic. — **fun·da·men·tal·ly** \-'ent-l-ē\ *adv.*

fu·ner·al \'fyün-r(-)əl\ *adj.* Of or relating to a funeral; suitable for a funeral; as, a *funeral* march; a *funeral* procession. — *n.* **1** The ceremonies preceding and accompanying the burial or cremation of a dead person. **2** A funeral procession.

fu·ne·re·al \fyü-'nir-ē-əl\ *adj.* Befitting a funeral; like a funeral; sad and solemn; gloomy; dismal. — **fu·ne·re·al·ly** \-ē-ə-lē\ *adv.*

fun·gi·cide \'fəng-gə-ˌsīd, 'fən-jə-\ *n.* Any substance that destroys fungi. — **fun·gi·cid·al** \ˌfəng-gə-'sīd-l, ˌfən-jə-\ *adj.*

fun·gous \'fəng-gəs\ *adj.* **1** Of or like fungi; as, a *fungous* growth. **2** Caused by a fungus; as, a *fungous* affection of the skin.

fun·gus \'fəng-gəs\ *n.; pl.* **fun·gi** \'fən-ˌjī, 'fəng-ˌgī\ or **fun·gus·es** \'fəng-gə-səz\. **1** Any of a group of flowerless plants containing no chlorophyll and growing on other plants or on decaying matter, as the molds, mildews, and mushrooms. **2** In medicine, a spongy growth, as one on the skin. — *adj.* Of, relating to, or like a fungus; fungous.

fu·nic·u·lar \fyü-'nik-yəl-r, fə-\ *n.* Also **funicular railway**. A cable railway; especially, a mountain railway on which each ascending car is counterbalanced in weight by a descending car.

fun·nel \'fən-l\ *n.* **1** A device, usually shaped like a hollow inverted cone with a narrow tube attached, for pouring liquids and powders into small-mouthed receptacles. **2** A smokestack; as, a steamship with two *funnels.* — *v.;* **fun·neled** or **fun·nelled; fun·nel·ing** or **fun·nel·ling.** To pass through or as if through a funnel.

funnel, 1

fun·ny \'fən-ē\ *adj.;* **fun·ni·er; fun·ni·est. 1** Causing laughter; comical; as, a *funny* story. **2** Strange; odd; queer; as, to hear a *funny* noise in the cellar. — *n.; pl.* **fun·nies.** Something funny; especially [in the plural], comic strips, as in a newspaper. — **fun·ni·ly** \'fən-l-ē\ *adv.*

funny bone. A place at the back of the elbow where the striking of a nerve causes a painful tingling sensation.

fur \'fər\ *n.* **1** A piece of the prepared pelt of any of certain animals, used in making, trimming, or lining garments. **2** An article of clothing made of or trimmed with such pieces. **3** The hairy coat of a mammal, especially when fine, soft, and thick. **4** Any furlike coating, as on the tongue. — *adj.* Relating to or made of fur; as, a *fur* coat. — *v.;* **furred; fur·ring.** To line, face, cover, or clothe with fur.

fur·be·low \'fərb-l-ˌō\ *n.* A flounce or ruffle; any showy trimming.

fur·bish \'fər-bish\ *v.* To make bright and new-looking by polishing; to restore to freshness and vigor; as, to *furbish* a sword. — **fur·bish·er,** *n.*

fu·ri·ous \'fyür-ē-əs\ *adj.* **1** Being in a fury; fierce; angry; as, a *furious* storm; to be *furious* with someone. **2** Rushing; violent; as, a *furious* assault. — **fu·ri·ous·ly,** *adv.*

furl \'fərl\ *v.* To wrap or roll close to or around something; to curl or fold; as, to *furl* a flag. — *n.* A furling; a coil, as of rope.

fur·long \'fər-ˌlȯng\ *n.* A measure of length equaling one eighth of a mile, or 220 yards.

fur·lough \'fər-ˌlō\ *n.* A leave of absence from duty, especially to a soldier. — *v.* To grant a furlough to; as, a soldier *furloughed* for 30 days.

fur·nace \'fər-nəs\ *n.* An enclosed place in which heat is produced, as for heating a house or for melting metals.

fur·nish \'fər-nish\ *v.* **1** To provide with what is needed or wanted; to equip; as, to *furnish* a house. **2** To supply; as, a stream that *furnishes* water power. — **fur·nish·er,** *n.*

fur·nish·ing \'fər-nish-ing\ *n.* **1** The supplying of furniture or fittings. **2** [in the plural] Furniture; things used in making a room or house ready to live in. **3** [in the plural] Articles of dress; as, boys' *furnishings.*

fur·ni·ture \'fər-nich-r\ *n.* **1** A supply of articles making up the fittings of something, as of an automobile or bed. **2** Movable articles, such as chairs and tables, used in furnishing a room.

fu·ror \'fyu̇r-ˌōr, -ˌȯr\ *n.* **1** Fury; rage; as, the *furor* of a storm at sea. **2** Wild excitement; as, the *furor* over a new discovery in medical science. **3** An object of widespread enthusiastic admiration; a craze; as, the *furor* of the moment among the younger set.

fu·rore \'fyu̇r-ˌōr, -ˌȯr\ *n.* Furor; especially, a craze or mania.

furred \'fərd\ *adj.* Bearing or wearing fur; trimmed or lined with fur.

fur·ri·er \'fər-ē-ər, 'fə-rē-\ *n.* A person who prepares or deals in furs.

fur·ring \'fər-ing\ *n.* **1** Fur trimmings or lining. **2** In building, the putting of thin wood, brick, or metal on a surface to level it. **3** The material used for this purpose.

fur·row \'fər-ō, 'fə-rō\ *n.* **1** A trench in the earth made by, or as if by, a plow. **2** Any narrow groove; a wrinkle; as, the *furrows* of age. — *v.* To make furrows in; to plow; to make wrinkles; as, a brow *furrowed* with care.

fur·ry \'fər-ē\ *adj.;* **fur·ri·er; fur·ri·est. 1** Of or like fur. **2** Covered with or dressed in fur.

fur·ther \'fər<u>th</u>-r\ *adj. in comparative degree.* [There is no positive degree for this adjective — see *far.*] **1** Farther; more distant; as, the *further* end of the street. **2** Additional; more; as, *further* trouble. — *adv.* **1** Farther; beyond the present or a particular point; to a greater extent or degree; as, to look no *further.* **2** In addition; furthermore. — *v.;* **fur·thered; fur·ther·ing** \-r(-)ing\. To help forward; to promote; as, to *further* a plan.

fur·ther·ance \'fər<u>th</u>-r(-)ən(t)s\ *n.* A furthering; advancement; as, the *furtherance* of a cause.

fur·ther·more \ˈfərth-r-ˌmōr, -ˌmȯr\ *adv.* Moreover; besides.

fur·ther·most \ˈfərth-r-ˌmōst\ *adj.* Most distant; most remote; furthest; as, the *furthermost* peak of the mountain range.

fur·thest \ˈfər-thəst\ *adj.* or *adv. in superlative degree.* [See *further* and *far.*] Farthest.

fur·tive \ˈfərt-iv\ *adj.* Done by stealth; sly; secret; as, a *furtive* look or manner. — **fur·tive·ly**, *adv.* — **fur·tive·ness**, *n.*

fu·ry \ˈfyu̇r-ē\ *n.; pl.* **fu·ries. 1** Violent anger; rage. **2** A person given to spells of rage. **3** Fierceness; violence; as, the *fury* of a storm.

furze \ˈfərz\ *n.* A prickly, mostly leafless, evergreen shrub of the pea family, with yellow flowers.

fuse \ˈfyüz\ *n.* **1** A cord soaked in some flammable substance or a tube or case filled with combustible matter, lighted to set off an explosive charge, as in firing a cannon or in blasting. **2** A piece of easily melted metal inserted in an electric circuit, intended to melt under a dangerously heavy current and thus break the circuit.

fuse \ˈfyüz\ *v.;* **fused**; **fus·ing. 1** To melt; to liquefy by heat; as, to *fuse* metals. **2** To unite or blend, as if melted together.

fu·see or **fu·zee** \fyü-ˈzē\ *n.* **1** A match not easily blown out after being lighted. **2** A flare used as a signal, especially on railroads.

fu·se·lage \ˈfyüs-l-ˌäzh, ˈfyüz-l-, -ˌäzh\ *n.* The long narrow body of an airplane, which holds the crew, passengers, and cargo, and to which the wings and tail are attached.

fus·i·ble \ˈfyü-zəb-l\ *adj.* Capable of being fused; especially, capable of being melted or liquefied with relative ease. Lead is a very *fusible* metal. — **fus·i·bil·i·ty** \ˌfyü-zə-ˈbil-ət-ē\ *n.*

fu·si·form \ˈfyü-zə-ˌfȯrm\ *adj.* Spindle-shaped; tapering at each end.

fu·sil·ier or **fu·sil·eer** \ˌfyüz-l-ˈir\ *n.* **1** A soldier armed with a light flintlock musket. **2** [in the plural] The name or title used by certain British regiments.

fu·sil·lade \ˌfyüs-l-ˈäd, ˌfyüz-, -ˈäd, -ˈȧd\ *n.* **1** A discharge of many firearms at the same time or a series of rapid discharges. **2** A series, as of questions or remarks, suggestive of gunfire in its rapidity.

fu·sion \ˈfyüzh-n\ *n.* **1** A fusing or melting together; as, the *fusion* of metals. **2** A blending or merging; as, the *fusion* of many nationalities in a large city. **3** Something formed by the fusing of different things; a union. **4** The union of atomic nuclei to form heavier nuclei that results in the release of atomic energy.

fusion bomb. A bomb in which nuclei of a light chemical element unite with a release of energy; especially, a hydrogen bomb.

fuss \ˈfəs\ *n.* A commotion, especially an unnecessary one; petty worry; bustle; stir; as, to make a *fuss* over nothing. — *v.* To bother; to make a commotion, especially about little things.

fussy \ˈfəs-ē\ *adj.;* **fuss·i·er**; **fuss·i·est. 1** Inclined to fuss; as, a *fussy* child. **2** Too particular; as, a person who is *fussy* about his clothes. **3** Showing or needing a great deal of work; as, a *fussy* dress. — **fuss·i·ly** \ˈfəs-l-ē\ *adv.*

fus·tian \ˈfəs-chən\ *n.* **1** Cotton and linen cloth. **2** Corduroy or velveteen. **3** Pompous language; bombast; as, a political speech full of rant and *fustian.*

fusty \ˈfəs-tē\ *adj.;* **fust·i·er**; **fust·i·est. 1** Moldy; musty. The empty room gave off a *fusty* odor. **2** Old-fashioned; like an old fogy.

fu·tile \ˈfyüt-l, ˈfyü-ˌtīl\ *adj.* **1** Having no result or effect; vain; useless; as, a *futile* struggle against overwhelming forces; to waste time in *futile* talk. **2** Unimportant; trivial; as, a round of *futile* pleasures. — **fu·tile·ly** \ˈfyüt-l-(l)ē, ˈfyü-ˌtīl-lē\ *adv.*

fu·til·i·ty \fyü-ˈtil-ət-ē\ *n.; pl.* **fu·til·i·ties. 1** Uselessness; as, to be at last convinced of the *futility* of continuing to fight. **2** Worthlessness; unimportance. Most people now and then have a feeling of their own *futility.*

fu·ture \ˈfyüch-r\ *adj.* [From medieval English, there borrowed from medieval French *futur*, there borrowed from Latin *futurus*, the future participle of *esse* meaning "to be".] **1** Coming after the present; that is to be or come hereafter; as, *future* events. **2** Expressing time yet to come; as, a verb in the *future* tense. — *n.* **1** Time that is to come; future time. **2** [in the plural] Things bought and sold for future delivery, especially commodities such as grain and cotton. **3** The future tense or a verb in that tense.

fu·ture·less \ˈfyüch-r-ləs\ *adj.* Without prospect of future success; as, an apparently *futureless* young man.

future perfect tense. The tense that in English is formed with *will have* and *shall have* and that indicates completion of an action earlier than a specified time that is still to come, as in "They *will have finished* dinner before we get there".

future tense. The tense that in English is formed with *will* and *shall* and that indicates action or occurrence at a time that is still to come, as in "I *shall go* tomorrow".

fu·tu·ri·ty \fyü-ˈtu̇r-ət-ē, -ˈtyu̇r-\ *n.; pl.* **fu·tu·ri·ties. 1** The state of being yet to come. **2** Future time; the future. **3** A future event.

fuze \ˈfyüz\ *n.* A fuse.

fuzee. Variant of *fusee.*

fuzz \ˈfəz\ *n.* Fine light particles or fibers; fluff; down.

fuzzy \ˈfəz-ē\ *adj.;* **fuzz·i·er**; **fuzz·i·est. 1** Having fuzz; covered with fuzz; as, a *fuzzy* caterpillar. **2** Indistinct; not clear; as, *fuzzy* outlines; *fuzzy* sounds.

-fy \ˌfī\. A suffix that can mean: to make or become, or to form or make into, as in *beautify, intensify, simplify, solidify.*

g \'jē\ *n.; pl.* **g's** \'jēz\. The seventh letter of the alphabet.

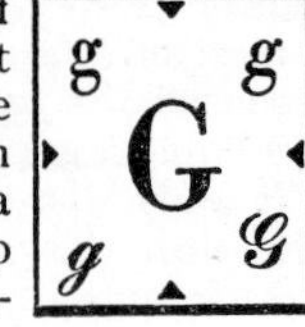

G \'jē\ *n.; pl.* **G's** \'jēz\. A unit of force equal to a person's weight and used to express the forces he experiences, as when he is in an airplane that is pulling out of a dive or that is making a sharp turn. The pilot of the plane experienced a force of three *G's*.

g. Abbreviation for *gram*.

gab \'gab\ *v.;* **gabbed; gab·bing.** To chatter; to gabble; as, to waste the morning *gabbing* with the neighbors. — *n.* Chatter.

gab·ar·dine \'gab-r-ˌdēn\ *n.* **1** A gaberdine. **2** A firm, durable fabric made of various fibers, having a twill weave and a smooth, hard finish, used for clothing. **3** A garment of this fabric, especially a coat or suit.

gab·ble \'gab-l\ *v.;* **gab·bled; gab·bling** \-l(-)ing\. To talk fast, or to talk without meaning; to jabber; to chatter. — *n.* Loud or rapid talk without meaning. — **gab·bler** \-l(-)ər\ *n.*

gab·er·dine \'gab-r-ˌdēn\ *n.* **1** A loose frock or coat. **2** The medieval Jewish gown or mantle.

ga·ble \'gāb-l\ *n.* **1** The triangular part of an outside wall of a building, formed by the sides of the roof sloping down from the ridgepole to the eaves. **2** A similar triangular space, as over a door or window. — **ga·bled** \'gāb-ld\ *adj.*

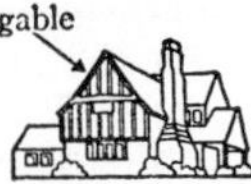

gable roof. A roof that forms a gable at each end.

gad \'gad\ *n.* A pointed stick; a goad.

gad \'gad\ *v.;* **gad·ded; gad·ding.** To roam about; to wander restlessly in search of pleasure or excitement. — **gad·der** \'gad-r\ *n.*

gad·about \'gad-ə-ˌbaủt\ *adj.* Gadding; roaming idly about; as, to lead a *gadabout* life. — *n.* A person who gads about.

gad·fly \'gad-ˌflī\ *n.; pl.* **gad·flies** \-ˌflīz\. A fly that bites, as a horsefly.

gadg·et \'gaj-ət\ *n.* A contrivance; a device; as, a *gadget* for peeling potatoes; a house filled with all the latest *gadgets*.

gaff \'gaf\ *n.* **1** A barbed spear or iron hook with a handle, used in lifting heavy fish from the water. **2** Something difficult to bear; as, a person unable to stand the *gaff*. **3** A spar along the top of a fore-and-aft sail. — *v.* To strike or hold with a gaff.

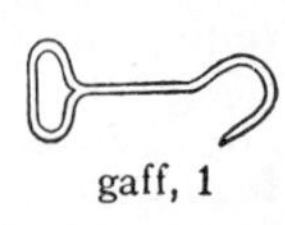
gaff, 1

gag \'gag\ *v.;* **gagged; gag·ging. 1** To prevent from speaking by stopping up the mouth. **2** To choke; to retch or strain as in vomiting; as, to *gag* on bitter medicine. — *n.* **1** A mouthful that chokes or that produces retching. **2** Something pushed into the mouth to prevent speech. **3** A joke; a practical joke.

gage \'gāj\. Variant of *gauge*.

gage \'gāj\ *n.* **1** A pledge, as a glove or cap thrown upon the ground, that one will appear to defend one's claims. **2** A challenge; a defiance.

gager. Variant of *gauger*.

gai·e·ty or **gay·e·ty** \'gā-ət-ē\ *n.; pl.* **gai·e·ties** or **gay·e·ties. 1** The state of being gay; gay spirits, actions, or talk. **2** Finery; show; as, *gaiety* in dress.

gai·ly or **gay·ly** \'gā-lē\ *adv.* **1** In a gay or lively manner; merrily; as, to talk *gaily*. **2** Brightly; in a fine and showy manner; as, *gaily* dressed or decorated.

gain \'gān\ *n.* **1** Profit or advantage; as, to share in the *gains*. **2** An increase or addition in amount or degree; as, a *gain* in weight. **3** The getting of something, as money; acquisition; as, the desire for *gain*. — *v.* **1** To get; to earn; to acquire; to win; as, to *gain* experience; to *gain* a victory. **2** To get by increases; to advance; to make progress; as, to *gain* in strength; to *gain* five pounds. **3** To reach; to arrive at; as, to *gain* the top of the hill.

gain·er \'gān-r\ *n.* **1** One that gains, profits, or wins an advantage; as, the best ground *gainer* on the football team. **2** In fancy diving, a back somersault made from the take-off position for a front dive.

gain·ful \'gān-fəl\ *adj.* Producing gain; profitable; paid; as, *gainful* employment. — **gain·ful·ly** \-fə-lē\ *adv.*

gain·say \'gān-'sā\ *v.;* **gain·said** \-'sād, -'sed\; **gain·say·ing.** To speak against; to contradict; to oppose; to deny; as, to *gainsay* the truth.

gait \'gāt\ *n.* A manner of walking or running; as, a slow *gait;* to recognize someone by his *gait*. — **gait·ed** \'gāt-əd\ *adj.*

gai·ter \'gāt-r\ *n.* **1** A covering of cloth or leather for the leg from knee to instep or for the ankle and instep. **2** An ankle-high shoe having pieces of elastic in the sides. **3** An overshoe reaching to the ankle or above and having a fabric upper.

gaiter, 1

gal. Abbreviation for *gallon*.

ga·la \'gā-lə, 'gal-ə\ *n.* A festival; a celebration; as, a welcoming *gala* for the visitors. — *adj.* Festive; suitable for festivities; as, a *gala* occasion; *gala* dress.

gal·axy \'gal-ək-sē\ *n.; pl.* **gal·ax·ies.** [From Late Latin *galaxias*, there borrowed from Greek, where it is a derivative of *gala* meaning "milk".] **1** A huge system or swarm of stars and other heavenly bodies occupying a vast region in space; especially, [with a capital] the Milky Way. **2** An assembly of brilliant or famous persons.

gale \'gāl\ *n.* **1** A strong wind. **2** An outburst; as, *gales* of laughter.

ga·le·na \gə-'lē-nə\ *n.* The chief ore of lead.

gall \'gȯl\ *n.* **1** Bile. **2** The gall bladder. **3** Bitterness; hatred; spite. **4** Impudence; brazen self-assurance.

gall \'gȯl\ *n.* A sore spot caused by rubbing or chafing, especially one on a horse's back. — *v.* **1** To make sore by chafing. **2** To annoy; to vex; to irritate; as, to be *galled* by repeated discourteous treatment. **3** To become sore or worn from chafing.

gall \'gȯl\ *n.* A swelling or growth on the tissues of plants, as on a twig or leaf, caused by the attacks of parasites, as the gallfly.

gal·lant \'gal-ənt *in sense 3;* gə-'lant *or* 'gal-ənt *in other senses*\ *adj.* **1** Showy; gay or smart in dress or appearance; as, a *gallant* display of spring flowers. **2** Stately in appearance or action; as, a *gallant* ship. **3** Noble; brave; daring; as, a *gallant* soldier; a *gallant* attempt. **4** Very polite and attentive to women; as, a *gallant* escort. — *n.* **1** A gay, lighthearted man of fashion. **2** A man who is gallant towards women. — **gal·lant·ly**, *adv.*

gal·lant·ry \'gal-ən-trē\ *n.; pl.* **gal·lant·ries. 1** *Archaic.* Gallant appearance. **2** Courage; bravery; as, the *gallantry* of troops in battle. **3** A gallant speech or act. **4** Courteous attentiveness towards women.

gall bladder. A muscular sac of membrane in which the bile produced by the liver is stored until needed.

gal·le·on \'gal-ē-ən, 'gal-yən\ *n.* A large sailing ship, often having three or four decks, of the time of Columbus and later, used for either war or commerce.

gal·lery \'gal-r(-)ē\ *n.; pl.* **gal·ler·ies. 1** A long narrow room, hall, or other passage, especially one having windows along one side. **2** A balcony, as in a theater or church; especially, the highest balcony in a theater or the people who sit in this balcony; as, to play to the *gallery.* **3** A gallerylike room or hall used for a special purpose, as for showing pictures or for target practice; as, a photograph *gallery;* a shooting *gallery.* **4** Any room for the exhibition of works of art. **5** In the southern United States, a veranda. **6** An underground passage, as in a mine or fort. **7** A body of spectators at a contest, as a golf match.

gal·ley \'gal-ē\ *n.; pl.* **gal·leys. 1** A large, low, usually single-decked ship propelled by oars and sails, used in ancient times and in the Middle Ages, chiefly in the Mediterranean Sea. **2** The kitchen of a ship. **3** An oblong tray to hold printer's type that has been set. **4** A proof (**galley proof**) from type in such a tray before it has been separated into pages.

galley

gall·fly \'gȯl-ˌflī\ *n.; pl.* **gall·flies** \-ˌflīz\. An insect that causes galls to form on plants by depositing its eggs in a puncture made in the bark or leaf.

Gal·lic \'gal-ik\ *adj.* Of or relating to ancient Gaul or to France.

gal·li·gas·kins \ˌgal-ē-'gas-kənz\ *n. pl.* **1** Loose wide breeches. **2** *Dial.* Gaiters; leggings.

gall·ing \'gȯl-ing\ *adj.* **1** Irritating. **2** Humiliating; as, to have the *galling* experience of being ridiculed in front of one's schoolmates. — **gall·ing·ly**, *adv.*

gal·li·vant \'gal-ə-ˌvant, ˌgal-ə-'vant\ *v.* **1** To act or play the gallant. **2** To travel or roam about for pleasure; to gad about.

gal·lon \'gal-ən\ *n.* A measure of quantity, especially of liquids, equal to four quarts.

gal·lop \'gal-əp\ *v.* **1** To go at or as if at a gallop; to run with a succession of springs or leaps; as, horses *galloping* across a field. **2** To ride a galloping horse. **3** To cause to gallop; as, to *gallop* a horse. — *n.* **1** A fast springing gait, especially of a horse, with all four feet off the ground at the same time once in each stride; the fastest gait of a horse. **2** A ride on a galloping horse.

gal·lows \'gal-ōz\ *n.; pl.* **gal·lows·es** \'gal-ō-zəz\ or **gal·lows. 1** A frame, usually of two posts and a crossbeam, from which criminals are hanged. **2** The punishment of hanging; as, to be sentenced to the *gallows.*

gall·stone \'gȯl-ˌstōn\ *n.* A hard pebblelike mass formed in the gall bladder or bile passages.

ga·lore \gə-'lōr, -'lȯr\ *adv.* In abundance; as, a Christmas dinner with good things *galore.*

ga·losh \gə-'läsh\ *n.* An overshoe for wear in snow or wet weather.

gal·van·ic \gal-'van-ik\ *adj.* **1** Of or relating to a direct current of electricity, especially from a battery. **2** Affecting or affected as if by an electric shock; electrifying; as, a man of *galvanic* energy; a discovery that had a *galvanic* effect on the world of science. — **gal·van·i·cal·ly** \-ik-l(-)ē\ *adv.*

gal·va·nism \'galv-n-ˌiz-m\ *n.* [Named in honor of Luigi *Galvani* (1737–1798), an Italian physicist who experimented with electricity.] **1** Electricity produced by chemical action in a battery. **2** The science that deals with electrical currents.

gal·va·nize \'galv-n-ˌīz\ *v.;* **gal·va·nized; gal·va·niz·ing. 1** To subject to the action of electrical currents. **2** To stimulate or excite as if by an electric shock; as, to be *galvanized* into action. **3** To coat with zinc in order to protect a surface, especially to prevent rust; as, *galvanized* iron.

gal·va·nom·e·ter \ˌgalv-n-'äm-ət-r\ *n.* An instrument for detecting the presence of a small electric current and determining its strength and direction.

gam·ble \'gam-bl\ *v.;* **gam·bled; gam·bling** \-bl(-)ing\. **1** To play, especially games of chance, for money or some other stake. **2** To bet, as on the outcome of a game or a race. **3** To take risks for the sake of uncertain gains. **4** To lose by gambling; as, to *gamble* away a small fortune. — *n.* Any risky undertaking.

gam·bler \'gam-blər\ *n.* One who gambles; especially, one who gambles a great deal, or who makes an occupation of gambling.

gam·bling \'gam-bl(-)ing\ *n.* The action of one

who gambles; especially, playing for money, as at cards or dice.

gam·boge \gam-'bōj\ *n.* An orange-red resin derived from certain tropical Asiatic trees and used as a yellow pigment by painters and in medicine as a cathartic.

gam·bol \'gam-bl\ *n.* [From French *gambade*, there borrowed from Italian *gambata*, a derivative of *gamba* meaning "leg".] A playful skipping or leaping about. — *v.;* **gam·boled** or **gam·bolled**; **gam·bol·ing** or **gam·bol·ling** \-bl-ing\. To skip about; to frisk; as, lambs *gamboling* in a pasture.

game \'gām\ *n.* **1** Sport of any kind; fun; as, to make *game* of someone. **2** An amusement; a diversion. Tag is a children's *game.* **3** A contest carried on according to set rules, for amusement, exercise, or reward; as, the *game* of baseball; to prefer *games* of skill to *games* of chance. **4** Materials for playing a game; as, to be given a *game* as a birthday present. **5** An undertaking or line of work thought of as like a game; as, the advertising *game.* **6** A scheme; a plan; as, diplomats trying to guess what each other's *game* is. **7** An animal or animals hunted for sport or for food; the flesh of such an animal considered as food. **8** A single contest lasting until a set limit is reached, as of time or points. **9** Manner of playing; as, to play a good defensive *game.*

— The words *play* and *sport* are synonyms of *game: play* is a term applying to almost any form of activity, whether physical or mental, intended to provide amusement and diversion; *sport* may apply to some form of pleasurable physical activity, usually carried on outdoors, either for developing skill and ability or for the enjoyment of friendly competition; *game* may indicate a controlled type of play in the form of a contest under fixed rules.

— *v.;* **gamed**; **gam·ing**. To play, as with cards or dice, for a stake; to gamble. — *adj.;* **gam·er**; **gam·est**. **1** Having a brave and unyielding spirit; plucky; as, a *game* fighter. **2** Of or relating to game, or the animals that are hunted; as, the *game* laws; *game* birds.

game \'gām\ *adj.* Lame; as, a *game* leg.

game·cock \'gām-ˌkäk\ *n.* A rooster trained for fighting.

game·keep·er \'gām-ˌkēp-r\ *n.* A person employed, as on a landed estate, to take care of game and to prevent unauthorized shooting and trapping.

game·ly \'gām-lē\ *adv.* Bravely; with pluck or spirit; as, to fight *gamely* on; to bear pain *gamely.*

game·ness \'gām-nəs\ *n.* Pluck; spirit.

game·some \'gām-səm\ *adj.* Gay; merry; playful.

game·ster \'gām-stər\ *n.* A gambler.

ga·mete \gə-'mēt, 'gam-ˌēt\ *n.* A matured sex cell or germ cell capable of uniting with another cell to form a new plant or animal.

ga·me·to·phyte \gə-'mēt-ə-ˌfīt\ *n.* An individual, in plants that have alternating sexual and asexual generations, of the generation that produces the gametes from which the asexual sporophyte develops.

game warden. An official whose duties are to enforce the laws regulating the shooting and trapping of game.

gam·in \'gam-ən\ *n.* A homeless boy who roams the streets.

gam·ing \'gā-ming\. Pres. part. of *game.* — *n.* Gambling.

gam·ma glob·u·lin \'gam-ə 'gläb-yə-lən\. A blood plasma protein that contains antibodies used against measles, hepatitis, and polio.

gam·ut \'gam-ət\ *n.* [From medieval Latin *gamma ut*, derived from *gamma* and *ut*, two notes of the medieval scale.] **1** The whole series of musical notes; the whole range of a voice or an instrument. **2** Any whole range or series; as, the *gamut* of human emotions.

gamy \'gā-mē\ *adj.;* **gam·i·er**; **gam·i·est**. **1** Game; plucky. **2** Having the flavor of game, especially when slightly tainted; as, *gamy* meat. — **gam·i·ly** \'gām-l-ē\ *adv.* — **gam·i·ness** \'gā-mē-nəs\ *n.*

gan·der \'gand-r\ *n.* A male goose.

gang \'gang\ *n.* **1** A number of persons working or going about together; as, a *gang* of laborers; a *gang* of boys in swimming. **2** A group of persons associated or acting together for lawless or criminal purposes; as, a *gang* of thieves. **3** Two or more similar implements arranged to work together in order to save time and labor; as, a *gang* of saws.

gang \'gang\ *v.* **1** To go about in a gang or group. Those girls usually *gang* together. **2** To set upon as a gang; to oppose or attack in large numbers. The crowd *ganged* the murderer as he was led from jail. — **gang up**. **1** To form into a gang; as, students *ganging up* around a jukebox. **2** To band together, especially for the purpose of opposing or attacking; as, small nations *ganging up* against a large one; spectators *ganging up* on a referee.

gan·gling \'gang-gling\ *adj.* Spindly and awkward; lanky; as, *gangling* boys still at the awkward age.

gan·gli·on \'gang-glē-ən\ *n.; pl.* **gan·gli·ons** \-glē-ənz\ or **gan·glia** \-glē-ə\. A mass of nerve tissue containing nerve cells; a nerve center.

gang·plank \'gang-ˌplangk\ *n.* A long narrow movable platform or bridge extending from the deck of a ship to the shore and used for boarding and leaving the ship.

gang plow. A plow with several shares or a number of plows joined together.

gan·grene \'gan(g)-ˌgrēn, -'grēn\ *n.* The dying of body tissue because of interference with its source of nourishment, as by an injury or disease shutting off the blood supply. — *v.;* **gan·grened**; **gan·gren·ing**. To cause gangrene; to be affected by gangrene. — **gan·gre·nous** \'gan(g)-grə-nəs\ *adj.*

gang·ster \'gang(k)st-r\ *n.* A person who belongs to a lawless or criminal gang.

gang·way \'gang-ˌwā\ *n.* **1** A passage into,

through, or out of any enclosed place. **2** A gangplank. — *interj.* Stand aside! Make way!

gan·net \'gan-ət\ *n.* A large web-footed sea bird that is a powerful flier and that plunges into the water for the fish on which it lives.

gan·try \'gan-trē\ *n.* A frame on side supports that spans or encloses something, as a rocket in preparation for launching.

gaol \'jāl\ *n. Chiefly British.* A jail. — **gaol·er**, *n.*

gap \'gap\ *n.* **1** An opening made by a break or a parting; a breach; a cleft. The earthquake left wide *gaps* in the streets. **2** A mountain pass. **3** Any break or separation; a blank space.

gape \'gāp, 'gap\ *v.;* **gaped**; **gap·ing**. **1** To open the mouth wide, especially in sleepiness or surprise. **2** To stare with open mouth. **3** To open or part widely, as the mouth of a cave. — *n.* A gaping, as a yawn or an openmouthed stare.

ga·rage \gə-'räzh, -'räj, -'ȧzh, -'ȧj\ *n.* **1** A building where automobiles are housed. **2** A repair shop for automobiles. — *v.;* **ga·raged**; **ga·rag·ing**. To keep or put in a garage; as, to *garage* a car.

garb \'gärb, 'gȧrb\ *n.* Fashion or style of dress; clothing; as, the proper *garb* for a picnic. — *v.* To clothe; to dress; as, to go *garbed* as a pirate.

gar·bage \'gär-bij, 'gȧr-\ *n.* Waste food, especially that thrown out from a kitchen.

gar·ble \'gärb-l, 'gȧrb-l\ *v.;* **gar·bled**; **gar·bling** \-l(-)ing\. **1** To tell only selected parts of; to confuse or spoil in telling; as, to *garble* a story. **2** To distort the sound of, as by transposing letters or syllables in a word or phrase.

gar·den \'gärd-n, 'gȧrd-n\ *n.* **1** A piece of ground in which fruits, flowers, or vegetables are grown. **2** An enclosure for the exhibition of plants or animals; as, a botanical *garden;* a zoological *garden.* — *v.;* **gar·dened**; **gar·den·ing** \-n(-)ing\. To make a garden; to work in a garden.

gar·den·er \'gärd-n(-)ər, 'gȧrd-\ *n.* A person who gardens; especially, a person hired to take care of a garden.

gar·de·nia \gär-'dēn-yə, gȧr-, -'dē-nē-ə\ *n.* [Named after Alexander *Garden* (1730–1791) a Scottish-American botanist.] **1** A shrub of the madder family with thick leathery lance-shaped leaves and very fragrant white or yellow flowers. **2** The flower of this shrub.

gar·den·ing \'gärd-n(-)ing, 'gȧrd-\ *n.* The laying out and cultivating of gardens.

gar·gle \'gärg-l, 'gȧrg-l\ *v.;* **gar·gled**; **gar·gling** \-l(-)ing\. To rinse the throat with a liquid kept in motion by air forced through it from the lungs. — *n.* Any liquid used in gargling.

gar·goyle \'gär-ˌgȯil, 'gȧr-\ *n.* A waterspout, often grotesquely carved, jutting out at the roof or eaves of a building.

gargoyle

gar·ish \'gar-ish, 'ger-\ *adj.* Extremely bright; glaring; gaudy; as, *garish* light; *garish* colors. — **gar·ish·ly**, *adv.*

gar·land \'gär-lənd, 'gȧr-\ *n.* A wreath or rope of leaves or flowers; as, a Christmas *garland* of evergreens. — *v.* To form into, or to decorate with, a garland or garlands.

garland

gar·lic \'gär-lik, 'gȧr-\ *n.* A strong-smelling, onionlike plant of the lily family, used in cooking. — **gar·licky** \-lik-ē\ *adj.*

gar·ment \'gär-mənt, 'gȧr-\ *n.* Any article of clothing. — *v.* To clothe.

gar·ner \'gärn-r, 'gȧrn-r\ *n.* **1** A storehouse for grain. **2** A store of anything. — *v.* To gather in; to store up; as, to *garner* grain; to *garner* a fortune.

gar·net \'gär-nət, 'gȧr-\ *n.* **1** A deep red mineral, used as a gem when transparent and of good color. **2** A deep-red color.

gar·nish \'gär-nish, 'gȧr-\ *v.* To decorate, especially food for serving at the table; as, fish *garnished* with lemon and parsley. — *n.* Something used in garnishing. — **gar·nish·er**, *n.*

gar·nish·ment \'gär-nish-mənt, 'gȧr-\ *n.* A garnish.

gar·ni·ture \'gär-nich-r, 'gȧr-\ *n.* A decoration; an embellishment.

gar·ret \'gar-ət\ *n.* The part of a house that is on the top floor just under the roof; an attic.

gar·ri·son \'gar-əs-n\ *n.* **1** A place in which troops are regularly stationed. **2** A body of troops stationed in a fort or a town. — *v.* **1** To furnish with troops for defense, as a fort or a town. **2** To protect with forts and soldiers; as, to *garrison* a frontier.

gar·rote \gə-'rōt, -'rät\ or **gar·rotte** \-'rät\ *n.* **1** A Spanish method of execution by strangulation with an iron collar tightened by a screw. **2** The iron collar used in this way. **3** A throttling or choking as if with a garrote, especially for the purpose of robbery. — *v.;* **gar·rot·ed** or **gar·rot·ted**; **gar·rot·ing** or **gar·rot·ting**. **1** To strangle with a garrote. **2** To throttle and rob.

gar·ru·lous \'gar-ə-ləs, -yə-ləs\ *adj.* Very talkative, especially about trifles; wordy. — For synonyms see *talkative.* — **gar·ru·li·ty** \gə-'rü-lət-ē\ *n.* — **gar·ru·lous·ly** \'gar-ə-ləs-lē, -yə-ləs-lē\ *adv.*

gar·ter \'gärt-r, 'gȧrt-r\ *n.* A band or strap worn to hold up a stocking or sock. — *v.* To fasten or support with a garter.

garter snake. Any of several harmless American snakes having longitudinal stripes along the back.

gas \'gas\ *n.* [An alteration of *chaos.*] **1** An airlike substance having no fixed shape and tending to expand without limit. Oxygen is a *gas* found in air. **2** Any such gas or a mixture of gases used as a fuel or as an anesthetic. *Gas* is used to heat many homes. **3** Any vapor, smoke, or fume that poisons the air or makes breathing difficult; as, coal *gas;* tear *gas.* **4** Empty, boasting, or humbugging talk. **5** Gasoline. — *v.;* **gassed**; **gas·sing**. **1** To treat with gas; to poison or injure with gas. **2** To supply with gas. **3** To talk in an idle or empty manner.

gas·e·ous \'gas-ē-əs, 'gash-əs\ *adj.* In the form of, like, or relating to gas. Steam is water in a *gaseous* state.

gash \'gash\ *v.* To make a long, deep cut in; as, to *gash* one's hand. — *n.* A long, deep cut, especially in flesh.

gas·house \'gas-ˌhau̇s\ *n.; pl.* **gas·hous·es** \-ˌhau̇-zəz\. A gasworks.

gas·ket \'gas-kət\ *n.* Material, such as asbestos, rubber, or metal used as packing, as for pistons or pipe joints.

gas·light \'gas-ˌlīt\ *n.* **1** The light made by burning illuminating gas. **2** A gas jet. **3** A lamp lighted by gas. — **gas·light·ed** \-ˌlīt-əd\ *adj.* — **gas·light·ing** \-ˌlīt-ing\ *n.* or *adj.*

gas·lit \'gas-ˌlit\ *adj.* Illuminated by gaslight; as, a *gaslit* room.

gas mask. A face covering to protect a person from poisonous gases.

gas·o·line or **gas·o·lene** \ˌgas-l-'ēn, 'gas-l-ˌēn\ *n.* An inflammable fluid used as a motor fuel and a cleaning material.

gasoline engine. An internal combustion engine using gasoline as fuel; especially, such an engine made as a separate power unit and used to drive other implements by a belt or chain.

gasp \'gasp\ *v.* **1** To breathe with difficulty; to pant; as, to be *gasping* at the end of a race. **2** To utter with quick, difficult breaths; as, to *gasp* out a cry for help. — *n.* **1** A gasping. **2** Something gasped out; as, a *gasp* of surprise or of fear. — **gasp·ing·ly**, *adv.*

gas station. A filling station.

gas·sy \'gas-ē\ *adj.;* **gas·si·er; gas·si·est.** Full of or like gas; as, a *gassy* odor.

gas·tric \'gas-trik\ *adj.* Of, relating to, or near the stomach; as, *gastric* glands.

gastric juice. The acid digestive fluid given off by glands in the walls of the stomach.

gas·tri·tis \gas-'trīt-əs\ *n.* Inflammation of the stomach, especially of its mucous membrane.

gas·tron·o·my \gas-'trän-ə-mē\ *n.* The art of good eating. — **gas·tro·nom·ic** \ˌgas-trə-'näm-ik\ or **gas·tro·nom·i·cal** \-ik-l\ *adj.*

gas·tro·pod \'gas-trə-ˌpäd\ *n.* Any mollusk having on the ventral surface of the body a muscular foot for locomotion and, usually, a spiral shell into which the body can be withdrawn. Snails, whelks, and slugs are *gastropods.*

gas·tru·la \'gas-trə-lə\ *n.; pl.* **gas·tru·las** \-ləz\ or **gas·tru·lae** \-ˌlē\. In embryos, a form in the early development, typically consisting of a double cup-shaped layer of cells produced by a folding in of the wall of the blastula.

gas·works \'gas-ˌwərks\ *n. pl.* A place where gas is manufactured — usually used as a singular.

gate \'gāt\ *n.* **1** An opening in a wall or fence; especially, such an opening with a movable frame or door for closing it. **2** A part of a fence or other barrier that opens and closes like a door; the frame or door that closes a gateway. **3** A structure having a passageway and towers, especially when designed for defense; as, the *gate* of a walled town. **4** Something like a gate in shape or use; as, a *gate* in a canal lock.

gate·way \'gāt-ˌwā\ *n.* **1** An opening for a gate in a wall or fence. **2** A passage into or out of a place.

gath·er \'gath-r\ *v.;* **gath·ered; gath·er·ing** \-r(-)ing\. **1** To bring together or come together; to collect; to assemble; as, to *gather* around a fireplace; to *gather* the pieces of a broken dish. **2** To pick out and collect; as, to *gather* fruit or flowers. **3** To gain gradually; as, to *gather* speed. **4** To summon up a reserve of something, as strength, preparatory to using it; as, to *gather* one's wits. **5** To get an impression; to understand; as, to *gather* from someone's manner that he is displeased. **6** To draw together in folds; as, to *gather* a skirt at the waist. **7** To come to a head, as a sore.

— The word *collect* is a synonym of *gather: gather* may suggest merely the coming or bringing together of many separate and often diverse objects; *collect* usually suggests a more careful selection or ordering of the objects brought together.

— *n.* One of the folds made by gathering; a pleat.

gath·er·er \'gath-r-r\ *n.* One that gathers.

gath·er·ing \'gath-r(-)ing\ *n.* **1** A coming together of people; an assembly. **2** A gather, as of cloth. **3** A boil; an abscess.

gauche \'gōsh\ *adj.* [From French, meaning literally "left-handed".] Awkward and inexperienced; especially, showing little knowledge of accepted social customs.

gau·cho \'gau̇-ˌchō\ *n.; pl.* **gau·chos.** A South American cowboy.

gaud \'gȯd\ *n.* A showy ornament; a trinket; as, necklaces, bracelets, and other *gauds.*

gaudy \'gȯd-ē, 'gäd-ē\ *adj.;* **gaud·i·er; gaud·i·est.** Gay and showy but in bad taste; flashy. — **gaud·i·ly** \'gȯd-l-ē, 'gäd-\ *adv.*

gauge or **gage** \'gāj\ *n.* **1** A measure; a standard measure. **2** An instrument for measuring, testing, or registering; as, a rain *gauge;* a steam *gauge.* **3** The interior diameter of the barrel of a shotgun expressed by the number of round lead bullets fitting it that are needed to make a pound; as, a ten-*gauge* shotgun. **4** The distance between the rails of a railroad. — *v.;* **gauged; gaug·ing.** **1** To measure exactly, as rainfall or wind. **2** To measure the character, capacity, or ability of; to estimate; to judge; as, to find someone very hard to *gauge;* to *gauge* public opinion.

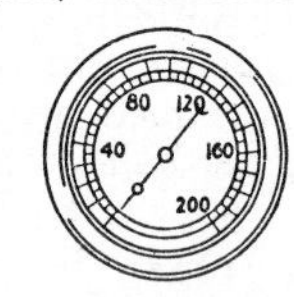

steam gauge

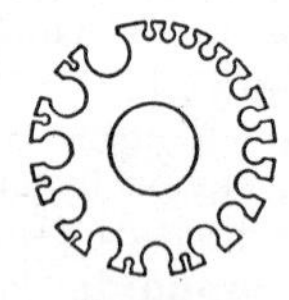
wire gauge

gaunt \'gȯnt, 'gänt\ *adj.* **1** Very thin and bony, as if from illness or starvation. **2** Desolate; grim; as, the *gaunt* walls of a prison; a countryside that is bare and *gaunt* in winter. — For synonyms see *thin.*

gaunt·let \'gȯnt-lət, 'gänt-\ *n.* **1** A glove worn as part of a suit of armor, made partly or wholly of small metal plates. **2** A glove with a flaring cuff that covers the wrist and part of the arm.

gaunt·let \'gȯnt-lət, 'gänt-\ *n.* A double file of persons armed with switches, clubs, or paddles with which to strike at those made to run the length of the file, originally as a punishment.

gauze \'gȯz\ *n.* [From French *gaze*, probably named after *Gaza*, city and region of Palestine.] A very thin transparent fabric. — **gauzy** \'gȯz-ē\ *adj.*

gave. Past tense of *give*.

gav·el \'gav-l\ *n.* A hammer or mallet, usually of wood, with which the person presiding calls a meeting to order.

ga·votte \gə-'vät\ *n.* **1** An old French dance, originally a country dance. **2** Music for this dance or in the same rhythm.

gawk \'gȯk\ *n.* A clumsy, stupid person. — *v.* To stare stupidly, like a gawk.

gawky \'gȯk-ē\ *adj.*; **gawk·i·er**; **gawk·i·est**. Awkward; clumsy; as, a *gawky* girl, all hands and feet.

gay \'gā\ *adj.*; **gay·er** \'gā-ər\; **gay·est** \-əst\. **1** Merry; lively; lighthearted. **2** Bright and showy; as, *gay* colors.

gayety. Variant of *gaiety*.

gayly. Variant of *gaily*.

gaze \'gāz\ *v.*; **gazed**; **gaz·ing**. To fix the eyes in a steady look; to look earnestly or eagerly at something.

— The words *stare* and *peer* are synonyms of *gaze*: *gaze* may describe fixed and prolonged attention, especially in wonder; *stare* usually indicates long, intent looking at something, either curiously, rudely, or vacantly; *peer* may suggest looking closely, as with partly closed eyes, or curiously and furtively, as from behind something.

— *n.* A long steady look. — **gaz·er** \'gāz-r\ *n.*

ga·zelle \gə-'zel\ *n.* A small, swift antelope with soft, bright eyes, noted for its graceful movements.

ga·zette \gə-'zet\ *n.* A newspaper; especially, a journal giving official information. — *v.*; **ga·zet·ted**; **ga·zet·ting**. To announce or publish in a gazette.

gaz·et·teer \ˌgaz-ə-'tir\ *n.* **1** A writer of news or an officer appointed to publish news. **2** A geographical dictionary.

gds. Abbreviation for *goods*.

gear \'gir\ *n.* **1** Equipment; tools; implements; as, camping *gear*. **2** In a machine, the parts or set of parts that fit and act together to cause motion, or to change speed or direction; as, the steering *gear* of an automobile. **3** Any one of these parts, such as a cogwheel. **4** The position the gears of a machine are in when they are ready to work; as, to shift into second *gear*. — *v.* **1** To provide with gears; to put in gear. **2** To be in gear; to come into gear.

gear·ing \'gir-ing\ *n.* **1** The action or manner of fitting a machine with a gear or gears. **2** The parts by which motion is transmitted in machinery.

gear shift. A mechanism by which transmission gears in a power-transmission system are engaged and disengaged.

gear·wheel \'gir-ˌhwēl\ *n.* or **gear wheel**. A wheel that gears with another piece; especially, a cogwheel.

gecko \'gek-ˌō\ *n.*; *pl.* **geck·os** or **geck·oes**. Any of a family of small harmless lizards with large eyes and vertical pupils.

gee \'jē\ *interj.* A command, as to a horse, to turn to the right.

geese. Pl. of *goose*.

Gei·ger count·er \'gīg-r 'kau̇nt-r\. An instrument used for detecting and measuring radioactivity.

gei·sha \'gā-shə, 'gē-\ *n.*; *pl.* **gei·sha** or **gei·shas**. A Japanese professional singing and dancing girl.

gel·a·tin or **gel·a·tine** \'jel-ət-n\ *n.* A substance obtained from the tissues of animals, eaten as food and also used for various other purposes, as in photography and dyeing.

ge·lat·i·nous \jə-'lat-n-əs\ *adj.* **1** Like jelly. **2** Of or containing gelatin.

geld·ing \'gel-ding\ *n.* A castrated animal, especially a horse.

gem \'jem\ *n.* **1** Any jewel; a precious stone cut and polished for ornament. **2** Anything prized for great beauty or perfection, especially when small or brief, as a poem. — *v.*; **gemmed**; **gem·ming**. To adorn with or as if with gems.

Gen. Abbreviation for *General*.

gen·darme \'zhän-ˌdärm, -ˌdȧrm\ *n.* In France and some other European countries, one of a police force armed and drilled as soldiers.

gen·der \'jend-r\ *n.* Any one of the several (in English three) grammatical classes of nouns and pronouns, of which one (**masculine gender**) consists largely or wholly of nouns and pronouns referring to male beings, one (**feminine gender**) largely or wholly of nouns and pronouns referring to female beings, and one (**neuter gender**) largely or wholly of nouns and pronouns referring to things that are neither male nor female.

gene \'jēn\ *n.* A small element within a chromosome concerned with the transmission and development of hereditary characters or traits.

ge·ne·al·o·gist \ˌjē-nē-'al-ə-jəst, ˌjen-ē-\ *n.* A person who traces the descent of persons or families.

ge·ne·al·o·gy \ˌjē-nē-'al-ə-jē, ˌjen-ē-\ *n.*; *pl.* **ge·ne·al·o·gies**. **1** A history of the descent of a person or family from an ancestor. **2** The descent of a person or family from an ancestor; a pedigree; lineage. **3** The study of family pedigrees. — **ge·ne·a·log·i·cal** \ˌjē-nē-ə-'läj-ik-l, ˌjen-ē-\ *adj.* — **ge·ne·a·log·i·cal·ly** \-ik-l-ē\ *adv.*

genera. Pl. of *genus*.

gen·er·al \'jen-r(-)əl\ *adj.* **1** Of or relating to the whole; not local; as, a *general* election. **2** Taken as a whole; as, the *general* body of citizens. **3** Relating to or covering all instances or individuals of a class or group; as, a *general* conclusion. **4** Not limited in meaning; not specific or in detail; as, a *general* outline. **5** Common to many; as, a *general* custom. **6** Not special; not specialized; as, a *general* store. **7** Not precise or definite; as, *general* comments. **8** Superior in rank; concerned with administrating or counseling — used as a second term in certain nonmilitary titles, as in *governor general* or *attorney general.* **—** *n.* An army officer of the highest rank; especially, in the United States Army, an officer who ranks next above a lieutenant general and next below a general of the army. — **in general**. Generally; for the most part.

gen·er·al·is·si·mo \\ˌjen-r(-)ə-ˈlis-m-ˌō\\ *n.; pl.* **gen·er·al·is·si·mos.** The chief commander, as of a joint military and naval force.

gen·er·al·i·ty \\ˌjen-r-ˈal-ət-ē\\ *n.; pl.* **gen·er·al·i·ties. 1** The condition or quality of being general. **2** A general law or principle; as, a *generality* based upon many specific instances. **3** A general or vague statement or phrase; as, to turn from empty *generalities* to a study of the facts. **4** The main body; the bulk; the greatest part; as, a statement that applies to the *generality* of mankind.

gen·er·al·i·za·tion \\ˌjen-r(-)ə-lə-ˈzāsh-n\\ *n.* **1** The mental activity in forming a general observation or statement upon the basis of particular instances. **2** A general observation or statement, as a law.

gen·er·al·ize \\ˈjen-r(-)ə-ˌlīz\\ *v.;* **gen·er·al·ized; gen·er·al·iz·ing. 1** To make general, as ideas. **2** To draw general conclusions from; as, to *generalize* one's experiences. **3** To reach a general conclusion, especially upon the basis of particular instances; as, to *generalize* about the symptoms of a disease.

gen·er·al·ly \\ˈjen-r(-)ə-lē, ˈjen-r-lē\\ *adv.* In a general way; usually; for the most part; as, a man who *generally* does good work.

general of the army. In the United States Army, a general of the highest grade, entitled to wear five stars.

gen·er·al·ship \\ˈjen-r(-)əl-ˌship\\ *n.* **1** Office or tenure of office of a general. **2** Military skill as shown by a general. **3** Leadership.

gen·er·ate \\ˈjen-r-ˌāt\\ *v.;* **gen·er·at·ed; gen·er·at·ing.** To produce; to cause to come into being; as, to *generate* electricity.

gen·er·a·tion \\ˌjen-r-ˈāsh-n\\ *n.* **1** One of the steps in a line of descent, or a person or persons representing it; as, a family that has lived in the same house for four *generations.* **2** The whole mass of people born at about the same time; as, the younger *generation.* **3** The average period of time between one generation and the next. **4** The action of generating; as, the *generation* of electricity.

gen·er·a·tive \\ˈjen-r-ˌāt-iv, -ət-iv\\ *adj.* **1** Of or relating to generation. **2** Having the power or function of generating or reproducing.

gen·er·a·tor \\ˈjen-r-ˌāt-r\\ *n.* **1** One that generates. **2** An apparatus in which vapor or gas is formed. **3** A machine that produces an electric current.

ge·ner·ic \\jə-ˈner-ik\\ *adj.* [From Latin *gener-*, stem of *genus*, and the English suffix *-ic* — see *genus.*] **1** Belonging to or characteristic of a genus or any class of related things; as, a *generic* name. **2** Not specific; general. — **ge·ner·i·cal·ly** \\-ik-l(-)ē\\ *adv.*

gen·er·os·i·ty \\ˌjen-r-ˈäs-ət-ē\\ *n.; pl.* **gen·er·os·i·ties. 1** Willingness or readiness to give or to share; liberality in spirit or act. **2** A generous act or gift.

gen·er·ous \\ˈjen-r(-)əs\\ *adj.* **1** Free in giving or sharing; liberal; unselfish; not mean or stingy; as, a *generous* giver. **2** High-minded; noble; as, to be *generous* in dealing with a defeated enemy. **3** Abundant; plentiful; ample; as, a *generous* supply. — **gen·er·ous·ly**, *adv.*

gen·e·sis \\ˈjen-ə-səs\\ *n.* The coming into existence of anything; origin; beginnings; as, the *genesis* of an idea; the *genesis* of the United States of America.

ge·net·ic \\jə-ˈnet-ik\\ *adj.* **1** Of or relating to the genesis of anything, or its origin and development. **2** Of or relating to genetics. — **ge·net·i·cal·ly** \\-ik-l(-)ē\\ *adv.*

ge·net·i·cist \\jə-ˈnet-ə-səst\\ *n.* A specialist in genetics.

ge·net·ics \\jə-ˈnet-iks\\ *n.* The branch of biology that deals with heredity and variation among related animals and plants.

ge·nial \\ˈjēn-yəl, ˈjē-nē-əl\\ *adj.* **1** Favorable to growth or comfort; as, a *genial* climate; a *genial* fire. **2** Cheerful and cheering; kindly; as, a *genial* host; a *genial* disposition. — **ge·nial·ly** \\ˈjēn-yə-lē, ˈjē-nē-ə-\\lē *adv.*

ge·ni·al·i·ty \\ˌjē-nē-ˈal-ət-ē, jēn-ˈyal-\\ *n.* The quality of being genial; especially, cheerful kindliness.

ge·nie \\ˈjē-nē\\ *n.* A magic spirit; especially, one of the genii, or jinn, of Arabian stories.

genii. A pl. of *genius.*

gen·i·tal \\ˈjen-ət-l\\ *adj.* Relating to generation or to the sexual organs.

gen·i·tive \\ˈjen-ət-iv\\ *n.* or **genitive case**. The case of a noun or pronoun that expresses primarily source or possession — in modern English commonly called *possessive* or *possessive case.*

gen·i·to·uri·nary \\ˌjen-ə-ˌtō-ˈyu̇r-ə-ˌner-ē\\ *adj.* Relating to the genital and urinary organs.

ge·nius \\ˈjēn-yəs, ˈjē-nē-əs\\ *n.; pl.* in senses 3 to 7, **ge·nius·es** \\ˈjēn-yə-səz, ˈjē-nē-ə-səz\\, in senses 1 and 2, **ge·nii** \\ˈjē-nē-ˌī\\. **1** An attendant spirit or protecting deity of the ancient Romans. **2** A genie; a jinni. **3** A person who influences another for good or ill; as, a man who seemed to be the evil *genius* of everyone he knew. **4** A natural ability or bent; as, to have a *genius* for keeping out of trouble. **5** A special or peculiar character or nature, as of a nation or people, a place or an age. **6** Extraordinary intellectual power, especially of invention; as, a man of *genius.* **7** A person having such ability; a highly gifted person.

gen·o·cide \\ˈjen-ə-ˌsīd\\ *n.* The deliberate, systematic extermination of a whole racial, religious, or cultural group. — **gen·o·cid·al** \\ˌjen-ə-ˈsīd-l\\ *adj.*

gent. Abbreviation for *gentleman.*

gen·teel \\jen-ˈtēl\\ *adj.* **1** Refined; polite; well-bred. **2** Stylish; fashionable; elegant. — **gen·teel·ly** \-'tēl-lē\ *adv.*

gen·tian \'jench-n\ *n.* A fall-flowering mountain plant with funnel-shaped or bell-shaped flowers usually blue in color.

gen·tile or **Gen·tile** \'jen-ˌtīl\ *n.* Any person who is not Jewish. — *adj.* **1** Of or relating to any people not Jewish. **2** Of or relating to Christians, as distinguished from Jews.

gen·til·i·ty \jen-'til-ət-ē\ *n.* **1** Good birth and family. **2** The qualities characteristic of a well-bred person. **3** Good manners.

gen·tle \'jent-l\ *adj.*; **gen·tler** \-l(-)ər\; **gen·tlest** \-l(-)əst\. **1** Wellborn; of good family. **2** Mild; not harsh or stern; as, a *gentle* manner. **3** Soft; soothing; light; as, a *gentle* murmur; a *gentle* touch. **4** Easily handled; not wild; as, a *gentle* horse. **5** Moderate; easy; as, a *gentle* slope.

gen·tle·folk \'jent-l-ˌfōk\ or **gen·tle·folks** \-ˌfōks\ *n. pl.* Persons of good family and breeding.

gen·tle·man \'jent-l-mən\ *n.; pl.* **gen·tle·men** \-mən\. **1** A man of good, though not noble, family. **2** A well-bred man of good education and good social position. **3** A man — used in the plural as a form of address in speaking to a group of men.

gen·tle·man·ly \'jent-l-mən-lē\ *adj.* Like a gentleman in nature, behavior, or appearance; befitting a gentleman; as, a very *gentlemanly* man; a *gentlemanly* occupation.

gen·tle·wom·an \'jent-l-ˌwu̇m-ən\ *n.; pl.* **gen·tle·wom·en** \-ˌwim-ən\. **1** A woman of good family or breeding. **2** A woman attending a lady of rank.

gen·tly \'jent-lē\ *adv.* In a gentle manner; softly; not harshly or roughly; not abruptly; as, to handle something *gently;* a path dropping *gently* down.

gen·try \'jen-trē\ *n.* **1** People of good birth, breeding, and education. **2** In England, the class of people between the nobility and the yeomanry. **3** People; especially, persons of a designated class.

gen·u·ine \'jen-yə-wən\ *adj.* **1** Real; actually what it seems to be; as, *genuine* gold; a *genuine* antique. **2** Sincere; honest; as, a *genuine* interest in classical music; a very *genuine* person. — **gen·u·ine·ly,** *adv.*

ge·nus \'jē-nəs\ *n.; pl.* **gen·era** \'jen-r-ə\, rarely **ge·nus·es** \'jē-nə-səz\. [From Latin, meaning "birth", "race", "kind".] A group of related things that can be divided into subordinate groups; especially, a group of plants or animals, ranking in classification below a family and above a species; as, a *genus* of birds.

ge·o·cen·tric \ˌjē-ō-'sen-trik\ *adj.* **1** Relating to or measured from the earth's center. **2** Relating to or having the earth as a center.

ge·og·ra·pher \jē-'äg-rəf-r\ *n.* A person skilled in geography.

ge·o·graph·ic \ˌjē-ə-'graf-ik\ or **ge·o·graph·i·cal** \-ik-l\ *adj.* Of or relating to geography; as, the *geographic* center of the United States; important *geographical* studies. — **ge·o·graph·i·cal·ly** \-ik-l(-)ē\ *adv.*

ge·og·ra·phy \jē-'äg-rə-fē\ *n.; pl.* **ge·og·ra·phies.** **1** The science that studies the natural features of the earth and its climate, products, and inhabitants. **2** The natural features of an area, as mountains, valleys, and rivers. **3** A book dealing with geography.

ge·o·log·ic \ˌjē-ə-'läj-ik\ or **ge·o·log·i·cal** \-ik-l\ *adj.* Of or relating to geology; as, a *geological* expedition; *geologic* time. — **ge·o·log·i·cal·ly** \-ik-l(-)ē\ *adv.*

ge·ol·o·gist \jē-'äl-ə-jəst\ *n.* A person skilled in geology.

ge·ol·o·gy \jē-'äl-ə-jē\ *n.* The science that studies the history of the earth and its life, especially as recorded in the rocks.

ge·o·met·ric \ˌjē-ə-'me-trik\ or **ge·o·met·ri·cal** \-trik-l\ *adj.* Based on the principles of or the figures used in geometry; as, *geometric* reasoning; *geometrical* designs. — **ge·o·met·ri·cal·ly** \-trik-l(-)ē\ *adv.*

ge·o·met·rid \ˌjē-ə-'me-trəd\ *n.* A large-winged moth the caterpillar of which is the measuring worm.

ge·om·e·try \jē-'äm-ə-trē\ *n.* The branch of mathematics that studies solid objects, surfaces, lines, and angles.

ge·o·pol·i·ti·cian \ˌjē-ˌō-ˌpäl-ə-'tish-n\ *n.* An expert or specialist in geopolitics.

ge·o·pol·i·tics \ˌjē-ˌō-'päl-ə-ˌtiks\ *n.* A science based upon the theory that domestic and foreign politics of a country are dependent upon physical geography. — **ge·o·po·lit·i·cal** \ˌjē-ˌō-pə-'lit-ik-l\ *adj.* — **ge·o·pol·i·tic** \-'päl-ə-ˌtik\ *adj.* — **ge·o·po·lit·i·cal·ly** \-pə-'lit-ik-l(-)ē\ *adv.*

ge·ra·ni·um \jə-'rā-nē-əm, -'rān-yəm\ *n.* **1** A common purple or pink wild flower with deeply cut leaves and bearing long beaklike pods. **2** A closely related herb distinguished by clusters of scarlet or white flowers having the sepals joined at the base into a hollow spur, used as a window plant.

geranium, 2

ger·fal·con or **gyr·fal·con** \'jər-ˌfalk-n, -ˌfȯ(l)k-n\ *n.* A large arctic falcon, more powerful but less active than the peregrine falcon.

germ \'jərm\ *n.* **1** A small mass of living substance that is capable of developing into an animal or plant, or into an organ or part; a seed. **2** Any of the harmful bacteria; a microbe. Milk is pasteurized to kill the *germs* in it. **3** That from which something springs or starts, as from a seed; as, the *germ* of an idea.

ger·man \'jər-mən\ *adj.* Having the same parents or grandparents; as, brothers-*german*; cousin-*german*.

Ger·man \'jər-mən\ *adj.* Of or relating to Germany. — *n.* **1** A native or inhabitant of Germany. **2** The language of Germany.

ger·mane \(ˌ)jər-'mān\ *adj.* Bearing significantly upon the case in hand; pertinent; as, a statement that is not *germane* to the topic being discussed.

Ger·man·ic \(ˌ)jər-ˈman-ik\ *adj.* **1** German. **2** Teutonic.

ger·ma·ni·um \jər-ˈmā-nē-əm\ *n.* A grayish-white, brittle, metallic element found in a few rare minerals.

German measles. A disease marked by red spots on the skin, like measles but much milder.

German silver. A silver-white alloy of copper, zinc, and nickel.

germ cell. A cell whose function is reproductive; one that is set apart from the rest of the body to develop, usually after union with another cell of the opposite sex, into a new individual.

ger·mi·cide \ˈjər-mə-ˌsīd\ *n.* A substance that destroys germs, especially disease germs. — **ger·mi·cid·al** \ˌjər-mə-ˈsīd-l\ *adj.*

ger·mi·nate \ˈjər-mə-ˌnāt\ *v.;* **ger·mi·nat·ed**; **ger·mi·nat·ing.** **1** To begin to grow or develop, as seeds; to sprout. **2** To cause to sprout or develop. — **ger·mi·na·tion** \ˌjər-mə-ˈnāsh-n\ *n.*

ger·ry·man·der \ˌjer-ē-ˈmand-r, ˈjer-ē-ˌmand-r; ˌger-, ˈger-\ *v.;* **ger·ry·man·dered**; **ger·ry·man·der·ing** \-r(-)ing\. To divide, as a state or county, into election districts in such a way as to give a political party an advantage over its opponents. — *n.* The action of gerrymandering.

ger·und \ˈjer-ənd\ *n.* In English grammar, the verb form ending in *-ing* used as a noun and at the same time capable of taking adverbial modifiers and having an object, as *eating* in "Doctors recommend eating food slowly".

ges·ta·tion \jes-ˈtāsh-n\ *n.* The action or period of carrying young in the uterus; pregnancy.

ges·tic·u·late \jes-ˈtik-yə-ˌlāt\ *v.;* **ges·tic·u·lat·ed**; **ges·tic·u·lat·ing.** To make gestures, especially when speaking. — **ges·tic·u·la·tor** \-ˌlāt-r\ *n.*

ges·tic·u·la·tion \(ˌ)jes-ˌtik-yə-ˈlāsh-n\ *n.* **1** The action of making gestures. **2** A gesture, as one made in showing strong feeling or in enforcing arguments.

ges·ture \ˈjes-chər\ *n.* **1** A motion of the body or limbs that expresses an idea or a feeling or that emphasizes a statement; as, to raise one's hand as a *gesture* of farewell. **2** The use of such motions as a means of expression; as, to resort to *gesture* and mimicry. **3** Something said or done merely for effect, as for the sake of courtesy; as, an empty *gesture.* — *v.;* **ges·tured**; **ges·tur·ing.** To make a gesture or gestures; to gesticulate.

get \(ˈ)get; *often* git, *without stress, when a heavily stressed adverb follows, as in "get up"*\ *v.;* **got** \(ˈ)gät\; **got** \(ˈ)gät\ or **got·ten** \ˈgät-n\; **get·ting.** **1** To obtain; to receive; to acquire; to buy; to earn; to win; as, to *get* a present or a prize; to *get* a loaf of bread for breakfast. **2** To arrive; as, to *get* home early. When did you *get* there? **3** To strike. The blow *got* him on the chin. **4** To establish communication with; as, to *get* a person on the telephone. **5** To go; to move; as, to be told to *get* out; to *get* about on crutches. **6** To become; as, to *get* sick or angry. It is *getting* warmer. **7** To catch, as a disease. **8** To capture or kill. The police *got* the criminal. **9** To puzzle; to baffle. The second question *got* all the contestants. **10** In certain sports, to catch a ball or to put out a player by catching a ball. The first baseman barely managed to *get* the runner. **11** To be obliged to — used only in the form *got* with *have, has,* or *had.* The children have *got* to go home. **12** To cause to be done; to bring into another condition; to undergo an experience that results in a change of condition; as, to *get* one's hair cut; to *get* one's feet wet. **13** To cause to move or be taken away; as, to *get* an intruder out of the house. **14** To prepare; as, to *get* dinner. **15** To persuade; as, to *get* someone to agree. — **get about.** To become known; to circulate. Rumors *get about.* — **get along. 1** To manage; as, to *get along* on a small salary. **2** To remain on friendly terms; as, to try to *get along* with everybody. — **get at. 1** To reach; to come at; to come to understand; as, to be unable to *get at* the meaning of a word. **2** To begin; to settle down to; as, to *get at* the day's work. — **get away with.** To accomplish without penalty; as, to *get away with* a practical joke. — **get back at.** To do something to in return; as, to *get back at* someone for playing a trick on one. — **get behind.** To take sides with; to support; as, to *get behind* the team. — **get in.** To allow for; to work in; as, to try to *get in* some tennis before dark. — **get off. 1** To utter; as, to *get off* a joke. **2** To escape; as, to *get off* without a scratch. — **get on.** To get along; to make out; as, to inquire how someone is *getting on.* — **get out.** To publish; as, to *get out* a newspaper. — **get over.** To recover from, as an illness.

get·a·way \ˈget-ə-ˌwā\ *n.* **1** The action or fact of getting away. **2** The action of starting or getting under way, as of horses in a race or an automobile starting from a dead stop.

get·up \ˈget-ˌəp\ *n.* **1** The manner in which the parts of a thing are combined; makeup. **2** A style of dress; a costume; as, an elaborate *getup.*

gew·gaw \ˈgyü-ˌgȯ\ *n.* A showy, useless trifle; a toy; a bauble.

gey·ser \ˈgīz-r\ *n.* [From Icelandic *Geysir,* the name of a hot spring in Iceland, meaning literally "gusher".] A spring that intermittently shoots up hot water and steam.

Gha·na·ian \ˈgän-ə-yən, ˈgän-yən\ or **Gha·nian** \ˈgän-yən\ *adj.* Of or relating to Ghana. — *n.* A native of Ghana.

ghast·ly \ˈgast-lē\ *adj.;* **ghast·li·er**; **ghast·li·est** **1** Horrible; shocking; as, a *ghastly* crime. **2** Like a ghost; deathlike; pale; as, a *ghastly* face. — *adv.* In a ghastly manner; with a deathlike appearance; as, to turn *ghastly* pale.

gher·kin \ˈgərk-n\ *n.* **1** The small oblong prickly fruit of a trailing West Indian cucumber vine, used for pickling. **2** Any small pickling cucumber

ghet·to \ˈget-ˌō\ *n.; pl.* **ghet·tos.** **1** The part of a European city in which Jews were required to live. **2** Any section of a city in which members of a racial group are segregated.

ghost \ˈgōst\ *n.* **1** The soul or spirit of a dead

person thought of as living in an unseen world or as appearing in physical form to living people. **2** A specter; a spook. **3** A faint shadowy likeness; as, to fail to get even a *ghost* of an idea of what the speaker meant.

ghost·ly \'gōst-lē\ *adj.;* **ghost·li·er**; **ghost·li·est.** Of a ghost; like a ghost or spirit; as, a *ghostly* shape; a *ghostly* silence.

ghost town. A town or city once flourishing and still standing but deserted by all but a few stragglers, often after exhaustion of some natural resource, as gold.

ghoul \'gül\ *n.* **1** An imaginary evil being that robs graves and feeds on corpses. **2** A person whose activities suggest those of a ghoul, as a blackmailer or a grave robber. — **ghoul·ish** \'gü-lish\ *adj.* — **ghoul·ish·ly,** *adv.*

GI or **G.I.** \'jē-'ī\ *adj.* [From an unofficial army abbreviation for *galvanized iron*, but understood to be an abbreviation of *government issue*.] **1** Provided by the quartermaster; as, *GI* shoes. **2** Strictly according to regulations or custom in the military service; as, a *GI* haircut; conduct not exactly *GI*. **3** Of or characteristic of enlisted servicemen; as, a *GI* joke. — *n.; pl.* **GIs, GI's, G.I.s,** or **G.I.'s** \-'īz\. Any enlisted man or woman in the United States armed services.

gi·ant \'jī-ənt\ *n.* **1** A mythical manlike monster of great size and strength. **2** A person, animal, plant, or thing that is very large or powerful. — *adj.* **1** Like a giant in size, strength, or power; gigantic. **2** In plant and animal names, describing a species that is huge in comparison with related or similar species.

gib·ber \'jib-r\ *v.;* **gib·bered**; **gib·ber·ing** \-r(-)ing\. To speak in a rapid confused way; to talk fluently and foolishly. — *n.* Gibberish.

gib·ber·ish \'jib-r(-)ish, 'gib-\ *n.* Rapid, confused talk.

gib·bet \'jib-ət\ *n.* A gallows on which in former times the bodies of executed criminals were hung in chains and allowed to remain as a warning to others. — *v.* **1** To execute by hanging. **2** To hang on a gibbet. **3** To hold up to public shame.

gib·bon \'gib-n\ *n.* A tailless ape of southeastern Asia and the East Indies, the smallest of the manlike apes, living entirely in treetops.

gib·bous \'gib-əs\ *adj.* **1** Rounded; convex — used of the moon between half moon and full moon. **2** Hunched; humpbacked.

gibe or **jibe** \'jīb\ *v.;* **gibed** or **jibed**; **gib·ing** or **jib·ing.** To mock at; to jeer; to make fun of. — *n.* A jeer; a taunt.

gib·let \'jib-lət\ *n.* One of the edible inner organs of a fowl, as the heart, liver, or gizzard.

gid·dy \'gid-ē\ *adj.;* **gid·di·er**; **gid·di·est.** **1** Having a feeling of whirling or reeling about; dizzy. **2** Causing dizziness; as, a *giddy* height. **3** Not serious; frivolous; fickle; as, a *giddy* girl.

gift \'gift\ *n.* **1** The act or power of giving; as, to have something in one's *gift*. **2** The thing that is given; a present. **3** A special ability; a talent; as, to have a *gift* for music. — For synonyms see *present*.

gift·ed \'gif-təd\ *adj.* Having great natural ability; talented; as, a special class for *gifted* children; an unusually *gifted* musician.

gig \'gig\ *n.* **1** A light two-wheeled carriage drawn by one horse. **2** A long light ship's boat; as, the captain's *gig*.

gi·gan·tic \jī-'gant-ik\ *adj.* Like a giant, as in size, weight, or strength; huge; as, a *gigantic* tree.

gig·gle \'gig-l\ *v.;* **gig·gled**; **gig·gling** \-l(-)ing\. To laugh with repeated short catches of the breath; to laugh in a silly manner. — *n.* A light silly laugh or titter. — **gig·gly** \'gig-l(-)ē\ *adj.*

Gi·la monster \'hē-lə\. A large orange and black poisonous lizard of Arizona and New Mexico.

gild \'gild\ *v.;* **gild·ed** \'gil-dəd\ or **gilt** \'gilt\; **gild·ing.** **1** To cover with a thin coating of gold; as, to *gild* a picture frame. **2** To make attractive; to ornament; to decorate; as, to *gild* a story

gild. Variant of *guild*.

gill \'jil\ *n.* A small liquid measure now fixed at a quarter of a pint.

gill \'gil\ *n.* **1** An organ of thin plates or threadlike processes by means of which fish breathe under water. **2** The flesh about the chin or jaw; as, looking rather pale around the *gills*.

gilt \'gilt\. A past tense and past part. of *gild*. — *n.* Gold, or something like gold, applied to a surface. — *adj.* Covered with gold or gilt; of gold color; as, a book with *gilt* edges.

gim·crack \'jim-ˌkrak\ *n.* A showy object of little use or value; a fancy trifle; a gewgaw. — *adj.* Showy but of little worth; as, *gimcrack* ornaments.

gim·let \'gim-lət\ *n.* A small tool for boring with a screwlike point and a handle set crosswise.

gimlet

gin \'jin\ *n.* [A shortened form of *geneva*, an altered form (due to confusion with the city of *Geneva*, Switzerland) of obsolete Dutch *genever* meaning literally "juniper".] An alcoholic liquor made from grain with added flavoring, as from juniper berries or orange peel.

gin \'jin\ *n.* [From medieval English *ginne*, a shortened form of Old French *engin*, the source of English *engine*.] **1** A trap for game. **2** A cotton gin. — *v.;* **ginned**; **gin·ning.** **1** To catch in a gin; to snare. **2** To separate seeds from cotton in a cotton gin.

gin·ger \'jinj-r\ *n.* **1** The sharp-tasting root of a tropical herb with a spike of yellowish-green purple-lipped flowers, dried and used for flavoring and as a medicine. **2** Spirit; mettle; as, a saddle horse that is full of *ginger*.

ginger ale. A nonalcoholic drink flavored with ginger.

gin·ger·bread \'jinj-r-ˌbred\ *n.* **1** A plain cake flavored with ginger and sweetened with molasses.

2 Something showy but in poor taste; especially, in architecture, excessive ornamentation serving no useful purpose.

gin·ger·ly \'jinj-r-lē\ *adv.* Very cautiously. — *adj.* Very cautious; as, to walk with *gingerly* steps.

gin·ger·snap \'jinj-r-ˌsnap\ *n.* A thin brittle cooky flavored with ginger.

gin·gery \'jinj-r-ē\ *adj.* **1** Having the characteristics or color of ginger; sharp; spicy. **2** Flavored with ginger.

ging·ham \'ging-m\ *n.* [From Malay *gingan* meaning literally "striped".] A fabric woven, usually from cotton yarn, in plain colors, checks, plaids, or stripes.

gink·go \'ging-ˌkō\ *n.; pl.* **gink·goes**. A large Chinese tree with leaves shaped like a fan and foul-smelling yellow fruit.

gin·ner \'jin-r\ *n.* A person who gins cotton.

gin rummy. A game of rummy in which a player whose cards are matched according to the rules scores a "gin", consisting of a 20-point bonus.

gin·seng \'jin-ˌseng\ *n.* **1** A perennial Chinese herb of a family of herbs, shrubs, trees, and vines, with small greenish flowers in a rounded cluster and a berrylike fruit. **2** A closely related North American herb. **3** The forked aromatic root of either herb used medicinally.

gipsy. Variant of *gypsy*.

gi·raffe \jə-'raf\ *n.* A cud-chewing, long-necked, spotted mammal of Africa, the tallest of four-footed animals.

gird \'gərd\ *v.;* **girt** \'gərt\ or **gird·ed**; **gird·ing. 1** To encircle or fasten, as with a belt or cord; to girdle; as, to *gird* on a sword. **2** To clothe or invest, as with strength. **3** To prepare; to brace; as, to *gird* oneself for a struggle.

gird·er \'gərd-r\ *n.* Any heavy, strong beam of wood or steel that supports the weight of a structure; as, the *girders* of a bridge.

gir·dle \'gərd-l\ *n.* **1** Something that encircles or binds, especially a belt or sash. **2** A light corset worn below the waistline. **3** A ring made by removing the bark around the trunk of a tree. — *v.;* **gir·dled**; **gir·dling** \-l(-)ing\. **1** To bind with or as if with a girdle, belt, or sash; to encircle. **2** To strip a ring of bark from a tree trunk. — **gir·dler** \'gərd-l(-)ər\ *n.*

girl \'gərl\ *n.* **1** A female child or young woman. **2** A female servant. **3** A sweetheart.

girl·hood \'gərl-ˌhu̇d\ *n.* The time or condition of being a girl.

girl·ish \'gər-lish\ *adj.* Like a girl; relating to girls or girlhood; as, *girlish* laughter. — **girl·ish·ly**, *adv.*

girl scout. A girl who is a member of the organization called "**Girl Scouts**", whose purpose is to develop healthy, active girls trained in good citizenship.

girt \'gərt\. A past tense and past part. of *gird*.

girt \'gərt\ *v.* **1** To gird; to equip, invest, or fasten by a girdle. **2** To encircle. **3** To fasten by means of a girth.

girth \'gərth\ *n.* **1** A band placed around the body of a horse or other animal, to which may be fastened a blanket, saddle, or pack. **2** The measure around the body, as at the waist; the distance around anything; as, a man of huge *girth;* the *girth* of a tree. **3** A girdle. — *v.* To bind with a girth; to put a girth on; as, to *girth* a horse.

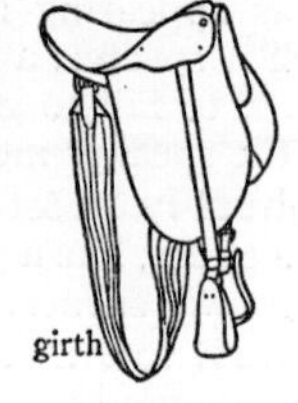
girth

gist \'jist\ *n.* The main point of a matter; the essence; the pith; as, to repeat only the *gist* of something one has read; the *gist* of a question.

give \'giv\ *v.;* **gave** \'gāv\; **giv·en** \'giv-n\; **giv·ing. 1** To hand over to be kept; to present; to deliver; as, to *give* a friend a Christmas present. The man *gave* himself up to the police. **2** To devote; to surrender; to apply; as, to *give* one's energies to a cause. **3** To pay; as, to *give* a fair price. **4** To utter; as, to *give* a yell; to *give* a speech. **5** To express in words; as, to *give* a reply. **6** To issue; as, to *give* a command. **7** To pronounce, as an opinion or sentence. **8** To award; as, to *give* a prize. **9** To furnish; to provide; as, a candle that *gives* light; to *give* a party. **10** To offer; as, to *give* a person one's hand. **11** To assign; as, to be *given* a good seat. **12** To cause to have; as, to *give* someone a lot of trouble. My brother *gave* me his cold. **13** To grant; to allow; as, to *give* permission. **14** To yield slightly; to move; to be springy; as, to feel the earth *give* underfoot. — **give away. 1** To perform the ceremony of delivering a bride to the bridegroom at a wedding. **2** To betray or disclose, as a secret. — **give in.** To yield; to succumb; as, to *give in* to a repeated request. — **give off.** To send forth; to emit, as steam or odor. — **give out. 1** To utter publicly; to publish; to announce. **2** To distribute; as, to *give out* handbills. **3** To become exhausted or used up; as, to realize that one's strength is *giving out.* The shipwrecked sailors' food *gave out.* — **give over.** To leave off; to quit; to abandon; as, to *give over* the habit of smoking. — **give tongue.** To begin barking, as hounds in the chase. — **give up. 1** To abandon; to surrender; to part with; to yield; as, to refuse to *give up* hope; to *give up* without a struggle. **2** To leave off; to cease from; as, to *give up* eating dessert. **3** To pronounce incurable, as a patient. **4** To cease from effort. The tired swimmer was about ready to *give up* when help reached him. — **give way. 1** To retreat. The troops *gave way* before the attacking enemy. **2** To break down; to yield to force or pressure. Many were drowned when the dam *gave way.* **3** To lose control of one's feelings. — *n.* A yielding; a giving way; springiness; as, to feel the *give* of the ground under one's feet.

give-and-take \'giv-n-'tāk\ *n.* An exchange, as of remarks or ideas, especially upon fair or equal terms.

give·a·way \'giv-ə-ˌwā\ *n.* A betrayal; a revealing, especially one made unintentionally; as, a remark that was a complete *giveaway* of the secret.

giv·en \'giv-n\ *adj.* **1** Disposed; inclined; as, one *given* to outbursts of temper. **2** Stated; fixed; as, at a *given* time. **3** In mathematics, granted or assumed.

given name. A Christian or first name.

giv·er \'giv-r\ *n.* A person who gives; a donor; as, a generous *giver* to charity.

giz·zard \'giz-rd\ *n.* The second stomach of birds, which has a tough horny lining for grinding food.

gla·cial \'glāsh-l\ *adj.* **1** Having to do with ice and its action; especially, relating to glaciers; as, *glacial* soil. **2** Of or relating to the Glacial period.

glacial epoch. **1** Any of those parts of geological time during which a much larger portion of the earth was covered by glaciers than at present. **2** The latest of the glacial epochs (the **Pleis·to·cene epoch** \'plīs-tə-ˌsēn\), during which Canada and the northern United States were largely covered with ice.

Glacial period. The period that includes the glacial epochs.

gla·cier \'glāsh-r\ *n.* A field of ice that moves slowly down a slope such as the side of a mountain or over a wide area of land.

glad \'glad\ *adj.;* **glad·der; glad·dest. 1** Happy; joyful; pleased; as, to be *glad* to see someone. **2** Bringing or arousing joy; as, *glad* tidings. **3** Gay; bright; as, dressed in *glad* colors.

glad·den \'glad-n\ *v.;* **glad·dened; glad·den·ing** \-n(-)ing\. To make or become glad.

glade \'glād\ *n.* A grassy open space in a forest.

glad·i·a·tor \'glad-ē-ˌāt-r\ *n.* [From Latin, meaning literally "swordsman", and derived from *gladius* meaning "sword" — see *gladiolus.*] **1** A man who fought with a sword to entertain the public in ancient Rome. **2** One that engages in any fierce combat or controversy. — **glad·i·a·to·ri·al** \ˌglad-ē-ə-'tōr-ē-əl, -'tȯr-\ *adj.*

glad·i·o·lus \ˌglad-ē-'ō-ləs\ *n.; pl.* **glad·i·o·li** \-'ō-ˌlī\ or **glad·i·o·lus·es** \-'ō-lə-səz\. [From Latin, meaning literally "short sword", a diminutive of *gladius* meaning "sword" — see *gladiator.*] **1** A summer-blooming plant of the iris family with stiff sword-shaped leaves and spikes of brilliantly colored irregular flowers. **2** A flower of this plant.

gladiolus

glad·ly \'glad-lē\ *adv.* Willingly; cheerfully; joyfully.

glad·ness \'glad-nəs\ *n.* Joy; happiness; as, a heart filled with *gladness.*

glad·some \'glad-səm\ *adj.* Giving or showing joy or gladness; gay; cheerful; as, a *gladsome* song; a *gladsome* holiday. — **glad·some·ly**, *adv.*

glam·or·ous \'glam-r(-)əs\ *adj.* Full of glamour; fascinating; alluring. — **glam·or·ous·ly**, *adv.*

glam·our or **glam·or** \'glam-r\ *n.* **1** Magic; charm; especially, false or deceptive charm; as, the *glamour* of faraway places; the *glamour* of war. **2** Alluring or fascinating personal attraction; as, the *glamour* of a movie star.

glance \'glan(t)s\ *v.;* **glanced; glanc·ing. 1** To strike at an angle and fly off to one side. The arrow *glanced* off the shield. **2** To give a quick or hasty look; as, to *glance* at one's watch; to *glance* up from a book. **3** To flash; to glint; as, polished metal *glancing* in the sun. — *n.* **1** An indirect or slanting hit or blow. **2** A quick look; a glimpse; as, a *glance* at the clock; a *glance* over one's shoulder. **3** A sudden movement producing a flash of light or a flash thus produced.

gland \'gland\ *n.* A structure in a living organism that prepares and secretes a product to be used by the organism or discharged from it, as saliva, sweat, bile, or shell.

glan·du·lar \'glanj-l-ər\ *adj.* **1** Bearing glands or gland cells. **2** Of, relating to, or like a gland or glands; as, *glandular* secretions; a *glandular* disorder.

glare \'glar, 'gler\ *v.;* **glared; glar·ing. 1** To shine with a dazzling light. **2** To be bright and intense, as certain colors. **3** To look fiercely or angrily. — *n.* **1** A bright, dazzling light; glitter. **2** A fierce look; an angry stare.

glare \'glar, 'gler\ *n.* A smooth glassy surface; as, a *glare* of ice. — *adj.* Smooth and bright; as, *glare* ice.

glar·ing \'glar-ing, 'gler-\ *adj.* **1** Dazzlingly bright; as, *glaring* sunlight; a *glaring* red. **2** Staring angrily; as, *glaring* eyes. **3** Very conspicuous; obvious; as, a *glaring* mistake. — **glar·ing·ly**, *adv.*

glary \'glar-ē, 'gler-ē\ *adj.;* **glar·i·er; glar·i·est.** Of a dazzling brightness; glaring.

glass \'glas\ *n.* **1** A hard, brittle, usually transparent substance, commonly made from sand heated with chemicals, and used for windows, tableware, and lenses, and in various forms for many other purposes. **2** Anything made of glass, as a mirror, a water tumbler, a lens, a barometer, or a telescope. **3** [in the plural] Eyeglasses; spectacles. **4** The contents of a glass; as, a *glass* of milk. — *adj.* Made of or relating to glass; as, a *glass* ornament. — *v.* To fit or protect with glass; as, to *glass* in a porch.

glass blowing. The art of shaping a mass of glass that has been softened by heat by blowing air into it through a tube. — **glass blower.**

glass·ful \'glas-ˌfu̇l\ *n.; pl.* **glass·fuls.** The contents of a glass; the amount a glass will hold.

glass·house \'glas-ˌhau̇s\ *n.; pl.* **glass·hous·es** \-ˌhau̇-zəz\. A greenhouse.

glass·ware \'glas-ˌwar, -ˌwer\ *n.* Articles made of glass.

glassy \'glas-ē\ *adj.;* **glass·i·er; glass·i·est. 1** Like glass, as in smoothness. **2** Dull; lifeless; as, to stare with *glassy* eyes. — **glass·i·ly** \'glas-l-ē\ *adv.*

glaze \'glāz\ *v.;* **glazed; glaz·ing. 1** To furnish or fit with glass; to put a pane or panes of glass in; as, to *glaze* a window. **2** To cover with a thin surface of glass or something resembling glass; as, to *glaze* pottery. **3** In cooking, to coat as with crystallized sugar. **4** To become glazed or glassy in appearance. — *n.* **1** A substance used for glazing. **2** The glasslike surface or coating of pottery or porcelain, especially when transparent.

gla·zier \'glāzh-r\ *n.* A person who sets glass in window frames.

gleam \'glēm\ *n.* A moderate brightness; a beam of light; a glow. — *v.* To send out gleams. Stars *gleamed* in the darkness.

glean \'glēn\ *v.* **1** To gather from a field or vineyard what has been left by the reapers. **2** To gather little by little; to collect with patient effort; as, to *glean* knowledge from books. — **glean·er**, *n.*

glean·ings \'glē-ningz\ *n. pl.* That which is collected by gleaning, especially grain left in the field by the reapers.

glee \'glē\ *n.* **1** An unaccompanied song for three or more solo voices. **2** Joy; merriment.

glee club. A chorus organized for singing part songs, especially as a social activity in a school or college.

glee·ful \'glēf-l\ *adj.* Merry; gay; joyous. — **glee·ful·ly** \'glēf-l-ē\ *adv.*

glen \'glen\ *n.* A small, secluded, narrow valley.

glib \'glib\ *adj.;* **glib·ber**; **glib·best**. Speaking or spoken with careless ease, often with not enough regard for the truth of what is said; as, a *glib* talker; a *glib* excuse. — **glib·ly**, *adv.*

glide \'glīd\ *v.;* **glid·ed**; **glid·ing**. **1** To move with a smooth, silent motion; as, a river *gliding* on. **2** In aviation, to descend smoothly and gradually with reduced engine power; as, to *glide* in for a landing. — *n.* **1** The act of gliding or moving smoothly; smooth, sliding motion. **2** In aviation, a gradual descent with reduced engine power. **3** In music, a slur.

glid·er \'glīd-r\ *n.* **1** One that glides. **2** An aircraft that resembles an airplane but that has no engine and depends on air currents to keep it in the air. **3** A porch or garden swing with a cushioned seat or couch suspended by links from an upright framework.

glim·mer \'glim-r\ *v.;* **glim·mered**; **glim·mer·ing** \-r(-)ing\. To shine faintly and unsteadily. — *n.* **1** A feeble and unsteady light. The old flashlight gave only a *glimmer*. **2** A faint perception or idea; an inkling; as, a *glimmer* of understanding. **3** A bit; as, a *glimmer* of hope.

glimpse \'glim(p)s\ *n.* **1** A short, hurried view; as, to catch a *glimpse* of something rushing by. **2** A faint idea; a glimmer. — *v.;* **glimpsed**; **glimps·ing**. To catch a quick view of.

glint \'glint\ *n.* A gleam; a flash; as, a *glint* of humor in a person's eye. — *v.* To flash; to gleam; as, polished metal *glinting* in the sun.

glis·ten \'glis-n\ *v.;* **glis·tened**; **glis·ten·ing** \-n(-)ing\. To sparkle or shine; especially, to shine with a soft sparkle or luster; as, eyes *glistening* with tears. — *n.* A glistening; a shining brightness.

glis·ter \'glist-r\ *v.;* **glis·tered**; **glis·ter·ing** \-r(-)ing\. To glitter; to sparkle. — *n.* Glitter.

glit·ter \'glit-r\ *v.* **1** To sparkle with bright light, especially with light that is harsh and cold. On a winter night the stars *glitter* in the sky. **2** To be very brilliant and showy; as, a *glittering* display of the newest fashions; a *glittering* career as an actress. — *n.* **1** A bright, sparkling light; brilliant sparkle. **2** Brilliant and splendid show; as, the *glitter* of the world of fashion. — **glit·tery** \'glit-r-ē\ *adj.*

gloam·ing \'glō-ming\ *n.* Twilight; dusk.

gloat \'glōt\ *v.* To look at or think about something with great satisfaction, especially with mean satisfaction or with greed; as, to *gloat* over a victory over an opponent; to *gloat* over a new toy.

glob·al \'glōb-l\ *adj.* **1** Like a globe; spherical. **2** Of or relating to the globe, or earth; world-wide; as, a *global* war. — **glob·al·ly** \'glōb-l-ē\ *adv.*

globe \'glōb\ *n.* **1** A round or nearly round object; a ball; a sphere; as, a lamp *globe*. **2** The earth — usually used with *the*. **3** A round model of the earth or heavens.

globe, 3

glob·u·lar \'gläb-yəl-r\ *adj.* **1** Globe-shaped; round. **2** Consisting of globules.

glob·ule \'gläb-ˌyül\ *n.* A small round particle; as, *globules* of water.

glock·en·spiel \'gläk-n-ˌs(h)pēl\ *n.* A musical instrument consisting of a series of metal bars tuned to the chromatic scale and played with two hammers.

gloom \'glüm\ *n.* **1** Partial or total darkness. **2** Depression of mind; low spirits. — For synonyms see *melancholy*. — *v.* **1** To look sullen; to frown. **2** To look dismal or low-spirited. **3** To become dark or threatening, as the sky.

gloomy \'glü-mē\ *adj.;* **gloom·i·er**; **gloom·i·est**. **1** Dusky; dim; as, a *gloomy* cave. **2** Melancholy; low-spirited; as, to feel *gloomy*. **3** Causing gloom; dismal; as, *gloomy* weather; *gloomy* news. — **gloom·i·ly** \'glüm-l-ē\ *adv.*

glo·ri·fi·ca·tion \ˌglōr-ə-fə-'kāsh-n, ˌglȯr-\ *n.* A glorifying or state of being glorified.

glo·ri·fy \'glōr-ə-ˌfī, 'glȯr-\ *v.;* **glo·ri·fied** \-ˌfīd\; **glo·ri·fy·ing**. **1** To worship; to adore; as, to *glorify* God. **2** To give the highest honor and praise to; to bestow glory upon; as, to *glorify* a hero. **3** To show in a very favorable way; to make seem glorious or splendid; especially, to represent as more splendid or important than is the fact; as, a story *glorifying* war; a street fight *glorified* by newsmen into a battle for freedom.

glo·ri·ous \'glōr-ē-əs, 'glȯr-\ *adj.* **1** Showing qualities or performing deeds that deserve glory; noble; as, a *glorious* hero; a *glorious* victory. **2** Splendid; magnificent; as, a *glorious* sunset. **3** Delightful; as, *glorious* weather; to have a *glorious* time. — **glo·ri·ous·ly**, *adv.*

glo·ry \'glōr-ē, 'glȯr-ē\ *n.; pl.* **glo·ries. 1** Praise, honor, and admiration given to a person by others; as, to win fame and *glory* as a soldier. **2** Something that brings honor, praise, or fame; as, the *glories* of Greece and Rome. **3** Brilliance; splendor; as, the moon in all its *glory*. **4** Heavenly bliss; heaven; as, with the saints in *glory*. **5** Height of prosperity or splendor; as, an aged actress remembering the days of her *glory*. — *v.;* **glo·ried** \-ēd\; **glo·ry·ing.** To rejoice; to be proud or boastful; as, to *glory* in one's strength.

gloss \'glȯs, 'gläs\ *n.* **1** Brightness from a smooth surface; luster; sheen. **2** An outwardly attractive appearance; outward show; as, a thin *gloss* of good manners. — *v.* **1** To give a gloss to. **2** To give an attractive appearance to, especially in order to conceal a weakness or defect; to smooth over; to explain away; as, to *gloss* over a mistake one has made. **3** To pass over lightly or quickly, especially in an attempt to ignore; as, to *gloss* over work that is distasteful.

glos·sa·ry \'gläs-r(-)ē, 'glȯs-\ *n.; pl.* **glos·sa·ries.** A list in the back of a book of the hard or unusual words found in the text; a dictionary of the special terms found in a particular field of study.

glossy \'glȯs-ē, 'gläs-ē\ *adj.;* **gloss·i·er; gloss·i·est.** Smooth and shining.

glot·tis \'glät-əs\ *n.* The opening between the vocal cords in the larynx.

glove \'gləv\ *n.* A covering for the hand, especially one made with a division for each finger. — **gloved** \'gləvd\ *adj.*

glov·er \'gləv-r\ *n.* A person who makes or sells gloves.

glow \'glō\ *v.* **1** To shine with an intense heat; to give off light and heat without flame. **2** To show strong bright color; as, a sunset *glowing* in the west. **3** To be or to look warm and flushed, as with exercise, feeling, or excitement; as, to *glow* with health; to *glow* with happiness. — *n.* **1** Light such as comes from something that is intensely hot but not flaming. **2** Brightness or warmth of color; as, a rosy *glow* of health; a golden *glow* in the sky. **3** A feeling of physical warmth, as from exercise; as, to be in a *glow*. **4** Warmth of feeling; as, a *glow* of pleasure.

glow·er \'glaủr\ *v.* To stare angrily; to scowl; to glare.

glow·worm \'glō-ˌwərm\ *n.* An insect or insect larva that gives off light.

gloze \'glōz\ *v.;* **glozed; gloz·ing.** To smooth over; to gloss; as, to *gloze* over a person's faults.

glu·cose \'glü-ˌkōs\ *n.* **1** A simple sugar occurring especially in the blood and in the fruits and saps of plants. **2** A light-colored syrup obtained chiefly from cornstarch.

glue \'glü\ *n.* **1** A substance made by boiling animal skins, bones, and hoofs, and used for sticking things together. **2** Any substance that is like glue in stickiness. — *v.;* **glued; glu·ing.** To make fast with or as if with glue; as, tiny snails *glued* to a water lily pad; to sit with eyes *glued* to a television screen.

glu·ey \'glü-ē\ *adj.;* **glu·i·er** \'glü-ē-ər\; **glu·i·est** \-ē-əst\. Covered with glue; sticky like glue.

glum \'gləm\ *adj.;* **glum·mer; glum·mest.** Silent and gloomy; dismal; sullen. — **glum·ly**, *adv.*

glut \'glət\ *v.;* **glut·ted; glut·ting. 1** To fill full; to satisfy to the limit or to excess; as, *glutted* with huge helpings of dessert. **2** To oversupply or overstock. The market was *glutted* with grapefruit. — *n.* A full supply or an oversupply.

glu·ten \'glüt-n\ *n.* The tough, gluey substance in the flour from certain grains, such as wheat, that holds together dough made from this flour and makes it sticky.

glu·ti·nous \'glüt-n-əs\ *adj.* Like glue; sticky.

glut·ton \'glət-n\ *n.* **1** A person who overeats. **2** A shaggy thickset flesh-eating mammal of northern Europe and Asia, similar to the wolverine.

glut·ton·ous \'glət-n-əs\ *adj.* Having the habit of eating to excess; greedy. — **glut·ton·ous·ly**, *adv.*

glut·tony \'glət-n-ē\ *n.; pl.* **glut·ton·ies.** Excess in eating.

glyc·er·in \'glis-r(-)ən\ or **glyc·er·ine** \-r(-)ən, -r-ˌēn\ *n.* Glycerol, especially for industrial use.

glyc·er·ol \'glis-r-ˌȯl, -ˌōl\ *n.* A sweet, colorless, syrupy liquid obtained from natural fats and oils, used in medicine, in toilet preparations, and in making explosives.

gly·co·gen \'glīk-əj-n\ *n.* A white, tasteless substance, the form in which carbohydrate is stored in the body tissues.

G-man \'jē-ˌman\ *n.; pl.* **G-men** \-ˌmen\. [An abbreviation for *Government man.*] A special agent of the Federal Bureau of Investigation of the United States.

gnarl \'närl, 'nårl\ *n.* A knot in wood; a large or hard knot on a tree.

gnarled \'närld, 'nårld\ *adj.* Full of knots or gnarls; rugged; twisted; as, a *gnarled* old oak; hands *gnarled* from years of labor.

gnash \'nash\ *v.* To strike or grind the teeth together, as in anger or pain.

gnat \'nat\ *n.* Any of various small two-winged flies, especially such as bite.

gnaw \'nȯ\ *v.;* **gnawed** \'nȯd\; **gnawed** \'nȯd\ or **gnawn** \'nȯn\; **gnaw·ing. 1** To bite repeatedly so as to wear away little by little; to bite or chew upon; as, to *gnaw* on a bone. **2** To produce by gnawing. Rats *gnawed* a hole in the wall. **3** To have an effect like gnawing with the teeth; as, the *gnawing* pain of hunger. — **gnaw·er**, *n.*

gnat

gneiss \'nīs\ *n.* A rock in layers, similar in composition to granite or feldspar.

gnome \'nōm\ *n.* One of an imaginary race of

dwarfs supposed to live inside the earth and guard treasure.

gnu \'nü, 'nyü\ *n.; pl.* **gnu** or **gnus**. An African antelope with large oxlike head, short mane, long tail, and horns that curve downward and outward and then upward.

go \'gō\ *v.;* **went** \'went\; **gone** \'gón\; **go·ing** \'gō-ing\. **1** To pass from one place or point to another; to move; to proceed; as, to *go* slowly; to *go* upstairs. **2** To move away; to leave; as, a place full of people coming and *going*. It is time to *go*. **3** To be guided or governed; as, a good rule to *go* by. **4** To pass away; to be spent; to be lost; to disappear; as, to get up in the morning and find that all the snow has *gone*. Money *goes* more easily than it comes. **5** To continue its course or action; to run; as, a machine that *goes* by electricity. That clock is not *going*. **6** To make its own special sound. How does a kitten *go?* **7** To happen in a given manner. Things *went* badly all day. **8** To extend along a certain way. This road *goes* to the city. **9** To put oneself. Mother *went* to great trouble for the children's party. **10** To participate equally in; as, to *go* halves with someone. **11** To be suitable; to harmonize; as, to wear a necktie that *goes* with one's suit. **12** To belong. This book *goes* on the top shelf. **13** To endure; to tolerate. I cannot *go* him. **14** To bet; to wager. — **go at.** To attack; to undertake energetically. — **go back on.** To abandon; to turn against; to betray; as, to *go back on* one's promise. — **go in for. 1** To make the object of one's work or studies; as, to *go in for* languages. **2** To indulge in; to take part in; as, to *go in for* a good time. — **go into. 1** To enter as a profession or business; as, to *go into* politics. **2** To pass into; to be affected by; as, to *go into* hysterics. **3** To speak of; to investigate; to discuss; as, to *go into* the cause of the accident. — **go off. 1** To explode; to be discharged. Dynamite *goes off* with a loud boom. **2** To progress to the end; to occur. The sports program *went off* as planned. **3** To give oneself up; as, to *go off* to sleep. — **go on. 1** To continue; to proceed. The road *goes on* for miles without a turn. **2** To keep talking. The speaker *went on* for hours. — **go out. 1** To become spread abroad; to be published. The story *went out* that the war was over. **2** To come to an end; to be extinguished. The light has *gone out*. **3** To end, as a year. **4** To take part in social affairs not at one's home; as, to *go out* every night in the week. **5** To be emotionally drawn. The father's heart *went out* to his son. **6** To go on strike. — **go over. 1** To read over; to review; to rehearse; as, to *go over* a part in a play before curtain time. **2** To examine and change if necessary; to revise; to retouch; as, to *go over* a piece of work in the hope of improving it. **3** To succeed; to be favorably received; as, to *go over* in a new job. — **go through. 1** To continue to the end; to persevere; as, to *go through* with the unpleasant job. **2** To examine thoroughly; to search. The police *went through* the captured man's belongings. **3** To suffer; to undergo; to experience; as, to *go through* a serious illness. **4** To spend completely; to exhaust; as, to *go through* a fortune. — **go under. 1** To be known or recognized by, as a name or title. **2** To be overwhelmed or defeated; to go to ruin; to fail. The business *went under* during the depression. — **go up. 1** To go to ruin; to be ruined. **2** To increase, as in price or number. — **go with. 1** To be connected or associated with. A cough sometimes *goes with* a severe cold. **2** To court. — *n.; pl.* **goes** \'gōz\. **1** Energy; spirit; as, a person with a great deal of snap and *go*. **2** The fashion; the rage. **3** A circumstance or situation; as, a bad *go*. **4** Something that turns out successfully; as, to make a *go* of selling insurance. **5** An attempt; a try; as, to have a *go* at farming. — **no go.** Useless; hopeless. This plan is *no go*. — **on the go** or **upon the go.** In a state of restless activity.

goad \'gōd\ *n.* **1** A pointed stick used to urge on an animal. **2** Something that urges a person on; a spur. — *v.* To urge on with or as if with a goad; as, to *goad* a person into fighting.

goal \'gōl\ *n.* **1** The point at which a race or journey is to end. **2** An aim; a purpose; as, to reach one's *goal* in life. **3** A place into, over, or through which the players in certain games try to drive something, as a ball, in order to score; a score made in this way.

goal·ie \'gō-lē\ *n.* A goalkeeper.

goal·keep·er \'gōl-ˌkēp-r\ *n.* or **goal tender**. In certain games, a player whose duty it is to defend the goal.

goat \'gōt\ *n.* **1** Any of certain hollow-horned, cud-chewing mammals related to the sheep but of lighter build, having backwardly arching horns, a short tail, and, usually, straight hair. **2** *Slang.* A person made to take the blame for another's fault or mistake; a scapegoat.

goa·tee \gō-'tē\ *n.* A man's beard on the chin, trimmed to a point.

goat·herd \'gōt-ˌhərd\ *n.* A person who tends goats.

goat·skin \'gōt-ˌskin\ *n.* The skin of a goat or a leather made from it.

goat·suck·er \'gōt-ˌsək-r\ *n.* Any of a group of long-winged, short-billed, wide-mouthed nocturnal birds, including the American whippoorwill and the nighthawks.

gob \'gäb\ *n.* A mass; a lump; as, a *gob* of mud.

gob \'gäb\ *n. Slang.* A sailor of the United States Navy.

gob·bet \'gäb-ət\ *n.* A lump; a mass.

gob·ble \'gäb-l\ *v.;* **gob·bled**; **gob·bling** \-l(-)ing\. To eat hastily or greedily; to gulp; as, to *gobble* one's food.

gob·ble \'gäb-l\ *n.* The throaty sound that a turkey makes. — *v.;* **gob·bled**; **gob·bling** \-l(-)ing\. To make the throaty sound characteristic of a turkey.

gob·bler \'gäb-lər\ *n.* A male turkey.

go-be·tween \'gō-bə-ˌtwēn\ *n.* A person who goes from one person to another as a messenger or a peacemaker; an intermediate agent.

gob·let \'gäb-lət\ *n.* A tall drinking glass with a foot and stem.

gob·lin \'gäb-lən\ *n.* An ugly imaginary creature with evil or mischievous ways.

goblet

go·cart \'gō-ˌkärt, -ˌkårt\ *n.* A baby carriage with small front wheels and a back that can be raised and lowered.

god \'gäd, 'gȯd\ *n.* **1** A being possessing more than human powers. Ancient peoples worshiped many *gods.* **2** Any natural or man-made physical object worshiped as divine; especially, an image or idol. **3** Anything held to be the most important thing in existence; as, to make a *god* of money. **4** [written with a capital letter] The Deity regarded as that holy and sovereign power creating and sustaining all things of the universe.

god·child \'gäd-ˌchīld, 'gȯd-\ *n.; pl.* **god·chil·dren** \-ˌchild-r(ə)n\. A person for whom another person stands as sponsor at baptism, promising to see that the baptized person receives a Christian training; a godson or goddaughter.

god·daugh·ter \'gäd-ˌdȯt-r, 'gȯd-\ *n.* A female godchild.

god·dess \'gäd-əs, 'gȯd-\ *n.* **1** A female god. **2** A woman who excites adoration for her great charm or beauty.

god·fa·ther \'gäd-ˌfäth-r, 'gȯd-, -fåth-r\ *n.* A man who stands as sponsor for a child at its baptism.

god·head \'gäd-ˌhed, 'gȯd-\ *n.* **1** Divine nature; divinity. **2** [with a capital] God.

god·less \'gäd-ləs, 'gȯd-\ *adj.* **1** Not acknowledging the existence of God. **2** Wicked; evil.

god·like \'gäd-ˌlīk, 'gȯd-\ *adj.* Like or suitable for a god or God; divine.

god·ly \'gäd-lē, 'gȯd-\ *adj.;* **god·li·er**; **god·li·est.** Religious; pious; devout; as, a *godly* man. — **god·li·ness** \-lē-nəs\ *n.*

god·moth·er \'gäd-ˌməth-r, 'gȯd-\ *n.* A woman who stands as sponsor for a child at its baptism.

god·par·ent \'gäd-ˌpar-ənt, 'gȯd-, -ˌper-\ *n.* A godfather or godmother.

God's acre. A cemetery or burial ground.

god·send \'gäd-ˌsend, 'gȯd-\ *n.* Some needed thing that comes unexpectedly, as if sent by God.

god·son \'gäd-ˌsən, 'gȯd-\ *n.* A male godchild.

God·speed \'gäd-'spēd, 'gȯd-\ *n.* A wish for success given to a person on parting from him.

goes \'gōz\. A form of the verb *go* showing present time, and used with "he", "she", or "it" or with words for which these stand.

go-get·ter \'gō-ˌget-r\ *n. Slang.* A very aggressive, enterprising person.

gog·gle \'gäg-l\ *v.;* **gog·gled**; **gog·gling** \-l(-)ing\. To stare with eyes bulging or to roll the eyes to one side or from side to side; as, to *goggle* at an unusual sight. When he heard the bad news, the old fellow *goggled* at me in dismay. — *n.* [in the plural] Large, tightly fitted eyeglasses with side shields, worn to protect the eyes, as from dust, sun, or wind.

gog·gle-eyed \'gäg-l-'īd\ *adj.* Having bulging or rolling eyes.

go·ing \'gō-ing\. Present part. of *go.* — *n.* **1** Departure; a leaving; as, to say good-by before *going.* **2** Condition of the road or ground. The *going* was good. — *adj.* Working; in operation; carrying on in its ordinary way; as, a *going* concern.

go·ings-on \'gō-ing-'zȯn, -'zän\ *n. pl.* **1** Happenings or instances of conduct not generally approved of; as, to be shocked by the *goings-on* next door. **2** Any actions or events; doings. The audience was amused by the *goings-on* in the play.

goi·ter \'gȯit-r\ *n.* A swelling on the front part of the throat associated with enlargement of the thyroid gland; also, a diseased condition characterized by this enlargement.

gold \'gōld\ *n.* **1** A precious yellow metal that is heavy and easily bent. **2** Gold money; wealth; riches. **3** The yellow color of the metal gold. — *adj.* **1** Made of gold. **2** Of the color of gold. **3** Payable in gold.

gold·brick \'gōl(d)-ˌbrik\ *n. Slang.* A person who manages to evade assigned work; a shirker. — *v. Slang.* To act as a goldbrick.

gold·en \'gōl-dən\ *adj.* **1** Like gold; made of or containing gold. **2** Of the color of gold; as, *golden* hair. **3** Precious; excellent; as, a *golden* opportunity. **4** Prosperous and happy; flourishing; as, the *golden* age of a civilization. **5** The fiftieth in a series of anniversaries or celebrations.

golden glow. A branched plant of the aster or thistle family, about four feet tall, with many-petaled yellow flowers.

golden mean. The course between extremes of any kind; neither too much nor too little.

gold·en·rod \'gōl-dən-ˌräd\ *n.* A stiff-stemmed herb of the aster family, about three feet high, with narrow heads of tiny yellow flowers most often in one-sided clusters.

golden rule. The rule, as stated in the teachings of Jesus, of doing to others as we would have them do to us.

gold-filled \'gōl(d)-'fild\ *adj.* Filled or covered with gold; as, a *gold-filled* bracelet.

gold·finch \'gōl(d)-ˌfinch\ *n.* **1** A European finch with a yellow patch on each wing. **2** An American finch that resembles the canary.

gold·fish \'gōl(d)-ˌfish\ *n.; pl.* **gold·fish** or **gold·fish·es.** A small, shiny, aquarium fish related to the carp, usually golden-yellow or orange in color.

gold leaf. A thin sheet of gold, used for gilding.

gold rush. A hastening of many people to newly discovered gold fields, as to California in 1849.

gold·smith \'gōl(d)-ˌsmith\ *n.* A person who makes things of gold.

golf \'gälf, 'gȯlf, 'gäf, 'gȯf\ *n.* An outdoor game in which the player uses wooden or metal clubs to hit a small hard rubber ball into a series of holes, usually nine or 18, with as few strokes as possible. — *v.* To play golf. — **golf·er**, *n.*

gon·do·la \'gän-də-lə, gän-'dō-lə\ *n.* **1** A long, narrow boat with high bow and stern used in the canals of Venice. **2** A railroad freight car with sides and a flat bottom but with no top. **3** A car attached to the underside of an airship, as a balloon.

gondola, 1

gon·do·lier \ˌgän-də-'lir\ *n.* A man who rows or poles a gondola.

gone \'gȯn\. Past part. of *go.* — *adj.* **1** Advanced; as, far *gone* in sleep. **2** Weak; as, a *gone* feeling from being hungry. — **gone on.** In love with; as, to be *gone on* the boy next door.

gong \'gȯng, 'gäng\ *n.* **1** A metallic disk that produces a harsh tone when struck. **2** A flat saucer-shaped bell.

gon·or·rhea or **gon·or·rhoea** \ˌgän-r-'ē-ə\ *n.* A contagious inflammatory disease of the genito-urinary tract.

goo·ber \'güb-r, 'gůb-r\ *n.* A peanut.

good \'gůd\ *adj.;* **bet·ter** \'bet-r\; **best** \'best\. **1** Suitable for its purpose; satisfactory; as, a *good* light for reading. **2** Over rather than under the required amount; full; thorough; as, a *good* day's work; a *good* dollar's worth. **3** Considerable; as, to go to a *good* deal of trouble; a *good* while. **4** Desirable; attractive; as, a *good* job; a *good* dinner. **5** Helpful; kind; friendly; as, a *good* neighbor; a man who is *good* to his family. **6** Well-behaved; as, a *good* boy. *Good* dog! **7** Honest and upright; as, a *good* man. **8** Sound and reliable; as, *good* advice; *good* sense. **9** Up to the standard; not bad; as, to do *good* work; a *good* drawing. — *n.* **1** Something that is good. **2** Welfare; benefit; as, to work for the *good* of the community. **3** Good people. The *good* shall prosper. **4** [in the plural] Wares; property; as, a stock of *goods;* all one's earthly *goods.* — **as good as.** In effect; practically; the same as. By the eighth inning the game was *as good as* won. — **for good** or **for good and all.** Fully; completely; permanently; as, finished *for good and all;* to leave *for good.*

good-by or **good-bye** also **good·by** or **good·bye** \gů(d)-'bī, gə(d)-\ *interj.* [A contraction of *God be with you.*] Farewell! — \gůd-\ *n.* [The plural of all forms is made with *s.*] A farewell; as, tearful *good-bys.*

Good Friday. The Friday before Easter, kept as the anniversary of the crucifixion of Christ.

good·heart·ed \'gůd-'härt-əd, -'hȧrt-\ *adj.* Having or showing a kind disposition.— **good·heart·ed·ly,** *adv.*

good-hu·mored \'gůd-'hyüm-rd, -'yüm-\ *adj.* Cheerful. — **good-hu·mored·ly,** *adv.*

good·ish \'gůd-ish\ *adj.* **1** Fairly good. **2** Considerable; as, a *goodish* distance.

good-look·ing \'gůd-'lůk-ing\ *adj.* Having a pleasing appearance; handsome; attractive; as, a *good-looking* man; a *good-looking* car.

good·ly \'gůd-lē\ *adj.;* **good·li·er**; **good·li·est.** **1** Of pleasing appearance, character, or quality; as, a *goodly* person; *goodly* land. **2** Large; considerable; as, a *goodly* number.

good·man \'gůd-mən\ *n.; pl.* **good·men** \-mən\. *Archaic.* **1** The master of a household. **2** A title equivalent to *Mister* given to persons under the rank of gentleman.

good-na·tured \'gůd-'nāch-rd\ *adj.* Having or showing a pleasant, kindly nature; especially, not easily offended.— **good-na·tured·ly,** *adv.*

good·ness \'gůd-nəs\ *n.* The quality or the condition of being good; excellence of character; virtue; kindness; generosity.

goods \'gůdz\ *n. pl.* **1** Articles of trade or commerce; wares; merchandise. **2** Personal property; as, to sell one's household *goods.* **3** Dry goods; especially, cloth for clothing; as, dress *goods.*

good-sized \'gůd-'sīzd\ *adj.* Large enough; fairly large.

good-tem·pered \'gůd-'temp-rd\ *adj.* Having a good temper; not easily annoyed or angered. — **good-tem·pered·ly,** *adv.*

good·wife \'gůd-ˌwīf\ *n.; pl.* **good·wives** \-ˌwīvz\. *Archaic* **1** The mistress of a household. **2** A title equivalent to *Mistress* (*Mrs.*).

good will or **good·will** \'gůd-'wil\ *n.* **1** Good intention. **2** Kindly feeling; friendliness. **3** The value of the trade a business has built up over a considerable time.

goody \'gůd-ē\ *n.; pl.* **good·ies.** Anything regarded as especially good. to eat, as a piece of candy. — *interj.* An exclamation of pleasure or delight.

goose \'güs\ *n.; pl.* **geese** \'gēs\. **1** A web-footed water bird of the same family as ducks and swans, resembling both these birds but larger than a duck and smaller than a swan. **2** A female goose, as distinguished from a gander. **3** The flesh of a goose used as food. **4** A silly person; a simpleton.

goose·ber·ry \'güs-ˌber-ē, 'güz-\ *n.; pl.* **goose·ber·ries.** The sour and usually hairy berry of a thorny shrub of the same family as the currant.

goose flesh \'güs\. A roughness of the skin caused by cold or fear.

goose·neck \'güs-ˌnek\ *n.* Anything curved like the neck of a goose, as an iron hook or the flexible tube of jointed metal in certain adjustable desk lamps.

goose step. A straight-legged, stiff-kneed marching step used by German soldiers on parade. — **goose-step** \'güs-ˌstep\ *v.*

go·pher \'gōf-r\ *n.* [Probably from American French *gaufre* meaning literally "honeycomb".] **1** A burrowing ratlike rodent with strong claws on the forefeet and very large outside cheek pouches. **2** A small striped ground squirrel found in the prairie region of the United States.

gore \'gōr, 'gȯr\ *n.* Blood; especially, clotted blood.

gore \'gōr, 'gȯr\ *n.* A tapering or three-cornered piece of material, as cloth or canvas, used to vary the width of a larger piece, as in a dress or sail. — *v.;* **gored**; **gor·ing**. To cut into a tapering or three-cornered form; to put a gore in.

gore \'gōr, 'gȯr\ *v.;* **gored**; **gor·ing**. To pierce or wound, as with a horn or tusk; as, to be *gored* by a bull.

gorge \'gȯrj\ *n.* **1** The throat. **2** A narrow passage, as one between two mountains; a ravine with steep, rocky walls. **3** A mass of matter that chokes up a passage; as, an ice *gorge* in a river. — *v.;* **gorged**; **gorg·ing**. To eat greedily until one has all one can hold.

gor·geous \'gȯr-jəs\ *adj.* Splendid; richly colored; magnificent; as, a *gorgeous* sunset. — **gor·geous·ly**, *adv.*

go·ril·la \gə-'ril-ə\ *n.* [From scientific Latin, derived from Greek *Gorrillai*, the name given to a tribe of hairy women described by an ancient Greek geographer.] The largest of the manlike apes and the nearest to man in structure.

gor·mand·ize \'gȯr-mən-ˌdīz\ *v.;* **gor·mand·ized**; **gor·mand·iz·ing**. To eat greedily or ravenously. — **gor·mand·iz·er**, *n.*

gorse \'gȯrs\ *n.* Furze.

gory \'gōr-ē, 'gȯr-ē\ *adj.;* **gor·i·er**; **gor·i·est**. Covered with gore; bloody; blood-stained.

gos·hawk \'gäs-ˌhȯk\ *n.* A large short-winged hawk noted for its powerful flight, activity, and courage.

gos·ling \'gäz-ling, 'gȯz-\ *n.* A young goose.

gos·pel \'gäsp-l\ *n.* [From Old English *godspel*, meaning literally "good tidings".] **1** The teachings of Christ and the apostles; as, to spread the *gospel*. **2** [with a capital] Any one of the first four books of the New Testament, each of which contains an account of the life and death of Jesus Christ. **3** Anything that is told or accepted as being absolutely true; as, to accept everything someone says as *gospel*. **4** Any guiding principle for action, as in social or political theory.

gos·sa·mer \'gäs-m-ər\ *n.* **1** A fine film of cobwebs floating in the air. **2** Any very thin, gauze-like fabric. — *adj.* Light and flimsy. — **gos·sa·mery**, *adj.*

gos·sip \'gäs-əp\ *n.* **1** A person who goes about tattling or telling news. **2** Idle talk; the news spread by a tattler; as, unkind *gossip;* harmless *gossip*. — *v.* To act as a gossip; to go about spreading news or rumors. — **gos·sip·er**, *n.* — **gos·sipy**, *adj.*

got. Past tense and past part. of *get*.

gotten. A past part. of *get*.

gouge \'gau̇j\ *n.* **1** A chisel with a curved blade for scooping or cutting holes. **2** A hole made with a gouge or as if with a gouge. — *v.;* **gouged**; **goug·ing**. **1** To scoop out with or as if with a gouge. **2** To defraud; to cheat. — **goug·er** \'gau̇j-r\ *n.*

gouge, 1

gou·lash \'gü-ˌläsh, -ˌlȧsh, -ˌlash\ *n.* A stew of beef or veal flavored with vegetables and paprika.

gourd \'gōrd, 'gȯrd, 'gu̇rd\ *n.* **1** The hard-shelled, many-seeded fruit of a vine related to the pumpkin, squash, cucumber, melon, and citron. **2** The vine bearing this fruit. **3** The cleaned, dried shell of this fruit, used for decoration or as a bottle, bowl, or dipper.

gour·mand \'gu̇r-ˌmänd, -mənd\ *n.* A person who takes great pleasure in fine food; an epicure.

gour·met \gu̇r-'mā, 'gu̇r-ˌmā\ *n.* A connoisseur in eating and drinking.

gout \'gau̇t\ *n.* **1** A drop or clot, as of blood. **2** A disease that attacks the joints of the body, causing painful swelling. — **gouty**, *adj.*

Gov. Abbreviation for *Governor*.

gov·ern \'gəv-rn\ *v.* **1** To direct; to control; to rule; as, to *govern* a country. **2** To regulate; to restrain; as, to *govern* one's temper. **3** To determine; to be a rule or law for. A former court decision *governs* this case. **4** To require to be in a certain case or mood. A transitive verb *governs* a noun in the objective case. **5** To require a certain case or mood. A transitive verb *governs* the objective case. — **gov·ern·a·ble**, *adj.*

gov·ern·ance \'gəv-r-nən(t)s\ *n.* The exercise of control; government.

gov·ern·ess \'gəv-r-nəs\ *n.* A woman who teaches and trains a child or children, especially in a private home.

gov·ern·ment \'gəv-r(n)-mənt\ *n.* **1** Control and direction of affairs, as of a city, state, or nation. **2** The method or system of control; especially, the established form of political rule; as, a country with a democratic *government*. **3** The function, office, or power of governing. The king gave over his *government* to the representative of the people. **4** The territory or country governed. **5** The persons making up the governing body; as, to wait to see what action the *government* will take. — **gov·ern·men·tal** \ˌgəv-r(n)-'ment-l\ *adj.* — **gov·ern·men·tal·ly** \-'ment-l-ē\ *adv.*

gov·er·nor \'gəv-n(-)ər, 'gəv-r-nər\ *n.* **1** A person who governs; especially, the chief executive of a state of the United States, or of a British colony. **2** *Slang*. One's employer. **3** *Slang*. One's father. **4** An automatic device attached to an engine for controlling its speed.

gov·er·nor·ship \'gəv-n(-)ər-ˌship, 'gəv-r-nər-\ *n.* **1** The office or position of a governor. **2** The function, authority, or term of a governor.

govt. Abbreviation for *government*.

gown \'gau̇n\ *n.* **1** A woman's dress; especially, one intended for wear on very important occasions; as, a dinner *gown;* a bridal *gown*. **2** A loose robe, as a dressing gown or a nightgown. **3** Any of various official robes worn by certain officers, as judges, by some clergymen, and on certain occasions, as commencement, by teachers and students. — *v.* To clothe in a gown; as, to be *gowned* in satin.

gr. Abbreviation for: **1** *gram.* **2** *grain.*

grab \'grab\ *v.;* **grabbed; grab·bing.** To snatch; to seize. — *n.* **1** A grabbing; something that is grabbed. **2** A device for clutching objects, as for lifting them. — **grab·ber,** *n.*

grace \'grās\ *n.* **1** Kindness; good will; favor; mercy; as, by the *grace* of God. **2** [in the plural] The state of being in favor; as, to be in someone's good *graces.* **3** A short prayer before or after a meal; as, to say *grace.* **4** A sense of what is right or proper; as, to accept criticism with good *grace;* to have the *grace* to admit a mistake. **5** [usually with a capital] A title given to a duke, a duchess, or an archbishop. **6** Temporary exemption, as from a penalty; as, to have three days' *grace.* **7** A pleasing and attractive quality, manner, or feature; as, social *graces.* **8** Easy, flowing action; beauty of movement. The fat man ran with surprising *grace.* **9** [in the plural with a capital] In Greek mythology, graceful and beautiful sister goddesses, usually three in number, who were intimates of the Muses. — *v.;* **graced; grac·ing.** **1** To honor; to favor; as, to be asked to *grace* a party with one's presence. **2** To adorn or to make more attractive; as, to *grace* a table with flowers.

grace·ful \'grās-fəl\ *adj.* **1** Showing grace or beauty in form or action; as, to have a *graceful* walk; a vase with *graceful* lines. **2** Nicely done; tactful; agreeable; as, a *graceful* refusal; a *graceful* speech of thanks. — **grace·ful·ly** \-fə-lē\ *adv.*

grace·less \'grās-ləs\ *adj.* Without grace, charm, or elegance; especially, showing lack of feeling for what is fitting; as, *graceless* behavior. — **grace·less·ly,** *adv.*

grace note. A note not essential to a melody or harmony but added as an ornamentation.

gra·cious \'grā-shəs\ *adj.* **1** Full of grace or charm; as, *gracious* houses; a *gracious* way of life. **2** Kindly; courteous; as, a *gracious* act; a *gracious* invitation. — **gra·cious·ly,** *adv.*

grack·le \'grak-l\ *n.* Any of certain American blackbirds with glossy feathers that show changeable green, purple, and bronze colors.

gra·da·tion \grā-'dāsh-n\ *n.* **1** A grading. **2** A series resulting from grading. **3** [in the plural] The steps, stages, or degrees in a graded series.

grade \'grād\ *n.* **1** A stage, step, or degree in any series, order, or rank. **2** Position in a scale of rank, of quality, or of order; as, to hold a high *grade* in the army; leather of the highest *grade.* **3** A class of things that are of the same rank, quality, or order. **4** A division of the school course, representing a year's work; as, to finish the fourth *grade.* **5** The group of pupils in such a division. **6** [in the plural] The elementary school system; as, to teach in the *grades.* **7** A mark or rating, as in school; as, to get a *grade* of 90 in a test. **8** The rate at which a road slopes upward or downward; a slope; as, a steep *grade.* — *v.;* **grad·ed; grad·ing.** **1** To arrange in grades; to sort; as, to *grade* apples; to *grade* colors. **2** To make level or evenly sloping; as, to *grade* a highway. **3** To give a grade to, or to assign to a grade; as, to *grade* a spelling test; to *grade* a pupil. **4** To form a series having only slight differences; as, colors that *grade* into one another.

grade crossing. A crossing or intersection of a railroad and a highway or another railroad on the same level or grade.

grad·er \'grād-r\ *n.* **1** One that grades. **2** A machine for grading earth and for shallow excavating.

grade school. A school divided into the first six, or sometimes into the first eight, grades of a twelve year public school course.

gra·di·ent \'grād-ē-ənt\ *n.* A slope; a grade.

grad·u·al \'graj-ə-wəl, 'graj-l\ *adj.* By steps or degrees; very slow or slight; as, a *gradual* change for the better. — **grad·u·al·ly** \'graj-l-ē, 'graj-ə-wə-lē\ *adv.*

grad·u·ate \'graj-ə-wət, -ˌwāt\ *adj.* **1** That has been graduated, as from college. **2** Of, relating to, or designed for graduates; as, *graduate* schools. — *n.* **1** One who has completed the required course of study in a college or school; as, a high school *graduate.* **2** A cup, tube, or flask marked with a scale for measuring contents. — \-ˌwāt\ *v.;* **grad·u·at·ed; grad·u·at·ing.** **1** To admit, at the close of a course of study, to a standing described by a diploma. Five members of the class were *graduated* with honors. **2** To become a graduate; to finish successfully the course of study in a school or college; as, to *graduate* from the state university; to *graduate* at the head of one's class. **3** To mark with degrees of measurement; as, to *graduate* a cup. — **grad·u·a·tor** \-ˌwāt-r\ *n.*

grad·u·a·tion \ˌgraj-ə-'wāsh-n\ *n.* **1** A graduating or a being graduated. **2** The ceremony or exercises marking the completion by a student of a required course of study at a school or college; commencement.

graft \'graft\ *v.* **1** To insert a shoot from one plant into another plant so they are joined and grow together. **2** To join one thing to another as if by grafting; as, to *graft* skin or bone. **3** To get money or some advantage by dishonest means. — *n.* **1** The act of grafting. **2** A shoot from one plant grafted upon another plant; a cion. **3** The point of insertion of a cion in a plant or tree. **4** In surgery, a piece of living tissue, as skin or bone, used in grafting. **5** The getting of money or advantage by dishonest means, especially through misuse of an official position. **6** The money, position, or other advantage gained in this way. — **graft·er,** *n.*

gra·ham \'grā-əm\ *adj.* [Named after Sylvester *Graham* (1794–1851), an American reformer who advocated the use of whole wheat flour.] Made of **graham flour,** an unsifted wheat flour; as, *graham* crackers.

grain \'grān\ *n.* **1** The seed or seedlike fruit of

cereal grasses, such as wheat, Indian corn, or oats. **2** Cereal grasses or plants. **3** Any small hard particle; as, a *grain* of sand. **4** A tiny amount; a bit; as, a *grain* of sense. **5** A unit in some systems of measuring weight. **6** The fibers that make up the substance of wood; the arrangement of these fibers or of the layers in a stone such as marble; as, to carve against the *grain;* a beautiful *grain.* **7** Temper; natural disposition; as, to be asked to do something that goes against one's *grain.* — *v.* To paint in imitation of the grain, as of wood or marble. — **grain·er**, *n.* — **grainy**, *adj.*

gram or **gramme** \\'gram\\ *n.* A unit of weight in the metric system equal to the weight of one cubic centimeter of water.

gra·mer·cy \\grə-'mər-sē\\ *interj. Archaic.* An exclamation, as of thanks or surprise.

gram·mar \\'gram-r\\ *n.* **1** The study that deals with the facts about classes of words, their relation to each other, and their use in sentences. **2** The manner of speaking or writing considered with reference to the rules of grammar, as in making subjects and predicates agree in person and number; as, to pay careful attention to one's *grammar.* **3** A book about grammar; as, a sixth-grade *grammar.*

gram·mar·i·an \\grə-'mer-ē-ən\\ *n.* A specialist in grammar.

grammar school. The school grades between those called primary and high school.

gram·mat·i·cal \\grə-'mat-ik-l\\ *adj.* **1** Having to do with or according to the rules of grammar. **2** Correct as regards grammar; as, a construction that is not *grammatical.* — **gram·mat·i·cal·ly** \\-ik-l(-)ē\\ *adv.*

gramme. Variant of *gram.*

gram·pus \\'gramp-əs\\ *n.; pl.* **gram·pus·es** \\-ə-səz\\. **1** A sea animal resembling a whale but having teeth in the lower jaw only. **2** A killer whale.

gra·na·ry \\'grān-r(-)ē, 'gran-\\ *n.; pl.* **gra·na·ries.** **1** A storehouse for grain. **2** A region that produces grain in great abundance; as, the *granary* of a nation.

grand \\'grand\\ *adj.* **1** Higher in rank than others of the same class; foremost; principal; as, the *grand* prize. **2** Great in size; as, *grand* mountains. **3** Inclusive; complete; as, a *grand* total. **4** Magnificent; splendid; showing wealth or high social standing; as, a very *grand* party; a *grand* lady. **5** Impressive; stately; noble; as, a *grand* view; a *grand* old man. **6** Very good; fine; as, *grand* weather; to have a *grand* time. **7** Belonging to the second generation before or after one's own, as in *grandfather* or *grandson.*

gran·dam \\'gran-ˌdam, 'grand-m\\ or **gran·dame** \\'gran-ˌdām, 'grand-m\\ *n.* An old woman; especially, a grandmother.

grand·aunt \\'gran-'dant, -'dȧnt\\ *n.* An aunt of one's father or mother; a great-aunt.

grand·child \\'gran-ˌchīld\\ *n.; pl.* **grand·chil·dren** \\-ˌchil-dr(ə)n\\. A son's or daughter's child.

grand·daugh·ter \\'gran-ˌdȯt-r\\ *n.* A son's or daughter's daughter.

gran·dee \\(')gran-'dē\\ *n.* A Spanish or Portuguese nobleman of high rank; any man of exalted rank or station in life.

gran·deur \\'granj-r, 'gran-ˌdyu̇r, 'gran-ˌju̇r\\ *n.* Greatness, as of power, position, or character; magnificence; sublimity; as, the *grandeur* of the Rocky Mountains.

grand·fa·ther \\'gran-ˌfät͟h-r, -ˌfȧt͟h-r\\ *n.* **1** A father's or mother's father. **2** Any forefather; as, in the days of our *grandfathers.* — **grand·fa·ther·ly**, *adj.*

grandfather clock or **grandfather's clock.** A large pendulum clock having a tall square columnlike case standing directly on the floor.

grandfather clock

gran·dil·o·quence \\gran-'dil-ə-kwən(t)s\\ *n.* The use of high-sounding language; pompous eloquence. — **gran·dil·o·quent** \\-kwənt\\ *adj.*

gran·di·ose \\'gran-dē-ˌōs, ˌgran-dē-'ōs\\ *adj.* **1** Impressive, especially because of size; imposing. **2** Grand or imposing in a pompous or affected manner.

grand jury. A jury that chiefly examines accusations of crime made against persons and, if the evidence warrants, makes formal charges on which the accused persons are later tried before a judge and ordinary jury.

grand·ly \\'gran-dlē\\ *adv.* In a grand manner.

grand·moth·er \\'gran-ˌmət͟h-r\\ *n.* **1** A father's or mother's mother. **2** Any female ancestor. — **grand·moth·er·ly**, *adj.*

grand·neph·ew \\'gran-'nef-ˌyü\\ *n.* A grandson of one's brother or sister.

grand·niece \\'gran-'nēs\\ *n.* A granddaughter of one's brother or sister.

grand opera. Opera in which all the words are set to music and sung to the accompaniment of an orchestra.

grand·par·ent \\'gran-ˌpar-ənt, -ˌper-\\ *n.* A parent's parent; a grandfather or grandmother.

grand·sire \\'gran-ˌsīr\\ *n.* **1** *Archaic.* A grandfather. **2** An ancestor or forefather. **3** An aged man.

grand·son \\'gran-ˌsən\\ *n.* A son's or daughter's son.

grand·stand \\'gran-ˌstand\\ *n.* The principal stand for spectators, as at an athletic field or racecourse.

grand·un·cle \\'gran-'dəngk-l\\ *n.* An uncle of one's father or mother; a great-uncle.

grange \\'grānj\\ *n.* **1** A farm; especially, a farmhouse with its various buildings. **2** One of the lodges of "Patrons of Husbandry", a secret association to further the interests of farmers. **3** [with a capital] The association itself.

grang·er \'grānj-r\ *n.* **1** A member of a grange or of the Grange. **2** A farmer.

gran·ite \'gran-ət\ *n.* A very hard rock that takes a high polish, much used for building and for monuments.

gran·ite·ware \'gran-ət-ˌwar, -ˌwer\ *n.* Enameled ware.

gran·ny \'gran-ē\ *n.; pl.* **gran·nies.** **1** Grandmother. **2** An old woman. **3** A fussy person.

granny knot. An insecure and easily jammed knot often made by the inexperienced instead of a square knot.

grant \'grant\ *v.* **1** To agree to; to allow; as, to *grant* a request. **2** To give; as, to *grant* permission; to *grant* a charter. **3** To admit as true something not yet proved; to concede; as, *granting* that this is so.

— The word *concede* is a synonym of *grant: grant* may suggest the generous giving, as to a person in a lower position, of something requested or sought that might have been withheld; *concede* usually suggests the giving in or yielding to a rightful claim or the reluctant acknowledgment of the truth or justice of such a claim.

— *n.* **1** The act of granting; a concession. **2** Anything granted or given; especially, a tract of land granted by a government.

grant·ee \(')grant-'ē\ *n.* One to whom a grant is made.

grant·or \'grant-r, (')grant-'ȯr\ *n.* The one by whom a grant is made.

gran·u·lar \'gran-yəl-r\ *adj.* **1** Consisting of or like grains or granules; as, a *granular* rock; *granular* leather. **2** Granulated; showing granulation, as the eyelids in trachoma.

gran·u·late \'gran-yə-ˌlāt\ *v.;* **gran·u·lat·ed; gran·u·lat·ing.** **1** To form or collect into grains or crystals; as, *granulated* sugar. **2** To raise in granules; to make rough on the surface. — **gran·u·lat·ed** \-ˌlāt-əd\ *adj.*

gran·u·la·tion \ˌgran-yə-'lāsh-n\ *n.* **1** A granulating or the condition of being granulated. **2** One of the small raised places of a granulated surface.

gran·ule \'gran-ˌyül\ *n.* A small grain or particle; as, *granules* of sugar.

grape \'grāp\ *n.* **1** A smooth-skinned juicy berry that grows in clusters on a woody vine in colors ranging from green or white to deep red, purple, or black. **2** A grapevine. **3** Grapeshot.

grape·fruit \'grāp-ˌfrüt\ *n.* A large fruit related to the orange and lemon, with bitter yellow rind and somewhat acid juicy pulp.

grape·shot \'grāp-ˌshät\ *n.* A cluster of small iron balls to be shot from a cannon.

grape sugar. A natural sugar found in ripe grapes; dextrose.

grape·vine \'grāp-ˌvīn\ *n.* **1** Any grape-bearing vine. **2** News or rumor conveyed by secret means or signals. **3** Also **grapevine telegraph.** The secret or underground system by which news or rumor is conveyed; as, a prison *grapevine.*

graph \'graf\ *n.* **1** A diagram that, by means of dots and lines, shows a system of relationships between things; as, a *graph* showing the rise and fall in temperature. **2** In mathematics, a curve or surface representing the relations of equations or functions. — *v.* To plot or trace, as a curve from its equation.

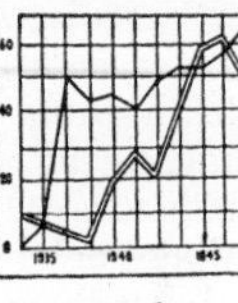
graph

graph·ic \'graf-ik\ or **graph·i·cal** \-ik-l\ *adj.* **1** Clearly and vividly told or described; as, a *graphic* account of an accident. **2** Of or relating to such arts (**graphic arts**) as painting, drawing, and printing. **3** Having to do with, or in the form of, a graph; as, a *graphic* record of the weather. — **graph·i·cal·ly** \-ik-l(-)ē\ *adv.*

graph·ite \'graf-ˌīt\ *n.* [From German *graphit,* derived from Greek *graphein,* meaning "to write".] A soft black carbon with a metallic luster, used in making lead pencils and as a lubricant.

grap·nel \'grap-nəl\ *n.* **1** A small anchor with four or five claws, or flukes. **2** A hooked iron for grappling objects, as under water.

grap·ple \'grap-l\ *v.;* **grap·pled; grap·pling** \-l(-)ing\. **1** To seize or hold with some implement, as a hook. **2** To seize one another; to struggle in or as if in a close fight; as, wrestlers *grappling* for a hold; to *grapple* with a problem. — *n.* **1** The act of grappling or seizing; a grip; a hold. **2** An implement used or designed for grappling.

grasp \'grasp\ *v.* **1** To make the motion of seizing; to clutch. A drowning man is said to *grasp* at a straw. **2** To seize and hold, as with the hand; to grip; as, to *grasp* a bat firmly with both hands. **3** To seize with the mind; to understand; as, to *grasp* a problem. — *n.* **1** The act of grasping; a grip of the hand; an embrace. **2** Possession; control; as, a land in the *grasp* of a tyrant. **3** The power of seizing and holding; reach; as, to have fame and fortune within one's *grasp.* **4** Understanding; knowledge; comprehension; as, to have a good *grasp* of fractions.

grasp·ing \'gras-ping\ *adj.* Greedy; avaricious; acquisitive. — **grasp·ing·ly,** *adv.*

grass \'gras\ *n.* **1** Green plant life eaten by grazing animals, especially that having leaves with narrow and spear-shaped blades. **2** Any of a family of plants characterized by their jointed, usually hollow, stems, narrow leaves, and fruit consisting of a seedlike grain. Wheat, Indian corn, bamboo, and sugar cane are all *grasses.* **3** Any grass-covered ground, as a lawn or a pasture. — *v.* **1** To graze, as cattle. **2** To cover with grass.

grass·hop·per \'gras-ˌhäp-r\ *n.* **1** Any of numerous leaping, plant-eating insects. **2** A light unarmed military airplane used especially for scouting and in helping to direct artillery fire.

grass·land \'gras-ˌland\ *n.* **1** A land area in which the vegetation consists chiefly of grasses. **2** Land kept in grass and used for pasture.

grassy \'gras-ē\ *adj.;* **grass·i·er; grass·i·est.** **1** Covered with grass. **2** Of or like grass.

grate \'grāt\ *v.;* **grat·ed; grat·ing. 1** To make into small particles by rubbing against something rough; as, to *grate* cheese. **2** To grind or rub against something with a rasping noise; as, a door that *grates* on its hinges. **3** To have a harsh or rasping effect; as, a noise that *grates* on one's nerves.

grate \'grāt\ *n.* **1** A frame containing parallel or crossed bars, as in a prison window. **2** A frame of iron bars for holding burning fuel, as in a furnace or a fireplace.

grate

grate, 1

grate·ful \'grāt-fəl\ *adj.* **1** Thankful; appreciative; as, to be *grateful* for a favor. **2** Pleasing; welcome; agreeable; as, a *grateful* breeze; the *grateful* shade of a great tree. **3** Expressing gratitude; as, to offer *grateful* thanks. — **grate·ful·ly** \-fə-lē\ *adv.*

grat·er \'grāt-r\ *n.* One that grates; especially, a tool or utensil with a rough surface for grating; as, a nutmeg *grater.*

grat·i·fi·ca·tion \ˌgrat-ə-fə-'kāsh-n\ *n.* **1** A gratifying or being gratified; satisfaction; as, desires not capable of *gratification* without great wealth. **2** Something that gratifies; a source of satisfaction or pleasure.

grat·i·fy \'grat-ə-ˌfī\ *v.;* **grat·i·fied** \-ˌfīd\; **grat·i·fy·ing. 1** To give pleasure or satisfaction to; as, a scene that *gratifies* the eye; to be *gratified* by news of a friend's recovery from an illness. **2** To satisfy; to humor; to oblige; as, parents who *gratify* every desire of their children.

— The words *indulge* and *humor* are synonyms of *gratify: gratify* usually suggests the giving of happiness, especially through the satisfaction of some important need or desire; *indulge* may refer to satisfying the unimportant or merely selfish desires of another, either through weakness or through too great eagerness to please; *humor* may suggest unusual compliance or attention to the changing moods or whims of another, sometimes patronizingly, sometimes for a selfish purpose.

grat·ing \'grāt-ing\ *n.* A partition, covering, or frame of parallel bars or crossed bars; a grate.

grat·ing \'grāt-ing\ *adj.* Harsh in sound; unpleasant.

gra·tis \'grāt-əs, 'grat-\ *adv.* or *adj.* For nothing; without charge; free; as, children under ten admitted *gratis.* On Sundays admission is *gratis.*

grat·i·tude \'grat-ə-ˌtüd, -ˌtyüd\ *n.* The condition of being grateful; thankfulness.

gra·tu·i·tous \grə-'tü-ət-əs, -'tyü-\ *adj.* **1** Given or obtained freely without regard to claim or merit. **2** Not called for by the circumstances; unwarranted; as, a *gratuitous* insult. — **gra·tu·i·tous·ly,** *adv.*

gra·tu·i·ty \grə-'tü-ət-ē, -'tyü-\ *n.; pl.* **gra·tu·i·ties.** Something given freely; especially, something given in return for a favor or service; a tip.

grave \'grāv\ *adj.;* **grav·er; grav·est. 1** Important; deserving serious consideration; as, a *grave* question. **2** Solemn; serious; earnest; as, a *grave* face; a *grave* manner. **3** Characterized by the tone or quality indicated by the grave accent. **4** Marked with the grave accent. — **grave·ly,** *adv.*

grave \'grāv\ *v.;* **graved** \'grāvd\; **grav·en** \'grāv-n\ or **graved; grav·ing** \'grā-ving\. **1** To carve or shape by cutting with a chisel; to sculpture; to engrave. **2** To impress deeply or indelibly on the mind; as, an event *graven* in one's memory.

grave \'grāv\ *n.* **1** A hole in the ground for burying a dead body. **2** Any place of burial; as, a watery *grave.* **3** Death; destruction; as, to go to an early *grave.*

grave accent. A mark [\`] used over certain vowels in some foreign languages to show their quality and used in English poetry to indicate that an ordinarily silent *e* in the ending *-ed* is to be pronounced \ə\, as in *wreathèd.*

grav·el \'grav-l\ *n.* **1** Small fragments of rock and pebbles, coarser than sand. **2** A deposit of small pebblelike bodies in the kidneys and urinary bladder. **3** The disease causing such a deposit. — *v.;* **grav·eled** or **grav·elled; grav·el·ing** or **grav·el·ling** \-l(-)ing\. To cover with gravel. — **grav·el·ly** \-l(-)ē\ *adj.*

grav·en \'grāv-n\ *adj.* Sculptured; engraved; as, a *graven* image.

grav·er \'grāv-r\ *n.* **1** An engraver; a sculptor. **2** A tool for cutting or engraving.

grave·stone \'grāv-ˌstōn\ *n.* A stone over a grave; a tombstone.

grave·yard \'grāv-ˌyärd, -ˌyȧrd\ *n.* A cemetery; a burial ground, as one beside a church.

grav·i·tate \'grav-ə-ˌtāt\ *v.;* **grav·i·tat·ed; grav·i·tat·ing. 1** To obey the law of gravitation. **2** To tend to move; to go; as, particles in a bottle of liquid that *gravitate* to the bottom. After the race people *gravitated* toward the winner.

grav·i·ta·tion \ˌgrav-ə-'tāsh-n\ *n.* **1** The action or process of gravitating. **2** The attraction or pull that tends to draw bodies together. The force of *gravitation* helps keep the planets in their courses around the sun. **3** The pull that tends to draw all objects on the earth down toward the center. An apple falls to the ground by the force of *gravitation.* **4** A going; a tendency to go; as, the *gravitation* of the crowd to the scene of the accident. — **grav·i·ta·tion·al** \-'tāsh-n(-)əl\ *adj.*

grav·i·ty \'grav-ət-ē\ *n.; pl.* **grav·i·ties. 1** The condition of being grave; importance; seriousness. Everyone sensed the *gravity* of the occasion. **2** Gravitation; especially, the attraction of bodies toward the center of the earth. **3** Weight. — **center of gravity.** The point in a body about which all the parts of the body exactly balance each other.

gra·vy \'grā-vē\ *n.; pl.* **gra·vies. 1** A sauce for meat, fish, or vegetables. **2** Also **dish gravy.** The juice that drips from meat in cooking. **3** *Slang.* Something got without effort; especially, illegal profit or graft.

gray or **grey** \'grā\ *adj.* **1** Of the color gray.

2 Dull; not bright; as, a *gray* shade of blue. **3** Cheerless; dismal; as, a *gray* day. The future looks *gray.* **4** Gray-haired; elderly; old. — *n.* Any color formed by blending black and white. — *v.* To make or become gray or grayish.

gray·beard or **grey·beard** \'grā-ˌbird\ *n.* **1** An old man. **2** A very wise or experienced man; as, young in years but a *graybeard* in politics.

gray·ish or **grey·ish** \'grā-ish\ *adj.* Somewhat gray.

gray·ling \'grā-ling\ *n.* **1** *pl.* **gray·ling** or **gray·lings.** A slender fresh-water fish similar in habits to the trout. **2** Any of certain gray and brown butterflies.

gray matter. **1** Nerve tissue, especially of the brain and spinal cord, containing nerve cells as well as fibers, and brownish gray in color. **2** Brains; intellect; as, a problem calling for the use of all one's *gray matter.*

graze \'grāz\ *v.;* **grazed; graz·ing.** **1** To feed or supply with grass or pasture; as, to *graze* sheep. **2** To eat grass; as, cattle *grazing* in the meadow.

graze \'grāz\ *v.;* **grazed; graz·ing.** **1** To rub or touch lightly in passing; to touch and glance off; as, to *graze* the curb with the wheel of a car. **2** To scratch or scrape by rubbing against something; as, to *graze* one's arm. — *n.* A grazing; a scrape or rub caused by grazing.

grease \'grēs\ *n.* **1** Animal fat, especially when soft. **2** Any thick oily substance. — \'grēs, 'grēz\ *v.;* **greased; greas·ing.** To smear with grease or fat; to lubricate; as, to *grease* a pan; to *grease* a car. — **greas·er** \'grēs-r, 'grēz-r\ *n.*

greasy \'grē-sē, -zē\ *adj.;* **greas·i·er; greas·i·est.** **1** Smeared with grease; containing grease; as, a *greasy* pan; *greasy* food. **2** Like grease or oil; smooth; slippery. — **greas·i·ly** \'grēs-l-ē, 'grēz-\ *adv.*

great \'grāt; *in the South, also* 'gret\ *adj.* **1** Large in size; big; not small or little. **2** Large in number; numerous; as, a *great* crowd. **3** Long-continued; as, a *great* while. **4** Much beyond the average or ordinary; mighty; heavy; intense; as, a *great* weight; to be in *great* pain. **5** Eminent; important; noble; distinguished; as, a *great* artist; *great* men. **6** Remarkable in knowledge of, or skill in, something; as, a boy who is *great* at diving. **7** Favorite; much used; as, a *great* joke of my father's. **8** Excellent; fine; as, a *great* time at the beach. **9** More distant in relationship by one generation; as, *great*-grandchildren; *great*-grandfather. **10** Grand; as, *great*-aunt.

great-aunt \'grāt-'ant, -'ȧnt\ *n.* A grandaunt.

great circle. A circle drawn on a sphere and having its plane passing through the center of the sphere, used in navigation to determine the shortest path between two places. — **great-cir·cle** \'grāt-ˌsərk-l\ *adj.*

great·coat \'grāt-ˌkōt\ *n.* A heavy overcoat.

great Dane \'dān\. A smooth-coated dog of a breed of massive size and great strength.

Great Divide. A chief mountain watershed, especially that of the Rocky Mountains.

great-grand·child \'grāt-'gran-ˌchīld\ *n.; pl.* **great-grand·chil·dren** \-ˌchild-r(ə)n\. A son's or daughter's grandson (**great-grand·son** \-ˌsən\) or granddaughter (**great-grand·daugh·ter** \-ˌdȯt-r\).

great-grand·par·ent \'grāt-'gran-ˌpar-ənt, -ˌper-\ *n.* A parent's grandfather (**great-grand·fa·ther** \-ˌfäth-r, -ˌfȧth-r\) or grandmother (**great-grand·moth·er** \-ˌməth-r\).

great·heart·ed \'grāt-'härt-əd, -'hȧrt-\ *adj.* **1** High-spirited; fearless. **2** Generous; noble.

great·ly \'grāt-lē\ *adv.* **1** In a great manner; nobly. **2** To a great extent or degree; very; much; as, a *greatly* exaggerated story; to be *greatly* missed.

great-neph·ew \'grāt-'nef-ˌyü\ *n.* A grandnephew.

great-niece \'grāt-'nēs\ *n.* A grandniece.

great-un·cle \'grāt-'əngk-l\ *n.* A granduncle.

greave \'grēv\ *n.* Armor for the leg below the knee.

grebe \'grēb\ *n.* Any of a family of swimming and diving birds closely related to the loons.

Gre·cian \'grēsh-n\ *adj.* or *n.* Greek.

greed \'grēd\ *n.* Greedy desire or longing, especially for wealth.

greedy \'grēd-ē\ *adj.;* **greed·i·er; greed·i·est.** **1** Having a keen appetite for food or drink; very hungry; as, a lion *greedy* for its prey. **2** Having an eager, and often selfish, desire or longing; as, to be *greedy* for praise. **3** Wanting more than one needs or more than one's fair share, as of food or wealth. — **greed·i·ly** \'grēd-l-ē\ *adv.*

Greek \'grēk\ *adj.* Of or relating to Greece. — *n.* **1** A native or inhabitant of Greece. **2** The language of Greece.

green \'grēn\ *adj.* **1** Of the color green. **2** Having a green growth; covered with grass; in leaf; as, *green* fields. **3** Without snow; mild; as, a *green* Christmas. **4** Grown above ground; leafy; as, *green* vegetables. **5** Having a sickly color; as, *green* with envy. **6** Not ripe; as, *green* bananas. **7** Not trained or experienced; as, a *green* assistant. **8** Not seasoned, dried, or cured; as, *green* lumber. — *n.* **1** The color in the rainbow between yellow and blue; the color of most growing plants. **2** A grassy plot; a common; as, the village *green.* **3** [in the plural] Green leaves and branches for decorations. **4** [in the plural] Vegetables used for food; as, salad *greens.*

green·back \'grēn-ˌbak\ *n.* A piece of United States paper money with a green back.

green·ery \'grēn-r-ē\ *n.; pl.* **green·er·ies.** Green plants, as shrubs, bushes, and vines; verdure.

green·gro·cer \'grēn-ˌgrōs-r\ *n.* A retailer of fresh vegetables and fruit. — **green·gro·cery** \-ˌgrōs-r(-)ē\ *n.*

green·horn \'grēn-ˌhȯrn\ *n.* An inexperienced person; a person easily tricked or cheated.

green·house \'grēn-ˌhau̇s\ *n.; pl.* **green·hous·es**

\-ˌhau̇-zəz\. A glass-enclosed building for growing plants; a hothouse.

green·ing \'grē-ning\ *n.* Any of several green-skinned apples.

green·ish \'grē-nish\ *adj.* Somewhat green.

green manure. **1** A herbaceous crop, as clover, plowed under while green to enrich the soil. **2** Fresh or undecayed barn manure.

green·sward \'grēn-ˌswȯrd\ *n.* Turf green with grass.

green thumb. An unusual ability to make plants grow.

green·wood \'grēn-ˌwu̇d\ *n.* A forest when the leaves are green, as in spring and summer.

greet \'grēt\ *v.* **1** To address in a friendly, courteous manner; to welcome; as, to *greet* a visitor at the door. **2** To receive with a show of feeling; as, to *greet* an announcement with cheers. **3** To appear or present itself to. A pretty scene *greeted* their eyes as the curtain rolled up.

greet·ing \'grēt-ing\ *n.* **1** The words or gesture of one who greets; especially, an expression of pleasure on meeting someone. **2** A friendly message from a person who is absent; as, a Christmas *greeting;* to remember to send birthday *greetings* to all one's friends. **3** The opening words of a letter, as *Dear Sir.*

gre·gar·i·ous \grə-'gar-ē-əs, -'ger-\ *adj.* Habitually living or moving in flocks or herds; tending to flock together. — **gre·gar·i·ous·ly,** *adv.*

Gre·go·ri·an calendar \grə-'gōr-ē-ən, -'gȯr-\. The calendar introduced by Pope Gregory XIII in 1582 and now in general use.

grem·lin \'grem-lən\ *n.* **1** One of the impish gnomes whom airmen blame when something goes wrong with their motors or instruments. **2** Any elf that upsets an action.

gre·nade \grə-'nād\ *n.* [From French, meaning literally "pomegranate", it resembling this fruit both in appearance and in being filled with pellets as a pomegranate is with seeds.] **1** A case filled with high explosive and made to be hurled, often by hand (**hand grenade**) against an enemy. **2** A glass containing chemicals, to be thrown and exploded, as for putting out a fire.

gren·a·dier \ˌgren-ə-'dir\ *n.* Originally, a soldier who carried and threw grenades; now, a member of one of certain special regiments or corps.

grenadier

grew. Past tense of *grow.*

grey. Variant of *gray.*

greybeard. Variant of *graybeard.*

grey·hound \'grā-ˌhau̇nd\ *n.* **1** A tall, graceful, and very swift dog with a smooth coat and keen eyesight. **2** A fast ocean-going passenger boat.

greyish. Variant of *grayish.*

grid \'grid\ *n.* **1** A grating or gridiron. **2** A perforated or ridged plate of lead for conducting current and holding the active material of storage battery plates. **3** An electrode consisting of a mesh or a spiral of fine wire placed between two other elements of an electron tube so as to control the amount of current that flows between them.

grid·dle \'grid-l\ *n.* A plate or pan, as of iron or aluminum, used for cooking. — *v.;* **grid·dled; grid·dling** \-l(-)ing\. To cook on a griddle.

grid·dle·cake \'grid-l-ˌkāk\ *n.* A cake made from a thin batter cooked on both sides on a griddle.

grid·i·ron \'grid-ˌīrn\ *n.* **1** A cooking utensil consisting of a small iron grate for broiling food. **2** Something like a gridiron, as a network of pipes, tracks, or streets. **3** A football field.

grief \'grēf\ *n.* **1** Deep sorrow; sadness; distress. **2** A cause of sorrow. **3** A mishap; disaster; failure; as, a boat that came to *grief* on the rocks.

griev·ance \'grēv-n(t)s\ *n.* A cause of uneasiness or annoyance; something to complain about; a real or imagined wrong or injustice; as, to discuss a *grievance* frankly with one's teacher.

grieve \'grēv\ *v.;* **grieved; griev·ing.** **1** To cause grief or sorrow to; to cause to suffer. It *grieved* the father to punish his son. **2** To feel grief; to sorrow; to mourn. The boy *grieved* over his lost dog.

griev·ous \'grē-vəs\ *adj.* **1** Causing suffering; distressing; severe; as, *grievous* news; a *grievous* wound. **2** Full of or expressing grief; as, a *grievous* cry. — **griev·ous·ly,** *adv.*

grif·fin or **grif·fon** \'grif-n\ *n.* An imaginary animal, half lion and half eagle.

grill \'gril\ *n.* **1** A gridiron for broiling food. **2** A broiling, as of food. **3** A dish of broiled meat or fish. **4** A room or restaurant serving broiled foods as its specialty. — *v.* **1** To broil on a grill. **2** To torment as if by broiling; to distress with continued questioning or examination; as, to *grill* a person suspected of a crime.

grill

grille or **grill** \'gril\ *n.* A lattice or grating forming an openwork barrier or protective covering, as for a door or window.

grill·work \'gril-ˌwərk\ *n.* Any of the work making up a grille or grilles; work resembling a grille; as, the *grillwork* of a car.

grim \'grim\ *adj.;* **grim·mer; grim·mest.** **1** Savage; fierce; cruel; as, *grim* wolves. **2** Harsh in appearance; stern; severe; as, a *grim* look. **3** Unyielding; as, *grim* determination. **4** Ghastly; frightful; as, *grim* tales about ghosts. — **grim·ly,** *adv.*

grim·ace \'grim-əs, grə-'mās\ *n.* A twisting of the face or features; as, the *grimaces* of a clown; a frightful *grimace.* — *v.;* **grim·aced; grim·ac·ing.** To distort the face; to make faces; as, to *grimace* with pain.

grime \'grīm\ *n.* Dirt rubbed into the skin or into any surface. — *v.;* **grimed; grim·ing.** To soil deeply.

grimy \'grī-mē\ *adj.;* **grim·i·er; grim·i·est.** Full of grime; very dirty.

grin \'grin\ *v.;* **grinned; grin·ning. 1** To draw back the lips and show the teeth, as in a broad smile. **2** To express by grinning; as, to *grin* approval. — *n.* The act of grinning; a wide smile.

grind \'grīnd\ *v.;* **ground** \'graund\; **grind·ing. 1** To make or be made into powder by rubbing; to crush into small bits; as, to *grind* wheat into flour. **2** To wear down, polish, or sharpen by friction; as, to *grind* an ax. **3** To rub together with a grating noise; to grit; as, to *grind* the teeth. **4** To burden with severe demands; to oppress; as, to *grind* the poor. **5** To operate or produce by turning a crank; as, to *grind* a hand organ; to *grind* out a tune. **6** To work hard or steadily; to produce in a laborious way; as, to *grind* out a composition. — *n.* **1** A grinding. **2** Steady hard work; as, to find one's lessons a *grind.* **3** *Slang.* A student who spends most of his time in hard, plodding study.

grind·er \'grīnd-r\ *n.* **1** One that grinds. **2** A molar tooth.

grind·er \'grīnd-r\ *n.* A large sandwich made of two slabs of bread cut lengthwise and filled with meat, usually spiced, and various relishes.

grind·stone \'grīn-ˌstōn\ *n.* A flat, round stone that turns on an axle and is used for sharpening tools and for smoothing and polishing.

grindstone

grip \'grip\ *n.* **1** A strong grasp or hold; as, a *grip* of the hand. **2** Strength or power in holding; as, the *grip* of a disease. **3** Mental grasp; as, to have a *grip* on the problem. **4** A special way of clasping the hand, as among members of a secret society. **5** A handle to help in grasping. **6** A small suitcase or traveling bag. — *v.;* **gripped; grip·ping. 1** To grasp firmly; to seize and hold tightly. **2** To hold closely the interest or attention of; as, a story that *grips* the reader.

gripe \'grīp\ *v.;* **griped; grip·ing. 1** To grip; especially, to seize and hold. **2** To distress or afflict. **3** To cause spasms of pain in the bowels. **4** To anger, irritate, or vex. **5** To complain. — *n.* **1** The act of griping or grasping; control. **2** Distress or affliction. **3** A pinching pain in the intestines. **4** A complaint.

grippe \'grip\ *n.* Influenza.

gris·ly \'griz-lē\ *adj.;* **gris·li·er; gris·li·est.** Horrible; ghastly; gruesome.

grist \'grist\ *n.* Grain to be ground or that is already ground.

gris·tle \'gris-l\ *n.* Cartilage; firm, elastic tissue. — **gris·tly** \'gris-lē\ *adv.*

grist·mill \'grist-ˌmil\ *n.* A mill for grinding grain.

grit \'grit\ *n.* **1** Rough, hard particles, especially of sand. **2** Firmness of mind or spirit; unyielding courage; as, a game that takes *grit* as well as ability. — *v.;* **grit·ted; grit·ting.** To grind; to grate; as, to *grit* the teeth.

grits \'grits\ *n. pl.* Hulled and coarsely ground grain.

grit·ty \'grit-ē\ *adj.;* **grit·ti·er; grit·ti·est. 1** Containing or seeming to contain rough particles or grit; resembling grit. Cornbread is *gritty.* **2** Courageously persistent; brave.

griz·zled \'griz-ld\ *adj.* Streaked or mixed with gray.

griz·zly \'griz-lē\ *adj.;* **griz·zli·er; griz·zli·est.** Grayish; grizzled. — *n.; pl.* **griz·zlies.** A grizzly bear.

grizzly bear. A large powerful bear of western North America, usually brownish yellow but sometimes having hair tipped with gray or white.

groan \'grōn\ *v.* **1** To make a deep, moaning sound. **2** To creak, as from a burden or strain; as, the *groaning* timbers of a sailing ship. The table *groaned* with food. **3** To utter or express with or as if with groans; as, to *groan* out a tale of woe. — *n.* A low, moaning sound.

gro·cer \'grōs-r\ *n.* A dealer in foodstuffs.

gro·cery \'grōs-r(-)ē\ *n.; pl.* **gro·cer·ies. 1** A retail grocer's store. **2** The trade or business of a grocer. **3** [in the plural] The foodstuffs sold by grocers.

grog \'gräg\ *n.* [Named after Old *Grog,* nickname for Admiral Edward Vernon (1684–1757) of the British Navy, who in 1740 issued an order to mix the sailors' ration of rum with water.] **1** An unsweetened mixture of a strong liquor, usually rum or whiskey, and water. **2** Any strong alcoholic liquor.

grog·gy \'gräg-ē\ *adj.;* **grog·gi·er; grog·gi·est.** Unsteady on the legs, as from intoxication, illness, shock, or lack of sleep; shaky; staggering. — **grog·gi·ly** \'gräg-l-ē\ *adv.*

groin \'gröin\ *n.* **1** The junction of the abdomen and the thigh or the part of the body about this junction. **2** In building, the curved line formed by the meeting of two vaults. — *v.* To build with groins; as, a *groined* and vaulted roof.

groom \'grüm, 'grům\ *n.* **1** A male servant, especially one in charge of horses. **2** A bridegroom. — *v.* **1** To take care of, tend, or clean; as, to *groom* a horse. **2** To make neat and tidy; as, a well-*groomed* person.

grooms·man \'grümz-mən, 'grůmz-\ *n.; pl.* **grooms·men** \-mən\. A male friend who attends a bridegroom at his wedding.

groove \'grüv\ *n.* **1** A channel or long hollow such as may be made by cutting or grinding; a worn path; a rut. **2** A fixed, unchanging way; as, a mind that runs in a *groove.* — *v.;* **grooved; groov·ing.** To form a groove in; as, to *groove* a board.

grope \'grōp\ *v.;* **groped; grop·ing. 1** To search for in the dark by feeling; as, to *grope* for the first step of a dark stairway. **2** To feel one's way; as, to *grope* along a wall. **3** To search mentally; as, to *grope* for the right word.

gros·beak \'grōs-ˌbēk\ *n.* Any of various finches with stout cone-shaped bills, as the **pine grosbeak** of cone-bearing forests, the **rose-breast·ed gros-**

beak \'rōz-ˌbres-təd\ of eastern North America, and the cardinal bird.

gross \'grōs\ *adj.* **1** Thick; rank; as, *gross* vegetation. **2** Whole; entire; total; as, *gross* earnings. **3** Coarse; vulgar; as, *gross* language. **4** Glaring; obvious; as, a *gross* error. **5** Shameful; as, a *gross* injustice. — *n.* **1** The main body; the whole before anything has been deducted. **2** *Pl.* **gross.** Twelve dozen; as, two *gross* of lead pencils. — **gross·ly,** *adv.*

grot \'grät\ *n.* A grotto.

gro·tesque \grō-'tesk\ *adj.* **1** Combining, as in a painting or poem, details that are never found together in nature and rarely in art; using distortion for the sake of artistic effect. **2** Queer and strange; absurdly awkward; fantastic; as, the *grotesque* appearance of a clown. — **gro·tesque·ly,** *adv.*

grot·to \'grät-ˌō\ *n.; pl.* **grot·toes** or **grot·tos.** **1** A cave; a cavern. **2** An artificial cavelike structure, as one in a garden.

grouch \'grau̇ch\ *n.* **1** A fit of bad temper or sulkiness. **2** A sulky person. — *v.* To sulk or grumble. — **grouch·i·ly** \-l-ē\ *adv.* — **grouchy** \-ē\ *adj.*

ground \'grau̇nd\. Past tense and past part. of *grind.*

ground \'grau̇nd\ *n.* **1** The surface of the earth; soil; as, to sit on the *ground;* dry *ground.* **2** A particular region or piece of land, as in *fairground* or *playground.* **3** Land; as, to own a house with a fair amount of *ground* around it. **4** [in the plural] The gardens and lawns around a house; as, well-kept *grounds.* **5** An area or distance; as, to gain *ground.* **6** The bottom of a body of water. The boat struck *ground.* **7** [in the plural] The material from a liquid that settles to the bottom; sediment; as, coffee *grounds.* **8** The basis on which anything rests; foundation; as, *ground* for complaint. **9** Basic belief; assumption; as, to shift one's *ground* in an argument. **10** The surface or background upon which anything is made or displayed; as, a picture on a gray *ground.* **11** In electricity, the connection made in grounding a circuit or the place to which the conductor leading to the earth is connected. — *v.* **1** To force or bring down to the ground; to keep on the ground; as, planes *grounded* by a storm. **2** To run aground or to cause to run aground; as, a boat *grounded* on a sand bar. **3** To base or establish; to fix or set; as, a house *grounded* on rock. **4** To instruct in basic knowledge or understanding; as, to be well-*grounded* in arithmetic. **5** To connect with the ground in a circuit; as, to *ground* an electric motor. — *adj.* On or near the ground; as, the *ground* floor.

ground hog. The woodchuck.

ground·less \'grau̇n-dləs\ *adj.* Without foundation or reason; as, *groundless* fears.

ground·ling \'grau̇n-dling\ *n.* **1** One that keeps close to the ground or bottom — used especially in referring to certain fishes. **2** A spectator in the pit of a theater. **3** A person of inferior taste.

ground pine. A mosslike flowerless herb related to the ferns, with long creeping stems and evergreen one-veined leaves.

ground plan. **1** A plan of the ground floor of a building. **2** Any first or basic plan.

ground squirrel. Any of numerous burrowing rodents, including the gopher and the chipmunk, differing from true squirrels in having cheek pouches and shorter fur.

ground swell. A broad, deep ocean swell, caused by a distant storm or earthquake.

ground water. Water within the earth, by which wells and springs are supplied.

ground·work \'grau̇n-ˌdwərk\ *n.* Foundation; basis.

group \'grüp\ *n.* **1** A number of persons or things considered as forming one whole; a small crowd; a cluster. **2** A number of objects having some relationship, resemblance, or common characteristic, as in the classification of plants or animals naturally related. — *v.* To arrange or combine in a group; as, to *group* children by their ages.

grou·per \'grüp-r\ *n.; pl.* **grou·pers** or **grou·per.** A large food fish of warm seas, related to the sea basses.

grouse \'grau̇s\ *n. sing. and pl.* A ground-dwelling game bird related to the domestic fowl, with plump body, strong feathered legs, and mottled plumage.

grove \'grōv\ *n.* A small wood; a group of trees without underbrush, planted or growing naturally; as, a picnic *grove;* an orange *grove.*

grov·el \'gräv-l, 'grəv-l\ *v.;* **grov·eled** or **grov·elled;** **grov·el·ing** or **grov·el·ling** \-l(-)ing\. To creep or lie face down on the ground, especially in fear or in the desire to please; to cringe.

grow \'grō\ *v.;* **grew** \'grü\; **grown** \'grōn\; **grow·ing.** **1** To spring up and develop to maturity; to thrive. **2** To be found naturally in some place. Rice *grows* in China. **3** To cause to grow; to cultivate; as, to *grow* flowers. **4** To increase or develop in any way; to extend; as, a city that is *growing* rapidly. **5** To come to be; to become; as, to *grow* pale. **6** To become united as if by growth; as, trees with limbs *grown* together. — **grow·er,** *n.*

growl \'grau̇l\ *v.* **1** To make a deep, throaty sound such as a dog makes. **2** To find fault; to grumble; to complain; as, to *growl* about the weather. **3** To make a rumbling noise like that of thunder. — *n.* **1** A deep, threatening sound. **2** A grumbling or muttered complaint. **3** A rumble.

grown \'grōn\ *adj.* Mature; having reached full growth; as, *grown* people.

grown-up \'grō-ˌnəp\ *adj.* Adult; of, for, or characteristic of adults; as, *grown-up* behavior; a book that is too *grown-up* for small children.

grown·up \'grō-ˌnəp\ *n.* An adult person.

growth \'grōth\ *n.* **1** The act of growing; increase; development. **2** A stage or condition in growing; size; as, a plant in full *growth.* **3** Anything that has grown or is growing; as, a thick *growth* of underbrush. **4** An abnormal formation of tissue, as a wart or tumor.

grub \'grəb\ *v.;* **grubbed**; **grub·bing.** **1** To dig; to root out by digging; as, to *grub* up roots. **2** To work hard; to drudge. **3** *Slang.* To eat. — *n.* **1** Any soft thick wormlike larva, especially of a beetle. **2** *Slang.* Food.

grub·by \'grəb-ē\ *adj.;* **grub·bi·er**; **grub·bi·est.** Grimy; dirty.

grub·stake \'grəb-ˌstāk\ *n.* Supplies or money furnished to a prospector on a promise of a share in his finds. — *v.;* **grub·staked**; **grub·stak·ing.** **1** To provide with a grubstake. **2** To support temporarily, as with food and lodging or funds; as, to *grubstake* a friend during a period of hard luck.

grudge \'grəj\ *v.;* **grudged**; **grudg·ing.** **1** To be unwilling to give; as, to *grudge* a penny to a beggar. **2** To want someone not to have something; to envy; as, to *grudge* a person his success. — *n.* A feeling of ill will or resentment aroused by real or fancied mistreatment or insult.

grudg·ing·ly \'grəj-ing-lē\ *adv.* In a grudging manner; unwillingly.

gru·el \'grü-əl\ *n.* A thin liquid food made by boiling cracked or ground grain in water or milk; thin porridge.

gru·el·ing or **gru·el·ling** \'grü-ə-ling\ *adj.* Requiring extreme effort; exhausting; as, a *grueling* race.

grue·some \'grüs-m\ *adj.* Horrifying and repulsive; ghastly; as, the *gruesome* sights of war. — **grue·some·ly**, *adv.*

gruff \'grəf\ *adj.* Rough in manner, speech, or look; harsh; as, a *gruff* reply; a *gruff* voice. — **gruff·ly**, *adv.*

grum·ble \'grəm-bl\ *v.;* **grum·bled**; **grum·bling** \-bl(-)ing\. **1** To murmur or mutter in discontent; as, to *grumble* about one's food. **2** To rumble. — *n.* **1** A rumbling; a muttered complaint. **2** A rumble. — **grum·bler** \-blər\ *n.*

grumpy \'grəmp-ē\ *adj.;* **grump·i·er**; **grump·i·est.** Surly; cross; irritable. — **grump·i·ly** \-l-ē\ *adv.*

grunt \'grənt\ *n.* **1** A deep short noise in the throat such as a hog makes. **2** Any of numerous sea fishes that make a grunting noise when taken from the water. — *v.* To make a grunt; to utter with a deep throaty sound; as, to *grunt* a reply.

g's. Pl. of *g.*

gua·no \'gwän-ˌō\ *n.; pl.* **gua·nos.** A substance composed chiefly of the excrement of sea birds, used as a fertilizer.

guar·an·tee \ˌgar-ən-'tē, ˌgär-, ˌgȧr-\ *n.* **1** A person who guarantees something; a guarantor. **2** The act of such a person. **3** An agreement by which a person guarantees something. **4** Something that is given or held as a security; a guaranty. **5** The person to whom something is guaranteed. — *v.;* **guar·an·teed**; **guar·an·tee·ing.** **1** To promise to answer for the debt or duty of another person; as, to *guarantee* that a loan will be repaid. **2** To make oneself responsible for something; to vouch for; to warrant; as, to *guarantee* the quality of goods sold. **3** To furnish security to; as, to *guarantee* a bank against loss.

guar·an·tor \'gar-ən-ˌtȯr, 'gär-, 'gȧr-, -tər\ *n.* A person who gives a guarantee.

guar·an·ty \'gar-ən-tē, 'gär-, 'gȧr-\ *n.;* **guar·an·ties.** **1** An agreement by which a person guarantees something; a guarantee. **2** Something given or held as a security.

guard \'gärd, 'gȧrd\ *v.* **1** To protect; to defend. **2** To watch over so as to restrain, control, or check; to stand or keep guard over; as, to *guard* a prisoner; to *guard* a fort. **3** To take precautions; as, to *guard* against catching cold. — *n.* **1** A position of defense, as in fencing and boxing. **2** The act or duty of keeping watch; as, to keep *guard.* **3** A person or a body of persons that guards against injury or danger; as, a coast *guard;* the *guards* at the gates of a defense plant. **4** A device giving protection, as against injury, soiling, or loss. **5** A player occupying a defensive or supporting position in certain games, as basketball and football. **6** [in the plural] Certain bodies of troops in the British army whose chief duty is to act as a personal guard for the sovereign.

guard

guard cell. Either of a pair of somewhat kidney-shaped cells on opposite sides of a plant stoma that can round out and close the stoma between them.

guard·ed \'gärd-əd, 'gȧrd-\ *adj.* **1** Protected. **2** Cautious; as, to give a *guarded* answer. — **guard·ed·ly**, *adv.*

guard·house \'gärd-ˌhau̇s, 'gȧrd-\ *n.; pl.* **guard·hous·es** \-ˌhau̇-zəz\. **1** A building occupied by a guard or used as a headquarters by soldiers on guard duty. **2** A military jail.

guard·i·an \'gärd-ē-ən, 'gȧrd-\ *n.* **1** A person who guards or preserves; a custodian or caretaker. **2** In law, one who has the care and management of the person and property of another, as of a child or an insane person. — *adj.* Acting as a protector; as, a *guardian* angel.

guard·room \'gärd-ˌrüm, -ˌru̇m\ *n.* **1** A room used by a military guard while on duty. **2** A room where military prisoners are confined.

guards·man \'gärdz-mən, 'gȧrdz-\ *n.; pl.* **guards·men** \-mən\. **1** A person who guards; a guard. **2** A member of any military body called Guards.

Gua·te·ma·lan \ˌgwät-m-'äl-ən, -'ȧl-\ *adj.* Of or relating to Guatemala. — *n.* A native or inhabitant of Guatemala.

gua·va \'gwäv-ə\ *n.* A tropical American tree of the myrtle family with a round or pear-shaped fruit used for making jelly and jam.

gu·ber·na·to·ri·al \ˌgüb-(r)n-ə-'tōr-ē-əl, ˌgyüb-, -'tȯr-\ *adj.* Of or relating to a governor; as, the forthcoming *gubernatorial* campaign.

gudg·eon \'gəj-n\ *n.* **1** A small European freshwater fish of the carp family. **2** A minnow. **3** A person easily deceived.

guer·ril·la or **gue·ril·la** \gə-'ril-ə\ *n.* [From Spanish *guerilla* meaning "little war", a diminutive of *guerra* meaning "war".] A member of a band of persons engaged in carrying on warfare, especially raiding, but not part of a regular army.

guess \\'ges\\ *v.* **1** To judge without certain knowledge; as, to *guess* at a person's weight. **2** To solve correctly with little or no evidence or information; to discover; as, to *guess* a riddle; to *guess* someone's thoughts. **3** To think; to suppose; to believe. I *guess* it is going to rain. — *n.* **1** A guessing. **2** An opinion formed by guessing, or without real evidence or knowledge; a surmise.

guess·work \\'ges-ˌwərk\\ *n.* Work done by guess and not accurately or scientifically; results obtained by guess.

guest \\'gest\\ *n.* **1** A visitor; a person entertained in one's house or at one's table. **2** A patron of a hotel, inn, or restaurant.

guf·faw \\ˌgə-'fȯ\\ *n.* A loud coarse burst of laughter. — *v.* To laugh noisily or coarsely.

guid·ance \\'gīd-n(t)s\\ *n.* A guiding or being guided; direction; something that serves as a guide; as, to read under the *guidance* of a teacher.

guide \\'gīd\\ *v.;* **guid·ed**; **guid·ing. 1** To act as a guide to; to show the way to; to lead; to conduct; to pilot; as, to *guide* visitors through the new school building; to *guide* a car through traffic. **2** To direct; to instruct; as, to *guide* a child in his choice of reading; to be *guided* by one's conscience. — *n.* **1** A person who guides, as one hired to conduct parties of tourists or hunters. **2** Anyone or anything that directs a person in his conduct or course of life; a model; a guiding principle. **3** A device for directing or steadying the motion of something, as on a machine. **4** A guidebook.

guide·book \\'gīd-ˌbu̇k\\ *n.* A handbook of information for travelers or sightseers.

guid·ed missile \\'gīd-əd\\. Any missile whose course may be changed during flight, as by radio signals or a built-in target seeking device.

guide·post \\'gīd-ˌpōst\\ *n.* A post, as at a crossroads, with an attached board giving directions about routes.

guide word. A word used as a guide or key. There is a *guide word* at the top of each column in your dictionary.

guild or **gild** \\'gild\\ *n.* **1** An association of persons with similar aims or common interests, formed for mutual aid and protection; as, a trade *guild* of the Middle Ages. **2** Any society or fellowship.

guild·hall \\'gild-ˌhȯl, -'hȯl\\ *n.* The hall where a guild regularly meets; a town hall.

guile \\'gīl\\ *n.* Crafty cunning; deceit; treachery; as, to gain one's ends by *guile.*

guile·ful \\'gīlf-l\\ *adj.* Full of guile; characterized by cunning, deceit, or treachery. — **guile·ful·ly** \\-l-ē\\ *adv.*

guile·less \\'gīl-ləs\\ *adj.* **1** Without deceit or cunning; as, a *guileless* smile. **2** Innocent; artless; unsophisticated. Only a *guileless* person could believe him.

guil·lo·tine \\'gil-ə-ˌtēn, 'gē-(y)ə-\\ *n.* [From French, there named after Joseph I. *Guillotin* (1738–1814), a French physician who advocated its use.] A machine for cutting off a person's head by means of a heavy blade sliding in two upright grooved posts. — *v.;* **guil·lo·tined**; **guil·lo·tin·ing.** To behead with a guillotine.

guillotine

guilt \\'gilt\\ *n.* **1** The fact of having committed an offense, especially one that is punishable by law; as, to prove a person's *guilt* by the evidence. **2** Guilty conduct; wickedness; as, to have a feeling of *guilt;* a life of *guilt* and shame.

guilty \\'gil-tē\\ *adj.;* **guilt·i·er**; **guilt·i·est. 1** Having committed an offense; responsible for a fault or a crime; as, found *guilty* of murder; to be *guilty* of bad manners. **2** Showing guilt; conscious of guilt; as, a *guilty* expression; a *guilty* feeling.

guin·ea \\'gin-ē\\ *n.* **1** An English gold coin, no longer issued, worth 21 shillings. **2** The sum of 21 shillings.

guin·ea fowl \\'gin-ē\\. A gray and white spotted game and farm bird closely related to the pheasants.

guinea hen. The female of the guinea fowl.

guinea pig. 1 A short-eared, short-tailed rodent about seven inches long, often kept as a pet and much used in scientific experiments, especially in medicine. **2** Any person or thing experimented on.

guise \\'gīz\\ *n.* **1** Appearance; dress or costume; as, to appear in the *guise* of a shepherd. **2** Cover; cloak; mask; as, under the *guise* of patriotism.

gui·tar \\gi-'tär, -'tär\\ *n.* A six-stringed musical instrument with a long neck and a body somewhat like that of a violin, played by plucking the strings with the fingers.

guitar

gulch \\'gəlch\\ *n.* A deep steep-sided ravine, especially one that is the bed of a stream.

gulf \\'gəlf\\ *n.* **1** A part of an ocean or sea extending into the land; as, the *Gulf* of Mexico. **2** A deep hollow in the earth; a chasm; an abyss. **3** A wide separation; as, a *gulf* between two brothers resulting from a great difference in age and interests.

gull \\'gəl\\ *v.* To deceive; to cheat; to trick. — *n.* A person who is easily cheated.

gull \\'gəl\\ *n.* A blue-gray or whitish water bird with a thick hooked bill, long wings, and webbed feet.

gul·let \\'gəl-ət\\ *n.* **1** The tube which leads from the back of the mouth to the stomach; the esophagus. **2** The throat.

gull·i·ble \\'gəl-əb-l\\ *adj.* Easily deceived. — **gull·i·bil·i·ty** \\ˌgəl-ə-'bil-ət-ē\\ *n.*

gul·ly \\'gəl-ē\\ *n.; pl.* **gul·lies.** A ditch or small ravine made by running water, as after heavy rains.

gulp \'gəlp\ *v.* **1** To swallow eagerly, or in large amounts at a time. **2** To keep back as if by swallowing; as, to *gulp* down a sob. **3** To catch the breath as if after a long drink. — *n.* A gulping; a swallow; as much as is swallowed at one time.

gum \'gəm\ *n.* The tissue along the jaws of animals which surrounds the necks of the teeth.

gum \'gəm\ *n.* **1** A sticky substance that comes out of many trees and plants and hardens when exposed to the air. **2** A gumlike substance, as glue or mucilage. **3** Chewing gum. **4** A gum tree. — *v.;* **gummed; gum·ming. 1** To smear, stick together, or stiffen with gum; as, to *gum* together the pieces of a broken vase. **2** To give out or form gum. **3** To make clogged or sticky as if with gum; as, a motor that has been allowed to *gum* up; a face *gummed* up with cold cream. — **gum the works** or **gum up the works.** To cause to stop or to function less efficiently.

gum ar·a·bic \'ar-ə-bik\. A plant gum obtained from certain tropical acacias and used in the preparation of inks and adhesives, in certain candies, and in pharmacy.

gum·bo \'gəm-ˌbō\ *n.; pl.* **gum·bos. 1** A soup thickened with okra pods. **2** The okra plant or its pods. **3** A soil which becomes very sticky when wet.

gum·boil \'gəm-ˌbȯil\ *n.* A small abscess on the gums.

gum·drop \'gəm-ˌdräp\ *n.* A gumlike candy made usually from corn syrup with cornstarch, gelatin, or gum arabic.

gum·my \'gəm-ē\ *adj.;* **gum·mi·er; gum·mi·est. 1** Consisting of, containing, or covered with gum. **2** Sticky.

gump·tion \'gəm(p)sh-n\ *n.* **1** Common sense; shrewdness. **2** Initiative; enterprise.

gum tree. Any of several trees that yield gum, as the sour gum, the sweet gum, and the eucalyptus.

gun \'gən\ *n.* **1** A tube of metal, mounted on a block or carriage, through which a heavy projectile, as a shell or a ball of iron, can be thrown out with great force by means of an explosive charge; a cannon. **2** Any portable firearm such as a rifle, shotgun, or pistol. **3** Any similar tube-shaped device for shooting or squirting; as, a grease *gun;* an air *gun.* **4** A discharge of a gun, as in a salute or as a signal; as, the starting *gun* of a race. — *v.;* **gunned; gun·ning. 1** To hunt with a gun. **2** To open up the throttle of a motor so as to increase the speed.

gun·boat \'gən-ˌbōt\ *n.* A small lightly armed vessel for use in shallow waters.

gun cotton. An explosive usually made by soaking cotton waste with nitric and sulfuric acids.

gun·fire \'gən-ˌfīr\ *n.* The firing of guns.

gun·lock \'gən-ˌläk\ *n.* The device on some firearms by which the charge is exploded.

gun·man \'gən-mən\ *n.; pl.* **gun·men** \-mən\. A man armed with a gun: especially, an armed thug.

gun metal. 1 A bronze once much used for making cannon, or a metal made to look like this. **2** A dull dark gray color.

gunned. Past tense and past part. of *gun.*

gunnel. Variant of *gunwale.*

gun·ner \'gən-r\ *n.* **1** A person who handles or has charge of a gun; as, the tail *gunner* in a bomber. **2** A hunter.

gun·nery \'gən-r-ē\ *n.* **1** The science that treats of the use of guns and the flight of projectiles fired from guns. **2** The practical use of big guns; as, practice in *gunnery.*

gun·ning \'gən-ing\. Pres. part. of *gun.* — *n.* Hunting with a gun.

gun·ny \'gən-ē\ *n.; pl.* **gun·nies. 1** A coarse cloth made from jute, used in making sacks. **2** Also **gunny sack.** A sack of this material.

gun·pow·der \'gən-ˌpau̇d-r\ *n.* An explosive powder used in guns and in blasting.

gun·shot \'gən-ˌshät\ *n.* **1** A shot fired from a gun. **2** The range of a gun. The hunter couldn't get within *gunshot* of the deer.

gun·smith \'gən-ˌsmith\ *n.* A person whose business is making and repairing firearms.

gun·stock \'gən-ˌstäk\ *n.* The wooden part of a firearm to which the barrel is fastened.

gun·wale or **gun·nel** \'gən-l\ *n.* The upper edge of a ship's or boat's side.

gup·py \'gəp-ē\ *n.; pl.* **gup·pies.** A small tropical minnow, often kept as an aquarium fish.

gur·gle \'gərg-l\ *v.;* **gur·gled; gur·gling** \-l(-)ing\. **1** To run or flow in a broken, irregular, noisy current. **2** To sound like a liquid flowing in this way; as, an infant *gurgling* in its crib. — *n.* A sound as of water flowing over stones; a gurgling.

gush \'gəsh\ *v.* **1** To burst forth or pour forth violently; to flow freely; as, oil *gushing* from a newly dug well. Tears *gushed* from the girl's eyes. **2** To make an exaggerated show of affection or enthusiasm. — *n.* A sudden, free pouring out of anything.

gush·er \'gəsh-r\ *n.* **1** A person or thing that gushes. **2** An oil well with a large flow; especially, one from which the oil spouts or flows freely of itself.

gus·set \'gəs-ət\ *n.* A triangular piece inserted, as into a garment or glove, to give width or strength.

gusset

gust \'gəst\ *n.* **1** A sudden brief blast of wind. **2** A sudden outburst of feeling, especially of temper.

gus·to \'gəs-ˌtō\ *n.* Keen appreciation; high relish or enjoyment; as, to eat with *gusto.*

gusty \'gəs-tē\ *adj.;* **gust·i·er; gust·i·est.** Marked by gusts; windy; as, a *gusty* day.

gut \'gət\ *n.* **1** An intestine; the alimentary canal, or a part of it. **2** The intestine of an animal prepared for some special use, as for stringing tennis rackets. **3** [in the plural] *Slang.* Grit; courage. — *v.;* **gut·ted**; **gut·ting**. **1** To remove the bowels from; as, to scale and *gut* a fish. **2** To destroy or remove the inside of. The fire *gutted* the building but left the walls standing.

gut·ta-per·cha \ˌgət-ə-ˈpərch-ə\ *n.* A hard, rather elastic substance resembling rubber, yielded by various Malaysian trees.

gut·ter \ˈgət-r\ *n.* **1** A channel worn by running water. **2** A channel at the eaves of a house or at a roadside for carrying off rain or water. **3** Any narrow channel or groove. — *v.* **1** To form gutters in. **2** To become channeled, as the rim of a burning candle. **3** To flow in streams.

gut·tur·al \ˈgət-r-əl, ˈgə-trəl\ *adj.* **1** Having to do with the throat. **2** Sounded or made in the throat; harsh; rasping; as, a *guttural* voice. **3** Formed with the back of the tongue touching or near the soft palate — used of sounds. — *n.* A guttural sound or utterance. — **gut·tur·al·ly** \ˈgət-r-ə-lē, ˈgə-trə-lē\ *adv.*

guy \ˈgī\ *n.* A rope, chain, or rod attached to something to steady it. — *v.;* **guyed**; **guy·ing**. To steady with a guy.

guy \ˈgī\ *n.* **1** A person of queer or grotesque appearance or dress. **2** A person; a fellow. — *v.;* **guyed**; **guy·ing**. To make fun of.

guz·zle \ˈgəz-l\ *v.;* **guz·zled**; **guz·zling** \-l(-)ing\. To drink greedily; to drink too much. — **guz·zler** \-l(-)ər\ *n.*

gym \ˈjim\ *n.* A gymnasium.

gym·na·si·um \jim-ˈnā-zē-əm\ *n.* A room or a building equipped for athletic exercises and for playing indoor athletic games.

gym·nast \ˈjim-ˌnast, -nəst\ *n.* A person who is skilled in gymnastics.

gym·nas·tics \jim-ˈnas-tiks\ *n. sing. and pl.* Physical exercises designed to develop or to exhibit skill, strength, and control in the use of the body. — **gym·nas·tic** \-tik\ *adj.*

gym·no·sperm \ˈjim-nə-ˌspərm\ *n.* Any plant having the seeds naked, or not enclosed in an ovary.

gyp \ˈjip\ *v.;* **gypped**; **gyp·ping**. *Slang.* To cheat; to swindle. — *n. Slang.* A cheat.

gyp·sum \ˈjips-m\ *n.* A colorless mineral occurring in crystals or in masses, used as a fertilizer and in making plaster of Paris.

gyp·sy or **gip·sy** \ˈjip-sē\ *n.; pl.* **gyp·sies** or **gip·sies**. [A shortened and altered form of *Egyptian* (gypsies previously having been regarded as coming from Egypt).] **1** A member of a wandering Caucasian people coming originally from India. **2** A member of any wandering dark-skinned family; a person who looks or lives like a gypsy. — *adj.* Having to do with gypsies; like a gypsy or gypsies.

gypsy moth. A moth whose caterpillar has a grayish mottled appearance and does great damage to fruit, shade, and forest trees.

gy·rate \ˈjī-ˌrāt\ *v.;* **gy·rat·ed**; **gy·rat·ing**. To revolve around a center; to rotate about an axis; to spin; to whirl. A top *gyrates.*

gy·ra·tion \jī-ˈrāsh-n\ *n.* **1** A whirling or spinning; rotation; revolution. **2** One of the whorls of a spiral shell.

gyrfalcon. Variant of *gerfalcon.*

gy·ro·com·pass \ˈjī-rō-ˌkəmp-əs, -ˌkämp-\ *n.* A compass in which the horizontal axis of a constantly spinning gyroscope points to the north, often used instead of a magnetic compass, as on ships, because metal in the vicinity does not interfere with its working.

gy·ro·scope \ˈjī-rə-ˌskōp\ *n.* A wheel or disk mounted to spin rapidly about an axis that is free to turn in various directions.

gyve \ˈjīv\ *n.* A shackle or fetter, as one placed on the leg of a prisoner. — *v.;* **gyved**; **gyv·ing**. To shackle; to fetter.

h \ˈāch\ *n.; pl.* **h's** \ˈā-chəz\. The eighth letter of the alphabet.

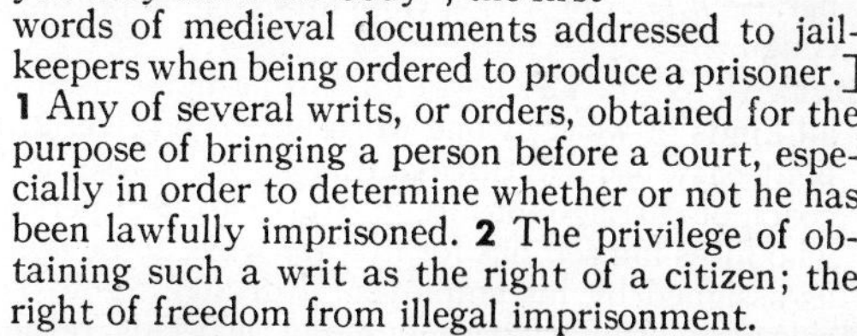

h. Abbreviation for *hour.*

ha \ˈhä, ˈhȧ\ *interj.* An exclamation, as of surprise, suspicion, joy, or triumph.

ha·be·as cor·pus \ˈhā-bē-əs ˈkȯrp-əs\. [From Latin, meaning, "that you may have the body", the first words of medieval documents addressed to jailkeepers when being ordered to produce a prisoner.] **1** Any of several writs, or orders, obtained for the purpose of bringing a person before a court, especially in order to determine whether or not he has been lawfully imprisoned. **2** The privilege of obtaining such a writ as the right of a citizen; the right of freedom from illegal imprisonment.

hab·er·dash·er \ˈhab-r-ˌdash-r\ *n.* A dealer in men's wear, as gloves, neckties, socks, and shirts.

hab·er·dash·ery \ˈhab-r-ˌdash-r(-)ē\ *n.; pl.* **hab·er·dash·er·ies**. **1** A haberdasher's shop. **2** The goods sold by a haberdasher.

hab·er·geon \ˈhab-rj-n\ *n.* **1** A jacket of mail, shorter than a hauberk. **2** A hauberk.

ha·bil·i·ment \hə-ˈbil-ə-mənt\ *n.* Clothing; as, muddy and torn *habiliments;* the *habiliment* of a beggar — used chiefly in the plural.

hab·it \ˈhab-ət\ *n.* **1** Dress; costume; as, a monk's *habit;* a riding *habit.* **2** The usual or characteristic way of acting, happening, or developing; way; as, to study the *habits* of a wild animal. Elm trees have a spreading *habit.* **3** An action or a way of acting or behaving that has been learned and has become fixed by many repetitions; as, the *habit* of smoking; to form good *habits* in childhood. **4** The ability or inclination to do something easily and without hesitation, acquired by constant repetition of an act or way of behaving; as, to act from force of *habit.*

hab·it·a·ble \'hab-ət-əb-l\ *adj.* Suitable or fit to live in; as, the *habitable* parts of the earth; a *habitable* house.

hab·it·ant \'hab-ə-tənt\ *n.* An inhabitant.

hab·i·tat \'hab-ə-ˌtat\ *n.* [From Latin, meaning "it dwells".] The place where a plant or an animal grows or lives naturally. The higher and drier parts of the western plains are the *habitat* of the prairie dog.

hab·i·ta·tion \ˌhab-ə-'tāsh-n\ *n.* **1** The act of inhabiting or dwelling. **2** A dwelling place; residence.

ha·bit·u·al \hə-'bich-ə-wəl\ *adj.* **1** According to habit; as, *habitual* tardiness. **2** Doing or acting by force of habit; as, a *habitual* smoker. **3** Usual; regular; as, a person's *habitual* topic of conversation. — For synonyms see *usual.* — **ha·bit·u·al·ly** \-'bich-l-ē, -ə-wə-lē\ *adv.*

ha·bit·u·ate \hə-'bich-ə-ˌwāt\ *v.;* **ha·bit·u·at·ed; ha·bit·u·at·ing.** To accustom; as, *habituated* to cold weather.

ha·chure \ha-'shu̇r\ *n.* A short line used in drawing and engraving, especially in shading and in representing different surfaces, as slopes of the ground on a map.

ha·ci·en·da \ˌ(h)äs-ē-'en-də, ˌ(h)ȧs-\ *n.* In Spanish America, a large estate, factory, or other establishment in the country; especially, a large cultivated farm with a good house; a landed estate.

hack \'hak\ *v.* **1** To cut roughly or jaggedly, as if by chopping. **2** To cough in a short, broken manner. — *n.* **1** A notch; cut; nick. **2** A short, broken cough.

hack \'hak\ *n.* **1** A horse for hire; a horse used in all kinds of work or one worn out in service. **2** A light easy usually three-gaited saddle horse. **3** A coach or carriage for hire. **4** A taxicab. **5** A person who hires himself out for literary work to be done as assigned by his employer; a drudge. — *v.* To ride at an ordinary pace, or along the roads, rather than across country. — *adj.* Done by a hack; as, *hack* work; *hack* writing.

hack·ber·ry \'hak-ˌber-ē\ *n.; pl.* **hack·ber·ries.** A tree related to the elm, with small greenish or blackish egg-shaped fruits.

hack·le \'hak-l\ *n.* **1** A comb for dressing fibers, as of flax or raw silk. **2** A long narrow feather on the neck of certain birds, especially the domestic fowl. **3** [in the plural] Bristles along the neck and back of a dog.

hack·ney \'hak-nē\ *n.; pl.* **hack·neys. 1** Any of a breed of compact English horses with very high stylish action. **2** A carriage for hire; a hack. — *adj.* **1** Let out for hire; as, a *hackney* coach. **2** Hackneyed.

hack·neyed \'hak-nēd\ *adj.* Worn out from too long or too much use; commonplace and ineffective; trite; as, a *hackneyed* expression.

hack·saw \'hak-ˌsȯ\ *n.* or **hack saw.** A fine-toothed, narrow-bladed saw stretched in a frame, for cutting metal.

hacksaw

had. Past tense and past part. of *have.*

had·dock \'had-ək\ *n.; pl.* **had·dock** or **had·docks.** A food fish related to the cod, but smaller.

ha·des \'hād-(ˌ)ēz\ *n.* **1** [with a capital] In Greek mythology, Pluto, the god of the lower world, or the lower world itself as the home of the dead. **2** Hell.

hadn't \'had-nt\. A contraction of *had not.*

hadst \(')hadst, (h)ədst\. An archaic form of *had,* used chiefly with *thou.*

haft \'haft\ *n.* A handle or hilt, as of a knife or a sword.

haft

hag \'hag\ *n.* **1** A witch. **2** An ugly old woman, especially one of an evil nature.

hag·gard \'hag-rd\ *adj.* Having the expression of a person who is suffering, as from great hunger, worry, or pain, or who is wasted with age; gaunt.

hag·gle \'hag-l\ *v.;* **hag·gled; hag·gling** \-l(-)ing\. **1** To cut roughly; to hack. **2** To dispute or argue, especially over a bargain or a price. — *n.* A haggling. — **hag·gler** \-l(-)ər\ *n.*

hail \'hāl\ *n.* **1** Small, roundish lumps of ice, formed from raindrops, that sometimes fall from the clouds during thunderstorms. **2** A shower or volley; as, a *hail* of bullets. — *v.* To fall as hail; to shower down like hail.

hail \'hāl\ *v.* **1** To greet; to welcome or salute, as with cheers; as, to *hail* the victor in a contest. **2** To call out to; as, to *hail* a taxi; to *hail* a ship. — **hail from.** To come from as one's home place or place of last departure. — *interj.* An exclamation expressing greeting or welcome. — *n.* **1** The act of hailing; a greeting; a salutation. **2** Hailing distance; as, within *hail.*

hail·stone \'hāl-ˌstōn\ *n.* A pellet of hail; a frozen drop of rain.

hail·storm \'hāl-ˌstȯrm\ *n.* A storm or shower accompanied with hail.

hair \'har, 'her\ *n.* **1** A slender threadlike growth from the skin of an animal, or the entire mass of such growths, such as makes up the fur or coat of an animal or grows on a person's head. **2** Something, as a fine process on a root or leaf, like a hair in slenderness. **3** A very small distance or amount; a hairbreadth. The speeding car missed a boy on a bicycle by only a *hair.* — **haired** \'hard, 'herd\ *adj.*

hair·breadth \'har-ˌbredth, 'her-\ *n.* Also **hairs-breadth** \'harz-, 'herz-\. The width of a hair; an extremely small distance. — *adj.* Very narrow; close; as, a *hairbreadth* escape.

hair·brush \'har-ˌbrəsh, 'her-\ *n.* A brush for the hair.

hair·cloth \'har-ˌklȯth, 'her-\ *n.; pl.* **hair·cloths** \-ˌklȯthz, -ˌklȯths\. A fabric of horsehair or camel's hair, used especially for covering upholstered furniture.

hair·cut \'har-ˌkət, 'her-\ *n.* The act, process, or style of cutting the hair; as, to wear a short *haircut.* — **hair·cut·ter**, *n.* — **hair·cut·ting**, *n.*

hair·do \'har-ˌdü, 'her-\ *n.; pl.* **hair·dos** \-ˌdüz\. A way of dressing or arranging a woman's hair; coiffure; as, the very latest in *hairdos.*

hair·dress·er \'har-ˌdres-r, 'her-\ *n.* A person who dresses or cuts hair, especially women's hair. — **hair·dress·ing**, *n.*

hair·less \'har-ləs, 'her-\ *adj.* Having no hair.

hair·line \'har-ˌlīn, 'her-\ *n.* **1** A very thin line. **2** The outline of the scalp or of the growth of hair on a head.

hair·pin \'har-ˌpin, 'her-\ *n.* A U-shaped pin for keeping the hair in place. — *adj.* U-shaped; sharply reversing direction in a sudden bend; as, *hairpin* curves on a mountain road.

hair·split·ter \'har-ˌsplit-r, 'her-\ *n.* A person who makes unnecessarily fine distinctions in reasoning or argument. — **hair·split·ting**, *n.*

hair·spring \'har-ˌspring, 'her-\ *n.* A very slender spring used in many instruments, especially in watches.

hairspring of a watch

hair trigger. A trigger adjusted so as to permit a firearm to be discharged by a very slight pressure.

hairy \'har-ē, 'her-ē\ *adj.;* **hair·i·er**; **hair·i·est**. **1** Bearing hair; covered with hair. **2** Of or like hair.

Hai·tian \'hāsh-n, 'hāt-ē-ən\ *adj.* Of or relating to Haiti. — *n.* A native or inhabitant of Haiti.

hal·berd \'halb-rd\ or **hal·bert** \'halb-rt\ *n.* A long-handled weapon that could be used both as a spear and as a battle-ax, used especially in the 15th and 16th centuries.

hal·cy·on \'hal-sē-ən\ *n.* A bird, possibly the kingfisher, that according to old fables nested on the sea in December and calmed the waves. — *adj.* Calm; peaceful; as, *halcyon* days.

hale \'hāl\ *v.;* **haled**; **hal·ing**. To pull or drag; to compel to go or come; as, a suspected thief *haled* into court.

hale \'hāl\ *adj.;* **hal·er**; **hal·est**. Strong and healthy; robust; as, a *hale* and hearty old man.

half \'haf, 'ȧf\ *n.; pl.* **halves** \'havz, 'ȧvz\. **1** One of two equal parts into which anything is or can be divided. **2** A part of anything that is about equal to the remainder; as, to offer someone the larger *half* of an apple. **3** Either of the two equal divisions of playing time in certain games, between which the players rest. — *adj.* **1** Being or equal to one of two equal parts; as, a *half* turn to the right; a *half* pound of butter. **2** About a half; partial; imperfect; as, a *half* truth. — *adv.* In an equal part or degree; by about a half; imperfectly; as, a biscuit only *half* done; to be *half* persuaded.

half·back \'haf-ˌbak, 'ȧf-\ *n.* One of the players stationed behind the line in some games, as football.

half-breed \'haf-ˌbrēd, 'ȧf-\ *n.* A person born of parents of different races; especially, in the United States, a child of one white parent and one Indian parent.

half brother. A brother related through one parent only.

half-caste \'haf-ˌkast, 'ȧf-\ *n.* **1** A person of mixed racial or cultural descent; especially, one of a group that is socially rejected because of mixed parentage.

half dollar. **1** Fifty cents; a half of a dollar. **2** A United States silver coin worth fifty cents.

half·heart·ed \'haf-'härt-əd, 'ȧf-, -'ȧrt-əd\ *adj.* Lacking spirit or interest. — **half·heart·ed·ly**, *adv.*

half-hour \'haf-'au̇r, 'ȧf-\ *n.* The mid-point of an hour; as, to hear the *half-hour* strike; to wait till the *half-hour.* — **half–hour·ly**, *adj.* or *adv.*

half-mast \'haf-'mast, 'ȧf-\ *n.* A point some distance, not necessarily halfway, down from the top of a mast or flagpole; as, flags flying at *half-mast.*

half·pen·ny \'hāp-n(-)ē\ *n.; pl.* **half·pence** \'hāp-n(t)s\ or **half·pen·nies** \'hāp-n(-)ēz\. Half of an English penny, or a coin of this value.

half sister. A sister related through one parent only.

half step. The difference in pitch between any two adjacent keys on a keyboard instrument; a semitone.

half tone. A semitone; a half step.

half-tone or **half·tone** \'haf-ˌtōn, 'ȧf-\ *n.* **1** A medium tint or tone in a painting, engraving, or photograph. **2** A picture done in half-tone.

half-track \'haf-ˌtrak, 'ȧf-\ *n.* **1** One of the endless-chain tracks used in place of rear wheels on one type of truck. **2** A truck or tractor having half-tracks and front wheels.

half·way \'haf-'wā, 'ȧf-\ *adj.* **1** At equal distance from the opposite ends or sides of anything; midway; as, to stop at the *halfway* mark. **2** Partial; incomplete; as, *halfway* measures. — *adv.* In the middle; at or to half the distance; partially; as, to open the door *halfway;* to be *halfway* satisfied.

half-wit \'haf-ˌwit, 'ȧf-\ *n.* A foolish person; a blockhead; a dunce. — **half-wit·ted** \-'wit-əd\ *adj.*

hal·i·but \'hal-ə-bət, 'häl-\ *n.; pl.* **hal·i·but**, sometimes **hal·i·buts**. [From medieval English *halybutte,* meaning literally "holy butt" (*butt* being a name applied to various flat fishes), probably because it was a popular item of the diet on holy fast days.] A food fish resembling the flounder, found in the North Atlantic.

hall \'hȯl\ *n.* **1** A large building used for public purposes; as, the city *hall.* **2** One of the buildings of a college or university set apart for a special purpose; as, Science *Hall;* the residence *halls.*

3 An assembly room; as, a lecture *hall.* 4 An entrance room in a house or public building. 5 A passageway or corridor.

hal·le·lu·jah or **hal·le·lu·iah** \ˌhal-ə-ˈlü-yə\ or **al·le·lu·ia** \ˌal-ə-\ *n.* or *interj.* Praise ye the Lord — used chiefly as an exclamation in songs of praise or thanks.

hall·mark \ˈhȯl-ˌmärk, -ˌmȧrk\ *n.* 1 The official stamp put on gold and silver articles at Goldsmith's Hall in London to certify their purity; any stamp similarly used. 2 Any sign of excellence, quality, or purity; as, a leader who has the *hallmark* of greatness in his face. — *v.* To put a hallmark on.

hal·loo \hə-ˈlü\ *n.; pl.* **hal·loos.** A shout; a hail. — *interj.* A shout to spur on an animal or to attract attention. — *v.;* **hal·looed; hal·loo·ing.** To shout.

hal·low \ˈhal-ō\ *v.* To make holy; to set apart for holy purposes; to treat or keep as sacred.

hal·lowed \ˈhal-ōd; *in the Lord's Prayer, also* ˈhal-ə-wəd\ *adj.* Made holy; regarded as holy; sacred; consecrated; as, *hallowed* ground.

Hal·low·een \ˌhal-ə-ˈwēn, ˌhäl-\ *n.* The evening preceding Allhallows or All Saints' Day; the evening of October 31.

hal·lu·ci·na·tion \hə-ˌlüs-n-ˈāsh-n\ *n.* 1 The perceiving of objects which do not exist or the experiencing of feelings which have no cause outside one's mind, usually the result of a nervous or mental disorder. 2 The object perceived or the feeling experienced.

hall·way \ˈhȯl-ˌwā\ *n.* 1 An entrance hall. 2 A passageway, usually one into which rooms open; a corridor.

ha·lo \ˈhā-ˌlō\ *n.; pl.* **ha·los** or **ha·loes.** 1 A circle of light around the sun or moon, caused by the presence of tiny ice crystals in the air. 2 A circle drawn or painted around the head of a person in a picture as a symbol of holiness. 3 The glory that surrounds anything idealized; as, the *halo* of heroism; the *halo* about old plantation life.

halo, 2

halt \ˈhȯlt\ *n.* A stop in marching or walking, or in any action; as, to call a *halt;* school activities coming to a complete *halt* during holidays. — *v.* 1 To stop marching. 2 To come or to bring to a stop. The policeman *halted* the speeding car.

halt \ˈhȯlt\ *adj. Archaic.* Lame; crippled. — *v.* 1 To walk lamely; to limp. 2 To be in doubt what to do; to hesitate. 3 To go along slowly and with frequent stops; as, *halting* speech. — **halt·ing·ly** \ˈhȯl-ting-lē\ *adv.*

hal·ter \ˈhȯlt-r\ *n.* 1 A rope or strap for leading or tying a horse or other animal. 2 A rope for hanging a person; a noose. 3 A woman's blouse, usually backless and fastened by straps around the neck and waist.

halve \ˈhav, ˈhȧv\ *v.;* **halved; halv·ing.** 1 To divide into two equal parts; to share equally; as, to *halve* an apple. 2 To reduce to one half; to decrease by one half; as, to *halve* a recipe for cookies.

halves. Pl. of *half.*

hal·yard \ˈhal-yərd\ *n.* A rope for raising and lowering yards, sails, or flags on a ship.

ham \ˈham\ *n.* 1 The thigh of an animal, especially of a hog, prepared for food. 2 [usually in the plural] The thigh and buttock. 3 A licensed operator of an amateur radio station.

ham·burg·er \ˈham-ˌbərg-r\ *n.* 1 Finely chopped or ground beef. 2 A sandwich made of a fried or broiled cake of this meat and, usually, a round flat roll.

ham·let \ˈham-lət\ *n.* A small village.

ham·mer \ˈham-r\ *n.* 1 A tool for driving or beating, as nails or metal, consisting of a head fastened crosswise to a handle. 2 Something resembling a hammer in shape or use; as a mallet used for striking the keys of a xylophone or the part of a gun that strikes the explosive charge in firing. 3 The outermost of the chain of three small bones in the ears of mammals. — *v.;* **ham·mered; ham·mer·ing** \-r(-)ing\. 1 To strike with a hammer; to beat with heavy blows. 2 To fasten with a hammer, as by nailing. 3 To produce by means of repeated blows; as, to *hammer* a ring out of metal. 4 To work long and hard at one thing; as, to *hammer* away at one's lessons.

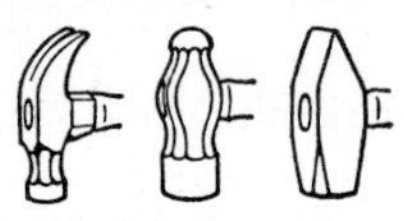
hammers

ham·mer·head \ˈham-r-ˌhed\ *n.* A shark about fifteen feet long, having the sides of the head extended in long flat outgrowths, at the ends of which the eyes are located.

ham·mock \ˈham-ək\ *n.* [From Spanish *hamaca,* there borrowed from an Indian word used in Haiti, where the Spaniards first encountered hammocks.] A swinging couch or bed, usually made of canvas or netting, hung from the ends by ropes.

ham·per \ˈhamp-r\ *n.* A large basket, usually with a cover; as, a clothes *hamper;* a picnic *hamper.*

ham·per \ˈhamp-r\ *v.;* **ham·pered; ham·per·ing** \-r(-)ing\. To keep from moving or acting freely; to hinder; to obstruct; as, to be *hampered* by heavy clothing; restrictions that *hampered* more than they helped.

picnic hamper

ham·ster \ˈham(p)st-r\ *n.* A thick-bodied, short-tailed rodent with large cheek pouches.

ham·string \ˈham-ˌstring\ *n.* 1 In man, either of two groups of tendons behind the knee. 2 In four-footed animals, the large tendon above and behind the hock. — *v.;* **ham·strung** \-ˌstrəng\; **ham·string·ing** \-ˌstring-ing\. 1 To disable by cutting the hamstring. 2 To disable in any way, especially by preventing free movement or activity.

hand \ˈhand\ *n.* 1 The end part of the arm, adapted for such acts as grasping and holding.

2 Possession; ownership; control; as, in the *hands* of the enemy. **3** A part or share in doing something; as, to take a *hand* in the work. **4** Side or aspect of a subject; as, on the one *hand* . . . on the other *hand*. **5** A pledge, especially of marriage; as, a young woman whose *hand* had been asked by a dozen men. **6** Ability; skill; as, to try one's *hand* at a game. **7** Handwriting; as, to write a clear *hand*. **8** The hand as a means of helping; as, to lend a *hand*. **9** A round of applause. The audience gave the speaker a good *hand*. **10** A hired worker; a laborer; as, a farm *hand*. **11** Source; as, to get the news at first *hand*. **12** Something resembling the hand of a person in appearance or use; as, the *hands* of a clock. **13** A hand's breadth, or four inches; as, a horse 15 *hands* high. **14** One round of a game of cards; the cards received by a player in one deal. — **at hand**. Near in time or place. — **on hand**. **1** In present possession; as, a stock of goods *on hand*. **2** In attendance; as, to be *on hand* at all times. — **out of hand**. Beyond control. — *v.* **1** To guide or assist with one's hand; as, to *hand* a lady into her car. **2** To give or pass by hand; as, to *hand* a paper to the teacher. — **hand down.** To pass along in succession; to transmit; as, a custom *handed down* from ancient times. — **hand over.** To give up control of; to surrender; as, to *hand over* one's watch to a robber. — *adj.* Of or relating to the hand; carried in the hand; operated by hand.

hand·bag \ˈhan(d)-ˌbag\ *n.* **1** A small bag used by women for carrying money and small articles. **2** A traveling bag smaller than an ordinary suitcase.

hand·ball \ˈhan(d)-ˌbȯl\ *n.* **1** A game played in a walled court or against a single wall or board by two to four players who use their hands in striking the ball. **2** The ball used in this game.

hand·bar·row \ˈhan(d)-ˌbar-ō\ *n.* A frame or flat barrow, without a wheel, carried by handles.

hand·bill \ˈhan(d)-ˌbil\ *n.* A printed sheet to be distributed by hand, as for advertising.

hand·book \ˈhan(d)-ˌbu̇k\ *n.* A small book of facts and other useful information, usually about a particular subject; a manual; a guidebook.

hand·car \ˈhan(d)-ˌkär, -ˌkȧr\ *n.* A small flat railroad car hand-propelled by a leverlike device, used chiefly by railroad workers.

hand·craft \ˈhan(d)-ˌkraft\ *n.* Handicraft.

hand·craft·ed \ˈhan(d)-ˌkraf-təd\ *adj.* Made by hand.

hand·cuff \ˈhan(d)-ˌkəf\ *n.* A rounded metal clasp that can be locked around a person's wrist, usually one of a pair connected by a short bar or chain. — *v.* To lock handcuffs on.

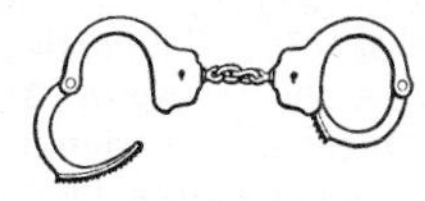
handcuffs

hand·ful \ˈhan(d)-ˌfu̇l\ *n.; pl.* **hand·fuls. 1** As much or as many as the hand will grasp or hold. **2** A small number; as, a bus carrying only a *handful* of passengers.

hand·i·cap \ˈhan-dē-ˌkap, -də-\ *n.* **1** A contest in which those who are more skilled are given some disadvantage to overcome and the less skilled are given some advantage. **2** The disadvantage or advantage given in such a contest. **3** Any disadvantage that makes progress or success more difficult. — *v.;* **hand·i·capped; hand·i·cap·ping.** To give or be a handicap to; to put at a disadvantage; to hinder; as, to be *handicapped* by poor health.

hand·i·craft \ˈhan-dē-ˌkraft\ *n.* Skilled work with the hands; an occupation, either trade or hobby, requiring skill with the hands, such as woodworking, weaving, or pottery; handcraft. — **hand·i·craft·er** \-ˌkraft-r\ *n.*

handier. Comparative of *handy*.

handiest. Superlative of *handy*.

hand·i·ly \ˈhan-də-lē\ *adv.* In a handy manner; conveniently; easily.

hand·i·work \ˈhan-dē-ˌwərk\ *n.* Work done by the hands; something one has made or done himself; as, an artist's pride in his *handiwork*.

hand·ker·chief \ˈhangk-r-chəf, -(ˌ)chif, -ˌchēf\ *n.; pl.* **hand·ker·chiefs** \-chəfs, -(ˌ)chifs, -ˌchēvz, -ˌchēfs, -chəvz, -(ˌ)chivz; *some say* -chəf *or* -(ˌ)chif *but* -ˌchēvz\. **1** A small piece of cloth, usually square, carried for wiping the face, nose or eyes. **2** A neckerchief.

han·dle \ˈhand-l\ *v.;* **han·dled; han·dling** \-l(-)ing\. **1** To touch, feel, or move with the hand. It isn't wise to *handle* objects in a china shop. **2** To deal with; to treat; to take care of; as, to understand how to *handle* children; to *handle* a dog like an expert. **3** To manage with the hands; as, to *handle* tools skillfully. **4** To control; to direct; as, an automobile that is easy to *handle*. **5** To deal or trade in; as, a store that *handles* toys and games. — *n.* That part of an object by which it is picked up or held when in use; as, the *handle* of an ax or of a teapot.

han·dle·bar \ˈhand-l-ˌbär, -ˌbȧr\ *n.* or **handle bar** [often in the plural]. A bar with a handle at each end for steering a bicycle or motorcycle.

hand lens. A magnifying glass to be held in the hands.

hand·made \ˈhan(d)-ˈmād\ *adj.* Made by hand, not by machine.

hand·maid \ˈhan(d)-ˌmād\ *n.* A female servant.

hand·maid·en \ˈhan(d)-ˌmād-n\ *n. Archaic.* A handmaid.

hand organ. A small musical instrument which plays tunes when cranked by hand.

hand·rail \ˈhan-ˌdrāl\ *n.* A rail to be grasped by the hand for support, as on a staircase; a railing serving as a guard.

hand·saw \ˈhan(d)-ˌsȯ\ *n.* A saw used with one hand.

hand·shake \ˈhan(d)-ˌshāk\ *n.* A clasping of the hands, usually the right hands, especially as a form of greeting or farewell or as a sign of agreement, as after bargaining.

hand·some \ˈhan(t)s-m\ *adj.;* **hand·som·er; hand·som·est. 1** Having a pleasing appearance; good-looking; as, a *handsome* person. **2** Considerable; ample; as, a *handsome* fortune. **3** Liberal; generous; as, a *handsome* allowance; a *handsome* tip. — **hand·some·ly**, *adv.*

hand·spike \'han(d)-ˌspīk\ *n.* A bar used as a lever, as in working a windlass on a boat.

hand·spring \'han(d)-ˌspring\ *n.* A feat of tumbling in which the body rotates forward or backward in full circle from a standing position, landing first on the hands and then on the feet.

hand-to-hand \'han(d)-tə-'hand\ *adj.* At close quarters; close together; as, a *hand-to-hand* fight.

hand-to-mouth \'han(d)-tə-'mau̇th\ *adj.* Using immediately what one acquires; thriftless; as, a *hand-to-mouth* existence.

hand·work \'han-ˌdwərk\ *n.* Work done by hand, not by machine.

hand·writ·ing \'han-ˌdrīt-ing\ *n.* Writing done by hand; especially, a person's own writing or style of writing; as, to know the *handwriting* of all one's friends.

handy \'han-dē\ *adj.;* **hand·i·er**; **hand·i·est. 1** Conveniently near; convenient for use; as, to keep a pencil and paper *handy;* a *handy* little book of facts. **2** Skillful in using the hands; as, to be *handy* with tools; a man who is *handy* around the house.

hang \'hang\ *v.;* **hung** \'həng\ or, with reference to death by hanging, **hanged** \'hangd\; **hang·ing** \'hang-ing\. **1** To fasten, or to be fastened, to something without any support from below; to suspend; as, to *hang* curtains; to *hang* up one's hat and coat. **2** To put to death or be put to death by hanging from a rope tied round the neck, as from a gallows; as, sentenced to be *hanged.* **3** To fasten so as to allow free motion forward and backward; as, to *hang* a door. **4** To cover, decorate, or furnish, as by hanging pictures or flags. **5** To droop; as, to *hang* one's head. **6** To hover. Evils *hung* over the country. **7** To rest; to depend. The results of the election *hung* on a single vote. **8** To linger or loiter; as, to *hang* about the school building after school hours. — **hang out.** To spend much time, through choice, in or at a place; as, to *hang out* in the drug store. — *n.* **1** The manner in which a thing hangs; as, the *hang* of a skirt. **2** Meaning; sense; as, to get the *hang* of an argument without difficulty. **3** Method of use; knack; as, to get the *hang* of steering a boat.

hang·ar \'hang-r, 'hang-gr\ *n.* A shelter for housing aircraft, especially airplanes.

hang·dog \'hang-ˌdȯg\ *adj.* Sneaking; ashamed; as, a *hangdog* look.

hang·er \'hang-r\ *n.* **1** One who hangs something; as, a paper *hanger.* **2** Something from which something else hangs; as, a coat *hanger.*

hang·er-on \'hang-r-'ȯn, -'än\ *n.; pl.* **hang·ers-on.** One who holds fast to an association with another person, place, or position, especially when he is no longer wanted; a dependent.

hang·ing \'hang-ing\ *n.* **1** The act of suspending. The *hanging* of the pictures took two hours. **2** Execution, as of a criminal, by suspending from a gallows. **3** [usually in the plural] Something that is hung, as drapery. — *adj.* **1** Suspended; leaning over or downward. **2** Situated on steeply sloping grounds; as, *hanging* gardens. **3** Intended for holding up a suspended object; as, the *hanging* post of a gate. **4** Punishable by death by hanging; as, a *hanging* offense.

hang·man \'hang-mən\ *n.; pl.* **hang·men** \-mən\. A person who hangs condemned criminals.

hang·nail \'hang-ˌnāl\ *n.* A bit of skin hanging loose at the side or base of a fingernail.

hang·out \'hang-ˌau̇t\ *n.* A place where one hangs out; any place in which a person by choice spends a great deal of time or which he visits repeatedly.

hank \'hangk\ *n.* A coil or loop; especially, a coil or skein of yarn.

han·ker \'hangk-r\ *v.;* **han·kered**; **han·ker·ing** \-r(-)ing\. To long; to have an eager or intense desire; as, to *hanker* after fame and fortune; to waste no time *hankering* for what one cannot have. — **han·ker·ing**, *n.*

han·som \'han(t)s-m\ *n.* or **hansom cab.** [Named after Joseph A. *Hansom* (1803–1882), an English architect, who invented it.] A light two-wheeled covered carriage with the driver's seat behind the body and almost level with its top.

hansom cab

Ha·nuk·kah \'hä-nə-kə\ *n.* The eight-day Jewish festival of lights celebrated in November or December to commemorate the rededication of the Temple in Jerusalem after the defeat of the Syrians in 165 B.C.

hap \'hap\ *n.* Chance; happening; luck. — *v.;* **happed**; **hap·ping.** To happen; to befall.

hap·haz·ard \'hap-'haz-rd\ *n.* Chance; accident; random; as, to leave a room with everything lying about at *haphazard;* events which occurred by *haphazard.* — *adj.* Accidental; random; decided by chance; as, a *haphazard* guess. — *adv.* In a chance or random manner; haphazardly; as, thrown together *haphazard.* — **hap·haz·ard·ly**, *adv.*

hap·less \'hap-ləs\ *adj.* Unlucky; as, a *hapless* person. — **hap·less·ly**, *adv.*

hap·ly \'hap-lē\ *adv. Archaic.* By chance; perhaps.

hap·pen \'hap-n, -m\ *v.;* **hap·pened** \-nd, -md\; **hap·pen·ing** \'hap-n(-)ing\. **1** To occur or come about by chance. As it *happened,* no one was in the building when the fire started. **2** To take place; to occur; as, to describe how an accident *happened;* a whole day during which nothing interesting *happened.* **3** To chance; as, to *happen* to meet an old friend. — **happen on** or **happen onto.** To come upon or meet by chance; as, to *happen on* the right path; to *happen onto* a friend in a crowd. — **happen to. 1** To befall or come to, especially by way of harm or injury. The child acted as if something had *happened to* him. **2** To become of; as, to wonder what has *happened to* old friends.

hap·pen·ing \'hap-n(-)ing\ *n.* Something that happens; an event; an occurrence.

hap·pi·ly \'hap-l-ē\ *adv.* **1** In a happy way; as, to laugh *happily;* to live *happily* ever after. **2** By good fortune; luckily. *Happily,* no one was injured in the crash.

hap·pi·ness \'hap-ē-nəs, -ə-nəs\ *n.* **1** Good fortune; prosperity; as, to wish someone every *happiness.* **2** The condition of being happy; contentment; gladness.

hap·py \'hap-ē\ *adj.;* **hap·pi·er; hap·pi·est. 1** Fortunate; lucky; as, to meet someone by a *happy* chance. **2** Fitting; suitable; apt; as, a *happy* choice for class president; a *happy* answer to a troublesome question. **3** Enjoying one's condition or circumstances; satisfied and content; as, a person who is *happy* in his work. **4** Joyous; as, *happy* laughter.

hap·py-go-lucky \'hap-ē-(ˌ)gō-'lək-ē\ *adj.* Trusting to luck; carefree.

ha·rangue \hə-'rang\ *n.* A noisy speech, especially one that is violent or scolding. — *v.;* **ha·rangued; ha·rangu·ing. 1** To address in a harangue. **2** To deliver a harangue; to talk at length in a noisy, scolding manner.

ha·rass \hə-'ras, 'har-əs\ *v.* **1** To weary or exhaust; to tire out by persistent efforts; to worry or annoy with repeated attacks. **2** To lay waste; to harry. — **ha·rass·ment** \-mənt\ *n.*

har·bin·ger \'härb-nj-r, 'hȧrb-\ *n.* A messenger sent on ahead; one that announces or shows what is coming; a forerunner; as, warm rains that come as *harbingers* of spring. — *v.* To be a harbinger of.

har·bor \'härb-r, 'hȧrb-r\ *n.* **1** A place of safety and comfort; a shelter. **2** Part of a body of water so protected by man or nature as to be a place of safety for ships; a port. — *v.;* **har·bored; har·bor·ing** \-r(-)ing\. **1** To give shelter, lodging, or refuge to; as, to *harbor* an escaped prisoner. **2** To hold in one's mind; as, to *harbor* suspicion; to *harbor* a grudge. **3** To take shelter; to lodge for a time, especially for safety or refuge.

har·bor·age \'härb-r(-)ij, 'hȧrb-\ *n.* Shelter; harbor.

hard \'härd, 'hȧrd\ *adj.* **1** Not easily cut, pierced, or divided into parts; not soft; as, the *hard* outer surface of the teeth. **2** Physically fit; hardy. Exercise makes the body *hard.* **3** Carried on diligently; as, hours of *hard* study. **4** Diligent; energetic; as, a *hard* worker. **5** Severe; harsh; as, *hard* words; a *hard* winter. **6** Not sympathetic; unkind; bitter; as, a *hard* heart; *hard* feelings. **7** Strong in alcohol; as, *hard* liquor. **8** Difficult to do or to bear; as, *hard* times; a *hard* problem in arithmetic. **9** Containing substances that prevent the forming of a lather with soap; as, to wash in *hard* water. **10** Pronounced in a way thought of as hard rather than soft, as *c* in *case* (contrasted with *cease*), *g* in *goose* (contrasted with *gem*), *s* in *this* (contrasted with *these*), *th* in *ether* (contrasted with *either*). — **hard of hearing.** Somewhat deaf. — *adv.* **1** With strain, energy, or great effort; as, to work *hard;* to try *hard* to win. **2** Tightly; firmly; as, to hold *hard* to something. **3** With or so as to involve pain, trouble, or difficulty; as, a *hard*-won victory. The boy knew that it would go *hard* with him if he were found out. — **hard by.** Close by; near. *Hard by* the school stood a church.

hard and fast. Rigidly binding; strict; as, a *hard and fast* rule.

hard-bit·ten \'härd-'bit-n, 'hȧrd-\ *adj.* **1** Having a hard bite — used of dogs. **2** Tough; dogged; as, a *hard-bitten* old campaigner.

hard-boiled \'härd-'bȯild, 'hȧrd-\ *adj.* **1** Boiled until both yolk and white have solidified — used of an egg. **2** Tough and severe in character; callous; unfeeling; as, a *hard-boiled* drill sergeant; a *hard-boiled* attitude toward everybody.

hard coal. Anthracite coal.

hard·en \'härd-n, 'hȧrd-n\ *v.;* **hard·ened; hard·en·ing** \-n(-)ing\. **1** To make or to become hard or harder. **2** To make or to become hardy or strong; as, muscles *hardened* by exercise. **3** To make or to become stubborn, unfeeling, or unsympathetic; as, to *harden* one's heart; to *harden* one's mind against all arguments.

hard·hack \'härd-ˌhak, 'hȧrd-\ *n.* An American shrub of the rose family with rusty, hairy leaves and clusters of small flowers, usually pink.

hard·head·ed \'härd-'hed-əd, 'hȧrd-\ *adj.* **1** Stubborn. **2** Having sound judgment; shrewd.

hard·heart·ed \'härd-'härt-əd, 'hȧrd-'hȧrt-\ *adj.* Unfeeling; unsympathetic; cruel. — **hard·heart·ed·ly,** *adv.*

har·di·hood \'härd-ē-ˌhu̇d, 'hȧrd-\ *n.* Boldness combined with firmness of mind; bravery.

har·di·ly \'härd-l-ē, 'hȧrd-\ *adv.* In a hardy manner; boldly; strongly.

har·di·ness \'härd-ē-nəs, 'hȧrd-\ *n.* Vigor; hardihood; hardy quality.

hard·ly \'härd-lē, 'hȧrd-\ *adv.* **1** Severely; harshly; as, to be *hardly* treated by fortune. **2** Scarcely; barely; only just; as, *hardly* to have time to catch a train; a place where it *hardly* ever rains. **3** Very probably not; as, a wish that will *hardly* come true. **4** With difficulty; as, *hardly* earned.

hard·ness \'härd-nəs, 'hȧrd-\ *n.* The quality or the condition of being hard.

hard·pan \'härd-ˌpan, 'hȧrd-\ *n.* **1** A cementlike layer in soils, often containing clay, which roots cannot easily penetrate. **2** Hard unbroken ground. **3** The fundamental part of anything; the basis.

hard·ship \'härd-ˌship, 'hȧrd-\ *n.* Something that is hard to bear, as a loss, injury, or suffering.

hard·tack \'härd-ˌtak, 'hȧrd-\ *n.* A hard biscuit baked in round cakes without salt, eaten by sailors on shipboard.

hard·ware \'härd-ˌwar, 'hȧrd-, -ˌwer\ *n.* Articles made of metal, as cutlery and cooking utensils, tools, metal building equipment, and parts of machines and appliances.

hard·wood \'härd-ˌwu̇d, 'hȧrd-\ *n.* **1** Any wood that is heavy, close-grained, and difficult to cut, saw, or trim. **2** In forestry, the wood of any broad-leaved tree as distinguished from that of any cone-bearing tree. — *adj.* **1** Having hardwood; as, *hardwood* trees. **2** Made of hardwood; as, *hardwood* floors.

har·dy \'härd-ē, 'hȧrd-ē\ *adj.;* **har·di·er**; **har·di·est.** **1** Bold; daring. **2** Able to endure fatigue or hardship; robust. **3** Not easily affected by severe weather; as, *hardy* plants.

hare \'har, 'her\ *n.* Any of various swift-footed, timid mammals with long ears and hind legs, divided upper lip, and a short tail that are related to the rabbits but bear young with fur and with eyes open at birth.

hare·bell \'har-ˌbel, 'her-\ *n.* A slender herb with bright blue bell-shaped flowers; the bluebell.

hare·brained \'har-'brānd, 'her-\ *adj.* Giddy; heedless.

hare·lip \'har-'lip, 'her-, -ˌlip\ *n.* A deformity in which the upper lip is split like that of a hare.

har·em \'har-əm, 'her-\ *n.* **1** The rooms assigned to the women in a Moslem house. **2** The women of a Moslem household.

hark \'härk, 'hȧrk\ *v.* To listen. — **hark back.** To go back to an earlier point; as, to *hark back* to something briefly mentioned before; an old soldier whose ideas on warfare *harked back* to his youth.

harken. Variant of *hearken.*

har·le·quin \'här-lə-kwən, 'hȧr-\ *n.* A clown. — *adj.* Resembling the typical costume of a harlequin; especially, of many colors and usually in a design composed of diamond-shaped figures; as, a *harlequin* border on a tablecloth.

har·lot \'här-lət, 'hȧr-\ *n.* A woman of loose morals; a prostitute.

harm \'härm, 'hȧrm\ *n.* **1** Injury; damage; hurt; as, to come through an accident without *harm.* **2** Evil; wrong; as, to mean no *harm.* — *v.* To injure; to damage; to cause harm to.

harm·ful \'härm-fəl, 'hȧrm-\ *adj.* Causing harm; injurious; hurtful. — **harm·ful·ly** \-fə-lē\ *adv.*

harm·less \'härm-ləs, 'hȧrm-\ *adj.* Not harmful or harming; without power to harm; as, a *harmless* snake; a *harmless* joke. — **harm·less·ly**, *adv.*

har·mon·ic \här-'män-ik, hȧr-\ *adj.* Having to do with musical harmony as opposed to melody or rhythm. — *n.* An overtone; especially, a flutelike tone produced, as on a violin, by lightly touching a vibrating string with the finger.

har·mon·i·ca \här-'män-ik-ə, hȧr-\ *n.* A small, flat wind instrument held in the hand and played by the mouth; a mouth organ.

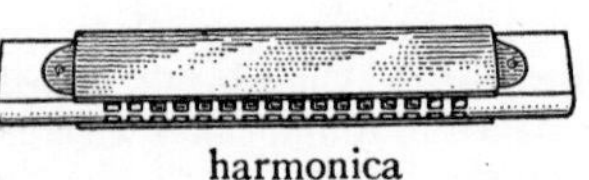
harmonica

har·mo·ni·ous \här-'mō-nē-əs, hȧr-\ *adj.* **1** Combining so as to produce a pleasing effect; as, *harmonious* colors; *harmonious* sounds. **2** Marked by harmony in action or feeling; as, a *harmonious* family; a *harmonious* discussion. **3** Pleasant-sounding; melodious; as, a *harmonious* voice; a *harmonious* song. — **har·mo·ni·ous·ly**, *adv.*

har·mo·nize \'här-mə-ˌnīz, 'hȧr-\ *v.;* **har·mo·nized**; **har·mo·niz·ing.** **1** To combine in a pleasing, agreeable manner; as, voices or colors that *harmonize.* **2** To bring into harmony or agreement; as, to *harmonize* the various wishes of a group. **3** To accompany with musical harmony; to provide with parts; as, to *harmonize* a melody.

har·mo·ny \'här-mə-nē, 'hȧr-\ *n.; pl.* **har·mo·nies.** **1** A combination or arrangement of things in such a way as to produce a pleasing effect; as, a picture showing *harmony* of color and design. **2** Agreement, as in opinions, manners, or interests; as, a meeting marked by *harmony;* to live in *harmony* with one's neighbors. **3** Musical agreement of sounds; tuneful sound. **4** The combination of musical tones into chords; the art of combining tones into chords and of connecting these chords according to certain rules.

har·ness \'här-nəs, 'hȧr-\ *n.* **1** The straps and fastenings placed on an animal used for pulling loads. **2** Any arrangement of straps resembling this; as, a dog *harness;* a baby *harness.* — *v.* **1** To put a harness on. **2** To equip with machinery so as to produce power; as, to *harness* a waterfall.

harp \'härp, 'hȧrp\ *n.* A musical instrument consisting of a triangular frame set with strings that are plucked by the fingers. — *v.* **1** To play on a harp. **2** To refer to something over and over again; as, to *harp* on someone's failings.

harp·er \'härp-r, 'hȧrp-r\ *n.* One who plays the harp; a minstrel.

harp·ist \'härp-əst, 'hȧrp-\ *n.* A harp player.

har·poon \här-'pün, hȧr-\ *n.* A barbed spear used for striking whales and large fish. — *v.* To strike or catch with a harpoon. — **har·poon·er**, *n.*

harpoon gun. A gun used for shooting a harpoon.

harp·si·chord \'härp-sə-ˌkȯrd, 'hȧrp-\ *n.* A harp-shaped, wire-stringed musical instrument with a keyboard, in use before the piano.

harpsichord

har·py \'härp-ē, 'hȧrp-ē\ *n.; pl.* **har·pies.** **1** A mythological creature, usually pictured as half woman and half bird and supposed to snatch away the souls of the dead. **2** A greedy or grasping person.

har·que·bus \'härk-wē-bəs, 'hȧrk-\ or **ar·que·bus** \'ärk-, 'ȧrk-\ *n.* A portable firearm of the 15th and 16th centuries, later replaced by the musket.

har·row \'har-ō\ *n.* A heavy frame set with metal teeth or disks, used in farming for breaking up soil and smoothing it over. — *v.* **1** To draw a harrow over. **2** To break as with a harrow; to wound; to distress. The story *harrowed* the feelings of those who heard it.

har·ry \'har-ē\ *v.;* **har·ried** \-ēd\; **har·ry·ing.** **1** To raid; to rob and lay waste. **2** To worry; to torment; as, *harried* by cares.

harsh \'härsh, 'hȧrsh\ *adj.* **1** Coarse; rough; as, a *harsh* fabric. **2** Not harmonious; as, a *harsh* sound; a *harsh* combination of colors. **3** Unduly rigorous;

severe; as, a *harsh* climate; *harsh* discipline. — **harsh·ly,** *adv.*

hart \'härt, 'hȧrt\ *n.* A stag; the male red deer, especially one over five years old.

har·te·beest \'härt-ə-ˌbēst, 'hȧrt-\ *n.* A large swift African antelope with ringed horns.

harts·horn \'härts-ˌhȯrn, 'hȧrts-\ *n.* A preparation of ammonia used as smelling salts.

har·um–scar·um \'har-əm-'skar-əm, 'her-əm-'sker-əm\ *adj.* Reckless; irresponsible; as, mischievous, *harum-scarum* boys. — *n.* A harum-scarum person.

har·vest \'här-vəst, 'hȧr-\ *n.* **1** The season when grains and fruits are gathered. **2** The gathering of a crop of any kind. **3** A crop, as of grain or fruit. — *v.* To reap or gather.

har·vest·er \'här-vəst-r, 'hȧr-\ *n.* A person or a thing that harvests; especially, a machine for harvesting field crops.

has \(')haz, (h)əz, z, s; *before "to", often* (')has\. A form of the verb *have* showing present time, and used with *he, she,* or *it* or with words for which these stand.

hash \'hash\ *v.* [From French *hacher* meaning "to chop up into small pieces", derived from *hache* meaning "ax" — see *hatchet.*] **1** To chop into small pieces and mix. **2** To make a mess of something; to bungle. — *n.* **1** A mixture of meat and vegetables, chopped, cooked, and served for food. **2** A mess; a jumble.

hash·ish \'hash-(ˌ)ēsh\ *n.* A preparation made from hemp, especially the dried flowers, chewed or smoked for its intoxicating effect.

hasn't \'haz-nt\. A contraction of *has not.*

hasp \'hasp\ *n.* A clasp or fastening, as for a door or lid; especially, a hinged metal clasp for the lid of a trunk.

has·sock \'has-ək\ *n.* **1** A clump of coarse grass. **2** A cushion used under the knees while praying. **3** A tightly stuffed cushion on legs or a large cushionlike stool used as a low seat or as a footrest.

hast \(')hast, (h)əst\. An archaic form of *have* used chiefly with *thou.*

haste \'hāst\ *n.* **1** Swiftness; speed; as, a matter requiring *haste.* **2** Hurry; rash speed in thought or action. *Haste* makes waste.

— The words *hurry* and *speed* are synonyms of *haste:* all three apply to quickness, but *haste* is likely to suggest eagerness or pressure of time that usually results in carelessness; *hurry* usually indicates haste that is accompanied by urgency, excitement, or confusion; *speed* places attention on the swiftness of action and often suggests smoothness or ease of movement.

— **in haste.** In a hurry. — **make haste.** To hurry. — *v.;* **hast·ed; hast·ing.** To hasten.

has·ten \'hās-n\ *v.;* **has·tened; has·ten·ing** \-n(-)ing\. **1** To drive or urge forward; to accelerate; to speed; as, to *hasten* one's pace at the sound of thunder. Rest in bed *hastens* recovery from many illnesses. **2** To hurry; to make haste; as, to *hasten* away; to *hasten* to correct a mistake.

hasty \'hās-tē\ *adj.;* **hast·i·er; hast·i·est. 1** Done or made quickly; hurried; as, to make a *hasty* trip to town. **2** Made, done, or decided without proper care and thought; as, to regret a *hasty* decision. **3** Quick-tempered; as, *hasty* words. — **hast·i·ly** \'hās-tə-lē\ *adv.*

hasty pudding. 1 A pudding or batter made by stirring flour or oatmeal into boiling water or milk. **2** Cornmeal mush.

hat \'hat\ *n.* A shaped covering for the head, usually with crown and brim. — **pass the hat.** To take up a collection. — **under one's hat.** In one's head; to oneself; secret.

hat·band \'hat-ˌband\ *n.* A band round the crown of a hat just above the brim.

hatch \'hach\ *n.* **1** The lower half of a door or gate that is divided in separately movable upper and lower sections. **2** An opening in the deck of a ship or in the floor or roof of a building. **3** The covering for such an opening.

hatch \'hach\ *v.* **1** To produce from an egg or eggs. The hen *hatched* ten chicks. **2** To come forth from the egg; as, chicks that have just *hatched.* **3** To produce young from. The sun *hatches* the turtle's eggs. **4** To think up and produce; to plot; to plan; as, to *hatch* some new ideas; to *hatch* a plot.

hatch \'hach\ *v.* To mark with hatching, as the shading in a picture.

hatch·ery \'hach-r(-)ē\ *n.; pl.* **hatch·er·ies.** A place for hatching eggs, especially those of hens or fish.

hatch·et \'hach-ət\ *n.* [From medieval English *hachet,* there borrowed from medieval French, and derived from *hache* meaning "ax" — see *hash.*] A short-handled ax with a hammer head, to be used with one hand.

hatchet

hatch·ing \'hach-ing\ *n.* **1** The making of fine lines drawn close together to show shading in a picture. **2** A mass of such lines.

hatch·way \'hach-ˌwā\ *n.* An opening in a deck or in the floor or roof of a building.

hate \'hāt\ *v.;* **hat·ed; hat·ing.** To dislike intensely; to feel an extreme aversion to; to detest.

— The words *detest* and *loathe* are synonyms of *hate: hate* usually suggests a strong and active feeling of extreme dislike sometimes accompanied by a certain amount of respect; *detest* may suggest an even stronger dislike but often lacks such active hostility as *hate; loathe* may indicate disgust and revulsion usually aroused by something offensive to one's feelings or sensitivities.

— *n.* Intense dislike; ill will; hatred. — **hat·er,** *n.*

hate·ful \'hāt-fəl\ *adj.* Arousing or deserving hate or hatred; detestable; as, a *hateful* crime. Cruelty is *hateful* to all decent people. — **hate·ful·ly** \-fə-lē\ *adv.*

hath \(')hath, (h)əth\. An archaic form of *has.*

ha·tred \'hā-trəd\ *n.* Strong dislike and ill will; hate.

hat·ter \'hat-r\ *n.* A person who makes or sells hats.

hau·berk \'hȯ-(ˌ)bərk\ *n.* A suit of armor consisting of a long tunic of linked metal rings.

haugh·ty \'hȯt-ē, 'hät-ē\ *adj.;* **haugh·ti·er; haugh·ti·est. 1** Proud and scornful; inclined to look down on others; arrogant. **2** Arising from or showing great pride; as, a *haughty* answer. — **haugh·ti·ly** \'hȯt-l-ē, 'hät-\ *adv.*

haul \'hȯl\ *v.* **1** To pull or draw with force; to drag; as, to *haul* a log; to *haul* on a rope. **2** To change the course of a ship, especially so as to sail closer to the wind. — **haul off. 1** In sailing, to change course. **2** To withdraw or draw back. **3** To draw back the arm to gain force for a blow. — *n.* **1** A dragging with force; a strong pull; a tug. **2** A single drawing of a net, as for fish. **3** Anything caught, taken, or won at or as if at a single drawing of a net; as, a burglar's *haul.* **4** The distance over which anything is hauled; as, a *haul* of three miles.

haunch \'hȯnch, 'hänch\ *n.* **1** The hip. **2** [in the plural] The hindquarters. **3** The leg and loin of an animal taken together; as, a *haunch* of venison.

haunt \'hȯnt, 'hänt\ *v.* **1** To go to over and over again; to visit repeatedly; as, to *haunt* the river on hot summer days. **2** To visit repeatedly in the form of a ghost or spirit. The dark old house was said to be *haunted* by its former owner, long since dead. **3** To come to mind frequently but vaguely; as, to be *haunted* by a strain of music heard only once. — *n.* **1** A place visited again and again; as, to know the favorite *haunts* of birds. **2** *Dial.* A ghost.

haut·boy \'(h)ō-ˌbȯi\ *n.* An oboe.

hau·teur \(h)ō-'tər, hȯ-\ *n.* Haughtiness; arrogance.

have \(')hav, (h)əv, v; *before "to", often* 'haf\ *v.;* **had** \(')had, (h)əd, d\; **hav·ing** \'hav-ing\. **1** To own; to possess; as, to *have* a car; to *have* authority. **2** To be forced or compelled; as, to *have* to stay home. **3** To bear; to give birth to or become the parent of; as, to *have* a baby. **4** To be in a certain relation to; as, to *have* the sun at one's back. **5** To hold or keep in the mind; as, to *have* doubts; to *have* an idea. **6** To experience; as, to *have* trouble; to *have* a good time. **7** To show or exercise; as, to *have* patience; to *have* mercy. **8** To obtain; to get; to receive; to accept; to take; as, something that can be *had* for the asking. Please *have* another piece of cake. **9** To permit; to allow. Let us *have* no more nonsense. I will not *have* it! **10** To cause to do or be done; to cause to be or go; as, to *have* one's hair cut; to *have* someone mow the lawn.

☞ The forms of *have* are regularly used as helping or auxiliary verbs with the past participle of other verbs. The leaves *have* fallen from the trees. The bird *has* flown away. It *had* rained during the morning. We shall *have* finished before long.

ha·ven \'hāv-n\ *n.* **1** A harbor; a port. **2** Any shelter or place of refuge.

haven't \'hav-nt\. A contraction of *have not.*

hav·er·sack \'hav-r-ˌsak\ *n.* [From French *havresac,* there borrowed from German *hafersack* meaning literally "oat bag", and so called because it was originally used to carry oats for the horses on journeys.] A bag or case, usually of canvas or leather, for carrying provisions on a march or hike.

hav·oc \'hav-ək\ *n.* Wide and general destruction; ruin; as, the *havoc* caused by an earthquake.

haw \'hȯ\ *n.* A hawthorn berry.

haw \'hȯ\ *interj.* A command, used in guiding teams without reins, to turn to the left. — *v.* To turn to the left.

haw \'hȯ\ *interj.* An exclamation expressing hesitation. — *v.* To hesitate in speaking, interjecting sounds like "haw"; as, to hem and *haw* over one's answer.

Ha·wai·ian \hə-'wī-ən, -'wä-yən, -'wȯ-yən\ *adj.* Of or relating to Hawaii. — *n.* **1** A native or inhabitant of Hawaii. **2** The native language of Hawaii.

hawk \'hȯk\ *n.* A bird of prey, smaller than most eagles, with strong hooked bill and sharp curved claws. — *v.* To hunt birds by means of trained hawks.

hawk \'hȯk\ *v.* **1** To make a harsh coughing sound, as in clearing the throat. **2** To raise by hawking, as phlegm. — *n.* A hawking.

hawk \'hȯk\ *v.* To offer goods for sale by crying them out in the public streets; as, to *hawk* vegetables and fruit.

hawk·er \'hȯk-r\ *n.* A falconer.

hawk·er \'hȯk-r\ *n.* One who sells goods, especially small wares, from place to place or by crying them out in the street; a peddler.

hawk·ing \'hȯk-ing\ *n.* Falconry.

haw·ser \'hȯz-r\ *n.* A large rope for towing or mooring a ship.

haw·thorn \'hȯ-ˌthȯrn\ *n.* Any of several spiny shrubs or small trees of the apple family, with shiny leaves, white, pink, or red fragrant flowers that are produced in spring or early summer, and small red berrylike fruits called *haws.*

hay \'hā\ *n.* Grass or other plants, as clover, cut and dried for use as fodder. — *v.* To cut grass for hay.

hay·cock \'hā-ˌkäk\ *n.* A cone-shaped pile or heap of hay.

hay fever. A catarrhal affection of the mucous membranes of the eyes, nose, and throat, caused chiefly by inhaled pollen of various plants.

hay·field \'hā-ˌfēld\ *n.* A field where grass for making hay is grown.

hay·fork \'hā-ˌfȯrk\ *n.* **1** A pitchfork. **2** A mechanically operated fork for loading or unloading hay.

hay·loft \'hā-ˌlȯft\ *n.* A loft in a barn or stable for storing hay.

hay·mow \'hā-ˌmaů\ *n.* **1** A mass or pile of hay laid up in a barn. **2** The part of a barn where hay is kept; a hayloft.

hay·rack \'hā-ˌrak\ *n.* A wide frame mounted on

a wagon and used for carrying large loads of hay or straw.

hay·rick \'hā-ˌrik\ *n.* A haystack.

hay·stack \'hā-ˌstak\ *n.* A large firmly-packed heap of hay kept in the open air.

hay·wire \'hā-ˌwīr\ *n.* Wire for tying up bales of hay or straw. — *adj. Slang.* Disorganized; in confusion. — **go haywire.** *Slang.* **1** To become completely disorganized. **2** To act as if crazy.

haz·ard \'haz-rd\ *n.* [From medieval English *hasard* meaning "a game played with dice", there borrowed from Old French, where it was borrowed from Arabic *al-zahr* meaning "the die".] **1** An old game of chance played with dice. **2** Chance; accident. **3** Risk; danger; peril; as, the *hazards* of war. **4** A source of danger; as, a fire *hazard.* **5** Any obstruction on a golf course. — *v.* To risk; to venture; as, to *hazard* one's life to prove one's courage; to *hazard* a guess.

haz·ard·ous \'haz-r-dəs\ *adj.* Dangerous; risky; as, a *hazardous* voyage; a *hazardous* business venture. — **haz·ard·ous·ly**, *adv.*

haze \'hāz\ *n.* **1** Light vapor or smoke in the air, interfering with vision but having little or no dampness. **2** A slightly clouded mental condition; a daze.

haze \'hāz\ *v.;* **hazed; haz·ing.** To force to perform ridiculous and humiliating tasks and stunts, as new students in a school or college or initiates in a club or fraternity.

ha·zel \'hāz-l\ *n.* **1** A shrub or small tree of the birch family that bears edible rounded nuts called *hazelnuts* or *filberts.* **2** A light brown color like that of hazelnuts.

ha·zel·nut \'hāz-l-(ˌ)nət\ *n.* **1** The nut of the hazel; a filbert. **2** The color hazel.

ha·zy \'hā-zē\ *adj.;* **ha·zi·er; ha·zi·est.** **1** Containing or partly concealed by haze; as, *hazy* air; the *hazy* outline of a distant hill. **2** Not clear in thought, meaning, or memory; vague; uncertain; as, a *hazy* idea; to be *hazy* on the subject of European geography. — **ha·zi·ly** \'hāz-l(-)ē\ *adv.*

H-bomb \'āch-ˌbäm\ *n.* A hydrogen bomb.

hd. Abbreviation for *head.*

hdqrs. Abbreviation for *headquarters.*

he \(')hē, ē\ *pron.* **1** The male person or animal mentioned before. **2** Any person; anyone. *He* who will may object.

head \'hed\ *n.* **1** The part of the body containing the brain, eyes, ears, nose, and mouth. **2** A picture or statue of this part of the body; as, a bronze *head* of Lincoln. **3** The side of a coin or medal bearing a head; as, *heads* or tails. **4** The mind; the understanding; as, a good *head* for figures. **5** Mental poise or balance; ability to think clearly; as, to keep one's *head* in time of danger. **6** An individual, especially when considered as one among a number — often used as a plural; as, thirty *head* of cattle. **7** Top, front, or upper part or position; as, the *head* of a bed; the *head* of a nail. **8** A person who is responsible for directing the actions and duties of others; as, the *head* of a company. **9** A headmaster of a school. **10** A position of leadership or command; as, the person at the *head* of the group. **11** Crisis. Events came to a *head.* **12** The part of a body of water farthest from the outlet; especially, the source of a body of flowing water; as, the *head* of the Nile River. **13** A body of water stored, as by damming a stream, in an elevated position so that it exerts pressure and when released will flow to a lower position, as to a water wheel, where it is needed. **14** The difference in elevation between a point where a fluid is and one where it is wanted, used as a measure of the energy available for the fluid to flow down or required to pump it up. **15** Pressure exerted by a fluid; as, getting up a good *head* of steam. **16** A compact mass, growing usually at the top of a stem, of leaves, as cabbage, or of leafstalks, as celery, or of flowers, as cauliflower. **17** The part of a boil or pimple at which it is likely to break. **18** The skin or membrane stretched across the frame of some percussion instruments, as a drum. — **out of one's head.** Delirious. — **over one's head.** **1** Beyond a person's ability to understand. **2** Ignoring or passing over one with a higher position. — *adj.* **1** Principal; as, a *head* cook. **2** Located at the head or front; as, *head* sails. **3** Coming from in front; as, a *head* wind. — *v.* **1** To be or put oneself at the head of; as, to *head* a revolt. **2** To lead, as in a race; to be or stand at the top or beginning of; as, to *head* the list. **3** To form a head, as a cabbage. **4** To go or point in a certain direction. A storm is *heading* this way — **head off.** To get in front of so as to stop or turn back; to turn aside; to check; as, to *head off* a runaway horse; to *head off* further argument.

head·ache \'hed-ˌāk\ *n.* **1** Pain in the head. **2** An annoying situation; an especially puzzling problem; a source of worry or trouble.

head·board \'hed-ˌbōrd, -ˌbȯrd\ *n.* The upright section forming the head of a bed.

head·dress \'he(d)-ˌdres\ *n.* A covering or ornament for the head.

head·ed \'hed-əd\ *adj.* **1** Having a head or heading. **2** Formed into a head; as, loosely-*headed* lettuce.

ancient Egyptian headdress

head·er \'hed-r\ *n.* **1** A fall or plunge headfirst. **2** A harvesting machine that cuts off the heads of grain and carries them up into a wagon.

head·first \'hed-'fərst\ *adv.* or *adj.* With the head foremost; headlong; as, to fall *headfirst* down the stairs; to rush *headfirst* into danger.

head·fore·most \'hed-'fōr-ˌmōst, -'fȯr-\ *adv.* or *adj.* Headfirst.

head·gear \'hed-ˌgir\ *n.* **1** A hat, bonnet, cap, or other headdress. **2** Harness for a horse's head.

headier. Comparative of *heady.*

headiest. Superlative of *heady.*

head·ing \'hed-ing\ *n.* That which stands at the

head, top, or beginning, as of a letter, a newspaper article, or a chapter in a book.

head·land \'hed-lənd\ *n.* A point of land jutting out into the sea; a cape or promontory.

head·less \'hed-ləs\ *adj.* **1** Having no head. **2** Without a leader. **3** Showing a lack of brains or prudence; foolish.

head·light \'hed-ˌlīt\ *n.* A light at the front of a vehicle, as a bicycle, an automobile, or a locomotive.

head·line \'hed-ˌlīn\ *n.* **1** A line at the top of a page, as in a book, giving a title or heading. **2** The title over an item or article in a newspaper.

head·long \'hed-'lȯng\ *adv.* **1** Headfirst. **2** Rashly; hastily; as, to dash *headlong* into traffic. — \-ˌlȯng\ *adj.* **1** Rash; hasty. **2** Plunging headfirst; as, a *headlong* dive into the water.

head·man \'hed-mən, -'man\ *n.; pl.* **head·men** \-mən, -'men\. A leader, as of a tribe, clan, or village; a chief.

head·mas·ter \'hed-ˌmast-r, -'mast-r\ *n.* In some schools, the head of the school; a principal.

head-on \'hed-ˌȯn, -ˌän\ *adj.* Having the head or front facing; head to head; front to front; as, a *head-on* collision.

head·phone \'hed-ˌfōn\ *n.* An earphone.

head·piece \'hed-ˌpēs\ *n.* **1** Any covering or fitting for the head, as a helmet, a hat, or an attachment with earphones. **2** The head; brains; understanding. **3** A decorative design at the head of a chapter.

head·quar·ters \'hed-ˌkwȯrt-rz, (')hed-'kwȯrt-\ *n. sing. and pl.* **1** The quarters or place occupied by a commanding officer of an army, a police force, or similar body. **2** Any center of authority or power; as, the *headquarters* of an insurance company.

head·ship \'hed-ˌship\ *n.* Chief authority; chief position.

heads·man \'hedz-mən\ *n.; pl.* **heads·men** \-mən\. An executioner who beheads condemned persons.

head·stand \'hed-ˌstand\ *n.* The gymnastic feat of standing on one's head, usually with support from the hands.

head·stone \'hed-ˌstōn\ *n.* A memorial stone placed at the head of a grave.

head·strong \'hed-ˌstrȯng\ *adj.* **1** Not easily controlled or managed; self-willed; stubborn; as, a *headstrong* child. **2** Moved or caused by stubbornness; as, a *headstrong* action. — For synonyms see *willful.*

head·wa·ters \'hed-ˌwȯt-rz, -ˌwät-\ *n.* The source and upper part of a stream.

head·way \'hed-ˌwā\ *n.* **1** Motion forward, as of a ship. **2** Progress. **3** Clear space, as under an arch, sufficient to allow easy passing underneath.

head·wind \'hed-ˌwind\ *n.* or **head wind.** A wind blowing in a direction directly opposite to the course of a ship or an aircraft.

head·work \'hed-ˌwərk\ *n.* Mental work or effort; thinking.

heady \'hed-ē\ *adj.;* **head·i·er; head·i·est. 1** Willful; rash. **2** Apt to affect or go to one's head; as, *heady* wine; a *heady* height.

heal \'hēl\ *v.* **1** To make healthy or whole; to cure; as, a wound that is hard to *heal;* a life devoted to *healing* the sick. **2** To grow healthy or whole; to return to a sound condition; as, a cut that *heals* slowly.

health \'helth\ *n.* **1** The condition of being well, or hale; freedom from illness or disease; as, to regain one's *health* rapidly after an illness. **2** The general condition of the body; as, to have good *health;* to be in poor *health.* **3** A wish of health and happiness; as, to drink a *health.*

health·ful \'helth-fəl\ *adj.* **1** Serving to build up health; good for the health; wholesome; as, *healthful* exercise. Milk is a *healthful* drink. **2** Enjoying health; sound; healthy. — For synonyms see *healthy.* — **health·ful·ly** \-fə-lē\ *adv.*

health·i·ly \'helth-l-ē\ *adv.* In a healthy manner.

healthy \'hel-thē\ *adj.;* **health·i·er; health·i·est. 1** Being sound and well; free from disease. **2** Showing health; as, a *healthy* complexion. **3** Aiding or building up health; wholesome; healthful; as, a *healthy* climate.

— The words *healthful* and *wholesome* are synonyms of *healthy: healthy* usually describes either something bringing about a good physical, mental, or moral condition or this condition itself; *healthful* applies especially to something producing good physical health, as adequate sleep and exercise, or proper food; *wholesome* usually suggests a sound mind, lively spirit, and, especially, good character, or anything helping to promote these.

heap \'hēp\ *n.* **1** A pile; a piled-up mass; as, a *heap* of earth; a rubbish *heap.* **2** A great amount or number; as, *heaps* of people; a *heap* of fun. — *v.* **1** To pile or collect in a heap; as, to *heap* up fallen leaves. **2** To give in large amounts; to load; as, to *heap* a plate with food. **3** To fill more than just barely full; as, a basket *heaped* to the brim.

hear \'hir\ *v.;* **heard** \'hərd\; **hear·ing** \'hir-ing\. **1** To take in through the ear; to gain knowledge of through the sense of hearing; as, to *hear* a car go by. **2** To have the faculty of taking in sounds through the ear. Some deaf persons cannot *hear* at all; others can *hear* slightly. **3** To give attention to; to listen to; as, to *hear* both sides of a story. **4** To examine or judge by listening to answers or explanations; as, to *hear* a recitation in class; to *hear* a case in a law court. **5** To receive information through or as if through the ear; to be told or informed; to get news of or from; as, to *hear* of a friend's illness; to *hear* from a cousin living abroad. — **hear·er,** *n.*

hear·ing \'hir-ing\ *n.* **1** The act or power of taking in sound through the ear; the sense by which a person hears; as, to have normal *hearing;* to be a bit hard of *hearing.* **2** A chance to be heard; as, to give both sides a fair *hearing.* **3** Distance within which sounds may be heard; as, to stay within *hearing.* **4** In law, a listening to arguments or proofs; in criminal cases, a preliminary examination of an accused person.

heark·en or **hark·en** \ˈhärk-n, ˈhȧrk-n\ *v.;* **heark·ened** or **hark·ened**; **heark·en·ing** or **hark·en·ing** \-n(-)ing\. To listen; to hark.

hear·say \ˈhir-ˌsā\ *n.* Something heard from another person but not known to be true; report; common talk or gossip.

hearse \ˈhərs\ *n.* [From the earlier meaning "coffin", this derived from medieval English *herse* meaning "a harrow-shaped frame for holding candles over a coffin", there derived from medieval French, meaning literally "harrow".] **1** *Archaic.* A bier. **2** A vehicle for carrying the dead to the grave.

heart \ˈhärt, ˈhȧrt\ *n.* **1** A hollow muscular organ of the body, the walls of which expand and contract so as to keep the blood moving through the arteries and veins. **2** The part nearest the center; as, the *heart* of a forest; the *heart* of a flower. **3** The most essential part of any body or system. **4** Anything resembling a heart in shape. **5** Human feelings; affection; kindness; as, a man seemingly without *heart.* **6** Courage; spirit; as, to take *heart.* **7** Mood; as, with a merry *heart.* **8** The real meaning; hidden meaning; as, to get to the *heart* of a subject. **9** Memory; as, to learn by *heart.* **10** A person loved or admired; as, dear *heart;* a sailing ship manned by a crew of stout *hearts.* **11** A playing card marked with red heart-shaped figures. **12** [in the plural] The suit made up of such cards or a game in which the object is to avoid taking cards belonging to this suit.

heart, 4

heart·ache \ˈhärt-ˌāk, ˈhȧrt-\ *n.* Sorrow; grief; anguish of mind.

heart·beat \ˈhärt-ˌbēt, ˈhȧrt-\ *n.* The throbbing movement or a single throbbing movement of the heart; as, to count one's *heartbeats.*

heart·break \ˈhärt-ˌbrāk, ˈhȧrt-\ *n.* Crushing sorrow or grief.

heart·break·ing \ˈhärt-ˌbrāk-ing, ˈhȧrt-\ *adj.* **1** Causing deep grief or sorrow; as, the *heartbreaking* cries of a child in pain. **2** Extremely trying or difficult; testing strength and courage to the full; as, the *heartbreaking* climb to the summit of a mountain. — **heart·break·ing·ly,** *adv.*

heart·bro·ken \ˈhärt-ˌbrōk-n, ˈhȧrt-\ *adj.* Overcome by sorrow. — **heart·bro·ken·ly,** *adv.*

heart·burn \ˈhärt-ˌbərn, ˈhȧrt-\ *n.* **1** A burning sensation about the heart, caused by acids rising from the stomach into the esophagus. **2** Also **heart·burn·ing.** Envy; jealousy.

heart·en \ˈhärt-n, ˈhȧrt-n\ *v.;* **heart·ened**; **heart·en·ing** \-n(-)ing\. To encourage; to cheer up; as, to be *heartened* by the confidence of a friend; *heartening* cheers from the stands.

heart·felt \ˈhärt-ˌfelt, ˈhȧrt-\ *adj.* Deeply felt; sincere; as, *heartfelt* thanks.

hearth \ˈhärth, ˈhȧrth\ *n.* **1** The floor of a fireplace. **2** A fireplace. **3** The fireside; the home. **4** The lowest part of a blast furnace, in which the molten metal and slag are collected.

hearth·side \ˈhärth-ˌsīd, ˈhȧrth-\ *n.* The part of a room close to the hearth; the fireside; the home.

hearth·stone \ˈhärth-ˌstōn, ˈhȧrth-\ *n.* A stone or paving forming a hearth; the fireside; the home.

heart·i·ly \ˈhärt-l-ē, ˈhȧrt-\ *adv.* **1** With sincerity, good will, zest, or enthusiasm; as, to set to work *heartily;* to eat *heartily.* **2** Cordially; as, to make a guest feel *heartily* welcome. **3** Completely; thoroughly; as, to be *heartily* sick of someone's complaints.

heart·land \ˈhärt-ˌland, ˈhȧrt-, -lənd\ *n.* A central land area, especially one thought of as economically and militarily self-sufficient and therefore able to control the land mass around it.

heart·less \ˈhärt-ləs, ˈhȧrt-\ *adj.* **1** Without courage, zeal, or spirit. **2** Without kindly feeling; without pity; unfeeling. — **heart·less·ly,** *adv.*

heart-rend·ing or **heart·rend·ing** \ˈhärt-ˌrending, ˈhȧrt-\ *adj.* Causing mental anguish or distress; as, a *heart-rending* cry. — **heart-rend·ing·ly** or **heart·rend·ing·ly,** *adv.*

hearts·ease or **heart's-ease** \ˈhärts-ˌēz, ˈhȧrts-\ *n.* **1** Peace of mind. **2** Any of several wild or garden flowers, as the wild pansy, a blue-flowered mint, and a variety of violet.

heart·sick \ˈhärt-ˌsik, ˈhȧrt-\ *adj.* Sick at heart; very unhappy; despondent.

heart·sore \ˈhärt-ˌsōr, ˈhȧrt-, -ˌsȯr\ *adj.* Grieved; showing grief.

heart·string \ˈhärt-ˌstring, ˈhȧrt-\ *n.* **1** A nerve once believed to sustain the heart. **2** [in the plural] The deepest emotions or affections; as, a story that tugged at one's *heartstrings.*

heart-to-heart \ˈhärt-tə-ˈhärt, ˈhȧrt-tə-ˈhȧrt\ *adj.* Sincere; frank.

heart-whole \ˈhärt-ˌhōl, ˈhȧrt-\ *adj.* **1** Having the affections free; not in love. **2** Sincere.

heart·wood \ˈhärt-ˌwu̇d, ˈhȧrt-\ *n.* The wood, usually darker colored, in the central part of the trunk of a tree.

hearty \ˈhärt-ē, ˈhȧrt-ē\ *adj.;* **heart·i·er**; **heart·i·est.** **1** Coming from the heart; sincere; cordial; as, a *hearty* welcome. **2** Energetic; as, a willing and *hearty* worker. **3** Strong; healthy; as, a hale and *hearty* old man. **4** Satisfying and abundant; as, a *hearty* meal. **5** Requiring or enjoying a good deal of food; as, a *hearty* appetite; a *hearty* eater. — *n.; pl.* **heart·ies.** In sailors' talk, a comrade; a sailor.

heat \ˈhēt\ *n.* **1** A form of energy that causes a body to rise in temperature. **2** High temperature; a period of hot weather; as, to stay inside during the *heat* of the day. **3** Warmth or intensity, as of feeling or activity; as, in the *heat* of anger; during the *heat* of an argument. **4** A single race in a contest that includes two or more races. — *v.* **1** To make hot; to become hot; as, to *heat* water. **2** To excite or inflame; to arouse; as, a *heated* quarrel. — **heat·ed·ly** \ˈhēt-əd-lē\ *adv.*

heat·er \'hēt-r\ *n.* A thing that heats, as a stove, furnace, or radiator.

heath \'hēth\ *n.* **1** An open level tract of land overgrown with low shrubs. **2** A low evergreen shrub having whorls of needlelike leaves and clusters of small white, pink, or yellow cup-shaped flowers, or any of a number of related woody plants, as arbutus, azalea, mountain laurel, or rhododendron.

hea·then \'hēth-n\ *n.; pl.* **hea·thens** or **hea·then.** **1** A person who does not acknowledge and worship the God of the Bible; a person who is neither Jewish, Christian, nor Moslem; a pagan. **2** An irreligious person. — *adj.* Pagan; having to do with heathens; as, *heathen* lands or customs.

hea·then·ish \'hēth-n-ish\ *adj.* Of or like the heathen.

heath·er \'heth-r\ *n.* An evergreen bush with small needle-like leaves, and flowers forming close, one-sided spikes, common on the heaths of Scotland and the north of England.

heat·ing element \'hēt-ing\. The part of an electrical heating appliance which changes electrical energy into heat by offering great resistance to the passage of an electrical current.

heat·stroke \'hēt-ˌstrōk\ *n.* Exhaustion or illness caused by exposure to excessive heat.

heave \'hēv\ *v.;* **heaved** \'hēvd\ or **hove** \'hōv\; **heav·ing.** **1** To lift; to raise with an effort; as, to *heave* a trunk onto a truck. **2** To throw; to cast; to hurl; as, to *heave* a rock. **3** To utter with an effort; as, to *heave* a sigh. **4** To rise and fall repeatedly, as the breast in deep breathing. **5** To be thrown up or raised. The ground *heaved* during the earthquake. — **heave in sight.** To seem to rise above the horizon and come into sight. — **heave to.** To bring a vessel to a stop. — *n.* **1** An effort to lift, raise, or move something. **2** A regular rising and falling, as of the breast with deep breathing.

heav·en \'hev-n\ *n.* **1** [usually in the plural] The sky; the place where the sun, moon and stars appear. **2** The dwelling place of God. **3** [with a capital] Providence. **4** Any place or condition of the greatest happiness, often regarded as the abode or condition of the blessed dead.

heav·en·ly \'hev-n-lē\ *adj.* **1** Of, relating to, or in heaven or the heavens; as, *heavenly* bodies such as the sun, moon, and stars. **2** Divine; sacred; blessed; as, *heavenly* grace. **3** Supremely delightful; as, a *heavenly* day.

heav·en·ward \'hev-n-wərd\ *adj.* or *adv.* Toward heaven.

heav·i·ly \'hev-l-ē\ *adv.* **1** With weight or as if with weight; as, to bear down *heavily;* to be *heavily* burdened with cares. **2** Slowly and laboriously; as, to breathe *heavily.* **3** Severely; as, *heavily* punished. **4** Thickly; as, a *heavily* populated district.

heavy \'hev-ē\ *adj.;* **heav·i·er; heav·i·est.** **1** Hard to lift or carry; weighty. **2** Not easy to bear; hard to endure; as, *heavy* troubles. **3** Deep; as, a *heavy* sleep. **4** Very large; unusual in amount; as, a *heavy* rain; *heavy* traffic. **5** Burdened; bowed down with grief; as, a *heavy* heart. **6** Gloomy; dull; as, *heavy* skies. **7** Not easily digested; as, *heavy* food. **8** Above the usual or standard weight; as, a *heavy* overcoat.

heavy water. Any water heavier than ordinary water; especially, water containing hydrogen that is twice as heavy as ordinary hydrogen.

heav·y·weight \'hev-ē-ˌwāt\ *n.* **1** A person or thing of more than average weight. **2** A wrestler or boxer in the heaviest of the classes; especially, one weighing 175 pounds or over.

He·brew \'hēb-ˌrü\ *adj.* Of or relating to Hebrews or Jews. — *n.* **1** An Israelite; a Jew. **2** The language of the ancient Hebrews, in which most of the Old Testament was written. **3** The modern form of this language; the official language of modern Israel.

heck·le \'hek-l\ *v.;* **heck·led; heck·ling** \-l(-)ing\. To interrupt with questions or comments, usually with the intention of annoying or hindering; to badger; as, to *heckle* an umpire or a public speaker.

hec·tic \'hek-tik\ *adj.* **1** Showing signs of suffering from a wasting disease, such as tuberculosis; feverish; as, a *hectic* flush. **2** Filled with excitement or confusion.

hec·tor \'hekt-r\ *v.;* **hec·tored; hec·tor·ing** \-r(-)ing\. To bully; to bluster.

he'd \(')hēd, ēd\. A contraction of *he had, he should,* or *he would.*

hedge \'hej\ *n.* **1** A thick growth of shrubbery; especially, one planted as a fence or boundary. **2** A barrier of any kind. — *v.;* **hedged; hedg·ing.** **1** To surround or protect with or as if with a hedge; as, to *hedge* a garden. **2** To obstruct, as with a barrier; as, to be *hedged* in with rules and regulations. **3** To avoid giving a direct or definite answer or a promise; as, to *hedge* when asked to support a candidate for office.

hedge·hog \'hej-ˌhȯg, -ˌhäg\ *n.* **1** A European insect-eating mammal having sharp spines mixed with the hair on its back and able to roll itself up into a spiny ball. **2** The porcupine.

hedge·hop \'hej-ˌhäp\ *v.;* **hedge·hopped; hedge-hop·ping.** To fly an airplane so low that it is sometimes necessary to climb to avoid such obstacles as trees or hedges.

hedge·row \'hej-ˌrō\ *n.* A row of shrubs or trees planted to enclose or separate fields; a hedge.

heed \'hēd\ *v.* To pay or give careful attention to; to take notice of; to mind; as, to *heed* advice; to *heed* a warning. — *n.* Notice; attention; as, to pay no *heed* to a warning.

heed·ful \'hēd-fəl\ *adj.* Mindful; taking heed; as, to be *heedful* of the rights of others. — **heed·ful·ly** \-fə-lē\ *adv.*

heed·less \'hēd-ləs\ *adj.* Taking no notice; without heed; careless; thoughtless; as, to be *heedless* of danger or of consequences; *heedless* drivers. — **heed·less·ly,** *adv.*

heel \'hēl\ *n.* **1** The back part of the human foot,

behind the arch and below the ankle; the corresponding part of an animal's limb. **2** The part of a stocking or shoe that covers the heel. **3** The solid part of a shoe that supports the heel. **4** Anything thought of as being like a heel, as the crust at the end of a loaf of bread or the back part of the bowl of a spoon. — *v.* To put a heel on, as a shoe.

heel \'hēl\ *v.* To lean to one side, as a ship; to tilt. — *n.* The action or the amount of heeling.

heft \'heft\ *n.* Weight. — *v.* **1** To heave; to lift. **2** To test the weight of something by lifting it.

hefty \'hef-tē\ *adj.*; **heft·i·er**; **heft·i·est.** Heavy; weighty.

heif·er \'hef-r\ *n.* A young cow; a cow that has not had a calf.

heigh-ho \'hī-'hō, 'hā-'hō\ *interj.* An exclamation expressing any of various emotions or states of mind from sadness and disappointment to satisfaction and good cheer.

height \'hīt, 'hītth\ *n.* **1** The condition of being raised up to some distance; the state of being high. **2** The measure of an object from its base to its top; as, a man six feet in *height.* The exact *height* of the mountain is not known. **3** The highest point or part; the summit. The enemy shelled the city from the surrounding *heights.* **4** The utmost degree; as, the *height* of foolishness. **5** The point of greatest intensity; climax; as, at the very *height* of a storm.

— The words *altitude* and *elevation* are synonyms of *height: height* is a general term that usually suggests the measurement of a thing from its lowest point to its highest; *altitude,* a more technical term, may indicate the distance of something above a given level, as sea level or ground level, and is likely to suggest extremely great distance; *elevation* is also technical and usually refers to the height to which a thing is or can be raised.

height·en \'hīt-n\ *v.*; **height·ened**; **height·en·ing** \-n(-)ing\. **1** To make or become high or higher. **2** To increase; to make more marked or outstanding; as, to *heighten* a contrast; the girl's embarrassment *heightened* the color in her face.

hei·nous \'hā-nəs\ *adj.* Wicked in the extreme, as a crime; atrocious; hateful. — **hei·nous·ly,** *adv.*

heir \'ar, 'er\ *n.* **1** A person who inherits or is entitled to inherit property. **2** A person who has legal claim to a title or a throne when the person holding it dies.

heir apparent; *pl.* **heirs apparent.** An heir who cannot legally be deprived of his right to succeed, as to a throne or a title, if he survives the present holder.

heir·ess \'ar-əs, 'er-\ *n.* A female heir, especially one who has inherited or will inherit great wealth.

heir·loom \'ar-,lüm, 'er-\ *n.* Any piece of personal property that is handed down by inheritance; especially, any such property owned by a family for several generations.

heir presumptive; *pl.* **heirs presumptive.** An heir who would succeed, as to a throne or a title, if the holder were to die at once but whose right to succeed could be lost through the birth of a nearer relative.

held. Past tense and past part. of *hold.*

hel·i·cop·ter \'hel-ə-,käpt-r, 'hē-lə-\ *n.* An aircraft that is supported in the air by propellers revolving on a vertical axis.

helicopter

he·li·o·graph \'hē-lē-ə-,graf, 'hēl-yə-\ *n.* An apparatus for signaling by means of the sun's rays reflected from a mirror. — *v.* To signal by means of a heliograph.

he·lio·trope \'hēl-yə-,trōp\ *n.* **1** A garden plant with hairy leaves and small fragrant white or purple flowers. **2** A reddish-purple color. **3** The scent of the garden heliotrope.

he·li·ot·ro·pism \,hē-lē-'ä-trə-,piz-m\ *n.* The natural turning of a plant or part of a plant away from or toward the sun's rays.

he·li·port \'hē-lə-,pōrt, 'hel-ə-, -,pȯrt\ *n.* An airport for helicopters.

he·li·um \'hē-lē-əm, 'hēl-yəm\ *n.* [From scientific Latin, there derived from Greek *helios* meaning "sun" and so called because it was first discovered in the sun's atmosphere.] A colorless gaseous chemical element separated from the natural gases with which it chiefly occurs and used in balloons and airships because it will not burn and because it is, next to hydrogen, the lightest gas.

hell \'hel\ *n.* **1** The abode of souls after death. **2** The place or state of punishment for the wicked after death; the home of evil spirits. **3** Any place or condition of misery or wickedness. **4** Anything that causes torment.

he'll \(')hēl, ēl\. A contraction of *he will* or *he shall.*

hell·ben·der \'hel-,bend-r\ *n.* A salamander common in the streams of the Ohio Valley.

hel·le·bore \'hel-ə-,bōr, -,bȯr\ *n.* **1** A plant related to the buttercup, with white, greenish, or purplish flowers, and roots that are dried and used in medicine. **2** A tall coarse herb of the lily family with a thick poisonous rootstock that in dried and powdered form is used as an insecticide.

Hel·lene \'hel-,ēn\ *n.* A Greek.

Hel·len·ic \hə-'len-ik, he-\ *adj.* Of or relating to the Hellenes, or Greeks; Greek.

hell·gram·mite \'hel-grə-,mīt\ *n.* The larva of a lacy-winged insect, found under stones in streams and used as a fish bait.

hell·ish \'hel-ish\ *adj.* Of hell; befitting hell; infernal; devilish. — **hell·ish·ly,** *adv.*

hel·lo \hə-'lō, he-\ *interj.* An exclamation used to call attention or to greet people, especially in telephoning.

helm \'helm\ *n.* **1** The steering apparatus of a ship, especially the tiller or wheel. **2** The place, position, or duty of one who is in command; as, to be at the *helm* of a growing business.

helm \'helm\ *n. Archaic.* A helmet.

hel·met \'hel-mət\ *n.* Any of various protective coverings for the head, as the headpiece of a suit of armor, a metal hat forming part of the battle dress of a soldier, a padded leather head covering worn by a football player or racing driver, or a cork-lined broad-brimmed hat worn as protection against the sun.

helms·man \'helmz-mən\ *n.; pl.* **helms·men** \-mən\. The man at the helm; the person who steers.

hel·ot \'hel-ət, 'hē-lət\ *n.* A slave; a serf; a bondman.

help \'help\ *v.* **1** To aid; to assist; as, to *help* someone home; to *help* with the dishes. **2** To furnish with relief, as from pain or disease; as, a medicine that *helps* a headache. **3** To prevent; to hinder; to avoid; as, a mistake that could not be *helped.* One cannot *help* noticing the change. **4** To serve; to give food to, as at table; as, to *help* oneself to butter. — *n.* **1** The act of helping; aid; assistance; as, to give *help;* to thank someone for his *help.* **2** The state of being helped; relief; as, a situation that is beyond *help.* **3** A person or a thing that helps; as, a *help* in time of trouble. **4** A hired helper or a whole body of hired helpers; as, to hire additional *help* in a business.

help·er \'help-r\ *n.* One that helps; an assistant; especially, a person who helps with manual labor; as, a plumber's *helper.*

help·ful \'help-fəl\ *adj.* Furnishing help; assisting; useful; as, a *helpful* neighbor; a *helpful* reference book. — **help·ful·ly** \-fə-lē\ *adv.*

help·ing \'help-ing\ *n.* **1** The act of one who helps. **2** A portion, as of food to which one is helped; a serving.

helping verb. An auxiliary verb.

help·less \'help-ləs\ *adj.* **1** Without help. **2** Unable to help or aid oneself; weak; defenseless. — **help·less·ly**, *adv.*

help·mate \'help-,māt\ or **help·meet** \-,mēt\ *n.* A helper; especially, a wife.

hel·ter-skel·ter \'helt-r-'skelt-r\ *adv.* In hurry and confusion; in disorder. — *adj.* Hurried and disorderly.

helve \'helv\ *n.* The handle of an ax, hatchet, or similar implement. — *v.;* **helved**; **helv·ing**. To fit with a helve.

hem \'hem\ *n.* A border of a garment or cloth; especially, one made by folding back an edge and sewing it down. — *v.;* **hemmed**; **hem·ming**. **1** To make a hem on; to finish with a hem; as, to *hem* a napkin. **2** To surround completely; to enclose and confine; as, a town *hemmed* in by flood waters; to feel *hemmed* about by restrictions.

hem \'hem\ *interj.* An exclamation used to call attention, to express doubt or hesitation, or to represent a clearing of the throat. — *v.;* **hemmed**; **hem·ming**. To make a sound somewhat like that made by a person clearing the throat; to hesitate in speaking; as, to *hem* and haw.

he·mip·ter·ous \he-'mipt-r-əs\ *adj.* Belonging to a large order of insects of which the bedbug and chinch bug are members, having flattened bodies, two pairs of wings, and heads equipped with piercing and sucking organs.

hem·i·sphere \'hem-ə-,sfir\ *n.* **1** The half of a sphere. **2** One of the halves of the earth as divided by the equator (**Northern Hemisphere** and **Southern Hemisphere**) or by a meridian (**Eastern Hemisphere** and **Western Hemisphere**). — **hem·i·spher·ic** \,hem-ə-'sfir-ik, -'sfer-\ or **hem·i·spher·i·cal** \-ik-l\ *adj.*

hem·lock \'hem-,läk\ *n.* **1** Any of several poisonous herbs having finely cut leaves and small white flowers. **2** An evergreen tree of the pine family with deeply furrowed bark and drooping branches bearing dark green foliage and backward-bending cones.

he·mo·glo·bin \'hē-mə-,glōb-n, ,hē-mə-'glōb-n\ *n.* An iron-containing substance that gives the red blood cells their color and that in the lungs combines loosely with oxygen which it carries to the body tissues and releases for their use.

he·mo·phil·ia \,hē-mə-'fil-ē-ə\ *n.* A tendency, usually hereditary, to uncontrollable bleeding even from slight wounds.

hem·or·rhage \'hem-r(-)ij\ *n.* In medicine, any discharge of blood from the blood vessels; especially, a discharge caused by injury.

hemp \'hemp\ *n.* A tall Asiatic plant related to the mulberry family, widely grown for its tough woody fiber, used in making cloth, matting, and rope, and for its flowers, from which hashish is made.

hemp·en \'hemp-n\ *adj.* Made of hemp; like hemp.

hem·stitch \'hem-,stich\ *v.* To ornament at the top of a hem by drawing out a few parallel threads and fastening the cross threads in a series of clusters. — *n.* Ornamental needlework done by hemstitching material, or the stitch used. — **hem·stitch·er**, *n.*

hen \'hen\ *n.* **1** The female of the domestic fowl. **2** The female of any bird.

hence \'hen(t)s\ *adv.* **1** *Archaic.* From this place. **2** From this time; as, a week *hence.* **3** As a result; therefore; for this reason — used as a conjunction.

hence·forth \'hen(t)s-,fōrth, -,fȯrth\ *adv.* From this time on.

hence·for·ward \(')hen(t)s-'fȯr-wərd\ *adv.* Henceforth.

hench·man \'hench-mən\ *n.; pl.* **hench·men** \-mən\. **1** A trusted follower or supporter. **2** A political follower, especially one serving for personal advantage.

hen·na \'hen-ə\ *n.* **1** A tropical shrub whose leaves yield a reddish-orange dye and a cosmetic for tinting the hair red. **2** A brown color of a reddish-orange shade. — *v.;* **hen·naed** \-əd\; **hen·na·ing**. To dye or tint with henna; as, *hennaed* hair.

hen·nery \'hen-r-ē\ *n.; pl.* **hen·ner·ies**. **1** A poultry farm. **2** An enclosure for keeping hens.

hen·pecked \'hen-,pekt\ *adj.* Ruled by one's wife;

nagged or constantly scolded by one's wife. — **hen·peck** \-ˌpek\ *v.*

he·pat·ic \hi-'pat-ik\ *adj.* [From Latin *hepaticus*, there borrowed from Greek, where it is derived from *hepar* meaning liver — see *hepatica.*] **1** Of or relating to the liver. **2** Affecting the liver. **3** Of or relating to a class of plants, the liverworts. — *n.* **1** A medicine affecting the liver. **2** A liverwort.

he·pat·i·ca \hi-'pat-ik-ə\ *n.* [From scientific Latin, there derived from Latin *hepaticus* meaning "of the liver", and so called from the liver-shaped leaves — see *hepatic.*] A hairy-stemmed woods plant that blooms with pink, white, blue, or purplish flowers in early spring.

hep·a·ti·tis \ˌhep-ə-'tīt-əs\ *n.* A virus disorder of the liver with fever and weakness.

hep·ta·gon \'hep-tə-ˌgän\ *n.* A figure with seven angles and seven sides.

hep·tag·o·nal \hep-'tag-n-əl\ *adj.* Having the form of a heptagon; seven-sided. — **hep·tag·o·nal·ly** \-ə-lē\ *adv.*

regular and irregular heptagons

her \(h)ər, r, 'hər\ *pron.* The form of the word *she* that is used as the object of a preposition or of a verb. — *adj.* Belonging to her; done by or to her; as, *her* doll; during *her* illness.

her·ald \'her-əld\ *n.* **1** An official in some countries who makes public announcements. **2** A person who has the care of genealogies and of the privileges of families to use coats of arms. **3** A person or thing that announces or foretells; a messenger. The robin is the *herald* of spring. — *v.* To give news of; to announce; to usher in.

he·ral·dic \hə-'ral-dik\ *adj.* Of or relating to heralds or to heraldry; as, *heraldic* emblems.

her·ald·ry \'her-əl-drē\ *n.; pl.* **her·ald·ries.** **1** The art or science of a herald; the science of tracing a person's family and determining what coat of arms he is entitled to have. **2** A coat of arms; a heraldic symbol. **3** Heraldic pomp or ceremony.

herb \'ərb, 'hərb\ *n.* **1** A plant that has more or less tender stalks and stems. **2** A plant used for making medicines and seasonings.

her·ba·ceous \hər-'bā-shəs\ *adj.* **1** Having a soft or fleshy, often green, stem. **2** Green and leaflike; as, *herbaceous* sepals.

herb·age \'ər-bij, 'hər-\ *n.* Herbs; green plants, especially those found in pastures; grass.

herb·al \'ərb-l, 'hərb-l\ *adj.* Relating to or made of herbs. — *n.* A book describing plants.

herb·al·ist \'ərb-l-əst, 'hərb-\ *n.* **1** A botanist. **2** A collector of herbs or a dealer in herbs.

her·bar·i·um \ˌhər-'ber-ē-əm\ *n.; pl.* **her·bar·i·ums** \-ē-əmz\ or **her·bar·ia** \-ē-ə\. **1** A collection of dried plants. **2** A room or building containing a collection of dried plants.

her·bi·vore \'hər-bə-ˌvōr, -ˌvȯr\ *n.* An animal feeding chiefly on herbage; especially, any of a group of mammals that feed mostly on herbage.

her·biv·o·rous \ˌhər-'biv-r(-)əs\ *adj.* Eating or living on plants. Cattle are *herbivorous.*

Her·cu·le·an \ˌhərk-yə-'lē-ən, ˌhər-'kyü-lē-ən\ *adj.* **1** Of or relating to Hercules. **2** [often with a small letter] Requiring or having the strength or size of Hercules; as, a statue of *Herculean* proportions; a *Herculean* task.

herd \'hərd\ *n.* **1** A number of beasts, especially of large animals, flocked together; as, a *herd* of cows. **2** People as a mass; a crowd. — *v.* **1** To join in a herd. **2** To form or put into a herd; to tend, lead, or drive as a herd; as, to *herd* cattle. — **herd·er,** *n.*

herds·man \'hərdz-mən\ *n.; pl.* **herds·men** \-mən\. A person who owns, keeps, or tends a flock or herd.

here \'hir\ *adv.* **1** In this place. Stand *here.* **2** To this place. Come *here.* **3** At this point; now. *Here* the game ended. *Here* goes! — *n.* This place. Let's get out of *here.* — *pron.* This. *Here's* to you.

here·about \'hir-ə-ˌbau̇t\ or **here·abouts** \-ˌbau̇ts\ *adv.* Near or around this place; near here; in this vicinity.

here·aft·er \hir-'aft-r\ *adv.* After this; in the future. — *n.* **1** The future. **2** The life after death.

here·by \hir-'bī, 'hir-ˌbī\ *adv.* By means of this.

he·red·i·tary \hə-'red-ə-ˌter-ē\ *adj.* **1** Passing from an ancestor to his heir; as, a *hereditary* title. **2** Holding an office or title by inheritance; as, a *hereditary* prince. **3** Capable of being passed from parent to child; as, a *hereditary* disease.

he·red·i·ty \hə-'red-ət-ē\ *n.; pl.* **he·red·i·ties.** **1** The sum of the characteristics of an individual derived from its ancestors. **2** The passing of characteristics from ancestors to a descendant.

here·in \hir-'in\ *adv.* In this.

here·of \hir-'əv, -'äv\ *adv.* Of this; concerning this.

here·on \hir-'ȯn, -'än\ *adv.* On or upon this.

her·e·sy \'her-ə-sē\ *n.; pl.* **her·e·sies.** **1** Religious opinion or teaching contrary to the fixed and accepted beliefs or doctrines of a church. **2** Any opinion contrary to a popular or generally accepted belief.

her·e·tic \'her-ə-ˌtik\ *n.* A person who believes or teaches something contrary to accepted beliefs, especially those of a church.

he·ret·i·cal \hə-'ret-ik-l\ *adj.* Containing heresy; of or characterized by heresy.

here·to·fore \'hirt-ə-ˌfōr, -ˌfȯr\ *adv.* Up to this time; formerly; in time past.

here·un·to \hir-'ən-tü, ˌhir-(ˌ)ən-'tü\ *adv.* To this; especially, to this document.

here·up·on \'hir-ə-ˌpȯn, -ˌpän\ *adv.* On this; hereon.

here·with \hir-'with, -'with\ *adv.* With this.

her·it·a·ble \'her-ət-əb-l\ *adj.* **1** Capable of being inherited. **2** Capable of inheriting. — **her·it·a·bil·i·ty** \ˌher-ət-ə-'bil-ət-ē\ *n.*

her·it·age \'her-ət-ij\ *n.* Something that is passed

on from one's ancestors; inheritance; birthright; as, our *heritage* of freedom.

her·maph·ro·dite \hər-'maf-rə-ˌdīt\ *n.* An animal or plant characterized by the presence of both male and female reproductive organs, a condition that is normal and functional in many plants and some lower animals but in the higher animals, including man, occurs only abnormally and with the organs imperfectly developed.

her·met·ic \hər-'met-ik\ *adj.* Made perfectly close or airtight. — **her·met·i·cal·ly** \-ik-l(-)ē\ *adv.*

her·mit \'hər-mət\ *n.* A person who lives apart from others, as for religious reasons.

her·mit·age \'hər-mət-ij\ *n.* A hermit's home; any secluded residence.

hermit crab. A small soft-bodied crab, common on most seacoasts, which lives in the empty shells of whelks and other gastropods.

her·nia \'hər-nē-ə, 'hərn-yə\ *n.* An abnormal protruding of a part through some opening in the cavity that normally contains it; especially, the protruding of a loop of the intestine through the walls of the abdomen.

he·ro \'hē-ˌrō, 'hir-ˌō\ *n.; pl.* **he·roes. 1** A man, especially a warrior, of the Greek epic or heroic age. **2** The chief male character in a story, play, or poem. **3** A person whose courageous life and deeds make him remembered and honored; as, the *heroes* of a nation's history. **4** A person who shows great courage; as, the *hero* of a disaster at sea.

he·ro·ic \hi-'rō-ik\ *adj.* **1** Of or about a hero or heroes; like or characteristic of heroes. **2** Brave; courageous; bold; daring; as, a *heroic* rescue. **3** Treating of heroes and their deeds; epic. **4** Larger than life size; very large; as, a *heroic* statue.

he·ro·i·cal \hi-'rō-ik-l\ *adj.* Heroic. — **he·ro·i·cal·ly** \-ik-l(-)ē\ *adv.*

he·ro·ics \hi-'rō-iks\ *n. pl.* **1** Extravagant display of heroic attitudes in actions or in words, especially when made chiefly for effect. **2** Heroic deeds.

her·o·in \'her-ə-wən\ *n.* A narcotic made from morphine.

her·o·ine \'her-ə-wən\ *n.* **1** A woman of courage and daring. **2** The chief female character in a story, poem, or play.

her·o·ism \'her-ə-ˌwiz-m\ *n.* Heroic qualities; heroic conduct; as, to receive a medal for *heroism* in war. — For synonyms see *courage*.

her·on \'her-ən\ *n.* A long-necked, long-legged wading bird having a long tapering bill, large wings, and soft plumage, as the **great blue heron,** a slaty-blue American species.

her·pe·tol·o·gy \ˌhərp-ə-'täl-ə-jē\ *n.* The study and classification of reptiles and amphibians. — **her·pe·tol·o·gist** \-jəst\ *n.*

her·ring \'her-ing\ *n.; pl.* **her·ring** or **her·rings.** A soft-finned, narrow-bodied food fish with forked tail, abundant in the north Atlantic Ocean.

her·ring·bone \'her-ing-ˌbōn\ *adj.* Resembling the pattern of a herring's spine; especially, arranged in rows of parallel lines that in any two successive rows slope at an angle to each other. — *n.* A herringbone arrangement or pattern. — *v.;* **her·ring·boned; her·ring·bon·ing. 1** To produce a herringbone pattern on a surface; to arrange in a herringbone pattern, as in piling lumber. **2** In skiing, to proceed by a method, as in going up a hill, that makes a herringbone pattern in the snow.

hers \'hərz\ *pron.* The form of the word *her* that is used to show possession when no noun follows. The book is *hers.*

her·self \(h)ər-'self, r-\ *pron.* **1** A form of the word *she* that is used to give emphasis or to show that the subject and object of a verb are the same person or thing. She *herself* did it. She hurt *herself.* **2** Her normal or true self. The girl did not seem *herself.*

he's \(')hēz, ēz\. A contraction of *he is* or *he has.*

hes·i·tance \'hez-ə-tən(t)s\ *n.* Hesitancy.

hes·i·tan·cy \'hez-ə-tən-sē\ *n.; pl.* **hes·i·tan·cies. 1** The quality or state of being hesitant; indecision. **2** The act of hesitating.

hes·i·tant \'hez-ə-tənt\ *adj.* Hesitating. — **hes·i·tant·ly,** *adv.*

hes·i·tate \'hez-ə-ˌtāt\ *v.;* **hes·i·tat·ed; hes·i·tat·ing. 1** To stop or pause because of forgetfulness, uncertainty, or inability to make up one's mind; as, to *hesitate* before answering. **2** To hold back because of scruples; to be reluctant; as, to *hesitate* to ask a favor. **3** To pause or falter in speaking; to stammer. — **hes·i·tat·ing** \-ˌtāt-ing\ *adj.* — **hes·i·tat·ing·ly,** *adv.*

hes·i·ta·tion \ˌhez-ə-'tāsh-n\ *n.* **1** The act of hesitating. **2** A pause, as from doubt, fear, or forgetfulness. **3** A faltering in speech; a stammering.

Hes·sian fly \'hesh-n\. A small two-winged fly or midge, the larvae of which suck the juices of wheat.

het·er·o·dox \'het-r-ə-ˌdäks, 'he-trə-\ *adj.* **1** Contrary to prevailing opinions, beliefs, or standards; not orthodox; especially, not orthodox in religion. **2** Holding or expressing beliefs or opinions that are not orthodox.

het·er·o·doxy \'het-r-ə-ˌdäks-ē, 'he-trə-\ *n.; pl.* **het·er·o·dox·ies. 1** The quality of being heterodox. **2** A heterodox opinion or doctrine.

het·er·o·ge·ne·ous \ˌhet-r-ə-'jē-nē-əs, ˌhe-trə-, -'jēn-yəs\ *adj.* Differing in kind; having unlike qualities; dissimilar; mixed; varied; not homogeneous; as, a *heterogeneous* society. A patchwork quilt is made of *heterogeneous* pieces of cloth. — **het·er·o·ge·ne·ous·ly,** *adv.*

hew \'hyü\ *v.;* **hewed** \'hyüd\; **hewed** \'hyüd\ or **hewn** \'hyün\; **hew·ing. 1** To chop or chop down; as, to *hew* logs; to *hew* trees. **2** To make or shape by cutting with an ax; as, to *hew* a beam; a cabin built of rough-*hewn* logs. — **hew·er** \'hyü-ər, 'hyủr\ *n.*

hex \'heks\ *n.* **1** A witch. **2** A magic spell; an enchantment; as, under a *hex;* to put a *hex* on an enemy. — *v.* To bewitch; to cast a spell over.

hex·a·gon \'heks-ə-ˌgän\ *n.* A figure with six angles and six sides.

hex·ag·o·nal \hek-'sag-n-əl\ *adj.* Having the form of a hexagon; six-sided. — **hex·ag·o·nal·ly** \-ə-lē\ *adv.*

hexagon

hex·am·e·ter \hek-'sam-ət-r\ *n.* In poetry, a line or verse having six metrical feet.

hey \'hā\ *interj.* An exclamation used to call attention or to express feelings such as surprise, joy, or wonder.

hey·day \'hā-ˌdā\ *n.* The time of greatest strength or vigor; as, a nation in the *heyday* of its power.

hi \'hī, 'hī-ē\ *interj.* An exclamation used as an informal greeting.

hi·a·tus \hī-'āt-əs\ *n.* **1** An opening; a gap, in space or in time; especially, a break occurring where a part is missing; as, a *hiatus* in an old manuscript. **2** A pause between two vowels each of which is to be distinctly pronounced, as in *co-operate.* **3** In radio and television, a summer vacation for a network program.

hi·ber·nate \'hīb-r-ˌnāt\ *v.;* **hi·ber·nat·ed; hi·ber·nat·ing.** To pass the winter hidden away, in a condition resembling sleep, as some animals do. — **hi·ber·na·tion** \ˌhīb-r-'nāsh-n\ *n.* — **hi·ber·na·tor** \'hīb-r-ˌnāt-r\ *n.*

hi·bis·cus \hi-'bis-kəs, hī-\ *n.* Any of a large group of shrubs and small trees of the mallow family with large, showy, bell-shaped flowers.

hic·cup or **hic·cough** \'hik-(ˌ)əp\ *n.* A gulping sound caused by sudden uncontrollable movements of muscles active in breathing. — *v.* To make a hiccup or hiccups; to have hiccups.

hick·o·ry \'hik-r(-)ē\ *n.; pl.* **hick·o·ries. 1** A tall North American tree of the walnut family, having a rough bark that peels off in strips, and bearing a hard-shelled edible nut (**hickory nut**). **2** The strong, tough, elastic wood of this tree.

hi·dal·go \hi-'dal-ˌgō\ *n.; pl.* **hi·dal·gos.** [From Spanish, there contracted from *hijo de algo* meaning literally "son of something".] A Spanish nobleman of the lower class of nobility.

hid·den hunger \'hid-n\. A deficiency caused by a diet that, even though full, is ill-balanced.

hide \'hīd\ *n.* The raw or dressed skin of an animal. — *v.;* **hid·ed; hid·ing. 1** To take the hide from. **2** To flog; to whip.

hide \'hīd\ *v.;* **hid** \'hid\; **hid·den** \'hid-n\ or **hid; hid·ing** \'hīd-ing\. **1** To put out of sight; to conceal; as, to *hide* a treasure. Squirrels *hide* nuts. **2** To keep from being known; as, to *hide* one's fear. **3** To keep from being seen; to obstruct the view of; as, clouds *hiding* the sun; a house *hidden* behind trees. **4** To keep or put oneself out of view; as, to *hide* in a closet.

hide-and-seek \ˌhīd-n-'sēk\ or **hide-and-go-seek** \-gō-'sēk\ *n.* A game in which the player who is "it" searches for the others, who have hidden themselves while he covered his eyes.

hide·bound \'hīd-ˌbau̇nd\ *adj.* **1** Having the skin adhering closely to the ribs and back — used of an animal. **2** Very obstinate and conservative in attitudes and opinions; narrow.

hid·e·ous \'hid-ē-əs\ *adj.* Horribly ugly; shocking and disgusting; frightful. — **hid·e·ous·ly,** *adv.*

hid·ing \'hīd-ing\ *n.* A flogging; a whipping.

hid·ing \'hīd-ing\ *n.* Concealment or a place of concealment; as, to go into *hiding.*

hie \'hī\ *v.;* **hied** \'hīd\; **hy·ing** or **hie·ing** \'hī-ing\. To hasten; to hurry.

hi·er·archy \'hī-ə-ˌrärk-ē, -ˌrȧrk-ē\ *n.; pl.* **hi·er·arch·ies. 1** A body of rulers, especially in a church, divided into ranks each of which is subordinate in authority to the one above. **2** A form of government in which the rulers are in ranks, each ruler being responsible to another in the rank above. **3** Any organization of persons or things according to rank or order of importance, or any series of persons or things classified in this way. — **hi·er·ar·chic** \ˌhī-ə-'rärk-ik, -'rȧrk-\ or **hi·er·ar·chi·cal** \-ik-l\ *adj.*

hi·er·o·glyph \'hī-ə-rə-ˌglif, 'hī-rə-\ *n.* A hieroglyphic.

hi·er·o·glyph·ic \ˌhī-ə-rə-'glif-ik, ˌhī-rə-\ *n.* **1** A character in the picture-writing of the ancient Egyptians or of certain other ancient peoples, as the Mexicans. **2** The method of writing in such characters. **3** Any obscure or unintelligible sign or symbol; [in the plural] any illegible writing.

hieroglyphics

hi-fi \'hī-'fī\ *n.* Short for *high fidelity.* — *adj.* Of, relating to, or characteristic of high fidelity; capable of faithful reproduction of sound; as, a *hi-fi* record player.

hig·gle·dy-pig·gle·dy \'hig-l-dē-'pig-l-dē\ *adv.* or *adj.* In confusion; topsy-turvy. — *n.; pl.* **hig·gle·dy-pig·gle·dies.** A confusion; a jumble.

high \'hī\ *adj.* **1** Reaching far above the ground or some other level; tall; lofty; as, a *high* building; a *high* mountain. **2** Reaching or extending upward from a certain level or point; as, a desk 30 inches *high.* **3** Advanced toward its fullness; as, *high* noon. **4** Above the average; beyond what is ordinary or usual; as, *high* prices; a *high* temperature. **5** Filled with joy; hilarious; as, in *high* spirits. **6** Chief; principal; of more than usual importance; above the average; as, a *high* priest; *high* rank. **7** Strong; powerful; as, *high* winds; *high* explosives. **8** Among the best; superior; as, *high* marks. **9** Complex in structure and physiology; as, the *higher* animals. **10** Pitched or sounding above some other sound; as, a *high* tone. **11** Dear in price; costly; as, fruit that is *high* for the time of year.
— The words *tall* and *lofty* are synonyms of *high: high* is a general word and usually describes something extending conspicuously far upward from its base, or something placed at a considerable height above the ground or above its usual level; *tall* generally suggests something that rises or grows high as compared with others of its kind; *lofty* is likely to suggest imposing height or qualities thought of

in terms of imposing height such as grandeur, dignity, or pride.

— *n.* **1** Something that is high, as a level, price, score, or speed; as, an all-time *high.* **2** The arrangement of gears in a transmission, as of an automobile, in such a position as to give the greatest speed to the propelling shaft. — *adv.* In or to a high degree or place; in a high manner; as, to live *high;* to fly *high.*

high and dry. **1** Out of the water; out of reach of the current or tide. **2** Out of the current of events, influence, or activity.

high·ball \'hī-ˌbȯl\ *n.* A drink of diluted alcoholic spirits served with ice in a tall glass.

high·born \'hī-'bȯrn\ *adj.* Of noble birth.

high·boy \'hī-ˌbȯi\ *n.* A piece of furniture consisting of a set of drawers mounted on a tablelike base or on a lowboy.

highboy

high·brow \'hī-ˌbraů\ *n.* A person of superior learning or culture; an intellectual person. — *adj.* Of, belonging to, or characteristic of a highbrow; as, *highbrow* attitudes.

high chair. A child's chair with long legs and a footrest.

high·fa·lu·tin \ˌhī-fə-'lüt-n\ or **high·fa·lu·ting** \-'lüt-n, -ing\ *adj.* High-flown; pretentious.

high fidelity. In electronics, the reproduction of sound with a high degree of faithfulness to the original, as by a radio or phonograph. — **high-fi·del·i·ty,** *adj.*

high-flown \'hī-'flōn\ *adj.* **1** Elevated; proud. **2** Not plain or simple; extravagant; as, *high-flown* language.

high frequency. In radio and television, any frequency in the range from 3 to 30 megacycles. — **high-fre·quen·cy,** *adj.*

high-grade \'hī-'grād\ *adj.* Of a grade rated as superior.

high·hand·ed \'hī-'han-dəd\ *adj.* Following one's own opinion or wishes; arbitrary; domineering. — **high·hand·ed·ly,** *adv.*

high-hat \'hī-'hat\ *n.* A snob. — *adj.* Characteristic of a high-hat; aristocratic; snobbish. — *v.;* **high-hat·ted; high-hat·ting.** To treat snobbishly; to act snobbishly.

high jinks \'jingks\. Wild or boisterous behavior.

high·land \'hī-lənd\ *n.* High or hilly country; a high plateau.

High·land·er \'hī-lənd-r\ *n.* **1** An inhabitant of the high regions of Scotland. **2** [in the plural] The Scottish regiments of the British army.

Highland fling. A Scottish folk dance performed usually by three or four dancers, and characterized by high kicking.

high·light \'hī-ˌlīt\ *n.* **1** One of the spots or areas on an object that reflect the most light. **2** The brightest spot in a painting or drawing. **3** Any event or scene of greatest interest; as, the *highlights* of a trip. — *v.;* **high·light·ed; high·light·ing.** **1** To throw a strong light upon. **2** To emphasize or make prominent in some way.

high·ly \'hī-lē\ *adv.* **1** In a high degree; extremely; very much; as, to be *highly* pleased; to come *highly* recommended. **2** With much approval; as, to speak *highly* of a person and his work.

high-mind·ed \'hī-'mīn-dəd\ *adj.* Having or showing high motives, thoughts, or feelings; idealistic; as, a *high-minded* man; a *high-minded* speech.

high·ness \'hī-nəs\ *n.* **1** The condition of being high; height. **2** [with a capital] A title of honor given to kings, princes, and others of high rank.

high-pres·sure \'hī-'presh-r\ *adj.* **1** Having a pressure much higher than normal air pressure. **2** Having a high atmospheric pressure as measured by a barometer. **3** Urgent; persistent; as, *high-pressure* salesmanship. — *v.;* **high-pres·sured; high-pres·sur·ing** \-r(-)ing\. To press a person with arguments and promises in order to persuade him to act according to one's wishes; as, to *high-pressure* a customer into buying.

high·road \'hī-ˌrōd\ *n.* A highway; a main road.

high school or **high·school** \'hī-ˌskül\ *n.* A school composed of the grades above those of the elementary school, and preparing students for college, business, or a trade.

high seas. The open sea or ocean; especially that part outside any country's jurisdiction.

high-sound·ing \'hī-'saůn-ding\ *adj.* Pompous or imposing in sound; as, *high-sounding* phrases.

high-spir·it·ed \'hī-'spir-ət-əd\ *adj.* **1** Bold; daring. **2** Animated; lively.

high-strung \'hī-'strəng\ *adj.* Highly sensitive or nervous.

high-test \'hī-ˌtest\ *adj.* Meeting a difficult test — used especially of certain gasolines that vaporize easily and thus enable an engine to start quickly in cold weather.

high tide. The tide of the sea when the water is at its highest flow.

high treason. Treason against the sovereign or the state.

high·way \'hī-ˌwā\ *n.* A main road; any public road.

high·way·man \'hī-ˌwā-mən\ *n.; pl.* **high·way·men** \-mən\. A person who robs travelers on a highway.

hike \'hīk\ *v.;* **hiked; hik·ing.** To take a long walk. — *n.* A long walk or tramp, especially in the country. — **hik·er,** *n.*

hi·lar·i·ous \hi-'lar-ē-əs, hī-, -'ler-\ *adj.* Noisily merry. — **hi·lar·i·ous·ly,** *adv.*

hi·lar·i·ty \hi-'lar-ət-ē, hī-\ *n.* Noisy merriment; hilarious behavior.

hill \'hil\ *n.* **1** An elevation of land, lower than a mountain, and usually rounded. **2** A little heap or mound of earth; as, *hills* made by ants. **3** A heap of earth around the root or roots of a plant; a plant or a cluster of plants so surrounded; as, a *hill* of potatoes or corn. — *v.* To make a hill; to surround with hills; as, to *hill* corn.

hill·bil·ly \'hil-ˌbil-ē\ *n.; pl.* **hill·bil·lies.** A backwoodsman or mountaineer, especially of the southern United States.

hill·man \'hil-mən\ *n.; pl.* **hill·men** \-mən\. **1** A man who lives in the hills; a mountaineer. **2** A man who climbs hills.

hill·ock \'hil-ək\ *n.* A small hill.

hill·side \'hil-ˌsīd\ *n.* The side of a hill.

hill·top \'hil-ˌtäp\ *n.* The top of a hill.

hilly \'hil-ē\ *adj.;* **hill·i·er; hill·i·est. 1** Having many hills; as, a *hilly* city; a *hilly* road. **2** Steep; as, a *hilly* climb.

hilt \'hilt\ *n.* A handle, as of a sword or dagger. — **up to the hilt.** To the limit; completely.

hi·lum \'hī-ləm\ *n.; pl.* **hi·la** \-lə\ or **hi·lums** \-ləmz\. In botany, the mark at the point of attachment of an ovule forming the eye, as of a bean.

him \im, (')him\ *pron.* The form of the word *he* that is used as the object of a preposition or of a verb.

him·self \(h)im-'self\ *pron.* **1** A form of the word *he* that is used to give emphasis or to show that the subject and object of a verb are the same person or thing. He *himself* did it. He hurt *himself.* **2** His normal or true self. The boy was not *himself* yesterday.

hind \'hīnd\ *n.* A farm hand.

hind \'hīnd\ *n.; pl.* **hinds** or **hind. 1** The female of the red deer. **2** Any of a number of spotted or speckled groupers.

hind \'hīnd\ *adj.;* **hind·er** \'hīnd-r\; **hind·most** \'hīn(d)-ˌmōst\ or **hind·er·most** \'hīnd-r-ˌmōst\. At the end or back; rear; as, the *hind* legs of a horse.

hind·er \'hīnd-r\ *adj.* Rear; posterior; hind.

hin·der \'hind-r\ *v.;* **hin·dered; hin·der·ing** \-r(-)ing\. To keep back or behind; to prevent starting, moving, or acting; to hamper. The ambulance was *hindered* by heavy traffic.

hind·most \'hīn(d)-ˌmōst\ or **hind·er·most** \'hīnd-r-ˌmōst\ *adj.* Farthest to the rear.

Hin·doo \'hin-ˌdü\ *adj.* Hindu. — *n.; pl.* **Hin·doos.** A Hindu; an Indian.

hind·quar·ter \'hīn(d)-ˌkwȯrt-r\ *n.* **1** The hind part of either half of a split carcass of beef, veal, lamb, or mutton. **2** [usually in the plural] The rear part or rump of an animal.

hin·drance \'hin-drən(t)s\ *n.* **1** A hindering; as, free from *hindrance.* **2** A person or a thing that hinders.

hind·sight \'hīn(d)-ˌsīt\ *n.* **1** The rear sight of a firearm. **2** Realization of the significance of an event only after it has taken place. *Hindsight* is easier than foresight.

Hin·du \'hin-ˌdü\ *adj.* **1** Of or relating to the people of India; Indian. **2** Of or relating to those people of India who follow the ancient religious and social system (**Hin·du·ism** \-ˌiz-m\) by which all men are divided by birth into castes. — *n.* **1** A native of India who accepts Hinduism. **2** A member of any of the native peoples of India.

hinge \'hinj\ *n.* **1** A jointed piece on which one surface, as a door, gate, or lid, turns or swings on another. **2** The joint in the shell of an oyster or clam. — *v.;* **hinged; hing·ing. 1** To furnish with or attach by a hinge or hinges. **2** To hang or turn as if on a hinge; to depend. The success of the plan *hinged* on this decision.

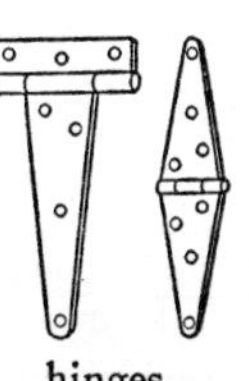
hinges

hinge joint. A joint between bones that permits motion only in one plane, as that between the humerus and the ulna.

hint \'hint\ *n.* A slight mention; an indirect suggestion or reminder; as, a *hint* of winter in the air. — *v.* To bring to mind by a hint; to make a hint; as, to *hint* at what one would like for Christmas.

hin·ter·land \'hint-r-ˌland\ *n.* **1** The region lying well inland from the coast. **2** A region far from cities or towns.

hip \'hip\ *interj.* An exclamation used to call to attention, as in beginning a cheer.

hip \'hip\ *n.* The part of the body that curves outward below the waist on either side formed by the side part of the pelvis and the upper part of the thigh.

hip \'hip\ *n.* The ripened fruit of a rosebush.

hip·bone \'hip-'bōn, -ˌbōn\ *n.* Either of two large compound bones that lie one on each side of the lower part of the trunk, providing points of attachment for the skeleton of the leg, and that fuse together in front and with the backbone in the rear to form a closed bony ring which supports the lower part of the trunk and the abdominal organs.

hip·po·drome \'hip-ə-ˌdrōm\ *n.* **1** In ancient times, an oval track for horse races and chariot races. **2** An arena for the staging of horse shows, rodeos, and circuses.

hip·po·pot·a·mus \ˌhip-ə-'pät-m-əs\ *n.; pl.* **hip·po·pot·a·mus·es** \-m-ə-səz\ or **hip·po·pot·a·mi** \-m-ˌī\. [From Latin, there borrowed from Greek *hippopotamos* meaning literally "river horse", from *hippos* meaning "horse" and *potamos* meaning "river".] A large thick-skinned hairless mammal allied to the hogs, living in African rivers and feeding on water plants, next to the elephant the largest existing four-footed animal.

hire \'hīr\ *n.* **1** Money paid or to be paid for services or for the use of something; wages or salary or rental price; as, to work for *hire;* a laborer worthy of his *hire.* **2** The act of hiring; rent; as, a truck for *hire;* to pay for the *hire* of a boat for one hour. — *v.;* **hired; hir·ing. 1** To employ for pay; as, to *hire* a servant. **2** To rent, lease, or let for money; as, to *hire* a car for the afternoon; to *hire* out boats to picnickers.

hire·ling \'hīr-ling\ *n.* A person who serves for wages; especially, one whose only interest in his work is the money he receives.

his \'hiz\ *pron.* Something or someone belonging

to him — used when no noun follows. The book is *his*. — \(h)iz, 'hiz\ *adj.* Belonging to him; done by or to him; as, *his* book; *his* fault.

hiss \'his\ *n.* **1** The sound made by drawing out the sound of the letter *s*, usually as a sign of dislike or contempt. **2** A sound like a prolonged *s* sound; as, the *hiss* of steam in a radiator. — *v.* **1** To make a hiss. Some snakes *hiss*. **2** To show dislike with a hiss; as, to *hiss* a speaker.

hist *a long* s *sound followed by a* t *sound, sometimes with a* p *sound at the beginning*\ *interj.* An exclamation used to call for silence or for attention, as to a sound.

his·ta·mine \'hist-m-ˌēn, -m-ən\ *n.* A compound occurring in many animal tissues that is believed to play an important part in allergic reactions, as hives and asthma, and in certain respiratory diseases.

his·to·ri·an \his-'tōr-ē-ən, -'tȯr-, -'tär-\ *n.* A person who writes histories or who knows much about history.

his·tor·ic \his-'tȯr-ik, -'tär-\ *adj.* Belonging to or connected with history; making history; as, a *historic* event; a *historic* old building.

his·tor·i·cal \his-'tȯr-ik-l, -'tär-\ *adj.* **1** Of or about history; based upon history; as, *historical* writings; a *historical* novel. **2** Known to be true; faithful to history; as, a *historical* fact. — **his·tor·i·cal·ly** \-ik-l(-)ē\ *adv.*

his·to·ry \'hist-r(-)ē\ *n.; pl.* **his·to·ries.** [From Latin *historia*, there borrowed from Greek, meaning "inquiry", "information gleaned by inquiry", "narrative", "history".] **1** The branch of knowledge that records and studies past events. **2** A written account of past events. **3** Any account of events; a narrative. **4** The events that provide the materials for a history; a series of events connected with someone or something; as, a house with a strange *history*.

his·tri·on·ic \ˌhis-trē-'än-ik\ *adj.* Of or relating to the stage or to actors; theatrical.

his·tri·on·ics \ˌhis-trē-'än-iks\ *n. pl.* **1** Dramatic presentation; theatricals. **2** Theatrical behavior.

hit \'hit\ *v.;* **hit**; **hit·ting.** **1** To strike or touch, especially with force; as, to *hit* a ball over the fence; to *hit* out with one's fists. **2** To strike something aimed at; not to miss; as, to *hit* a target with an arrow. **3** To knock; as, to *hit* one's head in falling. **4** To deliver; as, to *hit* a blow. **5** To come upon by chance or by searching; to discover; as, to *hit* upon the right answer. **6** To agree with; to suit; as, a song that just *hits* one's mood. **7** To affect as if by a blow; as, to be hard *hit* by a disappointment. **8** In an internal-combustion engine, to fire the charge in its cylinders; as, an engine that is *hitting* perfectly. — *n.* **1** A blow. **2** A successful blow or stroke; as, to make three *hits* out of five attempts. **3** In baseball, a stroke by which a batter reaches one or more bases without an opponent's error. **4** A great success; as, a song that immediately became a *hit*.

hit-and-miss \'hit-n-'mis\ *adj.* Hit-or-miss.

hitch \'hich\ *v.* **1** To move or pull with a jerk; as, to *hitch* a chair up to a table. **2** To fasten, as by a hook or knot; as, to *hitch* a horse to a tree. **3** To become entangled or caught. — *n.* **1** A jerky movement or pull; as, to give one's trousers a *hitch*. **2** A sudden stop; a halt; an unforeseen obstacle; as, a plan that went off without a *hitch*. **3** The connection between something towed, as a plow or trailer, and its mover, as a tractor, automobile, or animal. **4** A knot, especially one used for a temporary fastening, as by sailors.

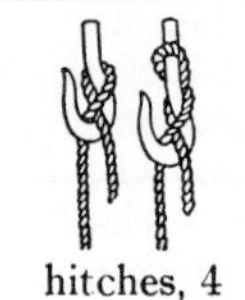

hitches, 4

hitch·hike \'hich-ˌhīk\ *v.;* **hitch·hiked**; **hitch·hik·ing.** To make one's way by getting rides in automobiles that overtake one on the road. — **hitch-hik·er** \-ˌhīk-r\ *n.*

hitch·ing post \'hich-ing\. A post to which horses are hitched.

hith·er \'hi<u>th</u>-r\ *adv.* To this place; here. — *adj.* Toward the person speaking; nearer.

hith·er·to \'hi<u>th</u>-r-ˌtü, ˌhi<u>th</u>-r-'tü\ *adv.* Up to the present; until now.

hith·er·ward \'hi<u>th</u>-r-wərd\ *adv.* Toward this place; hither.

hit-or-miss \'hit-r-'mis\ *adj.* Haphazard; random.

hit parade. A listing or presentation, as of popular songs or books, in order of current public preference.

hit·ter \'hit-r\ *n.* **1** One who hits. **2** In baseball, a batsman.

hive \'hīv\ *n.* **1** A box or other container for housing honey bees; a beehive. **2** The bees belonging to a hive; a swarm of bees. **3** A place swarming with busy people; a large number of busy people. — *v.;* **hived**; **hiv·ing.** **1** To collect into or cause to enter a beehive. **2** To store up in a hive, as honey. **3** To enter a hive together, as bees; to settle together in a hive.

hives \'hīvz\ *n.* A disease marked by an itching rash on the skin.

ho \'hō\ *interj.* **1** A cry, as of surprise or delight. **2** A call to attract attention or to give warning.

hoar \'hōr, 'hȯr\ *adj.* **1** White or light-gray; hoary. **2** White or gray with age. — *n.* Hoarfrost.

hoard \'hōrd, 'hȯrd\ *n.* A store or accumulation laid up; as, a *hoard* of coins. — *v.* To lay up; to store away; as, to *hoard* money.

hoar·frost \'hōr-ˌfrȯst, 'hȯr-\ *n.* A silvery-white icy deposit formed during cold, clear nights.

hoarhound. Variant of *horehound*.

hoarse \'hōrs, 'hȯrs\ *adj.* **1** Harsh in sound; as, a crow's *hoarse* caw. **2** Having a rough, grating voice, as when suffering from a cold. — **hoarse·ly**, *adv.*

hoary \'hōr-ē, 'hȯr-ē\ *adj.;* **hoar·i·er**; **hoar·i·est.** **1** White or gray, especially with age; as, *hoary* eyebrows. **2** Very old; ancient; as, sailors spinning *hoary* yarns about the sea.

hoax \'hōks\ *n.* A trick intended to fool or deceive; something false passed off or exhibited as genuine. — *v.* To fool by a hoax.

hob \'häb\ *n.* **1** A hobgoblin; a fairy; an elf. **2** Mischief or havoc; as, to raise *hob.* The storm played *hob* with the small boats in the harbor.

hob \'häb\ *n.* **1** A projection at the back or side of a fireplace on which something may be placed to be kept warm. **2** A peg or pin used as a target in certain games. **3** A hobnail.

hob·ble \'häb-l\ *v.;* **hob·bled**; **hob·bling** \-l(-)ing\. **1** To walk with a limp. **2** To make movement difficult by tying the legs; as, to *hobble* a horse. — *n.* **1** A limping walk. **2** A rope used to hobble an animal.

hob·ble·de·hoy \'häb-l-dē-ˌhȯi\ *n.* An awkward gawky fellow.

hob·by \'häb-ē\ *n.; pl.* **hob·bies.** An interest or activity which is outside a person's main occupation but to which he devotes much time for pleasure; as, the *hobby* of stamp collecting.

hob·by·horse \'häb-ē-ˌhȯrs\ *n.* A stick, sometimes with a horse's head, on which children pretend to ride; a toy horse; a rocking horse.

hob·gob·lin \'häb-ˌgäb-lən\ *n.* **1** A mischievous elf; a goblin. **2** A strange unreal being whom children fear; a bogey.

hob·nail \'häb-ˌnāl\ *n.* A short large-headed nail used to stud the soles and heels of certain heavy shoes as a protection against wear. — **hob·nailed** \-ˌnāld\ *adj.*

hob·nob \'häb-ˌnäb\ *v.;* **hob·nobbed**; **hob·nob·bing.** To associate familiarly; to be on intimate terms.

ho·bo \'hō-ˌbō\ *n.; pl.* **ho·bos** or **ho·boes.** A tramp.

hock \'häk\ *n.* The joint about midway between the foot and the thigh in a hind leg of a four-footed animal.

hock·ey \'häk-ē\ *n.* A game played in a field (**field hockey**) or on ice (**ice hockey**) in which two groups of players try to drive a ball or puck through opposite goals by hitting it with a curved or hooked stick.

ho·cus-po·cus \'hōk-əs-'pōk-əs\ *n.* **1** A set form of words used by those skilled in tricks of illusion. **2** A trick; any nonsense which serves as a means of deception.

hod \'häd\ *n.* **1** A long-handled wooden tray or trough used to carry mortar or bricks. **2** A bucket for holding or carrying coal.

hod, 1

hodge·podge \'häj-ˌpäj\ *n.* A mixture; a mess; a jumble.

hoe \'hō\ *n.* A farm or garden tool with a thin, flat blade attached at nearly a right angle to a long handle, used for weeding and hilling. — *v.;* **hoed**: **hoe·ing.** To loosen the soil with a hoe; to dig out the weeds around plants with a hoe; as, to *hoe* potatoes.

hoe·cake \'hō-ˌkāk\ *n.* A cake made of cornmeal, often baked on a griddle.

hog \'hȯg, 'häg\ *n.* **1** A swine; a full-grown pig; especially, an adult animal suitable for market. **2** A selfish, greedy, or filthy person. — *v.;* **hogged**; **hog·ging.** To take too much of something; to take more than a fitting number or amount of something; as, to *hog* all the best seats.

ho·gan \'hō-ˌgän, -ˌgȧn\ *n.* An earth-covered dwelling of the Navaho Indians.

hog·gish \'hȯg-ish, 'häg-\ *adj.* Like a hog; greedy. — **hog·gish·ly,** *adv.*

hog·nose snake \'hȯg-ˌnōz, 'häg-\ or **hog·nosed snake** \-ˌnōzd\. A moderate-sized, stout-bodied, harmless North American snake that dilates the neck, flattens the head, and hisses and blows when disturbed.

hogs·head \'hȯgz-ˌhed, 'hägz-, -əd\ *n.* **1** A very large cask. **2** A measure for liquids, especially one of 63 gallons.

hoist \'hȯist\ *v.* To raise; to lift up, especially with a tackle; as, to *hoist* a flag or a sail. — *n.* **1** A lift; a boost. **2** A lifting apparatus; especially, an elevator for heavy loads.

hold \'hōld\ *v.;* **held** \'held\; **hold·ing.** **1** To keep in one's possession or under one's control; not to let go; as, to *hold* a fort. **2** To receive and contain; as, a pail that *holds* a gallon. **3** To have in the grasp; to keep fixed in place; to support, secure, or fasten; as, to *hold* one's hat; a nail that will *hold* a picture. **4** To restrain; to check; as, to *hold* one's tongue. **5** To keep in mind; to have as one's belief; as, to *hold* an opinion. **6** To accept; as, to *hold* a theory. **7** To consider; to regard; as, to *hold* a person innocent. **8** To carry on by united action; as, to *hold* a meeting. **9** To maintain in a certain stated condition; as, to *hold* oneself erect. **10** To own; to possess or occupy; as, to *hold* property; to *hold* an office. **11** To remain steadfast or faithful; as, to *hold* to what one considers right. **12** To keep a grasp on something; to maintain a connection with something; to remain fast; as, to *hold* onto a rope. **13** To remain unbroken or unsubdued; not to give way. The football line *held* against each attack. **14** To be true. This rule *holds* in all cases. **15** To continue. The cold weather still *holds.* — **hold forth. 1** To offer; to put forward. **2** To speak in public; to preach. The speaker *held forth* on one small point until the listeners grew restless. — **hold good.** To remain valid. The reasoning *holds good* wherever it is applied. — **hold in.** To restrain; to curb; to restrain oneself. — **hold off.** To keep at a distance; to keep away; as, to *hold off* one's attackers. — **hold on. 1** To keep a hold. **2** To continue; to go on. **3** To wait; to stop. — **hold one's own. 1** To maintain one's position. **2** To remain in the same physical condition; to grow no worse. — **hold out. 1** To last; as, to make the food *hold out* as long as possible. **2** Not to yield or give way; as, to *hold out* as long as possible before admitting defeat. — **hold over.** To postpone; to keep for future action; as, to take up the question that was *held over* at the last meeting. — **hold the bag.** To be left empty-handed; to be left at a disadvantage. — **hold up. 1** To display; to exhibit. The student with the highest grades was *held up* as an example to others. **2** To stop in order to rob. **3** To stop or hinder the course of. The parade *held up* traffic for an hour. **4** To meet the requirements of a situation; to remain unbent or unbroken; as, to *hold up* under misfortunes. **5** To last; to wear; to continue; as, tires that *hold up* well under difficult driving conditions. — **hold water**. To be whole, sound, or consistent, especially in logic; as, an argument that will not *hold water*. — **hold with**. To agree with; to approve of; as, not to *hold with* the proposed plan. — *n.* **1** A stronghold. **2** Anything that holds, secures, or fastens something. **3** The act or manner of holding; seizure; grasp; as, to lose one's *hold* on a rope. **4** A manner of grasping the opponent in wrestling. **5** The authority to take or keep; power. The law has no *hold* over this man. **6** Something that may be grasped or held. **7** In music, a prolonged note or rest.

hold \'hōld\ *n.* The part of a ship below decks where the cargo is stored.

hold·back \'hōld-ˌbak\ *n.* **1** A hindrance; a check. **2** A device to enable a horse to back or hold back a vehicle.

hold·er \'hōld-r\ *n.* A person who holds or a thing used for holding something else.

hold·ing \'hōl-ding\ *n.* **1** Land held for any purpose, as for farming or residence. **2** Property of any kind, as in stocks.

hold·up \'hōl-ˌdəp\ *n.* **1** The action or period of holding up. **2** An attack for the purpose of robbery.

hole \'hōl\ *n.* **1** An opening into or through a thing; as, a *hole* in a wall; a *hole* in a stocking. **2** A hollow; a cavity; as, a *hole* in the road; a *hole* in a tooth. **3** A defect; as, to pick *holes* in a person's reasoning. **4** An embarrassing position. **5** A den or burrow; as, a rabbit *hole*. **6** In some games, as golf, a cavity into which a ball is to be played, or a score made in this way. **7** In golf, the distance from a tee to the corresponding hole. — *v.;* **holed**; **hol·ing**. **1** To make a hole or holes in. **2** To drive or put into a hole.

hol·i·day \'häl-ə-ˌdā\ *n.* [From Old English *hālig-daeg* meaning "holy day".] **1** A day of freedom from work; especially, such a day fixed by law. **2** [in the plural] A period of recreation or rest; as, during the Christmas *holidays*. **3** A vacation; as, to have a week's *holiday* at the seaside. — *adj.* Joyous; gay; as, in a *holiday* mood.

holier. Comparative of *holy*.

holiest. Superlative of *holy*.

ho·li·ness \'hō-lē-nəs\ *n.* **1** The quality or state of being holy. **2** [with a capital] A title of the pope.

hol·low \'häl-ō\ *adj.* **1** Having a hole inside; not solid throughout; as, a *hollow* ball; a *hollow* tree. **2** Sunken; not filled out; as, *hollow* cheeks. **3** Empty; hungry. **4** Having the sound of or like noise that comes from an empty place or from a cavity; as, a *hollow* roar. **5** Not sincere; not whole-hearted; as, *hollow* praise. **6** Worthless; as, a *hollow* victory. — *n.* A hollow place; a hole; a valley. — *v.* To make or become hollow; to make a hole or hollow in. — **hol·low·ly**, *adv.*

hol·ly \'häl-ē\ *n.; pl.* **hol·lies**. **1** An evergreen tree or shrub with prickly-edged shiny leaves and red berries, much used for Christmas decorations. **2** The foliage or branches of this tree.

holly: leaves and berries

hol·ly·hock \'häl-ē-ˌhäk, -ˌhòk\ *n.* A tall, leafy-stemmed Chinese herb of the mallow family, with large, coarse, rounded, usually hairy leaves and spikelike clusters of showy flowers.

holm oak \'hōm\. **1** An evergreen oak of southern Europe, having hollylike leaves. **2** The wood of this tree.

hol·o·caust \'häl-ə-ˌkòst, 'hō-lə-\ *n.* **1** A sacrificial offering, all of which is consumed by fire. **2** A complete or great destruction, especially by fire.

hol·o·graph \'häl-ə-ˌgraf, 'hō-lə-\ *n.* Any document wholly in the handwriting of its author.

hol·ster \'hōlst-r\ *n.* A leather case for a pistol, usually worn at the belt or attached to a saddle.

ho·ly \'hō-lē\ *adj.;* **ho·li·er**; **ho·li·est**. **1** Set apart for the service of God or of a divine being; sacred; hallowed; blessed for use in worship; as, a *holy* temple; a *holy* day. **2** Connected with sacred events; as, the *Holy* Land. **3** Saintly; godly; pious; as, *holy* men; a *holy* life. — *n.; pl.* **ho·lies**. A holy thing or place, as a sanctuary.

ho·ly·day \'hō-lē-ˌdā\ *n.* or **holy day**. A religious feast day.

Holy Father. A title of the pope.

Holy Ghost or **Holy Spirit**. The third person of the Trinity.

Holy Grail \'grāl\. In medieval legends, the dish, or the cup, used by Christ at the Last Supper.

Holy Land. Palestine.

ho·ly·stone \'hō-lē-ˌstōn\ *n.* A soft sandstone used to scrub the decks of ships. — *v.;* **ho·ly·stoned**; **ho·ly·ston·ing**. To scrub with a holystone.

Holy Week. The week before Easter.

Holy Writ. The Bible.

hom·age \'häm-ij, 'äm-\ *n.* **1** A ceremony in which a person pledged allegiance to a lord and became his vassal. **2** Anything done or given as an acknowledgment of a vassal's duty to his lord. **3** Respect; honor.

home \'hōm\ *n.* **1** The house in which one lives or in which one's family lives. **2** One's native land; the country or place where one lives or where one's ancestors lived. **3** The place where something is usually or naturally found; habitat; as, the *home* of the elephant. **4** A place where persons unable to care for themselves are taken care of; as, a *home* for old people. **5** The social unit formed by a family living together in one dwelling; as, a city of twenty thousand *homes*. **6** A dwelling house; as, new modern *homes* for sale. **7** In some games, the goal or point to be reached, as the **home plate** or **home base** in baseball. — *adj.* Of or relating to home; as, the *home* folks; *home* news. — *adv.* **1** At, in, or to one's home or country; as, to go or to write *home;* to stay *home.* **2** To the place where it belongs; as, to drive a nail *home.* — *v.;* **homed**; **hom·ing**. To go to, send to, or place in a home.

home economics. The study that deals with the care and management of a household; domestic science.

home·land \'hōm-ˌland\ *n.* Native land; fatherland.

home·less \'hōm-ləs\ *adj.* Having no home; as, a *homeless* kitten; a family left *homeless* by a fire.

home·like \'hōm-ˌlīk\ *adj.* Like home; comfortable; cozy; friendly.

home·ly \'hōm-lē\ *adj.;* **home·li·er**; **home·li·est**. **1** Characteristic of home life; plain; simple; as, *homely* meals. **2** Lacking polish or refinement; rude; as, *homely* manners. **3** Not handsome; as, a *homely* person.

home·made \'hō(m)-'mād\ *adj.* Made at home; not bought; as, *homemade* bread.

home·mak·er \'hōm-ˌmāk-r\ *n.* One who makes a home; a person whose occupation is managing a household and taking care of a family.

hom·er \'hōm-r\ *n.* **1** A home run. **2** A homing pigeon. — *v.* To make a home run.

home·room \'hōm-'rüm, -'rům\ *n.* or **home room**. The schoolroom in which a pupil keeps his books and to which he reports at the opening and closing of school each day.

home rule. The administration of their own government, especially local government, by the citizens of a politically dependent country, colony, or district.

home run. In baseball, a hit that enables the batter to make a complete circuit of the bases without the aid of an error by the opposing team.

home·sick \'hōm-ˌsik\ *adj.* Longing or pining for home.

home·spun \'hōm-ˌspən\ *adj.* Spun at home or made of yarn spun at home. — *n.* A cloth made of homespun yarn or of yarn resembling it; especially, a rough, loosely-woven woolen cloth.

home·stead \'hōm-ˌsted\ *n.* **1** A home and the land surrounding it. **2** In law, the land and buildings occupied by the owner as a home and protected by law from the claims of creditors.

home·stead·er \'hōm-ˌsted-r\ *n.* One who holds a homestead; especially, one who has acquired a homestead under laws (**homestead laws**) authorizing the sale of public lands in parcels of 160 acres to settlers.

home·stretch \'hōm-'strech\ *n.* The part of a racecourse between the last curve and the winning mark; the last part of any course, operation, or activity; as, a fund-raising drive now in the *homestretch.*

home·ward \'hōm-wərd\ *adv.* or *adj.* Toward or in the direction of home.

home·wards \'hōm-wərdz\ *adv.* Homeward.

home·work \'hōm-ˌwərk\ *n.* Work, especially school lessons, to be done at home.

homey \'hō-mē\ *adj.;* **hom·i·er**; **hom·i·est**. Homelike; cozy. — **home·y·ness**, *n.*

hom·i·cid·al \ˌhäm-ə-'sīd-l, ˌhō-mə-\ *adj.* Having or showing tendencies toward homicide; murderous. — **hom·i·cid·al·ly** \-l-ē\ *adv.*

hom·i·cide \'häm-ə-ˌsīd, 'hō-mə-\ *n.* **1** The killing of one human being by another. **2** A person who kills another person; especially, a murderer.

hom·i·ly \'häm-l-ē\ *n.; pl.* **hom·i·lies**. **1** A sermon. **2** A moral talk or writing.

hom·ing \'hō-ming\ *adj.* Home-returning; as, the *homing* instinct; *homing* pigeons.

homing pigeon. A pigeon trained to return home from a distance and used for carrying messages.

hom·i·ny \'häm-ə-nē\ *n.* [A shortened form of *rockahominy,* from an Indian word meaning "parched corn".] Hulled and, sometimes, coarsely broken corn, cooked and served as food.

ho·mo·ge·ne·ous \ˌhō-mə-'jē-nē-əs, ˌhäm-ə-, -'jēn-yəs\ *adj.* Made up of parts or elements that are the same or are closely related; having or showing few or no differences among its parts. — **ho·mo·ge·ne·ous·ly**, *adv.*

ho·mog·e·nize \hə-'mäj-n-ˌīz\ *v.;* **ho·mog·e·nized**; **ho·mog·e·niz·ing**. To make homogeneous; especially, to break up and reblend into a homogeneous whole, as milk by passing it through an apparatus that breaks up the globules of fat and shreds of casein.

hom·o·graph \'häm-ə-ˌgraf, 'hō-mə-\ *n.* One of two or more words alike in spelling but different in origin and meaning, as *fair* meaning "market" and *fair* meaning "beautiful".

ho·mol·o·gous \hə-'mäl-ə-gəs\ *adj.* **1** Having the same relative position, proportion, value, or structure. **2** In biology, corresponding in structure, as a bird's wing and a man's arm.

hom·o·nym \'häm-ə-ˌnim, 'hō-mə-\ *n.* A word having the same pronunciation as another word but a different meaning and, usually, spelling, as *bear* and *bare, coarse* and *course.*

hom·o·phon·ic \ˌhäm-ə-'fän-ik, ˌhō-mə-\ *adj.* **1** Having the same sound. **2** In music, having a single melodic voice part; not polyphonic.

Hon. Abbreviation for *Honorable.*

Hon·du·ran \hän-'dür-ən, -'dyür-\ *adj.* Of or relating to Honduras. — *n.* A native or inhabitant of Honduras.

hone \'hōn\ *n.* **1** A fine whetstone, especially for razors. **2** A tool for enlarging holes to precise measurements. — *v.;* **honed**; **hon·ing**. To sharpen, dress, or enlarge with or as if with a hone; as, to *hone* the cylinders of an engine; to *hone* a knife.

hon·est \'än-əst\ *adj.* **1** Fair and straightforward; trustworthy; truthful; as, an *honest* man. **2** Free from fraud; genuine; as, *honest* goods; *honest* weight. **3** Open; frank; as, an *honest* face.

— The word *sincere* is a synonym of *honest: honest* is likely to suggest conformity to what is true, often as a matter of habit; *sincere* usually indicates a genuine and heartfelt desire to conform to the truth or to express one's true feelings or nature.

hon·est·ly \'än-əst-lē\ *adv.* In an honest manner; with honesty.

hon·es·ty \'än-əs-tē\ *n.* Fairness and straightforwardness in conduct or speech; truthfulness; freedom from fraud or deceit.

hon·ey \'hən-ē\ *n.; pl.* **hon·eys. 1** A sweet sticky fluid made by bees from the liquid drawn from flowers. **2** A honeylike quality, as in a person's voice or words. **3** Sweet one — used as a term of affection.

hon·ey·bee \'hən-ē-ˌbē\ *n.* A honey-producing bee, living and breeding in organized communities, that is kept for its honey and wax.

hon·ey·comb \'hən-ē-ˌkōm\ *n.* **1** The mass of six-sided wax cells built by bees in their nests or hives for rearing young bees and storing honey. **2** Anything that looks like a honeycomb. **—** *v.* To make or become full of holes like a honeycomb; as, a mountain *honeycombed* with caves.

hon·ey·dew \'hən-ē-ˌdü, -ˌdyü\ *n.* A sugary liquid that is secreted by aphids or scale insects and often found as a deposit on the leaves of many plants.

honeydew melon. A sweet, smooth-skinned, white variety of muskmelon.

hon·eyed \'hən-ēd\ *adj.* **1** Abounding with honey; like honey; sweetened. **2** Sweet; flattering; as, *honeyed* words.

hon·ey·moon \'hən-ē-ˌmün\ *n.* The time immediately after marriage; the holiday spent by a couple after marriage. **—** *v.* To have a honeymoon.

hon·ey·suck·le \'hən-ē-ˌsək-l\ *n.* An upright shrub or woody climbing vine with fragrant white, yellow, or red tubular flowers.

honeysuckle

honk \'hängk, 'hȯngk\ *n.* The cry of a wild goose or any similar sound; as, the *honk* of a horn. **—** *v.* To make a honk.

hon·or \'än-r\ *n.* **1** Respect paid to or due to worth; reverence; as, a man held in *honor* by all who know him. **2** A mark of respect; a courtesy; a ceremonial showing of respect or esteem; as, to heap *honors* upon a victorious general. **3** A title or dignity conferred on a person. **4** [in the plural] Social courtesies; as, to do the *honors* at the table. **5** Purity; chastity. **6** A person who brings glory to others or to things associated with him; as, to be an *honor* to one's school. **7** Excellence of character; high moral worth; especially, loyalty to one's own ideals of behavior; as, a man of unquestionable *honor.* **8** [in the plural] High rank or marks in school or college. **9** [with a capital] A title of respect; as, his *Honor,* the judge. **—** *v.;* **hon·ored; hon·or·ing** \-r(-)ing\. **1** To regard or treat with honor; to respect; as, to *honor* one's parents. **2** To give honor or honors to. **3** In business, to accept and pay when due; as, to *honor* a note.

hon·or·a·ble \'än-r(-)əb-l, 'än-rb-l\ *adj.* **1** Worthy of honor; guided by principles of honor; as, an *honorable* man; *honorable* behavior. **2** Performed or accompanied with honor; as, an *honorable* burial; an *honorable* defeat. **3** Conferring honor; as, *honorable* wounds. **4** [with a capital] A title of respect given to certain officials and to some other persons. — **hon·or·a·bly** \-r(-)ə-blē, -r-blē\ *adv.*

hon·or·ary \'än-r-ˌer-ē\ *adj.* **1** Given or done as a sign of honor; as, to receive an *honorary* doctor's degree from a university. **2** Indicating a title or position held or awarded merely as an honor without requiring any service or without any pay. **3** Holding such a title or position; as, *honorary* chairman.

honor roll. A roll of names of persons deserving honors.

hood \'hu̇d\ *n.* **1** A soft covering, usually of cloth, for the head and neck, sometimes attached to a cloak or jacket. **2** Something like a hood in use or appearance, as a top on a carriage. **3** In machinery, the covering over parts of mechanisms; especially, the removable metal covering for an automobile engine. **4** The crest of a bird or animal. **—** *v.* To cover with or as if with a hood; to hide; to blind. — **hood·ed** \'hu̇d-əd\ *adj.*

-hood \ˌhu̇d\. A suffix that can mean: **1** A state of being or all the persons or things that are in this state, as in *boyhood, brotherhood, knighthood, neighborhood.* **2** A thing that is, as in *falsehood.*

hood \'hu̇d\ *n.* [A shortened form of *hoodlum.*] *Slang.* A gangster or racketeer, especially one who uses a gun or physical violence.

hood·lum \'hüd-ləm, 'hu̇d-\ *n.* **1** A young rowdy; a tough. **2** A gangster; a mobster.

hoo·doo \'hüd-ˌü\ *n.; pl.* **hoo·doos. 1** Voodoo. **2** One that brings bad luck. **—** *v.;* **hoo·dooed; hoo·doo·ing.** To be a hoodoo to; to bring bad luck to.

hood·wink \'hu̇d-ˌwingk\ *v.* **1** To blind by covering the eyes. **2** To deceive; to impose upon; as, *hoodwinked* by a confidence man.

hoof \'hu̇f, 'hüf\ *n.; pl.* **hoofs** \'hu̇fs, 'hüfs\ or **hooves** \'hu̇vz, 'hüvz\. **1** The covering of horn that protects the ends of the toes of some animals, as horses, oxen, and swine. **2** The foot as a whole, especially of the horse. **—** *v.* To walk; as, to *hoof* it to town. — **hoofed** \'hu̇ft, 'hüft\ *adj.*

hoof·beat \'hu̇f-ˌbēt, 'hüf-\ *n.* The rhythmic sound made by a horse's hoofs, as in galloping.

hook \'hu̇k\ *n.* **1** A curved device, as a piece of bent metal, for catching, holding, or pulling something. **2** A curved implement for cutting; as, a bush *hook.* **3** Something like a hook in shape or use, as a sharp bend in a road or stream. **4** In boxing, a short swinging blow delivered with the elbow bent and rigid. **5** In music, one of the cross strokes on certain notes. — **by hook or by crook.** One way or another; by any means. — **on one's own hook.** On one's own account or responsibility; by oneself. — **to get the hook.** To be removed; to be discharged, as from a job. **—** *v.* **1** To bend in the shape of a hook; as, to *hook* the arm. **2** To catch, seize, hold, or fasten with or as if with a hook.

3 To steal; to pilfer. 4 To pierce or strike with the horns, as cattle. 5 To be caught or fastened by or as if by a hook; as, a dress that *hooks.* 6 To draw, or make by drawing, loops of yarn or cloth through a backing of canvas or burlap with a hook designed for this purpose; as, to *hook* a rug.

hooked \'hu̇kt\ *adj.* 1 Shaped like a hook; furnished with a hook; as, a bird's *hooked* bill. 2 Made by hooking; as, a *hooked* rug.

hook·up \'hu̇k-ˌəp\ *n.* 1 A diagram, as of a radio set, showing the arrangement of the parts. 2 A combination of apparatus and circuits specially set up or connected, as for radio transmission and reception; as, a broadcast over a national *hookup.* 3 A connection; an alliance; as, a *hookup* between two countries.

hook·worm \'hu̇k-ˌwərm\ *n.* 1 Any of certain parasitic worms having hooks or spines about the mouth. 2 Also **hookworm disease.** A disease marked by paleness and weakness, caused by hookworms.

hoop \'hu̇p, 'hüp\ *n.* 1 A circular band of wood or metal used to hold together the staves of a barrel or tub; such a band used by children for rolling. 2 A circle, or framework of circles, of bone or wire used for spreading a skirt (**hoop skirt**). 3 An arch or wicket in croquet and other games. — *v.* To bind or fasten with a hoop or hoops.

hoose·gow \'hüs-ˌgau̇\ *n. Slang.* A jail; a lockup.

hoot \'hüt\ *n.* 1 A loud shout, especially of scorn or contempt. 2 The cry of an owl. — *v.* 1 To utter a hoot. 2 To attack or to show disapproval with hoots.

hooves. A pl. of *hoof.*

hop \'häp\ *v.;* **hopped; hop·ping.** 1 To move in short quick jumps, as birds or toads do. 2 To spring or jump on one foot. 3 To jump over; as, to *hop* a puddle. 4 To jump on; to catch; as, to *hop* a bus. — *n.* 1 A short quick leap or spring, especially on one leg. 2 A dance. 3 A flight in an aircraft, especially one stage in a long journey by air.

hop \'häp\ *n.* 1 A twining vine whose greenish flowers look like cones. 2 [in the plural] The dried conelike flowers of this plant, used chiefly in making beer and ale and in medicine. — *v.;* **hopped; hop·ping.** 1 To produce hops, as a plant. 2 To gather hops. 3 To flavor with hops.

hope \'hōp\ *n.* 1 The desire for something that a person believes can be obtained or expects he will get; as, to have *hope* of succeeding. 2 The thing that is desired. 3 A source of hope; a person or thing that gives promise of future benefit or blessing; as, a man who was the *hope* of his country. — *v.;* **hoped; hop·ing.** To have hope; to desire; to wish; as, to *hope* for the best; to *hope* to succeed.

hope·ful \'hōp-fəl\ *adj.* 1 Having hope; inclined to hope; as, to be of a *hopeful* turn of mind; to feel *hopeful* about the future. 2 Giving grounds for hope; arousing hope; promising; as, a *hopeful* sign; a *hopeful* prospect. — *n.* A young person considered promising or likely to succeed. — **hope·ful·ly** \-fə-lē\ *adv.*

hope·less \'hōp-ləs\ *adj.* 1 Without hope; despairing. 2 Giving no grounds for hope; as, a *hopeless* case; a *hopeless* illness. — **hope·less·ly,** *adv.*

hop·per \'häp-r\ *n.* 1 One that hops; especially, the larvae of a black two-winged fly that infests cheese. 2 Any of various leaping insects — used chiefly in compounds, as *grasshopper* and *leafhopper.* 3 A chute or box, often funnel-shaped, for feeding or passing on material.

hop·scotch \'häp-ˌskäch\ *n.* A child's game in which the players hop from one part to another of a figure drawn on the ground.

horde \'hōrd, 'hȯrd\ *n.* 1 A loosely organized group of wandering people. 2 Any crowd or multitude; as, a *horde* of ants. — *v.;* **hord·ed; hord·ing.** To form a horde.

hore·hound or **hoar·hound** \'hōr-ˌhau̇nd, 'hȯr-\ *n.* 1 An aromatic, bitter mint with hairy whitish leaves and small white flowers. 2 A candy flavored with an extract made from the horehound plant.

ho·ri·zon \hə-'rīz-n\ *n.* 1 The line where it seems as if the earth or sea meets the sky. 2 The limit or range of a person's outlook or experience. Reading broadens one's *horizons.*

hor·i·zon·tal \ˌhȯr-ə-'zänt-l, ˌhär-\ *adj.* On a level; parallel to the horizon. — *n.* Something that is horizontal, as a line or plane. — **hor·i·zon·tal·ly** \-l-ē\ *adv.*

hor·mone \'hȯr-ˌmōn\ *n.* 1 A chemical substance produced in a gland and carried by the blood to another part of the body whose activity it affects, usually through stimulation. 2 A comparable substance in a plant, carried by the sap. — **hor·mo·nal** \hȯr-'mōn-l\ *adj.*

horn \'hȯrn\ *n.* 1 One of the hard body growths on the head of many hoofed animals, including the true horns of cattle, goats, and sheep and the antlers of deer. 2 The material, keratin, of which true horns are composed, or a similar material, as that on the outside of a horse's hoof; as, a *horn*-handled knife. 3 Something made, or originally made, from a horn; as, a hunting *horn;* a powder *horn.* 4 Something shaped somewhat like a horn; as, a saddle *horn;* the *horns* of a crescent moon. 5 A musical wind instrument originally made of a horn and somewhat like a horn in shape, but now made of brass or other metal; as, a French *horn.* 6 A device for sounding a warning; as, an automobile *horn.* — *v.* To gore or toss with the horns.

horn·bill \'hȯrn-ˌbil\ *n.* Any of a family of Old World birds having enormous bills.

horn·book \'hȯrn-ˌbu̇k\ *n.* A child's primer consisting of a sheet of paper protected by a sheet of transparent horn.

horned \'hȯrnd\ *adj.* Having a horn or horns, or some hornlike growth.

horned owl. Any of various owls having conspicuous tufts of feathers on the head.

horned toad. Any of certain small harmless lizards having several hornlike spines on the head and a broad flat body covered with spiny scales.

hor·net \'hȯr-nət\ *n.* A large strong wasp, dark brown and yellow in color, that can give a severe sting.

horn of plenty. A cornucopia.

horn·pipe \'hȯrn-ˌpīp\ *n.* **1** A musical instrument formerly popular in Wales, consisting of a wooden pipe with a flaring end sometimes made of horn. **2** A lively sailors' dance originally accompanied by hornpipe playing; music for such a dance.

horny \'hȯr-nē\ *adj.;* **horn·i·er**; **horn·i·est**. **1** Made of horn or a similar substance. **2** Having horns. **3** Like horn; hard; callous.

ho·rol·o·ger \hȯ-'räl-əj-r\ *n.* A maker or seller of clocks and watches; a person skilled in horology.

ho·rol·o·gy \hȯ-'räl-ə-jē\ *n.* **1** The science of measuring time. **2** The art of making clocks or dials. — **ho·rol·o·gist** \-jəst\ *n.*

hor·o·scope \'hȯr-ə-ˌskōp, 'här-\ *n.* **1** The position of the stars at a particular time, as at the moment of a person's birth. **2** A diagram or plan that represents the twelve divisions of heaven used by astrologers in making predictions.

hor·ren·dous \hə-'ren-dəs\ *adj.* Fearful; frightful. — **hor·ren·dous·ly**, *adv.*

hor·ri·ble \'hȯr-əb-l, 'här-\ *adj.* Arousing horror; terrible; dreadful; shocking. — **hor·ri·bly** \-ə-blē\ *adv.*

hor·rid \'hȯr-əd, 'här-\ *adj.* **1** Hideous; shocking. **2** Rather objectionable; offensive; as, a child with *horrid* manners. — **hor·rid·ly**, *adv.*

hor·ri·fy \'hȯr-ə-ˌfī, 'här-\ *v.;* **hor·ri·fied** \-ˌfīd\; **hor·ri·fy·ing**. To cause a person to feel horror.

hor·ror \'hȯr-r, 'här-r\ *n.* **1** A painful feeling of great fear, dread, or intense dislike. **2** The condition of being horrible; as, the *horror* of war. **3** A person or thing that arouses horror.

hors d'oeuvre \ȯr-'dərv\ *n.; pl.* **hors d'oeuvres** \-'dərvz, -'dərv\. Any salt, tart, or savory appetizer served before a meal or as a first course.

horse \'hȯrs\ *n.* **1** A large solid-hoofed mammal having a mane and tail and feeding on grasses, long used as a work animal and for riding; especially, the male of this animal. **2** A frame that supports something, as wood while being cut or clothes while being dried. **3** A piece of gymnasium equipment used for vaulting exercises. **4** Soldiers on horseback; cavalry; as, a troop of *horse*. — *v.;* **horsed**; **hors·ing**. To provide with a horse or horses; to mount on a horse.

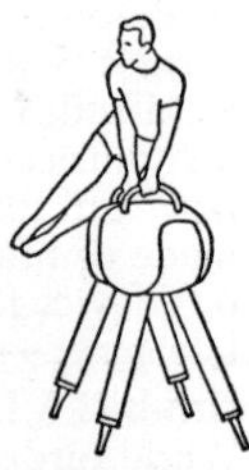

horse, 3

horse·back \'hȯrs-ˌbak\ *n.* The back of a horse. — *adv.* On the back of a horse.

horse·car \'hȯrs-ˌkär, -ˌkar\ *n.* **1** A car drawn by horses. **2** A car for transporting horses.

horse chestnut. [So called because the nut somewhat resembles a true chestnut, and because horse chestnuts were once used to treat horses for chest ailments.] **1** A tree with five or seven leaflets arranged like the fingers of the hand, sticky buds in spring, showy flowers in erect conical clusters, and large shiny seeds in round prickly burs. **2** The nutlike seed of this tree.

horse·fly \'hȯrs-ˌflī\ *n.; pl.* **horse·flies**. A swift two-winged fly, often large, the females of which suck the blood of animals.

horse·hair \'hȯrs-ˌhar, -ˌher\ *n.* **1** The hair of a horse, especially from the mane or tail. **2** Cloth made from horsehair. — *adj.* Made of horsehair; covered or stuffed with horsehair.

horse·hide \'hȯrs-ˌhīd\ *n.* A horse's hide or leather made from it.

horse latitudes. Either of two belts or regions in the neighborhood of 30° N. and 30° S. latitude, characterized by high pressure, calms, and light changeable winds.

horse·laugh \'hȯrs-ˌlaf, -ˌlȧf\ *n.* A loud boisterous laugh.

horse mackerel. Any of several large fishes; especially, the tuna.

horse·man \'hȯrs-mən\ *n.; pl.* **horse·men** \-mən\. **1** A horseback rider. **2** A person skilled in riding horseback or in caring for or managing horses.

horse·man·ship \'hȯrs-mən-ˌship\ *n.* **1** The art of managing horses. **2** Skill in riding or handling horses.

horse opera. *Slang.* A western movie, especially a thriller.

horse pistol. A large pistol formerly carried by horsemen.

horse·play \'hȯrs-ˌplā\ *n.* Rough, boisterous play.

horse·pow·er \'hȯrs-ˌpaur\ *n.* A unit for measuring the power of a machine to do work, numerically equal to 33,000 foot-pounds per minute or 550 foot-pounds per second.

horse-rad·ish \'hȯrs-ˌrad-ish\ *n.* **1** A tall coarse white-flowered herb of the mustard family whose fleshy, hot-tasting root is ground and eaten as a relish. **2** The relish made from this root.

horse sense. Practical common sense.

horse·shoe \'hȯrs(h)-ˌshü\ *n.* **1** A shoe for horses, consisting of a narrow curved iron plate that is nailed to the rim of a horse's hoof. **2** Something shaped like a horseshoe. **3** [in the plural] A game like quoits played with horseshoes or horseshoe-shaped pieces of metal. — *v.;* **horse·shoed**; **horse·shoe·ing**. To furnish or fit with a horseshoe or horseshoes. — **horse·sho·er** \-ˌshü-ər\ *n.*

horse·tail \'hȯrs-ˌtāl\ *n.* **1** The tail of a horse. **2** Any of a group of flowerless plants related to the ferns; especially, a leafless, flowerless weed with hollow grooved stems and whorls of threadlike branches.

horse·whip \'hȯrs-ˌhwip\ *n.* A whip for use in driving horses. — *v.;* **horse·whipped** or **horse·whipt** \-ˌhwipt\; **horse·whip·ping**. To whip with a horsewhip.

horse·wom·an \'hȯrs-ˌwu̇m-ən\ *n.; pl.* **horse·wom·en** \-ˌwim-ən\. **1** A woman horseback rider. **2** A woman skilled in riding horseback or in caring for or managing horses.

horsy \'hȯr-sē\ *adj.;* **hors·i·er**; **hors·i·est**. **1** Relating to horses. **2** Fond of or interested in horses, especially for riding, driving, and racing; as, the fashionable *horsy* set. **3** Characteristic of horsemen; as, *horsy* clothes; a *horsy* manner.

hor·ti·cul·tur·al \ˌhȯrt-ə-'kəlch-r(-)əl\ *adj.* Relating to horticulture; as, a county *horticultural* society; a *horticultural* exhibit.

hor·ti·cul·ture \'hȯrt-ə-ˌkəlch-r\ *n.* The science or art of growing fruits, vegetables, flowers, or ornamental plants; the cultivation of a garden or orchard. — **hor·ti·cul·tur·ist** \ˌhȯrt-ə-'kəlch-r-əst\ *n.*

ho·san·na \hō-'zan-ə\ *interj.* An exclamation of praise to the Lord or Saviour.

hose \'hōz\ *n.; pl.* **hose**. **1** A stocking or stockings. **2** About the year 1600, close-fitting coverings for the legs and waist, similar to tights and worn as an outer garment by men; later, knee breeches. **3** Flexible pipe or tubing for carrying water or other liquid; as, rubber *hose*. **4** *Pl.* **hos·es**. A length of such tubing with suitable fittings at the ends; as, a fire *hose*. — *v.;* **hosed**; **hos·ing**. To wet with a hose.

ho·siery \'hōzh-r(-)ē\ *n.* Hose; stockings or socks.

hos·pice \'häs-pəs\ *n.* An inn for travelers, especially one kept by monks.

hos·pit·a·ble \häs-'pit-əb-l, 'häs-ˌpit-\ *adj.* **1** Generous and kindly in receiving and entertaining guests. **2** Open and receptive; as, a mind *hospitable* to new ideas. — **hos·pit·a·bly** \-ə-blē\ *adv.*

hos·pi·tal \'häs-ˌpit-l\ *n.* An institution where the sick and injured are given medical or surgical care.

hos·pi·tal·i·ty \ˌhäs-pə-'tal-ət-ē\ *n.; pl.* **hos·pi·tal·i·ties**. Generous and kindly reception and treatment of guests and visitors.

hos·pi·tal·ize \'häs-ˌpit-l-ˌīz\ *v.;* **hos·pi·tal·ized**; **hos·pi·tal·iz·ing**. To place in a hospital for treatment. — **hos·pi·tal·i·za·tion** \ˌhäs-ˌpit-l-ə-'zāsh-n\ *n.*

host \'hōst\ *n.* An army; a great number; a throng.

host \'hōst\ *n.* **1** A person who entertains a guest. **2** A person who keeps an inn. **3** Any living animal or plant affording food or lodgment to a parasite.

Host \'hōst\ *n.* The bread or wafer consecrated in the Mass of the Roman Catholic Church.

hos·tage \'häs-tij\ *n.* A person given or held by one side or party in a conflict as a pledge that certain promises will be kept or terms met by the other side.

hos·tel \'häst-l\ *n.* **1** An inn. **2** *Chiefly British.* A lodginghouse, especially for students or other young people away from home. **3** One of a system of supervised overnight lodgings or shelters for use by young people, as on hiking or bicycling trips.

hos·tel·ry \'häst-l-rē\ *n.; pl.* **hos·tel·ries**. An inn; a hotel.

host·ess \'hōs-təs\ *n.* **1** A woman or girl who entertains a guest. **2** A woman who keeps an inn. **3** A woman who acts as host, as in receiving and arranging for the care of patrons in a restaurant.

hos·tile \'häst-l, 'häs-ˌtīl, 'häs-(ˌ)til\ *adj.* [From Latin *hostilis*, a derivative of *hostis* meaning "enemy".] **1** Belonging to an enemy; as, *hostile* troops. **2** Unfriendly; showing ill will; as, a *hostile* look or manner. — **hos·tile·ly** \'häst-l-(l)ē, 'häs-ˌtīl-lē, 'häs-(ˌ)ti(l)-lē\ *adv.*

hos·til·i·ty \häs-'til-ət-ē\ *n.; pl.* **hos·til·i·ties**. **1** Unfriendliness; enmity; ill will. **2** A hostile act. **3** [in the plural] Acts of warfare.

hos·tler \'(h)äs-lər\ *n.* **1** A person who takes care of horses at an inn or a stable. **2** Anyone who takes care of horses; a groom.

hot \'hät\ *adj.;* **hot·ter**; **hot·test**. **1** Having a high temperature or a temperature much above normal; more than warm; as, a *hot* stove; a *hot* day. **2** Marked by violent activity or feeling; as, a *hot* answer; a *hot* temper. **3** Excited; urgent; as, in *hot* haste. **4** Eagerly desirous; as, a radical politician who is *hot* for reform. **5** Pressing closely upon one; as, a *hot* pursuit. **6** Biting or sharp in taste; as, *hot* mustard. **7** Fresh; recent; as, news *hot* off the press. **8** Strong. The dogs picked up a *hot* scent. **9** Exciting in rhythm and mood and, often, in execution; as, *hot* music. **10** Played in this style. **11** *Slang.* Exciting warm admiration; as, a boxer who is not so *hot*. **12** Illegally obtained; as, *hot* goods. **13** Radioactive. **14** Dealing with radioactive material. — **hot·ly**, *adv.*

hot·bed \'hät-ˌbed\ *n.* **1** A bed of heated earth in a glass-covered frame for growing plants earlier than they can be grown in a garden. **2** A place favorable to the rapid growth of something; as, a *hotbed* of rebellion.

hotbed, 1

hot-blood·ed \'hät-'bləd-əd\ *adj.* Easily roused or excited.

hot·box \'hät-ˌbäks\ *n.* A journal bearing, as on a railroad car, overheated by friction.

hotch·potch \'häch-ˌpäch\ *n.* A mingled mass; a hodgepodge.

hot dog \'hät ˌdȯg\. A frankfurter, especially one served in a split roll.

ho·tel \hō-'tel, 'hō-ˌtel\ *n.* A place that provides lodging and usually meals for the public, especially for transients; an inn.

hot·head \'hät-ˌhed\ *n.* A hotheaded person.

hot·head·ed \'hät-'hed-əd\ *adj.* Hasty; rash; fiery. — **hot·head·ed·ly**, *adv.*

hot·house \'hät-ˌhau̇s\ *n.; pl.* **hot·hous·es** \-ˌhau̇-zəz\. A heated glass-enclosed house for raising plants.

hot rod. An automobile rebuilt or modified for high speed and fast acceleration.

hothouse

hotter. Comparative of *hot*.

hottest. Superlative of *hot*.

hound \'hau̇nd\ *n.* **1** A hunting dog of certain breeds with large drooping ears and voice of a deep tone that follow their prey by scent, as the bloodhound, foxhound, beagle, and dachshund. **2** A hunting dog of certain breeds that follow their prey by sight, as the greyhound and wolfhound. **3** A contemptible fellow. — *v.* To hunt or track with or as if with hounds; to pursue relentlessly.

hour \'aủr\ *n.* **1** One of the 24 divisions of a day; 60 minutes. **2** Fifteen degrees of longitude. **3** The time of day. What is the *hour?* **4** A fixed or particular time; as, lunch *hour.* **5** A measure of distance reckoned by the amount of time it takes to cover it; as, two *hours* distant. **6** In education, a classroom period; as, a fifty-minute *hour.*

hour·glass \'aủr-ˌglas\ *n.* A device for measuring time, in which a substance, as sand, runs from the upper into the lower part of a glass in a definite length of time, as an hour.

hour·ly \'aủr-lē\ *adv.* **1** Every hour; as, trains leaving *hourly* for the city. **2** Frequently. — *adj.* **1** Happening or done every hour; as, *hourly* train service. **2** Constant; continual.

house \'haủs\ *n.; pl.* **hous·es** \'haủ-zəz\. **1** A place built for human inhabitants. **2** Anything used by an animal for shelter, as a nest or a den. **3** A building for any special purpose; as, a tool *house.* **4** A household. **5** A family, especially a royal or princely family. **6** A body of persons assembled to discuss and make laws for a country or state, as the **House of Representatives**, the lower branch of the United States Congress and of certain state legislatures in the United States, and the **House of Commons**, the lower house, and the **House of Lords**, the upper house, of the Parliament of Great Britain and Northern Ireland. **7** The building or chamber where such a body of persons meets. **8** A theater or the audience in a theater; as, a full *house;* to play to a good *house.* **9** A place of business; a commercial firm; as, the *house* of Rothschild. — \'haủz\ *v.;* **housed** \'haủzd\; **hous·ing** \'haủ-zing\. To take or put into a house or under cover; to shelter; to provide a house or houses for. Volunteers helped to *house* the flood victims.

house·boat \'haủs-ˌbōt\ *n.* A boat used as a dwelling; especially, a large flat-bottomed boat with an upper structure like a house, used for cruising.

house·boy \'haủs-ˌbȯi\ *n.* A boy or man hired to act as a general household servant.

house·break \'haủs-ˌbrāk\ *v.;* **house·broke** \-ˌbrōk\; **house·bro·ken** \-ˌbrōk-n\; **house·break·ing.** To train an animal to control its excretions so that it can share the living quarters of human beings. — **house·bro·ken** \-ˌbrōk-n\ or **house·broke** \-ˌbrōk\ *adj.*

house·break·ing \'haủs-ˌbrāk-ing\ *n.* **1** The action of breaking into another person's house with the intention of committing a crime. **2** The action or process of training an animal to live in a house. — **house·break·er** \-ˌbrāk-r\ *n.*

house·fly \'haủs-ˌflī\ *n.; pl.* **house·flies.** A two-winged fly, common about dwelling houses, whose larvae, or maggots, hatch in decaying matter.

house·hold \'haủs-ˌhōld\ *n.* All the persons who live in one house; a family. — *adj.* **1** Of or relating to a household; domestic; as, *household* chores; *household* goods. **2** Familiar; common; as, great men whose names have become *household* words.

house·hold·er \'haủs-ˌhōld-r\ *n.* **1** One who occupies a house. **2** The head of a household or family.

house·keep·er \'haủs-ˌkēp-r\ *n.* A person who does or oversees the work of keeping house.

house·keep·ing \'haủs-ˌkēp-ing\ *n.* The care and management of a house and home affairs.

house·maid \'haủs-ˌmād\ *n.* A female household servant.

house·top \'haủs-ˌtäp\ *n.* A roof.

house·warm·ing \'haủs-ˌwȯr-ming\ *n.* A party given by or for those moving into a new house.

house·wife \'haủs-ˌwīf; *sense 2 is often* 'həz-əf, 'həs-\ *n.; pl.* **house·wives** \-ˌwīvz, -əfs\. **1** A woman whose chief occupation is keeping house in her own home. **2** A little bag or case for needles, thread, and pins.

house·wife·ly \'haủs-ˌwīf-lē\ *adj.* Relating to or befitting a housewife; domestic; thrifty. — *adv.* In a housewifely manner.

house·wif·ery \'haủs-ˌwīf-r(-)ē\ *n.* The work of a housewife; housekeeping.

house·work \'haủs-ˌwərk\ *n.* The work of keeping house, as sweeping, washing, and cooking.

hous·ing \'haủ-zing\ *n.* **1** The act of sheltering. **2** Something that shelters or covers; shelter; lodging; as, to find *housing* for the night. **3** Houses taken together; as, a community with insufficient *housing.* **4** A frame or other support for holding part of a machine in place. **5** The part of a mast that is below the deck of a boat.

hous·ing \'haủ-zing\ *n.* **1** A covering, especially an ornamental covering, for the back and sides of a horse. **2** [in the plural] Trappings.

hove. A past tense and past part. of *heave.*

hov·el \'həv-l, 'häv-l\ *n.* **1** A rough shed or shelter. **2** A small, poor house, cabin, or hut; especially, one that is dirty and in bad repair.

hov·er \'həv-r, 'häv-r\ *v.;* **hov·ered; hov·er·ing** \-r(-)ing\. **1** To hang fluttering in the air, or on the wing; to remain floating over a place or object; as, birds *hovering* over their nest. **2** To move to and fro near a place, especially as if watching or undecided what to do; as, suspicious characters *hovering* about the doors of a bank. **3** To waver in a situation whose outcome is uncertain; as, to lie for days *hovering* between life and death.

how \'haủ\ *adv.* **1** In what way; by what means; as, to study *how* plants grow. *How* was it done? **2** To what degree, number, or amount; as, to wonder *how* much something costs. *How* cold is it? **3** In what condition or state of health. *How* are you? **4** For what reason; why. *How* is it that you are here? **5** What. *How* about a game of tennis?

how·be·it \haủ-'bē-ət\ *conj. Archaic.* Be it as it may; nevertheless.

how·dah \'haů-ə\ *n.* A seat, usually covered, on the back of an elephant.

how·ev·er \haů-'ev-r\ *adv.* **1** In whatever way; by whatever means; to whatever extent. **2** Nevertheless; yet — often used as a conjunction.

how·itz·er \'haů-əts-r\ *n.* [From German *haubitze*, there borrowed from Czech *houfnice* originally meaning "catapult".] A short-barreled, relatively lightweight cannon used for firing shells at low speed in a high curving path.

howl \'haůl\ *v.* **1** To utter a loud, long, mournful cry, as a dog or wolf. **2** To make a wailing sound; as, wind *howling* through the trees. **3** To yell; to scream; to shout; as, to *howl* with rage; to *howl* with laughter. **4** To utter or to bring about with a howl; as, to *howl* a song; to *howl* down a speaker. **—** *n.* **1** The long, loud, mournful cry of a dog or wolf, or a similar sound. **2** A long wail; a wild yell.

howl·er \'haůl-r\ *n.* **1** One that howls. **2** An exceptionally stupid or ridiculous mistake.

how·so·ev·er \'haů-sə-'wev-r\ *adv.* **1** In whatever manner. **2** To whatever degree or extent.

hoy·den \'hȯid-n\ *n.* **1** A rude, ill-bred girl. **2** A tomboy. **—** *adj.* Boisterous; hoydenish; as, *hoyden* pranks not very becoming in a young woman. — **hoy·den·ish** \-ish\ *adj.*

h.p. Abbreviation for *horsepower.*

H.Q. Abbreviation for *headquarters.*

hr. Abbreviation for *hour.*

h's. Pl. of *h.*

ht. Abbreviation for *height.*

hub \'həb\ *n.* **1** The center of a wheel. **2** A center of activity.

hub

hub·bub \'həb-ˌəb\ *n.* An uproar; a din.

huck·le·ber·ry \'hək-l-ˌber-ē\ *n.; pl.* **huck·le·ber·ries.** **1** The edible, many-seeded black or blue-black berry of a bush related to the blueberry, differing from the blueberry in being more acid and having a shiny skin. **2** The bush bearing these berries.

huck·ster \'həkst-r\ *n.* **1** A peddler. **2** A mean, miserly person.

hud·dle \'həd-l\ *v.;* **hud·dled; hud·dling** \-l(-)ing\. **1** To crowd, push, or pile together; as, people *huddled* in a doorway out of the rain. **2** In football, to gather in a group to hear signals for the next play. **3** To curl or draw oneself together; as, a child lying *huddled* up in its bed; to *huddle* by a fire. **4** To drive or push hurriedly or in disorder. The police *huddled* the crowd away from the burning building. **—** *n.* **1** A number of persons or things crowded together in a confused way; a jumble. **2** In football, a gathering of players of a team to hear signals. **3** A secret conference.

hue \'hyü\ *n.* **1** Color; as, flowers of every *hue.* **2** A shade; a modification of a color. The red faded to a dingy *hue.*

hue and cry. Any shout or outcry of alarm, pursuit, attack, or objection; as, the *hue and cry* against an increase in taxes.

huff \'həf\ *n.* A sudden fit of anger or sulkiness.

huffy \'həf-ē\ *adj.;* **huff·i·er; huff·i·est. 1** Easily offended; touchy. **2** Offended; sulky. — **huff·i·ly** \-l-ē\ *adv.*

hug \'həg\ *v.;* **hugged; hug·ging. 1** To clasp a person or thing in one's arms; to embrace. **2** To cling to, as an idea or a habit. **3** To keep close to something; as, a ship *hugging* the shore. **—** *n.* A close embrace.

huge \'hyüj, 'yüj\ *adj.;* **hug·er; hug·est.** Very large; vast; enormous. — **huge·ly,** *adv.*

hug·ger·mug·ger \'həg-r-ˌməg-r\ *n.* Confusion; disorder.

hulk \'həlk\ *n.* **1** A heavy clumsy ship. **2** The body of an old ship, or of a wrecked ship, unfit for use at sea. **3** [in the plural] Ships built for or used as prisons; as, a thief condemned to the *hulks.* **4** A person or thing that is bulky or clumsy; as, a great *hulk* of a man.

hulk·ing \'həl-king\ *adj.* Bulky; heavy and clumsy; as, a great *hulking* fellow.

hull \'həl\ *n.* **1** The outside covering of a fruit or seed, as of corn or peas, or the cluster of small leaves clinging about one end of a fruit, as of a strawberry. **2** The outer frame of the main body of a ship, airship, or seaplane. **—** *v.* To remove the hulls from something; as, to *hull* peas.

hull

hul·la·ba·loo \'həl-ə-bə-ˌlü, -'lü\ *n.; pl.* **hul·la·ba·loos.** A great noise; an uproar.

hum \'həm\ *v.;* **hummed; hum·ming. 1** To utter a prolonged *m*-like sound with the mouth closed. **2** To buzz or drone, as a bee in flight. **3** To sing with closed lips; as, to *hum* a tune. **4** To bring to a certain condition by singing in this way; as, to *hum* a child to sleep. **5** To give forth a low murmur or a confused sound; as, a street *humming* with activity. **6** To be lively or active; as, to make things *hum.* **—** *n.* The act of humming or the prolonged, murmuring sound of humming.

hu·man \'hyü-mən, 'yü-\ *adj.* **1** Belonging or relating to man or mankind; having to do with or consisting of people; as, the *human* race; *human* nature. **2** Being a man, woman, or child; having human form or characteristics; as, a *human* being. It is only *human* to make mistakes.

— The word *humane* is a synonym of *human: human* may describe anything, especially an emotion or weakness, which is thought of as typical or characteristic of all mankind; *humane* usually refers to an attitude of compassion and sympathy for others, particularly for the lower animals.

— *n.* A human being.

hu·mane \hyü-'mān\ *adj.* **1** Having or showing the best qualities of human beings; gentle; kind; sympathetic; as, a *humane* judge. **2** Humanizing; as, *humane* studies.

— The word *merciful* is a synonym of *humane:*

humane usually suggests general kindness and sympathy for others; *merciful* is more likely to suggest leniency in situations where one might justly have been severe. — For other synonyms see *human*.

hu·mane·ly \hyü-'mān-lē\ *adv.* In a humane manner; with humanity.

hu·man·i·tar·i·an \(ˌ)hyü-ˌman-ə-'ter-ē-ən, (ˌ)yü-\ *n.* A person who is actively interested in promoting the welfare of all mankind; a philanthropist. — *adj.* Relating to or concerned with the welfare of human beings; benevolent; philanthropic.

hu·man·i·ty \hyü-'man-ət-ē, yü-\ *n.; pl.* **hu·man·i·ties.** **1** The quality of being human; human nature; the peculiar nature of man that marks him off from other beings. **2** The quality of being humane, or merciful and kindly; kindness; sympathy; as, an act of great *humanity*. **3** The human race; mankind. **4** [in the plural, with *the*] Studies such as literature and philosophy as contrasted with the physical and social sciences; especially, the classical languages and literatures.

hu·man·ize \'hyü-mə-ˌnīz, 'yü-\ *v.;* **hu·man·ized; hu·man·iz·ing.** **1** To adapt to human nature or use. **2** To make humane; to civilize or refine.

hu·man·kind \'hyü-mən-'kīnd, 'yü-\ *n.* Mankind; the human race.

hu·man·ly \'hyü-mən-lē, 'yü-\ *adv.* **1** In a human manner. **2** Within the power or experience of a human being; as, something that is not *humanly* possible.

hum·ble \'həm-bl, 'əm-\ *adj.;* **hum·bler** \-blər\; **hum·blest** \-bləst\. **1** Not bold or proud; meek; as, a *humble* man; a *humble* request. **2** Simple; low in rank or condition; lowly; as, a *humble* dwelling; a *humble* occupation. — *v.;* **hum·bled; hum·bling** \-bl(-)ing\. To make humble; to reduce the pride or power of; as, to *humble* oneself before others; to show no signs of being *humbled* by a defeat. — **hum·bly** \-blē\ *adv.*

hum·bug \'həm-ˌbəg\ *n.* A false or deceiving person or thing; a fraud; a sham. — *v.;* **hum·bugged; hum·bug·ging.** To deceive. — **hum·bug·gery** \-ˌbəg-r(-)ē\ *n.*

hum·drum \'həm-ˌdrəm\ *adj.* Dull; tiresome; monotonous.

hu·mer·us \'hyüm-r-əs\ *n.; pl.* **hu·meri** \-r-ˌī\ or **hu·mer·us·es** \-r-ə-səz\. **1** The bone of the upper part of the arm, from the shoulder to the elbow; a corresponding bone in the front limbs of other animals or in wings of birds. **2** The part of the limb containing this bone.

hu·mid \'hyü-məd, 'yü-\ *adj.* Damp; moist; as, a *humid* day; a *humid* climate.

hu·mid·i·fi·er \hyü-'mid-ə-ˌfīr, yü-\ *n.* Any device or apparatus for keeping the air moist.

hu·mid·i·fy \hyü-'mid-ə-ˌfī, yü-\ *v.;* **hu·mid·i·fied** \-ˌfīd\; **hu·mid·i·fy·ing.** To moisten; to dampen; especially, to increase the moisture content of the air, as of a room.

hu·mid·i·ty \hyü-'mid-ət-ē, yü-\ *n.; pl.* **hu·mid·i·ties.** Dampness; moisture; especially, the amount of moisture in the air. — **relative humidity.** The ratio of the amount of vapor present in the air to the greatest amount possible (called 100) at a given temperature.

hu·mi·dor \'hyü-mə-ˌdȯr\ *n.* A case or jar in which the air is kept properly humidified for storing cigars or tobacco.

hu·mil·i·ate \hyü-'mil-ē-ˌāt, yü-\ *v.;* **hu·mil·i·at·ed; hu·mil·i·at·ing.** To lower the pride or self-respect of; to humble; to mortify. Mother was *humiliated* by finding that she did not have food enough for her guests. — **hu·mil·i·at·ing·ly** \-ˌāt-ing-lē\ *adv.*

hu·mil·i·a·tion \(ˌ)hyü-ˌmil-ē-'āsh-n, (ˌ)yü-\ *n.* The action of humiliating or the condition or feeling of being humiliated.

hu·mil·i·ty \hyü-'mil-ət-ē, yü-\ *n.* Freedom from pride; meekness.

hummed. Past tense and past part. of *hum*.

humming. Pres. part. of *hum*.

hum·ming·bird \'həm-ing-ˌbərd\ *n.* A very small brilliantly-colored American bird related to the swifts, with wings that beat so rapidly that a humming sound is produced.

hum·mock \'həm-ək\ *n.* **1** A rounded mound of earth; a knoll. **2** A ridge or pile of ice, as on an ice field. — **hum·mocky** \-ə-kē\ *adj.*

hu·mor \'hyüm-r, 'yüm-r\ *n.* **1** State of mind; mood; as, to be in a good *humor*. **2** The funny side of things; as, the *humor* of a situation. **3** The power to see or tell about the funny side of things; a keen perception of the comic or the ridiculous; as, a writer famous for his *humor*. — For synonyms see *mood*. — *v.;* **hu·mored; hu·mor·ing** \-r(-)ing\. To yield to the wishes or comply with the mood of another person; as, to *humor* an invalid. — For synonyms see *gratify*.

hu·mor·ist \'hyüm-r-əst, 'yüm-\ *n.* A person who writes or talks with humor.

hu·mor·ous \'hyüm-r(-)əs, 'yüm-\ *adj.* Full of humor; amusing; funny. — **hu·mor·ous·ly,** *adv.*

hump \'həmp\ *n.* **1** A rounded bulge or lump, as on the back of a camel. **2** A mound or hummock. — *v.* **1** To make something hump-shaped; to hunch up into a hump; as, to *hump* up the earth around a transplanted tree. **2** *Slang.* To put into lively action; to exert; as, to *hump* oneself to catch a bus.

hump·back \'həmp-ˌbak\ *n.* **1** A crooked back; a humped back. **2** A hunchback. — **hump·backed** \-ˌbakt\ *adj.*

hu·mus \'hyü-məs\ *n.* [From Latin, meaning "ground", "earth", "soil".] A brown or black material formed by the partial decay of vegetable or animal matter; the portion of the soil composed of such matter.

hunch \'hənch\ *v.* **1** To push out or bend into a hump; as, to *hunch* one's shoulders. **2** To push or move oneself forward by jerks; as, to *hunch* nearer the fire. — *n.* **1** A hump or lump. **2** A feeling that a certain thing is going to happen; as, to have a *hunch* that the team will win.

hunch·back \'hənch-ˌbak\ *n.* **1** A crooked, rounded back; a back with a hunch or hump. **2** A person who has such a back. — **hunch·backed** \-ˌbakt\ *adj.*

hun·dred \'hən-drəd, -dərd\ *adj.* Ten times ten; ninety-nine and one more. — *n.* **1** The sum of ten tens; one hundred units or objects; five score. **2** The figure standing for a hundred units, as 100 or C.

hun·dred·fold \'hən-drəd-'fōld, -dərd-\ *adj.* or *adv.* A hundred times as much or as many.

hun·dredth \'hən-drədth, -dərdth\ *adj.* Next after the ninety-ninth. — *n.* One of a hundred equal parts.

hun·dred·weight \'hən-drəd-ˌwāt, -dərd-\ *n.; pl.* **hun·dred·weights** or **hun·dred·weight**. A unit of weight, commonly 100 pounds in the United States.

hung. A past tense and past part. of *hang.*

Hun·gar·i·an \həng-'ger-ē-ən\ *adj.* Of or relating to Hungary or its people or the language of the Magyars. — *n.* **1** A native or citizen of Hungary; especially, a Magyar. **2** The language of the Magyars.

hun·ger \'həng-gr\ *n.* **1** A desire or a need for food; an uneasy feeling or weakened condition resulting from lack of food. **2** Any strong or eager desire for something; a craving; as, a *hunger* for praise. — *v.;* **hun·gered; hun·ger·ing** \-gr(-)ing\. To feel hunger; to have eager desire; to long; as, to *hunger* for affection.

hunger strike. Refusal to eat enough to keep a person alive, as by a prisoner in an effort to obtain his demands.

hun·gry \'həng-grē\ *adj.;* **hun·gri·er; hun·gri·est. 1** Feeling or showing hunger; feeling or showing an intense desire; as, a face with a *hungry* look; to go to bed *hungry.* **2** Not rich or fertile; as, *hungry* soil. — **hun·gri·ly** \-grə-lē\ *adv.*

hunk \'həngk\ *n.* A piece or lump; as, a *hunk* of cheese.

hunt \'hənt\ *v.* **1** To follow or search for game for the purpose of capturing or killing; as, to *hunt* deer; to *hunt* in Africa. **2** To seek carefully; search for; as, to *hunt* bargains; to *hunt* for a lost book. **3** To search through in pursuit of game; as, to *hunt* a woods. **4** To use in hunting game; as, to raise a dog with the idea of *hunting* him. **5** To drive; to chase; as, to *hunt* a thief out of town. — *n.* **1** The act or practice of hunting. **2** A search. **3** A group of persons, with dogs and usually with horses, engaged in hunting; an association of hunters. **4** A district or region hunted over.

hunt·er \'hənt-r\ *n.* **1** A person who hunts; especially, one who hunts game. **2** A dog or a horse trained for hunting.

hunt·ing \'hənt-ing\ *n.* The act of one who hunts; especially, the pursuit of game.

hunt·ress \'hən-trəs\ *n.* A woman who hunts.

hunts·man \'hənts-mən\ *n.; pl.* **hunts·men** \-mən\. **1** A man who hunts; a hunter. **2** A man who manages a hunt and handles its dogs.

hur·dle \'hərd-l\ *n.* **1** A movable frame, as one made of twigs or canes, used for fencing land. **2** A barrier to be jumped in a race. **3** [in the plural] A race in which such barriers are used. **4** Any obstacle or difficulty to be overcome. — *v.;* **hur·dled; hur·dling** \-l(-)ing\. **1** To leap over while running, as a person leaps a hurdle in a race. **2** To overcome difficulties. — **hur·dler** \-lər\ *n.*

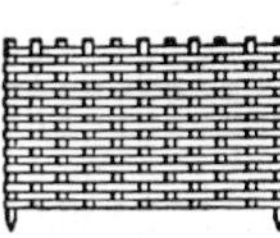
hurdle, 1

hur·dy-gur·dy \'hərd-ē-'gərd-ē\ *n.; pl.* **hur·dy-gur·dies**. Any musical instrument, as a hand organ, played by turning a crank.

hurl \'hərl\ *v.* **1** To throw violently; to fling; as, to *hurl* a spear. **2** In baseball, to pitch. — For synonyms see *throw.* — *n.* A violent throw; a fling. — **hurl·er**, *n.*

hurly-burly \'hər-lē-'bər-lē\ *n.; pl.* **hurly-burl·ies.** Tumult; uproar; noisy confusion.

hur·rah \hə-'rȯ, hü-, hu̇-, -'rä, -'rȧ\ or **hur·ray** \-'rā\ *interj.* An exclamation expressing joy, triumph, or approval. — *n.* A cheer; a shout of joy. — *v.* To cheer; to shout hurrahs.

hur·ri·cane \'hər-ə-ˌkān, 'hə-rə-ˌkān, 'hər-ək-n, 'hə-rək-n\ *n.* A violent windstorm of wide extent usually originating in the tropics, with winds from 75 to 100 miles an hour, heavy rain, and usually thunder and lightning.

hur·ried \'hər-ēd, 'hə-rēd\ *adj.* **1** Going or working at speed; as, the *hurried* atmosphere of a newspaper office. **2** Done in a hurry; hasty; as, a *hurried* visit; a *hurried* meal. — **hur·ried·ly** \'hər-əd-lē, 'hə-rəd-, 'hər-ēd-, 'hə-rēd-\ *adv.*

hur·ry \'hər-ē, 'hə-rē\ *v.;* **hur·ried** \'hər-ēd, 'hə-rēd\; **hur·ry·ing. 1** To move or act, or to make someone or something move or act, quickly or hastily; to hasten; as, to *hurry* home; to *hurry* a letter to the postoffice. **2** To urge on to greater speed; as, to refuse to be *hurried.* **3** To hasten the preparation or progress of; as, to *hurry* dinner; to *hurry* a job. — *n.; pl.* **hur·ries. 1** Quick motion; haste; rush. **2** Unnecessary haste or eagerness; need for haste. We can take our time; there's no *hurry.* — For synonyms see *haste.* — **in a hurry. 1** In great haste; as, a job done *in a hurry.* **2** Impatient; as, to be *in a hurry* to leave. **3** Soon; willingly; as, a mistake that he won't repeat *in a hurry.*

hurt \'hərt\ *v.;* **hurt; hurt·ing. 1** To cause or give physical pain or distress to; as, to try to lance a boil without *hurting* the patient. **2** To damage; to injure; to harm; as, to *hurt* one's arm. Water will *hurt* this cloth. **3** To wound the feelings of; to offend; as, to *hurt* someone with a thoughtless remark. **4** To give the sensation of pain; as, a tooth that *hurts.* — *n.* **1** A blow, bruise, or injury or the pain it causes. **2** Harm; damage; as, to intend no *hurt.*

hurt·ful \'hərt-fəl\ *adj.* Causing hurt or pain; harmful; injurious. — **hurt·ful·ly** \-fə-lē\ *adv.*

hur·tle \'hərt-l\ *v.;* **hur·tled; hur·tling** \-l(-)ing\. **1** To rush suddenly or violently. The rock *hurtled* down the hill. **2** To drive or throw violently; to fling.

hus·band \'həz-bənd\ *n.* [From Old English *husbonda* meaning "master of the house".] A man who has a wife; the male partner in a marriage. — *v.* To manage with thrift; to use carefully; as, to *husband* one's money.

hus·band·man \'həz-bən(d)-mən\ *n.; pl.* **hus·band·men** \-mən\. A farmer.

hus·band·ry \'həz-bən-drē\ *n.* **1** Wise management of household affairs; thrift; economy. **2** The business of a husbandman; farming. **3** The management of a person's business.

hush \'həsh\ *v.* **1** To make quiet, calm, or still; to soothe; as, to *hush* a baby to sleep. **2** To become or stay quiet. — **hush up.** To keep from becoming known or talked about; as, to *hush up* a scandal. — *n.* Stillness; quiet; as, the *hush* of the night.

hush pup·py \'həsh ˌpəp-ē\. A cornmeal bread, shaped into small cakes and fried in deep fat.

husk \'həsk\ *n.* **1** The outer covering of a fruit or seed, as of corn, grain, or coconuts. **2** The outside covering of anything, especially when rough or worthless. — *v.* To strip the husk from; as, to *husk* corn. — **husk·er,** *n.*

husk·ing \'həs-king\ *n.* or **husking bee.** A gathering of neighbors or friends to husk corn.

husky \'həs-kē\ *adj.;* **husk·i·er; husk·i·est.** **1** Abounding with husks; consisting of or resembling husks or a husk; as, a fruit with a *husky* shell. **2** Harsh or rough in tone; hoarse; as, a *husky* voice. **3** Strong; powerful; burly. — *n.; pl.* **husk·ies.** A husky person. — **husk·i·ly** \'həsk-l-ē\ *adv.*

hus·ky \'həs-kē\ *n.; pl.* **hus·kies.** [sometimes with a capital] An Eskimo dog.

hus·sar \ˌhə-'zär, -'zȧr\ *n.* A member of certain cavalry units in European armies, usually with brilliant uniforms.

hus·sy \'həz-ē, 'həs-ē\ *n.; pl.* **hus·sies.** [An altered form of *housewife,* its original meaning.] **1** A worthless woman or girl. **2** A pert or saucy girl.

hus·tings \'həs-tingz\ *n. pl.* Any place where political campaign speeches are made.

hus·tle \'həs-l\ *v.;* **hus·tled; hus·tling** \-l(-)ing\. **1** To push, crowd, or force forward roughly. The police *hustled* their prisoner off to jail. **2** To move or work rapidly and tirelessly; as, a worker who is able to *hustle* all day; a person who always *hustles* when he walks. — *n.* **1** The action of a person who hustles; a pushing or shoving. **2** Energy; energetic activity. — **hus·tler** \-lər\ *n.*

hut \'hət\ *n.* A small rude house or cabin.

hutch \'həch\ *n.* **1** A chest or a box for storage, as of grain. **2** A cage or coop; as, a rabbit *hutch.* **3** A hut; a hovel. **4** A cupboard or set of shelves for dishes, often with drawers for table linens and silver; a dresser.

huz·za \(ˌ)hə-'zä, -'zȧ\ *interj.* or *n.* Hurrah.

hy·a·cinth \'hī-ə-(ˌ)sin(t)th\ *n.; pl.* **hy·a·cinths** \-(ˌ)sints, -(ˌ)sin(t)ths\. A plant of the lily family, having a large deep bulb, grasslike leaves, and fragrant bell-shaped six-lobed flowers in a thick spike.

hy·brid \'hīb-rəd\ *n.* **1** The offspring of two animals or plants of different species or of different races, varieties, or strains within the same species. **2** Anything of mixed origin or composition. — *adj.* **1** Bred from two distinct species or from two distinct races, varieties, or strains; as, a *hybrid* rose. **2** Of mixed origin. — **hy·brid·ism** \-rə-ˌdiz-m\ *n.*

hy·brid·ize \'hīb-rə-ˌdīz\ *v.;* **hy·brid·ized; hy·brid·iz·ing.** To cause to produce a hybrid; to produce a hybrid, as by cross-pollination; to interbreed. — **hy·brid·i·za·tion** \ˌhīb-rə-də-'zāsh-n\ *n.*

hy·dra \'hīd-rə\ *n.; pl.* **hy·dras** \-rəz\ or **hy·drae** \'hī-ˌdrē\. A small aquatic animal related to the jellyfishes, having a body consisting of a simple tube with an adhesive platelike foot at one end and a mouth surrounded by tentacles at the other.

hy·dran·gea \hī-'drān-jə\ *n.* A bush with broad, pointed leaves and rounded clusters of white, bluish, or pinkish flowers.

hy·drant \'hīd-rənt\ *n.* A pipe with a valve and spout through which water may be drawn from the main pipes; as, a fire *hydrant.*

hy·drau·lic \hī-'drȯl-ik\ *adj.* **1** Having to do with hydraulics; carrying water; acting or done by means of water; as, *hydraulic* mining. **2** Becoming hard or firm under water; as, *hydraulic* cement. **3** Indicating a piece of machinery that operates by using the resistance offered when a body of liquid is forced through a small hole; as, *hydraulic* brakes.

hy·drau·lics \hī-'drȯl-iks\ *n.* The science that deals with facts about water or other fluid in motion, as in rivers and canals and in driving machinery.

hy·dro·car·bon \ˌhīd-rə-'kärb-n, -'kȧrb-n\ *n.* A compound consisting only of hydrogen and carbon, as benzine.

hy·dro·chlo·ric ac·id \'hīd-rə-ˌklōr-ik, -ˌklȯr-\. A strong, colorless acid usually made by the action of sulphuric acid on salt, normally present in dilute form in the stomach, and used commercially and in general chemical work; muriatic acid.

hy·dro·elec·tric \'hīd-rō-i-'lek-trik\ *adj.* [From English *hydro-* (a prefix meaning "water" and derived from Greek *hydor*) and *electric.*] Having to do with, or used in, making electricity by water power or steam; as, a *hydroelectric* power plant. — **hy·dro·elec·tric·i·ty** \ˌhīd-rō-i-ˌlek-'tris-ət-ē\ *n.*

hy·dro·gen \'hīd-rəj-n\ *n.* [From French *hydrogène* meaning literally "water producer" and named by 18th-century French scientists who thought of it primarily as a water-forming element, because when it is added to oxygen, which they considered the basic element, water is formed.] A gaseous element, colorless, odorless, tasteless, and lighter than any other known substance. — **hy·drog·e·nous** \hī-'dräj-n-əs\ *adj.*

hydrogen bomb. A bomb whose great power is

due to the sudden release of energy when the central portions of hydrogen atoms unite.

hydrogen per·ox·ide \pə-'räk-ˌsīd\. A colorless liquid used as a bleaching agent and as an antiseptic.

hydrogen sul·fide \'səl-ˌfīd\. A bad-smelling gas suggesting the odor of rotten eggs, found in many mineral waters.

hy·dro·graph·ic \ˌhīd-rə-'graf-ik\ or **hy·dro·graph·i·cal** \-ik-l\ *adj.* Of or relating to hydrography.

hy·drog·ra·phy \hī-'dräg-rə-fē\ *n.* **1** The study of seas, lakes, rivers, and other waters, especially with reference to their use by man. **2** The mapping and charting of bodies of water. — **hy·drog·ra·pher** \-rəf-r\ *n.*

hy·droid \'hī-ˌdrȯid\ *adj.* Of or relating to a hydrozoan; resembling the hydra; polyplike. — *n.* **1** A hydrozoan. **2** The polyp form of a hydrozoan as distinguished from the medusa, or free-swimming form.

hy·drom·e·ter \hī-'dräm-ət-r\ *n.* An instrument for measuring the specific gravity of a liquid.

hy·dro·pho·bia \ˌhīd-rə-'fō-bē-ə\ *n.* Rabies.

hy·dro·plane \'hīd-rə-ˌplān\ *n.* **1** A motorboat that glides on the surface of the water and at high speeds rises partly out of it. **2** An airplane built to take off from and alight upon water; a seaplane.

hydroplane, 2

hy·dro·pon·ics \ˌhīd-rə-'pän-iks\ *n.* The growing of plants, especially vegetables, without soil by immersing their roots in water containing the various substances necessary for growth.

hy·dro·sphere \'hīd-rə-ˌsfir\ *n.* **1** The water vapor that surrounds the earth as part of the atmosphere. **2** All the surface waters of the earth taken together.

hy·drot·ro·pism \hī-'drä-trə-ˌpiz-m\ *n.* The tendency of an organism or any of its parts, as the root of a plant, to turn towards moisture.

hy·dro·zo·an \ˌhīd-rə-'zō-ən\ *n.* Any member of a large class of water animals including the hydra and many jellyfishes and polyps.

hy·e·na \hī-'ē-nə\ *n.* A large and strong, but cowardly, flesh-eating animal of Asia and Africa, related to the dogs.

hy·giene \'hī-ˌjēn\ *n.* The science that deals with the preservation of health; a system of rules or principles for protecting and improving health.

hy·gi·en·ic \ˌhī-jē-'en-ik, hī-'jē-nik\ *adj.* **1** Of or relating to health or hygiene. **2** Sanitary. — **hy·gi·en·i·cal·ly** \-l(-)ē\ *adv.*

hy·gien·ist \'hī-ˌjē-nəst, 'hī-ˌjen-əst\ *n.* A person skilled in hygiene; especially, a person, usually a woman, trained professionally to clean teeth and to give instruction, as to school children, in the hygienic care of the teeth and mouth.

hy·gro·graph \'hīg-rə-ˌgraf\ *n.* An instrument for recording automatically variations in the amount of moisture in the air.

hy·grom·e·ter \hī-'gräm-ət-r\ *n.* An instrument for measuring the amount of moisture in the air.

hying. A pres. part. of *hie.*

hy·me·ne·al \ˌhī-mə-'nē-əl\ *adj.* [Named after *Hymen*, the ancient Greek god of marriage.] Of or relating to marriage.

hy·me·nop·ter·ous \ˌhī-mə-'näpt-r(-)əs\ *adj.* Belonging to a group of mostly four-winged and often highly social insects including the bees, wasps, and ants.

hymn \'him\ *n.* A song of praise or adoration, especially to God; a religious song.

hym·nal \'him-nəl\ *n.* A book of hymns.

hymn·book \'him-ˌbu̇k\ *n.* A hymnal.

hy·per·a·cid·i·ty \ˌhīp-r-ə-'sid-ət-ē\ *n.* An abnormally acid condition, as of the secretions of the stomach.

hy·per·bo·le \hī-'pərb-l-(ˌ)ē\ *n.* A figure of speech in which something is greatly exaggerated for effect, as in "I'm scared to death of spiders"; any greatly exaggerated statement.

hy·per·crit·i·cal \ˌhīp-r-'krit-ik-l\ *adj.* Too critical. — **hy·per·crit·i·cal·ly** \-ik-l(-)ē\ *adv.*

hy·per·sen·si·tiv·i·ty \ˌhīp-r-ˌsen(t)s-ə-'tiv-ət-ē\ *n.* An abnormal state in which the body has become unusually reactive to certain substances, as some pollens or foods, so that exposure to one of these substances causes distress, as from hives, sneezing, or asthma.

hy·per·ten·sion \ˌhīp-r-'tench-n\ *n.* **1** Abnormally high blood pressure. **2** A condition of extreme tension, as from anxiety, worry, or nervous strain.

hy·per·thy·roid·ism \ˌhīp-r-'thī-ˌrȯi-ˌdiz-m\ *n.* Excessive activity of the thyroid gland or the resulting abnormal state of health.

hy·pha \'hī-fə\ *n.; pl.* **hy·phas** \-fəz\ or **hy·phae** \-ˌfē\. One of the threadlike elements of the mycelium of a fungus.

hy·phen \'hīf-n\ *n.* A mark [-] used between the parts of some compound words, or between the syllables of a divided word, as at the end of a line. — *v.;* **hy·phened**; **hy·phen·ing** \-n(-)ing\. To connect or mark with a hyphen.

hy·phen·ate \'hīf-n-ˌāt\ *v.;* **hy·phen·at·ed**; **hy·phen·at·ing.** To hyphen. — **hy·phen·a·tion** \ˌhīf-n-'āsh-n\ *n.*

hyp·not·ic \hip-'nät-ik\ *adj.* **1** Causing or tending to cause sleep; as, a *hypnotic* drug. **2** Relating to hypnotism; under hypnotism; liable to hypnotism; as, *hypnotic* behavior; a *hypnotic* trance. — *n.* **1** Any agent, as a drug, that causes or tends to cause sleep; an opiate; a narcotic. **2** A person who is in a hypnotic state or in whom such a state can be easily induced. — **hyp·not·i·cal·ly** \-ik-l(-)ē\ *adv.*

hyp·no·tism \'hip-nə-ˌtiz-m\ *n.* The act or practice of putting a person or animal into a sleeplike condition, or trance, in which he is under the influence of someone else's suggestions or commands. — **hyp·no·tist** \-nət-əst\ *n.*

hyp·no·tize \'hip-nə-ˌtīz\ *v.;* **hyp·no·tized; hyp·no·tiz·ing.** To put into a hypnotic state; to affect by or as if by hypnotism.

hy·po \'hī-ˌpō\ *n.* [Short for (sodium) *hyposulfite.*] A crystalline salt, sodium hyposulfite (now usually called sodium thiosulfate), used in photography as a fixing agent.

hy·po \'hī-ˌpō\ *n.; pl.* **hy·pos.** A hypodermic.

hy·po·chon·dria \ˌhīp-ə-'kän-drē-ə\ *n.* Continued depression of mind or spirits, especially with undue anxiety over one's own health.

hy·po·chon·dri·ac \ˌhīp-ə-'kän-drē-ˌak\ *n.* A person affected with hypochondria.

hy·po·cot·yl \'hīp-ə-ˌkät-l\ *n.* The part of the stem below the cotyledons in the embryo of a seed plant.

hy·poc·ri·sy \hi-'päk-rə-sē\ *n.; pl.* **hy·poc·ri·sies.** The act or practice of pretending to be what one is not, or to feel what one does not feel; especially, a pretending to be better or more religious than one really is.

hyp·o·crite \'hip-ə-ˌkrit\ *n.* A person who pretends to be something other than he is or better than he really is; one who makes a false pretense of being virtuous or religious.

hyp·o·crit·i·cal \ˌhip-ə-'krit-ik-l\ *adj.* Of or relating to a hypocrite or hypocrisy; insincere. — **hyp·o·crit·i·cal·ly** \-ik-l(-)ē\ *adv.*

hy·po·der·mic \ˌhīp-ə-'dər-mik\ *adj.* Under the skin; as, a *hypodermic* administration of drugs.—*n.* **1** A hypodermic injection. **2** A hypodermic syringe. — **hy·po·der·mi·cal·ly** \-mik-l(-)ē\ *adv.*

hypodermic injection. An injection of a medicine or drug into the tissues under the skin by means of a small tubular syringe (**hypodermic syringe**) having a long hollow needlelike point (**hypodermic needle**).

hy·pot·e·nuse \hī-'pät-n-ˌyüs, -ˌyüz; -n-ˌüs, -ˌüz\ *n.* The side opposite the right angle in a right-angled triangle.

hy·poth·e·sis \hī-'päth-ə-səs\ *n.; pl.* **hy·poth·e·ses** \-ˌsēz\. Something not proved but assumed to be true for purposes of argument or further study or investigation.

hy·po·thet·i·cal \ˌhīp-ə-'thet-ik-l\ *adj.* Involving a hypothesis; assumed without proof to be true or to exist; supposed. — **hy·po·thet·i·cal·ly** \-ik-l(-)ē\ *adv.*

hy·po·thy·roid·ism \ˌhīp-ə-'thī-ˌrȯi-ˌdiz-m\ *n.* Deficient activity of the thyroid gland or the resulting abnormal state of health.

hys·sop \'his-əp\ *n.* **1** A low-growing woody European mint with aromatic leaves and blue flowers, once used as a medicine for bruises. **2** A plant whose twigs were sprinkled in ancient Jewish ceremonies as a purifying agent.

hys·ter·ia \his-'ter-ē-ə, -'tir-\ *n.* **1** A nervous disorder marked by loss of control over the emotions. **2** A wild uncontrolled outburst of emotion.

hys·ter·ic \his-'ter-ik\ *adj.* Hysterical.

hys·ter·i·cal \his-'ter-ik-l\ *adj.* **1** Relating to hysteria. **2** Affected by hysteria; as, a *hysterical* person. **3** Wildly emotional; as, *hysterical* laughter. — **hys·ter·i·cal·ly** \-ik-l(-)ē\ *adv.*

hys·ter·ics \his-'ter-iks\ *n.* A fit of uncontrolled nervousness or emotion; a fit of wild laughter or crying.

i \'ī\ *n.; pl.* **i's** \'īz\. **1** The ninth letter of the alphabet. **2** As a Roman numeral, 1.

I \(')ī\ *pron.* The speaker or writer himself.

I. Abbreviation for *island.*

-ial \ē-əl, yəl, -l\. Variant of *-al.*

iamb \'ī-ˌam(b)\ *n.; pl.* **iambs** \-ˌamz\. A metrical foot of two syllables, the first unaccented and the second accented, as in *display.*

iam·bic \ī-'am-bik\ *adj.* Consisting of an iamb or iambs; as, *iambic* verse; an *iambic* line. — *n.* **1** An iambic foot; an iamb. **2** A verse composed of iambs.

iam·bus \ī-'am-bəs\ *n.; pl.* **iam·bi** \-ˌbī\ or **iam·bus·es** \-bə-səz\. An iamb.

-ian \ē-ən, yən, -n\. Variant of *-an.*

ibex \'ī-ˌbeks\ *n.; pl.* **ibex** or **ibex·es.** A wild goat, especially the **Alpine ibex,** of the Old World, having large backward-curving horns with transverse ridges in front.

ibis \'ī-bəs\ *n.; pl.* **ibis** or **ibis·es.** Any of certain wading birds of the heron family, distinguished by a long, slender bill that curves downward.

-ible \əb-l\. Variant of *-able.*

-ic \ik, *sometimes* ˌik\ or **-ical** \ik-l\. A suffix that can mean: **1** Of the nature of, consisting of, characterized by, as in *angelic, iambic, historical.* **2** Of, belonging to, as in *heroic.* **3** After the manner of, characteristic of, resembling, as in *quixotic.* **4** Connected or dealing with, as in *aquatic, dramatic, domestic.* **5** Coming from, as in *volcanic.*
☞ In current English, the suffixes *-ic* and *-ical* are sometimes, but not always, interchangeable. For example, the words *philosophic* and *philosophical* are used interchangeably, as are *geographic* and *geographical.* But the words *comic* and *comical* are usually not interchangeable, a *comic* actor being one who acts in comedy, and a *comical* actor one about whom there is something funny or ludicrous.

ice \'īs\ *n.* **1** Frozen water. **2** A frozen dessert, especially one not containing cream; a sherbet. **3** A substance that looks like ice; as, camphor *ice.* **4** Icing; frosting, such as that on a cake. — *v.;* **iced; ic·ing. 1** To cover with or supply with ice; to change into ice. **2** To cover with icing, as a cake. **3** To cool; as, to *ice* lemonade. — *adj.* **1** Of ice; connected with or having to do with ice; as, an *ice* pack; *ice* cubes. **2** Used or done on ice; as, *ice* skates; *ice* hockey.

ice age. The glacial epoch.

ice·berg \'īs-ˌbərg\ *n.* [From Danish, Swedish, or Norwegian *isberg*, derived from *is* meaning "ice" and *berg* meaning "mountain".] A large mass of ice that has broken off from the end of a glacier and is floating in the sea.

ice·boat \'īs-ˌbōt\ *n.* **1** A boatlike frame on runners, propelled over ice by means of sails. **2** An icebreaker.

ice·bound \'īs-ˌbau̇nd\ *adj.* Surrounded or obstructed with ice; frozen in; as, an *icebound* river; an *icebound* ship.

ice·box \'īs-ˌbäks\ *n.* A box kept cool by ice, in which food may be kept.

ice·break·er \'īs-ˌbrāk-r\ *n.* A strong boat, as a steamer, used for breaking through ice, as in rivers and harbors.

ice cap \'īs-ˌkap\ A body of ice and snow that never melts away, moving in all directions from the center of an area.

ice cream \'īs 'krēm, ˌkrēm\. A frozen food usually containing cream, flavoring, sweetening, and eggs.

ice·house \'īs-ˌhau̇s\ *n.; pl.* **ice·hous·es** \-ˌhau̇-zəz\. A building for storing ice.

Ice·land·er \'īs-ˌland-r, -lənd-r\ *n.* A native of Iceland.

Ice·lan·dic \īs-'lan-dik\ *adj.* Of or relating to Iceland. — *n.* The language of the Icelanders.

ice·man \'īs-ˌman, -mən\ *n.; pl.* **ice·men** \-ˌmen, -mən\. One who sells and delivers ice.

ice pack. A large area of floating pieces of ice driven more or less closely together.

ice sheet \'īs(h) ˌshēt\. A very large icecap.

ice water. **1** Water cooled by ice. **2** Water formed by melting ice.

ich·thy·ol·o·gy \ˌik-thē-'äl-ə-jē\ *n.* The branch of zoology that treats of fishes. — **ich·thy·ol·o·gist** \-jəst\ *n.*

ici·cle \'ī-ˌsik-l\ *n.* A hanging pointed mass of ice formed from dripping water.

ic·ing \'ī-sing\ *n.* Frosting for cakes.

icon \'ī-ˌkän\ *n.; pl.* **icons** \'ī-ˌkänz\ or **ico·nes** \'īk-ə-ˌnēz\. **1** An image. **2** A picture of Christ, the Virgin Mary, or a saint.

icon·o·clast \ī-'kän-ə-ˌklast\ *n.* **1** A person who destroys icons or attacks the religious use of icons. **2** A person who attacks popular beliefs as false or mistaken. — **icon·o·clas·tic** \(ˌ)ī-ˌkän-ə-'klas-tik\ *adj.*

icon·o·scope \ī-'kän-ə-ˌskōp\ *n.* The cameralike device in television that transforms pictures into electrical impulses sent through the air.

icy \'ī-sē\ *adj.;* **ici·er**; **ici·est**. **1** Like ice; having much ice; covered with ice; cold; frosty; as, an *icy* road; an *icy* wind. **2** Cold and unfriendly; as, an *icy* stare. — **ici·ly** \'īs-l-ē\ *adv.*

I'd \(')īd\. Contraction of *I should, I would,* or *I had.*

idea \ī-'dē-ə, 'ī-(ˌ)dē-ə; *especially in the South, also* 'ī-dē\ *n.* **1** A plan of action; an intention. The boy's *idea* is to study law. **2** Something imagined or pictured in the mind; a notion; an opinion; a fancy; as, to form an *idea* of a foreign country from one's reading. **3** Meaning, explanation, or purpose. The *idea* of the game is to keep from getting caught.

ide·al \ī-'dē-əl, ī-'dēl\ *adj.* **1** Existing only in the mind; not real. **2** Perfect, or considered as perfect; as, an *ideal* place for a picnic; *ideal* weather. — *n.* An idea of something in its perfect form; a standard of perfection; a perfect type; as, to strive to live up to one's *ideals.* — For synonyms see *pattern.*

ide·al·ism \ī-'dē-ə-ˌliz-m\ *n.* **1** The practice of forming, or living according to, ideals. **2** The ability or tendency to see things as one believes they should be rather than as they are. — **ide·al·ist** \-ləst\ *n.* — **ide·al·is·tic** \(ˌ)ī-ˌdē-ə-'lis-tik\ *adj.*

ide·al·ize \ī-'dē-ə-ˌlīz\ *v.;* **ide·al·ized**; **ide·al·iz·ing.** To think of, or to represent, as ideal; as, to *idealize* life on a farm.

ide·al·ly \ī-'dē-ə-lē, ī-'dēl-lē\ *adv.* **1** In thought; mentally. **2** In agreement with an ideal; perfectly.

iden·ti·cal \ī-'dent-ik-l, ə-'dent-\ *adj.* **1** The very same; as, the *identical* book that was lost. **2** Exactly alike or equal. *Identical* awards were given to the winner in each class.

— The words *equivalent* and *equal* are synonyms of *identical* and all apply to one or both of two objects which do not differ from each other: *identical* may suggest complete agreement in all details; *equivalent* usually indicates that the objects considered amount to the same thing in such matters as quality, strength, or importance; *equal* may refer to objects that are the same in some specific way, particularly in number or amount.

iden·ti·cal·ly \ī-'dent-ik-l(-)ē, ə-'dent-\ *adv.* In an identical way.

identical twins. Twins, similar mentally and physically and always of the same sex, developed from a single fertilized egg cell by its complete division in the two-cell stage.

iden·ti·fi·ca·tion \ī-ˌdent-ə-fə-'kāsh-n, ə-ˌdent-\ *n.* An identifying or a being identified; as, to need *identification* in order to cash a check.

iden·ti·fy \ī-'dent-ə-ˌfī, ə-'dent-\ *v.;* **iden·ti·fied** \-ˌfīd\; **iden·ti·fy·ing.** **1** To prove that a person or thing is the same as one already known. The owner *identified* the watch as the one that was stolen from him. **2** To make, treat, or regard a thing as the same as something else; as, to *identify* patriotism with good citizenship. — **iden·ti·fi·a·ble** \-ˌfī-əb-l\ *adj.*

iden·ti·ty \ī-'dent-ət-ē, ə-'dent-\ *n.; pl.* **iden·ti·ties.** **1** The fact or condition of being identical; sameness; as, an *identity* of interests. **2** Distinctness as of character or appearance; individuality. Members of a mob often lose their *identity.* **3** The fact of being the same person or thing as one described or known to exist; as, to prove one's *identity.*

id·e·o·gram \'id-ē-ə-ˌgram, 'īd-ē-\ *n.* **1** A symbol

in the form of a picture, used as an original element of written communication; an early form of hieroglyph. **2** A written symbol representing an idea rather than a word, as the figure 3, which is referred to by different words in different languages.

id·e·o·graph \\'id-ē-ə-ˌgraf, 'īd-ē-\\ *n.* An ideogram.

ide·ol·o·gy \\ˌīd-ē-'äl-ə-jē, ˌid-ē-\\ *n.; pl.* **ide·ol·o·gies.** The ideas characteristic of a particular group, class, or party.

ides \\'īdz\\ *n. pl.* A certain day of the ancient Roman month, the fifteenth in March, May, July, and October, the thirteenth in other months.

id·i·o·cy \\'id-ē-ə-sē\\ *n.; pl.* **id·i·o·cies. 1** The condition of being an idiot; extreme lack of intelligence. **2** Extremely foolish behavior.

id·i·om \\'id-ē-əm\\ *n.* **1** The language or dialect peculiar to an individual, a group, a class, or a district; as, Shakespeare's *idiom;* doctors speaking in their professional *idiom.* **2** The characteristic form or structure of a language; as, to know the vocabulary of a foreign language but not its *idiom.* **3** An expression that cannot be understood from the meanings of its separate words but must be learned as a whole, as *to take cold* or *on no account.*

id·i·o·mat·ic \\ˌid-ē-ə-'mat-ik\\ *adj.* **1** Of or relating to idiom. **2** In accordance with a particular idiom. **3** Characterized by much use of idioms. — **id·i·o·mat·i·cal·ly** \\-ik-l(-)ē\\ *adv.*

id·i·o·syn·cra·sy \\ˌid-ē-ə-'sing-krə-sē\\ *n.; pl.* **id·i·o·syn·cra·sies.** A queer or unusual way, as of acting, thinking, or dressing; a peculiarity. — **id·i·o·syn·crat·ic** \\-ō-sin-'krat-ik\\ *adj.*

id·i·ot \\'id-ē-ət\\ *n.* **1** A feeble-minded person who is not capable of connected speech or of avoiding the common dangers of life. **2** A foolish or silly person.

id·i·ot·ic \\ˌid-ē-'ät-ik\\ *adj.* Senseless; very foolish. — **id·i·ot·i·cal·ly** \\-ik-l(-)ē\\ *adv.*

idle \\'īd-l\\ *adj.;* **idler** \\'īd-lər\\; **idlest** \\-ləst\\. **1** Not based on facts; worthless; as, *idle* rumor; mere *idle* talk. **2** Useless. It is *idle* to want what one cannot have. **3** Not employed; doing nothing; as, *idle* workmen; *idle* machines. **4** Lazy.

— The words *lazy* and *indolent* are synonyms of *idle: idle* usually refers to persons that are either temporarily or habitually without occupation or sometimes to objects temporarily unused; *lazy* suggests a strong dislike of work and a tendency to be constantly unoccupied or to dawdle in one's work; *indolent* generally indicates a love of bodily inactivity and a dislike of movement and exertion, whether physical or mental.

— *v.;* **idled; idling** \\-l(-)ing\\. **1** To spend time doing nothing; as, to *idle* while others work. **2** To waste; to spend in idleness; as, to *idle* one's time away. **3** To run, as an engine or a machine, without being connected for doing useful work. — **idly** \\'īd-lē\\ *adv.*

idler \\'īd-lər\\ *n.* An idle or lazy person.

idol \\'īd-l\\ *n.* **1** An image of a god made or used as an object of worship. **2** Any person or thing that is greatly loved and admired.

idol·a·ter \\ī-'däl-ət-r\\ *n.* **1** One that worships idols. **2** One that idolizes someone or something; a devoted admirer; an adorer.

idol·a·tress \\ī-'däl-ə-trəs\\ *n.* A female idolater.

idol·a·trous \\ī-'däl-ə-trəs\\ *adj.* **1** Of or relating to idolatry. **2** Given to idolatry. — **idol·a·trous·ly,** *adv.*

idol·a·try \\ī-'däl-ə-trē\\ *n.; pl.* **idol·a·tries. 1** The worship of idols. **2** Too much love or admiration for a person or thing.

idol·ize \\'īd-l-ˌīz\\ *v.;* **idol·ized; idol·iz·ing.** To make an idol of; to love or admire to excess.

idyl or **idyll** \\'īd-l\\ *n.* **1** A short description of country life, especially one written in a poetic style. **2** A scene or incident that is a fit subject for an idyl.

idyl·lic \\ī-'dil-ik\\ *adj.* Suitable for an idyl; having the charm of simplicity and naturalness. — **idyl·li·cal·ly** \\-ik-l(-)ē\\ *adv.*

-ie \\ē\\. A suffix used to form diminutives, as in *laddie* and *lassie.*

i.e. \\t͟hat 'iz *or* 'ī-'ē\\. [Abbreviated from Latin *id est* meaning "that is".] That is; that is to say.

if \\(')if, əf\\ *conj.* **1** In case that; supposing that. *If* it rains, there will be no picnic. **2** Whether. The man asked *if* his son was there. **3** Even though; as, an interesting *if* somewhat long story. — **as if.** As one would, or as would be the case, if. The boy ran *as if* someone were chasing him.

ig·loo \\'ig-ˌlü\\ *n.; pl.* **ig·loos.** [From an Eskimo word meaning "house".] An Eskimo hut, often dome-shaped and made of blocks of snow.

igloo

ig·ne·ous \\'ig-nē-əs\\ *adj.* **1** Relating to fire; like fire. **2** Resulting from or produced by the action of heat within the earth; especially, formed by the solidifying of melted material originating within the earth; as, *igneous* rocks.

ig·nite \\ig-'nīt\\ *v.;* **ig·nit·ed; ig·nit·ing. 1** To set on fire; to light; as, to *ignite* a piece of paper. **2** To catch fire; to begin to burn. Dry wood *ignites* quickly.

ig·ni·tion \\ig-'nish-n\\ *n.* **1** The act of igniting; a setting on fire; a lighting. **2** A means of setting on fire. **3** In internal-combustion engines, the process or means of igniting the fuel mixture, as by an electric spark.

ig·no·ble \\ig-'nōb-l\\ *adj.* **1** Not of noble birth. **2** Not honorable; base; mean; as, an *ignoble* act. — **ig·no·bly** \\-'nōb-lē\\ *adv.*

ig·no·min·i·ous \\ˌig-nə-'min-ē-əs\\ *adj.* Disgraced or disgraceful; dishonorable; as, an *ignominious* defeat. — **ig·no·min·i·ous·ly,** *adv.*

ig·no·miny \\'ig-nə-ˌmin-ē, ig-'näm-ə-nē\\ *n.; pl.* **ig·no·min·ies. 1** Disgrace or dishonor. **2** Something that deserves disgrace, as a person's conduct.

ig·no·ra·mus \ˌig-nə-ˈrā-məs\ *n.; pl.* **ig·no·ra·mus·es**. An ignorant person; a dunce.

ig·no·rance \ˈig-nər-ən(t)s\ *n.* The state of being ignorant; lack of knowledge.

ig·no·rant \ˈig-nər-ənt\ *adj.* **1** Having no knowledge or very little knowledge; not educated. **2** Not knowing; unaware; as, to be *ignorant* of the true facts. **3** Resulting from, or showing, lack of knowledge; as, an *ignorant* mistake.

— The word *illiterate* is a synonym of *ignorant: ignorant* generally indicates a lack of knowledge, either of general knowledge as acquired through experience and study, or of particular facts; *illiterate* usually describes persons who either do not know how to read and write or are far below the normal in education or learning.

ig·no·rant·ly \ˈig-nər-ənt-lē\ *adv.* In or through ignorance.

ig·nore \ig-ˈnōr, -ˈnȯr\ *v.;* **ig·nored**; **ig·nor·ing**. To refuse to take notice of; to disregard willfully. The speaker *ignored* the interruption.

i·gua·na \i-ˈgwän-ə, ē-\ *n.* A tropical American lizard, often six feet long, with a crest of erect scales along the back.

il-. A form of *in-* — used before *l*, as in *illogical* or *illumine.*

il·e·um \ˈil-ē-əm\ *n.* The part of the small intestine between the jejunum and the large intestine.

il·i·um \ˈil-ē-əm\ *n.; pl.* **il·ia** \-ē-ə\ or **il·i·ums** \-ē-əmz\. The back, upper one of three bones composing each hipbone.

ilk \ˈilk\ *n.* A family; a breed; a class; a kind — used chiefly in the phrase *of that ilk.*

ill \ˈil\ *adj.;* **worse** \ˈwərs\; **worst** \ˈwərst\. **1** Disagreeable; unfortunate; bad; as, *ill* luck. **2** Showing unfriendliness; unkind; as, *ill* will. **3** Not healthy; sick; as, an *ill* man. **4** Not right or proper; as, an *ill* use of power. — *adv.* In an ill manner; badly. — *n.* Evil; misfortune; sickness.

I'll \(ˈ)īl\. A contraction of *I shall* or *I will.*

ill–ad·vised \ˈil-əd-ˈvīzd\ *adj.* Unwise; as, an *ill-advised* act.

ill–bred \ˈil-ˈbred\ *adj.* Badly brought up.

il·le·gal \(ˈ)i(l)-ˈlē-gl\ *adj.* Not lawful. — **il·le·gal·i·ty** \ˌi(l)-lē-ˈgal-ət-ē\ *n.* — **il·le·gal·ly** \(ˈ)i(l)-ˈlēg-l-ē\ *adv.*

il·leg·i·ble \(ˈ)i(l)-ˈlej-əb-l\ *adj.* Not legible; impossible or very hard to read; as, *illegible* handwriting. — **il·leg·i·bil·i·ty** \(ˌ)i(l)-ˌlej-ə-ˈbil-ət-ē\ *n.* — **il·leg·i·bly** \(ˈ)i(l)-ˈlej-ə-blē\ *adv.*

il·le·git·i·mate \ˌi(l)-lə-ˈjit-m-ət\ *adj.* **1** Born of a father and mother who are not married. **2** Not logically reasoned; as, an *illegitimate* conclusion. **3** Not lawful. — **il·le·git·i·ma·cy** \-m-ə-sē\ *n.* — **il·le·git·i·mate·ly** \-m-ət-lē\ *adv.*

ill–fat·ed \ˈil-ˈfāt-əd\ *adj.* Doomed to misfortune or disaster; so beset with bad luck as to seem to have an evil fate; as, an *ill-fated* ship.

ill–fa·vored \ˈil-ˈfāv-rd\ *adj.* **1** Having a bad or unpleasing face; especially, evil-looking. **2** Offensive; disagreeable; unpleasant.

ill hu·mor \ˈil-ˈhyüm-r, -ˈyüm-r\. Moody crossness. — **ill–hu·mored** \-rd\ *adj.*

il·lib·er·al \(ˈ)i(l)-ˈlib-r(-)əl\ *adj.* **1** Not holding broad views; narrow in point of view. **2** Not generous; stingy.

il·lic·it \(ˈ)i(l)-ˈlis-ət\ *adj.* Not permitted; unlawful. — **il·lic·it·ly**, *adv.*

il·lim·it·able \(ˈ)i(l)-ˈlim-ət-əb-l\ *adj.* Incapable of being limited; boundless. — **il·lim·it·a·bly** \-ə-blē\ *adv.*

il·lit·er·a·cy \(ˈ)i(l)-ˈlit-r-ə-sē, -ˈli-trə-sē\ *n.; pl.* **il·lit·er·a·cies. 1** A lack of learning or knowledge; lack of ability to read and write. **2** An illiterate error in speech or writing.

il·lit·er·ate \(ˈ)i(l)-ˈlit-r-ət, -ˈli-trət\ *adj.* **1** Not knowing how to read or write. **2** Showing lack of education; as, *illiterate* speech. — *n.* A person who is illiterate. — **il·lit·er·ate·ly**, *adv.*

ill–judged \ˈil-ˈjəjd\ *adj.* Ill-advised; unwise.

ill–man·nered \ˈil-ˈman-rd\ *adj.* Not polite; discourteous; rude.

ill–na·tured \ˈil-ˈnāch-rd\ *adj.* Cross; surly. — **ill–na·tured·ly**, *adv.*

ill·ness \ˈil-nəs\ *n.* Sickness.

il·log·i·cal \(ˈ)i(l)-ˈläj-ik-l\ *adj.* Not according to good reasoning. — **il·log·i·cal·ly** \-ik-l(-)ē\ *adv.*

ill–spent \ˈil-ˈspent\ *adj.* Badly spent or used; as, an *ill-spent* life.

ill–starred \ˈil-ˈstärd, -ˈstȧrd\ *adj.* Born under or having one's affairs controlled by an evil star; ill-fated; unlucky; as, an *ill-starred* venture.

ill–suit·ed \ˈil-ˈsüt-əd\ *adj.* Not well adapted; unsuitable; not fitting.

ill–tem·pered \ˈil-ˈtemp-rd\ *adj.* Ill-natured; cross; quarrelsome. — **ill–tem·pered·ly**, *adv.*

ill–timed \ˈil-ˈtīmd\ *adj.* Done or coming at a bad time; inappropriate.

ill–treat \ˈil-ˈtrēt\ *v.* To treat cruelly or improperly; to abuse. — **ill–treat·ment** \-mənt\ *n.*

il·lu·mi·nate \i-ˈlü-mə-ˌnāt\ *v.;* **il·lu·mi·nat·ed**; **il·lu·mi·nat·ing. 1** To make light; to light up; to supply with light; as, to *illuminate* a building. **2** To make clear; to explain; as, to *illuminate* a social problem by relating it to everyday life. **3** To decorate, as a capital letter or the margin of a page, with designs or pictures in colors or gold, as in medieval manuscripts. — **il·lu·mi·na·tor** \-ˌnāt-r\ *n.*

il·lu·mi·na·tion \i-ˌlü-mə-ˈnāsh-n\ *n.* **1** An illuminating or the state of being illuminated; a supplying with light. **2** The light furnished; as, a lamp that provides proper *illumination* for reading. **3** Enlightenment. **4** Decoration, as of the margins and certain capital letters of a book or manuscript, in colors and gold.

il·lu·mine \i-ˈlü-mən\ *v.;* **il·lu·mined**; **il·lu·min·ing.** To illuminate.

ill–us·age \ˈil-ˈyü-sij, -zij\ *n.* Harsh, unkind, or abusive treatment.

ill–use \ˈil-ˈyüz\ *v.;* **ill–used**; **ill–us·ing.** To treat cruelly or badly.

il·lu·sion \i-ˈlüzh-n\ *n.* **1** A misleading image presented to the eye. **2** The state or fact of being led to accept as true something unreal or imagined. **3** A mistaken idea; as, the *illusions* of childhood about the world of grownups.

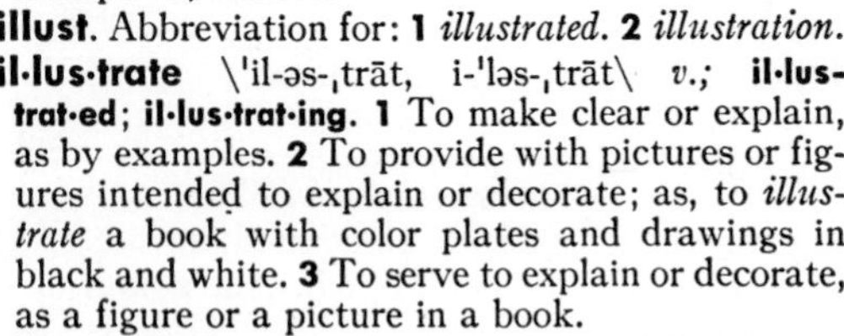

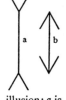

illusion; *a* is equal to *b* but seems longer

il·lu·sive \i-ˈlü-siv, -ziv\ *adj.* Deceiving through a false appearance; misleading; unreal. — **il·lu·sive·ly**, *adv.*

il·lu·so·ry \i-ˈlüs-r-ē, -ˈlüz-\ *adj.* Deceptive; illusive.

illust. Abbreviation for: **1** *illustrated.* **2** *illustration.*

il·lus·trate \ˈil-əs-ˌtrāt, i-ˈləs-ˌtrāt\ *v.;* **il·lus·trat·ed**; **il·lus·trat·ing.** **1** To make clear or explain, as by examples. **2** To provide with pictures or figures intended to explain or decorate; as, to *illustrate* a book with color plates and drawings in black and white. **3** To serve to explain or decorate, as a figure or a picture in a book.

il·lus·tra·tion \ˌil-əs-ˈtrāsh-n, i-ˌləs-\ *n.* **1** The act or process of furnishing with decorative or explanatory pictures or drawings. **2** An example or comparison that makes something more easily understood. **3** A picture or figure intended to explain or decorate, as a book or an article.

il·lus·tra·tive \i-ˈləs-trət-iv, -ˌtrāt-; ˈil-əs-ˌtrāt-iv\ *adj.* Illustrating or intended to illustrate; as, an *illustrative* diagram; a dictionary definition with *illustrative* examples. — **il·lus·tra·tive·ly**, *adv.*

il·lus·tra·tor \ˈil-əs-ˌtrāt-r, i-ˈləs-\ *n.* One that illustrates; especially, an artist who designs or makes illustrations for books and magazines.

il·lus·tri·ous \i-ˈləs-trē-əs\ *adj.* Eminent; renowned; famous.

ill will \ˈil-ˈwil\. Unfriendly or hostile feeling.

il·ly \ˈil-(l)ē\ *adv.* Badly, ill.

I'm \(ˈ)īm\. A contraction of *I am.*

im-. A form of *in-* used before *m*, *b*, or *p*, as in *immature, imbed, impatient.*

im·age \ˈim-ij\ *n.* **1** A likeness or imitation of a person or thing, sculptured, drawn, or painted; especially, a statue. **2** A person or thing that seems just like another; a counterpart; a copy; as, a child who is the *image* of his father. **3** Something seen in the mind; a mental picture. **4** A picture of an object as produced by a mirror or a lens. — *v.;* **im·aged**; **im·ag·ing.** **1** To show, picture, or describe in words. **2** To bring up before the imagination; to imagine; to fancy. **3** To reflect; to mirror, as water does.

im·ag·ery \ˈim-ij-r(-)ē\ *n.* **1** Images of objects taken collectively; statues; carved or sculptured figures. **2** Formation of mental images or the images thus formed. **3** Description through figures of speech or all the figures used in such description; as, the *imagery* of a poem.

imag·i·na·ble \i-ˈmaj-n(-)əb-l\ *adj.* Capable of being imagined; conceivable. — **imag·i·na·bly** \-n(-)ə-blē\ *adv.*

imag·i·nary \i-ˈmaj-n-ˌer-ē\ *adj.* Existing only in the imagination or fancy; not real.

imag·i·na·tion \i-ˌmaj-n-ˈāsh-n\ *n.* **1** The power of forming mental images of things not present to the senses; especially, the power to form pictures or conceptions of persons, scenes, or situations that one has not previously known or experienced. **2** A mental image; a creation of the mind.

imag·i·na·tive \i-ˈmaj-n(-)ət-iv, -n-ˌāt-iv\ *adj.* **1** Of or relating to the imagination. **2** Having a lively imagination; showing imagination; as, an *imaginative* child; an *imaginative* idea. — **imag·i·na·tive·ly**, *adv.*

imag·ine \i-ˈmaj-n\ *v.;* **imag·ined**; **imag·in·ing** \-n(-)ing\. **1** To produce by the imagination; to form a mental picture of; to picture to oneself; to fancy; as, to *imagine* how the house will look when it is finished. **2** To suppose; to guess; to think. I *imagine* there may be rain tonight.

ima·go \i-ˈmā-ˌgō, -ˈmä-\ *n.; pl.* **ima·goes** \-ˌgōz\ or **imag·i·nes** \i-ˈmaj-n-ˌēz\. An insect in its final adult, and usually winged, state.

im·bal·ance \(ˈ)im-ˈbal-ən(t)s\ *n.* Lack of balance; the state of being out of equilibrium or out of proportion.

im·be·cile \ˈim-bəs-l, -bə-ˌsil\ *adj.* **1** Mentally weak; feeble-minded. **2** Extremely stupid or foolish; as, an *imbecile* remark; the *imbecile* behavior of some motorists. — *n.* A feeble-minded person; especially, one incapable of earning a living but not so completely dependent on others as an idiot.

im·be·cil·i·ty \ˌim-bə-ˈsil-ət-ē\ *n.; pl.* **im·be·cil·i·ties.** **1** The condition of being imbecile; feeble-mindedness. **2** Foolishness or an instance of foolishness.

im·bed \im-ˈbed\ *v.;* **im·bed·ded**; **im·bed·ding.** To embed.

im·bibe \im-ˈbīb\ *v.;* **im·bibed**; **im·bib·ing.** **1** To drink or drink in. **2** To receive as if by drinking; to absorb; to assimilate. A sponge *imbibes* moisture. **3** To absorb into the mind and retain; as, to *imbibe* knowledge; to be guided by principles *imbibed* in childhood. — **im·bib·er**, *n.*

im·bi·bi·tion \ˌim-bə-ˈbish-n\ *n.* The act or process of imbibing; absorption; assimilation; especially, the taking up of fluid or of materials in solution, as by the substances of protoplasm or a cell wall.

im·bro·glio \im-ˈbrōl-ˌyō, -ˈbrȯl-\ *n.; pl.* **im·bro·glios.** [From Italian, meaning literally "entanglement".] **1** A difficult or complicated situation. **2** Any awkward or embarrassing state of things, as a serious misunderstanding.

im·bue \im-ˈbyü\ *v.;* **im·bued**; **im·bu·ing.** **1** To saturate, as with moisture or color; to tinge deeply; to dye. **2** To cause to become deeply impressed or penetrated; as, a leader able to *imbue* his followers with courage; men *imbued* with a desire to serve others.

im·i·tate \ˈim-ə-ˌtāt\ *v.;* **im·i·tat·ed**; **im·i·tat·ing.** **1** To follow as a pattern or model; to copy; as, to *imitate* one's father; to *imitate* someone's style of writing. **2** To be like; to resemble; as, paper finished to *imitate* leather. **3** To copy exactly; mimic; as, to *imitate* the barking of a dog.

— The words *mimic* and *mock* are synonyms of *imitate: imitate* may refer to the copying of a model, either an object or an action, in some general way or in some specific detail but allows for a good deal of variation; *mimic* applies especially to the copying of actions in as nearly exact a manner as possible and often suggests making fun of the original; *mock* nearly always suggests scornful and ridiculing imitation of another's words or actions.

im·i·ta·tion \ˌim-ə-ˈtāsh-n\ *n.* **1** The act of imitating; a copying; a mimicking. **2** A result of imitating; something made or produced as a copy of some other thing. — *adj.* Resembling something else of better quality; not real; as, *imitation* leather.

im·i·ta·tive \ˈim-ə-ˌtāt-iv, -tət-\ *adj.* **1** Marked by imitation; as, a composer whose music was largely *imitative; imitative* words such as "buzz" and "hum". **2** Inclined to imitate or copy. **3** Imitation.

im·i·ta·tor \ˈim-ə-ˌtāt-r\ *n.* One that imitates.

im·mac·u·late \i-ˈmak-yə-lət\ *adj.* **1** Without stain or blemish; pure. **2** Spotlessly clean; as, *immaculate* linen. — **im·mac·u·late·ly**, *adv.*

im·ma·te·ri·al \ˌim-ə-ˈtir-ē-əl\ *adj.* **1** Not consisting of material substance; spiritual. **2** Unimportant; trifling.

im·ma·ture \ˌim-ə-ˈtu̇r, -ˈtyu̇r\ *adj.* Not mature or fully developed; unripe; young. — **im·ma·ture·ly** \-lē\ *adv.* — **im·ma·tu·ri·ty** \-ˈtu̇r-ət-ē, -ˈtyu̇r-\ *n.*

im·mea·sur·a·ble \(ˈ)i(m)-ˈmezh-r(-)əb-l, -ˈmāzh-, -rb-l\ *adj.* Not capable of being measured; boundless; as, the *immeasurable* sea. — **im·mea·sur·a·bly** \-r(-)ə-blē, -r-blē\ *adv.*

im·me·di·a·cy \i-ˈmēd-ē-ə-sē\ *n.; pl.* **im·me·di·a·cies.** **1** The quality or state of being immediate, next in place or time, or urgent; as, the *immediacy* of a person's need. **2** That which is of immediate importance; as, the *immediacies* of daily life.

im·me·di·ate \i-ˈmēd-ē-ət; i-ˈmē-jit *is very common in British speech*\ *adj.* **1** Next in line or relationship; as, the king's *immediate* heir. **2** Closest in importance; as, one's *immediate* interest. **3** Acting directly and alone; as, an *immediate* cause of disease. **4** Not distant or separated; next; as, one's *immediate* neighbors. **5** Close in time; as, the *immediate* future. **6** Made or done at once; as, to ask for an *immediate* reply.

im·me·di·ate·ly \-lē\ *adv.* **1** Directly; with nothing between; as, the house *immediately* beyond this one. **2** Without delay; at once.

im·me·mo·ri·al \ˌim-ə-ˈmōr-ē-əl, -ˈmȯr-\ *adj.* Extending beyond the reach of memory or record. — **im·me·mo·ri·al·ly** \-ē-ə-lē\ *adv.*

im·mense \i-ˈmen(t)s\ *adj.* Very great; vast; huge. — **im·mense·ly** \-lē\ *adv.* — **im·men·si·ty** \i-ˈmen(t)s-ət-ē\ *n.*

im·merse \i-ˈmərs\ *v.;* **im·mersed; im·mers·ing.** **1** To plunge into a liquid. **2** To baptize by plunging in water. **3** To absorb; to engage or involve deeply; as, *immersed* in thought. — **im·mer·sion** \i-ˈmərzh-n, -ˈmərsh-n\ *n.*

im·mi·grant \ˈim-ə-grənt\ *n.* A person of foreign birth who enters a country to become a permanent resident.

im·mi·grate \ˈim-ə-ˌgrāt\ *v.;* **im·mi·grat·ed; im·mi·grat·ing.** To come into a foreign country to take up permanent residence there.

im·mi·gra·tion \ˌim-ə-ˈgrāsh-n\ *n.* **1** An immigrating. **2** The number of immigrants arriving during a given period.

im·mi·nence \ˈim-ə-nən(t)s\ *n.* **1** The quality or state of being imminent. **2** Something that is imminent; an impending evil or danger.

im·mi·nent \ˈim-ə-nənt\ *adj.* Threatening to occur immediately; near at hand; as, *imminent* danger. — **im·mi·nent·ly**, *adv.*

im·mo·bile \(ˈ)i(m)-ˈmōb-l, -ˈmō-ˌbēl\ *adj.* **1** Not capable of being moved; immovable. **2** Motionless. — **im·mo·bil·i·ty** \ˌi-(ˌ)mō-ˈbil-ət-ē\ *n.*

im·mo·bi·lize \i-ˈmōb-l-ˌīz\ *v.;* **im·mo·bi·lized; im·mo·bi·liz·ing.** To make immobile; as, to *immobilize* an injured joint with splints.

im·mod·er·ate \(ˈ)i(m)-ˈmäd-r(-)ət\ *adj.* Not moderate; excessive. — **im·mod·er·a·cy** \-r(-)ə-sē\ *n.* — **im·mod·er·ate·ly** \-r(-)ət-lē\ *adv.*

im·mod·est \(ˈ)i(m)-ˈmäd-əst\ *adj.* **1** Not modest or decent; as, *immodest* clothing. **2** Forward; bold; as, *immodest* boasting. — **im·mod·est·ly** \-əst-lē\ *adv.* — **im·mod·es·ty** \-əs-tē\ *n.*

im·mo·late \ˈim-l-ˌāt\ *v.;* **im·mo·lat·ed; im·mo·lat·ing.** To offer up as a sacrifice; especially, to kill as a sacrifice. — **im·mo·la·tion** \ˌim-l-ˈāsh-n\ *n.* — **im·mo·la·tor** \ˈim-l-ˌāt-r\ *n.*

im·mor·al \(ˈ)i(m)-ˈmȯr-əl, -ˈmär-\ *adj.* Not moral; wicked; lewd; lascivious. — **im·mor·al·ly** \-ə-lē\ *adv.*

im·mo·ral·i·ty \ˌi-ˌmȯ-ˈral-ət-ē, ˌim-r-ˈal-\ *n.; pl.* **im·mo·ral·i·ties.** **1** The condition of being immoral; immoral conduct; wickedness. **2** An immoral act.

im·mor·tal \(ˈ)i-ˈmȯrt-l\ *adj.* Not mortal; living or lasting forever; as, *immortal* fame. — *n.* **1** An immortal being; [in the plural] the gods. **2** A person whose fame is lasting; as, one of the *immortals* of baseball. — **im·mor·tal·ly** \-ˈmȯrt-l-ē\ *adv.*

im·mor·tal·i·ty \ˌi-ˌmȯr-ˈtal-ət-ē, ˌim-r-\ *n.* **1** The condition of being immortal; endless life; eternal existence. **2** Lasting fame or glory.

im·mor·tal·ize \i-ˈmȯrt-l-ˌīz\ *v.;* **im·mor·tal·ized; im·mor·tal·iz·ing.** To make immortal; as, a man *immortalized* by his writings.

im·mov·a·ble \(ˈ)i(m)-ˈmü-vəb-l\ *adj.* **1** Firmly fixed, settled, or fastened; as, the *immovable* mountains. **2** Steadfast; as, an *immovable* purpose. — **im·mov·a·bil·i·ty** \(ˌ)i-ˌmü-və-ˈbil-ət-ē\ *n.*

im·mune \i-ˈmyün\ *adj.* **1** Safe; protected; as, *immune* from attack or punishment. **2** Not susceptible to a disease or protected against it by vaccination or a previous attack.

im·mu·ni·ty \i-ˈmyü-nət-ē\ *n.; pl.* **im·mu·ni·ties.**

1 Freedom from any charge, tax, duty, or penalty. **2** Power of resisting a disease, resulting from vaccination or inoculation, a previous attack of the disease, or a natural resistance.

im·mu·nize \ˈim-yə-ˌnīz\ *v.;* **im·mu·nized; im·mu·niz·ing.** To make immune. — **im·mu·ni·za·tion** \ˌim-yə-nə-ˈzāsh-n, i-ˌmyü-\ *n.*

im·mu·nol·o·gy \ˌim-yə-ˈnäl-ə-jē\ *n.* The science treating of immunity to disease. — **im·mu·nol·o·gist** \-jəst\ *n.*

im·mure \i-ˈmyu̇r\ *v.;* **im·mured; im·mur·ing.** To enclose within or as if within walls; to imprison.

im·mu·ta·ble \i-ˈmyüt-əb-l\ *adj.* Unchangeable. — **im·mu·ta·bil·i·ty** \(ˌ)i-ˌmyüt-ə-ˈbil-ət-ē\ *n.* — **im·mu·ta·bly** \i-ˈmyüt-ə-blē\ *adv.*

imp \ˈimp\ *n.* **1** A small hateful and malicious spirit. **2** A mischievous child.

im·pact \ˈim-ˌpakt\ *n.* A striking together of two bodies; a collision.

im·pact·ed \im-ˈpak-təd\ *adj.* **1** Closely and firmly fixed in place as if by being wedged in. **2** In dentistry, wedged between the jawbone and another tooth and unable to erupt; as, an *impacted* wisdom tooth. — **im·pac·tion** \-ˈpaksh-n\ *n.*

im·pair \im-ˈpar, -ˈper\ *v.* To make less or weaken, as in quantity, value, or strength; as, to *impair* one's health by overwork. — **im·pair·ment,** *n.*

im·pale \im-ˈpāl\ *v.;* **im·paled; im·pal·ing. 1** To pierce with or as if with a sharp stake. **2** To torture or punish by fixing on a sharp stake. — **im·pale·ment,** *n.*

im·pal·pa·ble \(ˈ)im-ˈpal-pəb-l\ *adj.* **1** Incapable of being touched; intangible. **2** So fine or delicate as not to be easily perceived or understood; as, an *impalpable* difference between two shades of red. — **im·pal·pa·bil·i·ty** \(ˌ)im-ˌpal-pə-ˈbil-ət-ē\ *n.* — **im·pal·pa·bly** \(ˈ)im-ˈpal-pə-blē\ *adv.*

im·pan·el \im-ˈpan-l\ *v.;* **im·pan·eled** or **im·pan·elled; im·pan·el·ing** or **im·pan·el·ling** \-l(-)ing\. To enter in or on a panel or list; to enroll; as, to *impanel* a jury.

im·part \im-ˈpärt, -ˈpȧrt\ *v.* **1** To give, grant, or bestow a share of. The sun *imparts* warmth. **2** To tell; to make known; as, to *impart* information.

im·par·tial \(ˈ)im-ˈpärsh-l, -ˈpȧrsh-l\ *adj.* Not partial or biased; fair; just. — **im·par·ti·al·i·ty** \(ˌ)im-ˌpär-shē-ˈal-ət-ē, -ˌpȧr-\ *n.* — **im·par·tial·ly** \(ˈ)im-ˈpärsh-l-ē, -ˈpȧrsh-\ *adv.*

im·pass·a·ble \(ˈ)im-ˈpas-əb-l\ *adj.* Not capable of being passed, crossed, traveled, or circulated; as, roads made *impassable* by a storm; *impassable* paper money. — **im·pass·a·bil·i·ty** \(ˌ)im-ˌpas-ə-ˈbil-ət-ē\ *n.* — **im·pass·a·bly** \(ˈ)im-ˈpas-ə-blē\ *adv.*

im·passe \ˈim-ˌpas, im-ˈpas\ *n.* [French] **1** An impassable road or way. **2** A position or predicament from which there is no escape.

im·pas·si·ble \im-ˈpas-əb-l\ *adj.* Incapable of being emotionally moved or touched; unfeeling; as, a hardened, *impassible* criminal. — **im·pas·si·bil·i·ty** \(ˌ)im-ˌpas-ə-ˈbil-ət-ē\ *n.*

im·pas·sioned \im-ˈpash-nd\ *adj.* Filled with or moved by passion or zeal; showing strong feeling; as, an *impassioned* appeal for justice.

im·pas·sive \im-ˈpas-iv\ *adj.* Not feeling or not showing any emotion; indifferent; calm; as, an *impassive* expression on one's face. — **im·pas·sive·ly** \-əv-lē\ *adv.* — **im·pas·siv·i·ty** \ˌim-ˌpa-ˈsiv-ət-ē\ *n.*

im·pa·tience \(ˈ)im-ˈpāsh-n(t)s\ *n.* **1** The lack of patience; failure or inability to be patient, as when faced with pain, opposition, or delay. **2** Restless eagerness or desire; as, an *impatience* to get started.

im·pa·tient \(ˈ)im-ˈpāsh-nt\ *adj.* **1** Not patient; irritable; as, to be *impatient* with someone's mistakes. **2** Showing or arising from impatience; as, an *impatient* answer. **3** Restlessly eager; as, *impatient* to be on one's way. — **im·pa·tient·ly,** *adv.*

im·peach \im-ˈpēch\ *v.* **1** To bring official charges against a public officer for misconduct of his office. **2** To call into question; to throw discredit upon; as, to *impeach* a person's honesty; to *impeach* a witness. — **im·peach·a·ble,** *adj.* — **im·peach·ment,** *n.*

im·pec·ca·ble \im-ˈpek-əb-l\ *adj.* Free from fault or error; faultless. — **im·pec·ca·bly** \-ə-blē\ *adv.*

im·pe·cu·ni·ous \ˌim-pē-ˈkyü-nē-əs\ *adj.* Without money; poor.

im·pede \im-ˈpēd\ *v.;* **im·ped·ed; im·ped·ing.** [From Latin *impedire* meaning literally "to entangle or shackle the feet" and derived from the prefix *im-* meaning "in" and *ped-*, the stem of *pes* meaning "foot".] To obstruct; to hinder. The long parade *impeded* traffic.

im·ped·i·ment \im-ˈped-m-ənt\ *n.* **1** Anything that impedes, hinders, or obstructs. **2** A defect in speech.

im·pel \im-ˈpel\ *v.;* **im·pelled; im·pel·ling. 1** To drive or urge on; to compel; to force; as, to feel *impelled* to speak one's mind. **2** To give motion to; to propel; as, to *impel* water through a pipe. — **im·pel·ler** \im-ˈpel-r\ *n.*

im·pend \im-ˈpend\ *v.* **1** To hang over; to be suspended over; as, *impending* cliffs. **2** To threaten to occur immediately; to be imminent; as, warning of a danger that *impends.*

im·pend·ing \im-ˈpen-ding\ *adj.* Threatening to occur; approaching.

im·pen·e·tra·ble \(ˈ)im-ˈpen-ə-trəb-l\ *adj.* **1** Not capable of being penetrated, or pierced; as, *impenetrable* rock; an *impenetrable* jungle. **2** Incapable of being understood; as, an *impenetrable* mystery. — **im·pen·e·tra·bil·i·ty** \(ˌ)im-ˌpen-ə-trə-ˈbil-ət-ē\ *n.* — **im·pen·e·tra·bly** \(ˈ)im-ˈpen-ə-trə-blē\ *adv.*

im·pen·i·tent \(ˈ)im-ˈpen-ə-tənt\ *adj.* Not penitent; not sorry for having done wrong. — **im·pen·i·tence** \-tən(t)s\ *n.* — **im·pen·i·tent·ly** \-tənt-lē\ *adv.*

im·per·a·tive \im-ˈper-ət-iv\ *adj.* **1** In grammar, containing or expressing a command, request, or strong encouragement; as, an *imperative* sentence. **2** Commanding; authoritative; as, an *imperative* order; an *imperative* gesture. **3** Not to be avoided; compulsory; essential; as, an *imperative* duty. — *n.* **1** The imperative mood of a verb or a verb in this mood. **2** Something imperative; a command. — **im·per·a·tive·ly**, *adv.*

im·per·cep·ti·ble \ˌimp-r-ˈsep-təb-l\ *adj.* Not capable of being perceived by the senses or by the mind; so slight as not to be noticeable; as, an almost *imperceptible* difference. Color is *imperceptible* to the touch. — **im·per·cep·ti·bly** \-tə-blē\ *adv.*

im·per·fect \(ˈ)im-ˈpər-fikt\ *adj.* **1** Not perfect; faulty; incomplete; as, an *imperfect* copy of a painting. **2** In botany, having either stamens or pistils, but not both; as, an *imperfect* flower. **3** In grammar, especially of some foreign languages, indicating incomplete or continuing action or state in a time gone by; as, *imperfect* tense. — **im·per·fect·ly**, *adv.*

im·per·fec·tion \ˌimp-r-ˈfeksh-n\ *n.* **1** The condition of being imperfect. **2** A fault, deficiency, or blemish; as, reduced in price because of slight *imperfections.*

im·pe·ri·al \im-ˈpir-ē-əl\ *adj.* **1** Having to do with an empire or an emperor; as, *imperial* trade; an *imperial* decree. **2** Supreme in power; sovereign. **3** Of superior size or excellence. **4** Suitable to an emperor; royal; as, *imperial* splendor. — *n.* A small, sharply pointed beard. — **im·pe·ri·al·ly** \-ē-ə-lē\ *adv.*

im·pe·ri·al·ism \im-ˈpir-ē-ə-ˌliz-m\ *n.* **1** Imperial government or authority. **2** The policy of trying to extend the control, sovereignty, or territories of a nation. — **im·pe·ri·al·ist** \-ə-ləst\ *n.* or *adj.*

im·pe·ri·al·is·tic \im-ˌpir-ē-ə-ˈlis-tik\ *adj.* **1** Of or relating to imperialism. **2** Favoring imperialism; having or showing imperialist tendencies. — **im·pe·ri·al·is·ti·cal·ly** \-tik-l(-)ē\ *adv.*

imperial moth. A large yellow American moth with brown bands.

im·per·il \im-ˈper-əl\ *v.;* **im·per·iled** or **im·per·illed**; **im·per·il·ing** or **im·per·il·ling**. To bring into danger; as, to *imperil* the safety of others by reckless driving.

im·pe·ri·ous \im-ˈpir-ē-əs\ *adj.* **1** Commanding; domineering; haughty. **2** Urgent; imperative; compelling; as, *imperious* need. — **im·pe·ri·ous·ly**, *adv.*

im·per·ish·a·ble \(ˈ)im-ˈper-ish-əb-l\ *adj.* Not perishable; undying; indestructible; as, *imperishable* glory. — **im·per·ish·a·bly** \-ə-blē\ *adv.*

im·per·ma·nent \(ˈ)im-ˈpər-mə-nənt\ *adj.* Not permanent. — **im·per·ma·nent·ly**, *adv.*

im·per·me·a·ble \(ˈ)im-ˈpər-mē-əb-l\ *adj.* Not allowing passage, as of a liquid, through its substance; impervious. — **im·per·me·a·bil·i·ty** \(ˌ)im-ˌpər-mē-ə-ˈbil-ət-ē\ *n.* — **im·per·me·a·bly** \(ˈ)im-ˈpər-mē-ə-blē\ *adv.*

im·per·son·al \(ˈ)im-ˈpərs-n(-)əl\ *adj.* **1** Not referring to any particular person; as, an *impersonal* remark. **2** Not existing as a person; as, an *impersonal* power called fate. **3** Without any specified doer but with impersonal *it* as subject — used of certain verbs, as *rained* in "It rained yesterday".

im·per·son·ate \im-ˈpərs-n-ˌāt\ *v.;* **im·per·son·at·ed**; **im·per·son·at·ing**. **1** To act the part of or pretend to be some other person; as, to *impersonate* a circus barker. **2** To typify; to exemplify. — **im·per·son·a·tor** \-ˌāt-r\ *n.*

im·per·son·a·tion \im-ˌpərs-n-ˈāsh-n\ *n.* **1** The action of impersonating or the state of being impersonated. **2** A dramatic representation; an imitation, as of outstanding characteristics of a person.

im·per·ti·nence \im-ˈpərt-n(-)ən(t)s\ *n.* **1** Impudence; insolence. **2** An impudent act or remark.

im·per·ti·nent, *adj.* **1** \(ˈ)im-ˈpərt-n(-)ənt\ Not pertinent; not applicable or fitting; as, information that is *impertinent* to the problem. **2** \im-\ Rude; insolent; saucy; impudent. — **im·per·ti·nent·ly**, *adv.*

im·per·turb·a·ble \ˌimp-r-ˈtər-bəb-l\ *adj.* Not capable of being disturbed; calm; not easy to excite. — **im·per·turb·a·bil·i·ty** \-ˌtər-bə-ˈbil-ət-ē\ *n.* — **im·per·turb·a·bly** \-ˈtər-bə-blē\ *adv.*

im·per·vi·ous \im-ˈpər-vē-əs\ *adj.* Not capable of being penetrated or entered, as by light rays or moisture. Lead is *impervious* to X rays. — **im·per·vi·ous·ly**, *adv.*

im·pet·u·os·i·ty \(ˌ)im-ˌpech-ə-ˈwäs-ət-ē\ *n.; pl.* **im·pet·u·os·i·ties**. **1** The quality or state of being impetuous. **2** An impetuous action or impulse.

im·pet·u·ous \im-ˈpech-ə-wəs\ *adj.* **1** Rushing forcibly; violent; as, an *impetuous* current. **2** Violent and hasty in action; impulsive; as, a man of *impetuous* temper. — **im·pet·u·ous·ly**, *adv.*

im·pe·tus \ˈimp-ət-əs\ *n.* **1** Momentum. **2** Impulse; incentive; as, a person whose chief *impetus* is a desire for fame.

im·pi·e·ty \(ˈ)im-ˈpī-ət-ē\ *n.; pl.* **im·pi·e·ties**. **1** A lack of piety or reverence; ungodliness. **2** An impious act.

im·pinge \im-ˈpinj\ *v.;* **im·pinged**; **im·ping·ing**. **1** To strike or dash on or against something; to come sharply upon. Sound waves *impinge* upon the eardrum. **2** To encroach; to infringe; as, to *impinge* on another person's rights. — **im·pinge·ment**, *n.*

im·pi·ous \ˈimp-ē-əs, (ˈ)im-ˈpī-\ *adj.* Not pious; lacking due respect; profane. — **im·pi·ous·ly**, *adv.*

imp·ish \ˈimp-ish\ *adj.* Somewhat like an imp; especially, mischievous; as, an *impish* glance. — **imp·ish·ly**, *adv.*

im·plac·a·ble \(ˈ)im-ˈplak-əb-l, -ˈplāk-\ *adj.* Not capable of being pacified; as, an *implacable* enemy. — **im·plac·a·bly** \-ə-blē\ *adv.*

im·plant \im-ˈplant\ *v.* **1** To plant or set deeply and securely. **2** To fix firmly, as in the mind; as, to *implant* an idea. — **im·plan·ta·tion** \ˌim-ˌplan-ˈtāsh-n\ *n.*

im·ple·ment \ˈimp-lə-mənt\ *n.* A tool; a utensil; an

instrument; as, farm *implements.* — \-ˌment\ *v.* To give practical effect to; to carry out the terms or details of, as a treaty or a program; to put into practice.

im·pli·cate \ˈimp-lə-ˌkāt\ *v.;* **im·pli·cat·ed**; **im·pli·cat·ing.** To bring into connection; to involve. The accused man's confession *implicated* several other persons in the crime.

im·pli·ca·tion \ˌimp-lə-ˈkāsh-n\ *n.* **1** The act of implicating or the state of being implicated; involvement. **2** The act of implying or the state of being implied. **3** Something that is implied; something suggested but not expressed.

im·plic·it \im-ˈplis-ət\ *adj.* **1** Understood though not directly stated; as, an *implicit* agreement. **2** Complete; unquestioning; as, to have *implicit* confidence in a person. — **im·plic·it·ly**, *adv.*

im·plore \im-ˈplōr, -ˈplȯr\ *v.;* **im·plored**; **im·plor·ing.** To call upon, or for, earnestly; to beseech; to beg; as, to *implore* help.

im·ply \im-ˈplī\ *v.;* **im·plied** \-ˈplīd\; **im·ply·ing. 1** To include or involve as a natural or necessary though not expressly stated part or effect; as, military maneuvers *implying* threats of war. The rights of citizenship *imply* certain obligations. **2** To express indirectly; to suggest rather than say plainly; as, remarks that *implied* consent if not approval.

im·po·lite \ˌim-pə-ˈlīt\ *adj.* Not polite; discourteous; rude. — **im·po·lite·ly**, *adv.*

im·port \im-ˈpōrt, -ˈpȯrt; ˈim-ˌpōrt, -ˌpȯrt\ *v.* **1** To mean; to be of importance or consequence; to matter; as, events that *imported* little to the country as a whole. **2** To bring in or introduce from a foreign country, especially goods to be resold; as, to *import* coffee. — \ˈim-ˌpōrt, -ˌpȯrt\ *n.* **1** Meaning; as, to be uncertain of the *import* of what one has been told. **2** Importance; as, events of great *import.* **3** [usually in the plural] Something, especially goods, brought into a country from abroad.

im·por·tance \im-ˈpȯrt-n(t)s, -ən(t)s\ *n.* The condition of being important; significance; consequence.

im·por·tant \im-ˈpȯrt-nt, -ənt\ *adj.* **1** Having great meaning or influence; significant; weighty; as, *important* business; an *important* event. **2** Having considerable power or authority; as, an *important* official; an *important* man in his community. **3** Showing a feeling of personal importance; as, an *important* manner. — **im·por·tant·ly**, *adv.*

im·por·ta·tion \ˌim-ˌpōr-ˈtāsh-n, -ˌpȯr-\ *n.* **1** The act of bringing foreign goods into a country for sale or use. **2** Something that is imported; an import.

im·port·er \im-ˈpōrt-r, -ˈpȯrt-; ˈim-ˌpōrt-r, -ˌpȯrt-\ *n.* One that imports; especially, a person engaged in importing goods as a business.

im·por·tu·nate \im-ˈpȯrch-n-ət\ *adj.* Asking or asked repeatedly and urgently; persistent; urgent; as, an *importunate* beggar; an *importunate* request. — **im·por·tu·nate·ly**, *adv.*

im·por·tune \ˌimp-r-ˈtün, -ˈtyün; im-ˈpȯrch-n\ *v.;* **im·por·tuned**; **im·por·tun·ing.** To beg earnestly; to urge persistently.

im·por·tu·ni·ty \ˌimp-r-ˈtü-nət-ē, -ˈtyü-\ *n.; pl.* **im·por·tu·ni·ties.** Persistence in requests or demands.

im·pose \im-ˈpōz\ *v.;* **im·posed**; **im·pos·ing. 1** To put on as a charge or penalty; as, to *impose* a fine; to *impose* a tax on imports. **2** To use trickery or deception to get what one wants; as, to *impose* on an ignorant person. **3** To put a burden on; to take advantage of; as, to *impose* upon a friend's good nature.

im·pos·ing \im-ˈpō-zing\ *adj.* Impressive, as because of size, power, or dignity; as, an *imposing* building. — **im·pos·ing·ly**, *adv.*

im·po·si·tion \ˌimp-ə-ˈzish-n\ *n.* **1** The act of imposing. **2** Something that is imposed, as a levy or tax. **3** Any excessive, unduly burdensome requirement or demand. **4** A deception; a fraud; a trick.

im·pos·si·bil·i·ty \(ˌ)im-ˌpäs-ə-ˈbil-ət-ē\ *n.; pl.* **im·pos·si·bil·i·ties. 1** The condition of being impossible; as, the *impossibility* of finishing in the time allowed. **2** An impossible thing; something that cannot be.

im·pos·si·ble \(ˈ)im-ˈpäs-əb-l\ *adj.* **1** Not possible; not capable of being done or happening. **2** Completely impracticable or hopeless; as, to find oneself in an *impossible* situation. **3** Highly unsuitable; hopelessly unsatisfactory; out of the question; as, an *impossible* dress; an *impossible* person.

im·pos·si·bly \(ˈ)im-ˈpäs-ə-blē\ *adv.* In a way or to a degree that is or seems impossible; beyond belief, acceptance, or endurance; as, an *impossibly* hot day.

im·post \ˈim-ˌpōst\ *n.* A tax; especially, a customs duty.

im·pos·tor \im-ˈpäst-r\ *n.* A person who practices deceit; especially, one who represents himself as being someone else.

im·pos·ture \im-ˈpäs-chər\ *n.* The act or conduct of an impostor; fraud or a fraud; deception.

im·po·tence \ˈimp-ə-tən(t)s\ *n.* The condition of being impotent; lack of power; weakness or helplessness.

im·po·ten·cy \ˈimp-ə-tən-sē\ *n.* Impotence.

im·po·tent \ˈimp-ə-tənt\ *adj.* Lacking power, strength, or vigor; weak; helpless. — **im·po·tent·ly**, *adv.*

im·pound \im-ˈpau̇nd\ *v.* **1** To shut up in a pound, as stray dogs. **2** To seize and hold in legal custody; as, to *impound* certain funds pending decision of a case. **3** To collect for purposes of irrigation, as water in a reservoir.

im·pov·er·ish \im-ˈpäv-r(-)ish\ *v.* **1** To make poor; to reduce to poverty; as, an *impoverished* family. **2** To use up the strength, richness, or fertility of; as, *impoverished* soil. — **im·pov·er·ish·ment**, *n.*

im·prac·ti·ca·ble \(ˈ)im-ˈprak-tik-əb-l\ *adj.* Not practicable; difficult to put into practice or use;

as, an *impracticable* plan. — **im·prac·ti·ca·bil·i·ty** \(ˌ)im-ˌprak-tik-ə-ˈbil-ət-ē\ *n.* — **im·prac·ti·ca·bly** \(ˈ)im-ˈprak-tik-ə-blē\ *adv.*

im·prac·ti·cal \(ˈ)im-ˈprak-tik-l\ *adj.* **1** Not practical; as, a very *impractical* person. **2** Impracticable. — **im·prac·ti·cal·i·ty** \(ˌ)im-ˌprak-tə-ˈkal-ət-ē\ *n.*

im·pre·ca·tion \ˌimp-rə-ˈkāsh-n\ *n.* A curse.

im·preg·na·ble \im-ˈpreg-nəb-l\ *adj.* Incapable of being taken by assault; able to resist any attack; as, an *impregnable* fortress; *impregnable* defenses. — **im·preg·na·bil·i·ty** \(ˌ)im-ˌpreg-nə-ˈbil-ət-ē\ *n.*

im·preg·nate \im-ˈpreg-ˌnāt\ *v.;* **im·preg·nat·ed; im·preg·nat·ing. 1** To cause a substance to be filled or mixed thoroughly with another substance; as, to *impregnate* flavored water with carbon dioxide. **2** To make fruitful or fertile. **3** In biology, to introduce sperm cells into. — **im·preg·na·tion** \ˌim-(ˌ)preg-ˈnāsh-n\ *n.*

im·pre·sa·rio \ˌimp-rə-ˈsär-ē-ˌō, -ˈsar-, -ˈser-, -ˈsȧr-\ *n.; pl.* **im·pre·sa·ri·os.** The manager or conductor of an opera, concert, or ballet company.

im·press \im-ˈpres\ *v.* **1** To press, stamp, or print; as, to *impress* a name with a stamp. **2** To produce a clear impression of; as, a scene that *impressed* itself on the memory. **3** To influence or affect, especially strongly; as, to be favorably *impressed* by the new pupil's behavior. — \ˈim-ˌpres\ *n.* **1** A mark made by pressing; an imprint. **2** A result of influence; an impression. **3** A characteristic mark; stamp; as, the *impress* of a person's character on his work.

im·press \im-ˈpres\ *v.* **1** To seize for public service; especially, to force into naval service. **2** To enlist the aid or services of by strong argument or appeal; as, to *impress* helpers into a fund-raising campaign.

im·pres·sion \im-ˈpresh-n\ *n.* **1** The act or process of impressing. **2** A mark, stamp, or figure made by impressing. **3** A trait or characteristic resulting from indirect influence; an impress. **4** The influence or effect that something has on one's feeling, sense, or mind; as, to get a good *impression* of a new boy. No one likes to make a poor *impression* on others. **5** A vague recollection, belief, or opinion; as, to be under the *impression* that one has seen a person before. **6** A printed copy, as from type or from an engraved plate or block. **7** The whole number of copies, as of a book, printed for one issue; a printing.

im·pres·sion·a·ble \im-ˈpresh-n(-)əb-l\ *adj.* Sensitive to impressions; susceptible to outside influences; easily molded or affected.

im·pres·sion·ism \im-ˈpresh-n-ˌiz-m\ *n.* **1** A movement in modern art in which the artist tries to record momentary impressions of nature, especially the effects of light. **2** A style of musical composition designed to induce in the mind of the listener certain moods which in turn create descriptive impressions. — **im·pres·sion·ist** \-əst\ *n.* — **im·pres·sion·is·tic** \(ˌ)im-ˌpresh-n-ˈis-tik\ *adj.*

im·pres·sive \im-ˈpres-iv\ *adj.* Making, or tending to make, an impression; having the power to impress the mind or feelings; as, an *impressive* speech; an *impressive* record as an athlete. — **im·pres·sive·ly,** *adv.*

im·press·ment \im-ˈpres-mənt\ *n.* The act of seizing for public use or of impressing into public service.

im·print \im-ˈprint, ˈim-ˌprint\ *v.* **1** To stamp; to impress. **2** To mark or print, as letters on paper. **3** To fix firmly, as in the memory. — \ˈim-ˌprint\ *n.* **1** Something stamped or printed; an impression; as, the *imprint* of a foot. **2** The publisher's name, the date, and the place of publication, as printed on the title page of a book.

im·pris·on \im-ˈpriz-n\ *v.;* **im·pris·oned; im·pris·on·ing** \-n(-)ing\. To put in prison or jail; to confine. — **im·pris·on·ment** \-n-mənt\ *n.*

im·prob·a·ble \(ˈ)im-ˈpräb-əb-l\ *adj.* Not probable; not likely to be true or to occur. — **im·prob·a·bil·i·ty** \(ˌ)im-ˌpräb-ə-ˈbil-ət-ē\ *n.* — **im·prob·a·bly** \(ˈ)im-ˈpräb-ə-blē\ *adv.*

im·promp·tu \im-ˈpräm(p)-ˌtü, -ˌtyü\ *adv.* or *adj.* [From French, there borrowed from Latin *in promptu* meaning "in readiness", "at hand".] Offhand; without previous study; extemporaneous; as, an *impromptu* speech; an answer given *impromptu.*

im·prop·er \(ˈ)im-ˈpräp-r\ *adj.* **1** Not proper, fit, or suitable; as, *improper* dress for the occasion. **2** Incorrect; inaccurate. **3** Not in accordance with good taste or good manners; as, *improper* language.

— The words *indecent* and *indelicate* are synonyms of *improper: improper* usually describes something that violates conventionally accepted standards of conduct, particularly in etiquette or morals; *indecent* is likely to suggest something that is offensive to persons of high moral standards or good taste; *indelicate* usually refers to a violation of modesty or to coarseness and lack of tact, particularly in speech.

improper fraction. A fraction in which the numerator is greater than the denominator.

im·prop·er·ly \(ˈ)im-ˈpräp-r-lē\ *adv.* In an improper manner.

im·pro·pri·e·ty \ˌim-prə-ˈprī-ət-ē\ *n.; pl.* **im·pro·pri·e·ties. 1** The quality of being improper. **2** Something that is improper; an unsuitable or improper act. **3** An inaccuracy in the use of language.

im·prove \im-ˈprüv\ *v.;* **im·proved; im·prov·ing. 1** To make good use of; as, to *improve* the time by reading. **2** To grow better; to make better; as, to try to *improve* one's arithmetic; to *improve* in health. **3** To raise the value of land or property, as by building. **4** To make improvements; as, to *improve* on someone else's idea. — **im·prov·a·ble** \-ˈprü-vəb-l\ *adj.* — **im·prov·er** \-ˈprüv-r\ *n.*

im·prove·ment \im-ˈprüv-mənt\ *n.* **1** The action of improving. **2** The condition of being improved; as, to notice a marked *improvement* in someone's health. **3** A result of improving; something that improves the appearance or value of a thing; as, to add a number of *improvements* to an old house.

im·prov·i·dent \(')im-'präv-ə-dənt\ *adj.* Not providing for the future; thriftless. — **im·prov·i·dence** \-dən(t)s, -ˌden(t)s\ *n.* — **im·prov·i·dent·ly**, *adv.*

im·prov·i·sa·tion \(ˌ)im-ˌpräv-ə-'zāsh-n, ˌimp-rə-və-\ *n.* **1** The action or art of improvising. **2** Something that is improvised.

im·pro·vise \'imp-rə-ˌvīz, ˌimp-rə-'vīz\ *v.;* **im·pro·vised; im·pro·vis·ing. 1** To compose, recite, or sing something without previous study or preparation; as, to *improvise* on the piano. **2** To make, invent, or arrange offhand; as, to *improvise* a sail out of shirts. — **im·pro·vis·er**, *n.*

im·pru·dent \(')im-'prüd-nt\ *adj.* Not prudent; unwise; rash. — **im·pru·dence** \-n(t)s\ *n.* — **im·pru·dent·ly**, *adv.*

im·pu·dence \'imp-yə-dən(t)s\ *n.* Impudent behavior or speech; insolence; disrespect.

im·pu·dent \'imp-yə-dənt\ *adj.* Bold; saucy; showing contempt or disregard for others; insolent. — **im·pu·dent·ly**, *adv.*

im·pugn \im-'pyün\ *v.* To oppose or attack as false; to call into question; to doubt; as, to *impugn* the motives of an opponent.

im·pulse \'im-ˌpəls\ *n.* **1** A force that starts a body into motion; an impulsion. **2** The motion produced by such an impulsion. **3** A sudden arousing of the mind and spirit to do something; an inclination to act; as, to have an *impulse* to run away; to act on the *impulse* of the moment. **4** A change transmitted through nerves and muscles and resulting in greater or less activity, as of a part or organ.

im·pul·sion \im-'pəlsh-n\ *n.* **1** The action of impelling or the state of being impelled. **2** An impelling force. **3** A sudden inclination to do or not do something; an impulse.

im·pul·sive \im-'pəl-siv\ *adj.* **1** Having the power of driving or impelling. **2** Acting, or liable to act, on impulse; moved or caused by an impulse; impetuous; hasty. — **im·pul·sive·ly**, *adv.*

im·pu·ni·ty \im-'pyü-nət-ē\ *n.* Exemption or safety from punishment, harm, or loss. Boys soon learn that they cannot fight in school or in the schoolyard with *impunity.*

im·pure \(')im-'pyůr\ *adj.;* **im·pur·er; im·pur·est. 1** Not pure; unclean; dirty; as, *impure* water. **2** Mixed with some other, usually inferior, substance; as, *impure* drugs; *impure* metal. **3** Obscene; indecent. — **im·pure·ly**, *adv.*

im·pu·ri·ty \(')im-'pyůr-ət-ē\ *n.; pl.* **im·pu·ri·ties. 1** The condition of being impure. **2** A thing that is impure or that makes something else impure. Air-conditioning removes many of the *impurities* from air.

im·pute \im-'pyüt\ *v.;* **im·put·ed; im·put·ing.** To regard as responsible for; to give or charge either credit or blame to; to attribute; as, to *impute* a mistake to excusable ignorance. — **im·pu·ta·tion** \ˌimp-yə-'tāsh-n\ *n.*

in \(')in, ən, n\ *prep.* **1** Bounded or enclosed by; as, *in* a box; *in* town. **2** From among; out of; as, tallest *in* the class; one *in* a thousand. **3** During; as, *in* the morning; *in* childhood. **4** By way of; by means of; according to; with the form of; as, *in* French; *in* reply; *in* pencil. — \'in\ *adv.* **1** To or toward the inside; as, to go *in.* **2** Within a place; as, locked *in.* — *adj.* Being on the inside; going or coming toward the inside; as, an *in* train. — *n.* [usually in the plural] Those who are in an inside position, as in office or in power. — **ins and outs.** Nooks and corners; twists and turns; details.

in-. A prefix that can mean: in, within, into, or toward, as in *income, inside, indeed, inland.*

in-. A prefix that can mean: not, non-, or un-, as in *inactive, incombustible, insufficient.*

in. Abbreviation for *inch.*

in·a·bil·i·ty \ˌin-ə-'bil-ət-ē\ *n.* The condition of being unable; lack of ability, power, or means.

in·ac·ces·si·ble \ˌin-ik-'ses-əb-l, ˌi-ˌnak-\ *adj.* Not accessible. — **in·ac·ces·si·bil·i·ty** \-ˌses-ə-'bil-ət-ē\ *n.* — **in·ac·ces·si·bly** \-'ses-ə-blē\ *adv.*

in·ac·cu·ra·cy \(')i-'nak-yər-ə-sē\ *n.; pl.* **in·ac·cu·ra·cies. 1** Lack of accuracy. **2** A mistake; an error.

in·ac·cu·rate \(')i-'nak-yər-ət\ *adj.* Not accurate; not exact. — **in·ac·cu·rate·ly**, *adv.*

in·ac·tion \(')i-'naksh-n\ *n.* Lack of action; idleness.

in·ac·tive \(')i-'nak-tiv\ *adj.* Not active. — **in·ac·tive·ly**, *adv.* — **in·ac·tiv·i·ty** \ˌi-ˌnak-'tiv-ət-ē\ *n.*

in·ad·e·quate \(')i-'nad-ə-kwət\ *adj.* Not adequate; insufficient. — **in·ad·e·qua·cy** \-kwə-sē\ *n.* — **in·ad·e·quate·ly**, *adv.*

in·ad·mis·si·ble \ˌin-əd-'mis-əb-l\ *adj.* Not admissible.

in·ad·vert·ence \ˌin-əd-'vərt-n(t)s\ *n.* Inattention or a result of inattention; an oversight.

in·ad·vert·en·cy \ˌin-əd-'vərt-n-sē\ *n.* Inadvertence; inattention.

in·ad·vert·ent \ˌin-əd-'vərt-nt\ *adj.* Thoughtless; heedless; unintentional; as, an *inadvertent* personal remark. — **in·ad·vert·ent·ly**, *adv.*

in·ad·vis·a·ble \ˌin-əd-'vī-zəb-l\ *adj.* Not advisable; unwise. — **in·ad·vis·a·bil·i·ty** \-ˌvī-zə-'bil-ət-ē\ *n.*

in·a·lien·a·ble \i-'nāl-yə-nəb-l\ *adj.* Not capable of being taken away, given up, or transferred; as, the *inalienable* rights of a citizen. — **in·a·lien·a·bil·i·ty** \(ˌ)i-ˌnāl-yə-nə-'bil-ət-ē\ *n.* — **in·a·lien·a·bly** \i-'nāl-yə-nə-blē\ *adv.*

in·ane \i-'nān\ *adj.* Empty; silly; foolish. — **in·ane·ly**, *adv.*

in·an·i·mate \(')i-'nan-ə-mət\ *adj.* **1** Without life. Stones are *inanimate.* **2** Without animal life or consciousness; as, trees and other *inanimate* organisms. **3** Deprived of life or consciousness; as, the *inanimate* body of an accident victim. **4** Without spirit or animation; dull. — **in·an·i·mate·ly**, *adv.*

in·a·ni·tion \ˌin-ə-'nish-n\ *n.* Exhaustion from lack of food.

in·an·i·ty \i-'nan-ət-ē\ *n.; pl.* **in·an·i·ties. 1** The quality or condition of being inane; emptiness; silliness. **2** An inane, useless thing; especially, a senseless or foolish remark.

in·ap·pli·ca·ble \(ˈ)i-ˈnap-lə-kəb-l, ˌin-ə-ˈplik-əb-l\ *adj.* Not applicable; unsuitable. — **in·ap·pli·ca·bil·i·ty** \(ˌ)i-ˌnap-lə-kə-ˈbil-ət-ē, ˌin-ə-ˌplik-ə-\ *n.*

in·ap·pre·cia·ble \ˌin-ə-ˈprē-shəb-l\ *adj.* Not appreciable; very slight; as, an *inappreciable* change in the temperature. — **in·ap·pre·cia·bly** \-shə-blē\ *adv.*

in·ap·pro·pri·ate \ˌin-ə-ˈprō-prē-ət\ *adj.* Not appropriate; unsuitable; not proper. — **in·ap·pro·pri·ate·ly**, *adv.*

in·apt \(ˈ)i-ˈnapt\ *adj.* **1** Not suitable; as, an *inapt* reply. **2** Not skillful; not quick at learning. — **in·apt·ly**, *adv.*

in·ap·ti·tude \(ˈ)i-ˈnap-tə-ˌtüd, -ˌtyüd\ *n.* Lack of aptitude.

in·ar·tic·u·late \ˌi-ˌnär-ˈtik-yə-lət, ˌi-ˌnår-\ *adj.* **1** Not understandable as spoken words; as, *inarticulate* cries. **2** Not able to articulate, or utter intelligible sounds; dumb. **3** Not having the power of clear expression. **4** In zoology, not jointed or segmented. — **in·ar·tic·u·late·ly**, *adv.*

in·ar·tis·tic \ˌi-ˌnär-ˈtis-tik, ˌi-ˌnår-\ *adj.* Not artistic. — **in·ar·tis·ti·cal·ly** \-tik-l(-)ē\ *adv.*

in·as·much as \ˈin-əz-ˌməch əz\. In as much as; seeing that; since.

in·at·ten·tion \ˌin-ə-ˈtench-n\ *n.* Failure to pay attention.

in·at·ten·tive \ˌin-ə-ˈtent-iv\ *adj.* Not attentive. — **in·at·ten·tive·ly**, *adv.*

in·au·di·ble \(ˈ)i-ˈnȯd-əb-l\ *adj.* Not capable of being heard. — **in·au·di·bly** \-ə-blē\ *adv.*

in·au·gu·ral \i-ˈnȯg-yər-əl, -ˈnȯg-r(-)əl\ *adj.* Having to do with an inauguration; as, an *inaugural* ball. — *n.* An inaugural address.

in·au·gu·rate \i-ˈnȯg-yə-ˌrāt, -ˈnȯg-r-ˌāt\ *v.;* **in·au·gu·rat·ed**; **in·au·gu·rat·ing.** **1** To introduce into office with suitable ceremonies; to install; as, to *inaugurate* a president. **2** To celebrate the opening of; as, to *inaugurate* a new post office. **3** To commence or enter upon; to begin; as, to *inaugurate* a new policy or system.

in·au·gu·ra·tion \i-ˌnȯg-yə-ˈrāsh-n, -ˌnȯg-r-ˈāsh-n\ *n.* An inaugurating; especially, a ceremonial introduction into office.

in·aus·pi·cious \ˌi-(ˌ)nȯs-ˈpish-əs\ *adj.* Not auspicious; unlucky; unfavorable. — **in·aus·pi·cious·ly**, *adv.*

in·board \ˈin-ˌbōrd, -ˌbȯrd\ *adj.* or *adv.* **1** Inside the line of the hull of a boat; as, an *inboard* motor. **2** Toward the center line of a boat; as, deck cargo lashed well *inboard.*

in·born \ˈin-ˈbȯrn\ *adj.* Born in or with a person; natural; as, an *inborn* love of music.

in·bound \ˈin-ˈbau̇nd\ *adj.* Inward bound; as, *inbound* traffic.

in·bred \ˈin-ˈbred\ *adj.* **1** Bred within; inborn; as, an *inbred* sense of decency. **2** Produced by or subjected to inbreeding.

in·breed \ˈin-ˈbrēd\ *v.;* **in·bred** \-ˈbred\; **in·breed·ing.** To produce by or subject to inbreeding.

in·breed·ing \ˈin-ˌbrēd-ing\ *n.* The mating or breeding of closely related individuals; especially, the breeding of such individuals for the purpose of preserving favorable or eliminating unfavorable characteristics.

inc. Abbreviation for *incorporated.*

in·cal·cu·la·ble \(ˈ)in-ˈkalk-yə-ləb-l\ *adj.* **1** Not capable of being calculated; especially, too large or too numerous to be calculated. **2** Not capable of being known in advance; uncertain. — **in·cal·cu·la·bly** \-lə-blē\ *adv.*

in·can·des·cent \ˌin-kən-ˈdes-nt, -ˌkan-\ *adj.* White or glowing with intense heat; shining; brilliant. — **in·can·des·cence** \-n(t)s\ *n.*

incandescent lamp. A lamp whose light is produced by the glow of a heated substance, as of the filament that is heated by the current in an electric bulb.

incandescent lamp

in·can·ta·tion \ˌin-ˌkan-ˈtāsh-n\ *n.* **1** The use of charms or spells, usually spoken or chanted, in magic ceremonies. **2** A charm or spell thus used. **3** Any magic or sorcery.

in·ca·pa·bil·i·ty \(ˌ)in-ˌkāp-ə-ˈbil-ət-ē\ *n.* Lack of capability.

in·ca·pa·ble \(ˈ)in-ˈkāp-əb-l\ *adj.* **1** Not capable; not able; as, a workman who proved to be *incapable.* **2** Not of such a nature as to permit; as, *incapable* of measurement or description.
— The word *unable* is a synonym of *incapable: incapable* may apply to a person who by nature or training lacks, usually permanently, the necessary power to operate in some area of thinking or action; *unable* generally refers to a person who is prevented from performing a specific task by some hindrance either within himself or beyond his control and either temporary or permanent.

in·ca·pac·i·tate \ˌin-kə-ˈpas-ə-ˌtāt\ *v.;* **in·ca·pac·i·tat·ed**; **in·ca·pac·i·tat·ing.** To make incapable; to disable. The injury *incapacitated* the halfback for the rest of the season.

in·ca·pac·i·ty \ˌin-kə-ˈpas-ət-ē\ *n.; pl.* **in·ca·pac·i·ties.** Lack of ability or power; as, an *incapacity* for telling the truth.

in·car·cer·ate \in-ˈkärs-r-ˌāt, -ˈkårs-\ *v.;* **in·car·cer·at·ed**; **in·car·cer·at·ing.** To imprison; to confine. — **in·car·cer·a·tion** \(ˌ)in-ˌkärs-r-ˈāsh-n, -ˌkårs-\ *n.*

in·car·nate \(ˈ)in-ˈkär-nət, -ˈkår-, -ˌnāt\ *adj.* Embodied in flesh, especially in human form; represented in any concrete or actual form. — \-ˌnāt\ *v.;* **in·car·nat·ed**; **in·car·nat·ing.** To make incarnate.

in·car·na·tion \ˌin-ˌkär-ˈnāsh-n, -ˌkår-\ *n.* **1** The assuming or taking on of a concrete or actual form, especially of human form. **2** An incarnated being. **3** [with a capital] The union of Divinity with humanity in Jesus Christ.

in·case \in-ˈkās\ *v.;* **in·cased**; **in·cas·ing.** To enclose in or as if in a case. — **in·case·ment**, *n.*

in·cau·tious \(')in-'kȯsh-əs\ *adj.* Not cautious; rash. — **in·cau·tious·ly,** *adv.*

in·cen·di·ary \in-'sen-dē-ˌer-ē\ *adj.* **1** Having to do with the malicious burning of property. **2** Tending to arouse quarrels. **3** Having to do with explosives containing chemicals which ignite at the bursting of the shell. — *n.* **1** A person who maliciously sets fire to property. **2** A person who excites quarrels.

in·cense \in-'sen(t)s\ *v.;* **in·censed; in·cens·ing.** To make very angry.

in·cense \'in-ˌsen(t)s\ *n.* **1** Material, such as fragrant gums and spices, used to produce a perfume when burned. **2** The perfume or smoke so produced; any pleasing scent or fragrance.

in·cen·tive \in-'sent-iv\ *n.* Anything that arouses or spurs one on to action or effort; a stimulus.

in·ception \in-'sepsh-n\ *n.* The act or process of beginning; commencement; start; as, a campaign that was a success from the moment of its *inception.*

in·ces·sant \in-'ses-nt\ *adj.* Unceasing; continual; as, *incessant* rains. — **in·ces·sant·ly,** *adv.*

in·cest \'in-ˌsest\ *n.* The crime of cohabitation between persons so closely related that they are forbidden by law to marry, as parent and child or brother and sister.

inch \'inch\ *n.* [From Old English *yuce,* there borrowed from Latin *uncia* meaning literally "a twelfth" — see *ounce.*] A measure of length, the twelfth part of a foot. — *v.* To move, advance, or retire a little at a time; to move slowly; as, to *inch* along.

inch·worm \'inch-ˌwərm\ *n.* A measuring worm.

in·ci·dence \'in(t)s-ə-dən(t)s, -ˌden(t)s\ *n.* The range or scope of occurrence or effect; as, the *incidence* of a contagious disease.

in·ci·dent \'in(t)s-ə-dənt, -ˌdent\ *adj.* Liable to happen; apt to occur, especially in connection with some other event; as, difficulties *incident* to the trip. — *n.* **1** A happening; an event; an occurrence. **2** A slight or trifling event or matter.

in·ci·den·tal \ˌin(t)s-ə-'dent-l\ *adj.* **1** Occurring by chance; casual; as, an *incidental* remark. **2** Not having to do with the main part, object, or purpose; as, the *incidental* expenses of a trip. **3** Likely to happen along with something else; as, experiences *incidental* to school life. — *n.* [in the plural] Items of secondary importance. — **in·ci·den·tal·ly** \-'dent-l(-)ē\ *adv.*

in·cin·er·ate \in-'sin-r-ˌāt\ *v.;* **in·cin·er·at·ed; in·cin·er·at·ing.** To burn to ashes; to consume by fire. — **in·cin·er·a·tion** \in-ˌsin-r-'āsh-n\ *n.*

in·cin·er·a·tor \in-'sin-r-ˌāt-r\ *n.* One that incinerates; especially, a furnace or other receptacle designed for burning rubbish.

in·cip·i·ent \in-'sip-ē-ənt\ *adj.* Beginning, or beginning to show itself; as, an *incipient* smile. — **in·cip·i·ence** \-ən(t)s\ *n.*

in·cise \in-'sīz\ *v.;* **in·cised; in·cis·ing.** To cut into; to carve; to engrave.

in·cised \in-'sīzd\ *adj.* **1** Cut; carved; engraved; as, a name *incised* in stone. **2** Having the margin deeply and irregularly notched, as a leaf.

in·ci·sion \in-'sizh-n\ *n.* **1** The action of incising; especially, the action of cutting the skin or any part of the body in order to reach a diseased or injured region. **2** A cut; a gash.

in·ci·sive \in-'sī-siv\ *adj.* Cutting; penetrating; acute; as, an *incisive* comment. — **in·ci·sive·ly,** *adv.*

in·ci·sor \in-'sīz-r\ *n.* Any of the cutting teeth in front of the canines in either jaw.

incisor

in·cite \in-'sīt\ *v.;* **in·cit·ed; in·cit·ing.** To urge or stir to action; to rouse; as, to *incite* a mob to violence. — **in·cite·ment,** *n.*

in·ci·vil·i·ty \ˌin-sə-'vil-ət-ē\ *n.; pl.* **in·ci·vil·i·ties.** **1** Discourtesy; rudeness; impoliteness. **2** A rude or discourteous act.

in·clem·ent \(')in-'klem-ənt\ *adj.* **1** Not clement; harsh; severe. **2** Stormy; rough; as, *inclement* weather. — **in·clem·en·cy** \-ən-sē\ *n.* — **in·clem·ent·ly,** *adv.*

in·cli·na·tion \ˌin-klə-'nāsh-n\ *n.* **1** A natural leaning toward some thing or some course of action; a tendency; as, an *inclination* for sports; to follow one's *inclinations.* **2** A nod; a bow; as, an *inclination* of the head. **3** A leaning or bending away from a straight line; as, the *inclination* of the earth's axis. **4** An inclined surface; a slope.

in·cline \in-'klīn\ *v.;* **in·clined; in·clin·ing.** **1** To bend the head or body forward; to bow. **2** To lean in one's mind; to tend; to be favorable, as towards a person, an opinion, a course of action; as, to *incline* towards the second of two proposals. **3** To deviate from a line, direction, or course; to lean; to slope; to slant. **4** To cause to bend, bow, slope, or slant. **5** To influence, as in direction, course of action, or opinion. — \'in-ˌklīn\ *n.* A slope or slant. — **in·clin·a·ble** \in-'klī-nəb-l\ *adj.*

in·clined \in-'klīnd; *sense 2 is also* 'in-ˌklīnd\ *adj.* **1** Having inclination; feeling willingness; as, to be *inclined* to accept a story as true. **2** Sloping; slanting; as, an *inclined* plane.

in·close \in-'klōz\ *v.;* **in·closed; in·clos·ing.** To enclose.

in·clo·sure \in-'klōzh-r\ *n.* An enclosure.

in·clude \in-'klüd\ *v.;* **in·clud·ed; in·clud·ing.** To contain or take in as part or parts of a whole; as, ten days *including* today. The sale *included* the furniture as well as the house.

in·clu·sion \in-'klüzh-n\ *n.* **1** An including or a being included. **2** Something that is included.

in·clu·sive \in-'klü-siv, -ziv\ *adj.* Including; especially, including one or more limits; as, pages ten to twenty *inclusive; inclusive* of today. — **in·clu·sive·ly,** *adv.*

in·cog·ni·to \ˌin-ˌkäg-'nēt-ˌō, in-'käg-nə-ˌtō\ *adj.* or *adv.* [From Italian, meaning literally "unknown".] With one's identity concealed, as under an assumed name or title. The prince traveled *incognito.* — *n.; pl.* **in·cog·ni·tos.** The state or disguise of a person who is appearing or living incognito.

in·co·her·ence \ˌin-kō-ˈhir-ən(t)s\ *n.* **1** The quality or condition of being incoherent. **2** An incoherent statement.

in·co·her·ent \ˌin-kō-ˈhir-ənt\ *adj.* Not coherent; not clearly connected; rambling; as, an *incoherent* manner of speaking. — **in·co·her·ent·ly**, *adv.*

in·com·bus·ti·ble \ˌin-kəm-ˈbəs-təb-l\ *adj.* Not combustible; incapable of being burned. — *n.* An incombustible substance.

in·come \ˈin-ˌkəm\ *n.* The gain, usually figured in money, that comes in from labor, business, or property; receipts.

income tax. A tax on a person's income or on the excess over a certain amount.

in·com·ing \ˈin-ˌkəm-ing\ *adj.* Coming in; as, the *incoming* tide.

in·com·men·su·rate \ˌin-kə-ˈmen(t)s-r-ət, -ˈmench-r-ət\ *adj.* Not commensurate; especially, not adequate; not enough to satisfy; as, funds that are *incommensurate* with one's needs. — **in·com·men·su·rate·ly**, *adv.*

in·com·mode \ˌin-kə-ˈmōd\ *v.;* **in·com·mod·ed**; **in·com·mod·ing.** To trouble; to inconvenience; as, *incommoded* by lack of room.

in·com·mo·di·ous \ˌin-kə-ˈmōd-ē-əs\ *adj.* Not commodious.

in·com·mu·ni·ca·ble \ˌin-kə-ˈmyü-nə-kəb-l\ *adj.* Not capable of being communicated.

in·com·mu·ni·ca·do \ˌin-kə-ˌmyü-nə-ˈkäd-ˌō, -ˈkȧd-ˌō\ *adj.* Without means of communication with others; as, a prisoner held *incommunicado.*

in·com·mu·ni·ca·tive \ˌin-kə-ˈmyü-nə-ˌkāt-iv, -kət-iv\ *adj.* Not communicative; not sociable and friendly.

in·com·pa·ra·ble \(ˈ)in-ˈkämp-r(-)əb-l\ *adj.* Beyond comparison; without equal; matchless; as, an *incomparable* performance. — **in·com·pa·ra·bly** \-r(-)ə-blē\ *adv.*

in·com·pat·i·bil·i·ty \ˌin-kəm-ˌpat-ə-ˈbil-ət-ē\ *n.; pl.* **in·com·pat·i·bil·i·ties. 1** The quality or state of being incompatible. **2** An incompatible thing or quality.

in·com·pat·i·ble \ˌin-kəm-ˈpat-əb-l\ *adj.* Not capable of being brought together in a harmonious or agreeable relationship; as, conduct *incompatible* with a sense of honor; two persons temperamentally *incompatible.* — **in·com·pat·i·bly** \-ə-blē\ *adv.*

in·com·pe·tence \(ˈ)in-ˈkämp-ə-tən(t)s\ *n.* **1** Lack of ability. **2** Lack of legal qualification or fitness.

in·com·pe·ten·cy \(ˈ)in-ˈkämp-ə-tən-sē\ *n.* Incompetence.

in·com·pe·tent \(ˈ)in-ˈkämp-ə-tənt\ *adj.* **1** Not competent; lacking sufficient knowledge, skill, strength, or ability. **2** Not legally qualified. — *n.* An incompetent person. — **in·com·pe·tent·ly**, *adv.*

in·com·plete \ˌin-kəm-ˈplēt\ *adj.* Not complete; unfinished; imperfect. — **in·com·plete·ly**, *adv.*

in·com·pre·hen·si·ble \(ˌ)in-ˌkämp-rē-ˈhen(t)s-əb-l\ *adj.* Incapable of being comprehended; impossible to understand. — **in·com·pre·hen·si·bil·i·ty** \-ˌhen(t)s-ə-ˈbil-ət-ē\ *n.* — **in·com·pre·hen·si·bly** \-ˈhen(t)s-ə-blē\ *adv.*

in·con·ceiv·a·ble \ˌin-kən-ˈsē-vəb-l\ *adj.* Impossible to imagine or conceive; hard to believe; incredible; as, *inconceivable* wealth. — **in·con·ceiv·a·bly** \-və-blē\ *adv.*

in·con·clu·sive \ˌin-kən-ˈklü-siv, -ziv\ *adj.* Not conclusive; not leading to a definite result. — **in·con·clu·sive·ly**, *adv.*

in·con·gru·i·ty \ˌin-kən-ˈgrü-ət-ē, -ˌkän-\ *n.; pl.* **in·con·gru·i·ties. 1** The quality or state of being incongruous; lack of harmony; inconsistency. **2** Something that is incongruous.

in·con·gru·ous \(ˈ)in-ˈkäng-grü-əs\ *adj.* Not consistent with or suitable to the surroundings or associations; not harmonious, appropriate, or proper; out of place; as, *incongruous* colors. A grand piano makes an *incongruous* appearance in a log cabin. — **in·con·gru·ous·ly**, *adv.*

in·con·se·quen·tial \(ˌ)in-ˌkän(t)s-ə-ˈkwench-l\ *adj.* Of no consequence; not important. — **in·con·se·quen·tial·ly** \-ˈkwench-l-ē\ *adv.*

in·con·sid·er·a·ble \ˌin-kən-ˈsid-rb-l, -r(-)əb-l\ *adj.* Not worth considering; slight, trivial.

in·con·sid·er·ate \ˌin-kən-ˈsid-r-ət\ *adj.* Not considerate; careless of the rights and feelings of others. — **in·con·sid·er·ate·ly**, *adv.*

in·con·sist·en·cy \ˌin-kən-ˈsis-tən-sē\ *n.; pl.* **in·con·sist·en·cies. 1** The quality or state of being inconsistent. **2** Something that is inconsistent.

in·con·sist·ent \ˌin-kən-ˈsis-tənt\ *adj.* **1** Not consistent; not in agreement or harmony; as, a statement *inconsistent* with the facts. **2** Not logical in thought or actions; changeable; as, a very *inconsistent* man. — **in·con·sist·ent·ly**, *adv.*

in·con·sol·a·ble \ˌin-kən-ˈsō-ləb-l\ *adj.* Not capable of being consoled; grieved beyond comforting. — **in·con·sol·a·bly** \-lə-blē\ *adv.*

in·con·spic·u·ous \ˌin-kən-ˈspik-yə-wəs\ *adj.* Not conspicuous; not easily noticeable. — **in·con·spic·u·ous·ly**, *adv.*

in·con·stan·cy \(ˈ)in-ˈkän(t)s-tən-sē\ *n.* Lack of constancy; fickleness.

in·con·stant \(ˈ)in-ˈkän(t)s-tənt\ *adj.* Not constant; liable to sudden changes; changeable. — **in·con·stant·ly**, *adv.*

in·con·test·a·ble \ˌin-kən-ˈtes-təb-l\ *adj.* Not open to doubt or contest; indisputable; unquestionable. — **in·con·test·a·bly** \-tə-blē\ *adv.*

in·con·ti·nent \(ˈ)in-ˈkänt-n-ənt, -ˈkän-tə-nənt\ *adj.* Lacking in self-restraint, especially in the fulfillment of sensuous desires. — **in·con·ti·nence** \-ˈkänt-n-ən(t)s, -ˈkän-tə-nən(t)s\ *n.* — **in·con·ti·nent·ly**, *adv.*

in·con·tro·vert·i·ble \(ˌ)in-ˌkän-trə-ˈvərt-əb-l\ *adj.* Not capable of being disputed. — **in·con·tro·vert·i·bly** \-ə-blē\ *adv.*

in·con·ve·nience \ˌin-kən-ˈvēn-yən(t)s\ *n.* **1** The condition of not being convenient; lack of suitability for personal comfort; discomfort. **2** Something that causes discomfort or annoyance. — *v.;* **in·con·ve·nienced; in·con·ve·nienc·ing.** To cause inconvenience to; to trouble; to discomfort; as, to be *inconvenienced* by a delay.

in·con·ve·nient \ˌin-kən-ˈvēn-yənt\ *adj.* Not convenient; causing trouble or annoyance.— **in·con·ve·nient·ly,** *adv.*

in·cor·po·rate \in-ˈkȯrp-r(-)ət\ *adj.* Formed into a corporation; associated as a part of a corporation; incorporated; as, an *incorporate* municipality. — \-r-ˌāt\ *v.;* **in·cor·po·rat·ed; in·cor·po·rat·ing. 1** To join or unite closely into a single mass or body; to blend; as, to *incorporate* new ideas into a story. **2** To form into a legal corporation; to form a corporation; as, to *incorporate* a firm. **3** To give a material form to; as, to *incorporate* one's ideas in an essay. — **in·cor·po·ra·tion** \in-ˌkȯrp-r-ˈāsh-n\ *n.*

in·cor·po·rat·ed \in-ˈkȯrp-r-ˌāt-əd\ *adj.* United in one body; especially, formed into a corporation, as by charter.

in·cor·po·re·al \ˌin-ˌkȯr-ˈpōr-ē-əl, -ˈpȯr-\ *adj.* Not having a material body; as, *incorporeal* spirits. — **in·cor·po·re·al·ly** \-ē-ə-lē\ *adv.*

in·cor·rect \ˌin-kə-ˈrekt\ *adj.* **1** Not correct; not accurate or true; as, an *incorrect* answer. **2** Not proper or right; as, *incorrect* conduct. — **in·cor·rect·ly,** *adv.*

in·cor·ri·gi·ble \(ˈ)in-ˈkȯr-ə-jəb-l, -ˈkär-\ *adj.* **1** Bad beyond correction; incapable of being reformed; as, an *incorrigible* gambler. **2** Unruly; unmanageable; as, *incorrigible* children. — **in·cor·ri·gi·bil·i·ty** \(ˌ)in-ˌkȯr-ə-jə-ˈbil-ət-ē, -ˌkär-\ *n.* — **in·cor·ri·gi·bly** \(ˈ)in-ˈkȯr-ə-jə-blē, -ˈkär-\ *adv.*

in·cor·rupt·i·ble \ˌin-kə-ˈrəp-təb-l\ *adj.* **1** Not corruptible; not subject to decay. **2** Not capable of being morally corrupted; just and honest in character; as, an *incorruptible* judge. — **in·cor·rupt·i·bil·i·ty** \ˌin-kə-ˌrəp-tə-ˈbil-ət-ē\ *n.* — **in·cor·rupt·i·bly** \ˌin-kə-ˈrəp-tə-blē\ *adv.*

in·crease \in-ˈkrēs\ *v.;* **in·creased; in·creas·ing. 1** To make or to become greater, as in size, number, value, or power; as, to *increase* speed. Skill *increases* with practice. **2** To multiply by the production of young. Rabbits *increase* rapidly when their natural enemies are removed. — \ˈin-ˌkrēs, in-ˈkrēs\ *n.* **1** Addition or enlargement, as in size, number, value, or power; growth; as, the average yearly *increase* in population; to have an *increase* in weight. **2** Anything produced by increasing or growth. — **in·creas·er** \in-ˈkrēs-r\ *n.* — **in·creas·ing·ly** \in-ˈkrē-sing-lē\ *adv.*

in·cred·i·ble \(ˈ)in-ˈkred-əb-l\ *adj.* Too extraordinary or improbable to be believed; hard to believe; as, an *incredible* story; the *incredible* speed of a jet plane. — **in·cred·i·bil·i·ty** \(ˌ)in-ˌkred-ə-ˈbil-ət-ē\ *n.* — **in·cred·i·bly** \(ˈ)in-ˈkred-ə-blē\ *adv.*

in·cre·du·li·ty \ˌin-krē-ˈdü-lət-ē, -ˈdyü-\ *n.* The quality or state of not believing or of doubting; an instance of disbelieving.

in·cred·u·lous \(ˈ)in-ˈkrej-l-əs\ *adj.* **1** Not easily accepting as true; tending to disbelieve. **2** Showing or caused by lack of belief; as, to listen with an *incredulous* smile. — **in·cred·u·lous·ly,** *adv.*

in·cre·ment \ˈin(g)-krə-mənt\ *n.* **1** An increasing; increase. **2** Whatever is gained or added; especially, one of a series of regular additions; as, an *increment* of 300 dollars a year.

in·crim·i·nate \in-ˈkrim-ə-ˌnāt\ *v.;* **in·crim·i·nat·ed; in·crim·i·nat·ing.** To charge with or involve in a crime or fault; to accuse. The prisoner's confession *incriminated* one of his friends. — **in·crim·i·na·tion** \(ˌ)in-ˌkrim-ə-ˈnāsh-n\ *n.* — **in·crim·i·na·to·ry** \in-ˈkrim-ə-nə-ˌtōr-ē, -ˌtȯr-ē\ *adj.*

in·crust \in-ˈkrəst\ *v.* **1** To cover or coat with, or as if with, a crust; as, iron *incrusted* with rust; to *incrust* walls with marble. **2** To decorate a surface by inserting other material; as, a ring *incrusted* with diamonds.

in·crus·ta·tion \ˌin-ˌkrəs-ˈtāsh-n\ *n.* **1** An incrusting or a being incrusted. **2** A crust or hard coating.

in·cu·bate \ˈin(g)-kyə-ˌbāt\ *v.;* **in·cu·bat·ed; in·cu·bat·ing. 1** To sit upon eggs to hatch them by warmth. **2** To maintain, as eggs, embryos of animals, or bacteria, under conditions favorable for hatching or development. — **in·cu·ba·tion** \ˌin(g)-kyə-ˈbāsh-n\ *n.*

in·cu·ba·tor \ˈin(g)-kyə-ˌbāt-r\ *n.* **1** An apparatus that supplies enough heat to hatch eggs artificially. **2** Any similar apparatus, as one to help the growth of prematurely born babies or one for incubating bacteria.

in·cu·bus \ˈin(g)-kyə-bəs\ *n.* [From Late Latin, meaning "nightmare".] **1** A spirit supposed to work evil on persons in their sleep. **2** A nightmare. **3** A burden; anything oppressive; as, the *incubus* of debt.

in·cul·cate \in-ˈkəl-ˌkāt, ˈin-(ˌ)kəl-\ *v.;* **in·cul·cat·ed; in·cul·cat·ing.** To teach and impress upon the mind by frequent repetition. A sense of responsibility was *inculcated* in the girl early in her life.

in·cum·bent \in-ˈkəm-bənt\ *adj.* **1** Lying down; reclining. **2** Laid upon a person as a duty or obligation. It is *incumbent* on a person to do his best work. — *n.* The holder of an office or position.

in·cum·ber \in-ˈkəm-br\ *v.;* **in·cum·bered; in·cum·ber·ing** \-br(-)ing\. To encumber.

in·cum·brance \in-ˈkəm-brən(t)s\ *n.* Encumbrance.

in·cur \in-ˈkər\ *v.;* **in·curred; in·cur·ring.** To meet with, as something troublesome or harmful; to bring down upon oneself; as, to *incur* debts; to *incur* the dislike of a schoolmate.

in·cur·a·ble \(ˈ)in-ˈkyu̇r-əb-l\ *adj.* Not capable of being cured; as, an *incurable* disease. — *n.* A person suffering from a disease that is beyond cure. — **in·cur·a·bly** \-ə-blē\ *adv.*

in·cur·sion \in-ˈkərzh-n\ *n.* A sudden, usually temporary, invasion, as by a hostile force; a raid.

in·debt·ed \in-ˈdet-əd\ *adj.* Being in debt; owing something, as money, gratitude, or services.

in·debt·ed·ness \in-ˈdet-əd-nəs\ *n.* **1** The condition of being in debt or under obligation. **2** The amount owed; the sum of one's debts.

in·de·cen·cy \(ˈ)in-ˈdēs-n-sē\ *n.; pl.* **in·de·cen·cies.** **1** Lack of decency. **2** An indecent act or word.

in·de·cent \(ˈ)in-ˈdēs-nt\ *adj.* **1** Unbecoming; improper; as, a widow who remarried in *indecent* haste. **2** Morally offensive; not fit to be seen or heard; as, *indecent* talk. — For synonyms see *indelicate.* — **in·de·cent·ly,** *adv.*

in·de·ci·sion \ˌin-də-ˈsizh-n\ *n.* Slowness in deciding; hesitation or lack of firmness in making up one's mind.

in·de·ci·sive \ˌin-də-ˈsī-siv\ *adj.* **1** Not decisive or final; as, an *indecisive* battle. **2** Characterized by indecision; hesitating; uncertain; as, an *indecisive* person.

in·de·clin·a·ble \ˌin-də-ˈklī-nəb-l\ *adj.* Not declinable, as a word that does not change its form to show changes in number, case, tense, or gender.

in·dec·o·rous \(ˈ)in-ˈdek-r-əs; ˌin-də-ˈkōr-əs, -ˈkȯr-\ *adj.* Not decorous; improper; unbecoming. — **in·dec·o·rous·ly,** *adv.*

in·deed \in-ˈdēd\ *adv.* In fact; truly; to be sure. **—** *interj.* An exclamation expressing typically surprise or disbelief.

in·de·fat·i·ga·ble \ˌin-də-ˈfat-ig-əb-l\ *adj.* Capable of working a long time without tiring; not giving in to fatigue; tireless. — **in·de·fat·i·ga·bly** \-ə-blē\ *adv.*

in·de·fea·si·ble \ˌin-də-ˈfē-zəb-l\ *adj.* Not capable of being abolished or annulled; as, the *indefeasible* rights of a citizen. — **in·de·fea·si·bly** \-zə-blē\ *adv.*

in·de·fen·si·ble \ˌin-də-ˈfen(t)s-əb-l\ *adj.* Not capable of being defended; as, an *indefensible* position; *indefensible* conduct. — **in·de·fen·si·bly** \-ə-blē\ *adv.*

in·de·fin·a·ble \ˌin-də-ˈfī-nəb-l\ *adj.* Not capable of being defined or described exactly. — **in·de·fin·a·bly** \-nə-blē\ *adv.*

in·def·i·nite \(ˈ)in-ˈdef-n(-)ət\ *adj.* **1** Not clear or fixed in meaning or details; vague; as, to be *indefinite* about one's plans; to receive an *indefinite* answer to a question. **2** Not fixed or limited, as in amount or length; as, to go away for an *indefinite* period. **3** Unmeasured or unmeasurable; as, an *indefinite* number. **4** In grammar, not defining; denoting one of a class or number without saying which one. "Any" is an *indefinite* pronoun. — **in·def·i·nite·ly,** *adv.*

indefinite article. Either of the words *a* or *an,* used before a noun to show that the noun refers to any person or thing of the kind named, not to one in particular.

in·del·i·ble \in-ˈdel-əb-l\ *adj.* **1** Not capable of being erased, removed, or blotted out; as, *indelible* ink; an *indelible* impression. **2** Making marks not easily erased; as, an *indelible* pencil. — **in·del·i·bly** \-ə-blē\ *adv.*

in·del·i·ca·cy \(ˈ)in-ˈdel-ə-kə-sē\ *n.; pl.* **in·del·i·ca·cies.** **1** The quality of being indelicate; coarseness. **2** Any indelicate act or utterance.

in·del·i·cate \(ˈ)in-ˈdel-ik-ət\ *adj.* Not delicate; offensive to good manners or refined taste; immodest; coarse. — For synonyms see *improper.* — **in·del·i·cate·ly,** *adv.*

in·dem·ni·fy \in-ˈdem-nə-ˌfī\ *v.;* **in·dem·ni·fied** \-ˌfīd\; **in·dem·ni·fy·ing.** **1** To insure against; as, *indemnified* against any possible loss. **2** To make compensation to, as for a loss or damage suffered; to pay or repay; as, to *indemnify* the victims of a disaster at sea. **3** To make compensation for; to make good; as, to have one's losses in a disaster *indemnified.* — **in·dem·ni·fi·ca·tion** \-ˌdem-nə-fə-ˈkāsh-n\ *n.*

in·dem·ni·ty \in-ˈdem-nət-ē\ *n.; pl.* **in·dem·ni·ties.** **1** Protection from loss, damage, or injury; insurance. **2** Freedom or exemption from penalty for past offenses. **3** Money or other compensation paid for loss, damage, or injury suffered.

in·dent \in-ˈdent\ *v.* **1** To make a toothlike cut or cuts on an edge; to make jagged. Coves *indent* the lake shore. **2** To bind by an indenture; to indenture. **3** To write, type, or print the first word of a line in from the margin; as, to *indent* the beginning of a paragraph.

in·dent \in-ˈdent\ *v.* **1** To impress; to stamp or press in; as, to *indent* a pattern in metal. **2** To form a dent or dents in something.

in·den·ta·tion \ˌin-ˌden-ˈtāsh-n\ *n.* **1** An indenting. **2** A notch; a cut; as, *indentations* in a coast. **3** An indention. **4** A dent.

in·den·tion \in-ˈdench-n\ *n.* **1** An indenting; an indentation. **2** The action of setting in from the margin a line or lines, especially the first line of a paragraph. **3** The blank space left by such an action.

in·den·ture \in-ˈdench-r\ *n.* A written agreement; a contract, especially one that binds a person to the service of another. **—** *v.;* **in·den·tured; in·den·tur·ing** \-r(-)ing\. To bind by an indenture.

in·de·pend·ence \ˌin-də-ˈpen-dən(t)s\ *n.* **1** The state or condition of those who are independent; freedom from control by others; self-government. **2** Independent or sufficient means for supporting oneself.

Independence Day. A day set apart to celebrate the achieving of political independence or national sovereignty, as, in the United States, the Fourth of July.

in·de·pend·ent \ˌin-də-ˈpen-dənt\ *adj.* **1** Not under another's control or rule; self-governing; free; as, an *independent* nation. **2** Not having connections with any other or each other; separate; as, the same story told by *independent* witnesses. **3** Not supported by another; having or providing enough money to live upon; as, a person of *independent* means. **4** Not easily influenced; showing self-reliance; as, an *independent* mind. **5** Free; easy; bold; as, an *independent* manner. **6** Of a clause, having full meaning in itself and capable of standing alone as a simple sentence. **7** Not tied to a political party. **—** *n.* An independent person or thing; especially, a person who thinks and votes independently of party considerations in politics. — **in·de·pend·ent·ly**, *adv.*

in·de·scrib·a·ble \ˌin-də-ˈskrī-bəb-l\ *adj.* Incapable of being described; beyond description; as, *indescribable* beauty. — **in·de·scrib·a·bly** \-bə-blē\ *adv.*

in·de·struct·i·ble \ˌin-də-ˈstrək-təb-l\ *adj.* Incapable of being destroyed; strong and lasting. — **in·de·struct·i·bil·i·ty** \-ˌstrək-tə-ˈbil-ət-ē\ *n.* — **in·de·struct·i·bly** \-ˈstrək-tə-blē\ *adv.*

in·de·ter·min·a·ble \ˌin-də-ˈtər-mə-nəb-l\ *adj.* Not capable of being definitely known.

in·de·ter·mi·nate \ˌin-də-ˈtər-mə-nət\ *adj.* **1** Not definite, distinct, or precise; as, having only *indeterminate* plans for vacation. **2** Not leading to a definite end or result; as, an *indeterminate* debate. — **in·de·ter·mi·nate·ly**, *adv.*

in·dex \ˈin-ˌdeks\ *n.; pl.* **in·dex·es** \-ˌdeks-əz\ or **in·di·ces** \-də-ˌsēz\. **1** The finger next to the thumb (**index finger**); the forefinger. **2** A pointer or indicator, as a hand on a watch. **3** A sign; an indication; as, an *index* to character. **4** An alphabetized list, as of topics and names, in a book, with the pages where each is treated. **5** [Plural *indices*] In mathematics, the figure, letter, or expression showing the power or root of a quantity, as the figure *3* in a^3; an exponent. **6** In printing, a sign [☞] used to direct attention to a note or paragraph; a fist. — *v.* **1** To provide with or put into an index. **2** To be an index of something; to indicate.

In·dia ink \ˈin-dē-ə\. A black pigment of prepared lampblack or burned ivory, used for writing, drawing, and painting.

In·di·an \ˈin-dē-ən\ *adj.* [From *India* and the suffix *-an;* in sense 2, from Spanish *indiano, indio,* a name given (in the form *indio*) by Columbus to the natives of America because he thought he had reached the East Indies.] **1** Of or relating to India. **2** Of or relating to the native peoples found in America at the time of its discovery. — *n.* **1** A member of one of the native peoples of India. **2** A member of the native American race. **3** An American Indian language.

Indian club. A wooden club used in gymnastic exercises.

Indian corn. The seeds or kernels of a tall cereal plant with grasslike leaves, or the plant that bears these seeds; corn; maize.

Indian meal. Ground Indian corn, or maize.

Indian pudding. A pudding whose chief ingredients are Indian meal, milk, and molasses.

Indian summer. A period of mild weather in late autumn or early winter.

India paper. **1** A thin, delicate paper, as for prints of engravings. **2** A thin, tough printing paper.

India rubber. **1** Rubber. **2** A piece of very soft rubber used for erasing pencil marks.

in·di·cate \ˈin-də-ˌkāt\ *v.;* **in·di·cat·ed; in·di·cat·ing.** **1** To point out; to be a sign or index of or to something; to make known; as, to *indicate* what one wants. Those clouds *indicate* rain. **2** In medicine, to show by symptoms; to point to as the proper remedy or treatment.

in·di·ca·tion \ˌin-də-ˈkāsh-n\ *n.* **1** The act of indicating; a suggestion. **2** Something that indicates or points out; a sign.

in·dic·a·tive \in-ˈdik-ət-iv\ *adj.* **1** In grammar, belonging to or constituting the set of verb forms that are used regularly in simple declarative sentences and in questions that can be answered by simple declarative sentences. **2** Pointing out; giving a sign or indication of something that is not visible or obvious; suggestive; as, remarks *indicative* of resentment. — *n.* The indicative mood of a verb or a verb in this mood.

in·di·ca·tor \ˈin-də-ˌkāt-r\ *n.* A person or thing that indicates; a pointer, dial, or gauge.

indices. A pl. of *index.*

in·dict \in-ˈdīt\ *v.* **1** To charge with an offense. **2** In law, to bring in, or place on the record, an indictment against. — **in·dict·a·ble** \-ˈdīt-əb-l\ *adj.*

in·dict·ment \in-ˈdīt-mənt\ *n.* **1** The act or the legal process of indicting. **2** A formal written statement charging a person with an offense, drawn up by a prosecuting attorney and brought in by a grand jury after an inquiry.

in·dif·fer·ence \in-ˈdif-rn(t)s, -r(-)ən(t)s\ *n.* **1** The condition or the fact of being indifferent; lack of feeling for or against anything. **2** Lack of importance; as, a matter of *indifference* to everyone but oneself.

in·dif·fer·ent \in-ˈdif-rnt, -r(-)ənt\ *adj.* **1** Having no choice or preference; not interested in or concerned about something; as, to be *indifferent* to heat or cold; *indifferent* to the troubles of others. **2** Showing neither interest nor dislike. The audience was not so much bored as *indifferent.* **3** Neither good nor bad; as, *indifferent* health. **4** Of no great or special influence or value; not important; as, to spend the morning disposing of various *indifferent* matters.

in·dif·fer·ent·ly \in-ˈdif-rnt-lē, -r(-)ənt-\ *adv.* **1** With indifference; without interest, feeling, or concern. **2** Neither well nor badly; often, rather badly; as, to play golf well but tennis *indifferently.*

in·di·gence \ˈin-də-jən(t)s\ *n.* Poverty.

in·dig·e·nous \in-ˈdij-n-əs\ *adj.* Produced, growing, or living naturally in a region; native. — **in·dig·e·nous·ly**, *adv.*

in·di·gent \ˈin-də-jənt\ *adj.* Poor; needy.

in·di·gest·i·ble \ˌin-də-ˈjes-təb-l\ *adj.* Not digestible; not easily digested. — **in·di·gest·i·bil·i·ty** \-ˌjes-tə-ˈbil-ət-ē\ *n.*

in·di·ges·tion \ˌin-də-ˈjes-chən\ *n.* **1** Lack of digestion; incomplete or difficult digestion; dyspepsia. **2** Discomfort caused by slow or painful digestion.

in·dig·nant \in-ˈdig-nənt\ *adj.* Affected with indignation; angry because of the occurrence of something unfair or mean. — **in·dig·nant·ly**, *adv.*

in·dig·na·tion \ˌin-(ˌ)dig-ˈnāsh-n\ *n.* Anger aroused by something low, unworthy, or disgraceful.

in·dig·ni·ty \in-ˈdig-nət-ē\ *n.; pl.* **in·dig·ni·ties.** Anything said or done to a person which shows disrespect; offensive treatment; an insult.

in·di·go \ˈin-di-ˌgō\ *n.; pl.* **in·di·gos** or **in·di·goes.** [From Spanish *indigo,* there derived from Latin *indicum,* this having been borrowed from Greek *indikon,* a derivative of the adjective *Indikos* meaning "Indian", "from India".] **1** A blue dye now made artificially but formerly obtained from plants, especially from the **indigo plant**, a tropical shrub of the pea family. **2** Also **indigo blue.** A dark dull purplish blue.

in·di·rect \ˌin-də-ˈrekt, -dī-\ *adj.* **1** Not straight; not the shortest; as, an *indirect* route. **2** Not straightforward; roundabout; as, to achieve a purpose by *indirect* methods. **3** Not having a plainly seen connection; as, an *indirect* cause. **4** Not straight to the point; as, an *indirect* answer. **5** Stated essentially in the words of the original speaker but in the form of a dependent clause with appropriate changes in tense and person, as in "He said that he would come when I call him"; as, an *indirect* quotation; *indirect* discourse. — **in·di·rect·ly**, *adv.*

indirect object. A verb object that typically denotes the one to whom something is given, the one for whom something is done, or in some languages also the one from whom something is taken, as *me* in "He threw me the ball".

in·dis·creet \ˌin-dis-ˈkrēt\ *adj.* Not discreet; lacking good judgment or proper caution. — **in·dis·creet·ly**, *adv.*

in·dis·cre·tion \ˌin-dis-ˈkresh-n\ *n.* **1** Lack of discretion; imprudence. **2** An indiscreet act.

in·dis·crim·i·nate \ˌin-dis-ˈkrim-ə-nət\ *adj.* Showing lack of discrimination; not making careful distinction between persons or things; as, an *indiscriminate* reader; an *indiscriminate* attraction to everything new. — **in·dis·crim·i·nate·ly**, *adv.*

in·dis·pens·a·ble \ˌin-dis-ˈpen(t)s-əb-l\ *adj.* Absolutely necessary; as, an *indispensable* employee. Water is *indispensable* to man. — *n.* An indispens·ble person or thing. — **in·dis·pens·a·bil·i·ty** \-ˌpen(t)s-ə-ˈbil-ət-ē\ *n.* — **in·dis·pens·a·bly** \-ˈpen(t)s-ə-blē\ *adv.*

in·dis·posed \ˌin-dis-ˈpōzd\ *adj.* **1** Sick; ill; especially, slightly ill. **2** Unwilling; disinclined. The new pupil seemed *indisposed* to join in class activities.

in·dis·po·si·tion \(ˌ)in-ˌdis-pə-ˈzish-n\ *n.* **1** A slight illness. **2** Disinclination; unwillingness.

in·dis·put·a·ble \ˌin-dis-ˈpyüt-əb-l, (ˈ)in-ˈdis-pyət-\ *adj.* Not disputable. — **in·dis·put·a·bly** \-ə-blē\ *adv.*

in·dis·sol·u·ble \ˌin-di-ˈsäl-yəb-l\ *adj.* Not capable of being dissolved, undone, or broken up; as, an *indissoluble* bond. — **in·dis·sol·u·bil·i·ty** \-ˌsäl-yə-ˈbil-ət-ē\ *n.* — **in·dis·sol·u·bly** \-ˈsäl-yə-blē\ *adv.*

in·dis·tinct \ˌin-dis-ˈting(k)t\ *adj.* Not distinct; not clear; obscure; confused; blurred; as, *indistinct* writing; an *indistinct* recollection of what happened. — **in·dis·tinct·ly**, *adv.*

in·dis·tin·guish·a·ble \ˌin-dis-ˈting-gwish-əb-l\ *adj.* Not capable of being clearly distinguished. — **in·dis·tin·guish·a·bly** \-ə-blē\ *adv.*

in·dite \in-ˈdīt\ *v.;* **in·dit·ed**; **in·dit·ing.** To compose or to compose and write, as a letter.

in·di·vid·u·al \ˌin-də-ˈvij-ə-wəl, -ˈvij-l\ *n.* **1** A single member of a class or species; a particular person, animal, or thing. **2** A person; as, a very disagreeable *individual.* — *adj.* **1** Of or having to do with an individual; by or for an individual; as, *individual* effort; *individual* cups. **2** Particular; single; as, an *individual* case, not a general rule. **3** Having marked characteristics of its own; as, an *individual* style of dressing. — **in·di·vid·u·al·ly** \-ˈvij-l-ē, -ˈvij-ə-wə-lē\ *adv.*

in·di·vid·u·al·ism \ˌin-də-ˈvij-ə-wə-ˌliz-m, -ˈvij-l-ˌiz-m\ *n.* **1** Egoism. **2** The doctrine that the chief end of society is to promote the welfare of its individual members. **3** Any doctrine holding that the individual has certain political or economic rights with which the state must not interfere.

in·di·vid·u·al·ist \ˌin-də-ˈvij-ə-wə-ləst, -ˈvij-l-əst\ *n.* **1** A person who shows marked individuality or independence of others in thought or behavior. **2** A supporter of the doctrines of individualism. — **in·di·vid·u·al·is·tic** \ˌin-də-ˌvij-ə-wə-ˈlis-tik, -ˌvij-l-ˈis-tik\ *adj.*

in·di·vid·u·al·i·ty \ˌin-də-ˌvij-ə-ˈwal-ət-ē\ *n.; pl.* **in·di·vid·u·al·i·ties.** **1** The quality or qualities that mark one person or thing off from all others. **2** The condition of being individual, or having separate existence.

in·di·vid·u·al·ize \ˌin-də-ˈvij-ə-wə-ˌlīz, -ˈvij-l-ˌīz\ *v.;* **in·di·vid·u·al·ized**; **in·di·vid·u·al·iz·ing.** **1** To make individual in character; as, to *individualize* a work project so that each person does something he is suited for. **2** To treat or notice individually. The teacher *individualizes* each student's problems.

in·di·vis·i·ble \ˌin-də-ˈviz-əb-l\ *adj.* Not capable of being divided or separated. — **in·di·vis·i·bil·i·ty** \-ˌviz-ə-ˈbil-ət-ē\ *n.* — **in·di·vis·i·bly** \-ˈviz-ə-blē\ *adv.*

in·doc·tri·nate \in-ˈdäk-trə-ˌnāt\ *v.;* **in·doc·tri·nat·ed**; **in·doc·tri·nat·ing.** To instruct, as in the principles of learning; to teach a principle or doctrine to someone. — **in·doc·tri·na·tion** \(ˌ)in-ˌdäk-trə-ˈnāsh-n\ *n.*

in·do·lent \ˈin-də-lənt\ *adj.* Lazy; idle. — For synonyms see *idle.* — **in·do·lence** \-lən(t)s\ *n.* — **in·do·lent·ly** \-lənt-lē\ *adv.*

in·dom·i·ta·ble \in-ˈdäm-ət-əb-l\ *adj.* Unconquerable; as, an *indomitable* will. — **in·dom·i·ta·bly** \-ə-blē\ *adv.*

In·do·ne·sian \ˌin-də-ˈnēzh-n\ *adj.* Of or relating to Indonesia. — *n.* A native of Indonesia.

in·door \'in-ˌdōr, -ˌdȯr\ *adj.* Of or for the inside of a building; done, living, or used indoors; as, an *indoor* job.

in·doors \'in-'dōrz, -'dȯrz\ *adv.* In or into a building; as, games to be played *indoors.*

in·dorse \in-'dȯrs\ *v.;* **in·dorsed; in·dors·ing.** To endorse.

in·dorse·ment \in-'dȯrs-mənt\ *n.* Endorsement.

in·du·bi·ta·ble \in-'dü-bət-əb-l, -'dyü-\ *adj.* Too evident for doubt; unquestionable. — **in·du·bi·ta·bly** \-bət-ə-blē\ *adv.*

in·duce \in-'düs, -'dyüs\ *v.;* **in·duced; in·duc·ing. 1** To lead on to do something; to influence by persuasion. **2** To bring about; to cause; as, an illness *induced* by overwork. **3** To reach a conclusion by reasoning from particular instances to general principles. **4** To produce by induction, as an electric current.

in·duce·ment \in-'düs-mənt, -'dyüs-\ *n.* **1** The act of inducing. **2** Something that induces. A money-back guarantee is a good *inducement* to buy.

in·duct \in-'dəkt\ *v.* **1** To place in office; to install; as, to *induct* the new mayor. **2** To bring into military service in accordance with a draft law.

in·duc·tion \in-'dəksh-n\ *n.* **1** An inducting or bringing in; an installation. **2** The process by which an electrical conductor becomes electrified when near a charged body (**elec·tro·stat·ic induction** \i-'lek-trō-ˌstat-ik\). **3** The process by which a magnetizable body becomes magnetized when near a magnet or near a conductor carrying a varying current (**magnetic induction**). **4** The process by which an electric current is produced in a circuit, as by a magnet moving in the immediate vicinity (**electromagnetic induction**). **5** A reasoning from particular instances to a general conclusion; the conclusion so reached. **6** The formality by which a civilian is inducted into military service.

induction coil. An apparatus for transforming a direct current of electricity by induction into an alternating current of high potential.

in·duc·tive \in-'dək-tiv\ *adj.* Using or produced by induction; having to do with induction; as, the *inductive* method of reasoning. — **in·duc·tive·ly,** *adv.*

in·due \in-'dü, -'dyü\ *v.;* **in·dued; in·du·ing.** To endue.

in·dulge \in-'dəlj\ *v.;* **in·dulged; in·dulg·ing. 1** To be tolerant toward; to give way to; to humor; to gratify; as, to *indulge* one's appetite; to *indulge* a child. **2** To allow oneself to take pleasure; as, to *indulge* in teasing; to *indulge* in a new suit. — For synonyms see *gratify.*

in·dul·gence \in-'dəlj-n(t)s\ *n.* **1** An indulging. **2** An indulgent act: a favor granted. **3** Something indulged in. **4** In the Roman Catholic Church, a freeing, in whole or in part, from punishment in this world or in purgatory for a sin, by the saying of certain prayers or the performing of certain acts of piety.

in·dul·gent \in-'dəlj-nt\ *adj.* Indulging; not hard or severe toward those in one's charge; as, an *indulgent* parent. — **in·dul·gent·ly,** *adv.*

in·dus·tri·al \in-'dəs-trē-əl\ *adj.* Having to do with industries or with those working in industries. — **in·dus·tri·al·ly** \-trē-ə-lē\ *adv.*

in·dus·tri·al·ist \in-'dəs-trē-ə-ləst\ *n.* A person engaged in or connected with the development or operation of an industry or industries; a manufacturer.

in·dus·tri·al·ize \in-'dəs-trē-ə-ˌlīz\ *v.;* **in·dus·tri·al·ized; in·dus·tri·al·iz·ing.** To make industrial; to give over to industry; as, to *industrialize* a rural area. — **in·dus·tri·al·i·za·tion** \in-ˌdəs-trē-ə-lə-'zāsh-n\ *n.*

in·dus·tri·ous \in-'dəs-trē-əs\ *adj.* Showing industry; diligent; busy. — For synonyms see *busy.* — **in·dus·tri·ous·ly,** *adv.*

in·dus·try \'in-(ˌ)dəs-trē\ *n.; pl.* **in·dus·tries. 1** The habit of working hard and steadily; diligence. **2** Any branch of business or manufacture; business in general.

in·e·bri·ate \i-'nē-brē-ət, -brē-ˌāt\ *n.* A drunken person. — \-brē-ˌāt\ *v.;* **in·e·bri·at·ed; in·e·bri·at·ing.** To make drunk; to intoxicate.

in·ed·i·ble \(')i-'ned-əb-l\ *adj.* Not edible; not fit or safe to eat.

in·ef·fa·ble \i-'nef-əb-l\ *adj.* Beyond the power of language to describe; unutterable; as, *ineffable* bliss. — **in·ef·fa·bly** \-ə-blē\ *adv.*

in·ef·fec·tive \ˌin-ə-'fek-tiv\ *adj.* **1** Not effective; ineffectual; as, an *ineffective* law. **2** Not efficient; incapable. — **in·ef·fec·tive·ly,** *adv.*

in·ef·fec·tu·al \ˌin-ə-'fek-chə-wəl, -chəl\ *adj.* Not effectual; without effect; inefficient; useless; as, an *ineffectual* dose of medicine. — **in·ef·fec·tu·al·ly** \-chə-lē, -chə-wə-lē\ *adv.*

in·ef·fi·cien·cy \ˌin-ə-'fish-n-sē\ *n.* Lack of efficiency.

in·ef·fi·cient \ˌin-ə-'fish-nt\ *adj.* **1** Not producing the effect desired; not effective. **2** Not competent or capable; as, an *inefficient* workman. — **in·ef·fi·cient·ly,** *adv.*

in·el·e·gant \(')i-'nel-ə-gənt\ *adj.* Not elegant; lacking in grace or good taste; crude. — **in·el·e·gant·ly,** *adv.*

in·el·i·gi·ble \(')i-'nel-ə-jəb-l\ *adj.* Not eligible; not qualified, as for an office. — *n.* An ineligible person. — **in·el·i·gi·bil·i·ty** \(ˌ)i-ˌnel-ə-jə-'bil-ət-ē\ *n.*

in·ept \i-'nept\ *adj.* **1** Unsuited or unsuitable; especially, so inapt as to be absurd or foolish; as, an *inept* remark. **2** Lacking skill or aptitude to perform a particular task or to fill a particular role; as, a woman *inept* at housekeeping. **3** Generally inadequate or ineffectual; bungling; as, an *inept* person. — **in·ept·ly,** *adv.*

in·e·qual·i·ty \ˌin-ē-'kwäl-ət-ē\ *n.; pl.* **in·e·qual·i·ties. 1** The condition of being unequal; the fact of not being the same everywhere or at all times; as, *inequality* in prices. **2** Irregularity, as of a surface; as, the *inequalities* in a landscape.

in·eq·ui·ta·ble \(')i-'nek-wət-əb-l\ *adj.* Not just; unfair. — **in·eq·ui·ta·bly** \-wət-ə-blē\ *adv.*

in·e·rad·i·ca·ble \ˌin-ē-'rad-ə-kəb-l\ *adj.* That cannot be eradicated. — **in·e·rad·i·ca·bly** \-kə-blē\ *adv.*

in·ert \i-'nərt\ *adj.* [From Latin *inert-*, the stem of *iners*, meaning literally "unskilled".] **1** Powerless to move itself or to prevent being moved; as, an *inert* lump of clay. **2** Very slow to move or act; sluggish; lifeless. **3** Not contributing to an intended medicinal effect; as, *inert* ingredients in a cough medicine. — **in·ert·ly**, *adv.*

inert gas. A gas that does not react with other chemical elements.

in·er·tia \i-'nər-shə, -shē-ə\ *n.* **1** In physics, a tendency to remain at rest, or to continue in uniform motion in the same straight line or direction if not acted upon by some other force. **2** A disposition in a person not to move, act, or exert himself.

in·es·cap·a·ble \ˌin-ə-'skāp-əb-l\ *adj.* Incapable of being escaped; inevitable. — **in·es·cap·a·bly** \-ə-blē\ *adv.*

in·es·ti·ma·ble \(')i-'nest-m-əb-l\ *adj.* Above or beyond one's power to measure or to appreciate fully. — **in·es·ti·ma·bly** \-m-ə-blē\ *adv.*

in·ev·i·ta·ble \i-'nev-ət-əb-l\ *adj.* Bound to happen or come; not to be escaped or avoided; certain. — **in·ev·i·ta·bly** \-ət-ə-blē\ *adv.*

in·ex·act \ˌin-ig-'zakt\ *adj.* Not precisely correct; inaccurate. — **in·ex·act·ly**, *adv.*

in·ex·cus·a·ble \ˌin-iks-'kyü-zəb-l\ *adj.* Not to be excused; not justifiable; as, *inexcusable* rudeness. — **in·ex·cus·a·bly** \-zə-blē\ *adv.*

in·ex·haust·i·ble \ˌin-ig-'zȯs-təb-l\ *adj.* **1** Plentiful enough not to give out or be used up; unfailing; as, an *inexhaustible* supply. **2** Untiring. The Indian scout seemed *inexhaustible.* — **in·ex·haust·i·bly** \-tə-blē\ *adv.*

in·ex·o·ra·ble \i-'neks-r(-)əb-l, i-'negz-\ *adj.* Not moved by pleading or prayers; unyielding; relentless; as, an *inexorable* judge. — **in·ex·o·ra·bil·i·ty** \(ˌ)i-ˌneks-r(-)ə-'bil-ət-ē, (ˌ)i-ˌnegz-\ *n.* — **in·ex·o·ra·bly** \i-'neks-r(-)ə-blē, i-'negz-\ *adv.*

in·ex·pe·di·ent \ˌin-iks-'pēd-ē-ənt\ *adj.* Not suited to bring about a desired result; unwise. — **in·ex·pe·di·en·cy** \-ē-ən-sē\ *n.* — **in·ex·pe·di·ent·ly** \-ē-ənt-lē\ *adv.*

in·ex·pen·sive \ˌin-iks-'pen(t)s-iv\ *adj.* Not dear in price; cheap. — **in·ex·pen·sive·ly**, *adv.*

in·ex·pe·ri·ence \ˌin-iks-'pir-ē-ən(t)s\ *n.* Lack of experience or of personal knowledge gained by experience.

in·ex·pe·ri·enced \ˌin-iks-'pir-ē-ən(t)st\ *adj.* Without experience; without the skill or knowledge that comes from experience or practice.

in·ex·pert \(')i-'neks-(ˌ)pərt; ˌin-iks-'pərt, ˌi-ˌneks-\ *adj.* Not expert; unskilled; as, an *inexpert* workman. — **in·ex·pert·ly**, *adv.*

in·ex·pi·a·ble \(')i-'neks-pē-əb-l\ *adj.* Incapable of being atoned for; as, an *inexpiable* crime.

in·ex·plic·a·ble \ˌin-iks-'plik-əb-l, (')i-'neks-(ˌ)plik-\ *adj.* Incapable of being explained or accounted for; as, an *inexplicable* accident. — **in·ex·plic·a·bly** \-ə-blē\ *adv.*

in·ex·press·i·ble \ˌin-iks-'pres-əb-l\ *adj.* Beyond one's power to put in words; indescribable; as, *inexpressible* joy. — **in·ex·press·i·bly** \-ə-blē\ *adv.*

in·ex·pres·sive \ˌin-iks-'pres-iv\ *adj.* Not expressive.

in·ex·tin·guish·a·ble \ˌin-iks-'ting-gwish-əb-l\ *adj.* Incapable of being put out, as a fire; incapable of being subdued, as an emotional feeling. — **in·ex·tin·guish·a·bly** \-ə-blē\ *adv.*

in·ex·tric·a·ble \ˌin-iks-'trik-əb-l, (')i-'neks-(ˌ)trik-\ *adj.* **1** Forming a tangle from which one cannot free oneself. **2** Not capable of being disentangled. — **in·ex·tric·a·bly** \-ə-blē\ *adv.*

in·fal·li·ble \(')in-'fal-əb-l\ *adj.* **1** Not capable of being wrong; unerring. **2** Not liable to fail, deceive, or disappoint; sure; certain; as, an *infallible* remedy. — **in·fal·li·bil·i·ty** \(ˌ)in-ˌfal-ə-'bil-ət-ē\ *n.* — **in·fal·li·bly** \(')in-'fal-ə-blē\ *adv.*

in·fa·mous \'in-fə-məs\ *adj.* **1** Having an evil reputation; as, an *infamous* person. **2** Detestable; disgraceful; as, an *infamous* crime. — **in·fa·mous·ly**, *adv.*

in·fa·my \'in-fə-mē\ *n.; pl.* **in·fa·mies. 1** An evil reputation; public disgrace or dishonor. **2** The quality of being infamous. **3** An infamous deed.

in·fan·cy \'in-fən-sē\ *n.; pl.* **in·fan·cies. 1** Babyhood. **2** An early period of existence or development; as, in the *infancy* of our country.

in·fant \'in-fənt\ *n.* **1** A baby. **2** A minor; a person not yet 21 years of age. — *adj.* **1** Very young; not grown; in early development; as, an *infant* project. **2** Intended for babies or young children; as, *infant* food; an *infant* school.

in·fan·ti·cide \in-'fant-ə-ˌsīd\ *n.* **1** The killing of an infant. **2** One who kills an infant.

in·fan·tile \'in-fən-ˌtīl, -ˌtēl, -ˌtil, -təl\ *adj.* Of or relating to infants or infancy; babyish; childish; as, *infantile* diseases; *infantile* behavior. — For synonyms see *childlike.*

infantile paralysis. A disease, chiefly of infants and children, that affects the muscles, sometimes producing permanent injury; poliomyelitis.

in·fan·try \'in-fən-trē\ *n.; pl.* **in·fan·tries.** Soldiers armed and equipped for service on foot. — **in·fan·try·man** \-mən\ *n.*

in·fat·u·ate \in-'fach-ə-ˌwāt\ *v.;* **in·fat·u·at·ed; in·fat·u·at·ing.** To make a person experience a strong and passionate attraction or devotion to or interest in someone or something; especially, to inspire with a foolish and unrestrained passion.

in·fat·u·a·tion \in-ˌfach-ə-'wāsh-n\ *n.* **1** An infatuating or a being infatuated. **2** Something that infatuates.

in·fect \in-'fekt\ *v.* **1** To cause disease germs or bacteria to be present in or on; as, to *infect* a wound. **2** To contaminate; to taint. **3** To make ill by passing on a disease; as, to *infect* one's classmates with measles. **4** To cause to share one's feelings; as, to *infect* everyone with one's own enthusiasm.

in·fec·tion \in-'feksh-n\ *n.* **1** The act of infecting, as with a disease or with one's own mood or feeling. **2** The condition of being infected. **3** Any disease caused by germs. **4** Anything that infects.

in·fec·tious \in-'fek-shəs\ *adj.* Capable of infecting; as, an *infectious* disease; enthusiasm that is *infectious.* — **in·fec·tious·ly,** *adv.*

in·fe·lic·i·tous \ˌin-fə-'lis-ət-əs\ *adj.* **1** Unhappy; unfortunate; as, an *infelicitous* time. **2** Not apt; not suitably chosen for the occasion; as, an *infelicitous* word.

in·fe·lic·i·ty \ˌin-fə-'lis-ət-ē\ *n.;* **in·fe·lic·i·ties. 1** Unhappiness; wretchedness. **2** A lack of suitableness or aptness. **3** An inapt or inappropriate act or utterance.

in·fer \in-'fər\ *v.;* **in·ferred; in·fer·ring. 1** To come by reasoning to the idea that something is true or probable; to conclude from something known. By watching the sun and stars, early astronomers *inferred* that the earth was the center of the universe. **2** To surmise; to guess. The boy correctly *inferred* that his father would disapprove. — **in·fer·a·ble** \-əb-l\ *adj.*

in·fer·ence \'in-fərn(t)s, -fər-ən(t)s, -frən(t)s\ *n.* **1** The act of inferring. **2** Something that is inferred.

in·fe·ri·or \in-'fir-ē-ər\ *adj.* [From Latin, meaning literally "lower", the comparative of *inferus* meaning "below", "underneath" — see *infernal, inferno.*] **1** Lower, as in rank, importance, or degree. **2** Of poorer quality; not of a high grade; as, an *inferior* diamond. — *n.* A person or thing that is inferior, as in value or position.

in·fe·ri·or·i·ty \(ˌ)in-ˌfir-ē-'ȯr-ət-ē, -'är-\ *n.; pl.* **in·fe·ri·or·i·ties.** The state of being inferior.

in·fer·nal \in-'fərn-l\ *adj.* [From medieval English, there borrowed through French, from Late Latin *infernalis,* a derivative of *infernus* meaning "hell" — see *inferno, inferior.*] **1** Of or relating to hell; as, the *infernal* regions. **2** Suitable to hell; fiendish; as, *infernal* cruelty. — **in·fer·nal·ly** \-'fərn-l-ē\ *adv.*

in·fer·no \in-'fər-ˌnō\ *n.; pl.* **in·fer·nos.** [From Italian, there derived from Late Latin *infernus,* a derivative of Latin *infernus* meaning "lower", from *inferus* meaning "below", "underneath" — see *infernal, inferior.*] **1** Hell. **2** A place said or thought to be like hell.

in·fer·tile \(')in-'fərt-l\ *adj.* Not fertile; sterile; as, *infertile* eggs. — **in·fer·til·i·ty** \ˌin-(ˌ)fər-'til-ət-ē\ *n.*

in·fest \in-'fest\ *v.* To trouble or annoy by being present in great numbers; as, a building *infested* with rats.

in·fi·del \'in-fəd-l, -fə-ˌdel\ *adj.* **1** Non-Christian. **2** Opposing or unfaithful to Christianity. **3** Of or relating to infidels. — *n.* A person who does not believe in a certain religious faith; an unbeliever; especially, a non-Christian.

in·fi·del·i·ty \ˌin-fə-'del-ət-ē, ˌin-fī-\ *n.; pl.* **in·fi·del·i·ties. 1** Lack of faith in a particular religion. **2** Unfaithfulness, especially in a husband or wife.

in·field \'in-ˌfēld\ *n.* **1** The baseball diamond. **2** The players stationed on the diamond, also called **in·field·ers** \-ˌfēld-rz\.

in·fil·trate \in-'fil-ˌtrāt\ *v.;* **in·fil·trat·ed; in·fil·trat·ing. 1** To filter into or through something. **2** To pass into or through, as by filtering.

in·fil·tra·tion \ˌin-ˌfil-'trāsh-n\ *n.* **1** The act of infiltrating. **2** That which infiltrates.

in·fi·nite \'in-fə-nət\ *adj.* **1** Without limits of any kind; endless; as, *infinite* space. **2** Seeming to be without limits; vast; immense; inexhaustible; as, *infinite* patience; *infinite* wealth. — *n.* That which is infinite. — **the Infinite.** God. — **in·fi·nite·ly,** *adv.*

in·fin·i·tes·i·mal \ˌin-ˌfin-ə-'tes-m-əl, -'tez-\ *adj.* Very, very small; so little that it can hardly be measured. — **in·fin·i·tes·i·mal·ly** \-m-ə-lē\ *adv.*

in·fin·i·tive \in-'fin-ət-iv\ *n.* A form of the verb, commonly with *to,* serving as a noun and as a modifier and, at the same time, taking objects and qualifiers like a verb, as *go* in "planning to go to a movie" or *read* in "nothing to do but read".

in·fin·i·ty \in-'fin-ət-ē\ *n.; pl.* **in·fin·i·ties. 1** The quality of being infinite. **2** That which is infinite; an unlimited extent of space, time, or quantity. **3** Any indefinitely great number or amount.

in·firm \(')in-'fərm\ *adj.* **1** Not firm or sound physically; weak, especially from age; feeble. **2** Not solid or firmly fixed; insecure or shaky. — For synonyms see *weak.*

in·fir·ma·ry \in-'fərm-r(-)ē\ *n.; pl.* **in·fir·ma·ries.** A place for the sick or infirm; a hospital.

in·fir·mi·ty \in-'fər-mət-ē\ *n.; pl.* **in·fir·mi·ties. 1** The state of being infirm; weakness; frailty. **2** An instance of such infirmity, as a physical illness or weakness, or a defect in character.

in·flame \in-'flām\ *v.;* **in·flamed; in·flam·ing. 1** To cause to redden or grow hot, as from anger or excitement; as, a face *inflamed* with anger. **2** To excite to unnatural action or feeling; as, a speech that *inflamed* the mob. **3** To cause heat, redness, or swelling in a part of the body; as, infected tissue that has become *inflamed.*

in·flam·ma·ble \in-'flam-əb-l\ *adj.* **1** Easily set on fire; flammable. Gasoline is *inflammable.* **2** Easily inflamed; excitable; as, an *inflammable* temper.

in·flam·ma·tion \ˌin-flə-'māsh-n\ *n.* **1** The act of inflaming. **2** The state of being inflamed; especially, a diseased condition shown by redness or swelling of a part of the body.

in·flam·ma·to·ry \in-'flam-ə-ˌtōr-ē, -ˌtȯr-ē\ *adj.* **1** Exciting or tending to excite anger or disorder; as, a speech, obviously prejudiced and deliberately *inflammatory.* **2** In medicine, causing inflammation or accompanied by inflammation; as, an *inflammatory* disease.

in·flate \in-'flāt\ *v.;* **in·flat·ed; in·flat·ing. 1** To swell with air or gas; as, to *inflate* a balloon. **2** To puff up; to elate; as, *inflated* with a sense of your own importance. **3** To increase abnormally or unwisely, as prices, credit, or the amount of currency in circulation.

in·fla·tion \in-ˈflāsh-n\ *n.* **1** The act of inflating or the state of being inflated. **2** A great increase of money in circulation without any corresponding increase in business.

in·fla·tion·ary \in-ˈflāsh-n-ˌer-ē\ *adj.* Of or having to do with inflation; tending to cause inflation.

in·flect \in-ˈflekt\ *v.* **1** To vary the pitch of the voice. **2** To vary a word by inflection; to decline, as a noun, or conjugate, as a verb.

in·flec·tion \in-ˈfleksh-n\ *n.* **1** A change in the pitch or tone of a person's voice. **2** The change in the form of a word which shows its case, gender, number, person, tense, mood, voice or comparison. — **in·flec·tion·al** \-n(-)əl\ *adj.*

in·flex·i·ble \(ˈ)in-ˈfleks-əb-l\ *adj.* **1** Not easily bent or twisted; rigid; stiff; as, an *inflexible* cover on a notebook. **2** Firm; not easily influenced or persuaded; as, an *inflexible* judge. **3** Incapable of change; unalterable; as, the *inflexible* laws of nature. — **in·flex·i·bil·i·ty** \(ˌ) in-ˌfleks-ə-ˈbil-ət-ē\ *n.* — **in·flex·i·bly** \(ˈ)in-ˈfleks-ə-blē\ *adv.*

in·flict \in-ˈflikt\ *v.* **1** To give by striking or as if by striking; as, to *inflict* a blow; to *inflict* a wound. **2** To cause to bear or suffer; to impose; as, to *inflict* a penalty. — **in·flic·tion** \-ˈfliksh-n\ *n.*

in·flow \ˈin-ˌflō\ *n.* **1** The act of flowing in. **2** Something that flows in.

in·flu·ence \ˈin-ˌflü-ən(t)s\ *n.* **1** The act or power of bringing about a result without the use of force or authority; as, to use one's *influence* over others for good. Older people have great *influence* with children who like and trust them. **2** Power such as results from wealth, position, or character; as, a man of *influence* in the community. **3** A person or thing that has influence; as, good and bad *influences.* — *v.;* **in·flu·enced**; **in·flu·enc·ing.** To have an influence upon; to change or affect by influence; as, to be greatly *influenced* by an older friend. The weather *influences* our daily lives in many ways.

in·flu·en·tial \ˌin-ˌflü-ˈench-l\ *adj.* Having or exerting influence. — **in·flu·en·tial·ly** \-l-ē\ *adv.*

in·flu·en·za \ˌin-ˌflü-ˈen-zə\ *n.* **1** An acute, severe, infectious virus disease with fever, aches and pains, and respiratory inflammation. **2** Any of various infectious respiratory disorders.

in·flux \ˈin-ˌfləks\ *n.* A flowing in; inflow.

in·fold \in-ˈfōld\ *v.* To enfold.

in·form \in-ˈfȯrm\ *v.* **1** To let a person know something; to tell; to give knowledge to. **2** To tell so as to accuse or cast suspicion; as, to *inform* against a person to the police.

in·for·mal \(ˈ)in-ˈfȯrm-l\ *adj.* Without formality or ceremony; as, an *informal* party. — **in·for·mal·ly** \-l-ē\ *adv.*

in·for·mal·i·ty \ˌin-fȯr-ˈmal-ət-ē, ˌin-fər-\ *n.; pl.* **in·for·mal·i·ties.** **1** Absence of formality. **2** An informal act.

in·form·ant \in-ˈfȯr-mənt\ *n.* One giving information.

in·for·ma·tion \ˌin-fər-ˈmāsh-n\ *n.* **1** An informing; as, for your *information.* **2** News; as, to receive *information* about a lost dog. **3** Facts or knowledge gathered by study or observation; as, a book that is full of useful *information;* to have a great deal of *information* about American history. — **in·for·ma·tion·al** \-n(-)əl\ *adj.*

in·form·a·tive \in-ˈfȯr-mət-iv\ *adj.* Having power to inform; instructive; as, an *informative* magazine article.

in·form·er \in-ˈfȯrm-r\ *n.* One who informs; especially, a person who informs against someone else.

in·frac·tion \in-ˈfraksh-n\ *n.* A breaking, as of a rule.

in·fra·red \ˈin-frə-ˈred\ *adj.* Having to do with the invisible rays of light beyond the red end of the visible spectrum.

in·fre·quent \(ˈ)in-ˈfrēk-wənt\ *adj.* Seldom happening or found; rare. — **in·fre·quen·cy** \-wən-sē\ *n.* — **in·fre·quent·ly** \-wənt-lē\ *adv.*

in·fringe \in-ˈfrinj\ *v.;* **in·fringed**; **in·fring·ing.** **1** To fail to obey or heed; as, to *infringe* a law. **2** To go further than is right or fair to another; to trespass; as, to *infringe* upon a person's rights — **in·fringe·ment** \-ˈfrinj-mənt\ *n.* — **in·fring·er** \-ˈfrinj-r\ *n.*

in·fu·ri·ate \in-ˈfyu̇r-ē-ˌāt\ *v.;* **in·fu·ri·at·ed**; **in·fu·ri·at·ing.** To rouse to fury; to enrage.

in·fuse \in-ˈfyüz\ *v.;* **in·fused**; **in·fus·ing.** **1** To put in, as if by pouring; as, to *infuse* courage into one's followers. **2** To inspire; as, to *infuse* one's followers with courage. **3** To steep, as tea, without boiling.

in·fu·sion \in-ˈfyüzh-n\ *n.* **1** The action or process of infusing. **2** A substance extracted from another substance, especially from a plant material, by soaking in hot or cold water.

-ing \iŋ\. The suffix forming the present participle; as, *singing* birds.

-ing \iŋ\. A suffix that can mean: **1** The act or art of persons or things that, as in *Speaking comes before writing.* **2** A thing produced by one who, as in *shavings* or *sweepings.* **3** Things used in making or doing, as in *roofing* or *bedding.*

in·ge·nious \in-ˈjēn-yəs\ *adj.* Having or showing ability to solve problems or to plan or invent; skillful; cleverly made or done; as, an *ingenious* workman; an *ingenious* device. — **in·ge·nious·ly,** *adv.*

in·gé·nue or **in·ge·nue** \ˈan-jə-ˌnü, ˈan-zhə-, ˈän-\ *n.* **1** A simple artless girl or young woman. **2** An actress representing such a person.

in·ge·nu·i·ty \ˌinj-n-ˈü-ət-ē, -n-ˈyü-\ *n.; pl.* **in·ge·nu·i·ties.** Skill or cleverness in planning or inventing.

in·gen·u·ous \in-ˈjen-yə-wəs\ *adj.* **1** Free from reserve, disguise, or deceit; frank; open. **2** Innocent; naïve; artless; as, an *ingenuous* nature, free from deceit. — **in·gen·u·ous·ly,** *adv.*

in·gest \in-ˈjest\ *v.* To take in for digestion, as into the stomach. — **in·ges·tion** \-ˈjes-chən\ *n.*

in·gle·nook \ˈiŋ-gl-ˌnu̇k\ *n.* A chimney corner.

in·glo·ri·ous \(ˈ)in-ˈglōr-ē-əs, -ˈglȯr-\ *adj.* **1** Not bringing fame, honor, or glory. **2** Shameful; bringing disgrace; as, an *inglorious* defeat. — **in·glo·ri·ous·ly,** *adv.*

in·got \ˈing-gət\ *n.* A mass of metal cast into a block or bar for storage or transportation.

in·graft \(ˈ)in-ˈgraft\ *v.* To engraft.

in·grain \(ˈ)in-ˈgrān\ *v.* **1** To dye in or incorporate with the grain or texture; as, *ingrained* wood. **2** To instill deeply; to fix firmly within; to stamp indelibly; as, an *ingrained* habit. — \ˈin-ˌgrān\ *adj.* Ingrained; especially, dye in the fiber or yarn before being woven or knitted, as carpets. — *n.* Something ingrained; especially, an ingrain carpet or ingrain yarn.

in·grate \ˈin-ˌgrāt\ *n.* An ungrateful person.

in·gra·ti·ate \in-ˈgrā-shē-ˌāt\ *v.;* **in·gra·ti·at·ed; in·gra·ti·at·ing.** To bring or work oneself into another's favor. The new pupil quickly *ingratiated* himself with his classmates. — **in·gra·ti·at·ing·ly** \-ˌāt-ing-lē\ *adv.*

in·grat·i·tude \(ˈ)in-ˈgrat-ə-ˌtüd, -ˌtyüd\ *n.* Lack of gratitude or thankfulness.

in·gre·di·ent \in-ˈgrēd-ē-ənt\ *n.* One of the substances that make up a mixture; as, the *ingredients* of a cake.

in·gress \ˈin-ˌgres\ *n.* **1** The action of entering; entrance. **2** The power or liberty of entrance; as, to have free *ingress* to the circus grounds. **3** A place for entering; an entrance.

in·grow \(ˈ)in-ˈgrō\ *v.;* **in·grew** \-ˈgrü\; **in·grown** \-ˈgrōn\; **in·grow·ing.** To grow within or inward; as, an *ingrowing* toenail. — **in·grown** \ˈin-ˌgrōn\ *adj.*

in·gulf \in-ˈgəlf\ *v.* To engulf.

in·hab·it \in-ˈhab-ət\ *v.* To live or dwell in. — **in·hab·it·a·ble** \-əb-l\ *adj.*

in·hab·it·ant \in-ˈhab-ə-tənt\ *n.* One who lives permanently in a place.

in·hal·ant \in-ˈhā-lənt\ *n.* **1** An inhaler. **2** That which is to be inhaled, as a medicinal vapor.

in·ha·la·tion \ˌin-(h)ə-ˈlāsh-n\ *n.* **1** The act of inhaling. **2** Something to be inhaled; an inhalant.

in·ha·la·tor \ˈin-(h)ə-ˌlāt-r\ *n.* An apparatus providing a mixture of oxygen and carbon dioxide for artificial respiration.

in·hale \in-ˈhāl\ *v.;* **in·haled; in·hal·ing.** To draw into the lungs, as air, smoke, or vapor; to breathe in; as, to *inhale* and exhale; to *inhale* a fragrance.

in·hal·er \in-ˈhāl-r\ *n.* **1** A person who inhales. **2** A device for inhaling medicinal material.

in·har·mo·ni·ous \ˌin-ˌhär-ˈmō-nē-əs, -ˌhȧr-\ *adj.* Not in harmony; discordant. — **in·har·mo·ni·ous·ly,** *adv.*

in·her·ent \in-ˈhir-ənt, -ˈher-\ *adj.* Belonging to or being a part of the essential character of a person or thing; belonging by nature; as, an *inherent* sense of fair play. Fluidity is an *inherent* quality of gas. — **in·her·ent·ly,** *adv.*

in·her·it \in-ˈher-ət\ *v.* **1** To receive from a parent or ancestor; to come into possession of as a legal heir; as, to *inherit* property from an aunt. **2** To receive by birth; to acquire from an ancestor; as, to *inherit* the color of one's eyes from one's mother; to *inherit* a strong constitution. **3** To have handed on to one by a predecessor; as, problems *inherited* from the previous administration. — **in·her·i·tor** \-ət-r\ *n.*

in·her·it·ance \in-ˈher-ə-tən(t)s\ *n.* **1** The act of inheriting; as, money acquired by *inheritance.* **2** Something that is or may be inherited; a legacy; a heritage; as, to receive an *inheritance* of five thousand dollars; the priceless *inheritance* of good health.

in·hib·it \in-ˈhib-ət\ *v.* **1** To forbid; to prohibit. **2** To hold back; to check; to restrain; as, to learn to *inhibit* selfish impulses. The shy girl was greatly *inhibited* by the strangeness of her surroundings.

in·hi·bi·tion \ˌin-(h)ə-ˈbish-n\ *n.* **1** The act of inhibiting or the state of being inhibited; restraint; prohibition. **2** An inner force, as a fear, that prevents or impedes the free expression of one's thoughts or desires.

in·hos·pit·a·ble \ˌin-ˌhäs-ˈpit-əb-l, (ˈ)in-ˈhäs-ˌpit-\ *adj.* **1** Not showing kindness to guests or strangers. **2** Affording no shelter or food; as, mile after mile of *inhospitable* desert. — **in·hos·pit·a·bly** \-ə-blē\ *adv.*

in·hos·pi·tal·i·ty \(ˌ)in-ˌhäs-pə-ˈtal-ət-ē\ *n.* Lack of hospitality.

in·hu·man \(ˈ)in-ˈhyü-mən, (ˈ)in-ˈyü-\ *adj.* **1** Lacking human or humane feeling; brutal; cruel. **2** Unlike what is normally human; as, *inhuman* shrieks of pain. — **in·hu·man·ly,** *adv.*

in·hu·mane \ˌin-ˌhyü-ˈmān\ *adj.* Not humane; cruel; brutal.

in·hu·man·i·ty \ˌin-ˌhyü-ˈman-ət-ē, ˌin-ˌyü-\ *n.; pl.* **in·hu·man·i·ties. 1** Inhuman behavior; cruelty; brutality. **2** A cruel or brutal act.

in·im·i·cal \i-ˈnim-ik-l\ *adj.* **1** Unfriendly; hostile. **2** Adverse; unfavorable; harmful; as, habits *inimical* to health. — **in·im·i·cal·ly** \-ik-l(-)ē\ *adv.*

in·im·i·ta·ble \(ˈ)i-ˈnim-ət-əb-l\ *adj.* Not capable of being imitated; matchless. — **in·im·i·ta·bil·i·ty** \(ˌ)i-ˌnim-ət-ə-ˈbil-ət-ē\ *n.* — **in·im·i·ta·bly** \(ˈ)i-ˈnim-ət-ə-blē\ *adv.*

in·iq·ui·tous \i-ˈnik-wət-əs\ *adj.* Wicked; unjust. — **in·iq·ui·tous·ly,** *adv.*

in·iq·ui·ty \i-ˈnik-wət-ē\ *n.; pl.* **in·iq·ui·ties. 1** Great injustice; wickedness. **2** A wicked act or thing.

ini·tial \i-ˈnish-l\ *adj.* **1** Of or relating to the beginning; earliest; as, an *initial* effort; the *initial* stages of a disease. **2** Placed at the beginning; first; as, the *initial* letter of a word. — *n.* An initial letter, especially of a name; as, to have one's *initials* on a ring. — *v.;* **ini·tialed** or **ini·tialled; ini·tial·ing** or **ini·tial·ling** \-l(-)ing\. To put one's initial or initials on; as, to *initial* a note. — **ini·tial·ly** \-l(-)ē\ *adv.*

ini·ti·ate \i-ˈnish-ē-ˌāt\ *v.;* **ini·ti·at·ed; ini·ti·at·ing. 1** To begin; to originate; as, a policy *initiated* many years ago. **2** To teach a beginner the things he first needs to know; to introduce; as, to *initiate* a city boy into the mysteries of farming. **3** To admit into a club or society by special ceremonies. — \-ē-ət\ *n.* A person who is or who is to be initiated, as into a club or society. — **ini·ti·a·tor** \-ē-ˌāt-r\ *n.*

ini·ti·a·tion \i-ˌnish-ē-'āsh-n\ *n.* **1** An initiating or a being initiated; an introduction. **2** The ceremonies with which a person is made a member of a society or club.

ini·tia·tive \i-'nish-ət-iv\ *n.* **1** The power of seeing for oneself what ought to be done and of going ahead and doing it; as, a man who has great ability but lacks *initiative.* **2** A first step or movement; an act that originates or begins something; as, to take the *initiative* in becoming acquainted with a new pupil. **3** The process by which laws may be introduced or enacted directly by vote of the people — used chiefly with *the.*

in·ject \in-'jekt\ *v.* **1** To drive or force in; as, to *inject* fuel into an engine. **2** To throw in, as by way of suggestion or interruption; as, to *inject* a note of suspicion. **3** To force a fluid into a part of the body, as for relieving pain or protecting against disease. — **in·jec·tor** \-r\ *n.*

in·jec·tion \in-'jeksh-n\ *n.* **1** An injecting, as by means of a syringe. **2** Something that is injected, especially a liquid medicine injected under the skin or into a cavity of the body.

in·ju·di·cious \ˌin-jü-'dish-əs\ *adj.* Not judicious; unwise; indiscreet. — **in·ju·di·cious·ly**, *adv.*

in·junc·tion \in-'jəng(k)sh-n\ *n.* **1** An order not to do something; a command. **2** A court order requiring a party to do or to refrain from doing certain acts.

in·jure \'inj-r\ *v.;* **in·jured**; **in·jur·ing** \-r(-)ing\. To harm; to damage; to hurt; to wrong; to offend.

in·ju·ri·ous \in-'jůr-ē-əs\ *adj.* Causing injury; harmful. — **in·ju·ri·ous·ly**, *adv.*

in·ju·ry \'inj-r(-)ē\ *n.; pl.* **in·ju·ries.** **1** Harm or damage done or suffered. **2** Any act that injures.

in·jus·tice \(')in-'jəs-təs\ *n.* **1** A lack of fairness or justice; a violation of another person's rights. **2** An unjust act or deed; a wrong.

ink \'ingk\ *n.* **1** A fluid used for writing or printing. **2** The black fluid thrown out by certain mollusks, as the cuttlefish. — *v.* To put ink upon; as, to *ink* a rubber stamp. — **ink·er** \-r\ *n.*

ink·horn \'ingk-ˌhȯrn, 'ing-ˌkȯrn\ *n.* An old-fashioned inkwell usually made of horn. — *adj.* Bookish; as, *inkhorn* terms.

ink·ling \'ingk-ling\ *n.* A hint; a suggestion; a vague idea.

ink·stand \'ingk-ˌstand\ *n.* An inkwell or a device for holding ink and pens.

ink·well \'ingk-ˌwel\ *n.* A container for ink, as for use on a desk.

inky \'ingk-ē\ *adj.;* **ink·i·er**; **ink·i·est.** **1** Consisting of, using, or like ink. **2** Soiled with ink. **3** Of the color of ink; black.

in·laid \'in-ˌlād\ *adj.* Decorated with materials set into a surface to form an ornamental design; as, a table with an *inlaid* top.

in·land \'in-lənd, -ˌland\ *n.* The part of a country in from the coast or boundaries; the interior. — *adj.* **1** Not located near the coast or frontier. **2** Kept within a country or state; as, *inland* commerce. — *adv.* In or toward the inland.

in–law \'in-ˌlȯ\ *n.* A relative by marriage.

in·lay \(')in-'lā\ *v.;* **in·laid**; **in·lay·ing.** To set in so as to decorate a surface; to decorate by setting in other material; as, to *inlay* wood with ivory. — \'in-ˌlā\ *n.* **1** Inlaid work. **2** Material used in inlaying. **3** A filling for a tooth shaped to fit a prepared cavity and cemented into place.

in·let \'in-ˌlet, -lət\ *n.* **1** A way of entering. **2** A recess in a shore line; a narrow strip of water running into the land or between islands.

in·mate \'in-ˌmāt\ *n.* **1** One who lives in the same house or apartment with another. **2** A person kept in an institution, as a prison or asylum.

in·most \'in-ˌmōst\ *adj.* Deepest within; as, one's *inmost* feelings.

inn \'in\ *n.* **1** A public house that provides lodging and food for travelers; a hotel. **2** A tavern.

in·nate \i-'nāt\ *adj.* Inborn; natural; not learned from experience or training. — **in·nate·ly**, *adv.*

in·ner \'in-r\ *adj.* **1** Farther in; inside; interior; as, an *inner* room; the *inner* ear. **2** Near to a center, as of influence or importance; as, to belong to the *inner* circle. **3** Of or relating to the mind or spirit; as, *inner* thoughts; the *inner* life. **4** Not plain at first sight or thought; not obvious; as, *inner* meanings.

inner ear. A cavity in the temporal bone of vertebrates that contains sense organs concerned with the perception of sound and awareness of position in space.

in·ner·most \'in-r-ˌmōst\ *adj.* Farthest in; inmost.

in·ning \'in-ing\ *n.* **1** A turn at bat, as of one or both sides in baseball, or (in the form **in·nings**, *sing. and pl.*) of a side or a player in cricket; a turn at play. **2** A period during which a person or party is in power.

inn·keep·er \'in-ˌkēp-r\ *n.* One who keeps an inn.

in·no·cence \'in-ə-sən(t)s\ *n.* The quality or state of being innocent.

in·no·cent \'in-ə-sənt\ *adj.* **1** Free from sin; knowing nothing of evil; pure. **2** Free from guilt or blame; guiltless; as, an *innocent* bystander; to be found *innocent* of a crime. **3** Free from evil influence or effect; harmless; as, *innocent* fun. **4** Artless; simple; unsophisticated; as, *innocent* strangers in a big city. — For synonyms see *simple.* — *n.* An innocent person. — **in·no·cent·ly**, *adv.*

in·noc·u·ous \i-'näk-yə-wəs\ *adj.* Not injurious; harmless.

in·no·vate \'in-ə-ˌvāt\ *v.;* **in·no·vat·ed**; **in·no·vat·ing.** To make changes; to introduce novelties; to introduce as a novelty. — **in·no·va·tor** \-ˌvāt-r\ *n.*

in·no·va·tion \ˌin-ə-'vāsh-n\ *n.* **1** The action of

introducing something new. **2** A change made by bringing in something new. **3** The new thing that is introduced.

in·nu·en·do \ˌin-yə-ˈwen-ˌdō\ *n.; pl.* **in·nu·en·dos.** A slight reference to a person or thing not directly named; a hint; a suggestion, especially to someone's disadvantage.

in·nu·mer·a·ble \i-ˈnüm-r(-)əb-l, i-ˈnyüm-\ *adj.* Too many to be counted. — **in·nu·mer·a·bly** \-r(-)ə-blē\ *adv.*

in·oc·u·late \i-ˈnäk-yə-ˌlāt\ *v.;* **in·oc·u·lat·ed; in·oc·u·lat·ing.** [From medieval English *inoculaten* meaning "to graft a bud onto a tree", from Latin *inoculatus,* the past participle of *inoculare,* from the prefix *in-* meaning "in" and *oculus* meaning "bud", literally "eye".] **1** To give a disease, as to a person, in a mild form by inserting the causing agent of the disease into the body in order to prevent any other attack of the disease. **2** To introduce an agent, as a serum, into or onto something in order to prevent or to cure a disease. — **in·oc·u·la·tion** \i-ˌnäk-yə-ˈlāsh-n\ *n.* — **in·oc·u·la·tor** \i-ˈnäk-yə-ˌlāt-r\ *n.*

in·of·fen·sive \ˌin-ə-ˈfen(t)s-iv\ *adj.* Not offending; harmless. — **in·of·fen·sive·ly,** *adv.*

in·op·er·a·ble \(ˈ)i-ˈnäp-r(-)əb-l\ *adj.* **1** Not practicable. **2** In surgery, not suitable for operation.

in·op·er·a·tive \(ˈ)i-ˈnäp-r(-)ət-iv, -r-ˌāt-iv\ *adj.* Not in operation; producing no effect; as, a law that is *inoperative.*

in·op·por·tune \(ˌ)i-ˌnäp-r-ˈtün, -ˈtyün\ *adj.* Untimely; ill-timed. — **in·op·por·tune·ly,** *adv.*

in·or·di·nate \i-ˈnȯrd-n-ət\ *adj.* Not kept within bounds; excessive; as, an *inordinate* curiosity. — **in·or·di·nate·ly,** *adv.*

in·or·gan·ic \ˌi-ˌnȯr-ˈgan-ik\ *adj.* **1** Indicating or composed of matter that is not animal or vegetable; inanimate. **2** Indicating or relating to the branch of chemistry treating all substances except those called organic.

in·quest \ˈin-ˌkwest\ *n.* An official inquiry into the cause of a death; a judicial investigation.

in·quire \in-ˈkwīr\ *v.;* **in·quired; in·quir·ing. 1** To ask about; to ask; as, to *inquire* the way; to *inquire* about a person's health. **2** To make an examination or investigation; as, to *inquire* into the cause of a disastrous fire. — **in·quir·er** \-ˈkwīr-r\ *n.* — **in·quir·ing·ly** \-ˈkwīr-ing-lē\ *adv.*

in·quiry \in-ˈkwīr-ē, ˈin-ˌkwīr-ē, ˈin(g)-kwər-ē\ *n.; pl.* **in·quir·ies. 1** The act of inquiring or asking; as, to learn by *inquiry;* to make *inquiries* at the railroad station. **2** A search for truth or knowledge. **3** An examination by questioning; an investigation; as, a full *inquiry* into the causes of an accident. — For synonyms see *examination.*

in·qui·si·tion \ˌin(g)-kwə-ˈzish-n\ *n.* **1** An inquiring; an inquiry; especially, a judicial examination before a court. **2** [with a capital] A papal court appointed to search for heresy and heretics or any systematic effort to suppress heresy undertaken by this court with the help of the state — used especially with reference to such an attempt in the 15th and 16th centuries.

in·quis·i·tive \in-ˈkwiz-ət-iv\ *adv.* **1** Curious; interested in searching for truth or knowledge. **2** Asking too many questions about other people's business; too curious. — **in·quis·i·tive·ly,** *adv.*

in·quis·i·tor \in-ˈkwiz-ət-r\ *n.* An official investigator, as a coroner or a sheriff. — **in·quis·i·to·ri·al** \(ˌ)in-ˌkwiz-ə-ˈtōr-ē-əl, -ˈtȯr-\ *adj.*

in·road \ˈin-ˌrōd\ *n.* **1** A sudden invasion; a raid. **2** A forcible entrance; an encroachment; as, *inroads* upon one's time.

in·rush \ˈin-ˌrəsh\ *n.* A rushing in; an influx, as of water.

in·sane \(ˈ)in-ˈsān\ *adj.* **1** Not sane; unsound in mind; mad; crazy. **2** Showing evidence of an unsound mind; as, an *insane* look. **3** Used by or for the insane; as, an *insane* asylum. **4** Impractical; visionary; as, an *insane* attempt. — **in·sane·ly,** *adv.*

in·san·i·tary \(ˈ)in-ˈsan-ə-ˌter-ē\ *adj.* Not sanitary; unhealthy.

in·san·i·ty \in-ˈsan-ət-ē\ *n.; pl.* **in·san·i·ties. 1** The condition of being insane; mental illness. **2** Folly; senseless conduct; as, the sheer *insanity* of turning the corner at such high speed.

in·sa·tia·ble \in-ˈsā-shəb-l\ *adj.* That cannot be easily satisfied; as, an *insatiable* appetite. — **in·sa·tia·bly** \-shə-blē\ *adv.*

in·sa·ti·ate \in-ˈsā-shē-ət, -ˈsā-shət\ *adj.* Not easily satisfied; insatiable; as, an *insatiate* thirst for knowledge.

in·scribe \in-ˈskrīb\ *v.;* **in·scribed; in·scrib·ing. 1** To write upon; especially, to write upon so as to make a lasting record, as by engraving; as, a gravestone *inscribed* only with a name and a date. **2** To enter the name of, as upon a list; to enroll. **3** To dedicate, as a poem, in honor or memory of some person. **4** To stamp deeply; to impress; as, an unforgettable scene *inscribed* upon the mind.

in·scrip·tion \in-ˈskripsh-n\ *n.* Something that is inscribed; as, an *inscription* on a tombstone.

in·scru·ta·ble \in-ˈskrüt-əb-l\ *adj.* That cannot be searched into and understood; incomprehensible; as, an *inscrutable* mystery. Her face was an *inscrutable* mask. — **in·scru·ta·bly** \-ə-blē\ *adv.*

in·sect \ˈin-ˌsekt\ *n.* **1** A very small air-breathing

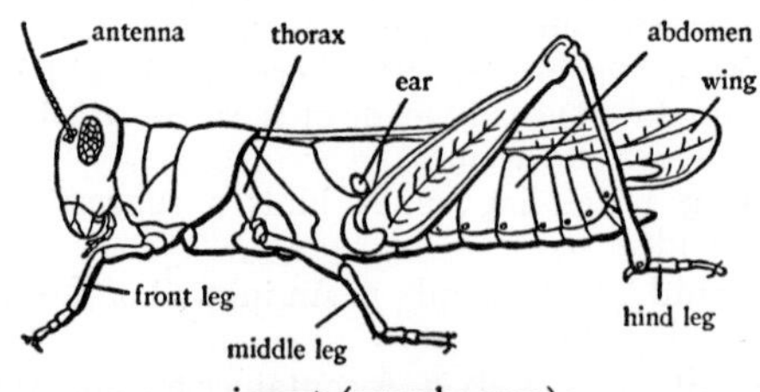

insect (grasshopper)

animal that has three pairs of jointed legs, a body formed of three parts, and, usually, one pair of feelers and one or two pairs of wings. Flies, bees, and beetles are true *insects.* **2** A similar animal not a true insect, as a spider.

in·sec·ti·cide \in-ˈsek-tə-ˌsīd\ *n.* A preparation for destroying insects.

in·se·cure \ˌin-sē-ˈkyu̇r\ *adj.* **1** Not confident or sure; uncertain. **2** Not well protected; exposed to danger. **3** Not tightly fastened; not fixed firmly in position; shaky. — **in·se·cure·ly** \-ˈkyu̇r-lē\ *adv.* — **in·se·cu·ri·ty** \-ˈkyu̇r-ət-ē\ *n.*

in·sen·sate \in-ˈsen-ˌsāt\ *adj.* **1** Inanimate; as, *insensate* clods. **2** Without sense; foolish. **3** Without feeling; harsh; brutal; as, *insensate* rage. — **in·sen·sate·ly,** *adv.*

in·sen·si·ble \(ˈ)in-ˈsen(t)s-əb-l\ *adj.* **1** Not able to feel, as pain, heat, or cold; as, hands *insensible* from the cold. **2** Unconscious; as, to be knocked *insensible* by a blow. **3** Not aware. The travelers were *insensible* of their danger. **4** Lacking in feelings; indifferent; as, to be *insensible* to the sufferings of others. **5** So small or so gradual as to be scarcely seen, heard, or felt; as, an *insensible* change in temperature. — **in·sen·si·bil·i·ty** \(ˌ)in-ˌsen(t)s-ə-ˈbil-ət-ē\ *n.* — **in·sen·si·bly** \(ˈ)in-ˈsen(t)s-ə-blē\ *adv.*

in·sen·si·tive \(ˈ)in-ˈsen(t)s-ət-iv\ *adj.* Not sensitive; without feeling; not quick to feel or to react.

in·sep·a·ra·ble \(ˈ)in-ˈsep-r(-)əb-l\ *adj.* Not capable of being separated or divided; as, *inseparable* friends. — **in·sep·a·ra·bil·i·ty** \(ˌ)in-ˌsep-r(-)ə-ˈbil-ət-ē\ *n.* — **in·sep·a·ra·bly** \(ˈ)in-ˈsep-r(-)ə-blē\ *adv.*

in·sert \in-ˈsərt\ *v.* To set so as to be within; to put in; as, to *insert* a comma between two words. — \ˈin-ˌsərt\ *n.* That which is inserted, as an extra sheet inserted between the pages of a newspaper or a panel of material inserted in a dress.

in·ser·tion \in-ˈsərsh-n\ *n.* **1** The act of inserting. **2** That which is inserted.

in·set \ˈin-ˌset\ *n.* Something inserted. — *v.;* **in·set; in·set·ting.** To insert.

in·shore \ˈin-ˈshōr, -ˈshȯr\ *adj.* or *adv.* Near, or moving toward, the shore; as, an *inshore* current; to be headed *inshore.*

in·side \(ˈ)in-ˈsīd, ˈin-ˌsīd\ *n.* **1** The inner side or surface; the part within; interior; as, the *inside* of a cup or a box. **2** [usually in the plural] The body's inward parts; especially, the entrails. — *adj.* **1** Having to do with the inside; lying on the inside; internal. **2** Employed or working indoors; as, an *inside* man. **3** Known only to a few persons familiar with conditions; as, *inside* information. — *prep.* Within; on the inside of. — \in-ˈsīd\ *adv.* On or in the inside; within.

in·sid·er \in-ˈsīd-r\ *n.* A person having firsthand information.

in·sid·i·ous \in-ˈsid-ē-əs\ *adj.* or *adv.* **1** Watching for a chance to trap someone; sly; treacherous. **2** Having a more serious effect than is apparent; as, an *insidious* disease.

in·sight \ˈin-ˌsīt\ *n.* The power or act of seeing into a situation; understanding; as, lacking in *insight;* a sudden *insight.*

in·sig·nia \in-ˈsig-nē-ə\ or **in·sig·ne** \-(ˌ)nē\ *n.; pl.* **in·sig·nia** or **in·sig·ni·as.** A distinguishing mark of authority, office, or honor; a badge; an emblem.

U.S. Army Medical Corps insignia

in·sig·nif·i·cant \ˌin-sig-ˈnif-ə-kənt\ *adj.* Not significant or important. — **in·sig·nif·i·cant·ly,** *adv.* — **in·sig·nif·i·cance** \-kən(t)s\ *n.*

in·sin·cere \ˌin-sin-ˈsir\ *adj.* Not sincere; deceitful; false. — **in·sin·cere·ly,** *adv.*

in·sin·cer·i·ty \ˌin-sin-ˈser-ət-ē, -ˈsir-\ *n.; pl.* **in·sin·cer·i·ties.** **1** The quality or state of being insincere. **2** An instance of being insincere.

in·sin·u·ate \in-ˈsin-yə-ˌwāt\ *v.;* **in·sin·u·at·ed; in·sin·u·at·ing.** **1** To work in or introduce gently and slowly, especially in an indirect or artful way; as, to *insinuate* oneself into a person's good graces. **2** To hint; to suggest; to imply.

in·sin·u·a·tion \in-ˌsin-yə-ˈwāsh-n\ *n.* **1** The act or process of insinuating. **2** An act or speech intended to gain favor. **3** An indirect hint or suggestion; especially, a suggestion designed to discredit the one referred to.

in·sip·id \in-ˈsip-əd\ *adj.* **1** Without taste or flavor; as, *insipid* food. **2** Lacking animation or spirit; uninteresting; dull; as, an *insipid* story about a priggish little girl. — **in·si·pid·i·ty** \ˌin-sə-ˈpid-ət-ē\ *n.*

in·sist \in-ˈsist\ *v.* To take a stand and refuse to give way; to be persistent; as, to *insist* on punctuality. We would have left much earlier if our host had not *insisted* that we stay.

in·sist·ence \in-ˈsis-tən(t)s\ *n.* **1** The act of insisting. **2** The quality or condition of being insistent; urgency; as, the *insistence* of a need.

in·sist·ent \in-ˈsis-tənt\ *adj.* Insisting; persistent; compelling attention. — **in·sist·ent·ly,** *adv.*

in·sole \ˈin-ˌsōl\ *n.* **1** The inside sole of a shoe. **2** A loose, thin inner sole, placed in a shoe for better fit or greater comfort.

in·so·lence \ˈin(t)s-l-ən(t)s\ *n.* Contemptuous or insulting behavior.

in·so·lent \ˈin(t)s-l-ənt\ *adj.* Haughty or contemptuous in behavior or language; insulting; overbearing. — **in·so·lent·ly,** *adv.*

in·sol·u·ble \(ˈ)in-ˈsäl-yəb-l\ *adj.* **1** Not to be solved or explained; as, an *insoluble* problem. **2** Impossible or very difficult to dissolve; as, a substance *insoluble* in water. — **in·sol·u·bil·i·ty** \(ˌ)in-ˌsäl-yə-ˈbil-ət-ē\ *n.*

in·sol·ven·cy \(ˈ)in-ˈsälv-n-sē\ *n.* The condition of being insolvent.

in·sol·vent \(ˈ)in-ˈsälv-nt\ *adj.* **1** Not able to pay one's debts. **2** Not sufficient to cover the charges against it; as, an *insolvent* estate.

in·som·nia \in-ˈsäm-nē-ə\ *n.* Prolonged inability to sleep; sleeplessness.

in·so·much \ˈin-sə-ˌməch\ *adv.* So much; to such

an extent or degree; so — usually followed by *that* or *as*.

in·spect \in-'spekt\ *v.* **1** To examine closely, as for judging quality or condition; as, to *inspect* foodstuffs. **2** To view and examine officially, as troops.

in·spec·tion \in-'speksh-n\ *n.* **1** An inspecting. **2** A careful, especially an official, examination. — For synonyms see *examination.*

in·spec·tor \in-'spekt-r\ *n.* **1** One that inspects. **2** A police officer ranking next below a superintendent or deputy superintendent.

in·spi·ra·tion \ˌin(t)s-pə-'rāsh-n\ *n.* **1** The action of breathing in. **2** A supernatural influence that fits those who come under it to receive divine truths and communicate them to others. **3** The act or power of arousing the thoughts or feelings; as, to feel the *inspiration* of music. **4** The condition or fact of being inspired; something inspired; as, an idea that was a pure *inspiration.* **5** A person or thing that has an inspiring influence.

in·spi·ra·tion·al \ˌin(t)s-pə-'rāsh-n(-)əl\ *adj.* **1** Produced by or moved by inspiration; inspired. **2** Of or relating to inspiration. **3** Communicating inspiration; inspiring. — **in·spi·ra·tion·al·ly** \-n(-)ə-lē\ *adv.*

in·spire \in-'spīr\ *v.;* **in·spired; in·spir·ing. 1** To breathe in; to inhale. **2** To affect with divine or otherwise supernatural inspiration or to cause to be done as a result of such inspiration; as, prophets *inspired* by God; the *inspired* writings of the Bible. **3** To influence as if by a higher or a divine power; as, an *inspired* performance by a musician. **4** To cause or arouse, as a thought or feeling; to affect with a thought or feeling; as, to *inspire* courage in a person; to *inspire* a person with fear. **5** To give inspiration to; to influence; to impel; as, to be *inspired* to great effort by the nearness of success. **6** To cause something to be said or written, usually through use of power or influence; as, an article about the president's health probably *inspired* by the opposing party.

in·spired \in-'spīrd\ *adj.* **1** Animated or affected by or as if by a higher or divine power. **2** Suggested by someone in a position of influence or power; as, an *inspired* newspaper article.

in·spir·it \in-'spir-ət\ *v.* To put spirit into; to animate; to hearten.

inst. Abbreviation for *instant.*

in·sta·bil·i·ty \ˌin-stə-'bil-ət-ē\ *n.* Lack of firmness or steadiness.

in·stall \in-'stȯl\ *v.;* **in·stalled; in·stall·ing. 1** To place in an office or rank; to introduce formally into office; as, to *install* the president of a club. **2** To give a place to; as, to *install* oneself in the best chair in the room. **3** To set up or fix in position for use or service; as, to *install* a television set; to *install* a sewage system for the whole town. — **in·stal·la·tion** \ˌin(t)s-tə-'lāsh-n\ *n.*

in·stall·ment or **in·stal·ment** \in-'stȯl-mənt\ *n.* The act of installing or the state of being installed; installation.

in·stall·ment or **in·stal·ment** \in-'stȯl-mənt\ *n.* **1** One of the parts into which a debt or a sum of money is divided for payment; as, to pay by *installments.* **2** One of several parts presented at intervals; as, the first *installment* of a magazine story.

installment plan. A system of paying for goods by installments.

in·stance \'in(t)s-tən(t)s\ *n.* **1** A suggestion; a request; as, to enter a contest at the *instance* of one's teacher. **2** An example; as, an *instance* of courage; for *instance.* **3** An occasion; a case; as, in the first *instance.* — *v.;* **in·stanced; in·stanc·ing.** To mention as a case or example; as, to *instance* an exception to the rule.

in·stant \'in(t)s-tənt\ *adj.* **1** Pressing; urgent; as, an *instant* need. **2** Present; current — used with dates to indicate the current month; as, the 10th *instant.* **3** Closely following in time; immediate; as, a drug that gives *instant* relief from pain. — *n.* A moment; a very short period of time.

in·stan·ta·ne·ous \ˌin(t)s-tən-'tā-nē-əs\ *adj.* Done or happening in an instant; done without delay; as, *instantaneous* action. — **in·stan·ta·ne·ous·ly,** *adv.*

in·stan·ter \in-'stant-r\ *adv.* Immediately.

in·stant·ly \'in(t)s-tənt-lē\ *adv.* Without delay; at once.

in·state \in-'stāt\ *v.;* **in·stat·ed; in·stat·ing.** To establish in a position or rank; to install.

in·stead \in-'sted\ *adv.* In place; as a substitute; as, to take this one *instead* of that; to take the other one *instead.*

in·step \'in-ˌstep\ *n.* **1** The arched middle part of the human foot in front of the ankle joint. **2** The part of a shoe or stocking over the instep.

instep

in·sti·gate \'in(t)s-tə-ˌgāt\ *v.;* **in·sti·gat·ed; in·sti·gat·ing.** To urge forward; to set on; to incite; as, to *instigate* an investigation. — **in·sti·ga·tion** \ˌin(t)s-tə-'gāsh-n\ *n.*

in·still or **in·stil** \in-'stil\ *v.;* **in·stilled; in·still·ing. 1** To drop in; to pour in drop by drop. **2** To introduce gradually, as if pouring drop by drop; as, a love of music carefully *instilled* in childhood.

in·stinct \'in-ˌsting(k)t\ *n.* **1** A natural aptitude or knack. **2** A natural inward impulse that leads a person or an animal to behave in a certain way; as, the web-building *instinct* of spiders. Fish swim by *instinct.* — \in-'sting(k)t\ *adj.* Filled or charged; as, a statue *instinct* with life and movement.

in·stinc·tive \in-'sting(k)-tiv\ *adj.* Of or relating to instinct; resulting from instinct; as, an *instinctive* action; an *instinctive* dislike. — **in·stinc·tive·ly,** *adv.*

in·sti·tute \'in(t)s-tə-ˌtüt, -ˌtyüt\ *v.;* **in·sti·tut·ed; in·sti·tut·ing. 1** To set up; to establish; to found; to organize; as, to *institute* a society. **2** To inaugurate; to begin; as, to *institute* an inquiry. — *n.* **1**

Something that is instituted. **2** An institution; an educational, scientific, or similar organization. **3** A building used for the work of such an organization.

in·sti·tu·tion \ˌin(t)s-tə-'tüsh-n, -'tyüsh-n\ *n.* **1** The act of instituting or establishing. **2** An established custom, practice, or law. The turkey dinner is a Thanksgiving *institution.* **3** An established society or corporation, especially a public one; as, educational and charitable *institutions.* A bank is a financial *institution.* **4** The building or buildings used by such an organization.

in·sti·tu·tion·al \ˌin(t)s-tə-'tüsh-n(-)əl, -'tyüsh-\ *adj.* **1** Of, relating to, or characteristic of instituting or establishing. **2** Of, relating to, or characteristic of an institution; as, *institutional* ceremonies; *institutional* management. — **in·sti·tu·tion·al·ize** \-n(-)ə-ˌlīz\ *v.* — **in·sti·tu·tion·al·ly** \-n(-)ə-lē\ *adv.*

in·struct \in-'strəkt\ *v.* [From Latin *instructus,* past participle of *instruere* meaning literally "to furnish", "to equip".] **1** To impart knowledge to; to teach. **2** To inform. The chairman failed to *instruct* one of the committee members that the meeting had been postponed. **3** To give directions or commands to. The teacher *instructed* the class to prepare for a test.

in·struc·tion \in-'strəksh-n\ *n.* **1** The act or practice of instructing. **2** A lesson or teaching; that which instructs. **3** [in the plural] Directions or commands; as, the *instructions* on a package.

in·struc·tive \in-'strək-tiv\ *adj.* Giving knowledge; serving to instruct or inform; as, an *instructive* experience. — **in·struc·tive·ly,** *adv.*

in·struc·tor \in-'strəkt-r\ *n.* A person who instructs; a teacher.

in·stru·ment \'in(t)s-trə-mənt\ *n.* **1** That by means of which something is done; a means. **2** A tool; a utensil; an implement; as, surgical *instruments.* **3** A device by which musical sounds are produced; as, a stringed *instrument;* a wind *instrument.* **4** A legal writing, as a deed or writ.

in·stru·men·tal \ˌin(t)s-trə-'ment-l\ *adj.* **1** Acting as an instrument or means; as, to be *instrumental* in sending a thief to jail. **2** Having to do with an instrument; designed for or performed with or on an instrument, especially a musical instrument; as, an unusual *instrumental* arrangement. — **in·stru·men·tal·ly** \-l-ē\ *adv.*

in·stru·men·tal·i·ty \ˌin(t)s-trə-ˌmen-'tal-ət-ē\ *n.; pl.* **in·stru·men·tal·i·ties.** **1** The quality or state of being instrumental. **2** A means or agency. Propaganda is now a major *instrumentality* in the waging of war.

in·stru·men·ta·tion \ˌin(t)s-trə-ˌmen-'tāsh-n\ *n.* The arrangement or composition of music for instruments.

in·sub·or·di·nate \ˌin-sə-'bȯrd-n(-)ət\ *adj.* Not submitting to authority; disobedient; rebellious. — **in·sub·or·di·nate·ly,** *adv.*

in·sub·or·di·na·tion \ˌin-sə-ˌbȯrd-n-'āsh-n\ *n.* Failure to obey authority.

in·sub·stan·tial \ˌin-səb-'stanch-l\ *adj.* **1** Not consisting of substance or matter; unreal; spectral. **2** Not substantial; flimsy.

in·suf·fer·a·ble \in-'səf-r(-)əb-l\ *adj.* Unbearable; as, *insufferable* wrongs. — **in·suf·fer·a·bly** \-r(-)ə-blē\ *adv.*

in·suf·fi·cien·cy \ˌin-sə-'fish-n-sē\ *n.; pl.* **in·suf·fi·cien·cies.** **1** The quality or state of being insufficient; as, the *insufficiency* of provisions. **2** A lack of something; a deficiency; as, an *insufficiency* in one's diet.

in·suf·fi·cient \ˌin-sə-'fish-nt\ *adj.* Not sufficient. — **in·suf·fi·cient·ly,** *adv.*

in·su·lar \'in(t)s-l-ər, 'in-shəl-r\ *adj.* [From Latin *insularis,* a derivative of *insula* meaning "island".] **1** Having to do with or like an island; found on or forming an island. **2** Isolated; detached. **3** Having to do with or like islanders. **4** Not liberal; narrow-minded. — **in·su·lar·i·ty** \ˌin(t)s-l-'ar-ət-ē, ˌin-shə-'lar-\ *n.*

in·su·late \'in(t)s-l-ˌāt\ *v.;* **in·su·lat·ed; in·su·lat·ing.** **1** To set or place apart; to isolate. **2** To separate by nonconductors, as to prevent the transfer of electricity, heat, or sound.

in·su·la·tion \ˌin(t)s-l-'āsh-n\ *n.* **1** The act of insulating or the state of being insulated. **2** That which is insulated. **3** Material used in insulating.

in·su·la·tor \'in(t)s-l-ˌāt-r\ *n.* That which insulates, as a substance or body, to prevent the transfer of electricity, heat, or sound.

insulators

in·su·lin \'in(t)s-l-ən\ *n.* A pancreatic hormone necessary for the normal utilization of sugar by the body.

in·sult \in-'səlt\ *v.* To be rude to; to treat with insolence, by word or act. — \'in-ˌsəlt\ *n.* An insulting act or speech.

in·su·per·a·ble \(')in-'süp-r(-)əb-l\ *adj.* Not capable of being overcome or passed over; as, an *insuperable* barrier. — **in·su·per·a·bly** \-r(-)ə-blē\ *adv.*

in·sup·port·a·ble \ˌin-sə-'pōrt-əb-l, -'pȯrt-\ *adj.* Not supportable; unendurable. — **in·sup·port·a·bly** \-ə-blē\ *adv.*

in·sur·a·ble \in-'shu̇r-əb-l\ *adj.* Capable of being insured, as against loss or death.

in·sur·ance \in-'shu̇r-ən(t)s; *in the South, often* 'in-ˌshu̇r-\ *n.* **1** The act of insuring; especially, a contract by which one party agrees to guarantee another against loss, as from fire, theft, damage, or death. **2** The business of making such contracts. **3** The money paid for insuring anything. **4** The amount for which anything is insured.

in·sure \in-'shu̇r\ *v.;* **in·sured; in·sur·ing.** **1** To give or obtain insurance on or for; as, to *insure* one's life; to *insure* a house against fire. **2** To make sure or safe; to guarantee; as, to do everything possible to *insure* the comfort of a guest.

in·sur·gent \in-'sərj-nt\ *adj.* Rising against authority; rebellious. — *n.* A person who revolts; a rebel. — **in·sur·gence** \-n(t)s\ *n.*

in·sur·mount·a·ble \(')in-sər-'maůnt-əb-l\ *adj.* Not capable of being surmounted or overcome; as, *insurmountable* difficulties. — **in·sur·mount·a·bly** \-ə-blē\ *adv.*

in·sur·rec·tion \ˌin(t)s-r-'eksh-n\ *n.* A revolt; a rebellion. — **in·sur·rec·tion·ary** \-n-ˌer-ē\ *adj.* — **in·sur·rec·tion·ist** \-n-əst\ *n.*

in·tact \in-'takt\ *adj.* Untouched, especially by anything that harms; uninjured; left complete or entire; whole.

in·take \'in-ˌtāk\ *n.* **1** A place where liquid or air is taken into something, as in a pump. **2** The act of taking in. **3** Something taken in.

in·tan·gi·ble \(')in-'tan-jəb-l\ *adj.* **1** Incapable of being touched. Light is *intangible.* **2** Incapable of being thought of as matter or substance; abstract. Good will is an *intangible* asset. — **in·tan·gi·bil·i·ty** \(ˌ)in-ˌtan-jə-'bil-ət-ē\ *n.* — **in·tan·gi·bly** \(')in-'tan-jə-blē\ *adv.*

in·te·ger \'int-əj-r\ *n.* A whole; especially, a whole number as distinguished from a fraction.

in·te·gral \'in-təg-rəl, in-'teg-, in-'tēg-\ *adj.* **1** Needed to make something complete; as, an *integral* part of the plan. **2** Composed of parts making a whole; complete; entire. **3** Having to do with integers. — *n.* A whole. — **in·te·gral·ly** \-rə-lē\ *adv.*

in·te·grate \'in-tə-ˌgrāt\ *v.;* **in·te·grat·ed; in·te·grat·ing.** To form or unite into one whole; to make complete; as, to integrate the plots of a play. — **in·te·gra·tion** \ˌin-tə-'grāsh-n\ *n.*

in·teg·ri·ty \in-'teg-rət-ē\ *n.; pl.* **in·teg·ri·ties. 1** The condition of being complete, undivided, or unbroken; wholeness; as, a war to preserve the *integrity* of an empire. **2** Soundness; purity. **3** Moral soundness; honesty; as, a man of *integrity.*

in·teg·u·ment \in-'teg-yə-mənt\ *n.* An external coating; skin. — **in·teg·u·men·ta·ry** \in-ˌteg-yə-'ment-r-ē, -'men-trē\ *adj.*

in·tel·lect \'int-l-ˌekt\ *n.* **1** The power of knowing; the ability to think. **2** The higher mental powers, as reasoning and judgment. **3** A mind or intelligence. **4** A person of great mental ability.

in·tel·lec·tu·al \ˌint-l-'ek-chə-wəl, -chəl\ *adj.* **1** Having to do with the intellect or understanding; performed by the intellect; as, *intellectual* processes. **2** Having intellect to a high degree; fond of and given to learning and thinking; as, an *intellectual* person. **3** Requiring study and thought; as, *intellectual* work. — *n.* An intellectual person. — **in·tel·lec·tu·al·ly** \-'ek-chə-lē, -'ek-chə-wə-lē\ *adv.*

in·tel·lec·tu·al·ism \ˌint-l-'ek-chə-ˌliz-m, -chə-wə-ˌliz-m\ *n.* **1** The quality of being intellectual. **2** Any philosophy or doctrine that emphasizes the importance of reason as a source of knowledge or as a test of truth. — **in·tel·lec·tu·al·ist** \-chə-ləst, -chə-wə-ləst\ *n.*

in·tel·lec·tu·al·i·ty \ˌint-l-ˌek-chə-'wal-ət-ē\ *n.* The quality of being intellectual; intellectual power.

in·tel·li·gence \in-'tel-ə-jən(t)s\ *n.* **1** The ability to learn and understand; as, a child's increase in *intelligence.* **2** The ability to deal with a new or trying situation; as, to possess the *intelligence* to solve the problem. **3** Information; news; as, to receive *intelligence* of enemy troop movements. **4** The getting or giving of information, especially secret information. **5** The persons engaged in obtaining information; secret service.

intelligence quotient. A number indicating the intelligence of a person, obtained by multiplying his mental age by 100 and dividing by his chronological age.

intelligence test. Any psychological test by which mental capacity can be estimated.

in·tel·li·gent \in-'tel-ə-jənt\ *adj.* Having or showing intelligence or intellect; as, an *intelligent* person; an *intelligent* question. — **in·tel·li·gent·ly,** *adv.*

in·tel·li·gen·tsia \(ˌ)in-ˌtel-ə-'jent-sē-ə, -'jench-ə, -'gent-sē-ə\ *n.* Intellectual people as a group; the educated class.

in·tel·li·gi·ble \in-'tel-ə-jəb-l\ *adj.* Capable of being understood; comprehensible. — **in·tel·li·gi·bil·i·ty** \(ˌ)in-ˌtel-ə-jə-'bil-ət-ē\ *n.* — **in·tel·li·gi·bly** \in-'tel-ə-jə-blē\ *adv.*

in·tem·per·ance \(')in-'temp-r(-)ən(t)s\ *n.* **1** The lack of moderation or self-restraint. **2** Any extreme indulgence; especially, excessive indulgence in intoxicating liquors.

in·tem·per·ate \(')in-'temp-r(-)ət\ *adj.* **1** Not moderate or mild; excessive; extreme; severe; as, *intemperate* weather. **2** Lacking or showing lack of restraint or self-control; as, *intemperate* language. **3** Indulging any appetite or desire to excess; especially, lacking self-restraint in the use of intoxicating liquors. — **in·tem·per·ate·ly,** *adv.*

in·tend \in-'tend\ *v.* To have in mind as a purpose or aim; to plan; as, to *intend* to do better work; to *intend* no harm.

in·tend·ed \in-'ten-dəd\ *adj.* **1** Intentional. **2** Betrothed; as, the woman's *intended* husband. — *n.* An intended husband or wife.

in·tense \in-'ten(t)s\ *adj.* **1** In an extreme degree; as, *intense* heat; *intense* pain. **2** Very earnest or intent; as, *intense* thought. **3** Feeling deeply; as, an *intense* person. — **in·tense·ly,** *adv.*

in·ten·si·fy \in-'ten(t)s-ə-ˌfī\ *v.;* **in·ten·si·fied** \-ˌfīd\; **in·ten·si·fy·ing.** To make intense or more intense; to heighten; as, to *intensify* one's efforts. — **in·ten·si·fi·ca·tion** \in-ˌten(t)s-ə-fə-'kāsh-n\ *n.* — **in·ten·si·fi·er** \in-'ten(t)s-ə-ˌfīr\ *n.*

in·ten·si·ty \in-'ten(t)s-ət-ē\ *n.; pl.* **in·ten·si·ties. 1** The condition of being intense; extreme strength or force; as, the *intensity* of heat or cold. **2** Degree or amount; as, the *intensity* of an electric current.

in·ten·sive \in-'ten(t)s-iv\ *adj.* **1** Thorough; marked by special effort; exhaustive; as, an *intensive* campaign to raise money; a few hours of *intensive* study. **2** Serving to give emphasis; as, the *intensive* pronoun in the sentence "He himself was present". — *n.* **1** Anything that intensifies. **2** An intensive word, as the adverb "very" in the phrase *very happy.*

in·tent \in-ˈtent\ *adj.* **1** Giving keen or eager attention; earnest; as, *intent* on a problem; an *intent* expression. **2** Closely occupied; determined; as, to be *intent* on having a good time. — **in·tent·ly,** *adv.*

in·tent \in-ˈtent\ *n.* Something that is intended; purpose; intention; as, to break into a house with *intent* to rob; to be uncertain of someone's *intent.*

in·ten·tion \in-ˈtench-n\ *n.* **1** A determination to act in a certain way; as, done without *intention.* **2** Purpose; end; aim; as, to be unable to carry out all one's *intentions.*

in·ten·tion·al \in-ˈtench-n(-)əl\ *adj.* Done on purpose; intended. — For synonyms see *voluntary.*— **in·ten·tion·al·ly** \-n(-)ə-lē\ *adv.*

in·ter \in-ˈtər\ *v.;* **in·terred; in·ter·ring.** To bury.

inter-. A prefix that can mean: **1** Between, among, together, as in *intermix* or *intertwine.* **2** Mutual or mutually, reciprocal or reciprocally, as in *intercommunication* and *interrelation.* **3** Between the parts or units of, as in *interscholastic* or *interurban.* **4** Placed or occurring between, as in *interlining.*

in·ter·act \ˌint-r-ˈakt\ *v.* To act upon each other. — **in·ter·ac·tion** \ˌint-r-ˈaksh-n\ *n.*

in·ter·breed \ˌint-r-ˈbrēd\ *v.;* **in·ter·bred** \-ˈbred\; **in·ter·breed·ing.** To breed together or cause to breed together, as in crossbreeding.

in·ter·cede \ˌint-r-ˈsēd\ *v.;* **in·ter·ced·ed; in·ter·ced·ing. 1** To act as a go-between between parties who are unfriendly. **2** To beg or plead in behalf of another; as, to *intercede* for a friend who is to be punished.

in·ter·cept \ˌint-r-ˈsept\ *v.* **1** To take or seize on the way, or before arrival at a destination; to stop the progress of; as, to *intercept* a letter; to *intercept* an enemy bomber. **2** To cut through; as, a line *intercepted* between points A and B.

in·ter·cep·tion \ˌint-r-ˈsepsh-n\ *n.* The act of intercepting or the state of being intercepted; as, the *interception* of a message.

in·ter·cep·tor \ˌint-r-ˈsept-r\ *n.* One that intercepts; especially, a defensive fighter plane of high rate of climb and speed, used for intercepting enemy airplanes.

in·ter·ces·sion \ˌint-r-ˈsesh-n\ *n.* The act of interceding. — **in·ter·ces·sor** \ˌint-r-ˈses-r\ *n.*

in·ter·change \ˌint-r-ˈchānj\ *v.;* **in·ter·changed; in·ter·chang·ing. 1** To change two persons or things about so that each takes the other's place; to give and receive; to exchange; as, to *interchange* seats; to *interchange* presents. **2** To alternate; to vary; as, to *interchange* work with play. — \ˈint-r-ˌchānj\ *n.* **1** An interchanging; an exchange. **2** A meeting or joining of two or more highways, usually on two levels, whereby turning traffic can leave one highway and enter another without interfering with the flow of traffic. **3** A place where one may enter or leave a toll road.

in·ter·change·a·ble \ˌint-r-ˈchān-jəb-l\ *adj.* Capable of being interchanged; as, *interchangeable* parts in a machine. — **in·ter·change·a·bly** \-jə-blē\ *adv.*

in·ter·col·le·giate \ˌint-r-kə-ˈlē-jət, -jē-ət\ *adj.* Existing, or carried on, between colleges; as, *intercollegiate* sports.

in·ter·com \ˈint-r-ˌkäm\ *n.* A two-way short-distance communication system with microphone and loud speaker at each end.

in·ter·com·mu·ni·cate \ˌint-r-kə-ˈmyü-nə-ˌkāt\ *v.;* **in·ter·com·mu·ni·cat·ed; in·ter·com·mu·ni·cat·ing.** To exchange communication with another. — **in·ter·com·mu·ni·ca·tion** \-ˌmyü-nə-ˈkāsh-n\ *n.*

in·ter·con·ti·nen·tal \ˌint-r-ˌkänt-n-ˈent-l, -ˌkän-tə-ˈnent-l\ *adj.* Between or among continents.

in·ter·course \ˈint-r-ˌkōrs, -ˌkȯrs\ *n.* Connection or dealings between persons or nations; relations.

in·ter·de·pend·ent \ˌint-r-dē-ˈpen-dənt\ *adj.* Depending upon one another. — **in·ter·de·pend·ence** \-dən(t)s\ *n.*

in·ter·dict \ˈint-r-ˌdikt\ *n.* An order that prohibits or forbids; especially, the prohibition, as by the pope, of such privileges as divine worship or the sacraments as a punishment for a crime. — \ˌint-r-ˈdikt\ *v.* To prohibit or forbid, especially by an interdict. — **in·ter·dic·tion** \ˌint-r-ˈdiksh-n\ *n.*

in·ter·est \ˈin-trəst, ˈint-r-ˌest, ˈint-rst, ˈin-ˌtrest, ˈint-r-əst\ *n.* **1** A share; part ownership; as, to have an *interest* in a factory. **2** That in which a person has or may have such an interest; business affairs; business; as, to invest money in mining *interests.* **3** Advantage; benefit; as, in the common *interest;* for one's own *interest.* **4** The money paid by a borrower for the use of borrowed money. **5** The persons interested in any particular business or kind of work, taken as a group; as, to get the views of the banking *interests.* **6** Heightened feeling accompanying special attention to something; as, to show an *interest* in geography. **7** Anything that arouses such special attention. — *v.* **1** To affect; to concern; to involve; as, to be financially *interested* in a factory. **2** To cause to have an interest or to take a share in something; as, to *interest* a friend in a plan to build a boat. **3** To hold the attention of; as, a boy whom nothing *interested* except ball.

in·ter·est·ed \see *interest*\ *adj.* **1** Having the attention occupied; having or showing interest; as, an *interested* listener. **2** Owning an interest or share.

in·ter·est·ing \see *interest*\ *adj.* Holding the attention; arousing interest.

in·ter·fere \ˌint-r-ˈfir\ *v.;* **in·ter·fered; in·ter·fer·ing. 1** To collide; to clash; to be in opposition; as, to let nothing *interfere* with business. **2** To take part in the affairs of others; to meddle. **3** To obstruct an opposing player illegally. **4** Of waves, as sound waves, to act upon one another.

in·ter·fer·ence \ˌint-r-ˈfir-ən(t)s\ *n.* **1** An interfering. **2** Something that interferes. **3** Confusion of received radio signals by undesired signals or electrical disturbances.

in·ter·fuse \ˌint-r-ˈfyüz\ *v.;* **in·ter·fused; in·ter·fus·ing. 1** To combine, as by fusing or blending; to intermingle. **2** To permeate; to pervade.

in·ter·im \'int-r-əm\ *n.* [From Latin, an adverb meaning "meanwhile", a derivative of *inter* meaning "between".] The meantime. — *adj.* Temporary; as, an *interim* president; an *interim* appointment.

in·te·ri·or \in-'tir-ē-ər\ *adj.* **1** Inside; inner; as, the *interior* parts of a clock. **2** Far from the limits, frontier, or shore; inland; as, the *interior* parts of a country. — *n.* **1** The interior part; the inside; as, the *interior* of a house; the *interior* of Africa. **2** The internal affairs of a state or nation; as, the Department of the *Interior.*

interj. Abbreviation *for interjection.*

in·ter·ject \ˌint-r-'jekt\ *v.* To throw in between; to insert; as, to *interject* a question or a remark.

in·ter·jec·tion \ˌint-r-'jeksh-n\ *n.* **1** An interjecting. **2** Something interjected. The speaker was interrupted several times by *interjections* from the audience. **3** A word or cry expressing sudden or strong feeling, as *ouch!* or *alas!*

in·ter·lace \ˌint-r-'lās\ *v.;* **in·ter·laced**; **in·ter·lac·ing.** To unite by or as if by lacing together; to twine or weave together; to cross as if woven; as, *interlacing* boughs.

in·ter·lard \ˌint-r-'lärd, -'lȧrd\ *v.* To insert or introduce at intervals; to intersperse; as, a speech *interlarded* with quotations.

in·ter·line \ˌint-r-'līn\ *v.;* **in·ter·lined**; **in·ter·lin·ing.** To write between the lines, as in making additions or corrections.

in·ter·line \ˌint-r-'līn\ *v.;* **in·ter·lined**; **in·ter·lin·ing.** To put a lining in under the ordinary lining, as of a coat.

in·ter·lin·e·ar \ˌint-r-'lin-ē-ər\ *adj.* Written between the lines; as, an *interlinear* translation of a text.

in·ter·lin·ing \ˌint-r-'lī-ning\ *n.* A lining under the ordinary lining of a garment.

in·ter·lock \ˌint-r-'läk\ *v.* To lock into one another; to interlace firmly; as, to *interlock* one's fingers; a series of rings *interlocking* to form a chain.

in·ter·lop·er \'int-r-ˌlōp-r\ *n.* A person who intrudes or interferes wrongly or officiously; an intruder.

in·ter·lude \'int-r-ˌlüd\ *n.* **1** Any performance given between the acts of a play. **2** A short piece of music, as one played between the acts of a play or the parts of a church service. **3** Any time, feature, or event, coming between other actions; as, an *interlude* of peace between wars.

in·ter·mar·riage \ˌint-r-'mar-ij\ *n.* Connection by marriage, as between two families, races, or religious groups.

in·ter·mar·ry \ˌint-r-'mar-ē\ *v.;* **in·ter·mar·ried** \-ēd\; **in·ter·mar·ry·ing.** To join or become connected by intermarriage.

in·ter·med·dle \ˌint-r-'med-l\ *v.;* **in·ter·med·dled**; **in·ter·med·dling** \-l(-)ing\. To meddle in the affairs of others; to meddle officiously.

in·ter·me·di·ary \ˌint-r-'mēd-ē-ˌer-ē\ *adj.* **1** Coming between; intermediate. **2** Acting as a mediator. — *n.; pl.* **in·ter·me·di·ar·ies** \-ˌer-ēz\. A go-between; a mediator.

in·ter·me·di·ate \ˌint-r-'mēd-ē-ət\ *adj.* Being in the middle; coming or done between; as, an *intermediate* grade. — *n.* One that is intermediate.

in·ter·ment \in-'tər-mənt\ *n.* Burial.

in·ter·mez·zo \ˌint-r-'met-ˌsō, -'med-ˌzō\ *n.; pl.* **in·ter·mez·zos** \-ˌsōz, -ˌzōz\ or **in·ter·mez·zi** \-(ˌ)sē, -(ˌ)zē\. **1** A short light musical piece suitable for playing between the acts of a serious drama or opera. **2** A short independent instrumental composition.

in·ter·mi·na·ble \in-'tər-mə-nəb-l\ *adj.* Endless or seeming to be endless; long-drawn-out; as, an *interminable* speech. — **in·ter·mi·na·bly** \-nə-blē\ *adv.*

in·ter·min·gle \ˌint-r-'ming-gl\ *v.;* **in·ter·min·gled**; **in·ter·min·gling** \-gl(-)ing\. To mingle or mix together.

in·ter·mis·sion \ˌint-r-'mish-n\ *n.* **1** Interruption; as, continuing without *intermission.* **2** A pause or interval, as between the acts of a play.

in·ter·mit \ˌint-r-'mit\ *v.;* **in·ter·mit·ted**; **in·ter·mit·ting.** To stop for a time; to discontinue at intervals and then continue again.

in·ter·mit·tent \ˌint-r-'mit-nt\ *adj.* Coming and going at intervals; starting, stopping, and starting again; as, an *intermittent* electric current; an *intermittent* fever. — **in·ter·mit·tent·ly**, *adv.*

in·ter·mix \ˌint-r-'miks\ *v.* To mix together. — **in·ter·mix·ture** \-'miks-chər\ *n.*

in·tern \'in-ˌtərn, in-'tərn\ *v.* **1** To detain and confine in a country or a place. In time of war a country *interns* persons suspected of being hostile to it. **2** To act as an intern, especially a medical intern.

in·tern or **in·terne** \'in-ˌtərn\ *n.* A person, especially a medical student who, upon completion of a required course of study, enters a period of practical training in preparation for independent work.

in·ter·nal \in-'tərn-l\ *adj.* **1** Enclosed; interior; inner. **2** Having to do with the inside of the body; as, *internal* medicine, *internal* injuries. **3** Having to do with affairs or interests within a country or organization; domestic; as, *internal* affairs. — **in·ter·nal·ly** \-'tərn-l-ē\ *adv.*

internal-combustion engine. An engine run by a fuel-air mixture ignited within the engine cylinder.

in·ter·na·tion·al \ˌint-r-'nash-n(-)əl\ *adj.* **1** Between or among nations; as, an *international* agreement. **2** Having to do with two or more nations; as, an *international* boundary. — **in·ter·na·tion·al·ly** \-n(-)ə-lē\ *adv.*

international date line. A hypothetical boundary line on or near the 180th meridian, fixed by international or general agreement as the place where each calendar day first begins.

in·ter·na·tion·al·ize \ˌint-r-'nash-n(-)ə-ˌlīz\ *v.;* **in·ter·na·tion·al·ized**; **in·ter·na·tion·al·iz·ing.** To make international; as, to *internationalize* a canal.

interne. Variant of the noun *intern*.

in·ter·nec·ine \ˌint-r-ˈnes-ˌēn, -ˈnē-ˌsīn\ *adj*. Deadly; especially, destroying both parties to a conflict; as, an *internecine* struggle for power.

in·tern·ment \in-ˈtərn-mənt\ *n*. The act of detaining or confining, as of an enemy alien, or the state of being so interned.

in·tern·ship \ˈin-ˌtərn-ˌship\ *n*. **1** The state of being an intern, especially a medical intern. **2** The period of practical training following a required course of study and preceding independent work in certain fields, as in medicine.

in·ter·phone \ˈint-r-ˌfōn\ *n*. A telephone system for intercommunication between points within a small area, as in an airplane or an office building.

in·ter·plan·e·tary \ˌint-r-ˈplan-ə-ˌter-ē\ *adj*. Between or in the regions of the planets; as, *interplanetary* travel.

in·ter·play \ˈint-r-ˌplā\ *n*. Mutual action or influence; interaction; as, an *interplay* of thought and feeling.

in·ter·po·late \in-ˈtərp-l-ˌāt\ *v*.; **in·ter·po·lat·ed**; **in·ter·po·lat·ing**. **1** To change, as something written, by inserting new material. **2** To insert; to interpose.

in·ter·po·la·tion \in-ˌtərp-l-ˈāsh-n\ *n*. **1** The act of interpolating or the state of being interpolated. **2** Something interpolated.

in·ter·pose \ˌint-r-ˈpōz\ *v*.; **in·ter·posed**; **in·ter·pos·ing**. **1** To place between. **2** To thrust in; to intrude; to interrupt. **3** To introduce between the parts of a conversation or argument. **4** To be or come between, as parties in a dispute; to intervene.

in·ter·po·si·tion \ˌint-r-pə-ˈzish-n\ *n*. **1** The act of interposing or the state of being interposed. **2** Something interposed.

in·ter·pret \in-ˈtərp-(r)ət\ *v*. **1** To explain or tell the meaning of; to translate; as, to *interpret* a dream; to *interpret* for a French-speaking visitor. **2** To understand according to one's own belief, judgment, or interest; as, to *interpret* an action as unfriendly. **3** To bring out the meaning or significance of. An actor *interprets* the characters he plays.

in·ter·pre·ta·tion \in-ˌtərp-(r)ə-ˈtāsh-n\ *n*. **1** An explanation; a translation; the meaning given by an interpreter. **2** A person's idea of the mood or meaning of an artistic work or subject, as shown by his performance or treatment of it.

in·ter·pre·ta·tive \in-ˈtərp-(r)ə-ˌtāt-iv\ or **in·ter·pre·tive** \in-ˈtərp-(r)ət-iv\ *adj*. Designed or fitted to interpret; explanatory; as, *interpretative* reporting; *interpretive* dancing.

in·ter·pret·er \in-ˈtərp-(r)ət-r\ *n*. A person who interprets; especially, one who translates for persons talking to each other in different languages.

in·ter·reg·num \ˌint-r-ˈ(r)eg-nəm\ *n*.; *pl*. **in·ter·reg·nums** \-nəmz\ or **in·ter·reg·na** \-nə\. [From Latin, composed of *inter* meaning "between" and *regnum* meaning "reign".] **1** The time during which a throne is vacant between two reigns. **2** A pause that interrupts a series of events.

in·ter·re·late \ˌint-r-(r)ē-ˈlāt\ *v*.; **in·ter·re·lat·ed**; **in·ter·re·lat·ing**. To relate two or more things to each other. — **in·ter·re·lat·ed** \-ˈlāt-əd\ *adj*. — **in·ter·re·la·tion** \-ˈlāsh-n\ *n*.

in·ter·ro·gate \in-ˈter-ə-ˌgāt\ *v*.; **in·ter·ro·gat·ed**; **in·ter·ro·gat·ing**. To question; especially, to examine by means of questions; as, to *interrogate* a prisoner of war. — **in·ter·ro·ga·tion** \in-ˌter-ə-ˈgāsh-n\ *n*. — **in·ter·ro·ga·tor** \in-ˈter-ə-ˌgāt-r\ *n*.

interrogation point or **interrogation mark**. A question mark.

in·ter·rog·a·tive \ˌint-r-ˈäg-ət-iv\ *adj*. Containing or expressing a question; as, an *interrogative* sentence; an *interrogative* pronoun. — *n*. A word used in asking questions, as *who, what, which*. — **in·ter·rog·a·tive·ly**, *adv*.

in·ter·rog·a·to·ry \ˌint-r-ˈäg-ə-ˌtōr-ē, -ˌtȯr-ē\ *adj*. Containing, expressing, or implying a question; as, an *interrogatory* tone of voice. — *n*.; *pl*. **in·ter·rog·a·to·ries**. A questioning; an inquiry.

in·ter·rupt \ˌint-r-ˈəpt\ *v*. **1** To break into or in between; to stop or hinder by breaking in; as, to *interrupt* a conversation; to *interrupt* production by a strike. **2** To break into something that is continuous or uniform. Not a hill *interrupted* the miles of plain.

in·ter·rup·tion \ˌint-r-ˈəpsh-n\ *n*. **1** An interrupting or a being interrupted. **2** A break; a stoppage. **3** An intermission; a pause.

in·ter·scho·las·tic \ˌint-r-skə-ˈlas-tik\ *adj*. Existing or carried on between schools.

in·ter·sect \ˌint-r-ˈsekt\ *v*. To cut or divide by passing through; to cut across; to meet and cross; as, where Main Street *intersects* Market.

in·ter·sec·tion \ˌint-r-ˈseksh-n\ *n*. **1** The action of intersecting. **2** The place or point where two or more things intersect; a crossing, as of streets; as, a busy *intersection*.

in·ter·space \ˈint-r-ˌspās\ *n*. An interval of space or time. — \ˌint-r-ˈspās\ *v*.; **in·ter·spaced**; **in·ter·spac·ing**. To put a space between. The book has photographs *interspaced* with drawings. — \ˈint-r-ˌspās\ *adj*. **1** In or between the regions of outer space; as, *interspace* travel. **2** Designed for use in or between the regions of outer space.

in·ter·sperse \ˌint-r-ˈspərs\ *v*.; **in·ter·spersed**; **in·ter·spers·ing**. **1** To scatter or set here and there among others; as, to *intersperse* pictures in a book. **2** To vary with things set about here and there; as, a serious talk *interspersed* with a few jokes. — **in·ter·sper·sion** \-ˈspərzh-n, -ˈspərsh-n\ *n*.

in·ter·state \ˈint-r-ˌstāt\ *adj*. Between states; as, *interstate* commerce.

in·ter·stel·lar \ˌint-r-ˈstel-r\ *adj*. Located among the stars; as, *interstellar* space.

in·ter·stice \in-ˈtərs-təs\ *n*.; *pl*. **in·ter·stic·es** \-tə-səz, -tə-ˌsēz\. A little space between one thing and another; a chink; a crevice. — **in·ter·sti·tial** \ˌint-r-ˈstish-l\ *adj*.

in·ter·twine \ˌint-r-ˈtwīn\ *v.;* **in·ter·twined; in·ter·twin·ing.** To twine one with another; to twist or lace together.

in·ter·twist \ˌint-r-ˈtwist\ *v.* To intertwine.

in·ter·ur·ban \ˌint-r-ˈərb-n\ *adj.* Running between towns or cities; as, an *interurban* bus line.

in·ter·val \ˈint-rv-l\ *n.* **1** A period of time between events; as, the *interval* between elections; an *interval* of three months. **2** A space or gap between things; as, the *interval* between two desks. **3** In music, difference in pitch between two tones. — **at intervals.** Coming or happening with intervals between.

in·ter·vene \ˌint-r-ˈvēn\ *v.;* **in·ter·vened; in·ter·ven·ing. 1** To happen or come in as an unrelated event. Rain *intervened* and we postponed the match. **2** To happen or come between points of time or between events. Only a second *intervened* between the flash and the report. **3** To come in or between in order to stop, settle, or change; as, to *intervene* in a quarrel. **4** To be or lie between; as, *intervening* mountains.

in·ter·ven·tion \ˌint-r-ˈvench-n\ *n.* **1** An intervening. **2** Any interference in order to influence others; especially, interference by one country in the affairs of another, as for settling a civil war.

in·ter·view \ˈint-r-ˌvyü\ *n.* **1** A meeting face to face, especially for the purpose of talking or consulting with someone. **2** A meeting between a representative of a newspaper or magazine and another person in order to get news or an article to be published. **3** The written account of such a meeting. — *v.* To have an interview with. — **in·ter·view·er** \-ˌvyü-ər\ *n.*

in·ter·weave \ˌint-r-ˈwēv\ *v.;* **in·ter·wove** \-ˈwōv\ or **in·ter·weaved** \-ˈwēvd\; **in·ter·wo·ven** \-ˈwōv-n\, **in·ter·wove,** or **in·ter·weaved; in·ter·weav·ing. 1** To weave together. **2** To mingle together; to connect closely; as, ideas *interwoven* in one's mind. — **in·ter·wo·ven,** *adj.*

in·tes·tate \in-ˈtes-ˌtāt, -tət\ *adj.* **1** Without having made a will; as, to die *intestate.* **2** Not disposed of by will. — **in·tes·ta·cy** \-ˈtes-tə-sē\ *n.*

in·tes·ti·nal \in-ˈtes-tən-l\ *adj.* Of or relating to the intestines.

intestinal juice. A fluid secreted by certain glands of the small intestine, containing digestive enzymes, mucus, salts, a hormone stimulating other glands, and water.

in·tes·tine \in-ˈtes-tən\ *adj.* Internal; domestic; as, *intestine* strife. — *n.* The lower tubelike part of the alimentary canal from stomach to anus, which helps to digest food and to discharge waste matter; the bowels.

in·ti·ma·cy \ˈin-tə-mə-sē\ *n.; pl.* **in·ti·ma·cies.** The state of being intimate or familiar; close friendship or association.

in·ti·mate \ˈin-tə-ˌmāt\ *v.;* **in·ti·mat·ed; in·ti·mat·ing. 1** To suggest; to hint. **2** To announce.

in·ti·mate \ˈin-tə-mət\ *adj.* **1** Innermost; very personal; private; as, *intimate* thoughts. **2** Close in one's personal relations; as, an *intimate* friend. **3** Thorough; as, *intimate* knowledge. — *n.* A close friend or associate. — **in·ti·mate·ly,** *adv.*

in·ti·ma·tion \ˌin-tə-ˈmāsh-n\ *n.* An intimating; something that is intimated; a suggestion; a hint; a statement.

in·tim·i·date \in-ˈtim-ə-ˌdāt\ *v.;* **in·tim·i·dat·ed; in·tim·i·dat·ing.** To make fearful; to frighten, as by threats. — **in·tim·i·da·tion** \in-ˌtim-ə-ˈdāsh-n\ *n.*

in·to \ˈin-tə, -tu̇, -tü\ *prep.* **1** To the inside of; within; as, to go *into* the house; to look *into* a matter. **2** To the place, condition, or form of; as, to burst *into* tears; divided *into* four parts.

in·tol·er·a·ble \(ˈ)in-ˈtäl-r(-)əb-l, -rb-l\ *adj.* Unbearable; as, *intolerable* heat. — **in·tol·er·a·bly** \-r(-)ə-blē, -r-blē\ *adv.*

in·tol·er·ance \(ˈ)in-ˈtäl-r-ən(t)s\ *n.* **1** The inability to bear or endure. **2** A refusal to allow others to hold their opinions or express their preferences; as, religious *intolerance.*

in·tol·er·ant \(ˈ)in-ˈtäl-r-ənt\ *adj.* Not tolerant; narrow-minded; illiberal. — **in·tol·er·ant·ly,** *adv.*

in·to·na·tion \ˌin-tə-ˈnāsh-n\ *n.* **1** The action of intoning, or musically reciting, as a chant or a psalm. **2** The action of sounding musical tones. **3** Something that is intoned. **4** The rise and fall in pitch of a person's voice.

in·tone \in-ˈtōn\ *v.;* **in·toned; in·ton·ing.** To recite musically or in one tone; to chant; as, to *intone* a church service.

in·tox·i·cant \in-ˈtäks-ə-kənt\ *adj.* Intoxicating. — *n.* Something that intoxicates; an intoxicating agent, as alcohol.

in·tox·i·cate \in-ˈtäks-ə-ˌkāt\ *v.;* **in·tox·i·cat·ed; in·tox·i·cat·ing.** [From medieval Latin *intoxicatus,* past participle of *intoxicare* meaning "to poison".] **1** To make drunk. **2** To make wildly excited; as, *intoxicated* with joy.

in·tox·i·ca·tion \in-ˌtäks-ə-ˈkāsh-n\ *n.* **1** In medicine, a poisoning. **2** Drunkenness. **3** A great excitement of mind.

intra-. A prefix that can mean: **1** Within, inside, as in *intramural, intrastate.* **2** In, into, as in *intravenous.*

in·trac·ta·ble \(ˈ)in-ˈtrak-təb-l\ *adj.* Not easily managed or taught; ungovernable; obstinate. — **in·trac·ta·bil·i·ty** \(ˌ)in-ˌtrak-tə-ˈbil-ət-ē\ *n.* — **in·trac·ta·bly** \(ˈ)in-ˈtrak-tə-blē\ *adv.*

in·tra·mu·ral \ˌin-trə-ˈmyu̇r-əl\ *adj.* Within the walls, as of a city or college; as, *intramural* athletics.

in·tran·si·tive \(ˈ)in-ˈtran(t)s-ət-iv, -ˈtran-zət-iv\ *adj.* Not transitive; especially, in grammar, not carrying or passing over to an object; expressing an action or state as limited to the doer or subject; as, an *intransitive* verb. — **in·tran·si·tive·ly,** *adv.*

in·tra·state \ˌin-trə-ˈstāt\ *adj.* Within the boundaries of a state.

in·tra·ve·nous \ˌin-trə-ˈvē-nəs\ *adj.* In or into a vein. — **in·tra·ve·nous·ly,** *adv.*

in·treat \in-ˈtrēt\ *v.* To entreat.

in·trench \in-ˈtrench\ *v.* To entrench. — **in·trench·ment** \-mənt\ *n.*

in·trep·id \in-ˈtrep-əd\ *adj.* Fearless; bold. — **in·tre·pid·i·ty** \ˌin-trə-ˈpid-ət-ē\ *n.*

in·tri·ca·cy \ˈin-trə-kə-sē\ *n.; pl.* **in·tri·ca·cies. 1** The condition of being intricate. **2** Something involved or complex; as, the *intricacies* of a plot.

in·tri·cate \ˈin-trik-ət\ *adj.* Difficult to follow, understand, or solve; complicated; as, the *intricate* wiring of a television set. — **in·tri·cate·ly,** *adv.*

in·trigue \in-ˈtrēg\ *v.;* **in·trigued; in·trigu·ing. 1** To plot; to scheme; to bring about by secret plotting. **2** To carry on a secret love affair. **3** To puzzle; to perplex. **4** To arouse the interest or curiosity of. The title of that book *intrigues* one. — \ˈin-ˌtrēg, in-ˈtrēg\ *n.* A plot; a secret scheme. — **in·trigu·er** \in-ˈtrēg-r\ *n.* — **in·trigu·ing·ly** \-ˈtrē-ging-lē\ *adv.*

in·trin·sic \in-ˈtrin-zik, -ˈtrin(t)s-ik\ *adj.* Belonging to the nature of a thing; essential; real. The lost ring has great sentimental but little *intrinsic* value. — **in·trin·si·cal·ly** \-zik-l(-)ē, -ik-l(-)ē\ *adv.*

in·tro·duce \ˌin-trə-ˈdüs, -ˈdyüs\ *v.;* **in·tro·duced; in·tro·duc·ing. 1** To bring into practice or use; as, to *introduce* a new fashion. **2** To lead or bring in; as, to *introduce* a person into a society; to *introduce* birds from other countries into America. **3** To cause to be acquainted; to make known; as, to *introduce* two of one's friends; to *introduce* the speaker to an audience. **4** To present or bring forward for discussion; as, to *introduce* a subject. **5** To put in, to insert. — **in·tro·duc·er** \-ˈdüs-r, -ˈdyüs-r\ *n.*

in·tro·duc·tion \ˌin-trə-ˈdəksh-n\ *n.* **1** The action of introducing. **2** Something that is introduced. **3** The part of a book that leads up to and explains what will be found in the main part; a preface; as, a textbook with an *introduction* and notes. **4** A book intended for beginners in a subject; a guide; as, an *introduction* to chemistry. **5** The action of making persons known to each other; as, to give two of one's friends an *introduction.*

in·tro·duc·to·ry \ˌin-trə-ˈdəkt-r(-)ē\ *adj.* Serving to introduce; leading to the main subject or business.

in·tro·spec·tion \ˌin-trə-ˈspeksh-n\ *n.* A looking inward; an examination of one's own thoughts or feelings. — **in·tro·spec·tive** \ˌin-trə-ˈspek-tiv\ *adj.* — **in·tro·spec·tive·ly,** *adv.*

in·tro·vert \ˈin-trə-ˌvərt\ *n.* A person who is more interested in thoughts and ideas than in people or action.

in·trude \in-ˈtrüd\ *v.;* **in·trud·ed; in·trud·ing. 1** To thrust or force something in or upon; as, to *intrude* one's views into a discussion. **2** To come or go in without invitation or welcome; to trespass; as, to *intrude* on a person's privacy; to apologize for *intruding.* — **in·trud·er** \-ˈtrüd-r\ *n.*

in·tru·sion \in-ˈtrüzh-n\ *n.* The act of intruding. — **in·tru·sive** \-ˈtrü-siv\ *adj.* — **in·tru·sive·ly,** *adv.*

in·trust \in-ˈtrəst\ *v.* To entrust.

in·tu·i·tion \ˌin-(ˌ)tü-ˈish-n, -(ˌ)tyü-\ *n.* **1** The power of knowing immediately and without conscious reasoning. **2** Something known or understood at once and without any effort of the mind; as, to act upon an *intuition.*

in·tu·i·tive \in-ˈtü-ət-iv, -ˈtyü-\ *adj.* **1** Knowing or understanding by intuition; as, an *intuitive* person. **2** Having or characterized by intuition; as, an *intuitive* mind. **3** Known or understood by intuition; as, *intuitive* knowledge. — **in·tu·i·tive·ly,** *adv.*

in·un·date \ˈin-ən-ˌdāt\ *v.;* **in·un·dat·ed; in·un·dat·ing.** To cover with or as with a flood; to overflow; to flood; as, to be *inundated* with Christmas cards.

in·un·da·tion \ˌin-ən-ˈdāsh-n\ *n.* **1** An overflowing or flooding. **2** A flood.

in·ure \i-ˈnu̇r, i-ˈnyu̇r\ *v.;* **in·ured; in·ur·ing. 1** To accustom; to harden. Living in Alaska had *inured* him to cold. **2** To become of advantage; as, the benefits that *inure* to our descendants.

in·vade \in-ˈvād\ *v.;* **in·vad·ed; in·vad·ing. 1** To enter in order to conquer or plunder. The enemy *invaded* the city. **2** To infringe on; to violate; as, to *invade* another's privacy. **3** To enter and gradually spread over or through, usually affecting adversely; as, stores *invading* residential sections; gangrene *invading* healthy tissue.

in·vad·er \in-ˈvād-r\ *n.* One that invades.

in·va·lid \ˈin-və-ləd\ *n.* [From French *invalide,* there borrowed from Latin *invalidus* meaning "weak".] A person who is weak and infirm, especially one disabled or incapacitated by chronic ill health. — *adj.* **1** Not well; infirm; sickly. **2** Suited for a sick person; as, an *invalid* diet. — \-ˌlid\ *v.* **1** To make or become invalid. **2** To classify, or dismiss from duty, as an invalid; as, wounded soldiers *invalided* home during the war.

in·val·id \(ˈ)in-ˈval-əd\ *adj.* [From Latin *invalidus* meaning "weak".] Having no force or effect; not valid; as, a license that is *invalid* unless signed by the person to whom it was issued. — **in·va·lid·i·ty** \ˌin-və-ˈlid-ət-ē\ *n.*

in·val·i·date \(ˈ)in-ˈval-ə-ˌdāt\ *v.;* **in·val·i·dat·ed; in·val·i·dat·ing.** To weaken or destroy the effect or value of; to nullify; as, to *invalidate* one's ballot by not following voting instructions.

in·val·u·a·ble \in-ˈval-yəb-l, -yə-wəb-l\ *adj.* Having value too great to be estimated; priceless. — **in·val·u·a·bly** \-yə-blē, -yə-wə-blē\ *adv.*

in·var·i·a·ble\(ˈ)in-ˈver-ē-əb-l, -ˈvar-\ *adj.* Never changing; unchangeable.

in·var·i·a·bly \(ˈ)in-ˈver-ē-ə-blē, -ˈvar-\ *adv.* Without change or exception; always; as, a person who is *invariably* pleasant.

in·va·sion \in-ˈvāzh-n\ *n.* An invading; especially, the entrance of an army into a country to conquer or plunder it.

in·vec·tive \in-ˈvek-tiv\ *n.* Condemnation written or spoken in a harsh or bitter tone; as, to attack the opposing candidate with *invective.*

in·veigh \in-ˈvā\ *v.* To make an attack with bitter words; as, to *inveigh* against the speed laws.

in·vei·gle \in-'vāg-l, -'vēg-l\ *v.;* **in·vei·gled; in·vei·gling** \-l(-)ing\. To lead on by wheedling; to win over by flattery; to entice by alluring promises; as, to *inveigle* a customer into a shop.

in·vent \in-'vent\ *v.* **1** To create in the imagination; to make up; as, to *invent* a story; to *invent* an excuse. **2** To discover by experiment; to produce for the first time. Do you know who *invented* the phonograph?

in·ven·tion \in-'vench-n\ *n.* **1** The power of inventing; skill in creating something new; as, a poet with *invention.* **2** Something invented, as a mechanical device or appliance. **3** A creation of the imagination; a falsehood. **4** The act of inventing; as, before the *invention* of gunpowder. **5** A musical composition imitative in style, usually short, and usually written for the piano or other keyboard instrument.

in·ven·tive \in-'vent-iv\ *adj.* Gifted with the skill and imagination to invent; original; as, a person with an *inventive* mind; an *inventive* genius.

in·ven·tor \in-'vent-r\ *n.* A person who invents, especially new appliances or new ways of doing things.

in·ven·to·ry \'in-vən-ˌtōr-ē, -ˌtȯr-ē\ *n.; pl.* **in·ven·to·ries.** A list of goods or valuables, with their estimated worth. — *v.;* **in·ven·to·ried** \-ēd\; **in·ven·to·ry·ing.** To make an inventory.

in·verse \(')in-'vərs, 'in-ˌvərs\ *adj.* Inverted; reversed. The letters of the word "was" in *inverse* order spell "saw". — *n.* Something that is inverse. — **in·verse·ly,** *adv.*

in·ver·sion \in-'vərzh-n\ *n.* **1** The act of inverting or the state of being inverted. **2** Something that is inverted.

in·vert \in-'vərt\ *v.* **1** To turn in an opposite direction; to turn upside down or inside out. *Invert* a figure six and it looks like a nine. **2** To reverse the order or position of.

in·ver·te·brate \(')in-'vərt-ə-brət, -ˌbrāt\ *adj.* Without a backbone, or spinal column. — *n.* An animal without a backbone.

in·vest \in-'vest\ *v.* **1** To surround or clothe as if with a garment; as, to *invest* an agent with full power; to *invest* an incident with mystery. **2** To install with appropriate ceremony in an office. **3** To put money into property or into a business enterprise, for income or profit. **4** To surround with troops or ships so as to prevent escape or entry; to besiege; as, a town *invested* from all sides by the enemy.

in·ves·ti·gate \in-'ves-tə-ˌgāt\ *v.;* **in·ves·ti·gat·ed; in·ves·ti·gat·ing.** To search into by inquiry, observation, and study of facts; as, to *investigate* the cause of a fire. — **in·ves·ti·ga·tive** \-ˌgāt-iv\ *adj.* — **in·ves·ti·ga·tor** \-ˌgāt-r\ *n.*

in·ves·ti·ga·tion \in-ˌves-tə-'gāsh-n\ *n.* An investigating; thorough inquiry or research; as, the *investigation* of an accident.

in·ves·ti·ture \in-'ves-tə-ˌchu̇r\ *n.* **1** The action of investing a person, especially with the robes of office; as, the *investiture* of a bishop. **2** Clothing; apparel.

in·vest·ment \in-'ves(t)-mənt\ *n.* **1** An investing or being invested; investiture. **2** The investing of money for income or profit. **3** The sum of money invested. **4** The property in which money is invested. **5** The surrounding of a place with military forces; siege.

in·ves·tor \in-'vest-r\ *n.* A person who invests money for income or profit.

in·vet·er·ate \in-'vet-r-ət, -'ve-trət\ *adj.* **1** Firmly established by age or by being long continued; deep-rooted. **2** Habitual; as, an *inveterate* smoker. — **in·vet·er·ate·ly,** *adv.*

in·vid·i·ous \in-'vid-ē-əs\ *adj.* Tending to arouse dislike, ill will, or envy; especially, discriminating unfairly between two things; as, an *invidious* comparison. Continual faultfinding often becomes *invidious.* — **in·vid·i·ous·ly,** *adv.*

in·vig·o·rate \in-'vig-r-ˌāt\ *v.;* **in·vig·o·rat·ed; in·vig·o·rat·ing.** To give vigor or energy to; to strengthen; to refresh. — **in·vig·o·ra·tion** \in-ˌvig-r-'āsh-n\ *n.*

in·vin·ci·ble \in-'vin(t)s-əb-l\ *adj.* Incapable of being conquered, overcome, or subdued; as, an *invincible* determination; an army that proved itself *invincible.* — **in·vin·ci·bil·i·ty** \in-ˌvin(t)s-ə-'bil-ət-ē\ *n.* — **in·vin·ci·bly** \in-'vin(t)s-ə-blē\ *adv.*

in·vi·o·la·ble \(')in-'vī-ə-ləb-l\ *adj.* **1** Too sacred to be violated; as, an *inviolable* oath. **2** Incapable of being harmed or destroyed by violence. — **in·vi·o·la·bil·i·ty** \(ˌ)in-ˌvī-ə-lə-'bil-ət-ē\ *n.* — **in·vi·o·la·bly** \(')in-'vī-ə-lə-blē\ *adv.*

in·vi·o·late \(')in-'vī-ə-lət\ *adj.* Not violated. — **in·vi·o·late·ly,** *adv.*

in·vis·i·ble \(')in-'viz-əb-l\ *adj.* **1** Not capable of being seen; as, *invisible* to the naked eye. The sun is often *invisible* on a cloudy day. **2** Not clear or distinct; hard to detect; as, an *invisible* stripe in cloth; *invisible* mending. — **in·vis·i·bil·i·ty** \(ˌ)in-ˌviz-ə-'bil-ət-ē\ *n.* — **in·vis·i·bly** \(')in-'viz-ə-blē\ *adv.*

in·vi·ta·tion \ˌin-və-'tāsh-n\ *n.* **1** The act of inviting. **2** The written, printed, or spoken expression by which a person is invited.

in·vite \in-'vīt\ *v.;* **in·vit·ed; in·vit·ing.** **1** To ask a person to come as a guest, or to do or take part in something. **2** To request; to ask for; as, to *invite* suggestions. **3** To induce; to attract; to encourage; as, behavior that *invites* criticism; quiet that *invited* sleep. — \'in-ˌvīt\ *n.* An invitation.

in·vit·ing \in-'vīt-ing\ *adj.* Tempting; attractive; as, the *inviting* prospect of a week end at the beach. — **in·vit·ing·ly,** *adv.*

in·vo·ca·tion \ˌin-və-'kāsh-n\ *n.* **1** An invoking; especially, a prayer or appeal for a blessing or for aid, as at the beginning of a religious service. **2** A formula for summoning a devil or a spirit.

in·voice \'in-ˌvȯis\ *n.* **1** An itemized statement of goods sent to a purchaser with a bill for the amount due. **2** A shipment of goods sent with such a statement and bill. — *v.;* **in·voiced**; **in·voic·ing.** To make an invoice of.

in·voke \in-'vōk\ *v.;* **in·voked**; **in·vok·ing. 1** To call on for aid or protection; to ask earnestly, as in prayer; as, to *invoke* God's blessing; to *invoke* aid. **2** To call forth by magic; to conjure; as, to *invoke* spirits. **3** To appeal to, or call attention to, as an authority or for support; as, to *invoke* a little-known law.

in·vol·un·tary \(')in-'väl-ən-ˌter-ē\ *adj.* **1** Not made or done willingly or from choice; unwilling; as, an *involuntary* surrender. **2** Not under the control of the will; as, the *involuntary* twitching of a muscle. Hiccups are *involuntary.* — **in·vol·un·tar·i·ly** \(ˌ)in-ˌväl-ən-'ter-ə-lē\ *adv.*

in·volve \in-'välv\ *v.;* **in·volved**; **in·volv·ing. 1** To draw a person into something; to entangle; to envelop; as, to *involve* a friend in one's own troubles. **2** To make difficult; to complicate; as, an *involved* account or explanation. **3** To include. One problem frequently *involves* others. **4** To demand; to require. Fine work *involves* great care. **5** To absorb; to occupy; as, deeply *involved* in a game of chess. — **in·volve·ment** \-mənt\ *n.*

in·vul·ner·a·ble \(')in-'vəl-nər-əb-l, -nərb-l\ *adj.* Not capable of being wounded; secure against attack. — **in·vul·ner·a·bil·i·ty** \(ˌ)in-ˌvəl-nər-ə-'bil-ət-ē\ *n.* — **in·vul·ner·a·bly** \(')in-'vəl-nər-ə-blē, -nər-blē\ *adv.*

in·ward \'in-wərd\ *adv.* **1** Toward the inside; toward the center. **2** Into or toward one's mind; as, to turn one's thoughts *inward.* — *adj.* **1** Inner; as, *inward* parts. **2** In or from the mind or soul; as, an *inward* belief. **3** Going toward the center; as, the *inward* flow.

in·ward·ly \'in-wərd-lē\ *adv.* **1** In the inner parts; as, to bleed *inwardly.* **2** In the heart or mind; mentally; privately; as, to be *inwardly* certain. **3** Towards the center or inside; inward; as, curving *inwardly.*

in·wards \'in-rdz, 'in-wərdz\ *n. pl.* The bowels.

in·wards \'in-wərdz\ *adv.* Inward.

in·wo·ven \'in-ˌwōv-n\ *adj.* Woven in or together; as, *inwoven* strands.

in·wrought \'in-ˌrȯt\ *adj.* **1** Worked in among other things; inwoven in a fabric; as, an *inwrought* design. **2** Adorned; decorated; as, silver *inwrought* with gold.

io·dide \'ī-ə-ˌdīd, -dəd\ *n.* A compound of iodine with another element or radical.

io·dine \'ī-ə-ˌdīn, -əd-n, -ə-ˌdēn\ *n.* **1** An element found widely in sea water and seaweeds and having various uses in commerce and medicine. **2** A preparation of iodine in the form of a brown liquid (**tincture of iodine**) used as an antiseptic.

io·dize \'ī-ə-ˌdīz\ *v.;* **io·dized**; **io·diz·ing.** To treat with iodine or an iodide; as, *iodized* salt.

io·do·form \ī-'ōd-ə-ˌfȯrm\ *n.* A crystalline, volatile compound used as a healing and antiseptic dressing for wounds and sores.

ion \'ī-ən, 'ī-ˌän\ *n.* An atom, group of atoms, or particle smaller than an atom carrying a charge that is either positive or negative, a positively charged ion being known as a **cat·ion** \'kat-ˌī-ən, -ˌī-ˌän\ and a negatively charged one as an **an·ion** \'an-ˌī-ən, -ˌī-ˌän\.

-ion. A suffix that can mean: **1** The act or process of, as in *execution* or *construction.* **2** An instance of, a result of, as in *eruption* or *decoration.* **3** The condition of being, as in *perfection* or *subjection.*

ion·ic \ī-'än-ik\ *adj.* Of, relating to, or existing in the form of ions or an ion.

Ion·ic \ī-'än-ik\ *adj.* Belonging to a style of Greek architecture whose chief feature was the scroll-like decoration of the capital.

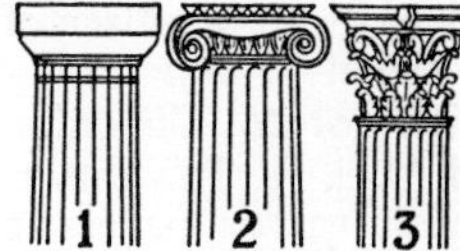

1 Doric capital, *2* Ionic capital, *3* Corinthian capital

ion·ize \'ī-ə-ˌnīz\ *v.;* **ion·ized**; **ion·iz·ing.** To convert wholly or partly into ions, as when a discharge of electricity or rays from radium pass through a gas or when an acid dissolves in water. — **ion·i·za·tion** \ˌī-ə-nə-'zāsh-n\ *n.* — **ion·iz·er** \'ī-ə-ˌnīz-r\ *n.*

ion·o·sphere \ī-'än-ə-ˌsfir\ *n.* The part of the earth's atmosphere beginning at an altitude of about 25 miles and extending outward 250 miles or more, containing free electrically charged particles by means of which radio waves are transmitted to great distances around the earth. — **ion·o·spher·ic** \ī-ˌän-ə-'sfir-ik, -'sfer-ik\ *adj.*

io·ta \ī-'ōt-ə\ *n.* [From Latin, there borrowed from Greek *iota,* the smallest letter of the Greek alphabet.] A tiny quantity or degree; as, a story that contained not an *iota* of truth.

I O U \'ī-ˌō-'yü\. [Abbreviated from *I owe you.*] A paper having on it the letters *I O U,* a specified sum, and a signature, given as evidence of debt.

I Q \'ī-'kyü\. Abbreviation for *intelligence quotient.*

ir-. A form of *in-* used before "r", as in *irradiate* or *irreverent.*

Ira·ni·an \i-'rā-nē-ən\ *adj.* Of or relating to Iran. — *n.* A native of Iran.

Iraqi \i-'räk-ē, i-'rak-ē\ *n.* **1** A native of Iraq. **2** The dialect of Arabic spoken in Iraq. — *adj.* Of or relating to Iraq.

Iraq·i·an \-ē-ən\ *adj.* Iraqi.

iras·ci·ble \i-'ras-əb-l, ī-'ras-\ *adj.* Easily angered; irritable. — **iras·ci·bil·i·ty** \i-ˌras-ə-'bil-ət-ē, (ˌ)ī-ˌras-\ *n.* — **iras·ci·bly** \i-'ras-ə-blē, ī-'ras-\ *adv.*

irate \ī-'rāt\ *adj.* Angry. — **irate·ly,** *adv.*

ire \'īr\ *n.* Anger; wrath. — *v.;* **ired**; **ir·ing.** To provoke ire; to anger; as, to be *ired* by the sales clerk's rude manner.

ire·ful \'īrf-l\ *adj.* Angry; wrathful. — **ire·ful·ly** \-l-ē\ *adv.*

ir·i·des·cence \ˌir-ə-'des-n(t)s\ *n.* A play or alternation of colors suggestive of a rainbow, as in a soap bubble or mother-of-pearl. — **ir·i·des·cent** \-nt\ *adj.* — **ir·i·des·cent·ly,** *adv.*

iris \'ī-rəs\ *n.; pl.* **iris·es** \-rə-səz\ or **ir·i·des** \'ir-ə-ˌdēz, 'ī-rə-\. [From Greek, meaning "circle of light or color", "iris", "rainbow".] **1** The colored part around the pupil of an eye. **2** A plant with swordlike leaves and flowers in six parts, three drooping and three upright.

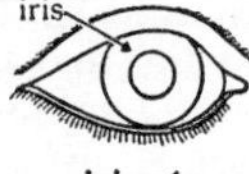

iris, 1

Irish \'ī-rish\ *adj.* Of or relating to Ireland, its people, or their speech. — *n.* **1** The Irish people — used as a plural with *the.* **2** The Celtic language of Ireland. **3** English as spoken in Ireland.

Irish·man \'ī-rish-mən\ *n.; pl.* **Irish·men** \-mən\. A native or a citizen of Ireland. — **Irish·wom·an** \-ˌwu̇m-ən\ *n.*

Irish potato. The ordinary white potato.

irk \'ərk\ *v.* To weary or trouble; to annoy. Carelessly written papers are likely to *irk* a teacher.

irk·some \'ərks-m\ *adj.* Tiresome; tedious; annoying; as, an *irksome* task. — **irk·some·ly,** *adv.*

iron \'īrn\ *n.* **1** A heavy, silver-white metal that rusts easily, is strongly attracted by magnets, and can be pressed or drawn into shape. **2** [usually in the plural] A chain of iron; a handcuff; as, to put a prisoner in *irons.* **3** Something, as a tool or instrument, made of iron; especially, an appliance, of iron or other metal, for pressing or smoothing cloth. — *adj.* **1** Made of iron; as, an *iron* fence. **2** Like iron in appearance or strength; as, an *iron* man; an *iron* will. — *v.* To smooth with a hot iron; as, to *iron* clothes. — **iron out.** To settle or solve satisfactorily; to reach an agreement on; to resolve; as, to *iron out* a problem; to *iron out* differences.

Iron Age. A period of human culture characterized by knowledge of iron and also by the use of brass implements, skill in pottery, and the use of domestic animals.

iron·clad \'īrn-ˌklad\ *adj.* **1** Covered with iron; as, an *ironclad* boat. **2** Very strict; as, an *ironclad* law. — *n.* An armored naval vessel.

iron curtain. A barrier or wall created by prohibition of free travel and by censorship, isolating a territory from outside contact and communication.

iron·i·cal \ī-'rän-ik-l\ or **iron·ic** \-ik\ *adj.* **1** Relating to or like irony; as, an *ironical* switch in a person's fortune. **2** Using irony; as, an *ironical* article attacking a political figure. — **iron·i·cal·ly** \-ik-l(-)ē\ *adv.*

iron lung. A boxlike device put around a person's chest to help him breathe by forcing air into and out of his lungs, as when the muscles do not work because of illness.

iron·mon·ger \'īrn-ˌməng-gr\ *n. Chiefly British.* A dealer in ironware or hardware. — **iron·mon·gery** \-gr(-)ē\ *n.*

iron·stone \'īrn-ˌstōn\ *n.* **1** Any hard, earthy ore of iron. **2** In full, **ironstone china.** A hard white pottery first made in England during the 18th century.

iron·ware \'īrn-ˌwar, -ˌwer\ *n.* Articles made of iron.

iron·weed \'īrn-ˌwēd\ *n.* A perennial weed of the thistle family, with heads of mostly red or purple tubular disk flowers in branched clusters.

iron·wood \'īrn-ˌwu̇d\ *n.* Any tree with strong, heavy wood or the wood itself.

iron·work \'īrn-ˌwərk\ *n.* **1** Work in iron; anything made of iron. **2** [in the plural] A building where iron is smelted or heavy iron or steel products are made — usually used as a singular. — **iron·work·er** \-ˌwərk-r\ *n.*

iro·ny \'ī-rə-nē\ *n.; pl.* **iro·nies.** **1** A kind of humor or sarcasm in which a person really means the opposite of what he says, as when words of praise are given but blame is meant. **2** An ironical utterance or expression. **3** A result contrary to what was expected; as, the *irony* of fate.

— The word *sarcasm* is a synonym of *irony: irony* generally refers to a manner of speaking or writing in which the meaning intended is the opposite of that apparently expressed, or to an often grimly humorous situation or state of affairs that is in some way the almost malicious opposite of what one expected, hoped for, or strove to bring about; *sarcasm* usually indicates a malicious sort of humor, often employing irony, intended to ridicule and hurt the person spoken to or spoken about.

ir·ra·di·ate \i-'rād-ē-ˌāt\ *v.;* **ir·ra·di·at·ed; ir·ra·di·at·ing.** **1** To throw rays of light on something; to illuminate; to brighten; to shine. **2** To radiate; to shed. **3** To treat by exposure to radiation, as of ultraviolet light. — **ir·ra·di·a·tion** \i-ˌrād-ē-'āsh-n\ *n.*

ir·ra·tion·al \(')i(r)-'rash-n(-)əl\ *adj.* **1** Without reasoning power. **2** Unreasonable; senseless; foolish; as, an *irrational* act; *irrational* fears. — **ir·ra·tion·al·ly** \-n(-)ə-lē\ *adv.* — **ir·ra·tion·al·i·ty** \(ˌ)i(r)-ˌrash-n-'al-ət-ē\ *n.*

irrational number. Any number that cannot be expressed as an integer or as the quotient of two integers — used especially of roots.

ir·re·claim·a·ble \ˌir-(r)ē-'klā-məb-l\ *adj.* Incapable of being reclaimed or reformed. — **ir·re·claim·a·bly** \-mə-blē\ *adv.*

ir·rec·on·cil·a·ble \(')i(r)-'rek-n-ˌsī-ləb-l\ *adj.* Not capable of being reconciled, adjusted, or pacified; as, *irreconcilable* enemies. — **ir·rec·on·cil·a·bly** \-ˌsī-lə-blē\ *adv.*

ir·re·cov·er·a·ble \ˌir-(r)ē-'kəv-r(-)əb-l\ *adj.* Not capable of being recovered, remedied, or regained. — **ir·re·cov·er·a·bly** \-r(-)ə-blē\ *adv.*

ir·re·deem·a·ble \ˌir-(r)ē-'dē-məb-l\ *adj.* **1** Not redeemable; especially, not convertible into gold or silver at the will of the holder; as, *irredeemable* paper money. **2** Beyond remedy; hopeless; as, *irredeemable* mistakes. — **ir·re·deem·a·bly** \-mə-blē\ *adv.*

ir·re·duc·i·ble \ˌir-(r)ē-'dü-səb-l, -'dyü-\ *adj.* Not reducible.

ir·re·fut·a·ble \ˌir-(r)ē-'fyüt-əb-l, (')i(r)-'ref-yət-əb-l\ *adj.* Not capable of being proved wrong; indisputable. — **ir·re·fut·a·bly** \-ə-blē\ *adv.*

ir·reg·u·lar \(')i(r)-'reg-yəl-r\ *adj.* **1** Not regular;

not according to rule, law, or custom; as, an *irregular* trial. **2** In grammar, not changing form according to the usual pattern to show change in meaning; strong. "Eat" is an *irregular* verb. **3** Not straight; uneven; not smooth; as, an *irregular* landscape. — **ir·reg·u·lar·ly**, *adv.*

ir·reg·u·lar·i·ty \(ˌ)i(r)-ˌreg-yə-'lar-ət-ē\ *n.; pl.* **ir·reg·u·lar·i·ties. 1** The condition of being irregular. **2** Something that is irregular.

ir·rel·e·vant \(')i(r)-'rel-ə-vənt\ *adj.* Not relevant; not applicable or to the point; foreign; as, an *irrelevant* remark. — **ir·rel·e·vance** \-vən(t)s\ or **ir·rel·e·van·cy** \-vən-sē\ *n.* — **ir·rel·e·vant·ly** \-vənt-lē\ *adv.*

ir·re·li·gious \ˌir-(r)ə-'lij-əs\ *adj.* Not religious. — **ir·re·li·gious·ly**, *adv.*

ir·re·me·di·a·ble \ˌir-(r)ē-'mēd-ē-əb-l\ *adj.* Not capable of being cured or remedied. — **ir·re·me·di·a·bly** \-ē-ə-blē\ *adv.*

ir·rep·a·ra·ble \(')i(r)-'rep-r(-)əb-l\ *adj.* Not capable of being repaired, recovered, regained, or remedied; as, an *irreparable* loss. — **ir·rep·a·ra·bly** \-r(-)ə-blē\ *adv.*

ir·re·place·a·ble \ˌir-(r)ē-'plā-səb-l\ *adj.* Not replaceable.

ir·re·press·i·ble \ˌir-(r)ē-'pres-əb-l\ *adj.* Not capable of being checked or held back; as, *irrepressible* laughter. — **ir·re·press·i·bil·i·ty** \-ˌpres-ə-'bil-ət-ē\ *n.* — **ir·re·press·i·bly** \-'pres-ə-blē\ *adv.*

ir·re·proach·a·ble \ˌir-(r)ē-'prō-chəb-l\ *adj.* Not reproachable; blameless. — **ir·re·proach·a·bly** \-chə-blē\ *adv.*

ir·re·sist·i·ble \ˌir-(r)ē-'zis-təb-l\ *adj.* Not to be resisted or opposed. — **ir·re·sist·i·bly** \-tə-blē\ *adv.*

ir·res·o·lute \(')i(r)-'rez-l-ˌüt\ *adj.* Not resolute; not decided or determined; wavering; hesitating; as, an *irresolute* answer. — **ir·res·o·lute·ly**, *adv.*

ir·res·o·lu·tion \(ˌ)i(r)-ˌrez-l-'üsh-n\ *n.* A lack of resolution; indecision.

ir·re·spec·tive of \ˌir-(r)ē-'spek-tiv əv\. Regardless of; without respect or regard to; as, *irrespective of* the differences between us.

ir·re·spec·tive·ly \ˌir-(r)ē-'spek-təv-lē\ *adv.* Without regard to other things; independently.

ir·re·spon·si·ble \ˌir-(r)ē-'spän(t)s-əb-l\ *adj.* **1** Not to be held responsible; as, an *irresponsible* child. **2** Having or showing little or no sense of responsibility; not trustworthy; as, an *irresponsible* employee, *irresponsible* behavior. — **ir·re·spon·si·bil·i·ty** \-ˌspän(t)s-ə-'bil-ət-ē\ *n.* — **ir·re·spon·si·bly** \-'spän(t)s-ə-blē\ *adv.*

ir·re·triev·a·ble \ˌir-(r)ē-'trē-vəb-l\ *adj.* Not capable of being recovered, regained, or remedied; as, an *irretrievable* mistake. — **ir·re·triev·a·bly** \-və-blē\ *adv.*

ir·rev·er·ence \(')i(r)-'rev-rn(t)s, -'rev-r(-)ən(t)s\ *n.* A lack of reverence; an irreverent act or utterance.

ir·rev·er·ent \(')i(r)-'rev-rnt, -'rev-r(-)ənt\ *adj.* Not reverent; not respectful. — **ir·rev·er·ent·ly**, *adv.*

ir·re·vers·i·ble \ˌir-(r)ē-'vər-səb-l\ *adj.* Incapable of being reversed. — **ir·re·vers·i·bly** \-sə-blē\ *adv.*

ir·rev·o·ca·ble \(')i(r)-'rev-ə-kəb-l\ *adj.* Not capable of being revoked or called back; final; as, an *irrevocable* decision. — **ir·rev·o·ca·bil·i·ty** \(ˌ)i(r)-ˌrev-ə-kə-'bil-ət-ē\ *n.* — **ir·rev·o·ca·bly** \(')i(r)-'rev-ə-kə-blē\ *adv.*

ir·ri·gate \'ir-ə-ˌgāt\ *v.;* **ir·ri·gat·ed; ir·ri·gat·ing. 1** To supply, as land or crops, with water by such means as canals, pipes, and flooding; to water. **2** To flush with a liquid, as a person's nose or ear. — **ir·ri·ga·tion** \ˌir-ə-'gāsh-n\ *n.*

ir·ri·ta·bil·i·ty \ˌir-ət-ə-'bil-ət-ē\ *n.; pl.* **ir·ri·ta·bil·i·ties. 1** The quality or state of being irritable; especially, the state in which one quickly becomes impatient or is quickly annoyed or angered. **2** The ability, as in living plants, animals, or cells, to respond to light, heat, and other stimuli, as by activity.

ir·ri·ta·ble \'ir-ət-əb-l\ *adj.* **1** Capable of being irritated; especially, easily angered or provoked; as, an *irritable* temper. **2** Easily upset; as, an *irritable* stomach. **3** In biology, responsive to stimuli, as a cell that moves away from heat. — **ir·ri·ta·bly** \-ə-blē\ *adv.*

ir·ri·tant \'ir-ə-tənt\ *adj.* Producing irritation or inflammation. — *n.* Something that irritates, excites, or produces irritation.

ir·ri·tate \'ir-ə-ˌtāt\ *v.;* **ir·ri·tat·ed; ir·ri·tat·ing. 1** To cause anger or impatience in; to annoy; to provoke. **2** To make unduly sensitive or sore; as, eyes *irritated* by smoke. **3** To stimulate; as, a muscle *irritated* to contract by the stimulus of heat.

— The words *exasperate* and *provoke* are synonyms of *irritate: irritate* usually suggests arousing annoyance and displeasure and a display of any feeling from momentary impatience to rage; *exasperate* may suggest such strong annoyance as to cause complete loss of temper, though often for only a short time; *provoke* may apply to irritating and annoying someone to such an extent as to incite him to immediate action.

ir·ri·tat·ing \'ir-ə-ˌtāt-ing\ *adj.* Provoking; causing displeasure. — **ir·ri·tat·ing·ly**, *adj.*

ir·ri·ta·tion \ˌir-ə-'tāsh-n\ *n.* **1** An irritating or a being irritated; as, to show *irritation* when pressed for an answer. **2** An oversensitiveness of an organ or part of the body.

ir·ri·ta·tive \'ir-ə-ˌtāt-iv\ *adj.* **1** Serving to irritate; irritating; as, an *irritative* agent. **2** Accompanied by irritation; produced by irritation; as, an *irritative* rash.

ir·rup·tion \i-'rəpsh-n\ *n.* A sudden, violent inrush; as, an *irruption* of water. — **ir·rup·tive** \i-'rəp-tiv\ *adj.*

is \(')iz, əz, z, s\. A form of the verb *be* showing present time and used with *he, she,* or *it* or with words for which these stand.

i's. Pl. of *i.*

is·chi·um \'is-kē-əm\ *n.; pl.* **is·chia** \-kē-ə\. The dorsal and posterior of the three principal bones composing either half of the pelvis. — **is·chi·al** \-kē-əl\ *adj.*

-ise. Variant of *-ize.*

-ish \ish\. A suffix that can mean: **1** Belonging to a stated nation, as in *Turkish.* **2** Of the nature of, characteristic of, as in *boyish* or *girlish.* **3** Having the bad qualities of, as in *childish.* **4** Suggestive of, resembling, as in *bookish.* **5** Somewhat, as in *whitish.*

isin·glass \'īz-n-ˌglas, 'ī-zing-ˌglas\ *n.* [An altered form (*-blas* being understood as English *glass*) of obsolete Dutch *huisenblas,* meaning literally "sturgeon's bladder".] **1** A pure gelatin from the air bladders of certain fishes. **2** Mica in thin sheets.

Is·lam \is-'läm, iz-, -'lam, -'lȧm, 'is-ˌ-, 'iz-ˌ-\ *n.* **1** The religion of the Moslems. **2** The whole body of Moslems or the countries they occupy. — **Is·lam·ic** \is-'läm-ik, iz-, -'lam-, -'lȧm-\ *adj.* — **Is·lam·ite** \'is-lə-ˌmīt, 'iz-\ *n.*

is·land \'ī-lənd\ *n.* **1** An area of land surrounded by water and smaller than a continent. **2** Anything suggestive of an island, as a safety zone in a street.

is·land·er \'ī-lənd-r\ *n.* A native or inhabitant of an island.

isle \'īl\ *n.* An island; a small island.

is·let \'ī-lət\ *n.* A little island.

islet of Lang·er·hans \'läng-r-ˌhän(t)s\. Any of the groups of small granular cells that secrete the hormone insulin and form the interlacing strands among the structures of the pancreas.

-ism \ˌiz-m\. A suffix that can mean: **1** The action of doing, as in *baptism.* **2** The manner or conduct that is characteristic of, as in *despotism* or *heroism.* **3** The condition of being, as in *barbarism* or *paganism.* **4** The belief or practice of, as in *realism* or *stoicism.* **5** An adherence or attachment to, as in *liberalism.* **6** A characteristic or peculiarity of expression, as in *colloquialism.* **7** An abnormal condition resulting from an excess of something, as in *alcoholism.*

ism \'iz-m\ *n.* A distinctive doctrine, ideal, system, or practice, especially when thought of disparagingly.

isn't \'iz-nt\. A contraction of *is not.*

iso·bar \'ī-sə-ˌbär, -ˌbȧr\ *n.* A line drawn on a map to indicate areas having the same atmospheric pressure at a given time or for a given period. — **iso·bar·ic** \ˌī-sə-'bar-ik\ *adj.*

iso·late \'īs-l-ˌāt, 'is-\ *v.;* **iso·lat·ed**; **iso·lat·ing.** To place or keep by itself; to separate; as, a town *isolated* by a blizzard; to *isolate* a person with a contagious disease. — **iso·la·tion** \ˌīs-l-'āsh-n, ˌis-\ *n.*

iso·la·tion·ism \ˌīs-l-'āsh-n-ˌiz-m, ˌis-l-\ *n.* The beliefs or practice of isolationists.

iso·la·tion·ist \ˌīs-l-'āsh-n-əst, ˌis-l-\ *n.* One who advocates isolation; especially, one who advocates a strictly followed national policy of not participating in alliances, engagements, or conflicts with other nations.

isos·ce·les \ī-'säs-l-ˌēz\ *adj.* Having two equal sides; as, an *isosceles* triangle.

iso·therm \'ī-sə-ˌthərm\ *n.* A line on a map joining points that have the same average temperature.

iso·tope \'ī-sə-ˌtōp, 'ī-zə-\ *n.* Any of the two or more forms of an element which differ slightly in weight and radioactivity.

Is·rae·li \iz-'rā-lē\ *adj.* Of or relating to the state of Israel. — *n.* An inhabitant of Israel.

Is·ra·el·ite \'iz-rē-ə-ˌlīt, -rə-ˌlīt\ *n.* A descendant of Israel, or Jacob; a Hebrew; a Jew.

is·su·ance \'ish-ə-wən(t)s\ *n.* The act of issuing or giving out; as, the *issuance* of an order.

is·sue \'ish-(ˌ)ü\ *n.* **1** A passing out; an exit; as, the *issue* of smoke from a chimney. **2** End; conclusion; outcome; as, the *issue* of a fight. **3** The act of sending out; delivery; as, the *issue* of an order. **4** Something sent out or delivered; as, one *issue* of a magazine. **5** A child or children; offspring; as, a man without *issue.* **6** A point in a debate or argument on which persons take opposite sides. — *v.;* **is·sued**; **is·su·ing. 1** To go, pass, or flow out; as, water *issuing* from a spring. **2** To result; to come as an effect; as, a quarrel that *issued* from a chance remark. **3** To give out officially; as, to *issue* a proclamation or an order. **4** To print and circulate; to publish; as, to *issue* a newspaper. **5** To give out, as for use; as, to *issue* winter uniforms.

-ist \əst\. A suffix that can mean: **1** One who does, one who makes a practice of, as in *theorist* or *bigamist.* **2** One who practices, as in *conversationalist.* **3** One particularly occupied with or skilled in, as in *physicist* or *humorist.* **4** One skilled in the use of, as in *organist* or *machinist.* **5** An advocate of; a supporter of, as in *socialist* or *atheist.*

isth·mus \'is-məs\ *n.; pl.* **isth·mus·es** \-mə-səz\ or **isth·mi** \-ˌmī\. A strip of land that connects two larger areas of land.

it \(')it, ət\ *pron.* **1** The act, thing, or matter mentioned before. **2** The state of affairs; things in general. *It* will go hard with him. — \'it\ *n.* In certain games, the player who has to catch the others.
☞ As a pronoun, *it* is used in special ways as the subject or object of verbs, as in "*It* snows", or "to foot *it* home".

Ital·ian \i-'tal-yən\ *adj.* Of or relating to Italy. — *n.* **1** A native or inhabitant of Italy. **2** The language of Italy.

ital·ic \i-'tal-ik, ī-'tal-\ *adj.* Referring to or having to do with type in which the letters slope up toward the right, as in *these words.* — *n.* **1** An italic letter. **2** [often in the plural] An italic type, or italic type in general. The last word in this sentence is printed in *italics.*

ital·i·cize \i-'tal-ə-ˌsīz, ī-'tal-\ *v.;* **ital·i·cized**; **ital·i·ciz·ing. 1** To print in italics. **2** To underline written letters or words with a single line.

itch \'ich\ *v.* **1** To have an uneasy sensation in the skin that arouses a desire to scratch. **2** To have a constant desire to do or say something; as, to be *itching* to ask a question. — *n.* **1** An itching contagious eruption of the skin. **2** A feeling in the skin like that caused by this eruption. **3** A constant, irritating desire; as, the *itch* to travel. — **itchy** \\'ich-ē\\ *adj.*

-ite \\ˌīt\\. A suffix that can mean: **1** A native or inhabitant of, as in *Israelite.* **2** A supporter or follower of, as in *laborite.* **3** An explosive or any of various other manufactured substances, as in *dynamite.* **4** A mineral or rock, as in *anthracite.*

item \\'īt-m\\ *n.* [From Latin, meaning "also", a word once frequently used in lists to introduce each new article, so that in time it came to mean "article".] **1** A separate part, as in a list or account; as, one *item* in a bill. **2** A piece of news or information; an article.

item·ize \\'īt-m-ˌīz\\ *v.;* **item·ized**; **item·iz·ing.** To state by items; as, to *itemize* one's expenses for the week.

it·er·ate \\'it-r-ˌāt\\ *v.;* **it·er·at·ed**; **it·er·at·ing.** To utter or do a second time or many times. — **it·er·a·tion** \\ˌit-r-'āsh-n\\ *n.* — **it·er·a·tive** \\'it-r-ˌāt-iv, -ət-iv\\ *adj.*

itin·er·ant \\ī-'tin-r-ənt, i-'tin-\\ *adj.* Wandering; as, an *itinerant* preacher.

itin·er·ary \\ī-'tin-r-ˌer-ē, i-'tin-\\ *adj.* Relating to a route, or journeying, or roads. — *n.; pl.* **itin·er·ar·ies. 1** A route followed during a journey. **2** A record of a journey. **3** A guidebook or an outline of a route.

-i·tion \\'ish-n\\. A suffix having the same meanings as *-ation.*

-i·tis \\'īt-əs\\. A suffix that can mean: an inflammatory disease, as in *bronchitis.*

its \\(ˌ)its, əts\\ *adj.* Of or belonging to it.

it's \\(ˌ)its, əts\\. A contraction of *it is* or *it has.*

it·self \\it-'self, ət-\\ *pron.* The form of the word *it* that is used to give emphasis or to show that the subject and object of a verb are the same thing; as, to shake the earth *itself.* The rabbit hid *itself.*

-i·ty \\ət-ē\\. A suffix that can mean: condition or quality, as in *acidity* or *felicity.*

-ive \\iv\\. A suffix that can mean: Having the nature or quality of, tending to, given to, as in *excessive, corrective.*

I've \\(')īv\\. A contraction of *I have.*

ivied \\'ī-vēd\\ *adj.* Overgrown with ivy.

ivo·ry \\'īv-r(-)ē\\ *n.; pl.* **ivo·ries. 1** The hard, creamy-white, bonelike substance of which elephant tusks are composed. **2** Any substance that is like ivory. **3** The color of ivory, a pale, creamy color or yellowed white. — *adj.* **1** Of or like ivory. **2** Of the color ivory.

ivy \\'ī-vē\\ *n.; pl.* **ivies. 1** Also **English ivy.** A climbing woody vine with evergreen leaves, small yellowish flowers, and black berries. **2** Any of various plants resembling the true ivy, as the Virginia creeper.

ivy, 1

-ize \\ˌīz\\. A suffix that can mean: **1** To subject to, as in *baptize* or *satirize.* **2** To make into, to cause to become, as in *dramatize, sterilize.* **3** To saturate, to combine with, to treat with, as in *oxidize, macadamize.*

j \\'jā\\ *n.; pl.* **j's** \\'jāz\\. The tenth letter of the alphabet.

jab \\'jab\\ *v.;* **jabbed**; **jab·bing.** To thrust quickly or abruptly, as with something sharp; to poke. — *n.* A jabbing; a poke.

jab·ber \\'jab-r\\ *v.;* **jab·bered**; **jab·ber·ing** \\-r(-)ing\\. To talk rapidly, indistinctly, or so as not to be understandable; to chatter. — *n.* Confused talk; chatter. — **jab·ber·er** \\'jab-r-r\\ *n.*

ja·bot \\zha-'bō, ja-'bō, 'zhab-ˌō, 'jab-ˌō\\ *n.* A ruffle or cascade, as of lace, that falls from the collar down the front of a dress or shirt.

jack \\'jak\\ *n.* [From the name *Jack,* which came to denote "man" in general and then various objects that do the work of men.] **1** [sometimes with a capital] An ordinary man; a fellow; a chap; as, a *jack* of all trades. **2** [often with a capital] A sailor. **3** The male of certain animals, as the donkey. **4** A jack rabbit. **5** A jackstone. **6** A device for turning a spit, as in roasting meat. **7** *Slang.* Money. **8** A bootjack. **9** The small ball used as a mark in the game of bowls. **10** Any one of the knaves in a pack of playing cards. **11** In electricity, a receptacle with connections to electric circuits, arranged for convenient plugging in. **12** A portable machine for exerting great pressure or for lifting a heavy body through a small distance. **13** A union jack. — *v.* **1** To move or lift by means of a jack; as, to *jack* up the front end of an automobile. **2** To raise; as, to *jack* up prices.

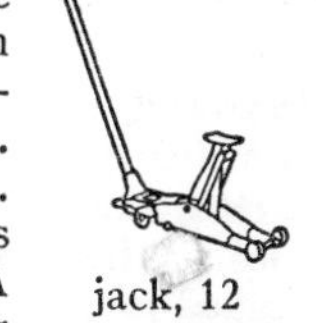

jack, 12

jack·al \\'jak-l, -ˌȯl\\ *n.* **1** A doglike wild animal that feeds on dead flesh and small animals. **2** One who slavishly performs servile or unpleasant work, often of a questionable nature, for another person.

jack·a·napes \\'jak-n-ˌāps\\ *n.* An impudent or conceited person.

jack·ass \\'jak-ˌas\\ *n.* **1** A male ass; a donkey. **2** A fool; a blockhead.

jack boot or **jack·boot** \\'jak-ˌbüt\\ *n.* A high boot reaching above the knee.

jack·daw \\'jak-ˌdȯ\\ *n.* A European bird somewhat like a crow.

jack·et \\'jak-ət\\ *n.* **1** A short coat. **2** A short coatlike garment, with or without sleeves. **3** A tough metal covering on a bullet or projectile. **4** A coating or covering of a nonconducting material used to prevent heat radiation. **5** A detachable outer paper wrapper on a bound book. **6** Any outer covering, as the skin of a potato.

jack-in-the-box \\'jak-n-t͟hə-ˌbäks\\ *n.* A child's

toy consisting of a box out of which a toy head springs when the lid is raised.

jack-in-the-pul·pit \'jak-n-t͟hə-'pu̇l-ˌpit, -'pəl-, -pət\ *n.* A plant that grows in moist shady woods and bears tiny yellowish flowers on a spike protected by a hoodlike leaf.

jack·knife \'jak-ˌnīf\ *n.; pl.* **jack·knives** \-ˌnīvz\. **1** A large pocketknife. **2** A fancy dive in which the diver, while in the air, assumes a position suggesting a slightly opened pocketknife. — *v.;* **jack-knifed; jack·knif·ing.** To double up like a jackknife.

jack-of-all-trades \ˌjak-əv-'ȯl-ˌtrādz\ *n.* A person who can do satisfactory work at many trades; a handy man.

jack-o'-lan·tern \'jak-l-ˌant-rn\ *n.* A lantern made of a pumpkin cut to look like a face.

jack·pot \'jak-ˌpät\ *n.* **1** In poker, a pot or pool that cannot be opened until a player has a pair of jacks or better. **2** A notable success or reward, often unexpected or unearned; as, to win the *jackpot.*

jack rab·bit \'jak ˌrab-ət\. A large hare of western North America with very long ears and long hind legs.

jack·screw \'jak-ˌskrü\ *n.* A jack using a screw for lifting or exerting pressure.

jack·stone \'jak-ˌstōn\ *n.* One of a set of five or six small metal pieces used in playing a game called **jack·stones** \-ˌstōnz\.

jack·straw \'jak-ˌstrȯ\ *n.* **1** One of a set of strips, as of wood, thrown in a heap in a game in which players attempt to remove a piece from the heap without disturbing other pieces. **2** [in the plural] The game played with these strips.

jade \'jād\ *n.* **1** A hard stone, commonly green, that takes a high polish and is used in making jewelry and other ornaments. **2** The color jade green.

jade \'jād\ *n.* **1** A horse; especially, a mean, tired, or worn-out horse. **2** A woman; especially, a disreputable woman. — *v.;* **jad·ed; jad·ing. 1** To tire or wear out from hard, tiresome work; to fatigue. **2** To dull; to surfeit. — **jad·ed** \'jād-əd\ *adj.*

jade green. A color varying from yellowish green to greenish yellow.

jag \'jag\ *n.* A sharp projecting part; as, a *jag* of rock. — *v.;* **jagged** \'jagd\; **jag·ging.** To make ragged; to notch.

jag \'jag\ *n.* **1** A small load, as of hay. **2** A drunken spree. — **to have a jag on.** *Slang.* To be drunk.

jag·ged \'jag-əd\ *adj.* Sharply notched; rough; as, a *jagged* edge. — **jag·ged·ly,** *adv.*

jag·uar \'jag-ˌwär, -ˌwȧr, -wər, 'jag-yə-\ *n.* A large brownish-yellow spotted animal of the cat family, having a larger head and thicker body than the puma, found from Texas to Paraguay.

jail \'jāl\ *n.* A building in which persons are kept as punishment or while they wait for a trial; a lockup; a prison. — *v.* To put or keep in a jail; to lock up a person.

jail·bird \'jāl-ˌbərd\ *n.* A prisoner in jail; one who has been in jail often or for a long time.

jail·er or **jail·or** \'jāl-r\ *n.* The keeper of a jail or prison.

ja·lopy or **ja·lop·py** \jə-'läp-ē\ *n.; pl.* **ja·lop·ies** or **ja·lop·pies.** A shabby old automobile or airplane.

jal·ou·sie \'jal-ə-sē\ *n.* A blind with slats sloping like louver boards to admit air and light and shut out rain and sun.

jam \'jam\ *v.;* **jammed; jam·ming. 1** To crowd, squeeze, or wedge; as, to *jam* one's cap into a pocket. **2** To push hard and suddenly into place; as, to *jam* a brake down; to *jam* one's hat on one's head. **3** To crush; to bruise; as, to *jam* one's finger in a door. **4** To cause to be wedged or stuck so as not to work; to fail to work as a result of becoming stuck; as, to *jam* a piece of machinery. The ejector of the rifle *jammed.* **5** To cause interference or confusion in radio or radar signals. — *n.* **1** A jamming. **2** A mass of people or objects crowded together; as, a traffic *jam;* a log *jam.*

jam \'jam\ *n.* A food made by boiling fruit with sugar until it is thick.

jamb or **jambe** \'jam\ *n.* An upright piece forming the side of an opening, as of a door.

jamb

jam·bo·ree \ˌjam-br-'ē\ *n.* **1** A noisy merrymaking. **2** A large gathering of boy scouts from different places.

jam session. A meeting of musicians for playing in impromptu style for their own entertainment.

Jan. Abbreviation for *January.*

jan·gle \'jang-gl\ *v.;* **jan·gled; jan·gling** \-gl(-)ing\. **1** To quarrel in words; to wrangle. **2** To sound discordantly; to cause to sound harshly, as bells out of tune. — *n.* **1** A noisy dispute. **2** A confused jingling; a discordant sound, as of bells.

jan·i·tor \'jan-ət-r\ *n.* **1** A doorkeeper; a porter. **2** A person who has the care of a building. — **jan-i·to·ri·al** \ˌjan-ə-'tōr-ē-əl, -'tȯr-\ *adj.*

jan·i·tress \'jan-ə-trəs\ *n.* A woman janitor.

Jan·u·ary \'jan-yə-ˌwer-ē\ *n.; pl.* **Jan·u·ar·ies.** [From medieval English, there borrowed from Latin *Januarius,* the first month of the ancient Roman year, derived from *Janus,* two-headed ancient Roman god of gates and doorways, thought of as presiding over the entrance of the new year.] The first month of the year, having 31 days.

ja·pan \jə-'pan\ *n.* **1** Any varnish giving a hard, glossy coating, as Japanese lacquer. **2** Varnished articles finished in the Japanese manner. — *adj.* Relating to or coated with japan. — *v.;* **ja·panned; ja·pan·ning.** To cover with japan; to lacquer.

Jap·a·nese \ˌjap-n-'ēz, -'ēs\ *adj.* Of or relating to Japan. — *n.* **1** *sing. and pl.* A native of Japan or a person descended from a native of Japan. **2** The language of Japan.

Japanese beetle. A stout-bodied green-and-brown beetle from Japan, the grubs of which feed on roots of grasses and the adults on foliage and fruits.

ja·pon·i·ca \jə-ˈpän-ik-ə\ *n.* The camellia.

jar \ˈjär, ˈjȧr\ *n.* **1** A broad-mouthed container of glass or earthenware. **2** Such a container and its contents; the contents of a jar; as, a *jar* of jam.

jar, 1

jar \ˈjär, ˈjȧr\ *v.; **jarred**; **jar·ring.*** **1** To make a harsh, grating sound; to make a discord. **2** To shake; as, to *jar* the table. **3** To affect with a harsh unpleasantness; as, a manner that *jars* on one; to *jar* the nerves. **4** To come into conflict; to clash; to quarrel; as, opinions that *jar*. — *n.* **1** A harsh sound; a rattle. **2** A jolt. **3** A quarrel; a dispute. **4** A painful effect; a shock, as to the nerves.

jar·di·niere \ˌjärd-n-ˈir, ˌjȧrd-\ *n.* An ornamental stand or pot for plants or flowers.

jar·gon \ˈjärg-n, ˈjȧrg-, -ˌän\ *n.* **1** Confused language; gibberish. **2** A speech or dialect resulting from a mixture of languages. **3** The special vocabulary of a science, art, sport, or trade; as, baseball *jargon*.

jas·mine \ˈjaz-mən\ *n.* An ornamental vine or shrub of the olive family cultivated for its fragrant white, yellow, or red flowers.

jas·per \ˈjasp-r\ *n.* **1** A cloudy stone, usually stained red, brown, or yellow, used for making vases and other ornamental objects. **2** A stone mentioned in the Bible, possibly dark green or opalescent.

ja·to unit \ˈjāt-ˌō\. [From the initial letters of *jet assisted take-off*.] A special rocket engine to help an airplane take off.

jaun·dice \ˈjȯn-dəs, ˈjän-\ *n.* **1** A disorder characterized by yellowness of the skin and eyeballs, owing to the presence of coloring matter from the bile. **2** A state of mind or point of view colored by jealousy, prejudice, or misfortune. — *v.;* **jaun·diced**; **jaun·dic·ing.** **1** To affect with jaundice. **2** To affect by prejudice or envy; as, *jaundiced* opinions.

jaunt \ˈjȯnt, ˈjänt\ *v.* To ramble here and there, especially for pleasure. — *n.* A short excursion for pleasure or recreation.

jaun·ty \ˈjȯnt-ē, ˈjänt-ē\ *adj.;* **jaun·ti·er**; **jaun·ti·est.** **1** Stylish; showy. **2** Gay and carefree; lively; as, a *jaunty* wave of the hand. — **jaun·ti·ly** \-l-ē\ *adv.*

Ja·va man \ˈjäv-ə, ˈjȧv-ə\. Pithecanthropus.

jav·elin \ˈjav-l(-)ən\ *n.* **1** A light spear. **2** A slender, metal-tipped, spearlike shaft of wood thrown for distance as an athletic feat.

jaw \ˈjȯ\ *n.* **1** The bony structure around the mouth, in which the teeth grow. **2** One of a pair of movable parts for holding or clamping; as, the *jaws* of a vise. **3** Anything suggesting an animal's jaw in form or action; mouth or entrance; as, the *jaws* of a mountain pass. — *v.* To scold.

jaw·bone \ˈjȯ-ˈbōn, -ˌbōn\ *n.* One of the bones of an animal's jaw, especially of the lower jaw.

jay \ˈjā\ *n.* A bird of the crow family, smaller and more graceful than a crow, and more brightly colored.

jay·walk \ˈjā-ˌwȯk\ *v.* To cross a street carelessly, paying no attention to traffic regulations. — **jay·walk·er**, *n.* — **jay·walk·ing**, *n.*

jazz \ˈjaz\ *n.* Music, especially dance music, marked by lively rhythms in which the accented notes often fall on beats that are not usually accented. — *adj.* Of, relating to, or characterized by jazz; as, a *jazz* band. — *v.* **1** To dance to or play jazz. **2** *Slang.* To make lively; as, to try to *jazz* up a dull evening.

jeal·ous \ˈjel-əs\ *adj.* **1** Demanding complete devotion. **2** Fearful or suspicious of a rival or competitor; feeling a spiteful envy toward someone more successful than oneself. **3** Suspicious that a person one loves is not faithful. **4** Watchful; careful; as, to be *jealous* of one's rights. — **jeal·ous·ly**, *adv.*

jeal·ousy \ˈjel-ə-sē\ *n.; pl.* **jeal·ous·ies.** The state of being jealous; ill feeling arising from distrust or envy of another. — For synonyms see *envy*.

jean \ˈjēn\ *n.; pl.* **jeans.** **1** A coarse heavy cotton cloth used especially for sportswear and work clothes. **2** [in the plural] Trousers or overalls, usually made of jean.

jeep \ˈjēp\ *n.* A small, powerful, general-purpose automobile developed for use by soldiers.

jeep

jeer \ˈjir\ *v.* To scoff at; to mock. — *n.* A rude or mocking speech or word. — **jeer·ing·ly**, *adv.*

je·june \jē-ˈjün\ *adj.* **1** Not nourishing. **2** Not satisfying; dull; as, a *jejune* story.

je·ju·num \jē-ˈjü-nəm\ *n.* The middle of the small intestine, between the duodenum and the ileum.

jel·ly \ˈjel-ē\ *n.; pl.* **jel·lies.** **1** A food that is soft, somewhat elastic, easily melted, and more or less transparent, made from fruit juice boiled with sugar, from meat juices, or from gelatin. **2** Any substance like jelly. — *v.;* **jel·lied** \-ēd\; **jel·ly·ing.** **1** To make into or become jelly. **2** To set in jelly; as, *jellied* tongue.

jel·ly·fish \ˈjel-ē-ˌfish\ *n.; pl.* **jel·ly·fish** \-ˌfish\ or **jel·ly·fish·es** \-ˌfish-əz\. A sea animal having a saucer-shaped body like jelly and no backbone.

jen·net \ˈjen-ət\ *n.* A small Spanish horse.

jen·ny \ˈjen-ē\ *n.; pl.* **jen·nies.** A female — often used with names of animals; as, *jenny* ass or *jenny* wren.

jeop·ard·ize \ˈjep-r-ˌdīz\ *v.;* **jeop·ard·ized**; **jeop·ard·iz·ing.** To expose to the danger of death, loss, or injury; to risk; as, to *jeopardize* the lives of brave men in battle; to *jeopardize* one's safety through carelessness.

jeop·ardy \ˈjep-r-dē\ *n.; pl.* **jeop·ard·ies.** Danger; peril; as, to put one's reputation in *jeopardy*.

jer·boa \jər-ˈbō-ə, jer-\ *n.* A nocturnal jumping rodent inhabiting arid regions of the Old World and having long hind legs, a long black-tipped tail, and a yellowish brown body with white underparts.

jerk \ˈjərk\ *v.* **1** To give a quick sharp pull or twist; to twitch; as, to *jerk* a rope. **2** To move with a jerk or with jerks; as, to *jerk* to attention; a car *jerking* to a stop. — *n.* **1** A short quick pull; a twitch. **2** A sudden involuntary muscular movement; a reflex; as, a knee *jerk*.

jerked \ˈjərkt\ *adj.* Cut into long strips and dried in the sun; as, *jerked* beef.

jer·kin \ˈjərk-n\ *n.* A jacket, usually close-fitting, either without sleeves or with extended shoulders.

jerky \ˈjərk-ē\ *adj.*; **jerk·i·er**; **jerk·i·est**. Moving by jerks or sudden starts and stops; as, a *jerky* bus. — **jerk·i·ly** \-l-ē\ *adv.*

jer·sey \ˈjər-zē\ *n.*; *pl.* **jer·seys**. [From *Jersey*, an island in the English Channel.] **1** A knitted fabric, usually of wool or cotton. **2** A knitted garment, especially a shirt or sweater.

jes·sa·mine \ˈjes-m-ən\ *n.* The jasmine.

jest \ˈjest\ *n.* **1** A joke. **2** Sport or fun; as, a truth spoken in *jest*. **3** An object of laughter; a butt of jokes. — *v.* To joke; to banter.

jest·er \ˈjest-r\ *n.* **1** A clown; a court fool. **2** A person given to jesting.

jet \ˈjet\ *n.* **1** A black coallike mineral used for beads, buttons, and other ornamental articles. **2** A deep shiny black color. — *adj.* **1** Made of jet. **2** Of the color of jet.

jet \ˈjet\ *n.* **1** A gush or sudden rush of liquid or gas through a narrow opening or nozzle; the liquid or gas that gushes forth. **2** A nozzle for the issue of gas, or liquid; as, a gas *jet*. **3** A jet airplane. — *v.*; **jet·ted**; **jet·ting**. To spurt; to gush out suddenly.

jet engine. An engine in which is produced a jet of gases and heated air that shoots out from the rear in a continuous stream.

jet plane or **jet airplane**. An airplane powered by a rearward jet from the engine, there being no propeller.

jet-pro·pelled \ˈjet-prə-ˈpeld\ *adj.* Driven by jet propulsion.

jet propulsion. The propelling of an airplane by means of engines that burn fuel inside of them and shoot air and hot gases rearward with the same kind of propelling force that drives an inflated toy balloon forward when air escapes through its neck.

jet plane

jet·sam \ˈjets-m\ *n.* Goods thrown overboard to lighten a vessel in distress; especially, such goods when washed ashore.

jet·ti·son \ˈjet-əs-n, -əz-n\ *n.* **1** The throwing overboard of goods, especially to lighten a boat in danger. **2** Jetsam. — *v.* **1** To throw goods overboard to lighten a boat in distress. **2** To cast away or aside; to discard.

jet·ty \ˈjet-ē\ *n.*; *pl.* **jet·ties**. **1** A pier built out into the water to influence the current or to protect a harbor. **2** A landing wharf.

Jew \ˈjü\ *n.* A descendant of the people who were led out of Egypt by Moses and who conquered Palestine in Biblical times. — **Jew·ish** \ˈjü-ish\ *adj.*

jew·el \ˈjü-əl\ *n.* **1** A costly ornament, as one of gold or silver set with precious stones, usually for personal wear. **2** A precious stone; a gem. **3** A bearing in a watch, formed of crystal or a precious stone. **4** A person or thing thought of as very precious. — *v.*; **jew·eled** or **jew·elled**; **jew·el·ing** or **jew·el·ling**. To dress, adorn, or supply with jewels, as a dress or watch.

jew·el·er or **jew·el·ler** \ˈjü-əl-r\ *n.* A person who makes or deals in jewelry.

jew·el·ry \ˈjü-əl-rē\ *n.* **1** The art or trade of a jeweler. **2** Jewels.

jew·fish \ˈjü-ˌfish\ *n.*; *pl.* **jew·fish** \-ˌfish\ or **jew·fish·es** \-ˌfish-əz\. A huge sluggish grouper of the sea-bass family, usually dusky green or brown and rough-scaled.

Jew·ry \ˈju̇r-ē, ˈjü-rē\ *n.*; *pl.* **Jew·ries**. **1** A district inhabited by Jews; a ghetto. **2** The Jewish people collectively.

jew's harp \ˈjüz ˌhärp, ˈjüs, ˌhȧrp\. A small musical instrument that, when placed between the teeth, gives tones from a bent metal tongue struck by the finger.

jib \ˈjib\ *n.* A three-cornered sail carried on a stay running from the bow to a point high on the foremast.

jibe \ˈjīb\ *v.*; **jibed**; **jib·ing**. **1** To shift suddenly from one side to the other, as a sail under certain conditions. **2** To change the course of a boat so that the sail jibes.

jibe \ˈjīb\ *v.*; **jibed**; **jib·ing**. To agree; as, two reports that *jibe*.

jibe \ˈjīb\. Variant of *gibe*.

jif·fy \ˈjif-ē\ *n.*; *pl.* **jif·fies**. A moment; an instant.

jig \ˈjig\ *v.*; **jigged**; **jig·ging**. **1** To sing, play, or dance as a jig. **2** To jerk up and down or to and fro. — *n.* **1** A lively springy dance in triple rhythm. **2** The music for such a dance. **3** A piece of sport; a trick — used especially in the phrase *The jig is up*, meaning "The game is ended" or "The time of reckoning has come". **4** Any of several devices used in fishing, as an imitation minnow made to be jerked through the water. **5** A hard steel device used to guide a tool, as a drill.

jig·ger \ˈjig-r\ *n.* **1** The chigoe. **2** The chigger.

jig·ger \ˈjig-r\ *n.* **1** One who jigs. **2** Any device; a contraption; a gadget. **3** A jig used in angling.

jig·gle \ˈjig-l\ *v.*; **jig·gled**; **jig·gling** \-l(-)ing\. To move with quick little jerks. — *n.* A light, jerky motion.

jig saw \ˈjig ˌsȯ\. A sawing machine used to cut curved and irregular lines or openwork patterns.

jig·saw puz·zle \ˈjig-ˌsȯ\. A puzzle made by sawing a picture into small pieces that may be fitted together.

jig saw

jilt \ˈjilt\ *v.* To cast aside someone,

as a lover, unfeelingly. — *n.* A person who jilts someone.

jim·my \'jim-ē\ *n.; pl.* **jim·mies.** A short crowbar used by burglars. — *v.;* **jim·mied** \-ēd\; **jim·my·ing.** To force open with or as if with a jimmy.

Jim·son weed \'jim(p)s-n\. A poisonous, bad-smelling weed of the potato family, with rank-smelling foliage and large white or violet trumpet-shaped flowers followed by prickly fruit.

jin·gle \'jing-gl\ *n.* **1** A sound as of metal striking lightly on metal. **2** A catchy repetition of sounds in a poem or a poem or verse having such sounds. — *v.;* **jin·gled; jin·gling** \-gl(-)ing\. **1** To make a light ringing sound; as, sleigh bells *jingling.* **2** To rhyme with a jingling effect. — **jin·gly** \'jing-gl(-)ē\ *adj.*

jin·go \'jing-,gō\ *n.; pl.* **jin·goes.** A person who favors a warlike policy in his country's relations with other countries.

jinn \'jin\ *n.* **1** Plural of *jinni.* **2** *pl.* **jinns.** A jinni.

jin·ni or **jin·nee** \ji-'nē\ *n.; pl.* **jinn** \'jin\. In Mohammedan belief, a good or evil creature made of flame and able to take any shape.

jin·rik·i·sha or **jin·rick·sha** \jin-'rik-,shȯ\ *n.* A small, two-wheeled covered carriage pulled by a man.

jinrikisha

jinx \'jingks\ *n.* A hoodoo.

jit·ney \'jit-nē\ *n.; pl.* **jit·neys.** *Slang.* **1** Five cents; a nickel. **2** An automobile that carries passengers for a small fare.

jit·ter·bug \'jit-r-,bəg\ *n.* A person who is intensely devoted to swing music and to dancing vigorously and with abandon to its rhythm. — *v.;* **jit·ter·bugged; jit·ter·bug·ging.** To play or dance to swing music.

jit·ters \'jit-rz\ *n. pl.* A feeling of extreme nervousness. — **jit·tery** \'jit-r-ē\ *adj.*

jiujitsu or **jiujutsu.** Variant of *jujitsu.*

jive \'jīv\ *n.* **1** The jargon peculiar to swing musicians and jitterbugs. **2** Any similar vocabulary of slang terms. **3** Swing music. **4** Jitterbug dance steps. — *v.;* **jived; jiv·ing. 1** To play swing music. **2** To jitterbug.

jo \'jō\ *n.; pl.* **joes.** *Scottish.* Sweetheart; darling.

job \'jäb\ *n.* **1** A piece of work, especially one done for a fixed price for the whole task. **2** A duty; a responsibility; as, to have the *job* of keeping the grass cut. **3** Work; employment; a position; as, a part-time *job.* — *adj.* Done by the job or piece; as, *job* work.

job·ber \'jäb-r\ *n.* **1** A person who buys goods and then sells them to other dealers; a middleman. **2** A person who does work by the job.

job lot. 1 A miscellaneous collection of goods for sale as a lot, usually to a retailer. **2** Any miscellaneous collection, usually of inferior quality.

jock·ey \'jäk-ē\ *n.; pl.* **jock·eys.** [From a Scottish form of the name *Jacky* — see *jack.*] A person who rides horses in races, especially as an occupation. — *v.;* **jock·eyed; jock·ey·ing. 1** To move or manage with skill, so as to obtain an advantage; as, sailboats *jockeying* for a favorable position in a race. **2** To outwit; to trick; to cheat; as, to *jockey* an old lady out of her life's savings. **3** To ride a horse as a jockey.

jo·cose \jō-'kōs\ *adj.* Merry; joking. — **jo·cose·ly,** *adv.*

joc·u·lar \'jäk-yəl-r\ *adj.* **1** Inclined to joke. **2** Said or done jokingly; sportive. — **joc·u·lar·ly** \'jäk-yəl-r-lē\ *adv.*

joc·u·lar·i·ty \,jäk-yə-'lar-ət-ē\ *n.; pl.* **joc·u·lar·i·ties. 1** Jocular quality. **2** A jocular remark.

joc·und \'jäk-nd, 'jōk-\ *adj.* Merry; cheerful; gay. — **joc·und·ly,** *adv.*

jodh·purs \'jäd-pərz\ *n. pl.* Riding breeches loose above the knee and tight-fitting below.

jog \'jäg\ *v.;* **jogged; jog·ging. 1** To push or shake a person in order to catch his attention; to jostle; to nudge. **2** To remind; as, to *jog* one's memory. **3** To move at a slow, jolting pace. — *n.* **1** A slight shake, push or jolt. **2** A slow, jolting pace; as, at a tired *jog.* **3** A part in a wall or line that sticks out or goes in; as, a *jog* in a building.

jog·gle \'jäg-l\ *v.;* **jog·gled; jog·gling** \-l(-)ing\. To shake slightly; to jog. — *n.* A jog.

John Doe \'jän 'dō\. A fictitious name for a party, real or fictitious, to any business or legal transaction.

john·ny·cake \'jän-ē-,kāk\ *n.* A bread made with corn meal, flour, eggs, and milk.

John·ny–jump–up \'jän-ē-'jəmp-,əp\ *n.* **1** A small-flowered pansy, as the wild pansy. **2** Any of several violets, as a bird's-foot violet.

join \'jȯin\ *v.* **1** To connect physically; to fasten or put together; as, to *join* the two ends of a rope; to *join* hands. **2** To unite by marriage. **3** To come together so as to be connected; as, the point where the roads *joined.* **4** To become a member of a group or organization; as, to *join* a hiking club. **5** To engage with others in an activity; as, to *join* in singing the national anthem. **6** To come into the presence of; as, to *join* a friend for lunch. **7** To adjoin; as, the field which *joins* this one.

join·er \'jȯin-r\ *n.* **1** One that joins. **2** A woodworker who finishes such things as doors, windows, and stairs.

joint \'jȯint\ *n.* **1** A part of an animal's body where two bones are joined, especially so as to allow motion; as, the *joint* at the knee. **2** A part in a plant where branches form; a node. **3** A point at which one part is joined to another; as, a *joint* in a water pipe. **4** The part between one joint and another; as, the upper *joint* of the arm. **5** A large piece of meat cut for roasting. — *adj.* **1** United; combined; as, a *joint* effort on the part of everybody. **2** Done by, shared, or having to do with two or more persons; as, a *joint* account in a bank. **3** Sharing with another; as, *joint* owner. — *v.* **1** To fit together. **2** To divide into joints; as, to *joint* meat. **3** To provide with a joint or joints.

joint·ly \'jȯint-lē\ *adv.* In a joint manner; together; as, owned *jointly* by husband and wife.

joist \\'jȯist\\ *n.* A small wood or metal beam laid crosswise in a building, as for supporting a floor.

floorboards

joists

joke \\'jōk\\ *n.* **1** Something said or done to draw a laugh; a jest. **2** Something done for fun, or without serious purpose. **3** An object of jokes; a laughingstock. — *v.;* **joked; jok·ing.** To make jokes; to jest. — **jok·ing·ly** \\'jōk-ing-lē\\ *adv.*

jok·er \\'jōk-r\\ *n.* **1** A person who jokes. **2** A part, as of an agreement, meaning something quite different from what it seems to mean and changing the apparent intention of the whole. **3** An extra card used in some card games.

jol·li·fi·ca·tion \\ˌjäl-ə-fə-'kāsh-n\\ *n.* A gay celebration; a party.

jol·li·ty \\'jäl-ət-ē\\ *n.; pl.* **jol·li·ties.** Gaiety; merriment.

jol·ly \\'jäl-ē\\ *adj.;* **jol·li·er; jol·li·est. 1** Full of life and laughter; full of fun; merry; as, a *jolly* old fellow. **2** Pleasant; agreeable; as, a *jolly* fire; *jolly* weather. — **jol·li·ly** \\'jäl-ə-lē\\ *adv.*

jolt \\'jōlt\\ *v.* To shake with short up-and-down movements, as a car moving along a rough road; to jar; to shake up. — *n.* A knock or blow; a sudden shock or jerk; a jolting or jerking motion.

jon·quil \\'jän(g)-kwəl\\ *n.* A plant with sword-shaped leaves and fragrant yellow or white flowers.

jonquil

Jor·da·ni·an \\jȯr-'dā-nē-ən\\ *n.* A native of Jordan. — *adj.* Of or relating to Jordan or its people.

Josh·ua tree \\'jäsh-ə-wə\\. A branched yucca of the southwestern United States, often 25 feet high, with short leaves and clustered greenish-white flowers.

jos·tle \\'jäs-l\\ *v.;* **jos·tled; jos·tling** \\-l(-)ing\\. To run or knock against so as to jar; to push roughly; to elbow; as, to be *jostled* by a crowd. — *n.* A crowding or bumping together; a jar.

jot \\'jät\\ *n.* The smallest particle; as, a tale with not a *jot* of truth in it. — *v.;* **jot·ted; jot·ting.** To make a note of; as, to *jot* down a telephone number.

jounce \\'jaủn(t)s\\ *v.;* **jounced; jounc·ing.** To jolt. — *n.* A jolt.

jour·nal \\'jərn-l\\ *n.* **1** A day-by-day record of things that happen; a diary. **2** A daily record, as of the acts of a lawmaking body or of business transactions. **3** A daily newspaper; a periodical; a magazine. **4** The part of a rotating shaft, axle, or spindle which turns in a bearing.

jour·nal·ism \\'jərn-l-ˌiz-m\\ *n.* The business of writing for, editing, or publishing newspapers or other periodicals.

jour·nal·ist \\'jərn-l-əst\\ *n.* An editor of, or writer for, a newspaper or other periodical.

jour·nal·is·tic \\ˌjərn-l-'is-tik\\ *adj.* Characteristic of journalism or journalists.

jour·ney \\'jər-nē\\ *n.; pl.* **jour·neys.** Travel from one place to another; a trip; as, a *journey* around the world; a day's *journey.*

— The words *trip* and *tour* are synonyms of *journey: journey* is a rather general term for a traveling from one place to another and carries no real implication of duration or distance or of the method of transportation; *trip* usually suggests a relatively short and direct journey, especially one taken for business or pleasure; *tour* is likely to indicate a leisurely and roundabout journey from place to place often without a definite route but ending back at the starting point and taken usually for pleasure.

— *v.;* **jour·neyed; jour·ney·ing.** To travel from place to place.

jour·ney·man \\'jər-nē-mən\\ *n.; pl.* **jour·ney·men** \\-mən\\. A worker who has learned a trade and works for another person, usually by the day.

joust \\'jaủst, 'jəst\\ *n.* A combat on horseback between two knights with lances. — *v.* To engage in a joust; to tilt.

jo·vi·al \\'jō-vē-əl, 'jōv-yəl\\ *adj.* Jolly; merry; full of fun. — **jo·vi·al·ly** \\'jō-vē-ə-lē, 'jōv-yə-lē\\ *adv.*

jo·vi·al·i·ty \\ˌjō-vē-'al-ət-ē\\ *n.* The quality or state of being jovial; jollity.

jowl \\'jaủl, 'jōl\\ *n.* **1** The jaw, especially the under jaw. **2** The cheek.

joy \\'jȯi\\ *v.* To take great pleasure in; to delight; to rejoice; as, to *joy* in the good fortune of a friend. — *n.* **1** A feeling of great pleasure or happiness such as comes from success, good fortune, or a sense of well-being; gladness. **2** Something that gives great pleasure or happiness; as, a *joy* to behold; a child who is a constant *joy* to his parents.

joy·ful \\'jȯif-l\\ *adj.* Filled with joy; having or causing joy; as, a *joyful* shout; *joyful* news. — **joy·ful·ly** \\'jȯif-l-ē\\ *adv.*

joy·less \\'jȯi-ləs\\ *adj.* Not having or causing joy.

joy·ous \\'jȯi-əs\\ *adj.* Glad; merry; joyful; causing joy; as, a *joyous* occasion. — **joy·ous·ly,** *adv.*

Jr. or **jr.** Abbreviation for *junior.*

j's. Pl. of *j.*

ju·bi·lant \\'jüb-l-ənt\\ *adj.* Noisily happy; showing great joy; exultant. — **ju·bi·lant·ly,** *adv.*

ju·bi·la·tion \\ˌjüb-l-'āsh-n\\ *n.* Rejoicing.

ju·bi·lee \\'jüb-l-ˌē, ˌjüb-l-'ē\\ *n.* **1** An anniversary, usually the 50th or 25th, of some event, or its celebration. **2** A period or an occasion of general joy and rejoicing; as, a *jubilee* to celebrate a victory. **3** Rejoicing; exultation.

Ju·da·ism \\'jüd-ə-ˌiz-m, 'jüd-ē-\\ *n.* **1** The religion of the Jews. **2** The practice of the Jewish ceremonies and customs.

judge \\'jəj\\ *n.* **1** A public officer having authority to decide questions brought before a court. **2** A person appointed to decide between two or more persons in a contest; an umpire. **3** A person having sufficient knowledge to decide on the value of something; as, a *judge* of paintings; a *judge* of cattle. — *v.;* **judged; judg·ing. 1** To hear and decide a case in court as a judge; to pass judgment on.

2 To reach a conclusion; to decide. 3 To criticize; as, to *judge* a person unkindly.

judg·ment or **judge·ment** \'jəj-mənt\ *n.* 1 The act of judging. 2 A decision or opinion given after judging. 3 The decision or sentence of a court. 4 Opinion. In his owner's *judgment* the dog would be a winner in the show. 5 The power of deciding wisely; as, a man of *judgment.*

ju·di·cial \jü-'dish-l\ *adj.* 1 Having to do with the courts or with judges. 2 Apt to form judgments and make decisions; critical; as, to take a *judicial* attitude. — **ju·di·cial·ly** \-'dish-l-ē\ *adv.*

ju·di·ci·ary \jü-'dish-ē-ˌer-ē, -'dish-r-ē\ *n.* 1 The branch of the government that has to do with courts of justice; the system of courts of justice. 2 The judges of the courts, considered as a body. — *adj.* Having to do with courts of justice, judges, or judicial methods; judicial.

ju·di·cious \jü-'dish-əs\ *adj.* Directed or governed by sound judgment; wise; as, a *judicious* course of action. — **ju·di·cious·ly,** *adv.*

ju·do \'jüd-ˌō\ *n.* The Japanese art of defending oneself by grasping or striking an opponent so that his own strength and weight are used against him.

jug \'jəg\ *n.* 1 A large earthenware container with a narrow mouth and a handle. 2 *Slang.* A jail. — *v.;* **jugged; jug·ging.** *Slang.* To put in jail.

jug, 1

jug·gle \'jəg-l\ *v.;* **jug·gled; jug·gling** \-l(-)ing\. 1 To perform the tricks of a juggler; especially, to throw into the air and catch a number of objects in rapid succession and according to a definite pattern. 2 To mix up things so as to trick or deceive; as, to *juggle* the figures in an account.

jug·gler \'jəg-lər\ *n.* 1 A person who entertains people by performing tricks requiring great skill with the hands. 2 A deceiver; a trickster.

jug·glery \'jəg-lər-ē\ *n.; pl.* **jug·gler·ies.** 1 The art or action of a juggler; sleight of hand. 2 Trickery.

Jugoslav. Variant of *Yugoslav.*

jug·u·lar \'jəg-yəl-r, 'jüg-\ *adj.* 1 Of or relating to the throat or neck. 2 Of or relating to the jugular vein. — *n.* One of the large veins (**jugular vein**) returning the blood from the head.

juice \'jüs\ *n.* 1 The liquid part that can be squeezed out of vegetables and fruits. 2 The fluid part of meat. 3 A medium, as electricity or gasoline, that supplies power.

juicy \'jü-sē\ *adj.;* **juic·i·er; juic·i·est.** 1 Having much juice. 2 Rich in interest; especially, racy. — **juic·i·ly** \'jüs-l-ē\ *adv.*

ju·jit·su or **jiu·jit·su** \jü-'jit-ˌsü\ or **jiu·jut·su** \jü-'jüt-ˌsü\ *n.* Judo.

juke·box \'jük-ˌbäks\ *n.* A cabinet containing an automatic player of phonograph records, any one of which may be played by depositing a coin in a slot.

ju·lep \'jü-ləp\ *n.* A beverage of brandy or whiskey with sugar, ice, and sprigs of mint.

Ju·ly \jü-'lī, jə-\ *n.; pl.* **Ju·lies.** [From medieval English *Julie,* there borrowed from Old French (as written and spoken in England) *Julie,* there derived from Latin *Julius,* the seventh month of the Roman year, named for Gaius *Julius* Caesar, who was born in this month.] The seventh month in the year, having 31 days.

jum·ble \'jəm-bl\ *v.;* **jum·bled; jum·bling** \-bl(-)ing\. To mix in a confused mass. — *n.* A disorderly mass or pile; as, a *jumble* of books and papers.

jum·bo \'jəm-ˌbō\ *n.; pl.* **jum·bos.** A big clumsy thing, animal, or person. — *adj.* Huge for a thing of its kind; as, *jumbo* peanuts.

jump \'jəmp\ *v.* 1 To spring into the air; to leap. 2 To rise sharply or suddenly. Prices *jumped.* 3 In checkers, to move over a square occupied by an opponent's man, capturing the man. 4 To leap over; as, to *jump* a ditch. 5 To come down upon and seize; as, to *jump* a mining claim. 6 To cause to leap or spring; as, to *jump* a horse over a hurdle. 7 To leap aboard; as, to *jump* a train. 8 To leave as if by a leap. The engine *jumped* the track. 9 To raise sharply or suddenly; as, to *jump* the price of gasoline. 10 To give a sudden movement; to start. — *n.* 1 A leap. 2 A sudden rise as if by a leap; as, a *jump* in price. 3 A distance passed over in a leap; as, to make a *jump* of six feet. 4 An advantage at the start, as in a race. 5 In checkers, a move made by jumping. 6 In athletic games, any contest featuring a leap; as, the high *jump.* 7 A sudden movement as if from fright; a start. — **jump·er** \'jəmp-r\ *n.*

jump·er \'jəmp-r\ *n.* 1 A loose blouse or jacket sometimes worn by workmen. 2 A sleeveless one-piece dress with or without a collar, usually worn over a blouse. 3 [in the plural] Rompers.

jumper, 2

jump·ing bean \'jəmp-ing 'bēn\. A seed of any of certain Mexican shrubs that tumbles about because of the movements of the larva of a small moth inside it.

jump·ing jack \ˌjak\. A toy figure of a man, jointed and made to jump or dance by means of strings.

jumpy \'jəmp-ē\ *adj.;* **jump·i·er; jump·i·est.** Nervous; irritable.

jun·co \'jəng-ˌkō\ *n.; pl.* **jun·cos** or **jun·coes.** A small pink-billed American finch with white feathers along the edges of the tail, as the **slate-col·ored junco,** or snowbird.

junc·tion \'jəng(k)sh-n\ *n.* 1 A joining or a being joined. 2 A place or point of meeting; as, a railroad *junction.*

junc·ture \'jəng(k)-chər\ *n.* 1 A joining; junction. 2 A joint; a connection; a seam; as, the *juncture* between two pieces of metal welded together. 3 A critical point of time; a combination of circumstances; a crisis.

June \'jün\ *n.* [From medieval English *June,* there

borrowed from Old French *juin,* there derived from Latin *Junius,* the sixth month of the Roman year.] The sixth month of the year, having 30 days.

June beetle or **June bug. 1** A large brown beetle that begins to fly about the first of June. **2** A large beetle of the southern United States that feeds on flowers.

jun·gle \'jəng-gl\ *n.* A thick or tangled growth of vegetation; a tract of land, especially in a tropical region, covered with such a growth.

jun·ior \'jün-yər\ *adj.* **1** Younger — used chiefly to indicate a son having the same name as his father. **2** Lower in standing or rank; as, a *junior* partner. **3** Composed of juniors; of or relating to juniors or the class containing the juniors; as, the *junior* class in school. — *n.* **1** A younger person. **2** A person lower in standing or rank. **3** A student in the third year of a four-year course of study.

junior high school. A school attended between the elementary school and the high school, usually including the seventh and eighth grades and the first year of high school.

ju·ni·per \'jü-nəp-r\ *n.* A low evergreen shrub or slender tree of the pine family, having blue berry-like fruit, as the common red cedar.

junk \'jəngk\ *n.* A type of sailing vessel common in China.

junk \'jəngk\ *n.* **1** Waste, such as old iron or paper; discarded articles; rubbish; trash. **2** Hard, salted beef served to sailors on shipboard. — *v.* To discard as worthless.

jun·ket \'jəngk-ət\ *n.* **1** A flavored sweetened milk jelly. **2** A feast; a banquet. **3** A trip or excursion at public expense. — *v.* **1** To feast; to banquet. **2** To go on an outing or excursion at public expense.

jun·ta \'hùn-tə, 'hün-tə, 'jənt-ə\ *n.* **1** A council, court, or committee for legislative or administrative purposes, as in Spain. **2** A junto.

jun·to \'jən-ˌtō\ *n.; pl.* **jun·tos.** A group of persons joined for a common purpose, as a political plot.

ju·ris·dic·tion \ˌjùr-əs-'diksh-n\ *n.* **1** The power and right to interpret and apply the law; as, the *jurisdiction* of the courts. **2** The authority of a sovereign; control. **3** The territory or limits within which authority may be exercised.

ju·ris·pru·dence \ˌjùr-əs-'prüd-n(t)s\ *n.* **1** The science that studies and explains law. **2** A system of laws. **3** A department of law.

ju·rist \'jùr-əst\ *n.* One having a thorough knowledge of law.

ju·ris·tic \jù-'ris-tik\ *adj.* **1** Of or relating to a jurist or to jurisprudence. **2** Relating to or recognized by law; legal.

ju·ror \'jùr-r, -ˌòr\ *n.* A member of a jury.

ju·ry \'jùr-ē\ *n.; pl.* **ju·ries. 1** A body of persons sworn to inquire into and test any question of fact, and to give their true answer, or verdict, according to the evidence presented before a court. **2** A committee that judges and awards prizes at exhibitions or contests.

ju·ry·man \'jùr-ē-mən\ *n.; pl.* **ju·ry·men** \-mən\. A juror.

just \'jəst\ *adj.* **1** Fair, impartial; as, a *just* punishment. **2** Lawful; legally right; as, a *just* claim. **3** Reasonable; well-founded; as, a *just* suspicion. **4** Exact; accurate; as, a *just* weight. — \(')jəst, (')jist, (')jest\ *adv.* **1** Exactly; precisely; as, *just* right. **2** Very recently; only a moment ago. The bell *just* rang. **3** By a very small space or a very short time; barely; as, *just* too late. The driver *just* managed to avoid an accident. **4** Simply; quite; as, *just* fine.

jus·tice \'jəs-təs\ *n.* **1** Just or righteous action, management, or treatment; deserved reward or punishment. **2** A judge. **3** The carrying out of law; as, a court of *justice.* **4** Rightfulness; as, the *justice* of a complaint.

justice of the peace. A local official authorized to try minor legal cases, and also to administer oaths and perform marriages.

jus·ti·fi·a·ble \'jəs-tə-ˌfī-əb-l\ *adj.* Capable of being justified, or shown to be just and fair. — **jus·ti·fi·a·bly** \-ə-blē\ *adv.*

jus·ti·fi·ca·tion \ˌjəs-tə-fə-'kāsh-n\ *n.* **1** The act of justifying or the state of being justified. **2** Something that justifies; a defense.

jus·ti·fy \'jəs-tə-ˌfī\ *v.;* **jus·ti·fied** \-ˌfīd\; **jus·ti·fy·ing. 1** To prove or show to be just, right, or reasonable; as, an act *justified* by the result. **2** To pronounce free from guilt or blame.

just·ly \'jəst-lē\ *adv.* In a just manner.

jut \'jət\ *v.;* **jut·ted; jut·ting.** To stick out, or up, or forward; to project; as, a rock *jutting* out.

jute \'jüt\ *n.* The fiber of a tropical plant, widely used for making sacks and string.

ju·ve·nile \'jüv-n-ˌīl, -n-əl, -n-ˌil\ *adj.* Young; immature; of or for young people. — *n.* **1** A young person. **2** An actor who plays youthful parts. **3** A book written for young people.

jux·ta·pose \'jəks-tə-ˌpōz\ *v.;* **jux·ta·posed; jux·ta·pos·ing.** To place side by side.

jux·ta·po·si·tion \ˌjəks-tə-pə-'zish-n\ *n.* A placing or being placed side by side.

k \'kā\ *n.; pl.* **k's** \'kāz\. The eleventh letter of the alphabet.

k *k* K *k* *K*

kai·ser \'kīz-r\ *n.* [From German, there borrowed from Latin *caesar.*] An emperor or monarch; especially, the emperor of Germany — used as a title.

kale \'kāl\ *n.* A hardy type of cabbage with wrinkled, loosely headed leaves.

ka·lei·do·scope \kə-'līd-ə-ˌskōp\ *n.* **1** A device containing loose bits of colored glass between two flat plates, and mirrors so placed that any change of position of the bits of glass is reflected in an endless variety of patterns. **2** Any changing pattern or scene. — **ka·lei·do·scop·ic** \kə-ˌlīd-ə-'skäp-ik\ *adj.*

kan·ga·roo \ˌkang-gr-'ü\ *n.; pl.* **kan·ga·roos.** A large leaping mammal of Australia with long powerful hind legs and a thick tail used as a support in standing or walking, the female having an abdominal pouch for carrying its young.

kangaroo rat. A pouched, burrowing rodent found in the dry regions of the western United States.

ka·o·lin \'kā-ə-lən\ *n.* A pure white clay used in making porcelain.

ka·pok \'kā-ˌpäk\ *n.* The mass of silky fibers around the seeds of the silk-cotton tree, used as filling for mattresses and life preservers.

kar·a·kul \'kar-ək-l\ *n.* **1** [usually with a capital] A hardy Asiatic sheep with wiry brown fur and a triangular mass of fat at the base of the tail. **2** The fur of newborn lambs of these sheep; caracul.

ka·ty·did \'kāt-ē-ˌdid\ *n.* A large, green, tree-dwelling insect related to the grasshopper and getting its name from the shrill sound which the male makes by scraping one forewing against the other.

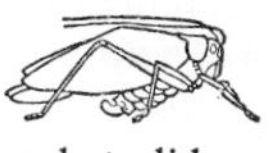
katydid

kay·ak \'kī-ˌak\ *n.* An Eskimo canoe made of a frame entirely covered with skins except for a small opening in the center where one or two paddlers may sit.

kayak

keel \'kēl\ *n.* **1** A timber or plate running lengthwise along the center of the bottom of a vessel and usually projecting from the bottom. **2** Something like a ship's keel in form or use. — *v.* **1** To provide with a keel. **2** To turn up the keel or bottom of; to turn over. — **keel over.** To upset; to fall suddenly, as in a faint or from a shock or blow.

keel·haul \'kēl-ˌhȯl\ *v.* **1** To haul under the keel of a ship as a punishment or torture. **2** To rebuke severely.

keel·son \'kels-n, 'kēls-n\ *n.* A structure running above and fastened to the keel of a ship in order to stiffen and strengthen its framework.

keen \'kēn\ *adj.* [From Old English *cene* meaning "brave", "bold", "fierce".] **1** Having a fine edge or point; sharp; as, a *keen* knife. **2** Cutting; stinging; severe; as, a *keen* wind. **3** Strong; acute; sharp; as, a *keen* sense of smell; *keen* eyesight. **4** Eager; enthusiastic; as, to be *keen* about baseball. **5** Having or showing mental sharpness; as, a *keen* mind; a *keen* question. — For synonyms see *sharp.* — **keen·ly,** *adv.*

keen \'kēn\ *n.* [From Irish *caoine.*] A lamentation, as for the dead, uttered in a loud, wailing voice; a wordless cry or wail. — *v.* To express grief with a keen.

keep \'kēp\ *v.;* **kept** \'kept\; **keep·ing. 1** To perform as a duty; to fulfill; to observe; as, to *keep* a promise; to *keep* a fast. **2** To guard; as, to *keep* someone from harm. **3** To take care of; as, to *keep* a war orphan. **4** To maintain; to continue doing something; as, to *keep* silence; to *keep* on working. **5** To have in one's service or at one's disposal; as, to *keep* a maid; to *keep* a car. **6** To maintain a record of, as events or transactions; as, to *keep* a diary; to *keep* books. **7** To have on hand for sale; as, to *keep* neckties. **8** To possess permanently; as, to *keep* what one has earned. **9** To hold; to detain; as, to *keep* a person in jail. **10** To hold back; to withhold; as, to *keep* a secret. **11** To remain in an unspoiled condition. Milk does not *keep* well in warm weather. **12** To refrain; as, to be unable to *keep* from talking. **13** To continue; as, to *keep* moving. — *n.* **1** A stronghold or fortress, especially one in a castle. **2** Maintenance; support; as, to pay for one's *keep.* **3** [in the plural] The right to keep something won; as, to play for *keeps.*

keep·er \'kēp-r\ *n.* A person who watches, guards, or takes care of something; a person in charge; a warden; a custodian.

keep·ing \'kēp-ing\ *n.* **1** Observance; as, the *keeping* of a holiday. **2** Care; charge; custody; as, in safe *keeping.* **3** Agreement; harmony; as, a remark not in *keeping* with good taste.

keep·sake \'kēp-ˌsāk\ *n.* Anything kept, or given to be kept, in memory of the giver.

keg \'keg, 'kag\ *n.* A barrel-shaped container, usually holding ten gallons or less.

kelp \'kelp\ *n.* **1** The ashes of seaweed, a source of iodine. **2** A large brown seaweed.

ken \'ken\ *n.* Sight; vision; understanding; as, beyond one's *ken.* — *v.;* **kenned; ken·ning.** *Archaic* or *dial.* To know; to understand.

ken·nel \'ken-l\ *n.* **1** A shelter for a dog. **2** [in the plural] A place where dogs are bred. — *v.;* **ken·neled** or **ken·nelled; ken·nel·ing** or **ken·nel·ling.** To put or keep in a kennel.

kept. Past tense and past part. of *keep.*

ker·a·tin \'ker-ə-tən\ *n.* A chemical substance forming the basis of such animal structures as horn, nails, hair and feathers.

ker·chief \'kər-chəf, -(ˌ)chif, -ˌchēf\ *n.; pl.* **ker·chiefs** \see *handkerchief* for pronunciation\. **1** A piece of cloth used as a head covering or worn as a scarf around the neck. **2** A handkerchief.

ker·nel \'kərn-l\ *n.* **1** The whole grain or seed of a cereal, as of wheat or corn. **2** The inner softer part of a seed, fruit stone, or nut; as, the *kernel* of a walnut; the *kernel* of a peach stone. **3** The most important or necessary part; heart; core; as, the *kernel* of an argument.

ker·o·sene \'ker-ə-ˌsēn, ˌker-ə-'sēn, 'kar-, ˌkar-\ *n.* A thin oil used for burning in lamps and oil stoves.

ketch \'kech\ *n.* A two-masted sailboat with the shorter mast just forward of the point at which the stern enters the water.

ketch

ketchup. Variant of *catsup.*

ket·tle \'ket-l\ *n.* A pot for boiling liquids; especially, a teakettle.

ket·tle·drum \'ket-l-ˌdrəm\ *n.* A brass or copper kettle-shaped drum with parchment stretched across the top, capable of being tuned to definite pitches.

key \'kē\ *n.* A low island or reef; as, the Florida *keys.*

key \'kē\ *n.* **1** An instrument by which the bolt of a lock, as on a gate or door, is turned. **2** Anything that gives or prevents entrance or possession; as, the *key* of a line of defenses. **3** A device like a key in form or use, as a cotter pin. **4** Something that explains or solves something; as, the *key* to a puzzle. **5** General tone or style; as, spoken in a sad *key.* **6** A keystone. **7** A small switch for opening or closing an electric circuit. **8** One of a number of levers, as on a piano or typewriter, by which an instrument is operated. **9** In music, a system of tones arranged in relation to a keynote from which the system is named; as, the *key* of C. — *v.;* **keyed; key·ing. 1** To put in tune with; to harmonize; as, to *key* one's mood to an occasion. **2** To regulate the pitch of; as, to *key* the strings of a violin. — **key up. 1** To raise in key, as by tightening the strings. **2** To make nervous or tense; as, all *keyed up* by the excitement.

key·board \'kē-ˌbōrd, -ˌbȯrd\ *n.* **1** A row of keys, as on a piano. **2** The whole arrangement of keys, as on a typewriter.

keyed \'kēd\ *adj.* **1** Provided with keys, as a musical instrument. **2** Strengthened by a key or keystone. **3** Set to a key, as a tune.

key·hole \'kē-ˌhōl\ *n.* A hole for receiving a key.

key·note \'kē-ˌnōt\ *n.* **1** In music, the first note of a scale; the fundamental tone of a key. **2** The fundamental fact; the central idea; as, the *keynote* of a lecture.

key·stone \'kē-ˌstōn\ *n.* **1** The wedge-shaped piece at the center of the top of an arch. **2** Something on which various other connected things depend

kg. Abbreviation for *kilogram.*

khaki \'kak-ē, 'käk-, 'ka̐k-\ *n.* **1** A dull yellowish-brown color. **2** A cotton cloth of this color; a uniform made of this cloth. — *adj.* Having the color of khaki; made of khaki.

khan \'kän, 'kan, 'ka̐n\ *n.* In certain Eastern countries, a caravansary or rest house.

khan \'kän, 'kan, 'ka̐n\ *n.* A title once used by certain rulers in Asia but now given to officials and other persons in countries such as Afghanistan and Iran.

khe·dive \kə-'dēv\ *n.* The title given from 1867 to 1914 to the Turkish governors of Egypt.

kibe \'kīb\ *n.* **1** A chilblain on the heel. **2** A sore on the hoof, as of a horse.

kib·itz·er \'kib-əts-r\ *n.* **1** A meddler; one who gives advice without being asked to do so. **2** One who watches a card game without playing and often without talking to the players. — **kib·itz** \-əts\ *v.*

kick \'kik\ *v.* **1** To strike out with the foot or feet, as in defense or at a ball in games. **2** To strike, thrust, or hit violently with the foot. **3** To object strongly; to protest; as, to *kick* because prices were raised. **4** To recoil, as a gun when fired. **5** In football, to score by kicking; as, to *kick* the point after touchdown. — *n.* **1** A blow with the foot or feet; the power or ability to kick. **2** Any movement resembling a kick, as the recoil of a gun. **3** A strong protest; a complaint; the grounds for complaint. **4** A stimulating effect; pleasurable excitement; a thrill. **5** In football, the action of kicking.

kick·off \'kik-ˌȯf\ *n.* In football, the action of starting play by kicking the ball from a fixed position near the center of the field.

kid \'kid\ *n.* **1** A young goat. **2** The flesh or skin of a kid; leather made of the skin of a kid. **3** A child; a youngster. — **kid·dish** \'kid-ish\ *adj.*

kid \'kid\ *v.;* **kid·ded; kid·ding. 1** To deceive or trick as a joke; to hoax; to humbug. **2** To make fun of; to jolly; to tease. — **kid·der,** *n.*

kid·nap \'kid-ˌnap\ *v.;* **kid·naped** \-ˌnapt\ or **kid·napped; kid·nap·ing** or **kid·nap·ping.** To carry away a person by unlawful force or by fraud, and against his will. — **kid·nap·er** or **kid·nap·per,** *n.*

kid·ney \'kid-nē\ *n.; pl.* **kid·neys. 1** One of a pair of bean-shaped glands, located in the back part of the abdomen near the spine, that produce urine, which then passes to the bladder. **2** The kidney of an animal, used as food.

kidney bean. 1 A common American bean cultivated either as a string bean or especially for its large dark-red kidney-shaped seed. **2** The vine whose seeds are kidney beans.

kid·skin \'kid-ˌskin\ *n.* The skin of a young goat, used in making leather goods, as gloves and footwear.

kill \'kil\ *v.* **1** To deprive of life; to put to death; to slay. **2** To destroy; to ruin; as, to *kill* all chance of success. **3** To use up; as, to *kill* time. **4** To defeat; as, to *kill* a proposed law. **5** In printing, to mark for omission; as, to *kill* a news story. **6** To cause to stop; as, to *kill* a motor.

— The words *slaughter* and *murder* are synonyms of *kill: kill* is a general term that refers to the taking of someone's life but suggests nothing about the manner of doing so; *slaughter* when referring to the death of persons usually indicates a brutal and savage killing as if in madness or frenzy and is often used of mass killing; *murder* generally refers to the deliberate killing of a person often after careful planning and deliberation and as the result of a definite motive on the part of the murderer.

— *n.* **1** The act of killing; as to close in for the *kill.* **2** An animal killed, especially as prey; as, a lion devouring its *kill.*

kill·deer \'kil-ˌdir\ *n.; pl.* **kill·deers** or **kill·deer.** Any one of several plovers, so called from their cry.

kill·er \'kil-r\ *n.* **1** A person, animal, or thing that kills. **2** The **killer whale,** which preys on large fish and seals, and sometimes attacks and kills whales larger than itself.

kiln \'kil(n)\ *n.* A furnace or oven for hardening, burning, or drying anything, as bricks or pottery. — *v.* To burn, bake, or dry in a kiln.

ki·lo \'kē-ˌlō, 'kil-ˌō\ *n.; pl.* **ki·los.** **1** A kilogram. **2** A kilometer.

kil·o·cy·cle \'kil-ə-ˌsīk-l\ *n.* 1,000 cycles, or complete reversals of direction of an alternating current, per second.

kil·o·gram or **kil·o·gramme** \'kil-ə-ˌgram\ *n.* [From French *kilogramme*, there derived irregularly from Greek *chilioi* meaning "thousand" and French *gramme* meaning "gram".] A unit of weight containing 1,000 grams and equal to 2.2046 pounds.

ki·lom·e·ter or **ki·lom·e·tre** \kə-'läm-ət-r, 'kil-ə-mēt-r\ *n.* A measure of length containing 1,000 meters and equal to 3,280.8 feet. — **kil·o·met·ric** \ˌkil-ə-'me-trik\ or **kil·o·met·ri·cal** \-trik-l\ *adj.*

kil·o·ton \'kil-ə-ˌtən\ *n.* **1** A thousand tons. **2** An explosive force equal to that of 1,000 tons of TNT — used especially in connection with an atomic bomb or a hydrogen bomb.

kil·o·watt \'kil-ə-ˌwät\ *n.* A unit of electrical power equal to 1,000 watts.

kil·o·watt-hour \'kil-ə-ˌwät-'au̇r\ *n.* A unit of work or energy equal to that done by one kilowatt acting for one hour.

kilt \'kilt\ *n.* **1** A knee-length, pleated skirt worn by men in the highlands of Scotland, and forming part of the uniform of certain regiments in the British army. **2** A skirt of similar design worn by girls and women. — *v.* **1** To tuck up, as a dress or skirt. **2** To equip with the kilt; as, a *kilted* regiment.

kil·ter \'kilt-r\ *n.* Proper condition; order — used chiefly in the phrase *out of kilter.*

ki·mo·no \kə-'mō-nə\ *n.; pl.* **ki·mo·nos.** **1** A loose gown or robe tied with a sash, worn as an outer garment by Japanese men and women. **2** A similar garment worn by women as a dressing gown. **3** A long, loose infant's robe fastened at the neck.

kin \'kin\ *n.* **1** A person's relatives taken together; kindred. **2** Family relationship; as, next of *kin.* — *adj.* Related.

-kin \kən, k-n\. A suffix meaning small or little, used to form diminutives, as in *lambkin.*

kind \'kīnd\ *n.* **1** A natural group or division; as, a bird of the hawk *kind.* **2** A sort; a variety; as, various *kinds* of people. **3** The quality or character of a thing; as, differences in *kind.* — **in kind. 1** In the same manner. **2** In goods or produce as distinguished from money; as, payment *in kind.* — **of a kind.** Of the same sort, class, or value.

kind \'kīnd\ *adj.* **1** Having the will to do good and to bring happiness to others; sympathetic; considerate; gentle. **2** Showing or growing out of gentleness or goodness of heart; as, a *kind* act.

kin·der·gar·ten \'kind-r-ˌgärt-n, -ˌgärd-, -ˌgȧrt-, -ˌgȧrd-\ *n.* A school or a class for very young children in which the teaching is done largely through activities based on the normal aptitudes and desire of the pupils for exercise and play.

kin·der·gart·ner \'kind-r-ˌgärt-nər, -ˌgärd-, -ˌgȧrt-, -ˌgȧrd-\ *n.* **1** A kindergarten teacher. **2** A kindergarten pupil.

kind·heart·ed \'kīnd-'härt-əd, -'hȧrt-\ *adj.* Having or showing a kind and sympathetic nature. — **kind·heart·ed·ly,** *adv.*

kin·dle \'kind-l\ *v.;* **kin·dled; kin·dling** \-l(-)ing\. **1** To set on fire or take fire; to start burning; to light; as, to *kindle* a fire. **2** To arouse; to provoke; to excite; as, to *kindle* a person's anger. **3** To begin to be excited; to grow warm and animated. **4** To light up as if with flame; as, with eyes *kindling.*

kind·li·ness \'kīn-(d)lē-nəs\ *n.* **1** The quality or state of being kind. **2** A kindly deed.

kin·dling \'kin-(d)ling\ *n.* Material, such as small pieces of soft wood, for starting a fire.

kind·ly \'kīn-(d)lē\ *adj.;* **kind·li·er; kind·li·est. 1** Sympathetic; kind. **2** Favorable; agreeable. — *adv.* In a kind manner; with good will.

kind·ness \'kīn(d)-nəs\ *n.* **1** Kind feeling; good will. **2** A kind act; an act of good will.

kin·dred \'kin-drəd\ *n.* **1** Family relationship; kinship. **2** Persons who are related to one another; relations collectively. — *adj.* **1** Belonging to the same kind; related. **2** Of like nature or character; as, persons with *kindred* likes and dislikes.

kine \'kīn\ *n. pl. Archaic and dial.* Cattle; cows.

kin·e·scope \'kin-ə-ˌskōp\ *n.* **1** A television picture tube. **2** A moving picture made from the image on this tube.

ki·net·ic \kə-'net-ik, kī-\ *adj.* Of, relating to, or due to motion.

kinetic energy. The energy that a thing, as a falling ball, has because of its motion.

ki·net·ics \kə-'net-iks, kī-\ *n.* The branch of physics treating of the effects of forces upon the motions of material bodies.

king \'king\ *n.* **1** A male ruler of a country, especially one who inherits his position and rules for life; a sovereign; the male monarch of any country called a kingdom. **2** One thought of as being like a king in power and position; as, an oil *king.* **3** A playing card that bears the picture of a king. **4** The chief piece in a game of chess. **5** In checkers, a piece that has reached the opponent's back row.

king·bird \'king-ˌbərd\ *n.* The tyrant flycatcher.

king·bolt \'king-ˌbōlt\ *n.* A vertical bolt by which the forward axle and wheel of a vehicle or the trucks of a railroad car are connected with the other parts.

king·dom \'kingd-m\ *n.* **1** A country whose ruler is called a king; the territory ruled by a king or a queen; a monarchy; a realm. **2** One of the three great divisions (**animal kingdom, vegetable kingdom, mineral kingdom**) into which all natural objects are grouped.

king·fish \'king-ˌfish\ *n.; pl.* **king·fish** or **king·fish·es. 1** The northern whiting. **2** A large food and game fish of the Florida coast, similar to and closely related to the Spanish mackerel.

king·fish·er \'king-ˌfish-r\ *n.* A bright-colored, usually crested bird with long straight bill and short tail, living chiefly on fish, as the slate-blue **belt·ed kingfisher** of the United States, which has a chestnut band across a white breast.

king·let \'king-lət\ *n.* **1** A king of a small country; a little or insignificant king. **2** A very small bird resembling the warblers with certain habits of the titmice, as the olive-green **gold·en-crowned king-let** of America.

king·ly \'king-lē\ *adj.;* **king·li·er; king·li·est.** Belonging to or suitable to a king; royal; regal. — *adv.* In a manner becoming to a king.

king·pin \'king-ˌpin\ *n.* **1** In bowling, a tall pin, the head pin, or the number 5 pin. **2** The chief person in a group or undertaking. **3** A kingbolt.

king·ship \'king-ˌship\ *n.* **1** The position, office, or dignity of a king. **2** Royal government. **3** The personality of a king; majesty.

king·size \'king-ˌsīz\ or **king·sized** \-ˌsīzd\ *adj.* **1** Longer than the regular or standard size. **2** Extra large.

king snake. A large, harmless snake of the southern United States, living chiefly on mice and rats.

kink \'kingk\ *n.* **1** A short, tight twist, loop, or curl, as in a rope or thread. **2** A cramp in some part of the body. **3** A peculiarity; a mental quirk or twist; a whim. — *v.* To wind into a kink; to form a kink. — **kinky** \'kingk-ē\ *adj.*

kin·ka·jou \'kingk-ə-ˌjü\ *n.* A slender long-tailed mammal of Central and South America, related to the raccoon.

kins·folk \'kinz-ˌfōk\ *n. pl.* Relatives; kindred; kin.

kin·ship \'kin-ˌship\ *n.* The condition of being kin; relationship.

kins·man \'kinz-mən\ *n.; pl.* **kins·men** \-mən\. A relative by birth or, sometimes, by marriage.

kins·wom·an \'kinz-ˌwu̇m-ən\ *n.; pl.* **kins·wom·en** \-ˌwim-ən\. A female relative by birth or, sometimes, by marriage.

ki·osk \kē-'äsk\ *n.* **1** A Turkish open summerhouse or pavilion. **2** A small, light structure having one or more open sides, as a newsstand or a bandstand.

kip·per \'kip-r\ *n.* A kippered salmon or herring. — *v.* To cure by salting and then drying or smoking.

kirk \'kərk, *Scottish* 'kirk\ *n. Scottish.* A church.

kir·tle \'kərt-l\ *n. Archaic.* A woman's dress, skirt, or petticoat.

kiss \'kis\ *v.* **1** To touch with the lips as a mark of affection or greeting. **2** To touch gently or lightly; as, wind gently *kissing* the trees. — *n.* **1** The act of kissing; a caress with the lips. **2** A gentle touch or contact. **3** A kind of candy. — **kiss·a·ble,** *adj.*

kit \'kit\ *n.* **1** A set of tools or implements; as, a carpenter's *kit;* a plumber's *kit.* **2** A collection of articles, especially one for personal use; as, a travel *kit;* a first-aid *kit.* **3** A set of parts to be assembled; as, a model-airplane *kit.* **4** Any packaged collection of related material; as, a *kit* of suggestions for window displays. **5** The box or bag containing such sets or collections.

kitch·en \'kich-n\ *n.* A room in which cooking is done.

kitch·en·ette \ˌkich-n-'et\ *n.* A very small kitchen, or an alcove or closet containing kitchen equipment.

kitchen police. **1** Enlisted men assigned to assist the cooks in a camp or other military establishment. **2** The duties performed by these men.

kitch·en·ware \'kich-n-ˌwar, -ˌwer\ *n.* Hardware for use in a kitchen.

kite \'kīt\ *n.* **1** Any of a number of hawks having long narrow wings and noted for their graceful flight. **2** A light frame, covered with paper or cloth and sometimes having a balancing tail, intended to be flown in the air at the end of a string.

kith \'kith\ *n.* Familiar friends and neighbors collectively; as, one's *kith* and kin.

kit·ten \'kit-n\ *n.* A young cat.

kit·ten·ish \'kit-n(-)ish\ *adj.* Like a kitten; playful.

kit·ti·wake \'kit-ē-ˌwāk\ *n.* Any of several gulls, white and pearl-gray in color, having a short stubby hind toe, black feet, and black-tipped wings.

kit·ty \'kit-ē\ *n.; pl.* **kit·ties.** A cat or kitten.

kit·ty-cor·ner \'kit-ē-'kȯrn-r\ *adj.* or *adv.* Cater-corner.

kit·ty-cor·nered \'kit-ē-'kȯrn-rd\ *adj.* or *adv.* Cater-cornered.

ki·wi \'kē-ˌwē\ *n.; pl.* **ki·wis.** A flightless bird of New Zealand, having a flat breastbone and grayish-brown plumage resembling hair.

klep·to·ma·nia \ˌklep-tə-'mā-nē-ə, -'mān-yə\ *n.* A persistent abnormal impulse to steal, especially when a person is not in need. — **klep·to·ma·ni·ac** \-'mā-nē-ˌak\ *n.*

klieg light or **kleig light** \'klēg\. An arc light of a type used in taking motion pictures.

km. Abbreviation for *kilometer.*

knack \'nak\ *n.* **1** Ability to do something easily, neatly, cleverly, or skillfully; aptness; as, a *knack* for using tools. **2** A clever or skillful way of doing something; trick; as, a task that is easy once you get the *knack* of it.

knap·sack \'nap-ˌsak\ *n.* A case of canvas or leather carried on the back, as by a traveler or hiker, for holding clothing and other necessaries.

knave \'nāv\ *n.* [From Old English *cnafa* meaning "boy", "boy servant".] **1** *Archaic.* A male servant. **2** A man of humble birth or position. **3** A tricky, deceitful person. **4** A playing card marked with the figure of a servant or soldier; a jack.

knav·ery \'nāv-r(-)ē\ *n.; pl.* **knav·er·ies.** **1** The practices of a knave; trickery; fraud. **2** A knavish or dishonest act.

knav·ish \'nā-vish\ *adj.* Having or showing the characteristics of a knave; dishonest; tricky. — **knav·ish·ly,** *adv.*

knead \'nēd\ *v.* **1** To work into a well-mixed mass by repeatedly drawing out and pressing together; as, to *knead* dough. **2** To form or shape as if by kneading; as, to *knead* a pillow. **3** To treat, as muscles or flesh, as if by kneading; to massage.

knee \'nē\ *n.* **1** The joint in the middle part of the leg. **2** The part of a garment that covers the knee; as, trousers with baggy *knees.*

knee·cap \'nē-ˌkap\ *n.* A thick, flat, movable bone forming the front part of the knee; the patella; the kneepan.

knee·hole \'nē-ˌhōl\ *n.* A space for the knees, as under a desk.

knee jerk. An involuntary kick produced by a light blow on the tendon below the knee.

kneel \'nēl\ *v.;* **knelt** \'nelt\ or **kneeled** \'nēld\; **kneel·ing.** To bend the knee; to go down or rest on the knee or knees.

knee·pan \'nē-ˌpan\ *n.* The patella; the kneecap.

knell \'nel\ *n.* **1** The stroke or sound of a bell, especially when rung slowly for a funeral. **2** A warning or indication of the passing away of anything. The invention of the automobile sounded the *knell* of the horse and carriage. **—** *v.* **1** To summon, announce, or proclaim by or as if by a knell. **2** To ring; especially, to toll a bell at a death or funeral. **3** To sound as a knell or as a warning.

knew. Past tense of *know.*

knick·er·bock·ers \'nik-r-ˌbäk-rz\ *n. pl.* Short loose breeches gathered at the knee.

knick·ers \'nik-rz\ *n. pl.* Knickerbockers.

knick·knack \'nik-ˌnak\ *n.* A small article of not much value, intended for ornament rather than use.

knickerbockers

knife \'nīf\ *n.; pl.* **knives** \'nīvz\. **1** A cutting instrument consisting of a thin, usually sharp blade fastened to a handle. **2** A weapon resembling a knife, as a dagger or short sword. **3** A cutting blade in a machine. **—** *v.;* **knifed; knif·ing.** To cut or stab with a knife.

knight \'nīt\ *n.* [From medieval English, meaning "servant", "military servant or follower", "knight", from Old English *cniht* meaning literally "boy".] **1** In feudal times, a mounted warrior serving a king or other superior, especially one who after a period of early service had been awarded a special military rank and been sworn to obey certain rules of conduct. **2** In modern times, a man honored by a sovereign for merit, in Great Britain ranking below a baronet but like a baronet having the title *Sir* before his name, as in *Sir* John Doe. **3** One of the pieces in the game of chess. **—** *v.* To make a person a knight; to raise to the rank of knight.

knight-er·rant \'nīt-'er-ənt\ *n.; pl.* **knights-er·rant.** A knight traveling in search of adventures in which to show his military skill and his nobility of character.

knight-er·rant·ry \'nīt-'er-ən-trē\ *n.; pl.* **knight-er·rant·ries. 1** The character or behavior of or befitting a knight-errant. **2** The practice of wandering in search of knightly adventures.

knight·hood \'nīt-ˌhu̇d\ *n.* **1** The rank of a knight. **2** The character of a knight or of knights in general. **3** The whole class or body of knights.

knight·ly \'nīt-lē\ *adj.* **1** Of or relating to a knight or knights; worthy of a knight; chivalrous. **2** Made up of knights. **—** *adv.* In a knightly manner.

knit \'nit\ *v.;* **knit** or **knit·ted; knit·ting. 1** To form a fabric by interlacing yarn or thread in connected loops with needles (**knit·ting nee·dles**); as, to *knit* a sweater. **2** To draw or come together closely as if knitted; to unite firmly; as, to wait for a broken bone to *knit.* **3** To wrinkle; as, to *knit* one's brows. **4** To bind closely by a tie of any kind; as, a group of people *knit* together by common interests. — **knit·ter,** *n.*

knit·ting \'nit-ing\ *n.* **1** The act of one who knits. **2** Work done or being done by one who knits.

knit·wear \'nit-ˌwar, -ˌwer\ *n.* Clothing made by knitting or from knitted fabrics.

knives. Pl. of *knife.*

knob \'näb\ *n.* **1** A rounded swelling, bunch, or mass; a lump. **2** A knoblike handle, as on a door or a drawer. **3** A rounded hill or mountain. — **knobbed** \'näbd\ *adj.* — **knob·by** \'näb-ē\ *adj.*

knock \'näk\ *v.* **1** To strike a sharp blow, as with something hard or with the fist; to rap. **2** To collide; to bump; to clash. **3** To make a pounding noise, as an automobile engine. **4** To find fault. — **knock about.** To travel about, especially in an irregular way. — **knock down. 1** To sell to the highest bidder at an auction. **2** To take apart or come apart, as for packing. — **knock off. 1** To leave off. **2** To cease from work. **3** To deduct; as, to *knock off* a dollar from the price. — **knock out. 1** To defeat; to overcome. **2** In boxing, to disable an opponent by knocking him down so that he cannot rise before the referee has counted ten seconds. **—** *n.* **1** A knocking; a sharp blow; a rap; as, a *knock* on the door. **2** A noise like that of a rap; as, a *knock* in a motor.

knock·down \'näk-ˌdau̇n\ *adj.* **1** Of such force as to knock one down. **2** Made so as to be capable of being taken apart, as for packing or shipping. **—** *n.* **1** That which knocks one down. **2** A knocking down, as of a boxer. **3** Something, as a piece of furniture, that comes apart for packing or shipping.

knock·er \'näk-r\ *n.* **1** A person or a thing that knocks. **2** A device for use in knocking at a door, consisting of a piece of metal, as a ring or knob, hinged to be lifted and let fall against the door.

door knocker

knock-kneed \'näk-'nēd\ *adj.* Having knees that bend in so as to touch each other in walking.

knock·out \'näk-ˌau̇t\ *adj.* Capable of knocking out; as, a *knockout* blow. **—** *n.* **1** The action of knocking out or the condition of being knocked out. **2** A knockout blow.

knoll \'nōl\ *n.* A little round hill.

knot \'nät\ *n.* **1** Any tie or fastening made with string, rope, or ribbon. **2** The lump or knob formed by the interlacing of parts of a string or rope. **3** A difficulty; a problem; a tangle. **4** A group or cluster; as, people standing about in *knots.* **5** A bond of union; as, the marriage *knot.* **6** A bow, cockade, or epaulet. **7** A lump; a knob, as in a muscle. **8** A node in a stem; a hard lump at the joint of a branch and the trunk. **9** A unit in which the speed of a moving ship is stated: one nautical mile, or 6,080.2 feet an hour; as, a speed of eight *knots.* — *v.;* **knot·ted**; **knot·ting.** **1** To form, or to tie into, a knot or knots. **2** To unite closely; to tangle, as string. **3** To make or knit knots for fringe or trimming.

overhand knot

loop knot

knot·hole \'nät-ˌhōl\ *n.* A hole, as in a board or a tree trunk, where a knot or a branch has come out.

knot·ted \'nät-əd\ *adj.* **1** Tied in or with a knot or knots; as, a *knotted* handkerchief. **2** Full of knots or knobs; gnarled; as, a *knotted* tree trunk. **3** Entangled; knotty. **4** Ornamented, as with knots or knobs.

knot·ty \'nät-ē\ *adj.;* **knot·ti·er**; **knot·ti·est.** **1** Full of knots; tied in knots; knotted; as, a *knotty* board. **2** Difficult; puzzling; as, a *knotty* problem.

knout \'nau̇t, 'nüt\ *n.* A whip for flogging criminals. — *v.* To flog with the knout.

know \'nō\ *v.;* **knew** \'nü, 'nyü\; **known** \'nōn\; **know·ing.** **1** To recognize as distinct from something else; as, to *know* someone by sight. **2** To be certain or sure; as, to *know* the earth is round. **3** To have in the mind with clear understanding; as, to *know* one's lessons. **4** To be acquainted with; as, to *know* all of one's schoolmates. **5** To have information about something; as, to ask someone who *knows.* **6** To have practical knowledge of; to be skilled in; as, to *know* cooking. — **know·a·ble** \'nō-əb-l\ *adj.* — **know·er** \'nō-ər\ *n.*

know-how \'nō-ˌhau̇\ *n.* Skill or competence in doing, making, or producing something.

know·ing \'nō-ing\ *adj.* **1** Intelligent; as, a very *knowing* child. **2** Artful; cunning; shrewd; as, a *knowing* rascal. **3** Having or showing special knowledge or information about something; as, a *knowing* look. — **know·ing·ly,** *adv.*

knowl·edge \'näl-ij\ *n.* **1** Understanding gained by actual experience; practical skill; as, a *knowledge* of carpentry. **2** The state of being aware of something or of having information; a range of information; as, not within my *knowledge.* **3** The act of understanding; clear perception of truth. **4** Something learned and kept in the mind; learning; enlightenment; as, a man of vast *knowledge* in the field of history.

known. Past part. of *know.*

know-noth·ing \'nō-ˌnəth-ing\ *n.* An ignoramus.

knuck·le \'nək-l\ *n.* **1** The rounded lump formed by the ends of two bones where they come together in a joint; especially, such lumps at the finger joints. **2** The knee of an animal, used for food; as, pig's *knuckles.* **3** Any of the connecting parts of a hinge through which a pin or rivet passes. — *v.;* **knuck·led**; **knuck·ling** \-l(-)ing\. **1** To place the knuckles on the ground in shooting a marble. **2** To yield; to submit. **3** To apply oneself earnestly; as, to *knuckle* down to the job.

knurl \'nərl\ *n.* **1** A knot in wood; a knob. **2** A ridge or one of a series of small beads on a metal surface, as on a circular nut, to aid in gripping it. — **knurly** \'nər-lē\ *adj.*

ko·a·la \kō-'äl-ə, -'ál-ə\ *n.* A tailless Australian animal with thick fur and long hairy ears, sharp claws for climbing, and a pouch like the kangaroo's for carrying its young.

kohl \'kōl\ *n.* A preparation used by women of the East to darken the edges of the eyelids.

kohl·rabi \kōl-'rab-ē, -'räb-, -'ráb-\ *n.; pl.* **kohl·rab·ies.** A plant that is a form of cabbage having an edible fleshy turnip-shaped stem eaten like cauliflower.

ko·la nut \'kō-lə\. The bitter nut of a tropical tree, containing much caffeine.

koo·doo or **ku·du** \'küd-ˌü\ *n.* A large African antelope, grayish brown with vertical white stripes on the sides, and with large ringed, spirally twisted horns.

kook·a·bur·ra \'ku̇k-ə-ˌbər-ə, -ˌbə-rə\ *n.* A kingfisher of Australia, about the size of a crow, with a call resembling loud laughter; the laughing jackass.

Ko·re·an \kə-'rē-ən\ *adj.* Of or relating to Korea. — *n.* **1** A native of Korea. **2** The language of Korea.

ko·sher \'kōsh-r\ *adj.* [From Hebrew *kasher* meaning "fit", "proper".] Approved or permitted by Jewish law; especially, denoting food that may be eaten as clean according to Jewish law.

kow·tow \(')kau̇-'tau̇\ *v.* **1** To kneel according to Chinese custom and knock one's forehead on the ground to show worship or deep respect. **2** To treat with slavish regard or obedience. — *n.* An act of kowtowing.

K.P. Abbreviation for *kitchen police.*

kraal \'kräl, 'král, 'król\ *n.* **1** A South African native village. **2** In South Africa, an enclosure for cattle or sheep.

krem·lin \'krem-lən\ *n.* The citadel of a Russian city, especially [with a capital] of Moscow.

k's. Pl. of *k.*

kudu. Variant of *koodoo.*

kud·zu \'ku̇d-ˌzü\ *n.* A trailing vine of China and Japan used for hay and forage, the stems of which yield a fiber.

kum·quat \'kəm-ˌkwät\ *n.* A citrus shrub bearing a small orangelike fruit, used especially for preserves.

kw. Abbreviation for *kilowatt.*

K.W.H. Abbreviation for *kilowatt-hour.*

l \'el\ *n.; pl.* **l's** \'elz\. **1** The twelfth letter of the alphabet. **2** As a Roman numeral, 50.

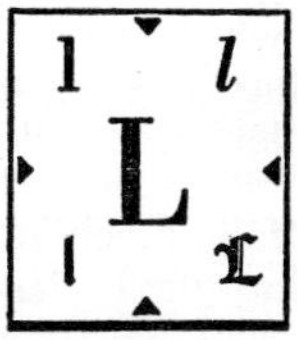

la \'lä, 'lȧ\ *n.* A syllable used in music to name the sixth note of the scale.

lab \'lab\ *n.* A laboratory.

la·bel \'lāb-l\ *n.* A slip of paper, cloth, or other material, attached to something and giving information about it, as contents, ownership, or destination; a tag. — *v.;* **la·beled** or **la·belled**; **la·bel·ing** or **la·bel·ling** \-l(-)ing\. **1** To attach a label or tag to; as, to *label* a package. **2** To describe or name as if by a label; as, to *label* a person as stingy.

la·bi·al \'lā-bē-əl\ *adj.* Of or relating to the lips.

la·bi·ate \'lā-bē-ət, -ˌāt\ *adj.* **1** Having a corolla divided into two unequal parts with one projecting over the other like lips, as in the snapdragon. **2** Of or relating to the mints.

la·bor \'lāb-r\ *n.* **1** Toil; work; as, rest from *labor.* **2** Something that requires toil or work; a task. **3** The services performed by skilled and unskilled workmen, as in manufacturing. **4** Workers as a body or class; as, the rights of *labor.* **5** The efforts and pain of childbirth. — *v.;* **la·bored**; **la·bor·ing** \-r(-)ing\. **1** To work; to toil; to exert oneself; to strive; as, to *labor* unceasingly; to *labor* to make a name for oneself. **2** To move slowly and heavily, as if with effort; as, a truck *laboring* up a hill. **3** To pitch and roll in the sea; as, a ship *laboring* in a storm. — For synonyms see *work.*

lab·o·ra·to·ry \'lab-r(-)ə-ˌtōr-ē, -ˌtȯr-ē\ *n.; pl.* **lab·o·ra·to·ries.** A room or building in which scientific experiments and tests are carried on, as in chemistry. — *adj.* Of or relating to a laboratory; used or done in a laboratory; as, *laboratory* equipment; a *laboratory* science.

Labor Day. The first Monday of September, set aside in most states of the United States as a legal holiday in honor of workingmen as a class.

la·bored \'lāb-rd\ *adj.* Produced or done with toil and difficulty; not easy or natural; as, *labored* breathing.

la·bor·er \'lāb-r-r\ *n.* One who works; a worker, especially on jobs requiring strength rather than skill.

la·bo·ri·ous \lə-'bōr-ē-əs, -'bȯr-\ *adj.* **1** Requiring hard work; as, a *laborious* task. **2** Hard-working; industrious. — **la·bo·ri·ous·ly,** *adv.*

la·bor·sav·ing \'lāb-r-ˌsā-ving\ *adj.* Adapted to replace or decrease human labor, especially manual labor; as, washing machines and other *laborsaving* devices.

labor union. An organization of workers formed to protect the rights and advance the interests of its members.

la·bur·num \lə-'bər-nəm\ *n.* A poisonous shrub of the pea family with three leaflets and bright-yellow flowers in hanging clusters.

lab·y·rinth \'lab-r-ˌin(t)th\ *n.* **1** A place full of passageways so arranged as to make it difficult for a person to find his way around; a maze. **2** Any confused or confusing condition. **3** The internal ear.

lab·y·rin·thine \ˌlab-r-'in(t)th-n\ *adj.* Like a labyrinth; very complicated or involved; intricate.

lac \'lak\ *n.* A resinous substance secreted by a certain scale insect, used in the manufacture of shellac, lacquers, and sealing wax.

lace \'lās\ *n.* **1** A string or cord passed through holes and used to draw or hold together opposite edges, as in shoes. **2** An ornamental braid used chiefly for trimming uniforms. **3** An openwork fabric of thread or cord, usually having an ornamental design. — *v.;* **laced**; **lac·ing.** **1** To fasten or join together with a lace or laces. **2** To decorate or trim with lace. **3** To interlace; to intertwine. **4** To beat; to lash.

lac·er·ate \'las-r-ˌāt\ *v.;* **lac·er·at·ed**; **lac·er·at·ing.** **1** To tear; to mangle; as, flesh *lacerated* by the teeth of a dog. **2** To afflict greatly; to harrow; as, a heart *lacerated* by grief.

lac·er·a·tion \ˌlas-r-'āsh-n\ *n.* **1** The action of lacerating. **2** A wound made by lacerating; a torn and ragged wound.

lace·wing \'lās-ˌwing\ *n.* A slender insect with four delicate, lacy wings and brilliant eyes.

lach·ry·mal or **lac·ri·mal** \'lak-rəm-l\ *adj.* Of or relating to tears or to the glands producing tears.

lach·ry·mose \'lak-rə-ˌmōs\ *adj.* **1** Shedding or given to shedding tears; tearful. **2** Tending to cause tears; sorrowful; as, a *lachrymose* story about a homeless orphan. — **lach·ry·mose·ly,** *adv.*

lacier. Comparative of *lacy.*

laciest. Superlative of *lacy.*

lac·i·ly \'lās-l-ē\ *adv.* In a manner suggesting lace.

lac·ing \'lā-sing\ *n.* **1** The action of one that laces. **2** Anything that serves to lace; a lace.

lack \'lak\ *n.* **1** The fact or state of being deficient or wanting; need. **2** That which is lacking; a thing needed. — *v.* To need, want, or be without or deficient in; as, to *lack* musical ability. Some countries *lack* natural resources.

lack·a·dai·si·cal \ˌlak-ə-'dā-zik-l\ *adj.* Languid; listless; as, a *lackadaisical* manner. — **lack·a·dai·si·cal·ly** \-zik-l(-)ē\ *adv.*

lack·ey \'lak-ē\ *n.; pl.* **lack·eys.** **1** A footman; a valet. **2** A toady.

lack·ing \'lak-ing\ *adj.* Needed; not present.

lack·lus·ter \'lak-ˌləst-r\ *adj.* Lacking luster or brightness; dull.

la·con·ic \lə-'kän-ik\ *adj.* Sparing of words; brief and to the point. — **la·con·i·cal·ly** \-ik-l(-)ē\ *adv.*

lac·quer \'lak-r\ *n.* **1** A varnish made of shellac and alcohol. **2** A natural varnish made from the sap of a sumac tree of China and Japan. **3** Articles, as trays, boxes, and vases, made of wood coated with lacquer. — *v.;* **lac·quered**; **lac·quer·ing** \-r(-)ing\. To coat with lacquer.

la·crosse \lə-'krȯs\ *n.* [From Canadian French *la crosse* meaning literally "the lacrosse racket", "the hooked stick".] An outdoor game of ball played with long-handled rackets by which a hard ball is caught, carried, and thrown.

lac·tase \'lak-ˌtās\ *n.* An enzyme that functions in digesting lactose and related sugars.

lac·te·al \'lak-tē-əl\ *adj.* **1** Relating to milk. **2** Consisting of or like milk; milky. **3** In anatomy, containing or carrying chyle. — *n.* One of the small vessels of the small intestine that convey the chyle from the intestine to the blood.

lac·tic \'lak-tik\ *adj.* Of or relating to milk; produced from sour milk or whey.

lactic acid. A colorless syrupy acid formed in the souring of milk and also manufactured in various ways.

lac·tose \'lak-ˌtōs\ *n.* A sugar present in milk, from which it can be separated by evaporation in the form of hard crystals.

lacy \'lā-sē\ *adj.;* **lac·i·er; lac·i·est. 1** Consisting of lace. **2** Resembling lace.

lad \'lad\ *n.* A boy; a youth.

lad·der \'lad-r\ *n.* **1** A device used for climbing, usually consisting of two long pieces of wood, rope, or metal, joined at short distances by horizontal crosspieces called *rounds* or *rungs.* **2** Something likened to a ladder in form or use, as a means by which one may achieve success; as, to start out in business at the very bottom of the *ladder.*

lad·die \'lad-ē\ *n.* A lad.

lade \'lād\ *v.;* **lad·ed** \'lād-əd\; **lad·ed** \'lād-əd\ or **lad·en** \'lād-n\; **lad·ing. 1** To load, as a vessel. **2** To dip, as with a ladle or dipper; to bail; to ladle.

lad·en \'lād-n\ *adj.* Loaded; burdened; as, a truck *laden* with gravel; a person *laden* with cares.

la·dle \'lād-l\ *n.* A long-handled cuplike spoon or dipper used in dipping. — *v.;* **la·dled; la·dling** \-l(-)ing\. To dip up; to take up and carry in a ladle; as, to *ladle* soup.

la·dy \'lād-ē\ *n.; pl.* **la·dies. 1** A woman of property, rank, or authority, having a standing equivalent to that of a lord. **2** [with a capital] Also **Our Lady.** The Virgin Mary. **3** A wife; as, officers and their *ladies.* **4** Any woman; especially, any well-bred woman considered as worthy of respect. **5** [with a capital] In the British Empire, the title of a woman having a certain rank, as a countess or baroness or the wife of a knight or baronet.

la·dy·bird \'lād-ē-ˌbərd\ *n.* or **ladybird beetle.** A small, roundish-backed, often brightly colored beetle that feeds on plant lice and aphids.

ladybird

la·dy·bug \'lād-ē-ˌbəg\ *n.* A ladybird.

la·dy·like \'lād-ē-ˌlīk\ *adj.* **1** Like a lady; well-bred. **2** Becoming or suitable to a lady; as, *ladylike* manners.

la·dy·love \'lād-ē-ˌləv\ *n.* A sweetheart.

la·dy·ship \'lād-ē-ˌship\ *n.* The rank or position of a lady — used with *her* or *your* to refer to or address one having the title of *Lady.*

la·dy's-slip·per \'lād-ē(z)-ˌslip-r\ or **la·dy-slip·per** \'lād-ē-\ *n.* A leafy-stemmed orchid plant from about one to two feet tall, with hairy, veined leaves and large drooping flowers, the lips of which form a sac somewhat resembling a slipper.

lag \'lag\ *v.;* **lagged; lag·ging.** To move slowly; to loiter; to fall behind; as, to *lag* behind the other hikers. — *n.* **1** The act of lagging; a slowing up; a falling behind. **2** The amount by which one lags.

lag·gard \'lag-rd\ *adj.* **1** Slow; loitering; as, *laggard* footsteps. **2** Backward; dull; as, a *laggard* child. — *n.* A person who lags.

lag·o·morph \'lag-ə-ˌmȯrf\ *n.* A member of a group of gnawing mammals differing from the rodents in having two pairs of upper incisors one behind the other, as the rabbit and the hare.

la·goon \lə-'gün\ *n.* A shallow channel, pond, or lake, especially one near the sea and connected with it.

laid. Past tense and past part. of *lay.*

lain. Past part. of *lie,* to recline.

lair \'lar, 'ler\ *n.* The bed of a wild beast.

laird \'lard, 'lerd\ *n. Scottish.* A landed proprietor.

lais·sez faire or **lais·ser faire** \ˌles-ˌā 'far, 'fer\. [From French, meaning literally "let do".] A policy or theory advocating noninterference by government, as in conditions of labor, commerce, or manufacturing. — **lais·sez-faire** or **lais·ser-faire** \ˌles-ˌā-'far, -'fer\ *adj.*

la·i·ty \'lā-ət-ē\ *n.; pl.* **la·i·ties. 1** Laymen as a group, especially as distinguished from the clergy. **2** Persons not of a certain profession, as law or medicine, as distinguished from those belonging to it.

lake \'lāk\ *n.* **1** A large inland body of standing water. **2** A widened part of a river. **3** A great pool of any liquid.

lamb \'lam\ *n.* **1** A young sheep. **2** The flesh of a lamb, used for food. **3** An innocent, weak, or gentle person. — *v.* To give birth to a lamb or lambs.

lam·baste \ˌlam-'bāst, -'bast\ *v.;* **lam·bast·ed; lam·bast·ing. 1** To beat; to strike. **2** To scold roughly.

lam·bent \'lam-bənt\ *adj.* **1** Playing lightly over a surface; wavering; flickering; as, a *lambent* flame. **2** Softly radiant; as, *lambent* eyes. **3** Having lightness and brilliance; as, *lambent* humor. — **lam·ben·cy** \-bən-sē\ *n.*

lamb·kin \'lam-kən\ *n.* A young lamb.

lamb·like \'lam-ˌlīk\ *adj.* Like a lamb; gentle; meek.

lam·bre·quin \'lam-br-kən, 'lam-brə-\ *n.* A drapery hanging from a shelf or from a casing above a window.

lamb·skin \'lam-ˌskin\ *n.* **1** A lamb's skin, especially one dressed with the wool on it. **2** Leather made from a lamb's skin.

lame \'lām\ *adj.;* **lam·er; lam·est. 1** Disabled in the leg or foot; crippled. **2** Weak; painful; as, a *lame* back. **3** Limping; halting; hobbling; as, a *lame* gait. **4** Unsatisfactory; as, a *lame* excuse. — *v.;* **lamed; lam·ing.** To make or become lame; as, to *lame* oneself in a fall. — **lame·ly,** *adv.*

la·ment \lə-'ment\ *v.* To express or feel sorrow for or about; to mourn greatly. — *n.* Grief or sorrow expressed, as in crying or complaints.

lam·en·ta·ble \'lam-ən-təb-l, lə-'ment-əb-l\ *adj.* **1** Mournful; full of grief. **2** Unfortunate; pitiable; as, a *lamentable* error; a *lamentable* remark. — **lam·en·ta·bly** \'lam-ən-tə-blē, lə-'ment-ə-blē\ *adv.*

lam·en·ta·tion \ˌlam-ən-'tāsh-n\ *n.* The act of lamenting or mourning; a wailing.

lam·i·nate \'lam-ə-ˌnāt\ *v.;* **lam·i·nat·ed; lam·i·nat·ing.** **1** To form, as metal, into a thin plate, as by rolling. **2** Of plastics, to make into a dense, tough solid by uniting separate layers, as of paper, fabric, or wood treated with a synthetic resin and applying heat and pressure. **3** Of glass, to unite two sheets by a layer of transparent plastic.

lamp \'lamp\ *n.* **1** A vessel with a wick for burning oil to produce light. **2** Any device that produces light or heat by electricity or gas; as, an electric *lamp.*

whale oil lamp

lamp·black \'lamp-ˌblak\ *n.* A finely powdered deep-black soot made by imperfectly burning oil or tar, used especially in paints and ink.

lamp·light \'lamp-ˌlīt\ *n.* The light given by a lamp.

lamp·light·er \'lamp-ˌlīt-r\ *n.* **1** One that lights a lamp; especially, a person employed to go about lighting street lights burning gas. **2** A small roll of paper or a splinter of wood for lighting lamps.

incandescent lamp

lam·poon \lam-'pün\ *n.* **1** A satire in writing, usually spiteful or abusive and directed against an individual. **2** A humorous, critical satire of any subject, as by a cartoon. — *v.* To satirize or ridicule humorously in a lampoon. — **lam·poon·er** \-r\ or **lam·poon·ist** \-əst\ *n.*

lamp·post \'lam(p)-ˌpōst\ *n.* A post, usually of iron, supporting a lamp, as for lighting a street.

lam·prey \'lam-prē\ *n.; pl.* **lam·preys.** A sea animal resembling an eel, with gill slits like those of a fish and a large, round, jawless sucker mouth.

lamp·shade \'lamp-ˌshād\ *n.* A device for softening or directing the light of a lamp.

lance \'lan(t)s\ *n.* **1** A long-handled weapon with a sharp steel head, formerly used by light-armed cavalry soldiers. **2** A soldier armed with a lance. **3** Any sharp-pointed implement suggesting a soldier's lance, as a surgeon's lancet. — *v.;* **lanced; lanc·ing.** To pierce or cut with a lance or lancet.

lanc·er \'lan(t)s-r\ *n.* **1** One who lances. **2** A cavalry soldier armed with a lance.

lan·cet \'lan(t)s-ət\ *n.* A sharp-pointed, two-edged surgical instrument.

land \'land\ *n.* **1** The solid part of the surface of the earth. **2** Any part of the earth's surface considered by itself, as a country or a farm. **3** The people of a country; a nation. **4** Ground; soil; as, wet *land.* — *v.* **1** To set on shore or to go ashore from a boat. **2** Of a ship, to stop at or near a place on shore. **3** To cause to reach or come to rest in a particular place; as, to *land* an arrow in the target. **4** To catch; as, to *land* a fish. **5** To win, secure or gain by effort; as, to *land* a good job; to *land* a thief in jail. **6** To come to ground or to bring to ground; as, to *land* an airplane. **7** Of a seaplane, to light on the surface of the water. **8** To reach the end of a course or a stage in a journey; to arrive.

land·ed \'lan-dəd\ *adj.* **1** Having an estate in land; as, *landed* proprietors. **2** Consisting of real estate; as, *landed* property.

land·hold·er \'land-ˌhōld-r\ *n.* A holder or owner of land.

land·ing \'lan-ding\ *n.* **1** The action of coming to land. **2** A place to land, as a wharf. **3** The level part of a staircase at the end of a flight of stairs or connecting one flight with another.

landing craft. Any of numerous naval craft specially designed for putting ashore troops or equipment.

landing field. A field where aircraft may land and take off.

landing net. A small, cone-shaped net used in fishing to take the captured fish from the water.

landing strip. An airstrip.

land·la·dy \'lan-ˌ(d)lād-ē\ *n.; pl.* **land·la·dies.** **1** A woman who owns land or houses that she rents. **2** A woman who runs an inn, lodginghouse, or boardinghouse.

land·locked \'lan-ˌ(d)läkt\ *adj.* **1** Shut in, or nearly shut in, by land; as, a *landlocked* harbor. **2** Shut off from the sea by some barrier; as, *landlocked* salmon.

land·lord \'lan-ˌ(d)lȯrd\ *n.* **1** The owner or holder of land or houses that he leases. **2** A man who runs an inn or lodginghouse.

land·lub·ber \'lan-ˌ(d)ləb-r\ *n.* In sailors' language, anyone who passes his life on land or anyone who is clumsy on shipboard.

land·mark \'lan(d)-ˌmärk, -ˌmȧrk\ *n.* **1** A stone, post, or tree that marks a boundary. **2** Any noticeable object on land that serves as a guide. **3** Any event that marks a turning point; as, *landmarks* in history.

land·own·er \'lan-ˌdōn-r\ *n.* An owner of land. — **land·own·er·ship** \-ˌdōn-r-ˌship\ *n.* — **land·own·ing** \-ˌdō-ning\ *n.* or *adj.*

land·scape \'lan(d)-ˌskāp\ *n.* **1** A stretch of land that can be seen in one glance. **2** A picture of natural scenery. — *v.;* **land·scaped; land·scap·ing.** To improve the natural beauties of a tract of land by grading, clearing, or gardening.

land·slide \'lan(d)-ˌslīd\ *n.* **1** The slipping down of a mass of rocks or earth on a steep slope. **2** The mass of rocks or earth that slides. **3** A great majority of votes for one side, as in an election; an overwhelming majority.

lands·man \'lan(d)z-mən\ *n.; pl.* **lands·men** \-mən\.

A person who lives or works on land; especially, one who knows little or nothing of the sea and ships.

land·ward \'lan-(d)wərd\ *adj.* Lying or being toward the land.

land·ward \'lan-(d)wərd\ or **land·wards** \-(d)wərdz\ *adv.* Toward the land.

lane \'lān\ *n.* **1** A narrow way or road, especially one between fences or hedges, not used as a highway; as, country *lanes.* **2** A special route, such as one that boats are supposed to follow in crossing an ocean. **3** A strip of roadway used for a single line of traffic.

lang·syne \'lang-'sīn, -'zīn\ *adv.* or *n. Scottish.* Long ago.

lan·guage \'lang-gwij\ *n.* **1** The speech of human beings. **2** The words and expressions used by a large group of people; a tongue; as, the English *language.* **3** The special words used by particular groups of people; as, the *language* of medicine or of sports. **4** Any means of expressing ideas or feelings; as, sign *language.* **5** Ability in the use of words; the form, style, or manner of using words; as, poetic or forceful *language.* **6** The study of a language or languages.

lan·guid \'lang-gwəd\ *adj.* Weak with weariness; drooping; dull, slow, or lacking in force; as, a *languid* voice; to walk with *languid* steps. — **lan·guid·ly,** *adv.*

lan·guish \'lang-gwish\ *v.* **1** To become weak or languid. **2** To lose strength or force; to waste away with longing; to pine; as, to *languish* in prison. **3** To appeal for sympathy by putting on a weary or sorrowful look. — **lan·guish·ment,** *n.*

lan·guor \'lang-(g)r\ *n.* **1** Weakness or weariness of body or mind. **2** A state of dreamy inactivity. — **lan·guor·ous** \-(g)r(-)əs\ *adj.*

lank \'langk\ *adj.* **1** Slender and thin; lean. **2** Of hair, without curl or wave. — **lank·ly,** *adv.*

lanky \'langk-ē\ *adj.;* **lank·i·er; lank·i·est.** Lank; tall, thin, and usually loose-jointed; as, a *lanky* boy. — **lank·i·ly** \-l-ē\ *adv.*

lan·o·lin \'lan-l-ən\ or **lan·o·line** \-ən, -ˌēn\ *n.* Purified fat or grease from wool, often mixed with water and used as a base in various preparations, as ointments and cosmetics.

lan·tern \'lant-rn\ *n.* A round or boxlike case for protecting a light.

lan·yard \'lan-yərd\ *n.* **1** A short rope or cord used as a fastening on ships. **2** A cord worn round the neck by sailors, often used for suspending a knife. **3** A cord with a hook at one end, used in firing certain types of cannon.

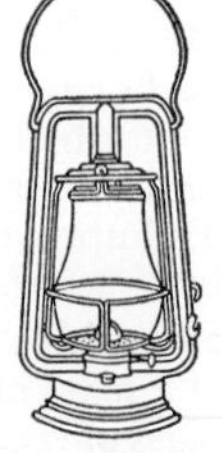
lantern

La·o·tian \lā-'ōsh-n, 'laủsh-n\ *adj.* Of or relating to Laos. — *n.* A native of Laos.

lap \'lap\ *n.* **1** A part of a garment that overlaps another; a flap, as the skirt of a coat. **2** The part of the clothing that is over the knees and thighs when a person sits down. **3** The front part of a person between the waist and the knees, when seated. **4** Circumstances; conditions — used in the phrase *the lap of luxury.*

lap \'lap\ *v.;* **lapped; lap·ping. 1** To fold; as, to *lap* cloth in making a seam. **2** *Dial.* To wrap. The mother *lapped* her coat around the child. **3** To lay a thing over or near to something else so as to partly cover it; to overlap; as, to *lap* one shingle over another. — *n.* **1** The part of anything that overlaps another part; the amount that overlaps. **2** One full circuit on a race track when the race consists of more than one circuit. **3** A stage in a journey. The first *lap* of the trip was over.

lap \'lap\ *v.;* **lapped; lap·ping. 1** To lick up, as liquid food, with a quick movement of the tongue. **2** To make a sound as if licking up liquid. **3** To wash against with a lapping sound, as water or waves. — *n.* The act or sound of lapping.

la·pel \lə-'pel\ *n.* The part of the front of a collar that is turned back; as, coat *lapels.*

lap·i·dary \'lap-ə-ˌder-ē\ *n.; pl.* **lap·i·dar·ies.** A person who cuts, polishes, and engraves precious stones.

lap·is laz·u·li \'lap-əs 'laz(h)-yə-ˌlī, -ˌlē\. A semiprecious stone of a deep blue color.

lap·pet \'lap-ət\ *n.* **1** A loose fold or flap of an article of clothing. **2** Anything lying in a fold or hanging down loosely, as a lobe of the ear or a flap of flesh.

lapse \'laps\ *n.* **1** A slight error; a slip, as of the tongue or pen. **2** A gradual slipping or falling away from a higher to a lower rank or condition; as, a *lapse* into laziness. **3** A gradual passing away, as of time. **4** The ending of a certain right or privilege by failure to meet certain requirements; as, the *lapse* of a magazine subscription. — *v.;* **lapsed; laps·ing. 1** To slip, pass, or fall gradually; as, to *lapse* into silence. **2** To fall into disuse, as a custom. **3** To end or cease, as insurance, or to pass to someone else, as property, because of failure to meet certain requirements.

lap·wing \'lap-ˌwing\ *n.* A crested plover, noted for its slow irregular flapping flight and its shrill wailing cry.

lar·board \'lärb-rd, 'lȧrb-; 'lär-ˌbōrd, 'lȧr-, -ˌbȯrd\ *n.* The left side of a ship to a person facing forward; port.

lar·ce·ny \'lärs-n(-)ē, 'lȧrs-\ *n.; pl.* **lar·ce·nies.** Theft; the unlawful carrying away of private property without the owner's consent.

larch \'lärch, 'lȧrch\ *n.* **1** A tree of the pine family that has cones but sheds its short needles. **2** The wood of this tree.

lard \'lärd, 'lȧrd\ *n.* The fat of a pig or hog; especially, the soft, white, melted fat from the abdomen. — *v.* **1** To insert pork or bacon into meat before cooking. **2** To smear with lard, fat, or grease. **3** To add to; especially, to enrich; as, a book *larded* with illustrations.

lard·er \ˈlärd-r, ˈlȧrd-r\ *n.* A place where meat and other foods are kept.

large \ˈlärj, ˈlȧrj\ *adj.;* **larg·er; larg·est.** Greater, bigger, more extended, or more powerful than usual; as, a *large* sum of money; a *large* house. — **at large. 1** At liberty; free; as, a criminal who is *at large.* **2** As a whole; in general; as, the public *at large.* **3** Representing a whole state or district; as, a congressman *at large.*

large intestine. The second major division of the intestine, consisting of the caecum, vermiform appendix, colon, and rectum.

large·ly \ˈlärj-lē, ˈlȧrj-\ *adv.* Generally; in the main; as, a story that is *largely* true.

lar·gess or **lar·gesse** \lär-ˈjes, lȧr-; ˈlär-ˌjes, ˈlȧr-\ *n.* **1** Liberal giving. **2** A generous gift.

lar·go \ˈlär-ˌgō, ˈlȧr-\ *adj.* or *adv.* In music, very slow. — *n.; pl.* **lar·gos.** A largo movement.

lar·i·at \ˈlar-ē-ət\ *n.* [From Spanish *la reata* meaning "the rope".] A rope for catching or tethering animals; a lasso.

lark \ˈlärk, ˈlȧrk\ *n.* **1** A small, mostly brownish songbird common in Europe, having the lower part of the leg covered with overlapping scales behind and in front; especially, the skylark. **2** Any of several similar birds.

lark \ˈlärk, ˈlȧrk\ *n.* A gay, lighthearted adventure, as a prank; a good time. — *v.* To frolic.

lark·spur \ˈlärk-ˌspər, ˈlȧrk-\ *n.* A plant that sometimes grows to be five feet tall, with erect clusters of blue, white, pink, or purplish flowers.

lar·va \ˈlär-və, ˈlȧr-\ *n.; pl.* **lar·vae** \-(ˌ)vē\ or **lar·vas** \-vəz\. A young animal basically unlike the adult of its kind, as a tadpole; especially, a wingless often wormlike young insect, as a caterpillar or maggot.

larvae

lar·val \ˈlärv-l, ˈlȧrv-l\ *adj.* Of, having to do with, or in the stage of, a larva.

lar·yn·gi·tis \ˌlar-ən-ˈjīt-əs\ *n.* Inflammation or soreness of the larynx.

lar·ynx \ˈlar-ingks\ *n.; pl.* **la·ryn·ges** \lə-ˈrin-ˌjēz\ or **lar·ynx·es** \ˈlar-ingks-əz\. The upper part of the windpipe, containing the vocal cords.

las·civ·i·ous \lə-ˈsiv-ē-əs, la-\ *adj.* Lustful; lewd. — **las·civ·i·ous·ly,** *adv.*

la·ser \ˈlā-zər\ *n.* A device that utilizes the natural oscillations of atoms to amplify or generate light waves.

lash \ˈlash\ *n.* **1** A blow with a whip or switch; any sudden, swinging blow. **2** The flexible part of a whip; anything used for whipping. **3** An eyelash. — *v.* **1** To whip. **2** To strike or drive as if with a lash; to move or beat like a lash. The lion *lashed* his tail. **3** To strike against with words; as, to *lash* out against an unfair practice.

lash \ˈlash\ *v.* To bind with a rope, cord, or chain.

lash·ing \ˈlash-ing\ *n.* **1** The act of one that lashes, or whips. **2** A whipping; a thrashing.

lash·ing \ˈlash-ing\ *n.* **1** The act of one that lashes, or binds. **2** Something used to bind or tie up.

lass \ˈlas\ *n.* A girl.

las·sie \ˈlas-ē\ *n.* A lass; a girl.

las·si·tude \ˈlas-ə-ˌtüd, -ˌtyüd\ *n.* The condition of being listless or weary; lack of energy; languor.

las·so \ˈlas-ˌō, la-ˈsü\ *n.; pl.* **las·sos** or **las·soes.** [From Spanish *lazo,* there derived from Latin *laqueus* meaning "noose", "snare".] A rope or long leather thong with a slipknot at the end, used for catching horses or other animals. — *v.;* **las·soed; las·so·ing.** To catch with a lasso.

lasso

last \ˈlast\ *n.* A foot-shaped block of wood or metal on which shoes are made or repaired. — *v.* To shape with a last.

last \ˈlast\ *adj.* A superlative of *late.* **1** Following all the rest; final; as, the *last* letter of the alphabet. **2** Next before the present; most recent; as, *last* week. **3** Lowest in rank or position; as, to be *last* in one's class. **4** Most unlikely; as, the *last* one to be suspected.

— The words *final* and *ultimate* are synonyms of *last: last* usually refers to something that comes at the end of a series and either implies that no more will follow or indicates merely the most recent in the series; *final* generally applies to something at the very end or closing of a series; *ultimate* may refer to an event that is the farthest distant in the future or the past, or to something that is the highest or most complete stage in a process of development.

— *adv.* **1** Latest; at the end. The dessert was served *last.* **2** At a time or occasion that is most recent. When did the doctor *last* call? — *n.* A person or thing that is last; the end of anything.

last \ˈlast\ *v.* To continue; to remain; to endure; to hold out.

last·ing \ˈlas-ting\ *adj.* Continuing for a long time; enduring.

— The words *permanent* and *durable* are synonyms of *lasting: lasting* usually describes something that seems to continue in existence or in effectiveness indefinitely or for a very long time; *permanent* may suggest something that is fixed or unalterable, as in a particular position or state, for an indefinitely long period or as long as it can resist decay or destruction; *durable* applies especially to objects or qualities that have an ability greater than others of their kind to resist forces tending to change or destroy.

last·ly \ˈlast-lē\ *adv.* In conclusion; in the last place.

Last Supper. The supper partaken of by Christ and his disciples on the night of his betrayal.

lat. Abbreviation for *latitude.*

latch \ˈlach\ *n.* A movable piece of metal or wood that holds a door, gate, or window closed. — *v.* To fasten by means of a latch.

latch·key \ˈlach-ˌkē\ *n.* **1** A key used to lift or pull back a latch on a door. **2** Any front-door key.

latch·string \ˈlach-ˌstring\ *n.* A string used to unfasten a latch on a door by lifting it.

late \'lāt\ *adj.;* **lat·er** \'lāt-r\ or **lat·ter** \'lat-r\; **lat·est** \'lāt-əst\ or **last** \'last\. **1** Coming or doing something after the usual or proper time; tardy. The train was an hour *late.* **2** Far advanced toward the end or close, as of a day or night; as, a *late* hour. **3** Having recently died or left a certain position; as, the *late* president. **4** Recent; as, a *late* invention. **5** Continuing or doing something after the usual time; as, a *late* show. — *adv.* **1** After the usual or proper time; after delay. Better *late* than never. **2** Far, as in the night, day, or week. **3** Not long ago; recently. — **of late.** Lately; recently.

late·com·er \'lāt-ˌkəm-r\ *n.* One who arrives late; a recent arrival.

la·teen \la-'tēn, lə-\ *adj.* Of or relating to a peculiar sailing rig of the Mediterranean, characterized by a triangular sail (**lateen sail**) attached by a long yard to a low mast.

Late Latin. Latin as used after the classic Latin had become a dead language for the people, from about A.D. 200 to A.D. 600.

late·ly \'lāt-lē\ *adv.* Not long ago; recently.

la·ten·cy \'lāt-n-sē\ *n.; pl.* **la·ten·cies.** The quality or state of being latent.

la·tent \'lāt-nt\ *adj.* Hidden; present, but not visible, active, or recognized; as, *latent* talent.
— The words *dormant* and *potential* are synonyms of *latent: latent* usually describes something that lies as if beneath a surface and is not visibly present except under close examination but may at any time emerge and develop in importance; *dormant* may suggest something that is inactive as if sleeping but that is capable of being awakened to action; *potential* usually refers to some quality or force that either does not exist or is undeveloped for the time being but because of surrounding conditions seems capable of being brought into existence or further developed.

la·tent·ly \'lāt-nt-lē\ *adv.* In a latent manner.

lat·er·al \'lat-r-əl, 'la-trəl\ *adj.* Having to do with the side; belonging on the side; at, toward, or coming from the side; as, the *lateral* branches of a tree; a *lateral* view. — *n.* Anything lateral. — **lat·er·al·ly** \'lat-r-ə-lē, 'la-trə-lē\ *adv.*

la·tex \'lā-ˌteks\ *n.; pl.* **la·tex·es** \'lā-ˌteks-əz\ or **lat·i·ces** \'lat-ə-ˌsēz\. [From Latin, meaning "liquid", "fluid".] A milky juice found in many plants. Rubber is made from a *latex.*

lath \'lath\ *n.; pl.* **laths** \'lathz, 'laths\. **1** A thin narrow strip of wood used as a base for plaster. **2** Sheet metal or wire cloth used as a substitute for wooden laths. **3** A number of laths together; lathwork. — *v.* To cover or line with laths. — **lath·er** \'lath-r\ *n.*

lathe \'lāth\ *n.* A machine in which a piece of material is held and turned while being shaped by a tool.

lath·er \'lath-r\ *n.* **1** The foam or froth made by mixing soap and water. **2** Foam from sweating; as, *lather* on a horse's back. — *v.;* **lath·ered; lath·er·ing** \-r(-)ing\. **1** To make lather; as, a soap that *lathers* well. **2** To spread lather on; as, to *lather* the face before shaving. — **lath·er·er** \'lath-r-r\ *n.* — **lath·ery** \-r-ē\ *adj.*

lath·ing \'lath-ing\ *n.* **1** The action or process of placing laths in position. **2** A number of laths together; lathwork.

lath·work \'lath-ˌwərk\ *n.* Lathing.

Lat·in \'lat-n\ *adj.* **1** Of or relating to ancient Rome, to its people, or to the language used by the Romans. **2** Of or relating to peoples or countries whose language and culture have descended from the ancient Roman. — *n.* **1** An inhabitant of ancient Latium, the territory surrounding Rome. **2** A person who lives in a Latin country. **3** The language of the ancient Romans.

Lat·in-Amer·i·can \'lat-n-ə-'mer-ək-n\ *adj.* Of or relating to any American nation in which the official or chief language is derived from Latin; relating to that part of the American continents lying south of the United States.

Latin American. A native or inhabitant of a Latin-American country; especially, one descended wholly or chiefly from European ancestors.

Lat·in·ist \'lat-n-əst\ *n.* A person with much knowledge of Latin.

Lat·in·ize \'lat-n-ˌīz\ *v.;* **Lat·in·ized; Lat·in·iz·ing.** **1** To translate into Latin. **2** To give something Latin characteristics or forms.

lat·ish \'lāt-ish\ *adj.* Somewhat late.

lat·i·tude \'lat-ə-ˌtüd, -ˌtyüd\ *n.* **1** Freedom from narrow limits, as in acting or speaking as one wishes. **2** A region or locality, especially as thought of with reference to distance from the equator; as, cold *latitudes.* **3** The distance north or south of the equator, measured in degrees (**degrees of latitude**).

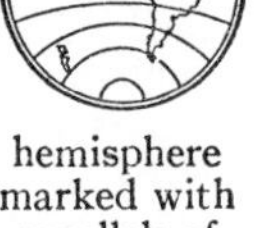
hemisphere marked with parallels of latitude

lat·ter \'lat-r\ *adj.* A comparative of *late.* **1** More recent; later; having to do with the end or a part toward the end; as, the *latter* part of the week. **2** The second of two things mentioned. The *latter* is the better book.

lat·ter·ly \'lat-r-lē\ *adv.* Lately; recently.

lat·tice \'lat-əs\ *n.* **1** A structure of thin strips of wood or metal crossed to form a network. **2** A window, door, or gate having latticed panels. — *v.;* **lat·ticed; lat·tic·ing.** To make into or like a lattice; to furnish with a lattice; as, a *latticed* window.

lat·tice·work \'lat-əs-ˌwərk\ *n.* **1** A lattice. **2** Lattices collectively; latticing.

Lat·vi·an \'lat-vē-ən\ *adj.* Of or relating to Latvia. — *n.* A native or inhabitant of Latvia.

laud \'lȯd\ *n.* Praise; especially, a hymn or song of praise. — *v.* To praise.

laud·a·ble \'lȯd-əb-l\ *adj.* Praiseworthy; commendable. — **laud·a·bly** \-ə-blē\ *adv.*

lau·da·num \'lȯd-n(-)əm\ *n.* Formerly, any of various preparations of opium; now, a solution of opium in alcohol.

lau·da·tion \lȯ-ˈdāsh-n\ *n.* **1** The act of lauding. **2** Praise.

laud·a·to·ry \ˈlȯd-ə-ˌtōr-ē, -ˌtȯr-ē\ *adj.* Expressing praise.

laugh \ˈlaf, ˈlȧf\ *v.* **1** To show amusement, joy, or scorn by smiling and making chuckling or other explosive sounds in the throat. **2** To influence a person in some way by laughter or scorn. **3** To express by laughing; to utter with laughter; as, to *laugh* one's agreement. — **laugh at. 1** To be amused by. **2** To make fun of; to ridicule. — **laugh off.** To dismiss with laughter or a pretense of laughter; as, to *laugh off* a disappointment. — *n.* **1** The act of laughing. **2** The sound of laughing. **3** Something provoking or deserving laughter.

laugh·a·ble \ˈlaf-əb-l, ˈlȧf-\ *adj.* Fitted to provoke laughter; comical; funny; ridiculous. — **laugh·a·bly** \-ə-blē\ *adv.*

laugh·ing \ˈlaf-ing, ˈlȧf-\ *adj.* Fit to be treated or accompanied with laughter — used in phrases such as *no laughing matter.*

laughing jackass. The kookaburra.

laugh·ing·ly \ˈlaf-ing-lē, ˈlȧf-\ *adv.* With a laugh; with laughter.

laugh·ing·stock \ˈlaf-ing-ˌstäk, ˈlȧf-\ *n.* A person or thing that is an object of ridicule.

laugh·ter \ˈlaft-r, ˈlȧft-r\ *n.* **1** The action of laughing. **2** The sound of laughing.

launch \ˈlȯnch, ˈlänch\ *v.* **1** To throw; to hurl; as, to *launch* a spear. **2** To cause to slide into the water; to set afloat; as, to *launch* a ship. **3** To shove or send off, especially with force; as, to *launch* an aircraft by catapult; to *launch* a rocket. **4** To start; to set in operation; as, to *launch* an attack. **5** To start off in some activity; as, to *launch* one's son on a business career. **6** To plunge; to move actively; as, to *launch* into a discussion. **7** To set out; as, to *launch* off alone. — *n.* An act or instance of launching.

launch \ˈlȯnch, ˈlänch\ *n.* **1** The largest boat carried by a ship of war. **2** An open or partly decked powerboat, used for pleasure or short-distance transportation.

launch, 2

launch·er \ˈlȯnch-r, ˈlänch-r\ *n.* **1** A device for firing a grenade from a rifle. **2** A device for launching a rocket or rocket shell.

launching pad. A noninflammable platform from which a rocket can be launched.

laun·der \ˈlȯnd-r, ˈländ-r\ *v.;* **laun·dered; laun·der·ing** \-r(-)ing\. **1** To wash, or wash and iron, as clothes. **2** To undergo laundering; as, fabrics guaranteed to *launder* well. — **laun·der·er** \-r-r\ *n.*

laun·dress \ˈlȯn-drəs, ˈlän-\ *n.* A woman whose work is laundering.

laun·dry \ˈlȯn-drē, ˈlän-\ *n.; pl.* **laun·dries** \-drēz\. **1** The action of laundering; a washing. **2** A place where clothes and other articles, as sheets, towels, and tablecloths, are washed and ironed. **3** Articles to be laundered.

laun·dry·man \ˈlȯn-drē-mən, ˈlän-\ *n.; pl.* **laun·dry·men** \-mən\. **1** A man who operates or works in a laundry. **2** A man who collects and delivers laundry.

laun·dry·wom·an \ˈlȯn-drē-ˌwu̇m-ən, ˈlän-\ *n.; pl.* **laun·dry·wom·en** \-ˌwim-ən\. A laundress.

lau·re·ate \ˈlȯr-ē-ət\ *adj.* Crowned with laurel; distinguished; marked with special honor, especially as a poet. — *n.* A poet laureate.

lau·rel \ˈlȯr-əl, ˈlär-\ *n.* **1** A small evergreen tree or shrub of southern Europe, the shiny stiff leaves of which were used by the ancient Greeks to make crowns for heroes and for the victors in various contests. **2** Any of a family of aromatic shrubs and trees including besides the true laurel the sassafras, spicebush, and cinnamon. **3** A bush or tree somewhat like the laurel, as the mountain laurel or the rhododendron. **4** A laurel crown; honor; fame.

mountain laurel

la·va \ˈläv-ə, ˈlav-ə, ˈlȧv-ə\ *n.* **1** Melted rock issuing from a volcano. **2** Melted volcanic rock that has cooled and hardened.

lav·a·to·ry \ˈlav-ə-ˌtōr-ē, -ˌtȯr-ē\ *n.; pl.* **lav·a·to·ries. 1** A basin or bowl for washing. **2** A room with conveniences for washing the hands and face, and often with a toilet. **3** A toilet.

lave \ˈlāv\ *v.;* **laved; lav·ing. 1** To wash; to bathe. **2** To wash or flow along or against; as, water *laving* the shore.

lav·en·der \ˈlav-nd-r\ *n.* **1** A plant with narrow, somewhat woolly leaves and spikes of small, sweet-smelling, lilac-purple flowers. **2** The dried leaves and flowers of this plant, used to perfume clothes and bed linen. **3** A pale bluish blue-red color; the color of lavender flowers.

lav·ish \ˈlav-ish\ *adj.* **1** Spending or giving more than is necessary; extravagant; as, to be *lavish* with money; *lavish* of praise. **2** Abundant; spent, produced, or given, freely; as, *lavish* gifts; *lavish* hospitality. — *v.* To spend or give freely; to squander; as, to *lavish* affection on a person. — **lav·ish·ly,** *adv.*

law \ˈlȯ\ *n.* [From Old English *lagu*, there borrowed from an older form of Old Norse *log* meaning "fate", "choice", "law".] **1** A rule of conduct or action laid down and enforced by the supreme governing authority in a community, as the legislature of a state or nation, or established by custom; an edict, statute, or ordinance. **2** The whole collection of such customs and rules; as, the *law* of the land. **3** A rule, principle, or formula of construction or procedure; as, the *laws* of poetry. **4** Any rule or principle stating something that always works in the same way under the same conditions; as, the *law* of gravity. **5** Trial in a court to determine what is just and right according to the laws; as, to go to *law*. **6** The science which deals with laws and their interpretation and application; as, to study *law*. **7** The profession of a lawyer; lawyers as a group.

law-abid·ing \'lȯ-ə-ˌbīd-ing\ *adj.* Obedient to the law.

law·break·er \'lȯ-ˌbrāk-r\ *n.* A person who breaks the law. — **law·break·ing** \-ˌbrāk-ing\ *n.* or *adj.*

law·ful \'lȯf-l\ *adj.* **1** Permitted by law; as, to admit only those having *lawful* business to transact. **2** Recognized by law; rightful; as, the *lawful* owner. — **law·ful·ly** \'lȯf-l(-)ē\ *adv.*

law·giv·er \'lȯ-ˌgiv-r\ *n.* **1** A person who gives a code of laws to a people, as Moses or Hammurabi. **2** A lawmaker.

law·less \'lȯ-ləs\ *adj.* **1** Having no laws; not based on or regulated by law; as, the *lawless* society of a new frontier. **2** Not controlled by existing law; unruly; disorderly; as, a *lawless* mob. — **law·less·ly**, *adv.*

law·mak·er \'lȯ-ˌmāk-r\ *n.* A person who has a part in framing laws; a legislator.

law·mak·ing \'lȯ-ˌmāk-ing\ *adj.* Making laws; legislative; as, a *lawmaking* branch of government. — *n.* The making of laws; legislation.

lawn \'lȯn, 'län\ *n.* A sheer linen or cotton fabric woven of very fine threads, used especially for handkerchiefs and dresses.

lawn \'lȯn, 'län\ *n.* Ground, especially around a house, covered with fine, closely mown grass.

lawn mower. A machine used to clip the grass on lawns.

law·suit \'lȯ-ˌsüt\ *n.* A case before a court of law.

law·yer \'lȯ-yər\ *n.* A person who has studied law; especially, one whose profession is advising others on legal matters and acting as attorney for them in lawsuits and other legal proceedings.

lax \'laks\ *adj.* **1** Loose; not firm or tight; as, a *lax* grip. **2** Not exact or strict; as, *lax* discipline. — **lax·ly**, *adv.*

lax·a·tive \'laks-ət-iv\ *n.* A medicine to loosen the bowels. — *adj.* Having a tendency to loosen or relax, especially to relieve from constipation.

lax·i·ty \'laks-ət-ē\ *n.; pl.* **lax·i·ties**. The condition of being lax; looseness; want of strictness; as, *laxity* in discipline.

lay \'lā\. Past tense of *lie,* to recline.

lay \'lā\ *n.* A song; a ballad.

lay \'lā\ *adj.* **1** Belonging to or having to do with people who are not clergymen; as, a *lay* church worker. **2** Not of or from a particular profession; not professional.

lay \'lā\ *v.;* **laid** \'lād\; **lay·ing**. **1** To bring down, as with force; as, trees *laid* low by the gale. **2** To put, place, or set; as, to *lay* one's hat on the table; to *lay* bricks. **3** To produce an egg, as a hen. **4** To bet on something; as, to *lay* a dollar on a number. **5** To calm; to quiet down; to cause to disappear; as, to *lay* one's fears. **6** To spread, as over a surface; as, to *lay* a pavement. **7** To prepare; to arrange; as, to *lay* plans; to *lay* a table for dinner. **8** To present a statement or claim as true; as, to *lay* claim to an estate. **9** To charge; to put; as, to *lay* a tax; to *lay* the blame on someone. — **lay down. 1** To discard; to give up; as, to *lay down* the cares of office. **2** To stake, as a wager. **3** To construct; as, to *lay down* a railroad. **4** To establish; to prescribe; as, a committee that *laid down* a code of behavior for students. **5** To assert or command positively; as, to *lay down* the law. — **lay hold of.** To seize; to grasp. — **lay off.** To dismiss or cease to employ; as, to *lay off* workers. — **lay on. 1** To apply or spread on a surface. **2** To strike; to beat; to attack. — **lay out. 1** To expend, as money. **2** To map out; to plan in detail. **3** To display; to exhibit; to *lay out* merchandise for sale. **4** To prepare a corpse for burial. — **lay up. 1** To store up. **2** To confine or disable, as with illness. — *n.* The way a thing lies in relation to something else; as, the *lay* of the land.

lay·er \'lā-ər, 'ler\ *n.* **1** A person or thing that lays something, as in *bricklayer*. **2** One thickness or fold of something laid over or under another; as, the top *layer* of a cake. **3** A branch or shoot of a plant that for purposes of propagation is bent down and covered with soil. — *v.* **1** To propagate plants by layering. **2** To cover with a layer.

lay·er·ing \'lā-ər-ing, 'ler-ing\ *n.* The production of new plants by surrounding a stem, usually partly cut through, with a rooting medium, as soil, until new roots have formed.

lay·ette \lā-'et\ *n.* A complete outfit for a newborn baby.

lay·man \'lā-mən\ *n.;* **lay·men** \-mən\. **1** A person who is not a clergyman. **2** A person who is not a member of a particular profession.

lay·off \'lā-ˌȯf\ *n.* The dismissing of workers for a temporary period; the period itself.

lay·out \'lā-ˌau̇t\ *n.* **1** Arrangement; plan; as, the *layout* of a house. **2** Something that is laid out; an outfit; as, a model train *layout*. **3** The way in which a piece of printed matter is arranged; as, the *layout* of a page; the *layout* of a book.

la·zy \'lā-zē\ *adj.;* **la·zi·er**; **la·zi·est**. **1** Not willing to act or work; idle; indolent. **2** Slow; sluggish; as, a *lazy* stream. — For synonyms see *idle*. — **la·zi·ly** \'lāz-l-ē\ *adv.*

lb. [Abbreviated from Latin *libra.*] Abbreviation for *pound.*

lea \'lē\ *n.* A pasture; a meadow.

leach \'lēch\ *v.* **1** To drain a liquid slowly through a material, as ashes, to obtain a substance that is dissolved and retained in the liquid. **2** To dissolve a substance in this manner.

lead \'led\ *n.* **1** A heavy, soft, gray, metallic element that is easily bent and shaped. **2** Something made of lead or an alloy of lead. **3** A mass of lead used to find the depth of water, as in a river or ocean; a plummet. **4** A thin strip of metal used to separate lines of type in printing. **5** Bullets or other ammunition; as, a shower of *lead*. **6** A long thin piece of graphite used in pencils. **7** [in the plural] Lead frames for windowpanes. — *v.;* **lead·ed** \'led-əd\; **lead·ing** \'led-ing\. **1** To cover, line, or weigh down something with lead. **2** To fix glass in position with lead. **3** To place lead between lines in printing.

lead \'lēd\ *v.;* **led** \'led\; **lead·ing** \'lēd-ing\. **1** To guide or conduct, as by going with or ahead of a person or thing, or by teaching, showing, or commanding; as, to *lead* a horse to water. **2** To be at the head because of ability or power; as, to *lead* an army. **3** To follow the course of; to spend; as, to *lead* a happy life. **4** To reach or go in a certain direction; as, a road *leading* to a city. **5** To begin a game, or a round of play in a game. — *n.* **1** Position at the front; leadership; as, to take the *lead* in making plans. **2** The distance that a person or thing is ahead; as, a five-yard *lead.* **3** Anything that acts as a guide or clue; as, *leads* in solving a crime. **4** The right to play first in a game; the card or piece so played. **5** An insulated electric conductor. **6** A brief summary introducing a newspaper article. **7** A role for a principal actor in a play; the actor who plays such a role.

lead·en \'led-n\ *adj.* **1** Made of lead; heavy as lead; as, a *leaden* weight. **2** Of the dull-gray color of lead; as, a *leaden* sky. **3** Dull; sluggish; cheerless; as, *leaden* spirits.

lead·er \'lēd-r\ *n.* **1** A person or thing that leads. **2** A guide. **3** A chief; a commander. **4** A horse placed in front of others in a team. **5** A pipe for conducting fluid. **6** A short line, as of gut, to attach the end of a fishline to the lure. **7** A chief article of trade, especially one sold at a low price to attract customers. **8** An editorial article.

lead·er·ship \'lēd-r-ˌship\ *n.* **1** The state of being a leader. **2** The skill or power to lead.

lead·ing \'lēd-ing\ *adj.* Guiding; directing; foremost; prominent; as, *leading* citizens.

leaf \'lēf\ *n.; pl.* **leaves** \'lēvz\. **1** One of the green, usually flat, thin parts that grow from the stem of a plant or tree. **2** A petal. **3** A single sheet of a book, making two pages. **4** A movable part of a table top, as a hinged end section (**drop leaf**) or a board to be inserted between the ends of an extension table. **5** Metal in a very thin sheet. — *v.* **1** To send forth leaves; to leave. **2** To turn the leaves of a book; as, to *leaf* through a book.

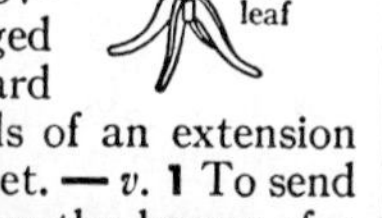

leaf·age \'lē-fij\ *n.* All the leaves on a plant or tree; foliage.

leaf·hop·per \'lēf-ˌhäp-r\ *n.* A leaping insect related to the cicadas and scale insects, which sucks the juices of plants.

leaf·let \'lēf-lət\ *n.* **1** One of the divisions of a compound leaf. **2** A small or young leaf. **3** A single sheet of paper, unfolded, or folded but not trimmed at the folds, and bearing print, as advertising or instructions.

leaf scar. A scar left on a plant when a leaf falls or is broken off.

leaf·stalk \'lēf-ˌstȯk\ *n.* A petiole.

leafy \'lē-fē\ *adj.;* **leaf·i·er**; **leaf·i·est.** Having, covered with, or like, leaves; as, a *leafy* bower; *leafy* vegetables.

league \'lēg\ *n.* A measure of distance, usually about three miles.

league \'lēg\ *n.* **1** An agreement between two or more nations, parties, or persons for the accomplishment of some purpose, as preservation of peace, mutual defense, or the advancement of trade and commerce. **2** Any union or alliance formed by such an agreement; the members of such an alliance taken collectively. **3** An association of athletic clubs, especially baseball clubs. — *v.;* **leagued**; **leagu·ing.** To unite in a league.

leak \'lēk\ *n.* **1** A crack or hole that accidentally lets fluid in or out; as, a *leak* in a boat. **2** Anything else that accidentally or secretly causes loss; as, a *leak* in the treasury. **3** The action of leaking; leakage. — *v.* **1** To let something, as a fluid, in or out accidentally; as, a kettle that *leaks.* **2** To enter or escape accidentally, or secretly; to become public. The secret *leaked* out. — **leaky** \'lēk-ē\ *adj.*

leak·age \'lēk-ij\ *n.* **1** A leaking; an entering or escaping through a leak. **2** The thing or amount that leaks in or out; as, *leakage* of gas.

leal \'lēl\ *adj. Archaic* or *Scottish.* Loyal; honest.

lean \'lēn\ *v.;* **leaned** \'lēnd\, sometimes **leant** \'lent\; **lean·ing. 1** To bend or tip from a straight position; as, a tree that *leans* dangerously. **2** To bend or stoop forward to receive support; to depend on; as, to *lean* on a cane. **3** To have a desire, interest, or tendency; as, to *lean* toward socialism. **4** To cause a thing to lean or incline; as, to *lean* a ladder against a wall. — *n.* The action of leaning; a slope; an inclination; as, a tree with a *lean* to the south.

lean \'lēn\ *adj.* **1** Lacking flesh or fat; thin; as, a *lean* horse. **2** Having little fat; as, *lean* meat. **3** Lacking, as in fullness or richness; scanty; small; as, a *lean* harvest; a *lean* supply. — For synonyms see *thin.* — *n.* Flesh that is chiefly muscle without fat.

lean·ing \'lē-ning\ *n.* The action or the condition of one that leans.

lean-to \'lēn-ˌtü\ *n.; pl.* **lean-tos. 1** A building having a roof with only one slope and usually joined to another building. **2** A rude shelter leaning against posts, rocks, or trees.

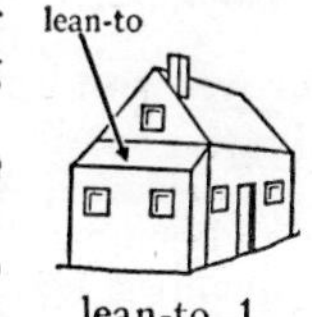

lean-to, 1

leap \'lēp\ *v.;* **leaped** or **leapt** \'lēpt, 'lept\; **leap·ing** \'lēp-ing\. **1** To spring off the ground; to jump; to vault; as, to *leap* upon a horse. **2** To spring or move suddenly as if by a jump; to move quickly; to beat fast; to throb; as, to *leap* with joy. **3** To jump, or to make another person or animal jump, over something; as, to *leap* a fence; to *leap* a horse over a ditch. — *n.* **1** The action of leaping; a jump or spring. **2** A place to be jumped over or the distance jumped; as, a five-foot *leap* over a stream. — **leap·er** \'lēp-r\ *n.*

leap·frog \'lēp-ˌfrȯg, -ˌfräg\ *n.* A game in which one person stoops down while another leaps over him.

leap year. A year containing 366 days (February 29 being added as the extra day) occurring whenever a calendar year is exactly divisible by four except at the end of a century, when the calendar year must be divisible by 400.

learn \'lərn\ *v.;* **learned** \'lərnd\ or **learnt** \'lərnt\; **learn·ing.** **1** To gain knowledge or understanding of, or skill in, as by study or instruction; as, to *learn* algebra. **2** To find out about; as, to *learn* the news too late. **3** To acquire knowledge or skill; as, eager to *learn.*

learn·ed \'lər-nəd\ *adj.* Possessing knowledge or learning; scholarly; as, a *learned* man.

learn·er \'lərn-r\ *n.* One who learns; one learning a kind of work.

learn·ing \'lər-ning\ *n.* **1** The gaining of knowledge or skill. **2** Knowledge or skill acquired by instruction or study.

lease \'lēs\ *v.;* **leased**; **leas·ing.** **1** To grant by lease; to let; as, to *lease* part of one's farm to a neighbor. **2** To take or hold by a lease. — *n.* **1** An agreement to hand over real estate for a period of time in exchange for rent or services. **2** The act of leasing real estate. **3** The period of time for which real estate is leased; as, a ten-year *lease* on a building.

leash \'lēsh\ *n.* A leather strap, a cord, or a chain to hold an animal. — *v.* To hold with a leash; to put on a leash; as, to *leash* a dog.

least \'lēst\ *adj.* A superlative form of *little.* Smallest; shortest; slightest; lowest; as, the *least* time possible. — *adv.* In the smallest or lowest degree. — *n.* The smallest or lowest, as in degree, amount, or value; as, not to care in the *least;* the *least* that can be said.

least common denominator. The least common multiple of the denominators of two or more fractions.

least·wise \'lēst-ˌwīz\ *adv.* At least.

leath·er \'le͟th-r\ *n.* **1** The skin of an animal, tanned or otherwise dressed for use; as, shoes of *leather.* **2** Something made of leather. — *adj.* Relating to, made of, or like leather; as, *leather* gloves. — *v.;* **leath·ered**; **leath·er·ing** \-r(-)ing\. To cover with leather.

leath·er·ette \ˌle͟th-r-'et\ *n.* [From *Leatherette,* a trademark.] A product that is colored, finished, and embossed in imitation of leather grains and qualities, used in bookbinding and in the manufacture of various fancy articles.

leath·ern \'le͟th-rn\ *adj.* Made of leather.

leath·ery \'le͟th-r(-)ē\ *adj.* Like leather; tough.

leave \'lēv\ *n.* **1** Permission; as, to ask *leave* to be absent. **2** The act of leaving and saying good-by; as, to take one's *leave.* **3** A period of time during which a person is allowed to be absent from his duties; as, to have an annual *leave* of 30 days.

leave \'lēv\ *v.;* **left** \'left\; **leav·ing** \'lē-ving\. **1** To allow or cause to remain behind; as, to *leave* one's books at home; to *leave* one's raincoat at school. **2** To deliver; as, to *leave* a book at the library. The postman *left* three letters. **3** To have remaining, as after death or subtraction; as, to *leave* a widow and two children. Taking 7 from 10 *leaves* 3. **4** To give by will; as, to *leave* property to one's wife. **5** To let stay without interference; as, to *leave* a kettle to boil; to *leave* someone alone. **6** To go away; as, to *leave* at ten o'clock; to *leave* for good. **7** To depart from; as, to *leave* the house. — **leave off**. To give up; to cease from; as, to *leave off* fooling and get to work.

leave \'lēv\ *v.;* **leaved**; **leav·ing.** To send forth leaves; to leaf.

leaved \'lēvd\ *adj.* Having leaves, especially of a kind mentioned — used chiefly in combinations, as in *smooth-leaved* or *four-leaved.*

leav·en \'lev-n\ *n.* **1** A fermenting substance, such as yeast. **2** A substance like baking powder, that makes dough or batter rise and become light while being cooked. **3** Anything that acts like a ferment in changing or lightening a whole mass; as, a *leaven* of good humor in a serious discussion; a *leaven* of common sense. — *v.;* **leav·ened**; **leav·en·ing** \-n(-)ing\. **1** To cause to ferment; to make light. **2** To mix leaven with; to introduce a leaven.

leaves. Pl. of *leaf.*

leave-tak·ing \'lēv-ˌtāk-ing\ *n.* The act of taking leave or saying good-by.

leav·ings \'lē-vingz\ *n. pl.* Things left over; as, the *leavings* of a meal.

Leb·a·nese \ˌleb-n-'ēz, -'ēs\ *adj.* Of or relating to Lebanon. — *n. sing. and pl.* A native or inhabitant of Lebanon.

lec·tern \'lekt-rn, 'lek-ˌtərn\ *n.* A stand used to hold an open book, especially one being read by a standing person; a reading desk, as in a church or on a lecture platform.

lec·ture \'lek-chər\ *n.* **1** An instructive talk or address; as, a *lecture* on birds. **2** A scolding; as, to get a *lecture* for being late. — *v.;* **lec·tured**; **lec·tur·ing.** **1** To give a lecture or lectures. **2** To instruct by lectures. **3** To scold. — **lec·tur·er** \-chər-r\ *n.*

led. Past tense and past part. of *lead.*

ledge \'lej\ *n.* **1** A projecting ridge or raised edge; as, the outer *ledge* of a window. **2** A narrow, flat, projecting shelf, as from a wall of rock. **3** A reef, especially one under water near a shore.

ledg·er \'lej-r\ *n.* In bookkeeping, the book in which accounts are kept in final form.

ledger line. A line added above or below the musical staff for notes that are too high or too low to be placed on the staff.

lee \'lē\ *n.* **1** The side protected from the wind; as, the *lee* of a mountain. **2** The side of a ship away from the point from which the wind blows. — *adj.* Of or relating to the lee; as, the *lee* side of a ship; the *lee* shore.

leech \'lēch\ *n.* **1** *Archaic.* A doctor. **2** A worm with flattened body showing external rings and having a sucker at each end by which it attaches itself to the bodies of animals and sucks their blood. **3** A person who clings to another in the hope of getting something from him.

leek \'lēk\ *n.* A cultivated plant of the lily family,

closely related to the onion but differing from the onion in having a slender bulb and solid stem.

leer \'lir\ *v.* To look with a leer. — *n.* A sly or sneering sidelong glance.

leery \'lir-ē\ *adj. Slang.* Suspicious; wary.

lees \'lēz\ *n. pl.* That which settles at the bottom, as of a cask of wine; dregs; sediment.

lee·ward \'lē-wərd, 'lü-ərd\ *adj.* Relating to or in the direction of the lee side. — *n.* The lee side. — *adv.* Toward the lee.

lee·way \'lē-ˌwā\ *n.* **1** The leeward drift of a ship caused by wind or tide. **2** The deviation of an aircraft to either side of its set course caused by currents of wind. **3** More time or room for action than is needed; margin; as, to allow enough *leeway*.

left \'left\ *adj.* **1** On the same side of the body as the heart; as, the *left* leg; the *left* hand. **2** Located so that the left side of the body is toward it; as, *left* field; the *left* wing of an army. — *n.* **1** The left side or the part on the left side. The house is on the *left.* **2** In some lawmaking bodies, the seats occupied by the liberal or radical members or the members occupying these seats. **3** Political liberals or radicals collectively or the beliefs they hold.

left \'left\. Past tense and past part. of *leave.*

left-hand \'left-ˌhand\ *adj.* **1** Situated on the left. **2** Left-handed; using, or done with, the left hand.

left-hand·ed \'left-'han-dəd\ *adj.* **1** Using the left hand more skillfully than the right hand. **2** Done or made with or for the left hand. **3** Awkward; clumsy; as, a *left-handed* compliment. **4** Having a structure with a counterclockwise turn or twist; as, a *left-handed* screw. — **left-hand·ed·ly** or **left-hand·ed,** *adv.*

left·over \'left-ˌōv-r\ *adj.* Left behind, undone, or unremoved. — *n.* Something left; especially, food remaining uneaten at a meal.

leg \'leg\ *n.* [From medieval English *leg, legge,* there borrowed from Old Norse *leggr* meaning "leg", "calf of the leg".] **1** One of those limbs of an animal that support the body and are used in walking and running; sometimes, the part of such a limb between the knee and the foot. **2** Something like a leg in shape or use; as, the *legs* of a table; the *legs* of a pair of compasses. **3** The part of a garment that covers the leg. **4** Either side of a triangle not the base or the hypotenuse. **5** A part or stage of a journey; as, the first *leg* of a trip. **6** The first event won in a sporting contest when a second is still necessary to decide the contest. — *v.;* **legged; leg·ging.** To walk or run; as, to *leg* it home.

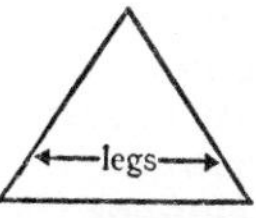

leg·a·cy \'leg-ə-sē\ *n.; pl.* **leg·a·cies. 1** Something left to a person by a will; an inheritance; a bequest. **2** Anything that has come to a person from an ancestor or a predecessor.

le·gal \'lēg-l\ *adj.* **1** Of or relating to law or lawyers; as, the *legal* profession; *legal* writings. **2** Based on law; as, a *legal* right. **3** Lawful; as, a *legal* act.

le·gal·i·ty \lē-'gal-ət-ē\ *n.; pl.* **le·gal·i·ties.** The quality or state of being legal; lawfulness.

le·gal·ize \'lēg-l-ˌīz\ *v.;* **le·gal·ized; le·gal·iz·ing. 1** To make legal, or lawful. **2** To give legal authority to, as to a document by having it notarized.

le·gal·ly \'lēg-l-ē\ *adv.* **1** In a legal manner. **2** According to law; under existing law; as, to be morally but not *legally* at fault.

legal tender. That currency, or money, which the law authorizes a person to use in paying a debt and requires a creditor to accept.

leg·ate \'leg-ət\ *n.* **1** An authorized representative of the pope. **2** An ambassador or envoy.

leg·a·tee \ˌleg-ə-'tē\ *n.* A person to whom a legacy is bequeathed.

le·ga·tion \lə-'gāsh-n\ *n.* **1** A legate and the persons associated with him; an envoy and his staff. **2** The official residence or the place of business of a diplomatic minister, especially of one not holding the rank of ambassador.

le·ga·to \lə-'gät-(ˌ)ō, -'gȧt-\ *adj.* In music, smooth and connected; with no breaks between successive tones. — *adv.* Smoothly.

leg·end \'lej-nd\ *n.* **1** An inscription, as on a coin. **2** The title beneath a picture. **3** A story coming down from the past that is widely accepted as true but cannot be proved to be so. **4** A body or group of such stories.

leg·end·ary \'lej-n-ˌder-ē\ *adj.* Of a legend; like a legend; consisting of legends; fabulous; fictional; as, *legendary* heroes; *legendary* writings.

leg·er·de·main \ˌlej-r-də-'mān\ *n.* **1** Sleight of hand. **2** Any artful trick.

legged \'legd\. Past tense and past part. of *leg.*

leg·ged \'leg-əd, 'legd\ *adj.* Having legs of a stated number or kind — used chiefly in combinations, as in *four-legged* or *bandy-legged.*

leg·ging \'leg-ing\. Pres. part. of *leg.*

leg·ging \'leg-n, 'leg-ing\ *n.* A long, heavy, outer stocking or gaiter; as, a child's *leggings* — used chiefly in the plural.

leg·horn \'leg-ˌhȯrn, 'leg-rn\ *n.* **1** A yellowish flat braided straw used in making hats. **2** A hat made of this straw. **3** A hardy domestic fowl of a Mediterranean breed, having smooth yellow legs and laying white eggs.

leg·i·ble \'lej-əb-l\ *adj.* Clear enough to be read; plain; easily read; as, *legible* writing. — **leg·i·bil·i·ty** \ˌlej-ə-'bil-ət-ē\ *n.* — **leg·i·bly** \'lej-ə-blē\ *adv.*

le·gion \'lēj-n\ *n.* **1** In ancient Rome, a body of from 3,000 to 6,000 soldiers, forming the chief army unit. **2** An army. **3** A very great number; as, to have a *legion* of admirers.

le·gion·ary \'lēj-n-ˌer-ē\ *adj.* Belonging to a legion; consisting of a legion or legions. — *n.; pl.* **le·gion·ar·ies.** A member of a legion.

le·gion·naire \ˌlēj-n-'ar, -'er\ *n.* A member of a legion, especially of a patriotic organization of military and naval veterans.

leg·is·late \'lej-əs-ˌlāt\ *v.;* **leg·is·lat·ed; leg·is·lat·ing. 1** To make or enact a law or laws. **2** To cause to be, become, or take a certain course of action by passing laws.

leg·is·la·tion \ˌlej-əs-ˈlāsh-n\ *n.* **1** The action of making laws. **2** The laws that are made.

leg·is·la·tive \ˈlej-əs-ˌlāt-iv\ *adj.* **1** Having the power or authority to make laws; as, the *legislative* branch of government. **2** Of, or having to do with, legislation or a legislature; as, a heavy *legislative* program.

leg·is·la·tor \ˈlej-əs-ˌlāt-r, -ˌlā-ˌtȯr\ *n.* A person who makes laws for a state or community; a lawmaker; a member of a legislature.

leg·is·la·ture \ˈlej-əs-ˌlāch-r\ *n.* The body of persons in a state having the power to make, alter, or repeal laws.

le·git·i·ma·cy \lə-ˈjit-m-ə-sē\ *n.* The quality or state of being legitimate.

le·git·i·mate \lə-ˈjit-m-ət\ *adj.* **1** Born of parents who are married; lawfully begotten; as, *legitimate* children. **2** According to law or to established requirements; lawful; as, a *legitimate* claim; a *legitimate* government. **3** In keeping with what is right; just; in accordance with standards permitted; as, to have a *legitimate* excuse for absence. — **le·git·i·mate·ly,** *adv.*

le·git·i·mize \lə-ˈjit-m-ˌīz\ *v.;* **le·git·i·mized; le·git·i·miz·ing.** To make legal or legitimate.

leg·man \ˈleg-ˌman\ *n.; pl.* **leg·men** \-ˌmen\. **1** A newspaperman who chiefly gathers information or sends reports from the scene of an occurrence. **2** A person who performs services for another person, as by gathering information or running errands for him.

leg·ume \ˈleg-ˌyüm, li-ˈgyüm\ *n.* **1** A table vegetable; especially, the fruit or seed of a leguminous plant used as a vegetable. **2** The one-celled pod that is the fruit of plants of the pea family and that when ripe splits along the upper seam between its two valves and discharges the seeds attached along the lower seam. **3** Any plant of the pea family; especially, one grown as food or as a crop to improve the soil.

le·gu·mi·nous \li-ˈgyü-mə-nəs, le-\ *adj.* Of, relating to, or being a legume and especially a legume-bearing plant.

leg·work \ˈleg-ˌwərk\ *n.* The work of a legman; as, to solve a case after months of dogged *legwork.*

lei \ˈlā, ˈlā-ē\ *n.; pl.* **le·is** \ˈlāz, ˈlā-ēz\. [Hawaiian.] A wreath or garland, as of flowers or leaves.

lei·sure \ˈlēzh-r, ˈlezh-r, ˈlāzh-r\ *n.* **1** Freedom from work; as, a time of *leisure.* **2** Time at one's command; ease; convenience; as, to do something at one's *leisure.* — *adj.* Unemployed; as, *leisure* hours.

lei·sure·ly \-lē\ *adj.* Slow and easy; unhurried; as, to go at a *leisurely* pace. — *adv.* In a leisurely manner.

lem·ming \ˈlem-ing\ *n.* Any of several small usually mostly tawny and black arctic rodents four or five inches long, with short tail, furry feet, and small ears.

lem·on \ˈlem-ən\ *n.* **1** The fruit of a stout thorny tree related to the orange, with yellow rind and sour, juicy center. **2** The tree that bears this fruit. **3** The color of ripe lemons. **4** *Slang.* Something worthless; a failure.

lem·on·ade \ˌlem-ə-ˈnād\ *n.* A drink made of lemon juice, sugar, and water.

le·mur \ˈlēm-r\ *n.* A tree-dwelling nocturnal mammal related to the monkeys but with a muzzle resembling that of a fox, large eyes, and soft fur.

lend \ˈlend\ *v.;* **lent** \ˈlent\; **lend·ing. 1** To allow the use of something on the condition that it or its equivalent be returned; as, to *lend* a book; to *lend* money. **2** To offer and give; as, to *lend* assistance. **3** To have the quality or nature that makes suitable; as, to have a voice that *lends* itself to singing in opera.

length \ˈleng(k)th\ *n.; pl.* **lengths** \ˈleng(k)ths, ˈlengks\. **1** The longest or the longer dimension of an object. A box has *length,* breadth, and depth. **2** The distance from end to end; as, a *length* of two feet. **3** The quality of being long; extent in time; as, the *length* of a story; the *length* of a visit. **4** A single piece or one of certain pieces that may be joined together; as, a *length* of pipe. **5** The sound of a vowel or syllable as it is affected by the time it takes to pronounce it. — **at length. 1** Very fully; as, to tell a story *at length.* **2** At the end; after a long time. *At length* the storm was over.

length·en \ˈleng(k)th-n\ *v.;* **length·ened; length·en·ing** \-n(-)ing\. To make or become longer; as, to *lengthen* a dress.

length·ways \ˈleng(k)th-ˌwāz\ *adv.* Lengthwise.

length·wise \ˈleng(k)th-ˌwīz\ *adv.* In the direction of the length; as, to turn a pillow *lengthwise.* — *adj.* Moved, placed, or directed lengthwise.

lengthy \ˈleng(k)th-ē\ *adj.;* **length·i·er; length·i·est.** Having length; very long; as, a *lengthy* speech. — **length·i·ly** \-ə-lē\ *adv.*

le·ni·ence \ˈlē-nē-ən(t)s, ˈlēn-yən(t)s\ *n.* Leniency.

le·ni·en·cy \ˈlē-nē-ən-sē, ˈlēn-yən-sē\ *n.* The quality or state of being lenient. — For synonyms see *mercy.*

le·ni·ent \ˈlē-nē-ənt, ˈlēn-yənt\ *adj.* Not harsh or severe; merciful. — **le·ni·ent·ly,** *adv.*

len·i·ty \ˈlen-ət-ē\ *n.; pl.* **len·i·ties. 1** Gentleness; kindness. **2** A kind act.

lens \ˈlenz\ *n.* [From Latin, meaning "lentil", the shape of which it resembles.] **1** A curved piece of glass or some other transparent substance, as one in eyeglasses, opera glasses, a microscope, or a camera, whose purpose is to change the direction of the rays of light passing through it so that they will come together and present a clear image. **2** A highly transparent, nearly spherical body in the eye that focuses rays of light upon the retina so as to form clear images.

lens

lent \ˈlent\. Past tense and past part. of *lend.*

Lent \ˈlent\ *n.* The 40 days, excluding Sundays, immediately preceding Easter, observed by many

Christians as a period of fasting and prayer in preparation for Easter.

lent·en \'lent-n\ *adj.* [usually with a capital] Of, relating to, or suitable to Lent.

len·til \'lent-l\ *n.* **1** A pod-bearing plant of the pea family grown for its seeds, which are cooked as a vegetable or ground into meal. **2** The seed of this plant.

len·to \'len-ˌtō\ *adj.* or *adv.* In music, slow.

le·o·nine \'lē-ə-ˌnīn\ *adj.* Of or like a lion; characteristic of lions.

leop·ard \'lep-rd\ *n.* A large and ferocious animal of the cat family, tawny or buff with black spots, inhabiting southern Asia and Africa.

lep·er \'lep-r\ *n.* A person who has leprosy.

lep·i·dop·ter·ous \ˌlep-ə-'däpt-r(-)əs\ *adj.* Belonging to an order of insects which consists of the butterflies and the moths, that when adult have four broad wings usually covered with minute, overlapping, often brightly colored scales.

lep·re·chaun \'lep-rə-ˌkän, -ˌkȯn\ *n.* In Irish folklore, a small fairy, especially a tricky old dwarf who, if caught, may reveal the hiding place of treasure.

lep·ro·sy \'lep-rə-sē\ *n.* An infectious disease found chiefly in the tropics and in the Orient, and marked by sores, loss of hair, and deformities.

lep·rous \'lep-rəs\ *adj.* Infected with, resembling, or relating to leprosy.

lese-maj·es·ty \'lēz-'maj-əs-tē\ *n.* [From French *lèse-majesté* meaning literally "injured majesty".] Any crime committed against the sovereign power; especially, an offense against the dignity of a ruler of a sovereign power.

le·sion \'lēzh-n\ *n.* **1** A hurt; an injury. **2** Any unhealthy change in the structure of an organ or other part of an animal or plant.

less \'les\ *adj.* A comparative of *little.* Not so much; as, *less* time. Pay *less* money. — *adv.* In a smaller or lower degree; as, to make the light *less* bright. — *prep.* Minus; with the subtraction of. Six *less* four leaves two. — *n.* **1** A smaller portion or quantity. **2** The inferior, younger, or smaller.

-less \ləs\. A suffix that can mean: **1** Without, not having, free from, as in *witless* or *painless.* **2** Beyond the range of, as in *countless.* **3** Unable or without the power to, as in *tireless* or *restless.*

les·see \(')les-'ē\ *n.* A person holding property under a lease.

less·en \'les-n\ *v.;* **less·ened; less·en·ing** \-n(-)ing\. To make or become less.

less·er \'les-r\ *adj.* A comparative of *little.* Less in importance; smaller; inferior.

les·son \'les-n\ *n.* **1** A portion of Scripture read in a church service. **2** A reading or exercise assigned to a pupil for study; as, to work on one's *lessons* in study hall. **3** A continuous period of instruction, usually an hour or less, in a particular skill or field of knowledge; as, music *lessons.* **4** Something learned or taught, especially something considered beneficial to the learner; as, a driver learning a *lesson* from an automobile accident; the *lesson* of a story.

les·sor \'les-ˌȯr, (')les-'ȯr\ *n.* A person who gives a lease.

lest \'lest\ *conj.* **1** For fear that. Take heed *lest* he escape. **2** That — after expressions of fear; as, to fear *lest* one fail one's friends.

let \'let\ *n.* A hindrance; an obstacle; as, to go ahead without *let* or hindrance.

let \'let\ *v.;* **let; let·ting. 1** To leave; to keep from interfering with; as, to *let* a person alone. **2** To rent; to lease; as, to *let* rooms. **3** To assign to another person; as, to *let* a contract for construction work. **4** To give leave; to permit. *Let* me do it. **5** To cause; as, to *let* a person know how one feels about something. **6** To cause to escape; as, to *let* blood. — **let be.** To leave untouched; to stop meddling with; to let alone. — **let down. 1** To forsake; to desert treacherously, as a friend. **2** To disappoint. — **let drive.** To aim a blow; to strike with violence. — **let fly.** To throw or drive with violence; to discharge. — **let go. 1** To loose hold of; to release. **2** To pass over; to neglect; to omit. **3** To let fly. — **let loose.** To remove restraint from. — **let off. 1** To discharge; to let fly, as a gun. **2** To release, as from an engagement or an obligation. — **let on. 1** *Chiefly dial.* To pretend; to give the impression; as, to *let on* that one has plenty of money. **2** To admit; to acknowledge; as, not to *let on* that one is guilty. — **let out. 1** To extend or loosen; to enlarge, as a garment. **2** To permit to run out, as a rope. **3** To allow or cause to move at a higher speed. **4** To lease; to assign by contract, as a job. **5** To tell; as, to *let out* a secret. **6** To be dismissed; as, after school *lets out.* — **let slide.** To let go; to neglect, as work. — **let the cat out of the bag.** To tell a secret.

-let \lət\. A suffix that can mean: **1** Little, as in *booklet* or *leaflet.* **2** An article for wear on, as in *armlet* or *wristlet.*

let·down \'let-ˌdau̇n\ *n.* **1** A slackening, as of speed or effort. **2** A disappointment.

le·thal \'lēth-l\ *adj.* Deadly; fatal.

le·thar·gic \lə-'thär-jik, -'thär-\ *adj.* **1** Of or relating to lethargy; affected with, causing, or resembling lethargy. **2** Unnaturally drowsy; dull; heavy.

leth·ar·gy \'leth-r-jē\ *n.; pl.* **leth·ar·gies. 1** Unnatural drowsiness; continued or deep sleep. **2** A state of inaction or indifference.

let's \(')lets\. A contraction of *let us.*

Lett \'let\ *n.* One of a people, closely related to the Lithuanians, dwelling chiefly in Latvia.

let·ter \'let-r\ *n.* **1** One of the characters of the alphabet; one of the symbols in writing or print that stand for speech sounds. **2** A written or printed communication, as one sent through the mail. **3** [usually in the plural] Literature; learning gained by reading; as, men of *letters.* **4** The exact meaning of the words; as, to follow the *letter* of the law. **5** In printing, a single type. — *v.* To mark with letters or words, as a poster. — **let·ter·er** \'let-r-r\ *n.*

let·tered \'let-rd\ *adj.* **1** Literate; educated. **2** Of or relating to learning or literature; learned. **3** Marked with letters; as, a *lettered* sign.

let·ter·head \'let-r-ˌhed\ *n.* **1** A heading printed on letter paper. **2** Paper having a printed heading.

let·ter·ing \'let-r-ing\ *n.* **1** The action or business of making or marking with letters. **2** The letters made.

let·ter–per·fect \'let-r-'pər-fikt\ *adj.* Knowing the words or lines, as of one's lesson or of one's part in a play, perfectly.

letter press. A press for copying letters.

let·ter·press \'let-r-ˌpres\ *n.* Print; printed reading matter.

letting. Pres. part. of *let.*

Lett·ish \'let-ish\ *adj.* Of or relating to the Letts. — *n.* The language of the Letts.

let·tuce \'let-əs\ *n.* A garden plant, the crisp leaves of which are used for salad.

let·up \'let-ˌəp\ *n.* A stop; a ceasing. It rained without *letup.*

leu·co·cyte \'lük-ə-ˌsīt\ *n.* A white or colorless blood cell.

leu·ke·mia \lü-'kē-mē-ə\ *n.* A cancerlike disease characterized by the production of an excessive number of white blood cells.

lev·ee \'lev-ē\ *n.* **1** An embankment along a shore to prevent flooding of low land. **2** A landing place; a pier.

lev·ee \'lev-ē; lə-'vē, -'vā\ *n.* **1** A reception, especially one held in the early morning. **2** Any gathering of guests.

lev·el \'lev-l\ *adj.* **1** Having a flat even surface; as, a *level* lawn. **2** On a line with the floor or even ground; horizontal; as, in a *level* position. **3** Of the same height or rank; on a line; even; as, to stand in water *level* with one's shoulders. **4** Steady and cool in judgment; as, to have a *level* head. — *n.* **1** An instrument used by surveyors to find a horizontal line. **2** A horizontal position. **3** A condition of fluids marked by a horizontal surface. Water seeks its own *level.* **4** A horizontal line taken as a point of measurement for height or distance; as, 200 feet above sea *level.* **5** A level surface; level ground; a level floor. **6** A step or stage in height, position, or rank; as, two boys on about the same *level* in arithmetic. — *v.;* **lev·eled** or **lev·elled**; **lev·el·ing** or **lev·el·ling** \-l(-)ing\. To make level; to make flat or even. — **level off. 1** To make level, flat, or even; to flatten. **2** To fly horizontally after a climb or a dive. The plane *leveled off* at 7500 feet.

lev·el·head·ed \'lev-l-'hed-əd\ *adj.* Having or showing common sense and sound judgment; sensible.

lev·er \'lev-r, 'lēv-r\ *n.* **1** A bar used to pry or move something firmly fixed. **2** A rigid piece capable of turning about a point or axis, the fulcrum, and having in each operation two or more other points where forces are applied, used for transmitting and changing force and motion. — *v.;* **lev·ered**; **lev·er·ing** \-r(-)ing\. To raise or move with a lever.

lev·er·age \'lev-r(-)ij, 'lēv-\ *n.* **1** The action of a lever. **2** The mechanical advantage or increase of power gained by or in the use of a lever.

le·vi·a·than \lə-'vī-ə-thən\ *n.* **1** A huge sea animal mentioned several times in the Bible and interpreted variously as a crocodile, a whale, and a dragon. **2** Something very large and powerful of its kind.

lev·i·ty \'lev-ət-ē\ *n.; pl.* **lev·i·ties.** Lack of earnestness in conduct or character; trifling gaiety; frivolity.

lev·u·lose \'lev-yə-ˌlōs\ *n.* The sweetest known sugar, occurring in honey and most sweet fruits.

levy \'lev-ē\ *n.; pl.* **lev·ies. 1** A collection, as of taxes, by legal authority. **2** A calling of troops into service; a conscripting. **3** Something that is levied, as a tax, a contribution, or a force of men called for military service. — *v.;* **lev·ied** \-ēd\; **lev·y·ing. 1** To collect legally, as taxes. **2** To raise or collect troops for service; to enroll into an army. **3** To carry on; to wage; as, to *levy* war on a neighboring country. **4** To impose; as, to *levy* a fine.

lewd \'lüd\ *adj.* Not chaste or pure; obscene; lustful. — **lewd·ly,** *adv.*

lex·i·cog·ra·pher \ˌleks-ə-'käg-rəf-r\ *n.* A writer or compiler of a dictionary.

lex·i·cog·ra·phy \ˌleks-ə-'käg-rə-fē\ *n.* The writing or compiling of dictionaries. — **lex·i·co·graph·ic** \-kō-'graf-ik\ or **lex·i·co·graph·i·cal** \-ik-l\ *adj.*

lex·i·con \'leks-ə-ˌkän, -ik-n\ *n.* A dictionary.

Ley·den jar \'līd-n\. A glass jar coated inside and outside with tin foil and topped by a brass knob communicating with the inside coating, used to accumulate electricity.

li·a·bil·i·ty \ˌlī-ə-'bil-ət-ē\ *n.; pl.* **li·a·bil·i·ties. 1** The state of being liable; as, the *liability* of a father for his son's debts; the greater *liability* of certain age groups to tuberculosis. **2** [in the plural] That for which a person is liable; total debts. **3** Something that is a drawback or disadvantage. Short stature is a *liability* in present-day basketball.

li·a·ble \'lī-əb-l; *sense 2 is also* 'līb-l\ *adj.* **1** Bound by law; obligated; responsible; as, to be *liable* for damage done to a neighbor's property; men *liable* for military service. **2** Exposed to or likely to experience something undesirable, as danger or accident; apt; likely; as, *liable* to slip; *liable* to be hurt.

li·ai·son \'lē-ə-ˌzän, lē-'ā-ˌzän\ *n.* **1** A connecting link; especially, a linking or coordinating of activities; as, an effective *liaison* between two departments of a business. **2** Intercommunication between two units of a military command or between two commands.

li·ar \'līr\ *n.* A person who tells lies.

li·ba·tion \lī-'bāsh-n\ *n.* The pouring out of a liquid, as wine, in honor of a god; the liquid poured out.

li·bel \'līb-l\ *n.* **1** In law, the action or the crime of injuring a person's reputation by means of something printed or written or by some visible representation, as a picture. **2** Any statement, either spoken or written, or any representation that gives an unjustly unfavorable impression of a person or thing. — *v.;* **li·beled** or **li·belled**; **li·bel·ing** or **li·bel·ling** \-l(-)ing\. To injure by a libel. — **li·bel·er** or **li·bel·ler** \-l(-)ər\ *n.*

li·bel·ous or **li·bel·lous** \'līb-l-əs\ *adj.* Containing or uttering a libel; as, a *libelous* statement.

lib·er·al \'lib-r(-)əl\ *adj.* **1** Generous; not stingy; as, a *liberal* giver. **2** Abundant; ample; large; as, a *liberal* amount. **3** Not strict; not narrow in one's ideas; broad-minded. **4** Broad; not restricted; as, a *liberal* education. **5** Not bound by generally accepted doctrines or beliefs; independent or showing independence in religious or political opinion; not conservative. — *n.* A person who is liberal in thought and principle. — **lib·er·al·ly** \-r(-)ə-lē\ *adv.*

liberal arts. The studies, as language and literature, philosophy, history, mathematics, and the pure sciences, that make up the curriculum of general academic or collegiate education as distinguished from technical or professional education.

lib·er·al·ism \'lib-r(-)ə-ˌliz-m\ *n.* Liberal principles and theories, as in religion or politics.

lib·er·al·i·ty \ˌlib-r-'al-ət-ē\ *n.; pl.* **lib·er·al·i·ties.** **1** Generosity. **2** Broad-mindedness; lack of prejudice.

lib·er·ate \'lib-r-ˌāt\ *v.;* **lib·er·at·ed**; **lib·er·at·ing.** **1** To free from bondage or restraint; to set at liberty; as, to *liberate* a prisoner; to *liberate* the mind from worry or from fear. **2** To free from combination, as gases; as, a chemical reaction *liberating* chlorine.

lib·er·a·tion \ˌlib-r-'āsh-n\ *n.* The act or action of setting free or the state of being set free.

lib·er·a·tor \'lib-r-ˌāt-r\ *n.* One who liberates; especially, one who liberates a country or a people from foreign control.

Li·be·ri·an \lī-'bir-ē-ən\ *adj* Of or relating to Liberia. — *n.* A native or inhabitant of Liberia.

lib·er·tine \'lib-r-ˌtēn\ *n.* A dissolute, immoral man.

lib·er·ty \'lib-rt-ē\ *n.; pl.* **lib·er·ties.** **1** The condition of those who are free and independent; freedom from slavery, imprisonment, or control by another. **2** Power to do what one pleases; freedom from restraint; as, to give a child some *liberty* to manage his own affairs. **3** Permission for a sailor to go ashore off duty for a certain number of hours. **4** Excessive freedom of action; the act of a person who is too free, or bold, or familiar; as, to take *liberties.* — **at liberty. 1** Not confined. **2** At leisure; not busy. **3** Free or having the right; as, *at liberty* to go or stay.

li·brar·i·an \lī-'brer-ē-ən\ *n.* A person in charge of a library.

li·brary \'lī-ˌbrer-ē\ *n.; pl.* **li·brar·ies.** [From medieval English *librarie,* there borrowed through French from medieval Latin *libraria,* a derivative of Latin *liber* meaning "book" — see *libretto.*] **1** A place where books are kept for use and not for sale. **2** A collection of books.

li·bret·to \lə-'bret-(ˌ)ō\ *n.; pl.* **li·bret·tos** \-(ˌ)ōz\ or **li·bret·ti** \-ē\. [From Italian, meaning literally "little book", a diminutive of *libro* meaning "book", derived from Latin *liber,* meaning literally "bark", out of which the Romans made books.] The text, or words, of an opera; the book containing this text.

Lib·y·an \'lib-ē-ən\ *adj.* Of or relating to Libya. — *n.* A native or inhabitant of Libya.

lice. Pl. of *louse.*

li·cense or **li·cence** \'līs-n(t)s\ *n.* **1** Permission, especially legal permission, to do something; a paper showing such permission; as, a driver's *license;* a marriage *license.* **2** Liberty of action, especially when carried too far; as, the difference between liberty and *license.* — *v.;* **li·censed** or **li·cenced**; **li·cens·ing** or **li·cenc·ing.** To permit or authorize by license; as, to be *licensed* to drive a car.

li·cen·tious \lī-'sench-əs\ *adj.* Loose and lawless in behavior; especially, lewd or lascivious. — **li·cen·tious·ly**, *adv.*

li·chen \'līk-n\ *n.* A gray-green, brown, or black flowerless plant found in flat irregular patches on rocks and bark and consisting of an alga and fungus living upon each other, the alga supplying the food and the fungus the salts and the moisture.

lick \'lik\ *v.* **1** To draw or pass the tongue over; as, to *lick* a spoon. **2** To touch or pass over like a tongue; as, flames *licking* a wall. **3** To beat; to whip; to defeat; to overcome. — *n.* **1** The act of licking; a stroke, as of a tongue or a brush; as, to give one's hair a few *licks.* **2** A small quantity; a little bit. **3** A place (**salt lick**) where salt is found on the surface and animals come to lick it up.

lic·o·rice \'lik-r(-)ish, -r(-)əs\ *n.* The dried root of a European plant or an extract made from it, used in making candies and medicines.

lid \'lid\ *n.* **1** A movable cover; as, the *lid* of a box; the *lid* of a saucepan. **2** An eyelid.

lie \'lī\ *n.* Something said or done in the hope of deceiving; a falsehood; an untruth. — *v.;* **lied** \'līd\; **ly·ing** \'lī-ing\. To tell or act a lie.

lie \'lī\ *v.;* **lay** \'lā\; **lain** \'lān\; **ly·ing** \'lī-ing\. **1** To stretch out or be stretched out, as on a bed or the ground; to recline. **2** To be or remain in a flat position; as, snow *lying* on the fields. **3** To have its location or place. Texas *lies* west of Florida. **4** To be or remain; to exist; as, machines *lying* idle. The remedy *lies* in complete rest. **5** To stretch out; to extend; as, the road *lying* straight ahead.

Liech·ten·stein·er \'lik-tən-ˌstīn-r\ *n.* A native or inhabitant of Liechtenstein. — **Liech·ten·stein** \-ˌstīn\ *adj.*

lief \'lēf, 'lēv\ *adj. Archaic.* Dear; beloved. — *adv.* Willingly. I would as *lief* go as stay.

liege \ˈlēj\ *adj.* **1** Having the right to receive service and allegiance; as, vassals and their *liege* lord. **2** Owing or giving service to a lord; as, a *liege* man. — *n.* **1** A feudal superior. **2** A vassal.

liege·man \ˈlēj-mən\ *n.; pl.* **liege·men** \-mən\. **1** A vassal. **2** A devoted or faithful follower.

li·en \ˈlēn, ˈlē-ən\ *n.* In law, a claim upon the property of another person until he has met a certain obligation, as a debt or the fulfillment of a duty.

lieu \ˈlü\ *n.* Place; stead; as, in *lieu* of.

Lieut. Abbreviation for *lieutenant.*

lieu·ten·an·cy \lü-ˈten-ən-sē\ *n.; pl.* **lieu·ten·an·cies.** The rank or position of lieutenant.

lieu·ten·ant \lü-ˈten-ənt\ *n.* **1** An officer who takes the place of an absent superior. **2** An army officer ranking next below a captain. **3** A naval officer ranking next below a lieutenant commander.

lieutenant colonel. An army officer ranking above a major and below a colonel.

lieutenant commander. A naval officer ranking above a lieutenant and below a commander.

lieutenant general. An army officer ranking below a general and above a major general.

lieutenant governor. 1 An officer of a state, next in rank to the governor. **2** An acting governor of a district or province under a governor general.

life \ˈlīf\ *n.; pl.* **lives** \ˈlīvz\. **1** The quality by which animals and plants differ from such things as rocks, earth, and water; a quality that animals and plants lose when they die. **2** The period during which a person or thing is alive or exists; that which happens during such a period; as, a short *life;* an interesting *life.* **3** A biography; as, a *life* of Lincoln. **4** A person; a living being; as, many *lives* being saved by quick action. **5** Liveliness; spirit; vigor; as, full of *life.* **6** A person who makes things lively; as, the *life* of the party. **7** A way or ways of living; as, to study the *life* of an ant; to choose the *life* of a scholar.

life·belt \ˈlīf-ˌbelt\ *n.* A life preserver in the form of a belt.

life·blood \ˈlīf-ˌbləd, -ˈbləd\ *n.* **1** The blood necessary to life. **2** That which gives strength and energy.

life·boat \ˈlīf-ˌbōt\ *n.* A strong buoyant boat especially designed for use in saving lives at sea.

life buoy. A ring, usually filled with cork or kapok, used to keep up persons in the water.

life cycle. The series of periods, forms, and modes of life through which an organism passes from the beginning of one individual, as in the egg, to the corresponding stage of its offspring.

life expectancy. The length of life of an individual or group that, after any specific age, is to be expected from the averages shown in mortality tables.

life·guard \ˈlīf-ˌgärd, -ˌgärd\ *n.* An expert swimmer employed at a bathing resort to safeguard bathers.

life jacket. A life preserver in the form of a sleeveless jacket.

life·less \ˈlīf-ləs\ *adj.* **1** Not living; deprived of life; dead; as, a *lifeless* body. **2** Not supporting life; as, a *lifeless* desert. **3** Spiritless; powerless; dull; as, a *lifeless* story. — **life·less·ly,** *adv.*

life·like \ˈlīf-ˌlīk\ *adj.* Accurately representing or imitating real life; as, a *lifelike* doll.

life·line \ˈlīf-ˌlīn\ *n.* **1** A line for saving life, as one shot over a boat in distress. **2** A line stretched along the deck or yards of a boat, to be clung to. **3** A rope stretched through surf for bathers to cling to. **4** A line attached to a diver's helmet, by which he is lowered and raised.

life·long \ˈlīf-ˌlȯng\ *adj.* Lasting through life; as, a *lifelong* friendship.

life preserver. Something used to keep a person from drowning, as a jacket lined with cork or capable of being inflated, or a buoyant belt or ring.

life preserver

life raft. A highly buoyant raft for use in lifesaving.

life·sav·ing \ˈlīf-ˌsā-ving\ *n.* The action of saving a life; especially, the work of a person (**life·sav·er** \-ˌsāv-r\) employed to save persons from drowning. — *adj.* Of or relating to lifesaving; used in or made for lifesaving.

life-sized \ˈlīf-ˌsīzd\ or **life-size** \-ˌsīz\ *adj.* Of natural size; of the size of the original; as, a *life-sized* statue.

life span or **life-span** \ˈlīf-ˌspan\ *n.* **1** The length of life of an individual. **2** The average length of life of a kind of living thing, especially in a particular environment. The *life span* of foxes in nature probably is not more than five years.

life·time \ˈlīf-ˌtīm\ *n.* The time that a life continues; the length of one's life.

life·work \ˈlīf-ˈwərk\ *n.* **1** The whole or chief work of one's life. **2** A work extending over a lifetime.

lift \ˈlift\ *v.* **1** To raise; to elevate. **2** To cause a rise, as in rank, condition, or spirit. **3** To steal; as, merchandise *lifted* by thieving shoppers. **4** To rise, or to appear to rise, as fog, clouds, or darkness. — For synonyms see *raise.* — *n.* **1** The action or result of lifting or raising. **2** An upward tilt; as, a proud *lift* of the head. **3** A load to be lifted; a burden; as, too heavy a *lift* for a child. **4** A feeling of being invigorated; elevation of spirit; as, to get a *lift* from the clear mountain air. **5** Assistance; aid; as, to give a friend a *lift* with his arithmetic. **6** A ride along one's way; as, to get a *lift* to school from a neighbor. **7** Lifting power, as of an automobile jack. **8** *Chiefly British.* An elevator. **9** One of the layers composing the heel of a shoe. **10** The extent or distance by which a thing rises or is raised; as, the *lift* of a canal lock. **11** The force developed by an aircraft that tends to raise it in the air. **12** Short for *airlift.* **13** An

lift, 9

aerial conveyor consisting of chairs or bars attached to an endless cable strung on towers, for carrying skiers up a slope.

lift·er \'lift-r\ *n.* One that lifts; something by means of which lifting is done.

lift–off \'lif-ˌtȯf \ *n.* A take-off by an airplane or rocket vehicle.

lig·a·ment \'lig-m-ənt\ *n.* A tough band of tissue or fibers that holds bones together or keeps an organ in place in the body.

lig·a·ture \'lig-əch-r, -ə-ˌchu̇r\ *n.* **1** A binding or tying. **2** Something that binds; a band or bandage. **3** In surgery, a thread or string for tying blood vessels, as to prevent bleeding.

light \'līt\ *n.* **1** The condition that enables us to see; the opposite of darkness. **2** Radiance coming from the sun, moon, fire, or lamp. Flames give *light.* **3** Something that helps the mind to understand; as, to throw *light* on a subject. **4** Public view or knowledge; as, facts brought to *light.* **5** A glow, as of the face; a brightness, as in the eyes. **6** A candle, lamp, star, or fire; as, city *lights;* coastal *lights.* **7** [in the plural] Means of informing oneself; ideas; understanding; as, a good man according to his *lights.* **8** A means by which light is let in, as a window. **9** That by which something, as a cigar, may be lighted. **10** An appearance from a particular point of view; as, to put a person in a false *light.* **11** A noteworthy person; an example; as, the leading *lights* of an age. **12** In physics, the radiant energy that, by its action upon the organs of vision, produces sight. **13** Energy, as in ultraviolet light or infrared light, that is practically invisible but otherwise like that enabling sight. — *adj.* **1** Having light; bright; as, a *light* room. **2** Not bright or deep in color; of a pale tint; as, *light* blue. **3** Blond; as, *light* hair. — *v.;* **light·ed** \'līt-əd\ or **lit** \'lit\; **light·ing. 1** To set fire to; to burn or cause to burn; to ignite; as, to *light* the gas; to *light* a fire. **2** To fill with light; to provide with lights; as, a town *lighted* by electricity. **3** To make or become bright; as, eyes *lighted* up with joy. **4** To attend with a light; as, to *light* a guest to his room.

light \'līt\ *adj.* **1** Having little weight; not heavy. **2** Not hard to bear, do, pay or digest; as, *light* punishment; *light* food. **3** Not strong or violent; as, a *light* breeze; a *light* touch. **4** Active or nimble in motion; as, *light* on one's feet. **5** Slight; moderate; as, a *light* case of measles. **6** Not burdened by care or suffering; happy; as, a *light* heart. **7** Not serious in theme or mood; as, a *light* novel. **8** Dizzy; giddy; as, a *light* head. **9** Well leavened; not soggy or heavy; as, a *light* dough. **10** Having a small percentage of alcohol; as, *light* wines. **11** Loose; easily reduced to dust; as, *light* soil. **12** Made to carry only a small load; as, a *light* wagon. **13** Weak — used of accent or stress. — *adv.* Lightly. — *v.;* **light·ed** \'līt-əd\ or **lit** \'lit\; **light·ing. 1** To dismount. **2** To descend and perch or settle. A bird *lit* on a branch. **3** To come by chance; as, to *light* upon an exciting book.

light·en \'līt-n\ *v.;* **light·ened; light·en·ing** \-n(-)ing\. **1** To make or grow light; to brighten. **2** To grow bright with flashes of lightning; as, to thunder and *lighten.*

light·en \'līt-n\ *v.;* **light·ened; light·en·ing** \-n(-)ing\. **1** To relieve of a load in whole or in part; to make lighter; as, to *lighten* a load. **2** To gladden.

light·er \'līt-r\ *n.* One that lights; as, a cigarette *lighter.*

ligh·ter \'līt-r\ *n.* A barge used to load or unload vessels not lying at wharves. — *v.* To carry by a lighter.

light·face \'līt-ˌfās\ *n.* In printing, a type having light, thin lines.

light–fin·gered \'līt-'fing-grd\ *adj.* Skillful in thieving, especially by picking pockets; thievish.

light–foot·ed \'līt-'fu̇t-əd\ *adj.* Having a light, springy step; nimble-footed.

light·head·ed \'līt-'hed-əd\ *adj.* **1** Dizzy; delirious. **2** Thoughtless; heedless.

light·heart·ed \'līt-'härt-əd, -'hȧrt-\ *adj.* Free from worry; gay; merry. — **light·heart·ed·ly,** *adv.*

light·house \'līt-ˌhau̇s\ *n.; pl.* **light·hous·es** \-ˌhau̇-zəz\. A tower with a powerful light at the top to guide navigators at night.

lighthouse

light·ing \'līt-ing\ *n.* **1** Lights and lighting equipment. **2** The light given by these; illumination. The *lighting* in the room is poor. **3** The arrangement of light parts and shaded parts in a picture.

light·ly \'līt-lē\ *adv.* In a light degree or manner.

light–mind·ed \'līt-'mīn-dəd\ *adj.* Frivolous; thoughtless; lacking in seriousness. — **light-mind·ed·ly,** *adv.*

light·ness \'līt-nəs\ *n.* **1** The quality, state, or degree of being light or lighted. **2** Lack of depth or dusky quality in color.

light·ness \'līt-nəs\ *n.* The quality or state of being light, or not heavy, severe, or serious.

light·ning \'līt-ning\ *n.* The flashing of light produced by a discharge of electricity from one cloud to another or from a cloud to the earth.

lightning arrester. A device for protecting electrical apparatus and radio and television sets from injury from lightning by carrying the discharges to the ground.

lightning bug. A firefly.

lightning rod. A metal rod set up on a building or a ship and connected with the earth or water below to decrease the chances of damage from lightning.

light opera. Opera in which some of the action and dialogue proceeds without musical setting.

lights \'līts\ *n. pl.* The lungs of animals.

light·ship \'līt-ˌship\ *n.* A vessel moored at a place dangerous to navigation and displaying a bright light or lights as a warning to sailors.

light·some \'līts-m\ *adj.* **1** Graceful; nimble. **2** Gay; cheerful. **3** Frivolous. — **light·some·ly,** *adv.*

light·weight \'līt-ˌwāt\ *adj.* Light in weight. — *n.* **1** A person of less than average weight. **2** In boxing, a man weighing between 127 and 135 pounds. **3** A person of little ability or importance.

light-year \'līt-ˌyir\ *n.* The distance over which light can travel in a year, approximately six trillion (6,000,000,000,000) miles. Most of the stars are more than 100 *light-years* away from the earth.

lig·nite \'lig-ˌnīt\ *n.* A brownish-black soft coal of slightly woody texture.

lik·a·ble or **like·a·ble** \'līk-əb-l\ *adj.* So pleasant or agreeable as to be liked.

like \'līk\ *adj.* **1** Similar; of the same or nearly the same kind; as, to have *like* tastes in clothing. **2** Similar to; resembling; as, a building *like* a fort. **3** Such as to promise or forecast. It looks *like* snow. **4** Inclined toward; as, to feel *like* taking a walk. **5** Characteristic of. It was just *like* him to do that. — *n.* A person or thing that is like another; an equal; as, never to see his *like* again. — *adv.* In the same way as; in a manner characteristic of; as, to act *like* a friend; working *like* a beaver.

-like \ˌlīk\. A suffix that can mean: **1** Having the characteristics of, as in *lifelike.* **2** Like that or those of, as in *doglike* devotion.

like \'līk\ *v.;* **liked; lik·ing. 1** To have a liking for; to enjoy; as, to *like* games. **2** To prefer; to choose; as, to do as one *likes.* — *n.* A liking; preference; as, to know a person's *likes* and dislikes.

like·li·hood \'līk-lē-ˌhu̇d\ *n.* Probability; a sign; an indication. There was small *likelihood* of getting lost.

like·ly \'līk-lē\ *adj.;* **like·li·er; like·li·est. 1** Expected by the person speaking because of something he sees or knows. It is *likely* to rain tonight. **2** Seeming like the truth; believable; as, a *likely* story. **3** Promising; as, a *likely* place to fish. — *adv.* In all probability; probably. You are very *likely* right.

lik·en \'līk-n\ *v.;* **lik·ened; lik·en·ing** \-n(-)ing\. To show to be alike or similar; to compare; as, to *liken* a star to a flower.

like·ness \'līk-nəs\ *n.* **1** Resemblance; as, a *likeness* between two sisters. **2** Appearance; as, in the *likeness* of a clown. **3** A representation, as in a portrait or a statue.

like·wise \'līk-ˌwīz\ *adv.* **1** In like manner; as, to do *likewise.* **2** Also; too. Think this over *likewise.*

lik·ing \'līk-ing\ *n.* Attraction toward some person or thing; fondness; preference.

li·lac \'lī-lək, -ˌlak, -ˌläk\ *n.* **1** A bush with large cone-shaped clusters of grayish-pink, purple, or white fragrant flowers; a lilac flower. **2** The pale violet or grayish-pink color of common lilacs.

lilac

lilt \'lilt\ *n.* **1** A gay lively tune. **2** A swinging movement; rhythm. — *v.* To sing gaily or rhythmically.

lily \'lil-ē\ *n.; pl.* **lil·ies.** A leafy-stemmed herb that grows from a bulb and has funnel-shaped white or bright-colored flowers, as the **Easter lily** and **tiger lily.** — *adj.* Like a lily; pure; white; pale; delicate.

lily

lily of the valley. A low herb usually having two oblong leaves and sweet-smelling bell-shaped white flowers on one side of the stem.

Li·ma bean or **li·ma bean** \'lī-mə\. A common variety of bean with broad flat seeds much used for food; the seed itself.

limb \'lim\ *n.* **1** A leg or arm; a wing. **2** A large branch growing out of the trunk of a tree; a bough.

lim·ber \'lim-br\ *adj.* Bending easily; supple; flexible; as, a *limber* willow twig; the *limber* body of an acrobat. — *v.;* **lim·bered; lim·ber·ing** \-br(-)ing\. To make limber; to make flexible. The pitcher *limbered* up his arm. — **lim·ber·ly,** *adv.*

lim·bo \'lim-ˌbō\ *n.* **1** [often with a capital] A supposed borderland of hell, believed by many to be the abode of souls neither condemned to hell nor admitted to heaven, especially of unbaptized infants and of righteous men who died before the coming of Christ. **2** A place of confinement. **3** A place of neglect; as, customs which are virtually in *limbo* now.

lime \'līm\ *n.* A white substance obtained from heating limestone, shells, or bones and used in making mortar, cement, fertilizers, and medicines. — *v.;* **limed; lim·ing.** To treat with lime; to apply lime to.

lime \'līm\ *n.* The linden or basswood.

lime \'līm\ *n.* **1** A fruit like the lemon, but smaller and with greenish-yellow rind. **2** The tree that bears this fruit.

lime·light \'līm-ˌlīt\ *n.* **1** A lighting device formerly used to cast a glaring white light on the stage or on a part of it. **2** The situation of a person who is much in the public eye.

lim·er·ick \'lim-r(-)ik\ *n.* [From *Will you come up to Limerick?*, the refrain for a kind of humorous verse, the reference being to *Limerick*, a city and county in Ireland.] A humorous or witty poem of five lines, the first, second, and fifth lines rhyming according to one scheme and the third and fourth according to another, with the last line containing a surprise meaning.

lime·stone \'līm-ˌstōn\ *n.* A kind of rock that is used for building and that yields lime when burned.

lime·wa·ter \'līm-ˌwȯt-r, -ˌwät-r\ *n.* A water solution of slaked lime, used in medicine and chemistry.

lim·it \'lim-ət\ *n.* **1** A boundary line; as, within the city *limits.* **2** A point beyond which a person or thing cannot go; as, the *limit* of one's power. — *v.* To apply a limit to; to set a limit or bounds for; as, to *limit* expenses to ten dollars.

lim·i·ta·tion \ˌlim-ə-'tāsh-n\ *n.* **1** The act of limiting or state of being limited. **2** Something that limits; a limit.

lim·it·ed \'lim-ət-əd\ *adj.* **1** Confined within limits; narrow; as, *limited* knowledge; *limited* range. **2** Of a railroad train, accommodating a restricted number or class of passengers. **3** Designating a government in which constitutional limitations are placed upon the powers of one or more of its branches; as, a *limited* monarchy.

lim·it·less \'lim-ət-ləs\ *adj.* Having no limits; without bounds.

limn \'lim\ *v.;* **limned** \'limd\; **limn·ing** \'lim-ing, 'lim-ning\. To draw or paint, as a picture; to portray. — **lim·ner** \'lim-nər, 'lim-r\ *n.*

lim·ou·sine \'lim-ə-ˌzēn, ˌlim-ə-'zēn\ *n.* **1** An automobile having an enclosed compartment for passengers and a driver's seat outside but covered by a roof. **2** A large automobile used as a bus.

limp \'limp\ *adj.* **1** Lacking body or stiffness; as, *limp*, wispy strands of hair; a *limp* shirt. **2** Lacking firmness or strength; as, to be *limp* with weariness. — **limp·ly**, *adv.*

limp \'limp\ *v.* **1** To walk lamely. **2** To proceed with difficulty. The ship *limped* into port. — *n.* A halt in one's walk; a limping. — **limp·er**, *n.*

lim·pet \'limp-ət\ *n.* A salt-water shellfish with low cone-shaped shell, found clinging to rock and timbers by its single, sucker-equipped foot, and used for food or fish bait.

lim·pid \'limp-əd\ *adj.* Clear; transparent; as, a *limpid* pool. — **lim·pid·i·ty** \lim-'pid-ət-ē\ *n.* — **lim·pid·ly** \'limp-əd-lē\ *adv.*

linch·pin \'linch-ˌpin\ *n.* A locking pin inserted crosswise through the end of an axle or shaft.

lin·den \'lin-dən\ *n.* A shade tree with heart-shaped toothed leaves, drooping clusters of yellowish white flowers, and small hard fruit; the basswood.

line \'līn\ *n.* **1** A thread, cord, or rope. **2** A cord or tape, as used in measuring or leveling. **3** The marked bounds or limits of a place; as, the town *line.* **4** One's fortune or lot. **5** The reins used in driving, as a horse. **6** Piping for carrying a fluid or steam. **7** The wire connecting one telegraph or telephone station with another. **8** Any long, narrow mark, as one drawn by a pencil; any long threadlike formation, as in rock; as, a chalk *line; lines* of trenches. **9** A straight mark, groove, or furrow. **10** In mathematics, something drawn that has length but neither breadth nor thickness. **11** Agreement; harmony; as, to bring ideas into *line.* **12** A wrinkle, as on the face. **13** An outline; a contour; as, the shore *line;* a boat's *lines.* **14** A plan for making or doing something; as, a play along the same *lines* as a novel. **15** A row of letters or words across a page or column; a verse of poetry. **16** A letter or note; as, to write a few *lines* home each week. **17** A course of conduct or thought; a method; as, a political *line;* in the *line* of duty. **18** A family or race; lineage; as, born of a royal *line.* **19** A row of similar things; as, a *line* of houses. **20** The direction followed by anything in motion; a road; a route; as, a *line* of flight. **21** A kind of business or occupation; one's special activity or interest. The salesman's *line* was toys. **22** A transportation system or a number of public conveyances under one management; as, a bus *line.* **23** The track and roadbed of a railroad. **24** On a map, a circle of latitude or longitude. **25** On a map, the equator, called **the line** or the **equinoctial line.** **26** [in the plural] The words of a part, as in a play; as, to learn one's *lines* before rehearsal. **27** A formation of troops or ships in which the individual units are abreast of each other. **28** The fighting units of an army as distinguished from the staff and supply units; as, an officer of the *line.* **29** A towline or a mooring rope on a boat. **30** A hose or pipe; as, a water *line.* **31** In trade, a supply of various grades and values of the same general class of articles. — *v.;* **lined; lin·ing.** **1** To mark with a line or lines. **2** To represent by lines, especially in outline; to portray; to outline. **3** To place or be placed in a line along. Crowds *lined* the streets. — **line up. 1** To bring into accurate adjustment to a line or into agreement with a standard; to align; as, to *line up* the front wheels of an automobile; to *line up* troops. **2** To take sides; as, to *line up* with a political organization. **3** To enlist; as, to *line up* new members for a club.

line \'līn\ *v.;* **lined; lin·ing. 1** To cover the inner surface of; as, to *line* a box with paper. **2** To serve as the lining or covering of. Pictures and banners *lined* the walls.

lin·e·age \'lin-ē-ij\ *n.* **1** The line of ancestors from whom a person is descended. **2** The line of descendants from a common ancestor; a race; family.

lin·e·al \'lin-ē-əl\ *adj.* **1** Linear; as, *lineal* measure. **2** Consisting of or being in a direct line of ancestry or descendants; as, a *lineal* descendant. **3** Hereditary; as, a *lineal* trait. — **lin·e·al·ly** \-ē-ə-lē\ *adv.*

lin·e·a·ment \'lin-ē-ə-mənt\ *n.* One of the outlines, features, or contours of a body or figure, especially of the face.

lin·e·ar \'lin-ē-ər\ *adj.* **1** Of or like a line or lines; consisting of lines. *Linear* measure is a measure of length. **2** Long and uniformly narrow, as the leaf of the hyacinth.

linear equation. In algebra, an equation of two first degree variables whose graph is a straight line.

linear measure. A measure of length or a system for such measurement.

line·man \'līn-mən\ *n.; pl.* **line·men** \-mən\. **1** One who carries the line, as in surveying. **2** A person who works on or repairs lines, as telephone lines. **3** In football, a player in the front line.

lin·en \'lin-ən\ *n.* **1** Thread or cloth made from flax. **2** Household articles, such as tablecloths or napkins, and clothing, such as collars and shirts, made of linen or a similar fabric. — *adj.* Made of linen.

line of force. An imaginary line serving as a convenience in indicating the direction in space in which an electric or magnetic force acts.

lin·er \'līn-r\ *n.* **1** One that lines or covers the inner surface of something. **2** Something used to line or back another part.

lin·er \'līn-r\ *n.* **1** One that draws lines. **2** A boat or aircraft of a regular transportation line; as, an ocean *liner*. **3** In baseball, a batted ball that flies through the air in a nearly straight line not far from the ground.

lines·man \'līnz-mən\ *n.; pl.* **lines·men** \-mən\. **1** A lineman. **2** One of the officials in a football game.

line-up or **line·up** \'lī-ˌnəp\ *n.* **1** A line of persons arranged for inspection, especially of suspects for identification. **2** A list of players, with their positions, who will take part in a game. **3** The players on such a list.

-ling \ling\. A suffix that can mean: **1** A person or thing concerned with or being, as in *worldling* or *underling*. **2** Young or little in size or importance, as in *princeling* or *duckling*.

lin·ger \'ling-gr\ *v.;* **lin·gered**; **lin·ger·ing** \-gr(-)ing\. To be slow in leaving or quitting anything; to delay; to loiter; as, to *linger* at the table after a meal is over.

— The word *loiter* is a synonym of *linger: linger* suggests remaining in a place after the expected time of departure, usually from fondness for the place or for something found there; *loiter* may indicate a lagging behind, especially while walking, in an aimless or lazy fashion, as from lack of any real purpose for hurrying on.

lin·ger·er \'ling-gr-r\ *n.* One that lingers.

lin·ge·rie \ˌlänj-r-'ē, ˌlanj-, -r-'ā\ *n.* [From French, meaning literally "linen goods", and derived from *linge* meaning "linen".] Underwear for women.

lin·go \'ling-ˌgō\ *n.; pl.* **lin·goes**. [From Provençal, meaning "tongue", "language", and derived from Latin *lingua*.] **1** A language; a dialect. **2** A foreign language or a manner of speech that seems strange.

lin·gual \'ling-gwəl\ *adj.* **1** Of or relating to the tongue or a part like a tongue. **2** Formed with the aid of the tongue, as the letter *t* or *d*.

lin·guist \'ling-gwəst\ *n.* **1** A person who is skilled in languages. **2** A person who is skilled in linguistics.

lin·guis·tic \ling-'gwis-tik\ *adj.* Of or relating to language or to the study of language. — **lin·guis·ti·cal·ly** \-tik-l(-)ē\ *adv.*

lin·guis·tics \ling-'gwis-tiks\ *n.* The study of human speech including the origin, structure, and changes in language or languages.

lin·i·ment \'lin-ə-mənt\ *n.* A liquid preparation rubbed on the body, as to relieve pain.

lin·ing \'lī-ning\ *n.* Something that lines the inner surface of anything; as, a coat *lining*.

link \'lingk\ *n.* **1** A single ring or division of a chain. **2** A bond or tie; a connection; as, the link of friendship. — *v.* To join with or as if with links; to unite; as, routes that *link* the East and West.

link·ing verb \'lingk-ing\. An intransitive verb that links the subject with a word or words in the predicate by expressing a state of being, as *is* in "This work *is* a pleasure" or *seems* in "The water *seems* warm".

links \'lingks\ *n. pl.* A golf course.

lin·net \'lin-ət\ *n.* A common, small, Old World finch, often kept as a cage bird.

li·no·le·um \lə-'nōl-yəm, -'nō-lē-əm\ *n.* [From Latin *linum* meaning "flax" and *oleum* meaning "oil".] A floor covering with a canvas back and a surface of hardened linseed oil and cork dust.

lin·seed \'lin-ˌsēd\ *n.* The seeds of flax.

linseed oil. A yellowish oil obtained from the seeds of flax, used in various products, as paints, soaps, and medicine.

lin·sey \'lin-zē\ *n.; pl.* **lin·seys**. Linsey-woolsey.

lin·sey-wool·sey \'lin-zē-'wu̇l-zē\ *n.; pl.* **lin·sey-wool·seys**. A coarse cloth made of linen and wool, or cotton and wool.

lint \'lint\ *n.* **1** Linen made into a soft, fleecy substance for use in dressing wounds. **2** Fine ravelings, fluff, or loose short fibers from yarn or fabrics.

lin·tel \'lint-l\ *n.* A horizontal piece or part across the top of an opening, as of a door, to carry the weight of the structure above it.

lintel

lint·er \'lint-r\ *n.* **1** A machine for removing fiber still remaining on cotton seed after ginning. **2** [in the plural] The fiber covering cottonseed after the longer fibers have been removed, used in making such products as cotton batting, rayon, and plastics.

li·on \'lī-ən\ *n.* **1** A large tawny flesh-eating animal of the cat family, with tufted tail, and, in the male, a shaggy mane, inhabiting Africa and southern Asia to western India. **2** A person like a lion, as in strength or courage. **3** A person who is regarded as an object of special interest; as, a literary *lion*.

li·on·ess \'lī-ə-nəs\ *n.* A female lion.

lip \'lip\ *n.* **1** Either of the two fleshy folds that surround the mouth. **2** The edge of a hollow vessel, especially where it flares slightly; as, the *lip* of a pitcher. **3** The protruding part of the irregular corolla of certain flowers, as the snapdragon, many mints, and most orchids. — *adj.* Coming from a person's lips only and not from his heart; not sincere; as, *lip* service.

li·pase \'lī-ˌpās, 'lip-ˌās\ *n.* An enzyme that helps the digestive system change fats to fatty acids and glycerol.

lip reading. Understanding of the words of a speaker by watching his lips rather than by hearing the sound of his voice.

lip·stick \'lip-ˌstik\ *n.* A rouge or a colorless ointment for the lips, put up in stick form.

liq·ue·fac·tion \ˌlik-wə-ˈfaksh-n\ *n.* **1** The act of making something liquid. **2** The state of being or becoming liquid.

liq·ue·fy \ˈlik-wə-ˌfī\ *v.;* **liq·ue·fied** \-ˌfīd\; **liq·ue·fy·ing.** **1** To reduce a solid substance or a gas to a liquid form; as, to *liquefy* air by pressure. **2** To become liquefied.

li·queur \li-ˈkər\ *n.* A highly flavored, usually sweetened, alcoholic liquor.

liq·uid \ˈlik-wəd\ *adj.* **1** Flowing freely like water; fluid. **2** Sounding smoothly; as, the *liquid* notes of a bird. **3** Consisting of cash or of things that can be quickly turned into cash; as, *liquid* assets of a business. **4** Of consonant sounds as *l* and *r*, smooth; flowing; like a vowel. — *n.* **1** A substance in a liquid state. **2** A liquid consonant.

liquid air. Air in a liquid state, used chiefly in refrigeration and prepared by subjecting air to very great pressure and then cooling it.

liq·ui·date \ˈlik-wə-ˌdāt\ *v.;* **liq·ui·dat·ed; liq·ui·dat·ing.** **1** To pay off, as a debt. **2** To settle the accounts of, as a business, and use the assets toward paying off the debts; to close up a business. **3** To do away with, get rid of, or destroy, as a person or thing regarded as undesirable or dangerous; especially, to destroy ruthlessly, and often secretly, as a political measure. — **liq·ui·da·tor** \-ˌdāt-r\ *n.*

liq·ui·da·tion \ˌlik-wə-ˈdāsh-n\ *n.* The act or process of liquidating or the state of being liquidated.

li·quid·i·ty \li-ˈkwid-ət-ē\ *n.* The quality or state of being liquid.

liq·uid·ize \ˈlik-wə-ˌdīz\ *v.;* **liq·uid·ized; liq·uid·iz·ing.** To make liquid. — **liq·uid·iz·er,** *n.*

liquid measure. A system of measures of volume for liquids; especially, the system in which four gills make one pint, two pints make one quart, and four quarts make one gallon.

liq·uor \ˈlik-r\ *n.* **1** Any liquid substance, as water, milk, juice, sap, or blood. **2** An alcoholic drink, especially one having a high alcoholic content, as brandy or whisky.

li·ra \ˈlir-ə, ˈlē-rə\ *n.; pl.* **li·re** \ˈlē-ˌrā\ or **li·ras** \ˈlir-əz, ˈlē-rəz\. A nickel coin and the monetary unit of Italy.

lisle \līl\ *n.* A hard twisted thread, originally of linen, now often of specially prepared cotton.

lisp \ˈlisp\ *v.* **1** To pronounce the letters *s* and *z* by giving them the sounds of *th.* **2** To speak imperfectly or falteringly, or in a childish manner. — *n.* **1** The act of lisping. **2** The habit of lisping. **3** A lisping sound.

lis·some or **lis·som** \ˈlis-m\ *adj.* **1** Bending easily; supple; limber. **2** Light and agile in movement; nimble.

list \ˈlist\ *n.* **1** A strip forming the border or selvage of cloth. **2** A strip or band of material, especially of cloth. **3** A stripe of color as on an animal's body. **4** A limit, or boundary, or an area enclosed by a boundary **5** [in the plural] The barriers of the field on which tournaments of knights were held, or the field itself or any similar field or arena. A roll, record, or catalogue of names or items. — **enter the lists.** To join in a contest. — *v.* **1** To put a list, or border, on. **2** To enter or enroll in a list or catalogue; as, to *list* names in alphabetical order.

list \ˈlist\ *v.;* **list·ed** or archaic **list; list·ed; list·ing.** **1** *Archaic.* To please; to suit; to incline to. **2** To lean to one side; to careen; as, a ship *listing* badly. — *n.* **1** *Archaic.* Inclination; wish. **2** A leaning over to one side, as of a boat; as, a *list* to starboard.

list \ˈlist\ *v. Archaic.* To listen; to hearken.

lis·ten \ˈlis-n\ *v.;* **lis·tened; lis·ten·ing** \-n(-)ing\. **1** To pay attention in order to hear; as, to *listen* for a signal; to *listen* to a new record. **2** To give heed; to follow advice; as, to *listen* to a warning. — **lis·ten·er** \-n(-)ər\ *n.*

list·less \ˈlist-ləs\ *adj.* Having no desire, interest, or wish to do things; indifferent; as, to be *listless* in one's work. — **list·less·ly,** *adv.*

lit. Past tense and past part. of *light.*

lit·a·ny \ˈlit-n-ē\ *n.; pl.* **lit·a·nies.** A form of prayer used in some churches; especially, a set form consisting of a series of supplications and responses said alternately by the clergyman and the congregation.

li·ter or **li·tre** \ˈlēt-r\ *n.* A measure of capacity in the metric system, equal to .9081 of a dry quart and 1.0567 liquid quarts.

lit·er·a·cy \ˈlit-r-ə-sē, ˈli-trə-sē\ *n.; pl.* **lit·er·a·cies.** The state of being literate; the ability to read and write.

lit·er·al \ˈlit-r-əl, ˈli-trəl\ *adj.* **1** Following the ordinary or usual meaning of the words; as, the *literal* meaning of a passage. **2** True to fact; accurate; not exaggerated; as, a *literal* account of what happened. **3** Following the exact words of the original; as, a *literal* translation from German. **4** Of or expressed by letters or alphabetic characters; as, a *literal* equation. **5** Tending to understand things according to their ordinary or usual meaning; matter-of-fact; as, to have a rather *literal* mind. — **lit·er·al·ly** \ˈlit-r-ə-lē, ˈli-trə-lē, ˈlit-r-lē\ *adv.*

lit·er·ary \ˈlit-r-ˌer-ē\ *adj.* **1** Of or relating to literature or the study or writing of literature. **2** Having great knowledge of or interest in literature.

lit·er·ate \ˈlit-r-ət, ˈli-trət\ *adj.* **1** Able to read and write; educated. **2** Versed in literature. — *n.* A person who can read and write.

lit·er·a·ture \ˈlit-r-ə-ˌchu̇r, ˈli-trə-, -ˌtyu̇r\ *n.* **1** The writing of literary works, as articles, pamphlets, and books, intended to have some permanent interest or value; especially, such writing done as a regular occupation. **2** The whole body of written and printed productions of a people, country, or language that have been preserved. **3** The part of the writings of a people or country that is especially notable for its form and expression. **4** The body of writings treating a given subject; as, the *literature* of music. **5** Any printed matter; as, advertising *literature.*

lithe \'līth, 'līth\ *adj.;* **lith·er**; **lith·est**. Capable of bending easily; limber; supple. — **lithe·ly**, *adv.*

lithe·some \'līth-səm, 'līths-m\ *adj.* Pliant; supple; lissome.

lith·i·um \'lith-ē-əm\ *n.* A soft silver-white metallic element, the lightest metal.

lith·o·graph \'lith-ə-ˌgraf\ *v.* To produce by the process of lithography. — *n.* A print made by lithography. — **li·thog·ra·pher** \li-'thäg-rəf-r, 'lith-ə-ˌgraf-r\ *n.*

li·thog·ra·phy \li-'thäg-rə-fē\ *n.* The art or process of putting writing or designs on stone, or on a metal plate, with an oily or greasy substance and of taking impressions from this in ink. — **lith·o·graph·ic** \ˌlith-ə-'graf-ik\ *adj.*

Lith·u·a·ni·an \ˌlith-(y)ə-'wā-nē-ən, -'wān-yən\ *adj.* Of or relating to Lithuania. — *n.* **1** A native or inhabitant of Lithuania. **2** The language of the Lithuanians.

lit·i·gant \'lit-ə-gənt\ *n.* A person engaged in a lawsuit.

lit·i·ga·tion \ˌlit-ə-'gāsh-n\ *n.* The taking of legal measures to establish one's claims or rights; as, *litigation* to settle the question of property boundaries.

lit·mus \'lit-məs\ *n.* A dyestuff obtained from certain lichens, that is turned red by an excess of acid and blue by an excess of alkali.

litmus paper. Paper colored with litmus.

litre. Variant of *liter*.

lit·ter \'lit-r\ *n.* **1** A covered and curtained couch, provided with shafts, used for carrying passengers. **2** A stretcher for carrying sick or wounded persons. **3** The young born at a single time, as to a dog or sow; as, a *litter* of pigs. **4** Material, such as straw or hay, used as bedding for animals. **5** Things scattered about in confusion; disorder. — *v.* **1** To cover with litter. Bits of paper *littered* the floor. **2** To cause to be in a disordered condition; as, a room *littered* with toys. **3** To bring forth a litter of young.

litter, 1

lit·tle \'lit-l\ *adj.;* **less** \'les\, **less·er** \'les-r\, or **lit·tler** \'lit-l(-)ər\; **least** \'lēst\ or **lit·tlest** \'lit-l(-)əst\. **1** Small in size or extent; as, a *little* body. **2** Short in duration; as, to spend *little* time. **3** Small in quantity; not much; as, *little* food to eat. **4** Small, as in dignity or power; as, a *little* matter. **5** Narrow; mean; not liberal or generous. — *adv.* In a very small quantity or degree; slightly. — *n.* Something that is small; as, *little* to be said.

lit·ur·gy \'lit-r-jē\ *n.; pl.* **lit·ur·gies**. The public rites and services of the Christian church, especially as contained in rituals.

liv·a·ble \'liv-əb-l\ *adj.* **1** Endurable. **2** Pleasant or suitable to live in or with.

live \'liv\ *v.;* **lived** \'livd\; **liv·ing**. **1** To be alive; to have life. **2** To continue in life; as, to *live* to a great age. **3** To get a living; as, to *live* by one's own efforts. **4** To feed; as, to *live* on grass and grain. **5** To pass life in a certain manner; as, to *live* in comfort or ease. **6** To dwell; as, to *live* in a town. **7** To continue in human memory or record; as, a piece of literature that has *lived* two thousand years. **8** To act according to; as, to *live* one's ideals.

live \'līv\ *adj.* **1** Alive; not dead. **2** Burning; glowing; as, *live* coals. **3** Not burned or exploded; as, a *live* cartridge. **4** Full of life; energetic; alert; as, a *live* salesman. **5** Of present and immediate interest; as, a *live* topic. **6** Charged with an electric current; as, a *live* wire. **7** Of or involving the presence of real people; as, a *live* audience. **8** Broadcast directly at the time of production; as, *live* television.

lived \'līvd, 'livd\ *adj.* Having life of the kind specified; as, long-*lived.*

live·li·hood \'līv-lē-ˌhu̇d\ *n.* The means of supporting life; support; as, an honest *livelihood.*

live·long \'liv-ˌlȯng\ *adj.* Whole; entire; long in passing; as, all the *livelong* day.

live·ly \'līv-lē\ *adj.;* **live·li·er**; **live·li·est**. **1** Full of life; active; as, a *lively* puppy. **2** Keen; vivid; as, a *lively* interest. **3** Animated; as, *lively* music; a *lively* debate. **4** Showing activity or vigor; as, a *lively* manner; a *lively* trade. **5** Rebounding quickly; as, a *lively* tennis ball.

liv·en \'līv-n\ *v.;* **liv·ened**; **liv·en·ing** \-n(-)ing\. To enliven.

live oak \'līv\. An evergreen oak with hard, durable wood; especially, one found in the southeastern states cultivated for its shelter and shade, and formerly much used in building ships.

liv·er \'liv-r\ *n.* **1** One that lives. **2** A resident.

liv·er \'liv-r\ *n.* **1** A large, dark-red organ of animal bodies that produces bile and causes changes in the blood. **2** The liver of certain animals, used as food.

liver fluke. A parasitic flatworm infesting the liver of many animals.

liv·er·ied \'liv-r(-)ēd\ *adj.* Wearing a livery.

liv·er·wort \'liv-r-ˌwərt, -ˌwȯrt\ *n.* A member of a class of dark-green flowerless plants found on rocks or bark in damp shady places.

liv·er·wurst \'liv-r-ˌwərst, -ˌwu̇rst\ *n.* A sausage consisting chiefly of liver.

liv·ery \'liv-r(-)ē\ *n.; pl.* **liv·er·ies**. **1** A special uniform worn by the servants of a wealthy household; as, a footman in *livery.* **2** The particular clothing worn to distinguish some association of persons; as, the *livery* of a school. **3** The feeding, care, and stabling of horses for pay; the keeping of horses and vehicles for hire. **4** A livery stable.

livery stable. A building where horses are stabled or where horses and vehicles are kept for hire.

lives. Pl. of *life.*

live·stock \'līv-ˌstäk\ *n.* Domestic animals on a farm, especially those kept for profit.

liv·id \'liv-əd\ *adj.* **1** Discolored like bruised flesh; black and blue. **2** Ashy pale.

liv·ing \'liv-ing\ *n.* **1** The fact of being alive. **2** The manner of life; as, right *living.* **3** A means of maintaining life; livelihood. — *adj.* **1** Alive; not dead;

as, *living* authors. **2** Active; not used up or outworn; as, *living* faith. **3** True to life; lively; as, the *living* image of his father. — **the living.** Those who are alive.

living room. A room in a dwelling house intended for general family use.

liz·ard \ˈliz-rd\ *n.* A reptile, commonly four-legged but including certain limbless forms, small or moderate-sized and having scaly skin, a longish body with tapering tail, five-clawed toes, and movable eyelids.

ll. Abbreviation for *lines.*

lla·ma \ˈläm-ə, ˈlȧm-ə, ˈyäm-ə, ˈyȧm-ə\ *n.; pl.* **lla·mas** or **lla·ma.** A South American cud-chewing, hoofed animal related to the camels but smaller and without a hump.

lla·no \ˈlän-ˌō, ˈlȧn-, ˈyän-, ˈyȧn-\ *n.; pl.* **lla·nos.** In Spanish America, a wide plain with or without vegetation.

lo \ˈlō\ *interj.* Behold! See!

load \ˈlōd\ *n.* **1** Anything heavy that is taken up and carried or is laid on or put in something to be carried; a burden; as, a big *load* for a small boy. **2** The quantity usually carried in such things as a car, cart, or vessel; as, ten *loads* of sand. **3** A weight or quantity of anything resting upon something else regarded as its support; as, a bridge capable of bearing *loads* up to ten tons. **4** Anything that burdens or weighs down the mind or spirit; as, a *load* of anxiety. **5** The charge for a firearm; as, a *load* of buckshot. **6** [in the plural] A great deal; very much; as, *loads* of fun. — *v.* **1** To lay a burden on; to furnish with a cargo; as, to *load* a truck. **2** To weigh down as with a burden; as, a mind *loaded* with care. **3** To place on or in something, as for carrying; as, to *load* hay; to *load* furniture into a van. **4** To receive or take on a load; as, ships engaged in *loading.* **5** To supply abundantly; as, to *load* a man with honors; to be *loaded* with wealth. **6** To increase in weight by the addition of a heavy substance; as, *loaded* dice, **7** To place a charge in; as, to *load* a rifle. — **load·er,** *n.*

loadstar. Variant of *lodestar.*

load·stone or **lode·stone** \ˈlōd-ˌstōn\ *n.* **1** A rock having magnetic properties. **2** Something that strongly attracts.

loaf \ˈlōf\ *n.; pl.* **loaves** \ˈlōvz\. **1** A regularly shaped mass of bread. **2** A shaped mass of cake or sugar. **3** A dish, as of minced meat, baked in the form of a loaf.

loaf \ˈlōf\ *v.* To spend time in idleness; to lounge; as, to *loaf* when one ought to be working; to *loaf* a whole afternoon away.

loaf·er \ˈlōf-r\ *n.* **1** One who loafs; a lazy person. **2** A man's or woman's low leather shoe with an upper resembling a moccasin but with a broad flat heel and the sole of a regular shoe.

loam \ˈlōm, ˈlüm\ *n.* A loose, easily crumbled soil that is composed of clay, sand, and decayed material, as leaves and grass. — *v.* To cover or fill with loam. — **loamy** \ˈlō-mē, ˈlü-\ *adj.*

loan \ˈlōn\ *n.* **1** The act of lending; permission to use; as, to ask the *loan* of a book. **2** Something that a person lends or borrows; especially, a sum of money lent or borrowed. — *v.* To lend.

loath or **loth** \ˈlōth, ˈlōth\ *adj.* Unwilling; reluctant. — **nothing loath.** Quite willing.

loathe \ˈlōth\ *v.;* **loathed; loath·ing.** To dislike greatly; to detest; to feel extreme disgust for or at; as, to *loathe* the smell of burning rubber. — For synonyms see *hate.*

loath·ing \ˈlō-thing\ *n.* Extreme disgust; a strong feeling of dislike or aversion.

loath·some \ˈlōths-m, ˈlōth-səm\ *adj.* Causing loathing; disgusting; as, a *loathsome* sight.

loaves. Pl. of *loaf.*

lob \ˈläb\ *v.;* **lobbed; lob·bing. 1** To throw or toss heavily or slowly; especially, in tennis, to return a ball in a high curve. **2** To go heavily or slowly, as a ball. — *n.* A ball or other object thrown or hit in a high curve.

lo·bate \ˈlō-ˌbāt\ or **lo·bat·ed** \-ˌbāt-əd\ *adj.* Having lobes or rounded divisions; as, a *lobate* leaf.

lob·by \ˈläb-ē\ *n.; pl.* **lob·bies. 1** A hall or passage, especially when serving also as a waiting room, as in a hotel. **2** The persons engaged in lobbying. — *v.;* **lob·bied** \-ēd\; **lob·by·ing. 1** To approach and talk with legislators in a lobby or elsewhere in an effort to influence legislation. **2** To urge or procure the passage of a bill by lobbying. — **lob·by·ist** \-ē-əst\ *n.*

lobe \ˈlōb\ *n.* A rounded projection or division of an organ or part; as, a *lobe* of a leaf; a *lobe* of the ear. — **lobed** \ˈlōbd\ *adj.*

lo·be·lia \lō-ˈbēl-yə\ *n.* A leafy-stemmed herb of a family having terminal clusters of flowers with three lobes of the corolla forming a lip and two lobes turned back, as the cardinal flower.

lob·lol·ly \ˈläb-ˌläl-ē\ *n.; pl.* **lob·lol·lies.** The loblolly pine.

loblolly pine. 1 A pine tree of the southern United States that has thick, flaky bark, long needles in threes, and spiny-tipped cones. **2** The coarse-grained wood of this tree.

lob·ster \ˈläb-stər\ *n.; pl.* **lob·sters** or **lob·ster.** A large salt-water crustacean used as food, with stalked eyes, five pairs of legs, the first pair of which are large claws or pincers, and a long abdomen.

lobster pot. A trap for catching lobsters.

lo·cal \ˈlōk-l\ *adj.* **1** Of or relating to place or position in space. **2** Relating to or occupying a particular place or places; not general or widespread; as, *local* news. **3** Making all the stops on its run; as, a *local* train. **4** Serving a single limited district; as, the *local* bus system; *local* telephone service. — *n.* **1** A local train or other public conveyance. **2** A local branch or chapter, as of a labor union. — **lo·cal·ly** \ˈlōk-l-ē\ *adv.*

local color. In a story or play, features and peculiarities that suggest a particular locality and its inhabitants.

lo·cale \lō-'kal\ *n.* A place or locality, especially with reference to a feature characteristic of it; as, the plants of this *locale.*

lo·cal·ism \'lōk-l-ˌiz-m\ *n.* **1** The inclination to be especially interested in the affairs of one's own locality. **2** A local manner of speech.

lo·cal·i·ty \lō-'kal-ət-ē\ *n.; pl.* **lo·cal·i·ties.** A particular district; a geographical place; a neighborhood.

lo·cal·ize \'lōk-l-ˌīz\ *v.;* **lo·cal·ized**; **lo·cal·iz·ing.** To make local; to fix in, or assign or confine to, a definite place or locality; as, a disease *localized* in a joint.

lo·cate \'lō-ˌkāt, lō-'kāt\ *v.;* **lo·cat·ed**; **lo·cat·ing.** **1** To state and fix exactly the place or limits of; as, to *locate* a mining claim. **2** To settle or establish in a particular spot; as, to *locate* a store on a corner. **3** To search for and discover; as, to *locate* the wrecked plane. **4** To assign a place to; as, to *locate* an event in history. **5** To refer to a place as the seat or origin of something; as, to *locate* a pain in a tooth. **6** To take up one's residence; to settle; as, to *locate* in the country.

lo·ca·tion \lō-'kāsh-n\ *n.* **1** The process of locating. **2** A situation; a place; especially, a locality of or for a building, as a residence or store. **3** A tract of land whose boundaries and purpose have been designated, as a mining claim. **4** A place outside a studio where a motion picture is filmed; as, made on *location* in the desert.

loch \'läk\ *n. Scottish.* A lake; an arm of the sea, especially one with a narrow entrance.

loci. Pl. of *locus.*

lock \'läk\ *n.* **1** A strand or ringlet of hair. **2** A tuft, as of hair, wool, or cotton.

lock \'läk\ *n.* **1** A fastening, as for a door, a trunk lid, or a drawer, operated by a bolt, key, or other device. **2** An enclosure, as in a canal, river, or dock, with gates at each end, used in raising or lowering boats as they pass from one level to another; as, the *locks* of the Panama Canal. **3** The mechanism of a firearm by which the charge is exploded. — *v.* **1** To fasten or be fastened, with a lock or locks; as, to *lock* a trunk. The door won't *lock.* **2** To confine; to shut in or out; as, to *lock* a person in a room. **3** To make fast by the linking together of parts; as, to *lock* arms.

lock, 1

lock·er \'läk-r\ *n.* **1** A drawer, cabinet, compartment, or chest for one's personal use. **2** An insulated compartment for storing food at a low temperature.

lock·et \'läk-ət\ *n.* A small ornamental case for a token, as a little picture or a lock of hair, usually worn on a necklace.

lock·jaw \'läk-ˌjȯ\ *n.* The disease tetanus; especially, the phase of the disease in which the upper and lower jaw are locked rigidly together.

lock·out \'läk-ˌau̇t\ *n.* The suspension of work or closing down of a plant by an employer during a labor dispute, in order to make his employees accept his terms.

lock·smith \'läk-ˌsmith\ *n.* A workman who makes or mends locks.

lock step. The marching in step of a body of men moving in a very close single file.

lock·up \'läk-ˌəp\ *n.* A jail; especially, a local jail where persons are held prior to a hearing.

lo·co·mo·tion \ˌlōk-ə-'mōsh-n\ *n.* The act or power of moving from place to place.

lo·co·mo·tive \ˌlōk-ə-'mōt-iv\ *n.* An engine that moves under its own power; especially, an engine that hauls cars on a railroad. — *adj.* **1** Of or relating to locomotion. **2** Having to do with an engine that moves under its own power.

lo·co·weed \'lō-ˌkō-ˌwēd\ *n.* Any of several herbs of the pea family, of the western United States, that cause a nervous disease (**lo·co disease** \'lō-ˌkō\) in cattle, horses, and sheep.

lo·cus \'lōk-əs\ *n.; pl.* **lo·ci** \'lō-ˌsī\. **1** A place; a locality. **2** The path of a point or curve moving according to some law in mathematics.

lo·cust \'lōk-əst\ *n.* **1** Any grasshopper; especially, one of a kind that travels in vast swarms and destroys almost all vegetation which lies in its path. **2** A cicada, as the **seventeen-year locust**, which spends from 13 to 17 years in an immature state, emerging as an adult for only a few weeks. **3** A North American tree of the pea family, with drooping clusters of fragrant flowers and a flat many-seeded pod. **4** The hard wood of this tree.

locust, 1

lo·cu·tion \lō-'kyüsh-n\ *n.* **1** The style of speaking; the manner of expression. **2** A particular form of expression; as, odd *locutions.*

lode \'lōd\ *n.* **1** A mass or strip of any mineral, as of gold or copper ore, that fills a crack in rock. **2** Any mass of ore in the earth or among rocks.

lode·star or **load·star** \'lōd-ˌstär, -ˌstȧr\ *n.* A star that leads; a guiding star; especially, the polestar.

lodestone. Variant of *loadstone.*

lodge \'läj\ *n.* **1** A dwelling place; a small house. **2** A house set apart for residence in the hunting or other special season. **3** A house on an estate, as for a caretaker. **4** In some organizations, the meeting place of a local branch or the members of such a branch; as, to attend a meeting at the *lodge.* **5** The den of a wild animal; as, a beaver's *lodge.* **6** A cabin, hut, or tent of the North American Indians; a wigwam; a tepee. **7** The regular occupants of such a lodge. — *v.;* **lodged**; **lodg·ing.** **1** To provide quarters for, especially temporarily; as, to *lodge* guests for the night. **2** To serve as a shelter for. Each tent is capable of *lodging* two campers. **3** To establish or settle (oneself) in a place. The troops *lodged* themselves in the captured fortification. **4** To dwell; to live; as, to *lodge* at a hotel.

5 To come to rest; to stop and stay. The bullet *lodged* in a tree. **6** To lay or place; as, to *lodge* a complaint with the police.

lodg·er \'läj-r\ *n.* One that lodges; especially, a person who occupies a rented room in another person's house.

lodg·ing \'läj-ing\ *n.* **1** A dwelling; especially, a temporary dwelling or sleeping place. **2** [in the plural] A room or rooms in the house of another person, rented as a dwelling place.

lodg·ing·house \'läj-ing-ˌhau̇s\ *n.* or **lodging house**; *pl.* **lodg·ing·hous·es** \-ˌhau̇-zəz\ or **lodging houses.** A house where lodgings are provided and rented.

lodg·ment or **lodge·ment** \'läj-mənt\ *n.* **1** A lodging place; lodgings. **2** The action or manner of lodging; especially, a placing, depositing, or coming to rest; the condition of being lodged; as, the *lodgment* of a balloon in a tree. **3** An accumulation of something lodged in a place; as, a *lodgment* of sticks and leaves in a gutter.

loess \'les, 'ləs\ *n.* A deposit of wind-borne, yellowish-brown loam found in large areas of North America, Europe, and Asia, that makes excellent soil where it is well watered.

loft \'lȯft\ *n.* **1** An upper room or upper story of a building; especially, an attic. **2** An upper room of a barn; a hayloft. **3** A gallery in a church or auditorium; as, the choir *loft.* **4** In golf, the backward slant of the face of a club, the action of lofting, or a lofting stroke. **—** *v.* In sports, to strike a ball so that it rises high in the air.

lofty \'lȯf-tē\ *adj.;* **loft·i·er; loft·i·est. 1** Rising high; towering; having imposing height; as, a *lofty* pine; a *lofty* mountain. **2** Proud; haughty; as, a person with a *lofty* air. **3** Of high rank or quality; as, *lofty* lineage. **4** High-minded; as, *lofty* ideals. — For synonyms see *high.*

log \'lȯg, 'läg\ *n.* **1** A bulky piece of unshaped timber; especially, a long piece of a tree trunk or of a large branch trimmed and ready for sawing. **2** An apparatus for measuring the rate of a ship's motion through the water, consisting of a block fastened to a line and run out from a reel. **3** The daily record of a ship's speed and progress. **4** The full record of a ship's voyage or of an aircraft's flight. **—** *adj.* Made from a log or built of logs; as, *log* cabins. **—** *v.;* **logged; log·ging. 1** To engage in cutting and transporting logs for timber. **2** To write down in a logbook. **3** To sail or move a distance shown in a ship's log; as, to *log* 350 miles in 24 hours.

lo·gan·ber·ry \'lōg-n-ˌber-ē\ *n.; pl.* **lo·gan·ber·ries.** [Named after James H. *Logan* (1841–1928), an American judge and horticulturist who first produced it.] The large red berry of an upright bush related to both the blackberry and the raspberry.

log·a·rithm \'lȯg-r-ˌith-m, 'läg-, -ˌith-m\ *n.* An exponent that expresses for a given number the times another number (in common logarithms 10) must be multiplied by itself to equal that given number. In the expression $10^3 = 1000$ the exponent 3 is the *logarithm* of 1000. **— log·a·rith·mic** \ˌlȯg-r-'ith-mik, ˌläg-, -'ith-\ *adj.*

log·book \'lȯg-ˌbu̇k, 'läg-\ *n.* **1** A book in which is written down the daily progress of a ship at sea, with notes on the weather and on events of the voyage. **2** Any book for keeping similar records, as of the flights of an aircraft; a log.

loge \'lōzh\ *n.* A box in a theater or opera house.

log·ger \'lȯg-r, 'läg-r\ *n.* **1** A workman employed in logging. **2** A machine for hauling and loading logs.

log·ger·head \'lȯg-r-ˌhed, 'läg-\ *n.* **1** A blockhead. **2** Also **loggerhead turtle.** A very large sea turtle of the warmer parts of the Atlantic Ocean. **— be at loggerheads.** To quarrel.

log·gia \'läj-ə, 'lȯj-, -ē-ə\ *n.; pl.* **log·gias** \-əz, -ē-əz\ or **log·gie** \'lȯj-ˌā\. A roofed gallery open on at least one side.

log·ging \'lȯg-ing, 'läg-\ *n.* The business of cutting down trees, cutting them into logs, and transporting them to a sawmill or to market.

log·ic \'läj-ik\ *n.* **1** The science that deals with the rules and tests of sound thinking and proof by reasoning. **2** Reasoning; especially, sound reasoning. There was no *logic* in that remark. **3** Connection, as of facts or events, in a way that seems reasonable; as, the *logic* of a situation.

log·i·cal \'läj-ik-l\ *adj.* **1** Of or relating to logic; used in logic. **2** According to the rules of logic; as, a *logical* argument. **3** Skilled in logic; as, a *logical* thinker. **4** According to what is reasonably expected; as, a *logical* result of an action. **— log·i·cal·ly** \-ik-l(-)ē\ *adv.*

lo·gi·cian \lō-'jish-n\ *n.* A person skilled in logic.

lo·gis·tics \lō-'jis-tiks, lə-\ *n.* The branch of military science that deals with the transportation, quartering, and supplying of troops in military operations. **— lo·gis·tic** \-tik\ or **lo·gis·ti·cal** \-tik-l\ *adj.*

log·roll·ing \'lȯg-ˌrō-ling, 'läg-\ *n.* **1** The rolling of logs in water by treading. **2** An arrangement by which one member of a congress or legislature agrees to vote for a bill backed by another member with the understanding that the favor will be returned.

lo·gy \'lō-gē\ *adj.;* **lo·gi·er; lo·gi·est.** Heavy or dull in motion or in thinking.

loin \'lȯin\ *n.* **1** The part of the body on either side of the spinal column, between the hip and the lower ribs. **2** A front part of a hind-quarter of beef, veal, lamb, mutton, or pork.

loin·cloth \'lȯin-ˌklȯth\ *n.* A simple garment consisting of a cloth worn around the loins.

loi·ter \'lȯit-r\ *v.;* **loi·tered; loi·ter·ing** \'lȯit-r-ing, 'lȯi-tring\. To lag behind; to be slow in moving. — For synonyms see *linger.* **— loi·ter·er** \'lȯit-r-r\ *n.*

loll \'läl\ *v.* **1** To hang or let hang loosely; to dangle; to droop. The dog's tongue *lolled* out of his mouth. **2** To move or sprawl in a lazy manner; to lounge; as, to *loll* in the sun.

lol·li·pop \'läl-ē-ˌpäp\ *n.* A sugar candy; especially, a lump of candy on a stick.

lone \'lōn\ *adj.* **1** Without company; solitary; as, a *lone* traveler. **2** Apart from other things of the kind; lonely; unfrequented; as, a *lone* island.

lone·li·ness \'lōn-lē-nəs\ *n.* **1** The quality or state of being lonely. **2** Depression or sadness because of being alone.

lone·ly \'lōn-lē\ *adj.;* **lone·li·er**; **lone·li·est.** **1** Without company; lone; as, a *lonely* hiker. **2** Unfrequented; desolate; as, a *lonely* spot. **3** Lonesome; as, to feel *lonely.*

lone·some \'lōn(t)s-m\ *adj.;* **lone·som·er**; **lone·som·est.** **1** Unfrequented; lonely; as, a *lonesome* road. **2** Conscious of and depressed by being without companions. — **lone·some·ly**, *adv.*

long \'lȯng\ *adj.;* **long·er** \'lȯng-gr\; **long·est** \'lȯng-gəst\. **1** Of great extent from end to end; not short. **2** Lasting for a considerable time; not brief; as, a *long* program at assembly. **3** Stretched out to a given measure, degree, or time; as, a yard *long;* an hour *long.* **4** Extending to what is distant, as in time or space; as, a *long* view of affairs. **5** Forming the greatest measurement in contrast to width or weight; as, a *long* body and short legs. **6** Of *a, e, i, o, oo, u,* pronounced as in *ale, eve, ice, old, food,* and *cube.* — *adv.* **1** For or during a long time. Have you been away *long?* **2** At a distant point of time; as, *long* before Columbus discovered America.

long \'lȯng\ *v.;* **longed** \'lȯngd\; **long·ing** \'lȯng-ing\. To wish for something earnestly, with deep feeling; to yearn; as, to *long* for ice skates; to *long* for home in the country.

long. Abbreviation for *longitude.*

long-ago \'lȯng-ə-'gō\ *adj.* Belonging to a time long past gone; as, a tale of *long-ago* knights and castles. — *n.* Time long before the present; as, in the *long-ago.*

long·boat \'lȯng-ˌbōt\ *n.* A large boat carried on a ship.

long·bow \'lȯng-ˌbō\ *n.* A wooden bow, usually five and a half to six feet long, discharged by hand.

lon·gev·i·ty \län-'jev-ət-ē, lȯn-\ *n.* **1** Long life; as, the *longevity* of redwoods; the *longevity* of turtles. **2** Length of life. The *longevity* of man has increased with the advance of medical knowledge.

long·hand \'lȯng-ˌhand\ *n.* Handwriting; not shorthand or typewriting.

long·horn \'lȯng-ˌhȯrn\ *n.* **1** An animal with long horns. **2** A steer or cow with very long horns, one of a breed formerly common in the southwestern United States.

longhorn, 2

long·ing \'lȯng-ing\ *n.* An eager desire; a craving or yearning; as, a *longing* to go back home again.

long·ing·ly \'lȯng-ing-lē\ *adv.* In a manner showing eager desire or yearning.

long·ish \'lȯng-ish\ *adj.* Somewhat long.

lon·gi·tude \'län-jə-ˌtüd, -ˌtyüd\ *n.* Distance measured by degrees or time east or west from a line, called the *prime meridian,* drawn between the North and South Poles and usually running through Greenwich, England. The *longitude* of New York is 74 degrees or about five hours west of Greenwich.

hemisphere marked with meridians of longitude

lon·gi·tu·di·nal \ˌlän-jə-'tüd-n(-)əl, -'tyüd-\ *adj.* **1** Of or relating to length. **2** Extended in length; placed or running lengthwise. — **lon·gi·tu·di·nal·ly** \-n(-)ə-lē\ *adv.*

long-lived \'lȯng-'līvd, -'livd\ *adj.* Living or lasting long.

long-range \'lȯng-'rānj\ *adj.* **1** Capable of shooting over great distances; as, a *long-range* gun. **2** Capable of traveling great distances; extending over great distances; as, *long-range* bombers; *long-range* travel. **3** Lasting over a long period; for or extending into a long period; considering or providing for the future; as, the *long-range* effects of better schools; *long-range* planning.

long·shore·man \'lȯng-'shōr-mən, -'shȯr-\ *n.; pl.* **long·shore·men** \-mən\. A laborer at a wharf who loads and unloads cargo.

long-suf·fer·ing \'lȯng-'səf-r(-)ing\ *n.* Long and patient endurance. — *adj.* Enduring something, as offense or sickness, long and patiently.

long-wind·ed \'lȯng-'win-dəd\ *adj.* Tediously long in speaking; as, a *long-winded* talker.

look \'lu̇k\ *v.* **1** To see. **2** To direct the eyes in order to see a particular thing; as, to *look* into a mirror. **3** To appear; to seem. It *looks* dangerous. **4** To pay attention; to take heed. *Look* to your steering. **5** To face in a certain direction; as, the house *looked* to the east. **6** To give a look to; as, to *look* a man in the eye. **7** To influence by one's gaze; as, to *look* down opposition. **8** To express by a glance; as, to *look* one's scorn. **9** To appear to be; as, to *look* one's age. — **look after.** To attend to; to take care of; as, to *look after* a child. — **look daggers.** To look threateningly. — **look down on.** To treat as an inferior; to despise. — **look down one's nose.** To look haughtily or disdainfully; as, to *look down one's nose* at a penniless relative. — **look for. 1** To expect; as, to *look for* a letter in the next mail. **2** To seek for; to search for. — **look forward to.** To anticipate with pleasure. — **look in.** To go in for a short call. The doctor *looked in* frequently. — **look into.** To inspect closely; to examine; as, to *look into* a problem. — **look on.** To be a spectator. — **look on** or **look upon.** To regard; to consider; to think of; as, to *look upon* the matter as of little importance. — **look out for. 1** To be on guard against; to beware of; as, to *look out for* cars in crossing the street. **2** To act on behalf of; to guard; as, to engage a lawyer to *look out for* one's interests. — **look over.** To inspect; to examine; as, to *look over* an account. — **look up.** To search for; to search out; as, to *look up* a word in a dictionary; to *look up* a friend in the city. — **look up to.** To respect. — *n.* **1** A glance, gaze, or stare. **2** An appearance or expression of the face; as, a healthy *look.*

look·er-on \ˌlu̇k-r-ˈȯn, -ˈän\ *n.; pl.* **look·ers-on.** A spectator.

look·ing glass \ˈlu̇k-ing ˌglas\. A mirror.

look·out \ˈlu̇k-ˌau̇t\ *n.* **1** A careful watch for an object or a happening; as, to be on the *lookout* for storm warnings. **2** The place, often an elevated place, from which such a watch is kept. **3** A person engaged in watching; especially, one assigned to watch, as on a ship. **4** A view; a prospect; an outlook. **5** An object of care; a proper matter of concern. What he does with his spare time is his *lookout,* not mine.

loom \ˈlüm\ *v.* **1** To come into sight in an unnaturally large, indistinct, or distorted form, as if through a haze. An iceberg *loomed* out of the fog. **2** To appear in an exaggerated or an impressively great form; as, a football player whose skill *loomed* large on the local team.

loom \ˈlüm\ *n.* A frame or machine for weaving together threads or yarns into cloth.

loon \ˈlün\ *n.* Any of several fish-eating diving birds, with webbed feet, black head, and white-spotted black back.

loo·ny \ˈlü-nē\ *adj.;* **loo·ni·er; loo·ni·est.** *Slang.* Crazy. — *n.; pl.* **loo·nies.** *Slang.* A crazy person.

loop \ˈlüp\ *n.* **1** A fold or doubling in a thread or rope, through which another thread or rope can be passed or into which a hook can be caught. **2** Any loop-shaped figure, bend, or course; as, a *loop* in a river. **3** A circular airplane maneuver involving flying upside down. **4** A complete electric circuit. — *v.* **1** To make a loop or loops in. **2** To make a loop or loops on or about; as, to *loop* a rope around a post. **3** Also **loop the loop.** To execute a loop in an airplane. **4** To crawl in the manner of a measuring worm.

loop·er \ˈlüp-r\ *n.* **1** One that loops. **2** A measuring worm.

loop·hole \ˈlüp-ˌhōl, ˈlü-ˌpōl\ *n.* **1** A small opening, as in the wall of a fort or blockhouse, through which a gun may be fired. **2** A means of escape; especially, a way of evading a law or regulation.

loophole

loose \ˈlüs\ *adj.;* **loos·er; loos·est.** **1** Not tightly set or fastened; as, a *loose* tooth; a *loose* board. **2** Not tightly drawn; slack; lax; as, a *loose* belt; to drive with *loose* reins. **3** Free; unattached; as, a boat *loose* from its moorings; a dog running *loose.* **4** Not brought together in a package or binding; as, *loose* coffee; *loose* sheets of paper. **5** Disconnected; random; as, *loose* paragraphs. **6** Having wide meshes; as, a cloth of *loose* weave. **7** Not exact, precise, or accurate; as, *loose* reasoning; a *loose* style of writing. **8** Lax in conduct; dissolute; immoral. — *adv.* Loosely; not tightly or rigidly. — *v.;* **loosed; loos·ing.** **1** To make loose; to unbind or untie. **2** To loosen; to relax; to slacken. **3** To set free. **4** To discharge from or as if from a weapon; as, to *loose* an arrow. — **loose·ly,** *adv.*

loos·en \ˈlüs-n\ *v.;* **loos·ened; loos·en·ing** \-n(-)ing\. **1** To let loose; to free. **2** To free from tightness or firmness. **3** To make less compact, as soil. **4** To allow to become less strict; as, to *loosen* discipline. **5** To become loose or looser.

loot \ˈlüt\ *n.* Plunder; booty; spoils. — *v.* **1** To plunder; as, to *loot* a captured city. **2** To rob, especially by dishonest practices; as, public funds *looted* by corrupt officials.

lop \ˈläp\ *v.;* **lopped; lop·ping.** **1** To cut branches from; to trim; as, to *lop* a tree. **2** To cut off, trim off, or shear off; as, to *lop* dead branches from a tree; *lopping* off loose threads.

lop \ˈläp\ *v.;* **lopped; lop·ping.** To hang downward; to droop; to flop or sway about. — *adj.* Hanging down; as, *lop* ears.

lope \ˈlōp\ *n.* An easy, bounding gait, like that of a running dog or wolf. — *v.;* **loped; lop·ing.** To run or move with a lope.

lop-eared \ˈläp-ˈird\ *adj.* Having hanging or drooping ears.

lop·sid·ed \ˈläp-ˈsīd-əd\ *adj.* Leaning to one side; not symmetrical; unbalanced. — **lop·sid·ed·ly,** *adv.*

lo·qua·cious \lō-ˈkwā-shəs\ *adj.* Talkative. — **lo·quac·i·ty** \-ˈkwas-ət-ē\ *n.*

lo·quat \ˈlō-ˌkwät, lō-ˈkwät\ *n.* A small Asiatic evergreen tree bearing a yellow fruit like a plum.

lord \ˈlȯrd\ *n.* [From Old English *hlaford* meaning literally "bread keeper", that is, "food dispenser".] **1** A person who has power or authority; a master. **2** [with a capital] The Supreme Being; God; Jesus Christ. **3** In the British Empire, a titled nobleman. **4** [usually with a capital] In the British Empire, the title prefixed to the names of certain noblemen and bishops and forming part of certain official titles; as, *Lord* Byron; the *lord* chamberlain. **5** In feudal times, the king or nobleman from whom a vassal had received land and to whom he owed allegiance. — **the Lords.** The House of Lords. — *v.* To act or rule in the manner of a lord; to domineer; as, to *lord* it over another person.

lord·ly \ˈlȯrd-lē\ *adj.;* **lord·li·er; lord·li·est.** Suitable for or like a lord; grand; proud; haughty; as, a *lordly* manner.

lord·ship \ˈlȯrd-ˌship\ *n.* **1** The rank or position of a lord — used with *his* or *your* to refer to or address one having the ranking title of *Lord.* **2** Rule; authority.

Lord's Prayer \ˈlȯrdz\. The prayer which Christ taught his disciples.

Lord's Supper. **1** The Last Supper. **2** The Eucharist.

lore \ˈlōr, ˈlȯr\ *n.* Knowledge; especially, knowledge about some particular subject; as, the *lore* of the sea; forest *lore.*

lor·gnette \lȯrn-ˈyet\ *n.* An eyeglass or eyeglasses on a handle.

lorn \ˈlȯrn\ *adj.* Left alone; forsaken; abandoned.

lor·ry \'lȯr-ē, 'lär-ē\ *n.; pl.* **lor·ries.** *British.* A large truck for carrying heavy material; as, a six-wheeled *lorry.*

lose \'lüz\ *v.;* **lost** \'lȯst\; **los·ing** \'lü-zing\. **1** To ruin; to destroy; as, a ship *lost* on the rocks. **2** To miss from one's possessions; to mislay; as, to *lose* a billfold; to *lose* a book. **3** To suffer the loss of; as, to *lose* money in a business deal; to *lose* one's eyesight. **4** To be deprived of, as by death or final separation; as, to *lose* a son. **5** To fail to use to the best advantage; as, to *lose* a day; to *lose* speed. **6** To fail to gain or win; to fail to achieve success; as, to *lose* a football game; to try hard but *lose.* **7** To fail to hear or understand; as, to *lose* part of what a person is saying. **8** To cause the loss of. The speech *lost* the candidate the election. **9** To fail to keep up or maintain; as, to *lose* hope; to *lose* interest. **10** To wander from; as, to *lose* one's way. **11** To fail to keep in sight or mind; as, to *lose* a person in a crowd. — **lose face.** To lose prestige. — **lose track of.** To fail to keep in touch with; as, to *lose track of* an old friend.

los·er \'lüz-r\ *n.* A person or thing that loses; as, being among the *losers* in a contest.

los·ing \'lü-zing\ *n.* The act of one who loses; as, the *losing* of a pet. — *adj.* That does not win; as, the *losing* team.

loss \'lȯs\ *n.* **1** Ruin; destruction; as, the *loss* of a ship. **2** Failure to keep in one's possession; as, the *loss* of property. **3** The harm resulting from losing something. The cancellation of the order was a great *loss* to the company. **4** Something that is mislaid or lost; the waste; as, money *losses; loss* from breakage. **5** Failure to win, get, or use to advantage; as, the *loss* of a battle; *loss* of time. — **at a loss.** Puzzled; unable; as, to be *at a loss* to explain the strange events.

lot \'lät\ *n.* **1** An object, such as a slip of paper bearing a name or number, a small stick, or a straw, used as one of several objects slightly different from one another, as in size or value, to be selected by chance in determining winners or losers or deciding a course to be followed; to draw *lots.* **2** The use of such objects to decide anything; as, to choose by *lot.* **3** That which comes to a person by this method of determining something; a share. It was my *lot* to wash the dishes. **4** Fortune; fate; as, to be satisfied with one's *lot.* **5** A piece or plot of land; as, a building *lot.* **6** A number of persons or things taken or considered together; as, a *lot* of stationery; goods in *lots.* **7** A considerable quantity; as, a *lot* of publication; a *lot* of cake for a small boy to eat.

loth. Variant of *loath.*

lo·tion \'lōsh-n\ *n.* A liquid containing oils or medicines and applied to the skin either as a healing agent or as a cosmetic.

lot·tery \'lät-r-ē, 'lä-trē\ *n.; pl.* **lot·ter·ies.** A drawing of lots in which prizes are given to the winning names or numbers; a scheme for distributing prizes by chance. There are many places in which *lotteries* are illegal.

lo·tus \'lōt-əs\ *n.* **1** A plant of the water-lily family with leaves up to two feet wide and cup-shaped flowers, as the yellow-flowered American lotus and the rose-colored East Indian lotus. **2** In Greek legend, a fruit that caused dreamy contentment and forgetfulness when eaten.

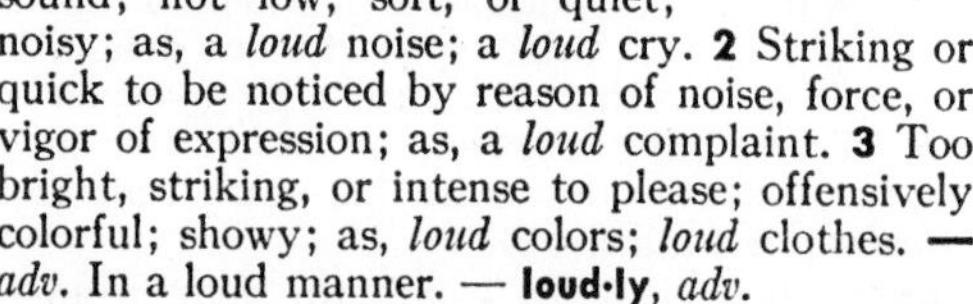

lotus

loud \'lau̇d\ *adj.* **1** Marked by intensity or relative intensity of sound; not low, soft, or quiet; noisy; as, a *loud* noise; a *loud* cry. **2** Striking or quick to be noticed by reason of noise, force, or vigor of expression; as, a *loud* complaint. **3** Too bright, striking, or intense to please; offensively colorful; showy; as, *loud* colors; *loud* clothes. — *adv.* In a loud manner. — **loud·ly,** *adv.*

loud·mouthed \'lau̇d-'mau̇t͟hd, -'mau̇tht\ *adj.* Having an offensively loud voice; talking in or having a noisy, blustering manner; as, a showy, *loudmouthed* person; a *loudmouthed* attempt to gain attention.

loud·speak·er \'lau̇d-'spēk-r\ *n.* A device, as on a radio, that produces sounds loud enough to be easily heard at a distance.

lounge \'lau̇nj\ *v.;* **lounged; loung·ing.** To move or act in a lazy, slow, or listless way; to stand, sit, or lie in a relaxed manner. — *n.* **1** A comfortable sitting room or place intended for lounging. **2** A sofa; a couch.

lour. Variant of *lower.*

louse \'lau̇s\ *n.; pl.* **lice** \'līs\. **1** A small wingless insect that lives on the bodies of warm-blooded animals and sucks blood. **2** Any of various small mostly parasitic arthropods.

wood louse

lousy \'lau̇-zē\ *adj.;* **lous·i·er; lous·i·est. 1** Infested with or as if with lice. **2** *Slang.* Disgusting; contemptible; as, a *lousy* way to act. **3** *Slang.* Poor; bad; as, a *lousy* speech. **4** *Slang.* Well supplied or provided, as with money.

lout \'lau̇t\ *n.* A stupid, clownish, or awkward person. — **lout·ish** \'lau̇t-ish\ *adj.* — **lout·ish·ly,** *adv.*

lou·ver \'lüv-r\ *n.* A louver board, or an opening or frame with louver boards fitted in; a slatted panel used for ventilation, for light control, or for decorative effect. — **lou·vered** \-rd\ *adj.*

louver board. 1 One of the sloping boards set to shed rain water outward, as in belfry windows. **2** A similar piece forming part of any slotted panel, as in a door or screen.

lov·a·ble \'ləv-əb-l\ *adj.* Having qualities that tend to make one loved; worthy of love. — **lov·a·bly** \-ə-blē\ *adv.*

love \'ləv\ *n.* **1** The feeling experienced when one is strongly attached or deeply devoted to another; especially, strong affection for one of the opposite sex. **2** A strong liking; a deep interest; as, *love* of learning; *love* of sports. **3** The object of affection; a sweetheart. **4** In certain games, as tennis, nothing; no points scored — used in counting the score — *v.;* **loved**; **lov·ing.** **1** To have or show warm affection for. **2** To take delight or pleasure in; as, to *love* reading. **3** To caress; to fondle.

love·bird \'ləv-ˌbərd\ *n.* Any of numerous rather small, usually largely green or gray parrots often kept as pets; especially, a budgerigar.

love knot. A knot or bow of ribbon as a token of love.

love·lorn \'ləv-ˌlȯrn\ *adj.* Deserted by one's love.

love·ly \'ləv-lē\ *adj.;* **love·li·er**; **love·li·est.** **1** Delicately beautiful; as, a *lovely* dress. **2** Beautiful in character. **3** Highly pleasing; as, a *lovely* view. — **love·li·ness** \-lē-nəs\ *n.*

lov·er \'ləv-r\ *n.* **1** A person, especially a man, who is in love. **2** [in the plural] Two persons in love with each other. **3** A person who is very fond of something; as, a *lover* of music.

love seat. A double chair, or a settee or sofa for two persons.

love·sick \'ləv-ˌsik\ *adj.* **1** Sick or unhappy because of love; as, a *lovesick* boy. **2** Expressing languishing love; as, a *lovesick* sigh.

lov·ing \'ləv-ing\ *adj.* Feeling or showing love; affectionate; as, *loving* care; a *loving* glance. — **lov·ing·ly**, *adv.*

low \'lō\ *v.* To make the calling sound of a cow; to moo. — *n.* A moo.

low \'lō\ *adj.* **1** Not high; not tall; as, a *low* building. **2** Lying below the usual level; going below the usual level; as, *low* ground; a *low* bow. **3** Of a dress, cut far down at the neck; as, a *low* evening gown. **4** Sounding below some other sound; deep; not loud; as, to sing a *low* note; a *low* whisper. **5** Near the horizon. The sun is *low.* **6** Inferior; commonplace; especially humble; as, people of *low* rank; to be of *low* birth. **7** Feeble; weak; as, left *low* by a fever. **8** Gloomy; depressed; dejected; as, in *low* spirits. **9** Less than usual, as in quantity or value; as, a *low* price; food of a *low* grade. **10** Bad-mannered; vulgar; as, a *low* person. **11** Unfavorable; poor; as, to have a *low* opinion of someone. **12** Not advanced in development or civilization; as, a *low* culture. — *adv.* **1** In or to a low position; in a low manner; near the ground; as, a plane flying *low.* **2** In poverty, disgrace, or subjection; as, to be brought *low* by financial failure. **3** Cheaply; as, to be forced to sell *low.* **4** With a low musical pitch or tone; as, to sing *low.* **5** Near the equator; near the horizon. — *n.* **1** Something that is low; as, a *low* price; a *low* score. **2** An area of low barometric pressure. **3** The arrangement of gears in the transmission, as of an automobile, in such a position as to transmit the greatest power from the engine to the propelling shaft.

low·boy \'lō-ˌbȯi\ *n.* A table with drawers, about three feet high.

low·bred \'lō-'bred\ *adj.* Vulgar; coarse; unrefined.

low-brow or **low·brow** \'lō-ˌbrau̇\ *n.* **1** A person who has a low brow or forehead. **2** A person without intellectual interests or cultivation; a person with low tastes. — *adj.* Lacking intellectual interests or cultivation; of low taste.

Low Countries. That part of Europe bordering on the North Sea and comprising the Netherlands, Belgium, and Luxembourg.

low·er or **lour** \'lau̇r\ *v.* **1** To frown; to look sullen. A portrait of an ancient ancestor *lowered* over the fireplace. **2** To be dark and threatening, as clouds. — *n.* A lowering look; a scowl.

low·er \'lōr, 'lō-ər\ *adj.* Comparative of *low.* **1** Below some other of two similar persons or things; as, a *lower* floor. **2** Not so far advanced; of less importance; as, the *lower* grades in school. **3** Less highly advanced in the scale of development through evolution; as, the *lower* animals. — *v.* **1** To let down; to pull down; as, to *lower* a line into the water; to *lower* a flag. **2** To make less, as in value or amount; as, to *lower* the price of eggs. **3** To humble; as, to *lower* one's pride. **4** To reduce the height of; as, to *lower* a wall. **5** To make the aim or direction lower; as, to *lower* the light beam on a car. **6** To reduce the height of; as, to *lower* a mast.

low·er·ing or **lour·ing** \'lau̇r-ing\ *adj.* Frowning; scowling; gloomy.

low·er·most \'lōr-ˌmōst, 'lō-ər-\ *adj.* Lowest.

low·er world \'lōr, 'lō-ər\. **1** The earth. **2** The world of the dead or of future punishment.

low frequency. In radio and television, any frequency in the range from 30 to 300 kilocycles. — **low-fre·quen·cy**, *adj.*

low·land \'lō-lənd\ *n.* Land that is low and flat with respect to the neighboring area; low or level country.

low·land·er \'lō-lənd-r\ *n.* A native or inhabitant of the lowlands.

low·ly \'lō-lē\ *adj.;* **low·li·er**; **low·li·est.** **1** Of low rank or station; modest; humble; as, the *lowly* dwelling of a hermit. **2** Inferior; secondary; as, *lowly* organisms of the insect world. — *adv.* Humbly; meekly.

low-pres·sure \'lō-'presh-r\ *adj.* **1** Having, employing, exerting, or operating under a low degree of pressure; as, *low-pressure* automobile tires. **2** Having a low atmospheric pressure as measured by a barometer.

low-spir·it·ed \'lō-'spir-ət-əd\ *adj.* Sad; depressed.

low tide. The farthest ebb of the tide.

loy·al \'lȯi-əl, 'lȯil\ *adj.* **1** Faithful to the lawful government or to the sovereign to whom one is subject. **2** True to any person or persons to whom one owes allegiance. — **loy·al·ly** \'lȯi-ə-lē\ *adv.*

loy·al·ist \'lȯi-ə-ləst\ *n.* A person who is loyal to his government or sovereign, especially in times of revolt.

loy·al·ty \'lȯi-əl-tē, 'lȯil-tē\ *n.;* *pl.* **loy·al·ties.** **1** Faithful adherence to one's government or sovereign. **2** Fidelity in thought and act, as to a friend.

— The word *allegiance* is a synonym of *loyalty: allegiance* usually suggests a rather formal relationship involving adherence and devotion, as of a vassal to his lord or of a citizen to his country; *loyalty* may suggest a more personal relationship characterized by steadfastness and faithfulness.

loz·enge \'läz-nj\ *n.* **1** A diamond-shaped figure. **2** Something small, flat, round, or diamond-shaped, as a cough drop.

lozenge

l's. Pl. of *l.*

Lt. Abbreviation for *lieutenant.*

ltd. Abbreviation for *limited.*

lub·ber \'ləb-r\ *n.* **1** A big clumsy fellow. **2** On a ship, an unskilled seaman. — **lub·ber·ly** \-r-lē\ *adj.* or *adv.*

lu·bri·cant \'lüb-rə-kənt\ *n.* Something that lubricates, such as oil or grease.

lu·bri·cate \'lüb-rə-ˌkāt\ *v.;* **lu·bri·cat·ed**; **lu·bri·cat·ing.** **1** To make smooth or slippery. **2** To apply oil or grease, as to parts that run together; as, a properly *lubricated* machine. — **lu·bri·ca·tion** \ˌlüb-rə-'kāsh-n\ *n.* — **lu·bri·ca·tor** \'lüb-rə-ˌkāt-r\ *n.*

lu·cent \'lüs-nt\ *adj.* **1** Shining; bright. **2** Clear; translucent.

lu·cid \'lü-səd\ *adj.* **1** Shining; bright. **2** Clear; as, a *lucid* stream of water. **3** Showing a sane and normal mental condition. Insane people often have *lucid* periods. **4** Easily understood; plain; as, a *lucid* explanation. — **lu·cid·ly,** *adv.*

lu·cid·i·ty \lü-'sid-ət-ē\ *n.* The quality or state of being lucid, especially in thought or expression; clearness.

Lu·ci·fer \'lü-səf-r\ *n.* [From Old English, there borrowed from Latin, meaning literally "light-bringing".] **1** The planet Venus when appearing as the morning star. **2** The Devil, who like the morning star in old stories fell from heaven. **3** [with a small letter] A friction match common in the 19th century.

luck \'lək\ *n.* **1** That which happens to a person apparently by chance; fortune; fate; chance; as, fortunate people who seem to have nothing but good *luck* in their lives. **2** The accidental way events occur; as, happening by pure *luck.* **3** Good luck; good fortune; as, to have *luck;* to be out of *luck.*

luck·i·ly \'lək-l-ē\ *adv.* By good luck; fortunately.

luck·less \'lək-ləs\ *adj.* Being without luck; having or marked by bad luck; unfortunate; as, a *luckless* day.

lucky \'lək-ē\ *adj.;* **luck·i·er**; **luck·i·est.** **1** Favored by luck; fortunate. **2** Producing a good result apparently by chance; as, a *lucky* hit. **3** Seeming to have a good influence; thought of as bringing good luck; as, a *lucky* coin.

lu·cra·tive \'lük-rət-iv\ *adj.* Bringing in good profits, especially in money; profitable; as, a *lucrative* profession. — **lu·cra·tive·ly,** *adv.*

lu·cre \'lük-r\ *n.* Gain in money or goods; profit; money — now used only of money or money-making when thought of as bad.

lu·di·crous \'lüd-ə-krəs\ *adj.* Laughable; ridiculous; comic. — **lu·di·crous·ly,** *adv.*

luff \'ləf\ *n.* The action of sailing a boat more nearly against the direct path of the wind. — *v.* To turn the bow of a boat toward the wind; to sail closer to the wind.

lug \'ləg\ *n.* **1** A small part projecting like an ear; especially, such a part used as a handle. **2** Any small projecting part.

lug \'ləg\ *v.;* **lugged**; **lug·ging.** To pull, haul, or drag along; to carry with difficulty or special effort, as something heavy or cumbersome.

lug·gage \'ləg-ij\ *n.* Baggage.

lug·ger \'ləg-r\ *n.* A boat carrying a lugsail or lugsails.

lug·sail \'ləg-ˌsāl, -səl\ *n.* A four-sided sail fastened at the top to a yard that hangs obliquely across a mast and is raised and lowered with the sail.

lu·gu·bri·ous \lə-'güb-rē-əs, lü-, -'gyüb-\ *adj.* Mournful, especially in an exaggerated or affected way; doleful. — **lu·gu·bri·ous·ly,** *adv.*

lug·worm \'ləg-ˌwərm\ *n.* A worm found along the seashore, having a row of tufted gills along each side of the back.

luke·warm \'lük-'wȯrm\ *adj.* **1** Neither hot nor cold; moderately warm; tepid; as, *lukewarm* water. **2** Not enthusiastic; indifferent; as, a suggestion that aroused only *lukewarm* interest.

lull \'ləl\ *v.* **1** To soothe to rest; to calm; to quiet. **2** To become gradually calm. — *n.* **1** A period of calm in the midst of a storm or of turmoil or confusion. **2** A period of inactivity; a pause; as, a *lull* in a conversation.

lull·a·by \'ləl-ə-ˌbī\ *n.;* **lull·a·bies.** A song to quiet babies or to lull them to sleep.

lum·ba·go \ˌləm-'bā-ˌgō\ *n.* Pain in the lower back and loins; rheumatism affecting the lumbar muscles.

lum·bar \'ləm-br\ *adj.* Of, relating to, or near the loins; as, a *lumbar* vertebra; the *lumbar* arteries.

lum·ber \'ləm-br\ *n.* **1** Timber; especially, timber sawed into boards or planks. **2** Useless, more or less bulky household stuff. — *v.;* **lum·bered**; **lum·ber·ing** \-br(-)ing\. **1** To fill with useless or old material; as, to *lumber* up a room. **2** To cut logs or to saw them into lumber for market.

lum·ber \'ləm-br\ *v.;* **lum·bered**; **lum·ber·ing** \-br(-)ing\. **1** To move heavily or clumsily along; as, a bear *lumbering* up the hill; a tractor *lumbering* across a field. **2** To rumble. — *n.* A noise as of one lumbering along; a rumble.

lum·ber·ing \'ləm-br(-)ing\ *n.* The business of cutting or getting timber or logs from the forest for lumber.

lum·ber·ing \'ləm-br(-)ing\ *adj.* **1** Clumsy; awkward. **2** Rumbling. — **lum·ber·ing·ly,** *adv.*

lum·ber·jack \'ləm-br-ˌjak\ *n.* A man who works at lumbering.

lum·ber·man \'ləm-br-mən\ *n.;* *pl.* **lum·ber·men** \-mən\. **1** A man who works at lumbering; a lumberjack. **2** A dealer in lumber.

lu·mi·nary \'lü-mə-ˌner-ē\ *n.;* *pl.* **lu·mi·nar·ies.** **1** A body that gives off natural light; especially, one of the heavenly bodies, as the sun or a star. **2** A person that can be likened to a celestial body because of the brightness of his fame; a star; a famous person; as, *luminaries* of the American theater.

lu·mi·nos·i·ty \ˌlü-mə-ˈnäs-ət-ē\ *n.; pl.* **lu·mi·nos·i·ties.** **1** The quality or state of being luminous. **2** Something luminous.

lu·mi·nous \ˈlü-mə-nəs\ *adj.* **1** Shining; bright. The sun is a *luminous* body. **2** Illuminated. **3** Easily understood; clear; illuminating; as, a *luminous* explanation. — **lu·mi·nous·ly,** *adv.*

lump \ˈləmp\ *n.* **1** A small, irregular mass; a hunk; as, a *lump* of coal; a *lump* of earth. **2** A swelling or growth; as, a *lump* on one's head. — *v.* **1** To form into a lump or lumps. **2** To group together; as, to *lump* several ideas into one paragraph. **3** To move or fall heavily; as, to go *lumping* down the road.

lump·ish \ˈləmp-ish\ *adj.* **1** Shapeless and heavy. **2** Sluggish; dull; as, a crude, *lumpish* person with no sense of humor. — **lump·ish·ly,** *adv.*

lumpy \ˈləmp-ē\ *adj.;* **lump·i·er; lump·i·est.** Having lumps; as, *lumpy* ground; *lumpy* gravy.

lu·na·cy \ˈlü-nə-sē\ *n.; pl.* **lu·na·cies.** **1** Insanity. **2** Great foolishness; craziness.

lu·nar \ˈlün-r\ *adj.* **1** Of or having to do with the moon; as, a *lunar* eclipse. **2** Like the moon; as, a *lunar* landscape of chasms and craters. **3** Measured by the revolutions of the moon; as, a *lunar* month.

lu·na·tic \ˈlü-nə-ˌtik\ *adj.* **1** Insane; crazy. **2** Set apart for, or used by, insane persons; as, a *lunatic* asylum. — *n.* An insane person.

lunch \ˈlənch\ *n.* **1** A light meal. **2** The regular midday meal. **3** Food prepared for lunch; as, a picnic *lunch.* — *v.* To take lunch; as, to *lunch* with friends.

lunch·eon \ˈlənch-n\ *n.* **1** Lunch. **2** A formal lunch.

lunch·room \ˈlənch-ˌrüm, -ˌru̇m\ *n.* **1** A restaurant specializing in food that is ready to serve or that can be quickly prepared. **2** A room, as in a school, where lunches brought from home may be eaten.

lung \ˈləng\ *n.* **1** One of the, usually two, organs that form the special breathing apparatus of air-breathing vertebrates. **2** A device to promote and facilitate breathing, as an iron lung.

lunge \ˈlənj\ *n.* **1** A sudden thrust with a sword or other weapon. **2** A sudden plunging forward; a leap. — *v.;* **lunged; lung·ing** \ˈlən-jing\. To make or cause to make a lunge.

lung·fish \ˈləng-ˌfish\ *n.; pl.* **lung·fish** or **lung·fish·es.** Any of several fishes that breathe with lunglike sacs as well as with gills.

lu·pine \ˈlüp-n\ *n.* **1** An herb of the pea family with white, yellow, blue, or purple flowers in long clusters, and flat pods with kidney-shaped seeds used in Europe as food. **2** The seed of this plant.

lurch \ˈlərch\ *n.* **1** A sudden roll of a ship to one side. **2** A swaying or staggering movement to one side. — *v.* To roll or sway suddenly to one side; to move with a lurch.

lurch \ˈlərch\ *n.* A helpless or difficult position; as, to be left in the *lurch.*

lure \ˈlu̇r\ *v.;* **lured; lur·ing.** **1** To draw or attract with a lure. **2** To tempt or lead away by offering some pleasure or advantage; to entice; as, to be *lured* by gold. — *n.* **1** An attraction; an enticement; as, the *lure* of a spring day. **2** A decoy or bait for animals.

lu·rid \ˈlu̇r-əd\ *adj.* **1** Having an unearthly paleness, as the yellowish gray luster that sometimes appears on an overcast sky. **2** Appearing like glowing fire seen through smoke; as, *lurid* flames. **3** Grimly terrible; sensational; as, a *lurid* story. — **lu·rid·ly,** *adv.*

lurk \ˈlərk\ *v.* **1** To stay in or about a place secretly. **2** To escape notice; to exist secretly. **3** To move secretly and without being noticed.

— The words *skulk* and *sneak* are synonyms of *lurk: lurk* usually suggests lying in wait in a place of concealment, as in an ambush; *skulk* has a strong suggestion of moving about stealthily with an evil intention or sometimes from cowardice and fear; *sneak* is likely to indicate a moving into or out of a place secretly by sly, underhanded, and deceptive methods.

lus·cious \ˈləsh-əs\ *adj.* **1** Very sweet and pleasing to taste and smell; as, a *luscious* strawberry. **2** Delightful to hear, see, or feel; as, *luscious* bells; *luscious* colors. — **lus·cious·ly,** *adv.*

lush \ˈləsh\ *adj.* **1** Juicy and fresh; as, *lush* grass. **2** Covered with luxuriant growth; as, *lush* valleys.

lust \ˈləst\ *n.* **1** Strong, passionate, sensual desire; especially, such desire when impure or immoral. **2** A longing or intense desire; as, a *lust* for gold. — *v.* To have a strong desire or lust.

lus·ter or **lus·tre** \ˈləst-r\ *n.* **1** A shine or sheen, as from reflected light; gloss; as, the *luster* of silk. **2** Brightness; glitter. **3** Glory; splendor; as, the *luster* of a famous name. **4** A fabric of wool or cotton with a lustrous surface. **5** A surface on pottery, sometimes iridescent and always metallic in appearance. — **lus·ter·less,** *adj.*

lust·ful \ˈləst-fəl\ *adj.* Excited by lust; showing lust. — **lust·ful·ly** \-fə-lē\ *adv.*

lus·trous \ˈləs-trəs\ *adj.* Having luster.

lusty \ˈləs-tē\ *adj.;* **lust·i·er; lust·i·est.** Healthy; sturdy; full of life and vigor. — **lust·i·ly** \ˈləs-tə-lē\ *adv.*

lute \ˈlüt\ *n.* A stringed musical instrument, common in olden days, played by plucking the strings with the fingers.

lute

Lux·em·bourg·er or **Lux·em·burg·er** \ˈlu̇ks-m-ˌbu̇rg-r, ˈləks-m-ˌbərg-r\ *n.* A native or inhabitant of Luxembourg.

Lux·em·bourg·i·an or **Lux·em·burg·i·an** \ˌlu̇ks-m-ˈbu̇r-gē-ən, ˌləks-m-ˈbər-\ *adj.* Of or relating to Luxembourg.

lux·u·ri·ant \(ˌ)ləg-'zhu̇r-ē-ənt, (ˌ)lək-'shu̇r-\ *adj.* **1** Growing plentifully or rankly, as vegetation. **2** Ornamented; lavish; profuse; as, *luxuriant* praise; a *luxuriant* imagination. — **lux·u·ri·ance** \-ē-ən(t)s\ *n.* — **lux·u·ri·ant·ly** \-ē-ənt-lē\ *adv.*

lux·u·ri·ate \(ˌ)ləg-'zhu̇r-ē-ˌāt, (ˌ)lək-'shu̇r-\ *v.;* **lux·u·ri·at·ed; lux·u·ri·at·ing. 1** To live luxuriously. **2** To take, or appear to take, great pleasure; to indulge freely; to revel; as, a writer who *luxuriates* in colorful description; to *luxuriate* in the warm sunshine.

lux·u·ri·ous \(ˌ)ləg-'zhu̇r-ē-əs, (ˌ)lək-'shu̇r-\ *adj.* **1** Of or relating to luxury. **2** Inclined to luxury; as, *luxurious* tastes. **3** Extravagantly elegant and comfortable; as, *luxurious* furnishings.

lux·u·ry \'ləksh-r(-)ē, 'ləgzh-\ *n.; pl.* **lux·u·ries. 1** Liberal use or possession of costly food, dress, or anything that pleases a person's appetite or desire; great ease or comfort; rich surroundings; as, to live in *luxury*. **2** Something desirable but costly or hard to get. A yacht is a *luxury* few can afford. **3** Something that adds to one's pleasure or comfort but is not absolutely necessary; as, to want only the necessities of life and a few minor *luxuries*.

lv. Abbreviation for: **1** *leave.* **2** *leaves.*

-ly \lē\. A suffix, used to form adjectives, that can mean: **1** Like in appearance or manner, characteristic of, as in *queenly* or *fatherly*. **2** Befitting, as in *manly* or *timely*. **3** Every, as in *hourly* or *weekly*.

-ly \lē\. A suffix, used to form adverbs, that can mean: **1** In a manner or way that is, as in *slowly* or *smilingly*. **2** Every, by the, once a, as in *hourly* or *weekly*.

ly·ce·um \lī-'sē-əm, 'lī-sē-əm\ *n.* **1** A building or room used for instruction by lectures. **2** An association providing educational or inspirational events, as lectures or concerts.

lye \'lī\ *n.* **1** A strong solution obtained from wood ashes, and formerly much used in making soap and in washing and cleaning. **2** Any strong alkaline solution.

ly·ing \'lī-ing\. Pres. part. of *lie.*

ly·ing \'lī-ing\ *n.* The telling of lies; untruthfulness. — *adj.* Untruthful; false.

lymph \'lim(p)f\ *n.* A nearly colorless fluid, chiefly blood plasma and colorless corpuscles, contained in the lymphatic vessels of the body.

lym·phat·ic \lim-'fat-ik\ *adj.* **1** Having to do with the lymph; containing or carrying lymph. **2** Lacking in healthful color; lacking energy; not easily aroused to activity. — *n.* A vessel of the body containing or carrying lymph.

lymph gland or **lymph node**. One of the masses of tissue occurring in association with the lymphatic vessels and giving rise to the colorless cells (**lym·pho·cytes** \'lim(p)f-ə-ˌsīts\) of the lymph.

lynch \'linch\ *v.* [Named after Charles *Lynch* (1736–1796), a Virginian planter and justice of the peace who presided over an irregular court that meted out hard punishments to British sympathizers during the American Revolution.] To put a suspected person to death without authority or trial.

lynx \'lingks\ *n.; pl.* **lynx·es** \'lingks-əz\ or **lynx** \'lingks\. Any of certain wildcats with rather long legs, a short stubby tail, and often, tufted ears.

lynx-eyed \'lingk-'sīd\ *adj.* Having very sharp sight.

ly·on·naise \'lī-ə-ˌnāz\ *adj.* Fried with sliced onion; as, *lyonnaise* potatoes.

lyre \'līr\ *n.* A stringed musical instrument used by the ancient Greeks.

lyre·bird \'līr-ˌbərd\ *n.* A singing Australian bird, the male of which has long tail feathers that can be spread out in the form of a lyre.

lyre

lyr·ic \'lir-ik\ *adj.* **1** Of or belonging to a lyre. **2** Like a song in form, feeling, or literary quality; expressing a poet's own feeling; as, *lyric* poetry. **3** In music, of a quality especially adapted for singing songs; as, a *lyric* voice. — *n.* **1** A lyric poem or song. **2** Words for a song.

lyr·i·cal \'lir-ik-l\ *adj.* Lyric; having a musical quality; like a song; as, a bird's *lyrical* call. — **lyr·i·cal·ly** \-ik-l(-)ē\ *adv.*

ly·sin \'līs-n\ *n.* Any of a class of substances capable of dissolving bacteria and blood corpuscles.

m \'em\ *n.; pl.* **m's** \'emz\. **1** The thirteenth letter of the alphabet. **2** As a Roman numeral, 1,000.

m *m* M *m* *M*

ma \'mä, 'mȯ, 'ma̐\ *n.; pl.* **mas.** Mamma.

ma'am \'mam, 'mäm, 'ma̐m, 'məm; *after "yes", also* -m\. A contraction of *madam.*

mac \'mak\ *n. British.* A mackintosh.

ma·ca·bre or **ma·ca·ber** \mə-'käb(-rə), -'ka̐b-\ *adj.* Relating to or like the "dance of death", in which Death, as a skeleton, leads other skeletons to the grave; gruesome; ghastly.

mac·ad·am \mə-'kad-m\ *n.* [Named after John L. *McAdam* (1756–1836), Scottish engineer who invented the macadamizing process.] **1** A roadway or pavement of small, closely packed, broken stone. **2** The broken stone used in macadamizing a roadway or pavement.

mac·ad·am·ize \mə-'kad-m-ˌīz\ *v.;* **mac·ad·am·ized; mac·ad·am·iz·ing.** To construct or surface, as a road, driveway, or pavement, by packing a layer of small broken stone on a well-drained earth roadbed.

ma·caque \mə-'kak, -'käk, -'ka̐k\ *n.* Any of several short-tailed monkeys of Asia and the East Indies.

mac·a·ro·ni \ˌmak-r-'ō-nē\ *n.; pl.* **mac·a·ro·nis** or

mac·a·ro·nies. **1** A food made chiefly of wheat flour paste dried in the form of tubes. **2** One of a class of young men in the 18th century who affected foreign ways; a dandy; a fop.

mac·a·roon \ˌmak-r-ˈün\ *n.* A small cake made of egg whites, sugar, and ground almonds or coconut.

ma·caw \mə-ˈkȯ\ *n.* A large harsh-voiced parrot with a long tail and brilliant plumage, native to Central and South America.

mace \ˈmās\ *n.* **1** A heavy spiked club used as a weapon in the Middle Ages. **2** A staff carried in front of or by certain officials as a sign of authority. **3** An official who carries a mace.

mace \ˈmās\ *n.* A spice consisting of the dried outer fibrous covering of the nutmeg.

mac·er·ate \ˈmas-r-ˌāt\ *v.;* **mac·er·at·ed**; **mac·er·at·ing.** **1** To waste away or cause to waste away. **2** To soften by steeping or soaking so as to separate the parts; to soften and wear away, as food in the process of digestion. — **mac·er·a·tion** \ˌmas-r-ˈāsh-n\ *n.*

Mach \ˈmäk, ˈmȧk\. Also **Mach number**. A number representing the ratio of the speed of a body to the speed of sound in the surrounding atmosphere.

ma·che·te \mə-ˈshet-ē, -ˈchet-ē; mə-ˈshet\ *n.* A large heavy knife, used especially in South and Central America and the West Indies for cutting cane and underbrush.

Mach·i·a·vel·li·an \ˌmak-ē-ə-ˈvel-ē-ən, -ˈvel-yən\ *adj.* [Named after Niccolo *Machiavelli* (1469–1527), Italian statesman and author of *The Prince.*] **1** Of or relating to the theory or doctrine that a ruler is justified in using any means whatever to keep himself in power. **2** Characterized by clever but dishonest conduct; crafty.

mach·i·nate \ˈmak-n-ˌāt\ *v.;* **mach·i·nat·ed**; **mach·i·nat·ing.** To plot; to contrive; especially, to plot to do harm. — **mach·i·na·tor** \-ˌāt-r\ *n.*

mach·i·na·tion \ˌmak-n-ˈāsh-n\ *n.* **1** The act of machinating, or planning and contriving, especially to do harm. **2** A scheme or plot to do harm.

ma·chine \mə-ˈshēn\ *n.* **1** A mechanical contrivance made by man. **2** A combination of mechanical parts, such as levers, gears, cogwheels, and pulleys, that serves to modify force and motion in such a way as to do some desired work; as, a hoisting *machine;* a sewing *machine.* **3** A vehicle or conveyance such as an automobile, airplane, or bicycle. **4** The organized group of persons controlling the activities of a political party; as, the party *machine.* — *adj.* **1** Characterized by the widespread use of machinery; as, the *machine* age. **2** Produced by or as if by machinery; as, *machine* products. — *v.;* **ma·chined**; **ma·chin·ing.** To shape by the use of a machine or machines.

machine gun. An automatic gun having a cooling device making it capable of continuous firing. — **ma·chine–gun**, *v.*

machine gun

ma·chin·ery \mə-ˈshēn-r(-)ē\ *n.* **1** Machines as a group; as, a factory and all its *machinery.* **2** The working parts of a machine, engine, or other device or instrument having moving parts; as, the *machinery* of a watch. **3** The organization or system by which something is done or kept going; as, the *machinery* of government.

machine shop. A workshop in which metal articles are machined and assembled.

machine tool. A machine, as a lathe or drill, that is operated by power and is partly or wholly automatic.

ma·chin·ist \mə-ˈshē-nəst\ *n.* A person who makes or works on machines and engines.

macintosh. Variant of *mackintosh.*

mack·er·el \ˈmak-r(-)əl\ *n.; pl.* **mack·er·el** or **mack·er·els.** **1** A North Atlantic food fish, green with blue bars above and silvery below. **2** Any of various related fishes, as the **frigate mackerel** and the **Spanish mackerel.**

mackerel sky. A sky covered with rows of clouds resembling the patterns on a mackerel's back.

mack·i·naw \ˈmak-n-ˌȯ\ *n.* or **Mack·i·naw coat.** A short, heavy, woolen plaid coat, reaching to about mid-thigh.

mackinaw

mack·in·tosh or **mac·in·tosh** \ˈmak-n-ˌtäsh\ *n.* [Named after Charles *Macintosh* (1766–1843), Scottish chemist who invented the waterproof material from which they were originally made.] A coat made from waterproofed fabric; a raincoat.

mac·ro·cosm \ˈmak-rə-ˌkäz-m\ *n.* The great world; the universe.

ma·cron \ˈmāk-ˌrän, ˈmak-, -rən\ *n.* A mark [¯] used in some books over *a, e, i, o, oo, u* to show that they are pronounced as in *age, even, side, bone, food, cube.*

mad \ˈmad\ *adj.;* **mad·der**; **mad·dest.** **1** Out of one's mind; crazy; insane. **2** Rash and foolish; as, a *mad* promise. **3** Furious; enraged; as, to make a bull *mad.* **4** Frantic; as, *mad* with pain. **5** Carried away by enthusiasm; as, *mad* about dancing. **6** Wildly gay; as, to be in a *mad* mood. **7** Having rabies; as, a *mad* dog. **8** Angry; displeased.

mad·am \ˈmad-m\ *n.; pl.* **mes·dames** \mā-ˈdäm, -ˈdam, -ˈdȧm\. A form of polite address to a lady. *Madam,* may I help you?

ma·dame \mə-ˈdam; *before a surname, also* ˈmad-m\ *n.; pl.* **mes·dames** \mā-ˈdäm, -ˈdam, -ˈdȧm\. My lady — often used as a title of respect in referring to distinguished women of foreign nationality.

mad·cap \ˈmad-ˌkap\ *adj.* Wild; reckless. — *n.* A madcap person.

mad·den \ˈmad-n\ *v.;* **mad·dened**; **mad·den·ing** \-n(-)ing\. To make or become mad; to enrage.

mad·den·ing \ˈmad-n(-)ing\ *adj.* Infuriating; irritating; as, a *maddening* habit. — **mad·den·ing·ly,** *adv.*

mad·der \ˈmad-r\ *n.* **1** An erect Old World herb with whorls of leaves and clusters of small yellow flowers followed by berries. **2** The red fleshy root of madder used in dyeing. **3** A dye made from or resembling that from madder.

made. Past tense and past part. of *make.*

ma·de·moi·selle \ˌmad-m(-)ə-'zel, mam-'zel\ *n.; pl.* **mes·de·moi·selles** \ˌmād-m(-)ə-'zel\. The French word for *Miss.*

made–up \'mād-'əp\ *adj.* **1** Falsely or fancifully invented; as, a *made-up* story. **2** Artificial; wearing too much makeup; as, to have a very *made-up* appearance. **3** Fully manufactured.

mad·house \'mad-ˌhau̇s\ *n.; pl.* **mad·hous·es** \-ˌhau̇-zəz\. **1** An asylum for insane persons. **2** A place or scene of confusion.

mad·ly \'mad-lē\ *adv.* In a mad manner.

mad·man \'mad-ˌman, -mən\ *n.; pl.* **mad·men** \-ˌmen, -mən\. A person who is mad or crazy; a lunatic.

mad·ness \'mad-nəs\ *n.* **1** Insanity. **2** Frenzy; rage. **3** Great folly.

ma·dras \mə-'dras, -'dräs, -'dras; 'mad-rəs\ *n.* A fine cotton fabric, usually corded or striped.

mad·ri·gal \'mad-rig-l\ *n.* **1** A poem, usually a love poem, that can be set to music. **2** The musical setting for such a poem. **3** Any part song or glee.

mael·strom \'māl-strəm\ *n.* **1** A whirlpool; especially, a whirlpool of great force and violence, dangerous to boats. **2** Any great turmoil; as, a *maelstrom* of emotions.

ma·e·stro \'mīs-ˌtrō, mä-'es-ˌtrō\ *n.; pl.* **ma·e·stros.** Master; a master in any art, especially music.

mag·a·zine \ˌmag-ə-'zēn, 'mag-ə-ˌzēn\ *n.* **1** A storehouse or warehouse, as for military supplies. **2** A place for keeping gunpowder in a fort or ship. **3** A chamber in a gun for holding cartridges. **4** A publication usually containing stories, articles, and poems and issued weekly or monthly.

magazine

ma·gen·ta \mə-'jent-ə\ *n.* **1** A deep-red dye. **2** A deep, bright, reddish-purple color.

mag·got \'mag-ət\ *n.* A soft-bodied, wormlike larva of an insect, as of a housefly, usually living in decaying matter.

mag·goty \'mag-ət-ē\ *adj.* Infested with maggots.

mag·ic \'maj-ik\ *n.* **1** The art of persons who claim to be able to do things by the help of supernatural creatures or by their own knowledge of nature's secrets. **2** Something that charms; any seemingly hidden or secret power; as, the *magic* of a voice; the *magic* of a great name. **3** Sleight of hand. — *adj.* **1** Of or having to do with magic. **2** Seemingly requiring more than human power; startling in performance; producing effects which seem supernatural; as, *magic* skill. **3** Having the powers or effects of magic; as, a *magic* land or scene.

mag·i·cal \'maj-ik-l\ *adj.* Magic. — **mag·i·cal·ly** \-ik-l(-)ē\ *adv.*

ma·gi·cian \mə-'jish-n\ *n.* **1** A person skilled in magic; a sorcerer. **2** A sleight-of-hand performer.

magic lantern. The name given to an early type of slide projector.

magic lantern

mag·is·te·ri·al \ˌmaj-əs-'tir-ē-əl\ *adj.* **1** Authoritative; commanding. **2** Of or relating to a magistrate, his office, or his duties.

mag·is·tra·cy \'maj-əs-trə-sē\ *n.; pl.* **mag·is·tra·cies. 1** The state of being a magistrate. **2** The position, duties, or jurisdiction of a magistrate. **3** Magistrates considered as a body.

mag·is·trate \'maj-əs-ˌtrāt, -trət\ *n.* **1** A person holding executive power in government. The President is our chief *magistrate.* **2** An official holding judicial power.

mag·na·nim·i·ty \ˌmag-nə-'nim-ət-ē\ *n.; pl.* **mag·na·nim·i·ties. 1** Nobility of character; high-mindedness. **2** Generosity. **3** A magnanimous act.

mag·nan·i·mous \mag-'nan-ə-məs\ *adj.* **1** High-minded; above all that is low or ignoble. **2** Generous; noble. — **mag·nan·i·mous·ly,** *adv.*

mag·nate \'mag-ˌnāt, -nət\ *n.* A person of rank, influence, or distinction.

mag·ne·sia \mag-'nē-shə, -zhə\ *n.* A light, earthy, white substance, a slightly alkaline compound of magnesium, used as a mild laxative.

mag·ne·si·um \mag-'nē-z(h)ē-əm, -zhəm\ *n.* A silver-white metallic element, lighter than aluminum and easily worked, that burns with a dazzling light and is much used in making lightweight articles.

mag·net \'mag-nət\ *n.* **1** A piece of some material that is able to attract iron; especially, a mass of iron or steel so treated that it has this property, as a **bar magnet** or a **horseshoe magnet. 2** Anything that attracts; as, the *magnet* of fame.

mag·net·ic \mag-'net-ik\ *adj.* **1** Having to do with a magnet; having the properties of a magnet. **2** Having to do with the earth's magnetism; as, the *magnetic* meridian. **3** Capable of being magnetized, as a piece of iron. **4** Gifted with great personal attractiveness; as, *magnetic* charm.

magnetic field. The portion of space near a magnetic body within which its forces can be detected.

magnetic needle. A narrow strip of magnetized steel that is free to swing, sometimes horizontally, sometimes vertically, to show the direction of the earth's magnetism.

magnetic pole. **1** Either of the two poles of a magnet. **2** Either of two places on the earth, one near the North Pole (**North Magnetic Pole**) and one near the South Pole (**South Magnetic Pole**) towards which there is magnetic attraction, the north-seeking end of a compass needle always pointing toward the North Magnetic Pole.

mag·net·ism \'mag-nə-ˌtiz-m\ *n.* **1** The power to attract, as possessed by a magnet. **2** The property of certain substances, as iron, that allows them to be magnetized, or made magnetic. **3** The power to attract the interest or affection of others; personal charm. **4** The science that deals with magnetic occurrences or conditions.

mag·net·ite \'mag-nə-ˌtīt\ *n.* An iron ore that is strongly attracted by a magnet and sometimes acts like a magnet.

mag·net·ize \'mag-nə-ˌtīz\ *v.;* **mag·net·ized; mag·net·iz·ing. 1** To cause to be magnetic; to make into a magnet. **2** To charm; to captivate.

mag·ne·to \mag-'nēt-(ˌ)ō\ *n.; pl.* **mag·ne·tos.** A small electric generator using permanent magnets; especially, such a generator used to produce sparks in an internal-combustion engine.

mag·ni·fi·ca·tion \ˌmag-nə-fə-'kāsh-n\ *n.* A magnifying; especially, the apparent enlargement of an object by an optical instrument.

mag·nif·i·cence \mag-'nif-ə-sən(t)s, məg-\ *n.* The quality or state of being magnificent; splendor; grandeur.

mag·nif·i·cent \mag-'nif-ə-sənt, məg-\ *adj.* **1** Splendid; richly ornamented; having grandeur and beauty; as, *magnificent* palaces; a *magnificent* view. **2** Exalted; noble; as, a *magnificent* character. — **mag·nif·i·cent·ly,** *adv.*

mag·ni·fy \'mag-nə-ˌfī\ *v.;* **mag·ni·fied** \-ˌfīd\; **mag·ni·fy·ing. 1** *Archaic.* To praise highly; to extol; to laud. **2** To make greater in size, either in fact or appearance. A microscope *magnifies* an object seen through it. **3** To exaggerate; as, to *magnify* a fault. — **mag·ni·fi·er** \-ˌfīr\ *n.*

mag·ni·fy·ing glass \'mag-nə-ˌfī-ing\. A lens that magnifies an object seen through it.

mag·nil·o·quent \mag-'nil-ə-kwənt\ *adj.* Speaking with a show of self-importance; bombastic; grandiloquent. — **mag·nil·o·quence** \-kwən(t)s\ *n.* — **mag·nil·o·quent·ly** \-kwənt-lē\ *adv.*

mag·ni·tude \'mag-nə-ˌtüd, -ˌtyüd\ *n.* **1** Greatness, as in size or extent; bigness. **2** Greatness in influence or effect; as, the *magnitude* of the plan or idea. **3** Size, whether great or small; quantity; number. **4** In astronomy, a degree of brightness, especially of a fixed star.

mag·no·lia \mag-'nōl-yə\ *n.* One of several trees or tall shrubs, having a cone-shaped fruit and showy white, pink, yellow, or purple flowers appearing before or sometimes with the leaves.

mag·num opus \'mag-nəm 'ōp-əs\. A great work; especially, a literary or artistic work of importance.

mag·pie \'mag-ˌpī\ *n.* **1** A noisy bird related to the jays, with long tapered tail and black and white plumage. **2** A person who chatters.

ma·guey \mə-'gā, 'mag-ˌwā\ *n.* **1** Any of several fleshy-leaved species of agave, especially one yielding pulque. **2** Any fiber-yielding agave, as the century plant.

Mag·yar \'mag-ˌyär, -ˌyår\ *n.* **1** One of the dominant people of Hungary, which they invaded and conquered at the close of the ninth century. **2** The language of the Magyars; Hungarian. — *adj.* Of or relating to the Magyars or Magyar.

ma·ha·ra·ja or **ma·ha·ra·jah** \ˌmä-hə-'räj-ə\ *n.* The title of certain Hindu princes, especially of the rulers of the chief native states.

ma·ha·ra·ni or **ma·ha·ra·nee** \ˌmä-hə-'rä-ˌnē\ *n.* The title of a queen or sovereign princess of a Hindu state.

ma·hat·ma \mə-'hät-mə, -'hat-\ *n.* [From Sanskrit *mahatman* meaning literally "great-souled", "wise".] In India, any individual regarded as unusually high-minded or self-sacrificing.

ma·hog·a·ny \mə-'häg-n-ē\ *n.; pl.* **ma·hog·a·nies. 1** The hard, reddish-brown wood of a tropical tree, used for furniture. **2** The tree that yields this wood. **3** The reddish-brown color of this wood.

Mahometan. Variant of *Mohammedan.*

maid \'mād\ *n.* **1** An unmarried girl or woman; usually, a young unmarried woman; a maiden. **2** A female servant.

maid·en \'mād-n\ *n.* An unmarried girl or woman. — *adj.* **1** Unmarried; as, a *maiden* aunt. **2** Of or relating to a maiden; suitable to or characteristic of a maiden; as, *maiden* grace. **3** First; earliest; as, a *maiden* speech. **4** Fresh; unused; as, *maiden* soil.

maid·en·hair \'mād-n-ˌhar, -ˌher\ *n.* or **maidenhair fern.** A fern with slender stems and delicate, much-divided, often feathery leaves.

maid·en·hood \'mād-n-ˌhůd\ *n.* The condition or time of being a maiden; virginity.

maid·en·ly \'mād-n-lē\ *adj.* Of or relating to a maiden or maidenhood; gentle; modest.

maid of honor. 1 An unmarried woman serving as the principal female attendant of a bride at her wedding. **2** An unmarried woman, usually of noble birth, who attends a queen or princess.

maid·serv·ant \'mād-ˌsərv-nt\ *n.* A female servant.

mail \'māl\ *n.* **1** A flexible network of small metal rings linked together for use as armor; as, a coat of *mail.* **2** The hard protective covering of various animals, as of a tortoise.

coat of mail

fragment of a coat of mail

mail \'māl\ *n.* **1** Anything, as letters and parcels, sent under public authority from one post office to another. **2** The whole system used in the public sending and delivery of letters and parcels; as, to do business by *mail.* **3** That which comes in the mail, especially in a single delivery. **4** That which carries mail, as a train, truck, or boat. — *v.* To send by mail; to put in the mail; to post. — **mail·a·ble,** *adj.*

mail·box \'māl-ˌbäks\ *n.* **1** A public box for the collection of mail. **2** A private box for the delivery of mail.

mailed \'māld\ *adj.* Protected by or armed with mail; as, a *mailed* fist.

mail·man \'māl-ˌman\ *n.; pl.* **mail·men** \-ˌmen\. A man who delivers mail or who collects mail from public mailboxes; a postman.

mail order. An order for goods that is received and filled by mail. — **mail-or·der,** *adj.*

maim \'mām\ *v.* To deprive of the use of a part of

the body, as a leg or an arm; to wound seriously; to cripple.

main \'mān\ *n.* **1** Physical strength; force; power; as, with might and *main.* **2** A broad stretch or expanse of land or sea; the mainland itself or the sea itself. **3** A principal line, duct, or pipe; as, a gas *main;* a water *main.* **4** A main or trunk line, as of a railroad. — **in the main.** For the most part. — *adj.* **1** First in such things as size, rank, or importance; as, the *main* thing to remember; the *main* street of a town. **2** Sheer; utter; as, by *main* force. **3** Of a clause, having full meaning in itself and capable of standing alone as a simple sentence but actually occurring as part of a larger sentence that includes also a subordinate clause or another main clause.

main·land \'mān-lənd, -ˌland\ *n.* A continent or the main part of a continent, as distinguished from an offshore island or, sometimes, from a cape or a peninsula.

main·ly \'mān-lē\ *adv.* Principally; chiefly; in the main.

main·mast \'mān-ˌmast, -məst\ *n.* The principal mast of a ship.

main·sail \'mān-ˌsāl, 'mān(t)s-l\ *n.* The principal sail on the mainmast of a ship.

main·sheet \'mān-ˌshēt\ *n.* A rope or sheet by which the mainsail of a vessel is trimmed and secured.

main·spring \'mān-ˌspring\ *n.* **1** The principal spring in a mechanism, as in a watch or clock. **2** The chief motive, cause, or force underlying or responsible for an action.

main·stay \'mān-ˌstā\ *n.* **1** The large strong rope running from the maintop of a ship, usually to the foot of the foremast. **2** Main support; as, the *mainstay* of the family.

main·tain \(')mān-'tān, mən-\ *v.* **1** To continue with; to carry on; as, to *maintain* a correspondence. **2** To keep possession of; as, to *maintain* one's balance on a bicycle. **3** To keep in any particular state or condition; as, to *maintain* a room exactly as it was years ago. **4** To keep up; as, to *maintain* a fence in good condition; to *maintain* one's health. **5** To support; as, to *maintain* a family. **6** To declare as true or capable of being proved; to defend by argument; as, to *maintain* that animals can reason. — **main·tain·a·ble,** *adj.*

main·te·nance \'mānt-n(-)ən(t)s, 'mān-tə-nən(t)s\ *n.* **1** The act of maintaining or the state of being maintained. The *maintenance* of law and order is the responsibility of the police. **2** That which maintains; a means of support; especially, a supply of necessities and conveniences; as, a salary sufficient to provide a *maintenance.* **3** Upkeep, as of property or machinery; as, workmen in charge of *maintenance.*

main·top \'mān-ˌtäp\ *n.* The platform around the head of the mainmast in certain sailing ships.

maize \'māz\ *n.* Indian corn; corn.

Maj. Abbreviation for *Major.*

ma·jes·tic \mə-'jes-tik\ *adj.* Stately and dignified; noble; grand. — **ma·jes·ti·cal·ly** \-tik-l(-)ē\ *adv.*

maj·es·ty \'maj-əs-tē\ *n.; pl.* **maj·es·ties. 1** Royal dignity or authority. **2** A sovereign. **3** A quality or state that inspires awe or reverence; grandeur; stateliness. **4** [with a capital] The title of a king, queen, emperor, or empress — used with a possessive pronoun; as, Your *Majesty.*

ma·jol·i·ca \mə-'jäl-ik-ə, -'yäl-\ *n.* Ornamented Italian pottery, glazed and richly colored.

ma·jor \'māj-r\ *adj.* **1** Greater, as in number, quantity, rank, or importance; as, the *major* part of the cost. **2** Making up the majority. The *major* vote in the election was cast for the conservative candidate. **3** Indicating a principal subject of study chosen by a student for a degree. **4** Indicating or relating to a musical scale having half steps between the third and fourth and the seventh and eighth tones. **5** Based harmoniously on such a scale; as, a *major* key; a *major* chord. — *n.* **1** A major course of study, as in college. **2** In the army, an officer next in rank above a captain and below a lieutenant colonel. — *v.* In a school or college, to take a certain subject as the chief study; as, to *major* in English.

ma·jor-do·mo \ˌmāj-r-'dō-ˌmō\ *n.; pl.* **ma·jor-do·mos.** A man in charge of a great household, especially of a royal establishment; a head steward.

major general. In the army, an officer ranking next above a brigadier general and next below a lieutenant general.

ma·jor·i·ty \mə-'jȯr-ət-ē, -'jär-\ *n.; pl.* **ma·jor·i·ties. 1** The quality or condition of being major or greater. **2** A number greater than half of a total; the amount by which the greater part exceeds the smaller part; as, winning by 51 to 49, a *majority* of two. **3** A group or party that makes up the greater part of a whole body of persons. The *majority* chose a leader. **4** The condition of being of full legal age; as, to reach one's *majority.* **5** The military rank and office of a major.

make \'māk\ *v.;* **made** \'mād\; **mak·ing** \'māk-ing\. **1** To build; to construct; to manufacture; as, to *make* a fence. **2** To bring about; to provide; to perform; to gain; to acquire; to reach; as, to *make* a noise; to *make* the next town before dark. **3** To frame or formulate in the mind; as, to *make* plans. **4** To constitute; to compose; as, a house *made* of brick. Two 2's *make* four. **5** To have the qualities that produce. Wool *makes* warm clothing. **6** To consider; to compute to be; as, to *make* it an even five dollars. He is not the fool you *make* him. **7** To understand; as, to be unable to *make* anything of the garbled story. **8** To cause to be or become; as, to *make* the facts known. The lieutenant was *made* a captain. **9** To prepare; to arrange; as, to *make* a bed. **10** To compel. The child was *made* to attend school. **11** To gain a place on; as, to *make* the football team. **12** To cause or assure the success of. His first important case *made* the budding lawyer. **13** To cause oneself to be in a stated condition; as, to *make* ready for the trip. **14** To act in a certain manner; as, to *make* merry. **15** To proceed; to go. The fugitives *made* for the hills. **16** To tend; to have effect. Careful plans *make* for the enjoyment of a trip. — **make as if** or **make as though.** To pretend that; to give the impression that; as, to *make as if* one is displeased. — **make away with. 1** To carry off; as, to *make away with* stolen goods. **2** To consume; as, to *make away with* the sandwiches. **3** To kill; to destroy. — **make believe.** To pretend; to feign. — **make good.** To fulfill; to prove; to succeed; as, to *make good* a promise; to *make good* on a job. — **make out. 1** To draw up or write; as, to *make out* a shopping list. **2** To see; to discern; as, to *make out* a street sign at a distance. **3** To succeed. — **make over. 1** To transfer the title of; as, to *make over* property to someone. **2** To alter; to refashion; as, to *make over* a dress. — **make sure.** To be or make certain. — **make the best of.** To consider or treat as favorably as possible; as, to *make the best of* a bad situation. — **make up. 1** To construct; to compose; as, to *make up* a poem. **2** To invent; to concoct; as, to *make up* an excuse. **3** To dress for a part, as an actor; to use cosmetics. **4** To become friends again, as after a quarrel. **5** To decide; as, to *make up* one's mind. **6** To compensate for something. — *n.* **1** The way in which a thing is made; the structure. The *make* was so poor the chair fell apart. **2** Kind or process of making or manufacturing; as, the *make* of car.

make-be·lieve \'māk-bə-ˌlēv\ *n.* A pretending to believe, as in children's play; a pretense. — *adj.* **1** Pretended; imaginary; as, a *make-believe* playmate. **2** Insincere.

mak·er \'māk-r\ *n.* **1** A person or thing that makes; as, a cake *maker.* **2** [with a capital] The Creator. **3** The person who signs a promissory note.

make·shift \'māk-ˌshift\ *n.* A person or thing temporarily substituting for another; a substitute. — *adj.* Serving as a substitute; as, using a crate as a *makeshift* table.

make·up \'māk-ˌəp\ *n.* **1** The way the parts or elements of anything are put together or joined; composition or manner of composition; as, last-minute changes in the *makeup* of the book. **2** Materials used in making up or in special costuming, such as wigs and cosmetics; as, to put on *makeup* for a play; a little girl too young to wear *makeup.* **3** Arrangement, as of headlines, stories, and pictures in a newspaper.

mak·ing \'māk-ing\. Pres. part. of *make.* — *n.* **1** The action of one that makes. **2** The process or means of advancement or success. Misfortune is sometimes the *making* of a man. **3** Material from which something can be developed. There is the *making* of a race horse in this colt. **4** [in the plural] The materials from which something can be made; as, to roll a cigarette from the *makings.*

mal-. A prefix that can mean: ill, badly, bad, or evil, as in *maladjusted, malnutrition, malpractice,* or *maltreat.*

mal·a·chite \'mal-ə-ˌkīt\ *n.* A green ore of copper used in a compact form as an ornamental mineral, as for table tops.

mal·ad·just·ed \ˌmal-ə-'jəs-təd\ *adj.* Not well or properly adjusted; especially, unhappy in one's surroundings. — **mal·ad·just·ment** \-'jəs(t)-mənt\ *n.*

mal·a·droit \ˌmal-ə-'drȯit\ *adj.* Awkward; clumsy. — **mal·a·droit·ly,** *adv.*

mal·a·dy \'mal-əd-ē\ *n.; pl.* **mal·a·dies.** Any disease of the body or mind; sickness.

ma·lar·ia \mə-'ler-ē-ə\ *n.* A disease marked by chills and fever and transmitted through the bite of a certain kind of mosquito. — **ma·lar·i·al** \-ē-əl\ *adj.*

Ma·lay \mə-'lā, 'mā-ˌlā\ *adj.* Of or relating to the Malay Peninsula or Malay Archipelago or to the Malays. — *n.* **1** A member of the dominant brown race of the Malay Peninsula and Malay Archipelago. **2** The language of the Malays.

Ma·lay·an \mə-'lā-ən\ *adj.* **1** Malay. **2** Of or relating to the Federation of Malaya. — *n.* **1** A Malay. **2** A native or inhabitant of the Federation of Malaya.

Ma·lay·sian \mə-'lāzh-n, -'lāsh-n\ *adj.* Of or relating to the Malay Archipelago. — *n.* A native of the Malay Archipelago.

mal·con·tent \'malk-n-ˌtent\ *adj.* Discontented. — *n.* A discontented person.

male \'māl\ *adj.* **1** Belonging to the sex that fathers young. **2** Suited to or characteristic of men; masculine. **3** Consisting of males; as, a *male* choir. **4** In botany, bearing only stamens; having stamens but no pistils. — *n.* **1** A male human being or animal. **2** A plant that accomplishes fertilization.

mal·e·dic·tion \ˌmal-ə-'diksh-n\ *n.* A prayer for harm to befall someone; a curse.

mal·e·fac·tor \'mal-ə-ˌfakt-r\ *n.* A person guilty of an evil deed; a criminal.

ma·lev·o·lent \mə-'lev-l-ənt\ *adj.* Having or showing ill will towards others; spiteful; wishing evil. — **ma·lev·o·lence** \-ən(t)s\ *n.*

mal·fea·sance \(')mal-'fēz-n(t)s\ *n.* **1** Wrongdoing; misconduct, especially in public office. **2** An illegal act, especially by an official.

mal·for·ma·tion \ˌmal-fȯr-'māsh-n\ *n.* A faulty or quite irregular formation or structure. — **mal-formed** \'mal-'fȯrmd\ *adj.*

mal·ice \'mal-əs\ *n.* **1** Ill will; strong desire that another suffer or be unhappy. **2** In law, the state of mind shown by an intention to commit an unlawful act. — **malice aforethought.** A deliberate intention to commit the act.

ma·li·cious \mə-'lish-əs\ *adj.* **1** Feeling strong ill will; mean and spiteful; wishing others evil. **2** Done or carried on with malice or caused by malice; as, *malicious* gossip. — **ma·li·cious·ly,** *adv.*

ma·lign \mə-'līn\ *adj.* **1** Moved by ill will towards others; wanting others to suffer harm and misfortune; malevolent. **2** Operating to injure or hurt; as, hindered by *malign* influences. — *v.* To speak evil of; to slander; to defame; as, to be *maligned* by one's enemies.

ma·lig·nan·cy \mə-'lig-nən-sē\ *n.; pl.* **ma·lig·nan·cies.** **1** The quality or state of being malignant. **2** A malignant tumor.

ma·lig·nant \mə-'lig-nənt\ *adj.* **1** Having an evil influence; malign. **2** Bent on doing harm; malicious. **3** In medicine, tending or threatening to cause death; as, a *malignant* disease; a *malignant* tumor. — **ma·lig·nant·ly,** *adv.*

ma·lign·er \mə-'līn-r\ *n.* One that maligns another.

ma·lig·ni·ty \mə-'lig-nət-ē\ *n.; pl.* **ma·lig·ni·ties.** **1** The quality or state of being malignant; malignancy. **2** [usually in the plural] Something, as an act or an event, that is malignant.

ma·lin·ger \mə-'ling-gr\ *v.;* **ma·lin·gered; ma·lin·ger·ing** \-gr(-)ing\. To pretend to be ill in order to avoid a duty or a task; to shirk. — **ma·lin·ger·er** \-gr-r\ *n.*

mall \'mȯl, 'mal\ *n.* A shaded walk; a promenade.

mall \'mȯl\. Variant of *maul.*

mal·lard \'mal-rd\ *n.; pl.* **mal·lards** or **mal·lard.** The common wild duck, from which domestic ducks are descended, especially the drake, which has a greenish-black head and neck, a white collar, and a bluish-purple band on the wings.

mal·le·a·ble \'mal-ē-əb-l, 'mal-(y)əb-l\ *adj.* **1** Capable of being beaten out, extended, or shaped by hammer blows or by the pressure of rollers; as, a *malleable* metal. **2** Adaptable; pliable. — **mal·le·a·bil·i·ty** \ˌmal-ē-ə-'bil-ət-ē, ˌmal-(y)ə-\ *n.*

mal·let \'mal-ət\ *n.* **1** A maul or hammer, usually one with a short handle and a cylinder-shaped head, used especially for driving other tools, as chisels. **2** A long-handled club with a cylindrical head, used in playing croquet. **3** A polo stick.

mal·low \'mal-ō\ *n.* **1** A common herb with pinkish or white flowers and a disk-shaped fruit composed of several sectors. **2** Also **dwarf mallow.** A trailing blue-flowered roundish-leaved weed. **3** Any of a family of plants, mostly herbs, of which the common mallow is typical, including the cotton, okra, hollyhock, and hibiscus.

mal·nour·ished \'mal-'nər-isht, -'nə-risht\ *adj.* Poorly nourished.

mal·nu·tri·tion \ˌmal-nü-'trish-n, -nyü-\ *n.* Faulty nutrition; as, a child suffering from *malnutrition.*

mal·o·dor·ous \'mal-'ōd-r-əs\ *adj.* Bad-smelling.

mal·prac·tice \'mal-'prak-təs\ *n.* Wrongful or negligent treatment or handling of a case, as by a doctor.

malt \'mȯlt\ *n.* **1** Grain, usually barley, steeped in water until it has sprouted. **2** Malt liquor, as beer or ale, produced by fermentation. **3** A drink flavored or treated with malt; as, a chocolate *malt.* — *v.* **1** To change into malt or into material like malt; as, to *malt* barley. **2** To make or treat with malt or malt extract; as, *malted* milk.

Mal·tese cat \(')mȯl-'tēz, -'tēs\. A bluish-gray variety of domestic cat.

Maltese cross. A cross with four arms of equal size that expand in width toward the outward ends, each of which is in the form of an indented V.

Maltese cross

malt·ose \'mȯl-ˌtōs\ *n.* A sugar, formed especially from starch by the action of enzymes, used in brewing and distilling.

mal·treat \'mal-'trēt\ *v.* To treat unkindly or roughly; to abuse; as, to *maltreat* animals. — **mal·treat·ment** \-mənt\ *n.*

ma·ma or **mam·ma** \'mäm-ə, 'måm-ə\ *n.* Mother.

mam·bo \'mäm-ˌbō, 'måm-\ *n.; pl.* **mam·bos.** **1** A usually fast dance of Haitian origin related to the rumba. **2** The fast, syncopated style of music for this dance.

mam·ma \'mam-ə\ *n.; pl.* **mam·mae** \'mam-ˌē\. A glandular organ for producing and giving milk, characteristic of all mammals but normally rudimentary in the male.

mam·mal \'mam-l\ *n.* An animal of the highest class among vertebrates, including man and other animals that nourish young with milk.

mam·ma·ry \'mam-r-ē\ *adj.* Of or relating to the mammae; as, the *mammary* glands.

mam·moth \'mam-əth\ *n.* A huge extinct hairy elephant, usually with tusks curving upward. — *adj.* Very large; huge; as, a *mammoth* ox.

mam·my \'mam-ē\ *n.; pl.* **mam·mies.** **1** Mother. **2** A Negro woman nurse.

mammoth

man \'man\ *n.; pl.* **men** \'men\. **1** A human being; a person; as, every *man* for himself. **2** The human race; mankind. *Man* is the highest of all animals. **3** A male human being; an adult male person; as, one *man* and a boy. **4** Anyone; a person — used with *a.* A *man* hardly knows what to believe. **5** A husband; as, *man* and wife. **6** An adult male servant or employee. **7** One of the pieces with which certain games, as chess or checkers, are played. — *v.;* **manned; man·ning.** **1** To supply with men or persons, as for service or defense; as, to *man* a boat; to *man* a fort. **2** To station men to take hold of and pull; as, to *man* a rope.

man·a·cle \'man-ik-l\ *n.* **1** A handcuff. **2** [usually in the plural] A fetter; a restraint; as, the *manacles* of servitude. — *v.;* **man·a·cled; man·a·cling** \-l(-)ing\. To put handcuffs on; to shackle.

man·age \'man-ij\ *v.;* **man·aged; man·ag·ing.** **1** To control and direct; to oversee and make decisions about; as, to *manage* a factory; to *manage* a team. **2** To bring about skillfully; to contrive; as, to *manage* an interview with the president. **3** To bring around to one's plans; to handle; as, to *manage* an unruly child. **4** To achieve one's purpose; to get along; as, to *manage* in spite of a handicap.

man·age·a·ble \'man-ij-əb-l\ *adj.* Easily managed; easily controlled or handled.

man·age·ment \'man-ij-mənt\ *n.* **1** A managing; direction; control; as, the *management* of a business; *management* of a boat. **2** Skillfulness in directing; ability to manage; as, good *management* in government. **3** The persons who manage. The *management* decided to close the store.

man·ag·er \'man-ij-r\ *n.* A person who manages, as the operation of a business. — **man·a·ge·ri·al** \ˌman-ə-'jir-ē-əl\ *adj.*

man-at-arms \'man-ət-'ärmz, -'årmz\ *n.; pl.* **men-at-arms** \'men-\. A soldier; especially, a heavily armed cavalry soldier.

man·a·tee \'man-ə-ˌtē\ *n.* A plant-eating mammal of West Indian coastal waters, resembling the dugong.

man·da·rin \'mand-r-ən, -ˌin\ *n.* **1** In the Chinese Empire, an official belonging to any of the nine grades of officials entitled to wear a distinguishing button on the hat; a high public official. **2** [with a capital] The form of the Chinese language accepted as standard for use officially and in schools; the chief dialect of Chinese. **3** Also **mandarin orange.** A tangerine.

man·date \'man-ˌdāt\ *n.* **1** A command; an order. **2** The instruction given by voters to their elected representatives, delegates, or governing bodies. **3** A commission granted by an organization of nations to a member nation to govern something, as a colony. **4** A mandated territory. — *v.;* **man·dat·ed**; **man·dat·ing.** To assign or administer under a mandate; as, *mandated* colonies.

man·da·to·ry \'man-də-ˌtōr-ē, -ˌtȯr-ē\ *adj.* **1** Containing a command; of the nature of a command. **2** Required; obligatory. **3** Of or relating to a mandate as granted by an organization of nations; as, *mandatory* powers.

man·di·ble \'man-dəb-l\ *n.* **1** A jaw, either upper or lower, especially of an animal having a well-developed beak, as a bird. **2** The bony skeleton of the lower jaw, especially when composed of a single bone. **3** Either the right or left of the forward pair of mouth appendages of arthropods, which often form strong biting jaws. — **man·dib·u·lar** \man-'dib-yəl-r\ *adj.*

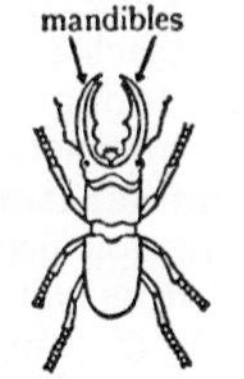

mandibles, 3

man·do·lin \'mand-l(-)ən, ˌmand-l-'in\ *n.* A stringed instrument with a deep pear-shaped body, a fretted neck, and from eight to twelve strings, played with a plectrum.

mandolin

man·drake \'man-ˌdrāk\ *n.* The May apple.

man·drel \'man-drəl\ *n.* **1** In machinery, an axle or spindle inserted into a piece of work having a hole in it, to support it while the piece is being machined. **2** A metal bar used as a core around which material may be cast, shaped, or molded.

man·drill \'man-drəl\ *n.* A large West African baboon having large red calloused areas on the rear quarters and, in the male, blue ridges on each side of the red-bridged nose.

mane \'mān\ *n.* The long heavy hair that grows along the necks of certain animals, as the horse and the lion.

ma·neu·ver \mə-'nüv-r, -'nyüv-r\ *n.* **1** A planned movement, as of troops or ships. **2** [in the plural] Military or naval exercises in time of peace for training purposes. **3** Skillful management or action; a clever move or succession of moves; as, to avoid a collision by a sudden *maneuver.* — *v.;* **ma·neu·vered** \-rd\; **ma·neu·ver·ing** \-r(-)ing\. **1** To move, as troops or ships, in a maneuver or in maneuvers. **2** To perform a maneuver. **3** To accomplish by a maneuver; as, to *maneuver* oneself out of an unpleasant situation; to *maneuver* a car through traffic. **4** To manage, especially skillfully; to manipulate; to handle; as, to *maneuver* things so as to gain one's ends.

ma·neu·ver·a·ble \mə-'nüv-r(-)əb-l, -'nyüv-\ *adj.* Capable of being maneuvered. — **ma·neu·ver·a·bil·i·ty** \mə-ˌnüv-r(-)ə-'bil-ət-ē, -ˌnyüv-\ *n.*

man·ful \'man-fəl\ *adj.* Brave; courageous; resolute. — **man·ful·ly** \-fə-lē\ *adv.*

man·ga·nese \'mang-gə-ˌnēs, -ˌnēz\ *n.* A grayish white metallic element that is soft when pure but ordinarily hard and brittle, resembling iron but not magnetic.

mange \'mānj\ *n.* Any of several forms of skin disease that cause itching and loss of hair in domestic animals and sometimes affect man.

man·ger \'mānj-r\ *n.* A trough or open box in which food for horses and cattle is placed.

man·gle \'mang-gl\ *v.;* **man·gled**; **man·gling** \-gl(-)ing\. **1** To cut, bruise, or hack with repeated blows, leaving ragged wounds; to cut or tear in a bungling manner. **2** To spoil in making or performing; as, to *mangle* a carefully prepared speech through nervousness. — **man·gler** \-glər\ *n.*

man·gle \'mang-gl\ *n.* A machine for smoothing cloth, as sheets, after washing by the pressure of heated rollers. — *v.;* **man·gled**; **man·gling** \-gl(-)ing\. To press or smooth with a mangle, as damp linen. — **man·gler** \-glər\ *n.*

man·go \'mang-ˌgō\ *n.; pl.* **man·goes** or **man·gos.** **1** An oblong tropical fruit having a thick yellowish red rind, a slightly acid juicy pulp, and a very large hard stone. **2** The tree of the sumac family that bears this fruit.

man·go·steen \'mang-gə-ˌstēn\ *n.* **1** A round tropical fruit having a reddish-brown rind and white, juicy flesh in sections like those of an orange. **2** The tree that bears this fruit, a resinous tree of the East Indies.

man·grove \'man(g)-ˌgrōv\ *n.* A low tropical tree, native to seacoasts, that sends forth from its trunk and branches aerial streamers which take root, forming thick tangled masses above ground.

mangy \'mān-jē\ *adj.;* **mang·i·er**; **mang·i·est.** **1** Having mange; caused by or like mange. **2** Shabby; seedy; as, to be unable to wear the *mangy* old coat another season.

man·han·dle \'man-ˌhand-l, ˌman-'hand-l\ *v.;* **man·han·dled; man·han·dling** \-l(-)ing\. To handle or treat roughly.

man·hole \'man-ˌhōl\ *n.* A hole, as one in a pavement or in tank or boiler through which a man may go.

man·hood \'man-ˌhu̇d\ *n.* **1** The state of being a male human being, especially an adult male. **2** Manliness; courage. **3** Men; as, the *manhood* of the nation.

man-hour \'man-'au̇r\ *n.* One hour of work by one man, used as a unit for various calculations in industry.

ma·nia \'mā-nē-ə, 'mān-yə\ *n.* **1** Insanity; madness; especially, insanity characterized by uncontrollable emotion or excitement. **2** Excessive enthusiasm; a craze.

ma·ni·ac \'mā-nē-ˌak\ *adj.* Insane; mad; maniacal; as, *maniac* rage. — *n.* A violently insane person; a madman.

ma·ni·a·cal \mə-'nī-ək-l\ *adj.* **1** Affected with madness. **2** Characteristic of a madman; maniac. — **ma·ni·a·cal·ly** \-ək-l(-)ē\ *adv.*

man·i·cure \'man-ə-ˌkyu̇r\ *n.* **1** A manicurist. **2** The care of the hands and fingernails. — *v.;* **man·i·cured; man·i·cur·ing.** To do manicure work on; especially, to trim and polish the fingernails; as, *manicured* hands.

man·i·cur·ist \'man-ə-ˌkyu̇r-əst\ *n.* A person whose work is to take care of the people's hands, especially their fingernails.

man·i·fest \'man-ə-ˌfest\ *adj.* Clear to the senses; easy to recognize; as, an announcement of a holiday received with *manifest* joy. — *v.* To show plainly; to display; as, to *manifest* one's disbelief in a fantastic tale of adventure; an act that clearly *manifested* willingness to co-operate. — *n.* A list of a ship's cargo, to be shown at a customhouse.

man·i·fes·ta·tion \ˌman-ə-fəs-'tāsh-n, -ə-fes-\ *n.* **1** The act of manifesting or making clear. **2** That which makes clear; a display; a demonstration; as, the first *manifestations* of spring.

man·i·fes·to \ˌman-ə-'fes-ˌtō\ *n.; pl.* **man·i·fes·toes** or **man·i·fes·tos.** A public declaration, as of a political group, stating a purpose or intention or explaining a policy.

man·i·fold \'man-ə-ˌfōld\ *adj.* **1** Many and varied; as, *manifold* activities. **2** Including different kinds, parts, or features; as, a *manifold* personality. **3** Consisting of or operating many of one kind joined together; as, a *manifold* bell pull. — *v.* To make several copies of; as, to *manifold* a letter. — *n.* **1** A copy, as of a letter, made by manifolding. **2** A pipe having several outlets for connecting one pipe with others. — **man·i·fold·ly,** *adv.*

man·i·kin or **man·ni·kin** \'man-ik-n\ *n.* **1** A little man; a dwarf. **2** A mannequin.

Ma·nila hemp \mə-'nil-ə\. The fiber obtained from the leaf stalk of a Philippine banana and used to make rope (**Manila rope**).

Manila paper. A tough brownish paper made originally from Manila hemp, used as a wrapping paper.

ma·nip·u·late \mə-'nip-yə-ˌlāt\ *v.;* **ma·nip·u·lat·ed; ma·nip·u·lat·ing.** **1** To treat or work with the hands, or by mechanical means, especially with skill; as, to *manipulate* the levers of a machine. **2** To manage skillfully; sometimes, to manage artfully or fraudulently; as, to *manipulate* accounts. — **ma·nip·u·la·tor** \-ˌlāt-r\ *n.*

ma·nip·u·lat·ion \mə-ˌnip-yə-'lāsh-n\ *n.* **1** The act of manipulating or the state of being manipulated; handling. **2** Skillful management, sometimes for dishonest purposes; as, a bank official accused of *manipulation* of its funds.

man·kind, *n.* **1** \'man-'kīnd, -ˌkīnd\ The human race. **2** \-ˌkīnd\ Men as distinguished from women.

man·like \'man-ˌlīk\ *adj.* Like a man or men; becoming to or belonging to a man or men; manly.

man·li·ness \'man-lē-nəs\ *n.* Manly character or behavior.

man·ly \'man-lē\ *adj.;* **man·li·er; man·li·est.** Having qualities that suit a man; especially, brave; honorable.

man-made \'man-'mād\ *adj.* Made by man, not by nature.

man·na \'man-ə\ *n.* **1** In the Bible, food that was supplied to the Israelites in the wilderness. **2** Something that, like manna, is much needed and joyfully received.

man·ne·quin \'man-ik-n\ *n.* **1** An artist's or tailor's jointed figure of the human body. **2** A woman hired to display gowns by wearing them.

man·ner \'man-r\ *n.* **1** A way of acting or proceeding; as, to speak in a serious *manner.* **2** A habit; a custom. It was the *manner* of the teacher to have each student recite daily. **3** [in the plural] Social rules of behavior. This novel is a study of *manners.* **4** [in the plural] Behavior; conduct; as, to teach children good *manners.* **5** A kind; a sort; as, to inquire what *manner* of person someone is. — **man·nered** \-rd\ *adj.*

man·ner·ism \'man-r-ˌiz-m\ *n.* A manner of expression used very much, especially in speech or writing; an action frequently repeated by a person, as smoothing one's hair or winking an eye.

man·ner·ly \'man-r-lē\ *adj.* Showing good manners; civil; polite; as, a *mannerly* child. — *adv.* Politely.

mannikin. Variant of *manikin.*

man·nish \'man-ish\ *adj.* Like a man; suitable to a man; manlike; as, a *mannish* voice; *mannish* clothes. — **man·nish·ly,** *adv.*

ma·noeu·vre \mə-'nüv-r, -'nyüv-r\ *n.* A maneuver. — *v.;* **ma·noeu·vred** \-rd\; **ma·noeu·vring** \-r(-)ing\. To maneuver.

man-of-war \'man-ə(v)-'wȯr\ *n.; pl.* **men-of-war** \'men-\. A warship.

man·or \'man-r\ *n.* A large landed estate, originally of a feudal lord. — **ma·no·ri·al** \mə-'nōr-ē-əl, -'nȯr-\ *adj.*

man-o'-war bird or **man-o'-war hawk** \'man-ə-

'wȯr\. Any of several long-winged, web-footed sea birds noted for their powers of flight and the habit of robbing other birds of fish.

man·pow·er \'man-ˌpaůr\ *n.* **1** The power available from or supplied by the physical efforts of persons. **2** The total supply of men and women available and fitted for service in any branch of industry and government.

man·sard roof \'man-ˌsärd, -ˌsȧrd\. A roof having two slopes on all sides, the lower slope being steeper than the upper one.

manse \'man(t)s\ *n.* A residence for a minister of a church; a parsonage.

man·serv·ant \'man-ˌsərv-nt\ *n.; pl.* **men·serv·ants** \'men-ˌsərv-n(t)s\. A male servant.

man·sion \'manch-n\ *n.* A large, stately house.

man·slaugh·ter \'man-ˌslȯt-r\ *n.* The unlawful killing of a person, especially when done without intention.

man·tel \'mant-l\ *n.* The beam, stone, arch, or shelf above a fireplace.

man·tel·piece \'mant-l-ˌpēs\ *n.* **1** The external finish or trim of a fireplace. **2** The shelf above a fireplace.

man·til·la \man-'til-ə\ *n.* **1** A woman's light cloak or cape. **2** A scarf or veil worn so as to cover the head and shoulders, but not the face, by women in Spain and some Spanish American countries.

man·tis \'mant-əs\ *n.; pl.* **man·tes** \'man-ˌtēz\ or **man·tis·es** \'mant-ə-səz\. An insect like a grasshopper, unusual for its strange form and for holding its stout forelegs like hands folded in prayer.

mantis

man·tle \'mant-l\ *n.* **1** A loose, sleeveless, or capelike outer garment or cloak. **2** Anything that covers or envelops; as, a *mantle* of snow. **3** A mesh sheath for use with a gas light and with certain oil lamps that when placed over the flame gives a glowing light. **4** In mollusks, the muscular fold of the body wall which lines the shell and bears the shell-secreting glands. — *v.;* **man·tled**; **man·tling** \-l(-)ing\. To cover or envelop, as with a mantle.

man·u·al \'man-yə-wəl, 'man-yəl\ *adj.* [From medieval English, there borrowed from Latin *manualis*, a derivative of *manus* meaning "hand".] Having to do with the hands; done or operated by the hands; as, *manual* dexterity; *manual* labor. — *n.* **1** A small book; a handbook; as, a scout *manual.* **2** In military use, a set exercise for the handling of a weapon. — **man·u·al·ly** \'man-yə-lē, -yə-wə-lē\ *adv.*

manual training. Training in work done with the hands, as woodworking.

man·u·fac·to·ry \ˌman-yə-'fakt-r(-)ē, ˌman-ə-\ *n.; pl.* **man·u·fac·to·ries.** A factory.

man·u·fac·ture \ˌman-yə-'fak-chər, ˌman-ə-\ *n.* [From French, there borrowed from medieval Latin *manufactura* meaning literally "work done by hand".] **1** The making of products, usually in large quantities, and especially by division of labor and the use of machinery. **2** The thing manufactured. **3** The production of anything by any means; as, the *manufacture* of blood in one's body. — *v.;* **man·u·fac·tured**; **man·u·fac·tur·ing. 1** To make something, usually in large quantities, and especially by systematic production and the use of machinery. **2** To work something into a useful form; as, to *manufacture* wool. **3** To invent; to fabricate; as, to *manufacture* an excuse.

man·u·fac·tur·er \ˌman-yə-'fak-chər-r, ˌman-ə-\ *n.* A person engaged in, or employing workmen in, manufacturing.

man·u·fac·tur·ing \ˌman-yə-'fak-chər-ing, ˌman-ə-\ *adj.* Engaged in manufacture; as, a *manufacturing* town. — *n.* The making of anything, especially by machinery.

man·u·mis·sion \ˌman-yə-'mish-n\ *n.* The act of freeing or the state of being freed from slavery.

man·u·mit \ˌman-yə-'mit\ *v.;* **man·u·mit·ted**; **man·u·mit·ting.** To release from slavery; to free.

ma·nure \mə-'nůr, -'nyůr\ *v.;* **ma·nured**; **ma·nur·ing.** To apply manure to; to enrich, as land, by application of a fertilizer. — *n.* A fertilizer; especially, the excrement of farm animals cleaned out of their pens; as, cow *manure.*

man·u·script \'man-yə-ˌskript\ *n.* **1** Something handwritten or typewritten, as a paper or book; as, the *manuscript* of a poem. **2** Handwriting, as distinguished from print.

many \'men-ē\ *adj.;* **more** \'mōr, 'mȯr\; **most** \'mōst\. Made up of a great number; numerous; not few; as, *many* flowers in a garden. — *n.* A large number; as, to see a good *many* familiar faces in the crowd. — *pron.* Many persons. *Many* went to the party.

map \'map\ *n.* **1** A picture or chart showing features of the earth's surface. **2** A similar picture of the sky. — *v.;* **mapped**; **map·ping. 1** To study and make a map of; as, to *map* the heavens. **2** To chart the course of; to plan in detail; as, to *map* out a route; to *map* out a campaign.

ma·ple \'māp-l\ *n.* **1** Any of a family of trees with three-lobed or fine-lobed leaves, a two-winged dry fruit, and a watery sap. **2** The hard, light-colored wood of these trees.

maple: fruit and leaf

maple sugar. A brown sugar usually molded into cakes, obtained by evaporating maple sap, especially sugar maple sap.

maple syrup. A syrup made by boiling down the sap of certain maples, especially the sugar maple.

mar \'mär, 'mȧr\ *v.;* **marred**; **mar·ring**. To damage; to spoil; to make a blemish on.

Mar. Abbreviation for *March.*

mar·a·bou \'mar-ə-ˌbü\ *n.* **1** A large African stork. **2** The long, soft, white wing and tail feathers of this bird, used as a trimming on hats and dresses.

3 A variety of raw silk or the thin fabric made from it.

ma·ra·ca \mə-'räk-ə, -'rak-ə, -'råk-ə\ *n.* A dried gourd, or a rattle resembling a gourd, containing dried seeds or pebbles, used as a percussion instrument.

mar·a·schi·no \ˌmar-ə-'skē-ˌnō, -'shē-\ *n.* A liqueur distilled from the juice of a bitter wild cherry.

maraschino cherries. Cherries preserved in maraschino or an imitation of it.

mar·a·thon \'mar-ə-ˌthän\ *n.* **1** A long-distance running race (**marathon race**). **2** Any endurance contest.

ma·raud \mə-'rȯd\ *v.* To rove about in search of plunder; to raid; as, *marauding* bands of Indians driven from their hunting grounds.

ma·raud·er \mə-'rȯd-r\ *n.* One who roves about in search of plunder.

mar·ble \'märb-l, 'mårb-l\ *n.* **1** A kind of limestone that can be highly polished and used for building and decorating. **2** A piece of marble; a work of art in marble. **3** A small ball, as of glass or clay, used by children in a game called **mar·bles** \'märb-lz, 'mårb-\. — *adj.* Like or imitating marble; made of marble. — *v.;* **mar·bled**; **mar·bling** \-l(-)ing\. To stain or make markings upon like marble; as, to *marble* the edges of a book.

mar·cel \mär-'sel, mår-\ *v.;* **mar·celled**; **mar·cel·ling.** To wave hair in deep grooves with a special curling iron. — *n.* Also **marcel wave.** A deep regular wave made by marcelling.

March \'märch, 'mårch\ *n.* [From medieval English, there borrowed from Old Norman French *Marche*, this derived from Latin *Martius* in *Martius mensis*, meaning literally "month of Mars", the Roman god of war.] The third month of the year, having 31 days.

march \'märch, 'mårch\ *n.* **1** A border or boundary; a frontier. **2** [in the plural] The borderlands between England and Scotland, and England and Wales.

march \'märch, 'mårch\ *v.* **1** To move or cause to move with regular steps; to move in step or in military order; as, to *march* in a parade. **2** To travel steadily; to progress. Science *marches* on. — *n.* **1** The act of marching; a regular, orderly movement; progress. **2** A regular, even step, especially by soldiers; as, to move at a *march.* **3** The amount of marching done at one time; as, a long day's *march.* **4** A piece of music, usually in 4/4 time, suitable for accompanying marching. — **march·er,** *n.*

mar·chion·ess \'märsh-n-əs, 'mårsh-\ *n.* **1** The wife or widow of an English marquis. **2** A woman who has in her own right a rank equal to that of an English marquis.

Mar·di gras \'märd-ē 'grä, 'mård-ē 'grå\. Shrove Tuesday, the last day before Lent, in some places celebrated as a day of merrymaking.

mare \'mar, 'mer\ *n.* The female of the horse and other members of the horse family as the ass and the zebra.

mar·ga·rine \'märj-r(-)ən, 'mårj-, -r-ˌēn\ *n.* A spread resembling butter, manufactured usually from a blend of refined oils, especially vegetable oils.

mar·gin \'märj-n, 'mårj-n\ *n.* **1** A border; an edge; as, the *margin* of a lake. **2** An extra amount, as of time or money, planned for use if needed; as, to allow a *margin* of five minutes. **3** The part of a page outside of the main body of printed or written matter. **4** The difference between the net sales and the cost of merchandise sold. **5** The return or reward from labor that just covers the cost of production. **6** Money or securities deposited by a customer with a broker to protect him from loss. **7** A transaction in the stock market in which the broker supplies part of the funds needed by the customer. — For synonyms see *border.* — *v.* To furnish with a margin; to border.

mar·gin·al \'märj-n(-)əl, 'mårj-\ *adj.* **1** Written or printed in the margin of a page; as, *marginal* notes. **2** Of, relating to, or situated at a border or margin. **3** Close to the lower limit of acceptability or worthwhile operation; as, *marginal* land; *marginal* housing.

mar·gue·rite \ˌmärg-r-'ēt, ˌmårg-, -yə-'rēt\ *n.* A plant of the aster family resembling a daisy.

mar·i·gold \'mar-ə-ˌgōld, 'mer-\ *n.* **1** A tropical American herb of the aster family, with yellow, red, or variegated flower heads. **2** A flower of this plant. **3** Any similar yellow-flowered herb, as the **bur marigold, marsh marigold,** and **pot marigold.**

mar·i·jua·na or **mar·i·hua·na** \ mar-ə-'(h)wän-ə\ *n.* The hemp or its dried leaves and flowers, which have narcotic properties.

ma·rim·ba \mə-'rim-bə\ *n.* A form of xylophone.

mar·i·nade \ˌmar-ə-'nād\ *n.* **1** A brine or pickle in which meat or fish is soaked before cooking to tenderize it or give it extra flavor. **2** Meat or fish soaked in such a pickle. — *v.;* **mar·i·nad·ed**; **mar·i·nad·ing.** To marinate.

mar·i·nate \'mar-ə-ˌnāt\ *v.;* **mar·i·nat·ed**; **mar·i·nat·ing. 1** To soak, as meat or fish, in a marinade. **2** To season ingredients for a salad, as lobster or chicken, by mixing them with a liquid salad dressing before adding mayonnaise.

ma·rine \mə-'rēn\ *adj.* **1** Of or relating to the sea or the ocean; as, *marine* paintings; *marine* plant life. **2** Of or relating to ships or the navigation of the seas; nautical; as, a *marine* chart. **3** Of or relating to the commerce of the sea; maritime; as, *marine* insurance. **4** Serving on shipboard, as certain soldiers. **5** Belonging or relating to the marines. — *n.* **1** A member of an organization trained as land soldiers for service in association with naval forces and often used as landing troops; [with a capital] a member of the United States Marine Corps. **2** Mercantile and naval shipping collectively; seagoing boats collectively.

mar·i·ner \'mar-ən-r\ *n.* A seaman or sailor.

mar·i·o·nette \ˌmar-ē-ə-ˈnet\ *n.* A puppet that can be made to move or act by means of strings or by hand.

marionette

mar·i·tal \ˈmar-ət-l\ *adj.* **1** Of or relating to a husband. **2** Of or relating to marriage; matrimonial.

mar·i·time \ˈmar-ə-ˌtīm\ *adj.* **1** Bordering on, living near, or situated near the ocean. **2** Having to do with ocean navigation or commerce; as, *maritime* law.

mar·jo·ram \ˈmärj-r-əm, ˈmȧrj-\ *n.* A hardy mint with creeping rootstock and small two-lipped purplish-pink flowers in dense heads; especially, **sweet marjoram**, a very fragrant mint the leaves of which are used as seasoning in cooking.

mark \ˈmärk, ˈmȧrk\ *n.* The money standard and a silver coin of Germany.

mark \ˈmärk, ˈmȧrk\ *n.* **1** A thing to aim at; a target; a goal. **2** An indication, as of character; a characteristic; a trait; as, a *mark* of friendship; a *mark* of character. **3** A label, brand, or seal put on an article, as to show the maker or owner or to certify quality; a trade-mark. **4** A written or printed sign, as a cross, made as a signature by a person unable to write. **5** A written or printed symbol; as, a question *mark*. **6** A scratch; a spot; a blemish; as, a blow that left a *mark*. **7** Importance; distinction; as, a man of *mark*. **8** A standard or limit; something that shows a limit or boundary; as, to come up to the *mark*. **9** A grade or score showing achievement or the quality of work or conduct; as, to receive good *marks* in school. **10** A conspicuous object serving as a guide for travelers; as, a *mark* for pilots. **11** Something, as a line or notch, designed to record position; as, a low-water *mark*. **12** The position at the starting line assigned to contestants, as in track athletics. — *v.* **1** To put a mark, sign, or figure on; as, to *mark* a package for quick delivery. **2** To bound, set apart, or show by or as if by a mark; as, to *mark* off one piece of land from the rest. **3** To form, as a figure, by making marks; as, to *mark* down a "5". **4** To furnish with natural marks of a specified kind; as, wings *marked* with white lines. **5** To give attention to; to observe; as, to *mark* what someone says. **6** To be a mark or sign of; to characterize or distinguish; as, a disease *marked* by fever. **7** To grade; to score; to correct; as, to *mark* test papers. **8** To put price signs on articles. **9** In games, to keep account of the points; to score. — **make one's mark.** To make an impression; to gain distinction. — **mark time.** **1** To keep the time of a marching step by moving the feet alternately without advancing. **2** To be active but without making any progress; to wait; to be still. — **mark·er**, *n.*

mark·down \ˈmärk-ˌdau̇n, ˈmȧrk-\ *n.* **1** A lowering of price. **2** An article lowered in price. **3** The amount by which the price of an article is lowered, as in a sale.

marked \ˈmärkt, ˈmȧrkt\ *adj.* **1** Having a mark or marks; distinguished by a mark. **2** Noticeable; conspicuous; as, a person who speaks with a *marked* accent. — **mark·ed·ly** \ˈmärk-əd-lē, ˈmȧrk-\ *adv.*

mar·ket \ˈmärk-ət, ˈmȧrk-\ *n.* **1** A meeting of people at a stated time and place to buy and sell things; the people at such a meeting. **2** A public place where such a sale is held. **3** A food store. **4** A region in which a thing can be sold; as, foreign *markets* for American cotton. **5** An opportunity for selling something; as, a good *market* for grain. — *v.* **1** To buy or sell in a market. **2** To offer for sale in a market; to sell.

mar·ket·a·ble \ˈmärk-ət-əb-l, ˈmȧrk-\ *adj.* **1** Fit to be offered for sale in a market; as, fruit so old that it was no longer *marketable*. **2** Wanted by purchasers; salable. — **mar·ket·a·bil·i·ty** \ˌmärk-ət-ə-ˈbil-ət-ē, ˌmȧrk-\ *n.*

market garden. A vegetable garden the produce of which is marketed.

market place. An open place or square in a town, where markets or public sales are held.

market value. The average value of a commodity in a given market over a short period of time; the price at which something can probably be bought or sold at the moment.

mark·ing \ˈmärk-ing, ˈmȧrk-\ *n.* A mark or marks made or showing upon something; especially, an arrangement of marks, as the colorings of an animal's coat or a bird's plumage.

marks·man \ˈmärks-mən, ˈmȧrks-\ *n.; pl.* **marks·men** \-mən\. One who shoots at a target; especially, one who shoots well.

marks·man·ship \ˈmärks-mən-ˌship, ˈmȧrks-\ *n.* **1** The art of shooting. **2** Skill in shooting; as, a man renowned for his *marksmanship*.

mark·up \ˈmärk-ˌəp, ˈmȧrk-\ *n.* **1** A raising of price. **2** An article raised in price. **3** The amount added to the cost price of an article in determining a selling price.

marl \ˈmärl, ˈmȧrl\ *n.* A soft crumbling soil consisting chiefly of clay and calcium carbonate, used as a fertilizer.

mar·lin \ˈmär-lən, ˈmȧr-\ *n.* Any of several large game fishes related to the sailfishes.

mar·line·spike or **mar·lin·spike** \ˈmär-lən-ˌspīk, ˈmȧr-\ *n.* A pointed iron tool used by sailors in splicing rope.

marlinespike

mar·ma·lade \ˈmärm-l-ˌād, ˈmȧrm-\ *n.* A thick jam, containing the pulp and often the sliced peel of the fruit from which it is made; as, orange *marmalade*.

mar·mo·re·al \mär-ˈmōr-ē-əl, mȧr-, -ˈmȯr-ē-əl\ *adj.* **1** Of or relating to marble. **2** Like marble in being cold, white, or smooth.

mar·mo·set \ˈmär-mə-ˌset, ˈmȧr-, -ˌzet\ *n.* A small monkey of South and Central America, with soft fur and a bushy, ringed tail.

mar·mot \ˈmär-mət, ˈmȧr-\ *n.* A short-legged

stout-bodied rodent with small ears, a bushy tail, and coarse fur; a woodchuck.

ma·roon \mə-'rün\ *v.* **1** To put ashore and abandon on a lonely island or coast, usually as a punishment. **2** To place or leave helpless and isolated; as, a family *marooned* by a flood.

ma·roon \mə-'rün\ *n.* A dull, dark, brownish red color.

mar·quee \mär-'kē, mår-\ *n.* **1** A tent set up to provide shade and shelter at an outdoor entertainment, as a bazaar or lawn fete. **2** A canopy projecting over an entrance, as of a theater or hotel.

mar·quess \'märk-wəs, 'mårk-\ *n.* A marquis.

mar·quis \'märk-wəs, 'mårk-; mär-'kē, mår-\ *n.* In England, a nobleman ranking above an earl and below a duke; in certain other European countries, a nobleman ranking next above a count.

mar·quise \mär-'kēz, mår-\ *n.* The wife or widow of a non-English marquis or a woman having a rank equal to that of a marquis.

mar·qui·sette \ˌmärk-(w)ə-'zet, ˌmårk-\ *n.* **1** A sheer somewhat lustrous cotton fabric of open weave, often used for curtains. **2** A sheer light silk or rayon fabric for dresses.

marred. Past tense and past part. of *mar.*

mar·riage \'mar-ij\ *n.* **1** The state of being married; the mutual relation of husband and wife. **2** The social institution in which a man and a woman enter into a special social and legal relationship for the purpose of making a home and raising a family. **3** The act of marrying. **4** A wedding ceremony, often with its accompanying celebration. **5** Any close or intimate union.

mar·riage·a·ble \'mar-ij-əb-l\ *adj.* Fitted for marriage, especially in age; as, a girl of *marriageable* age; a poor widow with four *marriageable* daughters.

mar·ried \'mar-ēd\ *adj.* **1** United in marriage; wedded; as, a young *married* couple; an old *married* man. **2** Of or relating to marriage; as, *married* life.

marring. Pres. part. of *mar.*

mar·row \'mar-ō\ *n.* **1** A soft tissue containing blood vessels and filling the cavities of most bones. **2** The inmost part; as, chilled to the *marrow.*

mar·row·bone \'mar-ō-ˌbōn\ *n.* A bone containing marrow.

mar·ry \'mar-ē\ *v.;* **mar·ried** \-ēd\; **mar·ry·ing. 1** To join as husband and wife according to the laws and customs of the time and place. **2** To take for husband or wife; as, to *marry* a soldier; to *marry* a childhood sweetheart. **3** To give in marriage; to permit or arrange the marriage of; as, to *marry* all one's daughters to rich men. **4** To enter into a marriage relationship. The couple decided to *marry* next month.

mar·ry \'mar-ē\ *interj. Archaic.* Indeed! In truth!

marsh \'märsh, 'mårsh\ *n.* An area of soft, wet land; a swamp; a bog.

mar·shal \'märsh-l, 'mårsh-l\ *n.* **1** A high official in a medieval royal household. **2** A general officer of the highest rank in some armies. **3** A person who regulates rank and order at ceremonies; as, the *marshal* of a parade. **4** Any of various officers concerned with the maintenance of law and order, as a federal officer having duties similar to those of a sheriff or, in some cities, the head of the police or fire department. — *v.;* **mar·shaled** or **mar·shalled; mar·shal·ing** or **mar·shal·ling** \-l(-)ing\. **1** To arrange in order; as, to *marshal* troops; to *marshal* one's facts for an argument. **2** To usher; to lead, especially with ceremony, as into the presence of a king.

marsh mallow. A perennial herb of the mallow family whose root is used in medicine.

marsh·mal·low \'märsh-ˌmel-ō, 'mårsh-, -ˌmal-\ *n.* A soft white gummy candy paste made originally from the root of the marsh mallow but now from corn syrup, sugar, starch, and gelatin.

marsh marigold. A swamp plant of the crowfoot family with bright yellow flowers; a cowslip.

marshy \'mär-shē, 'mår-\ *adj.;* **marsh·i·er; marsh·i·est.** Like a marsh; swampy.

mar·su·pi·al \mär-'süp-ē-əl, mår-\ *adj.* Having a pouch for carrying the young. Kangaroos and opossums are *marsupial* animals. — *n.* Any mammal having in the female an abdominal pouch formed by a fold of skin and used for carrying the young.

mart \'märt, 'mårt\ *n.* A market; a trading place.

mar·ten \'märt-n, 'mårt-n\ *n.* **1** A thin-bodied meat-eating mammal that has a long tail and very fine gray or brown fur. **2** The fur of this animal.

mar·tial \'märsh-l, 'mårsh-l\ *adj.* **1** Of, fitted for, or having to do with war; as, *martial* music. **2** Belonging to an army — used chiefly in *court-martial.* **3** Warlike.

— The words *warlike* and *military* are synonyms of *martial:* all three terms refer to war but *martial* usually suggests either the pomp, ceremony, and dignity often associated with war, or a lively eagerness to engage in battle; *warlike* is apt to indicate the very real and often unpleasant aspects of war or to describe persons or nations that have a hostile and fierce desire to fight; *military* usually applies to the armed forces, particularly land forces, to their activities and methods of operation, or to the appearance and attitude felt to be suitable to or typical of soldiers.

martial law. The law administered by the military power of a government when it has replaced the civil authority. In times of disaster, *martial law* is often invoked.

mar·tial·ly \'märsh-l-ē, 'mårsh-\ *adv.* In a martial manner.

Mar·tian \'märsh-n, 'mårsh-n\ *adj.* Of or relating to Mars, the god of war, or to the planet Mars. — *n.* One of the hypothetical natives of Mars.

mar·tin \'märt-n, 'mårt-n\ *n.* A swallow with a moderately forked tail, as the small European bluish black house swallow and in North America the large **purple martin.**

mar·ti·net \ˌmärt-n-'et, ˌmȧrt-\ *n.* A rigid disciplinarian.

mar·tin·gale \'märt-n-ˌgāl, 'mȧrt-\ *n.* A strap connecting a horse's girth to the bit or reins so as to hold down his head.

mar·tyr \'märt-r, 'mȧrt-r\ *n.* **1** A person who suffers greatly or dies rather than give up his religion or principles. **2** A person who suffers constantly, as from disease. — *v.* **1** To put to death for clinging to a belief, especially Christianity. **2** To torture.

mar·tyr·dom \'märt-r-dəm, 'mȧrt-\ *n.* **1** The sufferings and death of a martyr. **2** The condition of pain and distress; torture.

mar·vel \'märv-l, 'mȧrv-l\ *n.* Something that causes wonder or astonishment. The new bridge is a *marvel* of engineering. — *v.;* **mar·veled** or **mar·velled; mar·vel·ing** or **mar·vel·ling** \-l(-)ing\. To be struck with astonishment or wonder; as, to *marvel* at the speed of modern airplanes.

mar·vel·ous or **mar·vel·lous** \'märv-l(-)əs, 'mȧrv-\ *adj.* **1** Causing wonder or astonishment. **2** Wondrous; incredible. **3** Splendid. The children had a *marvelous* time at the party. — **mar·vel·ous·ly** or **mar·vel·lous·ly**, *adv.*

mas·cara \mas-'kar-ə\ *n.* A preparation for coloring the eyelashes.

mas·cot \'mas-ˌkät, -kət\ *n.* A person, animal, or thing supposed to bring good luck.

mas·cu·line \'mask-yə-lən\ *adj.* **1** Male; of the male sex; as, a *masculine* gathering. **2** Characteristic of men; belonging to men; as, a *masculine* voice. **3** Belonging to or relating to the class of words that ordinarily includes most nouns referring to male persons or animals and also in many languages a considerable number of nouns referring to things that are really neither male nor female. — **mas·cu·lin·i·ty** \ˌmask-yə-'lin-ət-ē\ *n.*

ma·ser \'māz-r\ *n.* A device that utilizes the natural oscillations of atoms to amplify or generate very short electromagnetic waves.

mash \'mash\ *n.* **1** Crushed malt or ground grain soaked and stirred in hot water. **2** A mixture of ground feeds, dry or moistened, for feeding livestock. **3** A soft pulpy mass of anything. — *v.* **1** To mix crushed malt or ground grain with water and to heat and stir this mixture in the preparation of wort. **2** To bring into a soft pulpy condition by beating or pressure. — **mash·er**, *n.*

mask \'mask\ *n.* **1** A cover for the face, as for disguise or protection; as, a Halloween mask; a baseball catcher's *mask.* **2** A device, usually covering the mouth and nose, either to aid in or prevent the inhaling of something, as a gas or spray. **3** A covering, as of gauze, for the mouth and nose to prevent droplets from being blown into the air. **4** Something that disguises or conceals; as, the *mask* of night. **5** One who wears a mask; a masker. **6** A sculptured face or face and neck or a copy of a face made by means of a mold in plaster or wax; as, a death *mask.* **7** A dramatic entertainment; a masque. — *v.* **1** To cover, as the face, for concealment or defense. **2** To disguise; to conceal; as, to *mask* one's real intentions.

mask, 1

masked \'maskt\ *adj.* **1** Wearing or using a mask or masks. **2** Characterized by or requiring the wearing of masks; as, a *masked* ball. **3** Concealed; hidden; as, a *masked* battery of machine guns.

masked ball. A fancy-dress ball at which those attending wear masks during the first part of the evening.

mask·er \'mask-r\ *n.* A person who wears a mask; a person who appears in disguise at a masquerade.

ma·son \'mās-n\ *n.* A person who builds or works with stone, brick, or cement.

ma·son·ry \'mās-n-rē\ *n.; pl.* **ma·son·ries. 1** The art, trade, or occupation of a mason. **2** The work of a mason; as, good *masonry.* **3** Something built of stone, brick, or concrete; as, a wall of *masonry.*

masque \'mask\ *n.* **1** A masquerade. **2** An old form of play in which the actors wore masks or a dramatic composition for such a play.

masqu·er \'mask-r\ *n.* A masker.

mas·quer·ade \ˌmask-r-'ād\ *n.* **1** A party, usually a dance, at which people wear masks and costumes. **2** A pretending by some form of disguise to be something one is not; as, a rich man's *masquerade* as a beggar. — *v.;* **mas·quer·ad·ed; mas·quer·ad·ing. 1** To take part in a masquerade. **2** To make a show of being what one is not. The man was arrested for *masquerading* as a policeman. — **mas·quer·ad·er**, *n.*

Mass \'mas\ *n.* **1** The sequence of prayers and ceremonies constituting the Eucharistic rite of the Roman Catholic Church. **2** The Eucharistic rite in certain other Christian churches. **3** Parts of the Mass set to music.

mass \'mas\ *n.* **1** An amount of matter, or the form of matter, that holds or clings together in one body; as, a *mass* of iron ore. **2** A large amount or number; as, a *mass* of treasure; a *mass* of people. **3** Size; bulk; as, an elephant's huge *mass.* **4** The main group; the most; as, the *mass* of people. **5** [in the plural] The common people. **6** In physics, a measure of the amount of matter in a body. — *adj.* Of, relating to, or for the mass or the masses; as, *mass* education. — *v.* To collect into a mass; as, to *mass* troops for an attack.

mas·sa·cre \'mas-ək-r\ *n.* The violent, cruel killing of a number of persons. — *v.;* **mas·sa·cred** \-rd\; **mas·sa·cring** \-r(-)ing\. To kill in a massacre; to slaughter.

mas·sage \mə-'säzh, -'sȧzh\ *n.* A method of treating the body by rubbing, kneading, and tapping as a remedy or to remove fat. — *v.;* **mas·saged; mas·sag·ing.** To treat by massage.

mas·seur \ma-'sər\ *n.* A man whose business is to massage people.

mas·seuse \ma-'süs, -'sərz, -'süz\ *n.* A woman whose business is to massage people.

mas·sive \'mas-iv\ *adj.* **1** Forming or consisting of a large mass; as, a *massive* landslide. **2** Large and bold; as, a *massive* forehead. **3** Impressive in scope or effect. The attorney presented *massive* evidence of the defendant's guilt. — **mas·sive·ly**, *adv.*

mass meeting. A large or general assembly of people.

mass production. The production of goods in large quantities by machinery. — **mass-pro-duced**, *adj.*

mast \'mast\ *n.* **1** A long pole or spar that rises into the air from the bottom of a boat and that supports the yards, booms, sails, and rigging. **2** Any tall, fixed, upright pole. — **before the mast**. In the position of a common sailor.

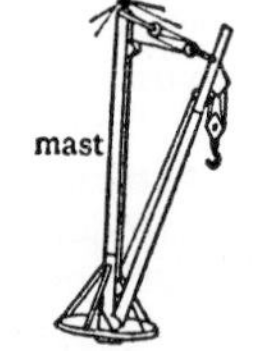

derrick mast

mas·ter \'mast-r\ *n.* **1** A person who has control or authority over the actions of other living beings; as, the dog's *master;* the *master* of a household. **2** A male teacher. **3** A person who has the use of or control over a lifeless thing; as, the *master* of a boat. **4** One who has control over a set of circumstances; as, to be *master* of one's fate; to be *master* of a situation. **5** Something that controls a person's thoughts or actions; as, to refuse to let money be one's *master*. **6** [with a capital] A title of respect, now usually used only before the name of a boy. **7** A person, as an artist or a workman, who is very skillful. **8** A painting or a statue by a great artist of former times. The picture was an old *master*. **9** A title or an advanced degree granted by a college or university; the person holding such a title or degree. — *v.;* **mas·tered**; **mas·ter·ing** \-r(-)ing\. **1** To get control of; to subdue; as, to *master* an enemy; to *master* an emotion. **2** To become skillful at; as, to *master* arithmetic. — *adj.* **1** Being a master; as, a *master* builder. **2** Principal; main; governing; as, a *master* plan. **3** Controlling the operation of other mechanisms; as, a *master* key for the doors of an apartment building; a *master* clock in a school building.

mas·ter·ful \'mast-rf-l\ *adj.* **1** Inclined to take control or dominate; as, a *masterful* person; *masterful* behavior. **2** Highly skillful; masterly; as, a *masterful* tennis player.

mas·ter·ful·ly \'mast-rf-l(-)ē\ *adv.* In a masterful way or manner.

mas·ter·ly \'mast-r-lē\ *adj.* Suitable to or like a master; showing knowledge or skill; as, a *masterly* plan. — *adv.* With the skill of a master.

master of ceremonies. A person who conducts a program, as on television, introducing performers, interviewing speakers, and tying together the various parts of the program.

mas·ter·piece \'mast-r-ˌpēs\ *n.* **1** Anything done or made with unusual skill. The painting was a *masterpiece*. **2** The greatest achievement of a person. The artist's *masterpiece* was a water color done during his later years.

mas·tery \'mast-r(-)ē\ *n.* **1** The position or authority of a master. **2** Victory, as in war or in a contest. **3** Skill or knowledge that makes a person master of something; as, *mastery* of a language.

mast·head \'mast-ˌhed, 'mas-ˌted\ *n.* The top of a mast.

mas·tic \'mas-tik\ *n.* The yellowish resin of a southern European tree, used as an astringent and as an ingredient in such products as varnish and lacquer.

mas·ti·cate \'mas-tə-ˌkāt\ *v.;* **mas·ti·cat·ed**; **mas·ti·cat·ing**. To grind or crush food with one's teeth before swallowing it; as, to be sure to *masticate* properly. — **mas·ti·ca·tion** \ˌmas-tə-'kāsh-n\ *n.*

mas·tiff \'mas-təf\ *n.* A very large, deep-chested, powerful dog with a smooth coat.

mas·to·don \'mas-tə-ˌdän, -dən\ *n.* A huge extinct animal that closely resembled the elephant.

mas·toid \'mas-ˌtȯid\ *n.* A somewhat conical outgrowth of the temporal bone of the skull that lies behind the ear and contains various small air-filled cavities which are sometimes the seat of a severe infection; the infection itself.

mat \'mat\ *n.* **1** A piece of coarse fabric made of woven or braided rushes, straw, or wool. **2** A piece of material in front of a door to wipe the shoes on. **3** Anything that grows thickly or is closely interwoven or snarled; as, a *mat* of weeds; a *mat* of hair on one's head. **4** A piece of material, such as leather, woven straw, or cloth, used under dishes or vases, or as an ornament. **5** A pad or cushion for gymnastics or wrestling. — *v.;* **mat·ted**; **mat·ting**. To cover with or as with a mat; to twist or interweave like a mat.

mat \'mat\ *n.* **1** A border for a picture, filling the space between the picture and its frame. **2** A dull finish; as, walls finished in *mat*.

mat·a·dor \'mat-ə-ˌdȯr\ *n.* In bullfights, the man appointed to kill the bull.

match \'mach\ *n.* **1** A wick or cord that is made to burn evenly and is used for lighting a charge of powder. **2** A short slender piece of wood or other material, tipped with a mixture that ignites when subjected to friction.

match \'mach\ *n.* **1** A person or thing that is equal to, or as good as, another thing; as, to be a *match* for the enemy. **2** A thing that is exactly like another thing. This cloth is a *match* for that. **3** Two persons or things that go well together. The curtains are a good *match* for the carpet. **4** A marriage; as, to make a good *match*. **5** A person to be considered as a marriage partner; as, to be a good *match* for a young executive. **6** A contest between two persons, teams, or the like; as, a tennis *match*. — *v.* **1** To meet as a competitor in a contest, usually victoriously; as, a player who *matched* all comers. **2** To place in competition against each other; as, to *match* two teams. **3** To choose something that is the same as another or goes well with it; as, to *match* colors. **4** To be the same, or to be suitable together. The colors *match*. **5** To marry. The king *matched* his daughter with a commoner. **6** To toss a coin so that it lands with the same side up as that of a coin held by another;

to flip coins with another person; to decide something by the way coins fall.

match·book \'mach-ˌbu̇k\ *n.* A small folder containing rows of paper matches.

match·less \'mach-ləs\ *adj.* Having no equal; better than anything of the same kind; as, a *matchless* gem; a *matchless* poem. — **match·less·ly,** *adv.*

match·lock \'mach-ˌläk\ *n.* An old form of gun in which the charge was lighted by a cord match.

match·mak·er \'mach-ˌmāk-r\ *n.* A person who arranges or attempts to bring about marriages.

mate \'māt\ *n.* **1** A companion; a comrade. **2** A husband or wife. **3** One of a pair of animals or birds, usually a male and female; as, a fox and his *mate.* **4** One of a pair of matched objects; as, a *mate* to a glove. **5** An officer who ranks next below the captain on a merchant ship. — *v.;* **mat·ed; mat·ing.** To join as mates; to match; to marry.

ma·te·ri·al \mə-'tir-ē-əl\ *adj.* **1** Having to do with or made of matter; physical; not spiritual. A baseball is a *material* thing. **2** Important. Food is *material* to one's health. **3** Having to do with a person's bodily needs or wants. Money buys *material* comforts. — *n.* **1** The substance or substances of which a thing is made; as, the raw *materials* of industry. **2** [in the plural] Tools; implements; supplies; as, the building *materials;* writing *materials.* **3** A fabric; cloth; as, dress *material.*

ma·te·ri·al·ism \mə-'tir-ē-ə-ˌliz-m\ *n.* **1** The theory that everything is matter or the result of matter and can be fully explained by physical science. **2** A tendency to attach too great importance to material things as money or comforts. — **ma·te·ri·al·ist** \-ə-ləst\ *n.* — **ma·te·ri·al·is·tic** \mə-ˌtir-ē-ə-'lis-tik\ *adj.*

ma·te·ri·al·ize \mə-'tir-ē-ə-ˌlīz\ *v.;* **ma·te·ri·al·ized; ma·te·ri·al·iz·ing. 1** To give something a physical form or to take on a physical form. **2** To become an actual fact; as, to find one's dreams *materialized.*

ma·te·ri·al·ly \mə-'tir-ē-ə-lē\ *adv.* **1** In regard to physical matter or substance. **2** In an important degree; as, to be *materially* influenced by something.

ma·ter·nal \mə-'tərn-l\ *adj.* **1** Having to do with a mother; motherly; as, *maternal* love. **2** Related through one's mother; as, one's *maternal* grandparents. — **ma·ter·nal·ly** \-'tərn-l-ē\ *adv.*

ma·ter·ni·ty \mə-'tər-nət-ē\ *n.* **1** The state of being a mother; motherhood. **2** Motherly character; motherliness.

math \'math\ Short for *mathematics.*

math·e·mat·i·cal \ˌmath-m-'at-ik-l\ *adj.* **1** Of or having to do with mathematics; as, a *mathematical* problem. **2** Accurate; as, *mathematical* precision. — **math·e·mat·i·cal·ly** \-ik-l(-)ē\ *adv.*

math·e·ma·ti·cian \ˌmath-m(-)ə-'tish-n\ *n.* A person skilled in mathematics.

math·e·mat·ics \ˌmath-m-'at-iks\ *n.* The science that studies and explains numbers, quantities, measurements, and the relations between them.

mat·i·nee \ˌmat-n-'ā\ *n.* A presentation of a play or some other entertainment in the daytime, especially in the afternoon.

mat·ing \'māt-ing\. Pres. part. of *mate.* — *n.* A pairing or matching; the act of becoming mates.

mat·ins \'mat-nz\ *n. pl.* **1** A collection of morning prayers making up the first of the seven parts of the breviary and recited either privately, as by a priest, or in common, as by a group of monks. **2** The morning prayer service in certain churches.

ma·tri·arch \'mā-trē-ˌärk, -ˌȧrk\ *n.* A woman who rules a family, group, or state; especially, a mother who is head and ruler of her family and descendants. — **ma·tri·ar·chal** \ˌmā-trē-'ärk-l, -'ȧrk-l\ *adj.*

ma·tri·archy \'mā-trē-ˌärk-ē, -ˌȧrk-ē\ *n.* **1** A family, group, or state ruled by a matriarch. **2** A form of social organization in which descent is traced in the female line and children belong to the mother's clan or family.

ma·tri·cide \'mā-trə-ˌsīd, 'ma-trə-\ *n.* **1** Murder of a mother by her child. **2** One who kills his mother. — **ma·tri·cid·al** \ˌmā-trə-'sīd-l, ˌma-trə-\ *adj.*

ma·tric·u·late \mə-'trik-yə-ˌlāt\ *v.;* **ma·tric·u·lat·ed; ma·tric·u·lat·ing.** To enroll, especially in a college or university. — **ma·tric·u·la·tion** \mə-ˌtrik-yə-'lāsh-n\ *n.*

mat·ri·mo·ni·al \ˌma-trə-'mō-nē-əl\ *adj.* Of or relating to marriage. — **mat·ri·mo·ni·al·ly** \-nē-ə-lē\ *adv.*

mat·ri·mo·ny \'ma-trə-ˌmō-nē\ *n.* Marriage.

ma·trix \'mā-triks, 'ma-\ *n.; pl.* **ma·tri·ces** \-trə-ˌsēz\ or **ma·trix·es** \-triks-əz\. **1** A place or an enclosing or surrounding substance within which something originates or develops, as a rock in which a mineral is embedded. **2** That which gives form, foundation, or origin to something else enclosed in it, as a mold for casting metal.

ma·tron \'mā-trən\ *n.* **1** A wife or a widow, especially one who has had children. **2** A woman who is in charge of the household affairs of an institution such as a hospital or a boarding school. **3** A woman who supervises women prisoners in a police station or jail. **4** A woman attendant, as in a bathhouse or ladies' room.

ma·tron·ly \'mā-trən-lē\ *adj.* Of or like a matron; suitable for a matron; as, *matronly* interests; a *matronly* manner.

matron of honor. A married woman serving as the principal attendant of a bride at a wedding.

mat·ted \'mat-əd\ *adj.* **1** Covered with mats. **2** Tangled closely together.

mat·ter \'mat-r\ *n.* **1** The substance things are made of; material or a particular kind of material; as, the gray *matter* of the brain; coloring *matter.* **2** A yellowish fluid found in sores and boils; pus. **3** An amount; a quantity; a space; as, a *matter* of five cents; a *matter* of one mile. **4** Something that has to be dealt with; a thing; as, a serious *matter;* personal *matters.* **5** A subject, as of an action, feeling, or discussion; as, a *matter* for careful thought. **6** A trouble; a difficulty. What is the *matter?* **7** In physics, whatever occupies space; that which is considered to make up the substance of the physical world. **8** Mail; as, first-class *matter.* **9** Printing or anything to be printed. **— *v.* 1** To be of importance. It does not *matter.* **2** To form or discharge pus.

matter of course. Something that may be expected or depended upon to happen as a natural, logical result of something else. — **mat·ter-of-course** \'mat-r-əv-'kōrs, -'kȯrs\ *adj.*

mat·ter-of-fact \'mat-r-ə(v)-'fakt\ *adj.* Sticking to fact; not fanciful; businesslike; commonplace. — **mat·ter-of-fact·ly,** *adv.*

mat·ting \'mat-ing\ *n.* **1** Materials for mats. **2** Mats taken collectively. **3** A fabric woven like mats, especially one of straw, grass, or similar fiber used as a floor covering.

mat·tock \'mat-ək\ *n.* An implement for digging consisting of a long wooden handle and a steel head, one end of which comes either to a point or to a cutting edge.

mattock heads

mat·tress \'ma-trəs\ *n.* A part of a bed made of a springy material such as hair, cotton, or molded rubber, incased in strong cloth and placed on the bed springs.

mat·u·ra·tion \ˌmach-r-'āsh-n\ *n.* **1** The process of becoming mature. **2** The process involving meiosis by which germ cells are readied for fertilization.

ma·ture \mə-'tu̇r, -'tyu̇r\ *adj.* **1** Fully grown; ripe. **2** Completely worked out; ready for use; perfected; as, a *mature* plan. **3** Of or relating to a fully developed state; as, a man of *mature* years; careful, *mature* thinking. **4** Due for payment, as a bond or a note. **— *v.;* ma·tured; ma·tur·ing. 1** To finish; to bring to maturity; as, to *mature* one's plans. **2** To grow to maturity. **3** To become payable, as a bond or a note. — **ma·ture·ly,** *adv.*

ma·tu·ri·ty \mə-'tu̇r-ət-ē, -'tyu̇r-\ *n.; pl.* **ma·tu·ri·ties. 1** Ripeness; full development. **2** A coming due; as, the date of *maturity* of a bond.

matz·oth \'mät-ˌsōs, 'mȧt-, -sə(s), -ˌsōth\ *n. pl.; sing.* **matzo** \-ˌsō, -sə\. Unleavened bread eaten at the Passover.

maud·lin \'mȯd-lən\ *adj.* **1** Weakly and excessively sentimental; as, a *maudlin* concern for the rights of thugs and scoundrels. **2** Drunk enough to weep over trifles; tearfully silly.

maul or **mall** \'mȯl\ *n.* Any of various heavy hammers, as for driving posts into the ground. **— *v.;* mauled** or **malled; maul·ing** or **mall·ing.** To beat and bruise; to handle roughly.

maun·der \'mȯnd-r, 'mänd-r\ *v.;* **maun·dered; maun·der·ing** \-r(-)ing\. **1** To wander slowly and idly; as, to *maunder* along looking in the store windows. **2** To mumble; to mutter.

mau·so·le·um \ˌmȯs-l-'ē-əm, ˌmȯz-\ *n.; pl.* **mau·so·le·ums** \-'ē-əmz\ or **mau·so·lea** \-'ē-ə\. [From Latin, there borrowed from Greek *mausoleion* meaning literally "tomb of Mausolus", Mausolus being an ancient king in Asia Minor in whose honor a magnificent tomb was erected.] A magnificent tomb.

mauve \'mōv, 'mȯv\ *n.* A color that is a soft shade of purple, violet, or purplish red.

mav·er·ick \'mav-r(-)ik\ *n.* **1** An unbranded animal, especially a motherless calf. **2** A rebellious and headstrong person who refuses to follow the leadership of his political party or his group and takes his own course.

ma·vis \'mā-vəs\ *n.* The song thrush of Europe.

maw \'mȯ\ *n.* **1** A stomach; in birds, the crop or craw. **2** A throat or jaws.

mawk·ish \'mȯk-ish\ *adj.* **1** Apt to disgust or nauseate. **2** Sickishly sentimental. — **mawk·ish·ly,** *adv.*

max·il·la \mak-'sil-ə\ *n.; pl.* **max·il·las** \-'sil-əz\ or **max·il·lae** \-'sil-ˌē\. **1** A bone on each side of the face, which bears the upper teeth. **2** In arthropods, either of the pair of mouth appendages immediately behind the mandibles. — **max·il·lary** \'maks-l-ˌer-ē\ *adj.* or *n.*

max·im \'maks-m\ *n.* A general truth or a rule of conduct expressed in a few words; as, the *maxim* "Honesty is the best policy."

max·i·mum \'maks-m-əm\ *n.; pl.* **max·i·mums** \-m-əmz\ or **max·i·ma** \-m-ə\. The highest point or greatest amount; as, to pay the *maximum.* **— *adj.*** The greatest possible in amount or degree; as, *maximum* efficiency.

may \'mā\ *v.; past tense* **might** \'mīt\. **1** Have or has permission to; am, is, or are allowed to. You *may* go if you like. **2** Have or has a chance to; am, is, or are somewhat likely to. It *may* rain. **3** It is wished or hoped that. *May* he live another hundred years!

May \'mā\ *n.* [From medieval English *Mai,* there borrowed from Old French, there derived from Latin *Maius,* probably named after *Maia,* an ancient Roman goddess.] The fifth month of the year, having 31 days.

May apple or **may·ap·ple** \'mā-ˌap-l\ *n.* **1** A North American woodland herb related to the barberry, with poisonous rootstock, leaves up to one foot in diameter, large, waxy white flowers, and yellow egg-shaped berries. **2** The fruit of this plant.

may·be \'mā-bē, 'meb-ē\ *adv.* Perhaps.

May Day. The first day of May, often celebrated by crowning a girl chosen as queen (**May queen**) with a garland of flowers and by dancing round a Maypole. — **May-day,** *adj.*

may·est \'mā-əst\. An archaic form of *may,* used chiefly with *thou.*

May·flow·er \'mā-ˌflau̇r\ *n.* Any of several plants that bloom in the spring, including the trailing arbutus, hepatica, and several of the anemones.

May fly. A slender delicate insect of a family living only a few hours in the adult stage; an ephemerid.

may·hap \mā-'hap, 'mā-ˌhap\ *adv. Archaic or Dial.* Perhaps.

may·hem \'mā-ˌhem, 'mā-əm\ *n.* **1** The maiming of a person in such a way as to deprive him of the ability to defend himself. **2** Any willful disfiguring of the body.

mayn't \'mā(-ə)nt\. A contraction of *may not.*

may·on·naise \ˌmā-ə-'nāz\ *n.* A dressing, as for salads, consisting chiefly of yolk of egg, vegetable oil, and vinegar beaten into a sauce.

may·or \'mā-ər, 'mer\ *n.* The highest official of a city or borough.

may·or·al·ty \'mā-ər-əl-tē, 'mer-əl-\ *n.; pl.* **may·or·al·ties.** The office or the term of office of a mayor.

May·pole \'mā-ˌpōl\ *n.* A tall pole wreathed with flowers, forming a center for sports on the first day of May.

mayst \'māst\. An archaic form of *may,* used chiefly with *thou.*

maze \'māz\ *n.* **1** A confusing network, as ot paths or passages; a labyrinth. **2** Confusion; as, a *maze* of ideas.

ma·zur·ka or **ma·zour·ka** \mə-'zərk-ə, -'zůrk-ə\ *n.* **1** A Polish dance in moderate triple time. **2** Music for this dance, usually in $\frac{3}{4}$ or $\frac{3}{8}$ time, slower in tempo than the waltz.

mazy \'mā-zē\ *adj.;* **maz·i·er**; **maz·i·est.** Like a maze; winding; confusing.

M.C. \'em-'sē\. Abbreviation for *Master of Ceremonies.* — *n.; pl.* **M.C.'s** \-'sēz\. A master of ceremonies. — *v.;* **M.C.'d** \-'sēd\; **M.C.'ing** \-'sē-ing\. To act as master of ceremonies; as, to *M.C.* a television show.

M.D. \'em-'dē\ *n.; pl.* **M.D.'s** \-'dēz\. [Abbreviation of medieval Latin *medicinae doctor* meaning "doctor of medicine".] A doctor; a physician.

mdse. Abbreviation for *merchandise.*

me \(')mē\ *pron.* The form of the word *I* that is used as the object of a preposition or as the direct object of a verb.

mead \'mēd\ *n.* A fermented drink made of water, honey, malt, and yeast.

mead \'mēd\ *n.* A meadow.

mead·ow \'med-ō\ *n.* A piece of land on which grass is grown for hay; any piece of land where grass and flowers grow.

meadow lark. Any of several North American birds about the size of a robin, with brown and buff upper parts and yellow breast.

mea·ger or **mea·gre** \'mēg-r\ *adj.* **1** Having little or no flesh; thin; lean. **2** Poor; insufficient; as, a *meager* harvest. — **mea·ger·ly** or **mea·gre·ly** \'mēg-r-lē\ *adv.*

meal \'mēl\ *n.* **1** Ground grain; especially, ground Indian corn. **2** Anything like meal.

meal \'mēl\ *n.* **1** The food eaten or prepared for eating at one time. **2** The action or time of eating; as, to be on time for *meals.*

meal·time \'mēl-ˌtīm\ *n.* The usual time for eating.

mealy \'mē-lē\ *adj.;* **meal·i·er**; **meal·i·est.** **1** Like meal; dry and crumbly; as, a *mealy* potato. **2** Containing or covered with meal or as if with meal; as, the *mealy* wings of an insect. **3** Mealymouthed.

meal·y·mouthed \'mē-lē-'maůt͟hd, -'maůtht\ *adj.* Using soft words; plausible but insincere.

mean \'mēn\ *v.;* **meant** \'ment\; **mean·ing** \'mē-ning\. **1** To have in mind as one's purpose; to intend; as, to *mean* to be kind. **2** To have as a sense; to indicate; to signify; to denote. The words do not *mean* that. **3** To have significance or importance; as, a man to whom fame and glory *meant* everything. **4** To intend for a particular purpose or use; as, a book *meant* for children. — **mean well.** To have good intentions.

mean \'mēn\ *adj.* **1** Humble; low; common. **2** Ordinary; inferior; as, a man of no *mean* ability. **3** Poor; shabby; as, to live in *mean* surroundings. **4** Not honorable or worthy; unkind; wicked. It is *mean* to take advantage of another's misfortunes. **5** Stingy; miserly. **6** Spiteful; malicious; nasty. **7** Vicious or troublesome, as a horse or dog.

mean \'mēn\ *adj.* **1** Holding a middle position; coming midway between extremes; as, to follow a *mean* course. **2** In mathematics, having an intermediate value between two extremes; average; as, a *mean* annual temperature. — *n.* **1** The middle point or course between extremes; moderation; as, to try to find and follow the *mean;* a happy *mean.* **2** In mathematics, a quantity having a middle value between several others; usually, the simple average (**arithmetical mean**) found by adding the quantities together and dividing by their number. **3** [in the plural] Something that helps a person to get what he wants; as, to use every *means* one can think of — used as singular or plural in construction. **4** [in the plural] Money or wealth; as, a man of *means.* **5** [in the plural] The second and third terms of a mathematical proposition. — **by all means.** Certainly; without fail. — **by any means.** In any way; at all. — **by means of.** Through the use of. — **by no means.** Not at all; certainly not.

me·an·der \mē-'and-r\ *n.* A turn or winding, as of a stream; a winding course. — *v.;* **me·an·dered**; **me·an·der·ing** \-r(-)ing\. **1** To wind or turn in a passage or course; as, a brook *meandering* through the fields. **2** To wander without aim or purpose; as, to *meander* around town.

mean·ing \'mē-ning\ *n.* **1** Intention; purpose; object. **2** That which is intended to be conveyed by an act or by words. **3** The sense in which a word or a statement is understood. **4** Significance; as, a silence that was full of *meaning.* — *adj.* Significant; as, a *meaning* look.

mean·ing·ful \'mē-ning-fəl\ *adj.* Having much meaning; significant. — **mean·ing·ful·ly** \-fə-lē\ *adv.*

mean·ing·less \'mē-ning-ləs\ *adj.* **1** Without sense or significance. **2** Without motive. — **mean·ing·less·ly,** *adv.*

mean·ing·ly \'mē-ning-lē\ *adv.* With special meaning; expressively.

mean·ly \'mēn-lē\ *adv.* **1** In a poor, humble, or shabby manner; as, *meanly* dressed. **2** In an ungenerous or ignoble manner.

mean·ness \'mēn-nəs\ *n.* **1** The quality or state of being low in station or ignoble in conduct. **2** A mean act.

meant. Past tense and past part. of *mean*.

mean·time \'mēn-ˌtīm\ *adv.* During the time coming between two events; in the interval; at the same time. — *n.* The time between two events.

mean·while \'mēn-ˌhwīl\ *adv.* or *n.* Meantime.

mea·sles \'mēz-lz\ *n.* **1** An acute contagious disease marked by fever and red spots on the skin. **2** Any of several similar but milder diseases, as German measles. **3** A disease of cattle and swine caused by the larvae of certain tapeworms. **4** [used as a plural] The larvae that cause measles in cattle and swine.

mea·sly \'mēz-l(-)ē\ *adj.;* **mea·sli·er**; **mea·sli·est**. **1** Infected with measles. **2** Like measles. **3** Insignificant; contemptible; as, to quarrel over a *measly* five cents.

mea·sur·a·ble \'mezh-r(-)əb-l, 'māzh-, -rb-l\ *adj.* Capable of being measured. — **mea·sur·a·bly** \-r(-)ə-blē, -r-blē\ *adv.*

mea·sure \'mezh-r, 'māzh-r\ *n.* **1** An extent or degree that is not excessive; as to be surprised beyond *measure.* **2** The dimensions, capacity, or quantity of anything as fixed by measuring; as, to give full *measure.* **3** Something, as a yardstick or a cup, used in measuring. **4** A unit used in measuring. A foot is a *measure* of length. **5** A system of measuring; as, liquid *measure.* **6** A means used to accomplish a purpose; as, to take *measures* to stop it. **7** A legislative act, bill, or law. **8** An extent, degree, or quantity; as, to succeed in large *measure.* **9** In music, the part of the staff between two adjacent bars; the group or grouping of beats between these bars. **10** Regulated movement or rhythm in music or poetry; as, a light, dancing *measure.* **11** A dance, especially a stately one. — *v.;* **mea·sured**; **mea·sur·ing** \-r(-)ing\. **1** To find out the extent, degree, or amount of something by comparing it with an accepted measurement; as, to *measure* cloth. **2** To estimate; as, to *measure* the distance with the eye. **3** To serve as a measure of. A thermometer *measures* temperature. **4** To bring into comparison; as, to *measure* one's skill against an opponent. **5** To turn out to be of a certain measurement, as in length or breadth. The cloth *measures* three yards.

measure, 3

mea·sured \'mezh-rd, 'māzh-\ *adj.* **1** Regulated or determined by a standard; uniform; even; as, to walk with *measured* steps. **2** Deliberate; calculated; as, to speak with *measured* bluntness. **3** Rhythmical; having meter; as, the *measured* cheering at the football game. — **mea·sured·ly**, *adv.*

mea·sure·less \'mezh-r-ləs, 'māzh-\ *adj.* Without measure; immeasurable.

mea·sure·ment \'mezh-r-mənt, 'māzh-\ *n.* **1** The act of measuring. **2** The extent, size, capacity, or amount of anything as fixed by measuring; as, the *measurements* of a room. **3** A system of measures.

mea·sur·ing worm \'mezh-r(-)ing, 'māzh-\. The larva of certain moths, having at each end of its body pairs of legs by which it progresses in a looping movement comparable to that used in measuring with a tape measure.

meat \'mēt\ *n.* **1** Food; anything eaten for nourishment. **2** The flesh of animals used as food, especially that of animals other than fish and poultry. **3** The food parts inside something such as a shell or husk; as, the *meat* of a coconut; nut *meats.*

meaty \'mēt-ē\ *adj.;* **meat·i·er**; **meat·i·est**. **1** Having much meat. **2** Resembling meat. **3** Full of matter for thought; solid; as, a *meaty* letter.

mec·ca \'mek-ə\ *n.* [From *Mecca*, Arabia, the holy city of the Moslems, and the goal of many pilgrimages.] A place considered extremely desirable, especially by a particular group of people; as, a university that is the *mecca* of chemistry students.

me·chan·ic \mə-'kan-ik\ *adj.* Requiring skill with the hands; as, the *mechanic* arts. — *n.* A person who practices any mechanic art; especially, a person who makes or repairs machines.

me·chan·i·cal \mə-'kan-ik-l\ *adj.* **1** Having to do with machinery; as, a course in *mechanical* engineering. **2** Made by machinery; machine-made. **3** Done or operated by a machine; as, a *mechanical* concrete mixer. **4** Produced as if by a machine; lacking a personal touch; as, to sing in a *mechanical* way. **5** Working by some machinery within itself; as, a *mechanical* toy. — **me·chan·i·cal·ly** \-ik-l(-)ē\ *adv.*

mechanical drawing. A method of drawing which makes use of such instruments as compasses, squares, and triangles in order to insure mathematical precision.

me·chan·ics \mə-'kan-iks\ *n. sing. and pl.* **1** The science that collects, studies, and explains facts about the action of forces on bodies. **2** The mechanical details of a process; as, the *mechanics* of running; the *mechanics* of writing plays.

mech·a·nism \'mek-n-ˌiz-m\ *n.* **1** A machine or mechanical device. **2** A process that is somewhat mechanical in nature. All animals have some sort of *mechanism* for digesting food. **3** The parts by which a machine operates as a mechanical unit; as, the *mechanism* of a watch. **4** The parts or steps by which a process occurs; as, the *mechanism* of democratic government.

mech·a·nize \'mek-n-ˌīz\ *v.;* **mech·a·nized**; **mech·a·niz·ing**. To make mechanical or like a machine; especially, to replace men by machines or to equip with motor vehicles; as, to *mechanize* an army.

med·al \'med-l\ *n.* A piece of metal like a coin with design and words in honor of something, as a special event, person, or deed. The soldier received a *medal* for bravery.

me·dal·lion \mə-'dal-yən\ *n.* **1** A large medal. **2** Something resembling a large medal, as a tablet or panel bearing a figure in relief or a wallpaper design.

med·dle \'med-l\ *v.;* **med·dled; med·dling** \-l(-)ing\. To interest oneself unnecessarily; to interfere; to pry; as, to *meddle* in another person's business.
— The word *tamper* is a synonym of *meddle: meddle* usually suggests rude and inquisitive prying into something that is not one's concern or responsibility and without asking permission to do so; *tamper* generally refers to deliberate and often dishonest altering or changing of something or to exerting improper influence in some situation that would be better left alone.

med·dler \'med-l(-)ər\ *n.* One that meddles.

med·dle·some \'med-ls-m\ *adj.* Inclined to meddle, as in other persons' affairs; curious.

media. A pl. of *medium.*

mediaeval. Variant of *medieval.*

me·di·al \'mēd-ē-əl\ *adj.* **1** Middle; median; intermediate; as, a *medial* zone. **2** Average; ordinary. — **me·di·al·ly** \-ē-ə-lē\ *adv.*

me·di·an \'mēd-ē-ən\ *n.* In a series, the item, as the number, line or point, that has as many numbers, lines, or points above as below it. In the series 1, 4, 5, 10, 20, the *median* is 5, but the average is 8. — *adj.* Being in the middle; medial; middle.

me·di·ate \'mēd-ē-ət\ *adj.* Acting through an intermediate agent or agency; not direct; as, the *mediate* connections between the foot accelerator and the carburetor in an automobile. — \-ˌāt\ *v.;* **me·di·at·ed; me·di·at·ing. 1** To settle by mediation. The management and the strikers agreed to *mediate* their dispute. **2** To act as a go-between. The president of the college *mediated* in the disagreement.

me·di·a·tion \ˌmēd-ē-'āsh-n\ *n.* **1** The action of mediating. **2** The plea made by one person or group on behalf of another.

me·di·a·tor \'mēd-ē-ˌāt-r\ *n.* A person, group, or country that acts as a go-between in a dispute in order to arrange a peaceful settlement.

me·di·a·to·ry \'mēd-ē-ə-ˌtōr-ē, -ˌtȯr-ē\ *adj.* Of, relating to, or of the nature of mediation.

med·i·ca·ble \'med-ə-kəb-l\ *adj.* Capable of being medicated, cured, or healed.

med·i·cal \'med-ik-l\ *adj.* Of or relating to the science of medicine or the treatment of disease. — **med·i·cal·ly** \-ik-l(-)ē\ *adv.*

me·dic·a·ment \mə-'dik-m-ənt\ *n.* A medicine or healing application.

med·i·cate \'med-ə-ˌkāt\ *v.;* **med·i·cat·ed; med·i·cat·ing. 1** To treat with medicine. **2** To impregnate with something medicinal; as, *medicated* soap.

med·i·ca·tion \ˌmed-ə-'kāsh-n\ *n.* **1** The action or process of medicating. **2** Medical treatment. **3** A medicament.

me·dic·i·nal \mə-'dis-n(-)əl\ *adj.* Having the power to check or cure disease; as, a *medicinal* plant. — **me·dic·i·nal·ly** \-'dis-n(-)ə-lē\ *adv.*

med·i·cine \'med-əs-n\ *n.* **1** The science that deals with the prevention, cure, or easing of disease. **2** That part of this science that is the business of the physician as distinguished from the surgeon. **3** Any substance used in treating disease. **4** Any object supposed to give control over natural or magical forces; a magical power; a magical rite.

medicine ball. A large, stuffed, leather-covered ball tossed and caught for exercise.

medicine man. Among the North American Indians and other primitive peoples, a person who claims he can cure diseases by potions and charms.

medicine show. A show in which medicine, often claimed to be a cure-all of Indian origin, is advertised and sold.

me·di·e·val or **me·di·ae·val** \ˌmēd-ē-'ēv-l, ˌmed-, ˌmid-; mē-'dēv-l, mi-, me-\ *adj.* Of, relating to, or characteristic of the Middle Ages.

me·di·o·cre \ˌmēd-ē-'ōk-r\ *adj.* Ordinary; commonplace; neither good nor bad.

me·di·oc·ri·ty \ˌmēd-ē-'äk-rət-ē\ *n.; pl.* **me·di·oc·ri·ties. 1** The quality or state of being mediocre. **2** A mediocre person.

med·i·tate \'med-ə-ˌtāt\ *v.;* **med·i·tat·ed; med·i·tat·ing. 1** To plan; to consider carefully; as, to *meditate* making a trip abroad. **2** To spend time in quiet thinking; to muse; to reflect.

med·i·ta·tion \ˌmed-ə-'tāsh-n\ *n.* Close and continued thought; pondering; reflection; as, to spend an hour in *meditation.* — **med·i·ta·tive** \'med-ə-ˌtāt-iv\ *adj.* — **med·i·ta·tive·ly**, *adv.*

Med·i·ter·ra·ne·an \ˌmed-ə-tə-'rā-nē-ən\ *adj.* Of or relating to the Mediterranean Sea, that lies between Europe and Africa, or to the lands or peoples around it.

Mediterranean fruit fly. A two-winged fly with black and white markings, native to the Mediterranean countries but now widely distributed.

me·di·um \'mēd-ē-əm\ *n.; pl.* **me·di·ums** \-ē-əmz\ or **me·dia** \-ē-ə\. **1** Something that is between or in the middle; a middle condition or degree. **2** A substance through which a force acts or through which something is transmitted. Air is the common *medium* of sound. **3** A surrounding substance; an environment. Slums are a poor *medium* for developing good citizens. **4** The means by which or through which anything is done; as, to advertise through the *medium* of television. Money is a *medium* of exchange. **5** A nourishing substance, such as broth or gelatin, that is used for growing bacteria. **6** A person through whom other persons seek to communicate with the spirits of the dead. — *adj.* **1** Intermediate in amount, quality, position, or degree. **2** Of stress or accent, like that on the last syllable of *penetrate* \'pen-ə-ˌtrāt\.

med·lar \'med-lər\ *n.* **1** A small hairy-leaved Eurasian tree of the apple family, with a fruit resembling a crab apple, eaten when decaying. **2** The fruit of this tree.

med·ley \'med-lē\ *n.; pl.* **med·leys. 1** A mixture; especially, a confused mixture; a jumble. **2** A musical composition made up of parts of other pieces.

me·dul·la \mə-'dəl-ə\ *n.; pl.* **me·dul·lae** \-'dəl-ˌē\ or **me·dul·las** \-'dəl-əz\. **1** The marrow of bones. **2** The deep or inner substance or tissue of an organ or part, as of a hair. **3** The medulla oblongata. **4** In botany, the pith. — **med·ul·lary** \'med-l-ˌer-ē, 'mej-l-\ *adj.*

medulla ob·lon·ga·ta \ˌäb-ˌlȯng-'gät-ə, -'gåt-ə\. The lowest or posterior part of the brain, tapering off into the spinal cord.

medullary ray. One of the fine rays of woody tissue extending from the center of the stem to the bark in plants having annual rings of growth.

me·du·sa \mə-'dü-sə, -'dyü-\ *n.; pl.* **me·du·sae** \-ˌsē\ or **me·du·sas** \-səz\. A jellyfish.

meed \'mēd\ *n.* Something given for merit; a reward; as, to receive one's *meed* of praise.

meek \'mēk\ *adj.* [From medieval English *meke,* there borrowed from Old Norse *mjukr* meaning literally "soft".] **1** Mild in temper; patient; long-suffering. **2** Lacking spirit or self-assurance; humble. — **meek·ly,** *adv.* — **meek·ness,** *n.*

meer·schaum \'mirsh-m, 'mir-ˌshȯm\ *n.* **1** A soft white lightweight mineral resembling a very fine clay, used especially for tobacco pipes. **2** A tobacco pipe made of this mineral.

meet \'mēt\ *v.;* **met** \'met\; **meet·ing** \'mēt-ing\. **1** To come upon or across; as, to *meet* an old friend by chance. **2** To go to the place where a person or thing is or will be; as, to *meet* a train; to arrange to *meet* a friend at four o'clock. **3** To join; to cross; as, where two roads *meet.* **4** To be seen, heard, or noticed by; as, a welcome sight to *meet* the eyes. **5** To fight against; to struggle with; as, to *meet* the enemy. **6** To endure; to experience; as, to *meet* failure bravely; to *meet* with bad luck. **7** To be enough; to satisfy; as, to *meet* the requirements. **8** To discharge or pay, as a debt or note. **9** To assemble or come together, as a club. — *n.* An assembly or meeting, especially for the purpose of engaging in sports; as, an athletic *meet.*

meet \'mēt\ *adj.* Proper; suitable; fitting. — **meet·ly,** *adv.*

meet·ing \'mēt-ing\ *n.* **1** The act of persons or things that meet; as, a chance *meeting* with a friend. **2** A coming together of a number of persons, usually at a stated time and place and for a known purpose; an assembly or gathering; as, the regular monthly *meeting* of the Science Club; a political *meeting.* **3** An assembly for religious worship; as, a Quaker *meeting.* **4** The place where two things come together; a junction.

meet·ing·house \'mēt-ing-ˌhau̇s\ *n.; pl.* **meet·ing·hous·es** \-ˌhau̇-zəz\. A building used for worship; a church.

meg·a·cy·cle \'meg-ə-ˌsīk-l\ *n.* One million cycles, or complete reversals of direction of an alternating current, per second; as, a radio frequency of 25 *megacycles.*

meg·a·lo·ma·nia \ˌmeg-l-ō-'mā-nē-ə, -'mān-yə\ *n.* A mental disorder in which the patient believes himself to be a person of great wealth or power. — **meg·a·lo·ma·ni·ac** \-'mā-nē-ˌak\ *n.*

meg·a·phone \'meg-ə-ˌfōn\ *n.* A device, usually in the form of a large funnel, used to direct sound and to increase its loudness.

megaphone

meg·a·ton \'meg-ə-ˌtən\ *n.* **1** A million tons. **2** An explosive force equal to that of one million tons of TNT — used especially in connection with hydrogen bombs.

mei·o·sis \mī-'ō-səs\ *n.* The process by which the number of chromosomes in a cell that will produce gametes is reduced to one half. — **mei·ot·ic** \-'ät-ik\ *adj.*

mel·an·cho·lia \ˌmel-ən-'kō-lē-ə\ *n.* A mental disorder in which the patient suffers from extreme depression of spirits and brooding.

mel·an·choly \'mel-ən-ˌkäl-ē\ *n.; pl.* **mel·an·chol·ies.** Depression of spirits; dejection; sadness; as, to be overtaken by a fit of *melancholy.*

— The words *dejection* and *gloom* are synonyms of *melancholy: melancholy* usually suggests a mood of sadness and pensiveness, sometimes without apparent cause; *dejection* may apply to a listless mood in which one feels let down and disheartened, and usually applies to a temporary condition coming from some natural or logical cause; *gloom* usually refers to an over-all condition or mood of profound sadness and despair from which it seems impossible to raise one's spirits.

— *adj.* **1** Low-spirited; depressed; dejected. **2** Causing sadness; as, a *melancholy* event. **3** Pensive; seriously thoughtful.

mé·lange \mā-'länzh\ *n.* [French.] A mixture; a medley.

mel·a·nin \'mel-ə-nən\ *n.* One of the dark pigments that make the skin of some people darker than that of others.

me·lee \'mā-ˌlā, mā-'lā\ *n.* A confused fight or struggle; a hand-to-hand fight among a number of persons.

mel·io·rate \'mēl-yər-ˌāt\ *v.;* **mel·io·rat·ed; mel·io·rat·ing.** To make or become better; to improve. — **mel·io·ra·tion** \ˌmēl-yər-'āsh-n\ *n.*

mel·io·ra·tive \'mēl-yər-ˌāt-iv\ *adj.* Tending to improve.

mel·lif·lu·ous \mə-'lif-lə-wəs\ *adj.* Smoothly flowing; as, *mellifluous* speech. — **mel·lif·lu·ous·ly,** *adv.*

mel·lo·phone \'mel-ə-ˌfōn\ *n.* An althorn in circular form.

mel·low \'mel-ō\ *adj.* **1** So ripe as to be soft and tender; as, a *mellow* peach. **2** Easily worked, as soil. **3** Mature; fully developed; made gentle or sweet by age; as, the *mellow* judgment that comes with great experience. **4** Clear, full, and pure; not coarse or rough; as, a *mellow* sound; a *mellow* color. **5** Not harsh or acid; as, a *mellow* wine. — *v.* To make or become mellow.

me·lo·de·on \mə-'lōd-ē-ən\ *n.* A small reed organ in which a suction bellows draws air inward through the reeds.

me·lod·ic \mə-'läd-ik\ *adj.* **1** Relating to melody.

2 Made up of melody. — **me·lod·i·cal·ly** \-ik-l(-)ē\ *adv.*

me·lo·di·ous \mə-'lōd-ē-əs\ *adj.* Having or producing melody; pleasing to the ear because of its melody; tuneful. — **me·lo·di·ous·ly,** *adv.*

mel·o·dra·ma \'mel-ə-ˌdräm-ə, -ˌdram-ə, -ˌdråm-ə\ *n.* **1** A play having a great deal of exciting action and appealing strongly to the emotions but ending happily; originally, such a play with music interspersed throughout. **2** Plays of this type taken collectively. **3** Events or conduct having characteristics of melodrama.

mel·o·dra·mat·ic \ˌmel-ə-drə-'mat-ik\ *adj.* **1** Relating to melodrama. **2** Like melodrama; suitable for melodrama; sensational. — **mel·o·dra·mat·i·cal·ly** \-ik-l(-)ē\ *adv.*

mel·o·dy \'mel-əd-ē\ *n.; pl.* **mel·o·dies. 1** A pleasing succession of sounds; tunefulness. **2** In music, a rhythmical series of tones of a given key so arranged as to make a pleasing effect; an air; a tune. **3** The leading part in a song or other composition.

mel·on \'mel-ən\ *n.* **1** Any of the varieties of the muskmelon. **2** A watermelon. **3** The flesh or pulp of a melon.

melt \'melt\ *v.* **1** To change from a solid to a liquid state, usually through the application of heat; as, to *melt* sugar. Snow *melts.* **2** To dissolve, as sugar in the mouth. **3** To grow less; to disappear as if by dissolving; as, clouds *melting* away. **4** To make or become gentle; to soften; as, kindness that *melts* the heart. **5** To lose distinct outline or shape; to blend; to merge; as, sky *melting* into sea.

melt·ing pot \'mel-ting\. **1** A container capable of withstanding great heat, in which something can be melted; a crucible. **2** A place, as a city or country, in which various nationalities or races live together and gradually blend into one community.

mel·ton \'melt-n\ *n.* A smooth heavy woolen cloth with a short nap, used for overcoats.

mem·ber \'mem-br\ *n.* **1** A part of a person, animal, or plant, as an arm, leg, leaf, or branch. **2** One of the persons or animals belonging to a group; as, a club *member.* **3** One part of a whole structure, as one of the parts of a bridge or one of the sides of an algebraic equation.

mem·ber·ship \'mem-br-ˌship\ *n.* **1** The condition of being a member. **2** The total number of members.

mem·brane \'mem-ˌbrān\ *n.* A thin, soft, flexible layer of tissue, as in a plant or in the body of a person or an animal. — **mem·bra·nous** \'mem-brə-nəs, -ˌbrā-nəs\ *adj.*

me·men·to \mə-'men-ˌtō\ *n.; pl.* **me·men·tos** or **me·men·toes.** A reminder; a souvenir; as, *mementos* of a trip.

memo \'mem-ˌō\ *n.; pl.* **mem·os.** A memorandum.

mem·oir \'mem-ˌwär, 'mēm-, -ˌwȯr\ *n.* **1** A story of the facts or experiences in a person's own life. **2** A story about any person or event, based on close knowledge or study.

mem·o·ra·bil·ia \ˌmem-r-ə-'bil-ē-ə\ *n. pl.* **1** Things worthy of being remembered. **2** The record of such things.

mem·o·ra·ble \'mem-r(-)əb-l\ *adj.* Worth remembering; not easily forgotten; as, *memorable* days at camp. — **mem·o·ra·bly** \-r(-)ə-blē\ *adv.*

mem·o·ran·dum \ˌmem-r-'and-m\ *n.; pl.* **mem·o·ran·dums** \-'and-mz\ or **mem·o·ran·da** \-'an-də\. An informal record of something; a few words jotted down to be kept as a reminder.

me·mo·ri·al \mə-'mōr-ē-əl, -'mȯr-\ *adj.* Keeping up the memory of a person or an event; as, a *memorial* service. — *n.* **1** Something by which the memory of a person or an event is kept, as a building, custom, or record. **2** A statement of facts presented to an official, usually with a petition.

Memorial Day. An American holiday set aside for honoring dead soldiers and sailors, falling in most states on May 30 but in some former Confederate states variously on April 26, May 10, May 30, and June 3.

me·mo·ri·al·ize \mə-'mōr-ē-ə-ˌlīz, -'mȯr-\ *v.;* **me·mo·ri·al·ized; me·mo·ri·al·iz·ing. 1** To address with a memorial. **2** To commemorate.

mem·o·rize \'mem-r-ˌīz\ *v.;* **mem·o·rized; mem·o·riz·ing.** To learn by heart; to commit to memory. — **mem·o·ri·za·tion** \ˌmem-r-ə-'zāsh-n\ *n.*

mem·o·ry \'mem-r(-)ē\ *n.; pl.* **mem·o·ries. 1** The action or power of remembering anything. A good *memory* helps in spelling. **2** The sum of what can be remembered. **3** The length of time that something is remembered; as, within *memory.* **4** Something remembered; as, a summer that left many pleasant *memories.* **5** Remembrance. **6** A part in an electronic computer in which information can be stored for use when needed.

— The words *remembrance* and *recollection* are synonyms of *memory: memory* may apply to the general ability of the mind to bring something from the past into present conscious thoughts, or to the thing brought into mind in this way; *remembrance* is likely to suggest a particular act of bringing something to mind, often something held in honor or having pleasant associations; *recollection* usually differs from *remembrance* in stressing a conscious and sometimes difficult effort to remember, and in suggesting little about one's attitude toward the thing remembered.

men. Pl. of *man.*

men·ace \'men-əs\ *n.* A threat; as, the *menace* of disease. — *v.;* **men·aced; men·ac·ing.** To threaten; as, a village *menaced* by a tiger. — **men·ac·ing·ly** \'men-ə-sing-lē\ *adv.*

mé·nage or **me·nage** \mā-'näzh, -'nȧzh\ *n.* [French.] A household; as, a *ménage* consisting of husband, wife, child, and governess.

me·nag·er·ie \mə-'naj-r(-)ē, -'nazh-\ *n.* **1** A place where animals are kept and trained, especially for exhibition. **2** A collection of caged wild animals.

men-at-arms. Pl. of *man-at-arms.*

mend \'mend\ *v.* **1** To improve or correct a thing in some way; as, to *mend* one's manners. **2** To repair; as, to *mend* shoes or socks. **3** To improve, as in health. A good rest will *mend* the tired old lady. — *n.* **1** The act of repairing or improving; as, to be on the *mend* after an illness. **2** A place mended; as, a neat *mend* in a sock. — **mend·er**, *n.*

men·da·cious \men-'dā-shəs\ *adj.* Given to falsehood; lying. — **men·da·cious·ly**, *adv.*

men·dac·i·ty \men-'das-ət-ē\ *n.; pl.* **men·dac·i·ties. 1** The state of being mendacious. **2** A lie.

men·di·cant \'men-də-kənt\ *adj.* **1** Making a practice of begging; as, a *mendicant* tramp. **2** Living by charity, as members of certain religious orders who originally lived by alms. — *n.* **1** A beggar. **2** A member of a mendicant order. — **men·di·can·cy** \-kən-sē\ *n.*

men·folk \'men-ˌfōk\ or **men·folks** \-ˌfōks\ *n. pl.* **1** Men in general. **2** The men of a family or community.

men·ha·den \men-'hād-n, mən-\ *n. sing. and pl.* A fish of the herring family, found off the Atlantic coast of the United States, and used for bait or converted into oil and fertilizer.

me·ni·al \'mē-nē-əl, 'mēn-yəl\ *adj.* Having to do with, or suitable for, a servant; as, *menial* tasks. — *n.* A servant. — **me·ni·al·ly** \'mē-nē-ə-lē, 'mēn-yə-lē\ *adv.*

me·nin·ges \mə-'nin-ˌjēz\ *n. pl.; sing.* **me·ninx** \'mē-ˌningks\. The three membranes which envelop the brain and spinal cord. — **me·nin·ge·al** \mə-'nin-jē-əl\ *adj.*

men·in·gi·tis \ˌmen-ən-'jīt-əs\ *n.* A disease in which a membrane of the brain or spinal cord becomes inflamed.

men-of-war. Pl. of *man-of-war.*

menservants. Pl. of *manservant.*

men·ses \'men-ˌsēz\ *n. pl.* The monthly flow of bloody fluid from the uterus.

men·stru·al \'men(t)s-trə-wəl, 'men(t)s-trəl\ *adj.* **1** Monthly. **2** Relating to the menses.

men·stru·ate \'men(t)s-trə-ˌwāt, 'men(t)s-ˌtrāt\ *v.;* **men·stru·at·ed; men·stru·at·ing.** To discharge the menses. — **men·stru·a·tion** \ˌmen(t)s-trə-'wāsh-n, men-'strāsh-n\ *n.*

men·su·ra·tion \ˌmen(t)s-r-'āsh-n, ˌmench-r-\ *n.* **1** The process or art of measuring. **2** The branch of mathematics that deals with the measurement or finding of lengths, areas, and volumes.

-ment \mənt\. A suffix that can mean: **1** Something that results from or is subject to, as in *embankment.* **2** A thing that does or causes, as in *entanglement.* **3** The act, process, or art of, as in *government.* **4** The condition of being, as in *amazement.*

men·tal \'ment-l\ *adj.* **1** Having to do with the mind; of the mind; as, *mental* ability; *mental* deficiency. **2** Carried on in the mind; as, *mental* arithmetic. **3** Affected with a deficiency or disorder of the mind; as, a *mental* patient. **4** For care of persons with deficient or disordered minds; as, a *mental* hospital.

mental age. A measure used in psychological testing which expresses an individual's mental ability in terms of the number of years it takes the average child to reach that same ability.

men·tal·i·ty \men-'tal-ət-ē\ *n.; pl.* **men·tal·i·ties.** Mental power; especially, keenness or breadth of mind.

men·tal·ly \'ment-l-ē\ *adv.* In the mind; in thought or in thinking; as, *mentally* keen.

men·thol \'men-ˌthȯl\ *n.* A white, soothing substance from oil of peppermint.

men·tho·lat·ed \'men(t)th-l-ˌāt-əd\ *adj.* Treated with or containing menthol.

men·tion \'mench-n\ *n.* A brief reference to something; a passing remark or remarks; as, to make *mention* of the fact that one has been ill. Any *mention* of his mistake will be very unwelcome to that boy. — *v.;* **men·tioned; men·tion·ing** \-n(-)ing\. To refer to; to discuss or speak about briefly; as, to *mention* a moving picture one has seen. Don't *mention* that boy to me. — **men·tion·a·ble** \-n(-)əb-l\ *adj.*

men·tor \'ment-r, 'men-ˌtȯr\ *n.* A wise and faithful adviser.

menu \'men-ˌyü, 'mān-\ *n.; pl.* **men·us.** [From French meaning literally "details" and derived from the adjective *menu* meaning "small".] **1** A list of dishes served at a meal; a bill of fare. **2** The dishes or kinds of food served.

me·ow \mē-'au̇\ *n.* The sound made by a cat or kitten. — *v.* To mew.

mer·can·tile \'mərk-n-ˌtēl, -ˌtīl\ *adj.* Of or relating to merchants or trade; as, a fleet of *mercantile* ships.

mer·ce·nary \'mərs-n-ˌer-ē\ *adj.* Doing something only for the pay or reward. — *n.; pl.* **mer·ce·nar·ies.** A soldier hired by a foreign nation to fight in its army.

mer·cer \'mərs-r\ *n. British.* A dealer in textiles, especially silk and other expensive fabrics.

mer·cer·ize \'mərs-r-ˌīz\ *v.;* **mer·cer·ized; mer·cer·iz·ing.** To treat cotton fiber or fabrics so that the fibers are strengthened, take dyes better, and often acquire a sheen.

mer·chan·dise \'mərch-n-ˌdīz, -ˌdīs\ *n.* The goods that are bought and sold in trade. — *v.;* **mer·chan·dised; mer·chan·dis·ing.** To trade or deal in; especially, to try to further sales or the use of merchandise or services by attractive presentation and publicity.

mer·chant \'mərch-nt\ *n.* **1** A person who carries on trade, especially on a large scale or with foreign countries. **2** A storekeeper. — *adj.* Relating to or used in trade; of the merchant marine; commercial.

mer·chant·man \'mərch-nt-mən, -ˌman\ *n.; pl.* **mer·chant·men** \-mən, -ˌmen\. A boat used especially in trading.

merchant marine. 1 The trading ships of a nation. **2** The persons manning such ships.

mer·ci·ful \'mər-sēf-l, -səf-l\ *adj.* Having or showing mercy; compassionate. — For synonyms see *humane.* — **mer·ci·ful·ly** \-l-ē\ *adv.*

mer·ci·less \ˈmər-sē-ləs, ˈmərs-l-əs\ *adj.* Without mercy; pitiless. — **mer·ci·less·ly,** *adv.*

mer·cu·ri·al \mər-ˈkyůr-ē-əl\ *adj.* **1** Having qualities associated with being born under the planet Mercury or attributed to the god Mercury; swift; clever; fickle; changeable. **2** Of, relating to, containing, or caused by the element mercury; as, *mercurial* medical preparations; a *mercurial* thermometer. — *n.* A drug containing mercury.

mer·cu·ric \mər-ˈkyůr-ik\ *adj.* Of, relating to, or containing mercury.

mer·cu·ry \ˈmərk-yər-ē, ˈmərk-r(-)ē\ *n.; pl.* **mer·cu·ries. 1** A messenger; a guide. **2** A heavy, silver-white metallic element, the only metal that is liquid at ordinary temperatures; quicksilver. **3** The column of mercury in a thermometer or barometer.

mer·cy \ˈmər-sē\ *n.; pl.* **mer·cies. 1** Kind and gentle treatment of an offender, an opponent, or some unfortunate person. **2** A kind, sympathetic manner or disposition; a willingness to forgive, to spare, or to help. **3** The power to be merciful; as, to throw oneself on an enemy's *mercy.* **4** An act of kindness; a blessing.

— The words *clemency* and *leniency* are synonyms of *mercy: mercy* usually refers to a compassionate and forgiving attitude on the part of a person who has the power or right to impose severe punishment on another; *clemency* may indicate a habit or policy of moderation and mildness in one whose duty it is to impose punishment for offences; *leniency* often indicates a deliberate overlooking of mistakes or an overindulgent acceptance of another's faults.

mere \ˈmir\ *n. Archaic* or *Dial.* A sheet of standing water; a lake or pool.

mere \ˈmir\ *adj.; superlative* **mer·est** \ˈmir-əst\. Only this, and nothing else; nothing more than; simple; as, a *mere* whisper; a *mere* child.

mere·ly \ˈmir-lē\ *adv.* Not otherwise than; simply; only.

mer·e·tri·cious \ˌmer-ə-ˈtrish-əs\ *adj.* Attracting by a display of showy but superficial and tawdry charms; falsely attractive. — **mer·e·tri·cious·ly,** *adv.*

mer·gan·ser \(ˌ)mər-ˈgan(t)s-r\ *n.; pl.* **mer·gan·sers** or **mer·gan·ser.** A fish-eating wild duck with a slender, hooked beak and, usually, a crested head.

merge \ˈmərj\ *v.;* **merged; merg·ing. 1** To be or cause to be swallowed up, combined, or absorbed in or within something else; to mingle; to blend; as, *merging* traffic. **2** To combine or unite, as two business firms into one.

merg·er \ˈmərj-r\ *n.* **1** The combining of business concerns or interests into one. **2** The resulting business unit.

me·rid·i·an \mə-ˈrid-ē-ən\ *adj.* **1** At or relating to midday. **2** Of or relating to a meridian. — *n.* **1** The highest apparent point reached by the sun or a star. **2** The highest point, as of success or importance; culmination. **3** An imaginary great circle on the earth's surface, passing through the North and South Poles and any given place between. **4** The half of such a circle included between the poles. **5** A representation of such a circle or half circle on a globe or map; any of a series of lines drawn at intervals due north and south or in the direction of the poles and numbered according to the degrees of longitude.

me·ringue \mə-ˈrang\ *n.* A mixture of beaten white of egg and sugar, put on pies or cakes and browned, or shaped into small cakes or shells and baked.

me·ri·no \mə-ˈrē-ˌnō\ *n.; pl.* **me·ri·nos. 1** A fine-wooled white sheep of a breed marked by the heavy twisted horns of the male. **2** A fine soft fabric resembling cashmere and originally made of the wool from this sheep. **3** A fine wool yarn.

merino

mer·it \ˈmer-ət\ *n.* **1** Due reward or punishment; especially, deserved reward; a mark or token of excellence or approval. **2** The condition or fact of deserving well or ill; desert; as, each according to his *merit.* **3** Worth; excellence; as, a suggestion having considerable *merit.* **4** A quality or act worthy of praise; as, an answer that at least had the *merit* of honesty. — *v.* To earn by service or performance; to deserve; as, a man who *merited* respect.

mer·i·to·ri·ous \ˌmer-ə-ˈtōr-ē-əs, -ˈtòr-\ *adj.* Deserving reward or honor; praiseworthy. — **mer·i·to·ri·ous·ly,** *adv.*

mer·maid \ˈmər-ˌmād\ *n.* [From medieval English *mermaide,* a compound formed from *mere* meaning "sea" and *maide* meaning "girl", "maid".] An imaginary sea creature usually represented with a woman's body and a fish's tail.

mer·man \ˈmər-ˌman, -mən\ *n.;* **mer·men** \-ˌmen, -mən\. An imaginary sea creature usually represented with a man's body and a fish's tail.

mer·ri·ment \ˈmer-ē-mənt, -ə-mənt\ *n.* Gaiety; mirth; fun.

mer·ry \ˈmer-ē\ *adj.;* **mer·ri·er; mer·ri·est. 1** Full of good humor and good spirits; laughingly gay. **2** Marked by gaiety or festivity; as, a *merry* Christmas. — **mer·ri·ly** \ˈmer-ə-lē\ *adv.*

mer·ry–an·drew \ˈmer-ē-ˈan-ˌdrü\ *n.* A clown; a buffoon.

mer·ry–go–round \ˈmer-ē-gō-ˌraůnd\ *n.* **1** A circular revolving platform fitted with seats and figures of animals on which people sit for a ride. **2** Any rapid round of activities; a whirl; as, a *merry-go-round* of parties.

merry-go-round

mer·ry·mak·ing \ˈmer-ē-ˌmāk-ing\ *adj.* Festive; jolly. — *n.* **1** The act of making merry; merriment. **2** A frolic; a festivity. — **mer·ry·mak·er** \-ˌmāk-r\ *n.*

me·sa \ˈmā-sə\ *n.* A flat-topped hill or small plateau with steep sides.

mes·cal \mes-ˈkal\ *n.* **1** A small, spineless cactus

having rounded stems or joints covered by tubercles with button-shaped tops. **2** A colorless liquor made from the pulp of this plant. **3** Any plant from which this liquor can be made.

mesdames. Pl. of *madam* or *madame.*

mesdemoiselles. Pl. of *mademoiselle.*

me·seems \mē-ˈsēmz\ *v.; past tense* **me·seemed** \-ˈsēmd\. *Archaic.* It seems to me.

mes·en·tery \ˈmes-n-ˌter-ē\ *n.; pl.* **mes·en·ter·ies.** The membranes or one of the membranes that envelop the intestines and connect them with the dorsal wall of the abdominal cavity. — **mes·en·ter·ic** \ˌmes-n-ˈter-ik\ *adj.*

mesh \ˈmesh\ *n.* **1** One of the open spaces formed by the threads of a net or the wires of a sieve or screen. **2** A net or network. **3** The coming or fitting together of the teeth of two sets of gears. — *v.* **1** To catch in, or as if in, meshes; to entangle. **2** To make something into a net or network. **3** To fit together or interlock, as the teeth of gears.

mes·mer·ism \ˈmez-mə-ˌriz-m, ˈmes-\ *n.* Hypnotism.

mes·mer·ize \ˈmez-mə-ˌrīz, ˈmes-\ *v.;* **mes·mer·ized; mes·mer·iz·ing.** To hypnotize.

mes·o·derm \ˈmes-ə-ˌdərm, ˈmez-\ *n.* The middle layer of cells of an animal in the embryonic stage, from which develop most of the muscular, skeletal, and connective tissues of the individual.

mes·on \ˈmes-ˌän, ˈmez-; ˈmē-ˌsän, -ˌzän\ *n.* A particle having a mass between that of the electron and the proton and being either positively or negatively charged or neutral.

mes·o·tron \ˈmes-ə-ˌträn, ˈmez-\ *n.* A meson.

mes·quite \mə-ˈskēt, me-\ *n.* A thorny, deep-rooted desert tree or shrub belonging to the mimosa family and found in the southwestern United States and Mexico.

mess \ˈmes\ *n.* **1** A quantity of food; a dish of soft or liquid food; as, a *mess* of porridge. **2** A group of people who regularly eat together; the meal they eat; as, to be absent from *mess.* **3** A confused heap; a state of confusion or disorder; as, to leave things in a *mess.* — *v.* **1** To supply with meals. **2** To eat regularly with a certain group. **3** To make a mess of. **4** To potter; to meddle; as, to *mess* about with machinery.

mes·sage \ˈmes-ij\ *n.* **1** Any information, notice, news, or instruction sent from one person to another. **2** A messenger's errand.

messeigneurs. Pl. of *monseigneur.*

mes·sen·ger \ˈmes-nj-r\ *n.* **1** A person or thing that carries a message or does an errand. **2** A herald; a forerunner; as, the *messengers* of spring.

Mes·si·ah \mə-ˈsī-ə\ *n.* **1** The expected king and deliverer of the Jews. **2** In Christian use, Jesus Christ. **3** [often with a small letter] Any deliverer or savior, especially of a whole people.

messieurs. Pl. of *monsieur.*

mess·mate \ˈmes-ˌmāt\ *n.* A member of a group of persons who regularly eat together.

Messrs. \ˈmes-rz\. Abbreviation of *Messieurs* — used as a plural of *Mr.*, as in *Messrs.* Brown, Smith, and Jones.

messy \ˈmes-ē\ *adj.;* **mess·i·er; mess·i·est.** Untidy; upset; as, a *messy* room.

mes·ti·za \mes-ˈtē-zə\ *n.; pl.* **mes·ti·zas.** A woman who is a mestizo.

mes·ti·zo \mes-ˈtē-ˌzō\ *n.; pl.* **mes·ti·zos.** A person of mixed blood; especially, one of Spanish and American Indian parentage.

met. Past tense and past part. of *meet.*

me·tab·o·lism \mə-ˈtab-l-ˌiz-m\ *n.* The sum of the processes by which protoplasm of plants and animals is built up and destroyed in furnishing energy for life. — **met·a·bol·ic** \ˌmet-ə-ˈbäl-ik\ *adj.*

met·a·car·pus \ˌmet-ə-ˈkärp-əs, -ˈkȧrp-əs\ *n.* The part of the hand or forefoot, especially the skeleton, between the carpus and the phalanges. — **met·a·car·pal** \-ˈkärp-l, -ˈkȧrp-l\ *adj.*

met·al \ˈmet-l\ *n.* **1** Any of certain substances, such as gold, tin, copper, or bronze, that have a peculiar shiny changeable color, are solid and heavy, are good conductors of electricity, and can be shaped and blended with other metals. **2** A simple metal like iron, distinguished from an alloy like bronze. **3** Material; temper; mettle; as, a man of stern *metal.* — *adj.* Made of metal.

me·tal·lic \mə-ˈtal-ik\ *adj.* Of, like, or having to do with metal; containing or made of metal.

met·al·lur·gy \ˈmet-l-ˌər-jē\ *n.* The science of extracting metals from their ores, refining them, and preparing them for use. — **met·al·lur·gi·cal** \ˌmet-l-ˈər-jik-l\ *adj.* — **met·al·lur·gist** \ˈmet-l-ˌər-jəst\ *n.*

met·al·work \ˈmet-l-ˌwərk\ *n.* **1** Metalworking. **2** Work, especially artistic work, made of metal.

met·al·work·er \ˈmet-l-ˌwərk-r\ *n.* One who makes or shapes things out of metal.

met·al·work·ing \ˈmet-l-ˌwərk-ing\ *n.* The process or occupation of making things from metal.

met·a·mor·phism \ˌmet-ə-ˈmȯr-ˌfiz-m\ *n.* **1** Metamorphosis. **2** A change in the structure of rock, especially a change to a more compact, more highly crystalline condition, produced by such forces as pressure, heat, and water. Marble is produced by the *metamorphism* of limestone. — **met·a·mor·phic** \-ˈmȯr-fik\ *adj.*

met·a·mor·phose \ˌmet-ə-ˈmȯr-ˌfōz, -ˌfōs\ *v.;* **met·a·mor·phosed; met·a·mor·phos·ing.** To change or cause to change in form.

met·a·mor·pho·sis \ˌmet-ə-ˈmȯr-fə-səs\ *n.; pl.* **met·a·mor·pho·ses** \-ˌsēz\. **1** A change of form, structure, or substance, especially by witchcraft or magic. **2** A striking alteration in appearance, character, or circumstances. **3** A fundamental and usually rather abrupt change in the form and often the habits of certain animals that occurs during the transformation of the larva into an adult, as the transformation of a tadpole into a frog or that of a wingless grub into a winged insect during pupation.

met·a·phor \ˈmet-ə-ˌfȯr, -əf-r\ *n.* A figure of speech by which two things are compared, not through the use of *like* or *as* but by speaking of one thing as if it were the other thing; as in "a sudden explosion of laughter".

met·a·phor·i·cal \ˌmet-ə-'fȯr-ik-l, -'fär-\ or **met·a·phor·ic** \-ik\ *adj.* Of or relating to a metaphor; made up of a metaphor. — **met·a·phor·i·cal·ly** \-ik-l(-)ē\ *adv.*

met·a·phys·i·cal \ˌmet-ə-'fiz-ik-l\ *adj.* **1** Of, relating to, or based on metaphysics. **2** Abstract; subtle. **3** Hard to understand. — **met·a·phys·i·cal·ly** \-ik-l(-)ē\ *adv.*

met·a·phys·ics \ˌmet-ə-'fiz-iks\ *n.* The part of philosophy concerned with the study of things in regard to their ultimate causes and their underlying but unseen nature; often, pure philosophy, as distinguished from branches of philosophy having a practical bearing, as logic.

met·a·tar·sus \ˌmet-ə-'tär-səs, -'tȧr-\ *n.; pl.* **met·a·tar·si** \-ˌsī\. The part of the foot, especially the skeleton, between the tarsus and the phalanges. — **met·a·tar·sal** \-'tärs-l, -'tȧrs-l\ *adj.*

met·a·zo·an \ˌmet-ə-'zō-ən\ *n.; pl.* **met·a·zo·ans.** Any of the great group of animals having a body composed of more than one cell.

mete \'mēt\ *v.;* **met·ed; met·ing.** To measure and distribute; to allot; as, to *mete* out punishment or reward.

me·te·or \'mēt-ē-ər, -ē-ˌȯr\ *n.* A shooting star; a small mass that travels through space at great speed and starts to burn as it enters the earth's atmosphere.

me·te·or·ic \ˌmēt-ē-'ȯr-ik, -'är-\ *adj.* **1** Of or having to do with a meteor or meteors; as, a *meteoric* shower. **2** Like a meteor in speed or brilliance; flashing and going out; as, a *meteoric* career.

me·te·or·ite \'mēt-ē-ə-ˌrīt\ *n.* A stony or metallic mass that falls to the earth from outer space.

me·te·o·ro·log·i·cal \ˌmēt-ē-ər-ə-'läj-ik-l\ or **me·te·o·ro·log·ic** \-ik\ *adj.* Of or relating to the atmosphere and its phenomena or to meteorology.

me·te·o·rol·o·gist \ˌmēt-ē-ə-'räl-ə-jəst\ *n.* A specialist in meteorology.

me·te·o·rol·o·gy \ˌmēt-ē-ə-'räl-ə-jē\ *n.* The science that collects, studies, and explains facts about the atmosphere, winds, and weather.

me·ter or **me·tre** \'mēt-r\ *n.* **1** Rhythm in poetry when it follows a definite pattern. **2** Rhythm in music. **3** A measure of length, equal to 39.37 inches, which is the basis of the metric system.

me·ter \'mēt-r\ *n.* An instrument for measuring and, usually, recording the amount of something; as, a gas *meter.*

meth·ane \'meth-ˌān\ *n.* An odorless flammable gas produced by decomposition of organic matter in marshes and mines, and also by distillation.

me·thinks \mē-'thingks\ *v.; past tense* **me·thought** \-'thȯt\. *Archaic.* It seems to me.

meth·od \'meth-əd\ *n.* **1** The regular way of doing something; as, a *method* of teaching. **2** Orderly arrangement; regularity; orderliness; as, a pupil whose work lacks *method.*

me·thod·i·cal \mə-'thäd-ik-l\ *adj.* Having or showing method; done with method; as, a *methodical* plan; a *methodical* worker. — **me·thod·i·cal·ly** \-ik-l(-)ē\ *adv.*

me·tic·u·lous \mə-'tik-yə-ləs\ *adj.* Careful or too careful in small details. — **me·tic·u·lous·ly**, *adv.*

metre. Variant of *meter.*

met·ric \'me-trik\ *adj.* **1** Having to do with measurement; especially, having to do with the metric system. **2** Having to do with poetic or musical meter; metrical.

met·ri·cal \'me-trik-l\ *adj.* **1** Having to do with meter, as in poetry or music; arranged in meter. **2** Having to do with measurement or the metric system; metric. — **met·ri·cal·ly** \-trik-l(-)ē\ *adv.*

metric system. A decimal system of weights and measures in which the meter is the unit of length and the gram is the unit of weight.

metric ton. A weight of 1000 kilograms, or 2204.6 pounds.

met·ro·nome \'me-trə-ˌnōm\ *n.* An instrument that ticks loudly to help a music pupil play in exact time. — **met·ro·nom·ic** \ˌme-trə-'näm-ik\ *adj.*

metronome

me·trop·o·lis \mə-'träp-l(-)əs\ *n.* [From Late Latin, there borrowed from Greek, meaning literally "mother city".] **1** The chief city or capital city of a country, state, or region. New York is an American *metropolis.* **2** Any very large city. **3** An important center; as, a *metropolis* of art.

met·ro·pol·i·tan \ˌme-trə-'päl-ət-n\ *adj.* Of, relating to, or being a metropolis; as, the *metropolitan* area. — *n.* A person who lives in a metropolis or large city; a person who has the manners or ideas of a metropolis.

met·tle \'met-l\ *n.* Temperament; courage; spirit; as, to prove one's *mettle.* — **on one's mettle.** Inspired to put forth one's best efforts.

met·tle·some \'met-ls-m\ *adj.* Full of mettle or spirit; fiery.

mew \'myü\ *n.* A sea gull.

mew \'myü\ *n.* **1** A cage, as for hawks or falcons. **2** [in the plural] A group of stables built around a courtyard — used as a singular. — *v.* To shut up in or as if in a cage.

mew \'myü\ *n.* The characteristic cry of a cat or kitten. — *v.* To utter a mew.

mewl \'myül\ *v.* To cry weakly; to whimper.

Mex·i·can \'meks-ik-n\ *adj.* Of or relating to Mexico. — *n.* A native or inhabitant of Mexico.

mez·za·nine \'mez-n-ˌēn\ *n.* An intermediate story in a building, usually coming between the first and second stories, and often extending over only part of the floor below.

mez·zo \'met-ˌsō, 'med-ˌzō\ *adj.* In music, moderate; not extreme; as, *mezzo* forte.

mez·zo-so·prano \'met-ˌsō-sə-'pran-ō, 'med-ˌzō-, -'prän-, -'prȧn-\ *n.; pl.* **mez·zo-so·pran·os. 1** In music, a woman's voice having a full, deep quality between that of the soprano and contralto. **2** A singer having such a voice.

mez·zo·tint \'met-ˌsō-ˌtint, 'med-ˌzō-\ *n.* **1** A process of engraving on copper or steel by scraping or burnishing a roughened surface to produce light and shade. **2** An engraving produced in this way.

mfg. Abbreviation for *manufacturing.*

mfr. Abbreviation for *manufacturer.*

mg. Abbreviation for *milligram.*

Mgr. Abbreviation for: **1** *manager.* **2** *Monseigneur.* **3** *Monsignor.*

mi \'mē\ *n.* A syllable used in music to name the third note of the scale.

mi. Abbreviation for *mile.*

mi·as·ma \mī-'az-mə, mē-'áz-\ *n.* **1** A harmful vapor formerly supposed to come from rotting matter or swamps, especially at night. **2** Any harmful influence or atmosphere.

mi·ca \'mīk-ə\ *n.* Any of certain minerals that may be separated easily into thin, often somewhat flexible and transparent sheets.

mice. Pl. of *mouse.*

Mich·ael·mas \'mik-l-məs\ *n.* September 29, the feast of the archangel Michael.

mi·crobe \'mīk-ˌrōb\ *n.* **1** A germ; a plant or animal so small that it can be seen only through a microscope. **2** A bacterium, especially one that causes disease. — **mi·cro·bi·al** \mī-'krō-bē-əl\ *adj.* — **mi·cro·bic** \mī-'krō-bik\ *adj.*

mi·cro·bi·ol·o·gist \ˌmīk-rō-bī-'äl-ə-jəst\ *n.* One who specializes in microbiology.

mi·cro·bi·ol·o·gy \ˌmīk-rō-bī-'äl-ə-jē\ *n.* A branch of biology that deals especially with microscopic forms of life, as bacteria, protozoans, and viruses. — **mi·cro·bi·o·log·ic** \-ˌbī-ə-'läj-ik\ *adj.* — **mi·cro·bi·o·log·i·cal** \-ik-l\ *adj.* — **mi·cro·bi·o·log·i·cal·ly** \-ik-l(-)ē\ *adv.*

mi·cro·cosm \'mīk-rə-ˌkäz-m\ *n.* A little world; especially, something, as man or a community, thought of as a miniature of the universe or as a world in itself.

mi·cro·film \'mīk-rə-ˌfilm\ *n.* A small-sized strip of film for making photographs that can be stored or shipped in small space. — *v.* To photograph on microfilm.

mi·cro·gram \'mīk-rō-ˌgram\ *n.* One millionth of a gram.

mi·crom·e·ter \mī-'kräm-ət-r\ *n.* **1** An instrument used with a telescope or microscope for measuring very small distances. **2** In full, **micrometer caliper.** A caliper having a screw with fine threads and a graduated head, used for exact measurement.

micrometer, 2

mi·cro-or·gan·ism \ˌmīk-rō-'órg-n-ˌiz-m\ *n.* Any organism of microscopic size or smaller; especially, a bacterium — also written *microörganism* or *microorganism.*

mi·cro·phone \'mīk-rə-ˌfōn\ *n.* An instrument used in increasing or transmitting sounds, especially one used in radio and television to receive sound and convert it into electrical waves.

mi·cro·scope \'mīk-rə-ˌskōp\ *n.* An optical instrument consisting of a lens or a combination of lenses for making enlarged or magnified images of minute objects.

microscope

mi·cro·scop·ic \ˌmīk-rə-'skäp-ik\ *adj.* **1** Of, relating to, or conducted with the microscope or microscopy; as, a *microscopic* examination. **2** Like a microscope; able to see very tiny objects. Some insects have *microscopic* vision. **3** Able to be seen only through a microscope; very small; as, a *microscopic* plant. — **mi·cro·scop·i·cal·ly** \-ik-l(-)ē\ *adv.*

mi·cros·co·py \mī-'kräs-kə-pē, 'mīk-rə-ˌskōp-ē\ *n.* The use of the microscope; investigation with the microscope. — **mi·cros·co·pist** \mī-'kräs-kə-pəst, 'mīk-rə-ˌskōp-əst\ *n.*

mi·cro·wave \'mīk-rō-ˌwāv\ *n.* Any radio wave between 1 and 100 centimeters in wave length.

mid \'mid\ *adj.; superlative* **mid·most** \'mid-ˌmōst\. Pointing out or being the middle part; middle.

mid- \(')mid\. A prefix that can mean: the middle or the middle part of the thing named, as in *midday* or *midsummer.*

'mid \(')mid\. Short for *amid.*

mid-air \'mid-'ar, -'er\ *n.* A position or point referred to as above the ground surface but low enough to be within a person's perception. The two planes collided in *mid-air.*

mid·day \'mid-ˌdā, -'dā\ *n.* The middle part of the day; noon. — *adj.* Of or relating to the middle of the day; as, a *midday* meal.

mid·dle \'mid-l\ *n.* **1** The point or part equally distant from the ends or sides; the center; as, the *middle* of a room. **2** The waist. The dressmaker will take in the dress around the *middle.* — *adj.* **1** Occupying or belonging to the middle; as, the *middle* house in a row. **2** Occupying any intermediate or halfway position; as, of *middle* size.

mid·dle-aged \'mid-l-'ājd\ *adj.* Being about the middle of the ordinary age of man.

Middle Ages. The period between ancient and modern times, from the fall of the Roman Empire in A.D. 476 to about 1400.

middle C. The note designated by the first ledger line below the treble staff and the first above the bass staff.

middle class. The large majority of the people of the United States and the United Kingdom that is now made up chiefly of business and professional men and women, and skilled wage earners.

middle ear. A small irregular membrane-lined cavity that is separated from the outer ear by the eardrum and that transmits sound waves picked up by the eardrum to the partition between the middle and inner ears.

Middle East. A region comprising southern and southwestern Asia and northeastern Africa, including the Near East and those countries extending to the borders of the Far East.

mid·dle·man \'mid-l-ˌman\ *n.; pl.* **mid·dle·men** \-ˌmen\. A go-between; especially, a person who deals in goods in any of the steps between the original producer and a retail merchant.

mid·dle·most \'mid-l-ˌmōst\ *adj.* Midmost.

mid·dle·weight \'mid-l-ˌwāt\ *n.* One of average weight; especially, in boxing and wrestling, one weighing between 147 and 160 pounds.

Middle West. The part of the United States from the Rocky Mountains to the Allegheny Mountains, north of the Ohio River and the southern boundaries of Missouri and Kansas. — **Middle Western.** — **Middle Westerner.**

mid·dling \'mid-ling\ *adj.* Of medium size, amount, or rank; neither good nor bad; as, a person of *middling* height. — *adv.* Moderately, rather; as, a *middling* good movie. — *n.* [usually in the plural] Any of various commodities of middle quality or size, as the medium-sized particles separated in the sifting of ground grain used in making the finest flour.

mid·dy \'mid-ē\ *n.; pl.* **mid·dies. 1** A midshipman. **2** Also **middy blouse.** A loose blouse with a collar cut wide and square in the back, worn by women and children.

midge \'mij\ *n.* Any very small fly or gnat.

midg·et \'mij-ət\ *n.* A very small person.

mid·land \'mid-lənd\ *n.* [usually in the plural] The inland or central part of a country. — *adj.* Inland.

mid·most \'mid-ˌmōst\ *adj.* Superlative of *mid.* In the exact middle.

mid·night \'mid-ˌnīt\ *n.* The middle of the night; twelve o'clock at night.

mid·rib \'mid-ˌrib\ *n.* The central vein of a leaf.

mid·riff \'mid-ˌrif\ *n.* A wall of muscle and sinew between the chest cavity and the abdomen; the diaphragm.

mid·ship·man \'mid-ˌship-mən, (')mid-'ship-\ *n.; pl.* **mid·ship·men** \-mən\. **1** In the British navy, a subordinate officer, usually a minor, who is being trained on shipboard for promotion to the rank of sublieutenant. **2** In the American navy, a student at the United States Naval Academy.

mid·ships \'mid-ˌships\ *adv.* Amidships.

midst \'midst\ *n.* The inside or central part; middle; as, a scream from the *midst* of the crowd; to be interrupted in the *midst* of one's homework. — *prep.* In the midst of; amidst.

mid·stream \'mid-'strēm\ *n.* The middle of a stream.

mid·sum·mer \'mid-'səm-r, -ˌsəm-r\ *n.* **1** The middle of summer. **2** The period about the summer solstice, or June 22.

mid·way \'mid-'wā\ *adv.* or *adj.* Halfway or about halfway; in or to the middle. — \'mid-ˌwā\ *n.* A central avenue at a fair or exposition, often used for side shows and other amusements.

mid·week \'mid-ˌwēk\ *n.* **1** The middle of the week. **2** [with a capital] Among Quakers, Wednesday. — **mid·week·ly** \'mid-ˌwēk-lē, (')mid-'wēk-lē\ *adj.*

Mid·west \'mid-'west\ *n.* The Middle West. — **Mid·west·ern** \-'west-rn\ *adj.* — **Mid·west·ern·er** \-'west-rn-r\ *n.*

mid·wife \'mid-ˌwīf\ *n.; pl.* **mid·wives** \-ˌwīvz\. A woman who helps other women in childbirth.

mid·wife·ry \'mid-ˌwīf-r(-)ē\ *n.* The art or the practice of assisting women in childbirth.

mid·win·ter \'mid-'wint-r, -ˌwint-r\ *n.* **1** The middle of winter. **2** The period about the winter solstice, or December 22.

mid·year \'mid-ˌyir\ *adj.* Occurring in the middle of a year, especially a school year. — *n.* **1** A midyear examination. **2** [in the plural] The period of midyear examinations.

mien \'mēn\ *n.* The manner, looks, or bearing of a person; appearance; air; as, a man of kindly *mien;* an aristocratic *mien.*

might \'mīt\. Past tense of *may.* **1** Had or would have permission to; was, were, or would be allowed to. I asked the teacher if I *might* leave early. **2** Was or were very slightly likely to; would be under certain circumstances likely to. He *might* help you if you asked him.

might \'mīt\ *n.* Power to do something; force or power of any kind; as, to hit a ball with all one's *might;* the *might* of Niagara Falls.

might·i·ly \'mīt-l-ē\ *adv.* **1** In a mighty manner; with great force, power, or effort; as, to strive *mightily* to win. **2** To a great degree; very much; as, *mightily* amused.

mightn't \'mīt-nt\. A contraction of *might not.*

mighty \'mīt-ē\ *adj.;* **might·i·er**; **might·i·est. 1** Powerful; strong; as, a *mighty* army. **2** Done by might; showing great power; as, *mighty* deeds. **3** Great, as in influence, result, or size; as, a *mighty* famine. — *adv.* Very; extremely; as, a *mighty* important message.

mi·gnon·ette \ˌmin-yə-'net\ *n.* A garden plant with long spikes of small, fragrant, greenish-white flowers.

mi·graine \'mī-ˌgrān\ *n.* A nervous headache, usually confined to one side of the head.

mi·grant \'mīg-rənt\ *adj.* Migrating; migratory. — *n.* A person, animal, or plant that migrates.

mi·grate \'mī-ˌgrāt\ *v.;* **mi·grat·ed**; **mi·grat·ing. 1** To move from one country or region to another with the intention of settling there. **2** To move periodically from one region or climate to another for feeding or breeding, as various birds.

mi·gra·tion \mī-'grāsh-n\ *n.* **1** The action of migrating. **2** An instance of migration. **3** A group of individuals that are migrating.

mi·gra·to·ry \'mīg-rə-ˌtōr-ē, -ˌtȯr-ē\ *adj.* **1** Of or relating to migration. **2** Migrating; especially, habitually or repeatedly migrating; as, *migratory* birds; *migratory* workers.

mi·ka·do \mə-'käd-ˌō, -'kȧd-\ *n.; pl.* **mi·ka·dos.** The emperor of Japan.

mike \'mīk\ *n.* A microphone.

milch \'milk, 'milch, 'milks\ *adj.* Giving milk; kept for milking; as, a *milch* cow.

mild \'mīld\ *adj.* **1** Gentle in nature or behavior; as, a *mild* man. **2** Expressive of gentleness; as, a *mild* manner. **3** Moderate; not severe or harsh; as, a *mild* winter; a *mild* case of measles. **4** Not strong or bitter to the taste; as, *mild* cheese. — **mild·ly,** *adv.*

mil·dew \'mil-ˌdü, -ˌdyü\ *n.* **1** A thin whitish growth produced on plants and other organic matter by fungi. **2** Any fungus that produces mildew. — *v.* To become covered with or affected by mildew.

mile \'mīl\ *n.* [From Old English *mil,* there borrowed from Latin *milia,* short for *milia pasuum* meaning "a thousand paces".] A measure of distance, the ordinary mile (**statute mile**) being 5,280 feet in length and the sea mile (**geographical mile** or **nautical mile**) about 6,080 feet in length.

mile·age \'mī-lij\ *n.* **1** An allowance for traveling expenses at a certain rate per mile. **2** Distance in miles. **3** Speed measured in miles. **4** The number of miles that something, as a car or tire, will travel before wearing out.

mile·post \'mīl-ˌpōst\ *n.* A post indicating the distance in miles from a stated point.

mil·er \'mīl-r\ *n.* A man or a horse specially qualified or trained to race a mile.

mile·stone \'mīl-ˌstōn\ *n.* **1** A stone serving as a milepost. **2** An important event in a person's life or in history.

mil·i·tant \'mil-ə-tənt\ *adj.* **1** Engaged in warfare; fighting. **2** Inclined to fight; warlike; aggressive. — **mil·i·tan·cy** \-tən-sē\ *adv.* — **mil·i·tant·ly,** *adv.*

mil·i·tar·i·ly \ˌmil-ə-'ter-ə-lē\ *adv.* **1** In a military manner. **2** From a military standpoint.

mil·i·ta·rism \'mil-ə-tə-ˌriz-m\ *n.* **1** Control or domination of a country by a military class. **2** A tendency to enforce one's demands by the use of military power. **3** A tendency or inclination towards maintaining large military forces in a high degree of readiness for action.

mil·i·ta·rist \'mil-ə-tər-əst\ *n.* **1** An expert in military matters. **2** A supporter of militarism.

mil·i·ta·ris·tic \ˌmil-ə-tə-'ris-tik\ *adj.* Of or relating to militarism or militarists. — **mil·i·ta·ris·ti·cal·ly** \-tik-l(-)ē\ *adv.*

mil·i·ta·rize \'mil-ə-tə-ˌrīz\ *v.;* **mil·i·ta·rized; mil·i·ta·riz·ing.** To bring into any condition of militarism. — **mil·i·ta·ri·za·tion** \ˌmil-ə-tər-ə-'zāsh-n\ *n.*

mil·i·tary \'mil-ə-ˌter-ē\ *adj.* **1** Of or relating to soldiers, armed forces in general, or war; as, *military* drill; *military* supplies. **2** Suitable for soldiers; characteristic of soldiers; as, a *military* appearance. **3** Made or done by soldiers; supported by armed force; as, a *military* government. For synonyms see *martial.* — *n.* Soldiers; the army.

military police. Soldiers who perform police duties.

mil·i·tate \'mil-ə-ˌtāt\ *v.;* **mil·i·tat·ed; mil·i·tat·ing.** To act; to operate; to have influence or effect — used of things, chiefly with *against.* A number of factors *militated* against our success.

mi·li·tia \mə-'lish-ə\ *n.* A body of citizens enrolled as a regular military force and receiving military training but not called into active service except in emergencies. — **mi·li·tia·man** \-mən\ *n.*

milk \'milk\ *n.* **1** A whitish fluid that nature provides in the bodies of female mammals for feeding their young. **2** This fluid pressed from the udders of such animals as cows and goats for human use. **3** A milklike juice; as, the *milk* of a coconut. — *v.* **1** To draw or press milk from the udder of; as, to *milk* a cow. **2** To draw or drain away the resources of; as, to *milk* a business.

milk·er \'milk-r\ *n.* **1** A person or a device that milks. **2** One that gives milk, as a cow; as, a good *milker.*

milkier. Comparative of *milky.*

milkiest. Superlative of *milky.*

milk·maid \'milk-ˌmād\ *n.* A woman or girl who milks cows or is employed in a dairy.

milk·man \'milk-ˌman\ *n.; pl.* **milk·men** \-ˌmen\. A man who sells or delivers milk.

milk of magnesia. A milk-white liquid, a preparation of magnesium in water, used as a laxative and as a medicine to counteract acidity.

milk shake or **milk·shake** \'milk-ˌshāk\ *n.* A drink made of milk or milk and egg, often with ice cream, flavored and shaken or beaten thoroughly.

milk snake. A small harmless gray snake with black-bordered blotches and an arrow-shaped spot on the head.

milk·sop \'milk-ˌsäp\ *n.* A timid, unmanly man or boy; a mollycoddle.

milk sugar. Lactose.

milk tooth. One of the first, temporary teeth of a young mammal, in man 20 in number.

milk·weed \'milk-ˌwēd\ *n.* Any of a number of related herbs and shrubs with milky juice and, usually, flowers in dense clusters.

milkweed

milky \'mil-kē\ *adj.;* **milk·i·er; milk·i·est. 1** Like milk; of the color of milk. **2** Consisting of or containing milk.

Milky Way. 1 The faintly luminous tract seen at night stretching across the sky, composed chiefly of a vast multitude of distant stars; the Galaxy. **2** [usually with small letters] Any of numerous similar aggregations of stars.

mill \'mil\ *n.* One tenth of a cent.

mill \'mil\ *n.* **1** A building in which grain is ground into flour. **2** A factory using machines; as, a steel *mill;* a cotton *mill.* **3** Any of various machines used in many ways, as for stamping coins, grinding coffee or pepper, or extracting juice from fruit, as apples. — *v.* **1** To grind; to shape or finish in a mill; as, to *mill* flour; to *mill* cloth. **2** To make a raised border or cut fine grooves around the edge of; as, to *mill* coins. **3** To make frothy by whipping or churning. **4** To circle about; to move around in a disorderly mass; as, cattle *milling* about.

mill·dam \'mil-ˌdam\ *n.* **1** The dam of a millpond. **2** A millpond.

mil·le·nary \'mil-ə-ˌner-ē, mi-'len-r-ē\ *adj.* Relating to or consisting of a thousand, especially a thousand years. — *n.; pl.* **mil·le·nar·ies. 1** A thousand. **2** A millennium. **3** One who believes in the millennium.

mil·len·ni·um \mi-'len-ē-əm\ *n.; pl.* **mil·len·nia** \-ē-ə\. **1** A thousand years; especially, a period of such length prophesied in the Bible as a time when there will be no sin or sorrow. **2** A thousandth anniversary. **3** Any period of great happiness. — **mil·len·ni·al** \-ē-əl\ *adj.*

mil·le·pede or **mil·li·pede** \'mil-ə-ˌpēd\ *n.* A small nonpoisonous animal with a long, slender, rounded body of many segments each of which, after the four in front, has two pairs of walking legs.

mill·er \'mil-r\ *n.* **1** A person who works in or runs a flour mill. **2** A moth whose wings seem to be covered with flour or dust.

mil·let \'mil-ət\ *n.* **1** An annual grass bearing clusters of small, shiny, almost white seeds, cultivated for hay or grain. **2** The seed of this plant.

mil·liard \'mil-ˌyärd, -ˌyȧrd\ *n. British.* A thousand million.

mil·li·bar \'mil-ə-ˌbär, -ˌbȧr\ *n.* A unit used in measuring atmospheric pressure and in reading the barometer, being equal to a certain tiny force acting on a square centimeter. An atmospheric pressure of 1,013 *millibars* is commonly referred to as a standard.

mil·li·gram or **mil·li·gramme** \'mil-ə-ˌgram\ *n.* A weight equal to one thousandth of a gram.

mil·li·me·ter or **mil·li·me·tre** \'mil-ə-ˌmēt-r\ *n.* A measure of length equal to one thousandth of a meter.

mil·li·ner \'mil-ən-r\ *n.* [From earlier *mylloner* meaning "vender of fancy goods" and derived from *Milan*, Italy, once famous for the manufacture of such materials.] A person who makes, trims, or sells women's hats.

mil·li·nery \'mil-ə-ˌner-ē\ *n.* **1** The business of a milliner. **2** The goods sold by a milliner.

mil·lion \'mil-yən\ *adj.* Numbering or consisting of a million. — *n.* **1** The number of ten hundred thousand, or a thousand thousand; 1,000,000. **2** A very great number; as, a *million* reasons.

mil·lion·aire \'mil-yə-ˌnar, -ˌner; ˌmil-yə-'nar, -'ner\ *n.* A person who is worth a million dollars or more.

mil·lionth \'mil-yən(t)th\ *adj.* Last in a series of a million; being one of a million equal parts. — *n.; pl.* **mil·lionths** \-yən(t)s, -yən(t)ths\. One of a million equal parts into which anything is or may be divided.

millipede. Variant of *millepede.*

mill·pond \'mil-ˌpänd\ *n.* A pond that supplies the water for running a mill.

mill·race \'mil-ˌrās\ *n.* **1** The canal in which water goes to a mill wheel. **2** The current of water that drives the mill wheel.

mill·stone \'mil-ˌstōn\ *n.* **1** One of two circular stones used for grinding grain. **2** A crushing burden; as, a *millstone* round one's neck.

mill·stream \'mil-ˌstrēm\ *n.* The stream in a millrace.

mill wheel. The water wheel that drives a mill.

mill·wright \'mil-ˌrīt\ *n.* One who builds mills, sets up mill machinery, or keeps mill machinery in repair.

milt \'milt\ *n.* The male reproductive glands of fishes when filled with secretion; the secretion itself.

mime \'mīm\ *n.* **1** A play or drama in which situations from life are imitated, usually in a farcical manner; the dialogue for such a play. **2** Acting by gestures and other movements of the body instead of through words; pantomime. **3** An actor in a mime; a mimic. — *v.;* **mimed; mim·ing. 1** To act in or as if in a mime. **2** To act out in the manner of a mime; to mimic.

mim·e·o·graph \'mim-ē-ə-ˌgraf\ *n.* A machine for making copies of typewritten or written matter by means of a stencil. — *v.* To copy by a mimeograph.

mim·ic \'mim-ik\ *v.;* **mim·icked** \-ikt\; **mim·ick·ing. 1** To copy or imitate very closely; to ridicule by imitating; to ape; as, to *mimic* a person's speech. **2** In biology, to assume a resemblance to, especially in form, coloring, or habit. — For synonyms see *imitate.* — *n.* A person who mimics. — *adj.* Not real; imitated; mock; as, a *mimic* battle.

mim·ic·ry \'mim-ik-rē\ *n.* **1** The act, art, or sport of mimicking. **2** The resemblance, as in form, coloring, or habit, to other animals or natural objects that some animals can show for their own concealment or protection.

mi·mo·sa \mə-'mō-sə, -zə\ *n.* A plant, bush, or tree that grows in warm regions and has round heads of small white or pink flowers.

min. Abbreviation for *minute.*

min·a·ret \ˌmin-r-'et\ *n.* A very tall slender tower of a mosque, from one of whose balconies the people are called to prayer.

minaret

mince \'min(t)s\ *v.;* **minced; minc·ing. 1** To cut into small pieces; to hash; as, to *mince* meat. **2** To weaken the force of; to act or speak in an unnaturally dainty way; as, to *mince* no words in answering the question. **3** To walk with short steps, or in a prim, unnatural manner. — *n.* The small bits into which something is cut up; especially, mincemeat.

mince·meat \'min(t)s-ˌmēt\ *n.* A mixture, used as a filling for pies, of finely chopped and cooked raisins, apples, suet, spices, and, usually, meat.

minc·ing \'min(t)s-ing\ *adj.* Dainty in an affected

way; as, *mincing* speech; *mincing* steps. — **minc·ing·ly**, *adv.*

mind \'mīnd\ *n.* **1** Memory; recollection; as, out of sight, out of *mind.* **2** That which a person thinks, wishes, intends, or feels; one's opinion, thoughts, wish, or purpose; as, to speak one's *mind;* to change one's *mind.* **3** A choice; a liking. The decision of the committee was not to my *mind.* **4** The part of a person that thinks, understands, wills, and feels; the power of thinking; intellect; brain; as, to have a fine *mind.* — *v.* **1** To remember; to recollect. **2** To heed; to pay attention; as, to *mind* what one is doing. **3** To object to; as, to *mind* having the window open. **4** To obey; as, to *mind* one's parents. **5** To take care of; as, to *mind* the children. **6** To be careful; to watch out. *Mind* the automobiles on the turnpike.

mind·ed \'mīn-dəd\ *adj.* **1** Having a particular kind of mind or interest, as in *narrow-minded* or *open-minded.* **2** Disposed; inclined; as, *minded* to do better next time.

mind·ful \'mīn(d)-fəl\ *adj.* Keeping in mind; having in mind; heedful; as, to be *mindful* of one's duty to others. — **mind·ful·ly** \-fə-lē\ *adv.*

mine \'mīn\ *pron.* The form of the word *I* used to show possession when no noun follows. That house is *mine.* — \(')mīn\ *adj.* An old or poetic form of *my* used before words beginning with a vowel sound or an "h" or when it follows its noun; as, *mine* eyes; mother *mine.*

mine \'mīn\ *n.* **1** A pit or tunnel from which minerals, such as coal, gold, or diamonds, are taken. **2** A deposit of ore. **3** A rich source; as, a book that is a *mine* of information. **4** A charge buried in the ground and set to explode when disturbed, as by an enemy soldier or vehicle. **5** An explosive charge placed in a case and sunk in the water to sink enemy ships. — *v.;* **mined**; **min·ing. 1** To dig a mine. **2** To obtain from a mine; as, to *mine* coal. **3** To work in a mine. **4** To burrow in the earth; to dig or form mines under a place; to lay mines; as, to *mine* a harbor.

min·er \'mī-nr\ *n.* One who mines; especially, one who works in a mine.

min·er·al \'min-r(-)əl\ *n.* A natural substance that is neither a plant nor an animal, as iron, gold, mercury, and petroleum. — *adj.* **1** Of, relating to, or of the nature of a mineral or minerals; inorganic. **2** Containing mineral salts or gases; as, *mineral* water.

min·er·al·ize \'min-r(-)ə-ˌlīz\ *v.;* **min·er·al·ized**; **min·er·al·iz·ing. 1** To transform a metal into an ore. **2** To petrify; as, *mineralized* bones. **3** To impregnate or supply with minerals; to change into mineral form; as, *mineralized* water.

min·er·al·o·gy \ˌmin-r-'al-ə-jē\ *n.* The science that collects and studies facts about minerals. — **min·er·al·o·gist** \-ə-jəst\ *n.* — **min·er·al·og·i·cal** \ˌmin-r(-)ə-'läj-ik-l\ *adj.*

mineral oil. 1 Any oil of mineral origin, as petroleum. **2** A refined petroleum oil having no color, odor, or taste that is used as a laxative.

mineral water. Any water naturally or artificially impregnated with mineral salts or gases.

min·gle \'ming-gl\ *v.;* **min·gled**; **min·gling** \-gl(-)ing\. **1** To bring or come together in a mixed mass; to mix; as, pleasure *mingled* with regret. The barking of dogs *mingled* with the children's laughter. **2** To come together, as persons by social ties; to join in company; to associate; as, to *mingle* with all sorts of people; to *mingle* in a crowd.

— The words *mix* and *blend* are synonyms of *mingle:* all of these refer to the combining of two or more parts into a whole; *mix* is the most general of these terms and may suggest a rather thorough combining in which the original elements may or may not be distinguishable; *mingle* usually indicates a looser joining in which the elements remain quite distinct; *blend* usually suggests a complete uniting, especially of similar things, so that the original parts cannot be separated or distinguished.

min·i·a·ture \'min-ē-ə-ˌchůr, -ˌtyůr, -ˌtůr; 'min-əch-r\ *n.* **1** A very small painting; especially, a very small portrait on ivory or metal. **2** The art of painting such small pictures. **3** Something much smaller than the usual or actual size; a very small model. — *adj.* Very small; on a very small scale; as, a *miniature* railroad.

miniature camera. A camera using film not wider than 35 millimeters.

min·i·mal \'min-əm-l\ *adj.* Relating to a minimum; least possible; as, a task accomplished with *minimal* inconveniences to everybody; *minimal* requirements.

min·i·mize \'min-ə-ˌmīz\ *v.;* **min·i·mized**; **min·i·miz·ing. 1** To make as small as possible; to reduce to a minimum; as, to *minimize* the chance of error. **2** To place a low estimate on the value, significance, or importance of; to belittle; to disparage; as, to *minimize* the achievements of a rival; to *minimize* the dangers of an adventure.

min·i·mum \'min-ə-məm\ *n.; pl.* **min·i·ma** \-mə\ or **min·i·mums** \-məmz\. **1** The lowest quantity or amount possible; as, to walk a *minimum* of three miles a day for exercise. **2** The lowest point reached or recorded. The thermometer registered its *minimum* for the year. — *adj.* Least or lowest.

min·ing \'mī-ning\ *n.* The action or business of working mines.

min·ion \'min-yən\ *n.* **1** A favorite; as, the *minion* of the king. **2** A person quick to do the bidding of his master; a groveling servant.

min·is·ter \'min-əst-r\ *n.* **1** A person authorized to conduct Christian worship and preach the gospel; especially, a Protestant clergyman. **2** A clergyman officiating or assisting at a service or administering a sacrament. **3** A person who represents his government in a foreign country. **4** In some countries, a government official with duties similar to those of a member of the president's cabinet in the United States. — *v.;* **min·is·tered**; **min·is·ter·ing** \-r(-)ing\. To serve; to attend; to render aid; as, to *minister* to the poor.

min·is·te·ri·al \ˌmin-əs-'tir-ē-əl\ *adj.* Of or relating to the office or conduct of a minister or to the ministry as a body in either church or government.

min·is·trant \'min-əs-trənt\ *adj.* Ministering; helping; aiding. — *n.* One who ministers or aids.

min·is·tra·tion \ˌmin-əs-'trāsh-n\ *n.* **1** The action of ministering, especially in religion. **2** The action of furnishing something; as, the *ministration* of food.

min·is·try \'min-əs-trē\ *n.; pl.* **min·is·tries. 1** The action of ministering. **2** The office or duties of a minister; the profession of a minister of religion; as, to study for the *ministry.* **3** The period during which a minister serves. **4** A body or group of ministers. **5** A government department headed by a minister; as, the *ministry* of foreign affairs. **6** The building containing the offices of such a department.

mink \'mingk\ *n.; pl.* **minks** or **mink. 1** A slender-bodied mammal resembling a weasel, with partially webbed feet and a somewhat bushy tail, living near water. **2** The soft fur of this animal, usually dark-brown in color.

min·now \'min-ō\ *n.; pl.* **min·nows** or **min·now. 1** Any small soft-finned freshwater bottom-feeding fish of the carp family, as the dace or shiner. **2** Any of various other small fish.

mi·nor \'mīn-r\ *adj.* **1** Less in size, importance, or value; smaller; inferior. **2** Not having reached the age of majority. **3** Making up the minority; as, the *minor* vote in an election. **4** Requiring of a student secondary concentration in a course or subject but less than required for a major subject. **5** Relating to a musical scale having half steps between the second and third, the fifth and sixth, and sometimes the seventh and eighth tones; based harmoniously on such a scale; as, a *minor* key; a *minor* chord. — *n.* **1** A person who has not yet reached his majority. **2** A minor subject or course of study. — *v.* To take the courses of one's minor subject; as, to *minor* in history.

mi·nor·i·ty \mə-'nȯr-ət-ē, mī-, -'när-\ *n.; pl.* **mi·nor·i·ties. 1** The condition of being a minor; the time during which a person is a minor. **2** The smaller number; especially, the number less than half of any total.

min·ster \'min(t)st-r\ *n.* **1** A church that is or once was attached to a monastery. **2** Any large church.

min·strel \'min(t)s-trəl\ *n.* **1** In the Middle Ages, a musical entertainer, especially one who sang to the accompaniment of a harp. **2** One of a group of entertainers, usually blacked in imitation of Negroes, who give a program of Negro melodies and jokes in a show called a **minstrel show.**

min·strel·sy \'min(t)s-trəl-sē\ *n.; pl.* **min·strel·sies. 1** The singing and playing of a minstrel. **2** A group of minstrels or a collection of their songs.

mint \'mint\ *n.* **1** Any of a number of fragrant plants yielding oils valued for flavoring, as the peppermint, spearmint, and catnip. **2** Any of a family of herbs and shrubs with square stems, opposite, fragrant leaves, commonly two-lipped flowers, as basil, rosemary, and salvia. **3** A piece of candy flavored with mint.

mint \'mint\ *n.* **1** A place where money is coined. **2** A great amount; as, a *mint* of money. — *v.* To stamp and make into money; as, to *mint* silver; to *mint* money.

mint·age \'mint-ij\ *n.* **1** The process of minting coin; coinage. **2** The cost of coining. **3** The stamp impressed upon a coin in minting.

min·u·end \'min-yə-ˌwend\ *n.* In arithmetic, the number from which another number is to be subtracted.

min·u·et \ˌmin-yə-'wet\ *n.* A slow, graceful dance, or music suitable for such a dance.

mi·nus \'mī-nəs\ *prep.* With the subtraction of; less. Seven *minus* four leaves three. — *adj.* **1** Showing that the following number is to be subtracted; as, the *minus* sign. **2** Negative; not positive; as, a *minus* quantity. **3** Lacking; deprived of; as, to be *minus* one's hat. **4** Being in the lower part of a graded evaluation; as, a grade of A *minus.* — *n.* **1** The minus sign [−]. **2** A minus quantity.

min·ute \'min-ət\ *n.* **1** A sixtieth part of an hour or of a degree; sixty seconds. **2** The distance a person can cover in a minute; as, to go to a school only ten *minutes* from one's home. **3** A memorandum or note, as of instructions. **4** [in the plural] The official record made of proceedings at a meeting.

mi·nute \mī-'nüt, mə-, -'nyüt\ *adj.;* **mi·nut·er; mi·nut·est. 1** Very small; tiny; as, the *minute* details; *minute* particles. **2** Of small importance; trifling; petty. The mayor attends personally even to the *minute* details of his office. **3** Having or paying attention to small details; as, a *minute* description. — **mi·nute·ly,** *adv.* — **mi·nute·ness,** *n.*

min·ute·man \'min-ət-ˌman\ *n.; pl.* **min·ute·men** \-ˌmen\. One of a group of armed American colonists who just before and during the War of Independence pledged themselves to be ready to fight at a minute's notice.

min·ute steak \'min-ət\. A small thin steak that can be quickly cooked.

mi·nu·tia \mə-'nü-shē-ə, mī-, -'nyü-\ *n.; pl.* **mi·nu·ti·ae** \-shē-ˌē\. A minute or very small detail — used chiefly in the plural.

minx \'mingks\ *n.* A saucy girl.

mir·a·cle \'mir-ək-l\ *n.* **1** An event or effect that cannot be explained by any known law of nature. **2** Anything so rare or unusual as to seem like a miracle; a marvel; a wonder.

miracle play. A drama popular in the Middle Ages, showing events in the life of a saint or martyr.

mi·rac·u·lous \mə-'rak-yə-ləs\ *adj.* **1** Of the nature of a miracle. **2** Like a miracle; marvelous. By a *miraculous* coincidence, the two friends unexpectedly met on the desert. **3** Working or able to work miracles; as, the oracle's claim of *miraculous* powers. — **mi·rac·u·lous·ly,** *adv.*

mi·rage \mə-'räzh, -'rȧzh\ *n.* A reflection, sometimes seen at sea or in the desert, of a distant object, usually presented upside down and somewhat distorted.

mire \'mīr\ *n.* Wet, spongy earth; soft, deep mud or slush. — *v.;* **mired**; **mir·ing. 1** To stick or cause to stick fast in mire. **2** To soil with mud; as, pedestrians *mired* by passing cars.

mir·ror \'mir-r\ *n.* **1** A glass backed with some reflecting substance, such as mercury; a looking glass. **2** Any smooth or polished surface that reflects an image. **3** Something that reflects a true likeness or gives a true description; as, an actress who is a *mirror* of fashion. — *v.* To reflect in or as if in a mirror.

mirth \'mərth\ *n.* Gay, cheerful laughter; jollity.

mirth·ful \'mərth-fəl\ *adj.* Full of, expressing, or producing mirth. — **mirth·ful·ly** \-fə-lē\ *adv.*

miry \'mīr-ē\ *adj.;* **mir·i·er**; **mir·i·est. 1** Marshy; boggy. **2** Muddy or slushy.

mis-. A prefix that can mean: **1** Amiss; wrongly; wrong, as in *mislead* or *misconstrue*. **2** Bad, as in *misconduct* or *misdeed*.

mis·ad·ven·ture \ˌmis-əd-'vench-r\ *n.* An unlucky adventure; misfortune.

mis·al·li·ance \ˌmis-ə-'lī-ən(t)s\ *n.* An improper or unsuitable alliance, especially in marriage.

mis·an·thrope \'mis-n-ˌthrōp\ or **mis·an·thro·pist** \mi-'san-thrə-pəst\ *n.* A person who dislikes and distrusts mankind.

mis·an·thro·py \mi-'san-thrə-pē\ *n.* A dislike or hatred of mankind. — **mis·an·throp·ic** \ˌmis-n-'thräp-ik\ *adj.*

mis·ap·ply \ˌmis-ə-'plī\ *v.;* **mis·ap·plied** \-'plīd\; **mis·ap·ply·ing.** To apply wrongly; as, to *misapply* a formula in mathematics. — **mis·ap·pli·ca·tion** \(ˌ)mis-ˌap-lə-'kāsh-n\ *n.*

mis·ap·pre·hend \(ˌ)mis-ˌap-rē-'hend\ *v.* To misunderstand. — **mis·ap·pre·hen·sion** \-'hench-n\ *n.*

mis·ap·pro·pri·ate \ˌmis-ə-'prō-prē-ˌāt\ *v.;* **mis·ap·pro·pri·at·ed**; **mis·ap·pro·pri·at·ing.** To appropriate wrongly; to misapply. — **mis·ap·pro·pri·a·tion** \-ˌprō-prē-'āsh-n\ *n.*

mis·be·got·ten \ˌmis-bē-'gät-n\ or **mis·be·got** \-'gät\ *adj.* Unlawfully or irregularly begotten; illegitimate.

mis·be·have \ˌmis-bē-'hāv\ *v.;* **mis·be·haved**; **mis·be·hav·ing.** To behave badly. — **mis·be·hav·ior** \-'hāv-yər\ *n.*

mis·be·lief \ˌmis-bə-'lēf\ *n.* A mistaken or false belief. — **mis·be·liev·er** \-'lēv-r\ *n.*

misc. Abbreviation for *miscellaneous*.

mis·cal·cu·late \(')mis-'kalk-yə-ˌlāt\ *v.;* **mis·cal·cu·lat·ed**; **mis·cal·cu·lat·ing.** To calculate wrongly. — **mis·cal·cu·la·tion** \(ˌ)mis-ˌkalk-yə-'lāsh-n\ *n.*

mis·call \(')mis-'kȯl\ *v.* To give a wrong name to; to call by a wrong or unsuitable name.

mis·car·riage \mis-'kar-ij\ *n.* **1** Mismanagement; a failure or mistake; as, a *miscarriage* of justice. **2** A failure to arrive; as, disappointed by the *miscarriage* of a letter. **3** A failure to carry properly; as, the *miscarriage* of goods by a trucking company. **4** The accidental separation of an unborn child from the body of its mother before it is capable of living independently; loss of a child through premature birth.

mis·car·ry \mis-'kar-ē\ *v.;* **mis·car·ried** \-ēd\; **mis·car·ry·ing. 1** To have a miscarriage; to give birth prematurely. **2** To fail of the intended purpose; to go wrong or go amiss; as, a plan that *miscarried*.

mis·cast \(')mis-'kast\ *v.;* **mis·cast**; **mis·cast·ing.** To cast in an unsuitable or inappropriate role, as in a play.

mis·ceg·e·na·tion \mi-ˌsej-n-'āsh-n, ˌmis-ə-jə-'nāsh-n\ *n.* Intermarriage or interbreeding between races.

mis·cel·la·ne·ous \ˌmis-l-'ā-nē-əs\ *adj.* Consisting of many things of different sorts; mixed; as, a *miscellaneous* collection; *miscellaneous* articles of clothing. — **mis·cel·la·ne·ous·ly,** *adv.*

mis·cel·la·ny \'mis-l-ˌā-nē\ *n.; pl.* **mis·cel·la·nies. 1** A mixture of various things. **2** [in the plural] Miscellaneous treatises, studies, or other pieces collected in one book.

mis·chance \(')mis-'chan(t)s\ *n.* **1** Ill luck. **2** A piece of ill luck; a mishap.

mis·chief \'mis-chəf\ *n.* **1** Harm; injury; damage. **2** A person or thing that annoys or vexes others in a trifling way. That child is a little *mischief*. **3** The conduct, acts, or disposition of such a person; as, a person who is always in *mischief*.

mis·chie·vous \'mis-chə-vəs\ *adj.* **1** Causing mischief; intended to do harm; as, *mischievous* gossip. **2** Causing, or inclined to cause, petty injury or annoyance; as, a *mischievous* youngster; a *mischievous* puppy. **3** Showing a spirit of mischief; as, *mischievous* behavior. — **mis·chie·vous·ly,** *adv.* — **mis·chie·vous·ness,** *n.*

mis·con·ceive \ˌmis-kən-'sēv\ *v.;* **mis·con·ceived**; **mis·con·ceiv·ing.** To interpret incorrectly; to misjudge. — **mis·con·cep·tion** \-'sepsh-n\ *n.*

mis·con·duct \(')mis-'kän-(ˌ)dəkt\ *n.* Wrong conduct; bad behavior; mismanagement. — \ˌmis-kən-'dəkt\ *v.* To mismanage.

mis·con·strue \ˌmis-kən-'strü\ *v.;* **mis·con·strued**; **mis·con·stru·ing.** To construe or understand wrongly; to misinterpret. — **mis·con·struc·tion** \-'strəksh-n\ *n.*

mis·count \(')mis-'kau̇nt\ *v.* To count incorrectly; to miscalculate. — *n.* A wrong count.

mis·cre·ant \'mis-krē-ənt\ *adj.* Having no conscience; villainous. — *n.* A villain; a wretch.

mis·cue \(')mis-'kyü\ *n.* **1** A stroke, as in billiards, in which the cue slips. **2** *Slang.* A mistake; a slip. — *v.;* **mis·cued**; **mis·cu·ing. 1** To make a miscue. **2** To miss one's cue in a play; to answer a wrong cue.

mis·deal \(')mis-'dēl\ *v.;* **mis·dealt** \-'delt\; **mis·deal·ing.** To deal or distribute wrongly, as cards. — *n.* A misdealing.

mis·deed \(')mis-'dēd\ *n.* A bad deed; a sin.

mis·de·mean·or \ˌmis-də-'mēn-r\ *n.* **1** A misdeed. **2** A crime less serious than a felony.

mis·di·rect \ˌmis-də-ˈrekt, -dī-\ *v.* To direct incorrectly. — **mis·di·rec·tion** \-ˈreksh-n\ *n.*

mis·do·ing \(ˈ)mis-ˈdü-ing\ *n.* Wrongdoing; a misdeed.

mi·ser \ˈmīz-r\ *n.* [From Latin, meaning "miserable", "wretched".] A grasping, mean person, especially one who lives miserably for the sake of hoarding money.

mis·er·a·ble \ˈmiz-rb-l, -r(-)əb-l\ *adj.* **1** Being in a state of misery or great unhappiness; wretched. **2** Causing misery or great discomfort; as, a *miserable* cold; *miserable* weather. **3** Arousing pity; lamentable; as, a *miserable,* homeless child. **4** Wretchedly bad; poor; paltry; as, a *miserable* dinner. — **mis·er·a·bly** \-r-blē, -r(-)ə-blē\ *adv.*

mi·ser·ly \ˈmīz-r-lē\ *adj.* Relating to, like, or characteristic of a miser; abnormally desirous of keeping what one has and of getting more. — **mi·ser·li·ness** \-lē-nəs\ *n.*

mis·ery \ˈmiz-r(-)ē\ *n.; pl.* **mis·er·ies. 1** A state of great distress; wretchedness or suffering due to poverty, pain, or unhappiness. **2** A wretched circumstance; a cause of misery; as, the *miseries* of a life in prison.

mis·fire \(ˈ)mis-ˈfīr\ *v.;* **mis·fired; mis·fir·ing. 1** To fail to go off, as a gun. **2** In an internal combustion engine, to have its explosive charge ignite at an improper time. — *n.* The action or an instance of misfiring.

mis·fit \(ˈ)mis-ˈfit\ *v.;* **mis·fit·ted; mis·fit·ting.** To fit badly. — *n.* **1** A poor fit. **2** Something that does not fit, as a coat. **3** A person poorly adjusted to his environment.

mis·for·tune \mis-ˈfȯrch-n, -ˈfȯr-(ˌ)chün\ *n.* **1** Bad fortune; ill luck. **2** An unfortunate condition or event; disaster.

— The word *adversity* is a synonym of *misfortune: misfortune* is a general term for bad luck and the circumstances brought about by it; *adversity* usually suggests a serious and continued misfortune that seems to pursue one.

mis·giv·ing \mis-ˈgiv-ing\ *n.* A fear that something bad is going to happen; a feeling of distrust or doubt; as, to have *misgivings* about one's future.

mis·gov·ern \(ˈ)mis-ˈgəv-rn\ *v.* To govern badly. — **mis·gov·ern·ment,** *n.*

mis·guide \(ˈ)mis-ˈgīd\ *v.;* **mis·guid·ed; mis·guid·ing.** To guide wrongly; to lead astray. — **mis·guid·ance** \-ˈgīd-n(t)s\ *n.*

mis·han·dle \(ˈ)mis-ˈhand-l\ *v.;* **mis·han·dled; mis·han·dling** \-l(-)ing\. To handle badly, wrongly, or roughly; to maltreat.

mis·hap \ˈmis-ˌhap, (ˈ)mis-ˈhap\ *n.* **1** Bad luck. **2** An unfortunate accident.

mis·in·form \ˌmis-n-ˈfȯrm\ *v.* To give false or incorrect information to. — **mis·in·for·ma·tion** \(ˌ)mis-ˌin-fər-ˈmāsh-n\ *n.*

mis·in·ter·pret \ˌmis-n-ˈtərp-(r)ət\ *v.* To understand or explain wrongly. — **mis·in·ter·pre·ta·tion** \-ˌtərp-(r)ə-ˈtāsh-n\ *n.*

mis·judge \(ˈ)mis-ˈjəj\ *v.;* **mis·judged; mis·judg·ing.** To judge wrongly or unjustly. — **mis·judg·ment** or **mis·judge·ment,** *n.*

mis·lay \(ˈ)mis-ˈlā\ *v.;* **mis·laid** \-ˈlād\; **mis·lay·ing.** To lay in a place later forgotten; to lose; as, to *mislay* a book. — For synonyms see *displace.*

mis·lead \(ˈ)mis-ˈlēd\ *v.;* **mis·led** \-ˈled\; **mis·lead·ing.** To lead into a wrong way; to lead astray; to lead into error; to deceive.

mis·lead·ing \(ˈ)mis-ˈlēd-ing\ *adj.* Giving the wrong impression; deceptive.

mis·like \(ˈ)mis-ˈlīk\ *v.;* **mis·liked; mis·lik·ing. 1** To displease. **2** To dislike. — *n.* Dislike; distaste.

mis·man·age \(ˈ)mis-ˈman-ij\ *v.;* **mis·man·aged; mis·man·ag·ing.** To manage badly or improperly. — **mis·man·age·ment,** *n.*

mis·match \(ˈ)mis-ˈmach\ *v.* To match unsuitably or badly, as in marriage. — *n.* The condition of being mismatched.

mis·mate \(ˈ)mis-ˈmāt\ *v.;* **mis·mat·ed; mis·mat·ing.** To mate unsuitably.

mis·name \(ˈ)mis-ˈnām\ *v.;* **mis·named; mis·nam·ing.** To call by the wrong name; to miscall.

mis·no·mer \(ˈ)mis-ˈnōm-r\ *n.* A wrong or unsuitable name.

mis·phrase \(ˈ)mis-ˈfrāz\ *v.;* **mis·phrased; mis·phras·ing.** To phrase poorly or wrongly.

mis·place \(ˈ)mis-ˈplās\ *v.;* **mis·placed; mis·plac·ing. 1** To put in a wrong place or position; as, to *misplace* a comma. **2** To mislay. — For synonyms see *displace.*

mis·play \(ˈ)mis-ˈplā\ *n.* A wrong play or move, as in a game.

mis·print \(ˈ)mis-ˈprint\ *v.* To print incorrectly. — *n.* A mistake in printing.

mis·pro·nounce \ˌmis-prə-ˈnau̇n(t)s\ *v.;* **mis·pro·nounced; mis·pro·nounc·ing.** To pronounce in a way regarded as incorrect. — **mis·pro·nun·ci·a·tion** \-ˌnən(t)s-ē-ˈāsh-n\ *n.*

mis·quote \(ˈ)mis-ˈkwōt\ *v.;* **mis·quot·ed; mis·quot·ing.** To quote incorrectly. — **mis·quo·ta·tion** \ˌmis-kwō-ˈtāsh-n\ *n.*

mis·read \(ˈ)mis-ˈrēd\ *v.;* **mis·read** \-ˈred\; **mis·read·ing** \-ˈrēd-ing\. **1** To read incorrectly. **2** To get a mistaken understanding of what one reads.

mis·rep·re·sent \(ˌ)mis-ˌrep-rē-ˈzent\ *v.* To represent incorrectly or unfairly; to give the wrong impression of. — **mis·rep·re·sen·ta·tion** \-zen-ˈtāsh-n\ *n.*

mis·rule \(ˈ)mis-ˈrül\ *v.;* **mis·ruled; mis·rul·ing.** To rule or govern badly. — *n.* **1** Bad government. **2** Disorder.

Miss \ˈmis\ *n.; pl.* **Miss·es** \ˈmis-əz\. **1** A title of courtesy used before the name of an unmarried girl or woman. **2** [with a small letter] A young girl; as, a saucy little *miss.*

miss \ˈmis\ *v.* **1** To fail to hit, catch, reach, or get; as, to *miss* a target; to *miss* the ball. **2** To escape; to avoid; as, to *miss* being hurt by a narrow margin. **3** To omit; to fail or neglect to have or attend; as, to *miss* one's lunch; to *miss* two days of school. **4** To be aware of the absence of; to feel the want or need of someone or something; as, to *miss* an absent friend. — *n.* The act of missing; failure to hit or catch; as, ten *misses* in a game; a near *miss.*

mis·sal \'mis-l\ *n.* The book containing the prayers to be said or sung in the Mass during the year.

mis·shap·en \(')mis(h)-'shāp-n\ *adj.* Formed or shaped badly; deformed; as, a *misshapen* foot.

mis·sile \'mis-l\ *n.* Any object, as a stone, arrow, bullet, or rocket, that is thrown or projected, usually so as to strike something at a distance; often, a guided missile or a ballistics missile.

miss·ing \'mis-ing\ *adj.* Absent; lost.

mis·sion \'mish-n\ *n.* **1** A group of persons sent by a government to represent it in a foreign country; as, a trade *mission;* a military *mission.* **2** The errand or task of such a group. **3** A group of missionaries or the place in which they live and work. **4** An organization for doing missionary work. **5** That which a person is fitted for or feels himself called upon to do; as, to have a *mission* in life. **6** A definite military task or errand, as one given to a plane or a group of planes for attacking an enemy.

mis·sion·ary \'mish-n-,er-ē\ *adj.* Of or having to do with missions, especially religious missions; as, a *missionary* society. — *n.; pl.* **mis·sion·ar·ies.** A person sent out to persuade people to accept the religion that he represents.

mis·sive \'mis-iv\ *n.* A letter or note.

mis·spell \(')mis-'spel\ *v.;* **mis·spelled** \-'speld\ or **mis·spelt** \-'spelt\; **mis·spell·ing.** To spell incorrectly.

mis·spend \(')mis-'spend\ *v.;* **mis·spent** \-'spent\; **mis·spend·ing.** To waste; to squander.

mis·state \(')mis-'stāt\ *v.;* **mis·stat·ed; mis·stat·ing.** To state incorrectly. — **mis·state·ment,** *n.*

mis·step \(')mis-'step\ *n.* A wrong step; a slip.

mist \'mist\ *n.* **1** Moisture hanging in the air, often falling as fine rain. **2** Anything that blurs or hinders vision; a haze; a film. — *v.* **1** To be or become misty; to form a mist. **2** To dim or blur, as with mist; as, eyes *misted* with tears.

mis·take \mə-'stāk\ *v.;* **mis·took** \mə-'stu̇k\; **mis·tak·en** \mə-'stāk-n\; **mis·tak·ing.** **1** To take in a wrong sense; to misunderstand; as, to *mistake* a remark. **2** To substitute wrongly, as one person for another; as, to *mistake* a visitor for the postman. **3** To fail to recognize or estimate correctly; as, to *mistake* the strength of an enemy. — *n.* An error; a misunderstanding; a blunder. — For synonyms see *error.*

mis·tak·en \mə-'stāk-n\ *adj.* **1** In error; having a wrong opinion; judging wrongly; as, to be *mistaken* about the time. **2** Wrong; incorrect; as, a *mistaken* idea. — **mis·tak·en·ly,** *adv.*

Mis·ter \'mist-r\ *n.* [An altered form of *master.*] A title of courtesy used before a man's name or the name of the office which he holds — generally written in its abbreviated form *Mr.;* as, *Mr.* Smith; *Mr.* President.

mistier. Comparative of *misty.*

mistiest. Superlative of *misty.*

mis·tle·toe \'mis-l-,tō\ *n.* A green plant with waxy white berries, which grows on the branches and trunks of trees.

mistletoe

mistook. Past tense of *mistake.*

mis·tral \'mis-trəl\ *n.* A violent, cold, and dry northerly wind of southern Europe.

mis·treat \(')mis-'trēt\ *v.* To treat badly; to abuse. — **mis·treat·ment,** *n.*

mis·tress \'mis-trəs; *sense 5 is* 'mis-əz, 'mis-əs, 'miz-əz, 'miz-əs, 'miz\ *n.* **1** A woman who has control or authority like that of a master; a head; as, the *mistress* of a household. **2** A woman illicitly living with or kept by a man to whom she is not married. **3** A woman teacher; as, a drawing *mistress.* **4** A woman especially skilled in anything. **5** [with a capital] A title of courtesy used before the name of a married woman — now used only in the abbreviated form *Mrs.*

mis·tri·al \(')mis-'trī-əl, -'trīl\ *n.* A trial legally of no effect because of some error in the proceedings.

mis·trust \(')mis-'trəst\ *n.* Lack of confidence or trust. — *v.* **1** To suspect. **2** To lack confidence in; as, to *mistrust* one's own abilities.

mis·trust·ful \(')mis-'trəst-fəl\ *adj.* Mistrusting or inclined to mistrust; suspicious. — **mis·trust·ful·ly** \-fə-lē\ *adv.*

misty \'mis-tē\ *adj.;* **mist·i·er; mist·i·est.** **1** Full of mist; as, to look down into a *misty* valley. **2** Blurred by, or as if by, mist; as, through *misty* eyes. **3** Vague; indistinct; as, a *misty* memory.

mis·un·der·stand \(,)mis-,ənd-r-'stand\ *v.;* **mis·un·der·stood** \-'stu̇d\; **mis·un·der·stand·ing.** To fail to understand; to take in a wrong sense or way.

mis·un·der·stand·ing \(,)mis-,ənd-r-'stan-ding\ *n.* **1** The act of one who misunderstands; a mistake of meaning. **2** A disagreement; a quarrel.

mis·use \(')mis(h)-'yüs\ *n.* Wrong or bad use; as, the *misuse* of a word in speaking; *misuse* of power. — \-'yüz\ *v.;* **mis·used; mis·us·ing.** **1** To use improperly; as, to *misuse* one's talents. **2** To treat badly or cruelly; to abuse; as, to *misuse* an animal.

mite \'mīt\ *n.* **1** Any of various tiny animals like spiders often living on plants, animals, and stored foods. **2** A very small coin or sum of money. **3** A very small object or creature; a bit; a tiny piece.

mi·ter or **mi·tre** \'mīt-r\ *n.* **1** The high, pointed headdress worn by bishops and abbots in church ceremonies. **2** The office or position of a bishop. **3** A miter joint. — *v.;* **mi·tered** or **mi·tred** \-rd\; **mi·ter·ing** or **mi·tring** \-r-ing\. **1** To invest with a miter; as, a *mitered* abbot. **2** To fit together in a miter joint. **3** In making a bed, to fold the bedclothes in such a way as to produce a miter-shaped corner.

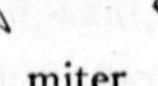

miter

miter joint or **mitre joint.** The joint or corner made by cutting the square edges of two boards at an angle and fitting them together.

mit·i·gate \'mit-ə-ˌgāt\ *v.;* **mit·i·gat·ed; mit·i·gat·ing.** To make or become less severe; as, to *mitigate* a punishment. — **mit·i·ga·tion** \ˌmit-ə-'gāsh-n\ *n.*

mi·to·sis \mī-'tō-səs\ *n.* **1** A process taking place in the nucleus of a dividing cell which results in the formation of two new nuclei, each having the same number of chromosomes as the parent nucleus. **2** A cell division in which mitosis occurs.

mitt \'mit\ *n.* **1** A glove without fingers; a mitten. **2** A glove protected on the palm side by a pad for use in playing baseball.

mit·ten \'mit-n\ *n.* A covering for the hand and wrist having one pocket for the fingers and another smaller one for the thumb.

mix \'miks\ *v.;* **mixed** or **mixt** \'mikst\; **mix·ing.** **1** To make into one mass by stirring together; to blend. **2** To make by blending different things; as, to *mix* a salad dressing. **3** To become one mass through blending. Oil will not *mix* with water. **4** To associate with others on friendly terms; as, to *mix* well in any company. **5** To confuse; as, to *mix* up facts. — For synonyms see *mingle.* — *n.* A commercial preparation of mixed ingredients; as, pancake *mix.* — **mix·er** \'miks-r\ *n.*

mixed \'mikst\ *adj.* **1** Made of mingled or blended ingredients; as, a *mixed* drink. **2** Made up of two or more kinds; as, *mixed* candies. **3** Made up of persons of both sexes; as, a *mixed* quartet. **4** Made up of a whole number and a fraction; as, the *mixed* number $1\frac{2}{3}$.

mix·ture \'miks-chər\ *n.* **1** The action of mixing. **2** Something mixed or being mixed; as, to add eggs to the *mixture.* **3** A cloth made of thread of different colors. **4** A preparation consisting of two or more ingredients or kinds; as, a smoking *mixture.* **5** Two or more substances mixed together but not chemically united and not necessarily present in definite proportions. Sand mixed with sugar forms a *mixture.*

mix-up \'mik-ˌsəp\ *n.* **1** A confusion; as, a *mix-up* about who was to meet the train. **2** A conflict; a fight.

miz·zen or **miz·en** \'miz-n\ *adj.* Of or relating to the mizzenmast. — *n.* **1** A fore-and-aft sail set on the mizzenmast. **2** A mizzenmast.

miz·zen·mast or **miz·en·mast** \'miz-n-ˌmast, -məst\ *n.* **1** The rear mast in a two-masted or three-masted boat. **2** The third mast in a boat with four or more masts.

Mlle.; *pl.* **Mlles.** Abbreviation for *Mademoiselle.*

mm. Abbreviation for *millimeter.*

Mme.; *pl.* **Mmes.** Abbreviation for *Madame* — sometimes used in the plural as a plural of *Mrs.*

mo. Abbreviation for *month.*

moan \'mōn\ *n.* **1** A low, drawn-out sound showing pain or grief. **2** A sound like a moan. — *v.* **1** To utter a moan or moans. **2** To complain; as, to *moan* about one's troubles. **3** To utter with moans.

moat \'mōt\ *n.* A deep, wide ditch, usually filled with water, around the walls of a castle or fortress; a ditch.

moat

mob \'mäb\ *n.* **1** The masses of people; the populace. **2** A disorderly or excited part of the populace; the rabble. **3** A crowd. — *v.;* **mobbed; mob·bing.** To crowd about in a disorderly way and attack or annoy. The crowd *mobbed* the actor for his autograph.

mo·bile \'mōb-l, 'mō-ˌbēl\ *adj.* **1** Movable; moving or flowing easily and readily; as, *mobile* liquids. **2** Changing quickly in expression; as, *mobile* features. **3** Capable of being readily moved; as, *mobile* troops. — \'mō-ˌbēl\ *n.* A sculpture, as of paper or wire, having movable parts that can be easily set in motion, as by a current of air. — **mo·bil·i·ty** \mō-'bil-ət-ē\ *n.*

mo·bi·lize \'mōb-l-ˌīz\ *v.;* **mo·bi·lized; mo·bi·liz·ing.** **1** To make mobile or movable; as, to *mobilize* a blood bank. **2** To assemble and make ready for active service, especially for war; as, to *mobilize* an army. **3** To undergo mobilization. The townspeople *mobilized* quickly to fight the forest fire. — **mo·bi·li·za·tion** \ˌmōb-l-ə-'zāsh-n\ *n.*

mob·ster \'mäb-stər\ *n.* A member of an organized criminal gang.

moc·ca·sin \'mäk-əs-n\ *n.* **1** A soft shoe without a heel and with its sole and sides made of one piece joined on top by a seam to a U-shaped piece across the front. **2** A water moccasin.

moccasin

moccasin flower. **1** A North American orchid with two large basal leaves and a solitary pink or sometimes white flower shaped like a moccasin. **2** Any lady's-slipper, especially one that is white with crimson stripes.

mock \'mäk, 'mȯk\ *v.* **1** To laugh at scornfully; to ridicule. **2** To defy; to disregard; as, to *mock* the law by willfully disobeying it. **3** To make fun of by mimicking. — For synonyms see *imitate.* — *n.* **1** The action of mocking; a sneer; a jibe. **2** An object of ridicule; as, to make a *mock* of a person. — *adj.* Not real; sham; as, *mock* grief; a *mock* battle. — **mock·er** \-r\ *n.* — **mock·ing·ly** \-ing-lē\ *adv.*

mock·ery \'mäk-r(-)ē, 'mȯk-\ *n.; pl.* **mock·er·ies.** **1** Insulting or contemptuous action or speech. The odd-looking invention drew forth a good deal of *mockery* from the townspeople. **2** Someone or something that is laughed at. **3** An insincere or a poor imitation. The actor's half-hearted performance was but a *mockery* of his great performances. **4** Ridiculously useless or unsuitable action. The noisy, ill-mannered audience made the speaker's efforts to be heard a *mockery.*

mock·ing·bird \'mäk-ing-ˌbərd, 'mȯk-\ *n.* A songbird of the southern United States, closely related to the catbird and thrashers, noted for the sweetness of its song and for its imitations of the notes of other birds.

mock orange. A hardy shrub related to the hydrangea, with large snowy-white flowers.

mock-up \'mäk-ˌəp, 'mȯk-\ *n.* A full-sized model built out of a suitable material; as plywood, cardboard, canvas, or clay, to the scale of the original or intended structure for the purpose of studying its operation or improving its design.

mode \'mōd\ *n.* **1** A manner of doing something; a method; a way; as, a *mode* of travel. **2** In grammar, the mood of a verb. **3** A popular style; a fashion; as, to dress in the *mode*.

mod·el \'mäd-l\ *n.* **1** A small but exact copy of a thing; as, a *model* of a ship. **2** A pattern or a figure of something that may be made; as, clay *models* for a statue. **3** A person who sets a good example; as, a *model* of politeness. **4** A person or thing that serves as an artist's pattern; especially, a person who poses for an artist. **5** A person who wears, in the presence of customers, garments that are for sale; especially, a mannequin in a dress shop. — For synonyms see *pattern*. — *adj.* **1** Serving as or worthy of being a model or pattern; as, a *model* student. **2** Being a miniature representation of something; as, a *model* airplane. — *v.;* **mod·eled** or **mod·elled**; **mod·el·ing** or **mod·el·ling** \-l(-)ing\. **1** To plan or shape after a pattern; as, a sports car *modeled* on a racing car. **2** To make a model or models; to mold; as, to *model* a dog in clay. **3** To act or serve as a model; as, to *model* for an artist. — **mod·el·er** or **mod·el·ler** \-l(-)ər\ *n.*

mod·er·ate \'mäd-r(-)ət\ *adj.* **1** Neither too much nor too little; not extreme; as, *moderate* heat. **2** Temperate; as, a person of *moderate* habits. **3** Reasonable; calm; as, *moderate* language. **4** Not extreme in opinion; as, *moderate* views. **5** Neither very good nor very bad; mediocre; ordinary; as, *moderate* success. — *n.* A person of moderate views, especially in politics. — \-r-ˌāt\ *v.;* **mod·er·at·ed**; **mod·er·at·ing.** **1** To make or become moderate or less extreme; as, to *moderate* a demand. **2** To preside over, direct, or regulate, as a public meeting.

mod·er·a·tion \ˌmäd-r-'āsh-n\ *n.* **1** The action of moderating. **2** The condition of being moderate or of keeping within proper bounds; as, to do everything in *moderation*.

mod·e·ra·to \ˌmäd-r-'ät-ō\ *adj.* In music, moderate — used as a direction to indicate tempo.

mod·er·a·tor \'mäd-r-ˌāt-r\ *n.* **1** One that moderates. **2** A presiding officer, as of a town meeting or of a presbytery or synod in the Presbyterian church.

mod·ern \'mäd-rn\ *adj.* **1** Of the present time or of times not long past; new-fashioned; as, *modern* schools. **2** Of the centuries after the Middle Ages; as, *modern* history. — *n.* A person of modern times; a person with modern ideas. — **mo·der·ni·ty** \mə-'dər-nət-ē, mä-\ *n.*

mod·ern·ism \'mäd-r-ˌniz-m\ *n.* A modern practice; especially, a modern usage, expression, or characteristic.

mod·ern·ist \'mäd-r-nəst\ *n.* **1** An admirer of modern ways, ideas, or fashions. **2** A person who advocates the teaching of modern subjects, as of the modern rather than the classical languages.

mod·ern·is·tic \ˌmäd-r-'nis-tik\ *adj.* Of, relating to, or characteristic of modernism or of modernists.

mod·ern·ize \'mäd-r-ˌnīz\ *v.;* **mod·ern·ized**; **mod·ern·iz·ing.** To make or become modern; to make conform to present usage, style, or taste; as, to *modernize* an old house. — **mod·ern·i·za·tion** \ˌmäd-r-nə-'zāsh-n\ *n.*

mod·est \'mäd-əst\ *adj.* **1** Having a moderate opinion of one's own good qualities and abilities; not boastful; as, a *modest* winner. **2** Showing moderation; not excessive; as, a *modest* request. **3** Pure in thought and conduct; decent; as, a *modest* girl. — **mod·est·ly**, *adv.*

mod·es·ty \'mäd-əs-tē\ *n.* The quality of being modest.

mod·i·cum \'mäd-ik-m, 'mōd-\ *n.* A limited quantity; a small amount; a little; as, an explanation that anyone with a *modicum* of intelligence should understand.

mod·i·fi·ca·tion \ˌmäd-ə-fə-'kāsh-n\ *n.* **1** A modifying or being modified. **2** Qualification or limitation; as, a *modification* of a statement made in haste. **3** Partial alteration; as, a *modification* of plans made earlier. **4** A change in an organism which is caused by the influence of its environment instead of being inherited.

mod·i·fi·er \'mäd-ə-ˌfīr\ *n.* A word, as an adjective or adverb, joined to another word to limit or qualify its meaning; a qualifier.

mod·i·fy \'mäd-ə-ˌfī\ *v.;* **mod·i·fied** \-ˌfīd\; **mod·i·fy·ing.** **1** To make changes in; as, to *modify* a plan. **2** To lower or reduce, as in extent or degree; to moderate; as, to *modify* a punishment. **3** To limit in meaning; to qualify. In the phrase "green gloves", "green" *modifies* "gloves".

mod·ish \'mōd-ish\ *adj.* Stylish. — **mod·ish·ly**, *adv.*

mod·u·late \'mäj-l-ˌāt\ *v.;* **mod·u·lat·ed**; **mod·u·lat·ing.** **1** To adjust or regulate to a certain proportion; especially, to soften or tone down. **2** To tune to a certain key or pitch; to vary in pitch; as, to *modulate* the voice. **3** In radio and television, to vary some quality of an electric wave in accordance with some quality of another electric wave; especially, to vary the frequency or amplitude of the carrier wave in accordance with the electric wave that carries the sound or sight. **4** In music, to pass from one key to another, usually in a gradual movement, especially by a melodious progression of chords.

mod·u·la·tion \ˌmäj-l-'āsh-n\ *n.* **1** A modulating; the extent or degree by which something is modulated. **2** In music, the changing from one key to another, especially without any break in the melody or chord succession. **3** In radio and television, variation of some quality of the carrier wave, as of the frequency, or number of vibrations per second (**frequency modulation**) or of the amplitude, or up-and-down extent (**amplitude modulation**), in accordance with the sound or sight that is to be transmitted.

Mo·gul \mō-'gəl, 'mōg-l, 'mō-ˌgəl\ *n.* **1** A person of the Mongolian race; especially, one of the Mongol conquerors of India or their descendants. **2** [with a small letter] A great personage; as, one of the *moguls* of the town.

mo·hair \'mō-ˌhar, -ˌher\ *n.* **1** Cloth made from the hair of the Angora goat. **2** A shiny cloth, usually of wool and cotton, imitating this cloth.

Mo·ham·med·an \mō-'ham-ə-dən, -'häm-, -'ham-\ or **Ma·hom·et·an** \mə-'häm-ət-n\ *adj.* or *n.* Moslem.

Mo·ham·med·an·ism \mō-'ham-ə-də-ˌniz-m, -'häm-, -'ham-\ *n.* The Moslem religion.

moi·e·ty \'mȯi-ət-ē\ *n.; pl.* **moi·e·ties. 1** One of two equal parts; a half. **2** About a half; a part.

moi·re or **moi·ré** \mȯ-'rā, mwä-\ *n.* Any fabric, especially silk, with a watered appearance.

moist \'mȯist\ *adj.* Slightly wet; damp; not dry; as, *moist* earth.

— The words *damp* and *dank* are synonyms of *moist: moist* usually refers to a very slight degree of wetness which is just enough to keep a thing from being called dry; *damp* may suggest a moderate wetness that is often disagreeable and depressing, though sometimes useful; *dank* almost always suggests a chill, penetrating, and highly unpleasant wetness that is often associated with mustiness and decay.

mois·ten \'mȯis-n\ *v.;* **mois·tened; mois·ten·ing** \-n(-)ing\. To make moist.

mois·ture \'mȯis-chər\ *n.* The small amount of liquid that causes moistness; dampness, in the air or on a surface.

mo·lar \'mōl-r\ *adj.* [From Latin *molaris* meaning literally "of a mill", "of a millstone", a derivative of *mola* meaning "mill", "millstone", this in turn being a derivative of *molare* meaning "to grind".] **1** Able or fitted to grind. **2** Of or relating to a molar. **—** *n.* A tooth with a broad surface adapted for grinding; a back tooth.

mo·las·ses \mə-'las-əz\ *n.* The thick brown syrup that drains from sugar as it is being manufactured.

mold or **mould** \'mōld\ *n.* **1** An often fuzzy growth produced by fungi living especially upon damp or decaying organic matter. **2** A fungus that forms mold. **—** *v.* To cover or fill with mold; to become moldy.

mold or **mould** \'mōld\ *n.* Light, rich, crumbly earth; soil containing decayed matter, as leaves.

mold or **mould** \'mōld\ *n.* **1** A hollow form from which something takes its shape; as, a candle *mold.* **2** Something shaped in a mold; as, a *mold* of ice cream. **—** *v.* **1** To knead into shape; as, to *mold* loaves of bread. **2** To form or to become formed in or as if in a mold; as, to *mold* butter.

mold·er or **mould·er** \'mōld-r\ *v.;* **mold·ered** or **mould·ered; mold·er·ing** or **mould·er·ing** \-r(-)ing\. To become like mold; to crumble into dust.

mold·ing or **mould·ing** \'mōl-ding\ *n.* **1** The act or work of a person who molds. **2** A strip of material having a shaped surface and used as a decoration, as on a wall or the edge of a table.

moldings

moldy or **mouldy** \'mōl-dē\ *adj.;* **mold·i·er** or **mould·i·er; mold·i·est** or **mould·i·est. 1** Overgrown with or containing mold; musty; as, *moldy* bread. **2** Of or like mold; as, *moldy* mass.

mole \'mōl\ *n.* A small permanent spot on the skin, usually brown and sometimes protruding.

mole \'mōl\ *n.* **1** A small burrowing mammal resembling a mouse and having very soft fur, concealed ears, and very tiny eyes. **2** Also **mole·skin** \-ˌskin\. The fur of the mole.

mole \'mōl\ *n.* A heavy masonry structure built in the sea as a breakwater or jetty.

mo·lec·u·lar \mə-'lek-yəl-r\ *adj.* Relating to molecules; produced by or consisting of molecules.

molecular weight. The weight of any molecule; the sum of the weights of the atoms contained in any molecule.

mol·e·cule \'mäl-ə-ˌkyül\ *n.* **1** The smallest portion of a substance retaining all the properties of the substance in a mass; as, a *molecule* of water. **2** Any very small particle.

mole·hill \'mōl-ˌhil\ *n.* **1** A little ridge of earth pushed up by moles as they burrow underground. **2** Any unimportant obstacle.

mo·lest \mō-'lest, mə-\ *v.* To injure or disturb by interfering; to annoy and harm. — **mo·les·ta·tion** \ˌmō-ˌles-'tāsh-n\ *n.*

mol·li·fy \'mäl-ə-ˌfī\ *v.;* **mol·li·fied** \-ˌfīd\; **mol·li·fy·ing.** To calm; to quiet; to soothe. — For synonyms see *pacify.* — **mol·li·fi·ca·tion** \ˌmäl-ə-fə-'kāsh-n\ *n.*

mol·lusk or **mol·lusc** \'mäl-əsk\ *n.* An invertebrate animal, usually with an outer shell, having a soft body not composed of segments, as an oyster, a snail, or a squid.

mol·ly·cod·dle \'mäl-ē-ˌkäd-l\ *n.* A person who is used to being coddled or petted; a pampered man or boy. **—** *v.;* **mol·ly·cod·dled; mol·ly·cod·dling** \-l(-)ing\. To pamper.

molt or **moult** \'mōlt\ *v.* To shed the hair, feathers, outer skin, or horns that will be replaced by a new growth. **—** *n.* The process of molting or the period of time during which molting occurs.

mol·ten \'mōlt-n\. Archaic past part. of *melt.* **—** *adj.* **1** Melted, as by intense heat; as, *molten* metal. **2** Made by melting and casting.

mol·to \'mōl-ˌtō\ *adv.* In music, much; very.

mo·lyb·de·num \mə-'lib-də-nəm\ *n.* A white metallic element used in steel alloys to give greater strength and hardness.

mo·ment \'mō-mənt\ *n.* **1** An instant; a very brief time; as, to vanish in a *moment.* **2** Importance. This is a matter of great *moment.*

mo·men·tar·i·ly \ˌmō-mən-'ter-ə-lē\ *adv.* **1** For a

moment; temporarily. The pain eased *momentarily.* **2** From moment to moment. The storm grew in force *momentarily.*

mo·men·tary \'mō-mən-ˌter-ē\ *adj.* Lasting only a moment; short-lived.

mo·ment·ly \'mō-mənt-lē\ *adv.* Momentarily.

mo·men·tous \mō-'ment-əs\ *adj.* Very important; as, a *momentous* decision. — **mo·men·tous·ly,** *adv.*

mo·men·tum \mō-'ment-m\ *n.* **1** The force that a moving body has because of its weight and motion. **2** Impetus.

Mon. Abbreviation for *Monday.*

Mon·a·can \'män-ək-n; mə-'näk-n, -'nȧk-\ *adj.* Of or relating to Monaco. — *n.* A native of Monaco.

mon·arch \'män-rk, -ˌärk, -ˌȧrk\ *n.* **1** A person who is the supreme ruler; a sovereign; a king, queen, or emperor. **2** Something that is likened to a monarch. The oak tree is the *monarch* of the forest. — **mo·nar·chal** \mə-'närk-l, -'nȧrk-l\ or **mo·nar·chi·al** \-'närk-ē-əl, -'nȧrk-\ *adj.*

mo·nar·chic \mə-'närk-ik, -'nȧrk-\ or **mo·nar·chi·cal** \-ik-l\ *adj.* Of or relating to a monarch or monarchy; favoring a monarchy.

mon·arch·ism \'män-r-ˌkiz-m\ *n.* **1** The system or principles of government under a monarch. **2** Belief in and support of such a form of government. — **mon·arch·ist** \-rk-əst\ *n.*

mon·archy \'män-rk-ē, -ˌärk-ē, -ˌȧrk-ē\ *n.; pl.* **mon·arch·ies.** **1** A state or country having a monarch. **2** Rule by a monarch. **3** The system of government under a monarch.

mon·as·tery \'män-əs-ˌter-ē\ *n.; pl.* **mon·as·ter·ies.** The building or group of buildings in which a community of religious persons, especially monks, live and carry on their work.

mo·nas·tic \mə-'nas-tik\ *adj.* **1** Of or relating to monks or monasteries. **2** Separated from worldly affairs; as, a *monastic* life.

mo·nas·ti·cism \mə-'nas-tə-ˌsiz-m\ *n.* The life or state of monks; the system or practice of living apart from the rest of the world for religious reasons, especially as members of a secluded community.

Mon·day \'mən-dē\ *n.* [From Old English *Monandaeg* meaning literally "day of the moon", and being a translation of Late Latin *Lunae dies.*] The second day of the week.

monecious. Variant of *monoecious.*

Mon·e·gasque \ˌmän-ə-'gask\ *adj.* or *n.* Monacan.

mon·e·tary \'män-ə-ˌter-ē, 'mən-\ *adj.* **1** Of or relating to coinage or currency. **2** Of or relating to money; pecuniary; as, the high *monetary* value of certain antiques.

mon·e·tize \'män-ə-ˌtīz, 'mən-\ *v.;* **mon·e·tized; mon·e·tiz·ing.** To give a standard value to as currency; as, to *monetize* silver. — **mon·e·ti·za·tion** \ˌmän-ət-ə-'zāsh-n, ˌmən-\ *n.*

mon·ey \'mən-ē\ *n.; pl.* **mon·eys** or **mon·ies.** **1** Metal, as gold, silver, or copper, coined or stamped and issued for use in buying and selling. **2** A stated amount of money. **3** Wealth reckoned in terms of money. **4** Any written or stamped certificate, such as a government paper note, lawfully used as money.

mon·ey·bag \'mən-ē-ˌbag\ *n.* **1** A bag for holding money. **2** [in the plural] A rich person.

mon·ey-chang·er \'mən-ē-ˌchānj-r\ *n.* One whose business is the exchanging of kinds or denominations of currency.

mon·eyed \'mən-ēd\ *adj.* Wealthy; rich.

money order. An order for the payment of money; especially, a government order sold at a post office and payable at another post office to a person or firm named.

Mon·gol \'mäng-gl, 'män-ˌgōl\ *adj.* Mongolian. — *n.* **1** A member of one of the native peoples of Mongolia. **2** The language of the Mongols. **3** A member of the Mongolian race.

Mon·go·lian \män(g)-'gōl-yən, -'gō-lē-ən\ *adj.* **1** Of or relating to Mongolia or the Mongols. **2** Of or relating to the division of mankind named the **Mongolian race**, comprising the peoples of nearly all Asia except Hindustan and the Moslem countries of the southwest. — *n.* **1** A member of the Mongolian race. **2** A member of one of the peoples of Mongolia. **3** The language of the Mongols.

Mon·gol·ism \'mäng-gl-ˌiz-m\ *n.* A malformation present from birth in which the child has slanting eyes, a large tongue, and a broad, short skull and is frequently of extremely low mentality.

Mon·gol·oid \'mäng-gl-ˌȯid\ *adj.* **1** Of or relating to the Mongolian race. **2** Having traits suggestive of the Mongolian race; as, *Mongoloid* features; a *Mongoloid* nose. — *n.* **1** A Mongolian. **2** A person having some Mongoloid traits.

mon·goose \'män(g)-ˌgüs\ *n.; pl.* **mon·goos·es.** A small mammal of India of the civet family that resembles the ferret in form and size and that kills poisonous snakes.

mon·grel \'məng-grəl, 'mäng-\ *n.* **1** The offspring of two or more breeds, as of dogs. **2** Any person or thing of mixed origin. — *adj.* **1** Of a mixed breed or race; as, a *mongrel* dog. **2** Of mixed character, origin, or kinds; as, a *mongrel* word.

mon·i·tor \'män-ət-r\ *n.* **1** A person who warns or advises. **2** A pupil, in a school, selected for special duties such as keeping order. **3** A heavily armored war vessel with low sides and one or more revolving gun turrets. **4** A person who monitors. **5** An apparatus used for monitoring. — *v.;* **mon·i·tored; mon·i·tor·ing** \-ət-r-ing, -ə-tring\. **1** To act as a monitor; as, to *monitor* the classrooms in the teacher's absence. **2** To use a receiving apparatus in order to check something, as a radio signal, a television channel, or a program for such characteristics as the quality of reception or the fidelity to a broadcasting band.

monk \'məngk\ *n.* A man who renounces the world for religious reasons; especially, one belonging to a religious order taking the monastic vows of poverty, chastity, and obedience and living in a monastery.

mon·key \'məngk-ē\ *n.; pl.* **mon·keys.** Any of a

number of animals found chiefly in tropical forests, resembling man and next to man in the scale of animals; especially, one of the smaller, longer-tailed forms, as distinguished from the apes. — *v.*; **mon·keyed**; **mon·key·ing**. To act or handle as a monkey does; to meddle. — **mon·key·ish** \-ē-ish\ *adj.*

mon·key·shine \'məngk-ē-ˌshīn\ *n. Slang.* A monkeyish trick, antic, or prank.

monkey wrench. A wrench for general use, having a straight handle, one fixed jaw set at right angles to the handle, and one adjustable jaw.

monkey wrench

monk·ish \'məngk-ish\ *adj.* Of or relating to monks; monastic.

monks·hood \'məngks-ˌhůd\ *n.* An herb of the crowfoot family, with poisonous juice and mostly blue or purple flowers shaped like hoods.

mono-. A prefix that can mean: **1** One, single, alone, as in *monoplane* or *monocotyledon.* **2** One atom or group, as in *monoxide.*

mon·o·chrome \'män-ə-ˌkrōm\ *n.* **1** A painting or drawing in a single hue. **2** The art or process of producing such a picture.

mon·o·cle \'män-ək-l\ *n.* An eyeglass for one eye. — **mon·o·cled** \-ək-ld\ *adj.*

mon·o·cot \'män-ə-ˌkät\ or **mon·o·cot·yl** \'män-ə-ˌkät-l\ *n.* A monocotyledon.

mon·o·cot·y·le·don \ˌmän-ə-ˌkät-l-'ēd-n\ *n.* Any seed plant having a single cotyledon and usually leaves with parallel veins and flower parts in threes, as the palms and the grasses. — **mon·o·cot·y·le·don·ous** \-'ēd-n-əs, -'ed-n-əs\ *adj.*

mo·noe·cious or **mo·ne·cious** \mə-'nē-shəs\ *adj.* In biology, having both male and female reproductive organs in the same individual; especially, in botany, having on the same plant flowers with stamens only and flowers with pistil only.

mo·nog·a·mous \mə-'näg-m-əs\ *adj.* Of or relating to monogamy; upholding or practicing monogamy.

mo·nog·a·my \mə-'näg-m-ē\ *n.* The condition of being married to only one person at a time. — **mo·nog·a·mist** \-m-əst\ *n.*

mon·o·gram \'män-ə-ˌgram\ *n.* A design composed of two or more letters, as a person's initials, interwoven or combined; as, a *monogram* on a towel.

mon·o·graph \'män-ə-ˌgraf\ *n.* A special treatise on a particular subject; especially, a scholarly or scientific paper printed in a journal or as a pamphlet.

mon·o·lith \'män-l-ˌith\ *n.* A single stone or block of stone shaped into a pillar, statue, or monument. — **mon·o·lith·ic** \ˌmän-l-'ith-ik\ *adj.*

mon·o·logue or **mon·o·log** \'män-l-ˌȯg\ *n.* **1** A dramatic scene in which one person speaks alone. **2** A drama performed by one actor. **3** A literary composition, as a poem, in the form of a soliloquy. **4** A long speech uttered by one person. — **mo·nol·o·gist** \mə-'näl-ə-jəst, 'män-l-ˌȯg-əst\ or **mon·o·logu·ist** \'män-l-ˌȯg-əst\ *n.*

mon·o·ma·nia \ˌmän-ə-'mā-nē-ə, -'mān-yə\ *n.* **1** A derangement of a person's mind limited to one idea or one group of ideas. **2** Such abnormal concentration on a single idea or object as to suggest mental derangement. — **mon·o·ma·ni·ac** \-'mā-nē-ˌak\ *n.*

mo·no·mi·al \mə-'nō-mē-əl\ *adj.* In algebra, having only one term. — *n.* An expression consisting of only one term.

mon·o·plane \'män-ə-ˌplān\ *n.* An airplane with only one main supporting surface.

mo·nop·o·list \mə-'näp-l-əst\ *n.* One who has a monopoly or favors monopoly. — **mo·nop·o·lis·tic** \mə-ˌnäp-l-'is-tik\ *adj.*

monoplane

mo·nop·o·lize \mə-'näp-l-ˌīz\ *v.*; **mo·nop·o·lized**; **mo·nop·o·liz·ing**. To acquire a monopoly of; as, to *monopolize* a conversation.

mo·nop·o·ly \mə-'näp-l(-)ē\ *n.*; *pl.* **mo·nop·o·lies.** **1** The exclusive control of the entire supply of any commodity or service. **2** Exclusive possession or control of anything; as, to have a *monopoly* on a person's time. **3** Any commodity the supply of which is under the control of one party. **4** Any person or corporation which has or acquires a monopoly.

mon·o·rail \'män-ə-ˌrāl\ *n.* **1** A single rail serving as a track for cars that are balanced upon it or suspended from it. **2** A railway having such a track.

mon·o·syl·la·ble \'män-ə-ˌsil-əb-l\ *n.* A word of one syllable. "Yes" and "no" are *monosyllables.* — **mon·o·syl·lab·ic** \ˌmän-ə-sə-'lab-ik\ *adj.*

mon·o·the·ism \'män-ə-(ˌ)thē-ˌiz-m\ *n.* The doctrine or belief that there is only one deity. — **mon·o·the·is·tic** \ˌmän-ə-thē-'is-tik\ *adj.*

mon·o·tone \'män-ə-ˌtōn\ *n.* **1** A succession of syllables, words, or sentences on one unvaried key or pitch; as, to speak in a *monotone.* **2** A single unvaried musical tone. **3** Sameness of tone or style; as, a poem written in *monotone.* **4** Sameness of color; as, engravings in *monotone.* **5** A person not able to produce musical intervals properly with the voice.

mo·not·o·nous \mə-'nät-n(-)əs\ *adj.* **1** Uttered in one unvarying tone. **2** Lacking variety; tiresome because of sameness; as, a *monotonous* voice; a *monotonous* ride. — **mo·not·o·nous·ly,** *adv.*

mo·not·o·ny \mə-'nät-n(-)ē\ *n.*; *pl.* **mo·not·o·nies.** **1** Sameness of tone or sound. **2** Lack of variety; especially, tiresome sameness; as, the *monotony* of the desert.

mon·o·treme \'män-ə-ˌtrēm\ *n.* An animal of the lowest order of mammals, as a duckbill.

mon·ox·ide \mə-'näk-ˌsīd\ *n.* An oxide containing only one oxygen atom in the molecule.

monoxide gas. Carbon monoxide.

mon·sei·gneur \ˌmän-ˌsān-'yər\ *n.*; *pl.* **mes·sei·gneurs** \ˌmā-ˌsān-'yər\. A French dignitary —

used [with a capital] as a title preceding a title of office or rank; as, *Monseigneur* the Archbishop.

mon·sieur \mə-'syə(r), -'sir\ *n.; pl.* **mes·sieurs** \mā-'syə(r), -'sir\. My lord; sir — used [with a capital] in France as a title corresponding to English *Mister*.

mon·si·gnor \män-'sēn-yər\ *n.; pl.* **mon·si·gno·ri** \ˌmän-ˌsēn-'yȯr-ē\. A title of honor borne by some Roman Catholic clergymen.

mon·soon \(')män-'sün\ *n.* **1** A wind in the Indian Ocean and Southern Asia that blows from the southwest from April to October, and from the northeast from October to April. **2** The rainy season that accompanies the southwest monsoon in India and adjacent areas.

mon·ster \'män(t)st-r\ *n.* **1** An animal or plant that differs greatly from the usual type. **2** An imaginary or a real animal with a strange or horrible form. **3** Any enormous animal or thing. **4** An extremely wicked or cruel person. — *adj.* Enormous; as, a *monster* commemorative edition of a newspaper.

mon·strance \'män(t)s-trən(t)s\ *n.* A vessel in which the consecrated bread of the Eucharist is exposed.

mon·stros·i·ty \män-'sträs-ət-ē\ *n.; pl.* **mon·stros·i·ties.** **1** The condition of being monstrous. **2** A monster.

mon·strous \'män(t)s-trəs\ *adj.* **1** Extraordinary because of size; huge; enormous; as, to grow to *monstrous* proportions. **2** Differing greatly from its natural form; abnormal; as, a *monstrous* kind of creature. **3** Very ugly or vicious; as, a *monstrous* crime. **4** Shockingly wrong. Isn't it *monstrous* that so many lives are lost in highway accidents?
— The words *tremendous* and *colossal* are synonyms of *monstrous: monstrous* usually describes something as being abnormal for its type, usually in greatness of size but often in shape or character as well; *tremendous* applies especially to something that inspires awe or fear because of its immensity of size or sometimes of importance; *colossal* may suggest something almost unimaginably huge or gigantic.

mon·strous·ly \'män(t)s-trəs-lē\ *adv.* In a monstrous manner.

month \'mən(t)th\ *n.; pl.* **months** \'mən(t)s, 'mən(t)ths\. [From Old English *monath*, a derivative of *mona* meaning "moon".] **1** One of the twelve portions (**calendar month**) into which the year is divided. **2** The period (**lunar month**) of a complete revolution of the moon; a period of 28 days.

month·ly \'mən(t)th-lē\ *adj.* **1** Continued during a month; in a month; as, the *monthly* revolution of the moon. **2** Done, happening, payable, or published once a month; as, a *monthly* visit; a *monthly* magazine. — *n.; pl.* **month·lies.** A magazine published once a month. — *adv.* Once a month; in every month.

mon·u·ment \'män-yə-mənt\ *n.* **1** Something that serves as a memorial; especially, a building, pillar, stone, or statue provided in memory of a person or event. **2** A work, saying, or deed that lasts or that is worth preserving. The book is a *monument* of scholarship.

mon·u·men·tal \ˌmän-yə-'ment-l\ *adj.* **1** Having to do with or suitable for a monument. **2** Like a monument; impressive and lasting; as, Shakespeare's *monumental* work. **3** As conspicuous as a monument; notable; colossal; as, *monumental* stupidity. — **mon·u·men·tal·ly** \-'ment-l-ē\ *adv.*

moo \'mü\ *n.; pl.* **moos.** The sound made by a cow. — *v.;* **mooed; moo·ing.** To make a moo; to low.

mood \'müd\ *n.* In grammar, one of the different forms that a verb can have in order to show whether the action or state that it expresses is to be thought of as a fact, a command, or a wish or possibility, the three moods in English being the indicative, the imperative, and the subjunctive.

mood \'müd\ *n.* A state or frame of mind; humor; disposition; as, to be in a good *mood.*
— The word *humor* is a synonym of *mood: mood* usually suggests a state of mind in which one particular emotion is felt very strongly and often to such an extent that it dominates one's actions for some time; *humor* can refer to a similar state of mind but generally suggests one dominated more by a whimsical or changeable emotion.

moody \'müd-ē\ *adj.;* **mood·i·er; mood·i·est.** **1** Subject to moods, especially to fits of depression or bad temper; as, a *moody* person. **2** Expressing a mood; showing a moody state of mind; as, a *moody* face. — **mood·i·ly** \-l-ē\ *adv.*

moon \'mün\ *n.* **1** The heavenly body that revolves about the earth from west to east in a little less than a calendar month and accompanies the earth in its yearly revolution about the sun. **2** A month. **3** Moonlight. **4** Something shaped like a moon, especially a crescent. **5** Any of the smaller bodies that revolve about a planet; a satellite; as, the *moons* of Jupiter and Saturn. — *v.* To wander about idly; to gaze about in a stupid or dreamy way.

moon·beam \'mün-ˌbēm\ *n.* A ray of light from the moon.

moon·fish \'mün-ˌfish\ *n.; pl.* **moon·fish** or **moon·fish·es.** A narrow, deep-bodied silvery fish of the southern coasts of North America.

moon·light \'mün-ˌlīt\ *n.* The light of the moon. — *adj.* **1** Of or having to do with moonlight. **2** Happening during or done by moonlight; moonlit; as, a *moonlight* walk.

moon·lit \'mün-ˌlit\ *adj.* Lighted by the moon; as, a *moonlit* night.

moon·shine \'mün-ˌshīn\ *n.* **1** Moonlight. **2** Empty show; foolishness; nonsense. **3** Liquor, especially whiskey, that has been illegally distilled.

moon·stone \'mün-ˌstōn\ *n.* A somewhat transparent stone with a pearly greenish or bluish luster, a variety of feldspar, used in jewelry.

moon-struck \'mün-ˌstrək\ *adj.* Mentally deranged; crazy.

moor \'mu̇r, 'mōr\ *n.* An area of open waste land, especially one covered with heather.

moor \'mu̇r, 'mōr\ *v.* To secure or fasten, as a vessel, in a place with cables, lines, or anchors.

moor·ings \'mu̇r-ingz, 'mōr-\ *n. pl.* **1** The anchors, cables, or lines used for mooring a boat. **2** A place where a boat is moored or may be moored.

moor·land \'mu̇r-lənd, 'mōr-, -ˌland\ *n.* Land consisting of a moor or moors.

moose \'müs\ *n. sing. and pl.* A large mammal of the deer family having humped shoulders and often weighing over 1000 pounds, found in the forests of Canada and the northern United States.

moose

moot \'müt\ *v.* To argue for and against; to bring up for discussion. — *adj.* Subject to argument or discussion; debatable; disputed; as, a *moot* question.

mop \'mäp\ *n.* **1** An implement for cleaning, made of a bundle of cloth or yarn fastened to a handle. **2** A similar device consisting of a sponge fastened to a handle. **3** Something likened to a mop; as, a tangled *mop* of hair. — *v.;* **mopped**; **mop·ping.** To rub or wipe with a mop or as if with a mop; as, to *mop* a floor; to *mop* one's forehead with a handkerchief. — **mop up. 1** To clean by mopping; to remove by mopping; as, to *mop up* a glass of spilled milk. **2** To finish; to make an end of; as, to have a few odd jobs to *mop up* before quitting.

mope \'mōp\ *v.;* **moped**; **mop·ing.** To be dull and without spirit. — *n.* **1** A dull, listless person. **2** [in the plural] Low spirits; as, a fit of the *mopes.*

mo·raine \mə-'rān\ *n.* An accumulation of earth and stones deposited by a glacier.

mor·al \'mȯr-əl, 'mär-\ *adj.* **1** Concerned with, or relating to, what is right and wrong in human behavior; as, *moral* problems; a *moral* code. **2** Serving to teach a lesson; as, a *moral* story. **3** Affecting standards of conduct; as, a *moral* influence. **4** Virtuous; good; as, a *moral* man; to lead a *moral* life. **5** Capable of right and wrong action. Man is a *moral* being. **6** Probable, but not proved; virtual; as, a *moral* certainty. — *n.* **1** [in the plural] Moral conduct; as, men of bad *morals.* **2** [in the plural] Moral teachings; moral principles. **3** The inner meaning of, or lesson to be learned from, a story or an experience.

mo·rale \mə-'ral\ *n.* Mental or moral condition, especially as affected by enthusiasm, spirit, or hope; as, the *morale* of an army; to build up *morale.*

mor·al·ist \'mȯr-ə-ləst, 'mär-\ *n.* **1** One who moralizes; a person who teaches, studies, or points out morals. **2** One who leads a moral life.

mor·al·is·tic \ˌmȯr-ə-'lis-tik, ˌmär-\ *adj.* **1** Teaching or pointing out morals; moralizing; as, a *moralistic* story. **2** Characteristic of moralists; as, a *moralistic* attitude towards the problems of youth. — **mor·al·is·ti·cal·ly** \-tik-l(-)ē\ *adv.*

mo·ral·i·ty \mə-'ral-ət-ē\ *n.; pl.* **mo·ral·i·ties.** **1** Moral quality or character; virtue; as, to judge the *morality* of an action. **2** Moral conduct; morals; as, standards of *morality.* **3** A system of morals; principles of conduct. **4** In full, **morality play.** An allegorical play of a type especially popular in the 15th and 16th centuries, in which the characters are personifications of various virtues and vices.

mor·al·ize \'mȯr-ə-ˌlīz, 'mär-\ *v.;* **mor·al·ized**; **mor·al·iz·ing. 1** To explain in a moral sense; to draw a moral from. **2** To make moral or morally better. **3** To make moral reflections; to talk or write in a moralistic way. — **mor·al·i·za·tion** \ˌmȯr-ə-lə-'zāsh-n, ˌmär-\ *n.*

mor·al·ly \'mȯr-ə-lē, 'mär-\ *adv.* **1** In a moral manner. **2** From a moral point of view; with respect to morality; as, to be *morally* bound. **3** According to what is probable; virtually; practically; as, an attempt that was *morally* certain to fail.

mo·rass \mə-'ras\ *n.* A marsh; a swamp.

mor·a·to·ri·um \ˌmȯr-ə-'tōr-ē-əm, ˌmär-, -'tȯr-\ *n.* A period during which a debtor has a legal right to delay paying a debt.

mo·ray \mə-'rā, 'mȯr-ˌā\ *n.* Any of a number of savage, often brightly colored eels found in all warm seas, especially in crevices about coral reefs.

mor·bid \'mȯr-bəd\ *adj.* **1** Not sound and healthful; diseased. **2** Characterized by gloomy or unwholesome ideas or feelings; as, to take a *morbid* interest in ghost stories. **3** Relating to disease. — **mor·bid·ly,** *adv.*

mor·bid·i·ty \mȯr-'bid-ət-ē\ *n.; pl.* **mor·bid·i·ties. 1** Morbid state or character. **2** Amount of disease; rate of sickness; as, a backward area, having extremely high *morbidity.*

mor·dant \'mȯrd-nt\ *adj.* Biting; sarcastic; as, a *mordant* criticism. — *n.* **1** A substance, such as an acid, that eats into metal, used in etching. **2** A substance used in dyeing to help produce a fixed color.

more \'mōr, 'mȯr\ *adj.* Used as the comparative of *many* and *much.* Additional; other; as, to buy *more* land. — *n.* A greater amount or number; an additional amount; as, to get *more* than one expected; to be too full to eat any *more.* — *adv.* **1** In or to a greater extent or degree; as, to feel *more* dead than alive. **2** In addition; moreover; as, to advance three yards *more.*

☞ *more* is used with some adjectives and adverbs to form the comparative degree; as, *more* active; *more* actively.

more·over \mōr-'ōv-r, mȯr-\ *adv.* Beyond what has been said; further; besides.

mo·res \'mȯr-ˌāz, -(ˌ)ēz\ *n. pl.* Customs; especially, fixed customs; conventions having the force of law.

mor·ga·nat·ic \ˌmȯrg-n-'at-ik\ *adj.* Of or relating to a marriage contracted by a person of royal or other high rank with one of inferior rank, in which the wife, if inferior, does not acquire the husband's rank and the children do not take or inherit the rank or property of the parent of higher rank.

morgue \'mȯrg\ *n.* **1** A place where the bodies of persons found dead are shown for identification. **2** A department of a newspaper office where miscellaneous material for reference is filed.

mor·i·bund \'mȯr-ə-(ˌ)bənd, 'mär-\ *adj.* In a dying condition; near death.

morn \'mȯrn\ *n.* Morning.

morn·ing \'mȯr-ning\ *n.* **1** The first or early part of the day; the forenoon. **2** The first or early part; as, the *morning* of life. **3** The dawn. — *adj.* Of or relating to the morning.

morn·ing–glo·ry \'mȯr-ning-ˌglōr-ē, -ˌglȯr-ē\ *n.; pl.* **morn·ing–glo·ries.** **1** A twining vine with large showy funnel-shaped flowers, purple, pink, or blue, that close in the sunshine. **2** Any of a family of twining vines, of which the morning glory is typical, with flowers shaped like funnels and having flaring outer margins, including the bindweeds and sweet potato.

morning-glory

morning star. Any of the planets Venus, Jupiter, Mars, Mercury, and Saturn, when it rises before the sun, especially Venus.

Mo·roc·can \mə-'räk-n\ *adj.* Of or relating to Morocco or its inhabitants. — *n.* A native or inhabitant of Morocco.

mo·roc·co \mə-'räk-ˌō\ *n.* A kind of fine leather which is made of goatskin tanned with sumac.

mo·ron \'mōr-ˌän, 'mȯr-\ *n.* A feeble-minded person whose mental ability is incapable of being developed beyond that of a normal child of from eight to 12 years. — **mo·ron·ic** \mə-'rän-ik\ *adj.*

mo·rose \mə-'rōs\ *adj.* Of a sour or gloomy temper; sullen. — **mo·rose·ly**, *adv.*

mor·phine \'mȯr-ˌfēn\ *n.* [From German *morphin*, named after *Morpheus*, the ancient Roman god of dreams.] A bitter, white, crystalline drug made from opium and used to deaden pain and to induce sleep.

mor·phol·o·gy \mȯr-'fäl-ə-jē\ *n.* The branch of biology dealing with the form and structure of animals and plants. — **mor·pho·log·ic** \ˌmȯr-fə-'läj-ik\ or **mor·pho·log·i·cal** \-ik-l\ *adj.*

mor·ris \'mȯr-əs, 'mär-\ *n.* or **morris dance.** A dance formerly common in England in pageants and games on May Day, performed by men in costume.

Mor·ris chair \'mȯr-əs, 'mär-\. An easy chair with adjustable back and removable cushions.

mor·row \'mär-ō\ *n.* **1** The next following day after the day specified. **2** Tomorrow.

Morse code or **Morse alphabet** \'mȯrs\. A system of signals used in telegraphing, invented by Samuel F. B. Morse and consisting of dots, dashes, and spaces.

mor·sel \'mȯrs-l\ *n.* **1** A small quantity; a little piece. **2** A small bit of tasty food.

mor·tal \'mȯrt-l\ *adj.* **1** Subject to death. All men are *mortal.* **2** Causing death; deadly; as, a *mortal* wound. **3** Making the person who commits it deserving of spiritual death; as, a *mortal* sin. **4** So severe as to be thought of as threatening death; as, *mortal* fear. **5** Fought to the death; as, *mortal* combat. **6** Wishing to kill; as, a *mortal* enemy. **7** Human; as, *mortal* power. **8** Of or relating to death or its occasion; fatal; as, condemned prisoners awaiting their *mortal* hour. — *n.* A human being.

mor·tal·i·ty \mȯr-'tal-ət-ē\ *n.* **1** The quality or state of being mortal. **2** The death of large numbers, as from war or disease. **3** The number or rate of deaths in a given time or community; the proportion of deaths to population; as, a period of low *mortality.*

mor·tal·ly \'mȯrt-l-ē\ *adv.* **1** Fatally; as, *mortally* wounded. **2** Very severely; extremely; as, *mortally* offended; *mortally* jealous.

mor·tar \'mȯrt-r\ *n.* **1** A strong bowl-shaped container in which substances are pounded or rubbed with a pestle. **2** A short light cannon used to throw shells high into the air.

mortar and pestle

mor·tar \'mȯrt-r\ *n.* A plastic building material that hardens, as one made of lime and cement mixed with sand and water and spread between bricks or stones to hold them together. — *v.* To plaster with mortar.

mor·tar·board \'mȯrt-r-ˌbōrd, -ˌbȯrd\ *n.* **1** A board for holding mortar while it is being applied. **2** An academic cap with a broad, projecting square top.

mort·gage \'mȯr-gij\ *n.* **1** A transfer of property as security for the payment of a debt, with the agreement that the transfer is void when the debt is paid. **2** The written agreement by which such a transfer is made. — *v.;* **mort·gaged**; **mort·gag·ing.** **1** To transfer by a mortgage; as, to *mortgage* a farm. **2** To make subject to a claim; to pledge; as, to *mortgage* one's future.

mort·gag·ee \ˌmȯr-gə-'jē\ *n.* One to whom property is transferred by a mortgage.

mort·ga·gor \ˌmȯr-gə-'jȯr, 'mȯr-gij-r\ *n.* One who mortgages his property.

mor·ti·cian \mȯr-'tish-n\ *n.* An undertaker.

mor·ti·fi·ca·tion \ˌmȯrt-ə-fə-'kāsh-n\ *n.* **1** Overcoming or disciplining of the physical passions and appetites through penance and self-denial. **2** Humiliation or shame caused by something that wounds the pride. Tears of *mortification* blinded the child's eyes. **3** The cause of such humiliation or shame. **4** Gangrene.

mor·ti·fy \'mȯrt-ə-ˌfī\ *v.;* **mor·ti·fied** \-ˌfīd\; **mor·ti·fy·ing.** **1** To humiliate; to shame. The child's naughtiness *mortified* the mother. **2** To decay. The injured foot had *mortified* and had to be cut off.

mor·tise or **mor·tice** \'mȯrt-əs\ *n.* A hole cut in a piece of wood or other material into which another piece, called a *tenon*, fits so as to form a joint. — *v.;* **mor·tised** or **mor·ticed**; **mor·tis·ing** or **mor·tic·ing.** **1** To join or fasten securely, especially by a tenon and mortise. **2** To cut a mortise in.

mor·tu·ary \'mȯr-chə-ˌwer-ē\ *n.; pl.* **mor·tu·ar·ies.** A place where dead bodies may be kept for a short time before burial. — *adj.* Having to do with burial, death, or mourning; as, a *mortuary* chapel.

mos. Abbreviation for *months.*

mo·sa·ic \mō-'zā-ik\ *n.* A surface decoration made by setting small pieces of glass or stone of different colors into some other material, so as to make patterns or pictures. — *adj.* **1** Consisting of mosaic; as, *mosaic* pavements. **2** Resembling mosaic.

Mos·lem \'mäz-ləm, 'mäs-\ *adj.* Of or relating to the religion or institutions founded by Mohammed. — *n.; pl.* **Mos·lems** or **Mos·lem.** A follower of Mohammed, the founder of Islam.

mosque \'mäsk\ *n.* A Moslem place of worship.

mos·qui·to \mə-'skēt-ō\ *n.; pl.* **mos·qui·toes.** A small two-winged insect, the female of which, with a proboscis like a needle, punctures the skin of people and animals to suck their blood.

mosquito

mosquito boat. A high-speed motorboat with torpedoes and with guns for protection against aircraft.

mosquito net. A net for keeping out mosquitoes.

moss \'mȯs\ *n.* [From Old English *mos* meaning "bog", "marsh".] **1** Any of a class of plants without flowers but with small, leafy, often tufted stems, growing in patches like a cushion and clinging to rocks, bark, or ground. **2** Any of various lichens or other plants resembling moss.

mossy \'mȯs-ē\ *adj.;* **moss·i·er; moss·i·est. 1** Of or like moss. **2** Covered with moss or something like moss.

most \'mōst\ *adj.* Superlative of *more,* used as the superlative of *many* and *much.* **1** The largest number of; the largest amount of. He has the *most* apples. She has the *most* paper. **2** Greatest in extent. Who has the *most* need of this? **3** Nearly all; as, *most* schools; *most* books. — *adv.* In the greatest degree; to the greatest extent; as, *most* necessary; *most* happily.

☞ The adverb *most* is placed before some adjectives and adverbs to form the superlative degree; as, *most* active; *most* rapidly.

-most \ˌmōst\. A suffix used in forming superlatives of certain adjectives and adverbs, as in *foremost, innermost,* and *topmost.*

most·ly \'mōst-lē\ *adv.* Chiefly; mainly.

mote \'mōt\ *n.* A small particle; a speck.

mo·tel \mō-'tel\ *n.* [Condensed from *motor hotel,* the *mot-* of *motor* being blended with the *-otel* of *hotel.*] An inn or a group of furnished cabins or attached cottages situated near a highway and offering lodgings and parking facilities for motorists.

moth \'mȯth\ *n.; pl.* **moths** \'mȯt͟hz, 'mȯths\. **1** Any insect related to the butterflies, but having a stouter body, smaller wings, less brilliant colors, and night-flying habits. **2** One of these insects with small yellowish wings and a larva that feeds on woolen cloth and furs.

moth·ball \'mȯth-ˌbȯl\ *n.* **1** A small ball, made of some substance such as camphor or naphthalene, that keeps moths away from clothing. **2** [in the plural] The condition of being stored or put away; as, a fleet put in *mothballs* after the war.

moth-eat·en \'mȯth-ˌēt-n\ *adj.* **1** Eaten into by moths. **2** Resembling cloth eaten into by moths.

moth·er \'mət͟h-r\ *n.* A slimy mass, composed of yeast cells and bacteria, that forms on the surface of fermenting alcoholic liquids and is added to wine or cider to produce vinegar.

moth·er \'mət͟h-r\ *n.* **1** A female parent. **2** The person or thing that gives rise to something else; the originator. Necessity is the *mother* of invention. **3** A woman in authority, as a nun in charge of a convent. — *v.;* **moth·ered; moth·er·ing** \-r(-)ing\. To be or act as a mother to. — *adj.* **1** Of or having to do with a mother; as, *mother* love. **2** Being in the relation of a mother to others; as, a *mother* church; a *mother* country. **3** Derived from, or as if from, a mother; as, a *mother* tongue.

moth·er·hood \'mət͟h-r-ˌhu̇d\ *n.* **1** The condition of being a mother. **2** The character or spirit of a mother. **3** Mothers; as, the *motherhood* of a nation.

moth·er-in-law \'mət͟h-r-ən-ˌlȯ\ *n.; pl.* **moth·ers-in-law.** The mother of one's husband or wife.

moth·er·land \'mət͟h-r-ˌland\ *n.* **1** One's native land. **2** The country where one's parents or ancestors were born.

moth·er·less \'mət͟h-r-ləs\ *adj.* **1** Having no living mother. **2** Having no known mother; lacking a mother's care and protection.

moth·er·ly \'mət͟h-r-lē\ *adj.* **1** Of or like a mother; as, a *motherly* old lady. **2** Showing the affection or concern of a mother; as, *motherly* love. — **moth·er·li·ness** \-lē-nəs\ *n.*

moth·er-of-pearl \'mət͟h-r-ə(v)-'pərl\ *n.* **1** The hard, pearly substance that forms the inside layer of pearl oysters, mussels, and similar shellfish. **2** This substance, or one resembling it, used in the manufacture of various articles, as buttons and knife handles.

Moth·er's Day \'mət͟h-rz\. The second Sunday in May, set aside in the United States and Canada for the honoring of mothers and motherhood.

mother tongue. 1 One's native language. **2** A language from which another language originates.

moth flakes. Flakes of the same composition and use as mothballs.

mo·tif \mō-'tēf\ *n.* **1** A theme, especially a dominant theme, in a work of literature or music; a principal feature in the subject matter of such a work; a motive. **2** A feature in a decoration or design; as, a flower *motif* in wallpaper.

mo·tion \'mōsh-n\ *n.* **1** The act or process of changing place or position; movement. **2** A suggestion or proposal, especially one made at a meeting; as, a *motion* to adjourn. — *v.;* **mo·tioned; mo·tion·ing**

\-n(-)ing\. To make a movement to show one's meaning; as, to *motion* the group to go on.

mo·tion·less \'mōsh-n-ləs\ *adj.* Without motion; still.

motion picture. **1** A series of pictures thrown on a screen so rapidly that they produce a continuous picture in which persons and things seem to move. **2** A play presented by means of such a series of pictures. — **mo·tion–pic·ture,** *adj.*

mo·ti·vate \'mōt-ə-ˌvāt\ *v.;* **mo·ti·vat·ed; mo·ti·vat·ing.** To provide with a motive; to induce; to incite. — **mo·ti·va·tion** \ˌmōt-ə-'vāsh-n\ *n.*

mo·tive \'mōt-iv\ *n.* **1** Anything that prompts one to do something. The boy's *motive* in running away was to avoid trouble. **2** In literature, art, and music, the guiding or controlling idea shown in a work; the theme. — For synonyms see *cause.* — *adj.* Causing motion; as, *motive* power.

mot·ley \'mät-lē\ *adj.* **1** Having various colors. **2** Of various mixed kinds or parts; as, a *motley* crowd; a *motley* collection of toys. — *n.* **1** A garment of mixed colors, once worn by jesters. **2** A mixture, as of diverse colors.

mo·tor \'mōt-r\ *n.* **1** A machine that produces motion or power for doing work; as, an electric *motor;* a gasoline *motor.* **2** A motorcar; an automobile. — *adj.* **1** Causing or setting up motion. **2** Equipped with or driven by a motor or motors. **3** Having to do with motion or with motors. — *v.* To travel by automobile.

mo·tor·boat \'mōt-r-ˌbōt\ *n.* A small boat run by a motor.

mo·tor·cade \'mōt-r-ˌkād\ *n.* A procession of automobiles or motorcycles.

mo·tor·car \'mōt-r-ˌkär, -ˌkȧr\ *n.* An automobile.

motor court. A motel.

mo·tor·cy·cle \'mōt-r-ˌsīk-l\ *n.* A two-wheeled motor vehicle having one or two saddles and sometimes a third wheel for the support of a sidecar. — **mo·tor·cy·clist** \-ˌsīk-l(-)əst\ *n.*

motorcycle

mo·tor·ist \'mōt-r-əst\ *n.* A person who travels by automobile.

mo·tor·ize \'mōt-r-ˌīz\ *v.;* **mo·tor·ized; mo·tor·iz·ing.** **1** To equip with a motor or motors. **2** To equip with motor vehicles for transportation; as, *motorized* soldiers.

mo·tor·man \'mōt-r-mən\ *n.; pl.* **mo·tor·men** \-mən\. A man who controls a motor or drives a motor vehicle; especially, the driver of a streetcar or an electric locomotive.

motor nerve. A nerve carrying impulses which cause a muscle to respond.

mot·tle \'mät-l\ *v.;* **mot·tled; mot·tling** \-l(-)ing\. To mark with spots; to spot; to blotch. — *n.* **1** A spot or blotch. **2** A pattern formed by spots, blotches, or other markings.

mot·tled \'mät-ld\ *adj.* Marked with spots or blotches of several colors or several shades; spotted; as, *mottled* marble.

mot·to \'mät-ˌō\ *n.; pl.* **mot·toes** or **mot·tos.** **1** A sentence, phrase, or word inscribed on something as suitable to its character or use; as, a *motto* on a state seal. **2** A short expression that suggests a guiding rule of conduct; a maxim.

mould. Variant of *mold.*

moulder. Variant of *molder.*

moulding. Variant of *molding.*

mouldy. Variant of *moldy.*

moult. Variant of *molt.*

mound \'mau̇nd\ *n.* **1** A small hill or heap of dirt, often one made by man to mark a grave or to act as a fort. **2** The place from which the pitcher throws, in the game of baseball. — *v.* To heap up into or like a mound.

mount \'mau̇nt\ *n.* A mountain; a high hill.

mount \'mau̇nt\ *v.* **1** To rise; to ascend; to climb; as, to *mount* a ladder. **2** To get upon something, as a platform; especially, to seat oneself on the back of a horse. **3** To furnish with animals for riding. The Arab *mounted* his troops on camels. **4** To increase in amount. Debts *mount* fast. **5** To prepare something for use by fastening in proper position or arrangement upon anything that preserves or supports it; to prepare for exhibition; as, to *mount* a picture on paper; to *mount* an engine. **6** To furnish with the necessary properties and scenery for presentation; as, to *mount* a play. **7** To place in position; as, to *mount* cannon to command an enemy position. **8** To post as a means of defense or observation; as, to *mount* a guard. — For synonyms see *ascend.* — *n.* That upon which a person or thing is mounted; especially, a saddle horse.

moun·tain \'mau̇nt-n\ *n.* **1** Any elevation higher than a hill. **2** Anything of great bulk; as, a *mountain* of mail.

moun·tain·eer \ˌmau̇nt-n-'ir\ *n.* **1** A person who lives in the mountains. **2** A mountain climber. — *v.* To climb mountains.

mountain goat. An antelope of the mountains of western North America that closely resembles a goat, with thick white hairy coat and slightly curved black horns.

mountain laurel. A North American evergreen shrub of the heath family, with glossy leaves and pink or white cup-shaped flowers.

mountain lion. A cougar.

moun·tain·ous \'mau̇nt-n(-)əs\ *adj.* **1** Having many mountains; as, *mountainous* country. **2** Resembling a mountain, especially in size; huge; as, *mountainous* waves.

mountain range. A series of mountains or mountain ridges closely related in direction and position.

mountain sheep. Any of various wild sheep inhabiting high mountains.

moun·tain·side \'mau̇nt-n-ˌsīd\ *n.* The side of a mountain.

moun·tain·top \'mau̇nt-n-ˌtäp\ *n.* The summit of a mountain.

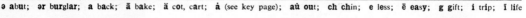

moun·te·bank \'mau̇nt-ə-ˌbangk\ *n.* **1** A person who sells quack medicines from a platform, as at fairs and festivals. **2** Any boastful pretender; a quack; a charlatan.

mount·ed \'maůnt-əd\ *adj.* **1** Seated or serving on horseback; as, *mounted* police. **2** Placed on a support; fastened in a suitable setting; as, a *mounted* gun; a *mounted* diamond.

mount·ing \'maůnt-ing\ *n.* **1** The act of a person who mounts. **2** Anything that serves as a mount; a support or frame, as for a machine or engine; a setting, as for a diamond.

mourn \'mōrn, 'mȯrn\ *v.* To feel or show grief or sorrow; to grieve; especially, to grieve over someone's death.

mourn·er \'mōrn-r, 'mȯrn-r\ *n.* One that mourns; especially, one who attends a funeral out of respect or affection for the dead person.

mourn·ful \'mōrn-fəl, 'mȯrn-\ *adj.* **1** Full of sorrow or sadness; expressing sorrow; as, a *mournful* face. **2** Causing sorrow; as, *mournful* news; a *mournful* story. — **mourn·ful·ly** \-fə-lē\ *adv.*

mourn·ing \'mōr-ning, 'mȯr-\ *n.* **1** The act of sorrowing. **2** An outward sign of grief for a person's death, as black clothes or a black arm band; as, to wear *mourning.* **3** A period of time during which such signs of grief are shown. — **in mourning**. Showing the outward signs and observing the conventions of mourning.

mourning dove. A wild dove of the United States, named from its mournful cry.

mouse \'maůs\ *n.; pl.* **mice** \'mīs\. **1** A small, usually grayish brown, soft-furred rodent found in houses throughout most of the world. **2** Any of numerous rodents resembling rats but much smaller. **3** A person without spirit or courage. — \'maůz, 'maůs\ *v.;* **moused; mous·ing. 1** To hunt mice. **2** To watch for slyly and carefully, as a cat for mice. **3** To move about softly, like a mouse.

mouse·hole \'maůs-ˌhōl\ *n.* A hole, as in a wall, made or used by a mouse; any very small hole.

mous·er \'maůz-r, 'maůs-r\ *n.* A cat that catches mice.

mouse·trap \'maůs-ˌtrap\ *n.* A trap for catching mice.

mousse \'müs\ *n.* [From French, meaning literally "froth", "foam".] Any of various dishes so prepared as to be light and spongy in texture; especially, a frozen dessert of sweetened and flavored whipped cream or thin cream and gelatin, frozen without stirring.

moustache. Variant of *mustache.*

mousy \'maůs-ē, 'maůz-ē\ *adj.;* **mous·i·er; mous·i·est. 1** Resembling a mouse, as in color. **2** Quiet, like a mouse. **3** Infested with mice; smelling of mice.

mouth \'maůth\ *n.; pl.* **mouths** \'maůt͟hz, 'maůths\. **1** The opening through which a person or an animal takes food or makes speech sounds; the cavity containing the tongue and teeth or its surrounding parts. **2** An opening that is like or likened to a mouth; as, the *mouth* of a cave; the *mouth* of a river. **3** A grimace; a face; as, to make a *mouth* at a staring stranger. — \'maůt͟h\ *v.* **1** To speak in a loud voice and in an unnatural, affected manner. **2** To take into or seize with the mouth.

mouth·ful \'maůth-ˌfůl\ *n.; pl.* **mouth·fuls.** As much as the mouth will hold, or as is put into the mouth at one time.

mouth organ. A harmonica.

mouth·piece \'maůth-ˌpēs\ *n.* **1** Something placed at or held in the mouth. **2** A part, as of certain instruments, to which the mouth is held; as, the *mouthpiece* of a clarinet; the *mouthpiece* of a telephone. **3** One, as a person or a newspaper, that speaks for a group or a party; a spokesman.

mouth·wash \'maůth-ˌwȯsh, -ˌwäsh\ *n.* A liquid preparation, usually antiseptic, for cleaning the mouth and teeth.

mov·a·ble or **move·a·ble** \'mü-vəb-l\ *adj.* **1** Capable of being moved; not fixed; as, *movable* desks. **2** Changing from one date to another. Easter is a *movable* holiday. — *n.* Something that can be moved, as a piece of clothing or kitchen equipment; especially [usually in the plural] furniture. — **mov·a·bly** or **move·a·bly** \-və-blē\ *adv.*

move \'müv\ *v.;* **moved; mov·ing. 1** To change the place or position of; to shift; as, to *move* one's chair closer to the window. **2** To go from one place to another; as, to *move* into the shade. **3** To set in motion; to stir; as, to *move* the head. **4** To influence; to cause a person to act or to make a decision; as, to *move* a person to change his mind. **5** To affect the feelings of. The sad story *moved* the children to tears. **6** To suggest; to recommend; especially, to propose something formally, as in a meeting; to present as a motion; to make an appeal; as, to *move* that the meeting adjourn; to *move* for a new trial. **7** To sell; as, to *move* one's stock of goods. **8** To change residence; to change place or position; to stir. **9** To turn; to work; to operate. The door is shut so tight that no one can *move* it. **10** To progress; to advance. **11** To carry on one's way of life or activities; as, to *move* in influential circles. **12** To depart; to go away. The policeman told the bystanders to *move* on. **13** In certain games, as chess and checkers, to transfer a piece from one place to another. **14** To act or to cause to act to empty themselves; as, medicine to *move* the bowels. — *n.* **1** The action of moving; a movement. **2** An action for carrying out a plan; a scheme; as, to make a shrewd *move.* **3** A moving from a fixed position; a change of place or residence. **4** The action of moving a piece, as at checkers, or a player's turn to move.

move·ment \'müv-mənt\ *n.* **1** A moving; a shift; as, to observe the *movement* of a star. **2** An emptying of the bowels or the matter emptied. **3** A program or a series of acts working toward some wished-for end; as, the boys' club *movement.* **4** [in the plural] Actions of a person or of a group of persons. The police had been watching the *movements* of the gang for weeks. **5** A delicate arrangement of wheels or other mechanism for causing a particular motion, such as that in a watch or clock. **6** A rhythm; a meter; as, a dance *movement.* **7** A section of a long piece of music; as, a *movement* of a symphony.

mov·er \'müv-r\ *n.* A person or thing that moves; especially, a person or company that moves the belongings of others from one home or place of business to another.

mov·ie \'mü-vē\ *n.* A motion picture.

mov·ing \'mü-ving\ *adj.* **1** Changing place or position; causing motion or action; as, to shoot at a *moving* target. **2** Having the power to affect the feelings or sympathies; as, a *moving* song. — **mov·ing·ly,** *adv.*

moving picture. A motion picture.

mow \'maủ\ *n.* **1** A heap or mass, as of hay or sheaves of grain; especially, such a heap stored in a barn. **2** The place in a barn for such storing.

mow \'mō\ *v.;* **mowed** \'mōd\; **mowed** \'mōd\ or **mown** \'mōn\; **mow·ing. 1** To cut down with a scythe or machine; as, to *mow* hay. **2** To cut off from, as grass or grain; as, to *mow* a lawn. **3** To cut down; to cause to fall in great numbers. The tackles *mowed* down our whole football team.

mow·er \'mōr, 'mō-ər\ *n.* **1** A person who mows. **2** A mowing machine.

mow·ing ma·chine \'mō-ing\. An implement with blades for cutting standing grass or grain.

M.P. Abbreviation for: **1** *Member of Parliament.* **2** *Military Police.*

mph or **m.p.h.** Abbreviation for *miles per hour.*

Mr. Abbreviation for *Mister.*

Mrs. Abbreviation for *Mistress* used as a title.

m's. Pl. of *m.*

MS. or **ms.** Abbreviation for *manuscript.*

Msgr. Abbreviation for *monsignor.*

MSS. or **mss.** Abbreviation for *manuscripts.*

MST. Abbreviation for *Mountain Standard Time.*

mt. Abbreviation for: **1** *mount.* **2** *mountain.*

mtn. Abbreviation for *mountain.*

much \'məch\ *adj.;* **more** \'mōr, 'mȯr\; **most** \'mōst\. Great in amount or extent. — *n.* A great quantity or amount; an indefinite amount. — *adv.* **1** To a great degree or extent; greatly; as, being *much* obliged. **2** Nearly; almost; as, a person looking *much* as he did years ago.

mu·ci·lage \'myüs-l(-)ij\ *n.* A soft, moist, gluey substance used to stick things together.

muck \'mək\ *n.* **1** Moist manure. **2** Decayed peat or black swamp earth, especially when used as fertilizer. **3** Filth; dirt; mud. — **mucky** \'mək-ē\ *adj.*

muck·rake \'mək-ˌrāk\ *v.;* **muck·raked; muck·rak·ing.** To seek out and expose, especially habitually, real or alleged corruption on the part of men in responsible positions, as in public office. — **muck·rak·er** \-ˌrāk-r\ *n.*

mu·cous \'myük-əs\ *adj.* **1** Like mucus; consisting of mucus; having to do with mucus; as, a *mucous* discharge. **2** Producing or giving off mucus.

mucous membrane. The membrane lining those cavities of the body that open directly or indirectly to its surface, as the alimentary and respiratory tracts.

mu·cus \'myük-əs\ *n.* **1** The slimy, slippery matter produced by mucous membranes, which it moistens and protects; as, to cough up *mucus.* **2** A similar substance secreted from the external surface of the body by some animals, as snails, slugs, and certain fishes.

mud \'məd\ *n.* Soft, wet earth or dirt.

mud·dle \'məd-l\ *v.;* **mud·dled; mud·dling** \-l(-)ing\. **1** To confuse or stupefy; as, to be *muddled* by too much advice; to be *muddled* by too much wine. **2** To mix up confusedly; as, to *muddle* the household accounts. **3** To bungle, as one's work. — *n.* A state of confusion; a tangle.

mud·dy \'məd-ē\ *adj.;* **mud·di·er; mud·di·est. 1** Having much mud; filled with mud; smeared with mud; as, a *muddy* pond; *muddy* shoes. **2** Similar to or looking like mud; as, a *muddy* color; *muddy* coffee. **3** Not clear or bright; dull or cloudy; as, a *muddy* varnish; a *muddy* complexion. **4** Confused; not clear in meaning; as, *muddy* thinking. — *v.;* **mud·died** \-ēd\; **mud·dy·ing. 1** To soil with mud; to dirty; as, to *muddy* one's clothes. **2** To cloud or fog; to make dull; as, to *muddy* a mirror.

mud·guard \'məd-ˌgärd, -ˌgȧrd\ *n.* A guard over a wheel to catch or deflect mud.

mud puppy. A large American salamander with external gills.

mud turtle. Any of a number of American freshwater tortoises.

muff \'məf\ *n.* **1** A soft, thick cover into which both hands may be thrust to protect them from cold. **2** One of a pair of covers for the ears to protect them from cold. **3** A clumsy failure; especially, in games, a failure to hold a ball when trying to catch it. — *v.* To handle awkwardly; to bungle.

muff, 1

muf·fin \'məf-n\ *n.* **1** A bread made of egg batter or yeast dough and baked in a small cup-shaped container. **2** A flat, round, raised biscuit (**English muffin**) baked on a griddle.

muf·fle \'məf-l\ *v.;* **muf·fled; muf·fling** \-l(-)ing\. **1** To wrap up so as to conceal or protect or to prevent seeing, hearing, or speaking. **2** To deaden the sound of; as, to *muffle* a cry.

muf·fler \'məf-lər\ *n.* **1** A scarf for the neck. **2** Something that deadens noises.

muf·ti \'məf-tē\ *n.* Ordinary clothes when worn by one usually dressed in a uniform.

mug \'məg\ *n.* **1** A flat-bottomed, straight-sided drinking cup with a handle, usually made of metal or thick earthenware. **2** The quantity a mug holds. **3** *Slang.* A face. — *v.;* **mugged; mug·ging. 1** To make a face; to grimace. **2** To photograph; especially, to photograph criminals.

mug

mug or **mugg** \'məg\ *v.;* **mugged**; **mug·ging**. To assault, especially in order to rob.

mug·gy \'məg-ē\ *adj.;* **mug·gi·er**; **mug·gi·est.** Warm, damp, and stifling; as, a *muggy* day in August.

Mu·ham·mad·an \mü-'ham-ə-dən, -'häm-, -'ham-\ *adj.* or *n.* Mohammedan.

mu·lat·to \mə-'lat-ō, myü-\ *n.; pl.* **mu·lat·toes.** A person with one Negro parent and one white parent; any person of mixed white and Negro descent.

mul·ber·ry \'məl-ˌber-ē\ *n.; pl.* **mul·ber·ries.** **1** A tree which bears edible dark-purple or white fruit much like the blackberry or the raspberry in appearance; also, the fruit of the mulberry tree. **2** A dark, reddish blue color.

mulch \'məlch\ *n.* A material, as straw, sawdust, leaves, or paper, spread upon the ground to protect the roots of plants from heat, cold, or drought, or to keep fruit clean. **—** *v.* To cover with mulch; as, to *mulch* the strawberry plants.

mulct \'məlkt\ *n.* A fine or penalty. **—** *v.* **1** To fine for an offense. **2** To deprive of, as by deceit or trickery or by way of punishment.

mule \'myül\ *n.* **1** An animal that is an offspring of a donkey and a horse. **2** A spinning machine; a spinning jenny.

mule \'myül\ *n.* A type of slipper in which the upper does not extend around the heel of the foot.

mule

mule deer. A long-eared deer of western North America, larger and more heavily built than the common white-tailed deer.

mule skinner. A driver of mules.

mu·le·teer \ˌmyü-lə-'tir\ *n.* A driver of mules.

mul·ish \'myü-lish\ *adj.* Like a mule; stubborn; as, a *mulish* person. — **mul·ish·ly**, *adv.*

mull \'məl\ *v.* To think; to ponder; as, to *mull* over an idea.

mull \'məl\ *v.* To heat, sweeten, and spice, as wine.

mul·lein or **mul·len** \'məl-ən\ *n.* A tall herb having coarse, woolly leaves, and spikes of yellow, white, or purplish flowers.

mul·let \'məl-ət\ *n.; pl.* **mul·lets** or **mul·let.** **1** A food fish, the **gray mullet**, living along most seacoasts, especially one kind, the **striped mullet**, that weighs up to 12 pounds. **2** A chiefly tropical fish, the **red mullet**, usually red or golden with a yellow band, that weighs up to three pounds. **3** Any of certain suckers.

mul·ti·cel·lu·lar \ˌməl-tə-'sel-yəl-r, -tē-, -ˌtī-\ *adj.* Having many cells.

mul·ti·col·ored \'məl-tə-ˌkəl-rd, -tē-\ *adj.* Having many colors.

mul·ti·far·i·ous \ˌməl-tə-'far-ē-əs, -'fer-\ *adj.* Of various kinds; many and varied; as, the *multifarious* complexities of language.

mul·ti·form \'məl-tə-ˌform\ *adj.* Having many forms, shapes, or appearances.

mul·ti·lat·er·al \ˌməl-tə-'lat-r-əl, -tē-, -ˌtī-, -'la-trəl\ *adj.* **1** Having many sides. **2** Participated in by more than two states; as, a *multilateral* treaty. — **mul·ti·lat·er·al·ly** \-'lat-r-ə-lē, -'la-trə-lē\ *adv.*

mul·ti·mil·lion·aire \ˌməl-tə-'mil-yə-ˌnar, -ˌner; -ˌmil-yə-'nar, -'ner\ *n.* A person having two or more million dollars or pounds.

mul·ti·ple \'məl-təp-l\ *adj.* **1** Containing or consisting of more than one; manifold; as, *multiple* ideas; *multiple* copies of a book. **2** In electricity, having a group of terminals that make a circuit available at a number of points. **—** *n.* The product of one number multiplied by another; a number that contains another an exact number of times without a remainder. 10 is a *multiple* of 5.

mul·ti·pli·cand \ˌməl-tə-plə-'kand\ *n.* A number that is multiplied by another number.

mul·ti·pli·ca·tion \ˌməl-tə-plə-'kāsh-n\ *n.* **1** The action or process of multiplying, or of increasing in number; as, the rapid *multiplication* of bacteria in decayed matter. **2** A short way of finding out what would be the result of adding a figure the number of times indicated by another figure. The *multiplication* of 7 by 3 gives 21.

mul·ti·plic·i·ty \ˌməl-tə-'plis-ət-ē\ *n.; pl.* **mul·ti·plic·i·ties.** **1** The quality of being multiple or various. **2** A great number; as, a *multiplicity* of thoughts.

mul·ti·pli·er \'məl-tə-ˌplīr\ *n.* **1** One that multiplies. **2** A number by which another number is multiplied.

mul·ti·ply \'məl-tə-ˌplī\ *v.;* **mul·ti·plied** \-ˌplīd\; **mul·ti·ply·ing.** **1** To increase in number; to make or become more numerous. Germs *multiply* rapidly. **2** To find the product of by means of multiplication; as, to *multiply* 7 by 8. **3** To perform the operation of multiplication.

mul·ti·stage \'məl-tə-ˌstāj, -tē-\ *adj.* Involving two or more steps or stages to complete a process.

mul·ti·tude \'məl-tə-ˌtüd, -ˌtyüd\ *n.* A crowd; a great number of persons or things.

— The words *crowd* and *throng* are synonyms of *multitude: multitude* usually suggests a comparatively large number of anything, especially of persons; *crowd* generally indicates a large number of persons gathered and pressed closely together without any particular order or arrangement; *throng* has a stronger suggestion than *crowd* of mass movement and a disorderly milling about.

mul·ti·tu·di·nous \ˌməl-tə-'tüd-n-əs, -'tyüd-\ *adj.* Consisting of a great multitude; as, a *multitudinous* gathering. — **mul·ti·tu·di·nous·ly**, *adv.*

mum \'məm\ *adj.* Silent; not speaking; as, to keep *mum* about a discovery.

mum·ble \'məm-bl\ *v.;* **mum·bled**; **mum·bling** \-bl(-)ing\. **1** To speak indistinctly, usually with lips partly closed; to mutter; as, to *mumble* one's words. **2** To chew gently with closed lips or with little use of the lips; as, a baby *mumbling* its food. **—** *n.* A low, confused, indistinct utterance. — **mum·bler** \-blər\ *n.* — **mum·bling·ly** \-bl(-)ing-lē\ *adv.*

mum·mer \'məm-r\ *n.* **1** A person who masks and

engages in merrymaking, as at Christmas time. **2** An actor.

mum·mery \'məm-r-ē\ *n.; pl.* **mum·mer·ies. 1** Masking and merrymaking, as by mummers. **2** Any ceremony regarded as ridiculous or too pompous.

mum·mi·fy \'məm-ē-ˌfī, -ə-ˌfī\ *v.;* **mum·mi·fied** \-ˌfīd\; **mum·mi·fy·ing. 1** To embalm and dry as a mummy. **2** To dry up, as skin, like a mummy. — **mum·mi·fi·ca·tion** \ˌməm-ē-fə-'kāsh-n, ˌməm-ə-\ *n.*

mum·my \'məm-ē\ *n.; pl.* **mum·mies. 1** A dead body embalmed by the ancient Egyptians. **2** Any dead body unusually well preserved.

mumps \'məmps\ *n.* An infectious disease marked by fever and the inflammation and swelling of certain glands, usually those around the jaw — used with a singular verb. *Mumps* is a common childhood disease.

munch \'mənch\ *v.* To chew, usually with a crunching sound; as, to *munch* on hard candy. — **muncher,** *n.*

mun·dane \'mən-ˌdān, ˌmən-'dān\ *adj.* Of or relating to the world; worldly; as, a man of *mundane* values.

mu·nic·i·pal \myü-'nis-əp-l\ *adj.* **1** Having local self-government. **2** Of, relating to, or characteristic of a municipality; as, a *municipal* court; a *municipal* building.

mu·nic·i·pal·i·ty \(ˌ)myü-ˌnis-ə-'pal-ət-ē\ *n.; pl.* **mu·nic·i·pal·i·ties.** A town, city, or other district having local self-government.

mu·nif·i·cence \myü-'nif-ə-sən(t)s\ *n.* Great generosity; liberality.

mu·nif·i·cent \myü-'nif-ə-sənt\ *adj.* Extremely liberal in giving; very generous. — **mu·nif·i·cent·ly,** *adv.*

mu·ni·tion \myü-'nish-n\ *n.* [usually in the plural] Ammunition; military supplies, equipment, and provisions; as, the *munitions* of war. — *v.* To provide with munitions.

mu·ral \'myůr-əl\ *adj.* Of or relating to a wall; on a wall; as, *mural* paintings. — *n.* A mural painting.

mur·der \'mərd-r\ *n.* The intentional and unlawful killing of a human being. — *v.;* **mur·dered; mur·der·ing** \-r(-)ing\. **1** To commit murder; to kill unlawfully. **2** To mutilate or spoil by wretched performance; as, to *murder* a song. — For synonyms see *kill.* — **mur·der·er** \-r-r\ *n.* — **mur·der·ess** \-r-əs\ *n.*

mur·der·ous \'mərd-r(-)əs\ *adj.* Of or relating to murder; causing murder or bloodshed; bloodthirsty; cruel; as, a *murderous* act; a *murderous* look. — **mur·der·ous·ly,** *adv.*

mu·ri·at·ic ac·id \'myůr-ē-ˌat-ik\. Hydrochloric acid.

murk \'mərk\ *n.* Darkness; gloom. — **murky** \'mərk-ē\ *adj.*

mur·mur \'mərm-r\ *n.* **1** A low, indistinct sound; as, the *murmur* of the wind; the *murmur* of voices. **2** A grumbled complaint. The boy accepted the scolding without a *murmur.* **3** An abnormal sound accompanying the heartbeat, as when the valves leak. — *v.;* **mur·mured; mur·mur·ing** \-r(-)ing\. To make a murmur; to speak in a murmur. — **mur·mur·er** \-r-r\ *n.*

mur·rain \'mər-ən, 'mə-rən\ *n.* A plague or pestilence, especially one affecting cattle.

mus·cat \'məs-ˌkat, -kət\ *n.* Any of several varieties of European grapes.

mus·ca·tel \ˌməs-kə-'tel\ *n.* A sweet wine made from muscat grapes.

mus·cle \'məs-l\ *n.* [From Latin *musculus* meaning literally "little mouse", rippling muscles having been thought to resemble scurrying mice.] **1** An organ of the body which produces motion. **2** The tissue of which this organ is made. **3** Muscular strength or development.

mus·cle-bound \'məs-l-ˌbaůnd\ *adj.* Having some of the muscles abnormally enlarged and lacking in elasticity, as from excessive athletic exercise.

mus·cu·lar \'məsk-yəl-r\ *adj.* **1** Having to do with muscles. **2** Performed by the muscles. **3** Brawny; strong.

mus·cu·la·ture \'məsk-yə-lə-ˌchůr\ *n.* The muscles of an animal or of some particular part of an animal.

muse \'myüz\ *v.;* **mused; mus·ing.** To ponder; to meditate; to consider carefully.

Muse \'myüz\ *n.* **1** One of the nine sister goddesses of song and poetry and of the arts and sciences. **2** [with a small letter] That which gives an artist or writer his creative inspiration or ideas.

mu·se·um \myü-'zē-əm, 'myü-ˌzē-əm\ *n.* A building, or part of one, in which are displayed objects of permanent interest in one or more of the arts or sciences.

mush \'məsh\ *n.* **1** Meal, especially Indian meal, boiled in water. **2** Anything soft and thick like mush. The skaters found the ice on the lake thawed to *mush.* **3** Sickly sentiment.

mush \'məsh\ *n.* A march across snow with sled and dogs. — *interj.* A cry to urge on sled dogs. — *v.* To travel across snow with a sled and dogs; as, to *mush* toward the trading post.

mush·er \'məsh-r\ *n.* One who drives a sled and team of dogs through the snow.

mush·room \'məsh-ˌrüm, -ˌrům\ *n.* A fungus shaped like an umbrella. — *adj.* **1** Having to do with mushrooms. **2** Like a mushroom in quick growth and decay; shaped like a mushroom. — *v.* To grow rapidly, like a mushroom.

mushrooms

mushy \'məsh-ē\ *adj.;* **mush·i·er; mush·i·est.** Soft, like mush; also, weakly sentimental; as, a *mushy* movie.

mu·sic \'myü-zik\ *n.* **1** The art of combining tones so that they are pleasing, expressive, or intelligible. **2** Compositions made according to the rules of this art. **3** The score of such a composition or compositions. Did you bring your *music* with you? **4** Sounds that have rhythm, harmony, and melody;

anything that gives the effect of music; as, the *music* of a brook.

mu·si·cal \'myü-zik-l\ *adj.* **1** Having to do with music or the writing or performance of music; as, *musical* instruments. **2** Having the pleasing qualities of music. **3** Fond of music; as, a *musical* family. **4** Set to music; accompanied by music. — *n.* **1** A musicale. **2** A musical comedy. — **mu·si·cal·ly** \-zik-l(-)ē\ *adv.*

musical comedy. A light dramatic production consisting of musical numbers and dialogue, usually with only a slight plot.

mu·si·cale \ˌmyü-zə-'kal\ *n.* A concert of music, usually at a private social gathering.

music box. A box or case containing apparatus which plays a tune or tunes automatically, especially one in which the apparatus is moved by clockwork.

mu·si·cian \myü-'zish-n\ *n.* A person who writes, sings, or plays music skillfully. — **mu·si·cian·ship** \-ˌship\ *n.*

musk \'məsk\ *n.* **1** A strong-smelling substance usually obtained from the male musk deer and used as the basis for many perfumes. **2** The odor of musk. — **musky** \'məs-kē\ *adj.*

musk deer. A small, hornless deer about three feet long and twenty inches tall, which lives in the high regions of central Asia.

mus·kel·lunge \'məsk-l-ˌənj\ *n. sing. and pl.* [From an Indian word meaning literally "big pike".] A large pike found especially in the Great Lakes.

mus·ket \'məs-kət\ *n.* A hand firearm formerly carried by infantry soldiers.

mus·ke·teer \ˌməs-kə-'tir\ *n.* A soldier armed with a musket.

mus·ket·ry \'məs-kə-trē\ *n.; pl.* **mus·ket·ries. 1** Muskets. **2** Musketeers. **3** The fire of muskets.

musketeer, French, 17th century

musk·mel·on \'məsk-ˌmel-ən\ *n.* A small round or oval and sometimes ridged melon of the gourd family having flesh of various colors as orange, green, or white; especially, a cantaloupe.

musk ox. A shaggy, dark-colored, horned and hoofed animal between a sheep and an ox in size, found in Greenland and the northern parts of North America.

musk·rat \'məsk-ˌrat\ *n.* **1** A North American water rat with dark glossy brown fur, webbed hind feet, and a long, scaly tail. **2** The fur of this animal.

Muslim. Variant of *Moslem.*

mus·lin \'məz-lən\ *n.* A cotton fabric of plain weave.

muss \'məs\ *n.* Disorder; confusion. — *v.* To rumple; as, to *muss* one's hair.

mus·sel \'məs-l\ *n.* **1** A salt-water mollusk with two black shells, much used in Europe as food. **2** Any of numerous two-valved freshwater mollusks of the central United States having shells with pearly inner linings used in making buttons.

mussy \'məs-ē\ *adj.;* **muss·i·er; muss·i·est.** Disordered; soiled; rumpled; as, *mussy* clothing.

must \(')məst\ *v.;* used without change of form as *pres.*, and sometimes *past, tense.* **1** Am, is, or are obliged or required to. A man *must* eat to live. **2** Was or were obliged to, required to, or compelled to. The teacher said that everyone *must* be quiet. The boy said that he *must* leave early. **3** Am, is, or are sure or nearly sure to. You *must* have read this before.

mus·tache or **mous·tache** \'məs-ˌtash, mə-'stash\ *n.* **1** The hair on man's upper lip. **2** Hair or bristles around the mouth of an animal, as a cat.

mus·ta·chio \mə-'stash-ē-ˌō, -'stash-ˌō\ *n.; pl.* **mus·ta·chi·os.** A mustache. — **mus·ta·chi·oed** \-ˌōd\ *adj.*

mus·tang \'məs-ˌtang\ *n.* A small, hardy, half-wild horse of western North America.

mus·tard \'məst-rd\ *n.* **1** A European herb with yellow flowers and long, narrow seed pods, cultivated for its seed. **2** A yellow powder of mustard seeds mixed with water for use as a seasoning and in poultices.

mustard gas. A poisonous gas having violent burning and blistering effects.

mustard plaster. A poultice prepared by spreading a paste made of mustard, flour, and cold water on cloth.

mus·ter \'məst-r\ *v.;* **mus·tered; mus·ter·ing** \-r(-)ing\. **1** To assemble, as troops or a ship's company, for roll call or inspection. **2** To collect and display; as, all the energy he could *muster.* — *n.* **1** An assembly of troops or a ship's company for roll call or inspection, or the total number of men assembled, or the roll call of these men. **2** Any assemblage of persons or things.

muster roll. A register of all the officers and men in a military body or a ship's company present or accounted for on the day of muster.

mustn't \'məs-nt\. A contraction of *must not.*

musty \'məs-tē\ *adj.;* **must·i·er; must·i·est. 1** Disagreeable in odor or taste from being long closed up in a damp place; moldy. **2** Spoiled by age; stale. **3** Dull; without spirit.

mu·ta·ble \'myüt-əb-l\ *adj.* **1** Capable of change in form or nature. **2** Changeable; fickle. — **mu·ta·bil·i·ty** \ˌmyüt-ə-'bil-ət-ē\ *n.*

mu·tant \'myüt-nt\ *n.* An individual resulting from mutation, differing from its parents in one or more well-marked characters.

mu·tate \'myü-ˌtāt\ *v.;* **mu·tat·ed; mu·tat·ing.** To alter; to undergo mutation.

mu·ta·tion \myü-'tāsh-n\ *n.* **1** Change; alteration in form or characteristics. **2** A sudden biological variation, the offspring differing from its parents in some well-marked character or characters. **3** The result of this process; a suddenly produced variation.

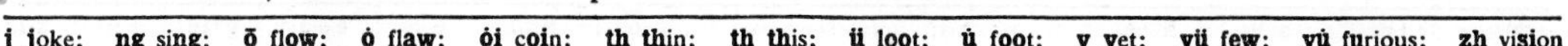

mute \'myüt\ *adj.* **1** Not speaking; silent; dumb; speechless. **2** Not pronounced, as the final *e* in many words. — For synonyms see *dumb.* — *n.* **1** A person who cannot or does not speak. **2** A person employed by undertakers to attend a funeral as a mourner. **3** Any device on a musical instrument which deadens, softens, or muffles its tone. **4** A letter representing no sound; a silent letter. — *v.;* **mut·ed; mut·ing.** To muffle or deaden the sound of, as by a mute.

mu·ti·late \'myüt-l-ˌāt\ *v.;* **mu·ti·lat·ed; mu·ti·lat·ing.** To cut off or remove a limb or an essential part of a person or thing; to cripple; to maim. — **mu·ti·la·tion** \ˌmyüt-l-'āsh-n\ *n.*

mu·ti·neer \ˌmyüt-n-'ir\ *n.* A person who is guilty of mutiny.

mu·ti·nous \'myüt-n(-)əs\ *adj.* Having or showing a disposition to mutiny; rebellious; unruly. — **mu·ti·nous·ly,** *adv.*

mu·ti·ny \'myüt-n(-)ē\ *n.; pl.* **mu·ti·nies.** Revolt against rightful authority, especially military or naval authority. — *v.;* **mu·ti·nied** \-n(-)ēd\; **mu·ti·ny·ing.** To take part in a mutiny.

mut·ter \'mət-r\ *v.;* **mut·tered; mut·ter·ing** \-r(-)ing\. **1** To utter indistinctly, as in complaining or grumbling; as, to *mutter* a reply. **2** To rumble; as, thunder *muttering* in the west. — *n.* A low, indistinct sound or utterance.

mut·ton \'mət-n\ *n.* [From medieval English *motoun,* there borrowed from Old French *moton* meaning "ram".] The flesh of a sheep used for food.

mut·ton·chop \'mət-n-ˌchäp\ *adj.* Having a form suggestive of a mutton chop, or roundish at one end and narrow and prolonged at the other — used especially of side whiskers (**mutton chops**).

mu·tu·al \'myü-chə-wəl, 'myüch-l\ *adj.* **1** Given and received back and forth between persons; as, *mutual* favors. **2** Having the same relation to another person as that person has to oneself; as, *mutual* enemies. **3** Owned, felt, or done by two or more persons jointly; joint; as, our *mutual* friend. — **mu·tu·al·ly** \'myüch-l-ē, 'myü-chə-wə-lē\ *adv.*

muz·zle \'məz-l\ *n.* **1** The nose and jaws of an animal, as a horse. **2** A covering for the nose and jaws of an animal to prevent it from biting; as, a *muzzle* for a dog. **3** The end or mouth of a gun, from which the missile is discharged. — *v.;* **muz·zled; muz·zling** \-l(-)ing\. **1** To bind or cover the muzzle of an animal to prevent biting. **2** To prevent from speaking; as, witnesses of a crime who were *muzzled* by fear.

muz·zle–load·er \'məz-l-'lōd-r\ *n.* A gun that is loaded through the muzzle. — **muz·zle–load·ing** \-ing\ *adj.*

my \(')mī, mə\ *adj.* Of or belonging to me; done by or to me; as, *my* head; *my* promotion.

my·ce·li·um \mī-'sē-lē-əm\ *n.; pl.* **my·ce·lia** \-lē-ə\ or **my·ce·li·ums** \-lē-əmz\. The vegetative part of the body of a fungus typically consisting of a mass of interwoven hyphas and often being submerged in another body, as of soil, a loaf of bread, or the tissues of a plant or animal host.

my·col·o·gy \mī-'käl-ə-jē\ *n.* The branch of botany dealing with fungi.

my·na or **my·nah** \'mī-nə\ *n.* A common bird of southeastern Asia allied to the starlings.

my·o·pia \mī-'ōp-ē-ə\ *n.* Nearsightedness; shortsightedness. — **my·op·ic** \-'äp-ik\ *adj.*

myr·i·ad \'mir-ē-əd\ *n.* **1** Ten thousand. **2** An indefinitely large number; an immense number; as, the *myriads* of stars of the Milky Way. — *adj.* Consisting of a very great but indefinite number; as, the *myriad* grains of sand in a single handful.

myr·i·a·pod \'mir-ē-ə-ˌpäd\ *n.* Any centipede or millepede.

myr·mi·don \'mər-mə-ˌdän, -mə-dən\ *n.* A subordinate who executes the orders of his superiors without concern or pity for those affected.

myrrh \'mər\ *n.* The dried juice of certain trees in the form of a fragrant brown gum, used in Biblical times as an ingredient of perfumes and incense and now in tooth powder and perfume.

myr·tle \'mərt-l\ *n.* **1** A common evergreen bushy shrub of southern Europe with oval to lance-shaped shining leaves, fragrant white or rosy flowers, and black berries. **2** Any of a family of chiefly tropical shrubs or trees of which the common myrtle is typical, as the eucalyptus and the guava. **3** The periwinkle.

my·self \mə-'self, mī-\ *pron.* **1** A form of the word *I* used to give emphasis or to show that the subject and object of a verb are the same person. I *myself* saw it. I hurt *myself.* **2** My true and natural self. After a short rest, I was *myself* again.

mys·te·ri·ous \mis-'tir-ē-əs\ *adj.* Of or relating to mystery; containing, suggesting, or implying a mystery; secret; hard to understand; as, *mysterious* ways of nature. — **mys·te·ri·ous·ly,** *adv.*

mys·tery \'mist-r(-)ē\ *n.; pl.* **mys·ter·ies.** **1** Something that has not been or cannot be explained; a secret that arouses curiosity. **2** A deep secret. The man's intentions were a *mystery* to everyone. **3** A religious doctrine that is beyond man's power to understand. **4** Also **mystery play.** A religious play, popular in the Middle Ages, representing Scriptural scenes, especially centering around Christ.

mys·tic \'mis-tik\ *adj.* **1** Of or relating to mysticism or mystics. **2** Mysterious; beyond understanding. **3** Giving a feeling of awe or wonder; as, the *mystic* beauty of the night. **4** Having magical qualities; as, *mystic* numbers. — *n.* A person who seeks direct knowledge of God through contemplation and prayer.

mys·ti·cal \'mis-tik-l\ *adj.* **1** Of or relating to ideas or meanings that only a mystic can understand; symbolical; as, *mystical* interpretations of the Bible. **2** Of or relating to communion with God through contemplation or inspiration; as, *mystical* rapture.

mys·ti·cism \'mis-tə-ˌsiz-m\ *n.* **1** The thought processes of a mystic; mystical thinking. **2** The belief that direct knowledge of God and of spiritual truth can be achieved by personal insight and inspiration. **3** Vague guessing about something; a belief without a sound basis.

mys·ti·fy \'mis-tə-ˌfī\ *v.;* **mys·ti·fied** \-ˌfīd\; **mys·ti·fy·ing.** **1** To make obscure or difficult to understand. **2** To puzzle; to perplex; as, strange actions that *mystified* everyone. — **mys·ti·fi·ca·tion** \ˌmis-tə-fə-'kāsh-n\ *n.*

myth \'mith\ *n.; pl.* **myths** \'miths\. **1** A legendary story used to describe a supernatural being or event or to explain certain customs or a religious belief or practice; as, the *myths* of ancient Greece. **2** A person or thing that exists only in one's imagination.

myth·i·cal \'mith-ik-l\ *adj.* **1** Based on, or described in, a myth; of the nature of a myth. Hercules is a *mythical* hero. **2** Imaginary; as, a person dreaming of his *mythical* castle. — **myth·i·cal·ly** \-ik-l(-)ē\ *adv.*

my·thol·o·gy \mi-'thäl-ə-jē\ *n.; pl.* **my·thol·o·gies.** **1** A collection of myths; as, *mythology* of ancient Greece. **2** The systematized knowledge of myths. — **myth·o·log·i·cal** \ˌmith-l-'äj-ik-l\ *adj.*

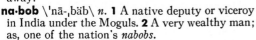

n \'en\ *n.; pl.* **n's** \'enz\. **1** The fourteenth letter of the alphabet. **2** In mathematics, an indefinite number.

N. Abbreviation for: **1** *north.* **2** *northern.*

n. Abbreviation for *noun.*

nab \'nab\ *v.;* **nabbed; nab·bing.** **1** To catch or seize; to arrest; as, to *nab* a fleeing criminal. **2** To snatch away.

na·bob \'nā-ˌbäb\ *n.* **1** A native deputy or viceroy in India under the Moguls. **2** A very wealthy man; as, one of the nation's *nabobs.*

na·celle \na-'sel\ *n.* An enclosed shelter on an aircraft for an engine or sometimes for members of the crew.

na·cre \'nāk-r\ *n.* Mother-of-pearl.

na·cre·ous \'nāk-rē-əs\ *adj.* Consisting of or resembling nacre; pearly.

na·dir \'nād-r, 'nā-ˌdir\ *n.* **1** The point of the heavens directly under the place where one stands; the point directly opposite the zenith. **2** The lowest point of anything, as the period of greatest poverty or shame; the time of greatest depression.

nag \'nag\ *n.* A horse; especially, one that is old and poor in appearance or condition.

nag \'nag\ *v.;* **nagged; nag·ging.** To annoy by finding fault; to torment by constant scolding or urging.

na·iad \'nā-əd, 'nī-, -ˌad\ *n.; pl.* **na·iads** \-ədz, -ˌadz\ or **na·ia·des** \-ə-ˌdēz\. In ancient mythology, a nymph believed to live in, and to give life to, lakes, rivers, springs, and fountains.

nail \'nāl\ *n.* **1** The horny scale or plate at the end of the fingers and toes of man, apes, and other animals. **2** A slender, pointed piece of metal used for driving into or through wood. — **on the nail.** Immediately; without delay. — *v.* **1** To fasten with a nail or nails. **2** To bind or hold; as to a promise. **3** To catch; to trap; as, to *nail* a thief.

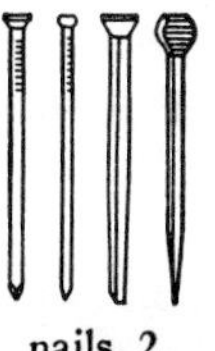

nails, 2

nail·brush \'nāl-ˌbrəsh\ *n.* A brush for cleaning the hands and fingernails.

nain·sook \'nān-ˌsu̇k\ *n.* A thin soft cotton fabric, a variety of muslin, originally made in India.

na·ïve or **na·ive** \nä-'ēv, nȧ-\ *adj.* **1** Simple and unaffected; artless; childlike. **2** Excessively artless or childlike; innocent to the degree of being foolish. — **na·ïve·ly** or **na·ive·ly,** *adv.*

na·ïv·e·té \nä-ˌē-və-'tā, nȧ-; ˌnä-ˌēv-'tā, ˌnȧ-\ *n.* **1** The quality of being naïve. **2** An instance of being naïve; an artless remark or action.

na·ked \'nāk-əd, 'nek-əd\ *adj.* **1** Having no clothes on; nude. **2** Not having its usual or natural covering, growth, or furnishing; bare; as, *naked* trees; *naked* walls. **3** Not in its case or sheath; as, a *naked* sword. **4** Without enveloping parts, as a bud without leaves or a seed that is not enclosed in an ovary. **5** Plain; stripped of anything misleading; as, the *naked* truth. **6** Not aided by artificial means; as, seen by the *naked* eye. — **na·ked·ly,** *adv.*

name \'nām\ *n.* **1** The title by which any person or thing is known. **2** A descriptive word, often disparaging, applied on account of a person's character or actions; as, to call somebody *names.* **3** Reputation; fame; as, to make a *name* for oneself in music. **4** A seeming, not really descriptive, title; title as distinguished from reality; as, to be friend in *name* only. — *v.;* **named; nam·ing.** **1** To give a name to; to call. **2** To refer to by name; to mention; as, to *name* a few books everybody should read. **3** To call by its right name; to identify; as, to *name* these flowers. **4** To speak about or mention; as, to *name* a price. **5** To choose; to appoint; to settle on; as, to *name* the day for a wedding. **6** To nominate, as for office. — *adj.* Recognized as of front rank; well-known; as, *name* brands; a *name* hand.

name·less \'nām-ləs\ *adj.* **1** Having no name. **2** Not marked with a name; as, a *nameless* grave. **3** Unknown; anonymous; as, a *nameless* hero; a *nameless* author. **4** Unnamable; not to be described; as, *nameless* fears. — **name·less·ly,** *adv.*

name·ly \'nām-lē\ *adv.* That is to say; as, the cat family, *namely,* lions, tigers, and similar animals.

name·sake \'nām-ˌsāk\ *n.* One who has the same name; especially, one named for another.

nan·keen or **nan·kin** \(')nan-'kēn\ *n.* [From *Nankeen,* older spelling of *Nanking,* China, where such cloth was first manufactured.] A strong, durable, naturally brownish yellow cotton cloth originally imported from China.

nap \'nap\ *v.;* **napped; nap·ping.** **1** To have a short sleep. **2** To be off one's guard; as, to be caught *napping* at the wrong moment. — *n.* A short sleep; a doze.

nap \'nap\ *n.* A downy surface of some woven cloths, as those made from wool. — **nap·py** \'nap-ē\ *adj.*

nape \'nāp, 'nap\ *n.* The back of the neck.

naph·tha \'naf-thə, 'nap-\ *n.* **1** Petroleum. **2** A product of petroleum, coal tar, or other thick oil, used in dry-cleaning clothing or burned as a fuel.

naph·tha·lene \'naf-thə-ˌlēn, 'nap-\ *n.* A chemical compound obtained from coal tar as white crystals and used in making various products, as dyes, explosives, and moth repellents.

nap·kin \'nap-kən\ *n.* **1** A small cloth or towel. **2** A small cloth for wiping lips and fingers after eating.

na·po·le·on \nə-'pōl-yən, -'pō-lē-ən\ *n.* **1** A gold twenty-franc piece formerly in use in France. **2** An oblong French pastry with a cream filling between layers of crust.

napped. Past tense and past part. of *nap.*

napping. Pres. part. of *nap.*

nar·cis·sus \när-'sis-əs, nȧr-\ *n.; pl.* **nar·cis·sus·es** \-'sis-ə-səz\ or **nar·cis·si** \-'sis-ˌī\. An herb of the family that includes the daffodil and jonquil, developing from a bulb and having erect narrow leaves and showy yellow, white, or two-colored flowers.

nar·cot·ic \när-'kät-ik, nȧr-\ *adj.* **1** Having the properties of a narcotic; as, a *narcotic* drug. **2** Of or relating to narcotics or their use. — *n.* **1** A drug, such as opium, that in moderate doses relieves pain and brings on sleep but in poisonous doses causes stupor, coma, or convulsions. **2** Something that soothes, relieves, or lulls.

na·res \'nar-(ˌ)ēz, 'ner-\ *n. pl.; sing.* **na·ris** \-əs\. The openings of the nose; the nostrils.

nar·rate \na-'rāt, 'nar-ˌāt\ *v.;* **nar·rat·ed; nar·rat·ing.** To tell, as a story; to give an account of; to relate. — **nar·ra·tor** \'nar-ˌāt-r, na-'rāt-r\ *n.*

nar·ra·tion \na-'rāsh-n\ *n.* **1** The action of telling about something; as, to listen to the *narration* of a person's troubles. **2** A story; a narrative.

nar·ra·tive \'nar-ət-iv\ *n.* **1** Something that is narrated; a story; a history of some event; an account. **2** The action of narrating; a telling or relating, as of a story. **3** The art or practice of narrating; as, a novelist who was a master of *narrative.*

— The words *account* and *recital* are synonyms of *narrative: narrative* usually refers to a factual reporting of a series of events, generally in the order in which they occurred; *account* is a more familiar term and may suggest a simple repetition of facts or of a single brief event; *recital* may indicate an elaborate and detailed narrative or a somewhat mechanical enumeration of facts as if they had been memorized.

— *adj.* Of the nature of narration; like a story; suitable for narration.

nar·row \'nar-ō\ *adj.* **1** Not wide or broad; as, a *narrow* street. **2** Of small scope or amount; limited; as, a *narrow* space; *narrow* circumstances. **3** Confining; penning in; as, to keep within *narrow* bounds. **4** Having only a slight margin; close; near; as, a *narrow* escape; to win by a *narrow* majority. **5** Not liberal or broad-minded; bigoted; as, to be *narrow* in one's opinions. — *v.* To lessen the width, range, or scope of; to contract; to restrict. The police gradually *narrowed* down the fugitive's means of escape to a single road. — *n.* [usually in the plural] A narrow passage, as in a river, lake, or sea. — **nar·row·ly,** *adv.*

nar·row–mind·ed \'nar-ō-'mīn-dəd\ *adj.* Not liberal or broad-minded; bigoted. — **nar·row–mind·ed·ly,** *adv.*

nar·whal \'när-wəl, 'nȧr-, -ˌwȯl\ *n.* An arctic sea mammal related to the dolphin, reaching about twenty feet in length, and having in the male a long ivory tusk.

na·sal \'nāz-l\ *adj.* **1** Of or relating to the nose. **2** Uttered with the mouth passage closed and the nose passage open, as *m, n,* and *ng,* or uttered with the nose passage as well as the mouth passage open, as certain vowels in French. **3** Having the quality of being uttered through the nose; as, to speak in a *nasal* tone. — *n.* A nasal sound, as *m, n,* and *ng.* — **na·sal·i·ty** \nā-'zal-ət-ē\ *n.* — **na·sal·ly** \'nāz-l-ē\ *adv.*

nas·tur·tium \nas-'tərsh-m, nəs-\ *n.* A soft-stemmed, usually climbing herb with pungent juice, roundish, prominently veined leaves attached in the middle of the blade, spurred red and yellow flowers, and a fruit with three seeds.

nas·ty \'nas-tē\ *adj.;* **nas·ti·er; nas·ti·est. 1** Very dirty or foul; filthy. **2** Indecent; vile. **3** Disagreeable; as, *nasty* weather. **4** Mean; ill-natured; dishonorable; as, a *nasty* temper; a *nasty* trick. **5** Harmful; dangerous; as, a *nasty* fall on the icy pavement. — **nas·ti·ly** \'nas-tə-lē\ *adv.* — **nas·ti·ness** \'nas-tē-nəs\ *n.*

na·tal \'nāt-l\ *adj.* Of or relating to a person's birth; as, one's *natal* day.

na·tion \'nāsh-n\ *n.* **1** The union of a people connected by ties of blood, a common language, a common religion, similar customs, or like political ideas. The Polish *nation* was long under Russian rule. **2** The people in a country united under a single independent government; an independent state; as, the American *nation.*

na·tion·al \'nash-n(-)əl\ *adj.* Of or having to do with a nation or independent state; as, *national* holidays. — *n.* A citizen or subject of a nation; as, protecting their *nationals* abroad. — **na·tion·al·ly** \-n(-)ə-lē\ *adv.*

national bank. A commercial bank organized under laws passed by Congress, and chartered by the national government.

National Guard. A militia force recruited, controlled, and partly maintained by the several states but subject to the call of the federal government.

na·tion·al·ism \'nash-n(-)ə-ˌliz-m\ *n.* **1** Devotion to national interests. **2** Devotion on the part of a dependent or disorganized people to the ideal of national unity and independence.

na·tion·al·ist \'nash-n(-)ə-ləst\ *n.* One who advocates nationalism. — *adj.* Of or relating to nationalism or nationalists. — **na·tion·al·is·tic** \ˌnash-n(-)ə-'lis-tik\ *adj.*

na·tion·al·i·ty \ˌnash-n-'al-ət-ē\ *n.; pl.* **na·tion·al·i·ties.** **1** The condition of being a nation; especially, political independence as a nation; as, a country that has attained *nationality.* **2** The fact of belonging to one particular nation by birth or citizenship; as, a person of British *nationality.* **3** The sense or feeling of being a people bound together by a common culture; nationalism. **4** A nation; as, the position of the smaller *nationalities* of the world.

na·tion·al·ize \'nash-n(-)ə-ˌlīz\ *v.;* **na·tion·al·ized; na·tion·al·iz·ing.** **1** To make national; to make a nation of. **2** To remove from private ownership and place under government control; as, to *nationalize* the railroads. — **na·tion·al·i·za·tion** \ˌnash-n(-)ə-lə-'zāsh-n\ *n.*

na·tion·wide \'nāsh-n-ˌwīd\ *adj.* Extending throughout the nation.

na·tive \'nāt-iv\ *adj.* **1** Inborn; natural; as, *native* genius. **2** Born in a particular place or country; as, *native* Americans. **3** Belonging to a person because of the place or circumstances of his birth; as, one's *native* land; one's *native* language. **4** Grown, produced, or having its origin in a particular region; as, *native* art; *native* fruit. **5** Natural; not artificially prepared; as, *native* salt.

— The word *aboriginal* is a synonym of *native: native* generally refers to a person born and often reared in a specified place, or to things that have their origin in such a place; *aboriginal* is nearly always applied to persons and indicates that they are the earliest known race of inhabitants of a particular place, often suggesting a primitive level of civilization.

— *n.* **1** A person who belongs to a particular country or place by right of birth. **2** A permanent inhabitant of a region. **3** An animal or plant produced in a certain region. **4** A product from nearby rather than from distant regions.

na·tiv·i·ty \nə-'tiv-ət-ē, nā-\ *n.; pl.* **na·tiv·i·ties.** **1** Birth; the time, place, or manner of a person's birth. **2** [with a capital] The birth of Jesus; Christmas Day.

natl. Abbreviation for *national.*

nat·ty \'nat-ē\ *adj.;* **nat·ti·er; nat·ti·est.** Trim, neat, and tidy; as, *natty* suits. — **nat·ti·ly** \'nat-l-ē\ *adv.*

nat·u·ral \'nach-r(-)əl\ *adj.* **1** Native; born in or with one; as, *natural* ability. **2** Being such by nature; born; as, a *natural* fool. **3** Born of unmarried parents; illegitimate; as, a *natural* son. **4** In keeping with the nature of the species; as, the *natural* food of dogs. **5** Human. It is not *natural* to hate one's son. **6** Of or in keeping with the laws of nature or the objects or operation of the physical world; as, *natural* causes; *natural* growth. **7** Not artificial; not made by man; as, *natural* silk; a person's *natural* complexion. **8** Not affected; simple and sincere; as, *natural* manners. **9** Lifelike. The people in the picture look *natural.* **10** In music, having neither sharps nor flats in the key signature or having a sharp or a flat changed in pitch by a natural sign. — *n.* **1** Also **natural sign.** In music, the sign [♮], which takes away the effect of a sharp or flat. **2** A note or tone affected by this sign. — **nat·u·ral·ness,** *n.*

natural barrier. Something in nature that obstructs the spread of people or animals, as an expanse of water or mountains.

natural gas. A gas that issues from the earth's crust through natural openings or bored wells, used industrially and as domestic fuel.

natural history. The study of animals, plants, and minerals.

nat·u·ral·ist \'nach-r(-)ə-ləst\ *n.* A person interested in or trained in the study of nature; especially, a student of animals or plants.

nat·u·ral·is·tic \ˌnach-r(-)ə-'lis-tik\ *adj.* Of, relating to, or closely resembling or reproducing nature; natural; realistic; as, a *naturalistic* painting.

nat·u·ral·ize \'nach-r(-)ə-ˌlīz\ *v.;* **nat·u·ral·ized; nat·u·ral·iz·ing.** **1** To give a foreign-born person the rights of citizenship. **2** To receive or adopt as native, natural, or vernacular; as, to *naturalize* a foreign word. **3** To cause to grow in a region to which it is not native, as fruit. — **nat·u·ral·i·za·tion** \ˌnach-r(-)ə-lə-'zāsh-n\ *n.*

nat·u·ral·ly \'nach-r(-)ə-lē, 'nach-r-lē\ *adv.* **1** By nature; by natural character or ability; as, to be *naturally* timid. **2** According to the laws of nature; as might be expected. One *naturally* dislikes being hurt. **3** Without artificial aid; without affectation; as, hair that curls *naturally;* to speak *naturally.* **4** In a lifelike manner; as, to paint flowers *naturally.*

natural resources. Materials found in nature, as mineral deposits and water affording power.

natural rights. Rights that are assumed to belong to man; especially, the right to life, liberty, and property and to participation in determining the form of government under which one lives.

natural science. The branches of knowledge dealing with natural objects, as biology, geology, mineralogy, physics, and chemistry.

natural selection. The natural process that results in the survival of those forms of animals and plants best adjusted to the conditions under which they live and the extinction of poorly adapted forms.

na·ture \'nāch-r\ *n.* **1** The peculiar quality or qualities; as, the *nature* of steel. **2** Kind, sort, or type; as, things of this *nature.* **3** Character or disposition; as, a man of generous *nature.* **4** [often with a capital] A power or set of forces referred to as controlling the universe; as, Mother *Nature.*

5 Natural feeling, especially as shown in one's attitude toward others; as, a man whose good *nature* is well known. **6** Man's native state; simple, primitive life; as, to return to *nature.* **7** The physical universe; as, the study of *nature.* **8** Life; the workings of a living body; as, to leave a cure to *nature.* **9** Natural scenery, as sky, sea, or trees.

naught \'nȯt, 'nät\ *n.* **1** The arithmetical character 0; zero. **2** Nought.

naugh·ty \'nȯt-ē, 'nät-ē\ *adj.;* **naugh·ti·er; naugh·ti·est.** Behaving badly or improperly; mischievous; disobedient. — **naugh·ti·ly** \'nȯt-l-ē, 'nät-\ *adv.* — **naugh·ti·ness** \-ē-nəs\ *n.*

nau·sea \'nȯsh-ə, 'nȯz-ē-ə, 'nȯs-ē-ə, 'nȯzh-ə\ *n.* [From Latin, there borrowed from Greek *nausia, nausie* meaning "seasickness" and derived from *naus* meaning "ship".] **1** Any sickness of the stomach marked by a desire to vomit. **2** Loathing; deep disgust.

nau·se·ate \'nȯsh-ē-ˌāt, 'nȯz-ē-, 'nȯs-ē-, 'nȯzh-ē-\ *v.;* **nau·se·at·ed; nau·se·at·ing.** **1** To affect or be affected with nausea; to sicken. **2** To cause loathing; to disgust.

nau·seous \'nȯsh-əs, 'nȯz-ē-əs, 'nȯs-ē-əs, 'nȯzh-əs\ *adj.* Nauseating. — **nau·seous·ly,** *adv.*

nau·ti·cal \'nȯt-ik-l\ *adj.* Of or relating to seamen, navigation, or ships. — **nau·ti·cal·ly** \-ik-l(-)ē\ *adv.*

nau·ti·lus \'nȯt-l-əs\ *n.; pl.* **nau·ti·lus·es** \-l-ə-səz\ or **nau·ti·li** \-l-ˌī\. **1** A mollusk of the South Pacific and Indian Oceans with a spiral shell divided into chambers and having an inner pearly layer; the **pearly nautilus.** **2** An eight-armed mollusk related to the octopus, the female of which has a fragile, papery, undivided shell; the **paper nautilus.**

na·val \'nāv-l\ *adj.* **1** Of or relating to a navy or warships; as, a *naval* shipyard; a *naval* officer. **2** Possessing a navy; as, a *naval* power.

nave \'nāv\ *n.* The hub of a wheel.

nave \'nāv\ *n.* The central part or main body of a church, running lengthwise from the main entrance.

nave

na·vel \'nāv-l\ *n.* A mark or depression in the middle of the abdomen marking the point where the umbilical cord was attached.

navel orange. A usually seedless orange with a small secondary fruit resembling a navel at one end.

navies. Pl. of *navy.*

nav·i·ga·ble \'nav-ig-əb-l\ *adj.* **1** Permitting passage of vessels; as, a *navigable* river. **2** Capable of being steered; as, a *navigable* balloon. — **nav·i·ga·bil·i·ty** \ˌnav-ig-ə-'bil-ət-ē\ *n.*

nav·i·gate \'nav-ə-ˌgāt\ *v.;* **nav·i·gat·ed; nav·i·gat·ing.** **1** To journey by water; to sail or manage a ship over or on; as, to *navigate* the Atlantic. **2** To direct one's course; to steer; as, a night so black it was almost impossible to *navigate.* **3** To conduct upon the water by the art or skill of seamen. **4** To operate, steer, or control the course of, as an airplane or airship.

nav·i·ga·tion \ˌnav-ə-'gāsh-n\ *n.* The act or art of navigating; especially, the science of fixing the course of a ship or aircraft through the use of calculations as to position and direction.

nav·i·ga·tor \'nav-ə-ˌgāt-r\ *n.* **1** One that sails the seas, especially as an explorer. **2** A person who directs the course of a ship or an aircraft.

nav·vy \'nav-ē\ *n.; pl.* **nav·vies.** An unskilled or common laborer.

na·vy \'nā-vē\ *n.; pl.* **na·vies.** **1** A fleet of ships. **2** The war vessels of a nation. **3** [usually with a capital] A nation's complete equipment and organization for war at sea. **4** Navy blue.

navy bean. A white-seeded variety of the common kidney bean.

navy blue. A very dark blue.

navy yard. A shore station for a navy, with facilities for building, equipping, and repairing warships.

na·wab \nə-'wäb\ *n.* **1** A nabob. **2** [with a capital] A title of certain Moslem princes.

nay \'nā\ *adv.* **1** *Archaic.* No — a negative answer. **2** Not this merely, but also; not only so, but; as, to believe, *nay,* to know that all will be well. — *n.* A reply of "no"; a negative vote or voter.

Naz·a·rene \ˌnaz-r-'ēn\ *adj.* Of or relating to Nazareth or the Nazarenes. — *n.* **1** A native or inhabitant of Nazareth; especially, with *the,* Jesus Christ. **2** A Christian.

N.B. or **n.b.** \'en-'bē\. [Abbreviated from Latin *nota bene* meaning "note well".] Consider or observe carefully — used in writing to call attention to a passage so marked.

N.C.O. Abbreviation for *noncommissioned officer.*

N.E. Abbreviation for *northeast.*

Ne·an·der·thal \nē-'and-r-ˌthȯl; nā-'änd-r-ˌtäl, -ˌtȧl\ *adj.* Of or relating to a type of prehistoric man intermediate between Java man and modern man, having a brain approximately as large as in modern man.

neap \'nēp\ *n.* or **neap tide.** A decrease in the height of high tide, occurring when the moon is at first or third quarter.

near \'nir\ *adv.* **1** At, within, or to, a short distance; close by in space or time. The enemy approached quite *near.* **2** Within little; almost; nearly; as, a dark brown that comes *near* to black. **3** Closely; as, a person who is *near* related to another. — *adj.* **1** Closely related; as, a *near* relative. **2** Close to one's interests or affection; intimate; as, one's *nearest* friend. **3** Not far away; as, in every country far and *near.* **4** Close; narrow; as, a *near* escape from death. **5** Left; as, the *near* horse of a team. **6** Closely imitated; not real but very like; as, *near* silk. **7** Direct; short; as, the *nearest* way. — *prep.* Near to or by; close to or upon; as, to stand *near* the edge of the cliff. — *v.* To draw near; to approach; as, to *near* home. — **near·ly,** *adv.* — **near·ness,** *n.*

near·by or **near-by** \'nir-ˌbī, -'bī\ *adj.* or *adv.* Close at hand; near.

Near East. The region extending from around the eastern end of the Mediterranean Sea to and including Iran.

near·sight·ed \'nir-'sīt-əd\ *adj.* Seeing distinctly at short distances only; shortsighted. — **near-sight·ed·ness,** *n.*

neat \'nēt\ *adj.* **1** Not mixed, adulterated, or diluted with anything; as, a *neat* liquor. **2** Simple and in good taste; as, a *neat* style. **3** Clever; skillful; as, a *neat* reply. **4** Orderly and cleanly; tidy; as, to keep one's house *neat.* — **neat·ly,** *adv.* — **neat·ness,** *n.*

'neath \'nēth\ *prep.* A contraction of *beneath.*

neat·herd \'nēt-ˌhərd\ *n.* [From medieval English *neetherde,* a compound made up of *neet* meaning "head of cattle" and *herde* meaning "herdsman".] A cowherd.

neb·u·la \'neb-yə-lə\ *n.; pl.* **neb·u·las** \-ləz\ or **neb·u·lae** \-ˌlē, -ˌlī\. A vast formation of matter in a gaseous or finely divided state that is visible in the sky on a clear night as a faintly bright mass resembling a cloud. — **neb·u·lar** \-yəl-r\ *adj.*

nebular hypothesis. A hypothesis that the stars and planets were formed out of nebular matter, as by a process of gradually cooling and contracting.

neb·u·lous \'neb-yə-ləs\ *adj.* **1** Of or resembling nebulas. **2** Cloudy; hazy; vague; as, an argument based on *nebulous* grounds. — **neb·u·lous·ly,** *adv.*

nec·es·sary \'nes-ə-ˌser-ē\ *adj.* **1** Positively needed; impossible to do without; indispensable; as, to lack the *necessary* tools. **2** Bound to be; bound to become; inevitable. **3** Logically unavoidable; absolutely certain; as, a *necessary* conclusion. — *n.; pl.* **nec·es·sar·ies** \-ˌser-ēz\. A necessary thing; something that is required; as, the *necessaries* of life. — **nec·es·sar·i·ly** \ˌnes-ə-'ser-ə-lē\ *adv.*

ne·ces·si·tate \nə-'ses-ə-ˌtāt\ *v.;* **ne·ces·si·tat·ed; ne·ces·si·tat·ing.** **1** To make necessary. Bad colds *necessitated* several absences from school. **2** To force; to compel. The overwhelming attack by the enemy *necessitated* the withdrawal of our troops.

ne·ces·si·ty \nə-'ses-ət-ē, -'ses-tē\ *n.; pl.* **ne·ces·si·ties.** **1** Very great need of help or relief; as, to call in case of *necessity.* **2** A very necessary thing; something badly needed. **3** Lack of necessary things; want; poverty. **4** Conditions that cannot be changed; as, to be compelled by *necessity.*

neck \'nek\ *n.* **1** The part of the body connecting the head and the trunk. **2** The parts of a garment covering or nearest to the neck. **3** Something like a neck in shape or position; as, the *neck* of a bottle; the *neck* of a guitar. — **neck and neck.** In racing, so nearly equal that one cannot be said to be ahead of the other; very close.

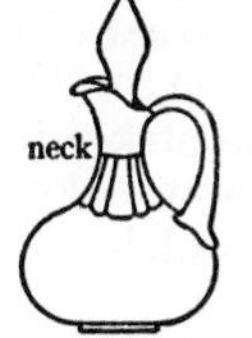

neck·er·chief \'nek-r-; *"-chief" as in "handkerchief"*\ *n.; pl.* **neck·er·chiefs.** A scarf for the neck.

neck·lace \'nek-ləs\ *n.* An ornamental chain or a string, as of jewels or beads, worn around the neck.

neck·line \'nek-ˌlīn\ *n.* The outline of the neck opening of a garment; as, a round *neckline.*

neck·piece \'nek-ˌpēs\ *n.* An article of wearing apparel, usually a scarf or fur piece, for the neck.

neck·tie \'nek-ˌtī\ *n.* A scarf, band or ribbon worn around the neck or collar and tied in front.

neck·wear \'nek-ˌwar, -ˌwer\ *n.* Articles worn around the neck, as scarves or neckties.

nec·ro·man·cy \'nek-rə-ˌman(t)s-ē\ *n.* **1** The art of revealing the future by pretended talk with the spirits. **2** Magic. — **nec·ro·man·cer** \-ˌman(t)s-r\ *n.*

nec·tar \'nekt-r\ *n.* In Greek mythology, a drink served to the gods.

nec·tar·ine \'nekt-r-ˌēn\ *n.* A smooth-skinned variety of peach.

nee or **née** \'nā\ *adj.* Born — used in introducing the maiden family name of a married woman, as in Mrs. John Jones, *nee* Smith.

need \'nēd\ *n.* **1** A condition requiring aid; as, to help those in *need.* **2** Lack of something required, wanted, or useful; as, to feel the *need* of a better education. **3** Poverty; want; as, a childhood spent in *need* and suffering. **4** Something required or felt to be required; as, our daily *needs.* — *v.* **1** To be in need of; to require; to want badly; as, to *need* food or sleep; to *need* an assistant. **2** To be required; to be under obligation. No one *need* reply to a question he thinks unfair.

need·ful \'nēd-fəl\ *adj.* Necessary; required.

needier. Comparative of *needy.*

neediest. Superlative of *needy.*

nee·dle \'nēd-l\ *n.* **1** A slender pointed sewing instrument, usually steel, with an eyehole for thread. **2** A thin rod or wire used in knitting; a hooked instrument used in crocheting. **3** A thin sharp-pointed piece of steel, sometimes with a tip, as of diamond or emerald, used in a phonograph to transmit vibrations. **4** Also **magnetic needle.** A slender bar of magnetized steel in a compass. **5** A pointed instrument used by doctors for puncturing or sewing tissues. **6** A needle-shaped leaf, as that of a pine. **7** Any needle-shaped object, as a pointed rock or an obelisk. — *v.;* **nee·dled; nee·dling** \-l(-)ing\. **1** To tease or annoy. **2** To incite to a desired action by repeated sharp gibes.

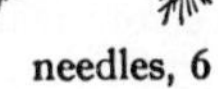
needles, 6

needle point. Needlework, usually of yarn, on a coarse, loosely woven cloth.

need·less \'nēd-ləs\ *adj.* Not needed; unnecessary. — **need·less·ly,** *adv.*

nee·dle·wom·an \'nēd-l-ˌwu̇m-ən\ *n.; pl.* **nee·dle·wom·en** \-ˌwim-ən\. A woman who does needlework.

nee·dle·work \'nēd-l-ˌwərk\ *n.* Work done with a needle; sewing; embroidery.

needn't \'nēd-nt\. A contraction of *need not.*

needs \'nēdz\ *adv.* Necessarily; of necessity —

used chiefly with *must.* A person must *needs* recognize his faults in order to overcome them.

needy \'nēd-ē\ *adj.;* **need·i·er**; **need·i·est**. In want; very poor.

ne'er \'ner\ *adv.* A contraction of *never.*

ne'er-do-well \'ner-(ˌ)dü-ˌwel\ *n.* One who is good for nothing; a worthless person.

ne·far·i·ous \nə-'far-ē-əs, -'fer-\ *adj.* Very wicked. — **ne·far·i·ous·ly**, *adv.*

ne·gate \nē-'gāt\ *v.;* **ne·gat·ed**; **ne·gat·ing**. To deny; to nullify.

ne·ga·tion \nē-'gāsh-n\ *n.* **1** A denying; a negative statement or answer. "Not" is a word used in *negation.* **2** A complete loss; an entire lack. Death is the *negation* of life.

neg·a·tive \'neg-ət-iv\ *adj.* **1** Expressing, showing, or implying denial; as, a *negative* reply. **2** Not having positive qualities; as, *negative* criticism. **3** Not conspicuous; as, a *negative* color. **4** Not affirming the presence of a particular germ or condition; as, *negative* results of a test for tuberculosis. **5** Of or relating to static electricity, as that generated on hard rubber by rubbing it with fur. **6** Of or relating to the electrical charge on a body that has more electrons than protons on its surface. **7** In a battery, of or relating to the electrode toward which the electric current flows in passing through the device being operated. **8** In mathematics, being a quantity that is to be subtracted or that is less than zero; minus; as, a *negative* number. **9** In photography, having the lights and shadows opposite to what they were in the original subject. — *n.* **1** A saying *no;* a negative word or statement. **2** The side that votes or argues against something. The debate was won by the *negative.* **3** In mathematics, a negative quantity or symbol. **4** The developed film or plate from which photographs are printed and which has the lights and shadows opposite to what they were in the thing or scene that was photographed. — *v.;* **neg·a·tived**; **neg·a·tiv·ing**. To vote against; to refuse to accept or approve. — **neg·a·tive·ly**, *adv.*

ne·glect \ni-'glekt\ *v.* **1** To treat as though of no importance; to fail to notice; to slight; as, to *neglect* a friend. **2** To fail to attend to or care for; as, to *neglect* one's work.

— The words *disregard* and *slight* are synonyms of *neglect: neglect* may indicate failure, whether deliberate or merely unintentional, to give proper attention to something deserving one's attention; *disregard* usually suggests deliberately overlooking some matter, often from a feeling that it is not worth one's notice; *slight* is likely to suggest a rude, scornful, and disdainful disregard.

— *n.* **1** A neglecting or a being neglected; a disregarding or slighting; as, a garden in a bad state of *neglect.* **2** Negligence; lack of due attention or care; as, to be criticized by one's superior for *neglect* of duty.

ne·glect·ful \ni-'glekt-fəl\ *adj.* Having the habit of neglecting things; careless; negligent. — **ne·glect·ful·ly** \-fə-lē\ *adv.*

neg·li·gee \ˌneg-lə-'zhā\ *n.* **1** A loose robe or dressing gown worn by women. **2** Informal attire.

neg·li·gence \'neg-lə-jən(t)s\ *n.* **1** A being negligent; neglect. **2** An action or instance of carelessness; failure to attend to something under one's charge.

neg·li·gent \'neg-lə-jənt\ *adj.* Guilty of neglect; inclined to neglect things; careless.

neg·li·gi·ble \'neg-lə-jəb-l\ *adj.* So unimportant as not to require or deserve attention; as, a *negligible* difference between two plans.

ne·go·tia·ble \ni-'gō-shəb-l\ *adj.* Capable of being negotiated; especially, capable of being passed from one person to another in return for money or its equivalent. — **ne·go·tia·bil·i·ty** \ni-ˌgō-shə-'bil-ət-ē\ *n.*

ne·go·ti·ate \ni-'gō-shē-ˌāt, -sē-ˌāt\ *v.;* **ne·go·ti·at·ed**; **ne·go·ti·at·ing**. **1** To have a discussion with another person or other persons for the purpose of reaching an agreement in some matter of business or politics; as, to *negotiate* for the purchase of a house; to *negotiate* a treaty. **2** In business, to give to another person in exchange for money or something else of value; as, to *negotiate* a check. **3** To succeed in getting through, along, around, or over; as, to *negotiate* a curve; to *negotiate* a fence. — **ne·go·ti·a·tion** \ni-ˌgō-shē-'āsh-n, -sē-'āsh-n\ *n.* — **ne·go·ti·a·tor** \ni-'gō-shē-ˌāt-r, -sē-ˌāt-r\ *n.*

Ne·gro \'nē-ˌgrō\ *n.; pl.* **Ne·groes**. **1** A person belonging to one of the black races native to Africa. **2** A colored person descended wholly or partly from these black races. — *adj.* Of or relating to Negroes.

Ne·groid \'nē-ˌgrȯid\ *adj.* Characteristic of or like the Negro or Negroes. — *n.* A person having some Negro blood or showing Negro traits.

ne·gus \'nē-gəs\ *n.* A beverage of wine, hot water, sugar, nutmeg, and lemon juice.

neigh \'nā\ *n.* The long, loud cry of a horse. — *v.* To utter a neigh.

neigh·bor \'nāb-r\ *n.* **1** A person who lives near another. **2** A person or thing near another; as, a skyscraper taller than any of its *neighbors.* **3** A fellow human being.

neigh·bor·hood \'nāb-r-ˌhu̇d\ *n.* **1** The condition of being neighbors; nearness in position. **2** A section of a town or city where people live who consider each other neighbors; as, the people in our *neighborhood.* **3** The people who live nearby, considered as a group. The whole *neighborhood* heard about it. **4** A place or region near; as, in the *neighborhood* of Baffin Island. **5** A number or amount near; as, in the *neighborhood* of 2000.

neigh·bor·ing \'nāb-r(-)ing\ *adj.* Living or being near; adjoining; adjacent; as, *neighboring* lots.

neigh·bor·ly \'nāb-r-lē\ *adj.* Befitting neighbors; friendly; as, *neighborly* help. — **neigh·bor·li·ness** \-lē-nəs\ *n.*

nei·ther \'nēth-r, 'nīth-r\ *adj.* Not either; as, *neither* hand. — *pron.* Not the one or the other. *Neither* was at home. — *conj.* **1** Not either — used before the first of two words, phrases, or clauses joined by *nor;* as, *neither* iron nor nickel. *Neither* the boys nor the girls knew where the ball was. **2** Nor yet. My friend did not go; *neither* did I.

nem·a·tode \'nem-ə-ˌtōd\ *adj.* Of or relating to a class of worms having cylindrical bodies not divided into segments. — *n.* A nematode worm; a roundworm.

nem·e·sis \'nem-ə-səs\ *n.; pl.* **nem·e·ses** \-ˌsēz\. [Named after *Nemesis*, the Greek goddess of revenge.] **1** One that avenges or punishes without mercy or that destroys inevitably; an agent of just punishment. **2** An act of just punishment; an unavoidable penalty.

ne·o·lith·ic \ˌnē-ə-'lith-ik\ *adj.* Of or relating to the stage (**Neolithic period**) of human culture marked by the use of polished stone implements and bows and arrows, and by the cultivation of grain and fruit trees.

ne·ol·o·gism \nē-'äl-ə-ˌjiz-m\ *n.* A new word or phrase.

ne·on \'nē-ˌän\ *n.* A colorless gaseous element found in very small quantities in the air, that gives a reddish glow in a vacuum tube and is used with other gases in a type of electric lamp (**neon lamp**) widely used for signs.

ne·o·phyte \'nē-ə-ˌfīt\ *n.* **1** A newly converted person; especially, a newly baptized Christian. **2** In the Roman Catholic Church, a newly ordained priest or a person who has just entered a convent. **3** A beginner; a novice.

Nep·a·lese \ˌnep-l-'ēz, -'ēs\ *adj.* Of or relating to Nepal. — *n. sing. and pl.* A native of Nepal.

ne·pen·the \nə-'pen(t)th-ē\ *n.* **1** A drug used by the ancients to dull pain or sorrow. **2** Anything that brings forgetfulness or relief from suffering.

neph·ew \'nef-ˌyü\ *n.* A son of one's brother or sister.

ne·phri·tis \nə-'frīt-əs\ *n.* Inflammation of the kidneys.

nep·o·tism \'nep-ə-ˌtiz-m\ *n.* Favoritism shown to relatives, as by appointment to business positions or political offices.

nep·tu·ni·um \nep-'tü-nē-əm, -'tyü-\ *n.* [Named after the planet *Neptune* by analogy with *uranium*, named after the planet *Uranus*.] A short-lived radioactive chemical element made from one form of uranium.

Ne·re·id \'nir-ē-əd\ *n.* **1** Any of the daughters of the ancient sea god Nereus. **2** [often with a small letter] Any sea nymph.

ner·va·tion \nər-'vāsh-n\ *n.* The arrangement of nerves, especially in leaves.

nerve \'nərv\ *n.* **1** One of the bands or strands chiefly of nerve fibers that connect the brain and spinal cord with every part of the body, carrying impulses. **2** Will power; endurance; as, a feat accomplished by sheer *nerve.* **3** [in the plural] Nervousness; loss of self-control; hysteria; as, an attack of *nerves.* **4** *Slang.* Impudence; boldness; audacity. **5** The sensitive pulp of a tooth. **6** A vein in a leaf. **7** A rib in an insect's wing. — **strain every nerve.** To put forth the utmost effort.

nerve cell. One of the cells that make up nervous tissue, as of the brain, and have one or more dendrites conducting impulses toward the cell, as from the eye or ear, and usually a single axon conducting impulses away from the cell, as to a muscle or gland.

nerve fiber. One of the axons or dendrites, usually covered by a sheath, that make up a nerve.

nerve·less \'nərv-ləs\ *adj.* **1** Lacking nerve; without strength or courage. **2** Having, or seeming to have, no nerves. — **nerve·less·ly**, *adv.*

nerv·ous \'nər-vəs\ *adj.* **1** Of or relating to the nerves or the nervous system; as, *nervous* tissue; *nervous* activity. **2** Having or showing disordered or easily stimulated nerves; as, a *nervous* twitching of the eye. **3** Easily agitated or upset; excitable; as, a high-strung, *nervous* child. **4** Fearful; timid; as, to be *nervous* in the dark; *nervous* about speaking in public. **5** Characterized by agitation or timidity; as, a *nervous* manner. — **nerv·ous·ly**, *adv.*

nerv·ous·ness \'nər-vəs-nəs\ *n.* The state of being nervous; weakness of the nerves; excitability· timidity.

nervous system. The system in the body of an animal that is concerned with receiving and transmitting stimuli and that consists of nerve cells and nerve fibers, the former largely massed in the brain, spinal cord, and certain ganglions, and the latter forming connections between the nerve cells and other body structures.

ner·vure \'nərv-yər\ *n.* **1** A vein in a leaf. **2** A rib in an insect's wing.

nervy \'nər-vē\ *adj.;* **nerv·i·er**; **nerv·i·est**. **1** *Slang.* Bold; audacious. **2** Requiring nerve; affecting the nerves; as, a *nervy* climb. **3** Having or showing courage. **4** *British.* Excitable; nervous.

-ness \nəs\. A suffix that can mean: the quality or condition of being, an act of being, or something that is or makes, as in the examples "in *sickness* and in health", "a man of great *kindness*", "an act of *kindness*", "to receive many *kindnesses* from a friend".

nest \'nest\ *n.* **1** The bed or shelter prepared by a bird for its eggs and young. **2** The place where the eggs of other animals, as insects, fishes, and turtles, are laid and hatched. **3** Any cozy home or snug retreat. **4** A haunt; a den; as, a *nest* of thieves. **5** The occupants of a nest. **6** A series of things, as boxes or bowls, each fitting into or under the next larger one. — *v.* **1** To build or occupy a nest. **2** To place in or as if in a nest.

nest egg. **1** An egg left in a nest to induce a hen to lay more eggs there. **2** A sum of money, kept as a reserve, or as the beginning of a fund.

nes·tle \'nes-l\ *v.;* **nes·tled**; **nes·tling** \-l(-)ing\. **1** To lie close and snug, as a bird in a nest; to cuddle up. **2** To settle as if in a nest; to provide with a nest or cozy retreat. The bird *nestled* its head under its wing. — **nes·tler** \-l(-)ər\ *n.*

nest·ling \'nes(t)-ling\ *n.* **1** A bird not yet able to leave its nest. **2** A young child.

net \'net\ *n.* **1** A fabric with a loose mesh made of intersecting cords or threads; especially, such a fabric used for catching something, as fish or butterflies. **2** Anything woven in loose meshes; as, a tennis *net;* a hair *net.* **3** Anything like a net that traps; as, to be caught in a *net* of lies. **4** A network, as of lines. — *v.;* **net·ted; net·ting. 1** To cover with a net or nets. **2** To capture in a net; to ensnare, as fish. **3** To make or form into a net. **4** In tennis, to strike the ball into the net.

net \'net\ *adj.* Remaining after every deduction has been made; reduced to its lowest amount; as, the *net* price. — *n.* A net amount, as of weight or profit. — *v.;* **net·ted; net·ting.** To gain or produce as clear profit; as, to *net* ten cents.

neth·er \'neth-r\ *adj.* Lower; situated below; as, the *nether* regions of the earth.

Neth·er·land·er \'neth-r-ˌland-r\ *n.* A native or inhabitant of the Netherlands.

Neth·er·land·ish \'neth-r-ˌlan-dish\ *adj.* Of or relating to the Netherlands or its people or language.

neth·er·most \'neth-r-ˌmōst\ *adj.* Lowest.

net·ting \'net-ing\ *n.* **1** The action or process of making nets or network. **2** The action of catching something, as fish, with a net or nets. **3** A fabric or piece of network.

net·tle \'net-l\ *n.* **1** A coarse herb with foliage covered with stinging hairs. **2** Any of a family of herbs with usually toothed leaves, often armed with stinging hairs, and having small, greenish flowers without petals and a dry fruit with one seed. — *v.;* **net·tled; net·tling** \-l(-)ing\. **1** To sting with nettles. **2** To annoy; to vex. His answer *nettled* me.

nettle, 2

net·work \'net-ˌwərk\ *n.* **1** A fabric or structure, as of ropes or wires, crossing one another at intervals and knotted or secured at the crossings. **2** Any arrangement of lines or channels that cross in the manner of a net; as, a *network* of roads. **3** A chain of radio or television stations.

neu·ral·gia \nü-'ral-jə, nə-, nyü-\ *n.* An acute pain that follows the course of a nerve; a condition marked by such pain. — **neu·ral·gic** \-jik\ *adj.*

neu·ri·tis \nü-'rīt-əs, nə-, nyü-\ *n.* Inflammation of a nerve or nerves.

neu·ron \'nü-ˌrän, 'nyü-\ *n.* A nerve cell with all its parts.

neu·ro·sis \nü-'rō-səs, nə-, nyü-\ *n.; pl.* **neu·ro·ses** \-ˌsēz\. A nervous disorder without a physical cause that is frequently characterized by such things as unreasonable fears and the unnecessary repetition of certain acts in otherwise normal persons.

neu·rot·ic \nü-'rät-ik, nə-, nyü-\ *adj.* Of or relating to neurosis. — *n.* **1** A person suffering from a neurosis. **2** An extremely nervous or high-strung person.

neu·ter \'nüt-r, 'nyüt-r\ *adj.* **1** In grammar, belonging to or having to do with the class of words that typically consists primarily of nouns and pronouns referring to things that are neither male nor female; as, a *neuter* noun; the *neuter* gender. **2** In biology, having no sex organs or having imperfectly developed sex organs. — *n.* **1** A word or a form of a word of the neuter gender. **2** The neuter gender. **3** One of the imperfectly developed females of certain insects, as ants and honeybees, that do the work of the community.

neu·tral \'nü-trəl, 'nyü-\ *adj.* **1** Not favoring either side in a quarrel, contest, or war. **2** Of or belonging to a neutral country; as, *neutral* ships. **3** Neither one thing nor the other; indifferent; as, a *neutral* character without great strengths or weaknesses. **4** Not decided in color; grayish. **5** In chemistry, neither acid nor base. — *n.* **1** A neutral person, nation, or vessel. **2** A neutral color or tone. **3** The position of the gears in which the motor imparts no motion, as to the wheels of an automobile. — **neu·tral·ly** \-trə-lē\ *adv.*

neu·tral·ism \'nü-trə-ˌliz-m, 'nyü-\ *n.* **1** Neutrality. **2** A policy of being neutral or nonpartisan in disputes or conflicts between major powers, as in a cold war.

neu·tral·i·ty \nü-'tral-ət-ē, nyü-\ *n.* **1** The quality or state of being neutral. **2** The condition of being neutral in time of war; as, to respect a nation's *neutrality* by letting her ships pass unmolested. **3** Neutralism.

neu·tral·ize \'nü-trə-ˌlīz, 'nyü-\ *v.;* **neu·tral·ized; neu·tral·iz·ing. 1** In chemistry, to destroy the peculiar properties of; as, to *neutralize* an acid with a base. **2** To make ineffective; to counteract; as, to *neutralize* the opposition by a clever move. **3** To make neutral; as, to *neutralize* a country. — **neu·tral·i·za·tion** \ˌnü-trə-lə-'zāsh-n, ˌnyü-\ *n.*

neu·tron \'nü-ˌträn, 'nyü-\ *n.* A particle, found in the nucleus of all atoms except ordinary hydrogen, which is slightly greater in mass than the proton and has no electrical charge.

nev·er \'nev-r\ *adv.* Not ever; at no time; not in any way; not at all.

nev·er·more \ˌnev-r-'mōr, -'mȯr\ *adv.* Never again.

nev·er·the·less \ˌnev-r-thə-'les\ *adv.* In spite of that; yet; however.

new \'nü, 'nyü; *in place names like "New York", often* nü *or* nyü *(without stress) or* nə *or* nyə\ *adj.* **1** Not old; recent; modern. **2** Not the same as the former; taking the place of one that came before; as, a *new* teacher. **3** Recently discovered or learned about; as, *new* lands. **4** Not formerly known or experienced; as, *new* feelings. **5** Not accustomed; as, a person *new* to her work. **6** Beginning as a repetition of some previous act or thing; as, a *new* moon; a *new* year. **7** Refreshed; regenerated. Vacation made a *new* man of him. **8** In a position or place for the first time; as, a *new* member.

— The words *novel* and *fresh* are synonyms of *new: new* is the most general of these terms and may describe anything not known, thought of, or experienced before, or anything only recently used or acquired; *novel* generally has a suggestion of something not only new but original and strikingly different from the usual; *fresh* is likely to apply to something still showing noticeable signs of newness or to something old but still keeping its original liveliness, brightness, energy, or novelty.

— *adv.* Newly; recently; freshly.

new·born \'nü-'bȯrn, 'nyü-\ *adj.* **1** Just lately born; having just lately come into existence; as, *newborn* lambs; a *newborn* hatred. **2** Born again; renewed; as, *newborn* hopes.

new·com·er \'nü-ˌkəm-r, 'nyü-, -'kəm-r\ *n.* One who has recently come to a place.

new·el \'nü-əl, 'nyü-\ *n.* **1** The upright post about which the steps of a circular staircase wind. **2** A post at the foot of a stairway or one at a landing.

newel

new·fan·gled \'nü-'fang-gld, 'nyü-\ *adj.* **1** Having a fondness for novelties or for new theories or fashions. **2** New, strange, and unusual; novel; as, *newfangled* ideas; a *newfangled* can opener.

new-fash·ioned \'nü-'fash-nd, 'nyü-\ *adj.* Made in a new fashion or lately come into fashion.

new look. The appearance or make-up of anything recently changed by extreme innovations. This year's car has a *new look.*

new·ly \'nü-lē, 'nyü-\ *adv.* **1** Lately; recently; as, a *newly* married couple; *newly* bought furniture. **2** Anew; afresh; as, to decide that a house should be *newly* furnished.

new·ness \'nü-nəs, 'nyü-\ *n.* The condition of being new; freshness.

news \'nüz, 'nyüz\ *n. pl.* used as a singular. **1** A report of something recent or, up to the time, unknown; as, to get *news* of an old friend; to have good *news* for someone. **2** A recent occurrence, or recent occurrences in general, especially of a kind that people wish to read about in a newspaper.

news·boy \'nüz-ˌbȯi, 'nyüz-\ *n.* A boy who sells or delivers newspapers.

news·cast \'nüz-ˌkast, 'nyüz-\ *n.* A broadcast of news over radio or television.

news·cast·er \'nüz-ˌkast-r, 'nyüz-\ *n.* **1** A person engaged to edit and broadcast news over radio or television. **2** A commentator. — **news·cast·ing** \-ˌkas-ting\ *n.*

newsier. Comparative of *newsy.*

newsiest. Superlative of *newsy.*

news·let·ter \'nüz-ˌlet-r, 'nyüz-\ *n.* A circular letter written or printed for the spreading of news.

news·man \'nüz-ˌman, 'nyüz-, -mən\ *n.; pl.* **news-men** \-ˌmen, -mən\. **1** A newspaperman. **2** A man who distributes or sells newspapers.

news·pa·per \'nüz-ˌpāp-r, 'nyüz-\ *n.* A publication consisting of several unbound sheets of printed paper, usually issued daily or weekly, providing its readers with news, the opinions of its editor and columnists, and advertisements.

news·pa·per·man \'nüz-ˌpāp-r-ˌman, 'nyüz-\ *n.; pl.* **news·pa·per·men** \-ˌmen\. A man who writes for or who owns or conducts a newspaper, especially a reporter or editor.

news·print \'nüz-ˌprint, 'nyüz-\ *n.* Cheap paper made chiefly from wood pulp and used mostly for newspapers.

news·reel \'nüz-ˌrēl, 'nyüz-\ *n.* A short motion picture showing current events.

news·room \'nüz-ˌrüm, 'nyüz-, -ˌrum\ *n.* **1** A room or place where newspapers and magazines are sold. **2** A reading room having newspapers and magazines.

news·stand \'nüz-ˌstand, 'nyüz-\ *n.* A stall or booth where magazines and newspapers are sold, especially one in the open air, as on a sidewalk.

news·wor·thy \'nüz-ˌwər-t͟hē, 'nyüz-\ *adj.* Sufficiently interesting to the average person to deserve reporting in a news article.

newsy \'nü-zē, 'nyü-\ *adj.;* **news·i·er; news·i·est.** Full of news or information about trivial things; as, a *newsy* letter.

newt \'nüt, 'nyüt\ *n.* A small salamander that has a tail adapted for swimming and lives chiefly in the water.

New Testament. The second of the two main divisions of the Bible, containing accounts of Christ's life and death and of the work done by his apostles after his death.

New World. The Western Hemisphere, including North America and South America.

New Year's Day or **New Year's.** The first day of a calendar year; January 1, celebrated as a holiday.

New Zea·land·er \nü 'zē-lənd-r, nyü\. A native or inhabitant of New Zealand.

next \'nekst\ *adj.* **1** Nearest; without any in between; as, the *next* house to ours. **2** The first after this; as, *next* Christmas. — *adv.* **1** In the nearest place, time, or order following. Do this part of the assignment *next.* **2** At the first time after this; as, when class *next* meets.

next door. **1** In the next house; as, the people *next door.* **2** Very close; as, a remark that was *next door* to an insult. — **next-door,** *adj.*

ni·a·cin \'nī-əs-n\ *n.* A vitamin found chiefly in protein foods, used in the treatment of pellagra.

nib \'nib\ *n.* **1** A pointed object; especially, the beak or bill of a bird. **2** The point of a pen.

nib, 2

nib·ble \'nib-l\ *v.;* **nib·bled; nib·bling** \-l(-)ing\. To bite at, taste, or eat away on lightly or bit by bit; as, to *nibble* a cracker. — *n.* A small or cautious bite.

Nic·a·ra·guan \ˌnik-r-'äg-wən, -'ág-\ *adj.* Of or relating to Nicaragua. — *n.* A native or inhabitant of Nicaragua.

nice \'nīs\ *adj.;* **nic·er; nic·est.** **1** Very particular about things, as appearance, manners, and food; refined. **2** Having the power to show or to feel small or fine differences between things; delicately sensitive; as, to have a *nice* ear for music. **3** Well-behaved; well-bred; as, to hope for *nice* people for neighbors. **4** Pleasing; as, a *nice* sunny room. — **nice·ly**, *adv.*

ni·ce·ty \'nī-sət-ē\ *n.; pl.* **ni·ce·ties. 1** A dainty, delicate, or elegant thing; as, to enjoy the *niceties* of life. **2** A small point; a fine detail; as, the *niceties* of table manners. **3** Careful attention to details; exactness. The greatest *nicety* is needed in making watches. **4** The point at which a thing is at its best; as, roasted to a *nicety.*

niche \'nich\ *n.* **1** A hollow recess in a wall for a statue or other ornament. **2** The place, work, or use for which a person or a thing is exactly fitted.

niche

nick \'nik\ *n.* **1** A notch or small groove; as, to file a *nick* in steel. **2** A broken place or chip; as, a *nick* in a cup. **3** The exactly right moment; as, in the *nick* of time. — *v.* **1** To make a nick or nicks in; as, to *nick* furniture. **2** To graze or touch lightly; as, to *nick* a can with a rifle bullet.

nick·el \'nik-l\ *n.* **1** A hard silver-white metallic element, used chiefly in alloys or for plating objects made of other metals. **2** A coin of the United States and Canada, made of copper and nickel and having the value of five cents. — *v.;* **nick·eled; nick·el·ing** \-l(-)ing\. To plate with nickel.

nick·el·o·de·on \ˌnik-l-'ōd-ē-ən\ *n.* A jukebox.

nick·er \'nik-r\ *n.* A whinny. — *v.;* **nick·ered; nick·er·ing** \-r(-)ing\. To whinny.

nick·name \'nik-ˌnām\ *n.* A name given a person or thing, as in affection, sport, or admiration. — *v.;* **nick·named; nick·nam·ing.** To give a nickname to.

nic·o·tine \'nik-ə-ˌtēn\ *n.* A poisonous substance found in small amounts in tobacco.

nic·o·tin·ic ac·id \'nik-ə-ˌtin-ik\. Niacin.

nic·ti·tat·ing mem·brane \'nik-tə-ˌtāt-ing\. A thin membrane found at the inner angle of the eye or beneath the lower eyelid of some animals, as the frog, and capable of being drawn across the eyeball.

niece \'nēs\ *n.* A daughter of one's brother or sister.

nig·gard \'nig-rd\ *n.* A mean, stingy person; a miser. — *adj.* Niggardly.

nig·gard·ly \'nig-rd-lē\ *adj.* **1** Stingy; miserly. **2** Characteristic of a niggard; as, a *niggardly* action; a *niggardly* offering. — *adv.* In a niggardly manner.

nigh \'nī\ *adj.* Near; close. — *adv.* Near in time or place.

night \'nīt\ *n.* **1** The time between dusk and dawn when there is no sunlight. **2** The beginning of darkness; nightfall. **3** The darkness of night. — *adj.* Of the night; for use at night; during the night; as, *night* hours; a *night* watchman.

night blindness. Subnormal vision at night or in a dim light, often caused by a deficiency in vitamin A.

night·cap \'nīt-ˌkap\ *n.* **1** A cap worn with night clothes. **2** A drink taken before going to bed.

night clothes. Any garments intended to be worn in bed; a nightgown, a nightshirt, or a pair of pajamas.

night club. A place of amusement open chiefly in the evening, usually serving alcoholic beverages and having a dance band or some other kind of entertainment.

night·fall \'nīt-ˌfȯl\ *n.* The close of the day; the coming of night; dusk.

night·gown \'nīt-ˌgau̇n\ *n.* A long, loose garment worn in bed.

night·hawk \'nīt-ˌhȯk\ *n.* **1** An insect-eating bird, flying mostly at twilight, that is related to and resembles the whippoorwill. **2** A person who habitually stays up late at night.

night·in·gale \'nīt-n-ˌgāl, 'nīt-in(g)-ˌgāl\ *n.* A reddish brown Old World bird of the thrush family, famous for its beautiful song.

night letter. A telegram sent at lower rates than an ordinary one in consideration of its being held and sent at night and not delivered until the following morning.

night·ly \'nīt-lē\ *adj.* Of or relating to nights; happening at night or every night; as, to read the children their *nightly* bedtime story. — *adv.* At or by night; every night. The mail is collected *nightly* from this box.

night·mare \'nīt-ˌmar, -ˌmer\ *n.* [From medieval English, meaning "a witch that oppressed sleeping people" and composed of *night* and *mare* meaning "witch".] **1** A condition during sleep when a person is extremely uneasy or fearful or has frightful dreams. **2** A horrible experience.

night·shade \'nīt-ˌshād\ *n.* An herb or shrub of the potato family with alternate leaves, white or purple or yellow flowers, and a many-seeded juicy berry, as belladonna or bittersweet.

night·shirt \'nīt-ˌshərt\ *n.* A garment worn in bed, usually shorter and of a plainer design than a nightgown.

night·time \'nīt-ˌtīm\ *n.* Night; the time from dusk to dawn.

nil \'nil\ *n.* Nothing; none at all. The girl's chances of swimming the channel were *nil.*

nim·ble \'nim-bl\ *adj.;* **nim·bler; nim·blest. 1** Quick and light in motion; agile; as, a *nimble* dancer. **2** Quick in understanding and learning; quick-witted; clever; as, a *nimble* mind. — **nim·bly** \-blē\ *adv.*

nim·bus \'nim-bəs\ *n.; pl.* **nim·bus·es** \-bə-səz\ or **nim·bi** \-ˌbī\. **1** A luminous cloud about a god or goddess when on earth. **2** In art, a circle or other indication of radiant light around the head of a divine or sacred figure. **3** The rain cloud, uniformly gray and extending over the whole sky.

nin·com·poop \'nin(g)-kəm-ˌpüp\ *n.* A fool; a simpleton.

nine \'nīn\ *adj.* One more than eight; as, *nine* weeks. — *n.* **1** The sum of six and three; nine units or objects. **2** The figure standing for nine units, as 9 or IX. **3** A baseball team.

nine·pins \'nīn-ˌpinz\ *n.* A game played on a bowling alley, in which wooden balls are rolled at nine bottle-shaped wooden pins set on end in the form of a truncated triangle.

nine·teen \'nīn(t)-'tēn\ *adj.* Nine plus ten; eighteen and one more. — *n.* **1** The sum of ten and nine; nineteen units or objects. **2** The figure standing for nineteen units, as 19 or XIX.

nine·teenth \'nīn(t)-'tēn(t)th\ *adj.* Next after the eighteenth. — *n.; pl.* **nine·teenths** \-'tēn(t)s, -'tēn(t)ths\. One of nineteen equal parts.

nine·ti·eth \'nīnt-ē-əth\ *adj.* Next after the eighty-ninth. — *n.* One of ninety equal parts.

nine·ty \'nīnt-ē\ *adj.* Nine times ten; eighty-nine and one more. — *n.; pl.* **nine·ties.** **1** The sum of nine tens; ninety units or objects. **2** The figure standing for ninety units, as 90 or XC.

nin·ny \'nin-ē\ *n.; pl.* **nin·nies.** A fool.

ninth \'nīn(t)th\ *adj.* Next after the eighth. — *n.; pl.* **ninths** \'nīn(t)s, 'nīn(t)ths\. One of nine equal parts.

nip \'nip\ *v.;* **nipped; nip·ping.** **1** To catch hold of and squeeze sharply between two surfaces, edges, or points; to pinch. **2** To cut off by pinching or clipping, as a shoot from a branch. **3** To sting or pierce with cold. **4** To check suddenly; to stop, as in growth or development, by or as if by pinching off; as, plans *nipped* in the bud. **5** To seize suddenly; to snatch. — *n.* **1** A pinch, bite, or peck. **2** Something that feels like a pinch; a sting or bite; as, a *nip* in the air on a cold morning.

nip \'nip\ *n.* A sip or small drink, as of liquor.

nip·per \'nip-r\ *n.* **1** One that nips. **2** [usually in the plural] Any of various devices for nipping, as a pair of pliers or pincers. **3** [in the plural] Handcuffs. **4** One of the large claws or pincers of a crab or lobster. **5** *British.* A small boy.

nippers, 2

nip·ple \'nip-l\ *n.* **1** The part of the breast from which a baby or a young animal sucks milk. **2** A thing like a nipple in form or use, as the rubber mouthpiece of a baby's nursing bottle.

Nip·pon·ese \ˌnip-n-'ēz, -'ēs\ *adj.* or *n.* Japanese.

nip·py \'nip-ē\ *adj.;* **nip·pi·er; nip·pi·est.** **1** Nipping; sharp; biting; as, a *nippy* wind. **2** Active; brisk; vigorous; as, an alert, *nippy* youngster.

nit \'nit\ *n.* The egg of a louse or similar insect; the insect itself when young.

ni·ter \'nīt-r\ *n.* **1** Potassium nitrate; saltpeter. **2** Sodium nitrate.

ni·trate \'nī-ˌtrāt\ *n.* A salt or ester of nitric acid derived by substitution of another element or radical for the hydrogen in the acid, as in **potassium nitrate**, an important chemical used in explosives, in which the hydrogen is replaced by potassium, or **sodium nitrate**, used chiefly as a fertilizer, in which the hydrogen is replaced by sodium.

ni·tric ac·id \'nī-trik\. A colorless, fuming, corrosive liquid made especially by the action of sulfuric acid on nitrates and having a variety of uses, as in the manufacture of explosives and of dyestuffs.

ni·tri·fy \'nī-trə-ˌfī\ *v.;* **ni·tri·fied** \-ˌfīd\; **ni·tri·fy·ing.** **1** To combine with nitrogen or a nitrogen compound. **2** To convert by oxidation into nitrous or nitric acid or their salts. — **ni·tri·fi·ca·tion** \ˌnī-trə-fə-'kāsh-n\ *n.*

ni·trite \'nī-ˌtrīt\ *n.* A salt or ester of nitrous acid.

ni·tro·gen \'nī-trəj-n\ *n.* A colorless, odorless, tasteless, gaseous element that makes up about four fifths of the atmosphere by volume and is a part of all living tissues.

nitrogen cycle. The continuous natural process by which nitrogen passes successively from the air into the soil, then into plants and into animals which eat the plants, and finally by decay of organisms back to the air.

ni·trog·e·nous \nī-'träj-n-əs\ *adj.* Of, relating to, or containing nitrogen.

ni·tro·glyc·er·in or **ni·tro·glyc·er·ine** \ˌnī-trō-'glis-r(-)ən\ *n.* A heavy, oily, explosive liquid, used especially in making dynamite.

ni·trous ac·id \'nī-trəs\. An acid that forms a series of salts or nitrites, but is itself known only in solution.

nitrous oxide. A colorless gas used as an anesthetic, especially in dentistry.

nit·wit \'nit-ˌwit\ *n. Slang.* A stupid person.

no *adv.* **1** \'nō\ Not; as, to plan to go whether or *no* it rains. **2** \'nō\ Not so. *No,* the door is not open. **3** \(')nō\ Not any; not at all; as, *no* more candy. — \'nō\ *n.; pl.* **noes** \'nōz\. **1** The act of saying "no"; a refusal by use of *no;* a denial. The boy heard his mother's *no.* **2** A vote or decision against something; [in the plural] those who vote in the negative. The *noes* have it. — \(')nō\ *adj.* Not any; not the least; as, *no* milk; *no* fear.

No. or **no.** [Abbreviated from Latin *numero* meaning "by number".] Number.

no·bil·i·ty \nō-'bil-ət-ē\ *n.; pl.* **no·bil·i·ties.** **1** The quality or state of being noble; as, *nobility* of character. **2** Noble rank; as, to confer *nobility* on a person. **3** The class or group of nobles; as, a member of the *nobility.*

no·ble \'nōb-l\ *adj.;* **no·bler; no·blest.** **1** Having a title and rank which is higher than that of other persons and which may be handed down from father to son. **2** Having dignity; being illustrious or eminent; as, a man of *noble* character. **3** Having excellent qualities; as, a *noble* dog. **4** Grand, especially in appearance; stately; imposing; as, a *noble* edifice. **5** Having or characterized by superiority of mind or character; magnanimous; lofty; as, *noble* sacrifices by a mother for her children. — *n.* A member of the nobility; a person of noble rank.

no·ble·man \'nōb-l-mən\ *n.; pl.* **no·ble·men** \-mən\. A peer; a member of the nobility. — **no·ble·wom·an** \-ˌwu̇m-ən\ *n.*

no·bly \'nōb-lē\ *adv.* **1** In a noble manner. **2** Of noble extraction; as, *nobly* born.

no·body \'nō-ˌbäd-ē, -bəd-ē\ *pron.* Not anybody. — *n.; pl.* **no·bod·ies.** A person of no importance.

noc·tur·nal \näk-'tərn-l\ *adj.* **1** Of or relating to night; done or occurring in the night; nightly; as, *nocturnal* trips. **2** Active at night; as, *nocturnal* insects. **3** Blooming at night, as certain plants. — **noc·tur·nal·ly** \-'tərn-l-ē\ *adv.*

noc·turne \'näk-ˌtərn\ *n.* **1** A musical composition dealing with or referring to night; especially, a dreamy or pensive piece of instrumental music; a serenade. **2** In painting, a night scene.

nod \'näd\ *v.;* **nod·ded; nod·ding. 1** To bend the head downward or forward, as in bowing or going to sleep, or as a way of answering "yes". **2** To move up and down. The tulips *nodded* in the breeze. **3** To show by a nod of the head; as, to *nod* agreement. **4** To let one's attention lapse for a moment; to make a slip or an error. — *n.* The action of nodding; as, a *nod* of the head.

nod·dle \'näd-l\ *n.* The head.

node \'nōd\ *n.* **1** A knot, knob, lump, or swelling; a nodule. **2** In botany, the joint of a stem or the point of insertion of a leaf or leaves. — **nod·al** \'nōd-l\ *adj.*

NODE

nod·ule \'näj-ˌül\ *n.* **1** A little lump or knob. **2** A tubercle on the roots of certain legumes. — **nod·u·lar** \'näj-l-ər\ *adj.*

no·el \nō-'el\ *n.* **1** A Christmas carol. **2** The shout of *noel,* made as a sign of joy. **3** [with a capital] Christmas.

nog·gin \'näg-n\ *n.* **1** A small mug. **2** A small quantity of drink, usually a gill.

noise \'nȯiz\ *n.* **1** Loud, confused, or senseless shouting; clamor. **2** Sound or a sound of any sort, especially if without agreeable musical quality. — *v.;* **noised; nois·ing.** To report; to spread by rumor. The gossip was *noised* about.

noise·less \'nȯiz-ləs\ *adj.* Making no noise; silent. — **noise·less·ly,** *adv.*

noise·mak·er \'nȯiz-ˌmāk-r\ *n.* A person or thing that makes noise; especially, a device, as a horn or clapper, for making noise at parties.

noi·some \'nȯis-m\ *adj.* **1** Harmful; unwholesome; as, a *noisome* pestilence. **2** Offensive, especially to the smell; disgusting. — **noi·some·ly,** *adv.*

noisy \'nȯi-zē\ *adj.;* **nois·i·er; nois·i·est.** Making loud noise; full of noises; loud; as, *noisy* children; a *noisy* city. — **nois·i·ly** \'nȯiz-l-ē\ *adv.*

no·mad \'nō-ˌmad\ *n.* A member of a tribe or people that has no fixed home, but wanders from place to place. — *adj.* Roving; wandering. — **no·mad·ic** \nō-'mad-ik\ *adj.* — **no·mad·ism** \'nō-ˌmad-ˌiz-m\ *n.*

nom de plume \ˌnäm də 'plüm\. [An English phrase coined from French words.] A pen name.

no·men·cla·ture \'nō-mən-ˌklāch-r, nō-'men-klə-ˌchu̇r\ *n.* The system of names used in any science or art or by any group or individual; especially, the names used in classifications.

nom·i·nal \'näm-ən-l\ *adj.* **1** Being something in name only; as, the *nominal* head of a department. **2** Very small; so little as to be not worth mentioning; as, a *nominal* price. — **nom·i·nal·ly** \-ən-l-ē\ *adv.*

nom·i·nate \'näm-ə-ˌnāt\ *v.;* **nom·i·nat·ed; nom·i·nat·ing.** To choose as a candidate for election or appointment; to propose for office; as, to *nominate* a man for president. — **nom·i·na·tor** \-ˌnāt-r\ *n.*

nom·i·na·tion \ˌnäm-ə-'nāsh-n\ *n.* **1** The action of nominating; the suggesting of a person for an office. **2** The state of being nominated; as, to win the *nomination.*

nom·i·na·tive \'näm-ə-ˌnāt-iv, -ə-nət-iv\ *n.* or **nominative case.** The case of a noun or pronoun when it is the subject of the verb or is in the predicate after a linking verb.

nom·i·nee \ˌnäm-ə-'nē\ *n.* A person who is named for an office, duty, or position.

non-. A prefix that can mean: not, un-, in-, as in *nonsense, nonresident,* or *nonbeliever.*

non·ac·cept·ance \ˌnän-ik-'sep-tən(t)s\ *n.* The failure or refusal to accept; the lack of acceptance.

non·a·ge·nar·i·an \ˌnän-əj-n-'er-ē-ən, ˌnō-nəj-\ *adj.* Ninety or between ninety and one hundred years old. — *n.* A person who is ninety or more but less than one hundred years old.

non·ag·gres·sion \ˌnän-ə-'gresh-n\ *n.* The absence or lack of aggression.

non·al·co·hol·ic \'nän-ˌal-kə-'hȯl-ik, -'häl-\ *adj.* Not containing alcohol.

non·be·liev·er \ˌnän-bə-'lēv-r\ *n.* A person who does not believe in or have faith in something; especially, one without religious convictions.

nonce \'nän(t)s\ *n.* The one, particular, or present occasion, use, or purpose. — **for the nonce.** For the special occasion; for the time being. — **nonce word.** A word invented for one occasion.

non·cha·lant \ˌnän-shə-'länt, -'lȧnt; 'nän-shə-ˌlänt, -lənt, -ˌlȧnt\ *adj.* Having a confident and easy manner; especially, unconcerned about drawing attention to oneself; coolly indifferent; as, to face an unfriendly crowd with *nonchalant* ease. — **non·cha·lance** \ˌnän-shə-'län(t)s, -'lȧn(t)s; 'nän-shə-ˌlän(t)s, -lən(t)s, -ˌlȧn(t)s\ *n.* — **non·cha·lant·ly,** *adv.*

non·com \'nän-ˌkäm\ *n.* A noncommissioned officer.

non·com·bat·ant \ˌnän-kəm-'bat-nt, 'nän-'käm-bə-tənt\ *n.* **1** A person in the armed forces whose duties do not include fighting, as a chaplain. **2** Any civilian.

non·com·bus·ti·ble \ˌnän-kəm-ˈbəs-təb-l\ *adj.* Not capable of being burned; as, a *noncombustible* drapery fabric.

non·com·mis·sioned of·fi·cer \ˈnän-kə-ˌmish-nd\. A subordinate officer, as a sergeant or corporal appointed from among the enlisted men by a commanding officer.

non·com·mit·tal \ˌnän-kə-ˈmit-l\ *adj.* Not telling or showing what a person thinks or has decided; as, a *noncommittal* answer. — **non·com·mit·tal·ly** \-ˈmit-l-ē\ *adv.*

non·con·duc·tor \ˌnän-kən-ˈdəkt-r\ *n.* A substance that is a very poor conductor, as of heat, electricity, or sound. — **non·con·duct·ing** \-ˈdək-ting\ *adj.*

non·con·form·ist \ˌnän-kən-ˈfȯr-məst\ *n.* A person who does not conform, especially to an established church. — **non·con·form·i·ty** \-ˈfȯr-mət-ē\ *n.*

non·dem·o·crat·ic \ˈnän-ˌdem-ə-ˈkrat-ik\ *adj.* Not democratic; not believing in democratic ideals and principles; not practicing democracy.

non·de·script \ˈnän-də-ˌskript, -ˈskript\ *adj.* Not easy to describe; of no particular class or kind; as, a *nondescript* house; a *nondescript* dog. — *n.* A person or thing not easily classified or of no particular class or kind.

none \ˈnən\ *pron.* **1** Not any. *None* of the old buildings have endured. **2** No one; not one. *None* of the family has gone to college. **3** Not any such thing or person. Half is better than *none.* — *adv.* Not at all; in no way; to no extent. Rescuers reached the man *none* too soon.

non·en·ti·ty \(ˈ)nän-ˈent-ət-ē\ *n.; pl.* **non·en·ti·ties. 1** A thing that does not exist or that exists only in the imagination. **2** A person or thing of little or no account.

non·es·sen·tial \ˌnän-ə-ˈsench-l\ *adj.* Not necessary or essential; not indispensable. — *n.* One that is not essential, necessary, or fundamental.

none·the·less \ˌnən-t͟hə-ˈles\ *adv.* Nevertheless.

non·ex·ist·ence \ˌnän-ig-ˈzis-tən(t)s\ *n.* The absence of existence. — **non·ex·ist·ent** \-tənt\ *adj.*

non·fic·tion \ˈnän-ˈfiksh-n\ *n.* Any literature that is not fictitious.

non·in·flam·ma·ble \ˌnän-in-ˈflam-əb-l\ *adj.* Not flammable.

non·in·ter·fer·ence \ˈnän-ˌint-r-ˈfir-ən(t)s\ *n.* A refraining from interfering.

non·in·tox·i·cant \ˌnän-in-ˈtäks-ə-kənt\ *adj.* Not intoxicating. — *n.* A beverage that does not intoxicate.

non·pa·reil \ˌnän-pə-ˈrel\ *adj.* Having no equal. — *n.* **1** Something that is unequalled in excellence; a paragon. **2** A brightly colored finch of the southern United States; the painted bunting.

non·par·ti·san \ˈnän-ˈpärt-əz-n, -ˈpärt-, -əs-n\ *adj.* Not partisan; not controlled by parties or influenced by party interests; as, a *nonpartisan* committee.

non·pay·ment \(ˈ)nän-ˈpā-mənt\ *n.* A lack of payment; the failure to make payment.

non·plus \ˈnän-ˈpləs\ *v.;* **non·plussed; non·plus·sing.** To puzzle; to stop; to make helpless, as by being perplexed.

non·poi·son·ous \(ˈ)nän-ˈpȯiz-n(-)əs\ *adj.* Having or containing no poison.

non·pro·duc·tive \ˌnän-prə-ˈdək-tiv\ *adj.* **1** Unproductive. **2** Not directly productive — used especially of labor that is not directly concerned with production.

non·prof·it \ˈnän-ˈpräf-ət\ *adj.* Not conducted or maintained for the purpose of making a profit; as, a *nonprofit* organization.

non·res·i·dent \ˈnän-ˈrez-ə-dənt, -ˈrez-dənt, -ə-ˌdent\ *adj.* Not living in a particular place; not making a home on one's own property. — *n.* A nonresident person. — **non·res·i·dence** \-ˈrez-ə-dən(t)s, -ˈrez-dən(t)s, -ə-ˌden(t)s\ *n.*

non·re·sist·ant \ˌnän-rē-ˈzis-tənt\ *adj.* Making no resistance. — *n.* A person who maintains or acts on the theory that authority or violence should not be resisted by force. — **non·re·sist·ance** \-tən(t)s\ *n.*

non·re·stric·tive \ˌnän-rē-ˈstrik-tiv\ *adj.* **1** Not serving or tending to restrict. **2** In grammar, not restricting or limiting the meaning of the word or words that it modifies; as, a *nonrestrictive* clause or phrase.

non·sec·tar·i·an \ˌnän-sek-ˈter-ē-ən\ *adj.* Not affiliated with any religious sect or creed.

non·sense \ˈnän-ˌsen(t)s, -sən(t)s\ *n.* **1** Foolish or meaningless words or actions. **2** Trifles; things of no importance or value. The children were told not to spend their money for *nonsense.* — **non·sen·si·cal** \nän-ˈsen(t)s-ik-l\ *adj.* — **non·sen·si·cal·ly** \-ik-l(-)ē\ *adv.*

non·skid \ˈnän-ˈskid\ *adj.* Specially constructed to resist skidding; as, *nonskid* tires.

non·stop \ˈnän-ˈstäp\ *adj.* or *adv.* Without a stop; as, a *nonstop* flight to London.

non·sup·port \ˌnän-sə-ˈpōrt, -ˈpȯrt\ *n.* Lack of support.

non·un·ion \ˈnän-ˈyün-yən\ *adj.* **1** Not belonging to a trade union; as, *nonunion* carpenters. **2** Not conforming to the requirements of a trade union; as, a *nonunion* organization. **3** Not favoring trade unions or their members; as, *nonunion* employers. — **non·un·ion·ism** \-yə-ˌniz-m\ *n.* — **non·un·ion·ist** \-yə-nəst\ *n.*

noo·dle \ˈnüd-l\ *n.* A food like macaroni but shaped into long flat strips like ribbon and made with egg — usually used in the plural.

nook \ˈnu̇k\ *n.* **1** An interior angle or corner formed usually by two walls; as, a chimney *nook.* **2** A sheltered or hidden place; a corner set apart from its surroundings; as, a shady *nook.*

noon \ˈnün\ *n.* The middle of the day; twelve o'clock in the daytime.

noon·day \ˈnün-ˌdā\ *adj.* Of noon; at noon; as, the *noonday* sun.

noon·tide \ˈnün-ˌtīd\ *n.* Noon.

noon·time \ˈnün-ˌtīm\ *n.* Noon.

noose \'nüs\ *n.* A loop with a slipknot, as in a lasso, that gets smaller and holds something within it more and more securely the harder the rope is pulled.

noose

nor \nər, (')nȯr\ *conj.* Or not; and not; no more — used between two words or groups of words that offer no choice and that are preceded by *neither;* as, neither hot *nor* cold.

norm \'nȯrm\ *n.* **1** A rule or standard; a model. **2** A standard of progress or achievement set for a group, representing usually the average attained by a large number of persons of the same class or age.

nor·mal \'nȯrm-l\ *adj.* **1** Of the regular or usual kind; standard; natural; as, *normal* behavior for children; *normal* rainfall. **2** Belonging to the average in intelligence or development. **3** Mentally sound; sane. — *n.* The usual degree or condition; average.

nor·mal·cy \'nȯrm-l-sē\ *n.* Normality.

nor·mal·i·ty \nȯr-'mal-ət-ē\ *n.* The state or quality of being normal.

nor·mal·ize \'nȯrm-l-ˌīz\ *v.;* **nor·mal·ized; nor·mal·iz·ing.** To make normal; to reduce to a norm.

nor·mal·ly \'nȯrm-l-ē\ *adv.* Naturally; regularly; according to standard; as, to grow *normally;* to progress *normally* in school.

normal school. A school for training persons to become teachers.

Nor·man \'nȯr-mən\ *adj.* Of or relating to the district of Normandy in France or to the Normans. — *n.* **1** A native of Normandy. **2** One of the Scandinavians who conquered Normandy in the 10th century. **3** One of the people of mixed Norman and French blood who conquered England in 1066.

Norse \'nȯrs\ *adj.* **1** Of or relating to ancient Scandinavia or the language of its inhabitants. **2** Of or relating to Norway. — *n.* **1** Scandinavians; especially, Norwegians — used as a plural with *the.* **2** The old Scandinavian languages (**Old Norse**). **3** The Norwegian language.

Norse·man \'nȯrs-mən\ *n.; pl.* **Norse·men** \-mən\. One of the ancient Scandinavians.

north \'nȯrth; *in compounds, as* "northeast", *also* 'nȯr *especially in the speech of seamen*\ *n.* **1** One of the four main points of the compass; the direction to the left of a person facing the rising sun. **2** Any country or region north of another. **3** [with a capital] That part of the United States lying north of the southern boundary of Pennsylvania and the Ohio River. — *adj.* **1** Situated at, in, or toward the north; as, the *north* end of town; a *north* window. **2** From the north; as, a *north* wind. — *adv.* Northward; as, to travel *north* five miles.

North Amer·i·can \ə-'mer-ək-n\ *adj.* Of or relating to the continent of North America. — *n.* A native or inhabitant of North America.

north·east \'nȯrth-'ēst\ *n.* **1** The point or direction halfway between north and east. **2** A part or region that lies in this direction. — *adj.* **1** Situated at, in, or toward the northeast; as, the *northeast* corner of a house. **2** From the northeast; as, a *northeast* wind. — *adv.* To or toward the northeast.

north·east·er \nȯrth-'ēst-r\ *n.* A storm or strong wind from the northeast.

north·east·er·ly \'nȯrth-'ēst-r-lē\ *adj.* **1** Situated, directed, or moving toward the northeast. **2** From the northeast. — *adv.* Toward the northeast.

north·east·ern \'nȯrth-'ēst-rn\ *adj.* **1** Of or relating to the northeast. **2** At, in, or toward the northeast. **3** From the northeast.

north·east·ward \'nȯrth-'ēst-wərd\ or **north·east·wards** \-wərdz\ *adv.* To or toward the northeast. — **north·east·ward·ly** \-wərd-lē\ *adj.* or *adv.*

north·east·ward \'nȯrth-'ēst-wərd\ *adj.* Going or facing toward the northeast.

north·er \'nȯrth-r\ *n.* A storm or wind from the north.

north·er·ly \'nȯrth-r-lē\ *adj.* **1** Situated, directed, or moving toward the north; as, a *northerly* direction. **2** From the north; as, a *northerly* wind. — *adv.* Toward the north.

north·ern \'nȯrth-rn\ *adj.* **1** Of or relating to the north. **2** At, in, or toward the north. **3** From the north. **4** [with a capital] Of or relating to the North, or northern part of the United States as contrasted with the South.

north·ern·er \'nȯrth-rn-r\ *n.* **1** A person native to or living in the north. **2** [usually with a capital] A person living in the northern part of the United States.

northern lights. Aurora borealis.

north·ern·most \'nȯrth-rn-ˌmōst\ *adj.* Farthest north; as, the *northernmost* region.

north·land \'nȯrth-ˌland, -lənd\ *n.* Land in the north; the north of a country or region.

North·man \'nȯrth-mən\ *n.; pl.* **North·men** \-mən\. A Norseman.

North Pole. The northernmost point of the earth; the northern end of the earth's axis.

North Star. The star toward which the earth's axis very nearly points; the polestar.

north·ward \'nȯrth-wərd\ or **north·wards** \-wərdz\ *adv.* To or toward the north. — **north·ward·ly** \-wərd-lē\ *adj.* or *adv.*

north·ward \'nȯrth-wərd\ *adj.* Going or facing toward the north.

north·west \'nȯrth-'west\ *n.* **1** The point or direction halfway between north and west. **2** A part or region that lies in this direction. — *adj.* **1** Situated at, in, or toward the northwest; as, the *northwest* corner. **2** From the northwest; as, a *northwest* wind. — *adv.* To or toward the northwest.

north·west·er \nȯrth-'west-r\ *n.* A storm or wind from the northwest.

north·west·er·ly \'nȯrth-'west-r-lē\ *adj.* **1** Situated, directed, or moving toward the northwest. **2** From the northwest. — *adv.* Toward the northwest.

north·west·ern \'nȯrth-'west-rn\ *adj.* **1** Of or relating to the northwest. **2** At, in, or toward the northwest. **3** From the northwest.

north·west·ward \'nȯrth-'west-wərd\ or **north·west·wards** \-wərdz\ *adv.* To or toward the northwest. — **north·west·ward·ly** \-wərd-lē\ *adj.* or *adv.*

north·west·ward \'nȯrth-'west-wərd\ *adj.* Going or facing toward the northwest.

Nor·we·gian \nȯr-'wēj-n\ *adj.* Of or relating to Norway. — *n.* **1** A native or inhabitant of Norway. **2** The language of Norway.

nose \'nōz\ *n.* **1** The part of a person's face or an animal's head that contains the nostrils. **2** The sense of smell. The dog has a good *nose.* **3** Something that resembles a nose, as a point, edge, or the front of an object; as, the *nose* of a plane. — *v.;* **nosed; nos·ing. 1** To smell; to discover by, or as if by smell; as, to *nose* out the enemy's hiding place. **2** To sniff; as, dogs *nosing* at the trail of a rabbit. **3** To touch or rub with the nose. The pony *nosed* its master's hand. **4** To pry or search, especially into other people's business. **5** To push or move with the nose or front forward. The train *nosed* its way into the station.

nose·bleed \'nōz-ˌblēd\ *n.* A bleeding at the nose.

nose dive. 1 A head-on dive in an airplane. **2** Any sharp, sudden drop, as in prices. — **nose-dive** \'nōz-ˌdīv\ *v.*

nose·gay \'nōz-ˌgā\ *n.* A bunch of flowers; a small bouquet.

nosegay

nos·tal·gia \näs-'tal-jə, nəs-\ *n.* A wistful yearning for something in the past.

nos·tal·gic \näs-'tal-jik, nəs-\ *adj.* **1** Of or relating to nostalgia. **2** Bringing nostalgia; as, *nostalgic* music; *nostalgic* memories. **3** Feeling nostalgia; as, *nostalgic* soldiers reading letters from home.

nos·tril \'näs-trəl, 'nȯs-\ *n.* Either of the outer openings of the nose, through which one breathes.

nos·trum \'näs-trəm, 'nȯs-\ *n.* **1** A medicine recommended by its preparer; especially, a quack medicine. **2** A pet remedy for some evil; as, a politician's *nostrum* for economic problems.

nosy \'nō-zē\ *adj.;* **nos·i·er; nos·i·est.** Inquisitive; given to prying into what does not concern one.

not \(')nät\ *adv.* A word, corresponding to "no", used with verbs. Our teacher is *not* here.

no·ta·ble \'nōt-əb-l\ *adj.* Worthy of note or notice; remarkable; as, a *notable* sight; a *notable* hero. — *n.* A person of note or great reputation. There were several *notables* at the party. — **no·ta·bly** \-ə-blē\ *adv.*

no·ta·rize \'nōt-r-ˌīz\ *v.;* **no·ta·rized; no·ta·riz·ing.** To make legally authentic through the use of the powers granted to a notary public.

no·ta·ry \'nōt-r-ē\ *n.; pl.* **no·ta·ries.** A public officer commissioned by a state governor to certify documents to make them legally authentic.

notary public; *pl.* **notaries public.** A notary.

no·ta·tion \nō-'tāsh-n\ *n.* **1** The act of noting. **2** An annotation; a note; as, to make *notations* on a small paper. **3** Any system of signs, marks, figures, or characters used to express facts, quantities, or actions in science or art; as, musical *notation.*

notch \'näch\ *n.* **1** A V-shaped cut in an edge or surface; a nick. **2** A narrow pass between two mountains. **3** A degree; a step; a peg; as, to turn up the volume of the radio a *notch.* — *v.* **1** To cut or make notches in. **2** To score, record, or tally; as, to *notch* up points for the team.

note \'nōt\ *n.* **1** A musical sound. **2** A cry, call, or sound; as, a bird's *note.* **3** A special tone in a person's words or voice; as, a *note* of fear. **4** Reputation; fame; as, a man of *note.* **5** A memorandum. **6** [usually in the plural] A record of impressions or incidents. **7** A written or printed comment or explanation. There are *notes* in the back of the book. **8** Notice; heed; as, to forget to take *note* of what time it is. **9** A short informal letter; as, to write a *note* to one's mother. **10** A formal diplomatic or official communication. **11** A written promise to pay. **12** A character in music that by its shape shows the length of time a tone is to be held, and by its place on the staff shows the pitch of a tone, as the **whole note,** 𝅝; **half note,** 𝅗𝅥; **quarter note,** ♩; **eighth note,** ♪. **13** A key of the piano. **14** A tone; as, a low *note.* — *v.;* **not·ed; not·ing. 1** To notice carefully; to heed. **2** To make a special mention of something. The teacher *noted* the children's good manners in her report to the principal. **3** To make a note; of to set down in writing; as, to *note* in one's diary the happenings of the day.

note·book \'nōt-ˌbu̇k\ *n.* A book for notes or memoranda.

not·ed \'nōt-əd\ *adj.* Specially marked or noticed; well-known; famous; as, a *noted* scientist. — **not·ed·ly,** *adv.*

note·wor·thy \'nōt-ˌwər-t͟hē\ *adj.* Worthy of note; remarkable.

noth·ing \'nəth-ing\ *pron.* Not anything; nought. There was *nothing* in the box. — *n.* **1** Something that does not exist; a nonentity; as, to try to make something out of *nothing.* **2** Something, as an event or a remark, that is of no account, value, or importance; as, a speech full of airy *nothings.* **3** A nobody. **4** The absence of all magnitude or quantity; a zero. — *adv.* In no degree; not at all; as, to be *nothing* loath to comply.

noth·ing·ness \'nəth-ing-nəs\ *n.* **1** The quality or state of being nothing. **2** Something nonexistent; worthlessness; as, metal reduced to *nothingness* by acid.

no·tice \'nōt-əs\ *n.* **1** An announcement; a warning. The dogs gave *notice* of a stranger's approach. **2** A notification from one person to another that the connection between them, usually a business connection, is to end at a certain time. **3** The act of remarking or observing; attention; heed; as, to bring a matter to someone's *notice.* **4** A written or printed sign giving information or warning. Read the *notice* on the door. **5** A written mention or announcement; as, a *notice* of a new book in the paper. — *v.;* **no·ticed; no·tic·ing. 1** To make mention of; to remark upon. In his latest speech the president *noticed* the need for more housing. **2** To take notice or note of; to observe; to pay attention to; as, to *notice* even the smallest details.

no·tice·a·ble \'nōt-ə-səb-l\ *adj.* **1** Capable of being noticed; as, a *noticeable* improvement. **2** Worthy of notice; as, a *noticeable* enthusiasm for art. **3** Likely to attract attention. The tear in the dress was not *noticeable.* — **no·tice·a·bly** \-sə-blē\ *adv.*

no·ti·fi·ca·tion \ˌnōt-ə-fə-'kāsh-n\ *n.* **1** A notifying; especially, the action of giving official notice or information. **2** Any written or printed matter that gives notice.

no·ti·fy \'nōt-ə-ˌfī\ *v.;* **no·ti·fied** \-ˌfīd\; **no·ti·fy·ing.** To give notice of; to inform by a notice; as, to *notify* the students of a meeting. — **no·ti·fi·er** \-ˌfīr\ *n.*

noting. Pres. part. of *note.*

no·tion \'nōsh-n\ *n.* **1** An idea; a conception; as, to have a *notion* of a poem's meaning. **2** A view; a theory or belief; an opinion. **3** A whim; a fancy; as, a sudden *notion* to go home. **4** [in the plural] Any of various small useful articles, as pins, needles, or thread.

no·tion·al \'nōsh-n(-)əl\ *adj.* **1** Existing in idea only; imaginary; unreal; as, a plan that never got beyond the *notional* stage. **2** Inclined to have foolish or visionary fancies or moods; as, a *notional* man.

no·to·chord \'nōt-ə-ˌkȯrd\ *n.* An elastic rod of cells that in the lowest vertebrates, and in the embryos of the higher vertebrates, forms a stiffening and supporting axis, or primitive backbone.

no·to·ri·e·ty \ˌnōt-r-'ī-ət-ē\ *n.; pl.* **no·to·ri·e·ties. 1** The state of being notorious. **2** A well-known person.

no·to·ri·ous \nō-'tōr-ē-əs, -'tȯr-\ *adj.* Widely known, especially in a bad sense; as, a *notorious* bully. — **no·to·ri·ous·ly,** *adv.*

not·with·stand·ing \ˌnät-with-'stan-ding, -wit͟h-\ *prep.* In spite of. The boy failed *notwithstanding* his skill. — *adv.* Nevertheless; yet. It snowed, but they skated *notwithstanding.*

nou·gat \'nü-gət\ *n.* A candy made with nuts, usually almonds, stirred into a sugar paste.

nought \'nȯt, 'nät\ *n.* Nothing. It came to *nought* in the end.

noun \'nau̇n\ *n.* A word that is the name of a person, place, thing, quality, idea, or action. — *adj.* Of a noun; playing the part of a noun; as, words with *noun* endings; a *noun* clause.

nour·ish \'nər-ish, 'nə-rish\ *v.* To promote growth; to supply with food; to feed; as, to *nourish* a friendship; to *nourish* the body properly.

nour·ish·ing \'nər-ish-ing, 'nə-rish-\ *adj.* Giving nourishment; nutritious; as, *nourishing* food.

nour·ish·ment \'nər-ish-mənt, 'nə-rish-\ *n.* Anything that nourishes; food.

Nov. Abbreviation for *November.*

no·va \'nō-və\ *n.; pl.* **no·vas** \-vəz\ or **no·vae** \-ˌvē, -ˌvī\. A star that suddenly increases greatly in brightness and then, within a few months or years, grows dim again.

nov·el \'näv-l\ *n.* A prose narrative somewhat longer than a short story, usually portraying imaginary characters and events. — *adj.* New; strange. — For synonyms see *new.*

nov·el·ette \ˌnäv-l-'et\ *n.* A short novel.

nov·el·ist \'näv-l-əst\ *n.* One who writes novels.

nov·el·ty \'näv-l-tē\ *n.; pl.* **nov·el·ties. 1** Newness and strangeness; as, the *novelty* of eating foreign foods. **2** Something new and strange. Riding was a *novelty* to her. **3** [often in the plural] A small, novel article, usually for personal or household use, often purchased as a gift.

No·vem·ber \nō-'vem-br\ *n.* [From Old English, there borrowed from Latin, where it designated the ninth month of the ancient Roman year and was derived from *novem* meaning "nine".] The eleventh month of the year, having 30 days.

no·ve·na \nō-'vē-nə\ *n.; pl.* **no·ve·nas** \-nəz\ or **no·ve·nae** \-ˌnē\. In the Roman Catholic Church, a devotion in which prayers are said for the same intention on nine successive days.

nov·ice \'näv-əs\ *n.* **1** A person who has entered a religious order but has not yet been officially accepted as a member. **2** A person newly received into the church or newly converted to Christianity. **3** A person who is new at something; a beginner; as, a *novice* at skating.

no·vi·tiate or **no·vi·ciate** \nō-'vish-ət, -'vish-ē-ət\ *n.* **1** The state or time of being a novice. **2** A place where novices are trained. **3** A novice; a beginner.

now \'nau̇\ *adv.* **1** At the present time; at this moment. The doctor is busy *now.* **2** Under present circumstances. The bridge is out and the river is rising; *now* what shall we do? **3** Immediately; promptly; soon. I shall go *now.* **4** A moment ago. The milkman was here just *now.* **5** At the time spoken of. *Now* the trouble began. — *conj.* Since, at, or by this time; seeing that — often used with *that. Now* that the rain is over, we can start. — *n.* The present time or moment; as, ten minutes from *now.* — **now and again** or **now and then.** From time to time; occasionally.

now·a·days \'nau̇-ə-ˌdāz\ *adv.* In these days; at the present time.

no·way \'nō-ˌwā\ or **no·ways** \-ˌwāz\ *adv.* Nowise.

no·where \'nō-ˌhwer\ *adv.* Not anywhere; in, at, or to no place. — **nowhere near.** Not nearly; as, *nowhere near* so good. — *n.* A place that does not exist; as, strange sounds that seemed to come from *nowhere.*

no·wise \'nō-ˌwīz\ *adv.* In no way; not at all.

nox·ious \'näk-shəs\ *adj.* Harmful or injurious, especially to health; unwholesome; as, *noxious* fumes.

noz·zle \'näz-l\ *n.* A small tube or spout attached to a pipe, hose, or bellows, usually as an outlet.

FIRE EXTINGUISHER
nozzle

n's. Pl. of *n.*

nth \'en(t)th\ *adj.* Of the indefinite number or size represented in mathematics by *n*. The expression 9^n is read "nine to the *nth* power". — **to the nth degree. 1** In mathematics, to an indefinite power. **2** To an extreme; as, cautious *to the nth degree.*

nu·ance \nü-'än(t)s, nyü-; 'nü-ˌän(t)s, 'nyü-\ *n.* A shade of difference; a delicate gradation or variation, as in color, tone, or meaning.

nub \'nəb\ *n.* **1** A knob; a lump. **2** The point or gist, as of an anecdote.

nub·bin \'nəb-n\ *n.* **1** A small or imperfect ear of corn. **2** Any small projecting bit.

nub·ble \'nəb-l\ *n.* A small knob or lump; a projecting bit, as of yarn in a rough-textured fabric. — **nub·bly** \'nəb-lē\ *adj.*

nu·cle·ar \'nük-lē-ər, 'nyük-\ *adj.* **1** Of or having to do with the nucleus of a cell; as, a *nuclear* membrane. **2** Of or having to do with the nucleus of an atom; as, *nuclear* physics; a *nuclear* scientist.

nuclear energy. Atomic energy.

nuclear reactor. An atomic pile.

nu·cle·on \'nük-lē-ˌän, 'nyük-\ *n.* Any of the particles that make up an atomic nucleus.

nu·cle·on·ics \ˌnük-lē-'än-iks, ˌnyük-\ *n.* The branch of physics that deals with nucleons and the phenomena of the atomic nucleus.

nu·cle·us \'nük-lē-əs, 'nyük-\ *n.; pl.* **nu·clei** \-lē-ˌī\ or **nu·cle·us·es** \-lē-ə-səz\. [From Latin, meaning "kernel", a diminutive of *nux* meaning "nut".] **1** The central mass or core; the focal point; as, men who were the *nucleus* of a new school of art. **2** The small, brighter, and denser part of the head of a comet. **3** A compact mass of protoplasm in a plant or animal cell that contains chromosomes and controls heredity and other vital processes. **4** The central portion of an atom, containing a positive charge equal to the negative charge of the electrons which surround it. **5** A group of nerve cell bodies.

nude \'nüd, 'nyüd\ *adj.* Bare; naked; unclothed. — *n.* **1** A nude or undraped figure; especially, a painting or a statue of such a figure. **2** The condition of being nude; as, in the *nude.*

nudge \'nəj\ *v.;* **nudged**; **nudg·ing**. To touch or push gently, as with the elbow, usually in order to attract attention. — *n.* A gentle push, as with the elbow.

nud·ism \'nüd-ˌiz-m, 'nyüd-\ *n.* The cult or practice of living in a nude state. — **nud·ist** \'nüd-əst, 'nyüd-\ *n.*

nu·di·ty \'nüd-ət-ē, 'nyüd-\ *n.* The condition or fact of being nude; nakedness.

nug·get \'nəg-ət\ *n.* A lump, especially of precious metal; as, a *nugget* of gold.

nui·sance \'nüs-n(t)s, 'nyüs-\ *n.* An annoying or troublesome person or thing.

null \'nəl\ *adj.* **1** Of no legal or binding force; invalid; void. **2** Amounting to nothing. **3** Of no consequence; insignificant. — **null and void**. Having no force, binding power, or validity.

nul·li·fi·ca·tion \ˌnəl-ə-fə-'kāsh-n\ *n.* **1** A nullifying or the state of being nullified. **2** [often with a capital] In United States history, the action of a state to impede or prevent the enforcement of a federal law within its territory.

nul·li·fy \'nəl-ə-ˌfī\ *v.;* **nul·li·fied** \-ˌfīd\; **nul·li·fy·ing**. **1** To destroy the legal effectiveness of; to annul. **2** To make of no value or importance; to destroy; as, a last-minute change that *nullified* all prior arrangements.

numb \'nəm\ *adj.* Without feeling; deadened; as, fingers *numb* with cold; a widow *numb* with grief. — *v.* To make numb. — **numb·ly** \'nəm-lē\ *adv.*

num·ber \'nəm-br\ *n.* **1** The total of persons, things, or units taken together; amount; sum; as, the *number* of people in a room. **2** A symbol, word, or character that represents such a total; a numeral; as, the *number* 5. **3** [in the plural] Arithmetic; as, a person skilled in *numbers.* **4** A particular numeral for telling one person or thing from another or others; as, a house *number;* a license *number.* **5** A group; many; as, to receive a *number* of presents. **6** One of a series of things; a part; as, the March *number* of a magazine; a *number* from a musical comedy. **7** In grammar, difference in form, as of nouns, pronouns, or verbs, to show reference to one or to more than one. A verb agrees in *number* with its subject. — *v.;* **numbered**; **num·ber·ing** \-br(-)ing\. **1** To count; as, so few they could be *numbered* on the fingers of one hand. **2** To give or apply a number to; as, to *number* the pages of a scrapbook. **3** To include with a group; to be one of a group; as, to be *numbered* among the guests. **4** To reduce to a small number. Vacation days are *numbered* now. **5** To contain; to equal in number. The class *numbers* 25. — **num·ber·er** \-br-r\ *n.*

num·ber·less \'nəm-br-ləs\ *adj.* Too many to count; innumerable; as, the *numberless* stars in the sky.

nu·mer·a·ble \'nüm-r(-)əb-l, 'nyüm-\ *adj.* Capable of being numbered or counted.

nu·mer·al \'nüm-r(-)əl, 'nyüm-\ *n.* **1** A word that expresses a number. Ten is a *numeral.* **2** A figure or character, or a group of figures or characters, used to express a number; as, the Arabic *numerals* 1, 2, 3; the Roman *numerals* I, II, III. **3** [in the plural] Numbers representing the graduation year of a student in high school or college, worn as a badge of distinction in some activity.

nu·mer·ate \'nüm-r-ˌāt, 'nyüm-\ *v.;* **nu·mer·at·ed**; **nu·mer·at·ing**. To count; to reckon; to enumerate.

nu·mer·a·tion \ˌnüm-r-'āsh-n, ˌnyüm-\ *n.* **1** The act, process, or method of numbering, counting, or reckoning. **2** The reading of numbers expressed in figures.

nu·mer·a·tor \'nüm-r-,āt-r, 'nyüm-\ *n.* **1** In arithmetic and algebra, the part of a fraction written above the line, which shows how many fractional parts are taken. 3 is the *numerator* of the fraction ⅗. **2** One that numbers.

nu·mer·i·cal \nü-'mer-ik-l, nyü-\ *adj.* Having to do with numbers; expressed by numbers; as, a *numerical* equation; *numerical* order. — **nu·mer·i·cal·ly** \-ik-l(-)ē\ *adv.*

nu·mer·ous \'nüm-r(-)əs, 'nyüm-\ *adj.* **1** Consisting of or including a great number; as, a *numerous* group of people. **2** Of or relating to a great number; many; as, to have been late on *numerous* occasions.

nu·mis·mat·ics \,nü-məz-'mat-iks, ,nyü-, -məs-\ *n.* The collection and study of coins and medals. — **nu·mis·ma·tist** \nü-'miz-mət-əst, nyü-\ *n.*

num·skull \'nəm-,skəl\ *n.* A stupid person; a dunce.

nun \'nən\ *n.* A member of a religious order of women, usually living in a convent or other religious community.

nun·cio \'nən(t)s-ē-,ō, 'nən-shē-,ō\ *n.; pl.* **nun·ci·os.** A permanent official representative of the pope at a foreign court or capital.

nun·nery \'nən-r(-)ē\ *n.; pl.* **nun·ner·ies. 1** A building or group of buildings used as a convent. **2** The community of nuns living in a convent.

nup·tial \'nəpsh-l, 'nəp-chəl\ *adj.* Of or relating to marriage or a wedding. — *n.* A marriage ceremony; a wedding — used in the plural.

nurse \'nərs\ *n.* **1** A woman who has the care of a young child or children. **2** A person trained to take care of sick persons and to assist doctors and surgeons; as, to study to be a *nurse.* **3** A worker ant or bee that takes care of the young. — *v.;* **nursed; nurs·ing. 1** To feed at the breast. **2** To take charge and care of, as a young child. **3** To tend, as an invalid. **4** To act or serve as a nurse; to be employed as a nurse. **5** To treat with special care; as, to *nurse* a plant along; to *nurse* a lame ankle. **6** To brood over in one's mind; as, to *nurse* grief; to *nurse* a grudge.

nurse·maid \'nərs-,mād\ *n.* A girl employed to tend children.

nurs·ery \'nərs-r(-)ē\ *n.; pl.* **nurs·er·ies. 1** A room in a house set aside for the special use and care of the small children in the family. **2** A place (**day nursery**) where small children may be left, as by working mothers, to be cared for during the day. **3** A place where young trees, shrubs, and vines are grown for transplanting or for use as stocks for grafting.

nurs·er·y·maid \'nərs-r(-)ē-,mād\ *n.* A nursemaid.

nurs·er·y·man \'nərs-r(-)ē-mən\ *n.; pl.* **nurs·er·y·men** \-mən\. A man who keeps or works in a plant nursery.

nursery rhyme. A short poem for small children.

nursery school. A school for children under kindergarten age.

nurs·ing \'nər-sing\. Pres. part. of *nurse.*

nursing bottle. A bottle with a rubber nipple, for feeding a baby.

nurs·ling \'nərs-ling\ *n.* **1** A child that is being nursed. **2** Any person or thing that is tended with special care.

nur·ture \'nərch-r\ *n.* **1** That which nourishes; food. **2** Care and training, as of a child; upbringing. — *v.;* **nur·tured; nur·tur·ing** \-r(-)ing\. **1** To feed and care for; as, to *nurture* a young plant. **2** To bring up and train; to educate.

nut \'nət\ *n.* **1** A dry fruit or seed that has a hard shell and a hard inner kernel. **2** The inner kernel of a nut. **3** A piece of metal that screws onto a bolt to tighten or hold something. **4** *Slang.* An insane person; one who is eccentric. **5** In stringed instruments, the ridge on the upper end of the finger board over which the strings pass.

nut, 3

nut·crack·er \'nət-,krak-r\ *n.* **1** An instrument for cracking the shells of nuts. **2** A bird of the crow family that lives largely on the seeds from pine cones.

nut·hatch \'nət-,hach\ *n.* A small insect-eating bird that creeps on tree trunks and branches in search of its food.

nut·meg \'nət-,meg\ *n.* **1** The small seed or nut of a tree grown in the East and West Indies and Brazil; the tree itself. **2** A spice made by grinding up or grating nutmeg seeds.

nu·tria \'nü-trē-ə, 'nyü-\ *n.* **1** A South American rodent, similar to the beaver, with webbed hind feet. **2** The light brown fur of this animal, plucked and blended to look like beaver.

nu·tri·ent \'nü-trē-ənt, 'nyü-\ *adj.* Nourishing. — *n.* A nutritious substance.

nu·tri·ment \'nü-trə-mənt, 'nyü-\ *n.* Nourishment.

nu·tri·tion \nü-'trish-n, nyü-\ *n.* **1** The act or process of nourishing or of being nourished; especially, the process by which a person, plant, or animal takes in and makes use of food substances. **2** Nourishment; food. — **nu·tri·tion·al** \-'trish-n(-)əl\ *adj.* — **nu·tri·tion·al·ly** \-n(-)ə-lē\ *adv.*

nu·tri·tious \nü-'trish-əs, nyü-\ *adj.* Useful as food; nourishing. Milk is *nutritious.* — **nu·tri·tious·ly,** *adv.*

nu·tri·tive \'nü-trət-iv, 'nyü-\ *adj.* **1** Having to do with nutrition. Digestion is a *nutritive* process. **2** Nutritious; nourishing. — **nu·tri·tive·ly,** *adv.*

nut·shell \'nət-,shel\ *n.* The shell of a nut. — **in a nutshell.** In a brief statement.

nut·ting \'nət-ing\ *n.* Gathering of nuts.

nut·ty \'nət-ē\ *adj.;* **nut·ti·er; nut·ti·est. 1** Containing nuts; full of nuts. **2** Like nuts; especially, tasting like nuts. **3** *Slang.* Mentally unbalanced; eccentric; zany; as, a *nutty* person; a *nutty* thing to do.

nuz·zle \'nəz-l\ *v.;* **nuz·zled; nuz·zling** \-l(-)ing\. **1** To push or rub with the nose. **2** To nestle; to lie close.

N.W. Abbreviation for *northwest.*

ny·lon \'nī-ˌlän\ *n.* A synthetic material derived from coal, air, and water, used in the making of such things as stockings, cloth, and brush bristles.

nymph \'nim(p)f\ *n.; pl.* **nymphs** \'nim(p)fs, 'nimps\. **1** One of a group of beautiful maidens said, in stories or poetry, to live in forests, streams, mountains, and other outdoor places. **2** A form of some insects before they are fully developed.

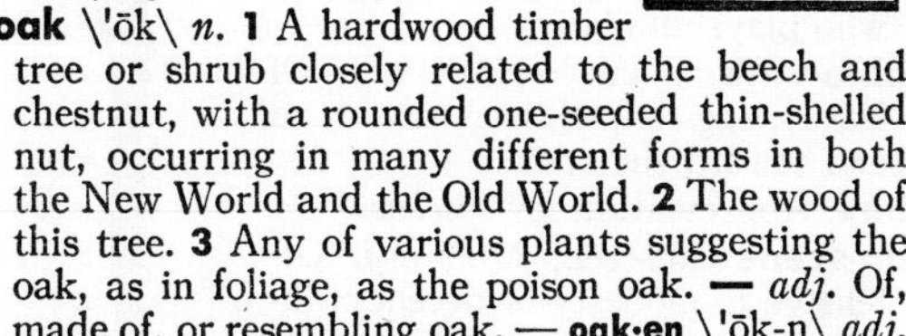

o \'ō\ *n.; pl.* **o's** \'ōz\. **1** The fifteenth letter of the alphabet. **2** A zero.

O \(')ō\. Variant of *oh.*

o' \ə\. A shortened form of *of* or *on,* as in *will-o'-the-wisp.*

oaf \'ōf\ *n.* A stupid or awkward person; a lubber. — **oaf·ish** \'ō-fish\ *adj.*

oak \'ōk\ *n.* **1** A hardwood timber tree or shrub closely related to the beech and chestnut, with a rounded one-seeded thin-shelled nut, occurring in many different forms in both the New World and the Old World. **2** The wood of this tree. **3** Any of various plants suggesting the oak, as in foliage, as the poison oak. — *adj.* Of, made of, or resembling oak. — **oak·en** \'ōk-n\ *adj.*

oa·kum \'ōk-m\ *n.* Loose fiber picked from old hemp ropes, used especially for calking boats.

oar \'ōr, 'ȯr\ *n.* **1** A long, slender, broad-bladed wooden implement for propelling or steering a boat. **2** An oarsman.

oar·lock \'ōr-ˌläk, 'ȯr-\ *n.* A support for an oar in rowing; a rowlock, especially the one in which a steering oar is worked.

oars·man \'ōrz-mən, 'ȯrz-\ *n.; pl.* **oars·men** \-mən\. One who uses an oar or oars; a rower.

oa·sis \ō-'ā-səs, 'ō-ə-\ *n.; pl.* **oa·ses** \-ˌsēz\. A fertile or green spot in a desert.

oarlock

oat \'ōt\ *n.* A cereal grain with long spikelets in loose clusters, cultivated for its grain (**oats**) which is used as a food for horses and yields a meal eaten as a cereal.

oat·en \'ōt-n\ *adj.* **1** Made of oats or oatmeal; as, *oaten* cakes. **2** Of the oat; made of an oat straw or stem.

oath \'ōth\ *n.; pl.* **oaths** \'ōt͟hz, 'ōths\. **1** A solemn appeal to God or to some revered person or thing to bear witness to the truth of one's word or the sacredness of a promise; as, under *oath* to tell the truth. **2** A careless or profane use of a sacred name, as God's.

oat·meal \'ōt-ˌmēl\ *n.* **1** Oats husked and crushed into coarse meal or flattened into flakes. **2** Porridge made from such meal or flakes.

ob·bli·ga·to \ˌäb-lə-'gät-ˌō\ *adj.* In music, usually in an accompaniment, required; necessary; not to be left out. — *n.; pl.* **ob·bli·ga·tos. 1** A prominent accompanying part, usually played by a single instrument; as, a violin *obbligato.* **2** Any accompanying part.

ob·du·ra·cy \'äb-dyər-ə-sē, -dər-; äb-'du̇r-ə-sē, -'dyu̇r-\ *n.* Quality of being obdurate.

ob·du·rate \'äb-dyər-ət, -dər-; äb-'du̇r-ət, -'dyu̇r-\ *adj.* **1** Hardhearted. **2** Unyielding; stubborn. — **ob·du·rate·ly,** *adv.*

obe·di·ence \ō-'bēd-ē-ən(t)s\ *n.* The act of obeying; willingness to obey.

obe·di·ent \ō-'bēd-ē-ənt\ *adj.* Willing to obey; inclined to mind. — **obe·di·ent·ly,** *adv.*

obei·sance \ō-'bās-n(t)s, ō-'bēs-\ *n.* **1** A movement of the body, as a bow, to show respect. **2** Deference; homage.

ob·e·lisk \'äb-l-ˌisk\ *n.* A four-sided pillar that tapers toward the top and ends in a pyramid.

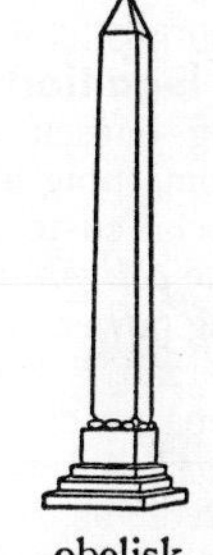

obelisk

obese \ō-'bēs\ *adj.* Excessively fat.

obes·i·ty \ō-'bē-sət-ē, ō-'bes-ət-ē\ *n.* Excessive fatness.

obey \ō-'bā\ *v.;* **obeyed; obey·ing. 1** To carry out the orders of someone; to mind; as, to *obey* one's parents. **2** To be ruled or regulated by; as, to *obey* common sense.

obit·u·ary \ō-'bich-ə-ˌwer-ē\ *n.; pl.* **obit·u·ar·ies.** A notice of a person's death, as in a newspaper. — *adj.* Of or relating to a death; recording a death; as, an *obituary* column.

ob·ject \əb-'jekt\ *v.* **1** To argue against or to be opposed to something; as, to *object* to a plan. **2** To put forward as a reason against some proposal or plan. The treasurer *objected* that the funds were already too low. — \'äb-jikt\ *n.* **1** Something that may be seen or felt. Tables and chairs are *objects.* **2** Something that arouses certain feelings, as of affection, hatred, or pity; as, a person who is an *object* of envy. **3** Aim; purpose. The *object* is to raise money. **4** A noun or pronoun denoting someone or something that receives or is affected by the action of a verb. **5** A noun or pronoun that completes the meaning of a preposition.

ob·jec·tion \əb-'jeksh-n\ *n.* **1** An objecting. **2** A reason for objecting or a feeling of disapproval; as, to have an *objection* to postponing the meeting.

ob·jec·tion·a·ble \əb-'jeksh-n(-)əb-l\ *adj.* Arousing objection; displeasing; offensive; as, *objectionable* language. — **ob·jec·tion·a·bly** \-n(-)ə-blē\ *adv.*

ob·jec·tive \əb-'jek-tiv\ *adj.* **1** Of or having to do with an object or end; as, to reach our *objective* point. **2** Outside of the mind and independent of it. Dragons have no *objective* existence. **3** Treating facts without allowing one's feelings to affect them; detached; impersonal; as, an *objective* editorial; an *objective* view of history. **4** In grammar, of, relating to, or constituting the case of the object of a verb or preposition. — *n.* **1** An end or aim of action; a goal; as, the *objective* of a lesson; a military *objective.* **2** Also **objective case.** The case of a noun or pronoun used as the object of a verb or preposition. **3** The lens or system of lenses, as in a microscope, nearest the object and forming an image of it. — **ob·jec·tive·ly,** *adv.*

ob·jec·tiv·i·ty \ˌäb-ˌjek-'tiv-ət-ē\ *n.* The state of being objective or free from prejudice.

ob·ject les·son \'äb-jikt\. A lesson taught by means of illustrative objects or concrete examples.

ob·jet d'art \ˌȯb-ˌzhā-'där, -'dȧr\ *n.; pl.* **objets d'art** *same*\. **1** An article of artistic value. **2** A curio.

ob·late \'äb-ˌlāt\ *adj.* Flattened or depressed at the poles, as a sphere; as, the *oblate* shape of the earth.

ob·la·tion \ə-'blāsh-n\ *n.* A religious offering, sacrifice, or gift.

ob·li·gate \'äb-lə-ˌgāt\ *v.;* **ob·li·gat·ed; ob·li·gat·ing.** To bring under obligation; to bind legally or morally; as, *obligated* to pay taxes.

ob·li·ga·tion \ˌäb-lə-'gāsh-n\ *n.* **1** The act of binding oneself to do something; an obligating. **2** Something a person is bound to do, as by law or social custom having the force of law; a duty; as, the *obligation* of supporting a family. **3** The binding power of a promise or contract. **4** Something a person is expected or feels it necessary to do to repay a courtesy; as, to have many social *obligations.* **5** Indebtedness for an act of kindness or a favor; as, to be under *obligation* to a friend.

oblig·a·to·ry \ə-'blig-ə-ˌtōr-ē, 'äb-lə-gə-, -ˌtȯr-ē\ *adj.* Legally or morally binding; required; as, a meeting at which attendance was *obligatory.*

oblige \ə-'blīj\ *v.;* **obliged; oblig·ing** \-'blī-jing\. **1** To force; to compel. Federal laws *oblige* citizens to pay taxes. **2** To bind by some favor; to place under a debt by doing a favor; as, to *oblige* an acquaintance by lending him money.

oblig·ing \ə-'blī-jing\ *adj.* Disposed to do favors; helpful; as, an *obliging* friend. — **oblig·ing·ly,** *adv.*

ob·lique \ə-'blēk, ə-'blīk\ *adj.* **1** Slanting; inclined; as, an *oblique* line. **2** Not direct or straightforward; as, *oblique* accusations; an *oblique* glance. — \ə-'blīk\ *v.;* **ob·liqued; ob·liqu·ing.** To march or advance obliquely; especially, to make a 45 degree turn when marching. — **ob·lique·ly,** *adv.*

oblique angle. An angle not a right angle; any acute or obtuse angle.

ob·liq·ui·ty \ə-'blik-wət-ē\ *n.; pl.* **ob·liq·ui·ties.** **1** The state of being oblique or not straight; crookedness. **2** Lack of moral uprightness.

ob·lit·er·ate \ə-'blit-r-ˌāt\ *v.;* **ob·lit·er·at·ed; ob·lit·er·at·ing.** To remove or destroy completely; to wipe out. The tide *obliterated* the marks on the sand. — **ob·lit·er·a·tion** \ə-ˌblit-r-'āsh-n\ *n.*

ob·liv·i·on \ə-'bliv-ē-ən\ *n.* **1** The act of forgetting or of losing awareness. **2** The state or fact of being forgotten; as, the *oblivion* that soon closes over most popular songs.

ob·liv·i·ous \ə-'bliv-ē-əs\ *adj.* Unconscious; unaware; forgetful; as, *oblivious* to the danger. — **ob·liv·i·ous·ly,** *adv.*

ob·long \'äb-ˌlȯng\ *adj.* Longer in one direction than in the other, with parallel sides; rectangular. — *n.* An oblong figure or object.

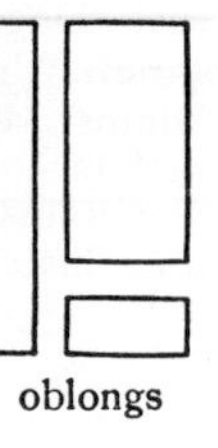

oblongs

ob·lo·quy \'äb-lə-kwē\ *n.; pl.* **ob·lo·quies** \-kwēz\. **1** Speech that criticizes or blames a person bitterly; slander; censure. **2** Disgrace; bad repute.

ob·nox·ious \əb-'näk-shəs, äb-\ *adj.* Extremely disagreeable; hateful. — **ob·nox·ious·ly,** *adv.*

oboe \'ō-ˌbō\ *n.* [From Italian, there borrowed from French *hautbois* meaning literally "high wood".] A musical instrument in the form of a slender cone-shaped tube with holes and keys, played by blowing into a reed mouthpiece.

oboe

obo·ist \'ō-ˌbō-əst\ *n.* A person who plays an oboe.

ob·o·vate \(')äb-'ō-ˌvāt\ *adj.* Of leaves, egg-shaped, with the broad end toward the apex.

obs. Abbreviation for *obsolete.*

ob·scene \əb-'sēn, äb-\ *adj.* Offensive to modesty or decency; indecent. — **ob·scene·ly,** *adv.*

ob·scen·i·ty \əb-'sen-ət-ē, äb-, -'sē-nət-ē\ *n.; pl.* **ob·scen·i·ties.** Quality of being obscene; obscene language or actions.

ob·scure \əb-'skyu̇r, äb-\ *adj.;* **ob·scur·er; ob·scur·est.** **1** Dark; gloomy. **2** Faraway; hidden; as, an *obscure* village. **3** Not clearly understood, seen, felt, or heard; as, an *obscure* passage in a book. **4** Not noticeable; inconspicuous; humble; as, an *obscure* family. — *v.;* **ob·scured; ob·scur·ing.** To make obscure; to darken; to hide; as, clouds *obscuring* the moon. — **ob·scure·ly,** *adv.*

ob·scu·ri·ty \əb-'skyu̇r-ət-ē, äb-\ *n.; pl.* **ob·scu·ri·ties.** **1** The state or quality of being obscure. **2** Someone or something obscure; as, the *obscurities* in a piece of writing.

ob·se·quies \'äb-sə-kwēz\ *n. pl.* The rites and ceremonies that go with burial; a funeral.

ob·se·qui·ous \əb-'sēk-wē-əs, äb-\ *adj.* Slavishly attentive to a person in authority; fawning. — **ob·se·qui·ous·ly,** *adv.*

ob·serv·a·ble \əb-'zər-vəb-l\ *adj.* **1** Necessarily or usually observed; as, forms *observable* in social intercourse. **2** Noticeable; as, an *observable* change in air pressure. — **ob·serv·a·bly** \-və-blē\ *adv.*

ob·serv·ance \əb-'zərv-n(t)s\ *n.* **1** The act or practice of following a rule, custom, or law; as, the *observance* of a holiday; *observance* of traffic regulations. **2** An act or ceremony, as of a religion; a custom; a form; as, *observances* of a church service. **3** Act of observing or noticing; observation; as, a new procedure worthy of study and *observance.*

ob·serv·ant \əb-'zərv-nt\ *adj.* **1** Watchful; attentive; as, an *observant* witness. **2** Careful; heedful; as, *observant* to avoid offense. — **ob·serv·ant·ly,** *adv.*

ob·ser·va·tion \ˌäb-sər-ˈvāsh-n, ˌäbz-r-\ *n.* **1** The act or power of seeing or fixing the mind upon something. **2** The gathering of information, as for scientific studies, by noting facts or occurrences; as, weather *observations.* **3** A conclusion drawn from observing; a view. **4** A remark; a comment. **5** The fact of being observed; as, to avoid *observation.* — For synonyms see *remark.* — *adj.* For use in making observations; as, an *observation* tower.

ob·serv·a·to·ry \əb-ˈzər-və-ˌtōr-ē, -ˌtȯr-ē\ *n.; pl.* **ob·serv·a·to·ries. 1** A place that has instruments for making observations of the stars and planets, and, sometimes, other natural phenomena. **2** A position or place affording a wide view.

ob·serve \əb-ˈzərv\ *v.;* **ob·served; ob·serv·ing. 1** To obey; to comply with; as, to *observe* the law. **2** To celebrate as a custom or rite; as, to *observe* the Sabbath. **3** To pay attention to; to watch; as, to *observe* a parade. **4** To perceive; to notice; as, to *observe* that a person is a good businessman. **5** To remark; to say. **6** To make an observation by scientific methods. — **ob·serv·ing·ly,** *adv.*

ob·serv·er \əb-ˈzərv-r\ *n.* A person who observes; especially, one whose duty it is to observe; as, a weather *observer.*

ob·sess \əb-ˈses\ *v.* To affect to an unreasonable degree; to haunt; as, *obsessed* by a fixed idea.

ob·ses·sion \əb-ˈsesh-n\ *n.* **1** A constant, unreasonable influence exerted upon one by a feeling or idea. **2** Such a feeling or idea.

ob·sid·i·an \əb-ˈsid-ē-ən\ *n.* A dark-colored natural glass formed by cooling of molten lava.

ob·so·les·cent \ˌäb-sə-ˈles-nt\ *adj.* Going out of use; becoming obsolete. — **ob·so·les·cence** \-ˈles-n(t)s\ *n.*

ob·so·lete \ˈäb-sə-ˌlēt, ˌäb-sə-ˈlēt\ *adj.* No longer in use; out of date; as, an *obsolete* word; an *obsolete* machine.

ob·sta·cle \ˈäb-(ˌ)stik-l\ *n.* Something that stands in the way or opposes; a hindrance; an obstruction.

ob·stet·ric \əb-ˈste-trik\ or **ob·stet·ri·cal** \-trik-l\ *adj.* Of or relating to obstetrics. — **ob·stet·ri·cal·ly** \-trik-l(-)ē\ *adv.*

ob·ste·tri·cian \ˌäb-stə-ˈtrish-n\ *n.* A physician specializing in obstetrics.

ob·stet·rics \əb-ˈste-triks\ *n.* The branch of medical science that deals with women before, during, and after childbirth.

ob·sti·na·cy \ˈäb-stə-nə-sē\ *n.; pl.* **ob·sti·na·cies. 1** A firm and usually unreasonable adherence to something, as an opinion or purpose. **2** A persistence in spite of efforts to remedy, relieve, or subdue; as, the *obstinacy* of a toothache. **3** An obstinate action.

ob·sti·nate \ˈäb-stə-nət\ *adj.* **1** Clinging, usually unreasonably, to an opinion, purpose, or course; stubborn. **2** Not easily subdued or removed; as, an *obstinate* fever. — **ob·sti·nate·ly,** *adv.*

ob·strep·er·ous \əb-ˈstrep-r(-)əs\ *adj.* Uncontrollably noisy; clamorous; unruly. — **ob·strep·er·ous·ly,** *adv.*

ob·struct \əb-ˈstrəkt\ *v.* **1** To block or stop up; to clog. The truck *obstructed* the narrow street. **2** To be in, or come in, the way of; to retard. The curtains *obstructed* the sunlight. **3** To shut off a view of; as, billboards *obstructing* the scenery. — **ob·struct·er** or **ob·struc·tor** \-ˈstrəkt-r\ *n.* — **ob·struc·tive** \-ˈstrək-tiv\ *adj.*

ob·struc·tion \əb-ˈstrəksh-n\ *n.* **1** An obstructing; the state of being obstructed. **2** A thing that hinders or impedes; an obstacle. Doctors removed the *obstruction* in the child's throat.

ob·struc·tion·ist \əb-ˈstrəksh-n-əst\ *n.* A person who hinders progress, especially in legislation. — **ob·struc·tion·ism** \-n-ˌiz-m\ *n.*

ob·tain \əb-ˈtān\ *v.* **1** To gain possession of; to get hold of with effort; to acquire; to procure; as, to *obtain* a raise in pay; to *obtain* a ticket. **2** To be recognized or established; to be common; as, customs that *obtain* only in certain parts of the country.

— The words *acquire* and *attain* are synonyms of *obtain: obtain* is a general term for the getting of anything, usually after searching or striving for a time; *acquire* may indicate a continuous or gradual getting or adding to one's possession, or may suggest gaining something indirectly or unexpectedly; *attain* usually refers to a reaching of an objective that is especially desirable and usually difficult to reach, as a lofty goal or the object of a great ambition.

ob·trude \əb-ˈtrüd\ *v.;* **ob·trud·ed; ob·trud·ing. 1** To thrust out; to expel. **2** To thrust foward or present without invitation or justification; as, to *obtrude* oneself upon the attention of a group. — **ob·tru·sion** \-ˈtrüzh-n\ *n.*

ob·tru·sive \əb-ˈtrü-siv\ *adj.* Inclined to obtrude; forward; pushing; intrusive. — **ob·tru·sive·ly,** *adv.*

ob·tuse \əb-ˈtüs, -ˈtyüs; ˈäb-ˌtüs, -ˌtyüs\ *adj.* **1** Not sharp or acute; blunt. **2** Not quick or keen of understanding or feeling; dull; as, a person too *obtuse* to grasp the meaning. — **ob·tuse·ly,** *adv.*

obtuse angle. An angle that is greater than a right angle and less than 180 degrees.

obtuse angle

ob·verse \ˈäb-ˌvərs, äb-ˈvərs\ *n.* **1** The side of something, as a coin or medal, bearing the principal design or lettering. **2** The front or principal surface of anything. **3** A counterpart.

ob·vi·ate \ˈäb-vē-ˌāt\ *v.;* **ob·vi·at·ed; ob·vi·at·ing.** To look forward to and arrange to take care of; to make unnecessary; as, to *obviate* an objection. — **ob·vi·a·tion** \ˌäb-vē-ˈāsh-n\ *n.*

ob·vi·ous \ˈäb-vē-əs\ *adj.* Easily found, seen, or understood; evident; as, an *obvious* place to hide something. — **ob·vi·ous·ly,** *adv.*

oc·a·ri·na \ˌäk-r-ˈē-nə\ *n.* A simple wind instrument or toy made in various sizes, having a mouthpiece and finger holes, and giving soft tones resembling those of a whistle.

oc·ca·sion \ə-ˈkāzh-n\ *n.* **1** A favorable opportunity; a good chance; as, to take the first *occasion* to write a letter home. **2** A time or a combination of circumstances affording ground or reason for something; as, to avoid the *occasion* of a quarrel. **3** An occurrence or a combination of circumstances that brings unexpected results; as, a chance remark that became the *occasion* of a dispute. **4** The time of an event; as, on the *occasion* of the wedding. **5** A special event or function; as, a great *occasion*. **6** A need; a necessity; as, to have *occasion* to travel. — *v.;* **oc·ca·sioned**; **oc·ca·sion·ing** \-n(-)ing\. To give occasion to; to cause; as, a remark that *occasioned* a laugh.

oc·ca·sion·al \ə-ˈkāzh-n(-)əl\ *adj.* **1** Happening now and then; met with now and then; as, a book in which there are *occasional* references to the war. **2** Used or meant for a special occasion or occasions; as, an *occasional* chair; an *occasional* poem. — **oc·ca·sion·al·ly** \-n(-)ə-lē\ *adv.*

Oc·ci·dent \ˈäks-ə-dənt, -ˌdent\ *n.* The West; Europe and the Western Hemisphere.

oc·ci·den·tal \ˌäks-ə-ˈdent-l\ *adj.* [usually with a capital] Of or relating to the Occident. — *n.* [with a capital] A person of the Western Hemisphere or Europe.

oc·cip·i·tal \äk-ˈsip-ət-l\ *adj.* Of or relating to the compound bone (**occipital bone**) forming the back part of the skull. — *n.* The occipital bone.

oc·clude \ə-ˈklüd, ä-\ *v.;* **oc·clud·ed**; **oc·clud·ing.** **1** To close; to obstruct. **2** To shut in or out, as by closing a passage. **3** In chemistry, to absorb — used especially of the absorbing of gases by certain substances, as iron.

oc·clu·sion \ə-ˈklüzh-n, ä-\ *n.* **1** The action of occluding or the state of being occluded. **2** The coming together of the opposing surfaces of the teeth of the two jaws.

oc·cult \ə-ˈkəlt, ˈäk-ˌəlt\ *adj.* **1** Of, relating to, or concerned with supernatural forces. Astrology and fortunetelling are *occult* arts. **2** Beyond understanding; mysterious.

oc·cult·ism \ə-ˈkəl-ˌtiz-m, ä-\ *n.* **1** Occult practices. **2** Belief in hidden or mysterious powers that may be controlled by humans.

oc·cu·pan·cy \ˈäk-yə-pən-sē\ *n.* The action of taking or holding possession; as, *occupancy* of a house.

oc·cu·pant \ˈäk-yə-pənt\ *n.* One that occupies something or takes or has possession of it.

oc·cu·pa·tion \ˌäk-yə-ˈpāsh-n\ *n.* **1** The action or process of occupying or the state of being occupied; occupancy. The invaders required two days to complete their *occupation*. **2** One's business or vocation; as, a tailor by *occupation*. — **oc·cu·pa·tion·al** \-ˈpāsh-n(-)əl\ *adj.*

oc·cu·py \ˈäk-yə-ˌpī\ *v.;* **oc·cu·pied** \-ˌpīd\; **oc·cu·py·ing.** **1** To take possession of a place, as by settling in it or conquering it; to keep conquered country under military control; as, to *occupy* enemy territory. **2** To take up the space or time of; to fill. The box *occupied* the whole top of the table. **3** To be in possession of; to hold, as an office. **4** To dwell in; as, to *occupy* a house. **5** To use; to employ; to busy; as, to *occupy* one's time usefully. — **oc·cu·pi·er** \-ˌpīr\ *n.*

oc·cur \ə-ˈkər\ *v.;* **oc·curred**; **oc·cur·ring** \ə-ˈkər-ing\. **1** To be found or met with; to appear; as, a disease that *occurs* among animals. **2** To happen; to take place; as, the place where the accident *occurred*. **3** To come into the mind; to suggest itself; as, an idea that *occurs* to one.

oc·cur·rence \ə-ˈkər-ən(t)s, ə-ˈkə-rən(t)s\ *n.* **1** An occurring; as, the *occurrence* of an earthquake. **2** An event; an incident; as, an unusual *occurrence*.

ocean \ˈōsh-n\ *n.* **1** The whole body of salt water that covers nearly three fourths of the earth. **2** One of the large bodies of water into which this body is divided. **3** A great expanse or quantity; as, the *ocean* of eternity. — **oce·an·ic** \ˌō-shē-ˈan-ik\ *adj.*

ocean·og·ra·phy \ˌōsh-n-ˈäg-rə-fē\ *n.* Geography of or dealing with the ocean. — **ocean·og·ra·pher** \-rəf-r\ *n.* — **ocean·o·graph·ic** \ˌōsh-n-ə-ˈgraf-ik\ *adj.*

oce·lot \ˈōs-l-ˌät, ˈäs-\ *n.; pl.* **oce·lots** or **oce·lot.** A large American forest cat, ranging southward from Texas, tawny yellow or gray with black markings.

ocher or **ochre** \ˈōk-r\ *n.* **1** An earthy, often impure ore of iron, usually red or yellow, used as a pigment in paints. **2** The color of ocher, especially of yellow ocher.

o'clock \ə-ˈkläk\. A shortened form of the phrase *of the clock.*

Oct. Abbreviation for *October.*

oc·ta·gon \ˈäk-tə-ˌgän\ *n.* A plane figure with eight angles and eight sides.

oc·tag·o·nal \äk-ˈtag-n-əl\ *adj.* Having the form of an octagon; eight-sided. — **oc·tag·o·nal·ly** \-n-ə-lē\ *adv.*

octagon

oc·tane num·ber or **oc·tane rat·ing** \ˈäk-ˌtān\. A number used to measure or indicate the antiknock properties of a liquid motor fuel, the higher this number the less the likelihood of knocking.

oc·tave \ˈäk-tiv, -təv, -ˌtāv\ *n.* **1** Any group of eight. **2** An interval of eight degrees or steps above or below a given musical note. **3** The whole series of notes, tones, or keys within this interval. **4** A tone or note at this interval. **5** A combination of two notes an octave apart.

oc·ta·vo \äk-ˈtā-ˌvō\ *n.; pl.* **oc·ta·vos.** **1** A book made of sheets of paper folded so that each sheet makes eight leaves. **2** A book size roughly that of a typical book made in this way. — *adj.* Having eight leaves to a sheet.

oc·tet or **oc·tette** \(ˈ)äk-ˈtet\ *n.* **1** A musical composition for eight voices or eight instruments.

2 The performers of such a composition. **3** Any group of eight.

Oc·to·ber \äk-'tōb-r\ *n.* [From Old English, there borrowed from Latin, where it designated the eighth month of the ancient Roman year and was derived from *octo* meaning "eight".] The tenth month of the year, having 31 days.

oc·to·ge·nar·i·an \ˌäk-təj-n-'er-ē-ən\ *adj.* Eighty or between eighty and ninety years old. — *n.* A person who is eighty or more but less than ninety years old.

oc·to·pus \'äk-tə-pəs, -ˌpůs\ *n.; pl.* **oc·to·pus·es** \-pə-sȯz, -ˌpůs-ȯz\ or **oc·to·pi** \-ˌpī\ **1** A sea mollusk having round the front of the head eight muscular arms, or tentacles, furnished with two rows of suckers, by means of which it holds on to its prey or to other objects. **2** Something suggestive of an octopus, especially a powerful, grasping organization with many branches.

oc·u·lar \'äk-yəl-r\ *adj.* **1** Of or relating to the eye or the eyesight. **2** Obtained or received by the sight; visual; as, *ocular* proof.

oc·u·list \'äk-yə-ləst\ *n.* **1** An ophthalmologist. **2** An optometrist.

odd \'äd\ *adj.* **1** Being only one of a pair or a set; as, an *odd* glove; a sofa and an *odd* chair or two. **2** Not divisible by two without leaving a remainder; not even; as, 1, 3, 5, and 7 are *odd* numbers. **3** Numbered with an odd number; as, an *odd* year. **4** Some more than the number mentioned; as, fifty *odd* years ago. **5** Being in addition to what is usual, regular, or accounted for; extra; occasional; as, *odd* jobs. **6** Unusual; strange; as, an *odd* way of behaving.

odd·i·ty \'äd-ət-ē\ *n.; pl.* **odd·i·ties.** **1** The quality or state of being odd or queer; strangeness; peculiarity. **2** An odd person, thing, or trait.

odd·ly \'äd-lē\ *adv.* In an odd manner; queerly; strangely.

odd·ment \'äd-mənt\ *n.* Something left over; a remnant; an extra thing or piece.

odds \'ädz\ *n. sing. and pl.* **1** Unequal things or conditions. **2** Difference. What's the *odds* whether we go or not? **3** A difference in favor of one thing over another; an advantage; probability. The *odds* are in favor of our team's winning. **4** An equalizing allowance made, especially in betting, to a contestant supposedly having less than an even chance of winning. — **at odds.** In disagreement; quarreling.

odds and ends. Miscellaneous things; oddments.

ode \'ōd\ *n.* A poem that expresses a noble feeling in dignified style.

odi·ous \'ōd-ē-əs\ *adj.* Causing hatred or strong dislike; worthy of hatred; disgustingly offensive. — **odi·ous·ly,** *adv.*

odi·um \'ōd-ē-əm\ *n.* **1** The condition of being generally hated; hatred. **2** The disgrace or shame attached to something considered hateful or low; as, the *odium* that has always been attached to disloyalty to one's country.

odor \'ōd-r\ *n.* **1** Any smell, whether pleasant or unpleasant; as, the *odor* of paint; the *odor* of lilacs. **2** A perfume. **3** Favor; repute; regard; as, to be in bad *odor.*

odor·if·er·ous \ˌōd-r-'if-r(-)əs\ *adj.* Having or bearing an odor, usually a sweet or pleasant odor; perfumed.

odor·ous \'ōd-r-əs\ *adj.* Having or giving off an odor, especially a sweet odor. — For synonyms see *fragrant.*

od·ys·sey \'äd-ə-sē\ *n.; pl.* **od·ys·seys.** [From the *Odyssey* of Homer, an ancient Greek epic poem describing the wanderings of Odysseus.] A long wandering or series of travels.

o'er \'ōr, 'ȯr\ *prep.* or *adv.* A contraction of *over.*

of \(')əv, ə, 'äv\ *prep.* **1** From as a consequence; through; as, to die *of* cold. **2** By as author or doer; as, the plays *of* Shakespeare. **3** Made from; containing or including; as, a rod *of* iron; a family *of* insects. **4** Specified as; as, the continent *of* America. **5** With reference to; about; as, to boast *of* one's skill. **6** In respect to; as, slow *of* speech. **7** Resulting in, or acting upon or toward; as, the commission *of* a crime. **8** Having as a distinguishing mark; as, a man *of* courage. **9** From, as the material or group from which a part is set aside; as, the flower *of* the family. **10** Relating to; belonging to; connected with; as, the path *of* the sun; the square root *of* a number.

off \'ȯf\ *adv.* **1** From a place or position; away; as, to march *off;* to live far *off.* **2** To a condition or point of ceasing, being completed, or lessening. The pain passed *off.* **3** Into a sleep; as, to drop *off* for a few minutes. **4** So as to be no longer attached or connected; as, to take *off* a coat; to peel *off* the skin of an orange. **5** So as to make less or cancel; as, to pay *off* a debt. **6** Away from one's regular work; as, to take a day *off.* **7** At a distance; away; as, only two weeks *off.* — *prep.* **1** Away from; so as to be no longer on; as, to take a dish *off* the table; a hole that is slightly *off* center. **2** Released or free from; as, to be *off* duty. **3** Below; below the standard of; as, ten per cent *off* the regular price; to be *off* one's game. **4** To seaward of; as, a ship two miles *off* shore. — *adj.* **1** Away; removed; as, to go with one's coat *off.* **2** Canceled; given up. The game is *off.* **3** Not working; not effective. The electricity is *off.* **4** Not true; not accurate; as, figures that are *off.* **5** Slight; faint; as, an *off* chance. **6** Provided for; as, to be well *off.* **7** Different from fact or below some standard; as, to be *off* in one's reckoning. **8** Inferior; as, an *off* grade of cotton. **9** Slack; as, the *off* season.

of·fal \'ȯf-l, 'äf-l\ *n.* **1** Waste or by-products separated in processing or making something; especially, the parts, as liver, heart, skin, hooves, removed from a meat animal. **2** Rubbish; garbage.

of·fence \ə-'fen(t)s\ *n.* Offense.

of·fend \ə-'fend\ *v.* **1** To sin; to commit a wrong. **2** To cause anger, dislike, or annoyance; to displease. Teasing *offends* some people.

of·fend·er \ə-'fend-r\ *n.* **1** A person who offends.

2 A person who breaks any law or rule. — **first offender.** A person who has not been charged with or convicted of any previous offenses.

of·fense \ə-ˈfen(t)s\ *n.* **1** An attack; an assault; as, weapons used for *offense.* **2** The act of offending or state of being offended; displeasure; as, capable of speaking the truth without *offense.* **3** A sin; a wrongdoing; as, to find willful deceit an *offense;* an *offense* requiring a trial by jury.

of·fen·sive \ə-ˈfen(t)s-iv\ *adj.* **1** Having to do with attack; made or suited for attack; as, *offensive* weapons. **2** Causing unpleasant sensations; as, *offensive* smells. **3** Causing displeasure or resentment; insulting; as, an *offensive* remark that angered. — *n.* **1** The state or position of one who is making an attack; an aggressive attitude; as, to be on the *offensive.* **2** An attack. The army launched its *offensive.* — **of·fen·sive·ly,** *adv.*

of·fer \ˈóf-r, ˈäf-r\ *v.;* **of·fered; of·fer·ing** \-r(-)ing\. **1** To present as an act of worship; to sacrifice. **2** To present for acceptance or rejection; to proffer. **3** To present for consideration; to suggest; to propose; as, to *offer* an opinion; to *offer* a vote of thanks. **4** To declare one's willingness; as, to *offer* to come to one's help. **5** To try to make, do, or inflict; as, to *offer* resistance. — *n.* **1** A proposal; a bid; the act of offering. **2** The condition of being offered.

of·fer·ing \ˈóf-r(-)ing, ˈäf-\ *n.* **1** The act of one who offers. **2** That which is offered. **3** A gift, as money collected from people at a church service. **4** A sacrifice made to God or a god.

of·fer·to·ry \ˈóf-r-ˌtōr-ē, ˈäf-, -ˌtór-ē\ *n.; pl.* **of·fer·to·ries. 1** That part of Communion in which bread and wine are offered to God before they are consecrated; the prayers or the music accompanying this portion of the service. **2** The collection taken up during a church service. **3** The music played or sung during the taking up of a collection in a church service.

off·hand \ˈóf-ˈhand\ *adv.* Without thought or preparation beforehand. — \ˈóf-ˌhand\ *adj.* Done or made offhand; casual; as, an *offhand* manner.

off·hand·ed \ˈóf-ˈhan-dəd\ *adj.* Offhand. — **off·hand·ed·ly,** *adv.*

of·fice \ˈóf-əs, ˈäf-\ *n.* **1** Something done for some-one else; a service. Through the *offices* of friends the class raised money. **2** A duty, job, or position; especially, a public position; as, the *office* of mayor. **3** A ceremony; a rite. **4** The place where a particular kind of business or service for others is done; as, a school *office;* a dentist's *office.* **5** The set prayer or prayers followed in a particular religious service; as, the *office* of the Mass.

of·fice·hold·er \ˈóf-əs-ˌhōld-r, ˈäf-\ *n.* One who holds an office, especially a government office.

of·fi·cer \ˈóf-əs-r, ˈäf-\ *n.* **1** A person who is chosen to assume specified responsibilities in the management of an organization; as, an *officer* of the camera club; an *officer* on the city council; a church *officer.* **2** A person who holds a position of command, as in the army or navy. **3** A policeman. — *v.* **1** To furnish an army or society with officers. **2** To command or direct as an officer.

of·fi·cial \ə-ˈfish-l\ *adj.* **1** Having to do with an office or officers; as, *official* duties. **2** Having authority to perform a service; as, an *official* referee for a football game. **3** Suitable to a person in office or authority; formal; as, an *official* greeting by the mayor. **4** Approved by the proper authority; as, an *official* language; an *official* newspaper. — *n.* A person in office; an officer.

of·fi·cial·dom \ə-ˈfish-l-dəm\ *n.* The whole class of officials.

of·fi·cial·ly \ə-ˈfish-l(-)ē\ *adv.* In an official manner.

of·fi·ci·ate \ə-ˈfish-ē-ˌāt\ *v.;* **of·fi·ci·at·ed; of·fi·ci·at·ing. 1** To perform a religious service. **2** To act as an officer in performing a duty.

of·fi·cious \ə-ˈfish-əs\ *adj.* Taking over duties or power without being asked or needed; meddlesome. — **of·fi·cious·ly,** *adv.*

off·ing \ˈóf-ing, ˈäf-\ *n.* **1** That part of the deep sea seen from the shore. **2** A distant place or time. There's trouble in the *offing.*

off·ish \ˈóf-ish\ *adj.* Inclined to be formal, stiff, or somewhat rude in manner. — **off·ish·ly,** *adv.*

off·set \ˈóf-ˌset\ *n.* **1** A thing that sets off, comes from, or is set off from, something. **2** An offshoot, as of a plant. **3** A sharp bend, as in a pipe, by which one part is turned aside out of line. — \óf-ˈset, ˈóf-ˌset\ *v.;* **off·set; off·set·ting.** To set off, balance, or make up for, something.

offset

off·shoot \ˈóf-ˌshüt\ *n.* **1** In plants, a branch of a main stem. **2** A side shoot or branch of anything.

off·shore \ˈóf-ˌshōr, -ˌshór\ *adj.* **1** Going from the shore toward the sea; as, an *offshore* breeze. **2** Located or done away from shore; as, *offshore* fisheries. — \-ˈshōr, -ˈshór\ *adv.* Away from the shore.

off·side or **off-side** \ˈóf-ˈsīd\ *adj.* In football, hockey, and other games, in such a position as to be barred by the rules from taking part in the play; especially, illegally in advance of the ball. — *n.* An action that results in a player or players being offside.

off·spring \ˈóf-ˌspring\ *n. sing. and pl.* A descendant of a person or animal; a child or children.

oft \ˈóft\ *adv. Archaic.* Often.

of·ten \ˈóf-n, -tən\ *adv.* Many times; frequently.

of·ten·times \ˈóf-n-ˌtīmz, ˈóf-tən-\ *adv.* Often.

oft·times \ˈóf(t)-ˌtīmz\ *adv. Archaic.* Oftentimes.

ogle \ˈōg-l\ *v.;* **ogled; ogling** \-l(-)ing\. To make eyes at a person; to stare in a flirtatious way. — *n.* An amorous or coquettish glance.

ogre \ˈōg-r\ *n.* **1** In fairy tales, a hideous giant or monster who eats human beings. **2** An ugly or cruel person. — **ogre·ish** or **ogrish** \ˈōg-r(-)ish\ *adj.*

oh or **O** \(ˈ)ō\ *interj.* An exclamation used to express various emotions, as surprise, sorrow, fear, or pain, and used also with little meaning before the name of a person spoken to.

ohm \\'ōm\\ *n.* [Named in honor of Georg S. *Ohm* (1787–1854), a German physicist who formulated an important law of electricity.] The practical unit of electrical resistance, being the resistance of a circuit in which a potential difference of one volt produces a current of one ampere. — **ohm·me·ter** \\'ōm-ˌ(m)ēt-r\\ *n.*

-oid \\ˌȯid\\. A suffix that can mean: like, resembling imperfectly, as in *anthropoid, Mongoloid, spheroid.*

oil \\'ȯil\\ *n.* **1** Any of a large class of combustible fatty or greasy substances, usually liquid, obtained from plants, animals, or minerals, and used for fuel, lighting, food, medicines, and in manufacturing processes; as, whale *oil;* crude *oil.* **2** Petroleum. **3** Any substance of oily consistency; as, *oil* of vitriol. **4** Artists' paint made with oil; as, to paint in *oils.* **5** A painting in oils. **—** *v.* To put oil on or in; as, to *oil* a machine. **—** *adj.* Of or like oil; having to do with oil or the production and distribution of oil. — **oil·er,** *n.*

oil·cloth \\'ȯil-ˌklȯth\\ *n.* Cloth treated with oil or paint so as to be waterproof, and used for such things as shelf and table coverings.

oil of vitriol. Concentrated sulfuric acid.

oil·skin \\'ȯil-ˌskin\\ *n.* **1** Cloth treated with oil so as to make it waterproof. **2** [in the plural] Clothing made of this material, as for sailors and fishermen.

oil well. A drilled or dug well from which petroleum is obtained.

oily \\'ȯi-lē\\ *adj.;* **oil·i·er; oil·i·est. 1** Of, relating to, or containing, oil. **2** Covered with oil. **3** Like oil. **4** Too smooth or suave in manner.

oint·ment \\'ȯint-mənt\\ *n.* A soft, greasy substance to be rubbed on the skin to heal, soften, or whiten it; a salve.

O.K. or **OK** \\'ō-'kā\\ *adv.* or *adj.* All right. **—** *v.;* **O.K.'d** or **OK'd** \\'ō-'kād\\; **O.K.'ing** or **OK'ing** \\'ō-'kā-ing\\. To put "O.K." on; to approve. **—** *n.; pl.* **O.K.'s** or **OK's** \\'ō-'kāz\\. Approval; as, to get an *O.K.* on a proposal.

oka·pi \\ō-'käp-ē, -'kȧp-ē\\ *n.; pl.* **oka·pis** or **oka·pi.** An animal of the African forests closely related to the giraffe.

okapi

okay \\'ō-'kā\\. Variant of *O.K.*

okra \\'ōk-rə\\ *n.* **1** A plant grown for its edible green pods, used in soups and stews. **2** The pods of this plant.

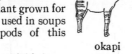

old \\'ōld\\ *adj.;* **old·er** \\'ōld-r\\ or **eld·er** \\'eld-r\\; **old·est** \\'ōl-dəst\\ or **eld·est** \\'el-dəst\\. **1** Not [illegible]oung, new, or recent; as, an *old* man; *old* gloves. [illegible] Having a certain age; as, ten years *old.* **3** Forn[illegible]; as, to visit one's *old* school. **4** Ancient; long [illegible]st; as, *old* times. **5** Of long standing; as, an *old* [illegible]om. **6** Belonging to, or having to do with, old[illegible]le; as, *old* eyes. **7** Being the earlier of two or [illegible]hings of the same kind or periods or stages of the same thing; as, the *Old* Testament; *Old* English.

— The words *elderly* and *venerable* are synonyms of *old: old* may apply to anything or anyone that has had long, or comparatively long, life or existence; *elderly* is used especially to describe persons who are somewhat old but not extremely so; *venerable* usually describes something of very great age that is worthy of reverence and respect because of its age, and applies more often to persons than to objects.

— *n.* Old time, or a former time; as, days of *old.*

old·en \\'ōl-dən\\ *adj.* Ancient; long past; as, *olden* times.

Old English. 1 The English language in the stage of its development that it passed through from about A.D. 450, when it was brought to England from the European continent by the Anglo-Saxons, to about 1100. **2** A style of printing in heavy black letters.

old-fash·ioned \\'ōl(d)-'fash-nd\\ *adj.* **1** Clinging to old ideas or customs; as, *old-fashioned* people. **2** Out of date; not in style; as, an *old-fashioned* hat.

Old French. The French language from about the 9th to the 16th centuries.

Old Glory. The flag of the United States.

old·ish \\'ōl-dish\\ *adj.* Somewhat old.

old maid. 1 An elderly woman who has never married. **2** A fussy, nervous, timid person. **3** A simple game of cards.

old·ster \\'ōl(d)-stər\\ *n.* An old or elderly person.

Old Testament. The first of the two chief divisions of the Bible, consisting of the books dealing with the history of the Hebrews before the time of Christ.

old-time \\'ōl(d)-ˌtīm\\ *adj.* Of or belonging to old or former times.

old-tim·er \\'ōl(d)-'tīm-r\\ *n.* **1** One who has lived or worked long in a place or has held the same position for a long time; one whose experience reaches far back. **2** An old-fashioned person or thing.

old-world \\'ōl-ˌ(d)wərld\\ *adj.* **1** Of or relating to ancient times or customs. **2** [written *Old World*] Of or relating to the Eastern Hemisphere, or **Old World.**

ole·an·der \\ˌō-lē-'and-r\\ *n.* A poisonous evergreen shrub with thick leathery leaves and fragrant white, red, or pink flowers.

ole·o·mar·ga·rine \\'ō-lē-ō-'märj-r(-)ən, -'mȧrj-, -r-ˌēn\\ or **ole·o·mar·ga·rin** \\-r(-)ən\\ *n.* A substance made from certain animal or vegetable fats and oils for use as a butter substitute.

ol·fac·to·ry \\äl-'fakt-r(-)ē, ōl-\\ *adj.* Of, relating to, or connected with the sense of smell; as, *olfactory* sensations; an *olfactory* nerve. **—** *n.; pl.* **ol·fac·to·ries.** An olfactory organ; the sense of smell itself — usually used in the plural.

olfactory nerve. A tract of nerve fibers connecting the olfactory organ of the nose with the brain.

ol·i·garch \'äl-ə-ˌgärk, -ˌgȧrk\ *n.* A member of an oligarchy.

ol·i·garchy \'äl-ə-ˌgärk-ē, -ˌgȧrk-ē\ *n.; pl.* **ol·i·garch·ies.** **1** A government in which the power is in the hands of a few persons. **2** A state having such a government. **3** The group of persons holding power in such a state.

ol·ive \'äl-iv, -əv\ *n.* **1** An Old World evergreen tree grown for its hard yellow wood and for its fruit, which is eaten both ripe and unripe and also yields a pale yellow non-drying oil (**olive oil**). **2** Any of a family of trees or shrubs of which the olive of commerce is typical. **3** The fruit or the wood of the olive tree. **4** Also **olive green.** The dull greenish yellow color of unripe olives.

olive branch. A branch of the olive tree, considered an emblem of peace; anything offered as a sign of peace.

Olym·pi·ad or **olym·pi·ad** \ō-'limp-ē-ˌad\ *n.* **1** The period of four, or in the reckoning of the ancient Greeks, five years from one Olympian festival to the next. **2** The celebration of the Olympic games. **3** The Olympian games or the Olympic games.

Olym·pi·an \ō-'limp-ē-ən\ *adj.* **1** Of or dwelling on Olympus; as, the *Olympian* gods. **2** Godlike; having power or dignity; awe-inspiring. **3** Of or relating to Olympia in ancient Greece. **—** *n.* A participator in the Olympian games or in the Olympic games.

Olym·pi·an games \ō-'limp-ē-ən\ or **Olym·pic games** \-'limp-ik\. **1** Games held in ancient Greece every fourth year from the year 776 B.C. **2** Usually *Olympic games.* A revival of the Olympian games, held every four years in a different country, beginning in Athens in 1896.

Olym·pic \ō-'limp-ik\ *adj.* Olympian. **—** *n.* [in the plural] Olympian games or Olympic games.

omega \ō-'meg-ə, ō-'mē-gə\ *n.* **1** The long *o*, the last letter of the Greek alphabet, often used to indicate something that is last in position or importance. **2** The last; the end.

om·e·let or **om·e·lette** \'äm-l(-)ət\ *n.* Eggs beaten with milk or water, cooked in a frying pan or on a grill, and folded over.

omen \'ō-mən\ *n.* An event or sign supposed to be a warning of some future occurrence; a portent.

om·i·nous \'äm-ə-nəs\ *adj.* Being or showing an omen; especially, foretelling evil; threatening; as, *ominous* events leading to war. — **om·i·nous·ly,** *adv.*

omis·sion \ō-'mish-n\ *n.* **1** An omitting or a being omitted. **2** Something omitted.

omit \ō-'mit\ *v.;* **omit·ted; omit·ting.** **1** To leave out; to fail to include; as, to *omit* a name from a list. **2** To leave undone; to neglect; as, to *omit* the dusting for a day.

om·ni·bus \'äm-nə-(ˌ)bəs\ *n.* [From French, where it is short for *voiture omnibus* meaning "vehicle for all", *omnibus* (meaning "for all") being a form of Latin *omnis* meaning "all".] **1** A large, usually four-wheeled passenger vehicle; a bus. **2** A collection containing reproductions of a number of works, especially of literature or music; an anthology. **—** *adj.* Of, relating to, or providing for many things or many classes of things at once; as, an *omnibus* bill passed by the legislature.

om·nip·o·tent \äm-'nip-ə-tənt\ *adj.* Unlimited in power or authority; all-powerful; almighty. **—** *n.* One who is all-powerful. — **the Omnipotent.** The Almighty; God. — **om·nip·o·tence** \-tən(t)s\ *n.* — **om·nip·o·tent·ly** \-tənt-lē\ *adv.*

om·ni·pres·ent \ˌäm-nə-'prez-nt\ *adj.* Present everywhere at once. — **om·ni·pres·ence** \-'prez-n(t)s\ *n.*

om·ni·scient \äm-'nish-nt\ *adj.* Knowing all things; very wise. — **om·ni·science** \-n(t)s\ *n.* — **om·ni·scient·ly** \-nt-lē\ *adv.*

om·ni·um-gath·er·um \'äm-nē-əm-'gath-r-əm\ *n.; pl.* **om·ni·um-gath·er·ums.** A collection of all sorts of things or persons.

om·ni·vore \'äm-nə-ˌvōr, -ˌvȯr\ *n.* An omnivorous animal; especially, any of a group of animals that eat both animal and vegetable food.

om·niv·o·rous \äm-'niv-r(-)əs\ *adj.* Eating everything; especially, eating both animal and vegetable food. — **om·niv·o·rous·ly,** *adv.*

on \(')ȯn, (')än\ *prep.* **1** Over and touching; as, a book *on* the table. **2** Near, touching, or connected with; as, a town *on* the river. **3** In connection with; engaged with; engaged in making; as, to work *on* a committee; to go *on* a tour. **4** With. It was stated *on* authority. **5** In or at a certain place, direction, time, or manner; during; as, the town *on* the right; *on* Monday. **6** At the time of; as, cash *on* delivery. **7** Under a certain condition; in a state or process of; as, *on* sale; *on* tap. **8** Down from above; to, toward, or against; as, to put the cover *on* a jar. **9** To the account of; about; as, to agree *on* a plan. **10** By means of; through; over; as, to talk *on* the telephone. **11** In addition to; as, to win game *on* game. **—** *adv.* **1** In or into the position of being on something; as, to put *on* a coat. **2** Toward something else; as, to look *on* while others do the work. **3** Forward; as, to go *on.* **4** In continuance; as, to sleep *on* in spite of the noise. **5** In or into use or action; as, to turn *on* the light; to bring *on* pneumonia. **—** *adj.* **1** In progress. The game is *on.* **2** In a position that allows unchecked flow; as, to leave a light switch *on.* **3** In action. The brake is *on.* **4** Arranged for; as, to have several things *on* for the weekend. **5** Aware, as of something concealed. **6** Willing to join, as in a venture.

once \'wən(t)s\ *adv.* **1** One time only. **2** At any one time; ever; on any occasion [illegible] as, if *once* the truth becomes known. **3** At some [illegible]ne time; especially, formerly. It was *once* don[illegible] that way. **—** *conj.* If ever; whenever; as, *once* [illegible]t is done, all will be well. **—** *adj.* That once w[illegible]er [illegible]rmer; as, the *once* mayor. **—** *n.* One time, or pa[illegible]ly time; as, just this *once.* — **at once.** **1** At [illegible]e time; simultaneously; as, several perso[illegible]g *at once.* **2** Immediately. Do it *at once* [illegible]forget.

on·com·ing \'ȯn-ˌkəm-ing, 'än-\ *adj.* Coming on; approaching; as, the *oncoming* traffic.

one \'wən, (ˌ)wən\ *adj.* **1** Being a single person or thing and no more; a single; as, *one* dollar; to be absent for *one* day. **2** Not divided; united; as, a crowd of people shouting with *one* voice. **3** A certain; some; as, *one* day last summer. **4** The same; as, all in *one* box. — *n.* **1** A single unit. **2** The figure standing for a single unit, as 1 or I. **3** A single person or thing. **4** Anything bearing the number one; especially, a one-dollar bill. — **at one.** In agreement. Our ideas are *at one.* — *pron.* **1** A certain person or thing that is not specified; as, *one* named Brown. **2** Anybody; any person or thing. *One* cannot be too careful.

one·ness \'wən-nəs\ *n.* Singleness; unity; sameness.

on·er·ous \'än-r-əs, 'ōn-\ *adj.* Burdensome; oppressive. — **on·er·ous·ly,** *adv.*

one·self \(ˌ)wən-'self\ *pron.* or **one's self** \ˌwən(z) 'self\. The form of the word *one* used to give emphasis or to show that the subject and object of a verb are the same. One sees *oneself* in a mirror. One should do it *one's self.*

one-sid·ed \'wən-'sīd-əd\ *adj.* **1** Having or on only one side; as, a *one-sided* argument. **2** Having one side larger, more prominent, or better developed. **3** Unequal; as, a *one-sided* game. **4** Limited to one side; partial; prejudiced; as, a *one-sided* point of view. — **one-sid·ed·ly,** *adv.*

one-way \'wən-ˌwā\ *adj.* Moving, or permitting motion or traffic, in only one direction.

on·ion \'ən-yən\ *n.* The strong-smelling bulb of a plant of the lily family, having a pungent flavor, commonly grown as a vegetable.

onion bulbs

on·look·er \'ȯn-ˌlu̇k-r, 'än-\ *n.* A person who looks on at anything, especially in a casual manner; a spectator. — **on·look·ing** \-ˌlu̇k-ing\ *adj.* or *n.*

on·ly \'ōn-lē\ *adj.* **1** Without others of the same kind; sole; as, an *only* child; the *only* boy in the group. **2** Chief; best; most suitable; as, the *only* man for the job. — *adv.* For no other reason; at no other time; solely; merely; as, to say *only* what one knows to be true; to fly *only* by night. — *conj.* Except that. The job would have been done, *only* there was not enough time.

on·o·mat·o·poe·ia \ˌän-ə-ˌmat-ə-'pē-ə, ō-ˌnäm-ət-ə-\ *n.* **1** Formation of words in imitation of natural sounds, as in *buzz, hiss, whippoorwill.* **2** The use of words whose sound suggests the sense, as in *the rumbling truck.* — **on·o·mat·o·poe·ic** \-'pē-ik\ or **on·o·mat·o·po·et·ic** \-pō-'et-ik\ *adj.*

on·rush \'ȯn-ˌrəsh, 'än-\ *n.* A rushing onward.

on·set \'ȯn-ˌset, 'än-\ *n.* **1** An attack. **2** A start or beginning; as, the *onset* of a disease.

on·shore \'ȯn-ˌshōr, 'än-, -ˌshȯr\ *adj.* Moving or directed toward the shore; as, an *onshore* breeze. — \-'shōr, -'shȯr\ *adv.* Toward the shore.

on·slaught \'ȯn-ˌslȯt, 'än-\ *n.* A furious attack.

on·to \'ȯn-tə, 'än-, -tu̇, -tü\ *prep.* On to; to a position on or against; upon.

on·ward \'ȯn-wərd, 'än-\ *adv.* **1** Forward; as, to press *onward.* **2** In front; as, a goal that lies farther *onward.* — *adj.* Going forward; as, the *onward* march of time.

on·wards \'ȯn-wərdz, 'än-\ *adv.* Onward.

on·yx \'än-iks\ *n.* A quartz stone having layers of different colors.

ooze \'üz\ *v.;* **oozed; ooz·ing.** To flow out slowly and quietly; to leak out gradually; as, sap *oozing* from a tree. — *n.* **1** That which oozes. **2** Soft mud; slime. — **oozy** \'ü-zē\ *adj.*

opac·i·ty \ō-'pas-ət-ē\ *n.; pl.* **opac·i·ties. 1** The condition of being opaque. **2** Obscurity of meaning. **3** Mental dullness.

opal \'ōp-l\ *n.* A stone having delicate, changeable colors.

opal·es·cent \ˌōp-l-'es-nt\ *adj.* Having colors like an opal. — **opal·es·cence** \-'es-n(t)s\ *n.*

opaque \ō-'pāk\ *adj.* **1** Not reflecting light; dark. **2** Not letting light through; not transparent. — **opaque·ly,** *adv.*

ope \'ōp\ *adj.* or *v. Archaic.* Open.

open \'ōp-n, -m\ *adj.* **1** Not shut, covered over, clogged, or stopped; as, an *open* door; an *open* bottle. **2** Not enclosed or capable of being enclosed or shut in; as, an *open* boat; an *open* field. **3** Free to be used or entered by all; as, an *open* contest. **4** Easy to enter, get through, or see; as, *open* country. **5** Not snowy; as, an *open* winter. **6** Not secret or hidden; public; frank; as, an *open* dislike; *open* defiance. **7** Spread out; extended; as, an *open* flower; an *open* umbrella. **8** Not decided; not certain; as, an *open* question. **9** Ready to listen to appeals or ideas; as, an *open* mind. — *v.;* **opened** \-nd, -md\; **open·ing** \'ōp-n(-)ing\. **1** To change or move from a shut position; to unfasten; to unfold or spread out; as, to *open* a book. **2** To lead to something else. The door *opens* on a terrace. **3** To break apart; to clear a thing, as of obstacles or difficulties; as, to *open* a road blocked with snow. The clouds *opened.* **4** To make or declare a thing ready for use; as, to *open* a new store. **5** To start; as, to *open* fire; to *open* negotiations. — *n.* Open space; the outdoors; open sea or air — used always with *the;* as, to go out in the *open.*

open air. The air out of doors.

open-air \'ōp-n-ˌar, -ˌer\ *adj.* Outdoor; as, an *open-air* theater.

open door. In international relations, equal and unrestricted opportunity for all countries in trade and business relations. — **open-door** \'ōp-n-ˌdōr, 'ōp-m-, -ˌdȯr\ *adj.*

open·er \'ōp-n(-)ər\ *n.* Someone or something that opens; as, a can *opener.*

open-eyed \'ōp-n-'īd\ *adj.* Having the eyes open as in wakefulness or in wonder; watchful; alert.

open-hand·ed \'ōp-n-'han-dəd\ *adj.* Generous; liberal. — **open-hand·ed·ly,** *adv.*

open-heart·ed \'ōp-n-'härt-əd, -'hårt-\ *adj.* Frank; generous. — **open-heart·ed·ly,** *adv.*

open-hearth \'ōp-n-ˌhärth, -ˌhårth\ *adj.* Relating to a process (**open-hearth process**) of making steel in a furnace that reflects the flame from the roof onto the material.

open house. Hospitality or entertainment for all who may come, with or without special invitation; an occasion on which such hospitality is offered.

open·ing \'ōp-n(-)iŋ\ *n.* **1** The act of opening; as, to attend the *opening* of a new school. **2** An open place; a clearing; a gap; a hole. **3** A start; a beginning. **4** An opportunity; a chance; as, to look for an *opening* in banking. **5** A move or a series of moves beginning certain games, as chess.

open·ly \'ōp-n-lē, 'ōp-m-\ *adv.* In an open or frank manner; as, to be *openly* defiant.

open-mind·ed \'ōp-n-'mīn-dəd, 'ōp-m-\ *adj.* Having a mind open to new ideas. — **open-mind·ed·ly,** *adv.*

open-mouthed \'ōp-n-'mau̇t͟hd, 'ōp-m-, -'mau̇tht\ *adj.* Having the mouth open; gaping; wide-mouthed; as, *open-mouthed* with amazement; standing dejected and *open-mouthed.*

open season. A period during which it is lawful to kill or catch game or fish protected at other times by law; as, the *open season* on ducks.

open secret. Something supposedly secret but in fact generally known.

open ses·a·me \'ses-m-ē\. [The magic words that opened the door to the robbers' cave in the story of *Ali Baba and the Forty Thieves.*] Something that opens or admits without fail; a magical key; as, an *open sesame* to success.

open shop. A shop or other place of business which employs both members and nonmembers of labor unions.

open·work \'ōp-n-ˌwərk, 'ōp-m-\ *n.* Anything made or any work done so that openings show through the fabric or material.

op·era \'äp-r(-)ə\ *n.* A play, usually with elaborate costumes and scenery, that is wholly or mostly sung with orchestral accompaniment.

opera. A pl. of *opus.*

opera glass or **opera glasses.** Small binoculars adapted for use at the opera or the theater.

opera glass

op·er·ate \'äp-r-ˌāt\ *v.;* **op·er·at·ed; op·er·at·ing. 1** To do work or labor; to act; to start and keep working; as, to *operate* a car. The machine *operates* smoothly. **2** To take effect; as, a medicine that *operates* quickly. **3** To conduct; to manage; as, to *operate* a small business. **4** To perform an operation on a person or animal.

op·er·at·ic \ˌäp-r-'at-ik\ *adj.* Of or like opera; relating to opera.

op·er·a·tion \ˌäp-r-'āsh-n\ *n.* **1** The act, process, method, or result of operating. **2** The use of power or influence; the working; as, the *operation* of a drug. **3** Any movement of troops or naval vessels made to carry out some plan. **4** A surgical procedure on the body of a living person or animal. **5** A process, as addition, of deriving one mathematical expression from others by rule.

op·er·a·tive \'äp-r(-)ət-iv, -r-ˌāt-iv\ *adj.* **1** Exerting force or influence; operating; as, the *operative* word in a sentence. **2** Producing the appropriate effect; as, an *operative* dose; an *operative* penalty. **3** Having to do with physical or mechanical operations; as, *operative* costs. **4** Engaged in or doing work; as, to be *operative* in an organization. — *n.* **1** A worker; especially, one employed in a mechanical industry. **2** A detective.

op·er·a·tor \'äp-r-ˌāt-r\ *n.* A person who operates; as, a radio *operator;* the *operator* of a dairy farm.

op·er·et·ta \ˌäp-r-'et-ə\ *n.* A short opera with a light, amusing plot and gay, tuneful music.

oph·thal·mia \äf-'thal-mē-ə, äp-\ *n.* An inflammation of the eye, especially of the mucous membrane which lines the inner surface of the eyelid and covers the front part of the eyeball.

oph·thal·mol·o·gist \ˌäf-ˌthal-'mäl-ə-jəst, ˌäp-\ *n.* A physician specializing in the diseases and disorders of the eye.

opi·ate \'ōp-ē-ət, -ē-ˌāt\ *n.* **1** Medicine which contains opium, used to bring sleep or rest. **2** Anything restful or soothing. — *adj.* **1** Containing opium. **2** Bringing sleep or causing rest, dullness, or lack of action.

opine \ō-'pīn\ *v.;* **opined; opin·ing.** To have or express an opinion.

opin·ion \ə-'pin-yən\ *n.* **1** A belief, stronger than an impression, but less strong than positive knowledge. **2** A judgment about a person or thing; as, to have a high *opinion* of someone. **3** A statement by an expert after careful study.

opin·ion·at·ed \ə-'pin-yə-ˌnāt-əd\ *adj.* Stubbornly holding to personal opinions.

opi·um \'ōp-ē-əm\ *n.* A drug from certain poppies used in medicine to bring sleep or dull pain but sometimes causing addiction.

opos·sum \ō-'päs-m\ *n.; pl.* **opos·sums** or **opos·sum.** A small American marsupial mammal that lives in trees and, when caught, acts as if dead.

op·po·nent \ə-'pō-nənt\ *n.* A person or thing that opposes another person or thing; a foe; a rival; an antagonist.

op·por·tune \ˌäp-r-'tün, -'tyün\ *adj.* Suitable; timely; as, an *opportune* moment to act. — **op·por·tune·ly,** *adv.*

op·por·tun·ism \ˌäp-r-'tü-ˌniz-m, -'tyü-\ *n.* The practice of taking advantage of opportunities or conditions, regardless of results; as, political *opportunism.* — **op·por·tun·ist** \-nəst\ *n.*

op·por·tu·ni·ty \ˌäp-r-'tü-nət-ē, -'tyü-\ *n.; pl.* **op·por·tu·ni·ties.** A suitable or convenient time to do something; a favorable chance; as, to have an *opportunity* to travel; to have little *opportunity* for recreation on school days.

op·pose \ə-ˈpōz\ *v.;* **op·posed; op·pos·ing.** **1** To put or set one person or thing against another. **2** To resist; to struggle against; as, to *oppose* a suggestion. — **be opposed to.** To be against; to disapprove of.

op·po·site \ˈäp-ə-zət, ˈäp-sət\ *adj.* **1** In front of; facing; as, the *opposite* side of the street. **2** Turned or moving in different directions; as, to travel by *opposite* routes. **3** As different as possible; contrary. Black is *opposite* to white. **4** Opposed; as, *opposite* sides of a question. — *n.* Any person or thing that is opposed, or very different. Soft is the *opposite* of hard. — **op·po·site·ly,** *adv.*

op·po·si·tion \ˌäp-ə-ˈzish-n\ *n.* **1** A setting opposite, or being set opposite. **2** The action of resisting anything; as, to offer *opposition* to a plan. **3** Any person or thing that opposes; especially, a political party opposed to the party in power.

op·press \ə-ˈpres\ *v.* **1** To weigh down; to burden in spirit as if with weight; as, to be *oppressed* by cares. **2** To crush by harsh rule; to treat cruelly or with too great severity; as, a country *oppressed* by a dictator's rule.

op·pres·sion \ə-ˈpresh-n\ *n.* **1** The act of oppressing or the state of being oppressed. **2** Cruel or unjust use of power or authority. **3** A sense of heaviness or obstruction in the body or mind; as, an *oppression* of spirits; a feeling of *oppression* in the chest.

op·pres·sive \ə-ˈpres-iv\ *adj.* **1** Unjustly severe, harsh, or burdensome; as, *oppressive* taxes. **2** Using oppression; tyrannical; cruel; as, *oppressive* rulers. **3** Causing a feeling of oppression; hard to bear; overpowering; as, *oppressive* heat. — **op·pres·sive·ly,** *adv.*

op·pres·sor \ə-ˈpres-r\ *n.* One that oppresses; especially, a cruel or unjust ruler.

op·pro·bri·ous \ə-ˈprōb-rē-əs\ *adj.* **1** Expressing opprobrium; abusive; reproachful; as, *opprobrious* words. **2** Bringing opprobrium; disgraceful; as, *opprobrious* behavior.

op·pro·bri·um \ə-ˈprōb-rē-əm\ *n.* **1** The disgrace that is brought by shameful behavior; infamy. **2** A cause of such disgrace.

op·tic \ˈäp-tik\ *adj.* Of or relating to the eye or to vision.

op·ti·cal \ˈäp-tik-l\ *adj.* **1** Relating to the science of optics. **2** Relating to vision; ocular; as, an *optical* illusion. **3** Made to help the eyesight, or to be used in examining the eyes; as, an *optical* instrument. — **op·ti·cal·ly** \-tik-l(-)ē\ *adv.*

op·ti·cian \äp-ˈtish-n\ *n.* A person who makes or sells eyeglasses and other optical instruments.

optic nerve. A sensory nerve transmitting visual impulses from the retina of the eye to the brain; the nerve of sight.

op·tics \ˈäp-tiks\ *n.* The science treating of the nature and properties of light, especially in relation to vision.

op·ti·mism \ˈäpt-m-ˌiz-m\ *n.* **1** Any belief that the world is the best possible or conceivable. **2** A natural inclination to be cheerful or hopeful about everything.

op·ti·mist \ˈäpt-m-əst\ *n.* A person given to optimism; one who sees all things as happening for the best; one who habitually looks on the bright side.

op·ti·mis·tic \ˌäpt-m-ˈis-tik\ *adj.* **1** Inclined to feel or believe that everything happens for the best; inclined to look on the bright side. **2** Cheerful; hopeful; as, to be *optimistic* about tomorrow's weather. — **op·ti·mis·ti·cal·ly** \-tik-l(-)ē\ *adv.*

op·ti·mum \ˈäpt-m-əm\ *n.; pl.* **op·ti·mums** \-m-əmz\ or **op·ti·ma** \-m-ə\. The best or most favorable quantity, degree, or condition. — *adj.* Most favorable for the end or purpose stated; best; as, *optimum* conditions of heat and moisture for growing orchids.

op·tion \ˈäpsh-n\ *n.* **1** The power or right to choose. Attending school is a matter in which children have no *option.* **2** That which is offered for choice or is chosen; as, to have music and art as *options* in the eighth grade. **3** The right to buy or sell something at a certain price during a stated period; as, to have a 90-day *option* on a house.

op·tion·al \ˈäpsh-n(-)əl\ *adj.* Permitting a choice; left to one's choice; not compulsory. — **op·tion·al·ly** \-n(-)ə-lē\ *adv.*

op·tom·e·trist \äp-ˈtäm-ə-trəst\ *n.* A person whose profession is the examination of the eyes for defects of vision and evidence of disease and the correction of defective vision by means other than drugs or surgery, usually the fitting of glasses. — **op·tom·e·try** \-ə-trē\ *n.*

op·u·lence \ˈäp-yə-lən(t)s\ *n.* **1** Wealth; riches. **2** Plenty; profusion.

op·u·lent \ˈäp-yə-lənt\ *adj.* **1** Wealthy. **2** Abundant; luxuriant; profuse; as, *opulent* vegetation; *opulent* harvests. — **op·u·lent·ly,** *adv.*

opus \ˈōp-əs\ *n.; pl.* **opus·es** \ˈōp-ə-səz\ or **opera** \ˈōp-r-ə, ˈäp-\. A work; especially, a musical composition or a set of compositions, often given an identifying number, usually in the order of its issue.

or \ər, r, (ˈ)ȯr\ *conj.* A word used: **1** To connect two words or groups of words that offer a choice; as, either fog *or* rain. **2** To connect two words or groups of words the second of which explains the first; as, a precipice *or* cliff; the bison *or* buffalo.

-or \ər; *sometimes* ˌȯr *or, especially in law terms,* ˈȯr\. A suffix that can mean: **1** Act, state, or quality, as in *error, fervor, pallor, rigor.* **2** A person or thing that, as in *actor, conductor, elevator, survivor.*

or·a·cle \ˈȯr-ək-l, ˈär-\ *n.* **1** In ancient Greece and Rome, the medium, as a priest or a priestess, through which a god supposedly revealed hidden knowledge or made known his purpose. **2** The place where such information was given out. **3** What was said by an oracle in reply to a question. **4** A person who gives very wise answers or advice. **5** Any wise or seemingly inspired answer or advice.

orac·u·lar \ȯ-ˈrak-yəl-r\ *adj.* **1** Of or relating to an oracle. **2** Like an oracle, as in wisdom, solemnity of manner, or obscurity. — **orac·u·lar·ly**, *adv.*

oral \'ōr-əl, 'ȯr-\ *adj.* **1** Spoken; using speech; not written; as, an *oral* agreement; an *oral* examination. **2** Of or relating to the mouth; as, *oral* hygiene.

— The word *verbal* is a synonym of *oral:* both of these terms refer to words and their use in communicating with others; *verbal* may apply to either written or spoken words; *oral* usually indicates spoken words only.

oral·ly \'ōr-ə-lē, 'ȯr-\ *adv.* **1** Through speech; as, to promise *orally* but not in writing. **2** Through the mouth; by mouth; as, a medicine for injection only, not to be taken *orally*.

or·ange \'ȯr-inj, 'är-, -ənj\ *n.* **1** The juicy, edible, yellow or reddish yellow fruit of an evergreen citrus tree with shiny leaves and fragrant, white flowers; the tree itself. **2** A reddish yellow color like that of a ripe orange.

or·ange·ade \ˌȯr-inj-'ād, ˌär-, -ənj-\ *n.* A drink made of orange juice, sugar, and water.

or·ange pe·koe \'pē-ˌkō\. A black tea from India and Ceylon.

orang·u·tan or **orang·ou·tang** \ə-'rang-ə-ˌtan(g)\ *n.* [From Malay *orang hutan* meaning literally "man of the forest".] A reddish brown anthropoid ape of the forests of Borneo and Sumatra, about two thirds as large as a gorilla.

ora·tion \ə-'rāsh-n\ *n.* A carefully prepared, dignified speech, especially one for a special occasion; as, a funeral *oration*.

or·a·tor \'ȯr-ət-r, 'är-\ *n.* One that delivers an oration; a public speaker, especially one who shows skill and power in speaking.

or·a·tor·i·cal \ˌȯr-ə-'tȯr-ik-l, ˌär-, -'tär-\ *adj.* **1** Of or relating to orators or oratory; as, an *oratorical* contest. **2** Suitable for an orator; as, an *oratorical* way of talking. — **or·a·tor·i·cal·ly** \-ik-l(-)ē\ *adv.*

or·a·to·rio \ˌȯr-ə-'tōr-ē-ˌō, ˌär-, -'tȯr-\ *n.; pl.* **or·a·to·ri·os.** A dramatic poem, usually on some subject taken from the Bible, set to music and sung by solo voices and chorus with orchestral accompaniment, but without scenery, costumes, or action.

or·a·to·ry \'ȯr-ə-ˌtōr-ē, 'är-, -ˌtȯr-ē\ *n.* **1** The art of speaking easily, powerfully, and skillfully in public. **2** Oratorical language.

or·a·to·ry \'ȯr-ə-ˌtōr-ē, 'är-, -ˌtȯr-ē\ *n.* A place set apart for prayer; a small chapel or room for private worship.

orb \'ȯrb\ *n.* A ball or globe; a sphere; especially, a heavenly body, as the sun or moon.

or·bit \'ȯr-bət\ *n.* **1** The eye socket. **2** The path taken by a heavenly body revolving around another body, as the earth around the sun, or by a man-made satellite, as one revolving around the earth. **3** Range or area of activity or influence; as, to move out of one's usual *orbit*. — *v.* **1** To revolve around; to travel in an orbit; as, a satellite *orbiting* the earth. **2** To travel in circles; to circle; as, a plane *orbiting* over a landing field. **3** To send up, as a man-made satellite from the earth, so as to revolve in an orbit.

or·bit·al \'ȯr-bət-l\ *adj.* Of or relating to an orbit; in an orbit; as, the *orbital* motion of the planets; an *orbital* rocket.

or·chard \'ȯrch-rd\ *n.* **1** A place where fruit trees are grown. **2** The trees in an orchard.

or·ches·tra \'ȯrk-əs-trə\ *n.* **1** A group of players on various musical instruments, especially stringed instruments. **2** The instruments used by an orchestra. **3** In a theater, the space used by a group of instrumental performers, usually just in front of the stage. **4** The front part or sometimes all of the main floor in a theater.

orchestra

orchestra, 3

or·ches·tral \ȯr-'kes-trəl\ *adj.* Having to do with, suitable for, or performed by an orchestra.

or·ches·trate \'ȯrk-əs-ˌtrāt\ *v.;* **or·ches·trat·ed; or·ches·trat·ing.** To arrange music for an orchestra.

or·ches·tra·tion \ˌȯrk-əs-'trāsh-n\ *n.* Arrangement or an arrangement of music for performance by an orchestra.

or·chid \'ȯrk-əd\ *n.* **1** Any of a large number of plants that have, usually, three-petaled flowers, with the middle petal enlarged into a lip and differing from the others in shape and color. **2** A flower of such a plant. **3** A soft, light purple color.

or·chis \'ȯrk-əs\ *n.* A member of the orchid family; especially, a plant of woodland areas of North America having spikes of irregular purple and white flowers.

or·dain \ȯr-'dān\ *v.* **1** To appoint, order, or decide upon; as, in the manner *ordained* by law. **2** To make a person a Christian minister or priest by a special ceremony.

or·deal \(')ȯr-'dēl, 'ȯr-ˌdēl\ *n.* **1** An old way of finding out the innocence or guilt of a person by requiring him to do some extremely dangerous thing, with failure or injury supposedly showing guilt. **2** Any severe test; a terrible experience.

or·der \'ȯrd-r\ *n.* **1** A group of people united in some formal way, as by living under the same religious rules, by having won the same distinction, or by loyalty to certain common interests and obligations; as, an *order* of monks; an *order* of knighthood. **2** The badge or insignia used by certain orders; as, to wear the Distinguished Service *Order*. **3** A rank or class in society; as, the lower *orders* of men. **4** A regular or harmonious arrangement; a system; as, the *order* of the seasons; alphabetical *order*. **5** The customary way of proceeding, as in a debate or a meeting; as, to raise a point of *order*. **6** General peace and quiet; a state of obedience to rules and regulations; as, to keep *order* in the classroom. **7** Normal condition; as, out of *order*. **8** The prevailing way of doing something in a particular period; as, the old *order* giving way to the new. **9** A command, rule, or authoritative direction; as, to obey *orders*. **10** A written direction to pay money to someone; as, to pay by money *order.* **11** A commission to buy, sell, or supply goods; as, an *order* for 500 blankets. **12** The things bought or sold; as, to ask the grocer to deliver the *order.* **13** A style of building or a type of column or pillar with the section of wall immediately above it; as, the three *orders* of Greek architecture. **14** One of the ranks or grades of the Christian ministry. **15** [usually in the plural] Also **holy orders.** The office or rank of priest; ordination to the priesthood. **16** A prescribed rite; an office; as, the *order* of confirmation. **17** A group of related animals or plants ranking in classification below a class and above a family. **18** Degree, as of a curve or equation. — **in order to.** For the purpose of. — **in order that.** For the purpose that. — **in short order.** Quickly; efficiently. — **on the order of.** Belonging to the class or kind of; as, cloth *on the order of* tweed. — **to order.** In fulfillment of an order given; as, shoes made *to order.*

— The word *system* is a synonym of *order: order* usually suggests a formal and regular arrangement of certain objects or actions, as in a harmonious or traditional pattern; *system* usually applies to a carefully planned and often complex arrangement that tries to establish the proper relationships between all the things brought together.

— *v.;* **or·dered**; **or·der·ing** \-r(-)ing\. **1** To put in order; to regulate; to dispose. **2** To give an order to; to command; to direct. **3** To give an order for; to place an order. **4** To put into a particular order; to arrange in a series or sequence.

or·der·ly \'ȯrd-r-lē\ *adj.* **1** In order; neat; as, an *orderly* room. **2** Obeying orders or rules; well-behaved; well-managed; as, an *orderly* meeting; *orderly* children. **3** Performed in good order; well-regulated; as, an *orderly* recitation by the class. — *n.; pl.* **or·der·lies.** **1** A soldier who attends a superior officer to carry orders and perform other services. **2** An attendant in a hospital who does general work. — **or·der·li·ness** \-lē-nəs\ *n.*

or·di·nal \'ȯrd-n(-)əl\ *adj.* Indicating order or succession. "First", "second", "third", etc. are *ordinal* numbers. — *n.* An ordinal number.

or·di·nance \'ȯrd-n(-)ən(t)s\ *n.* An order, decree, or law made by authority, especially one made by a town or city government.

or·di·nar·i·ly \,ȯrd-n-'er-ə-lē\ *adv.* **1** In an ordinary manner. **2** Usually; as, to go to bed *ordinarily* at nine o'clock.

or·di·nary \'ȯrd-n-,er-ē\ *adj.* **1** Usual; customary; regular; as, in the *ordinary* way of business; an *ordinary* day. **2** Neither good nor bad; not distinguished; as, an *ordinary* student. **3** Below the average; as, a very *ordinary* speech. — *n.; pl.* **or·di·nar·ies.** **1** Something that is ordinary, as in use or occurrence; as, a word usage that is out of the *ordinary.* **2** A tavern or eating house. — **in ordinary.** In actual and constant service.

or·di·nate \'ȯrd-n(-)ət\ *n.* **1** The distance of a point on a graph above or below the horizontal reference line, or abscissa. **2** The vertical reference line on a graph.

or·di·na·tion \,ȯrd-n-'āsh-n\ *n.* The act of ordaining or the condition of being ordained.

ord·nance \'ȯrd-nən(t)s\ *n.* Guns and ammunition for military use; especially, heavy guns; cannon.

or·dure \'ȯrj-r\ *n.* Dung; excrement.

ore \'ōr, 'ȯr\ *n.* Any material that is mined and worked to obtain the valuable metals that are a part of it; as, to get iron from iron *ore.*

or·gan \'ȯrg-n\ *n.* **1** Also **pipe organ.** A musical instrument played by means of one or more keyboards and having pipes sounded by air blown from a bellows. **2** Also **electric organ** or **electronic organ.** A musical instrument in which electric or electronic devices are employed to produce or amplify tones similar to those of a pipe organ. **3** A differentiated structure of a plant or animal that performs some specific function. Eyes are *organs* of sight. **4** Any means by which some important thing is done; as, courts of justice and other *organs* of government. **5** A medium of communication, as a newspaper.

pipe organ

or·gan·dy or **or·gan·die** \'ȯrg-n-dē\ *n.; pl.* **or·gan·dies.** A fine, thin muslin with a stiff finish, used especially for dresses and window curtains.

or·gan-grind·er \'ȯrg-n-,grīnd-r\ *n.* A person, especially a traveling street musician, who cranks a hand organ.

or·gan·ic \ȯr-'gan-ik\ *adj.* **1** Relating to an organ or a system of organs; especially, relating to the internal organs of the body. **2** Organized; as, an *organic* whole. **3** Belonging to the class of carbon compounds produced by plants and animals or related to or having the qualities of compounds of this class. Sugars, starches, and proteins are important *organic* compounds. **4** Of or relating to the branch of chemistry that deals with carbon and its compounds, especially with those that occur as a result of life processes. *Organic* chemistry could be called the chemistry of life. — **or·gan·i·cal·ly** \-ik-l(-)ē\ *adv.*

or·ga·nism \'ȯrg-n-,iz-m\ *n.* **1** An individual living being, as a person, animal, or plant, thought of as made up of a number of separate but related parts; as, the *organism* causing tuberculosis. **2** Anything that is like a living organism in having many related parts.

or·gan·ist \'ȯrg-n-əst\ *n.* A person who plays an organ.

or·ga·ni·za·tion \,ȯrg-n(-)ə-'zāsh-n\ *n.* **1** The act of organizing; as, to take part in the *organization* of a new club. **2** The condition or manner of being organized; as, to study the *organization* of the city government. **3** A group of persons united for some purpose; as, a business *organization;* charitable *organizations.*

or·ga·nize \'ȯrg-n-,īz\ *v.;* **or·ga·nized**; **or·ga·niz·ing.** To make separate parts into one united whole; to get a thing into working order; as, to *organize* a club; to *organize* a campaign to raise money.

or·ga·nized \'ȯrg-n-ˌīzd\ *adj.* **1** Having or based upon organization; as, *organized* labor; an *organized* effort. **2** Having or showing organic structure; as, certain highly *organized* plants and animals.

organ system. A group of organs acting in cooperation to perform a complex process, as digestion.

or·gy \'ȯr-jē\ *n.; pl.* **or·gies. 1** [usually in the plural] In ancient Greece and Rome, secret rites in honor of certain gods, often celebrated with wild singing and dancing. **2** Excessive indulgence in some activity.

ori·el \'ōr-ē-əl, 'ȯr-\ *n.* A curved or angular window built out from a wall, and sometimes supported by brackets; a bay window.

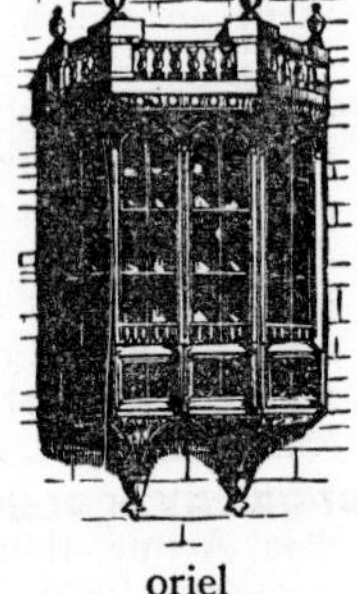
oriel

Ori·ent \'ōr-ē-ənt, 'ȯr-, -ˌent\ *n.* [From medieval English, there borrowed from medieval French, where it is derived from Latin *orient-*, the stem of *oriens* meaning "rising sun", "east", a noun made from the present participle of *oriri* meaning "to rise".] The East; the countries of Asia, especially of eastern Asia.

ori·ent \'ōr-ē-ˌent, 'ȯr-\ *v.* **1** To cause to face toward the east. **2** To set right; to give a sense of direction; to enable to deal with a new situation; as, to *orient* new students.

ori·en·tal \ˌōr-ē-'ent-l, ˌȯr-\ *adj.* [usually with a capital] Of or relating to the Orient; as, *Oriental* countries; an *oriental* rug. — *n.* [with a capital] A member of one of the native races of the Orient; especially, a Chinese or Japanese.

ori·en·tate \'ōr-ē-ən-ˌtāt, 'ȯr-\ *v.;* **ori·en·tat·ed; ori·en·tat·ing.** To orient.

ori·en·ta·tion \ˌōr-ē-ən-'tāsh-n, ˌȯr-\ *n.* **1** The act of orienting or the state of being oriented. **2** A knowledge of one's position with relation to environment or to some particular person, thing, or principle.

or·i·fice \'ȯr-ə-fəs, 'är-\ *n.* A mouth; an opening, as of a tube or pipe.

or·i·gin \'ȯr-əj-n, 'är-\ *n.* **1** The beginning, source, or cause of a thing. **2** A person's parentage or ancestry; birth.

orig·i·nal \ə-'rij-n(-)əl\ *adj.* **1** Of or relating to the origin or beginning; first; earliest; as, the *original* part of an old house; the *original* inhabitants. **2** Not copied from anything else; not translated; new; as, an *original* painting; an *original* idea. **3** Able to think up new things; inventive; as, an *original* mind. — *n.* A thing of which all similar things are copies; as, the *original* of a letter. — **orig·i·nal·ly** \-n(-)ə-lē\ *adv.*

orig·i·nal·i·ty \ə-ˌrij-n-'al-ət-ē\ *n.* **1** The quality of being original, or new; as, an idea that has *originality*. **2** Power or ability to do, think, or act in ways that are new; as, an artist of great *originality*.

orig·i·nate \ə-'rij-n-ˌāt\ *v.;* **orig·i·nat·ed; orig·i·nat·ing. 1** To begin a thing; to produce something new; as, to *originate* a game. **2** To begin; to come into existence; as, a custom that *originated* in ancient times. — **orig·i·na·tion** \ə-ˌrij-n-'āsh-n\ *n.*

orig·i·na·tor \ə-'rij-n-ˌāt-r\ *n.* One that originates.

ori·ole \'ōr-ē-ˌōl, 'ȯr-, -ē-əl\ *n.* **1** An Old World yellow and black bird related to the crow. **2** An American songbird related to the blackbird and bobolink, as the **Bal·ti·more oriole** \'bȯlt-m-ˌōr, -ˌȯr\, the male of which is orange and black, and the smaller **orchard oriole,** which is chestnut and black.

or·i·son \'ȯr-əs-n, 'är-, -əz-n\ *n.* A prayer.

or·na·ment \'ȯr-nə-mənt\ *n.* **1** Anything that adorns or adds beauty; a decoration; as, a table *ornament*. **2** Addition of something that beautifies; decoration; as, added by way of *ornament*. — \-ˌment\ *v.* To adorn; to decorate. — **or·na·men·ta·tion** \ˌȯr-nə-mən-'tāsh-n\ *n.*

or·na·men·tal \ˌȯr-nə-'ment-l\ *adj.* Serving to ornament; decorative; as, *ornamental* ironwork. — **or·na·men·tal·ly** \-'ment-l-ē\ *adv.*

or·nate \ȯr-'nāt\ *adj.* Decorated in an elaborate way. — **or·nate·ly,** *adv.* — **or·nate·ness,** *n.*

or·ni·thol·o·gist \ˌȯr-nə-'thäl-ə-jəst\ *n.* A person who studies birds.

or·ni·thol·o·gy \ˌȯr-nə-'thäl-ə-jē\ *n.* The study of birds. — **or·ni·tho·log·i·cal** \-thə-'läj-ik-l\ *adj.*

or·phan \'ȯrf-n\ *n.* A child whose parents are dead. — *adj.* For the use of orphans; as, an *orphan* asylum. — *v.;* **or·phaned; or·phan·ing** \-n(-)ing\. To cause to become an orphan; as, a man who was *orphaned* in childhood.

or·phan·age \'ȯrf-n(-)ij\ *n.* An institution for the care of orphans; a home for orphans.

or·ris \'ȯr-əs, 'är-\ *n.* **1** A European iris. **2** The rootstock of this plant.

or·ris·root \'ȯr-əs-ˌrüt, 'är-, -ˌru̇t\ *n.* The rootstock of the orris, powdered for use in such products as perfumes and dentifrices.

or·tho·don·tics \ˌȯr-thə-'dän-tiks\ or **or·tho·don·tia** \-'dänch-ə\ *n.* Dentistry dealing with the irregularity of teeth, especially the teeth of children. — **or·tho·don·tic** \-'dän-tik\ *adj.*

or·tho·dox \'ȯr-thə-ˌdäks\ *adj.* **1** Holding standard beliefs, especially religious beliefs; as, an *orthodox* Christian. **2** Approved as measuring up to some standard; usual; conventional; as, the *orthodox* style of dress for a church wedding. — **or·tho·doxy** \-ˌdäks-ē\ *n.*

or·tho·graph·ic \ˌȯr-thə-'graf-ik\ or **or·tho·graph·i·cal** \-ik-l\ *adj.* Of or relating to orthography. — **or·tho·graph·i·cal·ly** \-ik-l(-)ē\ *adv.*

or·thog·ra·phy \ȯr-'thäg-rə-fē\ *n.; pl.* **or·thog·ra·phies. 1** Correct spelling. **2** The study of letters and spelling. **3** A way or style of spelling; as, 17th century *orthography*.

or·tho·pe·dics \ˌȯr-thə-'pēd-iks\ *n.* Correction or

prevention of deformities, especially in children. — **or·tho·pe·dic** \-'pēd-ik\ *adj.* — **or·tho·pe·dist** \-'pēd-əst\ *n.*

or·thop·ter·ous \ȯr-'thäpt-r(-)əs\ *adj.* Belonging to an order of insects including the grasshoppers, locusts, and crickets which have biting mouth parts and, usually, two pairs of wings, the membranous hind wings folding under the front pair.

-ory \ˌōr-ē, ˌȯr-ē\. A suffix that can mean: **1** Having to do with; serving to, as in *prohibitory.* **2** The place of or for, as in *observatory.*

or·yx \'ȯr-iks, 'är-\ *n.; pl.* **or·yx·es** or **or·yx.** A large straight-horned African antelope.

o's. Pl. of *o.*

os·cil·late \'äs-l-ˌāt\ *v.;* **os·cil·lat·ed; os·cil·lat·ing. 1** To move or swing backward and forward like a pendulum; to fluctuate between fixed limits. **2** To waver between opposing beliefs or opinions.

os·cil·la·tion \ˌäs-l-'āsh-n\ *n.* **1** The act or fact of oscillating. **2** [in the plural] Fluctuations in an electric circuit, consisting of the flow of charges of electricity alternately in opposite directions but not at regular intervals.

os·cil·la·tor \'äs-l-ˌāt-r\ *n.* **1** A person or thing that oscillates. **2** Any device for producing electric oscillations; especially, a radio transmitter that produces radio waves.

os·cil·lo·scope \ə-'sil-ə-ˌskōp\ *n.* An instrument that records sound waves in the form of waves of light on a fluorescent screen.

os·cu·late \'äs-kyə-ˌlāt\ *v.;* **os·cu·lat·ed; os·cu·lat·ing.** To kiss. — **os·cu·la·tion** \ˌäs-kyə-'lāsh-n\ *n.*

osier \'ōzh-r\ *n.* **1** A willow tree with twigs that bend easily and are used for making articles, as furniture and baskets. **2** A twig of this tree.

os·mo·sis \äs-'mō-səs, äz-\ *n.* The passage of material, especially a solvent, through a partially permeable barrier from a region of higher to one of lower concentration, as through a plant or animal cell membrane. — **os·mot·ic** \-'mät-ik\ *adj.*

os·prey \'äs-prē, -ˌprā\ *n.; pl.* **os·preys** or **os·prey.** A large hawk that feeds chiefly on fish.

os·si·fy \'äs-ə-ˌfī\ *v.;* **os·si·fied** \-ˌfīd\; **os·si·fy·ing. 1** To change into bone; to form bone. **2** To become set. — **os·si·fi·ca·tion** \ˌäs-ə-fə-'kāsh-n\ *n.*

os·ten·si·ble \äs-'ten(t)s-əb-l, əs-\ *adj.* Shown outwardly; declared; apparent; as, his *ostensible* reason. — **os·ten·si·bly** \-ə-blē\ *adv.*

os·ten·ta·tion \ˌäs-tən-'tāsh-n\ *n.* Pretentious display; unnecessary show.

os·ten·ta·tious \ˌäs-tən-'tā-shəs\ *adj.* Marked by or fond of unnecessary display. — **os·ten·ta·tious·ly,** *adv.*

os·te·o·path \'äs-tē-ə-ˌpath\ *n.* A person who practices osteopathy.

os·te·op·a·thy \ˌäs-tē-'äp-ə-thē\ *n.* A method of treating diseases that places emphasis on manipulation, especially of bones, but does not exclude other treatment, as the use of medicine and surgery.

ost·ler \'äs-lər\ *n.* A stableman; a hostler.

os·tra·cism \'äs-trə-ˌsiz-m\ *n.* **1** In ancient Greece, a method of banishing a person temporarily, by popular vote without a trial, when he was considered politically dangerous to the state. **2** Exclusion of a person, by the action of a group of people, from association with the group.

os·tra·cize \'äs-trə-ˌsīz\ *v.;* **os·tra·cized; os·tra·ciz·ing.** [From Greek *ostrakizein* meaning "to vote to banish someone", and derived from *ostrakon* meaning "earthen vessel", "fragment of pottery", such fragments being used in the voting in ancient Greece.] To banish; to exclude from association with a group of people.

os·trich \'äs-trich, 'ȯs-, *sometimes* -trij\ *n.* A very large bird, often weighing 300 pounds, of Africa and Arabia, that is very swift-footed but is unable to fly.

oth·er \'əth-r\ *adj.* **1** Not the one or ones just mentioned or thought of; different; as, some *other* person; under *other* conditions. **2** Additional. There won't be room if *other* guests come. **3** Second; alternate; as, every *other* page. — *pron.* **1** The other one or ones; the remaining one; as, to lift one foot and then the *other.* **2** A different person; another; as, someone or *other;* to see what *others* do.

oth·er·wise \'əth-r-ˌwīz\ *adv.* **1** In another way; differently; in other ways; as, to hear *otherwise.* **2** In other respects; as, the *otherwise* busy street. **3** In different circumstances; else. The boy must have been ill, *otherwise* he would not have been absent.

ot·ter \'ät-r\ *n.; pl.* **ot·ters** or **ot·ter. 1** A fish-eating animal with webbed feet and dark brown fur that, when dressed, resembles the fur of a beaver. **2** The fur of this animal.

Ot·to·man \'ät-ə-mən\ *adj.* Turkish. — *n.; pl.* **Ot·to·mans** \-mənz\. **1** A Turk. **2** [with a small letter] A low padded stool; a footstool.

ouch \'au̇ch\ *interj.* An exclamation expressing sharp and sudden pain.

ought \'ȯt\ *v.* **1** To be bound or obligated by duty or conscience. Children *ought* to obey their parents. **2** To be ideally right or proper; as, a world that *ought* to be better than it is. **3** To be expected or probable; as, a disease that *ought* to be conquered soon; the team that *ought* to have won. **4** To require; to need; as, a shoe that *ought* to be mended.

☞ A past sense with *ought* is made clear by putting the following infinitive in the perfect tense; as, a party to which she *ought* to have gone.

oughtn't \'ȯt-nt\. A contraction of *ought not.*

ounce \'au̇n(t)s\ *n.* [From medieval English, there borrowed from medieval French, where it was derived from Latin *uncia* meaning literally "a twelfth" — see *inch.*] **1** The sixteenth part of a pound in common weight. **2** The twelfth part of a pound in the special systems used for weighing gold, silver, and drugs. **3** A small quantity; a little; as, an *ounce* of prevention.

our \(')är, (')au̇r, (')ar\ *adj.* Of or belonging to us; done, given, or felt by us; as, *our* house; *our* fault.

ours \'au̇rz, 'ärz, 'ȧrz\ *pron.* The form of the word *we* that is used to show possession when no noun follows. The book is *ours.*

our·selves \är-'selvz, au̇r-, ȧr-\ *pron.* A form of the word *we* or *us* used to give emphasis or to show that the subject and object of a verb are the same persons. We *ourselves* can do it. We have fooled *ourselves.*

-ous \əs\. A suffix that can mean: **1** Full of, abounding in, having, as in *poisonous, joyous.* **2** Like, resembling, as in *bulbous, riotous.*

ousel. Variant of *ouzel.*

oust \'au̇st\ *v.* To force or drive out, as from office or from possession of something; to expel; as, to *oust* a corrupt official.

out \'au̇t\ *adv.* **1** In a direction away from the inside or the center; as, to look *out* of a window. **2** Away, as from home, business, or proper place; as, to step *out.* **3** In a manner causing loss of power or control; as, to vote the party *out* of office. **4** Beyond the point of concealment or control; as, to let a secret *out.* **5** To the surface; as, a fish leaping *out* of the water. **6** To the point of being completed or exhausted; as, a plan that was well worked *out;* worn *out.* — *adj.* **1** Beyond the limits or range of; unusual; as, *out* of the ordinary; *out* sizes. **2** Moving or placed out; as, a ship three days *out* of port. **3** Not in place or position; as, a box with the bottom *out.* **4** Not at home; as, to be *out* for the evening. **5** Not burning; as, the fire is *out.* **6** Unconscious; as, a boxer who was *out.* **7** Ended; as, before the week is *out.* **8** No longer in fashion or use; as, a style that is *out.* **9** Made public; as, a secret that is *out;* the latest edition, *out* today. **10** No longer in office; as, a party that is *out.* **11** No longer in possession; as, *out* of milk; *out* of work. **12** In baseball, no longer at bat. — *n.* **1** [in the plural] A disagreement; as, to be at *outs* with someone. **2** In baseball, the act of putting a player out or the state or fact of having been put out. — *v.* To become public. It is said that the truth will *out.*

out-. A prefix that can mean: **1** Beyond the boundaries, outer, as in *outside, outbuilding.* **2** Away from the center or source, outward, as in *outburst, outbound.* **3** Passing beyond, exceeding, as in *outnumber, outrank.*

out-and-out \'au̇t-n-ˌau̇t\ *adj.* Complete; thoroughgoing; as, an *out-and-out* rascal.

out·bid \(')au̇t-'bid\ *v.;* **out·bid; out·bid·ding.** To make a higher bid or offer than.

out·board \'au̇t-ˌbōrd, -ˌbȯrd\ *adj.* Outside the line of the hull of a boat; as, *outboard* rigging. — *adv.* Toward the hull of a boat; nearer the side than the center; as, to swing the davits *outboard.* — **outboard motor.** An engine with a propeller attached, which can be fixed to the stern of a small boat.

out·bound \'au̇t-'bau̇nd\ *adj.* Outward bound; as, an *outbound* boat; *outbound* traffic.

out·brave \(')au̇t-'brāv\ *v.;* **out·braved; out·brav·ing.** **1** To face or resist defiantly; as, to *outbrave* the enemy. **2** To excel in bravery; as, to *outbrave* all the others in taking dangerous ski jumps.

out·break \'au̇t-ˌbrāk\ *n.* **1** A breaking out; as, at the *outbreak* of the war. **2** Something that breaks out, as an outburst of feeling, an epidemic, or a rebellion.

out·breed·ing \'au̇t-ˌbrēd-ing\ *n.* The breeding or mating of individuals or stocks that are relatively unrelated.

out·build·ing \'au̇t-ˌbil-ding\ *n.* A building separate from and smaller than the main one.

out·burst \'au̇t-ˌbərst\ *n.* A bursting out, as of gunfire or strong feeling.

out·cast \'au̇t-ˌkast\ *adj.* Cast out; exiled; rejected. — *n.* **1** One that is cast out, expelled, or exiled, as from home, society, or country. **2** A vagabond; a pariah.

out·caste \'au̇t-ˌkast\ *n.* Among the Hindus, one who has been expelled from his caste for violation of its rules or one not born into a caste, as an untouchable.

out·class \(')au̇t-'klas\ *v.* To excel; to surpass so decisively as to appear of a higher class; as, a football team that was hopelessly *outclassed.*

out·come \'au̇t-ˌkəm\ *n.* Result; consequence; as, the *outcome* of a contest.

out·crop \'au̇t-ˌkräp\ *n.* **1** The coming out of a layer of earth, or stratum, to the surface of the ground. **2** The part that appears in this manner. — *v.;* **out·cropped; out·crop·ping.** To come to the surface, as a stratum. — **out·crop·ping,** *n.*

out·cry \'au̇t-ˌkrī\ *n.; pl.* **out·cries.** A loud cry, as of distress or alarm.

out·dat·ed \(')au̇t-'dāt-əd\ *adj.* Out of fashion; outmoded.

out·dis·tance \(')au̇t-'dis-tən(t)s\ *v.;* **out·dis·tanced; out·dis·tanc·ing.** To go faster than; to leave behind; to outstrip.

out·do \(')au̇t-'dü\ *v.;* **out·did** \-'did\; **out·done** \-'dən\; **out·do·ing** \-'dü-ing\. To excel; to surpass.

out·door \'au̇t-ˌdōr, -ˌdȯr\ *adj.* Used, belonging, or done outside of houses or buildings; as, *outdoor* exercise.

out·doors \'au̇t-'dōrz, -'dȯrz\ *adv.* Outside a house or building; in or to the open; as, to play *outdoors.* — *n.* The open; the world exclusive of houses and buildings; as, to exercise in the great *outdoors.*

out·er \'au̇t-r\ *adj.* Being on the outside; external; farthest or farther from the interior; as, an *outer* wall; the *outer* layers of tissue.

outer ear. The outer, visible portion of the ear in higher vertebrates, whose function is to collect and direct sound waves toward the ear drum by means of the membrane-lined canal which extends from the external opening of the outer ear through the temporal bone.

out·er·most \'au̇t-r-ˌmōst\ *adj.* Farthest outward; as, the *outermost* reaches of space.

outer space. **1** The regions immediately outside the earth's atmosphere. **2** Interplanetary or interstellar space.

out·field \'au̇t-ˌfēld\ *n.* **1** The part of a baseball field between the foul lines and beyond the diamond. **2** Also **out·field·ers** \-ˌfēld-rz\. The players in the outfield.

out·fit \'au̇t-ˌfit\ *n.* **1** The articles forming the equipment for some special purpose; as, a camping *outfit;* a brand-new sports *outfit.* **2** A group of persons working together or associated in the same undertaking; as, soldiers belonging to the same *outfit.* — *v.;* **out·fit·ted**; **out·fit·ting**. To furnish with equipment; to equip; as, to *outfit* an expedition. — **out·fit·ter** \-ˌfit-r\ *n.*

out·flank \(ˈ)au̇t-'flangk\ *v.* To go, extend, or be beyond the flank or flanks of, as an army. The general maneuvered to *outflank* the enemy.

out·gen·er·al \(ˈ)au̇t-'jen-r(-)əl\ *v.;* **out·gen·er·aled** or **out·gen·er·alled**; **out·gen·er·al·ing** or **out·gen·er·al·ling**. To surpass in military skill or strategy; to outmaneuver.

out·go \'au̇t-ˌgō\ *n.; pl.* **out·goes**. Outlay; money spent. If a budget is to balance, income must equal *outgo.*

out·go·ing \'au̇t-ˌgō-ing\ *adj.* **1** Going out; departing; outward bound; as, an *outgoing* tide; an *outgoing* train. **2** Friendly; easy to approach; as, a very *outgoing* person.

out·grow \(ˈ)au̇t-'grō\ *v.;* **out·grew** \-'grü\; **out·grown** \-'grōn\; **out·grow·ing. 1** To grow larger than; to surpass in growing; as, a plant that *outgrows* another. **2** To grow out of or away from; to grow too large for; as, to *outgrow* one's clothes.

out·growth \'au̇t-ˌgrōth\ *n.* Something that grows out or develops from something else; an offshoot; a product; as, a plan that was the *outgrowth* of the committee's efforts.

out·guess \(ˈ)au̇t-'ges\ *v.* **1** To guess more accurately than. **2** To outwit.

out·house \'au̇t-ˌhau̇s\ *n.; pl.* **out·hous·es** \-ˌhau̇-zəz\. An outbuilding; especially, an outdoor toilet.

out·ing \'au̇t-ing\ *n.* A brief trip, especially in the open; on excursion; as, the annual Sunday School *outing.*

out·land·er \'au̇t-ˌland-r\ *n.* A foreigner; an alien; a stranger.

out·land·ish \'au̇t-'lan-dish\ *adj.* Of foreign appearance or manner; strange; unusual; as, *outlandish* clothes.

out·last \(ˈ)au̇t-'last\ *v.* To last longer than.

out·law \'au̇t-ˌlȯ\ *n.* **1** A person who is deprived of the protection of the law, as by his own illegal acts. **2** A lawless person; a fugitive from justice; a criminal. — *v.* **1** To deprive, as a known criminal, of the protection of the law. **2** To bar; to rule out as unfair or not lawful; as, to *outlaw* war. — **out·law·ry** \-ˌlȯ-rē\ *n.*

out·lay \'au̇t-ˌlā\ *n.* **1** The act of laying out, or spending, as money. **2** That which is spent, especially money.

out·let \'au̇t-ˌlet, -lət\ *n.* **1** A place or opening through which something is let out; a passage out; an exit. **2** A means or way of escape; as, an *outlet* for the emotions. **3** A place, as in a wall, at which an electrical device can be plugged into the wiring system. **4** In business, a market for a product or an agency, as a store or a dealer, through which a product is marketed.

out·line \'au̇t-ˌlīn\ *n.* **1** A line that traces or forms the outer limits of an object or figure and shows its shape. **2** A drawing or picture giving only the outlines of a thing; this method of drawing; as, to draw something in *outline.* **3** A brief statement or sketch of something, as a plan, a speech, or a composition, often in the form of a series of numbered main divisions and subdivisions. **4** A short summary of the chief points or features of a subject; as, an *outline* of world history. — *v.;* **out·lined**; **out·lin·ing. 1** To draw or trace the outline of. **2** To indicate by or as if by an outline; as, to *outline* a plan.

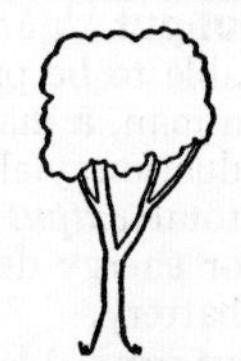
outline of tree

out·live \(ˈ)au̇t-'liv\ *v.;* **out·lived**; **out·liv·ing.** To live beyond, or longer than; to outlast; to survive.

out·look \'au̇t-ˌlu̇k\ *n.* **1** A place from which one watches; a lookout. **2** What is seen by a person who looks out; a view; as, the *outlook* from a window. **3** A particular way of thinking about or looking at a thing; as, a person with a broad *outlook.* **4** Prospect for the future; as, the *outlook* for business.

out·ly·ing \'au̇t-ˌlī-ing\ *adj.* Lying or located at a distance; far from a central point; remote; as, an *outlying* suburb.

out·ma·neu·ver \ˌau̇t-mə-'nüv-r, -'nyüv-r\ *v.;* **out·ma·neu·vered**; **out·ma·neu·ver·ing** \-r(-)ing\. To surpass in maneuvering; to get an advantage over by maneuvering.

out·ma·noeu·vre. Variant of *outmaneuver.*

out·mod·ed \(ˈ)au̇t-'mōd-əd\ *adj.* Left behind by changes in fashion; no longer accepted or approved; as, *outmoded* styles; *outmoded* beliefs.

out·most \'au̇t-ˌmōst\ *adj.* Farthest outward.

out·num·ber \(ˈ)au̇t-'nəm-br\ *v.;* **out·num·bered**; **out·num·ber·ing** \-br(-)ing\. To be more than in number. The boys in the class *outnumbered* the girls.

out-of-date \'au̇t-ə(v)-'dāt\ *adj.* No longer in use; outmoded; unfashionable; as, *out-of-date* clothes.

out-of-door \'au̇t-ə(v)-'dōr, -'dor\ *adj.* Outdoor.

out-of-doors \'au̇t-ə(v)-'dōrz, -'dȯrz\ *adj.* Outdoor. — *n.* Outdoors.

out-of-the-way \'au̇t-ə(v)-t͟hə-'wā\ *adj.* **1** Away from the lines of travel; off the beaten path; as, to live in an *out-of-the-way* village. **2** Not commonly found or met; unusual; as, a collection of *out-of-the-way* books about magic.

out·pa·tient \'au̇t-ˌpāsh-nt\ *n.* A person who receives treatment from a hospital without becoming a resident.

out·play \(ˈ)au̇t-'plā\ *v.* To play better than.

out·post \'aůt-ˌpōst\ *n.* **1** A soldier or soldiers stationed at some distance from a halted military force or a camp as a guard against enemy attack. **2** The position occupied by such a guard. **3** A settlement on a frontier; any outlying settlement.

out·pour·ing \'aůt-ˌpōr-ing, -ˌpȯr-\ *n.* A pouring out; an outburst, as of strong feeling.

out·put \'aůt-ˌpůt\ *n.* **1** The amount produced or able to be produced, usually in a stated time, by a man, a machine, a factory, or an industry; production; yield; as, the daily *output* of a factory; the total *output* of the nation's steel mills. **2** Power or energy delivered, as by an engine or a storage battery.

out·rage \'aůt-ˌrāj\ *n.* A violent or shameful wrong; a violation of right and decency. — *v.;* **out·raged**; **out·rag·ing.** To subject to violent injury or abuse; to offend against what is right, decent, or just.

out·ra·geous \aůt-'rā-jəs\ *adj.* Beyond all bounds of decency or justice; extremely offensive, insulting, or shameful; shocking; as, *outrageous* behavior. — **out·ra·geous·ly**, *adv.*

out·rank \(')aůt-'rangk\ *v.* To rank higher than; to exceed in importance.

out·rid·er \'aůt-ˌrīd-r\ *n.* A servant riding on a horse beside a carriage.

out·rig·ger \'aůt-ˌrig-r\ *n.* **1** Any projecting board or beam attached for temporary or special use, as to a ship's mast. **2** A projecting device fastened at the side or sides of a boat, as a canoe, to prevent upsetting. **3** A boat equipped with such a device.

out·right \(')aůt-'rīt\ *adv.* **1** At once; immediately; as, killed *outright.* **2** Completely and all at one time; in one transaction; as, to buy a business *outright.* **3** Openly; without restraint or concealment; as, to tell someone *outright* that he is at fault. — \'aůt-ˌrīt\ *adj.* **1** Direct; straightforward; as, a frank, *outright* manner; an *outright* refusal. **2** Complete; thorough; as, an instance of *outright* dishonesty.

out·run \(')aůt-'rən\ *v.;* **out·ran** \-'ran\; **out·run**; **out·run·ning.** **1** To run or travel faster than. **2** To get ahead of; to go beyond; to exceed; as, a readiness to spend money that far *outran* his ability to earn it.

out·sell \(')aůt-'sel\ *v.;* **out·sold** \-'sōld\; **out·sell·ing.** **1** To sell more than. **2** To surpass in salesmanship.

out·set \'aůt-ˌset\ *n.* A beginning; a start. From the *outset,* the discussion held everybody's attention.

out·shine \(')aůt-'shīn\ *v.;* **out·shone** \-'shōn, -'shän\; **out·shin·ing** \-'shī-ning\. To shine more brightly than; to excel; as, to *outshine* one's classmates in arithmetic.

out·side \(')aůt-'sīd, 'aůt-ˌsīd\ *n.* **1** The outer part, end, side, or surface; the exterior; as, the *outside* of a cup. **2** The furthest limit, as in number or length of time. It will take a week at the *outside.* — *adj.* **1** Of or on the outside; outer; as, the *outside* wall of a house. **2** Coming from without; not belonging to a place or group; as, *outside* influences. — *prep.* On the outside of; beyond the limits of; as, to wait *outside* the house. — \aůt-'sīd\ *adv.* On or to the outside; outdoors; as, to go *outside.*

out·sid·er \aůt-'sīd-r\ *n.* A person who does not belong to a particular group.

out·size \'aůt-ˌsīz, -'sīz\ *n.* A size larger than standard; especially, a ready-made article of dress larger than standard size. — *adj.* Also **out·sized** \-ˌsīzd, -'sīzd\. Larger than standard; very large; as, helicopters looking like *outsize* insects; an *outsize* job.

out·skirts \'aůt-ˌskərts\ *n. pl.* The outlying parts of a place or town; the edges or borders.

out·smart \(')aůt-'smärt, -'smȧrt\ *v.* To outwit.

outsold. Past tense and past part. of *outsell.*

out·spo·ken \'aůt-'spōk-n\ *adj.* Speaking or spoken openly or bluntly; frank; blunt; as, *outspoken* criticism; a very *outspoken* man.

out·spread \(')aůt-'spred\ *v.;* **out·spread**; **out·spread·ing.** To spread out or stretch out.

out·stand·ing \'aůt-'stan-ding\ *adj.* **1** Standing out clearly; notable; conspicuous; as, an *outstanding* talent. **2** Unpaid; as, an *outstanding* debt.

out·stand·ing·ly \'aůt-'stan-ding-lē\ *adv.* In a conspicuous or notable manner; as, to be *outstandingly* good in sports.

out·stretched \'aůt-'strecht\ *adj.* Stretched out or forth; as, *outstretched* arms.

out·strip \(')aůt-'strip\ *v.;* **out·stripped**; **out·strip·ping.** **1** To go faster than; to leave behind; as, to *outstrip* all others in a race. **2** To surpass; to excel.

out·ward \'aůt-wərd\ *adv.* **1** From the inside to the outside; out; away from a place; as, *outward* bound. **2** On the outside; outwardly. — *adj.* **1** On, of, or having to do with the outside; outer; as, *outward* appearances. **2** Outward bound; outgoing; as, an *outward* train. **3** Showing outwardly; visible; as, *outward* signs of character.

out·ward·ly \'aůt-wərd-lē\ *adv.* On the outside; on the surface; as, to be *outwardly* calm.

out·wards \'aůt-wərdz\ *adv.* Outward.

out·wear \(')aůt-'war, -'wer\ *v.;* **out·wore** \-'wōr, -'wȯr\; **out·worn** \-'wōrn, -'wȯrn\; **out·wear·ing.** To wear or last longer than; as, a fabric that *outwears* most others.

out·weigh \(')aůt-'wā\ *v.* **1** To be heavier than. **2** To be more important than; as, a fact that *outweighed* all the rest.

out·wit \(')aůt-'wit\ *v.;* **out·wit·ted**; **out·wit·ting.** To get the better of by cleverness.

out·work \'aůt-ˌwərk\ *n.* A less important defensive structure beyond the main body of a fortification. — \(')aůt-'wərk\ *v.* To exceed in working; to work more than.

out·worn \'aůt-'wōrn, -'wȯrn\ *adj.* Worn out; out-of-date; old; as, *outworn* clothes; *outworn* ideas.

ou·zel or **ou·sel** \'üz-l\ *n.* **1** A European thrush related to the blackbird. **2** Any of certain other thrushes.

ova Pl. of *ovum*.

oval \'ō-vl\ *adj.* Having the shape of a hen's egg; as, an *oval* figure. — *n.* Something oval.

oval

ova·ry \'ō-v-r(-)ē\ *n.; pl.* **ova·ries. 1** The organ of the body in female animals in which eggs are produced. **2** The part of a plant in which seeds are produced. — **ovar·i·an** \ō-'ver-ē-ən\ *adj.*

ovate \'ō-ˌvāt\ *adj.* Oval.

ova·tion \ō-'vāsh-n\ *n.* A public expression of praise; enthusiastic applause. The returning general was given an *ovation*.

ov·en \'əv-n\ *n.* A heated chamber, as in a stove, for baking, heating, or drying.

ov·en·bird \'əv-n-ˌbərd\ *n.* A large olive-green American warbler that builds a dome-shaped nest on the ground.

over \'ō-v-r\ *prep.* **1** Above in position; higher than. The sky is *over* us. **2** Above or superior to in authority; as, to preside *over* a meeting; to have an advantage *over* someone. **3** More than. The cost will be *over* five dollars. **4** Here and there upon the surface of; on or along the surface of; as, to wander *over* the earth; to skim *over* the ice. **5** Along the length of; as, to motor *over* a course. **6** Across; to the other side of; as, to jump *over* a brook. **7** During the time of; throughout; as, to read a book *over* the weekend. **8** During occupation with; as, chatting *over* the coffee cups. **9** On account of; as, to laugh *over* one's mistakes. **10** Beyond the top or edge of; down from; as, to fall *over* a cliff. **11** By means of; as, to hear the news *over* a radio. — *adv.* **1** Above; as, hanging directly *over*. **2** To the other side; across. The traitor went *over* to the enemy. **3** Away from an upright position. The tree fell *over*. **4** So as to bring the under part up or out; as, to turn a stone *over*. **5** Across the brim; down from the top, edge, or brim. The water in the glass ran *over*. **6** Beyond, above, or in excess of a certain quantity or limit; as, boys of 12 years or *over*. **7** From beginning to end; as, a dress covered *over* with jewels. **8** Again; as, to do the work *over*. — *adj.* **1** Upper; covering; superior; as, an *over* curtain. **2** Excessive; surplus. **3** Having reached the opposite side. The first boat is already *over*. **4** Ended. The play is *over*.

over-. A prefix that can mean: **1** Above in place or station; superior, as in *overhead*, *overlord*. **2** Across, on, or covering the surface, as in *overleap*, *overcloud*. **3** So as to exceed or surpass, to an excessive degree, as in *overtime*, *overeat*.

over·a·bun·dance \ˌō-v-r-ə-'bən-dən(t)s\ *n.* More than an abundance; an excess.

over·act \ˌō-v-r-'akt\ *v.* To exaggerate in acting; to overplay a role.

over·ac·tive \ˌō-v-r-'ak-tiv\ *adj.* Excessively active. — **over·ac·tiv·i·ty** \-ak-'tiv-ət-ē\ *n.*

over·all \'ō-v-r-'ȯl\ *adj.* Including everything; as, the *overall* expenses of a trip.

over·alls \'ō-v-r-ˌȯlz\ *n. pl.* Loose trousers, usually with a piece extending up to cover the chest, worn over other clothes to protect them from soiling.

overalls

over·anx·ious \ˌō-v-r-'ang(k)-shəs\ *adj.* Too anxious. — **over·anx·i·e·ty** \-ang-'zī-ət-ē\ *n.*

over·arm \'ō-v-r-ˌärm, -ˌårm\ *adj.* Done by raising the arm above the shoulder and lowering it in a forward sweeping motion; as, an *overarm* stroke in tennis.

overate. Past tense of *overeat*.

over·awe \ˌō-v-r-'ȯ\ *v.;* **over·awed; over·aw·ing.** To control or restrain by awe or fear; as, a mob *overawed* by courageous police.

over·bal·ance \ˌō-v-r-'bal-ən(t)s\ *v.;* **over·bal·anced; over·bal·anc·ing. 1** To have greater weight or importance than; to outweigh. **2** To lose balance or cause to lose balance. — *n.* **1** Excess of weight or value. **2** The state of being out of balance.

over·bear \ˌō-v-r-'bar, -'ber\ *v.;* **over·bore** \-'bōr, -'bȯr\; **over·borne** \-'bōrn, -'bȯrn\; **over·bear·ing. 1** To bear or carry down, as by too much weight; to overburden. **2** To domineer over; to overcome by insolence. **3** To bear fruit or offspring to excess. A tree permitted to *overbear* may produce inferior fruit.

over·bear·ing \ˌō-v-r-'bar-ing, -'ber-\ *adj.* Acting in a proud or domineering way towards other people; arrogant. — **over·bear·ing·ly**, *adv.*

over·bid \ˌō-v-r-'bid\ *v.;* **over·bid; over·bid·ding. 1** To outbid. **2** At cards, to bid more than the value of one's hand. — \'ō-v-r-ˌbid\ *n.* The act of overbidding or the amount that is overbid.

over·board \'ō-v-r-ˌbōrd, -ˌbȯrd\ *adv.* Over the side of a ship; from a ship into the water; as, to fall *overboard*.

over·bur·den \ˌō-v-r-'bərd-n\ *v.;* **over·bur·dened; over·bur·den·ing** \-n(-)ing\. To load too heavily.

overcame. Past tense of *overcome*.

over·cast \'ō-v-r-'kast\ *v.;* **over·cast** or **over·cast·ed; over·cast·ing. 1** To spread over so as to cover; especially, to cloud; to darken. **2** In sewing, to take long slanting stitches over the raw edge of a seam to prevent raveling. — *adj.* **1** Clouded over; gloomy. **2** Made with overcast stitches.

over·cau·tious \ˌō-v-r-'kȯsh-əs\ *adj.* Using or showing more caution than is necessary.

over·charge \ˌō-v-r-'chärj, -'chårj\ *v.;* **over·charged; over·charg·ing. 1** To load too heavily; to fill too full; as, an ancient cannon *overcharged* with powder and shot. **2** To charge too much. — \'ō-v-r-ˌchärj, -ˌchårj\ *n.* **1** An excessive burden. **2** A charge in an account that is either higher than agreed upon or is higher than justified for the goods.

over·cloud \ˌō-v-r-'klau̇d\ *v.* To overspread with

clouds; to become overspread with clouds; to darken.

over·coat \'ōv-r-ˌkōt\ *n.* A coat worn over a suit, especially in cold weather; a greatcoat; a topcoat.

over·come \ˌōv-r-'kəm\ *v.;* **over·came** \-'kām\; **over·come; over·com·ing. 1** To get the better of; to conquer; as, to *overcome* an enemy; to *overcome* temptation. **2** To make helpless or exhausted; as, to be *overcome* by gas.

over·con·fi·dence \ˌōv-r-'kän-fə-dən(t)s, -ˌden(t)s\ *n.* More confidence than is justified. — **over·con·fi·dent** \-dənt, -ˌdent\ *adj.*

over·crowd \ˌōv-r-'krau̇d\ *v.* To crowd too much for safety or comfort.

over·de·vel·op \ˌōv-r-də-'vel-əp\ *v.* **1** To develop excessively. **2** In photography, to subject an exposed plate or film too long to the developing process. — **over·de·vel·op·ment** \-mənt\ *n.*

over·do \ˌōv-r-'dü\ *v.;* **over·did** \-'did\; **over·done** \-'dən\; **over·do·ing** \-'dü-ing\. **1** To do too much; to tire oneself. **2** To exaggerate; as, to *overdo* praise. **3** To cook too much; as, meat that is *overdone.*

over·dose \'ōv-r-ˌdōs\ *n.* A dose that is too great. — \ˌōv-r-'dōs\ *v.;* **over·dosed; over·dos·ing.** To give an overdose to; to give too many doses to, as of medicine.

over·draft \'ōv-r-ˌdraft\ *n.* **1** A draft or current of air passing over a fire. **2** In banking, an overdrawing of an account or the amount overdrawn.

over·draw \ˌōv-r-'dro̊\ *v.;* **over·drew** \-'drü\; **over·drawn** \-'dro̊n\; **over·draw·ing. 1** To exaggerate. The child's account of his adventures was somewhat *overdrawn.* **2** To draw upon a bank account for more money than there is in it.

over·dress \ˌōv-r-'dres\ *v.* To dress too richly for an occasion. — \'ōv-r-ˌdres\ *n.* **1** An outer dress. **2** The condition of being overdressed.

over·drive \ˌōv-r-'drīv\ *v.;* **over·drove** \-'drōv\; **over·driv·en** \-'driv-n\; **over·driv·ing** \-'drī-ving\. **1** To drive too hard, too far, or beyond strength, as a horse. **2** To urge on or compel to exert too much effort; to overwork. **3** To drive an automobile, especially at night, at such speed that one cannot stop or guide it safely within the limits of vision or available space. — \'ōv-r-ˌdrīv\ *n.* An automotive gear mechanism so arranged as to provide a higher car speed for a specific engine speed than that provided by ordinary high gear.

over·due \ˌōv-r-'dü, -'dyü\ *adj.* Beyond the time due, as for arriving or paying; as, a train that is *overdue; overdue* bills.

over·ea·ger \ˌōv-r-'ēg-r\ *adj.* Too eager. — **over·ea·ger·ly,** *adv.*

over·eat \ˌōv-r-'ēt\ *v.;* **over·ate** \-'āt\; **over·eat·en** \-'ēt-n\; **over·eat·ing.** To eat too much or more than is good for one.

over·em·pha·size \ˌōv-r-'em(p)-fə-ˌsīz\ *v.;* **over·em·pha·sized; over·em·pha·siz·ing.** To emphasize too much. — **over·em·pha·sis** \-'em(p)-fə-səs\ *n.*

over·es·ti·mate \ˌōv-r-'est-m-ˌāt\ *v.;* **over·es·ti·mat·ed; over·es·ti·mat·ing.** To estimate too highly; to overvalue. — \-m-ət, -m-ˌāt\ *n.* An estimate that is too high. — **over·es·ti·ma·tion** \-ˌest-m-'āsh-n\ *n.*

over·ex·cite \ˌōv-r-ik-'sīt\ *v.;* **over·ex·cit·ed; over·ex·cit·ing.** To excite too much. — **over·ex·cite·ment** \-mənt\ *n.*

over·ex·ert \ˌōv-r-ig-'zərt\ *v.* To exert too much.

over·ex·er·tion \ˌōv-r-ig-'zərsh-n\ *n.* The action of overexerting; a spending of too much strength or energy; as, to collapse from *overexertion.*

over·ex·pose \ˌōv-r-iks-'pōz\ *v.;* **over·ex·posed; over·ex·pos·ing.** In photography, to expose for a longer time than is needed. — **over·ex·po·sure** \-'pōzh-r\ *n.*

over·feed \ˌōv-r-'fēd\ *v.;* **over·fed** \-'fed\; **over·feed·ing.** To feed too much.

over·fill \ˌōv-r-'fil\ *v.* To put or pour more into something than is called for or required; to fill something until it overflows.

over·flow \ˌōv-r-'flō\ *v.* **1** To flow over; to flood; to be filled to running over. The creek *overflows* each spring. **2** To spread over; to cover like water. Visitors *overflowed* the town. **3** To run over the edge or top of. The river *overflowed* its banks. **4** To more than fill. The crowd *overflowed* the hall. — \'ōv-r-ˌflō\ *n.* **1** A flood. **2** Something that overflows. **3** Something, as a pipe, that acts as an outlet or container for such an overflow.

over·gar·ment \'ōv-r-ˌgär-mənt, -ˌgȧr-\ *n.* An outer garment.

over·grow \ˌōv-r-'grō\ *v.;* **over·grew** \-'grü\; **over·grown** \-'grōn\; **over·grow·ing. 1** To grow over; to cover with growth or herbage; as, a wall *overgrown* with ivy. **2** To outgrow. The boy *overgrew* his clothes. **3** To grow beyond proper bounds, limits, or size; as, a city that is *overgrown;* an *overgrown* boy. — **over·grown** \-'grōn\ *adj.* — **over·growth** \'ōv-r-ˌgrōth\ *n.*

over·hand \'ōv-r-ˌhand\ *adj.* **1** Down from above; as, an *overhand* blow. **2** Played or playing with the hand grasping with palm downward or inward toward the body; as, an *overhand* stroke. **3** Over and over — used of sewing in which two edges are joined by passing each stitch over both edges. — *n.* An overhand stroke or the mastery of carrying out overhand strokes, as in tennis. — *adv.* In an overhand manner.

over·hang \ˌōv-r-'hang\ *v.;* **over·hung** \-'həng\; **over·hang·ing. 1** To hang over; to jut or project over something; especially, to hang over threateningly. Many tons of snow *overhung* the ravine. **2** To adorn with hangings; as, a path *overhung* with vines. — \'ōv-r-ˌhang\ *n.* A part that overhangs; as, the *overhang* of a roof.

overhang

over·haul \ˌōv-r-'ho̊l\ *v.* **1** To examine for places that need repair; to repair by replacing worn parts and by readjusting; as, to *overhaul* a motor. **2** To gain upon in a chase; to overtake — used especially of boats. — **over·haul·ing** \-ing\ *n.*

over·head \'ōv-r-'hed\ *adv.* Above one's head; aloft; as, a plane flying *overhead.* — \-ˌhed\ *adj.* **1** Operating or situated above or overhead; as, an *overhead* railroad. **2** Placed or passing overhead or over the head; as, an *overhead* wire. **3** In business, general and indirect. — \-ˌhed\ *n.* Also **overhead expenses.** The general expenses of a business, as rent, heat, and lighting.

over·hear \ˌōv-r-'hir\ *v.;* **over·heard** \-'hərd\; **over·hear·ing** \-'hir-ing\. To hear something said to someone else and not intended for one's own ears; as, to *overhear* a conversation in a crowded bus.

over·heat \ˌōv-r-'hēt\ *v.* To heat too much; to become too hot; as, an *overheated* motor; an *overheated* room.

overhung. Past tense and past part. of *overhang.*

over·in·dulge \ˌōv-r-in-'dəlj\ *v.;* **over·in·dulged; over·in·dulg·ing.** To indulge to excess.

over·in·dul·gence \ˌōv-r-in-'dəlj-n(t)s\ *n.* An excessive indulgence of one's self, as in intoxicating drink.

over·in·dul·gent \ˌōv-r-in-'dəlj-nt\ *adj.* Excessively indulgent, especially toward another person or persons.

over·joyed \ˌōv-r-'jȯid\ *adj.* Extremely joyful; highly delighted.

over·lad·en \ˌōv-r-'lād-n\ *adj.* Loaded with too great a cargo; overloaded.

overlaid. Past tense and past part. of *overlay.*

overlain. Past part. of *overlie.*

over·land \'ōv-r-ˌland, -lənd\ *adv.* By, upon, or across land; as, a messenger sent *overland.* — *adj.* Going or accomplished overland; as, an *overland* route.

over·lap \ˌōv-r-'lap\ *v.;* **over·lapped; over·lap·ping.** To place or be placed so that a part of one covers a part of another; to lap over. Shingles must *overlap* if a roof is to be watertight.

over·lay \ˌōv-r-'lā\. Past tense of *overlie.*

over·lay \ˌōv-r-'lā\ *v.;* **over·laid** \-'lād\; **over·lay·ing.** To lay over or across; to spread over. — \'ōv-r-ˌlā\ *n.* Something that is overlaid, as a veneer on wood.

over·leap \ˌōv-r-'lēp\ *v.;* **over·leaped** or **over·leapt** \-'lēpt, -'lept\; **over·leap·ing** \-'lēp-ing\. **1** To leap over or across; as, to *overleap* a ditch. **2** To exceed; to go beyond; to defeat by leaping too far; as, an argument that *overleaps* all reason.

over·lie \ˌōv-r-'lī\ *v.;* **over·lay** \-'lā\; **over·lain** \-'lān\; **over·ly·ing** \-'lī-ing\. To lie over or upon.

over·load \ˌōv-r-'lōd\ *v.* To put too great a load on; as, to *overload* a truck. — \'ōv-r-ˌlōd\ *n.* The amount that is beyond the proper load.

over·look \ˌōv-r-'lu̇k\ *v.* **1** To view, or to give a view of, from a higher position; as, a house that *overlooks* a valley. **2** To rise above; to overtop. **3** To watch over; to oversee. **4** To miss in looking over; to fail to note; as, to *overlook* a name on a list. **5** To pass over without notice or blame; to excuse; as, to *overlook* a mistake or a fault.

over·lord \'ōv-r-ˌlȯrd\ *n.* A person who is lord over another person or persons.

over·ly \'ōv-r-lē\ *adv.* Excessively; too.

over·mas·ter \ˌōv-r-'mast-r\ *v.;* **over·mas·tered; over·mas·ter·ing** \-r(-)ing\. To overpower; to subdue.

over·match \ˌōv-r-'mach\ *v.* **1** To match against too great ability or odds; as, a boxer who was badly *overmatched.* **2** To be more than a match for; to vanquish. Our troops *overmatched* the best the enemy could do.

over·much \'ōv-r-'məch\ *adj.* Too much. — *adv.* In too great a degree; too much. — *n.* An excess.

over·night \'ōv-r-'nīt\ *adv.* During the night; for the night; as, to stay *overnight.* — \-ˌnīt\ *adj.* **1** Done or lasting through the night; as, an *overnight* journey. **2** Staying for the night; as, an *overnight* guest. **3** For use on short trips; as, an *overnight* bag.

over·pass \ˌōv-r-'pas\ *v.* **1** To pass over or across. **2** To overcome; to excel. **3** To overlook; to disregard. — \'ōv-r-ˌpas\ *n.* A passageway, as a bridge or road, over a railroad, highway, or canal.

over·play \ˌōv-r-'plā\ *v.* **1** To surpass in playing. **2** To give too much emphasis or praise; to give too prominent a place; as, to *overplay* the importance of an insignificant item.

over·pow·er \ˌōv-r-'pau̇r\ *v.* **1** To overcome; to overwhelm; to conquer. **2** To affect intensely; as, to be *overpowered* by grief. **3** To supply with more power than is needed.

over·pow·er·ing \ˌōv-r-'pau̇r-ing\ *adj.* So strong as to overpower or overwhelm. — **over·pow·er·ing·ly,** *adv.*

over·price \ˌōv-r-'prīs\ *v.;* **over·priced; over·pric·ing.** To price something higher than it should be.

over·pro·duce \ˌōv-r-prə-'düs, -'dyüs\ *v.;* **over·pro·duced; over·pro·duc·ing.** To produce more than is needed or than can be sold profitably. — **over·pro·duc·tion** \-prə-'dəksh-n\ *n.*

over·proud \'ōv-r-'prau̇d\ *adj.* Excessively proud.

overran. Past tense of *overrun.*

over·rate \ˌōv-r-'(r)āt\ *v.;* **over·rat·ed; over·rat·ing.** To value, rate, or praise too highly; as, a book that is *overrated.*

over·reach \ˌōv-r-'(r)ēch\ *v.* **1** To reach above or beyond. **2** To spread over; as, trees that *overreach* the street. **3** To miss by reaching too far. **4** To strain oneself or defeat one's purpose by too great an effort. **5** To cheat; to trick; to outwit.

over·ride \ˌōv-r-'(r)īd\ *v.;* **over·rode** \-'(r)ōd\; **over·rid·den** \-'(r)id-n\; **over·rid·ing** \-'(r)īd-ing\. **1** To ride over or across; to trample down. The cavalry *overrode* the enemy soldiers. **2** To ride too much, as a horse. **3** To set aside; to disregard; to annul. The club members *overrode* their president's decision.

over·ripe \'ōv-r-'(r)īp\ *adj.* Beyond the condition of ripeness.

over·rule \ˌōv-r-'(r)ül\ *v.;* **over·ruled; over·rul·ing.** **1** To decide against. The chairman *overruled* the suggestion. **2** To reverse or set aside a decision or ruling made by someone having less authority.

over·run \ˌōv-r-ˈ(r)ən\ *v.;* **over·ran** \-ˈ(r)an\; **over-run; over·run·ning. 1** To run over; to overspread; as, a garden *overrun* with weeds. **2** To trample down. The escaped cattle *overran* the field of wheat. **3** To infest. Rats *overran* the ship. **4** To ravage; to lay waste. Pillagers *overran* the city. **5** To run further than; to go beyond; to exceed; as, to *overrun* a base. A radio program must not *overrun* the time allowed it. — \ˈōv-r-ˌ(r)ən\ *n.* **1** The action or an instance of overrunning. **2** The amount by which something overruns.

over·sea \ˈōv-r-ˌsē\ *adj.* Overseas. — \ˈōv-r-ˈsē\ *adv. Chiefly British.* Overseas.

over·seas \ˈōv-r-ˌsēz\ *adj.* Beyond the sea; for or from a place beyond the sea; foreign; as, *overseas* duty; *overseas* mail. — \ˈōv-r-ˈsēz\ *adv.* Over or across the sea.

over·see \ˌōv-r-ˈsē\ *v.;* **over·saw** \-ˈsȯ\; **over·seen** \-ˈsēn\; **over·see·ing.** To superintend; to supervise; to manage; as, to *oversee* a farm.

over·se·er \ˈōv-r-ˌsir, ˌōv-r-ˈsir\ *n.* A person whose business is to oversee something; a superintendent; a supervisor.

over·sen·si·tive \ˈōv-r-ˈsen(t)s-ət-iv\ *adj.* Too sensitive; extremely sensitive.

over·shad·ow \ˌōv-r-ˈshad-ō\ *v.* **1** To throw a shadow or shade over; to darken. **2** To tower above or over; to be more important than; to dominate. The excitement of winning *overshadowed* everything else.

over·shoe \ˈōv-r-ˌshü\ *n.* A protective outer shoe, as of rubber, especially for winter wear.

overshoe

over·shoot \ˌōv-r-ˈshüt\ *v.;* **over-shot** \-ˈshät\; **over·shoot·ing. 1** To pass swiftly beyond. The train *overshot* the platform. **2** To shoot over or beyond; as, to *overshoot* the target.

over·shot \ˈōv-r-ˌshät\ *adj.* **1** Having the upper jaw extending beyond the lower, as in some dogs. **2** Moved by water shooting over from above; as, an *overshot* water wheel.

over·sight \ˈōv-r-ˌsīt\ *n.* **1** The act or duty of overseeing; watchful care; supervision; as, to have the *oversight* of a piece of work. **2** An omission or error resulting from carelessness or haste.

over·size \ˈōv-r-ˌsīz\ *n.* A size larger than the usual or normal size; as, a truck tire that is an *oversize.* — \-ˈsīz\ *adj.* Also **over·sized** \-ˈsīzd\. Larger than the usual or normal size; as, an *oversize* shoe.

over·skirt \ˈōv-r-ˌskərt\ *n.* A shorter or draped skirt that falls over the upper part of a skirt.

over·sleep \ˌōv-r-ˈslēp\ *v.;* **over·slept** \-ˈslept\; **over·sleep·ing** \-ˈslēp-ing\. To sleep beyond the usual time for waking or beyond the time set for getting up.

over·spread \ˌōv-r-ˈspred\ *v.;* **over·spread; over-spread·ing.** To spread over or above; to extend over; as, branches *overspreading* a garden path.

over·state \ˌōv-r-ˈstāt\ *v.;* **over·stat·ed; over·stat-ing.** To state in too strong terms; to exaggerate. — **over·state·ment** \-mənt\ *n.*

over·stay \ˌōv-r-ˈstā\ *v.;* **over·stayed; over·stay-ing.** To stay beyond the time or limits of; as, to *overstay* one's welcome.

over·step \ˌōv-r-ˈstep\ *v.;* **over·stepped; over·step-ping.** To step over or beyond; to do more than is permitted by; as, to *overstep* one's authority.

over·stock \ˌōv-r-ˈstäk\ *v.* To stock too much or too many of; as, shelves *overstocked* with merchandise. — \ˈōv-r-ˌstäk\ *n.* An oversupply.

over·strung \ˌōv-r-ˈstrəng\ *adj.* Too high-strung; too sensitive; as, *overstrung* nerves.

over·stuff \ˌōv-r-ˈstəf\ *v.* **1** To stuff to excess. **2** To cover completely and deeply with upholstery; as, *overstuffed* furniture.

over·sub·scribe \ˌōv-r-səb-ˈskrīb\ *v.;* **over·sub-scribed; over·sub·scrib·ing.** To subscribe for more than is offered for sale, available, or asked for. The townspeople *oversubscribed* the required fund for a new school.

over·sup·ply \ˌōv-r-sə-ˈplī\ *v.;* **over·sup·plied** \-ˈplīd\; **over·sup·ply·ing.** To supply with an excess. — \ˈōv-r-sə-ˌplī\ *n.* An excessive supply.

overt \ˈō-(ˌ)vərt, ō-ˈvərt\ *adj.* Open to view; publicly known or seen; not secret. — **overt·ly,** *adv.*

over·take \ˌōv-r-ˈtāk\ *v.;* **over·took** \-ˈtu̇k\; **over-tak·en** \-ˈtāk-n\; **over·tak·ing. 1** To catch up with; as, to *overtake* the car ahead. **2** To come upon suddenly or unexpectedly; as, to be *overtaken* by rain.

over·tax \ˌōv-r-ˈtaks\ *v.* **1** To tax too much. **2** To put too great a burden or strain on.

over·throw \ˌōv-r-ˈthrō\ *v.;* **over·thrown** \-ˈthrōn\; **over·throw·ing. 1** To overturn; to upset; as, lawn furniture *overthrown* by the gale. **2** To defeat; as, a government *overthrown* by rebels. — \ˈōv-r-ˌthrō\ *n.* The action of overthrowing or the state of being overthrown; defeat; ruin; as, before the *overthrow* of the monarchy.

over·time \ˈōv-r-ˌtīm\ *n.* The time beyond or in addition to a certain set limit; especially, extra working time. — *adj.* or *adv.* Beyond a regular time limit; as, an *overtime* period in a basketball game. The men worked *overtime.* — \ˌōv-r-ˈtīm\ *v.;* **over·timed; over·tim·ing.** To exceed the proper limit in timing, as in taking a photograph.

over·tone \ˈōv-r-ˌtōn\ *n.* **1** One of the higher tones in a complex musical tone. **2** [usually in the plural] A richness of suggestion; an extra meaning. The news from abroad contained *overtones* of war.

overtook. Past tense of *overtake.*

over·top \ˌōv-r-ˈtäp\ *v.;* **over·topped; over·top·ping. 1** To rise above the top of; to tower above. **2** To surpass; to excel.

over·ture \ˈōv-r-ˌchu̇r, -rch-r, -r-ˌtu̇r, -r-ˌtyu̇r\ *n.* **1** An opening offer; a first proposal. The enemy made *overtures* of peace. **2** An orchestral composition that is the introduction to an oratorio, opera, or other long musical work; a composition in this style for concert performance.

over·turn \ˌōv-r-'tərn\ *v.* **1** To turn over; to upset. **2** To overthrow; to destroy. — \'ōv-r-ˌtərn\ *n.* **1** The action of overturning or the state of being overturned; as, an *overturn* of government. **2** A turnover; as, a fast *overturn* of the goods on a grocer's shelves.

over·use \ˌōv-r-'yüz\ *v.;* **over·used**; **over·us·ing.** To use too much; as, to *overuse* the word "awful". — \'ōv-r-'yüs\ *n.* Too much use; as, worn out from *overuse.*

over·val·ue \ˌōv-r-'val-(ˌ)yü, -yu̇\ *v.;* **over·val·ued**; **over·val·u·ing.** To place too high a value on. — **over·val·u·a·tion** \-ˌval-yə-'wāsh-n\ *n.*

over·view \'ōv-r-ˌvyü\ *n.* An over-all view.

over·ween·ing \ˌōv-r-'wē-ning\ *adj.* Too confident; arrogant; conceited; too pretentious. — **over·ween·ing·ly,** *adv.*

over·weigh \ˌōv-r-'wā\ *v.* To exceed in weight; to overbalance.

over·weight, *n.* **1** \'ōv-r-ˌwāt\ Weight over what is required or allowed by law or custom; extra weight. **2** \ˌōv-r-'wāt\ The weight that a person has over what is considered normal or proper for his age, size, and build; the condition of being too fat. — \ˌōv-r-'wāt\ *adj.* Weighing more than is normal, necessary, or allowed. — \ˌōv-r-'wāt\ *v.* To overload.

over·whelm \ˌōv-r-'hwelm\ *v.* **1** To cover over completely; to submerge. The boat was *overwhelmed* by a great wave. **2** To bear down upon so as to crush or destroy; to overpower; as, to *overwhelm* the enemy with the force of an attack; to be *overwhelmed* by emotion. — **over·whelm·ing** \-'hwel-ming\ *adj.* — **over·whelm·ing·ly,** *adv.*

over·wind \ˌōv-r-'wīnd\ *v.;* **over·wound** \-'wau̇nd\; **over·wind·ing.** To wind too tightly or too far; as, to *overwind* a watch spring.

over·work \ˌōv-r-'wərk\ *v.;* **over·worked** \-'wərkt\ or **over·wrought** \-'(r)ȯt\; **over·work·ing.** To work or to cause to work too much or too hard. — *n.* Too much work.

over·worked \ˌōv-r-'wərkt\ *adj.* **1** Made to work too much or too hard. **2** Used too frequently; stale; as, an *overworked* expression.

over·wrought \ˌōv-r-'(r)ȯt\ *adj.* **1** Overworked. **2** Overexcited; as, *overwrought* feelings. **3** Decorated all over or to excess, as armor.

ovi·duct \'ō-və-ˌdəkt\ *n.* A tube for the passage of eggs from the ovary of an animal.

ovi·form \'ō-və-ˌfȯrm\ *adj.* Having the shape of an egg.

ovip·a·rous \ō-'vip-r-əs\ *adj.* Producing eggs that hatch after leaving the body, as birds.

ovi·pos·i·tor \ˌō-və-'päz-ət-r\ *n.* A female abdominal organ for depositing eggs, common among insects and often functioning also as a boring apparatus for making a hole, as in the ground or a plant, in which the eggs are placed.

ovoid \'ō-ˌvȯid\ *adj.* Having the shape of an egg. — *n.* An ovoid body.

ovule \'ōv-ˌyül\ *n.* **1** The small body inside the ovary of a plant that after fertilization becomes a seed. **2** A small egg; an egg in an early stage of growth. — **ovu·lar** \'ōv-yəl-r\ *adj.*

ovum \'ō-vəm\ *n.; pl.* **ova** \'ō-və\. [From Latin, meaning "egg".] A female germ cell.

owe \'ō\ *v.;* **owed**; **ow·ing.** **1** To have or hold, as a feeling affecting one's attitude or behavior towards another; to bear; as, to *owe* a schoolmate a grudge. **2** To be under obligation to pay, give, or return; as, to *owe* money; to *owe* allegiance to one's country. **3** To be in debt to; as, to *owe* the grocer for food. **4** To be in debt. We still *owe* for things we bought years ago. **5** To be indebted or obliged for; to possess as something derived or given; as, to *owe* one's wealth to one's grandfather; to *owe* one's success to hard work.

ow·ing \'ō-ing\ *adj.* Due to be paid; owed; as, to have a number of bills *owing;* to claim no more than is *owing.* — **owing to.** Because of; as a result of; as, absent *owing to* illness.

owl \'au̇l\ *n.* A soft-feathered bird with large head and eyes, a short, hooked bill, and long sharp claws, active at night and living on rats and mice, insects, and small birds, American varieties including the brown and gray **barn owl,** the **great horned owl,** with conspicuous ear tufts, the small **screech owl,** and the **snowy owl,** white with dark spots.

owl·et \'au̇-lət\ *n.* A young or small owl.

owl·ish \'au̇-lish\ *adj.* Like or suggestive of an owl, as in solemnity or appearance of wisdom. — **owl·ish·ly,** *adv.*

own \'ōn\ *adj.* **1** Belonging to oneself or itself. The boy had his *own* room. **2** Directly or immediately related; as, to have two *own* brothers and two half brothers. First cousins are sometimes called *own* cousins. — **on one's own.** For or by oneself; without assistance or control. — *v.* **1** To possess; to have as one's own; to hold as property; as, to *own* a house. **2** To acknowledge or admit to be one's own; as, to *own* a fault. — **own to.** To admit; as, to *own to* being scared. — **own up.** To confess.

own·er \'ōn-r\ *n.* One that owns; a person who has legal title to property; as, the *owner* of a house; to return a lost pocketbook to its rightful *owner.*

own·er·ship \'ōn-r-ˌship\ *n.* The state or fact of being an owner.

ox \'äks\ *n.; pl.* **ox·en** \'äks-n\. **1** The full-grown castrated male of domestic cattle used for beef or as a draft animal. **2** Any of numerous large cud-chewing mammals that have hollow unbranched horns which are not shed and replaced and even-toed hoofed feet and that include domestic cattle, yaks, buffaloes, and others but not certain smaller related animals, as sheep and goats. **3** [in the plural] Domestic cattle collectively.

ox·blood \'äks-ˌbləd\ *n.* A deep, somewhat dull red color.

ox·bow \'äks-ˌbō\ *n.* **1** A U-shaped collar worn by a draft ox. **2** A U-shaped bend in a river.

ox·cart \'äks-ˌkärt, -ˌkȧrt\ *n.* A cart drawn by oxen.

ox·eye \'äk-ˌsī\ *n.* Any of several plants having flower heads with a conspicuous center disk surrounded by rays; especially, the oxeye daisy.

ox-eyed \'äk-'sīd\ *adj.* Having large round eyes like those of an ox.

ox·ford \'äks-fərd\ *n.* **1** A low shoe laced or tied over the instep. **2** A soft durable fabric often used for shirts, usually of cotton woven in a basket weave. **3** Oxford gray.

Oxford gray. A medium to very dark gray.

ox·heart \'äks-ˌhärt, -ˌhȧrt\ *n.* Any of several varieties of the sweet cherry.

ox·i·da·tion \ˌäks-ə-'dāsh-n\ *n.* **1** The process of oxidizing; the combining of oxygen with other substances, typically releasing heat, as in burning, or other forms of energy. **2** The state or result of being oxidized.

ox·ide \'äk-ˌsīd\ *n.* A compound of oxygen with another element or a radical.

ox·i·dize \'äks-ə-ˌdīz\ *v.;* **ox·i·dized**; **ox·i·diz·ing.** To combine with oxygen; to add oxygen to. Iron rusts because it is *oxidized* by exposure to the air. — **ox·i·di·za·tion** \ˌäks-ə-də-'zāsh-n\ *n.*

ox·y·gen \'äks-ij-n\ *n.* An odorless, colorless, tasteless, gaseous chemical element essential to life and forming about 21 per cent, by volume, of the air and $\frac{8}{9}$, by weight, of water.

ox·y·gen·ate \'äks-ij-n-ˌāt\ *v.;* **ox·y·gen·at·ed**; **ox·y·gen·at·ing.** To treat with oxygen; to combine with oxygen; to oxidize. — **ox·y·gen·a·tion** \ˌäks-ij-n-'āsh-n\ *n.*

oxygen helmet. A headgear through which oxygen is supplied to the wearer, as an airman or diver, from an attached container.

ox·y·gen·ize \'äks-ij-n-ˌīz\ *v.;* **ox·y·gen·ized**; **ox·y·gen·iz·ing.** To oxidize; to oxygenate.

oxygen mask. A device worn over the nose and mouth, as by airmen at high altitudes, through which oxygen is supplied from a storage tank.

oxygen tent. A small tent or canopy that can be placed over the bed of a sick person and filled with oxygen, used in the treatment of certain illnesses.

ox·y·he·mo·glo·bin \'äks-ē-ˌhē-mə-'glōb-n, ˌäks-ē-'hē-mə-ˌglōb-n\ *n.* A compound of hemoglobin with oxygen that is formed in the presence of abundant oxygen and is the chief mechanism for the transportation of oxygen from the air, as in the lungs, by way of the blood to the tissues.

oys·ter \'ȯist-r\ *n.* A soft gray shellfish with an irregular shell made up of two hinged parts, living on stony bottoms in shallow sea water and used as food.

oz. Abbreviation for *ounce.*

ozone \'ō-ˌzōn\ *n.* **1** A faintly blue form of oxygen with a peculiar odor like that of weak chlorine, produced by the silent discharge of electricity in air or oxygen and present in the air in small quantities. **2** Pure and refreshing air.

p \'pē\ *n.; pl.* **p's** \'pēz\. The sixteenth letter of the alphabet.

p. Abbreviation for *page.*

pa \'pä, 'pȯ, 'pȧ\ *n.; pl.* **pas.** Papa.

pace \'pās\ *n.* **1** A person's step. **2** The length of a step in walking; as, posts five *paces* apart. **3** A manner of walking; a gait; as, a swaggering *pace.* **4** The rate of movement; speed; as, where the broad river flows at a slow *pace.* **5** A particular gait of a horse in which the legs on the same side are moved at the same time. — *v.;* **paced**; **pac·ing.** **1** To walk with slow measured steps. **2** To measure by paces; as, to *pace* off 100 feet. **3** To move at a pace. The spotted horse was able to *pace* better than the bay.

pac·er \'pās-r\ *n.* One that paces; especially, a horse that uses a particular gait, the pace.

pach·y·derm \'pak-ə-ˌdərm\ *n.* Any of various thick-skinned hoofed mammals; especially, an elephant or a rhinoceros.

pa·cif·ic \pə-'sif-ik\ *adj.* **1** Making peace; suitable to make peace; as, *pacific* words that ended a quarrel. **2** Having a mild and calm nature; peaceable; as, a land inhabited by a quiet, *pacific* people. — **pa·cif·i·cal·ly** \-ik-l(-)ē\ *adv.*

Pa·cif·ic \pə-'sif-ik\ *adj.* Relating to or bordering upon the ocean that lies between Asia and Australia on the west and North and South America on the east.

pac·i·fi·ca·tion \ˌpas-ə-fə-'kāsh-n\ *n.* The act of pacifying or state of being pacified; a quieting to a peaceful condition.

pac·i·fi·er \'pas-ə-ˌfīr\ *n.* **1** One who pacifies. **2** An object, as a rubber ring, for babies to suck or bite upon to keep them quiet.

pac·i·fism \'pas-ə-ˌfiz-m\ *n.* Opposition to war or to the use of military force for any purpose. — **pac·i·fist** \-fəst\ *n.*

pac·i·fy \'pas-ə-ˌfī\ *v.;* **pac·i·fied** \-ˌfīd\; **pac·i·fy·ing.** To make peaceful or quiet; to calm; to soothe; as, to *pacify* an angry person; to *pacify* a crying baby.

— The words *mollify* and *appease* are synonyms of *pacify: pacify* generally indicates a quieting and a returning to order of a person or group of persons who are in a state of agitation or open hostility; *mollify* may suggest a calming of someone's anger or a soothing of hurt feelings; *appease* is likely to suggest the satisfaction of often unreasonable demands and a resulting feeling of contentment.

pack \'pak\ *n.* **1** A bundle prepared to be carried, especially on the back of a man or animal; as, a peddler's *pack.* **2** A group of like persons or animals; as, a *pack* of thieves; a *pack* of wolves. **3** A group of like articles, often of a specified number; as, a *pack* of cards; a *pack* of cigarettes. **4** A large area of floating pieces of ice driven closely together. **5** A method of packing; as, vacuum *pack.* **6** A cosmetic in paste form, applied to the face and left until dry as a beauty treatment. **7** A wrapping of wet or dry, hot or cold sheets used in treating an ill person. **8** Absorbent material, as gauze pads, used to make compresses, to plug body cavities in order to stop bleeding, and to apply medication; as, hot *packs* for an infected arm; a *pack* to stop a nosebleed. — *v.* **1** To place articles in, as for transportation or storage; as, to *pack* a suitcase; to *pack* a box. **2** To arrange closely and securely in a can, box, or bundle; as, to *pack* goods. **3** To crowd together; to fill full; to cram. The crowd *packed* the hall. **4** To form into a pack or packs. The ice is *packing* in the gorge. **5** To fill or cover so as to prevent passage of air or steam; as, to *pack* a joint in a pipe. **6** To send away; as, to *pack* a boy off to school. — *adj.* **1** Formed or forming into a pack or mass; as, *pack* ice. **2** Carrying or made to carry packs; as, a *pack* horse. **3** Made up of pack animals; as, a *pack* train.

pack \'pak\ *v.* To use unfair or dishonest means to fill a voting group with persons favorable to one's side; as, to *pack* a jury.

pack·age \'pak-ij\ *n.* **1** Something packed or wrapped, especially when made up to be taken or sent from one place to another; as, a department store that delivers *packages;* to open a *package* received in the mail. **2** The container for packaged goods; as, highways cluttered with empty *packages.* — *v.;* **pack·aged; pack·ag·ing.** To make up into a package; as, *packaged* tea.

package store. A store that sells alcoholic beverages only in containers that may not lawfully be opened on the premises.

pack animal. An animal, as a horse or donkey, used for carrying packs.

pack·er \'pak-r\ *n.* A person who packs, makes up bundles, or puts things in bundles; especially, a dealer who prepares and packs foods for the market; as, a meat *packer.*

pack·et \'pak-ət\ *n.* **1** A small pack or bundle. **2** A ship that carries passengers, mail, and goods, and has fixed days for sailing.

pack·ing \'pak-ing\ *n.* **1** The act or process of one who packs. **2** The putting up or preserving of meat and foods for future use. **3** Any material used to pack or fill up.

packing house. A building where meats or sometimes other foods are prepared for market.

packing plant. A packing house.

pack rat. A rat, especially a large bushy-tailed one of the Rocky Mountain area, that has large cheek pouches in which it carries food and sometimes other articles.

pack·sad·dle \'pak-ˌsad-l\ *n.* A saddle made especially to support the load on the back of a pack animal.

pack·thread \'pak-ˌthred\ *n.* Strong thread or narrow twine used especially for sewing or tying packs or parcels.

pact \'pakt\ *n.* An agreement; a compact.

pad \'pad\ *n.* The dull noise of soft footsteps. — *v.;* **pad·ded; pad·ding. 1** To travel on foot; to trudge. **2** To walk or run with steady dull footsteps. The cat *padded* away.

pad \'pad\ *n.* **1** A cushion; something soft or stuffed, like a cushion. **2** A tablet of writing or drawing paper. **3** A cushion of material that holds ink and is used in inking rubber stamps. **4** The foot of certain animals, such as foxes or hares. **5** A thickening of the skin on the soles of an animal's feet. **6** The floating leaf of a water plant. **7** A launching pad. — *v.;* **pad·ded; pad·ding. 1** To fill with stuffing; as, to *pad* a quilt. **2** To increase in size as if by stuffing; as, to *pad* a speech.

pad·ding \'pad-ing\ *n.* **1** The act of padding. **2** Soft material used to pad; stuffing. **3** Material of little or no value, added to fill space, as in a piece of writing or in a speech.

pad·dle \'pad-l\ *n.* **1** An implement used in moving and steering canoes and similar watercraft, like an oar but not held in an oarlock nor, usually, as long as an oar. **2** One of the broad boards at the outer rim of a water wheel or a paddle wheel of a boat. **3** A broad-bladed implement for stirring or mixing or, sometimes, for beating clothes in washing. **4** An instrument of punishment. **5** A small, racket-shaped bat used for hitting the ball in certain games; as, the *paddles* in a table tennis set. — *v.;* **pad·dled; pad·dling** \-l(-)ing\. **1** To use a paddle; to move with or as if with a paddle. **2** To stir, mix, or beat with a paddle. **3** To punish with or as if with a paddle.

pad·dle \'pad-l\ *v.;* **pad·dled; pad·dling** \-l(-)ing\. To dabble in water with the hands or feet; to wade.

paddle wheel. A wheel with paddles around its circumference, used in propelling a steam vessel.

pad·dock \'pad-ək\ *n.* **1** A small enclosed field or pasture, usually near a building, for housing or sheltering animals. **2** An enclosure near the stables, especially at a racecourse, in which horses are exercised.

pad·dy or **padi** \'pad-ē\ *n.* **1** Unhusked rice; rice when still growing or when first cut. **2** Any rice; as, time to sow *paddy.* **3** *pl.* **pad·dies.** A rice field; as, unplowed *paddies.*

pad·lock \'pad-ˌläk\ *n.* A removable lock with a hinged bow-shaped piece attached at one end so that the other end can be passed through a staple, as on a hasp, and then snapped into a catch in the lock. — *v.* To fasten with a padlock; to lock securely.

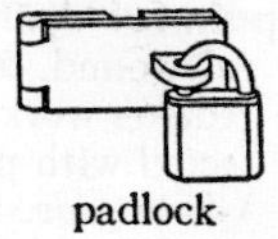
padlock

pa·dre \'päd-ˌrā, 'påd-\ *n.* [From Portuguese, meaning literally "father" — borrowed by the British from the Portuguese in India.] A priest.

pae·an \'pē-ən\ *n.* A song of joy, praise, or triumph.

pa·gan \'pāg-n\ *n.* **1** A person who worships strange gods or idols; a heathen. **2** An irreligious person. — *adj.* **1** Of or having to do with pagans; heathen. **2** Irreligious. — **pa·gan·ism** \-ˌiz-m\ *n.*

page \'pāj\ *n.* **1** Formerly, a boy in training for knighthood who served as an attendant to his master or mistress. **2** A boy attending a person of high degree. **3** A boy who carries messages, as in a hotel. **4** In the United States, a boy who waits on or aids members of a legislature. — *v.;* **paged; pag·ing. 1** To act as a page. **2** To seek out a person by calling his name aloud, as pages do in a hotel.

page \'pāj\ *n.* **1** One side of a printed or written leaf. **2** That which is printed or written on a page. Read the last three *pages* of the assignment carefully. **3** [often in the plural] A record; writing; as, the *pages* of history. **4** An event or circumstance that might fill a written page; as, an exciting *page* in a person's life. **5** A leaf, as of a book. — *v.;* **paged; pag·ing.** To mark or number the pages of.

pag·eant \'paj-nt\ *n.* **1** An elaborate exhibition or spectacle, as a parade with floats. **2** An entertainment consisting of scenes based on history or legend; as, a Christmas *pageant.*

pag·eant·ry \'paj-n-trē\ *n.; pl.* **pag·eant·ries. 1** The spectacles of a pageant; its floats or costumes. **2** A splendid display; pomp; show; as, the *pageantry* of a coronation ceremony.

pa·go·da \pə-'gōd-ə\ *n.* A many-storied oriental building, like a tower, usually a temple or a memorial.

pagoda

paid. Past tense and past part. of *pay.*

pail \'pāl\ *n.* **1** A container, usually round with arched handle, mainly for holding or carrying liquids; a bucket; as, a water *pail.* **2** A pailful.

pail·ful \'pāl-ˌfu̇l\ *n.; pl.* **pail·fuls.** The amount a pail holds.

pain \'pān\ *n.* **1** Punishment; penalty — now used only in certain phrases, as *under pain of death.* **2** Physical suffering usually associated with disease, injury, or other bodily disorder. **3** A basic bodily sensation caused by harmful stimuli, characterized by physical discomfort, and leading to attempts to escape its source. **4** Mental distress; sorrow; trouble. **5** [in the plural] Great care; labor; as, to take *pains.* — *v.* **1** To cause bodily pain or distress. **2** To give mental pain to; to grieve.

pain·ful \'pān-fəl\ *adj.* **1** Causing pain; as, a *painful* wound. **2** Requiring hard work or slow and tedious work; difficult; as, a *painful* task. **3** Affected with pain; as, a *painful* arm. — **pain·ful·ly** \-fə-lē\ *adv.*

pain·less \'pān-ləs\ *adj.* Free from pain; causing no pain; without pain. — **pain·less·ly,** *adv.*

pains·tak·ing \'pānz-ˌtāk-ing\ *n.* The act of taking pains. After much *painstaking,* the job was completed. — *adj.* **1** Taking pains; showing care; as, a *painstaking* workman. **2** Requiring painstaking; as, a *painstaking* task. — **pains·tak·ing·ly,** *adv.*

paint \'pānt\ *v.* **1** To represent on canvas, a wall, or other surface, by use of colors; to make a picture or design of by means of paints; as, to *paint* a dog on the wall. **2** To cover a surface with paint; as, to *paint* a wall; to *paint* a chair. **3** To put on or apply like paint; as, to *paint* a throat with iodine. **4** To practice the art of painting; as, to *paint* for a living. **5** To describe vividly; as, to *paint* a scene in words. — *n.* **1** A mixture of coloring matter and a suitable liquid that forms a dry coat when spread over a surface. **2** The dried film of paint on a surface; as, to scrape *paint* off the deck.

paint·brush \'pānt-ˌbrəsh\ *n.* **1** A brush for applying paint. **2** A parasitic herb, the painted cup.

paint·ed bun·ting \'pānt-əd\. A finch of the southern United States, the male of which has a blue head, bright red underparts, green back and wings, and a purple tail; a nonpareil.

painted cup. A parasitic herb of the figwort family with brightly colored bracts and spiked, tubular, two-lipped flowers.

paint·er \'pānt-r\ *n.* A cougar.

paint·er \'pānt-r\ *n.* A rope, usually at the bow, used for fastening a boat.

paint·er \'pānt-r\ *n.* **1** A person who paints pictures; an artist. **2** A person who applies paint to things.

paint·ing \'pānt-ing\ *n.* **1** Act of a person who paints. **2** A painted picture or design.

pair \'par, 'per\ *n.; pl.* **pairs** or, sometimes, **pair. 1** Two things of a kind, naturally matched or intended to be used together; as, a *pair* of gloves. **2** A single thing composed of two connected corresponding parts; as, a *pair* of scissors. **3** Two of a sort; a set of two; a couple; as, a *pair* of horses. **4** Two closely associated persons or animals; a mated couple, as of birds; a married or engaged couple. **5** *Chiefly dial.* A set; as, a *pair* of stairs. **6** Two persons on opposite sides, as in a legislature, who agree not to vote on a certain question during a specified time. — For synonyms see *couple.* — *v.;* **paired; pair·ing. 1** To unite or arrange in a pair or pairs; as, to *pair* off dancers. **2** To form a pair.

pa·ja·mas \pə-'jäm-əz, -'jam-, -'jȧm-\ *n. pl.* A set of garments for sleeping or lounging, consisting of a blouse or jacket and loose-fitting trousers.

Pak·i·stani \ˌpak-ə-'stan-ē, ˌpäk-ə-'stän-ē, ˌpȧk-ə-'stȧn-ē\ *adj.* Of or relating to Pakistan. — *n.* A native or inhabitant of Pakistan.

pal \'pal\ *n.* **1** A partner. **2** A comrade; a playmate. — *v.;* **palled; pal·ling.** To be a pal; to go as a pal; as, boys who *pal* around together.

pal·ace \'pal-əs\ *n.* **1** The official residence of a sovereign. **2** *British.* The residence of an archbishop or bishop. **3** A large and splendid house. **4** A large public building, as for a legislature or a high court.

pal·an·quin \ˌpal-ən-'kēn\ *n.* A conveyance, usually for one person, consisting of an enclosed or covered couch or seat carried on the shoulders of men by means of poles.

pal·at·a·ble \'pal-ət-əb-l\ *adj.* **1** Pleasant or agreeable to the taste; as, *palatable* food. **2** Acceptable; pleasing; as, *palatable* advice; a very *palatable* suggestion. — **pal·at·a·bly** \-ə-blē\ *adv.*

pal·ate \'pal-ət\ *n.* **1** The roof of the mouth, the front part, which is supported by bone, being the **hard palate** and the back part, consisting of a muscular fold, the **soft palate. 2** Taste; sense of taste. The food pleased his *palate.* **3** Mental taste or relish.

pa·la·tial \pə-'lāsh-l\ *adj.* Of, like, or fit for a palace; magnificent. — **pa·la·tial·ly** \-'lāsh-l-ē\ *adv.*

pal·a·tine \'pal-ə-ˌtīn\ *adj.* Of or relating to the palate.

pal·a·tine \'pal-ə-ˌtīn\ *adj.* **1** Of or relating to a palace; palatial. **2** Possessing royal rights in his own territory or belonging to a nobleman having such rights; as, a count *palatine;* a county *palatine.*

pa·lav·er \pə-'lav-r, -'läv-r, -'låv-r\ *n.* **1** In Africa, a talk or discussion, usually a long one, among or with natives; a conference; a debate. **2** Talk; especially, smoothly flowing idle or flattering talk. — *v.;* **pa·lav·ered**; **pa·lav·er·ing** \-r(-)ing\. To talk, especially idly or at great length.

pale \'pāl\ *adj.* **1** Lacking color or intensity of color; especially, not having the color of a person in good health; pallid; wan; as, to become *pale.* **2** Not bright or brilliant; as, a *pale* moon. **3** Light in color; as, *pale* pink. — *v.;* **paled**; **pal·ing. 1** To turn pale; to lose color. **2** To make dim or pale. — **pale·ly** \'pāl-lē\ *adv.* — **pale·ness** \-nəs\ *n.*

pale \'pāl\ *n.* **1** A stake or picket of a fence. **2** An enclosed place. **3** Limits; bounds; as, behavior outside the *pale* of common decency. **4** Formerly, a district or territory with clearly marked bounds or under particular control. — *v.;* **paled**; **pal·ing.** To enclose with or as if with pales; to fence.

pale·face \'pāl-ˌfās\ *n.* A white person — supposedly so-called by the American Indians.

pa·le·o·lith·ic \ˌpā-lē-ə-'lith-ik\ *adj.* Of or relating to the stage of human culture **(Paleolithic period)** characterized by the use of rough or chipped stone implements.

pa·le·on·tol·o·gy \ˌpā-lē-ˌän-'täl-ə-jē, -ən-\ *n.* The science treating of the life of past geologic periods as shown by fossil remains. — **pa·le·on·tol·o·gist** \-jəst\ *n.*

pal·ette \'pal-ət\ *n.* **1** A thin board or tablet, usually oval in shape and having a hole for the thumb at one end, used by a painter to lay and mix his colors on. **2** The colors that a painter lays on his palette.

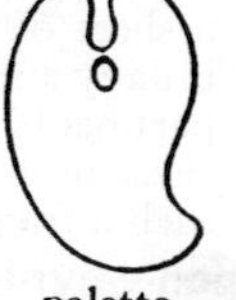
palette

pal·frey \'pòl-frē\ *n.; pl.* **palfreys.** A saddle horse for the road, as distinguished from a war horse; especially, a small saddle horse for ladies.

pal·ing \'pā-ling\ *n.* **1** A pale or picket. **2** Pales or a fence of pales.

pal·i·sade \ˌpal-ə-'sād\ *n.* **1** A high fence of stout pales or stakes, used as a defense. **2** A long, strong pointed stake set in the ground with others as a defensive barrier. **3** [usually in the plural] A line of prominent cliffs. — *v.;* **pal·i·sad·ed**; **pal·i·sad·ing.** To enclose or fortify with palisades.

pall \'pòl\ *n.* **1** A heavy cloth covering for a coffin, hearse, or tomb. **2** In the Roman Catholic Church, a chalice cover made of a square piece of cardboard covered with embroidered linen. **3** Something that covers, darkens, or produces a gloomy effect; as, a *pall* of smoke; a *pall* of silence.

pall \'pòl\ *v.* To become dull or uninteresting; to lose the ability to give pleasure.

pall·bear·er \'pòl-ˌbar-r, -ˌber-r\ *n.* A person who attends a coffin at a funeral; especially, one who helps to carry the coffin.

pal·let \'pal-ət\ *n.* A small, poor bed; a bed of straw; a bed on the floor.

pal·li·ate \'pal-ē-ˌāt\ *v.;* **pal·li·at·ed**; **pal·li·at·ing. 1** To make less severe; to ease without curing, as a disease. **2** To make seem less serious, as a fault; to try to excuse. — **pal·li·a·tion** \ˌpal-ē-'āsh-n\ *n.*

pal·li·a·tive \'pal-ē-ˌāt-iv, -ət-iv\ *adj.* Palliating. — *n.* Something that serves to palliate, as a medicine that relieves but does not cure. — **pal·li·a·tive·ly**, *adv.*

pal·lid \'pal-əd\ *adj.* Pale; especially, unhealthily pale. — **pal·lid·ly**, *adv.*

pal·lor \'pal-r\ *n.* Paleness, especially of the face; pallid appearance.

palm \'päm, 'påm\ *n.* **1** The under part of the hand between the fingers and the wrist. **2** A rough measure of length of about the width of the palm, or three to four inches. **3** Something resembling or corresponding to the palm of the hand, as the blade of an oar or paddle. — *v.* **1** To hide in the palm or about the hand; as, to *palm* a coin. **2** To get rid of by trickery or fraud; as, to *palm* off a worthless car on an unsuspecting buyer.

palm \'päm, 'pam\ *n.* **1** Any of a family of mostly tropical or subtropical woody plants or trees, usually having a round, often very tall, trunk topped by a crown of huge feathery or fan-shaped leaves, and including among well-known varieties the coconut palm, date palm, rattan palm, and royal palm. **2** A palm leaf; especially, one carried in a procession as a religious symbol, as on Palm Sunday, or, formerly, in celebration of a victory. **3** An emblem of success or victory; honors. Our team carried off the *palm.*

palm·er \'päm-r, 'påm-r\ *n.* In medieval England a person wearing two crossed leaves of palm as a sign that he had made a pilgrimage to the Holy Land.

pal·met·to \pal-'met-ō\ *n.; pl.* **pal·met·tos** or **pal·met·toes.** Any of several palms with fan-shaped leaves.

palm·is·try \'päm-əs-trē, 'påm-\ *n.* The art or

practice of telling fortunes by studying the markings of the palm of the hand. — **palm·ist** \-əst\ *n.*

Palm Sunday. The Sunday before Easter.

palmy \'päm-ē, 'pȧm-ē\ *adj.;* **palm·i·er**; **palm·i·est**. **1** Bearing palms; having palms; as, a *palmy* shore. **2** Like a palm; as, a *palmy* plant. **3** Flourishing; prosperous; as, ruins recalling the *palmy* days of ancient Rome.

pal·o·mi·no \ˌpal-ə-'mē-ˌnō\ *n.; pl.* **pal·o·mi·nos**. A slender-legged, short-bodied horse of a light tan or cream color with lighter colored mane and tail.

pal·pa·ble \'pal-pəb-l\ *adj.* **1** Capable of being touched or felt; tangible. **2** Easily visible or audible; as, a *palpable* sigh. **3** Easily understood or recognized; obvious; as, a *palpable* error. — **pal·pa·bly** \-pə-blē\ *adv.*

pal·pi·tate \'pal-pə-ˌtāt\ *v.;* **pal·pi·tat·ed**; **pal·pi·tat·ing**. **1** To beat rapidly; to pulsate violently, as the heart after abnormal exertion. **2** To throb, quiver, or tremble, as with excitement. — For synonyms see *throb*.

pal·pi·ta·tion \ˌpal-pə-'tāsh-n\ *n.* A rapid pulsation; a throbbing or quivering; especially, an abnormal, rapid beating of the heart, as from violent exertion or strong emotion.

pal·sy \'pȯl-zē\ *n.; pl.* **pal·sies**. **1** Paralysis. **2** An uncontrollable trembling or shaking, as of the head or hands. — *v.;* **pal·sied** \-zēd\; **pal·sy·ing**. To affect with or as if with palsy.

pal·ter \'pȯlt-r\ *v.;* **pal·tered**; **pal·ter·ing** \'pȯlt-r-ing, 'pȯl-tring\. **1** To act insincerely; to use deceit or trickery. **2** To haggle; to bargain, especially in a matter of duty or honor. — **pal·ter·er** \'pȯlt-r-r\ *n.*

pal·try \'pȯl-trē\ *adj.;* **pal·tri·er**; **pal·tri·est**. Petty; worthless; trifling.

pam·pas \'pam-pəz, -pəs\ *n. pl.* Wide treeless plains, especially of Argentina.

pam·per \'pamp-r\ *v.;* **pam·pered**; **pam·per·ing** \-r(-)ing\. To let a person have his own way; to supply with the best of everything; as, to *pamper* a sick child.

pam·phlet \'pam(p)-flət, 'pam-plət\ *n.* A book consisting of a few printed sheets, commonly with a paper cover.

pam·phle·teer \ˌpam(p)-flə-'tir, ˌpam-plə-\ *v.* To write and publish pamphlets. — *n.* A person who writes pamphlets or a pamphlet.

pan \'pan\ *n.* **1** A dish, usually broad, shallow, and open, used in cooking. **2** A vessel or article somewhat like such a dish; as, the *pans* of a pair of scales; a screening *pan* used by gold miners. **3** The hollow part in the lock of old guns that holds the priming. **4** A hard subsoil; a hardpan. — *v.;* **panned**; **pan·ning**. **1** In gold mining, to wash gravel in a pan. **2** To cook in a pan. **3** To yield gold or other precious metal in panning. The gravel *panned* out richly. **4** To yield a result; to turn out. The scheme *panned* out badly.

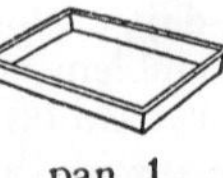

pan, 1

pan·a·cea \ˌpan-ə-'sē-ə\ *n.* A remedy for all diseases or troubles; a cure-all.

pan·a·ma \'pan-ə-ˌmȯ, -ˌmä, -ˌmȧ\ *n.* or **panama hat**. A hat of fine texture, made of hand-plaited leaves from an Ecuadorian tree.

Pan·a·ma·ni·an \ˌpan-ə-'mā-nē-ən\ *adj.* Of or relating to Panama. — *n.* A native or citizen of Panama.

Pan-Amer·i·can \ˌpan-ə-'mer-ək-n\ *adj.* Of or relating to both North America and South America or all Americans.

Pan-Amer·i·can·ism \ˌpan-ə-'mer-ək-n-ˌiz-m\ *n.* **1** The advocating of a political alliance of all American nations. **2** Co-operation among the American republics in political or economic matters.

pan·cake \'pan-ˌkāk\ *n.* **1** A griddlecake. **2** An abrupt landing by an airplane, with little or no run along the ground. — *v.;* **pan·caked**; **pan·cak·ing**. To level off an airplane as if for landing but too far up from the landing area so that the airplane stalls and drops abruptly with not enough forward movement for a normal landing.

pan·chro·mat·ic \ˌpan-krō-'mat-ik\ *adj.* Sensitive to light of all colors, as a photographic plate. — **pan·chro·ma·tism** \(')pan-'krō-mə-ˌtiz-m\ *n.*

pan·cre·as \'pan(g)-krē-əs\ *n.* A large gland near the stomach in the body of people and animals that discharges digestive enzymes into the intestines and insulin into the blood.

pan·cre·at·ic \ˌpan(g)-krē-'at-ik\ *adj.* Of or having to do with the pancreas.

pancreatic duct. The duct leading from the pancreas and opening into the duodenum.

pancreatic juice. An alkaline secretion given off by the pancreas that contains trypsin, amylopsin, and lipase and aids in digestion.

pan·da \'pan-də\ *n.* **1** An animal of the Himalayas, related to and much resembling the raccoon, reddish with black legs and a whitish face and bushy tail. **2** Also **giant panda**. A very rare large black and white animal of Tibet which has some resemblance to a bear.

pan·da·nus \pan-'dā-nəs\ *n.* Any of a genus of tropical Old World plants, the screw pines.

pan·de·mo·ni·um \ˌpand-m-'ō-nē-əm\ *n.* A wildly riotous place; a wild uproar.

pan·der \'pand-r\ *n.* **1** A go-between in a love intrigue. **2** A person who caters to another's base or depraved desires. — *v.;* **pan·dered**; **pan·der·ing** \-r(-)ing\. To act as a pander.

pane \'pān\ *n.* **1** A section or side of something, as one of the facets of a gem or one of the divisions of a sheet of postage stamps, in the United States usually a section of 100 stamps. **2** One of the compartments of a window or door, consisting of a sheet of glass in a frame. **3** The sheet of glass in such a frame.

pan·e·gyr·ic \ˌpan-ə-'jir-ik\ *n.* **1** A formal speech or article in praise of a person or event. **2** Formal praise. — **pan·e·gyr·i·cal** \-ik-l\ *adj.*

pan·e·gyr·ist \ˌpan-ə-'jir-əst\ *n.* A person who formally praises a person or event.

pan·el \'pan-l\ *n.* **1** A section or part of a wall, ceiling, or door, often sunk below the level of the frame; especially, a thin and usually rectangular board set in a frame, as in a door. **2** A thin, flat piece of wood on which a picture is painted. **3** A painting on such a surface. **4** A lengthwise strip or band sewn in a dress; as, an embroidered *panel* on a skirt. **5** A list or group of persons appointed for some service; especially, a group of persons called to serve on a jury. **6** A group of no less than three persons, often experts in various fields, conducting before an audience an unrehearsed discussion on a topic of interest, either to a special audience or to the general public; a similar group, usually of persons well-known to the public, acting as players in a quiz game or guessing game conducted by a master of ceremonies on a radio or television program. — *v.;* **pan·eled** or **pan·elled; pan·el·ing** or **pan·el·ling** \-l(-)ing\. To furnish, fit, trim, or decorate with panels; as, to *panel* a wall.

pan·el·ing or **pan·el·ling** \'pan-l(-)ing\ *n.* **1** Wood or other material made into panels. **2** Panels considered collectively.

pan·el·ist \'pan-l-əst\ *n.* A member of a panel for discussion or entertainment.

pang \'pang\ *n.* **1** A sudden sharp attack of pain; a throe. **2** A sudden sharp feeling of any emotion; as, a *pang* of regret.

pan·han·dle \'pan-ˌhand-l\ *n.* **1** The handle of a pan. **2** An arm or projection of land shaped like the handle of a pan.

pan·han·dle \'pan-ˌhand-l\ *v.;* **pan·han·dled; pan·han·dling** \-l(-)ing\. To approach people on the street and beg for money. — **pan·han·dler** \-lər\ *n.*

pan·ic \'pan-ik\ *n.* **1** A sudden, terrifying fright, especially without reasonable cause. **2** A sudden, widespread fear in financial circles, causing hurried selling of securities and a rapid fall in prices. — *v.;* **pan·icked** \-ikt\; **pan·ick·ing** \-ik-ing\. **1** To affect with panic; to be affected with panic; as, one who *panics* easily. **2** *Slang.* To call forth a show of appreciation on the part of someone. The comedian's performance *panicked* the audience. — **pan·icky** \'pan-ik-ē\ *adj.* — **pan·ic-strick·en** \'pan-ik-ˌstrik-n\ *adj.*

pan·i·cle \'pan-ik-l\ *n.* A flower cluster, loosely branched and often in the shape of a pyramid, in which the branches of the flowerless main stem are elongated clusters in the form of a raceme, blooming from the bottom toward the top and outward, as in the oat.

pan·nier \'pan-yər, 'pan-ē-ər\ *n.* **1** A large basket, especially one of wicker, carried on the back of an animal or the shoulder of a person. **2** A framework worn by women to expand their skirts at the hips. **3** An overskirt puffed out at the sides and back.

pan·o·ply \'pan-ə-plē\ *n.; pl.* **pan·o·plies. 1** A full suit of armor. **2** Anything defending or protecting completely by covering; anything forming a magnificent covering or environment. The automobiles in the parade were covered with *panoplies* of flowers and bunting. — **pan·o·plied** \-plēd\ *adj.*

pan·o·rama \ˌpan-r-'am-ə, -'äm-, -'ám-\ *n.* **1** A picture that is unrolled little by little as a person looks at it. **2** A clear, complete view in every direction. **3** A complete view or treatment of any subject; as, a *panorama* of history. — **pan·o·ram·ic** \-'am-ik\ *adj.*

pan·pipe \'pan-ˌpīp\ *n.* A wind instrument consisting of a series of hollow reeds or pipes of different lengths, closed at one end and bound together with the mouth pieces in an even row.

panpipe

pan·sy \'pan-zē\ *n.; pl.* **pan·sies.** [From medieval English *pensee,* there borrowed from medieval French *pensée,* meaning literally "thought".] A low-growing, commonly annual plant belonging to the violet group and derived from the wild pansy or Johnny-jump-up, with small purple and violet flowers and, in its various garden forms, with showy five-petaled flowers that are usually of cream, violet, or yellow.

pant \'pant\ *v.* **1** To breathe hard or quickly; to gasp; as, to *pant* from running. **2** To want intensely; to long. **3** To breathe or say quickly and with difficulty. — *n.* **1** One of a series of short, quick breaths, as after exercise; a gasp. **2** A puff, as of a steam engine.

pan·ta·lets or **pan·ta·lettes** \ˌpant-l-'ets\ *n. pl.* Long, loose drawers with ruffles around each ankle, worn by women and girls.

pan·ta·loon \ˌpant-l-'ün\ *n.* **1** A clown. **2** [in the plural] Trousers.

pan·the·ism \'pan(t)th-ē-ˌiz-m\ *n.* **1** Any doctrine or belief that the universe taken as a whole is God. **2** The worship of gods of various creeds or religions at one time, as at one period in ancient Rome.

pantalets

pan·ther \'pan(t)th-r\ *n.* **1** The leopard. **2** In America, the cougar.

pant·ies \'pant-ēz\ *n. pl.; sing.* **pant·ie** or **panty** \'pant-ē\. A child's or woman's undergarment covering the lower trunk, with a closed crotch and very short legs.

pan·to·mime \'pant-m-ˌīm\ *n.* **1** A performer skilled in the art of conveying emotions and ideas without the use of words. **2** A play in which the actors use few or no words. **3** Silent movements or facial expressions that show how a person feels about something. — *v.;* **pan·to·mimed; pan·to·mim·ing.** To represent by pantomime. — **pan·to·mim·ist** \-ˌī-məst, -ˌim-əst\ *n.*

pan·to·then·ic ac·id \ˌpant-ə-ˌthen-ik\. A substance in the vitamin-B complex that promotes growth, found especially in liver and yeast.

pan·try \'pan-trē\ *n.; pl.* **pan·tries.** A small room where food and dishes are kept.

pants \'pan(t)s\ *n. pl.* **1** Trousers. **2** Drawers; especially, panties.

pap \'pap\ *n.* A soft food, as gruel, for babies or sick persons.

pa·pa \'päp-ə, 'påp-ə\ *n.* Father.

pa·pa·cy \'pāp-ə-sē\ *n.; pl.* **pa·pa·cies. 1** The office or authority of the pope; the central government of the Roman Catholic Church. **2** The succession of popes; the papal line. **3** The term of a pope's reign.

pa·pal \'pāp-l\ *adj.* **1** Of or relating to the pope or the papacy. **2** Decreed or issued by the pope.

pa·paw or **paw·paw,** *n.* **1** \pə-'pȯ, pȯ-'pȯ\ The papaya. **2** \'päp-ˌȯ, 'pȯp-ˌȯ\ The oblong yellowish fruit, with many-seeded pulp, of a tree growing in the central and southern United States. **3** The tree itself.

pa·paya \pə-'pī-ə\ *n.* **1** A tropical tree having a crowning tuft of large deeply lobed leaves and large oblong fruit with yellow pulpy flesh, black seeds, and a thick rind. **2** The fruit of this tree.

pa·per \'pāp-r\ *n.* [From medieval English *papir,* there borrowed from medieval French *papier,* this derived from Latin *papyrus,* out of which the first paper was made — see *papyrus.*] **1** A pliable substance made in thin sheets from rags, wood, straw, or bark and used for many purposes, as to write or print on, to wrap things in, or to cover walls. **2** A sheet or piece of paper. A *paper* fell on the floor. **3** A piece of paper that contains a definite amount of something; as, a *paper* of pins. **4** Something printed or written on paper. She read a *paper* before her club. The pupils handed their *papers* to the teacher. **5** [in the plural] An official document that proves who a person is or what position he holds; as, an ambassador's *papers.* **6** A newspaper. **7** Wallpaper. **—** *v.;* **pa·pered; pa·per·ing** \-r(-)ing\. To furnish with paper; to cover or line with paper; as, to *paper* a room. **—** *adj.* **1** Having to do with paper; made of paper. **2** Dealing in, or used for, paper. **3** Like paper; papery; as, a nut with a *paper* shell. **4** Existing only as something written on paper; as, *paper* profits.

pa·per hang·er \'pāp-r ˌhang-r\ or **pa·per·er** \'pāp-r-r\ *n.* A person whose occupation is the applying of wallpaper to walls.

paper money. Engraved paper certificates which circulate in place of metallic money. Most modern countries find *paper money* more convenient than coins.

pa·per·weight \'pāp-r-ˌwāt\ *n.* An object used to hold down loose papers by its weight; as, an ornamental glass *paperweight.*

pa·pery \'pāp-r(-)ē\ *adj.* Like paper, as in being thin or flimsy.

pa·pier-mâ·ché \ˌpāp-r-mə-'shā, -ma-\ *n.* A substance made of paper pulp mixed with rosin, glue, or the like, which while wet can be shaped or molded into various articles, as masks or figurines, and when dry is hard and strong.

pa·pil·la \pə-'pil-ə\ *n.; pl.* **pa·pil·las** \-'pil-əz\ or **pa·pil·lae** \-'pil-ˌē, -ˌī\. Any small projection or part, as the nipple on a breast or the little nubs on the surface of the tongue.

pa·poose or **pap·poose** \pa-'püs, pə-\ *n.* A baby of North American Indian parents.

pa·pri·ka \pə-'prēk-ə, pa-\ *n.* The mild, red spice prepared from the ripe fruit of certain tropical American peppers, used more for its color than for its flavor.

pa·py·rus \pə-'pī-rəs\ *n.; pl.* **pa·py·rus·es** \-rə-səz\ or **pa·py·ri** \-ˌrī\. [From Latin, there borrowed from Greek *papyros,* where it was borrowed from Egyptian.] **1** A tall water plant found especially in Egypt, resembling the grasses but differing from the true grasses in having a solid stem. **2** A substance like paper made from the pith of this plant by the ancient Egyptians, Greeks, and Romans, and used by them to write on. **3** A writing on papyrus; especially, a scroll of papyrus with writing on it.

par \'pär, 'pår\ *n.* **1** The fixed value of the money unit of one country expressed in terms of the money unit of another country; as, to determine the present *par* of the English pound. **2** The value of a stock, bond, or other security as stated on its face; as, stock of $100 *par.* **3** An equally high level; as, two persons whose talents are on a *par.* **4** An accepted standard or normal level; as, to feel below *par.* **5** In golf, the number of strokes required to play a hole or round successfully according to course specifications. **—** *adj.* At or up to par; normal; as, the *par* value of a stock.

par·a·ble \'par-əb-l\ *n.* A short, simple story illustrating a moral attitude or a religious principle; as, the *parables* of Jesus.

pa·rab·o·la \pə-'rab-l-ə\ *n.* The curve formed by the intersection of a cone with a plane parallel to one of its sides; any curve resembling this one. A ball thrown high into the air will form a *parabola* in its flight.

par·a·chute \'par-ə-ˌshüt\ *n.* A large, folding device like an umbrella, made of a light fabric, such as silk or nylon, used in making a descent from airplanes high in the air. **—** *v.;* **par·a·chut·ed; par·a·chut·ing.** To jump or drop from an airplane with the aid of a parachute; as, troops *parachuting* from a plane; to *parachute* food to soldiers trapped in enemy territory. — **par·a·chut·ist** \-ˌshüt-əst\ *n.*

pa·rade \pə-'rād\ *n.* **1** Pompous show or display; as, a *parade* of one's wealth. **2** The formation of troops before an officer for inspection. **3** Any orderly movement of a group along a certain route; as, a circus *parade.* **4** A crowd of people promenading; as, the Easter *parade.* **—** *v.;* **pa·rad·ed; pa·rad·ing. 1** To show off; to display; as, to *parade* one's knowledge. **2** Of troops, to march in military formation, as for inspection. **3** To walk in an orderly group, along a certain route. The supporters of the candidate *paraded* along the main street in a campaign demonstration. **4** To exhibit oneself, as by walking in public; as, schoolgirls *parading* along the sidewalks during the noon hour.

par·a·digm \'par-ə-ˌdim, -ˌdīm\ *n.* **1** A model or pattern; as, an essay that is a *paradigm* of clear writing. **2** In grammar, an example of a conjugation or declension, showing a word in all its inflectional forms.

par·a·dise \ˈpar-ə-ˌdīs, -ˌdīz\ *n.* **1** [with a capital] The Garden of Eden. **2** Heaven. **3** A place or state of bliss.

par·a·dox \ˈpar-ə-ˌdäks\ *n.* **1** A statement that seems contrary to good sense, but may still be true. **2** Any fact or event that seems to have contrary or conflicting qualities within itself. **3** A person or thing full of contradictions or inconsistencies. — **par·a·dox·i·cal** \ˌpar-ə-ˈdäks-ik-l\ *adj.* — **par·a·dox·i·cal·ly** \-ik-l(-)ē\ *adv.*

par·af·fin \ˈpar-əf-n\ *n.* A white or colorless, tasteless, odorless wax made from wood, coal, or petroleum, and used in making candles, sealing foods, and waterproofing paper. — *v.* **1** To saturate with paraffin. **2** To apply paraffin to; as, to *paraffin* cheese to prevent its losing its moisture.

par·a·gon \ˈpar-ə-ˌgän, -əg-n\ *n.* A model of excellence or perfection; as, a *paragon* of beauty.

par·a·graph \ˈpar-ə-ˌgraf\ *n.* **1** A part of a piece of writing or a speech that develops in an organized manner one point of a subject or gives the words of one speaker. **2** A short written article, complete in one undivided section, as in a newspaper. — *v.* To divide into paragraphs; as, to *paragraph* a letter.

Par·a·guay·an \ˌpar-ə-ˈgwī-ən, -ˈgwā-\ *adj.* Of or relating to Paraguay. — *n.* A native of Paraguay.

par·a·keet or **par·ra·keet** \ˈpar-ə-ˌkēt\ *n.* A small parrot with a slender body and a long tail.

par·al·lel \ˈpar-ə-ˌlel, -ləl\ *adj.* **1** Lying or moving in the same direction but always the same distance apart; as, *parallel* lines. Train tracks are *parallel.* **2** Like; similar; as, *parallel* circumstances. — *n.* **1** A parallel line, curve, or surface. **2** Resemblance; likeness; similarity. **3** A comparison to show resemblance; as, to draw a *parallel.* **4** A thing or happening that is like another; as, an engine whose performance was without *parallel.* **5** An arrangement in an electrical system in which all positive poles are connected to one conductor and all negative poles to another — used chiefly in the phrase *in parallel.* **6** One of the imaginary circles on the earth's surface, parallel to the equator, that marks latitude; a line that represents this on a globe or map. — *v.;* **par·al·leled**; **par·al·lel·ing.** **1** To compare; as, to *parallel* the playwright's skill with Shakespeare's. **2** To correspond to; as, two events which *parallel* each other. **3** To extend in the same direction as. This highway *parallels* the river.

parallel lines

par·al·lel·e·pi·ped \ˌpar-ə-ˌlel-ə-ˈpīp-əd\ or **par·al·lel·e·pip·e·don** \-ˈpip-ə-ˌdän\ *n.* A six-sided prism whose faces are parallelograms.

par·al·lel·ism \ˈpar-ə-ˌlel-ˌiz-m, -lə-ˌliz-m\ *n.* Close similarity in construction of adjacent word groups, as for rhythm or effect, as in "What we anticipate seldom occurs; what we least expect generally happens".

par·al·lel·o·gram \ˌpar-ə-ˈlel-ə-ˌgram\ *n.* In geometry, a four-sided figure, the opposite sides of which are parallel and therefore equal.

parallelograms

pa·ral·y·sis \pə-ˈral-ə-səs\ *n.; pl.* **pa·ral·y·ses** \-ˌsēz\. Loss of the normal action of an organ or a part of the body; especially, loss of the power of voluntary movement and of the sensation of touch.

par·a·lyt·ic \ˌpar-ə-ˈlit-ik\ *adj.* Of or related to paralysis; like paralysis. — *n.* A person affected with paralysis.

par·a·lyze \ˈpar-ə-ˌlīz\ *v.;* **par·a·lyzed**; **par·a·lyz·ing.** **1** To affect with paralysis. **2** To destroy or lessen the effectiveness or activity of anything; as, a labor dispute that *paralyzed* the industry.

par·a·me·cium \ˌpar-ə-ˈmēsh-m, -ˈmē-s(h)ē-əm\ *n.; pl.* **par·a·me·ciums** \-ˈmēsh-mz, -ˈmē-s(h)ē-əmz\ or **par·a·me·cia** \-ˈmē-shə, -ˈmē-s(h)ē-ə\. A one-celled animal whose slipper-shaped body is provided with minute hairs, or cilia, by means of which it swims about.

par·a·mount \ˈpar-ə-ˌmau̇nt\ *adj.* Superior to all others; chief; supreme; as, an event of *paramount* importance.

par·a·noia \ˌpar-ə-ˈnȯi-ə\ *n.* A mental derangement characterized by feelings of persecution or by distorted ideas of one's own importance. — **par·a·noi·ac** \-ˈnȯi-ˌak\ *n.*

par·a·noid \ˈpar-ə-ˌnȯid\ *adj.* Of or relating to paranoia; having some of the symptoms associated with paranoia. — *n.* A person affected with paranoia or showing some of its symptoms.

par·a·pet \ˈpar-ə-pət, -ˌpet\ *n.* **1** A wall of earth or stone to protect soldiers; a breastwork. **2** A low wall or railing at the edge of a platform, roof, or bridge.

par·a·pher·na·lia \ˌpar-ə-fə-ˈnāl-yə, -əf-r-ˈnāl-\ *n. pl.* **1** Personal belongings, such as clothes. **2** Equipment; furnishings; apparatus.

par·a·phrase \ˈpar-ə-ˌfrāz\ *n.* A restatement of something, giving the meaning in different words. — *v.;* **par·a·phrased**; **par·a·phras·ing.** To make a paraphrase of; to give the meaning of something in different words.

par·a·site \ˈpar-ə-ˌsīt\ *n.* **1** A person who lives at the expense of another. **2** A plant or animal that lives in or on some other living creature, and gets food and sometimes shelter from it; as, the *parasite* mistletoe. Hookworm is caused by a *parasite.*

par·a·sit·ic \ˌpar-ə-ˈsit-ik\ *adj.* Of or relating to parasites; living on other organisms. — **par·a·sit·ism** \ˈpar-ə-ˌsīt-ˌiz-m\ *n.*

par·a·sol \ˈpar-ə-ˌsȯl\ *n.* A light umbrella used as a protection against the sun.

par·a·thy·roid gland \ˌpar-ə-ˈthī-ˌrȯid\. One of the several small oval glands near or embedded in the thyroid gland which secrete a hormone (**par·a·thor·mone** \-ˈthȯr-ˌmōn\) that is essential in the regulation of the calcium supply in the body.

par·a·troop·er \ˈpar-ə-ˌtrüp-r\ *n.* A member of a unit of paratroops.

par·a·troops \ˈpar-ə-ˌtrüps\ *n. pl.* Infantry soldiers specially trained and equipped to descend into enemy-held territory by parachute.

par·a·ty·phoid \ˌpar-ə-ˈtī-ˌfȯid\ *adj.* Of, relating to, or naming a disease (**paratyphoid fever**) that is caused by bacteria and resembles typhoid fever.

par·cel \ˈpärs-l, ˈpȧrs-l\ *n.* **1** A bundle or package. **2** A piece or part; as, a *parcel* of land. — *v.;* **par·celed** or **par·celled; par·cel·ing** or **par·cel·ling** \-l(-)ing\. **1** To divide and distribute by parts; as, to *parcel* out supplies. **2** To wrap up into a parcel.

parcel post \ˈpōst\. The branch of the post office that collects, carries, and delivers parcels.

parch \ˈpärch, ˈpȧrch\ *v.* **1** To scorch; to roast over a fire; as, to *parch* corn. **2** To dry up; to shrivel, as with heat. The ground was *parched* by the sun.

parch·ment \ˈpärch-mənt, ˈpȧrch-\ *n.* **1** The skin of sheep or goats, prepared so that it can be written on. **2** Any paper similar to parchment. **3** Something written on parchment.

par·don \ˈpärd-n, ˈpȧrd-n\ *v.;* **par·doned; par·don·ing** \-n(-)ing\. **1** To forgive; to excuse. **2** To free from punishment for a fault or crime. — *n.* **1** Forgiveness. **2** An official release from legal punishment. — For synonyms see *excuse.*

par·don·a·ble \ˈpärd-n(-)əb-l, ˈpȧrd-\ *adj.* That can be pardoned; excusable; as, a *pardonable* fault. — **par·don·a·bly** \-n(-)ə-blē\ *adv.*

pare \ˈpar, ˈper\ *v.;* **pared; par·ing. 1** To cut or shave off the outside or the ends of something; as, to *pare* an apple; to *pare* one's nails. **2** To reduce as if by cutting; as, to *pare* the cost.

pa·ren·chy·ma \pə-ˈrengk-m-ə\ *n.* **1** A tissue of higher plants consisting of thin-walled living cells that remain capable of cell division even when mature, that are agents of photosynthesis and storage, and that make up much of the substance of leaves and roots and the pulp of fruits as well as parts of stems and supporting structures. **2** The functional tissue of an animal organ, as a gland, as distinguished from its supporting tissue or framework.

par·ent \ˈpar-ənt, ˈper-\ *n.* **1** A father or mother. **2** Any animal or plant that produces offspring or seed. **3** A source or origin. Some scientists consider the sun the *parent* of our planetary system.

par·ent·age \ˈpar-ən-tij, ˈper-\ *n.* Descent from parents or ancestors; birth; as, a man of noble *parentage.*

pa·ren·tal \pə-ˈrent-l\ *adj.* Of, concerned with, or like parents; as, *parental* affection. — **pa·ren·tal·ly** \-l-ē\ *adv.*

pa·ren·the·sis \pə-ˈren(t)th-ə-səs\ *n.; pl.* **pa·ren·the·ses** \-ˌsēz\. **1** A word, phrase, or sentence put into the middle or at the end of a sentence to explain or comment on the thought. **2** One or both of the curved marks [( )] used in writing and printing to set off such a word, phrase, or sentence.

par·en·thet·ic \ˌpar-ən-ˈthet-ik\ *adj.* Using parentheses; expressed in parentheses; commenting or explaining; as, a *parenthetic* statement.

par·en·thet·i·cal \ˌpar-ən-ˈthet-ik-l\ *adj.* Parenthetic. — **par·en·thet·i·cal·ly** \-ik-l(-)ē\ *adv.*

par·ent·hood \ˈpar-ənt-ˌhu̇d, ˈper-\ *n.* State of being a parent.

par ex·cel·lence \ˈpär ˌeks-ə-ˈläns\. **1** Surpassingly; to the greatest extent; as, a section of a city that *par excellence* stands outside the law. **2** Of the first degree; beyond comparison; excellent; as, a cook *par excellence.*

par·fait \pär-ˈfā, pȧr-\ *n.* **1** A custard made from a syrup thickened with eggs and whipped cream and frozen without stirring. **2** A cold dessert made of layers of ice cream, syrup, fruit, and whipped cream.

pa·ri·ah \pə-ˈrī-ə\ *n.* A person or animal despised by everyone; an outcast.

par·ing \ˈpar-ing, ˈper-\ *n.* **1** The act of shaving off the outside or the ends of something. **2** The thing pared off; as, potato *parings.*

Par·is green \ˈpar-əs ˈgrēn\. A poisonous bright green powder containing arsenic, used as a pigment and as an insecticide.

par·ish \ˈpar-ish\ *n.* **1** A section of a diocese in charge of a priest or minister. **2** The persons who live in such a section and attend the parish church. **3** The members of any church. **4** In Louisiana, a division of the state corresponding to a county in other states.

pa·rish·ion·er \pə-ˈrish-n(-)ər\ *n.* An inhabitant of a parish or a member of its church.

par·i·ty \ˈpar-ət-ē\ *n.* The quality or state of being equal or equivalent; equality.

park \ˈpärk, ˈpȧrk\ *n.* **1** A large tract of ground around a great country house, kept as a recreation ground, as for walking and riding. **2** An area of land in or near a town or city, set aside for recreation or for ornament. **3** An area of land preserved in its natural state as a public property; as, Yellowstone *Park.* **4** Any open place where vehicles, as automobiles, are assembled and left unoccupied; as, a car *park.* — *v.* **1** To leave a vehicle standing on a street or in any open place; as, to *park* a car. **2** *Slang.* To place and leave for a time something to be removed later. You can *park* your books on that table.

par·ka \ˈpärk-ə, ˈpȧrk-ə\ *n.* A very warm jacket with a hood.

park·way \ˈpärk-ˌwā, ˈpȧrk-\ *n.* A wide road beautified with trees and grass.

parka

par·lance \ˈpär-lən(t)s, ˈpȧr-\ *n.* Speech; way of speaking; as, a police officer, in common *parlance* called a cop.

par·ley \ˈpär-lē, ˈpȧr-\ *n.; pl.* **par·leys.** A discussion; a conversation; especially, a conference with an enemy; as, a truce *parley.* — *v.* To confer, especially with an enemy about terms.

par·lia·ment \ˈpärl-ə-mənt, ˈpärl-yə-, ˈpȧrl-\ *n.*

1 A formal conference on public affairs; in history, any of a number of such conferences. 2 [often with a capital] In various countries, the assembly that constitutes the lawmaking branch of the government; as, the British *Parliament.*

par·lia·men·tar·i·an \ˌpärl-ə-ˌmen-'ter-ē-ən, ˌpärl-yə-, ˌpȧrl-, -mən-\ *n.* One with expert knowledge of rules and usages of parliamentary procedure.

par·lia·men·ta·ry \ˌpärl-ə-'ment-r-ē, ˌpärl-yə-, ˌpȧrl-, -'men-trē\ *adj.* 1 Of, relating to, or like a parliament. 2 According to the customs or rules of a parliament; as, *parliamentary* practice. 3 Having a parliament; organized with a parliament as a lawmaking body; as, a *parliamentary* form of government.

par·lor \'pärl-r, 'pȧrl-r\ *n.* 1 A sitting room in a private house, especially one for receiving guests; a living room. 2 A public room in an inn or hotel, separated from the main lounge or lobby and intended to offer semiprivacy to guests. 3 A room or group of rooms fitted up for use in a business that offers personal service or amusement; as, a beauty *parlor;* a billiard *parlor.*

parlor car. An extra-fare railroad car for day travel, having more comfortable accommodations than a coach.

par·lous \'pär-ləs, 'pȧr-\ *adj.* 1 *Archaic.* Perilous; risky. 2 Very bad; shocking; as, to consider the whole country in a *parlous* state.

pa·ro·chi·al \pə-'rōk-ē-əl\ *adj.* 1 Of or belonging to a parish. 2 Supported by a parish or by a religious body; as, a *parochial* school. 3 Confined to a small section such as a parish; narrow; limited; as, a man with a very *parochial* attitude on many questions. — **pa·ro·chi·al·ism** \-ē-ə-ˌliz-m\ *n.*

par·o·dy \'par-əd-ē\ *n.; pl.* **par·o·dies.** A piece of writing in which the language and style of an author are mimicked for comic effect or in ridicule. — *v.;* **par·o·died** \-ēd\; **par·o·dy·ing.** To write a parody of; to mimic; to burlesque. — **par·o·dist** \-əd-əst\ *n.*

pa·role \pə-'rōl\ *n.* 1 A solemn pledge or promise; especially, a promise given by a prisoner of war to carry out certain conditions in return for certain privileges, usually release from captivity. 2 The conditional release of a prisoner from a prison or jail before his sentence has ended. 3 The condition of being on parole. — *v.;* **pa·roled; pa·rol·ing.** To release on parole.

pa·rol·ee \pə-ˌrō-'lē, pə-'rō-(ˌ)lē, ˌpar-ə-'lē\ *n.* A person released on parole.

pa·rot·id \pə-'rät-əd\ *adj.* Relating to or in the region of a salivary gland (**parotid gland**) below and in front of the ear; as, the *parotid* duct.

par·ox·ysm \'par-ək-ˌsiz-m\ *n.* 1 A fit, attack, or increase of violence of a disease that occurs at intervals; as, a *paroxysm* of coughing. 2 Any sudden, violent action or burst of feeling; as, a *paroxysm* of rage.

par·quet \pär-'kā, pȧr-\ *n.* 1 A flooring of parquetry. 2 The lower floor of a theater, especially in front of the balcony.

par·quet·ry \'pärk-ə-trē, 'pȧrk-\ *n.* Fine woodwork inlaid, usually, in geometric patterns, used especially for floors.

parquetry

parrakeet. Variant of *parakeet.*

par·rot \'par-ət\ *n.* 1 A bright-colored tropical bird of a family characterized by a strong, hooked bill, toes arranged in pairs, two in front and two behind, and by the ability to mimic human speech. 2 A person who repeats words mechanically and without understanding. — *v.* To repeat mechanically.

par·ry \'par-ē\ *v.;* **par·ried** \-ēd\; **par·ry·ing.** 1 To ward off; to turn aside skillfully; as, to *parry* a blow. 2 To avoid; to evade; as, to *parry* an embarrassing question. — *n.; pl.* **par·ries.** A warding off or evading, as of a blow.

parse \'pärs, 'pȧrs, 'pärz, 'pȧrz\ *v.;* **parsed; pars·ing.** 1 To analyze a sentence, naming its parts and their relations to each other. 2 To give the part of speech of a word and explain its relation to other words in a sentence.

Par·si or **Par·see** \'pär-ˌsē, 'pȧr-\ *n.* A Zoroastrian descended from Persian refugees and settled in India.

par·si·mo·ni·ous \ˌpär-sə-'mō-nē-əs, ˌpȧr-\ *adj.* Extremely economical; stingy. — **par·si·mo·ni·ous·ly,** *adv.*

par·si·mo·ny \'pär-sə-ˌmō-nē, 'pȧr-\ *n.* Extreme frugality; stinginess.

pars·ley \'pärs-lē, 'pȧrs-\ *n.; pl.* **pars·leys.** A garden plant with crisp, curly leaves used in cooking and for decorating various dishes.

pars·nip \'pärs-nəp, 'pȧrs-\ *n.* 1 A strong-scented plant of the carrot family, grown for its edible fleshy white root. 2 The root of this plant.

par·son \'pärs-n, 'pȧrs-n\ *n.* [From medieval English *person* meaning both "parson" and "person" — see *person.*] 1 A minister in charge of a parish; the pastor of a church. 2 Any clergyman.

par·son·age \'pärs-n(-)ij, 'pȧrs-\ *n.* A house provided for the pastor by a parish or congregation.

part \'pärt, 'pȧrt\ *n.* 1 One of the portions into which anything is divided; something less than a whole; a piece, section, or share. 2 A spare piece or member for a machine. 3 [in the plural] An ability; a talent; as, a man of *parts.* 4 A quarter, as of a city; a district; a region. 5 A portion of an animal body; as, the mouth *parts.* 6 A person's share, duty, or concern; as, to do one's *part.* 7 One of the sides in a disagreement; as, to take someone's *part* in a quarrel. 8 The line where one parts or divides one's hair in combing it. 9 In music, one particular voice or instrument or the music for this voice or instrument. 10 A character in a play. 11 The words and actions of a character in a play.

— The words *portion* and *fragment* are synonyms of *part: part* is a general term for one of the divisions of a whole thing, sometimes a piece separated or partly separated from the rest of the whole; *portion* suggests one section of a group or collection rather than of a compact whole and is used especially when referring to something allotted as a share; *fragment* usually indicates a small part broken off and separated from the whole, sometimes suggesting that the remainder has been used up or lost.

— **for the most part.** In most cases; in the main. — **in good part.** Without offense; favorably; graciously; as, to take the criticism *in good part.* — **in part.** In some degree; partly. — **on one's part** or **on the part of.** Characterizing one's action or behavior; experienced or shown by; as, a change in attitude *on the part of* the voters. — **part and parcel.** An essential part; a constituting force. — *v.* **1** To divide into parts; as, to *part* a sheet of paper in the middle. **2** To hold apart; to intervene between; as, to *part* the fighting boys. **3** To break into pieces. The rope *parted* in the middle. **4** To go away; to depart. **5** To separate; to give up a connection of any kind. Grandfather refused to *part* with his ragged old sweater.

part. Abbreviation for *participle.*

par·take \pär-'tāk, pər-, pȧr-\ *v.;* **par·took** \-'tu̇k\; **par·tak·en** \-'tāk-n\; **par·tak·ing.** **1** To have a share or part; to take a portion of; as, to *partake* of a meal. **2** To have something of the character of. The sailors' action *partook* of mutiny.

— The words *participate* and *share* are synonyms of *partake: share* usually suggests the granting to another of the partial use, enjoyment, or possession of something one owns or the acceptance of this by the receiver; *participate* may indicate a taking part in some experience, enterprise, or activity in common with other persons; *partake* is likely to suggest the accepting or acquiring of a share in something, particularly food or drink.

par·tak·er \pär-'tāk-r, pər-, pȧr-\ *n.* One who takes a share or part of something.

par·tial \'pärsh-l, 'pȧrsh-l\ *adj.* **1** Favoring one side of a question over another; biased; as, *partial* in his judgment. **2** Fond of some person or thing; especially, foolishly fond; as, *partial* to ice cream sodas. **3** Of or relating to one part or portion only; not complete; as, *partial* deafness; a *partial* eclipse. — *n.* In music, a partial tone. — **par·tial·ly** \-l(-)ē\ *adv.*

par·ti·al·i·ty \ˌpär-shē-'al-ət-ē, ˌpȧr-; pär-'shal-, pȧr-\ *n.; pl.* **par·ti·al·i·ties.** **1** The quality or state of being partial; bias; prejudice; as, to show *partiality* in choosing the winner. **2** A particular fondness, taste, or liking; as, a *partiality* for baseball.

partial tone. One of the simple tones of which a complex musical tone is composed.

par·tic·i·pant \pər-'tis-ə-pənt, pär-, pȧr-\ *n.* A person who takes a part or share; a sharer; as, one of the *participants* in a game.

par·tic·i·pate \pər-'tis-ə-ˌpāt, pär-, pȧr-\ *v.;* **par·tic·i·pat·ed**; **par·tic·i·pat·ing.** To have a share in common with others; to share; to take part; as, to *participate* in a first-aid demonstration. — For synonyms see *partake.* — **par·tic·i·pa·tion** \-ˌtis-ə-'pāsh-n\ *n.* — **par·tic·i·pa·tor** \-'tis-ə-ˌpāt-r\ *n.*

par·ti·cip·i·al \ˌpärt-ə-'sip-ē-əl, ˌpȧrt-\ *adj.* Of, relating to, or including a participle; as, a *participial* phrase. — **par·ti·cip·i·al·ly** \-ē-ə-lē\ *adv.*

par·ti·ci·ple \'pärt-ə-ˌsip-l, 'pȧrt-; 'pärt-səp-l, 'pȧrt-\ *n.* A word formed from a verb and used partly like a verb and partly like an adjective, having the power to modify a noun, to take an object when active and transitive, and to be modified by an adverb, and sometimes having tense and voice.

par·ti·cle \'pärt-ik-l, 'pȧrt-\ *n.* **1** A very small part of matter; as, a *particle* of sand. **2** Any of the very small things of which all matter is composed. Atoms are considered as being made up of elementary *particles*, such as electrons and neutrons.

par·ti-col·ored \'pärt-ē-ˌkəl-rd, 'pȧrt-\ *adj.* Colored with different tints; variegated; as, a *particolored* costume.

par·tic·u·lar \pə(r)-'tik-yəl-r, pär-, pȧr-\ *adj.* **1** Of or relating to one or some but not all of the things called by the same name; individual; single; certain; as, the *particular* stars of a constellation. **2** Of or relating to a single person, class, or thing; as, one's own *particular* problem. **3** Noteworthy; special; as, no *particular* advantage. **4** Attentive to small details; precise; fastidious; as, a person who is *particular* about his clothes. — *n.* An individual fact, point, or item; as, full *particulars* of the accident. — **in particular.** **1** Especially; peculiarly; particularly. **2** Individually; in detail.

par·tic·u·lar·i·ty \pə(r)-ˌtik-yə-'lar-ət-ē, pär-, pȧr-\ *n.; pl.* **par·tic·u·lar·i·ties.** **1** Great care; attention to small things. **2** Carefulness of behavior or expression. **3** A peculiarity; a small detail.

par·tic·u·lar·ize \pə(r)-'tik-yəl-r-ˌīz, pär-, pȧr-\ *v.;* **par·tic·u·lar·ized**; **par·tic·u·lar·iz·ing.** **1** To give as a particular; as, to *particularize* each expenditure made during a trip. **2** To state in detail.

par·tic·u·lar·ly \pə(r)-'tik-yəl-r-lē, pär-, pȧr-, -'tik-yə-lē\ *adv.* **1** In a particular manner. **2** Especially; extremely; as, *particularly* anxious to go.

part·ing \'pärt-ing, 'pȧrt-\ *n.* **1** The action of separating; a division. **2** A place where a division or separation occurs; as, to reach the *parting* of the ways. **3** A leave-taking; as, to shake hands at *parting.* — *adj.* **1** Departing; as, the deepening shadows of *parting* day. **2** Dividing; separating; as, the *parting* insulation between two electric wires. **3** Given or done when departing; farewell; final; as, a *parting* kiss; a *parting* shot.

par·ti·san or **par·ti·zan** \'pärt-əz-n, 'pȧrt-, -əs-n\ *n.* **1** A person who takes the part of another; especially, a devoted adherent, as to a cause. **2** A member of a guerrilla force within enemy lines who impedes the enemy by sabotage and raids. — *adj.* Clinging to a party or faction, especially unreasoningly. — **par·ti·san·ship** \-ˌship\ *n.*

par·ti·ta \pär-'tēt-ə, pȧr-\ *n.* **1** An instrumental form of music consisting of a series of dances in the same or related keys, often with an elaborate prelude. **2** A set of musical variations.

par·ti·tion \pär-'tish-n, pər-, pȧr-\ *n.* **1** A division; a separation; as, the *partition* of a defeated country. **2** Something that divides or separates; especially, an interior wall dividing one part of a house from another. **3** A portion; a section or division. — *v.;* **par·ti·tioned**; **par·ti·tion·ing** \-n(-)ing\. **1** To divide into parts or shares; as, to *partition* an estate. **2** To divide into distinct parts, as by a line or wall; as, to *partition* off a basement.

part·ly \'pärt-lē, 'pȧrt-\ *adv.* In part; in some measure; partially; as, to be *partly* correct.

part·ner \'pärt-nər, 'pȧrt-\ *n.* **1** A person who shares something with another or others. **2** A husband or wife. **3** Either of a couple who dance together. **4** In games, one who plays on the same side or team with another person or other persons. **5** One of the members of a partnership.

part·ner·ship \'pärt-nər-ˌship, 'pȧrt-\ *n.* **1** The condition of being a partner; the relation between partners. **2** The contract by which a partnership is created. **3** A form of business organization in which the partners agree to share the profits and in which, often, each partner is individually liable for any losses.

part of speech. One of the classes (noun, adjective, pronoun, verb, adverb, preposition, conjunction, and interjection) into which words are traditionally and somewhat arbitrarily placed according to their function in a sentence.

partook. Past tense of *partake*.

par·tridge \'pär-trij, 'pȧr-\ *n.; pl.* **par·tridg·es** or **par·tridge**. **1** Any of several stout-bodied game birds, related to the domestic fowl. **2** In the northern United States, a ruffed grouse.

part song. A melody written to be sung in parts, usually four parts, and often without accompaniment.

par·ty \'pärt-ē, 'pȧrt-ē\ *n.; pl.* **par·ties**. **1** A group of persons who take one side of a question, or believe in one set of principles; especially, an organized political group whose purpose is the nomination and sponsoring of candidates for public office; as, both major *parties*. **2** A group of persons gathered together for pleasure or entertainment; the entertainment or gathering itself; as, a dinner *party*. **3** A part of a larger group assigned to some task; a detachment; as, a scouting *party*. **4** A person concerned in an affair; one who takes part in something; as, to be a *party* in a law suit.

— The word *faction* is a synonym of *party: party* usually suggests a relatively large group of persons holding a common set of political beliefs and principles and attempting to gain their desires through the election of their chosen candidates; *faction* is likely to indicate a smaller group, especially one that is quarrelsome and thoughtless of the public good in gaining its own selfish ends.

par value. Nominal value; face value.

par·ve·nu \'pär-və-ˌnü, 'pȧr-, -ˌnyü\ *n.; pl.* **par·ve·nus** \-ˌnüz, -ˌnyüz\. [From French, where it is derived from the past participle of *parvenir* meaning "to arrive", "to attain".] A person who has risen above the social position to which he was born, especially by the acquisition of wealth, and who is not accustomed to his new position; an upstart.

pa·sha \'päsh-ə, 'pȧsh-ə, 'pash-ə\ *n.* An honorary title, no longer used, that was placed after the name of high-ranking Turkish officers.

pass \'pas\ *n.* **1** An opening or way for passing along or through. **2** A gap in a mountain range.

pass \'pas\ *n.* **1** The act of passing; passage. **2** Accomplishment — now used only in archaic phrases, as *to come to pass.* **3** Condition of affairs; situation. Things have come to a strange *pass.* **4** A permit to go or come, such as a ticket or official order; as, a free *pass* on the railroad; a weekend *pass.* **5** A movement of the hand over, before, or along anything; as, a magician making a few *passes* over his hat before pulling out the rabbit. **6** In games, a transfer of the ball from one player to another. — *v.* **1** To go; to move; as, to *pass* by the house. Time *passes* quickly. **2** To move or cause to move from one place or condition to another. The business has *passed* into other hands. The man *passed* his business on to his son. **3** To go away; to depart. Sorrow *passes.* **4** To allow to go on; to go by, over, beyond, or through; as, to *pass* only those who have tickets; to *pass* a pupil into the next grade. **5** To advance a law through the steps necessary before it can be put into action. **6** To go successfully through, as an examination or inspection; as, to *pass* a test. **7** To move from one person to another; as, to *pass* a football; to *pass* a dollar bill. **8** To take place; to occur; as, the thoughts that *pass* within our minds. **9** To be recognized or generally known; as, to *pass* as an expert. **10** In card games, to decline to play or to bid. **11** To cause to be accepted; as, to *pass* oneself off as a war hero. — **pass away** or **pass on**. To die. — **pass out**. To lose consciousness; to faint.

pass·a·ble \'pas-əb-l\ *adj.* **1** Capable of being passed, traveled, or crossed; as, *passable* roads. **2** Tolerable; moderate; mediocre; as, a *passable* talent for acting. — **pass·a·bly** \-ə-blē\ *adv.*

pas·sage \'pas-ij\ *n.* **1** The act of passing, going, or proceeding. **2** A means of passing; a road; a way; a hall, lobby, or corridor. **3** A journey; a voyage; as, to have a smooth *passage* over the sea. **4** A right or permission to pass; as, *passage* at a reduced rate. **5** The enactment by a legislature of a bill into law. **6** A particular portion of something, as a speech, book, or musical composition.

pas·sage·way \'pas-ij-ˌwā\ *n.* A road or way by which a person or thing may pass; a passage; as, a dark *passageway* between two cellar rooms; a *passageway* between buildings.

pass·book \'pas-ˌbu̇k\ *n.* A depositor's book in which a bank enters his deposits and, sometimes, his withdrawals.

pas·sé \pa-'sā\ *adj.* [From French, meaning literally "past"; the past participle of *passer* meaning "to pass".] Out-of-date; behind the times; as, fashions that are now *passé.*

pas·sel \'pas-l\ *n. Dial.* A large number; a lot; as, a *passel* of cowboys riding the range.

pas·sen·ger \'pas-nj-r\ *n.* **1** A passerby; a wayfarer; as, a foot *passenger*. **2** A person who travels on some kind of public vehicle, as a boat or train.

passenger pigeon. A North American wild pigeon formerly abundant but now extinct.

pass·er \'pas-r\ *n.* One who passes.

pass·er-by \'pas-r-'bī\ *n.; pl.* **pass·ers-by**. One who passes by.

pass·ing \'pas-ing\ *adj.* **1** Going by, beyond, through, or away; as, the *passing* crowd. **2** Lasting only for a short time; not enduring; as, a *passing* fancy or wish. **3** Indicating satisfactory completion of an examination or course of study; as, a *passing* mark. **4** Given in passing; hasty; as, a *passing* glance. — *adv. Archaic.* Exceedingly; very; as, *passing* strange. — *n.* **1** The act of a person or thing that passes. **2** Departure; especially, death. **3** A means of passing; a ford.

pas·sion \'pash-n\ *n.* **1** [with a capital] The suffering of Christ on the cross, or between the night of the Last Supper and his death. **2** Strong feeling or emotion; as, to speak with *passion* for a cause in which one believes. **3** An outburst of feeling; as, to break into a furious *passion*. **4** [in the plural] The feelings; as, to curb the *passions* of a mob. **5** Rage; anger; as, to be goaded into an ungovernable *passion*. **6** Love for a person of the opposite sex, especially physical love. **7** A strong liking; a longing; as, a *passion* for music; a *passion* to speak the truth. **8** An object of one's love, liking, or longing. Red roses were the gardener's *passion*.

pas·sion·ate \'pash-n(-)ət\ *adj.* **1** Easily moved or excited; quick-tempered. **2** Ardent in feeling or desire; showing strong emotion; as, a *passionate* speech. — **pas·sion·ate·ly**, *adv.*

pas·sion·flow·er \'pash-n-ˌflaůr\ *n.* [So called from the resemblance of the corona of the flowers to a crown of thorns, this suggesting the passion or suffering of Christ.] Any of a genus of tropical climbing vines or erect herbs having showy symmetrical flowers.

Passion play. A play representing scenes connected with Christ's suffering and crucifixion.

pas·sive \'pas-iv\ *adj.* **1** Not active, but acted upon; as, *passive* spectators, not actors. **2** Enduring without resistance; patient; as, *passive* obedience. **3** In grammar, representing the subject as the receiver of the action expressed by the verb; as, a verb in the *passive* voice; the *passive* verb "was beaten" in "The team was badly beaten". — **pas·sive·ly**, *adv.*

pass·key \'pas-ˌkē\ *n.* **1** A key for opening two or more locks. **2** A private key.

Pass·over \'pas-ˌōv-r\ *n.* An annual Jewish feast commemorating that event spoken of in the Bible as the sparing, or passing over, of the Hebrews in Egypt when God killed the first-born children of the Egyptians.

pass·port \'pas-ˌpōrt, -ˌpȯrt\ *n.* **1** An official document issued upon request to a citizen desiring to travel abroad authorizing him to leave his own country and requesting protection for him abroad. **2** Something that gains admission or approval for its possessor; as, a friendship with a duke that was a *passport* to society.

pass·word \'pas-ˌwərd\ *n.* A secret word to be uttered by a person before he is allowed to pass, as through a line of guards; a countersign.

past \'past\ *adj.* **1** Of or relating to a former time; as, for a long time *past;* in times *past*. **2** Just gone by; just preceding; as, during the *past* year. **3** Expressing a time gone by; as, the *past* tenses of the verb. **4** No longer serving as; as, a *past* president. — *n.* **1** A former time or condition; as, in the *past*. **2** Past life or history; especially, a past life that is secret or mysterious; as, a man with a *past*. **3** The past tense or a verb in the past tense. — *adv.* By. A deer fled *past*. — *prep.* **1** Beyond in time or age; after; as, *past* ten o'clock. **2** Beyond in position or place; as, *past* the red barn. **3** Beyond the influence of; as, to be *past* feeling.

paste \'pāst\ *n.* **1** Dough; especially, dough rich in fat, for pastry. **2** Dough made of wheat flour and dried in tubes or strips; uncooked macaroni or noodles. **3** A smooth food product made by grinding certain substances and mixing them with some liquid; as, almond *paste;* sardine *paste*. **4** A soft candy with the consistency of gum. **5** A preparation of flour and water or starch and water, used for sticking things together. **6** Any soft doughy mixture, as a kind of wet clay used in making pottery or china. **7** A very brilliant glass used in imitating precious stones. — *v.;* **past·ed; past·ing. 1** To stick with paste or mucilage; as, to *paste* pictures in a scrapbook. **2** To cover by or as if by pasting; as, to *paste* a wall with advertisements. — **past·er** \'pāst-r\ *n.*

paste \'pāst\ *v.;* **past·ed; past·ing.** *Slang.* **1** To hit; to punch. **2** To defeat badly. — *n. Slang.* A pasting; a blow.

paste·board \'pāst-ˌbōrd, -ˌbȯrd\ *n.* A stiff material made of sheets of paper pasted together or of pulp pressed and dried.

pas·tel \(')pas-'tel\ *n.* **1** A paste made of ground color or colors, used for making crayons. **2** A crayon made from such a paste. **3** A drawing made with crayons of this kind. **4** Any of various soft pale colors. — \'pas-ˌtel\ *adj.* Light or pale in color; as, *pastel* shades of green.

pas·tern \'past-rn\ *n.* The part of the foot of a horse between the fetlock and the joint at the hoof.

pas·teur·i·za·tion \ˌpas-chər-ə-'zāsh-n, ˌpast-r-ə-\ *n.* Partial sterilization of a fluid, as milk or wine, by exposure to heat at a temperature which does not greatly affect its chemical composition, the standard for milk being 145° F. for 30 minutes, followed by rapid cooling to below 50° F.

pas·teur·ize \'pas-chər-ˌīz, 'past-r-\ *v.;* **pas·teur·ized; pas·teur·iz·ing.** [Named after Louis *Pasteur* (1822–1895), the French scientist who invented the process.] To subject to pasteurization.

pastier. Comparative of *pasty*.

pastiest. Superlative of *pasty*.

pas·time \ˈpas-ˌtīm\ *n.* Anything that helps to make time pass pleasantly.

past·i·ness \ˈpās-tē-nəs\ *n.* The quality or condition of being pasty; pasty consistency or appearance.

past master. **1** A former master, as of a fraternal society, a club, or a guild. **2** One who has had great experience; as, a *past master* in the art of borrowing money.

pas·tor \ˈpast-r\ *n.* A minister or priest in charge of a church or parish.

pas·to·ral \ˈpast-r(-)əl\ *adj.* **1** Of or relating to shepherds or to rural life or scenes. **2** Characteristic or suggestive of the life of shepherds or of peaceful rural life; as, *pastoral* simplicity. **3** Relating to the pastor of a church; as, *pastoral* duties. — *n.* **1** A piece of literature describing peaceful rural life. **2** A rural scene or picture. **3** A pastorale.

pas·to·rale \ˌpast-r-ˈal, -ˈäl(-ē), -ˈal(-ē)\ *n.* An instrumental piece of music of idyllic or rustic simplicity and sentiment.

pas·tor·ate \ˈpast-r(-)ət\ *n.* **1** The office or duties of a pastor. **2** The term of service of a pastor. **3** A body of pastors, as of a denomination or a region.

past participle. The participle that in English is usually formed by adding *-ed*, *-d*, *-t*, *-en*, or *-n* to the verb, or by change of vowel of the verb, and that indicates completed action, as in "Many hands were *raised*" or "The ball was *thrown*".

past perfect tense. The tense that in English is formed with *had* and that indicates completion of an action earlier than a specified past time, as in "When we opened the ice cream we found it *had melted*".

past·ry \ˈpās-trē\ *n.; pl.* **past·ries.** Articles of food such as pies, puffs, and tarts.

past tense. The tense that indicates action or state in a time gone by, as in "I *bought* the book" or "He *was writing* a letter".

pas·tur·age \ˈpas-chər-ij\ *n.* Pasture.

pas·ture \ˈpas-chər\ *n.* **1** Grass or other plants grown for feeding grazing animals. **2** Land or a piece of land on which animals graze. — *v.;* **pastured; pas·tur·ing.** **1** To feed on growing grass; to graze. **2** To put out to graze; as, to *pasture* sheep.

pas·ty \ˈpas-tē\ *n.; pl.* **pas·ties.** *Chiefly British.* A pie; especially, a meat pie.

pasty \ˈpās-tē\ *adj.;* **past·i·er; past·i·est.** Like paste, as in color or softness.

pat \ˈpat\ *v.;* **pat·ted; pat·ting.** **1** To strike or tap gently with a flat surface, as the hand. **2** To flatten, smooth, or shape by a pat or pats. **3** To caress or soothe with pats. **4** To fall or strike so as to make a light sound of beating or tapping. — *n.* **1** A light blow or tap with a flat instrument or with the fingers or palm; as, a *pat* on the back. **2** The sound of a pat or tap. **3** A small mass of something, especially butter, shaped by or as if by patting. — *adj.;* **pat·ter; pat·test.** **1** Exactly suitable; timely; as, a *pat* answer. **2** With every detail exactly right; as, to get a lesson down *pat*. **3** Fixed; steadfast; as, to stand *pat*.

patch \ˈpach\ *n.* **1** Something, especially a piece like the original material, used to mend or cover a hole, a torn place, or a weak spot. **2** A small piece, as of cloth, worn on the face to cover a defect; as, a man wearing a *patch* over one eye. **3** A bit or scrap of cloth. **4** A small area or plot distinguished from its surroundings; as, a *patch* of oats; a *patch* of snow. **5** A spot of color; a blotch; as, a *patch* of white on a dog's head. — *v.* **1** To mend or cover with a patch or patches. **2** To make out of patches; to put together hastily or clumsily. **3** To settle or adjust; as, to *patch* up a quarrel.

patch test. A test for determining a person's sensitiveness to an allergy-producing substance made by applying to the unbroken skin small pads soaked with the substance in question.

patch·work \ˈpach-ˌwərk\ *n.* Something made of patches, scraps, or odds and ends; especially, fancy work made of pieces of cloth of different shapes and colors. — *adj.* Of or covered with patchwork; as, a *patchwork* quilt.

patchy \ˈpach-ē\ *adj.;* **patch·i·er; patch·i·est.** Consisting of or marked by patches; resembling patchwork; spotty.

pate \ˈpāt\ *n.* The head; especially, the crown of the head.

pa·tel·la \pə-ˈtel-ə\ *n.; pl.* **pa·tel·las** \-ˈtel-əz\ or **pa·tel·lae** \-ˈtel-ˌē, -ˌī\. The kneecap.

pat·en \ˈpat-n\ *n.* **1** A shallow dish or plate; especially, a gold or silver plate used in the Eucharistic service. **2** A thin disk.

pat·ent, *adj.* **1** \ˈpat-nt, ˈpāt-\ Plain; evident; obvious; as, a *patent* lie. **2** \ˈpat-nt\ Patented; made by a patented process or protected by a patent. — \ˈpat-nt\ *n.* **1** An official document that grants a right or privilege. **2** An official document that secures to an inventor, for a period of years, the exclusive right to make, use, and sell his invention. **3** The right granted or obtained in this way. **4** Something patented; an article, device, or process on which a patent has been secured. — \ˈpat-nt\ *v.* To secure by patent; as, to *patent* a new fire alarm.

pat·en·tee \ˌpat-n-ˈtē\ *n.* One to whom a patent is granted.

pat·ent leather \ˈpat-nt\. A leather, usually black, with a hard, smooth, glossy surface finish.

pat·ent·ly \ˈpat-nt-lē, ˈpāt-\ *adv.* Plainly; obviously; as, a compliment that was *patently* sincere.

pat·ent medicine \ˈpat-nt\. A packaged medicine, usually protected by a trademark, put up for immediate use by the public in a package with a label bearing the name of the medicine, the manufacturer's name and address, and directions for its use.

pa·ter·nal \pə-ˈtərn-l\ *adj.* **1** Of or relating to a father; fatherly. **2** Received or inherited from a father. **3** Related through the father; as, a *paternal* grandfather. — **pa·ter·nal·ly** \-ˈtərn-l-ē\ *adv.*

pa·ter·nal·ism \pə-ˈtərn-l-ˌiz-m\ *n.* The principle

or practice of governing or of exercising authority, as over a group of employees, in a manner suggesting the care and control exercised by a father over his children.

pa·ter·ni·ty \pə-'tər-nət-ē\ *n.* **1** The state of being a father; fatherhood. **2** Descent from a father; male parentage.

pat·er·nos·ter \'pat-r-ˌnäst-r; 'pä-ˌter-'näs-ˌter, 'pȧ-\ *n.* [From Old English, there borrowed from medieval Latin, meaning literally "our father" and being the first two words of the Latin version of the Lord's Prayer.] **1** The Lord's Prayer. **2** One of the large beads on a rosary on which the Lord's Prayer is said.

path \'path\ *n.; pl.* **paths** \'pat͟hz\. **1** A track, usually made by foot travel; the way or track in which something moves; as, a *path* through a park; the *path* of a planet. **2** A track or roadway built for racing or riding; as, a bridle *path.* **3** A course or way of life or thought; as, *paths* of glory.

pa·thet·ic \pə-'thet-ik\ *adj.* Affecting or arousing tender feelings, as of pity or grief; as, a *pathetic* story. — **pa·thet·i·cal·ly** \-ik-l(-)ē\ *adv.*

path·find·er \'path-ˌfīnd-r\ *n.* One who discovers a way, especially a new route for travelers, by exploring previously untraveled regions.

path·o·gen \'path-əj-n, -ə-ˌjen\ or **path·o·gene** \-ə-ˌjēn\ *n.* A specific cause of disease, as a bacterium or a virus.

path·o·gen·ic \ˌpath-ə-'jen-ik\ *adj.* Causing disease; as, *pathogenic* bacteria.

path·o·log·ic \ˌpath-l-'äj-ik\ or **path·o·log·i·cal** \-ik-l\ *adj.* **1** Of or relating to pathology. **2** Diseased; altered by disease, as tissue. — **path·o·log·i·cal·ly** \-ik-l(-)ē\ *adv.*

pa·thol·o·gist \pa-'thäl-ə-jəst, pə-\ *n.* A specialist in pathology.

pa·thol·o·gy \pa-'thäl-ə-jē, pə-\ *n.* **1** The science that studies facts about diseases, their nature, causes, and spread. **2** The condition produced by disease, as of an organ of the body.

pa·thos \'pā-ˌthäs, -ˌthȯs\ *n.* The quality in an artistic or literary representation of life, or in life itself, which moves one to pity, sympathy, or sorrow.

path·way \'path-ˌwā\ *n.* A footpath; any path or course.

pa·tience \'pāsh-n(t)s\ *n.* **1** The state or quality of being patient; uncomplaining endurance, as of suffering or annoyance. **2** A card game.

— The words *forbearance* and *resignation* are synonyms of *patience: patience* generally indicates calmness and composure in enduring something disagreeable or painful or in awaiting a long-delayed outcome; *forbearance* may suggest a restraining of one's natural responses to annoyances and irritations or a tolerating of something that deserves blame or punishment; *resignation* may indicate an acceptance of suffering or evil as inescapable.

pa·tient \'pāsh-nt\ *adj.* **1** Bearing pains or annoyances without complaint; as, a *patient* invalid. **2** Showing calm self-control. **3** Constant; persevering; as, a *patient* worker. — *n.* A person under medical treatment. — **pa·tient·ly,** *adv.*

pat·io \'pat-ē-ˌō, 'pät-, 'pȧt-\ *n.; pl.* **pat·i·os.** **1** In Spain and Spanish-American countries, a courtyard of a building. **2** A flat paved area adjoining a house or other dwelling, used for recreation or rest.

pa·tois \'pa-ˌtwä, 'pä-, 'pȧ-\ *n.; pl.* **pa·tois** \-ˌtwäz\. **1** A dialect. **2** A highly restricted and localized speech that is not accepted as a dialect or a language and is often associated with illiteracy.

pa·tri·arch \'pā-trē-ˌärk, -ˌȧrk\ *n.* **1** A father at the head of a family in Biblical history before Moses. **2** A father who is head and ruler of his family and descendants. **3** A venerable old man. **4** One of certain bishops of highest rank and dignity in various churches. — **pa·tri·ar·chal** \ˌpā-trē-'ärk-l, -'ȧrk-l\ *adj.*

pa·tri·archy \'pā-trē-ˌärk-ē, -ˌȧrk-ē\ *n.; pl.* **pa·tri·arch·ies.** **1** A family, group, or state ruled by a patriarch. **2** A form of social organization in which descent is traced in the male line and children belong to the father's clan or family.

pa·tri·cian \pə-'trish-n\ *n.* **1** A member of the higher class of people in ancient Rome; a noble. **2** A person belonging to the higher classes by birth or position in life and distinguished by a high degree of cultivation; an aristocrat. — *adj.* Of or relating to a patrician; aristocratic.

pat·ri·mo·ny \'pa-trə-ˌmō-nē\ *n.; pl.* **pat·ri·mo·nies.** **1** An estate inherited from one's father or other ancestor; a heritage. **2** An ancient endowment, as of a church. — **pat·ri·mo·ni·al** \ˌpa-trə-'mō-nē-əl\ *adj.*

pa·tri·ot \'pā-trē-ət, -ˌät\ *n.* A person who loves his country and zealously supports it.

pa·tri·ot·ic \ˌpā-trē-'ät-ik\ *adj.* Of or befitting a patriot; having or showing patriotism. — **pa·tri·ot·i·cal·ly** \-ik-l(-)ē\ *adv.*

pa·tri·ot·ism \'pā-trē-ə-ˌtiz-m\ *n.* Love of one's own country and devotion to its welfare.

pa·trol \pə-'trōl\ *v.;* **pa·trolled** \-'trōld\; **pa·trol·ling** \-'trō-ling\. **1** To go the rounds of a district or section for the purpose of watching or protecting; to traverse, as a guard or policeman. **2** To go on an assigned military task as a patrol or as a member of one. — *n.* **1** A going of the rounds by a guard to insure greater safety; the guard itself; as, a coast *patrol.* **2** A detachment of military personnel employed for reconnaissance, security, or combat, as on foot or in airplanes. **3** A subdivision of a troop of boy scouts, consisting of eight scouts. — **pa·trol·ler** \-'trōl-r\ *n.*

pa·trol·man \pə-'trōl-mən\ *n.; pl.* **pa·trol·men** \-mən\. A policeman or other guard on patrol duty.

patrol wagon. A wagon used by policemen to transport prisoners.

pa·tron \'pā-trən\ *n.* [From medieval English

patroun, there borrowed from medieval French, where it was borrowed from Latin *patronus*, a derivative of *pater* meaning "father" — see *patroon*.] **1** A person who is chosen as a special guardian or protector; as, a *patron* of poets. **2** A person who gives generous support or approval; as, a *patron* of the arts. **3** A person designated as sponsor for a social or charitable affair. **4** A customer. **5** A saint (**patron saint**) to whom a church or society is dedicated. — **pa·tron·ess** \-trə-nəs\ *n.*

pat·ron·age \'pa-trə-nij, 'pā-\ *n.* **1** The office, function, or position of a patron. **2** The support or aid given by or asked of a patron. **3** A body of patrons, as of a shop or theater. **4** In politics, the control by officials of appointments to jobs, contracts, and favors.

pa·tron·ize \'pā-trə-ˌnīz, 'pa-\ *v.;* **pa·tron·ized; pa·tron·iz·ing. 1** To act as a patron to or of; to favor or support; as, to *patronize* the arts. **2** To do business with; as, to *patronize* a neighborhood store. **3** To treat with a superior air; to be condescending toward; as, to *patronize* one's equals. — **pa·tron·iz·ing·ly** \-ˌnī-zing-lē\ *adv.*

pa·troon \pə-'trün\ *n.* [From Dutch, meaning literally "patron", and borrowed in the medieval Dutch period from medieval French *patroun* or Latin *patronus* — see *patron*.] Under the old Dutch governments of New York and New Jersey, a proprietor of any of certain large tracts of land, with such administrative rights as that of holding court and fining tenants.

patted. Past tense and past part. of *pat.*

patter. Comparative of *pat.*

pat·ter \'pat-r\ *v.;* **pat·tered; pat·ter·ing.** To talk glibly; to chatter. — *n.* **1** A jargon, as of thieves. **2** The special language of any class or profession; as, legal *patter.* **3** Glib or rapid speech; chatter.

pat·ter \'pat-r\ *v.;* **pat·tered; pat·ter·ing.** To strike or move with a quick succession of light blows; as, rain *pattering* on a roof. — *n.* A quick succession of slight sounds or pats; as, the *patter* of children's feet.

pat·tern \'pat-rn\ *n.* **1** Anything meant to be imitated; anything fit to be copied; a model; as, one who is a *pattern* of behavior. **2** A model, guide, or set of guiding pieces for making things; as, a dressmaker's *pattern.* **3** A form or figure used in decoration; a design; as, chintz with a small *pattern.* **4** A natural formation or marking; as, a frost *pattern.* **5** A set of characteristics that are displayed repeatedly; as, to study behavior *patterns* in rats; the *pattern* of American industry; cultural *patterns* in a society.

— The words *model* and *ideal* are synonyms of *pattern· model* usually refers to a person or thing held up as a guide to one's conduct, usually one considered to be highly worthy of imitation by all; *ideal* may suggest either some real thing or a mental picture representing the highest standard which one can hope to attain; *pattern* usually applies to a carefully worked-out design to be followed in the making or doing of something, or to a complex set of relationships worth entering into in one's life.

— *v.* To design something after a pattern.

pattest. Superlative of *pat.*

patting. Pres. part. of *pat.*

pat·ty \'pat-ē\ *n.; pl.* **pat·ties. 1** A small pie or a pastry shell with its filling, usually of meat or fish. **2** A small flat cake of chopped food, especially ground meat; as, a hamburger *patty;* a fish *patty.* **3** Any piece of food that has been molded into a small flat cake; as, a mint *patty.*

pau·ci·ty \'pòs-ət-ē\ *n.* Smallness of number or amount; insufficiency; scarcity; as, a *paucity* of food; a *paucity* of experience.

paunch \'pònch, 'pänch\ *n.* **1** The belly. **2** The first stomach of a cud-chewing animal. **3** A large protruding belly; a potbelly.

paunchy \'pònch-ē, 'pänch-ē\ *adj.;* **paunch·i·er; paunch·i·est.** Having a large or protruding belly.

pau·per \'pòp-r\ *n.* A very poor person; especially, one that is supported by charity.

pau·per·ize \'pòp-r-ˌīz\ *v.;* **pau·per·ized; pau·per·iz·ing.** To make a pauper of. — **pau·per·ism** \-ˌiz-m\ *n.*

pause \'pòz\ *n.* **1** A temporary stop or rest. **2** Temporary inaction because of doubt or weariness. **3** Cause for stopping temporarily; as, a thought that gives one *pause.* **4** In music, a sign [𝄐 or 𝄑] above or below a note or rest to show that the note or rest is to be prolonged. — *v.;* **paused; paus·ing. 1** To make a pause; to stop for a time; as, to *pause* for lunch. **2** To remain for a time; to dwell; as, to *pause* on a high note; to *pause* on a point in a speech.

pa·vane or **pa·van** \pə-'vän, -'vȧn\ *n.* **1** A slow stately dance originating in southern Europe in the 16th century, usually performed by couples in ceremonial costume. **2** The music for this dance.

pave \'pāv\ *v.;* **paved; pav·ing. 1** To surface, as with stone or asphalt; as, to *pave* a street. **2** To make smooth or easy; as, to *pave* the way for those who come after.

pave·ment \'pāv-mənt\ *n.* **1** Material used in paving a surface. **2** A paved surface.

pa·vil·ion \pə-'vil-yən\ *n.* **1** A tent, especially a large one with a peaked or rounded top. **2** A lightly constructed, ornamented building, serving as a shelter in a park, garden, or athletic field. **3** A part of a building projecting from the main body of the structure. **4** A building either partly or completely detached from the main building or main group of buildings.

pavilion, 2

pav·ing \'pā-ving\ *n.* Pavement, or material for a pavement.

paw \'pò\ *n.* The foot of a quadruped having claws, as the lion, dog, or cat. — *v.* **1** To touch with a paw, usually clumsily. **2** To handle clumsily or rudely; as, merchandise *pawed* by customers. **3** To beat or scrape with the feet; as, a horse *pawing* the ground.

pawl \'pȯl\ *n.* A pivoted tongue or sliding bolt on one part of a machine adapted to fall into notches on another part, as a ratchet wheel, so as to permit motion in only one direction.

pawn \'pȯn, 'pän\ *n.* **1** The piece of the least value in a chess set. **2** Something of little value in itself but useful in gaining a desired end; as, to refuse to be a mere *pawn* in the hands of another.

pawn

pawn \'pȯn, 'pän\ *n.* **1** Something of value given as a pledge or guarantee. **2** The state of being pledged — usually used in the phrase *in pawn.* — *v.* To give or deposit in pledge; to put in pawn for a loan; as, to *pawn* one's watch.

pawn·bro·ker \'pȯn-ˌbrōk-r, 'pän-\ *n.* A person who makes a business of lending money on personal property pledged in his keeping.

pawpaw. Variant of *papaw.*

pay \'pā\ *v.;* **paid** \'pād\; **pay·ing. 1** To give, as money, in return for services received, or for something bought; as, to *pay* the taxi driver; to *pay* for a ticket. **2** To discharge a debt; as, to *pay* a tax. **3** To get even with; as, to *pay* someone back for an injury. **4** To give or offer freely; as, to *pay* a compliment; to *pay* attention. **5** To make or secure suitable return for expense or trouble; to be worth the effort or pains required. It *pays* to drive carefully.

— The words *compensate* and *remunerate* are synonyms of *pay: pay* is the most general of these terms, all of which suggest the giving of something, often money, in return for certain goods or services; *compensate* usually suggests the giving of something felt to balance or be roughly equivalent to whatever was received, or sometimes given to make up for a loss; *remunerate* may indicate the giving of some unexpected and often generous reward, more often in return for services or special kindnesses than for goods.

— **pay off. 1** To pay in full, sometimes through small payments made at intervals; as, to *pay off* a mortgage during a ten-year period of time. **2** To take revenge on; as, to *pay off* a person who has deceived one. **3** To be advantageous, even though difficult or trying; to be worth the effort. Sometimes studying *pays off.* — **pay out. 1** To give out in payment for something; as, a company that *pays out* large sums of money for supplies. **2** To get rid of by paying; to pay off; as, to *pay out* a debt. **3** [In this sense, *past tense and past part.* also **payed** \'pād\] To slacken and allow to run out, as a rope or chain; as, to *pay out* more cable. — **pay up.** To pay in full, especially debts that are overdue. — *n.* **1** The act of paying; payment; as, no work, no *pay.* **2** The state of being paid; employ; as, in the *pay* of the company. **3** Something that is paid; wages or salary; as, to receive one's *pay.* — For synonyms see *wage.*

pay·a·ble \'pā-əb-l\ *adj.* That can or must be paid; due; as, bills *payable.*

pay·load \'pā-ˌlōd\ *n.* The useful load carried by a vehicle, missile, or rocket in addition to what is needed for operation.

pay·mas·ter \'pā-ˌmast-r\ *n.* The person, especially the officer of a government or business firm, whose job it is to give out pay.

pay·ment \'pā-mənt\ *n.* **1** The act of paying; as, prompt *payment* of a debt. **2** Money given to discharge a debt; as, monthly *payments* on a radio set. **3** Pay; as, to receive *payment* for a day's work.

pay·off \'pā-ˌȯf\ *n.* **1** Payment, or sometimes repayment, at the outcome of an enterprise. **2** The climax or denouement of a story.

pay·roll \'pā-ˌrōl\ *n.* **1** A list of persons entitled to receive pay, together with the amounts due to each. **2** The amount of money necessary to pay those on such a list.

pd. Abbreviation for *paid.*

pea \'pē\ *n.; pl.* **peas** \'pēz\. **1** The round edible seed, rich in protein, that grows in the pod of a widely cultivated plant. **2** The plant bearing this seed. **3** The sweet pea.

peas

peace \'pēs\ *n.* **1** An agreement to end a war. **2** A state of public calmness; especially, the absence of war or public disturbance. **3** Mutual agreement of persons; as, to live in *peace* with one's neighbors. **4** Personal freedom from fears or emotional disturbances; as, a man's sense of *peace* and security. **5** Quiet; stillness; absence of noise; as, the *peace* of the woods.

peace·a·ble \'pē-səb-l\ *adj.* **1** Inclined toward peace; not quarrelsome. **2** Peaceful. — **peace·a·bly** \-sə-blē\ *adv.*

peace·ful \'pēs-fəl\ *adj.* **1** Liking peace; not easily provoked to argue or fight; as, a *peaceful* people; a *peaceful* man. **2** Calm; quiet; especially, not at war; as, a *peaceful* countryside; a *peaceful* country. **3** Not involving argument or fighting; as, to settle a difference by *peaceful* means. — **peace·ful·ly** \-fə-lē\ *adv.*

peace·mak·er \'pēs-ˌmāk-r\ *n.* A person who arranges a peace; one who settles an argument or stops a fight.

peace·time \'pēs-ˌtīm\ *n.* The period when a nation is not at war.

peach \'pēch\ *n.* **1** A sweet, juicy, round fruit that has a thin, downy skin, pulpy white or yellow flesh, and a hard, rough stone containing a single seed. **2** The tree bearing such a fruit. **3** The color of a ripe peach, a pale tint of yellowish pink.

pea·cock \'pē-ˌkäk\ *n.* A large domesticated bird having in the male rich blue coloring on the head, neck, and breast and very long tail feathers that it is capable of lifting and spreading into the shape of a fan, displaying brilliant green and gold feathers covered with spots resembling eyes.

pea·hen \'pē-ˌhen\ *n.* The female of the peacock.

peak \'pēk\ *n.* **1** A projecting point; as, to whip cream until it comes to a *peak.* **2** The top of a rise, hill, or mountain; often, a mountain itself; as, the *peak* of a hill; the solitary, snow-capped *peak* rising from the plain. **3** The projecting front part of a cap. **4** The point of maximum achievement, development, or activity; as, the *peak* of a person's career; the *peak* of the traffic rush.

peaked, *adj.* **1** \'pēkt, 'pēk-əd\ Pointed; as, a *peaked* roof. **2** \'pēk-əd\ Having sharpness of figure or features; thin; sickly; as, to look *peaked* after an illness.

peal \'pēl\ *n.* **1** A complete set of bells, such as is set in a large belfry. **2** A ringing of bells; especially, a ringing in sequence of all the bells in a belfry. **3** A loud sound or a series of loud sounds; as, a *peal* of laughter; a *peal* of thunder. **—** *v.* To give out peals or in peals; as, bells *pealing* in the distance; an organ *pealing* anthems.

pea·nut \'pē-(,)nət\ *n.* **1** A trailing plant of the bean family, whose pods ripen underground. **2** The oily seed of this plant which resembles a nut and is widely used for food.

pear \'par, 'per\ *n.* **1** The fleshy fruit of a tree related to the apple, commonly larger at the end opposite the stem. **2** The tree that bears this fruit.

pearl \'pərl\ *n.* **1** A small hard smooth body, very often white or light in color, and much valued as a gem, formed within the shell of the pearl oyster and certain other shellfish as a growth around some substance introduced from without, as a grain of sand. **2** Something likened to a pearl, as in shape, color, or value. **3** A simulated or artificial pearl; as, a doll's dress with *pearls* on the bodice. **4** Mother-of-pearl; as, buttons made of *pearl.* **5** The color of mother-of-pearl; a bluish gray. **—** *adj.* Of, like, or set with pearls.

pearl·er \'pərl-r\ *n.* **1** A person who dives for pearls or one who employs pearl divers. **2** A boat used in pearl fishing.

pearly \'pər-lē\ *adj.;* **pearl·i·er**; **pearl·i·est.** Like a pearl or mother-of-pearl, as in color or luster.

peas·ant \'pez-nt\ *n.* A country person; especially, in European countries, a small farmer or farm laborer.

peas·ant·ry \'pez-n-trē\ *n.* The whole body of peasants; as, a nation's *peasantry.*

peat \'pēt\ *n.* **1** A dark brown or black substance formed when certain plants partly decay in water, as in a bog or meadow. **2** A piece of this substance cut and dried for use as fuel. — **peaty** \'pēt-ē\ *adj.*

peb·ble \'peb-l\ *n.* A small, rounded stone. **—** *v.;* **peb·bled**; **peb·bling** \-l(-)ing\. **1** To furnish with or as if with pebbles; as, to *pebble* a walk. **2** To give leather, paper, or similar surfaces an irregular, pebbly surface.

peb·bly \'peb-l(-)ē\ *adj.;* **peb·bli·er**; **peb·bli·est.** **1** Having many pebbles; as, a *pebbly* beach. **2** Resembling pebbles; as, leather with a *pebbly* grain.

pe·can \pē-'kän, -'kan, -'kȧn; 'pē-,kan\ *n.* **1** A tree related to the hickories, of the southern and central United States. **2** The oval, thin-shelled, edible nut of this tree.

pec·ca·dil·lo \,pek-ə-'dil-,ō\ *n.; pl.* **pec·ca·dil·loes** or **pec·ca·dil·los.** A trifling fault; a slight offense; as, the *peccadilloes* of a high-spirited youth.

pec·ca·ry \'pek-r-ē\ *n.; pl.* **pec·ca·ries** or **pec·ca·ry.** A small, wild mammal having downward-curving tusks and resembling a pig, found from Texas to Paraguay.

peck \'pek\ *n.* **1** The fourth part of a bushel. **2** A great deal; a large quantity; as, a *peck* of trouble.

peck \'pek\ *v.* **1** To strike with the beak; to thrust the beak into; as, a woodpecker *pecking* a tree. **2** To strike with a pick or other sharp instrument, as in breaking up earth or ice. **3** To pick up food with the beak; as, a chicken *pecking* corn. **4** To bite daintily; to nibble; as, to *peck* at one's food. **—** *n.* **1** The act of pecking; a quick, sharp stroke, as with a beak or pick. **2** The mark made by pecking.

pec·tin \'pek-tən\ *n.* Any of certain water-soluble substances obtained especially from fruits and certain vegetables, causing fruit jellies to set.

pec·to·ral \'pekt-r-əl\ *adj.* Of, relating to, or situated in, on, or in the region of the breast or chest; as, the *pectoral* muscles; a *pectoral* fin.

p pectoral fin

pec·tose \'pek-,tōs\ *n.* Protopectin.

pec·u·late \'pek-yə-,lāt\ *v.;* **pec·u·lat·ed**; **pec·u·lat·ing.** To steal money, especially public funds, left in one's care. — **pec·u·la·tion** \,pek-yə-'lāsh-n\ *n.* — **pec·u·la·tor** \'pek-yə-,lāt-r\ *n.*

pe·cul·iar \pē-'kyül-yər\ *adj.* **1** One's own; privately owned; as, a man's own *peculiar* property. **2** Belonging to or characteristic of some one person, thing, or place; as, a custom *peculiar* to England. **3** Differing from the usual or normal; queer; eccentric; as, the *peculiar* appearance of the old hermit. — **pe·cul·iar·ly**, *adv.*

pe·cu·li·ar·i·ty \pē-,kyü-lē-'ar-ət-ē, -,kyül-'yar-\ *n.; pl.* **pe·cu·li·ar·i·ties.** **1** The quality or state of being peculiar; as, to recognize something from the *peculiarity* of its shape. **2** Something that is peculiar; a strange, odd, or queer trait or feature.

pe·cu·ni·ary \pē-'kyü-nē-,er-ē\ *adj.* **1** Consisting of money; taken or given in money; as, *pecuniary* aid; a *pecuniary* reward. **2** Of or relating to money; monetary; as, *pecuniary* policies.

ped·a·gogue or **ped·a·gog** \'ped-ə-,gäg\ *n.* A teacher of children; a schoolmaster; often, a dull, formal, and pedantic teacher.

ped·a·go·gy \'ped-ə-,gō-jē, -,gäj-ē\ *n.* **1** The art, practice, or profession of teaching; especially, systematized instruction in the principles and methods of teaching. **2** Instruction; teaching. — **ped·a·gog·ic** \,ped-ə-'gäj-ik, -'gō-jik\ or **ped·a·gog·i·cal** \-'gäj-ik-l, -'gō-jik-l\ *adj.* — **ped·a·gog·i·cal·ly** \-l(-)ē\ *adv.*

ped·al \'ped-l\ *adj.* **1** Of or relating to the foot or feet. **2** Of or relating to a pedal or treadle. — *n.* A lever worked by the foot or feet, as of a lathe or bicycle; especially, in an organ, one of the keys of the keyboard (**pedal keyboard**) operated by the feet. — *v.;* **ped·aled** or **ped·alled**; **ped·al·ing** or **ped·al·ling.** To use or work the pedal or pedals of something, as a bicycle. — **ped·al·er** or **ped·al·ler** \'ped-l-ər\ *n.*

ped·ant \'ped-nt\ *n.* A person who shows off his learning; a formal, uninspired teacher. — **pe·dan·tic** \pə-'dant-ik\ *adj.*

ped·ant·ry \'ped-n-trē\ *n.* The action of showing off one's knowledge or learning; excessive attention to bookish matters.

ped·dle \'ped-l\ *v.;* **ped·dled**; **ped·dling** \-l(-)ing\. **1** To go about, especially from house to house, with goods for sale. **2** To sell from place to place in small quantities; to hawk. **3** To sell in small amounts at retail prices.

ped·dler or **ped·lar** \'ped-l(-)ər\ *n.* One who peddles; a hawker; as, a fruit *peddler.*

ped·es·tal \'ped-əst-l\ *n.* **1** The support or base of a column. **2** The support of something, such as a statue, vase, or lamp. **3** A raised or superior position; a position of high regard or the state of being held in exceptionally high esteem; as, to place one's father on a *pedestal.*

pe·des·tri·an \pə-'des-trē-ən\ *adj.* **1** Of or relating to walking; going on foot. **2** Slow; dull; unimaginative; as, a *pedestrian* mind. — *n.* One who goes on foot. — **pe·des·tri·an·ism** \-ə-ˌniz-m\ *n.*

pe·di·a·tri·cian \ˌpēd-ē-ə-'trish-n\ *n.* A physician specializing in pediatrics.

pe·di·at·rics \ˌpēd-ē-'a-ˌtriks\ *n.* The medical science that deals with the hygiene and diseases of children.

ped·i·cure \'ped-ə-ˌkyůr\ *n.* **1** The care, especially professional care, of the feet and foot troubles; chiropody. **2** One who practices chiropody; a chiropodist. **3** A single treatment of the feet, toes, and toenails, as at a beauty parlor.

ped·i·gree \'ped-ə-ˌgrē\ *n.* [From medieval English *pedegre, pedegru,* there borrowed from medieval French *pié de grue* meaning literally 'crane's foot" and so called from the fancied resemblance of some diagrams of the branches of family trees to the shape of a crane's foot.] **1** A table or list showing the line of ancestors of a person or animal. **2** An ancestral line; lineage. — **ped·i·greed** \'ped-ə-ˌgrēd\ *adj.*

ped·i·ment \'ped-m-ənt\ *n.* **1** In ancient Greek architecture, the triangular space forming the gable of a roof. **2** A low, triangular decoration resembling a gable, as above a door.

pediments, 2

pedlar. Variant of *peddler.*

pe·dom·e·ter \pē-'däm-ət-r\ *n.* An instrument that measures the distance one covers in walking.

pe·dun·cle \'pē-ˌdəngk-l, pē-'dəngk-l\ *n.* A flower stalk; the main stalk of a flower cluster. — **pe·dun·cu·late** \pē-'dəngk-yə-lət\ *adj.*

peek \'pēk\ *v.* To peep; to look slyly or cautiously. — *n.* A glance; a peep.

peel \'pēl\ *v.* **1** To strip off the skin, bark, or rind of; as, to *peel* an apple. **2** To strip or tear off; as, to *peel* off one's coat. **3** To come off, as skin, bark, or rind does; to lose the skin, bark, or rind. — **peel off.** In aviation, to curve away from a flight formation and nose down for a dive at a target or for a landing. — *n.* The skin or rind of a fruit.

peel·ing \'pē-ling\ *n.* A piece or strip of skin, bark, or rind taken off; a peel.

peep \'pēp\ *v.* **1** To make a feeble, shrill sound such as a young bird makes. **2** To speak in a thin, weak voice or make a faint sound. — *n.* A chirp; a cheep.

peep \'pēp\ *v.* **1** To look through or as if through a small hole or a crack; to peek. **2** To show slightly; as, crocuses *peeping* through the grass. — *n.* **1** A brief look. **2** The first appearance; as, the *peep* of dawn.

peep·er \'pēp-r\ *n.* **1** One that peeps or chirps, as a young bird. **2** Any of certain frogs that make peeping sounds.

peep·er \'pēp-r\ *n.* **1** One who peeps; a prying person. **2** The eye.

peep·hole \'pēp-ˌhōl\ *n.* A hole or crack to peep through.

peep·ing Tom \'pēp-ing 'täm\. [Named after a legendary 11th century inhabitant of Coventry, England, who peeked at Lady Godiva as she rode naked through the streets in order to win tax relief from her husband, the Earl of Mercia, for the people of Coventry.] A person who spies into the windows of private dwellings; one who furtively watches others.

peep·show \'pēp-ˌshō\ *n.* or **peep show.** A small show or object that is exhibited, viewed through a small hole or a magnifying glass.

peer \'pir\ *v.* **1** To look curiously or closely; as, to *peer* into a box. **2** To come slightly into view; to peep out. The sun *peered* from behind a cloud. — For synonyms see *gaze.*

peer \'pir\ *n.* **1** A person of the same rank or character; an equal. **2** A member of one of the five ranks of the British nobility: duke, marquis, earl, viscount, baron.

peer·age \'pir-ij\ *n.* **1** The body of peers. **2** The rank or dignity of a peer. **3** A list or record of peers.

peer·ess \'pir-əs\ *n.* **1** The wife of a peer. **2** A woman who holds the rank of peer in her own right.

peer·less \'pir-ləs\ *adj.* Having no peer or equal; matchless. — **peer·less·ly,** *adv.*

peeve \'pēv\ *v.;* **peeved**; **peev·ing.** To make or become peevish or resentful. — *n.* **1** A peevish mood or attitude. **2** A cause of irritation; an annoyance.

pee·vish \'pē-vish\ *adj.* **1** Stubborn. **2** Fretful; complaining; as, a *peevish* remark; a *peevish* person.

— The words *fretful* and *cross* are synonyms of *peevish: peevish* generally describes a childish irritability and a tendency to express petty complaints; *fretful* may suggest constant worrisome complaint and whining peevishness; *cross* usually applies to the mood of an ill-humored, out-of-sorts person who is easily annoyed and is very difficult to please.

pee·vish·ly \'pē-vish-lē\ *adv.* In a peevish manner; fretfully; crossly.

pee·wee \'pē-ˌwē\ *n.* A very small person or thing.

peg \'peg\ *n.* **1** A small pointed piece of wood or metal, as one used to fasten together boards. **2** A projecting piece of wood or metal to hold things; as, a clothes *peg.* **3** A piece of wood to be driven into the ground to mark a boundary or to hold a rope; as, a tent *peg.* **4** A step or degree; as, to take a person down a *peg.* **5** One of the wooden or metal pins by turning which the pitch of a stringed instrument is adjusted. — *v.;* **pegged**; **peg·ging.** **1** To put a peg or pegs in; to fasten with pegs; as, to *peg* boards together; to *peg* a tent. **2** To mark out with pegs, as a boundary. **3** To work hard. The students *pegged* away at their lessons. **4** To count or score with pegs, as in the game of cribbage.

Pe·king man \'pē-ˌking\. An extinct species of man represented by a skull and parts of skeletons found in northeastern China near the city of Peking.

pe·koe \'pē-ˌkō\ *n.* A black tea made from small-sized tea leaves, especially in India and Ceylon.

pe·lag·ic \pə-'laj-ik\ *adj.* Of or relating to the ocean or open sea.

pelf \'pelf\ *n.* **1** Stolen property. **2** Money; riches; lucre.

pel·i·can \'pel-ik-n\ *n.* A large web-footed bird with a long bill on the under side of which is a great pouch used to scoop in fish for food.

pelican

pel·la·gra \pə-'lāg-rə, -'lag-\ *n.* A disease resulting primarily from an insufficient intake of niacin and characterized by a persistent skin rash, sore mouth, chronic diarrhea, and certain nervous or mental symptoms.

pel·let \'pel-ət\ *n.* **1** A little ball, as of food or medicine. **2** A ball, usually of stone, used as a missile in the Middle Ages. **3** A bullet; especially, one of a charge of small shot used in a shotgun.

pel·li·cle \'pel-ik-l\ *n.* A thin skin or film; a membrane.

pell-mell or **pell·mell** \'pel-'mel\ *adv.* **1** In confusion or disorder; as, toys scattered *pell-mell* about the room. **2** In very great haste; as, to run *pell-mell* down the street. — *adj.* **1** Marked by confusion or disorder. **2** Headlong.

pel·lu·cid \pə-'lü-səd\ *adj.* **1** Transparent; very clear. **2** Very clear in meaning. — **pel·lu·cid·ly,** *adv.*

pelt \'pelt\ *n.* A skin of an animal, especially a sheep, goat or fur-bearing animal.

pelt \'pelt\ *v.* **1** To strike with repeated blows, missiles, or words thought of as missiles; as, to be *pelted* with snowballs; *pelted* with questions by the reporters. **2** To hurl; to throw; as, to *pelt* snowballs. **3** To beat or pound; as, rain *pelting* a roof. — *n.* **1** A beating or striking, as of rain or sleet; as, the *pelt* of rain on a roof. **2** A rapid pace or rate — used especially in the phrase *full pelt.*

pel·vic \'pel-vik\ *adj.* Relating to the pelvis; in the region of the pelvis.

pel·vis \'pel-vəs\ *n.; pl.* **pel·vis·es** \-və-səz\ or **pel·ves** \-ˌvēz\. The basin-shaped part of the skeleton in man and some animals which is enclosed at the sides by the hipbones and to which the lower end of the spine is joined.

pem·mi·can \'pem-ik-n\ *n.* Dried meat pounded into fine bits and mixed with melted fat to form a paste.

pen \'pen\ *n.* **1** A small enclosure for animals. **2** Any small place of confinement or storage. — *v.;* **penned** \'pend\ or **pent** \'pent\; **pen·ning.** To shut in or as if in a pen; to coop up; to confine.

pen \'pen\ *n.* [From medieval English *penne,* there borrowed from Old French, meaning literally "feather", from which pens were formerly made.] **1** An instrument for writing or drawing with ink, consisting of a holder and a writing part (**pen point**) formerly made of a reed or of the quill of a goose or other bird but now usually of metal. **2** The writing part of a pen; a pen point. — *v.;* **penned**; **pen·ning.** To write by hand; as, to *pen* a letter.

pen \'pen\ *n. Slang.* A penitentiary.

pe·nal \'pēn-l\ *adj.* Of or relating to punishment; as, the *penal* laws; a *penal* institution.

pe·nal·ize \'pēn-l-ˌīz, 'pen-l-\ *v.;* **pe·nal·ized**; **pe·nal·iz·ing.** **1** To put a penalty on; to subject to a penalty; as, to *penalize* an athlete for a foul. **2** To place at a disadvantage; to handicap; as, to feel that one is *penalized* in the business world by one's youth.

pen·al·ty \'pen-l-tē\ *n.; pl.* **pen·al·ties.** **1** Punishment for a crime or offense. **2** Something forfeited when a person fails to do what he agreed to do. **3** In sports, a punishment or handicap imposed for breaking a rule.

pen·ance \'pen-ən(t)s\ *n.* **1** [often with a capital] The sacrament consisting of repentance for sin, confession to a priest, performance of such acts as he may require by way of satisfaction, and absolution. **2** Any act showing sorrow or repentance for sin.

pence. *British.* A pl. of *penny.*

pen·chant \'pench-nt\ *n.* [From French, meaning literally "bent", "inclination", and derived from the present participle of *pencher* meaning "to incline", "bend".] A strong attraction or liking; as, to have a *penchant* for winter sports; a *penchant* for jazz music.

pen·cil \'pen(t)s-l\ *n.* **1** A stick of black lead or colored material, usually incased in wood, plastic, or metal, for use in drawing or writing. **2** An object having the general shape or function of a pencil, as a stick of rouge. **3** A group of rays, as of light. — *v.;* **pen·ciled** or **pen·cilled**; **pen·cil·ing** or **pen·cil·ling** \-l(-)ing\. To sketch, write, or mark with a pencil.

pen·dant \'pen-dənt\ *n.* **1** Something hanging; especially, a freely hanging ornament, as an earring. **2** A companion piece or supplement. — *adj.* Pendent.

pen·dent \'pen-dənt\ *adj.* **1** Supported from above; hanging; overhanging. **2** Pending. **3** Jutting out; overhanging. — *n.* Pendant.

pend·ing \'pen-ding\ *adj.* Not yet decided; as, a question that is *pending.* — *prep.* During; until; as, *pending* a reply.

pen·du·lous \'penj-l-əs, 'pend-l-\ *adj.* **1** Hanging; suspended. **2** Swinging. — **pen·du·lous·ly**, *adv.*

pen·du·lum \'penj-l-əm, 'pend-l-\ *n.; pl.* **pen·du·lums**. A body so suspended from a fixed point as to swing freely to and fro under the combined action of gravity and momentum.

pendulum

pen·e·tra·ble \'pen-ə-trəb-l\ *adj.* Capable of being penetrated or pierced. — **pen·e·tra·bil·i·ty** \ˌpen-ə-trə-'bil-ət-ē\ *n.*

pen·e·trate \'pen-ə-ˌtrāt\ *v.;* **pen·e·trat·ed**; **pen·e·trat·ing**. **1** To enter into; to enter and pass through; to pierce; as, light *penetrating* darkness; troops *penetrating* an enemy line. **2** To move deeply; as, a sight that *penetrates* the heart. **3** To understand; as, ideas too difficult to *penetrate.* — **pen·e·tra·tive** \-ˌtrāt-iv\ *adj.*

pen·e·trat·ing \'pen-ə-ˌtrāt-ing\ *adj.* **1** Keen and quick; incisive; as, a very *penetrating* mind. **2** Biting and sharp; as, *penetrating* cold.

pen·e·tra·tion \ˌpen-ə-'trāsh-n\ *n.* **1** The act or process of penetrating; as, a deep *penetration* into enemy territory. **2** Sharp insight; acuteness; as, a statesman of great *penetration* in matters of politics.

pen·guin \'pen(g)-gwən\ *n.* A short-legged bird found chiefly in the cold regions of the Southern Hemisphere having, instead of wings, flippers which are used for swimming.

pen·i·cil·lin \ˌpen-ə-'sil-ən\ *n.* A substance extracted from a green mold and used in preventing bacteria from multiplying, as in an infected wound.

pen·i·cil·li·um \ˌpen-ə-'sil-ē-əm\ *n.; pl.* **pen·i·cil·li·ums** \-ē-əmz\ or **pen·i·cil·lia** \-ē-ə\. Any of a group of blue or green molds that grow on decaying fruit and cheese and certain other substances, one member of which is the source of penicillin.

pen·in·su·la \pə-'ninch-l-ə, -'nin(t)s-l(-)ə\ *n.* A portion of land nearly surrounded by water; any piece of land jutting out into the water.

pen·in·su·lar \pə-'ninch-l-ər, -'nin(t)s-l(-)ər\ *adj.* Of, having to do with, or like a peninsula.

pe·nis \'pē-nəs\ *n.; pl.* **pe·nis·es** \-nə-səz\ or **pe·nes** \-ˌnēz\. The male sex organ.

pen·i·tence \'pen-ə-tən(t)s\ *n.* Sorrow for one's sins or faults; repentance.

pen·i·tent \'pen-ə-tənt\ *adj.* Feeling sorrow for sins or offenses; repentant. — *n.* A penitent person; a person who is doing penance. — **pen·i·tent·ly**, *adv.*

pen·i·ten·tial \ˌpen-ə-'tench-l\ *adj.* Having to do with penitence or with penance. — **pen·i·ten·tial·ly** \-'tench-l-ē\ *adv.*

pen·i·ten·tia·ry \ˌpen-ə-'tench-r(-)ē\ *n.; pl.* **pen·i·ten·tia·ries**. A prison in which criminals are confined.

pen·knife \'pen-ˌnīf\ *n.; pl.* **pen·knives** \-ˌnīvz\. A small pocketknife.

pen·man \'pen-mən\ *n.; pl.* **pen·men** \-mən\. **1** A person who uses a pen; a writer. **2** A person skilled in penmanship.

pen·man·ship \'pen-mən-ˌship\ *n.* Writing with a pen; style or manner of handwriting.

pen name. An assumed name under which an author writes; a nom de plume.

pen·nant \'pen-ənt\ *n.* **1** A small flag used for decorating or signaling. **2** A flag that serves as an emblem of championship, especially in a sports contest; as, the baseball team that won the *pennant* in the state tournament.

pen·nate \'pen-ˌāt\ *adj.* Winged; feathered.

pen·ni·less \'pen-ē-ləs, 'pen-l-əs\ *adj.* Extremely poor; having no money, not even a penny.

pen·non \'pen-ən\ *n.* **1** A long triangular flag, especially one carried by a knight on his lance as an ensign. **2** Any flag or pennant.

pen·ny \'pen-ē\ *n.; pl.* **pen·nies** \'pen-ēz\ or **pence** \'pen(t)s\. **1** An English bronze coin worth $\frac{1}{12}$ of a shilling. **2** A cent. **3** A sum of money; as, to earn an honest *penny.*

penny arcade. A building containing various devices for entertainment, each originally costing a penny.

pen·ny·roy·al \ˌpen-ē-'ròi-əl, -'ròil; 'pen-ə-ˌrīl\ *n.* A plant of the mint family with strong-scented oval leaves and pinkish purple flowers.

pen·ny·weight \'pen-ē-ˌwāt\ *n.* A troy weight equivalent to $\frac{1}{20}$ of an ounce.

pen·ny-wise \'pen-ē-'wīz\ *adj.* Wise only in small matters.

pe·nol·o·gy \pē-'näl-ə-jē\ *n.* The branch of criminology dealing with prison management and the rehabilitation of criminals.

pen pal. A friend made and kept through correspondence, often without any face-to-face acquaintance; as, to learn about Mexico from a *pen pal* there.

pen·sion \'pench-n\ *n.* **1** An allowance made to a person retired from service; as, a *pension* for an old soldier. **2** A rooming house, boardinghouse, or boarding school, especially one in continental Europe. — *v.;* **pen·sioned; pen·sion·ing** \-n(-)ing\. To grant a pension to.

pen·sion·er \'pench-n(-)ər\ *n.* A person who is receiving, or living on, a pension.

pen·sive \'pen(t)s-iv\ *adj.* **1** Dreamily thoughtful; musing; as, a *pensive* mood. **2** Expressing or suggesting thoughtfulness with a trace of sadness; as, *pensive* language. — **pen·sive·ly,** *adv.*

pent \'pent\. A past tense and past participle of *pen,* to shut in. — *adj.* Penned or shut up; confined; as, *pent* breath suddenly released; *pent* up in narrow stretches of country.

pen·ta·gon \'pent-ə-ˌgän, 'pent-ē-\ *n.* A flat figure having five angles and five sides.

pen·tag·o·nal \pen-'tag-n-əl\ *adj.* Having five sides.

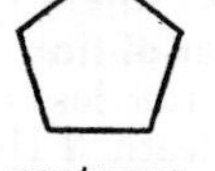
pentagon

pen·ta·he·dron \ˌpent-ə-'hēd-rən\ *n.* A solid figure with five faces.

pen·tam·e·ter \pen-'tam-ət-r\ *n.* In poetry, a line or verse having five metrical feet.

Pen·ta·teuch \'pent-ə-ˌtük, -ˌtyük\ *n.* The first five books of the Old Testament.

pen·tath·lon \pen-'tath-lən, -ˌlän\ *n.* An athletic contest in which each contestant participates in five events.

Pen·te·cost \'pent-ə-ˌkȯst, 'pent-ē-, -ˌkäst\ *n.* **1** A Jewish festival, celebrated seven weeks after the second day of the Passover; Shabuoth. **2** The seventh Sunday after Easter; Whitsunday. — **Pen·te·cos·tal** \ˌpent-ə-'kȯst-l, -'käst-l\ *adj.*

pent·house \'pent-ˌhau̇s\ *n.; pl.* **pent·hous·es** \-ˌhau̇-zəz\. **1** A roof or a shed attached to and sloping from a wall or building. **2** An apartment built on the roof of a building.

pen·tose \'pen-ˌtōs\ *n.* Any of a group of simple sugars containing five carbon atoms, found in plants and also in the animal body.

pe·nult \'pē-ˌnəlt\ *n.* The last syllable but one of a word.

pe·nul·ti·mate \pə-'nəlt-m-ət\ *adj.* **1** Last but one. **2** Of or belonging to the penult. — *n.* The penult.

pe·num·bra \pə-'nəm-brə\ *n.; pl.* **pe·num·bras** \-brəz\ or **pe·num·brae** \-ˌbrē, -ˌbrī\. **1** The partial shadow surrounding an umbra, or perfect shadow, as in an eclipse. **2** The shaded region around the dark central portion of a sunspot. — **pe·num·bral** \-brəl\ *adj.*

pe·nu·ri·ous \pə-'nu̇r-ē-əs, -'nyu̇r-\ *adj.* Excessively sparing in the use of money; stingy; miserly. — **pe·nu·ri·ous·ly,** *adv.*

pen·u·ry \'pen-yər-ē\ *n.* Extreme poverty.

pe·on \'pē-ˌän, -ən\ *n.* **1** In Spanish American countries and in the southwestern United States, a laborer, especially one who is unskilled and poorly paid. **2** A person bound to service for the payment of a debt. — **pe·on·age** \'pē-ə-nij\ *n.*

pe·o·ny \'pē-ə-nē, 'pī-nē\ *n.; pl.* **pe·o·nies. 1** A perennial garden plant with very large, usually double, red, pink, or white flowers. **2** A flower of this plant.

peo·ple \'pēp-l\ *n.* **1** A body of persons making up a race, tribe, or nation; as, the American *people.* **2** Men and women; persons. **3** The persons of some particular group or place; as, the *people* of this state. **4** Members of a family; kindred or, sometimes, ancestors; as, a man whose *people* were English. **5** The mass of persons in a community as distinguished from a nobility or aristocracy or other special classes. **6** The electorate; as, the *people's* choice. — *v.;* **peo·pled; peo·pling** \-l(-)ing\. To supply, stock, or fill with people or with inhabitants.

pep \'pep\ *n.* Brisk energy or liveliness. — *v.;* **pepped; pep·ping.** To give vigor to; to liven; as, something that *peps* a person up.

pep·lum \'pep-ləm\ *n.* A short overskirt attached to a blouse or skirt.

pep·per \'pep-r\ *n.* **1** A seasoning with a sharp taste, obtained from the berry of an East Indian plant; this plant itself. **2** Any of several tropical plants whose red berries are ground to make a similar seasoning. **3** A garden plant with a large fruit (**green pepper** or **sweet pepper**) that is sharp to the taste and is eaten as a vegetable or in salads. — *v.;* **pep·pered; pep·per·ing** \-r(-)ing\. **1** To season with or as if with pepper. **2** To shower shot or other missiles on; as, ducks *peppered* with shot.

pepper, 3

pep·per·corn \'pep-r-ˌkȯrn\ *n.* A dried berry of an East Indian pepper plant.

pep·per·mint \'pep-r-ˌmint\ *n.* **1** A fragrant, sharp-tasting mint with spikes of small pink flowers. **2** An oil obtained from this herb, used for flavoring. **3** Candy flavored with this oil.

pep·pery \'pep-r(-)ē\ *adj.* **1** Of or relating to pepper; sharp or hot to the taste. **2** Hot-tempered. **3** Fiery; stinging; as, *peppery* words.

pep·sin \'peps-n\ *n.* **1** An enzyme secreted by glands in the wall of the stomach of higher animals, which aids in the digestion of proteins. **2** A medicine made from this substance.

per \(ˌ)pər\ *prep.* **1** To or for each; as, a thousand dollars *per* year. **2** By direction or authorization of; according to. We are shipping 12 gross of pencils, *per* your order of June 1.

per·ad·ven·ture \ˌpər-əd-'vench-r, ˌper-\ *adv. Archaic.* Possibly; perhaps. — *n. Archaic.* Chance; doubt; uncertainty.

per·am·bu·late \pə-'ram-byə-ˌlāt\ *v.;* **per·am·bu·lat·ed; per·am·bu·lat·ing. 1** To walk through or over in order to inspect. **2** To walk about; to stroll.

per·am·bu·la·tion \pə-ˌram-byə-'lāsh-n\ *n.* A walk; a stroll.

per·am·bu·la·tor \pə-'ram-byə-ˌlāt-r\ *n.* A baby carriage.

per an·num \(ˌ)pər 'an-əm\. [Latin.] By the year; annually; as, earnings of five thousand *per annum.*

per·cale \pər-'kāl, 'pər-ˌkāl, pər-'kal\ *n.* A fine,

closely woven cotton fabric, widely used for sheets and pillowcases.

per cap·i·ta \(ˌ)pər 'kap-ət-ə\. [Latin, meaning "by heads".] To or for each person; as, the *per capita* wealth of a country.

per·ceive \pər-'sēv\ *v.;* **per·ceived**; **per·ceiv·ing. 1** To obtain knowledge or awareness of by the senses, as seeing, hearing, or feeling; as, to *perceive* that the air is colder. **2** To understand; to comprehend.

per cent \pər 'sent\ or **per cen·tum** \'sent-m\ [From Latin *per centum.*] By the hundred; in the hundred — used to express proportions, rates of interest, and similar relationships; as, to pay interest on a loan at the rate of five *per cent.*

per cent or **per·cent** \pər-'sent\ *n.* Parts, or specified number of parts, in every hundred; amount or quantity measured by the number of units as compared with one hundred; as, to calculate that 10 horses are one fifth or 20 *per cent* of 50 horses.

per·cen·tage \pər-'sent-ij\ *n.* A part or proportion of a whole expressed as so much or so many per cent.

per·cen·tile \pər-'sen-ˌtīl\ *n.* A measure widely used in educational testing which expresses an individual's standing in terms of the percentage of people falling below him. A person with a *percentile* of 75 has done as well as or better than 75 per cent of the people with whom he is being compared.

per·cep·ti·ble \pər-'sep-təb-l\ *adj.* Capable of being perceived or noticed; discernible; as, a change so slight as to be just *perceptible.* — **per·cep·ti·bly** \-tə-blē\ *adv.*

per·cep·tion \pər-'sepsh-n\ *n.* **1** The act or process of perceiving. **2** The power or ability to perceive; as, boys that differed in their *perception* of sound; a man of *perception* in financial matters. **3** The awareness of what is being perceived; as, to have a *perception* of blue when looking at the sky.

perch \'pərch\ *n.; pl.* **perch·es** or **perch. 1** A small freshwater, spiny-finned fish with olive-green back, yellow sides with dark bands, and vermillion lower fins. **2** A somewhat similar spiny-finned salt-water fish.

perch \'pərch\ *n.* **1** A pole or bar put up for birds to roost on; anything serving as a roost for birds. **2** Any raised seat or position. **3** A measure of length equal to a rod or, in square measure, to a square rod. — *v.* **1** To light or settle, as a bird; to rest on or as if on a perch; as, a bird *perching* on a limb. Flood victims *perched* on rooftops. **2** To place or set on or as if on a perch.

per·chance \pər-'chan(t)s\ *adv. Archaic.* **1** By chance. **2** Perhaps; possibly.

per·co·late \'pərk-l-ˌāt\ *v.;* **per·co·lat·ed**; **per·co·lat·ing. 1** To filter, as a liquid, through a porous substance. **2** To filter hot water repeatedly through ground coffee beans to make coffee. **3** To ooze through; to permeate. — **per·co·la·tion** \ˌpərk-l-'āsh-n\ *n.*

per·co·la·tor \'pərk-l-ˌāt-r\ *n.* Something that percolates; especially, a kind of pot for percolating coffee.

per·cus·sion \pər-'kəsh-n\ *n.* **1** The crashing together of two bodies; especially, the striking of a percussion cap to set off the charge in a gun. **2** The striking of sound waves against the eardrum; as, deafened by the *percussion.* **3** In medicine, the action of tapping the surface of the body to learn the condition of the parts beneath by the sound produced.

percussion cap. A small cap or container of explosive to be fired by a sharp forceful blow.

percussion instrument. A musical instrument sounded by tapping or striking, as a drum.

per di·em \(ˌ)pər 'dē-əm\. [Latin.] By the day.

per·di·tion \pər-'dish-n\ *n.* **1** Ruin; especially, utter loss of the soul or of final happiness after death. **2** Hell; damnation.

per·e·gri·nate \'per-ə-grə-ˌnāt\ *v.;* **per·e·gri·nat·ed**; **per·e·gri·nat·ing.** To travel; to journey from place to place. — **per·e·gri·na·tion** \ˌper-ə-grə-'nāsh-n\ *n.*

per·e·grine fal·con \'per-ə-grən\. A swift falcon, widely distributed, with dark bluish back, black head, and white underparts barred with black.

per·emp·to·ry \pə-'rem(p)t-r(-)ē\ *adj.* **1** In law, final; decisive; conclusive; as, a *peremptory* writ. **2** Impossible to deny or argue against; as, a *peremptory* statement. **3** Positive, especially in the expression of opinion. **4** Arrogant; as, a *peremptory* tone. — **per·emp·to·ri·ly** \-r(-)ə-lē\ *adv.*

per·en·ni·al \pə-'ren-ē-əl\ *adj.* **1** Lasting or continuing through the whole year; as, *perennial* springs. **2** Continuous; unceasing; as, *perennial* joy. **3** Living from year to year; as, a *perennial* plant. — *n.* A perennial plant. — **per·en·ni·al·ly** \-ē-ə-lē\ *adv.*

per·fect \'pər-fikt\ *adj.* **1** Lacking nothing essential; whole; complete; sound; as, a *perfect* set of teeth. **2** Thoroughly skilled or trained; meeting the highest standards of excellence; as, *perfect* manners. **3** Having no mistake, error, or flaw; as, a *perfect* diamond. **4** Exact; as, a *perfect* hexagon. **5** Pure; as, a *perfect* red. **6** Complete; unmitigated; as, a *perfect* fool. **7** In botany, having both stamens and pistil. **8** In grammar, expressing action as completed at the time of speaking or at a time spoken of; as, a verb in the *perfect* tense. — *n.* The perfect tense or a verb in that tense. — \pər-'fekt, 'pər-fikt\ *v.* To make perfect; to bring to a state of completion.

per·fect·i·ble \pər-'fek-təb-l\ *adj.* Capable of being perfected or of becoming perfect. — **per·fect·i·bil·i·ty** \pər-ˌfek-tə-'bil-ət-ē\ *n.*

per·fec·tion \pər-'feksh-n\ *n.* **1** Completeness in all parts or details. **2** The highest excellence or skill; as, to do something to *perfection.* **3** The action or process of perfecting. **4** Any quality or thing that is wholly excellent.

per·fec·tion·ist \pər-'feksh-n(-)əst\ *n.* A person who will not accept or be content with anything less than perfection.

per·fect·ly \'pər-fikt-lē\ *adv.* **1** In a perfect manner; completely; as, to spell a word *perfectly;* to understand *perfectly.* **2** Quite or altogether; as, to be *perfectly* willing.

per·fid·i·ous \pər-'fid-ē-əs\ *adj.* False to promises or trust; treacherous. — **per·fid·i·ous·ly**, *adv.*

per·fi·dy \'pər-fəd-ē\ *n.; pl.* **per·fi·dies.** A violation of a promise; faithlessness; treachery.

per·fo·rate \'pərf-r-ˌāt\ *v.;* **per·fo·rat·ed**; **per·fo·rat·ing.** To bore through; to pierce; especially, to make small holes in, as in sheets of postage stamps so that the stamps may be easily separated from one another. — **per·fo·ra·tor** \-ˌāt-r\ *n.*

per·fo·ra·tion \ˌpərf-r-'āsh-n\ *n.* **1** A piercing or a being pierced. **2** A hole made by boring or punching.

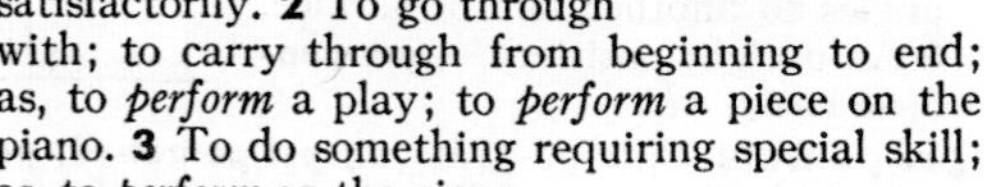
shoe with perforations

per·force \pər-'fōrs, -'fȯrs\ *adv.* By force of circumstances; of necessity; as, to go *perforce.*

per·form \pər-'fȯrm\ *v.* **1** To accomplish; to do; as, to *perform* a task; to *perform* one's duties satisfactorily. **2** To go through with; to carry through from beginning to end; as, to *perform* a play; to *perform* a piece on the piano. **3** To do something requiring special skill; as, to *perform* on the piano.

per·form·ance \pər-'fȯr-mən(t)s\ *n.* **1** The act of performing, or carrying out in action; as, the *performance* of one's duty. **2** Efficient working or operation, as of a motor; as, to test the *performance* of a new car. **3** A deed; a feat; as, an astonishing gymnastic *performance.* **4** A public entertainment, as a play presented on the stage, or a single presentation of such an entertainment.

per·form·er \pər-'fȯrm-r\ *n.* One that performs; especially, a person who performs in public as an entertainer or player.

per·fume \pər-'fyüm, 'pər-ˌfyüm\ *v.;* **per·fumed**; **per·fum·ing.** To add a pleasing smell to; to fill with a pleasing odor; as, to *perfume* a handkerchief. The flowers *perfume* the air. — \'pər-ˌfyüm, pər-'fyüm\ *n.* **1** A pleasing smell or odor; fragrance. **2** A fluid or other preparation used for perfuming.

per·fum·ery \pər-'fyüm-r(-)ē\ *n.; pl.* **per·fum·er·ies.** **1** A perfume; perfumes. **2** The business of preparing perfumes for sale. **3** A place where perfumes are prepared.

per·func·to·ry \pər-'fəngkt-r(-)ē\ *adj.* **1** Done unthinkingly and automatically. **2** Indifferent; showing no interest or zeal. — **per·func·to·ri·ly** \-r(-)ə-lē\ *adv.*

per·haps \pər-'(h)aps, 'praps\ *adv.* Possibly but not certainly; maybe.

per·i·anth \'per-ē-ˌan(t)th\ *n.* The part of a flower formed by the calyx and the corolla.

per·i·car·di·um \ˌper-ə-'kärd-ē-əm, -'kȧrd-\ *n.; pl.* **per·i·car·di·ums** \-ē-əmz\ or **per·i·car·dia** \-ē-ə\. The thin membrane which forms a conical sac around the heart and the roots of some blood vessels. — **per·i·car·di·ac** \-ē-ˌak\ *adj.*

per·i·gee \'per-ə-(ˌ)jē\ *n.* The point in the orbit of a satellite of the earth that is nearest to the earth.

per·il \'per-əl\ *n.* **1** Danger; exposure to injury, loss, or destruction; as, in *peril* of death. **2** A cause or source of danger; risk; as, the *perils* of the sea. — For synonyms see *danger.* — *v.;* **per·iled** or **per·illed**; **per·il·ing** or **per·il·ling.** To put in danger.

per·il·ous \'per-ə-ləs\ *adj.* Full of peril; dangerous; as, a *perilous* voyage. — **per·il·ous·ly**, *adv.*

pe·rim·e·ter \pə-'rim-ət-r\ *n.* The whole outer boundary of a body or figure; the measure around the sides of a figure.

pe·ri·od \'pir-ē-əd\ *n.* **1** A portion or division of time in which something is completed and is ready to begin again; as, tidal *periods.* **2** A portion of time marked by some stated characteristic; as, a *period* of cool weather. **3** A portion of time regarded as a stage or era in the history of something, as of a race or an art; as, the colonial *period.* **4** The punctuation point [.] that marks the end of a declarative sentence. **5** One of the divisions of a school day. **6** A distinct portion of playing time in some games. **7** A division of geologic time longer than an epoch and shorter than an era. **8** Menses.

pe·ri·od·ic \ˌpir-ē-'äd-ik\ *adj.* **1** Happening at regular stated times or at intervals; as, *periodic* visits to the dentist. **2** Happening occasionally; as, to make only *periodic* attempts at studying.

pe·ri·od·i·cal \ˌpir-ē-'äd-ik-l\ *adj.* **1** Periodic. **2** Published at regular intervals. — *n.* A periodical magazine. — **pe·ri·od·i·cal·ly** \-ik-l(-)ē\ *adv.*

per·i·os·te·um \ˌper-ē-'äs-tē-əm\ *n.* The membrane that covers a bone except at the end. — **per·i·os·te·al** \-tē-əl\ *adj.*

per·i·pa·tet·ic \ˌper-ə-pə-'tet-ik\ *adj.* Moving about from place to place; as, a *peripatetic* preacher.

pe·riph·er·al \pə-'rif-r(-)əl\ *adj.* Of or relating to a periphery or to any outermost extension; as, *peripheral* vision; to bring *peripheral* ideas into a discussion. — **pe·riph·er·al·ly** \-r(-)ə-lē\ *adv.*

pe·riph·ery \pə-'rif-r(-)ē\ *n.; pl.* **pe·riph·er·ies.** **1** The line bounding a rounded surface; especially, the circumference or perimeter of a circle, ellipse, or like figure. **2** The outermost part; the boundary; as, to live on the *periphery* of a large industrial city.

per·i·scope \'per-ə-ˌskōp\ *n.* An instrument made of a tube with lenses and mirrors on the top end that magnify a view and reflect it into another mirror at the bottom end, used by men on submarines and in trenches to view an area above without exposing themselves to danger.

per·ish \'per-ish\ *v.* To pass away completely; to be destroyed or ruined; to die; as, races that have *perished* from the earth.

per·ish·a·ble \'per-ish-əb-l\ *adj.* Easily spoiled; as, *perishable* foods.

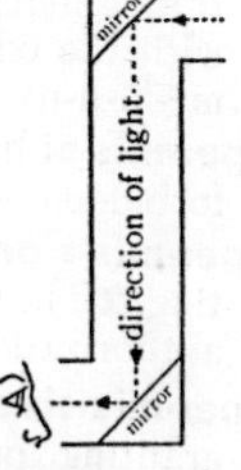

diagram of a periscope

per·i·stal·sis \ˌper-ə-ˈstȯl-səs, -ˈstal-\ *n.; pl.* **per·i·stal·ses** \-ˌsēz\. The contracting and expanding motion by which food is forced through the digestive canal. — **per·i·stal·tic** \-tik\ *adj.*

per·i·to·ne·um \ˌper-ə-tə-ˈnē-əm\ *n.; pl.* **per·i·to·ne·ums** \-ˈnē-əmz\ or **per·i·to·nea** \-ˈnē-ə\. In vertebrates, the smooth transparent membrane that lines the abdomen and covers the abdominal and pelvic organs. — **per·i·to·ne·al** \-ˈnē-əl\ *adj.*

per·i·to·ni·tis \ˌper-ə-tə-ˈnīt-əs\ *n.* Inflammation of the peritoneum.

per·i·wig \ˈper-ə-ˌwig\ *n.* A wig; especially, one, often of white or powdered hair, dressed in the pompadour style fashionable in the 18th century.

per·i·win·kle \ˈper-ə-ˌwingk-l\ *n.* **1** A small sea snail. **2** The shell of this snail.

per·i·win·kle \ˈper-ə-ˌwingk-l\ *n.* A trailing evergreen plant with shiny leathery leaves and blue or white flowers.

per·jure \ˈpərj-r\ *v.;* **per·jured**; **per·jur·ing** \-r(-)ing\. To make oneself guilty of perjury, especially by swearing to something one knows to be false when under oath to tell the truth.

per·ju·ry \ˈpərj-r(-)ē\ *n.; pl.* **per·ju·ries**. False swearing; conscious violation of one's oath to tell the truth.

perk \ˈpərk\ *v.* **1** To lift quickly, saucily, or boldly; as, a dog *perking* its ears. **2** To smarten one's appearance. — **perk up**. To be or become lively.

perky \ˈpərk-ē\ *adj.;* **perk·i·er**; **perk·i·est**. Jaunty; brisk; lively.

per·ma·nence \ˈpər-mə-nən(t)s\ *n.* The quality or condition of being permanent.

per·ma·nen·cy \ˈpər-mə-nən-sē\ *n.* Permanence.

per·ma·nent \ˈpər-mə-nənt\ *adj.* Lasting or intended to last for a very long time; not temporary; not changing; as, to have a *permanent* position in a business; the *permanent* population of a city. — For synonyms see *lasting*. — *n.* Also **permanent wave**. A long-lasting wave or curl in the hair produced by mechanical and chemical means. — **per·ma·nent·ly**, *adv.*

per·me·a·ble \ˈpər-mē-əb-l\ *adj.* Having pores or openings that permit liquids or gases to pass through. — **per·me·a·bil·i·ty** \ˌpər-mē-ə-ˈbil-ət-ē\ *n.*

per·me·ate \ˈpər-mē-ˌāt\ *v.;* **per·me·at·ed**; **per·me·at·ing**. **1** To pass through something which has pores or small openings or is of loose texture; to seep through. Water *permeates* sand. **2** To spread throughout; to pervade; as, a room *permeated* with the odor of tobacco. — **per·me·a·tion** \ˌpər-mē-ˈāsh-n\ *n.*

per·mis·si·ble \pər-ˈmis-əb-l\ *adj.* Permitted; not forbidden. — **per·mis·si·bly** \ə-blē\ *adv.*

per·mis·sion \pər-ˈmish-n\ *n.* **1** The act of permitting. **2** The consent of a person in authority; leave; authorization; as, to ask *permission* to leave.

per·mis·sive \pər-ˈmis-iv\ *adj.* **1** Permitting; granting permission; as, *permissive* legislation. **2** Allowed or allowable; as, within *permissive* limits. — **per·mis·sive·ly**, *adv.*

per·mit \pər-ˈmit\ *v.;* **per·mit·ted**; **per·mit·ting**. **1** To give permission; to allow; to consent to. **2** To make possible; to give an opportunity; as, if time *permits*. — \ˈpər-ˌmit, pər-ˈmit\ *n.* A written statement of permission, given by a person having authority; a license; as, a *permit* to keep a dog.

per·ni·cious \pər-ˈnish-əs\ *adj.* Very destructive or injurious; as, a *pernicious* disease; a *pernicious* habit.

pernickety. Variant of *persnickety*.

per·o·ra·tion \ˌper-ə-ˈrāsh-n\ *n.* The last part of a speech, in which an orator states his main points and makes an appeal to his audience.

per·ox·ide \pə-ˈräk-ˌsīd\ *n.* An oxide containing a high proportion of oxygen; especially, hydrogen peroxide. — *v.;* **per·ox·id·ed**; **per·ox·id·ing**. To bleach, as the hair, with peroxide.

per·pen·dic·u·lar \ˌpərp-n-ˈdik-yəl-r\ *adj.* **1** Exactly vertical and upright; as, a *perpendicular* wall. **2** Meeting another line at a right angle. — *n.* **1** A vertical line. **2** A line at right angles to another line or surface. **3** An upright position. — **per·pen·dic·u·lar·ly**, *adv.*

perpendicular
horizontal

per·pe·trate \ˈpər-pə-ˌtrāt\ *v.;* **per·pe·trat·ed**; **per·pe·trat·ing**. To do or perform; to be guilty of doing; to commit, as a crime. — **per·pe·tra·tion** \ˌpər-pə-ˈtrāsh-n\ *n.* — **per·pe·tra·tor** \ˈpər-pə-ˌtrāt-r\ *n.*

per·pet·u·al \pər-ˈpech-ə-wəl, -ˈpech-l\ *adj.* **1** Lasting forever; eternal. **2** Continuing without interruption; constant; as, to be in a *perpetual* flutter. — **per·pet·u·al·ly** \-ˈpech-l-ē, -ˈpech-ə-wə-lē\ *adv.*

per·pet·u·ate \per-ˈpech-ə-ˌwāt\ *v.;* **per·pet·u·at·ed**; **per·pet·u·at·ing**. To make perpetual; to give a lasting character or existence to. History *perpetuates* the fame of great men. — **per·pet·u·a·tion** \pər-ˌpech-ə-ˈwāsh-n\ *n.*

per·pe·tu·i·ty \ˌpər-pə-ˈtü-ət-ē, -ˈtyü-\ *n.* **1** Perpetual existence, duration, or possession; as, the *perpetuity* of laws. **2** Endless time; eternity.

per·plex \pər-ˈpleks\ *v.* **1** To disturb mentally; to bewilder; to confuse; to puzzle; as, to be *perplexed* by a problem. **2** To make complicated or difficult, as a problem. — For synonyms see *puzzle*.

per·plex·i·ty \pər-ˈpleks-ət-ē\ *n.; pl.* **per·plex·i·ties**. **1** The condition of being perplexed; a puzzled or anxious state of mind; bewilderment. **2** Something that perplexes; an anxiety.

per·qui·site \ˈpərk-wə-zət\ *n.* **1** A profit made from one's employment in addition to one's regular pay, especially such a profit when expected or promised. **2** A tip.

per·se·cute \ˈpər-sə-ˌkyüt\ *v.;* **per·se·cut·ed**; **per·se·cut·ing**. **1** To pursue in order to harm or destroy; to harass or cause to suffer, especially for religious or political reasons. **2** To annoy by repeated actions; as, to *persecute* helpless animals. — **per·se·cu·tor** \-ˌkyüt-r\ *n.*

per·se·cu·tion \ˌpər-sə-ˈkyüsh-n\ *n.* **1** The act or practice of persecuting; as, the *persecution* of the early Christians. **2** The state or condition of being persecuted; as, to flee from *persecution*.

per·se·ver·ance \ˌpər-sə-ˈvir-ən(t)s\ *n.* A persevering or the power of persevering; steadfastness; persistence.

per·se·vere \ˌpər-sə-ˈvir\ *v.;* **per·se·vered; per·se·ver·ing.** To keep at something in spite of difficulties, opposition, or discouragement; to persist.

per·se·ver·ing \ˌpər-sə-ˈvir-ing\ *adj.* Showing perseverance; persistent. — **per·se·ver·ing·ly,** *adv.*

Per·sian \ˈpərzh-n\ *adj.* Of or relating to Persia or Iran; Iranian. — *n.* A native or citizen of Persia or Iran.

per·si·flage \ˈpər-sə-ˌfläzh, ˈper-\ *n.* Banter; light jesting.

per·sim·mon \pər-ˈsim-ən\ *n.* **1** A tree of the ebony family, with hard fine wood, oblong leaves, small bell-shaped flowers, and an orange-red many-seeded fruit. **2** The fruit of this tree, which is sweet when fully ripe but puckers the mouth when eaten before then.

per·sist \pər-ˈsist, -ˈzist\ *v.* **1** To go on resolutely in spite of opposition, warnings, or pleas; to persevere. **2** To last on and on; to continue to exist; as, rain *persisting* for days.

per·sist·ence \pər-ˈsis-tən(t)s, -ˈzis-\ *n.* **1** The act or fact of persisting. **2** The quality of being persistent; the power of going on in spite of difficulties.

per·sist·ent \pər-ˈsis-tənt, -ˈzis-\ *adj.* **1** Persisting; lasting; as, a *persistent* cold. **2** Dogged; tenacious; as, a *persistent* salesman. — **per·sist·ent·ly,** *adv.*

per·snick·ety \pər-ˈsnik-ət-ē\ or **per·nick·ety** \pər-ˈnik-\ *adj.* Fussy about small details.

per·son \ˈpərs-n\ *n.* [From medieval English *persone,* there borrowed from Old French, where it was derived from Latin *persona* meaning originally "mask for the face".] **1** A human being; an individual. **2** The body of a human being; bodily appearance; as, to keep one's *person* neat. **3** Grammatical difference of form of a pronoun or a verb expressing reference to or action by or upon the person speaking (**first person**), the person spoken to (**second person**), or another person or thing spoken of (**third person**); one of the several forms differing in this manner. The plural pronoun of the first *person* is "we". — **in person.** In bodily presence; oneself; as, to go *in person*.

per·son·a·ble \ˈpərs-n(-)əb-l\ *adj.* Pleasing in appearance; attractive in manner.

per·son·age \ˈpərs-n(-)ij\ *n.* **1** A person of rank or distinction; a famous person. **2** A person. **3** A character in a book or play.

per·son·al \ˈpərs-n(-)əl\ *adj.* **1** Of or belonging to a person or persons; not public; not general; as, *personal* property. **2** Of the person or body; as, to pay great attention to one's *personal* appearance. **3** Relating to a particular person or his character or conduct; as, to make *personal* remarks. **4** For or directly to one particular person; private; as, a *personal* letter; a *personal* call; a *personal* pronoun. **5** Relating to oneself; as, *personal* pride. **6** Made or done in person; as, to give a matter *personal* attention; a *personal* appearance by a famous star. **7** In grammar, showing person. — *n.* A short newspaper paragraph, usually part of a column, relating to personal matters.

per·son·al·i·ty \ˌpərs-n-ˈal-ət-ē\ *n.; pl.* **per·son·al·i·ties.** **1** The state of being a person. **2** The characteristics or traits of a person that make him different from other persons; individuality. **3** Pleasing qualities of character; as, to lack *personality*. **4** A person who has such qualities; as, a great *personality*. **5** A personal remark; a slighting reference to a person; as, to use *personalities* in an argument.

per·son·al·ize \ˈpərs-n(-)ə-ˌlīz\ *v.;* **per·son·al·ized; per·son·al·iz·ing.** **1** To personify. **2** To make personal; as, *personalized* stationery.

per·son·al·ly \ˈpərs-n(-)ə-lē\ *adv.* **1** In person; as, to attend to the matter *personally*. **2** As a person; in personality; as, *personally* attractive but not very trustworthy. **3** For oneself; as far as oneself is concerned. *Personally,* I am against it.

personal pronoun. Any of a group of pronouns, as *I, me, you, him, they,* that distinguish or denote first, second, or third person.

per·son·al·ty \ˈpərs-n(-)əl-tē\ *n.; pl.* **per·son·al·ties.** Personal property as distinguished from real estate.

per·son·i·fi·ca·tion \pər-ˌsän-ə-fə-ˈkāsh-n\ *n.* **1** The act of personifying. **2** An imaginary being thought of as representing a thing or an idea. John Barleycorn is the *personification* of alcoholic liquor. **3** Embodiment; incarnation; perfect example; as, a child who was the *personification* of bad temper. **4** The figure of speech in which a lifeless object or abstract quality is spoken of as if alive, as in "a merry little brook laughing its way along".

per·son·i·fy \pər-ˈsän-ə-ˌfī\ *v.;* **per·son·i·fied** \-ˌfīd\; **per·son·i·fy·ing.** **1** To think of or represent as a person; as, to *personify* the forces of nature. In "Justice is blind", justice is *personified*. **2** To represent in a physical form. In the wild west the law was *personified* in the sheriff. **3** To serve as the perfect type or example of; as, a man who *personified* kindness.

per·son·nel \ˌpərs-n-ˈel\ *n.* The group of persons employed in some public service, or in a factory or office.

per·spec·tive \pər-ˈspek-tiv\ *n.* **1** The art of painting or drawing a scene so that objects in it have apparent depth and distance. **2** The power to see or think of things in their true relationship to each other. **3** The true relationship of objects or events to one another; as, to view the events of the last year in *perspective*. — *adj.* Of or relating to perspective, especially in art; done in perspective; as, a *perspective* drawing.

per·spi·ca·cious \ˌpər-spə-ˈkā-shəs\ *adj.* Having or showing keen understanding or discernment. — **per·spi·ca·cious·ly,** *adv.*

per·spi·cac·i·ty \ˌpər-spə-ˈkas-ət-ē\ *n.* The quality or state of being perspicacious; acuteness of understanding or discernment.

per·spi·cu·i·ty \ˌpər-spə-ˈkyü-ət-ē\ *n.* The quality of being easily understandable; clearness of expression or thought.

per·spic·u·ous \pər-ˈspik-yə-wəs\ *adj.* **1** Plain to the understanding; clear. **2** Expressing oneself clearly. — **per·spic·u·ous·ly,** *adv.*

per·spi·ra·tion \ˌpərsp-r-ˈāsh-n\ *n.* **1** The act of perspiring. **2** The salty fluid secreted by the sweat glands; sweat.

per·spire \pər-ˈspīr\ *v.;* **per·spired; per·spir·ing.** To excrete perspiration; to sweat.

per·suade \pər-ˈswād\ *v.;* **per·suad·ed; per·suad·ing.** To win over to a belief or to a course of action by argument or earnest request; to induce to do or believe something; as, a hard man to *persuade.*

per·sua·sion \pər-ˈswāzh-n\ *n.* **1** The act of persuading. **2** The power or ability to persuade; persuasive quality. **3** The state of being persuaded, or induced to believe or do something. **4** A way of believing; a belief; especially, a religious belief. **5** A group having the same religious beliefs.

per·sua·sive \pər-ˈswā-siv, -ziv\ *adj.* Tending to persuade; having the power or effect of persuading; as, a *persuasive* speech. — **per·sua·sive·ly,** *adv.*

pert \ˈpərt\ *adj.* **1** Saucily free in speech or actions; impudent; as, a *pert* reply. **2** Lively; active. — **pert·ly,** *adv.*

per·tain \pər-ˈtān\ *v.* **1** To belong to a person or thing as a part, quality, or function; as, the duties that *pertain* to an office. **2** To refer or relate to a person or thing; as, books *pertaining* to birds.

per·ti·na·cious \ˌpərt-n-ˈā-shəs\ *adj.* **1** Holding strongly to an opinion, purpose, or course of action. **2** Stubbornly persistent. — **per·ti·na·cious·ly** \-ˈā-shəs-lē\ *adv.* — **per·ti·nac·i·ty** \-ˈas-ət-ē\ *n.*

per·ti·nent \ˈpərt-n(-)ənt\ *adj.* Having to do with the subject or matter that is being considered; to the point; as, a *pertinent* suggestion. — **per·ti·nence** \-n(-)ən(t)s\ or **per·ti·nen·cy** \-n(-)ən-sē\ *n.* — **per·ti·nent·ly,** *adv.*

per·turb \pər-ˈtərb\ *v.* To disturb, especially in mind; to trouble; to agitate; as, *perturbing* news.

per·tur·ba·tion \ˌpərt-r-ˈbāsh-n, ˌpər-ˌtər-\ *n.* **1** A perturbing or a being perturbed; an agitation of mind. **2** A cause of disturbance or worry.

pe·ruke \pə-ˈrük\ *n.* A wig; a periwig.

pe·rus·al \pə-ˈrüz-l\ *n.* A perusing; a careful reading, as of a book.

pe·ruse \pə-ˈrüz\ *v.;* **pe·rused; pe·rus·ing.** To read; especially, to read carefully or critically.

Pe·ru·vi·an \pə-ˈrü-vē-ən\ *adj.* Of or relating to Peru. — *n.* A native or inhabitant of Peru.

Peruvian bark. Cinchona.

per·vade \pər-ˈvād\ *v.;* **per·vad·ed; per·vad·ing.** To pass through all parts of; to spread through. — **per·va·sion** \-ˈvāzh-n\ *n.*

per·va·sive \pər-ˈvā-siv, -ziv\ *adj.* Pervading; tending to spread around or through.

per·verse \pər-ˈvərs, ˈpər-ˌvərs\ *adj.* **1** Erring; wrong; corrupt. **2** Obstinate in being wrong; as, a *perverse* reluctance to correct one's faults. **3** Unreasonably contrary; willful; cranky. **4** Perverted. — For synonyms see *willful.* — **per·verse·ly,** *adv.*

per·ver·sion \pər-ˈvərzh-n\ *n.* **1** A turning from what is true or right to something that is wrong; a wrong form of something; a twisting; as, a *perversion* of the truth. **2** Abnormal sexual behavior.

per·ver·si·ty \pər-ˈvər-sət-ē\ *n.; pl.* **per·ver·si·ties.** An obstinate holding to something wrong.

per·vert \pər-ˈvərt\ *v.* **1** To turn away from the right, true, or regular course in, of, or to; to violate; as, to *pervert* the administering of justice. **2** To misinterpret; to misapply; as, to *pervert* another's words. **3** To lead astray; to corrupt. — \ˈpər-ˌvərt\ *n.* One who practices a form of sexual perversion.

per·vi·ous \ˈpər-vē-əs\ *adj.* Capable of being penetrated or permeated; as, *pervious* soil.

pes·ky \ˈpes-kē\ *adj.;* **pes·ki·er; pes·ki·est.** Annoying; troublesome.

pe·so \ˈpā-ˌsō, ˈpes-ˌō\ *n.; pl.* **pe·sos.** A coin of varying value used in Spain, the Spanish American countries, and the Philippines.

pes·si·mism \ˈpes-m-ˌiz-m, ˈpez-\ *n.* **1** A lack of hope that one's troubles will pass or that success or happiness will come. **2** A belief that evil is more common or powerful than good.

pes·si·mist \ˈpes-m-əst, ˈpez-\ *n.* A person who is characteristically pessimistic.

pes·si·mis·tic \ˌpes-m-ˈis-tik, ˌpez-\ *adj.* **1** Lacking in hope that one's troubles will end or that success or happiness will come; gloomy; as, to be *pessimistic* about the future. **2** Having the belief that evil is more common or powerful than good. — **pes·si·mis·ti·cal·ly** \-tik-l(-)ē\ *adv.*

pest \ˈpest\ *n.* **1** A contagious disease that spreads quickly and causes many deaths; especially, the plague. **2** A person who bothers or pesters others; anything that annoys. **3** Any very injurious or destructive insect.

pes·ter \ˈpest-r\ *v.;* **pes·tered; pes·ter·ing** \-r(-)ing\. To annoy; to bother.

pest·hole \ˈpest-ˌhōl\ *n.* A place in which pestilences are common.

pest·house \ˈpest-ˌhau̇s\ *n.; pl.* **pest·hous·es** \-ˌhau̇-zəz\. A house or hospital for those infected with contagious epidemic diseases.

pes·ti·cide \ˈpes-tə-ˌsīd\ *n.* Any substance, especially a chemical, used to destroy living plants or animals that are pests to man, animals, or crops.

pes·tif·er·ous \pes-ˈtif-r(-)əs\ *adj.* **1** Carrying infection; infected with a pestilential disease. **2** Harmful to peace, morals, or society; spreading vicious ideas. **3** Troublesome; annoying.

pes·ti·lence \ˈpes-tə-lən(t)s\ *n.* Any contagious epidemic disease that spreads quickly and is often fatal; especially, bubonic plague.

pes·ti·lent \ˈpes-tə-lənt\ *adj.* **1** Deadly; poisonous; as, a *pestilent* epidemic. **2** Harmful or injurious, as to peace or morals; as, the *pestilent* influence of the slums. **3** Pestering; troublesome; annoying; as, a *pestilent* child.

pes·ti·len·tial \ˌpes-tə-'lench-l\ *adj.* **1** Of or relating to pestilence. **2** Causing or likely to cause pestilence. **3** Morally harmful; vicious.

pes·tle \'pes-l, 'pest-l\ *n.* A pounding instrument used by druggists and others to crush substances to a powder or a mass. — *v.;* **pes·tled**; **pes·tling** \-l(-)ing\. To pound, crush, or pulverize with a pestle.

mortar and pestle

pet \'pet\ *n.* **1** An animal, as a cat, dog, bird, or fish, kept to be played with or enjoyed, especially for its color, song, grace, or antics. **2** A person who is given special treatment; a favorite. — *adj.* **1** Liked better than others; favorite. **2** Expressing fondness; as, a *pet* name. — *v.;* **pet·ted**; **pet·ting**. **1** To treat as a pet. **2** To fondle; to caress.

pet \'pet\ *n.* A peevish fit; a sulky mood.

pet·al \'pet-l\ *n.* One of the white or bright-colored leaves surrounding the stamen and pistil of a flower.

pet·aled or **pet·alled** \'pet-ld\ *adj.* **1** Having petals. **2** Resembling a petal or petals.

pe·tard \pə-'tärd, -'tȧrd\ *n.* A bomb consisting of a case filled with an explosive substance to be discharged against gates and walls.

pet·cock \'pet-ˌkäk\ *n.* or **pet cock**. A small faucet or valve, as for draining water from a radiator.

pe·ter \'pē-r\ *v.* To become exhausted; to fail. The conversation *petered* out.

pet·i·o·lar \'pet-ē-ˌōl-r\ *adj.* Relating to a petiole; originating from a petiole; as, a *petiolar* tendril.

pet·i·o·late \'pet-ē-ə-ˌlāt\ *adj.* Having a stalk or petiole; as, a *petiolate* leaf.

pet·i·ole \'pet-ē-ˌōl\ *n.* **1** The stem of a leaf. **2** A stalk, as the segment joining the abdomen and thorax in wasps.

pe·tite \pə-'tēt\ *adj.* Small.

pe·ti·tion \pə-'tish-n\ *n.* **1** A written request addressed to an official person or group of persons; as, a *petition* to Congress. **2** A prayer; a plea for aid. — *v.;* **pe·ti·tioned**; **pe·ti·tion·ing** \-n(-)ing\. **1** To make or send a petition to. **2** To ask for in a petition; as, to *petition* help.

ivy leaf showing *a* petiole, *b* blade

pet·it jury \'pet-ē\. A jury of twelve persons whose duty it is to hear and make a decision on the facts in a case brought to trial in a court.

pe·tits fours \pə-ˌtē(t) 'fōrz, ˌpet-ē, 'fȯrz\. Small sponge cakes or pound cakes cut into various shapes and iced, sometimes with decorative designs.

pet·rel \'pe-trəl\ *n.* A small, long-winged sea bird that flies far from land.

pet·ri·fac·tion \ˌpe-trə-'faksh-n\ *n.* **1** The act of petrifying or state of being petrified. **2** Something that is petrified.

pet·ri·fi·ca·tion \ˌpe-trə-fə-'kāsh-n\ *n.* Petrifaction.

pet·ri·fy \'pe-trə-ˌfī\ *v.;* **pet·ri·fied** \-ˌfīd\; **pet·ri·fy·ing**. **1** To change wood or animal matter into stone or a substance like stone; to turn as hard as stone; as, *petrified* trees. **2** To stun, as with fear.

pe·trog·ra·phy \pə-'träg-rə-fē\ *n.* The study of the origin and structure of rocks. — **pet·ro·graph·ic** \ˌpe-trə-'graf-ik\ *adj.*

pet·rol \'pe-trəl, -ˌträl\ *n. British.* Gasoline.

pet·ro·la·tum \ˌpe-trə-'lāt-m\ *n.* A tasteless, odorless, oily or greasy substance made from petroleum and used in ointments.

pe·tro·le·um \pə-'trō-lē-əm, -'trōl-yəm\ *n.* [From medieval Latin, meaning literally "rock oil".] A raw oil obtained from wells drilled in the ground and prepared for use in various forms, as gasoline, kerosene, and fuel oils.

petroleum jelly. A semisolid form of petrolatum.

pet·ti·coat \'pet-ē-ˌkōt\ *n.* A skirt worn under a dress or outer skirt. — *adj.* Of, or characteristic of, women; as, *petticoat* government.

pet·ti·fog·ger \'pet-ē-ˌfäg-r, -ˌfȯg-r\ *n.* **1** A lawyer who handles small cases in a tricky way. **2** Any person who makes unnecessarily fine distinctions or is overly concerned with trifles. — **pet·ti·fog·ging** \-ing\ *adj.*

pet·tish \'pet-ish\ *adj.* Fretful; peevish. — **pet·tish·ly**, *adv.*

pet·ty \'pet-ē\ *adj.;* **pet·ti·er**; **pet·ti·est**. **1** Small and of no great importance; trifling; as, *petty* faults. **2** Minor; inferior in rank; as, a *petty* prince.

petty cash. A cash fund kept on hand for the payment of minor items.

petty officer. In the navy, an enlisted man corresponding in rank to a noncommissioned officer in the army.

pet·u·lance \'pech-l-ən(t)s\ *n.* The quality or state of being petulant.

pet·u·lant \'pech-l-ənt\ *adj.* Easily put in a bad humor; peevish; fretful. — **pet·u·lant·ly**, *adv.*

pe·tu·nia \pə-'tün-yə, -'tyün-\ *n.* A garden plant about a foot tall, with funnel-shaped flowers of white, reddish, or purplish color.

petunia

pew \'pyü\ *n.* One of the benches set in rows in a church, for use by the worshipers.

pe·wee \'pē-ˌwē\ *n.* A phoebe or other small olive-green flycatcher; especially, the grayish olive **wood pewee**.

pew·ter \'pyüt-r\ *n.* **1** A metallic substance made of tin, copper, antimony, and other metals, used in making table utensils. **2** Utensils of pewter. — *adj.* Made of pewter; as, *pewter* ware.

pha·e·ton \'fā-ət-n, 'fāt-n\ *n.* [From French *phaéton*, named after *Phaethon*, a god who was noted for driving the chariot of the sun dangerously close to the earth.] **1** A light four-wheeled carriage having no sides in front of its seats. **2** An automobile designed much like a convertible.

pha·lanx \'fā-ˌlangks\ *n.; pl.* **pha·lanx·es** \-ˌlangks-əz\. **1** In ancient warfare, a body of heavily armed foot soldiers carrying lances and fighting in close ranks. **2** Any body of troops massed close together; a solid group of persons or things. **3** *pl.* **pha·lan·ges** \fə-'lan-ˌjēz\. In vertebrates, one of the bones of the fingers or toes.

phan·tasm \'fan-ˌtaz-m\ *n.* **1** A mental image in the form of an illusion, often resulting from a disordered mind; a fantasy. **2** A ghost; a specter. — **phan·tas·mal** \fan-'taz-məl\ *adj.*

phantasy. Variant of *fantasy.*

phan·tom \'fant-m\ *n.* **1** Something imagined; a delusion. The fugitive's sense of guilt filled the dark with pursuing *phantoms.* **2** A dim or ghostly image; a ghost; a figure resembling a ghost. **3** A person or thing that is not really what it seems or what it should be; a mere appearance; a shadow; as, a king with only the *phantom* of authority. **4** A representation of something ideal or abstract. — *adj.* Of the nature of a phantom; suggesting a phantom; unreal.

phar·aoh \'fer-ˌō, 'fā-ˌrō\ *n.* A title of the rulers of ancient Egypt.

phar·ma·ceu·tic \ˌfär-mə-'süt-ik, ˌfȧr-\ or **phar·ma·ceu·ti·cal** \-ik-l\ *adj.* Of or relating to pharmacy or to pharmacists.

phar·ma·cist \'fär-mə-səst, 'fȧr-\ *n.* A person who has studied pharmacy; especially, a druggist who makes up prescriptions.

phar·ma·col·o·gy \ˌfär-mə-'käl-ə-jē, ˌfȧr-\ *n.* The science of drugs, including their use in medicines. — **phar·ma·co·log·i·cal** \-kə-'läj-ik-l\ *adj.* — **phar·ma·col·o·gist** \-'käl-ə-jəst\ *n.*

phar·ma·co·poe·ia \ˌfär-mə-kə-'pē-(y)ə, ˌfȧr-\ *n.* **1** A book describing drugs, chemicals, and medicinal preparations. **2** A stock of drugs.

phar·ma·cy \'fär-mə-sē, 'fȧr-\ *n.; pl.* **phar·ma·cies. 1** The art or practice of mixing drugs according to a doctor's prescription. **2** A place of business of a pharmacist; a drugstore.

phar·ynx \'far-ingks\ *n.; pl.* **phar·ynx·es** \'far-ingks-əz\ or **pha·ryn·ges** \fə-'rin-ˌjēz\. A nearly vertical tubular space that lies behind the mouth, connects the mouth with the esophagus and the nasal passages with the trachea, and contains the openings of the Eustachian tubes.

phase \'fāz\ *n.* **1** The way that the moon or a planet looks to the eye at any time in its series of changes. The new moon and the full moon are two *phases* of the moon. **2** A step or part in a series of events or actions; a stage; a particular part or feature; as, the first *phase* of an experiment.

pheas·ant \'fez-nt\ *n.* **1** A large long-tailed game bird, brilliantly colored in the male, resembling the domestic fowl. **2** In the southern United States, a ruffed grouse.

phe·nol \'fē-ˌnōl, fē-'nōl\ *n.* Carbolic acid.

phe·nom·e·nal \fə-'näm-ən-l\ *adj.* Unusual; extraordinary; as, a *phenomenal* crowd. — **phe·nom·e·nal·ly** \-ən-l-ē\ *adv.*

phe·nom·e·non \fə-'näm-ə-ˌnän, -nən\ *n.; pl.* **phe·nom·e·na** \-ˌnä, -nə, -ˌnȧ\. **1** Any fact or event; especially, a fact or feature characteristic of something. Small factories are a common *phenomenon* in New England. **2** An outward sign of the ways of nature. **3** *pl.* **phe·nom·e·nons.** An extraordinary or unusual person or thing.

phi·al \'fī-əl, 'fīl\ *n.* A small bottle, as for medicines.

phi·lan·der \fə-'land-r\ *v.;* **phi·lan·dered; phi·lan·der·ing** \-r(-)ing\. **1** To make love to a woman to whom marriage is impossible, as because of an existing marriage, or with no intention of offering marriage. **2** To have many casual love affairs; to run after women. — **phi·lan·der·er** \-'land-r-r\ *n.*

phil·an·throp·ic \ˌfil-ən-'thräp-ik\ *adj.* Characterized by philanthropy; especially, having the purpose of helping people by giving generously, as to charities and education. — **phil·an·throp·i·cal·ly** \-ik-l(-)ē\ *adv.*

phi·lan·thro·pist \fə-'lan-thrə-pəst\ *n.* A philanthropic person.

phi·lan·thro·py \fə-'lan-thrə-pē\ *n.; pl.* **phi·lan·thro·pies. 1** Love for mankind or devotion to human welfare as shown by generous gifts. **2** An act or a gift of a philanthropist.

phil·a·tel·ic \ˌfil-ə-'tel-ik\ *adj.* Of or relating to philately.

phi·lat·e·ly \fə-'lat-l-ē\ *n.* The collection and study of various issues of postage stamps or stamped envelopes. — **phi·lat·e·list** \-l-əst\ *n.*

phil·har·mon·ic \ˌfil-r-'män-ik, ˌfil-ˌ(h)är-,-ˌ(h)ȧr-\ *adj.* **1** Loving harmony or music — now used only in names of orchestras or musical societies. **2** Of or relating to a philharmonic orchestra or society; as, a *philharmonic* concert.

Phil·ip·pine \'fil-ə-ˌpēn\ *adj.* Of or relating to the Philippine Islands or their inhabitants.

Phil·is·tine \'fil-ə-ˌstēn; fə-'lis-tən, -ˌtēn\ *n.* **1** A member of an ancient race that lived in the coastal regions of Palestine and conducted many raids against the Israelites. **2** [often with a small letter] A person who takes an attitude of smug indifference to art and literature and the cultural values they represent. **3** One who shows antagonism to any creative intellectual activity having no clear practical application. — *adj.* **1** Of or relating to the Philistines. **2** [often with a small letter] Having or showing the attitude of a philistine.

phil·o·den·dron \ˌfil-ə-'den-drən\ *n.* An indoor ornamental vine with heart-shaped green or green and white leaves.

phil·o·log·ic \ˌfil-ə-'läj-ik\ or **phil·o·log·i·cal** \-ik-l\ *adj.* Of or relating to philology. — **phil·o·log·i·cal·ly** \-ik-l(-)ē\ *adv.*

phi·lol·o·gy \fə-'läl-ə-jē\ *n.* The study of language, especially as a science. — **phi·lol·o·gist** \-jəst\ *n.*

phi·los·o·pher \fə-'läs-əf-r, -'läs-fər\ *n.* **1** A student of philosophy; a person who tries to understand the whole of life by means of reason. **2** One who attempts to practice the teachings of philosophy in the conduct of life; especially, one who practices fortitude and resignation.

phil·o·soph·i·cal \ˌfil-ə-'säf-ik-l, -'zäf-\ or **phil·o·soph·ic** \-ik\ *adj.* **1** Of or having to do with philosophy. **2** Calm; patient in the face of misfortune; as, to be *philosophical* about losing. — **phil·o·soph·i·cal·ly** \-ik-l(-)ē\ *adv.*

phi·los·o·phize \fə-'läs-ə-ˌfīz\ *v.;* **phi·los·o·phized**; **phi·los·o·phiz·ing.** To reason like a philosopher; to search into the reason and nature of things.

phi·los·o·phy \fə-'läs-ə-fē\ *n.; pl.* **phi·los·o·phies. 1** The study of the nature of knowledge, the principles of right and wrong, and the principles of value. **2** The philosophical teachings or principles of a man or group of men; as, Greek *philosophy.* **3** Wisdom or insight applied to life itself.

phil·ter or **phil·tre** \'filt-r\ *n.* A drug or charm supposed to make one person love another.

phlegm \'flem\ *n.* **1** Thick mucus, especially that which collects in the throat when a person is suffering from a cold. **2** Sluggishness of temperament. **3** Calmness; coolness.

phleg·mat·ic \fleg-'mat-ik\ *adj.* Not easily excited or aroused; slow to respond. — **phleg·mat·i·cal·ly** \-ik-l(-)ē\ *adv.*

phlo·em \'flō-ˌem\ *n.* The vascular tissue of higher plants that transports dissolved food material, contains sieve tubes, and lies mostly external to the cambium.

phlox \'fläks\ *n.* **1** A plant that bears clusters of white, purplish, reddish, or varicolored flowers. **2** The flower of this plant.

phlox

pho·bia \'fō-bē-ə\ *n.* An unreasonable, persistent fear of a particular thing.

phoe·be \'fē-bē\ *n.* A slightly crested American fly-catching bird that is grayish brown above and yellowish white below.

phoe·nix \'fē-niks\ *n.; pl.* **phoe·nix·es.** A legendary Arabian bird that according to the ancient Egyptians after a long life burns itself to death and comes to life again, fresh and young, out of its own ashes.

phone \'fōn\ *n.* A telephone. — *v.;* **phoned**; **phon·ing.** To telephone.

pho·net·ic \fə-'net-ik\ *adj.* **1** Of or relating to the voice or its use; of or relating to speech sounds. **2** Representing sounds, especially speech sounds; as, *phonetic* symbols. — **pho·net·i·cal** \-ik-l\ *adj.* — **pho·net·i·cal·ly** \-ik-l(-)ē\ *adv.*

pho·ne·ti·cian \ˌfō-nə-'tish-n, ˌfän-ə-\ *n.* A person skilled in phonetics.

pho·net·ics \fə-'net-iks\ *n.* The science of speech sounds, especially the study of their production, their qualities, as length, pitch, and stress, and their relations to spelling and pronunciation.

phon·ic \'fän-ik, 'fō-nik\ *adj.* **1** Of, relating to, or of the nature of sound, especially vocal sounds; phonetic. **2** Uttered with vocal tone; voiced.

phon·ics \'fän-iks, 'fō-niks\ *n.* A method of teaching beginners to read by teaching the phonetic value of letters, letter groups, and especially syllables.

pho·no·graph \'fō-nə-ˌgraf\ *n.* [From French *phonographe,* there formed from Greek *phone* meaning "sound", "voice" and *graphein* meaning "to write".] An instrument that reproduces sounds recorded on a grooved disk (a **phonograph record**). — **pho·no·graph·ic** \ˌfō-nə-'graf-ik\ *adj.* — **pho·no·graph·i·cal·ly** \-ik-l(-)ē\ *adv.*

pho·ny \'fō-nē\ *adj.;* **pho·ni·er**; **pho·ni·est.** *Slang.* False; fake. — *n.; pl.* **pho·nies.** *Slang.* A fake.

phos·phate \'fäs-ˌfāt\ *n.* **1** A chemical salt of phosphoric acid, much used in fertilizers, obtained from certain substances, as rocks and bones. **2** An effervescent drink made of fruit syrup, carbonated water, and a small amount of phosphoric acid.

phos·pho·res·cence \ˌfäs-fə-'res-n(t)s\ *n.* **1** The state or property of emitting light without heat, as shown by phosphorus. **2** The light so produced. **3** In physics, luminescence caused by the absorption of radiations, as X rays or ultraviolet light, and continuing for a noticeable time after these radiations have stopped. — **phos·pho·res·cent** \-'res-nt\ *adj.*

phos·phor·ic ac·id \'fäs-ˌfór-ik, -ˌfär-\. Any of three oxygen acids of phosphorus.

phos·pho·rous \'fäs-fər-əs, 'fäs-frəs\ *adj.* Of, relating to, resembling, or containing phosphorus.

phos·pho·rus \'fäs-fər-əs, 'fäs-frəs\ *n.* **1** A phosphorescent substance, especially one that glows in the dark. **2** A poisonous, active chemical element, usually obtained in the form of waxy, disagreeable-smelling crystals that glow in moist air.

pho·to \'fōt-ˌō\ *n.; pl.* **pho·tos.** A photograph.

pho·to·e·lec·tric cell \'fōt-ō-i-ˌlek-trik\. A cell or vacuum tube used to produce variations in an electric current in accordance with a varying light, as in the sound-producing part of a motion-picture projector or in a device for opening doors.

photo finish. In racing, a finish in which contestants are so close that a photograph of them as they cross the finish line has to be examined to determine the winner.

pho·to·gen·ic \ˌfōt-ə-'jen-ik, -'jē-nik\ *adj.* Suitable for being photographed; likely to look well in a photograph; as, a girl with a *photogenic* face. — **pho·to·gen·i·cal·ly** \-ik-l(-)ē\ *adv.*

pho·to·graph \'fōt-ə-ˌgraf\ *n.* [A compound formed in English from Greek *photos* meaning "light" and *graphein* meaning "to write".] A picture or likeness made by photography. — *v.* To take a picture of with a camera.

pho·tog·ra·pher \fə-'täg-rəf-r\ *n.* One who takes pictures with a camera.

pho·to·graph·ic \ˌfōt-ə-'graf-ik\ *adj.* **1** Of, relating to, or used in photography; as, a store for *photographic* supplies. **2** In art, representing or portraying life with the exactness of photography; as, a painter whose technique was almost *photographic.* — **pho·to·graph·i·cal·ly** \-ik-l(-)ē\ *adv.*

pho·tog·ra·phy \fə-ˈtäg-rə-fē\ *n.* The art or process of making pictures by the action of light on sensitized surfaces, as film or plates.

pho·to·play \ˈfōt-ə-ˌplā\ *n.* A motion picture.

pho·to·syn·the·sis \ˌfōt-ō-ˈsin(t)th-ə-səs\ *n.* The process by which plants that contain chlorophyll make carbohydrates from water and from the carbon dioxide of the air in the presence of light.

phras·al \ˈfrāz-l\ *adj.* Of, containing, or consisting of a phrase.

phrase \ˈfrāz\ *n.* **1** A brief expression, especially one often used. "Shiver my timbers" is a common *phrase* in old sea stories. **2** Any combination of words; a manner of expression; as, to answer in carefully chosen *phrases*. **3** In grammar, any group of two or more words forming a sense unit but not containing a subject and predicate; as, the adverbial prepositional *phrase* "with pleasure" in "to accept an invitation with pleasure"; the verb *phrase* "should have gone" in "We should have gone hours ago". **4** A short musical unit of a few measures. — *v.;* **phrased**; **phras·ing**. **1** To express in words; as, to *phrase* an idea well. **2** In music, to group notes into melodic phrases; to sing or play music according to the melodic phrases.

phra·se·ol·o·gy \ˌfrā-zē-ˈäl-ə-jē\ *n.* Manner of speaking or writing; diction; style.

phras·ing \ˈfrā-zing\ *n.* **1** Method of expression; phraseology. **2** The act, method, or result of grouping notes so as to form musical phrases.

phre·nol·o·gy \frə-ˈnäl-ə-jē\ *n.* A system for determining mental powers and other personal traits from a superficial study of the formation of the skull. — **phren·o·log·i·cal** \ˌfren-l-ˈäj-ik-l\ *adj.* — **phre·nol·o·gist** \frə-ˈnäl-ə-jəst\ *n.*

phthi·sis \ˈthī-səs, ˈtī-\ *n.* A wasting away or consumption of the bodily tissue; especially, tuberculosis of the lungs. — **phthis·i·cal** \ˈtiz-ik-l, ˈthī-sik-l\ *adj.*

phy·lac·tery \fə-ˈlakt-r(-)ē\ *n.; pl.* **phy·lac·ter·ies**. **1** Either of two small square leather boxes containing slips on which are written certain scriptural passages, worn by Jews, one on the head and one on the left arm, during morning prayer. **2** A reminder. **3** Anything worn as a charm.

phy·log·e·ny \fī-ˈläj-n-ē\ *n.; pl.* **phy·log·e·nies**. The race history of an animal or vegetable type. — **phy·lo·gen·ic** \ˌfī-lə-ˈjen-ik\ or **phy·lo·ge·net·ic** \-jə-ˈnet-ik\ *adj.*

phy·lum \ˈfī-ləm\ *n.; pl.* **phy·la** \-lə\. A group of animals or, more rarely, plants sharing one or more characteristics that set them apart from all other animals or plants and forming a primary division of the animal or plant kingdom.

phys·ic \ˈfiz-ik\ *n.* **1** *Archaic.* The profession of a doctor; medical science. **2** A remedy for disease; especially, medicine taken to cause the bowels to move; a cathartic. — *v.;* **phys·icked** \-ikt\; **phys·ick·ing** \-ik-ing\. To treat with medicine, especially a cathartic.

phys·i·cal \ˈfiz-ik-l\ *adj.* **1** Of or relating to nature or the laws of nature. **2** Of or relating to material things; not mental or spiritual. **3** Of or relating to natural science. **4** Of or relating to physics. **5** Of or relating to the body; bodily.

physical education. Instruction in the care and development of the body, ranging from simple calisthenic exercises to a course of study providing training in hygiene, gymnastics, and the performance and management of athletic games.

physical geography. Geography that treats of the exterior physical features and changes of the earth, in land, water, and air.

phys·i·cal·ly \ˈfiz-ik-l(-)ē\ *adv.* **1** With respect to nature and the laws of nature. **2** With respect to the body.

physical science. **1** Physics or a related science, as chemistry, geology, or astronomy. **2** Such sciences collectively.

phy·si·cian \fə-ˈzish-n\ *n.* A person whose profession it is to treat diseases, especially with medicines; a doctor of medicine.

phys·i·cist \ˈfiz-ə-səst\ *n.* A specialist in the science of physics.

phys·ics \ˈfiz-iks\ *n.* **1** The science that deals with the phenomena of inanimate matter and motion, including the subjects of mechanics, heat, light, electricity, and sound. **2** Physical composition, properties, or processes; as, the *physics* of sound.

phys·i·og·no·my \ˌfiz-ē-ˈäg-nə-mē, -ˈän-ə-mē\ *n.; pl.* **phys·i·og·no·mies**. **1** The art of discovering temperament and character from outward appearance, especially facial features. **2** The shape or appearance of the face; countenance.

phys·i·og·ra·phy \ˌfiz-ē-ˈäg-rə-fē\ *n.* Physical geography, especially of the land.

phys·i·o·log·i·cal \ˌfiz-ē-ə-ˈläj-ik-l\ or **phys·i·o·log·ic** \-ik\ *adj.* Of or relating to physiology. — **phys·i·o·log·i·cal·ly** \-ik-l(-)ē\ *adv.*

phys·i·ol·o·gist \ˌfiz-ē-ˈäl-ə-jəst\ *n.* A specialist in physiology.

phys·i·ol·o·gy \ˌfiz-ē-ˈäl-ə-jē\ *n.; pl.* **phys·i·ol·o·gies**. **1** The branch of biology dealing with the physical processes and activities of living animals and plants and their organs and tissues. **2** The life processes and activities collectively of a living organism or part of an organism.

phys·i·o·ther·a·py \ˌfiz-ē-ō-ˈther-ə-pē\ *n.* The treatment of disease or physical disability by physical and mechanical means, as by massage, regulated exercise, heat, or electricity.

phy·sique \fə-ˈzēk\ *n.* The build of a person's body; physical constitution.

pi \ˈpī\ *n.* **1** The 16th letter of the Greek alphabet, written Π or π, corresponding to English *p*. **2** This letter, used in mathematics to denote the ratio of the circumference of a circle to its diameter, the ratio being such that π is approximately equal to 3.1416.

pi or **pie** \ˈpī\ *n.; pl.* **pies**. **1** In printing, type that is upset, spilled, or otherwise jumbled. **2** A confusion; a jumble. — *v.;* **pied** \ˈpīd\; **pi·ing** or **pie·ing** \ˈpī-ing\. To jumble type, as by spilling.

pi·a·nis·si·mo \ˌpē-ə-ˈnis-m-ˌō\ *adj.* or *adv.* In music, very soft.

pi·an·ist \pē-ˈan-əst, ˈpē-ə-nəst\ *n.* A person who plays the piano.

pi·ano \pē-ˈan-ō\ *n.; pl.* **pi·an·os.** A large stringed musical instrument which is enclosed in a case and played from a keyboard that operates felt-covered hammers that strike strings or steel wires, producing musical tones, and which, according to the shape of the case and the arrangement of the strings, is called a **grand piano**, a **square piano**, or an **upright piano. —** \pē-ˈän-ō, -ˈȧn-ō\ *adj.* or *adv.* In music, soft; as, a *piano* passage in a composition.

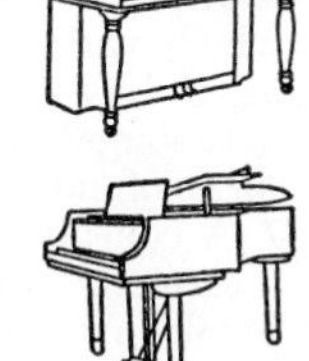
pianos

pi·an·o·forte \pē-ˈan-ə-ˌfōrt(-ē), -ˌfȯrt(-ē)\ *n.* A piano.

pi·az·za \pē-ˈaz-ə; *sense 1 is usually* pē-ˈat-sə\ *n.* **1** A large open square in an Italian town. **2** A roofed and arched gallery along one side of a house. **3** In the United States, a veranda; a porch.

pi·broch \ˈpē-ˌbräk\ *n.* An elaborate musical composition for the bagpipe, usually either martial or mournful in tone.

pi·ca \ˈpīk-ə\ *n.* A size of type frequently used on office typewriters.

pic·a·dor \ˈpik-ə-ˌdȯr\ *n.; pl.* **pic·a·dors** \-ˌdȯrz\ or **pic·a·do·res** \ˌpik-ə-ˈdȯr-ēz, -ˈdōr-ēz, -ās\. In a bullfight, a horseman with a lance who prods the bull in the neck muscles to weaken and tire him.

pic·a·yune \ˌpik-ē-ˈyün\ *adj.* [From the obsolete English name for a small coin worth 6¼ cents, from Louisiana French *picaillon.*] **1** Of small value; as, a *picayune* sum of money. **2** Petty; mean; as, a person who was inclined to be *picayune* about money matters.

pic·ca·lil·li \ˌpik-l-ˈil-ē\ *n.* A relish made of chopped vegetables and spices.

pic·co·lo \ˈpik-l-ˌō\ *n.; pl.* **pic·co·los.** A small, shrill flute whose tones are an octave higher than those of the ordinary flute.—**pic·co·lo·ist**\-ˌō-əst*n.*

piccolo

pick \ˈpik\ *n.* [Partly from Old English *pic* meaning "point", "pickax"; partly (especially sense 3) from modern English *pick,* the verb.] **1** A pickax. **2** A pointed instrument for picking or chipping; as, an ice *pick.* **3** A device for plucking the strings of an instrument, as a mandolin; a plectrum.

pick \ˈpik\ *v.* [Partly from medieval English *picken* "to pick" (related to Old English *pic* meaning "pickax"), partly from modern English *pick,* the preceding noun.] **1** To strike or work at with a pick or other pointed instrument; as, to *pick* rocks. **2** To make by picking; as, to *pick* a hole. **3** To clear of or free from something by or as if by plucking; as, to *pick* a chicken of its feathers; to *pick* a bone. **4** To gather; to pluck; as, to *pick* flowers; to *pick* apples. **5** To select; to choose; as, to *pick* a good book. **6** To pull apart; to separate; as, to *pick* cotton to remove the seeds. **7** To eat sparingly or daintily; as, to *pick* at one's dinner. **8** To pluck, as the strings of a musical instrument; as, to *pick* the strings of a mandolin. **9** To rob; as, to *pick* pockets. **10** To open by or as if by picking; as, to *pick* a lock. **11** To provoke; as, to *pick* a quarrel. — **pick on. 1** To choose or select for some unpleasant task; as, to *pick on* a boy to empty the trash. **2** To tease or annoy; as, a boy who never *picked on* anyone his own size. — **pick up. 1** To take up; as, to *pick up* a crying baby. **2** To tidy up; to straighten; as, to *pick up* the living room. **3** To get; as, to *pick up* a few things at the store. **4** To acquire by chance or without intending to; as, to *pick up* a habit. **5** To take in or along; as, a bus that *picks up* passengers. **6** To gather speed; as, a car that *picks up* quickly. **7** To improve; to get better; as, to *pick up* well after an illness; a boy whose arithmetic is *picking up.* **8** To get acquainted with a stranger without an introduction. — *n.* **1** The act of picking; that which has been picked at one time or place. **2** Choice; the choicest person or thing; as, the *pick* of the crop; to take one's *pick.*

pickaback. Variant of *piggyback.*

pick·a·nin·ny \ˈpik-ə-ˌnin-ē\ *n.; pl.* **pick·a·nin·nies.** A small colored child.

pick·ax or **pick·axe** \ˈpik-ˌaks\ *n.* A tool with a wooden handle and a curved or straight blade pointed at one or both ends, used by diggers and miners.

pickax

pick·er·el \ˈpik-r(-)əl\ *n.; pl.* **pick·er·el** or **pick·er·els.** A food fish of the eastern, southern, and central United States; a pike, especially of a small kind.

pick·er·el·weed \ˈpik-r(-)əl-ˌwēd\ *n.* An American water plant having a rootstock which grows in mud, thick arrow-shaped leaves, and blue flowers.

pick·et \ˈpik-ət\ *n.* **1** A pointed stake or post, as one used in making a fence. **2** A soldier or a detachment of soldiers posted to guard an army from surprise attack. **3** A person posted by a labor organization at a factory, shop, or other place of work where there is a strike. — *v.* **1** To fence in or enclose with pickets. **2** To tie to a picket; as, to *picket* a horse. **3** To guard as a picket. **4** To post labor pickets at or around; to walk or stand in front of as a picket; as, to *picket* a factory.

pick·le \ˈpik-l\ *n.* **1** A mixture of salt and water for preserving or corning meat or fish; brine. **2** Vinegar with or without spices, for preserving foods. **3** Any article of food, especially a cucumber, that has been preserved in a pickle. **4** A very unpleasant condition; a predicament; as, to get oneself in a *pickle.* — *v.;* **pick·led; pick·ling** \-l(-)ing\. To soak or steep in a pickle; to preserve by using a pickle; as, to *pickle* pork; *pickled* onions.

pick·pock·et \'pik-ˌpäk-ət\ *n.* A thief who steals out of pockets or purses.

pick·up \'pik-ˌəp\ *n.* **1** A picking up. **2** Improvement; as, a *pickup* in business. **3** Acceleration; as, an automobile with fast *pickup*. **4** A light truck used for collection and delivery. **5** An attachment on a phonograph for converting the recorded sound into electrical energy.

pic·nic \'pik-ˌnik\ *n.* **1** A party at which the food is usually provided by the picnickers and eaten outdoors. **2** *Slang.* Something that is easy or pleasant; as, a course that was a *picnic* for all the students. — *v.;* **pic·nicked** \-ˌnikt\; **pic·nick·ing** \-ˌnik-ing\. To go on a picnic; to have a picnic.

pic·nick·er \'pik-ˌnik-r\ *n.* One who picnics.

pi·cot \'pē-ˌkō\ *n.; pl.* **pi·cots** \-ˌkōz\. One of the small loops or points that form an edging, as on ribbon or lace.

pic·to·gram \'pik-tə-ˌgram\ *n.* **1** A pictograph. **2** A kind of graph, used to make statistics more colorful or more easily understood, in which pictures or symbols replace the usual lines or bars.

pic·to·graph \'pik-tə-ˌgraf\ *n.* **1** A symbol or hieroglyphic representing and expressing an idea; a series of such symbols. **2** Symbols or pictures which have been scratched, drawn, or painted, as on the walls of an ancient cave. — **pic·to·graph·ic** \ˌpik-tə-'graf-ik\ *adj.*

pic·to·ri·al \pik-'tōr-ē-əl, -'tȯr-\ *adj.* **1** Of or having to do with pictures; as, *pictorial* art. **2** Using pictures; illustrated; as, a *pictorial* magazine. **3** Like a picture in vividness; as, *pictorial* reporting. — **pic·to·ri·al·ly** \-ē-ə-lē\ *adv.*

pic·ture \'pik-chər\ *n.* **1** A representation of something real or imagined, as by photography, drawing, or engraving. **2** A very vivid description in words. **3** An image; a likeness; a copy; as, a boy who is the *picture* of his father. **4** A motion picture. **5** An image on the screen of a television set. — *v.;* **pic·tured**; **pic·tur·ing**. **1** To draw or paint a picture of. **2** To show as clearly as in a picture. Fear was *pictured* on the lost child's face. **3** To make a mental picture of; to imagine. — *adj.* **1** Of or having to do with pictures; illustrated with pictures; as, a *picture* book. **2** Made up of pictures; shown through pictures; as, *picture* puzzles.

pic·tur·esque \ˌpik-chə-'resk\ *adj.* Like a picture; suitable for a picture; unusual and charming; as, a *picturesque* village. — **pic·tur·esque·ly**, *adv.*

picture tube. The glass tube on the end of which the television picture is made.

picture writing. The art of recording events or expressing messages by pictures showing actions or events; the record or message made in this way.

pid·dling \'pid-l(-)ing\ *adj.* Insignificant; trifling; as, a *piddling* amount of money.

pie \'pī\ *n.* A magpie.

pie \'pī\ *n.* **1** A food consisting of a pastry crust and a filling, as of fruit or meat. **2** A layer cake with a thick filling, as of jam or custard.

pie \'pī\. Variant of *pi*.

pie·bald \'pī-ˌbȯld\ *adj.* Of two colors, especially black and white; mottled; as, a *piebald* horse. — *n.* A piebald animal, especially a horse.

piece \'pēs\ *n.* **1** A part cut, torn, or broken from a thing; a fragment; as, a *piece* of string. **2** One of a group, set, or mass of things; as, a *piece* of mail; a chess *piece*. **3** A portion marked off; as, a *piece* of land. **4** A single item, example, or instance; as, a *piece* of news. **5** A definite quantity or size in which various articles are made for sale or use; as, to buy goods by the *piece*. **6** A finished product; something made, composed, or written; as, a *piece* of music; a sculptor's most famous *piece*. **7** A coin; as, a fifty-cent *piece*. **8** A firearm, as a cannon. — **to come to pieces**. To fall apart; to break into pieces. — **to go to pieces**. To become emotionally or physically upset. She *went to pieces* at the bad news. — *v.;* **pieced**; **piec·ing**. **1** To mend, extend, or complete by a piece or pieces; as, to *piece* a garment. **2** To make by joining pieces. — *adj.* Made of pieces; as, a *piece* quilt.

piece·meal \'pēs-ˌmēl, -'mēl\ *adv.* **1** Piece by piece; little by little. **2** In or into pieces.

piece·work \'pēs-ˌwərk\ *n.* Work done and paid for at a rate based on the number of articles made rather than the time spent in making them. — **piece·work·er** \-ˌwərk-r\ *n.*

pie·crust \'pī-ˌkrəst\ *n.* The pastry shell of a pie.

pied \'pīd\ *adj.* Having two or more colors in blotches; variegated; piebald.

pied \'pīd\. Past tense and past part. of *pi*.

pied·mont \'pēd-ˌmänt\ *adj.* Lying or formed at the base of mountains; as, a *piedmont* plain. — *n.* A piedmont district or area.

pieing. A pres. part. of *pi*.

pie·plant \'pī-ˌplant\ *n.* Rhubarb.

pier \'pir\ *n.* **1** A support for a bridge span. **2** A structure built out into the water for use as a landing place or walk, or to protect or form a harbor. **3** A single pillar or a structure used to support something. **4** A mass of masonry, such as a buttress, used to strengthen a wall.

pier, 1

pierce \'pirs\ *v.;* **pierced**; **pierc·ing**. **1** To run into or through as a pointed instrument does; to stab. **2** To make a hole in or through. **3** To force or wedge a way into or through; as, to *pierce* the enemy's line. **4** To penetrate with the eye or mind; as, to *pierce* the mystery. — **pierc·ing·ly**, *adv.*

pi·e·ty \'pī-ət-ē\ *n.; pl.* **pi·e·ties**. **1** The quality or condition of being pious; loyal devotion to one's parents, family, or race. **2** Dutifulness in religion; reverence for God. **3** A pious act or expression.

pif·fle \'pif-l\ *n.* Trifling talk or action.

pig \'pig\ *n.* **1** A young hog. **2** A hog of any age. **3** Pork. **4** A person or animal compared to a pig because of greed, selfishness, or filth. **5** A casting of metal, especially of iron or lead, run directly from the smelting furnace into a mold. — *v.;* **pigged**; **pig·ging**. To bring forth pigs.

pi·geon \'pij-n\ *n.* A stout-bodied, short-legged bird with soft plumage and a cooing voice.

pi·geon·hole \'pij-n-ˌhōl\ *n.* **1** A hole or small place for pigeons to nest. **2** A small open compartment, as in a desk or cabinet, for keeping letters or papers. — *v.;* **pi·geon·holed**; **pi·geon·hol·ing**. **1** To place in or as if in the pigeonhole of a desk; to file. **2** To lay aside for an indefinite time; to shelve. **3** To classify.

pi·geon-toed \'pij-n-'tōd\ *adj.* Having the toes turned in.

pig·gery \'pig-r(-)ē\ *n.; pl.* **pig·ger·ies**. **1** A place where hogs are kept or bred. **2** Pigs collectively.

pig·gish \'pig-ish\ *adj.* Like a pig; especially, greedy or filthy. — **pig·gish·ly** \-lē\ *adv.*

pig·gy \'pig-ē\ *n.; pl.* **pig·gies**. A little pig.

pig·gy·back \'pig-ē-ˌbak\ or **pick·a·back** \'pik-ə-ˌbak\ *adv.* or *adj.* On the back or shoulders; as, to carry a child *piggyback*.

pig·head·ed \'pig-'hed-əd\ *adj.* Stubborn.

pig iron. Crude iron; the direct product of the blast furnace.

pig·ment \'pig-mənt\ *n.* **1** A substance that gives color to other substances; especially, a powder, mixed with a suitable liquid, used for giving color to paints and enamels. **2** The coloring matter in persons, animals, and plants. — **pig·men·tary** \'pig-mən-ˌter-ē\ *adj.*

pig·men·ta·tion \ˌpig-mən-'tāsh-n\ *n.* A coloring with pigment; a depositing of pigment; especially, in medicine, too great a depositing of pigment.

pigmy. Variant of *pygmy*.

pig·pen \'pig-ˌpen\ *n.* **1** A pen for pigs. **2** A dirty house or room.

pig·skin \'pig-ˌskin\ *n.* **1** The skin of a pig, or leather made of it. **2** A saddle. **3** A football.

pig·sty \'pig-ˌstī\ *n.; pl.* **pig·sties**. A pigpen.

pig·tail \'pig-ˌtāl\ *n.* **1** Tobacco in small twisted ropes or rolls. **2** A tight braid of hair hanging down from the back of the head; a queue.

pigtails, 2

piing. A pres. part. of *pi*.

pike \'pīk\ *n.* A sharp point or spike, as on a shield or buckler.

pike \'pīk\ *n.; pl.* **pike** or **pikes**. A long and slender large-mouthed freshwater fish.

pike \'pīk\ *n.* A weapon once used by foot soldiers, consisting of a wooden staff with a steel point.

pike \'pīk\ *n.* **1** A road that has, or once had, tollgates; a turnpike. **2** Any main road or highway.

pik·er \'pīk-r\ *n.* A person, especially a gambler or speculator, who does things in a cheap way.

pike·staff \'pīk-ˌstaf\ *n.; pl.* **pike·staves** \-ˌstavz, -ˌstāvz\. The shaft or staff to which the steel point of a pike is joined.

pi·las·ter \pə-'last-r\ *n.* An upright, rectangular slightly projecting column that ornaments or helps to support a wall.

pil·chard \'pilch-rd\ *n.; pl.* **pil·chards** or **pil·chard**. A fish of European coasts that is much used for food and that produces young that are marketed under the name *sardines*.

pile \'pīl\ *n.* **1** Hair; especially, short fine hair like fur. **2** A soft thick surface of some fabrics, made of raised loops that are cut and sheared.

pile \'pīl\ *n.* **1** A mass of things heaped together; a heap; as, a *pile* of stones; a *pile* of sand. **2** A heap of wood for burning a corpse or an object given as a sacrifice to the gods in ancient religious ceremonies. **3** An electric battery. **4** An atomic pile. — *v.;* **piled**; **pil·ing**. **1** To heap up; to stack, as firewood. **2** To fill; to load; as, to *pile* a table with food. **3** To move or press forward in a mass; to crowd; as, to *pile* into a car.

pile \'pīl\ *n.* A large wooden or metal stake or pointed post driven into the ground to help support a foundation or to resist pressure. — *v.;* **piled**; **pil·ing**. To drive piles into; to support with piles.

piled \'pīld\ *adj.* Having a pile; as, *piled* fabrics.

pile-driv·er \'pīl-ˌdrīv-r\ *n.* A machine for driving or hammering a pile into place, usually a high framework with a mechanism for raising a heavy weight that falls on the pile.

pil·fer \'pilf-r\ *v.;* **pil·fered**; **pil·fer·ing** \-r(-)ing\. To steal small amounts at a time or articles of small value. — **pil·fer·age** \-r(-)ij\ *n.* — **pil·fer·er** \-r-r\ *n.*

pil·grim \'pil-grəm\ *n.* **1** A wanderer; a traveler. **2** A person who travels, usually far, to a holy place or shrine as an act of religious devotion. **3** [with a capital] One of the 102 settlers who landed from the Mayflower at Plymouth colony in 1620.

pil·grim·age \'pil-grə-mij\ *n.* A journey made by a pilgrim.

pil·ing \'pī-ling\ *n.* **1** Piles or posts in general. **2** A structure of piles. **3** A timber pile; especially, one standing in water or within reach of tidewater, as for supporting a jetty.

pill \'pil\ *n.* **1** A medicine in the form of a small rounded mass to be swallowed whole. **2** *Slang.* A ball, especially a baseball or golf ball.

pil·lage \'pil-ij\ *n.* The act of looting or plundering, especially in war; plunder. — *v.;* **pil·laged**; **pil·lag·ing**. To loot; to plunder. The enemy *pillaged* the captured town. — **pil·lag·er** \-ij-r\ *n.*

pil·lar \'pil-r\ *n.* **1** An upright support, narrow as compared to its height, as for a roof; any vertical supporting structure. **2** A column or shaft standing alone, as for a monument. **3** Something suggesting a pillar; a main support; as, a *pillar* of local society. — **pil·lared** \-rd\ *adj.*

pill·box \'pil-ˌbäks\ *n.* **1** A small flat, usually round, box to hold pills. **2** A small, circular hat with a flat crown. **3** A low round concrete fortification containing machine guns.

pill bug. A wood louse that rolls into a ball when disturbed.

pil·lion \'pil-yən\ *n.* **1** A cushion or pad placed behind a saddle for an extra rider. **2** A passenger's saddle, as on a motorcycle.

pil·lo·ry \'pil-r-ē\ *n.; pl.* **pil·lo·ries**. **1** A device for punishing offenders publicly, consisting of a wooden frame having holes in which a person's head and hands could be locked. **2** Any means for exposing a person to public scorn or ridicule. — *v.;* **pil·lo·ried** \-r-ēd\; **pil·lo·ry·ing. 1** To put in a pillory. **2** To expose to public scorn or ridicule.

pil·low \'pil-ō\ *n.* A case that is filled with soft or springy material, as feathers, down, or sponge rubber, and used as a support or cushion for the head of a person lying down. — *v.* **1** To place on or as if on a pillow. **2** To serve as a pillow for.

pil·low·case \'pil-ō-ˌkās\ *n.* A removable covering for a pillow.

pi·lot \'pī-lət\ *n.* **1** A person who steers a ship. **2** A person qualified and licensed to conduct ships into and out of a port or in certain dangerous waters. **3** A guide; a leader. **4** The cowcatcher of a locomotive. **5** A person who flies or is qualified to fly an aircraft. **6** A part of a machine acting as a guide or control of another part. — *v.* To act as pilot of; to guide or lead. — *adj.* Serving on a small scale as a testing or trial device or unit; as, a *pilot* factory; a *pilot* technique.

pilot fish. A spiny-finned fish with narrow body and widely forked tail, often seen with a shark.

pi·lot·house \'pī-lət-ˌhau̇s\ *n.; pl.* **pi·lot·hous·es** \-ˌhau̇-zəz\. An enclosed place forward on the upper deck of a boat, sheltering the steering gear and the helmsman.

pi·mien·to \pə-'ment-ˌō, ˌpim-ē-'ent-ˌō\ or **pi·men·to** \pə-'ment-ˌō\ *n.; pl.* **pi·mien·tos** or **pi·men·tos. 1** The Spanish paprika plant. **2** The fleshy fruit of this plant, used as a vegetable.

pim·per·nel \'pimp-r-ˌnel, -rn-l\ *n.* A weedy herb related to the primrose, having flowers with a spreading five-lobed corolla; especially, the **scarlet pimpernel**, whose scarlet or purple flowers close at the approach of rainy or cloudy weather.

pim·ple \'pimp-l\ *n.* A very small, inflamed swelling of the skin, often containing pus; a small boil. — **pim·pled** \-ld\ *adj.* — **pim·ply** \-l(-)ē\ *adj.*

pin \'pin\ *n.* **1** A piece of rigid material such as wood or metal, often slender and pointed, used to fasten articles together or in place or to serve as a peg on which to hang things. **2** A small pointed piece of wire with a head, used for fastening or holding cloth or paper. **3** A thing of small value; a trifle. Not one of the prizes was worth a *pin.* **4** An ornament, such as a brooch or badge, fastened to the clothing by a pin; as, a girls' club *pin.* **5** The leg; as, to knock a person off his *pins.* **6** One of the wooden pieces set up to be struck by the ball in bowling. **7** In golf, the stick of the flag marking a hole. **8** A peg for regulating the tension of strings, as of a violin. — *v.;* **pinned**; **pin·ning. 1** To fasten, join, or pierce by or as if by a pin. **2** To hold as if by putting a pin through; as, to *pin* a person's arms to his sides; to *pin* a man down.

pin·a·fore \'pin-ə-ˌfōr, -ˌfȯr\ *n.* A sleeveless, usually square-necked garment worn as an apron or a dress by girls and women.

pi·ña·ta \pin-'yät-ə, -'yȧt-ə\ *n.* In Mexico, an elaborately decorated hanging container made of pottery or paper that holds gifts and candy and is broken on Christmas day.

pince-nez \'pan(t)s-ˌnā\ *n.* Eyeglasses clipped to the nose by a spring.

pin·cers \'pinch-rz, 'pin(t)s-rz\ *n. pl.* **1** An instrument with two handles and grasping jaws working on a pivot, used for gripping things. **2** The grasping or pinching claws of a lobster or a crab. **3** An offensive movement in which two forces of troops come together from different directions to isolate and crush an enemy.

pincers

pinch \'pinch\ *v.* **1** To squeeze between the finger and thumb or between the jaws of an instrument. **2** To squeeze painfully; as, to get a finger *pinched* in a door; shoes that *pinch.* **3** To cramp or contract; to make shriveled; as, a face *pinched* with cold. **4** To be economical; to be stingy; as, to *pinch* and save. **5** *Slang.* To steal. **6** *Slang.* To arrest; as, to be *pinched* for speeding. — *n.* **1** An emergency; a time of special need; a critical moment; as, good enough to be used in a *pinch.* **2** Painful pressure or stress; as, to feel the *pinch* of hunger. **3** The act of pinching; a nip or squeeze. **4** As much as may be picked up between the finger and the thumb; a small amount; as, a *pinch* of salt; a *pinch* of snuff. **5** *Slang.* A theft. **6** *Slang.* An arrest.

pinch·er \'pinch-r\ *n.* **1** One that pinches. **2** [in the plural] Pincers.

pinch hitter. 1 In baseball, a player sent in to bat for another player in an emergency, as when a hit is much needed. **2** Any person called upon to do another's work in an emergency. — **pinch-hit** \'pinch-'hit, -ˌhit\ *v.*

pin curl. A curl made usually by dampening a strand of hair with water or lotion, coiling it, and securing it by a hairpin or bobby pin.

pin·cush·ion \'pin-ˌku̇sh-n\ *n.* A small cushion in which pins may be stuck.

pine \'pīn\ *v.;* **pined**; **pin·ing. 1** To lose vigor, health, or weight through grief, worry, or other distress; as, to *pine* away. **2** To long; to yearn; to have a deep desire; as, to *pine* for home.

pine \'pīn\ *n.* **1** Any of several evergreen trees having temporary scaly leaves followed by narrow needles (**pine needles**) in clusters, cones (**pine cones**) with overlapping woody scales enclosing winged seeds, and durable wood that ranges from very soft to hard. **2** The wood of these trees. **3** Any tree of a family having needle-shaped or scaly leaves, cones with woody or fleshy scales, and fine-grained wood, as the spruces, firs, and hemlocks.

pin·e·al body or **pin·e·al gland** \'pin-ē-əl, 'pī-nē-əl\. A structure which is found in the brain of most animals having a skull and which evidently is a remnant of an important organ in early forms of life and was thought by some philosophers to be the seat of the soul in human beings.

pine·ap·ple \ˈpī-ˌnap-l\ *n.* **1** A tropical plant with stiff, spiny, sword-shaped leaves and a short flowering stalk that develops into a fleshy fruit. **2** The edible juicy fruit of this plant.

pineapple

pine tar. Tar distilled from pine wood and used in roofing, paints, and plastics and in medicinal preparations.

pin·feath·er \ˈpin-ˌfeth-r\ *n.* A feather that is not yet fully developed, especially one that is just coming through the skin.

ping-pong \ˈping-ˌpäng, -ˌpȯng\ *n.* [From *Ping-Pong*, a trademark.] Table tennis.

pin·hole \ˈpin-ˌhōl\ *n.* A tiny hole, as one made by a pin.

pin·ion \ˈpin-yən\ *n.* A gear with a small number of teeth designed to mesh with a larger wheel or rack; the smallest of a train of gear wheels.

pin·ion \ˈpin-yən\ *n.* **1** The end part of a bird's wing. **2** A wing. **3** A feather; a quill. — *v.* **1** To bind the wings or cut the pinion of a bird. **2** To disable or restrain by binding or holding the arms.

pink \ˈpingk\ *v.* **1** To cut or pierce cloth, leather, or paper in an ornamental pattern. **2** To cut the edge of a piece of fabric, as of a seam, in V-shaped notches in order to prevent fraying. **3** To stab, as with a sword.

pink \ˈpingk\ *n.* **1** Any plant of a family characterized by silvery leaves, thick joints, and flowers that form either singly or in small clusters. **2** The highest degree possible; as, in the *pink* of condition. **3** A light tint of red. — *adj.* Of the color pink; light red.

pink·eye \ˈpingk-ˌī\ *n.* A painful and infectious disease in which the inner surface of the eyelid and part of the eyeball become pinkish and sore.

pink·ish \ˈpingk-ish\ *adj.* Somewhat pink.

pin money. **1** Money given by a man to his wife for her own use. **2** Money for incidental expenses.

pin·nace \ˈpin-əs\ *n.* **1** A light sailing vessel that in former times was used as a tender. **2** Any of various ship's boats.

pin·na·cle \ˈpin-ik-l\ *n.* **1** An upright structure, as on a tower, generally ending in a small spire. **2** A lofty peak; a pointed summit. **3** The summit or highest point of anything; as, the *pinnacle* of success.

pinnacle

pin·nate \ˈpin-ˌāt, -ət\ *adj.* Having divisions of the blade, or leaflet, arranged along each side of the midrib; as, a *pinnate* leaf. — **pin·nate·ly**, *adv.*

pinned. Past tense of *pin.*

pinning. Pres. part. of *pin.*

pi·noch·le \ˈpē-ˌnək-l, -ˌnäk-l\ *n.* A card game which uses all cards above the eight in two decks.

pin·point \ˈpin-ˌpȯint\ *v.* To make something completely specific; to narrow down to one exact spot; as, to *pinpoint* a bombing target; to *pinpoint* the source of the trouble. — *adj.* Directed with extreme precision as if on a pin's point; as, *pinpoint* bombing.

pin-striped \ˈpin-ˌstrīpt\ *adj.* Having stripes so narrow that they appear to have been drawn with a pin point; as, a gray *pin-striped* suit.

pint \ˈpīnt\ *n.* A measure of capacity equal to half a quart, or four gills.

pin·to \ˈpin-ˌtō\ *adj.* Piebald; mottled; pied. — *n.; pl.* **pin·tos**. A piebald horse or pony.

pin·wale \ˈpin-ˌwāl\ *adj.* Made with extremely narrow wales; as, *pinwale* corduroy.

pin·wheel \ˈpin-ˌhwēl\ *n.* **1** A toy made of a stick with vanes on one end that rotate when they are blown upon or when the stick is moved rapidly. **2** A type of firework that rotates and makes a wheel of yellow or other-colored fire.

pin·worm \ˈpin-ˌwərm\ *n.* A small parasitic roundworm found chiefly in the cecum, as of man.

pi·o·neer \ˌpī-ə-ˈnir\ *n.* **1** A person who goes before, preparing the way for others to follow. **2** An early settler; a colonist. — *v.* **1** To open up, discover, or explore in advance. **2** To act as a pioneer for or in; as, to *pioneer* a cause.

pi·ous \ˈpī-əs\ *adj.* **1** Showing reverence toward God; religious; devout. **2** Done under the pretense of religion; as, a *pious* fraud. — **pi·ous·ly**, *adv.*

pip \ˈpip\ *n.* **1** A disease of birds. **2** A small scale that forms on the tip of the tongue as a symptom of this disease.

pip \ˈpip\ *n.* A small seed, as of an apple.

pip \ˈpip\ *v.;* **pipped**; **pip·ping**. **1** To chirp; to peep. **2** To break through the shell of the egg — used of birds. **3** To be broken by pipping; as, eggs starting to *pip.*

pip \ˈpip\ *n.* A spot of light on a radar screen that indicates the return of reflected radar waves.

pipe \ˈpīp\ *n.* **1** A musical instrument consisting of a tube of reed, wood, or metal, played by blowing. **2** Any tube producing a musical sound; as, an organ *pipe;* a pitch *pipe.* **3** [usually in the plural] The bagpipe. **4** The whistle, call, or note of a bird or an insect. **5** Any long tube or hollow body to conduct a substance, as water, steam, or gas. **6** A tube with a small bowl at one end, used for smoking tobacco. **7** A toy pipe for blowing bubbles. — *v.;* **piped**; **pip·ing**. **1** To play music on a pipe. **2** To speak in or have the shrill tone of a pipe. **3** To conduct or transfer by means of pipes; as, to *pipe* water. **4** To equip with pipes. **5** To call or direct by a boatswain's whistle.

pipe·fish \ˈpīp-ˌfish\ *n.; pl.* **pipe·fish** or **pipe·fish·es**. Any of certain long slender fishes belonging to the same family as the sea horses and characterized by a tube-shaped snout and a body covered with bony plates.

pipe·line \ˈpīp-ˌlīn\ *n.* A line of pipe with pumping machinery and equipment for carrying fluids, especially petroleum.

pip·er \'pīp-r\ *n.* One who plays on a pipe, especially a bagpipe.

pip·ing \'pīp-ing\ *n.* **1** The music or sound of a person or thing that pipes; as, the *piping* of frogs. **2** Pipes collectively; material for pipes. **3** A narrow fold of material, sometimes covering a cord, used to decorate edges or seams. — *adj.* **1** Playing on a musical pipe. **2** Making a high, shrill sound; high-pitched.

pip·ing hot \'pīp-ing 'hät\. So hot as to sizzle or hiss; very hot.

pip·it \'pip-ət\ *n.* A small bird resembling the larks and singing while flying.

pip·kin \'pip-kən\ *n.* **1** A small earthen pot, usually with a horizontal handle. **2** A similar vessel of metal, for cooking.

pip·pin \'pip-n\ *n.* An apple of any of a number of varieties.

pi·quant \'pēk-nt\ *adj.* **1** Pleasantly tart, sharp, or biting to the palate; as, a *piquant* sauce. **2** Pleasingly exciting to the mind; as, a *piquant* bit of gossip. **3** Having a lively, arch charm; as, a *piquant* face. — **pi·quan·cy** \-n-sē\ *n.*

pique \'pēk\ *n.* **1** Offense felt because of a slight or other injury to one's pride. **2** A fit of resentment or irritation from such an injury; as, to go off in a *pique.* — *v.;* **piqued**; **piqu·ing.** **1** To offend by injuring one's pride; to arouse resentment in. **2** To arouse or excite; as, to *pique* one's curiosity. **3** To pride (oneself).

pi·qué \pē-'kā\ *n.* A ribbed fabric, usually of cotton.

pi·ra·cy \'pī-rə-sē\ *n.; pl.* **pi·ra·cies.** **1** Robbery on the high seas. **2** The using of another's work or invention without permission.

pi·rate \'pī-rət\ *n.* A person who commits piracy, especially robbery on the high seas. — *v.;* **pi·rat·ed**; **pi·rat·ing.** To commit piracy upon; as, to *pirate* a ship; to *pirate* an invention.

pi·rat·i·cal \pī-'rat-ik-l\ or **pi·rat·ic** \-ik\ *adj.* **1** Of or like a pirate. **2** Of or like piracy. — **pi·rat·i·cal·ly** \-ik-l(-)ē\ *adv.*

pi·rogue \'pē-ˌrōg, pə-'rōg\ *n.* A dugout; any boat resembling a canoe.

pir·ou·ette \ˌpir-ə-'wet\ *n.* A whirling or turning on the toes. — *v.;* **pir·ou·et·ted**; **pir·ou·et·ting.** To whirl or turn on the toes.

pis·cine \'pis-ˌīn\ *adj.* Of, relating to, or like a fish.

pis·tach·io \pis-'tash-ē-ˌō, pis-'tash-ˌō\ *n.; pl.* **pis·tach·i·os.** **1** A small tree native to southern Europe and Asia Minor, or its nut, which contains one greenish edible seed. **2** The flavor of this nut. **3** The greenish color of this nut.

pis·til \'pist-l\ *n.* The seed-producing part of a flower, ordinarily consisting of stigma, style, and ovary; the female reproductive organ in a flower.

pis·til·late \'pist-l-ət, -ˌāt\ *adj.* Producing a pistil or pistils; especially, having a pistil or pistils but no stamens.

pis·tol \'pist-l\ *n.* [From French *pistole,* there borrowed from German, where it was borrowed from a Czech word meaning literally "pipe".] A short gun made to be aimed and fired with one hand.

pis·ton \'pis-tən\ *n.* **1** A sliding piece, usually a short cylinder moving back and forth inside a larger cylinder, moved by steam in steam engines and by explosion of the fuel in automobiles. **2** A sliding valve in certain wind instruments, which when pressed down serves to lower the pitch.

piston rod. A rod by which a piston is moved or by which it communicates motion.

pit \'pit\ *n.* The hard stone of certain fruits, as the cherry or peach. — *v.;* **pit·ted**; **pit·ting.** To remove the pits from; as, to *pit* cherries.

pit \'pit\ *n.* **1** A cavity or hole in the ground. **2** A pitfall for wild animals; a trap; a snare. **3** A deep place; an abyss; especially, hell, or a part of it. **4** A surface depression or hollow. The *pit* of the stomach is the depression below the lower end of the breastbone. **5** A scar left by a disease such as smallpox. **6** An enclosed place where animals, as cocks, are put to fight. **7** *British.* The cheaper downstairs seats of a theater or the spectators in these seats. — *v.;* **pit·ted**; **pit·ting.** **1** To put into a pit or hole. **2** To form pits in; as, a face *pitted* by smallpox. **3** To match one against another; as, to *pit* one's skill against an opponent's.

pit·a·pat \'pit-ē-'pat, -ə-'pat\ *adv.* With quick beats; in a flutter. My heart went *pitapat.* — *n.* A light repeated sound; a pattering.

pitch \'pich\ *n.* **1** A dark sticky substance left over from distilling tar or petroleum, used in manufacturing roofing paper, in calking seams, and in paving streets. **2** The resin from certain pines. — *v.* To cover or smear with pitch.

pitch \'pich\ *v.* **1** To place and set up or erect; as, to *pitch* a tent. **2** To throw, fling, hurl, or toss; as, to *pitch* hay. **3** In baseball, to throw the ball to the batter. **4** To plunge or fall, especially forward; as, to *pitch* from a cliff. **5** To slope; as, a lawn that *pitches* toward the street. **6** To fix or set at a particular pitch or level; as, to *pitch* a tune high or low. **7** Of ships and airplanes, to plunge so that the front and back ends alternately rise and fall. — **pitch in.** **1** To set to work energetically. **2** To begin eating. — **pitch into.** **1** To attack; to assail. **2** To scold vigorously. — *n.* **1** The action of pitching; a throw; a toss; as, in baseball, to hit the first *pitch.* **2** A plunging by bow and stern, as of a boat. **3** Something that is pitched. **4** A point or peak; as, at the highest *pitch* of success. **5** A slope or degree of slope; as, the *pitch* of a roof. **6** The distance apart of two things, especially in a series, as from center to center of two adjacent gear teeth. **7** The highness or lowness of sound or of a tone. **8** A standard of pitch used in tuning musical instruments.

pitch-and-toss \'pich-n-'tòs, -'täs\ *n.* A game in which the victor in pitching coins at a mark has first chance at tossing the pitched coins in the air and winning those that fall heads up.

pitch·blende \ˈpich-ˌblend\ *n.* A dark pitchy mineral that is a source of radium and uranium.

pitched battle \ˈpicht\. A full-scale battle in which the troops on both sides are arranged according to the rules of military science.

pitch·er \ˈpich-r\ *n.* **1** A container, usually with a handle and a lip, used for holding and pouring out liquids. **2** The amount held by a pitcher.

pitch·er \ˈpich-r\ *n.* **1** One that pitches. **2** In baseball, the player who throws the ball to the batter.

pitch·fork \ˈpich-ˌfȯrk\ *n.* A fork, usually long-handled, used in pitching hay or grain.

pitch pipe. A small pipe blown to indicate musical pitch, especially for singers.

pitchy \ˈpich-ē\ *adj.;* **pitch·i·er; pitch·i·est. 1** Like pitch. **2** Full of or smeared with pitch. **3** Black as pitch.

pitch pipe

pit·e·ous \ˈpit-ē-əs\ *adj.* Awakening pity; pitiful. — **pit·e·ous·ly**, *adv.*

pit·fall \ˈpit-ˌfȯl\ *n.* **1** A trap or snare; especially, a pit with the opening disguised for capturing animals. **2** A danger, difficulty, or error into which one may fall unknowingly.

pith \ˈpith\ *n.* **1** The loose spongy tissue occupying the center of the stem in certain plants. **2** The soft interior of a bone or feather. **3** Any loose tissue resembling pith; as, orange *pith.* **4** The important part; gist; as, the *pith* of the problem.

pith·e·can·thro·pus \ˌpith-ə-ˈkan(t)th-rə-pəs, -ˌkan-ˈthrōp-əs\ *n.* A prehistoric creature intermediate between modern man and the present anthropoid apes; Java man.

pith ray. A medullary ray.

pithy \ˈpith-ē\ *adj.;* **pith·i·er; pith·i·est. 1** Consisting of, or filled with, pith. **2** Short but to the point; as, a *pithy* remark. — **pith·i·ly** \ˈpith-l-ē\ *adv.*

pit·i·a·ble \ˈpit-ē-əb-l\ *adj.* **1** Deserving or arousing pity; lamentable. **2** Pitifully insignificant or mean; as, a *pitiable* show of skill. — **pit·i·a·bly** \-ē-ə-blē\ *adv.*

pit·i·ful \ˈpit-ēf-l, -əf-l\ *adj.* **1** Arousing pity or sympathy; as, a *pitiful* sight. **2** Deserving pitying contempt; pitiable; contemptible; as, a *pitiful* excuse. — **pit·i·ful·ly** \-l(-)ē\ *adv.*

pit·i·less \ˈpit-ē-ləs, ˈpit-l-əs\ *adj.* Without pity; merciless. — **pit·i·less·ly**, *adv.*

pit·tance \ˈpit-n(t)s\ *n.* A small portion, quantity, or allowance, especially of money.

pi·tu·i·tary \pə-ˈtü-ə-ˌter-ē, -ˈtyü-\ *adj.* Of or relating to a two-lobed gland (**pituitary gland**) which is attached to the gray matter of the brain and plays an important role in the regulation of the growth and reproductive processes of the body.

pit viper. Any of a group of venomous snakes including the rattlesnake and the copperhead.

pity \ˈpit-ē\ *n.* **1** A feeling of sympathy and sorrow for the sufferings or distress of others; compassion. **2** A reason or cause of pity, grief, or regret; something to be regretted. It is a *pity* to neglect opportunities.

— The words *sympathy* and *compassion* are synonyms of *pity: sympathy,* the most general of these terms, carries the idea of an ability to share another's feelings or understand his situation, and can suggest many attitudes ranging from friendly interest to deep tenderness for another; *pity* usually indicates a concern for the suffering of another, sometimes as if one felt the same suffering; *compassion* is like *pity* in suggesting a strong concern for or sharing in another's suffering but stresses strongly the desire to aid and comfort. — *v.;* **pit·ied** \-ēd\; **pit·y·ing**. To feel pity for.

piv·ot \ˈpiv-ət\ *n.* **1** A point or fixed pin on the end of which something turns. **2** That upon which something turns or depends; the central member, part, or point. — *v.* **1** To mount on, or furnish with, a pivot. **2** To turn on, or as if on, a pivot.

pivot

piv·ot·al \ˈpiv-ət-l\ *adj.* **1** Of or having to do with a pivot; as, a *pivotal* connection. **2** Crucial; of the first importance; as, the *pivotal* issue in an election. — **piv·ot·al·ly** \-ət-l-ē\ *adv.*

pixy or **pix·ie** \ˈpiks-ē\ *n.; pl.* **pix·ies**. A mischievous fairy or sprite.

piz·zi·ca·to \ˌpits-ə-ˈkät-ˌō, ˌpits-ē-, -ˈkȧt-ˌō\ *adj.* or *adv.* In music, plucked, not bowed — used as a direction for instruments of the violin family.

pk. Abbreviation for: **1** *peck.* **2** *peak.* **3** *park.*

pkg. Abbreviation for *package.*

pl. Abbreviation for *plural.*

plac·ard \ˈplak-ˌärd, -ˌȧrd, -rd\ *n.* A notice posted in a public place; a bill; a poster. — *v.* **1** To post placards on or in. **2** To announce by placards.

pla·cate \ˈplā-ˌkāt, ˈplak-ˌāt\ *v.;* **pla·cat·ed; pla·cat·ing**. To calm the anger of; to soothe or pacify.

place \ˈplās\ *n.* [From medieval English, there borrowed from Old French, where it was derived from Latin *platea* meaning "street", "area", "courtyard", and borrowed from Greek *plateia* meaning "street" — see *plaza.*] **1** Space; room; as, to make a *place* for the newcomer. **2** A region; a locality; a spot; as, a *place* on the map. **3** A village, town, or city; as, one's native *place.* **4** Any particular spot; as, a sore *place* on one's heel; to lose one's *place* in a book. **5** A space set aside for one's use, as a seat on an airplane. **6** A dwelling; as, a *place* in the country; to find a *place* in an apartment building. **7** Position, rank, or grade or the duties related to them; as, to know one's *place.* It is a teacher's *place* to correct her students. **8** A building or spot set apart for a special purpose; as, a *place* of worship. **9** A short street or court. **10** Position in the order of taking up matters; as, in the first *place.* **11** In arithmetic, the position of a figure in relation to others of a series; as, the first *place* after the decimal. **12** Stead; as, to wear mittens in *place* of gloves. **13** Situation; as, if I were in your *place.* **14** One of the first three positions at the finish of a horse race; especially, the second position. — **in place**. In the proper place. — **out of place**. **1** Not in the proper place. **2** Unsuitable; inappropriate; as, a remark that was *out of place*. — **to take place.** To occur; to happen; as, an event that *took place* in July. — *v.;* **placed; plac·ing. 1** To put in a certain place; to fix; to settle; as, to *place* a book on a shelf. **2** To identify by connecting with a certain place, time, or circumstance. The man looks familiar, but no one can *place* him. **3** To find a job for.

place kick. In football, a kicking of the ball after it has been placed on the ground. — **place-kick** \'plās-ˌkik\ *v.*

place·ment \'plās-mənt\ *n.* **1** A placing or a being placed. **2** The finding of employment for someone. **3** The assignment of students to the proper class or grade, as on the basis of tests. **4** A place kick.

pla·cen·ta \plə-'sent-ə\ *n.; pl.* **pla·cen·tas** \-'sent-əz\ or **pla·cen·tae** \-'sen-(ˌ)tē\. In most mammals, the structure to which the fetus is attached in the uterus and by which it is nourished. — **pla·cen·tal** \-'sent-l\ *adj.*

plac·er \'plas-r\ *n.* A place where gold is obtained by washing; a deposit of sand or gravel in the bed of a stream, containing gold or other valuable minerals.

plac·id \'plas-əd\ *adj.* Calm; undisturbed; quiet; as, a *placid* sea; *placid* sleep. — **pla·cid·i·ty** \pla-'sid-ət-ē\ *n.* — **plac·id·ly** \'plas-əd-lē\ *adv.*

plack·et \'plak-ət\ *n.* A slit or opening, as in a skirt, which fastens after the garment has been put on.

pla·gia·rism \'plāj-r-ˌiz-m, 'plā-jē-ə-ˌriz-m\ *n.* **1** The act of plagiarizing. **2** Something that has been plagiarized; as, a novel that was sheer *plagiarism*. — **pla·gia·rist** \'plāj-r-əst, 'plā-jē-ər-əst\ *n.*

pla·gia·rize \'plāj-r-ˌīz, 'plā-jē-ə-ˌrīz\ *v.;* **pla·gia·rized; pla·gia·riz·ing.** To steal and pass off as one's own the work of another; as, to *plagiarize* an invention; to *plagiarize* in writing a theme.

plague \'plāg\ *n.* **1** Anything that causes much suffering or trouble. **2** A nuisance; as, a child who was a little *plague*. **3** A contagious disease; an epidemic; especially, bubonic plague. — *v.;* **plagued; plagu·ing. 1** To strike or afflict with disease, great misfortune, or evil. **2** To vex; to tease.

plaid \'plad\ *n.* **1** A rectangular piece of cloth, usually of tartan, worn by both men and women in Scotland as a cloak. **2** A pattern like that of a Scottish tartan, consisting of rectangles formed by crossed lines of various widths and various colors. **3** Any fabric woven or printed with this pattern.

plaid, 2

plain \'plān\ *adj.* **1** Flat; level. **2** Open; clear; as, in *plain* view. **3** Easily understood; clear to the mind; as, in *plain* words. **4** Frank; outspoken; as, *plain* speaking. **5** Not luxurious or rich; simple; as, *plain* food. **6** Not handsome or beautiful; as, a *plain* woman. **7** Not highly born or educated; as, *plain* people. **8** Of simple weave or of solid color; as, a *plain* cloth. **9** Not especially difficult; not complicated; as, *plain* sewing. — *n.* **1** Level land; as, over hill and *plain*. **2** [in the plural] Broad stretches of level country; as, our western *plains*. — *adv.* In a plain manner; clearly. — **plain·ly,** *adv.*

plain-clothes man \(')plān-'klō(th)z mən, ˌman\. A detective or police officer who does not wear a uniform while on duty.

plains·man \'plānz-mən\ *n.; pl.* **plains·men** \-mən\. One who lives on the plains.

plain song or **plain chant.** A type of ancient religious chant which is rhythmical but not metrical and is sung in unison; especially, such a chant sung in services in the Roman Catholic Church.

plain-spo·ken \'plān-'spōk-n\ *adj.* Speaking or spoken plainly or bluntly; as, a *plain-spoken* man; a *plain-spoken* speech.

plaint \'plānt\ *n.* **1** A lamentation; a lament. **2** A complaint or protest.

plain·tiff \'plānt-əf\ *n.* The complaining party in a lawsuit; the one who begins a lawsuit to enforce his claims.

plain·tive \'plānt-iv\ *adj.* Expressing or suggesting sorrow; mournful; sad; as, a *plaintive* sigh. — **plain·tive·ly,** *adv.*

plait \'plat, 'plāt\ *n.* **1** A pleat. **2** A braid, as of hair. — *v.* **1** To pleat. **2** To braid, as hair. **3** To make by braiding; as, to *plait* a mat or a basket.

plan \'plan\ *n.* **1** A drawing or diagram showing the parts or outline of a thing. **2** A method or scheme of acting, doing, or arranging; as, a civil defense *plan;* vacation *plans.* — *v.;* **planned; planning. 1** To form a plan of or for; to show, as by a diagram. **2** To arrange the details beforehand; as, a party that was *planned* well. **3** To intend.

plane \'plān\ *n.* or **plane tree.** Any of several tall trees with light brown flaky bark, large five-lobed leaves, and a fruit that stays on all winter.

plane \'plān\ *adj.* **1** Level; flat; as, a *plane* surface. **2** Dealing with flat surfaces; as, *plane* geometry. — *n.* **1** A level or flat surface. **2** A level of development; a grade. **3** An airplane.

plane \'plān\ *n.* A tool with a blade set in that is used for smoothing or shaping wood. — *v.;* **planed; plan·ing. 1** To smooth or level off with a plane; as, to *plane* a board. **2** To remove with or as if with a plane.

plane

plan·et \'plan-ət\ *n.* Any heavenly body, except a comet or meteor, that revolves about the sun, or such a body revolving about the sun of another solar system.

plan·e·tar·i·um \ˌplan-ə-'ter-ē-əm\ *n.; pl.* **plan·e·tar·i·ums** \-ē-əmz\ or **plan·e·tar·ia** \-ē-ə\. **1** A model of the heavens showing stars and planets, especially one which can be projected on a dome-shaped ceiling. **2** A room or building containing a planetarium.

plan·e·tary \'plan-ə-ˌter-ē\ *adj.* **1** Having to do with planets. **2** Moving like a planet. **3** Of or relating to a system or chain of gear wheels, especially one making up an automobile transmission gear.

plan·e·toid \'plan-ə-ˌtȯid\ *n.* A body resembling a planet; an asteroid.

plank \'plangk\ *n.* **1** A heavy thick board. **2** One of the separate articles in the platform of a political party. **3** A gangplank. — *v.* **1** To cover or lay with planks; as, to *plank* a floor. **2** To lay down, as on a plank or table, with force; to slam down; to pay; as, to *plank* down money. **3** To cook and serve on a plank; as, to *plank* a steak.

plank·ton \'plang(k)t-n\ *n.* The floating plant and animal life of a body of water, made up chiefly of algae, protozoans, eggs, and larvae.

plan·ner \'plan-r\ *n.* A person who plans.

plant \'plant\ *n.* **1** Any member of the division of living things typically characterized by having a body which grows indefinitely and is stiffened by cellulose and by being made fast, as by roots in the soil, and that includes green plants which produce complex organic matter by photosynthesis and other plants, as fungi and bacteria, which lack this ability and depend like animals on organic matter for food. **2** The building, machinery, equipment, and fixtures used in the operating of a trade, business, or institution; as, a power *plant;* a hospital *plant.* **3** *Slang.* Something deliberately placed to trap wrongdoers or to cast suspicion on innocent persons; as, a *plant* to catch shoplifters. The police discovered the evidence was only a *plant.* — *v.* **1** To put or set in the ground to grow; as, to *plant* seeds in the spring. **2** To set firmly; to fix; as, to *plant* one's feet on solid ground. **3** To introduce as an idea or habit; as, a religion that had been *planted* years before. **4** To establish; to settle; as, to *plant* colonies. **5** To stock or provide with something; as, to *plant* a garden with flowers. **6** *Slang.* To land, as a blow; as, to *plant* a right to the jaw. **7** *Slang.* To place as a plant or false clue.

plan·tain \'plant-n\ *n.* Any of several common short-stemmed or stemless weeds having elliptic leaves with parallel veins and a long spike of tiny greenish flowers.

plan·tain \'plant-n\ *n.* A kind of banana plant having greenish fruit that is larger, less sweet, and more starchy than the ordinary banana; the fruit of this plant.

plan·ta·tion \plan-'tāsh-n\ *n.* **1** In history, a colony; as, the Virginia *plantation.* **2** A group of plants or trees planted and being tended; as, a sugar *plantation.* **3** A place planted; especially, an estate cultivated by laborers living on the grounds.

plant·er \'plant-r\ *n.* **1** A person or thing that plants or sows; as, a mechanical corn *planter.* **2** A person who owns or manages a plantation. **3** A pot, box, or tray for planting flowers.

plant louse. Any of various small insects that live and feed on plants.

plaque \'plak\ *n.* **1** A flat, thin plate of metal, clay, or ivory used for ornament, as on a wall. **2** An ornamental brooch or honorary badge.

plash \'plash\ *v.* To splash. — *n.* A splash.

plas·ma \'plaz-mə\ *n.* The watery part of lymph, milk, or, especially, blood.

plas·ter \'plast-r\ *n.* **1** A medicated or protective dressing made of cloth spread with a substance which adheres to the skin; as, an adhesive *plaster;* a mustard *plaster.* **2** A substance, usually of lime, water, and sand, that hardens when dry, used for coating walls and ceilings. **3** Plaster of paris. — *v.;* **plas·tered; plas·ter·ing** \-r(-)ing\. **1** To cover or smear with plaster; as, to *plaster* a wall. **2** To smear as if with plaster; as, a bicycle *plastered* with mud. **3** To paste or fasten on; as, to *plaster* the wall with posters. **4** To stick as if with paste; as, wet clothes *plastered* to a person's body. **5** To apply a plaster to, as to a wound.

plaster of par·is \ə(v) 'par-əs\. A white powdery substance that forms a quickly hardening paste used for making casts and moldings.

plas·tic \'plas-tik\ *adj.* **1** Giving form or fashion to a mass. A sculptor is a *plastic* artist. **2** Capable of being molded or modeled, as clay or wax. **3** Made of a plastic. — *n.* **1** Any substance capable of being molded. **2** A nonmetallic substance that is capable of being molded or cast during manufacture and that is solid in the finished state.

plas·tic·i·ty \plas-'tis-ət-ē\ *n.* The quality or state of being plastic.

plastic surgery. Surgery concerned with the repair or restoration of lost, injured, or deformed parts of the body.

plat \'plat\ *n.* **1** A small plot of ground. **2** A plan, map, or chart. — *v.;* **plat·ted; plat·ting.** To make a plat or plan of.

plate \'plāt\ *n.* **1** A thin, flat piece of any unbending material. **2** Metal in sheets; as, steel *plate.* **3** A piece of metal on which something is engraved or molded; as, a name *plate;* a license *plate.* **4** An illustration, especially one covering a full page of a book. **5** Platters, cups, and other household utensils made of or plated with gold or silver. **6** A shallow, usually round, dish. **7** Food placed on a plate; especially, the main course of a meal; as, a vegetable *plate;* two dollars a *plate.* **8** A dish used in churches for taking collections. **9** A bony or horny growth on the outside of some reptiles, fish, and animals. **10** One of the broad metal pieces of which armor is made. **11** The part of an artificial set of teeth that fits to the gums and serves as base for the teeth; any similar device, as for straightening irregular teeth. **12** In baseball, the area marked by a slab beside which a batter stands to bat and which must be touched by a player on completing a run. **13** A thin sheet of glass or metal coated with a chemical sensitive to light, on which a photograph is taken. **14** The electrode to which the electrons flow in an electron tube. **15** In printing, a page of type cast or molded in a form in which it can be printed from. — *v.;* **plat·ed; plat·ing.** **1** To cover or overlay with gold, silver, or other metal. **2** To arm with armor plate. **3** To make, as a page of type, into a plate to print from.

pla·teau \pla-'tō, plə-\ *n.; pl.* **pla·teaus.** A broad, flat tract of high land; a high plain.

plate·ful \'plāt-ˌfu̇l\ *n.; pl.* **plate·fuls** \-ˌfu̇lz\.

Enough food to fill a plate; the contents of a plate.

plate glass. A fine, quite clear glass poured in thick plates and rolled, ground, and polished.

plate·let \'plāt-lət\ *n.* A small plate-shaped body; especially, a blood cell smaller than a corpuscle that aids in the formation of a blood clot.

plat·form \'plat-ˌfȯrm\ *n.* **1** A level, usually raised, surface, as in a railway station; especially, a raised floor or stage, as in an auditorium. **2** A statement of principles, each of which is stated in a separate article, for which a group, especially a political party, stands; as, a *platform* including a strong civil rights plank. **3** Also **platform sole**. A built-up outside sole for a shoe, a quarter inch or more thick and usually having its edges covered with the material used in the upper.

plat·ing \'plāt-ing\ *n.* **1** A surface of metal plates, as in armor. **2** A thin coating of metal.

plat·i·num \'plat-n(-)əm\ *n.* A heavy grayish white metallic element that is hard to melt but easy to work, much used in jewelry.

plat·i·tude \'plat-ə-ˌtüd, -ˌtyüd\ *n.* **1** The quality or state of being commonplace or trite. **2** A remark that is flat, trite, or commonplace.

pla·toon \plə-'tün\ *n.* **1** A subdivision of a military company or troop, under a lieutenant. **2** A group of football players trained especially for offensive play or defensive play and intended to be sent into or withdrawn from the game as a body.

plat·ter \'plat-r\ *n.* A large plate or flat dish for serving meat or fish.

plat·y·pus \'plat-ə-pəs, -ˌpu̇s\ *n.; pl.* **plat·y·pus·es** \-pə-səz, -ˌpu̇s-əz\ or **plat·y·pi** \-ˌpī\. [A scientific Latin compound made from Greek *platys* meaning "broad", "flat" and *pous* meaning "foot".] The duckbill.

plau·dit \'plȯd-ət\ *n.* **1** An applauding, especially by clapping; a sound of applause. **2** Any strong expression of approval or praise.

plau·si·bil·i·ty \ˌplȯz-ə-'bil-ət-ē\ *n.; pl.* **plau·si·bil·i·ties. 1** The quality or state of being plausible. **2** Something that is plausible, or easy to believe.

plau·si·ble \'plȯz-əb-l\ *adj.* **1** Apparently reasonable or worthy of belief; as, a *plausible* excuse. **2** Seemingly trustworthy; inspiring confidence; persuasive; as, a very *plausible* liar. — **plau·si·bly** \-ə-blē\ *adv.*

play \'plā\ *v.;* **played; play·ing. 1** To move swiftly or lightly; as, shadows *playing* over water; leaves *playing* in the wind. **2** To engage in sport or recreation; to amuse oneself; as, to spend an hour or two *playing*. **3** To pretend; as, to *play* school. **4** To trifle; to toy; to finger; as, to *play* with a pencil. **5** To perform on a musical instrument; as, to *play* the piano; to *play* waltzes well. **6** To produce music; as, to listen to an organ *playing*. **7** To be performed; as, a new show *playing* for one week only. The music began to *play*. **8** To act; to behave; as, to *play* fair. **9** To act on or as if on the stage; as, to *play* a part. **10** To put or keep in action; as, to *play* a fish; to *play* a hose. **11** To engage in, as a game; as, to *play* baseball. **12** To do for amusement; as, to *play* a joke on a friend. **13** To bring about; as, to *play* hob; to *play* havoc with our plans. **14** To contend against in a game; as, to *play* the eighth grade in basketball. **15** To act or perform in, as a play, or to act the part of, as a character. — *n.* **1** Brisk motion; as, the *play* of a sword. **2** A literary composition portraying life and character through dialogue and action; a drama. **3** Exercise or action for amusement; a game; sport. **4** Fun; jest. **5** A particular series of actions in a game; as, a *play* in baseball. **6** A person's turn to take part in a game. **7** Action; conduct; as, fair *play;* foul *play*. **8** Activity; operation; as, the *play* of wit; to be in full *play*. **9** Freedom or room for movement or action; as, a jacket with not enough *play* in it. **10** Gambling; as, to lose a fortune at *play*. — **a play on words**. A pun. — For synonyms see *game*.

play·a·ble \'plā-əb-l\ *adj.* That can be played.

play-act·ing \'plā-ˌak-ting\ *n.* **1** Performance in theatrical productions. **2** Insincere behavior.

play·bill \'plā-ˌbil\ *n.* A poster advertising the performance of a play, usually announcing the cast of players.

play·boy \'plā-ˌbȯi\ *n.* A man whose chief interest is the pursuit of pleasure.

played out \'plād\. **1** Performed to the end; finished. **2** Exhausted; tired out.

play·er \'plā-ər\ *n.* **1** A contestant in a game. **2** An actor. **3** A musician. **4** A mechanical device for producing music, as from phonograph records.

play·fel·low \'plā-ˌfel-ō\ *n.* A playmate.

play·ful \'plāf-l\ *adj.* **1** Full of fun; fond of playing. **2** Humorous; not serious; as, a *playful* remark. — **play·ful·ly** \-l-ē\ *adv.*

play·ground \'plā-ˌgrau̇nd\ *n.* A piece of ground used for games and recreation, especially by children.

play·house \'plā-ˌhau̇s\ *n.; pl.* **play·hous·es** \-ˌhau̇-zəz\. **1** A theater. **2** A little house for children to play in.

playing. Pres. part. of *play*.

play·ing card \'plā-ing\. Any card used in playing games; especially, a card belonging to a set or pack of 52 divided into four suits called *hearts, diamonds, clubs*, and *spades*.

play·let \'plā-lət\ *n.* A little play.

play·mate \'plā-ˌmāt\ *n.* A companion in play; a playfellow.

play-off \'plā-ˌȯf\ *n.* A final contest, especially an extra contest, held to break a tie.

play·thing \'plā-ˌthing\ *n.* A toy.

play·wright \'plā-ˌrīt\ *n.* [A compound made from *play* and *wright* meaning "workman", "craftsman", a derivative from the stem of English *work* and unconnected with the word *write*.] A writer of plays.

plaza \'plaz-ə, 'pläz-, 'plȧz-\ *n.* [From Spanish, there derived from Latin *platea* meaning "street", "area", "courtyard" — see *place*.] A public square.

plea \'plē\ *n.* **1** An argument in defense; an excuse; as, a *plea* of insanity. **2** A prayer, entreaty, or appeal; as, a *plea* for mercy.

plead \'plēd\ *v.;* **plead·ed** \'plēd-əd\; **plead** \'pled\ or **pled** \'pled\; **plead·ing** \'plēd-ing\. **1** To argue for or against a claim; to argue at the bar; as, to *plead* a case before a jury; to *plead* for acquittal. **2** To answer to a charge; as, to *plead* guilty. **3** To offer as a defense, an excuse, or an apology; as, to *plead* sickness. **4** To entreat; to implore; as, to *plead* for another chance.

pleas·ant \'plez-nt\ *adj.* **1** That gives pleasure; agreeable; as, a *pleasant* day. **2** Having pleasing manners, behavior, or appearance; as, a *pleasant* person. — **pleas·ant·ly**, *adv.*

pleas·ant·ry \'plez-n-trē\ *n.; pl.* **pleas·ant·ries.** **1** Agreeable playfulness, especially in conversation. **2** A playful or humorous remark or action. **3** Any incidental polite remark offered as a token of good will, as in passing the time of day.

please \'plēz\ *v.;* **pleased**; **pleas·ing.** **1** To give pleasure or satisfaction; to gratify. **2** To be willing; to like; to think proper; to choose; as, to do as one *pleases;* if you *please.*

pleas·ing \'plē-zing\ *adj.* Giving pleasure; agreeable; as, *pleasing* colors. — **pleas·ing·ly**, *adv.*

plea·sur·a·ble \'plezh-r(-)əb-l, 'plāzh-\ *adj.* Capable of giving pleasure or satisfaction; pleasant; as, to regard writing as a *pleasurable* activity. — **plea·sur·a·bly** \-r(-)ə-blē\ *adv.*

plea·sure \'plezh-r, 'plāzh-r\ *n.* **1** A feeling of satisfaction; enjoyment; joy. **2** Will; choice; wish; as, to await someone's *pleasure.* **3** Something that pleases or delights; anything that entertains or amuses; sport; as, the *pleasures* of country life.

pleat \'plēt\ *n.* A flat fold, as of cloth; a plait. — *v.* To fold or crease in pleats; to plait.

ple·be·ian \plə-'bē-ən\ *n.* **1** A member of the lower class of people in ancient Rome. **2** Any person belonging to the lower classes by birth or by position in life. — *adj.* Of or relating to a plebeian; vulgar; common; as, *plebeian* manners.

pleb·i·scite \'pleb-ə-ˌsīt, -sət\ *n.* A popular vote by which the people of an entire country or a district indicate their wishes on some measure officially submitted to them.

plec·trum \'plek-trəm\ *n.; pl.* **plec·trums** \-trəmz\ or **plec·tra** \-trə\. A small, thin piece of ivory or metal used to pluck the strings of instruments such as the banjo and mandolin.

pled. A past tense and past part. of *plead.*

pledge \'plej\ *n.* **1** Something given or considered as a security for the fulfillment of a promise and, usually, liable to be forfeited if the promise is not kept. **2** The state of being given or held as a security; pawn; as, given in *pledge.* **3** Something considered as a token, sign, or evidence of something else; as, the exchange of rings as a *pledge* of friendship. **4** An assurance of goodwill given by drinking another's health; a toast. **5** A promise or agreement to do something. — *v.;* **pledged**; **pledg·ing.** **1** To give as a pledge; especially, to hand over or sign over as security for the repayment of a loan; to pawn. **2** To bind by a pledge; as, to *pledge* one's life to helping the sick. **3** To toast.

ple·na·ry \'plēn-r-ē, 'plen-\ *adj.* **1** Complete; full; as, *plenary* powers. **2** Including all entitled to attend; as, a *plenary* session of an assembly.

plen·i·po·ten·tia·ry \ˌplen-ə-pə-'tench-r(-)ē, -'ten-chē-ˌer-ē\ *n.; pl.* **plen·i·po·ten·tia·ries.** An agent, especially a diplomatic agent, with full authority to transact any business. — *adj.* Having full authority; as, minister *plenipotentiary.*

plen·i·tude \'plen-ə-ˌtüd, -ˌtyüd\ *n.* The quality or state of being full; fullness; abundance.

plen·te·ous \'plent-ē-əs\ *adj.* **1** Abundant; plentiful. **2** Yielding abundance; fruitful; as, the *plenteous* earth. — **plen·te·ous·ly**, *adv.*

plen·ti·ful \'plent-əf-l, -ēf-l\ *adj.* **1** Yielding or containing plenty; as, a *plentiful* table. **2** Existing in plenty; abundant. — **plen·ti·ful·ly** \-l-ē\ *adv.*

plen·ty \'plent-ē\ *n.* A full or abundant supply; enough and to spare; abundance. — *adj.* Plentiful; abundant. — *adv.* Quite; abundantly.

pleu·ra \'plůr-ə\ *n.; pl.* **pleu·ras** \-əz\ or **pleu·rae** \-ˌē, -ˌī\. The delicate membrane lining each half of the thorax of mammals and folded back over the surface of the lung. — **pleu·ral** \'plůr-əl\ *adj.*

pleu·ri·sy \'plůr-ə-sē\ *n.* Inflammation of the pleura, usually with fever, pain, and cough.

pleu·ro·coc·cus \ˌplůr-ə-'käk-əs\ *n.; pl.* **pleu·ro·coc·cus·es** \-'käk-ə-səz\ or **pleu·ro·coc·ci** \-'käk-ˌ(s)ī\. A one-celled green plant belonging to the algae and found growing as a green film, as on tree trunks, moist rocks, and flowerpots.

plex·us \'pleks-əs\ *n.; pl.* **plex·us·es** or **plex·us.** A network, especially of blood vessels or nerves.

pli·a·ble \'plī-əb-l\ *adj.* **1** Capable of being bent; flexible. **2** Easily influenced; as, a boy who was too *pliable* for his own good. — **pli·a·bil·i·ty** \ˌplī-ə-'bil-ət-ē\ *n.* — **pli·a·bly** \'plī-ə-blē\ *adv.*

pli·an·cy \'plī-ən-sē\ *n.* Pliant quality.

pli·ant \'plī-ənt\ *adj.* **1** Readily yielding without breaking; flexible. **2** Easily influenced; pliable; yielding; as, a *pliant* will. — **pli·ant·ly**, *adv.*

plied. Past tense and past part. of *ply.*

pli·ers \'plīrz\ *n. pl.* Small pincers with long jaws, used for bending or cutting wire or handling small objects.

pliers

plies. Pl. of *ply.*

plight \'plīt\ *n.* Condition or state, especially, a bad state; a predicament; as, an unhappy *plight* to be in.

plight \'plīt\ *v.* **1** To pledge, as one's faith, word, or honor. **2** To bind by a pledge; to betroth.

plinth \'plin(t)th\ *n.* **1** In architecture, the lowest part of the base of a column. **2** A block used as a base, as for a statue or vase.

P plinth, 1

plod \'pläd\ *v.;* **plod·ded**; **plod·ding.** **1** To move or travel slowly but steadily; to walk heavily; to trudge. **2** To work or study laboriously. — **plod·der**, *n.*

plot \'plät\ *n.* **1** A small area of ground; a lot. **2** A ground plan, as of a building or area; a map; a chart; a diagram. **3** A secret scheme; especially, a scheme having an evil intention; a conspiracy. **4** The events of a story as distinguished from the characters and setting; the plan or design of a play or novel. — *v.;* **plot·ted**; **plot·ting. 1** To make a plot, map, or plan of. **2** To draw a diagram or outline by marking and then connecting its principal points. **3** To plan; to scheme. — **plot·ter**, *n.*

plough \'plaů\ *n.* or *v. Chiefly British.* Plow. — **plough·boy** \-ˌbȯi\ *n.* — **plough·man** \-mən\ *n.* — **plough·share** \-ˌsher, -ˌshar\ *n.*

plov·er \'pləv-r, 'plōv-r\ *n.* Any one of several shore birds of the same family as the sandpipers but having shorter and stouter bills.

plow \'plaů\ *n.* **1** An implement used to cut, lift, and turn over soil and partly break it up. **2** An implement or a contrivance operating like a plow or suggesting a plow in appearance or use, as a snowplow. — *v.* **1** To turn up or break with or as if with a plow. **2** To till with a plow. **3** To clear with a snowplow; as, to *plow* a road. **4** To move through in the manner of a plow cutting a furrow; as, a ship *plowing* the waves. **5** To go laboriously and with effort; as, to *plow* through a book.

plow·boy \'plaů-ˌbȯi\ *n.* A boy who guides a plow or who assists by leading the horses.

plow·man \'plaů-mən\ *n.; pl.* **plow·men** \-mən\. **1** A man who guides a plow. **2** Any farm laborer.

plow·share \'plaů-ˌsher, -ˌshar\ *n.* That part of a plow which cuts the earth.

pluck \'plək\ *v.* **1** To pull off or out; to pick; as, to *pluck* grapes. **2** To strip off the feathers or hair of; as, to *pluck* a fowl. **3** To pull; to drag; as, to *pluck* a handkerchief from one's pocket. **4** To pull at sharply; to tug; to twitch; as, a child *plucking* its mother's skirts. **5** To make a musical instrument sound by pulling at the strings; to twang; as, to *pluck* the strings of a violin. — *n.* **1** The act of plucking; a pull; a twitch; a tug. **2** The heart, liver, lungs, and windpipe of an animal killed for food. **3** Spirit; courage.

plucky \'plək-ē\ *adj.;* **pluck·i·er**; **pluck·i·est.** Having or showing pluck; courageous; brave.

plug \'pləg\ *n.* **1** Any piece of wood, metal, or other substance used to stop or fill a hole; a stopper. **2** A worn-out horse. **3** A spark plug. **4** A device for making an electrical connection by insertion into a broken circuit. **5** A flat cake of tightly pressed tobacco leaves. **6** A cylindrical bait used in casting for fish. **7** Advertisement; favorable publicity. — *v.;* **plugged**; **plug·ging. 1** To stop or make tight with a plug; as, to *plug* up a hole. **2** *Slang.* To hit with a bullet; to shoot. **3** *Slang.* To keep steadily at work or in action; to plod; as, to *plug* along at a job. **4** To advertise widely; to give great publicity to; as, to *plug* a new song. — **plug in.** To make an electrical circuit by inserting a plug. — **plug·ger**, *n.*

plum \'pləm\ *n.* [From Old English *plume*, an altered form of Late Latin *pruna* — see *prune.*] **1** The fruit of any of various trees related to the peach and cherry, having a smooth skin and an unwrinkled stone. **2** The tree bearing this fruit. **3** A raisin, especially when used in puddings. **4** Something like a plum, as in shape and sweetness. **5** The dark purple color of some plums. **6** Something considered very choice.

plum·age \'plü-mij\ *n.* The entire clothing of feathers of a bird.

plumb \'pləm\ *n.* A little weight of lead or other heavy material attached to a line and used by builders to show a vertical direction. — **out of plumb** or **off plumb.** Not vertical. — *adj.* Also **plum.** Vertical. — *adv.* Also **plum. 1** Vertically; exactly. **2** Completely; quite; as, *plumb* crazy. — *v.* **1** To sound, adjust, or test with a plumb; as, to *plumb* a wall; to *plumb* the depths. **2** To fathom, as a secret.

plumb

plumb·er \'pləm-r\ *n.* A person who sells, fits, and repairs water and gas pipes and kitchen and bathroom fixtures.

plumb·ing \'pləm-ing\ *n.* **1** A plumber's work. **2** A system of pipes in a building, as for supplying or carrying off water.

plumb line. A line having at one end a weight or bob (**plumb bob**) and used to find out whether a thing is vertical or to measure the depth of water.

plume \'plüm\ *n.* **1** A feather; a tuft of fine feathers, as on an ostrich. **2** An ornamental feather or tuft of feathers, as on a helmet or a hat. **3** A token of honor or victory; a prize. — *v.;* **plumed**; **plum·ing. 1** To attach feathers to. **2** To arrange the feathers and make them neat; as, birds *pluming* themselves. **3** To be proud of (oneself); as, to *plume* oneself on one's skill in diving.

plume, 2

plum·met \'pləm-ət\ *n.* **1** A plumb. **2** A weight. — *v.* To drop or plunge straight down.

plump \'pləmp\ *adj.* Well rounded; well filled out; especially, chubby; fat. — *v.* To make or become plump; as, to *plump* up a pillow. — **plump·ly**, *adv.*

plump \'pləmp\ *v.* To drop, fall, or come in contact hard or suddenly; as, to *plump* down on a couch. — **plump for.** To come out for; to take a position in strong support of someone or something, as in an election. — *n.* A sudden plunge or fall. — *adv.* **1** Suddenly or hard; as, to fall *plump* on one's back on the ice. **2** Straight; directly; as, to run *plump* into trouble with a new bicycle. — *adj.* Abrupt; blunt; as, to give a *plump* "no".

plum pudding. A boiled spicy pudding containing raisins, currants, and other fruits and usually rich in fat.

plu·mule \'plü-ˌmyül\ *n.* **1** The primary bud of an embryo or germinating seed plant. **2** One of the soft fluffy feathers of which down is composed.

plun·der \'plənd-r\ *v.;* **plun·dered**; **plun·der·ing**

\-r(-)ing\. To rob, especially openly and by force, as in an invasion by an enemy force or a pirate raid; to pillage. — *n.* **1** The act of plundering, as during war. **2** Anything taken by robbery or force; booty. — **plun·der·er** \-r-r\ *n.*

plunge \'plənj\ *v.;* **plunged**; **plung·ing.** **1** To thrust or force, as into liquid or some other substance, or into a certain condition; as, to *plunge* a dagger in one's breast; to *plunge* a family into debt. **2** To leap or dive into water; as, to *plunge* in for a swim. **3** To rush with reckless haste; as, to *plunge* into activities. **4** To dip, descend, or move forward and downward rapidly or suddenly. The little boat *plunged* into the trough of the wave. **5** To bet large sums; to gamble heavily. — *n.* A sudden dive, rush, or leap.

plung·er \'plənj-r\ *n.* **1** Any person that plunges, as a diver or a reckless gambler. **2** A device, such as a piston in a pump, that acts with a plunging motion.

plunk \'pləngk\ *v.* **1** To make or cause to make a hollow metallic sound; as, to *plunk* the strings of a banjo. **2** To drop heavily; to plump; as, to *plunk* a suitcase on the bench. — *n.* The act or sound of plunking. — *adv.* With a plunk.

plu·ral \'plu̇r-əl\ *adj.* Indicating or meaning more than one. The word "boys" is a *plural* noun. — *n.* **1** A form of a word that is used to show that more than one person or thing is meant. **2** A word in the plural form. — **plu·ral·ly** \-ə-lē\ *adv.*

plu·ral·i·ty \plu̇-'ral-ət-ē\ *n.; pl.* **plu·ral·i·ties.** **1** The state of being plural or numerous. **2** The greater number or part. A *plurality* of the nations of the world want peace. **3** The fact of being chosen by the voters out of three or more candidates or measures when no one of them obtains more than half the total vote; as, to win an election by a *plurality*. **4** The excess of the number of votes received by one candidate over another, especially of the highest over the next highest; as, to win by a *plurality* of 4,000 votes.

plus \'pləs\ *prep.* [From Latin, meaning "more".] With the addition of; and; as, four *plus* two. — *adj.* **1** Indicating addition; as, the *plus* sign. **2** Indicating a greater value than usual. A *plus* is the best mark. **3** Having as an addition or gain. Now the family was *plus* a kitten. — *n.* **1** The plus sign [+]. **2** Anything added; something extra. **3** A positive quantity; an amount greater than zero.

plush \'pləsh\ *n.* A fabric like velvet but with a deeper and softer pile. — *adj.* **1** Made of plush; as, a *plush* sofa. **2** Very luxurious, expensive, or easy; as, a *plush* job; *plush* surroundings.

plu·to·crat \'plüt-ə-ˌkrat\ *n.* A person who has power or influence because he is wealthy; a member of the wealthy class. — **plu·to·crat·ic** \ˌplüt-ə-'krat-ik\ *adj.*

plu·to·ni·um \plü-'tō-nē-əm\ *n.* A radioactive element artificially produced from uranium atoms and used in the production of atomic energy.

ply \'plī\ *n.; pl.* **plies.** A fold, thickness, layer, or strand as in cloth, tires, or yarn — often used in combinations; as, *two-ply* yarn; *four-ply* tires.

ply \'plī\ *v.;* **plied** \'plīd\; **ply·ing.** **1** To use something steadily, or forcefully; as, to *ply* an ax. **2** To keep after a person about something; as, to *ply* a man with questions. **3** To keep supplying; as, to *ply* a guest with food. **4** To work hard and steadily; as, to *ply* one's trade. **5** To go back and forth. The ferry *plies* between the two cities.

ply·wood \'plī-ˌwu̇d\ *n.* Wood made by gluing together thin layers of veneer under heat and pressure.

P.M. or **p.m.** \'pē-'em\. [Abbreviated from Latin *post meridiem* meaning "after noon".] In the afternoon or evening; between noon and the following midnight; as, at 9 *P.M.*

pneu·mat·ic \nü-'mat-ik, nyü-\ *adj.* **1** Having to do with or using air or wind. **2** Moved by air pressure; as, a *pneumatic* tool. **3** Filled with air; as, *pneumatic* tires. — **pneu·mat·i·cal·ly** \-ik-l(-)ē\ *adv.*

pneu·mo·coc·cus \ˌnü-mə-'käk-əs, ˌnyü-\ *n.; pl.* **pneu·mo·coc·cus·es** \-'käk-ə-səz\ or **pneu·mo·coc·ci** \-'käk-ˌ(s)ī\. The bacterium which causes lobar pneumonia.

pneu·mo·graph \'nü-mə-ˌgraf, 'nyü-\ *n.* An instrument for recording the movements of the chest in breathing.

pneu·mo·nia \nü-'mōn-yə, nyü-\ *n.* A disease characterized by inflammation of the lungs and solidification of the tissue, the two main types being **lobar pneumonia**, an acute infection in which all or most of the lobe of a lung is involved, and **bronchial pneumonia**, an often chronic infection in which the area involved is more restricted.

P.O. \'pē-'ō\. Abbreviation for *Post Office.*

poach \'pōch\ *v.* To cook in hot liquid; especially, to cook an egg by dropping it from its shell into simmering water.

poach \'pōch\ *v.* To hunt or fish unlawfully on private property. — **poach·er,** *n.*

pock \'päk\ *n.* A small swelling on the skin similar to a pimple, as in chicken pox or smallpox; the mark it leaves.

pock·et \'päk-ət\ *n.* **1** A bag or pouch carried by a person; especially, a small pouch made as part of a garment and used for carrying money, keys, and other small articles on the person. **2** Money; wealth; as, to be out of *pocket.* **3** A place or thing like a pocket; as, a *pocket* of gold in a mine. **4** A condition of the air that causes an airplane to drop suddenly. **5** One of the pouches in a billiard table. — *v.* **1** To put something in or as **if in** a pocket; to take for oneself, especially dishonestly; as, to *pocket* the profits. **2** To put in a pocket; as, to *pocket* one's change; to *pocket* a billiard ball. **3** To receive quietly, as an insult, without seeming to be angry; to conceal, as pride or anger. — *adj.* **1** Small enough to fit in a pocket; small-sized; as, a *pocket* dictionary. **2** In, for, or from the pocket; as, *pocket* money.

pock·et·book \'päk-ət-ˌbu̇k\ *n.* **1** A case for carrying money or papers in the pocket; a wallet. **2** A purse; a handbag. **3** Money; income; as, a price suited to one's *pocketbook.*

pock·et·ful \'päk-ət-ˌfu̇l\ *n.; pl.* **pock·et·fuls.** As much or as many as a pocket will hold; as, a *pocketful* of change.

pock·et·knife \'päk-ət-ˌnīf\ *n.; pl.* **pock·et·knives** \-ˌnīvz\. A pocket-size knife with folding blade or blades; a jackknife.

pocket rat. A kangaroo rat.

pocket veto. A method of vetoing a bill passed by Congress by which the president fails to sign the bill before Congress adjourns.

pock-marked \'päk-ˌmärkt, -ˌmȧrkt\ *adj.* Scarred by pocks, as those left by smallpox.

pod \'päd\ *n.* **1** The seedcase or shell of certain plants, such as peas or beans. **2** The shell and seeds of such a plant; a legume. — *v.;* **pod·ded; pod·ding.** To produce pods.

pod

po·em \'pō-əm, -im, -ˌem\ *n.* A composition in verse; a rhythmical or metrical expression of a poet's thoughts or feelings written in verse; a piece of poetry.

po·e·sy \'pō-ə-zē, -sē\ *n. Archaic.* Poetry.

po·et \'pō-ət, -it\ *n.* A person who composes verses, poems, or poetry.

po·et·ess \'pō-ət-əs, 'pō-it-\ *n.* A woman who writes poetry.

po·et·ic \pō-'et-ik\ or **po·et·i·cal** \-ik-l\ *adj.* **1** Having to do with, belonging to, or suitable for, a poet or poetry. **2** Written in poetry; as, *poetical* works. **3** Used in poetry; as, *poetic* words. — **po·et·i·cal·ly** \-ik-l(-)ē\ *adv.*

poet laureate; *pl.* **poets laureate. 1** In England, a poet appointed by the sovereign to be a member of the royal household and to write poems for state occasions. **2** A poet thought of as the most outstanding of a locality; as, a local *poet laureate.*

po·et·ry \'pō-ə-trē, -i-trē\ *n.* **1** The art of telling stories, or expressing thoughts or feelings in metrical, rhythmical, or figurative language. **2** Literature of this kind; poems.

poi·gnant \'pȯin-yənt, 'pȯin-ənt\ *adj.* **1** Keen; sharp; piercing; severe; as, *poignant* pain. **2** Touching; moving; affecting the emotions deeply; as, a *poignant* story about homeless orphans. — **poi·gnan·cy** \-yən-sē, -ən-sē\ *n.*

poin·set·tia \pȯin-'set-ē-ə, -'set-ə\ *n.* [Named in honor of Joel R. *Poinsett* (1779–1851), an American diplomat and statesman who developed it from a Mexican wild flower.] A tropical plant, much used in Christmas decorations, with dark green foliage and brilliantly colored bracts that grow like petals around its small green flowers.

point \'pȯint\ *n.* **1** The tapering or sharp end of a thing, such as a pin, pencil, or sword; a tip or edge; as, a *point* of land. **2** A separate or particular part; a detail; a trait or feature, especially a valuable one; as, to make the *points* of the plan clear; to see many fine *points* in a person. **3** The chief part or meaning, as of a story or speech; the subject or topic; as, to keep to the *point;* to miss the *point.* **4** Aim or purpose; as, to gain one's *point.* **5** A single unit used in giving a value or score; as, a stock that is up one *point;* to get two *points* for each correct answer. **6** A place; a spot; a position; as, a starting *point.* **7** A position or condition arrived at; a degree or stage; as, the freezing *point;* to be on the *point* of leaving. **8** Either of two platinum or tungsten pieces in a distributor through which the circuit is made or broken. **9** A printed or written dot; a punctuation mark; especially, a period; a decimal point. **10** One of the 32 divisions into which a compass is divided. — **in point.** Pertinent; aptly illustrating; as, a case *in point.* — **to the point.** Apt; concise; as, a remark that was quite *to the point.* — *v.* **1** To put a point on anything; as, to *point* a pencil; to give force or importance to a thing; as, to *point* a lesson. **2** To punctuate. **3** To indicate something as by the finger, or by standing in a fixed position, as some dogs do in hunting. **4** To aim or direct; as, to *point* a gun. **5** To separate figures into groups by dots or points, especially by decimal points. **6** To face toward a certain direction. **7** To imply; to indicate; as, signs that *point* to a storm.

point-blank \'pȯint-ˌblangk\ *adj.* **1** So close to the target that a missile fired will travel straight to its mark without curving in its path; as, to fire from *point-blank* range. **2** Direct; prompt and plain-spoken; as, a *point-blank* refusal. — \-'blangk\ *adv.* In a point-blank manner; as, to refuse *point-blank.*

point·ed \'pȯint-əd\ *adj.* **1** Having a point. **2** Sharp; direct; as, a *pointed* remark. **3** Aimed at a particular person. — **point·ed·ly,** *adv.*

point·er \'pȯint-r\ *n.* **1** A thing that points. **2** A large, long-eared, short-haired hunting dog, usually white with colored spots, that hunts by scent and points game. **3** A hint; a tip; as, to get *pointers* on how to play a game. **4** [in the plural with a capital] The two stars in the Big Dipper which point to the North Star.

point·less \'pȯint-ləs\ *adj.* **1** Without a point; blunt; as, a *pointless* pencil. **2** Without meaning; as, a *pointless* remark.

point of view. Position from which something is viewed or considered.

poise \'pȯiz\ *v.;* **poised; pois·ing. 1** To balance; to hold or make firm or steady. **2** To hang or be held balanced. The bird *poised* in the air. — *n.* **1** The condition of being balanced; balance; steadiness. **2** Easy self-control and composure.

poi·son \'pȯiz-n\ *n.* **1** A substance that, if taken into the body, can injure or kill a living thing. **2** Anything that is harmful to a person's mind or morals. — *v.;* **poi·soned; poi·son·ing** \-n(-)ing\. **1** To put poison on or in something; as, to *poison* food. **2** To injure or kill by poison. **3** To corrupt; as, to *poison* a person's mind. — *adj.* Poisonous.

poi·son·ing \'pȯiz-n(-)ing\ *n.* The condition produced by poison.

poison ivy. A viny sumac with three leaflets, greenish flowers, white berries, and foliage and stems that when bruised and touched sometimes cause a rash on a person's skin.

poison ivy

poison oak. **1** Poison sumac. **2** A bushy poison ivy.

poi·son·ous \'pȯiz-n(-)əs\ *adj.* Containing poison; having or causing the effect of poison. — **poi·son·ous·ly**, *adv.*

poison sumac. A swamp shrub of the sumac family with seven to thirteen leaflets, greenish flowers, greenish white berries, and foliage and stems that when bruised and touched sometimes cause a skin eruption.

poke \'pōk\ *n. Dial.* A bag or sack.

poke \'pōk\ *v.;* **poked**; **pok·ing**. **1** To prod a person or thing. **2** To pry into things; as, to *poke* one's nose in the affairs of others. **3** To idle; to move lazily; as, to *poke* along. — *n.* **1** A nudge; a thrust. **2** A lazy or slow person.

poke bonnet. A bonnet with a projecting front.

pok·er \'pōk-r\ *n.* A metal rod used to stir a fire.

po·ker \'pōk-r\ *n.* A card game in which players bet on the value of the cards they hold.

poke·weed \'pōk-ˌwēd\ *n.* A plant with spikes of white flowers, a poisonous root, and purple berries.

pokeweed

poky or **pokey** \'pōk-ē\ *adj.;* **pok·i·er**; **pok·i·est**. **1** Small and cramped; as, a *poky* room. **2** Slow; dull; as, a *poky* person; a *poky* horse.

po·lar \'pōl-r\ *adj.* Having to do with a pole, as of a magnet; especially, lying near or coming from one of the poles of the earth.

polar bear. A large creamy-white bear of arctic regions.

polar bear

po·lar·i·ty \pō-'lar-ət-ē\ *n.* The condition of something that has electrical or magnetic poles.

po·lar·i·za·tion \ˌpōl-r-ə-'zāsh-n\ *n.* **1** The act of polarizing or the state of being polarized. **2** Polarity.

po·lar·ize \'pōl-r-ˌīz\ *v.;* **po·lar·ized**; **po·lar·iz·ing**. **1** To cause something, as a magnet, to develop poles. **2** To cause light to vibrate in certain directions only, instead of in all directions.

pole \'pōl\ *n.* A long slender piece of wood or metal; as, telephone *poles;* fishing *poles.* — *v.;* **poled**; **pol·ing**. To propel with a pole, as a boat.

pole \'pōl\ *n.* **1** Either end of an axis, as of a sphere; especially, either of the two ends of the earth's axis, the North Pole and South Pole. **2** Either of the two ends of a magnet or of the two terminals of an electric cell, battery, or dynamo.

Pole \'pōl\ *n.* A native or inhabitant of Poland.

pole·cat \'pōl-ˌkat\ *n.* **1** A small, dark, flesh-eating European animal, related to the weasel. **2** A skunk.

po·lem·ic \pə-'lem-ik\ or **po·lem·i·cal** \-ik-l\ *adj.* Attacking others' opinions or doctrines; controversial. — **po·lem·i·cal·ly** \-ik-l(-)ē\ *adv.*

po·lem·ic \pə-'lem-ik\ *n.* A polemic argument.

po·lem·ics \pə-'lem-iks\ *n.* The art or practice of refuting others' opinions or doctrines.

pole·star \'pōl-ˌstär, -ˌstår\ *n.* **1** The North Star. **2** A guiding principle; a lodestar.

pole vault. **1** A vault made with the aid of a pole. **2** An athletic event in which such a vault is performed for height or, sometimes, for distance.

po·lice \pə-'lēs\ *n.* **1** The department of government that prevents and investigates crimes, keeps order, and arrests lawbreakers; the members of this department, as in a city. **2** In the armed forces, soldiers appointed to keep order. — *v.;* **po·liced**; **po·lic·ing**. **1** To protect people or things and keep order. **2** To clean up, as a camp. — *adj.* Of, relating to, or done by the police.

police court. A court having jurisdiction over various minor offenses and authority to send cases involving serious offenses to a superior court.

po·lice·man \pə-'lēs-mən\ *n.; pl.* **po·lice·men** \-mən\. A man on a police force.

police state. A state in which the social, economic, and political activities of the people are under the arbitrary power of the government, often acting through a secret police force.

po·lice·wom·an \pə-'lēs-ˌwu̇m-ən\ *n.; pl.* **po·lice·wom·en** \-ˌwim-ən\. A woman on a police force.

pol·i·cy \'päl-ə-sē\ *n.; pl.* **pol·i·cies**. A course of action followed by a person, a group, or a government; as, the foreign *policy* of the United States; to learn that honesty is the best *policy.*

pol·i·cy \'päl-ə-sē\ *n.; pl.* **pol·i·cies**. A document which contains the agreement made by an insurance company with a person whose life or property is insured.

po·lio \'pō-lē-ˌō\ *n.* Poliomyelitis.

po·lio·my·e·li·tis \'pō-lē-ˌō-ˌmī-ə-'līt-əs\ *n.* A virus disease marked by inflammation of the nerve matter in the spinal cord, often causing paralysis; infantile paralysis.

pol·ish \'päl-ish\ *n.* **1** The act or process of polishing. **2** A smooth and glossy surface, often produced by rubbing. **3** Social good manners; refinement. **4** A preparation used to produce a gloss; as, shoe *polish.* — *v.* **1** To make smooth and glossy, usually by rubbing; as, to *polish* glass. **2** To refine or improve; as, to *polish* one's French.

Pol·ish \'pō-lish\ *adj.* Of or relating to Poland or its people. — *n.* The language of Poland.

po·lite \pə-'līt\ *adj.;* **po·lit·er**; **po·lit·est**. **1** Refined or cultivated; as, *polite* society. **2** Courteous; showing courtesy or good breeding; as, a *polite* answer. — **po·lite·ly**, *adv.*

pol·i·tic \'päl-ə-ˌtik\ *adj.* **1** Of or having to do with government. **2** Crafty; shrewd; as, a *politic* answer.

po·lit·i·cal \pə-'lit-ik-l\ *adj.* Of or having to do with politics, or the conduct of government. — **po·lit·i·cal·ly** \-ik-l(-)ē\ *adv.*

political science. The social science that deals with the government of states or nations.

pol·i·ti·cian \ˌpäl-ə-'tish-n\ *n.* **1** A person who is experienced in the science of government. **2** A person who is actively engaged in party politics.

pol·i·tics \'päl-ə-ˌtiks\ *n. sing. and pl.* **1** The science and art of government; the management of public affairs. **2** Activity in or management of affairs of state as influenced by political parties. **3** Activity in political parties. **4** Political opinion; as, a friend whose *politics* differ from one's own.

pol·ka \'pōl-kə, 'pōk-ə\ *n.* [From German, there borrowed from Czech, meaning literally "Polish woman".] **1** A lively hopping dance performed in couples. **2** The music for this dance.

pol·ka dot \'pōk-ə, 'pōl-kə\. A pattern of large evenly spaced dots, as in textile fabrics.

poll \'pōl\ *n.* **1** The head; the skull. **2** The casting or recording of the votes of a number of persons; as, the *poll* of the persons in the room. **3** The number of such votes, or the list of voters. **4** The place where votes are cast; as, to go to the *polls.* **5** A systematic canvass, as to discover opinions or political preferences. — *v.* **1** To enter in a list or register; to enroll. **2** To receive and count the votes of; as, to *poll* the jury. **3** To deposit one's vote or ballot. **4** To receive votes, as at an election. **5** To take an opinion poll.

pol·len \'päl-ən\ *n.* The particles in seed plants, usually in the form of a fine yellow dust, that fertilize the seeds.

pollen basket. A flat or hollow area bordered with stiff hairs on the hind leg of a bee in which it carries pollen to the hive or nest.

pol·li·nate \'päl-ə-ˌnāt\ *v.;* **pol·li·nat·ed**; **pol·li·nat·ing.** To perform pollination on.

pol·li·na·tion \ˌpäl-ə-'nāsh-n\ *n.* The transfer of pollen from the anthers of a plant to its pistil (**self-pollination**) or to the pistil of another plant (**cross-pollination**), resulting in the fertilization of the egg cell, which then ripens into seed.

pol·li·wog or **pol·ly·wog** \'päl-ē-ˌwäg\ *n.* A tadpole.

poll·ster \'pōlst-r\ *n.* One who designs, canvasses for, or interprets an opinion poll.

poll tax \'pōl\. A tax of so much per head or person, the payment of which is a requirement for voting in some states in the United States.

pol·lute \pə-'lüt\ *v.;* **pol·lut·ed**; **pol·lut·ing.** To make impure; to contaminate; as, to *pollute* a water supply. — **pol·lu·tion** \pə-'lüsh-n\ *n.*

po·lo \'pō-ˌlō\ *n.* A game played with a wooden ball and mallets having long flexible handles by players mounted on horseback.

pol·o·naise \ˌpäl-ə-'nāz, ˌpō-lə-\ *n.* **1** A stately Polish dance. **2** Music written for this dance.

pol·troon \päl-'trün\ *n.* A coward.

po·lyg·a·my \pə-'lig-m-ē\ *n.* The condition or fact of having at the same time more than one wife or, sometimes, husband. — **po·lyg·a·mist** \-m-əst\ *n.* — **po·lyg·a·mous** \-m-əs\ *adj.*

pol·y·glot \'päl-ē-ˌglät\ *adj.* **1** Speaking or writing many languages; as, a *polyglot* student. **2** Containing or made up of several languages.

pol·y·gon \'päl-ē-ˌgän\ *n.* In geometry, a figure having many angles, especially more than four.

polygons

pol·y·no·mi·al \ˌpäl-ē-'nō-mē-əl\ *n.* An algebraic expression having two or more terms, as $a^2 + 2ab - b^2$.

pol·yp \'päl-əp\ *n.* **1** A small sea animal having a hollow cylindrical body closed and attached at one end, and opening at the other with a mouth surrounded by tentacles. The coral and the sea anemone are *polyps.* **2** A projecting mass of overgrown mucous membrane.

pol·y·phon·ic \ˌpäl-ē-'fän-ik\ *adj.* Having several independent but harmonious melodies.

pol·y·syl·la·ble \'päl-ē-ˌsil-əb-l\ *n.* A word of many syllables, especially of more than three syllables. — **pol·y·syl·lab·ic** \ˌpäl-ē-sə-'lab-ik\ *adj.*

pol·y·tech·nic \ˌpäl-ə-'tek-nik\ *adj.* Of or devoted to instruction in many technical fields.

pol·y·the·ism \'päl-ē-(ˌ)thē-ˌiz-m\ *n.* Belief in the existence of many gods. — **pol·y·the·ist** \-ˌthē-əst\ *n.* — **pol·y·the·is·tic** \ˌpäl-ē-thē-'is-tik\ *adj.*

po·made \pə-'mäd, -'mād, -'mȧd\ *n.* A perfumed ointment, as one to help keep the hair in place, or one to soothe chapped lips.

pome \'pōm\ *n.* The fleshy fruit of certain trees and shrubs, as the apple or the pear.

pom·e·gran·ate \'päm-ə-ˌgran-ət, 'päm-ˌgran-, 'pəm-ˌgran-\ *n.* **1** A thick-skinned, many-seeded, reddish fruit about the size of an orange, with a crimson pulp of pleasant acid flavor. **2** The tropical tree which bears this fruit.

pom·mel \'pəm-l, 'päm-l\ *n.* A rounded, often ornamental knob, such as one on the handle of a sword, or one at the front and top of a saddle. — *v.;* **pom·meled** or **pom·melled**; **pom·mel·ing** or **pom·mel·ling** \-l(-)ing\. **1** To beat soundly, as with the pommel of a sword. **2** To beat with the fists.

pommel

pomp \'pämp\ *n.* **1** A show of magnificence; splendor; as, the *pomp* of a coronation ceremony. **2** Showy display; as, a person who loves *pomp.*

pom·pa·dour \'pämp-ə-ˌdōr, -ˌdȯr\ *n.* A style of dressing the hair high over the forehead; hair dressed in this style.

pom·pa·no \'pämp-n-ˌō, 'pəmp-\ *n.; pl.* **pom·pa·nos.** A spiny-finned food fish of the southern Atlantic and Gulf coasts, having a narrow body and forked tail.

pom·pon \'päm-ˌpän\ *n.* **1** A rounded tuft of silk, feathers, or wool, used as trimming on costumes, hats, or shoes. **2** A chrysanthemum with small rounded flower heads.

pomp·ous \'päm-pəs\ *adj.* **1** Making an appearance of importance or dignity; as, a *pompous* manner. **2** Of persons, self-important; as, a very *pompous* little man. — **pomp·ous·ly**, *adv.*

pon·cho \'pän-ˌchō\ *n.; pl.* **pon·chos. 1** A Spanish-American cloak, like a blanket with a slit in the middle for the head. **2** A similar garment made of waterproof material and used chiefly as a raincoat.

pond \'pänd\ *n.* A body of water, usually smaller than a lake.

pon·der \'pänd-r\ *v.;* **pon·dered; pon·der·ing** \-r(-)ing\. To consider carefully.

pon·der·ous \'pänd-r(-)əs\ *adj.* **1** Very heavy. **2** Not light or lively; dull; as, *ponderous* words.

pond lily. The water lily.

pond scum. Any of certain green algae that grow as floating mats of threads on still water.

pond·weed \'pän-ˌdwēd\ *n.* Any of several water plants with both submerged and floating leaves and spikes of greenish flowers.

pone \'pōn\ *n.* Corn pone.

pon·gee \(')pän-'jē\ *n.* **1** A thin soft fabric of Chinese origin made of brownish undyed silk. **2** A dyed silk fabric resembling this.

pon·iard \'pän-yərd\ *n.* A slender dagger.

pon·tiff \'pänt-əf\ *n.* **1** A bishop; especially, the pope. **2** Any of various high priests or chief religious figures. — **pon·tif·i·cal** \pän-'tif-ik-l\ *adj.*

pon·tif·i·cals \pän-'tif-ik-lz\ *n. pl.* The robes worn by a bishop when he officiates, as at a mass.

pon·tif·i·cate \pän-'tif-ik-ət\ *n.* The office or term of office of a pontiff.

pon·toon \(')pän-'tün\ *n.* **1** A small flat-bottomed boat. **2** A light frame or float used as one of the supports for a floating bridge (**pontoon bridge**). **3** One of the two floats attached to the bottom of an aircraft so that it will float on water.

pontoon

pontoon, 3

po·ny \'pō-nē\ *n.; pl.* **po·nies.** A small horse; especially, a horse of any of several very small but sturdy breeds.

pony express. A rapid-transit postal and express system across the western United States in 1860–61, using relays of horses to carry mails 1960 miles in 10 days.

poo·dle \'püd-l\ *n.* A pet dog of a highly intelligent breed, having wiry curled hair or long silky hair that is all one color.

poodle

pooh-pooh \'pü-'pü\ *v.* To scorn; to deride; as, to *pooh-pooh* the idea that a house is haunted.

pool \'pül\ *n.* **1** A small, rather deep body of water, usually fresh and either natural or artificial; as, the *pool* in the brook; a swimming *pool.* **2** A small body of standing liquid; a puddle. **3** A portable wading pool made of rubber or plastic.

pool \'pül\ *n.* **1** The stake played for in certain games. **2** A game played with solid balls and a cue on a large oblong table with six pockets. **3** In a venture shared by a number of persons, the total amount contributed by these persons toward the success of the venture; the group of persons sharing in the venture. **4** A combination of business interests for mutual profit; as, a railroad *pool.* — *v.* To put together in a common fund to be used for the mutual advantage of the persons interested. The brothers *pooled* their allowances.

poop \'püp\ *n.* A deck on a ship above the open deck and behind the mizzen.

poor \'pu̇r, 'pōr\ *adj.* **1** Lacking riches; needy. **2** Scanty; insufficient; as, a *poor* crop. **3** Not good in quality or workmanship. **4** Feeble; as, *poor* health. **5** Lacking fertility; as, *poor* land. **6** Unfavorable; uncomfortable. The patient had a *poor* day. **7** Lacking in signs of wealth or good taste; as, *poor* furnishings. **8** Not efficient, capable, or satisfactory; as, a *poor* carpenter. **9** Worthy of pity or sympathy. The *poor* child hurt herself. — **poor·ly**, *adv.*

poor·house \'pu̇r-ˌhau̇s, 'pōr-\ *n.; pl.* **poor·hous·es** \-ˌhau̇-zəz\. A house, maintained at public expense, to which people who cannot support themselves are sent.

pop \'päp\ *n.* **1** A small, sharp, explosive sound. **2** A shot from a rifle or pistol. **3** A bottled soft drink such as ginger ale or flavored soda water. — *v.;* **popped; pop·ping. 1** To make or cause a pop; to burst with a pop. **2** To go, come, push, or enter quickly or unexpectedly; as, to *pop* into bed. **3** To fire a gun. **4** To stick out; as, eyes *popping* with surprise. **5** To cause to burst open; as, to *pop* corn. — *adv.* Like or with a pop; suddenly.

pop·corn \'päp-ˌkȯrn\ *n.* Corn which swells up and bursts open into a white mass when heated.

pope \'pōp\ *n.* The bishop of Rome, the head of the Roman Catholic Church — often written with a capital.

pop·gun \'päp-ˌgən\ *n.* A toy gun that shoots with a popping sound.

pop·in·jay \'päp-n-ˌjā\ *n.* A vain, talkative, thoughtless person.

pop·lar \'päp-lər\ *n.* Any slender quick-growing tree of the willow family, including the aspens and the cottonwoods.

pop·lin \'päp-lən\ *n.* Silk or worsted cloth ribbed like corduroy.

pop·over \'päp-ˌōv-r\ *n.* A muffin made from batter rich in egg which expands during baking into an almost hollow shell.

pop·per \'päp-r\ *n.* **1** One that pops. **2** A device for popping corn.

pop·py \'päp-ē\ *n.; pl.* **pop·pies.** A hairy-stemmed plant with large showy flowers that are usually red, yellow, or white.

pop·u·lace \'päp-yə-ləs\ *n.* **1** The common people; the crowd. **2** The inhabitants of any particular place; as, a town with a peaceful *populace.*

pop·u·lar \'päp-yəl-r\ *adj.* **1** Having to do with, belonging to, or coming from the whole body of people; as, *popular* government; *popular* opinion. **2** Suitable to the average person; easy to understand; not expensive; as, *popular* science; *popular* prices. **3** Pleasing to many people; approved by many people; as, a *popular* game; a *popular* leader. — **pop·u·lar·ly**, *adv.*

pop·u·lar·i·ty \ˌpäp-yə-ˈlar-ət-ē\ *n.* The quality or condition of being popular.

pop·u·lar·ize \ˈpäp-yəl-r-ˌīz\ *v.;* **pop·u·lar·ized**; **pop·u·lar·iz·ing.** To make popular. — **pop·u·lar·i·za·tion** \ˌpäp-yəl-r-ə-ˈzāsh-n\ *n.*

pop·u·late \ˈpäp-yə-ˌlāt\ *v.;* **pop·u·lat·ed**; **pop·u·lat·ing.** To furnish with inhabitants.

pop·u·la·tion \ˌpäp-yə-ˈlāsh-n\ *n.* **1** The number of people in a country, city, or area; the people themselves. **2** The act or process of populating.

pop·u·lous \ˈpäp-yə-ləs\ *adj.* Thickly populated.

por·ce·lain \ˈpōrs-l(-)ən, ˈpȯrs-\ *n.* **1** Fine translucent ceramic ware, whiter and harder than ordinary earthenware, used variously in industry and especially in the manufacture of dishes; china. **2** An article or articles made of porcelain.

porch \ˈpōrch, ˈpȯrch\ *n.* A covered entrance to a building, often having a separate roof attached to the side of the house; a veranda.

por·cu·pine \ˈpȯrk-yə-ˌpīn\ *n.* A small mammal having stiff, sharp quills mingled with its hair.

pore \ˈpōr, ˈpȯr\ *v.;* **pored**; **por·ing.** To gaze, study, or think long or earnestly; as, to *pore* over a book.

pore \ˈpōr, ˈpȯr\ *n.* A tiny hole or opening, as in skin.

por·gy \ˈpȯr-gē\ *n.; pl.* **por·gies** or **por·gy.** Any of several food fishes of the Mediterranean Sea and the Atlantic Ocean.

pork \ˈpōrk, ˈpȯrk\ *n.* The flesh of pigs or hogs used as food.

pork·er \ˈpōrk-r, ˈpȯrk-r\ *n.* A pig or hog.

po·rous \ˈpōr-əs, ˈpȯr-əs\ *adj.* **1** Full of pores or tiny holes; as, *porous* wood. **2** Capable of absorbing liquids, as blotting paper.

por·phy·ry \ˈpȯrf-r-ē\ *n.; pl.* **por·phy·ries.** A dark red or purple Egyptian rock with white feldspar crystals embedded in it.

por·poise \ˈpȯrp-əs\ *n.; pl.* **por·pois·es** or **porpoise. 1** A sea animal somewhat like a small whale, with a blunt rounded snout. **2** A dolphin.

por·ridge \ˈpȯr-ij, ˈpär-\ *n.* A food made by boiling some vegetable or grain in water or milk until it thickens; as, oatmeal *porridge.*

por·rin·ger \ˈpȯr-ənj-r, ˈpär-\ *n.* A dish or small bowl from which liquid or partly liquid food is eaten.

porringer

port \ˈpōrt, ˈpȯrt\ *n.* [Named after the city of *Oporto*, Portugal, from which such wines were first shipped to England.] A strong, rich, usually dark red wine.

port \ˈpōrt, ˈpȯrt\ *n.* [From Old English, there borrowed from Latin *portus.*] **1** A harbor. **2** A place where ships may load and unload cargo.

port \ˈpōrt, ˈpȯrt\ *n.* [From medieval English *porte* meaning "gate", "porthole", there borrowed from medieval French, where it was derived from Latin *porta* meaning "door", "gate".] **1** An opening, as in machinery, for gas, steam, or water to go in or out. **2** A porthole.

port \ˈpōrt, ˈpȯrt\ *n.* [Probably derived from English *port* meaning "harbor", this side of the ship formerly being turned toward land when the ship was in dock.] The side of a ship on the left of a person looking from the stern to the bow. — *adj.* Of or having to do with the port side. — *v.* To turn the helm of a ship to port.

por·ta·ble \ˈpōrt-əb-l, ˈpȯrt-\ *adj.* Capable of being carried; easily moved from one place to another.

por·tage \ˈpōrt-ij, ˈpȯrt-\ *n.* **1** The carrying of boats or goods overland from one body of water to another. **2** The route taken.

por·tal \ˈpōrt-l, ˈpȯrt-l\ *n.* A door, gate, or entrance.

port·cul·lis \pōrt-ˈkəl-əs, pȯrt-\ *n.* A grating at the gateway of a castle or fortress that can be let down to prevent entrance.

portcullis

por·tend \pȯr-ˈtend, pōr-\ *v.* To give a sign or warning of something beforehand. The distant thunder *portended* a storm.

por·tent \ˈpȯr-ˌtent, ˈpōr-\ *n.* Anything that portends evil; a warning.

por·ten·tous \pȯr-ˈtent-əs, pōr-\ *adj.* **1** Ominous or threatening. **2** Very serious or solemn. **3** Wondrous; monstrous.

por·ter \ˈpōrt-r, pȯrt-r\ *n.* A doorkeeper.

por·ter \ˈpōrt-r, ˈpȯrt-r\ *n.* **1** A man who carries baggage, as at a hotel or a railroad station. **2** An attendant in a parlor car or sleeping car. **3** [A shortened form of *porter's ale*, probably so called because it was much drunk by porters and similar laborers in England.] A dark heavy beer.

por·ter·house \ˈpōrt-r-ˌhau̇s, ˈpȯrt-\ *n.* or **porterhouse steak.** A choice beefsteak with a large piece of tenderloin on a T-shaped bone.

port·fo·lio \pōrt-ˈfō-lē-ˌō, pȯrt-, -ˈfōl-ˌyō\ *n.; pl.* **port·fo·li·os.** A case for carrying papers or drawings without having to fold them.

port·hole \ˈpōrt-ˌhōl, ˈpȯrt-\ *n.* **1** An opening in the side of a ship. **2** An opening in a wall, as a loophole to shoot through.

por·ti·co \ˈpōrt-ə-ˌkō, ˈpȯrt-\ *n.; pl.* **por·ti·coes** or **por·ti·cos.** A covered walk; a row of columns supporting a roof, around or at the entrance of a building.

por·ti·ere \ˌpȯrt-ē-ˈer, pȯr-ˈtir, ˈpȯrt-ē-ər\ *n.* A curtain hung across a doorway.

por·tion \ˈpōrsh-n, ˈpȯrsh-n\ *n.* **1** A share; a part; as, a *portion* of time; a *portion* of food. **2** A dowry; as, a marriage *portion.* — For synonyms see *part.* — *v.;* **por·tioned**; **por·tion·ing** \-n(-)ing\. To divide or give out in shares or portions.

port·ly \ˈpōrt-lē, ˈpȯrt-\ *adj.;* **port·li·er**; **port·li·est.**

1 Dignified in appearance; stately. **2** Having a large and bulky body. — For synonyms see *stout.*

port·man·teau \pōrt-'man-ˌtō, pȯrt-\ *n. Chiefly British.* A suitcase or traveling bag.

por·trait \'pōr-trət, 'pȯr-, -ˌtrāt\ *n.* **1** A picture of a person. **2** A portrayal; as, a *portrait* of city life.

por·tray \pōr-'trā, pȯr-, pər-\ *v.* **1** To make a portrait of; to depict. **2** To picture in words; to describe vividly. **3** To represent by acting; as, to be chosen to *portray* George Washington in a pageant. — **por·tray·er** \-'trā-ər\ *n.*

por·tray·al \pōr-'trā-əl, pȯr-, pər-\ *n.* A portraying or describing; as, a great actor's famous *portrayal* of Hamlet; a painting that was a faithful *portrayal* of its subject.

Por·tu·guese \'pōrch-ə-ˌgēz, 'pȯrch-, -ˌgēs\ *adj.* Of or relating to Portugal, its people, or their language. — *n.* **1** A native or inhabitant of Portugal. **2** The people of Portugal — used as a plural with *the.* **3** The language of Portugal.

pose \'pōz\ *v.;* **posed**; **pos·ing.** **1** To propose, state, or set forth as a question or problem. **2** To hold or cause to hold a special position of the body, as for the painting of a picture or the taking of a photograph. **3** To pretend to be what one is not; as, to *pose* as a hero. — *n.* **1** A special position, as for the painting of a picture. **2** An assumed attitude; as, a person whose cheerfulness is a *pose.* — The word *posture* is a synonym of *pose: posture* generally refers to the normal relationship of the various parts of the body to each other as unconsciously assumed either in an active or in a relaxed state; *pose* has the suggestion of a bodily attitude consciously assumed to give some desired impression to the observer.

pos·er \'pōz-r\ *n.* **1** One that poses. **2** A baffling question.

po·seur \pō-'zər\ *n.* One who pretends to be what he is not.

po·si·tion \pə-'zish-n\ *n.* **1** The manner in which anything is placed or arranged. **2** Posture; as, to sit in an awkward *position.* **3** A way of looking at or considering things; as, to make one's *position* plain to everybody. **4** The place where a person or thing is; the situation; as, a map showing the *position* of the treasure. **5** Social or official rank; as, persons of *position.* **6** Employment; a job; as, to have a very good *position.* **7** Spot, place, or condition that gives one an advantage over a competitor; as, to maneuver for *position* in a race.

pos·i·tive \'päz-ət-iv, 'päz-tiv\ *adj.* **1** Definitely stated, as by some superior authority; as, *positive* orders. **2** Filled with confidence; certain; as, to be *positive* that one will win. **3** Overconfident; as, to have an annoyingly *positive* attitude. **4** Approving; affirmative; not negative; as, a *positive* answer. **5** Having a real position or effect; as, a *positive* influence for good in the school. **6** Showing the presence of the germ or condition in question; as, a *positive* test for tuberculosis. **7** Of or relating to static electricity as generated on fur by rubbing it on hard rubber. **8** Of or relating to the electrical charge on a body that has more protons than electrons on its surface. **9** In a dry cell, of or relating to the electrode to which the electric current flows from the device being operated. **10** In a storage battery, of or relating to the electrode from which the current flows to the device being operated. **11** Naming or relating to the form of an adjective or adverb that shows no degree of comparison. "Wise" is an adjective in the *positive* degree. **12** In mathematics, greater than zero; plus. **13** In photography, having the light and shade as existing in the original subject; as, a *positive* print. — *n.* **1** The positive degree of an adjective or adverb, or a form expressing it. **2** In photography, a positive picture or a print from a negative.

pos·i·tive·ly \'päz-ət-əv-lē, 'päz-təv-; *sense 2 is often* ˌpäz-ə-'tiv-lē\ *adv.* **1** In a positive way; as, to speak very *positively.* **2** Extremely; really; downright; as, *positively* rude.

pos·i·tron \'päz-ə-ˌträn\ *n.* A charge of positive electricity of exactly the same size as an electron.

pos·se \'päs-ē\ *n.* **1** A force of men called upon by a sheriff to aid him in his duty, as in pursuing a criminal. **2** A number of people temporarily organized to make a search, as for a lost child.

pos·sess \pə-'zes\ *v.* **1** To have and to hold as property; to own. **2** To have as part of one's character or physical make-up; as, to *possess* great strength. **3** To influence or control; as, to act as if *possessed* by an evil spirit. Rage *possessed* him.

pos·ses·sion \pə-'zesh-n\ *n.* **1** The act of possessing or holding as one's own; ownership; as, to be charged with the *possession* of stolen goods. **2** Something that is held as one's own property; something possessed; as, to guard one's *possessions;* the island *possessions* of the United States. **3** Domination by some idea or influence from outside oneself.

pos·ses·sive \pə-'zes-iv\ *adj.* **1** Showing the desire to possess or to keep; as, a child who is very *possessive* about his toys. **2** Of a word or group of words, expressing the idea of possession or some relation felt to be similar; as, a *possessive* adjective; a *possessive* pronoun. **3** Being in the possessive case. — *n.* **1** A word or group of words expressing the idea of possession or some relation felt to be similar. **2** Also **possessive case.** The case of a noun or pronoun denoting ownership; the genitive case, especially in English. **3** A word in the possessive case. — **pos·ses·sive·ly,** *adv.*

pos·ses·sor \pə-'zes-r\ *n.* A person who occupies, holds, owns, or controls.

pos·set \'päs-ət\ *n.* A hot spiced milk drink that has been curdled, as by wine or ale.

pos·si·bil·i·ty \ˌpäs-ə-'bil-ət-ē\ *n.; pl.* **pos·si·bil·i·ties.** **1** The fact of being possible; as, to face the *possibility* of failure. **2** Anything that is possible or that may happen.

pos·si·ble \'päs-əb-l\ *adj.* **1** Within the limits of one's ability; being something that can be done or brought about; as, a task *possible* only to skilled workmen. **2** Being something that may or may not occur; as, to plan against *possible* dangers. **3** Allowable; permitted. It is *possible* to see the patient only during visiting hours. **4** Able or fitted to be or to become; as, a *possible* site for a camp.

pos·si·bly \'päs-ə-blē\ *adv.* **1** By possible means; by any possibility; as, not *possibly* true. **2** Perhaps; maybe. The injured man may *possibly* recover.

pos·sum \'päs-m\. Short for *opossum.* — **to play possum.** To pretend, as sleep or illness, with the intention of deceiving.

post \'pōst\ *n.* A piece of something, as of timber or metal, fixed upright, especially as a support; a pillar; a prop; as, a fence *post.* — *v.* **1** To fasten to a post or other place used for public notices; to placard. **2** To fix public notices to or on; to publish or announce by or as if by a notice; as, advertisements *posted* on the windows of a vacant store. **3** To forbid persons from entering or using by putting up warning notices; as, to *post* a trout brook. **4** To enter on a list put up on a bulletin board; as, to *post* all arrivals and departures.

post \'pōst\ *n.* **1** The place at which a soldier is stationed, as while on sentry duty. **2** The place where a body of troops is stationed. **3** The body of troops at such a place. **4** A local subdivision of a veterans' organization. **5** A place, position, or office to which a person is appointed. **6** A trading settlement, as on a frontier. — *v.* To place or station at a post; as, to *post* a guard at a bridge.

post \'pōst\ *n.* **1** A courier or runner who carries messages or letters. **2** One of a series of stations for keeping horses for relays. **3** The sending of mail to or from a place; a delivery of mail; as, to expect a letter in the morning *post.* — *v.* **1** To travel with speed; to hurry. **2** To send by post, or mail; to mail; as, to *post* a letter. **3** To inform; as, to keep oneself *posted* on current events. **4** To rise and sink in the saddle in accordance with the motion of the horse, especially in trotting.

post-. A prefix that can mean: Later, or later than; subsequent, or subsequent to; as in *postscript, postgraduate, post-mortem.*

post·age \'pōs-tij\ *n.* The charge fixed by law for carrying something by mail, as a letter or parcel.

postage stamp. A government stamp put on articles sent by mail in payment of the postage.

post·al \'pōst-l\ *adj.* Of or relating to the post office or the handling of mail; as, a *postal* clerk. — *n.* A postal card.

postal card. **1** A card with a postage stamp printed on it, for sending by mail. **2** A postcard.

post·card \'pōs(t)-ˌkärd, -ˌkȧrd\ *n.* or **post card.** **1** Any private card that can be mailed when properly stamped. **2** A postal card.

post chaise. A four-wheeled, closed horse-drawn carriage for traveling rapidly.

post·date \(')pōs(t)-'dāt\ *v.;* **post·dat·ed; post·dat·ing.** To use a date later than the actual date; as, to *postdate* a check.

post·er \'pōst-r\ *n.* **1** A notice or advertisement intended to be posted in a public place. **2** A person who posts such notices; as, a bill *poster.*

pos·te·ri·or \päs-'tir-ē-ər, pōs-\ *adj.* **1** Later in time, order, or sequence. **2** Situated behind or toward the hinder end; hinder; as, the *posterior* legs of an insect. — *n.* The hinder parts of an animal's body; the buttocks — usually used in the plural.

pos·ter·i·ty \päs-'ter-ət-ē\ *n.* **1** The line of persons who are descended from one ancestor; descendants; offspring. **2** All future generations of men; collectively, future time; as, to hand customs down to *posterity.*

pos·tern \'pōst-rn, 'päst-\ *n.* A back door or gate; a private or side entrance. — *adj.* Situated at the back, rear, or side.

post·grad·u·ate \(')pōst-'graj-ə-wət, -ˌwāt\ *adj.* Of or relating to graduates or to studies carried on after graduation. — *n.* A student carrying on such studies.

post·haste \(')pōst-'hāst\ *n.* Speed in traveling, as of a messenger. — *adv.* With great speed; by the fastest means.

post·hole \'pōst-ˌhōl\ *n.* A hole for a post, especially a fence post.

post·hu·mous \'päs-chə-məs, päs-'tyü-məs, päs-'tü-\ *adj.* **1** Born after the death of the father; as, a *posthumous* son. **2** Published after the death of its author; as, a *posthumous* novel. **3** Following or occurring after one's death; as, *posthumous* fame. — **post·hu·mous·ly,** *adv.*

pos·til·ion or **pos·til·lion** \pōs-'til-yən, pəs-\ *n.* A person who rides the left-hand horse of a pair drawing a coach.

post·lude \'pōst-ˌlüd\ *n.* In music, a closing piece; especially, an organ solo played at the end of a church service.

post·man \'pōs(t)-mən, -ˌman\ *n.; pl.* **post·men** \-mən, -ˌmen\. A person who carries and delivers mail; a mailman; a letter carrier.

post·mark \'pōs(t)-ˌmärk, -ˌmȧrk\ *n.* Any mark officially put on a piece of mail; especially, a mark canceling the postage stamp and giving the date and place of sending. — *v.* To put a postmark on; to stamp with a postmark.

post·mas·ter \'pōs(t)-ˌmast-r\ *n.* A person in charge of a post office and the mails.

postmaster general; *pl.* **postmasters general.** The head of the post-office department of a government.

post·mis·tress \'pōs(t)-ˌmis-trəs\ *n.* A woman in charge of a post office.

post-mor·tem \(')pōs(t)-'mȯrt-m\ *adj.* [From Latin *post mortem* meaning "after death".] Occurring or done after death, as an examination of the body. — *n.* A post-mortem examination.

post office. **1** An office, under the charge of a government official, where mail is received, handled, and sent out. **2** The department of the government in charge of the mail.

post·paid \'pōs(t)-'pād\ *adj.* With the postage prepaid.

post·pone \(')pōs(t)-'pōn, pəs(t)-\ *v.;* **post·poned; post·pon·ing.** To put off till some later time; to delay. — **post·pone·ment,** *n.*

post road. A road over which the mail is carried or was formerly carried.

post·script \'pōs(t)-ˌskript\ *n.* [From Latin *postscriptum,* neuter of *postscriptus,* the past participle of *postscribere* meaning "to write after", "to add something in writing".] A note added to a finished letter or book.

pos·tu·late \'päs-chə-lət, -ˌlāt\ *n.* Anything taken for granted or assumed to be true and used as the basis for development of further laws or principles. — \-ˌlāt\ *v.;* **pos·tu·lat·ed; pos·tu·lat·ing.** To give as a postulate; to assume a thing to be true; as, to *postulate* that all men are created equal. — **pos·tu·la·tion** \ˌpäs-chə-'lāsh-n\ *n.*

pos·ture \'päs-chər\ *n.* The position of one part of the body with relation to other parts; the general way of holding the body; as, to do exercises to improve one's *posture.* — For synonyms see *pose.* — *v.;* **pos·tured; pos·tur·ing.** To take a particular posture; to pose.

post·war \'pōst-'wȯr\ *adj.* Coming after a war.

po·sy \'pō-zē\ *n.; pl.* **po·sies. 1** A brief inscription, as on a ring. **2** A flower. **3** A bunch of flowers; a bouquet.

pot \'pät\ *n.* **1** Any somewhat rounded vessel or container, often made of metal or earthenware, and used for many purposes; as, a stew *pot;* a watering *pot.* **2** The contents of a pot; the amount a pot will hold; as, a *pot* of soup. **3** A chimney pot. **4** A large sum of money. **5** The total of the bets at stake at any one time; as, to win the *pot* at poker. — *v.;* **pot·ted; pot·ting. 1** To place in a pot; as, to *pot* plants. **2** To preserve by placing in a sealed container, as a jar or can; to can; as, *potted* chicken.

pot·ash \'pät-ˌash\ *n.* A chemical made from wood ashes, used in making fertilizer and in various manufacturing processes.

po·tas·si·um \pə-'tas-ē-əm\ *n.* A soft, light, silver-white metallic element that occurs abundantly in nature, but always in combination with other substances.

po·ta·to \pə-'tāt-ō, pət-'āt-\ *n.; pl.* **po·ta·toes. 1** The sweet potato. **2** The thick, edible, underground tuber of a plant native to America; the plant that bears these tubers.

potato beetle or **potato bug.** A black and yellow beetle that feeds on the leaves of the potato.

potato chip. A thin slice of potato that has been fried in deep fat.

potato plant

pot·bel·ly \'pät-ˌbel-ē\ *n.; pl.* **pot·bel·lies.** A bulging or protruding belly. — **pot·bel·lied** \-ˌbel-ēd\ *adj.*

po·ten·cy \'pōt-n-sē\ *n.; pl.* **po·ten·cies.** The quality or condition of being potent; especially, ability or power to bring about a certain result.

po·tent \'pōt-nt\ *adj.* **1** Powerful; mighty; as, a *potent* ruler. **2** Very influential or effective; as, a *potent* argument. **3** Very effective chemically or medicinally; as, a *potent* medicine. — **po·tent·ly,** *adv.*

po·ten·tate \'pōt-n-ˌtāt\ *n.* A person who has great power; a ruler; a sovereign.

po·ten·tial \pə-'tench-l\ *adj.* Capable of becoming real; possible; as, to be aware of the *potential* dangers in a scheme. — For synonyms see *latent.* — *n.* **1** A possibility; potentiality. **2** The condition of electric charge at one place in relation to the charge at another place such that a current tends to flow between the two places when there is a difference between the amount of the charges.

potential energy. The amount of energy a thing has because of its position or because of the arrangement of its parts, as a weight raised to a height or a coiled spring.

po·ten·ti·al·i·ty \pə-ˌtench-ē-'al-ət-ē, ˌpō-ˌten-'chal-\ *n.; pl.* **po·ten·ti·al·i·ties. 1** The state of being possible, not actual; as, an event that is just a *potentiality.* **2** Possible future capacity; as, a young writer with great *potentiality.*

poth·er \'päth-r\ *n.* Disturbance; fuss; bother.

pot·herb \'pät-ˌərb, -ˌhərb\ *n.* Any herb whose leaves or stems are boiled for food, especially greens, as spinach, or used to season food, as mint.

pot·hole \'pät-ˌhōl\ *n.* Any large pit or hole, as in a river bed or road surface.

pot·hook \'pät-ˌhu̇k\ *n.* A hook, shaped like an S, used to suspend a pot over a fire.

po·tion \'pōsh-n\ *n.* A drink; a dose; especially, a dose of a liquid medicine or of a poison.

pot·luck \'pät-'lək\ *n.* Whatever happens to be ready for a meal; a simple, informal meal.

pot·pie \'pät-'pī\ *n.* Stewed meat or fowl served with a crust or dumplings.

pot·pour·ri \ˌpōp-r-'ē\ *n.* **1** A jar of spiced flower petals used to scent a room. **2** A mixture; a medley; a conglomeration.

pot shot. 1 A shot fired to get food and not just for sport. **2** A shot taken at random or at a target within easy reach.

pot·tage \'pät-ij\ *n. Archaic.* A dish of boiled vegetables, or vegetables and meat; a thick soup.

potted. Past tense and past part. of *pot.*

pot·ter \'pät-r\ *n.* A person who makes earthenware.

potter. Variant of *putter.*

pot·ter's field \'pät-rz\. A burial place for paupers, unknown persons, and criminals.

potter's wheel. A horizontal disk revolving on a vertical spindle, used by a potter in shaping clay.

pot·tery \'pät-r-ē, 'pä-trē\ *n.; pl.* **pot·ter·ies. 1** A place where earthen articles are made. **2** The art of a potter. **3** Things made by a potter from clay shaped while moist and then hardened by heat; especially, the coarser articles so made.

potter's wheel

potting. Pres. part. of *pot*.

pouch \'paůch\ *n.* **1** A bag or sack; as, a mail *pouch;* a tobacco *pouch.* **2** Something resembling such a pouch in shape; as, an old man with *pouches* under his eyes. **3** A bag or sac of folded skin or flesh, especially one for carrying the young, as on the abdomen of a kangaroo, or one for carrying food, as in the cheek of many animals of the rat family. — *v.* **1** To put into a pouch; to pocket. **2** To form a pouch; to shape like a pouch.

poul·tice \'pōl-təs\ *n.* A soft mixture, usually heated, spread on a cloth, and applied to a sore or inflamed part of the body to soothe or medicate it.

poul·try \'pōl-trē\ *n.* Domestic birds that furnish meat or eggs for human food, as chickens, turkeys, ducks, and geese.

pounce \'paůn(t)s\ *v.;* **pounced; pounc·ing. 1** To swoop down on and seize. The hawk *pounced* on a chicken. **2** To spring; to leap; as, a cat waiting to *pounce.* — *n.* A pouncing; a sudden swoop or spring, as of a bird or an animal.

pound \'paůnd\ *n.* **1** A public enclosure where stray animals are kept; as, a dog *pound.* **2** An enclosure for sheltering or trapping animals. **3** An area or enclosure within which fish are kept or caught.

pound \'paůnd\ *v.* **1** To crush to a powder or pulp by striking heavily again and again; as, to *pound* almonds into a paste. **2** To strike heavily over and over again, as with the fist or with a heavy instrument; to beat; to thump; to hammer; as, to *pound* a piano; a boxer who was really *pounding* his opponent. **3** To walk, run, or move heavily; as, horses *pounding* along the road. — *n.* A pounding; a heavy blow or a noise as of a heavy blow; a thud.

pound \'paůnd\ *n.* **1** A measure of weight equal to 16 ounces. **2** In the systems used for weighing precious metals and drugs, a measure of weight equal to 12 ounces. **3** Also **pound sterling**. A unit of money in Great Britain equal to 20 shillings. **4** A unit of money in many other countries, as Australia, Egypt, and Israel.

pound-fool·ish \'paůnd-'fü-lish\ *adj.* Foolish in dealing with large sums of money or important matters.

pour \'pōr, 'pȯr\ *v.* **1** To flow or to cause to flow in a stream; as, to *pour* the tea; tears *pouring* down a child's cheeks. **2** To let loose something without restraint; to express freely; as, to *pour* out one's troubles. **3** To rain very hard.

pout \'paůt\ *v.* To push out one's lips, as when displeased; to look sullen. — *n.* **1** A pouting. **2** A fit of bad humor.

pov·er·ty \'päv-rt-ē\ *n.* **1** The condition of being poor; want; need. **2** A lack of something desirable; poor quality; as, the *poverty* of the soil.

pov·er·ty-strick·en \'päv-rt-ē-ˌstrik-n\ *adj.* Very poor; destitute.

pow·der \'paůd-r\ *n.* **1** The fine particles made from a dry substance, as by pounding or crushing; dust. **2** Something made in or changed to the form of a powder; as, face *powder;* milk *powder.* **3** An explosive, such as gunpowder. — *v.;* **pow·dered; pow·der·ing** \-r(-)ing\. **1** To sprinkle with or as if with powder; as, streets *powdered* with snow. **2** To crush into powder; to pulverize. **3** To change to a powder; as, *powdered* milk. **4** To use or apply powder; as, to *powder* the baby.

powder blue. A delicate greenish-blue color. — **pow·der–blue**, *adj.*

powder horn. A container for gunpowder, especially a cow or ox horn used for this purpose.

powder horn

pow·dery \'paůd-r-ē\ *adj.* **1** Made of, or like powder; as, *powdery* snow. **2** Crumbly; as, *powdery* soil. **3** Sprinkled with powder; dusty.

pow·er \'paůr\ *n.* **1** The ability to act or to do; as, to lose the *power* to walk. **2** Control; authority; influence; as, to be in the *power* of an enemy. **3** A person or thing that has power or influence; a nation having control or influence among other nations; as, the great *powers;* a man who is a *power* in the business world. **4** Might; energy; vigor; as, a storm of tremendous *power.* **5** Force or energy used to do work; as, electric *power.* **6** In mathematics, the product obtained by multiplying a quantity by itself a specified number of times, as indicated by its exponent. **7** The number of times an optical instrument magnifies the apparent size of the object viewed.

— The words *energy* and *strength* are synonyms of *power: power* generally indicates an ability to act or be acted upon, whether this ability is mental or physical, and whether it is latent or actually exerted; in common use *energy* suggests the stored-up power used in or capable of being transformed into work; *strength* may indicate the power that is in someone or something as a result of certain qualities, as health, and that enables it to exert force or exhibit its energy through action.

— *adj.* Having to do with power; run by, producing, or supplying power; as, a *power* drill; a *power* plant.

pow·er·boat \'paůr-ˌbōt, -'bōt\ *n.* A boat moved by an engine or motor; a motorboat.

pow·er·ful \'paůrf-l\ *adj.* Full of, or having, power, strength, or influence; strong; mighty; effective. — **pow·er·ful·ly** \'paůrf-l(-)ē\ *adv.*

pow·er·house \'paůr-ˌhaůs\ *n.; pl.* **pow·er·hous·es** \-ˌhaů-zəz\. **1** A building in which power, especially electric power, is produced. **2** A source of power, energy, or influence; someone or something having unusual strength or energy.

pow·er·less \'paůr-ləs\ *adj.* Without power, force, or energy; unable to produce any effect.

pow·wow \'paů-ˌwaů\ *n.* **1** Among North American Indians, a priest or medicine man, or a noisy ceremony, especially one at which magic is practiced. **2** A conference of or with Indians. **3** Any noisy gathering; a conference or meeting. — *v.* To hold a powwow.

pox \'päks\ *n.* [An altered spelling of *pocks*, the plural of *pock*.] Any of various diseases that cause eruptions on the skin; as, chicken *pox*.

pp. Abbreviation for *pages.*

pr. Abbreviation for *pair.*

prac·ti·ca·ble \'prak-tik-əb-l\ *adj.* **1** Capable of being done, put into practice, or accomplished; feasible; as, a suggestion that was interesting but not *practicable.* **2** Usable; as, a *practicable* weapon. — **prac·ti·ca·bil·i·ty** \ˌprak-tik-ə-'bil-ət-ē\ *n.* — **prac·ti·ca·bly** \'prak-tik-ə-blē\ *adv.*

prac·ti·cal \'prak-tik-l\ *adj.* **1** Of or relating to action and practice rather than ideas or thought; as, to put a first-aid lesson to *practical* use. **2** Capable of being put to use or account; useful; as, a *practical* knowledge of carpentry. **3** Inclined to do things rather than just plan or think about them; as, a *practical* man with a lot of common sense. **4** In effect; virtual. The speech was so badly delivered that it was a *practical* failure. — **prac·ti·cal·i·ty** \ˌprak-tə-'kal-ət-ē\ *n.*

practical joke. A joke turning on something done rather than said; especially, a trick played on a person.

prac·ti·cal·ly \'prak-tik-l(-)ē\ *adv.* **1** Really; actually; as, *practically* worthless. **2** By experience or experiment; as, a self-educated man who is *practically* wise. **3** In actual practice or use; as, a medicine that is *practically* safe. **4** Almost entirely; to all practical purposes; as, *practically* friendless. **5** Within limits of usefulness.

prac·tice or **prac·tise** \'prak-təs\ *v.;* **prac·ticed** or **prac·tised**; **prac·tic·ing** or **prac·tis·ing.** **1** To do or perform often or habitually; as, to *practice* economy. **2** To do repeated exercises in, so as to learn or improve; as, to *practice* music. **3** To follow or work at as a profession; as, to *practice* medicine. **4** To teach by repeating; to train; to drill; as, to *practice* pupils in marching. — *n.* **1** Actual performance or application of knowledge; use; as, to put into *practice.* **2** Habit; custom; usage; as, the *practice* of rising early. **3** A usual way or method of doing something; as, evil *practices.* **4** Systematic exercise to gain skill. *Practice* makes perfect. **5** Practical acquaintance or skill acquired by such systematic exercise; as, a baseball player who is out of *practice.* **6** The carrying on of one's profession; as, the *practice* of law. **7** Professional business or work. The doctor sold his *practice.* — **prac·tic·er** or **prac·tis·er** \-təs-r\ *n.*

prac·ticed or **prac·tised** \'prak-təst\ *adj.* **1** Experienced; skilled. **2** Learned by practice.

prac·ti·tion·er \prak-'tish-n(-)ər\ *n.* A person who practices a profession, especially law or medicine.

prae·tor \'prēt-r\ *n.* In ancient Rome, a magistrate ranking next to a consul and having chiefly judicial duties.

prae·to·ri·an \prē-'tōr-ē-ən, -'tȯr-\ *adj.* **1** Of or relating to a Roman praetor. **2** Of or relating to the bodyguard of a Roman emperor; as, the *praetorian* guard. — *n.* A member of this guard.

prag·mat·ic \prag-'mat-ik\ *adj.* **1** Of or relating to the affairs of a community or state — used chiefly in the phrase **pragmatic sanction**, a solemn decree issued by the head of a state on a very important matter and having the force of fundamental law. **2** Pragmatical; practical. **3** Of or relating to pragmatism. **4** Concerned with practical values or consequences; as, to put a theory to a *pragmatic* test of its usefulness.

prag·mat·i·cal \prag-'mat-ik-l\ *adj.* Practical; matter-of-fact.

prag·mat·i·cal·ly \prag-'mat-ik-l(-)ē\ *adv.* In a pragmatic or a pragmatical manner.

prag·ma·tism \'prag-mə-ˌtiz-m\ *n.* **1** The quality or state of being pragmatic. **2** The doctrine that the purpose of thought and knowledge is to guide action and that the truth of any belief is to be judged by its practical consequences. — **prag·ma·tist** \-mət-əst\ *n.* or *adj.*

prai·rie \'prer-ē\ *n.* A large area of level or rolling grassland without trees.

prairie chicken. A grouse of the Mississippi valley with a patch of bare inflatable skin on the neck.

prairie dog. An American burrowing rodent about the size of a large squirrel, being related to the marmots and having a grayish or buff-colored body and a black-tipped tail.

prairie schoo·ner \'skün-r\. A long wagon that had sides and a rounded top of canvas, used by pioneers to cross the prairies.

prairie schooner

prairie wolf. A coyote.

praise \'prāz\ *v.;* **praised**; **prais·ing.** **1** To express approval of something; to extol; to commend; to applaud. **2** To glorify God or a saint, especially in song; to worship. — *n.* The act of praising; approval or honor given because of great worth.

praise·wor·thy \'prāz-ˌwər-t͟hē\ *adj.* Worthy of praise; laudable; as, *praiseworthy* action. — **praise·wor·thi·ly** \-ˌwərt͟h-l-ē\ *adv.*

pra·line \'prä-ˌlēn\ *n.* A candy of nut kernels in a crisp brown sugar coating.

prance \'pran(t)s\ *v.;* **pranced**; **pranc·ing.** **1** To spring from the hind legs or move by bounding in this way, as a horse. **2** To ride on a prancing horse; to ride gaily or proudly. **3** To swagger. — *n.* A prancing; a prancing movement. — **pranc·er** \'pran(t)s-r\ *n.*

prank \'prangk\ *n.* A gay or playful act; a practical joke; a trick; as, Halloween *pranks.* — **prank·ish** \-ish\ *adj.*

prank·ster \'prang(k)st-r\ *n.* A person that plays pranks.

prate \'prāt\ *v.;* **prat·ed**; **prat·ing.** To talk a great deal and to little purpose; to talk foolishly; to babble. — *n.* Worthless or foolish talk. — **prat·er** \'prāt-r\ *n.*

prat·tle \'prat-l\ *v.;* **prat·tled**; **prat·tling** \-l(-)ing\. To talk a great deal without much meaning; to prate; to chatter. — *n.* Trifling or childish talk. — **prat·tler** \-l(-)ər\ *n.*

prawn \'prȯn, 'prän\ *n.* An edible shellfish much like a shrimp, with long feelers and five pairs of legs.

pray \'prā\ *v.* **1** To ask earnestly; to beg; to implore; as, to *pray* a judge for mercy. **2** To say prayers, especially to God. — **I pray you** or **pray.** I beg of you; please. *Pray* be seated.

prayer \'prar, 'prer\ *n.* **1** A request; entreaty; as, a *prayer* for peace. **2** The act of praying to God or to an object of worship, as in adoration or entreaty. **3** The words of a prayer; as, a written *prayer*. **4** A form of religious service that is mostly prayers; as, evening *prayer*. **5** [in the plural] Hearty good wishes. My *prayers* go with you.

prayer·ful \'prarf-l, 'prerf-l\ *adj.* Devout; given to or characterized by prayers. — **prayer·ful·ly** \-l(-)ē\ *adv.*

prayer book. A book of prayers.

pray·ing mantis \'prā-ing\. A mantis.

pre-. A prefix that can mean: **1** Before in time, beforehand, in advance, as in *prearrange* or *precaution*. **2** Before in place, in front, as in *prefix* or *premolar*. **3** Prior to; existing before, as in *prewar*. **4** Preparatory to; prerequisite to, as in *premedical*.

preach \'prēch\ *v.* **1** To talk on a religious subject; to deliver a sermon. **2** To urge publicly; to advocate; as, to *preach* patience. **3** To deliver; as, to *preach* a sermon.

preach·er \'prēch-r\ *n.* A person who preaches; especially, a minister.

pre·am·ble \'prē-ˌam-bl, prē-'am-bl\ *n.* **1** An introductory portion or preface, as to a law, that often states the reasons and purpose for the matter that follows; as, the *preamble* to the Constitution. **2** An introductory fact or circumstance; a preliminary.

pre·ar·range \ˌprē-ə-'rānj\ *v.;* **pre·ar·ranged**; **pre·ar·rang·ing.** To arrange beforehand; as, to meet at a *prearranged* spot.

pre·car·i·ous \prē-'kar-ē-əs, -'ker-\ *adj.* Uncertain; not secure; depending on unknown conditions; as, *precarious* health; *precarious* fortunes. — **pre·car·i·ous·ly**, *adv.*

pre·cau·tion \prē-'kȯsh-n\ *n.* **1** Caution or care taken in advance. **2** Something done beforehand to prevent evil or bring about good results; as, to take all possible *precautions* against fire. — **pre·cau·tion·ary** \-ˌer-ē\ *adj.*

pre·cede \prē-'sēd\ *v.;* **pre·ced·ed**; **pre·ced·ing.** To be or go before, as in rank, importance, position, or time.

prec·e·dence \'pres-ə-dən(t)s, prē-'sēd-n(t)s\ or **prec·e·den·cy** \'pres-ə-dən-sē, prē-'sēd-n-sē\ *n.* A preceding, as in time, importance, or position.

prec·e·dent \'pres-ə-dənt\ *n.* Something that may serve as a rule or as a pattern to be followed in the future.

pre·ced·ing \prē-'sēd-ing\ *adj.* Going before; previous.

pre·cept \'prē-ˌsept\ *n.* Any principle or instruction taken as a rule of action or behavior; a guiding principle.

pre·cep·tor \prē-'sept-r\ *n.* **1** A teacher. **2** The principal of a school.

pre·cinct \'prē-ˌsing(k)t\ *n.* A district marked off from adjacent areas for administrative or electoral purposes; as, a police *precinct*.

pre·cious \'presh-əs\ *adj.* **1** Very valuable; as, diamonds, emeralds, and other *precious* stones. **2** Greatly loved; dear; cherished; as, *precious* memories. **3** Fastidiously refined; too elaborate; as, *precious* language. — For synonyms see *valuable*. — **pre·cious·ly**, *adv.*

prec·i·pice \'pres-ə-pəs\ *n.* A very steep and high face of rock or mountain; a cliff.

pre·cip·i·tate \prē-'sip-ət-ət, -ə-ˌtāt\ *adj.* Hasty; rash; as, *precipitate* action. — \-ə-ˌtāt\ *v.;* **pre·cip·i·tat·ed**; **pre·cip·i·tat·ing. 1** To throw or dash headlong, as from a precipice. **2** To cause to happen suddenly or unexpectedly; as, a misunderstanding that *precipitated* a quarrel. **3** To change from a vapor to a liquid, and fall as hail, mist, rain, sleet, or snow. **4** In chemistry, to separate or become separated from a solution. — \-ət-ət, -ə-ˌtāt\ *n.* In chemistry, a solid or crystalline substance that has separated from a solution; as, an isoluble *precipitate*. — **pre·cip·i·tate·ly** \-ət-ət-lē, -ə-ˌtāt-lē\ *adv.* — **pre·cip·i·ta·tor** \-ə-ˌtāt-r\ *n.*

pre·cip·i·ta·tion \prē-ˌsip-ə-'tāsh-n\ *n.* **1** A headlong rush or fall. **2** In chemistry, the process of precipitating from a solution. **3** Water that falls to the earth as hail, mist, rain, sleet, or snow; the amount of this water that falls.

pre·cip·i·tous \prē-'sip-ət-əs\ *adj.* **1** Steep like a precipice; having precipices; as, a *precipitous* trail. **2** Falling or flowing with a steep descent; very rapid; as, the *precipitous* rush of water. **3** Sudden; rash; as, a *precipitous* act. — **pre·cip·i·tous·ly**, *adv.*

pré·cis \prā-'sē\ *n.; pl.* **pré·cis** \-'sēz\. A concise summary or abstract.

pre·cise \prē-'sīs\ *adj.* **1** Definite; exactly stated or defined; as, *precise* rules; *precise* directions. **2** Distinct; clear and sharp in enunciation; as, to speak in a *precise* voice. **3** Accurate; very exact; as, *precise* scales; the *precise* time of arrival. **4** Conforming exactly to rules or customs; strict in behavior; as, a very *precise* person. — **pre·cise·ly**, *adv.*

pre·ci·sion \prē-'sizh-n\ *n.* The quality or condition of being precise or exact; accuracy.

pre·clude \prē-'klüd\ *v.;* **pre·clud·ed**; **pre·clud·ing.** To prevent; to make impossible; to keep from taking place.

pre·co·cious \prē-'kō-shəs\ *adj.* Having the skill or ability of one who is older or more experienced; showing early development of ability; as, a *precocious* child. — **pre·co·cious·ly**, *adv.*

pre·coc·i·ty \prē-'käs-ət-ē\ *n.* The quality or state of being precocious; very early development.

pre·con·ceive \ˌprēk-n-'sēv\ *v.;* **pre·con·ceived**; **pre·con·ceiv·ing.** To form an opinion of beforehand; as, *preconceived* ideas about foreign lands.

pre·con·cep·tion \ˌprēk-n-'sepsh-n\ *n.* An idea or opinion of something formed without real knowledge or experience of it.

pre·con·cert·ed \ˌprēk-n-'sərt-əd\ *adj.* Arranged or agreed upon in advance.

pre·cur·sor \prē-'kərs-r\ *n.* A forerunner.

pre·da·cious or **pre·da·ceous** \prē-'dā-shəs\ *adj.* Living by preying on others; predatory.

pre·date \(')prē-'dāt\ *v.;* **pre·dat·ed**; **pre·dat·ing.** To antedate.

pred·a·tor \'pred-ət-r, -ə-ˌtȯr\ *n.* A predatory organism; especially, a predatory bird or mammal.

pred·a·to·ry \'pred-ə-ˌtōr-ē, -ˌtȯr-ē\ *adj.* **1** Of or relating to plundering; characterized by plundering; as, *predatory* raids by a band of outlaws. **2** Living by preying upon other animals. Lions are *predatory* animals. **3** Destructive, as to crops; as, *predatory* insects.

pred·e·ces·sor \'pred-ə-ˌses-r, 'prēd-; ˌpred-ə-'ses-r, ˌprēd-\ *n.* **1** One that goes before; especially, a person who has held an office or position before another; as, to take over a position upon the resignation of one's *predecessor*. The new class president is better than his *predecessor*. **2** An ancestor; a forefather.

pre·des·ti·na·tion \(ˌ)prē-ˌdes-tə-'nāsh-n\ *n.* **1** The act of settling, as the fate of someone or something, beforehand. **2** Destiny; fate. **3** The doctrine held in some churches that God has predestined some persons to everlasting happiness and others to everlasting misery.

pre·des·tine \prē-'des-tən\ *v.;* **pre·des·tined**; **pre·des·tin·ing.** To settle beforehand, as a person's fate at the time of his birth; to foreordain.

pre·de·ter·mine \ˌprē-də-'tər-mən\ *v.;* **pre·de·ter·mined**; **pre·de·ter·min·ing.** To determine or settle beforehand; as, to meet at a *predetermined* time and place.

pre·dic·a·ment \prē-'dik-m-ənt\ *n.* A bad, unpleasant, or trying situation or position; a fix.

pred·i·cate \'pred-ə-ˌkāt\ *v.;* **pred·i·cat·ed**; **pred·i·cat·ing.** **1** To declare or proclaim; to assert. **2** To found or base; as, a proposal *predicated* upon the belief that sufficient support could be obtained. — \-ik-ət\ *n.* The word or group of words in a sentence or clause expressing what is said about the subject, as the verb phrase *has returned* in "The boy has returned". — \-ik-ət\ *adj.* Belonging to the predicate; as, the *predicate* adjective "strong" in "A lion is strong". In "His father is a doctor", "doctor" is a *predicate* noun; it is also a *predicate* nominative.

pred·i·ca·tive \'pred-ə-ˌkāt-iv\ *adj.* **1** Predicating or affirming. **2** In grammar, having the force of a predicate or belonging to the predicate. — **pred·i·ca·tive·ly**, *adv.*

pre·dict \prē-'dikt\ *v.* [From Latin *praedictus*, the past participle of *praedicere* meaning literally "to say beforehand".] To tell beforehand; to foretell; to prophesy; as, to *predict* the weather. — For synonyms see *foretell*. — **pre·dict·a·ble** \-'dik-təb-l\ *adj.*

pre·dic·tion \prē-'diksh-n\ *n.* **1** The act of predicting. **2** Something that is predicted.

pre·di·gest \ˌprē-dī-'jest, -də-'jest\ *v.* To digest beforehand; especially, to digest artificially by chemical action, as food prepared for use by babies or invalids. — **pre·di·ges·tion** \-də-'jes-chən, -dī-\ *n.*

pred·i·lec·tion \ˌpred-l-'eksh-n, ˌprēd-l-\ *n.* An inclination in favor of something in advance of knowledge of it; a partiality.

pre·dis·pose \ˌprē-dis-'pōz\ *v.;* **pre·dis·posed**; **pre·dis·pos·ing.** **1** To cause to incline beforehand, as to approve or disapprove of something of which one has no real knowledge. **2** To give a tendency to; as, an inherited weakness *predisposing* one to certain diseases. **3** To dispose of beforehand.

pre·dis·po·si·tion \(ˌ)prē-ˌdis-pə-'zish-n\ *n.* **1** The action of predisposing. **2** The condition of being predisposed; inclination or susceptibility.

pre·dom·i·nance \prē-'däm-ə-nən(t)s\ *n.* The quality or state of being predominant; superiority, as in strength or numbers; prevalence.

pre·dom·i·nant \prē-'däm-ə-nənt\ *adj.* Superior to others in number, strength, influence, authority, or importance; as, the *predominant* color in a dress. — **pre·dom·i·nant·ly**, *adv.*

pre·dom·i·nate \prē-'däm-ə-ˌnāt\ *v.;* **pre·dom·i·nat·ed**; **pre·dom·i·nat·ing.** **1** To be predominant; to be of greatest importance; to prevail; to rule. **2** To exceed others in number; as, a landscape in which low-growing shrubs *predominated*.

pre-em·i·nence \prē-'em-ə-nən(t)s\ *n.* The quality or state of being pre-eminent; special prominence; outstanding superiority.

pre-em·i·nent \prē-'em-ə-nənt\ *adj.* Eminent above others; very outstanding, especially in excellence; superior. — **pre-em·i·nent·ly**, *adv.*

pre-empt \prē-'em(p)t\ *v.* **1** To settle upon, as public land, with the right to purchase before others; to take by such a right. **2** To appropriate; to take before someone else can; as, to *pre-empt* a seat at the stadium. — **pre-emp·tion** \-'em(p)sh-n\ *n.*

preen \'prēn\ *v.* **1** To smooth with or as if with the beak. The peacock *preened* his feathers. **2** To make one's appearance neat and tidy.

pre-ex·ist \ˌprē-ig-'zist\ *v.* To exist before.

pre-ex·ist·ence \ˌprē-ig-'zis-tən(t)s\ *n.* Existence in a former state; especially, existence of the soul before its union with the body; as, a religion that preaches the doctrine of *pre-existence*. — **pre-ex·ist·ent** \-tənt\ *adj.*

pre·fab \'prē-'fab\ *n.* A prefabricated house or other structure.

pre·fab·ri·cate \(')prē-'fab-rə-ˌkāt\ *v.;* **pre·fab·ri·cat·ed**; **pre·fab·ri·cat·ing.** To manufacture all the parts of something in advance so that it can be built merely by putting together the parts. — **pre·fab·ri·ca·tion** \(ˌ)prē-ˌfab-rə-'kāsh-n\ *n.*

pref·ace \'pref-əs\ *n.* An introductory section, as at the beginning of a book; a prologue; a foreword. — *v.;* **pref·aced; pref·ac·ing.** To introduce by or commence with a preface; to furnish with a preface; as, to *preface* a book; to *preface* a speech with a few jokes.

pre·fect \'prē-ˌfekt\ *n.* **1** In ancient Rome, any of certain high officials at the head of a command or of a department of government. **2** A similar office in other ancient countries. **3** A president or chief magistrate or official. **4** In France, the chief administrative officer of a department. **5** A student monitor in certain schools.

pre·fec·ture \'prē-ˌfek-chər\ *n.* **1** The office, jurisdiction, term, or residence of a prefect. **2** A district governed by a prefect.

pre·fer \prē-'fər\ *v.;* **pre·ferred; pre·fer·ring. 1** To put in a higher position or rank; to advance; to promote; as, to *prefer* an officer to the rank of general. **2** To hold something in greater favor; to like better; as, to *prefer* chocolate. **3** To present for action; as, to *prefer* charges against a person.

pref·er·a·ble \'pref-r(-)əb-l\ *adj.* Deserving to be preferred; more desirable. — **pref·er·a·bly** \-r(-)ə-blē\ *adv.*

pref·er·ence \'pref-rn(t)s, -r(-)ən(t)s\ *n.* **1** A preferring or the condition of being preferred; a special liking for one person or thing rather than another. **2** The power or chance to choose; choice; as, to give the child his *preference.* **3** The thing or person that is preferred.

pref·er·en·tial \ˌpref-r-'ench-l\ *adj.* **1** Of or relating to preference. **2** Showing preference; as, *preferential* treatment. **3** Creating or employing preference; as, a *preferential* tariff. **4** Showing one's preference or order of choice, as of candidates in an election; as, a *preferential* ballot. — **pref·er·en·tial·ly** \-'ench-l-ē\ *adv.*

pre·fer·ment \prē-'fər-mənt\ *n.* **1** A preferring or advancing, as in office; promotion. **2** A position, appointment, or office of honor or profit.

pre·fig·ure \(')prē-'fig-yər, -'fig-r\ *v.;* **pre·fig·ured; pre·fig·ur·ing** \-yər-ing, -r(-)ing\. **1** To show, suggest, or announce by a previous type, form, or likeness; to foreshadow. Other religions *prefigured* the Christian Easter. **2** To picture or imagine beforehand; as, to *prefigure* the desolation of an atomic war. — **pre·fig·ur·a·tion** \(ˌ)prē-ˌfig-yə-'rāsh-n, -ˌfig-r-'āsh-n\ *n.*

pre·fix \'prē-ˌfiks, prē-'fiks\ *v.* To put at the beginning; to place before; as, to *prefix* a syllable to a word. — \'prē-ˌfiks\ *n.* Something put at the beginning; especially, one or more sounds or letters combined with the beginning of a word, as the syllable *un-* in "unnecessary".

preg·na·ble \'preg-nəb-l\ *adj.* Capable of being taken or captured; vulnerable.

preg·nan·cy \'preg-nən-sē\ *n.; pl.* **preg·nan·cies.** The condition of being pregnant.

preg·nant \'preg-nənt\ *adj.* **1** Having young in the uterus; carrying unborn offspring. **2** Full of ideas; fertile; inventive; as, a *pregnant* mind. **3** Full of meaning or significance; as, *pregnant* words. — **preg·nant·ly,** *adv.*

pre·heat \(')prē-'hēt\ *v.* To heat beforehand; as, to put a pie into a *preheated* oven.

pre·hen·sile \prē-'hen(t)s-l\ *adj.* Adapted for grasping, especially by wrapping around; as, the *prehensile* tail of certain monkeys.

pre·his·tor·ic \ˌprē-(h)is-'tȯr-ik, -'tär-\ *adj.* Of, relating to, or existing in the period before written history begins; as, *prehistoric* animals. — **pre·his·tor·i·cal** \-ik-l\ *adj.* — **pre·his·tor·i·cal·ly** \-ik-l(-)ē\ *adv.*

pre·judge \(')prē-'jəj\ *v.;* **pre·judged; pre·judg·ing.** To judge before full or sufficient examination; to pass judgment on beforehand. — **pre·judg·ment** or **pre·judge·ment** \-mənt\ *n.*

prej·u·dice \'prej-əd-əs\ *n.* **1** Injury or damage due to a judgment or action of another; as, to agree to something without *prejudice* to one's rights. **2** A judgment or opinion formed beforehand; a favoring or dislike of one side of a question for unfair reasons or without full knowledge of the facts; bias. — *v.;* **prej·u·diced; prej·u·dic·ing. 1** To hurt, harm, or damage by some judgment or action. **2** To cause to have a prejudice; to bias.

prej·u·di·cial \ˌprej-ə-'dish-l\ *adj.* Tending to injure or impair; hurtful; damaging. — **prej·u·di·cial·ly** \-'dish-l-ē\ *adv.*

prel·a·cy \'prel-ə-sē\ *n.; pl.* **prel·a·cies. 1** The station or dignity of a prelate. **2** Prelates as a body or class. **3** Church government by prelates.

prel·ate \'prel-ət\ *n.* A clergyman of high rank, as a bishop.

pre·lim·i·nary \prē-'lim-ə-ˌner-ē\ *adj.* Preceding the main part; introductory; as, the *preliminary* games before the championship playoffs. — *n.; pl.* **pre·lim·i·nar·ies.** Something preliminary, introductory, or preparatory; a preparatory step or action; [chiefly in the plural] a preliminary examination. — **pre·lim·i·nar·i·ly** \-ˌlim-ə-'ner-ə-lē\ *adv.*

prel·ude \'prel-ˌyüd, 'prel-ˌüd, 'prē-ˌlüd; *also, especially in senses 2 and 3,* 'prā-ˌlüd, 'prāl-ˌyüd\ *n.* **1** Something preceding and preparing for more important matter; a preface. The wind was a *prelude* to the storm. **2** A short musical piece, especially an introductory section, as of an opera. **3** A piece, especially an organ solo, played at the beginning of a church service. — *v.;* **prel·ud·ed; prel·ud·ing.** To give, play, or serve as a prelude to.

pre·ma·ture \ˌprē-mə-'tu̇r, -'tyu̇r, -'chu̇r\ *adj.* Happening, coming, existing, or done before the usual or proper time; too early; as, a *premature* fall of snow. — **pre·ma·ture·ly,** *adv.*

pre·med·i·cal \(')prē-'med-ik-l\ *adj.* Coming before medicine; especially, preceding and preparing for the regular study of medicine; as, the *premedical* course in a university.

pre·med·i·tate \(')prē-'med-ə-ˌtāt\ *v.;* **pre·med·i-**

tat·ed; **pre·med·i·tat·ing**. To think about and plan beforehand; to deliberate, as before acting or speaking; as, *premeditated* murder. — **pre·med·i·ta·tion** \(ˌ)prē-ˌmed-ə-ˈtāsh-n\ *n.*

pre·mier \prē-ˈmir, -ˈmyir, ˈprē-mē-ər; ˈprim-ē-ər, ˈprem-, -ē-ˌer\ *adj.* **1** First in position or importance; chief; leading. **2** First in time; earliest. — *n.* The first or chief minister of government; a prime minister.

pre·miere \prə-ˈmyer, pre-ˈmyer, prē-ˈmir\ *adj.* First; chief; as, a *premiere* performance. — *n.* A first performance, as of a play.

prem·ise \ˈprem-əs\ *n.* **1** A statement of fact, made as a basis for argument or reasoning. **2** [in the plural] In law, matters previously stated or set forth, as in a deed. **3** [in the plural] In law, the property transferred in a deed, as a piece of land or real estate; sometimes, a building; as, to insure the *premises.* — \ˈprem-əs, prē-ˈmīz\ *v.;* **prem·ised**; **prem·is·ing**. To set forth beforehand or as an introduction or explanation; to offer as premises, especially to an argument.

pre·mi·um \ˈprē-mē-əm\ *n.* [From Latin *praemium* meaning "booty", "profit", "reward".] **1** A prize to be gained by some special merit. **2** Something offered for the loan of money; a bonus. **3** A sum over and above the stated or par value of anything; as, to sell stock at a *premium.* **4** The amount paid for an insurance contract. — **at a premium**. Above par; unusually valuable; rare, or hard to get. Tickets were *at a premium.*

pre·mo·lar \(ˈ)prē-ˈmōl-r\ *n.* In man, a bicuspid tooth.

pre·mo·ni·tion \ˌprē-mə-ˈnish-n, ˌprem-ə-\ *n.* A previous warning or notice; foreboding; presentiment. — **pre·mon·i·to·ry** \prē-ˈmän-ə-ˌtōr-ē, -ˌtȯr-ē\ *adj.*

pre·na·tal \(ˈ)prē-ˈnāt-l\ *adj.* Before birth.

pre·oc·cu·pied \(ˈ)prē-ˈäk-yə-ˌpīd\ *adj.* **1** Lost in thought; absorbed; as, *preoccupied* by worries. **2** Already occupied. — **pre·oc·cu·pa·tion** \(ˌ)prē-ˌäk-yə-ˈpāsh-n\ *n.*

pre·oc·cu·py \(ˈ)prē-ˈäk-yə-ˌpī\ *v.;* **pre·oc·cu·pied** \-ˌpīd\; **pre·oc·cu·py·ing**. **1** To engage, occupy, or engross the attention of beforehand. **2** To take possession of before another.

pre·or·dain \ˌprē-ȯr-ˈdān\ *v.* To foreordain; to decree beforehand; as, a ceremony *preordained* by law. — **pre·or·di·na·tion** \(ˌ)prē-ˌȯrd-n-ˈāsh-n\ *n.*

prep. Abbreviation for *preposition.*

prepaid. Past tense and past part. of *prepay.*

prep·a·ra·tion \ˌprep-r-ˈāsh-n\ *n.* **1** The act or process of making ready in advance, for some special purpose. **2** Preparedness; readiness; as, in good *preparation* for war. **3** Something which prepares; as, to finish *preparations* for a journey. **4** Something which is prepared for a particular purpose; as, a medicinal *preparation.*

pre·par·a·to·ry \prē-ˈpar-ə-ˌtōr-ē, -ˌtȯr-ē\ *adj.* **1** Preparing, or serving to prepare, for something; as, *preparatory* training for a boxer. **2** Undergoing training or teaching for something which is to follow; being made ready; as, a *preparatory* student.

preparatory school. **1** A school, usually private, preparing students primarily for college. **2** In England, a school preparing young children for entrance into a public school.

pre·pare \prē-ˈpar, -ˈper\ *v.;* **pre·pared**; **pre·par·ing**. **1** To make ready beforehand for some particular purpose; as, to *prepare* for college. **2** To equip; as, to be *prepared* for a camping trip. **3** To make or form, usually for some special purpose; as, to *prepare* a medicine; to *prepare* meals.

pre·par·ed·ness \prē-ˈpar-əd-nəs, -ˈper-; -ˈpard-nəs, -ˈperd-\ *n.* The state of being prepared; especially, readiness of the armed forces to meet and counter any act of war.

pre·pay \(ˈ)prē-ˈpā\ *v.;* **pre·paid** \-ˈpād\; **pre·pay·ing**. To pay, or pay for, in advance; as, several *prepaid* shipments of rugs. — **pre·pay·ment** \-ˈpā-mənt\ *n.*

pre·pon·der·ance \prē-ˈpänd-r(-)ən(t)s\ *n.* **1** Excess or superiority, as of weight, influence, or numbers; as, a great *preponderance* of military power. **2** Majority; greatest amount; as, the *preponderance* of the evidence.

pre·pon·der·ant \prē-ˈpänd-r(-)ənt\ *adj.* Predominant; outweighing others; of the greatest importance. — **pre·pon·der·ant·ly**, *adv.*

prep·o·si·tion \ˌprep-ə-ˈzish-n\ *n.* A word that joins with a noun or a pronoun to form a phrase that typically modifies a noun, adjective, or verb and expresses a relation such as that of position, direction, or time; as *of* in "a piece of pie", *at* in "safe at home", or *to* in "children going to school".

prep·o·si·tion·al \ˌprep-ə-ˈzish-n(-)əl\ *adj.* Like or formed with a preposition; as, a *prepositional* phrase. — **prep·o·si·tion·al·ly** \-n(-)ə-lē\ *adv.*

pre·pos·sess \ˌprēp-ə-ˈzes\ *v.* **1** To possess or occupy before another. **2** To preoccupy the mind so as to preclude other thoughts; to bias; to prejudice, especially favorably.

pre·pos·sess·ing \ˌprēp-ə-ˈzes-ing\ *adj.* Inviting favor; attractive; as, a young man with a *prepossessing* manner. — **pre·pos·sess·ing·ly**, *adv.*

pre·pos·ses·sion \ˌprēp-ə-ˈzesh-n\ *n.* Preoccupation of the mind by an opinion or impression already formed; prejudice; bias.

pre·pos·ter·ous \prē-ˈpäst-r(-)əs\ *adj.* Contrary to common sense; foolish; absurd; as, a *preposterous* suggestion. — **pre·pos·ter·ous·ly**, *adv.*

prep school \ˈprep\. A preparatory school.

pre·req·ui·site \(ˈ)prē-ˈrek-wə-zət\ *adj.* Required beforehand; necessary as a preliminary to something else; as, to have completed all the *prerequisite* courses for one's major subject. — *n.* Something that is prerequisite.

pre·rog·a·tive \prē-ˈräg-ət-iv\ *n.* A superior privilege or advantage; especially, a right attached to an office or rank; as, a royal *prerogative.* It is a woman's *prerogative* to change her mind.

pres. Abbreviation for *present.*

pres·age \'pres-ij\ *n.* **1** An omen or sign. **2** A feeling that something is about to happen; a foreboding; a foreknowledge. **3** A prediction. — \'pres-ij, prē-'sāj\ *v.;* **pres·aged; pres·ag·ing. 1** To give an omen or sign of something; to indicate beforehand. Thunder in the distance *presaged* a storm. **2** To have a presentiment of; to forebode. **3** To foretell; to predict.

pres·by·ter \'prez-bət-r, 'pres-\ *n.* [From Late Latin — see *priest.*] **1** An elder in the early Christian church. **2** Formerly, a minister or an elder in a Presbyterian church.

pres·by·te·ri·an \ˌprez-bə-'tir-ē-ən, ˌpres-\ *adj.* Of or relating to a presbyter or to church government by presbyters.

pres·by·te·ri·an·ism \ˌprez-bə-'tir-ē-ə-ˌniz-m, ˌpres-\ *n.* **1** Church government by presbyters. **2** A belief in or an adherence to such government.

pres·by·tery \'prez-bə-ˌter-ē, 'pres-\ *n.; pl.* **pres·by·ter·ies. 1** In Presbyterian churches, a court consisting of the ministers and representative elders from the congregations within a district. **2** The jurisdiction of such a court. **3** The part of a church reserved for officiating priests. **4** A rectory, or priest's residence.

pre·school \'prē-'skül\ *adj.* Of or relating to the period in a child's life from infancy to about the age of five, ordinarily preceding attendance at school. — \'prē-ˌskül\ *n.* A kindergarten or nursery school where children of preschool age are entered for social and educational training.

pre·science \'prēsh-n(t)s, 'presh-\ *n.* A foreknowledge of events; a knowledge of the future. — **pre·scient** \-nt\ *adj.*

pre·scribe \prē-'skrīb\ *v.;* **pre·scribed; pre·scrib·ing. 1** To lay down as a guide, direction, or a rule of action; to order; to dictate; as, to *prescribe* longer hours of rest. **2** To order or direct the use of something as a remedy. The doctor *prescribed* hot drinks and rest. — **pre·scrib·er** \-'skrīb-r\ *n.*

pre·scrip·tion \prē-'skripsh-n\ *n.* **1** A prescribing. **2** A written direction or order for the preparation and use of a medicine. **3** The medicine prescribed. **4** The establishment of a claim or title by use during a time fixed by law. **5** The right or title thus acquired. — **pre·scrip·tive** \-'skrip-tiv\ *adj.*

pres·ence \'prez-n(t)s\ *n.* **1** The fact or condition of being in a certain place. No one noticed the stranger's *presence.* **2** The immediate nearness or vicinity of a person. **3** The sum of one's personal qualities; a person's appearance or bearing; as, a man of noble *presence.* **4** An apparition; a ghost.

presence of mind. The ability to think clearly and act quickly in an emergency or in a dangerous situation; unshaken calmness of thought.

pres·ent \'prez-nt\ *adj.* **1** Being before a person, in his sight, or near at hand; being at a certain place and not elsewhere. The pupils are all *present.* **2** Not past or future; now going on or existing; as, *present* plans. **3** Typically expressing action or state in the time that now is or the time of speaking or writing, habitual action, or general truth; as, the *present* tense of a verb. — *n.* **1** The present time; as, a book that reviews the progress of science from its beginnings to the *present.* **2** The present tense or a verb in it. **3** In law, a deed, a lease, or other writing.

pre·sent \prē-'zent\ *v.* **1** To introduce one person to another; to take oneself into another's presence; to introduce formally; as, to *present* oneself before the chairman. **2** To bring before the public; as, to *present* a play. **3** To make a gift to; as, to *present* someone with a gold watch. **4** To give as a gift; as, to *present* a gold watch to someone. **5** To show; to display; to offer to view; as, a person who *presents* a fine appearance. **6** To submit for consideration or action; as, to *present* a plan.

pres·ent \'prez-nt\ *n.* Anything that is given or presented; a gift; as, Christmas *presents.*

— The words *gift* and *donation* are synonyms of *present: gift* may apply to anything of value given to another person for his use or enjoyment with no thought of receiving anything in return; *present* most often suggests something given as a compliment or as an expression of one's affection or admiration; *donation* usually refers to a sum of money given to some public, religious, or charitable organization and often, especially if a large sum, presented publicly in the name of the donor.

pre·sent·a·ble \prē-'zent-əb-l\ *adj.* **1** Capable of being presented or displayed. Details of the plan are so disorganized that they are not *presentable* to the committee. **2** In a condition to pass inspection; as, to make a room *presentable.* **3** Satisfying or pleasing in appearance.

pre·sen·ta·tion \ˌprē-ˌzen-'tāsh-n, ˌprez-n-, ˌprēz-n-\ *n.* **1** A presenting or a being presented. **2** A formal introduction of one person to another. **3** A presenting or offering of something; a giving; as, a *presentation* of a watch. **4** A representation; an exhibition; a showing; as, a *presentation* of a play. **5** Something that is presented; a present; a gift.

pres·ent-day \'prez-nt-ˌdā\ *adj.* Now existing or occurring; current.

pre·sen·ti·ment \prē-'zent-m-ənt\ *n.* A feeling, especially of fear, that something will happen; a premonition.

pres·ent·ly \'prez-nt-lē\ *adv.* **1** *Dial.* At once; immediately. **2** Soon; shortly; before long.

pre·sent·ment \prē-'zent-mənt\ *n.* **1** A presenting or a being presented. **2** A setting forth to view or notice. **3** Something that is presented or exhibited.

pres·ent participle \'prez-nt\. The participle that in English is formed by adding *-ing* to the verb and that indicates action in progress, as in "He is *going*".

present perfect tense. The tense that in English is formed with *have* or *has* and that indicates action completed at the time of speaking or writing, as in "The train *has arrived*"

present tense. The tense that typically indicates action or state in the time that now is or the time of speaking or writing, habitual action, or general truth, as in "I *write*", "Spring *is coming*", "He *goes* home every Saturday", or "Air *expands* when heated".

pres·er·va·tion \ˌprez-r-ˈvāsh-n\ *n.* **1** A preserving or a being preserved. **2** Safekeeping; a keeping of something from injury or decay.

pre·serv·a·tive \prē-ˈzər-vət-iv\ *adj.* Having the power of preserving; tending to preserve. — *n.* A preservative substance or agent.

pre·serve \prē-ˈzərv\ *v.;* **pre·served**; **pre·serv·ing. 1** To keep or save from injury or ruin; to protect. **2** To keep from decaying. **3** To can, pickle, or otherwise prepare fruits or vegetables for keeping; as, *preserved* peaches. **4** To maintain; to keep up; as, to *preserve* silence. — *n.* **1** Whole fruits canned or made into jams, or jellies; as, raspberry *preserves.* **2** A place in which some part of nature, as wildlife or trees, is preserved, as for sport or for food. — **pre·serv·a·ble** \-ˈzər-vəb-l\ *adj.* — **pre·serv·er** \-ˈzərv-r\ *n.*

pre·side \prē-ˈzīd\ *v.;* **pre·sid·ed**; **pre·sid·ing. 1** To occupy the place of authority, as of president. **2** To act as chairman of a meeting. **3** To occupy the leading place, especially as the director or featured performer at a concert; as, to *preside* over an orchestra; to *preside* at the piano.

pres·i·den·cy \ˈprez-ə-dən-sē, ˈprez-dən-, -ə-ˌden-sē\ *n.; pl.* **pres·i·den·cies. 1** The office of president. **2** The term during which a president holds office.

pres·i·dent \ˈprez-ə-dənt, ˈprez-dənt, -ə-ˌdent\ *n.* **1** A person who presides over a meeting. **2** The chief officer of a company or society. **3** [often with a capital] The chief executive officer of a modern republic.

pres·i·den·tial \ˌprez-ə-ˈdench-l\ *adj.* Of or relating to a president or presidency; as, a *presidential* appointment; a *presidential* candidate.

pre·sid·i·um \prə-ˈsid-ē-əm, -ˈzid-\ *n.* In the Soviet Union, any permanent administrative committee, especially of the government.

press \ˈpres\ *v.* **1** To force into service, especially military or naval service. **2** To use in a way not in accordance with the nature of the thing used; as, a knife *pressed* to do duty as a screwdriver.

press \ˈpres\ *v.* **1** To act upon by steady pushing; to bear upon; to squeeze. **2** To force; to compel; as, to be *pressed* by business to return. **3** To affect as if with a weight or burden; to distress; as, hard *pressed* by poverty. **4** To squeeze so as to force out the juice or contents of; as, to *press* oranges. **5** To squeeze out; as, to *press* juice from grapes. **6** To flatten out or smooth by bearing down upon; especially, to smooth by ironing; as, to *press* clothes. **7** To request earnestly; to urge strongly; as, to *press* someone to go along. **8** To urge on; as, to *press* a horse to greater speed. **9** To lay stress upon; to emphasize; to urge; as, to *press* a point in an argument. **10** To move insistently; as, to *press* forward. **11** To bear down; as, to *press* on a blister. **12** To require speed or haste in action. Time *presses.* — *n.* **1** A crowd; a throng. **2** The act of pressing; pressure. **3** Any machine by which material is stamped or pressed into some shape. **4** Any machine for making impressions, especially on paper, from an inked surface, as of types. **5** A place or building containing such a machine or machines. **6** A closet or case for holding clothing; as, a clothes *press.* **7** Newspapers and magazines collectively.

copying press

press agent. A person engaged by another person or by an organization to get publicity, as through articles in the press, for his employer.

press·er \ˈpres-r\ *n.* One that presses.

press·ing \ˈpres-ing\ *adj.* Urgent; demanding immediate attention. — **press·ing·ly,** *adv.*

press·man \ˈpres-mən\ *n.; pl.* **press·men** \-mən\. A man who operates or has charge of a press.

pres·sure \ˈpresh-r\ *n.* **1** The action of pressing; as, done by slow steady *pressure.* **2** The condition of being pressed; as, kept under *pressure.* **3** A painful feeling of weight or burden; oppression; distress. **4** Any burdensome or restricting force or influence; as, the *pressure* of taxes; the constant *pressures* of modern life. **5** Urgency, as of business. **6** The force exerted by a body over the surface of another body; especially, such force exerted by air, steam, or gas; as, atmospheric *pressure;* the *pressure* of steam in a boiler.

pressure cooker. A utensil for cooking or preserving foods by the action of steam held under pressure.

pres·sur·ize \ˈpresh-r-ˌīz\ *v.;* **pres·sur·ized**; **pres·sur·iz·ing.** To maintain an inside atmospheric pressure, as in the sealed cabin of an aircraft, nearly equal to the normal pressure at ground level. — **pres·sur·i·za·tion** \ˌpresh-r-ə-ˈzāsh-n\ *n.*

pres·ti·dig·i·ta·tion \ˌpres-tə-ˌdij-ə-ˈtāsh-n\ *n.* The art of the stage magician; sleight of hand. — **pres·ti·dig·i·ta·tor** \-ˈdij-ə-ˌtāt-r\ *n.*

pres·tige \(ˈ)pres-ˈtēzh, -ˈtēj\ *n.* Importance in the estimation of others resulting from one's achievements, rank in society, or associations; standing among one's fellows; distinction.

pres·to \ˈpres-ˌtō\ *adv.* **1** Quickly. **2** In music, at a rapid pace. — *adj.* Performed at a rapid pace.

pre·sum·a·ble \prē-ˈzü-məb-l\ *adj.* That may be taken for granted; probable. — **pre·sum·a·bly** \-mə-blē\ *adv.*

pre·sume \prē-ˈzüm\ *v.;* **pre·sumed**; **pre·sum·ing. 1** To undertake without leave or clear justification; to dare; to venture; as, to *presume* to question the authority of a superior. **2** To suppose to be true without proof. Our law *presumes* all persons charged with crime to be innocent until they are proved guilty. **3** To act or behave boldly without reason for doing so; especially, to take liberties; as, to *presume* upon another's time.

pre·sum·ed·ly \prē-ˈzü-məd-lē\ *adv.* Presumably.

pre·sum·ing \prē-ˈzü-ming\ *adj.* Presumptuous; forward.

pre·sump·tion \prē-ˈzəm(p)sh-n\ *n.* **1** Presumptuous quality or state of mind; too great pride, hope, or confidence. **2** Strong grounds for believing something to be so in spite of lack of proof. **3** A conclusion reached on such grounds; something that is believed to be so but not proved.

pre·sump·tive \prē-ˈzəm(p)-tiv\ *adj.* **1** Based on presumption; as, *presumptive* evidence. **2** Presumed to be so, as in *heir presumptive.* — **pre·sump·tive·ly**, *adv.*

pre·sump·tu·ous \prē-ˈzəm(p)-chə-wəs, -ˈzəm(p)-chəs\ *adj.* Too proud, self-confident, or forward; taking undue liberties; presuming. — **pre·sump·tu·ous·ly**, *adv.*

pre·sup·pose \ˌprē-sə-ˈpōz\ *v.;* **pre·sup·posed**; **pre·sup·pos·ing.** To suppose beforehand; to take for granted; as, a biology book that *presupposes* a knowledge of general science in its readers. — **pre·sup·po·si·tion** \(ˌ)prē-ˌsəp-ə-ˈzish-n\ *n.*

pre·tend \prē-ˈtend\ *v.* **1** To make believe; to sham. Let's *pretend* we're pirates. **2** To represent falsely; to put forward as true something that is not true; as, to *pretend* friendship. **3** To lay claim, as to a throne or to a title.

pre·tend·er \prē-ˈtend-r\ *n.* A person who pretends; especially, one who claims.

pre·tense or **pre·tence** \prē-ˈten(t)s, ˈprē-ˌten(t)s\ *n.* **1** A claim; a stated or implied assertion. **2** Display; show, especially dishonest show; as, a man entirely free from *pretense.* **3** An aim; attempt; as, no *pretense* at completeness. **4** Pretext; excuse. What was his *pretense* this time? **5** Deception; false show; as, under a *pretense* of illness.

pre·ten·sion \prē-ˈtench-n\ *n.* **1** A pretext. **2** A claim; especially, a claim to something admirable; as, a ne'er-do-well with *pretensions* to great knowledge. **3** Sham; lack of honesty; pretentiousness; as, a man who was all *pretension.*

pre·ten·tious \prē-ˈtench-əs\ *adj.* **1** Making or having claims, as to excellence or worth; showy; ostentatious; as, a *pretentious* house. **2** Ambitious; as, a *pretentious* project. — **pre·ten·tious·ly**, *adv.*

pret·er·it or **pret·er·ite** \ˈpret-r-ət\ *adj.* In grammar, especially of some foreign languages, past; expressing action or state in a time gone by but not indicating whether the action is viewed as complete or incomplete; as, the *preterit* tense. — *n.* The preterit tense or a verb in it.

pre·ter·nat·u·ral \ˌprēt-r-ˈnach-r(-)əl\ *adj.* Beyond what is natural or normal; especially, strange and not easily explained but not miraculous.

pre·text \ˈprē-ˌtekst\ *n.* A purpose stated in order to conceal the true purpose; a pretense.

pret·ty \ˈprit-ē, ˈpůrt-ē\ *adj.;* **pret·ti·er**; **pret·ti·est.** [From Old English *praettig* meaning "sly", "cunning", "smart".] Delicately or gracefully pleasing; attractive to the eye or ear; as, a *pretty* face; a *pretty* tune. — *n.; pl.* **pret·ties.** A pretty or dainty person or thing. — \ˈpůrt-ē, pərt-ē, ˈprit-ē\ *adv.* In some degree; rather; fairly; as, *pretty* good; *pretty* sure. — **pret·ti·ly** \ˈprit-l-ē\ *adv.*

pret·zel \ˈprets-l\ *n.* A brittle cracker that is twisted, glazed, and salted on the surface.

pretzel

pre·vail \prē-ˈvāl\ *v.* **1** To triumph; to win a victory; as, to *prevail* over one's enemies. **2** To succeed; to become successful or effective. Hard work and brains are bound to *prevail.* **3** To urge successfully; to persuade; as, to *prevail* upon a person to play the piano. **4** To be or become usual, common, or widespread, as a belief or a custom.

pre·vail·ing \prē-ˈvā-ling\ *adj.* **1** Having influence or power; effective. **2** Current; widespread; most frequent; as, the *prevailing* customs; an area where the *prevailing* winds are trade winds.

prev·a·lent \ˈprev-l(-)ənt\ *adj.* Generally or extensively existing; occurring often or over a wide area. — **prev·a·lence** \-l(-)ən(t)s\ *n.*

pre·var·i·cate \prē-ˈvar-ə-ˌkāt\ *v.;* **pre·var·i·cat·ed**; **pre·var·i·cat·ing.** To wander from the truth; to speak evasively; to lie. — **pre·var·i·ca·tor** \-ˌkāt-r\ *n.*

pre·var·i·ca·tion \prē-ˌvar-ə-ˈkāsh-n\ *n.* A departing from the truth; a falsehood.

pre·vent \prē-ˈvent\ *v.* To keep from happening; to hinder; to stop; as, to *prevent* accidents. Rain *prevented* the plane from taking off. — **pre·vent·a·ble** or **pre·vent·i·ble** \-əb-l\ *adj.*

pre·vent·a·tive \prē-ˈvent-ət-iv\ *adj.* or *n.* Preventive.

pre·ven·tion \prē-ˈvench-n\ *n.* **1** The act of preventing or thwarting. **2** That which prevents something from happening.

pre·ven·tive \prē-ˈvent-iv\ *adj.* Tending or used to prevent; precautionary; as, to take *preventive* measures against disease. — *n.* A preventive measure; something that prevents; as, vaccines and other *preventives.*

pre·view \ˈprē-ˌvyü\ *n.* **1** A showing of something, as a motion picture or a collection of paintings, before it is put on public exhibition. **2** Also **pre·vue** \ˈprē-ˌvyü\. A showing of small parts from a motion picture advertised for future appearance. — *v.* To see or show beforehand.

pre·vi·ous \ˈprē-vē-əs\ *adj.* Earlier; former; as, a *previous* lesson. — **pre·vi·ous·ly**, *adv.*

pre·war \ˈprē-ˈwȯr\ *adj.* Of or relating to the period before a war; as, *prewar* prices.

prey \ˈprā\ *n.* **1** Any animal hunted or killed by another animal for food. **2** A person seized or influenced by another person; a victim. **3** The act of seizing or pouncing upon, as to kill for food; as, birds of *prey.* — *v.* **1** To raid, as a place or ship, for booty; to plunder. **2** To hunt, seize, or devour anything; as, cats *prey* upon robins. **3** To have a harmful or wasting effect. Fear *preys* on the mind.

price \ˈprīs\ *n.* [ME *pris* meaning "prize", "price", and borrowed from Old French, where it is derived from Latin *pretium* meaning "worth", "value" — see *prize.*] **1** Value; worth; as, gems of great *price*. **2** The quantity of one thing, especially money, given or asked in payment for something else. **3** A reward. **4** The cost at which something is done; as, to win a victory at the *price* of many lives.

— The word *charge* is a synonym of *price:* both these terms refer to whatever is given or asked as payment for something else; *price* usually applies to the cost of goods or commodities; *charge* is likely to refer to the cost of services, as delivery or postage.

— *v.;* **priced**; **pric·ing**. **1** To set a price on a thing. **2** To ask the price of a thing.

price·less \'prīs-ləs\ *adj.* **1** Too valuable to have a price; not to be bought at any price. **2** Very amusing or absurd; as, a *priceless* remark.

prick \'prik\ *n.* **1** A mark made by a pointed instrument; a point; a dot; especially, a tiny hole or wound; as, a pin *prick*. **2** Something sharp or pointed. **3** A pricking or a sensation of being pricked; a stinging pain; as, to feel the *prick* of conscience. — *v.* **1** To pierce slightly with something sharp or pointed. **2** To sting, as with remorse; to make repentant and regretful. The thief's conscience *pricked* him. **3** To urge on a horse by spurs. **4** To point upwards; to raise. The horse *pricked* up his ears. — **prick up one's ears.** To begin to listen alertly.

prick·er \'prik-r\ *n.* **1** One that pricks. **2** A thorn; a prickle; a spine.

prick·le \'prik-l\ *n.* **1** A small, sharp point; a thorn or spine. **2** A pricking sensation. — *v.;* **prick·led**; **prick·ling** \-l(-)ing\. To prick; to tingle.

prick·ly \'prik-lē\ *adj.;* **prick·li·er**; **prick·li·est.** **1** Full of or covered with prickles, as blackberry bushes. **2** Pricking; stinging; as, a *prickly* sensation.

prickly heat. An inflammation around the sweat ducts, causing pimples, itching, and tingling.

prickly pear. **1** Any of several flat-jointed cactus plants. **2** The pear-shaped, edible, pulpy fruit of one of these plants.

pride \'prīd\ *n.* **1** Too high an opinion of one's own ability or worth; a feeling of being better than others. **2** A proper favorable feeling of one's own worth or acts; self-respect; as, to take *pride* in doing good work. **3** A sense of pleasure that comes from some act or possession; as, to take *pride* in a son's high marks. **4** Anything of which a person is proud. The boy's bicycle was his *pride* and joy.

— The words *vanity* and *conceit* are synonyms of *pride: pride* may suggest either a justifiable appreciation of one's own worth, abilities, and high ideals, or an exaggeratedly high opinion of oneself and a resulting contempt for persons felt to be beneath one; *vanity* usually indicates a self-centered attitude, particularly with regard to one's appearance and accomplishments, and a desire to be noticed and admired by others; *conceit* usually suggests a strong feeling of superiority to others and a refusal to acknowledge one's weaknesses and failings.

— *v.;* **prid·ed**; **prid·ing**. To indulge (oneself) in pride; as, to *pride* oneself on one's memory.

priest \'prēst\ *n.* [From Old English *preost*, there borrowed from Late Latin *presbyter* meaning "elder" and borrowed from Greek *presbyteros* — see *presbyter*.] A person who has the authority to conduct religious rites.

priest·ess \'prēs-təs\ *n.* A woman priest, especially of the ancient pagans.

priest·hood \'prēst-ˌhůd, 'prēs-ˌtůd\ *n.* **1** The office or the duties of a priest. **2** Priests collectively.

priest·ly \'prēst-lē\ *adj.* Of or relating to priests; befitting or becoming a priest.

prig \'prig\ *n.* A self-sufficient person who irritates others by being too careful or rigid about things, as speech or manners. — **prig·gery** \'prig-r-ē\ *n.* — **prig·gish** \'prig-ish\ *adj.* — **prig·gish·ly**, *adv.*

prim \'prim\ *adj.;* **prim·mer**; **prim·mest.** Very particular, or too particular, as about one's appearance or conduct; as, a *prim* old lady.

pri·ma·cy \'prī-mə-sē\ *n.; pl.* **pri·ma·cies.** **1** The condition of being first, as in time, place, or rank. **2** The office, status, or dignity of a bishop of the highest rank. **3** In the Roman Catholic church, the supreme power of the pope, or bishop of Rome, over the bishops of all other sees.

pri·ma don·na \ˌprim-ə 'dän-ə, ˌprē-mə\; *pl.* **pri·ma don·nas.** **1** A principal female singer, as in an opera. **2** A self-centered, vain, temperamental person, especially a woman.

pri·mal \'prīm-l\ *adj.* **1** First; original. **2** Most important; chief.

pri·mar·i·ly \prī-'mer-ə-lē\ *adv.* In the first place; originally; fundamentally.

pri·mary \'prī-ˌmer-ē, 'prīm-r(-)ē\ *adj.* [From Latin *primarius* meaning literally "of first rank" and derived from *primus* meaning "first" — see *primer*.] **1** First in order of time or development; primitive; original; as, the *primary* meaning of a word. **2** First in importance; chief; principal; as, *primary* reasons; *primary* planets. **3** First in order, especially as being preparatory to something higher; as, the *primary* grades in school. **4** Basic; fundamental; from which other divisions or combinations are made; as, *primary* colors. **5** In an induction coil or transformer, of or relating to the inducing current or its circuit. **6** Of or relating to the principal feathers of a bird's wing, borne on the outer joint. **7** Of stress or accent, like that on the first syllable of *penetrate* \'pen-ə-ˌtrāt\. — *n.; pl.* **pri·mar·ies.** **1** A primary election. **2** One of the primary colors. **3** A planet as distinguished from its satellites. **4** In electricity, a primary coil. **5** A primary feather or quill.

primary colors. A set of colors, from which all other colors may be described or made up, as a set consisting of red, yellow, green and blue, together with black and white.

primary election. A preliminary election in which voters directly nominate for office the candidates of their own party.

pri·mate \'prī-ˌmāt, -mət\ *n.* **1** A bishop, usually an archbishop, who is the highest in rank and dignity in a group of dioceses or in a nation. **2** One of an order of mammals consisting of man and the apes, monkeys, marmosets, and lemurs.

prime \'prīm\ *n.* **1** The first part of anything; the earliest stage. **2** The spring of life; youth. **3** The period in life when a person is best in health, looks, or strength; as, a man in his *prime.* **4** The best thing or part; as, the *prime* of the flock. **5** Any of the first set of usually 60 equal parts into which a unit, especially a degree, is divided; a minute. **6** The accent [′] used to denote such a fraction and for other purposes, as a′ in algebra. **7** A prime number. — *adj.* **1** First in time or order; original; as, the *prime* cost. **2** First in importance, rank, or quality; as, the *prime* minister; *prime* beef. **3** Divisible by no number except itself or 1. The number "7" is a *prime* number. — *v.;* **primed; prim·ing. 1** To put a thing into working condition by doing some necessary operation first; as, to *prime* a pump by pouring water into it. **2** To apply the first color or coating, as in painting. **3** To prepare, instruct, or coach beforehand; as, to *prime* a witness before he testifies. — **prime·ly,** *adv.*

prime meridian. A meridian from whose intersection with the equator longitude is counted both east and west.

prime minister. In many countries, the chief officer of the government; a premier.

prim·er \'prīm-r\ *n.* **1** A person or thing that primes something, as a cap containing powder to ignite an explosive. **2** Any substance, as paint or sizing, used or intended for use as priming.

prim·er \'prim-r\ *n.* [From medieval English where it was used to name a prayer book (from which children also learned to read), there borrowed from medieval Latin *primarium,* from the neuter of Latin *primarius* "of first rank", "primary" — see *primary.*] **1** A small book for teaching children to read. **2** A book of first instructions on any subject.

pri·me·val \prī-'mēv-l\ *adj.* Belonging to the first ages; primal; as, a *primeval* forest. — **pri·me·val·ly** \-'mēv-l-ē\ *adv.*

prim·ing \'prī-ming\ *n.* **1** The act of a person who primes something, as a pump. **2** The powder or other material used to fire a charge, as in a gun. **3** A first coating, as of paint, varnish, or sizing, laid on a surface to prepare it for finishing coats.

prim·i·tive \'prim-ət-iv\ *adj.* **1** Original; first; belonging to very early times; as, *primitive* men. **2** Like or representing early times; characterized by the rudeness or simplicity of early times; as, to live in a *primitive* manner; *primitive* tools. — *n.* **1** An artist or a work of art of a primitive period. **2** The algebraic or geometric form from which another is derived. — **prim·i·tive·ly,** *adv.*

prim·ly \'prim-lē\ *adv.* In a prim manner.

pri·mo·gen·i·ture \ˌprī-mō-'jen-əch-r\ *n.* **1** The state or fact of being the first-born of the children of the same parents. **2** The right of the first-born child to inherit his father's property; especially, an exclusive right of inheritance belonging to an eldest son.

pri·mor·di·al \prī-'mȯrd-ē-əl\ *adj* **1** First created; existing at the beginning; as, *primordial* matter. **2** First in order; primary; fundamental; as, *primordial* rights. — **pri·mor·di·al·ly** \-ē-ə-lē\ *adv.*

primp \'primp\ *v.* To dress up; to preen.

prim·rose \'prim-ˌrōz\ *n.* A perennial plant six to eight inches tall with large spoon-shaped leaves growing from the base of the stem and showy, often yellow or pink flowers on stalks having no leaves. — *adj.* **1** Of or like the primrose; flowery; gay. **2** Pale reddish yellow in color.

primrose

prin. Abbreviation for *principal.*

prince \'prin(t)s\ *n.* **1** A sovereign; a ruler. **2** A title given to the son of a sovereign or to other members of a royal family. **3** In many European countries, a nobleman of high rank. **4** A person who is very important or successful in his profession or class; as, a merchant *prince.*

prince con·sort \'kän-ˌsȯrt\. The husband of a queen who reigns in her own right.

prince·ling \'prin(t)s-ling\ *n.* A prince of little power or importance.

prince·ly \'prin(t)s-lē\ *adj.;* **prince·li·er; prince·li·est. 1** Of or relating to a prince; royal; as, *princely* birth. **2** Befitting a prince; noble; magnificent; as, *princely* manners; a *princely* sum.

prin·cess \'prin(t)s-əs, -ˌes, prin(t)s-'es\ *n.* **1** *Archaic.* A female sovereign; any woman ruler. **2** A daughter or granddaughter of a monarch; any female member of a royal family. **3** The wife of a prince.

princess royal. The eldest daughter of a sovereign.

prin·ci·pal \'prin(t)s-əp-l\ *adj.* Highest in rank, power, or importance; main; chief. — *n.* **1** A leader, chief, or head. **2** A sum of money used to earn interest or other income. **3** A chief official in a school; especially, the head of an elementary school or high school. **4** In law, a person who employs another to act for him. **5** A person who actually commits a crime, as distinguished from an accessory.

prin·ci·pal·i·ty \ˌprin(t)s-ə-'pal-ət-ē\ *n.; pl.* **prin·ci·pal·i·ties.** A territory ruled by a prince or one giving a prince his title.

prin·ci·pal·ly \'prin(t)s-əp-l(-)ē\ *adv.* Chiefly; mainly; primarily.

principal parts. In grammar, the forms of a verb from which other forms can be derived, in English including the present tense, past tense, and past participle as, *sing, sang, sung.*

prin·ci·ple \'prin(t)s-əp-l\ *n.* **1** Ultimate source or origin; as, to trace all things to the *principles,* matter and energy. **2** A truth that is the basis of other truths or theories; as, scientific *principles.* **3** A rule of moral conduct; as, a man of high *prin-*

ciples. **4** Loyalty to such rules; honor; as, to show oneself to be without *principle.* **5** Any constituent that gives a substance its essential properties; as, the active *principle* of a drug. **6** A law of nature or a scientific rule by which a machine or device is made to work; the way anything works or is made; as, a machine that works by the *principle* of the lever; the *principle* of magnetism.

prink \'pringk\ *v.* To dress up; to dress for show; to primp.

print \'print\ *n.* **1** A mark made by pressure; as, the *print* of a finger on a glass. **2** A stamp or die for molding or something that has received an impression from such a stamp or mold; as, a *print* of butter. **3** Printed form; as, to put a manuscript into *print.* **4** Printed matter, as newspapers or books. **5** Printed letters; impression taken from type; as, clear *print.* **6** A picture, copy, or design taken from an engraving or from a photographic negative. **7** Cloth upon which a design is stamped; as, a cotton *print.* — *v.* **1** To fix, put, stamp, or impress something into or on a thing. **2** To produce impressions made with type or engraved plates. **3** To publish; as, to *print* a paper; to have a book *printed.* **4** To stamp, as cloth or paper, with a design or picture by pressure. **5** To write in unconnected letters like those made by a printing press; as, to *print* one's name; to be able to *print* but not write. **6** To make from a photographic negative; as, to have some snapshots *printed.*

print·a·ble \'print-əb-l\ *adj.* **1** Capable of being printed or of being printed from. **2** Worthy or fit to be printed.

print·er \'print-r\ *n.* **1** One that prints. **2** One whose business is printing books, magazines, or newspapers. **3** One who works at printing; especially, one who sets type. **4** A device used for printing, as for making prints from photographic negatives.

print·er's dev·il \'print-rz ˌdev-l\. An apprentice or an errand boy in a printing office.

print·ing \'print-ing\ *n.* **1** The act of one that prints. **2** The business or occupation of a printer. **3** That which is printed by a press; printed words. **4** An amount printed in one continuous or prearranged operation of a press. **5** Letters printed by hand in the form of types.

printing press. A machine by which printing is done, as on paper or a similar surface, from types, wood blocks, or plates.

pri·or \'prīr\ *n.* The head of a priory of men.

pri·or \'prīr\ *adj.* Preceding in order of time; being or happening before something else; previous; as, a *prior* engagement. — **prior to.** Before; earlier than; as, *prior to* graduation.

pri·or·ess \'prīr-əs\ *n.* The head of a priory of women.

pri·or·i·ty \prī-'ȯr-ət-ē, -'är-\ *n.; pl.* **pri·or·i·ties.** **1** The quality of being prior, or coming before another person or thing, in time or importance. **2** Order of preference based on urgency, importance, or merit; the possession of certain rights or advantages over others. In time of war top *priority* is given government contracts.

pri·o·ry \'prīr-ē\ *n.; pl.* **pri·o·ries.** A house of a religious order, as a monastery or a convent, ranking next below an abbey.

prism \'priz-m\ *n.* **1** A solid whose ends, or bases, are similar, equal, and parallel polygons and whose faces are parallelograms. **2** A solid object, usually of glass or crystal and often three-sided, that reflects light and breaks it up into rainbow colors.

prism

pris·mat·ic \priz-'mat-ik\ *adj.* **1** Of, like, or relating to a prism; as, a *prismatic* lens; *prismatic* form. **2** Formed by the refraction of light through a transparent prism; as, *prismatic* colors; *prismatic* effects. **3** Highly colored; brilliant. — **pris·mat·i·cal·ly** \-ik-l(-)ē\ *adv.*

pris·on \'priz-n\ *n.* **1** A place or state of confinement, especially for criminals; as, to be sentenced to *prison* for ten years. **2** A building or group of buildings for the confinement of criminals.

pris·on·er \'priz-n(-)ər\ *n.* **1** A person under arrest, in custody, or in prison. **2** A person captured in war; a captive.

pris·tine \'pris-ˌtēn, pris-'tēn\ *adj.* Of or relating to the earliest period or condition; original; primitive; especially, having the purity or freshness of the original state.

prith·ee \'prith-ē\ *interj.* [A shortened and altered form of *I pray thee.*] *Archaic.* An exclamation of request.

pri·va·cy \'prī-və-sē\ *n.; pl.* **pri·va·cies.** **1** The condition of being apart from all other people; seclusion; as, lodgings desirable because of their *privacy.* **2** Secrecy; as, to talk together in *privacy.*

pri·vate \'prī-vət\ *adj.* **1** Concerning or for the use of a single person, company, or special group; personal; not public; as, *private* property. **2** Offering privacy; secluded; as, a *private* office. **3** Not holding any public office; as, a *private* citizen. **4** Not under public control; as, a *private* school. **5** Not publicly known; secret; as, *private* meetings. — *n.* A soldier of the lowest rank. — **in private.** Secretly.

pri·va·teer \ˌprī-və-'tir\ *n.* **1** An armed private ship permitted by its government to make war on ships of an enemy country. **2** The commander or a member of the crew of such a ship. — *v.* To cruise in or as a privateer. — **pri·va·teers·man** \-'tirz-mən\ *n.*

pri·vate·ly \'prī-vət-lē\ *adv.* In a private way; unofficially; confidentially.

pri·va·tion \prī-'vāsh-n\ *n.* The state of being deprived of something that is needed; lack of a necessity or necessities; hardship; want; extreme need. War causes severe *privations* among people.

priv·et \'priv-ət\ *n.* A branching shrub with small white flowers, related to the olive and widely used for hedges.

priv·i·lege \'priv-l(-)ij\ *n.* **1** A right or liberty granted as an advantage or favor, especially to some and not to others. **2** Any of various rights guaranteed to all persons under modern constitutional governments. — *v.;* **priv·i·leged**; **priv·i·leg·ing**. To grant a special right or liberty to; as, *privileged* groups; to be *privileged* to meet the president.

priv·i·ly \'priv-l-ē\ *adv.* Secretly.

privy \'priv-ē\ *adj. Archaic.* For private or personal use; as, a *privy* chamber. — **privy to**. Having secret knowledge of; especially, admitted as one sharing in a secret; as, to be *privy to* the details of a conspiracy. — *n.; pl.* **priv·ies**. A toilet or water closet; especially, an outhouse.

prize \'prīz\ *v.;* **prized**; **priz·ing**. [From medieval English *prisen*, there borrowed from medieval French *prisier*, *preisier*, derived from Late Latin *pretiare*, a derivative of *pretium* meaning "worth", "value" — see *price*.] **1** To set a value on. **2** To value highly; as, to *prize* a picture. — *n.* **1** Something won or to be won in a competition or lottery. **2** Any valuable possession. — *adj.* **1** Given a prize; as, a *prize* essay. **2** Worthy of a prize; as, a *prize* student. **3** Given as a prize; as, a *prize* medal.

prize \'prīz\ *n.* [From medieval English *prise*, there borrowed from Old French, meaning literally "taking", "grasping", a derivative of the past participle of *prendre* meaning "to take", "to capture".] **1** The act of capturing or taking. **2** A person or thing captured or seized. **3** In law, the capture of anything in war or the property captured.

prize \'prīz\ *v.;* **prized**; **priz·ing**. [From obsolete English *prize* meaning "crowbar", from medieval English *prise*, there borrowed from Old French, meaning literally "taking", "grasping".] To press, force, or raise, especially with a lever; to pry.

prize fight. A boxing match, especially between professionals fighting for pay. — **prize fighter**.

pro \'prō\ *adv.* [Latin.] For; on the affirmative side; as, to argue *pro* and con. — *n.* **1** One who takes the affirmative side. **2** An argument or a vote on the affirmative side.

pro \'prō\ *n.; pl.* **pros**. A professional; especially, a professional athlete.

pro-. A prefix that can mean: **1** Forward, onward, further, as in *proceed*, *prolong*, *propel*. **2** In place or stead of, as in *proconsul* or *pronoun*. **3** For, in favor of, as in *pro-American*.

pro-. A prefix that can mean: **1** Before in position, in front of, as in *proscenium*. **2** Before in time, occurring before, as in *prologue*.

prob·a·bil·i·ty \ˌpräb-ə-'bil-ət-ē\ *n.; pl.* **prob·a·bil·i·ties**. **1** The quality or condition of being probable; a likelihood. **2** Something that is or appears probable or likely.

prob·a·ble \'präb-əb-l\ *adj.* **1** Supported by evidence strong enough to make it likely, though not certain, to be true; as, a hypothesis that is *probable*. **2** Likely to happen or to have happened; being such as may or might be real or true. — **prob·a·bly** \'präb-ə-blē, 'präb-lē\ *adv.*

pro·bate \'prō-ˌbāt\ *adj.* Of or relating to a probate or a probate court. — *n.* In law, official proof, especially that submitted in a special court (**probate court**) as evidence of the last will and testament of a deceased person. — *v.;* **pro·bat·ed**; **pro·bat·ing**. To submit official proof of, as a will, before a probate court.

pro·ba·tion \prō-'bāsh-n\ *n.* **1** The action of proving; proof. **2** Any proceeding for the purpose of determining fitness; trial or a period of trial; as, to be hired on *probation*. — **pro·ba·tion·al** \-n(-)əl\ or **pro·ba·tion·ary** \-n-ˌer-ē\ *adj.*

pro·ba·tion·er \prō-'bāsh-n(-)ər\ *n.* A person who is undergoing probation or is on trial, as a newly admitted student nurse or a convicted person released on a suspended sentence.

probation officer. A court officer appointed to supervise and receive regular reports from persons whose sentences are suspended.

probe \'prōb\ *n.* **1** A slender instrument for examining a cavity, as a wound. **2** A searching examination; especially, an inquiry to discover evidence of wrongdoing; as, a legislative *probe*. **3** A device used to penetrate outer space or to send back information from it or from a celestial body. — *v.;* **probed**; **prob·ing**. **1** To examine with or as if with a probe. **2** To investigate thoroughly, as a person's motives.

probe, 1

pro·bi·ty \'prō-bət-ē, 'präb-ət-ē\ *n.* Honesty; uprightness.

prob·lem \'präb-ləm, -ˌlem\ *n.* **1** A question to be worked out or solved. **2** A question, matter, or person that is hard to understand or deal with. **3** In mathematics, something to be worked out or solved; as, a *problem* in arithmetic. — *adj.* **1** Dealing with a problem or problems; especially, having a plot presenting a problem of human conduct or social justice; as, a *problem* novel or play. **2** Difficult to deal with because unruly or poorly adjusted; as, a *problem* child.

prob·lem·at·ic \ˌpräb-lə-'mat-ik\ or **prob·lem·at·i·cal** \-ik-l\ *adj.* Having the nature of a problem; difficult and uncertain; puzzling. — **prob·lem·at·i·cal·ly** \-ik-l(-)ē\ *adv.*

pro·bos·cis \prō-'bäs-əs\ *n.; pl.* **pro·bos·cis·es** \-'bäs-ə-səz\ or **pro·bos·ci·des** \-ə-ˌdēz\. **1** The trunk of an elephant. **2** The snout of other animals in which it is unusually long and flexible, as in the shrew or tapir. **3** In many invertebrates, a coiled tubular sucking organ, as in the mosquito.

pro·caine \'prō-ˌkān\ *n.* A drug resembling cocaine, used as a local anesthetic.

pro·ce·dure \prə-'sēj-r\ *n.* **1** The manner or method of proceeding in a process or a course of action; as, the strict observance of legal *procedure*. **2** An action or series of actions; the continuance or progress of a process or action. Climbing high mountains is a slow *procedure*.

pro·ceed \prə-'sēd\ *v.* **1** To move, pass, or go forward or onward; to advance; to continue; as, to *proceed* to the next part of the test. **2** To come out of something as from a source. Light *proceeds* from the sun. **3** To go or act by an orderly method; to begin and carry on a series of acts; as, to *proceed* on sound principles.

pro·ceed·ing \prə-'sēd-ing\ *n.* **1** A procedure. **2** An act or step in a course of business or conduct; a transaction; as, an illegal *proceeding.* **3** [in the plural] The record of the business of a society or meeting.

pro·ceeds \'prō-ˌsēdz\ *n. pl.* The money or profit that comes from a property or a business deal; especially, the amount realized from a sale.

proc·ess \'präs-ˌes, -əs, 'prō-ˌses\ *n.; pl.* **proc·ess·es** \'präs-ˌes-əz, -ə-səz; 'prō-ˌses-əz, -sə-səz; 'präs-ə-ˌsēz\ **1** The action of proceeding; a progress; an advance; as, in the *process* of time. **2** Any fact or event that shows a continuous change in time; as, the *process* of growth. **3** A series of actions, motions, or operations leading to some result; as, a *process* of manufacture. **4** In biology, any prominent projection or part; an outgrowth; as, a bony *process.* **5** In law, an order in writing or a summons in a legal action, by which a court carries out its authority. — *v.* To subject something to a special process or treatment before it is used; as, to *process* butter. — *adj.* Made according to a special process; as, *process* cheese.

pro·ces·sion \prə-'sesh-n\ *n.* **1** A progression, as of a series; a continuous course; as, in the *procession* of life. **2** A group, as of persons or vehicles, moving onward in an orderly manner; a parade; as, a funeral *procession.*

pro·ces·sion·al \prə-'sesh-n(-)əl\ *n.* **1** A hymn sung during a church procession, as when the choir enters the church at the beginning of a service. **2** A book containing hymns and prayers for religious processions. — *adj.* Of, relating to, or moving in or as if in a procession.

proc·es·sor \'präs-ˌes-r, -əs-r, 'prō-ˌses-r\ *n.* One that processes.

pro·claim \prō-'klām\ *v.* To announce publicly; to declare; as, to *proclaim* a holiday. The prince was *proclaimed* king. — **pro·claim·er** \-r\ *n.*

proc·la·ma·tion \ˌpräk-lə-'māsh-n\ *n.* **1** The action of proclaiming; an official publication; as, the *proclamation* of a new law. **2** Something that is proclaimed.

pro·cliv·i·ty \prō-'kliv-ət-ē\ *n.; pl.* **pro·cliv·i·ties.** A tendency or inclination, as of the mind or temperament; a disposition; as, a boy with a marked *proclivity* towards laziness.

pro·con·sul \(')prō-'kän(t)s-l\ *n.* **1** An official in ancient Rome who performed the duties of a consul, as in a province, but was not himself a consul. **2** *Chiefly British.* The governor of a colony.

pro·cras·ti·nate \prō-'kras-tə-ˌnāt\ *v.;* **pro·cras·ti·nat·ed; pro·cras·ti·nat·ing.** To put things off from day to day; to keep postponing something supposed to be done. — **pro·cras·ti·na·tor** \-ˌnāt-r\ *n.*

pro·cras·ti·na·tion \prō-ˌkras-tə-'nāsh-n\ *n.* The act or the habit of delaying or of putting things off.

proc·tor \'präkt-r\ *n.* An officer in a school or college who enforces obedience to regulations, as in a dormitory or at an examination. — *v.;* **proc·tored; proc·tor·ing** \-r(-)ing\. To act as proctor.

pro·cur·a·ble \prō-'kyůr-əb-l\ *adj.* Capable of being procured; obtainable.

proc·u·ra·tor \'präk-yə-ˌrāt-r, 'prōk-\ *n.* Any of various imperial administrators in ancient Rome.

pro·cure \prō-'kyůr\ *v.;* **pro·cured; pro·cur·ing. 1** To obtain; to acquire; to get. **2** To cause or bring about; as, to *procure* the downfall of an enemy. — **pro·cure·ment,** *n.*

prod \'präd\ *v.;* **prod·ded; prod·ding. 1** To thrust a pointed thing into; to poke or prick with something sharp or blunt. **2** To arouse a person or animal to action; as, to *prod* a lazy student. — *n.* **1** A prodding; a sharp reminder or reproof; a dig. **2** A pointed thing for prodding.

prod·i·gal \'präd-ig-l\ *adj.* **1** Recklessly extravagant; as, a *prodigal* spender. **2** Wasteful; lavish; as, *prodigal* entertainment. — *n.* A spendthrift. — **prod·i·gal·ly** \-ig-l(-)ē\ *adv.*

prod·i·gal·i·ty \ˌpräd-ə-'gal-ət-ē\ *n.; pl.* **prod·i·gal·i·ties.** Extravagance in expenditure; excessive liberality; waste.

pro·di·gious \prə-'dij-əs\ *adj.* **1** Huge, as in size or amount; vast; as, *prodigious* costs. **2** Marvelous; amazing; monstrous. — **pro·di·gious·ly,** *adv.*

prod·i·gy \'präd-ə-jē\ *n.; pl.* **prod·i·gies. 1** *Archaic.* Something that is out of the ordinary course of nature; a marvel or wonder, especially one taken as an omen; as, comets and other *prodigies* of nature. **2** An amazing instance, deed, or performance; as, an exhibition of weight lifting that was a *prodigy* of strength and skill. **3** A highly gifted or precocious child.

pro·duce \prə-'düs, -'dyüs\ *v.;* **pro·duced; pro·duc·ing. 1** To bring to view; to show or exhibit; as, to *produce* a play; to *produce* evidence. **2** To bring forth; to bear; as, a tree that *produces* apples. **3** To yield; to cause to accrue. Money loaned at interest *produces* an income. **4** To make or manufacture; as, a city that *produces* steel. **5** To bring about or lead to something; as, actions that *produce* results.

prod·uce \'präd-ˌüs, 'prōd-, -ˌyüs\ *n.* The thing or amount produced; the yield or product; as, farm *produce.*

pro·duc·er \prə-'düs-r, -'dyüs-r\ *n.* **1** One that produces; especially, one who produces goods for human consumption, as by agriculture or manufacture. **2** One who finances or supervises the production of something, as a motion picture, play, or radio or television program.

pro·duc·i·ble \prə-'dü-səb-l, -'dyü-\ *adj.* Capable of being produced.

prod·uct \'präd-(ˌ)əkt\ *n.* **1** Anything that is produced, as by manufacture, labor, thought, or growth; as, to sell a new *product.* **2** The amount, quantity, or total produced. **3** The figure or amount that results from multiplying together two or more figures. The *product* of 3 and 5 is 15.

pro·duc·tion \prə-'dəksh-n\ *n.* **1** The action or process of producing; as, mass *production.* **2** Anything produced; a product; especially, a literary or artistic work; as, an amateur stage *production.* **3** The producing of goods having economic value.

pro·duc·tive \prə-'dək-tiv\ *adj.* **1** Having the power to produce or create anything; fertile; as, *productive* soil. **2** Effective in bringing forth or forward; as, an age *productive* of great men. **3** Yielding or furnishing results; profitable; as, a business venture that proved to be highly *productive.* **4** Yielding or engaged in the production of wealth. — **pro·duc·tive·ly** \-lē\ *adv.* — **pro·duc·tive·ness** \-nəs\ or **pro·duc·tiv·i·ty** \(ˌ)prō-ˌdək-'tiv-ət-ē, ˌpräd-ˌək-, prə-ˌdək-\ *n.*

Prof. Abbreviation for *Professor.*

prof·a·na·tion \ˌpräf-n-'āsh-n\ *n.* The action of profaning or violating, especially sacred things; desecration.

pro·fane \prō-'fān\ *v.;* **pro·faned; pro·fan·ing.** [From medieval English *prophane,* there borrowed from medieval French, where it was borrowed from Latin *profanus* meaning literally "in front of (outside) the temple".] **1** To violate or treat with irreverence, abuse, or contempt; to desecrate. **2** To put a thing to a wrong, unworthy or vulgar use; to debase. — *adj.* **1** Not holy or sacred; not concerned with or suitable for religion or religious purposes; secular; as, *profane* history. **2** Not sanctified; as, the *profane* rites of the heathen. **3** Having the effect of profaning something that is worthy of reverence; blasphemous; using oaths; as, *profane* language. — **pro·fane·ly** \-lē\ *adv.* — **pro·fan·er** \-'fān-r\ *n.*

pro·fan·i·ty \prō-'fan-ət-ē\ *n.; pl.* **pro·fan·i·ties.** **1** The quality or condition of being profane; irreverence. **2** Profane language or acts.

pro·fess \prə-'fes\ *v.* **1** To declare openly; as, to *profess* complete confidence in a friend's honesty. **2** To lay claim to something, as an ability, knowledge, or position, especially without really having it; as, a man who *professed* to be a gentleman; to *profess* to know a great deal about mountain climbing. **3** To follow as a calling or profession; as, to *profess* the law. **4** To confess one's faith in, especially a religion; as, to *profess* Christianity.

pro·fessed \prə-'fest\ *adj.* **1** Openly declared whether truly or falsely; self-stated; as, a *professed* hater of jazz music. **2** Having taken the vows of a religious order, as a monk or nun.

pro·fess·ed·ly \prə-'fes-əd-lē\ *adv.* According to one's own declaration; apparently; supposedly.

pro·fes·sion \prə-'fesh-n\ *n.* **1** An open declaration; as, a *profession* of religious faith. **2** A religious system or a religious body. **3** An occupation that is not primarily commercial, mechanical, or agricultural and that requires special education, as medicine, law, the ministry, or teaching; a calling. **4** The people engaged in such an occupation; as, the attitude of the medical *profession.* **5** The taking of the vows of a religious order, as by a monk or nun. — For synonyms see *trade.*

pro·fes·sion·al \prə-'fesh-n(-)əl\ *adj.* **1** Of or relating to a profession. Doctors, lawyers, and teachers are *professional* people. **2** Engaging in an activity, as a sport, for money rather than for fun; as, a *professional* football player. **3** Engaged in by professionals; as, *professional* baseball. — *n.* A person who engages in anything for gain rather than for sport or recreation alone; a professional worker of any kind. — **pro·fes·sion·al·ly** \-n(-)ə-lē\ *adv.*

pro·fes·sor \prə-'fes-r\ *n.* **1** A person who professes or openly declares his beliefs, especially in matters of religion; as, a *professor* of Christianity. **2** A lecturer or teacher of the highest rank in an advanced school; as, a college *professor;* a *professor* of mathematics.

pro·fes·so·ri·al \ˌprō-fə-'sōr-ē-əl, ˌpräf-ə-, -'sór-\ *adj.* **1** Of or relating to a professor; as, *professorial* duties. **2** Characteristic of a professor; as, a *professorial* manner. — **pro·fes·so·ri·al·ly** \-ē-ə-lē\ *adv.*

pro·fes·sor·ship \prə-'fes-r-ˌship\ *n.* The position held by a professor in a college or university.

prof·fer \'präf-r\ *v.;* **prof·fered; prof·fer·ing** \-r(-)ing\. To offer for acceptance; to tender. — *n.* An offer.

pro·fi·cien·cy \prə-'fish-n-sē\ *n.; pl.* **pro·fi·cien·cies.** The quality or state of being proficient; an advanced degree of ability or accomplishment; skill.

pro·fi·cient \prə-'fish-nt\ *adj.* Having thorough knowledge or training; skilled; expert; as, a *proficient* pianist; to be very *proficient* in French. — **pro·fi·cient·ly,** *adv.*

pro·file \'prō-ˌfīl\ *n.* **1** A head, or the outline of a face, seen or drawn from the side. **2** An outline; a contour; as, the *profile* of a hill seen against the sky.

profile

prof·it \'präf-ət\ *n.* **1** Valuable results; the gain, advantage, or benefit of something; as, to find *profit* in the study of foreign languages. **2** The gain after all the expenses are subtracted from the total amount received; as, a business that shows a *profit* of 100 dollars a week. — *v.* **1** To be of use or advantage; to be of service to; to benefit; as, a business transaction that *profited* no one. **2** To gain; to derive benefit; as, to *profit* by experience.

prof·it·a·ble \'präf-ət-əb-l, 'präf-təb-l\ *adj.* Yielding or bringing profit or gain; lucrative; useful; as, a *profitable* business. — For synonyms see *beneficial.* — **prof·it·a·bly** \'präf-ət-ə-blē, 'präf-tə-blē\ *adv.*

prof·i·teer \ˌpräf-ə-'tir\ *n.* A person who makes an unreasonable or unjust profit, as by taking advantage of his country's needs in wartime. — *v.* To act as a profiteer. — **prof·i·teer·ing,** *n.*

prof·li·ga·cy \'präf-lə-gə-sē\ *n.* The quality or state of being profligate; loose character or conduct.

prof·li·gate \'präf-lig-ət\ *adj.* **1** Loose, as in character or morals; dissipated. **2** Extremely wasteful; prodigal. — *n.* A profligate person. — **prof·li·gate·ly,** *adv.*

pro·found \prə-'faünd\ *adj.* **1** Intellectually deep; thorough; as, a *profound* scholar. **2** Coming from a depth; deep-seated; as, *profound* sighs. **3** Deeply felt; intense; as, *profound* respect. **4** Bending low in respect or honor; as, a *profound* bow. — **pro·found·ly,** *adv.*

pro·fun·di·ty \prə-'fən-dət-ē\ *n.; pl.* **pro·fun·di·ties.** **1** Depth; profoundness. **2** Something that is profound or deep; especially, a profound problem or theory.

pro·fuse \prə-'fyüs\ *adj.;* **pro·fus·er; pro·fus·est.** **1** Pouring forth liberally; exceedingly or excessively generous; prodigal; as, to give with a *profuse* hand. **2** Bountiful; lavish; as, to offer *profuse* apologies. — **pro·fuse·ly,** *adv.*

pro·fu·sion \prə-'fyüzh-n\ *n.* **1** Profuse or lavish expenditure. **2** Abundance; plenty; lavish supply; as, the *profusion* of flowers in the garden.

pro·gen·i·tor \prō-'jen-ət-r\ *n.* A direct ancestor; a forefather.

prog·e·ny \'präj-n-ē\ *n.; pl.* **prog·e·nies.** Descendants or a descendant; children; offspring.

prog·no·sis \präg-'nō-səs\ *n.; pl.* **prog·no·ses** \-ˌsēz\. **1** A forecast of the course of a disease. **2** The outlook given by such a forecast.

prog·nos·tic \präg-'näs-tik\ *n.* **1** A sign; an omen. **2** A forecast; a prognostication. — *adj.* Indicating something future by signs or symptoms.

prog·nos·ti·cate \präg-'näs-tə-ˌkāt\ *v.;* **prog·nos·ti·cat·ed; prog·nos·ti·cat·ing.** To foretell from signs or symptoms; to prophesy; to predict. — **prog·nos·ti·ca·tor** \-ˌkāt-r\ *n.*

prog·nos·ti·ca·tion \(ˌ)präg-ˌnäs-tə-'kāsh-n\ *n.* **1** A prediction; a forecast; a prophecy. **2** Something that foretells; a sign.

pro·gram \'prō-ˌgram, -grəm\ *n.* **1** A brief statement or written outline of something, as of a concert or play; as, a theater *program.* **2** A performance; as, a television *program.* **3** A plan of action; as, a work *program.*

prog·ress \'präg-rəs, -ˌres\ *n.* **1** Movement forward; an onward course; as, a ship's *progress.* **2** An advance to an objective; a going or getting ahead; as, to make *progress* in a fog. **3** Growth or development; as, the rapid *progress* of science.

pro·gress \prə-'gres\ *v.* **1** To move forward; to proceed. **2** To make progress; to improve.

pro·gres·sion \prə-'gresh-n\ *n.* **1** The action of progressing, or moving forward; as, a snail's manner of *progression.* **2** A continuous and connected series, as of acts, events, or steps; a sequence; as, the rapid *progression* of incidents in a play. **3** In mathematics, a series that has a first but no last element, especially one in which any intermediate element is related by a uniform law to the other elements. In the **arithmetical progression** 1, 3, 5, 7, etc., the elements progress by a constant difference of 2, while in the **geometric progression** 2, 6, 18, 54, etc., the elements progress by a constant factor of 3.

pro·gres·sive \prə-'gres-iv\ *adj.* **1** Moving forward or onward; advancing; as, the *progressive* movement of the hands of a clock. **2** Occurring by successive stages; as, a *progressive* series; *progressive* promotions. **3** Of, relating to, or showing progress or gradual improvement; as, a patient's *progressive* recovery from a disease. **4** Favoring or striving for progress, as in politics. **5** Accepting or making use of new ideas, inventions, or opportunities; as, a *progressive* race; *progressive* ideas. **6** In grammar, expressing action as in progress or being continued either at the time of speaking or writing or at another time referred to, as the verb phrase *was sleeping* in "The child was sleeping when the storm broke". — *n.* **1** A person who is progressive, especially in political policy. **2** A progressive tense or a verb form in such a tense. — **pro·gres·sive·ly,** *adv.*

pro·hib·it \prō-'hib-ət\ *v.* **1** To forbid by authority; as, to *prohibit* parking of cars on the street. **2** To stop or prevent; to hinder. The high walls *prohibit* escape.

pro·hi·bi·tion \ˌprō-ə-'bish-n\ *n.* **1** The action of prohibiting. **2** A declaration or order forbidding something. **3** The forbidding by law of the sale, and sometimes the manufacture and transportation, of alcoholic liquors as beverages.

pro·hi·bi·tion·ist \ˌprō-ə-'bish-n(-)əst\ *n.* A person who is in favor of prohibiting the manufacture and sale of alcoholic liquors as beverages.

pro·hib·i·tive \prō-'hib-ət-iv\ or **pro·hib·i·to·ry** \-ə-ˌtōr-ē, -ˌtȯr-ē\ *adj.* Serving or tending to prohibit; as, *prohibitive* prices; *prohibitory* legislation.

pro·ject \prə-'jekt\ *v.* **1** To throw or cast forward, as bodies, substances, or heat; to shoot forth. The sun *projects* gases. **2** To devise; to contrive; to scheme; as, to *project* a plan. **3** To stick out; to jut out; to extend beyond a certain line. The roof *projects* two feet beyond the side of the house. **4** To cause to fall on a surface; to cause to stand out distinctly against a background; as, to *project* a shadow; to *project* motion pictures on a screen.

proj·ect \'präj-ˌekt, -ikt\ *n.* **1** A plan; a scheme; a proposal. **2** A planned undertaking, as in research. **3** A school problem or unit of work that requires the doing or making of something that illustrates principles already taught or that leads to a student's finding out those principles for himself. **4** A group of houses or apartment buildings constructed and arranged according to a single plan, especially one built with government help to provide low-cost housing.

pro·jec·tile \prə-'jekt-l\ *n.* **1** An object, especially a missile, projected by an exterior force and maintaining its motion by inertia. **2** A rocket, especially a rocket missile, or a guided missile.

pro·jec·tion \prə-'jeksh-n\ *n.* **1** The action of projecting. **2** A jutting out. **3** A part that juts out. The *projection* of the roof protects the side of the house from rain. **4** The action or process of projecting something on a surface, as a picture on a screen. **5** The picture formed in this way.

pro·jec·tor \prə-'jekt-r\ *n.* **1** A person who forms projects; especially, a schemer; a promoter. **2** A machine for projecting images on a screen.

pro·le·tar·i·an \ˌprō-lə-'ter-ē-ən\ *adj.* Of or relating to the proletarians. — *n.* **1** One of the poorest and lowest class in a community or state. **2** One of the wage-earning class; especially, a laborer for day wages who has no capital.

pro·le·tar·i·at \ˌprō-lə-'ter-ē-ət\ *n.* Proletarians collectively; the proletarian class.

pro·lif·ic \prə-'lif-ik\ *adj.* **1** Producing young or fruit abundantly; reproductive; fruitful; as, a *prolific* orchard. **2** Highly inventive; productive; as, a *prolific* brain. **3** Causing fruitfulness; characterized by fruitfulness; as, a *prolific* growing season. — **pro·lif·i·cal·ly** \-ik-l(-)ē\ *adv.*

pro·lix \prō-'liks, 'prō-(ˌ)liks\ *adj.* Continued or drawn out too long, as by too many words; wordy; long-winded. — **pro·lix·i·ty** \prō-'liks-ət-ē\ *n.*

pro·logue or **pro·log** \'prō-ˌlȯg\ *n.* **1** The preface or introduction to a story, poem, or performance. **2** A person who speaks the prologue, as to a play. **3** An act or event that serves as an introduction.

pro·long \prə-'lȯng\ *v.* **1** To make a thing longer than usual; to continue or lengthen in time; to draw out; as, to *prolong* a person's life; the *prolonged* whistle of a train. **2** To lengthen in extent or range; as, to *prolong* a line.

pro·lon·ga·tion \ˌprō-ˌlȯng-'gāsh-n\ *n.* **1** A lengthening in space or time; a prolonging. **2** Something that prolongs or is prolonged.

prom \'präm\ *n.* [A shortened form of *promenade.*] A ball or dance, especially in college.

prom·e·nade \ˌpräm-ə-'nād, -'näd, -'nȧd\ *n.* **1** A walk, especially in a public place, for pleasure, display, or exercise. **2** A place for walking; a public walk. **3** A march participated in by the guests at the opening of a formal ball. **4** A ball or dance. — *v.;* **prom·e·nad·ed**; **prom·e·nad·ing**. To engage in a promenade; to take a promenade.

prom·i·nence \'präm-ə-nən(t)s\ *n.* **1** The quality, condition, or fact of being prominent; distinction; as, a person of *prominence.* **2** Something prominent, as a mountain; a projection.

prom·i·nent \'präm-ə-nənt\ *adj.* **1** Projecting; sticking out beyond a surface or a line; jutting. **2** Attracting attention, as by size or position; conspicuous. **3** Well-known; leading; outstanding. — The word *conspicuous* is a synonym of *prominent: prominent,* when applied to an object or a part of an object, usually indicates that it stands out noticeably from its surroundings, as in size, position, or color; when applied to a person, *prominent* usually suggests qualities that mark him as exceeding and usually superior to others, as in social position, worth, or reputation; *conspicuous* may describe something as being so outstanding that it cannot escape notice, often more notice than it deserves.

prom·i·nent·ly \'präm-ə-nənt-lē\ *adv.* In a prominent or noticeable manner; outstandingly.

prom·is·cu·i·ty \ˌpräm-əs-'kyü-ət-ē, ˌprō-ˌmis-\ *n.; pl.* **prom·is·cu·i·ties.** **1** A miscellaneous mixture or mingling of persons or things. **2** Promiscuous sexual behavior.

pro·mis·cu·ous \prə-'mis-kyə-wəs\ *adj.* **1** Mixed; composed of all sorts of persons and things. **2** Done or said without regard or distinction; not restricted to one person or class; as, to give *promiscuous* praise. **3** Haphazard; irregular; as, *promiscuous* eating habits. — **pro·mis·cu·ous·ly**, *adv.*

prom·ise \'präm-əs\ *n.* **1** A pledge; a statement assuring someone that the person making the statement will do or not do something; as, a *promise* to pay within a month. **2** Something that is promised. **3** A cause or ground for hope or expectation, especially of success or distinction. These plans give *promise* of success. — *v.;* **prom·ised**; **prom·is·ing.** **1** To give a promise about one's own actions; as, to *promise* to pay within a month. **2** To assure someone about a thing that does not depend on one's own actions. The people will come, I *promise* you. **3** To give reason for expecting something. The clouds *promise* rain.

prom·ised land \'präm-əst\. [From the promised land of the Bible, the land of Canaan, which Jehovah promised to Abraham and his descendants.] A better place that one hopes to reach or a better condition that one hopes to attain.

prom·is·ing \'präm-ə-sing\ *adj.* Full of promise; giving hope or assurance, as of success; as, a *promising* pupil. — **prom·is·ing·ly**, *adv.*

prom·is·so·ry \'präm-ə-ˌsōr-ē, -ˌsȯr-ē\ *adj.* Containing a promise, as in **promissory note**, a written promise to pay a person a sum of money on demand or on a certain date.

prom·on·to·ry \'präm-ən-ˌtōr-ē, -ˌtȯr-ē\ *n.; pl.* **prom·on·to·ries.** A high point of land or rock jutting out into the sea; a headland.

pro·mote \prə-'mōt\ *v.;* **pro·mot·ed**; **pro·mot·ing.** **1** To advance a person in position, rank, or honor; to elevate; as, to *promote* pupils to a higher grade. **2** To contribute to the growth, success, or development of something; to further; to encourage. Good food *promotes* health. **3** To take the first steps in organizing something, as a business.

pro·mot·er \prə-'mōt-r\ *n.* **1** One that promotes or advances something; an encourager; a lobbyist. **2** A person who alone or with others organizes a company or any other business undertaking.

pro·mo·tion \prə-'mōsh-n\ *n.* **1** The act of promoting or state of being promoted; as, to help in the *promotion* of the school athletic program. **2** Advancement in rank or position or an instance of this; as, to receive a *promotion.* — **pro·mo·tion·al** \-'mōsh-n(-)əl\ *adj.*

prompt \'präm(p)t\ *adj.* **1** Quick and ready to act; as, *prompt* to answer. **2** On time; punctual; as, to be *prompt* in arriving. **3** Done at once; given without delay; as, *prompt* aid. — *v.* **1** To move a person to action. Curiosity *prompted* him to ask the question. **2** To remind a person of something forgotten or poorly learned, as by suggesting the next few words in a speech; as, to *prompt* an actor. **3** To suggest; to inspire. Pride *prompted* the act.

prompt·er \'präm(p)t-r\ *n.* **1** A person who reminds another of the words to be spoken next, as in a play. **2** In square dancing, a caller.

promp·ti·tude \'präm(p)-tə-ˌtüd, -ˌtyüd\ *n.* The quality or habit of being prompt; quickness.

prompt·ly \'präm(p)t-lē\ *adv.* At once; on time; as, to answer *promptly;* to arrive *promptly.*

prom·ul·gate \'präm-l-ˌgāt, prō-'məl-\ *v.;* **prom·ul·gat·ed; prom·ul·gat·ing.** To make known or declare; to proclaim; especially, in church usage, to announce a dogma. — **prom·ul·ga·tion** \ˌpräm-l-'gāsh-n, ˌprō-(ˌ)məl-\ *n.*

pron. Abbreviation for: **1** *pronoun.* **2** *pronunciation.*

prone \'prōn\ *adj.* **1** Having a tendency or inclination; disposed; as, *prone* to laziness. **2** Lying on the belly, or face downwards; as, *prone* on the sand. **3** Not erect; lying down; flattened out on a surface. The wind blew the trees *prone.*

prong \'pròng, 'präng\ *n.* **1** One of the sharp points, or tines, of a fork. **2** A slender projecting part, as a point of an antler. — **pronged** \'pròngd, 'prängd\ *adj.*

prong·horn \'pròng-ˌhòrn, 'präng-\ *n.* A cud-chewing animal resembling an antelope and found on the treeless parts of the western United States and Mexico.

pronghorn

pro·nom·i·nal \prō-'näm-ən-l\ *adj.* **1** Of, being, or having to do with a pronoun. **2** Like a pronoun; having a meaning that resembles that of a pronoun in identifying or specifying without describing. In "come here" the adverb "here" is *pronominal.* — **pro·nom·i·nal·ly** \-ən-l-ē\ *adv.*

pro·noun \'prō-ˌnaùn\ *n.* A word used as a substitute for a noun, as *it* in "The stone hit the window and broke it".

pro·nounce \prə-'naùn(t)s\ *v.;* **pro·nounced; pro·nounc·ing.** **1** To utter officially or solemnly; to declare. The minister *pronounced* them man and wife. **2** To assert as an opinion; as, to *pronounce* the book a success. **3** To speak aloud, especially with correct sound and accent; as, to practice *pronouncing* a foreign language.

pro·nounced \prə-'naùn(t)st\ *adj.* Strongly marked; emphatic; conspicuous; as, a *pronounced* change for the better. — **pro·nounc·ed·ly** \-'naùn(t)s-əd-lē\ *adv.*

pro·nounce·ment \prə-'naùn(t)s-mənt\ *n.* A declaration; a formal announcement.

pro·nun·ci·a·tion \prə-ˌnən(t)s-ē-'āsh-n\ *n.* The act or manner of pronouncing a word or words.

proof \'prüf\ *n.* **1** Evidence of the truth or correctness of something; as, to find *proof* of a statement. **2** The means by which something is proved; a test, check or trial. **3** Strength of alcoholic liquor with reference to a standard of alcoholic content. Whiskey that is 100 *proof* is 50 per cent pure alcohol. **4** A test made from a photographic negative. **5** A trial printing from type, for correction and examination; as, to read newspaper *proof.* — *adj.* Able to resist or keep out; not affected by — used chiefly in combinations, as in *waterproof* or *fireproof.*

proof·read \'prüf-ˌrēd\ *v.;* **proof·read** \-ˌred\; **proof·read·ing** \-ˌrēd-\. To read and make corrections, as in printer's proof; as, to *proofread* a composition.

proof·read·er \'prüf-ˌrēd-r\ *n.* A person who reads and makes corrections in printer's proof.

prop \'präp\ *v.;* **propped; prop·ping.** **1** To hold up or keep from falling or slipping by placing a support under or against; as, to *prop* a clothesline; to *prop* up a broken chair. **2** To help, encourage, or support. — *n.* A person or thing that props.

prop·a·gan·da \ˌpräp-ə-'gan-də, ˌprōp-ə-\ *n.* **1** Any organized group or movement for spreading particular ideas, beliefs, or information. **2** A methodical spreading of such ideas, beliefs, or information. **3** The ideas, beliefs, or information spread in this way. — **prop·a·gan·dist** \-dəst\ *n.*

prop·a·gan·dize \ˌpräp-ə-'gan-ˌdīz, ˌprōp-ə-\ *v.;* **prop·a·gan·dized; prop·a·gan·diz·ing.** **1** To spread propaganda. **2** To influence or attempt to influence by propaganda.

prop·a·gate \'präp-ə-ˌgāt\ *v.;* **prop·a·gat·ed; prop·a·gat·ing.** **1** To have offspring or to cause to have offspring; to increase the numbers of, as a kind of organism, by a natural process of reproduction or by grafting, by dividing, or by cuttings; as, to *propagate* a species of winter apple. Rabbits *propagate* rapidly. **2** To extend the action of; to transmit; to diffuse; as, to *propagate* sound. **3** To spread or cause to spread, as an idea or belief from one person to another; as, to *propagate* a religious faith; to *propagate* fears. — **prop·a·ga·tion** \ˌpräp-ə-'gāsh-n\ *n.*

pro·pel \prə-'pel\ *v.;* **pro·pelled; pro·pel·ling.** **1** To push or drive, usually forward or onward. A bicycle is *propelled* by pedals, a rowboat by oars. **2** To give an impelling motive to; to urge ahead.

pro·pel·lent \prə-'pel-ənt\ *n.* A propelling agent, as an explosive for propelling projectiles or fuel plus an oxidizing agent used by a rocket engine.

pro·pel·lent \prə-'pel-ənt\ *adj.* Able or tending to propel; driving forward. — *n.* Something that propels.

pro·pel·ler \prə-'pel-r\ *n.* One that propels; especially, a device consisting of a hub fitted with blades, which when made to revolve by an engine is used to drive steamships, power boats, and certain types of airplanes.

pro·pen·si·ty \prə-'pen(t)s-ət-ē\ *n.; pl.* **pro·pen·si·ties.** A natural inclination or liking; a bent; as, a *propensity* for drawing.

prop·er \'präp-r\ *adj.* **1** *Archaic.* One's own; belonging to oneself. **2** Being a necessary or natural part of something; peculiar; distinctive; especially, appropriate because natural. **3** In an exact and accurate sense; strictly so called. England *proper* is about the size of Pennsylvania. **4** Suitable; right; fit; as, *proper* clothes for an occasion; the *proper* words for expressing one's thanks. **5** Obeying the social rules; conforming to accepted standards; decent; as, *proper* conduct. **6** Special to a particular day or festival, as prayers for a certain church service.

proper adjective. An adjective formed from a proper noun.

proper fraction. A fraction in which the numerator is less, or of lower degree, than the denominator.

prop·er·ly \'präp-r-lē\ *adv.* **1** In a suitable or fit manner; as, to behave *properly* in church. **2** Rightly; strictly in accordance with fact; correctly; as, goods not *properly* labeled. *Properly* speaking, whales are not fish.

proper noun. A noun that names a particular person, place, or thing, as *John, America, January,* the *Monitor.*

prop·er·tied \'präp-rt-ēd\ *adj.* Owning property, especially much property.

prop·er·ty \'präp-rt-ē\ *n.; pl.* **prop·er·ties. 1** A special quality or characteristic of a thing; a quality or attribute common to all things called by the same name. Sweetness is a *property* of sugar. **2** Anything that is owned, as land, goods, or money. **3** A piece of real estate, with or without a house; as, to own a *property* in the suburbs. **4** Ownership. **5** [usually in the plural] An article to be used on the stage during a play or on the set of a motion picture except the artificial scenery or the costumes of the actors.

proph·e·cy \'präf-ə-sē\ *n.; pl.* **proph·e·cies. 1** The foretelling of the future; as, to have the gift of *prophecy.* **2** That which is foretold by a prophet. **3** Anything foretold of the future; a prediction.

proph·e·sy \'präf-ə-ˌsī\ *v.;* **proph·e·sied** \-ˌsīd\; **proph·e·sy·ing. 1** To speak or write as a prophet; to utter with or as if with divine inspiration. **2** To foretell or predict future events; as, to *prophesy* bad weather. — For synonyms see *foretell.*

proph·et \'präf-ət\ *n.* **1** A person inspired by God to speak for him; one who declares publicly that which he believes has been divinely revealed to him, as a religious message or a warning for the future. **2** A person who prophesies or predicts.

proph·et·ess \'präf-ət-əs\ *n.* A woman who makes prophecies.

pro·phet·ic \prə-'fet-ik\ *adj.* **1** Of or relating to a prophet or prophecy; as, *prophetic* insight. **2** Containing prophecy or prophecies; as, the *prophetic* books of the Bible. — **pro·phet·i·cal·ly** \-ik-l(-)ē\ *adv.*

pro·pi·ti·ate \prə-'pish-ē-ˌāt\ *v.;* **pro·pi·ti·at·ed; pro·pi·ti·at·ing.** To appease; to gain or regain the favor or good will of; as, primitive men *propitiating* the angry gods with sacrifices. — **pro·pi·ti·a·tion** \-ˌpish-ē-'āsh-n\ *n.* — **pro·pi·ti·a·to·ry** \-'pish-ē-ə-ˌtōr-ē, -ˌtȯr-ē\ *adj.*

pro·pi·tious \prə-'pish-əs\ *adj.* **1** Favorably disposed. The fates are *propitious.* **2** Promising; favorable; of good omen; as, *propitious* signs. **3** Opportune; likely to produce good results; as, the *propitious* moment for asking a favor.

prop·o·lis \'präp-l-əs\ *n.* A brownish, waxy, resinous material collected by bees from the buds of trees and used as a cement.

pro·por·tion \prə-'pōrsh-n, -'pȯrsh-n\ *n.* **1** The size, number, or amount of one thing or group of things as compared to the size, number, or amount of another thing or group of things. The *proportion* of boys to girls in our class is three to one. **2** [in the plural] Dimensions; the length and width, or length, breadth, and height. The *proportions* of this room are very good. **3** A balanced or pleasing arrangement; as, to be out of *proportion.* **4** Fair or just share. Each did his *proportion* of the work. **5** In mathematics, the equality of ratios; as, the *proportion* a/b = c/d. — *v.;* **pro·por·tioned; pro·por·tion·ing** \-n(-)ing\. **1** To fix or determine the proportion of one thing to another thing or things. **2** To form or arrange symmetrically.

pro·por·tion·al \prə-'pōrsh-n(-)əl, -'pȯrsh-\ *adj.* **1** Determined with reference to proportions; as, *proportional* representation in the legislature. **2** Proportionate; in proportion; as, wages that are *proportional* to ability. **3** In mathematics, having the same or a constant ratio. — **pro·por·tion·al·ly** \-n(-)ə-lē\ *adv.*

pro·por·tion·ate \prə-'pōrsh-n(-)ət, -'pȯrsh-\ *adj.* In proportion to something else; proportional. The results were not *proportionate* to our efforts. — **pro·por·tion·ate·ly,** *adv.*

pro·pos·al \prə-'pōz-l\ *n.* **1** A proposing or setting forth for consideration. **2** Something proposed; a plan. **3** An offer of marriage.

pro·pose \prə-'pōz\ *v.;* **pro·posed; pro·pos·ing. 1** To offer for consideration or discussion; to suggest; as, to *propose* terms of peace. **2** To have as a plan; to make plans; to intend; as, to *propose* to buy a new house. **3** To offer as a toast; to suggest drinking as a toast. **4** To name; to nominate; as, to *propose* someone for membership in the club. **5** To make an offer of marriage.

prop·o·si·tion \ˌpräp-ə-'zish-n\ *n.* **1** A statement to be proved, explained, or discussed. **2** That which is proposed; a proposal. **3** An undertaking or venture, especially in business.

pro·pound \prə-'pau̇nd\ *v.* To offer for consideration; to propose. — **pro·pound·er,** *n.*

propped. Past tense and past part. of *prop.*

propping. Pres. part. of *prop.*

pro·pri·e·tary \prə-'prī-ə-ˌter-ē\ *n.; pl.* **pro·pri·e·tar·ies. 1** A proprietor; an owner; especially, in

American history, the owner of a **proprietary colony**, a colony granted to a person or persons with full powers of government. **2** A body of property owners. — *adj.* **1** Of, relating to, or owned by a proprietary or a proprietor; as, *proprietary* control; *proprietary* rights. **2** Privately owned; as, a *proprietary* hospital. **3** Made and sold by a manufacturer having the exclusive right of manufacture and sale; as, a *proprietary* medicine.

pro·pri·e·tor \prə-'prī-ət-r\ *n.* **1** One who holds something as his property or possession; an owner; as, the *proprietor* of a store. **2** In American history, a proprietary. — **pro·pri·e·tor·ship** \-ˌship\ *n.*

pro·pri·e·tress \prə-'prī-ə-trəs\ *n.* A female proprietor.

pro·pri·e·ty \prə-'prī-ət-ē\ *n.; pl.* **pro·pri·e·ties.** **1** The quality of being proper. **2** Correctness in manners or behavior; politeness; as, to behave with *propriety.* **3** [in the plural] The rules and customs of good or polite society.

pro·pul·sion \prə-'pəlsh-n\ *n.* **1** Act or process of propelling. **2** Something that propels; a driving or operating power; as, jet *propulsion.* — **pro·pul·sive** \-'pəl-siv\ *adj.*

pro ra·ta \(')prō 'rāt-ə, 'rät-ə, 'rȧt-ə\. [From Latin *pro rata (parte)* meaning "according to a calculated part".] In proportion; proportionately; according to share or liability.

pro·rate \(')prō-'rāt\ *v.;* **pro·rat·ed**; **pro·rat·ing.** To divide or distribute proportionally; to assess pro rata.

pro·sa·ic \prō-'zā-ik\ *adj.* **1** Of or pertaining to prose; especially, characteristic of prose rather than poetry. **2** Plain and unimaginative; not exciting; dull. — **pro·sa·i·cal·ly** \-ik-l(-)ē\ *adv.*

pro·scribe \prō-'skrīb\ *v.;* **pro·scribed**; **pro·scrib·ing.** **1** To put outside the protection of the law; to outlaw. **2** To denounce and condemn; to prohibit. — **pro·scrip·tion** \-'skripsh-n\ *n.*

prose \'prōz\ *n.* **1** The ordinary language of men in speaking or, especially, in writing; written language not having the characteristics of poetry. **2** That which is prosaic or matter-of-fact in quality or character; as, the unending *prose* of daily life. — *adj.* **1** Of or having to do with prose; as, *prose* works. **2** Prosaic; dull; ordinary; as, the *prose* sorts of men, with little imagination.

pros·e·cute \'präs-ə-ˌkyüt\ *v.;* **pros·e·cut·ed**; **pros·e·cut·ing.** **1** To follow up to the end; to keep at; to persist in carrying on; as, to *prosecute* our war efforts strongly. **2** To seek to punish through an appeal to the courts; to carry on a legal action against an accused person to prove his guilt.

pros·e·cu·tion \ˌpräs-ə-'kyüsh-n\ *n.* **1** A prosecuting; as, in the *prosecution* of the plans. **2** The starting and carrying on of a suit in court. **3** The party bringing charges of crime or serious misdeeds against a person being tried. **4** In a criminal case, the state's lawyers.

pros·e·cu·tor \'präs-ə-ˌkyüt-r\ *n.* **1** One who prosecutes. **2** One who begins an official prosecution before a court. **3** A public prosecuting attorney.

pros·e·lyte \'präs-l-ˌīt\ *n.* A new convert; a person won over, as to another religion or a political belief. — *v.;* **pros·e·lyt·ed**; **pros·e·lyt·ing.** To convert; to make a proselyte of.

pros·e·ly·tize \'präs-l-ə-ˌtīz\ *v.;* **pros·e·ly·tized**; **pros·e·ly·tiz·ing.** To proselyte.

pros·o·dy \'präs-əd-ē\ *n.* The science or art of versification; the study of poetic forms, including feet and meters, types of stanzas and poems, and rhymes and rhyming schemes.

pros·pect \'präs-ˌpekt\ *n.* **1** A wide view; a far-reaching scene; as, a *prospect* of sea and land. **2** Act of looking forward; anticipation. **3** That which is hoped for; a probable result; as, to have little *prospect* of success. **4** A person who may be a contestant, run for an office, become a customer; as, a party's best *prospect* for president. — *v.* To explore a place, as for ore or oil.

pro·spec·tive \prəs-'pek-tiv, präs-, 'präs-ˌpek-\ *adj.* **1** Expected; likely to come about; as, the *prospective* benefits of a new law. **2** Likely to be or become; as, a *prospective* bride. — **pro·spec·tive·ly**, *adv.*

pros·pec·tor \'präs-ˌpekt-r\ *n.* One who explores a region for valuable deposits, as of metals or oil.

pro·spec·tus \prəs-'pek-təs\ *n.* A statement, usually in printed form, giving advance information, as about a business venture to people who are likely to be investors in it.

pros·per \'präsp-r\ *v.;* **pros·pered**; **pros·per·ing** \-r(-)ing\. **1** To turn out well; to succeed; to become strong or flourishing. **2** To make successful.

pros·per·i·ty \präs-'per-ət-ē\ *n.; pl.* **pros·per·i·ties.** The state of being prosperous or successful.

pros·per·ous \'präsp-r(-)əs\ *adj.* Prospering; marked by prosperity; successful; flourishing; as, a *prosperous* region; a *prosperous* business.

pros·ti·tute \'präs-tə-ˌtüt, -ˌtyüt\ *v.;* **pros·ti·tut·ed**; **pros·ti·tut·ing.** To devote to unworthy or base purposes; as, to *prostitute* one's talents. — *n.* A woman who offers herself for immoral sexual relations for money; a harlot. — **pros·ti·tu·tion** \ˌpräs-tə-'tüsh-n, -'tyüsh-n\ *n.*

pros·trate \'präs-ˌtrāt, -trət\ *adj.* **1** Bending forward or lying at full length with face on the ground. **2** Lying flat and outstretched; trailing. **3** Thrown to the ground; weak and powerless, as though overthrown; as, the hurricane left trees *prostrate;* a mother *prostrate* with grief. — \-ˌtrāt\ *v.;* **pros·trat·ed**; **pros·trat·ing.** **1** To throw or bend down in a prostrate position. **2** To bring to a weak and powerless condition.

pros·tra·tion \präs-'trāsh-n\ *n.* **1** The act of prostrating or the condition of being prostrated. **2** Complete exhaustion or dejection; as, heat *prostration;* nervous *prostration.*

prosy \'prō-zē\ *adj.;* **pros·i·er**; **pros·i·est.** **1** Of or relating to prose; prosaic. **2** Dull; tedious.

pro·te·an \'prōt-ē-ən, prō-'tē-ən\ *adj.* [A derivative of *Proteus*, a sea god of Greek mythology who could change his shape at will.] Easily taking different shapes or forms; extremely variable. An amoeba is a *protean* form of life.

pro·tect \prə-'tekt\ *v.* To cover or defend from something that would destroy or injure; to guard.

pro·tec·tion \prə-'teksh-n\ *n.* **1** The act of protecting; the condition of being protected; as, to be under police *protection.* **2** A protecting person or thing. Dark glasses are a *protection* from the sun. **3** A document guaranteeing safe-conduct, as a passport. **4** Government or support of a weak nation or people by a strong nation; the relation of a protecting power to a protectorate. **5** The freeing of a domestic producer from foreign competition by levying high tariffs on imported goods.

pro·tec·tive \prə-'tek-tiv\ *adj.* **1** Giving protection; self-protecting; as, a *protective* shell. **2** Based on or relating to economic protection; as, a *protective* tariff.

protective coloration. Coloring which blends an animal with its background so that it is less easily seen by its enemies.

pro·tec·tor \prə-'tekt-r\ *n.* **1** One who protects; a defender; guardian. **2** Something that protects; a guard; as, a chest *protector.* **3** A person who rules a kingdom until the sovereign becomes of age; a regent.

pro·tec·tor·ate \prə-'tekt-r(-)ət\ *n.* **1** Government by a protector. **2** A political relationship in which a strong nation protects and shares in the government of a weak nation; the period of time during which this relationship continues.

pro·té·gé \'prōt-ə-ˌzhā\ *n.* [From French, there formed from the past participle of *protéger* meaning "to protect".] A person who is under the care and protection of another.

pro·tein \'prō-ˌtēn, 'prōt-ē-ən\ *n.* A substance found in all living cells which is an essential element in human and animal diet and is supplied especially by such foods as meat, eggs, and milk.

pro tem·po·re \(')prō 'temp-r-(ˌ)ē\. [Latin.] For the time being; temporarily.

pro·test \prə-'test\ *v.* **1** To declare positively; to assert; to state. The accused man *protested* his innocence. **2** To object strongly; to make a protest against. The boys *protested* the umpire's decision. — \'prō-ˌtest\ *n.* A speech, letter, or petition stating an objection or complaint.

prot·es·tant \'prät-əs-tənt; *sense 2 of n. and sense 1 of adj. are also* prə-'tes-tənt\ *n.* **1** [with a capital] A member of one of the Christian churches that separated from the Roman Catholic Church in the 16th century or of a church deriving from them. **2** A person who protests. — *adj.* **1** Making a protest. **2** [with a capital] Of or having to do with Protestants.

prot·es·ta·tion \ˌprät-əs-'tāsh-n, ˌprōt-\ *n.* A protesting; an open avowal; as, his *protestations* of friendship.

pro·to·col \'prōt-ə-ˌkȯl, -ˌkäl\ *n.* **1** An original copy or record, as of a document, transaction, or experiment. **2** The rigid code of etiquette prescribing the forms and procedures for various ceremonies and social functions in government, military, and diplomatic circles.

pro·ton \'prō-ˌtän\ *n.* The very small charge of positive electricity that forms one part of an atom.

pro·to·pec·tin \'prōt-ə-ˌpek-tən\ *n.* The insoluble form in which pectin occurs naturally.

pro·to·plasm \'prōt-ə-ˌplaz-m\ *n.* The essential living substance of the cell body and nucleus of all plant and animal cells, usually a sticky translucent material holding fine granules in suspension. — **pro·to·plas·mic** \ˌprōt-ə-'plaz-mik\ *adj.*

pro·to·plast \'prōt-ə-ˌplast\ *n.* The contents of a protoplasmic cell considered as a unit.

pro·to·type \'prōt-ə-ˌtīp\ *n.* **1** An original or model after which anything is copied; a pattern· as, the *prototype* of new aircraft. **2** In biology an ancestral form.

pro·to·zo·an \ˌprōt-ə-'zō-ən\ *n.* Any of a group of microscopic animals in which the body consists, usually, of a single cell and in which reproduction occurs by the splitting of the cell into two individuals. — *adj.* Of or relating to protozoans.

pro·tract \prō-'trakt\ *v.* **1** To lengthen in time; to draw out; as, *protracted* discussion. **2** In surveying, to lay down the lines and angles of, as with a scale and protractor; to plot. **3** In zoology, to extend or protrude. — **pro·trac·tion** \-'traksh-n\ *n.*

pro·trac·tor \prō-'trakt-r\ *n.* **1** One that protracts, prolongs, or delays. **2** An instrument used in drawing for laying down and measuring angles.

pro·trude \prō-'trüd\ *v.;* **pro·trud·ed**; **pro·trud·ing.** To stick out; to project; as, to *protrude* one's tongue. — **pro·tru·sion** \-'trüzh-n\ *n.*

pro·tu·ber·ance \prō-'tüb-r-ən(t)s, -'tyüb-\ *n.* A protruding; a bulging or sticking out; a bulge.

pro·tu·ber·ant \prō-'tüb-r-ənt, -'tyüb-\ *adj.* Bulging or extending beyond the surrounding surface or area; swelling; sticking out; as, a very *protuberant* chin. — **pro·tu·ber·ant·ly,** *adv.*

proud \'prau̇d\ *adj.* **1** Having or showing a feeling that one is better than others; haughty; arrogant; conceited; self-satisfied; as, *proud* ladies; a *proud* manner. **2** Having a feeling of delight or satisfaction; highly pleased. The father was *proud* of his heroic son. **3** Having proper pride; self-respecting; as, to be too *proud* to ask favors. **4** Spirited; courageous; as, a *proud* steed; cadets marching with a *proud* step. — **proud·ly,** *adv.*

prove \'prüv\ *v.;* **proved**; **proved** \'prüvd\ or **prov·en** \'prüv-n\; **prov·ing.** **1** To test something; as, to *prove* the strength of gunpowder. **2** To convince others of the truth of something; to demonstrate; to show. **3** To show to be genuine or valid; as, to *prove* a will. **4** To test the answer to, and to check the means of solving, an arithmetic problem.

prov·en·der \'präv-nd-r\ *n.* Dry food for domestic animals; feed, as hay or oats.

prov·erb \'präv-ˌərb, 'präv-rb\ *n.* A popular maxim; an adage. "All work and no play makes Jack a dull boy" is an often quoted *proverb.*

pro·ver·bi·al \prə-ˈvər-bē-əl\ *adj.* **1** Of, relating to, or of the nature of a proverb; as, a *proverbial* saying. **2** That has become a proverb; commonly spoken of. The old man's wisdom had become *proverbial.* — **pro·ver·bi·al·ly** \-bē-ə-lē\ *adv.*

pro·vide \prə-ˈvīd\ *v.;* **pro·vid·ed**; **pro·vid·ing.** [From medieval English *providen,* there borrowed from Latin *providere,* a compound composed of *pro* meaning "for" and *videre* meaning "to see".] **1** To look out for in advance; to make provision for; as, to *provide* for a child's education. **2** To supply; to furnish. Cows *provide* milk. **3** To make as a condition; to stipulate. The contract *provides* a penalty for late delivery. — **pro·vid·er,** *n.*

pro·vid·ed \prə-ˈvīd-əd\ *conj.* On condition; if. We shall go, *provided* the day is pleasant.

prov·i·dence \ˈpräv-ə-dən(t)s, -ˌden(t)s\ *n.* **1** [with a capital] God, as the guide and protector of man. **2** An instance of divine or providential help. **3** Prudence; thrift.

prov·i·dent \ˈpräv-ə-dənt\ *adj.* **1** Making provision for the future. **2** Prudent; frugal; thrifty. — **prov·i·dent·ly,** *adv.*

prov·i·den·tial \ˌpräv-ə-ˈdench-l\ *adj.* **1** Of or relating to Providence; as, *providential* guidance. **2** Fortunate; timely; lucky; as, a *providential* escape. — **prov·i·den·tial·ly** \-ˈdench-l-ē\ *adv.*

prov·ince \ˈpräv-n(t)s\ *n.* **1** In ancient Roman history, a district far from Rome brought under Roman government. **2** A division, usually large, of a country made for purposes of local government; especially, one of the divisions of the Dominion of Canada. **3** [usually in the plural] The part or parts of a country far from the capital or chief city. **4** Proper sphere of activity; limits of authority; as, a decision not within one's *province* to make. **5** A group of dioceses over which an archbishop presides.

pro·vin·cial \prə-ˈvinch-l\ *adj.* **1** Of, relating to, or characteristic of, a province or provinces. **2** Of narrow or limited interests; not broad or liberal; as, a *provincial* attitude. **3** Lacking the polish and refinement of urban society; countrified; as, *provincial* manners. — *n.* A person who lives in or comes from the provinces.

pro·vin·cial·ism \prə-ˈvinch-l-ˌiz-m\ *n.* **1** The quality or state of being provincial. **2** A provincial custom, fashion, or characteristic; especially, a word or expression, or a manner of speaking, peculiar to a part or parts of a country remote from its capital or chief city.

pro·vin·ci·al·i·ty \prə-ˌvinch-ē-ˈal-ət-ē\ *n.* Provincialism.

pro·vin·cial·ly \prə-ˈvinch-l-ē\ *adv.* In a provincial manner.

prov·ing ground \ˈprü-ving\. An area used for testing weapons, as shells, rockets, and missiles.

pro·vi·sion \prə-ˈvizh-n\ *n.* **1** The act of providing; as, to see to the *provision* of transportation for a journey; to make *provision* for the future. **2** A stock or store of food; as, to lay in *provisions* for a holiday; a dealer in *provisions.* **3** A condition; a stipulation; as, the *provisions* of a contract. — *v.;* **pro·vi·sioned**; **pro·vi·sion·ing** \-n(-)ing\. To supply with provisions.

pro·vi·sion·al \prə-ˈvizh-n(-)əl\ *adj.* Serving for the time being; not permanent; temporary; as, a *provisional* government; *provisional* arrangements. — **pro·vi·sion·al·ly** \-n(-)ə-lē\ *adv.*

pro·vi·so \prə-ˈvī-ˌzō\ *n.; pl.* **pro·vi·sos** or **pro·vi·soes.** **1** A sentence or clause in a legal document, as a will or a contract, in which a condition is stated. **2** Any conditional stipulation; a provision; as, to be given a bicycle with the *proviso* that one must keep it in good repair.

prov·o·ca·tion \ˌpräv-ə-ˈkāsh-n\ *n.* **1** The act of provoking; as, to be responsible for the *provocation* of a quarrel. **2** A cause of anger or quarreling; as, to become angry at the smallest *provocation.*

pro·voc·a·tive \prə-ˈväk-ət-iv\ *adj.* Serving or tending to provoke or arouse, as interest, curiosity, or anger; as, a *provocative* book; a *provocative* remark. — **pro·voc·a·tive·ly,** *adv.*

pro·voke \prə-ˈvōk\ *v.;* **pro·voked**; **pro·vok·ing.** **1** To arouse to action or feeling; especially, to excite to anger; as, to *provoke* one's father. **2** To bring about; to stir up; as, to *provoke* an argument. — For synonyms see *irritate.*

pro·vok·ing \prə-ˈvōk-ing\ *adj.* Causing mild anger; annoying; irritating; as, a *provoking* delay. — **pro·vok·ing·ly,** *adv.*

pro·vost \ˈprō-ˌvōst, ˈpräv-əst, ˈprō-vəst\ *n.* **1** A superintendent; the official head, as of some Scottish cities or of some English colleges. **2** A high administrative officer in some American colleges.

prow \ˈpraủ\ *n.* **1** The forward end or part of a ship; the bow. **2** Something resembling the bow of a ship, as the front part of an airship.

prow

prow·ess \ˈpraủ-əs\ *n.* **1** Great bravery; conspicuous courage; valor. **2** Great skill or ability; as, athletic *prowess.*

prowl \ˈpraủl\ *v.* **1** To move about stealthily, as a wild animal hunting prey. **2** To wander; as, to *prowl* around to see the sights. — *n.* The act of prowling, as for prey; as, wild animals on the *prowl.* — **prowl·er,** *n.*

prowl car \ˈpraủl\. A squad car.

prox. Abbreviation for *proximo.*

prox·im·i·ty \präk-ˈsim-ət-ē\ *n.* Nearness in time, place, order, or relationship; closeness; as, a house that was very noisy because of the *proximity* of an airfield.

prox·i·mo \ˈpräks-m-ˌō\ *adv.* In or of the next month after the present; as, a bill falling due on the 10th *proximo.*

proxy \ˈpräks-ē\ *n.; pl.* **prox·ies.** **1** Authority held by one person to act for another, as in voting. **2** A person holding such authority. **3** A written paper giving a person such authority.

prude \ˈprüd\ *n.* A person, especially a woman, who is exaggeratedly or affectedly modest in speech, behavior, and dress and is oversensitive to slight violations of accepted rules of decorous behavior.

pru·dence \'prüd-n(t)s\ *n.* **1** The ability to govern and discipline oneself by means of one's reason. **2** Skill and good judgment in managing affairs.

pru·dent \'prüd-nt\ *adj.* **1** Wise and careful in action or judgment. **2** Cautious in one's conduct and methods; not rash. — **pru·dent·ly**, *adv.*

pru·den·tial \prü-'dench-l\ *adj.* **1** Resulting from prudence; characterized by prudence. **2** Using prudence or good judgment. — **pru·den·tial·ly** \-'dench-l-ē\ *adv.*

prud·ery \'prüd-r-ē\ *n.; pl.* **prud·er·ies.** **1** The quality or state of being prudish; exaggerated or priggish modesty. **2** A prudish remark or act.

prud·ish \'prüd-ish\ *adj.* Like or characteristic of a prude; showing prudery. — **prud·ish·ly**, *adv.*

prune \'prün\ *n.* A plum of any variety that can be dried without fermenting; the plum so dried.

prune \'prün\ *v.;* **pruned**; **prun·ing.** To preen; to prink.

prune \'prün\ *v.;* **pruned**; **prun·ing.** **1** To cut off the dead or unwanted branches, twigs, or parts of a bush or tree; to trim; as, to *prune* rosebushes. **2** To cut off or out all useless parts, as unnecessary words or phrases. — **prun·er** \'prün-r\ *n.*

pru·ri·ent \'prür-ē-ənt\ *adj.* Having or revealing indecent desires or thoughts; lewd. — **pru·ri·ence** \-ən(t)s\ *n.* — **pru·ri·ent·ly**, *adv.*

prus·sic acid \'prəs-ik\. A poisonous volatile acid having a peach-blossom odor, used as an insecticide.

pry \'prī\ *n.; pl.* **pries** \'prīz\. A lever used for prying. — *v.;* **pried** \'prīd\; **pry·ing.** **1** To raise, open, or move, or try to do so, with a lever; as, to *pry* off a tight lid. **2** To get at with great difficulty; as, to try to *pry* a secret out of a person.

pry \'prī\ *v.;* **pried** \'prīd\; **pry·ing.** To look curiously or inquisitively; to peep; to peer searchingly; to snoop. — *n.* A person who pries.

P.S. \'pē-'es\. Abbreviation for *postscript.*

p's. Pl. of *p.*

psalm \'säm, 'såm\ *n.* **1** A sacred song or poem; a hymn. **2** [with a capital] One of the hymns that make up one book of the Old Testament.

psalm·ist \'säm-əst, 'såm-\ *n.* A writer or composer of sacred songs.

psalm·o·dy \'säm-əd-ē, 'såm-\ *n.; pl.* **psalm·o·dies.** **1** The singing of psalms or sacred songs in worship. **2** Psalms collectively or a collection of psalms.

Psal·ter \'sólt-r\ *n.* **1** The Book of Psalms of the Old Testament, especially when separately printed. **2** The part of a prayer book or breviary containing the Psalms.

psal·tery \'sólt-r-ē\ *n.; pl.* **psal·ter·ies.** **1** An ancient stringed instrument resembling a zither. **2** [with a capital] The Psalter.

pseu·do \'süd-,ō\ *adj.* Sham; pretended; false; spurious; deceptively resembling; as, a *pseudo* poet — used commonly also, especially in modern science, as a prefix with a variety of meanings all related to the meanings of the adjective.

pseu·do·nym \'süd-n-,im\ *n.* A fictitious name used for a time, as by an author; a pen name.

pseu·do·pod \'süd-ə-,päd\ *n.* A pseudopodium.

pseu·do·po·di·um \,süd-ə-'pōd-ē-əm\ *n.; pl.* **pseu·do·po·dia** \-ē-ə\. A part of a cell that is temporarily protruded by moving cytoplasm, as in the amoeba, and that helps to move the cell and to take in its food.

pshaw \'shó\ *interj.* An exclamation of disgust, contempt, or impatience.

psit·ta·co·sis \,sit-ə-'kō-səs\ *n.* A contagious wasting disease of birds, especially parrots, that is communicable to man.

PST. Abbreviation for *Pacific Standard Time.*

psy·che \'sīk-ē\ *n.* The soul, mind, or mental life of a person.

psy·chi·at·ric \,sīk-ē-'a-trik\ *adj.* Of or relating to psychiatry. — **psy·chi·at·ri·cal·ly** \-trik-l(-)ē\ *adv.*

psy·chi·a·trist \sə-'kī-ə-trəst, sī-\ *n.* A specialist in psychiatry.

psy·chi·a·try \sə-'kī-ə-trē, sī-\ *n.* The branch of medicine dealing with mental disorders.

psy·chic \'sīk-ik\ *adj.* **1** Of or relating to a person's soul, mind, or mental life. **2** Not physical; not to be explained by knowledge of natural laws. **3** Sensitive to influences or forces supposedly exerted from beyond the natural world. — *n.* A person supposedly sensitive to supernatural forces; a psychic medium. — **psy·chi·cal** \-ik-l\ *adj.* — **psy·chi·cal·ly** \-ik-l(-)ē\ *adv.*

psy·cho·anal·y·sis \,sīk-,ō-ə-'nal-ə-səs\ *n.; pl.* **psy·cho·anal·y·ses** \-,sēz\. A method of explaining and treating emotional disorders that emphasizes the importance of the patient's talking freely about himself while under treatment, especially about early childhood memories and experiences and about his dreams. — **psy·cho·an·a·lyt·ic** \-,an-l-'it-ik\ or **psy·cho·an·a·lyt·i·cal** \-ik-l\ *adj.* — **psy·cho·an·a·lyt·i·cal·ly** \-ik-l(-)ē\ *adv.*

psy·cho·an·a·lyst \,sīk-,ō-'an-l-əst\ *n.* A specialist in psychoanalysis.

psy·cho·an·a·lyze \,sīk-,ō-'an-l-,īz\ *v.;* **psy·cho·an·a·lyzed**; **psy·cho·an·a·lyz·ing.** To give or subject to psychoanalytic treatment.

psy·cho·log·i·cal \,sīk-l-'äj-ik-l\ *adj.* **1** Of or relating to the science of psychology; as, *psychological* experiments. **2** Of or relating to a person's mental and emotional make-up; as, an event that did much *psychological* damage to the small boy. **3** Intended to affect morale as by weakening that of an enemy; as, *psychological* warfare. — **psy·cho·log·i·cal·ly** \-ik-l(-)ē\ *adv.*

psy·chol·o·gist \sī-'käl-ə-jəst\ *n.* A specialist in psychology.

psy·chol·o·gy \sī-'käl-ə-jē\ *n.; pl.* **psy·chol·o·gies.** [From scientific Latin *psychologia*, a compound derived from Greek *psyche* meaning "mind", "soul", and *-logia* meaning "study of".] **1** The science that studies mental activity and behavior, especially in human beings. **2** A characteristic way of thinking or behaving; as, to understand a person's *psychology*.

psy·cho·path·ic \ˌsīk-ˌō-ˈpath-ik\ *adj.* **1** Of or relating to mental disease or disorder. **2** Susceptible to or having mental disease or derangement.

psy·cho·pa·thol·o·gy \ˌsīk-ō-pa-ˈthäl-ə-jē, -pə-\ *n.* The science that investigates mental disorders from a psychological point of view.

psy·cho·sis \sī-ˈkō-səs\ *n.; pl.* **psy·cho·ses** \-ˌsēz\. Mental disease; any serious mental derangement.

pt. Abbreviation for: **1** part. **2** pint. **3** point.

P.T.A. \ˈpē-ˌtē-ˈā\. Abbreviation for *Parent-Teacher Association.*

ptar·mi·gan \ˈtär-mig-n, ˈtȧr-\ *n.; pl.* **ptar·mi·gans** or **ptar·mi·gan.** Any of various species of grouse of northern regions, with completely feathered feet.

pte·rid·o·phyte \tə-ˈrid-ə-ˌfīt, ˈter-ə-dō-\ *n.* Any of a phylum of plants including the ferns and their allies.

pter·o·dac·tyl \ˌter-ə-ˈdakt-l\ *n.* An extinct flying reptile having a featherless membrane extending from the body and forming the supporting surface of the wings.

pto·maine \ˈtō-ˌmān, tō-ˈmān\ *n.* Any of certain complex organic compounds produced by bacteria during the putrefaction of nitrogen-containing materials and formerly thought to cause ptomaine poisoning.

ptomaine poisoning. Any severe stomach and intestinal disturbance caused by eating food that has been contaminated, as with certain bacteria or their poisonous products or with chemical sprays.

pty·a·lin \ˈtī-ə-lən\ *n.* An enzyme in the saliva of man that helps to change starch into sugar that can be absorbed in the body.

pub \ˈpəb\ *n. British.* A public house.

pu·ber·ty \ˈpyüb-rt-ē\ *n.* The age at which a boy or a girl undergoes a physical change that marks the beginning of manhood or womanhood, often legally fixed at 14 years for boys and 12 for girls.

pu·bic \ˈpyü-bik\ *adj.* Of or relating to the lower middle part of the abdomen or the pubis.

pu·bis \ˈpyü-bəs\ *n.; pl.* **pu·bes** \-ˌbēz\. The front one of the three bones that compose each hipbone.

pub·lic \ˈpəb-lik\ *adj.* **1** Of or relating to the people; belonging to or affecting a nation, state, or community; not private; as, *public* opinion. **2** Open to all; not limited in use, enjoyment, or admission; serving everybody; for the use of the public; as, a *public* meeting; a *public* library. **3** Not kept secret; generally known. The story became *public.* **4** Engaged in activities that bring or keep a person prominently before the people at large; as, men in *public* life. **5** Having a position, especially an official position, representing the people at large; as, the *public* prosecutor. — *n.* **1** The people of a nation, state, or community; persons in general; as, a lecture that is open to the *public.* **2** A particular group or body of people; as, an artist's *public.* — **pub·lic·ly,** *adv.*

pub·lic-ad·dress system. An apparatus, including one or more loud-speakers, for reproducing sound so that it may be heard by a large audience, as in an auditorium or out of doors.

pub·li·can \ˈpəb-lik-n\ *n.* **1** In ancient Rome, a tax collector. **2** *British.* A keeper of a public house.

pub·li·ca·tion \ˌpəb-lə-ˈkāsh-n\ *n.* **1** A publishing or a being published; public notification; as, the *publication* of a new traffic law. **2** The issuing to the public of copies of something, as a book or engraving. **3** The business of printing and issuing such works. **4** Something that is published, as a book, magazine, or pamphlet offered for sale or public notice.

public house. Any inn or hotel; especially, *British,* a place where liquors are sold by the glass, to be drunk on the premises.

pub·li·cist \ˈpəb-lə-səst\ *n.* **1** A person who is skilled in or who writes on international law. **2** A writer, as a journalist, on matters of public policy or public interest. **3** An agent in charge of publicity, as for a business. **4** A spokesman or agitator, as for a cause or a point of view.

pub·lic·i·ty \(ˌ)pəb-ˈlis-ət-ē\ *n.* **1** The condition of being public or publicly known. **2** Advertising of any kind. **3** Information with a news value designed to further the interests of a place, person, or cause; as, *publicity* for a school play. **4** Any action or matter that gains public attention or the attention gained by such action or matter; as, to like *publicity.*

pub·li·cize \ˈpəb-lə-ˌsīz\ *v.;* **pub·li·cized; pub·li·ciz·ing.** To give publicity to.

public school. **1** In England, any of various select endowed schools that give a liberal education and prepare students for the universities. **2** An elementary or secondary school maintained by local government.

public servant. **1** An officer or employee of a government. **2** An individual or corporation that provides a public service, as by supplying gas, electricity, or water.

public utility. A business organization supplying products or services that are used by the public, as gas and electricity, and that are subject to government regulation.

public works. Works constructed with public funds for public use or enjoyment, as roads, dams, docks, and canals.

pub·lish \ˈpəb-lish\ *v.* **1** To make public announcement of; to make known to people in general; to proclaim; as, to *publish* one's opinions far and wide. **2** To bring before the public for sale or distribution; to issue in printed form; as, to *publish* a newspaper.

pub·lish·er \ˈpəb-lish-r\ *n.* One that publishes something; especially, one that issues something from the press and offers it for sale or circulation, as books, magazines, or newspapers.

puck \'pək\ *n.* **1** [often with a capital] A mischievous sprite; a tricky household fairy. **2** A hard rubber disk used in the game of hockey.

puck·er \'pək-r\ *v.;* **puck·ered; puck·er·ing** \-r(-)ing\. To draw up into folds or wrinkles; as, to *pucker* one's forehead. The cloth *puckered* in shrinking. — *n.* A fold or wrinkle caused by puckering.

pud·ding \'pu̇d-ing\ *n.* A dessert having flour or some other starch as a foundation, with other ingredients, as milk, sugar, eggs, and flavoring, added.

pudding stone. A rock made up of rounded fragments varying from small pebbles to large boulders, in a natural cement, as of hardened clay or silica.

pud·dle \'pəd-l\ *n.* **1** A small pool of liquid, especially dirty or muddy water. **2** A mass of clay or clay and sand that has been worked when wet until water will not pass through it. — *v.;* **pud·dled; pud·dling** \-l(-)ing\. **1** To cover with puddles. **2** To make a puddle of, as clay.

pudgy \'pəj-ē\ *adj.;* **pudg·i·er; pudg·i·est.** Short and plump; dumpy.

pu·eb·lo \pü-'eb-ˌlō, 'pweb-\ *n.; pl.* **pu·eb·los.** **1** One of the Indian villages in Arizona or New Mexico, built of stone or adobe, often several stories high. **2** Any Indian village of the southwestern United States.

pu·er·ile \'pyu̇-ər-əl, 'pyu̇r-əl\ *adj.* Childish; silly; as, a *puerile* remark. — **pu·er·il·i·ty** \ˌpyu̇-ə-'ril-ət-ē\ *n.*

Puer·to Ri·can \ˌpōrt-ə 'rēk-n, ˌpȯrt-ə, ˌpwert-ə\ *adj.* Of or relating to Puerto Rico. — *n.* A native or inhabitant of Puerto Rico.

puff \'pəf\ *n.* **1** A quick, short letting out of the breath; any short, sudden discharge, as of air, smoke, or steam; as, *puffs* from a locomotive. **2** A very light pastry that has puffed out in cooking. **3** A soft pad for applying powder, as to the skin. **4** A thick light quilt filled with wool or down. **5** A swelling, as from a bruise. **6** A series of large, loose gathers; as, a dress with *puffs* at the hip. — *v.* **1** To blow in puffs or whiffs; to let out puffs, as of breath or smoke; as, to *puff* at a pipe; to pant and *puff.* **2** To move, run, or speak while letting out puffs; as, to *puff* up a hill. **3** To fill or become full, as with wind; to stick out; to swell; as, to *puff* out one's cheeks.

puff adder. A thick-bodied, extremely poisonous African snake that can swell its body greatly when irritated.

puff·ball \'pəf-ˌbȯl\ *n.* Any of various, mostly edible, round fungi that discharge ripe spores in a cloud resembling smoke when they are disturbed.

puff·er \'pəf-r\ *n.* **1** One that puffs. **2** Any of various fishes that can inflate their bodies with air.

puf·fin \'pəf-n\ *n.* A sea bird of the same family as the auk, about a foot long, with a short neck and a deep, grooved bill having marks of different colors.

puffy \'pəf-ē\ *adj.;* **puff·i·er; puff·i·est.** **1** Blowing or breathing with puffs; puffing. **2** Swollen or distended; as, a *puffy* ankle. **3** Soft and very light; as, a *puffy* cushion.

pug \'pəg\ *n.* **1** A small, stocky, usually short-haired dog having a massive round head, a blunt, square muzzle, and a tightly curled tail. **2** A nose (**pug nose**) turning up at the tip and usually short and thick.

pug

pu·gi·list \'pyüj-l-əst\ *n.* One who fights with his fists; a boxer. — **pu·gi·lis·tic** \ˌpyüj-l-'is-tik\ *adj.*

pug·na·cious \ˌpəg-'nā-shəs\ *adj.* Fond of fighting; quarrelsome; as, a *pugnacious* dog. — **pug·na·cious·ly,** *adv.* — **pug·nac·i·ty** \-'nas-ət-ē\ *n.*

pu·is·sance \'pyü-ə-sən(t)s, pyü-'is-n(t)s\ *n.* Power; might; as, a knight whose *puissance* was often tried in battle. — **pu·is·sant** \-ə-sənt, -'is-nt\ *adj.*

pule \'pyül\ *v.;* **puled; pul·ing.** To whimper; to whine; as, a *puling* infant.

pull \'pu̇l\ *v.* **1** To use force so as to draw or try to draw near; to tug; as, to *pull* on a rope. **2** To move or get under way. The train *pulled* out of the station. **3** To gather with the hands; to pluck; as, to *pull* radishes. **4** To extract; as, to *pull* a tooth. **5** To draw apart; to tear; as, to *pull* a flower to pieces. **6** To stretch; to work by stretching; as, to *pull* taffy. **7** *Slang.* To draw out; as, to *pull* a gun. **8** To strain; as, to *pull* a tendon. — **pull oneself together.** To regain one's composure; to calm down. — **pull through.** To come successfully through, as danger, an illness, or troubles; as, a boy who was badly hurt, but is expected to *pull through.* — *n.* **1** Act of pulling; as, two *pulls* of a bell. **2** The force of something that pulls; as, to feel the *pull* of a hand. **3** A hard climb; as, a long *pull* up the hill. **4** A knob, cord, or handle for pulling something; as, a bell *pull.* **5** *Slang.* Influence; special favor; as, to use *pull* to get a certain job. — **pull·er,** *n.*

pul·let \'pu̇l-ət\ *n.* A young hen, especially one less than a year old.

pul·ley \'pu̇l-ē\ *n.; pl.* **pul·leys.** A wheel with a grooved rim in which a belt, rope, or chain runs, used in running a machine, in lifting, or in changing the direction of a pulling force.

Pull·man car or **Pull·man** \'pu̇l-mən\ *n.* [Named after George M. *Pullman* (1831–1897), the American inventor who first designed such cars.] **1** A sleeping car. **2** A parlor car.

pull·over \'pu̇l-ˌōv-r\ *n.* A sweater or blouse that is put on by pulling it over the head.

pul·mo·nary \'pu̇l-mə-ˌner-ē, 'pəl-\ *adj.* **1** Relating to or affecting the lungs. **2** Having lungs.

pulp \'pəlp\ *n.* **1** The soft juicy or fleshy part of a fruit or vegetable; as, the *pulp* of an apple. **2** A mass of vegetable matter from which the moisture has been squeezed. **3** The soft, sensitive tissue that fills the central cavity of a tooth. **4** A soft moist mass; especially, a mass of ground rag or wood fibers softened in water and used in making paper.

5 [usually in the plural] A magazine printed on rough-surfaced paper, especially, one featuring sensational articles. — *v.* To reduce to pulp.

pul·pit \ˈpu̇l-ˌpit, ˈpəl-, -pət\ *n.* **1** An elevated place in which a clergyman stands at a religious service, especially while preaching. **2** Preachers as a class; preaching; as, the power of the *pulpit.*

pulp·wood \ˈpəlp-ˌwu̇d\ *n.* The wood of certain trees, as spruces and aspens, used in making paper.

pulpy \ˈpəl-pē\ *adj.;* **pulp·i·er**; **pulp·i·est**. Like pulp; consisting of pulp.

pul·que \ˈpül-ˌkā, -kē\ *n.* A fermented drink made in Mexico from the juice of the maguey.

pul·sate \ˈpəl-ˌsāt\ *v.;* **pul·sat·ed**; **pul·sat·ing**. To have or show a beat or pulse; to throb.

pul·sa·tion \ˌpəl-ˈsāsh-n\ *n.* A throbbing or vibrating; a beat; a throb.

pulse \ˈpəls\ *n.* The seeds of various plants of the pea family, as peas, beans, and lentils, which are used as food; one of these plants.

pulse \ˈpəls\ *n.* **1** Also **pulse beat**. The throbbing of the arteries caused by the contractions of the heart. **2** A rhythmical beating or throbbing. — *v.;* **pulsed**; **puls·ing**. To throb; to beat.

pul·ver·ize \ˈpəlv-r-ˌīz\ *v.;* **pul·ver·ized**; **pul·ver·iz·ing**. **1** To reduce or be reduced into a powder or dust, as by beating or grinding. **2** To demolish as if by pulverizing; to smash to pieces.

pu·ma \ˈpyü-mə, ˈpü-\ *n.; pl.* **pu·mas** or **pu·ma**. A cougar.

pum·ice \ˈpəm-əs\ *n.* or **pumice stone**. A very light porous volcanic glass used, especially powdered, for cleaning, polishing, and smoothing.

pum·mel \ˈpəm-l\ *v.;* **pum·meled** or **pum·melled**; **pum·mel·ing** or **pum·mel·ling** \-l(-)ing\. To beat, as with the fists or a stick; to pommel.

pump \ˈpəmp\ *n.* A low shoe not fastened on, gripping the foot only at the toe and heel.

pump \ˈpəmp\ *n.* A device for raising, transferring, or compressing fluids or gases, operating usually by suction or pressure or both; as, a water *pump;* an air *pump.* — *v.* **1** To raise, transfer, or compress by means of a pump; as, to *pump* up water. **2** To free, as from water or air, by the use of a pump; as, to *pump* a boat dry. **3** To fill by means of a pump; as, to *pump* up a tire. **4** To draw, force, or drive onward in the manner of a pump. The heart *pumps* blood into the arteries. **5** To move up and down like a pump handle; as, to *pump* the hand of a friend. **6** To subject to persistent questioning to find out something; to draw out by such questioning; as, to *pump* a secret out; to *pump* someone for information. — **pump·er**, *n.*

hand pump for water

pum·per·nick·el \ˈpəmp-r-ˌnik-l\ *n.* [From German, where it was originally a term of abuse for people, and probably applied to the bread because it is hard to digest.] A dark and somewhat sour rye bread.

pump·kin \ˈpəngk-n, ˈpəm(p)-kən\ *n.* **1** A large, round, orange or yellow fruit of a vine of the gourd family, widely used as food. **2** The prickly, hairy vine that bears this fruit.

pump·kin·seed \ˈpəngk-n-ˌsēd, ˈpəm(p)-kən-\ *n.* Any of various small fresh-water sunfishes, especially one with a red spot on the gill cover.

pun \ˈpən\ *n.* A play on words of the same sound but different meanings or on different meanings or applications of a single word. — *v.;* **punned**; **punning**. To make a pun.

punch \ˈpənch\ *n.* A drink made of various, usually many, ingredients and often flavored with wine or distilled liquor.

punch \ˈpənch\ *v.* **1** To prod with a stick; to poke; to drive or herd; as, to *punch* cattle. **2** To strike with the fist. **3** To press or strike a key or button of, as in order to print or record; as, to *punch* a typewriter; to *punch* a time clock. **4** To pierce or stamp with a punch. The conductor *punched* our tickets. — *n.* **1** A blow with the fist; as, a *punch* on the head. **2** A tool for piercing, pricking, stamping, or cutting. **3** Effective force; as, a team that was well trained but lacked *punch.* — **punch·er**, *n.*

punch, *n.* 2

punch card \ˈpənch\ or **punched card** \ˈpəncht\. A card for recording information by means of holes punched in particular positions each of which has its own significance, for use in various electrically operated machines, as automatic sorting machines or accounting equipment.

pun·cheon \ˈpənch-n\ *n.* A large cask, typically holding about twice as much as a barrel.

punc·til·io \ˌpəng(k)-ˈtil-ē-ˌō\ *n.; pl.* **punc·til·i·os**. **1** A fine point or detail, as of manners, conduct, or dress; a formality. **2** Careful observance of proper forms, as in dress or manners.

punc·til·i·ous \ˌpəng(k)-ˈtil-ē-əs\ *adj.* Very attentive to the fine points of conduct and manners; as, to be *punctilious* about keeping one's engagements. — **punc·til·i·ous·ly**, *adv.*

punc·tu·al \ˈpəng(k)-chə-wəl, -chəl\ *adj.* Arriving, or doing some appointed thing, exactly at the right time; prompt; especially, not late.

punc·tu·al·i·ty \ˌpəng(k)-chə-ˈwal-ət-ē\ *n.* The quality or fact of being punctual, especially in keeping appointments.

punc·tu·al·ly \ˈpəng(k)-chə-lē, -chə-wə-lē\ *adv.* On time; promptly.

punc·tu·ate \ˈpəng(k)-chə-ˌwāt\ *v.;* **punc·tu·at·ed**; **punc·tu·at·ing**. **1** To mark or divide, as a sentence, with punctuation marks. **2** To interrupt at intervals; as, a speech *punctuated* by a harsh cough.

punc·tu·a·tion \ˌpəng(k)-chə-ˈwāsh-n\ *n.* **1** The act of punctuating. **2** The division of sentences, clauses, and phrases by means of certain marks (**punctuation marks**), especially the period, comma, semicolon, and colon, in order to help make meaning clear by showing the structure of sentence parts; as, to study *punctuation* in school.

punc·ture \'pəng(k)-chər\ *n.* **1** The act of puncturing. **2** A hole or a slight wound resulting from puncturing; as, a slight *puncture* of the skin; a tire with a *puncture.* — *v.;* **punc·tured**; **punc·tur·ing.** **1** To pierce with something pointed; to prick. A nail *punctured* the tire. **2** To get a puncture in, as a tire. **3** To take the force or life out of something; to destroy; as, to *puncture* a person's hopes. — **punc·tur·a·ble** \-chər-əb-l\ *adj.*

pun·gen·cy \'pənj-n-sē\ *n.* The quality or state of being pungent; sharpness, as of taste or smell; keenness, as of feeling.

pun·gent \'pənj-nt\ *adj.* **1** Causing a sharp or biting sensation, as through the taste or smell. Mustard is *pungent.* **2** Sharply stimulating to the mind; as, a *pungent* criticism; *pungent* wit. — **pun·gent·ly**, *adv.*

punier. Comparative of *puny.*

puniest. Superlative of *puny.*

pun·ish \'pən-ish\ *v.* **1** To cause to suffer, as by enduring pain or loss of freedom or privileges, for an offense committed; to chastise; as, to *punish* criminals with imprisonment; to *punish* a child for disobedience. **2** To inflict punishment for, as a fault or crime; as, to *punish* treason with death. **3** To deal with or handle severely or roughly; as, a boxer badly *punished* by his opponent.

pun·ish·a·ble \'pən-ish-əb-l\ *adj.* Deserving punishment; liable to punishment.

pun·ish·ment \'pən-ish-mənt\ *n.* **1** The act of punishing or the state or fact of being punished. A prison is a place of confinement for persons undergoing *punishment* for criminal acts. **2** The penalty for a fault or crime; as, the *punishment* for speeding. **3** Severe, rough, or disastrous treatment; as, trees showing the effects of *punishment* by a heavy storm.

pu·ni·tive \'pyü-nət-iv\ *adj.* **1** Of or relating to punishment or penalties; as, *punitive* law. **2** Intended to inflict punishment; as, a *punitive* expedition against outlaws.

punk \'pəngk\ *n.* **1** Partly decayed, crumbly wood useful as tinder. **2** A spongy substance made from parts of certain fungi for use as tinder, as in lighting fireworks.

punk \'pəngk\ *adj. Slang.* **1** Very bad; poor; inferior. **2** In poor health; miserable.

punt \'pənt\ *n.* **1** *Chiefly British.* A flat-bottomed boat with square ends, usually propelled with a pole. **2** The act or an instance of punting a football. — *v.* **1** To propel, as a punt, by pushing with a pole. **2** To travel or carry in a punt. **3** To kick a football before it touches the ground after dropping it from the hands. — **punt·er**, *n.*

pu·ny \'pyü-nē\ *adj.;* **pu·ni·er**; **pu·ni·est**. Much smaller or slighter than it should be; weak in power, size, or importance; as, a *puny* child.

pup \'pəp\ *n.* **1** A young dog; a puppy. **2** A young seal.

pu·pa \'pyüp-ə\ *n.; pl.* **pu·pas** \'pyüp-əz\ or **pu·pae** \'pyü-ˌpē\. An insect, as a moth, bee, or beetle, in the stage of development in which it is in a case or cocoon changing from a larva to an adult. —**pu·pal** \'pyüp-l\ *adj.*

pu·pate \'pyü-ˌpāt\ *v.;* **pu·pat·ed**; **pu·pat·ing.** To become a pupa. — **pu·pa·tion** \pyü-'pāsh-n\ *n.*

pu·pil \'pyüp-l\ *n.* The small opening in the center of the iris which appears like a black spot in the middle of the eye and contracts and expands according to the degree of light.

pu·pil \'pyüp-l\ *n.* A boy or girl in school; any person under the care of a teacher.

pu·pil·age \'pyüp-l-ij\ *n.* The state or time of being a pupil.

pup·pet \'pəp-ət\ *n.* **1** A doll. **2** A doll, or a similar figure representing a person or animal, moved by wires or strings or by the hands from behind the scenes, as in a dance or a little play (**puppet show**); a marionette. **3** A person who does blindly what another wishes done, as a member of a government (**puppet government**) kept in office and acting at the direction of a foreign power.

pup·py \'pəp-ē\ *n.; pl.* **pup·pies.** **1** A young dog. **2** A silly youth.

pur·blind \'pər-ˌblīnd\ *adj.* Lacking in vision, insight, or understanding — formerly used to indicate total or partial physical blindness.

pur·chase \'pərch-əs\ *v.;* **pur·chased**; **pur·chas·ing.** To buy for a price; as, to *purchase* a house; men who *purchased* freedom dearly. — *n.* **1** The act of purchasing; as, the *purchase* of supplies. **2** Something purchased; as, an extravagant *purchase.* **3** A secure hold or grasp or place to stand. The climber could not get a *purchase* on the ledge. — **pur·chas·a·ble** \'pərch-ə-səb-l\ *adj.* — **pur·chas·er** \-əs-r\ *n.*

pure \'pyu̇r\ *adj.;* **pur·er**; **pur·est.** **1** Not mixed with anything else; free from everything that might taint or lower the quality; as, *pure* water; *pure* French. **2** Free from sin; innocent; chaste. **3** Mere; absolute; nothing other than; as, *pure* nonsense. **4** Abstract; theoretical; as, *pure* science.

pure·bred \'pyu̇r-'bred\ *adj.* Belonging to a recognized breed kept pure for many generations.

pu·rée \pyə-'rā\ *n.* Food boiled to a pulp and forced through a sieve; a soup thickened with such food; as, tomato *purée.*

pure·ly \'pyu̇r-lē\ *adv.* Completely; entirely.

pur·ga·tive \'pər-gət-iv\ *adj.* Tending to act as a purge or a laxative. — *n.* A purge; a cathartic.

pur·ga·to·ry \'pər-gə-ˌtōr-ē, -ˌtȯr-ē\ *n.* In the teachings of the Roman Catholic Church, an intermediate state after death in which the souls of those who die in God's grace are purified of their sins by suffering.

purge \'pərj\ *v.;* **purged**; **purg·ing.** **1** To cleanse; to purify; especially, to free from sin or guilt. **2** To clear the bowels by the use of a medicine. — *n.* **1** A purging; a cleansing. **2** A cathartic.

pu·ri·fi·ca·tion \ˌpyu̇r-ə-fə-'kāsh-n\ *n.* The act of purifying or a being purified; the act or process of removing impure, harmful, or foreign matter.

pu·ri·fy \'pyůr-ə-ˌfī\ *v.;* **pu·ri·fied** \-ˌfīd\; **pu·ri·fy·ing. 1** To make pure; to free from impurities. Most cities find it necessary to *purify* their water supplies. **2** To cleanse spiritually.

Pu·rim \'pu̇r-(ˌ)im\ *n.* An annual Jewish festival, observed in February or March, commemorating the deliverance of the Jews from the massacre plotted by Haman.

pur·ist \'pyůr-əst\ *n.* A person who is very particular about purity or nicety, especially in language.

pu·ri·tan \'pyůr-ət-n\ *n.* [From the *Puritans,* a name applied to the members of various religious sects in England and America in the 16th and 17th centuries who are renowned for their strict moral codes and who were so called because they wished to "purify" the existing church.] A person who preaches or openly follows a much stricter moral code than that which prevails in his time. — **pu·ri·tan·i·cal** \ˌpyůr-ə-'tan-ik-l\ or **pu·ri·tan·ic** \-'tan-ik\ *adj.* — **pu·ri·tan·i·cal·ly** \-ik-l(-)ē\ *adv.*

pu·ri·ty \'pyůr-ət-ē\ *n.* **1** Freedom from impurities; cleanness; as, the *purity* of a water supply. **2** Freedom from guilt or sin; as, *purity* of life. **3** Freedom from all elements considered inappropriate in any way, as grammatical errors, unidiomatic expressions, substandard language such as slang, and, sometimes, foreign or newly coined words; as, *purity* of style in writing.

purl \'pərl\ *v.* To invert the stitches in knitting.

purl \'pərl\ *v.* **1** To run swiftly around, as a small stream flowing among rocks. **2** To make a murmuring sound, as the waters of a brook. — *n.* **1** A purling stream; a rill. **2** A murmuring sound.

pur·lieu \'pərl-ˌ(y)ü\ *n.* **1** An outlying or adjacent district. **2** [in the plural] Environs; outskirts, as of a city or town.

pur·loin \(ˌ)pər-'lȯin, 'pər-ˌlȯin\ *v.* To steal; to filch. — **pur·loin·er,** *n.*

pur·ple \'pərp-l\ *n.* **1** A color which is a combination of blue and red, including many shades, such as violet and lavender. **2** Imperial or regal rank or power; high station; as, born to the *purple.* — *v.;* **pur·pled; pur·pling** \-l(-)ing\. To make or become purple. — *adj.* Of the color purple.

pur·plish \'pərp-l(-)ish\ *adj.* Somewhat purple.

pur·port \(ˌ)pər-'pōrt, -'pȯrt\ *v.* To give the impression of being; to claim; to profess; as, a medicine *purporting* to cure all ills. — \'pər-ˌpōrt, -ˌpȯrt\ *n.* Meaning; import; gist; as, the *purport* of the conversation.

pur·pose \'pərp-əs\ *v.;* **pur·posed; pur·pos·ing.** To have as one's intention; to resolve to do or bring about. — *n.* **1** Aim; design; intention; as, a knife sharp enough to serve one's *purpose.* **2** That which is purposed; the end aimed at or attained; as, to work hard but to little *purpose.* — **on purpose.** Purposely; intentionally.

pur·pose·ful \'pərp-əs-fəl\ *adj.* Having a purpose; guided by a definite aim. — **pur·pose·ful·ly** \-fə-lē\ *adv.*

pur·pose·ly \'pərp-əs-lē\ *adv.* With a clear or known purpose; intentionally.

purr or **pur** \'pər\ *v.;* **purred; purr·ing.** To make a low murmuring sound such as that made by a contented cat. — *n.* The sound of purring.

purse \'pərs\ *n.* **1** A bag or pouch for money. **2** A woman's handbag or pocketbook. **3** The contents of a purse; money; as, to have a lean *purse.* **4** A sum of money offered as a prize or collected as a present; as, a *purse* for a retiring pastor. — *v.;* **pursed; purs·ing. 1** To put into a purse; to pocket. **2** To pucker; to draw together; as, to *purse* one's lips.

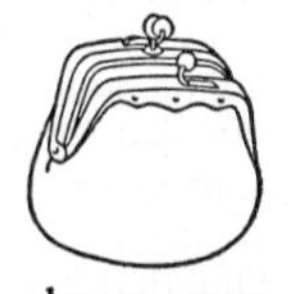
change purse

purs·er \'pərs-r\ *n.* A clerk on a passenger vessel who keeps the accounts.

purs·lane \'pərs-lən, -ˌlān\ *n.* A fleshy-leaved trailing plant with bright yellow flowers, mainly regarded as a troublesome weed but sometimes eaten as a vegetable or in salads.

pur·su·ance \pər-'sü-ən(t)s\ *n.* The act of pursuing or carrying out; as, in *pursuance* of his plans.

pur·su·ant \pər-'sü-ənt\ *adj.* In consequence; according; as, *pursuant* to your instructions.

pur·sue \pər 'sü\ *v.;* **pur·sued; pur·su·ing. 1** To follow after; to chase. The dogs *pursued* the fox. **2** To seek; to try to obtain; as, to *pursue* pleasure. **3** To follow with an end in view; to proceed with; to continue; as, to *pursue* a wise course. **4** To follow as a trade or profession; as, to *pursue* law or medicine. — For synonyms see *follow.* — **pur·su·er** \-'sü-ər\ *n.*

pur·suit \pər-'süt\ *n.* **1** Act of pursuing; as, *pursuit* of a retreating enemy. **2** An occupation; as, to choose a *pursuit* that interests one.

pur·vey \pər-'vā\ *v.* To supply, as provisions. — **pur·vey·ance** \-'vā-ən(t)s\ *n.*

pur·vey·or \pər-'vā-ər\ *n.* A person who supplies, especially provisions; a caterer.

pus \'pəs\ *n.* Yellowish white creamy matter, chiefly dead tissue, leucocytes, and bacteria, produced by an abscess or boil.

push \'pu̇sh\ *v.* **1** To use force so as to drive or move away; to shove. **2** To thrust forward, downward, or outward; to press against; as, a tree *pushing* its roots deep in the soil. **3** To press forward; to urge on; to drive ahead; as, to *push* a task to completion. **4** To bear hard upon so as to involve in difficulty; as, to be *pushed* for funds. — **push off. 1** To move away from shore in a boat by pushing. **2** To start; to set out. — *n.* **1** A pushing movement or force; a shove; as, to give the car a *push.* **2** Energy; a capacity for hard work; aggressiveness; as, a person who is listless and lacks *push.* — **push·er,** *n.*

push button. A small button or knob that, when pushed, operates something, as a switch or a bell, by closing an electric circuit. — **push-but·ton,** *adj.*

push-but·ton warfare. Warfare carried on from afar by means of weapons that are more or less self-operating after once being set in operation by or as if by pressing a push button.

push·cart \'pu̇sh-ˌkärt, -ˌkȧrt\ *n.* A cart pushed by hand, especially one used by street vendors.

pu·sil·la·nim·i·ty \ˌpyüs-l-ə-'nim-ət-ē\ *n.* The quality or condition of being pusillanimous; cowardice.

pu·sil·lan·i·mous \ˌpyüs-l-'an-ə-məs\ *adj.* **1** Lacking in manly strength or spirit; cowardly. **2** Showing or resulting from lack of courage and weakness of spirit. — **pu·sil·lan·i·mous·ly,** *adv.*

push·over \'pu̇sh-ˌōv-r\ *n.* **1** An opponent easy to defeat or incapable of effective resistance. **2** One that is either unwilling or too gullible to resist the power of a particular attraction or appeal. **3** An action or problem that offers no difficulties; a cinch.

puss \'pu̇s\ *n.* **1** A cat. **2** A girl; a young woman.

puss \'pu̇s\ *n. Slang.* The face; the mouth.

pus·sy \'pəs-ē\ *adj.;* **pus·si·er; pus·si·est.** Containing pus; like pus.

pussy \'pu̇s-ē\ *n.; pl.* **puss·ies. 1** Also **puss·y·cat** \-ˌkat\. A cat. **2** A catkin of a pussy willow.

puss·y·foot \'pu̇s-ē-ˌfu̇t\ *v.* **1** To move cautiously or stealthily. **2** To keep from taking a decided or definite stand, as in a controversy; to hedge.

pussy wil·low \'pu̇s-ē ˌwil-ō, 'wil-ō\. A willow bush or tree that bears spikes of flowers in the form of silky grayish catkins.

pussy willow

pus·tu·lar \'pəs-chəl-r\ *adj.* **1** Of, relating to, or of the nature of pustules; as, *pustular* eruptions on the skin. **2** Covered with elevations resembling pustules, as a leaf.

pus·tule \'pəs-ˌchül\ *n.* **1** A small elevation of the skin having an inflamed base and containing pus. **2** Any small elevation resembling a pimple or blister.

put \'pu̇t\ *v.;* **put; put·ting. 1** To thrust; to push. The trees *put* forth their leaves in the spring. **2** To throw overhand with a pushing motion; as, to *put* the shot. **3** To bring into a position; to place; to lay; to set. *Put* the book on the table. **4** To bring into a certain state; to cause to be or become; as, to *put* things in order; to *put* one's mind at rest. **5** To force; to drive; to urge; as, to *put* the enemy to flight; to *put* a person to work. **6** To give, as a quality, meaning, or price, to a thing; to attach; to assign; as, to *put* a value on a ring; to *put* a wrong interpretation on a statement. **7** To state so as to set before the mind; to express; as, to *put* ideas clearly. **8** To go; to proceed; as, to *put* out to sea in a small boat. — **put about.** To change direction; to turn back or around, as a ship. — **put across. 1** To carry out a trick or a deceitful plan at someone's expense; as, to *put across* the sale of worthless stock. **2** To communicate successfully. The teacher *put across* his point by use of a drawing on the blackboard. — **put by. 1** To turn, set, or push aside; to reject. **2** To lay aside; to store up; as, to *put by* money. — **put down. 1** To suppress; as, to *put down* a revolt. **2** To make a written record of; to enter in a list; as, to *put down* the things needed from the store. **3** To sink; to drill; to dig; as, to *put down* a well. — **put in. 1** To enter a harbor or place of shelter; to conduct into harbor. **2** To devote; to spend; as, to *put in* one's time at odd jobs. — **put in for. 1** To make a request or claim for; as, to *put in for* a share of the profits. **2** To offer oneself for; to become a candidate for; as, to *put in for* the position of head usher. — **put off. 1** To lay aside; to remove; to take off; as, to *put off* one's clothes. **2** To turn aside; to hinder; to baffle; as, to *put off* a question with an evasive answer. **3** To delay; to postpone; as, to *put off* answering a letter. **4** To push from land, as a boat; to leave land. — **put on. 1** To set to work; to put into action; to turn on; as, to *put on* steam. **2** To cause to depend or subsist on; as, to be *put on* a strict diet by the doctor. **3** To add to; to overload; as, to *put on* the price; to *put on* weight. **4** To pretend; to assume; as, to *put on* airs. **5** To prepare and show; as, to *put on* a play. — **put out. 1** To destroy the sight of; as, to *put out* a person's eyes. **2** To extinguish; as, to *put out* a fire. **3** To place at interest; to invest; to loan; as, to *put out* money on mortgages. **4** To provoke; to displease; to offend; to inconvenience; as, to be *put out* by an insulting remark. **5** In baseball, to cause a batter to terminate his turn at bat; to prevent a runner on the bases from continuing his progress toward home plate. — **put over. 1** To defer; to postpone. The case was *put over* until tomorrow by the judge. **2** To succeed in getting something done or accepted, as a plan. — **put through.** To carry or cause to be brought to completion; as, to *put through* a traffic regulation; to *put through* a telephone call or connection. — **put to it.** To distress; to press hard; to perplex. Even the experts were *put to it* to find an answer. — **put up. 1** To offer publicly, especially at auction; as, to *put up* goods for sale. **2** To preserve; to pickle; to can; as, to *put up* jam. **3** To put away; to place out of sight. The children were told to *put up* their toys. **4** To raise; to erect; to build; as, to *put up* a tent. **5** To give lodging to; to take lodgings; as, to *put up* travelers. **6** To nominate. **7** To pack; to make into a bundle or parcel; as, to *put up* a lunch. **8** To pay; as, to *put up* one's share. **9** To offer; to present; to confront one with; as, to *put up* a bluff; to *put up* a struggle. — **put upon.** To deceive; to impose upon; to trick; as, to feel *put upon* by being expected to work overtime. — **put up to.** To encourage toward; to set about; to incite; as, a boy *put up to* stealing by his older companions. — **put up with.** To endure without complaint; to tolerate.

put \'pu̇t\ *n.* The action of putting; a thrust; a push; a throw.

put-out \'pu̇t-ˌau̇t\ *n.* In baseball, the action of putting a player out.

pu·tre·fac·tion \ˌpyü-trə-'faksh-n\ *n.* The rotting of animal or vegetable matter. — **pu·tre·fac·tive** \-'fak-tiv\ *adj.*

pu·tre·fy \'pyü-trə-ˌfī\ *v.;* **pu·tre·fied** \-ˌfīd\; **pu·tre·fy·ing.** To make putrid; to become putrid; to decompose; to rot.

pu·tres·cent \pyü-'tres-nt\ *adj.* Becoming putrid; rotting. — **pu·tres·cence** \-n(t)s\ *n.*

pu·trid \'pyü-trəd\ *adj.* **1** Rotten; decayed; as, *putrid* flesh. **2** Coming from decayed matter; foul; as, a *putrid* smell. **3** Corrupt.

putt \'pət\ *n.* [From a Scottish variant of English *put.*] In golf, a short stroke made to play the ball into the hole. — *v.* To make a putt.

put·tee \ˌpə-'tē, pu̇-\ *n.* **1** A strip of woolen or cotton cloth wound spirally around the lower leg. **2** A leather gaiter or legging.

putt·er \'pət-r\ *n.* **1** In golf, a person who putts. **2** A golf club with a short shaft and almost perpendicular face, used in putting.

put·ter \'pu̇t-r\ *n.* **1** One that puts; as a *putter* of questions. **2** One who puts the shot.

put·ter \'pət-r\ or **pot·ter** \'pät-r\ *v.* To busy oneself with trifles; to work first at one thing and then at another with little purpose or energy; as, to spend the morning *puttering* about the house. — **put·ter·er** or **pot·ter·er** \-r-r\ *n.*

put·ty \'pət-ē\ *n.; pl.* **put·ties.** A soft cement, as for holding glass in a window frame, made usually of whiting and boiled linseed oil. — *v.;* **put·tied** \-ēd\; **put·ty·ing.** To cement or seal up with putty.

puz·zle \'pəz-l\ *v.;* **puz·zled; puz·zling** \-l(-)ing\. **1** To perplex; to confuse; to bewilder. The boy's condition *puzzled* the doctor. **2** To solve by thought or by clever guesswork; as, to *puzzle* out a mystery.

— The words *perplex* and *bewilder* are synonyms of *puzzle: puzzle* may suggest some complication that is difficult to understand or explain and that causes temporary mental confusion; *perplex* usually has the suggestion of worry and disturbance, as well as puzzlement; *bewilder* is likely to suggest an even more serious mental disturbance and such complete disorder and confusion that it may become difficult to act or make decisions.

— *n.* **1** The condition of being puzzled; perplexity. **2** Something that perplexes; a difficult problem. **3** A toy, mechanical device, or problem designed to test one's cleverness or ingenuity; as, a jigsaw *puzzle.* — **puz·zler** \-l(-)ər\ *n.*

puz·zle·ment \'pəz-l-mənt\ *n.* **1** Puzzled state; perplexity. **2** Something that perplexes; a puzzle.

pyg·my or **pig·my** \'pig-mē\ *n.; pl.* **pyg·mies** or **pig·mies.** [From the *Pygmies,* a fabled race of small people of the ancient world supposed to inhabit the upper Nile Valley, borrowed from Latin *Pygmaei,* there borrowed from Greek *Pygmaioi.*] **1** [often with a capital] A member of any of various groups or tribes of people of central Africa averaging under five feet in height. **2** A person or thing very small for its kind; a dwarf. — *adj.* Dwarfish; very small.

py·ja·mas \pə-'jäm-əz, 'jam-, -'jȧm-\ *n. pl. Chiefly British.* Pajamas.

py·lon \'pī-ˌlän\ *n.* **1** A gateway; especially, in Egyptian architecture, one composed of two flat-topped pyramids and a crosspiece. **2** A tower which serves as a support for a long span of wire. **3** A tower or post that marks the proper course of flight for an airplane.

py·lo·rus \pī-'lōr-əs, pə-, -'lȯr-\ *n.* The opening from the stomach into the intestine. — **py·lor·ic** \-'lȯr-ik, -'lär-\ *adj.*

py·or·rhea or **py·or·rhoea** \ˌpī-ə-'rē-ə\ *n.* A disease of the sockets of the teeth in which the gums become inflamed, pus forms, and the teeth gradually loosen.

pyr·a·mid \'pir-ə-ˌmid\ *n.* **1** A massive structure, usually with a square base and four triangular faces meeting at a point, used for tombs, as in ancient Egypt. **2** Something that has a shape similar to a pyramid. **3** In geometry, any solid having for its base a plane figure with three or more angles and for its sides three or more triangles which meet to form the vertex. — *v.* To build up in the form of a pyramid; to heap up.

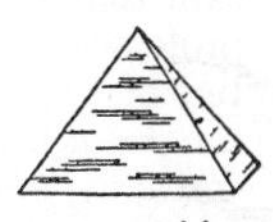
pyramid

py·ram·i·dal \pə-'ram-əd-l, ˌpir-ə-'mid-l\ *adj.* Of or relating to a pyramid; shaped like a pyramid.

pyre \'pīr\ *n.* **1** A funeral pile consisting of a heap of wood for burning a dead body. **2** Any pile to be burned.

py·re·thrum \pī-'rē-thrəm, -'reth-rəm\ *n.* **1** Any of several chrysanthemums, some grown for their showy flowers, others for the insecticides they yield. **2** An insecticide from a pyrethrum.

pyr·i·dox·ine \ˌpir-ə-'däk-ˌsēn\ *n.* A vitamin that prevents convulsions and diseases of the skin, found especially in wheat germ, yeast, and meat — called also *vitamin* B_6.

py·ri·tes \pə-'rīt-ˌēz, pī-; 'pī-ˌrīts\ *n.* Any of several metallic-looking compounds of sulfur and another element, as iron, copper, or tin.

py·ro·ma·nia \ˌpī-rə-'mā-nē-ə\ *n.* A mental disorder characterized by a persistent impulse to set something on fire.

py·ro·ma·ni·ac \ˌpī-rə-'mā-nē-ˌak\ *n.* A person suffering from pyromania.

py·ro·tech·nics \ˌpī-rə-'tek-niks\ *n. sing. and pl.* **1** The art of making fireworks; the use or display of fireworks. **2** A spectacular display, as of wit or oratory. — **py·ro·tech·nic** \-nik\ or **py·ro·tech·ni·cal** \-nik-l\ *adj.*

py·rox·y·lin \pī-'räks-l-ən\ *n.* A flammable substance resembling cotton, produced chemically from cellulose and used in the manufacture of various products, as celluloid, lacquer, and certain explosives.

py·thon \'pī-ˌthän, 'pīth-n\ *n.* [Named after *Python,* a huge serpent in Greek mythology that was slain by the god Apollo.] **1** A huge, nonpoisonous Old World snake that, like the boa, crushes its prey. **2** Any large snake, as the boa or anaconda.

q \'kyü\ *n.; pl.* **q's** \'kyüz\. The 17th letter of the alphabet.

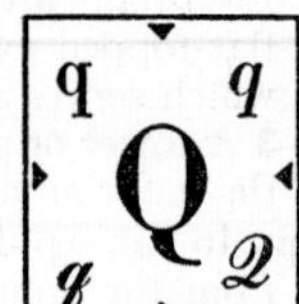

Q.E.D. \'kyü-ˌē-'dē\. [Abbreviated from Latin *quod erat demonstrandum.*] Which was to be demonstrated.

qr. Abbreviation for: **1** *quarter.* **2** *quire.*

qt. Abbreviation for *quart.*

quack \'kwak\ *v.* To utter a quack. — *n.* The cry of a duck, or a sound like it.

quack \'kwak\ *n.* **1** A person engaged, legally or illegally, in the practice of medicine who boastfully pretends to have professional knowledge and skill that he does not possess. **2** Any person who professes to have great knowledge or skill in matters of which he knows little or nothing; a charlatan. — *adj.* Being a quack; pretending to cure diseases; as, *quack* remedies; a *quack* doctor.

quack·ery \'kwak-r(-)ē\ *n.; pl.* **quack·er·ies.** The practices or the pretensions of a quack.

quad \'kwäd\ *n.* A quadrangle, as on a campus.

quad·ran·gle \'kwäd-ˌrang-gl\ *n.* **1** A plane figure having four angles and four sides; any figure having four angles. **2** A four-sided enclosure, especially when surrounded by buildings. **3** The buildings enclosing such a quadrangle. — **quad·ran·gu·lar** \kwäd-'rang-gyəl-r\ *adj.*

quad·rant \'kwäd-rənt\ *n.* **1** The quarter of a circle, an arc of 90 degrees, or the area bounded by such an arc and two radii. **2** An instrument for measuring altitudes, as in astronomy or surveying.

Q, Q, quadrants, 1

quad·rat·ic \kwäd-'rat-ik\ *adj.* **1** Square. **2** In algebra, having terms of the second degree but none of higher degree, as in **quadratic equation**, an equation in which the highest power of the unknown is a square. — *n.* A quadratic expression or equation.

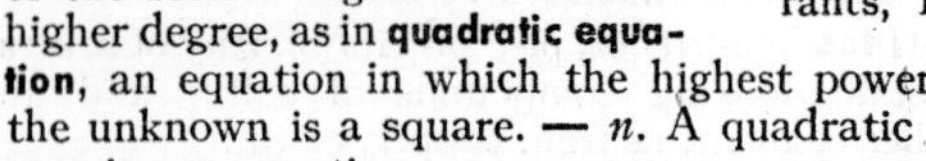

quad·rat·ics \kwäd-'rat-iks\ *n.* The branch of algebra treating of quadratic equations.

quad·ren·ni·al \kwäd-'ren-ē-əl\ *adj.* **1** Including a period of four years; lasting through four years. **2** Occurring once in four years. — **quad·ren·ni·al·ly** \-ē-ə-lē\ *adv.*

quad·ri·ceps \'kwäd-rə-ˌseps\ *n.* In full **quadriceps ex·ten·sor** \iks-'ten(t)s-r\. The great extensor muscle of the front of the thigh.

quad·ri·lat·er·al \ˌkwäd-rə-'lat-r-əl, -'la-trəl\ *adj.* Having four sides and four angles; quadrangular. — *n.* A plane figure of four sides and four angles; a quadrangle.

qua·drille \kwä-'dril, k(w)ə-\ *n.* A square dance for four couples or music for this dance.

quadrilaterals

quad·ril·lion \kwäd-'ril-yən\ *n.* In the United States, one thousand trillions; in Great Britain, one million trillions.

quad·ri·no·mi·al \ˌkwäd-rə-'nō-mē-əl\ *n.* In algebra, an expression consisting of four terms. — *adj.* Having four terms.

quad·ru·ped \'kwäd-rə-ˌped\ *n.* An animal having four feet. — *adj.* Having four feet.

quad·ru·ple \(')kwäd-'rüp-l, 'kwäd-(ˌ)rəp-l\ *adj.* **1** Consisting of four; fourfold. **2** Taken in groups of four. **3** In music, having four beats to the measure, the first and third being accented. — *adv.* Fourfold. — *n.* An amount four times as great as another. — *v.;* **quad·ru·pled; quad·ru·pling** \-l(-)ing\. **1** To multiply by four; to increase fourfold. **2** To total four times as many as.

quad·rup·let \(')kwäd-'rəp-lət, -'rüp-, 'kwäd-rə-plət\ *n.* **1** A group of four of the same kind. **2** One of four offspring, especially children, born at one birth.

quaff \'kwäf, 'kwaf\ *v.* To drink deeply or repeatedly.

quag·mire \'kwag-ˌmīr, 'kwäg-\ *n.* Soft, miry land that yields and shakes under the foot; a bog; a marsh.

qua·hog \'kwȯ-ˌhȯg, 'k(w)ō-, -ˌhäg\ *n.* A round thick-shelled American clam.

quail \'kwāl\ *v.* To lose courage; to shrink from fear; to cower; as, to *quail* before an attack; to *quail* at the thought of playing the violin in public.

quail \'kwāl\ *n.; pl.* **quail** or **quails. 1** Any of numerous stout-bodied and short-winged migratory game birds of Europe, Asia, and Africa. **2** In America, any of several small game birds most of which are also called *partridge;* especially, in the northern and eastern states, the bobwhite.

quaint \'kwānt\ *adj.* Strange; peculiar; especially, strange but pleasing, as because of suggestions of old customs or things; as, a *quaint* old-fashioned house. — **quaint·ly,** *adv.*

quake \'kwāk\ *v.;* **quaked; quak·ing. 1** To shake, vibrate, or quiver, as from a violent convulsion or from not being solid, as a swamp. The earth shook and *quaked.* **2** To shudder or tremble, as with fear or cold. — *n.* A trembling; a quivering; especially, an earthquake.

quak·er \'kwāk-r\ *n.* **1** One that quakes. **2** [with a capital] A member of a religious sect called the Society of Friends; a Friend.

qual·i·fi·ca·tion \ˌkwäl-ə-fə-'kāsh-n\ *n.* **1** The act of qualifying or an instance of qualifying. **2** The state of being qualified. **3** Any special skill, knowledge, or ability that fits a person for a certain work or position; fitness; as, to lack the *qualifications* for a job. **4** Limitation; as, to agree without *qualification.*

qual·i·fied \'kwäl-ə-ˌfīd\ *adj.* **1** Having the necessary skill, knowledge, or ability to do something; fitted; as, to be *qualified* for a job. **2** Limited or modified in some way; as, to give one's *qualified* agreement.

qual·i·fi·er \'kwäl-ə-ˌfīr\ *n.* **1** A person or thing that qualifies. **2** In grammar, a word joined to another word to limit its meaning; a modifier.

qual·i·fy \'kwäl-ə-ˌfī\ *v.;* **qual·i·fied** \-ˌfīd\; **qual·i·fy·ing.** **1** To make less general or more definite in meaning; to restrict the application of; to modify; to limit; as, to *qualify* a statement. Adjectives *qualify* nouns. **2** To make less harsh or strict; to soften; as, to *qualify* a punishment. **3** To reduce the strength of, as liquors. **4** To fit by training, skill, or ability for some special purpose; as, to *qualify* oneself to be a doctor. **5** To be fit, as for an office. **6** To show the skill or ability necessary to be on a team or take part in a contest, as through preliminary contests.

qual·i·ta·tive \'kwäl-ə-ˌtāt-iv\ *adj.* Relating to or concerned with quality or qualities. — **qual·i·ta·tive·ly,** *adv.*

qual·i·ty \'kwäl-ət-ē\ *n.; pl.* **qual·i·ties.** **1** True or essential nature. **2** Any mark or characteristic by which a thing or class of things is distinguished or identified; any of the marks of a person's or thing's nature or condition; an attribute; as, a man's good and bad *qualities.* Hardness is a *quality* of steel. **3** Class, kind, or grade; as, a fine *quality* of yarn. **4** Excellence. Fine silks prove their *quality.* **5** *Archaic.* Superior birth or position; high rank; as, people of *quality.* **6** *Archaic.* Persons of high birth or rank; as, the *quality* of the town. **7** That characteristic of a tone by which it can be distinguished from another tone of the same pitch and loudness.

qualm \'kwäm, 'kwȯm, 'kwȧm\ *n.* **1** A sudden attack of illness, faintness, or pain; especially, a sudden attack of nausea. **2** A sudden fear or misgiving. **3** A feeling of doubt or hesitation in matters of conscience; a scruple.

qualm·ish \'kwäm-ish, 'kwȯm-, 'kwȧm-\ *adj.* **1** Feeling qualms, especially of nausea. **2** Like a qualm; as, a sudden *qualmish* doubt. **3** Likely to produce qualms. — **qualm·ish·ly,** *adv.*

quan·da·ry \'kwänd-r(-)ē\ *n.; pl.* **quan·da·ries.** A state of perplexity or doubt; a dilemma.

quan·ti·ta·tive \'kwänt-ə-ˌtāt-iv\ *adj.* Relating to or concerned with quantity or quantities. — **quan·ti·ta·tive·ly,** *adv.*

quan·ti·ty \'kwänt-ət-ē\ *n.; pl.* **quan·ti·ties.** **1** An amount or portion; as, a small *quantity* of fuel. **2** A great amount; as, to buy food in *quantity.*

quar·an·tine \'kwȯr-ən-ˌtēn, 'kwär-\ *n.* [From Italian *quarantina,* a derivative of *quaranta* meaning "forty", the extent of the quarantine having been formerly forty days.] **1** The prevention of a ship suspected of infection from having any contact with a port until the danger of contagion has passed. **2** The keeping of a person away from others because he has a contagious disease or has been exposed to one. **3** A place, usually a hospital, where persons are kept in quarantine. — *v.;* **quar·an·tined; quar·an·tin·ing.** To put in quarantine; to hold in quarantine.

quar·rel \'kwȯr(-ə)l, 'kwär(-ə)l\ *n.* **1** A cause to be defended; as, to have a just *quarrel.* **2** A disagreement; especially, an angry dispute. — For synonyms see *dispute.* — *v.;* **quar·reled** or **quar·relled; quar·rel·ing** or **quar·rel·ling.** **1** To find fault; to complain; as, to *quarrel* with one's lot. **2** To have a disagreement or misunderstanding; to dispute angrily; as, to make up after *quarreling.*

quar·rel·some \-səm\ *adj.* Inclined to quarrel; likely to get into arguments and fights.

quar·ry \'kwȯr-ē, 'kwär-ē\ *n.; pl.* **quar·ries.** The object of a hunt; game, especially when hunted with hawks; prey.

quar·ry \'kwȯr-ē, 'kwär-ē\ *n.; pl.* **quar·ries.** An open excavation, as for getting building stone, slate, or limestone. — *v.;* **quar·ried** \-ēd\; **quar·ry·ing.** **1** To dig or take from a quarry; as, to *quarry* marble. **2** To make a quarry in; as, to *quarry* land.

quart \'kwȯrt\ *n.* **1** A measure of capacity, equal to a quarter of a gallon, or two pints. **2** A vessel or measure containing a quart.

quar·ter \'kwȯrt-r\ *n.* **1** A fourth part or portion of anything. **2** Twenty-five cents, one fourth of a dollar. **3** A silver coin of this value. **4** In some schools, a term of study. **5** A fourth of an hour; the moment marking this; as, a bell ringing on the *quarter.* **6** One leg of a four-legged animal with the parts near it. **7** Place; region; district; as, all *quarters* of the globe; the foreign *quarter* of a city. **8** Proper station; assigned position; especially, in the navy, battle station. **9** [in the plural] A place in which to live; temporary residence; as, the winter *quarters* of the army. **10** Mercy; as, to show no *quarter* to the enemy. — **at close quarters.** In close contact; at short range. — *v.* **1** To divide into four equal parts. **2** To divide into parts either more or less than four; as, to *quarter* an orange. **3** To dismember; as, a prisoner who was hanged and *quartered* by the enemy. **4** To shelter; to furnish lodging, especially to soldiers. — *adj.* Consisting of, or equal to, a quarter.

quar·ter·back \'kwȯrt-r-ˌbak\ *n.* A backfield player in football who calls the signals and directs the offensive play of his team.

quarter day. A day regarded as beginning a quarter of a year, when quarterly payments come due.

quar·ter-deck \'kwȯrt-r-ˌdek\ *n.* An aft part of the upper deck of a vessel reserved for special purposes, as for ceremonies.

quar·ter·ly \'kwȯrt-r-lē\ *adv.* Once in a quarter of a year, especially at the beginning or end of a quarter; as, dividends paid *quarterly.* — *adj.* **1** Containing a fourth part. **2** Coming during, or at the end of, each quarter; as, *quarterly* payments of insurance premiums. — *n.; pl.* **quar·ter·lies.** A magazine published once a quarter.

quar·ter·mas·ter \'kwȯrt-r-ˌmast-r\ *n.* **1** In the army, an officer who provides quarters and supplies for troops. **2** On a ship, a petty officer who attends to steering and signals.

quarter section. In land surveying in the United States and Canada, a tract of land half a mile square, containing 160 acres.

quar·ter·staff \'kwȯrt-r-ˌstaf\ *n.; pl.* **quar·ter·staves** \-ˌstavz, -ˌstāvz\. A long stout staff, formerly used as a weapon.

quar·tet or **quar·tette** \(')kwȯr-'tet\ *n.* **1** A group of four persons or things. **2** A group of four singers or players. **3** A musical composition written for four voices or four instruments.

quar·to \'kwȯrt-ˌō\ *adj.* Of the size of one fourth of a sheet of printing paper. — *n.; pl.* **quar·tos.** A book of quarto size, or about 9½ by 12½ inches.

quartz \'kwȯrts\ *n.* A common mineral, often found in the form of colorless transparent crystals but sometimes brightly colored, as in amethysts, agates, and jaspers.

quartz·ite \'kwȯrt-ˌsīt\ *n.* A closely packed granular rock composed of quartz.

quash \'kwäsh\ *v.* **1** In law, to annul or make void. **2** To suppress; to quell.

qua·si \'kwā-ˌzī, 'kwäz-ē, 'kwā-ˌsī\ *adj.* or *adv.* As if; as though; in a certain sense or degree; seeming; as, a *quasi* bargain; *quasi*-respectable society.

quat·rain \'kwä-ˌtrān\ *n.* A stanza of four lines.

qua·ver \'kwāv-r\ *v.;* **qua·vered; qua·ver·ing** \-r(-)ing\. **1** To tremble; to quiver. **2** To speak in trembling, uncertain tones; as, a voice that *quavered.* **3** In music, to trill. — *n.* **1** A trembling or shaky tone. **2** A melodic trill, as in singing. — **qua·very** \-r(-)ē\ *adj.*

quay \'kē, 'kwā, 'kā\ *n.* A landing place, often of stone; a wharf.

quea·sy \'kwē-zē\ *adj.;* **quea·si·er; quea·si·est.** **1** Presenting difficulties; hazardous. **2** Nauseated; sick at one's stomach. **3** Uneasy; uncomfortable; as, *queasy* about his debts.

queen \'kwēn\ *n.* [From Old English *cwen* meaning "woman", "wife", "queen".] **1** A wife of a king. **2** A female ruler; as, *Queen* Elizabeth. **3** A woman with high rank, power, or attraction; as, a society *queen.* **4** The fully developed adult female of bees, ants, and termites whose function is the laying of eggs. **5** A playing card with a picture of a queen on it. **6** One of the pieces in the game of chess. — *v.* To make a queen of.

Queen Anne's lace \kwēn 'anz 'lās\. The wild carrot, which has delicate white blossoms appearing in a large flat-topped cluster.

Queen Anne's lace

queen·ly \'kwēn-lē\ *adj.* Like or suitable to a queen.

queen mother. The widowed mother of a reigning monarch.

queer \'kwir\ *adj.* **1** Peculiar; odd; strange. **2** *Slang.* Not genuine; counterfeit. — *v.* To defeat the success or effect of; to spoil; as, to *queer* their plans by interfering. — **queer·ly,** *adv.*

quell \'kwel\ *v.* **1** To overpower; to subdue; as, to *quell* a riot. **2** To quiet; to allay; as, to *quell* a fear.

quench \'kwench\ *v.* **1** To put out, as a fire; as, to *quench* the flames. **2** To subdue; to suppress; as, a love easily *quenched.* **3** To end by satisfying; as, to *quench* one's thirst. — **quench·a·ble** \-əb-l\ *adj.* — **quench·er** \-r\ *n.*

quer·u·lous \'kwer-(y)ə-ləs\ *adj.* **1** Constantly finding fault; complaining. **2** Fretful; whining; as, a *querulous* child. — **quer·u·lous·ly,** *adv.*

que·ry \'kwir-ē, 'kwer-ē\ *n.; pl.* **que·ries.** An inquiry to be answered; a question. — *v.;* **que·ried** \-ēd\; **que·ry·ing.** **1** To ask questions about something; to inquire into or ask about. **2** To question the truth or correctness of; as, to *query* a statement.

quest \'kwest\ *n.* **1** A search after anything; an attempt to find or obtain; as, in *quest* of fame. **2** In old stories, a knightly expedition. — *v.* To make a search; to go on a quest.

ques·tion \'kwes-chən\ *n.* **1** The act of asking; inquiry; as, to examine a witness by *question.* **2** Something asked; a query. **3** Objection; dispute; as, true beyond *question.* **4** A subject of argument or inquiry; a matter to be inquired into; as, an important *question* of the day. **5** A proposal to be voted on; as, to put the *question* to the members. — **out of the question.** Not worthy of consideration; not to be thought of. — *v.* **1** To ask questions of; to inquire; to query; as, to *question* a witness. **2** To be uncertain of; to doubt; as, to *question* the wisdom of the plan. **3** To make objection to; to dispute; as, to *question* the man's right to vote. — **ques·tion·ing·ly** \-chə-ning-lē\ *adv.*

ques·tion·a·ble \'kwes-chə-nəb-l\ *adj.* **1** Open to doubt; not sure or decided. It is *questionable* that students spend enough time on their studies. **2** Not of good character or reputation; as, a *questionable* neighborhood. — **ques·tion·a·bly** \-nə-blē\ *adv.*

question mark. The mark of punctuation [?] used to show a direct question.

ques·tion·naire \ˌkwes-chə-'nar, -'ner; 'kwes-chə-ˌnar, -ˌner\ *n.* A set of questions to be asked of a number of persons usually in order to gather statistics, as on opinions, facts, or knowledge.

quet·zal or **que·zal** \ket-'säl, -'sal, -'sȧl\ *n.* A Central American bird with narrow crest and brilliant plumage, and, in the male, tail feathers often over two feet in length.

queue \'kyü\ *n.* [From French, meaning literally "tail".] **1** A pigtail. **2** A waiting line; as, a *queue* at a ticket window. — *v.;* **queued; queu·ing** or **queue·ing.** **1** To braid the hair in a queue. **2** To form a waiting line; as, to *queue* up for tickets.

quib·ble \'kwib-l\ *n.* A shifting from the main issue in an argument, as by using a word in a double meaning or stressing some unimportant detail; an equivocation. — *v.;* **quib·bled; quib·bling** \-l(-)ing\. To evade the issue in an argument; to equivocate. — **quib·bler** \-l(-)ər\ *n.*

quick \'kwik\ *adj.* **1** *Archaic.* Living. **2** Swift; rapid; speedy; as, to go at a *quick* trot. **3** Alert; as, a *quick* wit. **4** Hasty; passionate; as, a *quick* temper. **5** Sensitive; as, a *quick* ear for music. — *adv.* In a quick manner; hastily; at once. — *n.* **1** Living persons as a group; as, the *quick* and the dead. **2** Sensitive living flesh; as, to bite one's nails to the *quick.* **3** A vital or inmost part; the heart or center; as, words that cut to the *quick.*

quick·en \'kwik-n\ *v.;* **quick·ened; quick·en·ing** \-n(-)ing\. **1** To make alive; to revive, as from near death. **2** To excite; to arouse. The story *quickened* the interest of the group. **3** To increase in speed; to hurry; as, to *quicken* one's steps.

quick-freeze \'kwik-'frēz\ *v.;* **quick-froze** \-'frōz\; **quick-fro·zen** \-'frōz-n\; **quick-freez·ing.** To preserve food by freezing it so rapidly that its flavor is not lost when it is thawed out.

quick·ie \'kwik-ē\ *n. Slang.* Something produced, made, or done in much less than the usual time.

quick·lime \'kwik-ˌlīm\ *n.* A caustic white substance composed of calcium and oxygen, made by heating limestone or shells, and used in various ways, as in agriculture and in the production of mortar and cement.

quick·ly \'kwik-lē\ *adv.* Promptly; rapidly; speedily.

quick·sand \'kwik-ˌsand\ *n.* A deep mass of loose sand mixed with water, dangerous because persons and heavy objects sink in it.

quick·sil·ver \'kwik-ˌsilv-r\ *n.* The metallic element mercury.

quick-tem·pered \'kwik-'temp-rd\ *adj.* Quick to lose temper; likely to flare up in anger.

quick-wit·ted \'kwik-'wit-əd\ *adj.* Mentally alert.

quid \'kwid\ *n.* A lump, as of tobacco, for chewing.

qui·es·cent \kwī-'es-nt, kwē-\ *adj.* At rest; still; motionless. — **qui·es·cence** \-n(t)s\ *n.* — **qui·es·cent·ly,** *adv.*

qui·et \'kwī-ət\ *adj.* **1** In a state of rest or calm; without motion. **2** Free from noise or disturbance; as, *quiet* afternoons; *quiet* sleep. **3** Gentle; mild; as, a *quiet* disposition. **4** Not excited, anxious, or stirred up; peaceful; as, a *quiet* life. **5** Not loud in color or showy in style; as, a *quiet* dress. **6** Secluded; as, a *quiet* nook. — *n.* The state or condition of being quiet. — *v.* **1** To calm; to pacify; as, to *quiet* a crying baby. **2** To become or grow quiet. The audience *quieted* when the curtain rose. — *adv.* In a quiet, peaceful, or smooth manner. — **qui·et·ly,** *adv.*

qui·e·tude \'kwī-ə-ˌtüd, -ˌtyüd\ *n.* The condition of being quiet; peace; repose.

qui·e·tus \kwī-'ēt-əs\ *n.* **1** The final freeing of a person from something, as from a debt, from an office or duty, or from life itself. **2** That which quiets, calms, or ends life or activity; as, to put the *quietus* on a scandal.

quill \'kwil\ *n.* **1** A large stiff feather. **2** The end of a feather which is attached to the bird. **3** A spine of the hedgehog or porcupine. **4** A pen made from a feather.

quilt \'kwilt\ *n.* A bed covering made of two pieces of material, with a filling of wool, cotton, or down, stitched together in some ornamental pattern or design. — *v.* To stitch or sew together, as in making a quilt.

quilt·ing \'kwil-ting\ *n.* **1** The act of a person or machine that quilts something. **2** Quilted material; material for quilts.

quince \'kwin(t)s\ *n.* **1** A hard yellow apple-shaped acid fruit used in making marmalade, jelly, and preserves. **2** The tree or shrub that bears this fruit.

quince

qui·nine \'kwī-ˌnīn\ *n.* **1** A bitter white crystalline substance extracted from cinchona bark. **2** Any of several drugs prepared from this substance, especially one used as a remedy for fever.

quin·quen·ni·al \kwin-'kwen-ē-əl\ *adj.* **1** Occurring once in five years or at the end of five years. **2** Lasting five years.

quin·sy \'kwin-zē\ *n.* A severe inflammation of the throat or adjacent parts with swelling and fever; tonsillitis with the formation of pus.

quint \'kwint\. Short for *quintuplet.*

quin·tal \'kwint-l\ *n.* A hundredweight.

quint·es·sence \kwin-'tes-n(t)s\ *n.* **1** The purest form of something; as, the *quintessence* of beauty. **2** The most highly perfected type or example; as, manners that were the *quintessence* of courtesy.

quin·tet or **quin·tette** \(')kwin-'tet\ *n.* **1** A piece of music written for five voices or five instruments. **2** The performers of such a composition. **3** Any group of five.

quin·til·lion \kwin-'til-yən\ *n.* **1** In the United States, one thousand quadrillions. **2** In Great Britain, one million quadrillions.

quin·tup·let \(')kwin-'təp-lət, -'tüp-, -'tyüp-, 'kwint-ə-plət\ *n.* **1** A group of five of the same kind. **2** [usually in the plural] One of a group of five offspring, especially children, born at one birth.

quip \'kwip\ *n.* **1** A bantering or, sometimes, cutting joke. **2** A bright and witty saying. — *v.;* **quipped; quip·ping.** To make quips.

quire \'kwīr\ *n.* A collection of 24, or sometimes 25, sheets of paper of the same size and quality.

quirk \'kwərk\ *n.* **1** A sudden turn, twist, or curve, as a flourish in writing. **2** A sudden turn of the mind; an unpredictable shift. **3** An individual peculiarity.

quirt \'kwərt\ *n.* A riding whip with a short handle and a lash of braided rawhide.

quis·ling \'kwiz-ling\ *n.* [Named after Vidkun *Quisling* (1887–1945), a Norwegian politician who collaborated with Germany in its conquest of Norway (1940) and who headed the Norwegian puppet government from 1940 to 1945.] A traitor, especially one who aids the invader of his country, often serving as his chief agent or governor.

quit \'kwit\ *v.;* **quit·ted** or **quit; quit·ting.** **1** To pay something owed; to meet a claim; to repay a debt. **2** To leave; as, to *quit* the house. **3** To let go; to surrender. The outnumbered soldiers were forced to *quit* the fort. **4** To discontinue; as, to *quit* a job. **5** To stop doing something; as, to *quit* talking. — *adj.* Free; clear; released from obligation; as, to be *quit* of all debt.

quite \'kwīt\ *adv.* **1** Completely; wholly; entirely;

as, *quite* finished. **2** Positively; really; as, to be *quite* sure. **3** Rather; as, to live *quite* near.

quits \'kwits\ *adj.* Equal or even; on even terms, as by repaying a debt, returning a favor, or retaliating for an injury. After the loan was repaid, the boys were *quits.* — **call it quits. 1** To stop whatever one has been doing. **2** To cease efforts, as to prove one's superiority to another; especially, to agree to let a dispute or quarrel end.

quit·tance \'kwit-n(t)s\ *n.* **1** A discharge from a debt or an obligation. **2** The document stating such discharge. **3** A repayment; a return.

quit·ter \'kwit-r\ *n.* A person who quits or shirks; one who gives up without a fight.

quiv·er \'kwiv-r\ *v.;* **quiv·ered; quiv·er·ing** \-r(-)ing\. To move with a slight, trembling motion. The tall grass *quivered* in the breeze. — *n.* A quivering; a tremor.

quiv·er \'kwiv-r\ *n.* **1** A case for carrying arrows. **2** The arrows in such a case.

quix·ot·ic \kwik-'sät-ik\ *adj.* [Named after Don *Quixote,* the absurdly chivalric hero of the famous Spanish novel *Don Quixote* by Miguel de Cervantes Saavedra (1547–1616).] **1** Like or characteristic of Don Quixote. **2** Idealistic; impractical. — **quix·ot·i·cal·ly** \-ik-l(-)ē\ *adv.*

quiz \'kwiz\ *n.; pl.* **quiz·zes** \-əz\. A questioning; especially, a short or informal classroom examination or test; as, a *quiz* in history. — *v.;* **quizzed; quiz·zing.** To question closely; to examine by questions. — **quiz·zer** \'kwiz-r\ *n.*

quiz show or **quiz program.** A show, as on television, in which contestants are given questions to answer or tasks to perform and usually are awarded a prize for each success.

quiz·zi·cal \'kwiz-ik-l\ *adj.* **1** Odd; queer; funny. **2** Questioning; bantering; teasing. — **quiz·zi·cal·ly** \-ik-l(-)ē\ *adv.*

quoit \'kwȯit, 'kwāt, 'kȯit\ *n.* A flattened ring, as of iron, to be pitched at a fixed peg in a game called **quoits.**

quon·dam \'kwänd-m, 'kwän-ˌdam\ *adj.* Former. The *quondam* clerk is now manager.

quo·rum \'kwōr-əm, 'kwȯr-\ *n.* The number of members of a body or society, generally more than half, needed at a meeting to transact business officially or legally.

quo·ta \'kwōt-ə\ *n.* The part or share, forming a definite proportion of the whole, assigned individually to each member of a group; as, the *quota* of troops and money required of a district.

quot·a·ble \'kwōt-əb-l\ *adj.* Capable of being quoted; worth quoting.

quo·ta·tion \kwō-'tāsh-n\ *n.* **1** The act of quoting or citing. **2** Something that is quoted or cited; as, a *quotation* from the Bible. **3** In business, the naming or publishing of the current price of a stock, bond, or commodity or the price named.

quotation mark. 1 One of the double marks [" "] used to show the beginning and end of a direct quotation or of a title, as of a short story or song. **2** One of the single marks [' '] commonly used to indicate a quotation within a quotation but sometimes used in place of double quotation marks.

quote \'kwōt\ *v.;* **quot·ed; quot·ing. 1** To name as an authority for a statement or an opinion; as, to *quote* the President. **2** To repeat a passage from an author; to give as an illustration. **3** In business, to name the current price of something, as a bond or commodity. — *n.* **1** A quotation. **2** A quotation mark.

quoth \'kwōth\ *v. Archaic.* Said; spoke — used in the first and third persons and always placed before the subject, as in "*quoth* he".

quo·tient \'kwōsh-nt\ *n.* In arithmetic, the number resulting from the division of one number by another.

r \'är, 'ȧr\ *n.; pl.* **r's** \'ärz, 'ȧrz\. The 18th letter of the alphabet.

rab·bet \'rab-ət\ *n.* A groove or recess cut in the edge or face of a surface, especially to receive the edge of another surface, as a panel. — *v.* **1** To cut a rabbet in. **2** To join the edges of, as boards, by a rabbet.

rab·bi \'rab-ˌī\ *n.; pl.* **rab·bis** or **rab·bies. 1** [with a capital] Teacher; master — used as a title of respect for Jewish religious teachers. **2** A Jewish religious teacher, especially one serving as spiritual leader of a congregation.

rab·bin·i·cal \rə-'bin-ik-l, ra-\ *adj.* Of or relating to rabbis; as, *rabbinical* studies.

rab·bit \'rab-ət\ *n.* Any of various gnawing mammals resembling the related hares but usually smaller and with shorter ears and having young that are naked and helpless at birth.

rab·ble \'rab-l\ *n.* **1** A noisy and unruly crowd; a mob. **2** Any body of people looked down upon by other people as ignorant and disorderly; as, to be contemptuous of the *rabble.*

rab·id \'rab-əd\ *adj.* **1** Extremely violent; furious; raging; as, *rabid* with anger. **2** Going to extremes in one's opinions; as, a *rabid* baseball fan. **3** Affected with rabies; as, a *rabid* dog. — **rab·id·ly,** *adv.*

ra·bies \'rā-bēz\ *n.* An acute disease of the central nervous system of warm-blooded animals, transmitted through virus-infected saliva, usually by the bite of a rabid animal, and always fatal when untreated; hydrophobia.

rac·coon or **ra·coon** \(')ra-'kün\ *n.* **1** A small North American flesh-eating mammal with grayish fur and a bushy ringed tail, living largely in trees and active at night. **2** The fur of this animal.

race \'rās\ *n.* **1** A strong or rapid current of water or the channel or passage for such a current; especially, a current of water used for industrial purposes, as in mining or for turning the wheel of a mill. **2** A contest of speed, as in running or sailing. **3** [in the plural] A meeting for holding a series of contests in running, especially between horses. **4** Any contest for some desired end, as for election to some political office. **5** A track or channel in which something rolls or slides. — *v.;* **raced; racing. 1** To run in a race; to take part in a contest of speed. **2** To run swiftly; to rush. **3** To take part in a race against; as, to *race* the champion. **4** To cause to compete in a race; as, to *race* a horse. **5** To run or cause to run too fast, as an engine.

race \'rās\ *n.* **1** The descendants of a common ancestor; a family, tribe, nation, or people, supposed to belong to the same stock; as, the chief *races* of men. **2** The condition of being one of a special stock or of a particular group or family; the features or qualities belonging to a stock or group of people. **3** In biology, a group of animals or plants distinguished from the other groups within a species by constant characteristics but not sufficiently distinct to make a new species. **4** A division of mankind possessing constant traits that characterize it as a distinct human type and are transmitted from generation to generation.

race·course \'rās-ˌkōrs, -ˌkȯrs\ *n.* A race track.

race·horse \-ˌhȯrs\ *n.* A horse bred or kept for racing.

ra·ceme \rā-'sēm, rə-\ *n.* A long flower cluster in which the individual flowers grow along a main stem, opening successively from the bottom of the cluster toward the top.

raceme of lily of the valley

rac·er \'rās-r\ *n.* **1** One that races. **2** A variety of the American blacksnake.

race track. A track on which horse or dog races are run; a racecourse.

ra·chis \'rāk-əs\ *n.; pl.* **ra·chis·es** \'rāk-ə-səz\ or **rach·i·des** \'rak-ə-ˌdēz, 'rāk-ə-\. **1** The main axis of a flower cluster; the main stalk of a compound leaf. **2** The outer part of the shaft of a feather.

ra·cial \'rāsh-l\ *adj.* Of or relating to a race. — **ra·cial·ly** \'rāsh-l-ē\ *adv.*

rac·i·ly \'rās-l-ē\ *adv.* In a racy manner.

rac·i·ness \'rā-sē-nəs\ *n.* Racy quality.

rac·ism \'rā-ˌsiz-m\ *n.* **1** Belief that certain races of men are by birth and nature superior to others. **2** Discrimination against the members of one or more races based upon such belief. **3** Any form of race hatred and discrimination. — **rac·ist** \-səst\ *n.*

rack \'rak\ *n.* Destruction; as, *rack* and ruin.

rack \'rak\ *v.* To go at a rack. — *n.* A gait of a horse, either pace or single-foot.

rack \'rak\ *n.* **1** A framework for holding fodder for cattle. **2** A machine once used for torturing people, consisting of a frame on which the victims were fastened and their limbs stretched. **3** A framework on or in which articles may be placed for keeping or for display; as, a clothes *rack;* a magazine *rack.* **4** A frame fitted to a wagon or truck for carrying hay, straw, or grain. **5** A bar with teeth on one face for meshing with those of a pinion. — *v.* **1** To stretch or strain by force; to torture as if on a rack; to torment; as, to be *racked* by a cough. **2** To place on or in a rack.

rack·et \'rak-ət\ *n.* **1** A light bat one end of which is a handle and the other an oval frame with catgut tightly stretched across it. **2** [in the plural] A game played with ball and rackets in a four-walled court. — **rack·et·er** \-ət-r\ *n.*

rack·et \'rak-ət\ *n.* **1** A confused noise; din; uproar. **2** Strain, as of a continuing ordeal or activity; as, to be unable to stand the *racket.* **3** A dishonest scheme, especially one for obtaining money either by cheating or through threats of violence. **4** *Slang.* An occupation. — *v.* To make a racket; be noisy. — **rack·ety** \-ət-ē\ *adj.*

rack·e·teer \ˌrak-ə-'tir\ *n.* A person who alone or in combination forces others, especially businessmen, to pay him money or grant him certain advantages, usually by threats of violence or of unlawful interference. — **rack·e·teer·ing** \-ing\ *n.*

racoon. Variant of *raccoon.*

rac·quet \'rak-ət\ *n.* **1** A racket, or bat. **2** [in the plural] The game of rackets.

racy \'rā-sē\ *adj.;* **rac·i·er; rac·i·est. 1** Having the quality of a thing in its natural form; fresh; unspoiled; full-flavored. **2** Full of life, vigor, or zest; spirited; as, a *racy* style of writing. **3** Slightly indecent or improper; suggestive; as, *racy* jokes.

ra·dar \'rād-ˌär, -ˌår\ *n.* [Formed from the following italicized letters of its full name: *ra*dio *d*etecting *a*nd *r*anging.] A device that sends out a powerful beam of radio waves that when reflected back to it from a distant object indicate the position and direction of motion of the object.

ra·dar·scope \'rād-ˌär-ˌskōp, -ˌår-\ *n.* The part of a radar apparatus on which the spots of light appear that indicate the position and direction of motion of distant objects.

ra·di·al \'rād-ē-əl\ *adj.* **1** Arranged like rays coming from a common center. **2** In anatomy, relating to or in the region of the radius. — **ra·di·al·ly** \-ē-ə-lē\ *adv.*

ra·di·ance \'rād-ē-ən(t)s\ or **ra·di·an·cy** \'rād-ē-ən-sē\ *n.* Brilliance; vivid brightness.

ra·di·ant \'rād-ē-ənt\ *adj.* **1** Giving out or reflecting rays of light; shining; as, the *radiant* sun. **2** Beaming or glowing, as with joy, happiness, or energy; as, *radiant* youth. **3** Emitted or transmitted by radiation, as in **radiant energy**, the energy in waves, especially light waves, radio waves, and X rays. — **ra·di·ant·ly,** *adv.*

ra·di·ate \'rād-ē-ˌāt\ *v.;* **ra·di·at·ed; ra·di·at·ing. 1** To send out rays; to shine. **2** To come forth in the form of rays. Light *radiates* from shining bodies. **3** To spread around as from a center. — \-ˌāt, -ət\ *adj.* **1** Having ray flowers, as the aster. **2** In zoology, having similar parts arranged radially about a central axis.

ra·di·a·tion \ˌrād-ē-ˈāsh-n\ *n.* **1** A radiating; especially, the giving off of radiant energy. **2** That which is radiated, as radiant energy or the particles released by changes in the nuclei of atoms, as in the explosion of an atom bomb.

ra·di·a·tor \ˈrād-ē-ˌāt-r\ *n.* Something that radiates; especially, a device to heat surrounding air, as in a room, or to cool an object, as an engine.

rad·i·cal \ˈrad-ik-l\ *adj.* **1** Of or relating to a root; proceeding directly from a root. **2** Fundamental; extreme; as, a *radical* change. **3** Of or relating to political radicals. — *n.* **1** A root; a fundamental element. **2** In politics, a person who favors rapid and sweeping changes in laws and government. **3** In mathematics, a radical sign. **4** In chemistry, a group of atoms that can be replaced by a single atom or remain unchanged through a series of reactions. — **rad·i·cal·ly** \-ik-l(-)ē\ *adv.*

radical sign. In mathematics, the sign [√] placed before an expression to indicate that its root is to be extracted.

rad·i·cand \ˌrad-ə-ˈkand\ *n.* The quantity under a radical sign.

ra·dio \ˈrād-ē-ˌō\ *n.; pl.* **ra·di·os**. [A shortened form of *radiotelegraphy*, this being compounded from Latin *radius* (meaning "staff", "radius", "ray") and English *telegraphy* — see *radium, radius, ray.*] **1** The sending or receiving of signals by means of electric waves — commonly used to refer to the transmitting of sound. **2** A radio receiving set. **3** A radio message. **4** The field or business of radio broadcasting. — *adj.* **1** Of or relating to the waves used in radio. **2** Having to do with or used in radio. — *v.;* **ra·di·oed**; **ra·di·o·ing**. To send or communicate by radio.

ra·di·o·ac·tive \ˈrād-ē-ˌō-ˈak-tiv\ *adj.* Having the property of radioactivity.

ra·di·o·ac·tiv·i·ty \ˈrād-ē-ˌō-ˌak-ˈtiv-ət-ē\ *n.* **1** The sending out of radioactive rays. **2** The property of certain substances, as radium, uranium, and thorium that causes them to emit rays and particles.

radio astronomy. Astronomy dealing with electric waves received by a special device (**ra·di·o·tel·e·scope** \ˈrād-ē-ˌō-ˈtel-ə-ˌskōp\) from outside the earth's atmosphere.

radio frequency. Any radio-wave frequency between 10 kilocycles and 300,000 megacycles per second.

ra·di·o·gram \ˈrād-ē-ə-ˌgram\ *n.* **1** A radiograph. **2** A message sent by wireless telegraphy.

ra·di·o·graph \ˈrād-ē-ə-ˌgraf\ *n.* A photograph made by radiation other than light; an X ray.

ra·di·o·tel·e·phone \ˌrād-ē-ˌō-ˈtel-ə-ˌfōn\ *n.* A telephone that utilizes radio waves instead of connecting wires. — **ra·di·o·te·leph·o·ny** \-tə-ˈlef-n-ē\ *n.*

radio wave. An electric wave used in communicating by radio, television, or radar.

rad·ish \ˈrad-ish\ *n.* The edible fleshy root of a plant of the mustard family; also, the plant itself.

ra·di·um \ˈrād-ē-əm\ *n.* [A scientific Latin word derived from Latin *radius* meaning "staff", "radius", "ray" — see *radio, radius, ray.*] An intensely radioactive element found in minute quantities in pitchblende and some other minerals.

ra·di·us \ˈrād-ē-əs\ *n.; pl.* **ra·dii** \-ē-ˌī\ or **ra·di·us·es** \-ē-ə-səz\. [From Latin, meaning "staff", "radius", "ray" — see *radio, radium, ray.*] **1** A straight line extending from the center of a circle to the circumference, or from the center of a sphere to the surface; half of a diameter. **2** An area bounded by certain definite limits; as, within a *radius* of one mile from the school. **3** The anterior of the two bones in the forearm, on the same side as the thumb, or a corresponding part of the front limb of other vertebrates above fishes.

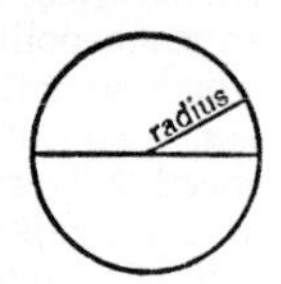

raf·fia \ˈraf-ē-ə\ *n.* Fiber from the **raffia palm**, a tree native to Madagascar, used especially for hats and baskets.

raf·fle \ˈraf-l\ *n.* A form of lottery. — *v.;* **raf·fled**; **raf·fling** \-l(-)ing\. To dispose of by a raffle.

raft \ˈraft\ *n.* A large amount of anything; a lot.

raft \ˈraft\ *n.* **1** A number of logs or pieces of timber, fastened together to serve as a float. **2** A buoyant, usually flat-topped object, as those used for recreation and for life saving. — *v.* To make a raft; to use a raft; to transport by raft.

raf·ter \ˈraft-r\ *n.* A supporting timber of a roof.

rag \ˈrag\ *n.* **1** A waste piece of cloth torn or cut off. **2** Any worthless bit of old cloth. **3** [usually in the plural] Tattered clothing; as, to dress in *rags.*

rag·a·muf·fin \ˈrag-ə-ˌməf-n\ *n.* A tattered, ragged person, especially a child.

rage \ˈrāj\ *n.* **1** Violent passion; anger; fury. **2** Violence, as of the sea or wind. **3** Something that is sought after. Puzzles were all the *rage* that winter. — *v.;* **raged**; **rag·ing** \ˈrā-jing\. **1** To be furiously angry. **2** To be violent, as a storm. **3** To continue because out of control, as an epidemic.

rag·ged \ˈrag-əd\ *adj.* **1** Rough; jagged; as, a *ragged* rock. **2** Torn; tattered; as, *ragged* clothes. **3** Wearing ragged clothes; as, a *ragged* stranger. **4** Faulty; not well performed or done; as, *ragged* workmanship. — **rag·ged·ly**, *adv.*

rag·lan \ˈrag-lən\ *n.* An overcoat with sleeves (**raglan sleeves**) sewn in with diagonal seams extending from the neck to below the armpit.

ra·gout \ra-ˈgü\ *n.* A highly seasoned meat stew with vegetables.

rag·time \ˈrag-ˌtīm\ *n.* Rhythm in which the melody has the accented notes falling on beats that are not usually accented.

rag·weed \ˈrag-ˌwēd\ *n.* A common coarse weed related to the thistle, whose pollen is irritating to the eyes and nasal passages of some persons.

raid \ˈrād\ *n.* **1** A sudden attack or invasion, especially by troops or aircraft as a military operation; as, an air *raid;* a night *raid.* **2** A sudden attack by police, as to seize illegal goods. **3** A sudden or determined movement or rush, as to get to something, to use it, or to get something out of it; as, a *raid* on the icebox. — *v.* To make a raid on. — **raid·er,** *n.*

rail \'rāl\ *n.; pl.* **rails** or **rail.** Any of a family of small wading birds related to the cranes.

rail \'rāl\ *v.* To scold or complain in harsh or bitter language; as, to *rail* against the party in power.

rail \'rāl\ *n.* **1** A bar of timber or metal extending from one support to another as a guard or barrier, as in a fence. **2** A bar, usually of rolled steel, forming a track for wheeled vehicles. **3** A railway; a railroad; as, to travel by *rail.* — *v.* To provide with rails; to fence; as, to *rail* in a space.

rail·ing \'rā-ling\ *n.* **1** A barrier, as a fence or a balustrade, consisting of rails and their supports. **2** Rails in general. **3** Material for making rails.

rail·lery \'rāl-r-ē\ *n.; pl.* **rail·ler·ies. 1** Ridicule uttered jokingly; banter. **2** A bantering act.

rail·road \'rāl-ˌrōd\ *n.* **1** A permanent road or way that has parallel steel rails that make a track for cars. **2** Such a road together with the lands, buildings, locomotives, cars, and other equipment belonging with it. — *v.* **1** To work on a railroad or as part of a railroad system. **2** To transport by railroad. **3** To put through with great haste and little consideration; as, to *railroad* a bill through Congress. **4** *Slang.* To get rid of by sending to prison on a false charge.

rail·road·er \'rāl-ˌrōd-r\ *n.* A railroad worker.

rail·way \'rāl-ˌwā\ *n.* **1** A railroad; especially, a railroad for light traffic; as, a street *railway.* **2** Any track providing a runway for wheels.

rai·ment \'rā-mənt\ *n.* Clothing; garments.

rain \'rān\ *n.* **1** Water falling in drops from the clouds. **2** The descent of such drops. **3** A shower of rain; a rainfall; as, a drizzling *rain.* **4** [in the plural] The rainy season. **5** A shower of numerous objects; as, a *rain* of bullets. — *v.* **1** To fall in drops from the clouds. **2** To send down rain. **3** To fall thick and fast. Bullets *rained* down on the troops. **4** To send like rain. Fortune had *rained* blessings on them.

rain·bow \'rān-ˌbō\ *n.* An arc showing the colors of the spectrum and formed by refraction and reflection of sunshine on rain, mist, or spray.

rain·coat \'rān-ˌkōt\ *n.* A coat, waterproof or nearly waterproof, worn for protection from rain.

rain·drop \'rān-ˌdräp\ *n.* A drop of rain.

rain·fall \'rān-ˌfȯl\ *n.* A fall of rain, especially the amount that falls measured in inches of depth.

rain·mak·er \'rān-ˌmāk-r\ *n.* **1** A tribal magician who seeks to cause rain by ritual. **2** A person who seeds clouds with chemicals to produce rain.

rain·spout \'rān-ˌspau̇t\ *n.* A waterspout.

rain·storm \'rān-ˌstȯrm\ *n.* A storm of rain.

rain water. Water falling or fallen as rain.

rainy \'rā-nē\ *adj.;* **rain·i·er; rain·i·est.** Having much rain; showery; wet; as, a *rainy* season.

raise \'rāz\ *v.;* **raised; rais·ing. 1** To cause to rise; to lift; as, to *raise* a window; to *raise* one's hand. **2** To give life to; to arouse; as, enough noise to *raise* the dead. **3** To build; as, to *raise* a monument. **4** To collect; as, to *raise* money. **5** To breed or grow; as, to *raise* cattle; to *raise* corn. **6** To give rise to; to occasion. The child's remark *raised* a laugh. **7** To bring to notice; to utter or express; as, to *raise* an objection. **8** To elevate; to advance; as, to *raise* a man to a higher office. **9** To increase the strength of; to intensify; to heighten; as, to *raise* one's voice. **10** To increase in size or amount; as, to *raise* a price. **11** To make light or spongy, as bread. **12** To end as if by lifting away; as, to *raise* a siege. **13** In card playing, to increase a bid or wager or to wager more than another player.

— The words *lift* and *elevate* are synonyms of *raise: lift* usually suggests moving something to a higher position than it formerly occupied, often by overcoming the resistance of weight; *raise* is like *lift* but can also indicate the placing of something, as a pole or wall, in the upright position that it was intended to have; *elevate* may suggest placing something in a high or lofty position, as a person in a high political or social position, or the bringing of something, as a person's standards or tastes, to a condition thought of as high and noble.

— *n.* **1** An increase in amount, as of a bid or wager. **2** An increase in pay.

rais·er \'rāz-r\ *n.* One that raises something; as, a cattle *raiser.*

rai·sin \'rāz-n\ *n.* A dried sweet grape of certain varieties.

ra·ja or **ra·jah** \'räj-ə\ *n.* In India, a prince, king, or minor chief.

rake \'rāk\ *v.;* **raked; rak·ing.** To slant, as a mast or funnel of a boat. — *n.* A slant or slope away from the perpendicular; as, the *rake* of a mast.

rake \'rāk\ *n.* A long-handled garden tool having a bar with teeth or prongs. — *v.;* **raked; rak·ing. 1** To scrape together or along with or as if with a rake; as, to *rake* the leaves together. **2** To smooth with a rake; as, to *rake* the soil just spaded. **3** To gather with much effort; to scrape together; as, barely able to *rake* up enough to pay the rent. **4** To search minutely; to ransack; as, to *rake* the records for evidence. **5** To sweep with shot. The guns *raked* the enemy's ship.

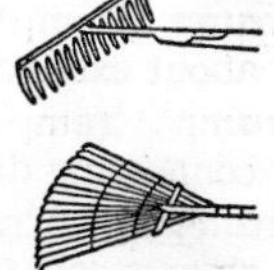

rakes

rake \'rāk\ *n.* A dissipated or dissolute man.

rake-off \'rāk-ˌȯf\ *n.* A commission or profit, often unlawful, received by one party in a business deal.

rak·ish \'rāk-ish\ *adj.* **1** Having a smart appearance that indicates speed; as, a *rakish* boat. **2** Jaunty; showy; sporty; as, a hat set at a *rakish* angle. — **rak·ish·ly,** *adv.*

ral·ly \'ral-ē\ *v.;* **ral·lied** \-ēd\; **ral·ly·ing. 1** To collect and reduce to order; to reunite. The general *rallied* his troops. **2** To come together in active support; to unite in action. **3** To revive, as in health or strength. **4** To engage in a rally. The team *rallied* and won by two points. — *n.; pl.* **ral-**

lies. **1** The action of rallying. **2** A mass meeting to arouse enthusiasm; as, a football *rally;* a political *rally.* **3** In tennis and other games, a series of strokes interchanged before a point is won.

ram \'ram\ *n.* **1** A male sheep. **2** A machine of war used for battering walls. **3** A pointed beak on the prow of a vessel for piercing an enemy ship. **4** A weight, as in a pile driver. — *v.;* **rammed; ram·ming. 1** To force, press, or drive; as, to *ram* piles into the earth; to *ram* ideas into students' minds. **2** To stuff; to cram; as, to *ram* clothes into a trunk; to *ram* tobacco into a pipe. **3** To butt or strike against violently.

ram, 1

ram·ble \'ram-bl\ *v.;* **ram·bled; ram·bling** \-bl(-)ing\. **1** To go aimlessly from place to place; to wander; to roam; as, to *ramble* about the city. **2** To talk or write in an irregular or pointless way. **3** To grow at random; to spread out widely, as a vine; to extend. — *n.* A long walk; a hike.

ram·bler \'ram-blər\ *n.* **1** One that rambles. **2** Any climbing rose, especially the **crimson rambler.**

ram·i·fi·ca·tion \ˌram-ə-fə-'kāsh-n\ *n.* **1** The action or process of branching; especially, in botany, an arrangement of branches. **2** A branch or offshoot from a main stock or channel; as, the *ramifications* of an artery. **3** Something that springs from or arises in another thing in the manner of a branch; as, all the *ramifications* of a problem.

ram·i·fy \'ram-ə-ˌfī\ *v.;* **ram·i·fied** \-ˌfīd\; **ram·i·fy·ing.** To spread out into branches or divisions.

ram·jet engine \'ram-ˌjet\. A jet engine having in its forward end an opening so that there is a ramming, or compressing, effect produced on the air taken in while the engine is in motion.

ram·mer \'ram-r\ *n.* One that rams; especially, a ramming instrument.

ramp \'ramp\ *v.* **1** To rage; to rant. **2** To rush about excitedly.

ramp \'ramp\ *n.* A sloping passage or roadway connecting different levels.

ram·page \'ram-ˌpāj\ *n.* A fit of violent actions; riotous behavior; as, to go on a *rampage.* — \'ram-ˌpāj, (')ram-'pāj\ *v.;* **ram·paged; ram·pag·ing.** To rush about or storm wildly or excitedly.

ramp·ant \'ram-pənt, -ˌpant\ *adj.* **1** In heraldry, rearing upon the hind legs with forelegs extended. **2** Threatening or unrestrained in manner or action; as, a *rampant* mob. **3** Unchecked in growth or spread, as a disease. — **ramp·ant·ly,** *adv.*

ram·part \'ram-ˌpärt, -ˌpȧrt, -pərt\ *n.* A broad embankment round a place; a barrier; a bulwark.

ram·rod \'ram-ˌräd\ *n.* **1** A long rod used for ramming down the charge in muzzle-loading firearms. **2** A cleaning rod for small arms.

ram·shack·le \'ram-ˌshak-l\ *adj.* Rickety.

ran. Past tense of *run.*

ranch \'ranch\ *n.* **1** An establishment for the grazing and rearing of horses, cattle, or sheep; especially, the buildings and other structures of such an establishment. **2** A large farm; as, a fruit *ranch.* — *v.* To live or work on a ranch.

ranch·er \'ranch-r\ *n.* A person who ranches.

ranch house. A one-story house, usually with an informal interior plan and a low-pitched roof.

ranch·man \'ranch-mən\ *n.; pl.* **ranch·men** \-mən\. A rancher.

ran·cid \'ran(t)s-əd\ *adj.* Having the strong disagreeable smell or taste resulting from decay.

ran·cor \'rangk-r\ *n.* Strong ill will; intense hatred or spite. — **ran·cor·ous** \-r(-)əs\ *adj.*

ran·dom \'rand-m\ *adj.* Aimless; chance; haphazard; as, a *random* shot; *random* thoughts. — **at random.** Without special aim or method.

rang. A past tense of *ring.*

range \'rānj\ *v.;* **ranged; rang·ing** \'rān-jing\. **1** To set in rows or a row; to border with a row; as, a road *ranged* with trees. **2** To set in place among others of the same kind; as, to *range* oneself with the enemy. **3** To correspond in direction and line; as, villages *ranging* the coast line. **4** To rove over or through. Chickens *ranged* the yard. **5** To vary within limits. The temperature *ranged* from 50 to 90 degrees. — *n.* **1** A series of things in a line; a row; as, a mountain *range.* **2** A place for roving; especially, open grazing land; any stretch of open country. Cattle graze on the western *ranges.* **3** A cooking stove. **4** Distance or space covered; scope; reach; as, a subject beyond the *range* of the course; a voice of wide *range.* **5** The distance a weapon will shoot; the distance between weapon and target. **6** A place where shooting is practiced; as, a rifle *range.* **7** A variation within limits; as, a great *range* in prices.

rang·er \'rānj-r\ *n.* **1** In England, the keeper of a royal park or forest. **2** A rover; a wanderer. **3** A member of an organized patrol. **4** A warden who patrols forest lands.

rangy \'rān-jē\ *adj.;* **rang·i·er; rang·i·est. 1** Long-legged and slender; as, a *rangy* horse. **2** Having room for ranging; spacious.

rank \'rangk\ *adj.* **1** Strong and vigorous in growth, especially coarse growth; as, *rank* weeds. **2** Covered with a vigorous growth; as, *rank* meadows. **3** Offensively gross or coarse. **4** Unpleasantly strong-smelling; rancid. **5** Extreme; utter; as, *rank* dishonesty. — **rank·ly,** *adv.*

rank \'rangk\ *n.* **1** A row; a line; as, *ranks* of houses. **2** A line of soldiers ranged side by side; as, *rank* and file. **3** A group of individuals classed together; as, the *ranks* of the American farmer. **4** Relative position or order; standing. His *rank* was fifth in terms of size. **5** Official grade, as in the army or navy; as, to have the *rank* of general. **6** Position in regard to merit; as, a musician of the highest *rank.* **7** High position; as, a man of *rank.* **8** [in the plural] The whole body of private soldiers in an army; as, a man who rose from the *ranks.* — *v.* **1** To arrange in a line or lines. **2** To assign to or place in ranks; as, to *rank* the compositions from best to poorest. **3** To range or be in a class;

to class; as, to *rank* first in one's class. **4** To rate above; to outrank. A captain *ranks* a lieutenant.

ran·kle \'rangk-l\ *v.;* **ran·kled; ran·kling** \-l(-)ing\. **1** To fester, as a wound; to become or continue to be inflamed. **2** To produce a festering effect; as, a splinter that *rankled* in the flesh. **3** To vex or make angry or bitter; as, criticism that *rankled.*

ran·sack \'ran-ˌsak, -'sak\ *v.* **1** To search thoroughly; to rummage. **2** To search through and rob.

ran·som \'ran(t)s-m\ *n.* **1** The freeing or rescue of a captive by payment of money; as, the *ransom* of a captive from bandits. **2** Money paid or asked for the freedom of a captive. — *v.* To free from captivity by the payment of a ransom.

rant \'rant\ *v.* **1** To talk noisily, excitedly, or wildly; as, to *rant* and rave in anger. **2** To scold violently; as, to *rant* at a troublesome child.

rap \'rap\ *v.;* **rapped; rap·ping. 1** To give a quick, sharp blow; to knock; as, to *rap* on the door. **2** To utter suddenly with force; as, to *rap* out an order. — *n.* A knock; a quick, sharp blow.

ra·pa·cious \rə-'pā-shəs\ *adj.* **1** Given to taking what one wants; excessively greedy; predatory. **2** Ravenous. — **ra·pa·cious·ly,** *adv.*

ra·pac·i·ty \rə-'pas-ət-ē\ *n.* The quality of being rapacious.

rape \'rāp\ *n.* An herb grown for forage and for its seeds, which are used as bird food and also yield an oil used as a lubricant.

rape \'rāp\ *v.;* **raped; rap·ing** \'rāp-ing\. To commit rape upon; to ravish. — *n.* **1** A seizing by force; a stealing. **2** Unlawful sexual intercourse with a woman against her will.

rap·id \'rap-əd\ *adj.* Very fast; swift. — *n.* [in the plural] A place in a stream where the current flows very fast and usually over obstructions, as rocks or pebbles. — **rap·id·ly,** *adv.*

ra·pid·i·ty \rə-'pid-ət-ē, ra-\ *n.* Swiftness; speed.

ra·pi·er \'rāp-ē-ər\ *n.* A straight two-edged sword with a narrow pointed blade.

rap·ine \'rap-n\ *n.* The seizing and carrying away of something by force; pillage; plunder.

rap·port \ra-'pōr, -'pȯr\ *n.* Relationship between people which makes communication possible or easy; as, an actor able to establish *rapport* with his audience; a governor in *rapport* with his advisers.

rapier

rap·scal·lion \rap-'skal-yən\ *n.* A scamp; a rascal.

rapt \'rapt\ *adj.* Showing complete delight or interest; absorbed; as, to listen with *rapt* attention.

rap·ture \'rap-chər\ *n.* A deep, joyous feeling; ecstasy; utter delight.

rap·tur·ous \'rap-chər-əs\ *adj.* Filled with rapture or delight. — **rap·tur·ous·ly,** *adv.*

rare \'rar, 'rer\ *adj.* Of meat, cooked so as not to lose the red or pink color in the center.

rare \'rar, 'rer\ *adj.* **1** Not thick or dense; thin; as, the *rare* atmosphere at high altitudes. **2** Unusually fine; excellent; splendid; as, a *rare* treat. **3** Seldom occurring or found; very uncommon.

— The word *scarce* is a synonym of *rare: rare* usually applies to an object or quality of which only a few examples are to be found and which is therefore especially cherished or valued; *scarce* may apply to something that for the time being is in too short supply to meet the demand for it.

rare·bit \'rar-bət, 'rer-\ *n.* A dish of melted cheese and other ingredients served on toast or crackers.

rar·e·fac·tion \ˌrar-ə-'faksh-n, ˌrer-\ *n.* The act or process of rarefying; the state of being rarefied.

rar·e·fy \'rar-ə-ˌfī, 'rer-\ *v.;* **rar·e·fied** \-ˌfīd\; **rar·e·fy·ing.** To make or become less dense; to become rare. The air is *rarefied* in the mountains.

rare·ly \'rar-lē, 'rer-\ *adv.* **1** Seldom. **2** Finely; with rare skill. **3** Unusually; as, *rarely* beautiful.

rar·i·ty \'rar-ət-ē, 'rer-\ *n.; pl.* **rar·i·ties. 1** Thinness; as, the *rarity* of the atmosphere at great heights. **2** Scarcity; as, the *rarity* of genius. **3** Something rare. Black pearls are *rarities.*

ras·cal \'rask-l\ *n.* A mean, tricky fellow; a dishonest person; a rogue — often used, especially to or of children, as a term of affection.

ras·cal·i·ty \ras-'kal-ət-ē\ *n.; pl.* **ras·cal·i·ties.** The act, actions, or character of a rascal.

ras·cal·ly \'rask-l-ē\ *adj.* Characteristic of a rascal; mean; dishonest; as, a *rascally* trick.

rash \'rash\ *n.* A breaking out of the skin with red spots, as in measles; an eruption.

rash \'rash\ *adj.* **1** Too hasty in speech or action, or in making decisions; reckless; venturesome. **2** Showing undue disregard for consequences; as, a *rash* act; to live to regret a *rash* promise.

rash·er \'rash-r\ *n.* A thin slice of bacon, or sometimes of ham, cut for broiling or frying.

rash·ly \'rash-lē\ *adv.* In a rash manner; without due consideration.

rash·ness \'rash-nəs\ *n.* Recklessness.

rasp \'rasp\ *v.* **1** To rub with or as if with a rough file; to file; as, to *rasp* off a rough edge. **2** To grate harshly upon, as upon one's nerves; to irritate; as, a *rasping* voice. **3** To speak or utter in a grating tone. — *n.* **1** A coarse file with sharp points instead of raised lines forming the grating surface. **2** A rasping sound or sensation.

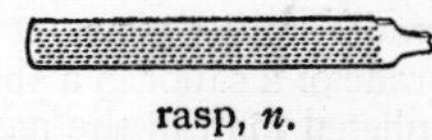

rasp, *n.*

rasp·ber·ry \'raz-ˌber-ē, -bər-ē\ *n.; pl.* **rasp·ber·ries. 1** The seedy fruit of certain brambles related to the blackberry but having rounder and smaller fruits. **2** The plant that bears this fruit. **3** *Slang.* A sound of contempt made with pursed lips.

rat \'rat\ *n.* **1** A scaly-tailed, gnawing rodent with brown, black, white, or gray fur, distinguished from the mouse chiefly by its large size and by differences in the teeth. **2** A person who deserts a cause or betrays his fellows. — *v.;* **rat·ted; rat·ting. 1** To betray or forsake one's associates for one's own advantage. **2** To hunt or catch rats.

ratch·et \'rach-ət\ *n.* **1** A movable metal arm that fits into the divisions of a notched bar (**ratch** \'rach\) or notched wheel (**ratchet wheel**) to produce motion forward or prevent motion backward; a pawl. **2** A device composed of a ratchet wheel and pawl.

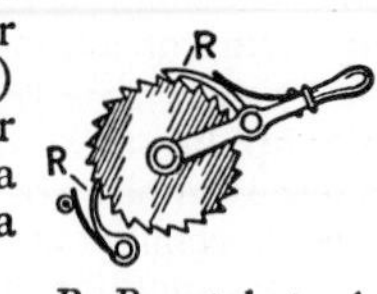

R, *R*, ratchets, 1

rate \'rāt\ *v.;* **rat·ed**; **rat·ing.** To scold violently; to berate.

rate \'rāt\ *n.* **1** Quantity or degree of a thing measured in terms of some accepted standard, usually per unit of something else; as, a *rate* of 40 miles an hour. **2** An amount of payment or charge measured by its relation to some other amount; as, interest at the *rate* of six per cent. **3** A charge, payment, or price set according to a fixed scale; as, postal *rates;* summer *rates.* **4** Rating; rank; class; as, first *rate;* second *rate.* — **at any rate. 1** Anyhow. **2** In any case. — *v.;* **rat·ed**; **rat·ing. 1** To consider; to regard; as, to be *rated* a good pianist. **2** To set an estimate or value on; as, to *rate* houses and land for tax purposes. **3** To settle the rank, class, or position of; as, to *rate* a seaman; to *rate* a ship. **4** To have a rating or rank; to be classed; as, to *rate* high in one's classes. **5** To deserve; to be qualified for; as, to *rate* a promotion.

rath·er \'ra*th*-r, 'rä*th*-, 'rə*th*-, 'rȧ*th*-\ *adv.* **1** More willingly; preferably. I would *rather* not go. **2** On the contrary; instead. Things did not turn out well; *rather*, they turned out very badly. **3** More exactly; more properly; preferably from a certain point of view; as, to be pitied *rather* than blamed; in the morning, or, *rather*, in the early afternoon. **4** Somewhat; as, *rather* cold.

rat·i·fi·ca·tion \ˌrat-ə-fə-'kāsh-n\ *n.* The act of ratifying or the state of being ratified; confirmation; as, the *ratification* of a treaty.

rat·i·fy \'rat-ə-ˌfī\ *v.;* **rat·i·fied** \-ˌfīd\; **rat·i·fy·ing.** To approve and accept, especially officially, as a treaty; to confirm. — **rat·i·fi·er** \-ˌfīr\ *n.*

rat·ing \'rāt-ing\ *n.* A scolding.

rat·ing \'rāt-ing\ *n.* **1** Classification according to grade; rank; class. **2** The relative standing or grade of a sailor in a ship's company. **3** *British.* An enlisted man in the navy.

ra·tio \'rā-ˌshō, -shē-ˌō\ *n.; pl.* **ra·tios.** [From Latin, meaning "reckoning", "relationship", "reason" — see *ration, reason.*] **1** A relation, either fixed or approximate, between things or to another thing, in number, quantity, or degree; rate; proportion; as, the *ratio* of eggs to butter in a cake; an island on which women outnumbered men in the *ratio* of three to one. **2** In mathematics, the quotient of one number divided by another. The *ratio* of 6 to 3 is expressed also as 6:3, 6/3, and 2; the *ratio* of *a* to *b* is expressed also as *a:b* and *a/b.*

rat·i·o·ci·na·tion \ˌrat-ē-ˌōs-n-'āsh-n, -ˌäs-\ *n.* Exact, careful thinking; reasoning.

ra·tion \'rash-n, 'rāsh-n\ *n.* [From French, there borrowed from Latin *ration-*, the stem of *ratio* meaning "reckoning", "relationship", "reason" — see *ratio, reason.*] **1** An allowance of provisions; an allotment or share, especially as determined by supply, as during wartime. **2** The daily food allowance for one person or one animal. — *v.;* **ra·tioned**; **ra·tion·ing** \-n(-)ing\. **1** To supply with rations. **2** To fix or limit, by law or official order, the amount of something, as food, clothing, or fuel, that can be bought by a person at one time.

ra·tio·nal \'rash-n(-)əl\ *adj.* **1** Having the ability to reason or understand; reasoning. Man is a *rational* creature. **2** Of or relating to the reason; based on or showing reason; as, *rational* thinking; a *rational* explanation of a mystery. **3** Not absurd or foolish; sensible; sane; as, *rational* behavior; a man who did not seem to be quite *rational.*

ra·tio·nal·ist \'rash-n(-)ə-ləst\ *n.* A person who bases his opinions upon reasoning and judges all theories and beliefs according to their reasonableness. — **ra·tio·nal·ism** \-ˌliz-m\ *n.* — **ra·tio·nal·is·tic** \ˌrash-n(-)ə-'lis-tik\ *adj.*

ra·tio·nal·i·ty \ˌrash-n-'al-ət-ē\ *n.* The quality or state of being rational.

ra·tio·nal·ize \'rash-n(-)ə-ˌlīz\ *v.;* **ra·tio·nal·ized**; **ra·tio·nal·iz·ing. 1** To make rational or reasonable. **2** To provide a rational explanation of, as of a myth. **3** To give a rational appearance to; especially, to find explanations of one's actions or desires that are favorable to oneself. **4** In mathematics, to free from irrational expressions. — **ra·tio·nal·i·za·tion** \ˌrash-n(-)ə-lə-'zāsh-n\ *n.*

ra·tio·nal·ly \'rash-n(-)ə-lē\ *adv.* In a rational way.

rational number. An integer or the quotient of two integers.

rat·line or **rat·lin** \'rat-lən\ *n.* **1** One of the cross ropes attached to the shrouds of a ship and forming the steps of a rope ladder. **2** The tarred line used in these ropes.

ratlines

rats·bane \'rats-ˌbān\ *n.* Rat poison.

rat·tan \ra-'tan, rə-\ *n.* **1** Also **rattan palm.** A climbing palm with tough stems that sometimes grow 600 feet long. **2** A portion of one of these stems used in various ways, as for walking sticks, for cord, or in making furniture.

rat·ter \'rat-r\ *n.* **1** A person who deserts or betrays his associates for his own advantage. **2** A person hired to catch rats. **3** A rat-catching cat or dog.

rat·tle \'rat-l\ *v.;* **rat·tled**; **rat·tling** \-l(-)ing\. **1** To make or give out a series of short, sharp sounds, as those made by one hard thing hitting another; to clatter; as, windows *rattling* in a storm. **2** To cause to rattle; to shake. **3** To move with a clatter; as, to *rattle* down the road in a jalopy. **4** To say or do in a brisk way, especially with a clatter; as, to *rattle* off a lesson. **5** To confuse; to upset; as, to be *rattled* by persistent questioning. — *n.* **1** A series of short, sharp sounds; a

rattle, *n.* 3

clatter; as, the *rattle* of hail on a roof. **2** A device, as a toy, for making a rattling sound. **3** A rattling organ at the end of a rattlesnake's tail, made up of horny joints. **4** A noise in the throat caused by air passing through mucus — used especially in the phrase *death rattle*.

rat·tler \'rat-l(-)ər\ *n.* A rattlesnake.

rat·tle·snake \'rat-l-ˌsnāk\ *n.* A poisonous American snake having at the end of the tail horny interlocking joints which rattle when shaken.

rat·tle·trap \'rat-l-ˌtrap\ *n.* A rickety vehicle.

rat·tling \'rat-l(-)ing\ *adj.* Lively; brisk; fast; good; as, a *rattling* argument.

rau·cous \'rȯk-əs\ *adj.* Hoarse; harsh; shrill; as, a *raucous* voice. — **rau·cous·ly**, *adv.*

rav·age \'rav-ij\ *v.;* **rav·aged**; **rav·ag·ing.** To lay waste and plunder; to destroy; to ruin; as, a country *ravaged* by an enemy; a body *ravaged* by disease. — *n.* **1** The action of laying waste. **2** Ruin; havoc; devastation. — **rav·ag·er** \-ij-r\ *n.*

rave \'rāv\ *v.;* **raved**; **rav·ing. 1** To talk wildly, as in delirium. **2** To storm; to rage. **3** To talk enthusiastically about something.

rav·el \'rav-l\ *v.;* **rav·eled** or **rav·elled**; **rav·el·ing** or **rav·el·ling** \-l(-)ing\. **1** To unravel; to untwist; to unwind; to fray. **2** To make plain or understandable; to undo the complexities of; as, to *ravel* out a problem. — *n.* Something that is raveled.

rav·el·ing or **rav·el·ling** \'rav-l(-)ing\ *n.* Something that is raveled or frayed; especially, a thread raveled out of a fabric.

ra·ven \'rāv-n\ *n.* A glossy black bird related to the crow, being about two feet long and having pointed throat feathers, and inhabiting northern regions. — *adj.* Black and glossy like a raven's feathers; as, *raven* hair.

rav·en·ing \'rav-n(-)ing\ *adj.* Greedy; rapacious.

rav·en·ous \'rav-n-əs\ *adj.* **1** Greedy; rapacious. **2** Eager for food; very hungry. — **rav·en·ous·ly**, *adv.*

ra·vine \rə-'vēn\ *n.* A depression worn out by running water, larger than a gully and smaller than a valley; especially, a deep gorge.

rav·ish \'rav-ish\ *v.* **1** To take possession of and carry away by force. **2** To carry away with emotion. **3** To rape. — **rav·ish·ing·ly**, *adv.*

raw \'rȯ\ *adj.* **1** Not cooked; as, *raw* meat. **2** In the natural state; not changed by processes of preparation, manufacture, or refining; as, *raw* steel; *raw* sugar. **3** Not spun or twisted; as, *raw* silk. **4** Not diluted; as, *raw* alcohol. **5** Not tanned; as, *raw* hides. **6** Inexperienced; untrained; as, a *raw* recruit. **7** Not pasteurized; as, *raw* milk. **8** With the skin rubbed or torn off; open; as, a *raw* sore. **9** Disagreeably damp or cold; bleak. **10** *Slang.* Unfair; crude; as, a *raw* deal. — **raw·ly**, *adv.*

raw·boned \'rȯ-'bōnd\ *adj.* Thin; lean; gaunt.

raw·hide \'rȯ-ˌhīd\ *n.* **1** The untanned skin of cattle. **2** A whip made of this untanned skin.

raw material. 1 Material in its natural state that is suitable for manufacture or development. **2** Human beings thought of as like such material; as, the *raw material* for a good soldier.

ray \'rā\ *n.* Any of numerous flat, broad fish that live on the sea bottom and have their eyes on the upper surface of their bodies, as the skate and the sting ray.

ray \'rā\ *n.* [From medieval English, there borrowed from medieval French *rai*, this derived from Latin *radius* meaning "staff", "radius", "ray" — see *radio, radium, radius.*] **1** A beam of light or heat, especially one that seems to come from a bright or shining object; as, *rays* of sunlight. **2** A tiny bit; a particle; as, not one *ray* of truth in the story. **3** Something like a ray, as the arm of a starfish. **4** A beam of light or radiant energy. **5** A stream of radioactive particles traveling in the same line. — *v.* To give off rays; to expose to rays.

ray·on \'rā-ˌän\ *n.* **1** A fiber made by forcing a solution of chemically treated cellulose through tiny holes and then drying the filaments. **2** A fabric made from this fiber, much used for clothing.

raze \'rāz\ *v.;* **razed**; **raz·ing.** To level or ruin by destroying everything above the ground.

ra·zor \'rāz-r\ *n.* A sharp cutting instrument used to shave off hair.

razz \'raz\ *v.* To ridicule with the intent of embarrassing, usually in fun.

razors

R.D. \'är-'dē, 'är-\. Abbreviation for *rural delivery.*

rd. Abbreviation for: **1** *road.* **2** *rod.*

re \'rā\ *n.* A syllable used in music to name the second note of the scale.

re-. A prefix that can mean: **1** Toward a former position, back, backwards, as in *retrace, recall.* **2** Again, as in *rebuild, restate, reassurance* — used freely to mean either "once again" or "over and over again".

reach \'rēch\ *v.* **1** To stretch out; to extend; as, to *reach* out a hand to help. **2** To touch, move, or seize by extending some part of the body, especially the hand, or something held in the hand. The boy could not *reach* the apple on the tree. **3** To extend to; to stretch to. This land *reaches* the river. **4** To arrive at; to come to; as, to *reach* home safely; to *reach* an understanding. **5** To influence or impress. Nobody seemed able to *reach* the disobedient boy. — *n.* **1** The act of reaching, especially as if to grasp something. **2** An expanse; a stretch; as, long *reaches* of meadow. **3** The power to grasp.

re·act \rē-'akt\ *v.* **1** To act in return; to have a return effect or influence. A child's home life and school life *react* upon each other. **2** To act in response, as to stimulation or to an influence; to respond; as, a boy who *reacts* badly to criticism. **3** To undergo chemical change.

re-act \'rē-'akt\ *v.* To act over again, as a play.

re·ac·tion \rē-'aksh-n\ *n.* **1** A return effect of an action upon the person or thing that originally started the action. **2** A movement or tendency toward movement in an opposite direction; especially, in politics, a movement toward a former political or social policy. **3** An action, feeling, or attitude caused by some influence; an effect of stimulation; a response; as, to show the desired *reaction* to a certain treatment. **4** A chemical change; a chemical process or its result. **5** A specific effect, as in vaccinations or in tests for showing the presence of disease.

re·ac·tion·ary \rē-'aksh-n-,er-ē\ *adj.* Having to do with, showing, or favoring a return to an older political order; as, a *reactionary* movement. — *n.; pl.* **re·ac·tion·ar·ies.** A reactionary person.

re·ac·tive \rē-'ak-tiv\ *adj.* **1** Of or relating to reaction. **2** Reacting or tending to react.

re·ac·tor \rē-'akt-r\ *n.* **1** One that reacts. **2** An individual who reacts positively to a foreign substance, especially in a test for a disease. **3** An atomic pile.

read \'rēd\ *v.;* **read** \'red\; **read·ing** \'rēd-ing\. **1** To go over something, as a book, with understanding of its letters and symbols. **2** To utter aloud words that are written. *Read* the story to the class. **3** To learn or be informed of something by reading; to get to know by observing. Scouts *read* the signs of nature. **4** To discover the meaning of something; as, to *read* a riddle. **5** To foretell; as, to *read* the future. **6** To put into something a meaning that may or may not actually be there; as, to *read* guilt in the boy's manner. **7** To make a special study of, as by reading; as, to *read* law. **8** To register, as a machine or instrument; to indicate. **9** To consist of, as something written or printed, in phrasing or meaning. How does the contract *read?* — **read between the lines.** To understand more than is said or written.

read \'red\ *adj.* Taught or informed by reading; as, a well-*read* man; widely *read* in history.

read·a·ble \'rēd-əb-l\ *adj.* **1** Legible; as, *readable* handwriting. **2** Interesting to read; as, a *readable* account of a journey. — **read·a·bil·i·ty** \,rēd-ə-'bil-ət-ē\ *n.* — **read·a·bly** \'rēd-ə-blē\ *adv.*

read·er \'rēd-r\ *n.* **1** A person who reads; as, a great *reader* of mystery stories. **2** A book for instruction and practice in reading.

read·i·ly \'red-l-ē\ *adv.* **1** Without delay or objection. **2** Promptly; quickly. **3** Easily.

read·i·ness \'red-ē-nəs\ *n.* **1** Promptness; as, a *readiness* in answering. **2** Preparedness; as, in *readiness* for flight.

read·ing \'rēd-ing\ *n.* **1** The act of one who reads. **2** Something that is read. **3** Written or printed matter meant to be read. **4** Manner of rendering something written, as a musical composition or a dramatic role. **5** The meaning put on what one sees. The teacher's *reading* of the boy's character was accurate. **6** That which is registered, as on a gauge. The thermometer *reading* was 70 degrees.

re·ad·just \,rē-ə-'jəst\ *v.* To make a new adjustment. — **re·ad·just·ment** \,rē-ə-'jəs(t)-mənt\ *n.*

ready \'red-ē\ *adj.;* **read·i·er**; **read·i·est. 1** Prepared for use or action. Dinner is *ready.* **2** Probably about to; likely; as, to be *ready* to cry. **3** Willing; as, *ready* to give aid. **4** Quick; prompt; as, a *ready* answer. **5** Available; handy; as, *ready* money. — *v.;* **read·ied** \-ēd\; **read·y·ing.** To make ready; to prepare.

ready-made \'red-ē-'mād\ *adj.* **1** Already made up for general sale; not made to order; as, a *ready-made* suit. **2** Lacking originality; as, *ready-made* ideas.

re·a·gent \rē-'āj-nt\ *n.* A substance which acts in a known way under certain conditions and which is therefore used, as in chemistry, to test or measure other substances, as for purity or quality.

re·al \rā-'äl, -'ál\ *n.; pl.* **re·als** \-'älz, -'álz\ or **re·a·les** \-'ä-,lās, -'á-,lās\. The former silver coin unit of the Spanish monetary system, eight of which made the peso or dollar.

re·al \'rē-əl, 'rēl, 'ril\ *adj.* **1** Actually being or existing; actual; not imaginary; as, *real* life. **2** Genuine; true; not artificial.

real estate. Property in houses and land.

re·al·ism \'rē-ə-,liz-m\ *n.* **1** The belief that objects we perceive through our senses are real and have an existence outside our own minds. **2** The disposition to see situations or difficulties in the light of facts and to deal with them practically. **3** In literature and art, the representation of things as they are in life. — **re·al·ist** \-ləst\ *n.*

re·al·is·tic \,rē-ə-'lis-tik\ *adj.* **1** True to life or nature; as, a *realistic* painting. **2** Having or showing an inclination to face facts and to deal with them sensibly. — **re·al·is·ti·cal·ly** \-tik-l(-)ē\ *adv.*

re·al·i·ty \rē-'al-ət-ē\ *n.; pl.* **re·al·i·ties. 1** Actual existence; genuineness; as, to doubt the *reality* of sea serpents. **2** Someone or something real or actual; as, the *realities* of life. **3** In art, the characteristic of being true to life or to fact.

re·al·ize \'rē-ə-,līz\ *v.;* **re·al·ized**; **re·al·iz·ing. 1** To make actual; to accomplish; as, to *realize* a lifelong ambition. **2** To convert into money; as, to *realize* all one's tangible assets. **3** To obtain or acquire; to gain; as, to *realize* a large profit. **4** To be aware of; as, to *realize* one's danger. — **re·al·i·za·tion** \,rē-ə-lə-'zāsh-n\ *n.*

re·al·ly \'rē-ə-lē, 'rē-lē, 'ril-ē\ *adv.* Actually; in truth; in fact.

realm \'relm\ *n.* **1** A kingdom. **2** A region; a domain; as, the *realm* of fancy.

re·al·ty \'rē-əl-tē\ *n.* Real estate.

ream \'rēm\ *n.* **1** A quantity of paper, usually 480 sheets but sometimes 472, 500, or 516. **2** [in the plural] A very large amount of something written or printed; as, *reams* of notes.

ream \'rēm\ *v.* **1** To widen the opening of, as a hole, by beveling the edges. **2** To enlarge, clean, or clear with a reamer.

ream·er \'rēm-r\ *n.* **1** Any of various rotating tools with cutting edges for enlarging or shaping a hole. **2** A juice extractor with a ridged and pointed center rising from a shallow dish.

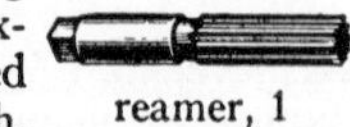
reamer, 1

re·an·i·mate \(ˈ)rē-ˈan-ə-ˌmāt\ *v.;* **re·an·i·mat·ed; re·an·i·mat·ing.** To give life to anew; to revive.

reap \ˈrēp\ *v.* **1** To cut, as grain, with a sickle, scythe, or machine; to gather, as a harvest, by cutting. **2** To gain as a reward; as, to *reap* the benefit of years of hard work. **3** To clear of a crop by cutting off the grain; as, to *reap* a field.

reap·er \ˈrēp-r\ *n.* One that reaps; especially, any of various machines for reaping grain.

re·ap·pear \ˌrē-ə-ˈpir\ *v.* To appear again.

rear \ˈrir\ *n.* **1** The division of an army, fleet, or other fighting force that is behind all the rest. **2** The back of anything; as, the *rear* of a building. **3** The space or position behind or at the back of anything; as, to move to the *rear.* — *adj.* In, at, or near the rear; as, the *rear* view of the house.

rear \ˈrir\ *v.* **1** To raise or set upright; as, to *rear* a pole. **2** To erect by building; to construct; as, to *rear* a house. **3** To lift or seem to lift upwards. The city *rears* its tall buildings. **4** To breed and raise; as, to *rear* cattle. **5** To bring up, as children. **6** To stand up on the hind legs, as a horse.

rear admiral. A naval officer of the rank next above a captain.

re·arm \(ˈ)rē-ˈärm, -ˈårm\ *v.* To furnish with weapons again; to begin to carry weapons again. — **re·ar·ma·ment** \(ˈ)rē-ˈär-mə-mənt, -ˈår-\ *n.*

rear·ward \ˈrir-wərd\ *adj.* In, at, or toward the rear. — *adv.* Also **rear·wards** \-wərdz\. To the rear.

rea·son \ˈrēz-n\ *n.* [From medieval English *resoun,* there borrowed from Old French *raison,* this derived from Latin *ration-,* the stem of *ratio* meaning "reckoning", "relationship", "reason" — see *ratio, ration.*] **1** A ground or motive for an action, belief, or conclusion. His religious faith is the *reason* for his charity. **2** An explanation, especially in defense of something done; a justification; as, to have a good *reason* for not doing one's homework. **3** The power to think; intellect. Man has *reason* while animals do not. **4** The ability to think clearly and intelligently; especially, the ability to think in a systematic and logical way. **5** A sound mind; sanity; sense. Have you lost your *reason?* — For synonyms see *cause.* — *v.;* **rea·soned; rea·son·ing** \-n(-)ing\. **1** To talk persuasively or to present reasons in order to cause a change of mind; as, to *reason* with someone for hours. **2** To use one's reason or to think in a logical way or manner.

rea·son·a·ble \ˈrēz-n(-)əb-l\ *adj.* **1** Able to use reason. Man is a *reasonable* being. **2** Just; fair; sensible; as, a *reasonable* request. **3** Moderately priced.

rea·son·a·bly \ˈrēz-n(-)ə-blē\ *adv.* **1** In a fair or reasonable way; as, to treat someone *reasonably.* **2** Moderately; as, played *reasonably* well.

rea·son·ing \ˈrēz-n(-)ing\ *n.* **1** The process of relating facts to each other so as to arrive at a conclusion; thinking. **2** The reasons or proofs that result from thinking. That *reasoning* sounds correct.

re·as·sure \ˌrē-ə-ˈshu̇r\ *v.;* **re·as·sured; re·as·sur·ing.** To comfort; to free from fear; to restore confidence. — **re·as·sur·ance** \-ˈshu̇r-ən(t)s\ *n.*

reave \ˈrēv\ *v.;* **reaved** \ˈrēvd\ or **reft** \ˈreft\; **reav·ing.** *Archaic.* To rob or plunder.

re·a·wak·en \ˌrē-ə-ˈwāk-n\ *v.;* **re·a·wak·ened; re·a·wak·en·ing** \-n(-)ing\. To awaken again.

re·bate \ˈrē-ˌbāt\ *n.* A reduction in cost in the form of something paid back. — *v.;* **re·bat·ed; re·bat·ing.** To make a rebate; to give a rebate.

re·bel \rē-ˈbel\ *v.;* **re·belled; re·bel·ling.** **1** To resist the authority of one's government by force. **2** To be insubordinate; to resist authority.

reb·el \ˈreb-l\ *adj.* Of or relating to rebels or rebellions; rebellious; as, *rebel* forces. — *n.* A person who rebels against authority.

re·bel·lion \rē-ˈbel-yən\ *n.* **1** An uprising; a revolt. **2** Open resistance to authority.

re·bel·lious \rē-ˈbel-yəs\ *adj.* **1** Engaged in rebellion. **2** Inclined to resist or disobey authority; insubordinate. — **re·bel·lious·ly,** *adv.*

re·birth \(ˈ)rē-ˈbərth\ *n.* **1** A new or second birth. **2** A revival; a renewal.

re·born \ˈrē-ˈbȯrn\ *adj.* Born again; revived.

re·bound \(ˈ)rē-ˈbau̇nd\ *v.* To spring back on striking something; to bounce back. The ball *rebounded* from the wall. — \ˈrē-ˌbau̇nd\ *n.* A springing back; as, to catch a ball on the *rebound.*

re·buff \rē-ˈbəf\ *n.* **1** An abrupt refusal to meet an advance or offer; a snub. **2** Any sharp check; a repulse. — *v.* **1** To snub. **2** To drive or beat back.

re·buke \rē-ˈbyük\ *v.;* **re·buked; re·buk·ing.** To scold or criticize severely.

— The word *admonish* is a synonym of *rebuke: rebuke* usually suggests a rather sharp and stern expression of disapproval intended to put an immediate stop to undesirable behavior; *admonish* suggests far less severity and usually indicates a gentle and friendly warning or advising of another person to reconsider his manner of conduct.

— *n.* A scolding; a severe criticism.

re·bus \ˈrē-bəs\ *n.* [From Latin, meaning "by things", a form of *res* meaning "thing".] **1** The representation of words or phrases by means of pictures of objects whose names resemble those of the words or phrases. **2** A riddle or puzzle composed of such pictures.

re·but \rē-ˈbət\ *v.;* **re·but·ted; re·but·ting.** To contradict, especially formally, as in a debate; to offer facts and arguments to disprove something.

re·but·tal \rē-ˈbət-l\ *n.* The act of rebutting.

re·cal·ci·trant \rē-ˈkal-sə-trənt\ *adj.* Rebellious; obstinately disobedient. — **re·cal·ci·trance** \-trən(t)s\ *n.*

re·call \rē-ˈkȯl\ *v.* **1** To cause to come back by calling; to ask to come back. **2** To remember; to call back to mind; as, to *recall* an address. **3** To cancel something, as a law; to revoke; to do away with; as, to *recall* an order. — \rē-ˈkȯl, ˈrē-ˌkȯl\ *n.* **1** A calling back; a summons to return; as, the *recall* of a messenger. **2** A calling back to mind. **3** The action of canceling or revoking; an annulment; as, a decision that is now beyond *recall.* **4** The process by which a public official may be removed from office by a vote of the people.

re·cant \rē-'kant\ *v.* To withdraw or take back formally or publicly, as a statement of opinion or belief; to disown; to disclaim; to repudiate. — **re·can·ta·tion** \ˌrē-ˌkan-'tāsh-n\ *n.*

re·cap \(')rē-'kap\ *v.;* **re·capped**; **re·cap·ping**. To cement, mold, and vulcanize a strip of rubber upon the surface of the tread of a worn automobile tire. — \'rē-ˌkap\ *n.* A recapped tire.

re·ca·pit·u·late \ˌrēk-ə-'pich-l-ˌāt\ *v.;* **re·ca·pit·u·lat·ed**; **re·ca·pit·u·lat·ing**. To repeat or restate in a few words; to give a summary. — **re·ca·pit·u·la·tion** \-ˌpich-l-'āsh-n\ *n.*

re·cap·ture \'rē-'kap-chər\ *n.* A capturing again; as, the *recapture* of escaped prisoners. — \'rē-'kap-chər; *sense 2 is* (')rē-\ *v.;* **re·cap·tured**; **re·cap·tur·ing**. **1** To capture again. **2** To remember; as, to *recapture* the days of one's youth.

re·cast \(')rē-'kast\ *v.* **1** To throw again after hauling in, as a fishing line or net. **2** To cast or found anew; to remold or remodel; as, to *recast* a cannon. **3** To arrange in a new or different form; as, to *recast* a sentence. **4** To provide a new set of actors for; as, to *recast* a play. — \'rē-ˌkast\ *n.* **1** The action of recasting. **2** The product of recasting.

recd. Abbreviation for *received.*

re·cede \rē-'sēd\ *v.;* **re·ced·ed**; **re·ced·ing**. **1** To move back or away; to withdraw, especially from view; to retreat; to retire. The tide *recedes.* **2** To fall or slant back; as, a *receding* forehead.

re·ceipt \rē-'sēt\ *n.* **1** A cooking recipe. **2** The act of receiving; as, on *receipt* of your letter. **3** [usually in the plural] Something taken in, in contrast to something paid out; as, to record the day's *receipts.* **4** A written acknowledgment of goods or money received. Get a *receipt* when you pay a bill. — *v.* To mark as paid; as, to *receipt* a bill.

re·ceiv·a·ble \rē-'sē-vəb-l\ *adj.* **1** Capable of being received; especially, acceptable as legal. **2** That is to be received, as money due on bills sent out.

re·ceive \rē-'sēv\ *v.;* **re·ceived**; **re·ceiv·ing**. **1** To take or get something that is given, paid, or sent; as, to *receive* the money; to *receive* a letter. **2** To permit to enter one's household or company; to welcome; to greet; as, to *receive* friends. The king *received* the ambassador at court. **3** To hold a reception; as, to *receive* from four to six o'clock. **4** To undergo an experience or a certain kind of treatment; as, to *receive* a shock. **5** To change incoming electric waves into sounds or pictures; as, a radio or television set that *receives* well. — For synonyms see *take.*

re·ceiv·er \rē-'sēv-r\ *n.* **1** One that receives or takes in. **2** That portion of an apparatus, as a telephone or a radio, by which electric currents or waves are converted into signals which can be seen or heard. **3** In law, a person appointed to take control of property that is involved in a lawsuit or of a business that is bankrupt or is being reorganized.

receiver

re·ceiv·er·ship \rē-'sēv-r-ˌship\ *n.* **1** In law, the office or duties of a receiver. **2** The condition of being in the hands of a receiver.

re·cent \'rēs-nt\ *adj.* Lately made, created, or used; of the present time or time just past; as, *recent* events; a *recent* illness. — **re·cent·ly**, *adv.*

re·cep·ta·cle \rē-'sep-tik-l\ *n.* **1** Something used to receive and contain smaller objects; a container. **2** The enlarged and thickened end of a stem on which a flower grows. **3** A permanently fixed electrical fitting to which other devices are connected, as a socket for a light bulb.

re·cep·tion \rē-'sepsh-n\ *n.* **1** The act or manner of receiving, welcoming, or accepting; as, to get a warm *reception.* **2** A party, especially one where guests are formally welcomed; as, a wedding *reception.* **3** The process or manner of receiving on radio or television.

re·cep·tion·ist \rē-'sepsh-n(-)əst\ *n.* An office employee, usually a woman, who greets callers, answers questions, and arranges appointments.

re·cep·tive \rē-'sep-tiv\ *adj.* **1** Able or inclined to take in, hold, contain, or receive. **2** Ready and willing to listen and learn. — **re·cep·tive·ly**, *adv.*

re·cep·tor \rē-'sept-r\ *n.* A cell or group of cells which receives stimuli; a sense organ.

re·cess \'rē-ˌses, rē-'ses\ *n.* **1** A space or little hollow set back, as from the main line of a coast or mountain range. **2** In a room, an alcove; a niche. **3** [often in the plural] A place of seclusion or privacy; a secret or hidden part; as, the inner *recesses* of the soul. **4** A short time during which work stops. — *v.* **1** To put into a recess; to hide; as, a *recessed* bed. **2** To make a recess in; as, to *recess* a wall. **3** To take a recess, or short rest.

re·ces·sion \rē-'sesh-n\ *n.* **1** The act or fact of receding or withdrawing. **2** The departing procession of clergy and choir at the end of a church service. **3** A downward turn in business activity or the period of such a downward turn.

re·ces·sive \rē-'ses-iv\ *adj.* **1** Tending to go back; receding. **2** In biology, reappearing in fewer offspring than a contrasting characteristic. — *n.* **1** A recessive characteristic. **2** A plant or animal possessing recessive characteristics.

rec·i·pe \'res-ə-(ˌ)pē\ *n.* [From Latin, meaning "take!", the imperative form of *recipere* meaning "to take", "to receive" used by physicians at the head of prescriptions.] **1** Directions for mixing ingredients in cooking. **2** A set of instructions for obtaining any result; as, a *recipe* for happiness.

re·cip·i·ent \rē-'sip-ē-ənt\ *n.* One that receives; as, the *recipient* of many honors.

re·cip·ro·cal \rē-'sip-rək-l\ *adj.* **1** Mutual; shared; done or felt equally by both sides; as, *reciprocal* affection. **2** Related to each other in such a way that one completes the other or is the equivalent of the other. — *n.* Of a number in mathematics, the result obtained by dividing that number into 1. — **re·cip·ro·cal·ly** \-rək-l-ē\ *adv.*

re·cip·ro·cate \rē-'sip-rə-ˌkāt\ *v.;* **re·cip·ro·cat·ed**;

re·cip·ro·cat·ing \-ˌkāt-ing\. **1** To move forward and backward alternately, as the piston in some engines. **2** To make a return for something done or given; to return a favor or a compliment. **3** To give and return mutually; to exchange. — **re·cip·ro·ca·tion** \rē-ˌsip-rə-ˈkāsh-n\ *n.*

rec·i·proc·i·ty \ˌres-ə-ˈpräs-ət-ē\ *n.; pl.* **rec·i·proc·i·ties.** **1** Mutual dependence, co-operation, or exchange between persons, groups, or states. **2** International policy by which special commercial advantages are granted to one country in return for special advantages granted by another.

re·cit·al \rē-ˈsīt-l\ *n.* **1** A reciting; a story told in detail; as, the *recital* of his troubles. **2** A repeating of another's words. **3** A program of one kind of music, vocal or instrumental; as, a piano *recital.* **4** A public performance by pupils, as music or dancing pupils. — For synonyms see *narrative.*

rec·i·ta·tion \ˌres-ə-ˈtāsh-n\ *n.* **1** A reciting; a recital. **2** The delivery before an audience of something that has been memorized; that which is recited, as a poem or a play. **3** A class exercise in which pupils answer questions orally on a lesson they have studied; any class exercise.

rec·i·ta·tive \ˌres(-ə)-tə-ˈtēv\ *n.* A kind of singing in which the words are spoken with the music rather than actually sung; a piece of music meant for such recitation.

re·cite \rē-ˈsīt\ *v.;* **re·cit·ed**; **re·cit·ing.** **1** To repeat, as something studied or memorized; as, to *recite* a poem. **2** To tell in detail; to relate; as, to *recite* the story of one's misfortunes. **3** To answer questions about a lesson, as to a teacher.

reck \ˈrek\ *v. Archaic.* **1** To care; to mind. **2** To be of interest; to matter.

reck·less \ˈrek-ləs\ *adj.* Heedless; careless; rash. — **reck·less·ly**, *adv.*

reck·on \ˈrek-n\ *v.;* **reck·oned**; **reck·on·ing** \-n(-)ing\. **1** To count; to compute; as, to *reckon* the days till Christmas. **2** To consider; to regard; to class; as, to be *reckoned* among the leaders. **3** To think; to suppose. The boy *reckoned* he hadn't much chance to win. **4** To make up an account; as, to *reckon* a bill. **5** To depend; to count; as, to *reckon* on support. — **reck·on·er** \-n(-)ər\ *n.*

reck·on·ing \ˈrek-n(-)ing\ *n.* **1** The act of a person who reckons; a count; a calculation. **2** An account of one's conduct; as, to call a man to a *reckoning* at last. **3** The calculation of a ship's position, or the position so determined.

re·claim \rē-ˈklām\ *v.* **1** To call back to a moral life; to reform; as, to *reclaim* sinners. **2** To change to a desirable condition or state, as by labor or cultivation; as, to *reclaim* a swamp. **3** To obtain something useful or valuable from waste. — **re·claim·a·ble** \-ˈklā-məb-l\ *adj.* — **re·claim·er** \-ˈklām-r\ *n.*

rec·la·ma·tion \ˌrek-lə-ˈmāsh-n\ *n.* The act or process of reclaiming or the state of being reclaimed.

re·cline \rē-ˈklīn\ *v.;* **re·clined**; **re·clin·ing.** To lean or cause to lean; to lie down; to rest.

rec·luse \ˈrek-ˌlüs, rē-ˈklüs\ *n.* A person who lives away from others, as a hermit.

rec·og·ni·tion \ˌrek-ig-ˈnish-n\ *n.* **1** The act of recognizing; as, her *recognition* of the old man. **2** Attention or notice, usually favorable. **3** Acknowledgment of something done or given, as by making an award; as, to receive a medal in *recognition* of bravery. **4** Formal acknowledgment of the political existence of a government or nation.

re·cog·ni·zance \rē-ˈkäg-nə-zən(t)s\ *n.* In law, a recorded promise to do something, as to appear in court or to keep the peace.

rec·og·nize \ˈrek-ig-ˌnīz\ *v.;* **rec·og·nized**; **rec·og·niz·ing.** **1** To know again; to remember knowing; as, to *recognize* a person. **2** To consent to admit; to acknowledge; as, to *recognize* one's own faults. **3** To take approving notice of something; as, to *recognize* an act of bravery by the award of a medal. **4** To make some sign to show acquaintance; as, to *recognize* someone with a nod. **5** To acknowledge as one entitled to be heard at a meeting. The chair *recognizes* the delegate from Illinois. **6** To grant recognition to. — **rec·og·niz·a·ble** \-ˌnī-zəb-l\ *adj.* — **rec·og·niz·a·bly** \-zə-blē\ *adv.*

re·coil \rē-ˈkȯil\ *v.* **1** To retreat; to draw back; as, to *recoil* in horror. **2** To spring back; to fly back into its former position, as a released spring. — \rē-ˈkȯil, ˈrē-ˌkȯil\ *n.* **1** The act of recoiling; a rebound; a drawing back. **2** A springing back, as of a discharged gun or a spring. **3** The distance through which something, as a spring, recoils.

rec·ol·lect \ˌrek-l-ˈekt\ *v.* To call to mind; to remember; as, to *recollect* what happened.

rec·ol·lec·tion \ˌrek-l-ˈeksh-n\ *n.* **1** The act of recalling something to mind. **2** The time within which things can be remembered; memory; as, the coldest year within *recollection.* **3** Something remembered; as, my earliest *recollections.* — For synonyms see *memory.*

rec·om·mend \ˌrek-m-ˈend\ *v.* **1** To make a statement in praise of someone or something; as, to *recommend* a person for a position. **2** To put forward as one's advice, as one's choice, or as having one's support; as, to *recommend* that the matter be dropped. **3** To cause to receive favorable attention; as, a man *recommended* by his good manners.

rec·om·men·da·tion \ˌrek-m-ən-ˈdāsh-n, -m-ˌen-\ *n.* **1** The act of recommending. **2** Something that recommends; as, a written *recommendation.* **3** A thing or course of action recommended.

rec·om·pense \ˈrek-m-ˌpen(t)s\ *v.;* **rec·om·pensed**; **rec·om·pens·ing.** To give an equivalent return for; to make up for; to compensate, as for a loss. — *n.* Payment; return; as, *recompense* for labor.

rec·on·cile \ˈrek-n-ˌsīl\ *v.;* **rec·on·ciled**; **rec·on·cil·ing.** **1** To make friendly again; as, to *reconcile* friends who have quarreled. **2** To settle; to adjust; as, to *reconcile* differences of opinion. **3** To make agree; as, a story that cannot be *reconciled* with the facts. **4** To make willing to accept; to make content; as, to *reconcile* oneself to a loss. — **rec·on·cile·ment** \-mənt\ *n.* — **rec·on·cil·er** \-ˌsīl-r\ *n.*

rec·on·cil·i·a·tion \ˌrek-n-ˌsil-ē-'āsh-n\ *n.* **1** The act of restoring or the state of being restored to friendship. **2** Settlement or explanation of differences.

rec·on·dite \'rek-n-ˌdīt, rē-'kän-\ *adj.* **1** Hidden from sight; concealed. **2** Difficult to understand.

re·con·di·tion \ˌrēk-n-'dish-n\ *v.;* **re·con·di·tioned; re·con·di·tion·ing** \-n(-)ing\. To put something worn into serviceable condition again.

re·con·nais·sance \rē-'kän-ə-zən(t)s, -sən(t)s\ *n.* An examination or survey of a region or territory; especially, such a survey made by the military to obtain information, as about enemy troops.

re·con·noi·ter or **re·con·noi·tre** \ˌrēk-n-'ȯit-r, ˌrek-n-\ *v.;* **re·con·noi·tered** or **re·con·noi·tred** \-'ȯit-rd\; **re·con·noi·ter·ing** or **re·con·noi·tring** \-'ȯit-r(-)ing\. To make a reconnaissance; to survey, especially in preparation for military action.

re·con·struct \ˌrēk-n-'strəkt\ *v.* To construct again; to rebuild; to remodel.

re·con·struc·tion \ˌrēk-n-'strəksh-n\ *n.* **1** The act of constructing again. **2** Something that has been reconstructed. **3** [with a capital] The process of reorganizing the governments of the southern states after the Civil War and re-establishing their relations with the national government.

re·cord \rē-'kȯrd\ *v.* **1** To set down, as in writing or printing; as, to *record* a vote; to *record* a name and address in a register. **2** To preserve an account of or information about; as, events *recorded* in history. **3** To register, as on a chart or graph; to show; to indicate. The seismograph *records* earthquakes. **4** To register transformed sounds by means of impressions on a receptive surface, as a disk or a magnetic tape or wire, for later reproduction. **5** To admit of reproduction, as on a phonograph record; as, a voice that *records* well.

rec·ord \'rek-rd, -ˌȯrd\ *n.* **1** The act of recording or the fact of being recorded. **2** Something written to preserve an account; as, a court *record.* **3** The known facts about anything, as about a man's life. The student's *record* was good. **4** The best that has ever been done in a particular competition. The runner broke the *record.* **5** A disk on which sounds are recorded for reproduction at will. — \'rek-rd\ *adj.* Setting a record; outstanding among other things like it; as, a *record* crop.

re·cord·er \rē-'kȯrd-r\ *n.* **1** A person who makes or keeps official records; as, a court *recorder;* a *recorder* of deeds. **2** In some cities, a judge of certain courts. **3** An instrument for recording sounds; as, a tape *recorder.* **4** A vertical flute with a whistle mouthpiece and eight finger holes. **5** One who sings or plays for a phonographic recording.

recorder, 4

re·cord·ing \rē-'kȯrd-ing\ *n.* **1** A transcribing of sound, especially music or speech, so that it can be reproduced, as onto a phonograph record. **2** A record of sound; especially, a phonograph record.

rec·ord player \'rek-rd\. An electrical instrument for playing phonograph records either through the loudspeaker of a radio set to which it may be attached or through its own loudspeaker.

re·count \rē-'kau̇nt\ *v.* To relate in detail; to tell all about; as, to *recount* an adventure.

re-count \'rē-'kau̇nt\ *v.* To count again.

re·count \'rē-'kau̇nt, -ˌkau̇nt\ *n.* A second or further count, as of votes in an election.

re·coup \rē-'küp\ *v.* **1** To make up for; to recover; as, to *recoup* a loss in business. **2** To reimburse; to compensate; as, to *recoup* a person for losses.

re·course \'rē-ˌkōrs, -ˌkȯrs; rē-'kōrs, -'kȯrs\ *n.* **1** A turning for assistance or protection; resort; as, to have *recourse* to the law to settle a dispute. **2** That to which one turns for assistance or protection.

re·cov·er \rē-'kəv-r\ *v.;* **re·cov·ered; re·cov·er·ing** \-r(-)ing\. **1** To get again; to win back; to regain; as, to *recover* a lost ball. **2** To regain health, consciousness, or self-control. **3** To bring (oneself) back to a normal condition, as after losing one's balance. **4** To make up for; as, to *recover* lost time.

re-cov·er \'rē-'kəv-r\ *v.;* **re-cov·ered; re-cov·er·ing** \-r(-)ing\. To cover again or anew.

re·cov·ery \rē-'kəv-r(-)ē\ *n.; pl.* **re·cov·er·ies. 1** The act of getting back something that was lost or stolen. **2** A return, as to health, good spirits, or prosperity; restoration to any normal condition.

rec·re·ant \'rek-rē-ənt\ *adj.* **1** Cowardly; weakly; yielding. **2** Unfaithful to duty or allegiance; false; traitorous. — *n.* **1** A coward. **2** A traitor.

rec·re·ate \'rek-rē-ˌāt\ *v.;* **rec·re·at·ed; rec·re·at·ing. 1** To give fresh life to. **2** To take recreation.

re-cre·ate \ˌrēk-rē-'āt\ *v.;* **re-cre·at·ed; re-cre·at·ing.** To create anew. — **re-cre·a·tion** \-'āsh-n\ *n.*

rec·re·a·tion \ˌrek-rē-'āsh-n\ *n.* **1** A refreshing, as of strength or spirits after work or anxiety. **2** A game, exercise, or diversion. His *recreation* was tennis. — **rec·re·a·tion·al** \-'āsh-n(-)əl\ *adj.*

re·crim·i·nate \rē-'krim-ə-ˌnāt\ *v.;* **re·crim·i·nat·ed; re·crim·i·nat·ing.** To make an accusation against an accuser; to accuse in return.

re·crim·i·na·tion \rē-ˌkrim-ə-'nāsh-n\ *n.* **1** The act of recriminating. **2** An accusation made by an accused person against the one who accused him.

re·cru·des·cence \ˌrēk-rü-'des-n(t)s\ *n.* A renewal or breaking out again, especially of something unhealthful or dangerous; as, a *recrudescence* of an epidemic disease. — **re·cru·des·cent** \-nt\ *adj.*

re·cruit \rē-'krüt\ *v.* **1** To form or strengthen an organization by enlisting members or followers; as, to *recruit* an army; to *recruit* a political force. **2** To enlist new soldiers. The army is *recruiting.* **3** To restore or regain, as health or strength; to recuperate. — *n.* A newly enlisted member of a country's armed forces. — **re·cruit·er,** *n.*

rec·tal \'rekt-l\ *adj.* Of or relating to the rectum.

rec·tan·gle \'rek-ˌtang-gl\ *n.* A four-sided figure with four right angles.

rec·tan·gu·lar \rek-'tang-gyəl-r\ *adj.* Shaped like a rectangle. — **rec·tan·gu·lar·ly,** *adv.*

rec·ti·fy \'rek-tə-ˌfī\ *v.;* **rec·ti·fied** \-ˌfīd\; **rec·ti·fy·ing. 1** To make or set right; to correct. **2** To purify or refine, especially by repeated distillation. **3** To convert into a direct current, as an alternating or oscillating current. — **rec·ti·fi·ca·tion** \ˌrek-tə-fə-ˈkāsh-n\ *n.* — **rec·ti·fi·er** \ˈrek-tə-ˌfīr\ *n.*

rec·ti·lin·e·ar \ˌrek-tə-ˈlin-ē-ər\ *adj.* **1** Moving in or forming a straight line. **2** Formed or bounded by straight lines.

rec·ti·tude \ˈrek-tə-ˌtüd, -ˌtyüd\ *n.* Strict observance of standards of honesty and integrity and of the moral code; upright conduct.

rec·tor \ˈrekt-r\ *n.* **1** A clergyman who is in charge of a church or parish. **2** The priest in charge of certain Roman Catholic religious houses for men. **3** The head of certain universities or schools.

rec·to·ry \ˈrekt-r(-)ē\ *n.; pl.* **rec·to·ries.** A rector's residence.

rec·tum \ˈrekt-m\ *n.* The lower end of the intestine.

re·cum·bent \rē-ˈkəm-bənt\ *adj.* Reclining; lying down.

re·cu·per·ate \rē-ˈkyüp-r-ˌāt, -ˈküp-\ *v.;* **re·cu·per·at·ed; re·cu·per·at·ing. 1** To recover or regain, especially health or strength; to convalesce. **2** To recover from a financial loss.

re·cu·per·a·tion \rē-ˌkyüp-r-ˈāsh-n, -ˌküp-\ *n.* The process of recuperating.

re·cu·per·a·tive \rē-ˈkyüp-r-ˌāt-iv, -ˈküp-, -r(-)ət-iv\ *adj.* **1** Of or relating to recuperation. **2** Helping recuperation.

re·cur \rē-ˈkər\ *v.;* **re·curred; re·cur·ring** \-ˈkər-ing\. **1** To go or come back in thought or discussion; as, to *recur* to the subject of an earlier conversation. **2** To come again into the mind; as, a childhood memory that *recurred* over and over again. **3** To occur or appear again; as, a fever that *recurred.*

re·cur·rence \rē-ˈkər-ən(t)s, -ˈkə-rən(t)s\ *n.* **1** The act of recurring. **2** The state of being recurrent. **3** A repetition; a return.

re·cur·rent \rē-ˈkər-ənt, -ˈkə-rənt\ *adj.* **1** Returning from time to time; recurring; as, a *recurrent* fever. **2** Running or turning back in direction, as a nerve or vein. — **re·cur·rent·ly,** *adv.*

red \ˈred\ *n.* **1** Any of several colors ranging from the hue of blood to that of the ruby; any color of the spectrum lying between orange and violet. **2** Any pigment or dye that colors red. **3** [usually with a capital] A revolutionary in politics; especially, a communist. — *adj.* **1** Of the color or hue of red. **2** [usually with a capital] Revolutionary in politics; especially, of or relating to the U.S.S.R. or to communism; as, the *Red* army.

red·bird \ˈred-ˌbərd\ *n.* Any of various red-colored birds, as the cardinal or the scarlet tanager.

red blood cell. One of the colored cells of the blood of vertebrates, containing the hemoglobin and carrying oxygen from the respiratory organs to the tissues.

red·breast \ˈred-ˌbrest\ *n.* A robin.

red·cap \ˈred-ˌkap\ *n.* A railroad-station porter.

red·coat \ˈred-ˌkōt\ *n.* A British soldier.

red cross. 1 A red-colored cross on a white background, used as a badge for hospitals and for neutrals helping the sick and wounded in war areas. **2** [with a capital] A service, usually a national society, for relieving sufferings in war or disaster.

red deer. The common stag of Europe.

red·den \ˈred-n\ *v.;* **red·dened; red·den·ing** \-n(-)ing\. **1** To make red or reddish. **2** To become red or reddish; to blush or flush.

red·dish \ˈred-ish\ *adj.* Somewhat red.

re·dec·o·rate \(ˈ)rē-ˈdek-r-ˌāt\ *v.;* **re·dec·o·rat·ed; re·dec·o·rat·ing. 1** To restore to its previous state of decoration; to renew the decorations of. **2** To give different decorations to; to change the decorations. — **re·dec·o·ra·tion** \(ˌ)rē-ˌdek-r-ˈāsh-n\ *n.*

re·deem \rē-ˈdēm\ *v.* **1** To buy back or off; especially, to gain or regain possession of by payment of money due, as on a mortgage or note. **2** To liberate or rescue, as from bondage, by paying ransom. **3** To make amends for; to offset; to atone for; as, to *redeem* a mistake. **4** To make good; to fulfill; as, to *redeem* a promise. **5** To rescue and deliver from sin and its penalties. — **redeem oneself.** To make amends for a fault or shortcoming; to make good after a poor start. — **re·deem·a·ble** \-ˈdē-məb-l\ *adj.*

re·deem·er \rē-ˈdēm-r\ *n.* A person who redeems; especially [with a capital], Jesus Christ.

re·demp·tion \rē-ˈdem(p)sh-n\ *n.* **1** The action of redeeming; a ransom; a rescue; a deliverance. **2** Something that redeems. **3** Salvation. — **re·demp·tive** \-ˈdem(p)-tiv\ *adj.* — **re·demp·to·ry** \-ˈdem(p)t-r-ē\ *adj.*

red-hand·ed \ˈred-ˈhan-dəd\ *adj.* Having hands red with blood; in the very act of crime.

red·head \ˈred-ˌhed\ *n.* **1** A person with red hair. **2** A diving wild duck related to the canvasback but with brighter plumage.

red·head·ed \ˈred-ˈhed-əd\ *adj.* **1** Having red or reddish hair. **2** Having a red or reddish head.

red-hot \ˈred-ˈhät\ *adj.* **1** Red from intense heat. **2** Excited; fiery; as, a *red-hot* debate. **3** Very fresh; new; as, *red-hot* news.

re·dis·cov·er \ˌrē-dis-ˈkəv-r\ *v.;* **re·dis·cov·ered; re·dis·cov·er·ing** \-r(-)ing\. To discover again or anew.

red-let·ter \ˈred-ˌlet-r\ *adj.* Memorable, especially in a happy or joyful way; as, a *red-letter* day.

red man. A North American Indian.

red·o·lent \ˈred-l-ənt\ *adj.* **1** Having a sweet odor; fragrant; as, a *redolent* breeze. **2** Suggestive in odor or atmosphere; as, perfume *redolent* of spring. **3** Filled; imbued; as, in a voice *redolent* with contempt. — **red·o·lence** \-ən(t)s\ *n.*

re·dou·ble \(ˈ)rē-ˈdəb-l\ *v.;* **re·dou·bled; re·dou·bling** \-l(-)ing\. **1** To double or to become doubled, as in size, amount, or degree; as, to *redouble* one's efforts. **2** To double back. The fox *redoubled* on his tracks.

re·doubt \rē-ˈdau̇t\ *n.* A small, often temporary, fortification, as for defending a hilltop.

re·doubt·a·ble \rē-ˈdau̇t-əb-l\ *adj.* Arousing fear or dread; as, a *redoubtable* warrior.

re·dound \rē-'daůnd\ *v.* To be reflected back, especially so as to bring credit or discredit to a person or thing; to have a result or effect; as, actions that *redound* to a man's credit.

red pepper. Cayenne pepper.

red·poll \'red-ˌpōl\ *n.* Any of several finches with streaky plumage, the males having a red crown.

re·dress \rē-'dres\ *v.* **1** To set right, as a wrong; to make amends for; to remedy; to relieve. **2** To correct or amend, as a fault. — \rē-'dres, 'rē-ˌdres\ *n.* A redressing or something done to redress or correct; as, to seek *redress* in the courts.

red·skin \'red-ˌskin\ *n.* A North American Indian.

red·start \'red-ˌstärt, -ˌstȧrt\ *n.* **1** A red-tailed European thrush. **2** An American fly-catching warbler.

red tape. **1** Tape used in public offices for tying up documents. **2** Official routine; unnecessary official delay. — **red-tape,** *adj.*

re·duce \rē-'düs, -'dyüs\ *v.;* **re·duced; re·duc·ing. 1** To diminish or lessen, especially in bulk, amount, or extent; as, to *reduce* expenses; to *reduce* weight. **2** To bring down; to lower, as to an inferior grade, rank, or value, or to a disagreeable condition; as, to *reduce* a soldier in rank; to be *reduced* to tears. **3** To bring to terms; to conquer; as, to *reduce* a fort. **4** To bring into a certain order, arrangement, classification, or form; as, to *reduce* grammar to rules. **5** To bring to a certain condition, as by grinding or pounding; as, to *reduce* chalk to powder. **6** In arithmetic, to change the denominations of a quantity or the form of an expression without changing the value; as, to *reduce* a fraction to its lowest terms; to *reduce* hours to minutes. **7** In surgery, to correct, as a fracture, by bringing displaced or broken parts back into their normal positions. — **re·duc·er** \-'düs-r, -'dyüs-r\ *n.* — **re·duc·i·ble** \-'dü-səb-l, -'dyü-\ *adj.*

re·duc·tion \rē-'dəksh-n\ *n.* **1** A reducing or the condition of being reduced. **2** The amount by which something is reduced in price. **3** Something made by reducing, as a copy of a picture.

reduction division. Cell division in which meiosis occurs.

re·dun·dance \rē-'dən-dən(t)s\ *n.* Redundancy.

re·dun·dan·cy \rē-'dən-dən-sē\ *n.; pl.* **re·dun·dan·cies. 1** The quality or condition of being redundant. **2** Something that is redundant or in excess. **3** The use of surplus words.

re·dun·dant \rē-'dən-dənt\ *adj.* **1** More than what is natural, usual, or necessary; superfluous. **2** Using more words than are necessary; especially, repetitious. — **re·dun·dant·ly,** *adv.*

re·du·pli·ca·tion \(ˌ)rē-ˌdüp-lə-'kāsh-n, -ˌdyüp-\ *n.* **1** The action of reduplicating or state of being reduplicated. **2** A result of reduplicating. — **re·du·pli·ca·tive** \rē-'düp-lə-ˌkāt-iv, -'dyüp-\ *adj.*

red·wing \'red-ˌwing\ *n.* **1** A red-winged European thrush. **2** The red-winged blackbird.

red·wood \'red-ˌwůd\ *n.* **1** Any tree yielding a red dye or having wood of a red or reddish color. **2** A timber tree of California having foliage resembling that of the hemlock and bearing numerous small oblong cones. **3** The brownish red wood of this tree.

re-echo \(')rē-'ek-ˌō\ *v.* To echo back; to reverberate. Thunder *re-echoed* through the valley. — *n.; pl.* **re-ech·oes.** The echo of an echo; a second echo.

reed \'rēd\ *n.* **1** Also **reed grass.** Any of various tall grasses resembling bamboo or their slender, often jointed, stems. **2** A musical instrument with a mouthpiece and finger holes, made of the hollow joint of a plant. **3** A thin elastic strip of cane, wood, or metal fastened to the mouthpiece or over an air opening in certain musical instruments, such as the clarinet or the accordion, and set in vibration by the breath or an air current.

reedy \'rēd-ē\ *adj.;* **reed·i·er; reed·i·est. 1** Having a great many reeds; covered with reeds. **2** Like a reed; especially, long and slender. **3** Having the quality of a reed instrument in tone.

reef \'rēf\ *n.* A ridge of rocks or sand at or near the surface of the water.

reef \'rēf\ *n.* **1** The part of a sail taken in or let out in regulating size. **2** The reduction in sail area made by reefing. — *v.* **1** To reduce a sail by rolling or folding a part of it. **2** To lower or bring inboard a spar, as a topmast or bowsprit.

reef·er \'rēf-r\ *n.* **1** One who reefs. **2** A close-fitting, usually double-breasted jacket of thick cloth.

reek \'rēk\ *n.* A warm, damp, ill-smelling vapor; a fume. — *v.* To give forth reek; to fume; to steam.

reel \'rēl\ *n.* **1** A lively Scottish dance. **2** Music for this dance. **3** The Virginia reel.

reel \'rēl\ *n.* **1** A device that can be revolved, on which something is wound, as yarn, thread, wire, or hose. **2** A small revolvable wheel for the butt end of a fishing rod, on which the line is wound. **3** A quantity of something, as thread, wire, or paper, wound on a reel; as, two *reels* of wire. **4** A spool on which a photographic film is wound. **5** A strip of motion-picture film wound on a spool. — *v.* **1** To wind upon a reel; as, to *reel* silk. **2** To draw by the use of a reel; as, to *reel* in a fish.

reel \'rēl\ *v.* **1** To whirl around; to be dizzy. **2** To give way; to fall back; to waver. **3** To stagger or sway dizzily. — *n.* A reeling motion.

re·en·try \(')rē-'en-trē\ *n.* A new or second entry; especially, a return to the earth's atmosphere after travel in space.

re·fec·to·ry \rē-'fekt-r(-)ē\ *n.; pl.* **re·fec·to·ries.** A dining hall, especially in a monastery or convent.

re·fer \rē-'fər\ *v.;* **re·ferred; re·fer·ring.** [From medieval English *referren,* there borrowed from Latin *referre* meaning literally "to carry back".] **1** To place in a certain class so far as cause, relationship, or source is concerned; as, to *refer* the defeat to poor training. **2** To send or direct to some person or place, as for treatment, help, or information; as, to *refer* a boy to a dictionary. **3** To go for information, advice, or aid; as, to *refer* to the telephone book for a number. **4** To have relation; to relate. The asterisk *refers* to a footnote. **5** To submit or hand over to someone else; as, to *refer* a problem to the teacher. **6** To direct attention; to speak of or mention. — For synonyms see *allude*. — **ref·er·a·ble** \'ref-r(-)əb-l, rē-'fər-əb-l\ *adj.*

ref·er·ee \ˌref-r-'ē\ *n.* **1** A person to whom a thing is referred for decision; an arbitrator; especially, an attorney appointed to act as an officer of the court in reporting on something referred to him in a lawsuit. **2** An umpire in certain games. — *v.;* **ref·er·eed**; **ref·er·ee·ing**. To act as referee.

ref·er·ence \'ref-rn(t)s, -r(-)ən(t)s\ *n.* **1** The action of referring or of being referred. **2** A relation; a connection; a respect; as, with *reference* to what was said. **3** A sign or direction referring a reader to another passage or book; as, a *reference* in the footnote. **4** A remark referring to something; an allusion. There are many *references* to our city in this book. **5** Consultation, especially for obtaining facts; as, a book to be used for *reference* — often used as an adjective; as, *reference* books. **6** A person of whom questions can be asked about the character or ability of another person. **7** A written statement about someone's character or ability.

ref·er·en·dum \ˌref-r-'end-m\ *n.; pl.* **ref·er·en·dums** \-'end-mz\ or **ref·er·en·da** \-'en-də\. **1** The practice of referring laws or proposed laws directly to the people for approval or rejection by vote. **2** The right of the people to pass upon laws. **3** The vote by which the people pass upon laws.

re·fill \'rē-ˌfil\ *n.* Something intended to fill again; as, a *refill* for a loose-leaf notebook; a *refill* of a prescription. — \(')rē-'fil\ *v.* To fill again. — **re·fill·a·ble** \(')rē-'fil-əb-l\ *adj.*

re·fine \rē-'fīn\ *v.;* **re·fined**; **re·fin·ing**. **1** To free from worthless matter; to make pure; as, to *refine* gold. **2** To become free from impurities, coarseness, or vulgarity. **3** To improve or perfect; to make better; as, to *refine* upon another's invention; to *refine* one's manners. — **re·fin·er** \-'fīn-r\ *n.* — **re·fine·ment** \-'fīn-mənt\ *n.*

re·fined \rē-'fīnd\ *adj.* **1** Freed from impurities; pure; as, *refined* gold; *refined* sugar. **2** Well-bred; cultured; as, *refined* manners. **3** Subtle; carried to a fine point; as, *refined* cruelty.

re·fin·ery \rē-'fīn-r(-)ē\ *n.; pl.* **re·fin·er·ies**. A building and equipment for refining, as oil or sugar.

re·fit \(')rē-'fit\ *v.;* **re·fit·ted**; **re·fit·ting**. To get ready for use again; to fit out or equip again; as, to *refit* a ship for service.

re·flect \rē-'flekt\ *v.* **1** To bend or throw back waves of light, sound, or heat. A polished surface *reflects* light. **2** To give back an image or likeness of, as a mirror does. **3** To bring as a result. The boy's scholarship *reflects* credit on his school. **4** To cast reproach or blame. Our bad conduct *reflects* upon our training. **5** To think seriously and carefully; to meditate. — **re·flec·tion** \rē-'fleksh-n\ *n.*

re·flec·tive \rē-'flek-tiv\ *adj.* **1** That reflects; especially, given or disposed to reflect or ponder over problems. **2** Of, relating to, or caused by reflection; reflected. — **re·flec·tive·ly**, *adv.*

re·flec·tor \rē-'flekt-r\ *n.* One that reflects; especially, a polished surface, often curved, for reflecting light or heat.

re·flex \'rē-ˌfleks\ *adj.* **1** Bent or turned back; reversed in direction. **2** Of light, reflected. **3** In physiology, produced by reflex action. — *n.* **1** A mirrored image; a likeness; a copy. **2** In physiology, an involuntary response made by a process (**reflex action**) by which a nervous impulse travels over a path (**reflex arc**) running inward from a receptor, as a sense organ, through a nerve center, and then outward to an effector, as a muscle.

re·flex·ive \rē-'fleks-iv\ *adj.* **1** Reflex. **2** Expressing the idea that the performer of an action is also the one upon whom the action is performed, as the pronoun "myself" in "I have cut myself". — *n.* A reflexive pronoun or verb.

re·for·est \(')rē-'fȯr-əst, -'fär-\ *v.* To renew forest growth by planting seeds or young trees. — **re·for·est·a·tion** \(ˌ)rē-ˌfȯr-əs-'tāsh-n, -ˌfär-\ *n.*

re·form \rē-'fȯrm\ *v.* **1** To make better or improve by removal of faults; as, to *reform* a prisoner. **2** To correct or improve one's own character or habits. — *n.* Improvement in what is bad or corrupt; an instance of such improvement. — **re·form·a·ble** \-'fȯr-məb-l\ *adj.*

re-form \'rē-'fȯrm\ *v.* To form again or anew.

ref·or·ma·tion \ˌref-r-'māsh-n\ *n.* **1** The act of reforming or the condition of being reformed; improvement. **2** [usually with a capital] The movement for certain changes in the Roman Catholic Church that began in Europe in the late 16th century and resulted in the formation of the various Protestant churches.

re·form·a·to·ry \rē-'fȯr-mə-ˌtōr-ē, -ˌtȯr-ē\ *adj.* Aiming at reformation; intended to reform. — *n.; pl.* **re·form·a·to·ries**. A penal institution, especially one for reforming young offenders or women.

re·form·er \rē-'fȯrm-r\ *n.* One who seeks to bring about reform, as in religious or political practices.

re·fract \rē-'frakt\ *v.* To subject to refraction.

re·frac·tion \rē-'fraksh-n\ *n.* The bending of a ray, as of light when it passes slantingly from one medium into another in which its speed is different, as when light passes from air into water. — **re·frac·tive** \-'frak-tiv\ *adj.*

re·frac·to·ry \rē-'frakt-r-ē\ *adj.* **1** Obstinate; stubborn; unmanageable. **2** Resisting ordinary treatment; hard to work or change; as, *refractory* ore. — **re·frac·to·ri·ly** \-r-ə-lē\ *adv.*

re·frain \rē-'frān\ *v.* To hold oneself back from doing or saying something.

re·frain \rē-'frān\ *n.* A phrase or verse repeated regularly in a poem or song.

re·fresh \rē-'fresh\ *v.* **1** To make or become fresh or fresher. Sleep *refreshes* the body. **2** To revive; to renew; as, to *refresh* one's memory of a book. **3** To give or supply refreshment. **4** To take refreshment. — **re·fresh·er**, *n.* — **re·fresh·ing·ly**, *adv.*

re·fresh·ment \rē-'fresh-mənt\ *n.* **1** The act of refreshing or the state of being refreshed. **2** That which refreshes; especially, food or drink; [in the plural] a light meal; as, *refreshments* at a party.

re·frig·er·ant \rē-'frij-r-ənt\ *n.* A substance, as ice, ammonia, or carbon dioxide, used in refrigeration.

re·frig·er·ate \rē-'frij-r-ˌāt\ *v.;* **re·frig·er·at·ed; re·frig·er·at·ing.** To make or keep cold or cool; to freeze or chill for preservation, as food.

re·frig·er·a·tion \rē-ˌfrij-r-'āsh-n\ *n.* The act or process of refrigerating, especially by means of mechanical, electrical, or gas devices.

re·frig·er·a·tor \rē-'frij-r-ˌāt-r\ *n.* A box or room for keeping food or other articles cool; especially, one equipped with an engine designed to lower temperatures quickly.

reft. A past tense and past part. of *reave.*

ref·uge \'ref-ˌyüj\ *n.* **1** Shelter or protection, as from danger, distress, or annoyance; as, to take *refuge* with a friend. **2** A shelter; a place of protection; as, a *refuge* from a storm.

ref·u·gee \'ref-yə-ˌjē, ˌref-yə-'jē\ *n.* A person who flees for safety, especially to a foreign country.

re·ful·gence \rē-'fəlj-n(t)s\ or **re·ful·gen·cy** \-n-sē\ *n.* Brightness; splendor; radiance. — **re·ful·gent** \-'fəlj-nt\ *adj.* — **re·ful·gent·ly,** *adv.*

re·fund \rē-'fənd, 'rē-ˌfənd\ *v.* To give back; to repay; as, to *refund* the cost. — \'rē-ˌfənd\ *n.* **1** A refunding; a repayment. **2** The amount refunded.

re·fur·bish \(')rē-'fər-bish\ *v.* To brighten; to freshen; to make as if new.

re·fus·al \rē-'fyüz-l\ *n.* **1** The act of refusing; a rejection, as of an offer. **2** A right either to refuse or to take something before it is offered to others; an option; as, to have the *refusal* of a house.

re·fuse \rē-'fyüz\ *v.;* **re·fused; re·fus·ing.** **1** To declare oneself not willing to take; as, to *refuse* a job. **2** To declare oneself not willing to do or give; as, to *refuse* to help. — For synonyms see *decline.*

ref·use \'ref-ˌyüs, -ˌyüz\ *n.* Worthless material; material to be thrown away; rubbish; waste.

re·fute \rē-'fyüt\ *v.;* **re·fut·ed; re·fut·ing.** To prove something wrong by argument or evidence; to prove to be false; as, to *refute* the testimony of a witness. — **re·fut·a·ble** \rē-'fyüt-əb-l, 'ref-yət-əb-l\ *adj.* — **ref·u·ta·tion** \ˌref-yə-'tāsh-n\ *n.*

re·gain \(')rē-'gān\ *v.* **1** To gain or get again; to get back; as, to *regain* one's health. **2** To get back to; to reach again; as, to *regain* the shore.

re·gal \'rēg-l\ *adj.* Of or relating to a king; suitable to or resembling a king; royal; stately; splendid. — **re·gal·ly** \'rēg-l-ē\ *adv.*

re·gale \rē-'gāl\ *v.;* **re·galed; re·gal·ing.** To feast or entertain; as, to *regale* oneself with delicious food; to *regale* an audience with stories.

re·ga·lia \rē-'gāl-yə\ *n. pl.* **1** The emblems and symbols of royalty, as the crown and scepter. **2** The insignia of any office or order. **3** Finery; special dress; as, Sunday *regalia.*

re·gard \rē-'gärd, -'gȧrd\ *v.* **1** To look at, especially attentively; to gaze upon; as, to *regard* someone with curiosity. **2** To observe closely; to pay attention to; to obey; to heed; as, to *regard* advice; to *regard* the law. **3** To think well of; to care for; as, to *regard* someone highly. **4** To consider; as, one who is *regarded* as a fine teacher. — **as regards.** Regarding; as, complete agreement *as regards* methods. — *n.* **1** A look; a glance; a gaze. **2** Consideration; heed; care; concern; as, a decent *regard* for the rights of others. **3** Respect; esteem; as, to hold a man in high *regard.* **4** [in the plural] An expression of such respect, or affection; as, to send one's *regards.* — **in regard to** or **with regard to.** With respect or relation to.

re·gard·ful \rē-'gärd-fəl, -'gȧrd-\ *adj.* **1** Observant; attentive. **2** Respectful.

re·gard·ing \rē-'gärd-ing, -'gȧrd-\ *prep.* Concerning; respecting.

re·gard·less \rē-'gärd-ləs, -'gȧrd-\ *adj.* Having or taking no regard or heed; heedless; careless; as, to plunge ahead *regardless* of consequences. — **re·gard·less·ly,** *adv.*

re·gat·ta \rē-'gät-ə, -'gat-, -'gȧt-\ *n.* A rowing or sailing race, or a series of such races.

re·gen·cy \'rēj-n-sē\ *n.; pl.* **re·gen·cies.** **1** The office or powers of a regent. **2** A body of regents. **3** The period during which a regent governs.

re·gen·er·ate \rē-'jen-r-ət\ *adj.* Regenerated, especially spiritually. — \-ˌāt\ *v.;* **re·gen·er·at·ed; re·gen·er·at·ing.** **1** To cause to be reborn spiritually. **2** To reform completely in character and habits; as, the difficulty of *regenerating* criminals. **3** To grow anew, as a body part, by formation of new tissue. **4** To give new life to; to revive; as, land *regenerated* by rotation of crops. **5** To increase the amplification of radio signals by electron tubes in which a part of the outgoing current acts upon the incoming signal so as to increase the amplification. — **re·gen·er·a·tion** \(ˌ)rē-ˌjen-r-'āsh-n\ *n.* — **re·gen·er·a·tive** \rē-'jen-r-ˌāt-iv, -r(-)ət-iv\ *adj.* — **re·gen·er·a·tor** \rē-'jen-r-ˌāt-r\ *n.*

re·gent \'rēj-nt\ *adj.* Acting as a regent. — *n.* **1** A person who rules a kingdom during the childhood, absence, or disability of the sovereign. **2** A member of a governing body, as in certain universities.

reg·i·cide \'rej-ə-ˌsīd\ *n.* **1** One who kills a king, especially his own king. **2** The murder of a king.

re·gime or **ré·gime** \rā-'zhēm, rə-\ *n.* **1** A method of rule or management; as, the school *regime.* **2** A system of living. **3** The existing political or social system.

reg·i·men \'rej-m-ən, -ˌen\ *n.* **1** A way of governing; an administration. **2** Any systematic course or treatment intended to benefit by continued operation, as a diet to reduce a person's weight.

reg·i·ment \'rej-m-ənt\ *n.* A body of soldiers, often consisting of three battalions and commanded by a colonel. — \-ˌent\ *v.* **1** To organize into groups or units, especially for central control. **2** To subject to strict orders; to make uniform; as, a government that *regiments* its subjects. — **reg·i·men·tal** \ˌrej-m-'ent-l\ *adj.* — **reg·i·men·ta·tion** \ˌrej-m-ən-'tāsh-n, -ˌen-\ *n.*

reg·i·men·tals \ˌrej-m-'ent-lz\ *n. pl.* A regimental uniform; military dress.

re·gion \'rēj-n\ *n.* **1** A large tract of land; a country; a district. **2** A space; an indefinite area. **3** A part or area of the body; as, in the *region* of the lungs. — **re·gion·al** \-n(-)əl\ *adj.* — **re·gion·al·ly** \-n(-)ə-lē\ *adv.*

reg·is·ter \'rej-əst-r\ *n.* **1** A written record or list containing regular entries of items or details; a book for such a record; as, a public *register* of births, marriages, and deaths; a school *register.* **2** A device, as in a floor or wall, for regulating the flow of heated air from a furnace. **3** Something which registers or records; as, a cash *register.* **4** The range of a voice or instrument. — *v.;* **reg·is·tered; reg·is·ter·ing** \-r(-)ing\. **1** To enroll; to enter one's name in a list; as, to *register* at a hotel; to *register* for an English class. **2** To enter officially in a register; as, to *register* a will. **3** To record automatically; to indicate. The thermometer *registered* 10 degrees below zero. **4** To secure special care and protection for something mailed by having it recorded and paying extra postage. **5** To show an emotion by facial expression or by actions.

cash register

reg·is·trar \'rej-əs-ˌträr, -ˌtrȧr\ *n.* **1** One who keeps a register. **2** An official at a school charged with registering students and maintaining records.

reg·is·tra·tion \ˌrej-əs-'trāsh-n\ *n.* **1** The act of registering or enrolling. **2** An entry in a register. **3** The number of persons registered; enrollment.

reg·is·try \'rej-əs-trē\ *n.; pl.* **reg·is·tries. 1** A registering; an enrollment. **2** The condition or fact of being entered on an official record book. **3** A place where a register is kept. **4** A register or official record book or an entry in such a book.

re·gress \rē-'gres\ *v.* To recede; to go backward. — **re·gres·sion** \-'gresh-n\ *n.*

re·gret \rē-'gret\ *v.;* **re·gret·ted; re·gret·ting. 1** To remember with sorrow or grief; to mourn the loss or death of. **2** To be or feel sorry for. — *n.* **1** Pain or sorrow on account of something past, with a wish that it had been different. **2** An expression of sorrow or disappointment; especially [in the plural] a note politely declining an invitation.

re·gret·ful \rē-'gret-fəl\ *adj.* Feeling or showing regret; sorry. — **re·gret·ful·ly** \-fə-lē\ *adv.*

re·gret·ta·ble \rē-'gret-əb-l\ *adj.* Deserving or demanding regret. — **re·gret·ta·bly** \-ə-blē\ *adv.*

reg·u·lar \'reg-yəl-r\ *adj.* **1** Belonging to a religious order; living in a religious community; under a religious rule; as, a *regular* priest. **2** Formed, built, or arranged according to some rule, law, principle, or type; even in form or structure; as, a *regular* design; *regular* features. **3** Steady or even in speed, practice, or occurrence; orderly; as, a *regular* pulse; *regular* habits. **4** Made, selected, or conducted according to rules or customs; as, a *regular* meeting. **5** Properly fitted or qualified; as, a *regular* member. **6** Thorough; complete; as, a *regular* scoundrel. **7** In grammar, conforming to the usual manner of making inflectional forms; as, a *regular* verb. **8** Belonging to or relating to the permanent standing army (**regular army**). — *n.* A member of the regular army.

reg·u·lar·i·ty \ˌreg-yə-'lar-ət-ē\ *n.; pl.* **reg·u·lar·i·ties.** The condition or quality of being regular.

reg·u·lar·ly \'reg-yəl-r-lē\ *adv.* **1** In a regular, orderly, methodical way. **2** At regular intervals; as, he sees his dentist *regularly.*

reg·u·late \'reg-yə-ˌlāt\ *v.;* **reg·u·lat·ed; reg·u·lat·ing. 1** To govern or direct according to rule; to bring under the control of authority; as, to *regulate* prices. **2** To put in good order; to make regular; as, to *regulate* one's habits. **3** To adjust so as to work accurately or regularly; as, to *regulate* a clock. — **reg·u·la·tor** \-ˌlāt-r\ *n.*

reg·u·la·tion \ˌreg-yə-'lāsh-n\ *n.* **1** The act of regulating or the state of being regulated. **2** A rule or restriction; regulating principle or law. — *adj.* Prescribed by regulations.

re·gur·gi·tate \(')rē-'gər-jə-ˌtāt\ *v.;* **re·gur·gi·tat·ed; re·gur·gi·tat·ing.** To throw or be thrown back or out again, as incompletely digested food. — **re·gur·gi·ta·tion** \(ˌ)rē-ˌgər-jə-'tāsh-n\ *n.*

re·ha·bil·i·tate \ˌrē-(h)ə-'bil-ə-ˌtāt\ *v.;* **re·ha·bil·i·tat·ed; re·ha·bil·i·tat·ing. 1** To restore to a former right, rank, or status. **2** To repair or renovate; as, to *rehabilitate* slum areas. **3** To equip to lead useful lives, as criminals or handicapped persons. — **re·ha·bil·i·ta·tion** \-ˌbil-ə-'tāsh-n\ *n.*

re·hash \(')rē-'hash\ *v.* To use again in a new form; to restate, as an argument. — *n.* A rehashing. His second book is a *rehash* of his first.

re·hears·al \rē-'hərs-l\ *n.* A rehearsing; especially, a preparatory performance prior to public appearance.

re·hearse \rē-'hərs\ *v.;* **re·hearsed; re·hears·ing. 1** To repeat or tell over; as, to *rehearse* the day's events. **2** To practice in private in preparation for a public performance. **3** To train or instruct by rehearsal, as a cast.

reign \'rān\ *n.* **1** The authority or rule of a king, emperor, or other sovereign. **2** The time during which a sovereign rules. — *v.* **1** To preside as a sovereign. **2** To hold sway; to prevail; as, in times when ignorance *reigned.*

re·im·burse \ˌrē-əm-'bərs\ *v.;* **re·im·bursed; re·im·burs·ing.** To pay back; to make restitution. — **re·im·burse·ment** \-mənt\ *n.*

rein \'rān\ *n.* **1** The strap of a bridle, fastened to the bit, to govern a horse or other animal. **2** [usually in the plural] Controlling or guiding power; as, the *reins* of government. — *v.* To check, stop, or direct by or as if by reins; to control; to restrain. — **give rein to.** To give freedom to; as, to *give rein to* the imagination.

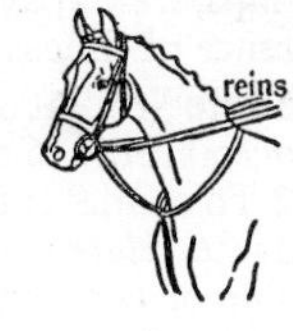

re·in·car·nate \ˌrē-ən-'kär-ˌnāt, -'kȧr-\ *v.;* **re·in·car·nat·ed; re·in·car·nat·ing.** To give a new body or form to.

re·in·car·na·tion \(ˌ)rē-ˌin-ˌkär-'nāsh-n, -ˌkȧr-\ *n.*

1 The belief that the souls of the dead return to earth again and again and assume new forms or bodies. 2 A rebirth of a soul in a new body or form.

rein·deer \'rān-ˌdir\ *n. sing. and pl.* A large-hoofed deer with antlers in both sexes, found in northern regions and used as a draft animal.

re·in·force \ˌrē-ən-'fōrs, -'fȯrs\ *v.;* **re·in·forced; re·in·forc·ing.** 1 To strengthen with new force, assistance, material, or support; as, to *reinforce* a wall. 2 To strengthen with additional troops or ships.

re·in·force·ment \ˌrē-ən-'fōrs-mənt, -'fȯrs-\ *n.* 1 The act of reinforcing; the condition of being reinforced. 2 Something that reinforces; especially [in the plural] additional troops or ships.

re·in·state \ˌrē-ən-'stāt\ *v.;* **re·in·stat·ed; re·in·stat·ing.** To place again in possession or in a former position; as, to *reinstate* an official. — **re·in·state·ment** \-mənt\ *n.*

re·it·er·ate \(')rē-'it-r-ˌāt\ *v.;* **re·it·er·at·ed; re·it·er·at·ing.** To repeat; to say or do over again or repeatedly. — **re·it·er·a·tion** \(ˌ)rē-ˌit-r-'āsh-n\ *n.*

re·ject \rē-'jekt\ *v.* 1 To refuse to acknowledge, believe, or receive. 2 To throw away as useless or unsatisfactory; to discard. 3 To refuse to grant or consider. — For synonyms see *decline.* — \'rē-ˌjekt\ *n.* A person or thing rejected, especially as unsatisfactory; as, factory *rejects;* army *rejects.*

re·jec·tion \rē-'jeksh-n\ *n.* 1 The act of rejecting or the state of being rejected. 2 Something that is rejected; a reject.

re·joice \rē-'jȯis\ *v.;* **re·joiced; re·joic·ing.** 1 To give joy to; to gladden; as, news that *rejoices* the heart. 2 To feel joy or great delight; as, to *rejoice* over a friend's good fortune.

re·joic·ing \rē-'jȯi-sing\ *n.* Joy; delight.

re·join, *v.* 1 \(')rē-'jȯin\ To join again; to return to; as, to *rejoin* one's family after a week in camp. 2 \rē-\ To say as an answer; to reply; to retort.

re·join·der \rē-'jȯind-r\ *n.* An answer; a retort.

re·ju·ve·nate \rē-'jüv-n-ˌāt\ *v.;* **re·ju·ve·nat·ed; re·ju·ve·nat·ing.** To make young or youthful again; to give new vigor to. — **re·ju·ve·na·tion** \-ˌjüv-n-'āsh-n\ *n.*

re·lapse \rē-'laps\ *v.;* **re·lapsed; re·laps·ing.** 1 To slip or fall back into a former condition after a change for the better; especially, to become ill again after a period of improvement. 2 To sink; to lapse; as, to *relapse* into unconsciousness. — \rē-'laps, 'rē-ˌlaps\ *n.* A relapsing; especially, a recurrence of illness after a period of improvement.

re·late \rē-'lāt\ *v.;* **re·lat·ed; re·lat·ing.** 1 To give an account of; to narrate; to tell; as, to *relate* a story. 2 To connect; to establish a relationship between; as, to *relate* cause and effect. 3 To have relationship or connection; to refer; to belong.

re·lat·ed \rē-'lāt-əd\ *adj.* 1 Connected in some understood way; as, pneumonia and *related* diseases; bees and the closely *related* wasps. 2 Connected by reason of belonging to the same family; as, to be *related* to the mayor; *related* by marriage.

re·la·tion \rē-'lāsh-n\ *n.* 1 The act of relating or telling. 2 An account; a recital. 3 A related person; a relative. 4 Connection by blood or marriage; relationship; kinship. 5 The state of being related or connected; connection; as, the *relation* of master to servant. 6 Reference; respect; as, in *relation* to this matter. 7 The state of being mutually interested or concerned, as in a social or business way; as, to have a friendly *relation* with one's neighbors. 8 [in the plural] Dealings; affairs; as, a country's foreign *relations.*

re·la·tion·ship \rē-'lāsh-n-ˌship\ *n.* 1 The state of being related in any way; connection. 2 Connection by blood or marriage; kinship.

rel·a·tive \'rel-ət-iv\ *adj.* 1 Referring; belonging; as, arguments *relative* to the subject. 2 Comparative; not absolute or independent; as, the *relative* value of two objects. 3 Dependent for meaning on relationship to something else. "Far" and "near" are *relative* terms. 4 Referring to an antecedent; introducing a subordinate clause (**relative clause**) qualifying an expressed or understood antecedent; as, the *relative* pronoun "which" in "the cat which killed the rat". 5 Having the same key signature — used of major and minor keys and scales. — *n.* 1 A person connected with another by blood or marriage; a relation. 2 A relative pronoun.

rel·a·tive·ly \'rel-ət-əv-lē\ *adv.* In relation or respect to something else; comparatively.

rel·a·tiv·i·ty \ˌrel-ə-'tiv-ət-ē\ *n.* 1 The state of being relative. 2 A mathematically developed theory based upon the proposition that when two bodies are moving with a uniform velocity in a straight line, it is impossible for an observer on one to learn anything about the motion of the other except that there is relative motion.

re·la·tor \rē-'lāt-r\ *n.* One that relates; a narrator.

re·lax \rē-'laks\ *v.* 1 To make or become less firm, rigid, or tense; to slacken; as, to *relax* one's attention. 2 To make less severe or strict; as, to *relax* discipline. 3 To seek recreation and rest; as, a fine way to *relax* after a hard day's work. — **re·lax·a·tion** \(ˌ)rē-ˌlak-'sāsh-n\ *n.*

re·lay \'rē-ˌlā\ *n.* 1 A fresh supply, as of horses or men, arranged to relieve others at various stages, as in a journey or a race. 2 An electromagnetic device by which the opening or closing of one circuit operates another device, as a switch in another circuit. — \'rē-ˌlā, rē-'lā\ *v.;* **re·layed; re·lay·ing.** 1 To pass on by or as if by relays; as, to *relay* the news of the disaster. 2 To control or operate by an electrical relay.

relay race. A race between teams of runners each of whom runs only a portion of the whole distance.

re·lease \rē-'lēs\ *v.;* **re·leased; re·leas·ing.** 1 To let loose; as, to *release* a spring. 2 To set free; as, to *release* a bird from a cage. 3 To relieve, as from pain, trouble, or obligation. 4 To permit, at a certain date, the publication, sale, exhibition, or public performance of something; as, to *release* a news story; to *release* a moving picture. — *n.* 1 A deliverance or relief, as from care, pain, or trouble.

2 A discharge from an obligation, as a debt; a giving up of a right or claim. 3 The act of freeing; the condition of being liberated or freed; as, a *release* from prison. 4 The document granting such a liberation. 5 Any legal statement by which a legal right is given up. 6 A device for letting loose or freeing something fixed or held; as, the shutter *release* on a camera. 7 A releasing, as of news or a statement for publication or circulation.

rel·e·gate \'rel-ə-ˌgāt\ *v.;* **rel·e·gat·ed; rel·e·gat·ing.** 1 To exile; to banish. 2 To remove or dismiss a person or thing to a less important or prominent place; as, to *relegate* some old books to the attic. 3 To hand over to someone else to do; to delegate. — **rel·e·ga·tion** \ˌrel-ə-'gāsh-n\ *n.*

re·lent \rē-'lent\ *v.* To become less stern, hard, or cruel; to soften in temper.

re·lent·less \rē-'lent-ləs\ *adj.* Without mercy or pity; harsh. — **re·lent·less·ly,** *adv.*

rel·e·vance \'rel-ə-vən(t)s\ *n.* Relevancy.

rel·e·van·cy \'rel-ə-vən-sē\ *n.; pl.* **rel·e·van·cies.** The state of being relevant.

rel·e·vant \'rel-ə-vənt\ *adj.* Having something to do with the case being considered; pertinent; as, a *relevant* question. — **rel·e·vant·ly,** *adv.*

re·li·a·ble \rē-'lī-əb-l\ *adj.* Fit to be trusted or relied upon; dependable. — **re·li·a·bil·i·ty** \-ˌlī-ə-'bil-ət-ē\ *n.* — **re·li·a·bly** \-'lī-ə-blē\ *adv.*

re·li·ance \rē-'lī-ən(t)s\ *n.* 1 A relying or depending on a person or thing; confidence; trust; as, *reliance* on a friend. 2 A person or thing relied upon; a mainstay. — **re·li·ant** \-ənt\ *adj.*

rel·ic \'rel-ik\ *n.* 1 An object regarded with reverence or respect because it is associated with Christ or a saint. 2 [in the plural] Ruins. 3 A survival; a remaining trace; as, Indian *relics.*

rel·ict \'rel-ikt\ *n.* A widow.

relied. Past tense and past part. of *rely.*

re·lief \rē-'lēf\ *n.* 1 The act of relieving or the condition of being relieved; removal of a burden, pain, or discomfort. 2 Aid; assistance; help in time of difficulty or danger; as, *relief* sent to a flooded city. 3 Release from duty; especially, the replacing of a sentinel by another one. 4 The person who takes someone else's place on duty. 5 A projection from the background, as of figures in sculpture or of mountains on a map; sharpness of outline. 6 A work of art with such raised figures. 7 In drawing and painting, the appearance of projection above the background, given by lines and shading.

relief map. A model, or a map drawn in perspective, in which its inequalities of surface are shown in relief.

re·lieve \rē-'lēv\ *v.;* **re·lieved; re·liev·ing.** 1 To free wholly or partly from any burden, pain, discomfort, or trouble; as, to *relieve* distress. 2 To aid, especially the poor and needy. 3 To release from a post or duty; as, to *relieve* a sentry. 4 To take away the sameness or monotony of; as, a black dress *relieved* by a white collar. 5 To put in relief, to give prominence to, or to set off by contrast, as in sculpture or painting.

re·li·gion \rē-'lij-n\ *n.* 1 The serving of God or a supreme reality with worshipful devotion. 2 A system of faith and worship; one of the churches or denominations. 3 Belief in the existence and power of God, a god, or gods.

re·li·gious \rē-'lij-əs\ *adj.* 1 Of or relating to religion or religions. 2 Devoted to the service of God, a god, or gods; pious; devout. 3 Faithful; dependable; as, to perform one's duties with *religious* regularity. — *n. sing. and pl.* A member of a religious order. — **re·li·gious·ly,** *adv.*

re·lin·quish \rē-'ling-kwish\ *v.* 1 To withdraw from; to abandon; to quit. 2 To renounce a claim to. — **re·lin·quish·ment** \-mənt\ *n.*

rel·i·quary \'rel-ə-ˌkwer-ē\ *n.; pl.* **rel·i·quar·ies.** A small box or shrine in which sacred relics are kept.

rel·ish \'rel-ish\ *n.* 1 A pleasing, appetizing taste. 2 A small bit added for flavor; a dash. 3 Personal liking; as, to have no *relish* for hard work. 4 Keen enjoyment of food or of anything; as, to eat with *relish.* 5 A highly seasoned sauce, as one made of pickles or mustard, eaten with other food to add flavor. — *v.* 1 To enjoy; to like very much; as, to *relish* a good joke. 2 To eat with relish; to like the taste of; as, to *relish* one's food.

re·live \(')rē-'liv\ *v.;* **re·lived; re·liv·ing.** To experience again, as in memory.

re·load \(')rē-'lōd\ *v.* To load again.

re·lo·cate \(')rē-'lō-ˌkāt, ˌrē-lō-'kāt\ *v.;* **re·lo·cat·ed; re·lo·cat·ing.** 1 To locate again. 2 To move to a new location; as, to *relocate* a factory. — **re·lo·ca·tion** \ˌrē-lō-'kāsh-n\ *n.*

re·luc·tance \rē-'lək-tən(t)s\ *n.* The state of being reluctant; unwillingness.

re·luc·tant \rē-'lək-tənt\ *adj.* 1 Unwilling; as, to be *reluctant* to answer. 2 Showing hesitation or unwillingness; as, *reluctant* obedience. — **re·luc·tant·ly,** *adv.*

re·ly \rē-'lī\ *v.;* **re·lied** \-'līd\; **re·ly·ing.** To place one's trust or confidence; to depend; as, to *rely* on a friend; to *rely* on one's own judgment.

re·main \rē-'mān\ *v.* 1 To be left after other things have been removed or destroyed. Little *remained* after the fire. 2 To be left as yet to be done or considered; as, a fact that *remains* to be proved. 3 To stay after others have gone. Few *remained* to listen. 4 To continue unchanged in place, form, or condition; as, to *remain* single. The weather *remained* the same.

re·main·der \rē-'mānd-r\ *n.* 1 The part that remains; the number remaining. Some went by bus, the *remainder* went by train. 2 That which is left after subtraction. 3 In division, the undivided part which is less than the divisor.

re·mains \rē-'mānz\ *n. pl.* 1 Something that remains; as, the *remains* of a meal. 2 A dead body; a corpse.

re·make \(')rē-'māk\ *v.;* **re·made** \-'mād\; **re·mak·ing** \-'māk-ing\. To make again or anew. — \'rē-

ˌmāk\ *n.* Something that has been made again; as, a movie that is a *remake* of one popular years ago.

re·mand \rē-ˈmand\ *v.* To send or send back, as a prisoner to jail to await trial, or a case from a higher to a lower court. — *n.* **1** The act of remanding or the state of being remanded. **2** A remanded prisoner.

re·mark \rē-ˈmärk, -ˈmȧrk\ *v.* **1** To take notice of; to observe. **2** To state; to say; as, to *remark* that it is time to leave. — *n.* **1** A passing comment or observation. The speaker's *remarks* on modern poetry were well received. **2** A casual comment or statement; as, a *remark* about the weather.

— The words *observation* and *comment* are synonyms of *remark: remark* usually refers to a rather casual expression of opinion or of some passing thought, generally not one intended as a final decision or judgment; *observation* may indicate a more carefully considered opinion of some matter, as after close examination of it; *comment* is likely to suggest a remark or an observation made to serve as an explanation, interpretation, or criticism.

re·mark·a·ble \rē-ˈmärk-ə-bəl, -ˈmȧrk-\ *adj.* Worthy of being remarked or noticed; unusual; extraordinary. — **re·mark·a·bly** \-ə-blē\ *adv.*

re·me·di·a·ble \rē-ˈmēd-ē-əb-l\ *adj.* Capable of being remedied. — **re·me·di·a·bly** \-ē-ə-blē\ *adv.*

re·me·di·al \rē-ˈmēd-ē-əl\ *adj.* Intended to remedy or improve; as, to take *remedial* measures; *remedial* reading courses. — **re·me·di·al·ly** \-ē-ə-lē\ *adv.*

rem·e·dy \ˈrem-əd-ē\ *n.; pl.* **rem·e·dies. 1** A medicine or any form of treatment that cures or relieves. **2** Something that corrects an evil, rights a wrong, or makes up for a loss. — *v.;* **rem·e·died** \-ēd\; **rem·e·dy·ing.** To provide or serve as a remedy for; to cure; to relieve; to correct.

re·mem·ber \rē-ˈmem-br\ *v.;* **re·mem·bered; re·mem·ber·ing** \-br(-)ing\. **1** To have something come to mind again; to recollect; as, to *remember* the event. **2** To keep in mind so as to give attention to; as, to *remember* friends at Christmas. **3** To keep from forgetting; as, to *remember* to do an errand. **4** To retain in one's memory. *Remember* this well! **5** To recall to the mind of another· as, to *remember* one person to another.

re·mem·brance \rē-ˈmem-br(-)ən(t)s\ *n.* **1** The act of remembering; something remembered; as, a vivid *remembrance.* **2** The state or fact of being remembered; as, to hold someone in fond *remembrance.* **3** A gift; a souvenir. **4** [in the plural] Greetings. — For synonyms see *memory.*

re·mind \rē-ˈmīnd\ *v.* To put a person in mind of something; to cause to remember; as, to *remind* a child that it is bedtime. — **re·mind·er** \-ˈmīnd-r\ *n.*

rem·i·nisce \ˌrem-ə-ˈnis\ *v.;* **rem·i·nisced; rem·i·nisc·ing.** To indulge in reminiscence.

rem·i·nis·cence \ˌrem-ə-ˈnis-n(t)s\ *n.* **1** The recalling or telling of a past experience; as, a *reminiscence* of early childhood. **2** [in the plural] An account of one's memorable experiences.

rem·i·nis·cent \ˌrem-ə-ˈnis-nt\ *adj.* **1** Of or relating to reminiscence; indulging in reminiscence. **2** That reminds one, as of something seen or known before; as, a city *reminiscent* of one's home.

re·miss \rē-ˈmis\ *adj.* Negligent; careless; showing neglect or lack of attention.

re·mis·sion \rē-ˈmish-n\ *n.* **1** The act of freeing from just punishment; as, the *remission* of sins. **2** The cancellation or giving up of something, as a claim. **3** A lessening in intensity, as of heat or cold.

re·mit \rē-ˈmit\ *v.;* **re·mit·ted; re·mit·ting. 1** To forgive; to pardon. **2** To slacken; to lessen, as in strictness or intensity. **3** To refrain from exacting or enforcing; as, to *remit* a penalty. **4** To send, especially money due on a bill or debt.

re·mit·tance \rē-ˈmit-n(t)s\ *n.* **1** The sending, as of money or bills, especially to a distance. **2** Money sent in payment of a bill or debt.

rem·nant \ˈrem-nənt\ *n.* **1** That which remains or is left over; as, a *remnant* of cloth. **2** A surviving trace; as, the *remnants* of a great civilization.

re·mod·el \(ˈ)rē-ˈmäd-l\ *v.;* **re·mod·eled** or **re·mod·elled; re·mod·el·ing** or **re·mod·el·ling** \-l(-)ing\. **1** To model again. **2** To rebuild in part, especially so as to introduce changes from a former style or plan; to make over; as, to *remodel* an old house.

re·mon·strance \rē-ˈmän(t)s-trən(t)s\ *n.* **1** The act of remonstrating. **2** A protest; an objection.

re·mon·strate \rē-ˈmän-ˌstrāt\ *v.;* **re·mon·strat·ed; re·mon·strat·ing.** To plead in opposition to something; to speak in reproof; to object; to protest; as, to *remonstrate* with a pupil for being disorderly.

re·morse \rē-ˈmȯrs\ *n.* Deep regret for one's sins or for acts that wrong others; distress aroused by a sense of guilt.

re·morse·ful \rē-ˈmȯrs-fəl\ *adj.* Feeling or expressing remorse. — **re·morse·ful·ly** \-fə-lē\ *adv.*

re·morse·less \rē-ˈmȯrs-ləs\ *adj.* Without remorse or pity; merciless. — **re·morse·less·ly,** *adv.*

re·mote \rē-ˈmōt\ *adj.;* **re·mot·er; re·mot·est. 1** Far off in place or time; not near or recent; as, *remote* countries; *remote* ages. **2** Out of the way; secluded; as, a *remote* valley. **3** Not closely connected or related; as, a *remote* kinsman. **4** Slight; not obvious or striking; as, *remote* likeness between two girls. **5** Apart; aloof; as, to keep oneself *remote* from one's fellows. **6** Operated or operating from a distance; as, *remote* control. — **re·mote·ly,** *adv.*

re·mount \(ˈ)rē-ˈmau̇nt\ *v.* To mount again. — \(ˈ)rē-ˈmau̇nt, ˈrē-ˌmau̇nt\ *n.* A fresh horse to take the place of one disabled or exhausted.

re·mov·a·ble \rē-ˈmü-vəb-l\ *adj.* Capable of being removed.

re·mov·al \rē-ˈmüv-l\ *n.* **1** The act of taking away or the fact of being taken away. **2** A change of residence. **3** Dismissal, as from an official position.

re·move \rē-ˈmüv\ *v.;* **re·moved; re·mov·ing. 1** To change the location of; to transfer. **2** To move by lifting or taking off; as, to *remove* one's hat; to *remove* a glove. **3** To dismiss; to discharge; as, to *remove* a dishonest official. **4** To get rid of; to take or put away; as, to *remove* a fire hazard. **5** To change one's location, especially one's place of residence. — *n.* **1** A transfer from one location to another; a move. **2** A step or degree in or as if in a scale. — **re·mov·er** \-ˈmüv-r\ *n.*

re·moved \rē-ˈmüvd\ *adj.* **1** Distant; far away; as, a town far *removed* from large cities. **2** Distant in relationship — used to show the relationship of cousins. The children of one's first cousin are one's first cousins once *removed.*

re·mu·ner·ate \rē-ˈmyün-r-ˌāt\ *v.;* **re·mu·ner·at·ed; re·mu·ner·at·ing.** To pay, as for services rendered or work done. — For synonyms see *pay.*

re·mu·ner·a·tion \rē-ˌmyün-r-ˈāsh-n\ *n.* Payment; compensation.

re·mu·ner·a·tive \rē-ˈmyün-r-ˌāt-iv, -r(-)ət-iv\ *adj.* Serving to remunerate; gainful; profitable.

ren·ais·sance \ˌren-ə-ˈsän(t)s, -ˈzän(t)s; ˈren-ə-ˌsän(t)s, -ˌzän(t)s\ *n.* **1** A new birth or revival; especially [with a capital] the period of European history between the 14th and 16th centuries, marked by a revival of interest in ancient art and literature. **2** Any period marked by new vigor.

re·nal \ˈrēn-l\ *adj.* Of, relating to, or in the region of the kidneys.

re·nas·cence \rē-ˈnas-n(t)s, -ˈnās-\ *n.* **1** A rebirth or revival; a renaissance. **2** [with a capital] The Renaissance. — **re·nas·cent** \-nt\ *adj.*

rend \ˈrend\ *v.;* **rent** \ˈrent\; **rend·ing.** **1** To take forcibly from its place; to wrench. **2** To tear apart by great force; to split. **3** To affect as if by tearing or splitting; as, a country *rent* by civil war.

ren·der \ˈrend-r\ *v.;* **ren·dered; ren·der·ing** \-r(-)ing\. **1** To deliver; to give. **2** To melt down; to clarify by melting; as, to *render* lard. **3** To give up; to surrender; as, to *render* one's life; to *render* a city to a conquering army. **4** To give in return; as, to *render* thanks. **5** To present a statement of; to bring to a person's attention; as, to *render* a bill. **6** To cause to be or become; to make; as, to *render* a person helpless. **7** To furnish; to contribute; as, to *render* aid. **8** To present or perform by playing or singing; as, to *render* a song. **9** To translate; as, to *render* Latin into English.

ren·dez·vous \ˈrän-dē-ˌvü, -də-\ *n.; pl.* **ren·dez·vous** \-ˌvüz\. [From medieval French, there formed from *rendez vous!* meaning "present yourself!", "betake yourself!".] **1** A place set for a meeting. **2** A meeting by appointment; as, to arrange a *rendezvous.*— *v.;* **ren·dez·voused** \-ˌvüd\; **ren·dez·vous·ing** \-ˌvü-ing\. To assemble or meet, especially by appointment.

ren·di·tion \ren-ˈdish-n\ *n.* Any act or result of rendering.

ren·e·gade \ˈren-ē-ˌgād\ *n.* **1** One who deserts a faith, cause, principle, or party. **2** A turncoat; a traitor.

re·nege \rē-ˈnig, -ˈneg\ *v.;* **re·neged; re·neg·ing.** **1** In card playing, to violate a rule of the game by failing to play a card of the same suit when able to do so. **2** To fail to keep one's promise.

re·new \rē-ˈnü, -ˈnyü\ *v.* **1** To make new again; to restore to freshness or vigor. A rest *renewed* the traveler's strength. **2** To restore to existence; to re-establish; to recreate; to rebuild; as, to *renew* the old splendor of a palace. **3** To repeat; to go over again; as, to *renew* a complaint. **4** To revive; to become new or as if new; as, to *renew* the thoughts and sentiments of one's youth. **5** To begin again; to resume; as, to *renew* one's efforts. **6** To put in a fresh supply of; to replace; as, to *renew* the water in a tank; to *renew* one's equipment. **7** To grant or obtain an extension of; to continue in force for a fresh period; as, to *renew* a lease; to *renew* a subscription.

re·new·al \rē-ˈnü-əl, -ˈnyü-\ *n.* The act of renewing or state of being renewed.

ren·net \ˈren-ət\ *n.* **1** The contents of the stomach of an unweaned calf or other animal or the lining membrane of the stomach, used for curdling milk. **2** Anything used to curdle milk. **3** Rennin.

ren·nin \ˈren-ən\ *n.* An enzyme that curdles milk.

re·nounce \rē-ˈnau̇n(t)s\ *v.;* **re·nounced; re·nounc·ing.** **1** To give up, abandon, or resign. The king *renounced* the throne. **2** To cast off; to disown. The angry father *renounced* his son. — **re·nounce·ment** \-mənt\ *n.*

ren·o·vate \ˈren-ə-ˌvāt\ *v.;* **ren·o·vat·ed; ren·o·vat·ing.** To make like new again; to put in good condition again; to repair; as, to *renovate* a run-down house. — **ren·o·va·tion** \ˌren-ə-ˈvāsh-n\ *n.* — **ren·o·va·tor** \ˈren-ə-ˌvāt-r\ *n.*

re·nown \rē-ˈnau̇n\ *n.* Widespread fame; illustrious reputation. — **re·nowned** \rē-ˈnau̇nd\ *adj.*

rent \ˈrent\. Past tense and past part. of *rend.* — *n.* An opening made by rending, as a tear in cloth.

rent \ˈrent\ *n.* Money paid for the use of another's property; especially, money paid by a tenant to his landlord for the use of land or buildings. — *v.* **1** To take and hold under an agreement to pay rent. **2** To give possession and use of in return for rent. **3** To be leased or let. The room *rents* for ten dollars a week. — **rent·a·ble** \-əb-l\ *adj.*

rent·al \ˈrent-l\ *n.* The total amount of rent. — *adj.* Of or relating to rent; as, *rental* value.

rent·er \ˈrent-r\ *n.* One that rents; especially, a tenant.

re·nun·ci·a·tion \rē-ˌnən(t)s-ē-ˈāsh-n\ *n.* The act or an instance of renouncing; a renouncement.

re·or·ga·ni·za·tion \(ˌ)rē-ˌórg-n(-)ə-ˈzāsh-n\ *n.* **1** A reorganizing or a being reorganized. **2** The reconstruction of a business concern, especially when undertaken because of failure or likelihood of failure under the existing organization.

re·or·ga·nize \(ˈ)rē-ˈórg-n-ˌīz\ *v.;* **re·or·ga·nized; re·or·ga·niz·ing.** To organize again or anew; especially, to bring about a reorganization, as of a business concern. — **re·or·ga·niz·er** \-ˌīz-r\ *n.*

Rep. Abbreviation for: **1** *Representative.* **2** *Republic.* **3** *Republican.*

repaid. Past tense and past part. of *repay.*

re·pair \rē-ˈpar, -ˈper\ *v.* To go; to betake oneself; as, to *repair* to an inner office for greater privacy.

re·pair \rē-'par, -'per\ *v.* **1** To restore to good condition; as, to *repair* a broken toy. **2** To remedy, heal, or mend; as, to *repair* a wrong; to *repair* a broken leg. — *n.* **1** The action or process of repairing; as, to make *repairs.* **2** The result of repairing. This tire shows three *repairs.* **3** Good or sound condition; as, a house in *repair.* **4** Condition with respect to soundness or need of repairing; as, a house in bad *repair.* — **re·pair·a·ble** \-əb l\ *adj.* — **re·pair·er** \-r\ *n.*

re·pair·man \rē-'par-mən, -'per-, -ˌman\ *n.; pl.* **re·pair·men** \-mən, -ˌmen\. One whose occupation is to make repairs or readjustments, especially in a mechanism.

rep·a·ra·ble \'rep-r(-)əb-l\ *adj.* Capable of being repaired, remedied, or made good.

rep·a·ra·tion \ˌrep-r-'āsh-n\ *n.* **1** The action or process of repairing or restoring; the state of being repaired or restored. **2** A making amends for a wrong or injury done; a compensation. **3** The amends made for a wrong or injury; [in the plural] money paid in compensation, as by one country to another for damages in war.

rep·ar·tee \ˌrep-r-'tē, ˌrep-ˌär-, -ˌȧr-\ *n.* **1** A clever, witty reply. **2** The making of such replies.

re·past \rē-'past\ *n.* A meal; a feast.

re·pa·tri·ate \(')rē-'pā-trē-ˌāt, -'pa-trē-\ *v.;* **re·pa·tri·at·ed; re·pa·tri·at·ing.** To send or bring back to one's own country or to the country of which one is a citizen; as, to *repatriate* prisoners of war. — **re·pa·tri·a·tion** \(ˌ)rē-ˌpā-trē-'āsh-n, -ˌpa-trē-\ *n.*

re·pay \(')rē-'pā\ *v.;* **re·paid** \-'pād\; **re·pay·ing. 1** To pay back; to make a return for; as, to *repay* a loan; to *repay* a kindness. **2** To pay back to; to compensate; as, to feel well *repaid.* — **re·pay·a·ble** \-əb-l\ *adj.* — **re·pay·ment** \-mənt\ *n.*

re·peal \rē-'pēl\ *v.* To recall or revoke; to do away with, as a law. — *n.* A repealing; revocation.

re·peat \rē-'pēt\ *v.* **1** To say or state again; to reiterate; as, to *repeat* a question. **2** To say from memory; to recite; as, to *repeat* a poem. **3** To say or utter after another person; as, to *repeat* an oath of office. **4** To make or do again; as, to *repeat* a mistake. **5** To tell to others; as, to *repeat* a secret. — **repeat oneself.** To do or say what one has already said. — *n.* **1** A repeating; a repetition. **2** Something repeated or to be repeated, as a passage in music or a second order of goods.

re·peat·ed \rē-'pēt-əd\ *adj.* Done or happening again and again; frequent. — **re·peat·ed·ly,** *adv.*

re·peat·er \rē-'pēt-r\ *n.* **1** One that repeats. **2** A person who violates law by voting more than once in an election. **3** A student repeating a course in a school or college. **4** A gun that fires several times without reloading. **5** A watch that strikes the time when a spring is pressed.

re·pel \rē-'pel\ *v.;* **re·pelled; re·pel·ling. 1** To drive back or away; to force to retreat; as, to *repel* the enemy. **2** To reject; to refuse to receive or consider; as, to *repel* a suggestion. **3** To cause to turn away, as in dislike or disgust; as, a sight that *repelled* everyone. **4** To resist; to keep out; as, cloth treated to *repel* water.

re·pel·lent \rē-'pel-ənt\ *adj.* Repelling or tending to repel. — *n.* Something intended to repel, as a lotion to repel insects.

re·pent \rē-'pent\ *v.* **1** To feel sorrow for one's sins and to determine to do what is right. **2** To feel sorry for or dissatisfied with something one has done; to regret; as, to *repent* a rash decision.

re·pent·ance \rē-'pent-n(t)s\ *n.* A feeling of regret for something done or said; especially, regret or sorrow for sin.

re·pent·ant \rē-'pent-nt\ *adj.* Feeling or showing repentance. — **re·pent·ant·ly,** *adv.*

re·peo·ple \(')rē-'pēp-l\ *v.;* **re·peo·pled; re·peo·pling** \-l(-)ing\. **1** To people anew. **2** To stock again, as with animals.

re·per·cus·sion \ˌrēp-r-'kəsh-n, ˌrep-r-\ *n.* **1** A rebound or recoil. **2** A reflection of sound; a reverberation. **3** A reaction to something done or said.

rep·er·toire \'rep-ə-ˌtwär, 'rep-r-\ *n.* A list of all the things, as plays or parts in plays, operas or operatic roles, or musical pieces, which a company or a person has rehearsed and is prepared to perform.

rep·er·to·ry \'rep-ə-ˌtōr-ē, 'rep-r-, -ˌtȯr-ē\ *n.; pl.* **rep·er·to·ries. 1** A stock or store; a collection; as, a *repertory* of unusual skills. **2** A repertoire.

rep·e·ti·tion \ˌrep-ə-'tish-n\ *n.* **1** The act of repeating; a saying, doing, or happening again or repeatedly. **2** Something repeated.

rep·e·ti·tious \ˌrep-ə-'tish-əs\ *adj.* **1** Containing repetition. **2** Repeating so much or so often as to be tiresome. — **rep·e·ti·tious·ly,** *adv.*

re·pet·i·tive \rē-'pet-ət-iv\ *adj.* Repetitious.

re·phrase \(')rē-'frāz\ *v.;* **re·phrased; re·phras·ing.** To phrase over again in a different form.

re·pine \rē-'pīn\ *v.;* **re·pined; re·pin·ing.** To be discontented; to fret; to complain.

re·place \rē-'plās\ *v.;* **re·placed; re·plac·ing. 1** To put back in its proper or former place; as, to *replace* a card in a file. **2** To take the place of; to supplant. Paper money has *replaced* gold coins. **3** To fill the place of; to supply an equivalent for; as, to *replace* a broken dish.

re·place·ment \rē-'plās-mənt\ *n.* **1** The act of replacing or the state of being replaced. **2** Someone or something that replaces another.

re·plen·ish \rē-'plen-ish\ *v.* To fill again; to bring back to a condition of being full or complete. — **re·plen·ish·ment** \-mənt\ *n.*

re·plete \rē-'plēt\ *adj.* **1** Filled to capacity; full; especially, full of food. **2** Fully supplied or provided; as, a book *replete* with illustrations.

re·ple·tion \rē-'plēsh-n\ *n.* The state of being replete, especially with food; as, to eat to *repletion.*

rep·li·ca \'rep-lik-ə\ *n.* **1** A reproduction or copy of a picture or statue, especially by the artist who made the original. **2** Any very close copy.

re·ply \rē-'plī\ *v.;* **re·plied** \-'plīd\; **re·ply·ing.** To make answer; to respond. — *n.; pl.* **re·plies. 1** An answer; a response. **2** The act of replying.

re·port \rē-ˈpōrt, -ˈpȯrt\ *v.* **1** To give an account, as of some incident or of one's activities. **2** To give an account of in a newspaper article; as, to *report* a baseball game. **3** To make a charge of misconduct against; as, to *report* a schoolmate. **4** To present oneself; as, to *report* for duty; to *report* at the office. **5** To make known to the proper authorities; as, to *report* a fire. **6** In parliamentary use, to return or present, as a matter officially referred to a committee, with conclusions and recommendations. — *n.* **1** An account; as, a first-hand *report* of an accident. **2** An official statement, as of a pupil's marks. **3** Common talk; rumor; as, idle *report.* **4** Reputation; as, a man of good *report.* **5** An explosive noise; as, the *report* of a gun. — **re·port·a·ble** \-əb-l\ *adj.*

re·port·er \rē-ˈpōrt-r, -ˈpȯrt-r\ *n.* A person who reports; especially, one who reports or gathers news for a magazine or newspaper.

re·pose \rē-ˈpōz\ *v.;* **re·posed; re·pos·ing.** To place, as trust or hope; as, to *repose* trust in a friend.

re·pose \rē-ˈpōz\ *v.;* **re·posed; re·pos·ing. 1** To lay at rest; to put in a restful position; as, to *repose* one's head on a cushion. **2** To lie at rest; to take rest; as, *reposing* on the couch. — *n.* **1** Rest; sleep; as, a night's *repose.* **2** A state of freedom from all that excites or disturbs; peace; calm.

re·pose·ful \rē-ˈpōz-fəl\ *adj.* Calm; quiet.

re·pos·i·to·ry \rē-ˈpäz-ə-ˌtōr-ē, -ˌtȯr-ē\ *n.; pl.* **re·pos·i·to·ries.** A place where something valuable is put for safekeeping.

re·pos·sess \ˌrēp-ə-ˈzes\ *v.* To regain possession of. — **re·pos·ses·sion** \-ˈzesh-n\ *n.*

rep·re·hend \ˌrep-rē-ˈhend\ *v.* To blame; to censure; to reprimand.

rep·re·hen·si·ble \ˌrep-rē-ˈhen(t)s-əb-l\ *adj.* Deserving blame or censure; blameworthy. — **rep·re·hen·si·bly** \-ə-blē\ *adv.*

rep·re·sent \ˌrep-rē-ˈzent\ *v.* **1** To present a picture, image, or likeness of; to portray. This picture *represents* a scene at King Arthur's court. **2** To serve as a sign or symbol of. The flag *represents* our country. **3** To stand in place of; to act or speak for; as, a lawyer *representing* his client. **4** To make a statement about with the purpose of influencing action or judgment; as, to *represent* oneself as very poor. **5** To act in place of a person or body of persons. We elect men and women to *represent* us in Congress. **6** To be a member or example of. These ten men *represent* ten nationalities.

rep·re·sen·ta·tion \ˌrep-rē-zen-ˈtāsh-n\ *n.* **1** The act of representing. **2** A picture, statue, or likeness. **3** A sign, emblem, or symbol that stands in place of something. The symbols in the pronunciations in this book are *representations* of sounds. **4** The state of being represented in a legislature.

rep·re·sent·a·tive \ˌrep-rē-ˈzent-ət-iv\ *adj.* **1** Representing; giving a likeness; portraying; as, a painting *representative* of a battle. **2** Being or acting as the agent for another; as, a *representative* committee. **3** Serving as a good example of a class; characteristic; typical; as, a *representative* housewife. **4** Founded on the principle of representation; carried on by elected representatives; as, a *representative* government. — *n.* **1** A person or thing that represents. **2** A person who represents his district or state in a lawmaking body; especially, a member of the lower house of a legislature.

re·press \rē-ˈpres\ *v.* **1** To keep down by or as if by pressure; to restrain. **2** In psychology, to subject to repression. — **re·press·i·ble** \-əb-l\ *adj.*

re·pres·sion \rē-ˈpresh-n\ *n.* **1** A repressing or a being repressed. **2** In psychology, a process by which wishes or impulses that cannot be satisfied are kept from conscious awareness. — **re·pres·sive** \-ˈpres-iv\ *adj.*

re·prieve \rē-ˈprēv\ *v.;* **re·prieved; re·priev·ing. 1** To delay the punishment of; especially, to postpone the execution of sentence on a condemned person. **2** To give temporary relief to. — *n.* **1** The act of reprieving or state of being reprieved. **2** A temporary escape, as from pain or death.

rep·ri·mand \ˈrep-rə-ˌmand\ *n.* A severe or formal reproof. — *v.* To reprove severely, especially officially.

re·print \(ˈ)rē-ˈprint\ *v.* To print again; to print another edition of. — \ˈrē-ˌprint\ *n.* Something reprinted; a new impression of a printed work.

re·pris·al \rē-ˈprīz-l\ *n.* **1** The use of force short of war by one nation against another in retaliation for damage or loss suffered; as, economic *reprisals.* **2** Any act of retaliation, especially in war.

re·proach \rē-ˈprōch\ *v.* To blame; to find fault with. — *n.* **1** Something which deserves blame; a cause of shame. **2** Censure or blame; a rebuke; a scolding.

re·proach·ful \rē-ˈprōch-fəl\ *adj.* Expressing disapproval or reproach; as, a *reproachful* glance. — **re·proach·ful·ly** \-fə-lē\ *adv.*

rep·ro·bate \ˈrep-rə-ˌbāt\ *adj.* Vicious; corrupt. — *n.* A complete scoundrel; a reprobate person. — *v.;* **rep·ro·bat·ed; rep·ro·bat·ing.** To condemn.

rep·ro·ba·tion \ˌrep-rə-ˈbāsh-n\ *n.* Severe disapproval; condemnation.

re·pro·duce \ˌrēp-rə-ˈdüs, -ˈdyüs\ *v.;* **re·pro·duced; re·pro·duc·ing. 1** To produce again; to cause to exist again. **2** Of a plant or animal, to produce another living thing like itself; to bear offspring. **3** To copy; to make an image or imitation of; as, to *reproduce* a photograph. **4** To present again, as a play. **5** To recite from memory; as, to *reproduce* a poem perfectly. — **re·pro·duc·er** \-ˈdüs-r, -ˈdyüs-r\ *n.* — **re·pro·duc·i·ble** \-ˈdü-səb-l, -ˈdyü-\ *adj.*

re·pro·duc·tion \ˌrēp-rə-ˈdəksh-n\ *n.* **1** The act or process of reproducing. **2** A copy; as, a good *reproduction* of a painting. **3** The process by which living things give rise to others of the same kind.

re·pro·duc·tive \ˌrēp-rə-ˈdək-tiv\ *adj.* **1** That reproduces or tends to reproduce. **2** Of or relating to reproduction. — **re·pro·duc·tive·ly,** *adv.*

re·proof \rē-ˈprüf\ *n.* **1** Blame or censure for a fault; as, a word of *reproof.* **2** A reproachful speech, look, or action; a rebuke.

re·prov·al \rē-'prüv-l\ *n.* Reproof; censure.

re·prove \rē-'prüv\ *v.;* **re·proved; re·prov·ing.** To censure; to scold; as, to *reprove* a child. — **re·prov·er** \-'prüv-r\ *n.*

rep·tile \'rept-l, 'rep-ˌtīl\ *n.* **1** A cold-blooded, air-breathing vertebrate that has a dry scaly skin and crawls on its belly or on short legs. Snakes, lizards, and turtles are *reptiles.* **2** A low, mean person. — *adj.* **1** Creeping; crawling. **2** Of or relating to a reptile or reptiles. — **rep·til·i·an** \rep-'til-ē-ən\ *adj.*

re·pub·lic \rē-'pəb-lik\ *n.* **1** A state or country in which supreme governing power is held by the citizens having the right to vote and is exercised by representatives elected by and responsible to the voters. **2** The form of government by which such a country is governed.

re·pub·li·can \rē-'pəb-lik-n\ *adj.* **1** Of or relating to a republic; as, a *republican* form of government. **2** [with a capital] Of or relating to the Republican Party. — *n.* **1** A person who favors a republican form of government. **2** [with a capital] A member of the Republican Party.

re·pu·di·ate \rē-'pyüd-ē-ˌāt\ *v.;* **re·pu·di·at·ed; re·pu·di·at·ing.** **1** To cast off or disown, as a child. **2** To refuse to acknowledge as true or just, as a claim. **3** To refuse to pay, as debts. — **re·pu·di·a·tion** \-ˌpyüd-ē-'āsh-n\ *n.*

re·pug·nance \rē-'pəg-nən(t)s\ *n.* Deep-rooted dislike; aversion; loathing.

re·pug·nant \rē-'pəg-nənt\ *adj.* **1** Opposed; contrary; incompatible; as, punishments *repugnant* to the spirit of the law. **2** Distasteful; repulsive.

re·pulse \rē-'pəls\ *v.;* **re·pulsed; re·puls·ing.** **1** To repel; to beat or drive back; as, to *repulse* the enemy. **2** To repel by unkindness or coldness; to rebuff. **3** To disgust; to cause a feeling of repulsion in. — *n.* **1** The act of repulsing or fact of being repulsed. **2** A setback; a check. The army suffered a *repulse.* **3** Refusal; denial; rebuff.

re·pul·sion \rē-'pəlsh-n\ *n.* **1** A repulsing or a being repulsed; a rebuff; a rejection. **2** A feeling of extreme dislike; repugnance. **3** In physics, the act of repelling or the force with which bodies repel one another.

re·pul·sive \rē-'pəl-siv\ *adj.* **1** Serving or able to repel or repulse. **2** Causing disgust; offensive. — **re·pul·sive·ly,** *adv.*

rep·u·ta·ble \'rep-yət-əb-l\ *adj.* Having a good reputation; respected. — **rep·u·ta·bly** \-ə-blē\ *adv.*

rep·u·ta·tion \ˌrep-yə-'tāsh-n\ *n.* **1** The quality of a thing, or the character of a person, as seen or judged by people in general. **2** Recognition by other people of some characteristic or ability; as, to have the *reputation* of being clever. **3** Good name; a place in public esteem; as, to lose one's *reputation.* **4** Fame; as, a world-wide *reputation.*

re·pute \rē-'pyüt\ *v.;* **re·put·ed; re·put·ing.** To believe; to consider; as, a man *reputed* to be a millionaire. — *n.* **1** Reputation; as, to know a man by *repute.* **2** Fame; note; as, a scientist of *repute.*

re·put·ed \rē-'pyüt-əd\ *adj.* **1** Having repute; as, a highly *reputed* lawyer. **2** Popularly supposed; as, a *reputed* success. — **re·put·ed·ly,** *adv.*

re·quest \rē-'kwest\ *n.* **1** An asking for something; a petition; an entreaty; as, a *request* for aid. **2** Something asked for; as, to grant every *request.* **3** The condition of being requested. Tickets are available upon *request.* **4** Demand; as, a book that is a great *request.* — *v.* **1** To ask for; as, to *request* a loan. **2** To make a request to or of; as, to *request* a person to sing. — For synonyms see *ask.*

req·ui·em \'rek-wē-əm, 'rāk-, 'rēk-\ *n.* **1** [usually with a capital] In the Roman Catholic Church, a Mass for a dead person or persons or a musical setting for such a Mass. **2** Any musical service or hymn in honor of the dead.

re·quire \rē-'kwīr\ *v.;* **re·quired; re·quir·ing.** **1** To demand; to order; to command. The law *requires* drivers to observe traffic lights. **2** To need; to call for; as, a trick that *requires* skill.

re·quire·ment \rē-'kwīr-mənt\ *n.* **1** A requiring. **2** Something, as a condition or quality, required; as, to comply with all *requirements.* **3** A necessity; a need. Sleep is a *requirement* for health.

req·ui·site \'rek-wə-zət\ *adj.* Required; necessary; essential; as, conditions *requisite* for success. — *n.* Something needed; a requirement; as, a list of all the *requisites* for the trip. — **req·ui·site·ly,** *adv.*

req·ui·si·tion \ˌrek-wə-'zish-n\ *n.* **1** The act of requiring or demanding. **2** An authoritative or formal demand or application; as, a *requisition* for army supplies. **3** The condition of being demanded or put into use. Every car was in *requisition.* — *v.;* **req·ui·si·tioned; req·ui·si·tion·ing** \-n(-)ing\. To make a requisition for or on; as, to *requisition* food for troops; to *requisition* a town for food.

re·quit·al \rē-'kwīt-l\ *n.* **1** The act of requiting or state of being requited; as, to suffer without hope of *requital.* **2** Something given in return or retaliation.

re·quite \rē-'kwīt\ *v.;* **re·quit·ed; re·quit·ing.** **1** To repay, as a benefit or an injury; to make a return or retaliation for; as, to *requite* evil with good. **2** To repay, as a person, for a benefit or an injury; to reward; to retaliate upon; as, to *requite* a person handsomely for his services.

re·run \(')rē-'rən\ *v.;* **re·ran** \-'ran\; **re·run; re·run·ning.** To run again. — \'rē-ˌrən\ *n.* **1** A rerunning; especially, the showing of a motion picture again after its first run. **2** A picture that is rerun.

re·sale \(')rē-'sāl\ *n.* The act of selling again.

re·scind \rē-'sind\ *v.* **1** To cancel; to annul; as, to *rescind* a decision. **2** To repeal, as a law.

res·cue \'res-ˌkyü\ *v.;* **res·cued; res·cu·ing.** To free from confinement, danger, or evil. — *n.* A rescuing. — **res·cu·er** \-ˌkyü-ər, -ˌkyůr\ *n.*

re·search \rē-'sərch, 'rē-ˌsərch\ *n.* Careful search; especially, critical study or investigation in seeking new knowledge; as, scientific *research.* — *v.* To make researches. — **re·search·er** \-r\ *n.*

re·sem·blance \rē-'zem-blən(t)s\ *n.* The quality or condition of resembling; a likeness or a point of likeness; as, a *resemblance* between father and son.

re·sem·ble \rē-'zem-bl\ *v.;* **re·sem·bled; re·sem·bling** \-bl(-)ing\. To be like or similar to.

re·sent \rē-'zent\ *v.* To feel or express annoyance or ill will over; as, to *resent* all criticism.

re·sent·ful \rē-'zent-fəl\ *adj.* Feeling or showing resentment; inclined to feel resentment. — **re·sent·ful·ly** \-fə-lē\ *adv.*

re·sent·ment \rē-'zent-mənt\ *n.* A feeling of indignant displeasure and ill will because of something regarded as a wrong, an insult, or neglect.

res·er·va·tion \ˌrez-r-'vāsh-n\ *n.* **1** The act of reserving. **2** An arrangement to have something, as a room in a hotel or a seat on a train, held for one's use. **3** Something reserved for a special use; especially, a tract of public lands so reserved; as, an Indian *reservation.* **4** A limiting condition; an exception; as, to agree without *reservations.*

re·serve \rē-'zərv\ *v.;* **re·served; re·serv·ing. 1** To keep in store for future or special use. **2** To hold back and not give over; to keep for oneself; as, to *reserve* the right to cancel an order. **3** To arrange to have set aside or held for one's use; as, to *reserve* a room in a hotel. — *n.* **1** The state of being reserved; as, to have plenty of food in *reserve.* **2** Something reserved; a stock or store; an extra supply; as, to have a *reserve* of cash for emergencies; a nation's oil *reserves.* **3** A tract of land set apart for some special purpose; a reservation; as, a forest *reserve.* **4** [usually in the plural] A force of troops held back for use in an emergency; reinforcements; as, to bring up the *reserves.* **5** The military or naval forces of a country not in active service but liable to be called upon when needed. **6** That part of the assets of a bank kept in cash or in a form easily turned into cash, ready to meet demands. **7** That part of the earnings of a business set aside for emergencies. **8** A tendency to hold back or not to show one's thoughts or feelings; restraint; as, to speak without *reserve.* — *adj.* Being or forming a reserve; as, *reserve* troops.

re·served \rē-'zərvd\ *adj.* **1** Set aside for future or special use. **2** Restrained in words or actions; reticent. — **re·serv·ed·ly** \-'zər-vəd-lē\ *adv.*

re·serv·ist \rē-'zər-vəst\ *n.* A member of a military, naval, or air reserve.

res·er·voir \'rez-əv-ˌwär, -ˌ(w)ȯr, -ˌȯi, -ˌwȧr, 'rez-rv-\ *n.* **1** A place where something is stored for use, as the part of an oil lamp where the supply of oil is held; especially, an artificial lake or system of lakes in which water is collected and kept for future use, as by a city. **2** A reserve; a store.

re·set \(')rē-'set\ *v.;* **re·set; re·set·ting.** To set again or anew. — \(')rē-'set, 'rē-ˌset\ *n.* A thing reset.

re·set·tle \(')rē-'set-l\ *v.;* **re·set·tled; re·set·tling** \-l(-)ing\. To settle again or anew. — **re·set·tle·ment** \-l-mənt\ *n.*

re·shape \(')rē-'shāp\ *v.;* **re·shaped; re·shap·ing.** To shape again; especially, to give a new shape to.

re·side \rē-'zīd\ *v.;* **re·sid·ed; re·sid·ing. 1** To make one's home; to live; to dwell. **2** To be present or fixed as a quality, a right, or a power; to exist. The power of veto *resides* in the president.

res·i·dence \'rez-ə-dən(t)s, 'rez-dən(t)s, -ə-ˌden(t)s\ *n.* **1** The act or fact of residing in a place as a dweller or in discharge of a duty; as, physicians in *residence* in a hospital; *residence* abroad. **2** The house in which a family lives. **3** The period of a person's residing in a place.

res·i·den·cy \'rez-ə-dən-sē, 'rez-dən-sē, -ə-ˌden(t)s-ē\ *n.; pl.* **res·i·den·cies. 1** The residence of, or the territory under, a diplomatic resident. **2** The position or rank of a resident physician.

res·i·dent \'rez-ə-dənt, 'rez-dənt, -ə-ˌdent\ *adj.* **1** Living in a place for some length of time; residing. **2** Living in a place while discharging official duties; as, a *resident* physician of a hospital. **3** Of birds, not migratory. — *n.* **1** A person who resides in a place. **2** A diplomatic representative having governing powers, as in a protectorate. **3** A resident physician.

res·i·den·tial \ˌrez-ə-'dench-l\ *adj.* **1** Used as a residence or by residents; as, a *residential* hotel. **2** Adapted to or occupied by residences; as, a *residential* section in a city.

re·sid·u·al \rē-'zij-ə-wəl, -'zij-l\ *adj.* Being or forming a residue; remaining; left over.

re·sid·u·ary \rē-'zij-ə-ˌwer-ē\ *adj.* **1** Residual. **2** Of or relating to the residue of an estate.

res·i·due \'rez-ə-ˌdü, -ˌdyü\ *n.* **1** That which remains after a part has been taken away. **2** The part of a dead person's estate that remains after all debts and specific bequests have been paid.

re·sign \rē-'zīn\ *v.* **1** To give up by a formal or official act; as, to *resign* an office. **2** To give up an office or position. **3** To commit or give over or up; to submit or yield deliberately; as, to *resign* oneself to a disappointment.

res·ig·na·tion \ˌrez-ig-'nāsh-n\ *n.* **1** An act of resigning. **2** A letter or written statement that gives notice of this act. **3** The quality or the feeling of a person who is resigned; quiet or patient submission or acceptance. — For synonyms see *patience.*

re·signed \rē-'zīnd\ *adj.* Submitting patiently, as to loss, sorrow, or misfortune; submissive; uncomplaining. — **re·sign·ed·ly** \-'zī-nəd-lē\ *adv.*

re·sil·ience \rē-'zil-yən(t)s\ or **re·sil·ien·cy** \-yən-sē\ *n.* The ability of a body to rebound, recoil, or resume its original size and shape after being compressed, bent, or stretched; elasticity.

re·sil·ient \rē-'zil-yənt\ *adj.* **1** Having resilience; rebounding; recoiling. **2** Having the power of quick recovery; buoyant; as, *resilient* spirits.

res·in \'rez-n\ *n.* **1** Any of various yellowish or brownish organic substances obtained from the gum or sap of trees such as the pine; especially, rosin. **2** Any artificial product having most of the properties of the natural resins.

res·in·ous \'rez-n(-)əs\ *adj.* **1** Of or like resin. **2** Containing resin.

re·sist \rē-'zist\ *v.* **1** To be able to repel, ward off, or prevent; as, strong enough to *resist* disease.

2 To fight against; to oppose; as, to *resist* arrest. **3** To withstand the action of; as, a surface able to *resist* acids; stain-*resisting* steel.

re·sist·ance \rē-'zis-tən(t)s\ *n.* **1** The act of resisting. **2** The ability to resist. **3** Any force that opposes or hinders. **4** The opposition offered by a substance to the passage through it of an electric current. **5** The organized underground movement of a conquered country, made up of groups of persons engaged in sabotage and secret operations against occupation forces.

re·sist·ant \rē-'zis-tənt\ *adj.* Resisting; as, fire-*resistant* materials.

re·sist·i·ble \rē-'zis-təb-l\ *adj.* Capable of being resisted. — **re·sist·i·bil·i·ty** \-ˌzis-tə-'bil-ət-ē\ *n.*

re·sist·less \rē-'zist-ləs\ *adj.* **1** Incapable of being resisted; irresistible. **2** Having no power to resist. — **re·sist·less·ly**, *adv.*

re·sis·tor \rē-'zist-r\ *n.* A device offering electrical resistance.

res·o·lute \'rez-l-ˌüt\ *adj.* Not to be moved from one's purpose; determined; resolved; firm. — **res·o·lute·ly**, *adv.*

res·o·lu·tion \ˌrez-l-'üsh-n\ *n.* **1** The action of resolving. **2** The action of solving; an answer; a solution. **3** The quality of being resolute; determination; perseverance. **4** Something resolved or decided on; a fixed determination; as, New Year *resolutions.* **5** A statement expressing the feelings, wishes, or decisions of a group.

re·solve \rē-'zälv\ *v.;* **re·solved; re·solv·ing. 1** To change by breaking up or separating; to transform. Boiling water *resolves* itself into steam. **2** To solve; to find an answer to; as, to *resolve* a difficulty. **3** To decide or determine; to form a purpose; as, to *resolve* to work harder. **4** To make or pass a resolution. The legislature *resolved* to adjourn. — *n.* **1** Something that has been resolved; a resolution. **2** The quality of being resolute; determination. — **re·solv·a·ble** \-'zäl-vəb-l\ *adj.*

re·solved \rē-'zälvd\ *adj.* Determined; resolute. — **re·solv·ed·ly** \-'zäl-vəd-lē\ *adv.*

res·o·nance \'rez-n(-)ən(t)s\ *n.* **1** The quality or condition of being resonant. **2** The state of adjustment of an electric circuit, as of a radio receiving apparatus tuned to a particular station, that permits the greatest flow of current of a particular frequency. **3** A prolonging or increase of sound due to vibration of a body caused by waves from another vibrating body. **4** A vibrating quality of a voice sound. **5** A fullness and richness of a musical tone resulting from additional vibration, as from the body of a violin.

res·o·nant \'rez-n(-)ənt\ *adj.* **1** Resounding; ringing; echoing. **2** Intensified and enriched by resonance; as, a *resonant* baritone. **3** Of, relating to, or showing resonance. — **res·o·nant·ly**, *adv.*

res·o·na·tor \'rez-n-ˌāt-r\ *n.* Anything that resounds or exhibits resonance.

re·sort \rē-'zȯrt\ *v.* **1** To go; to visit; especially, to visit often or as a habit; as, to *resort* to the beach regularly all summer. **2** To go for help or relief; to have recourse; as, to *resort* to force. — *n.* **1** Someone or something resorted to for help; a resource; a refuge; as, a last *resort.* **2** The action of turning to for help; as, to have *resort* to force. **3** A frequent or general visiting; as, our usual place of *resort* on Saturdays. **4** A popular place for entertainment or recreation; as, a summer *resort.*

re·sound \rē-'zau̇nd\ *v.* **1** To be filled with sound; to ring; to echo. The hall *resounded* with cheers. **2** To sound or make sound loudly. The organ *resounded* through the hall. **3** To be proclaimed; to be re-echoed; as, a hero whose fame *resounded* far and wide. — **re·sound·ing·ly**, *adv.*

re·source \'rē-ˌsōrs, -ˌsȯrs; rē-'sōrs, -'sȯrs, -'zōrs, -'zȯrs\ *n.* **1** A new or a reserve source of supply or support. **2** [in the plural] A usable stock or supply, as of money, products, power, or energy. America has great natural *resources.* **3** The possibility of relief or recovery; as, left helpless without *resource.* **4** The ability to meet and handle situations; resourcefulness. **5** A means of handling a situation or of getting out of difficulty.

re·source·ful \rē-'sōrs-fəl, -'sȯrs-, -'zōrs-, -'zȯrs-\ *adj.* Able to meet situations; capable of devising ways and means. — **re·source·ful·ness**, *n.*

re·spect \rē-'spekt\ *v.* **1** To honor; to think highly of and treat courteously; as, to *respect* one's parents. **2** To heed; to refrain from intruding upon; as, to *respect* a person's privacy. **3** To have reference to. — *n.* **1** Relation; reference; as, to write with *respect* to the plans. **2** Esteem; high regard; as, to have great *respect* for a person. **3** [in the plural] An expression of respect; regards; as, to send one's *respects.* **4** A detail; a particular; as, to fail in several *respects.* — **re·spect·er** \-r\ *n.*

re·spect·a·bil·i·ty \rē-ˌspek-tə-'bil-ət-ē\ *n.; pl.* **re·spect·a·bil·i·ties. 1** The quality or state of being respectable. **2** [in the plural] Decencies; conventions.

re·spect·a·ble \rē-'spek-təb-l\ *adj.* **1** Worthy of respect; respected; as, a *respectable* authority. **2** Decent in behavior or character; behaving according to customs or conventions; as, *respectable* society. **3** Fairly large or good; as, a *respectable* number. **4** Fit to be seen; presentable. The coat is old but *respectable.* — **re·spect·a·bly** \-tə-blē\ *adv.*

re·spect·ful \rē-'spekt-fəl\ *adj.* Marked by or showing respect. — **re·spect·ful·ly** \-fə-lē\ *adv.*

re·spect·ing \rē-'spek-ting\ *prep.* With regard to.

re·spect·ive \rē-'spek-tiv\ *adj.* Relating to each individual of a number; each to each; as, returning to their *respective* homes.

re·spect·ive·ly \rē-'spek-təv-lē\ *adv.* As relating to each; each in the order given.

re·spell \(')rē-'spel\ *v.* To spell again; to spell in a different way; as, to *respell* words to show pronunciation. — **re·spell·ing**, *n.*

res·pi·ra·tion \ˌresp-r-'āsh-n\ *n.* **1** The act or process of breathing; inspiration and expiration. **2** The process by which a plant or animal absorbs oxygen and gives off products, as carbon dioxide, that are formed in the tissues by oxidation.

res·pi·ra·tor \'resp-r-ˌāt-r\ *n.* **1** A device covering the mouth or nose, used to prevent the inhalation of harmful vapors, or to allow the inhalation of medicated vapors, as anesthetics. **2** A device used in artificial respiration.

respirator, 1

res·pi·ra·to·ry \'resp-r(-)ə-ˌtōr-ē, rē-'spīr-ə-, -ˌtȯr-ē\ *adj.* Of or relating to respiration; used for respiration; as, *respiratory* organs.

re·spire \rē-'spīr\ *v.;* **re·spired; re·spir·ing.** To breathe.

res·pite \'res-pət, -ˌpīt\ *n.* **1** A putting off; a delay. **2** A time of rest from work or relief from suffering; as, *respite* from toil.

re·splen·dent \rē-'splen-dənt\ *adj.* Shining brilliantly; gloriously bright; splendid. The queen stood *resplendent* in her jewels. — **re·splen·dence** \-dən(t)s\ *n.* — **re·splen·dent·ly,** *adv.*

re·spond \rē-'spänd\ *v.* **1** To make a response; to answer; to reply. **2** To act in response; to react.

re·sponse \rē-'spän(t)s\ *n.* **1** Act of replying; an answer. **2** Words said or sung by the people or choir in a religious service. **3** Any reaction to stimulation in a plant or animal.

re·spon·si·bil·i·ty \rē-ˌspän(t)s-ə-'bil-ət-ē\ *n.; pl.* **re·spon·si·bil·i·ties. 1** The condition or quality of being responsible. **2** Reliability; trustworthiness. **3** Something for which a person is responsible; a care; a duty.

re·spon·si·ble \rē-'spän(t)s-əb-l\ *adj.* **1** Liable to be called upon to give satisfaction, as for losses or misdeeds; answerable; as, *responsible* for the damage. **2** Able to fulfill one's obligations; trustworthy; reliable; as, to prove *responsible.* **3** Requiring a person to take charge of or be trusted with important matters; as, a *responsible* job. **4** Able to choose for oneself between right and wrong. — **re·spon·si·bly** \-ə-blē\ *adv.*

re·spon·sive \rē-'spän(t)s-iv\ *adj.* **1** Responding; answering. **2** Ready or quick to respond or to react in a sympathetic way. **3** Said or sung alternately by the clergyman and the congregation; as, a *responsive* reading. — **re·spon·sive·ly,** *adv.*

rest \'rest\ *n.* **1** A place of shelter or lodging; as, a sailors' *rest.* **2** Sleep; slumber; as, to take one's *rest.* **3** Freedom from work or activity; quiet; tranquillity. **4** The state of being motionless or inactive. **5** Something on which another thing leans for support; a stand; a support, as for a rifle. **6** In music, a silence equivalent in duration to a note of the same name; a character indicating this silence. — *v.* **1** To get rest by lying down; to sleep. **2** To lie dead. **3** To cease from action, motion, or exertion; to be still. **4** To give rest or repose to; as, to *rest* oneself on a couch. **5** To be attached or supported; to lean or cause to lean for support. **6** To fix or be fixed in trust or confidence; as, to *rest* one's hopes on another's promise. **7** To depend. The success of the flight *rests* on the wind. **8** In law, to stop introducing new evidence voluntarily.

rests, 6: from left to right: whole, half, quarters, eighth, sixteenth, thirty-second, sixty-fourth

rest \'rest\ *n.* That which is left over; the remainder; the others — used with *the.*

re·state \(')rē-'stāt\ *v.;* **re·stat·ed; re·stat·ing.** To state again; to express in another way; as, to *restate* a question. — **re·state·ment** \-mənt\ *n.*

res·tau·rant \'rest-r(-)ənt, -r-ˌänt, -rnt, -r-ˌånt\ *n.* [From French, there formed from the present participle of *restaurer* meaning "to restore".] A public eating house.

res·tau·ra·teur \ˌrest-r-ə-'tər\ *n.* A restaurant keeper.

rest·ful \'rest-fəl\ *adj.* **1** Giving rest; as, a *restful* chair. **2** Quiet; giving a feeling of rest; as, a *restful* scene. — **rest·ful·ly** \-fə-lē\ *adv.*

res·ti·tu·tion \ˌres-tə-'tüsh-n, -'tyüsh-n\ *n.* The restoring of anything to its rightful owner or the giving of an equivalent, as for loss or damage; as, to make *restitution* for property damage.

res·tive \'res-tiv\ *adj.* **1** Stubbornly resisting control; balky; as, a *restive* horse. **2** Uneasy; fidgety. The crowd grew *restive.* — **res·tive·ly,** *adv.*

rest·less \'res(t)-ləs\ *adj.* **1** Without rest; giving no rest; uneasy; as, a *restless* night. **2** Never resting or settled; always moving. — **rest·less·ly,** *adv.*

res·to·ra·tion \ˌrest-r-'āsh-n\ *n.* **1** The act of restoring or the state or fact of being restored. **2** Something that has been restored; especially, a representation of an original form, as of a fossil animal or of a building.

re·stor·a·tive \rē-'stōr-ət-iv, -'stȯr-\ *adj.* Of or relating to restoration; having the power to restore; as, a *restorative* medicine. — *n.* Something that restores, as to consciousness or health.

re·store \rē-'stōr, -'stȯr\ *v.;* **re·stored; re·stor·ing. 1** To give back; to return; as, to *restore* stolen goods. **2** To re-establish; to put back into existence or use; as, to *restore* harmony between two groups. **3** To bring or put back; to put again in possession; as, to *restore* a person to health; to *restore* a king to a throne. **4** To bring back to or put back into the former or original state; to repair; to renew; as, to *restore* an old statue. — **re·stor·er** \-'stōr-r, -'stȯr-r\ *n.*

re·strain \rē-'strān\ *v.* **1** To hold back from doing something; to keep in check; to curb; as, to *restrain* one's anger. **2** To limit or restrict, as power or trade. **3** To place under restraint or arrest; to deprive of liberty, as the mentally ill. — **re·strain·a·ble** \-'strā-nəb-l\ *adj.* — **re·strain·er** \-'strān-r\ *n.*

re·strained \rē-'strānd\ *adj.* Marked by restraint; disciplined; without excess or extravagance. — **re·strain·ed·ly** \-'strā-nəd-lē\ *adv.*

re·straint \rē-'strānt\ *n.* **1** The action of restraining. **2** The state of being restrained; as, held in *restraint.* **3** A means of restraining; a restraining force or influence. **4** Control over one's thoughts or feelings; reserve; constraint; as, to show *restraint* in one's manner.

re·strict \rē-'strikt\ *v.* To keep within bounds; to limit; as, a *restricted* diet. — **re·strict·ed,** *adj.*

re·stric·tion \rē-'striksh-n\ *n.* **1** The action of restricting or the state of being restricted. **2** A law or rule that restricts.

re·stric·tive \rē-'strik-tiv\ *adj.* **1** Serving to restrict; as, *restrictive* regulations. **2** In grammar, restricting or limiting the meaning of the word or words that it modifies; as, a *restrictive* clause or phrase. — **re·stric·tive·ly,** *adv.*

re·string \(')rē-'string\ *v.;* **re·strung** \-'strəng\; **re·string·ing.** To string again, as a tennis racket.

re·sult \rē-'zəlt\ *v.* **1** To come about as an effect. Disease *results* from infection. **2** To have as an effect; to finish; to end. The disease *results* in death. — *n.* **1** Something that results; an effect; a consequence; as, the *results* of the war. **2** A good effect. The treatment brought *results.* **3** An answer to an example or a problem; something found by investigation; as, a *result* obtained by adding.

re·sult·ant \rē-'zəlt-nt\ *adj.* Resulting; following as a consequence. — *n.* In physics, a single force equal to two or more specified forces and therefore able to produce the same effect upon a body as the joint action of the forces.

re·sume \rē-'züm\ *v.;* **re·sumed; re·sum·ing. 1** To take again; to occupy again; as, to *resume* one's seat. **2** To begin again or go back to, as after an interruption; as, to *resume* a game.

ré·su·mé \ˌrez-ə-'mā, ˌrā-zə-\ *n.* A summing up; a condensed statement.

re·sump·tion \rē-'zəm(p)sh-n\ *n.* The action of resuming; as, *resumption* of work.

re·sur·gence \rē-'sərj-n(t)s\ *n.* A rising again into life or activity. — **re·sur·gent** \-'sərj-nt\ *adj.*

res·ur·rect \ˌrez-r-'ekt\ *v.* **1** To raise from the dead; to bring back to life. **2** To bring to view or into use again; as, to *resurrect* an old song.

res·ur·rec·tion \ˌrez-r-'eksh-n\ *n.* **1** The action of resurrecting. **2** [with a capital] The rising of Christ from the dead. **3** A restoration, as of strength or vigor; a bringing back, as into view or use.

re·sus·ci·tate \rē-'səs-ə-ˌtāt\ *v.;* **re·sus·ci·tat·ed; re·sus·ci·tat·ing.** To revive from unconsciousness or apparent death. — **re·sus·ci·ta·tion** \-ˌsəs-ə-'tāsh-n\ *n.* — **re·sus·ci·ta·tive** \-'səs-ə-ˌtāt-iv\ *adj.*

ret \'ret\ *v.;* **ret·ted; ret·ting.** To soak or expose to moisture, as flax, hemp, or timber.

re·tail \'rē-ˌtāl\ *n.* The sale of goods directly to the consumer. — *adj.* **1** Of or relating to the retailing of goods. **2** Engaged in retailing; as, a *retail* grocer. — *v.* **1** To sell at retail. **2** \rē-'tāl\ To relate in detail or to one person after another; as, to *retail* gossip. — **re·tail·er** \'rē-ˌtāl-r, rē-'tāl-r\ *n.*

re·tain \rē-'tān\ *v.* **1** To keep in a fixed place or condition. Some metals *retain* heat for hours. **2** To hold in possession or use; as, to *retain* knowledge. **3** To employ by paying a retainer. — **re·tain·a·ble** \-'tā-nəb-l\ *adj.*

re·tain·er \rē-'tān-r\ *n.* A fee paid to engage services, especially of a lawyer.

re·tain·er \rē-'tān-r\ *n.* **1** One that retains. **2** A servant or follower in a wealthy household.

re·take \(')rē-'tāk\ *v.;* **re·took** \-'tu̇k\; **re·tak·en** \-'tāk-n\; **re·tak·ing. 1** To take or receive again. **2** To photograph again. — \'rē-ˌtāk\ *n.* A retaking of a scene, as in a motion picture.

re·tal·i·ate \rē-'tal-ē-ˌāt\ *v.;* **re·tal·i·at·ed; re·tal·i·at·ing.** To return like for like, especially evil for evil; to make requital. — **re·tal·i·a·tion** \-ˌtal-ē-'āsh-n\ *n.* — **re·tal·ia·to·ry** \-'tal-yə-ˌtōr-ē, -'tal-ē-ə-, -ˌtȯr-ē\ *adj.*

re·tard \rē-'tärd, -'tȧrd\ *v.* To slow up; to keep back, hinder, or delay. — For synonyms see *delay.* — **re·tar·da·tion** \ˌrē-ˌtär-'dāsh-n, -ˌtȧr-\ *n.*

retch \'rech\ *v.* To vomit or try to vomit.

re·ten·tion \rē-'tench-n\ *n.* The act of retaining or state of being retained.

re·ten·tive \rē-'tent-iv\ *adj.* Having ability to retain; especially, having a good memory.

ret·i·cence \'ret-ə-sən(t)s\ *n.* Reticent nature; the quality of being secretive.

ret·i·cent \'ret-ə-sənt\ *adj.* Inclined to be silent or secretive; uncommunicative. — **ret·i·cent·ly,** *adv.*

ret·i·na \'ret-n-ə\ *n.;* *pl.* **ret·i·nas** \-n-əz\ or **ret·i·nae** \-n-ˌē\. The sensitive membrane in the back part of the eye that receives the image formed by the lens and is connected with the brain by the optic nerve. — **ret·i·nal** \-n-əl\ *adj.*

ret·i·nue \'ret-n-ˌü, -ˌyü\ *n.* The servants, followers, or attendants of a distinguished person.

re·tire \rē-'tīr\ *v.;* **re·tired; re·tir·ing. 1** To withdraw; to retreat. The troops *retired.* **2** To give up or cause to give up an office or position. **3** To go to bed. **4** To withdraw from circulation, as bonds. **5** In games, as baseball, to put out a player or side.

re·tired \rē-'tīrd\ *adj.* **1** Quiet; hidden; secret; as, a *retired* spot in the woods. **2** Withdrawn from active duties or business. **3** Received by, or due to, a person who has retired; as, *retired* pay.

re·tire·ment \rē-'tīr-mənt\ *n.* **1** The act of retiring or state of being retired.

re·tir·ing \rē-'tīr-ing\ *adj.* Shy; reserved.

retook. Past tense of *retake.*

re·tort \rē-'tȯrt\ *v.* **1** To answer back; to reply angrily or sharply. **2** To reply, as to an argument, with a counter argument. — *n.* A quick, witty, sarcastic, or angry reply, especially one that turns the first speaker's words against him.

re·tort \rē-'tȯrt\ *n.* A vessel used in laboratories for distilling or decomposing substances by heat.

re·touch \(')rē-'təch\ *v.* To touch or work again; to touch up something so as to improve it; as, to *retouch* a photograph.

re·trace, *v.;* **re·traced; re·trac·ing. 1** \(')rē-'trās\ To trace over again, as a drawing. **2** \rē-\ To trace the early history of something. **3** \(ˈ)rē-\ To go over again in a reverse direction, as one's way.

re·tract \rē-ˈtrakt\ *v.* **1** To draw or pull back or in. A cat can *retract* its claws. **2** To withdraw, as an offer, a statement, or an accusation; to take back.

re·tract·a·ble \rē-ˈtrak-təb-l\ *adj.* Capable of being drawn up, back, or in.

re·trac·tile \rē-ˈtrakt-l\ *adj.* **1** Retractable. **2** Showing retraction.

re·trac·tion \rē-ˈtraksh-n\ *n.* **1** The act of retracting or the condition of being retracted. **2** A statement retracting something previously said or published. **3** Power to retract.

re·trac·tor \rē-ˈtrakt-r\ *n.* One that retracts, as a muscle that draws in or back an organ or part.

re·tread \(ˈ)rē-ˈtred\ *v.;* **re·tread·ed**; **re·tread·ing.** To put a new tread on. — \ˈrē-ˌtred\ *n.* A retreaded tire.

re·treat \rē-ˈtrēt\ *n.* **1** The act of withdrawing from what is dangerous, difficult, or disagreeable. **2** A withdrawal, especially a forced withdrawal, of troops or ships from the enemy. **3** The signal for a withdrawal of troops or ships. **4** A signal given in the army by drum, trumpet, or bugle after evening roll call or parade. **5** A place where people can go for safety, quiet, or rest; a refuge. — *v.* To make a retreat; to withdraw.

re·trench \rē-ˈtrench\ *v.* To reduce; to cut down; to economize. — **re·trench·ment** \-mənt\ *n.*

re·tri·al \(ˈ)rē-ˈtrī-əl, -ˈtrīl\ *n.* A second trial.

ret·ri·bu·tion \ˌre-trə-ˈbyüsh-n\ *n.* Something given in payment for an offense; punishment.

re·trib·u·tive \rē-ˈtrib-yət-iv\ *adj.* Of or relating to retribution; bringing retribution.

re·trib·u·to·ry \rē-ˈtrib-yə-ˌtōr-ē, -ˌtȯr-ē\ *adj.* Retributive.

re·trieve \rē-ˈtrēv\ *v.;* **re·trieved**; **re·triev·ing.** **1** To find and bring in killed or wounded game; as, a dog that *retrieves* well. **2** To recover, restore, or repair, as a loss or damage; to make good; as, to *retrieve* a damaged reputation.

re·triev·er \rē-ˈtrēv-r\ *n.* A dog used for retrieving game; especially, any of several dogs with water-resistant coats bred for this purpose.

ret·ro·ac·tive \ˌre-trō-ˈak-tiv, ˌrē-\ *adj.* Intended to apply or take effect at a date in the past.

ret·ro·grade \ˈre-trə-ˌgrād\ *adj.* **1** Going or inclined to go from a better to a worse state; degenerating. **2** Having a backward direction, motion, or tendency. — *v.;* **ret·ro·grad·ed**; **ret·ro·grad·ing.** **1** To go or appear to go backward; to recede. **2** To decline; to degenerate; to retrogress.

ret·ro·gress \ˌre-trə-ˈgres, ˌrē-\ *v.* To move backwards; to revert to an earlier state or condition. — **ret·ro·gres·sion** \-ˈgresh-n\ *n.*

ret·ro·spect \ˈre-trə-ˌspekt, ˈrē-\ *n.* A looking back on things past; a thinking of past events.

ret·ro·spec·tion \ˌre-trə-ˈspeksh-n, ˌrē-\ *n.* **1** The act or power of recalling the past. **2** A review of past events.

ret·ro·spec·tive \ˌre-trə-ˈspek-tiv, ˌrē-\ *adj.* **1** Directed backwards or toward the past; as, a *retrospective* view. **2** Characterized by or given to retrospection. — **ret·ro·spec·tive·ly**, *adv.*

retted. Past tense and past part. of *ret.*

retting. Pres. part. of *ret.*

re·turn \rē-ˈtərn\ *v.* **1** To come or go back. **2** To reply; to answer. "I'll not do it", he *returned.* **3** To make a report, especially officially, by submitting a statement. The jury *returned* a verdict. **4** To elect, as to a legislature; as, a candidate *returned* by a large majority. **5** To bring, carry, send, or put back; to restore; as, to *return* a book to the library. **6** To yield; to produce. The farm *returned* a poor crop. **7** To repay; as, to *return* borrowed money. **8** To send or say in response or reply; as, to *return* thanks. — *n.* **1** The act of a person or thing that returns; a going or coming back; as, to await someone's *return.* **2** The act of bringing, taking, or sending something back. **3** A person or thing that returns or is returned. **4** The profit gained from labor or a business deal; as, a good *return* on an investment. **5** An account or report; as, election *returns.* — *adj.* Having to do with a return; as, a *return* ticket; a *return* game.

re·turn·a·ble \rē-ˈtər-nəb-l\ *adj.* **1** That may be returned; as, *returnable* bottles. **2** That must be returned; as, a library book *returnable* in two weeks.

re·union \rē-ˈyün-yən\ *n.* **1** The act of reuniting or the state of being reunited. **2** A reuniting of persons after separation; as, a class *reunion.*

re·unite \ˌrē-yü-ˈnīt\ *v.;* **re·unit·ed**; **re·unit·ing.** To come or bring together after a separation.

Rev. Abbreviation for *Reverend.*

rev \ˈrev\ *n.* A revolution of a motor. — *v.;* **revved**; **rev·ving.** To increase, or sometimes decrease, the speed of; as, to *rev* up a motor.

re·vamp \(ˈ)rē-ˈvamp\ *v.* To repair, especially by giving a new form or appearance to old materials.

re·veal \rē-ˈvēl\ *v.* **1** To make known; to explain, tell, or show; as, to *reveal* a secret. **2** To open up to view; as, a doorway *revealing* a comfortable room.

rev·eil·le \ˈrev-l-ē\ *n.* [From French imperative *reveillez!* meaning "wake up!".] A signal sounded at about sunrise on a bugle or drum to call soldiers or sailors to duty.

rev·el \ˈrev-l\ *v.;* **rev·eled** or **rev·elled**; **rev·el·ing** or **rev·el·ling** \-l(-)ing\. **1** To be gay and noisy. **2** To take great delight in something; as, to *revel* in a good ball game. — *n.* A noisy or merry celebration. — **rev·el·er** or **rev·el·ler** \-l(-)ər\ *n.*

rev·e·la·tion \ˌrev-l-ˈāsh-n\ *n.* **1** A revealing to others of something previously unknown to them; a disclosure. **2** That which is revealed. **3** [with a capital] The last book of the Bible.

rev·el·ry \ˈrev-l-rē\ *n.; pl.* **rev·el·ries.** Reveling; boisterous merrymaking.

re·venge \rē-ˈvenj\ *v.;* **re·venged**; **re·veng·ing.** To inflict harm or injury in return for a wrong; to exact satisfaction; to avenge. — *n.* **1** The act of revenging; desire to return evil for evil. **2** An opportunity for getting satisfaction, as a return match with an opponent who has defeated one.

rev·e·nue \'rev-n-ˌü, -n-ˌyü\ *n.* **1** Income received from any source. **2** Government income, as from taxes and duties.

re·ver·ber·ate \rē-'vərb-r-ˌāt\ *v.;* **re·ver·ber·at·ed; re·ver·ber·at·ing.** To resound; to echo. The shot *reverberated* among the hills. — **re·ver·ber·a·tion** \-ˌvərb-r-'āsh-n\ *n.*

re·vere \rē-'vir\ *v.;* **re·vered; re·ver·ing.** To honor and respect; to venerate.

rev·er·ence \'rev-rn(t)s, -r(-)ən(t)s\ *n.* **1** Honor and respect mixed with love and awe. **2** A sign of respect, as a bow or curtsy. — *v.;* **rev·er·enced; rev·er·enc·ing.** To regard with reverence.

rev·er·end \'rev-rnd, -r(-)ənd\ *adj.* Worthy of honor or respect — used with a capital as a title for clergymen.

rev·er·ent \'rev-rnt, -r(-)ənt\ *adj.* Very respectful; showing reverence. — **rev·er·ent·ly,** *adv.*

rev·er·en·tial \ˌrev-r-'ench-l\ *adj.* Reverent. — **rev·er·en·tial·ly** \-'ench-l-ē\ *adv.*

rev·er·ie or **rev·ery** \'rev-r(-)ē\ *n.; pl.* **rev·er·ies.** **1** The condition of being lost in thought; as, to sit in dreamy *reverie.* **2** A daydream.

re·vers·al \rē-'vərs-l\ *n.* The act or the process of reversing.

re·verse \rē-'vərs\ *adj.* **1** Turned back so as to move or face in an opposite direction; opposite or contrary; as, *reverse* order. **2** Causing movement backward; as, a *reverse* gear. — *n.* **1** That which is directly contrary to something else; the opposite. **2** A complete change, as from better to worse; a defeat; a loss. **3** The back; as, the *reverse* of a coin. **4** In machinery, a reverse gear or motion; as, to put a car in *reverse.* — *v.;* **re·versed; re·vers·ing.** **1** To turn a thing upside down, inside out, or completely around; as, to *reverse* the cloth. **2** To set aside or change; as, to *reverse* the jury's decision. **3** To cause to go in an opposite direction; to put into reverse, as a car. — **re·vers·er** \-'vərs-r\ *n.*

re·vers·i·ble \rē-'vər-səb-l\ *adj.* Capable of reversing or being reversed. — **re·vers·i·bly** \-sə-blē\ *adv.*

re·ver·sion \rē-'vərzh-n\ *n.* **1** A right of future possession, as of property or a title. **2** The act of reverting, as to a former faith. **3** In biology, a return toward some ancestral type; a throwback.

re·vert \rē-'vərt\ *v.* **1** To return; to come or go back. **2** To undergo reversion.

revery. Variant of *reverie.*

re·view \rē-'vyü\ *v.* **1** To look at a thing again; to study or examine again; as, to *review* a lesson. **2** To make a formal inspection, as of troops. **3** To write a criticism of, as a book or play. **4** To look back on; as, to *review* accomplishments. — *n.* **1** A general examination or summary of a period or topic; as, a *review* of today's news. **2** A repetition of a lesson at a later date. **3** A critical judgment, as of a book or play; a periodical publishing such articles. **4** A revue. **5** An inspection. — **re·view·er** \-'vyü-ər, -'vyu̇r\ *n.*

re·vile \rē-'vīl\ *v.;* **re·viled; re·vil·ing.** To subject to abuse, especially by loud scolding; to rail at.

re·vise \rē-'vīz\ *v.;* **re·vised; re·vis·ing.** **1** To look over something written, in order to improve or correct it; as, to *revise* printer's proofs. **2** To make a new version of; as, to *revise* a textbook. **3** To change; to amend; as, to *revise* an opinion; to *revise* a law. — **re·vis·er** or **re·vi·sor** \-'vīz-r\ *n.*

re·vi·sion \rē-'vizh-n\ *n.* **1** A revising; an examination to correct or improve. **2** A revised version.

re·viv·al \rē-'vīv-l\ *n.* **1** A reviving of interest, as in art, literature, or religion. **2** A new publication or presentation, as of a book or play. **3** A renewed flourishing; as, a *revival* of business. **4** A meeting or series of meetings conducted by a preacher to arouse religious emotions or to make converts.

re·viv·al·ist \rē-'vīv-l-əst\ *n.* One who conducts revivals.

re·vive \rē-'vīv\ *v.;* **re·vived; re·viv·ing.** **1** To bring back or come back to life, consciousness, or activity; to make or become fresh or strong again. **2** To bring back into use; as, to *revive* an old fashion. — **re·viv·er** \-'vīv-r\ *n.*

rev·o·ca·ble \'rev-ə-kəb-l\ *adj.* Capable of being revoked.

rev·o·ca·tion \ˌrev-ə-'kāsh-n\ *n.* The act of revoking; a repeal or annulment, as of a law or a decree.

re·voke \rē-'vōk\ *v.;* **re·voked; re·vok·ing.** **1** To put an end to by withdrawing, repealing, or canceling, as a law, order, or privilege; to annul; as, to have a driver's license *revoked* for reckless driving. **2** In card playing, to make a revoke. — *n.* In card playing, a failure to follow suit when able to do so.

re·volt \rē-'vōlt; *sometimes,* -'vȯlt\ *n.* **1** The act of rising up against established authority; rebellion; as, a people in *revolt* against a tyrant. **2** An uprising. — *v.* **1** To rebel. **2** To be, or to cause to be, disgusted or shocked.

re·volt·ing \-ing\ *adj.* Extremely offensive; disgusting. — **re·volt·ing·ly,** *adv.*

rev·o·lu·tion \ˌrev-l-'üsh-n\ *n.* **1** The action or motion of revolving; turning round a center or axis; rotation. **2** The action or motion of a heavenly body in going round in an orbit, or the time taken in such a course. **3** A single complete turn, as of a wheel or a phonograph record. **4** A complete or radical change, as in thinking or in manner of living or working; as, a *revolution* in education. **5** [often with a capital] A complete and radical change in a system of government brought about by the people of a country, especially by war or rebellion.

rev·o·lu·tion·ary \ˌrev-l-'üsh-n-ˌer-ē\ *adj.* Of or relating to revolution; tending toward, or desiring, revolution; causing a revolution; as, *revolutionary* ideas; a *revolutionary* invention. — *n.; pl.* **rev·o·lu·tion·ar·ies.** A revolutionist.

Revolutionary War. The American Revolution.

rev·o·lu·tion·ist \ˌrev-l-'üsh-n-əst\ *n.* One who takes part in a revolution or believes in revolution as a means of change; a revolutionary.

rev·o·lu·tion·ize \ˌrev-l-'üsh-n-ˌīz\ *v.;* **rev·o·lu-**

tion·ized; **rev·o·lu·tion·iz·ing.** To change completely; to cause to be entirely different; as, to *revolutionize* a manufacturing process; the airplane has *revolutionized* overseas travel.

re·volve \rē-ˈvälv\ *v.;* **re·volved**; **re·volv·ing. 1** To turn over and over in the mind; to reflect upon; as, to *revolve* an idea. **2** To go in a circular course around an axis or in a curved path around some center. **3** To cause to turn round; to turn; to rotate, as a wheel. **4** To come around again; to recur. Seasons, years, and centuries all *revolve.* **5** To circulate; as, an idea *revolving* in the mind.

re·volv·er \rē-ˈvälv-r\ *n.* One that revolves; especially, a pistol having a revolving cylinder holding several cartridges which may be discharged in succession.

re·vue \rē-ˈvyü\ *n.* A theatrical entertainment consisting of a number of scenes in which events of the past year, especially plays, are burlesqued, together with dancing and singing and specialty acts.

re·vul·sion \rē-ˈvəlsh-n\ *n.* **1** A strong pulling or drawing back or away. **2** A violent change of feeling; especially, a strong sudden reaction or change in feeling.

re·ward \rē-ˈwȯrd\ *v.* To make a suitable return for something, especially for some service, achievement, or merit; to repay. — *n.* Something given or offered in return for some service; especially, money offered for the return of something lost or stolen or for the capture of a criminal.

re·word \(ˈ)rē-ˈwərd\ *v.* To state in different words; as, to *reword* a question.

re·write \(ˈ)rē-ˈrīt\ *v.;* **re·wrote** \-ˈrōt\; **re·writ·ten** \-ˈrit-n\. **1** To write over again, especially in a different form. **2** To put into form for publication in a newspaper material turned in by a reporter. — \ˈrē-ˌrīt\ *n.* A rewritten newspaper article.

R.F.D. \ˈär-ˌef-ˈdē, ˈär-\. Abbreviation for *Rural Free Delivery.*

rhap·so·dy \ˈrap-səd-ē\ *n.; pl.* **rhap·so·dies. 1** An expression, either spoken or written, of extravagant praise or ecstasy. **2** A musical composition of irregular form. — **rhap·sod·ic** \rap-ˈsäd-ik\ or **rhap·sod·i·cal** \-ik-l\ *adj.*

rhea \ˈrē-ə\ *n.* A three-toed South American ostrich, smaller than the African ostrich.

rhe·o·stat \ˈrē-ə-ˌstat\ *n.* A device for regulating electric current by use of variable resistances.

rhet·o·ric \ˈret-r-ik\ *n.* The art of speaking or writing effectively; especially, the art of writing prose. — **rhe·tor·i·cal** \rə-ˈtȯr-ik-l, -ˈtär-\ *adj.*

rhetorical question. A question asked merely for effect and with no answer expected.

rheum \ˈrüm\ *n.* A watery discharge, especially from the eyes or nose. — **rheumy** \ˈrü-mē\ *adj.*

rheu·mat·ic \rü-ˈmat-ik\ *adj.* Of, relating to, afflicted with, or caused by rheumatism. — *n.* **1** A person who has rheumatism. **2** [in the plural] *Dial.* Rheumatism.

rheu·ma·tism \ˈrü-mə-ˌtiz-m, ˈru̇m-ə-\ *n.* Any of various conditions affecting the muscles, joints, and fibrous tissues of the body and marked by pain, inflammation, and, sometimes, crippling.

rhine·stone \ˈrīn-ˌstōn\ *n.* A brilliant, colorless imitation diamond made of glass or paste.

rhi·no \ˈrī-ˌnō\ *n.; pl.* **rhi·nos.** A rhinoceros.

rhi·noc·er·os \rī-ˈnäs-r(-)əs\ *n.; pl.* **rhi·noc·er·os·es** or **rhi·noc·er·os.** A large, thick-skinned, three-toed animal of Africa and Asia, with one or two heavy upright horns on the snout.

rhi·zome \ˈrī-ˌzōm\ *n.* An elongated horizontal underground stem that sends out leafy shoots from the upper side and roots from the lower side; a rootstock.

rho·do·den·dron \ˌrōd-ə-ˈden-drən\ *n.* A bush or tree that has glossy, usually evergreen, oval leaves and clusters of white, pink, or purplish flowers.

rhom·boid \ˈräm-ˌbȯid\ *n.* A parallelogram in which the angles are oblique and the adjacent sides are unequal. — *adj.* Shaped like a rhomboid or a rhombus.

rhom·bus \ˈräm-bəs\ *n.; pl.* **rhom·bus·es** \-bə-səz\ or **rhom·bi** \-ˌbī\. Any equilateral parallelogram that is not a square.

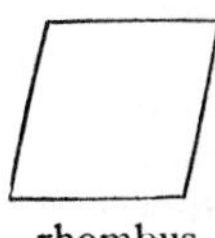
rhombus

rhu·barb \ˈrü-ˌbärb, -ˌbȧrb\ *n.* **1** A plant with broad green leaves and thick, juicy, pinkish stems which are used for food. **2** *Slang.* A heated dispute or controversy, especially on the playing field during a game.

rhumba. Variant of *rumba.*

rhyme or **rime** \ˈrīm\ *n.* **1** Correspondence or similarity in two or more words or lines of verse of final sounds beginning with an accented vowel, as in *play* and *say* or *await* and *sedate.* **2** One of the words whose sounds agree in this way. "Season" is a *rhyme* for "reason." **3** Verse composition in rhyme; poetry. — *v.;* **rhymed** or **rimed**; **rhym·ing** or **rim·ing. 1** To make rhymes; to write poetry. **2** To end with a similar sound. "Cat" *rhymes* with "rat". — **rhym·er** or **rim·er** \ˈrīm-r\ *n.*

rhythm \ˈrith-m\ *n.* **1** The flow of rising and falling sounds in language, produced in verse by a regular recurrence of heavy and light, or stressed and unstressed, syllables; cadence. **2** The effect gained by the use of such cadence. **3** In music, a flow of sound marked by accented beats coming at regular intervals. **4** Any movement in which some action or element recurs regularly; as, the *rhythm* of breathing.

rhyth·mic \ˈrith-mik\ or **rhyth·mi·cal** \-mik-l\ *adj.* Marked by rhythm; showing rhythm. — **rhyth·mi·cal·ly** \-mik-l(-)ē\ *adv.*

rib \ˈrib\ *n.* **1** One of the series of curved bones that are joined in pairs to the spine of man and animals, and help to stiffen the body wall. **2** Something that is like a rib in shape or use, as a cross timber in the frame of a boat. **3** One of the parallel ridges in a knitted or woven fabric. **4** One of the primary veins of a leaf or a nerve in an insect's wing. — *v.;* **ribbed**; **rib·bing. 1** To furnish or strengthen with ribs. **2** To mark with ridges; as, a *ribbed* fabric. **3** *Slang.* To make fun of; to tease.

rib·ald \'rib-ld\ *adj.* Coarse, offensive, or obscene in language; as, a *ribald* joke.

rib·ald·ry \'rib-l-drē\ *n.; pl.* **rib·ald·ries.** Ribald language.

rib·bon \'rib-n\ *n.* **1** A narrow strip of cloth, as velvet or silk, used for trimming or for badges; as, hair *ribbons.* **2** A narrow strip or shred; [in the plural] tatters; as, torn to *ribbons.* **3** An inked tape for a typewriter. — **rib·boned** \-nd\ *adj.*

ri·bo·fla·vin \ˌrī-bə-'flāv-n\ *n.* A substance of the vitamin-B complex that promotes growth, found especially in whey, green leaves, yeast, liver, and heart — called also *vitamin* B_2.

rice \'rīs\ *n.* **1** An annual marsh grass three to four feet high cultivated in warm regions. **2** The seed or grain of this grass, used for food.

rice

rice·bird \'rīs-ˌbərd\ *n.* Any of several small birds common in rice fields; especially, in the southern United States, the bobolink.

ric·er \'rīs-r\ *n.* A form of potato masher in which the cooked vegetable is pressed through small holes.

rich \'rich\ *adj.* **1** Wealthy; well supplied with money or property; as, a *rich* person. **2** Costly; valuable; as, *rich* robes. **3** Highly seasoned, fatty, oily, or sweet; as, *rich* cake; a *rich* meal. **4** Deep and pleasing in color; vivid; as, a *rich* green. **5** Mellow and full in tone; as, a *rich* voice. **6** High in combustible content; as, a *rich* mixture of gas and air. **7** Plentiful; abundant; as, a *rich* crop. **8** Yielding large returns; fertile; fruitful; as, a *rich* mine; *rich* soil. **9** Humorous; entertaining; laughable. — **rich·ly** \-lē\ *adv.*

rich·es \'rich-əz\ *n. pl.* Wealth.

rick \'rik\ *n.* A stack, as of hay or grain, in the open air. — *v.* To heap up in ricks.

rick·ets \'rik-əts\ *n.* A deficiency disease, usually of children, marked by soft deformed bones and due to lack of vitamin D, calcium, and phosphorus.

rick·ett·sia \ri-'ket-sē-ə\ *n.; pl.* **rick·ett·si·as** \-sē-əz\ or **rick·ett·si·ae** \-sē-ˌē\. Any of various microorganisms that live usually in cells of insects and ticks but can cause serious diseases in persons.

rick·ety \'rik-ət-ē\ *adj.* **1** Affected with rickets. **2** Feeble; shaky; as, a *rickety* wagon.

rick·sha or **rick·shaw** \'rik-ˌshȯ\ *n.* A jinrikisha.

ric·o·chet \'rik-ə-ˌshā, ˌrik-ə-'shā\ *n.* A glancing rebound or skipping, as of a bullet along the ground. — *v.;* **ric·o·cheted** \-ˌshād, -'shād\; **ric·o·chet·ing** \-ˌshā-ing, -'shā-ing\. To skip with glancing rebounds, as a bullet.

rid \'rid\ *v.;* **rid** or **rid·ded**; **rid·ding.** To free; to clear; as, to *rid* a dog of fleas. — **be rid of** or **get rid of. 1** To be or become free from. **2** To dispose of.

rid·dance \'rid-n(t)s\ *n.* The act of ridding or the state of being rid of.

rid·den \'rid-n\. Past part. of *ride.* — *adj.* Dominated by; pressed down by; as, disease-*ridden.*

rid·dle \'rid-l\ *n.* A sieve with coarse meshes. — *v.;* **rid·dled**; **rid·dling** \-l(-)ing\. **1** To sift with a riddle. **2** To fill full of holes so as to make like a riddle; as, a boat *riddled* with shot.

rid·dle \'rid-l\ *n.* A puzzling question or statement whose answer is to be guessed; an enigma; a conundrum. — *v.;* **rid·dled**; **rid·dling** \-l(-)ing\. **1** To speak in riddles. **2** To explain; to solve.

ride \'rīd\ *v.;* **rode** \'rōd\; **rid·den** \'rid-n\; **rid·ing** \'rīd-ing\. **1** To go or be carried along on an animal's back or in or on a vehicle, as a boat, automobile, or airplane. **2** To sit on and control so as to be carried along; as, to *ride* a horse. **3** To float or move on the water; as, a boat *riding* at anchor. **4** To carry; to bear along. The team *rode* the coach off the field on their shoulders. **5** To support and carry its rider; as, a car that *rides* well. **6** To torment by constant nagging or teasing. — *n.* The act or fact of riding; a journey on an animal or on or in a vehicle.

rid·er \'rīd-r\ *n.* **1** A person who rides. **2** An addition to a document, often attached on a separate piece of paper. **3** An additional clause, often dealing with an unrelated subject, attached to a bill during its passage through a l wmaking body.

ridge \'rij\ *n.* **1** The back, especially the top of the back, of a four-footed animal. **2** A range of hills or mountains. **3** A raised line or strip; as, *ridges* of earth left in plowing. **4** The line made where two sloping surfaces come together; as, the *ridge* of a roof. — *v.;* **ridged**; **ridg·ing. 1** To form into a ridge or ridges. **2** To mark with ridges.

ridge·pole \'rij-ˌpōl\ *n.* The highest horizontal timber or pole in a sloping roof, to which the upper ends of the rafters are fastened.

ridgepole

ridgy \'rij-ē\ *adj.;* **ridg·i·er**; **ridg·i·est.** Having or rising in a ridge or ridges.

rid·i·cule \'rid-ə-ˌkyül\ *n.* Remarks or actions intended to make people laugh at a person or thing. — *v.;* **rid·i·culed**; **rid·i·cul·ing.** To make fun of; to laugh at, especially mockingly.

ri·dic·u·lous \rə-'dik-yə-ləs\ *adj.* Arousing or deserving ridicule; absurd. — For synonyms see *comical.* — **ri·dic·u·lous·ly**, *adv.*

rife \'rīf\ *adj.* Widespread; common; abounding. Rumors of a disaster were *rife.*

riff·raff \'rif-ˌraf\ *n.* **1** Trash. **2** The rabble.

ri·fle \'rīf-l\ *v.;* **ri·fled**; **ri·fling** \-l(-)ing\. **1** To ransack and rob or plunder. **2** To steal.

ri·fle \'rīf-l\ *v.;* **ri·fled**; **ri·fling** \-l(-)ing\. To groove the inside of a gun barrel with winding channels in order to increase the accuracy of fire. — *n.* A firearm with a rifled barrel; especially, such a firearm fired from the shoulder.

ri·fle·man \'rīf-l-mən\ *n.; pl.* **ri·fle·men** \-mən\. **1** A soldier armed with a rifle. **2** A person skilled in shooting with a rifle.

ri·fler \'rīf-l(-)ər\ *n.* One that rifles; a robber.

ri·fle·ry \'rīf-l-rē\ *n.* **1** Rifle fire. **2** Rifle shooting, especially at targets for practice.

rift \'rift\ *n.* An opening made by splitting or separation; a break; a cleft; a fissure; as, a *rift* in a bank of clouds. — *v.* To split; to divide.

rig \'rig\ *v.;* **rigged; rig·ging. 1** To fit with rigging, as a ship, or to fit the rigging of a ship, as to the masts and spars. **2** To outfit; to equip; to put in order for use; as, to *rig* up a cosy shelter. **3** To dress or clothe; as, to be *rigged* out in one's Sunday clothes. — *n.* **1** The definite shape, number, and arrangement of the sails and masts of a certain type of ship; as, a fore-and-aft *rig;* a schooner *rig.* **2** Clothes or dress, especially of an unusual type; as, a sports *rig.* **3** A carriage with its horse or horses. **4** Any equipment, outfit, or apparatus adopted for a special purpose. — **rig·ger,** *n.*

rig·ging \'rig-ing\ *n.* **1** The ropes and chains that hold and move the masts, sails, and spars of a ship. **2** Tackle; gear.

right \'rīt\ *adj.* **1** Straight; as, a *right* line. **2** Upright; perpendicular; having the axis perpendicular to the base; as, a *right* cone. **3** Suitable; proper; favorable; most convenient; as, to pick the *right* man for a job. **4** Just; upright. It is *right* to obey the law. **5** Conforming to fact or reason; not mistaken or wrong; correct; as the *right* answer to a problem. **6** Physically or mentally well. The child did not feel *right.* **7** Made to be placed or worn outward; as, the *right* side of a rug. **8** On the side of the body opposite the heart; located to the right of the body; as, the *right* hand. **9** Of or relating to a side corresponding to the right of the human body; as, the *right* side of the road. — *adv.* **1** In a right or straight line; directly; immediately; as, to stand *right* in front of someone. **2** Conforming to the standard of justice and duty; as, to live *right.* **3** In a suitable or proper manner. The players won because their coach had instructed them *right.* **4** According to fact or truth; truly; correctly; as, to tell a story *right.* **5** Exactly; precisely; as, *right* here and now. **6** In a great degree; extremely; very; as, to be *right* valiant; the *right* reverend. **7** Toward the right hand. The car turned *right* at the bridge. — **right along.** Without letup; continuously; as, to work *right along.* — **right away.** At once. — **right off.** Right away. — *n.* **1** Something that is right; something that is in keeping with moral law or that meets the approval of one's conscience. **2** Just action or decision; justice; as, to petition as a matter of *right.* **3** A power or privilege to which one has a natural, legal, or moral claim; as, the *right* to vote. **4** The side or part that is on or toward the right side. On the *right* was a deep hole. **5** In some lawmaking bodies, the seats occupied by the conservative members or the members occupying these seats. **6** Political conservatives collectively or the beliefs they hold. — **by right** or **by rights.** Rightly; properly. *By rights,* the job should be done over. — **to rights.** In order; as, to put a room *to rights.* — *v.* **1** To bring or restore a thing to the proper position; to set or become upright; as, to *right* a capsized boat. **2** To return (oneself) to one's balance or footing. The runner tripped but *righted* himself. **3** To do justice to; to restore rights to; as, to *right* the oppressed. **4** To avenge; to vindicate. **5** To make right something that has been wrong; to adjust; to correct. **6** To set in order; as, to *right* a room.

right angle. An angle formed by two lines that are perpendicular to each other. Watch hands at three o'clock form a *right angle.* — **right-an·gled** \'rīt-'ang-gld\ *adj.*

right angle

righ·teous \'rī-chəs\ *adj.* Doing or conforming to that which is right; free from wrong, guilt, or sin; just; worthy. — **righ·teous·ly,** *adv.*

right·ful \'rīt-fəl\ *adj.* **1** Conforming to what is right; just; fair; as, a *rightful* decision. **2** Having a legally right or just claim; as, the *rightful* owner. **3** Belonging or held by a legally just claim; as, a *rightful* inheritance. — **right·ful·ly** \-fə-lē\ *adv.*

right-hand \'rīt-ˌhand\ *adj.* **1** Being on the right; nearer the right hand than the left. **2** Right-handed. **3** Chiefly relied on; as, the president's *right-hand* man.

right-hand·ed \'rīt-'han-dəd\ *adj.* **1** Using the right hand more skillfully than the left. **2** Done or made with or for the right hand. **3** Having a structure with a clockwise turn or twist. — **right-hand·ed·ly** or **right-hand·ed,** *adv.*

right·ly \'rīt-lē\ *adv.* **1** Justly. **2** Properly; suitably. **3** Correctly; exactly.

right of way. 1 A right of passage over another person's land. **2** The land occupied by a railroad for its tracks; a strip of land, occupied by a public road or by a power transmission line. **3** The right of certain traffic to proceed ahead of other traffic.

right triangle. A triangle one of whose angles is a right angle.

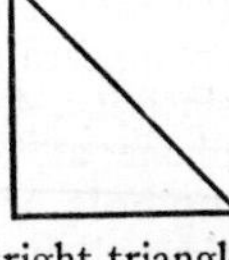
right triangle

rig·id \'rij-əd\ *adj.* **1** Firm; stiff; not flexible; as, *rigid* as a statue. **2** Strict; as, *rigid* rules. **3** Precise; accurate; as, *rigid* reasoning. — **ri·gid·i·ty** \ri-'jid-ət-ē\ *n.* — **rig·id·ly** \'rij-əd-lē\ *adv.*

rig·ma·role \'rig-m(-)ə-ˌrōl\ *n.* Confused, meaningless, or foolish talk.

rig·or \'rig-r\ *n.* **1** The condition of being stiff or rigid. **2** Strictness; harshness; severity; as, the *rigors* of a northern winter. **3** A severe shuddering, as in a chill.

rig·or·ous \'rig-r(-)əs\ *adj.* Strict; harsh; severe. — **rig·or·ous·ly,** *adv.*

rile \'rīl\ *v.;* **riled; ril·ing.** To roil.

rill \'ril\ *n.* A very small brook; a rivulet.

rim \'rim\ *n.* **1** A border or edge, usually of something curving or circular; as, the *rim* of a cup. **2** The outer, circular part of a wheel, as of an automobile. — *v.;* **rimmed; rim·ming. 1** To furnish with a rim. **2** To go or be run around the rim of.

rime \'rīm\ *n.* **1** White frost; hoar frost. **2** A covering or deposit resembling white frost; as, salt *rime* on rocks of the seacoast. — **rimy** \'rī-mē\ *adj.*

rime \'rīm\. Variant of *rhyme.*

rind \'rīnd, 'rīn\ *n.* A firm outer covering, as the peel of fruit or the skin of bacon.

rin·der·pest \'rind-r-ˌpest\ *n.* An acute virus infection of cattle and, sometimes, sheep and goats.

ring \'ring\ *n.* **1** A circular band, often of precious metal set with gems, worn usually on a finger as an ornament or token. **2** Any circular band used for holding or fastening; as, a napkin *ring;* a key *ring.* **3** Anything circular, as an object, figure, or arrangement; as, a *ring* of smoke. **4** A combination of persons formed for some, often corrupt, purpose; as, a gambling *ring.* **5** A place for a contest or display; as, a boxing *ring;* a rodeo *ring.* **6** One of the circular marks seen in the cross section of most tree trunks, marking the annual growth of spring and summer wood. — *v.;* **ringed; ring·ing** \'ring-ing\. **1** To surround with or as if with a ring; to encircle. **2** To provide with a ring or rings. **3** In games such as quoits, to throw the ring exactly over the mark. **4** To form or take the shape of a ring.

ring \'ring\ *v.;* **rang** \'rang\ or **rung** \'rəng\; **rung; ring·ing** \'ring-ing\. **1** To sound clearly when struck, as a bell, coin, or other metallic object; to resound. Swords *rang* on the helmets. **2** To cause something to make a clear, metallic sound by striking; as, to *ring* the bell. **3** To be filled with a ringing sound; as, ears *ringing* from the explosion. **4** To fill or be filled with talk or rumors. The land *rang* with the news of the battle. **5** To announce or call by or as if by ringing; as, to *ring* an alarm; to *ring* for the maid. **6** To have a particular quality, as of truth or falsity; as, a story that *rings* true. — *n.* **1** A sound made by or as if by a metal object that has been struck; as, the *ring* of steel against stone. **2** Any loud resounding noise; as, the *ring* of their shouts. **3** A characteristic sound or appearance; as, a story that had the *ring* of sincerity. **4** The sounding of a bell, as of a telephone; as, to hang up after five *rings.*

ring·bolt \'ring-ˌbōlt\ *n.* A bolt with a ring through one end.

ring·er \'ring-r\ *n.* One that rings or surrounds, as a quoit that falls right over the peg.

ring·er \'ring-r\ *n.* **1** One that rings, as a bell or chime. **2** One that enters a competition under a false name. **3** One that closely resembles another.

ring·lead·er \'ring-ˌlēd-r\ *n.* A leader, especially of a group of persons who cause trouble.

ring·let \'ring-lət\ *n.* **1** A small ring. **2** A curl.

ring·mas·ter \'ring-ˌmast-r\ *n.* A person in charge of performances within a ring, as at a circus.

ring·worm \'ring-ˌwərm\ *n.* A contagious skin disease, caused by fungi and characterized by ring-shaped discolored patches.

rink \'ringk\ *n.* An area, usually enclosed, used for skating or as a playing field in some games.

rinse \'rin(t)s\ *v.;* **rinsed; rins·ing. 1** To wash lightly with water. **2** To remove something, as dirt or excess soap, by washing lightly, especially in water. **3** To color or condition the hair with a rinse. — *n.* **1** A rinsing; a light washing. **2** A preparation for coloring or conditioning the hair.

ri·ot \'rī-ət\ *n.* **1** Noisy, disorderly conduct; uproar. **2** A disturbance of the peace by a number of persons gathered to gain some purpose by unlawful, violent means. **3** A vivid and confused display; as, a *riot* of color. **4** *Slang.* Someone or something that is very amusing. — *v.* **1** To take part in a riot. **2** To create a riot. — **ri·ot·er** \-r\ *n.*

ri·ot·ous \'rī-ət-əs\ *adj.* **1** Engaged in or involving riot. **2** Of the nature of a riot; noisy; tumultuous. — **ri·ot·ous·ly**, *adv.*

rip \'rip\ *v.;* **ripped; rip·ping. 1** To divide or separate by cutting or tearing; to cut or tear roughly or quickly. **2** To become torn. This cloth *rips* easily. **3** To saw or split lengthwise of the grain; as, to *rip* a board. — For synonyms see *tear.* — *n.* A torn place made by ripping; a tear.

rip \'rip\ *n.* A body of water made rough by the meeting of opposing currents or tides.

rip cord. The cord which is pulled by a jumper to open his parachute.

ripe \'rīp\ *adj.;* **rip·er; rip·est. 1** Ready to be picked or harvested; mature; as, *ripe* fruit. **2** In the best condition for use; mellow; as, *ripe* cheese. **3** Fully developed; as, *ripe* minds. **4** Ready; prepared; as, plans *ripe* for action. — **ripe·ly**, *adv.*

rip·en \'rīp-n\ *v.;* **rip·ened; rip·en·ing** \-n(-)ing\. To grow or make ripe.

rip·ple \'rip-l\ *v.;* **rip·pled; rip·pling** \-l(-)ing\. **1** To form little waves, as a stream in passing over a rough, shallow place. **2** To make a sound like water running over a shallow place. Laughter *rippled* through the crowd. — *n.* **1** A little wave or a series of little waves. **2** A sound of rippling.

rip·saw \'rip-ˌsȯ\ *n.* A saw with coarse teeth used for cutting wood in the direction of the grain.

rise \'rīz\ *v.;* **rose** \'rōz\; **ris·en** \'riz-n\; **ris·ing** \'rī-zing\. **1** To move to a higher position; to climb; to mount upward. The sun *rose.* **2** To extend upward. The hill *rises* to a great height. **3** To come to life after dying. Christ is *risen.* **4** To reach a higher level, position, rank, or office. **5** To do one's best to overcome a difficulty; as, to *rise* to every emergency. **6** To get up or stand up from kneeling, lying, or sitting. **7** To rebel. The barons *rose* against the king. **8** To increase, as in price, degree, or loudness; as, *rising* anger. **9** To happen; to come about; to begin. A rumor *rose.* **10** To come into sight. Land *rose* on the left. **11** To have a source or origin. This river *rises* in the hills. **12** To swell or puff up; as, to let the dough *rise.* — *n.* **1** The act of rising; ascent. **2** An upward slope or a part that slopes upward; as, the *rise* of a roof. **3** A piece of land higher than its surroundings. **4** An increase or advance, as in price, value, or fame. **5** The source of a thing; origin; as, the *rise* of a stream.

ris·er \'rīz-r\ *n.* **1** One that rises; as, an early *riser.* **2** The upright piece of a step in a stairway.

ris·i·bil·i·ty \ˌriz-ə-'bil-ət-ē\ *n.; pl.* **ris·i·bil·i·ties.** **1** The ability or tendency to laugh. **2** [in the plural] A person's sense of humor.

ris·i·ble \'riz-əb-l\ *adj.* **1** Having the ability to laugh; disposed to laugh. **2** Of or relating to laughter; used in laughter; as, *risible* muscles.

risk \'risk\ *n.* Exposure to possible loss or injury; danger; peril. — For synonyms see *danger.* **—** *v.* **1** To expose to danger or injury; as, to *risk* one's life. **2** To take the risk of; as, to *risk* danger.

risky \'ris-kē\ *adj.;* **risk·i·er; risk·i·est.** Dangerous; having or accompanied by risk or danger.

ris·qué \ris-'kā\ *adj.* Verging upon the indelicate or improper; as, *risqué* stories.

rite \'rīt\ *n.* A prescribed form for conducting a ceremony. — For synonyms see *ceremony.*

rit·u·al \'rich-ə-wəl, 'rich-l\ *adj.* Having to do with rites or rituals. **—** *n.* **1** The form of worship established by custom or law; as, the Jewish *ritual.* **2** The fixed forms or traditional acts that are used in a ceremony; as, an initiation *ritual.* **3** A book containing ceremonial forms. — **rit·u·al·ly** \'rich-l-ē, -ə-wə-lē\ *adv.*

ri·val \'rīv-l\ *n.* **1** One of two or more persons trying to get something only one of them can have; a competitor; as, a business *rival.* **2** One that matches another in the possession of certain important qualities. **—** *adj.* Having the same claims or purposes; competing. **—** *v.;* **ri·valed** or **ri·valled; ri·val·ing** or **ri·val·ling** \-l(-)ing\. **1** To be in competition with. **2** To strive to equal or excel. **3** To equal or match.

ri·val·ry \'rīv-l-rē\ *n.; pl.* **ri·val·ries.** The act of rivaling; the state of being a rival; competition.

rive \'rīv\ *v.;* **rived** \'rīvd\; **rived** \'rīvd\ or **riv·en** \'riv-n\; **riv·ing** \'rī-ving\. **1** To tear apart. **2** To split.

riv·er \'riv-r\ *n.* **1** A natural stream of water larger than a brook or creek. **2** A large stream; a copious flow; as, a *river* of oil.

riv·er·side \'riv-r-ˌsīd\ *n.* The side or bank of a river. **—** *adj.* Situated at the side of a river.

riv·et \'riv-ət\ *n.* A nail or bolt for fastening things together, the headless end of which is beaten down into a head after being passed through the things to be joined. **—** *v.* **1** To fasten with a rivet. **2** To fasten firmly, as the attention or a glance. — **riv·et·er** \-ət-r\ *n.*

rivets

riv·u·let \'riv-yə-lət\ *n.* A small stream.

rm. Abbreviation for: **1** *ream.* **2** *room.*

RNA \ˌär-ˌen-'ā, ˌär-\. An organic substance related to DNA and active in building protoplasm.

roach \'rōch\ *n.* A cockroach.

roach \'rōch\ *n.; pl.* **roach** or **roach·es.** A European freshwater fish of the carp family.

road \'rōd\ *n.* **1** An open way or public passage for vehicles and persons; a highway. **2** A way or path; as, the *road* to success. **3** [often in the plural] An anchorage for ships, less sheltered than a harbor.

road·bed \'rōd-ˌbed\ *n.* The underlying material and surface of a railroad track or highway.

road·block \'rōd-ˌbläk\ *n.* **1** A road barricade built at a point that can be covered by heavy fire from a defending army. **2** Any road barricade.

road runner. A swift-running long-tailed bird of the southwestern United States.

road·side \'rōd-ˌsīd\ *n.* The side of a road or the land along it. **—** *adj.* Situated at the side of a road.

road·stead \'rōd-ˌsted\ *n.* A protected place where ships may anchor.

road·ster \'rōd-stər\ *n.* **1** A horse for driving, or light work. **2** An open car with one cross seat.

road·way \'rōd-ˌwā\ *n.* A road; a highway.

roam \'rōm\ *v.* To go from place to place with no certain purpose or direction; to wander.

roan \'rōn\ *adj.* Having the basic color, as bay, chestnut, red, or brown, mixed with gray or white — used of the coats of animals. **—** *n.* **1** Roan color. **2** A roan horse.

roar \'rōr, 'ròr\ *v.* **1** To shout or bellow with a loud, full sound. **2** To make a loud, confused sound, as wind or waves. **3** To be boisterous or noisy; especially, to laugh uproariously. **—** *n.* A roaring; a prolonged shout, bellow, or loud noise.

roast \'rōst\ *v.* **1** To cook something by dry heat, as over an open fire, in hot ashes, or in an oven; as, to *roast* meat. **2** To dry or parch by exposure to heat, as coffee beans. **3** To be in the process of being cooked or dried by fire. **—** *n.* **1** A piece of roasted meat or a piece of meat for roasting; as, a *roast* of pork. **2** An outing for roasting food; as, a corn *roast.* **—** *adj.* Roasted; as, *roast* beef.

roast·er \'rōst-r\ *n.* **1** One that roasts. **2** A pan, especially with a cover, for roasting. **3** Something, as a chicken, of a size suitable for roasting.

rob \'räb\ *v.;* **robbed; rob·bing. 1** To steal from by force; to plunder; to commit robbery; as, to *rob* a store. **2** To deprive someone of something.

rob·ber \'räb-r\ *n.* One who robs; a thief.

rob·bery \'räb-r(-)ē\ *n.; pl.* **rob·ber·ies.** The act or an instance of robbing; theft.

robe \'rōb\ *n.* **1** A long flowing garment. **2** A wrap or covering thrown over the lower part of one's body; as, a lap *robe.* **—** *v.;* **robed; rob·ing.** To put a robe on; to dress; as, *robed* in white.

rob·in \'räb-n\ *n.* **1** In Europe, a small thrush with yellowish red breast. **2** In America, a larger thrush with dull reddish breast and under parts.

ro·bot \'rō-bət, -ˌbät\ *n.* A machine made to act somewhat like a living person; an automaton.

robot bomb. A small, pilotless, self-steering, jet-propelled airplane, heavily loaded with explosives, which descends as an aerial bomb.

ro·bust \rō-'bəst, 'rō-ˌbəst\ *adj.* **1** Strong and healthy; sturdy. **2** Requiring strength or vigor; as, *robust* work. — For synonyms see *strong.*

roc \'räk\ *n.* A fabulous bird of Arabia so huge that it carried off elephants to feed its young.

rock \'räk\ *v.* **1** To move, as in a cradle; to lull or quiet; as, to *rock* a baby to sleep. **2** To sway or move back and forth. An earthquake *rocked* the town. — *n.* A rocking; a rocking motion.

rock \'räk\ *n.* **1** Solid mineral matter occurring in large masses in nature. **2** A mass of such material, as a boulder or a cliff. **3** Something firm or protecting like a rock.

rock·er \'räk-r\ *n.* **1** A person who rocks. **2** One of the curved pieces of wood or metal on which a chair or cradle rocks. **3** Any of various things that have rockers or work with a rocking motion, as a **rock·ing chair** \'räk-ing\.

rock·et \'räk-ət\ *n.* **1** A firework that shoots high into the air and then bursts in a shower of sparks; a skyrocket. **2** A jet engine that carries its own oxygen for burning the fuel and is therefore able to run without the oxygen of the air. **3** A rocket-propelled bomb or missile. — *v.* To move very swiftly, like a rocket.

rock·et·ry \'räk-ə-trē\ *n.* The science that studies and experiments with rockets and their uses.

rock·ing horse \'räk-ing\. A toy horse mounted on rockers.

rock salt. Common salt in solid chunks.

rock wool. A fibrous insulating material resembling natural wool in color and texture, made by blowing steam through melted rock or slag.

rocky \'räk-ē\ *adj.;* **rock·i·er**; **rock·i·est.** **1** Full of rocks; consisting of rock. **2** Like a rock; hard.

rocky \'räk-ē\ *adj.;* **rock·i·er**; **rock·i·est.** Wobbly; tottering; shaky.

ro·co·co \rə-'kōk-ˌō\ *n.* An ornate style of decoration making much use of curved lines and designs composed of shells, scrolls, and leaves.

rod \'räd\ *n.* **1** A straight, slender stick or bar; as, a curtain *rod.* **2** Anything shaped like a rod. **3** A fishing pole. **4** A stick used to whip a person. **5** A measure of length equal to 5½ yards or 16½ feet.

rode. Past tense of *ride.*

ro·dent \'rōd-nt\ *n.* One of a group of animals that have long, sharp, front teeth used for gnawing. Rats, squirrels, mice, and beavers are *rodents.*

ro·deo \'rōd-ē-ˌō, rō-'dā-ˌō\ *n.; pl.* **ro·de·os.** **1** A roundup of cattle. **2** A cowboy exhibition featuring such things as riding, roping, and branding.

roe \'rō\ *n.* **1** The roe deer. **2** A doe.

roe \'rō\ *n.* The eggs of fishes, especially while still bound together in a membrane.

roe·buck \'rō-ˌbək\ *n.* A male roe deer.

roe deer. A small nimble deer of Europe and Asia that has erect antlers forked at the tip and is reddish brown in summer and grayish in winter.

Roent·gen ray \'rent-gən, 'rənt-\. [Named after Wilhelm K. *Roentgen* (1845–1923), the German physicist who discovered X rays.] X ray.

rogue \'rōg\ *n.* **1** A dishonest person; a cheat. **2** A scamp; a rascal. **3** A mischievous person. The baby is a little *rogue.* **4** In full, **rogue elephant.** A vicious elephant that roams alone.

rogu·ery \'rōg-r-ē\ *n.; pl.* **rogu·er·ies.** **1** The practices of a rogue; cheating; fraud. **2** Playful trickery; mischievousness.

rogues' gallery \'rōgz\. A file kept by the police of photographs of persons arrested as criminals.

rogu·ish \'rō-gish\ *adj.* **1** Tricky; dishonest. **2** Mischievous; arch. — **rogu·ish·ly**, *adv.*

roil \'rīl, 'ròil\ *v.* **1** To make cloudy or muddy by stirring up sediment; as, to *roil* the water of a brook. **2** To rouse the temper of; to vex; to irritate.

rois·ter \'ròist-r\ *v.;* **rois·tered**; **rois·ter·ing** \-r(-)ing\. **1** To bluster or swagger. **2** To make merry in a boisterous way. — **rois·ter·er** \-r-r\ *n.*

role or **rôle** \'rōl\ *n.* **1** A part or a character played by an actor in a play. **2** A part or function assumed by anyone; as, to take on the *role* of cook.

roll \'rōl\ *v.* **1** To move by turning over and over along a surface without sliding. The ball *rolled* away. **2** To revolve by turning over and over. **3** To move or be moved on wheels or rollers. The cart *rolls* easily. **4** To wrap into a rounded or a cylindrical mass; as, to *roll* up a sheet of paper; to *roll* clay into a ball. **5** To trill; as, to *roll* one's r's. **6** To utter or sound in a loud, rumbling tone. Thunder *rolled* in the west. **7** To beat with rapid, continuous strokes, as a drum. **8** To drive or move forward with an easy motion, as if on wheels. The river keeps *rolling* along to the sea. **9** To press or level out with a roller, as pastry or steel. **10** To sway or rock from side to side; as, a ship *rolling* in a stormy sea. The sailor walked with a *rolling* gait. **11** To have a rising and falling surface; as, *rolling* land. — *n.* **1** The act of rolling or the state of being rolled; a rolling motion or movement. **2** Something that rolls; a roller. **3** Something that is rolled or rounded; as, a *roll* of cloth. **4** A list; especially, a list of persons who are present or who might be present; as, to call the *roll.* **5** A heavy, echoing sound, or a flow of such sounds; as, the *roll* of a drum. **6** A swell on a surface; as, a *roll* of skin. **7** A rolled biscuit, cake, or piece of bread. **8** *Slang.* Paper money rolled into a wad; money.

roll call. **1** The act of calling a list of names, as of soldiers or members of a class. **2** The time or the signal for such a call.

roll·er \'rōl-r\ *n.* **1** A heavy device with one or more broad wheels, used to make ground level and firm; as, a steam *roller.* **2** A wheel, as of a caster or a roller skate. **3** A rubber cylinder for spreading ink. **4** Either of the revolving cylinders between which clothes pass in a wringer or mangle. **5** A stick on which to roll up a map or curtain. **6** A kind of pigeon that somersaults backward in flight; a tumbler. **7** A canary with a soft, trilling song. **8** A long, heavy wave or billow. **9** One who rolls something.

roller, 2

roller bearing. A bearing in which a revolving part turns on rollers held in a circular frame or cage.

roll·er coast·er \'rōl-r, 'rō-lē\. A circular railway on which small open cars travel round sharp curves and up and down steep inclines.

roll·er skate \ˈrōl-r\. A skate that has wheels instead of a runner. — **roll·er-skate,** *v.*

rol·lick \ˈräl-ik\ *v.* To frolic; to romp.

rol·lick·ing \ˈräl-ik-ing\ *adj.* Boisterously jolly.

roll·ing mill \ˈrō-ling\. A place where iron or steel is rolled into bars or plates.

rolling pin. A cylinder of wood or other material used for rolling out dough or paste.

rolling stock. Railroad cars and locomotives.

ro·ly-po·ly \ˈrō-lē-ˈpō-lē\ *n.; pl.* **ro·ly-po·lies. 1** A baked or steamed pudding made of dough spread with fruit or jam and rolled before cooking. **2** A roly-poly person or thing. **—** *adj.* Short and plump.

Ro·man \ˈrō-mən\ *adj.* **1** Of or relating to Rome, especially ancient Rome. **2** Having to do with the Roman Catholic Church. **3** [usually with a small letter] Naming an upright printer's type, the type in which this definition is printed. **—** *n.* **1** A native or citizen of Rome. **2** [usually with a small letter] Roman type, print, or letters.

Roman candle. A candle-shaped firework that gives off a continuous shower of sparks and sends out balls or stars of fire at intervals.

ro·mance \rō-ˈman(t)s, ˈrō-ˌman(t)s\ *n.* **1** A tale of noble deeds and strange adventures, especially one of knights and noble ladies. **2** A novel of adventure. **3** A love story. **4** Picturesque, colorful, or adventurous appeal; as, the *romance* of the old West. **5** A love affair. **6** Something made up or not truthful; as, an explanation that was pure *romance.* **—** *v.;* **ro·manced; ro·manc·ing. 1** To write or tell romances. **2** To have romantic fancies. — **ro·manc·er** \rō-ˈman(t)s-r, ˈrō-ˌman(t)s-r\ *n.*

Ro·mance lan·guag·es \ˈrō-ˌman(t)s\. The languages, as French, Spanish, and Italian, that developed from the Latin spoken by the Romans.

Ro·man·esque \ˌrō-mə-ˈnesk\ *adj.* Of or relating to a style of architecture, developed in Italy and western Europe during the Middle Ages, which used columns, a round arch and vault, and profuse ornamentation. **—** *n.* The Romanesque style.

Ro·ma·nian \rō-ˈmā-nē-ən, rü-, -ˈmān-yən\ *adj.* Of or relating to Romania. **—** *n.* **1** A native or inhabitant of Romania. **2** The language of Romania.

Roman numerals. The numerals in the Roman system of writing numbers, of which the following are the most common: I = 1; V = 5; X = 10; L = 50; C = 100; D = 500; M = 1000.

ro·man·tic \rō-ˈmant-ik\ *adj.* **1** Having to do with romance; fanciful; unreal. **2** Inclined to be sentimental and impractical; as, a *romantic* girl. **3** Showing fancy and imagination; as, *romantic* poetry. **4** Having a mysterious charm; as, a *romantic* spot. **5** Created by or associated with feelings of love; as, a *romantic* attachment. — **ro·man·ti·cal·ly** \-ik-l(-)ē\ *adv.*

ro·man·ti·cism \rō-ˈmant-ə-ˌsiz-m\ *n.* Inclination toward romance; romantic characteristics, principles, or spirit. — **ro·man·ti·cist** \-ə-səst\ *n.*

romp \ˈrämp\ *n.* **1** A frolic; rough or noisy play. **2** A person, especially a girl, fond of romping. **—** *v.* To play very actively or boisterously.

romp·ers \ˈrämp-rz\ *n.* A one-piece garment worn by small children.

ron·deau \ˈrän-ˌdō\ *n.; pl.* **ron·deaux** \-ˌdōz\. A kind of verse of French origin in which the first few words of the poem make up the refrain.

ron·do \ˈrän-ˌdō\ *n.; pl.* **ron·dos. 1** A musical composition or movement in which the principal theme recurs several times, with contrasting themes in between. **2** A rondeau.

rood \ˈrüd\ *n.* **1** A cross or crucifix. **2** A square measure, usually equal to one fourth of an acre.

roof \ˈrüf, ˈru̇f\ *n.* **1** The cover of a building. **2** Anything like a roof in position or use. **—** *v.* To provide with a roof. — **roof·er** \-r\ *n.*

roof·ing \ˈrü-fing, ˈru̇f-ing\ *n.* **1** The act of covering with a roof. **2** Materials for a roof.

roof·top \ˈrüf-ˌtäp, ˈru̇f-\ *n.* The outer surface of a roof.

roof·tree \ˈrüf-ˌtrē, ˈru̇f-\ *n.* A ridgepole.

rook \ˈru̇k\ *n.* One of the pieces in the game of chess; a castle.

rook \ˈru̇k\ *n.* **1** A glossy black European bird of the crow family. **2** A cheat. **—** *v.* To cheat.

rook

rook·ery \ˈru̇k-r-ē\ *n.; pl.* **rook·er·ies. 1** The breeding place of a colony of rooks or of certain other birds, as herons or penguins. **2** The breeding ground of seals. **3** A dilapidated building or group of buildings with many occupants.

rook·ie \ˈru̇k-ē\ *n. Slang.* A new recruit; a novice.

room \ˈrüm, ˈru̇m\ *n.* **1** Extent of space; especially, unobstructed space; as, to need *room* to grow in; enough *room* for everybody. **2** Space set apart by walls; a chamber; an apartment; as, a dining *room;* a spare *room.* **3** The people in a room. The whole *room* applauded. **4** Opportunity; chance; as, a schedule of work that left little *room* for recreation. **—** *v.* To occupy a room or rooms; to lodge.

room·er \ˈrüm-r, ˈru̇m-r\ *n.* One who rents a room in another's house; a lodger.

room·ette \rü-ˈmet, ru̇-\ *n.* A small private single bedroom in certain types of Pullman cars.

room·ing house \ˈrü-ming, ˈru̇m-ing\. A house in which rooms are rented; a lodginghouse.

room·mate \ˈrüm-ˌmāt, ˈru̇m-\ *n.* A person with whom one shares a room or rooms.

roomy \ˈrü-mē, ˈru̇m-ē\ *adj.;* **room·i·er; room·i·est.** Having plenty of room; as, a *roomy* house.

roost \ˈrüst\ *n.* Any support on which birds rest; a perch. **—** *v.* To sit or rest, as fowls on a perch.

roost·er \ˈrüst-r\ *n.* The male domestic fowl; a cock.

root \ˈrüt, ˈru̇t\ *v.* **1** To dig up the earth with the snout, as a pig does. **2** To poke around; to dig down in order to find something; as, to *root* around in a bureau drawer.

root \ˈrüt, ˈru̇t\ *v.* To cheer, as for an athletic team. — **root·er** \-r\ *n.*

root \'rüt, 'ru̇t\ *n.* **1** In higher plants (as ferns and seed plants), a leafless part, usually underground, that absorbs and stores substances necessary to the plant's growth and often serves to anchor and support it. **2** Any underground part of a plant, as a tuber; especially, an edible part, as a carrot or radish. **3** Something like a root in use or position, especially as a source of support or growth; as, the *root* of a fingernail. **4** The part of something by which it is attached; as, the *root* of a tooth. **5** The part from which anything grows or springs; the source. Love of money has been called the *root* of all evil. **6** The lowest part; the basic or most important part; as, to get to the *root* of a matter. **7** A word or part of a word from which other words are made by adding a prefix or suffix. "Hold" is the *root* of "holder". **8** A quantity which when multiplied by itself a certain number of times produces another quantity or power. 3 is the third *root* of 27 and 27 is the third power of 3. — *v.* **1** To enter the earth, as roots do; to take root and begin to grow. The plant *rooted* quickly. **2** To be or become settled; as, to be *rooted* in the place where one lives. **3** To plant firmly; to settle deeply; as, a *rooted* dislike of fuss. **4** To tear up by the root; to remove entirely; as, to *root* out a fault.

root beer. A soft drink made from juices extracted from various roots.

root hair. A tubular outgrowth from near the tip of a growing rootlet, through which water and minerals are absorbed from the soil.

root·let \'rüt-lət, 'ru̇t-\ *n.* A small root; one of the small branches of a growing root.

root·stock \'rüt-ˌstäk, 'ru̇t-\ *n.* A rhizome.

rope \'rōp\ *n.* **1** A large, stout cord made of strands, as of fiber or wire, twisted or braided together. **2** A hangman's noose; death or punishment by hanging. **3** A string of things braided or twisted together; as, a *rope* of daisies. **4** A lasso; a lariat. **5** Liberty; freedom to do as one wishes; latitude — used especially in such phrases as "to let a person have all the *rope* he wants". — *v.;* **roped; rop·ing. 1** To bind, fasten, or tie with a rope or cord. **2** To separate or divide by means of a rope; as, to *rope* off a street. **3** To lasso, as a steer or horse. **4** To draw as if with a rope; to lure; to inveigle; as, to *rope* in customers. **5** To be formed into a rope; to twist in the shape of rope; to draw out into a filament or thread, as thick syrup. — **rop·er** \'rōp-r\ *n.*

rope·walk \'rōp-ˌwȯk\ *n.* A long covered walk, building, or room where ropes are manufactured.

rope·walk·er \'rōp-ˌwȯk-r\ *n.* An acrobat who walks a rope.

ropy \'rōp-ē\ *adj.;* **rop·i·er; rop·i·est. 1** Forming sticky threads, as syrup. **2** Resembling rope.

ro·sa·ceous \rō-'zā-shəs\ *adj.* **1** Belonging to the family of which the rose is a member. **2** Having the color or shape of a rose.

ro·sa·ry \'rōz-r(-)ē\ *n.; pl.* **ro·sa·ries.** A string of beads used in counting prayers, especially prayers to the Virgin Mary.

rose \'rōz\ *n.* **1** A prickly plant having two, three, or four pairs of leaflets with an odd leaflet at the end of each leaf and showy fragrant flowers, single or five-petaled in the wild state but usually double in cultivation. **2** [in the plural] The plants, as the strawberry and spirea, that belong to the same natural family as the rose and that usually are herbs or shrubs having alternate leaves and five-petaled regular flowers, with fleshy fruits, as in the strawberry, or dry fruits, as in the spirea. **3** Something resembling a rose, as a fixture that supports or surrounds an electric-light wire. **4** A perforated nozzle for delivering water in fine jets. **5** The color of a rose, deep pink or pale cardinal. **6** A form in which gems are cut or a gem cut in this form.

rose \'rōz\. Past tense of *rise.*

ro·se·ate \'rō-zē-ət\ *adj.* **1** Full of, consisting of, or made from roses; rosy. **2** Like a rose; especially, tinged with the color rose; as, a *roseate* dawn. **3** Optimistic; pleasing; as, having a *roseate* view of his worth.

rose·bud \'rōz-ˌbəd\ *n.* The flower of a rose before it opens or when only partly open.

rose·bush \'rōz-ˌbu̇sh\ *n.* A shrubby rose plant.

rose mallow. Any of several plants related to the mallows and having rose-colored flowers, as the hibiscus and certain hollyhocks.

rose·mary \'rōz-ˌmer-ē\ *n.; pl.* **rose·mar·ies.** A fragrant evergreen shrub of the same natural family as the mints, whose leaves are used in cooking and in perfume.

ro·sette \rō-'zet\ *n.* **1** An ornament, as of cloth or paper, suggesting the array of petals of a rose. **2** In architecture, a circular ornament filled with representations of leaves. **3** In botany, a very short stem bearing a circular cluster of close-set leaves, as in the dandelion.

rosette, 1

rose·wood \'rōz-ˌwu̇d\ *n.* **1** A dark-red or purplish tropical wood streaked with black, valuable for furniture. **2** The tree that furnishes this wood.

Rosh Ha·sha·nah \ˌrōsh hə-'shän-ə, ˌräsh, -'shȯn-ə\. The Jewish New Year, observed as a religious holiday in September or October.

ros·i·ly \'rōz-l-ē\ *adv.* In a rosy manner.

ros·in \'räz-n, 'rȯz-n\ *n.* A brittle yellow or brownish resin made from turpentine. — *v.;* **ros·ined; ros·in·ing** \-n(-)ing\. To rub with rosin, as the bow of a violin.

ros·ter \'räst-r\ *n.* A roll; a list.

ros·trum \'räs-trəm\ *n.; pl.* **ros·trums** \-trəmz\ or **ros·tra** \-trə\. [From Latin, meaning literally "beak", "prow of a ship"; so called from the *Rostra* (plural), a speakers' platform in ancient Rome that was adorned with the prows of captured ships.] **1** A stage or platform for public speaking; a pulpit. **2** In anatomy, a part resembling a bird's beak. — **ros·tral** \-trəl\ *adj.*

rosy \'rō-zē\ *adj.;* **ros·i·er; ros·i·est. 1** Like a rose in color or beauty; blooming; as, a *rosy* face. **2** Made of or decorated with roses. **3** Hopeful; promising.

rot \'rät\ *v.;* **rot·ted; rot·ting. 1** To decay or cause to decay; to spoil. The apples *rotted* in the barrels. **2** To soak or expose to moisture, as flax, in order to separate the fiber; to ret. — *n.* **1** The process of rotting or the condition of being rotten; decay. **2** Something that is rotting or rotten; a rotten portion; as, to cut the *rot* out of an apple. **3** *Slang.* Nonsense; rubbish. **4** Any disease characterized by the breaking down of tissue in plants or animals; especially, an area affected by broken-down tissue, as in the hoof of an animal or a tree trunk.

ro·ta·ry \'rōt-r-ē\ *adj.* Turning, as a wheel on its axis; having parts that rotate. — *n.; pl.* **ro·ta·ries.** A road junction formed around a central circular plot about which traffic moves in one direction.

ro·tate \'rō-ˌtāt\ *v.;* **ro·tat·ed; ro·tat·ing. 1** To turn round an axis, as a wheel does; to revolve. The earth *rotates* on its axis. **2** To do something in turn; to pass in a series. The seasons *rotate.* **3** To vary in succession the crops grown on one plot of land; as, to *rotate* alfalfa and corn. — **ro·ta·tor** \-ˌtāt-r\ *n.*

ro·ta·tion \rō-'tāsh-n\ *n.* **1** The act of rotating. **2** Any return or succession in a series.

ro·ta·to·ry \'rōt-ə-ˌtōr-ē, -ˌtȯr-ē\ *adj.* **1** Of or relating to rotation. **2** Going or following in rotation.

rote \'rōt\ *n.* **1** A fixed course or routine. **2** Learning by heart without attention to the meaning.

ro·ti·fer \'rōt-əf-r\ *n.* One of a class of minute water animals having at one end a disc with circles of cilia which in motion look like revolving wheels.

ro·tor \'rōt-r\ *n.* **1** A part that revolves in a stationary part. **2** A complete system of rotating blades that supplies all or most of the lift supporting a helicopter.

rotor, 2

rotor plane. Any aircraft supported in the air chiefly by rotating blades, as a helicopter.

rot·ten \'rät-n\ *adj.* **1** Spoiled; as, *rotten* eggs. **2** Not firm or safe; unsound; as, *rotten* timbers. **3** Corrupt. **4** Disagreeable; as, *rotten* weather.

ro·tund \rō-'tənd\ *adj.* Round or rounded out; plump. — **ro·tun·di·ty** \-'tən-dət-ē\ *n.*

ro·tun·da \rō-'tən-də\ *n.* **1** A round building, especially one with a dome. **2** A large round room.

rouble. Variant of *ruble.*

rouge \'rüzh\ *n.* **1** A red powder that is used as a pigment and for polishing. **2** Any of various cosmetics, as of powder, paste, or liquid, used to give color to the cheeks or lips. — *v.;* **rouged; roug·ing.** To put rouge on.

rough \'rəf\ *adj.* **1** Having an uneven surface; not smooth; not calm; as, a *rough* sea; *rough* cloth. **2** Coarse or rugged; crude. **3** Incomplete; unfinished; approximate; not exact; as, a *rough* drawing; a *rough* estimate. **4** Not gentle; harsh; as, *rough* treatment; *rough* play. — *n.* **1** A rowdy; a ruffian. **2** That which is rough or unrefined; as, a golf ball lost in the *rough.* — *v.* **1** To roughen; to rumple. **2** To shape or make roughly; as, to *rough* out a plan. — **rough it.** To live without comfort.

rough·age \'rəf-ij\ *n.* Any rough or coarse substance; especially, coarse, bulky food having much indigestible material.

rough·en \'rəf-n\ *v.;* **rough·ened; rough·en·ing** \-n(-)ing\. To make or become rough.

rough·hew \'rəf-'hyü\ *v.;* **rough·hewed** \-'hyüd\; **rough·hewed** \-'hyüd\ or **rough·hewn** \-'hyün\; **rough·hew·ing. 1** To hew, as timber, roughly and without smoothing. **2** To form crudely or roughly.

rough·ly \'rəf-lē\ *adv.* **1** In a rough manner. **2** Approximately; not exactly.

rough·rid·er \'rəf-'rīd-r\ *n.* One who breaks horses to the saddle or who rides little-trained horses.

rough·shod \'rəf-'shäd\ *adj.* Having shoes with points or calks; as, a *roughshod* horse. — **ride roughshod over.** To treat roughly or without consideration; to domineer.

rou·lette \rü-'let\ *n.* **1** A gambling game in which a wheel (**roulette wheel**) is spun. **2** A toothed wheel used to make dots or small holes.

Rou·ma·nian \rü-'mā-nē-ən, rō-, -'mān-yən\ *adj.* or *n.* Romanian.

round \'raůnd\ *adj.* **1** Ball-shaped; spherical. **2** Ring-shaped; circular. **3** Circular in cross sections; cylindrical, as a rifle barrel. **4** Curved; not pointed; as, *round* handwriting; a *round* arch. **5** Formed or moving in a circle; as, a *round* dance. **6** Full; without fractions; approximate; in even units, such as tens or hundreds; as, to give a figure in *round* numbers; a *round* dozen. **7** Large; generous in quantity, size, or amount; as, a *round* helping; a good *round* sum of money. **8** Complete; done or made by going through a series of points with a return at last to the starting point; as, a *round* trip. — *n.* **1** Anything round, as a circle, ring, or globe. **2** A course ending where it began; travel over a route which returns to the starting point. The mailman made his *round.* **3** An act or course of action performed or taken by a number of persons in turn or together; as, a *round* of applause. **4** A series; a cycle; as, a *round* of pleasures. **5** A rounded or curved part of anything, as a rung of a ladder. **6** A cut of beef from a cow's thigh. **7** One of the periods into which a boxing match is divided. **8** One shot fired by each soldier or gun. Each side fired two *rounds.* **9** Ammunition for one shot. **10** A song in which the singers begin one after another and sing the same melody and words. **11** A complete game in a contest between two or more persons; as, a *round* of golf. **12** The condition of being round or circular; roundness. — **in the round. 1** Of sculptured figures, giving the full form on all sides; not in relief. **2** Of a theater, having its stage in the center, surrounded by the audience. — *v.* **1** To make or grow round; as, to *round* a snowball. **2** To bring to a finish; to complete; as, to *round* out a career. **3** To fill to roundness or fullness of form or perfection; as, a well-*rounded* figure; to *round* out a plan. **4** To develop; as, to *round* into manhood. **5** To go round a corner or point; as, to *round* a turn. **6** To pronounce, as a vowel, with the lips drawn into a rounded opening. — **round**

off. In mathematics, to reduce to an approximate expression; as, to *round off* 8.197 to 8.20. — **round up. 1** To collect cattle by riding round them and driving them in. **2** To gather in, as scattered persons. — *prep.* **1** In a circle about; so as to encircle; around; as, to travel *round* the world. **2** So as to include each person or place in turn. The message was passed *round* the group. **3** About; as, to write a story *round* the life of an explorer. — *adv.* **1** With a circular course; with a circular or whirling movement; as, a wheel turning *round* and *round.* **2** To each one of a group in turn; as, enough to go *round.* **3** From beginning to end; through; throughout; as, to work the year *round.* **4** In circumference; as, a circle six feet *round.* **5** All about; on all sides; as, to look *round* carefully; an unbroken view for miles *round.* **6** In or toward the opposite direction; as, to turn *round* and go home.

round·about \\'raủn-də-ˌbaủt\\ *n.* **1** *Chiefly British.* A merry-go-round. **2** A roundabout way, method, or expression. **3** A short close-fitting jacket for men and boys, popular in the 19th century. — *adj.* **1** Indirect; not following the straightest route. **2** Round about; surrounding.

round dance. 1 A country dance in which the participants form a ring, sometimes separating into couples. **2** Any dance characterized by circular movements, as distinguished from a square dance.

roun·de·lay \\'raủn-də-ˌlā\\ *n.* **1** A song in which one part is repeated over and over again. **2** A round dance.

round·house \\'raủnd-ˌhaủs\\ *n.; pl.* **round·hous·es** \\-ˌhaủ-zəz\\. **1** A circular building in which locomotives are housed and repaired. **2** A cabin on the after part of the deck of old sailing ships.

round·ish \\'raủn-dish\\ *adj.* Somewhat round.

round·ly \\'raủn-(d)lē\\ *adv.* **1** Wholly; thoroughly; as, to deny a charge *roundly.* **2** Sharply; severely; as, to scold someone *roundly.* **3** In round numbers; as, speaking *roundly,* about fifty.

round rob·in \\'räb-n\\. **1** A petition or a letter, usually one making a protest or a complaint, with signatures in a circle so as not to show who signed first. **2** A tournament in which each contestant is matched against every other contestant. **3** A letter sent in turn from one member of a group to another, each making an addition.

round–shoul·dered \\'raủnd-'shōld-rd\\ *adj.* Having the shoulders stooping or bent forward.

round table. A meeting of a group of persons for discussion of questions of mutual interest; the persons meeting for such a purpose.

round·up \\'raủn-ˌdəp\\ *n.* **1** The gathering together of cattle on the range by riding around them and driving them in. **2** Any gathering together of scattered persons or things.

round·worm \\'raủn-ˌdwərm\\ *n.* Any of several worms having an unsegmented cylindrical body; a nematode worm.

rouse \\'raủz\\ *v.;* **roused; rous·ing. 1** To startle from a hiding place, as a bird or animal. **2** To wake from sleep. **3** To excite to activity; to stir up. — *n.* **1** A rousing; a sudden start, as from a state of inactivity. **2** A signal for action.

roust·about \\'raủs-tə-ˌbaủt\\ *n.* **1** A general laborer, as around wharves, mines, or oilfields. **2** A handy man on a ranch.

rout \\'raủt\\ *v.* **1** To root or root up, as a pig. **2** To scoop out, with or as if with a gouging tool.

rout \\'raủt\\ *n.* **1** The state of being broken up and put to disordered flight, as by a victorious enemy; as, an army put to *rout.* **2** The act of defeating and breaking up an enemy force; total defeat. **3** Disturbance; riot; trouble. **4** *Archaic.* A fashionable assembly; especially, a large evening party. — *v.* To put to rout; to defeat utterly.

route \\'rüt, 'raủt\\ *n.* The course or way which is or is to be traveled; as, the most direct *route* across the country; a delivery *route.* — *v.;* **rout·ed; rout·ing. 1** To send, forward, or transport by a certain route; as, to *route* traffic around the center of a city. **2** To arrange and direct the course of procedure of, as a series of operations in a factory.

rou·tine \\(')rü-'tēn\\ *n.* **1** A round or series of activities, as of business or pleasure, regularly or often performed. **2** Any regular course of action followed by habit or custom. — *also* 'rü-ˌtēn\\ *adj.* **1** Like part of a routine, as of an activity. **2** Done or happening regularly; as, a *routine* inspection.

rove \\'rōv\\ *v.;* **roved; rov·ing.** To wander over or through; to go or move without definite direction; to ramble; to roam; as, to *rove* about the countryside. Pirates once *roved* the seas.

rov·er \\'rōv-r\\ *n.* **1** A pirate or a pirate ship. **2** One that roams about; a wanderer.

row \\'raủ\\ *n.* A noisy quarrel; a brawl; a fuss. — *v.* To engage in a row; to quarrel.

row \\'rō\\ *v.* **1** To propel along the surface of water with oars; as, to *row* a boat. **2** To use oars in propelling a boat; as, to *row* for exercise. **3** To carry in a boat propelled by using oars; as, to *row* someone across a lake. **4** To match strength and skill in rowing against another; to meet in a rowing contest. — *n.* A rowing; an excursion in a rowboat.

row \\'rō\\ *n.* A series of persons or things in a line; a rank; a file; as, a *row* of houses.

row·boat \\'rō-ˌbōt\\ *n.* A boat for rowing by oars.

row·dy \\'raủd-ē\\ *n.; pl.* **row·dies.** A person who customarily gets into rows; one who is rough or coarse in behavior. — *adj.;* **row·di·er; row·di·est.** Characteristic of a rowdy; like a rowdy.

row·el \\'raủ-əl, 'raủl\\ *n.* A small sharp-pointed wheel on some spurs, used to prick a horse. — *v.;* **row·eled** or **row·elled; row·el·ing** or **row·el·ling.** To spur.

rowel

row·er \\'rōr, 'rō-ər\\ *n.* A person who rows a boat.

row·lock \\'rō-ˌläk, 'rəl-ək\\ *n.* An oarlock.

roy·al \\'rȯi-əl, 'rȯil\\ *adj.* [From medieval English, there borrowed from medieval French *roial,* where it was derived from Latin *regalis* — see *regal.*] **1** Of or relating to a king or queen or the government of a kingdom; as, the *royal* crown; the *royal* navy. **2** Holding a charter granted by a sovereign; as, a *royal* colony. **3** Suitable for a king; magnificent; as, a *royal* welcome. — *n.* A small sail, the highest regularly carried on a square-rigged ship.

roy·al·ist \'rȯi-ə-ləst\ *n.* **1** A supporter of a king, as during a time of civil war. **2** A believer in monarchy as a system of government.

royal jelly. A special food, derived from the salivary glands, fed by the workers to the larvae of queen bees.

roy·al·ly \'rȯi-ə-lē\ *adv.* In a royal manner.

royal palm. A tall, graceful palm widely planted as an ornamental tree in tropical regions.

roy·al·ty \'rȯi-əl-tē, 'rȯil-tē\ *n.; pl.* **roy·al·ties. 1** The state or condition of being royal. **2** A king, queen, or other royal person; royal persons as a group; as, in the presence of *royalty*. **3** A share of the profit from something claimed by its owner or creator for allowing someone else to make, sell, or use it; especially, a payment made to the owner of a patent or copyright for the use of it.

r.p.m. \'är-ˌpē-'em, 'ȧr-\. Abbreviation for *revolutions per minute.*

R.R. Abbreviation for: **1** *railroad.* **2** *rural route.*

r's. Pl. of *r.*

R.S.V.P. \ˌär-ˌes-ˌvē-'pē, ˌȧr-\. [Abbreviated from French *répondez, s'il vous plaît,* meaning "please reply".] An abbreviation often used at the end of a formal invitation to request a reply.

rt. Abbreviation for *right.*

rte. Abbreviation for *route.*

rub \'rəb\ *v.;* **rubbed; rub·bing. 1** To use pressure and friction on a body or object, as with the palm of the hand. **2** To scour, polish, erase, or smear by rubbing; as, to *rub* up silver; to *rub* out an error. **3** To move or cause to move with pressure and friction; as, to *rub* against the table. **4** To fret or chafe with friction. New shoes sometimes *rub.* — *n.* **1** A rubbing. **2** A place roughened or injured by rubbing. **3** That which rubs; a hindrance or obstruction. **4** Something that hurts the feelings, as a sarcastic remark.

rub·ber \'rəb-r\ *n.* **1** One that rubs, as in polishing. **2** Something used in rubbing, as an eraser. **3** An elastic substance made from the juice of certain tropical plants. **4** Something made of rubber, as a low overshoe or an elastic band (**rubber band**). — **rub·bery** \-r(-)ē\ *adj.*

rub·ber \'rəb-r\ *n.* The odd game that breaks a tie; a contest to be decided by the winning of two out of three games.

rub·ber·ize \'rəb-r-ˌīz\ *v.;* **rub·ber·ized; rub·ber·iz·ing.** To coat or impregnate with rubber or a rubber preparation; as, *rubberized* raincoats.

rub·bish \'rəb-ish\ *n.* Anything worthless; trash.

rub·ble \'rəb-l\ *n.* **1** Rough, broken stones or bricks used in coarse masonry. **2** Rough stone as it comes from the quarry. **3** Any mass of rough, broken pieces; as, a town bombed to *rubble.*

rub·down \'rəb-ˌdau̇n\ *n.* A brisk rubbing of the body, as after a bath.

ru·bi·cund \'rü-bə-(ˌ)kənd\ *adj.* Reddish; ruddy.

ru·ble or **rou·ble** \'rüb-l\ *n.* The monetary unit of the U.S.S.R.

ru·bric \'rüb-rik\ *n.* **1** A rule for conducting a religious service. **2** Any established form or practice.

ru·by \'rü-bē\ *n.; pl.* **ru·bies. 1** A precious stone of a clear deep red color. **2** The color of the ruby.

ruck·sack \'rək-ˌsak, 'ru̇k-\ *n.* A loose flat bag supported on the back by straps over the shoulders; a knapsack.

rud·der \'rəd-r\ *n.* **1** A flat piece of wood or metal attached to the stern of a boat for steering it. **2** A similar piece attached to the rear of an aircraft.

rudder, 1

rud·dy \'rəd-ē\ *adj.;* **rud·di·er; rud·di·est.** Reddish in color; as, a *ruddy* complexion.

rude \'rüd\ *adj.* **1** Roughly made; as, a *rude* shelter. **2** Impolite; discourteous; as, a *rude* remark. — **rude·ly,** *adv.*

ru·di·ment \'rüd-m-ənt\ *n.* **1** Something in a beginning, undeveloped stage. Young birds have only *rudiments* of feathers. **2** The most elementary knowledge of anything; as, the *rudiments* of Latin.

ru·di·men·ta·ry \ˌrüd-m-'ent-r-ē, -'en-trē\ *adj.* **1** Of or relating to rudiments; elementary. **2** Imperfectly developed; immature.

rue \'rü\ *n.* A woody plant with yellow flowers, a strong smell, and bitter-tasting leaves.

rue \'rü\ *v.;* **rued; ru·ing.** To regret; to wish undone. — *n.* Regret; disappointment.

rue·ful \'rüf-l\ *adj.* **1** Expressing mild sorrow or regret; as, a *rueful* smile. **2** Mournful; sorrowful. — **rue·ful·ly** \-l(-)ē\ *adv.*

ruff \'rəf\ *n.* **1** A stiff round collar of pleated muslin or linen, worn by men and women in the 16th and 17th centuries. **2** A fringe of hair or feathers on the neck of an animal or bird; as, a dog with a white *ruff.* — **ruffed** \'rəft\ *adj.*

ruff, 1

ruffed grouse. A grouse with tufts of shiny black feathers on the sides of the neck, in the northern United States called *partridge* and in the southern United States called *pheasant.*

ruf·fi·an \'rəf-ē-ən\ *n.* A person of habitually brutal, cruel, and violent behavior.

ruf·fle \'rəf-l\ *v.;* **ruf·fled; ruf·fling** \-l(-)ing\. **1** To draw into or arrange in pleats, folds, or gathers. **2** To provide with pleats, folds, or gathers. **3** To erect, as hair or feathers, into something like a ruff. The cat *ruffled* its fur in anger. **4** To disturb, as the surface of water; to roughen. The wind *ruffled* the surface of the pond. **5** To annoy; to irritate. — *n.* **1** A strip of lace or cloth pleated or gathered on one edge and used as a trimming. **2** A ruff. **3** The state of being annoyed. **4** A ripple.

ruf·fle \'rəf-l\ *n.* A low vibrating beat of a drum.

rug \'rəg\ *n.* A piece of thick, heavy fabric, usually with a nap or pile, as one used for a floor covering.

Rug·by \'rəg-bē\ *n.* or **Rugby football.** [Named after *Rugby* school, Rugby, Warwickshire, England, where it was first played.] A football game played by teams of 15 players.

rug·ged \'rəg-əd\ *adj.* **1** Having an extremely rough, uneven surface; as, a *rugged* terrain. **2** Harsh; hard; stern; as, *rugged* times. **3** Stormy; wild. **4** Robust; sturdy; vigorous.

ru·in \'rü-ən, -(ˌ)in\ *n.* **1** Complete loss or destruction, as of health or prosperity. **2** Something that causes, or the action of causing, such destruction. Sudden wealth was the man's *ruin.* **3** Something that has fallen to worthlessness from decay or destruction; especially [in the plural], the remains of a destroyed building or city; as, to dig among the Roman *ruins.* **4** The state of being worthless or destroyed; as, to go to *ruin.* — *v.* **1** To bring to ruin; to destroy. **2** To damage or spoil.

ru·in·a·tion \ˌrü-ə-'nāsh-n\ *n.* **1** A ruining or a being ruined; destruction; ruin. **2** Something that causes ruin. Drink was his *ruination.*

ruing. Pres. part. of *rue.*

ru·in·ous \'rü-ə-nəs\ *adj.* **1** Causing, or likely to cause, ruin; destructive; extremely harmful. **2** Ruined; in ruins. — **ru·in·ous·ly,** *adv.*

rule \'rül\ *n.* **1** A guide or principle laid down to govern action or behavior; a regulation; as, the *rules* of good conduct; the *rules* of the game. **2** The usual or systematic method or way of doing something; the usual thing. It is the *rule* at home to rise at seven. **3** A governing or controlling. The king's *rule* was brutal and merciless. **4** The time during which a particular rule is in power; a reign. There was peace throughout the king's *rule.* **5** A straight strip, as of wood or metal, usually marked in inches and feet, used as a guide in drawing straight lines or for measuring; a ruler. **6** A ruled line on paper. **7** The laws laid down by the founder of a religious order; as, the *rule* of St. Dominic. **8** In law, an order or direction made by a court. **9** In mathematics, a method laid down for performing an operation. — **as a rule.** Usually; ordinarily; as, a child who behaves well *as a rule.* — *v.;* **ruled; rul·ing. 1** To govern; to manage; to control. **2** To form the main or controlling quality of something. Common sense *ruled* the advice the teacher gave. **3** To give as a considered decision or verdict. The court *ruled* that the testimony must be removed from the record. **4** To mark with straight lines, especially with the aid of a ruler; as, to *rule* paper. **5** To have power or command; to exercise supreme authority. A king *rules* over the country. — **rule out.** To decide against; to exclude; to eliminate.

rule of thumb. A rough measurement or calculation; a judgment based on practical experience rather than on scientific knowledge.

rul·er \'rül-r\ *n.* **1** A person who rules; a sovereign. **2** A straight-edged strip, as of wood or metal, used as a guide in drawing straight lines or for measuring; a rule.

rul·ing \'rü-ling\ *n.* **1** The action of a person who rules; government. **2** The drawing of ruled lines. **3** A ruled line. **4** A decision of a judge or court, especially on a point of law. — *adj.* Controlling; main; chief; as, a person's *ruling* ambition.

rum \'rəm\ *n.* **1** An alcoholic liquor made from molasses or sugar cane. **2** Alcoholic liquor in general.

rum \'rəm\ *adj. Slang.* Queer; odd.

Ru·ma·nian \rü-'mā-nē-ən, rō-, -'mān-yən\ *adj.* or *n.* Romanian.

rum·ba or **rhum·ba** \'rəm-bə, 'ru̇m-\ *n.* A Cuban Negro dance or an imitation of it.

rum·ble \'rəm-bl\ *v.;* **rum·bled; rum·bling** \-bl(-)ing\. **1** To make a low, heavy, rolling sound. Thunder *rumbled* in the distance. **2** To travel or move with a heavy, rolling sound. The cart *rumbled* away. **3** To utter in a low, rolling voice. — *n.* A low, continuous, rolling sound, as of thunder.

rumble seat. A seat in the rear deck of an automobile, not covered by the top.

ru·men \'rü-mən\ *n.; pl.* **ru·mens** \-mənz\ or **ru·mi·na** \-mə-nə\. The first stomach of cud-chewing animals in which food is stored before chewing.

ru·mi·nant \'rü-mə-nənt\ *adj.* **1** Cud-chewing. Cows, goats, and sheep are *ruminant* animals. **2** Meditative. — *n.* A cud-chewing animal.

ru·mi·nate \'rü-mə-ˌnāt\ *v.;* **ru·mi·nat·ed; ru·mi·nat·ing. 1** To chew the cud; to chew again what has been chewed slightly and swallowed. **2** To ponder; to meditate. — **ru·mi·na·tion** \ˌrü-mə-'nāsh-n\ *n.* — **ru·mi·na·tive** \'rü-mə-ˌnāt-iv\ *adj.*

rum·mage \'rəm-ij\ *n.* A search in which everything is turned over or looked into; as, a *rummage* in a drawer. — *v.;* **rum·maged; rum·mag·ing. 1** To search by moving or turning everything over; as, to *rummage* around in a closet. **2** To bring to light by or as if by a thorough search.

rummage sale. A sale of donated odds and ends.

rum·my \'rəm-ē\ *n.* A card game in which the object is to be the first to match all one's cards into sets or sequences of three or more by drawing from and discarding on a common pile of cards.

ru·mor \'rüm-r\ *n.* **1** A popular story; common talk. **2** A current report without any known authority for its truth; as, the *rumor* that the governor is going to resign. — *v.;* **ru·mored; ru·mor·ing** \-r(-)ing\. To tell or spread by rumor.

rump \'rəmp\ *n.* **1** The back part of an animal's body where the hips and thighs join, generally including the buttocks. **2** A cut of beef between the sirloin and the round.

rum·ple \'rəmp-l\ *v.;* **rum·pled; rum·pling** \-l(-)ing. To wrinkle; to muss; to crumple.

rum·pus \'rəmp-əs\ *n.* A disturbance; a noisy confusion; a fracas.

rumpus room. A room set apart in a home, usually in the basement, and suitably furnished for parties, for playing games, and for other recreation.

run \'rən\ *v.;* **ran** \'ran\; **run; run·ning. 1** To go fast by moving one's legs more rapidly than in walking. **2** To move or cause to move swiftly or smoothly; as, an automobile that *runs* better after being greased. **3** To go; to go back and forth; to ply. The bus *runs* to town every hour. **4** To pass out freely or loosely; as, to let a cable *run* to its full length. **5** To flee. The thieves *ran* as soon as they saw the police. **6** To make or be a candidate; as, to *run* for president. **7** To move in schools, as fish. The salmon are *running.* **8** To turn, as a wheel. **9** To extend. The child's memory does not *run* back that far. **10** To do something by or as if by running; as, to *run* a race; to *run* errands. **11** To grow, increase, or develop. The report *ran* to 60 pages before it was finished. **12** To cause to enter; to thrust; as, to *run* a nail into one's foot. **13** To push forth; to project; as, to *run* out the gangplank. **14** To smuggle; as, to *run* liquor. **15** To meet with or incur; as, to *run* a risk. **16** To manage; to operate; as, to *run* a business; to *run* a machine. **17** To have a course or direction. The boundary *runs* east from here. **18** To sew, as a seam, usually with small, even stitches. **19** To pour; as, to *run* cake batter into a pan. **20** To bring or come to a stated condition by or as if by running; as, to *run* a company into debt. The well *ran* dry. **21** To discharge matter. The child's nose is *running.* **22** To spread or dissolve, as a dyed color in washing. **23** To become fluid; to flow, as sap or blood. **24** To continue in existence, force, or operation. The contract *runs* for five years. **25** To keep in action or motion; to proceed continuously; as, a motor that *runs* day and night. **26** To continue to be of a stated character, size, extent, or value. This year's potato crop is *running* ten per cent above normal. **27** To gad about; to roam; as, children who *run* the streets all day. **28** To be worded. The passage *runs* as follows. **29** To creep or climb up or along; as, a vine that *runs* along the fence. The fire *ran* along the roof. **30** To ravel lengthwise, as in knitted goods or stockings, because of a broken or faulty stitch. **31** To keep recurring in one's mind, as ideas or tunes. **32** To trace; as, to *run* a rumor back to its source. **33** To slide or put in place; as, to *run* cards into a filing case. **34** To compete with by, or as if by, running, as in a foot race or a political contest. **35** To allow something, as a bill, to mount up before paying; as, to *run* a bill at the grocery store. — **run across.** To meet or come upon by chance. — **run after.** To seek the company of. — **run away with.** To outdo in competition. Although she lacked experience, the young actress *ran away with* the play. — **run down. 1** To run against and knock down, as with an automobile. **2** To pursue and capture, as a criminal. **3** To speak disparagingly of. **4** To stop running or operating because the motive power is exhausted, as a clock or watch. **5** To decline in condition; as, a farm that has been permitted to *run down* badly; a person who is badly *run down.* — **run in. 1** To insert, as a paragraph in a story. **2** *Slang.* To place under arrest. — **run into. 1** To come in collision with. **2** To meet unexpectedly. — **run off. 1** To print. **2** To cause to be run or played to a finish, as a race or other contest. — **run on. 1** To keep talking. The children *ran on* endlessly about what they saw at the circus. **2** To continue a line of print without a break, as at the end of a definition. — **run out.** To come to an end, as a lease. — **run out of.** To exhaust the supply of. — **run over. 1** To ride or drive over. **2** To look at or examine hurriedly. **3** To exceed; to be more than enough. **4** To overflow. — **run short.** To lack enough of something, as supplies; to be or become insufficient in amount. — **run through. 1** To consume wastefully. The boy *ran through* his allowance in a short time. **2** To pierce. — *n.* **1** The action of running. **2** An unbroken series, as of performances of a play or successful shots in a game; a succession; a continued period; as, a *run* of luck. The town has had a *run* of fires. **3** A brook; a rivulet. **4** Something that runs during a certain time; as, a *run* of salmon; the first *run* of sap in a sugar orchard. **5** The usual or normal kind; as, the ordinary *run* of people. **6** The operation of a machine or business; as, to learn the *run* of things. **7** The amount of work turned out during a period of operation. The first *run* broke all production records. **8** The time or distance over which something runs; as, the night *run* of a train. **9** A place in which animals are allowed to run; as, a sheep *run.* **10** Freedom to range or roam at will. The children were given the *run* of the place. **11** A course; a passage, as in time; as, in the long *run.* **12** A trip; a journey; as, to make a quick *run* to town. **13** A lengthwise ravel in knitted goods, as stockings. **14** A contest, especially one that is hard-fought. **15** In baseball and cricket, a unit of scoring, made by covering a required course. — **in the long run.** In the course of time, use, or experience; eventually. — **on the run. 1** In haste; engaged in continuous rapid work or activity; as, to be *on the run* from morning till night. **2** Headed for defeat; at a disadvantage; as, to have one's opponent *on the run* in an argument.

run·about \'rən-ə-ˌbau̇t\ *n.* **1** A person who runs about. **2** A light open wagon. **3** A light open automobile or motorboat.

run·around or **run–around** \'rən-ə-ˌrau̇nd\ *n.* The planned, deceptive referring of a person to other persons or departments; a replying evasively.

run·away \'rən-ə-ˌwā\ *n.* **1** A person who flees from danger, duty, or punishment; a fugitive. **2** A running away, especially of a horse or team. **3** A horse that is running away. — *adj.* **1** Running away; as, a *runaway* slave. **2** Done by running away or during flight; as, a *runaway* marriage. **3** Won by a long lead; decisive; as, a *runaway* victory.

run–down \'rən-'dau̇n\ *adj.* **1** Dilapidated; neglected; going to ruin. **2** In poor health; worn-out. **3** Stopped for lack of winding, as a clock.

rune \'rün\ *n.* **1** Any of the characters or signs of the alphabet formerly used by the Teutonic peoples. **2** Mystery; magic. **3** [in the plural] Old Finnish or Old Norse poetry in runes. — **ru·nic** \'rü-nik\ *adj.*

rung \'rəng\ *n.* **1** A stick, often rounded, placed as a cross piece between the legs of a chair. **2** A round of a ladder. **3** A spoke of a wheel.

rung \'rəng\. A past tense and the past part. of *ring,* meaning to sound something.

run-in \'rən-ˌin\ *n.* Something inserted, as a paragraph in printed matter, or a derived or related word or phrase within a main vocabulary entry. In this dictionary "saffron yellow" is a *run-in* at the main entry "saffron".

run·let \'rən-lət\ *n.* A brook; a runnel.

run·nel \'rən-l\ *n.* A rivulet; a brook.

run·ner \'rən-r\ *n.* **1** A person or thing that runs, as a racer, a race horse, or a messenger. **2** A manager; an operator. **3** A thin piece or part on or in which something slides; as, the *runners* of a sled. **4** A long narrow strip, as of carpet. **5** A lengthwise ravel in a stocking; a run. **6** A slender creeping branch of a plant, which roots at the end or at the joints to form new plants. **7** A plant that spreads in this way.

runner, 3

run·ner-up \'rən-r-ˌəp\ *n.* The competitor in a contest who finishes next to the winner.

run·ning \'rən-ing\ *n.* **1** The act of a person or thing that runs. *Running* is good exercise. **2** Management; operation; care; as, to be responsible for the actual *running* of a business. — *adj.* **1** Moving by or as if by running; as, *running* water. **2** Continuous; as, *running* rifle fire. **3** Successive; as, five days *running.* **4** Flowing; smooth; easy; as, *running* handwriting. **5** Having to do with a run or the act of running; as, a *running* start; the *running* time of a train. **6** Discharging matter; as, a *running* sore.

running board. A footboard, as one at the side of an automobile or a locomotive.

running knot or **running noose.** A slipknot.

running title. The title of a book, as printed at the top of the left-hand pages or, sometimes, of all pages.

run·off \'rən-ˌöf\ *n.* **1** Water that is removed from soil by drainage. **2** A final contest to decide a previous indecisive contest or contests.

run-on \'rən-ˌön, -ˌän\ *adj.* That is run on or appended to something else, especially in printed matter; as, a *run-on* entry in a dictionary. — *n.* That which is run on. In this dictionary "runty" is a *run-on* at "runt".

run-on sentence. A group of words put together so as to express two or more complete thoughts but written and punctuated as if one sentence.

runt \'rənt\ *n.* An unusually small person or animal. — **runty** \'rənt-ē\ *adj.*

run·way \'rən-ˌwā\ *n.* **1** A path beaten by animals in going to and from their feeding grounds. **2** An enclosure for animals, especially poultry. **3** A track or way, as for wheeled vehicles or for the landing and taking off of airplanes.

ru·pee \rü-'pē, 'rü-ˌpē\ *n.* The monetary unit of India.

rup·ture \'rəp-chər\ *n.* **1** A breaking apart or the state of being broken apart; as, the *rupture* of a blood vessel. **2** Open hostility or warfare; as, a *rupture* between nations. **3** The sticking out of an organ or body part through a break in the wall surrounding it; a hernia. — *v.;* **rup·tured; rup·tur·ing. 1** To break; to burst; as, to *rupture* a vein. **2** To produce a rupture in a person.

ru·ral \'rür-əl\ *adj.* Of or relating to the country or country people; as, *rural* life.

— The word *rustic* is a synonym of *rural:* both of these terms apply to things having to do with the country or country life; *rural* may suggest life in the open countrysides and farmlands, particularly the more pleasant or romantic aspects of this life; *rustic* usually suggests its coarser, less civilized, but often picturesque, aspects, especially as contrasted with the refinements of city life.

rural delivery or **rural free delivery.** The free delivery of mail on routes in country districts.

rural route. A route in a rural free delivery system.

ruse \'rüs, 'rüz\ *n.* A trick; an artifice.

rush \'rəsh\ *n.* A tufted marsh plant, the hollow stems of which are used for chair seats and mats.

rush \'rəsh\ *v.* **1** To go, move, carry, or push forward with haste or violence. **2** To act or move without preparation. **3** To attack; to charge. — *n.* **1** A violent forward motion; as, a *rush* of wind. **2** A crowding together of people at a place; as, a gold *rush.* **3** Hurried activity; as, a *rush* of business. — *adj.* Demanding haste; as, a *rush* order.

rusk \'rəsk\ *n.* Any bread, sweet or plain, that is prepared and baked and then sliced and baked again until it is dry and hard.

rus·set \'rəs-ət\ *n.* **1** A dull brown color of a reddish or yellowish tone. **2** A winter apple with a russet skin. — *adj.* Russet colored.

Rus·sian \'rəsh-n\ *adj.* Of or relating to Russia or the U.S.S.R. — *n.* **1** A native or inhabitant of Russia or the U.S.S.R. **2** The language of Russia.

rust \'rəst\ *n.* **1** The reddish coating that forms on iron and other metals exposed to the air. **2** The deep reddish-orange color of rust. **3** A plant disease caused by fungi that makes spots on plants; as, wheat *rust.* — *v.* **1** To make or become rusty. **2** To be affected with plant rust. **3** To weaken or corrupt by idleness or inaction.

rus·tic \'rəs-tik\ *adj.* **1** Having to do with the country; rural; as, *rustic* scenes. **2** Awkward; unpolished; as, *rustic* manners. **3** Suited to the country; plain; simple; as, a *rustic* bridge. — For synonyms see *rural.* — *n.* A country person. — **rus·ti·cal·ly** \-tik-l(-)ē\ *adv.*

rus·tic·i·ty \ˌrəs-'tis-ət-ē\ *n.; pl.* **rus·tic·i·ties.** The quality or state of being rustic; simplicity.

rus·tle \'rəs-l\ *v.;* **rus·tled; rus·tling** \-l(-)ing\. To stir so as to make a series of small sounds like the shaking of straw or the swishing of silk. — *n.* A rustling sound. — **rus·tler** \-lər\ *n.*

rus·tle \'rəs-l\ *v.;* **rus·tled; rus·tling** \-l(-)ing\. **1** *Slang.* To act with or get by a show of energetic activity. **2** To steal, as cattle. — **rus·tler** \-lər\ *n.*

rusty \'rəs-tē\ *adj.;* **rust·i·er; rust·i·est. 1** Rusted; covered with rust; damaged by rust; like rust; as, a *rusty* nail. **2** Weakened, as in strength or skill; as, *rusty* from lack of practice. **3** Of the color rust.

rut \'rət\ *n.* **1** A track or groove, as one worn by the wheels of vehicles. **2** A usual or fixed way of doing something from which one is not easily moved; as, to fall into a *rut.* — *v.;* **rut·ted; rut·ting.** To make a rut or ruts in. — **rut·ty** \'rət-ē\ *adj.*

ru·ta·ba·ga \ˌrüt-ə-'bā-gə\ *n.* A variety of turnip with a large, elongated, yellowish root.

ruth·less \'rüth-ləs\ *adj.* Having no pity; cruel; showing no mercy. — **ruth·less·ly,** *adv.*

-ry \rē\. A form of the suffix *-ery,* as in *chemistry, peasantry, rivalry.*

Ry. Abbreviation for *railway.*

rye \'rī\ *n.* **1** A hardy bluish green grass cultivated for grain or hay. **2** The seeds or grain of this plant.

s \'es\ *n.; pl.* **s's** \'es-əz\. The nineteenth letter of the alphabet.

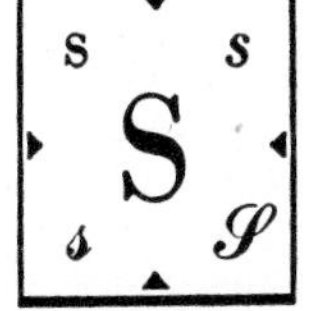

S. Abbreviation for: **1** *south.* **2** *southern.*

Sab·bath \'sab-əth\ *n.* **1** The seventh day of the week observed from sundown on Friday until sundown on Saturday as a day of rest and worship by Jews and some Christians. **2** Among most Christians, Sunday.

sab·bat·i·cal \sə-'bat-ik-l\ *adj.* **1** [often with a capital] Of or suited to the Sabbath. **2** Of the nature of the Sabbath or a similar recurring period of rest, as in **sabbatical year,** a leave of absence granted to a college professor every seventh year.

sa·ber or **sa·bre** \'sāb-r\ *n.* A cavalry sword with a curved blade.

sa·ber-toothed tiger \'sāb-r-ˌtütht, -ˌtüt͟hd\. Any of various prehistoric mammals of the cat family having long curved upper canine teeth.

Sa·bin vaccine \'sāb-n\. A polio vaccine given orally.

sa·ble \'sāb-l\ *n.* **1** A dark brown, meat-eating animal of northern Europe and Asia, highly valued for its fur, or a related North American animal. **2** The fur of the sable. **3** A black color.

sab·o·tage \'sab-ə-ˌtäzh, -ˌtȧzh\ *n.* [From French, there derived from *saboter* meaning "to work carelessly", "to perform sabotage", literally, "to wear wooden shoes", and derived from *sabot* meaning 'wooden shoe".] **1** The destruction of an employer's property or the hindering of manufacturing by discontented workmen. **2** Any destructive act performed by enemy sympathizers to hinder a nation's war or defense effort. — *v.;* **sab·o·taged; sab·o·tag·ing.** To practice sabotage on; to destroy.

sab·o·teur \ˌsab-ə-'tər, -'tu̇r\ *n.* One who engages in sabotage.

sac \'sak\ *n.* A structure in a plant or animal resembling a bag or pouch, often containing fluid.

sac·cha·rin \'sak-r(-)ən\ *n.* A very sweet white sugar substitute made from coal tar.

sac·cha·rine \'sak-r(-)ən, -r-ˌēn, -r-ˌīn\ *adj.* **1** Of sugar or of the nature of sugar; sweet; yielding sugar. **2** Sickeningly sweet; as, a *saccharine* smile.

sac·er·do·tal \ˌsas-r-'dōt-l, ˌsak-r-\ *adj.* Priestly. — **sac·er·do·tal·ly** \-'dōt-l-ē\ *adv.*

sa·chem \'sāch-m\ *n.* An Indian tribal chief.

sa·chet \sa-'shā\ *n.* A small bag or pad filled with perfumed powder.

sack \'sak\ *n.* The plundering of a city by its conquerors. — *v.* To plunder; to pillage.

sack \'sak\ *n.* **1** A container of flexible material for holding goods; a bag. **2** The quantity contained in a sack; as, a *sack* of flour. **3** *Slang.* Dismissal; discharge. — *v.* **1** To put into a sack. **2** *Slang.* To dismiss; to discharge.

sack·cloth \'sak-ˌklȯth\ *n.* **1** Coarse cloth, as that used for making sacks. **2** The traditional garb of mourning and penitence in the Bible.

sack·ing \'sak-ing\ *n.* Strong, coarse cloth from which sacks are made.

sacque \'sak\ *n.* A loose, lightweight jacket; especially, an infant's short jacket fastened at the neck.

sac·ra·ment \'sak-rə-mənt\ *n.* **1** A religious act, ceremony, or practice that is considered especially sacred in Christian worship; especially, the Eucharist or Holy Communion. **2** [with a capital] In the Roman Catholic Church, the consecrated Host. — **sac·ra·men·tal** \ˌsak-rə-'ment-l\ *adj.*

sa·cred \'sāk-rəd\ *adj.* **1** Set apart in honor of someone, as a god; as, a mountain *sacred* to Jupiter. **2** Holy; as, the *sacred* name of Jesus. **3** Religious; as, *sacred* songs. **4** Not to be violated or misused; as, a *sacred* right. — **sa·cred·ly,** *adv.*

sac·ri·fice \'sak-rə-ˌfīs, -fəs, -ˌfīz\ *n.* **1** The act or ceremony of making an offering to God or a god, especially on an altar. **2** Something offered up as a religious act. **3** An unselfish giving up; as, a *sacrifice* of one's time to help others. **4** A loss of profit; as, goods sold at a *sacrifice.* — \-ˌfīs, -ˌfīz\ *v.;* **sac·ri·ficed; sac·ri·fic·ing. 1** To offer up or to kill as a sacrifice. **2** To make a sacrifice; as, to *sacrifice* one's life for one's country. **3** To sell at a loss.

sac·ri·fi·cial \ˌsak-rə-'fish-l\ *adj.* Of or relating to sacrifice. — **sac·ri·fi·cial·ly** \-'fish-l-ē\ *adv.*

sac·ri·lege \'sak-rə-lij\ *n.* The crime of stealing, misusing, or profaning anything holy or sacred. — **sac·ri·le·gious** \ˌsak-rə-'lij-əs, -'lē-jəs\ *adj.*

sac·ris·ty \'sak-rəs-tē\ *n.; pl.* **sac·ris·ties.** A church room where vestments and altar vessels are kept.

sac·ro·sanct \'sak-rō-ˌsangkt\ *adj.* Most sacred.

sa·crum \'sāk-rəm, 'sak-\ *n.; pl.* **sa·crums** \-rəmz\ or **sa·cra** \-rə\. The part of the backbone connected with, or forming a part of, the pelvis.

sad \'sad\ *adj.;* **sad·der; sad·dest. 1** Filled with sorrow or unhappiness; grieving. **2** Causing sorrow or gloom; depressing; as, a *sad* accident.

sad·den \'sad-n\ *v.;* **sad·dened; sad·den·ing** \-n(-)ing\. To make or become sad.

sad·dle \'sad-l\ *n.* **1** A leather-covered, padded seat for a rider on horseback or on a bicycle. **2** A padded part of a harness, worn on a horse's back under a strap that encircles his body. **3** A cut of meat, as of mutton, lamb, or veal, consisting of the whole upper back of the animal including both loins; such a piece roasted. **4** A ridge of land connecting two higher elevations. **5** Anything or part of a thing that resembles a saddle in shape, position, or use, as a piece of leather covering the back part of a book's binding. — **in the saddle.** In command; in a position to command. — *v.;* **sad·dled; sad·dling** \-l(-)ing\. **1** To put a saddle upon; as, to *saddle* a horse. **2** To burden; as, to *saddle* a man with debt.

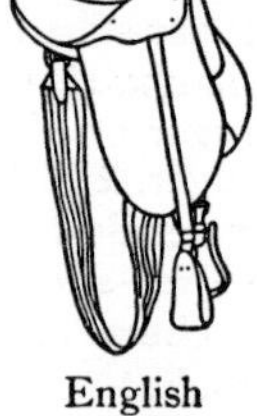
English saddle

sad·dle·bag \'sad-l-ˌbag\ *n.* A bag, usually one of a pair, carried hanging from the side of a saddle.

sad·dle·bow \'sad-l-ˌbō\ *n.* The arch in the front of a saddle.

sad·dler \'sad-lər\ *n.* A person who makes, repairs, or sells saddles and other horse equipment.

sad·dlery \'sad-lər-ē\ *n.; pl.* **sad·dler·ies.** The work or the shop or the merchandise of a saddler.

sad·dle·tree \'sad-l-ˌtrē\ *n.* The frame of a saddle.

sad·ly \'sad-lē\ *adv.* In a sad manner or way.

sa·fa·ri \sə-'fär-ē, -'far-ē, -'får-ē\ *n.; pl.* **sa·fa·ris.** A hunting expedition in eastern Africa.

safe \'sāf\ *adj.;* **saf·er; saf·est. 1** Free from danger or risk; as, to bank one's money to keep it *safe.* **2** Not harmed; unhurt. **3** Giving protection or security against danger or harm; as, a *safe* harbor. **4** Without risk of error or failure; as, a *safe* guess. **5** Reliable; trustworthy; as, a *safe* guide. **6** Incapable of doing harm; securely in custody. — *n.* A place for keeping things safe; especially, a steel chest for money and valuables.

safe-con·duct \'sāf-'kän-(ˌ)dəkt\ *n.* **1** Protection given a person passing through enemy or foreign country. **2** A pass permitting such passage.

safe·guard \'sāf-ˌgärd, -ˌgård\ *n.* Something that protects and gives safety; a defense. — *v.* To protect; to keep safe; as, to *safeguard* one's health.

safe·keep·ing \'sāf-'kēp-ing\ *n.* A keeping in safety; protection; care; custody.

safe·ly \'sāf-lē\ *adv.* In a safe manner; with safety.

safe·ty \'sāf-tē\ *n.; pl.* **safe·ties. 1** Freedom from danger; security; as, laws to ensure the *safety* of citizens. **2** Dependability; reliability; as, the *safety* of a bridge. **3** A device on a firearm to prevent accidental discharge. **4** The putting down of a football by a player behind his own goal line after it has been impelled or carried there by his own side. — *adj.* **1** Made or planned to ensure safety; as, a *safety* razor; a *safety* zone; a traffic *safety* crusade.

safety glass. 1 Glass that resists shattering, consisting of two sheets of glass with a sheet of transparent plastic between them. **2** Wired glass.

safety match. A match that can be struck only on a specially prepared surface.

safety pin. A pin made in the form of a clasp with a guard covering its point.

safety valve. 1 A valve that opens automatically, as to let out steam from a boiler when pressure becomes too great for safety. **2** An outlet for pent-up energy or emotion.

saf·fron \'saf-rən\ *n.* **1** A substance of a deep orange color obtained from the flower of an autumn-blooming crocus and used to flavor and color foods. **2** The crocus from which this substance is obtained. **3** Usually **saffron yellow.** A bright orange color.

saffron, 2

sag \'sag\ *v.;* **sagged; sag·ging. 1** To droop below the natural or right level; to bend down in the middle; as, a *sagging* rope. **2** To lose firmness or vigor; as, *sagging* cheeks; *sagging* spirits. **3** To fall gradually, as prices. — *n.* **1** A sagging part. **2** An instance or an amount of sagging.

sa·ga \'säg-ə, 'sag-, 'såg-\ *n.* [From Old Norse, meaning "story", "tale".] **1** A story, real or imaginary, of a hero or heroes of Iceland. **2** Any story of heroic deeds; as, a *saga* of war.

sa·ga·cious \sə-'gā-shəs\ *adj.* Quick and shrewd in understanding and judging.

sa·gac·i·ty \sə-'gas-ət-ē\ *n.; pl.* **sa·gac·i·ties.** The quality of being sagacious; especially, shrewdness.

sag·a·more \'sag-m-ˌōr, -ˌȯr\ *n.* A chief in certain North American Indian tribes; a sachem.

sage \'sāj\ *n.* **1** A garden herb with strong-smelling grayish green leaves. **2** The sagebrush.

sage \'sāj\ *adj.;* **sag·er; sag·est.** Wise; prudent. — *n.* A very wise man. — **sage·ly,** *adv.*

sage·brush \'sāj-ˌbrəsh\ *n.* A low-growing shrub with bitter juice and a smell like that of sage, found on the western plains.

sa·go \'sā-ˌgō\ *n.; pl.* **sa·gos.** A powdered or granulated edible starch made chiefly from the pith of an East Indian palm (**sago palm**).

sa·gua·ro \sə-'wär-ō, -'gwär-ō\ *n.; pl.* **sa·gua·ros.** A giant spiny cactus found in the southwestern states and in Mexico.

said. Past tense and past part. of *say.*

sail \'sāl\ *n.* **1** A three-sided or four-sided piece of canvas or cloth by means of which the wind is used to move boats through the water or over ice. **2** Sails; as, to proceed under full *sail.* **3** A sailing vessel; any vessel; as, to sight a *sail.* **4** Something like a sail, such as a wing or a fin. **5** A voyage or trip on a sailing vessel. — **set sail.** To begin a boat trip. — *v.* **1** To travel on a sailboat. **2** To travel or begin to travel by water; as, to *sail* for England. **3** To move or pass over by ship; as, to *sail* the Atlantic. **4** To take trips in a sailboat. **5** To manage or direct the motion of a vessel. **6** To glide through the air, as a bird. — **sail·ing** \'sā-ling\ *n.*

sail·boat \'sāl-ˌbōt\ *n.* A boat equipped with sails.

sail·cloth \'sāl-ˌklȯth\ *n.* A heavy canvas or duck material used for tents and sails.

sail·fish \'sāl-ˌfish\ *n.; pl.* **sail·fish** or **sail·fish·es.** A West Indian fish related to the swordfish but having scales, teeth, and a very large dorsal fin.

sail·or \'sāl-r\ *n.* **1** A person who sails; a seaman. **2** A person considered with respect to his ability to withstand seasickness; as, a good *sailor.*

sail·plane \'sāl-ˌplān\ *n.* A glider so light that it is able to rise in an upward air current.

saint \'sānt; *when a name follows,* (ˌ)sānt *or* sənt\ *n.* **1** A holy and godly person; especially, such a person who is canonized. **2** A person who is sweet-tempered or self-sacrificing. — *v.* To make a saint of; to canonize.

Saint An·drew's cross \'an-ˌdrüz\. A cross shaped like the letter X.

Saint Ber·nard \bər-'närd, -'nȧrd\. A large powerful dog bred especially in the Swiss Alps.

saint·ed \'sānt-əd\ *adj.* Being a saint; saintly.

saint·hood \'sānt-ˌhu̇d\ *n.* **1** Saintly state. **2** Saints taken as a group; all the saints.

saint·ly \'sānt-lē\ *adj.;* **saint·li·er**; **saint·li·est.** Like a saint; holy; pious.

Saint Vi·tus's dance \'vīt-əs(-əz)\. A nervous disorder characterized by spasmodic twitching.

saith \(')seth, 'sā-əth\. An archaic form of *says.*

sake \'sāk\ *n.* **1** Purpose; motive; end; as, to work for the *sake* of keeping busy. **2** Good, advantage, or well-being; as, for one's country's *sake.*

sa·laam \sə-'läm, -'lȧm\ *n.* A ceremonious Oriental greeting; a very low bow with the hand on the forehead. — *v.* To make a low bow.

sal·a·ble or **sale·a·ble** \'sā-ləb-l\ *adj.* **1** Fit to be sold. **2** Likely to be bought; easy to sell. — **sal·a·bil·i·ty** or **sale·a·bil·i·ty** \ˌsā-lə-'bil-ət-ē\ *n.*

sal·ad \'sal-əd\ *n.* **1** A cold dish generally of raw green vegetables, served with oil, vinegar, and seasonings. **2** Any cold dish of meat, shellfish, fruit, or vegetables, served singly or in combinations, with a dressing.

sal·a·man·der \'sal-ə-ˌmand-r\ *n.* Any of numerous amphibians that resemble the lizard but have a soft, moist skin and no scales.

sal·a·ried \'sal-r(-)ēd\ *adj.* **1** Receiving a salary. **2** Yielding a salary; as, a *salaried* position.

sal·a·ry \'sal-r(-)ē\ *n.; pl.* **sal·a·ries.** Money paid at regular intervals, as monthly, for work done.

sale \'sāl\ *n.* **1** The act or business of selling; an exchange of goods or property for money; as, to make *sales.* **2** The purpose of selling or being sold; as, a house offered for *sale.* **3** An auction. **4** A selling of goods at reduced prices; as, a clearance *sale.*

sales·man \'sālz-mən\ *n.; pl.* **sales·men** \-mən\. A person whose occupation is selling.

sales·man·ship \'sālz-mən-ˌship\ *n.* The art or skill of being a salesman; ability in selling goods.

sales·wom·an \'sālz-ˌwu̇m-ən\ *n.; pl.* **sales·wom·en** \-ˌwim-ən\. A woman engaged in selling.

sa·lient \'sāl-yənt, 'sā-lē-ənt\ *adj.* **1** Leaping; jumping. **2** Projecting; as, a *salient* angle. **3** Conspicuous; important. — **sa·lient·ly,** *adv.*

sa·line \'sā-ˌlīn, -ˌlēn; *sense 1 of noun is usually* sə-'lēn\ *adj.* **1** Consisting of or containing salt. **2** Of or like salt; salty. — *n.* **1** A natural deposit of any soluble salt. **2** A metallic salt, especially one with a cathartic action. — **sa·lin·i·ty** \sā-'lin-ət-ē, sə-\ *n.*

sa·li·va \sə-'lī-və\ *n.* The watery fluid secreted by glands (**salivary glands**) discharging into the mouth; spit. — **sal·i·vary** \'sal-ə-ˌver-ē\ *adj.*

sal·i·vate \'sal-ə-ˌvāt\ *v.;* **sal·i·vat·ed**; **sal·i·vat·ing.** To secrete saliva, especially in large amounts. — **sal·i·va·tion** \ˌsal-ə-'vāsh-n\ *n.*

Salk vaccine \'sȯ(l)k\. A polio vaccine given by injection.

sal·low \'sal-ō\ *adj.* Of a pale, yellowish, sickly color; as, *sallow* skin. — *v.* To make sallow.

sal·ly \'sal-ē\ *n.; pl.* **sal·lies.** **1** A rushing or bursting forth, especially one by soldiers on their besiegers. **2** A flash of wit; a witty remark. **3** A sallying forth; a jaunt. — *v.;* **sal·lied** \-ēd\; **sal·ly·ing.** To rush forth; to go out, as for a walk.

salm·on \'sam-ən\ *n.; pl.* **salm·on,** rarely **salm·ons.** **1** A large soft-finned food fish with pinkish or reddish flesh, living in coastal waters and going up rivers to lay its eggs. **2** Also **salmon pink.** The light reddish orange color of the flesh of some salmon.

sa·lon \sə-'län, sa-\ *n.* [French.] **1** A large drawing room. **2** A reception held in a salon or the guests attending. **3** An apartment for the exhibition of works of art or the exhibition itself.

sa·loon \sə-'lün\ *n.* [An altered form of French *salon.*] **1** A public room used for some designated purpose; as, the first-class dining *saloon* of a ship. **2** A tavern; a bar.

sal·si·fy \'sal-sə-fē\ *n.* A purple-flowered plant with a long fleshy white-skinned edible root.

sal so·da \'sal 'sōd-ə\. Washing soda.

salt \'sȯlt\ *n.* **1** Sodium chloride, a colorless or white crystalline substance used to season and preserve meats and fish. **2** A saltcellar. **3** [in the plural] Any mineral salt or mixture of salts used as a laxative or cathartic. **4** [in the plural] Smelling salts. **5** A chemical compound derived from an acid by replacement of all or part of the hydrogen by a metallic or other positively charged ion. **6** A sailor. — **with a grain of salt.** With some doubt or reservation. — *adj.* **1** Salted; salty; briny. **2** Coming from, living in, or covered by salt or sea water. — *v.* To preserve, season, treat, or feed with salt. — **salt away** or **salt down.** **1** To pack in salt. **2** To save, or invest safely, as money.

salt·cel·lar \'sȯlt-ˌsel-r\ *n.* A small container for salt, used at the table.

salt·pe·ter or **salt·pe·tre** \(')sȯlt-'pēt-r\ *n.* **1** A chemical used in explosives and in preserving meat; potassium nitrate. **2** Also **Chile saltpeter.** A chemical used chiefly for fertilizer; sodium nitrate.

salt-wa·ter \'sölt-,wöt-r, -,wät-r\ *adj.* Of, relating to, containing, or existing in salt water.

salty \'söl-tē\ *adj.;* **salt·i·er**; **salt·i·est.** Of or containing salt; tasting of or like salt.

sa·lu·bri·ous \sə-'lüb-rē-əs\ *adj.* Healthful; pleasantly invigorating; as, *salubrious* air. — **sa·lu·bri·ous·ly,** *adv.*

sal·u·tary \'sal-yə-,ter-ē\ *adj.* **1** Promoting health; as, *salutary* exercise. **2** Beneficial; as, *salutary* advice.

sal·u·ta·tion \,sal-yə-'tāsh-n\ *n.* **1** The act of saluting or greeting. **2** The words used in greeting, as "Dear Sir", in a letter.

sa·lu·ta·to·ri·an \sə-,lüt-ə-'tōr-ē-ən, -'tör-\ *n.* The graduating student who makes the salutatory address at the graduation ceremonies.

sa·lu·ta·to·ry \sə-'lüt-ə-,tōr-ē, -,tör-ē\ *adj.* Welcoming; speaking a welcome. — *n.; pl.* **sa·lu·ta·to·ries.** An address of greeting.

sa·lute \sə-'lüt\ *v.;* **sa·lut·ed**; **sa·lut·ing. 1** To greet with courteous words or with a bow. **2** In the army or navy, to honor, as a person, a nation, or a festival, by a discharge of cannon or a dipping of the colors. **3** To make the required sign of respect to a superior officer. — *n.* The act of saluting; especially, the position or gesture of a person saluting.

Sal·va·dor·an \,sal-və-'dör-ən\ or **Sal·va·dor·i·an** \-'dör-ē-ən\ *adj.* Of or relating to El Salvador or its people. — *n.* A native or citizen of El Salvador.

sal·vage \'sal-vij\ *n.* **1** Money paid for saving a wrecked or endangered ship, its cargo, or passengers. **2** The act of saving a ship; the saving of possessions in danger of being lost. **3** That which is saved or recovered, as from a wreck or fire. — *v.;* **sal·vaged**; **sal·vag·ing.** To rescue, save, or recover, as from wreckage or ruin.

sal·va·tion \sal-'vāsh-n\ *n.* **1** The saving of a person from the power and the effects of sin. **2** The saving from danger or evil; as, the *salvation* of a country. **3** That which saves, preserves, redeems.

salve \'sav, 'säv\ *n.* An oily or waxy substance applied to the skin to heal or soothe wounds or sores. — *v.;* **salved**; **salv·ing.** To quiet or soothe with or as if with a salve.

sal·ver \'salv-r\ *n.* A small tray.

sal·via \'sal-vē-ə\ *n.* An herb of the mint family; especially, a cultivated species with scarlet flowers.

sal·vo \'sal-,vō\ *n.; pl.* **sal·vos** or **sal·voes. 1** In the army, a discharge of one gun after another in a battery. **2** In the navy, a simultaneous discharge of two or more guns at the same target. **3** A burst of shouts or cheers.

sam·ba \'säm-bə, 'sam-, 'säm-\ *n.* A Brazilian dance of fast tempo.

Sam Browne belt \'sam ,braün\. A belt made of leather or heavy cotton webbing that is supported by a strap going over the right shoulder.

same \'sām\ *adj.* **1** Not another; not different; identical; as, to live in the *same* house all one's life. **2** Very much alike; similar; of one kind; as, to eat the *same* breakfast every day. **3** Unchanged; as, a boy who is always the *same.* — *adv.* In the same way; as, two words that are pronounced the *same.* — *pron.* The same person or thing.

sam·o·var \'sam-ə-,vär, -,vär\ *n.* [From Russian, meaning literally "self-boiler".] A Russian urn, often of brass, for making tea.

sam·pan \'sam-,pan\ *n.* Any of various small boats used in the harbors and rivers of China and Japan.

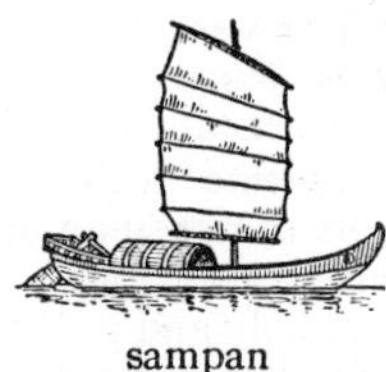
sampan

sam·ple \'samp-l\ *n.* A part or piece that shows the quality of the whole; as, a *sample* of cloth. — *v.;* **sam·pled**; **sam·pling** \-l(-)ing\. To judge the quality of by a sample; to test.

sam·pler \'samp-lər\ *n.* A piece of needlework done as an example of skill, especially one showing embroidered letters or verses.

san·a·to·ri·um \,san-ə-'tōr-ē-əm, -'tör-\ *n.; pl.* **san·a·to·ri·ums** \-ē-əmz\ or **san·a·to·ria** \-ē-ə\. An institution for the care and treatment of convalescents and the chronically ill.

sanc·ti·fy \'sang(k)-tə-,fī\ *v.;* **sanc·ti·fied** \-,fīd\; **sanc·ti·fy·ing. 1** To set apart as sacred; to consecrate. **2** To make free from sin; to purify. — **sanc·ti·fi·ca·tion** \,sang(k)-tə-fə-'kāsh-n\ *n.*

sanc·ti·mo·ni·ous \,sang(k)-tə-'mō-nē-əs\ *adj.* Hypocritically pious. — **sanc·ti·mo·ni·ous·ly,** *adv.*

sanc·tion \'sang(k)sh-n\ *n.* **1** Consent; confirmation; especially, solemn or official approval. **2** A measure employed against a nation breaking international law; as, economic *sanctions.* — *v.;* **sanc·tioned**; **sanc·tion·ing** \-n(-)ing\. To approve; to ratify.

sanc·ti·ty \'sang(k)-tət-ē\ *n.; pl.* **sanc·ti·ties. 1** Holiness; saintliness. **2** Sacredness; religious or moral binding force; as, the *sanctity* of an oath.

sanc·tu·ary \'sang(k)-chə-,wer-ē\ *n.; pl.* **sanc·tu·ar·ies. 1** A holy or sacred place. **2** A building for religious worship. **3** The most sacred part of any building for religious worship. **4** A refuge for wildlife where predators are controlled and hunting is illegal. **5** Protection; refuge; safety.

sanc·tum \'sang(k)t-m\ *n.; pl.* **sanc·tums** \-mz\ or **sanc·ta** \'sang(k)-tə\. **1** A sacred place. **2** A place where one can be in strict privacy; a study.

sand \'sand\ *n.* **1** Small loose bits or grains produced by the wearing away or breaking up of rock. **2** [usually in the plural] A tract, region, or deposit of sand; a beach. **3** The sand in an hourglass or a grain of it that symbolizes a moment or interval of time; as, the *sands* of life. **4** *Slang.* Courage; grit. — *v.* **1** To sprinkle with sand. **2** To fill with sand. **3** To add sand to. **4** To smooth or scour by rubbing with sand or sandpaper.

san·dal \'sand-l\ *n.* **1** A shoe consisting of a sole strapped to the foot. **2** A low or open slipper held in place by a strap or straps. — **san·daled** or **san·dalled** \-ld\ *adj.*

san·dal·wood \'sand-l-ˌwu̇d\ *n.* The fragrant, yellowish heartwood of an Asiatic tree, used in carving and cabinet work; also, the tree itself.

sand·bag \'san(d)-ˌbag\ *n.* **1** A bag filled with sand, used as ballast or as part of a fortification wall or of a temporary dam. **2** A small bag of sand used as a weapon. — *v.;* **sand·bagged**; **sand·bag·ging.** **1** To bank or stop up with sandbags. **2** To hit or stun with a sandbag.

sand·bank \'san(d)-ˌbangk\ *n.* A ridge of sand.

sand·bar \'san(d)-ˌbär, -ˌbȧr\ *n.* A ridge of sand formed in water by tides or currents.

sand·blast \'san(d)-ˌblast\ *n.* A stream of sand forced through a tube by air or steam to cut, engrave, or clean stone or other hard materials. — *v.* To engrave, cut, or clean with a sandblast.

sand·box \'san(d)-ˌbäks\ *n.* A box for holding sand.

sand dollar. Any flat circular sea urchin that lives chiefly in shallow water and on sandy bottoms.

sand·er \'sand-r\ *n.* A device for sanding or a person who operates such a device.

sand flea. A flea found in sandy places.

sand·glass \'san(d)-ˌglas\ *n.* An hourglass.

sand·hog \'sand-ˌhȯg, -ˌhäg\ *n.* One who works, usually in a caisson, in underwater tunnels.

sand·lot \'san(d)-ˌlät\ *n.* A sandy or vacant lot, as used by children for unorganized sports. — *adj.* Of or relating to the sports played on sandlots.

sand·man \'san(d)-ˌman\ *n.* An imaginary person who is supposed to make children sleepy.

sand·pa·per \'san(d)-ˌpāp-r\ *n.* Paper with sand glued on one side, used in rubbing surfaces to smooth or polish them. — *v.;* **sand·pa·pered**; **sand·pa·per·ing** \-r(-)ing\. To rub with sandpaper.

sand·pile \'san(d)-ˌpīl\ *n.* A pile of sand, as for children to play in.

sand·pip·er \'san(d)-ˌpīp-r\ *n.* A slender, short-tailed wading bird, smaller than the related plovers, snipes, and woodcocks and having a longer and soft-tipped bill.

sand·stone \'san(d)-ˌstōn\ *n.* Rock made of sand held together by a natural cement.

sand·storm \'san(d)-ˌstȯrm\ *n.* A storm of wind that drives clouds of sand, as in a desert.

sand table. A table with raised edges to hold sand, as for molding.

sand·wich \'san-ˌ(d)wich\ *n.* Two slices of bread placed one on the other with a filling, as of meat or cheese, between them. — *v.* **1** To make into a sandwich. **2** To put between two other things; as, a valley *sandwiched* between mountains.

sandwich man. A man with two advertising boards, one hung in front of him and one behind.

sand·wort \'san-ˌ(d)wərt, -ˌ(d)wȯrt\ *n.* Any low, tufted chickweed growing in sandy or gritty soil.

sandy \'san-dē\ *adj.;* **sand·i·er**; **sand·i·est.** **1** Consisting of or containing sand. **2** Of the reddish yellow color of sand; as, *sandy* hair.

sane \'sān\ *adj.;* **san·er**; **san·est.** Mentally healthy; sound; rational; sensible. — **sane·ly**, *adv.*

sang. Past tense of *sing.*

san·gui·nary \'sang-gwə-ˌner-ē\ *adj.* **1** Bloody; as, a *sanguinary* battle. **2** Bloodthirsty; murderous.

san·guine \'sang-gwən\ *adj.* **1** Red like blood; ruddy; as, a *sanguine* complexion. **2** Cheerful; hopeful; as, a *sanguine* disposition. **3** Confident; as, *sanguine* of success. **4** Sanguinary. — **san·guine·ly**, *adv.*

san·i·tar·i·um \ˌsan-ə-'ter-ē-əm\ *n.; pl.* **san·i·tar·i·ums** \-ē-əmz\ or **san·i·tar·ia** \-ē-ə\. A sanatorium.

san·i·tary \'san-ə-ˌter-ē\ *adj.* **1** Of or relating to health; hygienic; as, *sanitary* laws. **2** Free from filth, infection, or other dangers to health.

san·i·ta·tion \ˌsan-ə-'tāsh-n\ *n.* The study and use of sanitary measures for the prevention of disease.

san·i·ty \'san-ət-ē\ *n.* Soundness of mind.

sank. Past tense of *sink.*

San Mar·i·nese \ˌsan ˌmar-ə-'nēz, -'nēs\ *adj.* Of or relating to San Marino. — *n. pl.* The people of San Marino.

sans \(')sanz\ *prep. Archaic.* Without.

San·ta Claus \'sant-ə ˌklȯz, 'sant-ē\. [From Dutch *Sinterklaas* or *Sant Nikolaas*, that is, Saint Nicholas, the patron saint of children, a 4th century bishop of Asia Minor whose name day (December 6) was celebrated by the Dutch in the Hudson valley in colonial America by giving gifts to children.] Christmas personified.

sap \'sap\ *n.* **1** The watery part of plants; especially, the solution of foods and nutrients circulating in the vascular system of higher plants. **2** *Slang.* A saphead.

sap \'sap\ *v.;* **sapped**; **sap·ping.** **1** To destroy by undermining. Heavy tides *sapped* the sea wall. **2** To weaken gradually. His long illness *sapped* his strength.

sap·head \'sap-ˌhed\ *n.* A simpleton.

sa·pi·ence \'sāp-ē-ən(t)s, 'sap-\ *n.* Wisdom.

sa·pi·ent \'sāp-ē-ənt, 'sap-\ *adj.* Wise; discerning. — **sa·pi·ent·ly**, *adv.*

sap·ling \'sap-ling\ *n.* A young tree.

sap·o·dil·la \ˌsap-ə-'dil-ə\ *n.* A tropical American evergreen tree with hard reddish wood, an edible brownish berry, and a sap that yields chicle.

sa·pon·i·fy \sə-'pän-ə-ˌfī\ *v.;* **sa·pon·i·fied** \-ˌfīd\; **sa·pon·i·fy·ing.** To convert into soap. — **sa·pon·i·fi·ca·tion** \sə-ˌpän-ə-fə-'kāsh-n\ *n.*

sap·per \'sap-r\ *n.* A military engineer who digs trenches and constructs fortifications.

sap·phire \'saf-ˌīr\ *n.* **1** A transparent, bright blue precious stone. **2** The color of this stone.

sap·py \'sap-ē\ *adj.;* **sap·pi·er**; **sap·pi·est.** **1** Full of sap; vigorous. **2** *Slang.* Silly; foolishly sentimental.

sap·ro·phyte \'sap-rə-ˌfīt\ *n.* Any organism living upon dead or decaying organic matter. — **sap·ro·phyt·ic** \ˌsap-rə-'fit-ik\ *adj.*

sap·suck·er \'sap-ˌsək-r\ *n.* Any of several small American woodpeckers that feed partly on sap.

sap·wood \'sap-ˌwu̇d\ *n.* The young, living wood just beneath the bark of a tree.

sar·casm \'sär-ˌkaz-m, 'sȧr-\ *n.* **1** A cutting remark; a bitter rebuke. **2** The use of sharp, stinging remarks expressing contempt, often made in the form of irony. — For synonyms see *irony*.

sar·cas·tic \sär-'kas-tik, sȧr-\ *adj.* **1** Having the habit of sarcasm. **2** Containing sarcasm; as, a *sarcastic* remark. — **sar·cas·ti·cal·ly** \-tik-l(-)ē\ *adv.*

sar·co·ma \sär-'kō-mə, sȧr-\ *n.; pl.* **sar·co·mas** \-məz\ or **sar·co·ma·ta** \-mət-ə\. A malignant growth of bone, cartilage, or muscle.

sar·coph·a·gus \sär-'käf-ə-gəs, sȧr-\ *n.; pl.* **sar·coph·a·gus·es** \-gə-səz\ or **sar·coph·a·gi** \-ˌgī, -ˌjī\. [From Latin, there borrowed from Greek *sarkophagos* meaning literally "flesh-eater" and applied originally to a kind of limestone that disintegrated bodies and then to coffins made of this stone.] A stone coffin; any large coffin exposed to view in the open air or in a tomb.

sar·dine \(')sär-'dēn, (')sȧr-\ *n.; pl.* **sar·dines** or **sar·dine.** A young, very small fish, often preserved in oil and used for food.

sar·don·ic \sär-'dän-ik, sȧr-\ *adj.* Scornful; mocking; sneering. — **sar·don·i·cal·ly** \-ik-l(-)ē\ *adv.*

sar·do·nyx \'särd-n-(ˌ)iks, 'sȧrd-\ *n.* Onyx having layers of carnelian.

sar·gas·so \sär-'gas-ˌō, sȧr-\ *n.; pl.* **sar·gas·sos.** A greenish brown seaweed of the Atlantic Ocean.

sar·gas·sum \sär-'gas-m, sȧr-\ *n.* Sargasso.

sa·ri \'sär-ē, 'sȧr-ē\ *n.* A woman's dress much used in India, consisting of a long cloth wrapped round and draped on the body.

sa·rong \sə-'rȯng, -'räng\ *n.* A long strip of cloth wrapped round the body like a skirt, worn by both men and women in the Malay Archipelago.

sar·sa·pa·ril·la \ˌsas-(ə-)pə-'ril-ə, ˌsärs-, ˌsȧrs-\ *n.* **1** The dried roots of a tropical American woody plant, used in medicine and for flavoring. **2** The plant itself. **3** Soda water flavored with sarsaparilla.

sar·to·ri·al \sär-'tōr-ē-əl, sȧr-, -'tȯr-\ *adj.* Of or relating to a tailor or tailoring.

sash \'sash\ *n.; pl.* **sash·es** or, collectively, **sash.** **1** In a door or window, a frame for a pane of glass. **2** The movable part of a window.

sash
sash, 2

sash \'sash\ *n.* A broad band, as of silk, worn around the waist or over the shoulder.

sas·sa·fras \'sas-ə-ˌfras\ *n.* **1** A tree of the laurel family with fragrant yellow flowers and blue-black berries. **2** The dried bark of the root of this tree, used in medicine and for flavoring.

sassy \'sas-ē\ *adj.;* **sass·i·er; sass·i·est.** *Dial.* Saucy.

sat. Past tense and past part. of *sit.*

Sat. Abbreviation for *Saturday.*

Sa·tan \'sāt-n\ *n.* **1** The evil spirit that tempts men to sin; the Devil. **2** [often with a small letter] A cruel and wicked person; a devil; a fiend.

sa·tan·ic \sə-'tan-ik, sā-\ *adj.* Of, relating to, or like Satan; devilish; fiendish. — **sa·tan·i·cal·ly** \-ik-l(-)ē\ *adv.*

satch·el \'sach-l\ *n.* A small bag of leather or heavy cloth for carrying clothes or books.

sate \'sāt\ *v.;* **sat·ed; sat·ing.** **1** To satisfy to the full. **2** To satiate.

sa·teen \sa-'tēn\ *n.* A cotton fabric finished with a glossy surface to resemble satin.

sat·el·lite \'sat-l-ˌīt\ *n.* **1** An attendant of a prince or other great person. **2** In astronomy, a smaller body that revolves around a planet. **3** A man-made vehicle designed to be sent out from the earth to revolve around the earth or the moon. **4** A country dominated by a powerful neighboring country in politics and trade.

sa·ti·ate \'sā-shē-ˌāt\ *v.;* **sa·ti·at·ed; sa·ti·at·ing.** To fill beyond natural desire; to stuff; to glut.

sa·ti·e·ty \sə-'tī-ət-ē\ *n.* The condition of being satiated; as, to eat to *satiety.*

sat·in \'sat-n\ *n.* A closely woven cloth of silk, rayon, or nylon with a smooth shiny surface and a dull back. — *adj.* **1** Of satin. **2** Like satin; satiny.

sat·in·et \ˌsat-n-'et\ *n.* A cheap, thin satin or imitation satin.

sat·in·wood \'sat-n-ˌwu̇d\ *n.* **1** A hard yellowish brown wood with a satiny luster. **2** Any of several trees yielding such wood, especially a mahogany of the East Indies.

sat·iny \'sat-n-ē\ *adj.* **1** Of satin. **2** Like satin; soft, smooth, and shiny; lustrous.

sat·ire \'sa-ˌtīr\ *n.* **1** A literary work holding up to scorn and ridicule persons, ideas, or practices regarded as evil or foolish. **2** Biting wit or sarcasm used in exposing and attacking faults and follies.

sa·tir·ic \sə-'tir-ik\ or **sa·tir·i·cal** \-ik-l\ *adj.* **1** Of or relating to satire. **2** Usually *satirical.* Given to the use of satire. — **sa·tir·i·cal·ly** \-ik-l(-)ē\ *adv.*

sat·i·rist \'sat-r-əst\ *n.* A writer of satires.

sat·i·rize \'sat-r-ˌīz\ *v.;* **sat·i·rized; sat·i·riz·ing.** To attack in or as if in a satire; to hold up to ridicule.

sat·is·fac·tion \ˌsat-əs-'faksh-n\ *n.* **1** The act of satisfying or the state of being satisfied. **2** Something that satisfies, as an apology or compensation.

sat·is·fac·to·ry \ˌsat-əs-'fakt-r(-)ē\ *adj.* Satisfying or sufficient or adequate to satisfy. — **sat·is·fac·to·ri·ly** \-'fakt-r(-)ə-lē\ *adv.*

sat·is·fy \'sat-əs-ˌfī\ *v.;* **sat·is·fied** \-ˌfīd\; **sat·is·fy·ing.** **1** To supply what is wanted or expected; to gratify; as, to *satisfy* the baby with his bottle. **2** To quiet; to appease; as, to *satisfy* one's hunger. **3** To give what is due to; to pay or pay off; to discharge; as, to *satisfy* a creditor; to *satisfy* a claim. **4** To convince; as, to be *satisfied* of his innocence. **5** To answer convincingly; as, to *satisfy* all objections. **6** To meet a requirement; to fulfill a condition. — **sat·is·fy·ing·ly** \-ˌfī-ing-lē\ *adv.*

sa·trap \'sā-ˌtrap, 'sa-trəp\ *n.* **1** The governor of a province in ancient Persia. **2** A subordinate ruler; especially, a tyrannical or cruel subordinate ruler.

sat·u·ra·ble \'sach-r(-)əb-l\ *adj.* Capable of saturation. — **sat·u·ra·bil·i·ty** \ˌsach-r(-)ə-'bil-ət-ē\ *n.*

sat·u·rate \'sach-r-ˌāt\ *v.;* **sat·u·rat·ed; sat·u·rat·ing. 1** To cause to become soaked through and through. **2** To treat, fill, or charge to the point (**saturation point**) where no more can be absorbed or held in solution or suspension.

sat·u·rat·ed \'sach-r-ˌāt-əd\ *adj.* **1** In a state of saturation. **2** Of colors, not diluted with white.

sat·u·ra·tion \ˌsach-r-'āsh-n\ *n.* The act or process of saturating or the state of being saturated.

Sat·ur·day \'sat-r-dē\ *n.* [From Old English *Saeterdaeg, Saeternesdaeg,* a translation of Latin *Saturni dies* meaning literally "day of Saturn" (the planet).] The seventh day of the week.

sat·ur·na·lia \ˌsat-r-'nāl-yə\ *n. pl.* **1** [with a capital] An ancient Roman festival held in honor of Saturn, the god of the seed sowing. **2** An occasion or a period marked by a great amount of vice and crime or by excessive lack of restraint in behavior.

sat·ur·nine \'sat-r-ˌnīn\ *adj.* Gloomy; grave.

sat·yr \'sat-r, 'sāt-r\ *n.* **1** A forest god in Greek mythology, having a horse's ears and tail, and given to boisterous pleasures. **2** A man whose habits are suggestive of a satyr.

sauce \'sȯs\ *n.* **1** A tasty mixture, often liquid, to be added to food for extra flavor. **2** Stewed fruit; as, apple *sauce.* **3** \'sas, 'sȯs\ Impudence; sauciness. — *v.;* **sauced; sauc·ing. 1** \'sȯs\ To add sauce to; to season; to flavor. **2** \'sas, 'sȯs\ To be saucy or impudent to.

sauce·pan \'sȯs-ˌpan\ *n.* A cooking utensil with a handle, used for stewing and boiling.

sau·cer \'sȯs-r\ *n.* **1** A small shallow dish on which to set a cup. **2** Any of various objects resembling a saucer.

saucy, *adj.;* **sauc·i·er; sauc·i·est. 1** \'sas-ē, 'sȯs-ē\ Bold; disrespectful; as, a *saucy* child. **2** \'sȯs-ē\ Amusingly pert; as, a *saucy* smile. **3** \'sȯs-ē, 'sas-ē\ Smart; trim; as, a *saucy* hat.

sauer·kraut \'saůr-ˌkraůt\ *n.* [From German, meaning literally "sour cabbage".] Finely cut cabbage fermented in brine.

saun·ter \'sȯnt-r, 'sänt-r\ *v.;* **saun·tered; saun·ter·ing** \-r(-)ing\. To walk about slowly and idly.

sau·ri·an \'sȯr-ē-ən\ *n.* A long-bodied four-limbed reptile, as a lizard or a dinosaur.

sau·sage \'sȯs-ij\ *n.* **1** Pork or other meat minced and highly seasoned. **2** A roll of this in a casing.

sau·té \sō-'tā, sȯ-\ *v.;* **sau·téed; sau·té·ing.** To fry quickly in shallow fat. — *n.* A sautéed dish.

sav·age \'sav-ij\ *adj.* **1** Wild; not tamed. **2** Uncivilized; barbarous. **3** Cruel and brutal; fierce. — *n.* **1** A savage person. **2** One who is not civilized. — **sav·age·ly,** *adv.*

sav·age·ry \'sav-ij-r(-)ē\ *n.; pl.* **sav·age·ries. 1** Savage disposition or action; cruelty. **2** The state or condition of being savage.

sa·van·na or **sa·van·nah** \sə-'van-ə\ *n.* A treeless plain; an open grassland of warm regions.

sa·vant \sa-'vän(t), 'sav-nt\ *n.* A scholar.

save \'sāv\ *v.;* **saved; sav·ing. 1** To make safe; to rescue from danger. **2** To guard; to protect; as, to *save* fruits from spoiling. **3** To keep; to lay by or aside; as, to *save* money. **4** To deliver from the power or effects of sin. **5** To keep from spending; as, to *save* money by walking. **6** To avoid unnecessary waste or expense. — **sav·er** \'sāv-r\ *n.*

save \'sāv\ *prep.* Except; as, to be on time regularly, *save* on one occasion.

sav·ing \'sā-ving\ *adj.* **1** Rescuing; redeeming; making safe. **2** Economical; thrifty. **3** Making up for something else; as, a *saving* sense of humor. — *n.* **1** The act of rescuing; as, the *saving* of lives. **2** Something saved; especially [in the plural] money saved over a period of time.

sav·ings bank \'sā-vingz\. A bank that receives small deposits and pays compound interest.

sav·ior or **sav·iour** \'sāv-yər\ *n.* **1** One who saves from ruin or danger. **2** [with a capital] In Christian use, Jesus Christ.

sa·vor \'sāv-r\ *n.* **1** The taste and odor of a thing; as, the *savor* of roast meat. **2** Distinctive quality; smack. — *v.;* **sa·vored; sa·vor·ing** \-r(-)ing\. **1** To flavor. **2** To taste or smell with pleasure. **3** To have the flavor of; to smack.

sa·vory \'sāv-r(-)ē\ *adj.;* **sa·vor·i·er; sa·vor·i·est.** Pleasing to the taste or smell; as, *savory* sausages.

sa·vory \'sāv-r(-)ē\ *n.* An herb of the mint family, dried and powdered for use as a seasoning.

saw \'sȯ\ *n.* A common saying; a proverb.

saw \'sȯ\ *n.* **1** A tool or instrument with a tooth-edged cutting blade. **2** A machine that operates a toothed blade. — *v.;* **sawed** \'sȯd\; **sawed** \'sȯd\ or **sawn** \'sȯn\; **saw·ing. 1** To cut or shape with a saw. **2** To slice through with motions like those of one using a saw.

saw \'sȯ\. Past tense of *see.*

saw·buck \'sȯ-ˌbək\ *n.* A sawhorse.

saw·dust \'sȯ-(ˌ)dəst\ *n.* Fine particles, as of wood, which fall from something being sawed.

saw·fly \'sȯ-ˌflī\ *n.; pl.* **saw·flies.** Any of numerous insects related to the wasps and bees and having females usually with a pair of organs for making incisions in leaves or stems for laying her eggs.

saw·horse \'sȯ-ˌhȯrs\ *n.* A frame or rack on which wood is rested while being sawed by hand.

saw·mill \'sȯ-ˌmil\ *n.* **1** A mill having machinery for sawing logs. **2** A machine for sawing logs.

saw·yer \'sȯ-yər\ *n.* One who saws timber.

sax·horn \'saks-ˌhȯrn\ *n.* [Named after Antoine Joseph (also known as Adolphe) *Sax* (1814–1894), the Belgian maker of musical instruments who invented it — see *saxophone.*] A brass horn with a loud, full sound, much used in military bands.

sax·i·frage \'saks-ə-frij\ *n.* Any of a group of plants with showy five-parted flowers and often with leaves growing in tufts close to the ground.

sax·o·phone \'saks-ə-ˌfōn\ *n.* [Named after A. J. *Sax,* its inventor — see *saxhorn.*] A musical instrument in the form of a bent cone-shaped metal tube with finger keys and a reed mouthpiece like that of the clarinet.

say \'sā\ *v.;* **said** \(')sed, səd\; **say·ing** \'sā-ing\. **1** To express in words; to utter; to tell. **2** To state as one's opinion or decision; to declare; to announce; as, to be unable to *say* when school will close. **3** To repeat; to recite; as, to *say* one's prayers. **4** To state as common opinion or belief. **—** *n.* **1** That which a person says or wishes to say. **2** The power of deciding.

say·ing \'sā-ing\ *n.* A proverb; a saw.

says \(')sez, səz\. A form of the word *say* showing present time and used with *he, she,* or *it,* or with words for which these stand — used also informally with *I.*

say–so \'sā-ˌsō\ *n.; pl.* **say–sos. 1** A claim; an assertion. **2** Authority; right of final decision.

scab \'skab\ *n.* **1** A crust that forms over a sore or wound. **2** A disease of animals or plants marked by the formation of spots resembling crusts; as, potato *scab.* **3** One who takes the place of a striking workman. **—** *v.;* **scabbed; scab·bing. 1** To become covered with a scab. **2** To work as a scab.

scab·bard \'skab-rd\ *n.* A protective case, or sheath, for the blade of a sword or dagger.

scab·by \'skab-ē\ *adj.;* **scab·bi·er; scab·bi·est. 1** Covered with scabs; consisting of scabs. **2** Diseased with the scab. **3** Mean; contemptible.

sca·bies \'skā-bēz\ *n.* An itch caused by mites living as parasites under the skin; mange.

scaf·fold \'skaf-ld, -ˌōld\ *n.* **1** An elevated platform built as a support for workmen and their tools and materials, as in building or painting. **2** A platform on which a criminal is executed.

scaf·fold·ing \'skaf-l-ding, -ˌōl-ding\ *n.* A scaffold or group of scaffolds; materials for scaffolds.

scal·a·wag \'skal-ə-ˌwag, 'skal-ē-\ *n.* **1** A rascal; a scamp. **2** A white Southerner who favored the Republican party following the Civil War.

scald \'skȯld\ *v.* **1** To burn with or as if with hot liquid or steam; as, to *scald* one's hand. **2** To pour very hot water over; as, to *scald* dishes. **3** To bring to a heat just below the boiling point; as, to *scald* milk. **—** *n.* A burn caused by scalding.

scale \'skāl\ *n.* **1** Either pan of a balance. **2** [usually in the plural] A balance itself. **3** Any device for weighing. **—** *v.;* **scaled; scal·ing. 1** To weigh or be weighed in scales. **2** To have a weight of; to weigh.

scale \'skāl\ *n.* **1** A small hard plate forming part of the outside body covering of certain animals, as fish and snakes. **2** Any thin layer resembling the scale of a fish, as one of the tiny leaves which protect a bud (**bud scale**). **3** One of the small dry pieces of skin shed in some diseases. **4** A scale insect. **—** *v.;* **scaled; scal·ing. 1** To strip or clear of scales; as, to *scale* fish. **2** To shed scales. **3** To break or peel off in pieces like scales.

scale \'skāl\ *n.* **1** A ladder; a series of steps. **2** Anything divided into regular spaces; as, the *scale* on a thermometer; a ruler is a *scale.* **3** A basis for a system of numbering; as, the decimal *scale.* **4** A graduated series; as, the *scale* of prices. **5** The size of a picture, plan, or model of a thing in proportion to the size of the thing itself. **6** A relative size or degree; as, to do things on a large *scale.* **7** A standard by which something can be measured or judged. **8** In music, a graduated series of tones going up or down in pitch according to a scheme of intervals. **—** *v.;* **scaled; scal·ing. 1** To climb by or as if by a ladder or a series of steps; to ascend. **2** To arrange in a scale or graded series. **3** To reduce according to some fixed ratio; as, to *scale* down prices.

scale insect. Any of many small insects related to the aphids, whose young suck the juices of plants.

sca·lene \'skā-ˌlēn, skā-'lēn\ *adj.* **1** Having sides and angles unequal; as, a *scalene* triangle. **2** Having the axis leaning toward the base; as, a *scalene* cone.

scal·lion \'skal-yən\ *n.* A leek.

scal·lop \'skäl-əp, 'skal-\ *n.* **1** A shellfish whose rounded shell has two parts, or valves, each of which is ribbed. **2** One of the rounded or angular divisions forming an edge like that of a scallop shell in lace or embroidery. **—** *v.* **1** To embroider, cut, or edge with scallops; as, to *scallop* a collar. **2** To bake with crumbs, butter, and milk; as, *scalloped* oysters.

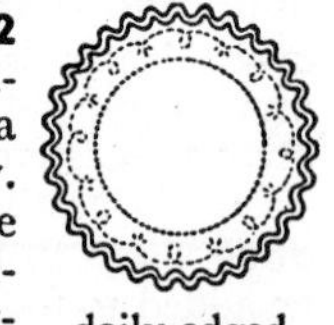
doily edged with scallops

scalp \'skalp\ *n.* **1** The part of the skin and flesh of the head usually covered with hair. **2** Part of this skin cut off as a sign of victory, as by American Indians in warfare. **—** *v.* **1** To remove the scalp by cutting or tearing. **2** To buy and sell so as to make small quick profits. **3** To buy up, as tickets for a theater, so as to sell at higher than the official price. — **scalp·er** \-r\ *n.*

scal·pel \'skalp-l, (')skal-'pel\ *n.* A small straight knife with a thin sharp blade, used by surgeons.

scaly \'skā-lē\ *adj.;* **scal·i·er; scal·i·est. 1** Covered with scales. **2** Coming off in flakes; as, a soft *scaly* stone. **3** Infested with scale insects.

scamp \'skamp\ *n.* A worthless fellow; a rascal. **—** *v.* To perform hastily; to skimp.

scam·per \'skamp-r\ *v.;* **scam·pered; scam·per·ing** \-r(-)ing\. To run or move lightly and hurriedly. **—** *n.* A scampering; a quick run.

scan \'skan\ *v.;* **scanned; scan·ning. 1** To read or mark verses so as to show their divisions into feet. **2** To reveal a definite metrical pattern; as, verse that *scans* easily. **3** To look over point by point; to examine closely. **4** To look over hastily.

scan·dal \'skand-l\ *n.* **1** Offense caused by something considered morally wrong. **2** Shame; disgrace. **3** Something that is a disgrace. **4** Malicious, lying gossip; spiteful talk.

scan·dal·ize \'skand-l-ˌīz\ *v.;* **scan·dal·ized; scan·dal·iz·ing.** To shock the moral sense. Her cruelty to the child *scandalized* the neighbors.

scan·dal·mon·ger \'skand-l-ˌməng-gr\ *n.* A person who spreads scandal.

scan·dal·ous \'skand-l(-)əs\ *adj.* **1** Scandalizing; offensive; disgraceful; as, *scandalous* behavior.

2 Spreading scandal; defamatory; as, a *scandalous* story. — **scan·dal·ous·ly**, *adv.*

Scan·di·na·vi·an \ˌskan-də-ˈnā-vē-ən\ *adj.* Of or relating to the peninsula occupied by Norway and Sweden or to the countries of Norway, Sweden, Denmark, or Iceland. — *n.* **1** A native or inhabitant of Norway, Sweden, Denmark, or Iceland. **2** The languages of the people of Norway, Sweden, Denmark, and Iceland.

scan·ning \ˈskan-ing\ *n.* **1** In television, the process of breaking up a picture into a series of lines of varying dark and light and of reproducing the picture at the receiving set by a corresponding series of lines. **2** In radar, the process of directing the electric waves that detect objects or the process by which objects cause an image or other effect in the receiver.

scan·sion\ ˈskanch-n\ *n.* The scanning of verse.

scant \ˈskant\ *adj.* **1** Scanty; as, a *scant* lunch. **2** Just short of; not quite full; as, a *scant* quart of milk. **3** Having an insufficient supply; as, *scant* of money. — *v.* To skimp; to stint. — **scant·ly**, *adv.*

scant·ling \ˈskant-ling\ *n.* A small piece of lumber; especially, one of the upright pieces in the frame of a house; a stud.

scanty \ˈskant-ē\ *adj.;* **scant·i·er**; **scant·i·est**. **1** Barely enough; meager; lacking size or extent. **2** Less than is needed; insufficient. — **scant·i·ly** \-l-ē\ *adv.*

scape \ˈskāp\ *n.* **1** A leafless stalk supporting a flower, which begins at or beneath the surface of the ground, as in the tulip. **2** In zoology, a shaft, as of a feather.

scape·goat \ˈskāp-ˌgōt\ *n.* One bearing the blame for something others have done.

scape·grace \ˈskāp-ˌgrās\ *n.* A rascal.

scap·u·la \ˈskap-yə-lə\ *n.; pl.* **scap·u·las** \-ləz\ or **scap·u·lae** \-ˌlē\. The shoulder blade. — **scap·u·lar** \-yəl-r\ *adj.*

scar \ˈskär, ˈskȧr\ *n.* **1** A mark left after a wound or sore has healed. **2** An ugly or disfiguring mark, as on furniture. **3** The lasting effect of some unhappy experience; as, to bear the *scars* of prison. — *v.;* **scarred**; **scar·ring**. To mark or become marked with a scar; to leave a scar.

scar·ab \ˈskar-əb\ *n.* **1** A large black or nearly black beetle regarded by the ancient Egyptians as symbolic of resurrection and immortality. **2** An ornament or a gem made to represent this beetle.

scar·a·bae·us \ˌskar-ə-ˈbē-əs\ *n.; pl.* **scar·a·bae·us·es** \-ˈbē-ə-səz\ or **scar·a·baei** \-ˈbē-ˌī\. A scarab.

scarce \ˈskers\ *adj.;* **scarc·er**; **scarc·est**. Not plentiful; uncommon. — For synonyms see *rare.*

scarce·ly \ˈskers-lē\ *adv.* **1** Barely; only just. **2** Certainly not; very probably not.

scar·ci·ty \ˈsker-sət-ē\ *n.; pl.* **scar·ci·ties**. The condition of being scarce; a very small supply.

scare \ˈsker\ *v.;* **scared**; **scar·ing**. **1** To frighten suddenly; to startle. **2** To be scared; to take alarm; as, to *scare* easily. — *n.* A sudden fright.

scare·crow \ˈsker-ˌkrō\ *n.* **1** An object, usually suggesting a human figure, set up to scare away birds and animals that might destroy crops. **2** A ragged, dirty person who looks like such a figure.

scarf \ˈskärf, ˈskȧrf\ *n.; pl.* **scarves** \-rvz\ or **scarfs** \-rfs\. **1** A long band of cloth worn loosely around the neck, over the shoulders, or on the head. **2** A necktie. **3** A long narrow strip of cloth used as a cover, as on a bureau or a sideboard.

scarf·skin \ˈskärf-ˌskin, ˈskȧrf-\ *n.* The epidermis.

scar·i·fy \ˈsker-ə-ˌfī\ *v.;* **scar·i·fied** \-ˌfīd\; **scar·i·fy·ing**. **1** To scratch; to cut the skin of. **2** To wound or lacerate, as the feelings.

scar·la·ti·na \ˌskär-lə-ˈtē-nə, ˌskȧr-\ *n.* Scarlet fever, especially in a mild form.

scar·let \ˈskär-lət, ˈskȧr-\ *n.* **1** A very bright red color with a tinge of yellow or orange. **2** Scarlet cloth or clothes. — *adj.* Of the color scarlet.

scarlet fever. A contagious disease marked by sore throat, a high fever, and a scarlet rash.

scarlet runner. A high-climbing tropical American bean with red flowers and red-and-black seeds.

scarlet tanager. A common American tanager, the male of which is scarlet with black wings.

scarp \ˈskärp, ˈskȧrp\ *n.* **1** The inner side of a ditch or moat around a fort. **2** A steep descent. — *v.* To cut down vertically or into a steep slope.

scarred. Past tense and past part. of *scar.*

scarring. Pres. part. of *scar.*

scarves. A pl. of *scarf.*

scary \ˈsker-ē\ *adj.;* **scar·i·er**; **scar·i·est**. **1** Easily scared; timid. **2** Causing fright.

scathe·less \ˈskāth-ləs\ *adj.* Unhurt.

scath·ing \ˈskā-thing\ *adj.* Hurtful; bitterly severe; as, a *scathing* rebuke. — **scath·ing·ly**, *adv.*

scat·ter \ˈskat-r\ *v.* **1** To throw, cast, or sow here and there; as, to *scatter* grass seed. **2** To separate and go in different directions. The crowd *scattered.*

scat·ter·brain \ˈskat-r-ˌbrān\ or **scat·ter·brains** \-ˌbrānz\ *n.* A person unable to keep his mind on one thing. — **scat·ter·brained** \-ˌbrānd\ *adj.*

scat·ter·ing \ˈskat-r-ing\ *adj.* Found or placed far apart or at irregular intervals. — *n.* A small number or quantity placed or found here and there. Only a *scattering* of people attended the concert.

scav·en·ger \ˈskav-nj-r\ *n.* **1** A person who removes rubbish and waste from the streets. **2** Any animal that lives largely on refuse.

sce·na·rio \sə-ˈnar-ē-ˌō, -ˈner-, -ˈnär-, -ˈnȧr-\ *n.; pl.* **sce·na·ri·os**. **1** A summary of the plot of a play or an opera. **2** A written version of the story of a motion picture, giving details of the action, scene by scene, to be followed by the cast and director.

sce·na·rist \-əst\ *n.* A writer of scenarios.

scene \ˈsēn\ *n.* **1** A division of an act in a play. **2** A single happening or incident in a play or story. **3** The place and time of the action in a play or story; setting. **4** The place or circumstances in which any incident or event takes place. **5** [usually in the plural] Stage scenery; as, to change *scenes.* **6** Something that attracts or holds one's gaze; a view; as, a beautiful winter *scene.* **7** A show of feeling, as of anger; as, to make a *scene*.

scen·ery \'sēn-r(-)ē\ *n.; pl.* **scen·er·ies. 1** The painted scenes used upon a stage and the furnishings that go with them. **2** Outdoor scenes or views in general; as, mountain *scenery*.

sce·nic \'sē-nik\ *adj.* **1** Of or relating to scenery; picturesque; as, *scenic* effects; a *scenic* route. **2** Representing an action or event in pictured form; as, a *scenic* frieze.

scent \'sent\ *v.* **1** To become aware of or to trace by means of the sense of smell; to smell. The dog *scented* a rabbit. **2** To get a hint of; to discover the existence of; as, to *scent* trouble. **3** To fill with an odor; to perfume; as, to *scent* a handkerchief. — *n.* **1** A smell; a fragrant odor. **2** An odor left by some animal or person or given forth, as by flowers, at a distance. The dogs followed the fox's *scent.* **3** Sense of smell. **4** A course followed in search of something; as, to be thrown off the *scent.* **5** Perfume; as, a bottle of *scent.*

scep·ter or **scep·tre** \'sept-r\ *n.* A staff borne by a ruler as a sign of authority.

sceptic. Variant of *skeptic.*

scepticism. Variant of *skepticism.*

sched·ule \'skej-ˌül, 'skej-l\ *n.* **1** A written or printed formal list or statement of details. **2** A timetable; as, a *schedule* of trains. — *v.;* **sched·uled; sched·ul·ing.** To form into a schedule; to add to a schedule.

sche·mat·ic \skē-'mat-ik\ *adj.* Of or relating to a scheme, plan, or diagram; diagrammatic. — **sche·mat·i·cal·ly** \-ik-l(-)ē\ *adv.*

scheme \'skēm\ *n.* **1** A plan or program of something to be done; a project. **2** A secret plan; a plot. **3** A systematic design; as, the color *scheme* of a room. — *v.;* **schemed; schem·ing.** To form a scheme. — **schem·er** \'skēm-r\ *n.*

Schick test \'shik\. A test to discover if a person is susceptible to diphtheria.

schism \'s(k)iz-m\ *n.* Division or separation, especially in a church.

schis·mat·ic \s(k)iz-'mat-ik\ *adj.* Of or having to do with schism; causing schism. — *n.* A person who creates or takes part in a schism.

schol·ar \'skäl-r\ *n.* **1** A student in a school; a pupil. **2** A holder of a scholarship. **3** One who has engaged in advanced study and knows a great deal about one or more subjects. — **schol·ar·ly,** *adv.*

schol·ar·ship \'skäl-r-ˌship\ *n.* **1** The qualities of a scholar; learning. **2** A foundation or endowment to help deserving students. **3** An allowance made to a student to help him further his studies.

scho·las·tic \skə-'las-tik\ *adj.* Having to do with schools, pupils, education, or scholarship. — **scho·las·ti·cal·ly** \-tik-l(-)ē\ *adv.*

school \'skül\ *n.* A large number of one kind of fish or water animals swimming together; a shoal; as, a *school* of mackerel.

school \'skül\ *n.* **1** A place for teaching and learning; as, public *schools;* a music *school.* **2** The body of teachers and pupils in such a place. The whole *school* has measles. **3** A session of school; as, no *school* today. **4** A schoolhouse. **5** A division for specialized study within a university; as, the law *school;* the *school* of medicine. **6** A body of persons who share the same opinions and beliefs; as, the modern French *school* of painting. — *v.* To teach; to train; to drill; as, to *school* a horse.

school·bag \'skül-ˌbag\ *n.* A bag designed for carrying schoolbooks.

school board. A board in charge of local public schools.

school·book \'skül-ˌbu̇k\ *n.* A school textbook.

school·boy \'skül-ˌbȯi\ *n.* A boy in school.

school·fel·low \'skül-ˌfel-ō\ *n.* A schoolmate.

school·girl \'skül-ˌgərl\ *n.* A girl in school.

school·house \'skül-ˌhau̇s\ *n.; pl.* **school·hous·es** \-ˌhau̇-zəz\. A building used for a school.

school·ing \'skü-ling\ *n.* School education.

school·mas·ter \'skül-ˌmast-r\ *n.* A man who has charge of a school or teaches in a school.

school·mate \'skül-ˌmāt\ *n.* A fellow pupil.

school·mis·tress \'skül-ˌmis-trəs\ *n.* A woman who has charge of a school or teaches in a school.

school·room \'skül-ˌrüm, -ˌru̇m\ *n.* A classroom.

school·teach·er \'skül-ˌtēch-r\ *n.* A person who teaches in a school.

school·work \'skül-ˌwərk\ *n.* Lessons done in classes at school or assigned to be done at home.

school·yard \'skül-ˌyärd, -ˌyȧrd\ *n.* The playground of a school.

schoo·ner \'skün-r\ *n.* A fore-and-aft rigged vessel with two or more masts.

schooner

schot·tische or **schot·tish** \'shät-ish\ *n.* **1** A round dance resembling the polka but slower. **2** Music for this dance.

schwa \'shwä\ *n.* **1** The unstressed sound used for the first and third *a*'s of the word *banana.* **2** The pronunciation symbol [ə], widely used for this sound and also often used for the stressed sound of *u* in *bundle.*

sci·at·ic \sī-'at-ik\ *adj.* Of or relating to the hip; affecting the hip.

sci·at·i·ca \sī-'at-ik-ə\ *n.* **1** Inflammation of the **sciatic nerve,** a nerve running down the back of the thigh. **2** Any pain in or near the hip.

sci·ence \'sī-ən(t)s\ *n.* [From medieval English *siens, science,* there borrowed from medieval French *science,* where it was derived from Latin *scientia* meaning "knowledge".] **1** Systematized knowledge. **2** Art or skill; as, the *science* of boxing. **3** A branch of study concerned with observing and classifying facts and attempting to make up general laws about them. Physics is a *science.*

sci·en·tif·ic \ˌsī-ən-'tif-ik\ *adj.* **1** Having to do with science or scientists. **2** Using or applying the laws of science; as, *scientific* farming. — **sci·en·tif·i·cal·ly** \-ik-l(-)ē\ *adv.*

sci·en·tist \'sī-ən-təst\ *n.* A person versed in science or engaged in scientific work.

scim·i·tar \'sim-ət-r, -ə-ˌtär, -ə-ˌtȧr\ or **scim·i·ter** \'sim-ət-r\ *n.* A sword with a curved blade, used chiefly in Moslem countries.

scimitar

scin·til·la \(ˈ)sin-'til-ə\ *n.* [From Latin, meaning literally "spark".] A spark or trace.

scin·til·late \'sint-l-ˌāt\ *v.;* **scin·til·lat·ed; scin·til·lat·ing. 1** To give off sparks: to sparkle. **2** To flash or gleam by or as if by emitting sparks; as, *scintillating* wit. — **scin·til·la·tion** \ˌsint-l-'āsh-n\ *n.*

sci·on \'sī-ən\ *n.* **1** A part of a plant that will yield above-ground parts when grafted to a stock. **2** A descendant; as, a *scion* of a royal family.

scis·sors \'siz-rz\ *n. pl.* A cutting instrument having two blades fastened together so that the sharp edges slide against each other.

scle·ra \'sklir-ə\ *n.* The dense white or bluish white tissue that covers that portion of the eyeball not covered by the cornea.

scle·ro·sis \sklə-'rō-səs\ *n.; pl.* **scle·ro·ses** \-ˌsēz\. In medicine, hardening of an organ or part, usually resulting from an abnormal increase in the connective tissue.

scle·rot·ic \sklə-'rät-ik\ *adj.* Of or relating to the sclera or to sclerosis. — *n.* The sclera.

scoff \'skäf, 'skȯf\ *n.* An expression of scorn or contempt. — *v.* To show contempt by jeering or ridiculing. — **scoff·er** \-r\ *n.*

scold \'skōld\ *n.* A person who scolds constantly. — *v.* **1** To rebuke sternly or harshly; as, to *scold* a child. **2** To find fault; to speak in an angry way.

sconce \'skän(t)s\ *n.* A candlestick or group of candlesticks fastened to a wall.

scone \'skōn, 'skän\ *n.* A little cake or muffin; especially, a rich baking-powder biscuit.

scoop \'skü̇p\ *n.* **1** A large shovel, as for shoveling coal. **2** A tool or utensil shaped like a shovel for digging into a soft substance and lifting out a portion; as, a flour *scoop.* **3** The act of scooping; a motion made with or as if with a scoop. **4** A hole made by scooping. **5** The publishing or broadcasting of news before competitors. — *v.* **1** To take out or up with or as if with a scoop. **2** To make hollow. **3** To get a scoop on, as a rival paper.

scoop, 2

scoot \'sküt\ *v.* To move off quickly and suddenly; to dart. — *n.* A darting or scooting.

scoot·er \'sküt-r\ *n.* **1** A flat-bottomed sailboat with steel runners, for sailing through the water or over ice. **2** A vehicle consisting of a narrow board mounted on two wheels, one at each end, and guided by a handle attached to the front wheel.

scope \'skōp\ *n.* **1** Room for growth or expansion; chance to develop. **2** Extent covered, reached, or viewed; range; as, a subject broad in *scope.*

scor·bu·tic \skȯr-'byüt-ik\ *adj.* Of or relating to scurvy; like scurvy; diseased with scurvy.

scorch \'skȯrch\ *v.* **1** To burn on the surface; as, to *scorch* a cloth in ironing. **2** To burn so as to brown; as, a lawn *scorched* by the hot sun. **3** To hurt or embarrass, as with sarcasm.

— The words *singe* and *char* are synonyms of *scorch:* all of these terms refer to some degree of burning; *singe* usually suggests a very light burning, as from a quick passing over a flame, that results in only slight damage, as to skin or hair; *scorch* suggests a superficial burning that results in only slight discoloration of the exposed area; *char* indicates a serious degree of burning that reduces the burned area to carbon or cinder.

scorch·er \'skȯrch-r\ *n.* One that scorches; especially, a very hot day.

score \'skōr, 'skȯr\ *n.* **1** A line such as a cut, a scratch, or a slash. **2** Amount owed; debt; account; as, to pay one's *score.* **3** An obligation or injury kept in mind for repayment; as, to settle an old *score.* **4** Account; reason; as, absent on the *score* of illness. **5** A record, as of plays, errors, and points made or lost in a game. **6** The number of points made in a game. **7** The number twenty; as, a *score* of boys. **8** Grade; mark; as, to get a high *score* on a test. **9** The music of a composition, with the parts for all the different instruments or voices written on staffs one above another. — *v.;* **scored; scor·ing. 1** To set down in an account; to record. **2** To keep the score in a game. **3** To tally; as, to *score* twice in the first inning. **4** To win; as, to *score* a great success. **5** To orchestrate or arrange music. **6** To grade; to mark; as, to *score* an examination. **7** To cut or mark with a line, scratch, or notch. — **scor·er** \'skōr-r, 'skȯr-r\ *n.*

scorn \'skȯrn\ *n.* **1** A feeling of anger and disgust; bitter contempt; disdain; derision. **2** A person or thing held in contempt or derision; as, to be the *scorn* of honest persons. **3** Words or actions expressing disdain, contempt, or derision. — *v.* To hold in scorn; to refuse or reject with contempt; as, to *scorn* a bribe. — **scorn·er** \-r\ *n.*

scorn·ful \'skȯrn-fəl\ *adj.* Feeling or showing scorn; contemptuous; disdainful; as, to be *scornful* of weakness; a *scornful* laugh. — For synonyms see *contemptuous.* — **scorn·ful·ly** \-fə-lē\ *adv.*

scor·pi·on \'skȯrp-ē-ən\ *n.* **1** Any of various arachnids with a narrow, segmented tail having a sting at the tip. **2** Something that stirs one to action.

Scot \'skät\ *n.* A Scotsman.

scotch \'skäch\ *v.* **1** To cut superficially; to gash; to wound. **2** To make harmless temporarily, as by wounding or crippling. **3** To crush; to stamp out.

Scotch \'skäch\ *adj.* Of or relating to Scotland. — *n.* **1** The people of Scotland. **2** English as spoken in Scotland. **3** A whisky distilled in Scotland, especially from malted barley.

Scotch·man \'skäch-mən\ *n.; pl.* **Scotch·men** \-mən\. A Scotsman.

sco·ter \'skōt-r\ *n.* A sea duck of the northern coasts of the Old and New Worlds; a coot.

scot-free \'skät-'frē\ *adj.* [Compounded from obsolete English *scot* meaning "tax" and English *free.*] Without being hurt or having to pay; clear· safe; as, to get off *scot-free.*

Scots \'skäts\ *adj. and n.* Scotch.

Scots·man \'skäts-mən\ *n.; pl.* **Scots·men** \-mən\. A native or inhabitant of Scotland.

Scot·tish \'skät-ish\ *adj. and n.* Scotch.

scoun·drel \'skau̇n-drəl\ *n.* A wicked rascal.

scoun·drel·ly \'skau̇n-drə-lē\ *adj.* Of, relating to, or characteristic of a scoundrel.

scour \'skau̇r\ *v.* **1** To run swiftly or move sweepingly, especially in pursuit or search of something. **2** To go through carefully in search of something; as, to *scour* the woods for a lost child.

scour \'skau̇r\ *v.* **1** To rub hard, as with a gritty substance, in order to clean; as, to *scour* knives. **2** To free from impurities, as if by rubbing; to sweep away, as by a flood; to flush. **3** To become clean and bright by rubbing; as, a pan that *scours* easily. — *n.* A scouring. — **scour·er** \-r\ *n.*

scourge \'skərj, 'skōrj, 'skȯrj\ *v.;* **scourged; scourg·ing. 1** To whip; to lash; to flog. **2** To inflict severe suffering upon; as, a country *scourged* by famine. — *n.* **1** A lash or whip. **2** Any means of punishment. **3** An affliction, as a plague.

scout \'skau̇t\ *v.* **1** To go about in search of information; to watch or follow in the manner of a scout; to spy. **2** To look; to search; as, to *scout* about for firewood. **3** To serve as a boy or girl scout. — *n.* **1** One sent out to observe and gather information about an enemy force. **2** The act of scouting; as, to be on the *scout.* **3** A member of the Boy Scouts or Girl Scouts. **4** Fellow· chap.

scout \'skau̇t\ *v.* To reject completely; to treat as absurd; to scorn; as, to *scout* a suggestion.

scout·ing \'skau̇t-ing\ *n.* **1** The act of one who scouts. **2** The activities of boy and girl scouts.

scout·mas·ter \'skau̇t-ˌmast-r\ *n.* The leader of a troop of boy scouts.

scow \'skau̇\ *n.* A large flat-bottomed boat with square ends, used chiefly for loading and unloading ships and for carrying refuse.

scowl \'skau̇l\ *v.* To draw down the eyebrows, as in frowning; to look sullen or angry. — *n.* A wrinkling of the brows in ill humor; an angry look.

scrab·ble \'skrab-l\ *v.;* **scrab·bled; scrab·bling** \-l(-)ing\. **1** To scratch or scrape as with hands or paws; as, children *scrabbling* in the sand for shells. **2** To work wearily or long; as, to *scrabble* for a living. **3** To scramble. — *n.* A scrabbling; a scramble.

scrag \'skrag\ *n.* One that is lean and tough.

scrag·gly \'skrag-l(-)ē\ *adj.* Irregular; unkempt.

scram·ble \'skram-bl\ *v.;* **scram·bled; scram·bling** \-bl(-)ing\. **1** To move or climb on hands and knees or in a stumbling way. **2** To strive or struggle for something; as, to *scramble* for a seat. **3** To cook the mixed whites and yolks of eggs by stirring them while frying. **4** To mix together in disorder; as, to *scramble* the letters in a word. — *n.* **1** A scrambling; a confused jostling struggle. **2** An emergency takeoff, as of fighter planes.

scram·bler \'skram-blər\ *n.* One that scrambles.

scrap \'skrap\ *n.* **1** A small bit; a fragment. **2** Discarded material; waste; refuse; as, table *scraps.* **3** Discarded metal; as, to pay good prices for *scrap.* — *v.;* **scrapped; scrap·ping. 1** To discard as useless; as, to *scrap* an old car. **2** To make into scrap. — *adj.* Made up of scrap; as, *scrap* iron. — **scrap·per** \'skrap-r\ *n.*

scrap \'skrap\ *n.* A fight; a quarrel. — *v.;* **scrapped; scrap·ping.** To fight; to quarrel. — **scrap·per** \'skrap-r\ *n.*

scrap·book \'skrap-ˌbu̇k\ *n.* A blank book for mementos, as clippings and pictures.

scrape \'skrāp\ *v.;* **scraped; scrap·ing. 1** To remove by drawing a knife over again and again; as, to *scrape* off rust. **2** To clean or smooth by rubbing. **3** To rub so as to make a grating noise; to scuff; as, to *scrape* the curb with a car; to *scrape* one's feet. **4** To gather with difficulty and little by little; as, to *scrape* together a few dollars. — *n.* **1** The act of scraping; a grating sound. **2** A line or scratch. **3** A trying situation. — **scrap·er** \'skrāp-r\ *n.*

scrap·ple \'skrap-l\ *n.* A dish, served sliced and lightly fried, made of pork scraps, corn meal, and seasonings cooked together and set in a mold.

scratch \'skrach\ *v.* **1** To scrape or rub with claws, nails, or an instrument; as, to be *scratched* by a cat; to *scratch* one's head. **2** To mark a surface with something sharp or rough. **3** To withdraw; as, to *scratch* a horse from a race. **4** To make a scraping noise. **5** To erase; to cancel; as, to *scratch* out a name. **6** To scribble; to scrawl. — *n.* **1** The act of scratching. **2** A mark or line made by scratching. **3** The line from which contestants start in a race; a beginning with nothing; as, to start from *scratch.*

scratch test. A test for determining a person's susceptibility to allergies, made by rubbing an extract of the allergy-producing substance into small breaks or scratches made in the skin.

scratchy \'skrach-ē\ *adj.;* **scratch·i·er; scratch·i·est. 1** Making a scratching noise; as, a *scratchy* pen. **2** Showing scratches. **3** Uneven; straggling. — **scratch·i·ly** \-l-ē\ *adv.*

scrawl \'skrȯl\ *v.* To write hastily and carelessly; to scribble. — *n.* Something written carelessly or without skill. — **scrawly** \'skrȯl-ē\ *adj.*

scrawny \'skrȯn-ē\ *adj.;* **scrawn·i·er; scrawn·i·est.** Thin; lean; skinny.

scream \'skrēm\ *v.* **1** To cry out loudly and shrilly, as in fright, pain, or anger. **2** To have an alarming or startling effect; as, headlines that *scream* about a disaster. — *n.* A loud, shrill, prolonged cry.

scream·ing \'skrē-ming\ *adj.* **1** Uttering screams. **2** Like a scream. **3** Causing screams, as of laughter; as, a *screaming* comedy. — **scream·ing·ly** \-lē\ *adv.*

screech \'skrēch\ *v.* To utter a shrill and piercing cry; to shriek; to scream harshly. — *n.* A shrill harsh scream or a similar sound.

screen \'skrēn\ *n.* **1** A curtain or partition used to hide or to protect; as, a fire *screen;* a window *screen.* **2** A sieve set in a frame, for separating finer parts from coarser parts, as of sand. **3** The curtain or wall on which motion pictures are projected; motion pictures in general. **4** The part of a television set on which the picture appears. — *v.* **1** To separate by a screen or screens. **2** To hide or shield with or as with a screen. **3** To sift through a screen. **4** To sort people, as for physical fitness or for a particular ability.

screen·ing \'skrē-ning\ *n.* **1** The act of one who screens. **2** [in the plural] Material that has been screened. **3** Material for making screens.

screw \'skrü\ *n.* **1** A nail-shaped or rod-shaped piece of metal with a continuous ridge, or thread, winding spirally around its length, used for fastening and holding pieces together. **2** A spiral. **3** *British.* A small twisted paper packet, as of tobacco or pepper. **4** A screw propeller. **5** The thread of a screw. **6** The act of screwing tight; a twist; as, to give a *screw* to a cork. — *v.* **1** To turn as a screw does; to twist. **2** To attach by means of a screw; as, to *screw* a bracket to a wall. **3** To tighten by turning something threaded like a screw; as, to *screw* on the top of a jar. **4** To make tense; as, to *screw* up one's nerve.

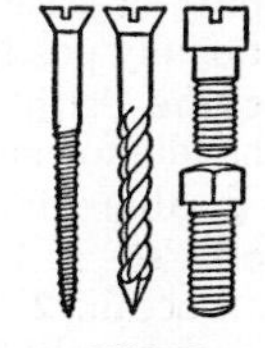

screws

screw·ball \'skrü-ˌbȯl\ *n. Slang.* A person whose ideas or actions are very queer or eccentric. — *adj. Slang.* Crazily eccentric; as, a *screwball* idea.

screw·driv·er \'skrü-ˌdrīv-r\ *n.* or **screw driver.** A tool for turning screws.

screw·eye \'skrü-ˌī\ *n.* A screw having a head in the form of a loop.

screw pine. Any of a number of tropical trees and shrubs of the islands of the Indian and Pacific oceans having stiff spiral leaves; a pandanus.

screw propeller. A spindled hub with twisted radiating blades, for propelling airplanes or steamboats.

scrib·ble \'skrib-l\ *v.;* **scrib·bled; scrib·bling** \-l(-)ing\. To write hastily or carelessly. — *n.* Something scribbled. — **scrib·bler** \'skrib-lər\ *n.*

scribe \'skrīb\ *n.* **1** A person who copies writing; especially, before the invention of printing, a person who copied manuscripts. **2** An official writer acting usually as a clerk. **3** A teacher of the ancient Jewish law. — *v.;* **scribed; scrib·ing.** To mark, as wood or metal to be cut, by scratching with a pointed instrument.

scrim·mage \'skrim-ij\ *n.* **1** A confused struggle. **2** In football, the play that follows the snapping back of the ball. — *v.;* **scrim·maged; scrim·mag·ing.** To engage in a scrimmage.

scrimp \'skrimp\ *v.* **1** To make too small, short, or scanty; to skimp. **2** To economize.

scrip \'skrip\ *n.* **1** A certificate showing that the holder is entitled to something, as stocks or land. **2** A piece of paper money formerly issued by the United States for an amount less than a dollar.

script \'skript\ *n.* **1** Letters and figures as written by hand; handwriting. **2** A printing type made in imitation of handwriting. **3** The manuscript of a play. **4** The typed text and description of a motion picture, including the scenario, a synopsis of the plot, and the cast. **5** The written text of the lines to be said by a radio or television performer.

scrip·to·ri·um \skrip-'tōr-ē-əm, -'tȯr-\ *n.; pl.* **scrip·to·ri·ums** \-ē-əmz\ or **scrip·to·ria** \-ē-ə\. A room in a monastery for the use of the scribes.

scrip·tur·al \'skrip-chər-əl\ *adj.* Of or relating to the Scriptures; according to the Scriptures; Biblical. — **scrip·tur·al·ly** \-ə-lē\ *adv.*

scrip·ture \'skrip-chər\ *n.* **1** *Archaic.* Anything written. **2** [with a capital] The books of the Old and New Testament or of either of them; the Bible. **3** Any writing regarded as sacred.

scrive·ner \'skriv-n(-)ər\ *n.* **1** A scribe; a clerk; a secretary. **2** An author; a writer.

scrod \'skräd\ *n.* A young fish, especially cod, cut in strips for cooking.

scrof·u·la \'skräf-yə-lə\ *n.* A tuberculous condition marked by enlargement of glands under the skin, especially of the face and neck. — **scrof·u·lous** \-yə-ləs\ *adj.*

scroll \'skrōl\ *n.* **1** A roll of paper or parchment; especially, one on which something is written or engraved. **2** An ornament like a roll of paper, especially one loosely or only partly rolled.

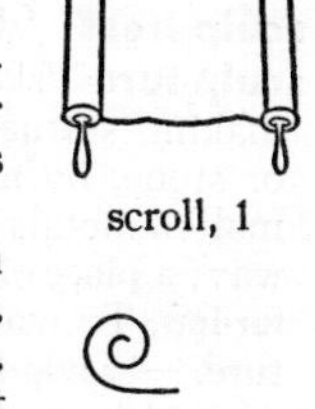

scroll, 1

scrolls, 2

scroll·work \'skrōl-ˌwərk\ *n.* Ornamental work, as in metal or wood, having a scroll or scrolls as its chief feature.

scrub \'skrəb\ *n.* **1** A thick growth of small or stunted shrubs or trees. **2** An undersized person or thing. **3** A player in a sport who does not belong to the regular team or group. **4** In stockbreeding, an inferior animal of mixed parentage. — *adj.* **1** Undersized; inferior; stunted; as, a *scrub* oak. **2** Made up of or played by scrubs; as, a *scrub* team or game. — **scrub·by** \'skrəb-ē\ *adj.*

scrub \'skrəb\ *v.;* **scrubbed; scrub·bing.** To rub hard in washing; to wash by rubbing; as, to *scrub* a floor. — *n.* The action or process of scrubbing.

scruff \'skrəf\ *n.* The loose skin of the back of the neck; nape.

scru·ple \'skrüp-l\ *n.* **1** A small part; a minute portion or amount; as, a second plan not one *scruple* better than the first. **2** A unit of weight used by druggists. **3** A point of conscience or honor that makes one uneasy or the uneasiness thus caused; as, a player not troubled by *scruples.* — *v.;* **scru·pled; scru·pling** \-l(-)ing\. To have scruples.

scru·pu·lous \'skrüp-yə-ləs\ *adj.* Having scruples; showing careful regard for what is right; as, *scrupulous* honesty. — **scru·pu·lous·ly,** *adv.*

scru·ti·nize \'skrüt-n-ˌīz\ *v.;* **scru·ti·nized; scru·ti-**

niz·ing. To examine very closely or critically.

scru·ti·ny \'skrüt-n(-)ē\ *n.; pl.* **scru·ti·nies.** A close examination; a careful looking over.

scud \'skəd\ *v.;* **scud·ded; scud·ding.** To move or run swiftly; as, sailboats *scudding* out to sea; clouds *scudding* across the moon. — *n.* **1** A scudding. **2** Light clouds driven by the wind.

scuff \'skəf\ *v.* **1** To shuffle; to scrape; as, to *scuff* one's feet on the ground. **2** To become rough or scratched through wear. Soft leather *scuffs* easily. — *n.* The action or noise of scuffing.

scuf·fle \'skəf-l\ *v.;* **scuf·fled; scuf·fling** \-l(-)ing\. **1** To struggle in a confused way at close quarters. **2** To shuffle one's feet; to scuff. — *n.* A rough, confused struggle or fight. — **scuf·fler** \'skəf-lər\ *n.*

scull \'skəl\ *n.* **1** An oar used in propelling a boat by a person standing at the stern. **2** One of a pair of short oars. **3** A boat, usually for racing, propelled by one or more pairs of sculls. — *v.* To move a boat by means of a scull or sculls. — **scull·er** \-r\ *n.*

scul·lery \'skəl-r(-)ē\ *n.; pl.* **scul·ler·ies. 1** A place where cooking utensils are cleaned and kept. **2** A room near the kitchen where vegetables and meats are prepared for cooking.

scul·lion \'skəl-yən\ *n.* **1** A cook's assistant; a dishwasher. **2** A menial person; a wretch.

scul·pin \'skəlp-n\ *n.* A spiny, large-headed, broad-mouthed fish of the North Atlantic.

sculp·tor \'skəlpt-r\ *n.* One who sculptures.

sculp·tress \'skəlp-trəs\ *n.* A female sculptor.

sculp·ture \'skəlp-chər\ *n.* **1** The act or process of making statues by carving or chiseling, as wood or stone, by modeling, as clay, or by casting, as molten metals or plaster. **2** Work produced in this way; a piece of such work. — *v.;* **sculp·tured; sculp·tur·ing.** To make sculptures; to adorn with sculpture. — **sculp·tur·al** \-chər-əl\ *adj.*

scum \'skəm\ *n.* **1** A film of matter that rises to the top of a liquid that is boiling or fermenting. **2** A slimy coating on stagnant water. **3** People regarded as making up a very low class; rabble. **4** Pond scum. — **scum·my** \'skəm-ē\ *adj.*

scup·per \'skəp-r\ *n.* An opening in the bulwarks of a boat through which water drains overboard.

scup·per·nong \'skəp-r-ˌnȯng, -ˌnäng\ *n.* **1** A large yellowish green plum-flavored grape of the southern United States. **2** Wine made from this grape.

scurf \'skərf\ *n.* **1** Thin dry scales given off by the skin, especially in an abnormal skin condition. **2** Any substance that sticks to a surface in flakes.

scur·ri·lous \'skər-ə-ləs, 'skə-rə-\ *adj.* Coarse; abusive; obscene. — **scur·ril·i·ty** \skə-'ril-ət-ē\ *n.* — **scur·ri·lous·ly** \'skər-ə-ləs-lē, 'skə-rə-\ *adv.*

scur·ry \'skər-ē, 'skə-rē\ *v.;* **scur·ried** \'skər-ēd, 'skə-rēd\; **scur·ry·ing.** To scamper. The squirrel *scurried* up a tree. — *n.* A scurrying.

scur·vy \'skər-vē\ *adj.;* **scur·vi·er; scur·vi·est.** Contemptible; mean. — **scur·vi·ly** \'skərv-l-ē\ *adv.*

scur·vy \'skər-vē\ *n.* A deficiency disease caused by lack of vitamin C, once common among sailors on long voyages.

scut \'skət\ *n.* The short erect tail of an animal, especially of a hare or a rabbit.

scutch·eon \'skəch-n\ *n.* An escutcheon.

scut·tle \'skət-l\ *n.* A pail for carrying coal.

scut·tle \'skət-l\ *v.;* **scut·tled; scut·tling** \-l(-)ing\. To run hurriedly from view; to scurry.

scut·tle \'skət-l\ *n.* A small opening with a lid or cover, as in the roof of a house, or in the deck, side, or bottom of a ship. — *v.;* **scut·tled; scut·tling** \-l(-)ing\. To sink a boat intentionally by cutting holes or by opening valves to let in water.

scut·tle·butt \'skət-l-ˌbət\ *n.* [From *scuttlebutt* meaning "drinking fountain on a ship", originally a butt or cask of water, where the sailors traditionally gossiped.] *Slang.* Rumor; gossip.

scythe \'sīth\ *n.* A curved blade with a long curved handle for mowing grass or grain by hand.

S.E. Abbreviation for *southeast.*

sea \'sē\ *n.* **1** A body of salt water not as large as an ocean. **2** A large inland body of water, either fresh or salt. **3** The ocean. **4** Rough water; a heavy wave or swell; as, a high *sea.* **5** Something suggesting the sea, as in vastness; as, a *sea* of faces. — **at sea. 1** On the sea. **2** Confused; bewildered.

sea anemone. A polyp that suggests a flower because of its shape, its bright colors, and the many tentacles around its mouth.

sea·board \'sē-ˌbōrd, -ˌbȯrd\ *n.* The seacoast or land bordering it.

sea·coast \'sē-ˌkōst\ *n.* The shore of the sea.

sea cow. 1 Any large swimming mammal that feeds on seaweed, as the manatee. **2** A walrus.

sea cucumber. A sea animal related to the starfishes and sea urchins, having a long flexible muscular body that looks somewhat like a cucumber.

sea dog. 1 A dogfish. **2** Also **sea calf.** The common seal. **3** An experienced sailor.

sea·far·er \'sē-ˌfar-r, -ˌfer-r\ *n.* One who travels over the ocean; especially, a mariner.

sea·far·ing \'sē-ˌfar-ing, -ˌfer-\ *n.* Traveling over the sea as work or as recreation; the sailor's calling. — *adj.* Of, given to, or employed in seafaring.

sea food. Edible salt-water fish or shellfish.

sea·girt \'sē-ˌgərt\ *adj.* Surrounded by the sea.

sea·go·ing \'sē-ˌgō-ing\ *adj.* Made for sea travel; seafaring; as, *seagoing* ships; *seagoing* men.

sea gull. A gull that frequents the sea.

sea horse. 1 A mythological animal half horse and half fish. **2** A walrus. **3** A small long-snouted fish that is covered with bony plates and has a head suggestive of a horse's head.

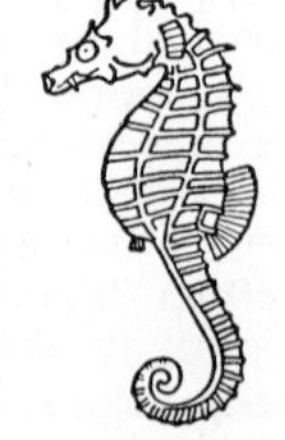
sea horse, 3

seal \'sēl\ *n.* **1** A flesh-eating marine mammal found chiefly in cold regions, and hunted for its fur, hide, or oil. **2** The fur of this animal; sealskin. **3** A leather made from the skin of a seal. — *v.* To hunt seals. — **seal·er** \-r\ *n.*

seal \'sēl\ *n.* **1** A device having a cut or raised design or figure that can be stamped or pressed into wax or paper; as, the corporation's official *seal.* **2** The piece of wax, often stamped with a design, placed on a letter or package to close it. **3** Something which is a proof of a document's genuineness, such as a stamped design bearing an emblem. **4** A stamp which may be used in sealing a letter or package; as, a Christmas *seal.* **5** Something which makes safe or secure, such as a pledge; as, under *seal* of secrecy. **6** Any device used to close something securely, as the rubber ring on a fruit jar. — *v.* **1** To mark or stamp with a seal. **2** To close with or as if with a seal; as, to *seal* one's lips. **3** To glue shut, as a letter. **4** To hold tightly; to close. A ship *sealed* in ice. **5** To determine finally. His fate was *sealed.* — **seal·er** \-r\ *n.*

sea legs. Ability to walk steadily on a ship at sea; freedom from seasickness.

sea level. The height of the surface of the sea midway between the average high and low tides.

sea lily. A small, cup-shaped sea animal that clings to rocks by means of a jointed stalk.

seal·ing wax \ˈsē-ling\. A substance, made of resin and shellac and easily molded when warm, used to seal documents and letters.

sea lion. A large, eared seal of the Pacific Ocean.

seal·skin \ˈsēl-ˌskin\ *n.* **1** The fur or pelt of a fur seal. **2** A garment made of this fur.

seam \ˈsēm\ *n.* **1** The fold, line, or groove made by sewing together or joining two edges or two pieces of material; as, the *seams* of a skirt; the *seams* of a boat. **2** A layer, as of a mineral or metal; as, a *seam* of coal. **3** A wrinkle; a furrow. — *v.* **1** To join by a seam. **2** To line or wrinkle; as, a face *seamed* by age.

sea·man \ˈsē-mən\ *n.; pl.* **sea·men** \-mən\. **1** A person who helps in the handling of a ship at sea. **2** A sailor who is not an officer.

sea·man·like \ˈsē-mən-ˌlīk\ *adj.* Characteristic of a good seaman.

sea·man·ship \ˈsē-mən-ˌship\ *n.* The art, or skill in the art, of handling and running a ship.

sea mew. A sea gull.

sea mile. A nautical mile.

seam·stress \ˈsēm(p)-strəs\ *n.* A woman who sews; especially, one who sews for a living.

seamy \ˈsē-mē\ *adj.;* **seam·i·er; seam·i·est. 1** Having or showing seams; seamed. **2** Less presentable; worse; as, the *seamy* side of life.

sé·ance \ˈsā-ˌän(t)s\ *n.* **1** A sitting; a meeting for discussion. **2** A spiritualist meeting.

sea·plane \ˈsē-ˌplān\ *n.* An airplane which is so designed that it can rise from or land on water.

sea·port \ˈsē-ˌpōrt, -ˌpȯrt\ *n.* A port, harbor, or town accessible to seagoing vessels.

sear \ˈsir\ *v.* **1** To dry by heat; to wither. **2** To burn, scorch, or brown, especially on the surface, as in cooking meat. **3** To brand with a heated iron. **4** To harden, as in feeling; to make callous.

search \ˈsərch\ *v.* **1** To go through or look over carefully, hunting for something. **2** To look in the pockets or the clothing of, for something hidden. — *n.* The act of searching or seeking out; as, the never-ending *search* for truth. — **search·er** \-r\ *n.*

search·ing \ˈsərch-ing\ *adj.* **1** That explores or examines deeply or thoroughly; as, a *searching* look; *searching* questions. **2** Penetrating; piercing; as, *searching* cold. — **search·ing·ly,** *adv.*

search·light \ˈsərch-ˌlīt\ *n.* **1** A lamp for shining a beam of bright light on objects at a distance, usually designed to be swiveled about. **2** The beam of light projected by such a lamp.

search warrant. A warrant authorizing a search of a house or other place, as for stolen goods.

sea rover. A pirate or pirate ship.

sea·scape \ˈsē-ˌskāp\ *n.* **1** A view of or over the sea. **2** A picture of a scene at sea.

sea serpent. 1 A huge marine animal resembling a snake, often reported to have been seen at sea. **2** Any of a number of poisonous snakes of the Indian and Pacific oceans marked by a flattened oar-shaped tail and small scales on the under side.

sea shell. The shell of any shell-bearing marine animal; especially, the shell of a marine mollusk.

sea·shore \ˈsē-ˌshōr, -ˌshȯr\ *n.* The land on the edge of the sea; the shore; the seacoast.

sea·sick \ˈsē-ˌsik\ *adj.* Nauseated by the pitching or rolling of a ship. — **sea·sick·ness** \-nəs\ *n.*

sea·side \ˈsē-ˌsīd\ *n.* The seacoast.

sea·son \ˈsēz-n\ *n.* **1** A period in which a special type of agricultural work is carried on; as, the harvest *season.* **2** The proper or suitable time or occasion; as, a few precautions taken in *season.* **3** One of the four divisions of the year, spring, summer, autumn, or winter. **4** A period of time that has some special character; as, the Christmas *season;* the baseball *season.* — **in season. 1** At the right or fitting time. **2** At the stage of greatest fitness, as for use or marketing. **3** Of game and fish, subject to being legally hunted or caught. — *v.;* **sea·soned; sea·son·ing** \-n(-)ing\. **1** To make pleasant to the taste by the use of seasoning. **2** To make or become ready for use, as by aging or drying; to cure; as, to *season* lumber. **3** To accustom; to make used; as, an old man *seasoned* to misfortune; a *seasoned* traveler.

sea·son·a·ble \ˈsēz-n(-)əb-l\ *adj.* Timely; as, *seasonable* weather. — **sea·son·a·bly** \-n(-)ə-blē\ *adv.*

sea·son·al \ˈsēz-n(-)əl\ *adj.* Of a season or seasons; coming at a particular season; as, *seasonal* crops. — **sea·son·al·ly** \-n(-)ə-lē\ *adv.*

sea·son·ing \ˈsēz-n(-)ing\ *n.* Something that seasons, as salt or pepper.

seat \ˈsēt\ *n.* **1** The manner of sitting, as on horseback; as, a rider with a fine *seat.* **2** The place at which a person sits. **3** An article of furniture to sit on, as a chair. **4** The part of such an article on which a person sits. **5** The part of the body on which a person sits; the corresponding part of the clothing, as of a pair of trousers. **6** A place that serves as a capital or a center; as, a *seat* of learning; a county *seat.* **7** A right to sit as a member in a legislature. — *v.* **1** To place in or on a seat; as, to *seat* guests. **2** To provide seats for; as, a hall *seat-*

ing 800. **3** To put a seat in or repair the seat of.

sea urchin. A spiny animal that lives on the sea bottom between rocks or buries itself in sand.

sea wall. An embankment or wall to protect the shore from erosion or to act as a breakwater.

sea·ward \'sē-wərd\ *n.* The direction away from land and out to the sea. — *adj.* **1** Directed or located toward the sea. **2** From the sea; as, a *seaward* breeze. — *adv.* Toward the sea.

sea·wards \'sē-wərdz\ *adv.* Seaward.

sea·way \'sē-ˌwā\ *n.* **1** A rough sea — chiefly in the phrase *in a seaway.* **2** The forward motion of a ship; headway. **3** A route over the sea. **4** A deep inland waterway that admits ocean shipping.

sea·weed \'sē-ˌwēd\ *n.* A plant growing in the sea; especially, one of the salt-water algae, as kelp.

sea·wor·thy \'sē-ˌwər-t͟hē\ *adj.* Fit or safe for a sea voyage; as, a *seaworthy* ship.

se·ba·ceous \sə-'bā-shəs\ *adj.* Of, relating to, or secreting fat; as, *sebaceous* glands.

sec. Abbreviation for: **1** *secant.* **2** *second.* **3** *secretary.* **4** *section.*

se·cant \'sē-ˌkant, 'sēk-nt\ *adj.* Cutting; as, a *secant* line. — *n.* **1** In geometry, a line that cuts another; especially, a straight line that cuts a curved line in two or more places. **2** With reference to an acute angle in a right triangle, the ratio of the hypotenuse to the side adjacent to that angle.

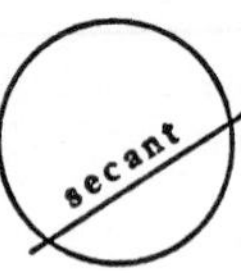

se·cede \sē-'sēd\ *v.;* **se·ced·ed; se·ced·ing.** To withdraw formally from an organized body, especially a political body. — **se·ced·er** \-'sēd-r\ *n.*

se·ces·sion \sē-'sesh-n\ *n.* **1** The act of seceding; a formal withdrawal. **2** [with a capital] The withdrawal of the 11 southern states from the Union at the start of the Civil War.

se·clude \sē-'klüd\ *v.;* **se·clud·ed; se·clud·ing.** To keep away from others; to shut off alone.

se·clu·sion \sē-'klüzh-n\ *n.* **1** The state or fact of being secluded; isolation. **2** A secluded place. — **se·clu·sive** \-'klü-siv, -ziv\ *adj.*

sec·ond \'sek-nd, *before consonants often* 'sek-n\ *n.* **1** A sixtieth part of a minute, either of time or of a degree. **2** A moment; an instant.

sec·ond \'sek-nd, *before consonants often* 'sek-n\ *adj.* **1** Coming or happening after the first; as, the *second* time. **2** Next lower than the first; as, *second* prize. **3** Similar to the first; another; as, a *second* Lincoln. **4** Lower in pitch; as, *second* sopranos; *second* violin. — *adv.* In the second place or rank. — *n.* **1** One that is second, as in place, time, or rank. **2** One who aids another in a duel or prize fight. **3** An imperfect or second-rate article of merchandise; as, a sale of *seconds* in sheets. — *v.* **1** To act as a second, as in a duel. **2** To give support to a motion or nomination so that it may be debated or voted on.

sec·ond·ary \'sek-n-ˌder-ē\ *adj.* **1** Second in rank, value, or occurrence; inferior; lesser. **2** Derived from or dependent on that which is primary or original. **3** Coming after the primary; higher than the elementary; as, *secondary* school. **4** In an induction coil or transformer, of or relating to the induced current or its circuit; as, a *secondary* coil. **5** Of feathers or quills, borne on the second joint of a bird's wing. **6** Of stress or accent, like that on the last syllable of *penetrate* \'pen-ə-trāt\. — *n.; pl.* **sec·ond·ar·ies.** One that is secondary, as a circuit or a feather. — **sec·ond·ar·i·ly** \ˌsek-n-'der-ə-lē\ *adv.*

sec·ond-class \'sek-n(d)-'klas\ *adj.* **1** Of or relating to a class below the first; as, *second-class* mail. **2** Second-rate; mediocre.

sec·ond·hand \'sek-n(d)-'hand\ *adj.* **1** Not original; taken from someone else; as, *secondhand* information. **2** Not new; having had a previous owner; as, a *secondhand* car. **3** Selling used goods; as, a *secondhand* store.

sec·ond·ly \'sek-nd-lē\ *adv.* In the second place.

sec·ond-rate \'sek-n-'(d)rāt\ *adj.* Of second or inferior quality or value. — **sec·ond-rat·er** \-'(d)rāt-r\ *n.*

se·cre·cy \'sēk-rə-sē\ *n.; pl.* **se·cre·cies.** **1** The state or quality of being secret; privacy; concealment. **2** The action or the fact of keeping a secret.

se·cret \'sēk-rət\ *adj.* **1** Hidden from the knowledge of others. **2** Working in secrecy; engaged in detecting or spying; as, a *secret* agent. **3** Secluded; retired; as, a *secret* valley. — *n.* **1** Something kept or intended to be kept secret. **2** Something not explainable; as, nature's *secrets.* **3** Secrecy; as, to meet in *secret.* **4** The key to the solution of something; as, the *secret* of success. — **se·cret·ly,** *adv.*

sec·re·tar·i·at \ˌsek-rə-'ter-ē-ət\ *n.* **1** The staff and offices of an official executive or administrative agency headed by a secretary or a secretary-general. **2** The secretarial staff of some groups.

sec·re·tary \'sek-rə-ˌter-ē\ *n.; pl.* **sec·re·tar·ies.** **1** A person who is employed to take care of records and letters of a private or confidential nature; a confidential clerk. **2** An officer of a business corporation or society who has charge of the correspondence and records. **3** A government official in charge of the affairs of a department; as, the *Secretary* of State. **4** A writing desk, especially one with a top section for books. — **sec·re·tar·i·al** \ˌsek-rə-'ter-ē-əl\ *adj.*

secretary, 4

secretary-general, *n.; pl.* **secretaries-general.** A chief or superior secretary, as of an official agency.

sec·re·tar·y·ship \'sek-rə-ˌter-ē-ˌship\ *n.* The office or position of a secretary.

se·crete, *v.;* **se·cret·ed; se·cret·ing.** **1** \sē-'krēt, 'sēk-rət\ To conceal; to hide; as, to *secrete* stolen goods. **2** \sē-'krēt\ To produce and discharge; as, glands that *secrete* saliva. — **se·cre·tor,** *n.*

se·cre·tion \sē-'krēsh-n\ *n.* **1** A concealing or hiding. **2** In biology, the act or process of secreting or the substance secreted. Sweat is a *secretion.*

se·cre·tive \'sēk-rət-iv, sē-'krēt-\ *adj.* Not frank or open. — **se·cre·tive·ly**, *adv.*

secret service. The detective service of a government. The *secret service* investigates counterfeiting.

sect \'sekt\ *n.* **1** A group having a common leader or doctrine; a following; a school. **2** A religious group made up of dissenters from a parent church. **3** A religious denomination.

sec·tar·i·an \sek-'ter-ē-ən\ *adj.* Of or relating to a sect or group; denominational. — *n.* **1** A dissenter from an established church. **2** A member of a sect.

sec·tion \'seksh-n\ *n.* **1** A part cut off or separated; as, a *section* of an orange. **2** A part of a written work; as, a chapter divided into *sections.* **3** The appearance that a thing has or would have if cut straight through. **4** A part of a country, people, or community. **5** A part, as of a bookcase, that may be assembled with other parts. **6** One of the portions, of one square mile each, into which public lands in the United States are divided. **7** A portion of railroad track under the charge of one group of workmen. — *v.;* **sec·tioned; sec·tion·ing** \-n(-)ing\. **1** To cut into sections. **2** To represent in section, as by a drawing.

sec·tion·al \'seksh-n(-)əl\ *adj.* **1** Of or relating to a section; characteristic of a section; as, *sectional* interests. **2** Consisting of or divided into sections; as, a *sectional* sofa. — **sec·tion·al·ly** \-n(-)ə-lē\ *adv.*

sec·tion·al·ism \'seksh-n(-)ə-,liz-m\ *n.* Undue devotion to the interests of one part of the country.

sec·tor \'sekt-r\ *n.* **1** In geometry, the part of a circle included between two radii. **2** An area assigned to a military commander to defend.

sec·u·lar \'sek-yəl-r\ *adj.* **1** Not under church control; nonreligious; as, *secular* education. **2** Not sacred; not religious; as, *secular* music. **3** Not regular; not bound by the rules of a religious order; as, *secular* priests. — **sec·u·lar·ly**, *adv.*

se·cure \sē-'kyůr\ *adj.* **1** Easy in mind; not worried. **2** Safe; as, a *secure* foundation. **3** Certain; assured. — *v.;* **se·cured; se·cur·ing. 1** To make safe; to guard. **2** To assure payment of; as, to *secure* a loan. **3** To fasten tightly. **4** To acquire; to obtain; as, to *secure* information. — **se·cure·ly**, *adv.*

se·cu·ri·ty \sē-'kyůr-ət-ē\ *n.; pl.* **se·cu·ri·ties. 1** The state of being secure; safety; protection. **2** Something given as a pledge of payment. **3** [usually in the plural] An evidence of debt or property; especially, a stock or bond certificate.

se·dan \sə-'dan\ *n.* **1** Also **sedan chair.** A covered chair used as a vehicle for one person, and usually carried on poles by two men. **2** A closed automobile seating four or more persons and having two or four doors and full-width front and rear seats.

sedan, 1

se·date \sē-'dāt\ *adj.* Quiet; calm; sober; as, *sedate* manners; too *sedate* for her age. — **se·date·ly**, *adv.*

sed·a·tive \'sed-ət-iv\ *adj.* Soothing; relieving pain. — *n.* A sedative remedy.

sed·en·tary \'sed-n-,ter-ē\ *adj.* **1** Characterized by sitting; requiring sitting; as, *sedentary* work. **2** Not migratory. **3** Given to much sitting.

sedge \'sej\ *n.* A tufted, grasslike marsh herb.

sed·i·ment \'sed-m-ənt\ *n.* **1** The material from a liquid that settles to the bottom; the dregs. **2** Material, such as stones and sand, deposited by a river where the current is slow.

sed·i·men·ta·ry \,sed-m-'ent-r-ē, -'en-trē\ *adj.* **1** Of, relating to, or containing sediment. **2** Formed from sediment; as, *sedimentary* rock.

sed·i·men·ta·tion \,sed-m-ən-'tāsh-n\ *n.* The act or process of depositing sediment.

se·di·tion \sē-'dish-n\ *n.* The arousing of resistance to lawful authority. — **se·di·tious** \-'dish-əs\ *adj.*

se·duce \sē-'düs, -'dyüs\ *v.;* **se·duced; se·duc·ing.** To persuade to do wrong; to lead astray; as, *seduced* into crime. — **se·duc·er** \-'düs-r, -'dyüs-r\ *n.*

se·duc·tion \sē-'dəksh-n\ *n.* **1** Enticement to evil or wrongdoing. **2** A temptation.

se·duc·tive \sē-'dək-tiv\ *adj.* Tending to seduce; alluring; tempting. — **se·duc·tive·ly**, *adv.*

sed·u·lous \'sej-l-əs\ *adj.* Diligent in one's work; faithful; assiduous. — **sed·u·lous·ly**, *adv.*

see \'sē\ *n.* **1** The city in which a bishop's church is located. **2** A diocese.

see \'sē\ *v.;* **saw** \'sȯ\; **seen** \'sēn\; **see·ing. 1** To perceive by the eye; to look at; to have the power of sight; as, a person who cannot *see.* **2** To make sure; as, to *see* that nothing is lost. **3** To attend to; to look after; to take care of; as, to *see* to the order at once. **4** To escort; as, to *see* a person to the train. **5** To meet and talk with; to visit; as, to *see* a sick friend. **6** To understand; as, to *see* the point. **7** To undergo; to experience. The captain *saw* service overseas. **8** To know or determine by investigation. The mechanic will *see* what the trouble is with the car. **9** To look. *See!* The boat is coming. — **see out.** To continue with until the end; to see through. — **see through. 1** To detect the hidden purpose of, as a scheme. **2** To see out; to help or guide until a difficulty is solved.

seed \'sēd\ *n.; pl.* **seed** or **seeds. 1** The grains of plants used for sowing, or one of these grains. **2** A miniature dormant plant in a protective coating, often with food, capable of developing under suitable conditions into a plant like the one that produced it. **3** Any small fruit forming with its seed a single grain; as, grass *seed.* **4** Descendants; as, the *seed* of David. **5** The source for anything; the origin; as, the *seeds* of discontent. — **go to seed. 1** To develop seed. **2** To become worn out, shabby, or ineffective. — *v.* **1** To spread seed over. **2** To bear or shed seeds. **3** To take the seeds out of; as, to *seed* grapes. **4** In arranging a sports tournament, to distribute the names of the better contestants so that they will not meet each other in the early rounds. **5** To treat a cloud with particles of a substance to produce condensation that will result in the precipitation of rain or snow.

seed·bed \'sēd-ˌbed\ *n.* **1** The surface soil of land prepared for planting seed. **2** A bed for growth of plants that will later be transplanted.

seed·case \'sēd-ˌkās\ *n.* Any dry, hollow fruit, such as a pod, that contains seeds.

seed·coat \'sēd-ˌkōt\ *n.* The external coating or skin of a seed.

seed·er \'sēd-r\ *n.* **1** A machine for planting or sowing seeds. **2** A device for seeding fruit.

seed·less \'sēd-ləs\ *adj.* Having no seeds; as, *seedless* grapes.

seed·ling \'sēd-ling\ *n.* A plant grown from seed; especially, a young tree.

seed plant. Any plant that bears seeds.

seeds·man \'sēdz-mən\ *n.; pl.* **seeds·men** \-mən\. **1** A sower of seed. **2** A dealer in seeds.

seedy \'sēd-ē\ *adj.;* **seed·i·er**; **seed·i·est.** **1** Full of seeds. **2** Gone to seed. **3** Worn out; shabby.

see·ing \'sē-ing\ *n.* The power of vision; sight. — *adj.* Having sight or insight. — *conj.* Inasmuch as.

seek \'sēk\ *v.;* **sought** \'sȯt\; **seek·ing.** **1** To try to reach, find, or come to; as, to *seek* help. **2** To ask for; to request. **3** To try to get or obtain; as, to *seek* employment. **4** To try; to attempt; as, to *seek* to find a way. — **seek·er** \'sēk-r\ *n.*

seem \'sēm\ *v.* **1** To appear; to look to be; as, to *seem* pleased. **2** To appear to exist. There *seems* no reason for worry. **3** To appear to a person's own mind or opinion. I *seem* to remember you.

seem·ing \'sē-ming\ *adj.* Apparent; pretended; as, *seeming* friendship.

seem·ing·ly \'sē-ming-lē\ *adv.* As it seems; apparently; as, a *seemingly* deserted town.

seem·ly \'sēm-lē\ *adj.;* **seem·li·er**; **seem·li·est.** **1** Pleasant to look at. **2** Fitting; proper; suitable; as, to reply in a *seemly* way. — *adv.* Becomingly.

seen. Past part. of *see.*

seep \'sēp\ *v.* To leak through fine pores and cracks; to ooze. Water *seeped* through the wall.

seep·age \'sēp-ij\ *n.* **1** The action or process of seeping. **2** Fluid that has seeped.

seer, *n.* **1** \'sē-ər\ One who sees. **2** \'sir\ A person who foresees or foretells events; a prophet.

seer·suck·er \'sir-ˌsək-r\ *n.* A light fabric, usually with alternating plain and puckered stripes.

see·saw \'sē-ˌsȯ\ *n.* **1** A children's game of riding on the ends of a plank balanced in the middle, one end going up while the other goes down. **2** The plank itself. **3** An action or motion like that of a seesaw. — *adj.* Moving up and down or back and forth. — *v.* **1** To ride on a seesaw. **2** To move like a seesaw. **3** To take the lead in a race alternately.

seethe \'sē<u>th</u>\ *v.;* **seethed**; **seeth·ing.** **1** *Archaic.* To boil or stew. **2** To move with a boiling or violently agitated motion; as, the *seething* water of the rapids. **3** To be in a state of upset or confusion.

seg·ment \'seg-mənt\ *n.* **1** Any of the parts into which a thing is divided or naturally separates; a section. **2** A part cut off from a geometrical figure, as a circle or sphere, by means of a line or plane. — \-ˌment\ *v.* To divide into segments.

seg·men·ta·tion \ˌseg-mən-'tāsh-n\ *n.* **1** The act or process of dividing into segments. **2** In biology, the formation of many cells from a single cell.

se·go \'sē-ˌgō\ *n.; pl.* **se·gos.** Also **sego lily.** A lily of the western United States with a large tulip-shaped white flower and an edible bulb.

seg·re·gate \'seg-rə-ˌgāt\ *v.;* **seg·re·gat·ed**; **seg·re·gat·ing.** **1** To separate; to set apart from others; to isolate. **2** To separate from the general mass and collect together, as in crystallization.

seg·re·ga·tion \ˌseg-rə-'gāsh-n\ *n.* **1** The act of segregating or the state of being segregated. **2** Separation of a particular class of persons, as a racial group, from the main body of a community.

seg·re·ga·tion·ist \ˌseg-rə-'gāsh-n(-)əst\ *n.* One who believes in segregation, especially of races.

sei·gneur \sān-'yər\ *n.* A lord; a seignior.

sei·gnior \'sān-yər, -ˌyȯr\ *n.* **1** A lord; especially, the lord of a manor; a feudal lord. **2** A title of respect, corresponding to *Sir.*

sei·gniory \'sān-yər-ē\ *n.; pl.* **sei·gnior·ies.** The territory ruled by a lord, especially a feudal lord.

seine \'sān\ *n.* A large fishing net kept hanging vertically in the water by weights. — *v.;* **seined**; **sein·ing.** To catch or fish with a seine.

seis·mic \'sīz-mik\ *adj.* **1** Of or relating to earthquakes. **2** Caused by or like an earthquake.

seis·mo·gram \'sīz-mə-ˌgram\ *n.* The record of an earth tremor made by a seismograph.

seis·mo·graph \'sīz-mə-ˌgraf\ *n.* An apparatus for recording the intensity, direction, and duration of earthquakes. — **seis·mo·graph·ic** \ˌsīz-mə-'graf-ik\ *adj.* — **seis·mog·ra·phy** \sīz-'mäg-rə-fē\ *n.*

seis·mol·o·gist \sīz-'mäl-ə-jəst\ *n.* A specialist in seismology.

seis·mol·o·gy \sīz-'mäl-ə-jē\ *n.* The study of earthquakes. — **seis·mo·log·i·cal** \ˌsīz-mə-'läj-ik-l\ *adj.*

seize \'sēz\ *v.;* **seized**; **seiz·ing.** **1** To take possession of by force; as, to *seize* a fortress. **2** To take hold of suddenly or with force; to clutch; to grasp. **3** To understand; to comprehend; as, to *seize* an idea quickly. **4** To take prisoner; to arrest. **5** To bind together by lashing, as with small cord; as, to *seize* two ropes. **6** To affect, as with fever. — **seize on** or **seize upon.** To clutch or clutch at.

sei·zure \'sēzh-r\ *n.* **1** The act of seizing or the state of being seized. **2** A sudden illness.

sel·dom \'seld-m\ *adv.* Not often; rarely.

se·lect \sə-'lekt\ *adj.* **1** Carefully chosen. **2** Choice; exclusive; as, a *select* hotel. — *v.* To take by preference from among several; to choose.

se·lec·tion \sə-'leksh-n\ *n.* **1** The act of selecting; choice. **2** A thing chosen or a collection of things chosen. **3** In biology, any process that tends to prevent certain individuals or groups of organisms from surviving while allowing others to do so.

se·lec·tive \sə-'lek-tiv\ *adj.* **1** Of, relating to, or characterized by selection; selecting or tending to select. **2** In radio, having the ability to be tuned to desired stations without interference from unwanted signals; as, a highly *selective* receiving set. — **se·lec·tiv·i·ty** \sə-ˌlek-'tiv-ət-ē, ˌsē-ˌlek-\ *n.*

se·lect·man \sə-'lekt-mən\ *n.; pl.* **se·lect·men** \-mən\. One of a board of town officials elected annually in some of the New England states.

se·lec·tor \sə-'lekt-r\ *n.* **1** A person who selects. **2** A mechanical or electrical selecting device.

se·le·ni·um \sə-'lē-nē-əm\ *n.* A nonmetallic chemical element used in photoelectric devices because of its property of conducting electricity in accordance with the amount of light falling upon it.

self \'self\ *n.; pl.* **selves** \'selvz\. **1** A person regarded as an individual apart from everyone else; as, a man's *self.* **2** A particular side of a person's character; as, one's better *self.* **3** Personal interest or advantage; as, without thought of *self.* ☞ *self* is often used as a prefix meaning: **1** Of oneself, as in *self*-control. **2** By oneself or by something in itself, as in *self*-inflicted, *self*-winding. **3** To or toward oneself, as in *self*-addressed. **4** For or on oneself, as in *self*-respect, *self*-reliance. **5** With or in oneself, as in *self*-confidence.

self-act·ing \'self-'ak-ting\ *adj.* Acting or capable of acting of or by itself; automatic.

self-ad·dressed \'self-ə-'drest\ *adj.* Addressed for return to the sender, as an envelope.

self-as·ser·tion \'self-ə-'sərsh-n\ *n.* Insistence upon one's own rights, claims, or ideas. — **self-as·sert·ive** \-ə-'sərt-iv\ *adj.*

self-as·sur·ance \'self-ə-'shůr-ən(t)s\ *n.* Self-confidence. — **self-as·sured** \-ə-'shůrd\ *adj.*

self-cen·tered \'self-'sent-rd\ *adj.* Interested chiefly in one's own self: selfish.

self-com·mand \'self-kə-'mand\ *n.* Self-control.

self-con·ceit \'self-kən-'sēt\ *n.* Too high an opinion of oneself and one's abilities; excessive pride; vanity; conceit. — **self-con·ceit·ed** \-'sēt-əd\ *adj.*

self-con·fi·dence \'self-'kän-fə-dən(t)s, -ˌden(t)s\ *n.* Confidence in one's own powers and abilities.

self-con·fi·dent \'self-'kän-fə-dənt, -ˌdent\ *adj.* Sure, or too sure, of oneself or of one's own ability. — **self-con·fi·dent·ly,** *adv.*

self-con·scious \'self-'känch-əs\ *adj.* Too much aware of oneself and of one's feelings or appearance when in the presence of other people; embarrassed. — **self-con·scious·ly,** *adv.* — **self-con·scious·ness,** *n.*

self-con·tained \'self-kən-'tānd\ *adj.* **1** Sufficient in itself; complete in itself. **2** Showing self-control; not impulsive. **3** Not talkative.

self-con·trol \'self-kən-'trōl\ *n.* Control of one's own feelings or acts; restraint exercised over oneself. — **self-con·trolled** \-'trōld\ *adj.*

self-de·fense \'self-də-'fen(t)s\ *n.* The act of defending oneself or one's property.

self-de·ni·al \'self-də-'nī-əl, -'nīl\ *n.* The act of refraining from gratifying one's own desires; going without something that one wants or needs. — **self-de·ny·ing** \-'nī-ing\ *adj.*

self-de·ter·mi·na·tion \'self-də-ˌtər-mə-'nāsh-n\ *n.* **1** The act or power of deciding things for oneself. **2** Decision by the people of a territorial unit as to the form of government they shall have.

self-es·teem \'self-ə-'stēm\ *n.* **1** Self-respect. **2** Self-conceit.

self-ev·i·dent \'self-'ev-ə-dənt, -ˌdent\ *adj.* Evident or plain without proof or argument; needing no proof. — **self-ev·i·dent·ly,** *adv.*

self-ex·plan·a·to·ry \'self-iks-'plan-ə-ˌtōr-ē, -ˌtȯr-ē\ *adj.* Understandable without explanation.

self-ex·pres·sion \'self-iks-'presh-n\ *n.* The expression of one's personality, especially through an art form, as poetry, music, or dancing.

self-gov·ern·ment \'self-'gəv-r(n)-mənt\ *n.* **1** Self-control. **2** Government by action of the people; especially, democratic government. — **self-gov·ern·ing** \-'gəv-r-ning\ *adj.*

self·heal \'self-ˌhēl\ *n.* A low-growing blue-flowered mint supposed to have healing properties.

self-help \'self-'help\ *n.* The act of aiding or providing for oneself without assistance from others.

self-im·por·tant \'self-im-'pȯrt-nt, -ənt\ *adj.* Showing an exaggerated opinion of one's own importance. — **self-im·por·tance** \-n(t)s, -ən(t)s\ *n.*

self-in·duced \'self-in-'düst, -'dyüst\ *adj.* **1** Induced by oneself or by itself. **2** Produced by self-induction.

self-in·duc·tion \'self-in-'dəksh-n\ *n.* The inducing of an electromotive force in a circuit by a varying current in the same circuit.

self-in·flict·ed \'self-in-'flik-təd\ *adj.* Inflicted, as a wound, on one by oneself.

self-in·ter·est \'self-'in-trəst, -'int-r-ˌest, -'int-rst, -'in-ˌtrest, -'int-r-əst\ *n.* **1** One's own interest or advantage. **2** Concern with one's own personal advantage regardless of the interests of others.

self·ish \'sel-fish\ *adj.* **1** Taking care of one's own interests without regard for those of others. **2** Arising from selfishness; as, *selfish* pleasures. — **self·ish·ly,** *adv.* — **self·ish·ness,** *n.*

self·less \'self-ləs\ *adj.* Having or showing no concern with self; unselfish. — **self·less·ly,** *adv.*

self-made \'self-'mād\ *adj.* **1** Made by oneself or by itself. **2** Having risen from poverty or low position by one's own efforts; as, a *self-made* man.

self-mov·ing \'self-'mü-ving\ *adj.* Moving or able to move by power within itself.

self-pos·sessed \'self-pə-'zest\ *adj.* Having or showing control of one's feelings and behavior.

self-pos·ses·sion \'self-pə-'zesh-n\ *n.* Self-control; presence of mind; composure.

self-pres·er·va·tion \'self-ˌprez-r-'vāsh-n\ *n.* The keeping of oneself from destruction, injury, or loss.

self-re·li·ance \'self-rē-'lī-ən(t)s\ *n.* Dependence on one's own efforts; confidence in one's own powers and judgment. — **self-re·li·ant** \-ənt\ *adj.*

self-re·proach \'self-rē-'prōch\ *n.* The act of reproaching or blaming oneself.

self-re·spect \'self-rē-'spekt\ *n.* Respect for oneself; proper regard for one's character and standing. — **self-re·spect·ing** \-'spek-ting\ *adj.*

self-re·straint \'self-rē-'strānt\ *n.* Self-control.

self-righ·teous \'self-'rī-chəs\ *adj.* Righteous, just, and upright in one's own opinion; sure of one's own goodness. — **self-righ·teous·ly,** *adv.*

self-ris·ing \'self-'rī-zing\ *adj.* Containing leaven and needing no added leaven for rising, as a flour.

self-sac·ri·fice \'self-'sak-rə-ˌfīs, -fəs, -ˌfīz\ *n.* Sacrifice of oneself or one's desires or interests for the benefit of others or for reasons of conscience. — **self-sac·ri·fic·ing** \-ˌfī-sing, -ˌfī-zing\ *adj.*

self·same \'self-ˌsām\ *adj.* Exactly the same; as, dressed in the *selfsame* clothes as yesterday.

self-sat·is·fac·tion \'self-ˌsat-əs-'faksh-n\ *n.* The state of being pleased with oneself or with one's abilities or accomplishments.

self-sat·is·fied \'self-'sat-əs-ˌfīd\ *adj.* Feeling or showing self-satisfaction; self-complacent.

self-seek·er \'self-'sēk-r\ *n.* One who is mainly or unduly concerned with seeking his own interest or advantage. — **self-seek·ing** \-ing\ *n.* or *adj.*

self-serv·ice \'self-'sər-vəs\ *n.* The serving of oneself, as in a cafeteria or a supermarket.

self-start·er \'self-'stärt-r, -'stärt-r\ *n.* An automatic device, as an electric motor, for starting an internal-combustion engine.

self-styled \'self-'stīld\ *adj.* So called or named by oneself; as, a *self-styled* patriot.

self-suf·fi·cient \'self-sə-'fish-nt\ *adj.* **1** Needing no help from other people; independent. **2** Self-important. — **self-suf·fi·cien·cy** \-'fish-n-sē\ *n.*

self-sup·port \'self-sə-'pōrt, -'pȯrt\ *n.* Unaided support of oneself or itself.

self-taught \'self-'tȯt\ *adj.* Taught by oneself; having little or no formal instruction.

self-will \'self-'wil\ *n.* Obstinacy; stubbornness.

self-willed \'self-'wild\ *adj.* Obstinate.

self-wind·ing \'self-'wīn-ding\ *adj.* Wound automatically.

sell \'sel\ *v.;* **sold** \'sōld\; **sell·ing.** [From Old English *sellan* meaning literally "to give".] **1** To betray, as a person or duty. The traitors *sold* their king to the enemy. **2** To exchange something in return for money or something else of value; as, to *sell* fish. **3** To be sold or priced. Corn *sells* high. — The words *vend* and *barter* are synonyms of *sell: sell* usually refers to the transferring of property from one person to another for a fixed price with payments generally made in money; *vend* applies especially to the peddling of small articles or commodities, as by an individual selling in the streets or by an automatic machine; *barter* generally indicates the exchange of one type of goods for an equivalent value in another type of goods.

sell·er \'sel-r\ *n.* **1** A person who sells goods. **2** A thing that sells well or to a specified extent.

sel·vage or **sel·vedge** \'sel-vij\ *n.* The edge of cloth so woven that it will not ravel.

selves. Pl. of *self.*

se·man·tics \sə-'mant-iks\ *n.* The study of meanings and changes of meaning, especially of words.

sem·a·phore \'sem-ə-ˌfōr, -ˌfȯr\ *n.* **1** Any apparatus for sending visual signals that consists of one or more arms attached to an upright post and capable of being turned into different positions; as, a marine *semaphore;* a railroad *semaphore.* **2** Signaling by a semaphore or by flags held in both hands in positions like those of the arms of a two-arm semaphore. — *v.;* **sem·a·phored; sem·a·phor·ing.** To signal by semaphore.

semaphore signals

sem·blance \'sem-blən(t)s\ *n.* Outward appearance; a likeness; an image.

se·men \'sē-mən\ *n.* The fluid produced in the male reproductive organs and containing the spermatozoa.

se·mes·ter \sə-'mest-r\ *n.* Half an academic year; a school term.

semi-. A prefix that can mean: **1** About half, partly, incompletely, as in *semidivine, semitropical.* **2** Precisely half, as in *semicircle.* **3** Coming twice in each period named, as in *semiannual.*

sem·i·an·nu·al \'sem-ē-'an-yə-wəl, 'sem-ī-, -'an-yəl\ *adj.* Occurring twice each year. — **sem·i·an·nu·al·ly** \-'an-yə-lē, -'an-yə-wə-lē\ *adv.*

sem·i·cir·cle \'sem-ē-ˌsərk-l\ *n.* Half of a circle.

sem·i·cir·cu·lar \'sem-ē-'sərk-yəl-r\ *adj.* Having the form of a semicircle.

semicircle

semicircular canal. Any of the loop-shaped tubular parts in the inner ear of animals having a backbone.

sem·i·co·lon \'sem-ē-ˌkō-lən\ *n.* A mark of punctuation [;] that can be used: **1** Between parts of a sentence that require a more distinct separation than would be shown by a comma. **2** To give transition between main clauses when there is no connective. **3** To separate phrases and clauses containing commas.

sem·i·di·vine \'sem-ē-də-'vīn, 'sem-ī-\ *adj.* Partly divine; part god, part mortal.

sem·i·fi·nal \'sem-ē-'fīn-l, 'sem-ī-\ *adj.* Coming immediately before the final round in a tournament. — *n.* **1** A semifinal match or game. **2** [in the plural] A semifinal round.

sem·i·month·ly \'sem-ē-'mən(t)th-lē, 'sem-ī-\ *adj.* Coming twice in a month. — *adv.* Twice a month.

sem·i·nal \'sem-ən-l\ *adj.* Relating to, containing, or consisting of seeds or semen.

sem·i·nary \'sem-ə-ˌner-ē\ *n.; pl.* **sem·i·nar·ies. 1** A private school of high-school rank. **2** An institution for training clergymen.

sem·i·pre·cious \'sem-ē-'presh-əs, 'sem-ī-\ *adj.* Of gems, not equal to those of the highest value.

sem·i·pri·vate \'sem-ē-'prī-vət, 'sem-ī-\ *adj.* Shared with only a few others; as, a *semiprivate* room in a hospital. — **sem·i·pri·va·cy** \-və-sē\ *n.*

sem·i·skilled \'sem-ē-'skild, 'sem-ī-\ *adj.* Skilled only to a certain degree; as, *semiskilled* workmen.

sem·i·soft \'sem-ē-'sȯft, 'sem-ī-\ *adj.* Partially soft.

sem·i·sol·id \'sem-ē-'säl-əd, 'sem-ī-\ *adj.* Partially solid.

Sem·ite \'sem-ˌīt\ *n.* A member of a division of the Caucasian race which includes chiefly the Jews and Arabs. — **Se·mit·ic** \sə-'mit-ik\ *adj.*

sem·i·tone \'sem-ē-ˌtōn\ *n.* In music, a half step.

sem·i·trop·i·cal \'sem-ē-'träp-ik-l, 'sem-ī-\ *adj.* Partly tropical; subtropical; as, a *semitropical* city.

sem·i·week·ly \'sem-ē-'wēk-lē, 'sem-ī-\ *adj.* Happening twice in a week. — *adv.* Twice a week.

Sen. Abbreviation for: **1** *Senate.* **2** *Senator.*

sen·ate \'sen-ət\ *n.* [From medieval English *senat,* there borrowed from Old French, there derived from Latin *senatus,* a derivative of *senex* meaning "old" — see *senior.*] **1** [with a capital] The upper and smaller branch of some legislatures. **2** An official lawmaking group or council.

sen·a·tor \'sen-ət-r\ *n.* A member of a senate.

sen·a·to·ri·al \ˌsen-ə-'tōr-ē-əl, -'tȯr-\ *adj.* Having to do with a senator or senate.

send \'send\ *v.;* **sent** \'sent\; **send·ing. 1** To cause to go; to dispatch; to transmit; as, to *send* a pupil home; to *send* a letter. **2** To cause to happen or come; to give or inflict. Fate often *sends* hardships.

sen·es·chal \'sen-əsh-l\ *n.* An agent or bailiff who managed a lord's estate in feudal times.

se·nile \'sē-ˌnīl, 'sen-ˌīl\ *adj.* **1** Of or relating to old age; resulting from old age; as, *senile* weaknesses. **2** Having the infirmities sometimes characteristic of old age; as, a *senile* woman. — *n.* A senile person.

se·nil·i·ty \sə-'nil-ət-ē\ *n.* The quality or state of being senile; foolishness caused by old age.

sen·ior \'sēn-yər\ *adj.* [From medieval English, there borrowed from Latin, where it is the comparative of *senex* meaning "old" — see *senate.*] **1** Older — used chiefly to indicate a father having the same name as his son. **2** Higher in rank or office. **3** Having to do with the last year of high school or college. — *n.* One who is senior.

sen·ior·i·ty \sēn-'yȯr-ət-ē, -'yär-\ *n.; pl.* **sen·ior·i·ties. 1** The quality or state of being senior. **2** The status obtained by length of service.

sen·na \'sen-ə\ *n.* **1** Any of various cassias with pinnate leaves and often with showy yellow flowers; especially, one that is used in medicine. **2** The dried leaflets of a senna used in medicine as a purgative.

sen·sa·tion \sen-'sāsh-n, sən-\ *n.* **1** The direct result of stimulating a sense organ; as, a *sensation* of heat. **2** A condition of excitement. **3** That which causes such a condition. The play was a *sensation.*

sen·sa·tion·al \sen-'sāsh-n(-)əl, sən-\ *adj.* **1** Having to do with the senses or with sensation. **2** Exciting unusual interest or feeling; as, *sensational* news. — **sen·sa·tion·al·ly** \-n(-)ə-lē\ *adv.*

sense \'sen(t)s\ *n.* **1** A power to perceive physical objects or conditions by means of certain organs (**sense organs**) or body mechanisms, as the eye or the nerve ends. **2** The function of the perceptive organs or mechanisms of the body; as, the *sense* of sight. **3** A particular sensation; as, a *sense* of tiredness. **4** A feeling; as, a *sense* of shame. **5** Awareness; consciousness; as, a *sense* of danger. **6** Intellectual appreciation; as, a *sense* of humor. **7** Intelligence; judgment; especially, good judgment. **8** Good reason or excuse. There is no *sense* in waiting. **9** Meaning; especially, one of the meanings a word may bear. **10** Import; intention; as, to get the *sense* of the speaker's words. — *v.;* **sensed; sens·ing.** To feel, realize, or understand indirectly.

sense·less \'sen(t)s-ləs\ *adj.* **1** Unconscious; as, to be knocked *senseless.* **2** Stupid; meaningless; silly; as, a *senseless* act. — **sense·less·ly,** *adv.*

sen·si·bil·i·ty \ˌsen(t)s-ə-'bil-ət-ē\ *n.; pl.* **sen·si·bil·i·ties. 1** The ability to receive or feel sensations. **2** The emotion or feeling of which a person is capable; sensitivity or responsiveness.

sen·si·ble \'sen(t)s-əb-l\ *adj.* **1** Capable of being known by the senses; able to be perceived; as, *sensible* objects; a *sensible* difference in weight. **2** Capable of seeing or perceiving. The ear is *sensible* to sounds. **3** Aware. **4** Having good sense; intelligent. — **sen·si·bly** \-ə-blē\ *adv.*

sen·si·tive \'sen(t)s-ət-iv\ *adj.* **1** Having sense or feeling; as, a *sensitive* animal. **2** Easily or strongly affected or hurt; as, a *sensitive* child. **3** Readily changed or affected by the action of a certain thing; as, *sensitive* to light. **4** Capable of indicating very small differences; as, *sensitive* scales. **5** In radio, high in sensitivity. — **sen·si·tive·ly,** *adv.*

sensitive plant. Any of various American tropical and greenhouse mimosas with numerous leaflets that close tightly at the touch.

sen·si·tiv·i·ty \ˌsen(t)s-ə-'tiv-ət-ē\ *n.; pl.* **sen·si·tiv·i·ties. 1** The quality or state of being sensitive or responsive. **2** In radio, the degree to which a receiving set responds to incoming waves.

sen·si·tize \'sen(t)s-ə-ˌtīz\ *v.;* **sen·si·tized; sen·si·tiz·ing. 1** To make sensitive, as photographic paper. **2** To make allergic.

sen·so·ry \'sen(t)s-r(-)ē\ *adj.* **1** Having to do with sensation or the senses. **2** Carrying nerve impulses from the sense organs; as, *sensory* nerves.

sen·su·al \'sench-ə-wəl\ *adj.* **1** Relating to the senses; satisfying or pleasing to the senses. **2** Given to indulging the appetites; voluptuous.

sen·su·al·i·ty \ˌsench-ə-'wal-ət-ē\ *n.; pl.* **sen·su·al·i·ties.** The quality or state of being sensual.

sen·su·ous \'sench-ə-wəs\ *adj.* Having to do with the senses or with things perceived by the senses; as, *sensuous* pleasure. — **sen·su·ous·ly,** *adv.*

sent. Past tense and past part. of *send.*

sen·tence \'sent-n(t)s, -nz\ *n.* **1** A decision; judgment. The judge passed *sentence* on the man. **2** A judicial decree; in criminal courts, the order by which a court imposes punishment upon a person found guilty. **3** The punishment so imposed; as, to serve a *sentence* for robbery. **4** A group of words put together so as to express a complete thought. — *v.;* **sen·tenced; sen·tenc·ing.** To pass sentence on; to assign punishment to.

sentence fragment. A part of a sentence, usually

a phrase or a dependent clause, written and punctuated as if it were a complete sentence.

sen·ten·tious \(ˈ)sen-ˈtench-əs\ *adj.* **1** Concise and forceful; pithy. **2** Containing, using, or inclined to use high-sounding, empty phrases or pompous sayings. — **sen·ten·tious·ly,** *adv.*

sen·tient \ˈsench-nt, -ē-ənt\ *adj.* Capable of feeling; conscious of sense impressions. The lowest of *sentient* creatures.— **sen·tience** \-n(t)s, -ē-ən(t)s\ *n.*

sen·ti·ment \ˈsent-m-ənt\ *n.* **1** Emotion; feeling; especially, tender feelings. **2** Thought or mental attitude influenced by feeling; as, a strong religious *sentiment.* **3** A view, opinion, or judgment.

sen·ti·men·tal \ˌsent-m-ˈent-l\ *adj.* **1** Of the nature of or influenced strongly by sentiment. **2** Having or showing too much sentiment; pretending more tender feeling than one actually has. **3** Primarily affecting the emotions; as, *sentimental* music. — **sen·ti·men·tal·ly** \-ˈent-l-ē\ *adv.*

sen·ti·men·tal·ist \ˌsent-m-ˈent-l-əst\ *n.* A person who characteristically favors or indulges in sentiment. — **sen·ti·men·tal·ism** \-l-ˌiz-m\ *n.*

sen·ti·men·tal·i·ty \ˌsent-m-ˌen-ˈtal-ət-ē, -m-ən-\ *n.; pl.* **sen·ti·men·tal·i·ties.** The quality or condition of being sentimental, especially to excess.

sen·ti·nel \ˈsent-n(-)əl\ *n.* A sentry.

sen·try \ˈsen-trē\ *n.; pl.* **sen·tries.** A person, especially a soldier, standing guard; a sentinel.

se·pal \ˈsēp-l, ˈsep-l\ *n.* A leaflike part or division of the calyx of a flower.

sep·a·ra·ble \ˈsep-r(-)əb-l\ *adj.* Capable of being separated or distinguished. — **sep·a·ra·bil·i·ty** \ˌsep-r(-)ə-ˈbil-ət-ē\ *n.* — **sep·a·ra·bly** \ˈsep-r(-)ə-blē\ *adv.*

sepal

sep·a·rate \ˈsep-r-ˌāt\ *v.;* **sep·a·rat·ed; sep·a·rat·ing. 1** To disunite; to take apart; to sever; as, to *separate* the leaves of a book. **2** To keep apart by something intervening; to occupy the space between two or more things; as, twin cities *separated* by a river. **3** To cease to be together; to part. **4** To come apart; to become detached. **5** To become disengaged as a separate body; as, crystals *separating* out from a solution. — \ˈsep-r(-)ət\ *adj.* **1** Not connected; not united or associated; as, two *separate* apartments. **2** Divided from another or others. **3** Being apart from others; solitary. **4** Relating to one only; not shared; as, to live in *separate* rooms. **5** Single; particular; as, the *separate* pieces of a puzzle. — **sep·a·rate·ly** \ˈsep-r(-)ət-lē\ *adv.*

sep·a·ra·tion \ˌsep-r-ˈāsh-n\ *n.* **1** A separating; a condition of being separated. **2** A point or line of division. **3** A divorce. **4** A formal separating of husband and wife by agreement but without divorce. — **sep·a·ra·tive** \ˈsep-r-ˌāt-iv, -r(-)ət-\ *adj.*

sep·a·ra·tist \ˈsep-r-ˌāt-əst, -r(-)ət-\ *n.* An advocate of separation, as from a church or party.

sep·a·ra·tor \ˈsep-r-ˌāt-r\ *n.* One that separates, as a machine for separating cream from milk.

se·pia \ˈsēp-ē-ə\ *n.; pl.* **se·pi·as** \-ē-əz\ or **se·pi·ae** \-ē-ˌē\. **1** A cuttlefish having long lateral fins and an internal shell. **2** A brown pigment prepared from the black secretion of various cuttlefish. **3** The dark reddish brown color of sepia. — *adj.* Of the color of sepia; made of or done in sepia.

se·poy \ˈsē-ˌpȯi\ *n.* A native of India employed as a soldier in the service of a European power.

sep·sis \ˈsep-səs\ *n.* A poisoned condition resulting from the spread of bacteria or poisonous products from a center of infection.

Sept. Abbreviation for *September.*

septa. A pl. of *septum.*

Sep·tem·ber \sep-ˈtem-br, səp-\ *n.* [From Old English, there borrowed from Latin, where it designated the seventh month of the ancient Roman year and was derived from *septem* meaning "seven".] The ninth month of the year, containing 30 days.

sep·tet or **sep·tette** \(ˈ)sep-ˈtet\ *n.* **1** A set of seven persons or things; as, a *septet* of singers. **2** A musical composition for seven instruments or voices.

sep·tic \ˈsep-tik\ *adj.* **1** Of, relating to, or causing putrefaction. **2** Produced by putrefaction or by disease germs; as, *septic* poisoning.

septic tank. A tank in which the solid matter of sewage is deposited and decomposed by bacteria.

sep·tu·a·ge·nar·i·an \(ˌ)sep-ˌtü-əj-n-ˈer-ē-ən\ *adj.* Seventy or between seventy and eighty years old. — *n.* A septuagenarian person.

sep·tum \ˈsept-m\ *n.; pl.* **sep·tums** \-mz\ or **sep·ta** \ˈsep-tə\. A dividing partition, especially between two cavities or masses of softer body tissue.

sep·ul·cher or **sep·ul·chre** \ˈsep-lk-r\ *n.* A grave; a tomb; a burial vault. — *v.;* **sep·ul·chered** or **sep·ul·chred** \-rd\; **sep·ul·cher·ing** or **sep·ul·chring** \-r(-)ing\. To bury; to entomb.

se·pul·chral \sə-ˈpəl-krəl\ *adj.* **1** Of or relating to burial, the grave, or monuments to the dead; as, a *sepulchral* stone. **2** Dismal; gloomy.

sep·ul·ture \ˈsep-lch-r\ *n.* **1** The action of burying; interment. **2** A sepulcher.

se·quel \ˈsēk-wəl\ *n.* **1** An event that follows or comes afterwards; a result. **2** A book that continues a story begun in another.

se·quence \ˈsēk-wən(t)s, ˈsē-ˌkwen(t)s\ *n.* **1** The condition or fact of coming after something else. **2** A result; a sequel. **3** A series having continuity and connection. **4** The order of events in time.

se·quent \ˈsēk-wənt\ *adj.* Following in time or as an effect. — *n.* That which follows or results.

se·ques·ter \sē-ˈkwest-r\ *v.;* **se·ques·tered; se·ques·ter·ing** \-r(-)ing\. **1** To set apart; to retire; to withdraw. **2** In law, to take possession of, as a person's property, until a demand is satisfied.

se·ques·tra·tion \ˌsēk-wəs-ˈtrāsh-n\ *n.* The act of sequestering or the state of being sequestered.

se·quin \ˈsēk-wən\ *n.* A spangle used as an ornament on clothes.

se·quoia \sē-ˈkwȯi-ə\ *n.* **1** A tree of California that grows about 300 feet tall and has pointed leaves and small oval cones. **2** The redwood.

sera. A pl. of *serum.*

se·ra·glio \sə-'räl-ˌyō, -'ral-, -'ràl-\ *n.; pl.* **se·ra·glios** \-ˌyōz\ or **se·ra·gli** \-(ˌ)yē\. A harem.

se·ra·pe \sə-'räp-ē, -'ràp-ē\ *n.* A blanket worn as an outer garment by some Spanish Americans.

ser·aph \'ser-əf\ *n.; pl.* **ser·a·phim** \-ə-ˌfim\ or **ser·aphs** \-əfs\. An angel of a very high order. — **se·raph·ic** \sə-'raf-ik\ or **se·raph·i·cal** \-ik-l\ *adj.*

sere \'sir\ *adj.* Dry; withered.

ser·e·nade \ˌser-ə-'nād\ *n.* Music as sung or played in the open air at night, usually to please a woman. — *v.;* **ser·e·nad·ed**; **ser·e·nad·ing.** To sing or play a serenade. — **ser·e·nad·er** \-'nād-r\ *n.*

se·rene \sə-'rēn\ *adj.* **1** Clear; as, *serene* skies. **2** Calm; as, a *serene* manner. — **se·rene·ly**, *adv.*

se·ren·i·ty \sə-'ren-ət-ē\ *n.* The quality or condition of being serene; calm; composure.

serf \'sərf\ *n.* A peasant laborer bound to the land and subject to the will of its owner; a slave.

serf·dom \'sərf-dəm\ *n.* The quality, state, or fact of being a serf.

serge \'sərj\ *n.* Woolen cloth woven with raised diagonal lines, used especially for suits and coats.

ser·geant \'särj-nt, 'sàrj-\ *n.* **1** A sergeant at arms. **2** A police officer ranking next below a captain or, sometimes, a lieutenant. **3** A noncommissioned army officer ranking next above a corporal.

sergeant at arms. An officer of a court of law or a lawmaking body appointed to keep order.

se·ri·al \'sir-ē-əl\ *adj.* Arranged in, or appearing in, parts or numbers that follow regularly in a series; as, a *serial* story. — *n.* **1** A serial publication. **2** A story or other writing appearing in successive installments. — **se·ri·al·ly** \-ē-ə-lē\ *adv.*

se·ries \'sir-ēz\ *n. sing. and pl.* **1** A number of things or events arranged in order and connected by being alike in some way; as, a *series* of games. **2** The arrangement of connecting the separate parts of an electrical circuit successively end to end to form a single path for the current.

se·ri·ous \'sir-ē-əs\ *adj.* **1** Solemn; thoughtful; earnest. **2** Requiring much thought or work; as, a *serious* task. **3** Dangerous; harmful; as, a *serious* illness. — **se·ri·ous·ly**, *adv.*

ser·mon \'sər-mən\ *n.* **1** A public speech, usually by a priest or minister, for the purpose of giving religious instruction. **2** A serious talk to a person about his conduct or duty.

se·rous \'sir-əs\ *adj.* **1** Thin; watery; like serum. **2** Of or relating to serum.

ser·pent \'sərp-nt\ *n.* **1** A snake, especially, a large snake. **2** An evil, sly, or crafty person.

ser·pen·tine \'sərp-n-ˌtēn, -ˌtīn\ *adj.* **1** Of or like a serpent. **2** Winding or turning one way and another; as, a *serpentine* path in the woods.

ser·pen·tine \'sərp-n-ˌtēn\ *n.* A mineral or rock, usually dull-green and often mottled.

ser·rate \'ser-ˌāt\ or **ser·rat·ed** \-ˌāt-əd\ *adj.* Having a saw-toothed edge, as many tree leaves.

ser·ried \'ser-ēd\ *adj.* Closely pressed together, as soldiers in ranks.

se·rum \'sir-əm\ *n.; pl.* **se·rums** \-əmz\ or **se·ra** \-ə\. **1** The watery part of an animal fluid remaining after coagulation. **2** The watery part of blood, especially when containing immune bodies and used as an injection to protect from disease.

serv·ant \'sərv-nt\ *n.* **1** A person hired to perform household or personal services. **2** A government employee; as, a civil *servant.* **3** One who willingly follows or works for another person or for a cause.

serve \'sərv\ *v.;* **served**; **serv·ing.** **1** To act as a servant; to be a servant of. **2** To worship or obey; as, to *serve* God. **3** To perform the official duties of a position; as, to *serve* as a juror. **4** To do duty as a soldier or sailor. **5** To benefit; to promote the welfare of. Scientists *serve* the world. **6** To spend a period of time in doing something; as, to *serve* a jail sentence. **7** To provide people with food, as at a table or counter. **8** To wait on customers in a store. **9** To supply or furnish, as with light and heat. **10** To be useful, helpful, or satisfactory; to suit; as, when the time *serves.* A tree may *serve* as a shelter. **11** To be enough for. A pie that will *serve* eight people. **12** In tennis and some other games, to put the ball in play. **13** In law, to deliver or execute; as, to *serve* a summons. **14** To treat; to behave oneself towards; as, to *serve* another ill. — *n.* In some games, as tennis, the serving of a ball; a turn at serving; the ball served.

serv·er \'sərv-r\ *n.* **1** A person who serves. **2** Something used in serving, as a tray for food.

serv·ice \'sər-vəs\ *n.* **1** The occupation or condition of a servant; as, to be in *service* as a cook. **2** The act, fact, or means, of serving; as, to render *service.* **3** Duty done or demanded; as, two hours of *service* per day. **4** Spiritual serving, as shown by obedience, good works, and love. **5** An official religious duty; a religious rite; as, the marriage *service.* **6** The performance of official or professional duties; the results of these duties; as, to give medical *service.* **7** A branch of public employment, or the persons employed in it; as, civil *service.* **8** Military or naval duty, organization, or performance. **9** A set of dishes or silverware. **10** Help; benefit. **11** The supplying of some public need; as, bus *service.* **12** Care or maintenance of a product. **13** In tennis, a serve. — *v.;* **serv·iced**; **serv·ic·ing.** To do repair or maintenance work on, as a car.

serv·ice·a·ble \'sər-və-səb-l\ *adj.* **1** Prepared for, or capable of, service; useful. **2** Fit for use or service. **3** Lasting or wearing well in use. — **serv·ice·a·bil·i·ty** \ˌsər-və-sə-'bil-ət-ē\ *n.*

serv·ice·man \'sər-vəs-ˌman, -mən\ *n.; pl.* **serv·ice·men** \-ˌmen, -mən\. One in military service.

service station. A place that supplies vehicles, as with gasoline and oil, and may do servicing.

ser·vi·ette \ˌsər-vē-'et\ *n.* A table napkin.

ser·vile \'sərv-l, 'sər-ˌvīl\ *adj.* **1** Relating to a slave or slaves; consisting of slaves. **2** Like or suited to a slave or servant; as, a *servile* manner; *servile* work. — **ser·vile·ly** \'sərv-l-(l)ē, 'sər-ˌvīl-lē\ *adv.*

ser·vil·i·ty \(ˌ)sər-'vil-ət-ē\ *n.; pl.* **ser·vil·i·ties.** The quality, state, or an instance of being servile.

ser·vi·tor \'sər-vət-r\ *n.* A servant; an attendant.

ser·vi·tude \'sər-və-ˌtüd, -ˌtyüd\ *n.* **1** Slavery; bondage. **2** Service required as a penalty for crime.

ses·a·me \'ses-m-ē\ *n.* **1** A hairy herb of the East Indies or its small flattish seeds (**sesame seed**), which are used as food. **2** Same as *open sesame.*

ses·qui·cen·ten·ni·al \ˌses-kwə-sen-'ten-ē-əl\ *adj.* Of or relating to a century and a half. — *n.* The 150th anniversary or its celebration.

ses·sile \'ses-l\ *adj.* Attached directly by the base; not raised on a stalk; as, *sessile* leaves.

ses·sion \'sesh-n\ *n.* **1** One meeting, as of court or school. **2** A series of meetings; as, a *session* of Congress. **3** The period of such a meeting or series.

set \'set\ *v.;* **set; set·ting. 1** To cause to sit; as, to *set* a hen on eggs. **2** To sit, as hens on eggs. **3** To put or fix in any place, condition, or position; as, to *set* a dish on the table. **4** To fix or settle; as, to *set* a price. **5** To furnish as an example to be followed; to establish; as, to *set* the pace. **6** To cause to be, become, or do; as, to *set* a prisoner free. **7** To start; as, to *set* a fire. **8** To pass below the horizon, as the sun. **9** To direct; as, to *set* one's steps toward school. **10** To arrange; to adjust; as, to *set* a watch; to *set* type for a book. **11** To fix in a setting or frame; as, a ring *set* with diamonds. **12** To value; to rate; to estimate; as, to *set* the loss at two thousand dollars. **13** To fix firmly; as, to *set* one's jaw. **14** To harden or solidify; as, to wait for cement to *set.* This jelly *sets* quickly. **15** To fit, as words to music or music to words. **16** To incline; to flow; as, a current that *sets* to the north. — **set about.** To begin to do. — **set aside. 1** To discard; to dismiss from the mind. **2** To reserve. **3** To annul. — **set back.** To hinder. — **set down.** To put in writing; as, to *set down* a poem on paper. — **set forth. 1** To make known; as, to *set forth* an idea. **2** To start out; as, to *set forth* on a journey. — **set in.** To begin. Winter *set in* early. — **set off. 1** To serve as a contrast; as, dark eyes *set off* by a pale face. **2** To separate from a whole. **3** To begin or cause to begin; as, to be *set off* laughing. **4** To explode, as dynamite. — **set on** or **set upon. 1** To attack. **2** To urge to attack or pursue. — **set out. 1** To start on a course, journey, or career. **2** To state; to describe; as, to *set out* the plan in detail. — **set to.** To go to work earnestly; as, to *set to* and finish a job. — **set up. 1** To raise, as a cry. **2** To begin, establish, or organize. — *adj.* **1** Fixed by authority; as, a *set* rule. **2** Intentional; carefully thought out and expressed; as, of *set* purpose. **3** Stubborn; as, *set* in one's ways. **4** Fixed; rigid; as, a *set* smile. **5** Formed; made; built; as, a heavy-*set* man. **6** Built in; as, a *set* tub for washing. — *n.* **1** Form; build; as, the *set* of one's shoulders. **2** Direction or course; as, the *set* of the wind. **3** A number of things of the same kind that belong or are used together; as, a *set* of dishes. **4** A group of persons joined by common interests; as, the bicycling *set.* **5** Any artificial setting for a scene of a play or a motion picture. **6** A radio or television receiver.

se·ta \'sēt-ə\ *n.; pl.* **se·tas** \'sēt-əz\ or **se·tae** \'sē-ˌtē\. In biology, a slender, bristlelike organ or part.

set·back \'set-ˌbak\ *n.* An unexpected reverse.

set·tee \se-'tē\ *n.* A long bench or sofa with a back and arms.

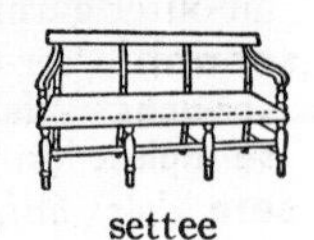
settee

set·ter \'set-r\ *n.* **1** A person or thing that sets. **2** One of a breed of long-haired hunting dogs trained to stand stiffly and point when a game bird is nearby.

set·ting \'set-ing\ *n.* **1** The act of a person or thing that sets; as, the *setting* of type. **2** That in which something is set or mounted; as, a gold *setting* for a ruby. **3** The background, as of time and place, of the action of a story or play; scenery; surroundings. **4** The music composed for a poem. **5** The eggs that a hen sits on for hatching at one time.

set·tle \'set-l\ *n.* A long wooden bench with arms and a high solid back.

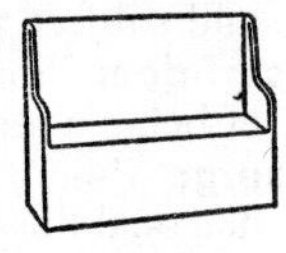
settle

set·tle \'set-l\ *v.;* **set·tled; set·tling** \-l(-)ing\. **1** To place so as to stay; to place in a fixed condition; as, to *settle* oneself in a chair. **2** To establish residence in; to colonize; as, those who *settled* the West. **3** To make one's home; as, to *settle* in the country. **4** To alight. The birds *settled* on the roof. **5** To sink gradually to a lower level, as the foundations of a house. **6** To sink, as in a liquid. **7** To apply oneself; as, to *settle* down to work. **8** To fix by agreement, as a price. **9** To bestow or give possession of legally. He *settled* property on his wife. **10** To put in order or adjustment, as one's room. **11** To calm; as, to *settle* one's nerves. **12** To decide; as, to *settle* a question. **13** To pay in full, as a bill. **14** To adjust differences; as, to *settle* a quarrel.

set·tle·ment \'set-l-mənt\ *n.* **1** The act of settling; the condition of being settled. **2** The amount settled; as, a *settlement* of ten thousand dollars. **3** Payment, as of a bill. **4** Colonizing. **5** A place or region newly settled. **6** A small village. **7** Also **settlement house.** An institution that renders educational, recreational, and other community service to people in a crowded part of a city.

set·tler \'set-l(-)ər\ *n.* A person who settles in a new region; a colonist.

set·up \'set-ˌəp\ *n.* The way in which something is set up; organization; arrangement.

sev·en \'sev-n\ *adj.* One more than six. — *n.* **1** The sum of four and three; seven units or objects. **2** A figure standing for seven units, as 7 or VII.

seven seas. All the waters or oceans of the world.

sev·en·teen \'sev-n-'tēn\ *adj.* Ten and seven; one more than sixteen. — *n.* **1** The sum of ten and seven; seventeen units or objects. **2** A figure standing for seventeen units, as 17 or XVII.

sev·en·teenth \'sev-n-'tēn(t)th\ *adj.* Next after the sixteenth. — *n.; pl.* **sev·en·teenths** \-'tēn(t)s, -'tēn(t)ths\. One of seventeen equal parts.

sev·enth \'sev-n(t)th\ *adj.* Next after the sixth. — *n.; pl.* **sev·enths** \-n(t)s, -n(t)ths\. One of seven equal parts.

sev·en·ti·eth \'sev-n-tē-əth\ *adj.* Next after the sixty-ninth. — *n.* One of seventy equal parts.

sev·en·ty \'sev-n-tē\ *adj.* Seven times ten; one more than sixty-nine. — *n.; pl.* **sev·en·ties. 1** The sum of seven tens; seventy units or objects. **2** A figure standing for seventy units, as 70 or LXX.

sev·er \'sev-r\ *v.;* **sev·ered; sev·er·ing** \-r(-)ing\. **1** To separate two or more persons, things, or ideas; to divide; to disunite, as by cutting or tearing. **2** To cut or break apart. The cable *severed* in the middle. — **sev·er·a·ble** \-r(-)əb-l\ *adj.*

sev·er·al \'sev-r(-)əl\ *adj.* **1** Individual; respective. The travelers went their *several* ways. **2** Different; as, two *several* items. **3** Consisting of more than two but not very many; as, *several* pieces.

sev·er·al·ly \'sev-r(-)ə-lē\ *adv.* **1** Separately; one at a time; each by itself; as, to acknowledge gifts *severally*. **2** Respectively. Police, teachers, and principal *severally* questioned the accused boy.

sev·er·ance \'sev-r(-)ən(t)s\ *n.* A severing or a being severed; a division; a separation.

se·vere \sə-'vir\ *adj.;* **se·ver·er; se·ver·est. 1** Serious in feeling or manner; grave; austere. **2** Very strict; harsh. **3** Not using unnecessary ornament; plain; as, a *severe* style. **4** Sharp; extreme; as, *severe* pain. **5** Hard to endure; as, a *severe* test. — **se·vere·ly,** *adv.*

se·ver·i·ty \sə-'ver-ət-ē\ *n.; pl.* **se·ver·i·ties. 1** The quality or condition of being severe; as, the *severity* of the winter. **2** Extreme strictness; harshness. **3** Painful or distressing nature; as, the *severity* of his illness. **4** Cruel treatment or punishment.

sew \'sō\ *v.;* **sewed; sewed** \'sōd\ or **sewn** \'sōn\; **sew·ing. 1** To join or fasten by stitches; as, to *sew* up a rip; to *sew* a dress. **2** To work with needle and thread. — **sew·er** \'sōr, 'sō-ər\ *n.*

sew·age \'sü-ij\ *n.* Waste liquids and solid matter carried off by sewers.

sew·er \'sü-ər, 'su̇r\ *n.* A covered, usually underground, drain to carry off water and waste.

sew·er·age \'sü-ər-ij, 'su̇r-ij\ *n.* **1** The removal and disposal of sewage and surface water by sewers. **2** A system of sewers. **3** Sewage.

sew·ing \'sō-ing\ *n.* **1** The action or occupation of one who sews. **2** Material to be sewed.

sewing machine. A machine for sewing.

sewn. A past part. of *sew.*

sex \'seks\ *n.* **1** One of the two divisions of living things distinguished as male and female; males or females taken as a class. **2** The sum of the characteristics which determine whether a living organism is male or female; the character of being either male or female.

sex·a·ge·nar·i·an \ˌseks-əj-n-'er-ē-ən\ *adj.* Sixty or between sixty and seventy years old. — *n.* A person who is sixty or more but less than seventy.

sex cell. An egg cell or a sperm cell.

sex·tant \'seks-tənt\ *n.* An instrument for measuring angular distances, used in navigation to observe the altitude of the sun or stars above the horizon.

sex·tet or **sex·tette** \(')seks-'tet\ *n.* **1** A musical composition for six voices or six instruments; the performers of such a composition. **2** Any group or set of six.

sex·ton \'seks-tən\ *n.* A member of a church staff whose duties include care of the buildings and property and the ringing of the bell for services.

sex·tu·ple \(')seks-'tüp-l, 'seks-(ˌ)təp-l\ *adj.* **1** Consisting of six; six times. **2** In music, having six beats to the measure. — *v.;* **sex·tu·pled; sex·tu·pling** \-l(-)ing\. To multiply by six.

sex·u·al \'sek-shə-wəl, 'seksh-l\ *adj.* **1** Relating to or associated with sex. **2** In biology, having sex. — **sex·u·al·ly** \'seksh-l(-)ē, 'sek-shə-wə-lē\ *adv.*

Sgt. Abbreviation for *Sergeant.*

shab·by \'shab-ē\ *adj.;* **shab·bi·er; shab·bi·est. 1** Threadbare and faded from wear; worn out. **2** Dressed in worn clothes. **3** Mean; low; as, *shabby* treatment. — **shab·bi·ly** \-l-ē\ *adv.*

Sha·bu·oth \shə-'vü-ˌōs, -əs, -ˌōt(h)\ *n.* An annual Jewish holiday celebrated seven weeks after the second day of the Passover as a harvest festival and also to commemorate the revelation of the Ten Commandments at Mt. Sinai; Pentecost.

shack \'shak\ *n.* A hut; a shanty.

shack·le \'shak-l\ *n.* **1** Something that confines the legs or arms so as to prevent their free motion; especially, a manacle or a fetter. **2** Something which prevents free action, as if by fetters; as, the *shackles* of superstition. **3** Any device for making something fast or secure. — *v.;* **shack·led; shack·ling** \-l(-)ing\. **1** To put shackles on. **2** To hinder; to impede. — **shack·ler** \-l(-)ər\ *n.*

shad \'shad\ *n. sing. and pl.* Any of several food fish of the Atlantic, like herring, but with deeper bodies, which ascend rivers in the spring to spawn.

shade \'shād\ *n.* **1** Partial darkness or obscurity caused by something obstructing the rays of light. **2** Space sheltered from light or heat, especially from the sun. **3** A secluded place. **4** A degree of color or a special variety of a color; the degree, especially of darkness, of a color; as, four *shades* of brown. Maroon is a *shade* of red. **5** A very small difference, variation, or degree of thought, belief, or expression; as, *shades* of meaning. **6** [in the plural] The shadows which gather as darkness falls. **7** Spirit; ghost. **8** A thing that shades; a screen; a shelter. **9** An adjustable screen, usually on a roller, used to shut out or regulate the light. **10** In painting or drawing, the representation of a shaded surface, as by darker pigment or closely drawn lines. — *v.;* **shad·ed; shad·ing. 1** To shelter from light or heat; to screen. **2** To darken; to obscure. **3** To mark with degrees of light or color; as, to *shade* a drawing. **4** To undergo or show slight differences or variations of color, value, or meaning.

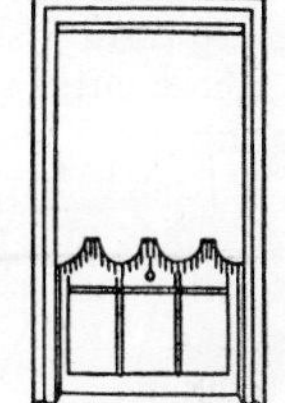
window shade

shad·ow \'shad-ō\ *n.* **1** The shade which results when an opaque object comes between a source of light and any broad surface; the image thus made; as, a *shadow* on the wall. **2** Protecting cover; shelter. **3** A small degree or portion; as, beyond a *shadow* of a doubt. **4** A gloomy influence. The accident cast a *shadow* over their happiness. **5** A shadowy form; a reflected image in a mirror or in water. **6** A specter; a ghost. **7** A constant companion. **8** A person who, as spy or detective, follows like a shadow. **9** A shaded portion of a picture. — *v.* **1** To cut off light from; to throw a shadow upon. **2** To make obscure, dim, or dark; to cloud. **3** To represent faintly; to foreshadow. **4** To follow and watch closely. **5** To mark with different degrees of light; to shade.

shad·owy \ˈshad-ə-wē\ *adj.* **1** Like a shadow; unreal. **2** Full of shadow.

shady \ˈshād-ē\ *adj.;* **shad·i·er**; **shad·i·est.** **1** Abounding in or giving shade; as, a *shady* nook. **2** Questionable; disreputable; as, a *shady* act.

shaft \ˈshaft\ *n.; pl.* **shafts** \ˈshaf(t)s; *in sense 4, also* ˈshavz\. **1** The long handle of a spear or similar weapon; a spear; a lance. **2** The slender stem of an arrow; an arrow. **3** A pole; a flagstaff. **4** One of two poles between which a horse is hitched to pull a wagon or carriage. **5** A narrow beam, as of light. **6** A barb, as of ridicule. **7** Something that is suggestive of the stem of an arrow or spear; a long slender part, especially when round, such as the stem of a tree. **8** The handle of certain tools or instruments. **9** A column or other tall monument. **10** A vertical opening or passage through the floors of a building; as, an air *shaft.* **11** A bar to support rotating pieces of machinery, such as pulleys. **12** In mining, an opening made for finding or mining ore. **13** The stem of a feather.

shag \ˈshag\ *n.* **1** Coarse, matted wool or hair; as, the *shag* of a woolly dog. **2** The long, coarse nap of cloth. **3** A matted or tangled mass; as, a *shag* of weeds. **4** A strong, coarse, shredded tobacco.

shag·bark \ˈshag-ˌbärk, -ˌbȧrk\ *n.* A hickory tree whose outer shaggy bark peels off in long strips.

shag·gy \ˈshag-ē\ *adj.;* **shag·gi·er**; **shag·gi·est.** **1** Rough with or as if with long hair or wool. **2** Thick and rough; tangled; as, *shaggy* hair.

shah \ˈshä, ˈshȯ, ˈshȧ\ *n.* The sovereign of Iran.

shake \ˈshāk\ *v.;* **shook** \ˈshu̇k\; **shak·en** \ˈshāk-n\; **shak·ing.** **1** To tremble or make tremble; to quiver; as, to *shake* with cold. The speaker's voice *shook* with emotion. **2** To become unsteady; to vibrate; to totter; as, to feel a boat *shake* in a storm. **3** To be moved, to fall, or to cause to fall or disappear by or as if by a shake; as, to *shake* off anxiety. **4** To become convulsed; as, to *shake* with laughter. **5** To make less firm; to weaken; as, to have one's confidence *shaken.* **6** To move back and forth or to and fro; to brandish, wave, or flourish; as, to *shake* a branch; to *shake* one's head. **7** To clasp as in greeting; as, to *shake* a person's hand. — *n.* **1** The action of shaking. **2** A moment; as, to be ready in a *shake.* **3** A quivering or trembling.

shak·er \ˈshāk-r\ *n.* One that shakes or is used in shaking something; as, a salt *shaker.*

shake-up \ˈshāk-ˌəp\ *n.* **1** The action or process of shaking, stirring up, or jarring, as by physical shock. **2** A reorganization, as in a department, resulting in change of personnel.

shako \ˈshak-ˌō, ˈshāk-ˌō\ *n.; pl.* **shak·os.** A stiff military cap with a high crown and a plume.

shaky \ˈshāk-ē\ *adj.;* **shak·i·er**; **shak·i·est.** **1** Easily shaken; tottering; unsound; as, a *shaky* fence; a *shaky* argument. **2** Trembling; tremulous; as, a *shaky* voice. **3** Lacking stability; unsettled; as, *shaky* in one's belief. **4** Questionable; uncertain; unreliable.

shale \ˈshāl\ *n.* Rock formed of densely packed clay or mud that splits easily into layers.

shall \shəl, (ˈ)shal\ *v.; past tense* **should** \shəd, (ˈ)shu̇d\. **1** Am or are going to or expecting to; as, I *shall* write today. **2** Is or are obliged, destined, certain, or compelled to; must. They *shall* not pass.

shal·lop \ˈshal-əp\ *n.* A light open boat.

shal·low \ˈshal-ō\ *adj.* **1** Not deep; having little depth. **2** Not deep intellectually; superficial. — *n.* A shallow place in a body of water.

shalt \shəlt, (ˈ)shalt\. An archaic form of *shall* — used chiefly with *thou.*

sham \ˈsham\ *n.* **1** Anything resembling an article of household linen and used in its place or to cover it; as, a pillow *sham.* **2** A fraud; a substitute; an imitation. — *adj.* **1** False; pretended; unreal; as, a *sham* battle. **2** Made or used as an imitation; as, *sham* jewelry. — *v.;* **shammed**; **sham·ming.** To pretend; to fake; as, to *sham* illness.

sham·ble \ˈsham-bl\ *v.;* **sham·bled**; **sham·bling** \-bl(-)ing\. To walk awkwardly and unsteadily; to shuffle along. — *n.* A shambling gait.

sham·bles \ˈsham-blz\ *n. pl.* **1** A slaughterhouse. **2** A scene of slaughter or destruction.

shame \ˈshām\ *n.* **1** A painful feeling of guilt caused by having done something wrong, improper, or immodest. **2** Disgrace; dishonor. **3** Something that brings disgrace or reproach. — *v.;* **shamed**; **sham·ing.** **1** To make ashamed; to humiliate. **2** To dishonor; to disgrace. **3** To bring or drive by shame; as, to *shame* a person into confessing.

shame·faced \ˈshām-ˈfāst\ *adj.* **1** Modest; shy. **2** Ashamed. — **shame·fac·ed·ly** \-ˈfā-səd-lē, -ˈfāst-lē\ *adv.*

shame·ful \ˈshām-fəl\ *adj.* **1** Bringing shame or disgrace; disgraceful; as, *shameful* behavior. **2** Arousing a feeling of shame; indecent; as, a *shameful* sight. — **shame·ful·ly** \-fə-lē\ *adv.*

shame·less \ˈshām-ləs\ *adj.* Without shame; brazen; impudent. — **shame·less·ly**, *adv.*

sham·poo \(ˈ)sham-ˈpü\ *v.;* **sham·pooed**; **sham·poo·ing.** **1** To cleanse and rub the hair and scalp with soap and water or with a special preparation; to give such a treatment to a person. **2** To give a similar cleansing to an object, as a rug or upholstery. — *n.; pl.* **sham·poos.** **1** A shampooing. **2** A preparation to be used in shampooing.

sham·rock \'sham-ˌräk\ *n.* [From Irish *seamrog,* the diminutive of *seamar,* meaning "clover", "trefoil", "honeysuckle".] Any of various three-leaved plants used as a national emblem by the Irish, as wood sorrel or certain varieties of clover.

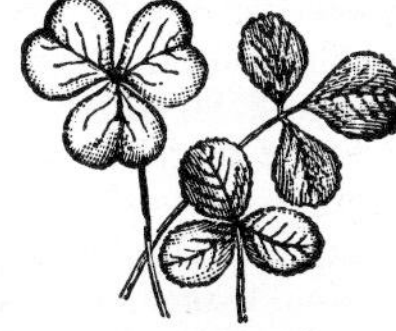
shamrocks

shang·hai \(')shang-'hī\ *v.;* **shang·haied; shang·hai·ing. 1** To make helpless, as by drugs or alcohol, and put on a ship, as a sailor. **2** To bring by deceit and force.

shank \'shangk\ *n.* **1** The lower part of the leg; in man, the shin; in animals, the corresponding part. **2** A cut of beef from the upper foreleg. **3** The leg. **4** The part of a tool connecting the acting part to another part by which it is operated. **5** The part of a shoe sole beneath the instep.

shan't \'shant\. A contraction of *shall not.*

shan·ty \'shant-ē\ *n.; pl.* **shan·ties.** A small roughly built shelter or cabin; a hut; a shack.

shape \'shāp\ *n.* **1** Form; external appearance; as, the *shape* of a ball; made in a box *shape.* **2** Bodily outline, especially of the trunk; figure; as, to lose one's *shape.* **3** A vague appearance; as, dim *shapes* in a fog. **4** Definite arrangement and form; as, taking *shape.* **5** Condition; as, in good *shape.* **6** A thing having a particular form or figure. — *v.;* **shaped; shap·ing. 1** To form or create; to mold; to fashion; as, to *shape* a plan. **2** To give a shape to. **3** To take on an especially definite shape; to develop, as a plan. — **shaped** \'shāpt\ *adj.*

shape·less \'shāp-ləs\ *adj.* **1** Without shape. **2** Without regular shape. — **shape·less·ly,** *adv.*

shape·ly \'shāp-lē\ *adj.;* **shape·li·er; shape·li·est.** Well-formed; well-proportioned; trim.

shard \'shärd, 'shȧrd\ *n.* A fragment of pottery.

share \'sher, 'shar\ *n.* A plowshare.

share \'sher, 'shar\ *n.* **1** A portion belonging to one person; a fair portion; as, to have one's *share* of good luck. **2** The part given or belonging to one of a number of persons owning something together. **3** Any of the equal portions or interests into which the property of a corporation is divided. — *v.;* **shared; shar·ing. 1** To divide and distribute in portions; as, to *share* one's lunch. **2** To use, experience, or enjoy with others; as, to *share* a room. **3** To take a part. — For synonyms see *partake.*

share·crop·per \'sher-ˌkräp-r, 'shar-\ *n.* A farmer who works land for a landlord in return for a share of the value of the crop. — **share·crop** \-ˌkräp\ *v.*

share·hold·er \'sher-ˌhōld-r, 'shar-\ *n.* A person who owns shares, especially of stock, in a company.

shark \'shärk, 'shȧrk\ *n.* A very active tough-skinned fish of warm seas, destructive of other fish and sometimes, in its larger varieties having triangular saw-edged teeth, dangerous to man.

shark \'shärk, 'shȧrk\ *n.* **1** A greedy, crafty person who takes advantage of the needs of others; as, a loan *shark.* **2** A person who excels, especially in a particular line; as, he can be a *shark* at arithmetic.

shark·skin \'shärk-ˌskin, 'shȧrk-\ *n.* **1** The skin of a shark or leather made from it. **2** A cloth with a hard sleek finish.

sharp \'shärp, 'shȧrp\ *adj.* **1** Having a very thin edge or fine point; not blunt or dull; keen. **2** Ending in a point or edge; not rounded; angular; as, a *sharp* peak. **3** Steep; abrupt; as, a *sharp* curve. **4** Well-defined; distinct; as, a *sharp* outline. **5** Affecting the senses as if pointed or cutting; as, a *sharp* taste. **6** Cold; as, *sharp* weather. **7** Very trying to the feelings; piercing; as, *sharp* pain. **8** Cutting; biting; showing rebuke or anger; as, a *sharp* reply. **9** Keen in spirit or action; as, a *sharp* student. **10** Having quick perception; as, a *sharp* eye. **11** Eager; keen; as, a *sharp* appetite. **12** Violent; as, a *sharp* clash. **13** Brisk; active; as, a *sharp* run. **14** Very attentive; as, to keep a *sharp* watch. **15** Quick-witted; clever; witty. **16** In music, above the true pitch; especially, higher by a half step.
— The words *keen* and *acute* are synonyms of *sharp:* used of objects, *sharp* may apply to either an edge or a point that cuts or pierces easily or quickly, or to a curve, bend, or outline that is distinct; *keen* usually applies to a sharp edge and rarely to a point; *acute* applies especially to an angle, tip, or end formed by lines meeting sharply. Referring to things which affect senses or to pleasures and pains, *sharp* suggests an unpleasantly cutting or biting quality; *keen* may indicate a bracing, zestful quality which is very pleasurable or may apply to an intensity, as of pain; *acute* may suggest the most intense, severe pain or the strongest pleasure. Applied to qualities of the mind and personality, these three terms differ little.
— *adv.* **1** In a sharp manner; as, to turn *sharp* left. **2** To a point or thin edge. **3** Precisely; exactly; as, at ten o'clock *sharp.* **4** Briskly; quickly; abruptly. **5** In music, higher than the true pitch. — *n.* **1** An expert. **2** A sharper. **3** In music, a sharp tone or note, or a sign [♯] that means that the pitch of a tone or note is to be made higher by a half step. — *v.* In music, to raise in pitch by a half step; to sing or play above the true pitch.

sharp·en \'shärp-n, 'shȧrp-n\ *v.;* **sharp·ened; sharp·en·ing** \-n(-)ing\. To make or become sharp or sharper. — **sharp·en·er** \-n(-)ər\ *n.*

sharp·er \'shärp-r, 'shȧrp-r\ *n.* A swindler; a cheat.

sharp·ie \'shärp-ē, 'shȧrp-ē\ *n.* A long flat-bottomed boat with one or two masts each carrying a triangular sail.

sharp·ly \'shärp-lē, 'shȧrp-\ *adv.* In a sharp way.

sharp·shoot·er \'shärp-ˌshüt-r, 'shȧrp-\ *n.* A person skilled in shooting; a good marksman. — **sharp·shoot·ing** \-ˌshüt-ing\ *n.*

sharp-wit·ted \'shärp-'wit-əd, 'shȧrp-\ *adj.* Having a quick, keen mind.

shat·ter \'shat-r\ *v.* **1** To dash, burst, or part violently into fragments; to break at once into pieces. **2** To damage; to wreck; to disorder; as, a *shattered* mind; a ship *shattered* by a storm.

shat·ter·proof \'shat-r-'prüf\ *adj.* Proof against shattering; as, *shatterproof* glass.

shave \'shāv\ *v.;* **shaved**; **shaved** \'shāvd\ or **shav·en** \'shāv-n\; **shav·ing. 1** To cut or pare off by means of a razor or other edged instrument; especially, to remove hair close to the skin with a razor. **2** To make bare or smooth by cutting the hair from; as, to *shave* the face. **3** To cut off closely; as, a lawn *shaven* close. **4** To cut off thin slices from, as from a board with a plane. **5** To pass close to; to skim along or near the surface of, with or without touching. — *n.* **1** A tool for cutting thin slices or shavings, as of wood. **2** An act of shaving, especially the beard. **3** A narrow escape; as, a close *shave.*

shav·er \'shāv-r\ *n.* **1** A person who shaves. **2** A tool or machine for shaving; especially, an electric razor. **3** A lad; a youngster.

shave·tail \'shāv-ˌtāl\ *n.* **1** An untrained mule. **2** *Slang.* A newly appointed second lieutenant.

shav·ing \'shā-ving\ *n.* A thin slice or strip pared off with a cutting tool; as, wood or ice *shavings.*

shawl \'shȯl\ *n.* A square or oblong piece of woven or knitted fabric used especially by women as a loose covering for the head or shoulders.

shay \'shā\ *n.* A chaise.

she \(')shē\ *pron.* **1** The female person or animal, or the thing thought of as feminine, mentioned before. **2** Any woman or girl.

sheaf \'shēf\ *n.; pl.* **sheaves** \'shēvz\ or, sometimes, **sheafs** \'shēfs\. **1** A bundle of stalks and ears of grain. **2** Any collection of things either bound together or loose; as, a *sheaf* of arrows; a *sheaf* of papers. — *v.* To gather and bind into a sheaf.

sheaf of wheat

shear \'shir\ *v.;* **sheared**; **sheared** \'shird\ or **shorn** \'shōrn, 'shȯrn\; **shear·ing. 1** To cut the hair from; to shave. **2** To cut or clip, especially wool from sheep. **3** To deprive of by or as if by cutting off; as, *shorn* of his power. **4** To cut with shears or scissors; as, to *shear* a metal sheet in two. — **shear·er** \'shir-r\ *n.*

shears \'shirz\ *n. pl.* Large strong scissors.

sheath \'shēth\ *n.; pl.* **sheaths** \'shēt͟hz, 'shēths\. **1** A case, as for the blade of a sword or hunting knife. **2** Any covering like a sheath in form or use, as the outer wings of a beetle. — *v.* To sheathe.

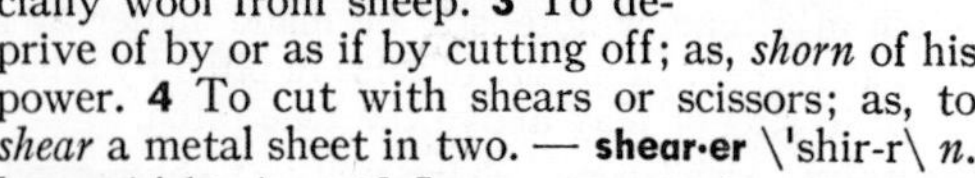

sheath, 1

sheathe \'shēt͟h\ *v.;* **sheathed**; **sheath·ing. 1** To put into a sheath; as, to *sheathe* one's sword. **2** To cover with something which guards or protects; as, to *sheathe* a ship's bottom with copper. — **sheath·er** \'shēt͟h-r, 'shēth-r\ *n.*

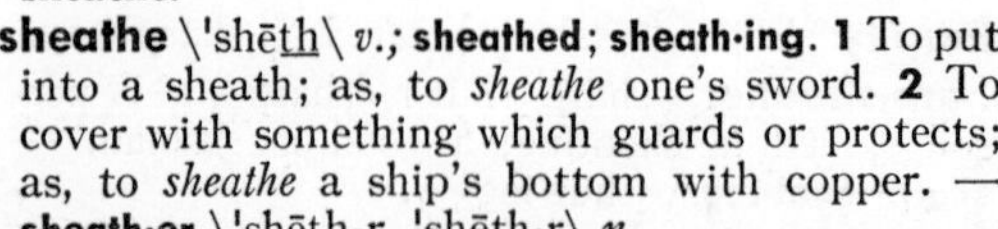

sheath knife. A knife carried in a sheath.

sheave \'shēv\ *v.;* **sheaved**; **sheav·ing.** To gather and tie up stalks of grain, as wheat, into a sheaf.

sheaves. A pl. of *sheaf.*

shed \'shed\ *n.* A structure built for shelter or storage; as, the old stable is now a tool *shed.*

shed \'shed\ *v.;* **shed**; **shed·ding. 1** To pour forth or down in drops; to pour out or forth; as, to *shed* tears. **2** To cause to flow from a cut or wound; as, to *shed* blood. **3** To spread abroad. The sun *sheds* light and heat. **4** To throw off. Raincoats *shed* water. **5** To cast aside, as some natural covering. A snake *sheds* its skin. — **shed·der** \'shed-r\ *n.*

she'd \(')shēd\. A contraction of *she had* or *she would.*

sheen \'shēn\ *n.* Brightness; glitter; gloss; as, the *sheen* of satin.

sheep \'shēp\ *n. sing. and pl.* **1** An animal related to the goat, bred and raised for its flesh, its fleece, and its skin. **2** Any timid, defenseless person. **3** Sheepskin; as, a book bound in *sheep.*

sheep·cote \'shēp-ˌkōt, -ˌkät\ *n.* A sheepfold.

sheep dog. A dog used to tend sheep.

sheep·fold \'shēp-ˌfōld\ *n.* A fold or pen for sheep.

sheep·herd·er \'shēp-ˌhərd-r\ *n.* One who herds sheep. — **sheep·herd·ing** \-ing\ *n.* or *adj.*

sheep·ish \'shēp-ish\ *adj.* **1** Like a sheep, as in meekness or stupidity. **2** Embarrassed, especially when found out in a fault. — **sheep·ish·ly**, *adv.*

sheep·skin \'shēp-ˌskin\ *n.* **1** The skin of a sheep; a leather prepared from such a skin; a parchment. **2** A diploma, as one given at graduation.

sheer \'shir\ *adj.* **1** Pure and unqualified; utter; as, *sheer* nonsense. **2** Taken or acting apart from everything else; as, by *sheer* force. **3** Very steep; almost straight up and down; as, a *sheer* cliff. **4** Very thin or transparent; as, a *sheer* curtain or veil. — *adv.* **1** Completely; absolutely. **2** Straight up or down; perpendicularly. — **sheer·ly**, *adv.*

sheer \'shir\ *v.* To turn aside from a course; to swerve; as, to *sheer* off. — *n.* A change in a course.

sheet \'shēt\ *n.* **1** A broad piece of cloth, especially one used on a bed next to the body. **2** A broad piece of paper, as for writing or printing. **3** A printed paper, as a newspaper or magazine; [in the plural] the unbound pages of a book. **4** Any broad surface; as, a *sheet* of water. **5** Anything that is very thin as compared with its length and width; as, a *sheet* of iron. **6** A complete printing of stamps on a single piece of paper as it leaves the press and before it is cut into panes. — *v.* To wrap in a sheet; to cover with or furnish with a sheet or sheets.

sheet \'shēt\ *n.* **1** [often in the plural] A rope or chain that is used to adjust the angle at which the sail of a boat is set to catch the wind. **2** [in the plural] The spaces at the bow (**fore·sheets** \'fōr-ˌshēts, 'fȯr-\) or at the stern (**stern sheets**) of an open boat that are not occupied by the thwarts. — *v.* To haul by means of a sheet — used only in *to sheet home,* to haul a square sail so that it is set flat to the wind.

sheets

sheet·ing \'shēt-ing\ *n.* **1** The action or process of forming into or covering with sheets. **2** Material made into sheets or suitable for sheets.

sheet lightning. Diffused lightning occurring in a form resembling a sheet.

sheet metal. Metal in the form of a sheet.

sheet music. A musical score for piano, or the words and music of a song, published separately on unbound sheets.

sheik or **sheikh**, *n.* [From Arabic *shaykh*, meaning literally "old man".] **1** \'shēk, 'shāk\ An Arab chief — used also as an Arabic title of respect. **2** \'shēk\ *Slang.* A man who is supposedly irresistibly attractive to women.

shek·el \'shek-l\ *n.* [From Hebrew *sheqel*, a derivative of *shagal*, meaning "to weigh".] **1** An ancient unit of weight or money. **2** A coin having this weight.

shel·drake \'shel-ˌdrāk\ *n.; pl.* **shel·drakes** or **shel·drake. 1** An Old World, chiefly black and white duck that resembles a goose and that nests in burrows. **2** Any merganser.

shelf \'shelf\ *n.; pl.* **shelves** \'shelvz\. **1** A usually long and narrow piece of board or metal, fastened to a wall to hold things. **2** The books or other contents of a shelf. **3** A ledge, as of rock; a reef or shoal. — **on the shelf.** Put aside as of no present use.

shell \'shel\ *n.* **1** A hard, rigid, or tough outer covering of certain animals, as a turtle, an oyster, or a beetle; the outer covering of an egg, especially a bird's egg; the outer covering of certain nuts, fruits, and seeds; a nutshell, pod, or husk. **2** Shell material or shells collectively, especially of mollusks, turtles, or tortoises; tortoise shell. **3** Something resembling a shell, as in shape, position, or material; as, the *shell* of a boat; a pastry *shell.* **4** A metal or paper case that holds the explosive charge and the shot or projectile to be fired from a rifle, shotgun, or cannon. **5** A light long racing boat wide enough to accommodate one oarsman on each seat. — *v.* **1** To take out of the shell or husk; as, to *shell* peas. **2** To separate the kernels of corn or oats from the cob or husk. **3** To shoot shells at; to bombard. **4** To cast the shell; to fall out of the pod or husk. Nuts *shell* in falling.

she'll \(')shēl\. A contraction of *she will* or *she shall.*

shel·lac \shə-'lak\ *n.* **1** Purified lac, as used in varnishes. **2** A preparation of lac dissolved in alcohol, used in filling wood or as a varnish. — *v.;* **shel·lacked**; **shel·lack·ing. 1** To coat or treat with shellac. **2** *Slang.* To beat; to defeat.

shell·bark \'shel-ˌbärk, -ˌbȧrk\ *n.* The shagbark.

shelled \'sheld\ *adj.* **1** Having a shell; covered with shell. Oysters and snails are *shelled* animals. **2** Taken from the shell; as, *shelled* walnuts.

shell·fire \'shel-'fīr\ *n.* The firing of shells.

shell·fish \'shel-ˌfish\ *n.; pl.* **shell·fish** or **shell·fish·es.** Any water animal with an outer shell, especially one used for food, as the oyster, scallop, crab, or shrimp.

shell·proof \'shel-'prüf\ *adj.* Proof against shells or bombs.

shell shock. A nervous condition, like hysteria, as of soldiers under the strain of war. — **shell·shock** \'shel-ˌshäk\ *v.* — **shell·shocked** \-ˌshäkt\ *adj.*

shel·ter \'shelt-r\ *n.* **1** Anything that covers or protects. **2** The state of being protected; refuge; as, to take *shelter* from a storm. — *v.;* **shel·tered**; **shel·ter·ing** \'shelt-r-ing, 'shel-tring\. **1** To be a shelter for; to protect; to shield. **2** To take shelter. — **shel·ter·er** \'shelt-r-r\ *n.*

shelve \'shelv\ *v.;* **shelved**; **shelv·ing. 1** To incline; to slope, especially gradually. The stream bed *shelves* up toward both banks. **2** To furnish with shelves. **3** To place or store on shelves. **4** To dismiss from service or use; to put off or aside.

shelves. Pl. of *shelf.*

shep·herd \'shep-rd\ *n.* **1** A herder of sheep. **2** A pastor. — *v.* To guard as a shepherd guards his sheep; to herd, lead, or drive as one does sheep.

shepherd dog. A sheep dog; a collie.

shep·herd·ess \'shep-r-dəs\ *n.* A woman who takes care of sheep.

sher·bet \'shər-bət\ *n.* **1** A drink made of sweetened fruit juice. **2** A frozen dessert of fruit juice and milk, white of egg, or gelatin.

sher·iff \'sher-əf\ *n.* The chief law-enforcing officer of a county.

sher·ry \'sher-ē\ *n.; pl.* **sher·ries.** A still wine, light tan to brown in color.

she's \(')shēz\. A contraction of *she is* or *she has.*

shew \'shō\ *v.;* **shewed** \'shōd\; **shewn** \'shōn\; **shew·ing.** To show.

shib·bo·leth \'shib-l-əth, -ˌeth\ *n.* A watchword, as of a party, class, or religious sect; a pet phrase.

shied. Past tense and past part. of *shy.*

shield \'shēld\ *n.* **1** A broad piece of defensive armor consisting of a plate of metal, wood, or leather, carried on the arm or in the hand to protect oneself in battle. **2** Anyone or anything serving as a defense or shelter. **3** Something shaped like a shield, as an ornamental carving. — *v.* To cover with or as if with a shield; to protect.

shier. A comparative of *shy.*

shiest. A superlative of *shy.*

shift \'shift\ *v.* **1** To exchange one thing for another or others, usually of the same kind. **2** To change or remove from one person or place to another. **3** To get along; to manage; as, to *shift* for oneself. **4** To change gears, as in operating an automobile. — *n.* **1** The act of shifting; a transfer. **2** A change in direction; as, a *shift* in the wind. **3** An effort, especially one that is successful in spite of difficulties; as, to make *shift.* **4** A scheme or trick used to accomplish a purpose. **5** A group who work together, alternating with other groups, or the period which one such group works.

shift·less \'shift-ləs\ *adj.* Lacking in means to an end because lazy or inefficient. — **shift·less·ly**, *adv.*

shifty \'shif-tē\ *adj.;* **shift·i·er**; **shift·i·est. 1** Tricky; not to be relied upon. **2** Indicating a tricky nature; tending to shift; as, *shifty* eyes.

shil·le·lagh or **shil·la·lah** \shə-'lā-lē\ *n. Irish.* A club; a cudgel.

shil·ling \'shil-ing\ *n.* A British silver coin worth 12 pence.

shil·ly–shal·ly \'shil-ē-ˌshal-ē\ *v.;* **shil·ly–shal·lied** \-ēd\; **shil·ly–shal·ly·ing.** To be undecided; to hesitate. — *n.* Hesitation; wavering.

shily. Variant of *shyly.*

shim·mer \'shim-r\ *v.;* **shim·mered; shim·mer·ing** \-r(-)ing\. To shine with a wavering light; to glimmer. — *n.* A shimmering. — **shim·mery** \-r-ē\ *adj.*

shim·my \'shim-ē\ *n.; pl.* **shim·mies. 1** A jazz dance characterized by rapid shaking movements of the body. **2** Abnormal vibration, as in the front wheels of a car. — *v.;* **shim·mied** \-ēd\; **shim·my·ing. 1** To dance the shimmy. **2** To undergo shimmy.

shin \'shin\ *n.* The front part of the leg below the knee. — *v.;* **shinned; shin·ning.** To climb, as a pole or tree, by grasping with arms and legs and hitching oneself gradually upward.

shin·bone \'shin-'bōn, -ˌbōn\ *n.* The tibia.

shin·dig \'shin-ˌdig\ *n.* A festivity, dance, or party.

shine \'shīn\ *v.;* **shone** \'shōn, 'shän\ or **shined** \'shīnd\; **shin·ing. 1** To give light. **2** To be glossy; to gleam. **3** To make glossy; to clean and polish. **4** To be splendid or brilliant; to show brilliant mental power; as, to *shine* in conversation. — *n.* **1** Radiance; brightness. **2** Luster; sheen. **3** Sunshine; fair weather; as, rain or *shine.* **4** A liking; a fancy; as, to take a *shine* to a new acquaintance. **5** A polish, as one given to shoes.

shin·er \'shīn-r\ *n.* **1** One that shines; especially, a small silvery fresh-water American fish related to the carp. **2** *Slang.* A black eye.

shin·gle \'shing-gl\ *n. Chiefly British.* **1** Very coarse pebbly gravel on the seashore. **2** A place, as a beach, strewn with such gravel.

shin·gle \'shing-gl\ *n.* **1** A piece of board or of other material, as asbestos, cut with one end thinner than the other, used for covering roofs or walls in overlapping rows. **2** A sign, as on a doctor's or lawyer's office. **3** A short haircut. — *v.;* **shin·gled; shin·gling** \-gl(-)ing\. **1** To cover with shingles. **2** To give a shingle to; as, *shingled* hair.

shingles, 1

shin·gles \'shing-glz\ *n.* A virus disease marked by inflammation of a ganglion and by pain and skin eruption along the course of a nerve arising from the ganglion.

shin·ing \'shī-ning\ *adj.* **1** Giving forth or reflecting light, especially steadily; radiant. **2** Splendid; brilliant; as, a *shining* example of heroism. — For synonyms see *bright.* — **shin·ing·ly,** *adv.*

shin·ny or **shin·ney** \'shin-ē\ *n.* A simple form of hockey played by schoolboys with a curved stick and a ball or a block of wood.

shin·ny \'shin-ē\ *v.;* **shin·nied** \-ēd\; **shin·ny·ing.** To shin; as, to *shinny* up a tree.

shiny \'shī-nē\ *adj.;* **shin·i·er; shin·i·est. 1** Bright; radiant. **2** Polished; glossy.

ship \'ship\ *n.* **1** A large seagoing boat. **2** The officers and crew of a ship; a ship's company. **3** An airship or airplane. **4** A vehicle for traveling beyond the earth's atmosphere; as, a rocket *ship.* — *v.;* **shipped; ship·ping. 1** To put or receive on board a vessel for transportation. **2** To transport, whether by ship or by train, truck, or other conveyance. **3** To take into a ship or boat; as, to *ship* oars. **4** To place in position for use on a ship or boat; as, to *ship* the rudder. **5** To take a job, or hire a person for a job, on a ship.

-ship \ˌship\. A suffix that can mean: **1** State or quality of, as in *friendship.* **2** Office, dignity, or rank of, as in *lordship* or *professorship.* **3** Art or skill of, as in *marksmanship.* **4** Something made of or formed by, as in *membership* or *township.*

ship biscuit. Hardtack.

ship·board \'ship-ˌbōrd, -ˌbȯrd\ *n.* **1** A ship's side. **2** A ship; as, on *shipboard.*

ship·build·er \'ship-ˌbild-r\ *n.* One who designs or builds ships. — **ship·build·ing** \-ˌbil-ding\ *n.*

ship·load \'ship-'lōd, -ˌlōd\ *n.* The load or cargo of a ship.

ship·mas·ter \'ship-ˌmast-r\ *n.* The master, or captain, of a merchant ship.

ship·mate \'ship-ˌmāt\ *n.* A fellow sailor.

ship·ment \'ship-mənt\ *n.* **1** The act or process of shipping or sending goods by any method of transportation. **2** The goods shipped.

ship·own·er \'ship-ˌōn-r\ *n.* The owner of a ship.

ship·per \'ship-r\ *n.* A person who ships or sends goods by any form of transportation.

ship·ping \'ship-ing\ *n.* **1** The act or business of one who ships goods. **2** Ships gathered in one place; as, the *shipping* in the harbor. **3** The ships belonging to one nation; as, United States *shipping.*

ship·shape \'ship-'shāp\ *adj.* Arranged in a way suitable for a ship; trim; tidy; neat. — *adv.* In a shipshape or seamanlike manner.

ship·worm \'ship-ˌwərm\ *n.* A long-bodied salt-water clam that burrows in submerged wood.

ship·wreck \'ship-ˌrek\ *n.* **1** A wrecked ship or its parts; wreckage. **2** The loss or destruction of a ship, as by sinking or being driven on shore or on rocks. **3** Ruin; total loss or failure. — *v.* **1** To destroy, as a ship at sea; to wreck. **2** To cause to undergo shipwreck; as, sailors *shipwrecked* in war.

ship·wright \'ship-ˌrīt\ *n.* A man who works on the building or repair of ships.

ship·yard \'ship-ˌyärd, -ˌyȧrd\ *n.* A place where ships are built or repaired.

shire \'shīr\ *n.* A territorial division of England, usually identical with a county.

shirk \'shərk\ *v.* To get out of doing what one ought to do; to avoid one's duty. — **shirk·er** \-r\ *n.*

shirr \'shər\ *n.* A series of close, parallel, stitched lines, sewed in such a way as to make a gather between the lines. — *v.* **1** To make a shirr or shirrs in. **2** To break eggs into a dish with cream or crumbs and bake in the oven or cook in hot water.

shirt \'shərt\ *n.* **1** A loose upper garment with a collar, short or long sleeves, and usually a front opening, worn with trousers or a skirt and with or without a jacket. **2** A close-fitting, collarless, knitted upper garment pulled on over the head and made with short or long sleeves for wear as an outer garment, undergarment, or undershirt.

shirt·ing \'shərt-ing\ *n.* Cloth for shirts.

shirt·waist \'shərt-ˌwāst\ *n.* A woman's or child's blouse, usually tucked in at the waist.

shiv·er \'shiv-r\ *n.* One of the small pieces of splinters into which a brittle material, as glass, may break. — *v.;* **shiv·ered; shiv·er·ing** \-r(-)ing\. To break into many small pieces; to splinter.

shiv·er \'shiv-r\ *v.;* **shiv·ered; shiv·er·ing** \-r(-)ing\. To tremble; to quiver; to quake, as from cold or fear. — *n.* A trembling; a quiver.

shiv·ery \'shiv-r(-)ē\ *adj.* Inclined to, characterized by, or causing shivering or trembling.

shoal \'shōl\ *n.* A large number, especially of fish, gathered together; a school of fish. — *v.* To throng; to swim in shoals.

shoal \'shōl\ *adj.* Having little depth; shallow; as, *shoal* water. — *n.* **1** A place where a sea, lake, or river is shallow. **2** A sand bank or bar just below the surface of the water. — *v.* To become shallow gradually. The water begins to *shoal* at this spot.

shoat or **shote** \'shōt\ *n.* A young pig.

shock \'shäk\ *n.* A bunch of sheaves of grain or of cut stalks of corn set upright in the field. — *v.* To make up into a shock or shocks.

shock \'shäk\ *n.* **1** The sudden, violent collision of bodies in a fight; as, the *shock* of battle. **2** Any collision, or violent shake or jar; as, an earthquake *shock.* **3** Any sudden and violent agitation of mind or feelings. **4** The effect of a charge of electricity passing through the body of a man or animal. **5** A condition of great weakness, restlessness, and rapid breathing, such as often results from wounds, blows, or loss of blood. — *v.* **1** To surprise, terrify, or disgust. The man's violence *shocked* his friends. **2** To cause to undergo a physical or nervous shock. **3** To drive into or out of, as if by a shock; as, to be *shocked* into action.

shock \'shäk\ *n.* A thick bushy mass, as of hair.

shock ab·sorb·er \əb-'sörb-r, -'zörb-r\. Something that lessens the effect of sudden impulses or shocks, especially to the wheels of a vehicle.

shock·ing \'shäk-ing\ *adj.* Causing horror or disgust; as, a *shocking* offense. — **shock·ing·ly**, *adv.*

shod. Past tense and past part. of *shoe.*

shod·dy \'shäd-ē\ *n.; pl.* **shod·dies.** Cloth made from reclaimed wool. — *adj.;* **shod·di·er; shod·di·est. 1** Made of shoddy; as, a *shoddy* coat. **2** Pretending to have qualities not actually possessed; sham. **3** Low; mean; shabby; as, a *shoddy* trick.

shoe \'shü\ *n.* **1** A covering for the human foot, having a thick and somewhat stiff sole and heel, and a lighter upper. **2** Something that resembles a shoe, as in appearance or use, as a horseshoe, the runner of a sled, or the part of a brake (**brake shoe**) that presses on the wheel of a vehicle. **3** The outside casing of an automobile tire. — *v.;* **shod** \'shäd\; **shoe·ing. 1** To put a shoe on; to furnish with shoes. **2** To cover, as for protection against wear; as, to *shoe* a sleigh runner with steel.

shoe·black \'shü-ˌblak\ *n.* A bootblack.

shoe·horn \'shü-ˌhörn\ *n.* A curved blade used to make the heel of a shoe slip on easily.

shoe·lace \'shü-ˌlās\ *n.* A shoestring.

shoe·mak·er \'shü-ˌmāk-r\ *n.* A person who makes or repairs shoes.

shoe·string \'shü-ˌstring\ *n.* **1** A string for holding together the opposite edges of a shoe. **2** A very small sum of money; as, to live on a *shoestring.*

shoe tree. A form for keeping shoes in shape.

sho·gun \'shō-ˌgən, 'shōg-n\ *n.* A title of the military governors formerly very powerful in Japan.

shone. Past tense and past part. of *shine.*

shoo \'shü\ *interj.* An exclamation used to frighten away animals or chickens. — *v.;* **shooed; shoo·ing.** To drive away, as by crying "shoo".

shook. Past tense of *shake.*

shoot \'shüt\ *v.;* **shot** \'shät\; **shoot·ing** \'shüt-ing\. **1** To move, rush, or let fly forcibly; as, to *shoot* past on skis; to *shoot* an arrow. **2** To strike with something propelled from a gun or a bow; especially, to hit or kill with a missile from a gun; as, to *shoot* a deer. **3** To cause a missile to be driven forth from; to discharge a gun or other weapon; as, to *shoot* a gun; to *shoot* at a target. **4** Of a gun or bow, to send a missile. **5** To propel with a snap of the thumb or finger; as, to *shoot* marbles. **6** To push into or out of a catch; as, to *shoot* a bolt in a door. **7** To push forward; to stick out. The toad *shot* out its tongue. **8** To pass rapidly along; as, to *shoot* the rapids in a canoe; to feel a pain *shoot* down one's arm. **9** To take the altitude of; as, to *shoot* a star. **10** To stream or spurt out. Liquid *shot* from the fire extinguisher. **11** To throw or cast; as, to *shoot* dice. **12** In making motion pictures, to photograph; as, to *shoot* a scene. **13** In games, to throw or hit, as a ball or puck, toward the goal. **14** To spring or grow up rapidly. — *n.* **1** A hunting party. **2** A new growth of a root or branch.

shoot·er \'shüt-r\ *n.* One that shoots — used often in combinations, as *sharpshooter, six-shooter.*

shoot·ing star \'shüt-ing\. A meteor.

shop \'shäp\ *n.* **1** A store. **2** A place of business employing workmen, especially one that specializes in making or repairing things; a factory. **3** A room in a school for giving specialized instruction in manual skills. **4** The instruction given in such a place; as, to do well in *shop.* **5** The details of a person's occupation as a subject for conversation; as, to talk *shop.* — *v.;* **shopped; shop·ping.** To visit shops in order to look over or purchase goods.

shop·keep·er \'shäp-ˌkēp-r\ *n.* A storekeeper.

shop·lift·er \'shäp-ˌlift-r\ *n.* One who steals goods for sale in a store. — **shop·lift·ing** \-ˌlif-ting\ *n.*

shop·man \'shäp-mən\ *n.; pl.* **shop·men** \-mən\. One who works in a shop.

shop·per \'shäp-r\ *n.* **1** One who shops. **2** One who buys goods, especially at retail, for others.

shop·worn \'shäp-ˌwōrn, -ˌwȯrn\ *adj.* Somewhat worn or marred by having been kept in a shop.

shore \'shōr, 'shȯr\ *n.* A prop or support placed beneath or against anything to support it. — *v.;* **shored**; **shor·ing.** To support with one or more bracing timbers.

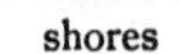
shores

shore \'shōr, 'shȯr\ *n.* The land along the edge of a body of water; especially, seacoast.
— The words *beach* and *bank* are synonyms of *shore: shore* is a general term for the land lying along the edge of a lake, a river, or especially a sea, and often suggests seacoast resorts for pleasure and vacationing; *beach* usually indicates a stretch of seashore or lake shore covered by sand or pebbles washed up by the water and often calls to mind a place for swimming and sunbathing; *bank* generally refers to the steeply rising edge of a stream or river.

shore·line \'shōr-ˌlīn, 'shȯr-\ *n.* The line where a body of water touches the shore.

shore patrol. Police of the United States Navy.

shorn. A past part. of *shear.*

short \'shȯrt\ *adj.* **1** Not long or tall; as, a *short* dress; a *short* man. **2** Not great in distance; as, a *short* journey. **3** Brief in time; as, a *short* delay. **4** Not retentive; as, a *short* memory. **5** Payable at an early date; as, a *short* credit. **6** Cut down to a brief length; sometimes, rudely brief; curt; as, a *short* answer. **7** Not coming up to the regular standard; as, to give *short* measure. **8** Less in amount than expected or called for. The cash in his pocket was *short* three dollars. **9** Not reaching the goal or mark. The arrow landed 50 yards *short.* **10** Less than; not equal to; as, to be little *short* of perfect; all measures *short* of war. **11** Insufficiently furnished; not having enough; as, to be *short* of money. **12** Flaky or crumbly because rich in fat; as, a *short* piecrust. **13** Of *a, e, i, o, oo, u,* pronounced as in *add, end, ill, odd, foot,* and *up,* respectively. — *n.* **1** Something that is shorter than the usual or regular length. **2** [in the plural] Light-weight pants with legs reaching part way to the knee, some suited for underwear, some for wear as informal outer garments. **3** A short circuit. **4** [in the plural] A wheat milling by-product that contains the wheat germ, fine bran, and some flour. — **in short.** In brief; in few words. — *adv.* **1** Abruptly; as, to stop *short.* **2** So as to reach less than the expected distance; as, to fall *short.*

short·age \'shȯrt-ij\ *n.* A lack in the amount needed; a deficit; as, a *shortage* in the accounts.

short·cake \'shȯrt-ˌkāk\ *n.* A dessert made usually of very short baking powder biscuit dough, baked and served with sweetened fruit.

short circuit. An electric circuit through a small resistance, especially one formed when the insulation is worn off the wires and a greater flow of current passes through than would normally do so. — **short–cir·cuit,** *v.*

short·com·ing \'shȯrt-'kəm-ing\ *n.* A fault.

short cut. **1** A route more direct than that usually taken. **2** A quicker way of doing something.

short·en \'shȯrt-n\ *v.;* **short·ened**; **short·en·ing** \-n(-)ing\. To make or become short or shorter.

short·en·ing \'shȯrt-n(-)ing\ *n.* **1** A making or becoming short or shorter. **2** Any fat used in baking.

short·hand \'shȯrt-ˌhand\ *n.* A method of rapid writing by using characters or symbols for sounds or words; stenography.

short·hand·ed \'shȯrt-'han-dəd\ *adj.* Short of the regular number of workers or helpers.

short·horn \'shȯrt-ˌhȯrn\ *n.* A short-horned animal; especially, a steer or cow of a short-horned breed of cattle.

short–lived \'shȯrt-'līvd, -'livd\ *adj.* Not living or lasting long.

short·ly \'shȯrt-lē\ *adv.* **1** In a short time; soon. **2** In a few words; briefly. **3** Abruptly; curtly.

short–sight·ed \'shȯrt-'sīt-əd\ *adj.* **1** Not able to see far; nearsighted; myopic. **2** Lacking foresight.

short·stop \'shȯrt-ˌstäp\ *n.* In baseball, a player stationed between second base and third base.

short–tem·pered \'shȯrt-'temp-rd\ *adj.* Having a quick temper; easily angered.

short wave. A radio wave of sixty-meter length or less, used especially in long-distance broadcasting. — **short–wave,** *adj.*

shot \'shät\ *n.; pl.* **shots** or, in senses 3, 13, 14, **shot.** **1** The action of shooting. **2** A discharge of a gun or cannon. **3** A missile made to be discharged from a gun or cannon. **4** Something thrown or let fly with force. **5** A remark made so as to have a telling effect. **6** An attempt; a try; as, to take another *shot* at that job. **7** An injection of medicine into the body; as, penicillin *shots.* **8** A single drink of liquor; as, a *shot* of whiskey. **9** The flight of a missile or the distance it travels; range; as, to be within rifle *shot.* **10** A reckoning to be paid; a bill; as, to pay the *shot.* **11** A person who shoots. That man is a good *shot.* **12** In games, a stroke or throw, often at a goal. **13** A ball-shaped weight used in a throwing contest. **14** A small round ball of lead fired along with others like it from a gun. **15** The film of a motion-picture scene or the scene itself. — **not by a long shot.** Absolutely not; not at all.

shot \'shät\. Past tense and past part. of *shoot.* — *adj.* **1** Woven, as silk, or dyed, as a silk or cotton fabric so as to be changeable in color. **2** *Slang.* Drunk. **3** *Slang.* Worn out; used up. — **shot through.** Filled; liberally intermixed.

shote. Variant of *shoat.*

shot·gun \'shät-ˌgən\ *n.* A gun with a smooth bore, used to fire small shot at short range.

shotgun

shot–put \'shät-ˌpu̇t\ *n.* A field event consisting in putting the shot for distance.

should \shəd, (')shu̇d\. Past tense of *shall.* **1** Was or were going to or expecting to. I wrote that I *should* leave the next day. **2** Ought to. You *should* have let me know. **3** Happen or happens to; as, if it *should* snow. **4** Would; would then. I *should* be a fool, were I to do that. **5** Were to. If you *should* yield now, you would lose all. **6** Might; as, until he *should* prove his innocence.

shoul·der \'shōld-r\ *n.* **1** The part of the body of a person or animal where the arm or foreleg joins the body. **2** The part of a coat or dress at the wearer's shoulder. **3** A part that resembles a person's shoulder; as, the *shoulder* of a bottle. **4** The edge of a road. **5** A cut of meat that includes the upper joint of the foreleg with part of the neck and chest. — *v.;* **shoul·dered; shoul·der·ing** \-r(-)ing\. **1** To push or thrust with or as if with a shoulder. **2** To take upon one's shoulders; to bear.

shoulder blade. The flat triangular bone of the shoulder jointed to the bone of the upper arm.

shoulder strap. 1 A strap worn over the shoulder to hold up a garment. **2** A strip worn on the shoulder of a military uniform to show rank.

shouldn't \'shu̇d-nt\. A contraction of *should not.*

shouldst \shədst, (')shu̇dst\. An archaic form of *should,* used chiefly with *thou.*

shout \'shau̇t\ *v.* To utter a sudden, loud cry, as of joy, pain, or sorrow. — *n.* A sudden, loud cry; a loud burst of voices. — **shout·er** \-r\ *n.*

shove \'shəv\ *v.;* **shoved; shov·ing. 1** To push with steady force. **2** To push carelessly or rudely; as, to *shove* a person out of the way. — **shove off. 1** To move away from shore by pushing. **2** To depart; to set out. — *n.* A shoving; a forcible push.

shov·el \'shəv-l\ *n.* **1** An implement consisting of a plate or scoop attached to a long handle, used for lifting and throwing loose material, as snow, earth, grain, or coal. **2** As much as a shovel will hold; a shovelful; as, to toss up a *shovel* of earth. — *v.;* **shov·eled** or **shov·elled; shov·el·ing** or **shov·el·ling** \-l(-)ing\. **1** To lift or throw with a shovel. **2** To dig or clean out with a shovel; as, to *shovel* a ditch. **3** To throw or carry roughly, as if with a shovel; as, to *shovel* food into one's mouth.

shovel, 1

shov·el·er or **shov·el·ler** \'shəv-l(-)ər\ *n.* **1** A person who shovels. **2** A common river duck having a very large and broad bill.

shov·el·ful \'shəv-l-ˌfu̇l\ *n.; pl.* **shov·el·fuls.** The amount held by a shovel.

show \'shō\ *v.;* **showed** \'shōd\; **shown** \'shōn\ or **showed; show·ing. 1** To place in sight; to exhibit; to display. **2** To reveal; as, to *show* oneself a coward. **3** To grant; to bestow. The king *showed* no mercy. **4** To teach; to instruct; as, to *show* one how to knit. **5** To prove; as, to *show* that one is right. **6** To direct; to usher; to guide; as, to *show* a visitor to the door; to *show* one's friends around the town. **7** To appear. Anger *showed* in his face. **8** To be noticeable; as, a patch that hardly *shows.* **9** To be third, or at least third, in a horse race. — **show off.** To make a display of one's abilities or possessions. — **show up. 1** To expose, especially to ridicule. **2** To appear, especially to advantage; to stand out. **3** To arrive or be present, especially at an appointed time or place. — *n.* **1** The act of showing or the thing shown; exhibition; display; as, a hobby *show.* **2** A pretense; as, a *show* of friendship. **3** Proud display; parade; as, a great *show* of wealth. **4** A theatrical performance. **5** In horse racing, third place in a race. — **for show.** For the sake of the impression made.

show·boat \'shō-ˌbōt\ *n.* A steamboat, as a Mississippi river boat, used as a traveling theater.

show·case \'shō-ˌkās\ *n.* A glass case or box for display of articles, as in a store or museum.

show·down \'shō-ˌdau̇n\ *n.* A definite or final disclosure, as of facts or intentions, especially in answer to a challenge.

show·er \'shau̇r\ *n.* **1** A short fall of rain over a small area. **2** Something like or suggesting a brief fall of rain; as, a *shower* of tears; a *shower* of sparks. **3** A party where gifts are given, as to a bride. **4** A shower bath. — *v.* **1** To wet with fine spray or drops. **2** To fall in a shower. **3** To give freely; as, to *shower* a person with presents. **4** To take a shower bath. — **show·ery** \'shau̇r-ē\ *adj.*

shower bath. 1 A bath in which water is sprayed from overhead. **2** The apparatus for such a bath.

show·man \'shō-mən\ *n.; pl.* **show·men** \-mən\. **1** A person who exhibits or helps to exhibit a show. **2** One who is good at showing or presenting things to their best advantage.

show·man·ship \'shō-mən-ˌship\ *n.* The art or ability of a showman; a gift for display.

shown. A past part. of *show.*

show-off \'shō-ˌȯf\ *n.* **1** The act of showing off. **2** One who shows off.

show·place \'shō-ˌplās\ *n.* A place, as a district, an estate, or a building, exhibited or suitable for exhibition because of its beauty or elegance.

show·room \'shō-ˌrüm, -ˌru̇m\ *n.* A room used for the display of merchandise or of samples.

showy \'shō-ē\ *adj.;* **show·i·er; show·i·est.** Making an attractive show; striking; as, *showy* clothes.

shrank. Past tense of *shrink.*

shrap·nel \'shrap-nəl\ *n.* **1** A shell designed to burst and scatter fragments of the shell case and the metal balls it contains. **2** Shell fragments.

shred \'shred\ *n.* **1** A long, narrow piece torn or cut off; a strip; as, a *shred* of cloth. **2** A fragment or particle. — *v.;* **shred** or **shred·ded; shred·ding.** To cut or tear into shreds.

shrew \'shrü\ *n.* **1** A small mouselike mammal with long pointed snout, tiny eyes, and velvety fur, living on insects and worms. **2** A woman who scolds or quarrels constantly.

shrewd \'shrüd\ *adj.* Able in practical affairs; sharp-witted; keen; clever; as, a *shrewd* observer; a *shrewd* reply. — **shrewd·ly,** *adv.*

shrew·ish \'shrü-ish\ *adj.* Having the qualities of a shrew; scolding. — **shrew·ish·ly,** *adv.*

shriek \'shrēk\ *v.* **1** To utter a sharp, shrill cry; to scream. **2** To utter sharply or shrilly; as, to *shriek* an answer. — *n.* A sharp, shrill cry or a sound resembling this; as, the *shriek* of a locomotive.

shrift \'shrift\ *n. Archaic.* The confession of sins to a priest or the hearing of a confession by a priest.

shrike \'shrīk\ *n.* Any of numerous chiefly gray or brownish, black-winged birds with a notched bill hooked at the tip, as a butcherbird.

shrill \'shril\ *adj.* **1** Having or giving out a sharp, high sound; as, a *shrill* whistle. **2** Accompanied by sharp, high sounds; as, *shrill* gaiety. — *adv.* In a shrill tone. — *v.* **1** To make a shrill sound. **2** To utter in a shrill tone. — **shril·ly** \'shril-lē\ *adv.*

shrimp \'shrimp\ *n.; pl.* **shrimp** or **shrimps. 1** A small salt-water crustacean resembling a crayfish, used as food. **2** [Plural *shrimps.*] A small person. — *v.* To catch or fish for shrimp.

shrine \'shrīn\ *n.* **1** A case or box for sacred relics, such as the bones of saints. **2** The tomb of a saint or other holy person. **3** A place or object that is considered sacred.

shrink \'shringk\ *v.;* **shrank** \'shrangk\ or **shrunk** \'shrəngk\; **shrunk** \'shrəngk\ or **shrunk·en** \'shrəngk-n\; **shrink·ing. 1** To withdraw or move away, as in fear or pain; to cower. **2** To make or become smaller. The sweater *shrank* when it was washed. **3** To refuse to take action, as from fear or disgust; as, to *shrink* from a quarrel. **4** To cause to shrink, as cloth. — *n.* A shrinking.

shrink·age \'shringk-ij\ *n.* **1** The action of shrinking. **2** The amount by which something shrinks.

shrive \'shrīv\ *v.;* **shrived** \'shrīvd\ or **shrove** \'shrōv\; **shriv·en** \'shriv-n\ or **shrived; shriv·ing** \'shrī-ving\. *Archaic.* **1** To hear the confession of. **2** To pardon the sins of in confession.

shriv·el \'shriv-l\ *v.;* **shriv·eled** or **shriv·elled; shriv·el·ing** or **shriv·el·ling** \-l(-)ing\. To wrinkle; to shrink and wither; as, a *shriveled* old man.

shroud \'shraůd\ *n.* **1** The cloth placed over or around a dead body; a winding sheet. **2** Something that covers or shelters like a garment. **3** A rope, usually one of a pair, that goes from the masthead of a boat to the side to support the mast. — *v.* To cover with or as if with a shroud; to conceal.

shroud, 3

shrove \'shrōv\. A past tense of *shrive.*

Shrove Tuesday \'shrōv\. The day before Ash Wednesday.

shrub \'shrəb\ *n.* A plant smaller than a tree, with woody stems and low-growing branches; a bush.

shrub·bery \'shrəb-r(-)ē\ *n.; pl.* **shrub·ber·ies.** Shrubs collectively.

shrub·by \'shrəb-ē\ *adj.;* **shrub·bi·er; shrub·bi·est. 1** Covered with shrubs. **2** Consisting of shrubs. **3** Like a shrub or shrubs in size or growth.

shrug \'shrəg\ *v.;* **shrugged; shrug·ging.** To draw or hunch up the shoulders, as with dislike, doubt, or uncertainty. — *n.* The act of shrugging.

shrunk. A past tense and past part. of *shrink.*

shrunk·en \'shrəngk-n\. A past part. of *shrink.* — *adj.* Seemingly grown smaller; shriveled.

shuck \'shək\ *n.* **1** A shell, husk, or pod, as of nuts, corn, or peas. **2** The shell of an oyster or clam. — *v.* To remove the shuck from.

shucks \'shəks\ *interj.* An exclamation expressing annoyance or disappointment.

shud·der \'shəd-r\ *v.;* **shud·dered; shud·der·ing** \-r(-)ing\. To tremble or shake, as from fear or horror; to quake; to shiver. — *n.* A trembling.

shuf·fle \'shəf-l\ *v.;* **shuf·fled; shuf·fling** \-l(-)ing\. **1** To mix in a disorderly mass; as, odds and ends *shuffled* in a drawer. **2** To mix cards by changing their order in the pack. **3** To move one's feet or dance with a clumsy, dragging gait. **4** To shift from place to place; as, to *shuffle* chairs. — *n.* **1** The act of shuffling, as cards. **2** A turn, or the right, to shuffle the cards. **3** A dance done with a sliding dragging motion. — **shuf·fler** \-l(-)ər\ *n.*

shuf·fle·board \'shəf-l-ˌbōrd, -ˌbȯrd\ *n.* **1** A game in which disks are pushed along a flat surface, as the deck of a ship, in an attempt to reach certain marks. **2** A board marked for playing this game.

shun \'shən\ *v.;* **shunned; shun·ning.** To avoid deliberately; to keep clear of.

shunt \'shənt\ *v.* **1** To move aside; to shift; as, to *shunt* cattle into a corral. **2** To switch railroad cars from one track to another. — **shunt·er** \-r\ *n.*

shut \'shət\ *v.;* **shut; shut·ting. 1** To close, as by bringing parts together. **2** To forbid entrance to; to bar. **3** To confine; to imprison.

shut·down \'shət-ˌdaůn\ *n.* A shutting down, as of a factory; a closing.

shut-in \'shət-ˌin\ *adj.* Confined to one's home, as by illness. — *n.* An invalid.

shut·out \'shət-ˌaůt\ *n.* **1** A lockout. **2** A game in which the losing side scores no points at all.

shut·ter \'shət-r\ *n.* **1** One that shuts. **2** A movable cover for a window; a blind. **3** The part of a camera that opens and closes to expose the film.

shutters, 2

shut·tle \'shət-l\ *n.* **1** In weaving, an instrument used to carry the thread back and forth from side to side through the threads that run lengthwise. **2** In a sewing machine, a thread holder that slides or rotates to carry the lower thread up to the top thread to make a stitch. **3** Also **shuttle train.** A train that goes back and forth over a short route. **4** A number of airplanes going back and forth between two places or from point to point of a triangle. — *v.;* **shut·tled; shut·tling** \-l(-)ing\. **1** To move back and forth like a shuttle. **2** To go by a shuttle.

shut·tle·cock \'shət-l-ˌkäk\ *n.* A cork stuck with feathers which is batted back and forth both in badminton and in battledore and shuttlecock.

shy \'shī\ *adj.;* **shi·er** or **shy·er** \'shīr\; **shi·est** or **shy·est** \'shī-əst\. **1** Easily frightened; timid; bashful. **2** Scant; lacking; as, to be *shy* of ready money. — The words *bashful* and *diffident* are synonyms of *shy: shy* suggests a tendency to be reserved and shrinking in dealing with or approaching other persons, and to withdraw from group activities, as well as a desire to be as inconspicuous as possible; *bashful* usually refers to a frightened, hesitant, and awkward shyness often typical of small children and some adolescents; *diffident* may refer to a tendency to withdraw resulting from a lack of self-confidence, distrust of one's abilities, or from great self-consciousness.

— *v.;* **shied** \'shīd\; **shy·ing. 1** To draw back; to recoil. **2** To start suddenly aside in fright, as a horse. — *n.; pl.* **shies** \'shīz\. A sudden start aside.

shy \'shī\ *v.;* **shied** \'shīd\; **shy·ing.** To fling; to throw sideways with a snapping motion; as, to *shy* stones. — *n.; pl.* **shies** \'shīz\. A throw; a fling.

shy·ly \'shī-lē\ *adv.* In a shy way or manner.

si \'sē\ *n.* A syllable used in music to name the seventh note of the scale; ti.

Si·a·mese \ˌsī-ə-'mēz, -'mēs\ *adj.* Of or relating to Thailand (formerly Siam), its people, or their language. — *n.* **1** A native of Thailand. **2** The language of Thailand.

Siamese twins. [So called from a famous pair of such twins, Chang and Eng (1811–1874), who were born in Thailand (then Siam).] Twins born joined together.

sib·i·lant \'sib-l-ənt\ *adj.* Making a hissing sound; especially, in phonetics, uttered with a hissing sound. — *n.* A sibilant speech sound or the symbol standing for it. *S* and *sh* are *sibilants.*

sib·yl \'sib-l\ *n.* A prophetess.

sick \'sik\ *adj.* **1** Affected with disease; ill; not well. **2** Having to do with illness or with someone who is ill, as in *sickbed.* **3** Accompanied by an inclination to vomit; nauseated. **4** Mentally unsound; not completely sane; as, *sick* fancies. **5** Filled with sorrow or longing; as, to be *sick* at heart. **6** Tired from having had too much of something; as, to be *sick* of candy. **7** Pale; wan; as, a *sick* color. — *n.* Sick persons.

sick bay. A section on a ship used as a hospital.

sick·bed \'sik-ˌbed\ *n.* The bed of a sick person.

sick·en \'sik-n\ *v.;* **sick·ened; sick·en·ing** \-n(-)ing\. To make or become sick.

sick·ish \'sik-ish\ *adj.* **1** Somewhat sick. **2** Somewhat sickening. — **sick·ish·ly,** *adv.*

sick·le \'sik-l\ *n.* An agricultural tool with a sharp, curved metal blade and a short handle.

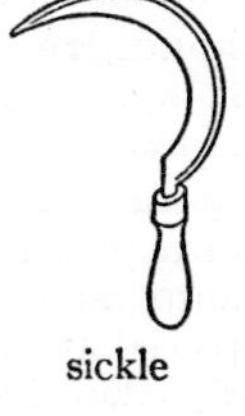
sickle

sick·ly \'sik-lē\ *adj.;* **sick·li·er; sick·li·est. 1** Somewhat sick; usually or often ailing; as, a *sickly* child. **2** Caused by sickness; as, a *sickly* complexion. **3** Associated with sickness; as, a *sickly* appetite. **4** Appearing as if sick; weak; pale; as, a *sickly* color; a *sickly* light. **5** Sickening; as, a *sickly* taste.

sick·ness \'sik-nəs\ *n.* **1** Illness; poor health. **2** A disease; an ailment. **3** Nausea; vomiting.

sick·room \'sik-ˌrüm, -ˌru̇m\ *n.* A room in which there is a sick person.

side \'sīd\ *n.* **1** A surface forming a border or face of an object; especially, one of the longer surfaces, as contrasted with an end. **2** An outer part or surface; as, one *side* of the paper. **3** The right or left part of the trunk of the body; as, a pain in one's *side.* **4** The space beside one. **5** A slope, as of a hill. **6** A place beyond a central point or line; as, to set something to one *side.* **7** Any position viewed as opposite to another; as, one *side* of a question. **8** The party, as a person, group or team, that supports either of these positions. **9** A line of descent traced from either parent. — *adj.* **1** Of or relating to a side or sides; being on or toward the side; as, *side* arms. **2** Directed from or toward the side; as, a *side* glance. **3** Indirect; not main; incidental; as, a *side* issue. — *v.;* **sid·ed; sid·ing. 1** To take the same side; as, to *side* with one's brother in the argument. **2** To furnish with siding.

side arms. Weapons worn at the side or in a belt, as a pistol and sword.

side·board \'sīd-ˌbōrd, -ˌbȯrd\ *n.* A piece of dining-room furniture with drawers and compartments for dishes, silverware, and table linen.

side·burns \'sīd-ˌbərnz\ *n. pl.* Short side whiskers.

side·car \'sīd-ˌkär, -ˌkår\ *n.* A one-wheeled car attached to the side of a motorcycle.

sid·ed \'sīd-əd\ *adj.* Having a side or sides — used chiefly in combinations, as in *lopsided, one-sided.*

side·light \'sīd-ˌlīt\ *n.* **1** Light from the side. **2** Incidental information about a subject. **3** A lamp or light on the side of something.

side·line \'sīd-ˌlīn\ *n.* **1** A line of goods sold in addition to one's main article of trade. **2** A line marking a side of a playing area; the space just outside these lines. **3** The standpoint of persons not directly participating or concerned.

side·long \'sīd-ˌlȯng\ *adv.* **1** Obliquely; as, to glance *sidelong.* **2** On the side; as, to lay a thing *sidelong.* — *adj.* **1** Slanting; lying on one side. **2** Directed sideways; as, a *sidelong* glance.

si·de·re·al \sī-'dir-ē-əl\ *adj.* **1** Of or relating to the stars or constellations. **2** Measured by the apparent motion of fixed stars; as, a *sidereal* day.

sid·er·ite \'sid-r-ˌīt\ *n.* Natural iron carbonate.

side·sad·dle \'sīd-ˌsad-l\ *n.* A woman's saddle in which the rider sits with both legs on the same side of the horse.

side·show \'sīd-ˌshō\ *n.* A small show near or accompanying a main exhibition, as of a circus.

side·slip \'sīd-ˌslip\ *v.;* **side·slipped; side·slip·ping.** To slip to one side; to skid. — *n.* The action of slipping to one side, as by an airplane.

side step. 1 A step aside, as to avoid a blow. **2** A step taken sideways, as in climbing on skis.

side·step \'sīd-ˌstep\ *v.;* **side·stepped; side·step·ping. 1** To take a side step. **2** To avoid by a step to the side, as a blow. **3** To avoid meeting issues.

He is adept at *sidestepping* awkward questions.

side·stroke \'sīd-ˌstrōk\ *n.* A stroke made by a swimmer while lying on his side, in which the arms are moved alternately forward and backward while the legs are moved in a way resembling the opening and closing of scissors.

side·swipe \'sīd-ˌswīp\ *v.;* **side·swiped**; **side-swip·ing.** To strike lightly along the side.

side·track \'sīd-ˌtrak\ *v.* **1** To transfer from a main railroad line to a siding; as, to *sidetrack* a train. **2** To turn aside from a main purpose or use; as, to *sidetrack* the conversation. — *n.* A siding.

side·walk \'sīd-ˌwȯk\ *n.* A walk, usually paved, at the side of a street or road.

side·ward \'sīd-wərd\ *adj.* or *adv.* To one side.

side·wards \'sīd-wərdz\ *adv.* Sideward.

side·ways \'sīd-ˌwāz\ *adv.* **1** From the side; as, viewed *sideways.* **2** With one side to the front; as, turned *sideways.* **3** To, toward, or at one side; as, to glance *sideways.* — *adj.* Moving, directed, or turned toward one side; as, a *sideways* glance.

side·winder \'sīd-ˌwīnd-r\ *n.* **1** Any of several rattlesnakes. **2** *Slang.* A heavy swinging blow from the side.

side·wise \'sīd-ˌwīz\ *adv.* or *adj.* Sideways.

sid·ing \'sīd-ing\. Pres. part. of *side.* — *n.* **1** A short railroad track connected with the main track by switches at one or more points. **2** Material used to cover the sides of a building.

si·dle \'sīd-l\ *v.;* **si·dled**; **si·dling** \-l(-)ing\. To go or move with one side forward; to move sideways.

siege \'sēj\ *n.* **1** A besieging of a fortified place. **2** A continued attempt to gain possession of something. **3** A long, wearying time; a persistent attack; as, to recover from a *siege* of the flu.

si·en·na \sē-'en-ə\ *n.* An earthy substance, brownish yellow when raw and orange-red or reddish brown when burnt, used as a pigment.

si·er·ra \sē-'er-ə\ *n.* [From Spanish, meaning literally "saw" and derived from Latin *serra.*] A range of mountains with jagged peaks.

si·es·ta \sē-'es-tə\ *n.* A short sleep or rest, especially at midday.

sieve \'siv\ *n.* A utensil with meshes that let the finer particles of a substance go through; as, a *sieve* for gravel; a flour *sieve.*

sieve

sieve tube. 1 A tube, characteristic of phloem tissue, that consists of an end-to-end series of thin-walled living cells (**sieve cells**) having no nucleus when mature. **2** A sieve cell.

sift \'sift\ *v.* **1** To pass or cause to pass through a sieve. **2** To separate with or as if with a sieve. **3** To examine carefully, as evidence. **4** To scatter by or as if by sifting. — **sift·er** \-r\ *n.*

sigh \'sī\ *v.* **1** To take a long, deep, audible breath, especially as an expression of grief or weariness. **2** To grieve; to lament; to yearn; as, to *sigh* for old friends. **3** To make a sound like sighing. The wind *sighed* in the trees. — *n.* **1** The act of sighing. **2** A sound like a sigh. **sigh·er** \'sīr\ *n.*

sight \'sīt\ *n.* **1** A view; a spectacle; as, a beautiful *sight.* **2** Something that is worth seeing, or that is peculiar or funny. **3** The ability to see; eyesight. **4** The act of seeing or looking; as, to know a person by *sight.* **5** Inspection; as, a letter intended for the teacher's *sight* only. **6** A device, as a small metal bead on a gun barrel, that aids the eye in aiming. **7** An aim or observation taken by means of such a device. **8** A view; a glimpse; as, to catch *sight* of a friend. **9** Presence within the field of vision; as, unable to bear the *sight* of someone. **10** The distance a person can see; as, out of *sight.* **11** A position from which a person can see a certain thing; as, in *sight* of land. — *v.* **1** To get sight of. **2** To look at through or as if through a sight. **3** To aim by means of a sight.

sight·less \'sīt-ləs\ *adj.* Lacking sight; blind.

sight·ly \'sīt-lē\ *adj.* **1** Pleasing to the sight; handsome. **2** Affording a good view.

sight–see·ing \'sīt-ˌsē-ing\ *n.* Going about to see things and places of interest. — *adj.* Engaged in or used for sight-seeing. — **sight–se·er** \-ˌsē-ər\ *n.*

sign \'sīn\ *n.* **1** Something that stands for something else; a symbol; as, the *sign* of the cross. **2** A motion, action, or gesture that expresses something; as, to beckon as a *sign* to go. **3** A publicly displayed notice; as, a "For Sale" *sign;* a road *sign.* **4** Something that shows the existence of a thing. Snow is a *sign* of winter. **5** Something that indicates what is to come; an omen. **6** A trace; as, no *signs* of life. **7** In mathematics, any symbol that gives information of some kind about a value or the operation to be performed on it. — *v.* **1** To make or place a sign on something. **2** To write one's name on something; as, to *sign* a letter. **3** To make known by gestures instead of talk. **4** To hire by getting a person's signature. — **sign off.** To announce the end of television or radio broadcasting for the day and stop transmitting. — **sign on.** To engage oneself for work by signing a register.

sig·nal \'sig-nəl\ *n.* **1** A sign, event, or word that serves to start some action. The whistle was a *signal* to run. **2** Something that stirs to action or starts action. One blow was the *signal* for a general fight. **3** A sign that gives notice of something· as, a traffic *signal.* **4** In radio and television, the group of electric waves that is transmitted and produces the effect heard or seen. — *adj.* **1** Unusual; extraordinary; as, a *signal* act of bravery. **2** Used for signaling; as, a *signal* light. — *v.;* **sig·naled** or **sig·nalled**; **sig·nal·ing** or **sig·nal·ling.** To communicate by signals. — **sig·nal·ly** \-nə-lē\ *adv.*

sig·nal·ize \'sig-nə-ˌlīz\ *v.;* **sig·nal·ized**; **sig·nal·iz·ing.** To mark; to indicate; especially, to make noteworthy; to distinguish.

sig·na·ture \'sig-nə-ˌchu̇r, -nəch-r\ *n.* **1** The name of a person written in his own handwriting; an autograph. **2** In music, either of the two signs placed at the beginning of a staff, the first or **key signature** indicating the key, and the second or **time signature** indicating the time or meter.

sign·board \'sīn-ˌbōrd, -ˌbȯrd\ *n.* A board for a notice or sign.

signed \'sīnd\ *adj.* **1** Bearing a signature; as, a *signed* document. **2** Having a sign; especially, in algebra, having a positive or negative sign.

sign·er \'sīn-r\ *n.* A person who signs.

sig·net \'sig-nət\ *n.* A seal, especially one used to mark an official document.

sig·nif·i·cance \sig-'nif-ə-kən(t)s\ *n.* **1** What is meant; meaning. **2** Importance; consequence.

sig·nif·i·cant \sig-'nif-ə-kənt\ *adj.* **1** Meaningful; expressive; as, a *significant* gesture with the hand. **2** Important; momentous; as, a *significant* step toward world peace. — **sig·nif·i·cant·ly**, *adv.*

sig·ni·fi·ca·tion \ˌsig-nə-fə-'kāsh-n\ *n.* **1** A signifying, as by signs. **2** Meaning; import.

sig·ni·fy \'sig-nə-ˌfī\ *v.;* **sig·ni·fied** \-ˌfīd\; **sig·ni·fy·ing.** **1** To show by a sign; to make known. **2** To mean; to have significance or importance.

sign·post \'sīn-ˌpōst\ *n.* A post with a sign on it.

si·lage \'sī-lij\ *n.* Chopped fodder, as the stalks and leaves of corn, fermented in a silo.

si·lence \'sī-lən(t)s\ *n.* **1** The state of keeping or being silent. **2** Secrecy, as about one's plans. **3** Quietness; stillness; as, the *silence* of night. — *v.;* **si·lenced**; **si·lenc·ing.** **1** To stop the noise of someone or something. **2** To suppress, as objections. — *interj.* Be silent! Be still!

si·lenc·er \'sī-lən(t)s-r\ *n.* One that silences, as the muffler of an internal combustion engine.

si·lent \'sī-lənt\ *adj.* **1** Not speaking; not talkative. **2** Free from noise or sound; still. **3** Uncommunicative. The boy was *silent* about that part of his plan. **4** Performed or borne without sound; as, *silent* prayer; *silent* grief. **5** Not pronounced. The "e" in "came" is *silent.*

— The word *taciturn* is a synonym of *silent: silent* may suggest a habitual tendency to say no more than is absolutely necessary or may refer to the use of only a few words on some particular occasion, as from cautiousness; *taciturn* usually indicates a deep-seated temperamental dislike of communicating with others and is apt to suggest a sullen, unsociable nature.

sil·hou·ette \ˌsil-ə-'wet\ *n.* **1** A drawing or picture of the outline of an object, filled in with a solid color, usually black. **2** A profile or outline of this kind, as a person's shadow. — *v.;* **sil·hou·et·ted**; **sil·hou·et·ting.** **1** To represent by a silhouette. **2** To show or appear as a silhouette; as, an airplane *silhouetted* against the sunset.

silhouette

sil·i·ca \'sil-ik-ə\ *n.* A mineral substance occurring in such forms as opal and quartz.

sil·i·cate \'sil-ik-ət, -ə-ˌkāt\ *n.* A compound regarded as a salt or ester of one of various acids containing silicon (**si·lic·ic acids** \sə-'lis-ik\).

sil·i·con \'sil-ik-n\ *n.* A nonmetallic element that occurs in nature only in combination.

sil·i·co·sis \ˌsil-ə-'kō-səs\ *n.* A disease of the lungs caused by inhaling silica or quartz dust.

silk \'silk\ *n.* **1** A fine, strong, glossy fiber produced by certain worms for their cocoons or nests and used for making into thread and cloth. **2** Thread, cloth, or a garment made from this fiber. **3** A thread or a fiber like silk, as in a spider's web. **4** Something like silk, as the styles on ears of corn. — *adj.* Of or relating to silk; like silk.

silk–cot·ton tree \'silk-'kät-n ˌtrē\. Any of a number of tropical trees having seeds surrounded by a soft substance called **silk cotton**; especially, the one whose fiber is kapok.

silk·en \'silk-n\ *adj.* **1** Of, relating to, or made of silk; as, a *silken* gown. **2** Silky; as, *silken* hair.

silk moth. The silkworm moth.

silk·worm \'silk-ˌwərm\ *n.* The caterpillar of certain moths, which spins a strong silk in making its cocoon.

silkworm and moth

silky \'sil-kē\ *adj.;* **silk·i·er**; **silk·i·est.** **1** Silken. **2** In botany, covered with soft hairs pressed close to the surface, as certain leaves. — **silk·i·ness** \'sil-kē-nəs\ *n.*

sill \'sil\ *n.* **1** A horizontal piece or slab, as of wood or stone, that forms the foundation of a structure, as in a house or bridge. **2** The timber or stone at the foot of a door; the threshold. **3** The timber or stone on which a window frame stands or the lowest piece in a window frame.

sil·ly \'sil-ē\ *adj.;* **sil·li·er**; **sil·li·est.** [From Old English *saelig* meaning "happy".] **1** Feebleminded. **2** Foolish; unwise. **3** Absurd; stupid.

si·lo \'sī-ˌlō\ *n.; pl.* **si·los.** A pit or trench, or a building, usually tower-shaped and made of wood, concrete, or metal, where silage is stored.

barn with silo

silt \'silt\ *n.* **1** Fine soil or earth; especially, particles of such soil floating in water, as in a river or pond. **2** A deposit of such material, as by a river in flood. — *v.* To choke, fill, cover, or block with silt. The channel *silts* up. — **silty** \'sil-tē\ *adj.*

silvan. Variant of *sylvan.*

sil·ver \'silv-r\ *n.* **1** A soft, white, metallic element that takes a high polish, used for money, for jewelry and ornaments, and for table utensils. **2** Coin made of silver; silver money. **3** Silverware; as, table *silver.* **4** Anything having the luster or appearance of silver. **5** The grayish white color of the metal silver. — *adj.* **1** Made of, or coated or plated with silver. **2** Of the color of silver. **3** Like silver, as in being shiny, precious, or soft and clear in sound; as, to have a *silver* tongue. **4** Twenty-fifth in a series of anniversaries or celebrations; as, a *silver* wedding anniversary. — *v.;* **sil·vered**; **sil·ver·ing** \-r(-)ing\. **1** To coat or color with or as if with silver. **2** To become the color of silver.

sil·ver·fish \'silv-r-ˌfish\ *n.; pl.* **sil·ver·fish** or **sil-**

ver·fish·es. 1 Any of various silvery fishes, as the tarpon or certain goldfish. 2 A small wingless insect found in buildings, often injurious to sized paper or starched clothes.

silver nitrate. A chemical substance composed of silver, nitrogen, and oxygen, used especially in antiseptics and in photography.

sil·ver-plat·ed \'silv-r-'plāt-əd\ *adj.* Coated with silver.

sil·ver·smith \'silv-r-ˌsmith\ *n.* A person who makes articles of silver or similar metals.

sil·ver·ware \'silv-r-ˌwar, -ˌwer\ *n.* Articles made of silver, silver plate, or metal resembling silver.

sil·very \'silv-r(-)ē\ *adj.* 1 Having the color or luster of silver. 2 Having the clear soft tone of silver.

sim·i·an \'sim-ē-ən\ *adj.* Of, belonging to, or like the apes or monkeys. — *n.* Any ape or monkey.

sim·i·lar \'sim-l-ər\ *adj.* 1 Like or alike. 2 Of geometric figures, alike in shape but differing in size and position. — **sim·i·lar·ly,** *adv.*

sim·i·lar·i·ty \ˌsim-l-'ar-ət-ē\ *n.; pl.* **sim·i·lar·i·ties.** 1 Likeness; resemblance. 2 A point in which things are similar. The two books have many *similarities.*

sim·i·le \'sim-l-(ˌ)ē\ *n.* A figure of speech in which the word *as* or *like* is used to compare things different in kind or quality, as in "as bold as a lion".

si·mil·i·tude \sə-'mil-ə-ˌtüd, -ˌtyüd\ *n.* 1 Similarity; resemblance. 2 A simile. 3 A facsimile.

sim·mer \'sim-r\ *v.;* **sim·mered; sim·mer·ing** \-r(-)ing\. 1 To be on the point of boiling; to boil gently. 2 To be on the point of expressing one's feelings violently; as, to *simmer* with anger. — **simmer down.** To calm down. — *n.* The condition of simmering; as, to bring to a *simmer.*

si·mo·ny \'sī-mə-nē, 'sim-ə-\ *n.* The crime of buying or selling positions in the church or clergy.

si·moom \sə-'müm\ or **si·moon** \-'mün\ *n.* A strong, hot, dust-laden wind that blows occasionally near desert regions, as in Arabia.

sim·per \'simp-r\ *v.;* **sim·pered; sim·per·ing** \-r(-)ing\. To smile in a silly manner; as, *simpering* girls. — *n.* An affected, silly smile; a smirk.

sim·ple \'simp-l\ *adj.;* **sim·pler** \-l(-)ər\; **simplest** \-l(-)əst\. 1 Not mixed or compounded with anything else; as, a *simple* substance. 2 Mere; as, the *simple* truth. 3 Not complex; as, a *simple* machine. 4 Not hard to understand or solve. 5 Sincere; straightforward. 6 Not elaborate; without ornament; as, a *simple* dress. 7 Without much variety or luxury. 8 Foolish or ignorant.
— The words *innocent* and *unsophisticated* are synonyms of *simple: simple* generally refers to a complete lack of deceitfulness in a person's character, thought, or speech, and usually suggests naturalness as well; *innocent* usually indicates the lack of knowledge of evil, sometimes even of the common dangers of life, and accompanying trustfulness and openness; *unsophisticated* stresses the lack of experience in worldly matters and the resulting lack of poise, shrewdness, or discretion.

sim·ple-mind·ed \'simp-l-'mīn-dəd\ *adj.* 1 Not subtle; undesigning. 2 Lacking sense; foolish.

simple sentence. A sentence containing only one clause.

sim·ple·ton \'simp-l-tən\ *n.* A silly person; a fool.

sim·plic·i·ty \sim-'plis-ət-ē\ *n.; pl.* **sim·plic·i·ties.** 1 The quality or state of being simple. 2 Honesty; straightforwardness. 3 Plainness in manners or way of life. 4 Foolishness.

sim·pli·fy \'simp-lə-ˌfī\ *v.;* **sim·pli·fied** \-ˌfīd\; **sim·pli·fy·ing.** To make simple or simpler. — **sim·pli·fi·ca·tion** \ˌsimp-lə-fə-'kāsh-n\ *n.*

sim·ply \'simp-lē\ *adv.* 1 In a clear and easy way. 2 Plainly; as, *simply* dressed. 3 Merely; only; as, to ask a question *simply* out of curiosity. 4 Really; truly; absolutely; as, *simply* glorious weather.

sim·u·late \'sim-yə-ˌlāt\ *v.;* **sim·u·lat·ed; sim·u·lat·ing.** To imitate or feign; to pretend; as, *simulated* pearls; a *simulated* interest in engines.

si·mul·ta·ne·ous \ˌsīm-l-'tā-nē-əs, ˌsim-l-\ *adj.* Taking place or operating at the same time; as, *simultaneous* events. — **si·mul·ta·ne·ous·ly,** *adv.*

simultaneous equations. Two or more algebraic equations so related that they are satisfied by the same set of values for the unknowns.

sin \'sin\ *n.* 1 A breaking of God's law or will. 2 Any offense or wrongdoing. — *v.;* **sinned; sin·ning.** To commit a sin; to do that which is wrong.

since \(')sin(t)s\ *adv.* 1 From a past time until now. He has kept it ever *since.* 2 In the time between a certain past time and now. He left here and has *since* gone to Chicago. 3 Before now; ago; as, clothes that have long *since* gone out of style. — *prep.* In or during the time that followed; from the time of; as, to have felt sick ever *since* breakfast. — *conj.* 1 At some time in the past after or later than. The building had been torn down *since* he visited the city. 2 From the time when; as, friends *since* they were children. 3 Seeing that; because. *Since* it rained, there was no picnic.

sin·cere \sin-'sir\ *adj.* 1 Honest; straightforward. 2 Genuine; real; as, a *sincere* interest in learning. — For synonyms see *honest.* — **sin·cere·ly,** *adv.*

sin·cer·i·ty \sin-'ser-ət-ē, -'sir-\ *n.* The quality or state of being sincere; honesty; genuineness.

sine \'sīn\ *n.* The ratio of the side opposite an acute angle in a right triangle to the hypotenuse.

si·ne·cure \'sī-nə-ˌkyůr, 'sin-ə-\ *n.* A well-paid position or job that has little work attached to it.

sin·ew \'sin-(ˌ)yü, 'sin-(ˌ)ü\ *n.* 1 A tough cord or band that connects a muscle with some other part, as with a bone; a tendon. 2 A tendon used as a thread or cord; as, sewed with reindeer *sinews.* 3 Strength; muscular power; nervous energy.

sin·ewy \'sin-(y)ə-wē\ *adj.* 1 Having many sinews; tough; stringy; as, a *sinewy* piece of meat. 2 Strong; powerful; as, *sinewy* arms.

sin·ful \'sin-fəl\ *adj.* Tainted with or full of sin; wicked. — **sin·ful·ly** \-fə-lē\ *adv.*

sing \'sing\ *v.;* **sang** \'sang\ or **sung** \'səng\; **sung; sing·ing** \'sing-ing\. 1 To produce musical sounds by means of one's voice; as, to *sing* for joy. **2** To utter with musical sounds; as, to *sing* a song. **3** To make pleasing, musical sounds, as birds. **4** To make a slight, shrill sound; as, a kettle *singing* on the stove. **5** To tell a story in poetry. **6** To express with enthusiasm; as, to *sing* someone's praises. **7** To hum, buzz, or ring, as the ears. **8** To chant; to intone; as, to *sing* Mass. **9** To do something with, or by means of, song; as, to *sing* a baby to sleep. — *n.* **1** A singing, especially in company with others; as, a community *sing.* **2** A slight, shrill sound as of a bullet in flight.

sing. Abbreviation for *singular.*

singe \'sinj\ *v.;* **singed; singe·ing** \'sin-jing\. **1** To burn or scorch the ends or outside of. **2** To remove the hair or down from, as a plucked chicken, by passing over a flame. — *n.* A slight scorching of the surface. — For synonyms see *scorch.*

sing·er \'sing-r\ *n.* **1** One who sings, especially before the public. **2** A singing bird. **3** A poet.

Sin·gha·lese \ˌsing-gə-'lēz, -'lēs\ or **Sin·ha·lese** \ˌsin-(h)ə-\ *adj.* **1** Of or relating to the principal race of Ceylon. **2** Ceylonese. — *n. sing. and pl.* **1** A member of the Singhalese race. **2** The language of the Singhalese.

sin·gle \'sing-gl\ *adj.* **1** One only; as, a *single* thread. **2** Unmarried. **3** Taken part in by one, or by one on each side; as, to fight in *single* combat. **4** For the use of only one person or family; separate; as, a *single* house. **5** Having only one row of petals; as, a *single* rose. **6** Simple; honest; sincere. — *n.* **1** One individual person or thing. **2** In baseball, a base hit. **3** [usually in the plural] In tennis, a game or match between two players. — *v.;* **sin·gled; sin·gling** \-l(-)ing\. **1** To select from among a number; as, to be *singled* out for praise. **2** In baseball, to make a base hit.

single file. A line of persons or things arranged one behind another.

sin·gle-foot \'sing-gl-ˌfu̇t\ *n.* A gait of the horse in which each foot strikes singly and there are alternately one and two feet on the ground. — *v.* To proceed by means of the single-foot.

sin·gle·hand·ed \'sing-gl-'han-dəd\ *adj.* **1** Done by one person or with one hand. **2** Working alone; lacking help. — **sin·gle·hand·ed·ly,** *adv.*

sin·gle·heart·ed \'sing-gl-'härt-əd, -'hȧrt-\ *adj.* Sincere; straightforward. — **sin·gle·heart·ed·ly,** *adv.*

sin·gle-mind·ed \'sing-gl-'mīn-dəd\ *adj.* **1** Sincere; singlehearted. **2** Having a single purpose.

sin·gle·ness \'sing-gl-nəs\ *n.* **1** The quality or state of being single, especially in mind or purpose. **2** The unmarried state.

sin·gle·stick \'sing-gl-ˌstik\ *n.* **1** A stick about 40 inches long, usually with a guard near the handle, used in fencing. **2** Fencing with singlesticks.

sin·glet \'sing-glət\ *n. Chiefly British.* An undershirt or jersey.

sin·gle·tree \'sing-gl-(ˌ)trē\ *n.* The pivoted or swinging bar of a horse-drawn carriage or wagon, to which the traces are attached; a whippletree.

sin·gly \'sing-glē\ *adv.* **1** Individually; separately; one by one; one at a time. **2** Singlehandedly.

sing·song \'sing-ˌsȯng\ *n.* A monotonous rhythm or a monotonous rise and fall of pitch. — *adj.* Having a monotonous rhythm.

sin·gu·lar \'sing-gyəl-r\ *adj.* **1** Of or relating to a single person, thing, or instance. **2** Strange; unusual; queer; as, a woman of *singular* dress and manners. **3** Exceptional; as, *singular* devotion to duty. **4** In grammar, indicating or meaning one, not more than one; as, the *singular* number. — *n.* **1** A form of a word used to show that only one person or thing is meant. **2** A word in the singular form. — **sin·gu·lar·ly,** *adv.*

sin·gu·lar·i·ty \ˌsing-gyə-'lar-ət-ē\ *n.; pl.* **sin·gu·lar·i·ties.** **1** The quality or state of being singular. **2** Something that is singular; a peculiarity.

Sinhalese. Variant of *Singhalese.*

sin·is·ter \'sin-əst-r\ *adj.* [From medieval English *sinistre,* there borrowed from Latin *sinister* meaning literally "on the left".] Threatening evil; evil.

sink \'singk\ *v.;* **sank** \'sangk\ or **sunk** \'səngk\; **sunk; sink·ing.** **1** To move or cause to move downwards; to become submerged or swallowed up; as, to feel one's feet *sinking* into mud. The ship *sank.* **2** To fall or descend lower and lower. The sun *sank* behind the hills. **3** To fall gradually; to settle. The lake *sank* a foot. **4** To become lower or poorer. The invalid was *sinking* rapidly. **5** To become hollowed, as the cheeks of an aging person. **6** To make a hole and fix something in it; as, to *sink* a well. **7** To make a lasting impression; as, an experience that *sank* deep. **8** To seep. The rain *sank* into the earth. **9** To invest, as money, often unwisely. — *n.* **1** A drain to carry off dirty water. **2** A basin, usually with water faucets and a drain, fixed to a wall, or floor, as of a kitchen. **3** A foul or filthy place. — **sink·a·ble,** *adj.*

sink·er \'singk-r\ *n.* **1** One that sinks, as a weight for sinking a fishing line. **2** *Slang.* A doughnut.

sink·hole \'singk-ˌhōl\ *n.* A hollow place in which drainage collects.

sink·ing fund \'singk-ing\. The total of sums of money set apart at intervals, as by a company, to pay a debt or for other purposes.

sin·ner \'sin-r\ *n.* One who sins, especially habitually or without repentance.

sin·u·os·i·ty \ˌsin-yə-'wäs-ət-ē\ *n.; pl.* **sin·u·os·i·ties.** **1** The quality or state of being sinuous. **2** Something that is sinuous; a winding turn.

sin·u·ous \'sin-yə-wəs\ *adj.* Bending in and out; winding. — **sin·u·ous·ly,** *adv.*

si·nus \'sī-nəs\ *n.* A hollow or cavity; especially, one of several in the skull connected with the nose.

si·nus·i·tis \ˌsī-nə-'sīt-əs\ *n.* Inflammation of a sinus.

-sion. A suffix having the same meanings as "-tion", as in *compulsion, explosion, submersion.*

sip \'sip\ *v.;* **sipped; sip·ping.** To drink little by little; to take small drinks of; as, to *sip* hot milk. — *n.* **1** The act of sipping. **2** A taste.

si·phon \'sīf-n\ *n.* **1** A bent pipe or tube through which a liquid can be drawn, by means of air pressure, up and over the edge of one container and into another container placed at a lower level. **2** Also **siphon bottle.** A bottle containing soda water under pressure and having a valve on top by which the contents can be discharged. **3** A tubular organ for drawing in or expelling fluids, as in some shellfish and octopuses. — *v.;* **si·phoned**; **si·phon·ing** \-n(-)ing\. To draw off or pass off by means of a siphon.

siphon, 1

sir \(')sər\ *n.* **1** [with a capital] A title put before the given name of a knight or a baronet; as, *Sir* John Doe. **2** A title of respect used in addressing a man without using his name.

sire \'sīr\ *n.* **1** A title of respect formerly used in the same way as *sir*, but now used only in addressing a king. **2** A father; a male ancestor. **3** The male parent of an animal. — *v.;* **sired**; **sir·ing.** To father; as, a colt *sired* by a very famous horse.

si·ren \'sī-rən\ *n.* **1** A woman in ancient Greek and Roman stories thought of as being able to lure a sailor and his ship to destruction on a rock or reef by her sweet singing. **2** Someone or something charming but dangerous. **3** A whistle or horn used for sounding signals, especially of warning; as, an air-raid *siren*. **4** One of a group of eel-shaped amphibians having small forelimbs and permanent external gills as well as lungs. **5** Any of a group of aquatic mammals, as the dugong or manatee.

sir·loin \'sər-ˌlȯin\ *n.* [From medieval French *surlonge* meaning literally "above the loin".] A cut of beef taken from the part just in front of the rump.

si·roc·co \sə-'räk-ˌō\ *n.; pl.* **si·roc·cos. 1** A hot dust-laden wind that blows across the Mediterranean Sea from the Libyan deserts. **2** A warm, moist, oppressive, southeast wind affecting that area. **3** Any hot or warm wind of cyclonic origin.

sir·rah \'sir-ə\ *n. Archaic.* A term of address — used chiefly to express contempt, scorn, or anger.

sirup. Variant of *syrup*.

sis·al \'sīs-l, 'sīz-l\ *n.* **1** Also **sisal hemp.** A long, strong white fiber obtained from a West Indian agave plant and used to make ropes and twine. **2** The plant that yields this fiber.

sis·sy \'sis-ē\ *n.; pl.* **sis·sies.** A weak, soft, or cowardly boy or man.

sis·ter \'sist-r\ *n.* **1** A girl or woman related to a person by having the same parents. **2** A member of a religious society of women. **3** One of the same kind regarded as nearly related; as, to think of botany as the *sister* of zoology. **4** *British.* A senior nurse, as in a hospital.

sis·ter·hood \'sist-r-ˌhu̇d\ *n.* **1** The state or relation of being a sister. **2** A community or society of sisters; especially, a society of women religious. **3** A group of things with common characteristics.

sis·ter-in-law \'sist-r-ən-ˌlȯ\ *n.; pl.* **sis·ters-in-law. 1** The sister of one's husband or wife. **2** The wife of one's brother.

sis·ter·ly \'sist-r-lē\ *adj.* Like or becoming a sister; as, *sisterly* affection.

sit \'sit\ *v.;* **sat** \'sat\; **sit·ting. 1** To rest upon the buttocks; to occupy a seat; as, to *sit* in a chair. **2** To perch or roost with the body drawn up close, as an owl on a branch; to squat. **3** To occupy a seat as a member; as, to *sit* in Congress. **4** To hold a session. **5** To cover and warm eggs for hatching. **6** To pose for a certain purpose; as, to *sit* for a portrait. **7** To be located; to lie; to rest. The vase *sits* on the table. **8** To seat or cause to be seated; as, to *sit* oneself down. **9** To baby-sit.

sit-down \'sit-ˌdau̇n\ *n.* or **sit-down strike.** A strike in which the workers stop work and refuse to leave their places of employment.

site \'sīt\ *n.* The location of something, as a town, a monument, a camp, or a significant event; as, the *site* of a famous battle; a good camp *site*.

sit·ter \'sit-r\ *n.* **1** One that sits. **2** A baby sitter.

sit·ting \'sit-ing\ *n.* **1** The act or position of a person who sits, as for a portrait; the time occupied in such a sitting. **2** A brooding over, or the time of brooding over, eggs. **3** The eggs a fowl sits on for one hatching. **4** A session; as, the first *sitting* of a society. — *adj.* **1** That sits; as, a *sitting* duck. **2** For sitting; as, a *sitting* position; a *sitting* room.

sit·u·at·ed \'sich-ə-ˌwāt-əd\ *adj.* **1** Located; as, a house *situated* on a hill. **2** Placed; fixed; as, to be nicely *situated* financially.

sit·u·a·tion \ˌsich-ə-'wāsh-n\ *n.* **1** A place; a location; as, a good *situation* for a camp. **2** Position in regard to job, money, or personal relationships. **3** A combination of circumstances; a state of affairs; as, an embarrassing *situation*. **4** A job.

six \'siks\ *adj.* One more than five. — *n.* **1** The sum of one and five; six units or objects. **2** The figure standing for six units, as 6 or VI.

six·pence \'siks-pən(t)s\ *n.* An English silver coin worth half a shilling.

six-shoot·er \'sik(s)-'shüt-r\ *n.* A revolver that can be fired six times without reloading.

six·teen \'siks-'tēn\ *adj.* Six and ten; one more than fifteen. — *n.* **1** The sum of six and ten; sixteen units or objects. **2** The figure standing for sixteen units, as 16 or XVI.

six·teenth \'siks-'tēn(t)th\ *adj.* Next after the fifteenth. — *n.; pl.* **six·teenths** \-'tēn(t)s, -'tēn(t)ths\ One of sixteen equal parts.

sixth \'siks(t)th, 'sikst\ *adj.* Next after the fifth. — *n.* One of six equal parts.

six·ti·eth \'siks-tē-əth\ *adj.* Next after the fifty-ninth. — *n.* One of sixty equal parts.

six·ty \'siks-tē\ *adj.* Six times ten; one more than fifty-nine. — *n.; pl.* **six·ties. 1** The sum of six tens; sixty units or objects. **2** The figure standing for sixty units, as 60 or LX.

siz·a·ble or **size·a·ble** \'sī-zəb-l\ *adj.* Somewhat large; as, a *sizable* increase in pay. — **siz·a·bly** or **size·a·bly** \-zə-blē\ *adv.*

size \\'sīz\\ *n.* **1** Amount of space occupied; bulk. **2** The measurements of a thing; dimensions; as, the *size* of a book. **3** One of a set of standard measurements in which many manufactured articles are made; as, to wear *size* six in gloves. **4** True state of affairs. That's about the *size* of it. — *v.;* **sized**; **siz·ing**. **1** To adjust, grade, or classify according to size; as, to *size* eggs. **2** To size up. — **size up**. To form an opinion or estimate of.

size \\'sīz\\ *n.* A gluey material, as a preparation of glue, flour, or shellac, used as a filler, stiffener, or adhesive. — *v.;* **sized**; **siz·ing**. To apply size to.

siz·zle \\'siz-l\\ *v.;* **siz·zled**; **siz·zling** \\-l(-)ing\\. To make a hissing or sputtering sound while frying or broiling. — *n.* A sizzling. — **siz·zler** \\-l(-)ər\\ *n.*

skate \\'skāt\\ *n.* Any of numerous rays with broadly developed fins.

skate \\'skāt\\ *n.* **1** A metal runner fitting the sole of the shoe or a fixed combination of shoe and metal runner, used for gliding swiftly over ice. **2** A roller skate. — *v.;* **skat·ed**; **skat·ing**. To glide on skates; to slide or move as if on skates. — **skat·er** \\'skāt-r\\ *n.*

ice skate

skein \\'skān\\ *n.* A loose coil of yarn or thread.

skel·e·tal \\'skel-ət-l\\ *adj.* Of or relating to a skeleton; of the nature of a skeleton.

skel·e·ton \\'skel-ət-n\\ *n.* **1** The bony framework of a vertebrate, as a man, a bird, or a fish. **2** A framework; as, the steel *skeleton* of a building.

skeleton key. A key made to open many locks.

skep·tic or **scep·tic** \\'skep-tik\\ *n.* A person slow to believe or ready to question; a doubter.

skep·ti·cal or **scep·ti·cal** \\'skep-tik-l\\ *adj.* Inclined to doubt; having or showing doubt. — **skep·ti·cal·ly** or **scep·ti·cal·ly** \\-tik-l(-)e\\ *adv.*

skep·ti·cism or **scep·ti·cism** \\'skep-tə-ˌsiz-m\\ *n.* The attitude of a skeptic; a state of doubt.

sketch \\'skech\\ *n.* **1** An outline or drawing showing the main features of something to be written, painted, or built. **2** A descriptive short story or a little play. — *v.* **1** To make or draw a sketch of. **2** To present in outline. — **sketch·er** \\-r\\ *n.*

sketchy \\'skech-ē\\ *adj.;* **sketch·i·er**; **sketch·i·est**. Like a sketch; roughly outlined; vague.

skew \\'skyü\\ *v.* To make or do on a slant; to turn or place at an angle. — *adj.* Slanting; distorted. — *n.* A deviation from a straight line; a slant.

skew·er \\'skyü-ər, 'skyu̇r\\ *n.* A pin for fastening meat to a spit or holding it together while cooking. — *v.* To pierce or hold with or as if with a skewer.

ski \\'skē\\ *n.; pl.* **skis** \\'skēz\\ or **ski** \\'skē\\. [From Norwegian, there derived from Old Norse *skith* meaning literally "piece of wood".] One of a pair of strips of wood, metal, or plastic fastened one to each foot and used in gliding over snow. — *v.;* **skied** \\'skēd\\ **ski·ing** \\'skē-ing\\. To glide on skis. — **ski·er** \\'skē-ər\\ *n.*

skid \\'skid\\ *n.* **1** A log or plank for supporting something above the ground; as, to put a boat on *skids*. **2** One of the logs, planks, or rails, along which something heavy is rolled or pushed. **3** Any device that slows up or retards movement, as one placed under a carriage wheel; a drag. **4** A runner used as part of the landing gear of an airplane. **5** The act of skidding; a slide. — *v.;* **skid·ded**; **skid·ding**. **1** To roll or slide on skids. **2** To slide sideways, as a car on an icy road.

skiff \\'skif\\ *n.* **1** A small, light rowboat. **2** A sailboat light enough to be rowed.

skill \\'skil\\ *n.* **1** Ability that comes from training or practice; as, *skill* in building campfires. **2** A particular art or science; a developed or acquired ability; as, the *skills* of swimming and diving.

skilled \\'skild\\ *adj.* **1** Having skill; expert; as, a *skilled* mason. **2** Requiring skill; as, a *skilled* trade.

skil·let \\'skil-ət\\ *n.* A frying pan; a spider.

skillet

skill·ful or **skil·ful** \\'skilf-l\\ *adj.* Having or showing skill; expert; as, a *skillful* craftsman; a *skillful* piece of work.
— The word *expert* is a synonym of *skillful: skillful* usually refers to highly developed dexterity and speed in executing or performing some task, especially one requiring training and muscular control; *expert* is likely to indicate exceptional and extraordinary ability and proficiency in a particular field of activity or learning.

skill·ful·ly or **skil·ful·ly** \\'skilf-l-ē\\ *adv.* In a skillful manner.

skim \\'skim\\ *v.;* **skimmed**; **skim·ming**. **1** To remove the top part of a liquid, often a film or scum; as, to *skim* the cream off milk. **2** To read through rapidly to learn the main ideas or to find something. **3** To pass swiftly or lightly over; to glide. Gulls *skim* the water. **4** To throw a stone so that it skips along the surface of the water. — *n.* The action of skimming. — *adj.* Skimmed, as milk.

skim·mer \\'skim-r\\ *n.* **1** One that skims. **2** A small strainer with a long handle, used in skimming liquids. **3** Any of several long-winged sea birds, that fly with the lower mandible in the water so as to skim out small sea animals.

skim milk. Milk with the cream removed.

skimp \\'skimp\\ *v.* **1** To scrimp; to use something very sparingly; as, to *skimp* and save. **2** To do or make carelessly or inefficiently; to scamp.

skimpy \\'skimp-ē\\ *adj.;* **skimp·i·er**; **skimp·i·est**. **1** Scanty. **2** Stingy; miserly.

skin \\'skin\\ *n.* **1** The outer usually tough and flexible layer of an animal body. **2** A person's life; as, to save one's *skin*. **3** An outer layer of a plant or plant part, as of a fruit. **4** Something that is like skin or is made of skin; as, the *skin* of a drum. **5** A container made of skin, used for liquids. — *v.;* **skinned**; **skin·ning**. **1** To remove or lose the skin from; to peel; as, to *skin* one's knee. **2** *Slang.* To cheat; to fleece. — **skin·ner** \\'skin-r\\ *n.*

skin diving. The sport of submerging usually without a diving helmet but with a breathing device.

skin·flint \\'skin-ˌflint\\ *n.* A person who is very hard and grasping in money matters.

skin·ny \'skin-ē\ *adj.;* **skin·ni·er; skin·ni·est. 1** Like skin; as, a *skinny* tissue. **2** Very thin; lean.

skip \'skip\ *v.;* **skipped; skip·ping. 1** To move lightly with leaps and bounds; especially, to move with a skip or skips; as, to *skip* down the street. **2** To omit, as parts in reading, studying, or other activities; as, to read a story without *skipping;* to *skip* lunch. **3** To run away suddenly; as, to *skip* out of town. **4** To leap lightly over. **5** To skim; as, to *skip* stones. **6** To pass to the grade beyond the next higher; as, to *skip* third grade. — *n.* **1** The action of skipping. **2** An omission. **3** A leap; a light bound or spring; a gait, as of children, marked by alternating hops and steps.

skip·per \'skip-r\ *n.* The captain of a fishing or small trading boat; the master of any boat.

skip·per \'skip-r\ *n.* **1** One that skips. **2** A small stout-bodied butterfly that has a short swift flight. **3** Any of various skipping insects.

skirl \'skirl, 'skərl\ *v. Scottish.* To sound shrilly, as a bagpipe. — *n. Scottish.* A shrill sound.

skir·mish \'skər-mish\ *n.* **1** A minor fight between small bodies of troops. **2** Any slight contest. — *v.* To engage in a skirmish. — **skir·mish·er** \-r\ *n.*

skirt \'skərt\ *n.* **1** A woman's garment or the part of a garment that hangs below the waist; as, the *skirt* of a dress. **2** [in the plural] The outer edge; the border; the outskirts. **3** A piece hanging down like a skirt; as, the *skirts* of a saddle. **4** *Slang.* A girl or a woman. — *v.* To go around the edge of.

skit \'skit\ *n.* A brief sketch usually in play form.

skit·ter \'skit-r\ *v.* To pass or glide lightly or hurriedly; to skip along a surface.

skit·tish \'skit-ish\ *adj.* **1** Lively in nature or in action; frivolous. **2** Easily frightened — used chiefly of horses. **3** Coy; shy. — **skit·tish·ly,** *adv.*

skit·tles \'skit-lz\ *n. pl.* A form of ninepins that sometimes uses wooden disks instead of balls.

skul·dug·gery \ˌskəl-'dəg-r(-)ē\ *n.* Trickery; plotting; dishonesty.

skulk \'skəlk\ *v.* To hide or move in a sneaking way. — For synonyms see *lurk.* — **skulk·er** \-r\ *n.*

skull \'skəl\ *n.* **1** The bony framework of the head. **2** The head.

skull·cap \'skəl-ˌkap\ *n.* A cap fitting the top of the head; especially, a brimless cap worn indoors.

skunk \'skəngk\ *n.* **1** A North American animal, related to the weasels and minks, that can eject a fluid having an extremely offensive odor. **2** A contemptible person. — *v. Slang.* To defeat in a game in such a way that the opponent fails to score.

skunk cabbage. An unpleasant-smelling broad-leaved marsh herb.

sky \'skī\ *n.; pl.* **skies. 1** The upper air; the vast arch or dome which seems to spread over the earth. **2** Heaven; as, the angels in the *sky.* **3** Weather; climate. The weatherman predicts sunny *skies* for tomorrow. — **sky·ey** \'skī-ē\ *adj.*

sky blue. The color of the midsummer sky at noon on a clear day.

sky·lark \'skī-ˌlärk, -ˌlȧrk\ *n.* The common Old World lark, which sings as it rises in almost perpendicular flight. — *v.* To play wild pranks.

sky·light \'skī-ˌlīt\ *n.* A window or group of windows in a roof or ceiling.

skylight

sky·line \'skī-ˌlīn\ *n.* **1** The line where earth and sky, or water and sky, seem to meet; the horizon. **2** An outline against the sky; as, the *skyline* of a mountain range.

sky·rock·et \'skī-ˌräk-ət\ *n.* A firework that flies rapidly upward, usually leaving a fiery trail, and explodes high in the air. — *v.* To rise like a skyrocket. Prices *skyrocketed* during the war.

sky·sail \'skī-ˌsāl, 'skīs-l\ *n.* The sail above the royal on a square-rigged boat.

sky·scrap·er \'skī-ˌskrāp-r\ *n.* A very tall building.

sky·ward \'skī-wərd\ *adj.* or *adv.* Toward the sky.

sky·wards \'skī-wərdz\ *adv.* Skyward.

sky·way \'skī-ˌwā\ *n.* A charted route for aircraft.

sky·writ·ing \'skī-ˌrīt-ing\ *n.* The formation of words or tracery in the sky by means of vapor released from an airplane. — **sky·writ·er** \-r\ *n.*

slab \'slab\ *n.* **1** A flat thick piece or slice of anything; as, a stone *slab;* a *slab* of bread. **2** The outside piece, with or without bark, cut from a log.

slack \'slak\ *adj.* **1** Careless or neglectful. **2** Lacking vitality; slow; sluggish; as, a *slack* pace. **3** Not tight, taut, or firm; loose; as, a *slack* rope. **4** Lacking in firmness of character. **5** Showing little activity; not busy; as, a *slack* season. — *v.* To make or become looser, slower, or less energetic; to slacken. — *n.* **1** A loose-hanging part, as of a rope or sail. **2** A dull season in business. **3** [in the plural] Long loose trousers for informal wear. — *adv.* Slackly.

slack·en \'slak-n\ *v.;* **slack·ened; slack·en·ing** \-n(-)ing\. **1** To make slower or less energetic; to slow up or slow down; as, to *slacken* one's speed; to *slacken* one's efforts. **2** To make less taut.

slack·er \'slak-r\ *n.* One who shirks work or evades an obligation, especially military service.

slack·ly \'slak-lē\ *adv.* In a slack manner; loosely.

slag \'slag\ *n.* **1** Waste left after the melting of ores and the separation of the metal from them. **2** Volcanic lava resembling cinders. — **slag·gy,** *adj.*

slain. Past part. of *slay.*

slake \'slāk; *when used of lime, often* 'slak\ *v.;* **slaked; slak·ing. 1** To slacken. **2** *Archaic.* To relieve, as pain. **3** To quench, as thirst. **4** To cause solid lime to crumble by treatment with water or exposure to air. **5** To become slaked.

slam \'slam\ *n.* In a card game such as bridge, the winning of every trick in a deal (**grand slam**) or of all but one (**little slam** or **small slam**).

slam \'slam\ *v.;* **slammed; slam·ming. 1** To shut noisily and forcibly; to close with a bang. **2** To put or place forcibly or hurriedly; as, to *slam* down the money. **3** To criticize severely. — *n.* **1** A heavy impact; a banging noise. **2** A severe criticism.

slan·der \'sland-r\ *n.* **1** A statement tending to injure the reputation of another and deliberately made with this intention. **2** The crime of hurting a person's reputation by making false statements about him in public. — *v.;* **slan·dered**; **slan·der·ing** \-r(-)ing\. To utter slander against. — **slan·der·er** \-r-r\ *n.* — **slan·der·ous** \-r(-)əs\ *adj.*

slang \'slang\ *n.* **1** The special language of a particular class of persons or of a particular trade, occupation, or pursuit; as, thieves' *slang;* baseball *slang.* **2** Words and expressions used especially in very informal speaking or writing, usually short-lived, and consisting mostly of coined words, shortened words, and words or phrases used in exaggerated or humorous senses.

slangy \'slang-ē\ *adj.;* **slang·i·er**; **slang·i·est.** **1** Containing slang or much slang; as, *slangy* speech. **2** Addicted to the use of slang.

slant \'slant\ *adj.* Not level or erect in line; inclined; sloping; slanted; as, *slant* rays of light; *slant* lines. — *n.* **1** A slanting direction, line, or plane; a slope. The hill has a sharp *slant.* **2** A way of looking at something; an attitude, opinion, or view; as, a new *slant* on a problem. — *v.* To lie or move along a line that is not straight up and down or straight across; to slope. The roof *slants.*

slant·ways \'slant-ˌwāz\ *adv.* Slantwise.

slant·wise \'slant-ˌwīz\ *adv.* So as to slant; obliquely. — *adj.* Slanting; oblique.

slap \'slap\ *n.* A blow given with something flat, as with the open hand. — *adv.* Directly and suddenly; as, to come *slap* up against a wall. — *v.;* **slapped**; **slap·ping.** **1** To give a slap or slaps to, often as a punishment or a rebuff. **2** To put, place, or throw with careless haste or with the force or the sound of slapping; as, to *slap* one's hat on.

slap·dash \'slap-ˌdash\ *adv.* or *adj.* Done with, or characterized by, careless haste or force.

slap·jack \'slap-ˌjak\ *n.* **1** A griddlecake; a flapjack. **2** A child's card game.

slap·stick \'slap-ˌstik\ *n.* **1** A device made of two flat sticks fastened so as to make a loud noise when used to strike a person. **2** Use of this device or similar devices on the stage to produce a comic effect; comedy characterized by such use. — *adj.* Using slapstick; as, *slapstick* comedy.

slash \'slash\ *v.* **1** To cut by sweeping and aimless blows; to gash. **2** To whip or strike with or as if with a cane. **3** To criticize without mercy. **4** To cut slits in, as a skirt, to reveal a color beneath. **5** To cut down; to reduce; as, to *slash* prices. — *n.* **1** The act of slashing. **2** A long cut or slit. **3** A reduction, as in prices.

slat \'slat\ *n.* A thin narrow bar of wood, plastic, or metal; as, the *slats* of a blind. — **slat·ted**, *adj.*

slate \'slāt\ *n.* **1** A fine-grained, usually blue-gray rock which splits into thin layers or plates, used for roofing and blackboards. **2** A framed piece of slate used to write on. **3** Something written on or as if on a slate, as a list of candidates for office, or a record of a person's deeds; as, to read the *slate* of nominees; to have a clean *slate.* **4** The dark bluish gray color of slate. — *v.;* **slat·ed**; **slat·ing.** **1** To cover with shingles of slate, as a roof. **2** To register on or as if on a slate; as, a matter *slated* to come up next week. — **slaty** \'slāt-ē\ *adj.*

slat·tern \'slat-rn\ *n.* An untidy, slovenly woman. — **slat·tern·ly**, *adj.* or *adv.*

slaugh·ter \'slȯt-r\ *n.* **1** The butchering of animals for food. **2** Destruction of many lives, as in war. — *v.* To butcher; to massacre. — For synonyms see *kill.* — **slaugh·ter·er** \-r-r\ *n.*

slaugh·ter·house \'slȯt-r-ˌhau̇s\ *n.; pl.* **slaugh·ter·hous·es** \-ˌhau̇-zəz\. A building where animals are butchered for food.

Slav \'släv, 'slav, 'slȧv\ *n.* A person speaking a Slavic language as his native tongue or coming from a region where Slavic languages are spoken.

slave \'slāv\ *n.* **1** A person who is owned by another and can be sold at his master's will. **2** One who is like a slave in not being his own master; as, to be a *slave* to alcohol. **3** A drudge. — *v.;* **slaved**; **slav·ing.** To work as hard as a slave; to drudge.

slave·hold·er \'slāv-ˌhōld-r\ *n.* One who owns slaves. — **slave·hold·ing** \-ˌhōl-ding\ *adj.* or *n.*

slav·er \'slav-r, 'slāv-r\ *v.;* **slav·ered**; **slav·er·ing** \-r(-)ing\. To drool; to slobber. — *n.* Saliva drooling from the mouth; drivel.

slav·er \'slāv-r\ *n.* **1** A ship that carries people to be sold into slavery. **2** A person trading in slaves.

slav·ery \'slāv-r(-)ē\ *n.* **1** Long-continued and tiring labor; drudgery. **2** The state of being a slave; bondage. **3** The custom of owning slaves.

Slav·ic \'slav-ik, 'släv-, 'slȧv-\ *adj.* Of or relating to the principal peoples and languages of Bulgaria, Czechoslovakia, Poland, Russia, and Yugoslavia. — *n.* The group of related Slavic languages.

slav·ish \'slā-vish\ *adj.* **1** Of or characteristic of slaves; servile. **2** Showing lack of freedom or independence; as, *slavish* obedience. — **slav·ish·ly**, *adv.*

slaw \'slȯ\ *n.* Sliced cabbage served as a salad.

slay \'slā\ *v.;* **slew** \'slü\; **slain** \'slān\; **slay·ing.** To kill. — **slay·er** \'slā-ər\ *n.*

slea·zy \'slē-zē, 'slā-\ *adj.;* **slea·zi·er**; **slea·zi·est.** Not firmly or closely woven; flimsy.

sled \'sled\ *n.* **1** A vehicle on runners for carrying goods, especially over snow. **2** A small vehicle on runners for sliding on snow and ice. — *v.;* **sled·ded**; **sled·ding.** To ride or carry on a sled.

sledge \'slej\ *n.* Also **sledge hammer.** A large, heavy hammer, usually used with both hands.

sledge \'slej\ *n.* A strong, heavy vehicle with or without runners used for carrying heavy loads. — *v.;* **sledged**; **sledg·ing.** To go or carry by sledge.

sleek \'slēk\ *v.* To make bright and smooth by rubbing, polishing, or brushing; to freshen and tidy up; as, to *sleek* a horse's coat. — *adj.* Smooth; glossy; as, *sleek* hair. — **sleek·ly**, *adv.*

sleep \'slēp\ *n.* **1** The state of not being awake; slumber; as, a night's *sleep.* **2** A condition of inactivity like sleep; as, the *sleep* of hibernating animals. **3** Death. — *v.;* **slept** \'slept\; **sleep·ing** **1** To take rest in sleep; to be or lie asleep. **2** To be inactive, numb, or quiet as if asleep. **3** To provide sleeping space for; as, a boat that *sleeps* fourteen.

sleep·er \'slēp-r\ *n.* **1** A sleeping person. **2** Also **sleep·ing car** \'slēp-ing\. A railway coach with berths for night travel. **3** A beam or timber used to support something on or near the ground level. **4** Anything unpromising and long unnoticed that suddenly attains value or importance.

sleep·ing bag \'slēp-ing\. A bag, usually waterproof and warmly padded, to sleep in outdoors.

sleeping sickness. **1** A serious disease prevalent in parts of Africa, transmitted by the bite of the tsetse fly. **2** Either of two forms of an insect-transmitted virus disease existing in the United States and affecting horses or people.

sleep·less \'slēp-ləs\ *adj.* **1** Without sleep; as, a *sleepless* night. **2** Alert. — **sleep·less·ly,** *adv.*

sleep·walk·er \'slēp-ˌwȯk-r\ *n.* A person who walks in his sleep. — **sleep·walk·ing** \-ing\ *n.*

sleepy \'slēp-ē\ *adj.;* **sleep·i·er**; **sleep·i·est.** **1** Ready to fall asleep; drowsy. **2** Inactive and quiet; as, a *sleepy* village. — **sleep·i·ly** \-l-ē\ *adv.*

sleet \'slēt\ *n.* **1** Partly frozen rain; a mixture of rain and snow. **2** The icy coating formed by freezing rain. — *v.* To shower sleet. — **sleety,** *adj.*

sleeve \'slēv\ *n.* **1** The part of a garment covering the arm. **2** Something like a sleeve in shape or use; a tubular part fitting over another part.

sleigh \'slā\ *n.* A vehicle on runners for use on snow or ice. — *v.* To drive or travel in a sleigh.

sleight \'slīt\ *n.* **1** An artifice; a trick. **2** Skill.

sleight of hand \'slīt ə(v) 'hand\. A trick requiring skillful use of the hands; the art of deceiving an audience by such tricks.

slen·der \'slend-r\ *adj.* **1** Thin; slim. **2** Not strong or great; weak; small; feeble; as, a *slender* hope. **3** Insufficient; meager; as, a *slender* income. — **slen·der·ly,** *adv.*

slept. Past tense and past part. of *sleep.*

sleuth \'slüth\ *n.* **1** Also **sleuth·hound** \-ˌhau̇nd\. A hound that tracks by scent. **2** A detective.

slew \'slü\ *v.* To turn or twist; to slue. — *n.* A twisting or turning.

slew or **slue** \'slü\ *n.* A large number; a lot; as, a whole *slew* of people.

slew \'slü\. Past tense of *slay.*

slice \'slīs\ *n.* **1** A thin flat piece cut off from something; as, a *slice* of bread; a *slice* of meat. **2** A knife with a wedge-shaped blade, as for serving fish. — *v.;* **sliced**; **slic·ing.** **1** To cut into slices; as, to *slice* a loaf of bread. **2** To cut into and across with a knife; as, to *slice* open a squash. **3** To remove a slice from; to cut as a slice; as, to *slice* off a piece of meat. — **slic·er** \'slīs-r\ *n.*

slick \'slik\ *v.* To make sleek or smooth; as, to *slick* down one's hair. — *adj.* **1** Sleek. **2** Clever; tricky; as, a *slick* manner. **3** Slippery, as with oil or grease; as, a *slick* road. — *n.* **1** A smooth surface of water, as caused by a film of oil. **2** Also **slick paper.** A magazine printed on heavy paper with a glossy finish. — *adv.* In a slick manner.

slick·er \'slik-r\ *n.* **1** A long, loose, unfitted raincoat, often of oilskin or plastic. **2** A sly, clever, tricky person; as, a city *slicker.*

slide \'slīd\ *v.;* **slid** \'slid\; **slid** \'slid\ or **slid·den** \'slid-n\; **slid·ing** \'slīd-ing\. **1** To move or cause to move smoothly over a surface; to glide; to slip; as, to *slide* a dish across the table. The pen *slides* smoothly over the paper. **2** To slip and fall by a loss of footing, balance, or support. The package *slid* from the woman's hands. **3** To move with great smoothness and ease. The car *slid* rapidly up the hill. **4** To pass so as not to be noticed; to slip by, out, or in; as, to *slide* into one's seat. — *n.* **1** The act or motion of sliding. **2** A loosened mass that slides; as, a rock *slide.* **3** A surface down which a person or thing slides. **4** Something that operates or adjusts by sliding, as a cover for an opening. **5** A transparent picture that can be thrown on a screen by means of a projecting device (**slide projector**). **6** A glass plate on which is placed an object to be examined under a microscope.

slide fastener. A fastener consisting of two rows of metal or plastic teeth on strips of tape for binding to the edges of an opening, as of a garment, and having a sliding piece that closes the opening by drawing the teeth into interlocking position.

slide rule. An instrument consisting of a ruler with a sliding scale along its middle, used for mathematical calculations.

slier. A comparative of *sly.*

sliest. A superlative of *sly.*

slight \'slīt\ *adj.* **1** Slender; slim; as, a trim, *slight* figure. **2** Frail. **3** Small, especially in amount; as, a *slight* odor. **4** Not worth noticing; trivial; as, a *slight* wound. — *v.* To treat as slight, or unimportant; to neglect; to ignore impolitely. — For synonyms see *neglect.* — *n.* A slighting or a being slighted; a snub. — **slight·ing·ly,** *adv.*

slight·ly \'slīt-lē\ *adv.* **1** In a slight manner; lightly; not sturdily; as, *slightly* built. **2** To a slight degree; somewhat; as, to know a person only *slightly.*

slily. Variant of *slyly.*

slim \'slim\ *adj.;* **slim·mer**; **slim·mest.** **1** Slender; thin; slight; as, a *slim* body. **2** Scanty; slight; as, a *slim* attendance; a *slim* chance. — **slim·ly,** *adv.*

slime \'slīm\ *n.* **1** Soft slippery mud; mire. **2** Any moist slippery substance, as that on the skins of slugs, land snails, and some fishes.

slimy \'slī-mē\ *adj.;* **slim·i·er**; **slim·i·est.** Having the feel or appearance of, or covered with slime.

sling \'sling\ *n.* **1** A short strap with a string attached at each end, used for hurling stones and other missiles. **2** A slingshot. — *v.;* **slung** \'sləng\; **sling·ing** \'sling-ing\. **1** To hurl with a sling; as, to *sling* stones. **2** To fling or toss; to throw casually.

sling \'sling\ *n.* A device, as a rope or chain, by which something is supported, lifted, or carried; as, a *sling* on a rifle; to have one's arm in a *sling.* — *v.;* **slung** \'sləng\; **sling·ing** \'sling-ing\. **1** To put in a sling; to carry or suspend by means of a sling. **2** To be suspended from; as, a knapsack worn *slung* over the shoulder; a hammock *slung* from a tree; a ship's lifeboat *slung* from davits.

sling·shot \'sling-ˌshät\ *n.* A forked stick with an elastic band attached for shooting small stones.

slink \'slingk\ *v.;* **slunk** \'sləngk\; **slink·ing.** To move or go stealthily; to creep along, as in fear.

slip \'slip\ *v.;* **slipped; slip·ping. 1** To go or pass without attracting attention; as, to *slip* out of a room. **2** To let pass or escape unnoticed; as, to *slip* a stitch in knitting. **3** To escape, as from one's mouth or memory; as, a remark that just *slipped* out; a name that *slips* one's mind. **4** To slide along smoothly; to glide. **5** To slide from its proper place or from one's grasp. The knife *slipped.* **6** To slide so as to fall or lose balance; as, to *slip* on a banana peel. **7** To cause to slide; to put, pass, insert easily or quickly; as, to *slip* into a dress; to *slip* one's foot into a shoe. **8** To fall into error. There are times when one's judgment *slips.* — **slip up.** To make a mistake or a failure. — *n.* **1** A berth for a ship between two piers. **2** The act of slipping; as, a *slip* on the ice. **3** An eluding; a getting away; as, to give one's pursuers the *slip.* **4** A small mistake; a blunder; as, a *slip* of the pen. **5** A slight wrongdoing; as, to excuse a *slip.* **6** A covering that slips on or off easily; as, a pillow *slip.* **7** A one-piece garment of dress length worn as underwear by women.

slip \'slip\ *n.* **1** A small shoot or twig cut for grafting or planting. **2** A young, slender person; as, a *slip* of a girl. **3** A long narrow strip, as of paper. **4** A piece of paper used for a memorandum or note. — *v.;* **slipped; slip·ping.** To take slips or cuttings from a plant; as, to *slip* a geranium.

slip·knot \'slip-ˌnät\ *n.* A knot made by tying the end of a line around the line itself to form a loop, so that the size of the loop may be changed by sliding the knot along the line.

slipknot

slip·per \'slip-r\ *n.* A light, low shoe, without laces, which is easily slipped on or off.

slip·pered \'slip-rd\ *adj.* Wearing slippers.

slip·pery \'slip-r(-)ē\ *adj.;* **slip·per·i·er; slip·per·i·est. 1** Having a surface smooth enough to cause one to slide or lose one's hold; as, a *slippery* floor. **2** Not worthy of trust; tricky; unreliable.

slip·shod \'slip-'shäd\ *adj.* Very careless; slovenly.

slit \'slit\ *v.;* **slit; slit·ting. 1** To make a slit in; to slash; to cut. **2** To cut off; to cut away; to sever. — *n.* **1** A long, narrow cut. **2** A long, narrow opening, as in a wall. — **slit·ter** \'slit-r\ *n.*

slith·er \'slith-r\ *v.;* **slith·ered; slith·er·ing** \-r(-)ing\. **1** To slide, as down a gravelly slope. **2** To move as if slipping or sliding, as a snake.

sliv·er \'sliv-r; *sense 2 is usually* 'slīv-r\ *n.* **1** A long slender piece cut or torn off; a splinter. **2** A strand of raw cotton or other fiber as it comes from the combing machine. — *v.;* **sliv·ered; sliv·er·ing** \-r(-)ing\. To split or break into slivers.

slob \'släb\ *n.* A dull, slovenly, or clumsy person.

slob·ber \'släb-r\ *v.;* **slob·bered; slob·ber·ing** \-r(-)ing\. **1** To let saliva or liquid dribble from the mouth, as a young child; to drool. **2** To show feeling to excess; to gush. — *n.* **1** Dripping saliva. **2** Silly, excessive show of feeling. — **slob·bery** \-r(-)ē\ *adj.*

sloe \'slō\ *n.* The tart bluish black fruit of the blackthorn, used to flavor gin.

slog \'släg\ *v.;* **slogged; slog·ging. 1** To hit heavily. **2** To plod doggedly on, as through mud.

slo·gan \'slōg-n\ *n.* [From Scottish Celtic *sluaghghairm* meaning literally "army yell".] **1** A war cry; a word or phrase that calls to battle. **2** A word or phrase used by a party, a group, or a business to attract attention.

sloop \'slüp\ *n.* A sailing boat with one mast and a fore-and-aft mainsail and jib.

slop \'släp\ *n.* **1** Spilled liquid. **2** Kitchen refuse or garbage. **3** Dirty waste water. **4** Thin, tasteless drink or liquid food. — *v.;* **slopped; slop·ping. 1** To spill over; as, to *slop* milk from a glass. **2** To feed with slop; as, to *slop* the pigs.

sloop

slope \'slōp\ *v.;* **sloped; slop·ing.** To take a slanting direction; to slant; to incline. — *n.* **1** A slanting surface, as a hillside. **2** A slanting position or direction, or the amount of such slant. The roof has a *slope* of 15 feet. **3** The part of a continent draining its waters into a particular ocean; as, the Pacific *slope.*

slop·py \'släp-ē\ *adj.;* **slop·pi·er; slop·pi·est. 1** Wet so as to spatter easily; wet as with standing water, slush, or slop. **2** Careless; slovenly.

slosh \'släsh\ *v.* To move through with splashing.

slot \'slät\ *n.* A narrow opening; as, a mail *slot.* — *v.;* **slot·ted; slot·ting.** To cut a slot in.

sloth \'slȯth, 'slōth\ *n.* **1** Laziness. **2** Any of several slow-moving mammals of Central and South America related to the armadillos, living in trees and eating leaves, shoots, and fruits.

sloth·ful \'slȯth-fəl, 'slōth-\ *adj.* Lazy; sluggish; indolent. — **sloth·ful·ly** \-fə-lē\ *adv.*

slouch \'slau̇ch\ *n.* **1** A lazy slovenly fellow; a loafer. **2** A drooping of the head and body. **3** A droop, as of a hat brim. — *v.* To move, walk, or sit with a slouch. — **slouchy,** *adj.*

slough \'slau̇, 'slü\ *n.* **1** A marshy or muddy place; a swamp. **2** A discouraged or dejected state.

slough \'sləf\ *n.* **1** The outer skin, as shed by a snake. **2** Something that may be cast off, as a bad habit. **3** The dead part that separates from living tissues, as in a healing wound. — *v.* **1** To be shed or cast off, as diseased tissue. **2** To shed or cast off, as a habit or a condition. **3** To fall off; to decline. Business *sloughs* off periodically. **4** To separate in the form of dead matter from living tissue.

Slo·vak \'slō-ˌväk, -ˌvak, -ˌvȧk\ *adj.* Of or relating to the Slovaks. — *n.* **1** One of a northern Slavic people of central Czechoslovakia. **2** The language of the Slovaks. — **Slo·vak·i·an** \slō-'väk-ē-ən, -'vak-, -'vȧk-\ *adj.* or *n.*

slov·en \'sləv-n\ *n.* A person who is habitually untidy, especially in dress; a slipshod person.

slov·en·ly \'sləv-n-lē\ *adj.;* **slov·en·li·er; slov·en·li·est. 1** Personally untidy; careless; slipshod. **2** Characteristic of a sloven. — *adv.* In a slovenly manner.

slow \'slō\ *adj.* **1** Dull in mind; stupid; as, a *slow* pupil. **2** Not willing to hurry or to be active; sluggish; as, a *slow* worker. **3** Not quickly aroused or excited; as, *slow* to anger. **4** Moving, flowing, or going at less than the usual speed or without much speed; as, a *slow* train; *slow* music. **5** Taking more than the usual time. The baby's growth has been *slow.* **6** Registering behind or below the correct time, weight, or measure. My watch is *slow.* **7** Not lively; dull and unprogressive; as, a *slow* town. **8** Possessing qualities that hinder or prevent rapid progress or play; as, a *slow* race track. — *v.* **1** To make slow; to retard; to delay. **2** To go slower. — **slow·ly,** *adv.*

slow·poke \'slō-ˌpōk\ *n.* A very slow person.

slue \'slü\ *n.* A marsh or slough.

slue \'slü\ *v.;* **slued; slu·ing.** To turn, twist, or swing about, especially out of a course; to veer. — *n.* The act or process of sluing a body.

slue \'slü\. Variant of *slew,* a large number.

slug \'sləg\ *n.* **1** A slow-moving animal somewhat like a snail without a shell or with a very slight shell, found in damp places, especially around decaying wood. **2** Any smooth larva or caterpillar of a sawfly or moth which creeps like a snail.

slug \'sləg\ *n.* **1** A roughly shaped lump of metal used as a missile in a gun. **2** A bullet, especially after being fired. **3** A strip of metal used by printers for spacing or a line of type cast in one piece. **4** A small blank disk used as a coin, as in a machine.

slug \'sləg\ *n.* A heavy blow, as with the fist. — *v.;* **slugged; slug·ging.** To hit hard, as with the fist or a bat. — **slug·ger** \'sləg-r\ *n.*

slug·gard \'sləg-rd\ *n.* A lazy person. — *adj.* Sluggish; lazy.

slug·gish \'sləg-ish\ *adj.* Slow and inactive in movement or action by habit or condition. — **slug·gish·ly,** *adv.*

sluice \'slüs\ *n.* **1** An artificial passage for water with a gate for controlling its flow or changing its direction. **2** A body of water held back by a gate or a stream flowing through a gate. **3** A water gate or other device for controlling the flow of water. **4** A channel that carries off surplus water. **5** A long inclined trough, as for washing gold-bearing earth or for floating logs to a saw mill. — *v.;* **sluiced; sluic·ing. 1** To draw off by or through a sluice, as a stream. **2** To wash in a stream of water running through a sluice. **3** To drench, wash, or flush with running water.

slum \'sləm\ *n.* A thickly populated section of a city marked by crowded streets, dirty run-down houses, and generally wretched living conditions. — *v.;* **slummed; slum·ming.** To visit slums.

slum·ber \'sləm-br\ *v.;* **slum·bered; slum·ber·ing** \-br(-)ing\. **1** To sleep. **2** To be in a state suggesting sleep, as one of complete inactivity. — *n.* Sleep or a sleeplike state. — **slum·ber·er** \-br-r\ *n.*

slum·ber·ous or **slum·brous** \'sləm-br(-)əs\ *adj.* **1** Slumbering; sleepy. **2** Inviting sleep.

slump \'sləmp\ *v.* **1** To fall in a heap as in a collapse; as, to *slump* to the floor. **2** To hold a drooping posture; to slouch; as, to *slump* in one's chair. **3** To decline sharply. Prices *slumped.* — *n.* The act or fact of slumping; especially, a marked decline, as in prices or values or in business.

slung. Past tense and past part. of *sling.*

slunk. Past tense and past part. of *slink.*

slur \'slər\ *v.;* **slurred; slur·ring.** To blacken the good name of; to defame. — *n.* **1** A reproach; a stigma. **2** A slighting remark; an aspersion.

slur \'slər\ *v.;* **slurred; slur·ring. 1** To pass over quickly giving little attention to; to fail to bring out clearly; as, to *slur* over some facts. **2** In music, to perform two or more successive notes of different pitch in a smooth or connected way; also, to mark such notes with a slur. **3** To speak so that sounds or words become indistinct; to enunciate obscurely. — *n.* **1** In music, a curved line [‿ or ⁀] connecting notes to be sung or performed without a break; also, the combination of two or more slurred tones. **2** A slurred sound in speech.

slush \'sləsh\ *n.* **1** Partly melted snow. **2** Highly sentimental, silly talk or writing; drivel.

slushy \'sləsh-ē\ *adj.;* **slush·i·er; slush·i·est. 1** Having much slush. **2** Of or like slush.

slut \'slət\ *n.* **1** A dirty, slovenly woman. **2** An immoral woman. — **slut·tish** \'slət-ish\ *adj.*

sly \'slī\ *adj.;* **sli·er** or **sly·er** \'slīr\; **sli·est** or **sly·est** \'slī-əst\. **1** Acting or working secretly or stealthily; crafty and cunning, especially in a mean, underhanded way. **2** Done by stealth or craft; as, *sly* tricks. **3** Roguish; artful; as, a *sly* jest. — For synonyms see *cunning.* — **on the sly.** Secretly; underhandedly; slyly.

sly·ly or **sli·ly** \'slī-lē\ *adv.* In a sly manner.

smack \'smak\ *n.* Characteristic taste or flavor. — *v.* To have a certain flavor, trace, or suggestion; as, actions that *smacked* of tyranny.

smack \'smak\ *n.* **1** A quick sharp noise made by the lips, as in enjoyment of some taste or food. **2** A loud kiss. **3** A noisy slap or blow. — *v.* **1** To open and close the lips noisily while eating and drinking. **2** To slap. — *adv.* Squarely and sharply; as, to run *smack* into a tree.

smack \'smak\ *n.* A sailboat, such as a sloop, used in fishing and coasting.

small \'smȯl\ *adj.* **1** Little in size. **2** Few in numbers or members; as, a *small* crowd; a *small* list. **3** Little in amount; low; as, a *small* supply. **4** Not very much; as, *small* success. **5** Unimportant; as, a *small* matter. **6** Not having a large business; as, *small* dealers. **7** Gentle; soft; as, a *small* voice. **8** Not generous; mean; as, a *small* nature. **9** Made up of small units; as, *small* change. **10** Humble; as, a *small* beginning. **11** Humiliated; humbled. He felt very *small* to be caught cheating. **12** Naming letters that are not capital letters. — *n.* The small part of a thing; as, the *small* of the back.

small arms. Arms carried on the person and fired by hand; portable firearms.

small intestine. The first major division of the intestine, consisting of the duodenum, jejunum, and ileum.

small·pox \'smȯl-ˌpäks\ *n.* A contagious disease marked by fever and skin eruptions.

smart \'smärt, 'smȧrt\ *v.* **1** To cause a stinging pain; to feel such a pain. **2** To feel or endure distress, remorse, or embarrassment; as, to *smart* under criticism. — *adj.* **1** Causing smarting; stinging; severe; as, a *smart* thrashing. **2** Very active and able; as, a *smart* salesman. **3** Quick to learn or do; clever; as, a *smart* pupil. **4** Brightly amusing; witty; as, a *smart* talker. **5** Somewhat impudent; saucy; as, to give a *smart* retort. **6** Fashionable; stylish. — *n.* A smarting pain. — **smart·ly**, *adv.*

smart·en \'smärt-n, 'smȧrt-n\ *v.;* **smart·ened**; **smart·en·ing** \-n(-)ing\. To make smart or smarter; to freshen; as, to *smarten* up a dress.

smash \'smash\ *v.* **1** To break or be broken into pieces by violence, as by hitting or dropping. **2** To destroy utterly; to break up, in, or down; to wreck; as, to *smash* an enemy force; to *smash* in a door. **3** To move forward with force and crashing effect; as, to *smash* into the car ahead. **4** To go to pieces; to collapse. — *n.* **1** The act or sound of smashing. **2** The state of being smashed; ruin. **3** A collision or a wreck caused by a collision.

smash·up \'smash-ˌəp\ *n.* A smash; especially, a collision resulting in a wreck.

smat·ter·ing \'smat-r-ing\ *n.* Slight or superficial knowledge; as, to have a *smattering* of French.

smear \'smir\ *n.* **1** A spot made by an oily or greasy substance or by dirt; a daub; a smudge. **2** A smearing, or blackening of a person's reputation. **3** Material smeared on a surface, as of a microscope slide or of a medium for cultivating bacteria. — *v.* **1** To spread all over or in patches with something oily, greasy, or sticky. **2** To smudge. **3** To blacken the reputation of; to defame. **4** In sports, to defeat by a wide margin.

smeary \'smir-ē\ *adj.;* **smear·i·er**; **smear·i·est**. **1** Smeared. **2** Tending to smear; as, *smeary* wax.

smell \'smel\ *v.;* **smelled** \'smeld\ or **smelt** \'smelt\; **smell·ing**. **1** To become aware of by means of certain nerves leading from the nose to the brain; to get or inhale the odor or scent of. **2** To detect or become aware of as if by the sense of smell; as, to *smell* mischief; to *smell* out a secret. **3** To have an odor; to give forth an aroma; as, to *smell* sweet; to *smell* of roses. **4** To have an offensive odor. — *n.* **1** The sense by which one smells. **2** Odor; scent; aroma. **3** An act of smelling.

smell·ing salts \'smel-ing\. A strong-smelling chemical preparation used to relieve faintness.

smelly \'smel-ē\ *adj.;* **smell·i·er**; **smell·i·est**. Having a smell; especially, having a bad smell.

smelt \'smelt\ *n.; pl.* **smelts** or **smelt**. A very small food fish of coastal waters, resembling a trout.

smelt \'smelt\ *v.* To melt or fuse, as ore, usually in order to separate the metal; to refine.

smelt \'smelt\. A past tense and past part. of *smell.*

smelt·er \'smelt-r\ *n.* **1** A person who smelts ore. **2** A place where smelting is done.

smile \'smīl\ *v.;* **smiled**; **smil·ing**. **1** To show a smile or look with a smile. **2** To show by a smile; as, to *smile* approval. **3** To look with amusement or ridicule; as, to *smile* at one's clumsy efforts. **4** To look as cheerful, bright, gay, or encouraging as a person who smiles. The weather *smiled* on our plans. — *n.* A change of facial expression in which the eyes brighten and the lips open or curve slightly upward; an expression of amusement, pleasure, approval, or sometimes scorn.

smirch \'smərch\ *v.* **1** To smear with something that stains or dirties; to soil. **2** To disgrace or dishonor, as a reputation. — *n.* A stain; a smear.

smirk \'smərk\ *v.* To wear a self-conscious or conceited smile; to simper. — *n.* An affected smile.

smite \'smīt\ *v.;* **smote** \'smōt\; **smit·ten** \'smit-n\, **smit** \'smit\, or **smote**; **smit·ing** \'smīt-ing\. **1** To strike hard, especially with the hand or a weapon; as, to *smite* a foe like the heroes of old. **2** To affect as if by striking hard; as, *smitten* with terror. The boy's conscience *smote* him. — **smit·er** \'smīt-r\ *n.*

smith \'smith\ *n.* One who forges with a hammer; a worker in metals; especially, a blacksmith.

smith·er·eens \ˌsmith-r-'ēnz\ *n. pl.* Fragments.

smithy \'smith-ē, 'smith-ē\ *n.; pl.* **smith·ies**. The workshop of a smith, especially a blacksmith.

smock \'smäk\ *n.* A light, loose garment worn over the clothes as a protection from dirt. — *v.* **1** To clothe in a smock. **2** To embroider by sewing in small, regularly spaced gathers (**smock·ing**).

smog \'smäg\ *n.* A fog made heavier and darker by the smoke of a city.

smoke \'smōk\ *n.* **1** The gas of burning materials, as coal or wood, made visible by particles of soot floating in it. **2** A mass or column of smoke. **3** The act of smoking a cigar, pipe, or cigarette. **4** Something as unsubstantial as smoke; as, plans that went up in *smoke.* **5** Something to be smoked, as a cigar or a cigarette. — *v.;* **smoked**; **smok·ing**. **1** To give forth smoke. The chimney *smokes.* **2** To inhale and exhale the fumes of burning tobacco. **3** To drive away by smoke; as, to *smoke* out a woodchuck. **4** To cure, as meat, or fish, with smoke. **5** To blacken or discolor with smoke.

smoke·house \'smōk-ˌhau̇s\ *n.; pl.* **smoke·hous·es** \-ˌhau̇-zəz\. A building where meat or fish is cured by being held in dense smoke.

smoke·less \'smōk-ləs\ *adj.* Making or having little or no smoke; as, *smokeless* powder.

smok·er \'smōk-r\ *n.* **1** One that smokes. **2** A railroad car or compartment where smoking is permitted. **3** A social gathering for men.

smoke screen. A curtain of heavy smoke used as a concealing screen, as for a ship or a fleet.

smoke·stack \'smōk-ˌstak\ *n.* A chimney, as on a ship, locomotive, or factory.

smoke tree. A small tree bearing clusters of minute flowers suggesting a cloud of smoke.

smoky \'smōk-ē\ *adj.;* **smok·i·er; smok·i·est. 1** Giving off smoke, especially in large amounts. **2** Like smoke in nature or appearance; as, a *smoky* fog; *smoky* pearl buttons. **3** Filled with smoke.

smol·der or **smoul·der** \'smōld-r\ *n.* Smoke; smudge. — *v.;* **smol·dered** or **smoul·dered; smol·der·ing** or **smoul·der·ing** \-r(-)ing\. **1** To burn and smoke without flame. Green wood *smolders.* **2** To burn inwardly. Anger *smoldered* in his heart.

smooth \'smüth\ *adj.* **1** Not rough or uneven in surface; as, a *smooth* board. **2** Without hair, either naturally or as a result of shaving. **3** Not jerky, jarring, or jolting; as, the *smooth* flight of a gull. **4** Pleasantly soft or even; calm; as, a *smooth* tone of voice. **5** Fluent in speech and agreeable in manner. **6** Having its surface leveled by wear or use; as, a *smooth* tire. — *adv.* Smoothly. — *v.* **1** To make smooth. **2** To soothe, especially with flattery. **3** To polish, refine, or soften, as one's manners. **4** To free from difficulty; to make easy; as, to *smooth* one's way. — **smooth·ly,** *adv.*

smooth·bore \'smüth-ˌbōr, -ˌbȯr\ *adj.* Having a bore without rifling. — *n.* A smoothbore gun.

smote. Past tense of *smite.*

smoth·er \'sməth-r\ *n.* A thick, stifling smoke or fog. — *v.;* **smoth·ered; smoth·er·ing** \-r(-)ing\. **1** To destroy by depriving of air; to suffocate. **2** To be suffocated. **3** To cover up; to suppress; as, to *smother* a yawn; to *smother* a revolt.

smudge \'sməj\ *n.* **1** Thick or suffocating smoke. **2** A fire made to smoke, as for driving away mosquitoes or protecting fruit from frost. **3** A dirty mark or spot made by rubbing or smearing; as, a *smudge* on a drawing. — *v.;* **smudged; smudg·ing. 1** To make a smudge or dirty smear. **2** To smoke or protect by a smudge. — **smudgy** \'sməj-ē\ *adj.*

smug \'sməg\ *adj.;* **smug·ger; smug·gest.** Highly self-satisfied. — **smug·ly** \-lē\ *adv.*

smug·gle \'sməg-l\ *v.;* **smug·gled; smug·gling** \-l(-)ing\. **1** To export or import secretly and unlawfully, as to avoid paying duty; as, to *smuggle* jewels. **2** To take, bring, or introduce secretly or stealthily. — **smug·gler** \'sməg-lər\ *n.*

smut \'smət\ *n.* **1** Something that smudges, as soot or coal dust. **2** A spot made by such matter. **3** Indecent language or jokes; obscenity. **4** Any of certain destructive diseases of plants, especially cereals, producing black masses of spores. **5** The fungus causing any of these diseases. — *v.;* **smut·ted; smut·ting. 1** To stain or taint with smut. **2** To be affected by smut. The wheat will soon *smut.*

smut·ty \'smət-ē\ *adj.;* **smut·ti·er; smut·ti·est. 1** Soiled, as with soot; dirty; smudgy. **2** Affected with smut fungus. **3** Obscene; indecent.

snack \'snak\ *n.* A light meal.

snaf·fle \'snaf-l\ *n.* Also **snaffle bit.** A jointed bridle bit. — *v.;* **snaf·fled; snaf·fling** \-l(-)ing\. To restrain with or as if with a snaffle.

snag \'snag\ *n.* **1** A stump of a cut or broken branch, especially when embedded under water and not visible from the surface. **2** An uneven or broken projection from a smooth or finished surface. **3** A concealed or unexpected difficulty or hindrance. — *v.;* **snagged; snag·ging.** To catch on or as if on a snag.

snag·gle·tooth \'snag-l-ˌtüth\ *n.* An irregular, broken, or projecting tooth. — **snag·gle-toothed** \-'tütht, -'tüthd\ *adj.*

snail \'snāl\ *n.* **1** A small, slow-moving mollusk having a well-developed spiral shell into which it can withdraw; especially one living mostly on land. **2** A slow-moving person.

snake \'snāk\ *n.* **1** Any of numerous long-bodied, limbless, crawling reptiles, living on large insects or small animals and birds. **2** A contemptible or treacherous person. — *v.;* **snaked; snak·ing. 1** To drag or draw forcibly or at full length, as a log. **2** To crawl or move like a snake.

snake·skin \'snāk-ˌskin\ *n.* **1** The skin of a snake. **2** Leather made from the skin of a snake.

snaky \'snāk-ē\ *adj.;* **snak·i·er; snak·i·est. 1** Of or like a snake or snakes. **2** Abounding in snakes.

snap \'snap\ *v.;* **snapped; snap·ping. 1** To grasp or grasp at suddenly with the teeth; to bite or try to bite. **2** To utter harsh or angry words; as, to *snap* at a naughty child. **3** To break short or in two, especially with a cracking sound. A twig *snapped.* **4** To give way to heavy strain; as, to feel one's nerves *snap.* **5** To give or cause a sharp, crackling noise, as a fire. **6** To close, shut, or fit with a snap or click; as, to *snap* the lock shut. **7** To flash. The girl's eyes *snapped.* **8** To take quickly or at once; to snatch or seize; as, to *snap* up a bargain; to *snap* at a chance. **9** To speak to sharply; to interrupt with a cutting or crushing remark; as to *snap* a person up. **10** To cause to crack, click, or make a report; as, to *snap* one's fingers. **11** To throw with a quick motion; as, to *snap* a ball. **12** To take a snapshot of. — *n.* **1** The action or sound of snapping; a biting, snatching, sudden breaking, or cracking. **2** Something that is easy, as a job or a course of study. **3** A bit; as, not to care a *snap.* **4** A sharp noise or report, as one caused by a snapping on or off; as, a *snap* of the fingers. **5** A period of cold weather. **6** A fastening or a lock that closes with a click; as, the *snap* on a purse. **7** Energy, as of speech or movement; smartness. **8** A thin, brittle cookie or wafer. — *adj.* **1** Done or made suddenly; as, a *snap* judgment. **2** Closing with a snap; as, a *snap* fastener.

snap·drag·on \'snap-ˌdrag-n\ *n.* **1** A garden plant of the same natural family as the figworts, with long spikes of white, reddish, or yellowish flowers. **2** A game in which raisins are snatched from burning brandy and eaten.

snap·per \'snap-r\ *n.* **1** One that snaps; as, a device at the end of a whiplash that snaps or cracks when the lash is jerked. **2** A snapping turtle. **3** Any of numerous marine food fishes resembling the bass.

snap·ping turtle \'snap-ing\. A large American

water turtle that catches its prey with a snap of the jaws.

snap·pish \'snap-ish\ *adj.* **1** Inclined to snap. **2** Irritable; ill-tempered. — **snap·pish·ly**, *adv.*

snap·py \'snap-ē\ *adj.;* **snap·pi·er**; **snap·pi·est.** **1** Snappish. **2** Full of snap; lively; quick; smart.

snap·shot \'snap-ˌshät\ *n.* A photograph taken with fast camera action; especially, an informal photograph taken by an amateur.

snare \'snar, 'sner\ *n.* **1** A trap, often consisting of a noose, for catching small animals or birds. **2** Anything by which a person is attracted into trouble. — *v.;* **snared**; **snar·ing.** **1** To catch in a snare or as if in a snare; to trap. **2** To lure.

snare drum \'snar 'drəm, 'sner\. A small double-headed drum with strings of catgut (**snares**) stretched across its lower head.

snares

snare drum

snarl \'snärl, 'snårl\ *n.* **1** A tangle or knot, especially of hair, thread, or string. **2** Any tangled situation or condition; as, a traffic *snarl.* — *v.* To get into a tangle.

snarl \'snärl, 'snårl\ *v.* **1** To growl with a snapping or showing of the teeth, as a dog. **2** To express one's anger in rough, surly language; to utter with a snarl; as, to *snarl* a reply. — *n.* A surly, angry growl or utterance. — **snarl·er** \-r\ *n.*

snatch \'snach\ *v.* **1** To seize or try to seize something suddenly. **2** To grasp or take suddenly or hastily· to grab. — *n.* **1** A quick catching or grabbing. **2** A short period; as, to sleep in *snatches.* **3** A brief bit; as, *snatches* of song. — **snatch·er** \-r\ *n.*

sneak \'snēk\ *v.* To move, act, bring, or put in a sly, secret. or furtive way. — For synonyms see *lurk.* — *n.* **1** A mean, sly person. **2** The act or an instance of sneaking. — **sneaky** \'snēk-ē\ *adj.*

sneak·er \'snēk-r\ *n.* **1** One that sneaks; a sneak. **2** [in the plural] Rubber-soled shoes, usually with canvas uppers.

sneak·ing \'snēk-ing\ *adj.* **1** Furtive; sly. **2** Not clearly felt or openly stated; as, a *sneaking* suspicion. — **sneak·ing·ly**, *adv.*

sneer \'snir\ *v.* **1** To smile with a contemptuous expression. **2** To speak or write with a sneer. — *n.* A contemptuous smile; a scoff; a gibe.

sneeze \'snēz\ *v.;* **sneezed**; **sneez·ing.** To force the breath out through the nose in a sudden and violent involuntary expiration. — *n.* A sneezing. — **sneez·er** \'snēz-r\ *n.*

snick·er \'snik-r\ *v.;* **snick·ered**; **snick·er·ing** \-r(-)ing\. To giggle. — *n.* A snickering; a giggle.

sniff \'snif\ *v.* **1** To draw quick, short breaths through the nose, as in smelling something or in expressing disgust or disdain. **2** To smell something by sniffing; as, to *sniff* a flower. — *n.* **1** The act or sound of sniffing. **2** That which is sniffed.

snif·fle \'snif-l\ *v.;* **snif·fled**; **snif·fling** \-l(-)ing\. **1** To sniff loudly and repeatedly. **2** To whimper or snuffle. — *n.* A snuffle.

snig·ger \'snig-r\ *v.;* **snig·gered**; **snig·ger·ing** \-r(-)ing\. To giggle. — *n.* A giggle.

snip \'snip\ *v.;* **snipped**; **snip·ping.** To cut or take off in one stroke or with a series of quick strokes; to clip. — *n.* **1** A single cut, as with shears; a clip. **2** A small bit cut off. **3** A small person or thing.

snipe \'snīp\ *n.* A long-billed bird that lives in marshes. — *v.;* **sniped**; **snip·ing.** To shoot at individual enemy soldiers, especially when mass fighting is not taking place. — **snip·er** \'snīp-r\ *n.*

snip·py \'snip-ē\ *adj.;* **snip·pi·er**; **snip·pi·est.** **1** Unduly brief or curt. **2** Somewhat haughty.

sniv·el \'sniv-l\ *v.;* **sniv·eled** or **sniv·elled**; **sniv·el·ing** or **sniv·el·ling** \-l(-)ing\. **1** To have a running nose. **2** To snuffle. **3** To whine. — *n.* **1** Mucus in or from the nose. **2** A sniffling or snuffling. — **sniv·el·er** \-l(-)ər\ *n.*

snob \'snäb\ *n.* A person who imitates, admires, or seeks friendship with people who are of higher rank or position than himself and looks down on people whom he considers his inferiors.

snob·bery \'snäb-r(-)ē\ *n.* The quality of being snobbish; snobbish conduct.

snob·bish \'snäb-ish\ *adj.* Characteristic of a snob; like or befitting a snob. — **snob·bish·ly**, *adv.*

snood \'snüd\ *n.* **1** A band or ribbon worn by a young woman around her head. **2** A coarse net worn by women to hold the hair at the back of the head. — *v.* To hold with a snood.

snoop \'snüp\ *v.* To look or pry in a sneaking way. — *n.* A prying person. — **snoop·er** \-r\ *n.*

snooty \'snüt-ē\ *adj.;* **snoot·i·er**; **snoot·i·est.** Haughtily contemptuous· arrogant.

snooze \'snüz\ *n.* A short sleep; a nap. — *v.;* **snoozed**; **snooz·ing.** To fall asleep; to take a nap.

snore \'snōr, 'snȯr\ *v.;* **snored**; **snor·ing.** To breathe with a rough, hoarse noise while sleeping. — *n.* The act or noise of snoring. — **snor·er** \-r\ *n.*

snor·kel \'snȯrk-l\ *n.* [From German *schnorchel,* an adaptation of a German dialect word meaning "snout".] **1** A tube or tubes that can be extended above the surface of the water to supply air to and remove exhaust from a submerged diesel-powered submarine. **2** A tube used by swimmers for breathing with the head under water. — *v.;* **snor·keled**; **snor·kel·ing** \-l(-)ing\. To use a snorkel.

snort \'snȯrt\ *v.* **1** To force the air violently through the nose as horses sometimes do. **2** To make a similar sound, as in laughter or disgust. — *n.* The act or the sound of snorting.

snout \'snau̇t\ *n.* **1** The long nose of an animal, as of a pig; the front part of the head of an animal. **2** Any nose, especially when large or prominent. **3** Something that resembles a snout.

snow \'snō\ *n.* **1** Small flakes of frozen water formed in the air. **2** The falling of such flakes, or a mass of them fallen to earth. **3** Small light or dark spots in a television image caused by electrical interference. — *v.* **1** To fall, scatter, or shower down in or as if in snow. **2** To cover or shut in with snow or as if with snow.

snow·ball \'snō-ˌbȯl\ *n.* **1** A round mass of snow. **2** A bush with ball-shaped clusters of white flowers. — *v.* **1** To throw snowballs at. **2** To increase in size, as a snowball rolled in snow.

snow·bank \'snō-ˌbangk\ *n.* A bank of snow.

snow·bird \'snō-ˌbərd\ *n.* **1** Also **snow bunting.** A bird about the size of a sparrow, mostly white in color. **2** The slate-colored junco.

snow-blind \'snō-ˌblīnd\ *adj.* Affected with **snow blindness**, a temporary loss of sight caused by the glare of ultraviolet rays reflected from snow.

snow·bound \'snō-'bau̇nd\ *adj.* Shut in by snow.

snow·drift \'snō-ˌdrift\ *n.* A bank of drifted snow.

snow·drop \'snō-ˌdräp\ *n.* An early-blooming European plant of the same family as the amaryllis that bears nodding white flowers.

snow·fall \'snō-ˌfȯl\ *n.* **1** A fall of snow. **2** The amount of snow that falls in a single storm or in a certain period of time.

snow·flake \'snō-ˌflāk\ *n.* A flake of snow.

snow·man \'snō-ˌman\ *n.; pl.* **snow·men** \-ˌmen\. Snow shaped to resemble a person.

snow·plow \'snō-ˌplau̇\ *n.* A plow, or any device that works like a plow, for clearing away snow.

snow·shoe \'snō-ˌshü\ *n.* A light oval frame of wood strung with rawhide leather, worn under the shoe to prevent sinking down into soft snow. — *v.;* **snow·shoed**; **snow·shoe·ing**. To go on snowshoes.

snowshoes

snowshoe rabbit. A hare which is white in winter and brownish with white feet in summer, native to the northwestern United States and Canada.

snow·slide \'snō-ˌslīd\ *n.* The slipping down of a mass of snow, as on a mountain slope.

snow·storm \'snō-ˌstȯrm\ *n.* A heavy fall of snow, especially one accompanied by wind.

snowy \'snō-ē\ *adj.;* **snow·i·er**; **snow·i·est.** **1** Having, or covered with, snow. **2** White, like snow.

snub \'snəb\ *v.;* **snubbed**; **snub·bing.** **1** To check or stop with a sharp reply or remark. **2** To check suddenly while running out, as a rope or chain. **3** To check the motion of, as a boat, by snubbing a rope. **4** To slight purposely; to treat rudely. — *n.* **1** An intentional slight. **2** A checking of motion, as of a boat. — *adj.;* **snub·ber**; **snub·best.** Slightly turned up and flattened at the end, as the nose.

snub·ber \'snəb-r\ *n.* One that snubs; especially, a device for snubbing.

snuff \'snəf\ *n.* The charred end of the wick of a candle. — *v.* **1** To cut or pinch off a snuff. **2** To put out a flame. **3** To end; as, a life *snuffed* out.

snuff \'snəf\ *v.* **1** To draw in, or to inhale forcibly, through the nose; to sniff. **2** To take snuff through the nose. — *n.* **1** The act of snuffing. **2** Powdered tobacco to be snuffed up the nose.

snuff·box \'snəf-ˌbäks\ *n.* A small box for snuff.

snuff·er \'snəf-r\ *n.* One that snuffs or that snuffs out a light; especially [in the plural] a device for clipping off and holding the snuff of a candle.

snuf·fle \'snəf-l\ *v.;* **snuf·fled**; **snuf·fling** \-l(-)ing\. To breathe noisily through the nose; to sniffle. — *n.* A snuffling sound. — **snuf·fler** \-l(-)ər\ *n.*

snug \'snəg\ *adj.;* **snug·ger**; **snug·gest.** **1** Seaworthy and well-equipped; as, a *snug* ship. **2** Comfortable and secure; as, a good night to be *snug* at home. **3** Cozy; as, a *snug* little room. **4** Small but sufficient; nice; tidy; as, a *snug* fortune. **5** Hidden; concealed; as, to lie *snug*, away from prying eyes. **6** Tight; not loose; as, a *snug* fit. — *adv.* Snugly.

snug·gery \'snəg-r-ē\ *n.; pl.* **snug·ger·ies.** A snug place; especially, a den.

snug·gle \'snəg-l\ *v.;* **snug·gled**; **snug·gling** \-l(-)ing\. To curl up comfortably; as, to *snuggle* down in bed. — *n.* The action of snuggling.

snug·ly \'snəg-lē\ *adv.* **1** Comfortably; cozily; warmly; as, to tuck a child *snugly* in bed. **2** Tightly; as, a coat that fits a bit too *snugly*.

so \(')sō, *in some senses* sə *when a stressed syllable follows without pause*\ *adv.* **1** In the indicated way; in the indicated condition; like this; like that. Hold the knife *so.* The man had been very strong as a youth and was still *so.* **2** In accordance with the facts. The story we heard turned out not to be *so.* **3** To the indicated degree. They wanted fifty dollars but we could not pay *so* much. **4** To a high degree; extremely; very. This book is *so* interesting. **5** In such a way. Plan your work *so* that you have time to rest after lunch. **6** To such a degree. He walked *so* fast that he got there ahead of me. **7** For this reason; therefore. He had a fever and *so* he had to go to bed. **8** Likewise; also — followed by *do*, *does*, or *did* with its subject. You like sports and *so* do I. — *conj.* **1** Provided that; on condition that; if only — often preceded by *just.* I don't care who goes hungry, just *so* I get enough to eat. **2** In order that — often followed by *that.* Be quiet *so* he can sleep. Move over *so* that I can see. — *pron.* **1** Approximately that; as, to read a page or *so.* **2** The same. The man was a coward and remained *so.*

so \'sō\ *n.* A syllable used in music to name the fifth note of the scale; sol.

soak \'sōk\ *v.* **1** To make or become wet through. **2** To penetrate through pores or tiny holes. Rain *soaks* into the ground. **3** To put in a liquid so as to soften or steep; as, to *soak* a paint brush overnight. **4** To draw in or suck up; to absorb. A sponge *soaked* up water. **5** *Slang.* To punch. **6** *Slang.* To charge, as a customer, too high a price for something. — *n.* **1** The act or process of soaking or state of being soaked. **2** *Slang.* A drunkard.

so-and-so \'sō-ən-ˌsō\ *n.; pl.* **so-and-sos.** Someone or something not specifically named.

soap \'sōp\ *n.* A substance, usually made by the action of alkali on fat, that dissolves in water and is used for washing. — *v.* To rub with soap.

soap·ber·ry \'sōp-ˌber-ē\ *n.; pl.* **soap·ber·ries.** Any of various chiefly tropical trees, shrubs, or vines bearing berries that can be used as a substitute for soap; especially, the chinaberry.

soap·box \'sōp-ˌbäks\ *n.* **1** A box for holding soap.

2 A packing box used as a platform, as by a street orator (**soapbox orator**).

soapbox derby. A downhill race for children's homemade racing cars without pedals or motors.

soap opera. [So called from the fact that many such programs are sponsored by soap manufacturing companies.] A radio or television serial drama performed on a daytime commercial program.

soap·stone \'sōp-ˌstōn\ *n.* A soft stone having a soapy or greasy feeling.

soap·suds \'sōp-ˌsədz\ *n. pl.* Bubbles and foam forming on water containing soap.

soapy \'sōp-ē\ *adj.;* **soap·i·er; soap·i·est. 1** Smeared with soap; lathered. **2** Containing soapsuds. **3** Like soap; suggesting soap; greasy.

soar \'sōr, 'sȯr\ *v.* **1** To fly upward on or as if on wings. **2** To rise, as in thought, imagination, or spirits, far above the common or usual level. **3** To move through the air, as a glider, without engine power and without loss of altitude.

sob \'säb\ *v.;* **sobbed; sob·bing. 1** To weep with heavings of the chest, or with catching in the throat. **2** To bring about by sobbing; as, to *sob* oneself to sleep. **3** To make a sound like that of sobbing. — *n.* The act or sound of sobbing.

so·ber \'sōb-r\ *adj.* **1** Not drinking too much; temperate in the use of alcoholic drinks. **2** Not drunk. **3** Serious or grave in mood or expression; solemn; as, a *sober* child. **4** Not affected by emotion or prejudice; calm; well-balanced; as, *sober* judgment. — *v.;* **so·bered; so·ber·ing** \-r(-)ing\. To make or become sober. — **so·ber·ly,** *adv.*

so·bri·e·ty \sə-'brī-ət-ē\ *n.* The state or fact of being sober.

so·bri·quet \'sōb-rə-ˌkā\ *n.* A nickname.

so-called \'sō-'kȯld\ *adj.* Generally, but perhaps inaccurately, called thus; as, this *so-called* hero.

soc·cer \'säk-r\ *n.* [A shortened and altered form of *association football,* its original name.] A game played between two teams of eleven men each with a round football which is either kicked toward a goal or driven or blocked by any part of the body except the hands and arms.

so·cia·bil·i·ty \ˌsō-shə-'bil-ət-ē\ *n.* Sociable character or behavior; friendly social relations.

so·cia·ble \'sō-shəb-l\ *adj.* Friendly; marked by pleasant social relations. — *n.* A friendly party; a social. — **so·cia·bly** \-shə-blē\ *adv.*

so·cial \'sōsh-l\ *adj.* **1** Marked by or given up to sociability. **2** Naturally living or growing in groups or communities. Bees are *social* insects. **3** Of or relating to fashionable society; as, a *social* leader. **4** Of or relating to human beings as a closely knit group; as, *social* science. **5** Of or concerned with the welfare of human beings; as, *social* service. **6** Of or relating to human beings in their physical contacts; as, *social* hygiene; *social* diseases. **7** Socialistic. — *n.* A social gathering; a sociable.

so·cial·ism \'sōsh-l-ˌiz-m\ *n.* A political and economic theory or system of social organization based on government ownership, management, and control of the essential means of production, distribution, and exchange.

so·cial·ist \'sōsh-l(-)əst\ *n.* A person who believes in or practices socialism. — *adj.* Socialistic.

so·cial·is·tic \ˌsōsh-l-'is-tik\ *adj.* **1** Of, relating to, or based upon socialism. **2** Favoring socialism. — **so·cial·is·ti·cal·ly** \-tik-l(-)ē\ *adv.*

so·cial·ite \'sōsh-l-ˌīt\ *n.* A person who is prominent in fashionable society.

so·cial·ize \'sōsh-l-ˌīz\ *v.;* **so·cial·ized; so·cial·iz·ing. 1** To make social; especially, to train so as to develop the qualities essential to group living. **2** To adapt to social needs and uses. **3** To regulate according to the theory or practice of socialism; to place under government control. **4** To take part in the social life around one.

so·cial·ly \'sōsh-l(-)ē\ *adv.* In a social way or manner; with respect to society.

social science. 1 The science that deals with human society or its elements, as family, state, or race, and with man's relations and institutions as a member of an organized community. **2** One of a group of studies dealing with special phases of human society, as economics or sociology.

social security. Protection of citizens by a government program against the major hazards of the functioning of the national economy; especially, benefits received under an old-age pension system insuring an income to many classes of citizens on loss of personal earning power.

social studies. The studies dealing with human relationships and the institutions of human society, as history, civics, economics, and geography.

so·ci·e·ty \sə-'sī-ət-ē\ *n.; pl.* **so·ci·e·ties. 1** Companionship with one's fellows; company. **2** The social order, or community life, considered as a system within which the individual lives; as, rural *society.* **3** People in general; as, to work for the benefit of *society.* **4** An association of persons for some purpose; as, a mutual benefit *society.* **5** Any part of a community regarded as a unit distinguished by certain interests or standards; especially, the group or set of fashionable persons.

so·ci·o·log·i·cal \ˌsō-s(h)ē-ə-'läj-ik-l\ *adj.* Of or relating to sociology. — **so·ci·o·log·i·cal·ly** \-ik-l(-)ē\ *adv.*

so·ci·ol·o·gist \ˌsō-s(h)ē-'äl-ə-jəst\ *n.* A specialist in sociology.

so·ci·ol·o·gy \ˌsō-s(h)ē-'äl-ə-jē\ *n.* The social science that studies the origin and development of society and the forms, institutions, and functions of human groups.

sock \'säk\ *n.* A stocking with a short leg.

sock \'säk\ *v. Slang.* **1** To strike or hurl hard. **2** To deliver a blow to. — *n. Slang.* A hard blow. — *adv. Slang.* Directly; as, to be hit *sock* in the face.

sock·et \'säk-ət\ *n.* An opening or hollow that receives and holds something; as, the eye *socket.*

sod \'säd\ *n.* **1** The layer of the soil filled with roots, as of grass and herbs; turf. **2** A piece of this turf cut or pulled off. **3** The grass-covered earth.

— *v.;* **sod·ded**; **sod·ding.** To cover or fill with sods.

so·da \'sōd-ə\ *n.* **1** Sodium carbonate; washing soda. **2** Sodium bicarbonate; baking soda. **3** Sodium hydroxide; caustic soda. **4** Soda water. **5** Soda water with ice cream and a flavoring syrup.

soda biscuit. 1 A biscuit leavened with baking soda and sour milk or buttermilk. **2** A soda cracker.

soda cracker. A lightly baked crisp cracker made from yeast dough neutralized with baking soda.

soda fountain. 1 An apparatus for drawing soda water. **2** A counter where soda water, soft drinks, sundaes, and similar things are served.

so·dal·i·ty \sō-'dal-ət-ē\ *n.; pl.* **so·dal·i·ties.** An association; a fellowship of men or women; especially, a devotional or charitable association of Roman Catholic laymen.

soda water. A beverage of water to which carbon dioxide and often flavoring have been added.

sod·den \'säd-n\ *adj.* **1** Dull; as, *sodden* faces. **2** Soaked. **3** Heavy or soggy; as, *sodden* biscuits.

so·di·um \'sōd-ē-əm\ *n.* A soft, waxy, silver-white metallic element, chemically very active and found abundantly in nature, always in combination.

sodium bicarbonate. Bicarbonate of soda.

sodium carbonate. A strong-tasting salt used in making soap, in softening water, in scouring and bleaching, and in medicine and photography.

sodium chloride. Common salt; table salt.

sodium fluoride. A white crystalline salt used as an antiseptic and in fluoridation of drinking water.

sodium hy·drox·ide \hī-'dräk-ˌsīd\. A white brittle solid used in making soap, rayon, and paper, and in bleaching; caustic soda.

sodium hy·po·sul·fite \ˌhīp-ə-'səl-ˌfīt\. **1** Sodium thiosulfate. **2** A crystalline salt used in dyeing and bleaching.

sodium nitrate. A colorless salt used as a fertilizer and in making potassium nitrate, or saltpeter, and nitric acid; Chile saltpeter.

sodium thi·o·sul·fate \ˌthī-ə-'səl-ˌfāt\. A crystalline salt used in photography for fixing; hypo.

so·fa \'sō-fə\ *n.* An upholstered couch with a back and arms.

soft \'sȯft\ *adj.* **1** Restful, peaceful, mild, or gentle. **2** Not loud; as, a *soft* voice. **3** Gentle in action; moderate; as, *soft* breezes. **4** Kind; tolerant; easily moved; as, a *soft* heart. **5** Not hard, solid, or firm; as, *soft* wood. **6** Not in condition to endure prolonged exercise or hardships. **7** Gently curved; as, *soft* outlines. **8** Not containing certain substances that prevent lathering. Rain is *soft* water. **9** Pronounced in a way thought of as soft rather than hard, as *c* in *cease* (contrasted with *case*), *g* in *gem* (contrasted with *goose*), *s* in *these* (contrasted with *this*) *th* in *ether* (contrasted with *either*). **10** Not alcoholic; as, *soft* drinks. — *adv.* Softly; quietly.

soft·ball \'sȯf(t)-ˌbȯl\ *n.* A modified form of baseball, played with a softer, larger ball and on a smaller diamond.

soft coal. Bituminous coal.

sof·ten \'sȯf-n\ *v.;* **sof·tened**; **sof·ten·ing** \-n(-)ing\. To make or become soft or softer. — **sof·ten·er,** *n.*

soft·heart·ed \'sȯft-'härt-əd, -'hårt-\ *adj.* Tenderhearted. — **soft·heart·ed·ly,** *adv.*

soft·ly \'sȯft-lē\ *adv.* In a soft way; quietly; gently.

soft·wood \'sȯft-ˌwu̇d\ *n.* **1** Any easily worked wood of light texture. **2** In forestry, the wood of any coniferous tree whether physically hard or soft.

softy \'sȯf-tē\ *n.; pl.* **soft·ies. 1** A silly or sentimental person. **2** A weakling.

sog·gy \'säg-ē\ *adj.;* **sog·gi·er**; **sog·gi·est.** Heavy and damp; as, *soggy* ground.

soil \'sȯil\ *v.* To make or become dirty or corrupt. White clothes *soil* easily. — *n.* That which soils.

soil \'sȯil\ *n.* **1** Firm land; earth. **2** The loose surface material of the earth in which plants grow. **3** Any substance in which something may take root and grow. Slums are fertile *soil* for crime.

so·journ \'sō-ˌjərn, sō-'jərn\ *v.* To dwell temporarily. — *n.* A temporary stay. — **so·journ·er,** *n.*

sol \'sōl\ *n.* A syllable used in music to name the fifth note of the scale.

sol·ace \'säl-əs\ *n.* Comfort; consolation. — *v.;* **sol·aced**; **sol·ac·ing. 1** To comfort; to soothe; to allay. **2** To cheer; to divert.

so·lar \'sōl-r\ *adj.* **1** Of, from, or having to do with the sun; as, the *solar* system. **2** Measured by the sun; as, a *solar* year. **3** Produced or operated by the sun's heat; as, a *solar* engine; a *solar* battery.

so·lar·i·um \sō-'ler-ē-əm\ *n.; pl.* **so·lar·i·ums** \-ē-əmz\ or **so·lar·ia** \-ē-ə\. A sunroom.

so·lar plex·us \ˌsōl-r 'pleks-əs\. **1** A plexus of nerves in the abdomen, behind the stomach. **2** The pit of the stomach.

solar system. The sun and the planets, comets, and meteors which revolve around it.

sold. Past tense and past part. of *sell.*

sol·der \'säd-r, 'sȯd-r\ *n.* **1** A metal used when melted to join or mend metals. **2** Anything that unites or mends. — *v.;* **sol·dered**; **sol·der·ing** \-r(-)ing\. To join together by or as if by solder.

sol·dier \'sōlj-r\ *n.* **1** A man in military service, especially one who is not a commissioned officer. **2** A worker in any cause. **3** In most termites and certain ants, one of a class of wingless individuals with large heads and jaws. — *v.* To serve as a soldier. — **sol·dier·ly,** *adj.*

sol·diery \'sōlj-r-ē\ *n.; pl.* **sol·dier·ies.** A body of soldiers.

sole \'sōl\ *n.* **1** The under surface of the foot. **2** The bottom of a shoe or boot. — *v.;* **soled**; **sol·ing.** To furnish with a sole; as, to have shoes *soled.*

sole \'sōl\ *n.* Any of various flatfishes that have small mouths and small closely set eyes.

sole \'sōl\ *adj.* **1** Single; only; one; as, the *sole* heir to a fortune. **2** Belonging or granted to the one person or group named; as, *sole* fishing rights.

sol·e·cism \'säl-ə-ˌsiz-m\ *n.* **1** A combination of words that do not properly belong together in the same construction; a minor blunder in speech. **2** A breach of etiquette or good manners.

sole·ly \'sōl-(l)ē\ *adv.* **1** Singly; alone. **2** Entirely; wholly; as, done *solely* for money.

sol·emn \'säl-əm\ *adj.* **1** Celebrated with religious rites or ceremony; sacred. **2** Formal; stately; as, a *solemn* procession. **3** Done or made seriously and thoughtfully; as, a *solemn* promise. **4** Grave; sober; earnest. **5** Somber; gloomy; as, a robe of *solemn* black. — **sol·emn·ly,** *adv.*

so·lem·ni·ty \sə-'lem-nət-ē\ *n.; pl.* **so·lem·ni·ties.** **1** A solemn ceremony or rite; a solemn event, day, or speech. **2** Seriousness; formal dignity.

sol·em·nize \'säl-əm-ˌnīz\ *v.;* **sol·em·nized; sol·em·niz·ing.** **1** To observe or honor solemnly. **2** To perform with solemn ceremony, as a marriage. — **sol·em·ni·za·tion** \ˌsäl-əm-nə-'zāsh-n\ *n.*

so·lic·it \sə-'lis-ət\ *v.* **1** To entreat; to beg; to approach with a request for something. **2** To appeal for; as, to *solicit* money for a hospital. **3** To tempt; to lure. — **so·lic·i·ta·tion** \sə-ˌlis-ə-'tāsh-n\ *n.*

so·lic·i·tor \sə-'lis-ət-r\ *n.* **1** One that solicits; as, a *solicitor* of advertising space. **2** *British.* A lawyer. **3** The law officer of a city, town, or government.

so·lic·it·ous \sə-'lis-ət-əs\ *adj.* **1** Full of concern; as, *solicitous* about one's health. **2** Eager; anxiously willing; as, *solicitous* to please.

so·lic·i·tude \sə-'lis-ə-ˌtüd, -ˌtyüd\ *n.* The state of being solicitous; anxious concern.

sol·id \'säl-əd\ *adj.* **1** Having its interior filled with matter; not hollow; as, a *solid* iron bar. **2** Having the three dimensions of length, breadth, and thickness; cubic. **3** Compact; not loose; as, a *solid* mass of rock. **4** Rigid; hard; thick; neither liquid nor gaseous; as, *solid* ice. **5** Strong; firm; reliable; as, a *solid* chair; a *solid* citizen. **6** All of one material, kind, or color; as, *solid* gold. **7** Without a break, interruption, or change; as, a *solid* panel. **8** Serious; not light or trivial; as, *solid* reading. **9** Having parts joined without a hyphen; unbroken — used of words. **10** Without an interruption; as, three *solid* hours. **11** United, as in feeling or voting; as, the *solid* South. — *n.* **1** Something with length, breadth, and thickness. **2** A solid substance; anything not flowing. — **sol·id·ly,** *adv.*

sol·i·dar·i·ty \ˌsäl-ə-'dar-ət-ē\ *n.; pl.* **sol·i·dar·i·ties.** A unity of interests or opinions in a group.

so·lid·i·fy \sə-'lid-ə-ˌfī\ *v.;* **so·lid·i·fied** \-ˌfīd\; **so·lid·i·fy·ing.** To make or become solid or hard; to crystallize; as, to wait until the concrete *solidifies.* — **so·lid·i·fi·ca·tion** \sə-ˌlid-ə-fə-'kāsh-n\ *n.*

so·lid·i·ty \sə-'lid-ət-ē\ *n.; pl.* **so·lid·i·ties.** The quality or state of being solid; hardness.

so·lil·o·quize \sə-'lil-ə-ˌkwīz\ *v.;* **so·lil·o·quized; so·lil·o·quiz·ing.** To utter a soliloquy; to talk to oneself. — **so·lil·o·quiz·er** \-ˌkwīz-r\ *n.*

so·lil·o·quy \sə-'lil-ə-kwē\ *n.; pl.* **so·lil·o·quies.** **1** The action of talking to oneself. **2** A dramatic monologue that gives the effect of being the character's unspoken thoughts.

sol·i·taire \'säl-ə-ˌtar, -ˌter\ *n.* **1** A single gem set alone. **2** A card game played by one person.

sol·i·tary \'säl-ə-ˌter-ē\ *adj.* **1** All alone; as, a *solitary* traveler. **2** Seldom visited; lonely. **3** Single; sole; only; as, not a *solitary* case.

sol·i·tude \'säl-ə-ˌtüd, -ˌtyüd\ *n.* **1** The condition of being alone; loneliness. **2** A lonely place.

so·lo \'sō-ˌlō\ *n.; pl.* **so·los.** [From Italian, there derived from *solo* meaning "alone", this derived from Latin *solus.*] **1** A tune or a whole piece played or sung by one person with or without accompaniment. **2** A piece of music written to be played or sung by one person. **3** Any action in which there is only one performer, as a dance or a flight in an airplane. — *adj.* **1** Performing a solo; performed as a solo; alone; as, a *solo* dancer; a *solo* flight. **2** Written to be performed by one voice or instrument; as, a *solo* part. — *adv.* Alone; as, to fly *solo.* — *v.;* **so·loed; so·lo·ing.** To perform by oneself; especially, to fly solo in an airplane.

so·lo·ist \'sō-lə-wəst, -ˌlō-əst\ *n.* A person who performs a solo.

so·lon \'sō-lən, -ˌlän\ *n.* [Named after *Solon* (about 638–about 559 B.C.), a famous lawgiver of ancient Greece.] **1** A lawmaker. **2** A wise man.

sol·stice \'säl-stəs, 'sōl-, 'sȯl-\ *n.* **1** The point in the apparent path of the sun at which the sun is farthest from the equator, either north (**summer solstice**) or south (**winter solstice**). **2** The time of the year when the sun passes one of the solstices, about June 22 and December 22.

sol·u·bil·i·ty \ˌsäl-yə-'bil-ət-ē\ *n.; pl.* **sol·u·bil·i·ties.** The quality or state of being soluble.

sol·u·ble \'säl-yəb-l\ *adj.* **1** Capable of being dissolved in a fluid; as, *soluble* powder. **2** Capable of being solved or explained; solvable.

sol·ute \'säl-ˌyüt\ *n.* A dissolved substance.

so·lu·tion \sə-'lüsh-n\ *n.* **1** The act or process of solving or of finding a way out. **2** An answer obtained in solving a problem. **3** The act or process by which a solid, liquid, or gaseous substance is dissolved and mixed with another substance, usually a liquid, forming a mixture consisting apparently of only one substance. **4** A mixture formed by this process; especially, a liquid in which something has been dissolved. **5** The condition of being dissolved. **6** The process by which the root or roots of an algebraic equation are found.

solv·a·ble \'säl-vəb-l\ *adj.* Capable of being solved. — **solv·a·bil·i·ty** \ˌsäl-və-'bil-ət-ē\ *n.*

solve \'sälv\ *v.;* **solved; solv·ing.** To clear up, as something that is difficult or vague; to find the answer to or solution of, as a problem, a mystery, or a difficulty. — **solv·er** \'sälv-r\ *n.*

sol·ven·cy \'sälv-n-sē\ *n.; pl.* **sol·ven·cies.** The condition or fact of being able to pay one's debts.

sol·vent \'sälv-nt\ *adj.* **1** Able to pay all legal debts. **2** Dissolving or able to dissolve; as, the *solvent* action of water. — *n.* A substance, usually a liquid, capable of dissolving something.

so·mat·ic \sō-'mat-ik\ *adj.* **1** Of or relating to the body. **2** Of or relating to the wall of the body.

somatic cell. Any cell of an animal or plant other than a germ cell.

som·ber \'säm-br\ *adj.* **1** Dark and gloomy; dull; as, a *somber* brown; a *somber* sky. **2** Serious; grave; as, a *somber* mood. — **som·ber·ly**, *adv.*

som·bre·ro \səm-'brer-ˌō\ *n.; pl.* **som·bre·ros.** [From Spanish, meaning "hat", literally "shade-giver", and derived from *sombra* meaning "shade".] A broad-brimmed hat, usually of felt, originally worn in Spain and Spanish America.

sombrero

-some. An adjective suffix that can mean: **1** Like, much the same as, as in *burdensome.* **2** Inclined to, as in *frolicsome* or *quarrelsome.* **3** Having to a considerable degree, as in *mettlesome.*

-some. A noun suffix that can mean: In all, together, a group of, as in *foursome* or *twosome.*

some \'səm *or* ˌsəm, *but in sense 2 of the adjective* səm, *without stress*\ *adj.* **1** A certain; one; a certain unknown or not specified; as, *some* evening next week. **2** Of unspecified number or amount, extent, or degree; as, to buy *some* potatoes and *some* flour. *Some* violence occurred. **3** A minority of. *Some* people don't like ice cream. **4** More or less; just about. There are *some* ten houses on the street. **5** *Slang.* That is important or outstanding. That was *some* party last night. — *pron.* **1** Some one; as, *some* of these days. **2** Any indefinite portion; as, to catch a lot of fish but let *some* go.

some·body \'səm-ˌbäd-ē, -bəd-ē\ *pron.* Some person of no certain identity; someone. — *n.; pl.* **some·bod·ies.** A person of importance.

some·day \'səm-ˌdā\ *adv.* At some future time.

some·how \'səm-ˌhau̇\ *adv.* By some means.

some·one \'səm-(ˌ)wən\ *pron.* Some person; somebody. — *n.* A somebody.

som·er·sault \'səm-r-ˌsȯlt\ *n.* A leap, fall, or dive in which a person turns his heels over his head. — *v.* To turn a somersault.

som·er·set \'səm-r-ˌset\ *n.* or *v.* Somersault.

some·thing \'səm(p)-thing\ *n.* **1** Some undetermined or unremembered thing; a thing that is not decided, settled, or understood. *Something* must be done. **2** A thing or amount that is definite but not named; as, *something* to work for.

some·time \'səm-ˌtīm\ *adv.* **1** At one time or another in the future. **2** At a time not known or not named; as, *sometime* last night. — *adj.* Former; as, the *sometime* mayor of the city.

some·times \'səm-ˌtīmz\ *adv.* Occasionally.

some·what \'səm-ˌhwät, -ˌhwət\ *n.* **1** Some part, amount, or degree; as, to feel *somewhat* of another person's embarrassment. **2** One that has some of the character or quality of another. The play was *somewhat* of a bore. — *adv.* A little; in some degree; to some extent; as, to be *somewhat* tired.

some·where \'səm-ˌhwer\ *adv.* In, at, or to a place or point not known or not named. — *n.* An unnamed place. The shot came from *somewhere* near.

som·nam·bu·list \säm-'nam-byə-ləst\ *n.* A sleepwalker. — **som·nam·bu·lism** \-ˌliz-m\ *n.*

som·no·lence \'säm-nə-lən(t)s\ *n.* The state of being somnolent; sleepiness; drowsiness.

som·no·lent \'säm-nə-lənt\ *adj.* Sleepy; drowsy.

son \'sən\ *n.* **1** A boy or man thought of in relation to his father or mother. **2** A male descendant; [in the plural] descendants in general. **3** [with a capital] Jesus Christ, especially as the second person of the Trinity. **4** A man or boy thought of as a child of something, as of a country, race, religion, or occupation; as, hardy *sons* of the soil.

so·nar \'sō-ˌnär, -ˌnȧr\ *n.* An apparatus that detects the presence and location of submerged objects, as submarines, by reflected vibrations.

so·na·ta \sə-'nät-ə, -'nȧt-ə\ *n.* A musical composition for one or two instruments, usually in three or four movements that differ in rhythm and mood but are related in key.

song \'sȯng\ *n.* **1** Something that is sung; singing; vocal music. **2** Poetical composition; poetry; as, a person born with the gift of *song.* **3** A short poem set, or suited to be set, to music; a lyrical poem. **4** A musical setting for a poem or ballad. **5** An instrumental composition having the characteristics of vocal music. **6** A trifle; as, sold for a *song.*

song·bird \'sȯng-ˌbərd\ *n.* A bird that sings.

song·book \'sȯng-ˌbu̇k\ *n.* A collection of songs; a book of hymns or other vocal music.

song·fest \'sȯng-ˌfest\ *n.* An informal session of group singing of popular songs.

song sparrow. A common sparrow of eastern North America noted for its sweet cheerful song.

song·ster \'sȯng(k)st-r\ *n.* **1** A man who sings. **2** A songbird.

song·stress \'sȯng(k)-strəs\ *n.* A woman singer.

son·ic \'sän-ik\ *adj.* **1** Of, relating to, or using sound waves; as, a *sonic* altimeter. **2** Of or relating to the speed of sound in air, about 1087 feet per second or about 738 miles per hour.

sonic barrier. The sound barrier.

son-in-law \'sən-ən-ˌlȯ\ *n.; pl.* **sons-in-law.** The husband of one's daughter.

son·net \'sän-ət\ *n.* A poem having 14 iambic pentameter lines and a restricted rhyme scheme.

son·ne·teer \ˌsän-ə-'tir\ *n.* A composer of sonnets.

son·ny \'sən-ē\ *n.* Little son — used familiarly.

son·o·rous \'sän-r-əs, sə-'nōr-əs, -'nȯr-\ *adj.* **1** Sounding when struck; as, *sonorous* metals. **2** Loud, deep, or rich in sound; as, a *sonorous* voice. **3** Impressive; high-sounding. *Sonorous* phrases.

soon \'sün, 'su̇n\ *adv.* **1** At once; without delay. **2** Shortly after; before long. **3** Promptly; quickly. **4** Before the usual time; early. **5** Readily; willingly. The children would as *soon* go now as later.

soot \'su̇t, 'sət, 'süt\ *n.* A black powder formed when something is burned; the fine powder that colors smoke.

sooth \'süth\ *n. Archaic.* Truth.

soothe \'süt͟h\ *v.;* **soothed; sooth·ing. 1** To calm, quiet, or comfort. **2** To ease, as pain.

sooth·say·er \'süth-ˌsā-ər\ *n.* A person who claims

to foretell events. — **sooth·say·ing** \-ing\ *n.*

sooty \'su̇t-ē, 'sət-ē, 'süt-ē\ *adj.;* **soot·i·er**; **soot·i·est.** Soiled with or as if with soot; black.

sop \'säp\ *v.;* **sopped**; **sop·ping.** **1** To dip in a liquid; as, to *sop* bread in milk. **2** To make something wet or soggy; to soak; to wet; as, to *sop* a dirty floor with soapy water. **3** To mop up; as, to *sop* up the spilled milk. — *n.* **1** Any food softened in liquid, as bread dipped in milk or gravy. **2** Something given to pacify or win favor, as a gift.

soph·ism \'säf-ˌiz-m\ *n.* An unsound, misleading argument that, on the surface, seems reasonable.

soph·ist \'säf-əst\ *n.* One who uses sophisms.

so·phis·tic \sə-'fis-tik\ or **so·phis·ti·cal** \-tik-l\ *adj.* Clever and subtle but misleading. — **so·phis·ti·cal·ly** \-tik-l(-)ē\ *adv.*

so·phis·ti·cate \sə-'fis-tə-ˌkāt\ *v.;* **so·phis·ti·cat·ed**; **so·phis·ti·cat·ing.** To cause to become sophisticated. — \-tik-ət, -tə-ˌkāt\ *n.* A sophisticated person.

so·phis·ti·cat·ed \sə-'fis-tə-ˌkāt-əd\ *adj.* **1** Made worldly-wise by experience; having lost one's naturalness, simplicity, or genuineness. **2** Of a kind or quality that interests sophisticates.

so·phis·ti·ca·tion \sə-ˌfis-tə-'kāsh-n\ *n.* The quality or state of being sophisticated.

soph·is·try \'säf-əs-trē\ *n.; pl.* **soph·ist·ries.** **1** Subtle and misleading reasoning. **2** A sophism.

soph·o·more \'säf-ˌmōr, -ˌmȯr; 'säf-m-ˌōr, -ˌȯr\ *n.* A person in the second year of a four-year course at college or high school.

soph·o·mor·ic \ˌsäf-m-'ōr-ik, -'ȯr-\ *adj.* **1** Of or relating to a sophomore. **2** Conceited and overconfident but poorly informed and immature.

sop·o·rif·ic \ˌsäp-r-'if-ik, ˌsōp-r-\ *adj.* **1** Causing or tending to cause sleep; as, a *soporific* drug. **2** Sleepy; drowsy. — *n.* A drug or medicine that causes sleep. — **sop·o·rif·i·cal·ly** \-ik-l(-)ē\ *adv.*

sop·py \'säp-ē\ *adj.;* **sop·pi·er**; **sop·pi·est.** Soaked; very wet; sloppy.

so·prano \sə-'pran-ō, -'prän-, -'prȧn-\ *n.; pl.* **so·pran·os.** [From Italian, there derived from *soprano* meaning "highest".] **1** The highest quality of voice, usually covering two or more octaves up from middle C. **2** A part sung by this voice. **3** A soprano singer. — *adj.* Of or relating to a soprano voice, part, or quality.

sor·cer·er \'sȯrs-r-r\ *n.* One who practices sorcery.

sor·cer·ess \'sȯrs-r(-)əs\ *n.* A woman sorcerer.

sor·cery \'sȯrs-r(-)ē\ *n.; pl.* **sor·cer·ies.** Witchcraft; the use of magic and enchantments.

sor·did \'sȯrd-əd\ *adj.* **1** Filthy; dirty; as, *sordid* surroundings. **2** Vile; base; as, a *sordid* life. **3** Miserly; niggardly. — **sor·did·ly**, *adv.*

sore \'sōr, 'sȯr\ *adj.;* **sor·er**; **sor·est.** **1** Severe; intense; as, *sore* need. **2** Painful; inflamed; infected; as, a *sore* hand. **3** Causing painful thoughts, distress, or irritation; as, a *sore* subject for discussion. **4** Angry or resentful. — *n.* **1** A bruised spot on the body, especially one where the skin is broken. **2** An infected wound or cut; a boil.

sore·ly \'sōr-lē, 'sȯr-\ *adv.* In a sore manner; painfully; severely; extremely.

sor·ghum \'sȯrg-m\ *n.* **1** A plant similar to Indian corn, of which one type, **sor·go** \'sȯr-ˌgō\, is cultivated for forage and syrup, others for forage and grain. **2** Syrup from sorgo.

sori. A pl. of *sorus.*

so·ror·i·ty \sə-'rȯr-ət-ē, -'rär-\ *n.; pl.* **so·ror·i·ties.** A society or club of women, usually associated with a college or university.

sor·rel \'sȯr-əl, 'sär-\ *n.* Any of several weeds of the buckwheat family; especially, the bitter-tasting **sheep sorrel.**

sor·rel \'sȯr-əl, 'sär-\ *n.* **1** A yellowish or reddish brown. **2** An animal, as a horse, of this color.

sor·row \'sär-ō\ *n.* **1** Suffering or sadness, as from loss or disappointment. **2** Repentance for wrong done. **3** A cause of grief. — *v.* To grieve; to mourn.

sor·row·ful \'sär-əf-l\ *adj.* **1** Feeling sorrow. **2** Arousing sorrow. — **sor·row·ful·ly** \-əf-l(-)ē\ *adv.*

sor·ry \'sär-ē\ *adj.;* **sor·ri·er**; **sor·ri·est.** **1** Causing sorrow; distressing. **2** Feeling repentance. **3** Dismal; gloomy. **4** Poor; contemptible; pitiful.

sort \'sȯrt\ *n.* **1** A group of persons or things that resemble each other; a kind or class; as, all *sorts* of people. **2** Type of person. The new pupil was not a bad *sort.* — **out of sorts.** **1** Irritable. **2** Ill. — *v.* To separate and arrange; as, to *sort* mail.

sor·tie \'sȯrt-ē, 'sȯr-ˌtē\ *n.* **1** A sally of troops from a besieged place against the besiegers. **2** One mission or attack made by a single military airplane.

so·rus \'sōr-əs, 'sȯr-\ *n.; pl.* **so·rus·es** \-ə-səz\ or **so·ri** \'sōr-ˌī, 'sȯr-\. In ferns, a spore cluster forming one of the dots on the under side of the fertile fronds.

SOS \'es-ˌō-'es\. The international code signal of distress for use by ships and aircraft.

so-so \'sō-'sō\ *adj.* Neither very good nor very bad; middling. — *adv.* Tolerably; passably.

sot \'sät\ *n.* A drunkard. — **sot·tish** \'sät-ish\ *adj.*

sot·to vo·ce \ˌsät-ō 'vō-chē\. [From Italian, meaning literally "under (one's) voice".] Under the breath; in an undertone; privately.

sou \'sü\ *n.* A French bronze coin of the period before 1914, worth one twentieth of a franc.

souf·flé \sü-'flā\ *n.* A delicate spongy hot dish lightened in baking by stiffly beaten egg white.

sough \'səf, 'sau̇\ *n.* A hollow moaning, murmuring, or sighing sound, as of the wind through trees. — *v.* To make a sough; to sigh.

sought. Past tense and past part. of *seek.*

soul \'sōl\ *n.* **1** That spiritual part of man believed to give life to his body, and in many religions regarded as immortal. **2** Man's moral and emotional nature; as, to feel one's *soul* rebel against cruelty. **3** The essential part of anything. **4** The leader; the moving spirit; as, the *soul* of a party. **5** Embodiment; as, a man who was the *soul* of honor. **6** A human being; a person; as, a kind *soul.* **7** A disembodied spirit.

soul·ful \'sōlf-l\ *adj.* Filled with or expressing deep feeling or emotion. — **soul·ful·ly** \-l-ē\ *adv.*

soul·less \'sōl-ləs\ *adj.* Having no soul; mean; ignoble. — **soul·less·ly,** *adv.*

sound \'saůnd\ *adj.* **1** Free from flaw, defect, or decay. **2** Healthy; as, a *sound* mind in a *sound* body. **3** Firm; strong; safe; secure; as, a *sound* business. **4** Solid; as, *sound* rock. **5** Not faulty; right; as, a *sound* argument. **6** Showing good sense; wise; as, *sound* advice. **7** Honorable; honest; as, *sound* principles. **8** Thorough; as, a *sound* beating. **9** Undisturbed; deep; as, a *sound* sleep.

sound \'saůnd\ *n.* **1** A long passage of water, wider than a strait, often connecting two larger bodies of water or forming a channel between the mainland and an island. **2** The air bladder of a fish.

sound \'saůnd\ *v.* **1** To measure the depth of water, as by a line. **2** To try to find the thoughts or motives of a person; as, to *sound* someone out on his intentions. **3** To dive straight toward the bottom, as a fish when hooked. — **sound·er** \-r\ *n.*

sound \'saůnd\ *n.* **1** The sensation of hearing. **2** That which is heard; a noise. **3** In physics, the energy of a vibration that causes the sensation of hearing. **4** A tone or noise of a special quality or kind; as, a *sound* of rejoicing. **5** A mental impression; implication. This excuse has a suspicious *sound.* **6** Noise without meaning; mere noise. **7** Hearing distance; as, within *sound* of my voice. **8** One of the noises which together make up human speech; as, the *sound* represented by the letters *th* in *this.* — *v.* **1** To make or cause to make a sound or noise. **2** To produce the sound of. *Sound* the word endings clearly. **3** To order or proclaim by sound, as on a bugle; as, to *sound* a retreat. **4** To give a certain impression when heard or read. The story *sounds* false. **5** To celebrate or honor by or as if by sounds; as, to *sound* a hero's praise. **6** To examine something by causing it to emit sounds.

sound barrier. The sudden large increase in resistance that the air offers to an airplane whose speed nears the speed of sound.

sound·board \'saůn(d)-ˌbōrd, -ˌbȯrd\ *n.* A sounding board.

sound·er \'saůnd-r\ *n.* One that sounds; especially, an instrument used in telegraphy for recording sounds.

sound·ing \'saůn-ding\ *adj.* Making or giving off sound; loud and full in sound; resonant; ringing.

sound·ing \'saůn-ding\ *n.* **1** The act of one that sounds. **2** Measurement of depth of water by a weighted line (**sounding line**); the depth of water thus sounded. **3** [in the plural] Any part of the sea where a sounding line will reach bottom.

sounding board. **1** A thin resonant board so placed in a stringed musical instrument as to reinforce its tones by sympathetic vibration. **2** A structure placed behind or over a platform to direct sound towards an audience.

sound·less \'saůn-(d)ləs\ *adj.* Making no sound. — **sound·less·ly,** *adv.*

sound·ly \'saůn-(d)lē\ *adv.* In a sound manner; as, a *soundly* built ship; sleeping *soundly.*

sound·ness \'saůn(d)-nəs\ *n.* The quality or state of being sound, as in health or judgment.

sound·proof \'saůn(d)-'prüf\ *adj.* Impervious to sound; as, a *soundproof* room. — *v.* To make soundproof. — **sound·proof·ing** \-'prü-fing\ *n.*

sound waves. Vibrations traveling through the air or other substance and affecting the ear as sound.

soup \'süp\ *n.* A liquid food consisting usually of a meat broth with or without vegetables or a cream sauce mixed with strained vegetables.

soup \'süp\ *n. Slang.* Engine power; horsepower. — **soup up.** To boost the power and speed of.

sour \'saůr\ *adj.* **1** Having an acid or tart taste, like vinegar. **2** Changed, as by fermentation, so as to be acid or like acid; spoiled; as, *sour* milk. **3** Unpleasant; disagreeable; as, a *sour* look. **4** Acid; as, *sour* soil. — *v.* To become, or cause to become, sour. — *n.* **1** Something which is sour, acid, or rancid. **2** An acid beverage; as, a whisky *sour.*

source \'sōrs, 'sȯrs\ *n.* **1** The beginning of a stream of water. **2** Beginning or origin or place of beginning or origin; as, the *source* of his ideas. **3** A person, book, or document that supplies information.

sour gum. **1** A gum tree related to the dogwood, with small blue-black stone fruits. **2** The tupelo.

sour·ly \'saůr-lē\ *adv.* In a sour manner; especially, disagreeably or with displeasure.

souse \'saůs\ *n.* **1** Something steeped in pickle, as pigs' feet. **2** Brine. **3** A sousing. **4** *Slang.* A drunkard. — *v.;* **soused; sous·ing.** **1** To pickle. **2** To drench. **3** *Slang.* To make or become drunk.

south \'saůth; *in compounds, as* "southeast", *also* 'saů *especially in the speech of seamen*\ *n.* **1** One of the four main points of the compass; the direction to the right of a person facing the rising sun. **2** Any region south of another. **3** [with a capital] That part of the United States that lies south of Pennsylvania and the Ohio River. — *adj.* **1** Going or facing toward the south; situated at or in the south; as, the *south* side of the city. **2** Coming from the south; as, a *south* wind. — *adv.* Southward.

South Af·ri·can \'af-rik-n\ *adj.* Of or relating to South Africa, especially the Union of South Africa. — *n.* A native or inhabitant of South Africa.

South A·mer·i·can \ə-'mer-ək-n\ *adj.* Of or relating to the continent of South America. — *n.* A native or inhabitant of South America.

south·east \'saůth-'ēst\ *n.* **1** The direction halfway between south and east. **2** A part or region that lies in this direction. — *adj.* **1** Going or facing toward the southeast. **2** Coming from the southeast. — *adv.* Toward the southeast.

south·east·er \saůth-'ēst-r\ *n.* A storm, gale, or strong wind from the southeast.

south·east·er·ly \'saůth-'ēst-r-lē\ *adj.* **1** Situated, directed, or moving toward the southeast. **2** Coming from the southeast. — *adv.* Toward the southeast.

south·east·ern \'saůth-'ēst-rn\ *adj.* **1** Of or relating to the southeast. **2** Going or facing toward the southeast. **3** Coming from the southeast.

south·east·ward \'sau̇th-'ēst-wərd\ or **south-east·wards** \-wərdz\ *adv.* To or toward the southeast. — **south·east·ward·ly** \-wərd-lē\ *adj.* or *adv.*

south·east·ward \'sau̇th-'ēst-wərd\ *adj.* Going or facing toward the southeast.

south·er·ly \'sə_th_-r-lē\ *adj.* **1** Situated, directed, or moving toward the south. **2** Coming from the south. — *adv.* Toward the south; southward.

south·ern \'sə_th_-rn\ *adj.* **1** Of or relating to the south. **2** [with a capital] Of or relating to the South. **3** Going or facing toward the south. **4** Coming from the south.

Southern Cross. **1** A group of four bright stars in the southern sky situated as if at the ends of a Latin cross. **2** The constellation Crux, in which these stars are the brightest.

south·ern·er \'sə_th_-rn-r\ *n.* A person native to or living in the southern part of a country or region, especially [with a capital] of the southern United States.

south·ern·most \'sə_th_-rn-ˌmōst\ *adj.* Most south.

south·land \'sau̇th-ˌland, -lənd\ *n.* Land to the south; the southern part of a region or country.

south·paw \'sau̇th-ˌpȯ\ *adj.* In sports, left-handed. — *n.* A left-handed player.

South Pole. The southernmost point of the earth; the southern end of the earth's axis.

south·ward \'sau̇th-wərd\ or **south·wards** \-wərdz\ *adv.* To or toward the south; as, to travel *southward.* — **south·ward·ly** \-wərd-lē\ *adj.* or *adv.*

south·ward \'sau̇th-wərd\ *adj.* Going or facing toward the south.

south·west \'sau̇th-'west\ *n.* **1** The direction halfway between south and west. **2** A part or region that lies in this direction. — *adj.* **1** Going or facing toward the southwest. **2** Coming from the southwest. — *adv.* Toward the southwest.

south·west·er \sau̇th-'west-r\ *n.* A storm, gale, or strong wind from the southwest.

south·west·er·ly \'sau̇th-'west-r-lē\ *adj.* **1** Situated, directed, or moving toward the southwest. **2** Coming from the southwest. — *adv.* Toward the southwest.

south·west·ern \'sau̇th-'west-rn\ *adj.* **1** Of or relating to the southwest. **2** Going or facing toward the southwest. **3** Coming from the southwest.

south·west·ward \'sau̇th-'west-wərd\ or **south-west·wards** \-wərdz\ *adv.* To or toward the southwest. — **south·west·ward·ly** \-wərd-lē\ *adj.* or *adv.*

south·west·ward \'sau̇th-'west-wərd\ *adj.* Going or facing toward the southwest.

sou·ve·nir \'sü̇v-n-ˌir, ˌsüv-n-'ir\ *n.* Something that serves as a reminder; a keepsake.

sou'·west·er \sau̇-'west-r\ *n.* **1** A southwester. **2** A waterproof hat with a broad flap at the back, made usually of heavy oiled cloth or painted canvas.

sov·er·eign \'säv-r(-)ən, 'säv-rn, 'səv-\ *adj.* **1** Chief or highest; as, our *sovereign* interest; a citizen's *sovereign* duty. **2** Supreme in power or authority; reigning; as, a *sovereign* prince. **3** Having independent authority; as, a *sovereign* state. **4** Effectual; excellent; as, a *sovereign* remedy for colds. — *n.* **1** A person, as a king, or body of persons holding supreme authority in a state. **2** A British gold coin equal to one pound sterling.

sov·er·eign·ty \'säv-r(-)ən-tē, 'säv-rn-tē, 'səv-\ *n.; pl.* **sov·er·eign·ties.** **1** The condition of being sovereign or a sovereign. **2** The position or rule of a sovereign. **3** Supreme political authority.

so·vi·et \'sō-vē-ˌet, -ət, 'säv-ē-\ *n.* [From Russian *sovyet* meaning "council".] **1** A council. **2** Either of two local governing bodies (**village soviets, town soviets**) in the Union of Soviet Socialist Republics. **3** Any of various similar socialistic bodies. **4** [with a capital and *the*] The Union of Soviet Socialist Republics or [in the plural] the people, leaders, or armed forces of the U.S.S.R. — *adj.* **1** Of or relating to soviets or sovietism. **2** [with a capital] Of or relating to the U.S.S.R.

so·vi·et·ism \'sō-vē-ˌet-ˌiz-m, -ət-ˌiz-m, 'säv-ē-\ *n.* **1** Government by soviets. **2** Communism.

so·vi·et·ize \'sō-vē-ˌet-ˌīz, -ət-ˌīz, 'säv-ē-\ *v.;* **so·vi·et·ized; so·vi·et·iz·ing.** To change or convert to a government by a soviet or soviets.

sow \'sau̇\ *n.* A female hog.

sow \'sō\ *v.;* **sowed** \'sōd\; **sown** \'sōn\ or **sowed**; **sow·ing.** **1** To scatter, as seed upon the earth. **2** To scatter seed over. **3** To spread abroad; as, to *sow* discontent. — **sow·er** \'sōr, 'sō-ər\ *n.*

sow·bug \'sau̇-ˌbəg\ *n.* A wood louse.

soy \'sȯi\ *n.* **1** A Chinese and Japanese sauce made from fermented soybeans. **2** The soybean.

so·ya \'sȯi-(y)ə\ *n.* or **soya bean.** The soybean.

soy·bean \'sȯi-'bēn\ *n.* A bushy, hairy plant from Asia, grown for feed, forage, and soil improvement, and for its round edible seeds.

SP. Abbreviation for *shore patrol.*

spa \'spä, 'spȯ, 'spå\ *n.* [Named after *Spa*, a town near Liége, Belgium, famous for its mineral springs.] **1** A mineral spring. **2** A locality or a resort having mineral springs.

space \'spās\ *n.* **1** The limitless area through which the earth, sun, moon, and stars move. **2** Some part of this limitless area; as, the *space* between two hills; the *space* in a box. **3** A definite place, as a seat on a plane; accommodations. **4** An empty place. **5** An empty place marked off for a certain purpose; as, a parking *space.* **6** A period of time; as, after a long *space.* **7** Lines or pages in a newspaper or periodical; as, advertising *space.* **8** In music, one of the parallel open places of the staff. **9** The regions beyond the earth's atmosphere; outer space. — *v.;* **spaced; spac·ing.** To arrange with spaces between; to place at intervals.

space·craft \'spās-ˌkraft\ *n.* A spaceship.

space·man \'spās-ˌman\ *n.; pl.* **space·men** \-ˌmen\. **1** A traveler in a spaceship. **2** A dweller in outer space. **3** A person engaged in any of various fields bearing on flight through outer space.

space medicine. A branch of medicine concerned especially with the study of physiological and psychological disorders expected to arise during travel in outer space.

space·ship, *n.* or **space ship** \'spās(h)-ˌship\. A proposed aircraft for travel in outer space.

space station. A proposed manned artificial satellite which would revolve around the earth and serve as an observation station and as a base for further travel into more distant space.

space suit. **1** A pressurized suit for wear in very high altitude flying. **2** Any fanciful costume imagined to be worn by dwellers in outer space.

spa·cious \'spā-shəs\ *adj.* Very large in extent; roomy; as, a *spacious* room; a *spacious* house.

spade \'spād\ *n.* A tool for turning over earth, heavier than a shovel and adapted for being pushed into the ground by the foot. — *v.;* **spad·ed**; **spad·ing.** To dig with a spade.

spade \'spād\ *n.* [From Spanish *espada* meaning literally "sword", the shape of one of the marks distinguishing suits on Spanish playing cards.] **1** A playing card bearing a black figure resembling a sharp-pointed spade. **2** [in the plural] The suit of cards bearing this figure.

spa·ghet·ti \spə-'get-ē\ *n.* A food paste made chiefly of wheat flour shaped in long thin cords.

spake. A past tense of *speak.*

span \'span\ *n.* **1** The space from the end of the thumb to the end of the little finger when the hand is stretched wide open — considered in English measure as being 9 inches. **2** A limited portion of time; as, the *span* of life. **3** The spread of an arch, a beam, a truss, or a girder from one support to another. **4** A pair of work animals driven together. — *v.;* **spanned**; **span·ning.** **1** To measure by the hand stretched wide open. **2** To reach across. A bridge *spans* the river.

span \'span\. A past tense of *spin.*

span·gle \'spang-gl\ *n.* **1** A small piece of shining metal used as an ornament, especially on a dress or fabric. **2** Any little sparkling thing. — *v.;* **span·gled**; **span·gling** \-gl(-)ing\. To set or sprinkle with or as if with spangles.

Span·iard \'span-yərd\ *n.* A native or citizen of Spain.

span·iel \'span-yəl\ *n.* [From medieval English *spaynel,* there borrowed from medieval French *espaignol* meaning literally "Spanish (dog)".] A dog of any of numerous small or medium-sized breeds with short legs, wavy hair, and drooping ears, including the **field spaniels**, as the cocker spaniel, the **water spaniels**, and the **English toy spaniels.**

a spaniel

Span·ish \'span-ish\ *adj.* Of or relating to Spain. — *n.* **1** The people of Spain; the Spaniards — used as a plural with *the.* **2** The chief language of Spain and of Spanish American countries.

Spanish Amer·i·can \ə-'mer-ək-n\ *adj.* Of or relating to Mexico and the countries of Central and South America in which Spanish is the national language. — *n.* A native or inhabitant of a Spanish American country.

Span·ish-Amer·i·can \'span-ish-ə-'mer-ək-n\ *adj.* Of or relating to Spain and America, especially Spain and the United States; as, *Spanish-American* relations; the *Spanish-American* War.

Spanish Main. **1** The mainland of Spanish America; especially, the northern coast of South America. **2** The Caribbean Sea.

spank \'spangk\ *v.* To strike the rump or buttocks of, usually with the open hand. — *n.* A spanking; a slap, especially on the buttocks.

spank·er \'spangk-r\ *n.* **1** The fore-and-aft sail on the mast nearest the stern of a square-rigged ship. **2** The last mast and sail on a schooner of more than four masts.

spank·ing \'spangk-ing\ *adj.* Moving with a quick, lively pace; brisk; lively.

span·ner \'span-r\ *n.* **1** One that spans. **2** A tool having a socket or jaw at each end for turning nuts and bolts or pipe; a wrench.

spar \'spär, 'spȧr\ *n.* Any of various nonmetallic, somewhat lustrous minerals usually able to be split readily in certain directions.

spar \'spär, 'spȧr\ *n.* **1** A long piece of wood or metal to which a sail is fastened, as a mast, boom, or yard. **2** A main, supporting, lengthwise beam in parts of an airplane, especially a wing.

spar \'spär, 'spȧr\ *v.;* **sparred**; **spar·ring.** **1** To box with the fists; especially, to box cautiously and skillfully. **2** To contest in words; to wrangle.

spare \'spar, 'sper\ *v.;* **spared**; **spar·ing.** **1** To refrain from; to avoid; as, to *spare* no cost. **2** To free from; as, to be *spared* the labor. **3** To use very little or rarely; as, to *spare* the rod and spoil the child. **4** To give away something out of a supply that is more than enough. **5** To show mercy to; as, to *spare* the women and children. **6** To do without; as, to be unable to *spare* even a dollar. — *adj.;* **spar·er**; **spar·est.** **1** Held in reserve; as, a *spare* tire. **2** Being over and above what is needed; as, *spare* time. **3** Lean; gaunt; thin; as, of *spare* build. **4** Scanty; frugal; as, a *spare* diet. — *n.* **1** Something that has not been used or spent. **2** A spare or duplicate piece or part, as an automobile tire. **3** In bowling, the knocking down of all the pins in two bowls or the score made by this action. — **spare·ly**, *adv.*

spare·rib \'spar-ˌrib, 'sper-\ *n.* A cut of pork, consisting of the close-trimmed ends of the ribs.

spar·ing \'spar-ing, 'sper-\ *adj.* Saving; frugal; scanty. — **spar·ing·ly**, *adv.*

spark \'spärk, 'spȧrk\ *n.* **1** A small particle of fire. **2** Anything resembling such a burning particle. **3** The flash of light that accompanies an electric discharge between two conductors. **4** The discharge of electricity in a spark plug or the mechanism that controls this discharge. **5** Anything that, like a spark, may be kindled into fire or into life or action. Not a *spark* of life was found on the island. — *v.* **1** To produce a spark or sparks; to flash out like a spark. **2** To spur to energetic, determined action, especially a group or team.

spark \'spärk, 'spȧrk\ *n.* **1** A brisk, showy, gay man. **2** A lover; a beau. — *v.* To court.

spar·kle \'spärk-l, 'spȧrk-l\ *v.;* **spar·kled**; **spar·kling** \-l(-)ing\. **1** To throw off sparks of light or fire; to flash; to twinkle. **2** To bubble; as, a *sparkling* wine. **3** To be lively or active. The conversation *sparkled* with humor. — *n.* **1** A flash; a spark; glitter; as, the *sparkle* of a diamond. **2** Brilliance; liveliness; as, the *sparkle* of a witty play.

spar·kler \'spärk-lər, 'spȧrk-\ *n.* One that sparkles, as a firework or a brilliant gem.

spark plug. **1** A plug, fitting in the top of the cylinder, whose electric spark ignites the explosive mixture in an internal-combustion engine. **2** A member of a group who spurs his fellow members to spirited action.

spar·row \'spar-ō\ *n.* **1** Also **house sparrow.** A small brownish or brown-gray finch with a short, stout bill; the English sparrow. **2** Any of numerous finches somewhat resembling the house sparrow in size and in having plumage streaked with shades of gray and brown, as the song sparrow.

sparrow hawk. A small North American falcon, rusty red and bluish gray above and yellowish white below.

sparse \'spärs, 'spȧrs\ *adj.;* **spars·er**; **spars·est.** Not thickly grown or settled. — **sparse·ly** \-lē\ *adv.* — **spar·si·ty** \'spär-sət-ē, 'spȧr-\ *n.*

Spar·tan \'spärt-n, 'spȧrt-n\ *adj.* **1** Of or relating to Sparta. **2** Hardy; undaunted; severe; as, *Spartan* courage. — *n.* **1** A citizen of Sparta. **2** A person of great courage and bravery.

spasm \'spaz-m\ *n.* **1** A sudden uncontrolled drawing together of muscles or a muscle. **2** Any sudden, violent, and temporary effort or feeling.

spas·mod·ic \spaz-'mäd-ik\ *adj.* **1** Of, relating to, or affected by a spasm; as, *spasmodic* breathing. **2** Going by fits and starts; fitful; as, *spasmodic* energy. — **spas·mod·i·cal·ly** \-ik-l(-)ē\ *adv.*

spas·tic \'spas-tik\ *adj.* Of or relating to muscular spasm, as in **spastic paralysis**, an affliction in which there is prolonged muscular contraction. — *n.* A person suffering from spastic paralysis.

spat \'spat\ *n.* A young oyster or oysters. — *v.;* **spat·ted**; **spat·ting**. To spawn, as oysters.

spat \'spat\ *n.* A short cloth or leather gaiter.

spat \'spat\ *v.;* **spat·ted**; **spat·ting.** **1** To strike with a smacking sound. **2** To dispute; to quarrel. — *n.* **1** A light slap or the sound it makes. **2** A petty quarrel; a dispute.

spat \'spat\. A past tense and past part. of *spit*, to throw out from the mouth.

spa·tial \'spāsh-l\ *adj.* Of or relating to space; occupying or occurring in space. — **spa·tial·ly**, *adv.*

spat·ter \'spat-r\ *v.* **1** To splash with a liquid; to spot or soil by splashing. **2** To scatter by splashing; as, to *spatter* mud. **3** To cover with splashes and spots. **4** To spurt in scattered drops. **5** To drop with a sound like rain. — *n.* **1** The action or sound of spattering; a splashing. **2** A drop or splash spattered on something.

spat·u·la \'spach-l-ə\ *n.* An instrument resembling a knife, with a flat, thin, flexible blade for spreading, as artist's paint, for handling powdered drugs, or for general kitchen use.

spatulas

spav·in \'spav-n\ *n.* A disease of horses that causes bony enlargement of the hock. — **spav·ined** \-nd\ *adj.*

spawn \'spȯn, 'spän\ *v.* **1** To produce or deposit eggs, as fish. **2** To produce young in vast quantities. — *n.* **1** The eggs of water animals that produce many small eggs. **2** Any product or offspring.

spay \'spā\ *v.;* **spayed**; **spay·ing.** To remove the ovaries of, as of a female dog or cat.

speak \'spēk\ *v.;* **spoke** \'spōk\ or, archaic, **spake** \'spāk\; **spo·ken** \'spōk-n\; or, archaic, **spoke**; **speak·ing.** **1** To utter words with the ordinary voice; to talk. **2** To utter by means of words; as, to *speak* the truth. **3** To address a gathering. **4** To mention in speech or writing. **5** To carry a meaning as if by speech; as, clothes that *spoke* of poverty. **6** To sound, as does a bugle or a rifle. **7** To use in talking; as, to *speak* French. — **speak for.** **1** To speak in behalf of; to represent the opinions of. **2** To engage; to apply for. — **speak out.** **1** To speak loudly and distinctly. **2** To speak freely. — **speak to.** To reprove; to rebuke. — **speak up.** To speak out. — **speak well for.** To be evidence in favor of. — **speak with.** To talk to.

speak·er \'spēk-r\ *n.* **1** One that speaks; especially, a person who makes a public address. **2** [with a capital] The presiding officer of certain legislative bodies, usually a lower or popular house as the House of Representatives. **3** A loudspeaker.

speak·er·ship \'spēk-r-ˌship\ *n.* The position of speaker, especially of a legislative body.

speak·ing \'spēk-ing\ *adj.* **1** Uttering speech; used for uttering or conveying speech; as, a pleasant *speaking* voice. **2** Seeming to be capable of speech; lifelike; expressive, as, *speaking* eyes; a *speaking* likeness. — *n.* The act or art of one who speaks, especially in public; oratory.

spear \'spir\ *n.* **1** A weapon with a long shaft and sharp head or blade, for throwing or thrusting. **2** A sharp-pointed implement with barbs, used for catching large fish by stabbing them under water. **3** A shoot or sprout, as of grass or asparagus. — *v.* **1** To pierce or strike with or as if with a spear. **2** To shoot into a long stem, as a plant.

spear·head \'spir-ˌhed\ *n.* **1** The head or point of a spear. **2** The foremost point, person, or body, as in an attack, drive, or undertaking. — *v.* To serve as spearhead of, as of an attack.

spear·man \'spir-mən\ *n.;* *pl.* **spear·men** \-mən\. A person, especially a soldier, armed with a spear.

spear·mint \'spir-ˌmint\ *n.* The common garden mint, cultivated for use in flavoring and for its aromatic oil.

spe·cial \'spesh-l\ *adj.* **1** Uncommon; extraordinary; as, a *special* occasion. **2** Having superiority in some way, as in power or importance; as, a *special* ambassador. **3** Individual; unique; as, a *special* case. **4** Particularly favored; dear; as, a *special* friend. **5** Meant for a particular purpose or use; as, a *special* diet. — *n.* A special person or thing, as a special edition, train, or sale.

spe·cial·ist \'spesh-l(-)əst\ *n.* One who devotes himself to a special branch or activity in his business, profession, or studies; as, an eye *specialist.*

spe·cial·i·za·tion \ˌspesh-l-ə-'zāsh-n\ *n.* **1** The action or process of specializing; limiting of one's attention or study to a single business, activity, or interest. **2** The state of being specialized; especially, the state or fact of having developed or having been changed, as an organism or part, to suit special conditions or to serve a special purpose.

spe·cial·ize \'spesh-l-ˌīz\ *v.;* **spe·cial·ized; spe·cial·iz·ing. 1** To limit one's attention or energy to one business, subject, or study; as, to *specialize* in jet airplanes. **2** To undergo or cause to undergo specialization; as, *specialized* sense organs.

spe·cial·ly \'spesh-l(-)ē\ *adv.* In a special manner or degree.

spe·cial·ty \'spesh-l-tē\ *n.; pl.* **spe·cial·ties. 1** Something with a special quality or characteristic or made to serve a special purpose; as, a store that sells only *specialties.* **2** A special accomplishment. Pancakes were the cook's *specialty.* **3** That in which one specializes or has special knowledge.

spe·cie \'spē-shē, -sē\ *n.* Coin, usually of gold or silver; money in the form of coins.

spe·cies \'spē-(ˌ)shēz, -(ˌ)sēz\ *n. sing. and pl.* [From Latin, meaning literally "look", "appearance".] **1** A sort; a variety; as, a *species* of dishonesty. **2** One of the subordinate classes into which a larger class is divided. Quartz is a *species* of rock. **3** In biology, a group of plants or animals that have distinctive characteristics in common and that may reproduce their characteristics in their offspring, ranking as a group in classification below a genus and above a variety.

spec·i·fi·a·ble \'spes-ə-ˌfī-əb-l\ *adj.* Capable of being specified.

spe·cif·ic \spə-'sif-ik\ *adj.* **1** Of or relating to a species. **2** Definite; particular; exact; as, a *specific* date. **3** In medicine, curing by some special fitness, as a drug, or caused by a particular germ or virus, as a disease. — *n.* **1** Something peculiarly adapted to its purpose. **2** In medicine, a specific remedy.

spe·cif·i·cal·ly \spə-'sif-ik-l(-)ē\ *adv.* **1** With reference to species. **2** Definitely; precisely.

spec·i·fi·ca·tion \ˌspes-ə-fə-'kāsh-n\ *n.* **1** The act of making specific; a precise naming of particulars. **2** Something that is specified; a single specified item. **3** [usually in the plural] A description of work to be done or materials to be used.

specific gravity. A measure of the heaviness of a substance determined by comparing the weight of a quantity of this substance with the weight of an equal quantity of some standard, usually water for solids and liquids and air or hydrogen for gases. Thus 19, the *specific gravity* of gold, expresses the fact that, bulk for bulk, gold weighs nineteen times as much as water.

spec·i·fy \'spes-ə-ˌfī\ *v.;* **spec·i·fied** \-ˌfīd\; **spec·i·fy·ing. 1** To mention or name exactly or in detail; as, to *specify* the reason for absence. **2** To include as an item in a specification.

spec·i·men \'spes-m-ən\ *n.* **1** A piece of something or a single unit of a group of similar things that shows what the whole thing or group is like; a sample. **2** A person; as, a tough *specimen.*

spe·cious \'spē-shəs\ *adj.* Apparently but not really fair, just, or right; appearing well at first view; as, a *specious* argument. — **spe·cious·ly,** *adv.*

speck \'spek\ *n.* **1** A small spot or blemish, especially from or of dirt or decay; as, *specks* of dust. **2** A small piece or bit; a particle. — *v.* To produce specks in or on; as, a washing *specked* with soot.

speck·le \'spek-l\ *n.* A little speck; a spot or mark, as of color. — *v.;* **speck·led; speck·ling** \-l(-)ing\. To mark with speckles; as, a *speckled* trout.

specs \'speks\ *n. pl.* Spectacles; glasses.

spec·ta·cle \'spek-tik-l\ *n.* **1** Something exhibited to view, especially as being unusual or notable. **2** An impressive public display, as a pageant, designed to appeal to the eye, as through its proportions or color. **3** [in the plural] A pair of glasses held in place by side pieces passing over the ears.

spectacles, 3

spec·ta·cled \'spek-tik-ld\ *adj.* **1** Wearing spectacles. **2** In zoology, having spots or patches suggesting spectacles.

spec·tac·u·lar \spek-'tak-yəl-r, spək-\ *adj.* Of, relating to, or of the nature of a spectacle; striking; showy; sensational. — *n.* **1** That which is spectacular; as, an exhibition of skill close to the *spectacular.* **2** A lavishly produced performance, as on television, intended to appeal especially to the eye. — **spec·tac·u·lar·ly**, *adv.*

spec·ta·tor \'spek-ˌtāt-r\ *n.* One who looks on; an onlooker, as at an exhibition, play, or game.

spec·ter \'spekt-r\ *n.* A visible disembodied spirit; ghost or ghostly figure; an apparition.

spectra. A pl. of *spectrum.*

spec·tral \'spek-trəl\ *adj.* **1** Of or relating to a specter or specters. **2** Like a specter; ghostly; as, a *spectral* figure. **3** Of, relating to, or made by the spectrum or a spectrum; as, *spectral* colors.

spec·tro·graph \'spek-t(r)ə-ˌgraf\ *n.* **1** An apparatus for photographing or mapping a spectrum. **2** A picture of a spectrum. — **spec·tro·graph·ic** \ˌspek-t(r)ə-'graf-ik\ *adj.* — **spec·tro·graph·i·cal·ly** \-ik-l(-)ē\ *adv.*

spec·tro·scope \'spek-trə-ˌskōp\ *n.* An optical instrument for forming spectrums, as that of the sunlight or those produced by various flames. — **spec·tro·scop·ic** \ˌspek-trə-'skäp-ik\ *adj.* — **spec·tro·scop·i·cal·ly** \-ik-l(-)ē\ *adv.*

spec·trum \'spek-trəm\ *n.; pl.* **spec·trums** \-trəmz\ or **spec·tra** \-trə\. The series of images formed when a beam of light or, in general, radiant energy is separated into its different rays so that the component waves are arranged in the order of their wave lengths; the group of colors (red, orange, yellow, green, blue, indigo, and violet) seen when light passes through a prism and falls on a surface, or when sunlight is affected by drops of water, as in a rainbow.

spec·u·late \'spek-yə-ˌlāt\ *v.;* **spec·u·lat·ed; spec·u·lat·ing.** **1** To ponder; to meditate. **2** To conjecture; to guess. **3** To engage in speculation.

spec·u·la·tion \ˌspek-yə-'lāsh-n\ *n.* **1** Thought; meditation. **2** An unfounded conclusion; a guess. **3** A venture in which a large profit may be made if a considerable risk is taken.

spec·u·la·tive \'spek-yə-ˌlāt-iv, -lət-iv\ *adj.* **1** Thoughtful; meditative; as, a man of a *speculative* turn of mind. **2** Theoretical; as, *speculative* thinking; a *speculative* conclusion. **3** Of, relating to, or engaged in speculation; of the nature of a speculation. — **spec·u·la·tive·ly,** *adv.*

spec·u·la·tor \'spek-yə-ˌlāt-r\ *n.* A person who speculates, as in real estate or securities.

sped. A past tense and past part. of *speed.*

speech \'spēch\ *n.* **1** The uttering of understandable sounds or words; the power of speaking. **2** The act or manner of speaking. **3** Something spoken; talk. **4** A public or formal talk; as, a *speech* on politics. **5** A language; a dialect.

speech·less \'spēch-ləs\ *adj.* **1** Lacking or deprived of the power of speaking. **2** Not speaking for a time; silent; as, to be *speechless* with surprise. — For synonyms see *dumb.* — **speech·less·ly,** *adv.*

speed \'spēd\ *n.* **1** *Archaic.* Success; as, to wish a person good *speed.* **2** Swiftness; rapidity; rate of motion; as, to drive at top *speed.* **3** A transmission gear, as in an automobile. — *v.;* **sped** \'sped\ or **speed·ed; speed·ing.** **1** To hurry; to hasten; to move rapidly. **2** To go or drive at too great speed. **3** To further; to advance; to aid. **4** To wish godspeed to; as, to *speed* the parting guest. **5** To increase the speed of; as, to *speed* up a motor. — For synonyms see *haste.*

speed·boat \'spēd-ˌbōt\ *n.* A launch or powerboat designed for high speed.

speed·er \'spēd-r\ *n.* One that speeds; especially, a person who exceeds the legal speed limit.

speed·i·ly \'spēd-l-ē\ *adv.* **1** Rapidly; quickly. **2** Promptly; soon.

speed·om·e·ter \spē-'däm-ət-r\ *n.* An instrument that measures speed or one that measures speed and distance, as in an automobile.

speed·way \'spēd-ˌwā\ *n.* A road on which more than ordinary speed is allowed.

speed·well \'spēd-ˌwel\ *n.* Any of several creeping plants with mostly oblong, toothed leaves and blue or white flowers.

speedy \'spēd-ē\ *adj.;* **speed·i·er; speed·i·est.** Marked by speed; fast; as, a *speedy* trip.

spell \'spel\ *v.* **1** To take the place of someone for a time; to relieve; as, to *spell* a person at shoveling. **2** To allow rest to. The man *spelled* his horse. — *n.* **1** The relief of one person by another in any work or duty. **2** One's turn at work or duty. **3** A period of rest from work or duty. **4** A short time, as a few minutes, few hours, or few months; as, a hot *spell.* **5** The period of time occupied as by illness, faintness, laughter, or crying. **6** A fit, as of illness.

spell \'spel\ *n.* [From Old English, meaning "story", "speech", "news".] **1** A spoken word or group of words supposed to have magic power; a charm. **2** Magic influence; as, an evil *spell.*

spell \'spel\ *v.;* **spelled** \'speld, 'spelt\ or **spelt** \'spelt\; **spell·ing.** **1** To name, write, or print in order the letters of, especially the correct letters; as, to *spell* a word. **2** To constitute the letters of. C-a-t *spells* "cat". **3** To mean; to signify. Such an act would *spell* ruin for the country. **4** To read slowly with or as if with difficulty; as, to *spell* out the page. **5** To spell a word or words.

spell·bind \'spel-ˌbīnd\ *v.;* **spell·bound** \-ˌbaůnd\; **spell·bind·ing.** To hold by or as if by a spell; to charm. — **spell·bind·er** \-ˌbīnd-r\ *n.*

spell·er \'spel-r\ *n.* **1** A person who spells. **2** A book with exercises for teaching how to spell.

spell·ing \'spel-ing\ *n.* **1** The action of a person who spells. **2** The formation of words by letters.

spelling bee or **spelling match.** A contest of skill in spelling words.

spend \'spend\ *v.;* **spent** \'spent\; **spend·ing.** **1** To use up in any way; to expend. **2** To use wastefully. **3** To pass; as, to *spend* the winter in the city.

spend·thrift \'spen(d)-ˌthrift\ *n.* A person who spends lavishly or wastefully. — *adj.* Wasteful.

spent \'spent\ *adj.* With force or strength exhausted; as, a *spent* runner; a *spent* bullet.

sperm \'spərm\ *n.* **1** A fluid that is produced by male animals and contains the living bodies (**sperm cells**) that fertilize the eggs of a female. **2** Short for *spermaceti.* **3** Sperm oil.

sper·ma·ce·ti \ˌspər-mə-'sēt-ē, -'set-ē\ *n.* A white, waxy solid separating from the oil of certain sea-dwelling mammals, as the sperm whale and the dolphin, used in making candles and ointments.

sper·ma·to·phyte \'spər-mət-ə-ˌfīt, (ˌ)spər-'mat-ə-\ *n.* A plant that produces seeds.

sper·ma·to·zo·on \ˌspər-mət-ə-'zō-ˌän, (ˌ)spər-ˌmat-ə-, -'zō-ən\ *n.; pl.* **sper·ma·to·zo·ons** \-'zō-ˌänz, -ənz\ or **sper·ma·to·zoa** \-'zō-ə\. A male animal's sperm cell, which fertilizes the egg.

sperm whale. A large, toothed whale of warm seas, having in its head a closed cavity containing spermaceti and a lubricant oil (**sperm oil**).

spew \'spyü\ *v.* To vomit; to pour forth.

sp. gr. Abbreviation for *specific gravity.*

sphag·num \'sfag-nəm\ *n.* **1** Any of a group of peat-forming mosses. **2** A mass of these plants used variously, as for surgical dressings.

sphere \'sfir\ *n.* **1** A figure so shaped that every point on its surface is an equal distance from the center of the figure; a ball. **2** Any globe or ball-shaped body, especially a heavenly body. **3** A globe that represents the earth. **4** A circuit or range of action, knowledge, or influence; a field; as, a subject outside one's *sphere*. **5** Social rank, position, or class. **6** The atmosphere; the heavens.

spher·i·cal \'sfir-ik-l, 'sfer-\ *adj.* **1** Sphere-shaped; round. **2** Of or relating to a sphere; as, *spherical* geometry. — **spher·i·cal·ly** \-ik-l(-)ē\ *adv.*

sphe·roid \'sfir-ˌȯid\ *n.* A figure resembling a sphere but not perfectly round. — **sphe·roi·dal** \sfi-'rȯid-l\ *adj.*

sphinc·ter \'sfing(k)t-r\ *n.* A ring of contractile muscle surrounding an opening of the body.

sphinx \'sfingks\ *n.; pl.* **sphinx·es** \'sfingks-əz\ or **sphin·ges** \'sfin-ˌjēz\. **1** In stories, a monster having a lion's body, wings, and the head and bust of a woman. **2** A figure having the body of a lion and the head of a man, a ram, or a hawk. **3** A person whose character and motives are hard to understand.

sphinx, 2

spice \'spīs\ *n.* **1** Any of various flavorings used to season food, made from plant substances, as dried berries, seeds, buds, or bark. **2** Any sharp flavoring; something that adds interest and relish. — *v.;* **spiced**; **spic·ing.** To season with or as if with spices; as, a speech *spiced* with humor.

spice·bush \'spīs-ˌbu̇sh\ *n.* A fragrant swamp and woods shrub related to the laurels, with small yellow flowers blooming before the leaves unfold.

spick-and-span \'spik-n-'span\ *adj.* New and fresh; neat and tidy.

spic·ule \'spik-ˌyül\ *n.* **1** A slender, pointed body, especially of bony material. **2** In botany, a spikelet. **3** One of the slender, pointed bodies supporting the tissues of certain invertebrates, as sponges.

spicy \'spī-sē\ *adj.;* **spic·i·er**; **spic·i·est.** **1** Flavored with or containing spice; aromatic. **2** Having the quality of spice; as, a *spicy* taste. **3** Sharp; keen; as, a *spicy* debate. **4** Improper; somewhat scandalous; as, *spicy* jokes; *spicy* gossip.

spi·der \'spīd-r\ *n.* **1** [From Old English *spithra* meaning literally "spinner".] A wingless animal, related to the scorpions and mites, resembling a true insect except that it has eight legs instead of six and its body is divided into two parts instead of three. **2** A cast-iron frying pan, originally with legs. **3** A tripod to support pots or pans over a fire.

spi·der·web \'spīd-r-ˌweb\ *n.* Also **spider web.** **1** The silken web formed by most spiders, the threads of which are made of a sticky fluid formed in glands in the abdomen and discharged through small openings in the spinnerets. **2** Anything like a spiderweb in appearance or function.

spi·dery \'spīd-r-ē\ *adj.* **1** Like a spider; long and thin like the legs of a spider. **2** Resembling a spider web. **3** Full of spiders.

spied. Past tense and past part. of *spy*.

spig·ot \'spig-ət, 'spik-\ *n.* **1** A pin or peg used to stop the vent in a cask. **2** A device for controlling the flow of liquid, as from a barrel. **3** A faucet.

spike \'spīk\ *n.* **1** An ear of grain. **2** A long, usually rather narrow flower cluster in which the blossoms grow very close to a central stem.

spike \'spīk\ *n.* **1** Any of various pointed, usually rather slender objects; especially, a very large nail. **2** Anything shaped like a very large nail, as an unbranched antler of a young deer. **3** Metal pieces or points worn on the bottom of a player's shoes in some games or sports to prevent slipping. — *v.;* **spiked**; **spik·ing.** **1** To fasten or furnish with spikes. **2** To pierce or cut with or as if with a spike. **3** To put an end to something; to block; as, to *spike* a rumor. **4** To disable a cannon, as by driving a spike into the vent.

spikes, 3

spike·let \'spīk-lət\ *n.* In botany, a small spike, especially one of the clusters forming the flower of the grasses and sedges.

spike·nard \'spīk-ˌnärd, -ˌnȧrd\ *n.* **1** A fragrant ointment of the ancients. **2** An East Indian aromatic plant that was possibly its source.

spiky \'spīk-ē\ *adj.;* **spik·i·er**; **spik·i·est.** **1** Like a spike; pointed. **2** Furnished or armed with spikes.

spile \'spīl\ *n.* **1** A small plug used to stop a hole, as in a cask. **2** A small spout inserted in a tree to carry sap, as from a sugar maple. **3** A pile, as used in soft ground as one of the supports for a building.

spill \'spil\ *n.* A slender piece, as a small roll of paper used for lighting a fire or a pipe.

spill \'spil\ *v.;* **spilled** \'spild, 'spilt\ or **spilt** \'spilt\; **spill·ing.** **1** Accidentally to cause or allow to fall, flow, or run out; to lose; as, to *spill* water from a pitcher. **2** To fall or run out and so be wasted. The milk *spilled*. **3** To cause intentionally to run out; to shed; as, to *spill* blood. **4** To let become known, as news; to allow to leak out, as secrets. — *n.* **1** The act of spilling or state of being spilled. **2** An accidental fall or drop, as from a bicycle. **3** Something that is spilled. **4** A spillway.

spill·way \'spil-ˌwā\ *n.* A passage for surplus water, as in a reservoir or a river; a dam or part of a dam over which water flows.

spin \'spin\ *v.;* **spun** \'spən\ or, archaic, **span** \'span\; **spin·ning.** **1** To draw out and twist into threads, by hand or machinery; as, to *spin* flax. **2** Of spiders or silkworms, to form silk threads, a web, or a cocoon by ejecting from the body a sticky, rapidly hardening fluid. **3** To extend to a great length; to prolong; as, to *spin* a story. **4** To make, shape, or produce in a form suggestive of thread, as if by spinning; as, *spun* glass; *spun* molasses. **5** To twirl or whirl rapidly; as, to *spin* a top. **6** To feel as if whirling, as one's head when dizzy. **7** To move swiftly on wheels. — *n.* **1** The act of spinning; as, the *spin* of a top. **2** A fast ride.

spin·ach \'spin-ich\ *n.* **1** An annual plant that is grown for its edible leaves. **2** The leaves of this plant cooked for food.

spi·nal \'spīn-l\ *adj.* Relating to or near the spine.

spinal column. The series of small connected

bones forming the backbone; the spine.

spinal cord. The thick cord of nervous tissue extending along and protected by the backbone, giving off pairs of nerves (**spinal nerves**) to various parts of the trunk and limbs and carrying nervous impulses to and from the brain.

spin·dle \ˈspind-l\ *n.* **1** A slender rod or stick, often tapering at each end, by which thread is twisted in spinning and on which it is wound. **2** Any slender pin or rod, as a long spike on which to stick papers temporarily; especially, a slender rod that turns or on which something turns, as an axle or shaft. — *v.;* **spin·dled; spin·dling** \-l(-)ing\. **1** To become too tall and thin. The plant *spindled* and died. **2** To shape like a spindle.

spin·dling \ˈspind-l(-)ing\ *adj.* Long and thin; tall and thin; especially, too tall and thin.

spin·dly \ˈspind-l(-)ē\ *adj.;* **spin·dli·er; spin·dli·est.** Spindling.

spin·drift \ˈspin-ˌdrift\ *n.* Spray blown from waves.

spine \ˈspīn\ *n.* **1** A stiff sharp-pointed outgrowth on a plant or animal, as on the thistle or the porcupine. **2** The spinal column; the backbone. **3** Anything that looks like or serves as a backbone.

spine·less \ˈspīn-ləs\ *adj.* **1** Lacking a spine; invertebrate. **2** Lacking thorns or prickles. **3** Lacking spirit or courage. — **spine·less·ly,** *adv.*

spin·et \ˈspin-ət\ *n.* **1** A small form of harpsichord no longer in use. **2** A small upright piano.

spin·na·ker \ˈspin-ik-r\ *n.* A large three-cornered sail set on a long light pole, used on some yachts when running before the wind.

spin·ner \ˈspin-r\ *n.* **1** One that spins. **2** A fishing lure that revolves when drawn through the water.

spin·ner·et \ˌspin-r-ˈet\ *n.* **1** An organ for producing a thread of silk from the secretion of the silk glands, as in spiders and certain caterpillars. **2** A sieve through which the cellulose solution is passed for forming into rayon filaments.

spin·ning jen·ny \ˈspin-ing ˌjen-ē\. A machine with many spindles for spinning wool or cotton.

spinning wheel. A machine for spinning yarn or thread by means of a single spindle driven by a wheel that is itself driven by hand or foot.

spinning wheel

spi·nose \ˈspī-ˌnōs\ *adj.* Having spines; full of spines; thorny. — **spi·nose·ly,** *adv.*

spi·nous \ˈspī-nəs\ *adj.* **1** Shaped like a spine or thorn. **2** Spinose; spiny.

spin·ster \ˈspin(t)st-r\ *n.* **1** A woman who spins. **2** An unmarried woman; especially, an older unmarried woman.

spiny \ˈspī-nē\ *adj.;* **spin·i·er; spin·i·est.** Having spines; covered with spines; prickly; thorny.

spir·a·cle \ˈspir-ək-l, ˈspī-rək-l\ *n.* A breathing hole, as in a whale's head; a vent.

spi·raea or **spi·rea** \spī-ˈrē-ə\ *n.* Any of a group of shrubs with dense clusters of small white or pink five-petaled flowers.

spi·ral \ˈspī-rəl\ *adj.* **1** Coiling around a central point in circles that grow constantly larger; as, a *spiral* spring. **2** Moving like the thread of a screw; corkscrew. — *n.* **1** Anything that has a spiral form. **2** A single coil in a spiral object; a spire. — *v.;* **spi·raled** or **spi·ralled; spi·ral·ing** or **spi·ral·ling.** To form into a spiral; to move in a spiral course. — **spi·ral·ly** \-rə-lē\ *adv.*

spiral

spire \ˈspīr\ *n.* **1** A spiral; a coil. **2** The upper part of a spirally formed shell.

spire \ˈspīr\ *n.* **1** A slender, tapering blade or stalk, as of grass. **2** A sharp, pointed tip, as of a deer's horn. **3** A pointed roof surmounting a tower or something like a tower. **4** A steeple.

spi·ril·lum \spī-ˈril-əm\ *n.; pl.* **spi·ril·lums** \-ˈril-əmz\ or **spi·ril·la** \-ˈril-ə\. **1** Any of certain long curved bacteria having tufted ends. **2** Any spiral thread-shaped microscopic organism.

spir·it \ˈspir-ət\ *n.* **1** A life-giving force; especially, a force within man which moves his body with life, energy, and power; the soul. **2** [with a capital and often with *the*] The Holy Ghost. **3** A supernatural being; a ghost; especially, a supernatural being thought of as entering into and controlling a person. **4** [often in the plural] Mood; disposition; as, in good *spirits.* **5** Liveliness; enthusiasm; courage; as, to answer with *spirit.* **6** Real meaning; as, the *spirit* of the law. **7** An emotion, frame of mind, or inclination governing one's actions; as, school *spirit.* **8** A person; as, a bold *spirit.* **9** [often in the plural] Any distilled alcoholic liquor. **10** An alcoholic solution that evaporates easily. — *v.* **1** To animate; to encourage. **2** To carry rapidly and secretly, as if by the aid of spirits.

spir·it·ed \ˈspir-ət-əd\ *adj.* Full of spirit, courage, or energy; lively; animated. — **spir·it·ed·ly,** *adv.*

spir·it·less \ˈspir-ət-ləs\ *adj.* Without spirit; lifeless; dejected; depressed. — **spir·it·less·ly,** *adv.*

spirit level. A level using a bubble in alcohol as an indicator.

spir·it·u·al \ˈspir-ə-chə-wəl, ˈspir-əch-l\ *adj.* **1** Of or relating to man's spirit or soul; not bodily or material. **2** Characterized by purity of soul and devotion to religion. **3** Of or relating to the church or sacred things; sacred; religious. — *n.* A religious song originating among the Negroes of the southern United States, characterized by a strongly marked rhythm, deep emotional feeling, and repetition and simplicity of words and melody.

spir·it·u·al·ism \ˈspir-ə-chə-wə-ˌliz-m, -əch-l-ˌiz-m\ *n.* **1** Spirituality. **2** The belief that the spirits of the dead communicate with the living.

spir·it·u·al·ist \ˈspir-ə-chə-wə-ləst, -əch-l-əst\ *n.* A person who believes in spiritualism. — **spir·it·u·al·is·tic** \ˌspir-ə-chə-wə-ˈlis-tik, -əch-l-ˈis-tik\ *adj.*

spir·it·u·al·ly \ˈspir-əch-l-ē, -ə-chə-wə-lē\ *adv.* In a spiritual way; with reference to things of the spirit.

spir·it·u·ous \ˈspir-ə-chə-wəs, -ə-chəs\ *adj.* Containing alcohol produced by distillation; alcoholic; as, *spirituous* liquors.

spi·ro·chete \'spī-rə-ˌkēt\ *n.* Any of certain slender spiral-shaped bacteria.

spi·ro·gy·ra \ˌspī-rə-'jī-rə\ *n.* Any of a number of green algae with spiral chlorophyll bands.

spirt \'spərt\ *v.* or *n.* Spurt.

spit \'spit\ *n.* **1** A thin pointed iron rod for holding meat over a fire. **2** A small point of land that runs out into a body of water. — *v.;* **spit·ted; spit·ting.** To pierce with a spit or fix on a spit, as meat.

barbecue spit

spit \'spit\ *v.;* **spat** \'spat\ or **spit; spit·ting. 1** To throw out saliva from the mouth. **2** To throw out; to send forth. The fire is *spitting* sparks. **3** To make a noise like the sound of spitting, as a cat when angry. **4** To rain or snow slightly. — *n.* **1** Saliva; spittle. **2** The act of spitting. **3** A frothy secretion produced by spittle insects. **4** Perfect likeness. The boy was the *spit* and image of his father.

spite \'spīt\ *n.* Dislike or hatred for another person, with a wish to annoy, anger, or defeat; petty malice. — **in spite of.** In defiance of; notwithstanding; despite. — *v.;* **spit·ed; spit·ing.** To treat with spite; to annoy or injure out of spite.

spite·ful \'spīt-fəl\ *adj.* Filled with spite or showing spite; malicious. — **spite·ful·ly** \-fə-lē\ *adv.*

spit·fire \'spit-ˌfīr\ *n.* A quick-tempered person.

spit·tle \'spit-l\ *n.* **1** Saliva; spit. **2** A frothy fluid secreted by certain insects (**spittle insects**).

spit·toon \spi-'tün\ *n.* A receptacle to spit in; especially, a low round receptacle of metal or earthenware with a funnel-shaped top; a cuspidor.

splash \'splash\ *v.* **1** To strike liquid and cause it to move and scatter roughly; as, to *splash* water or mud. **2** To wet or soil by dashing water or mud on; to spatter; as, to be *splashed* by a passing car. **3** To move or strike with a splashing noise; as, to *splash* through a puddle. — *n.* **1** Liquid splashed or a spot made by it; as, a *splash* of mud. **2** The sound of liquid being splashed. **3** An act of splashing. — **splash·er,** *n.* — **splashy,** *adj.*

splat \'splat\ *n.* A single flat piece of wood set vertically in the center of a chair back.

splat·ter \'splat-r\ *v.* To spatter. — *n.* A spatter.

splay \'splā\ *v.* **1** To spread out; to open out. **2** To make slanting, as the side of a door or window. — *n.* A slope, as of the sides of a door or window. — *adj.* Spread out; turned outward; as, *splay*-toed.

spleen \'splēn\ *n.* **1** A ductless organ containing many blood vessels, located near the stomach or intestine in most vertebrates, and having some connection with nutrition. **2** Spite; malice; hatred.

splen·did \'splen-dəd\ *adj.* **1** Having or showing splendor; glorious; as, a *splendid* palace. **2** Excellent; as, a *splendid* idea. — **splen·did·ly,** *adv.*

splen·dor \'splend-r\ *n.* **1** Brilliance; as, the *splendor* of the sun. **2** Magnificence; glory.

sple·net·ic \splə-'net-ik\ *adj.* **1** Relating to the spleen. **2** Spiteful. — **sple·net·i·cal·ly** \-ik-l(-)ē\ *adv.*

splice \'splīs\ *v.;* **spliced; splic·ing. 1** To unite, as two ropes, by weaving the strands together. **2** To unite, as rails or timbers, by lapping the ends together and making them fast. — *n.* A joining or joint made by splicing. — **splic·er** \'splīs-r\ *n.*

splint \'splint\ *n.* **1** A splinter. **2** A thin flexible strip of wood interwoven with others, as in making a chair seat or basket. **3** A device made of stiff material for keeping in proper position a broken or displaced bone in a limb. — *v.* To fasten or confine with splints, to support or brace with splints.

splin·ter \'splint-r\ *n.* A thin sharp piece, as of wood, glass, bone, split off lengthwise; a sliver. — *v.* To break into splinters. — **splin·tery,** *adj.*

split \'split\ *v.;* **split; split·ting. 1** To divide, as by cutting or cracking, lengthwise or from end to end; as, to *split* a log. **2** To burst or break apart or in pieces; as, to *split* a rock. **3** To divide into shares or parts; as, to *split* the cost of an outing. — **split hairs.** To make very fine, or too fine, distinctions. — *n.* **1** A crack or lengthwise break. **2** A division; as, a *split* in a political party. **3** The feat of going down to the floor so that the legs extend in a straight line in opposite directions. — *adj.* Divided; as, a *split* decision. — **split·ter,** *n.*

split infinitive. An infinitive with a modifier between the *to* and the verb, as in *to really learn.*

split·ting \'split-ing\ *adj.* That splits; rending; piercing; very severe; as, a *splitting* headache.

splotch \'spläch\ *n.* A spot, stain, or smear. — *v.* To cover with splotches. — **splotchy,** *adj.*

splurge \'splərj\ *n.* A showy display. — *v.;* **splurged; splurg·ing. 1** To make a showy display. **2** To indulge oneself extravagantly.

splut·ter \'splət-r\ *v.* **1** To sputter. **2** To talk hastily and indistinctly, as when angry. — *n.* A spluttering noise. — **splut·ter·er** \-r-r\ *n.*

spoil \'spȯil\ *v.;* **spoiled** \'spȯild, 'spȯilt\ or **spoilt** \'spȯilt\; **spoil·ing. 1** To plunder; to rob. **2** To decay or to lose freshness, value, or usefulness through being kept too long. **3** To damage or destroy the use or value of; to injure; to ruin. **4** To damage the character or disposition of, as by pampering; as, to *spoil* a child. — *n.* **1** Things taken by violence; booty. **2** [in the plural] Public offices, and their salaries and fees, as the property of a successful political party. — **spoil·er,** *n.*

spoil·age \'spȯi-lij\ *n.* **1** The act of spoiling. **2** That which is spoiled or wasted.

spoke \'spōk\ *n.* **1** One of the bars or rods extending from the hub of a wheel to the rim, which they support. **2** A rung of a ladder; a round. — *v.;* **spoked; spok·ing.** To furnish with spokes.

spoke

spoke \'spōk\. Past tense of *speak.*

spo·ken \'spōk-n\. A past part. of *speak.* — *adj.* **1** Uttered; as, the *spoken* word. **2** Speaking; as, a well-*spoken* man.

spoke·shave \'spōk-ˌshāv\ *n.* A two-handled tool

that is used for planing curved pieces of wood.

spokes·man \'spōks-mən\ *n.; pl.* **spokes·men** \-mən\. A person who speaks as a representative, as of another person or of a group.

spo·li·a·tion \ˌspō-lē-'āsh-n\ *n.* A plundering, especially in war. — **spo·li·a·tor** \'spō-lē-ˌāt-r\ *n.*

sponge \'spənj\ *n.* **1** The springy, porous mass of fiber forming the skeleton of certain animals living in colonies in warm seas. **2** One of the animals or a colony of the animals that have such skeletons. **3** A piece of this substance or a manufactured product, as one of rubber or plastic, having a similar elastic, porous quality. **4** The act of bathing or wiping with a sponge. **5** One that lives upon others; a parasite. **6** Any spongy substance, such as raised dough. **7** A pad of cotton or gauze used in surgical operations. — *v.;* **sponged**; **spong·ing** \'spən-jing\. **1** To bathe, clean, or wipe with a sponge. **2** To absorb with a sponge or like a sponge. **3** To live or eat at another's expense. **4** To fish for sponges. — **spong·er** \'spənj-r\ *n.*

spongy \'spən-jē\ *adj.;* **spong·i·er**; **spong·i·est.** Like a sponge, in appearance or in absorbency; soft and full of holes; not firm or solid.

spon·sor \'spän(t)s-r\ *n.* **1** A person who takes the responsibility for some other person or thing. **2** A godfather or a godmother. **3** A person or an organization that pays for or plans and carries out a project or activity. **4** A person or an organization that pays the cost of a radio or television program. — *v.;* **spon·sored**; **spon·sor·ing** \-r(-)ing\. To act as sponsor for.

spon·ta·ne·i·ty \ˌspänt-ə-'nē-ət-ē\ *n.* The quality or state of being spontaneous; spontaneous action.

spon·ta·ne·ous \spän-'tā-nē-əs\ *adj.* **1** Done, said, or produced freely and naturally; as, *spontaneous* laughter. **2** Acting or taking place without external force or cause. — **spon·ta·ne·ous·ly**, *adv.*

spontaneous combustion. The bursting into flame of a substance by the heat it produces within itself through chemical action.

spook \'spük, 'spu̇k\ *n.* A ghost; a specter.

spooky \'spük-ē, 'spu̇k-ē\ *adj.;* **spook·i·er**; **spook·i·est.** **1** Like a spook; as, a *spooky* figure. **2** Suggesting the presence of spooks; as, a *spooky* place.

spool \'spül\ *n.* A small cylinder with rimmed or ridged ends, on which thread or wire is wound. — *v.* To wind on a spool.

spoon \'spün\ *n.* **1** A utensil with a shallow bowl and a handle, used in cooking and eating. **2** Something resembling a spoon, as a curved piece of metal used as a fishing lure. **3** A golf club with a wooden head. — *v.* **1** To take up in or as if in a spoon. **2** To shape like the bowl of a spoon. **3** To make love in a silly, demonstrative way.

spoon·bill \'spün-ˌbil\ *n.* A long-legged wading bird having the bill flattened at the tip.

spoon·ful \'spün-ˌfu̇l\ *n.; pl.* **spoon·fuls.** As much as a spoon can hold.

spoor \'spu̇r\ *n.* A track or trail of a wild animal.

spo·rad·ic \spə-'rad-ik\ *adj.* Occurring in scattered single instances; as, *sporadic* outbreaks of influenza. — **spo·rad·i·cal·ly** \-ik-l(-)ē\ *adv.*

spo·ran·gi·um \spə-'ran-jē-əm\ *n.; pl.* **spo·ran·gi·ums** \-jē-əmz\ or **spo·ran·gia** \-jē-ə\. The sac in which asexual spores are produced; a spore case.

spore \'spōr, 'spȯr\ *n.* A rounded microscopic body, usually consisting of a single cell, that is discharged by some plants, as ferns, lichens, algae, and mosses, and by some bacteria and protozoans, and grows to be a new plant or animal. — *v.;* **spored**; **spor·ing.** To form or develop spores.

spore case. The sporangium.

spo·ro·phyll or **spo·ro·phyl** \'spōr-ə-ˌfil, 'spȯr-\ *n.* A spore-bearing leaf.

spo·ro·phyte \'spōr-ə-ˌfīt, 'spȯr-\ *n.* In plants having alternating sexual and asexual generations, the individual or generation that bears asexual spores.

spor·ran \'spär-ən\ *n.* A pouch made of skin with the hair or fur on, worn in front of the kilt by Scottish Highlanders in full dress.

sport \'spōrt, 'spȯrt\ *n.* **1** That which diverts or amuses; pastime; diversion. **2** A particular kind of game or amusement; as, indoor and outdoor *sports.* **3** Fun; jest; mockery; as, done in *sport.* **4** A butt; a laughingstock; as, to be the *sport* of one's fellows. **5** A person who takes things in a spirit of fun or fair play, as if abiding by the rules of a game. **6** A person devoted to gay pleasures and amusements, or one inclined to take risks and chances. **7** In biology, a sudden spontaneous deviation or variation from type; a mutation. — For synonyms see *game.* — *v.* **1** To play; to frolic. **2** To speak or act in fun or jest. **3** To display by using or wearing; as, to *sport* a new suit. — *adj.* Also **sports.** Of, relating to, or suitable for sports.

sport·ing \'spōrt-ing, 'spȯrt-\ *adj.* **1** Having to do with sports; taking part in sports. **2** Showing sportsmanship; fair and generous. **3** Suitable for use or wear in sports; as, *sporting* goods. **4** Involving risk as in sports; as, a *sporting* chance.

sport·ive \'spōrt-iv, 'spȯrt-\ *adj.* Playful; frolicsome; merry. — **sport·ive·ly**, *adv.*

sports·cast \'spōrts-ˌkast, 'spȯrts-\ *n.* A broadcast dealing with sports events. — **sports·cast·er**, *n.*

sports·man \'spōrts-mən, 'spȯrts-\ *n.; pl.* **sports·men** \-mən\. **1** A person who takes part or is interested in sports, especially outdoor sports. **2** A person who abides by the rules and chances of the game and is a good loser and a modest winner.

sports·man·like \'spōrts-mən-ˌlīk, 'spȯrts-\ *adj.* Like a sportsman; befitting a good sportsman.

sports·man·ship \'spōrts-mən-ˌship, 'spȯrts-\ *n.* Skill in or devotion to sports; especially, conduct befitting a good sportsman.

sports·wear \'spōrts-ˌwar, 'spȯrts-, -ˌwer\ *n.* Clothes suitable for engaging in or watching sports.

sporty \'spōrt-ē, 'spȯrt-ē\ *adj.;* **sport·i·er**; **sport·i·est.** Characteristic of a sport; gay; smart; flashy.

spot \'spät\ *n.* **1** A mark; a blot; a stain. **2** A blemish or stain on character or reputation. **3** A small part that is different, as in color, from the main part of something; as, a leopard's *spots.* **4** A place; a location; as, a good *spot* for a camp. — **on the spot. 1** Immediately; before going elsewhere. **2** At the place where action is required. **3** In a position of disadvantage or danger. — *v.;* **spot·ted; spot·ting. 1** To mark or be marked with spots; to stain or be stained; as, cloth that *spots* easily. **2** To blemish or disgrace, as a reputation. **3** To recognize; to detect; to pick out; as, to *spot* a friend in a crowd. **4** To set or place on a certain spot. **5** To allow as a handicap; as, to *spot* an opponent five points. — *adj.* **1** Paid or ready for payment on delivery; as, *spot* cash. **2** Made between radio or television programs; as, *spot* announcements.

spot·less \'spät-ləs\ *adj.* Without spot or blemish. — **spot·less·ly,** *adv.*

spot·light \'spät-ˌlīt\ *n.* **1** A spot or circle of light used to show up a single person or thing. **2** An electric lamp for throwing a brilliant beam of light, as on a stage. **3** Conspicuous public notice. — *v.* **1** To light up with a spotlight. **2** To bring to public notice; to emphasize.

spot·ted \'spät-əd\ *adj.* **1** Marked with spots; as, the *spotted* coat of a leopard. **2** Blemished; stained, as a person's character. **3** Characterized by the appearance of spots; as, *spotted* fever.

spot·ter \'spät-r\ *n.* One who spots, as a civilian watcher who must report all approaching aircraft.

spot·ty \'spät-ē\ *adj.;* **spot·ti·er; spot·ti·est. 1** Spotted. **2** Good in spots; uneven; as, *spotty* class work; a *spotty* performance.

spouse \'spau̇s, 'spau̇z\ *n.* A husband or a wife.

spout \'spau̇t\ *v.* **1** To throw out forcibly, as liquids; to squirt. **2** To flow out with force; as, flames *spouting* from a volcano. **3** To speak or recite, especially pompously. — *n.* **1** A tube, pipe, or hole through which anything spouts. **2** A jet of liquid; especially, a waterspout.

sprain \'sprān\ *v.* To injure the muscles or tear the ligaments, as of a joint, by a sudden wrenching; as, to *sprain* one's ankle. — *n.* **1** The action of spraining. **2** The condition resulting from spraining.

sprang. A past tense of *spring.*

sprat \'sprat\ *n.* **1** A small European herring. **2** Any of a number of small fishes, as the anchovy.

sprawl \'sprȯl\ *v.* **1** To lie or sit with one's limbs spread out ungracefully, as after a fall. **2** To spread out irregularly; as, a *sprawling* city. — *n.* The action or posture of sprawling.

spray \'sprā\ *n.* A flat mass of small branches with foliage, flowers, or fruit; as, *sprays* of holly.

spray \'sprā\ *n.* **1** Liquid flying in fine drops or particles, like water blown from a wave. **2** A jet of fine vapor, as from an atomizer. **3** An instrument for applying a spray of liquid or vapor. **4** The substance applied by such an instrument. — *v.* **1** To scatter or let fall in a spray; as, to *spray* paint. **2** To throw spray upon. The waves *sprayed* the children. **3** To treat with a spray; as, to *spray* an orchard. — **spray·er** \'sprā-ər\ *n.*

spray gun. A device for spraying paints and varnishes.

spray gun

spread \'spred\ *v.;* **spread; spread·ing. 1** To scatter or strew; to distribute over a surface; as, to *spread* fertilizer. **2** To extend; to stretch out; to open out; as, sails *spreading* in the wind; a tree *spreading* its branches. **3** To stretch forth or apart; to force or push apart; as, to *spread* one's fingers. **4** To make known far and wide; as, to *spread* news. **5** To distribute over a time or among many persons; as, to *spread* work to make it last. **6** To pass on from person to person; to transmit. Flies *spread* disease. **7** To cover or overlay; as, to *spread* a floor with rugs. **8** To cover with a thin even layer; as, to *spread* the bread. **9** To prepare for a meal; to set forth food for; as, to *spread* a table; to *spread* a banquet. **10** To record; as, to *spread* a motion on the minutes of a meeting. — *n.* **1** The act of spreading; expansion or distribution; as, the *spread* of education. **2** The extent or area of something spread out; as, the *spread* of a bird's wings. **3** A cloth used to cover a table or a bed. **4** Anything used to spread on bread, as cheese. **5** A meal that is substantial but usually informal; a feast. — **spread·er,** *n.*

spree \'sprē\ *n.* **1** A frolic. **2** A period of drinking or of drunkenness.

sprier. A comparative of *spry.*

spriest. A superlative of *spry.*

sprig \'sprig\ *n.* **1** A small shoot or twig. **2** An ornament or design resembling a twig. — **sprigged** \'sprigd\ *adj.*

spright·ly \'sprīt-lē\ *adj.;* **spright·li·er; spright·li·est.** Full of life; brisk; gay.

spring \'spring\ *v.;* **sprang** \'sprang\ or **sprung** \'sprəng\; **sprung; spring·ing** \'spring-ing\. **1** To leap; to bound. **2** To spurt or dart out. **3** To jump up, as from sleep. **4** To be elastic or resilient. **5** To shoot up or shoot out; to arise; as, grass *springing* up; new cities *springing* from the plains. **6** To fly back into position, as a bent bow when released. **7** To warp; as, a plank that had *sprung.* **8** To tower, as a spire above a roof. **9** To start, as an arch, from the top of a wall or pier and round upward. **10** To crack or split. The boat's seams have *sprung.* **11** To develop, as a leak. The ship has *sprung* a leak. **12** To make known suddenly; as, to *spring* a surprise. **13** To cause to close suddenly; as, to *spring* a trap. — *n.* **1** A leap or jump or the distance covered by a leap. **2** A flowing up of water from the earth; as, a lake fed by *springs.* **3** A cause, origin, or motive; as, the *springs* of one's behavior. **4** The season of the year between winter and summer, in which plants begin to grow or put forth foliage. **5** An elastic body or device that recovers its original shape when it is released

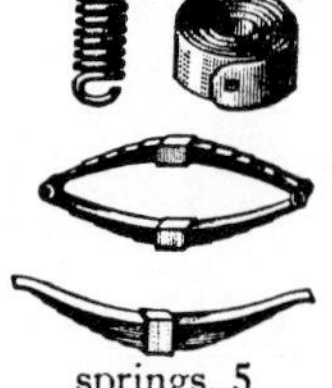
springs, 5

after being forced out of shape. **6** The quality of being elastic; elasticity; vigor; energy.

spring·board \'spring-ˌbōrd, -ˌbȯrd\ *n.* **1** A springy board used in various exercises in springing, jumping, and vaulting. **2** A diving board.

spring·er \'spring-r\ *n.* **1** One that springs. **2** In full, **springer spaniel.** A hunting dog noted for its ability to flush game.

spring fever. A lazy listless feeling common in the first warm days of spring.

spring·house \'spring-ˌhau̇s\ *n.; pl.* **spring·hous·es** \-ˌhau̇-zəz\. A small structure built over a spring and used as a cooling place, as for milk.

spring·tide \'spring-ˌtīd\ *n.* Springtime.

spring tide. A greater than usual tide occurring at each new moon and full moon.

spring·time \'spring-ˌtīm\ *n.* The spring season.

springy \'spring-ē\ *adj.;* **spring·i·er; spring·i·est.** Like a spring; elastic; as, a *springy* step.

sprin·kle \'springk-l\ *v.;* **sprin·kled; sprin·kling** \-l(-)ing\. **1** To scatter in or as if in drops or particles; as, to *sprinkle* water. **2** To scatter small drops or particles over; as, to *sprinkle* with sugar. **3** To rain lightly. — *n.* A sprinkling; especially, a light rain. — **sprin·kler** \'springk-lər\ *n.*

sprint \'sprint\ *v.* To run at top speed. — *n.* A short, fast run.

sprint·er \'sprint-r\ *n.* One that sprints.

sprit \'sprit\ *n.* A pole or spar that diagonally crosses and supports a fore-and-aft sail (**sprit·sail** \'sprit-ˌsāl, 'sprits-l\).

sprite \'sprīt\ *n.* An elf; a fairy; a goblin.

sprock·et \'spräk-ət\ *n.* **1** A tooth or projection on the rim of a wheel (**sprocket wheel**) shaped so as to interlock with the links of a chain. **2** A sprocket wheel.

sprocket

sprout \'sprau̇t\ *v.* **1** To push out or bring forth new shoots. **2** To grow rapidly like young shoots. **3** To cause to sprout. Rain *sprouts* seed. **4** *Dial.* To strip the sprouts from. — *n.* **1** The shoot of a plant. **2** [in the plural] Brussels sprouts.

spruce \'sprüs\ *n.* **1** A pyramid-shaped evergreen tree related to the pines, with a dense foliage of needle-shaped leaves, drooping cones, and light, soft wood. **2** The wood of this tree.

spruce \'sprüs\ *adj.;* **spruc·er; spruc·est.** Neat and smart; trim. — **spruce up.** To make or become neat and smart in appearance. — **spruce·ly,** *adv.*

sprung. A past tense and past part. of *spring.*

spry \'sprī\ *adj.;* **spri·er** or **spry·er** \'sprīr\; **spri·est** or **spry·est** \'sprī-əst\. Nimble; active; brisk. — **spry·ly** \'sprī-lē\ *adv.*

spud \'spəd\ *n.* **1** A sharp, narrow spade used for digging up large roots of weeds. **2** A potato. — *v.;* **spud·ded; spud·ding.** To dig with a spud.

spume \'spyüm\ *n.* Froth; foam; especially, sea foam. — *v.;* **spumed; spum·ing.** To froth; to foam.

spun \'spən\. Past tense and past part. of *spin.*

spun glass. Glass drawn into a thread while liquid.

spunk \'spəngk\ *n.* Spirit; courage; pluck.

spunky \'spəngk-ē\ *adj.;* **spunk·i·er; spunk·i·est.** Plucky; spirited.

spur \'spər\ *n.* **1** A pointed device fastened to a horseman's boot, for urging on a horse. **2** Anything that stirs or urges to action; a stimulus. **3** In botany, a hollow projecting part of a corolla or calyx, as in the flowers of larkspur. **4** Any stiff, sharp spine, as on a bird's wing or leg. **5** A ridge or crag extending sidewise from a mountain. **6** A short branch of railway track connected at only one end to a main line. — **on the spur of the moment.** On a hasty impulse; without previous plan or preparation. — *v.;* **spurred; spur·ring. 1** To prick with spurs. **2** To urge; to stimulate. **3** To put spurs on, as a boot. **4** To spur on one's horse.

spu·ri·ous \'spyu̇r-ē-əs\ *adj.* Counterfeit; false.

spurn \'spərn\ *v.* **1** To kick aside. **2** To reject with contempt. — *n.* **1** A kick. **2** A disdainful rejection.

spurred \'spərd\ *adj.* Wearing spurs; having a spur.

spurt \'spərt\ *v.* **1** To gush or force out suddenly or violently. Water *spurted* through the cracks. **2** To make a spurt. — *n.* **1** A sudden gushing forth; as, a *spurt* of flame. **2** A sudden increase of energy or exertion; as, to put on a *spurt.*

sput·ter \'spət-r\ *v.* **1** To spit in small scattered particles, as in careless or rapid speaking. **2** To speak hastily and indistinctly. **3** To throw out something, as jets of steam or fire, with a noise like that made by someone sputtering. — *n.* **1** The act or sound of sputtering. **2** Confused, excited talk.

spu·tum \'spyüt-m\ *n.* **1** Spittle; saliva. **2** A thick discharge from the lungs and throat.

spy \'spī\ *v.;* **spied** \'spīd\; **spy·ing. 1** To watch, inspect, or examine secretly; to play the part of a spy. **2** To catch sight of something that is at a distance or in hiding; to see. **3** To discover by close examination. — *n.; pl.* **spies. 1** A person who watches the conduct of others, especially secretly. **2** A person who tries secretly to obtain information for one country in the territory of another, usually hostile, country.

spy·glass \'spī-ˌglas\ *n.* A small telescope.

sq. Abbreviation for *square.*

squab \'skwäb\ *n.* A young pigeon or similar bird.

squab·ble \'skwäb-l\ *v.;* **squab·bled; squab·bling** \-l(-)ing\. To quarrel noisily, especially about trifles; to wrangle. — *n.* A petty quarrel.

squad \'skwäd\ *n.* **1** A small unit of soldiers grouped for drill, inspection, or other purposes. **2** Any relatively small group of persons engaged in some common effort; as, a football *squad.*

squad car. A police cruiser; a prowl car.

squad·ron \'skwäd-rən\ *n.* **1** Any group in regular formation. **2** A cavalry unit consisting of two or more troops with a headquarters troop. **3** A group of naval vessels consisting of one or more divisions, usually four ships each, of a fleet; also, a group of ships assigned to a special station or duty. **4** An air fleet or a division of an air fleet consisting of several groups of planes.

squal·id \'skwäl-əd\ *adj.* **1** Dirty from neglect; filthy. **2** Mean; poverty-stricken. — **squal·id·ly,** *adv.*

squall \'skwȯl\ *n.* A sudden violent gust of wind, often with rain or snow. — *v.* To blow a squall.

squall \'skwȯl\ *v.* To cry out loudly; to scream violently. — *n.* A harsh cry; a squawk.

squally \'skwȯl-ē\ *adj.;* **squall·i·er; squall·i·est.** Having many sudden, brief storms; gusty.

squal·or \'skwäl-r, *also* 'skwāl-r\ *n.* Squalid state.

squan·der \'skwänd-r\ *v.;* **squan·dered; squan·der·ing** \-r(-)ing\. To spend foolishly or wastefully.

square \'skwar, 'skwer\ *n.* **1** A flat figure that has four equal sides and four right angles. **2** Something of or like this form; as, the *squares* of a checkerboard. **3** An area bounded by four streets or the distance along one side of such an area. **4** An open place or area where two or more streets meet. **5** An instrument having at least one right angle and two or more straight edges, used in laying out or testing work that must be square. **6** The product of a number or quantity multiplied by itself. 25 is the *square* of 5. — **on the square. 1** At right angles. **2** In an open, fair manner; honestly. — *v.;* **squared; squar·ing. 1** To make square; to form with four equal sides and right angles or with right angles and straight lines or with flat surfaces. **2** To cause to show the form or approximate form of a right angle; as, to *square* one's shoulders. **3** To conform or agree. The man's actions *squared* with his beliefs. **4** To make even; to settle; as, to *square* accounts. **5** To bribe; to fix; as, to try to *square* a traffic officer. **6** To multiply a number by itself. 9 *squared* is 81. **7** To mark off in squares; as, *squared* paper. — **square off.** To assume the position of a boxer ready to fight. — **square oneself. 1** To put oneself right, as by smoothing over something one has done. **2** To get even. — **square up. 1** To settle an account. **2** To face up; to square off. — *adj.* **1** Having four equal sides and four right angles. **2** Forming a right angle; as, a *square* corner. **3** Squared, or multiplied by itself; converted into a square unit of area having the same length of side. **4** Having a shape broad for its height; as, a man of *square* build. **5** Plain; as, a *square* refusal. **6** Just; honest; as, a *square* deal. **7** Even; leaving no balance; as, to get one's accounts *square.* **8** Hearty; as, three *square* meals a day. — **square·ly,** *adv.*

square dance. Any dance in which the dancers are arranged in a square or other set form.

square knot. A common knot in which the ends and the standing parts are together and parallel to each other.

square knot

square measure. 1 The measure of areas in square units, as square feet. **2** A system of such units.

square-rigged \'skwar-'rigd, 'skwer-\ *adj.* Having the principal sails extended on yards fastened to the masts horizontally and at their center.

square-rig·ger \'skwar-'rig-r, 'skwer-\ *n.* A square-rigged ship.

square root. In mathematics, a number or quantity obtained by dividing a number or quantity into its two equal factors. The *square root* of 16 is 4.

squar·ish \'skwar-ish, 'skwer-\ *adj.* Somewhat square in form or appearance.

squash \'skwäsh\ *n.* A large green or yellow fruit that grows on a vine, with flesh which is cooked and served as a vegetable or used as filling for pies.

squash \'skwäsh\ *v.* **1** To beat or press into a pulp or a flat mass; to crush. **2** To suppress; to put down; as, to *squash* a revolt. **3** To become crushed or mashed, as from pressure or by falling heavily. **4** To squelch. — *n.* **1** A sudden fall of a heavy, soft body or the sound of such a fall. **2** A crushed mass. **3** A squelching sound. **4** A game played with a racket and a rubber ball in a walled court.

squash bug. A large ill-smelling black sucking insect injurious to squash vines.

squashy \'skwäsh-ē\ *adj.;* **squash·i·er; squash·i·est.** Easily squashed or crushed; soft.

squat \'skwät\ *v.;* **squat·ted** or **squat; squat·ting. 1** To sit on one's heels; to crouch. **2** To cause to crouch. **3** To settle without any right on land, especially unoccupied land, that one does not own. **4** To settle on public land with a view to acquiring title to it. — *adj.;* **squat·ter; squat·test. 1** Crouching. **2** Short and thick; as, a *squat* figure. — *n.* **1** The act of squatting. **2** A squatting position. — **squat·ter** \'skwät-r\ *n.*

squat·ty \'skwät-ē\ *adj.;* **squat·ti·er; squat·ti·est.** Squat; thickset; dumpy.

squaw \'skwȯ\ *n.* An American Indian woman.

squawk \'skwȯk\ *v.* **1** To utter a harsh, abrupt scream, as a chicken. **2** To complain; to object; to find fault. — *n.* **1** The act or noise of squawking. **2** A complaint. — **squawk·er,** *n.*

squaw man. A white man married to an Indian woman and, usually, living as one of her tribe.

squeak \'skwēk\ *v.* **1** To make a sharp, shrill cry or sound like that of a mouse; as, a *squeaking* door. **2** To utter or speak in a shrill, piping tone. **3** To betray a secret; to squeal. — *n.* A sharp, shrill cry or sound. — **squeaky** \'skwēk-ē\ *adj.*

squeal \'skwēl\ *v.* **1** To utter a long, sharp, shrill cry. **2** To complain. **3** To betray, especially by giving information to the police. — *n.* An act or instance of squealing. — **squeal·er,** *n.*

squeam·ish \'skwē-mish\ *adj.* **1** Fastidious; easily nauseated. **2** Prudish. — **squeam·ish·ly,** *adv.*

squee·gee \'skwē-ˌjē\ *n.* A device consisting of a strip of rubber at one end of a handle, used for drying a flat surface by pressing off excess liquid.

squeeze \'skwēz\ *v.;* **squeezed; squeez·ing. 1** To press together from the opposite sides or parts. **2** To get by squeezing; as, to *squeeze* juice from a lemon. **3** To force by squeezing; as, to *squeeze* oneself into a box. **4** To pass, or make one's way, by pressing; as, to *squeeze* through. **5** To oppress, as with burdens or taxes. — *n.* **1** A squeezing; a pressure, as in a crowd. **2** A firm pressing of another's hand. **3** A hug. — **squeez·er** \'skwēz-r\ *n.*

squelch \'skwelch\ *n.* **1** A sound of or as of walking in mud. **2** A crushing retort. — *v.* **1** To fall or step on so as to crush. **2** To suppress, as a revolt. **3** To make a squelching sound.

squib \'skwib\ *n.* **1** Something, as a paper tube or ball, filled with powder to burn and, often, explode. **2** A broken firecracker that fizzes and burns. **3** A brief witty or sarcastic writing or speech.

squid \'skwid\ *n.* A ten-armed cephalopod similar to the cuttlefish but having a tapering body and a tail fin on each side.

squint \'skwint\ *adj.* Cross-eyed. — *v.* **1** To peer or look with the eyes partly closed, as in bright light. **2** To look obliquely or with a furtive glance. **3** To be cross-eyed. — *n.* **1** A squinting. **2** The condition of being cross-eyed. — **squinty** \'skwint-ē\ *adj.*

squire \'skwīr\ *n.* **1** A person who carried the shield and armor of a knight. **2** A title of courtesy often given to a justice of the peace or, in England, to a country landowner. **3** A male attendant or escort. — *v.;* **squired**; **squir·ing.** To escort.

squirm \'skwərm\ *v.* To twist about like an eel; to wriggle; to writhe. — **squirmy** \'skwər-mē\ *adj.*

squir·rel \'skwərl, 'skwər-əl, 'skwə-rəl\ *n.* **1** A small, slender, gnawing animal having a long bushy tail and strong hind legs for leaping, as the common red and gray squirrels. **2** The fur of this animal.

squirt \'skwərt\ *v.* To throw out liquid in a thin stream; to spurt. — *n.* **1** The act of squirting. **2** A small forcible stream of liquid. **3** An instrument, as a syringe, for squirting a liquid.

Sr. or **sr.** Abbreviation for *senior.*

S.S. Abbreviation for *steamship.*

s's. Pl. of *s.*

St. Abbreviation for: **1** *Saint.* **2** *Strait.* **3** *Street.*

stab \'stab\ *v.;* **stabbed**; **stab·bing.** **1** To pierce with a pointed weapon. **2** To thrust or drive a pointed implement; as, to *stab* a fork into meat. **3** To wound as if with a pointed weapon; as, *stabbed* by the harsh words. — *n.* **1** A wound made by stabbing. **2** An attempt; a try; as, to make a *stab* at it. — **stab·ber** \'stab-r\ *n.*

sta·bil·i·ty \stə-'bil-ət-ē\ *n.* **1** The quality or condition of being stable; steadiness; constancy. **2** The property that causes a body to return to its original condition when disturbed, as in balance.

sta·bi·lize \'stāb-l-ˌīz\ *v.;* **sta·bi·lized**; **sta·bi·liz·ing.** To make stable or firm; as, a device for *stabilizing* aircraft; to hold steady; as, to *stabilize* prices. — **sta·bi·li·za·tion** \ˌstāb-l-ə-'zāsh-n\ *n.*

sta·bi·liz·er \'stāb-l-ˌīz-r\ *n.* One that stabilizes, as a mechanical device or a fixed surface for stabilizing the motion of an aircraft.

sta·ble \'stāb-l\ *adj.;* **sta·bler** \-l(-)ər\; **sta·blest** \-l(-)əst\. **1** Firmly established; not easily moved or overthrown; as, a *stable* government. **2** Steady in purpose; firm; unwavering. **3** Lasting; enduring. **4** In chemistry, not decomposing readily.

sta·ble \'stāb-l\ *n.* **1** A building in which horses or cattle are fed and sheltered. **2** The horses of a certain racing stable collectively. **3** A group of athletes, especially professional athletes, under one manager. — *v.;* **sta·bled**; **sta·bling** \-l(-)ing\. To put, keep, or lodge in or as if in a stable.

sta·ble·man \'stāb-l-mən\ *n.; pl.* **sta·ble·men** \-mən\. A worker around a stable; a hostler.

stac·ca·to \stə-'kät-ˌō, -'kȧt-ˌō\ *adj.* In music, disconnected; marked by short, clear-cut playing or singing of tones or chords; as, *staccato* notes; a *staccato* passage. — *adv.* In a staccato manner.

stack \'stak\ *n.* **1** A large usually cone-shaped pile, as of hay, straw, or grain. **2** A pile of objects one on top of the other; as, a *stack* of dishes. **3** A vertical pipe for carrying off smoke or vapor; a chimney; a smokestack. **4** A rack with shelves for storing books. **5** A number of rifles arranged together to stand in the form of a pyramid. — *v.* To pile up; to form a stack.

sta·di·um \'stād-ē-əm\ *n.; pl.* **sta·di·ums** \-ē-əmz\ or **sta·dia** \-ē-ə\. **1** In ancient Greece, a course for foot races, with tiers of seats for spectators **2** A similar modern structure used for athletic games.

staff \'staf\ *n.; pl.* **staves** \'stavz, 'stāvz\ or **staffs** \'stafs\. **1** A pole, stick, rod, or bar used as a support or as a sign of authority; as, a flag hanging limp on its *staff;* a bishop's *staff.* **2** The long handle of certain weapons, as the lance and the pike. **3** That which props or sustains. Bread is the *staff* of life. **4** [Plural *staffs*] A group of persons serving as assistants to or employees under a chief; as, a hospital *staff.* **5** [Plural *staffs*] A group of officers or aides appointed to attend upon a civil executive. **6** [Plural *staffs*] A body of military officers not having command but having administrative duties. **7** The five horizontal lines, with their spaces, on which music is written; a stave. — *v.* To supply with a staff.

stag \'stag\ *n.* **1** The adult male of the red deer or of other large deer, as the caribou. **2** A man at a social gathering unaccompanied by a woman. — *adj.* Of or for men only; as, a *stag* dinner.

stage \'stāj\ *n.* **1** A platform or scaffold. **2** The raised flooring in a theater on which plays are acted. **3** The theater, the theatrical profession, or the drama. **4** A place where anything is publicly shown; the scene of any noted action, event, or career. **5** A place of rest on a traveled road; a station. **6** A stagecoach. **7** The distance between two places of rest on a road; as, to travel by easy *stages.* **8** A degree of advance in a journey or in any undertaking, process, or development; as, a *stage* in a disease. **9** One of several periods in the development and growth of many animals or plants; as, the pupa *stage.* — *v.;* **staged**; **stag·ing.** To exhibit on or as if on a stage; as, to *stage* a play.

stage·coach \'stāj-ˌkōch\ *n.* A horse-drawn passenger and mail coach running between stations.

stage·hand \'stāj-ˌhand\ *n.* A theater worker who handles scenery and assists the stage manager.

stage–struck \'stāj-ˌstrək\ *adj.* Fascinated by the theater; especially, longing to become an actor.

stage whisper. A loud whisper by an actor, audible to the spectators but supposed not to be heard by persons on the stage; any similar whisper.

stag·ger \'stag-r\ *v.;* **stag·gered**; **stag·ger·ing** \-r(-)ing\. **1** To move unsteadily from side to side as if about to fall; to reel. **2** To cause to reel or totter. **3** To begin to doubt and waver; to become less confident. **4** To cause to doubt, waver, or hesitate. **5** To place or arrange in a zigzag or alternate but regular way. — *n.* **1** A reeling or tottering movement. **2** [in the plural] Also **blind staggers.** A disease of horses and other animals, marked by reeling, unsteady gait, or falling.

stag·hound \'stag-ˌhau̇nd\ *n.* A hound of a nearly extinct breed used for hunting large animals.

stag·ing \'stā-jing\ *n.* **1** Scaffolding. **2** The act, method, or art of putting a play on the stage.

stag·nant \'stag-nənt\ *adj.* **1** Not flowing; especially, foul from want of motion; as, a *stagnant* pool. **2** Not active or brisk; dull.

stag·nate \'stag-ˌnāt\ *v.;* **stag·nat·ed**; **stag·nat·ing.** To be or become stagnant. — **stag·na·tion** \stag-'nāsh-n\ *n.*

staid \'stād\ *adj.* **1** Settled; fixed; as, *staid* opinion. **2** Sober; serious; sedate.

stain \'stān\ *v.* **1** To discolor with foreign matter; to spot; as, to *stain* a tablecloth with coffee. **2** To taint or spot with guilt or disgrace. **3** To give color to, especially to wood, paper, or glass by processes affecting the material itself; to dye. **4** To give or receive a stain; as, material that *stains* easily. — *n.* **1** A discoloration; a spot. **2** A taint of guilt; a blemish. **3** A pigment used in staining.

stain·less steel \'stān-ləs\. Steel alloyed with chromium and highly resistant to stain, rust, and corrosion.

stair \'star, 'ster\ *n.* **1** Any step of a series of steps for going up or down to a different level. **2** [usually in the plural] A flight of steps.

stair·case \'star-ˌkās, 'ster-\ *n.* A flight of stairs with the supporting framework and banisters.

stair·way \'star-ˌwā, 'ster-\ *n.* A staircase.

stake \'stāk\ *n.* **1** A pointed piece of wood or other material driven, or to be driven, into the ground. **2** A post or support to which a person who is to be burned is tied; death by such burning. **3** Something which is staked for gain or loss; as, to play cards for high *stakes.* **4** The prize in any contest. **5** A share or interest; as, a *stake* in the business. **6** A grubstake. — **at stake.** Risked; in a position to be lost or won. — *v.;* **staked**; **stak·ing.** **1** To mark the limits of by stakes; as, to *stake* off a lot. **2** To fasten or support with stakes; as, to *stake* up flowers. **3** To risk; to bet. **4** To grubstake.

sta·lac·tite \stə-'lak-ˌtīt\ *n.* **1** An icicle-shaped object hanging from the roof or side of a cave, formed by the partial evaporation of dripping water containing dissolved calcium carbonate. **2** A similar formation of other material, as of lava.

sta·lag·mite \stə-'lag-ˌmīt\ *n.* **1** A deposit like an inverted stalactite found on the floor of a cave. **2** A similar deposit of other material.

stale \'stāl\ *adj.;* **stal·er**; **stal·est.** **1** Tasteless or unpalatable from age. **2** Not new; not freshly made. **3** Worn out by use or familiarity; trite; as, a *stale* joke. **4** Having decreased vigor; as, a boxer *stale* from overtraining. — *v.;* **staled**; **stal·ing.** To grow or become stale.

stale·mate \'stāl-ˌmāt\ *n.* **1** In chess, a position in which a player who is not in check cannot move except into check. **2** A drawn contest; a deadlock. — *v.;* **stale·mat·ed**; **stale·mat·ing.** To subject to a stalemate; to bring to a standstill.

stalk \'stȯk\ *n.* **1** The stem of a plant. **2** Something that is like the stem of a plant, as the slender, movable part to which a lobster's eye is attached.

stalk \'stȯk\ *v.* **1** To approach or hunt stealthily; as, to *stalk* deer. **2** To walk with haughty or pompous bearing. **3** To pass from place to place; to spread. Famine *stalked* the land. — *n.* **1** The act or process of stalking. **2** A slow, haughty walk.

stalked \'stȯkt\ *adj.* Having, or carried on, a stalk.

stalk·ing-horse \'stȯk-ing-ˌhȯrs\ *n.* **1** A horse, or figure like a horse, behind which a hunter stalks game. **2** A mask; a pretense.

stall \'stȯl\ *n.* **1** A compartment, usually in a stable, for one animal, as a cow or a horse. **2** A small compartment or booth in which business is conducted; a bench or table on which articles are exposed, as for sale; as, a butcher's *stall;* a *stall* at a fair. **3** One of the compartments in a pew; as, the choir *stalls.* **4** *Chiefly British.* One of the front seats in the orchestra of a theater. **5** Of an airplane, the fact or condition of being stalled. — *v.* **1** To put or keep in a stall. **2** To stop or cause to stop, usually without intention, as an engine.

stall \'stȯl\ *n.* Something used or done to cause delay. — *v.* To stave off; to cause a delay on purpose; to evade or deceive; as, to *stall* for time; to *stall* off questions.

stal·lion \'stal-yən\ *n.* A male horse.

stal·wart \'stȯl-wərt\ *adj.* Stout; strong; brave; as, a *stalwart* guard. — *n.* **1** A stalwart person. **2** An unwavering supporter, as in politics.

sta·men \'stā-mən\ *n.* The part in the center of a flower, consisting of the anther and the filament, that bears the pollen.

stamen

stam·i·na \'stam-ə-nə\ *n.* Vigor; endurance.

stam·i·nate \'stam-ə-nət\ *adj.* Having or producing stamens; especially, having stamens but no pistils.

stam·mer \'stam-r\ *v.;* **stam·mered**; **stam·mer·ing** \-r(-)ing\. To hesitate or falter in speaking; to stutter; as, to *stammer* an excuse. — *n.* A stammering; a stutter. — **stam·mer·er** \-r-r\ *n.*

stamp \'stamp; *in verb senses 1 and 2, and in corresponding noun senses, also* 'stämp *or* 'stȯmp\ *v.* **1** To strike or beat forcibly with the bottom of the foot. **2** To walk heavily and noisily. **3** To impress or imprint with a mark. **4** To cut out, indent, or form with a die or stamp. **5** To indicate as by a mark or stamp; to mark. Frankness *stamped* his character. **6** To crush into a powder, as ore. **7** To put a stamp on. — *n.* **1** The act of stamping. **2** Something that stamps, as an instrument or a die. **3** The mark or impression made by stamping. **4** An official slip of paper, or a mark or seal placed on a thing, as to show that a tax has been paid. **5** A distinctive sign; as, the *stamp* of genius.

stam·pede \(')stam-'pēd\ *n.* [From Mexican Spanish *estampida* meaning literally "crash", "explosion".] **1** A wild, headlong running away of a number of animals. **2** A sudden rush of a group of people. — *v.;* **stam·ped·ed; stam·ped·ing. 1** To run away or cause to run away as a group. **2** To act together or cause to act together suddenly and without thought.

stance \'stan(t)s\ *n.* Way of standing; posture.

stanch or **staunch** \'stȯnch, 'stänch, 'stȧnch\ *v.* [usually *stanch*] To stop or check the flow of something, especially of blood; as, to *stanch* a cut. — *adj.* [usually *staunch*] Firm; steadfast.

stan·chion \'stanch-n\ *n.* **1** An upright bar, post, or support. **2** A device which fits loosely around an animal's neck and limits forward and backward motion. — *v.;* **stan·chioned; stan·chion·ing** \-n(-)ing\. To provide with or fasten by stanchions.

stand \'stand\ *v.;* **stood** \'stu̇d\; **stand·ing. 1** To be in or to take an upright position. **2** To be in a certain position. The house *stood* on a hill. **3** To set upright. **4** To remain unchanged. **5** To submit to; to undergo; as, to *stand* trial. **6** To pause or stop; to remain inactive. **7** To be fixed or steadfast, as in defense; as, to *stand* for democracy. **8** To act in opposition or resistance; as, to *stand* against the enemy. **9** To have a relative position or rank in a graded scale. Where do we *stand?* **10** *Chiefly British.* To be a candidate; to run. **11** To pay for; as, to *stand* the cost of dinner. — **stand by. 1** To be near or present. **2** To defend; to support. **3** To be or get ready. — **stand for. 1** To represent; to be a symbol for. **2** To permit; to put up with. — **stand guard.** To keep watch. — **stand out. 1** To project; to be noticeable. **2** To persist, as in demanding or in opposing something; as, to *stand out* against a new ruling. — **stand to reason.** To be obvious in light of the facts. — **stand up for. 1** To support; to defend. **2** To be a sponsor for. — *n.* **1** The act of standing. **2** A halt, especially for defense or resistance; as, to make a *stand.* **3** A place or post where one stands; a station. **4** A firm belief or decision; as, to take a *stand* on an issue. **5** A raised platform. **6** [often in the plural] A tier of seats from which a race or a game may be watched. **7** A stall or booth for business; as, a peanut *stand.* **8** Something on or in which an object may be placed for support; as, an umbrella *stand.* **9** A group of plants or trees growing on a given area. **10** On a theatrical tour, any of the stops made to give a performance.

stand·ard \'stand-rd\ *n.* **1** A figure adopted as an emblem by an organized body of people. The eagle was the *standard* of the Roman legion. **2** The personal flag of the ruler of a state; a banner. **3** Something set up as a rule for measuring or as a model; as, a *standard* of weight or quantity; *standards* of good manners. **4** A structure that serves as a support; as, a lamp *standard.* — *adj.* **1** Used as or agreeing with a standard for comparison or judgment; as, *standard* weights. **2** Having recognized, lasting value; as, *standard* authors.

stand·ard-bear·er \'stand-rd-ˌbar-r, -ˌber-r\ *n.* **1** An officer or soldier who bears a standard. **2** The leader of any organization, party, or movement.

stand·ard·ize \'stand-r-ˌdīz\ *v.;* **stand·ard·ized; stand·ard·iz·ing.** To make conform to a standard. — **stand·ard·i·za·tion** \ˌstand-r-də-'zāsh-n\ *n.*

standard time. The time established by law or by general usage over a region or country, as any of the four official standards of time in the United States: **Eastern, Central, Mountain,** and **Pacific.**

stand-by \'stan(d)-ˌbī\ *n.* One that can be relied upon in time of need.

stand-in \'stan-ˌdin\ *n.* Someone employed to stand in the place of a motion-picture actor or actress until lights and cameras are ready.

stand·ing \'stan-ding\ *adj.* **1** Upright or erect; as, *standing* grain. **2** At rest; not flowing; stagnant; as, a *standing* pool. **3** Remaining at the same level or amount for an indefinite period; as, a *standing* offer of $1,000. **4** Permanent; as, a *standing* army. **5** Done from a standing position; as, a *standing* jump. — *n.* **1** The action of one that stands; a stand; a stance. **2** Length of service; duration. **3** Position or rank; reputation.

standing part. The part of a rope around which turns are taken in tying a knot.

stand·point \'stan(d)-ˌpȯint\ *n.* A basis for judgment; a mental position from which things are viewed and judged.

stand·still \'stan(d)-ˌstil\ *n.* A stop; a state of rest.

stank. A past tense of *stink.*

stan·za \'stan-zə\ *n.* A group of lines forming a division of a poem; a verse. — **stan·za·ic** \stan-'zā-ik\ *adj.*

staph·y·lo·coc·cus \ˌstaf-l-ō-'käk-əs\ *n.; pl.* **staph·y·lo·coc·cus·es** \-'käk-ə-səz\ or **staph·y·lo·coc·ci** \-'käk-ˌ(s)ī\. Any of a group of bacteria that tend to grow in clusters like bunches of grapes and are usually parasites on the skin and mucous membranes. — **staph·y·lo·coc·cic** \-'käk-sik\ *adj.*

sta·ple \'stāp-l\ *n.* **1** A U-shaped piece of metal with sharp points to be driven into something firm, like wood, as to hold a hook or a pin. **2** A similarly shaped piece of thin wire to be driven through papers and bent over at the ends to fasten them together. — *v.;* **sta·pled; sta·pling** \-l(-)ing\. To fasten by a staple or staples.

staples, 1.

sta·ple \'stāp-l\ *n.* **1** A chief commodity or product. **2** A staple food. **3** A fiber of raw wool, cotton, or flax. — *adj.* **1** Established in commerce; settled; as, a *staple* trade. **2** Regularly produced in large quantities; as, *staple* goods. **3** Principal; chief; as, *staple* foods.

sta·pler \'stāp-lər\ *n.* A machine that staples.

star \'stär, 'stȧr\ *n.* **1** Any of the luminous bodies seen in the heavens; especially, one of those heavenly bodies which are visible at night as apparently fixed points of light but are actually distant bodies like our sun. **2** In astrology, a star supposed to influence one's fortune; destiny; as, born under a lucky *star.* **3** A figure with five or more points, representing a star. **4** Something like or suggesting a star, as an asterisk or a star-shaped object used as an insignia. **5** A person standing out among his fellows; as, one of the brightest *stars* in the legal profession. **6** An actor who plays the leading part in a play or a motion picture. — *v.;* **starred; star·ring. 1** To set or adorn with stars or spangles. **2** To mark with a figure of a star as being superior. **3** To mark with an asterisk. **4** To shine; to be brilliant or prominent. **5** To be a star in a play. **6** To present or advertise as a star, as an actor. — *adj.* Being a star; chief; leading.

stars, 3

star·board \'stärb-rd, 'stȧrb-; 'stär-ˌbōrd, 'stȧr-, -ˌbȯrd\ *n.* The side of a ship on the right of a person who stands on board facing the bow. — *adj.* Relating to the starboard. — *adv.* Toward the starboard side. — *v.* To put or move to starboard.

starch \'stärch, 'stȧrch\ *n.* **1** A white, odorless, tasteless, granular or powdery carbohydrate occurring widely in plants, especially corn and potatoes, an important element of food, and having various household and commercial uses. **2** A stiff, formal manner. **3** *Slang.* Energy; vigor; vim. — *v.* To stiffen with or as if with starch.

starchy \'stärch-ē, 'stȧrch-ē\ *adj.;* **starch·i·er; starch·i·est. 1** Like starch; containing starch. **2** Starched. **3** Stiff or formal in manner.

stare \'star, 'ster\ *v.;* **stared; star·ing. 1** To gaze or look fixedly; as, to *stare* at a stranger. **2** To be very conspicuous, as because of brilliance; as, *staring* colors. — For synonyms see *gaze.* — *n.* The act of staring; a fixed look. — **star·er** \'star-r, 'ster-r\ *n.*

star·fish \'stär-ˌfish, 'stȧr-\ *n.; pl.* **star·fish** or **star·fish·es.** A sea animal with a star-shaped body, related to the sea urchins.

star·gaze \'stär-ˌgāz, 'stȧr-\ *v.;* **star·gazed; star·gaz·ing. 1** To gaze at stars. **2** To stare absent-mindedly; to daydream. — **star·gaz·er** \-ˌgāz-r\ *n.*

stark \'stärk, 'stȧrk\ *adj.* **1** Stiff; motionless; as, *stark* in death. **2** Harsh; rough; violent; as, *stark* weather. **3** Severe; stern. **4** Barren; desolate; as, a *stark* landscape. **5** Sheer; utter; as, *stark* nonsense. — *adv.* Wholly; entirely; quite; as, *stark* mad.

star·less \'stär-ləs, 'stȧr-\ *adj.* Without stars; without visible stars. — **star·less·ly,** *adv.*

star·let \'stär-lət, 'stȧr-\ *n.* **1** A little star. **2** A young motion-picture actress being coached and publicized for possible starring roles.

star·light \'stär-ˌlīt, 'stȧr-\ *n.* The light given by the stars. — *adj.* Lighted by the stars.

star·ling \'stär-ling, 'stȧr-\ *n.* A bird about the size of a robin, with dark brown plumage that turns greenish black in summer, yellowish white spots, and a short, blunt tail.

star·lit \'stär-ˌlit, 'stȧr-\ *adj.* Lighted by the stars.

starred \'stärd, 'stȧrd\ *adj.* **1** Adorned with or as if with stars. **2** Marked with a star or an asterisk. **3** Affected in fortune by the stars.

star·ry \'stär-ē, 'stȧr-ē\ *adj.* **1** Of or relating to the stars. **2** Studded with stars. **3** Shining like stars. **4** Arranged in rays like those of a star.

Stars and Bars. The first flag of the Confederate States of America.

Stars and Stripes. The flag of the United States.

star-span·gled \'stär-ˌspang-gld, 'stȧr-\ *adj.* Spangled or studded with stars.

start \'stärt, 'stȧrt\ *v.* **1** To move suddenly and quickly; to give an involuntary convulsive twitch; to jump; as, to *start* in surprise. **2** To cause to start; as, to *start* a rabbit. **3** To protrude or seem to protrude; as, eyes *starting* from their sockets. **4** To set out; to commence; to begin; to go; as, to *start* to school. **5** To cause to move or act; to set going, running, or flowing; as, to *start* a motor. **6** To work loose. The nail has *started.* **7** To open up, as a topic or subject; as, to *start* a discussion. **8** To enter in a contest, as a horse race. — *n.* **1** The act or an instance of starting. **2** A brief effort or action; as, by fits and *starts.* **3** A sudden impulse. **4** The beginning of a journey or of a course of action. **5** The place of beginning; the point of departure. **6** A lead at the beginning, as of a race.

start·er \'stärt-r, 'stȧrt-r\ *n.* **1** A person or thing that starts something; as, the *starter* of an automobile; the official *starter* for a race. **2** A person or animal that begins a race.

star·tle \'stärt-l, 'stȧrt-l\ *v.;* **star·tled; star·tling** \-l(-)ing\. To start or move suddenly, as in alarm, surprise, or fear; to frighten momentarily.

star·va·tion \stär-'vāsh-n, stȧr-\ *n.* The act of starving, or the condition of being starved.

starve \'stärv, 'stȧrv\ *v.;* **starved; starv·ing.** [From Old English *steorfan* meaning "to die".] **1** To die of hunger. **2** To suffer extreme hunger. **3** To cause to die from hunger. **4** To distress or subdue by famine; as, to *starve* a besieged town. **5** To suffer need of any kind; as, a child *starving* for affection.

starve·ling \'stärv-ling, 'stȧrv-\ *n.* A person, animal, or plant that is thin or weak from lack of food.

stash \'stash\ *v.* To hide or store for future use.

state \'stāt\ *n.* **1** Manner or condition of being; as, the *state* of affairs now; the three *states* of matter. **2** Condition of mind; as, a *state* of fear. **3** A condition befitting a person of rank or wealth; as, to travel in *state.* **4** Any body of people occupying a definite territory and politically organized under one government, especially an independent government. **5** [often with a capital] One of the political units that are joined by federation to form a united government, as in the United States. **6** The territory or the government of a sovereign state or of one of the units joined in a sovereign state.

state \'stāt\ *v.;* **stat·ed**; **stat·ing**. **1** To fix; to settle; to establish; as, at *stated* intervals; a *stated* meeting of a board of trustees. **2** To formulate or utter in words; to tell or express; as, to *state* an opinion.

state·craft \'stāt-ˌkraft\ *n.* Skill in conducting state affairs; statesmanship.

state·hood \'stāt-ˌhu̇d\ *n.* The condition of being a state, especially of the United States.

state·house \'stāt-ˌhau̇s\ *n.; pl.* **state·hous·es** \-ˌhau̇-zəz\. A state capitol.

state·ly \'stāt-lē\ *adj.;* **state·li·er**; **state·li·est**. Having or showing lofty dignity; dignified; majestic.

state·ment \'stāt-mənt\ *n.* **1** The act of stating. **2** Something that is stated; a narrative; a report; an account. **3** A brief summarized record of a financial account; as, a monthly bank *statement.*

state·room \'stāt-ˌrüm, -ˌru̇m\ *n.* A private cabin or room on a ship or on a railroad car.

state·side \'stāt-ˌsīd\ *adj.* Of or relating to the United States as regarded from outside its continental limits; as, the latest *stateside* news; *stateside* mail. — *adv.* In or to the United States.

states·man \'stāts-mən\ *n.; pl.* **states·men** \-mən\. A person engaged in fixing the policies and conducting the affairs of a government; especially, one having unusual wisdom in such matters.

states·man·like \'stāts-mən-ˌlīk\ *adj.* Befitting a statesman.

states·man·ly \'stāts-mən-lē\ *adj.* Statesmanlike.

states·man·ship \'stāts-mən-ˌship\ *n.* The qualities, methods, or skill of a statesman.

state·wide \'stāt-'wīd\ *adj.* Including all parts of a state; as, a *statewide* spelling contest.

stat·ic \'stat-ik\ *adj.* **1** Acting by weight alone; without motion; as, *static* pressure. **2** Relating to bodies or forces that are at rest or that balance each other. **3** Resting; not moving; not active. **4** In electricity, of, relating to, or producing stationary charges such as are generated by rubbing hard rubber with fur. **5** In radio, relating to or caused by static. — *n.* In radio, a crackling noise caused by electrical disturbances in the air.

sta·tion \'stāsh-n\ *n.* **1** The spot or place where a person or thing officially or characteristically stands; as, a sentry's *station.* **2** A regular stopping place on a railroad or bus line; a depot. **3** In Australia and New Zealand, a stock farm or ranch; as, a sheep *station.* **4** A place where a fleet is assigned for duty. **5** A military post. **6** Social standing or rank. **7** A place for receiving or transmitting by radio or television. — *v.;* **sta·tioned**; **sta·tion·ing** \-n(-)ing\. To assign to a station.

sta·tion·ary \'stāsh-n-ˌer-ē\ *adj.* **1** Fixed in a certain place or post; as, a *stationary* engine; *stationary* laundry tubs. **2** Not changing; fixed.

sta·tion·er \'stāsh-n(-)ər\ *n.* A dealer in writing paper, pens and pencils, notebooks and diaries, calendars, and other desk and office supplies.

sta·tion·ery \'stāsh-n-ˌer-ē\ *n.* Writing paper and envelopes.

station wagon. An automobile, for passengers or light hauling, with a rear panel that opens and one or more folding, removable rear seats.

sta·tis·ti·cal \stə-'tis-tik-l\ *adj.* Of or relating to statistics. — **sta·tis·ti·cal·ly** \-tik-l(-)ē\ *adv.*

stat·is·ti·cian \ˌstat-ə-'stish-n\ *n.* A person skilled or engaged in compiling and interpreting statistics.

sta·tis·tics \stə-'tis-tiks\ *n. sing. and pl.* **1** Systematic collection and classification of facts or instances as a basis for study or for drawing general conclusions. **2** Facts so collected and arranged.

stat·u·ary \'stach-ə-ˌwer-ē\ *n.; pl.* **stat·u·ar·ies**. **1** Sculpture. **2** A collection of statues.

stat·ue \'stach-(ˌ)ü\ *n.* The image or likeness of a person or animal, often life-size or larger, sculptured in a solid substance, as marble or bronze.

stat·u·esque \ˌstach-ə-'wesk\ *adj.* Suggesting a statue, as in great size, dignity, or classic form.

stat·ure \'stach-r\ *n.* **1** The natural height of a person; as, a man of average *stature.* **2** Development; growth; as, to reach man's *stature.*

sta·tus \'stāt-əs, 'stat-\ *n.* **1** The state, position, or rank of a person with reference to others; standing. **2** Condition; situation; as, the economic *status* of a country.

stat·ute \'stach-(ˌ)üt, -ət\ *n.* A man-made law.

stat·u·to·ry \'stach-ə-ˌtōr-ē, -ˌtȯr-ē\ *adj.* **1** Of, relating to, or of the nature of a statute. **2** Fixed by statute. **3** Punishable by statute.

staunch or **stanch** \'stȯnch, 'stänch, 'stȧnch\ *v.* [usually *stanch*] To check the flow of, as blood from a wound. — *adj.* [usually *staunch*] **1** Watertight; sound; as, a *staunch* ship. **2** Firm; strong; as, *staunch* foundations. **3** Firm in principle; loyal; steadfast. — **staunch·ly** or **stanch·ly**, *adv.*

stave \'stāv\ *n.* [A new singular that developed irregularly from *staves,* the plural of *staff.*] **1** A stick; a staff. **2** Any of a number of narrow strips of wood placed edge to edge to form the sides or lining of a barrel or keg. **3** A set of verses, as of a song; a stanza. **4** In music, a staff. — *v.;* **staved** \'stāvd\ or **stove** \'stōv\; **stav·ing** \'stā-ving\. **1** To break in the sides of; as, to *stave* in a boat. **2** To keep at a distance; as, to *stave* off trouble.

staves. **1** \'stavz, 'stāvz\ A pl. of *staff.* **2** \'stāvz\ Pl. of *stave.*

stay \'stā\ *n.* A strong rope or wire, as one used to support a mast. — *v.* To fasten with stays.

stay \'stā\ *v.* **1** To prop or hold up. **2** To satisfy for a time; as, to *stay* one's hunger. **3** To endure; to last. — *n.* **1** A support. **2** [in the plural] A corset.

stay \'stā\ *v.* **1** To wait; to delay. **2** To remain; to dwell; as, to *stay* at a small hotel. **3** To stand still; not to change position; as, to *stay* quietly in one spot. **4** To check; to restrain; as, to *stay* one's hand. — *n.* **1** The act of staying or stopping; a halt. **2** The act of remaining; as, a *stay* in town.

stay·sail \'stā-ˌsāl, 'stās-l\ *n.* A sail set on a stay.

stead \'sted\ *n.* **1** Place that another has had, has at present, or might have; as, to act in another person's *stead.* **2** Advantage; service. His knowledge of the sea stood him in good *stead.*

stead·fast \'sted-ˌfast\ *adj.* **1** Firmly established; resolute; as, *steadfast* troops. **2** Not changing; constant; steady; as, a *steadfast* purpose. — **stead-fast·ly** or **sted·fast·ly**, *adv.*

steady \'sted-ē\ *adj.;* **stead·i·er**; **stead·i·est.** **1** Firm in position; not tottering or shaking. **2** Direct; unfaltering; unswerving. **3** Not nervous or easily scared; calm. **4** Constant; not fickle or changing. **5** Regular; uniform; as, a *steady* breeze. **6** Well-ordered; as, *steady* habits. — *v.;* **stead·ied** \-ēd\; **stead·y·ing.** To make or become steady.

steak \'stāk\ *n.* **1** A slice of meat cut from the fleshy part of a beef. **2** A similar slice cut from another animal or from fish; as, ham *steak.*

steal \'stēl\ *v.;* **stole** \'stōl\; **sto·len** \'stō-lən\; **steal·ing.** **1** To take and carry away wrongfully something that belongs to another; to rob. **2** To get for oneself slyly or secretly; as, to *steal* a nap. **3** To take possession of gradually. **4** To move or go slyly or secretly. **5** In baseball, to advance a base without the aid of a hit or an error. — *n.* **1** An act of stealing. **2** Something stolen.

stealth \'stelth\ *n.* Sly or underhand action.

stealthy \'stel-thē\ *adj.;* **stealth·i·er**; **stealth·i·est.** Acting slyly or secretly; done in a sly manner.

steam \'stēm\ *n.* **1** The vapor into which water is changed when heated to the boiling point; as, to heat houses by *steam.* **2** Power; force; energy. The boys let off *steam* by running. **3** The mist formed when water vapor cools; as, *steam* on a window. — *v.* **1** To send forth steam or vapor. **2** To rise or pass off in the form of vapor. **3** To expose to steam; as, *steamed* clams. **4** To move or travel by the power of steam. — *adj.* Using, driven by, or conducting steam.

steam·boat \'stēm-ˌbōt\ *n.* A steam-driven boat.

steam·er \'stēm-r\ *n.* **1** Something driven by steam, as an engine or vehicle; especially, a steamboat. **2** A vessel in which something is steamed.

steam fitter. A workman who installs or repairs steam pipes and their fittings.

steam·roll·er \'stēm-'rōl-r\ *n.* **1** A steam-driven machine with wide heavy rollers for pressing down and smoothing roads. **2** Any power or force that crushes opposition. — *v.* To roll or crush with or as if with a steamroller.

steam·ship \'stēm-ˌship\ *n.* A steam-driven ship.

steam shovel. A large machine that excavates earth with a bucket attached to a crane.

steamy \'stē-mē\ *adj.;* **steam·i·er**; **steam·i·est.** **1** Of steam; like steam. **2** Full of or giving off steam.

ste·ap·sin \stē-'aps-n\ *n.* A lipase from the pancreas.

steed \'stēd\ *n.* A horse, especially a spirited horse.

steel \'stēl\ *n.* **1** A hard, tough metal made by treating iron with intense heat and mixing carbon with it. **2** An instrument or implement of steel; especially a weapon of steel, as a sword or dagger. **3** Such implements or weapons collectively. **4** A piece of steel, as for striking sparks from flint. **5** A hard cold quality like that of steel; as, a man of *steel.* — *adj.* Made of, or like, steel. — *v.* **1** To edge with steel; as, to *steel* an ax. **2** To make like steel; to make bold, strong, or able to resist.

steel·head \'stēl-ˌhed\ *n.* A rainbow trout especially in its silvery seagoing form.

steel wool. An abrasive material made of fine steel shavings, used for cleaning or polishing.

steel·work \'stēl-ˌwərk\ *n.* **1** Any work in steel or of steel. **2** [in the plural] A mill where steel is made. — **steel·work·er** \-ˌwərk-r\ *n.*

steely \'stē-lē\ *adj.;* **steel·i·er**; **steel·i·est.** **1** Made of steel. **2** Like steel, as in hardness or color.

steel·yard \'stēl-ˌyärd, -ˌyȧrd\ *n.* A form of balance on which the thing to be weighed is hung from the shorter arm of a lever and is balanced by a weight that slides along the longer arm, which is marked with a scale.

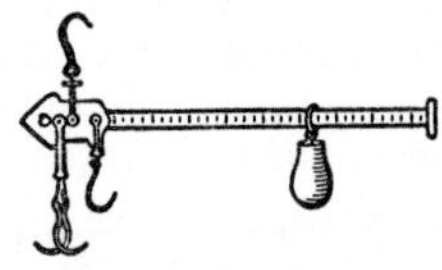
steelyard

steep \'stēp\ *adj.* **1** Having a slope running up or down at a sharp angle; almost perpendicular; as, a *steep* hill. **2** Very great or high; extreme; as, *steep* prices.

steep \'stēp\ *v.* **1** To extract the essence of by soaking; as, to *steep* tea. **2** To undergo this process. **3** To saturate; as, *steeped* in learning.

steep·en \'stēp-n\ *v.;* **steep·ened**; **steep·en·ing** \-n(-)ing\. To make or become steeper.

stee·ple \'stēp-l\ *n.* **1** A tall tapering structure, usually topped with a spire, on top of a church tower. **2** A church tower. — **stee·pled** \-ld\ *adj.*

stee·ple·chase \'stēp-l-ˌchās\ *n.* **1** A race across country by horsemen. **2** A race on a course with hedges, walls, and other obstacles.

stee·ple·jack \'stēp-l-ˌjak\ *n.* A repairman who works on steeples and other high structures.

steep·ly \'stēp-lē\ *adv.* In a steep manner; sharply.

steer \'stir\ *n.* **1** The castrated male of domestic cattle; especially, one raised for beef.

steer \'stir\ *v.* **1** To direct the course of, as by a rudder or wheel; as, to *steer* a boat. **2** To guide; to control; to manage. **3** To be steered; to take a direction or course; to obey the helm or wheel.

steer·age \'stir-ij\ *n.* **1** The art or practice of steering. **2** The effect of the helm on a boat. **3** The lowest-fare accommodation of a passenger ship.

steer·ing wheel \'stir-ing\. A wheel by which something, as a ship or automobile, is steered.

steers·man \'stirz-mən\ *n.; pl.* **steers·men** \-mən\. A person who steers; a helmsman.

stein \'stīn\ *n.* An earthenware beer mug.

stel·lar \'stel-r\ *adj.* Of or relating to stars; like a star, as in shape or brilliancy.

stem \'stem\ *n.* **1** The main trunk of a tree or other plant. **2** Any part of a plant that develops buds and shoots instead of roots; any part that supports leaves, flowers, or fruit; a stalk. **3** Anything resembling or likened to the stem of a plant; as, the *stem* of a pipe. **4** The prow of a ship. **5** The stock, or a branch, of a family. **6** That part of an inflected word which remains unchanged throughout a given inflection. — *v.;* **stemmed**; **stem·ming.** **1** To remove the stem from; as, to *stem* cherries. **2** To grow out or develop like the stems of a plant.

stem \'stem\ *v.;* **stemmed**; **stem·ming. 1** To stop or dam up, as a river. **2** To check as if by damming; to stanch; as, to *stem* a flow of blood.

stem \'stem\ *v.;* **stemmed**; **stem·ming.** To make headway against. The ship *stemmed* the tide.

stench \'stench\ *n.* A stink.

sten·cil \'sten(t)s-l\ *n.* **1** A piece of material having letters or designs cut through it so that an impression can be left upon another surface by applying ink or paint across the parts cut away. **2** A pattern or design made with a stencil. — *v.;* **sten·ciled** or **sten·cilled**; **sten·cil·ing** or **sten·cil·ling** \-l(-)ing\. To mark with a stencil.

ste·nog·ra·pher \stə-'näg-rəf-r\ *n.* A person skilled in or employed to do stenography.

sten·o·graph·ic \ˌsten-ə-'graf-ik\ *adj.* **1** Of or relating to stenography. **2** Done or made by stenography. — **sten·o·graph·i·cal·ly** \-ik-l(-)ē\ *adv.*

ste·nog·ra·phy \stə-'näg-rə-fē\ *n.* The art of writing in shorthand, especially from dictation.

sten·to·ri·an \sten-'tōr-ē-ən, -'tȯr-\ *adj.* Extremely loud; as, a *stentorian* voice.

step \'step\ *n.* **1** An advance or a movement made by raising one foot and placing it down in another spot. **2** A rest or place for the foot in going up or down, as a stair. **3** A rank, degree, or stage in a series; as, one *step* nearer graduation. **4** The distance covered by one movement of the foot in walking or running; as, a *step* of three feet. **5** A very short distance; as, only a *step* away. **6** A footstep; as, to follow in another's *steps.* **7** Manner of walking; as, to know a man by his *step.* **8** Measure; action; as, to take *steps* to help matters. **9** Any combination of foot and body movements which forms part of a dance; as, a waltz *step.* **10** In music, a scale or staff degree or the interval between two adjoining degrees of the staff or two successive notes of the scale; especially, a whole step. — **in step.** Stepping in accord with others or in time to music; in accord; in unison. — **keep step. 1** To walk or mark time in step. **2** To progress at the same rate. — **out of step.** Not in step; not in accord. — *v.;* **stepped**; **step·ping. 1** To move in any direction by a step or steps. **2** To go on foot; to walk. **3** To move rapidly; as, to *step* along at sixty miles an hour. **4** To obtain something with little or no effort; as, to *step* into a good job. **5** To press down with the foot. **6** To measure by stepping. **7** To change by or as if by a series of regulated steps; as, to *step* up production. — **step down. 1** To give up a position, often in favor of another. **2** To decrease or retard. — **step out. 1** To go outdoors. **2** To stride along vigorously. **3** To depart from one's usual routine; especially, to indulge in some unusually extravagant recreation or entertainment. — **step up. 1** To step forward or to the front; to move up; to become prominent. **2** To increase or augment, as in rate or volume.

step·broth·er \'step-ˌbrəth-r\ *n.* A son of one's stepfather or stepmother by a previous marriage.

step·child \'step-ˌchīld\ *n.; pl.* **step·chil·dren** \-ˌchild-r(ə)n\. A child of one's husband or wife by a former marriage; a **step·daugh·ter** \-ˌdȯt-r\ or **step·son** \-ˌsən\.

step·fa·ther \'step-ˌfäth-r, -ˌfȧth-r\ *n.* The husband of one's mother by her remarriage.

step·lad·der \'step-ˌlad-r\ *n.* A light portable set of steps, especially one with flat, broad steps.

stepladder

step·moth·er \'step-ˌməth-r\ *n.* The wife of one's father by his remarriage.

steppe \'step\ *n.* A vast tract of flat, almost treeless country of southeastern Europe and west central Asia.

step·ping·stone \'step-ing-ˌstōn\ *n.* **1** A stone projecting above the surface of water or mud, on which to step in walking, as in crossing a stream. **2** A means, especially of progress; as, a *steppingstone* to success.

step rocket. A rocket the sections of which are fired successively.

step·sis·ter \'step-ˌsist-r\ *n.* A daughter of one's stepfather or stepmother by a previous marriage.

ster·e·op·ti·con \ˌster-ē-'äp-tik-n, ˌstir-, -tə-ˌkän\ *n.* A lantern for showing pictures, as photographs, upon a screen by means of a strong light.

ster·e·o·scope \'ster-ē-ə-ˌskōp, 'stir-\ *n.* An optical instrument that blends two slightly different pictures of the same subject to produce a three-dimensional effect. — **ster·e·o·scop·ic** \ˌster-ē-ə-'skäp-ik, ˌstir-\ *adj.* — **ster·e·o·scop·i·cal·ly** \-ik-l(-)ē\ *adv.*

ster·e·o·type \'ster-ē-ə-ˌtīp, 'stir-\ *n.* **1** A solid metal plate with a relief surface from which a page, such as one in a newspaper, may be reproduced. **2** Anything repeated or reproduced without change; anything conforming to a fixed or general pattern; as, *stereotypes* of behavior. — *v.;* **ster·e·o·typed**; **ster·e·o·typ·ing. 1** To make stereotypes of, as a book. **2** To repeat without change; to fix in lasting form. — **ster·e·o·typ·er** \-ˌtīp-r\ *n.*

ster·e·o·typed \'ster-ē-ə-ˌtīpt, 'stir-\ *adj.* Always the same; lacking originality.

ster·ile \'ster-əl\ *adj.* **1** Not able to bear fruit, crops, or offspring; barren; not fertile; as, *sterile* soil. **2** Free from living germs; disinfected; as, a *sterile* gauze pad. — **ste·ril·i·ty** \stə-'ril-ət-ē\ *n.*

ster·i·lize \'ster-ə-ˌlīz\ *v.;* **ster·i·lized**; **ster·i·liz·ing.** To make sterile; to treat so as to be free from germs. — **ster·i·li·za·tion** \ˌster-ə-lə-'zāsh-n\ *n.*

ster·i·liz·er \'ster-ə-ˌlīz-r\ *n.* One that sterilizes; especially, an apparatus for sterilizing.

ster·ling \'stər-ling\ *n.* **1** British money. **2** The standard of fineness of lawful British coin. **3** Silver of the same proportion of pure metal as a British silver coin (**sterling silver**); articles made of sterling silver. — *adj.* **1** Of or relating to sterling. **2** Made of sterling silver. **3** Of full value; genuine.

stern \'stərn\ *adj.* **1** Hard and severe in nature or manner; as, a *stern* judge. **2** Not inviting or attractive; forbidding; grim. **3** Showing severity; harsh. **4** Stout; resolute. — **stern·ly**, *adv.*

stern \'stərn\ *n.* **1** The rear end of a boat. **2** The hinder part of anything.

stern·most \'stərn-ˌmōst\ *adj.* Farthest astern.

ster·num \'stər-nəm\ *n.; pl.* **ster·nums** \-nəmz\ or **ster·na** \-nə\. The bone or cartilage connecting the ribs in front in most vertebrates above fishes; the breastbone.

steth·o·scope \'steth-ə-ˌskōp, 'steth-\ *n.* An instrument used by doctors for listening to sounds produced in the body, especially in the chest.

ste·ve·dore \'stē-və-ˌdōr, -ˌdȯr\ *n.* A person whose work is to load and unload boats in port.

stew \'stü, 'styü\ *v.* **1** To boil slowly; to cook in liquid at a low heat. **2** To worry. — *n.* **1** A dish of meat and vegetables prepared by stewing. **2** An upset state; as, to be in a *stew* over nothing.

stew·ard \'stü-ərd, 'styü-; 'stu̇rd, 'styu̇rd\ *n.* **1** A manager of a large home, an estate, or a club. **2** A person who supervises the provision and distribution of food, as in a club or ship. **3** An employee who serves passengers on boats or airplanes.

stew·ard·ess \'stü-ərd-əs, 'styü-; 'stu̇rd-əs, 'styu̇rd-\ *n.* A female steward.

stick \'stik\ *n.* **1** A cut or broken branch or twig, especially when dry and dead. **2** A long narrow wooden rod, staff, club, or implement. **3** Something like a stick in shape or use; as, a *stick* of dynamite. **4** A person who is dull and lifeless. **5** A stab, as with a knife. **6** The vertical lever by which certain controls of an airplane are operated. — *v.;* **stuck** \'stək\; **stick·ing. 1** To stab; to prick. **2** To kill by piercing. **3** To push out, up, into, or under; to thrust; as, to *stick* up one's hand; to *stick* a needle into one's finger. **4** To fasten by or on a point; to fasten by thrusting in; as, to *stick* a flower in a buttonhole. **5** To adhere to a surface. **6** To place; as, to *stick* a cap on one's head. **7** To puzzle. One question *stuck* all the students. **8** To hold fast; to keep close; as, to *stick* to one's friends. **9** To remain fast; to become immovable. The car *stuck* in the mud. **10** To be held back, as by fear or hesitation; as, to *stick* at nothing to gain one's end. **11** To apply oneself industriously; as, to *stick* to a task. **12** To protrude. The shoot *sticks* through the soil. — **stick up. 1** To take a stand; to argue; to offer defense; as, to *stick up* for one's rights. **2** To hold up, as at the point of a gun; to rob.

stick·er \'stik-r\ *n.* **1** One that sticks, as a pointed implement. **2** A gummed label. **3** A thorn; a bur.

stick·le \'stik-l\ *v.;* **stick·led**; **stick·ling** \-l(-)ing\. **1** To fight obstinately for something, often on very slight grounds. **2** To hesitate because of objections, such as a point of conscience or honor. — **stick·ler** \-l(-)ər\ *n.*

stick·le·back \'stik-l-ˌbak\ *n.* A small scaleless nest-building fish with sharp spines on the back.

stick·pin \'stik-ˌpin\ *n.* An ornamental pin to be stuck into a necktie.

stick·tight \'stik-ˌtīt\ *n.* The bur marigold.

stick–up \'stik-ˌəp\ *n.* A holdup; a robbery.

sticky \'stik-ē\ *adj.;* **stick·i·er**; **stick·i·est. 1** Gluey; adhesive. **2** Hot and muggy; as, a *sticky* day.

stiff \'stif\ *adj.* **1** Not easily bent; rigid; as, a *stiff* book cover. **2** Not easily moved; not limber; as, *stiff* joints. **3** Not flowing easily; thick and heavy; as, *stiff* glue. **4** Stubborn; hard-fought. **5** Strong and powerful; as, a *stiff* wind. **6** Not natural and easy; formal; as, a *stiff* manner. **7** Very hard to understand or perform; difficult. **8** Harsh; severe; as, a *stiff* sentence. **9** High; steep; as, *stiff* prices. — **stiff·ly**, *adv.*

stiff·en \'stif-n\ *v.;* **stiff·ened**; **stiff·en·ing** \-n(-)ing\. To make or become stiff.

sti·fle \'stīf-l\ *v.;* **sti·fled**; **sti·fling** \-l(-)ing\. **1** To smother; to choke; to suffocate. **2** To hold back by force of will; as, to *stifle* one's anger. **3** To keep down; to silence; as, to *stifle* opposition.

stig·ma \'stig-mə\ *n.; pl.* **stig·ma·ta** \stig-'mät-ə, 'stig-mət-ə, stig-'mȧt-ə\ or, especially in senses 1 and 3, **stig·mas** \'stig-məz\. **1** A mark of disgrace or reproach; as, unable to live down the *stigma* of a term in prison. **2** [in the plural *stigmata*] Marks resembling the wounds on the crucified body of Christ. **3** A knob at the tip of a pistil that receives the pollen causing seeds to develop in a flower. **4** In medicine, a red speck on the skin.

stig·ma·tize \'stig-mə-ˌtīz\ *v.;* **stig·ma·tized**; **stig·ma·tiz·ing.** To mark with a stigma; to brand by calling disgraceful, shameful, or unworthy.

stile \'stīl\ *n.* **1** A step or set of steps used for crossing a fence or wall. **2** A turnstile.

sti·let·to \stə-'let-ˌō\ *n.; pl.* **sti·let·tos** or **sti·let·toes. 1** A slender, pointed dagger. **2** A pointed instrument for making eyelet holes.

still \'stil\ *adj.* **1** Inactive; motionless; as, *still* water. **2** Quiet; soundless; as, a *still* night. **3** Hushed; silent. The children were *still.* **4** Not sparkling or effervescent; as, *still* wine. **5** Of a photograph, not showing motion. — *n.* **1** A still time; stillness. **2** A still photograph. — *v.;* **stilled**; **still·ing.** To make or become still; to quiet.

still \'stil\ *adv.* **1** *Archaic.* Always; ever. **2** Up to this or that time; as yet. **3** Even after that; in spite of what happened. Although he had been told otherwise, he *still* believed the news. **4** Even more than that; even. Try to do *still* better. — *conj.* However; nevertheless.

still \'stil\ *n.* **1** An apparatus for distilling liquids, especially alcoholic liquors. **2** A distillery.

still·born \'stil-'bȯrn\ *adj.* Born dead.

still life. A drawing or painting of an inanimate object or objects, as fruit, pottery, or flowers.

still·ness \'stil-nəs\ *n.* Quiet; silence; calm.

stilly \'stil-ē\ *adj.;* **still·i·er**; **still·i·est**. Still; calm.

stilt \'stilt\ *n.* **1** One of a pair of tall poles each of which has a high step or loop to raise the foot above the ground in walking. **2** A tall post or log used as a support for a shed or for a pier or other structure built over water.

stilts

stilt·ed \'stil-təd\ *adj.* Elevated as if on stilts; stiffly formal; not easy and natural; as, a *stilted* speech.

stim·u·lant \'stim-yə-lənt\ *adj.* Serving to stimulate; acting as a stimulant. — *n.* **1** Something that stimulates, as a stimulating medicine or beverage. **2** An alcoholic drink.

stim·u·late \'stim-yə-ˌlāt\ *v.;* **stim·u·lat·ed**; **stim·u·lat·ing**. To arouse to action or to increased activity; to excite, arouse, or animate.

stim·u·la·tion \ˌstim-yə-'lāsh-n\ *n.* **1** The action of stimulating. **2** The condition of being stimulated.

stim·u·lus \'stim-yə-ləs\ *n.; pl.* **stim·u·lus·es** \-lə-səz\ or **stim·u·li** \-ˌlī, -ˌlē\. **1** Something that stirs to action or that induces activity; an incentive. **2** Anything that causes a temporary increase of activity in a living body or any of its parts.

sting \'sting\ *v.;* **stung** \'stəng\; **sting·ing** \'sting-ing\. **1** To prick painfully; to cause a keen burning pain or smarting sensation; as, to be *stung* by a bee. **2** To feel a burning or smarting pain. **3** To cause to suffer keenly; as, to be *stung* by criticism. **4** To stimulate or urge on; as, to be *stung* into renewed activity. — *n.* **1** The act of stinging. **2** A sore or pain caused by stinging. **3** A mark left by something that stings. **4** Stinging force or quality. **5** An organ by which some insects and fishes defend themselves. **6** In some plants, a hair that secretes a stinging fluid. — **sting·er** \'sting-r\ *n.*

sting ray. A very flat fish with one or more stinging spines near the base of its tail.

stin·gy \'stin-jē\ *adj.;* **stin·gi·er**; **stin·gi·est**. **1** Unwilling to give or spend; mean about sharing or parting with anything. **2** Scanty; as, a *stingy* meal. — **stin·gi·ly** \'stinj-l-ē\ *adv.* — **stin·gi·ness** \'stin-jē-nəs\ *n.*

stink \'stingk\ *v.;* **stank** \'stangk\ or **stunk** \'stəngk\; **stunk**; **stink·ing**. **1** To give forth a strong and offensive smell. **2** To cause to have a stink; as, to *stink* up a room. **3** To cause or affect by a stink. **4** *Slang.* To be no good or of very poor quality. — *n.* **1** A disgusting odor; a stench. **2** A public outcry against something offensive.

stint \'stint\ *v.* **1** To limit in share or portion; to cut short in amount; as, to *stint* the children's milk. **2** To be sparing or frugal. — *n.* **1** A person's share, especially of work; a set task; as, one's daily *stint* of dishwashing. **2** The act of stinting; restraint; limit; as, to give without *stint.*

stipe \'stīp\ *n.* A short stalk, especially one supporting a fern frond or the cap of a mushroom.

sti·pend \'stī-ˌpend, 'stīp-nd\ *n.* Salary or other settled compensation; as, a clergyman's *stipend.*

stip·ple \stip-l\ *v.;* **stip·pled**; **stip·pling** \-l(-)ing\. **1** To engrave by means of dots instead of lines. **2** To depict, as in paint or ink, by short touches that produce together an even, softly graded shadow. — *n.* **1** Painting by stippling. **2** The effect so produced. — **stip·pler** \-l(-)ər\ *n.*

stip·u·late \'stip-yə-ˌlāt\ *v.;* **stip·u·lat·ed**; **stip·u·lat·ing**. To make an agreement; to arrange as part of an agreement; especially, to demand or insist on as a condition in an agreement.

stip·u·la·tion \ˌstip-yə-'lāsh-n\ *n.* **1** The act of stipulating. **2** Something that is stipulated.

stip·ule \'stip-ˌyül\ *n.* One of the pair of small leaflike parts at the base of the leaf in many plants.

stir \'stər\ *v.;* **stirred**; **stir·ring**. **1** To change position; to move even slightly; to budge. **2** To set in motion or activity, as by beating or poking. **3** To be active or busy; as, to be up and *stirring* by daybreak. **4** To mix or dissolve, as by circular motion of a spoon or fork. **5** To arouse; to excite; as, to *stir* up anger. — *n.* **1** The act of stirring; a stirring movement. **2** The state of being stirred up.

stir·ring \'stər-ing\ *adj.* **1** Active; busy. **2** Lively; rousing; inspiring; exciting; as, a *stirring* song.

stir·rup \'stər-əp, 'stə-rəp, 'stir-əp\ *n.* A small light frame, often of metal and used in pairs, hung by straps from a saddle and serving as a support for the foot of a horseback rider.

stirrups

stirrup bone. The innermost of the chain of small bones in the ears of mammals.

stitch \'stich\ *n.* **1** One of the series of loops formed by or over a needle in sewing. **2** In crocheting or knitting, a single turn of thread around a needle. **3** A particular arrangement of stitches. **4** A sharp, sudden pain. A *stitch* in one's side. — *v.* **1** To make stitches in. **2** To sew.

stoat \'stōt\ *n.* The European ermine, especially in its brown summer coat.

stock \'stäk\ *n.* **1** A stump or block of wood. **2** A part of a thing that serves as its support or handle; as, the *stock* of a gun; the *stock* of a whip. **3** The main stem of a plant; the trunk. **4** The original ancestor, from which others have descended. **5** Lineage; ancestry; as, to come of good *stock.* **6** A strain, race, or group of animals or plants closely related by descent, within the same species. **7** Livestock; cattle; farm animals. **8** The whole supply or amount on hand. **9** The sum of money or capital that is invested in a business. **10** The total of shares in a company or corporation, represented by certificates of ownership. **11** Raw material; as, paper *stock.* **12** A rich extract, as of meat, used as a basis for soups and gravies. **13** [in the plural] An old instrument of punishment, consisting of a wooden frame with holes in which the wrists or ankles of offenders could be confined. **14** [in the plural] The frame or timbers on which a ship rests while being built. **15** A stock company or the plays presented by it. **16** A close-fitting wide band of cloth for the neck. **17** A garden herb with fragrant four-petaled flowers. **18** In grafting, the stem or plant in which a cion is inserted. — *v.* **1** To furnish with stock or a stock. **2** To keep on hand; as, to *stock* canned foods. — *adj.* **1** Of or relating to stock; as, a *stock* farm. **2** Kept in stock; as, *stock* sizes. **3** Constantly repeated; as, *stock* remarks.

stock·ade \(ˈ)stä-ˈkād\ *n.* **1** A line of strong posts set in the ground to form a defense. **2** A pen or enclosure so made. — *v.;* **stock·ad·ed**; **stock·ad·ing.** To fortify or surround with a stockade.

stock·bro·ker \ˈstäk-ˌbrōk-r\ *n.* A person who executes orders to buy and sell shares of stock.

stock company. **1** A business whose capital is represented by stock. **2** A theatrical company organized to present a repertory of plays and made up of actors able to play many parts.

stock exchange. **1** A place where the buying and selling of shares of stock is carried on. **2** An association of stockbrokers.

stock·hold·er \ˈstäk-ˌhōld-r\ *n.* An owner of stock in a company.

stock·ing \ˈstäk-ing\ *n.* A close-fitting knitted or woven covering for the foot and leg.

stocking cap. A long knitted cone-shaped cap, sometimes with a tassel at the top.

stocking cap

stock·man \ˈstäk-mən\ *n.; pl.* **stock·men** \-mən\. An owner or breeder of livestock; one in charge of livestock; a rancher; a herder.

stock·pile \ˈstäk-ˌpīl\ *n.* A reserve supply of a material accumulated within a country as a safeguard against a shortage, especially in an emergency. — *v.;* **stock·piled**; **stock·pil·ing.** To accumulate a stockpile of; as, to *stockpile* uranium.

stock·room \ˈstäk-ˌrüm, -ˌru̇m\ *n.* A storage place for supplies or goods used in a business.

stock-still \ˈstäk-ˈstil\ *adj.* Very still; motionless.

stocky \ˈstäk-ē\ *adj.;* **stock·i·er**; **stock·i·est.** Short and thick; thickset; sturdy.

stock·yard \ˈstäk-ˌyärd, -ˌyȧrd\ *n.* A yard for keeping livestock, especially for slaughter.

stodgy \ˈstäj-ē\ *adj.;* **stodg·i·er**; **stodg·i·est.** **1** Short and thickset; as, a *stodgy* figure. **2** Dull; as, a *stodgy* book. **3** Unappetizing; as, *stodgy* food.

sto·ic \ˈstō-ik\ *n.* One who is indifferent to both pain and pleasure or who suffers without complaint. — **sto·i·cism** \-ə-ˌsiz-m\ *n.*

sto·ic \ˈstō-ik\ or **sto·i·cal** \-ik-l\ *adj.* Like a stoic. — **sto·i·cal·ly** \-ik-l(-)ē\ *adv.*

stoke \ˈstōk\ *v.;* **stoked**; **stok·ing.** **1** To poke or stir up, as a fire. **2** To fuel, as a furnace or boiler.

stoke·hold \ˈstōk-ˌhōld\ *n.* A ship's boiler room.

stoke·hole \ˈstōk-ˌhōl\ *n.* **1** The opening through which fuel is put into a furnace. **2** The space in front of a furnace.

stok·er \ˈstōk-r\ *n.* One that feeds a furnace.

stole \ˈstōl\ *n.* **1** A long narrow band worn round the neck by priests and bishops in ceremonies. **2** A woman's garment consisting of a long band of fur or cloth worn round the neck and shoulders.

stole \ˈstōl\. Past tense of *steal.*

stolen. Past part. of *steal.*

stol·id \ˈstäl-əd\ *adj.* Showing little or no feeling; not easily excited; impassive. — **stol·id·ly**, *adv.*

sto·lon \ˈstō-lən\ *n.* **1** A slender branch or shoot growing at or near the base of a plant and developing a bud and root at its tip, from which a new plant grows. **2** In zoology, an extension of a body wall, from which buds are developed.

sto·ma \ˈstō-mə\ *n.; pl.* **sto·mas** \-məz\ or **sto·ma·ta** \-mət-ə\. Any of various tiny openings for the passage of gases and moisture, as in the under surface of leaves.

stom·ach \ˈstəm-ək, -ik\ *n.* **1** The pouch into which food goes after it leaves the mouth and has passed down the throat. **2** Abdomen; belly. **3** Appetite; desire; as, no *stomach* for a quarrel. — *v.* To bear; to endure; as, unable to *stomach* the smell. — **sto·mach·ic** \stə-ˈmak-ik\ *adj.*

stom·ach·er \ˈstəm-ək-r, -ik-r\ *n.* An ornamental covering for the chest formerly worn by women.

stomp \ˈstämp, ˈstȯmp\ *v.* **1** To strike forcibly with the bottom of the foot. **2** To bring down forcibly on the ground; as, to *stomp* one's foot with rage. **3** To walk heavily and noisily. — *n.* The action or sound of stomping.

stone \ˈstōn\ *n.* **1** Earth or mineral matter hardened in a mass. **2** A piece of rock not as fine as gravel; as, to throw *stones.* **3** Rock as a material, especially for building. **4** A piece of rock used for some special purpose, as for a monument at a grave. **5** A jewel; a gem; as, precious *stones.* **6** The hard seed of some fruits, as a peach or plum. **7** *pl.* **stone.** An English measure of weight equaling fourteen pounds. **8** A stony mass sometimes present in diseased organs, as the bladder or kidney. — *v.;* **stoned**; **ston·ing.** **1** To pelt with stones. **2** To remove the stones or seeds of. — *adj.* **1** Of, relating to, or consisting of stone; as, a *stone* wall. **2** Made of stoneware. — *adv.* Absolutely; completely; as, *stone* deaf.

Stone Age. The oldest period in which man is known to have existed; the age of stone tools.

stone·cut·ter \ˈstōn-ˌkət-r\ *n.* One that cuts or dresses stone. — **stone·cut·ting** \-ing\ *n.*

stone·ma·son \ˈstōn-ˌmās-n\ *n.* A mason who works or builds in stone.

stone·ware \ˈstōn-ˌwar, -ˌwer\ *n.* Vessels of heavy earthenware, as jugs and jars.

stone·work \ˈstōn-ˌwərk\ *n.* **1** The work of cutting, dressing, and shaping stones, as in masonry. **2** The stones thus prepared. — **stone·work·er**, *n.*

stony \ˈstō-nē\ *adj.;* **ston·i·er**; **ston·i·est.** **1** Having many stones; as, *stony* soil. **2** Like stone.

stood. Past tense and past part. of *stand.*

stooge \ˈstüj\ *n.* **1** An actor who, usually by questions, prepares the way for a comedian's jokes. **2** One who slavishly follows or serves another.

stool \'stül\ *n.* **1** A single seat without a back. **2** A footstool. **3** A seat used in emptying the bowels. **4** A discharge from the bowels.

stool pigeon. **1** A pigeon used to trap other pigeons. **2** A person used as a spy by the police.

stoop \'stüp\ *v.* **1** To bend over. **2** To carry the head and shoulders or the upper part of the body bent forward. **3** To descend to doing something that is beneath one; as, to *stoop* to lying. — *n.* The action of stooping; a stooping posture.

stoop \'stüp\ *n.* A small porch at a house door.

stop \'stäp\ *v.;* **stopped; stop·ping.** **1** To close an opening by filling or blocking it; as, to *stop* one's ears with cotton. **2** To check; to restrain; as, to *stop* a person from going. **3** To halt the movement or progress of; as, to *stop* the car. **4** To instruct one's banker not to honor or pay; as, to *stop* payment on a check. **5** To regulate the pitch of the tone of a musical instrument, as by pressing a violin string with the finger. **6** To cease; to come to an end. **7** To make a visit; to stay; as, to *stop* with friends for a week. — *n.* **1** The action of stopping or the state of being stopped; a halt. **2** A stay; a short halt in a trip; as, to make a *stop* for lunch. **3** A stopping place. **4** A stopper. **5** A punctuation mark; especially, a period. **6** In music, any means by which the pitch of the tone of an instrument is changed; a knob in an organ by which the player controls a set of pipes. **7** A device for stopping or limiting motion; as, a door held open by a *stop.* **8** A consonant formed by a complete momentary stoppage in the breath passage, as *p, b, t, d, k, g.*

stop·gap \'stäp-ˌgap\ *n.* Something that fills a gap, such as a temporary job.

stop·light \'stäp-ˌlīt\ *n.* **1** A signal light used in controlling traffic. **2** A rear light on an automobile that shows red when the brakes are applied.

stop·over \'stäp-ˌōv-r\ *n.* An interruption of a journey for a short stay or the place stayed at.

stop·page \'stäp-ij\ *n.* The action of stopping or the state of being stopped; an obstruction.

stop·per \'stäp-r\ *n.* A cork, plug, or bung used to stop openings. — *v.;* **stop·pered; stop·per·ing** \-r(-)ing\. To close or secure with a stopper.

stop·ple \'stäp-l\ *n.* A stopper.

stop watch. A watch, used especially by those keeping time in athletic contests, with hands which can be started or stopped by pressing a small button.

stor·age \'stōr-ij, 'stȯr-\ *n.* **1** The act of storing. **2** The state of being stored or the place in which things are stored. **3** The cost of storing.

storage battery. A battery in which electricity is generated by chemical action and which may be restored to a charged condition by passing a current through it in a direction opposite to the flow of current when the battery is being used.

store \'stōr, 'stȯr\ *v.;* **stored; stor·ing.** **1** To stock up; to supply for future use; as, to *store* up sugar. **2** To put in a place for safekeeping; as, to *store* one's goods in a warehouse. — *n.* **1** [in the plural] Accumulated supplies, as of food; as, a ship's *stores.* **2** Something stored; a stock; as, a *store* of good jokes. **3** A place where goods are sold; a shop. **4** The state of being ready; as, a surprise in *store.*

store·house \'stōr-ˌhaủs, 'stȯr-\ *n.; pl.* **store·hous·es** \-ˌhaủ-zəz\. **1** A building for storing goods. **2** A place having a large supply; a rich source.

store·keep·er \'stōr-ˌkēp-r, 'stȯr-\ *n.* **1** One who is in charge of stores. **2** One who keeps a store or shop.

store·room \'stōr-ˌrüm, 'stȯr-, -ˌrủm\ *n.* A room for storing things not in use.

sto·ried \'stōr-ēd, 'stȯr-\ *adj.* Celebrated in story.

sto·ried \'stōr-ēd, 'stȯr-\ *adj.* Having stories, or floors; as, a three-*storied* house.

stork \'stȯrk\ *n.* Any of various large, mostly Old World wading birds having a long stout bill.

storm \'stȯrm\ *n.* **1** Disturbance of the atmosphere accompanied by wind, rain, snow, hail, sleet, or thunder and lightning; a heavy fall of rain, snow, or hail. **2** A shower of objects; as, a *storm* of arrows. **3** A violent outbreak; as, a *storm* of anger. **4** A determined mass attack by soldiers; as, to take a place by *storm.* — *v.* **1** To blow hard; to rain, snow, or hail heavily. **2** To rage; to be violently angry. **3** To rush violently. The mob *stormed* through the streets. **4** To assault by storm.

storm·bound \'stȯrm-'baủnd\ *adj.* Isolated by a storm; stopped or delayed by a storm.

stormy \'stȯr-mē\ *adj.;* **storm·i·er; storm·i·est.** **1** Characterized by a storm or by storms. **2** Angry and excited; as, a *stormy* meeting.

stormy petrel. **1** Any of certain small petrels found in the north Atlantic and Mediterranean, believed to be active before a storm. **2** Anyone who is fond of strife or is believed to bring trouble.

sto·ry \'stōr-ē, 'stȯr-ē\ *n.; pl.* **sto·ries.** The set of rooms or the area making up one level of a building; a floor; as, a house with three *stories.*

sto·ry \'stōr-ē, 'stȯr-ē\ *n.; pl.* **sto·ries.** [From medieval English, meaning "narrative", "history" and borrowed from Old French *estoire, estorie,* there derived from Latin *historia.*] **1** A telling of a happening or a series of happenings; as, the *story* of one's life. **2** A narrative in prose or verse; a tale; as, a fairy *story.* **3** The plot of a narrative. **4** A falsehood; a fib.

sto·ry·tell·er \'stōr-ē-ˌtel-r, 'stȯr-ē-\ *n.* **1** One who tells narrative stories. **2** A fibber; a teller of falsehoods. — **sto·ry·tell·ing** \-ing\ *n.*

stoup \'stüp\ *n.* **1** A drinking vessel; as, a *stoup* of wine. **2** A font or basin for holy water.

stout \'staủt\ *adj.* **1** Strong, brave, and firm, as in character or purpose. **2** Physically strong; robust. **3** Fleshy; fat. **4** Tough; firm; as, a *stout* stick. — The words *portly* and *burly* are synonyms of *stout: stout* generally applies to a person who is

thickset and fleshy, though usually not so heavy as to be called fat; *portly* suggests heaviness of body accompanied by a dignified and imposing appearance; *burly* usually suggests such strength and muscular development as to give a heavy, massive appearance to the body.
— *n.* A strong dark beer.

stout·heart·ed \'staůt-'härt-əd, -'hȧrt-\ *adj.* Brave. — **stout·heart·ed·ly**, *adv.*

stove \'stōv\ *n.* An apparatus for supplying heat for cooking or for warmth.

stove \'stōv\. A past tense and past part. of *stave.*

stove·pipe \'stōv-ˌpīp\ *n.* **1** A metal pipe for carrying off smoke from a stove. **2** A tall silk hat.

stow \'stō\ *v.* **1** To place or arrange compactly; to pack; as, to *stow* freight. **2** To put away; to hide.

stow·a·way \'stō-ə-ˌwā\ *n.* One who hides, as in a ship, to obtain passage.

strad·dle \'strad-l\ *v.;* **strad·dled**; **strad·dling** \-l(-)ing\. **1** To stand, sit, or walk with the legs spread wide apart. **2** To stand, sit, or ride astride of. **3** To favor or seem to favor both sides in a dispute or contest; to refuse to take sides; as, to *straddle* an issue. — *n.* **1** A straddling. **2** The position of one who straddles. — **strad·dler** \-l(-)ər\ *n.*

strafe \'strāf\ *v.;* **strafed**; **straf·ing**. **1** To inflict damage upon, as by heavy gunfire. **2** To machine-gun from a low-flying airplane.

strag·gle \'strag-l\ *v.;* **strag·gled**; **strag·gling** \-l(-)ing\. **1** To wander away or become separated from one's companions or party; to stray or loiter behind. **2** To trail off from the usual course; to spread far and unevenly. — **strag·gler** \-l(-)ər\ *n.*

straight \'strāt\ *adj.* **1** Following the same direction throughout its length; direct. **2** Not wandering from the main point; as, *straight* thinking. **3** Honest; upright; as, *straight* dealings. **4** Correct or in order; as, to find all accounts *straight.* **5** Unmixed or undiluted; not modified; as, *straight* whiskey. **6** Making no exceptions in one's support of a party; as, to vote a *straight* ticket. **7** Having or costing a fixed price; as, cigars that are 20 cents *straight.* — *adv.* **1** In a straight line; without turning or twisting. **2** Without departing from what is right or correct; straightforwardly; truly.

straight·a·way \'strāt-ə-ˌwā\ *adj.* Proceeding in a straight line. — *n.* A straight course or a straight part of a course.

straight·edge \'strāt-ˌej\ *n.* A strip of wood, metal, or plastic having one edge reliably straight, used for drawing straight lines and for testing lines and surfaces for straightness.

straight·en \'strāt-n\ *v.;* **straight·ened**; **straight·en·ing** \-n(-)ing\. **1** To make or become straight. **2** To put in order; as, to *straighten* a room. — **straight·en·er** \-n(-)ər\ *n.*

straight-faced \'strāt-'fāst\ *adj.* Showing no signs of emotion, especially amusement.

straight·for·ward \(')strāt-'fȯr-wərd\ *adj.* Speaking, acting, or spoken frankly and openly; direct and candid; as, a *straightforward* reply. — *adv.* Also **straight·for·wards** \-wərdz\. In a straightforward manner. — **straight·for·ward·ly**, *adv.*

straight·way \'strāt-ˌwā\ *adv.* Immediately.

strain \'strān\ *n.* **1** Family; race; stock. **2** A quality or disposition that runs through a family or race. **3** A streak; a trace; as, humor with a *strain* of sadness in it. **4** In biology, a group of animals or plants not sufficiently distinguished to make a separate breed or variety. **5** General tone; as, remarks all in the same *strain.* **6** An air; a melody.

strain \'strān\ *v.* **1** To draw tight or taut; as, to *strain* a rope. **2** To exert to the utmost; as, to *strain* one's eyes to see. **3** To stretch beyond its proper limit; as, to *strain* the truth. **4** To injure or weaken by wrenching or by overuse; as, to *strain* a muscle. **5** To be stretched, pulled, or used to the utmost; as, muscles *straining* under a load. **6** To make violent efforts; as, to *strain* to lift a heavy box. **7** To hug; to press; as, to *strain* a child to one's breast. **8** To pass through a sieve or cloth; as, to *strain* orange juice. — *n.* **1** The act of straining. **2** The state of being strained. **3** Overwork or worry. **4** A sprain; a wrench.

strained \'strānd\ *adj.* **1** Forced; as, a *strained* smile. **2** Pushed by antagonism near to open conflict; as, *strained* relations between countries.

strain·er \'strān-r\ *n.* Something used for straining, as a sieve or a filter.

strainer

strait \'strāt\ *adj.* **1** *Archaic.* Narrow; rigid; strict. **2** Limited in resources; straitened. — *n.* **1** A narrow channel connecting two bodies of water — often used in the plural with a singular meaning. **2** [usually in the plural] A position of great difficulty; distress; need; as, in dire *straits.*

strait·en \'strāt-n\ *v.;* **strait·ened**; **strait·en·ing** \-n(-)ing\. **1** *Archaic.* To narrow or to confine within narrow limits. **2** To limit or restrict, especially in resources; to distress financially — chiefly in the phrase *in straitened circumstances.*

strait jack·et \'strāt ˌjak-ət\. A strong tight coat used to restrain violent prisoners or patients.

strait-laced \'strāt-'lāst\ *adj.* Very strict in matters relating to morality; puritanical; prudish.

strake \'strāk\ *n.* One breadth of planks or plates along the length of the bottom or sides of a boat.

strand \'strand\ *n.* A shore; especially, the seashore. — *v.* **1** To run aground, as a ship. **2** To place in a position which one cannot leave.

strand \'strand\ *n.* **1** One of the threads, strings, or wires twisted to make a cord, rope, or cable. **2** The rope, cord, or cable into which these strands are twisted. **3** A string, as of pearls or beads. **4** A tress of hair.

strands

strange \'strānj\ *adj.;* **strang·er**; **strang·est**. **1** *Archaic.* Foreign. **2** Of or relating to some other person or thing. The cuckoo lays her eggs in a *strange* nest. **3** Exciting surprise or wonder because not usual; queer; as, *strange* clothes. **4** Unfamiliar; as, *strange* surroundings. **5** Shy; ill at ease; as, to feel *strange* on one's first day in school. — **strange·ly**, *adv.*

stran·ger \'strānj-r\ *n.* **1** A person not in the place where his home is. **2** A person with whom one is not acquainted. **3** One not familiar with something specified; as, a *stranger* to trigonometry.

stran·gle \'strang-gl\ *v.;* **stran·gled; stran·gling** \-gl(-)ing\. **1** To choke to death by squeezing the throat. **2** To stifle, choke, or suffocate in any way. — **stran·gler** \-glər\ *n.*

stran·gle·hold \'strang-gl-ˌhōld\ *n.* **1** Also **strangle hold.** A hold in wrestling by which one's opponent is choked. **2** Any force or influence that chokes or suppresses development or expression.

stran·gu·la·tion \ˌstrang-gyə-'lāsh-n\ *n.* The act of strangling or the state of being strangled.

strap \'strap\ *n.* **1** A narrow strip of some flexible material, as leather, used for binding or fastening. **2** Something consisting of, serving as, or resembling a strap; as, a shoulder *strap.* — *v.;* **strapped; strap·ping. 1** To fasten or bind with a strap. **2** To beat with a strap. **3** To strop.

strap·ping \'strap-ing\ *adj.* Large; strong; robust.

strata. A pl. of *stratum.*

strat·a·gem \'strat-əj-m\ *n.* **1** A trick in war for deceiving the enemy. **2** Any trick used to deceive.

stra·te·gic \strə-'tē-jik\ *adj.* **1** Of or relating to strategy; marked by strategy. **2** Important in strategy. **3** Advantageous; as, in a *strategic* position. — **stra·te·gi·cal·ly** \-jik-l(-)ē\ *adv.*

strat·e·gist \'strat-ə-jəst\ *n.* One skilled in strategy.

strat·e·gy \'strat-ə-jē\ *n.; pl.* **strat·e·gies. 1** The science and art of employing the armed strength of a country to gain victory in war; especially, the planning and directing of large-scale military maneuvers and operations leading to this end. **2** An instance of such planning and direction. **3** The use of stratagems; maneuvering.

strat·i·fy \'strat-ə-ˌfī\ *v.;* **strat·i·fied** \-ˌfīd\; **strat·i·fy·ing.** To form, deposit, or arrange in strata, as rock. — **strat·i·fi·ca·tion** \ˌstrat-ə-fə-'kāsh-n\ *n.*

strat·o·sphere \'strat-ə-ˌsfir\ *n.* The upper portion of the atmosphere, more than seven miles above the earth, where temperature changes little and clouds of water never form. — **strat·o·spher·ic** \ˌstrat-ə-'sfir-ik, -'sfer-ik\ *adj.*

stra·tum \'strāt-m, 'strat-m\ *n.; pl.* **stra·ta** \-ə\ or **stra·tums** \-mz\. **1** A layer of a substance, especially one having parallel layers of other kinds lying above or below or both above and below it. **2** A level of culture. **3** A group representing a stage of development in a culture or society.

stra·tus \'strāt-əs\ *n.; pl.* **stra·ti** \'strāt-ˌī\. A cloud form extending horizontally over a relatively large area at an altitude of from 2000 to 7000 feet.

straw \'strȯ\ *n.* **1** The stalks of grain after the grain has been threshed off. **2** A single stalk of grain. **3** A thing of small worth; a trifle. **4** A thing made of or shaped like a straw, as a slender tube for sucking up a beverage. — *adj.* **1** Made of straw. **2** Of the light yellow color of dry straw.

straw·ber·ry \'strȯ-ˌber-ē, 'strȯb-r(-)ē\ *n.; pl.* **straw·ber·ries. 1** The edible juicy red pulpy fruit of a low herb (**strawberry vine**) with white flowers and long slender runners. **2** A strawberry vine.

strawberries

straw vote. An unofficial vote taken to show the strength of candidates or issues.

stray \'strā\ *v.* **1** To wander away from a road or course. **2** To wander from company, restraint, or the proper limits; to go astray. — *n.* One that has strayed. — *adj.* **1** Wandering; as, a *stray* dog. **2** Incidental; as, a *stray* remark.

streak \'strēk\ *n.* **1** A line or mark of a different color or texture from its background; a stripe; a vein; as, a *streak* of ore; a *streak* of lightning. **2** A trace; a strain; a trait; as, a man with quite a *streak* of humor; a wild *streak.* **3** A layer; as, a *streak* of fat in meat. — *v.* **1** To form streaks on. **2** To go like a streak of lightning.

streaky \'strēk-ē\ *adj.;* **streak·i·er; streak·i·est. 1** Marked with streaks. **2** Uneven; variable.

stream \'strēm\ *n.* **1** A current or course of water, as a brook or river. **2** Any course of running liquid; as, a *stream* of blood. **3** Any steady flow, as of water, air, or gas. **4** Anything moving in a continued succession of parts; as, a *stream* of words; a *stream* of cars. — *v.* **1** To issue and flow in a stream. **2** To cause to flow; as, eyes *streaming* tears. **3** To pour out streams of liquid. **4** To pass swiftly. A meteor *streamed* across the sky. **5** To stretch out in length; as, hair *streaming* in the wind. **6** To move forward in a steady stream.

stream·er \'strēm-r\ *n.* **1** A long narrow banner or flag that floats in the wind. **2** A long flowing ribbon on a dress or hat. **3** A column of light shooting upward from the horizon, as in the aurora borealis. **4** An extension from the sun seen during eclipses. **5** A newspaper headline running the width of a page.

stream·let \'strēm-lət\ *n.* A small stream.

stream·line \'strēm-'līn\ *adj.* **1** Having a surface or body made so as to give an unbroken flow of air, gas, or water around it; as, a *streamline* body for an automobile; a *streamline* train. **2** Designed for easy or efficient use; as, a *streamline* filing system. — *v.;* **stream·lined; stream·lin·ing.** To design or construct with a streamline form.

stream·lin·er \'strēm-'līn-r\ *n.* A streamlined train, bus, or airplane.

street \'strēt\ *n.* **1** A public way or thoroughfare, especially in a city, town, or village, usually including the sidewalks or footpaths on both sides and often the bordering houses or lots. **2** The occupants of a street. The whole *street* was curious.

street·car \'strēt-ˌkär, -ˌkȧr\ *n.* A passenger car running on rails on the public streets.

strength \'streng(k)th\ *n.* **1** The quality or condition of being strong; power; force. **2** Power to resist force; as, the *strength* of a rope. **3** Power to resist attacks. **4** Effective power, as of a government. **5** Intensity or degree, as of light or color. **6** Capacity to produce an effect, as of drugs or liquors. **7** Force as measured in numbers; as, the *strength* of an army. **8** One regarded as affording strength; support. The widow's children were her *strength.* — For synonyms see *power.*

strength·en \'streng(k)th-n\ *v.;* **strength·ened; strength·en·ing** \-n(-)ing\. To make, grow, or become stronger. — **strength·en·er** \-n(-)ər\ *n.*

stren·u·ous \'stren-yə-wəs\ *adj.* **1** Ardent; vigorous; unusually energetic; as, a *strenuous* supporter. **2** Marked by or requiring great expenditure of energy; as, a *strenuous* trip. — **stren·u·ous·ly,** *adv.*

strep·to·coc·cus \ˌstrep-tə-'käk-əs\ *n.; pl.* **strep·to·coc·cus·es** \-'käk-ə-səz\ or **strep·to·coc·ci** \-'käk-ˌ(s)ī\. Any of a number of spherical bacteria occurring in pairs or chains, some causing disease.

strep·to·my·cin \ˌstrep-tə-'mīs-n\ *n.* An antibiotic used especially against tuberculosis.

stress \'stres\ *v.* **1** To put pressure on; to strain. **2** To accent; as, to *stress* the second syllable. **3** To emphasize. — *n.* **1** Pressure; strain. **2** Urgency; emphasis; as, to lay *stress* on algebra. **3** Accent, as given to a speech sound or to a note in music.

stress mark. A mark used to indicate stress, as one placed before or after a written syllable in the respelling of a word to show that this syllable is to be accented in speaking; an accent mark.

stretch \'strech\ *v.* **1** To reach out; to extend, as one's limbs or body. **2** To draw out or extend; as, to *stretch* rubber. **3** To reach or cause to reach, as from one point to another; as, to *stretch* a wire between two posts. **4** To extend too far; as, a suit *stretched* out of shape. **5** To exaggerate; as, to *stretch* the truth. **6** To extend without breaking or tearing. — *n.* **1** The act of stretching. **2** Extension, especially to the point of straining. **3** A continuous line or surface. **4** The extent to which anything may be stretched. **5** Either of the sides of a race track with curving ends. **6** A walk; as, a *stretch* in the park. **7** A term of imprisonment. — *adj.* Stretchable; as, *stretch* socks. — **stretch·a·ble,** *adj.*

stretch·er \'strech-r\ *n.* **1** One that stretches; especially, a device for stretching or expanding something, as curtains. **2** A bedlike arrangement for carrying disabled persons. **3** A rod or bar extending between two legs of a chair or table.

strew \'strü\ *v.;* **strewed** \'strüd\; **strewed** \'strüd\ or **strewn** \'strün\; **strew·ing. 1** To scatter; to spread by scattering. **2** To cover by or as if by scattering something over.

stri·at·ed \'strī-ˌāt-əd\ *adj.* Marked with parallel lines or bands. — **stri·a·tion** \strī-'āsh-n\ *n.*

strick·en \'strik-n\. A past part. of *strike.* — *adj.* Affected by illness, wounds, grief, or disaster.

strict \'strikt\ *adj.* **1** Governing or governed by exact rules; severe; rigorous; as, *strict* discipline. **2** Accurate; precise; as, the *strict* truth. **3** Close and careful; as, to keep a *strict* watch. — **strict·ly** \'strik(t)-lē\ *adv.*

stric·ture \'strik-chər\ *n.* **1** An unnatural binding or contraction of a passage in the body, as the esophagus. **2** An adverse criticism.

stride \'strīd\ *v.;* **strode** \'strōd\; **strid·den** \'strid-n\; **strid·ing** \'strīd-ing\. **1** To walk or run with long regular strides. **2** To walk over, through, or along with long and measured steps; as, to *stride* a ditch. **3** To straddle; as, to *stride* a fence. — *n.* **1** A long step, or the distance measured by such a step; as, a manly *stride.* **2** An advance; as, great *strides* in the treatment of disease. **3** A regular stepping, as of a horse in walking or running.

stri·dent \'strīd-nt\ *adj.* Harsh-sounding; shrill; rasping. — **stri·dent·ly,** *adv.*

strid·u·late \'strij-l-ˌāt\ *v.;* **strid·u·lat·ed; strid·u·lat·ing.** To make a shrill creaking noise, as male crickets and grasshoppers, by scraping a roughened area on one forewing with the edge of the other. — **strid·u·la·tion** \ˌstrij-l-'āsh-n\ *n*

strife \'strīf\ *n.* Conflict; fighting; quarreling.

strike \'strīk\ *v.;* **struck** \'strək\; **struck** \'strək\ or **strick·en** \'strik-n\; **strik·ing. 1** To touch or hit with some force. **2** To collide with; to run into. **3** To injure or destroy as if by collision. Lightning *struck* the barn. **4** Of a hawk or a snake, to sink the talons or fangs into something; of a fish, to seize the bait. **5** To give or inflict, as a blow. **6** To knock; to dash; as, waves *striking* against a shore. **7** To cause or produce by or as if by a stroke or blow; as, to *strike* a light; to *strike* fear into the enemy. **8** To cause to burn by striking or rubbing; as, to *strike* a match. **9** To impress, as a coin or medal, with a die or punch. **10** To pierce or enter, or to cause to pierce or enter; to thrust, as a tree its roots. **11** To affect suddenly, as if by a blow; as, to be *struck* blind. **12** To affect in a particular way. The sight *strikes* one as strange. **13** To sound or indicate by sounding. **14** To come upon or meet with; as, to *strike* on a good idea. **15** To catch and hold the admiration and affection of; as, to be *struck* by the girl's beauty. **16** To reach by figuring or reckoning; as, to *strike* an average. **17** To lower, take down, or take apart; as, to strike a flag; to *strike* the tents. **18** To remove or cancel, as by the stroke of a pen. **19** To assume; as, to *strike* an attitude. **20** To go; to proceed; as, to *strike* across the field. **21** To go on strike. **22** To make an urgent request of; as, to *strike* a friend for a loan. — **strike off. 1** To erase, as from a list. **2** To separate, as by a blow. — **strike out. 1** To cross out; to erase. **2** To start suddenly; as, to *strike out* at a sharp pace. **3** In baseball, to be put out or cause to be put out for not batting the ball fairly in three chances during a turn at bat. — **strike up. 1** To begin to sing, sound, or play. **2** To form or enter upon suddenly, as a friendship. — *n.* **1** The act of striking. **2** The act of a body of workmen in quitting work together in order to force some change in the conditions of their employment. **3** A sudden finding of rich ore in mining, or of oil in drilling. **4** Any sudden success or good fortune; as, a lucky *strike.* **5** The act of striking the bait. **6** In baseball, any striking by the batter at a pitched ball in which he does not hit the ball; also, any act which under the rules is regarded the same as a failure to hit a good pitched ball. **7** In bowling, the knocking down of all the pins with the first ball; the score thus made. — **on strike.** Taking part in a workmen's strike.

strike·break·er \'strīk-ˌbrāk-r\ *n.* A person hired to help break up a strike of workmen.

strike-out \'strīk-ˌau̇t\ *n.* The act or an instance of striking out a batter in baseball.

strik·er \'strīk-r\ *n.* **1** One that strikes; as, the *striker* of a clock. **2** A workman who is on strike.

strik·ing \'strīk-ing\ *adj.* Attracting attention; remarkable; as, a *striking* fact. — **strik·ing·ly,** *adv.*

string \'string\ *n.* **1** A thin cord used for fastening or tying up things. **2** A thread or cord strung with a number of objects; as, a *string* of pearls. **3** A line or series of things arranged as if strung together; as, a *string* of automobiles. **4** A group of players or contestants ranked according to skill; as, to be on the third *string* of a football squad. **5** The race horses or polo ponies belonging to one owner. **6** The cord, usually of gut or wire, of a stringed instrument. **7** [in the plural] The stringed instruments of an orchestra. **8** A fiber, as the tough fiber connecting the halves of a string-bean pod. **9** [in the plural] Conditions attached to a deal or an offer; as, an agreement with no *strings* attached. — *v.;* **strung** \'strəng\; **string·ing** \'string-ing\. **1** To furnish with a string or strings. **2** To adjust or tune, as the strings of a musical instrument; to tighten; to make tense. **3** To thread on or as on a string. **4** To take the strings out of; as, to *string* beans. **5** To tie, hang, or fasten by a string. **6** To stretch out or extend like a string. **7** *Slang.* To fool; to josh. — **string up.** To hang; to lynch.

string bean. 1 A variety of bean grown for its pods, which are edible when young. **2** One of these pods.

stringed instrument \'stringd\. A musical instrument, as a violin, mandolin, harp, or piano, sounded by plucking, striking, or drawing a bow over a set of tightly drawn strings.

strin·gent \'strinj-nt\ *adj.* **1** Strict; severe; as, *stringent* rules; *stringent* requirements. **2** Convincing; forceful; as, a *stringent* argument. — **strin·gen·cy** \-n-sē\ *n.* — **strin·gent·ly** \-nt-lē\ *adv.*

string·er \'string-r\ *n.* **1** A person or thing that strings. **2** A long horizontal timber used for support or strengthening in building, as under a floor.

stringy \'string-ē\ *adj.;* **string·i·er; string·i·est. 1** Containing many strings; fibrous; as, *stringy* meat. **2** Capable of being drawn out into a long string; as, *stringy* molasses. **3** Having its parts strung out; not compact; as, a *stringy* sentence. **4** Thin and long in build; as, a *stringy* horse.

strip \'strip\ *v.;* **stripped; strip·ping. 1** To remove, as a covering or clothing. **2** To take off one's clothes. **3** To skin or peel; as, to *strip* a tree of bark. **4** To make bare or clear, as by cutting or grazing. **5** To break the thread from a nut or bolt; to break the teeth from a gear. **6** To plunder; to pillage; to loot; as, the troops *stripped* the captured town. — **strip·per** \'strip-r\ *n.*

strip \'strip\ *n.* A long narrow flat piece; as, a *strip* of bacon; a *strip* of ground.

stripe \'strīp\ *n.* **1** A line or long narrow division or section of anything different in color or material from the background. **2** A long narrow bruise made by a blow, as from a whip. **3** A blow, as with a whip. **4** Type; as, men of the same *stripe.* — *v.;* **striped; strip·ing.** To mark with stripes.

striped \'strīpt, 'strīp-əd\ *adj.* Having stripes.

strip·ling \'strip-ling\ *n.* A youth just passing from boyhood to manhood.

strive \'strīv\ *v.;* **strove** \'strōv\; **striv·en** \'striv-n\; **striv·ing** \'strī-ving\. **1** To try hard; to make efforts; as, to *strive* to win. **2** To struggle against, with, or for something; to contend.

strode. Past tense of *stride.*

stroke \'strōk\ *n.* **1** The action or result of striking; a blow. **2** A sudden action suggesting a blow; as, a *stroke* of lightning; *stroke* of luck. **3** A feeling or condition as if one had been struck; especially, a sudden attack of disease; as, to suffer a *stroke* of apoplexy. **4** A great effort to do something. **5** The thing accomplished by such an effort; as, not to do a *stroke* of work. **6** The sound of striking, especially of a clock; as, at the *stroke* of ten. **7** One of a series of movements made to get through or over a resisting medium; as, the *stroke* of an oar. **8** A single movement with or as if with a tool, as a pen. **9** The result, as a mark, made by such a movement. **10** A rower nearest the stern of a boat who sets the rate of rowing for all the oarsmen. **11** The movement in either direction of a piston or piston rod. — For synonyms see *blow.*

stroke \'strōk\ *v.;* **stroked; strok·ing. 1** To rub gently, especially in one direction, as a cat's fur. **2** To row as stroke of or set the stroke for a boat.

stroll \'strōl\ *v.* **1** To wander about on foot; to rove; especially, to ramble idly or leisurely; as, a *strolling* musician. **2** To walk leisurely along or about. — *n.* A leisurely walk; a ramble.

stroll·er \'strōl-r\ *n.* **1** One who strolls or saunters. **2** Any of various carriages for babies.

strong \'stro̊ng\ *adj.;* **strong·er** \'stro̊ng-gr\; **strong·est** \'stro̊ng-gəst\. **1** Having great physical power; as, a *strong* swimmer. **2** Healthy; tough; robust; as, a *strong* baby. **3** Having or showing moral or intellectual power, vigor, or endurance; as, a man of *strong* character. **4** Having great numbers or wealth; as, *strong* armies. **5** Great in degree or quality; not mild or weak; as, *strong* tea; a *strong* dislike. **6** Containing a large proportion of alcohol; as, *strong* liquors. **7** Powerful; forceful; as, a *strong* wind. **8** Not easily broken or damaged; as, *strong* timbers. **9** Forming the past tense by a change in the root vowel but without the addition of a suffix and the past participle usually by the addition of the suffix *-en,* with or without a change in the root vowel; irregular; as, a *strong* verb. **10** Of stress or accent, like that on the first syllable of *penetrate* \'pen-ə-ˌtrāt\. — *adv.* Strongly; as, *strong*-growing, *strong*-willed. — **strong·ly**, *adv.*

strong·hold \'strȯng-ˌhōld\ *n.* A fortified place.

stron·tium \'strănch-(ē-)əm, 'strănt-ē-əm\ *n.* A metallic element that resembles calcium and that may, in one of its radioactive forms, as **strontium 90**, result from a nuclear explosion and become one of the harmful parts of fall-out.

strop \'străp\ *n.* A strap; especially, a strap for sharpening a razor. — *v.;* **stropped**; **strop·ping**. To sharpen, as a razor, on a strop.

stro·phe \'strō-fē\ *n.* A division of a poem; a stanza. — **stroph·ic** \'străf-ik, 'strō-fik\ *adj.*

strove. Past tense of *strive.*

struck. Past tense and past part. of *strike.*

struc·tur·al \'strək-chər-əl, 'strəksh-r(-)əl\ *adj.* Of or relating to structure; used in construction. — **struc·tur·al·ly** \-ə-lē\ *adv.*

struc·ture \'strək-chər\ *n.* **1** The manner in which anything is built; construction; form. **2** Something built, as a house or a dam. **3** The arrangement or relationship of parts, organs, or elements.

strug·gle \'strəg-l\ *v.;* **strug·gled**; **strug·gling** \-l(-)ing\. To put forth great effort; to strive hard; as, to *struggle* for a living. — *n.* **1** A great effort; as, a *struggle* to keep one's footing. **2** A contest; a fight; strife. — **strug·gler** \-l(-)ər\ *n.*

strum \'strəm\ *v.;* **strummed**; **strum·ming**. To play on a stringed instrument idly or unskillfully.

strung. Past tense and past part. of *string.*

strut \'strət\ *v.;* **strut·ted**; **strut·ting**. To walk with a proud or haughty gait; to swagger. — *n.* **1** A strutting; a proud, haughty gait. **2** A bar or brace used to resist lengthwise pressure.

strut

strych·nine \'strik-ˌnīn, -nən, -ˌnēn\ *n.* A bitter, very poisonous substance obtained from certain plants, used as a rat poison and in medicine.

stub \'stəb\ *n.* **1** A tree stump. **2** The short blunt end of anything after the larger part has been broken off or used up; as, the *stub* of a pencil. **3** In a checkbook, a small part of each leaf kept in the book as a memorandum of the items that were on the detached check; a receipt. — *v.* **stubbed**; **stub·bing**. To strike, as one's foot or toe, against something. — **stub·by** \'stəb-ē\ *adj.*

stub·ble \'stəb-l\ *n.* **1** The stumps of grain left in the ground, as after reaping. **2** Any rough growth resembling stubble. — **stub·bly** \-l(-)ē\ *adj.*

stub·born \'stəb-rn\ *adj.* **1** Having a firm idea or purpose; determined; especially, obstinate; as, *stubborn* as a mule. **2** Done or continued in an obstinate or persistent manner; as, a *stubborn* refusal. **3** Difficult to handle, manage, or treat; as, *stubborn* hair. — **stub·born·ly**, *adv.*

stuc·co \'stək-ˌō\ *n.; pl.* **stuc·coes** or **stuc·cos**. A plaster for coating walls. — *v.;* **stuc·coed** \-ˌōd\; **stuc·co·ing**. To cover or decorate with stucco.

stuck. Past tense and past part. of *stick.*

stuck-up \'stək-'əp\ *adj.* Conceited; vain.

stud \'stəd\ *n.* A collection of horses kept for breeding or the place at which they are kept.

stud \'stəd\ *n.* **1** A nail with a large head, used chiefly for ornament; an ornamental knob. **2** A detachable device resembling a button, used as a fastener or for ornament; as, shirt *studs.* **3** A scantling; especially, one of the upright pieces of lumber to which lath or boards are nailed in a partition or wall. — *v.;* **stud·ded**; **stud·ding**. **1** To supply with studs. **2** To ornament with or as if with studs or knobs; to set with objects that stand out. **3** To set thickly together; as, a sky *studded* with stars.

stu·dent \'stüd-(ə)nt, 'styüd-\ *n.* **1** A learner; a scholar; especially, one who attends a school or college. **2** One who studies; a careful, systematic observer; as, a *student* of life.

stud·ied \'stəd-ēd\ *adj.* **1** Made the subject of study. **2** Planned; intentional; as, a *studied* insult.

stu·dio \'stüd-ē-ˌō, 'styüd-\ *n.; pl.* **stu·di·os**. **1** A place where an artist works. **2** A place where motion pictures are made. **3** A place from which radio or television programs are broadcast.

stu·di·ous \'stüd-ē-əs, 'styüd-\ *adj.* **1** Devoted to and fond of study. **2** Diligent; careful; thoughtful; as, a *studious* effort to give satisfaction. — **stu·di·ous·ly**, *adv.*

study \'stəd-ē\ *n.; pl.* **stud·ies**. **1** The application of the mind to gain knowledge or to find out something. **2** The action or process of finding out about something; as, the *study* of a disease. **3** Any branch of learning, as mathematics. **4** Deep or puzzled thought; as, absorbed in *study.* **5** A room especially for study or writing. **6** Something made or done, as a written report, as the result of careful investigation; as, a *study* of juvenile delinquency. — *v.;* **stud·ied** \-ēd\; **stud·y·ing**. **1** To apply the mind to books or learning. **2** To ponder; to meditate; as, to *study* a question carefully before answering. **3** To make the subject of study; as, to *study* music. **4** To strive intelligently. A good salesman *studies* to please his customers.

stuff \'stəf\ *n.* **1** Raw material out of which something is or may be made; any material; as, to buy *stuff* for a new dress. **2** The basic element of a person or thing; the essence; as, a man who lacks the *stuff* of success. **3** Any matter, solid, liquid, or gaseous. **4** Goods; personal property; especially, furniture, household goods, or baggage. **5** Fabric of any kind. **6** Worthless material; nonsense; trash. — *v.* **1** To fill by crowding something into; as, to *stuff* a cushion. **2** To fill the skin of; as, to *stuff* an owl for mounting. **3** To fill too full; to fill the stomach of. **4** To put fraudulent votes into; as, to *stuff* a ballot box. **5** In cookery, to fill with stuffing; as, to *stuff* a turkey.

stuff·ing \'stəf-ing\ *n.* The material used in filling up anything; especially, a mixture, as of bread crumbs and seasonings, used to stuff meat or poultry.

stuffy \'stəf-ē\ *adj.;* **stuff·i·er**; **stuff·i·est**. **1** Needing fresh air; close. **2** Feeling choked up, as from a cold. **3** Sulky. **4** Old-fashioned. **5** Straitlaced.

stul·ti·fy \'stəl-tə-ˌfī\ *v.;* **stul·ti·fied** \-ˌfīd\; **stul·ti·fy·ing.** To make or cause to appear ridiculous.

stum·ble \'stəm-bl\ *v.;* **stum·bled; stum·bling** \-bl(-)ing\. **1** To trip in walking or running. **2** To walk unsteadily. **3** To speak or act in a blundering or clumsy manner. **4** To happen by chance; as, he *stumbled* on a discovery. — *n.* **1** The action of tripping. **2** A blunder. — **stum·bler** \-blər\ *n.*

stum·bling block \'stəm-bl(-)ing\. Something that makes one stumble; an obstacle; a hindrance.

stump \'stəmp\ *n.* **1** The part of a tree that remains in the ground after the trunk is cut down. **2** The part of an arm, leg, or tooth that remains after the rest is removed. **3** A butt; a stub. **4** A heavy tramping sound; a clump. **5** A platform from which a politician speaks. — *v.* **1** To walk stiffly and clumsily. **2** To give someone a task he cannot perform or a problem he cannot solve; as, to *stump* the experts. **3** To dare; to challenge. **4** To travel over a region making political speeches.

stumpy \'stəmp-ē\ *adj.;* **stump·i·er; stump·i·est. 1** Full of stumps. **2** Short and thick.

stun \'stən\ *v.;* **stunned; stun·ning. 1** To make dizzy or senseless by a blow. **2** To daze; to stupefy; as, to be *stunned* by the bad news.

stung. Past tense and past part. of *sting.*

stunk. A past tense and past part. of *stink.*

stun·ning \'stən-ing\ *adj.* **1** Having the effect of stunning; as, a *stunning* blow. **2** Striking; unusually pretty; as, a *stunning* dress. — **stun·ning·ly,** *adv.*

stunt \'stənt\ *n.* An unusual performance or feat, especially one done to attract attention; as, acrobatic *stunts.* — *v.* To perform stunts; especially, to perform difficult maneuvers with an airplane.

stunt \'stənt\ *v.* To hinder from normal growth or progress; to dwarf; as, to *stunt* a tree.

stu·pe·fac·tion \ˌstüp-ə-'faksh-n, ˌstyüp-\ *n.* **1** A condition of being stupefied or stunned. **2** Great astonishment or bewilderment.

stu·pe·fy \'stüp-ə-ˌfī, 'styüp-\ *v.;* **stu·pe·fied** \-ˌfīd\; **stu·pe·fy·ing. 1** To make stupid, dull, or numb, as by drugs. **2** To astonish.

stu·pen·dous \stü-'pen-dəs, styü-\ *adj.* Wonderful; amazing, especially because of great size or height. — **stu·pen·dous·ly,** *adv.*

stu·pid \'stüp-əd, 'styüp-\ *adj.* **1** Very dull of mind; lacking sense. **2** Showing or resulting from dullness of mind; as, a *stupid* act. — **stu·pid·ly,** *adv.*

stu·pid·i·ty \stü-'pid-ət-ē, styü-\ *n.; pl.* **stu·pid·i·ties. 1** The quality or state of being stupid. **2** A stupid thought, action, or remark.

stu·por \'stüp-r, 'styüp-r\ *n.* A condition in which the senses or feelings are dulled.

stur·dy \'stərd-ē\ *adj.;* **stur·di·er; stur·di·est. 1** Resolute; firm; unyielding; as, a *sturdy* defense. **2** Strong; robust; as, a *sturdy* ship; a *sturdy* boy.

stur·geon \'stərj-n\ *n.; pl.* **stur·geon** or **stur·geons.** A large food fish with tough skin and rows of bony plates, whose roe is made into caviar and air bladder into isinglass.

stut·ter \'stət-r\ *v.* To speak or say jerkily, with involuntary repetition of sounds. — *n.* The action of one who stutters. — **stut·ter·er** \-r-r\ *n.*

sty \'stī\ *n.; pl.* **sties. 1** A pigpen. **2** A filthy place.

sty or **stye** \'stī\ *n.; pl.* **sties** or **styes.** An inflamed swelling on the edge of an eyelid.

style \'stīl\ *n.* **1** A way of speaking or writing; a characteristic manner of expression, as of a person, group, or period; as, Stevenson's clear *style.* **2** A distinctive manner of doing something; as, the batter's *style* of holding his bat; a pianist's *style* in playing. **3** A method or manner that is thought elegant or in accord with some standard; fashion; as, to dine in *style.* The dress is out of *style.* **4** In botany, a slender continuation of the ovary, bearing the stigma at the end. — *v.;* **styled; styl·ing. 1** To name or call; as, a self-*styled* patriot. **2** To design in or make conform to an accepted style or a new style; as, to *style* hats.

style

style, 4

styl·ish \'stī-lish\ *adj.* Having style; fashionable. — **styl·ish·ly,** *adv.*

styl·ist \'stī-ləst\ *n.* **1** A person who is a master or a model of style, as in writing. **2** One who styles or advises on matters of style. — **sty·lis·tic** \stī-'lis-tik\ *adj.* — **sty·lis·ti·cal·ly** \-tik-l(-)ē\ *adv.*

sty·lus \'stī-ləs\ *n.* A pointed instrument used by the ancients for writing on wax tablets.

styp·tic \'stip-tik\ *adj.* Stopping bleeding; astringent. — *n.* A styptic medicine.

sua·sion \'swāzh-n\ *n.* A persuading; persuasion; as, to use moral *suasion.* — **sua·sive** \'swā-siv\ *adj.*

suave \'swäv, 'swȧv\ *adj.* Persuasively pleasing; smoothly polite and agreeable. — **suave·ly** \'swäv-lē, 'swȧv-\ *adv.* — **suav·i·ty** \'swäv-ət-ē, 'swȧv-\ *n.*

sub \'səb\ *n.* **1** A submarine. **2** A substitute. — *v.;* **subbed; sub·bing.** To act as a substitute.

sub-. A prefix that can mean: **1** Under or beneath, as in place, rank, or quality, as in *submarine* or *subnormal.* **2** Bordering upon, slightly, almost, as in *subacid* or *subarctic.* **3** By or forming a further division, as in *subcommittee* or *subdivision.*

sub·ac·id \'səb-'as-əd\ *adj.* Moderately acid or sour. — **sub·ac·id·ly,** *adv.*

sub·al·tern \sə-'bȯlt-rn\ *n.* A commissioned military officer below a captain.

sub·arc·tic \'səb-'är(k)t-ik, -'ȧr(k)t-\ *adj.* **1** Located near arctic regions. **2** Having climate and conditions of life similar to those found near arctic regions.

sub·com·mit·tee \'səb-kə-ˌmit-ē\ *n.* A part or division of a larger committee.

sub·con·scious \'səb-'känch-əs\ *adj.* Being in one's mind but beneath the level of full consciousness; carried on more or less unconsciously by the mind; as, *subconscious* desires. — *n.* A part of the mind thought of as being the center of subconscious thought. — **sub·con·scious·ly,** *adv.*

sub·cu·ta·ne·ous \ˌsəb-kyü-'tā-nē-əs\ *adj.* Given or used under the skin; being or living under the skin; as, *subcutaneous* injection; *subcutaneous* fat;

a *subcutaneous* parasite. — **sub·cu·ta·ne·ous·ly**, *adv.*

sub·di·vide \ˌsəb-də-'vīd\ *v.;* **sub·di·vid·ed**; **sub·di·vid·ing.** To divide the parts of into more parts; especially, to divide a tract of land into lots to sell before developing or improving them.

sub·di·vi·sion \'səb-də-ˌvizh-n\ *n.* **1** The act of subdividing. **2** One of the parts into which something is subdivided; especially, a tract of land which has been divided into building lots.

sub·due \səb-'dü, -'dyü\ *v.;* **sub·dued**; **sub·du·ing.** **1** To conquer; to vanquish; as, to *subdue* the enemy. **2** To reduce; to soften; as, a *subdued* light.

sub·head \'səb-ˌhed\ or **sub·head·ing** \-ing\ *n.* A heading of a subdivision, as in an outline.

sub·ject \'səb-jikt\ *adj.* **1** Under the power or rule of another; as, *subject* people. **2** Owing allegiance to a particular monarch or state. **3** Exposed; liable; as, a valley *subject* to floods. **4** Dependent upon or exposed to some action that might take place; as, a bill *subject* to the approval of the president. — *n.* **1** A person under the authority or control of another. **2** A person who is subject to a monarch or state. **3** A person or animal operated on or experimented with. **4** The thing or person concerning which anything is said or done; theme; topic. **5** A branch of learning. Geography is a *subject* taught in this school. **6** The word or group of words about which the predicate makes a statement, as the word *children* in the sentence "Children enjoy vacations". — \səb-'jekt\ *v.* **1** To bring under control or rule; to subdue. **2** To expose; to make liable. Selfishness *subjects* a person to criticism. **3** To cause to undergo; to submit; as, to *subject* a person to a test.

sub·jec·tion \səb-'jeksh-n\ *n.* **1** The act of subjecting or subduing; subjugation. **2** The state of being subject; as, *subjection* to the laws.

sub·jec·tive \səb-'jek-tiv\ *adj.* **1** Of or relative to a subject. **2** Belonging to or concerned with one's own mind, in contrast to what is outside, or objective; personal. — **sub·jec·tive·ly**, *adv.* — **sub·jec·tiv·i·ty** \ˌsəb-ˌjek-'tiv-ət-ē\ *n.*

sub·join \'səb-'jȯin\ *v.* To annex; to append.

sub·ju·gate \'səb-jə-ˌgāt\ *v.;* **sub·ju·gat·ed**; **sub·ju·gat·ing.** **1** To bring under control; to conquer by force; to subdue. **2** To make subject. — **sub·ju·ga·tion** \ˌsəb-jə-'gāsh-n\ *n.*

sub·junc·tive \səb-'jəng(k)-tiv\ *adj.* In grammar, belonging to or constituting the set of verb forms that are used in referring to an action or state not as a fact but as conditional or possible or a matter of doubt or desire. — *n.* The subjunctive mood of a verb or a verb in this mood.

sub·lease \'səb-ˌlēs\ *n.* A lease given to another person by the tenant of a rented property. — *v.;* **sub·leased**; **sub·leas·ing.** To give or take a sublease on, as a house or piece of land.

sub·let \'səb-ˌlet\ *v.;* **sub·let**; **sub·let·ting.** **1** To sublease. **2** To turn over, as work to be done or goods to be supplied, to another.

sub·lieu·ten·ant \ˌsəb-lü-'ten-ənt\ *n.* *Chiefly British.* An officer ranking next below a lieutenant.

sub·li·mate \'səb-lə-ˌmāt\ *v.;* **sub·li·mat·ed**; **sub·li·mat·ing.** **1** To cause to sublime; as, to *sublimate* sulfur. **2** To purify; to refine; especially, to direct, as desires and impulses, from a lower to a higher level. — \-ˌmāt, -mət\ *n.* In chemistry, a substance obtained by subliming. — **sub·li·ma·tion** \ˌsəb-lə-'māsh-n\ *n.*

sub·lime \sə-'blīm\ *adj.* **1** Very great or noble; as, *sublime* truths. **2** Producing a feeling of great beauty or reverence; as, *sublime* music. — *v.;* **sub·limed**; **sub·lim·ing.** **1** To exalt; to heighten. **2** To purify; to refine. **3** In chemistry, to pass from a solid to a gaseous state and back to solid form without apparently passing through a liquid state. — **sub·lime·ly**, *adv.*

sub·lim·i·nal \ˌsəb-'lim-ən-l\ *adj.* **1** Subconscious. **2** Too weak to be perceived or felt; as, a *subliminal* stimulus. — **sub·lim·i·nal·ly** \-ən-l-ē\ *adv.*

sub·lim·i·ty \sə-'blim-ət-ē\ *n.; pl.* **sub·lim·i·ties.** **1** The quality or state of being sublime. **2** An instance of being sublime; that which is sublime.

sub·ma·chine gun \ˌsəb-mə-'shēn\. A lightweight automatic or semiautomatic portable firearm designed usually to be fired from the shoulder.

sub·ma·rine \'səb-mə-ˌrēn, ˌsəb-mə-'rēn\ *adj.* Being, acting, growing, or used under water in the sea. — *n.* A naval vessel armed with torpedoes and able to operate either on or under the surface of the water. — *v.;* **sub·ma·rined**; **sub·ma·rin·ing.** To attack or sink by a submarine.

sub·ma·rin·er \ˌsəb-mə-'rēn-r\ *n.* A sailor serving on a submarine.

sub·merge \səb-'mərj\ *v.;* **sub·merged**; **sub·merg·ing.** **1** To put under or plunge into water; to sink. **2** To cover or become covered with or as if with water; to inundate. — **sub·mer·gence** \-'mərj-n(t)s\ *n.* — **sub·merg·i·ble** \-'mər-jəb-l\ *adj.*

sub·merse \səb-'mərs\ *v.;* **sub·mersed**; **sub·mers·ing.** To submerge.

sub·mers·i·ble \səb-'mər-səb-l\ *adj.* **1** Capable of being submersed; submergible. **2** Capable of operating or functioning while submersed.

sub·mer·sion \səb-'mərzh-n, -'mərsh-n\ *n.* **1** The action of submerging or state of being submerged. **2** A condition resulting from being submerged.

sub·mis·sion \səb-'mish-n\ *n.* **1** The act of submitting, especially to power or authority. **2** Submissive behavior. **3** The act of submitting something, as for consideration or inspection.

sub·mis·sive \səb-'mis-iv\ *adj.* Inclined or willing to submit to others; yielding; meek. — **sub·mis·sive·ly**, *adv.*

sub·mit \səb-'mit\ *v.;* **sub·mit·ted**; **sub·mit·ting.** **1** To give over or leave to the judgment or approval of someone else; to refer; as, to *submit* an issue for arbitration; to *submit* a plan for consideration. **2** To put forward or give, as an opinion, reason, or idea. **3** To yield to power or authority; to surrender.

sub·nor·mal \'səb-'nȯrm-l\ *adj.* Falling below the normal; less than normal.

sub·or·di·nate \sə-'bȯrd-n(-)ət\ *adj.* **1** Placed in a lower order or rank; as, a *subordinate* officer. **2** Lower in order, rank, or importance; as, a *subordinate* position. **3** Giving due obedience; submissive to authority. **4** Also **sub·or·di·nat·ing** \-n-ˌāt-iŋ\. In grammar, joining word groups of lower or dependent rank to others in a sentence; as, a *subordinating* conjunction. **5** Of a clause, dependent. — *n.* One that is lower in rank or importance than another. — \-n-ˌāt\ *v.*; **sub·or·di·nat·ed**; **sub·or·di·nat·ing.** To make subordinate. — **sub·or·di·na·tion** \sə-ˌbȯrd-n-'āsh-n\ *n.*

sub·poe·na or **sub·pe·na** \sə-'pē-nə\ *n.* A writ ordering a person to appear in court, under penalty if he fails to do so. — *v.*; **sub·poe·naed** or **sub·pe·naed** \-nəd\; **sub·poe·na·ing** or **sub·pe·na·ing.** To summon by, or serve with, a subpoena.

sub·scribe \səb-'skrīb\ *v.*; **sub·scribed**; **sub·scrib·ing.** **1** To sign one's name to a document. **2** To promise to give by writing one's name with the amount promised; as, to *subscribe* ten dollars. **3** To place an order with payment or promise to pay, as for a magazine. **4** To approve; as, to *subscribe* to an idea. — **sub·scrib·er** \-'skrīb-r\ *n.*

sub·script \'səb-ˌskript\ *n.* In mathematics, a symbol written slightly below another symbol and used to distinguish it from others in its class.

sub·scrip·tion \səb-'skripsh-n\ *n.* **1** The act of subscribing. **2** The thing or amount subscribed.

sub·se·quent \'səb-sə-ˌkwent, -kwənt\ *adj.* Following in time or order. — **sub·se·quent·ly**, *adv.*

sub·ser·vi·ent \səb-'sər-vē-ənt\ *adj.* **1** Useful in an inferior place or way. **2** Servile; obsequious; as, a *subservient* manner. — **sub·ser·vi·ence** \-ən(t)s\ *n.*

sub·side \səb-'sīd\ *v.*; **sub·sid·ed**; **sub·sid·ing.** **1** To sink or fall to the bottom. The dregs *subsided.* **2** To become lower. The flood *subsided.* **3** To become quiet; to grow less. The pain *subsided.* — **sub·sid·ence** \səb-'sīd-n(t)s, 'səb-sə-dən(t)s\ *n.*

sub·sid·i·ary \səb-'sid-ē-ˌer-ē\ *adj.* **1** Furnishing aid, especially in a subordinate capacity; auxiliary; secondary; as, a *subsidiary* stream. **2** Of or relating to subsidy; aiding or aided by a subsidy; as, *subsidiary* payments. — *n.*; *pl.* **sub·sid·i·ar·ies.** **1** One that contributes aid or supplies; an auxiliary. **2** A company controlled by another company which owns a majority of its capital stock.

sub·si·dize \'səb-sə-ˌdīz, -zə-\ *v.*; **sub·si·dized**; **sub·si·diz·ing.** To aid or furnish with a subsidy. — **sub·si·di·za·tion** \ˌsəb-səd-ə-'zāsh-n, -zəd-ə-\ *n.*

sub·si·dy \'səb-səd-ē, -zəd-ē\ *n.*; *pl.* **sub·si·dies.** **1** Financial aid. **2** A government grant of money given to assist a private business whose operation is considered essential to the public interest.

sub·sist \səb-'sist\ *v.* **1** To exist; to continue living or being. **2** To be maintained with food and clothing; to support or be supported; as, to *subsist* on charity. **3** To continue in a certain state.

sub·sist·ence \səb-'sis-tən(t)s\ *n.* **1** The act or condition of subsisting; existence. **2** Means of support; livelihood.

sub·soil \'səb-ˌsȯil\ *n.* The layer of earth that lies just under the soil on the surface.

sub·stance \'səb-stən(t)s\ *n.* **1** The real part of a thing; the essence. **2** The essential meaning; as, the *substance* of a speech. **3** The material of which a thing is made. **4** Property; wealth.

sub·stand·ard \'səb-'stand-rd\ *adj.* Falling below a standard, as one fixed by law or by custom.

sub·stan·tial \səb-'stanch-l\ *adj.* **1** Having to do with the main part of anything; important; essential. **2** Real; true; as, the *substantial* facts. **3** Having or made of good substance; strong; firm. **4** Rather wealthy and of good reputation; as, *substantial* citizens. **5** Large; considerable; as, a *substantial* sum; a *substantial* meal. — **sub·stan·tial·ly** \-l(-)ē\ *adv.*

sub·stan·ti·ate \səb-'stanch-ē-ˌāt\ *v.*; **sub·stan·ti·at·ed**; **sub·stan·ti·at·ing.** **1** To provide evidence for; to prove; as, to *substantiate* one's claims in court. **2** To give substance or body to; to embody. — **sub·stan·ti·a·tion** \-ˌstanch-ē-'āsh-n\ *n.*

sub·stan·tive \'səb-stən-tiv\ *adj.* **1** Considerable; as, a *substantive* share of the profits. **2** In grammar, expressing existence. The verb "to be" is a *substantive* verb. — *n.* In grammar, a noun or a word used as a noun. — **sub·stan·tive·ly**, *adv.*

sub·sta·tion \'səb-ˌstāsh-n\ *n.* A station subordinate to another station, as a post-office branch.

sub·sti·tute \'səb-stə-ˌtüt, -ˌtyüt\ *n.* A person or thing replacing another. — *v.*; **sub·sti·tut·ed**; **sub·sti·tut·ing.** To put, serve, or use in place of another person or thing; to take the place of another.

sub·sti·tu·tion \ˌsəb-stə-'tüsh-n, -'tyüsh-n\ *n.* The act or process of substituting one for another.

sub·stra·tum \'səb-'strāt-m, -'strat-m\ *n.*; *pl.* **sub·stra·tums** \-mz\ or **sub·stra·ta** \-ə\. **1** That which is laid under; a foundation. **2** Subsoil.

sub·ter·fuge \'səb-tər-ˌfyüj\ *n.* A device, as a plan or trick, used to avoid some unpleasant circumstance, as to escape blame; a tricky evasion.

sub·ter·ra·ne·an \ˌsəb-tə-'rā-nē-ən\ *adj.* **1** Lying or being under the surface of the earth. **2** Hidden; secret; as, *subterranean* schemes.

sub·tle \'sət-l\ *adj.*; **sub·tler** \-l(-)ər\; **sub·tlest** \-l(-)əst\. **1** Thin; delicate; hardly noticeable; elusive; as, a *subtle* fragrance. **2** Marked by very fine distinctions or by sharp analysis; shrewd; keen; as, *subtle* questions; *subtle* reasoning. **3** Clever; sly; as, *subtle* flattery. — **sub·tly** \-l(-)ē, -l-lē\ *adv.*

sub·tle·ty \'sət-l-tē\ *n.*; *pl.* **sub·tle·ties.** **1** The quality or state of being subtle. **2** Something subtle.

sub·top·ic \'səb-ˌtäp-ik\ *n.* A secondary or less important topic, as in a composition or speech.

sub·tract \səb-'trakt\ *v.* To take away, as one part or number from another; to deduct.

sub·trac·tion \səb-'traksh-n\ *n.* The act or process or an instance of subtracting, especially one number or quantity from another.

sub·tra·hend \'səb-trə-ˌhend\ *n.* A number or quantity to be subtracted from another.

sub·trop·i·cal \'səb-'träp-ik-l\ *adj.* Bordering on

the tropics, or like or coming from the regions (**sub·trop·ics** \-iks\) bordering on the tropics.

sub·urb \'səb-ˌərb\ *n.* **1** An outlying part of a city or town. **2** A smaller place near a large city; [in the plural with *the*] districts, especially residential districts, lying on the outskirts of a city.

sub·ur·ban \sə-'bərb-n\ *adj.* Of, relating to, located in, or typical of, the suburbs.

sub·ur·ban·ite \sə-'bərb-n-ˌīt\ *n.* A person living in the suburbs.

sub·ver·sion \səb-'vərzh-n, -'vərsh-n\ *n.* **1** The act of subverting or state of being subverted. **2** That which subverts or is intended to subvert, especially an existing government or traditional beliefs or loyalties.

sub·ver·sive \səb-'vər-siv, -ziv\ *adj.* Tending or designed to subvert. — **sub·ver·sive·ly**, *adv.*

sub·vert \səb-'vərt\ *v.* **1** To overthrow or overturn; to ruin. **2** To undermine the morals, loyalty, or faith of; to corrupt.

sub·vis·i·ble \'səb-'viz-əb-l\ *adj.* Invisible unless magnified.

sub·way \'səb-ˌwā\ *n.* **1** An underground passage. **2** An underground electric railway.

suc·ceed \sək-'sēd\ *v.* **1** To follow; to come after. Night *succeeds* day. **2** To take the throne or assume power after the death or removal of someone else. The prince *succeeded* his father. **3** To get possession of a thing next; as, to *succeed* to the ownership. **4** To be successful. The plan *succeeded.*

suc·cess \sək-'ses\ *n.* **1** Satisfactory completion of something. **2** The gaining of wealth or fame. **3** One that is successful. The play was a *success.*

suc·cess·ful \sək-'ses-fəl\ *adj.* Resulting favorably; achieving, ending in, or having gained success. — **suc·cess·ful·ly** \-fə-lē\ *adv.*

suc·ces·sion \sək-'sesh-n\ *n.* **1** The order, action, or right of succeeding to a throne, title, or property. **2** A repeated following of one person or thing after another. **3** A series of persons or things that follow one after another.

suc·ces·sive \sək-'ses-iv\ *adj.* Following in order and without gaps; consecutive; as, to be absent on four *successive* days. — **suc·ces·sive·ly**, *adv.*

suc·ces·sor \sək-'ses-r\ *n.* One that follows; especially, a person who succeeds to a title or office.

suc·cinct \(ˌ)sək-'sing(k)t\ *adj.* Concise; brief; short. — **suc·cinct·ly**, *adv.*

suc·cor \'sək-r\ *n.* Aid; help; relief. — *v.;* **succored**; **suc·cor·ing** \-r(-)ing\. To aid; to help.

suc·co·tash \'sək-ə-ˌtash\ *n.* Beans and kernels of corn cooked together.

suc·cu·lent \'sək-yə-lənt\ *adj.* **1** Juicy. **2** In botany, having a fleshy stem or leaves, as most cacti. — **suc·cu·lence** \-lən(t)s\ *n.* — **suc·cu·lent·ly**, *adv.*

suc·cumb \sə-'kəm\ *v.* **1** To give way or yield to force or pressure. **2** To die.

such \(')səch, sich\ *adj.* **1** Of the same kind; of this or that kind. All *such* books are interesting. **2** Of the kind to be indicated; as, *such* changes as seem necessary. **3** Having a quality of a degree to be indicated. The runner ran at *such* speed that he won the race. **4** So great; so superior; so inferior. *Such* a storm! — \'səch\ *pron.* **1** Such a person or thing; such persons or things. *Such* is life. **2** This or that which has already been stated. *Such* was the man's decision.

suck \'sək\ *v.* **1** To draw in, as a liquid, with the mouth. **2** To draw liquid from by action of the mouth; as, to *suck* an orange. **3** To hold in the mouth and draw upon or lick with the tongue and lips; as, to *suck* a lollipop. **4** To draw in by suction; to absorb. Plants *suck* moisture from the soil.

suck·er \'sək-r\ *n.* **1** One that sucks. **2** A person who is easily deceived or tricked. **3** In various animals, a part of the body used for sucking or for clinging to something by suction. **4** Any of numerous freshwater fishes related to the carps but having usually thick, soft lips for sucking in food. **5** A secondary shoot from the roots or lower part of a plant. **6** A lollipop.

suck·le \'sək-l\ *v.;* **suck·led**; **suck·ling** \-l(-)ing\. **1** To nurse at the breast or udder. **2** To rear.

suck·ling \'sək-ling\ *n.* An unweaned child or animal.

su·crose \'sü-ˌkrōs\ *n.* Cane or beet sugar.

suc·tion \'səksh-n\ *n.* **1** The action or process of sucking; the capacity for sucking. **2** The drawing of something, as liquid or dust, into a space by drawing air out. Vacuum cleaners work by *suction.* **3** The drawing force exerted in this process.

Su·da·nese \ˌsüd-(ə)n-'ēz, -'ēs\ *adj.* Of or relating to Sudan. — *n. sing. and pl.* A native or inhabitant of Sudan.

sud·den \'səd-n\ *adj.* **1** Happening quickly and unexpectedly; as, *sudden* death. **2** Hasty; quick; as, a *sudden* decision. **3** Met with unexpectedly; as, a *sudden* turn in the road. **4** Hastily or quickly done or accomplished; as, a *sudden* cure. — **all of a sudden**. Suddenly. — **sud·den·ly**, *adv.*

suds \'sədz\ *n. pl.* Soapy water, especially when foamy.

sue \'sü\ *v.;* **sued**; **su·ing**. **1** To make a request; to ask; as, to *sue* for peace. **2** To seek justice or right by bringing a matter to a court of law.

suede \'swād\ *n.* [Originally used in the phrase *suède gloves*, a partial translation of French *gants de Suède* meaning literally "gloves from Sweden".] **1** A tanned skin with the flesh side rubbed into a nap. **2** Also **suede cloth**. A fabric, as of wool, cotton, or rayon, finished with a short, smooth nap.

su·et \'sü-ət\ *n.* The hard fat about the kidneys and loins in beef and mutton.

suf·fer \'səf-r\ *v.;* **suf·fered**; **suf·fer·ing** \-r(-)ing\. **1** To feel or endure pain. **2** To experience; to undergo; as, to *suffer* a defeat. **3** To bear loss or damage. The man's business *suffered* during his illness. **4** To allow; to permit.

suf·fer·ance \'səf-r(-)ən(t)s\ *n.* **1** Consent or approval not given openly but only implied by lack of objection. **2** The power or ability to endure;

endurance; as, woes that are beyond *sufferance*.

suf·fer·ing \'səf-r(-)ing\ *n*. Pain; misery; hardship.

suf·fice \sə-'fīs\ *v*.; **suf·ficed**; **suf·fic·ing**. **1** To be sufficient; to be sufficient for; to satisfy.

suf·fi·cien·cy \sə-'fish-n-sē\ *n*.; *pl*. **suf·fi·cien·cies**. **1** A sufficient means to meet one's needs; as, a comfortable *sufficiency* for life. **2** Enough. Everyone at the table received a *sufficiency*.

suf·fi·cient \sə-'fish-nt\ *adj*. Enough; as, *sufficient* food. — **suf·fi·cient·ly**, *adv*.

suf·fix \'səf-ˌiks, (ˌ)sə-'fiks\ *v*. To add to the end; to attach as a suffix. — \'səf-ˌiks\ *n*. One or more letters or syllables added to the end of a word to modify its meaning, as *-s* in *songs*, *-er* in *helper*, or *-ish* in *sweetish*.

suf·fo·cate \'səf-ə-ˌkāt\ *v*.; **suf·fo·cat·ed**; **suf·fo·cat·ing**. **1** To kill by stopping the breath; to stifle; to choke. **2** To be choked, stifled, or smothered. **3** To have or to cause to have a feeling of smothering. — **suf·fo·ca·tion** \ˌsəf-ə-'kāsh-n\ *n*.

suf·frage \'səf-rij\ *n*. **1** A vote for or against something. **2** The right to vote; the franchise.

suf·frag·ist \'səf-rə-jəst\ *n*. A person who favors extending voting rights, especially to women.

suf·fuse \sə-'fyüz\ *v*.; **suf·fused**; **suf·fus·ing**. To spread over, as with a fluid or color. A blush *suffused* the girl's cheeks. — **suf·fu·sion** \-'fyüzh-n\ *n*.

sug·ar \'shu̇g-r\ *n*. **1** A sweet substance obtained from sugar cane, sugar beets, or maple syrup. **2** Any of a number of sweet substances obtained from grapes (**grape sugar**), corn (**corn sugar**), or milk (**milk sugar**). — *v*.; **sug·ared**; **sug·ar·ing** \-r(-)ing\. **1** To mix, cover, or sprinkle with sugar. **2** To make something less hard to take or bear; to sweeten; as, to *sugar* advice with flattery. **3** To change to crystals of sugar, as candy or icing when cooked too long.

sugar beet. A beet with a white root from which sugar is made.

sug·ar·bush \'shu̇g-r-ˌbu̇sh\ *n*. A sugar orchard.

sugar cane. A tall, strong tropical grass with broad ribbon-shaped leaves and a jointed stem from the juice of which sugar is made.

sug·ar-coat \'shu̇g-r-'kōt\ *v*. **1** To coat with sugar. **2** To make attractive or agreeable on the surface; as, to *sugar-coat* an unpleasant truth. — **sug·ar-coat·ing** \-ing\ *n*.

sugar cane

sugar orchard. A grove of tall yellow-flowered maple trees (**sugar maples**) from whose sap maple sugar is made.

sug·ar·plum \'shu̇g-r-ˌpləm\ *n*. A sweetmeat; a piece of candy.

sug·ary \'shu̇g-r(-)ē\ *adj*. Like, containing, or consisting of sugar; tasting of sugar; sweet.

sug·gest \sə(g)-'jest\ *v*. **1** To put a thought, plan, or desire into a person's mind; to propose as an idea or possibility; as, to *suggest* going for a walk. **2** To bring something else to mind through close connection; as, that smoke *suggests* a forest fire.

sug·gest·i·ble \sə(g)-'jes-təb-l\ *adj*. **1** Easily influenced by suggestion. **2** Capable of being suggested. — **sug·gest·i·bil·i·ty** \-ˌjes-tə-'bil-ət-ē\ *n*.

sug·ges·tion \sə(g)-'jes-chən\ *n*. **1** A suggesting; a proposal of something as an idea or possibility. **2** Something that is suggested. **3** A trace; a hint; as, a *suggestion* of impatience in a person's voice.

sug·ges·tive \sə(g)-'jes-tiv\ *adj*. Tending to suggest something, often something improper. — **sug·ges·tive·ly**, *adv*.

su·i·cide \'sü-ə-ˌsīd\ *n*. **1** The action of killing oneself purposely. **2** A person who kills himself purposely. — **su·i·cid·al** \ˌsü-ə-'sīd-l\ *adj*. — **su·i·cid·al·ly** \-'sīd-l-ē\ *adv*.

suit \'süt\ *n*. **1** The action of suing; an entreaty; especially, a wooing. **2** A number of things used together; a set; as, a *suit* of clothes. **3** One of the four sets of cards in a pack of playing cards. **4** In law, an action or process in a court for the recovery of a right or claim. — *v*. **1** To answer the desires or needs of; to please. Music that *suits* us may not please others. **2** To fit or be fitted; to accord; as, to *suit* the action to the word; a color that *suits* one's complexion.

suit·a·ble \'süt-əb-l\ *adj*. Capable of suiting; appropriate; proper; fitting; as, *suitable* clothes for a picnic. — For synonyms see *fit*. — **suit·a·bil·i·ty** \ˌsüt-ə-'bil-ət-ē\ *n*. — **suit·a·bly** \'süt-ə-blē\ *adv*.

suit·case \'süt-ˌkās\ *n*. A flat oblong traveling bag.

suite, *n*. **1** \'swēt\ A company of attendants; as, an ambassador's *suite*. **2** \'swēt, 'süt\ A number of things that make up a series or a set; as, a *suite* of rooms. **3** \'swēt\ A musical composition consisting of a series of dances. **4** \'swēt\ A modern instrumental composition in several movements.

suit·ing \'süt-ing\ *n*. Fabric for suits of clothes.

suit·or \'süt-r\ *n*. **1** A person who sues. **2** A man who seeks the hand of a woman in marriage.

Suk·koth \'su̇k-ˌōs, -əs, -ˌōt(h)\ *n*. An annual Jewish holiday celebrated in September or October as a harvest festival of thanksgiving and also to commemorate the tabernacles used by the Israelites during their wanderings in the wilderness.

sul·fa or **sul·pha** \'səl-fə\ *adj*. Of or relating to a group of synthetic drugs (**sulfa drugs**) used in treating infections. — *n*. A sulfa drug.

sul·fur or **sul·phur** \'səlf-r\ *n*. A yellow element found widely in nature, free or combined, burning in air with a blue flame to form a choking gas.

sulfur dioxide or **sulphur dioxide**. A heavy, strong-smelling gas used in making sulfuric acid, in bleaching, and as a preservative.

sul·fu·ric or **sul·phu·ric** \ˌsəl-'fyu̇r-ik\ *adj*. Of, relating to, or containing sulfur.

sulfuric acid or **sulphuric acid**. A heavy, corrosive, oily liquid used especially in making fertilizers, chemicals, and petroleum products.

sul·fu·rous or **sul·phu·rous** \'səlf-r-əs; *sense 1 is also* ˌsəl-'fyu̇r-əs\ *adj*. **1** Of, relating to, or containing sulfur; like sulfur. **2** Fiery; inflamed; as, *sulphurous* language; a long, *sulphurous* sermon.

sulk \'səlk\ *v.* To be sullen; to become moodily silent or ill-humored. — *n.* A sullen mood — usually in the plural; as, to have a case of the *sulks*.

sulky \'səl-kē\ *adj.;* **sulk·i·er; sulk·i·est. 1** Inclined to sulk; given to fits of sulking. **2** Sullen; gloomy; as, a *sulky* voice. — *n.; pl.* **sulk·ies.** A light two-wheeled carriage for one person.

sul·len \'səl-ən\ *adj.* **1** Not sociable; gloomily silent; sulky. **2** Gloomy; dismal; as, a *sullen* autumn day. — **sul·len·ly,** *adv.*

sul·ly \'səl-ē\ *v.;* **sul·lied** \-ēd\; **sul·ly·ing.** To make or become soiled; to smirch; to foul.

sul·tan \'səlt-n; su̇l-'tän, -'tȧn\ *n.* A ruler, especially of a Moslem state.

sul·tana \ˌsəl-'tan-ə\ *n.* **1** The wife, mother, sister, or daughter of a sultan. **2** A pale yellow seedless grape grown as a source of raisins.

sul·tan·ate \'səlt-n-ət, -ˌāt\ *n.* The rule, territory, or rank of a sultan.

sul·try \'səl-trē\ *adj.;* **sul·tri·er; sul·tri·est. 1** Very hot and humid. **2** Burning hot; as, a *sultry* sun.

sum \'səm\ *n.* **1** An amount; a quantity of money; as, a *sum* of one hundred dollars. **2** The whole amount; as, the *sum* of man's experience. **3** A summary; the chief points or thoughts when taken together; as, the *sum* of the evidence. **4** The result of adding two or more numbers or quantities. **5** Any problem in arithmetic. — *v.;* **summed; sum·ming. 1** To find the sum of. **2** To summarize; as, to *sum* up the evidence.

su·mac or **su·mach** \'shü-ˌmak, 'sü-\ *n.* **1** A shrub or small tree with feathery green leaves changing to brilliant red in autumn and tapering clusters of flowers that are followed by red or whitish berries. **2** A material used in tanning and dyeing, made of the leaves and other parts of sumac.

smooth sumac

sum·mar·i·ly \(ˌ)sə-'mer-ə-lē, 'səm-r-ə-lē\ *adv.* In a summary manner; without delay or formality.

sum·ma·rize \'səm-r-ˌīz\ *v.;* **sum·ma·rized; sum·ma·riz·ing.** To make a summary of.

sum·ma·ry \'səm-r-ē\ *adj.* **1** Expressing or covering the main points briefly; concise; summed up; as, a *summary* account. **2** Done without delay or formality; quickly carried out; as, a *summary* procedure. — *n.; pl.* **sum·ma·ries.** A concise statement of the main points, as in a book.

sum·ma·tion \(ˌ)sə-'māsh-n\ *n.* **1** The act of summing up; as, the *summation* of evidence by a lawyer. **2** An aggregate; a total; a sum.

sum·mer \'səm-r\ *n.* The season of the year in any region when the sun shines there most directly; the warmest season. — *v.;* **sum·mered; sum·mer·ing** \-r(-)ing\. To pass the summer.

sum·mer·house \'səm-r-ˌhau̇s\ *n.; pl.* **sum·mer·hous·es** \-ˌhau̇-zəz\. A rustic covered structure in a garden or park, to provide shade in hot weather.

sum·mer·time \'səm-r-ˌtīm\ *n.* Summer.

summer time. *Chiefly British.* Daylight-saving time.

sum·mery \'səm-r-ē\ *adj.* Like or fit for summer.

sum·mit \'səm-ət\ *n.* **1** The top; the peak, as of a mountain. **2** The highest degree; the utmost height; as, a leader at the *summit* of his power.

sum·mon \'səm-ən\ *v.* **1** To call or invite to a meeting; to order to convene; as, to *summon* a legislature. **2** To call; to send for; as, to *summon* a messenger. **3** To order to appear before a court of law; as, to *summon* a witness. **4** To arouse or stir to activity; as, to *summon* one's courage.

sum·mons \'səm-ənz\ *n.; pl.* **sum·mons·es** \-ən-zəz\. **1** The act of summoning. **2** A signal that summons. **3** A written official order to appear before a court of law. — *v.* To issue or take out a legal summons against; to summon.

sump \'səmp\ *n.* A pit or reservoir serving as a receptacle or as a drain for fluids.

sump·tu·ous \'səm(p)-chə-wəs, 'səm(p)-chəs\ *adj.* Costly; involving large expense; luxurious; splendid; as, a *sumptuous* feast. — **sump·tu·ous·ly,** *adv.*

sun \'sən\ *n.* **1** The shining heavenly body round which the earth and other planets revolve and from which they receive light and heat. **2** Sunshine; as, to go out into the *sun*. **3** A heavenly body like our sun that is the center of a system of planets. **4** Any object that is like a sun. — *v.;* **sunned; sun·ning.** To expose to the sun's rays.

Sun. Abbreviation for *Sunday*.

sun·bath \'sən-ˌbath\ *n.; pl.* **sun·baths** \-ˌbat͟hz\. Exposure of the body to the sun's rays. — **sun·bath·er** \-ˌbāt͟h-r\ *n.* — **sun·bath·ing** \-ˌbā-t͟hing\ *n.*

sun·beam \'sən-ˌbēm\ *n.* A ray of sunlight.

sun·bon·net \'sən-ˌbän-ət\ *n.* A bonnet with a wide brim framing the face and usually a ruffle at the back to protect from the sun.

sunbonnet

sun·burn \'sən-ˌbərn\ *n.* A burning of the skin, caused by exposure to the sun's rays; the red or brown color so caused. — *v.;* **sun·burned** \-ˌbərnd\ or **sun·burnt** \-ˌbərnt\; **sun·burn·ing.** To burn by the sun; discolor by the sun; to tan.

sun·burst \'sən-ˌbərst\ *n.* **1** A burst of sunlight, especially through a break in the clouds. **2** A representation of a sun surrounded by rays.

sun·dae \'sən-dē\ *n.* A dish of ice cream with a topping, as of crushed fruit, syrup, or nuts.

Sun·day \'sən-dē\ *n.* [From Old English *Sunnandaeg* "day of the sun".] The first day of the week.

Sunday school. A school held on Sunday for religious instruction.

sun·der \'sənd-r\ *v.;* **sun·dered; sun·der·ing** \-r(-)ing\. To break or force apart; to separate; to divide. — **in sunder.** Into parts; apart.

sun·di·al \'sən-ˌdī-əl, -ˌdīl\ *n.* A device to show the time of day by the position of the shadow cast on a plate or disk, typically by an upright pin.

sun·down \'sən-ˌdau̇n\ *n.* Sunset.

sun·dries \'sən-drēz\ *n. pl.* Miscellaneous small articles or items.

sun·dry \'sən-drē\ *adj.* Several; various; miscellaneous; as, for *sundry* reasons.

sun·fish \'sən-ˌfish\ *n.; pl.* **sun·fish** or **sun·fish·es. 1** A large sea fish with a very deep, short, and flat body, high fins, and a small mouth. **2** A small American freshwater fish like a perch, usually of very bright metallic colors.

sun·flow·er \'sən-ˌflau̇r\ *n.* **1** Any of several tall American herbs with large dark-centered yellow-rayed flowers. **2** A flower of one of these plants.

sung. A past tense and past part. of *sing.*

sun·glass \'sən-ˌglas\ *n.* **1** A burning glass. **2** [in the plural] Spectacles made of glass that protects the eyes from the glare of the sun.

sunk. A past tense and past part. of *sink.*

sunk·en \'səngk-n\ *adj.* **1** Sunk; hollow; depressed; as, a *sunken* garden; *sunken* cheeks. **2** Lying on the sea or river bottom; as, *sunken* treasure.

sun lamp. An electric lamp designed to produce ultraviolet rays some of which are of the same wave lengths as those in sunlight.

sun·light \'sən-ˌlīt\ *n.* The light of the sun.

sun·lit \'sən-ˌlit\ *adj.* Lighted by the sun.

sun·ny \'sən-ē\ *adj.;* **sun·ni·er; sun·ni·est. 1** Bright with sunshine; as, a *sunny* day; a *sunny* room. **2** Merry; bright; as, a *sunny* smile.

sun·rise \'sən-ˌrīz\ *n.* **1** The apparent rising of the sun above the horizon. **2** The time at which the sun rises. **3** The light and color at this time.

sun·room \'sən-ˌrüm, -ˌru̇m\ *n.* A glass-enclosed porch or living room with a sunny exposure.

sun·set \'sən-ˌsət\ *n.* **1** The apparent descent of the sun below the horizon. **2** The time at which the sun sets. **3** The light and color that appear at this time.

sun·shade \'sən-ˌshād\ *n.* **1** A parasol. **2** An awning.

sun·shine \'sən-ˌshīn\ *n.* **1** The sun's light or rays. **2** The warmth and light given by the sun's rays or a spot warmed and lighted by them. **3** Happiness; cheer. — **sun·shiny** \-ˌshī-nē\ *adj.*

sun·spot \'sən-ˌspät\ *n.* One of the dark spots that appear from time to time on the sun, usually visible only with a telescope, but frequently accompanied by magnetic storms on the earth.

sun·stroke \'sən-ˌstrōk\ *n.* An illness caused by overexposure to the sun or to excessive heat.

sun·tan \'sən-ˌtan\ *n.* **1** A tan resulting from exposure of the skin to the sun's rays or to those of a sun lamp. **2** A yellowish red-brown color. — **sun-tanned** \-ˌtand\ *adj.*

sun·up \'sən-ˌəp\ *n.* Sunrise.

sup \'səp\ *v.;* **supped; sup·ping. 1** To sip; to sip liquid or liquid food. **2** To eat supper. — *n.* A sip.

super-. A prefix that can mean: **1** Situated or placed over or above, as in *superscribe, superstructure.* **2** One that surpasses others of its kind, as in *supermarket, superhuman.* **3** Very, in excess, great or greatly, as in *superabundant, superfine.*

su·per·a·bun·dant \'süp-r-ə-'bən-dənt\ *adj.* Being more than enough; abounding in great plenty; profuse. — **su·per·a·bun·dance** \-dən(t)s\ *n.*

su·per·an·nu·ate \ˌsüp-r-'an-yə-ˌwāt\ *v.;* **su·per·an·nu·at·ed; su·per·an·nu·at·ing.** To retire and give a pension to because of old age or infirmity. — **su·per·an·nu·a·tion** \ˌsüp-r-ˌan-yə-'wāsh-n\ *n.*

su·per·an·nu·at·ed \ˌsüp-r-'an-yə-ˌwāt-əd\ *adj.* **1** Retired on a pension. **2** Too old for work or service.

su·perb \sü-'pərb\ *adj.* **1** Noble; majestic. **2** Rich in appearance; splendid; as, *superb* gems. **3** Of highest quality; supremely good; as, *superb* acting. — **su·perb·ly**, *adv.*

su·per·car·go \'süp-r-'kär-ˌgō, -'kȧr-\ *n.; pl.* **su·per·car·goes** or **su·per·car·gos.** An officer in charge of commercial affairs on a voyage of a ship.

su·per·charg·er \'süp-r-ˌchärj-r, -ˌchȧrj-r\ *n.* A device, as on automobile or airplane engines, for increasing the air supply to the cylinders, as for high-speed operation.

su·per·cil·i·ous \ˌsüp-r-'sil-ē-əs\ *adj.* Haughty; proud and contemptuous.

su·per·cool \'süp-r-'kül\ *v.* In chemistry, to cool below the freezing point without solidification.

su·per·fi·cial \ˌsüp-r-'fish-l\ *adj.* **1** Having to do with the surface or appearance only; as, a *superficial* cut. **2** Shallow; hasty; not profound or thorough. — **su·per·fi·cial·ly** \-'fish-l-ē\ *adv.*

su·per·fi·ci·al·i·ty \ˌsüp-r-ˌfish-ē-'al-ət-ē\ *n.; pl.* **su·per·fi·ci·al·i·ties. 1** The quality or state of being superficial. **2** Something superficial, as a remark.

su·per·fine \'süp-r-'fīn\ *adj.* **1** Very delicate or refined; too nice. **2** Extra fine; very fine.

su·per·flu·i·ty \ˌsüp-r-'flü-ət-ē\ *n.; pl.* **su·per·flu·i·ties. 1** Superabundance, as of wealth or possessions. **2** An excess; an oversupply.

su·per·flu·ous \sü-'pər-flə-wəs\ *adj.* More than is needed or desired; unnecessary; surplus. — **su·per·flu·ous·ly**, *adv.*

su·per·high·way \'süp-r-'hī-ˌwā\ *n.* A highway with four or more lanes for fast-moving traffic.

su·per·hu·man \'süp-r-'hü-mən, -'yü-\ *adj.* **1** Above the human; divine. **2** Beyond normal human power; as, *superhuman* strength.

su·per·in·tend \ˌsüp-r(-)ən-'tend\ *v.* To oversee and direct; to supervise.

su·per·in·tend·ence \ˌsüp-r(-)ən-'ten-dən(t)s\ or **su·per·in·ten·den·cy** \-dən-sē\ *n.* The act or duty of superintending or overseeing.

su·per·in·tend·ent \ˌsüp-r(-)ən-'ten-dənt\ *n.* A person who oversees or manages anything; as, a building *superintendent; superintendent* of schools.

su·pe·ri·or \sə-'pir-ē-ər\ *adj.* **1** Higher in rank, importance, numbers, or quality. **2** Better than most; as, a machine *superior* in every way. **3** Courageously indifferent; as, *superior* to pain. **4** Feeling or showing that one feels that one is better or more important than others; arrogant; as, a *superior* smile. **5** Covering or including more things; more comprehensive. A genus is *superior* to a species. — *n.* **1** One who is above another or others.

2 The head of a monastery or convent.

su·pe·ri·or·i·ty \sə-ˌpir-ē-'ór-ət-ē, -'är-\ *n.* The quality or state of being superior.

su·per·la·tive \sə-'pər-lət-iv\ *adj.* **1** Better than all others; supreme; as, apples with a *superlative* flavor. **2** Expressing the highest degree of an adjective or adverb. — *n.* **1** The superlative degree of an adjective or adverb. "Worst" is the *superlative* of "bad". **2** The utmost degree of something; the acme. — **su·per·la·tive·ly**, *adv.*

su·per·man \'süp-r-ˌman\ *n.; pl.* **su·per·men** \-ˌmen\. A man with superhuman powers.

su·per·mar·ket \'süp-r-ˌmärk-ət, -ˌmȧrk-\ *n.* A large market in which one usually serves oneself.

su·per·nal \sü-'pərn-l\ *adj.* **1** Being or coming from above, as from heaven or from the sky. **2** Of heavenly or spiritual character; celestial.

su·per·nat·u·ral \'süp-r-'nach-r(-)əl\ *adj.* Of or having to do with something outside of nature or beyond the visible and observable universe. — **su·per·nat·u·ral·ly** \-r(-)ə-lē\ *adv.*

su·per·nu·mer·ary \ˌsüp-r-'nüm-r-ˌer-ē, -'nyüm-\ *adj.* Exceeding a necessary or expected number or quantity; superfluous; extra. — *n.; pl.* **su·per·nu·mer·ar·ies. 1** An extra or superfluous person or thing. **2** A person hired to appear in a play or movie as one of a large crowd or mob; an extra.

su·per·scribe \'süp-r-ˌskrīb\ *v.;* **su·per·scribed; su·per·scrib·ing.** To write or engrave something on the outside or top of; especially, to address, as a letter. — **su·per·scrip·tion** \ˌsüp-r-'skripsh-n\ *n.*

su·per·sede \ˌsüp-r-'sēd\ *v.;* **su·per·sed·ed; su·per·sed·ing.** To take the place or position of something else; to replace.

su·per·son·ic \'süp-r-'sän-ik\ *adj.* **1** Having speed greater than that of sound; as, a *supersonic* jet plane. **2** Of or relating to speeds greater than the speed of sound; as, a *supersonic* wind tunnel.

su·per·sti·tion \ˌsüp-r-'stish-n\ *n.* An unreasonable attitude toward that which is not understood or is beyond human comprehension; unreasoning fear of nature; belief in magic and witchcraft.

su·per·sti·tious \ˌsüp-r-'stish-əs\ *adj.* Having to do with, showing, or influenced by, superstition. — **su·per·sti·tious·ly**, *adv.*

su·per·struc·ture \'süp-r-ˌstrək-chər\ *n.* Any structure built on top of some other structure.

su·per·vise \'süp-r-ˌvīz\ *v.;* **su·per·vised; su·per·vis·ing.** To oversee and direct; to superintend.

su·per·vi·sion \ˌsüp-r-'vizh-n\ *n.* The act of supervising; management.

su·per·vi·sor \'süp-r-ˌvīz-r\ *n.* **1** One who supervises. **2** One who has charge of a special subject or of the teachers of that subject.

su·per·vi·so·ry \ˌsüp-r-'vīz-r(-)ē\ *adj.* Of or relating to supervision.

su·pine \sü-'pīn\ *adj.* **1** Lying on the back with the face upward. **2** Sluggish; lazy. — **su·pine·ly**, *adv.*

sup·per \'səp-r\ *n.* **1** The evening meal, especially when the main meal is eaten at noon. **2** A late meal, as one served at the close of a party.

sup·plant \sə-'plant\ *v.* **1** To take another's place, as by force or trickery. **2** To replace; to supersede.

sup·ple \'səp-l\ *adj.;* **sup·pler** \-l(-)ər\; **sup·plest** \-l(-)əst\. **1** Not breaking or creasing when bent; flexible; as, *supple* leather. **2** Limber; lithe. **3** Adaptable; as, a *supple* mind.

sup·ple·ment \'səp-lə-mənt\ *n.* Something that supplies a want or makes an addition; as, diet *supplements;* the *supplement* at the back of the book. — \-ˌment\ *v.* To add to; to fill a lack in; as, to *supplement* one's allowance by doing errands. — **sup·ple·men·tal** \ˌsəp-lə-'ment-l\ *adj.*

sup·ple·men·ta·ry \ˌsəp-lə-'ment-r-ē, -'men-trē\ *adj.* Added as a supplement; additional.

sup·pli·ant \'səp-lē-ənt\ *adj.* Supplicating. — *n.* One who supplicates. — **sup·pli·ant·ly**, *adv.*

sup·pli·cant \'səp-lə-kənt\ *adj.* Supplicating; asking humbly. — *n.* A suppliant.

sup·pli·cate \'səp-lə-ˌkāt\ *v.;* **sup·pli·cat·ed; sup·pli·cat·ing.** To make earnest entreaty; to ask humbly and sincerely; especially, to implore God.

sup·pli·ca·tion \ˌsəp-lə-'kāsh-n\ *n.* The act of supplicating; earnest, urgent, humble entreaty.

sup·ply \sə-'plī\ *v.;* **sup·plied** \-'plīd\; **sup·ply·ing. 1** To add something that is lacking. **2** To fill; to satisfy; as, enough to *supply* the demand. **3** To furnish or provide. — *n.; pl.* **sup·plies. 1** The act of supplying. **2** Something supplied; as, a *supply* of food for a camping trip. **3** The amount, especially of a commodity, available. Good harvests increased the *supply* of grain. **4** [usually in the plural] Food, clothing, or arms set aside to be distributed when needed. — **sup·pli·er** \-'plīr\ *n.*

sup·port \sə-'pōrt, -'pȯrt\ *v.* **1** To hold up; to keep from sinking or falling. **2** To endure; to bear; to tolerate; as, unable to *support* their taunts. **3** To side with; to back up. **4** To provide with food, clothing, and shelter. — *n.* **1** Something that supports; a prop. **2** The act of supporting; the state of being supported. — **sup·port·a·ble**, *adj.*

sup·port·er \sə-'pōrt-r, -'pȯrt-r\ *n.* One that supports; especially, an adherent or advocate.

sup·pose \sə-'pōz\ *v.;* **sup·posed; sup·pos·ing. 1** To take as true or as a fact for the sake of argument. *Suppose* the book is wrong, what then? **2** To believe; to think. I *suppose* he is honest. **3** To conjecture; to guess. Do you *suppose* it will rain tomorrow? — **be supposed to.** To be expected, required, or obliged to; to have to; ought to. I *am supposed to* go to that party.

sup·posed \sə-'pōzd\ *adj.* Accepted as being true, often wrongly. — **sup·pos·ed·ly** \-'pō-zəd-lē\ *adv.*

sup·po·si·tion \ˌsəp-ə-'zish-n\ *n.* **1** The act of supposing. **2** Something that is supposed.

sup·press \sə-'pres\ *v.* **1** To put down; to quell; to crush; as, to *suppress* a revolt. **2** To keep from being known. **3** To stop the publication or circulation of. **4** To hold back; to repress; as, to *suppress* laughter. — **sup·press·er** or **sup·pres·sor** \-'pres-r\ *n.* — **sup·pres·sion** \-'presh-n\ *n.*

sup·pu·rate \'səp-yə-ˌrāt\ *v.;* **sup·pu·rat·ed; sup-**

pu·rat·ing. To form or give off pus. — **sup·pu·ra·tive** \-ˌrāt-iv\ *adj.*

su·pra·re·nal \ˈsüp-rə-ˈrēn-l\ *adj.* Adrenal. — *n.* An adrenal gland.

su·prem·a·cy \sə-ˈprem-ə-sē\ *n.* **1** Supreme power or authority. **2** The condition of being supreme.

su·preme \sə-ˈprēm\ *adj.* [From Latin *supremus*, the superlative of *superus* meaning "situated above", "upper" and derived from *super* meaning "over", "above".] **1** Highest in rank, authority, or power. **2** The greatest or highest possible; utmost. **3** Ultimate; final. The *supreme* sacrifice is the giving up of one's life. — **su·preme·ly**, *adv.*

Supreme Being. God.

Supreme Court. **1** The highest court in the United States, consisting of a chief justice and eight associate justices. **2** A similar body in many states.

supt. Abbreviation for *superintendent*.

sur·cease \ˈsər-ˌsēs\ *n. Archaic.* A ceasing; an end.

sur·charge \ˈsər-ˌchärj, -ˌchårj\ *v.;* **sur·charged**; **sur·charg·ing**. **1** To overcharge. **2** To overload. **3** To fill to excess. **4** To print or write a surcharge on; as, a *surcharged* postage stamp. — *n.* **1** A charge over the usual or normal rate. **2** An excessive load or burden. **3** An additional printing on a postage stamp giving it a new value or use.

sur·cin·gle \ˈsər-ˌsing-gl\ *n.* A belt or band passing over a saddle, or over anything on a horse's back, to bind it fast.

sur·coat \ˈsər-ˌkōt\ *n.* An outer coat or cloak, especially one worn by a knight over his armor.

sure \ˈshůr\ *adj.;* **sur·er**; **sur·est**. **1** Steadfast; firm; as, a *sure* footing; a *sure* faith. **2** Having no doubt; confident; as, *sure* that one is right. **3** Entirely trustworthy; dependable. **4** Bound to happen; assured. **5** Bound; certain; as, *sure* to fail. — **for sure**. For certain; surely; without doubt. — **to be sure**. Surely; certainly. — *adv.* Surely.

sure-fire \ˈshůr-ˈfīr\ *adj.* Certain; dependable.

sure-foot·ed \ˈshůr-ˈfůt-əd\ *adj.* Not liable to stumble or fall. — **sure-foot·ed·ly**, *adv.*

sure·ly \ˈshůr-lē\ *adv.* **1** In a sure manner; firmly. **2** Undoubtedly; certainly.

sure·ty \ˈshůr-ət-ē, ˈshůrt-ē\ *n.; pl.* **sure·ties**. **1** Sure knowledge; certainty. **2** Something that confirms or makes sure; security against loss or damage; a guarantee; as, *surety* for a loan. **3** One who becomes a guarantor for another.

surf \ˈsərf\ *n.* The swell of the sea that breaks upon the shore. — *v.* To bathe in or ride the surf.

sur·face \ˈsər-fəs\ *n.* **1** The outside of an object or body. **2** Outside appearance. **3** In geometry, that which has length and breadth but no thickness. **4** An airfoil. — *adj.* **1** Relating to or at a surface; acting on a surface. **2** Not deep or real; superficial; as, *surface* friendship. — *v.;* **sur·faced**; **sur·fac·ing**. **1** To give a surface to; as, to *surface* a new road. **2** To make smooth, as lumber by planing; to finish, as by polishing. **3** To come to the surface. The submarine *surfaced*. — **sur·fac·er** \-fəs-r\ *n.*

surf·board \ˈsərf-ˌbōrd, -ˌbȯrd\ *n.* A board for riding the surf. — *v.* To ride the surf on a surfboard.

surf·boat \ˈsərf-ˌbōt\ *n.* A strongly built boat for use in heavy surf.

sur·feit \ˈsər-fət\ *n.* **1** An excess; an overabundance. **2** A feeling of sickness or dislike caused by too much of something, especially food or drink. — *v.* To supply, as with food or pleasures, to such excess as to cause disgust or illness.

surge \ˈsərj\ *n.* **1** A great rolling swell of water. **2** A rolling or sweeping onward like that of a wave; as, a *surge* of feeling; a *surge* of people. — *v.;* **surged**; **surg·ing**. To rise or move in surges; as, *surging* waves.

sur·geon \ˈsərj-n\ *n.* One who practices surgery.

sur·gery \ˈsərj-r(-)ē\ *n.; pl.* **sur·ger·ies**. **1** Medical science concerned with the correction of physical defects, the repair and healing of injuries, and the treatment of diseased conditions through operations. **2** The work done by a surgeon.

sur·gi·cal \ˈsər-jik-l\ *adj.* Of or relating to surgery or surgeons. — **sur·gi·cal·ly** \-jik-l(-)ē\ *adv.*

sur·ly \ˈsər-lē\ *adj.;* **sur·li·er**; **sur·li·est**. Rude and abrupt; cross; ill-natured.

sur·mise \sər-ˈmīz\ *v.;* **sur·mised**; **sur·mis·ing**. To infer without proof; to guess. — \sər-ˈmīz, ˈsər-ˌmīz\ *n.* A guess; a conjecture.

sur·mount \sər-ˈmaůnt\ *v.* **1** To conquer or overcome, as an obstacle. **2** To lie at the top of; to top. — **sur·mount·a·ble**, *adj.*

sur·name \ˈsər-ˌnām\ *n.* **1** *Archaic.* An additional name, as in Catherine *the Great*. **2** A family name; a last name. — *v.;* **sur·named**; **sur·nam·ing**. To give a surname to; to call by a surname; as, Lorenzo, *surnamed* the Magnificent.

sur·pass \sər-ˈpas\ *v.* **1** To be greater, better, or stronger than someone or something else; to exceed; to excel. **2** To go beyond the reach, powers, or capacity of. — **sur·pass·a·ble**, *adj.*

sur·plice \ˈsərp-ləs\ *n.* A priest's outer vestment of white linen, usually worn over a cassock.

sur·plus \ˈsərp-(ˌ)ləs\ *n.* An amount or quantity left over; an excess. — *adj.* Being a surplus.

sur·prise \sə(r)-ˈprīz\ *v.;* **sur·prised**; **sur·pris·ing**. **1** To seize by attacking unexpectedly; as, to *surprise* a fort. **2** To come upon unexpectedly; to take unawares. **3** To cause wonder by being different from what is expected. **4** To bring about by means of a surprise; as, to *surprise* a confession out of a suspected thief. — *n.* **1** An act of coming upon someone or something unexpectedly. **2** Something surprising. The gift was a *surprise*. **3** The state of being surprised; astonishment; amazement. *Surprise* kept him silent.

sur·pris·ing \sə(r)-ˈprī-zing\ *adj.* Astonishing; amazing; remarkable. — **sur·pris·ing·ly**, *adv.*

sur·ren·der \sə-ˈrend-r\ *v.;* **sur·ren·dered**; **sur·ren·der·ing** \-r(-)ing\. To give over into the power of another; to yield possession of, especially under compulsion. — *n.* The giving of oneself or something into the power of another person or thing.

sur·rep·ti·tious \ˌsər-əp-ˈtish-əs, ˌsə-rəp-\ *adj.* Done, made, or acquired by stealth or in secret; stealthy; secret. — **sur·rep·ti·tious·ly**, *adv.*

sur·rey \ˈsər-ē, ˈsə-rē\ *n.; pl.* **sur·reys.** A four-wheeled, two-seated carriage.

sur·ro·gate \ˈsər-ə-ˌgāt, ˈsə-rə-, -gət\ *n.* **1** A deputy; a substitute. **2** A judge who has jurisdiction over the administration of estates, the probate of wills, and the appointment of guardians.

sur·round \sə-ˈraůnd\ *v.* **1** To enclose on all sides; to encircle; as, land *surrounded* by water; troops *surrounded* by the enemy. **2** To form the environment of; as, to be *surrounded* by luxury.

sur·round·ings \sə-ˈraůn-dingz\ *n. pl.* The conditions around a person; environment.

sur·tax \ˈsər-ˌtaks\ *n.* An additional tax over and above a general tax.

sur·veil·lance \sər-ˈvā-lən(t)s, -ˈvāl-yən(t)s\ *n.* Close watch; as, kept under constant *surveillance.*

sur·vey \(ˌ)sər-ˈvā, ˈsər-ˌvā\ *v.* **1** To look over and examine closely. **2** To determine the form, extent, or position of a piece of land; to make a survey of. **3** To view or study as a whole. — \ˈsər-ˌvā, (ˌ)sər-ˈvā\ *n.* **1** The action or an instance of surveying. **2** Something that is surveyed. **3** A careful examination to learn certain facts; as, a *survey* of the school system. **4** A history or description that covers much material by bare outlines; as, a *survey* of world history. **5** The process of finding out and making a record of the outline, measurements, and position of any part of the earth's surface, especially by use of geometry and trigonometry. **6** A measured plan and description, as of a portion of land or of a road.

sur·vey·ing \(ˌ)sər-ˈvā-ing\ *n.* The act or occupation of a surveyor; the branch of mathematics that teaches the art of measuring and representing the earth's surface accurately.

sur·vey·or \(ˌ)sər-ˈvā-ər\ *n.* **1** One who surveys. **2** A person whose occupation is surveying land.

sur·viv·al \sər-ˈvīv-l\ *n.* **1** A remaining alive; a continuing to exist, especially after others of the kind have passed away. **2** Something that lives on or lasts after others like it have gone.

sur·vive \sər-ˈvīv\ *v.;* **sur·vived**; **sur·viv·ing.** **1** To remain alive. **2** To live on; to continue to exist; as, a quaint custom that had *survived* from a time long past. **3** To live longer than; to outlast; as, to *survive* a flood; to *survive* one's father.

sur·vi·vor \sər-ˈvīv-r\ *n.* One that survives.

sus·cep·ti·ble \sə-ˈsep-təb-l\ *adj.* **1** Of such a nature as to permit or admit; as, words *susceptible* of being misunderstood. **2** Having little resistance; as, a person *susceptible* to colds. **3** Easily affected or impressed. — **sus·cep·ti·bil·i·ty** \-ˌsəp-tə-ˈbil-ət-ē\ *n.* — **sus·cep·ti·bly** \-ˈsep-tə-blē\ *adv.*

sus·pect \ˈsəs-ˌpekt, sə-ˈspekt\ *adj.* Regarded with suspicion; distrusted; suspected; as, a person whose honesty is *suspect.* — \ˈsəs-ˌpekt\ *n.* A person or thing suspected. — \sə-ˈspekt\ *v.* **1** To doubt; to distrust; as, to *suspect* a person's sincerity. **2** To imagine to be guilty, without proof. **3** To surmise; to guess.

sus·pend \sə-ˈspend\ *v.* **1** To bar temporarily from any privilege or office; as, to *suspend* a student from school. **2** To stop or do away with for a time; to withhold; as, to *suspend* publication. **3** To cease for a time from operation or activity. **4** To hang; as, to *suspend* a ball by a thread. **5** To keep from falling or sinking through force of gravity; as, dust *suspended* in the air.

sus·pend·ers \sə-ˈspend-rz\ *n. pl.* Two supporting straps that pass over the shoulders and are attached to trousers or a skirt.

sus·pense \sə-ˈspen(t)s\ *n.* Uncertainty, anxiety, or worry as to the result of something.

sus·pen·sion \sə-ˈspench-n\ *n.* **1** A suspending or a being suspended. **2** Temporary forced withdrawal from a privilege or office. **3** A temporary removal of a rule or condition. **4** A device by which something is suspended. **5** The state of a solid when its particles are mixed with but undissolved in a gas, liquid, or another solid. **6** A mixture of two substances one of which is in this state.

suspension bridge. A bridge that has its roadway suspended from cables.

sus·pi·cion \sə-ˈspish-n\ *n.* **1** A suspecting or a being suspected. **2** An impression or feeling that something is wrong; doubt; distrust. **3** A slight trace; as, a boy with just a *suspicion* of dirt behind his ears. — For synonyms see *doubt.*

sus·pi·cious \sə-ˈspish-əs\ *adj.* **1** Open or liable to suspicion; such as to arouse distrust; as, *suspicious* actions. **2** Inclined to suspect or distrust. **3** Showing distrust. — **sus·pi·cious·ly**, *adv.*

sus·tain \sə-ˈstān\ *v.* **1** To provide for the support of something; as, food to *sustain* an army. **2** To keep up; to prolong; as, to *sustain* a note in singing. **3** To support or prop up; as, the pillars that *sustain* the roof. **4** To keep from sinking or giving way; to buoy up; as, to be *sustained* by hope. **5** To suffer; to undergo; as, to *sustain* an injury. **6** To make certain; to prove; to confirm. — **sus·tain·a·ble** \-ˈstā-nəb-l\ *adj.* — **sus·tain·er** \-ˈstān-r\ *n.*

sus·te·nance \ˈsəs-tə-nən(t)s\ *n.* **1** A means of support; especially, food or nourishment. **2** The action of sustaining or a being sustained.

su·ture \ˈsüch-r\ *n.* **1** A strand, as of silk or wire, used in surgery to join parts of the body. **2** The act of joining, as the edges of a wound, by sewing. **3** A line or seam, as between bones of the skull, along which parts unite.

su·zer·ain \ˈsüz-r-ən, -r-ˌān\ *n.* **1** A feudal lord; an overlord. **2** A nation that has political control over another nation. — **su·zer·ain·ty** \-r(-)ən-tē\ *n.*

svelte \ˈsvelt\ *adj.* Slender; lissome.

S.W. Abbreviation for *southwest.*

swab \ˈswäb\ *v.;* **swabbed**; **swab·bing.** To wipe or clean with or as if with a swab; as, to *swab* a cut with iodine; to *swab* a deck. — *n.* **1** A mop, especially a rope mop. **2** A small piece of soft material, usually on the end of a small stick, used to apply medicine or to remove a discharge from sores or wounds. **3** A specimen collected in this way for testing. **4** A sponge attached to the end of a rod to clean the bore of a gun.

swad·dle \ˈswäd-l\ *v.;* **swad·dled**; **swad·dling** \-l(-)ing\. To bind a newborn infant in bands of cloth, or **swaddling clothes**; to wrap up, as in bandages. — *n.* Something used for swaddling.

swag \ˈswag\ *n. Slang.* Loot; plunder.

swag·ger \ˈswag-r\ *v.;* **swag·gered**; **swag·ger·ing** \-r(-)ing\. **1** To walk with a conceited strut. **2** To boast or brag in a noisy way. — *n.* A conceited way of walking or talking. — **swag·ger·er** \-r-r\ *n.*

swain \ˈswān\ *n.* A rustic lover.

swal·low \ˈswäl-ō\ *n.* Any bird of a family with long pointed wings and, generally, forked tails, noted for graceful flight and regular migrations.

swal·low \ˈswäl-ō\ *v.* **1** To take into the stomach through the mouth and throat. **2** To take in as if in this way; as, a ship *swallowed* by the sea. **3** To accept without investigation or question. **4** To take back; to retract; as, to *swallow* one's words. **5** To keep from expressing or showing; as, to *swallow* one's pride. **6** To put up with; to bear. — *n.* **1** The action of swallowing. **2** As much as is swallowed at one time.

swal·low·tail \ˈswäl-ō-ˌtāl\ *n.* **1** A swallow's tail or a tail similarly forked and tapering. **2** Any of a number of large bright-colored butterflies. — **swal·low-tailed** \-ˈtāld\ *adj.*

swam. Past tense of *swim.*

swamp \ˈswämp, ˈswȯmp\ *n.* Wet, spongy land; a marsh. — *v.* **1** To cause to capsize in water or fill with water and sink. **2** To fill with water; to sink after filling with water. **3** To overwhelm; as, to be *swamped* with work. — **swampy** \ˈswämp-ē, ˈswȯmp-ē\ *adj.*

swan \ˈswän\ *n.* A heavy-bodied but graceful water bird with a long, curving neck.

swan's-down \ˈswänz-ˌdaůn\ *n.* **1** The down of the swan. **2** Usually **swans·down.** A soft, thick cloth of wool mixed with silk, rayon, or cotton.

swan song. **1** A song that a dying swan is said to sing. **2** A last effort, event, or piece of work.

swap \ˈswäp\ *v.;* **swapped**; **swap·ping**. To exchange; to trade; to barter. — *n.* A trade.

sward \ˈswȯrd\ *n.* A grassy surface; turf.

swarm \ˈswȯrm\ *n.* **1** A large number of honeybees with a queen that leave a hive together to form a new colony elsewhere; a hive of bees. **2** A large crowd in motion; a throng; a horde; as, a *swarm* of people. — *v.* **1** Of bees, to collect in a swarm and fly off to form a new colony. **2** To migrate, move, or gather in a swarm or a large crowd; to throng. **3** To contain a swarm; to be filled or covered with a swarm of something.

swarthy \ˈswȯr-t͟hē, -thē\ *adj.;* **swarth·i·er**; **swarth·i·est.** Dark in color or complexion; dusky.

swash \ˈswäsh, ˈswȯsh\ *v.* To move or strike with a splashing sound; to splash; as, to *swash* water around in a pail. — *n.* **1** The splashing of water against something. **2** The sound of splashing.

swash·buck·ler \ˈswäsh-ˌbək-lər, ˈswȯsh-\ *n.* A boasting soldier; a braggart. — **swash·buck·ling** \-ˌbək-l(-)ing\ *adj.* or *n.*

swas·ti·ka \ˈswäs-tik-ə, swä-ˈstēk-ə\ *n.* A symbol in the shape of a cross with the ends of the arms bent at right angles.

swat \ˈswät\ *v.;* **swat·ted**; **swat·ting.** To hit hard. — *n.* A hard blow. — **swat·ter** \ˈswät-r\ *n.*

swath \ˈswäth, ˈswät͟h\ or **swathe** \ˈswät͟h\ *n.* **1** A row, strip, or stripe. **2** The sweep of a scythe or a mowing machine. **3** A single continuous course cut in mowing. **4** A row of cut grass or grain.

swathe \ˈswät͟h\ *v.;* **swathed**; **swath·ing.** **1** To swaddle. **2** To wrap around in the manner of a bandage. **3** To cover or envelop. Fog *swathed* the river. — *n.* A bandage; a band.

sway \ˈswā\ *v.* **1** To swing back and forth or from side to side. **2** To bend or be bent to one side; to lean; to incline. **3** To cause to swing from side to side. **4** To influence; as, to *sway* an audience by a speech. — *n.* **1** A swaying or a being swayed. **2** A controlling influence; rule; governing power.

sway-backed \ˈswā-ˌbakt\ or **sway-back** \-ˌbak\ *adj.* Having an unusually hollow or sagged back; as, a *sway-backed* horse.

swear \ˈswar, ˈswer\ *v.;* **swore** \ˈswōr, ˈswȯr\; **sworn** \ˈswōrn, ˈswȯrn\; **swear·ing.** **1** To take an oath, as upon the Bible. **2** To declare, promise, or pledge solemnly; to vow; as, to *swear* allegiance. **3** To bind by a solemn promise; as, to *swear* to secrecy. **4** To administer an oath to; as, to *swear* a witness; to *swear* in an official. **5** To use profane language. — **swear by.** **1** To take an oath by. **2** To have complete confidence in. — **swear off.** To vow to give up, as a bad habit.

sweat \ˈswet\ *v.;* **sweat** or **sweat·ed**; **sweat·ing.** **1** To give off perceptible salty moisture through the pores of the skin; to perspire. **2** To give off moisture, as green plants closely packed. **3** To form drops of moisture. Stones *sweat* at night. **4** To work so that one perspires; to work hard; as, to *sweat* over a lesson. **5** To soak with sweat; as, to *sweat* a collar. **6** To get rid of or lose by perspiring; as, to *sweat* out a fever. **7** To overwork; as, a factory that *sweats* its employees. — *n.* **1** Moisture given off in sweating; perspiration. **2** A condition or a spell of sweating; as, to be in a *sweat.*

sweat·er \ˈswet-r\ *n.* **1** One that sweats. **2** A knitted or crocheted jacket, jumper, or blouse.

sweat gland. A gland that secretes perspiration through the pores of the skin.

sweat shirt. A loose, closely knit pullover, worn by athletes before and after exercising.

sweat·shop \ˈswet-ˌshäp\ *n.* A shop or factory in which workers are employed for long hours at low wages and under unhealthy conditions.

sweaty \ˈswet-ē\ *adj.;* **sweat·i·er**; **sweat·i·est.** **1** Wet or stained with sweat; smelling of sweat. **2** Causing sweat; as, a *sweaty* day

Swede \'swēd\ *n.* **1** One of the people of Sweden. **2** [often with a small letter] A rutabaga.

Swed·ish \'swēd-ish\ *adj.* Of or relating to Sweden. — *n.* **1** The people of Sweden — used as a plural, usually with *the.* **2** The language of Sweden.

sweep \'swēp\ *v.;* **swept** \'swept\; **sweep·ing.** **1** To brush away or off. **2** To remove by brushing with a broom. **3** To clean by brushing with or as if with a broom. **4** To strip or clear by blows or gusts. The storm *swept* the decks clean. **5** To move across with swiftness, force, or destruction; as, a raging torrent *swept* the fields. **6** To gather or take up with a single swift movement. **7** To touch a surface with an action or result like that of a brush. The musician's fingers *swept* the piano keys. **8** To move across, extend across, or cover a wide range; as, to *sweep* the horizon with a glance. **9** To move with a stately air; as, to *sweep* from a room. — *n.* **1** The act of sweeping; a clearing out as if with a broom; as, to make a clean *sweep.* **2** A sweeping movement. **3** A single stroke; as, at one *sweep.* **4** Range; scope; as, the whole *sweep* of human knowledge. **5** A curve; a bend; as, the *sweep* of an arch. **6** A person who sweeps; as, a chimney *sweep.* **7** A long oar. **8** A long pole pivoted on a high post and used to raise and lower a bucket in a well. **9** [often in the plural] A sweepstakes.

sweep·er \'swēp-r\ *n.* One that sweeps.

sweep·ing \'swēp-ing\ *n.* **1** The act of one that sweeps. **2** [in the plural] Things collected by sweeping, as scraps or dirt. — *adj.* **1** That sweeps; as, a *sweeping* gust of wind. **2** Of great extent or wide range; as, a *sweeping* statement; a *sweeping* victory. — **sweep·ing·ly,** *adv.*

sweep·stakes \'swēp-ˌstāks\ *n. sing. and pl.* **1** Also **sweep·stake** \-ˌstāk\. A horse race in which the stakes are put up by the owners of the horses in the race; the entire sum of the stakes in such a race, usually awarded by agreement to the winner. **2** A lottery based on a sweepstakes.

sweet \'swēt\ *adj.* **1** Having an agreeable taste like that of sugar. **2** Dear; beloved. **3** Fresh in taste; not stale; not salt; as, *sweet* butter. **4** Having a relatively large sugar content. **5** Of soil, not acid. **6** Fragrant; as, a *sweet* smell. **7** Soft; melodious; as, *sweet* music. **8** Attractive; pleasing; as, a *sweet* face. **9** Kindly; mild; as, a *sweet* disposition. **10** Of a motor, smooth-running and quiet. — *adv.* Sweetly. — *n.* **1** Something sweet. **2** *Chiefly British.* A sweet dish served for dessert. **3** [in the plural] Confectionery; candy. **4** A dearly beloved person. **5** Sweet quality; sweetness.

sweet·bread \'swēt-ˌbred\ *n.* The thymus or pancreas of certain animals, as calves or lambs.

sweet·bri·er or **sweet·bri·ar** \'swēt-ˌbrīr\ *n.* A European rose with stout prickles and single pink flowers.

sweet corn. A variety of Indian corn with kernels having a high sugar content when immature.

sweet·en \'swēt-n\ *v.;* **sweet·ened; sweet·en·ing** \-n(-)ing\. **1** To make sweet. **2** To become sweet. — **sweet·en·er** \-n(-)ər\ *n.*

sweet·en·ing \'swēt-n(-)ing\ *n.* **1** The act or process of making sweet. **2** That which sweetens.

sweet gum. A North American tree with leaves resembling maple and turning scarlet in autumn, prickly globe-shaped fruits, and hard wood.

sweet·heart \'swēt-ˌhärt, -ˌhȧrt\ *n.* A loved person; a lover.

sweet·ish \'swēt-ish\ *adj.* Somewhat sweet.

sweet·ly \'swēt-lē\ *adv.* In a sweet or pleasing manner; as, to sing *sweetly.*

sweet·meat \'swēt-ˌmēt\ *n.* Any delicacy rich in sugar; especially, a piece of candy or candied fruit.

sweet pea. **1** A cultivated garden plant with slender climbing stems and large fragrant flowers of many colors. **2** The flower of this plant.

sweet potato. **1** A tropical vine related to the morning-glory, with variously shaped leaves and purplish flowers. **2** The large, sweet, mealy root of this vine, cooked and eaten as a vegetable.

sweet Wil·liam or **sweet wil·liam** \'swēt 'wil-yəm\. A variety of pink whose many-colored flowers grow in thick, flat clusters.

swell \'swel\ *v.;* **swelled** \'sweld\; **swelled** \'sweld\ or **swol·len** \'swō-lən\; **swell·ing.** **1** To grow or make bigger. **2** To extend upward or outward; to bulge. **3** To fill or be filled with an emotion; as, a heart *swelling* with gratitude. **4** To increase gradually in loudness. — *n.* **1** An increase in size, quantity, or value. **2** A long rolling wave. **3** In music, an increase and decrease of sound, or the sign showing this [< >]. **4** A device in an organ for controlling loudness. **5** A fashionable person. — *adj.* **1** Stylish. **2** Excellent; first-rate.

swell·ing \'swel-ing\ *n.* The condition of being swollen; an abnormal enlargement, usually caused by inflammation.

swel·ter \'swelt-r\ *v.;* **swel·tered; swel·ter·ing** \'swelt-r-ing, 'swel-tring\. To suffer from the heat; to sweat; as, to *swelter* in the jungle.

swel·ter·ing \'swelt-r-ing, 'swel-tring\ *adj.* That causes one to swelter. — **swel·ter·ing·ly,** *adv.*

swept. Past tense and past part. of *sweep.*

swept-back \'swep(t)-ˌbak\ *adj.* **1** Of airplane wings, slanting toward the tail of the plane to form an acute angle with the body. **2** Of aircraft, having swept-back wings.

swerve \'swərv\ *v.;* **swerved; swerv·ing.** To go out of a straight line; to turn aside; as, to *swerve* to avoid hitting an oncoming car. — *n.* A swerving.

swift \'swift\ *adj.* **1** Moving or able to move with great speed; as, a *swift* horse. **2** Happening or done quickly; as, a *swift* transaction. — *adv.* Swiftly. — *n.* An insect-eating bird related to the hummingbird and mostly sooty black with long narrow wings. — **swift·ly,** *adv.*

swig \'swig\ *n.* A long drink. — *v.;* **swigged; swig·ging.** To drink in long gulps.

swill \'swil\ *v.* **1** To wash or rinse; to drench. **2** To drink or swallow greedily; to guzzle. — *n.* **1** Kitchen refuse mixed with a liquid and fed to hogs.

2 Garbage. **3** The swilling of liquor; a swig.

swim \\'swim\\ *v.;* **swam** \\'swam\\; **swum** \\'swəm\\; **swim·ming. 1** To move through or in water by moving arms, legs, fins, or tail. **2** To glide smoothly and quietly. **3** To be covered or surrounded with or as if with a liquid; as, meat *swimming* in gravy. **4** To cross by swimming; as, to *swim* the river. — *n.* The act of swimming. — **in the swim.** In the main current of activity; up on the latest fashion or interest; as, to get back *in the swim* after an illness; an extremely popular boy who was really *in the swim.* — **swim·mer** \\'swim-r\\ *n.*

swim \\'swim\\ *v.;* **swam** \\'swam\\; **swum** \\'swəm\\; **swim·ming. 1** To be dizzy. My head is *swimming.* **2** To move or seem to move dizzily.

swim fins. Fan-shaped plastic or rubber devices worn strapped to the feet of swimmers.

swim·ming \\'swim-ing\\ *n.* The act or sport of swimming and diving. — *adj.* **1** That swims; capable of swimming; as, *swimming* birds. **2** Used in or for swimming; as, a *swimming* suit.

swim·ming·ly \\'swim-ing-lē\\ *adv.* In an easy, smooth manner; as, to get along *swimmingly.*

swin·dle \\'swind-l\\ *v.;* **swin·dled; swin·dling** \\-l(-)ing\\. To get money or property from by fraud or deceit; to cheat or defraud. — *n.* An act of swindling; a cheating. — **swin·dler** \\'swin-dlər\\ *n.*

swine \\'swīn\\ *n. sing. and pl.* **1** Any of a group of short-legged hoofed mammals with thick bristly skin and a long mobile snout, including the domestic hog. **2** An especially contemptible person.

swine·herd \\'swīn-ˌhərd\\ *n.* A herder of swine.

swing \\'swing\\ *v.;* **swung** \\'swəng\\; **swing·ing. 1** To move rapidly in a sweeping curve; as, to *swing* a bat. **2** To throw or toss in a circle or back and forth; as, to *swing* a lasso. **3** To sway to and fro. **4** To hang or be hung so as to move freely back and forth or in a curve; as, to *swing* a hammock between two trees. **5** To pivot; move or turn around on or as if on hinges; as, to *swing* troops into line. **6** To march or walk with free, swaying movements. **7** To manage or handle successfully; as, to *swing* the job. — *n.* **1** The act of swinging. **2** A swinging movement, blow, or rhythm. **3** The distance through which something swings; as, the *swing* of the pendulum. **4** A swinging seat hung by overhead ropes. **5** In full, **swing music.** A style of jazz in which the melody is freely interpreted and improvised on by the individual players within a steadily maintained and usually lively rhythm.

swin·ish \\'swī-nish\\ *adj.* Of or like a swine; suitable to a swine; beastly. — **swin·ish·ly,** *adv.*

swipe \\'swīp\\ *n.* A blow delivered with a long, sweeping motion. — *v.;* **swiped; swip·ing. 1** To strike with a swipe. **2** To snatch; to steal.

swirl \\'swərl\\ *v.* To move with a whirling motion; to whirl; to eddy. — *n.* A whirl; an eddy.

swish \\'swish\\ *v.* **1** To make a rustling or hissing sound. **2** To move with a swish. — *n.* A sound like that made by a whip rapidly cutting the air.

Swiss \\'swis\\ *adj.* Of or relating to Switzerland. — *n. sing. and pl.* A native or inhabitant of Switzerland.

Swiss chard. Chard.

switch \\'swich\\ *n.* **1** A slender, flexible whip, rod, or twig. **2** The end of the tail of some animals, such as cows. **3** A device for making, breaking, or changing the connections in an electric circuit. **4** A device for adjusting the rails of a track so that a train or streetcar may be turned from the track on which it is running to another track. **5** A blow with a switch or whip. **6** The act of turning an electric switch or a railway switch. **7** A change or shift from one thing to another; as, a *switch* in one's opinions. — *v.* **1** To strike or whip with a switch. **2** To swing or whisk. **3** To turn, shift, or change by operating a switch. **4** To change or shift.

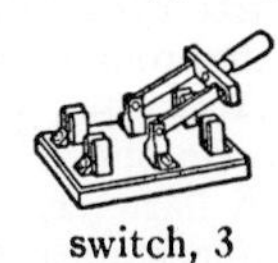
switch, 3

switch·back \\'swich-ˌbak\\ *n.* A zigzag road or arrangement of tracks for overcoming a steep grade.

switch·board \\'swich-ˌbōrd, -ˌbȯrd\\ *n.* An apparatus consisting of a board or panel on which are mounted electric switches so arranged that a number of circuits may be connected, combined, and controlled, as in a telephone exchange.

switch·man \\'swich-mən\\ *n.; pl.* **switch·men** \\-mən\\. One who attends a railroad switch.

swiv·el \\'swiv-l\\ *n.* A thing fastened on another thing in such a way that either can turn while the other remains fixed; especially, a part or piece that turns on a bolt or pin; as, a chair mounted on a *swivel.* — *v.;* **swiv·eled** or **swiv·elled; swiv·el·ing** or **swiv·el·ling** \\-l(-)ing\\. To swing or turn on or as if on a swivel.

swivel chair. A chair with a swiveling seat.

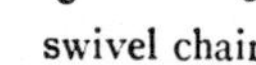
swivel chair

swollen. A past part. of *swell.*

swoon \\'swün\\ *v.* To faint. — *n.* A faint.

swoop \\'swüp\\ *v.* To descend, or to pounce suddenly, like a hawk attacking its prey. — *n.* A sudden descent or attack, as of a hawk.

sword \\'sōrd, 'sȯrd\\ *n.* **1** A weapon having a long and usually sharp-pointed and sharp-edged blade. **2** Something that kills or punishes as effectively as a sword. **3** Military power or the use of it; war.

sword·fish \\'sōrd-ˌfish, 'sȯrd-\\ *n.; pl.* **sword·fish** or **sword·fish·es.** A very large ocean food fish having a long swordlike beak formed by the bones of the upper jaw.

sword·play \\'sōrd-ˌplā, 'sȯrd-\\ *n.* The art or skill of using a sword, especially in fencing.

swords·man \\'sōrdz-mən, 'sȯrdz-\\ *n.; pl.* **swords·men** \\-mən\\. **1** One who fights with a sword. **2** One skilled in the use of the sword; a fencer.

swore. Past tense of *swear.*

sworn. Past part. of *swear.*

swum. Past part. of *swim.*

swung. Past tense and past part. of *swing.*

syc·a·more \'sik-m-ˌōr, -ˌȯr\ *n.* **1** The common fig tree (**sycamore fig**) of Egypt and Asia Minor. **2** A maple tree of Europe and Asia. **3** A broad-leaved tree with light-brown, flaky bark, and round fruits like buttons; the American plane tree.

sycamore: leaves and fruit

syc·o·phant \'sik-ə-fənt, 'sīk-\ *n.* A flatterer, especially of great or important people.

syl·lab·ic \sə-'lab-ik\ *adj.* **1** Of or relating to a syllable or syllables; as, *syllabic* division; *syllabic* accent. **2** Forming a syllable, as the *a* in *apex*. — **syl·lab·i·cal·ly** \-ik-l(-)ē\ *adv.*

syl·lab·i·cate \sə-'lab-ə-ˌkāt\ *v.;* **syl·lab·i·cat·ed**; **syl·lab·i·cat·ing.** To form or divide into syllables.

syl·lab·i·ca·tion \sə-ˌlab-ə-'kāsh-n\ *n.* The forming of syllables; the division of words into syllables.

syllabic consonant. A consonant that is the nearest approach to a vowel in a syllable, as the \l\ in \'bat-l\ (*battle*) or the \n\ in \'līs-n(t)s\ (*license*).

syl·lab·i·fy \sə-'lab-ə-ˌfī\ *v.;* **syl·lab·i·fied** \-ˌfīd\; **syl·lab·i·fy·ing.** To syllabicate. — **syl·lab·i·fi·ca·tion** \-ˌlab-ə-fə-'kāsh-n\ *n.*

syl·la·ble \'sil-əb-l\ *n.* **1** One of the parts into which spoken words break when sounds called consonants come between sounds called vowels, as in \'en-ē\ (*any*), and sometimes when a vowel follows a vowel or a consonant follows a consonant, as in \'kā-ˌäs\ (*chaos*), \'bat-l\ (*battle*). **2** One or more letters of the alphabet that stand for such a part of a spoken word. **3** One of the parts into which spelled words are sometimes divided to show a place where a writer may divide a word.

syl·la·bus \'sil-ə-bəs\ *n.; pl.* **syl·la·bus·es** \-bə-səz\ or **syl·la·bi** \-ˌbī\. A summary of chief topics and sometimes of subtopics, as of a course of study.

syl·lo·gism \'sil-ə-ˌjiz-m\ *n.* A brief form for stating an argument or instance of reasoning from the general to the particular, consisting of two statements and a conclusion that must be true if these two statements are true, as in the example: All lawbreakers deserve punishment; AB is a lawbreaker; therefore AB deserves punishment.

sylph \'silf\ *n.* **1** An imaginary being inhabiting the air. **2** A slender, graceful woman.

syl·van or **sil·van** \'silv-n\ *adj.* [A compound made from Latin *silva*, *sylva* meaning "forest" and the English adjective suffix *-an*.] **1** Of or relating to the woods or forests. **2** Characteristic of the forest. **3** Abounding in woods or forests.

sym·bi·o·sis \ˌsim-ˌbī-'ō-səs, -bē-\ *n.* The living together of two dissimilar animals or plants, or an animal and a plant, in intimate association, especially one that is advantageous or even necessary to either or both. — **sym·bi·ot·ic** \-'ät-ik\ *adj.*

sym·bol \'sim-bl\ *n.* **1** That which stands for something else; something concrete that represents or suggests another thing that cannot in itself be represented or visualized; an emblem. The cross is the *symbol* of Christianity. **2** A letter, character, or sign used instead of a word or words, as to represent a quantity, position, relationship, direction, or something to be done. The sign + is the *symbol* for addition. — For synonyms see *emblem.*

sym·bol·ic \sim-'bäl-ik\ or **sym·bol·i·cal** \-ik-l\ *adj.* **1** Of, relating to, or using symbols or symbolism; as, a *symbolic* meaning; *symbolic* art. **2** Having the function or significance of a symbol; as, a *symbolic* figure. — **sym·bol·i·cal·ly** \-ik-l(-)ē\ *adv.*

sym·bol·ism \'sim-bl-ˌiz-m\ *n.* **1** Representation by means of symbols or emblems. **2** Symbols used, as by a church in its rites.

sym·bol·ize \'sim-bl-ˌīz\ *v.;* **sym·bol·ized**; **sym·bol·iz·ing.** **1** To serve as a symbol of; to typify; to stand for. A lion *symbolizes* courage. **2** To use symbols; to represent by a symbol or symbols.

sym·met·ric \sə-'me-trik\ *adj.* Symmetrical.

sym·met·ri·cal \sə-'me-trik-l\ *adj.* Having or showing symmetry. — **sym·met·ri·cal·ly** \-trik-l(-)ē\ *adv.*

sym·me·try \'sim-ə-trē\ *n.; pl.* **sym·me·tries.** **1** Correspondence in size, shape, and position of parts that are on opposite sides of a dividing line or plane or distributed about a center or axis. **2** Regular and harmonious arrangement of parts.

sym·pa·thet·ic \ˌsimp-ə-'thet-ik\ *adj.* **1** Fitting one's mood or disposition; congenial; as, a *sympathetic* atmosphere. **2** Feeling sympathy; possessed of a tendency to sympathize. **3** Relating to, showing, or arising from sympathy; as, a *sympathetic* strike of factory workers. **4** Favorably inclined or disposed. **5** In physics, of or relating to a vibration produced in one body by vibrations of the same rate in a neighboring body. **6** Of or relating to the part of the nervous system that regulates certain involuntary activities in the body, as the beating of the heart. — **sym·pa·thet·i·cal·ly** \-ik-l(-)ē\ *adv.*

sym·pa·thize \'simp-ə-ˌthīz\ *v.;* **sym·pa·thized**; **sym·pa·thiz·ing.** **1** To feel or show pity or compassion. **2** To understand by putting oneself in another's place; as, to *sympathize* with a child's fear of the dark. **3** To understand and share or approve of; as, to *sympathize* with a friend's ambitions.

sym·pa·thy \'simp-ə-thē\ *n.; pl.* **sym·pa·thies.** **1** An agreement or harmony of likes, interests, or aims, forming a bond of good will; as, the *sympathy* between friends. **2** The entering into and sharing the feelings, interests, or aims of another, or the ability to do this. **3** Compassion; pity; as, to have *sympathy* for the poor. **4** An inclination to agree with or support; as, to have no *sympathy* with a proposed plan. **5** An expression of sorrow for another's loss, grief, or misfortune. — For synonyms see *pity.*

sym·phon·ic \sim-'fän-ik\ *adj.* **1** Of or relating to harmony, as of sounds or colors; as, the *symphonic* murmur of night sounds. **2** Of, relating to, or in the manner of a symphony.

sym·pho·ny \'sim(p)-fə-nē\ *n.; pl.* **sym·pho·nies.** **1** A harmony, as of many sounds or colors; as, a *symphony* of bird calls; a *symphony* of roses. **2** A long musical composition consisting usually of four main divisions each with a different rhythm, time, and theme, composed for a full orchestra. **3** Also **symphony orchestra**. A large orchestra that plays symphonies and similar compositions.

sym·po·si·um \sim-'pō-zē-əm, -'pōzh-m\ *n.; pl.* **sym·po·si·ums** \-'pō-zē-əmz, -'pōzh-mz\ or **sym·po·sia** \-'pō-zē-ə, -'pōzh-ə\. **1** A conference at which a particular topic is discussed and opinions gathered. **2** A collection of opinions on a subject.

symp·tom \'sim(p)-təm\ *n.* **1** A noticeable change in the structure or functions of a human being, animal, or plant, indicating the presence of disease. **2** An indication; a sign; as, *symptoms* of fear.

symp·tom·at·ic \ˌsim(p)-tə-'mat-ik\ *adj.* Being a symptom; characteristic; indicative.

syn. Abbreviation for *synonym.*

syn·a·gogue \'sin-ə-ˌgäg\ *n.* **1** An assembly of Jews organized chiefly for worship. **2** A Jewish house of worship.

syn·apse \'sin-ˌaps\ *n.* The point at which a nervous impulse passes from one neuron to another.

syn·chro·nize \'sin(g)-krə-ˌnīz\ *v.;* **syn·chro·nized**; **syn·chro·niz·ing. 1** To happen at the same time; to agree in time. **2** To cause to agree in time; to represent, arrange, or tabulate according to dates or time; as, to *synchronize* the events of European history. **3** To make synchronous in operation, as two gears. — **syn·chro·ni·za·tion** \ˌsin(g)-krə-nə-'zāsh-n\ *n.* — **syn·chro·niz·er** \'sin(g)-krə-ˌnīz-r\ *n.*

syn·chro·nous \'sin(g)-krə-nəs\ *adj.* **1** Happening at the same time; simultaneous. **2** Working, moving, or occurring together at the same rate and at the proper time with respect to each other. — **syn·chro·nous·ly,** *adv.*

syn·co·pate \'sin(g)-kə-ˌpāt\ *v.;* **syn·co·pat·ed**; **syn·co·pat·ing. 1** To shorten a word by syncopation. **2** In music, to modify by syncopation.

syn·co·pa·tion \ˌsin(g)-kə-'pāsh-n\ *n.* **1** The loss or cutting out of one or more sounds or letters from the middle of a word. **2** A syncopated word. "Laundress" is a *syncopation* of "launderess". **3** In music, the placing of accented notes on beats that are not usually accented, as in jazz. **4** Music that has syncopation.

syn·di·cate \'sin-dik-ət\ *n.* **1** An association of persons authorized to carry out a financial or industrial undertaking. **2** A business concern that sells material, as photographs, comic strips, and special articles, for publication in the press on specified dates. — \'sin-də-ˌkāt\ *v.;* **syn·di·cat·ed**; **syn·di·cat·ing. 1** To combine into a syndicate; to manage as a syndicate. **2** To publish through a syndicate, as of newspapers; as, to *syndicate* a story.

syn·od \'sin-əd\ *n.* **1** A church council. **2** An assembly or council; a meeting or convention.

syn·o·nym \'sin-ə-ˌnim\ *n.* One of two or more words of the same language having the same or nearly the same meaning in all or certain senses. "Talk" is a *synonym* of the word "speak".

syn·on·y·mous \sə-'nän-ə-məs\ *adj.* **1** Being a synonym or being synonyms. **2** Having the same or nearly the same meaning as another word.

syn·op·sis \sə-'näp-səs\ *n.; pl.* **syn·op·ses** \-ˌsēz\. A general view of a whole subject; a condensed statement; a summary; an abstract; as, a *synopsis* of a play. — **syn·op·tic** \sə-'näp-tik\ *adj.*

syn·tac·tic \sin-'tak-tik\ or **syn·tac·ti·cal** \-tik-l\ *adj.* Of or relating to syntax; according to the rules of syntax. — **syn·tac·ti·cal·ly** \-tik-l(-)ē\ *adv.*

syn·tax \'sin-ˌtaks\ *n.* Sentence structure; the relation to one another of the words in a sentence.

syn·the·sis \'sin(t)th-ə-səs\ *n.; pl.* **syn·the·ses** \-ˌsēz\. **1** The combination of parts into a whole; the making of something complex out of separate or simple elements. **2** The whole so formed.

syn·the·size \'sin(t)th-ə-ˌsīz\ *v.;* **syn·the·sized**; **syn·the·siz·ing.** To produce by synthesis.

syn·thet·ic \sin-'thet-ik\ *adj.* **1** Of or relating to synthesis. **2** Formed by artificial means; artificial; as, *synthetic* silk. — **syn·thet·i·cal·ly** \-ik-l(-)ē\ *adv.*

syph·i·lis \'sif-l-əs\ *n.* A chronic contagious disease, ordinarily venereal, caused by a spirochete. — **syph·i·lit·ic** \ˌsif-l-'it-ik\ *adj.*

sy·phon \'sīf-n\ *n.* or *v.* Siphon.

Syr·i·an \'sir-ē-ən\ *adj.* Of or relating to Syria. — *n.* A native or inhabitant of Syria.

sy·rin·ga \sə-'ring-gə\ *n.* [From scientific Latin, there borrowed from Greek *syring-*, the stem of *syrinx* meaning "pipe", "tube", and so called because the stems of some species were formerly used for pipe stems.] A garden shrub related to the hydrangea, with white or creamy, often fragrant flowers; the mock orange.

syringa

sy·ringe \sə-'rinj, 'sir-inj\ *n.* A small hand pump with a nozzle or hollow needle, used for cleansing wounds or injecting liquids into the body. — *v.;* **sy·ringed**; **sy·ring·ing.** To cleanse with a syringe.

syr·up or **sir·up** \'sər-əp, 'sir-\ *n.* **1** A thick, sticky liquid, usually sweet, made from concentrated juices of fruits or herbs. **2** A thick solution of sugar and water boiled together, sometimes flavored or medicated. — **syr·upy** or **sir·upy** \-ə-pē\ *adj.*

sys·tem \'sist-m\ *n.* **1** A group of objects or units so combined as to form a whole and operate or move interdependently and in harmony; as, a railroad *system.* **2** The body considered as a whole. The disease affected his entire *system.* **3** A group of organs of the body that carry on a function necessary for life; as, the nervous *system.* **4** A scheme or method of governing or arranging; a method of procedure or classification. **5** Regular method or order. — For synonyms see *order.*

sys·tem·at·ic \ˌsist-m-'at-ik\ *adj.* **1** Being or forming a system; systematized; as, a *systematic* course of study. **2** Having or using a system; methodical; orderly. **3** Carrying out a plan with thoroughness or regularity; as, *systematic* efforts. — **sys·tem·at·i·cal·ly** \-ik-l(-)ē\ *adv.*

sys·tem·a·tize \'sist-m-ə-ˌtīz\ *v.;* **sys·tem·a·tized; sys·tem·a·tiz·ing.** To make into a system; to arrange according to a system.

sys·tem·ic \sis-'tem-ik\ *adj.* Of or relating to the body as a whole; as, a *systemic* disease.

sys·to·le \'sis-tə-(ˌ)lē\ *n.* The contraction of the heart, forcing the blood onward and keeping up its circulation. — **sys·tol·ic** \sis-'täl-ik\ *adj.*

t \'tē\ *n.; pl.* **t's** \'tēz\. The twentieth letter of the alphabet. — **to a T.** Precisely; exactly; perfectly.

tab \'tab\ *n.* **1** A small flap, strip, or tag attached to something, as for fastening or covering, pulling, or hanging up; as, pockets with *tabs;* an index *tab.* **2** Account; check; especially, a strict watch or check — used chiefly in the phrase *keep tabs on.* — *v.;* **tabbed; tab·bing.** To provide or ornament with tabs; as, *tabbed* pockets.

tab·ard \'tab-rd\ *n.* **1** A cloak worn by knights. **2** A herald's garment displaying the arms of his lord.

tab·by \'tab-ē\ *n.; pl.* **tab·bies. 1** A yellowish gray domestic cat banded and varied with black. **2** Any domestic cat; especially, a female cat.

tab·er·nac·le \'tab-r-ˌnak-l\ *n.* **1** A temporary shelter; a tent. **2** [with a capital] A structure of wood hung with curtains, used in worship by the Jews in their wanderings under Moses. **3** A Jewish temple or place of worship. **4** A locked container for the consecrated bread used in the Mass. **5** A church, especially one with a large auditorium.

ta·ble \'tāb-l\ *n.* **1** A flat piece of solid material, as stone, with a smooth surface; a plate; a tablet; a panel. **2** [in the plural] Certain laws inscribed on tables. **3** A piece of furniture having a smooth flat top fixed on legs. **4** Such a table provided with food. **5** The people around a table. **6** Food placed on a table to be eaten; as, to set a good *table.* **7** A condensed statement in list form; as, a *table* of contents. **8** Any collection and arrangement in condensed form for ready reference; as, a *table* of weights and measures. **9** [in the plural] The multiplication and other common tables of school arithmetic. — *v.;* **ta·bled; ta·bling** \-l(-)ing\. **1** To tabulate. **2** To lay on a table, as money or cards. **3** To place, as a motion or bill, on the table of the presiding officer of a meeting and thus remove it temporarily or indefinitely from discussion.

tab·leau \'tab-ˌlō, tab-'lō\ *n.; pl.* **tab·leaus** or **tab·leaux** \-ˌlōz, -'lōz\. A lifelike representation, often of a scene or event, by an appropriate grouping of persons who remain silent and motionless.

ta·ble·cloth \'tāb-l-ˌklȯth\ *n.; pl.* **ta·ble·cloths** \-ˌklȯt͟hz, -ˌklȯths\. A cloth for covering a table.

ta·ble d'hôte \ˌtäb-l 'dōt, ˌtab-l, ˌtȧb-l\. **1** A common table for guests at a hotel. **2** A meal in a restaurant or hotel served at a fixed price.

ta·ble·land \'tāb-l-ˌ(l)and\ *n.* A plateau.

ta·ble·spoon \'tāb-l-ˌspün\ *n.* A large spoon used for serving at table and as a measure.

ta·ble·spoon·ful \'tāb-l-'spün-ˌfu̇l, -ˌspün-\ *n.; pl.* **ta·ble·spoon·fuls.** As much as a tablespoon will hold, ordinarily one half fluid ounce.

tab·let \'tab-lət\ *n.* **1** A thin flat slab of stiff material used for writing, painting, drawing, or carving. **2** A thin slab, usually of marble or bronze, fastened to a wall to bear inscriptions; as, a memorial *tablet.* **3** A number of sheets of writing paper fastened at the top or side. **4** A flattish cake of compressed or molded solid matter, as soap. **5** A small flat solid mass of a medicinal substance, usually disk-shaped; as, aspirin *tablets.*

table tennis. A game resembling tennis played on a table with small bats and a celluloid ball.

ta·ble·ware \'tāb-l-ˌwar, -ˌwer\ *n.* Knives, forks, spoons, and dishes for use at the table.

tab·loid \'tab-ˌlȯid\ *adj.* Shaped into small compact units; condensed; as, medicine in *tabloid* form; *tabloid* information. — *n.* A small newspaper often sensational in its treatment of news and profusely illustrated with photographs.

ta·boo or **ta·bu** \ta-'bü, tə-\ *adj.* **1** Set apart or made sacred by taboo. **2** Forbidden by taboo; as, practices that are *taboo* in polite society. — *n.; pl.* **ta·boos** or **ta·bus. 1** A sacred order, common in certain primitive cultures, forbidding certain things, words, or acts. **2** A restriction imposed by social convention. — *v.;* **ta·booed** or **ta·bued; ta·boo·ing** or **ta·bu·ing.** To place under a taboo; to prohibit.

ta·bor \'tāb-r\ *n.* A small drum with only one head, used as an accompaniment to a pipe or fife and played by the same person.

tab·u·lar \'tab-yəl-r\ *adj.* **1** Having a flat surface like a table. **2** Arranged or entered in tabulated form; as, *tabular* statistics. **3** Printed or written in columns and reading across. — **tab·u·lar·ly,** *adv.*

tab·u·late \'tab-yə-ˌlāt\ *v.;* **tab·u·lat·ed; tab·u·lat·ing.** To put in the form of a table or tables; arrange in, or reduce to, a schedule or list. — **tab·u·la·tion** \ˌtab-yə-'lāsh-n\ *n.*

tab·u·la·tor \'tab-yə-ˌlāt-r\ *n.* **1** One that tabulates. **2** An attachment to a typewriter, for arranging figures in columns.

ta·chis·to·scope \tə-'kis-tə-ˌskōp\ *n.* An apparatus for exposing to view for brief periods, usually one fifth of a second or less, various visual stimuli, as objects, colors, figures, and letters.

ta·chom·e·ter \tə-'käm-ət-r\ *n.* Any of a number of instruments for indicating speed; especially, an instrument for measuring revolutions per minute, as of an engine.

tac·it \'tas-ət\ *adj.* Silent; unspoken; implied or indicated; as, *tacit* consent. — **tac·it·ly,** *adv.*

tac·i·turn \'tas-ə-ˌtərn\ *adj.* Habitually silent. — For synonyms see *silent.* — **tac·i·turn·ly,** *adv.*

tac·i·tur·ni·ty \ˌtas-ə-'tər-nət-ē\ *n.* Habitual silence or reserve in speaking.

tack \'tak\ *n.* **1** A small, short, sharp-pointed nail, usually with a broad, flat head, for fastening some light object or material to a solid surface; as, a carpet *tack*. **2** A rope used to hold in place the forward lower corner of the lowest sail on any square-rigged mast of a vessel. **3** The lower forward corner of a fore-and-aft sail. **4** The direction a vessel is sailing as shown by the way the sails are trimmed; the run of a vessel as trimmed in one way; as, on the port *tack*. **5** A change of course from one tack to another. **6** A zigzag movement on land. **7** A course or method of action. He is on the wrong *tack*. **8** A slight sewing or fastening, as by basting. — *v.* **1** To fasten with tacks; as, to *tack* down a carpet. **2** To fasten together loosely; to baste. **3** To change from one tack to another; to sail a course by making a series of tacks. **4** To pursue a zigzag course; to shift abruptly, as in attitude or policy.

tacks, 1

tack·le \'tak-l, *by seamen often* 'tāk-l\ *n.* **1** Instruments or apparatus used for work or play; gear; equipment; as, fishing *tackle*. **2** The rigging of a ship. **3** An arrangement of ropes and pulleys for hoisting or pulling heavy objects. **4** The act of tackling in football, or seizing and stopping a runner carrying the ball. **5** In football, either of two positions or players between the guards and the ends. — *v.*; **tack·led**; **tack·ling** \-l(-)ing\. **1** To attach or fasten with or as if with tackle. **2** To seize with the intention of stopping, as in football. **3** to try to do or to solve; as, to *tackle* a new job. — **tack·ler** \-l(-)ər\ *n.*

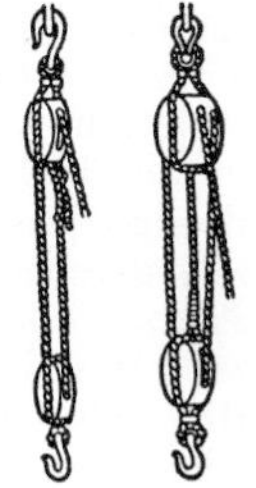

tackles, 3

tact \'takt\ *n.* A keen understanding of how to act in getting along with others; especially, the ability to deal with others without offending them.

tact·ful \'takt-fəl\ *adj.* Having or showing tact; as, a *tactful* person. — **tact·ful·ly** \-fə-lē\ *adv.*

tac·tic \'tak-tik\ *n.* **1** Tactics. **2** A tactical device; a maneuver.

tac·ti·cal \'tak-tik-l\ *adj.* **1** Of or relating to military or naval tactics; as, *tactical* exercises. **2** Relating to or showing orderly planning to accomplish a purpose; as, a debater's *tactical* arrangement of his arguments. **3** Skillful or showing skill in maneuvering. — **tac·ti·cal·ly** \-tik-l(-)ē\ *adv.*

tac·ti·cian \tak-'tish-n\ *n.* One skilled in tactics.

tac·tics \'tak-tiks\ *n.* **1** [usually used as a singular] The art of arranging and moving troops or ships in action to use them to best advantage. **2** [usually used as a plural] Any method of procedure; especially, skillful devices for gaining one's end; as, to use unfair *tactics* to win.

tac·tile \'takt-l, 'tak-ˌtīl\ *adj.* Of or relating to the sense of touch.

tact·less \'tak(t)-ləs\ *adj.* Having or showing no tact. — **tact·less·ly**, *adv.*

tad·pole \'tad-ˌpōl\ *n.* [From medieval English *taddepol* meaning literally "toad head".] The immature form of frogs and toads, living in water and typically having a long tail.

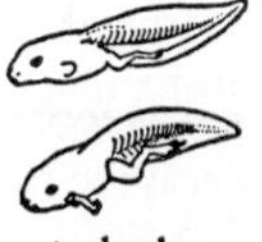

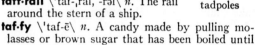

tadpoles

taf·fe·ta \'taf-ət-ə\ *n.* **1** A fine, smooth, glossy silk fabric made of tightly twisted yarn. **2** A similar fabric of linen or other fiber.

taff·rail \'taf-ˌrāl, -rəl\ *n.* The rail around the stern of a ship.

taf·fy \'taf-ē\ *n.* A candy made by pulling molasses or brown sugar that has been boiled until very thick.

tag \'tag\ *n.* **1** A loose end; a rag or tatter. **2** A small flap or tab fixed or hanging on something; as, a price *tag*. **3** A metal binder on the end of a string. **4** Something added at the end of a speech or writing, as an old saying to give point to the whole. — *v.*; **tagged**; **tag·ging**. **1** To put a tag on. **2** To follow closely; to tail.

tag \'tag\ *n.* A children's game in which one player is "it" and chases the others until he touches one of them, who then becomes "it". — *v.*; **tagged**; **tag·ging**. To touch, as in tag.

tail \'tāl\ *n.* **1** The rear end, or a lengthened growth extending from the rear end, of the body of an animal. **2** Something that in shape, appearance, or position is like an animal's tail; as, the *tail* of a coat; the *tail* of a kite. **3** The back; the rear; the end; as, the *tail* of an airplane. **4** [often in the plural] The side or end of a coin opposite the head. **5** [in the plural] A man's dress coat having long tails; full evening dress. — *adj.* **1** Hindmost. **2** Coming from the rear; as, a *tail* wind. — *v.* **1** To furnish with a tail. **2** To follow closely as if forming part of a tail; to shadow.

tail·board \'tāl-ˌbōrd, -ˌbȯrd\ *n.* A tail gate.

tail·first \'tāl-'fərst\ or **tail·fore·most** \'tāl-'fōr-ˌmōst, -'fȯr-\ *adv.* With the end or back foremost.

tail gate. A board at the back end of a vehicle, as a station wagon, that can be let down for loading and unloading.

tail·gate \'tāl-ˌgāt\ *v.* To drive dangerously close behind another vehicle.

tail·less \'tāl-ləs\ *adj.* Having no tail.

tail·light \'tāl-ˌlīt\ *n.* A light at the rear end of a vehicle, especially an automobile.

tai·lor \'tāl-r\ *n.* A person whose business is the making of men's or women's outer garments. — *v.*; **tai·lored**; **tai·lor·ing** \-r(-)ing\. To make as the work of a tailor or as a tailor makes clothing.

tai·lor–made \'tāl-r-'mād\ *adj.* **1** Made by or as if by a tailor; especially, characterized by precise fit and simplicity of style. **2** Made or seeming to have been made to suit a particular need.

tail·piece \'tāl-ˌpēs\ *n.* Any of various things attached at a rear or lower end, as an ornament at the bottom of a printed page or a triangular piece of wood at the lower end of a violin, to which the strings are fastened.

tail pipe. A pipe for the exhaust of gases generated by an internal-combustion engine.

tail–pipe burner. An afterburner.

tail spin. A maneuver or course of an airplane sharply downward while revolving on its own axis.

taint \'tānt\ *v.* **1** To contaminate; to poison; to infect. **2** To stain; as, to *taint* one's reputation. **3** To decay; to putrefy; as, *tainted* meat. — *n.* **1** A stain. **2** A corrupting influence.

take \'tāk\ *v.;* **took** \'tůk\; **tak·en** \'tāk-n\; **tak·ing.** **1** To lay hold of; to grasp; as, to *take* a person's hand. **2** To capture; as, to *take* a fort. **3** To win; as, to *take* first prize; to *take* every game. **4** To get possession of, as by buying or renting; as, to *take* a house. **5** To seize and affect; as, to be *taken* with a fever. **6** To charm; to delight; as, to be much *taken* with a new acquaintance. **7** To extract; as, to *take* material from an encyclopedia. **8** To remove; to subtract; as, to *take* 78 from 112. **9** To find out; as, to *take* a patient's temperature. **10** To select; to choose. **11** To assume; as, to *take* office. **12** To absorb. This cloth *takes* dye well. **13** To catch or contract, as a disease. **14** To accept; as, to *take* advice. **15** To introduce into the body; as, to *take* medicine. **16** To submit to; as, to *take* one's punishment. **17** To subscribe for. **18** To understand; as, to *take* a nod to mean "yes". **19** To feel; as, to *take* pride in one's work; to *take* offense. **20** In grammar, to be formed or used with; as, a noun that *takes* an "s" in the plural. This verb *takes* an object. **21** To convey, conduct, or carry; as, to *take* a parcel to the post office. **22** To make use of; to occupy; as, to *take* a chair. **23** To need; to require; as, a job that *takes* a lot of time. **24** To make; as, to *take* a photograph. **25** To do; to perform; as, to *take* a walk. **26** To have effect, as by adherence or absorption; as, a dye that *takes* well. **27** To betake oneself, as, to *take* to one's heels.
— The words *receive* and *accept* are synonyms of *take:* all three terms refer more strongly to the kind of attitude than to the action one takes toward something one gets or is given or that comes or is allowed to come into relationship with one; *receive* suggests a passive attitude in which one neither welcomes nor rejects; *accept* generally adds the suggestion of receiving with pleasure or at least with silent consent; *take* usually indicates an active getting or a welcoming or making no active protest against something that is offered, conferred upon, or sometimes inflicted upon one.
— **take after.** To look like; to resemble. The baby *takes after* its father. — **take back. 1** To take possession of again. **2** To withdraw; to retract; as, to *take back* a rude remark. — **take down. 1** To bring down; to lower; as, to *take down* a flag. **2** To take apart; as, to *take down* a cannon. **3** To write down. **4** To humble. — **take in. 1** To admit; as, to *take in* new members. **2** To make smaller by drawing in; as, to *take in* a dress. **3** To include. The camp *took in* several acres. **4** To grasp the meaning of; as, to *take in* the situation at a glance. **5** To cheat; to deceive. **6** To go to; to visit; as, to *take in* the sights of the city. — **take off. 1** To remove, as one's hat. **2** To deduct, as part of a price. **3** To mimic; to burlesque. **4** To start off or away suddenly, as a runner; to begin a leap or spring, as a jumper; to begin flight by leaving the surface of the land or water, as a bird, airplane, or rocket. — **take on. 1** To add, as flesh; as, to *take on* weight. **2** To put aboard, as a ship; as, to *take on* cargo. **3** To assume, as an appearance or quality; as, to *take on* dignity with age. **4** To undertake; to tackle; as, to *take on* a new job. **5** To hire; as, to *take on* more workmen. **6** To behave or talk excitedly; to show one's feelings. — **take place.** To happen; to occur. — **take to.** To be drawn to or attracted by; to form a liking for. — **take up. 1** To begin; to undertake; as, to *take up* swimming. **2** To remove or reduce; as, to *take up* the slack in a rope. — *n.* **1** The action of taking. **2** The amount or number taken; as, a large *take* of fish. **3** A successful inoculation, as in vaccination. **4** A part of a motion picture photographed at one time, without interruption.

take–off \'tāk-ˌȯf\ *n.* **1** An imitation, especially one that burlesques the original. **2** The action or process of taking off from the ground, as by an athlete making a jump or an airplane rising into the air. **3** The spot or place at which one takes off.

tak·ing \'tāk-ing\ *n.* That which is taken or received; especially [in the plural], receipts of money; as, the *takings* from a bazaar. — *adj.* **1** Attractive; as, *taking* ways. **2** Contagious; catching.

talc \'talk\ *n.* A soft whitish, grayish, or greenish mineral, much like soap to the touch, used in making such articles as toilet powder (**tal·cum powder** \'talk-m\), soap, and lubricants.

tale \'tāl\ *n.* **1** An oral relation or recital; as, a *tale* of woe. **2** A story, often short and about an imaginary event; as, a fairy *tale*. **3** A false story; a lie. **4** A piece of harmful gossip. All sorts of *tales* were going around about him. **5** A total; as, the whole *tale* of plays presented during the season.

tale·bear·er \'tāl-ˌbar-r, -ˌber-r\ *n.* A person who spreads gossip. — **tale·bear·ing** \-ing\ *adj.* or *n.*

tal·ent\'tal-ənt\ *n.* **1** An ancient weight and money unit varying in value according to time and place. **2** The combination of abilities and powers that a person has; especially, superior natural ability. **3** A natural gift for mastering some skill; as, a *talent* for art. **4** Persons of ability and skill; as, to recruit *talent*. — For synonyms see *ability*.

tal·ent·ed \'tal-ən-təd\ *adj.* Having natural ability; gifted; skilled; as, a *talented* pianist.

tal·is·man \'tal-əs-mən, -əz-\ *n.; pl.* **tal·is·mans.** A ring or stone, carved with symbols and supposed to have magical powers; a charm.

talk \'tȯk\ *v.* **1** To speak. **2** To communicate in any way; as, to *talk* by signs. **3** To gossip. **4** To confer; to consult. **5** To speak of; to discuss; as, to *talk* business. **6** To use, as a foreign language, in speech; as, to *talk* French. **7** To influence by talking; as, to *talk* a person into doing something. — *n.* **1** Speech; spoken words. **2** Ordinary conversation; often, an informal speech. **3** A conference; as, international *talks.* **4** Rumor; gossip. **5** A person or thing talked about; as, the *talk* of the town. — **talk·er** \'tȯk-r\ *n.*

talk·a·tive \'tȯk-ət-iv\ *adj.* Fond of talking; talking a great deal.
— The words *garrulous* and *voluble* are synonyms of *talkative: talkative* usually applies to one who is always ready to engage in talk; *garrulous* generally suggests a rambling, often foolish and tedious, talkativeness; *voluble* suggests talk that is unrestrained in flow and seemingly endless.

talk·ing-to \'tȯk-ing-ˌtü\ *n.; pl.* **talk·ing-tos** \-ˌtüz\. A scolding.

tall \'tȯl\ *adj.* **1** High or of a stated height; as, a *tall* tree; a boy five feet *tall.* **2** Exaggerated; as, a *tall* story. — For synonyms see *lofty.*

tal·lith \'täl-əs, 'tȧl-; 'tal-əth\ *n.* A fringed shawl or scarf worn over the head or shoulders by Jewish men, usually during morning prayer.

tal·low \'tal-ō\ *n.* **1** Animal fat; especially, suet. **2** Fat, as of cows, melted and used variously, as in making soap or candles. — *adj.* Made of tallow.

tal·ly \'tal-ē\ *n.; pl.* **tal·lies. 1** Anything on which a count or score is kept. **2** A reckoning; a score. **3** A label or tag with marks of identification. **4** A match; correspondence of two things with one another. — *v.;* **tal·lied** \-ēd\; **tal·ly·ing. 1** To keep a reckoning of; to count. **2** To make a tally; to score. **3** To match; to agree.

tal·ly·ho \ˌtal-ē-'hō\ *interj.* A huntsman's call given on sighting a fox. — *n.; pl.* **tal·ly·hos.** A large coach or carriage drawn by four horses.

tal·on \'tal-ən\ *n.* The claw of an animal, especially a bird of prey.

ta·lus \'tā-ləs\ *n.; pl.* **ta·lus·es** \-lə-səz\ or **ta·li** \-ˌlī\. The ankle or the bone of the ankle.

ta·lus \'tā-ləs\ *n.* Rock debris at the base of a cliff.

talons

tam·a·rack \'tam-r-ˌak\ *n.* Any of several American larch trees.

tam·a·rind \'tam-r-ˌind\ *n.* A tropical tree with leaves resembling feathers, hard yellowish wood, and red-striped yellow flowers; also, its pod.

tam·bou·rine \ˌtam-br-'ēn\ *n.* A small shallow drum open at one side and having loose metallic disks around the edge, played by shaking or striking with the hand.

tambourine

tame \'tām\ *adj.;* **tam·er; tam·est. 1** Made useful and obedient to man; domesticated. **2** Not like a wild animal; gentle; not afraid of man; as, *tame* deer in a park. **3** Lacking in spirit or interest; dull. — *v.;* **tamed; tam·ing. 1** To make or become tame, gentle, or obedient; to domesticate. **2** To break the spirit of; to subdue; as, to *tame* lions. — **tam·a·ble** or **tame·a·ble** \'tā-məb-l\ *adj.* — **tame·ly** \'tām-lē\ *adv.* — **tam·er** \'tām-r\ *n.*

tam-o'-shan·ter \ˌtam-ə-'shant-r\ *n.* [Named after *Tam o' Shanter*, the hero of the poem of the same name by Robert Burns (1759–1796), Scottish poet.] A Scottish cap resembling a beret.

tamp \'tamp\ *v.* **1** In blasting, to fill the hole over the charge, as with earth. **2** To drive in or down by repeated taps or blows. — **tamp·er,** *n.*

tam·per \'tamp-r\ *v.;* **tam·pered; tam·per·ing** \-r(-)ing\. **1** To plot; to use bribery; as, to *tamper* with a witness. **2** To meddle. — For synonyms see *meddle.* — **tam·per·er** \-r-r\ *n.*

tan \'tan\ *n.* **1** Tanbark. **2** The brown color of the skin caused by exposure to the sun. **3** A light yellowish brown color, as beige or fawn. — *adj.* Of the color tan. — *v.;* **tanned; tan·ning. 1** To make hide into leather by soaking in tannin. **2** To make or become tan in color. **3** To thrash; to beat.

tan. Abbreviation for *tangent.*

tan·a·ger \'tan-ij-r\ *n.* Any of a family of American singing birds related to the finches.

tan·bark \'tan-ˌbärk, -ˌbȧrk\ *n.* Bark that contains tannin, used in tanning hides.

tan·dem \'tand-m\ *adv.* One behind another. — *n.* **1** A two-seated carriage drawn by horses harnessed tandem. **2** A set of persons, things, or parts arranged one behind another, as a team of horses or a bicycle for two riders. **3** Tandem arrangement. — *adj.* Arranged tandem; as, a *tandem* bicycle.

tang \'tang\ *n.* **1** A shank on a tool, as a file, to connect with a handle. **2** A strong taste; a sharp flavor or smell; as, the *tang* of salt air.

tan·gent \'tanj-nt\ *adj.* Touching, especially at a single point; in geometry, meeting a curve or surface but not cutting it; as, a line, curve, or surface *tangent* to another. — *n.* **1** A tangent line, curve, or surface. **2** With reference to an acute angle in a right triangle, the ratio of the side opposite that angle to the side that, excluding the hypotenuse, is adjacent to the angle. **3** An abrupt change of course. — **tan·gen·tial** \tan-'jench-l\ *adj.* — **tan·gen·tial·ly** \-l-ē\ *adv.*

tan·ge·rine \'tanj-r-ˌēn\ *n.* A reddish yellow Chinese orange with a loose rind and sweet pulp.

tan·gi·ble \'tan-jəb-l\ *adj.* **1** Capable of being touched; capable of being felt when touched; solid and substantial. **2** Capable of being understood and appreciated; real; actual; as, *tangible* benefits. — *n.* [in the plural] Material things of determinable value; tangible assets. — **tan·gi·bil·i·ty** \ˌtan-jə-'bil-ət-ē\ *n.* — **tan·gi·bly** \'tan-jə-blē\ *adv.*

tan·gle \'tang-gl\ *v.;* **tan·gled; tan·gling** \-gl(-)ing\. **1** To involve so as to hamper or embarrass; to be or become entangled; as, hopelessly *tangled* in argument. **2** To twist or become twisted together into a mass hard to straighten out again; to entangle. — *n.* **1** A confused condition or mass; a tangled knot of threads or cords. **2** A condition of confusion; a muddle.

tan·go \'tang-ˌgō\ *n.; pl.* **tan·gos.** Any of several dances of Spanish American origin having a variety of steps and postures; especially, a dance distinguished by low dips and twisting steps on the toes. — *v.;* **tan·goed; tan·go·ing.** To dance a tango.

tank \'tangk\ *n.* **1** A large basin, cistern, or other artificial container for a liquid; as, a gasoline *tank.* **2** An armored, self-propelled vehicle armed with powerful guns and capable of attacking the enemy over rough ground. — *v.* To put or store in a tank.

tank·ard \'tangk-rd\ *n.* A tall, one-handled drinking vessel, often of pewter and having a lid.

tankard

tank·er \'tangk-r\ *n.* A steel cargo boat fitted with tanks, as for carrying oil or gasoline.

tan·ner \'tan-r\ *n.* A person whose business is the tanning of hides.

tan·nery \'tan-r-ē\ *n.; pl.* **tan·ner·ies.** A place where the work of tanning is carried on.

tan·nin \'tan-ən\ *n.* Also **tan·nic acid** \'tan-ik\. An acid commonly made from the bark of certain oaks or the leaves and flower clusters of sumac and used in tanning and dyeing and as an astringent.

tan·sy \'tan-zē\ *n.; pl.* **tan·sies.** A strong-smelling, bitter-tasting weedy herb related to the thistles, with divided leaves and yellow flowers.

tan·ta·lize \'tant-l-ˌīz\ *v.;* **tan·ta·lized; tan·ta·liz·ing.** [Named after *Tantalus,* a king of Greek mythology who was condemned to stand hungry and thirsty everlastingly in sight of food and water that he could not reach.] To tease, as by presenting to the view something desirable but out of reach. — **tan·ta·liz·er** \'tant-l-ˌīz-r\ *n.*

tan·ta·mount \'tant-m-ˌau̇nt\ *adj.* Equal in value, meaning, or effect; as, a statement that is *tantamount* to an admission of guilt.

tan·trum \'tan-trəm\ *n.* A fit of bad temper.

tap \'tap\ *v.;* **tapped; tap·ping. 1** To strike, knock, or rap lightly. **2** To give a light blow or blows, as with the feet or a cane. **3** To make, as a hole, by striking lightly again and again. A woodpecker *tapped* a hole in the tree. — *n.* **1** A light blow. **2** A partial sole put over a worn sole on a shoe.

tap \'tap\ *n.* **1** A faucet; a cock; a spigot. **2** A hole or pipe through which liquor is drawn. **3** In an electric circuit, a point where a connection may be made. — **on tap. 1** Ready to be drawn; as, beer *on tap.* **2** On hand; available; as, to have plenty of good ideas *on tap.* — *v.;* **tapped; tap·ping. 1** To let out, cause to flow, or make available, as by piercing or by drawing out a plug; as, to *tap* a cask of wine. **2** To pierce, open, or break into so as to draw something out; as, to *tap* maple trees. **3** To pierce or connect as if to draw something off; as, to *tap* telephone wires.

tap, 1

tap dance. A dance tapped out audibly with the feet. — **tap-dance,** *v.*

tape \'tāp\ *n.* **1** A narrow band of cotton or linen; as, adhesive *tape.* **2** A narrow strip or band of material, such as paper, steel, or plastic; as, a cash-register *tape;* a recording made on magnetic *tape.* **3** A string stretched above the finishing line in a race. — *v.;* **taped; tap·ing. 1** To fasten or tie with tape; to cover with tape; as, to *tape* an electric wire. **2** To measure with a tape measure.

tape measure. A tape marked off, usually in inches, and used for measuring.

ta·per \'tāp-r\ *n.* **1** A long waxed wick to be lighted and used as a candle. **2** A small light. **3** The rate by which a cone diminishes in diameter toward its point. — *v.;* **ta·pered; ta·per·ing** \-r(-)ing\. **1** To make or become gradually smaller toward the end. **2** To grow gradually less and less; as, to *taper* off.

tap·es·try \'tap-əs-trē\ *n.; pl.* **tap·es·tries.** A heavy, decorative fabric used as a wall hanging, carpet, or furniture covering. — **tap·es·tried** \-trēd\ *adj.*

tape·worm \'tāp-ˌwərm\ *n.* A long flat worm that, when adult, is parasitic in man and many animals.

tap·i·o·ca \ˌtap-ē-'ōk-ə\ *n.* Grains or flakes of starch obtained from cassava roots, used in making puddings and as a thickening in soups.

ta·pir \'tāp-r\ *n.* A large, hoofed animal with a long, flexible snout, a very short tail, and stout legs, found in South and Central American forests.

tap·room \'tap-ˌrüm, -ˌru̇m\ *n.* A room where liquors are kept on tap.

tap·root \'tap-ˌrüt, -ˌru̇t\ *n.* On a plant, a main root which grows straight downward, giving off small side roots.

taps \'taps\ *n. pl.* [A shortened form of *taptoo,* an old form of *tattoo* — see *tattoo.*] A signal, by drum, bugle, or trumpet, to put out all lights and go to bed.

tap·ster \'tap-stər\ *n.* A person employed to draw liquor in a taproom.

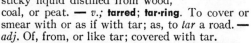

taproot

tar \'tär, 'tȧr\ *n.* A thick, dark, sticky liquid distilled from wood, coal, or peat. — *v.;* **tarred; tar·ring.** To cover or smear with or as if with tar; as, to *tar* a road. — *adj.* Of, from, or like tar; covered with tar.

tar \'tär, 'tȧr\ *n.* [A shortened form of *tarpaulin,* formerly also used to mean "sailor".] A sailor.

ta·ran·tu·la \tə-'ranch-l(-)ə\ *n.* **1** A large European spider whose bite was once thought to cause an uncontrollable desire to dance. **2** A large hairy spider of western North America and the tropics.

tar·dy \'tärd-ē, 'tȧrd-ē\ *adj.;* **tar·di·er; tar·di·est. 1** Moving with a slow pace. **2** Late; not on time, punctual, or ready. — **tar·di·ly** \-l-ē\ *adv.*

tare \'tar, 'ter\ *n.* In the Bible, a weed found in fields of grain.

tare \'tar, 'ter\ *n.* A deduction of weight made to allow for the weight of a container or vehicle.

tar·get \'tär-gət, 'tȧr-\ *n.* **1** A mark to aim at, as in rifle shooting. **2** An objective. **3** A person or thing that is made the object of criticisms or jokes.

tar·iff \'tar-əf\ *n.* **1** A schedule of duties imposed by a government upon goods coming into, or, sometimes, going out from a country. **2** The duty, or the rate of duty, imposed in such a schedule.

3 A schedule of rates or charges; as, a freight *tariff.*

tar·la·tan \ˈtär-lə-tən, ˈtȧr-, -lət-n\ *n.* A thin, stiff, transparent muslin.

tarn \ˈtärn, ˈtȧrn\ *n.* A small mountain lake.

tar·nish \ˈtär-nish, ˈtȧr-\ *v.* To make or become dull, dim, or discolored. Silver *tarnishes.* — *n.* The state of being tarnished; discoloration.

ta·ro \ˈtär-ˌō, ˈtar-, ˈtȧr-\ *n.; pl.* **ta·ros. 1** A plant grown throughout the tropics for its edible starchy rootstock. **2** The rootstock of this plant.

tar·pau·lin \tär-ˈpȯl-ən, tȧr-; ˈtärp-l-ən, ˈtȧrp-\ *n.* **1** A sheet of waterproofed canvas used especially for covering the hatches of ships. **2** A hat or coat made of waterproofed canvas.

tar·pon \ˈtärp-n, ˈtȧrp-n\ *n.; pl.* **tar·pons** or **tar·pon.** A large silvery game fish of the Florida coasts.

tar·ry \ˈtär-ē, ˈtȧr-ē\ *adj.* Of or like tar; covered with tar.

tar·ry \ˈtar-ē\ *v.;* **tar·ried** \-ēd\; **tar·ry·ing. 1** To delay; to linger. **2** To stay in a place; to wait.

tar·sal \ˈtärs-l, ˈtȧrs-l\ *adj.* Of or relating to the tarsus. — *n.* A tarsal bone.

tar·sus \ˈtär-səs, ˈtȧr-\ *n.; pl.* **tar·sus·es** \-sə-səz\ or **tar·si** \-ˌsī, -ˌsē\. **1** The ankle of a vertebrate; the small bones that support this part. **2** The shank of a bird's leg. **3** The foot of an insect.

tart \ˈtärt, ˈtȧrt\ *adj.* **1** Sour or sharp to the taste; as, a *tart* grapefruit. **2** Keen; biting; as, *tart* words.

tart \ˈtärt, ˈtȧrt\ *n.* **1** A small pie or shell of pastry containing a filling, as jelly, custard, or fruit. **2** *British.* Any fruit pie.

tar·tan \ˈtärt-n, ˈtȧrt-n\ *n.* **1** Woolen cloth woven in a plaid pattern, used in the Scottish national costume. **2** Any similarly designed material.

tar·tar \ˈtärt-r, ˈtȧrt-r\ *n.* **1** A substance existing in the juice of grapes and deposited on the inside of wine casks as a reddish crust or sediment. **2** Cream of tartar. **3** A hard crust of saliva, food, and lime deposits that forms on the teeth.

task \ˈtask\ *n.* A piece of work, especially as assigned by another person. — **to take to task.** To scold or censure. — *v.* To load down with work.

task·mas·ter \ˈtask-ˌmast-r\ *n.* One who sets a task or work for another or others.

tas·sel \ˈtas-l, ˈtȯs-l, ˈtäs-l\ *n.* **1** A hanging ornament that ends in a tuft of loose threads or strings and is fastened to something, as a cushion, a curtain, a hat, or a dress. **2** Something resembling a tassel; as, the *tassel* of Indian corn. — *v.;* **tas·seled** or **tas·selled; tas·sel·ing** or **tas·sel·ling** \-l(-)ing\. **1** To adorn with tassels; to put tassels on. **2** To put forth tassels.

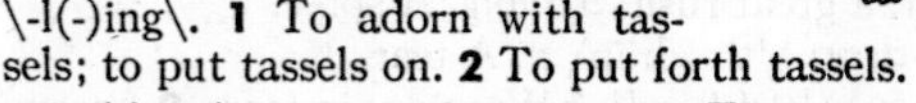

tassel

taste \ˈtāst\ *v.;* **tast·ed; tast·ing. 1** To test something by touching it with the tongue, or by taking a small quantity of it into the mouth. **2** To eat or drink a little of something in order to find its flavor or quality. **3** To undergo; to experience; as, to *taste* the joy of flying. **4** To have a certain flavor. This milk *tastes* sour. — *n.* **1** A small piece of something taken into the mouth, as for testing its flavor. **2** The sense by which the flavor of substances is learned by contact with certain groups of cells (**taste buds**) on the tongue. **3** Flavor; savor. **4** A fondness; a liking; as, a *taste* for music. **5** The power of appreciating beauty or excellence, as of music or literature; as, a man of *taste.* **6** Esthetic quality; style; as, decorations in bad *taste.*

taste·ful \ˈtāst-fəl\ *adj.* Having or showing good taste; artistic; as, a *tasteful* color scheme. — **taste·ful·ly** \-fə-lē\ *adv.*

taste·less \ˈtāst-ləs\ *adj.* **1** Having no taste or flavor; flat. **2** Not in good taste; not artistic; as, *tasteless* decorations. — **taste·less·ly,** *adv.*

tasty \ˈtās-tē\ *adj.;* **tast·i·er; tast·i·est. 1** Pleasing to the taste. **2** Showing good taste; artistic.

tat \ˈtat\ *v.;* **tat·ted; tat·ting.** To work at tatting; to make by tatting.

tat·ter \ˈtat-r\ *n.* **1** A rag or a torn and hanging piece of cloth. **2** [in the plural] Ragged or worn-out clothing; as, dressed in *tatters.*

tat·tered \ˈtat-rd\ *adj.* **1** Ragged; torn in shreds; as, a *tattered* flag. **2** Dressed in ragged clothes.

tat·ting \ˈtat-ing\ *n.* **1** Knotted lace made from cotton or linen thread wound on a shuttle. **2** The process of making this lace.

tat·tle \ˈtat-l\ *v.;* **tat·tled; tat·tling** \-l(-)ing\. **1** To chatter. **2** To tell tales or secrets; to gossip. — *n.* Idle talk; chatter; gossip. — **tat·tler** \-l(-)ər\ *n.*

tat·tle·tale \ˈtat-l-ˌtāl\ *n.* A person who tattles.

tat·too \(ˈ)ta-ˈtü\ *n.* [From older *taptoo,* this borrowed from Dutch *taptoe* meaning literally "tap in", that is "put the tap in the keg, stop drinking and go to bed" — see *taps.*] **1** A signal, as on a drum or bugle, given shortly before taps to warn soldiers and sailors to go to their quarters. **2** A beating of a drum; a rapping or knocking.

tat·too \(ˈ)ta-ˈtü\ *v.;* **tat·tooed; tat·too·ing.** To mark or color the skin with permanent marks forming some kind of pattern or figure. — *n.; pl.* **tat·toos.** A mark or figure made by tattooing.

taught. Past tense and past part. of *teach.*

taunt \ˈtȯnt, ˈtänt\ *v.* To tease with insults; to jeer at; to ridicule and mock. The boys *taunted* the losing team. — *n.* A spiteful, jeering remark.

taupe \ˈtōp\ *n.* A dark grayish brown color.

taut \ˈtȯt\ *adj.* **1** Tightly drawn; not slack, as, a *taut* rope. **2** Trim; neat; shipshape. **3** Strained; tense; as, *taut* nerves. — **taut·ly,** *adv.*

tau·tol·o·gy \tȯ-ˈtäl-ə-jē\ *n.; pl.* **tau·tol·o·gies. 1** A needless repetition of the same meaning. **2** An instance of such repetition, as in *audible to the ear.* — **tau·to·log·i·cal** \ˌtȯt-l-ˈäj-ik-l\ *adj.*

tav·ern \ˈtav-rn\ *n.* **1** A house where liquors are sold for drinking on the premises. **2** An inn.

taw \ˈtȯ\ *n.* **1** A marble used in shooting in a game of marbles. **2** A game of marbles. **3** Also **taw·line** \-ˌlīn\. The line from which marbles are shot.

taw·dry \ˈtȯd-rē, ˈtäd-\ *adj.;* **taw·dri·er; taw·dri·est.** Showy but in bad taste; cheap and gaudy.

taw·ny \'tȯn-ē, 'tän-ē\ *adj.;* **taw·ni·er; taw·ni·est.** Yellowish brown in color; tan.

tax \'taks\ *v.* **1** To determine by judicial ruling the amount of; as, to *tax* the costs of a trial. **2** To require to pay a tax. **3** To cause a strain upon; as, to *tax* one's strength. — *n.* **1** A charge, usually of money, laid upon a person or upon a property to raise funds for the costs of government; a duty. **2** Something that is a strain; an effort, task, or duty that makes heavy demands.

tax·a·ble \'taks-əb-l\ *adj.* Subject to taxation.

tax·a·tion \(')tak-'sāsh-n\ *n.* **1** The act of laying or imposing a tax or taxes. **2** A tax; a levy; the money from taxes.

taxi \'taks-ē\ *n.; pl.* **tax·is.** A taxicab. — *v.;* **tax·ied** \-ēd\; **tax·i·ing** or **tax·y·ing** \'taks-ē-ing\. **1** To ride in or go by a taxicab. **2** Of an airplane, to run along the ground or water under its own power when starting or coming in after a landing.

tax·i·cab \'taks-ē-ˌkab\ *n.* A motor car that carries passengers for a fare, determined usually by the distance traveled and often shown by a meter.

tax·i·der·my \'taks-ə-ˌdər-mē\ *n.* The art of preparing, stuffing, and mounting skins of animals. — **tax·i·der·mist** \-məst\ *n.*

tax·on·o·my \tak-'sän-ə-mē\ *n.* **1** Classification, especially of plants and animals according to their natural relationships. **2** The branch of biology dealing with such classification. — **tax·o·nom·ic** \ˌtaks-ə-'näm-ik\ *adj.* — **tax·on·o·mist** \tak-'sän-ə-məst\ *n.*

tax·pay·er \'taks-ˌpā-ər, -ˌper\ *n.* A person who pays a tax or taxes.

tbs. Abbreviation for *tablespoon.*

tea \'tē\ *n.* **1** A shrub related to the camellia, with lance-shaped leaves and fragrant white flowers, grown mainly in China, Japan, India, and Ceylon. **2** The leaves and leaf buds of this plant, cured for use in making a drink by being steeped in boiling water. **3** The drink made in this way. **4** Any of various other drinks; especially, a drink made from the leaves of any of numerous other plants more or less like tea; as, sage *tea.* **5** A late afternoon serving of tea and a light meal. **6** An afternoon party or reception at which tea is served.

tea: leaves and blossoms

tea·ber·ry \'tē-ˌber-ē\ *n.; pl.* **tea·ber·ries.** The wintergreen.

teach \'tēch\ *v.;* **taught** \'tȯt\; **teach·ing. 1** To assist in learning how to do something; to show how; as, to *teach* a child to read. **2** To guide the studies of; to instruct; as, to *teach* the senior class. **3** To give lessons in; to instruct pupils in; as, to *teach* music. **4** To be a teacher. **5** To make learn; to cause to know; as, to be *taught* by experience.

teach·a·ble \'tē-chəb-l\ *adj.* **1** Capable of being taught; especially, apt and willing to learn; as, a very *teachable* child. **2** Capable of being used for teaching. — **teach·a·bil·i·ty** \ˌtē-chə-'bil-ət-ē\ *n.*

teach·er \'tēch-r\ *n.* One that teaches; especially, one whose occupation is to teach; an instructor.

teach·ing \'tē-ching\ *n.* **1** The work or the profession of a teacher. **2** Something that is taught.

tea·cup \'tē-ˌkəp\ *n.* **1** A cup for tea. **2** The amount held by a teacup.

teacup with saucer

teak \'tēk\ *n.* **1** A tall timber tree of the East Indies yielding a somewhat hard and very durable yellowish brown wood. **2** Also **teak·wood** \-ˌwu̇d\. The wood of this tree.

tea·ket·tle \'tē-ˌket-l\ *n.* A kettle with a spout used for boiling water in making tea.

teal \'tēl\ *n.* A small short-necked river duck, very swift in flight.

team \'tēm\ *n.* **1** Two or more animals, as horses or oxen, harnessed to the same thing, as a wagon or plow. **2** Two or more persons associated for work or play, as those on one side in a game; as, a baseball *team.* — *v.* **1** To yoke or join in a team. **2** To join together as a team or group; as, to *team* up for a game. **3** To be a teamster.

team·mate \'tēm-ˌmāt\ *n.* A fellow team member.

team·ster \'tēm(p)-stər\ *n.* **1** A driver of a team or truck. **2** One who is in the business of hauling.

team·work \'tēm-ˌwərk\ *n.* The work or activity of a number of persons acting in close association as members of a unit. *Teamwork* won the game.

tea·pot \'tē-ˌpät\ *n.* A pot with a spout for making and serving tea.

teapot

tear \'tir\ *n.* **1** A drop of the salty liquid that keeps the eye and the inner eyelids moist. **2** Something in the form of a tear, as a solid transparent drop or bead of certain balsams or resins. — **in tears.** Weeping.

tear \'tar, 'ter\ *v.;* **tore** \'tōr, 'tȯr\; **torn** \'tōrn, 'tȯrn\; **tear·ing. 1** To separate or pull apart by force; as, to *tear* up cloth for bandages; to *tear* a coat. **2** To make by ripping or piercing; as, to *tear* a hole in a shirt. **3** To cut deeply and jaggedly; as, to *tear* the skin. **4** To divide by opposing forces; as, a mind *torn* by doubts; a nation *torn* by strife. **5** To cause to suffer painfully; as, to be *torn* by grief. **6** To break or yank away with force. **7** To move or act with violence or with extreme haste; as, to *tear* down the street; to *tear* into a friend for being late. — *n.* **1** The act of tearing. **2** The result of tearing; as, a house showing considerable wear and *tear.* **3** A torn place; a rent. **4** A violent passion; a great rush. **5** *Slang.* A spree.

tear·drop \'tir-ˌdräp\ *n.* A tear.

tear·ful \'tirf-l\ *adj.* **1** Weeping; in tears. **2** Accompanied by or causing tears; as, a *tearful* story. — **tear·ful·ly** \-l(-)ē\ *adv.*

tear gas \'tir\. A gas that when dispersed in the air blinds the eyes with tears, used as a weapon.

tea·room \'tē-ˌrüm, -ˌru̇m\ *n.* A small restaurant serving light meals.

tease \'tēz\ *v.;* **teased**; **teas·ing.** **1** To comb, as wool or flax, so as to disentangle and separate the fibers. **2** To scratch the surface of, as cloth, so as to raise a nap. **3** To irritate or annoy, as by joking remarks or by repeated requests or begging; to plague. **4** To practice teasing. — *n.* **1** The act of teasing or the state of being teased. **2** One who teases or plagues. — **teas·er** \'tēz-r\ *n.*

tea·sel \'tēz-l\ *n.* **1** A coarse herb resembling the thistle. **2** A dried flower head of this plant, formerly used in cloth manufacture to raise a nap on woolen cloth. **3** Any instrument for raising a nap on cloth. — *v.;* **tea·seled** or **tea·selled**; **tea·sel·ing** or **tea·sel·ling** \-l(-)ing\. To use a teasel on.

tea·spoon \'tē-ˌspün\ *n.* A spoon used in stirring and sipping tea and coffee.

tea·spoon·ful \'tē-'spün-ˌfu̇l, -ˌspün-\ *n.; pl.* **tea·spoon·fuls.** As much as a teaspoon will hold, about one third of a tablespoonful.

teat \'tit, 'tēt\ *n.* A nipple through which milk is drawn from a breast or udder.

tech·nic \'tek-nik, (')tek-'nēk\ *n.* A technique.

tech·ni·cal \'tek-nik-l\ *adj.* **1** Of or relating to practical knowledge or skill or the methods of a special field, as a trade, craft, industry, business, science, or profession; as, a *technical* school. **2** Used only in a particular field or activity; as, *technical* words. **3** Of or relating to technique; as, *technical* skill. — **tech·ni·cal·ly** \-nik-l(-)ē\ *adv.*

tech·ni·cal·i·ty \ˌtek-nə-'kal-ət-ē\ *n.; pl.* **tech·ni·cal·i·ties.** **1** The quality or state of being technical. **2** A point or detail known only to or of interest only to a specialist in a profession.

tech·ni·cian \tek-'nish-n\ *n.* A person skilled in technical details or in a technique.

tech·nics \'tek-niks, (')tek-'nēks\ *n.* **1** Technical procedures or the study of them. **2** Technology.

tech·nique \(')tek-'nēk\ *n.* **1** The things that a person needs to know and practice in order to become skillful in an activity; as, to study the *technique* of painting. **2** A special procedure developed or used for a specific purpose, as in science.

tech·nol·o·gy \tek-'näl-ə-jē\ *n.* **1** The science that deals with industrial arts, as engineering. **2** Applied science. — **tech·no·log·ic** \ˌtek-nə-'läj-ik\ or **tech·no·log·i·cal** \-ik-l\ *adj.* — **tech·no·log·i·cal·ly** \-ik-l(-)ē\ *adv.* — **tech·nol·o·gist** \tek-'näl-ə-jəst\ *n.*

te·di·ous \'tēd-ē-əs, 'tē-jəs\ *adj.* Tiresome; boring; as, a *tedious* speech. — **te·di·ous·ly**, *adv.*

te·di·um \'tēd-ē-əm\ *n.* Tiresomeness; boredom.

tee \'tē\ *n.* **1** The mark aimed at in some throwing games. **2** In golf, the place from which the ball is struck in starting play on a hole; also, a tiny mound or a small peg with concave top, on which the ball is set to be struck. — **to a tee.** Exactly; precisely. This suits me *to a tee.* — *v.;* **teed**; **tee·ing.** To place on a tee. — **tee off.** To drive a golf ball from a tee.

teem \'tēm\ *v.* To be full to the point of overflowing; to abound. The river *teems* with fish.

teen-age \'tēn-ˌāj\ *adj.* **1** Of or relating to young people in their teens. **2** Characteristic of or for young people in their teens.

teen-ag·er \'tēn-ˌāj-r\ *n.* A teen-age person.

teens \'tēnz\ *n. pl.* The years of a person's age from 13 through 19.

teepee. Variant of *tepee.*

tee shirt \'tē\. A T shirt.

tee·ter \'tēt-r\ *v.* To seesaw; to waver or wobble. — *n.* A seesaw.

tee·ter-tot·ter \'tēt-r-ˌtät-r\ *n.* or *v.* Seesaw.

teeth. Plural of *tooth.*

teethe \'tēth\ *v.;* **teethed** \'tēthd\; **teeth·ing** \'tē-thing\. To grow teeth; to cut one's teeth.

teg·u·ment \'teg-yə-mənt\ *n.* An integument. — **teg·u·men·ta·ry** \ˌteg-yə-'ment-r-ē, -'men-trē\ *adj.*

tel·e·cast \'tel-ə-ˌkast\ *v.;* **tel·e·cast** or **tel·e·cast·ed**; **tel·e·cast·ing.** To broadcast by television. — *n.* A broadcast by television. — **tel·e·cast·er,** *n.*

tel·e·gen·ic \ˌtel-ə-'jen-ik, -'jē-nik\ *adj.* Having attractive qualities that show up well in television.

tel·e·gram \'tel-ə-ˌgram; *in the South, also* -grəm\ *n.* A message sent by telegraph.

tel·e·graph \'tel-ə-ˌgraf\ *n.* An electric device or system for sending messages by a code over wires. — *v.* To send by telegraph; to send a telegram to. — **tel·e·graph·ic** \ˌtel-ə-'graf-ik\ *adj.* — **tel·e·graph·i·cal·ly** \-ik-l(-)ē\ *adv.*

te·leg·ra·pher \tə-'leg-rəf-r\ *n.* An operator of a telegraph.

te·leg·ra·phy \tə-'leg-rə-fē\ *n.* The use or operation of a telegraph apparatus or system.

te·lep·a·thy \tə-'lep-ə-thē\ *n.* Apparent communication from one mind to another without the use of speech or signs. — **tel·e·path·ic** \ˌtel-ə-'path-ik\ *adj.* — **tel·e·path·i·cal·ly** \-ik-l(-)ē\ *adv.*

tel·e·phone \'tel-ə-ˌfōn\ *n.* An instrument for receiving and reproducing sounds, as of the human voice, transmitted from a distance, over wires, by means of electricity. — *v.;* **tel·e·phoned**; **tel·e·phon·ing.** To send or communicate by telephone; to speak to by telephone; to call on the telephone.

telephone

tel·e·phon·ic \ˌtel-ə-'fän-ik\ *adj.* **1** Conveying sound to a distance. **2** Of or relating to the telephone; by telephone.

te·leph·o·ny \tə-'lef-n-ē\ *n.* The electrical transmission, with or without wires, of speech and other sounds between widely removed points; especially, such transmission between telephones.

tel·e·pho·to \'tel-ə-ˌfōt-ˌō\ *adj.* **1** Telephotographic. **2** Relating to a camera lens (**telephoto lens**) giving a large image of a distant object.

tel·e·pho·to·graph \ˌtel-ə-'fōt-ə-ˌgraf\ *n.* A picture made or reproduced by telephotography. — *v.* To use a telephoto lens or camera.

tel·e·pho·to·graph·ic \ˌtel-ə-ˌfōt-ə-'graf-ik\ *adj.* Of or relating to telephotography. — **tel·e·pho·to·graph·i·cal·ly** \-ik-l(-)ē\ *adv.*

tel·e·pho·tog·ra·phy \ˌtel-ə-fə-ˈtäg-rə-fē\ *n.* **1** The photographing of distant objects, usually with a camera having a telephoto lens. **2** The art or process of transmitting and reproducing pictures by telegraphic methods.

tel·e·print·er \ˈtel-ə-ˌprint-r\ *n.* A teletypewriter.

tel·e·scope \ˈtel-ə-ˌskōp\ *n.* A long tube-shaped optical instrument used in viewing or photographing distant objects, as stars. — *v.;* **tel·e·scoped**; **tel·e·scop·ing. 1** To slide or cause to slide together, one object or part passing within another, as sections of a portable telescope. **2** To run through after colliding. The engine *telescoped* the rear car of the forward train.

tel·e·scop·ic \ˌtel-ə-ˈskäp-ik\ *adj.* **1** Of or relating to a telescope. **2** Seen or discoverable only by telescope; as, *telescopic* stars. **3** Having the power to see clearly at great distances. **4** Capable of being telescoped; collapsible. — **tel·e·scop·i·cal·ly** \-ik-l(-)ē\ *adv.*

tel·e·type·writ·er \ˈtel-ə-ˈtīp-ˌrīt-r\ *n.* A form of printing telegraph which automatically records messages like a typewriter.

tel·e·view \ˈtel-ə-ˌvyü\ *v.* To observe or watch on a television screen. — **tel·e·view·er** \-ˌvyü-ər\ *n.*

tel·e·vise \ˈtel-ə-ˌvīz\ *v.;* **tel·e·vised**; **tel·e·viz·ing.** To send or receive by television.

tel·e·vi·sion \ˈtel-ə-ˌvizh-n\ *n.* **1** The sending and reproduction of a view or scene by any device that converts light rays into electrical waves and then converts these back into visible light rays. **2** An apparatus for receiving images by television; a television receiving set. **3** The field or business of broadcasting by television.

tell \ˈtel\ *v.;* **told** \ˈtōld\; **tell·ing. 1** To mention or say one by one; to count; as, twenty persons all *told;* to *tell* one's beads. **2** To report; to give an account of; to relate in detail; as, to *tell* a story. **3** To say; to speak; as, to *tell* a lie. **4** To make known; as, to *tell* a secret. **5** To inform. **6** To find out; to come to know; as, to *tell* time. **7** To command; as, to *tell* a person to go. **8** To have effect. Lack of sleep soon *tells* on one. **9** To be a talebearer; as, to *tell* on a schoolmate. **10** To serve as evidence; as, smiles *telling* of success.

tell·er \ˈtel-r\ *n.* **1** A person who tells; an informer, narrator, or describer; as, a *teller* of tales. **2** A person who counts or reckons, as votes in a legislative body. **3** A bank employee who receives and pays out money.

tell·ing \ˈtel-ing\ *adj.* Having a marked effect; as, a *telling* speech. — **tell·ing·ly**, *adv.*

tell·tale \ˈtel-ˌtāl\ *n.* **1** A talebearer. **2** An outward sign of something kept secret; an indication. — *adj.* **1** Talebearing. **2** Revealing; as, a *telltale* frown.

tel·lu·ri·um \tə-ˈlu̇r-ē-əm\ *n.* A nonmetallic chemical element resembling sulfur, usually occurring combined with metals.

te·mer·i·ty \tə-ˈmer-ət-ē\ *n.* Rashness; audacity.

tem·per \ˈtemp-r\ *v.;* **tem·pered**; **tem·per·ing** \-r(-)ing\. **1** To moderate; to soften; to mollify; as, to *temper* justice with mercy. **2** To control by reducing; to subdue; as, to *temper* one's anger. **3** To bring to the desired consistency or texture, as artist's paint or clay. **4** To bring to the desired hardness by heating and cooling, as steel. **5** To be or become tempered. — *n.* **1** The hardness or toughness of a substance, as of a metal. **2** A disposition or frame of mind; as, a fiery *temper.* **3** Calmness; self-control; as, to lose one's *temper.* **4** A state of anger; as, to show *temper.*

tem·per·a·ment \ˈtemp-r(-)ə-mənt\ *n.* A person's disposition as it affects what he says or does.

tem·per·a·men·tal \ˌtemp-r(-)ə-ˈment-l\ *adj.* **1** Of or relating to temperament; constitutional; as, a person who has a *temperamental* dislike of quarreling and violence. **2** Having or showing a nervous, sensitive temperament; excitable; as, *temperamental* artists. — **tem·per·a·men·tal·ly** \-ˈment-l-ē\ *adv.*

tem·per·ance \ˈtemp-r(-)ən(t)s\ *n.* **1** The practicing of moderation, as in eating. **2** Moderation in or complete avoidance of the use of intoxicants.

tem·per·ate \ˈtemp-r(-)ət\ *adj.* **1** Moderate; not excessive; as, *temperate* heat. **2** Moderate in satisfying one's needs or desires. **3** Showing self-control; restrained; as, *temperate* speech. **4** Seldom or never drinking intoxicating liquors. **5** Neither too hot nor too cold. — **tem·per·ate·ly**, *adv.*

tem·per·a·ture \ˈtemp-r-ˌchu̇r, ˈtemp-ə-, ˈtemp-r(-)ə-, -chər\ *n.* **1** The degree of hotness or coldness of something, as of air, water, or the body, as shown by a thermometer. Today's *temperature* is 70 degrees. **2** A fever; as, to have a *temperature.*

tem·pered \ˈtemp-rd\ *adj.* **1** Having a particular kind of temper; as, a bad-*tempered* boy. **2** Moderated; especially, hardened or toughened by special treatment; as, *tempered* steel.

tem·pest \ˈtemp-əst\ *n.* **1** A high wind, especially with rain, snow, or hail. **2** Any violent commotion.

tem·pes·tu·ous \(ˈ)tem-ˈpes-chə-wəs\ *adj.* Violent; stormy. — **tem·pes·tu·ous·ly**, *adv.*

tem·ple \ˈtemp-l\ *n.* The space between the eye and the forehead and the upper part of the ear.

tem·ple \ˈtemp-l\ *n.* **1** A building for worship. **2** [with a capital] One of three successive buildings erected in ancient Jerusalem for the worship of God.

tem·po \ˈtem-ˌpō\ *n.; pl.* **tem·pos** \-ˌpōz\ or **tem·pi** \-(ˌ)pē\. [From Italian, meaning literally "time" and derived from Latin *tempus.*] **1** The rate of speed at which a musical composition is played or sung. **2** Rhythm; rate of activity in general.

tem·po·ral \ˈtemp-r(-)əl\ *adj.* In anatomy, of or relating to the temple or temples.

tem·po·ral \ˈtemp-r(-)əl\ *adj.* **1** Not lasting forever; not eternal. **2** Earthly; worldly; not spiritual or religious. — **tem·po·ral·ly** \-r(-)ə-lē\ *adv.*

tem·po·rary \ˈtemp-r-ˌer-ē\ *adj.* Lasting for a time only; not permanent; as, a *temporary* job. — **tem·po·rar·i·ly** \ˌtemp-r-ˈer-ə-lē\ *adv.*

tem·po·rize \'temp-r-ˌīz\ *v.;* **tem·po·rized; tem·po·riz·ing. 1** To adjust oneself to the time or the occasion. **2** To give in for a time to avoid trouble or to gain time. — **tem·po·ri·za·tion** \ˌtemp-r-ə-'zāsh-n\ *n.* — **tem·po·riz·er** \'temp-r-ˌīz-r\ *n.*

tempt \'tem(p)t\ *v.* **1** To lead or try to lead into evil; to incite to wrongdoing. **2** To entice; to lure; as, to be *tempted* by good food. **3** To provoke; to arouse to action or anger. — **tempt·er,** *n.*

temp·ta·tion \tem(p)-'tāsh-n\ *n.* **1** A tempting or a being tempted. **2** Something that tempts.

tempt·ing \'tem(p)-ting\ *adj.* Capable of enticing or alluring. — **tempt·ing·ly,** *adv.*

tempt·ress \'tem(p)-trəs\ *n.* A woman tempter.

ten \'ten\ *adj.* One more than nine. — *n.* **1** The sum of five and five; ten units. **2** The figure standing for ten units, as 10 or X.

ten·a·ble \'ten-əb-l\ *adj.* Capable of being held, maintained, or defended; as, a *tenable* argument. — **ten·a·bil·i·ty** \ˌten-ə-'bil-ət-ē\ *n.*

te·na·cious \tə-'nā-shəs\ *adj.* **1** Holding fast; as, *tenacious* of one's rights. **2** Apt to retain; retentive; as, a *tenacious* memory. **3** Cohesive; tough. Steel is a *tenacious* metal. **4** Adhesive; sticking; as, *tenacious* burs. — **te·na·cious·ly,** *adv.*

te·nac·i·ty \tə-'nas-ət-ē\ *n.* The quality or state of being tenacious; persistency.

ten·an·cy \'ten-ən-sē\ *n.; pl.* **ten·an·cies. 1** A holding, as by a lease, of a property belonging to another; tenure. **2** A property held in this way.

ten·ant \'ten-ənt\ *n.* **1** One who occupies or uses a piece of land or a building in return for paying rent. **2** An occupant; a dweller; as, feathered *tenants* of the woods. — *v.* To occupy as tenant.

ten·ant·ry \'ten-ən-trē\ *n.; pl.* **ten·ant·ries. 1** The condition of being a tenant. **2** A group of tenants, as on an estate.

Ten Commandments. According to the Bible, the ten laws summarizing God's commands, given to Moses at Mount Sinai.

tend \'tend\ *v.* **1** To pay attention; as, to *tend* strictly to business. **2** To take care of; to attend to; to cultivate, as plants. **3** To have charge of as caretaker or overseer. **4** To manage or superintend the operation of; as, to *tend* a machine.

tend \'tend\ *v.* **1** To move or turn in a certain direction; to lead. The road *tends* to the right. **2** To have a tendency; to incline; to be likely; as, a boy who *tends* to slouch.

tend·en·cy \'ten-dən-sē\ *n.; pl.* **tend·en·cies. 1** A direction or course toward something; a drift; a trend; as, a *tendency* toward peaceful settlement of international problems. **2** A natural inclination; a bent; a leaning; as, a *tendency* towards laziness.

tend·er \'tend-r\ *n.* **1** A person or thing that tends another. **2** A boat that carries passengers or freight to a larger vessel. **3** A car attached to a locomotive for carrying a supply of fuel or water.

ten·der \'tend-r\ *v.;* **ten·dered; ten·der·ing** \-r(-)ing\. **1** To offer in payment; as, to *tender* the exact amount of a bill. **2** To present for acceptance; to offer; to give formally; as, to *tender* an apology. — *n.* **1** A formal offer; a proposal. **2** An offer of a contract, as for work to be done or goods supplied. **3** The thing offered; especially, legal tender.

ten·der \'tend-r\ *adj.* **1** Not hard or tough; easily broken or cut; as, a *tender* steak. **2** Not strong or hardened physically; delicate; as, a *tender* plant. **3** Having or showing love or affection; kind and sympathetic; as, a *tender* look. **4** Easily hurt; very sensitive; as, a *tender* nerve. **5** Gentle; as, *tender* care. **6** Considerate; careful; as, to be *tender* of another's feelings. **7** Requiring gentle handling; as, a *tender* subject. — **ten·der·ly,** *adv.*

ten·der·foot \'tend-r-ˌfu̇t\ *n.; pl.* **ten·der·feet** \-ˌfēt\. **1** A person who is not hardened to a rough out-of-door life; especially, a newcomer in a recent settlement, as on a frontier. **2** A boy scout or girl scout of the beginning class.

ten·der·heart·ed \'tend-r-'härt-əd, -'hȧrt-\ *adj.* Easily moved to love, pity, or sorrow.

ten·der·loin \'tend-r-ˌlȯin\ *n.* A strip of very tender meat on either side of the backbone, sold as a separate cut of beef or pork.

ten·don \'ten-dən\ *n.* A tough cord or band of fibrous tissue connecting a muscle to some other part, such as a bone, and transmitting the force exerted by the muscle; a sinew.

ten·dril \'ten-drəl\ *n.* **1** A slender, leafless, coiling stem by which some climbing plants, as grapevines, fasten themselves to a support. **2** Something that curls like a tendril; as, *tendrils* of hair.

ten·e·ment \'ten-ə-mənt\ *n.* **1** A dwelling house; as, lands and *tenements.* **2** A house or an apartment rented or for rent. **3** Also **tenement house.** A building, especially in the poorer part of a city, with living quarters for a great many families. **4** Habitation.

ten·et \'ten-ət\ *n.* A belief, dogma, or principle.

ten·fold \'ten-ˌfōld, -'fōld\ *adj.* or *adv.* Having ten parts; ten times as much or as many.

ten·nis \'ten-əs\ *n.* Any of several games in which a ball is driven back and forth over a net with a racket (**tennis racket**); especially, **lawn tennis,** played on an open court (**tennis court**) usually of turf or clay.

ten·on \'ten-ən\ *n.* A projection, made by cutting away the wood around it, for insertion into a mortice to make a joint. — *v.* **1** To cut to form a tenon. **2** To join by or as if by a tenon.

ten·or \'ten-r\ *n.* **1** General direction or course; trend; tendency; as, to have the *tenor* of one's life disturbed. **2** General drift of thought; general meaning; purport; as, the *tenor* of an argument. **3** The highest adult male singing voice. **4** The part written for this voice. **5** A singer or an instrument having such a voice, part, or range.

ten·pins \'ten-ˌpinz\ *n.* A game like ninepins but using ten wooden pins set to form a triangle.

tense \'ten(t)s\ *n.* A distinctive form or set of forms of a verb used to show the time of the action or occurrence that the verb expresses. The past *tense* of "run" is "ran".

tense \'ten(t)s\ *adj.* **1** Stretched tight; strained; as, *tense* muscles. **2** Feeling, showing, or marked by strain, especially nervous strain; not relaxed or easy; as, *tense* nerves. — *v.;* **tensed**; **tens·ing**. To make or become tense. — **tense·ly**, *adv.*

ten·sile \'ten(t)s-l\ *adj.* **1** Capable of being stretched or strained without breaking or bending. **2** Of or relating to tension; as, *tensile* strength.

ten·sion \'tench-n\ *n.* **1** The action of straining or stretching or the condition of being tightly stretched or strained. **2** Mental strain; intensity of feeling or effort. **3** Nervous anxiety; worry; tenseness. **4** Strained relations; as, *tension* between the two countries. **5** Voltage; as, a high-*tension* wire.

ten·si·ty \'ten(t)s-ət-ē\ *n.* Tense condition.

ten·sor \'ten(t)s-r\ *n.* A muscle that stretches a part or makes it tense.

tent \'tent\ *n.* A portable shelter of skins or strong cloth, as canvas, stretched and supported by poles. — *v.* **1** To live in a tent; to encamp. **2** Something suggesting a tent, as a screen placed over the bed of a sick person to retain vapors being administered; as, an oxygen *tent.*

tent, 1

ten·ta·cle \'tent-ik-l\ *n.* **1** One of the long, flexible processes about the head or mouth of certain animals, insects, and fishes, for feeling, grasping, or moving. **2** A sensitive hair on a plant.

ten·ta·tive \'tent-ət-iv\ *adj.* Done as an experiment; made or offered for trial; not fully worked out. — **ten·ta·tive·ly**, *adv.*

tent·er \'tent-r\ *n.* One that occupies a tent.

ten·ter \'tent-r\ *n.* A frame for stretching cloth so that it may dry even and square. — *v.* To stretch on a tenter.

ten·ter·hook \'tent-r-ˌhu̇k\ *n.* A sharp hook used for fastening cloth on a tenter. — **on tenterhooks**. In a state of great strain, suspense, or anxiety.

tenth \'ten(t)th\ *adj.* Next after the ninth. — *n. pl.* **tenths** \'ten(t)s, 'ten(t)ths\. One of ten equal parts.

ten·u·ous \'ten-yə-wəs\ *adj.* **1** Thin; slender; as, *tenuous* filaments. **2** Rare or light, as fluids; not dense. **3** Not substantial; flimsy; as, *tenuous* arguments. — **ten·u·ous·ly**, *adv.*

ten·ure \'ten-yər\ *n.* **1** The act or right of holding property, especially real estate, of a superior, as in feudal times. **2** The holding, or having possession or use of, a position or office; as, laws governing *tenure* of public office. **3** The period during which something is held.

te·pee or **tee·pee** \'tēp-(ˌ)ē\ *n.* The conical tent used by some American Indians.

tep·id \'tep-əd\ *adj.* Lukewarm; as, *tepid* water.

term \'tərm\ *n.* **1** *Archaic.* A limit; a boundary; an end. **2** A limited or definite extent of time; the time for which anything lasts; especially, a period of time fixed by law, or custom; as, a school *term.* The mayor served three *terms.* **3** A word; especially, a word or an expression used in a very definite, limited sense, as in a science, art, or profession; as, a botanical *term.* **4** [usually in the plural] The points or provisions offered for acceptance or agreed upon in making a contract or treaty, or mentioned in a will; conditions. **5** One of the three parts of a syllogism. **6** [in the plural] Agreement about conditions; as, to come to *terms.* **7** [in the plural] Mutual relationship; footing; as, to be on good *terms.* **8** In mathematics, a member of a compound quantity, as *ab* or *cd* in $ab + cd$, or of a proportion or ratio. — *v.* To apply a term to; to name.

ter·ma·gant \'tər-mə-gənt\ *n.* A boisterous, quarrelsome woman. — *adj.* Noisy; quarrelsome.

ter·mi·na·ble \'tər-mə-nəb-l\ *adj.* Subject to being terminated.

ter·mi·nal \'tər-mən-l\ *adj.* **1** Of or relating to a term, or an end, boundary, or terminus; forming a terminus. **2** Of or relating to a term, or fixed period of time; occurring in a term or in every term. **3** Occurring at the end. **4** In botany, growing at the end of a branch or stem; as, a *terminal* bud. — *n.* **1** The end, extremity, or termination of anything. **2** A device fastened to the end of an electric wire or cable to make connections easy. **3** The end of a division or line of a railroad; a terminus; especially, the railroad station at a terminus. — **ter·mi·nal·ly** \-mən-l-ē\ *adv.*

ter·mi·nate \'tər-mə-ˌnāt\ *v.;* **ter·mi·nat·ed**; **ter·mi·nat·ing**. **1** To form a boundary of; to bound. **2** To be bounded; to end. **3** To set or put an end or limit to. **4** To come to an end; to cease. — **ter·mi·na·tion** \ˌtər-mə-'nāsh-n\ *n.* — **ter·mi·na·tor** \'tər-mə-ˌnāt-r\ *n.*

ter·mi·nol·o·gy \ˌtər-mə-'näl-ə-jē\ *n.; pl.* **ter·mi·nol·o·gies**. The technical or special terms or words used in any field, as a business, profession, art, or science; as, the *terminology* of law.

ter·mi·nus \'tər-mə-nəs\ *n.; pl.* **ter·mi·nus·es** \-nə-səz\ or **ter·mi·ni** \-ˌnī\. **1** A boundary stone or post. **2** The end; goal. **3** Either end of a railroad or other transportation line or the buildings there.

ter·mite \'tər-ˌmīt\ *n.* A pale colored, biting and chewing insect resembling an ant, living in large colonies and feeding on wood.

termite

tern \'tərn\ *n.* A swift-flying fishing bird like a gull, common throughout the world.

ter·race \'ter-əs\ *n.* **1** A raised level or platform of earth, supported on one or more sides by a bank of turf or rock and often arranged as one of a series on a slope. **2** A row of houses along the side or top of rising ground or a street with such a row of houses. **3** An open area, usually paved, connected with a house and used as an outdoor living area; a patio. — *v.;* **ter·raced**; **ter·rac·ing**. To form into or furnish with a terrace or terraces.

ter·ra cot·ta \ˌter-ə ˈkät-ə\. [From Italian, meaning literally "baked earth".] **1** Glazed or unglazed baked earthenware. **2** The dull reddish brown color of typical terra cotta. — **ter·ra-cot·ta**, *adj.*

ter·ra fir·ma \ˌter-ə ˈfər-mə\. [Latin.] Firm or solid earth.

ter·rain \tə-ˈrān, te-\ *n.* Land, especially a visible stretch of land, considered with respect to its surface features; as, a rough *terrain.*

ter·ra·pin \ˈter-əp-n, ˈtar-\ *n.* An edible North American turtle living both in fresh and in brackish water.

ter·rar·i·um \tə-ˈrer-ē-əm\ *n.* **1** An enclosure, usually a box with glass sides, for keeping or raising small land animals indoors. **2** A small glass-enclosed indoor garden.

ter·res·tri·al \tə-ˈres-trē-əl\ *adj.* **1** Of or making up the earth; as, a *terrestrial* globe. **2** Earthly; worldly; not heavenly; as, *terrestrial* concerns. **3** Of the land; living on land and not in water, trees, or the air; as, *terrestrial* animals.

ter·ri·ble \ˈter-əb-l\ *adj.* **1** Causing or such as to cause terror; fearful; dreadful. **2** Hard to bear; distressing; excessive; extreme; very bad; as, *terrible* heat. — **ter·ri·bly** \-ə-blē\ *adv.*

ter·ri·er \ˈter-ē-ər\ *n.* A dog originally used by hunters to dig small game out of holes but now commonly kept as a pet and belonging either to a long-legged and short-bodied type including, in addition to the **fox terrier**, the **bull terrier**, **Welsh terrier**, **Irish terrier**, and **Aire·dale** \ˈar-ˌdāl, ˈer-\, or to a long-bodied and short-legged type represented by the **Scottish terrier**, **Sea·ley·ham terrier** \ˈsē-lē-ˌham, -lē-əm\ and **Skye terrier** \ˈskī\.

ter·rif·ic \tə-ˈrif-ik\ *adj.* **1** Terrifying. **2** Very great; tremendous. — **ter·rif·i·cal·ly** \-ik-l(-)ē\ *adv.*

ter·ri·fy \ˈter-ə-ˌfī\ *v.;* **ter·ri·fied** \-ˌfīd\; **ter·ri·fy·ing.** To fill with terror.

ter·ri·to·ri·al \ˌter-ə-ˈtōr-ē-əl, -ˈtȯr-\ *adj.* **1** Of or relating to territory; as, *territorial* claims. **2** [often with a capital] Of or relating to all or any of the territories of the United States; as, a *territorial* government. **3** Organized primarily for territorial defense; as, a *territorial* army. — *n. British.* A member of a territorial military force.

ter·ri·to·ry \ˈter-ə-ˌtōr-ē, -ˌtȯr-ē\ *n.; pl.* **ter·ri·to·ries.** **1** Land belonging to or controlled by a government or ruler. **2** A region; a district; especially, an area taken over by or assigned to a particular person or group; as, a salesman's *territory.* **3** [with a capital] A dependent country or part of a country; especially, a United States possession not yet a state. **4** The home area that an animal, as a bird, occupies and defends against intruders.

ter·ror \ˈter-r\ *n.* **1** Extreme fear; very great fright or dread. **2** A cause of extreme fear.

ter·ror·ism \ˈter-r-ˌiz-m\ *n.* The arousing of fear by threats or acts of violence, as in order to rule or to overthrow those in power. — **ter·ror·ist** \-əst\ *n.*

ter·ror·ize \ˈter-r-ˌīz\ *v.;* **ter·ror·ized**; **ter·ror·iz·ing.** To terrify by violence or threat of violence.

terse \ˈtərs\ *adj.* Using as few words as possible without loss of force or clearness; brief and effective; concise. — **terse·ly**, *adv.*

ter·ti·ary \ˈtər-shē-ˌer-ē\ *adj.* Of the third order, rank, or importance.

test \ˈtest\ *n.* **1** An examination or trial that shows up or measures how good or bad or how strong or weak a person or thing is. **2** A procedure or reaction used to distinguish or determine the presence of a particular substance or condition; as, a *test* for starch; a skin *test* for allergies. **3** A school examination. — For synonyms see *trial.* — *v.* To make a test of; to put to a test; as, to *test* one's strength.

tes·ta \ˈtes-tə\ *n.; pl.* **tes·tas** \-təz\ or **tes·tae** \-ˌtē, -ˌtī\. The hard external coating of a seed.

tes·ta·ment \ˈtest-m-ənt\ *n.* **1** [with a capital] One of the two parts of the Bible, the Old Testament or New Testamant; especially, the New Testament. **2** A legal paper stating how a person wishes his property distributed after his death; a will.

tes·ta·men·ta·ry \ˌtest-m-ˈent-r-ē, -ˈen-trē\ *adj.* Of or relating to a will or the administration of a will.

tes·ta·tor \ˈtes-ˌtāt-r\ *n.* A person making a will or who has died leaving a valid will or testament.

tes·ta·trix \tes-ˈtā-triks\ *n.* A woman testator.

test·er \ˈtest-r\ *n.* One that tests.

tes·ter \ˈtest-r, ˈtēst-r\ *n.* A canopy over a bed or a pulpit.

tes·ti·cle \ˈtes-tik-l\ *n.* A testis.

tes·ti·fy \ˈtes-tə-ˌfī\ *v.;* **tes·ti·fied** \-ˌfīd\; **tes·ti·fy·ing.** **1** To make a solemn statement of what is personally known or believed to be true; to give evidence; to declare solemnly, as under oath; as, to *testify* in court. **2** To give outward proof; to serve as a sign of; as, smiles *testifying* contentment.

tes·ti·mo·ni·al \ˌtest-m-ˈō-nē-əl\ *n.* **1** A letter or other writing testifying to a person's good character or ability or to the value of something. **2** A token of regard or esteem, as a gift or a reception given to a person in acknowledgment of services rendered. — *adj.* Being a testimonial; given or done as a testimonial; as, a *testimonial* dinner.

tes·ti·mo·ny \ˈtest-m-ˌō-nē\ *n.; pl.* **tes·ti·mo·nies.** **1** A statement made, especially in court, by a witness sworn to tell the truth. **2** Authoritative statements; as, the *testimony* of historians. **3** An outward proof or sign; evidence. **4** An open profession or declaration, as of one's religious faith.

tes·tis \ˈtes-təs\ *n.; pl.* **tes·tes** \-ˌtēz\. The male reproductive gland, in which the spermatozoa are produced.

test pilot. A pilot employed to test new aircraft.

test tube. A tube of thin glass closed at one end.

tes·ty \ˈtes-tē\ *adj.;* **tes·ti·er**; **tes·ti·est.** Short-tempered; easily angered; irritable.

tet·a·nus \ˈtet-n-əs\ *n.* **1** An infectious disease in which there is stiffness of the neck muscles with locking of the jaws, caused by a germ which enters the blood through a wound. **2** The state of a muscle undergoing continued contraction.

tête-à-tête \ˌtāt-ə-ˈtāt\ *adj.* [From French, meaning literally "head to head".] Being face to face; between two persons only; private; confidential. — *adv.* Together in private; privately. — *n.* A private conversation between two persons.

teth·er \'teth-r\ *n.* A rope or chain fastening an animal so that it can feed or wander only within its range. — **at the end of one's tether.** At the limit of one's power or resources. — *v.;* **teth·ered; teth·er·ing** \-r(-)ing\. To fasten with a tether.

tet·ra·chord \'te-trə-ˌkȯrd\ *n.* A diatonic series of four tones; half an octave.

tet·ra·he·dron \ˌte-trə-'hēd-rən\ *n.* A solid figure with four faces; a triangular pyramid.

te·tram·e·ter \te-'tram-ət-r\ *n.* A verse or line of four metrical feet.

Teu·ton \'tüt-n, 'tyüt-n\ *n.* **1** A member of an ancient German tribe. **2** A member of the Teutonic race; especially, a German. — *adj.* Teutonic.

Teu·ton·ic \tü-'tän-ik, tyü-\ *adj.* **1** Of or relating to the Teutons, the blond race characteristic of northern Europe. **2** Of or relating to the group of languages that includes German and the Scandinavian tongues. — *n.* The Teutonic languages.

text \'tekst\ *n.* **1** The actual words of an author's work as distinguished from illustrations, notes, or comments. **2** A verse or passage from the Bible chosen as the subject of a sermon. **3** The topic of any speech or writing; the subject.

text·book \'teks(t)-ˌbu̇k\ *n.* A book used by pupils in preparing lessons; any book designed for use as a basis of instruction.

tex·tile \'teks-ˌtīl, 'tekst-l\ *adj.* **1** Of or relating to weaving or to woven fabrics. **2** Made by weaving; as, a *textile* fabric. — *n.* A woven fabric.

tex·tu·al \'teks-chə-wəl\ *adj.* Of, in, or relating to the text; as, *textual* errors. — **tex·tu·al·ly** \-wə-lē\ *adv.*

tex·ture \'teks-chər\ *n.* **1** The characteristics of a fabric resulting from the yarn used and the method of weaving. **2** The arrangement of the particles of a body or a substance, as of minerals or bones; composition; as, rock of very soft *texture.*

-th or after a vowel **-eth**. A suffix used to form ordinal numbers, as in *tenth, twentieth, 9th, 150th.*

Thai \'tī\ *adj.* **1** Of or relating to a group of related peoples in Burma and Thailand. **2** Of or relating to Thailand; Siamese. — *n.* **1** The Thai people of Burma and Thailand. **2** A native of Thailand. **3** The language of the Thais or of Thailand.

thal·lo·phyte \'thal-ə-ˌfīt\ *n.* Any plant of the group including algae, bacteria, fungi, and lichens.

than \thən, (')than\ *conj.* **1** Used after an adjective or adverb in the comparative degree to introduce the second part of a comparison expressing inequality. The tree is higher *than* the house. **2** Used after "other" or a word of similar meaning to express a difference of kind, manner, or identity; as, adults other *than* parents.

thane \'thān\ *n.* In feudal England, one of a class of free attendants on a lord.

thank \'thangk\ *n.* **1** *Archaic.* Kindly or grateful thought; gratitude. **2** [in the plural] An expression of gratitude, as for a gift, favor, service, or courtesy. — **thanks to.** On account of. *Thanks to* that bit of carelessness, the ladder slipped. — *v.* To express or show one's gratitude or pleasure at something given to or done for him.

thank·ful \'thangk-fəl\ *adj.* Feeling or showing thanks; grateful. — **thank·ful·ly** \-fə-lē\ *adv.*

thank·less \'thangk-ləs\ *adj.* **1** Not giving thanks; ungrateful. **2** Not receiving thanks; unappreciated; as, a *thankless* task. — **thank·less·ly,** *adv.*

thanks·giv·ing \(')thangks-'giv-ing\ *n.* **1** The act of giving thanks, especially to God. **2** A prayer expressing gratitude. **3** [with a capital] In full, **Thanksgiving Day.** A day, usually the last Thursday in November, set apart by proclamation of the President of the United States as a legal holiday for public thanksgiving to God.

that, *pron.* **1** \(')that\ As a demonstrative pronoun; *pl.* **those** \(')thōz\. The person or thing mentioned or understood from the context; as, to recognize a voice as *that* of a friend — used also in opposition to *this* to mean the one farther away or first mentioned. **2** \thət\ As a relative pronoun; *sing. and pl.* Who; which; as, the one *that* answers first; books *that* everybody reads. — \(')that\ *adj.; pl.* **those** \(')thōz\. That is being pointed out or referred to as at a distance. Take *that* seat. — \thət\ *conj.* **1** Used to introduce a clause that is the object, subject, or predicate nominative of a verb; as, to know *that* one can do a job. *That* he has succeeded is undeniable. The reason for his absence is *that* he is not well. **2** Used alone or after "so" or "in order" to introduce a clause indicating purpose; as, to save money so *that* one can buy a bicycle. **3** Used after an expression including the word "so" or "such" to introduce a clause indicating result. The letter was so heavy *that* it required extra postage. **4** Used to introduce a clause or sentence expressing a wish or a cause of surprise or indignation. Oh *that* he would come! To think *that* he could deceive me so! — \'that\ *adv.* To the indicated extent; so; so very; as, not *that* old. The price is four dollars, and I don't want to pay *that* much.

thatch \'thach\ *n.* A roof or covering, for a house or hut, made of straw, rushes, reeds, or coconut or palm leaves. — *v.* To cover with thatch.

thaw \'thȯ\ *v.* **1** To melt or cause to melt or grow soft. The ice on the pond is *thawing.* **2** To become so warm or mild as to melt ice or snow. It *thawed* early this year. **3** To grow less cold in manner; to become more friendly. — *n.* **1** The action or process of thawing. **2** A period of weather warm enough to melt ice and snow.

the \thə, thē; *sense 5 is often* 'thē\ *adj.* or *definite article.* **1** One in particular; one especially pointed out. Here is *the* man you want. **2** One already spoken of. Please give me *the* book. **3** One that is near in space, time, or thought; as, news of *the* day. **4** One that forms or is thought of as forming a class with no other members; as, *the* Lord; *the* sky;

the sun; *the* Nile. **5** One having no equal; as, *the* poet of his time. **6** One that is most familiar or best known; as, *the* president. **7** Each; every; as, ten cents *the* copy. **8** A person or thing considered as typical of his or its class; as, hard as *the* diamond. **9** His, hers, its, or one's; as, pleasing to *the* eye; leading her by *the* hand. **10** All those that are; as, *the* Germans; *the* wise. **11** That which is; as, *the* beautiful. — *adv.* To what extent; to that extent; as, *the* sooner *the* better.

the·a·ter or **the·a·tre** \'thē-ət-r, 'thi-\ *n.* **1** A place in which plays or moving pictures are presented. **2** A place or area where some important action is carried on; as, a *theater* of war. **3** Dramas; the drama; as, the *theater* of Shakespeare's time. **4** A place like a theater in form or use.

the·at·ri·cal \thē-'a-trik-l\ *adj.* **1** Of or relating to the theater or the drama. **2** Like that in the theater; not natural and simple; artificial; showy; as, in a *theatrical* voice. — *n.* [usually in the plural] A dramatic performance, especially by amateurs. — **the·at·ri·cal·ly** \-trik-l(-)ē\ *adv.*

thee \(')th̲ē\ *pron.* The form of the word *thou* that is used as the object of a verb or of a preposition.

theft \'theft\ *n.* The act of stealing.

their \th̲ər, (')th̲er, (')th̲ar\ *adj.* Belonging to them; done by or to them; as, *their* clothes; during *their* absence; *their* mistakes.

theirs \'th̲erz, 'th̲arz\ *pron.* The form of the word *their* that is used to show possession when no noun follows. The books are *theirs.*

the·ism \'thē-ˌiz-m\ *n.* Belief in the existence of a god or gods; especially, belief in the existence of God as creator and ruler of the universe. — **the·ist** \-əst\ *n.* — **the·is·tic** \thē-'is-tik\ *adj.*

them \(th̲)əm, m, (')th̲em\ *pron.* The form of the word *they* that is used as object of a verb or of a preposition.

the·mat·ic \thē-'mat-ik\ *adj.* Of or relating to a theme or themes. — **the·mat·i·cal·ly** \-ik-l(-)ē\ *adv.*

theme \'thēm\ *n.* **1** A subject of discourse or discussion; a topic. **2** A short composition written as a school exercise. **3** In music, a short melody used as a basis for variation and development. **4** A melody used to identify a radio or television program.

them·selves \th̲əm-'selvz, th̲em-\ *pron.* **1** A form of the word *they* that is used to give emphasis or to show that the subject and object of a verb are the same persons or things. They *themselves* did it. They hurt *themselves.* **2** Their normal or true selves. They were not *themselves* that day.

then \(')th̲en\ *adv.* **1** At that time. It was *then* believed the world was flat. **2** Soon after; afterwards; next. The flash came first, *then* the sound. **3** If that is the case. Well, *then,* we must ask him. **4** Consequently; accordingly. If you saw him do it, *then* you should say so. — **now and then.** Occasionally. — **now then.** An expression used to call attention or to give a warning. — \'th̲en\ *n.* That time. We shall rest till *then.*

thence \'th̲en(t)s, 'then(t)s\ *adv.* **1** From that place; as, to go *thence* to sea. **2** From that time; thereafter; as, one year *thence.* From that part; therefore. It was a hopeless, *thence* helpless case.

thence·forth \'th̲en(t)s-ˌfōrth, 'then(t)s-, -ˌfȯrth\ *adv.* From that time on; thereafter.

thence·for·ward \th̲en(t)s-'fȯr-wərd, then(t)s-\ *adv.* Onward from that place or, especially, time.

the·oc·ra·cy \thē-'äk-rə-sē\ *n.; pl.* **the·oc·ra·cies.** **1** Government by priests or ministers. **2** A state so governed. — **the·o·crat·ic** \ˌthē-ə-'krat-ik\ *adj.*

the·od·o·lite \thē-'äd-l-ˌīt\ *n.* A surveying instrument for measuring horizontal and vertical angles.

the·o·lo·gian \ˌthē-ə-'lōj-n\ *n.* A person trained or versed in theology.

the·o·log·i·cal \ˌthē-ə-'läj-ik-l\ *adj.* Of or relating to theology. — **the·o·log·i·cal·ly** \-ik-l(-)ē\ *adv.*

the·ol·o·gy \thē-'äl-ə-jē\ *n.; pl.* **the·ol·o·gies.** **1** Knowledge of God and the supernatural; religious knowledge. **2** The study of religion and religious beliefs. **3** A system of religious beliefs.

the·o·rem \'thē-ər-əm, 'thir-əm\ *n.* **1** An established principle or law, as in a science. **2** A general statement in mathematics that has been proved or is to be proved. **3** A statement of mathematical relations expressed in a formula or by symbols.

the·o·ret·i·cal \ˌthē-ə-'ret-ik-l\ *adj.* **1** Relating to theory; not proved; as, a purely *theoretical* explanation. **2** Not practical; not applied; as, *theoretical* science. **3** Existing principally in theory; not really effective or existent; as, a *theoretical* right to appeal to a higher court. **4** Given to theorizing. — **the·o·ret·i·cal·ly** \-ik-l(-)ē\ *adv.*

the·o·rist \'thē-ər-əst, 'thir-əst\ *n.* A theorizer.

the·o·rize \'thē-ə-ˌrīz\ *v.;* **the·o·rized; the·o·riz·ing.** To form an opinion of what is likely to be true; to form theories. — **the·o·riz·er** \-ˌrīz-r\ *n.*

the·o·ry \'thē-ər-ē, 'thir-ē\ *n.; pl.* **the·o·ries.** **1** The general principles drawn from any body of facts, as in science; pure science as distinguished from applied science. **2** The principles governing a certain practice, as of a profession or an art; as, the *theory* of medicine. **3** A careful and plausible explanation which covers known facts; an opinion offered as possibly but not positively true; as, an expert's *theory* of the explosion.

ther·a·peu·tic \ˌther-ə-'pyüt-ik\ *adj.* Having to do with remedies and healing; curative.

ther·a·peu·tics \ˌther-ə-'pyüt-iks\ *n.* The branch of medical science dealing with the use of remedies.

ther·a·py \'ther-ə-pē\ *n.; pl.* **ther·a·pies.** The treatment of disease; therapeutics. — **ther·a·pist** \-pəst\ *n.*

there \'th̲ar, 'th̲er\ *adv.* **1** In or at that place. The train will stop *there.* **2** To or into that place; thither. Take the basket *there* and leave it. **3** At that point or stage. *There* the lecture became hard to follow. **4** In that matter or circumstance; in that respect. You were correct *there.* — *interj.* An exclamation used to express encouragement, approval, or satisfaction, and also comfort or dismay. *There!* I knew you could do it.

☞ *there* \pronounced thər, (ˌ)thar, or (ˌ)ther\ is often used to introduce a sentence in which the subject comes after the verb. *There* are four children in our family. *There* was a storm today.

there·a·bouts \'thar-ə-ˌbau̇ts, 'ther-\ or **there·a·bout** \-ˌbau̇t\ *adv.* **1** Near that place. It happened *thereabouts.* **2** Near that number or quantity; nearly; as, twenty people or *thereabouts.*

there·aft·er \thar-'aft-r, ther-\ *adv.* After that; afterwards. The stranger was not seen *thereafter.*

there·at \thar-'at, ther-\ *adv.* **1** At that place or point; there. **2** On that account; at that occurrence. He was ignored and angered *thereat.*

there·by \thar-'bī, 'thar-ˌbī, (')ther-\ *adv.* **1** By that means. The chief *thereby* made an enemy. **2** Connected with that. *Thereby* hangs a tale. **3** Thereabouts. The miller was at the mill or *thereby.* **4** By it; in possession of it; as, to come *thereby* honestly.

there·for \thar-'fȯr, ther-\ *adv.* For it; in return for it; as, to give one's reasons *therefor.*

there·fore \'thar-ˌfōr, 'ther-, -ˌfȯr\ *adv.* For that reason; consequently; hence.

there·from \thar-'frəm, ther-, -'främ\ *adv.* From that; from it; as, to learn much *therefrom.*

there·in \thar-'in, ther-\ *adv.* **1** In or into that place, time, or thing; as, the sea and all that is *therein.* **2** In that matter or respect. *Therein* we do not agree.

there·of \thar-'əv, ther-, -'äv\ *adv.* **1** Of that; of it. The man took the bread and ate *thereof.* **2** From that cause; therefrom. The soldier's wound was so deep that he died *thereof.*

there·on \thar-'ȯn, ther-, -'än\ *adv.* **1** On that; as, a table with a basket set *thereon.* **2** Thereupon.

there's \thərz, (ˌ)tharz, (ˌ)therz\. A contraction of *there is.*

there·to \thar-'tü, ther-\ *adv.* To that; as, the conditions *thereto* attached.

there·to·fore \'thart-ə-ˌfōr, 'thert-, -ˌfȯr\ *adv.* Up to that time.

there·un·to \thar-'ən-ˌtü, ther-; ˌthar-(ˌ)ən-'tü, ˌther-\ *adv.* Thereto; in addition; besides.

there·up·on \'thar-ə-ˌpȯn, 'ther-, -ˌpän\ *adv.* **1** Upon that; thereon; as, to disagree *thereupon.* **2** On account of that; therefore. The child ate too much candy and *thereupon* was sick. **3** Immediately after that; at once. The visitor pressed the button and *thereupon* the bell rang.

there·with \thar-'with, ther-, -'with\ *adv.* **1** With that; as, to lead a simple life and be happy *therewith.* **2** Thereupon; thereat.

there·with·al \ˌthar-wi-'thȯl, ˌther-, -'thȯl\ *adv.* **1** Over and above; besides; moreover. **2** With that; therewith.

ther·mal \'thərm-l\ or **ther·mic** \'thər-mik\ *adj.* Of or relating to heat; warm; hot.

ther·mo·dy·nam·ics \ˌthər-mō-dī-'nam-iks\ *n.* The science that deals with the relations between heat and other forms of energy, especially mechanical energy. — **ther·mo·dy·nam·ic** \-ik\ *adj.*

ther·mom·e·ter \thə(r)-'mäm-ət-r\ *n.* An instrument for measuring temperature, commonly by means of the expansion or contraction of mercury or alcohol as indicated by its rise or fall in a thin glass tube.

thermometer

ther·mo·nu·cle·ar \ˌthər-mō-'nük-lē-ər, -'nyük-\ *adj.* Relating to changes in the nuclei of atoms requiring unusually high temperatures, as in the hydrogen bomb.

ther·mo·stat \'thər-mə-ˌstat\ *n.* A device that automatically controls temperature, as by regulating a flow of liquid fuel or gas. — **ther·mo·stat·ic** \ˌthər-mə-'stat-ik\ *adj.* — **ther·mo·stat·i·cal·ly** \-ik-l(-)ē\ *adv.*

these. Plural of *this.*

the·sis \'thē-səs\ *n.; pl.* **the·ses** \-ˌsēz\. **1** A proposition, especially one to be proved or debated. **2** An essay or dissertation offered by a candidate for a college degree.

thews \'thüz, 'thyüz\ *n. pl.* Muscles; sinews.

they \(')thā\. Plural of *he, she,* or *it.*

they'd \(')thād\. A contraction of *they had* or *they would.*

they'll \(')thāl\. A contraction of *they will* or *they shall.*

they're \(')ther, (')thā-ər\. A contraction of *they are.*

they've \(')thāv\. A contraction of *they have.*

thi·a·mine \'thī-ə-mən, -ˌmēn\ or **thi·a·min** \-mən\ *n.* A vitamin found especially in cereals, nuts, yeast, and animal food products, used in the treatment of beriberi.

thick \'thik\ *adj.* **1** Having relatively great depth or extent from one of its surfaces to the opposite surface; not thin or slender; as, a *thick* slice. **2** Measuring through from one surface to its opposite; as, a book an inch *thick.* **3** Crowded; filled closely; as, a *thick* forest. **4** Dense; having great density; as, a *thick* fog; *thick* syrup. **5** Not clear. The air was *thick* with smoke. **6** Dull; stupid. **7** Husky; hoarse; as, a *thick* voice. **8** Falling fast; frequent; rapid. *Thick* snow fell all day. **9** Very friendly; intimate. — *n.* The time or place where something is thickest or most intense; as, in the *thick* of battle. — *adv.* Thickly. — **thick·ly,** *adv.*

thick·en \'thik-n\ *v.;* **thick·ened; thick·en·ing** \-n(-)ing\. To make or become thick or thicker.

thick·et \'thik-ət\ *n.* A thick growth of shrubbery, small trees, or underbrush.

thick·ness \'thik-nəs\ *n.* **1** The quality or state of being thick. **2** The depth or extent from one surface of an object to the opposite surface. **3** A layer; a sheet; as, several *thicknesses* of padding.

thick·set \'thik-'set\ *adj.* **1** Closely placed or planted. **2** Short and stout; stocky.

thick-skinned \'thik-'skind\ *adj.* **1** Having a thick skin. **2** Not sensitive; callous, as to criticism.

thief \'thēf\ *n.; pl.* **thieves** \'thēvz\. One who steals. — **thiev·ish** \'thē-vish\ *adj.* — **thiev·ish·ly,** *adv.*

thieve \'thēv\ *v.;* **thieved**; **thiev·ing.** To steal.

thiev·ery \'thēv-r(-)ē\ *n.; pl.* **thiev·er·ies.** The action of stealing; theft.

thigh \'thī\ *n.* The part of a person's leg or of the hind leg of a lower vertebrate between the knee and the trunk.

thigh·bone \'thī-'bōn, -ˌbōn\ *n.* The single bone extending from the hipbone to the knee; the femur.

thim·ble \'thim-bl\ *n.* [From Old English *thymel,* a derivative of *thuma* meaning "thumb".] A cap, cover, or broad ring used in sewing to protect the finger that pushes the needle.

thin \'thin\ *adj.;* **thin·ner**; **thin·nest. 1** Having relatively little depth; slender; not thick. **2** Not closely set or placed; sparse; scant; as, *thin* hair. **3** Not dense, or not dense enough; as, *thin* mountain air. **4** Watery; as, a *thin* syrup. **5** Lacking in strength, fullness, or richness; as, a *thin* voice. **6** Easily seen through; flimsy; slight; as, a *thin* excuse.

— The words *lean* and *gaunt* are synonyms of *thin: thin* is a general term for a person having no excess flesh or fat and often less than is desirable for good health; *lean* may suggest such a lack of fat as to cause an angular, rather than a pleasantly curving, appearance of the body, but may also suggest the tough, wiry, agile frame typical of some athletes; *gaunt* is likely to suggest boniness and an emaciated, undernourished appearance.

thin \'thin\ *v.;* **thinned**; **thin·ning.** To make or become thin or thinner. — **thin·ly,** *adv.* — **thin·ner,** *n.*

thine \(')thīn\ *pron.* The possessive form of *thou* used when no noun follows. The book is *thine.* — *adj.* The form of *thy* used before a vowel or *h.* Give *thine* answer.

thing \'thing\ *n.* **1** [in the plural] The state of affairs. *Things* grew worse. **2** A happening or deed; as, to hope to do great *things.* **3** The product, end, or aim of effort or activity; as, a boy who is handy at making *things.* **4** Anything at all; whatever exists; an object; an object as opposed to a living being. A book is a *thing,* not a person. **5** A substance or material; as, to like sweet *things.* **6** An article of clothing; as, to put on one's *things.* **7** [in the plural] Possessions; belongings; as, to gather one's *things* together. **8** A detail; an item. **9** A creature; a person; as, the poor little *thing.*

think \'thingk\ *v.;* **thought** \'thȯt\; **think·ing. 1** To form in the mind; to imagine; to conceive; as, to *think* noble thoughts. **2** To have an opinion of something; to believe. **3** To believe possible or likely; to suppose. I *think* it will rain. **4** To determine by reflecting; to reason; as, to try to *think* what to do. **5** To have in mind; to be mindful, conscious, or concerned; as, to *think* of oneself first. **6** To hold a view or views. **7** To have or form an opinion, mental picture, or notion; as, to try to *think* of the old man as he must have been when young. — **think·a·ble** \'thingk-əb-l\ *adj.* — **think·er** \-r\ *n.*

thin-skinned \'thin-'skind\ *adj.* **1** Having a thin skin. **2** Sensitive; easily affected, as by criticism.

third \'thərd\ *adj.* Next after the second. — *n.* One of three equal parts.

third degree Severe treatment of a prisoner by the police in order to get an admission.

third estate. The common people.

third·ly \'thərd-lē\ *adv.* In the third place.

thirst \'thərst\ *n.* **1** A sensation of dryness in the mouth and throat, with a craving for liquids; the condition that produces this feeling; as, a feverish *thirst.* **2** Any strong desire; a craving; as, a *thirst* for knowledge. — *v.* **1** To feel thirst; to crave drink. **2** To have a strong desire; to long.

thirsty \'thərs-tē\ *adj.;* **thirst·i·er**; **thirst·i·est. 1** Feeling thirst. **2** Dry; needing moisture; as, *thirsty* fields. — **thirst·i·ly** \-tə-lē\ *adv.*

thir·teen \'thər(t)-'tēn\ *adj.* Ten and three; one more than twelve. — *n.* **1** The sum of ten and three; thirteen units. **2** A figure standing for thirteen units, as 13 or XIII.

thir·teenth \'thər(t)-'tēn(t)th\ *adj.* Next after the twelfth. — *n.; pl.* **thir·teenths** \-'tēn(t)s, -'tēn(t)ths\. One of thirteen equal parts.

thir·ti·eth \'thərt-ē-əth\ *adj.* Next after the twenty-ninth. — *n.* One of thirty equal parts.

thir·ty \'thərt-ē\ *adj.* Three times ten; one more than twenty-nine. — *n.; pl.* **thir·ties. 1** The sum of three tens; thirty units. **2** A figure standing for thirty units, as 30 or XXX.

this \(')this, thəs\ *pron.; pl.* **these** \(')thēz\. The person or thing present, near, or just mentioned. *These* are friendly people. — *adj.* That is present, near, or just referred to; as, *this* book.

this·tle \'this-l\ *n.* **1** A tall prickly herb with spiny-margined leaves and tight heads of yellowish or purplish flowers. **2** Any herb of a family of which the thistle and aster are typical, having close heads of tubular flowers in a central disk and bearing a dry one-seeded fruit usually crowned with scales, bristles, or hairs. — **this·tly** \-l(-)ē\ *adj.*

thistle

this·tle·down \'this-l-ˌdau̇n\ *n.* The down from the ripe flower head of a thistle.

thith·er \'thith-r, 'thith-r\ *adv.* To that place; there. — *adj.* Away from the speaker; further.

tho. Variant of *though.*

thole \'thōl\ *n.* Also **thole·pin** \-ˌpin\. A pin set in the gunwale of a boat as a pivot for an oar.

thong \'thȯng, 'thäng\ *n.* A strip of leather, especially one used for fastening something.

tho·rax \'thōr-ˌaks, 'thȯr-\ *n.; pl.* **tho·rax·es** \-ˌaks-əz\ or **tho·ra·ces** \thə-'rā-ˌsēz\. **1** The part of the body of man and other mammals that lies between the neck and the abdomen and is supported by the ribs and breastbone. **2** The cavity inside this part of the body, containing the heart, lungs, and esophagus. **3** In insects, the middle of the three divisions of the body. — **tho·rac·ic** \thə-'ras-ik\ *adj.*

tho·ri·um \'thōr-ē-əm, 'thȯr-\ *n.* A rare radioactive metallic element occurring in certain minerals.

thorn \'thȯrn\ *n.* **1** A short, hard, sharp-pointed woody spine formed from a leafless branch on a plant, as on a rose. **2** A bush or tree that has thorns, as a hawthorn. **3** Something that hurts; a cause of distress or irritation. The boy's behavior was a *thorn* in his father's side.

thorny \'thȯr-nē\ *adj.;* **thorn·i·er; thorn·i·est. 1** Full of or covered with thorns; spiny. **2** Difficult; vexatious; as, a *thorny* problem.

tho·ron \'thōr-ˌän, 'thȯr-\ *n.* A gaseous radioactive chemical element formed from thorium.

thor·ough \'thər-ō, 'thə-rō\ *adj.* **1** Complete; as, a *thorough* success. **2** Being completely a certain thing. **3** Painstaking; careful about details.

thor·ough·bred \'thər-ə-ˌbred, 'thə-rə-\ *adj.* **1** [sometimes with a capital] Being of the breed of horses called Thoroughbreds. **2** Purebred. **3** Graceful, high-spirited, and elegant; characterized by good breeding and culture; as, a *thoroughbred* lady. — *n.* **1** [with a capital] A horse of a breed developed especially for racing. **2** A purebred animal. **3** A thoroughbred person.

thor·ough·fare \'thər-ə-ˌfar, 'thə-rə-, -ˌfer\ *n.* **1** A public way, connecting two streets; a street or road open at both ends. **2** A main road; a busy street.

thor·ough·go·ing \'thər-ə-ˌgō-ing, 'thə-rə-\ *adj.* Leaving nothing untouched or undone; thorough.

thor·ough·ly \'thər-ə-lē, 'thə-rə-\ *adv.* **1** Carefully; painstakingly. **2** Fully; very much; as, a picnic that everyone *thoroughly* enjoyed.

thorp or **thorpe** \'thȯrp\ *n.* A group of houses in the country; a hamlet.

those. Plural of *that.*

thou \(')thau̇\ *pron.* The person being spoken to; you — now used only in solemn or poetical style.

though or **tho** \(')thō\ *conj.* **1** Notwithstanding that; despite the fact that. *Though* it was raining, he went for a walk. **2** Even if; even supposing; as, determined to tell the truth *though* he should die for it. — **as though.** As if; looked *as though* he had seen a ghost. — \'thō\ *adv.* However; all the same; as, not for long, *though.*

thought \'thȯt\ *n.* **1** The act or process of thinking; use of the mind. **2** The power of thinking, especially of reasoning and judging. **3** The power to imagine or realize; as, beauty beyond *thought.* **4** A product of thinking; an idea, fancy, or intention; as, a pleasant *thought.* **5** Careful attention; heed. **6** Reflection; mental absorption. **7** A little; a trifle; as, just a *thought* more careful.

thought \'thȯt\. Past tense and past part. of *think.*

thought·ful \'thȯt-fəl\ *adj.* **1** Showing depth of thought; as, a *thoughtful* answer. **2** Mindful of others; considerate. **3** Pensive; meditative; as, a *thoughtful* look. — **thought·ful·ly** \-fə-lē\ *adv.*

thought·less \'thȯt-ləs\ *adj.* **1** Not giving thought; not careful. A *thoughtless* worker makes mistakes. **2** Heedless; reckless; rash; as, a *thoughtless* act. **3** Not considerate of other people. *Thoughtless* remarks often hurt others. — **thought·less·ly,** *adv.*

thou·sand \'thau̇z-n(d)\ *adj.* Ten hundred. — *n.* **1** The sum of ten hundreds; one thousand units or objects. **2** The figure standing for one thousand units, as 1000 or M.

thou·sand·fold \'thau̇z-n(d)-ˌfōld, -'fōld\ *adj.* or *adv.* A thousand times as much or as many.

thou·sandth \'thau̇z-n(t)th\ *adj.* Next after the nine hundred and ninety-ninth. — *n.; pl.* **thou·sandths** \-n(t)s, -n(t)ths\. One of one thousand equal parts.

thrall \'thrȯl\ *n.* **1** *Archaic.* A slave. **2** Thralldom. **3** Moral or mental bondage.

thrall·dom or **thral·dom** \'thrȯld-m\ *n.* A state of servitude; slavery; bondage.

thrash \'thrash\ *v.* **1** To thresh. **2** To go over again and again; as, to *thrash* out the details of a plan. **3** To beat soundly; to flog. **4** To move or stir violently, in the manner of a rapidly moving flail; as, to *thrash* around in the water. — *n.* A thrashing, as of the legs in certain strokes used in swimming.

thrash·er \'thrash-r\ *n.* **1** One that thrashes. **2** A thresher shark. **3** A long-tailed singing and mimicking bird resembling a thrush, as the **brown thrasher**, brown above and streaked below.

thread \'thred\ *n.* **1** A thin continuous filament; especially, a thin, fine cord made by twisting together strands of spun material, as cotton, flax, or silk, and used for sewing or weaving. **2** Anything resembling or suggestive of a thread used in sewing; as, a *thread* of light. **3** A line of reasoning or train of thought that connects the parts in a sequence of ideas or events. The storyteller lost the *thread* of his story. **4** The ridge or groove that winds around a screw; also, one complete turn of this ridge. — *v.* **1** To pass a thread through, as the eye of a needle. **2** To pass through like a thread; as, rock *threaded* with gold. **3** To go or make one's way carefully among obstacles; as, to *thread* through the crowd in the streets. **4** To string together; as, to *thread* beads. **5** To form a thread on or in; as, to *thread* a screw. **6** To spin a fine filament when dropped, as boiling syrup from the edge of a spoon. — **thread·er,** *n.*

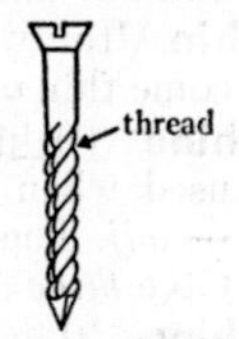

thread, 4

thread·bare \'thred-ˌbar, -ˌber\ *adj.* **1** Having the nap worn off so that the threads show; shabby; as, a *threadbare* rug. **2** With the freshness worn off; without interest; as, a dull, *threadbare* subject.

thready \'thred-ē\ *adj.;* **thread·i·er; thread·i·est. 1** Very thin or slender. **2** Very thin or slight; as, a *thready* voice. **3** Consisting of, containing, or covered with threads or filaments.

threat \'thret\ *n.* **1** The expression of an intention to do harm to another; as, to utter a *threat.* **2** A threatening; a danger or a sign of danger; as, spring rains bringing with them a *threat* of floods.

threat·en \'thret-n\ *v.;* **threat·ened; threat·en·ing**

\-n(-)ing\. **1** To utter threats; to make threats against; as, to *threaten* trespassers. **2** To give warning of, as by a threat or sign; as, clouds *threatening* rain. **3** To give signs of trouble to come. **4** To announce as intended or possible; as, to *threaten* to buy a new car. — **threat·en·ing·ly**, *adv.*

three \'thrē\ *adj.* Two and one more. — *n.* **1** The sum of two and one; three units or objects. **2** The figure standing for three units, as 3 or III.

three-deck·er \'thrē-'dek-r\ *n.* **1** A ship having three decks; a warship carrying guns on three decks. **2** Anything having three floors, tiers, or layers.

three-di·men·sion·al \'thrēd-m-'ench-n(-)əl, 'thrē-dī-'mench-\ *adj.* **1** Of, having, or relating to three dimensions; as, *three-dimensional* space. **2** Giving the illusion of depth or varying distances, as certain photographs and moving pictures.

three·fold \'thrē-ˌfōld, -'fōld\ *adj.* or *adv.* Having three parts; three times as much or as many.

three·pence \'thrip-n(t)s, 'thrəp-, 'threp-\ *n.* The sum of three pence or an English coin of this value.

three·pen·ny \'thrē-ˌpen-ē; 'thrip-n-ē, 'thrəp-, 'threp-\ *adj.* **1** Costing or worth threepence. **2** Of little value; poor; mean.

three R's. Reading, writing, and arithmetic.

three·score \'thrē-ˌskōr, -ˌskȯr\ *adj.* Sixty.

three·some \'thrēs-m\ *n.* **1** Something, as a game, in which three persons participate. **2** The three players in such a game. **3** Any group of three.

thren·o·dy \'thren-əd-ē\ *n.; pl.* **thren·o·dies.** A song of lament or sorrow; a dirge.

thresh \'thrash, 'thresh\ *v.* **1** To beat out grain from straw. **2** To thrash; as, to *thresh* the matter over; to *thresh* about on one's bed.

thresh·er \'thrash-r, 'thresh-r\ *n.* **1** A person that threshes. **2** A machine that threshes grain. **3** Also **thresher shark.** A large shark having a great tail reputedly used to thresh the water to stir up fish.

thresh·old \'thresh-ˌ(h)ōld\ *n.* **1** The sill of a door. **2** An entrance; beginning; outset; as, at the *threshold* of an adventure. **3** The point or level at which a physiological or psychological effect begins to be produced; as, below the *threshold* of consciousness.

threw. Past tense of *throw.*

thrice \'thrīs\ *adv.* **1** Three times. **2** In a threefold manner or degree; greatly; as, *thrice*-blessed.

thrift \'thrift\ *n.* **1** Economical management; frugality. **2** Vigorous growth, as of a plant. **3** A tufted stemless herb having heads of pink or white flowers, growing on mountains and seacoasts.

thrift·less \'thrift-ləs\ *adj.* Lacking thrift; wasteful. — **thrift·less·ly**, *adv.*

thrifty \'thrif-tē\ *adj.;* **thrift·i·er; thrift·i·est. 1** Inclined to save; saving. **2** Thriving through industry and frugality; prosperous. **3** Thriving; as, a *thrifty* plant. — For synonyms see *frugal.*

thrill \'thril\ *v.* **1** To affect or become affected emotionally as if by something that pierces; to have or cause to have a shivering, throbbing, or tingling feeling; as, to *thrill* with excitement. **2** To tremble; to vibrate; as, a voice that *thrilled* with feeling. — *n.* **1** A sensation of being thrilled; a quivering excitement. **2** A shaking or trembling; especially, an abnormal quiver or tremor. **3** A cause of thrilling; as a story that was full of *thrills.*

thrill·er \'thril-r\ *n.* One that thrills; especially, a sensational play or story.

thrips \'thrips\ *n.* A tiny sucking insect with narrow fringed wings, feeding mostly on plant juices.

thrive \'thrīv\ *v.;* **throve** \'thrōv\ or **thrived** \'thrīvd\; **thrived** \'thrīvd\ or **thriv·en** \'thriv-n\; **thriv·ing** \'thrī-ving\. **1** To win success by hard work, thrift, and good management. **2** To prosper by any means; to be successful. **3** To grow vigorously.

thro' \(')thrü\. Short for *through.*

throat \'thrōt\ *n.* **1** The part of the neck in front of the backbone. **2** The passage from the mouth to the stomach and lungs; as, to have a sore *throat.* **3** An entrance or a narrow part of anything; as, the *throat* of a vase. — **throat·ed** \-əd\ *adj.*

throaty \'thrōt-ē\ *adj.;* **throat·i·er; throat·i·est. 1** Uttered or produced from low in the throat; as, a *throaty* voice. **2** Heavy, thick, and deep, as if from the throat; as, the *throaty* notes of a horn.

throb \'thräb\ *v.;* **throbbed; throb·bing. 1** To beat, as the human pulse does; to pulsate; to vibrate. **2** To beat fast or hard; to pound; to palpitate. — The word *palpitate* is a synonym of *throb:* both terms refer to a rhythmic movement or vibration similar to that of the heart and circulatory system in the body; *throb* usually refers to any abnormally strong or insistent beating or pulsating, as from intense pain; *palpitate* generally suggests a rapid throbbing, often, a fluttering or quivering. — *n.* A beat or pulsation, as of the heart.

throe \'thrō\ *n.* Extreme pain or a violent spasm of pain; anguish; agony. — **in the throes of.** In the midst of struggling or contending with.

throm·bo·sis \thräm-'bō-səs\ *n.* The formation of a clot (**throm·bus** \'thräm-bəs\) in the heart or in a blood vessel during life.

throne \'thrōn\ *n.* **1** A decorated chair, often one having a canopy and raised on a platform, used as by a king or bishop on special occasions; a chair of state. **2** The power and dignity of a ruler; supreme rank or position. — *v.;* **throned; thron·ing.** To place on a throne; to enthrone.

throng \'thrȯng, 'thräng\ *n.* A great number assembled together; a crowd. — For synonyms see *multitude.* — *v.* **1** To crowd together. Thousands *thronged* to see the game. **2** To crowd into; as, to *throng* a stadium.

thros·tle \'thräs-l\ *n. Dial.* A thrush.

throt·tle \'thrät-l\ *n.* **1** The throat or windpipe. **2** A valve regulating the volume of steam or of fuel, as gasoline, delivered to the cylinders of an engine. **3** A lever or pedal operating such a valve. — *v.;* **throt·tled; throt·tling** \-l(-)ing\. **1** To choke; to strangle. **2** To stop or check, as the flow of fuel to an engine by closing a valve; to reduce the speed of an engine by this means.

through or **thru** \(')thrü\ *prep.* **1** In at one side and out at the opposite side of; as, *through* a gate. **2** Into and beyond; as, a road *through* town. **3** Among; in the midst of; as, walking *through* the trees. **4** During; from the beginning to the end of; as, *through* the night. **5** By means of; as, to do something *through* strength alone. **6** By way of; as, to go out *through* the window. **7** Over the whole surface or extent of; as, all *through* the country. **8** By reason of; because of; as, to hide *through* fear. — *adv.* **1** From one side or end to an opposite one. The bullet pierced his arm *through.* **2** All the way. The parcel was shipped *through* to Chicago. **3** From beginning to end; to completion; as, to read the book *through.* **4** Thoroughly; as, to be wet *through.* — *adj.* **1** Having both entrance and exit; as, a *through* street. **2** Finished; done; as, to be *through* at five o'clock. **3** Reaching or going from one end of a route to the other without change; as, *through* transportation. **4** Having to do with such transportation; as, a *through* ticket.

through·out \thrü-'aüt\ *prep.* **1** In or to every part of; as, *throughout* the house. **2** During the whole time of; as, *throughout* the evening. — *adv.* From beginning to end; in every part; as, to remain loyal *throughout;* of one color *throughout.*

through·way or **thru·way** \'thrü-ˌwā\ *n.* A superhighway; an expressway.

throve. A past tense of *thrive.*

throw \'thrō\ *v.;* **threw** \'thrü\; **thrown** \'thrōn\; **throw·ing.** **1** To twist two or more fibers to form one thread. **2** To fling, hurl, toss, or cast, especially with a quick forward motion of the arm at shoulder level or higher. **3** To fling or cast in any way. The girl *threw* a glance at her mother. **4** To cause to fall; as, to *throw* an opponent at wrestling. **5** To put in a certain condition or position; as, to be *thrown* out of work. **6** To put on or take off hastily; as, to *throw* on a coat. **7** To shed. A snake *throws* its skin. **8** To move quickly; as, to *throw* in reinforcements. **9** To move, as a switch or a lever. **10** *Slang.* To act as host for; to give; as, to *throw* a party.

—The words *hurl* and *fling* are synonyms of *throw: throw* is a general term for propelling something through the air, as with the arm; *hurl* usually suggests a forceful throwing that propels the object quickly and for a long distance; *fling* suggests more force and violence in throwing and often carelessness brought about by strong feeling, as anger, annoyance, or haste and excitement.

— **throw away.** **1** To discard. **2** To waste, as an opportunity. — **throw back.** **1** To retort. **2** To revert to an ancestral type. — **throw in.** **1** To contribute. **2** To add, as something extra to clinch a bargain. — **throw off.** **1** To free oneself of, as a disease. **2** To utter or produce offhand. — **throw open.** **1** To open suddenly and widely. **2** To remove restrictions from; as, to *throw open* a meeting for general discussion. — **throw out.** **1** To throw away; to discard. **2** To send or give forth; to utter. **3** In baseball, to assist by a throw in putting a player out. — **throw over.** To abandon, as a person or his cause; to forsake. — **throw up.** **1** To vomit. **2** To construct hastily. **3** To raise suddenly, as the hands. **4** To bring up or mention in a scornful or jeering way; as, to *throw up* to a man a past mistake. — *n.* **1** The act of throwing, flinging, or hurling; a cast. **2** A light wrap for warmth or decoration. **3** The distance something is or may be thrown; as, a stone's *throw.* **4** A way of throwing an opponent in wrestling.

throw·back \'thrō-ˌbak\ *n.* A reverting to an ancestral type or to an earlier stage of civilization.

thrown. Past part. of *throw.*

thru. Variant of *through.*

thrum \'thrəm\ *v.;* **thrummed**; **thrum·ming.** **1** To strum; as, to *thrum* a banjo. **2** To sound with a repeated monotonous hum; as, *thrumming* telephone wires. — *n.* The sound of thrumming.

thrush \'thrəsh\ *n.* Any of numerous insect-eating songbirds, usually of a plain color but sometimes with spotted or differently colored under parts, as the European blackbird and **song thrush** and the common robin, the sweet-singing **wood thrush**, and the retiring **hermit thrush** in America.

thrust \'thrəst\ *v.;* **thrust**; **thrust·ing.** **1** To push or drive with force; to shove; as, to *thrust* a person aside. **2** To stab or pierce. **3** To push forth or extend, as the roots of a plant. — *n.* **1** A hard push. **2** A stab. **3** An attack, as by military forces into enemy-held territory. **4** The force exerted endwise through a propeller shaft. **5** The forwardly directed reaction force produced by a jet discharged rearward from a nozzle. **6** The outward pressure of one part of a construction against another.

thruway. Variant of *throughway.*

thud \'thəd\ *n.* **1** A blow. **2** A dull thump. — *v.;* **thud·ded**; **thud·ding.** To move or strike so as to make a thud. The book *thudded* onto the floor.

thug \'thəg\ *n.* A ruffian; an assassin; a tough.

thu·li·um \'thü-lē-əm, 'thyü-\ *n.* A rare metallic chemical element.

thumb \'thəm\ *n.* **1** The short thick finger of the human hand next to the forefinger. **2** The part of a glove that covers the thumb. — *v.* **1** To touch or turn with or as if with the thumb; as, to *thumb* the pages of a book. **2** To soil or wear with the thumb by frequent handling; as, a well-*thumbed* book. **3** To ask for or obtain, as a ride in a passing car, by signaling with the thumb.

thumb·nail \'thəm-ˌnāl, -'nāl\ *n.* The nail of the thumb. — *adj.* Of the size of a thumbnail; small; brief; as, a *thumbnail* description.

thumb·screw \'thəm-ˌskrü\ *n.* **1** A screw having a head made to be turned by the thumb and forefinger. **2** An old instrument of torture.

thumb·tack \'thəm-ˌtak\ *n.* A tack with a broad head, for pressing in with the thumb.

thump \'thəmp\ *n.* **1** A blow or knock, as with something blunt or heavy. **2** The sound made by such a blow. — *v.* **1** To strike, beat, or fall with a thump; to pound; to knock. **2** To beat; to thrash.

thun·der \'thənd-r\ *n.* **1** The loud crashing or rolling noise that follows lightning and is caused by the sudden expansion of the air in the path of the electrical discharge. **2** Any sound likened to thunder; as, a *thunder* of applause. — *v.;* **thundered; thun·der·ing** \-r(-)ing\. **1** To produce thunder. **2** To make a noise like thunder. **3** To utter loudly; to roar.

thun·der·bolt \'thənd-r-ˌbōlt\ *n.* One discharge of lightning with the accompanying thunder.

thun·der·clap \'thənd-r-ˌklap\ *n.* **1** A crash of thunder. **2** Anything sudden and startling.

thun·der·cloud \'thənd-r-ˌklau̇d\ *n.* A dark storm cloud that produces lightning and thunder.

thun·der·head \'thənd-r-ˌhed\ *n.* A rounded mass of dark storm cloud; a thundercloud.

thun·der·ous \'thənd-r(-)əs\ *adj.* Producing thunder; as loud as thunder. — **thun·der·ous·ly,** *adv.*

thun·der·show·er \'thənd-r-ˌshau̇r\ or **thun·der·storm** \-ˌstȯrm\ *n.* A shower or storm accompanied with thunder and lightning.

thun·der·struck \'thənd-r-ˌstrək\ *adj.* Stunned, as if struck by a thunderbolt; astounded.

Thur. or **Thurs.** Abbreviation for *Thursday.*

Thurs·day \'thərz-dē\ *n.* [From Old English *Thunresdaeg, Thurresdaeg* meaning literally "Thunor's day" and named after *Thunor,* the Germanic god of thunder.] The fifth day of the week.

thus \'t͟həs\ *adv.* **1** In this or that way. **2** Because of this; therefore. **3** To this degree or extent; to this point; as, a mild winter *thus* far.

thwack \'thwak\ *v.* To whack. — *n.* A blow made with something flat; a whack; a bang.

thwart \'thwȯrt\ *adj.* Situated or placed across something; oblique. — *adv.* Athwart. — *n.* A rower's seat crosswise in a boat. — *v.* **1** To oppose or baffle, as a purpose. **2** To frustrate; to block; to defeat. Enemy attacks were *thwarted* repeatedly.

thy \(')t͟hī\ *adj.* A form of *thou* expressing possession; as, *thy* neighbor.

thyme \'tīm, 'thīm\ *n.* Any of several mints with a pleasantly sharp smell and taste, used for seasoning, especially the common **wild thyme.**

thy·mus \'thī-məs\ *n.* A gland, present in the throat of most young vertebrates, that is thought to function as a ductless gland and that tends to disappear in later life.

thy·roid \'thī-ˌrȯid\ *adj.* Of or obtained from a large ductless gland (**thyroid gland**) in the neck that produces a hormone that influences growth. — *n.* **1** The thyroid gland. **2** Medicine prepared from the thyroid gland of certain food animals.

thy·self \t͟hī-'self\ *pron.* A form of *thy* that may be added after *thou,* used to give emphasis or to show that the subject and object of a verb are the same. Thou *thyself* must decide. Save *thyself.*

ti \'tē\ *n.* A syllable used in music to name the seventh note of the scale; si.

ti·ara \tē-'ar-ə, -'er-, -'är-, -'ȧr-\ *n.* **1** A three-tiered crown worn by the Pope. **2** A crown-shaped ornament for the head; as, a pearl *tiara.*

Ti·bet·an \tə-'bet-n\ *adj.* Of or relating to Tibet. — *n.* **1** A native of Tibet. **2** The language of the Tibetans.

tib·ia \'tib-ē-ə\ *n.; pl.* **tib·i·as** \-ē-əz\ or **tib·i·ae** \-ē-ˌē, -ē-ˌī\. The inner of the two bones between the knee and the ankle in the leg of a person or in the hind leg of a lower vertebrate.

tic \'tik\ *n.* A twitching of certain facial muscles.

tick \'tik\ *n.* **1** Any of numerous blood-sucking, eight-legged animals, related to the spiders, that attach themselves to man and animals, as the **cattle tick** and **dog tick. 2** Any of certain wingless blood-sucking insects, as the **sheep tick.**

tick \'tik\ *n.* **1** A case for a mattress or pillow, made usually of ticking. **2** A mattress.

tick \'tik\ *n.* **1** A light, quick click, as of a clock. **2** A little mark to call attention to something. — *v.* **1** To make a tick or ticks, as a watch. **2** To count or record with a tick or ticks; as, a meter *ticking* up taxi fare. **3** To mark or check with a tick.

tick \'tik\ *n.* Credit; trust; as, to buy a suit on *tick.*

tick·er \'tik-r\ *n.* **1** One that ticks, as a watch. **2** A telegraph sounder. **3** *Slang.* The heart. **4** A telegraph instrument that prints off stock quotations on a paper tape (**ticker tape**).

tick·et \'tik-ət\ *n.* **1** A card or slip of paper giving its holder a right or privilege; as, a theater *ticket.* **2** A card or slip of paper serving as a notice or record; as, to be given a *ticket* for speeding. **3** A tag, a label; as, a price *ticket.* **4** A list of candidates to be voted for. — *v.* To put a ticket or label on.

tick·ing \'tik-ing\ *n.* A strong cloth, usually striped, used to make mattress and pillow covers.

tick·le \'tik-l\ *v.;* **tick·led; tick·ling** \-l(-)ing\. **1** To have an uneasy tingling sensation. **2** To excite agreeably; to please; as, food that *tickles* the palate. **3** To touch so as to cause an uneasy tingling or to arouse laughter accompanied with wriggling movements of the body. **4** To amuse. — *n.* A tickling or a tickling sensation.

tick·ler \'tik-l(-)ər\ *n.* **1** One that tickles. **2** A device for tickling persons' faces and necks, as at a party. **3** A device for reminding, as a book or file in a bank to show payments or amounts due.

tick·lish \'tik-l(-)ish\ *adj.* **1** Sensitive to tickling. **2** Not firm or steady; as, a *ticklish* foothold. **3** Easily disturbed or irritated; as, to be *ticklish* about personal questions. **4** Needing to be treated with care; delicate; as, a *ticklish* situation. — **tick·lish·ly,** *adv.*

tid·al \'tīd-l\ *adj.* Of or relating to tides; having tides; as, *tidal* waters; a *tidal* river.

tidal wave. A great wave that rolls in from the sea, as from an earthquake or hurricane.

tid·bit \'tid-ˌbit\ *n.* **1** A choice bit of anything eatable. **2** A very interesting bit of news or gossip.

tide \'tīd\ *n.* [From Old English *tid* meaning "time".] **1** The rising and falling of the surface of the ocean caused twice daily by the attraction of the sun and the moon. **2** The flow of the tide. **3** A surge; as, a *tide* of anger. **4** Something that normally rises and falls; as, the *tides* of fortune. — *v.;* **tid·ed**; **tid·ing**. To help along over a difficulty; as, money to *tide* one over.

tide·land \'tīd-ˌland, -lənd\ *n.* Land that is flooded during high tide.

tid·ings \'tīd-ingz\ *n.* **1** A piece of news; a message. **2** [in the plural] News; as, good *tidings*.

ti·dy \'tīd-ē\ *adj.;* **ti·di·er**; **ti·di·est**. **1** Neat; orderly; as, a *tidy* room. **2** Fair-sized; as, a *tidy* fortune. — *v.;* **ti·died** \-ēd\; **ti·dy·ing**. To make things neat or tidy. — *n.; pl.* **ti·dies**. A piece of needlework to protect the back or arms of a chair from wear.

tie \'tī\ *v.;* **tied** \'tīd\; **ty·ing** or **tie·ing** \'tī-ing\. **1** To fasten with a rope or cord; as, to *tie* a horse to a tree. **2** To unite firmly; as, people *tied* together by the same beliefs. **3** To confine; as, to be *tied* by sickness to one's bed. **4** To secure by a cord or lace that is drawn up and knotted; as, to *tie* one's shoes. **5** To form a knot or bow in something, as a necktie. **6** To make by tying, as a bow. **7** To make the same score as someone else in a contest. **8** In music, to connect notes by a tie. — *n.* **1** A band, rope, cord, or lace used for tying. **2** Something that joins one thing to another; a bond; as, family *ties*. **3** Something knotted when worn; especially, a necktie. **4** [in the plural] Low shoes fastened by laces. **5** An equality in numbers, as of votes or points. **6** In music, a curved line joining two notes of the same pitch to denote a single tone to be held through the time value of the two notes. **7** One of the cross supports to which railroad rails are fastened.

ti·er \'tīr\ *n.* A person or thing that ties.

tier \'tir\ *n.* A row, rank, or layer; especially, one of two or more rows arranged one above and behind another, as of seats in a grandstand.

tie-up \'tī-ˌəp\ *n.* **1** A suspension of activity, as one caused by a strike of employees or a failure of machinery. **2** A connection.

tiff \'tif\ *n.* A slight fit of anger; a petty quarrel.

ti·ger \'tīg-r\ *n.* **1** A large Asiatic flesh-eating animal of the cat family, of a tawny color with black stripes. **2** A yell at the end of a round of cheers.

tiger beetle. A swift-flying beetle of sandy regions whose larvae live in tunnels in the soil awaiting insect prey.

tiger cat. **1** Any of various wildcats. **2** A domestic cat with markings like those of a tiger.

ti·ger·ish \'tīg-r(-)ish\ *adj.* Of, relating to, or like a tiger or tigers; especially, fierce; cruel.

tiger lily. A common lily having large nodding orange-colored flowers spotted with black or purple.

tiger moth. A moth of a family having stout bodies and broad striped or spotted wings.

tiger shark. Any of several large banded and spotted sharks.

tight \'tīt\ *adj.* **1** So close in structure or fit as not to permit the passage of a liquid or fluid; not leaky; as, a *tight* roof. **2** Held, bound, or fastened firmly; hard to move. **3** Not loose; taut; as, a *tight* rope. **4** Close-fitting; too small for comfort. **5** Difficult to get through or out of; as, to be in a *tight* place. **6** Stingy. **7** Hard to get; scarce. **8** *Slang*. Intoxicated. — *adv.* Tightly; firmly. Shut the door *tight*.

tight·en \'tīt-n\ *v.;* **tight·ened**; **tight·en·ing** \-n(-)ing\. To make or become tight or tighter.

tight-fist·ed \'tīt-'fis-təd\ *adj.* Stingy.

tight-lipped \'tīt-'lipt\ *adj.* Taciturn; silent.

tight·ly \'tīt-lē\ *adv.* In a tight manner.

tight·rope \'tīt-ˌrōp, -'rōp\ *n.* A tight-stretched rope on which acrobats perform.

tights \'tīts\ *n. pl.* A close-fitting garment, usually covering the legs and lower part of the body.

tight·wad \'tīt-ˌwäd\ *n. Slang.* A stingy person.

tight·wire \'tīt-ˌwīr, -'wīr\ *n.* A tightrope made of wire.

ti·gress \'tīg-rəs\ *n.* A female tiger.

tike. Variant of *tyke*.

til·de \'til-də\ *n.* A mark [~] used in English chiefly over *n* in words from Spanish, as *cañon*, to indicate that the *n* is pronounced *ny*\.

tile \'tīl\ *n.* **1** A plate or thin piece, as of stone, concrete, asphalt, or rubber, used as a covering, as for roofs, floors, and walls. **2** Tiles collectively. **3** An earthenware pipe used for a drain. — *v.;* **tiled**; **til·ing**. To cover with tiles. — **til·er** \'tīl-r\ *n.*

til·ing \'tī-ling\ *n.* **1** The action of one who tiles. **2** Tiles collectively. **3** A surface of tiles.

till \tl, təl, til\ *prep.* Throughout the whole time to a certain time; until; as, to sleep *till* noon. — *conj.* **1** Up to the time when a certain thing happens. Study *till* the bell rings. **2** At any time before; unless at some future time. Do not stop *till* you are told to.

till \'til\ *v.* To plow and plant and raise crops from; to cultivate. — **till·a·ble** \-əb-l\ *adj.* — **till·er** \-r\ *n.*

till \'til\ *n.* A drawer or other receptacle for money.

till·age \'til-ij\ *n.* The process of tilling land.

til·ler \'til-r\ *n.* A lever used for turning the rudder of a boat from side to side.

til·ler·man \'til-r-mən\ *n.; pl.* **til·ler·men** \-mən\. One in charge of a tiller.

tiller: *a* tiller; *b* rudder

tilt \'tilt\ *v.* **1** To cause to slope; to tip; as, to *tilt* one's head back. **2** To make a rush against or to charge, as in a tournament; to joust. — *n.* **1** A joust. **2** Any encounter bringing about a sharp collision or conflict. **3** The action of tilting; the state of being tilted. — **full tilt** or **at full tilt**. At full speed.

tilth \'tilth\ *n.* **1** The action of tilling; cultivation of the soil. **2** Tilled land or its condition.

tim·ber \'tim-br\ *n.* **1** Wood for use in making something. **2** A squared piece of wood. **3** Wooded land from which timber is produced. — *v.;* **tim·bered**; **tim·ber·ing** \-br(-)ing\. To furnish, frame, support, or cover with timbers.

tim·bered \'tim-brd\ *adj.* Furnished with, made of, or covered with timbers or timber.

tim·ber·land \'tim-br-ˌland\ *n.* Wooded land.

timber line. On mountains and in very cold regions, the line above which there are no trees.

timber wolf. A large gray North American wolf.

tim·bre \'tam-br, 'tim-\ *n.* The quality of tone distinguishing one voice or instrument from another.

tim·brel \'tim-brəl\ *n.* A small hand drum.

time \'tīm\ *n.* **1** The period during which an action, process, or condition continues; as, done in an hour's *time.* **2** The period, moment, or point when something occurs. **3** The customary, fixed, or appointed moment or hour for something to happen; as, to arrive on *time.* **4** The proper season; the fitting moment. Now is the *time* to buy. **5** A term; as, to serve one's *time* in the army. **6** A period set apart from others, as in the course of history; an era; an age; as, ancient *times.* **7** An exact moment, hour, day, or year as determined by the clock or calendar. **8** One of a number of occasions or repeated actions; as, to write a sentence ten *times.* **9** A multiplying of a number by another number. Four *times* four is sixteen. **10** The whole series of days, years, and ages without reference to any one point or period; as, for all *time.* **11** Credit; trust; as, to buy goods on *time.* **12** [usually in the plural] Conditions during a specified period, especially the present. **13** One's experience during a particular period; as, to have a good *time* at a party. **14** The method of reckoning the passage of the hours; as, standard *time.* **15** The length of the period required for or used in an action, as a race. **16** In music, the grouping of rhythmic beats in equal measures; rhythm; tempo. — **at the same time.** However; nevertheless. — **at times.** Now and then; at intervals. — **behind the times.** Not up to date. — **from time to time.** Occasionally. — **in time. 1** Early enough; as, to arrive *in time* for the meeting. **2** In the course of time; eventually. **3** In correct rhythm or tempo. — **on time. 1** Punctual; punctually. **2** On a time payment plan; on credit. — *v.;* **timed; tim·ing. 1** To arrange, fix, or choose a time for; to schedule. **2** To cause to agree or move together in rhythm or tempo. **3** To give a proper time or measure to; as, to *time* the length of a speech. **4** To find or record the rate of speed of.

time clock. A clock that mechanically records the times of arrival and departure of workers.

time-hon·ored \'tīm-ˌän-rd\ *adj.* Honored or respected because of age or long-established usage.

time·keep·er \'tīm-ˌkēp-r\ *n.* A person or thing that keeps or records time.

time·less \'tīm-ləs\ *adj.* **1** Unending; eternal. **2** Unaffected by time; as, *timeless* music.

time·ly \'tīm-lē\ *adj.;* **time·li·er; time·li·est.** Coming at just the right time; as, *timely* aid.

time·piece \'tīm-ˌpēs\ *n.* A clock, watch, or other device to measure the passage of time.

tim·er \'tīm-r\ *n.* **1** One that times. **2** A distributor on an internal-combustion engine.

time·ta·ble \'tīm-ˌtāb-l\ *n.* A list of the times when certain things are to take place; a schedule.

time·worn \'tīm-ˌwōrn, -ˌwȯrn\ *adj.* Worn or impaired by time; out of date; as, a *timeworn* phrase.

time zone. A geographical region within which the same standard time is used.

tim·id \'tim-əd\ *adj.* Feeling or showing a lack of courage or self-confidence; shy. — **tim·id·ly,** *adv.* — **ti·mid·i·ty** \tə-'mid-ət-ē\ *n.*

tim·ing \'tī-ming\ *n.* **1** The regulating of the time of a public presentation, as a speech or a play, so as to increase the favorable effect of the performance. **2** In sports, the regulating of an action to cause it to reach its greatest effect at the right instant. **3** The regulating of a machine so that its parts work together at the right instant.

tim·or·ous \'tim-r(-)əs\ *adj.* Timid; fearful.

tim·o·thy \'tim-ə-thē\ *n.* [Named after *Timothy* Hanson, an 18th century American who introduced the grass into the Carolinas.] A grass with long round spikes, grown for hay.

tim·pa·ni or **tym·pa·ni** \'timp-n-(ˌ)ē\ *n. pl.* Kettledrums, especially a set played by one performer.

tin \'tin\ *n.* **1** A soft, bluish white metallic element used chiefly in combination with or as a coating for other metals, as in making tin plate. **2** Tin plate or a container made of it. — *v.;* **tinned; tinning. 1** To coat with tin. **2** To pack in a tin container; to can.

tin can. *Slang.* A naval destroyer.

tinc·ture \'ting(k)-chər\ *n.* **1** A substance that colors, dyes, or stains; a tinge. **2** A slight mixture; a trace; as, a *tincture* of hostility in his voice. **3** A solution of a medicinal substance in alcohol; as, *tincture* of iodine.

tin·der \'tind-r\ *n.* Something that very easily catches fire, especially from a slight spark.

tin·der·box \'tind-r-ˌbäks\ *n.* A box for tinder, usually with a flint and steel for striking a spark.

tine \'tīn\ *n.* A prong, as of a fork.

ting \'ting\ *n.* A high-pitched sound, as from a light stroke on glass. — *v.;* **tinged** \'tingd\; **tinging** \'ting-ing\. To make a ting.

tinge \'tinj\ *v.;* **tinged** \'tinjd\; **tinge·ing** or **ting·ing** \'tin-jing\. **1** To color slightly; to tint. **2** To give a trace of a quality, as flavor or odor, to something; as, meat *tinged* with garlic. — *n.* A slight coloring, flavor, or quality; a trace.

tin·gle \'ting-gl\ *v.;* **tin·gled; tin·gling** \-gl(-)ing\. **1** To feel a stinging, prickling, or thrilling sensation, as from cold or excitement. **2** To cause or produce such a sensation. **3** To be alive; to pulse. The story *tingles* with suspense. — *n.* A tingling sensation or condition; as, a *tingle* of excitement.

tink·er \'tingk-r\ *n.* **1** A person whose business is the mending of pots, pans, and kettles. **2** A man who can do various small repair jobs. — *v.;* **tinkered; tink·er·ing** \-r(-)ing\. **1** To do or work in the manner of a tinker. **2** To try unskillfully to repair or improve; to patch up. **3** To busy oneself; to potter. — **tink·er·er** \-r-r\ *n.*

tin·kle \'tingk-l\ *v.;* **tin·kled; tin·kling** \-l(-)ing\. To make or cause to make clinking sounds; as, ice cubes *tinkling* in a glass. — *n.* A tinkling sound.

tin·ny \'tin-ē\ *adj.;* **tin·ni·er; tin·ni·est. 1** Thin, hard, and brittle, like tin. **2** Sounding like tin; as, a *tinny* piano. **3** Tasting of tin, as food from a can.

tin·plate \'tin-'plāt\ *n.* Thin iron or steel covered with tin.

tin·sel \'tin(t)s-l\ *n.* **1** A sparkling metallic or metal-coated material made in sheets, strips, or threads for trimming. **2** Something that seems valuable but is not really so; cheap and gaudy decoration. — *adj.* Made of or covered with tinsel; cheap; gaudy. — *v.;* **tin·seled** or **tin·selled; tin·sel·ing** or **tin·sel·ling** \-l(-)ing\. **1** To decorate with tinsel. **2** To make gaudy or deceptively bright.

tin·smith \'tin-ˌsmith\ *n.* A worker in tin.

tint \'tint\ *n.* **1** A slight coloring; a tinge; as, a white without a *tint* of yellow. **2** A light color or shade; as, pale *tints* of red. — *v.* To color slightly.

tin·ware \'tin-ˌwar, -ˌwer\ *n.* Articles of tinplate.

ti·ny \'tī-nē\ *adj.;* **ti·ni·er; ti·ni·est.** Very small.

-tion. A suffix that can mean: **1** The action of, as in *contention.* **2** An instance of, a result of, as in *deception.* **3** The condition of being, as in *caution.*

tip \'tip\ *v.;* **tipped; tip·ping. 1** To overturn; to upset; as, to *tip* over a glass. **2** To tilt; to raise one end or side of. **3** To raise and tilt forward in greeting; as, to *tip* one's hat. — *n.* A slanting position.

tip \'tip\ *n.* **1** The pointed or rounded end of anything; an end. **2** A part or piece fitted on the end of something; as, the *tip,* or nozzle, of a hose. — *v.;* **tipped; tip·ping.** To put a tip on.

tip \'tip\ *v.;* **tipped; tip·ping. 1** In certain sports, as baseball, to hit the ball a glancing blow with the bat. **2** To give a tip to; as, to *tip* soldiers off that an attack is coming. **3** To give a gratuity to. — *n.* **1** A light blow; a tap. **2** Information given to a person privately; as, a *tip* on a horse race. **3** A gratuity.

ti·pi \'tēp-(ˌ)ē\ *n.* A tepee.

tip·pet \'tip-ət\ *n.* **1** A long hanging part of a garment, as on a sleeve or cape. **2** A long scarf, especially of fur.

tip·ple \'tip-l\ *v.;* **tip·pled; tip·pling** \-l(-)ing\. To drink liquor frequently or in small portions. — *n.* Liquor. — **tip·pler** \-l(-)ər\ *n.*

tip·sy \'tip-sē\ *adj.;* **tip·si·er; tip·si·est.** Somewhat drunk. — **tip·si·ly** \'tips-l-ē\ *adv.*

tip·toe \'tip-ˌtō, -'tō\ *n.* The tip, or end, of a toe; as, to walk on one's *tiptoes.* — *v.;* **tip·toed** \-ˌtōd, -'tōd\; **tip·toe·ing.** To step or walk on one's tiptoes.

tip·top \'tip-'täp, -ˌtäp\ *n.* The very top; the highest point. — *adj.* **1** At the top or highest point; as, the *tiptop* peak. **2** First-rate; fine; as, to feel *tiptop.*

ti·rade \tī-'rād, 'tī-ˌrād\ *n.* A long, violent, scolding speech.

tire \'tīr\ *v.;* **tired; tir·ing. 1** To make or become weary; to exhaust; to fatigue. **2** To wear out the patience, liking, or attention of; to bore.

— The words *fatigue* and *exhaust* are synonyms of *tire: tire* has the general suggestion of losing or causing one to lose all energy, strength, endurance, resolution, or patience, as from overwork, loss of sleep, or boredom; *fatigue* usually suggests great weariness caused by excessive effort or strain or sometimes by extreme boredom, and a reluctance to make further effort; *exhaust* is the strongest of these terms and indicates such an utter draining or using up of energy that both the mind and body are left completely unable to exert effort in any direction.

tire \'tīr\ *n.* A hoop or band, as of rubber or steel, that forms the tread of a wheel, as of a vehicle.

tired \'tīrd\ *adj.* Fatigued. — **tired·ly** \-lē\ *adv.*

tire·less \'tīr-ləs\ *adj.* Not becoming tired; not wearying. — **tire·less·ly,** *adv.*

tire·some \'tīrs-m\ *adj.* Boring; tedious; as, a *tiresome* speech. — **tire·some·ly,** *adv.*

'tis \(')tiz, təz\. A contraction of *it is.*

tis·sue \'tish-(ˌ)ü\ *n.* **1** A very thin fabric; a fine gauze. **2** A network or web; as, a *tissue* of lies. **3** Cells of one or more kinds, together with the substance uniting or enclosing them, forming one of the structural materials and performing a particular function in a person, a lower animal, or a plant; as, muscular *tissue.* **4** In full, **tissue paper.** A very thin soft paper.

tit \'tit\ *n.* **1** A titmouse. **2** Any of several other small birds, as the **wren tit** or **thrush tit.**

tit \'tit\ *n.* A teat; a nipple.

ti·tan \'tīt-n\ *n.* **1** [with a capital] One of a group of gods in Greek legend, who ruled until overthrown by the gods of Olympus. **2** Any person gigantic in size, power, or achievement.

ti·tan·ic \tī-'tan-ik\ *adj.* Vast in size, force, or power.

tit·bit \'tit-ˌbit\ *n.* A tidbit.

tithe \'tīth\ *v.;* **tithed; tith·ing** \'tī-thing\. **1** To pay or give a tithe. **2** To levy a tax of one tenth. — *n.* **1** A tenth part. **2** A tenth part of one's income or produce paid as a tax or contribution to church or charity. — **tith·er** \'tīth-r\ *n.*

tit·il·late \'tit-l-ˌāt\ *v.;* **tit·il·lated; tit·il·lat·ing. 1** To tickle. **2** To excite agreeably. — **tit·il·la·tion** \ˌtit-l-'āsh-n\ *n.*

tit·lark \'tit-ˌlärk, -ˌlȧrk\ *n.* A pipit.

ti·tle \'tīt-l\ *n.* **1** A right; especially, a legal right to the ownership of property or the document (**title deed**) that is evidence of such ownership. **2** The name given to a production, as a book, song, or painting. **3** A term showing a person's rank or office or one used as a mark of respect, as *Mr., Doctor, Lord.* **4** Championship.

ti·tled \'tīt-ld\ *adj.* Having a title of nobility.

title page. The page, as in a book, bearing the title.

title role. The character that gives a play its name.

tit·mouse \'tit-ˌmau̇s\ *n.; pl.* **tit·mice** \-ˌmīs\. A small insect-eating gray, black, and white bird.

tit·ter \'tit-r\ *v.* To snicker; to giggle. — *n.* A giggle.

tit·tle \'tit-l\ *n.* **1** A small mark placed over a letter in writing or printing, as the dot over *i.* **2** A very tiny bit; the smallest particle; a jot.

tit·tle-tat·tle \'tit-l-ˌtat-l\ *n.* Gossip. — *v.;* **tit·tle-**

tat·tled; **tit·tle–tat·tling** \-ˌtat-l(-)ing\. To gossip.

tit·u·lar \'tich-l-ər\ *adj.* **1** Having, or having to do with, a title. **2** Existing in title or name only; not actual; nominal; as, a *titular* head of a nation.

tiz·zy \'tiz-ē\ *n.; pl.* **tiz·zies.** A highly and foolishly excited state of mind.

TNT \'tē-ˌen-'tē\. A high explosive in the form of pale yellow or brownish crystals.

to \tə, tu̇, (')tü\ *prep.* **1** In the direction of and reaching; as, to walk *to* the station every day. **2** In a direction toward; directed toward; as, to break down while driving *to* town. **3** Next to; close against; upon; as, oil applied *to* a lock. **4** Aiming at; for the making of; as, a means *to* an end. **5** So as to become or bring about; as, beaten *to* death. **6** Accompanying; in harmony with. Sing *to* the music. **7** Intended for; fitting; as, a key *to* the desk. **8** Forming a part of; as, the trousers *to* this suit. **9** In honor of; as, a toast *to* a bride. **10** Composing; making up; as, two pints *to* a quart. **11** During; in; as, five strokes *to* a second. **12** In comparison with; as, a game won ten *to* six. **13** Within the range of; as, *to* my knowledge. **14** Until; before; as, quarter *to* six. **15** As far as; so as to reach in amount or degree; as, up *to* a dollar. **16** For receiving; as, open *to* everyone. **17** Affecting; as, a blow *to* one's pride. **18** For no one except; as, a room *to* oneself. **19** In accordance or compliance with; as, not *to* my taste. **20** Concerning; as regards. That is nothing *to* me. — \'tü\ *adv.* **1** In one direction contrasted with another; as, *to* and fro. **2** Forward; as, a hat wrong side *to.* **3** In or into position, contact, or agreement. Pull the door *to.* **4** To consciousness or realization. Fresh air will bring her *to.* **5** To the matter in hand. Fall *to,* men! ☞ *to* is used with the infinitive of verbs to express various relations, as purpose, result, action, possibility, or character, or simply as a sign of the infinitive form; as, running fast *to* win the race; beginning *to* rain; a house *to* sell; *to* be or not *to* be.

toad \'tōd\ *n.* A tailless leaping amphibian somewhat like a frog but usually living on land.

toad·stool \'tōd-ˌstül\ *n.* A fleshy fungus with an umbrella-shaped cap; a mushroom; especially, a poisonous mushroom.

toady \'tōd-ē\ *n.; pl.* **toad·ies.** A person who flatters or fawns upon another in the hope of receiving favors. — *v.;* **toad·ied** \-ēd\; **toad·y·ing.** To play the toady; to fawn upon or flatter for favors.

to-and-fro \'tü-ən-'frō\ *adj.* Forward and backward; as, a *to-and-fro* motion.

toast \'tōst\ *v.* **1** To dry and brown, as bread, by heat. **2** To warm thoroughly at or as if at a fire; as, *toasted* in the sun. — *n.* Sliced bread toasted.

toast \'tōst\ *n.* **1** A person whose health is drunk; something to which persons drink. **2** The act of suggesting someone or something to be drunk to or of drinking to the person or thing proposed. — *v.* To drink to the health of or in honor of.

toast·er \'tōst-r\ *n.* A person or thing that toasts; especially, a device for toasting bread.

toast·mas·ter \'tōst-ˌmast-r\ *n.* A person who presides and introduces the after-dinner speakers at a banquet.

to·bac·co \tə-'bak-ō\ *n.; pl.* **to·bac·cos.** **1** A tall annual plant covered with short sticky hairs and bearing broad leaves and white or pink tube-shaped flowers. **2** The product made from the dried leaves of this plant, used for smoking or chewing, or as snuff.

tobacco

to·bac·co·nist \tə-'bak-n-əst\ *n.* A dealer in tobacco.

to·bog·gan \tə-'bäg-n\ *n.* A long, flat-bottomed sled without runners, curved up at the front end. — *v.;* **to·bog·ganed**; **to·bog·gan·ning** \-n(-)ing\. **1** To slide on or as if on a toboggan. **2** To decline suddenly in value, as stocks.

toc·sin \'täks-n\ *n.* An alarm bell or the ringing of an alarm bell; any warning signal.

to·day or **to-day** \tə-'dā\ *adv.* **1** On or for this day. **2** At the present time; nowadays. — *n.* The present day, time, or age.

tod·dle \'täd-l\ *v.;* **tod·dled**; **tod·dling** \-l(-)ing\. To walk with short tottering steps, as a small child does. — *n.* A toddling gait. — **tod·dler** \-l(-)ər\ *n.*

tod·dy \'täd-ē\ *n.; pl.* **tod·dies.** **1** The sap of various palms. **2** A sweetened mixture of a strong alcoholic liquor, as whiskey, and hot water.

to-do \tə-'dü\ *n.; pl.* **to-dos** \-'düz\. Commotion; fuss; bustle.

toe \'tō\ *n.* **1** One of the separate parts of the front end of a foot. **2** The front end or part of the foot, as distinguished from the heel. **3** Anything worn on or attached to a toe or toes, as the front part of a shoe or stocking. **4** Anything that suggests the toe of a foot; as, the *toe* of a golf club; the *toe* of Italy. — *v.;* **toed** \'tōd\; **toe·ing.** **1** To touch, reach, or kick with the toe or toes; as, to *toe* a line. **2** To drive in at a slant, as a nail. **3** To stand or walk with the toes in a certain position.

toed \'tōd\ *adj.* **1** Having a toe or toes; especially, of a number or kind. **2** Driven in obliquely.

toe·nail \'tō-ˌnāl, -'nāl\ *n.* The hard covering at the end of a toe. — *v.* To fasten by toed nails.

tof·fee or **tof·fy** \'tȯf-ē, 'täf-ē\ *n.* Taffy.

tog \'täg\ *v.;* **togged**; **tog·ging.** To put togs on; to dress; as, *togged* out in the latest fashion.

to·ga \'tō-gə\ *n.* **1** A loose outer garment worn in public by citizens of ancient Rome. **2** A distinctive robe, as that of a judge. — **to·gaed** \-gəd\ *adj.*

to·geth·er \tə-'geth-r\ *adv.* **1** In or into one group, body, or place; as, gathered *together.* **2** In or into association, union, or contact with each other; as, in business *together;* the doors banged *together.* **3** At one time. They all cheered *together.* **4** In succession; without intermission; as, to work for four hours *to-*

toga, 1

gether. **5** In agreement; as, to get *together* on a plan.

tog·gery \'täg-r(-)ē\ *n.; pl.* **tog·ger·ies.** Clothes.

tog·gle \'täg-l\ *n.* **1** Any crosspiece attached to the end of, or to a loop in, a rope, chain, or belt to prevent slipping or to serve as a fastening or as a grip for tightening. **2** A toggle joint. — *v.;* **tog·gled; tog·gling** \-l(-)ing\. **1** To fasten with or as if with a toggle. **2** To furnish with a toggle.

toggle joint. A device consisting of two bars jointed together end to end but not in line, so that when a force is applied to the joint tending to straighten it, pressure will be exerted on the parts fixed at the ends of the bars.

togs \'tägz\ *n. pl.* Clothes; as, skiing *togs.*

toil \'tȯil\ *v.* To work very hard; to labor. — *n.* Hard work. — For synonyms see *work.* — **toil·er** \'tȯil-r\ *n.*

toil \'tȯil\ *n.* **1** *Archaic.* A net for trapping game. **2** [usually in the plural] Any net, trap, or snare.

toi·let \'tȯi-lət\ *n.* **1** The act or process of dressing or grooming the person. **2** A water closet.

toi·let·ry \'tȯi-lə-trē\ *n.; pl.* **toi·let·ries.** An article or preparation used in making one's toilet.

toilet water. A perfumed liquid used after bathing.

toil·some \'tȯils-m\ *adj.* Requiring toil; causing fatigue; laborious. — **toil·some·ly,** *adv.*

toil·worn \'tȯil-ˌwōrn, -ˌwȯrn\ *adj.* Worn out with toil; bearing the marks of much toil.

to·ken \'tōk-n\ *n.* **1** A sign; a symbol. Black clothing is a *token* of grief. **2** A symbolic act or thing. A white flag is a *token* of surrender. **3** Something given or shown as a symbol of one's identity, right, or authority. **4** A souvenir; a keepsake. **5** A metal ticket used as a fare. For synonyms see *emblem.*

told. Past tense and past part. of *tell.*

tol·er·a·ble \'täl-r(-)əb-l, -rb-l\ *adj.* **1** Capable of being endured; bearable; as, heat that is scarcely *tolerable.* **2** Fairly good; moderately satisfactory. — **tol·er·a·bly** \-r(-)ə-blē, -r-blē\ *adv.*

tol·er·ance \'täl-r-ən(t)s\ *n.* **1** The act or practice of tolerating or the quality of being tolerant; the ability and disposition to tolerate opinions, practices, or habits differing from one's own without accepting them or changing one's own. **2** A specific allowance for error, as in weighing or measuring, or for variation from a standard, as in coinage. **3** The capacity of the body to endure or resist the effects of certain things, as poisons and drugs.

tol·er·ant \'täl-r-ənt\ *adj.* Inclined to tolerate; showing tolerance. — **tol·er·ant·ly,** *adv.*

tol·er·ate \'täl-r-ˌāt\ *v.;* **tol·er·at·ed; tol·er·at·ing.** **1** To allow a thing to be done or to exist without making any move to stop it; to put up with; to endure; as, insolence too great to be *tolerated.* **2** To show tolerance, as to a drug.

tol·er·a·tion \ˌtäl-r-'āsh-n\ *n.* The act or practice of tolerating; especially, opinions and practices which differ from one's own.

toll \'tōl\ *n.* **1** A tax paid for a privilege, as for using a highway or bridge. **2** A charge for a service, as for a long-distance telephone call (**toll call**). **3** Something taken as if a toll, as a number of casualties.

toll \'tōl\ *v.* **1** To pull a bell so as to sound a summons or signal, as slowly to announce a death. **2** To sound or strike. The clock *tolled* six. **3** To announce by tolling, as a death; to summon by tolling. — *n.* The sound of a bell tolling.

toll·gate \'tōl-ˌgāt\ *n.* A gate, as one across a road or the entrance to a bridge, where toll is collected.

toll·house \'tōl-ˌhau̇s\ *n.; pl.* **toll·hous·es** \-ˌhau̇-zəz\. **1** *British.* A town hall. **2** A house where a tollkeeper is stationed, as at a tollgate.

toll·keep·er \'tōl-ˌkēp-r\ *n.* The keeper of a tollgate or tollhouse.

tom·a·hawk \'täm-ə-ˌhȯk, -ē-ˌhȯk\ *n.* A light North American Indian ax or hatchet. — *v.* To cut, strike, or kill with a tomahawk.

to·ma·to \tə-'māt-ō, -'mȧt-, -'mät-\ *n.; pl.* **to·ma·toes.** **1** A plant of the same family as the potato, with hairy stem and leaves and yellow flowers. **2** The red or yellow edible fruit of this plant.

tomb \'tüm\ *n.* **1** A grave. **2** A vault for the dead.

tom·boy \'täm-ˌbȯi\ *n.* A girl who plays active, boisterous games. — **tom·boy·ish** \-ish\ *adj.*

tomb·stone \'tüm-ˌstōn\ *n.* A gravestone.

tom·cat \'täm-ˌkat\ *n.* A male cat.

tome \'tōm\ *n.* A book; especially, a large book.

tom·fool·ery \(')täm-'fül-r(-)ē\ *n.; pl.* **tom·fool·er·ies.** Foolish action; nonsense.

to·mor·row \tə-'mär-ō\ *adv.* On or for the day after today. — *n.* The day after today.

tom-tom \'täm-ˌtäm\ *n.* A drum made to be beaten with the hands.

ton \'tən\ *n.* A measure of weight equal either to 2000 pounds (**short ton**) or 2240 pounds (**long ton**), the short ton being more commonly used in the United States and Canada.

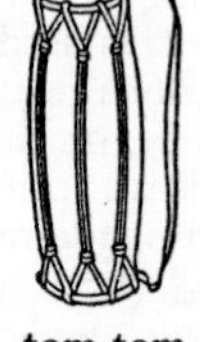
tom-tom

ton·al \'tōn-l\ *adj.* Of or relating to musical tone. — **ton·al·ly** \-l-ē\ *adv.*

to·nal·i·ty \tō-'nal-ət-ē\ *n.; pl.* **to·nal·i·ties.** **1** Tonal quality; especially, the character that a musical composition has because of its key or through the relationship of its tones and chords to the keynote. **2** The arrangement of tones or tints; color scheme.

tone \'tōn\ *n.* **1** Quality of vocal or musical sound. **2** A style or manner of speaking or writing; as, to reply in a friendly *tone.* **3** A general character, quality, or trend; as, a school noted for its studious *tone.* **4** Color quality or value; any tint or shade of color; as, decorated in soft *tones.* **5** A color that modifies another; as, gray with a blue *tone.* **6** The musical pitch of a sound. **7** A healthy state of the body or of its parts. **8** In painting, the general, usually harmonious, effect of light and shade with color; as, a picture that has *tone.* — *v.;* **toned; ton·ing.** **1** To give tone or a tone to. **2** To take on a tone, as a color quality or a tint. **3** To harmonize in color. Gray *tones* with many colors. — **tone**

down. To give a lower tone to; to moderate; to soften; as, to *tone down* one's voice. — **tone up.** To raise the tone of; to strengthen; to invigorate.

tongs \'täŋgz, 'tòŋgz\ *n. pl.* Any of numerous devices for taking hold of something, as a cake of ice or a hot coal.

tongs

tongue \'təŋ\ *n.* **1** An organ of the mouth that is present in most vertebrates and that in man is an organ of speech and the chief organ of taste. **2** The flesh of the tongue of an animal, as a beef, used as food. **3** The power of communication through speech; as, to hold one's *tongue.* **4** A language; as, foreign *tongues.* **5** The manner of speaking, as with respect to tone, sense, or intention; as, a smooth *tongue.* **6** Something like an animal's tongue in shape, position, motion, or use, as a jet of flame, the flap of leather under the lacing in a shoe, the clapper of a bell, or the rib on the edge of a board to fit into a groove. — *v.;* **tongued** \'təŋd\; **tongu·ing** \'təŋ-iŋ\. **1** To cut a tongue on; as, to *tongue* a board. **2** In music, to produce tones by tonguing. — **tongued,** *adj.*

tongue-tied \'təŋ-ˌtīd\ *adj.* Unable to speak clearly or freely, as from abnormal growth of the membrane under the tongue or from shyness.

tongu·ing \'təŋ-iŋ\ *n.* The production of quick staccato notes by means of the tongue, as in playing a flute or cornet.

ton·ic \'tän-ik\ *adj.* **1** Invigorating; refreshing; bracing; as, *tonic* air. **2** Of or relating to tones or sounds. **3** In music, of or relating to the keynote; as, the *tonic* chord. — *n.* **1** A medicine that has a tonic effect. **2** In music, the keynote.

to·nic·i·ty \tō-'nis-ət-ē\ *n.* The quality of having tone; especially, health; vigor; muscular elasticity.

to·night \tə-'nīt\ *adv.* On this present night. — *n.* The present or the coming night.

ton·nage \'tən-ij\ *n.* **1** A duty on boats, based on tons carried. **2** Boats collectively in terms of their carrying capacity in tons. **3** The weight in tons that can be carried, as by a boat or train. **4** Total weight in tons, as in transportation or mining.

ton·sil \'tän(t)s-l\ *n.* One of a pair of oval masses of spongy tissue at the back of the mouth.

ton·sil·lec·to·my \ˌtän(t)s-l-'ekt-m-ē\ *n.; pl.* **ton·sil·lec·to·mies.** Removal of the tonsils by surgery.

ton·sil·li·tis \ˌtän(t)s-l-'īt-əs\ *n.* Inflammation of the tonsils.

ton·so·ri·al \tän-'sōr-ē-əl, -'sòr-\ *adj.* Of or relating to a barber or his work.

ton·sure \'tänch-r\ *n.* **1** The action of clipping the hair; the shaving of the head, as of a candidate for clerical orders. **2** The shaven crown of the head, especially as worn by certain monks.

too \(')tü\ *adv.* **1** Also; in addition. The children are invited to come *too.* **2** More than is needed or desired. The speech was *too* long. **3** To such a degree as to be regrettable or shameful. This is going *too* far. **4** Very; as, to be only *too* glad to help.

took. Past tense of *take.*

tool \'tül\ *n.* **1** An instrument for doing work by hand, as a saw, file, knife, or wrench. **2** A person used for some purpose; a dupe. **3** A thing used for some purpose. Money is a *tool.* **4** The cutting or shaping part in a machine. — *v.* To shape, form, or finish with a tool; to letter or ornament, as a book cover, with a heated tool.

toot \'tüt\ *v.* To blow or sound, as a horn or whistle, in short rapid blasts. — *n.* A sound made by tooting. — **toot·er** \-r\ *n.*

tooth \'tüth\ *n.; pl.* **teeth** \'tēth\. **1** One of the hard bony projections from the jaws of most vertebrates, used for seizing and chewing food, and as weapons. **2** Any of various hard, sharp, usually horny processes about the mouth of many invertebrates. **3** Any projection suggestive of the tooth of an animal, in shape, arrangement, or function; as, the *teeth* of a saw; a *tooth* on a comb. **4** One of the projections on the rim of a cogwheel; a cog. **5** Something that pierces or cuts as a tooth does; as, the *teeth* of the wind. — \'tüth, 'tü<u>th</u>\ *v.* To furnish with teeth.

tooth·ache \'tüth-ˌāk\ *n.* Pain in a tooth.

tooth·brush \'tüth-ˌbrəsh\ *n.* A brush for cleaning the teeth.

toothed \'tütht, 'tü<u>th</u>d\ *adj.* **1** Having teeth, especially of a kind or number mentioned. **2** Having projecting points; notched; jagged.

tooth·paste \'tüth-ˌpāst\ *n.* A cream dentifrice.

tooth·pick \'tüth-ˌpik\ *n.* A small pointed stick for picking particles from between the teeth.

tooth·some \'tüths-m\ *adj.* Pleasing to the taste.

top \'täp\ *n.* **1** The highest part, point, or level of a thing; the upper end, edge, or surface. **2** The stalk and leaves of a plant, especially one with edible roots; as, beet *tops.* **3** The part of a flat thing that is thought of as the head or beginning and opposite to the foot; as, the *top* of a page. **4** The highest degree or rank; as, at the *top* of the class. **5** A platform high up on the lower mast of a ship, serving to spread the topmast rigging. **6** A forward spin given to a ball by striking it on or near the top. — *v.;* **topped; top·ping. 1** To cut or trim the top of, as a tree. **2** To cap or cover; to put or be on top; as, to *top* a pie with meringue. **3** To reach or exceed, as in height, weight, or amount. **4** To surmount, as an obstacle. **5** To do or be better than all others; to excel; as, to *top* the team in hits. — **top off.** To complete by adding a top; to end or finish. — *adj.* At or on the top; highest.

top \'täp\ *n.* A child's toy having a point on which it can be made to spin.

to·paz \'tō-ˌpaz\ *n.* **1** A mineral, usually yellow, classed as a gem when found in transparent crystals. **2** A gem resembling the true topaz, as a yellow sapphire.

top boot. A high boot, often with a band of light-colored leather around the top.

top·coat \'täp-ˌkōt\ *n.* A lightweight overcoat.

top·er \'tōp-r\ *n.* A drunkard.

top·gal·lant \(')täp-'gal-ənt, tə-'gal-ənt\ *adj.* Situated next above the topmast. — *n.* A topgallant mast or sail.

top hat. A man's silk-covered hat with a tall crown.

top-heavy \'täp-ˌhev-ē\ *adj.* Having the top part too heavy for the lower part.

top·ic \'täp-ik\ *n.* **1** A phrase used as a heading or summary, as in an outlined argument or composition. **2** The subject, as of a talk; a theme.

top·i·cal \'täp-ik-l\ *adj.* **1** Of or relating to a topic or topics; as, a *topical* outline. **2** Relating to the topics of the day; referring to local or current events. — **top·i·cal·ly** \-ik-l(-)ē\ *adv.*

topic sentence. A sentence stating the main thought of a paragraph or larger unit of a composition.

top·knot \'täp-ˌnät\ *n.* A crest of feathers or hair on the top of the head.

top·mast \'täp-ˌmast, -məst\ *n.* The second mast above the deck.

top·most \'täp-ˌmōst\ *adj.* Uppermost.

top·notch \'täp-'näch\ *adj.* Of highest quality.

to·pog·ra·pher \tə-'päg-rəf-r\ *n.* One who makes topographic surveys or is skilled in topography.

top·o·graph·ic \ˌtäp-ə-'graf-ik, ˌtōp-\ or **top·o·graph·i·cal** \-ik-l\ *adj.* **1** Of or relating to topography; as, a *topographical* survey. **2** Showing the topography of a region; as, a *topographic* map. — **top·o·graph·i·cal·ly** \-ik-l(-)ē\ *adv.*

to·pog·ra·phy \tə-'päg-rə-fē\ *n.; pl.* **to·pog·ra·phies.** **1** The art or practice of detailing on maps or charts the physical features of a region. **2** The outline of the surface of a place, showing its relief, or inequalities in height, and position of features, as roads, streams, lakes, towns, and cities.

top·ple \'täp-l\ *v.;* **top·pled**; **top·pling** \-l(-)ing\. **1** To fall forward because or as if too heavy at the top; to tumble; as, to *topple* out of a tree. **2** To push over; to overturn. The storm *toppled* trees.

top·sail \'täp-ˌsāl, 'täps-l\ *n.* In square rig, the sail next above the lowest sail on a mast; in fore-and-aft rig, a sail above the gaff.

top·side \'täp-'sīd\ *n.* The outer surface of a ship's hull, on either side, above the water line — usually used in the plural. — *adv.* On deck; above.

top·soil \'täp-ˌsȯil\ *n.* Surface soil.

top·sy-tur·vy \'täp-sē-'tər-vē\ *adv.* Upside down; in confusion. — *adj.;* **top·sy-tur·vi·er**; **top·sy-tur·vi·est.** Turned upside down; confused; disordered. — *n.* A topsy-turvy condition.

toque \'tōk\ *n.* A small round hat, usually without a brim.

tor \'tȯr\ *n.* A high, craggy hill; a rocky peak.

torch \'tȯrch\ *n.* **1** A flaming light made of something that burns brightly, as resinous wood, and usually carried in the hand. **2** Something that flames or illuminates like a torch; as, to pass along the *torch* of freedom. **3** Any of various portable devices for producing a hot flame. **4** *Chiefly British.* A flashlight.

torch·bear·er \'tȯrch-ˌbar-r, -ˌber-r\ *n.* One that carries a torch.

torch·light \'tȯrch-ˌlīt\ *n.* The light of a torch.

tore. Past tense of *tear.*

tor·e·a·dor \'tȯr-ē-ə-ˌdȯr\ *n.* A man who fights bulls in an arena for public entertainment.

tor·ment \tȯr-'ment, 'tȯr-ˌment\ *v.* **1** To distress with intense physical suffering or mental anguish; as, *tormented* by disease. **2** To tease; as, to *torment* a person with silly questions. — \'tȯr-ˌment\ *n.* **1** Anguish of body or mind; distress; as, the *torment* of a toothache. **2** Something that causes pain or vexation. Waiting was a *torment.* — **tor·men·tor** or **tor·ment·er** \tȯr-'ment-r, 'tȯr-ˌment-r\ *n.*

torn. Past part. of *tear.*

tor·na·do \tȯr-'nād-ˌō\ *n.; pl.* **tor·na·does.** A violent whirling wind accompanied by a funnel-shaped cloud that reaches to the ground and moves over the land in a narrow path.

tor·pe·do \tȯr-'pēd-ˌō\ *n.; pl.* **tor·pe·does.** **1** A fish of the ray family with a pair of organs near the head capable of giving its prey an electric shock. **2** A cigar-shaped metal case filled with an explosive and made so that it directs and propels itself under water. **3** A submarine mine. **4** Any case filled with explosive. **5** A small firework which explodes when struck. **6** A bit of explosive clasped to a railroad rail to give a signal when run over. — *v.;* **tor·pe·doed**; **tor·pe·do·ing.** To attack with or destroy by a torpedo, as a ship.

torpedo boat. A small fast war vessel designed for discharging torpedoes against enemy ships.

tor·pid \'tȯrp-əd\ *adj.* **1** Having lost motion or power of feeling or exertion, as a hibernating animal; dormant. **2** Dull; sluggish; listless; as, a *torpid* mind. — **tor·pid·ly,** *adv.*

tor·por \'tȯrp-r\ *n.* **1** Temporary loss or suspension of motion or feeling; sluggishness; as, the *torpor* of bears in winter. **2** Dullness; apathy.

tor·rent \'tȯr-ənt, 'tär-\ *n.* **1** A rushing stream, as of water or lava. **2** A violent or rapid flow or flood, as of words; as, a *torrent* of abuse. **3** A downpour.

tor·ren·tial \tə-'rench-l\ *adj.* Of or relating to a torrent; having the character of a torrent; as, *torrential* rains. — **tor·ren·tial·ly** \-'rench-l-ē\ *adv.*

tor·rid \'tȯr-əd, 'tär-\ *adj.* Exposed to tropical heat; dry and hot; scorching; parching.

tor·sion \'tȯrsh-n\ *n.* A turning or twisting; the state of being twisted.

tor·so \'tȯr-ˌsō\ *n.; pl.* **tor·sos.** [From Italian, meaning literally "stalk".] **1** The trunk of a statue that has no head or limbs. **2** The human trunk.

tor·til·la \tȯr-'tē-(y)ə\ *n.* A flat thin unleavened cake baked on a heated stone or iron.

tor·toise \'tȯrt-əs\ *n.* A turtle; especially, a turtle living wholly or mostly on land.

tor·toise·shell \'tȯrt-əs(h)-ˌshel\ *n.* The horny material that forms plates covering the shell of a turtle. — *adj.* Made of tortoiseshell or having its spotted brown and yellow coloring.

tor·tu·ous \'tȯr-chə-wəs\ *adj.* **1** Full of twists or curves; winding; crooked; as, a *tortuous* stream. **2** Confusingly roundabout. — **tor·tu·ous·ly**, *adv.*

tor·ture \'tȯrch-r\ *n.* **1** The inflicting of severe pain, especially to punish or obtain a confession. **2** Extreme pain; agony. — *v.;* **tor·tured**; **tor·tur·ing** \-r(-)ing\. **1** To subject to torture. **2** To be a cause of anguish to; to cause to suffer acutely. **3** To wrench or twist; as, trees *tortured* by wind. **4** To distort; to use or pronounce words incorrectly; as, to *torture* a language. — **tor·tur·er** \'tȯrch-r-r\ *n.*

To·ry \'tōr-ē, 'tȯr-ē\ *n.; pl.* **To·ries. 1** In English politics, a Conservative party member. **2** A loyalist who during the American Revolution favored the British. **3** [often with a small letter] An extreme conservative.

toss \'tȯs, 'täs\ *v.* **1** To keep throwing here and there or backward and forward; to cause to pitch or roll. Waves *tossed* the ship about. **2** To throw with a quick, light motion; as, to *toss* a ball into the air. **3** To lift up with a sudden motion; as, to *toss* the head. **4** To be tossed. The light canoe is *tossing* on the waves. **5** To be restless; to fling oneself about; as, to *toss* in one's sleep. **6** To stir or mix lightly; as, to *toss* a salad. — *n.* **1** A tossing; a pitch; a tossup. **2** A tossing distance.

toss·up \'tȯs-ˌəp, 'täs-\ *n.* **1** A tossing up, as of a coin to determine a chance. **2** An even chance.

tot \'tät\ *n.* A little child.

to·tal \'tōt-l\ *adj.* **1** Of or relating to the whole of a thing; as, a *total* eclipse of the sun. **2** Making up the whole; entire. **3** Complete; utter; as, *total* ruin. **4** Making use of every means to carry out a planned program; as, *total* defense; *total* war. — *n.* The whole; the sum. — *v.;* **to·taled** or **to·talled**; **to·tal·ing** or **to·tal·ling. 1** To find the total of; to add. **2** To amount to. The gifts *totaled* $120. — **to·tal·ly** \'tōt-l-ē\ *adv.*

to·tal·i·tar·i·an \(ˌ)tō-ˌtal-ə-'ter-ē-ən\ *adj.* Of or relating to government control by a political group that denies representation to other political groups and assumes control of all human activities.

to·tal·i·ty \tō-'tal-ət-ē\ *n.; pl.* **to·tal·i·ties.** The whole sum or amount; wholeness.

tote \'tōt\ *v.;* **tot·ed**; **tot·ing.** To carry; to haul; to transport; as, to *tote* the supplies to camp.

to·tem \'tōt-m\ *n.* **1** An animal, plant, or an inanimate object regarded by some tribal peoples as closely related to a certain family or clan. **2** A symbol or representation, such as a **totem pole**, of such a thing. — **to·tem·ic** \tō-'tem-ik\ *adj.*

tot·ter \'tät-r\ *v.* **1** To shake, tremble, or rock as if about to fall; to be unsteady. **2** To walk unsteadily; as, to *totter* with age. — **tot·tery** \-r-ē\ *adj.*

tou·can \'tü-ˌkan, tü-'kan\ *n.* A bright-colored bird of tropical America with a very large beak.

touch \'təch\ *v.* **1** To feel, as with fingers or hands. **2** To be or bring into contact with; as, to *touch* one's hand to one's hat. **3** To hit lightly. **4** To eat, drink, use, or take. I never *touch* tobacco. **5** To be or come next to; to join or border on. **6** To disturb; to harm. No one will *touch* you. **7** To make slightly unbalanced mentally. The man acts as if he were *touched.* **8** To blemish or spoil slightly. Frost *touched* the fruit. **9** To mention; to refer to; as, to *touch* on many subjects. **10** To come up to or to compare with. This boat does not *touch* ours for speed. **11** To improve a thing with or as if with light strokes of a brush or pencil; as, to *touch* up a picture. **12** To give a faint tint or expression to something. A smile *touched* her lips. **13** To concern; as, a matter that *touches* one's interest. **14** To stop at a point on shore. The ship *touched* at many ports. **15** To affect the feelings; to stir to pity or remorse; as, to be *touched* by the plea for help. — *n.* **1** A light stroke, tap, or blow. **2** The action or feeling of touching or being touched. **3** The sense by which pressure is felt; as, soft to the *touch.* **4** An impression or mark; a small trace; a dash; as, a *touch* of spring in the air; a *touch* of color. **5** A special method or skill; as, the *touch* of a professional. **6** Communication or close relationship; the condition of keeping abreast; as, in *touch* with friends; to be out of *touch* with the news. **7** A manner or style of striking the keys of a musical instrument; as, a firm *touch.* **8** A light attack of a disease. — **touch·a·ble** \-əb-l\ *adj.* — **touch·er** \-r\ *n.*

touch·down \'təch-ˌdau̇n\ *n.* A score made in football by being in possession of the ball on or over the opponents' goal line when the ball is declared dead.

touch·ing \'təch-ing\ *adj.* Arousing tenderness or compassion; pathetic. — **touch·ing·ly**, *adv.*

touch·stone \'təch-ˌstōn\ *n.* **1** A black stone used to test the purity of gold and silver by the streak left on the stone when rubbed by the metal. **2** Any test for judging something.

touchy \'təch-ē\ *adj.;* **touch·i·er**; **touch·i·est.** Sensitive to criticism; easily offended.

tough \'təf\ *adj.* **1** Able to undergo great strain; flexible and not brittle; as, *tough* fibers. **2** Not easily chewed; as, *tough* meat. **3** Able to stand hard work and hardship; robust; as, a *tough* body. **4** Hard to influence; stubborn; as, a *tough* bargainer. **5** Hardened in vice; rowdy; lawless; as, a *tough* neighborhood. **6** Very difficult; as, a *tough* problem. **7** Threatening with force; using force or compulsion; as, a *tough* policy toward those who disobey. — *n.* A ruffian; a rowdy. — **tough·ly**, *adv.*

tough·en \'təf-n\ *v.;* **tough·ened**; **tough·en·ing** \-n(-)ing\. To make or become tough or tougher.

tou·pee \tü-'pā\ *n.* A small wig for a bald spot.

tour \'tu̇r\ *n.* A trip or excursion, especially one in which one returns to one's starting point; as, a *tour* of the city. — For synonyms see *journey.* — *v.* To make a tour of; to travel as a tourist.

tour·ist \'tu̇r-əst\ *n.* One who travels for pleasure.

tourist court. A motel.

tour·ma·line \'tu̇rm-l-ən, -ˌēn\ *n.* A mineral that is valued as a gem when transparent, usually black, but sometimes blue, red, green, brown, or colorless.

tour·na·ment \'tu̇r-nə-mənt, 'tər-, 'tȯr-\ *n.* **1** A

contest of skill and courage between armored knights fighting with blunted lances or swords; a joust; a tilt. **2** A series of such knightly contests occurring at a particular time and place. **3** A series of athletic contests, sports events, or games for a championship; as, a tennis *tournament*.

tour·ney \'tůr-nē\ *n.; pl.* **tour·neys.** A tournament. — *v.;* **tour·neyed; tour·ney·ing.** To perform in a tournament.

tour·ni·quet \'tůr-nə-kət, 'tər-\ *n.* A device for stopping or checking bleeding made of a bandage twisted tight with a stick or of a piece of rubber tubing.

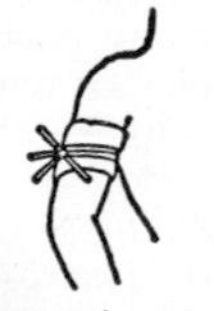
tourniquet

tou·sle \'taůz-l\ *v.;* **tou·sled; tou·sling** \-l(-)ing\. To put into disorder; to rumple; to muss; as, *tousled* hair. — *n.* A tousled mass; a tousled condition.

tout \'taůt\ *v.* **1** To solicit or canvass for patronage, trade, or votes, or other support. **2** *Chiefly British.* To spy about at racing stables and race tracks to get information to be used in betting. **3** To provide tips on racehorses. **4** To praise highly or extravagantly. — *n.* A person who touts.

tow \'tō\ *v.* To draw or pull along behind; as, to *tow* a wrecked car. — *n.* **1** An act or instance of towing or the fact or condition of being towed. **2** A line or rope for towing. **3** Anything that tows or is towed; especially, a tugboat or a barge. — **in tow. 1** Drawn by a towline. **2** As if drawn by a towline; in the position of a follower.

tow \'tō\ *n.* **1** The coarse broken parts of flax, hemp, or jute left when the finer fibers have been combed out. **2** Yarn spun from these broken fibers.

tow·age \'tō-ij\ *n.* **1** The act of towing. **2** The cost of towing.

to·ward \'tōrd, 'tȯrd, 'twōrd, 'twȯrd, tə-'wȯrd\ *adj.* **1** Approaching; imminent. A battle was *toward.* **2** *Archaic.* Ready to learn or do; willing; as, a *toward* youth. — *prep.* **1** In the direction of; as, walking *toward* the river. **2** So as to face; as, to turn a chair *toward* the window. **3** Just before; close to; as, *toward* noon. **4** As a share of; for the payment of; as, to save *toward* an education. **5** Designed for; looking to; aiming at; as, efforts *toward* patching up a quarrel.

to·wards \'tōrdz, 'tȯrdz, 'twōrdz, 'twȯrdz, tə-'wȯrdz\ *prep.* Toward.

tow·boat \'tō-ˌbōt\ *n.* **1** A boat for towing other boats; a tug. **2** A powerful river boat for pushing forward barges lashed together. **3** A boat designed to be towed.

tow·cloth \'tō-ˌklȯth\ *n.; pl.* **tow·cloths** \-ˌklȯt͟hz, -ˌklȯths\. A fabric made of spun tow.

tow·el \'taů-əl, 'taůl\ *n.* A cloth or piece of absorbent paper for wiping and drying anything wet. — *v.;* **tow·eled** or **tow·elled; tow·el·ing** or **tow·el·ling.** To rub or dry with a towel.

tow·el·ing or **tow·el·ling** \'taů-ə-ling, 'taůl-ing\ *n.* Cloth or paper for towels.

tow·er \'taůr\ *n.* **1** A building or structure that is higher than its length or width or is high by position, either standing by itself, as a campanile, or attached to a larger structure, as a church belfry; as, a signal *tower;* a water *tower.* **2** Such a structure used as a defense; a citadel; a stronghold. **3** A tall framework or mast resembling a tower; as, a radio *tower.* — *v.* To reach or rise to a great height above others. — **tow·ered** \'taůrd\ *adj.*

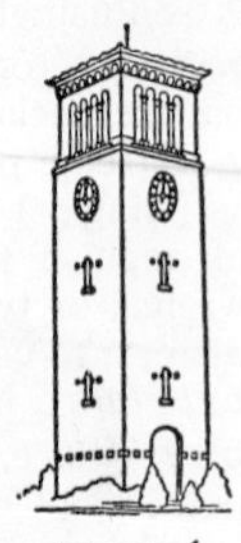
tower, 1

tow·head \'tō-ˌhed\ *n.* A person having soft whitish hair. — **tow·head·ed** \-'hed-əd\ *adj.*

tow·line \'tō-ˌlīn\ *n.* A line used in towing.

town \'taůn\ *n.* **1** A populated place larger than a village but not incorporated as a city. **2** Any large closely populated place, as a city or a borough. **3** In England, a village with a regular fair or market. **4** In New England, an incorporated community in which a general assembly of qualified voters elects all town officials and decides all matters of local government. **5** In some parts of the United States, a unit of rural administration more or less like a New England town; a township. **6** The townspeople; the voters of a town. **7** The city as contrasted with the country; city life.

town clerk. An official who keeps the town records.

town crier. A town officer who makes proclamations.

town hall. A public building used for public offices and for town meetings.

town meeting. A meeting of the voters of a town for the transaction of public business.

towns·folk \'taůnz-ˌfōk\ *n. pl.* Townspeople.

town·ship \'taůn-ˌship\ *n.* **1** A section or district, usually a division of a county, having certain powers of local government. **2** In surveys of United States public lands, a division six miles square.

towns·man \'taůnz-mən\ *n.; pl.* **towns·men** \-mən\. **1** An inhabitant of a town. **2** A town-bred man. **3** One of the same town as another.

towns·peo·ple \'taůnz-ˌpēp-l\ *n. pl.* **1** The inhabitants of a town. **2** People bred or living in towns.

tow·path \'tō-ˌpath\ *n.; pl.* **tow·paths** \-ˌpat͟hz\. A path by a canal, for men or animals towing boats.

tow·rope \'tō-ˌrōp\ *n.* A rope used in towing.

tox·e·mia or **tox·ae·mia** \täk-'sē-mē-ə\ *n.* Blood poisoning caused by toxins. — **tox·e·mic** or **tox·ae·mic** \-'sē-mik\ *adj.*

tox·ic \'täks-ik\ *adj.* Of, relating to, or caused or affected by a toxin; poisonous.

tox·ic·i·ty \täk-'sis-ət-ē\ *n.; pl.* **tox·ic·i·ties.** The quality, state, or degree of being toxic.

tox·i·col·o·gy \ˌtäks-ə-'käl-ə-jē\ *n.* The science that deals with poisons and their antidotes. — **tox·i·co·log·i·cal** \ˌtäks-ə-kə-'läj-ik-l\ *adj.* — **tox·i·col·o·gist** \-'käl-ə-jəst\ *n.*

tox·in \'täks-n\ *n.* A poison produced by plants,

by animals, as certain snakes and insects, or by germs, as in diphtheria or tetanus.

tox·in–an·ti·tox·in \'täks-n-'ant-ē-ˌtäks-n\ *n.* A mixture of the toxin and antitoxin for a particular disease, used in immunizing against this disease.

tox·oid \'täk-ˌsȯid\ *n.* A toxin, as of tetanus, treated so as to destroy its poisonous effects while leaving it still capable of causing the formation of antibodies when injected into the body.

toy \'tȯi\ *n.* **1** Something that is of small or no real value or importance; a trifle; a trinket. **2** A plaything. **3** Something small of its kind, as a dog (**toy dog**) of various small breeds. — *v.* To amuse oneself; to trifle; to play; as, to *toy* with an idea.

toy·on \'tȯi-ˌän\ *n.* An ornamental evergreen shrub of the North American Pacific coast, having white flowers followed by bright red berries.

tp. Abbreviation for *township.*

trace \'trās\ *n.* **1** A mark left by a person or thing in passing; a footprint; a track. **2** A sign or evidence of some past thing; a vestige; as, *traces* of an ancient city. **3** Something traced, as a line. **4** A very small amount; as, a *trace* of color. — *v.*; **traced**; **trac·ing.** **1** To draw; to mark out; to sketch. **2** To form, as letters; to write carefully. **3** To copy, as a drawing, on a transparent sheet of paper laid over it. **4** To record in the form of a graph, as the heart action. **5** To adorn with tracery; as, *traced* windows. **6** To follow, pursue, or track. **7** To study out or follow the development or progress of a thing; to outline; as to *trace* one's ancestry.

trace \'trās\ *n.* One of two straps, chains, or ropes of a harness that fasten a horse to a vehicle.

trace·a·ble \'trā-səb-l\ *adj.* **1** Capable of being traced. **2** Attributable; due; as, a failure *traceable* to plain laziness. — **trace·a·bly** \-sə-blē\ *adv.*

trac·er \'trās-r\ *n.* **1** One employed to trace missing articles or persons or an inquiry sent out for such. **2** A device, as a pointed wheel mounted in a handle, used to transfer patterns to cloth. **3** An element or an atom having a peculiarity, as radioactivity, by which it can be traced through chemical reactions or biological processes. **4** A small firework attached to a projectile, as a bullet (**tracer bullet**), to mark its flight by a trail.

trac·ery \'trās-r(-)ē\ *n.*; *pl.* **trac·er·ies.** **1** Ornamental work with branching or interlacing lines used in architectural decoration. **2** Any interlacing of lines suggestive of such tracery, as a pattern of frost on a window.

tracery, 1

tra·chea \'trāk-ē-ə\ *n.*; *pl.* **tra·che·as** \-ē-əz\ or **tra·che·ae** \-ē-ˌē, -ē-ˌī\. **1** In vertebrates, the main tube by which air passes to and from the lungs; the windpipe. **2** In insects and myriapods, one of the air-conveying tubes within the thorax and abdomen.

tra·che·al \'trāk-ē-əl\ *adj.* Of or relating to the trachea; like a trachea; having a trachea.

tra·che·id \'trāk-ē-əd, 'trāk-ˌēd\ *n.* A long water-conducting cell with tapering, closed ends and thickened walls, found in xylem and especially characteristic of cone-bearing plants.

tra·cho·ma \trə-'kō-mə\ *n.* A contagious disease of an eye membrane, sometimes causing blindness.

trac·ing \'trā-sing\ *n.* **1** The act of one that traces. **2** Anything that is traced, as a copy.

track \'trak\ *n.* **1** A mark left in passing, as of a foot or a tire; a sign; a trace. **2** A path, route, or road; a trail; as, the *track* of a comet. **3** Awareness or notice of something in regard to a person or thing; as, to lose *track* of a friend. **4** A course laid out for racing. **5** Sports performed on a running track; also, track sports and field events together; as, to excel in *track*. **6** A way for certain wheeled vehicles; as, a railroad *track*. **7** One of the two endless-chain treads on which a tank runs. — **in one's tracks.** In one's footprints; at the exact spot where one is at the moment; as, to drop *in one's tracks*. — **make tracks.** To go very fast. — **off the track.** Having left the right track; gone astray; away from the matter under consideration. — *v.* **1** To follow the tracks of; to trail. **2** To trace by following signs of any kind; to search for. **3** To pass over; to traverse, as a desert. **4** To make tracks upon or with; as, to *track* a floor with mud. — **track·er**, *n.*

track·less \'trak-ləs\ *adj.* **1** Having no tracks or footprints. **2** Not running on tracks or rails.

track meet. A series of athletic contests in track sports, usually including field events.

tract \'trakt\ *n.* A pamphlet, especially on a religious or political subject, written to persuade its readers to a certain belief or course of action.

tract \'trakt\ *n.* **1** An expanse; an area or region, often one not definitely bounded. **2** In the body, a system of parts or organs that serve some special purpose; as, the digestive *tract.*

trac·ta·ble \'trak-təb-l\ *adj.* **1** Easily led or controlled; as, *tractable* children. **2** Easily worked; as, *tractable* metal. — **trac·ta·bil·i·ty** \ˌtrak-tə-'bil-ət-ē\ *n.* — **trac·ta·bly** \'trak-tə-blē\ *adv.*

trac·tion \'traksh-n\ *n.* **1** The action or process of drawing or pulling or the state of being drawn. **2** The drawing of something along a surface, as of a wagon by horses. **3** The power used to draw something along; as, electric *traction*. **4** The friction that holds something on a surface on which it is moving, as a wheel on a rail.

trac·tor \'trakt-r\ *n.* **1** A self-propelled vehicle with large rear-drive wheels or tracks as on a tank, used to draw farm machines. **2** A motor truck with a short chassis, used to haul a trailer. **3** An airplane having its propeller forward of the wings.

tractor, 1

trade \'trād\ *n.* **1** [usually in the plural] A trade wind. **2** The skilled work at which

one regularly makes a living; a craft. **3** The act or business of buying and selling goods; commerce. **4** All persons in the same kind of business; as, the automobile *trade.* **5** Customers; as, to wait on *trade.* **6** An exchange of one article for another. — The words *craft, business,* and *profession* are synonyms of *trade: trade* is applied chiefly to an occupation that involves skilled manual or mechanical labor and the use of machinery and tools; *craft* is close to *trade* but has a stronger suggestion of training and skill and sometimes indicates greater freedom for creativeness by the craftsman; *business* applies especially to transactions or enterprises that are primarily commercial, as the production, manufacture, or especially the sale of a commodity, the providing of services, or the management of money or money matters; *profession* generally suggests an occupation requiring considerable study and training followed by examination of one's qualifications for the occupation and usually suggests a certain devotion to standards and ideals upheld in the practice.
— *v.;* trad·ed; trad·ing. 1 To carry on a business of bartering or buying and selling. **2** To make one's purchases; to deal; as, to *trade* at the new store. **3** To profit by taking an unfair advantage; as, to *trade* on someone's fears. **4** To exchange; to swap.

trade-in \\'trād-ˌin\\ *n.* Something given in trade, usually as part payment of the price of another.

trade·mark \\'trād-ˌmärk, -ˌmȧrk\\ *n.* **1** A word, mark, or picture, or a combination of these, used to identify and protect the goods of a certain manufacturer or merchant. **2** Something by which a person or thing may be recognized. **—** *v.* **1** To label with a trademark. **2** To register the trademark of.

trade name. 1 The name by which an article is called in its own trade. **2** Also **trademark name.** The name used by a manufacturer or merchant to identify and protect an article sold by him. **3** The name under which a firm does business.

trad·er \\'trād-r\\ *n.* **1** A person who trades. **2** A ship engaged in trade.

trade school. A school where trades are taught.

trades·man \\'trādz-mən\\ *n.; pl.* **trades·men** \\-mən\\. A person who trades; a shopkeeper.

trades·peo·ple \\'trādz-ˌpēp-l\\ *n. pl.* Tradesmen.

trade-un·ion \\'trād-ˌyün-yən\\ or **trades-un·ion** \\'trādz-\\ *n.* **1** A labor union organized within a particular trade or craft. **2** Any labor union. — **trade-un·ion·ist** or **trades-un·ion·ist** \\-yə-nəst\\ *n.*

trade wind. A wind blowing almost continually in the same course, from northeast to southwest in the region north of the equator and from southeast to northwest in that south of the equator.

trad·ing post \\'trād-ing\\. A station or store of a trader or trading company established in a sparsely settled region.

tra·di·tion \\trə-'dish-n\\ *n.* **1** The handing down of information, beliefs, or customs orally from one generation to another. **2** Something thus handed down. — **tra·di·tion·al** \\-n(-)əl\\ *adj.*

tra·duce \\trə-'düs, -'dyüs\\ *v.;* **tra·duced; tra·duc·ing.** To slander. — **tra·duc·er** \\-'düs-r, -'dyüs-r\\ *n.*

traf·fic \\'traf-ik\\ *n.* **1** The business of carrying passengers or goods; as, the tourist *traffic.* **2** The business of buying and selling; trade; commerce. **3** Dealings; familiarity; as, to have no *traffic* with the enemy. **4** The persons or goods carried by train, boat, or airplane, or passing along a road, river, or air route; the motions or activity of such persons or carriers; as, heavy holiday *traffic.* **—** *v.;* **traf·ficked** \\-ikt\\; **traf·fick·ing** \\-ik-ing\\. **1** To buy, sell, or barter; to trade. **2** To deal, especially in a dishonest way; as, to *traffic* with criminals. — **traf·fick·er** \\-ik-r\\ *n.*

traffic circle. A rotary.

traffic light. A signal light to regulate traffic.

tra·ge·di·an \\trə-'jēd-ē-ən\\ *n.* **1** A person who writes tragedy. **2** An actor who plays in tragedies.

trag·e·dy \\'traj-əd-ē\\ *n.; pl.* **trag·e·dies. 1** A literary composition, especially a play, that arouses pity or terror by a series of sad events and ends unhappily. **2** A tragic event or series of events.

trag·ic \\'traj-ik\\ *adj.* **1** Of or relating to tragedy; having the nature or character of tragedy or the tragic; as, a *tragic* story. **2** Awful; unfortunate. War is a *tragic* thing. — **trag·i·cal·ly** \\-ik-l(-)ē\\ *adv.*

trail \\'trāl\\ *v.* **1** To drag or draw along behind. The runaway horse *trailed* its reins. **2** To lag behind. The horse *trailed* in the race. **3** To carry or bring along. The boy disliked to *trail* his sister around with him. **4** To follow in the tracks of; to pursue. **5** To hang or let hang so as to touch the ground; as, a *trailing* skirt. **6** To grow to such a length as to droop over. **7** To form a trail; to straggle. Smoke *trailed* from the chimney. **8** To dwindle. The sound *trailed* off. **—** *n.* **1** Something that trails or is trailed; as, a *trail* of smoke. **2** A track left by something that has been trailed; as, a *trail* of blood. **3** A scent. The dogs followed a false *trail.* **4** A path through wooded or wild country.

trail·er \\'trāl-r\\ *n.* One that trails; especially, a vehicle hauled by a motor car.

train \\'trān\\ *n.* **1** Something that trails; especially, a part of a woman's gown. **2** A number of followers or attendants; as, a prince and his *train.* **3** A moving line or file; a procession; as, a wagon *train.* **4** A sequence, as of ideas; as, a *train* of thought. **5** A series, as of wheels and pinions for transmitting motion. **6** Results; accompanying circumstances. War brings many evils in its *train.* **7** A connected line of railway cars hauled by a locomotive. **—** *v.* **1** To cause to grow as desired; as, to *train* ivy along a wall. **2** To educate; to bring up; as, children who have been carefully *trained.* **3** To teach; to instruct; as, to *train* radio operators. **4** To make or become fit; as, to *train* for a race. **5** To aim or point at a target, as a cannon. — **train·a·ble** \\'trā-nəb-l\\ *adj.* — **train·er** \\'trān-r\\ *n.* — **train·ee** \\trā-'nē\\ *n.*

train·ing \\'trā-ning\\ *n.* **1** The course followed by one who trains or is being trained; as, to take nursing *training.* **2** The condition of one who has trained for a test or contest. — For synonyms see *education.* — *adj.* **1** Used in or for training; as, a *training* camp. **2** Providing training.

train oil. Oil from blubber, as of whales.

trait \'trāt\ *n.* A quality of character; a characteristic. — For synonyms see *characteristic.*

trai·tor \'trāt-r\ *n.* A person who betrays, as his cause or a friend; one guilty of treason.

trai·tor·ous \'trāt-r-əs, 'trā-trəs\ *adj.* **1** Guilty of treason; capable of treason. **2** Consisting of treason; of the nature of treason.

trai·tress \'trā-trəs\ *n.* A female traitor.

tra·jec·to·ry \trə-'jekt-r(-)ē\ *n.; pl.* **tra·jec·to·ries.** The curve that a body describes in space, as an artillery shell or as a planet in its orbit.

tram \'tram\ *n.* **1** *British.* A streetcar. **2** A cart or wagon running on rails, as in a mine. **3** The carriage of an overhead conveyer.

tram·mel \'tram-l\ *n.* **1** A net for birds or fish. **2** [usually in the plural] Something that hinders movement; restraint; entanglement; check. **3** An adjustable hook for hanging a kettle over an open fire. — *v.;* **tram·meled** or **tram·melled; tram·mel·ing** or **tram·mel·ling** \-l(-)ing\. **1** To hold as in a net; as, to be *trammeled* up in responsibilities. **2** To prevent the free movement of; to hamper.

tramp \'tramp\ *v.* **1** To walk heavily. **2** To tread or stamp upon; to trample; as, to *tramp* soil down. **3** To walk about or through; as, to *tramp* the streets. — *n.* **1** One that tramps; especially, a shiftless person who tramps from place to place. **2** A journey on foot. **3** The sounds made by tramping; as, the *tramp* of marching feet. **4** A ship that takes cargo to and from any port. — **tramp·er,** *n.*

tram·ple \'tramp-l\ *v.;* **tram·pled; tram·pling** \-l(-)ing\. **1** To tramp or tread heavily so as to bruise, crush, or injure. **2** To tread underfoot; to stamp on. **3** To inflict pain, injury, or loss by heartless treatment; as, to *trample* upon one's feelings. — *n.* The action or sound of trampling.

tram·po·lin \'tramp-l-ən\ or **tram·po·line** \-l-ˌēn\ *n.* A heavy net or sheet of canvas stretched on a metal frame, used as a springboard by acrobats.

tram·way \'tram-ˌwā\ *n.* **1** A road or way for trams. **2** *British.* A streetcar line.

trance \'tran(t)s\ *n.* **1** A daze; a stupor. **2** A condition of complete abstraction of mind or spirit, as in certain kinds of religious experience. **3** A sleep-like state caused by sickness or hypnotism.

tran·quil \'tran(g)-kwəl\ *adj.;* **tran·quil·er** or **tran·quil·ler; tran·quil·est** or **tran·quil·lest.** Very calm and quiet; undisturbed. — **tran·quil·ly** \-kwə-lē\ *adv.*

tran·quil·ize or **tran·quil·lize** \'tran(g)-kwə-ˌlīz\ *v.;* **tran·quil·ized** or **tran·quil·lized; tran·quil·iz·ing** or **tran·quil·liz·ing.** To make or become tranquil. — **tran·quil·iz·er** or **tran·quil·liz·er** \-ˌlīz-r\ *n.*

tran·quil·li·ty or **tran·quil·i·ty** \tran(g)-'kwil-ət-ē\ *n.* Calmness; quiet; composure.

trans-. A prefix that can mean: **1** Over, across, beyond, as in *translucent.* **2** Into a changed form or condition, as in *transform.* **3** On or to the other side of, as in *transatlantic.*

trans·act \tran(t)s-'akt, tranz-\ *v.* **1** To carry through; to bring about; as, to *transact* a sale of property. **2** To carry on; to conduct; as, to *transact* business. — **trans·ac·tor** \-'akt-r\ *n.*

trans·ac·tion \tran(t)s-'aksh-n, tranz-\ *n.* **1** The action of transacting. **2** That which is transacted, as a business deal. **3** [used in the plural] The records of the proceedings of a society.

trans·at·lan·tic \ˌtran(t)s-ət-'lant-ik, ˌtranz-\ *adj.* **1** Lying beyond or across the Atlantic ocean. **2** Crossing the Atlantic.

tran·scend \tran-'send\ *v.* **1** To be above or beyond; to exceed; as, a book that *transcends* one's power to understand. **2** To be greatly superior to; to surpass; as, a poem *transcending* all others.

tran·scend·ent \tran-'sen-dənt\ *adj.* Extraordinary; surpassing; superior. — **tran·scend·ent·ly,** *adv.*

tran·scen·den·tal \ˌtran-ˌsen-'dent-l, ˌtran(t)s-n-\ *adj.* **1** Transcendent. **2** Lying beyond one's power to know through the senses or experience; far removed from practical affairs or human comprehension. — **tran·scen·den·tal·ly** \-'dent-l-ē\ *adv.*

trans·con·ti·nen·tal \'tran(t)s-ˌkänt-n-'ent-l, -ˌkän-tə-'nent-l\ *adj.* **1** Crossing a continent. **2** Being on the other side of a continent.

tran·scribe \tran-'skrīb\ *v.;* **tran·scribed; tran·scrib·ing. 1** To write a copy of. **2** To copy by longhand or typewriter from shorthand. **3** In music, to make a transcription of. **4** To represent speech sounds by using phonetic signs. **5** To broadcast by electrical transcription. — **tran·scrib·er** \-'skrīb-r\ *n.*

tran·script \'tran-ˌskript\ *n.* **1** A written or typewritten copy; as, a *transcript* of a record. **2** Any copy or imitation.

tran·scrip·tion \tran-'skripsh-n\ *n.* **1** The action of transcribing. **2** A copy; a transcript. **3** An arrangement of a musical composition for some other instrument or voice than that for which it was originally written. **4** Also **electrical transcription.** Reproduction over a radio system of material previously prepared for the purpose and recorded.

tran·sept \'tran-ˌsept\ *n.* **1** In a church with a floor plan suggesting a cross, the part corresponding to the crosspiece. **2** Either end of this part of a church; as, the north *transept.*

trans·fer \tran(t)s-'fər, 'tran(t)s-ˌfər\ *v.;* **trans·ferred; trans·fer·ring. 1** To cause to pass from one owner to another; to convey. **2** To move from one place to another; to transport. **3** To print by impressing a picture or drawing from one surface upon another surface; as, to *transfer* designs on china. **4** To change from one streetcar, bus, or railway line to another. — \'tran(t)s-ˌfər\ *n.* **1** The act or process of transferring or the state of being transferred. **2** A person or thing that is transferred. **3** Something printed or to be printed in reverse from one surface to another. **4** A ticket permitting a passenger to transfer. **5** A place along a transportation line where one can transfer. — **trans·fer·a·ble** \tran(t)s-'fər-əb-l, 'tran(t)s-ˌfər-\ *adj.*

trans·fer·ence \tran(t)s-'fər-ən(t)s\ *n.* The act of transferring; passage; transfer.

trans·fig·u·ra·tion \(ˌ)tran(t)s-ˌfig-yə-'rāsh-n, -ˌfig-r-'āsh-n\ *n.* **1** A change of form or appearance. **2** [with a capital] The supernatural change in the personal appearance of Jesus that took place on the mountain; a church festival held on August 6 commemorating this.

trans·fig·ure \tran(t)s-'fig-yər, -'fig-r\ *v.;* **trans·fig·ured**; **trans·fig·ur·ing** \-yər-ing, -r(-)ing\. **1** To change the appearance or form of; to transform. **2** To make bright or radiant; to illumine; to exalt; to glorify; as, a face *transfigured* with joy.

trans·fix \tran(t)s-'fiks\ *v.* **1** To pierce through with or as if with a pointed weapon. **2** To hold fixed or motionless as if pierced through.

trans·form \tran(t)s-'fȯrm\ *v.* **1** To change in outward appearance; as, city streets *transformed* by snow. **2** To change completely in structure, composition, or nature; to convert. The caterpillar is *transformed* into a butterfly. **3** To change one form of energy into another; as, to *transform* water power into electric power. **4** To change an electric current in voltage, from high to low or low to high, or in type, from alternating to direct or direct to alternating. **5** To change the form of, as an algebraic expression or geometrical figure without altering the value or meaning.

trans·for·ma·tion \ˌtran(t)s-fər-'māsh-n\ *n.* **1** A transforming; a complete change of form, structure, composition, or condition. **2** A wig or a fringe of false hair for wear by women.

trans·form·er \tran(t)s-'fȯrm-r\ *n.* One that transforms; especially, an apparatus for changing an electric current into one of higher or lower voltage without changing the current energy.

trans·fuse \tran(t)s-'fyüz\ *v.;* **trans·fused**; **trans·fus·ing.** To cause transfusion; especially, to perform a blood transfusion.

trans·fu·sion \tran(t)s-'fyüzh-n\ *n.* The act of passing one thing into another; especially, a **blood transfusion**, the operation of passing blood taken from one person into the blood vessels of another.

trans·gress \tran(t)s-'gres, tranz-\ *v.* **1** To go beyond the limits set by; to break, as a law; to sin against. **2** To go beyond; to exceed. The sea *transgressed* its bounds. **3** To sin; to break the law. — **trans·gres·sor** \-'gres-r\ *n.*

trans·gres·sion \tran(t)s-'gresh-n, tranz-\ *n.* A transgressing; a violation of a law, a convention, or a command; a trespass; a sin.

tran·ship \tran-'ship\ *v.;* **tran·shipped**; **tran·ship·ping.** To transship. — **tran·ship·ment** \-mənt\ *n.*

tran·sient \'tranch-nt\ *adj.* **1** Not lasting or staying long; as, a hotel that accepts *transient* guests. **2** Changing in form or appearance; shifting; as, a *transient* scene. — *n.* A transient guest or boarder. — **tran·sient·ly**, *adv.*

tran·sis·tor \tran-'zist-r, -'sist-r\ *n.* A very small electronic device similar in its uses to the electron tube.

tran·sit \'tran(t)s-ət, 'tran-zət\ *n.* **1** Passage through or over; travel from one point to another; as, rapid *transit.* **2** The act or process of carrying from one point to another; transportation; as, goods lost in *transit.* **3** The passage of a celestial body over the meridian of a place or through the field of a telescope. **4** The passage of a smaller celestial body across the disk of a larger one. **5** A surveyor's instrument for measuring angles; a form of theodolite (**transit theodolite**). — *v.* To pass in transit; to make a transit across.

surveyor's transit

tran·si·tion \tran(t)s-'ish-n, tranz-\ *n.* **1** A passing from one state, condition, form, or stage of development to another; change; as, *transitions* in the weather. **2** A smooth passing from one subject to another; as, careful *transitions* in writing. **3** In music, a modulation; a change of key.

tran·si·tion·al \tran(t)s-'ish-n(-)əl, tranz-\ *adj.* Of or relating to transition; making or resulting from a transition; characterized by transition. — **tran·si·tion·al·ly** \-n(-)ə-lē\ *adv.*

tran·si·tive \'tran(t)s-ət-iv, 'tran-zət-\ *adj.* **1** Being or forming a transition; transitional. **2** In grammar, expressing an action or state as not limited to the doer or subject but directed upon an object. In the sentence "He writes books", the verb "writes" is *transitive.* — **tran·si·tive·ly**, *adv.*

tran·si·to·ry \'tran-zə-ˌtōr-ē, 'tran(t)s-ə-, -ˌtȯr-ē\ *adj.* Lasting only a short time; transient. — **tran·si·to·ri·ly** \ˌtran-zə-'tōr-ə-lē, ˌtran(t)s-ə-, -'tȯr-\ *adv.*

trans·late \tran(t)s-'lāt, tranz-\ *v.;* **trans·lat·ed**; **trans·lat·ing.** **1** To remove from one place or condition to another; to transfer, as a bishop from one see to another; especially, to remove or carry off to heaven while still living. **2** To turn from one language into another; as, to *translate* a French poem into English. **3** To carry over from one medium into another; as, to *translate* thought into action. — **trans·lat·a·ble** \-'lāt-əb-l\ *adj.*

trans·la·tion \tran(t)s-'lāsh-n, tranz-\ *n.* **1** The act or process of translating. **2** The result produced by translating; as, *translations* of the Bible.

trans·la·tor \tran(t)s-'lāt-r, tranz-\ *n.* One that translates, especially from another language.

trans·lu·cence \tran(t)s-'lüs-n(t)s, tranz-\ or **trans·lu·cen·cy** \-'lüs-n-sē\ *n.* The quality or state of being translucent.

trans·lu·cent \tran(t)s-'lüs-nt, tranz-\ *adj.* **1** Shining or glowing through. **2** Allowing rays of light to pass through without being fully transparent. — **trans·lu·cent·ly**, *adv.*

trans·mi·gra·tion \ˌtran(t)s-ˌmī-'grāsh-n, ˌtranz-\ *n.* **1** The changing of one's home from one country to another. **2** The passing of a soul into another body after death.

trans·mis·si·ble \tran(t)s-'mis-əb-l, tranz-\ *adj.* Capable of being transmitted.

trans·mis·sion \tran(t)s-'mish-n, tranz-\ *n.* **1** A

transmitting, as of a disease or of electric power. **2** Something that is transmitted. **3** The mechanism by which the power is transmitted from the engine to the axle that gives motion to a car. **4** The passage of radio waves in space between transmitting and receiving stations.

trans·mit \tran(t)s-'mit, tranz-\ *v.;* **trans·mit·ted; trans·mit·ting.** **1** To transfer from one person or place to another. **2** To hand down; as, to *transmit* a secret process from father to son. **3** To pass or cause to pass through space or some other medium; as, to *transmit* sound by telephone. Glass *transmits* light. **4** To send out by means of radio waves. — **trans·mit·tal** \-'mit-l\ *n.* — **trans·mit·ti·ble** \-'mit-əb-l\ *adj.*

trans·mit·ter \tran(t)s-'mit-r, tranz-\ *n.* **1** One that transmits; as, a *transmitter* of disease. **2** The instrument of a telegraph system that sends out messages. **3** The part of a telephone, including the mouthpiece and what is behind it, that picks up sound waves and sends them over the wire. **4** The apparatus that sends out radio and television waves or the building in which it is housed.

trans·mute \tran(t)s-'myüt, tranz-\ *v.;* **trans·mut·ed; trans·mut·ing.** To change from one nature, form, or substance into another; to convert. — **trans·mu·ta·tion** \ˌtran(t)s-myü-'tāsh-n, ˌtranz-\ *n.*

trans·oce·an·ic \(ˌ)tran(t)s-ˌō-shē-'an-ik, (ˌ)tranz-\ *adj.* Lying beyond the ocean; crossing the ocean; as, *transoceanic* airplane routes.

tran·som \'tran(t)s-m\ *n.* **1** A piece that lies crosswise in a structure, as in the frame of a window or of a door that has a window above it. **2** A window above a door or other window.

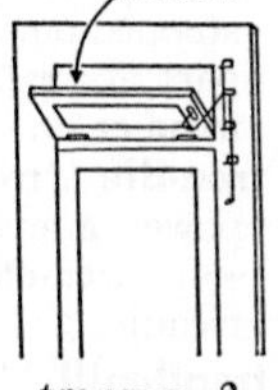

transom, 2

tran·son·ic \tran-'sän-ik\ *adj.* Of or relating to a speed about the same as that of sound in air — often used in aeronautics in referring to speeds from 600 to 900 miles per hour.

trans·pa·cif·ic \ˌtran(t)s-pə-'sif-ik\ *adj.* **1** Lying beyond or across the Pacific Ocean. **2** Crossing the Pacific.

trans·par·en·cy \tran(t)s-'par-ən-sē, -'per-\ *n.; pl.* **trans·par·en·cies.** **1** Also **trans·par·ence** \-ən(t)s\. The quality or state of being transparent. **2** Something transparent, as a picture on glass.

trans·par·ent \tran(t)s-'par-ənt, -'per-\ *adj.* **1** Transmitting light so that bodies can be clearly seen through; as, *transparent* glass. **2** Fine or sheer enough to be seen through. Gauze is *transparent.* **3** Easily understood; clear; as, a *transparent* statement. **4** Easily detected; perfectly evident; as, a *transparent* scheme. — **trans·par·ent·ly,** *adv.*

tran·spi·ra·tion \ˌtran(t)s-pə-'rāsh-n\ *n.* The action or process of transpiring, as in the passing of moisture through the skin or from the surface of green tissues in plants.

tran·spire \tran(t)s-'pīr\ *v.;* **tran·spired; tran·spir·ing.** **1** To pass by transpiration. **2** To leak out. What happened in the secret meeting has never *transpired.* **3** To happen; to take place.

trans·plant \tran(t)s-'plant\ *v.* **1** To remove and reset in another location; as, to *transplant* seedlings. **2** To cause to settle elsewhere. **3** To remove tissue from one individual or part and plant it for growth in another. — **trans·plan·ta·tion** \ˌtran(t)s-ˌplan-'tāsh-n\ *n.* — **trans·plant·er** \tran(t)s-'plant-r\ *n.*

trans·port \tran(t)s-'pōrt, -'pȯrt\ *v.* **1** To convey from one place to another; as, to *transport* goods. **2** To punish by conveying into exile. **3** To carry away with strong emotion; as, to be *transported* by glorious music. — \'tran(t)s-ˌpōrt, -ˌpȯrt\ *n.* **1** Conveyance, as of goods or soldiers; transportation; carriage. **2** A vehicle or vessel used in transporting; especially, a ship used in transporting troops and supplies. **3** Someone or something transported. **4** A joyous emotion; ecstasy; as, *transports* of joy. — **trans·port·a·ble** \tran(t)s-'pōrt-əb-l, -'pȯrt-\ *adj.*

trans·por·ta·tion \ˌtran(t)s-pər-'tāsh-n\ *n.* **1** A transporting or a being transported. **2** The business of transporting passengers or goods; systems or methods of transporting; as, money invested in *transportation.* **3** The ticket or pass needed for a journey; as, to secure *transportation* for a trip.

trans·pose \tran(t)s-'pōz\ *v.;* **trans·posed; trans·pos·ing.** **1** To change the order or position of. *Transpose* the *i* and the *a* in "lair" and make "liar". **2** In algebra, to change the sign of a term and bring the term from one side of an equation to the other. **3** To write or perform in a different key in music; as, to *transpose* a song. — **trans·pos·al** \-'pōz-l\ *n.* — **trans·pos·er** \-'pōz-r\ *n.* — **trans·po·si·tion** \ˌtran(t)s-pə-'zish-n\ *n.*

trans·ship \tran-'ship\ *v.;* **trans·shipped; trans·ship·ping.** To transfer for further transportation from one ship or conveyance to another. — **trans·ship·ment** \-mənt\ *n.*

tran·sub·stan·ti·a·tion \ˌtran-səb-ˌstanch-ē-'āsh-n\ *n.* The doctrine, as in the Roman Catholic Church, that the consecrated bread and wine in the Eucharist are changed in substance but not in appearance into the body and blood of Christ.

trans·ver·sal \tran(t)s-'vərs-l, tranz-\ *adj.* Running or lying across; transverse. — *n.* In geometry, a line that intersects any system of lines. — **trans·ver·sal·ly** \-'vərs-l-ē\ *adv.*

trans·verse \'tran(t)s-'vərs, 'tranz-, -ˌvərs\ *adj.* Lying or being across; set crosswise; as, the *transverse* pieces in a window frame. — *n.* Something that is transverse. — **trans·verse·ly,** *adv.*

trap \'trap\ *n.* **1** A device for catching animals; a snare; a pitfall; especially, a steel device with jaws that snap shut when a spring is released. **2** Something by or in which an unsuspecting person may be suddenly caught, injured, or captured; as, to lead an enemy into a *trap.* **3** A device that allows something to

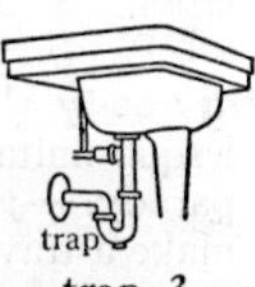

trap, 3

pass through but keeps other things out. A *trap* in a drain allows water to pass downward but prevents sewer gas from passing upward. **4** [in the plural] Musical instruments played by striking, as drums, bells, or cymbals. **5** A device for throwing objects into the air to be shot at. **6** A two-wheeled, one-horse carriage with springs. **7** A trap door. — *v.;* **trapped; trap·ping. 1** To catch in a trap; as, to *trap* game. **2** To provide with a trap; as, to *trap* a drain. **3** To be engaged in trapping animals, especially for their fur.

trap door. A lifting or sliding door covering an opening in a floor or roof.

tra·peze \tra-'pēz\ *n.* A swing high above the ground, used by acrobats and athletes.

trap·e·zoid \'trap-ə-ˌzȯid\ *n.* A four-sided plane figure with two parallel sides.

trap·per \'trap-r\ *n.* A person who traps; especially, one who traps animals for their furs.

trap·pings \'trap-ingz\ *n. pl.* **1** Ornamental cloths or coverings for a horse, especially a saddle horse. **2** Ornaments; decorations.

trap·shoot·ing \'trap-ˌshüt-ing\ *n.* Shooting at targets thrown into the air by a trap.

trash \'trash\ *n.* **1** Worthless things; rubbish; refuse. **2** Something or someone judged to be worthless or contemptible. — **trashy** \'trash-ē\ *adj.*

trash farming. A method of farming in which the soil is harrowed or plowed in such a way that stubble or other vegetation is left on the surface to act as a mulch and prevent erosion.

tra·vail \trə-'vāl, 'trav-ˌāl\ *n.* **1** Toil; especially, painful effort. **2** The pain of childbirth. **3** Agony; suffering. — *v.* To undergo the pains of childbirth.

trav·el \'trav-l\ *v.;* **trav·eled** or **trav·elled; trav·el·ing** or **trav·el·ling** \-l(-)ing\. **1** To journey from place to place or to a distant place. **2** To journey from place to place selling or taking orders. **3** To move; to be transmitted; as, light waves *travel* fast. **4** To journey over or through; to traverse. — *n.* **1** The action, recreation, or business of a person who travels. **2** [usually in the plural] A journey; a trip; a tour; as, a book of *travels.* **3** The number of persons or vehicles traveling; traffic. *Travel* is heavy.

trav·eled or **trav·elled** \'trav-ld\ *adj.* **1** Having done much traveling. **2** Used by travelers.

trav·el·er or **trav·el·ler** \'trav-l(-)ər\ *n.* One that travels.

trav·e·logue or **trav·e·log** \'trav-l-ˌȯg\ *n.* A lecture, usually illustrated, on travel.

trav·erse \'trav-rs\ *n.* Something that crosses. — *adj.* Placed or laid crosswise; transverse.

tra·verse \trə-'vərs\ *v.;* **tra·versed; tra·vers·ing. 1** To pass through or across. **2** To cross and recross, as in patrolling. — **tra·vers·a·ble** \-'vərsəb-l\ *adj.* — **tra·vers·er** \-'vərs-r\ *n.*

trav·es·ty \'trav-əs-tē\ *n.; pl.* **trav·es·ties.** A burlesque imitation; a grotesque likeness; a comical parody. — *v.;* **trav·es·tied** \-tēd\; **trav·es·ty·ing.** To make a travesty of; to parody; to burlesque.

tra·vois \trə-'vȯi\ or **tra·voise** \-'vȯiz\ *n.; pl.* **tra·vois** \-'vȯiz\ or **tra·vois·es** \-'vȯi-zəz\. [From Canadian French *travail* meaning literally "frame", "sling".] An Indian vehicle consisting of two trailing poles serving as shafts and bearing a platform or net for the load.

trawl \'trȯl\ *n.* **1** A heavy fish net dragged along the bottom of the sea. **2** A long fishing line having many short lines bearing hooks attached to it. — *v.* To fish or catch with a trawl line or net.

trawl·er \'trȯl-r\ *n.* **1** A person who trawls. **2** A boat used in trawling.

tray \'trā\ *n.* An open receptacle with a flat bottom and a low rim, for holding or carrying articles; as, a waiter's *tray;* the *trays* of a trunk.

treach·er·ous \'trech-r(-)əs\ *adj.* **1** Guilty of or inclined to treachery. **2** Giving a false appearance of safety. — **treach·er·ous·ly,** *adv.*

treach·ery \'trech-r(-)ē\ *n.; pl.* **treach·er·ies.** Faithless behavior toward someone or something one is supposed to aid; violation of allegiance, as to one's country, or of confidence, as of a friend.

trea·cle \'trēk-l\ *n. British.* Molasses.

tread \'tred\ *v.;* **trod** \'träd\; **trod·den** \'träd-n\ or **trod; tread·ing. 1** To walk on or over; as, to *tread* the deck of a ship. **2** To perform by stepping or dancing; as, to *tread* a measure. **3** To walk. **4** To tramp down; as, to *tread* a path through a field. **5** To trample; to step; as, to *tread* on a flower bed. — *n.* **1** A mark or rut left by or as if by treading; a trail of footprints or wheel marks. **2** The action, manner, or sound of treading; as, to know a person's *tread.* **3** The part of a thing that is trodden or stepped on, as the horizontal part of a step. **4** The part of a wheel or tire that bears on a surface. — **tread·er,** *n.*

trea·dle \'tred-l\ *n.* In a machine driven by foot power, a lever or other device worked by the foot. — *v.;* **trea·dled; trea·dling** \-l(-)ing\. To operate a treadle.

tread·mill \'tred-ˌmil\ *n.* **1** A device moved by persons treading on steps set around the rim of a wide wheel or by animals walking on an endless belt. **2** A dull series of chores; any monotonous routine.

trea·son \'trēz-n\ *n.* The betrayal of one's country; especially, the offense of trying to overthrow the government to which one owes allegiance or to bring about its defeat in war.

trea·son·a·ble \'trēz-n(-)əb-l\ *adj.* Involving treason; consisting of treason; treasonous; as, *treasonable* acts. — **trea·son·a·bly** \-n(-)ə-blē\ *adv.*

trea·son·ous \'trēz-n(-)əs\ *adj.* Treasonable. — **trea·son·ous·ly,** *adv.*

trea·sure \'trezh-r, 'trāzh-r\ *n.* **1** Money or other valuables kept as a reserve or hoarded up. **2** Something or someone valued highly. — *v.;* **trea·sured; trea·sur·ing** \-r(-)ing\. To keep as precious; as, to *treasure* a present.

trea·sur·er \'trezh-r-r, 'trāzh-\ *n.* A person trusted with charge of a treasure or treasures or a treasury; especially, an officer of a club or a business who has charge of money taken in and money paid out.

trea·sure trove \'trezh-r ˌtrōv, 'trāzh-r\. **1** Treasure found buried in the ground or otherwise hidden away and of unknown ownership. **2** A discovery, or something discovered, that is full of things to be treasured.

trea·sury \'trezh-r(-)ē, 'trāzh-\ *n.; pl.* **trea·sur·ies.** **1** A place where stores of wealth are kept. **2** Any place where money is taken in and given out. **3** [often with a capital] The department of a government that has charge of its finances. **4** Someone or something, as a book, thought of as a repository for treasures; as, a *treasury* of poems.

treat \'trēt\ *v.* **1** To negotiate; to consider terms of settlement; to deal; as, agents appointed to *treat* with the enemy. **2** To deal with in writing or speaking; to discuss; as, books *treating* of insects. **3** To handle, deal with, or represent in a specified way; as, to *treat* a mistake as if it were a crime. **4** To behave or act toward; as, to *treat* a dog kindly. **5** To furnish another's entertainment or food. **6** To care for medically; as, to *treat* a cold. **7** To subject to some action, as of a chemical; as, to *treat* soil with lime. — *n.* **1** A free entertainment; food, drink, or amusement paid for by another. **2** Anything that affords pleasure or amusement.

trea·tise \'trēt-əs\ *n.* A book or an article treating of a subject systematically; as, a *treatise* on war.

treat·ment \'trēt-mənt\ *n.* **1** The act or manner of treating; as, a disease that responded quickly to *treatment.* **2** An instance of a particular kind of treatment; as, a heat *treatment.*

trea·ty \'trēt-ē\ *n.; pl.* **trea·ties.** A pact especially negotiated between two or more nations.

tre·ble \'treb-l\ *adj.* **1** Having three parts or uses. **2** Triple in number or amount. **3** Soprano. **4** High-pitched; shrill. — *n.* **1** A high-pitched, shrill voice or sound. **2** Soprano. **3** A soprano singer or instrument. — *v.;* **tre·bled; tre·bling** \-l(-)ing\. To make or become three times as much, as many, or as great; as, to *treble* one's fortune. — **tre·bly** \'treb-lē\ *adv.*

tree \'trē\ *n.* **1** A large woody perennial plant commonly 10 feet or more high, with a single main stem, or trunk, and a head of branches and leaves. **2** A treelike shrub or bush. **3** A piece of timber; a wooden pole, bar, stake, stick, or lever forming a part of a structure or implement, as in *whippletree.* **4** Something shaped like a tree, as a diagram (**family tree**) showing all the branches of a family. **5** A shoe tree. — *v.;* **treed; tree·ing.** **1** To drive up a tree. The cat was *treed.* **2** To take refuge in a tree. **3** To furnish with trees. **4** To place upon or fit with a shoe tree.

tree fern. A tall tropical fern resembling a tree, with a woody trunk and a crown of large, often feathery fronds.

tree frog. **1** A tree toad. **2** An Old World tree-dwelling frog having toes with suckers.

tree toad. A tree-dwelling amphibian with sucking disks on its toes, a loud piping voice, and power to change color.

tree·top \'trē-ˌtäp\ *n.* The top part of a tree.

tre·foil \'trē-ˌfȯil, 'tref-ˌȯil\ *n.* **1** The clover. **2** Any related three-leaved plant resembling clover. **3** An ornamental design that has three leaflike parts.

trefoil, 3

trek \'trek\ *v.;* **trekked; trek·king.** **1** In South Africa, to draw or pull; as, a wagon *trekked* by oxen. **2** To travel by ox wagon; to migrate in wagons or a wagon train. **3** To travel slowly or painfully. — *n.* A trekking; a migration; a journey. — **trek·ker** \'trek-r\ *n.*

trel·lis \'trel-əs\ *n.* A frame or lattice used as a screen or as a support for climbing plants. — *v.* **1** To provide with a trellis. **2** To train on a trellis, as vines. **3** To cross or interlace as in a trellis.

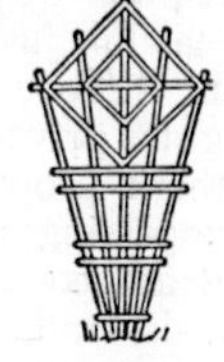

trellis

trem·a·tode \'trem-ə-ˌtōd\ *n.* Any of a class of parasitic flatworms that includes the flukes and related worms.

trem·ble \'trem-bl\ *v.;* **trem·bled; trem·bling** \-bl(-)ing\. **1** To shiver; to shudder. **2** To move as if shaken; to quiver; to quake. **3** To feel fear; as, to *tremble* for the safety of a friend. — *n.* A fit of trembling. — **trem·bler** \-bl(-)ər\ *n.* — **trem·bly** \-bl(-)ē\ *adj.*

tre·men·dous \trə-'men-dəs\ *adj.* **1** Such as may excite trembling; terrifying. **2** Astonishingly large, great, or powerful; extraordinary. — For synonyms see *monstrous.* — **tre·men·dous·ly,** *adv.*

trem·o·lo \'trem-l-ˌō\ *n.; pl.* **trem·o·los.** **1** A rapid wavering or fluttering of a tone or chord, producing a tremulous effect. **2** A device in an organ for producing this effect.

trem·or \'trem-r, 'trēm-r\ *n.* **1** A trembling or shaking, especially from disease or weakness. **2** A quivering or vibrating motion, as of the earth or of leaves. **3** A nervous thrill.

trem·u·lous \'trem-yə-ləs\ *adj.* **1** Quivering; shaking; as, a *tremulous* voice. **2** Fearful; timid. **3** Caused by trembling; unsteady; as, a *tremulous* smile.

trench \'trench\ *v.* **1** To cut trenches in. **2** To drain by trenches. **3** To protect with or as if with trenches. **4** To trespass; to encroach; as, to *trench* upon another's rights. — *n.* **1** A long, narrow cut in land; a ditch. **2** A long ditch protected by a bank of earth thrown before it, used to shelter soldiers.

trench·ant \'trench-nt\ *adj.* **1** Having a sharp edge or point; cutting; piercing; as, a *trenchant* blade; *trenchant* sarcasm. **2** Penetrating; acute; sharply clear; as, a *trenchant* analysis of a situation. **3** Keen; mentally energetic. — **trench·ant·ly,** *adv.*

trench coat. **1** A waterproof overcoat with a removable woolen lining. **2** A raincoat made in the style of this overcoat.

trench·er \'trench-r\ *n.* **1** A wooden board or platter on which food formerly was carved or served; any platter. **2** *Archaic.* Food; a trencher of food.

trench·er \'trench-r\ *n.* One that trenches; especially, a person who digs trenches.

trench·er·man \'trench-r-mən\ *n.; pl.* **trench·er·men** \-mən\. **1** An eater or feeder; especially, a hearty eater. **2** A hanger-on; a sponger.

trench mouth. [So called from its having been common among soldiers in the trenches during World War I.] A destructive infectious inflammation of the mouth.

trend \'trend\ *v.* To take a particular direction; to tend. — *n.* Drift; tendency; as, the *trend* of opinion.

trep·i·da·tion \ˌtrep-ə-'dāsh-n\ *n.* **1** A quaking or trembling. **2** A state of alarm; fear.

tres·pass \'tres-pəs, -ˌpas\ *v.* **1** To go beyond what is lawful, just, or right; to commit an offense; to sin. **2** To encroach or intrude, as on another's rights, privacy, or privileges. **3** To go onto another's property unlawfully. — *n.* **1** The act of trespassing; an offense; a sin. **2** In law, an unlawful act committed with force upon the person, goods, land, or rights of another. — **tres·pass·er,** *n.*

tress \'tres\ *n.* **1** A braid, plait, or long lock of hair. **2** [in the plural] A woman's hair.

tres·tle \'tres-l\ *n.* **1** A braced frame, consisting usually of a horizontal piece with spreading legs at each end, that supports something, as a table top or drawing board. **2** A braced framework of timbers or steel for carrying a road or railroad over a depression.

trey \'trā\ *n.* A card or die with three spots.

tri-. A prefix that can mean: **1** Having three or three parts, three times, into three, as in *tricycle, trisect.* **2** Every third, as in *trimonthly.*

tri·ad \'trī-ˌad\ *n.* **1** A union of three closely related persons or things. **2** In music, a chord consisting of a tone and the tones at the intervals of a third and a fifth above it.

tri·al \'trī-əl, 'trīl\ *n.* **1** The action of testing. **2** A test of strength, patience, or faith; something that afflicts. **3** A temporary use to determine quality; as, to give a soap a *trial.* **4** The hearing and judgment of a case in a law court. — *adj.* **1** Of or relating to a legal trial. **2** Used for testing; as, a *trial* race. **3** Furnished as a sample for a trial.

— The words *experiment* and *test* are synonyms of *trial: experiment* usually suggests some process intended to discover a new fact or to verify or demonstrate something already known; *trial* generally stresses the proof of something, as the worth, goodness, or innocence of a person or thing, by experience or by examination of evidence; *test* usually refers to a critical trial of anything, as by close examination of it in use or by comparison with some fixed standard.

tri·an·gle \'trī-ˌang-gl\ *n.* **1** A figure that has three sides and three angles. **2** Any object that has three sides and three angles. **3** A musical instrument, made of a steel rod bent in the shape of a triangle with one open angle, which hangs on a string and is sounded by striking with a small metal rod.

tri·an·gu·lar \trī-'ang-gyəl-r\ *adj.* **1** Of or relating to a triangle. **2** Of or having three parts or persons; as, a *triangular* business agreement. — **tri·an·gu·lar·i·ty** \(ˌ)trī-ˌang-yə-'lar-ət-ē\ *n.* — **tri·an·gu·lar·ly** \trī-'ang-gyəl-r-lē\ *adj.*

tribe \'trīb\ *n.* **1** A group of people, especially with primitive ways, who believe themselves to come from a common stock and who act as a unit, often under a chief. **2** A group of persons having something in common, as golf fans. **3** A group of related plants or animals; as, the cat *tribe.* — **trib·al** \'trīb-l\ *adj.*

tribes·man \'trībz-mən\ *n.; pl.* **tribes·men** \-mən\. A member of a tribe.

trib·u·la·tion \ˌtrib-yə-'lāsh-n\ *n.* **1** Distress caused by trouble or sorrow. **2** A trial; a trouble.

tri·bu·nal \trī-'byün-l, tri-\ *n.* **1** The seat of a judge. **2** A court of justice. **3** Something that decides or judges; as, the *tribunal* of public opinion.

trib·une \'trib-ˌyün, tri-'byün\ *n.* **1** In ancient Rome, an official or magistrate, especially one whose duty was to protect citizens of the common class from unfair treatment by magistrates of the noble class. **2** Any defender of the people.

trib·u·tary \'trib-yə-ˌter-ē\ *n.; pl.* **trib·u·tar·ies. 1** A ruler or nation that pays tribute. **2** A stream that flows into a larger stream or into a lake. — *adj.* **1** Paying tribute to another; under the power of another; as, *tributary* nations. **2** Paid as tribute; as, *tributary* gifts to the conqueror. **3** Flowing into a larger stream or into a lake.

trib·ute \'trib-ˌyüt, -yət\ *n.* **1** A payment made by one ruler or nation to another to show submission or to secure peace or protection. **2** A tax to raise money for this payment. **3** The obligation to pay tribute. Nations under *tribute.* **4** Praise; credit; as, to pay *tribute* to a man's honesty.

trice \'trīs\ *v.;* **triced; tric·ing.** To haul up and lash with a small rope, as a sail. — *n.* An instant; a moment. — used in the phrase "in a trice".

tri·ceps \'trī-ˌseps\ *n.; pl.* **tri·ceps·es** \-ˌsep-səz\. A muscle with three heads; especially, a large muscle in the back part of the upper arm.

tri·chi·na \trə-'kī-nə\ *n.; pl.* **tri·chi·nas** \-nəz\ or **tri·chi·nae** \-ˌnē\. A small slender roundworm whose larva lives in certain muscles of mammals, especially swine, and can infect man.

trich·i·no·sis \ˌtrik-n-'ō-səs\ *n.* The disease caused by trichinas. — **trich·i·nous** \'trik-n-əs\ *adj.*

trick \'trik\ *n.* **1** Something intended to deceive or cheat; a sly, mean act or habit. **2** A mischievous act; a prank. **3** A foolish or stupid action. That's a fine *trick.* **4** A clever or skillful act intended to amuse. **5** The knack; as, the *trick* of skating. **6** A habit; a mannerism; as, a *trick* of stuttering. **7** A turn or spell of duty; as, the night *trick.* **8** In card playing, the cards played in one round. — *v.* **1** To deceive by cunning or fraud; to cheat. **2** To dress; to decorate; as, *tricked* out in one's best.

trick·ery \'trik-r(-)ē\ *n.; pl.* **trick·er·ies.** The use of tricks to deceive; deception.

trick·le \'trik-l\ *v.;* **trick·led; trick·ling** \-l(-)ing\.

To run or fall in drops; to flow in a thin, slow stream; as, rain *trickling* down the pane. The brook *trickled* over the rocks. — *n.* A dribble.

trick·ster \'trikst-r\ *n.* A cheat.

tricky \'trik-ē\ *adj.;* **trick·i·er**; **trick·i·est.** **1** Inclined to or showing trickery; as, a *tricky* person. **2** Requiring skill or cleverness; as, a *tricky* puzzle.

tri·col·or \'trī-ˌkəl-r\ *n.* A three-colored flag.

tri·cy·cle \'trī-ˌsik-l\ *n.* A light three-wheeled vehicle moved by pedals or hand levers.

tri·dent \'trīd-nt\ *n.* A three-pointed spear. — *adj.* Having three teeth or points.

tried \'trīd\. Past tense and past part. of *try.* — *adj.* Proved; tested; trustworthy; as, a *tried* friend.

tri·en·ni·al \trī-'en-ē-əl\ *adj.* **1** Continuing for three years. **2** Happening or appearing once in three years. — *n.* A triennial event.

tri·fle \'trīf-l\ *n.* **1** A thing of little value; a bauble. **2** A small amount. **3** A sponge cake covered with whipped cream or soft custard. — *v.;* **tri·fled**; **tri·fling** \-l(-)ing\. **1** To talk jokingly or mockingly, so as to deceive. **2** To toy or play with something; to fidget. **3** To flirt; to play; as, to *trifle* with feelings. **4** To spend or waste on trifles. — **tri·fler** \-l(-)ər\ *n.*

tri·fling \'trīf-l(-)ing\ *adj.* **1** Frivolous; lacking in seriousness; as, *trifling* talk. **2** Unimportant; trivial; of little value. — *n.* **1** The act of one who trifles. **2** A waste of time. — **tri·fling·ly,** *adv.*

trig \'trig\. Short for *trigonometry.*

trig·ger \'trig-r\ *n.* A movable lever attached to a catch that when released by pressure allows a mechanism to go into action; especially, the part of the lock of a firearm that releases the hammer and so fires the gun. — *v.;* **trig·gered**; **trig·ger·ing** \-r(-)ing\. **1** To cause the explosion of; to fire. **2** To set off; to start; as, a mistake in judgment that *triggered* off a war.

trig·o·no·met·ric \ˌtrig-n-ə-'me-trik\ or **trig·o·no·met·ri·cal** \-'me-trik-l\ *adj.* Of or relating to trigonometry; performed by the rules of trigonometry. — **trig·o·no·met·ri·cal·ly** \-trik-l(-)ē\ *adv.*

trig·o·nom·e·try \ˌtrig-n-'äm-ə-trē\ *n.* The branch of mathematics that treats of the relations between the sides and angles of triangles.

tri·lat·er·al \(')trī-'lat-r-əl, -'la-trəl\ *adj.* Three-sided. — **tri·lat·er·al·ly** \-'lat-r-ə-lē, -'la-trə-lē\ *adv.*

trill \'tril\ *n.* **1** The rapid vibration of one organ of speech against another, as of the tongue against the ridge just above and behind the upper front teeth. **2** A speech sound made by such vibration, as *r* in many languages. **3** A letter or a word pronounced with a trill. **4** In music, the rapid changing back and forth of two notes of slightly different pitch. **5** A sound like a musical trill; a warble; as, the *trill* of birds. — *v.* **1** To utter a trill; to utter with a trill. **2** To sing or play with a trill.

tril·lion \'tril-yən\ *n.* In American and French numbering, a thousand billions; in English and German numbering, a million billions.

tril·li·um \'tril-ē-əm\ *n.* Any of several herbs related to the lily of the valley, with a short rootstock, and a single three-petaled flower set above three pointed leaves.

tri·lo·bate \(')trī-'lō-ˌbāt\ *adj.* Having three lobes.

tri·lo·bite \'trī-lə-ˌbīt\ *n.* An extinct arthropod having an oval body divided by longitudinal furrows on the back into three lobes.

tril·o·gy \'tril-ə-jē\ *n.; pl.* **tril·o·gies.** A set of three musical or literary compositions, as operas, plays, or novels that, though each is complete in itself, form a connected or related series.

trim \'trim\ *v.;* **trimmed**; **trim·ming.** **1** To make neat and trim; as, to *trim* the shelves. **2** To cut or clip; as, to *trim* the hair. **3** To decorate; as, to *trim* a hat. **4** To defeat; as, to *trim* an opponent. **5** To arrange the cargo, passengers, and ballast of a boat so that it will balance well in the water. **6** To arrange in order for sailing; as, to *trim* the sails. **7** To keep a balance between two parties. — *n.* **1** Order; as, to put a house in good *trim.* **2** Something that is cut off; as, the *trim* from wallpaper. **3** The woodwork around the openings of a house. **4** The readiness of a ship for sailing; the position of a boat in the water. — *adj.;* **trim·mer**; **trim·mest.** Neat, compact, and orderly; spruce and smart. — **trim·mer,** *n.* — **trim·ly,** *adv.*

trim·e·ter \'trim-ət-r\ *n.* A verse or line of three metrical feet.

trim·ming \'trim-ing\ *n.* **1** The action of one that trims. **2** A beating; a defeat. **3** [often in the plural] Something that trims, ornaments, or completes; as, the *trimming* on a hat; turkey and *trimmings.* **4** [in the plural] Parts removed by cutting. — *adj.* That trims or is used by one who trims.

tri·month·ly \(')trī-'mən(t)th-lē\ *adj.* Occurring, done, or coming once in three months.

trin·i·ty \'trin-ət-ē\ *n.; pl.* **trin·i·ties.** **1** [with a capital] The union of three persons, Father, Son, and Holy Ghost, in one divine being, or Godhead. **2** Any union of three.

trin·ket \'tringk-ət\ *n.* **1** A small ornament, as a jewel or ring. **2** A thing of small value; a trifle; toy.

tri·no·mi·al \(')trī-'nō-mē-əl\ *adj.* Consisting of three terms or names. — *n.* **1** In algebra, an expression consisting of three terms connected by the sign plus (+) or minus (−), or both. **2** In biology, a scientific name consisting of three words, the first denoting the genus, the second the species, and the third the variety.

trio \'trē-ˌō\ *n.; pl.* **tri·os.** **1** Three persons or things that go together; a set of three. **2** A musical composition for three voices or instruments; the singers or players of it. **3** A division in musical composition originally intended for three instruments.

trip \'trip\ *v.;* **tripped**; **trip·ping.** **1** To move with light quick steps; to skip. **2** To perform lightly, as a dance. **3** To catch one's foot while walking or running; to stumble or cause to stumble. **4** To make a mistake; to slip. **5** To release, as a catch on a door or machine. — *n.* **1** A journey; as, a European *trip.* **2** A false step; a stumble. **3** A tripping of an opponent, as in wrestling. **4** A releasing, as of a catch. **5** A device for tripping a catch. — For synonyms see *journey.*

tri·par·tite \(')trī-'pär-ˌtīt, -'pȧr-\ *adj.* **1** Divided into three parts. **2** Having three corresponding parts or copies. **3** Made between three parties.

tripe \'trīp\ *n.* **1** A part of the stomach of a cud-chewing animal, such as a cow, used for food. **2** *Slang.* Something worthless and, often, offensive.

trip·ham·mer \'trip-ˌham-r\ *n.* A massive hammer raised by machinery and then tripped to fall on the work below.

tri·ple \'trip-l\ *adj.* **1** Threefold; as, a *triple* mirror; a *triple* play. **2** Multiplied by three; three times repeated; treble. — *n.* A three-base hit in baseball. — *v.;* **tri·pled**; **tri·pling** \-l(-)ing\. **1** To make three times as great; to multiply by three. **2** To make a three-base hit in baseball.

tri·plet \'trip-lət\ *n.* **1** Three related or united things. **2** One of three offspring born at one birth; [in the plural] a group of three such offspring. **3** A group of three musical notes played or sung in the time of two notes of the same time value.

tri·plex \'trip-ˌleks, 'trī-ˌpleks\ *adj.* Triple; threefold. — *n.* Something that is triplex.

trip·li·cate \'trip-lik-ət\ *adj.* Triple; especially, made in three identical copies. — *n.* **1** Each of a triplicate set. **2** Triplicate form; as, a contract printed in *triplicate.* — \-lə-ˌkāt\ *v.;* **trip·li·cat·ed**; **trip·li·cat·ing.** To make in triplicate.

tri·ply \'trip-lē\ *adv.* In a triple degree; to a triple amount.

tri·pod \'trī-ˌpäd\ *n.* **1** Any object, as a stool, table, or kettle, standing on three legs. **2** A three-legged stand, as for a camera or machine gun. — *adj.* Having or supported on three legs.

tripped. Past tense and past part. of *trip.*

trip·per \'trip-r\ *n.* **1** *Chiefly British.* A tourist. **2** A tripping device or mechanism.

trip·ping \'trip-ing\ *adj.* Stepping lightly and quickly; quick; nimble. — **trip·ping·ly**, *adv.*

tri·reme \'trī-ˌrēm\ *n.* A galley with three banks of oars.

tri·sect \'trī-ˌsekt, trī-'sekt\ *v.* **1** To cut or divide into three parts. **2** In geometry, to divide into three equal parts, as an angle.

tri·syl·lab·ic \ˌtrī-sə-'lab-ik\ *adj.* Having three syllables. — **tri·syl·lab·i·cal·ly** \-ik-l(-)ē\ *adv.*

tri·syl·la·ble \(')trī-'sil-əb-l\ *n.* A word of three syllables.

trite \'trīt\ *adj.* So common that the novelty has worn off; stale; hackneyed; as, a *trite* remark.

trit·i·um \'trit-ē-əm, 'trish-ē-\ *n.* A form of hydrogen three times as heavy as ordinary hydrogen.

trit·u·rate \'trich-r-ˌāt\ *v.;* **trit·u·rat·ed**; **trit·u·rat·ing.** To rub, grind, or crush into a fine powder; to pulverize. — \-r-ət\ *n.* A triturated substance. — **trit·u·ra·tion** \ˌtrich-r-'āsh-n\ *n.*

tri·umph \'trī-əm(p)f\ *n.; pl.* **tri·umphs** \-əm(p)fs, -əmps\. **1** A ceremony held in ancient Rome in honor of a victorious general. **2** A state of joy or exultation for a success or victory. **3** Victory; success. — For synonyms see *victory.* — *v.* **1** To celebrate victory or success. **2** To obtain victory; to be successful; to prevail.

tri·um·phal \trī-'əm(p)-fəl\ *adj.* Of or relating to a triumph; in honor of a triumph.

tri·um·phant \trī-'əm(p)-fənt\ *adj.* **1** Rejoicing for, or celebrating, victory or success; exultant. **2** Victorious; conquering. — **tri·um·phant·ly**, *adv.*

tri·um·vir \trī-'əm-vər\ *n.; pl.* **tri·um·virs** \-vərz\ or **tri·um·vi·ri** \-və-ˌrī\. One of three men sharing public office and authority in ancient Rome.

tri·um·vi·rate \trī-'əm-vər-ət, -və-ˌrāt\ *n.* **1** The office or term of a triumvir. **2** Government by three persons who share authority and responsibility. **3** A group of three persons who share power or office.

triv·et \'triv-ət\ *n.* **1** A three-legged metal stand or support, especially one for holding a kettle near the fire; a tripod. **2** An ornamental metal plate on very short legs, used under a hot dish to protect the table.

trivet, 1

triv·ia \'triv-ē-ə\ *n. pl.* Trifles; unimportant matters.

triv·i·al \'triv-ē-əl\ *adj.* Unimportant; trifling; as, a *trivial* error; a *trivial* remark. — **triv·i·al·ly** \-ē-ə-lē\ *adv.*

triv·i·al·i·ty \ˌtriv-ē-'al-ət-ē\ *n.; pl.* **triv·i·al·i·ties.** **1** The quality or state of being trivial; unimportance. **2** Something that is trivial; a trifle.

tri·week·ly \(')trī-'wēk-lē\ *adj.* **1** Occurring or appearing every three weeks. **2** Occurring or appearing three times a week. — *adv.* **1** Once in three weeks. **2** Three times a week. — *n.; pl.* **tri·week·lies.** A triweekly publication.

tro·chee \'trō-(ˌ)kē\ *n.* A metrical foot of two syllables, the first accented and the second unaccented, as in *beggar.*

trod. Past tense and a past part. of *tread.*

trodden. A past part. of *tread.*

troll \'trōl\ *n.* In stories, a giant or a dwarf that lives in caves or hills.

troll \'trōl\ *v.* **1** To sing the parts of a song one after another, as of a round. **2** To sing loudly. **3** To fish with a lure or hook and bait drawn through the water, as behind a moving boat. — *n.* A song sung in parts one after another. — **troll·er**, *n.*

trol·ley or **trol·ly** \'träl-ē\ *n.; pl.* **trol·leys** or **trol·lies.** **1** A wheeled truck that runs on an overhead rail or track and supports a load. **2** A device to carry current from a wire to an electrically driven vehicle. **3** An electric car; a trolley car.

trolley bus or **trolley coach.** A bus powered by electric power from two overhead wires.

trolley car. A passenger car that runs on tracks and gets its electric power by a trolley; a streetcar.

trom·bone \(')träm-'bōn, (ˌ)trəm-\ *n.* [From Italian, meaning literally "big trumpet".] A musical instrument in the form of a curved tube, one part of which is made to slide back and forth in order to change pitch.

troop \'trüp\ *n.* **1** A collection; a company; as, a *troop* of children. **2** [usually in the plural] Soldiers collectively. **3** A group of boy scouts or of girl scouts consisting typically of sixteen to thirty-two scouts, or two to four patrols. **4** A section of a cavalry squadron, commanded by a captain. — *v.* To move or gather in crowds.

troop·er \'trüp-r\ *n.* **1** A cavalryman. **2** A cavalry horse. **3** A mounted policeman.

troop·ship \'trüp-ˌship\ *n.* A ship for carrying troops; a transport.

tro·phy \'trō-fē\ *n.; pl.* **tro·phies. 1** A memorial of victory; as, a golf *trophy.* **2** Something kept as a souvenir; a memento. — **tro·phied** \-fēd\ *adj.*

trop·ic \'träp-ik\ *n.* **1** Either of two parallels of the earth's latitude, one 23 degrees and 27 minutes north of the equator and one 23 degrees and 27 minutes south of the equator. **2** [in the plural and often written with a capital letter] The region lying between these two parallels of latitude. — or **trop·i·cal** \-ik-l\ *adj.* Of or relating to, like, or occurring in the tropics. — **trop·i·cal·ly** \-ik-l(-)ē\ *adv.*

tro·pism \'trō-ˌpiz-m\ *n.* An involuntary turning of a plant or animal or its parts toward a stimulus, as light. — **tro·pis·tic** \trō-'pis-tik\ *adj.*

trot \'trät\ *v.;* **trot·ted; trot·ting. 1** To go, as a horse, by moving a front foot and the opposite hind foot at the same time. **2** To run; to jog; to hurry. **3** To cause to go at a trot; as, to *trot* a horse. — *n.* **1** The gait of horses when trotting. **2** The sound made by a trotting horse. **3** A pace between a walk and a run. — **trot·ter** \'trät-r\ *n.*

troth \'trȯth, 'trōth\ *n.* **1** Faith; pledged faith; as, to plight one's *troth.* **2** Truth. It is so, by my *troth.* — \'trȯth, 'trō<u>th</u>\ *v.* To pledge; to betroth.

trou·ba·dour \'trü-bə-ˌdōr, -ˌdȯr, -ˌdůr\ *n.* A poet-musician of medieval France and Italy.

trou·ble \'trəb-l\ *v.;* **trou·bled; trou·bling** \-l(-)ing\. **1** To stir up; to agitate; as, *troubled* waves. **2** To worry; as, to be *troubled* by someone's absence. **3** To cause pain; to harm; to afflict physically. **4** To cause inconvenience. **5** To take pains; to make an effort. — *n.* **1** Uneasiness; annoyance. **2** Something or someone that causes distress; bother. **3** Civil disorder; unrest; agitation. **4** Pains; exertion; as, to take the *trouble* to check. **5** A condition of ill health.

trou·ble·some \'trəb-ls-m\ *adj.* Giving trouble; disturbing; bothersome; as, a *troublesome* tooth.

trou·blous \'trəb-ləs\ *adj.* **1** Full of trouble; restless; upset; as, *troublous* seas. **2** Troublesome.

trough \'trȯf\ *n.; pl.* **troughs** \'trȯfs, 'trȯvz\. **1** A long, shallow, open container, especially one for water or fodder for livestock. **2** A channel for water; a gutter, as under the eaves of a roof. **3** Any long channel or hollow, as between waves or hills.

trounce \'traůn(t)s\ *v.;* **trounced; trounc·ing.** To beat; to thrash; to defeat severely.

troupe \'trüp\ *n.* A company or troop, especially of performers on the stage. — **troup·er** \'trüp-r\ *n.*

trou·sers \'traůz-rz\ *n. pl.* An outer garment extending from the waist to the knee or to the ankle and covering each leg separately.

trous·seau \'trü-ˌsō\ *n.; pl.* **trous·seaus** \-ˌsōz\ or **trous·seaux** \-ˌsōz\. [From French, meaning literally "little bundle", a diminutive of *trousse* meaning "bundle".] A bride's personal outfit, as of clothes.

trout \'traůt\ *n.; pl.* **trout** or **trouts. 1** Any of certain food and game fishes, mostly of fresh waters, related to the salmon but usually smaller and often speckled with dark colors, as the **brook trout, brown trout,** or **rainbow trout. 2** Any of various fishes thought to resemble trout.

trow \'trō\ *v. Archaic.* To think; to suppose.

trow·el \'traů-əl, 'traůl\ *n.* **1** Any of various small hand tools consisting of a flat blade with a handle, used for spreading and smoothing mortar or plaster. **2** A small hand tool with a curved blade used by gardeners.

trowel, 1

troy \'trȯi\ *adj.* Of or relating to the system (**troy weight**) of weights commonly used for precious metals and gems. — *n.* Troy weight.

tru·ant \'trü-ənt\ *n.* **1** One that stays away, as from work, duty, or school, without leave. — **tru·an·cy** \'trü-ən-sē\ *n.*

truant officer. A school officer whose duty is to investigate and deal with cases of truancy.

truce \'trüs\ *n.* **1** An interruption of warfare by mutual agreement; an armistice. **2** A temporary rest.

truck \'trək\ *v.* To exchange goods; to barter; to peddle. — *n.* **1** Business; dealings. Have no *truck* with dishonest traders. **2** Small goods or merchandise; especially, vegetables raised for market. **3** Small articles of little value; rubbish.

truck \'trək\ *n.* **1** A small wooden cap at the top of a flagpole or mast. **2** Any of numerous vehicles for carrying heavy articles, as a small flat-topped car on wheels, a two-wheeled barrow with long handles, or a strong, heavy wagon or automobile. **3** A swiveling carriage with springs, and one or more pairs of wheels, used to carry an end of a railroad or electric car. — *v.* To carry on or by a truck.

truck, 2

truck·er \'trək-r\ *n.* A person who drives a truck or whose business is to carry goods on a truck.

truck farm. A farm growing vegetables for market.

truck·ing \'trək-ing\ *n.* **1** A bartering. **2** Truck farming. **3** Driving or transportation by truck.

truck·le \'trək-l\ *v.;* **truck·led; truck·ling** \-l(-)ing\. To give in slavishly to the will of another.

truck·le bed \'trək-l\. A trundle bed.

truc·u·lent \'trək-yə-lənt\ *adj.* Fierce; savage. — **truc·u·lence** \-lən(t)s\ *n.* — **truc·u·lent·ly,** *adv.*

trudge \'trəj\ *v.;* **trudged**; **trudg·ing**. To walk or march steadily; especially, to walk wearily or with an effort. — *n.* A long walk. — **trudg·er** \'trəj-r\ *n.*

trudg·en \'trəj-n\ *n.* Also **trudgen stroke**. A swimming stroke in which a double overarm motion is combined with a scissors kick.

true \'trü\ *adj.;* **tru·er** \'trü-ər\; **tru·est** \-əst\. **1** Faithful; loyal. **2** *Archaic.* Honest; just; upright. **3** To be relied on; certain. **4** Accurate; correct; as, a *true* story. **5** Sincere; as, *true* friendship. **6** Properly so called; genuine. Lichens have no *true* stems. **7** Rightful; as, the *true* owner. **8** Placed or formed accurately; as, a *true* square. **9** Steady, as a wind; not veering. — *adv.* Faithfully; truthfully; accurately; truly. — *n.* **1** That which is true; reality; as, the good and the *true.* **2** The state of being true or of fitting accurately. — *v.;* **trued**; **tru·ing**. To bring something to its exact correct condition as to place, position, or shape.

true-blue \'trü-'blü\ *adj.* [Originally applied to the Scottish Presbyterians of the 17th century, who had adopted blue as their distinctive color.] Loyal; dependable. — *n.* A true-blue person.

truf·fle \'trəf-l, 'trüf-l\ *n.* An underground fungus having a blackish fruit eaten as a delicacy.

tru·ism \'trü-ˌiz-m\ *n.* An obvious truth.

tru·ly \'trü-lē\ *adv.* **1** In a true manner; honestly; accurately. **2** In fact; in truth; really.

trump \'trəmp\ *n.* A trumpet or the sound of a trumpet; as, till the last *trump* blows.

trump \'trəmp\ *n.* **1** A playing card belonging to a suit any card of which will for the time being take any card of the other suits. **2** The suit thus ranking highest. **3** A fine, dependable person. — *v.* To play a trump on. — **trump up**. To make up falsely; as, a *trumped up* excuse.

trump·ery \'trəmp-r(-)ē\ *n.; pl.* **trump·er·ies**. Cheap ornamentation. — *adj.* Showy but useless; trashy.

trum·pet \'trəmp-ət\ *n.* **1** A wind instrument in the form of a long curved metal tube with finger valves and a cup-shaped mouthpiece. **2** A trumpeter. **3** A trumpet-shaped instrument that intensifies sound; as, an ear *trumpet.* **4** A sound, as of a trumpet. — *v.* **1** To sound on a trumpet or as if on a trumpet. **2** To noise abroad; as, to *trumpet* the news.

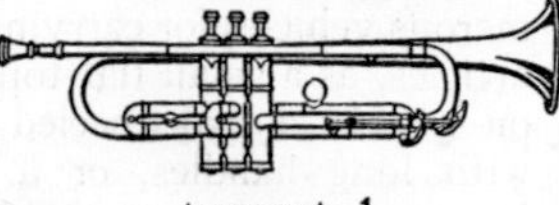
trumpet, 1

trumpet creeper or **trumpet vine**. A woody vine having red trumpet-shaped flowers.

trum·pet·er \'trəmp-ət-r\ *n.* **1** A person who blows a trumpet. **2** A long-legged, long-necked South American bird related to the cranes and having a loud prolonged cry. **3** Also **trumpeter swan**. A North American wild swan noted for its sonorous cry.

trun·cate \'trəng-ˌkāt\ *v.;* **trun·cat·ed**; **trun·cat·ing**. To cut off; to lop; to lessen by cutting. — *adj.* Cut off; having the end square or even, as if by cutting; lacking an apex or a point; as, a *truncate* leaf. — **trun·ca·tion** \ˌtrəng-'kāsh-n\ *n.*

trun·cheon \'trənch-n\ *n.* **1** *Archaic.* A short staff or cudgel. **2** A staff of office or authority. **3** A policeman's club. — *v.* To beat with a club.

trun·dle \'trənd-l\ *n.* **1** A little wheel; a caster. **2** A small-wheeled cart or hand truck. **3** A trundle bed. **4** A rolling motion, as of something on wheels, or the sound of such motion. — *v.;* **trun·dled**; **trun·dling** \-l(-)ing\. To roll, as a hoop or something on small wheels; as, to *trundle* a wheelbarrow.

trundle bed. A bed on casters, low enough to be pushed under another bed when not in use; a truckle bed.

trunk \'trəngk\ *n.* **1** The main stem or body of a tree, without branches or roots. **2** The body of a man or animal, apart from the head, arms, and legs. **3** The main body of anything; as, the *trunk* of an artery. **4** The long round muscular nose of an elephant. **5** A box or chest for holding clothes or other goods, especially for traveling. **6** A long box or pipe serving as a conveyer, as of water or air. **7** The enclosed space in the rear of an automobile for carrying articles, as tools or luggage. **8** [in the plural] In full **trunk hose**. Short full breeches worn in the 16th and 17th centuries. **9** [in the plural] Short breeches worn by athletes and swimmers. — *adj.* Relating to a main railroad, telegraph, telephone, or other line; as, a *trunk* call; a *trunk* line.

truss \'trəs\ *v.* **1** To pack into a bundle. **2** To bind or tie firmly; as, to *truss* a turkey for cooking. **3** To strengthen or stiffen, as a girder, by a brace. — *n.* **1** A bundle; a pack. **2** A measured quantity of hay (56 or 60 lbs.) or of straw (36 lbs.). **3** A rigid framework of beams, bars, or rods; as, a *truss* for a roof. **4** A support for a weakened part of the body.

trust \'trəst\ *n.* **1** Reliance; faith; confidence; as, a man worthy of *trust.* **2** Confident hope. **3** The person or thing trusted. God is our *trust.* **4** Custody; care. **5** Credit; as, to sell on *trust.* **6** Something which is put in one's care or charge. Public office is a public *trust.* **7** A legal right or interest in a property which one does not actually own; as, income received under a *trust* established by one's father. **8** Property held and managed by one person or concern, as a bank or trust company, for the benefit of another; as, houses and lands that were part of a *trust.* **9** An organization controlling the operations of a number of independently owned companies, especially so as to influence prices and eliminate competition. **10** Any large business that has or seems to have a monopoly or the power to control prices. — *v.* **1** To have confidence or faith; as, to *trust* in God. **2** To have faith in; as, to *trust* your friends. **3** To give into the care or charge of a person; to entrust; as, to *trust* a child to its grandmother. **4** To expect; to hope. **5** To believe. **6** To sell to in confidence that one will be paid later; to give credit to.

trust company. **1** Any corporation formed for the purpose of acting as trustee. **2** A bank organized under state laws for handling trusts and also performing all banking functions except the issuing of bank notes.

trus·tee \'trəs-'tē\ *n.* A person holding property in trust; one who has legal responsibility for keeping or managing property belonging to another person or to an organization.

trus·tee·ship \'trəs-'tē-ˌship\ *n.* **1** The office or function of a trustee. **2** Supervisory control of the administration of a certain territory (**trust territory**) entrusted to a member nation or nations by the United Nations. **3** A trust territory.

trust·ful \'trəst-fəl\ *adj.* Trusting or ready to trust; confiding. — **trust·ful·ly** \-fə-lē\ *adv.*

trust·ing \'trəs-ting\ *adj.* Having trust, faith, or confidence; trustful. — **trust·ing·ly**, *adv.*

trust·wor·thy \'trəst-ˌwər-t͟hē\ *adj.* Worthy of trust. — **trust·wor·thi·ness** \-ˌwər-t͟hē-nəs\ *n.*

trusty \'trəs-tē\ *adj.;* **trust·i·er**; **trust·i·est**. **1** Trustful. **2** Deserving confidence; reliable; trustworthy. — *n.* A trusty or trusted person; a convict considered trustworthy and given special privileges.

truth \'trüth\ *n.; pl.* **truths** \'trüt͟hz, 'trüths\. **1** *Archaic.* Loyalty; fidelity. **2** Sincerity and honesty in character, action, and speech. **3** Agreement with the facts; as, to doubt the *truth* of a statement. **4** An accepted fact, principle, or law; as, the basic *truths* of life. — **in truth**. In fact; really; actually; truly.

truth·ful \'trüth-fəl\ *adj.* **1** Having the habit of telling the truth; as, a *truthful* child. **2** Accurate; as, a *truthful* account. — **truth·ful·ly** \-fə-lē\ *adv.*

try \'trī\ *v.;* **tried** \'trīd\; **try·ing**. **1** To make an effort to do something; to attempt; to endeavor. **2** To make a test or trial of; to test; as, to *try* one's luck; to *try* the door. **3** To experiment with; to find out about by using; as, to *try* a new medicine. **4** To put to harmful use or test; to strain. Very strong light *tries* the eyes. **5** To cause suffering or worry to; to annoy; to be trying to. Excessive teasing *tries* one. **6** To examine and investigate by regular legal process; to hold a trial of; as, to *try* by jury. — **try and**. To try to. — **try for**. To try to come to or to attain or obtain. — **try on**. To put on, as a garment, to test the fit. — **try out**. **1** To test. **2** To be a contestant, as for a place on a team. — *n.; pl.* **tries** \'trīz\. An attempt.

try·ing \'trī-ing\ *adj.* Causing distress or annoyance; hard to put up with; as, a *trying* experience.

try-on \'trī-ˌȯn, -ˌän\ *n.* A trying on.

try·out \'trī-ˌau̇t\ *n.* **1** A chance to show one's fitness, as for a place on a team or a part in a play. **2** A preliminary performance, as of a play, or experimental test or demonstration, as of a machine.

tryp·sin \'trips-n\ *n.* An enzyme in pancreatic juice that helps to digest proteins.

tryst \'trist, 'trīst\ *n.* **1** An appointment for a meeting. **2** A place (**tryst·ing place** \'tris-ting, 'trīs-\) appointed for a meeting.

t's. Pl. of *t.*

tsar \'z-, 'ts-\. Variant of *czar.*

tsar·i·na \z-, ts-\. Variant of *czarina.*

tset·se \'(t)set-sē, 'tet-, '(t)sēt-, 'tēt-\ *n.* or **tsetse fly**. A two-winged African fly that by its bite conveys a tiny parasitic one-celled animal causing a fatal disease in cattle and sleeping sickness in man.

T shirt. **1** A man's or boy's undershirt with very short sleeves and collarless neck, to be pulled on over the head. **2** A similarly styled man's or woman's knit shirt for outer wear.

tsp. Abbreviation for *teaspoon.*

T square. A T-shaped ruler used for drawing parallel lines, the crosspiece or head sliding along the edge of a drawing board as guide.

tub \'təb\ *n.* **1** A wide, low vessel, usually about the size of a half barrel. **2** A container for water used for washing or bathing; a bathtub. **3** A wash; a bath; as, a hot *tub.* **4** The quantity that a tub will hold. **5** A small keg or cask. — *v.;* **tubbed**; **tubbing**. To wash or bathe in a tub.

tu·ba \'tü-bə, 'tyü-\ *n.* A large deep-toned saxhorn.

tube \'tüb, 'tyüb\ *n.* **1** A round, hollow pipe; as, bronchial *tubes;* a rubber *tube.* **2** A round metal container from which paste may be squeezed as needed. **3** An electron tube. **4** A tunnel for an underground railway or one for automotive vehicles. **5** An underground railway (**tube railway**).

tu·ber \'tüb-r, 'tyüb-r\ *n.* A short, fleshy, usually underground stem or shoot, bearing buds or eyes, as the potato.

tu·ber·cle \'tüb-rk-l, 'tyüb-\ *n.* **1** A small rounded growth, as on an animal or plant. **2** A small rounded diseased growth in an organ or the skin, especially one caused by tuberculosis.

tu·ber·cu·lar \tə-'bərk-yəl-r, tü-, tyü-\ *adj.* **1** Of or relating to a tubercle; having tubercles. **2** Having or caused by tuberculosis; tuberculous.

tu·ber·cu·lin \tə-'bərk-yə-lən, tü-, tyü-\ *n.* A preparation containing substances from tuberculosis germs, used in a test (**tuberculin test**) for tuberculosis.

tu·ber·cu·lo·sis \tə-ˌbərk-yə-'lō-səs, tü-, tyü-\ *n.* An infectious disease characterized by formation of tubercles and the wasting away of tissues, often in the lungs. — **tu·ber·cu·lous** \-'bərk-yə-ləs\ *adj.*

tube·rose \'tüb-ˌrōz, 'tyüb-\ *n.* A plant, of the same natural family as the amaryllis, that grows from a bulb and is cultivated for its spike of fragrant white flowers.

tu·ber·ous \'tüb-r-əs, 'tyüb-\ *adj.* **1** Covered with knobby prominences. **2** Consisting of or bearing a tuber or tubers. **3** Like a tuber.

tub·ing \'tü-bing, 'tyü-\ *n.* **1** A series of tubes. **2** Material for tubes.

tu·bu·lar \'tüb-yəl-r, 'tyüb-\ *adj.* **1** Having the form of a tube. **2** Consisting of a tube.

tu·bule \'tü-ˌbyül, 'tyü-\ *n.* A small tube.

tuck \'tək\ *v.* **1** To pull into a fold or folds and fasten; as, to *tuck* up one's sleeves. **2** To fold in the loose or hanging ends of; as, to *tuck* in a blanket. **3** To cover or wrap snugly; as, to *tuck* oneself up in bed. **4** To put a thing where it can be held snugly or tightly. **5** To make a tuck in. — *n.* **1** A sewed fold, as in a garment. **2** Energy. That race uphill took all the *tuck* out of the boys.

tuck·er \'tək-r\ *n.* **1** One that tucks. **2** A strip, as of linen or lace, folded across the breast or attached to the neck of a woman's dress.

tuck·er \'tək-r\ *v.;* **tuck·ered; tuck·er·ing** \-r(-)ing\. To tire; as, to be *tuckered* out by hard work.

Tues. Abbreviation for *Tuesday.*

Tues·day \'tüz-dē, 'tyüz-\ *n.* [From Old English *Tiwesdaeg* meaning literally "Tiw's day", and named after *Tiw*, the old Germanic god of war.] The third day of the week.

tuft \'təft\ *n.* **1** A small cluster of long, flexible parts or outgrowths, as hairs or feathers; as, a bird with a *tuft* on its head. **2** A cluster; a clump. — *v.;* **tuft·ed** \'təf-təd\; **tuft·ing** \-ting\ **1** To furnish or ornament with a tuft. **2** To fasten padding, as in a cushion or mattress, by stitching it here and there with a tuft, as of threads.

tug \'təg\ *v.;* **tugged; tug·ging. 1** To pull hard; to strain; as, to *tug* at a rope. **2** To drag; to haul; as, to *tug* a car out of the mud. **3** To tow with a tugboat. — *n.* **1** A hard pull; a strain. **2** A trace, or drawing strap, of a harness. **3** A tugboat.

tug·boat \'təg-ˌbōt\ *n.* A strongly built, powerful boat used for towing.

tug of war. A contest between two groups of persons, each pulling on a rope in opposite directions.

tu·i·tion \tü-'ish-n, tyü-\ *n.* **1** Instruction; tutelage; as, 20 students under her *tuition.* **2** The price paid for instruction; a payment for instruction.

tu·la·re·mia \ˌtül-r-'ē-mē-ə, ˌtyül-\ *n.* An infectious disease of wild and domestic animals and man that resembles typhoid.

tu·lip \'tü-ləp, 'tyü-\ *n.* **1** A spring-flowering plant of the same natural family as the lily, growing from a bulb and having a large, cup-shaped flower. **2** The flower or bulb of this plant.

tulip tree. 1 A North American forest tree of the same natural family as the magnolia, with broad blunt leaves deeply notched at the tip and greenish yellow tulip-shaped flowers. **2** The soft white wood (**tulip wood**) of this tree, used especially by cabinetmakers.

tulle \'tül\ *n.* Fine net, usually of silk.

tum·ble \'təm-bl\ *v.;* **tum·bled; tum·bling** \-bl(-)ing\. **1** To perform acrobatic feats, such as somersaults or hand springs. **2** To fall suddenly or violently; to pitch down; to collapse. **3** To roll or toss about. **4** To throw down or over; as, to *tumble* rocks down a steep bank. **5** To move or go in a hasty confused manner. The children *tumbled* into the boat. **6** To throw carelessly in a heap or here and there. **7** To disorder; to muss up. — **tumble to.** *Slang.* To come to understand; to become aware of; as, to *tumble to* a person's real intentions. — *n.* **1** A tumbling. **2** A disordered condition.

tum·ble·bug \'təm-bl-ˌbəg\ *n.* A large, stout-bodied beetle that rolls dung into small balls, buries them in the ground, and lays its eggs in them.

tum·ble-down \'təm-bl-ˌdau̇n\ *adj.* Ready to fall down; dilapidated; as, a *tumble-down* old building.

tum·bler \'təm-blər\ *n.* **1** One that tumbles. **2** A drinking glass without a foot or stem, or the amount it will hold. **3** A pigeon having the habit of turning backward somersaults in flight. **4** A movable part of a lock, which must be adjusted, as by a key, before the lock will open.

tum·ble·weed \'təm-bl-ˌwēd\ *n.* A plant that breaks away from its roots in autumn and is blown about by the wind.

tum·brel or **tum·bril** \'təm-brəl\ *n.* A farmer's cart used during the French Revolution to carry condemned persons to the guillotine.

tu·mid \'tü-məd, 'tyü-\ *adj.* **1** Swollen, especially from disease; as, *tumid* flesh. **2** Pompous; swollen in style; as, *tumid* speech. — **tu·mid·ly,** *adv.*

tu·mor \'tüm-r, 'tyüm-r\ *n.* A swollen part; especially, an abnormal mass of tissue growing without obvious cause from cells of pre-existing tissue.

tump \'təmp\ *v.* To drag or carry by a tumpline.

tump·line \'təmp-ˌlīn\ *n.* A sling formed by a strap passing over the forehead or the chest, used for carrying a pack on the back or in hauling a load over the ground.

tu·mult \'tü-ˌməlt, 'tyü-\ *n.* **1** Violent commotion or disturbance, as of a crowd of people, with uproar and confusion. **2** Violent agitation of mind.

tu·mul·tu·ous \tü-'məl-chə-wəs, tə-, tyü-, -'məl-chəs\ *adj.* Characterized by tumult. — **tu·mul·tu·ous·ly** \-'məl-chəs-lē, -chə-wəs-\ *adv.*

tu·mu·lus \'tüm-yə-ləs, 'tyüm-\ *n.; pl.* **tu·mu·li** \-ˌlī\. An artificial mound, especially over a grave; a barrow.

tun \'tən\ *n.* **1** A large cask for liquids, especially wine. **2** The capacity of a tun as a varying liquid measure, formerly 252 gallons for legal purposes.

tu·na \'tü-nə, 'tyü-\ *n.; pl.* **tu·na** or **tu·nas.** Any of several large active sea fishes related to the mackerels and valued as food and sport fishes.

tun·a·ble or **tune·a·ble** \'tü-nəb-l, 'tyü-\ *adj.* **1** Capable of being tuned. **2** Tuneful.

tun·dra \'tən-drə, 'tün-\ *n.* A treeless plain of northern arctic regions.

tune \'tün, 'tyün\ *n.* **1** A succession of pleasing musical tones; a melody; an air. **2** The musical setting of a song; as, a hymn *tune.* **3** In condition to give tones of the proper pitch. The piano was not in *tune.* **4** Agreement; harmony; as, in *tune* with the times. — *v.;* **tuned; tun·ing. 1** To adjust, as a musical instrument, to a given pitch. **2** To adjust a radio or television set so as to receive clearly. **3** To put in top operating condition; as, to *tune* an engine. — **tune in.** To adjust a receiving apparatus so as to hear the signals from a particular transmitting station. — **tune out.** To adjust a receiving apparatus so as not to receive, as an unwanted signal.

tune·ful \'tün-fəl, 'tyün-\ *adj.* Melodious; harmonious; as, a *tuneful* song. — **tune·ful·ly** \-fə-lē\ *adv.*

tun·er \'tün-r, 'tyün-r\ *n.* **1** A person who tunes

something; as, a piano *tuner*. **2** Something used for or in tuning, as the part of a radio receiving set consisting of the circuit or circuits used to tune in.

tung \'təng\ *n.* A Chinese tree cultivated for its nuts, each of which contains two to four oily seeds yielding a powerful drying oil (**tung oil**).

tung·sten \'təng-stən\ *n.* [From Swedish, meaning literally "heavy stone".] A hard, heavy metallic chemical element used for electric-light filaments and as an alloy in making steel.

tu·nic \'tü-nik, 'tyü-\ *n.* **1** An undergarment worn by the ancient Romans, reaching to or below the knees and girdled at the waist. **2** A blouse or coat reaching to or just below the hips. **3** An enveloping membrane or layer of tissue, as in the onion.

tun·ing fork \'tü-ning, 'tyü-\. A steel instrument consisting of two prongs and a handle, which gives a fixed tone when struck.

Tu·ni·sian \tü-'nēzh-n, tyü-, -'nizh-n\ *adj.* Of or relating to Tunisia or the city of Tunis. — *n.* A native or inhabitant of Tunisia or Tunis.

tun·nel \'tən-l\ *n.* **1** An underground passage, as for a railroad. **2** A burrow. — *v.;* **tun·neled** or **tun·nelled**; **tun·nel·ing** or **tun·nel·ling**. **1** To make a tunnel under. **2** To construct a tunnel.

tun·ny \'tən-ē\ *n.; pl.* **tun·ny** or **tun·nies**. A tuna; especially, a large oily coarse-fleshed food and game fish of the Atlantic Ocean.

tu·pe·lo \'tüp-l-ˌō, 'tyüp-\ *n.; pl.* **tu·pe·los**. A North American hardwood tree related to the dogwood, with drooping branches, brilliant autumn foliage, and blue-black fruit in clusters.

tup·pence \'təp-n(t)s\ *n.* Twopence.

tur·ban \'tərb-n\ *n.* **1** An Eastern headdress for men, consisting of a cap with a scarf wound around it. **2** A woman's hat with no brim or with brim turned back close to the crown. — **tur·baned** \-nd\ *adj.*

turban, 1

tur·bid \'tər-bəd\ *adj.* **1** Having the sediment or bottom disturbed; roiled; muddy; as, *turbid* waters. **2** Confused, as in thought or feeling; not clear. — **tur·bid·i·ty** \tər-'bid-ət-ē\ *n.* — **tur·bid·ly** \'tər-bəd-lē\ *adv.*

tur·bi·nate \'tərb-n-ət\ *adj.* **1** Shaped like an inverted cone or a child's top; as, a *turbinate* shell. **2** Rolled in a spiral; scroll-like — used of the thin bony plates (**tur·bi·nat·ed bones** \-n-ˌāt-əd\) on the walls of the nasal passages.

tur·bine \'tərb-n, 'tər-ˌbīn\ *n.* An engine whose central driving shaft is fitted with vanes whirled around by the pressure of water, steam, or air.

tur·bo·gen·er·a·tor \ˌtər-(ˌ)bō-'jen-r-ˌāt-r\ *n.* A turbine-driven generator.

tur·bo·jet engine \'tər-bō-ˌjet\. A jet engine having a turbine-driven air-compressing device for supplying air to burn the fuel.

tur·bo·prop engine \'tər-bō-ˌpräp\ or **tur·bo-prop-jet engine** \-'präp-ˌjet\. A turbo-propeller engine.

tur·bo-pro·pel·ler engine \'tər-(ˌ)bō-prə-'pel-r\. A jet engine having a turbine-driven propeller, designed to produce thrust principally by means of the propeller, with additional thrust obtained from the hot exhaust gases that issue in a jet.

tur·bot \'tər-bət\ *n.* **1** A large European edible flatfish. **2** Any somewhat similar flounder.

tur·bu·lence \'tərb-yə-lən(t)s\ or **tur·bu·len·cy** \-lən-sē\ *n.* A turbulent condition.

tur·bu·lent \'tərb-yə-lənt\ *adj.* **1** Causing or given to causing violence, discontent, or disturbances. **2** Being in violent commotion; excited or confused; tumultuous; disturbed. — **tur·bu·lent·ly**, *adv.*

tu·reen \tə-'rēn, tü-, tyü-\ *n.* A large soup dish.

tureen

turf \'tərf\ *n.; pl.* **turfs** \'tərfs\ or **turves** \'tərvz\. **1** The upper layer of earth filled with grass roots and decayed plant material in a lawn or grassy area; sod. **2** A piece or slab of this earth. **3** Peat, especially when prepared for fuel. **4** The track or course for horse racing or horse racing as a sport — usually with *the*. — **turfy** \'tər-fē\ *adj.*

tur·gid \'tər-jəd\ *adj.* **1** Distended by some internal force or agent; swollen. **2** High-sounding; pompous; as, a *turgid* style of writing. — **tur·gid·i·ty** \tər-'jid-ət-ē\ *n.* — **tur·gid·ly** \'tər-jəd-lē\ *adv.*

tur·gor \'tərg-r\ *n.* Turgid state; turgidity; especially, in biology, the state of being normally distended; the firmness and tension given to living cells by the pressure of the fluid that they contain.

Turk \'tərk\ *n.* **1** A member of certain Asian peoples of northern and western Asia and eastern Europe. **2** A native or inhabitant of Turkey.

tur·key \'tərk-ē\ *n.; pl.* **tur·keys**. [A former name for the guinea fowl (with which the turkey was confused in the 17th century), which was introduced into Europe from Africa by way of Turkey.] **1** A large domesticated fowl related to the pheasant, originally native to North America; its flesh used as food. **2** *Slang.* A show, as a play or moving picture, that turns out a failure.

turkey cock. **1** A male turkey. **2** A strutting, pompous person.

Turk·ish \'tərk-ish\ *adj.* Of or relating to Turkey. — *n.* **1** The Turkish people — used as a plural with *the*. **2** The language of Turkey.

turkish towel. A towel, usually of cotton, having surfaces formed by raised loops or a thick pile.

tur·moil \'tər-ˌmȯil\ *n.* Physical or mental agitation or confusion; turbulence; tumult.

turn \'tərn\ *v.* **1** To revolve; to rotate. **2** To consider from various points of view; as, to *turn* something over in one's mind. **3** To form in a lathe. **4** To do or make skillfully; as, to *turn* a sentence. **5** To reverse; to put or be put upside down or inside out; as, to *turn* a shirt collar. **6** To upset, as the stomach or the mind. **7** To depend; to hinge. The story *turns* on this event. **8** To go or move or make something else go or move in a certain direction. **9** To twist, as a key. **10** To move through an arc, so as to show another side; as, to *turn* a page. **11** To go beyond or around; to pass; as, to *turn* a corner; to have just *turned* ten. **12** To change; as, a tadpole about to *turn* into a frog. **13** To make or become sour. **14** To translate; as, to *turn* French into English. **15** To direct or take a direction. — **turn away. 1** To leave or start to leave. **2** To reject the application of. — **turn back. 1** To go back; to return. **2** To fold in a reverse direction. — **turn down. 1** To fold down. **2** To place face downward. **3** To lower, as a light or the sound of a radio. **4** To refuse to accept. — **turn in. 1** To send in; to hand in. **2** To bend inward. **3** To go to bed. — **turn out. 1** To expel; to dismiss. **2** To put out, as a light. **3** To turn inside out. **4** To empty, as a room of furniture for cleaning. **5** To bend outward. **6** To come or go to; as, to *turn out* for a football game. **7** To result; as, a plan that *turned out* well. **8** To make; to produce; as, a factory that *turns out* shoes. **9** To get up from bed. — **turn over. 1** To upset; to overturn. **2** To give up; to hand over. **3** To think over. **4** To handle in business; to buy and then sell in a certain amount. — **turn to. 1** To set to work; to apply oneself. **2** To refer to; to consult; to go to for assistance. — **turn up. 1** To fold up, so as to bring the bottom on top or so as to shorten. **2** To find or be found, as something lost. **3** To appear; as, to *turn up* at a meeting. **4** To increase in brightness or loudness; as, to *turn up* a radio. **5** To happen; to occur. Something always *turns up* to interfere. **6** To give an upward curve or direction to; to tilt upwards. — *n.* **1** A rotation; a revolution; as, the *turn* of a wheel. **2** A twist or coil, as of rope round a post. **3** A short walk or ride; as, a *turn* around the block. **4** A change, or the point where the change occurs; as, a *turn* in the road; a *turn* for the better in an illness. **5** A deed; an act; as, a good *turn*. **6** An opportunity; an assigned place in a series or group; as, to take *turns*. **7** Particular form, shape, or style; as, new *turns* to old stories. **8** A nervous start or shock; as, to give one a *turn*. **9** Special ability; bent; inclination; as, a curious *turn* of mind. **10** A short act on the stage, as in vaudeville.

turn·buck·le \'tərn-ˌbək-l\ *n.* A link with a screw thread at each end or with a swivel at one end and a screw thread at the other, used to tighten a rod or stay or to unite the ends of two rods.

turn·coat \'tərn-ˌkōt\ *n.* A person who abandons his party or his principles; a renegade.

turn·down \'tərn-ˌdau̇n\ *n.* **1** A turning down. **2** Something turned down. — *adj.* Made to be worn turned down; as, a *turndown* collar.

tur·nip \'tər-nəp\ *n.* **1** A plant of the mustard family with a thick white or yellow edible root. **2** This root.

turn·key \'tərn-ˌkē\ *n.; pl.* **turn·keys.** A person in charge of the keys of a prison.

turn·off \'tər-ˌnȯf\ *n.* **1** A turning off. **2** A place where one turns off.

turn·out \'tər-ˌnau̇t\ *n.* **1** A gathering, as of persons; as, a good *turnout* at the game. **2** A carriage with its horse or horses. **3** An outfit of clothes; a costume. **4** A clearing out and cleaning, as of a room. **5** A widened space in a narrow road for vehicles to pass. **6** A railroad siding. **7** Yield; output.

turn·over \'tər-ˌnōv-r\ *n.* **1** An upset; a spill. **2** A shift, as in opinion. **3** A reorganization, as of personnel. **4** A pie or tart with one half of the crust turned over the other. **5** Any part turned or folded over, as the flap of an envelope. **6** The amount of business done or work accomplished; the rate at which material is processed. **7** The buying, selling, and replacing of goods considered as a single complete process; as, the annual *turnover* in shoes. **8** The number of employees hired in a given time to replace those leaving or discharged. — *adj.* Made with a part that turns over.

turn·pike \'tərn-ˌpīk\ *n.* **1** A tollgate. **2** A road (**turnpike road**) that has or once had tollgates.

turn·spit \'tərn-ˌspit\ *n.* One that turns a spit.

turn·stile \'tərn-ˌstīl\ *n.* **1** A post with four arms pivoted on it, set in a passageway or in a barrier so that persons, but not cattle or horses, may pass through by turning these arms. **2** Such a device to register the number of persons passing through or to bar passage until released by deposit of a coin.

turn·ta·ble \'tərn-ˌtāb-l\ *n.* **1** A revolving platform for turning a locomotive. **2** The rotating disk on which a phonograph record is played.

tur·pen·tine \'tərp-n-ˌtīn\ *n.* **1** A mixture of oil and resin obtained from pine trees. **2** An oil distilled from this mixture and used in paint.

tur·pi·tude \'tər-pə-ˌtüd, -ˌtyüd\ *n.* Depravity.

tur·quoise \'tər-ˌk(w)ȯiz\ *n.* **1** A blue to greenish gray stone. **2** A light greenish blue gem made from this stone. **3** The color of the gem turquoise.

tur·ret \'tər-ət, 'tə-rət, 'tu̇r-ət\ *n.* **1** A little tower, often at a corner of a building. **2** A low tower, armored and usually revolving, in which heavy guns are mounted. — **tur·ret·ed,** *adj.*

tur·tle \'tərt-l\ *n. Archaic.* A turtledove.

tur·tle \'tərt-l\ *n.* **1** A horny-beaked four-limbed land, freshwater, or sea reptile having the trunk enclosed in a bony shell. **2** The flesh of any of several turtles used for food.

tur·tle·dove \'tərt-l-ˌdəv\ *n.* A wild dove; especially, a European dove noted for its cooing note and its seemingly affectionate ways.

turves. A plural of *turf.*

tush \'təsh\ *n.* A tusk.

tusk \'təsk\ *n.* **1** A long, greatly enlarged tooth in such animals as the elephant, walrus, and wild boar, usually growing in pairs and used in digging and fighting. **2** A protruding tooth. — *v.* To dig up or gore with the tusk. — **tusked** \'təskt\ *adj.*

tus·sle \'təs-l\ *v.;* **tus·sled; tus·sling** \-l(-)ing\. To struggle, as in sport; to scuffle. — *n.* A tussling.

tus·sock \'təs-ək\ *n.* A tuft, as of grass or twigs.

tut *as a word,* 'tət; *the actual sound represented by the spelling* "tut" *is made by placing the tip of the tongue against the roof of the mouth and suddenly sucking in air*\ *interj.* An exclamation of impatience or rebuke.

tu·te·lage \'tüt-l-ij, 'tyüt-\ *n.* **1** The action of guarding or protecting. **2** Instruction.

tu·te·lary \'tüt-l-ˌer-ē, 'tyüt-\ *adj.* **1** Having the guardianship of a person or thing; as, a *tutelary* goddess. **2** Of or relating to a guardian.

tu·tor \'tüt-r, 'tyüt-r\ *n.* A person in charge of the instruction of another person, as a private teacher or, in certain colleges, a teacher ranking below an instructor. — *v.* **1** To teach; as, to *tutor* a boy in French. **2** To take lessons, especially privately. — **tu·to·ri·al** \tü-'tōr-ē-əl, tyü-, -'tȯr-\ *adj.*

tux·e·do \ˌtək-'sēd-ō\ *n.; pl.* **tux·e·dos** or **tux·e·does. 1** A usually black jacket with notched silk lapels and without tails, used for semiformal wear. **2** A semiformal suit having such a jacket.

TV \'tē-'vē\. Abbreviation for *television.*

twad·dle \'twäd-l\ *n.* Nonsense. — *v.;* **twad·dled**; **twad·dling** \-l(-)ing\. To talk or write twaddle.

twain \'twān\ *n.* Two; as, broken in *twain.*

twang \'twang\ *v.* **1** To make a twang, as by plucking a banjo string. **2** To speak with a twang. — *n.* **1** A harsh, quick, ringing sound, as of a bowstring pulled and released. **2** A tone of voice produced by speaking through the nose or a way of uttering words that is characteristic of such a tone.

tweak \'twēk\ *v.* To pinch and pull, as the nose, with a sudden jerk; to twitch. — *n.* A sharp twist.

tweed \'twēd\ *n.* **1** A soft, heavy cloth, usually of wool, woven in small patterns of one or more colors. **2** [in the plural] Tweed clothing.

tweet \'twēt\ *n.* A low chirping note. — *v* To chirp.

tweez·ers \'twēz-rz\ *n. pl.* A small instrument, like pincers, for grasping or pulling.

twelfth \'twelft(h)\ *adj.* Next after the eleventh. — *n.; pl.* **twelfths** \'twelf(t)s, 'twelfths\. One of twelve equal parts.

twelve \'twelv\ *adj.* One more than eleven. — *n.* **1** The sum of eleven and one; twelve units. **2** The figure standing for twelve units, as 12 or XII.

twelve·month \'twelv-ˌmən(t)th\ *n.; pl.* **twelve-months** \-ˌmən(t)s, -ˌmən(t)ths\. A year.

twen·ti·eth \'twent-ē-əth\ *adj.* Next after the nineteenth. — *n.* One of twenty equal parts.

twen·ty \'twent-ē\ *adj.; pl.* **twen·ties**. Two times ten; one more than nineteen. — *n.* **1** The sum of ten and ten; twenty units; a score. **2** The figure standing for twenty units, as 20 or XX.

twice \'twīs\ *adv.* **1** Two times; once and again; as, to write *twice* in one week. **2** Doubly; as, to be *twice* as lucky as someone else.

twid·dle \'twid-l\ *v.;* **twid·dled**; **twid·dling** \-l(-)ing\. To touch lightly; to play with; to twirl; as, to *twiddle* a pencil; to *twiddle* one's thumbs. — *n.* A slight twirling motion with the fingers.

twig \'twig\ *n.* A small branch.

twi·light \'twī-ˌlīt\ *n.* **1** The dim light from the sky just before sunrise or after sunset. **2** A faint or dim light. — *adj.* **1** Of or relating to twilight. **2** Dimly lighted; shaded; as, a *twilight* room.

twill \'twil\ *n.* **1** A pattern of slanting lines or ribs made in weaving. **2** A fabric woven with this pattern. — *v.* To weave so as to produce a twill.

twin \'twin\ *adj.* **1** Made up of two distinct, closely related, and equal parts; double. **2** Consisting of or being a pair; as, *twin* beds. **3** Being a twin or twins. — *n.* **1** One of two persons or things resembling each other. **2** One of two persons or animals born at the same birth. — *v.;* **twinned**; **twin·ning. 1** To bring forth twins. **2** To be born at the same birth; to be coupled with another.

twine \'twīn\ *n.* **1** A strong thread or string of two or three strands twisted together. **2** A winding or interlacing; a tangle; as, a *twine* of ivy. — *v.;* **twined**; **twin·ing. 1** To twist together; as, to *twine* a wreath of flowers. **2** To wind or coil.

twinge \'twinj\ *v.;* **twinged**; **twing·ing** \'twin-jing\. To suffer a twinge. — *n.* A sudden, sharp pain in body or mind; as, a *twinge* of conscience.

twin·kle \'twingk-l\ *v.;* **twin·kled**; **twin·kling** \-l(-)ing\. **1** To wink; to blink. **2** To sparkle or flicker. **3** To appear every now and then while moving rapidly, as the feet in dancing. — *n.* **1** A wink; as, a *twinkle* in one's eye. **2** A sparkle or flash; a flicker. **3** A moment; a twinkling.

twin·kling \'twingk-l(-)ing\ *n.* **1** A wink; a twinkle. **2** An instant; a moment; as, to vanish in a *twinkling.*

twirl \'twərl\ *v.* **1** To turn rapidly; to spin; as, to *twirl* a key on a chain. **2** To twist; as, a man *twirling* his mustache. **3** In baseball, to pitch. — *n.* **1** A twirling. **2** A twist; a coil; a winding. — **twirl·er**, *n.*

twist \'twist\ *v.* **1** To unite, as strands, by winding one around another. **2** To wind; as, to *twist* a rope round a post. **3** To turn; as, to *twist* about in a chair. **4** To turn so as to sprain or hurt; as, to *twist* one's ankle. **5** To distort the shape of by turning; as, to *twist* a knife by using it as a screwdriver. **6** To turn from the true form or meaning; as, to *twist* a statement. — *n.* **1** Something made by winding together, as thread. **2** Tobacco in a thick twisted roll. **3** The action or manner of twisting; a condition of being twisted. **4** A knot; a bending; as, the *twists* in a rope. **5** The action of giving a twisting motion, as to a pitched ball; a twirl.

twist·er \'twist-r\ *n.* **1** One that twists. **2** In baseball, a curve. **3** A tornado; a waterspout.

twit \'twit\ *v.;* **twit·ted**; **twit·ting**. To taunt or tease a person by reminding him of a fault or misfortune. — *n.* A twitting; a taunt.

twitch \'twich\ *v.* To pull, yank, jerk, or snatch. — *n.* **1** A short, quick tug. **2** A jerking, as of the muscles.

twit·ter \'twit-r\ *v.* **1** To make a series of sharp little sounds, like chirps of swallows. **2** To titter; to giggle. **3** To show by action or speech that one is slightly nervous or upset. The ladies *twittered* with excitement. **4** To utter with a twitter. — *n.* **1** A twittering. **2** A slight nervous upset.

two \'tü\ *adj.* One more than one. — *n.* **1** The sum of one and one; two units. **2** The figure standing for two units, as 2 or II.

two-faced \'tü-'fāst\ *adj.* **1** Having two faces. **2** Not sincere; double-dealing; false.

two·fold \'tü-ˌfōld\ *adj.* Twice as much or as many; double. — \-'fōld\ *adv.* To twice as much or as many; doubly; as, to increase *twofold.*

two·pence \'təp-n(t)s\ *n.* The sum of two pence.

two·pen·ny \'tü-ˌpen-ē, 'təp-n-ē\ *adj.* **1** Of the value of twopence. **2** Cheap; inferior.

two·some \'tüs-m\ *n.* A couple; a pair. — *adj.* Consisting of two; done by two.

two-step \'tü-ˌstep\ *n.* **1** A ballroom dance performed with a sliding step in march or polka time. **2** Music for this dance.

-ty. A suffix that can mean: tens, ten times, as in *sixty.*

-ty. A suffix that can mean: quality, state, as in *entirety* or *loyalty.*

ty·coon \(')tī-'kün\ *n.* **1** A term applied to a Japanese shogun by foreigners in the 19th century. **2** A powerful businessman or industrialist.

tying. A present part. of *tie.*

tyke or **tike** \'tīk\ *n.* **1** A dog; a cur. **2** A lively or mischievous child. **3** A small child.

tympani. Variant of *timpani.*

tym·pan·ic \tim-'pan-ik\ *adj.* **1** Like a drum. **2** Of or relating to the middle ear or the eardrum.

tym·pa·num \'timp-n-əm\ *n.; pl.* **tym·pa·nums** \-n-əmz\ or **tym·pa·na** \-n-ə\. **1** The cavity forming the middle part of the ear. **2** The eardrum.

type \'tīp\ *n.* **1** The general form, character, or structure that is common to a number of individuals, persons, or things and that sets them off as a class or kind; as, the seedless *type* of orange. **2** A class, kind, or group set apart by common form or structure, as a genus or species. **3** A particular class or order; as, criminals of a dangerous *type.* **4** A kind; a sort; as, that *type* of thing. **5** A person or thing that exemplifies certain qualities. The characters in this story are *types.* **6** A rectangular block, usually of metal, that has its face so shaped as to produce, in printing, a letter, figure, or other character. **7** A group or series of such blocks or letters or figures printed from them; as, a paragraph printed in small *type.* — *v.;* **typed**; **typ·ing.** **1** To produce a copy of; to represent; to typify. **2** To typewrite. **3** To determine the type of, as blood.

types, 6

type·set·ter \'tīp-ˌset-r\ *n.* One that sets printing type. — **type·set·ting** \-ing\ *n.* or *adj.*

type·write \'tīp-ˌrīt\ *v.;* **type·wrote** \-ˌrōt\; **type·writ·ten** \-ˌrit-n\; **type·writ·ing** \-ˌrīt-ing\. To write with a typewriter.

type·writ·er \'tīp-ˌrīt-r\ *n.* **1** A machine for writing letters, figures, or other characters similar to those produced by printers' types. **2** A typist.

type·writ·ing \'tīp-ˌrīt-ing\ *n.* **1** The art of using a typewriter. **2** Writing done with a typewriter.

ty·phoid \'tī-ˌfȯid\ *adj.* Of or relating to **typhoid fever**, an infectious fever caused by a bacterium (**typhoid bacillus**) taken into the body with food or drink. — \-ˌfȯid, -'fȯid\ *n.* Typhoid fever.

ty·phoon \(')tī-'fün\ *n.* A tropical cyclone.

ty·phus \'tī-fəs\ *n.* An infectious disease transmitted by the bites of fleas and lice.

typ·i·cal \'tip-ik-l\ *adj.* Showing the qualities that mark a type of person, animal, plant, or thing; as, a *typical* tourist. — **typ·i·cal·ly** \-ik-l(-)ē\ *adv.*

typ·i·fy \'tip-ə-ˌfī\ *v.;* **typ·i·fied** \-ˌfīd\; **typ·i·fy·ing.** To have the essential or common characteristics of; to be the type of; to be a good example of.

typ·ist \'tīp-əst\ *n.* One who operates a typewriter.

ty·pog·ra·pher \tī-'päg-rəf-r\ *n.* A printer or one who designs or arranges printing.

ty·pog·ra·phy \tī-'päg-rə-fē\ *n.* The use of type for printing; especially, the style or arrangement of matter printed from type. — **ty·po·graph·ic** \ˌtīp-ə-'graf-ik\ or **ty·po·graph·i·cal** \-ik-l\ *adj.* — **ty·po·graph·i·cal·ly** \-ik-l(-)ē\ *adv.*

ty·ran·ni·cal \tə-'ran-ik-l, tī-\ *adj.* Also **ty·ran·nic** \-ik\. Of or relating to a tyrant; despotic. — **ty·ran·ni·cal·ly** \-ik-l(-)ē\ *adv.*

tyr·an·nize \'tir-ə-ˌnīz\ *v.;* **tyr·an·nized**; **tyr·an·niz·ing.** To act as a tyrant.

ty·ran·no·sau·rus \tə-ˌran-ə-'sȯr-əs\ *n.; pl.* **ty·ran·no·sau·rus·es** \-'sȯr-ə-səz\ or **ty·ran·no·sau·ri** \-'sȯr-ˌī\. An extinct American flesh-eating dinosaur having small forelegs and walking on its hind legs.

tyr·an·nous \'tir-ə-nəs\ *adj.* Tyrannical; despotic. — **tyr·an·nous·ly**, *adv.*

tyr·an·ny \'tir-ə-nē\ *n.; pl.* **tyr·an·nies.** **1** The rule or authority of a tyrant; government by a tyrant. **2** A cruel domineering or bullying act; harsh and cruel behavior or treatment.

ty·rant \'tī-rənt\ *n.* **1** An absolute ruler. **2** A cruel or brutal ruler. **3** Any oppressor.

tyrant flycatcher. An American flycatcher with flattened bill hooked at the tip; a kingbird.

ty·ro \'tī-ˌrō\ *n.; pl.* **ty·ros.** A beginner in learning; a novice.

u \'yü\ *n.; pl.* **u's** \'yüz\. The twenty-first letter of the alphabet.

U u U u u

ubiq·ui·tous \yü-'bik-wət-əs\ *adj.* Existing or being everywhere at the same time; omnipresent; as, the *ubiquitous* atom. — **ubiq·ui·tous·ly**, *adv.*

ubiq·ui·ty \yü-'bik-wət-ē\ *n.* An existing or being everywhere at the same time; omnipresence.

U-boat \'yü-'bōt\ *n.* A German submarine.

ud·der \'əd-r\ *n.* A large, bag-shaped milk gland having teats, as in cows.

ugh *stands for various sounds our symbols cannot represent*\ *interj.* An exclamation expressing disgust or horror.

ug·ly \'əg-lē\ *adj.;* **ug·li·er; ug·li·est.** **1** Unpleasant to the sight; unsightly; hideous. **2** So evil as to be hideous; as, *ugly* crimes. **3** Likely to cause trouble; difficult; as, an *ugly* situation. **4** Ill-natured; quarrelsome. — **ug·li·ness** \-lē-nəs\ *n.*

UHF. Abbreviation for *ultrahigh frequency.*

ukase \yü-'kās\ *n.* **1** A Russian imperial order. **2** Any decree.

uku·le·le \ˌyük-l-'ā-lē\ *n.* [From Hawaiian *'ukulele* meaning literally "flea".] A small four-stringed musical instrument played with the fingers or a pick.

ukulele

ul·cer \'əls-r\ *n.* **1** An open sore in which tissue breaks down and which is slow to heal. **2** Anything that weakens and corrupts.

ul·cer·ate \'əls-r-ˌāt\ *v.;* **ul·cer·at·ed; ul·cer·at·ing.** To cause or become affected with an ulcer; as, an *ulcerated* wound. — **ul·cer·a·tion** \ˌəls-r-'āsh-n\ *n.*

ul·cer·ous \'əls-r(-)əs\ *adj.* **1** Of or relating to ulcers. **2** Affected with an ulcer. — **ul·cer·ous·ly,** *adv.*

ul·na \'əl-nə\ *n.; pl.* **ul·nas** \-nəz\ or **ul·nae** \-ˌnē\. The inner of the two bones of the forearm or a corresponding part of the forelimb of vertebrates above fishes. — **ul·nar** \-nər\ *adj.*

ul·ster \'əlst-r\ *n.* A long loose overcoat.

ult. Abbreviation for *ultimo.*

ul·te·ri·or \ˌəl-'tir-ē-ər\ *adj.* **1** Situated beyond or on the farther side. **2** Lying farther away; more remote. **3** Going beyond what is openly said or shown; as, *ulterior* motives. — **ul·te·ri·or·ly,** *adv.*

ul·ti·ma \'əlt-m-ə\ *n.* The last syllable of a word.

ul·ti·mate \'əlt-m-ət\ *adj.* **1** The most distant in space or time; as, the *ultimate* reaches of the sky. **2** Last; final; as, *ultimate* truth. **3** Not capable of further division or separation; basic. The atom is no longer regarded as the *ultimate* particle of matter. **4** Fundamental; absolute. **5** Maximum; as, a test for *ultimate* strain. — For synonyms see *last.* — *n.* Something which is ultimate, final, or basic.

ul·ti·mate·ly \'əlt-m-ət-lē\ *adv.* Finally; at last.

ul·ti·ma·tum \ˌəlt-m-'āt-m, -'ät-m, -'àt-m\ *n.; pl.* **ul·ti·ma·tums** \-mz\ or **ul·ti·ma·ta** \-ə\. A final proposition or condition, especially as offered by one of the parties negotiating a settlement.

ul·ti·mo \'əlt-m-ˌō\ *adv.* In the month previous.

ul·tra \'əl-trə\ *adj.* Going beyond fit or expected limits; extreme; as, *ultra* measures.

ultra-. A prefix that can mean: **1** Beyond, above, as in *ultrasonic.* **2** Excessively; beyond what is ordinary, natural, or proper, as in *ultramodern.*

ul·tra·high frequency \'əl-trə-ˌhī\. In radio and television, any frequency in the range from 300 to 3000 megacycles.

ul·tra·ma·rine \ˌəl-trə-mə-'rēn\ *adj.* Situated beyond the sea. — *n.* **1** A deep blue pigment. **2** Also **ultramarine blue.** A very bright deep blue color.

ul·tra·mod·ern \'əl-trə-'mäd-rn\ *adj.* Extremely or excessively modern in idea, style, or tendency.

ul·tra·short wave \'əl-trə-ˌshȯrt\. In radio and television, a wave below 10 meters in length and having a frequency above 30 megacycles.

ul·tra·son·ic \'əl-trə-'sän-ik\ *adj.* Supersonic.

ul·tra·vi·o·let \'əl-trə-'vī-ə-lət\ *adj.* Of or relating to the invisible rays of light next to the violet in the spectrum.

um·bel \'əm-bl\ *n.* A flat-topped or ball-shaped flower cluster in which the stalks of the individual flowers all grow from one point on the main stem, like the ribs of an umbrella, as in the carrot family. — **um·bel·lar** \'əm-bl-ər, ˌəm-'bel-r\ *adj.* — **um·bel·late** \'əm-bl-ˌāt, ˌəm-'bel-ət\ *adj.*

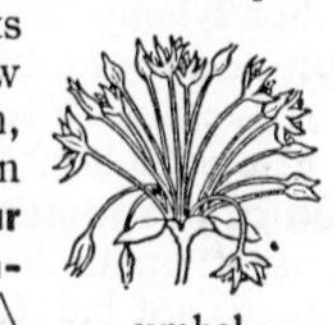
umbel

um·ber \'əm-br\ *n.* **1** A brown earth valued as a pigment. **2** The brown color produced by the use of this pigment, as in **burnt umber.**

um·bil·i·cal cord \ˌəm-'bil-ik-l\. The cord extending from the navel and joining the fetus of a mammal with the placenta.

um·bil·i·cus \ˌəm-'bil-ə-kəs\ *n.; pl.* **um·bil·i·ci** \-ə-ˌsī\. **1** The scar on the abdomen where the umbilical cord was attached; the navel. **2** In botany, the hilum. — **um·bil·i·cal** \-'bil-ik-l\ *adj.*

um·bra \'əm-brə\ *n.; pl.* **um·bras** \-brəz\ or **um·brae** \-ˌbrē\. **1** A shade; a shadow. **2** In astronomy, the cone-shaped shadow thrown by a planet or satellite on the side away from the sun. **3** The central dark portion of a sunspot.

um·brage \'əm-brij\ *n.* **1** Shade. **2** Resentment; offense; as, to take *umbrage* at a remark.

um·brel·la \ˌəm-'brel-ə\ *n.* [From Italian *ombrella* meaning literally "little shade".] A fabric covering stretched over ribs of wood or metal and fastened to a rod or stick, carried as a protection against rain or sun.

umbrella tree. An American magnolia with large oblong pointed leaves clustered at branch ends.

umi·ak \'ü-mē-ˌak\ *n.* An open Eskimo boat.

um·laut \'ům-ˌlaůt\ *n.* **1** A change in the sound of a vowel brought about by a sound following it in a word. **2** The two dots [¨] used in certain languages to indicate such a change.

um·pire \'əm-ˌpīr\ *n.* A person selected to give a decision on a disputed question; especially, a person chosen to rule on the plays of a game, such as baseball. — *v.* To officiate as an umpire.

un-. A verb-forming prefix that can mean: **1** To do the contrary or reverse of, as in *unbolt, unbutton.* **2** To deprive of, remove from, or free or release from, as in *unburden, unearth, unhorse.* **3** Completely, as in *unloose.*

un-. A prefix that can be added to almost any adjective or adverb, and to a few nouns, and that has the meaning *not,* as in *unbroken, unskillfully.*
☞ Some compounds of *un-* express little if anything more than a simple denial of the idea expressed by the word to which *un-* is added. Others

express some positive idea, especially one of opposition to or contrast with the word to which *un-* is added. Some words that may reasonably be considered to belong to the first type are given in a selective list at the foot of the page; a sufficient idea of their meaning can be gained by substituting *not* for *un-*; corresponding adverbs and nouns in *-ly* and *-ness* may be freely formed.

un·a·ble \'ən-'āb-l\ *adj.* Not able; incapable. — For synonyms see *incapable.*

un·ac·count·a·ble \ˌən-ə-'kaủnt-əb-l\ *adj.* **1** Not responsible. **2** Not to be explained; strange. — **un·ac·count·a·bly** \-ə-blē\ *adv.*

un·ac·cus·tomed \ˌən-ə-'kəst-md\ *adj.* **1** Unusual; unfamiliar; as, *unaccustomed* scenes. **2** Not used; not habituated; as, *unaccustomed* to travel.

un·ad·vised \ˌən-əd-'vīzd\ *adj.* **1** Not advised; especially, indiscreet; rash. **2** Without having advice. — **un·ad·vis·ed·ly** \-'vī-zəd-lē\ *adv.*

un·af·fect·ed \ˌən-ə-'fek-təd\ *adj.* **1** Not moved, changed, or influenced. **2** Free from affectation; simple; genuine; sincere; natural. — **un·af·fect·ed·ly**, *adv.*

un–Amer·i·can \ˌən-ə-'mer-ək-n\ *adj.* Not characteristic of or consistent with American principles or customs.

una·nim·i·ty \ˌyü-nə-'nim-ət-ē\ *n.* Complete agreement, as in opinion or policy.

unan·i·mous \yü-'nan-ə-məs\ *adj.* **1** Being of one mind; agreeing completely. **2** Assented to by all; as, a *unanimous* vote. — **unan·i·mous·ly**, *adv.*

un·arm \'ən-'ärm, -'årm\ *v.* To disarm.

un·armed \'ən-'ärmd, -'årmd\ *adj.* Not armed or armored; having no weapons.

un·as·sail·a·ble \ˌən-ə-'sā-ləb-l\ *adj.* Not assailable; not open to being successfully attacked or contested. — **un·as·sail·a·bly** \-lə-blē\ *adv.*

un·as·sum·ing \ˌən-ə-'sü-ming\ *adj.* Not putting on airs; modest; retiring. — **un·as·sum·ing·ly**, *adv.*

un·a·vail·ing \ˌən-ə-'vā-ling\ *adj.* Of no avail; not successful; vain. — **un·a·vail·ing·ly**, *adv.*

un·a·ware \ˌən-ə-'war, -'wer\ *adj.* Not aware; not noticing; ignorant. — *adv.* Unawares.

un·a·wares \ˌən-ə-'warz, -'werz\ *adv.* **1** Without warning; by surprise; as, to be taken *unawares.* **2** Without knowing; unintentionally.

un·bal·anced \'ən-'bal-ən(t)st\ *adj.* **1** Not in equilibrium, as a scale. **2** Not adjusted so as to make credits equal to debits, as an account. **3** Disordered; insane; as, an *unbalanced* mind.

un·bar \'ən-'bär, -'bår\ *v.;* **un·barred**; **un·bar·ring.** To remove a bar or bars from; to unbolt.

un·beat·a·ble \'ən-'bēt-əb-l\ *adj.* That cannot be defeated.

un·be·com·ing \ˌən-bē-'kəm-ing\ *adj.* Not becoming; unsuitable; improper. — **un·be·com·ing·ly,** *adv.*

un·be·known \ˌən-bē-'nōn\ or **un·be·knownst** \-'nōn(t)st\ *adj.* Unknown.

un·be·lief \ˌən-bə-'lēf\ *n.* The withholding of belief; an absence of belief; doubt; skepticism.

— The word *disbelief* is a synonym of *unbelief: unbelief* usually indicates nothing more than the lack of a positive belief in or acceptance of something, particularly of some religious matter; *disbelief* suggests a positive rejection of what is stated because of some proof or evidence against it.

un·be·liev·a·ble \ˌən-bə-'lē-vəb-l\ *adj.* Too improbable for belief. — **un·be·liev·a·bly** \-və-blē\ *adv.*

un·be·liev·er \ˌən-bə-'lēv-r\ *n.* **1** One who does not believe; a doubter. **2** One who does not believe in a particular religious faith; an infidel.

un·bend \'ən-'bend\ *v.;* **un·bent** \-'bent\; **un·bend·ing.** **1** To free from being bent; to make or allow to become straight. **2** To unfasten, as sails from the spars; to untie. **3** To make or become less stiff or more affable; to relax.

un·bend·ing \'ən-'ben-ding\ *adj.* Formal and distant in manner; inflexible.

un·bid·den \'ən-'bid-n\ *adj.* **1** Not commanded; not ordered. **2** Not invited; as, an *unbidden* guest.

un·bind \'ən-'bīnd\ *v.;* **un·bound** \-'baủnd\; **un·bind·ing.** To untie; to unfasten.

un·blush·ing \'ən-'bləsh-ing\ *adj.* Not blushing; shameless. — **un·blush·ing·ly**, *adv.*

un·bolt \'ən-'bōlt\ *v.* To withdraw a bolt from; to open; to unfasten.

un·bolt·ed \'ən-'bōl-təd\ *adj.* Not sifted; coarse.

un·born \'ən-'bôrn\ *adj.* Not born; not yet born; future; as, *unborn* generations.

un·bos·om \'ən-'bủz-m\ *v.* To disclose or reveal, as secret thoughts or feelings; to confess; to free (oneself) by confessing; as, to *unbosom* oneself to a friend.

un·bound·ed \'ən-'baủn-dəd\ *adj.* Having no bounds or limits; as, *unbounded* space; *unbounded* enthusiasm.

☞ See **un-**, *not*, and following note.

un·a·bashed
un·a·bat·ed
un·a·bridged
un·ac·cent·ed
un·ac·cept·a·ble
un·ac·com·mo·dat·ing
un·ac·com·pa·nied
un·ac·quaint·ed
un·a·dapt·a·ble
un·a·dorned
un·a·dul·ter·at·ed
un·a·fraid
un·aid·ed
un·al·ien·a·ble
un·a·like
un·al·loyed
un·al·ter·a·ble
un·al·tered
un·al·ter·ing
un·am·big·u·ous
un·am·bi·tious
un·a·mi·a·ble
un·an·chored
un·an·nounced
un·an·swer·a·ble
un·ap·peal·ing
un·ap·pe·tiz·ing
un·ap·pre·ci·at·ed
un·ap·pre·cia·tive
un·ap·proach·a·ble
un·ap·proved
un·ar·tis·tic
un·a·shamed
un·a·sham·ed·ly
un·asked
un·as·sist·ed
un·at·tached
un·at·tain·a·ble
un·at·tend·ed
un·at·trac·tive
un·au·tho·rized
un·a·vail·a·ble
un·a·venged
un·a·void·a·ble
un·baked
un·bap·tized
un·bear·a·ble
un·beat·en
un·be·liev·ing
un·bi·ased
un·bi·assed
un·bleached
un·blem·ished
un·blessed
un·blest
un·bound

un·bowed \'ən-'baud\ *adj.* Not bent; not subdued or conquered.

un·braid \'ən-'brād\ *v.* To separate the strands of.

un·bro·ken \'ən-'brōk-n\ *adj.* **1** Not damaged; whole. **2** Not subdued or tamed; as, an *unbroken* colt. **3** Not interrupted; continuous; as, an *unbroken* row of trees; *unbroken* sleep.

un·buck·le \'ən-'bək-l\ *v.;* **un·buck·led**; **un·buck·ling** \-l(-)ing\. To unfasten the buckle or buckles of, as a shoe or a belt.

un·bur·den \'ən-'bərd-n\ *v.;* **un·bur·dened**; **un·bur·den·ing** \-n(-)ing\. To relieve from a burden or from something burdensome, as by confession.

un·but·ton \'ən-'bət-n\ *v.;* **un·but·toned**; **un·but·ton·ing** \-n(-)ing\. To unfasten the button or buttons of, as a garment.

un·called–for \'ən-'kȯld-ˌfȯr\ *adj.* Not called for; not needed or wanted; not proper; as, an *uncalled-for* remark.

un·can·ny \'ən-'kan-ē, ˌən-\ *adj.* Ghostly; weird; mysterious. — **un·can·ni·ly** \-'kan-l-ē\ *adv.*

un·cap \'ən-'kap\ *v.;* **un·capped**; **un·cap·ping**. To remove the cap from.

un·cer·e·mo·ni·ous \'ən-ˌser-ə-'mō-nē-əs\ *adj.* Lacking, or acting without, ordinary courtesy. — **un·cer·e·mo·ni·ous·ly**, *adv.*

un·cer·tain \'ən-'sərt-n\ *adj.* **1** Not determined or fixed; as, an *uncertain* quantity. **2** Subject to chance or change; not dependable; as, an *uncertain* temper. **3** Not sure; as, to be *uncertain* of the truth. **4** Not definitely known. — **un·cer·tain·ly**, *adv.*

un·cer·tain·ty \'ən-'sərt-n-tē\ *n.; pl.* **un·cer·tain·ties**. **1** Lack of certainty; doubt. **2** Something that is uncertain.

un·char·i·ta·ble \'ən-'char-ət-əb-l\ *adj.* Not charitable; especially, severe in judging others. — **un·char·i·ta·bly** \-ə-blē\ *adv.*

un·chris·tian \'ən-'kris-chən\ *adj.* **1** Heathen; pagan. **2** Not in accordance with the Christian spirit. **3** Uncivilized; barbarous.

un·cial \'ənch-l\ *adj.* Relating to, or written in, a form of script with rounded letters used in early manuscripts. — *n.* An uncial letter; uncial writing.

un·civ·il \'ən-'siv-l\ *adj.* Not civil; impolite; discourteous; rude. — **un·civ·il·ly** \-'siv-l-(l)ē\ *adv.*

un·civ·i·lized \'ən-'siv-l-ˌīzd\ *adj.* Not civilized; savage; barbarous.

un·clad \'ən-'klad\ *adj.* Not clothed; undressed; naked.

un·clasp \'ən-'klasp\ *v.* To release from a clasp.

un·cle \'əngk-l\ *n.* **1** The brother of one's father or mother. **2** The husband of one's aunt.

un·clean \'ən-'klēn\ *adj.* **1** Dirty; filthy. **2** Disgusting; indecent; impure. — **un·clean·ness**, *n.*

un·clean·ly \'ən-'klen-lē\ *adj.* Dirty; filthy. — **un·clean·li·ness** \-lē-nəs\ *n.*

un·clench \'ən-'klench\ or **un·clinch** \-'klinch\ *v.* To relax or force open a clenched hand.

Un·cle Sam \'əngk-l 'sam\. [From *U.S.*, the abbreviation for *United States.*] The United States government.

un·cloak \'ən-'klōk\ *v.* **1** To take off a cloak; to remove a cloak from. **2** To reveal; to disclose.

un·close \'ən-'klōz\ *v.;* **un·closed**; **un·clos·ing.** To open.

un·clothe \'ən-'klōth\ *v.;* **un·clothed**; **un·cloth·ing** \-'klō-thing\. To strip of clothes or a covering.

un·coil \'ən-'kȯil\ *v.* To open the coils of; to unwind.

un·com·mu·ni·ca·tive \ˌən-kə-'myü-nə-ˌkāt-iv, -kət-iv\ *adj.* Not inclined to talk or to give out information; reticent.

un·com·pro·mis·ing \'ən-'käm-prə-ˌmī-zing\ *adj.* Not making any compromise; refusing to admit any exception; unyielding. — **un·com·pro·mis·ing·ly**, *adv.*

un·con·cern \ˌən-kən-'sərn\ *n.* **1** Lack or absence of excessive concern; freedom from anxiety. **2** Lack or absence of interest; indifference.

un·con·cerned \ˌən-kən-'sərnd\ *adj.* **1** Not involved; not having any part or interest. **2** Not anxious or upset; free of worry. — **un·con·cern·ed·ly** \-'sər-nəd-lē\ *adv.*

un·con·di·tion·al \ˌən-kən-'dish-n(-)əl\ *adj.* Not having any conditions or exceptions; not limited; absolute. — **un·con·di·tion·al·ly** \-n(-)ə-lē\ *adv.*

un·con·di·tioned \ˌən-kən-'dish-nd\ *adj.* **1** Not subject to conditions. **2** Not acquired or learned; natural; instinctive.

un·con·quer·a·ble \'ən-'käŋk-r(-)əb-l\ *adj.* That cannot be conquered or overcome. — **un·con·quer·a·bly** \-r(-)ə-blē\ *adv.*

un·con·scion·a·ble \'ən-'känch-n(-)əb-l\ *adj.* **1** Not being in accordance with what is right or just; unreasonable; excessive. **2** Not guided or controlled by conscience. — **un·con·scion·a·bly** \-n(-)ə-blē\ *adv.*

un·con·scious \'ən-'känch-əs\ *adj.* **1** Having lost consciousness; as, to be knocked *unconscious* by a

☞ See **un-**, *not*, and following note.
un·brand·ed
un·break·a·ble
un·bri·dled
un·broth·er·ly
un·bruised
un·bur·ied
un·burn·a·ble
un·burned
un·burnt
un·busi·ness·like
un·can·celed
un·can·celled
un·cared–for
un·ceas·ing
un·cen·sored
un·chained
un·chal·lenged
un·change·a·ble
un·changed
un·chang·ing
un·chart·ed
un·chaste
un·checked
un·claimed
un·clas·si·fied
un·cleared
un·clothed
un·cloud·ed
un·coat·ed
un·col·lect·ed
un·col·lect·i·ble
un·col·ored
un·com·fort·a·ble
un·com·fort·ed
un·com·mon
un·com·pan·ion·a·ble
un·com·plain·ing
un·com·plet·ed
un·com·pli·men·ta·ry
un·com·pre·hend·ing
un·con·cealed
un·con·fined
un·con·firmed
un·con·gen·ial
un·con·nect·ed
un·con·quered

fall. **2** Not aware; as, to be *unconscious* of having made a mistake. **3** Not realized by oneself; done without knowing; as, an *unconscious* mistake; *unconscious* humor. — *n.* That part of one's mental life of which one is not conscious; the sum of one's unconscious mental activity. — **un·con·scious·ly,** *adv.* — **un·con·scious·ness,** *n.*

un·con·sti·tu·tion·al \ˈən-ˌkän(t)s-tə-ˈtüsh-n(-)əl, -ˈtyüsh-\ *adj.* Not constitutional; being contrary to the constitution, as of a country. — **un·con·sti·tu·tion·al·i·ty** \-ˌtüsh-n-ˈal-ət-ē, -ˌtyüsh-\ *n.*

un·con·ven·tion·al \ˌən-kən-ˈvench-n(-)əl\ *adj.* Not conventional; not being in accordance with or bound by convention; free from conventionality. — **un·con·ven·tion·al·i·ty** \-ˌvench-n-ˈal-ət-ē\ *n.* — **un·con·ven·tion·al·ly** \-ˈvench-n(-)ə-lē\ *adv.*

un·count·ed \ˈən-ˈkau̇nt-əd\ *adj.* **1** Not counted. **2** Innumerable; countless.

un·cou·ple \ˈən-ˈkəp-l\ *v.;* **un·cou·pled; un·cou·pling** \-l(-)ing\. **1** To loose, as hunting dogs from their leashes. **2** To disconnect; as, to *uncouple* railroad cars.

un·couth \ˈən-ˈküth, ˌən-\ *adj.* [From Old English *uncuth* meaning "unknown", "strange".] **1** Strange, awkward, and clumsy in shape or appearance. **2** Vulgar in conduct or speech; rude.

un·cov·er \ˈən-ˈkəv-r\ *v.;* **un·cov·ered; un·cov·er·ing** \-r(-)ing\. **1** To lay bare; to expose to view by removing some object or material that covers; as, to *uncover* the walls of an ancient city. **2** To make known; to disclose; as, to *uncover* a plot. **3** To take off one's hat or cap, especially in respect.

un·cross \ˈən-ˈkrȯs\ *v.* To move or change so as no longer to be crossed; as, to *uncross* one's legs.

unc·tion \ˈəng(k)sh-n\ *n.* **1** The action of anointing. **2** An excessive smoothness of speech with pretended emotion.

unc·tu·ous \ˈəng(k)-chə-wəs, -chəs\ *adj.* **1** Like an ointment; oily; fatty. **2** Full of unction in speech and manner; especially, insincerely smooth. — **unc·tu·ous·ly** \-chəs-lē, -chə-wəs-\ *adv.*

un·curl \ˈən-ˈkərl\ *v.* To straighten out from a curled position.

un·daunt·ed \ˈən-ˈdȯnt-əd, -ˈdänt-\ *adj.* Not daunted; not discouraged or dismayed; fearless. — **un·daunt·ed·ly,** *adv.*

un·de·ceive \ˌən-dē-ˈsēv\ *v.;* **un·de·ceived; un·de·ceiv·ing.** To free from deception; to disillusion.

un·de·cid·ed \ˌən-dē-ˈsīd-əd\ *adj.* **1** Not yet decided; not settled. **2** Not having decided; wavering; uncertain what to do. — **un·de·cid·ed·ly,** *adv.*

un·de·mon·stra·tive \ˌən-dē-ˈmän-strət-iv\ *adj.* Restrained in the expression of feelings; reserved.

un·de·ni·a·ble \ˌən-dē-ˈnī-əb-l\ *adj.* That cannot be denied; incontestable; beyond doubt or question. — **un·de·ni·a·bly** \-ə-blē\ *adv.*

un·der \ˈənd-r\ *prep.* **1** Below or beneath; lower than and overhung by; as, to burrow *under* the house; to sit *under* a tree. **2** Below the surface of or inside of; as, to swim *under* water; to wear a sweater *under* a coat. **3** Subject to, led by, or controlled by; as, *under* penalty of the law; to fight *under* a brave general; to act *under* orders. **4** Undergoing or suffering the effect or action of; as, *under* an anesthetic. **5** Below; lower than, as in size, weight, number, or rank; as, to sell a car *under* the list price; slightly *under* six feet. — *adv.* In a lower position; below; beneath. — *adj.* **1** Lower in position, rank, or degree. **2** Normally facing downward; as, the *under* surface of a leaf.

under-. A prefix that can mean: **1** Below or beneath in place, order, or rank, as in *underfoot, underline, underpass, underwear.* **2** Below or less than a standard or than others, insufficient or insufficiently, imperfect or imperfectly, as in *underage, undernourished, underpay.*

un·der·age \ˈənd-r-ˈāj\ *adj.* Of less than mature age or a required age.

un·der·arm \ˈənd-r-ˌärm, -ˌȧrm\ *adj.* **1** Located under or on the underside of the arm; as, an *underarm* seam. **2** Underhand; as, an *underarm* throw. — \-ˈärm, -ˈȧrm\ *adv.* With an underarm motion.

un·der·bid \ˌənd-r-ˈbid\ *v.;* **un·der·bid; un·der·bid·ding.** To bid less than another.

un·der·bred \ˌənd-r-ˈbred\ *adj.* **1** Not of good breeding; ill-bred. **2** Not purebred.

un·der·brush \ˈənd-r-ˌbrəsh\ *n.* Shrubs and small trees growing among large trees; undergrowth.

un·der·car·riage \ˈənd-r-ˌkar-ij\ *n.* **1** The supporting framework, as of an automobile. **2** The landing structure of an aircraft.

un·der·charge \ˌənd-r-ˈchärj, -ˈchȧrj\ *v.;* **un·der·charged; un·der·charg·ing. 1** To charge too little, as for goods or services. **2** To load with too small a charge, as of an explosive.

un·der·clothes \ˈənd-r-ˌklō(th)z\ *n. pl.* Clothes worn under other clothes; underwear.

un·der·cloth·ing \-ˌklō-thing\ *n.* Underclothes.

un·der·coat \ˈənd-r-ˌkōt\ *n.* **1** A coat worn under another. **2** A growth of short hair or fur partly concealed by longer hair, as on a dog. **3** A coat of paint under another. **4** A paint for this purpose. — *v.* To provide with an undercoat.

☞ See **un-**, *not*, and following note.

un·con·strained
un·con·sumed
un·con·tam·i·nat·ed
un·con·tra·dict·ed
un·con·trol·la·ble
un·con·trolled
un·con·vinced
un·con·vinc·ing
un·cooked
un–co–op·er·a·tive
un–co–or·di·nat·ed
un·cork
un·corked
un·cor·rect·ed
un·cor·rob·o·rat·ed
un·cor·rupt·ed
un·cour·te·ous
un·crit·i·cal
un·crowd·ed
un·crowned
un·crys·tal·lized
un·cul·ti·vat·ed
un·cul·tured
un·cured
un·cut
un·dam·aged
un·dat·ed
un·de·clared
un·dec·o·rat·ed
un·de·feat·ed
un·de·fend·ed
un·de·filed
un·de·fin·a·ble
un·de·fined
un·dem·o·crat·ic
un·de·nom·i·na·tion·al
un·de·pend·a·ble

un·der·cov·er \'ənd-r-ˌkəv-r\ *adj.* Acting or done in secret; as, an *undercover* agent.

un·der·cur·rent \'ənd-r-ˌkər-ənt, -ˌkə-rənt\ *n.* **1** A current below the upper currents or below the surface, as of a body of water. **2** A hidden or underlying tendency of feeling or opinion.

un·der·cut \ˌənd-r-'kət\ *v.;* **un·der·cut; un·der·cut·ting. 1** To cut away the underpart of. **2** To cut or cut away from underneath. **3** To offer to sell or work at a lower price or rate than others. — \'ənd-r-ˌkət\ *n.* An undercutting or a part so cut away.

un·der·de·vel·op \ˌənd-r-də-'vel-əp\ *v.* To develop to a point below that which is usual or required.

un·der·dog \'ənd-r-ˌdȯg\ *n.* **1** The losing dog in a fight. **2** The loser in any struggle.

un·der·done \ˌənd-r-'dən\ *adj.* Not cooked long enough; rare.

un·der·es·ti·mate \ˌənd-r-'est-m-ˌāt\ *v.;* **un·der·es·ti·mat·ed; un·der·es·ti·mat·ing.** To evaluate below the proper value, amount, number, or size. — \-m-ət, -m-ˌāt\ *n.* An estimate that is too low. — **un·der·es·ti·ma·tion** \-ˌest-m-'āsh-n\ *n.*

un·der·ex·pose \ˌənd-r-iks-'pōz\ *v.;* **un·der·ex·posed; un·der·ex·pos·ing.** In photography, to expose for too short a time. — **un·der·ex·po·sure** \-'pōzh-r\ *n.*

un·der·feed \ˌənd-r-'fēd\ *v.;* **un·der·fed** \-'fed\; **un·der·feed·ing. 1** To feed with too little food. **2** To supply with fuel, as a furnace, from below.

un·der·foot \'ənd-r-'fu̇t\ *adv.* **1** Under the feet; as, flowers trampled *underfoot.* **2** Close about one's feet; in the way; as, a puppy always *underfoot.*

un·der·gar·ment \'ənd-r-ˌgär-mənt, -ˌgår-\ *n.* An article of underwear.

un·der·go \ˌənd-r-'gō\ *v.;* **un·der·went** \-'went\; **un·der·gone** \-'gȯn\; **un·der·go·ing** \-'gō-ing\. **1** To be subjected to; to suffer the force or effect of; as, to *undergo* an operation. **2** To pass through; to experience; as, to *undergo* a great change.

un·der·grad·u·ate \ˌənd-r-'graj-ə-wət, -ˌwāt\ *n.* A student in a university or college who has not finished his course and been granted a degree.

un·der·ground \'ənd-r-'grau̇nd\ *adv.* **1** Beneath the surface of the earth. **2** In secret. — \-ˌgrau̇nd\ *adj.* **1** Being, done, or taking place underground; as, an *underground* passage. **2** Secret; as, an *underground* political movement. — \-ˌgrau̇nd\ *n.* **1** A space under the surface of the ground; especially, an underground railway. **2** A secret political movement or group; especially, an organized body working in secret to overthrow those in power.

un·der·growth \'ənd-r-ˌgrōth\ *n.* Underbrush.

un·der·hand \'ənd-r-ˌhand\ *adj.* **1** Throwing or thrown with the hand swinging downward and kept lower than the shoulder; as, an *underhand* toss of a ball. **2** Unfairly deceptive or sly; as, to win a game by *underhand* means. — *adv.* **1** With an underhand motion; as, to throw a ball *underhand.* **2** Secretly; by fraud; underhandedly.

un·der·hand·ed \'ənd-r-'han-dəd\ *adj.* Underhand; deceitful. — **un·der·hand·ed·ly,** *adv.*

un·der·lie \ˌənd-r-'lī\ *v.;* **un·der·lay** \-'lā\; **un·der·lain** \-'lān\; **un·der·ly·ing** \-'lī-ing\. **1** To be situated under. **2** To be at the basis of; to form the base of; as, *underlying* principles.

un·der·line \'ənd-r-ˌlīn, ˌənd-r-'līn\ *v.;* **un·der·lined; un·der·lin·ing. 1** To draw a line under; to underscore. **2** To emphasize.

un·der·ly·ing \'ənd-r-ˌlī-ing\ *adj.* Fundamental; basic; as, *underlying* principles.

un·der·mine \ˌənd-r-'mīn\ *v.;* **un·der·mined; un·der·min·ing. 1** To dig out or wear away the supporting earth beneath; as, to *undermine* a wall. **2** To weaken or wear away secretly or gradually; as, to *undermine* a government.

un·der·neath \ˌənd-r-'nēth\ *adv.* or *prep.* Beneath; below; under.

un·der·nour·ish \ˌənd-r-'nər-ish, -'nə-rish\ *v.* To supply with insufficient nourishment. — **un·der·nour·ish·ment** \-mənt\ *n.*

un·der·part \'ənd-r-ˌpärt, -ˌpårt\ *n.* A part lying on the lower side, especially of a bird or animal.

un·der·pass \'ənd-r-ˌpas\ *n.* A passage underneath, as one for a road passing under a railroad.

un·der·pay \ˌənd-r-'pā\ *v.;* **un·der·paid** \-'pād\; **un·der·pay·ing.** To pay too little.

un·der·pin·ning \'ənd-r-ˌpin-ing\ *n.* **1** Supporting material worked in beneath a wall already constructed. **2** [in the plural] A person's legs.

un·der·priv·i·leged \ˌənd-r-'priv-l(-)ijd\ *adj.* Having fewer privileges than others; poor.

un·der·rate \ˌənd-r-'(r)āt\ *v.;* **un·der·rat·ed; un·der·rat·ing.** To rate or value too low.

un·der·score \'ənd-r-ˌskōr, -ˌskȯr\ *v.;* **un·der·scored; un·der·scor·ing. 1** To underline; as, to *underscore* all the nouns in a sentence. **2** To emphasize. — *n.* An underscoring; an underscored line.

un·der·sea \ˌənd-r-'sē, 'ənd-r-ˌsē\ *adj.* Being, carried on, or used beneath the surface of the sea; as, *undersea* life. — \'ənd-r-'sē\ *adv.* Underseas.

un·der·seas \'ənd-r-'sēz\ *adv.* Beneath the surface of the sea.

un·der·sec·re·tary \ˌənd-r-'sek-rə-ˌter-ē\ *n.; pl.* **un·der·sec·re·tar·ies.** A subordinate secretary; especially, an assistant secretary immediately under the principal secretary of a department of government.

un·der·sell \ˌənd-r-'sel\ *v.;* **un·der·sold** \-'sōld\; **un·der·sell·ing.** To sell cheaper than is usual.

un·der·shirt \'ənd-r-ˌshərt\ *n.* A close fitting shirt worn as an undergarment.

un·der·shoot \ˌənd-r-'shüt\ *v.;* **un·der·shot** \-'shät\; **un·der·shoot·ing.** To shoot short of a mark, as an airplane making a landing.

un·der·shot \'ənd-r-ˌshät\ *adj.* **1** Having the lower front teeth projecting beyond the upper ones when the mouth is closed, as in the bulldog. **2** Moved by water passing beneath, as a water wheel.

un·der·side \'ənd-r-ˌsīd\ *n.* The side underneath.

un·der·sign \ˌənd-r-'sīn\ *v.* To write one's name at the end or foot of, as a letter. — **the un·der·signed** \'ənd-r-ˌsīnd\. The signer or signers.

un·der·sized \'ənd-r-'sīzd\ *adj.* Smaller than is usual or standard.

un·der·skirt \'ənd-r-ˌskərt\ *n.* A petticoat.

un·der·slung \'ənd-r-ˌsləng\ *adj.* Suspended below the axles — used of the frame of an automobile.

undersold. Past tense and past part. of *undersell.*

un·der·stand \ˌənd-r-'stand\ *v.;* **un·der·stood** \-'stu̇d\; **un·der·stand·ing. 1** To grasp the meaning of; to comprehend. **2** To have thorough acquaintance with; as, to *understand* the arts. **3** To gather; to infer. I *understand* that he will come today. **4** To interpret; to explain; as, to *understand* the letter to be a refusal. **5** To have a sympathetic attitude. **6** To accept as settled. It is *understood* that I shall pay. **7** In grammar, to supply in thought as if present. The object of a verb may be *understood* rather than expressed.

un·der·stand·a·ble \ˌənd-r-'stan-dəb-l\ *adj.* Capable of being readily understood. — **un·der·stand·a·bly** \-də-blē\ *adv.*

un·der·stand·ing \ˌənd-r-'stan-ding\ *n.* **1** Knowledge and ability to apply judgment; intelligence; as, to act according to one's *understanding* of one's duty. **2** Ability to comprehend and judge; as, a man of *understanding.* **3** Agreement of opinion; a mutual agreement; as, an *understanding* between France and England over trade. — *adj.* **1** Knowing; intelligent. **2** Sympathetic; tolerant. — **un·der·stand·ing·ly,** *adv.*

un·der·state \ˌənd-r-'stāt\ *v.;* **un·der·stat·ed; un·der·stat·ing.** To state less strongly than might truthfully have been done. — **un·der·state·ment,** *n.*

understood. Past tense and past part. of *understand.*

un·der·study \'ənd-r-ˌstəd-ē\ *v.;* **un·der·stud·ied** \-ēd\; **un·der·stud·y·ing.** To study another actor's part in order to be his substitute in an emergency. — *n.; pl.* **un·der·stud·ies.** One that understudies.

un·der·take \ˌənd-r-'tāk\ *v.;* **un·der·took** \-'tu̇k\; **un·der·tak·en** \-'tāk-n\; **un·der·tak·ing. 1** To take upon oneself as a task; to enter upon; as, to *undertake* a journey. **2** To agree to perform; to contract; as, to *undertake* to deliver a package. **3** To guarantee; to promise.

un·der·tak·er \'ənd-r-ˌtāk-r\ *n.* A person whose business is to prepare the dead for burial and to take charge of funerals.

un·der·tak·ing \ˌənd-r-'tāk-ing, 'ənd-r-ˌtāk-\ *n.* **1** The act of a person who undertakes anything. **2** The business of an undertaker. **3** Anything undertaken. **4** A promise; a guarantee.

un·der·tone \'ənd-r-ˌtōn\ *n.* **1** A low or subdued tone. **2** A subdued color, as one seen through and modifying another color.

undertook. Past tense of *undertake.*

un·der·tow \'ənd-r-ˌtō\ *n.* A current beneath the surface of the water that moves away from or along the shore while the surface water above it moves toward the shore.

un·der·val·ue \ˌənd-r-'val-(ˌ)yü, -yu̇\ *v.;* **un·der·val·ued; un·der·val·u·ing. 1** To value below the real worth. **2** To set little value on. — **un·der·val·u·a·tion** \-ˌval-yə-'wāsh-n\ *n.*

un·der·wa·ter \'ənd-r-ˌwȯt-r, -ˌwät-r\ *adj.* Being, done, or used below the surface of the water.

un·der·wear \'ənd-r-ˌwar, -ˌwer\ *n.* Underclothes.

un·der·weight \ˌənd-r-'wāt\ *n.* Weight below normal or required weight. — *adj.* Weighing less than is normal or required.

underwent. Past tense of *undergo.*

un·der·wood \'ənd-r-ˌwu̇d\ *n.* Underbrush.

un·der·world \'ənd-r-ˌwərld\ *n.* **1** The earth. **2** In some legends, the place of departed souls. **3** The side of the globe opposite to oneself. **4** The lawless people; especially, the criminals in large cities.

un·der·write \ˌənd-r-'(r)īt\ *v.;* **un·der·wrote** \-'(r)ōt\; **un·der·writ·ten** \-'(r)it-n\; **un·der·writ·ing** \-'(r)īt-ing\. **1** To write under something else. **2** To insure, as life or property, by setting one's name to an insurance policy. **3** To agree to purchase on a fixed date, as an issue of bonds. **4** To agree to pay the cost or any unpaid balance. — **un·der·writ·er** \'ənd-r-ˌ(r)īt-r\ *n.*

un·de·sir·a·ble \ˌən-dē-'zīr-əb-l\ *adj.* **1** Not desirable. **2** Objectionable, as on grounds of past record or present behavior. — *n.* An undesirable person. — **un·de·sir·a·bly** \-ə-blē\ *adv.*

undid. Past tense of *undo.*

un·dis·tin·guished \ˌən-dis-'ting-gwisht\ *adj.* Not distinguished; ordinary; commonplace.

un·do \'ən-'dü\ *v.;* **un·did** \-'did\ **un·done** \-'dən\; **un·do·ing** \-'dü-ing\. **1** To open; to unfasten; as, to *undo* a knot; to *undo* a parcel. **2** To bring to nothing; to reverse, as work that has been done; to make as if never done; to destroy. **3** To bring to ruin. — **un·do·er** \-'dü-ər\ *n.*

un·do·ing \'ən-'dü-ing\ *n.* **1** A reversal of what is done. **2** Ruin or a cause of ruin.

un·done \'ən-'dən\ *adj.* **1** Not performed; not finished; neglected. **2** Ruined; brought to nothing.

un·doubt·ed \'ən-'dau̇t-əd\ *adj.* Not doubted; not called into question; certain; as, *undoubted* proof of guilt.

un·doubt·ed·ly \'ən-'dau̇t-əd-lē\ *adv.* Beyond doubt; certainly.

un·dreamed-of \'ən-'drēmd-ˌəv, -ˌäv\ or **un·dreamt-of** \'ən-'drem(p)t-\ *adj.* Not dreamed of; not thought of; as, *undreamed-of* dangers.

☞ See **un-**, *not,* and following note.

un·de·served
un·de·serv·ing
un·des·ig·nat·ed
un·de·vel·oped
un·di·gest·ed
un·dig·ni·fied
un·di·lut·ed
un·di·min·ished
un·dimmed
un·dip·lo·mat·ic
un·di·rect·ed
un·dis·ci·plined
un·dis·cov·ered
un·dis·guised
un·dis·mayed
un·dis·put·ed
un·dis·solved
un·dis·tin·guish·a·ble
un·dis·turbed
un·di·vid·ed
un·do·mes·ti·cat·ed
un·dou·bled
un·dra·mat·ic
un·draped

un·dress \'ən-'dres\ *v.* To take off clothes or covering; to disrobe. — *n.* **1** Loose, informal clothing. **2** Ordinary dress as contrasted with full dress.

un·due \'ən-'dü, -'dyü\ *adj.* **1** Not yet owed. **2** Not right; not lawful or legal. **3** Not agreeing with a rule or standard; excessive; extreme; as, *undue* harshness. — **un·du·ly** \'ən-'dü-lē, -'dyü-\ *adv.*

un·du·lant \'ənj-l-ənt, 'ən-dyə-lənt, 'ənd-l-ənt\ *adj.* Undulating.

undulant fever. A long-persisting bacterial disease characterized by an undulating fever, profuse perspiration, and pain and swelling in the joints.

un·du·late \'ənj-l-ˌāt, 'ən-dyə-ˌlāt, 'ənd-l-ˌāt\ *v.;* **un·du·lat·ed; un·du·lat·ing. 1** To move in waves; to rise and fall or swing to and fro with a wavy motion. **2** To show a wavy surface. — **un·du·la·tion** \ˌənj-l-'āsh-n, ˌən-dyə-'lāsh-n, ˌənd-l-'āsh-n\ *n.*

un·dy·ing \'ən-'dī-ing\ *adj.* Not dying; unending; eternal; immortal.

un·earth \'ən-'ərth\ *v.* **1** To drive or draw from the earth; to dig up; as, to *unearth* buried treasure. **2** To bring to light; to discover, as a secret.

un·earth·ly \'ən-'ərth-lē\ *adj.* **1** Not of or belonging to the earth. **2** Supernatural; weird; terrifying.

un·easy \'ən-'ē-zē\ *adj.;* **un·eas·i·er; un·eas·i·est. 1** Not easy in manner; awkward; as, to be *uneasy* among strangers. **2** Restless; disturbed by pain or worry. Rain made the crew *uneasy.* — **un·eas·i·ly** \-'ēz-l(-)ē\ *adv.* — **un·eas·i·ness** \-'ē-zē-nəs\ *n.*

un·em·ploy·a·ble \ˌən-im-'plȯi-əb-l\ *adj.* Not capable of being employed; especially, not capable of holding a job. — *n.* An unemployable person.

un·em·ploy·ment \ˌən-im-'plȯi-mənt\ *n.* The state of being out of work; lack of employment.

un·end·ing \'ən-'en-ding\ *adj.* Having no ending; endless. — **un·end·ing·ly,** *adv.*

un·e·qual \'ən-'ēk-wəl\ *adj.* **1** Not alike, as in size, amount, number, or value. **2** Not well balanced or matched. **3** Irregular. **4** Not adequate; insufficient; as, to be *unequal* to a task. — **un·e·qual·ly** \-wə-lē\ *adv.*

un·e·qualed or **un·e·qualled** \'ən-'ēk-wəld\ *adj.* Unmatched; unparalleled; surpassing.

un·e·quiv·o·cal \ˌən-ē-'kwiv-ək-l\ *adj.* Not doubtful or ambiguous; clear. — **un·e·quiv·o·cal·ly** \-ək-l(-)ē\ *adv.*

un·err·ing \'ən-'ər-ing, -'er-\ *adj.* Making no errors; certain; unfailing. — **un·err·ing·ly,** *adv.*

un·e·vent·ful \ˌən-ē-'vent-fəl\ *adj.* Not eventful; lacking interesting or noteworthy happenings; as, an *uneventful* vacation. — **un·e·vent·ful·ly** \-fə-lē\ *adv.*

un·ex·am·pled \ˌən-ig-'zamp-ld\ *adj.* Having no precedent or parallel; having no similar case.

un·ex·cep·tion·a·ble \ˌən-ik-'sepsh-n(-)əb-l\ *adj.* Not liable to any exception or objection; beyond criticism. — **un·ex·cep·tion·a·bly** \-n(-)ə-blē\ *adv.*

un·ex·cep·tion·al \ˌən-ik-'sepsh-n(-)əl\ *adj.* Not exceptional; usual; ordinary. — **un·ex·cep·tion·al·ly** \-n(-)ə-lē\ *adv.*

un·ex·pect·ed \ˌən-iks-'pek-təd\ *adj.* Not expected; sudden; as, an *unexpected* guest. — **un·ex·pect·ed·ly,** *adv.*

un·fail·ing \'ən-'fā-ling\ *adj.* **1** Not flagging; not decreasing; not yielding; as, *unfailing* support. **2** Inexhaustible; as, an *unfailing* supply. **3** Infallible. — **un·fail·ing·ly,** *adv.*

un·fair \'ən-'far, -'fer\ *adj.* **1** Using or involving trickery or deceit; dishonest. **2** Not just or reasonable. — **un·fair·ly,** *adv.*

un·fa·mil·iar \ˌən-fə-'mil-yər\ *adj.* **1** Not well known; strange; as, *unfamiliar* customs; an *unfamiliar* face. **2** Not acquainted or well acquainted; as, *unfamiliar* with foreign customs. — **un·fa·mil·iar·i·ty** \-ˌmil-'yar-ət-ē, -ˌmil-ē-'ar-\ *n.*

un·fas·ten \'ən-'fas-n\ *v.;* **un·fas·tened; un·fas·ten·ing** \-n(-)ing\. To make or become loose; to undo; to detach; to untie.

un·feel·ing \'ən-'fē-ling\ *adj.* Lacking feeling; especially, harsh; cruel; as, an *unfeeling* master. — **un·feel·ing·ly,** *adv.*

un·feigned \'ən-'fānd\ *adj.* Not feigned; not hypocritical; genuine. — **un·feign·ed·ly** \-'fā-nəd-lē\ *adv.*

un·fet·ter \'ən-'fet-r\ *v.* To remove the fetters from; to free from bonds.

un·fit \'ən-'fit\ *adj.* Not fit; not fitted.

un·fit \'ən-'fit\ *v.;* **un·fit·ted; un·fit·ting.** To make unfit; to disable; to disqualify.

un·fledged \'ən-'flejd\ *adj.* Not fledged, or feathered; not fully developed; immature.

un·fold \'ən-'fōld\ *v.* **1** To open the folds of; to open up, as a newspaper. **2** To lay open to view; to reveal; to disclose; as, to *unfold* a plan. **3** To open

☞ See **un-**, *not*, and following note.

un·dressed
un·drink·a·ble
un·du·ti·ful
un·dyed
un·earned
un·eat·a·ble
un·eat·en
un·ec·o·nom·i·cal
un·ed·u·cat·ed
un·e·mo·tion·al
un·em·pha·sized
un·em·phat·ic
un·em·ployed
un·en·closed
un·en·dorsed
un·en·dur·a·ble
un·en·force·a·ble
un·en·forced
un·en·gaged
un·en·joy·a·ble
un·en·ter·pris·ing
un·en·vi·a·ble
un·e·quipped
un·es·sen·tial
un·eth·i·cal
un·e·ven
un·ex·ag·ger·at·ed
un·ex·celled
un·ex·cit·ed
un·ex·cit·ing
un·ex·pe·ri·enced
un·ex·pired
un·ex·plain·a·ble
un·ex·plained
un·ex·plod·ed
un·ex·plored
un·ex·posed
un·ex·pressed
un·ex·pres·sive
un·fad·ing
un·faith·ful
un·fal·ter·ing
un·fash·ion·a·ble
un·fath·om·a·ble
un·fath·omed
un·fa·vor·a·ble
un·feath·ered
un·fed
un·fed·er·at·ed
un·felt
un·fenced
un·fer·ment·ed
un·fer·ti·lized
un·fet·tered
un·fil·i·al
un·filled
un·fil·tered
un·fin·ish·a·ble
un·fin·ished
un·flag·ging
un·flat·ter·ing
un·fla·vored
un·flinch·ing

or become developed; as, buds *unfold* in the sun.

un·for·get·ta·ble \ˌən-fər-ˈget-əb-l\ *adj.* Not to be forgotten; lasting in memory. — **un·for·get·ta·bly** \-ə-blē\ *adv.*

un·formed \ˈən-ˈfȯrmd\ *adj.* Not regularly formed; shapeless.

un·for·tu·nate \ˈən-ˈfȯrch-n(-)ət\ *adj.* Not fortunate; unlucky. — *n.* An unfortunate person. — **un·for·tu·nate·ly**, *adv.*

un·found·ed \ˈən-ˈfaůn-dəd\ *adj.* Lacking foundation; baseless; as, an *unfounded* accusation.

un·friend·ly \ˈən-ˈfren (d)lē\ *adj.* **1** Not friendly; not kind; hostile; as, an *unfriendly* greeting. **2** Not favorable.

un·fruit·ful \ˈən-ˈfrüt-fəl\ *adj.* **1** Not bearing fruit or offspring. **2** Not producing a desired result; not resulting in gain; as, *unfruitful* efforts. — **un·fruit·ful·ly** \-fə-lē\ *adv.*

un·furl \ˈən-ˈfərl\ *v.* To loose from a furled state; to unfold; to open or spread; as, to *unfurl* sails; to *unfurl* a flag.

un·gain·ly \ˈən-ˈgān-lē\ *adj.* Clumsy; awkward, as, an *ungainly* walk. — *adv.* In an ungainly manner.

un·god·ly \ˈən-ˈgäd-lē, -ˈgȯd-\ *adj.* Not godly; wicked; sinful.

un·gov·ern·a·ble \ˈən-ˈgəv-r-nəb-l\ *adj.* Not capable of being governed, ruled, or restrained; unbridled; as, an *ungovernable* temper. — **un·gov·ern·a·bly** \-nə-blē\ *adv.*

un·grate·ful \ˈən-ˈgrāt-fəl\ *adj.* **1** Not thankful for favors. **2** Not pleasing; disagreeable. — **un·grate·ful·ly** \-fə-lē\ *adv.*

un·ground·ed \ˈən-ˈgraůn-dəd\ *adj.* **1** Unfounded; baseless. **2** Not instructed or informed.

un·gual \ˈəng-gwəl\ *adj.* Of or relating to, like, or bearing a nail, claw, or hoof.

un·guent \ˈəng-gwənt, ˈənj-nt\ *n.* An ointment for sores or burns; a salve.

un·gu·la \ˈəng-gyə-lə\ *n.; pl.* **un·gu·las** \-ləz\ or **un·gu·lae** \-ˌlē\. **1** A hoof. **2** A claw or nail.

un·gu·late \ˈəng-gyə-lət\ *adj.* Having hoofs. — *n.* A hoofed mammal.

un·hand \ˈən-ˈhand\ *v.* To let go; to let out of one's grasp.

un·handy \ˈən-ˈhan-dē\ *adj.;* **un·hand·i·er**; **un·hand·i·est.** Not skillful; clumsy; awkward.

un·hap·py \ˈən-ˈhap-ē\ *adj.;* **un·hap·pi·er**; **un·hap·pi·est.** **1** Not fortunate; unlucky; as, the result of an *unhappy* mistake. **2** Not cheerful; sad; miserable. **3** Inappropriate; as, an *unhappy* color combination. — **un·hap·pi·ly** \ˈən-ˈhap-l-ē\ *adv.* — **un·hap·pi·ness** \-ˈhap-ē-nəs, -ə-nəs\ *n.*

un·har·ness \ˈən-ˈhär-nəs, -ˈhȧr-\ *v.* **1** To remove the harness from, as a horse; to free from harness or gear. **2** To disarm; to take off armor.

un·heard \ˈən-ˈhərd\ *adj.* Not heard; not granted a hearing.

un·heard-of \ˈən-ˈhərd-ˌəv, -ˌäv\ *adj.* Not heard of; not known to exist; having no precedent.

un·hinge \ˈən-ˈhinj\ *v.;* **un·hinged**; **un·hing·ing.** **1** To take from the hinges, as a door. **2** To make unstable; to unsettle, as, one's mind; as, *unhinged* by grief.

un·hitch \ˈən-ˈhich\ *v.* To free from being hitched; to unfasten; to loose.

un·ho·ly \ˈən-ˈhō-lē\ *adj.;* **un·ho·li·er**; **un·ho·li·est.** Not holy; profane; wicked.

un·hook \ˈən-ˈhůk\ *v.* To loose or become loosed from a hook.

un·horse \ˈən-ˈhȯrs\ *v.;* **un·horsed**; **un·hors·ing.** **1** To throw or cause to fall from a horse; as, an *unhorsed* rider. **2** To take a horse from; as, to *unhorse* a carriage.

uni·cam·er·al \ˌyü-nə-ˈkam-r(-)əl\ *adj.* Having a single house or chamber, as a legislature.

uni·cel·lu·lar \ˌyü-nə-ˈsel-yəl-r\ *adj.* In biology, having or consisting of a single cell; one-celled.

uni·corn \ˈyü-nə-ˌkȯrn\ *n.* A fabulous animal resembling a horse with one horn growing from its forehead.

unicorn

uni·fi·ca·tion \ˌyü-nə-fə-ˈkāsh-n\ *n.* The act, process, or result of unifying; the state of being unified.

uni·form \ˈyü-nə-ˌfȯrm\ *adj.* **1** Having always the same form, manner, or degree; not varying or variable; not changing; as, a *uniform* temperature. **2** Of the same form with others; alike; as, buildings of *uniform* style. — *n.* A uniform dress worn by persons in the same service. — *v.* To clothe with a uniform. — **uni·form·ly**, *adv.*

uni·form·i·ty \ˌyü-nə-ˈfȯr-mət-ē\ *n.* The state of being uniform; absence of variation; sameness.

uni·fy \ˈyü-nə-ˌfī\ *v.;* **uni·fied** \-ˌfīd\; **uni·fy·ing.** To become or cause to become one; to unite.

uni·lat·er·al \ˌyü-nə-ˈlat-r-əl, -ˈla-trəl\ *adj.* **1** Of, on, having, or affecting one side only. **2** Done, made, or undertaken by one of two or more parties. — **uni·lat·er·al·ly** \-ˈlat-r-ə-lē, -ˈla-trə-lē\ *adv.*

☞ See **un-**, *not*, and following note.	**un·for·ti·fied**	**un·grace·ful**	**un·hard·ened**	**un·hes·i·tat·ing**
un·forced	**un·fre·quent·ed**	**un·gra·cious**	**un·harmed**	**un·hin·dered**
un·fore·seen	**un·ful·filled**	**un·grad·ed**	**un·har·nessed**	**un·hon·ored**
un·for·est·ed	**un·fur·nished**	**un·gram·mat·i·cal**	**un·hatched**	**un·hoped-for**
un·for·giv·a·ble	**un·gen·er·ous**	**un·grudg·ing**	**un·health·ful**	**un·hur·ried**
un·for·giv·en	**un·gen·tle**	**un·guard·ed**	**un·healthy**	**un·hurt**
un·for·giv·ing	**un·gen·tle·man·ly**	**un·hal·lowed**	**un·heed·ed**	**un·hy·gi·en·ic**
un·for·got·ten	**un·glazed**	**un·ham·pered**	**un·heed·ing**	**un·i·den·ti·fied**
	un·gov·erned	**un·hand·some**	**un·her·ald·ed**	**un·id·i·o·mat·ic**

un·im·peach·a·ble \ˌən im-ˈpē-chəb-l\ *adj.* Not to be called in question; not liable to accusation; blameless; as, a man of *unimpeachable* loyalty. — **un·im·peach·a·bly** \-chə-blē\ *adv.*

un·ion \ˈyün-yən\ *n.* **1** The uniting of two or more things into one, or the state of being so united; combination; junction. **2** Something formed by combination; a confederation; a league. **3** A device serving as an emblem of union, as on a national flag. **4** A labor union. **5** Any device for connecting machine parts; a coupling for pipes. — **the Union.** The United States of America.

un·ion·ism \ˈyün-yə-ˌniz-m\ *n.* Belief in the principles of union or a union.

un·ion·ist \ˈyün-yə-nəst\ *n.* **1** One who advocates or promotes union. **2** A supporter of a labor union. **3** [with a capital] A supporter of the federal union of the United States, as in the Civil War.

un·ion·ize \ˈyün-yə-ˌnīz\ *v.;* **un·ion·ized; un·ion·iz·ing. 1** To form into a union. **2** To cause to become a member of a labor union. — **un·ion·i·za·tion**\ˌyün-yə-nə-ˈzāsh-n\ *n.*

union jack. 1 A flag consisting of that part of a national flag that signifies union, as a United States flag consisting of a blue field with one white star for each state. **2** [usually with capitals] The national flag of the United Kingdom.

unique \yü-ˈnēk\ *adj.* **1** Being the only one of its kind. **2** Very unusual; notable. — **unique·ly,** *adv.*

uni·sex·u·al \ˌyü-nə-ˈsek-shə-wəl, -ˈseksh-l\ *adj.* Having only male or only female reproductive organs.

uni·son \ˈyü-nəs-n, -nəz-n\ *n.* **1** Sameness or identity in pitch; a pitch level common to more than one voice. **2** The condition of being tuned or sounded at the same pitch; as, to sing in *unison* rather than in harmony. **3** Exact agreement; accord; as, all are in *unison* on the next move.

unit \ˈyü-nət\ *n.* **1** A single thing or person, or a smaller group taken as a member of a larger group. **2** In mathematics, the least whole number; one. **3** A definite amount, quantity, or value taken as a standard of measurement. The franc is the *unit* of French money. **4** A basic number of lessons to be studied or amount of work to be done.

uni·tary \ˈyü-nə-ˌter-ē\ *adj.* **1** Of or relating to a unit or units. **2** Of or relating to unity. **3** Having the character of a unit; not divided.

unite \yü-ˈnīt\ *v.;* **unit·ed; unit·ing. 1** To put or join together so as to make one; to combine. **2** To join, especially by a legal or moral bond, as nations by a treaty. **3** To join in an act; as, to *unite* in prayer. — **unit·er** \-ˈnīt-r\ *n.*

uni·ty \ˈyü-nət-ē\ *n.; pl.* **uni·ties. 1** The state of being one; singleness; oneness. **2** Concord; harmony. **3** Continuity without change; as, *unity* of purpose and effort. **4** Any definite mathematical quantity or combination of quantities taken as one or for which 1 is made to stand in a calculation. **5** Reference of all the parts of an artistic or literary composition to a single main idea; singleness of effect or style.

uni·valve \ˈyü-nə-ˌvalv\ *adj.* Also **uni·valved** \-ˌvalvd\. Having one valve only. — *n.* A univalve mollusk shell or a mollusk having such a shell.

uni·ver·sal \ˌyü-nə-ˈvərs-l\ *adj.* **1** Including or affecting all; unlimited; general; as, a *universal* rule. **2** Present everywhere; as, *universal* as the air. **3** Total; entire; as, the *universal* world. **4** Used or being for use among all; as, a *universal* language. — **uni·ver·sal·ly** \-ˈvərs-l(-)ē\ *adv.*

uni·ver·sal·i·ty \ˌyü-nə-(ˌ)vər-ˈsal-ət-ē\ *n.; pl.* **uni·ver·sal·i·ties.** The quality or state of being universal, as in range, occurrence, or appeal.

universal joint or **universal coupling.** A joint or coupling permitting swiveling or turning at many angles, as in the ball-and-socket joint.

uni·verse \ˈyü-nə-ˌvərs\ *n.* [From medieval French *univers,* there borrowed from Latin *universum,* where it is derived from the neuter of *universus* meaning "entire", "whole", literally, "turned into one".] All created things, including earth and stars, viewed as one system or whole.

uni·ver·si·ty \ˌyü-nə-ˈvər-sət-ē, -ˈvərs-tē\ *n.; pl.* **uni·ver·si·ties.** An institution of higher learning authorized to grant degrees in various special fields, as law, medicine, and theology, as well as in the arts and sciences generally.

un·kempt \ˈən-ˈkem(p)t, ˌən-\ *adj.* **1** Not combed; disheveled; uncared for. **2** Rough; not refined.

un·know·a·ble \ˈən-ˈnō-əb-l\ *adj.* That cannot be known or comprehended.

un·known \ˈən-ˈnōn\ *adj.* **1** Not known; as, the *unknown* events of the future. **2** Strange; unfamiliar; as, *unknown* lands and peoples. — *n.* Someone that is unknown; that which is unknown.

un·lace \ˈən-ˈlās\ *v.;* **un·laced; un·lac·ing.** To loose by undoing a lacing; as, to *unlace* a shoe.

un·lash \ˈən-ˈlash\ *v.* To untie the lashing of.

un·latch \ˈən-ˈlach\ *v.* To release a latch in order to open; to leave a latch unset in order to make opening easier.

un·law·ful \ˈən-ˈlȯf-l\ *adj.* **1** Not lawful; contrary to law; illegal. **2** Illegitimate. — **un·law·ful·ly** \-ˈlȯf-l(-)ē\ *adv.*

un·learn \ˈən-ˈlərn\ *v.;* **un·learned** \-ˈlərnd\ or **un·learnt** \-ˈlərnt\; **un·learn·ing. 1** To put out of one's memory. **2** To learn the contrary of, as something

☞ See **un-**, *not*, and following note.
un·im·ag·i·na·ble
un·im·ag·i·na·tive
un·im·paired
un·im·por·tant
un·im·pres·sive
un·im·proved
un·in·formed
un·in·hab·it·a·ble
un·in·hab·it·ed
un·in·i·ti·at·ed
un·in·jured
un·in·spired
un·in·tel·li·gent
un·in·tel·li·gi·ble
un·in·ten·tion·al
un·in·ter·est·ed
un·in·ter·est·ing
un·in·ter·rupt·ed
un·in·vit·ed
un·in·vit·ing
un·joint·ed
un·just
un·jus·ti·fi·a·ble
un·jus·ti·fied
un·kind
un·kind·ly
un·knight·ly
un·know·ing
un·la·beled
un·la·belled
un·la·dy·like
un·laid
un·la·ment·ed

learned incorrectly; as, to *unlearn* poor habits.

un·learned, *adj.* **1** \'ən-'lər-nəd\ Not learned; uneducated; illiterate; as, a good but *unlearned* man. **2** \-'lərnd\ Not learned by study; not known; as, lessons *unlearned* by many. **3** Not learned by previous experience, as nest building by a bird.

un·leash \'ən-'lēsh\ *v.* To free from or as if from a leash; as, to *unleash* a dog. The storm *unleashed* its fury on the mountain.

un·less \(,)ən-'les\ *conj.* If not; except that. The project will fail *unless* everyone works hard.

un·let·tered \'ən-'let-rd\ *adj.* **1** Not educated. **2** Illiterate.

un·load \'ən-'lōd\ *v.* **1** To take the load or cargo from, as a ship. **2** To remove the charge from, as a gun. **3** To relieve from anything troublesome; as, to *unload* one's mind of worries.

un·lock \'ən-'läk\ *v.* **1** To unfasten by opening the lock of, as a chest. **2** To open; to undo. **3** To disclose; to reveal; as, to *unlock* the secrets of nature.

un·looked–for \'ən-'lu̇kt-,fȯr\ *adj.* Unexpected.

un·loose \'ən-'lüs\ *v.;* **un·loosed**; **un·loos·ing**. To loose; to let loose; to set free.

un·loos·en \'ən-'lüs-n\ *v.;* **un·loos·ened**; **un·loos·en·ing** \-n(-)ing\. To loosen; to unloose.

un·love·ly \'ən-'ləv-lē\ *adj.* Without charm or appeal; not amiable; disagreeable; as, an *unlovely* disposition.

un·man \'ən-'man\ *v.;* **un·manned**; **un·man·ning**. **1** To deprive of manly courage. **2** To deprive of men.

un·man·ner·ly \'ən-'man-r-lē\ *adj.* Rude; impolite. — *adv.* Rudely; discourteously.

un·mask \'ən-'mask\ *v.* **1** To strip of a mask or a disguise; to expose; as, to *unmask* a traitor. **2** To take off one's own disguise, as at a masquerade.

un·mean·ing \'ən-'mē-ning\ *adj.* Having no meaning; senseless.

un·men·tion·a·ble \'ən-'mench-n(-)əb-l\ *adj.* Not fit or proper to be talked about.

un·mis·tak·a·ble \,ən-mə-'stāk-əb-l\ *adj.* Not capable of being mistaken or misunderstood; clear; plain; evident. — **un·mis·tak·a·bly** \-ə-blē\ *adv.*

un·mit·i·gat·ed \'ən-'mit-ə-,gāt-əd\ *adj.* **1** Not softened or lessened. **2** Absolute; downright; as, an *unmitigated* liar; *unmitigated* impudence. — **un·mit·i·gat·ed·ly**, *adv.*

un·moor \'ən-'mu̇r, -'mōr\ *v.* To loose from moorings or anchorage.

un·mor·al \'ən-'mȯr-əl, -'mär-\ *adj.* Having no moral quality or relation; neither moral nor immoral. — **un·mor·al·ly** \-ə-lē\ *adv.*

un·moved \'ən-'müvd\ *adj.* **1** Not moved; remaining in the same place. **2** Firm; resolute; unshaken; as *unmoved* in his purpose. **3** Calm; not disturbed emotionally; as, seeming *unmoved* by the sad news.

un·nam·a·ble or **un·name·a·ble** \'ən-'nā-məb-l\ *adj.* That cannot be named or described.

un·nat·u·ral \'ən-'nach-r(-)əl\ *adj.* **1** Not being in accordance with nature or with a normal course of events. **2** Not being in accordance with normal feelings or behavior; abnormal. **3** Artificial; contrived. — **un·nat·u·ral·ly** \-r(-)ə-lē, -r-lē\ *adv.*

un·nerve \'ən-'nərv\ *v.;* **un·nerved**; **un·nerv·ing**. To deprive of nerve, courage, or self-control.

un·num·bered \'ən-'nəm-brd\ *adj.* **1** Not counted or estimated; innumerable. **2** Not marked with a number.

un·ob·tru·sive \,ən-əb-'trü-siv\ *adj.* Not obtrusive; not drawing attention; inconspicuous. — **un·ob·tru·sive·ly**, *adv.*

un·or·ga·nized \'ən-'ȯrg-n-,īzd\ *adj.* **1** Not brought into a well-ordered whole. **2** Not having the characteristics of a living organism. **3** Not organized into unions; as, *unorganized* labor.

un·pack \'ən-'pak\ *v.* **1** To separate and remove things packed. **2** To open and remove the contents of; as, to *unpack* a trunk.

un·paired \'ən-'pard, -'perd\ *adj.* Not matched or mated; especially, in zoology, having no mate on the opposite side.

un·par·al·leled \'ən-'par-ə-,leld, -ləld\ *adj.* Having no parallel or equal; unequaled; unmatched.

un·par·lia·men·ta·ry \'ən-,pärl-ə-'ment-r-ē, -,pärl-yə-, ,pȧrl-, -'men-trē\ *adj.* Contrary to parliamentary practice.

☞ See **un-**, *not*, and following note.	**un·lucky**	**un·milled**	**un·neigh·bor·ly**	**un·o·pened**
un·leav·ened	**un·man·age·a·ble**	**un·mind·ful**	**un·not·ed**	**un·op·posed**
un·li·censed	**un·man·ly**	**un·mixed**	**un·no·tice·a·ble**	**un·or·dained**
un·light·ed	**un·manned**	**un·mod·i·fied**	**un·no·ticed**	**un·o·rig·i·nal**
un·lik·a·ble	**un·mapped**	**un·mo·lest·ed**	**un·ob·jec·tion·a·ble**	**un·or·tho·dox**
un·like	**un·marked**	**un·mount·ed**	**un·o·blig·ing**	**un·os·ten·ta·tious**
un·like·a·ble	**un·mar·ried**	**un·mov·a·ble**	**un·ob·scured**	**un·owned**
un·like·ly	**un·mas·tered**	**un·move·a·ble**	**un·ob·serv·ant**	**un·paid**
un·lim·it·ed	**un·matched**	**un·muf·fled**	**un·ob·served**	**un·paint·ed**
un·lined	**un·meant**	**un·mu·si·cal**	**un·ob·serv·ing**	**un·pal·at·a·ble**
un·lit	**un·mea·sured**	**un·muz·zled**	**un·ob·struct·ed**	**un·par·don·a·ble**
un·lobed	**un·me·lo·di·ous**	**un·named**	**un·ob·tain·a·ble**	**un·pa·tri·ot·ic**
un·lov·a·ble	**un·men·tioned**	**un·nat·u·ral·ized**	**un·ob·tru·sive**	**un·paved**
un·loved	**un·mer·ci·ful**	**un·nav·i·ga·ble**	**un·oc·cu·pied**	**un·peo·pled**
un·lov·ing	**un·mer·it·ed**	**un·nec·es·sary**	**un·of·fend·ing**	**un·per·ceived**
	un·mil·i·tary	**un·ne·go·tia·ble**	**un·of·fi·cial**	**un·per·turbed**

un·pin \'ən-'pin\ *v.;* **un·pinned; un·pin·ning.** To remove a pin or pins from; to unfasten.

un·pleas·ant \'ən-'plez-nt\ *adj.* Not pleasant; disagreeable; distasteful. — **un·pleas·ant·ly,** *adv.* — **un·pleas·ant·ness,** *n.*

un·plumbed \'ən-'pləmd\ *adj.* **1** Not supplied with plumbing. **2** Not measured or tested with a plumb or plummet; not explored as to depth.

un·pop·u·lar \'ən-'päp-yəl-r\ *adj.* Not popular; viewed or received unfavorably; disliked by many people. — **un·pop·u·lar·i·ty** \-ˌpäp-yə-'lar-ət-ē\ *n.*

un·prec·e·dent·ed \'ən-'pres-ə-ˌdent-əd\ *adj.* Having no precedent or example; novel; new. — **un·prec·e·dent·ed·ly,** *adv.*

un·pre·tend·ing \ˌən-prē-'ten-ding\ *adj.* Not pretending; especially, unpretentious.

un·pre·ten·tious \ˌən-prē-'tench-əs\ *adj.* Not pretentious; not showy or pompous; simple; modest. — **un·pre·ten·tious·ly,** *adv.*

un·prin·ci·pled \'ən-'prin(t)s-əp-ld\ *adj.* Not having right moral principles; unscrupulous.

un·print·a·ble \'ən-'print-əb-l\ *adj.* Not fit to be printed.

un·pro·fes·sion·al \ˌən-prə-'fesh-n(-)əl\ *adj.* Not professional; especially, not conforming to the standards of one's profession. — **un·pro·fes·sion·al·ly** \-n(-)ə-lē\ *adv.*

un·qual·i·fied \'ən-'kwäl-ə-ˌfīd\ *adj.* **1** Not having necessary qualifications. **2** Not restricted or limited by reservations; as, to give one's *unqualified* approval. — **un·qual·i·fied·ly,** *adv.*

un·ques·tion·a·ble \'ən-'kwes-chə-nəb-l\ *adj.* **1** Not questionable; indisputable; as, an *unquestionable* title to property. **2** Acknowledged as beyond question or doubt; as, a man of *unquestionable* integrity. — **un·ques·tion·a·bly** \-nə-blē\ *adv.*

un·qui·et \'ən-'kwī-ət\ *adj.* Not quiet; agitated; disturbed; restless; uneasy.

un·quote \'ən-'kwōt\ *v.;* **un·quot·ed; un·quot·ing.** To end a quotation — used especially in reading aloud and in telegrams.

un·rav·el \'ən-'rav-l\ *v.;* **un·rav·eled** or **un·rav·elled; un·rav·el·ing** or **un·rav·el·ling** \-l(-)ing\. **1** To disentangle; to separate the threads of; as, to *unravel* a snarl. **2** To clear from some difficulty; to solve, as a mystery. **3** To become unraveled.

un·read \'ən-'red\ *adj.* **1** Not read. **2** Not well-read; uneducated.

un·rea·son·ing \'ən-'rēz-n(-)ing\ *adj.* Not reasoning; especially, not using or showing the use of reason as a guide or control; as, *unreasoning* fear.

un·reel \'ən-'rēl\ *v.* To unwind from a reel.

un·re·gen·er·ate \ˌən-rē-'jen-r-ət\ *adj.* Not reborn spiritually; not at peace with God; sinful; wicked.

un·re·lent·ing \ˌən-rē-'lent-ing\ *adj.* **1** Not yielding; hard; stern; severe. **2** Not letting up; not relaxing or slackening. — **un·re·lent·ing·ly,** *adv.*

un·re·mit·ting \ˌən-rē-'mit-ing\ *adj.* Not stopping· unceasing; persevering. — **un·re·mit·ting·ly,** *adv.*

un·re·served \ˌən-rē-'zərvd\ *adj.* **1** Not held in reserve; not kept back. **2** Having or showing no reserve in manner or speech. — **un·re·serv·ed·ly** \-'zər-vəd-lē\ *adv.*

un·rest \'ən-'rest\ *n.* **1** Lack of rest or repose. **2** A state of uneasiness or disquiet among a populace with an apparent danger of rebellion.

un·re·straint \ˌən-rē-'strānt\ *n.* Lack of restraint.

un·righ·teous \'ən-'rī-chəs\ *adj.* **1** Wicked; sinful. **2** Unjust. — **un·righ·teous·ly,** *adv.*

un·ri·valed or **un·ri·valled** \'ən-'rīv-ld\ *adj.* Having no rival; unequaled.

un·roll \'ən-'rōl\ *v.* **1** To open, as something that is rolled up. **2** To display; to disclose. **3** To become unrolled or spread out; to unfold. A great vista of snowcapped mountains *unrolled* before their eyes.

un·round·ed \'ən-'raůn-dəd\ *adj.* Not rounded; especially, of a speech sound, pronounced with the lips not rounded.

un·ruled \'ən-'rüld\ *adj.* **1** Not governed or controlled. **2** Not marked with lines; as, *unruled* paper.

un·ruly \'ən-'rü-lē\ *adj.* Not yielding readily to

☞ See **un-**, *not*, and following note.

un·pit·ied
un·pleas·ing
un·po·et·ic
un·pol·ished
un·prac·ti·cal
un·prac·ticed
un·pre·dict·a·ble
un·prej·u·diced
un·pre·med·i·tat·ed
un·pre·pared
un·pre·pos·sess·ing
un·pre·sent·a·ble
un·pressed
un·pre·vent·a·ble
un·priv·i·leged
un·pro·cur·a·ble
un·pro·duc·tive
un·pro·faned
un·prof·it·a·ble
un·pro·gres·sive
un·prom·is·ing
un·pro·nounce·a·ble
un·pro·nounced
un·pro·pi·tious
un·pro·tect·ed
un·proved
un·prov·en
un·pro·voked
un·pub·lished
un·pun·ished
un·quench·a·ble
un·ques·tioned
un·ques·tion·ing
un·quot·a·ble
un·raised
un·ranked
un·rat·ed
un·rat·i·fied
un·read·a·ble
un·ready
un·re·al
un·re·al·is·tic
un·re·al·ized
un·rea·son·a·ble
un·rea·soned
un·rec·og·niz·a·ble
un·rec·og·nized
un·rec·on·cil·a·ble
un·rec·on·ciled
un·re·cord·ed
un·re·deem·a·ble
un·re·deemed
un·re·fined
un·re·flect·ed
un·re·flect·ing
un·re·formed
un·reg·is·tered
un·reg·u·lat·ed
un·re·lat·ed
un·re·laxed
un·re·li·a·ble
un·re·lieved
un·re·li·gious
un·re·mem·bered
un·re·mu·ner·at·ed
un·re·mu·ner·a·tive
un·rent·ed
un·re·pent·ant
un·re·port·ed
un·rep·re·sent·a·tive
un·rep·re·sent·ed
un·re·pressed
un·re·proved
un·re·quit·ed
un·re·sist·ed
un·re·sist·ing
un·re·solved
un·re·spon·sive
un·rest·ful
un·re·strained
un·re·strict·ed
un·re·turned
un·re·vealed
un·re·ward·ed
un·re·ward·ing
un·rhymed
un·rimed
un·ripe
un·rip·ened
un·roast·ed
un·ro·man·tic
un·ruf·fled

rule or restraint; uncontrollable; as, an *unruly* temper; an *unruly* horse.

un·sad·dle \'ən-'sad-l\ *v.;* **un·sad·dled; un·sad·dling** \-l(-)ing\. **1** To take the saddle from. **2** To unhorse.

un·sa·vory \'ən-'sāv-r(-)ē\ *adj.* **1** Having little or no taste. **2** Having a bad taste or smell. **3** Morally offensive. — **un·sa·vor·i·ly** \-r(-)ə-lē\ *adv.*

un·say \'ən-'sā\ *v.;* **un·said** \-'sed\ ; **un·say·ing** \-'sā-ing\. To take back something said; to retract; to withdraw.

un·scathed \'ən-'skāthd\ *adj.* Completely unharmed; uninjured.

un·scram·ble \'ən-'skram-bl\ *v.;* **un·scram·bled; un·scram·bling** \-bl(-)ing\. To bring order into, or restore to the original order, something scrambled or mixed up; as, to *unscramble* a code message.

un·screw \'ən-'skrü\ *v.* **1** To draw the screw or screws from. **2** To loosen or withdraw by turning.

un·scru·pu·lous \'ən-'skrüp-yə-ləs\ *adj.* Not scrupulous; unprincipled. — **un·scru·pu·lous·ly,** *adv.*

un·seal \'ən-'sēl\ *v.* To break or remove the seal or sealing of; to open.

un·sea·son·a·ble \'ən-'sēz-n(-)əb-l\ *adj.* Not seasonable; happening or coming at the wrong time; untimely. — **un·sea·son·a·bly** \-n(-)ə-blē\ *adv.*

un·seat \'ən-'sēt\ *v.* **1** To throw from one's seat, as on horseback. **2** To remove from a seat; especially, to deprive of the right to sit as a member of a legislative body.

un·seem·ly \'ən-'sēm-lē\ *adj.* Not seemly; unbecoming; indecent. — *adv.* In an unseemly manner.

un·self·ish \'ən-'sel-fish\ *adj.* Not selfish; generous; altruistic. — **un·self·ish·ly,** *adv.*

un·set·tle \'ən-'set-l\ *v.;* **un·set·tled; un·set·tling** \-l(-)ing\. To move or loosen from a settled state; to displace; to disturb.

un·set·tled \'ən-'set-ld\ *adj.* **1** Not settled; not fixed, as in position or character; as, *unsettled* weather. **2** Disturbed; not calm; as, *unsettled* waters. **3** Not decided in mind; undetermined; as, to be *unsettled* what to do. **4** Not paid; as, an *unsettled* account. **5** Not occupied by settlers; as, an *unsettled* region.

un·shaped \'ən-'shāpt\ *adj.* Not shaped; shapeless or misshapen.

un·shap·en \'ən-'shāp-n\ *adj.* Unshaped. — **un·shap·en·ly,** *adv.*

un·sheathe \'ən-'shēth\ *v.;* **un·sheathed; un·sheath·ing.** To draw from or as from a sheath or scabbard; as, to *unsheathe* a sword.

un·ship \'ən-'ship\ *v.;* **un·shipped; un·ship·ping.** **1** To remove from a ship. **2** To remove, as an oar, from the position occupied when in use.

un·shod \'ən-'shäd\ *adj.* Not wearing shoes.

un·sight·ly \'ən-'sīt-lē\ *adj.* Unpleasant to the sight; ugly; as, an *unsightly* scar.

un·snarl \'ən-'snärl, -'snȧrl\ *v.* To remove snarls from; to untangle.

un·so·phis·ti·cat·ed \ˌən-sə-'fis-tə-ˌkāt-əd\ *adj.* **1** Not worldly-wise. **2** Simple; innocent. — For synonyms see *simple.* — **un·so·phis·ti·ca·tion** \-ˌfis-tə-'kāsh-n\ *n.*

un·sought \'ən-'sȯt\ *adj.* Not sought; not searched for or asked for; not obtained by effort; as, *unsought* honors.

un·sound \'ən-'saůnd\ *adj.* **1** Not healthy or whole. **2** Not valid or true; as, *unsound* reasoning. **3** Not mentally normal; not wholly sane; as, of *unsound* mind. **4** Not firmly made or fixed; as, an *unsound* scaffolding. **5** Of sleep, not profound; not deep and restful. — **un·sound·ly,** *adv.*

un·spar·ing \'ən-'spar-ing, -'sper-\ *adj.* **1** Not frugal or saving; lavish; generous. **2** Not merciful or forgiving.

un·speak·a·ble \'ən-'spēk-əb-l\ *adj.* **1** Impossible to express in words. **2** Extremely bad; as, *unspeakable* conduct. — **un·speak·a·bly** \-ə-blē\ *adv.*

un·step \'ən-'step\ *v.;* **un·stepped; un·step·ping.** To remove, as a mast, from its frame or block.

un·strap \'ən-'strap\ *v.;* **un·strapped; un·strap·ping.** To loose from a strap or straps.

un·string \'ən-'string\ *v.;* **un·strung** \-'strəng\; **un·string·ing** \-'string-ing\. **1** To remove the strings of, as a harp. **2** To take from a string, as beads.

un·strung \'ən-'strəng\ *adj.* **1** Having the strings loose or detached. **2** Nervously tired; anxious.

un·stud·ied \'ən-'stəd-ēd\ *adj.* **1** Not acquired by study. **2** Not studied or planned with a certain effect in mind; natural; unforced.

un·sub·stan·tial \ˌən-səb-'stanch-l\ *adj.* **1** Lacking substance; flimsy. **2** Having no physical or real

☞ See **un-**, *not*, and following note.

un·safe	**un·scent·ed**	**un·shake·a·ble**	**un·skimmed**	**un·spoiled**
un·said	**un·schol·ar·ly**	**un·shak·en**	**un·skinned**	**un·spoilt**
un·sal·a·ble	**un·schooled**	**un·shav·en**	**un·slaked**	**un·spo·ken**
un·sale·a·ble	**un·sci·en·tif·ic**	**un·shed**	**un·smil·ing**	**un·sports·man·like**
un·salt·ed	**un·screened**	**un·shel·tered**	**un·so·cia·ble**	**un·spot·ted**
un·sanc·ti·fied	**un·sea·soned**	**un·shorn**	**un·so·cial**	**un·sta·ble**
un·san·i·tary	**un·sea·wor·thy**	**un·shrink·a·ble**	**un·sold**	**un·stained**
un·sat·is·fac·to·ry	**un·see·ing**	**un·shrink·ing**	**un·sol·dier·ly**	**un·states·man·like**
un·sat·is·fied	**un·seen**	**un·sift·ed**	**un·so·lic·it·ed**	**un·steady**
un·sat·is·fy·ing	**un·seg·ment·ed**	**un·sink·a·ble**	**un·solv·a·ble**	**un·stint·ed**
un·sat·u·rat·ed	**un·sen·ti·men·tal**	**un·sis·ter·ly**	**un·solved**	**un·stint·ing**
un·scarred	**un·serv·ice·a·ble**	**un·skil·ful**	**un·sort·ed**	**un·stitched**
	un·shad·ed	**un·skilled**	**un·spec·i·fied**	**un·stressed**
	un·shak·a·ble	**un·skill·ful**	**un·spent**	**un·sub·dued**

existence; unreal. — **un·sub·stan·tial·ly** \-l(-)ē\ *adv.*

un·sung \'ən-'səng\ *adj.* **1** Not sung. **2** Not celebrated in song or verse; as, *unsung* heroes.

un·tan·gle \'ən-'tang-gl\ *v.;* **un·tan·gled**; **un·tan·gling** \-gl(-)ing\. **1** To remove a tangle or tangles from; to disentangle. **2** To straighten out or resolve, as something complex or confused.

un·taught \'ən-'tȯt\ *adj.* **1** Not taught; not instructed; ignorant. **2** Not gained through instruction; natural; spontaneous.

un·think·a·ble \'ən-'thingk-əb-l\ *adj.* Not to be thought of or considered as possible; as, cruelty *unthinkable* in a decent human being.

un·think·ing \'ən-'thingk-ing\ *adj.* Not thinking; especially, thoughtless; careless. — **un·think·ing·ly**, *adv.*

un·thought-of \'ən-'thȯt-ˌəv, -ˌäv\ *adj.* Not thought of; not considered; not imagined.

un·tie \'ən-'tī\ *v.;* **un·tied** \-'tīd\; **un·ty·ing** or **un·tie·ing** \-'tī-ing\. **1** To loosen, as something knotted; to undo. **2** To free from fastening or restraint; to let loose; as, to *untie* a horse.

un·til \(ˌ)ən-'til, (ˌ)ən-tl\ *prep.* Up to; up to the time of; as, to stay *until* evening. — *conj.* **1** Till such time as; up to the time that or when; as, to play outdoors *until* it grows dark. **2** So long or so far that; to the point or degree that; as, to cheer *until* one is hoarse.

un·time·ly \'ən-'tīm-lē\ *adj.* Not timely; done or happening at an unusual or improper time; unseasonable. — *adv.* Out of the natural or usual time; especially, too early or too soon; prematurely.

un·tir·ing \'ən-'tīr-ing\ *adj.* Not becoming or making tired; especially, tireless; unceasing; as, *untiring* efforts to help. — **un·tir·ing·ly**, *adv.*

un·to \'ən-tə, -tu̇, -tü\ *prep. Archaic.* To; — not used to introduce infinitives.

un·told \'ən-'tōld\ *adj.* **1** Not told; not revealed; as, *untold* secrets; a story yet *untold.* **2** Not counted; vast; numberless; as, *untold* resources.

un·touch·a·ble \'ən-'təch-əb-l\ *adj.* Forbidden to be touched. — *n.* A member of the lowest social class in India, whose touch is believed to defile members of higher castes.

un·to·ward \ˌən-'tōrd, -'tȯrd, -'twōrd, -'twȯrd, -tə-'wȯrd\ *adj.* **1** Difficult to manage; stubborn; willful; as, an *untoward* child. **2** Inconvenient; troublesome; awkward; as, an *untoward* accident; an *untoward* encounter. — **un·to·ward·ly**, *adv.*

un·tram·meled or **un·tram·melled** \'ən-'tram-ld\ *adj.* Not bound or fettered; not under restraint; free.

un·truth \'ən-'trüth\ *n.; pl.* **un·truths** \-'trü*th*z, -'trüths\. **1** Lack of truth; falsity. **2** A falsehood; a lie.

un·tu·tored \'ən-'tüt-rd, -'tyüt-\ *adj.* Untaught; unlearned; ignorant.

un·twine \'ən-'twīn\ *v.;* **un·twined**; **un·twin·ing.** To unwind; to disentangle.

un·twist \'ən-'twist\ *v.* To separate and open, as twisted threads; to turn in a reverse direction, as a twisted object.

untying. Present part. of *untie.*

un·ut·ter·a·ble \'ən-'ət-r-əb-l\ *adj.* **1** Not capable of being pronounced; unpronounceable. **2** Not capable of being put into words; inexpressible; — **un·ut·ter·a·bly** \-ə-blē\ *adv.*

un·var·nished \'ən-'vär-nisht, -'vȧr-\ *adj.* **1** Not varnished. **2** Not embellished; not heightened or exaggerated; plain; as, the *unvarnished* truth.

un·veil \'ən-'vāl\ *v.* **1** To remove a veil or covering from; to disclose; as, to *unveil* a statue. **2** To remove a veil; to reveal oneself.

un·voiced \'ən-'vȯist\ *adj.* **1** Not expressed; unspoken. **2** Pronounced with the vocal cords not vibrating.

un·war·rant·a·ble \'ən-'wȯr-ən-təb-l, -'wär-\ *adj.* Not justifiable; undefensible. — **un·war·rant·a·bly** \-tə-blē\ *adv.*

un·well \'ən-'wel\ *adj.* Sick; ill; ailing.

un·wept \'ən-'wept\ *adj.* **1** Not shed, as tears. **2** Not wept for or over; not mourned.

un·wieldy \'ən-'wēl-dē\ *adj.* Not easily handled or managed because of size or weight; awkward;

☞ See **un-**, *not*, and following note.

un·sub·stan·ti·at·ed
un·suc·cess·ful
un·suit·a·ble
un·suit·ed
un·sul·lied
un·su·per·vised
un·sup·port·a·ble
un·sup·port·ed
un·sure
un·sur·mount·a·ble
un·sur·pass·a·ble
un·sur·passed
un·sur·veyed
un·sus·cep·ti·ble
un·sus·pect·ed
un·sus·pect·ing
un·sus·pi·cious
un·sweet·ened
un·swept
un·swerv·ing
un·sym·met·ri·cal
un·sym·pa·thet·ic
un·sys·tem·at·ic
un·sys·tem·at·i·cal
un·tact·ful
un·taint·ed
un·tam·a·ble
un·tame·a·ble
un·tamed
un·tanned
un·tar·nished
un·tax·a·ble
un·taxed
un·teach·a·ble
un·ten·a·ble
un·ten·ant·ed
un·ter·ri·fied
un·test·ed
un·thank·ful
un·thrifty
un·ti·dy
un·tilled
un·ti·tled
un·touched
un·trained
un·tram·pled
un·trav·eled
un·trav·elled
un·treat·ed
un·tried
un·trimmed
un·trod
un·trod·den
un·trou·bled
un·true
un·trust·wor·thy
un·truth·ful
un·us·a·ble
un·used
un·u·su·al
un·ut·tered
un·vac·ci·nat·ed
un·val·ued
un·var·ied
un·var·y·ing
un·ven·ti·lat·ed
un·ver·i·fi·a·ble
un·ver·i·fied
un·versed
un·vis·it·ed
un·want·ed
un·war·like
un·war·rant·ed
un·wary
un·washed
un·watched
un·wa·ver·ing
un·weaned
un·wea·ried
un·wea·ry·ing
un·weath·ered
un·wed
un·wed·ded
un·wel·come
un·whole·some
un·wife·ly
un·will·ing
un·winc·ing

clumsy; cumbersome; as, an *unwieldy* tool.

un·wind \'ən-'wīnd\ *v.;* **un·wound** \-'waůnd\; **un·wind·ing.** **1** To undo something that is wound; to loose from coils. **2** To become unwound; to be capable of being unwound.

un·wise \'ən-'wīz\ *adj.* Not wise; foolish. — **un·wise·ly,** *adv.*

un·wit·ting \'ən-'wit-ing\ *adj.* Not knowing; unaware; not intentional. — **un·wit·ting·ly,** *adv.*

un·wont·ed \'ən-'wȯnt-əd, -'wōnt-\ *adj.* Not wonted; not common or usual; unaccustomed. — **un·wont·ed·ly,** *adv.*

un·wound \'ən-'waůnd\ *adj.* Past tense and past part. of *unwind.*

un·wrap \'ən-'rap\ *v.;* **un·wrapped; un·wrap·ping.** **1** To free from wrappings; to undo, as a parcel. **2** To become open or undone, as something wrapped or folded.

un·writ·ten \'ən-'rit-n\ *adj.* **1** Not written; not put in writing; oral; traditional; as, an *unwritten* law. **2** Not written on; blank.

un·yoke \'ən-'yōk\ *v.;* **un·yoked; un·yok·ing.** **1** To free from a yoke, as oxen. **2** To separate or disconnect.

un·zip \'ən-'zip\ *v.;* **un·zipped; un·zip·ping.** To open, as a slide fastener or something fastened with a slide fastener; as, to *unzip* a briefcase.

up \'əp\ *adv.* **1** From a lower to a higher position; in a direction opposite to down; as, to hold *up* one's hand. **2** Into an erect or upright position; as, to stand *up.* **3** Out of the ground or water; as, to pull *up* weeds. **4** To or toward an advanced or improved condition; as, to bring *up* a child; to come *up* in business. **5** Into sight, view, or knowledge. The missing ring turned *up.* **6** Into activity; as, to stir *up* a fire. **7** To or in search of the source; as, to follow *up* a clue. **8** To the end or limit; completely; as, to eat *up* all the food on the plate. The house burned *up.* **9** To pieces; as, to blow *up* a bridge. **10** Tightly; as, to seal *up* a package. **11** So as to approach, arrive at, overtake, or remain even with a certain person, point, or time; as, to catch *up* with a friend; to keep *up* with the times. **12** Aside; by; as, to lay *up* money. **13** In baseball, at bat. **14** In tennis, each; apiece. **15** Ahead. At the end the winner was three games *up.* — *prep.* **1** To, toward, or near the top of; as, to climb *up* a ladder. **2** Toward the source or the northern part of; as, to sail *up* a river. **3** Toward the higher or farther end of; as, to walk *up* a street. **4** Toward or in the interior of; as, to move *up* state. — *adj.* **1** Moving or inclining toward a higher level; as, an *up* grade. **2** Above the horizon, ground, or level. The corn is *up.* **3** Out of bed; as, *up* early in the morning. **4** In a higher or the highest position; as, *up* in one's class at school. **5** Well-informed; skilled; as, *up* on the latest news. **6** Ended. The time is *up.* **7** Advanced in amount or scale. Prices are *up.* **8** Ahead of one's opponent; as, to be one point *up* in a match. **9** Beginning action; in the process of contributing; as, *up* to some deviltry. — *n.* **1** An upward course or slope. **2** A rise in fortune; prosperity; as, to have one's *ups* and downs. — *v.;* **upped; up·ping.** **1** To raise or rouse oneself up. **2** To raise or lift up; to haul up. **3** To increase; to advance; as, to *up* the prices.

up·beat \'əp-ˌbēt\ *n.* An unaccented beat; especially, the last beat of a measure.

up·braid \ˌəp-'brād\ *v.* To scold; reprove.

up·bring·ing \'əp-ˌbring-ing\ *n.* The raising and training, as of children.

up·draft \'əp-ˌdraft\ *n.* An upward movement of gas or air.

up·end \ˌəp-'end\ *v.* To set, stand, or rise on end.

up·grade \'əp-ˌgrād\ *n.* **1** An upward grade or slope. **2** A step toward a better state or position. Trade is on the *upgrade.* — *v.;* **up·grad·ed; up·grad·ing.** To raise to a higher grade or position.

up·growth \'əp-ˌgrōth\ *n.* **1** The process of growing up; a developing. **2** A result of upward growth or development.

up·heav·al \ˌəp-'hēv-l\ *n.* **1** A violent uplifting, as of the ground during an earthquake. **2** A sudden, violent change; as, revolutions and similar *upheavals* in government.

upheld. Past tense and past part. of *uphold.*

up·hill \'əp-'hil\ *adv.* Upwards on or as if on a hillside; as, to walk *uphill.* — \-ˌhil\ *n.* An ascent; rising ground. — \-ˌhil\ *adj.* **1** Going up; rising; steep. **2** Full of difficulty; as, an *uphill* struggle.

up·hold \ˌəp-'hōld\ *v.;* **up·held** \-'held\; **up·hold·ing.** **1** To hold up; to lift. **2** To support; to keep from falling or giving way; to sustain; as, to *uphold* tradition. The appeals court *upheld* the verdict of the lower *court.* — **up·hold·er,** *n.*

up·hol·ster \(ˌ)əp-'hōlst-r\ *v.;* **up·hol·stered; up·hol·ster·ing** \-r(-)ing\. To provide, especially a seat, with padding, springs, and covering fabrics. — **up·hol·ster·er** \-r-r\ *n.*

up·hol·stery \(ˌ)əp-'hōlst-r(-)ē\ *n.; pl.* **up·hol·ster·ies.** **1** Materials used in upholstering. **2** The work or business of an upholsterer.

up·keep \'əp-ˌkēp\ *n.* The action or cost of keeping something in good condition or in good repair.

up·land \'əp-lənd, -ˌland\ *n.* **1** Land higher than the other parts of a region. **2** High land away from the coast or a river.

up·lift \ˌəp-'lift\ *v.* **1** To lift or raise aloft; to elevate. **2** To improve morally, mentally, or physically. — \'əp-ˌlift\ *n.* **1** An uplifting. **2** An upheaval in the earth. **3** Moral or social improvement or a movement to make such improvement.

up·most \'əp-ˌmōst\ *adj.* Uppermost.

up·on \ə-'pȯn, -'pän, -pən\ *prep.* On.

up·per \'əp-r\ *adj.* **1** Higher; as, *upper* ground; the

☞ See **un-**, *not,* and following note. **un·wink·ing**	**un·wit·nessed** **un·wom·an·ly** **un·work·a·ble**	**un·work·man·like** **un·world·ly** **un·worn**	**un·wor·thy** **un·wound** **un·wound·ed**	**un·wo·ven** **un·wrin·kled** **un·yield·ing**

upper house of Congress. **2** Farther up; toward the interior; as, the *upper* Amazon. **3** Worn outside other clothing or above the waist; as, *upper* garments. — *n.* An upper part; especially, one of the parts of a shoe above the sole. — **on one's uppers.** At the end of one's means. — **the upper hand.** A position of control or advantage; the mastery.

up·per·cut \'əp-r-ˌkət\ *n.* In boxing, a short-arm swinging blow directed upward. — *v.;* **up·per·cut; up·per·cut·ting.** To strike or hit with an uppercut.

up·per·most \'əp-r-ˌmōst\ *adj.* **1** Highest up; topmost. **2** Nearest to one's attention; as, something that is *uppermost* in one's thoughts.

up·raise \ˌəp-'rāz\ *v.;* **up·raised; up·rais·ing.** To raise up; as, with arms *upraised.*

up·rear \ˌəp-'rir\ *v.* To raise up; to rear.

up·right \'əp-ˌrīt\ *adj.* **1** Standing, growing, or set so as to point straight upwards; erect. **2** Morally straight or correct; honorable; just; as, an *upright* man. — *n.* **1** An upright or vertical position. **2** Something that stands upright. — **up·right·ly,** *adv.* — **up·right·ness,** *n.*

up·rise \ˌəp-'rīz\ *v.;* **up·rose** \-'rōz\; **up·ris·en** \-'riz-n\; **up·ris·ing** \-'rī-zing\. **1** To rise up, as from sleep. **2** To have an upward direction.

up·ris·ing \'əp-ˌrī-zing\ *n.* **1** A rising up. **2** A sudden revolt; a rebellion.

up·roar \'əp-ˌrōr, -ˌrȯr\ *n.* A great disturbance and noise; noisy confusion.

up·roar·i·ous \ˌəp-'rōr-ē-əs, -'rȯr-\ *adj.* Making or accompanied by uproar. — **up·roar·i·ous·ly,** *adv.*

up·root \ˌəp-'rüt, -'ru̇t\ *v.* **1** To pull up by the roots. **2** To root out; to get completely rid of.

up·set \ˌəp-'set\ *v.;* **up·set; up·set·ting.** **1** To turn upside down or on its side; as, to *upset* a glass of milk. **2** To disarrange; to force to give up or change entirely. The accident *upset* our plans. **3** To disturb emotionally; as, to be *upset* easily. **4** To make sick. The baby's food *upset* his stomach. — \ˌəp-'set, 'əp-ˌset\ *adj.* **1** Turned upside down or on its side; as, an *upset* canoe. **2** Unsettled; disturbed; nervous; as, an *upset* stomach. — \'əp-ˌset\ *n.* The action of upsetting or the state of being upset.

up·shot \'əp-ˌshät\ *n.* The outcome or the final result; as, the *upshot* of the matter.

up·side \'əp-ˌsīd\ *n.* The upper side.

up·side down \'əp-ˌsīd 'dau̇n\. **1** With the upper side under or down. **2** In confusion; topsy-turvy.

up·stairs \'əp-'starz, -'sterz\ *adv.* Up the stairs; to a floor above. Please go *upstairs.* — *adj.* Located in or on a floor above; as, an *upstairs* room. — *n.* The part of a building above the ground story.

up·stand·ing \ˌəp-'stan-ding\ *adj.* **1** Erect. **2** Straightforward; honest.

up·start \'əp-ˌstärt, -ˌstȧrt\ *n.* **1** A person who has risen suddenly to wealth or power and is conceited about his success. **2** A person who claims more personal importance than he deserves.

up·state \'əp-'stāt\ *adj.* Of or from the part of a state outside of a large city, especially to the north. — *n.* An upstate region; especially, northern New York. — **up·stat·er** \-'stāt-r\ *n.*

up·stream \'əp-'strēm\ *adv.* Toward the source of a stream; against the current of a stream.

up·swing \'əp-ˌswing\ *n.* A swinging upward; an improvement; as, an *upswing* in the stock market.

up·thrust \'əp-ˌthrəst\ *n.* An upward thrust; especially, an uplift of part of the earth's crust.

up-to-date \'əp-tə-'dāt\ *adj.* **1** Of the present time; of the latest style. **2** Keeping up with progress in knowledge or change in fashions.

up·town \'əp-'tau̇n\ *adv.* To or in the upper part of a town especially as contrasted with the downtown or business section. — *adj.* Situated in or belonging to the upper part of a town or city.

up·turn \'əp-ˌtərn\ *v.* **1** To turn over; as, an *upturned* boat. **2** To turn or direct upward; as, *upturned* faces.

up·ward \'əp-wərd\ *adv.* **1** In a direction from lower to higher; as, to look *upward.* **2** To an upper place, rank, condition, or period; as, to advance from the position of office boy *upward.* **3** Toward the source or origin; as, to explore a river from its mouth *upward.* **4** On top; in the higher position; as, to lie with the face *upward.* **5** More; above; over; as, towns of 10,000 persons and *upward.* **6** Toward a higher value or price; as, from five dollars *upward.* — *adj.* Directed upward; located upward; as, an *upward* course. — **up·ward·ly,** *adv.*

up·wards \'əp-wərdz\ *adv.* Upward.

upwards of. More than; in excess of; as, *upwards of* twenty persons.

ura·ni·um \yu̇-'rā-nē-əm\ *n.* [From scientific Latin, there named after the planet *Uranus.*] A radioactive metallic element certain isotopes of which are used in producing atomic energy.

ur·ban \'ərb-n\ *adj.* Of or relating to a city; characteristic of or making up a city or cities.

ur·bane \ˌər-'bān\ *adj.* Courteous; polite. — **ur·bane·ly,** *adv.*

ur·ban·i·ty \ˌər-'ban-ət-ē\ *n.; pl.* **ur·ban·i·ties.** Courtesy; politeness.

ur·chin \'ərch-n\ *n.* A small boy; especially, a pert, mischievous boy of the streets.

urea \yu̇-'rē-ə, 'yu̇r-ē-ə\ *n.* A compound that is one of the chief solids in urine.

ure·mia or **urae·mia** \yu̇-'rē-mē-ə\ *n.* The accumulation in the blood of substances that are ordinarily passed off in the urine, producing a poisoned condition. — **ure·mic** or **urae·mic** \-mik\ *adj.*

ure·ter \yu̇-'rēt-r, 'yu̇r-ət-\ *n.* A duct that carries the urine from a kidney to the bladder or cloaca.

ure·thra \yu̇-'rē-thrə\ *n.; pl.* **ure·thras** \-thrəz\ or **ure·thrae** \-ˌthrē\. A canal that in most mammals carries off urine from the bladder and in the male is also a sperm duct. — **ure·thral** \-thrəl\ *adj.*

urge \'ərj\ *v.;* **urged; urg·ing.** **1** To argue earnestly for; to plead in behalf of. **2** To try to persuade to greater exertion; as, to *urge* on a runner. **3** To entreat; as, to *urge* a guest to stay. — *n.* **1** The action of urging. **2** A force or impulse that urges or drives.

ur·gen·cy \'ərj-n-sē\ *n.; pl.* **ur·gen·cies.** The quality or state of being urgent.

ur·gent \'ərj-nt\ *adj.* **1** Urging insistently; as, *urgent* with his advice. **2** Calling for immediate attention; as, an *urgent* need. — **ur·gent·ly,** *adv.*

uric \'yu̇r-ik\ *adj.* Of or relating to urine; obtained from urine, as **uric acid,** a white, odorless, nearly insoluble acid present in urine.

uri·nal \'yu̇r-ən-l\ *n.* A receptacle for urine.

uri·nal·y·sis \ˌyu̇r-ə-'nal-ə-səs\ *n.; pl.* **uri·nal·y·ses** \-ˌsēz\. The analysis of urine.

uri·nary \'yu̇r-ə-ˌner-ē\ *adj.* **1** Of, relating to, or occurring in body organs for the excretion and removal of urine. **2** Of, relating to, or for urine.

uri·nate \'yu̇r-ə-ˌnāt\ *v.;* **uri·nat·ing; uri·nat·ed.** To discharge urine. — **uri·na·tion** \ˌyu̇r-ə-'nāsh-n\ *n.*

urine \'yu̇r-ən\ *n.* Waste material excreted by the kidney, in mammals a yellowish liquid and in birds and reptiles usually whitish and semisolid.

urn \'ərn\ *n.* **1** A jar or vase, usually one broad at the top, with rounded body narrowing downward, and resting on a base. **2** A receptacle for the ashes of the dead. **3** A closed receptacle with a heating device and a tap, used for making and serving coffee or tea.

urn, 1

Uru·guay·an \ˌyu̇r-ə-'gwī-ən, ˌu̇r-, -'gwā-\ *adj.* Of or relating to Uruguay. — *n.* A native or citizen of Uruguay.

us \(ˈ)əs\ *pron.* The form of the word *we* that is used as the object of a preposition or as an indirect object or a direct object of a verb.

urn, 3

U.S. \'yü-'es\. Abbreviation for *United States.*

u's. Pl. of *u.*

U.S.A. \'yü-ˌes-'ā\. Abbreviation for *United States of America.*

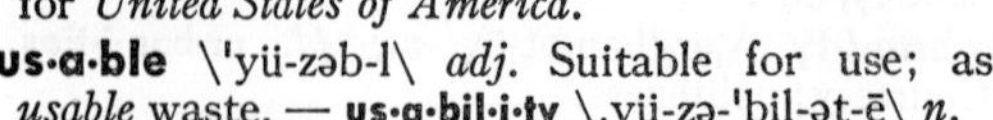

us·a·ble \'yü-zəb-l\ *adj.* Suitable for use; as, *usable* waste. — **us·a·bil·i·ty** \ˌyü-zə-'bil-ət-ē\ *n.*

us·age \'yü-sij, -zij\ *n.* **1** The way in which something is usually done or said; the customary use, as of a word. **2** Treatment; as, careless *usage.*

use \'yüz\ *v.;* **used; us·ing. 1** To make a practice of following, exercising, doing or speaking; as, to *use* care. **2** To employ for a special purpose; to put into use; as, to *use* a shovel. **3** To treat; to behave toward; as, to *use* a horse cruelly. **4** To partake of; to indulge in; as, I never *use* tobacco. — **used to** \'yüs-tə, -tu̇, -(ˌ)tü\. Was or were habitually prone to; formerly made it a practice to; continued to until some time in the past; as, forgetting how we *used to* quarrel as children; where the school *used* to stand. — \'yüs\ *n.* **1** The action or practice of using. Muscles develop by *use.* **2** The state of being used. The book is in *use.* **3** The way in which something is used; usage; treatment. **4** Reason for using; need; as, no *use* for a coat. **5** End gained by using; advantage; as, no *use* in crying. **6** The method of using; as, to teach the *use* of tools. — **us·er** \'yüz-r\ *n.*

used, *adj.* **1** \'yüzd\ That has been used or worn; secondhand; as, a *used* car. **2** \'yüst\ Having an approving or indifferent attitude as a result of habit or experience; as, to be *used* to flying.

use·ful \'yüs-fəl\ *adj.* Giving good use; serviceable; helpful. — **use·ful·ly** \-fə-lē\ *adv.*

use·less \'yüs-ləs\ *adj.* Having or being of no use; unserviceable. — **use·less·ly,** *adv.*

ush·er \'əsh-r\ *n.* A person who conducts other persons to their seats, as in a church. — *v.;* **ush·ered; ush·er·ing** \-r(-)ing\. **1** To serve as an usher; to conduct; to escort. **2** To appear to escort or bring. Storms *ushered* in the spring.

usu·al \'yü-zhə-wəl, 'yüzh-l\ *adj.* In common use; customary; habitual; as, in the *usual* way.

— The words *customary* and *habitual* are synonyms of *usual: usual* describes something that occurs so frequently in the normal course of events that it seems in no way strange or conspicuous; *customary* generally describes whatever is in accordance with the characteristic practices or conventions of a particular individual or community; *habitual* usually refers to something that has settled by constant repetition into a habit.

usu·al·ly \'yüzh-l(-)ē, 'yü-zhə-wə-lē\ *adv.* In the usual manner; customarily; as, *usually* on time.

usu·rer \'yüzh-r-r\ *n.* One who lends money, especially at an excessively high rate of interest.

usu·ri·ous \yü-'zhu̇r-ē-əs\ *adj.* Asking, taking, or involving an excessively high rate of interest for the use of money; as, a *usurious* contract.

usurp \yü-'sərp, -'zərp\ *v.* To seize and hold by force and without right; as, to *usurp* a throne. — **usur·pa·tion** \ˌyüs-r-'pāsh-n, ˌyüz-r-\ *n.*

usurp·er \yü-'sərp-r, -'zərp-r\ *n.* One who usurps, as position or power, especially sovereign power.

usu·ry \'yüzh-r(-)ē\ *n.; pl.* **usu·ries. 1** The lending of money with an interest charge for its use. **2** An excessive rate or amount of interest charged, especially interest above an established legal rate.

uten·sil \yü-'ten(t)s-l\ *n.* A container, a tool, or an instrument used in doing a particular kind of work.

uter·us \'yüt-r-əs\ *n.; pl.* **uter·us·es** \-r-ə-səz\ or **uteri** \-r-ˌī\. In female mammals, an organ in the body for holding and usually for nourishing the fetus; womb. — **uter·ine** \-r-ən, -r-ˌīn\ *adj.*

util·i·tar·i·an \(ˌ)yü-ˌtil-ə-'ter-ē-ən\ *adj.* Of or relating to utility; aiming at usefulness rather than beauty; serving a useful purpose.

util·i·ty \yü-'til-ət-ē\ *n.; pl.* **util·i·ties. 1** Usefulness; practical value; ways in which a thing can be made useful or put to use; as, the *utility* of certain scientific laws. **2** A business organization, as an electric-light or gas company (**public utility**) supplying some widespread service to the public.

uti·lize \'yüt-l-ˌīz\ *v.;* **uti·lized; uti·liz·ing.** To make use of; especially, to use for a practical purpose; as, to *utilize* water power. — **uti·liz·a·ble** \-ˌī-zəb-l\ *adj.* — **uti·li·za·tion** \ˌyüt-l-ə-'zāsh-n\ *n.*

ut·most \'ət-ˌmōst\ *adj.* **1** Farthest away; most distant. **2** Highest or greatest possible: extreme; as, to be in the *utmost* misery. — *n.* The utmost limit of effort or strength.

uto·pia \yü-'tōp-ē-ə\ *n.* [From *Utopia*, an imaginary island described in the book of the same name (1516), written in Latin by Sir Thomas More (1478–1535), English statesman and author.] **1** An imaginary place in which everything is perfect. **2** An unworkable scheme for solving social and political problems. — **uto·pi·an** \-ē-ən\ *adj.* or *n.*

ut·ter \'ət-r\ *adj.* Complete; total; entire; as, *utter* ruin. — **ut·ter·ly**, *adv.*

ut·ter \'ət-r\ *v.* To express in spoken words; to speak; as, to *utter* words of wisdom.

ut·ter·ance \'ət-r-ən(t)s\ *n.* **1** An expressing in speech; as, to give *utterance* to one's thoughts. **2** A way or manner of speaking; as, feeble *utterance*. **3** Something that is uttered; a statement.

ut·ter·most \'ət-r-ˌmōst\ *adj.* Extreme; utmost. — *n.* The most possible; the utmost.

uvu·la \'yüv-yə-lə\ *n.* The fleshy lobe hanging down from the back part of the roof of the mouth. — **uvu·lar** \-yəl-r\ *adj.*

v \'vē\ *n.; pl.* **v's** \'vēz\. **1** The twenty-second letter of the alphabet. **2** As a Roman numeral, 5.

v. Abbreviation for *verb.*

va·can·cy \'vāk-n-sē\ *n.; pl.* **va·can·cies. 1** A vacating, as of an office or position. **2** The state of being vacant. **3** A vacant apartment, office, position; as, two *vacancies* in this building. **4** The time something stands vacant. **5** Empty space; as, to stare into *vacancy*.

va·cant \'vāk-nt\ *adj.* **1** Without an occupant; empty, as of buildings; as, no position *vacant;* a *vacant* chair. **2** Free from business or care; leisure; as, a few *vacant* hours. **3** Brainless; foolish; as, a *vacant* stare; a *vacant* laugh. — For synonyms see *empty.*

va·cant·ly \'vāk-nt-lē\ *adv.* In a vacant manner.

va·cate \'vā-ˌkāt, vā-'kāt\ *v.;* **va·cat·ed; va·cat·ing. 1** To annul; to make void; as, to *vacate* an agreement. **2** To make vacant; to leave empty; as, to *vacate* a building; to *vacate* a position.

va·ca·tion \vā-'kāsh-n, və-\ *n.* A period of rest and recreation from work of any sort; a holiday. — *v.;* **va·ca·tioned; va·ca·tion·ing** \-n(-)ing\. To take or spend a vacation; as, to *vacation* in July.

va·ca·tion·ist \vā-'kāsh-n(-)əst, və-\ *n.* A person taking a vacation.

vac·ci·nate \'vaks-n-ˌāt\ *v.;* **vac·ci·nat·ed; vac·ci·nat·ing. 1** To inoculate with cowpox vaccine to protect against smallpox. **2** To inoculate with any vaccine.

vac·ci·na·tion \ˌvaks-n-'āsh-n\ *n.* **1** The act of vaccinating. **2** The scar left by vaccinating.

vac·ci·na·tor \'vaks-n-ˌāt-r\ *n.* **1** One who gives a vaccination. **2** An instrument used in vaccinating.

vac·cine \(')vak-'sēn, 'vak-ˌsēn\ *n.* A substance inoculated to produce or increase immunity to a disease; as, polio *vaccine.*

vac·il·late \'vas-l-ˌāt\ *v.;* **vac·il·lat·ed; vac·il·lat·ing. 1** To waver; to fluctuate; as, a *vacillating* stock market. **2** To incline first to one opinion and then to another. — **vac·il·la·tion** \ˌvas-l-'āsh-n\ *n.*

va·cu·i·ty \va-'kyü-ət-ē\ *n.; pl.* **va·cu·i·ties. 1** An empty space. **2** Emptiness; hollowness. **3** Vacancy of mind. **4** A senseless or foolish remark.

vac·u·ous \'vak-yə-wəs\ *adj.* **1** Empty. **2** Foolish; inane; as, a *vacuous* remark. — **vac·u·ous·ly**, *adv.*

vac·u·um \'vak-yəm, -yə-wəm\ *n.; pl.* **vac·u·ums** \-yəmz, -yə-wəmz\ or **vac·ua** \-yə-wə\. [From Latin, where it was derived from the neuter of the adjective *vacuus* meaning "empty".] **1** A perfectly empty space. **2** A space inside a closed vessel from which most of the air has been pumped. — *adj.* **1** Enclosing a vacuum, as in **vacuum bottle**, a double-walled bottle with a vacuum between the outer and inner walls used to keep the contents hot or cold, or in **vacuum tube**, a small sealed container from which the air has been drawn so that electrical current can be made to pass freely between metal wires, plates, or shields within the tube. **2** Operated by suction, as in **vacuum cleaner.** — *v.* To use a vacuum cleaner upon.

vag·a·bond \'vag-ə-ˌbänd\ *adj.* **1** Wandering from place to place; homeless. **2** Following a wandering course; as, a *vagabond* route. — *n.* A person of vagabond habits or character; a tramp.

va·ga·ry \'vāg-r-ē; və-'ger-ē, -'gar-ē\ *n.; pl.* **va·ga·ries.** An odd idea; a whim; a caprice.

va·gi·na \və-'jī-nə\ *n.; pl.* **va·gi·nas** \-nəz\ or **va·gi·nae** \-ˌnē\. In female mammals, a canal that leads out from the uterus. — **va·gi·nal** \və-'jīn-l, 'vaj-n-əl\ *adj.*

vag·i·nate \'vaj-n-ˌāt\ *adj.* Having a sheath or sheathing part, as some grasses.

va·gran·cy \'vāg-rən-sē\ *n.; pl.* **va·gran·cies. 1** The state or condition of a vagrant. **2** A vagrant idea or notion; as, occasional *vagrancies* of the mind.

va·grant \'vāg-rənt\ *n.* An idle wanderer; a tramp. — *adj.* **1** Wandering aimlessly; homeless and roving; as, *vagrant* gypsy life. **2** Following no fixed course; capricious; as, *vagrant* thoughts.

vague \'vāg\ *adj.;* **vagu·er; vagu·est. 1** Not clear; indistinct; hazy; as, a *vague* shape in the dark. **2** Not clearly felt or understood; as, a *vague* unrest; a *vague* idea. — **vague·ly**, *adv.*

vain \'vān\ *adj.* **1** Worthless; as, *vain* promises. **2** Futile; as, a *vain* attempt. **3** Proud of one's looks or abilities; conceited. — **in vain.** To no purpose. He has not lived *in vain.* — **vain·ly**, *adv.*

vain·glo·ri·ous \'vān-'glōr-ē-əs, -'glȯr-\ *adj.* Feeling or showing undue pride in one's own accomplishments; boastful. — **vain·glo·ri·ous·ly**, *adv.*

vain·glo·ry \'vān-ˌglōr-ē, -ˌglȯr-ē\ *n.* Too great pride in oneself and one's deeds; boastfulness.

val·ance \'val-ən(t)s\ *n.* A short decorative drapery across the top of a window or windows.

vale \'vāl\ *n.* A valley.

val·e·dic·to·ri·an \ˌval-ə-ˌdik-'tōr-ē-ən, -'tȯr-\ *n.* In high schools and colleges, the student, usually ranking first in scholarship, who gives the valedictory address at graduation exercises.

val·e·dic·to·ry \ˌval-ə-'dikt-r(-)ē\ *adj.* Bidding farewell; as, a *valedictory* address. — *n.* A farewell address.

val·en·tine \'val-ən-ˌtīn\ *n.* **1** A sweetheart, especially one chosen or complimented on **Saint Valentine's Day,** February 14. **2** A card or gift sent as a greeting on this day.

va·le·ri·an \və-'lir-ē-ən\ *n.* **1** A perennial herb with flat-topped clusters of flowers, the dried roots and rootstock of which make up a drug used as a sedative. **2** The drug made from this plant.

val·et \'val-ət, (')val-'ā\ *n.* A manservant or hotel employee who takes care of a man's clothes and performs personal services.

val·iant \'val-yənt\ *adj.* **1** Boldly brave; courageous; as, a *valiant* leader. **2** Valorous; heroic; as, *valiant* fighting. — **val·iant·ly,** *adv.*

val·id \'val-əd\ *adj.* **1** Founded on truth or fact; well-grounded; as, *valid* reasons. **2** Binding in law; sound; as, a *valid* contract. — **val·id·ly,** *adv.*

val·i·date \'val-ə-ˌdāt\ *v.;* **val·i·dat·ed; val·i·dat·ing. 1** To make valid. **2** To confirm; to substantiate. — **val·i·da·tion** \ˌval-ə-'dāsh-n\ *n.*

va·lid·i·ty \və-'lid-ət-ē\ *n.; pl.* **va·lid·i·ties.** The quality, condition, or fact of being valid.

va·lise \və-'lēs\ *n.* A satchel.

valise

val·ley \'val-ē\ *n.; pl.* **val·leys.** A tract of lowland nearly surrounded by hills or mountains; as, a river *valley.*

val·or \'val-r\ *n.* Personal bravery; courage.

val·or·ous \'val-r-əs\ *adj.* Having or showing valor; brave; heroic. — **val·or·ous·ly,** *adv.*

val·u·a·ble \'val-yəb-l, -yə-wəb-l\ *adj.* **1** Having money value; being worth a great deal of money; as, a *valuable* ring. **2** Full of worth; precious; as, a *valuable* friend; *valuable* information.

— The word *precious* is a synonym of *valuable: valuable* commonly describes something that is particularly useful to or prized by the owner or that seems likely to bring him a profit, as through bringing a high price when sold; *precious* generally indicates something of extremely great worth or high price either because of its rareness or because of one's deep emotional attachment to it.

— *n.* A precious possession; a thing of value; as, to keep one's *valuables* in a safe. — **val·u·a·bly** \'val-yə-blē, -yə-wə-blē\ *adv.*

val·u·a·tion \ˌval-yə-'wāsh-n\ *n.* **1** The act of evaluating; an appraisal; as, the *valuation* of an estate. **2** The value as estimated; an appraised price; as, a house with a high *valuation.*

val·ue \'val-(ˌ)yü, -yu̇\ *n.* **1** A fair return in an exchange, as of money for goods; as, to get full *value* for one's money. **2** Worth in money; fair price; as, the market *value* of a house. **3** Real worth; importance; benefit; advantage; as, to appreciate the *value* of an education. **4** The distinctive quality of a sound in speech; as, phonetic *value.* **5** The brilliance or luminosity of a color. **6** In art, the relation of one part to another with respect to lightness and darkness. **7** The relative length of a tone or note in music. — *v.;* **val·ued; val·u·ing. 1** To estimate the worth of; to fix the money value of; as, to *value* a property at ten thousand dollars. **2** To appreciate; as, to *value* books.

valve \'valv\ *n.* **1** A natural or artificial closing which controls the flow of a liquid or gas; especially, a hinged lid or flap that opens outward when there is pressure from behind and closes when that pressure is removed. **2** In botany, one of the pieces into which a splitting pod or capsule separates; as, the two *valves* of the pea pod. **3** A device in some musical instruments, as horns and trumpets, for quickly varying the tube length in order to change the tone. **4** A device, as an electron tube, that permits the flow of electric current in one direction only. **5** One of two hinged shells, as of an oyster or clam.

valve, 1

val·vu·lar \'valv-yəl-r\ *adj.* **1** Of or relating to a valve; especially, in medicine, relating to the valves of the heart. **2** Containing or opening by valves.

vamp \'vamp\ *n.* The part of a shoe or boot above the sole and welt and in front of the ankle seam; an upper. — *v.* To provide with a vamp.

vam·pire \'vam-ˌpīr\ *n.* **1** In folklore, a blood-sucking ghost that wanders at night. **2** A person who lives by preying on other people. **3** Also **vampire bat.** A South American bat that sucks the blood of animals. **4** Any of several bats with a leaf-like membrane on the nose, erroneously supposed to suck blood.

van \'van\ *n.* **1** The front part of an army, fleet, or other advancing body; the leading unit in a formation. **2** Those at the front of any line or movement.

van \'van\ *n.* [A shortened form of *caravan.*] **1** A large enclosed truck, especially one for moving furniture and other household effects. **2** *British.* A closed railway car for baggage.

va·na·di·um \və-'nād-ē-əm\ *n.* A soft bright metallic element used with steel in making a strong tough metal called **vanadium steel.**

van·dal \'vand-l\ *n.* A person who is addicted to vandalism.

van·dal·ism \'vand-l-ˌiz-m\ *n.* Reckless destructiveness; willful and senseless destruction.

vane \'vān\ *n.* **1** A thin, flat device attached to something high to show which way the wind blows; a weathervane; a weathercock. **2** Any flat extended surface attached to an axis and moved by the wind or by water or other fluid; as, the *vanes* of a windmill; the *vanes* of a propeller. **3** The flat, expanded part, or web, of a feather.

van·guard \'van-ˌgärd, -ˌgȧrd\ *n.* **1** The troops that march in the front of an army; the van. **2** One that is at the forefront, as of a movement.

va·nil·la \və-'nil-ə\ *n.* **1** A tropical American orchid with thick fleshy leaves and slender pods (**vanilla beans**) that resemble beans. **2** A flavoring extract made from the pods of this plant.

van·ish \'van-ish\ *v.* **1** To pass quickly from sight; to disappear. **2** To pass completely from existence; as, civilizations that have *vanished.*

van·i·ty \'van-ət-ē\ *n.; pl.* **van·i·ties. 1** That which is vain, empty, or useless. **2** The quality or state of being vain or futile; worthlessness. **3** The quality of being vain or conceited; conceit. **4** In full, **vanity box** or **vanity case.** A small box containing powder, a puff, and a mirror; a compact. — For synonyms see *pride.*

van·quish \'van(g)-kwish\ *v.* To conquer; to defeat.

van·tage \'vant-ij\ *n.* **1** Superiority, as in position or equipment. **2** An advantageous position or state of affairs. **3** A favorable opportunity.

vap·id \'vap-əd\ *adj.* Having lost its spirit, life, or zest; insipid; tasteless; dull. — **vap·id·ly,** *adv.*

va·por \'vāp-r\ *n.* **1** Fine particles of matter floating in the air and clouding it, as fog or smoke. **2** In physics, any substance in a gaseous state. **3** Something insubstantial or fleeting.

va·por·ize \'vāp-r-ˌīz\ *v.;* **va·por·ized; va·por·iz·ing.** To turn from a liquid or solid into a vapor.

va·que·ro \vä-'ker-ˌō, vȧ-\ *n.; pl.* **va·que·ros.** In the Southwest, a cowboy or herdsman.

var·i·a·ble \'ver-ē-əb-l, 'var-\ *adj.* **1** Able or inclined to vary; subject to variation; changeable. **2** Fickle; inconstant. **3** In biology, not true to type; as, a *variable* species. — *n.* **1** That which is variable; a thing that may vary. **2** In mathematics, a quantity that may assume a succession of values. **3** In experimental science, a measurable aspect of an experiment that has different values under different conditions. — **va·ri·a·bil·i·ty** \ˌver-ē-ə-'bil-ət-ē, ˌvar-\ *n.*

var·i·ance \'ver-ē-ən(t)s, 'var-\ *n.* **1** Variation or a degree of variation; deviation. **2** A disagreement; a dispute.

var·i·ant \'ver-ē-ənt, 'var-\ *adj.* **1** Differing from others of its kind or class, especially from another or others regarded as representing a norm, standard, or type. **2** Being one of two or more similar but not identical forms with the same meaning; as, a *variant* spelling. — *n.* Something that is variant, as an alternative spelling of a word.

var·i·a·tion \ˌver-ē-'āsh-n, ˌvar-\ *n.* **1** A varying or a result of varying; something which is different. **2** Extent of change or difference; as, a *variation* of thirty degrees in the temperature during the day. **3** In biology, divergence in characteristics from those typical or usual in the species or from those of the parents. **4** In music, the repetition of a theme or melody with ornamental notes or modifications, as in rhythm or time.

var·i·col·ored \'ver-ē-ˌkəl-rd, 'var-\ *adj.* Having various colors.

var·i·cose \'var-ə-ˌkōs, 'ver-\ *adj.* Irregularly swollen; as, *varicose* veins.

var·ied \'ver-ēd, 'var-\ *adj.* **1** Changed; altered. **2** Having many varieties or kinds; of many sorts; as, a man of *varied* interests. **3** Marked with different colors, as the coats of many animals.

var·ie·gat·ed \'ver-ə-ˌgāt-əd, 'ver-ē-ə-, 'var-\ *adj.* **1** Having patches, stripes, or marks of different colors; as, *variegated* flowers. **2** Full of variety; as, a *variegated* career. — **var·ie·ga·tion** \ˌver-ə-'gāsh-n, ˌver-ē-ə-, ˌvar-\ *n.*

va·ri·e·ty \və-'rī-ət-ē\ *n.; pl.* **va·ri·e·ties. 1** A mixture of different things; a change from the usual; as, to feel the need of some *variety* in one's life. **2** A varied assortment; as, a shop offering a great *variety* of silks. **3** A particular kind; as, a new *variety* of cake. **4** Entertainment such as is given in a **variety show,** a presentation consisting of a series of different kinds of acts, as songs, dances, acrobatics, and comedy. **5** In biology, a group of animals or plants within a species which are distinguished from other groups by characteristics not constant enough or too trivial to distinguish species.

var·i·ous \'ver-ē-əs, 'var-\ *adj.* **1** Not all alike; varied; as, the *various* colors of the rainbow. **2** Having varied characteristics; many-sided; as, *various* duties in an office. **3** Many and different; several; as, *various* schemes. — **var·i·ous·ly,** *adv.*

var·let \'vär-lət, 'vȧr-\ *n.* **1** *Archaic.* An attendant. **2** A scoundrel.

var·nish \'vär-nish, 'vȧr-\ *v.* To cover with or as if with varnish. — *n.* **1** A liquid which is spread like paint and forms a hard glossy coating. **2** The glaze given by varnishing. **3** Outside show; gloss.

var·si·ty \'vär-sət-ē\ *n.; pl.* **var·si·ties.** [A shortened and altered form of *university.*] A team in any sport or activity chosen to represent a school, college, or university as its first team.

vary \'ver-ē, 'var-ē\ *v.;* **var·ied** \-ēd\; **var·y·ing. 1** To make or become different; to change. **2** To make of different kinds; as, to *vary* one's meals. **3** To be different; as, laws that *vary* from state to state. **4** In biology, to show or undergo variation.

vase \'vās, 'vāz\ *n.* An ornamental jar, usually rounded in shape and deeper than it is wide.

vas·e·line \ˌvas-l-'ēn\ *n.* [From *Vaseline,* a trademark.] A yellowish white ointment or salve prepared from petroleum; petroleum jelly.

vas·sal \'vas-l\ *n.* **1** In feudal times, a person who placed himself under the protection of another, to whom he swore allegiance as his lord. **2** One that is in a position like that of a vassal.

vas·sal·age \'vas-l-ij\ *n.* **1** The condition of being a vassal. **2** Homage and loyalty due a lord from his vassal. **3** A politically dependent territory.

vast \'vast\ *adj.* **1** Of great extent or huge bulk; immense. **2** Very great in numbers, quantity, or amount. **3** Very great, as in intensity or range; as, a *vast* difference. — **vast·ly,** *adv.*

vasty \'vas-tē\ *adj.* Vast; immense.

vat \'vat\ *n.* A large container for liquids; a large cistern, tank, tub, or barrel; as, a *vat* for dye.

vau·de·ville \'vȯd-əv-l, -ə-ˌvil, 'vōd-ˌvil, 'vȯd-ˌvil\ *n.* A theatrical entertainment featuring songs, dances, and sketches.

vault \'vȯlt\ *n.* **1** An arched structure forming a ceiling or roof. **2** An arch suggesting a vault, such as the sky; as, the blue *vault* above us. **3** A room for storage or safekeeping; as, a bank *vault.* **4** A burial chamber. — *v.* To make with a vault; as, to *vault* a ceiling.

vault, 1

vault \'vȯlt\ *n.* A jump or bound; especially, a leap over or upon something, made by the aid of the hands or a pole. — *v.* To make a vault; to jump.

vault·ing \'vȯl-ting\ *adj.* **1** That vaults. **2** Arrogant; too pretentious; as, *vaulting* ambition.

vaunt \'vȯnt, 'vänt\ *v.* To brag or boast. — *n.* A brag; a boast.

veal \'vēl\ *n.* The flesh of a calf used as meat.

vec·tor \'vekt-r\ *n.* In biology, an organism, as an insect, that carries and transmits disease.

veer \'vir\ *v.* To change in direction; to turn; to shift; as, the wind *veered.* — *n.* A change of course.

veg·e·ta·ble \'vej-təb-l, -ət-əb-l\ *adj.* **1** Of or having to do with plants. Trees, herbs, and grasses belong to the *vegetable* kingdom. **2** Obtained from plants; as, *vegetable* oils; *vegetable* colors. — *n.* A plant, especially one used for human food.

veg·e·tar·i·an \ˌvej-ə-'ter-ē-ən\ *n.* A person who does not eat meat.

veg·e·tate \'vej-ə-ˌtāt\ *v.;* **veg·e·tat·ed; veg·e·tat·ing.** To grow in the manner of a plant; especially, to do little but eat and grow.

veg·e·ta·tion \ˌvej-ə-'tāsh-n\ *n.* **1** The act of vegetating. **2** Plant life.

ve·he·mence \'vē-ə-mən(t)s\ *n.* The quality or state of being vehement; force; fury, fervor.

ve·he·ment \'vē-ə-mənt\ *adj.* **1** Acting or moving with great force or violence. **2** Very ardent, eager, or angry; impetuous. — **ve·he·ment·ly,** *adv.*

ve·hi·cle \'vē-ˌ(h)ik-l, 'vē-ək-l\ *n.* **1** Anything used to carry persons or objects from place to place; a conveyance. **2** Any medium through which something is expressed, transferred, or applied.

ve·hic·u·lar \vē-'hik-yəl-r\ *adj.* Of or relating to a vehicle or vehicles; as, *vehicular* traffic.

veil \'vāl\ *n.* **1** A cloth curtain or covering used to hide or to limit the view of something; as, the *veil* of the temple. **2** Something which covers like a veil; as, a *veil* of darkness. **3** A thin gauzy fabric worn over the head and shoulders, or one worn to cover or partly cover the face; as, a bride's *veil;* a nun's *veil.* **4** The vows or the life of a nun; as, to take the *veil.* — *v.* To cover with or as if with a veil; as, to *veil* the face; to *veil* one's intentions.

veil·ing \'vā-ling\ *n.* A veil; material for veils.

vein \'vān\ *n.* **1** A streak, line, or wavy band of another color or texture, appearing in substances such as marble and wood. **2** Anything of distinctive character considered as running through something else; a strain; as, a *vein* of humor. **3** One of the branching blood vessels that carry the blood back to the heart. **4** One of the threadlike branching vascular bundles that form the framework of the leaf of a plant; a nerve. **5** One of the thickened ribs that stiffen the wings of insects. **6** A fissure in rock filled with mineral matter; as, a *vein* of gold. — *v.* To form or mark with veins.

vein·ing \'vā-ning\ *n.* **1** A system or pattern of veins; venation. **2** A streak or streaking.

veld or **veldt** \'felt, 'velt\ *n.* A South African tract of grassy land, sometimes with scattered trees or shrubs.

vel·lum \'vel-əm\ *n.* **1** A fine-grained skin of a lamb, kid, or calf, prepared for writing upon or for binding books. **2** A paper or binding manufactured to resemble real vellum.

ve·loc·i·pede \və-'läs-ə-ˌpēd\ *n.* [From French *vélocipède,* there compounded from Latin *veloc-* (the stem of *velox* meaning "swift") and Latin *ped-,* the stem of *pes* meaning "foot".] **1** A vehicle like a bicycle but smaller and having two rear wheels; a tricycle. **2** An old form of bicycle.

ve·loc·i·ty \və-'läs-ət-ē\ *n.; pl.* **ve·loc·i·ties.** The speed at which a thing moves; rapidity; swiftness.

ve·lours or **ve·lour** \və-'lu̇r\ *n.; pl.* **ve·lours** \-'lu̇rz\. Any of various fabrics finished to have a surface like that of velvet.

ve·lum \'vē-ləm\ *n.* A membranous partition likened to a veil or curtain; especially, the soft palate.

vel·vet \'vel-vət\ *n.* **1** A silk fabric with a thick soft surface, or pile, of short erect threads. **2** A similar fabric with a silk pile and a back of rayon, cotton, linen, or other fiber. — *adj.* **1** Soft as velvet. **2** Made of or covered with velvet.

vel·ve·teen \ˌvel-və-'tēn\ *n.* A fabric woven like velvet but entirely of cotton.

vel·vety \'vel-vət-ē\ *adj.* Soft and smooth as velvet, as to the sight, touch, or taste; like velvet.

ve·na ca·va \ˌvē-nə 'kä-və, 'kā-, 'kȧ-\; *pl.* **ve·nae ca·vae** \ˌvē-(ˌ)nē 'kä-(ˌ)vē, 'kā-, 'kȧ-\. One of the large veins by which, in air-breathing vertebrates, the blood is returned to the heart.

ve·nal \'vēn-l\ *adj.* **1** Willing to take bribes; open to corrupt influences. **2** Influenced by bribery; corrupt; as, *venal* conduct. — **ve·nal·ly** \-l-ē\ *adv.*

ve·nal·i·ty \vē-'nal-ət-ē\ *n.; pl.* **ve·nal·i·ties.** The quality or state of being venal.

ve·na·tion \vē-'nāsh-n\ *n.* The arrangement or system of veins, as in the wing of an insect.

vend \'vend\ *v.* To sell or offer for sale; as, to *vend* fruit. — For synonyms see *sell.* — **vend·er** \-r\ *n.*

ven·det·ta \ven-'det-ə\ *n.* A feud in which the family of a murdered man try to take vengeance by killing the murderer or his relatives.

ven·dor \'vend-r\ *n.* A seller; a vender.

ve·neer \və-'nir\ *n.* **1** A thin layer or sheet of a material; especially, a thin layer of a valuable or beautiful wood glued as a finishing surface to a cheaper wood. **2** Any one of the layers glued together to give stiffness and strength to plywood. **3** Something that shows on the surface but does not go deep. The man's politeness was but a *veneer.* — *v.* To cover with a veneer.

ven·er·a·ble \'ven-r(-)əb-l, -rb-l\ *adj.* Worthy of veneration; meriting honor or respect because of virtues, great age, historical, or religious importance; as, a *venerable* old man. — For synonyms see *old.* — **ven·er·a·bil·i·ty** \ˌven-r(-)ə-'bil-ət-ē\ *n.* — **ven·er·a·bly** \'ven-r(-)ə-blē, -r-blē\ *adv.*

ven·er·ate \'ven-r-ˌāt\ *v.;* **ven·er·at·ed; ven·er·at·ing.** To regard as venerable; to revere.

ven·er·a·tion \ˌven-r-'āsh-n\ *n.* **1** The act of venerating or the state of being venerated; as, the *veneration* of saints. **2** A feeling of reverence or deep respect; devotion. — **ven·er·a·tor** \'ven-r-ˌāt-r\ *n.*

ve·ne·re·al \və-'nir-ē-əl\ *adj.* Of or relating to sexual intercourse or to diseases transmitted by it.

Ve·ne·tian blind \və-'nēsh-n\. A blind having thin slats that can be set to overlap to keep out light or tipped to let light come in between them.

Venetian blind

Ven·e·zu·e·lan \ˌven-ə-zə-'wā-lən, -'wē-\ *adj.* Of or relating to Venezuela. — *n.* A native or inhabitant of Venezuela.

venge·ance \'venj-n(t)s\ *n.* **1** Punishment in return for an injury or offense; the act of avenging; as, victims of the king's *vengeance.* **2** Revenge; as, to take *vengeance* on one's enemy. **3** Great force; a display of energy; as, to set to work with a *vengeance.*

venge·ful \'venj-fəl\ *adj.* Filled with a desire for revenge. — **venge·ful·ly** \-fə-lē\ *adv.*

ve·ni·al \'vē-nē-əl, 'vēn-yəl\ *adj.* Easily forgiven; pardonable; not serious; as, a *venial* sin.

ve·ni·re \və-'nīr-ē, -'nir-ē\ *n.* A writ summoning persons to appear in court to serve as jurors.

ve·ni·re·man \və-'nīr-ē-mən, -'nir-\ *n.; pl.* **ve·ni·re·men** \-mən\. A juror summoned by a venire.

ven·i·son \'ven-əs-n, -əz-n\ *n.* The meat of a deer.

ven·om \'ven-əm\ *n.* **1** The poison that certain animals, as snakes, scorpions, and bees, secrete and transmit by biting or stinging. **2** Spite; malice.

ven·om·ous \'ven-ə-məs\ *adj.* **1** Filled with venom; poisonous. **2** Full of spite, malice, or envy; as, *venomous* words. — **ven·om·ous·ly,** *adv.*

ve·nous \'vē-nəs\ *adj.* Of or relating to a vein.

vent \'vent\ *n.* **1** A small hole or opening for passage or escape, as of a fluid or gas. **2** An opening for ventilation, as in the wall of a room. **3** A letting out; expression; as, to give *vent* to one's wrath. **4** The opening of the intestine on the surface of the body, as in birds and fishes. **5** The opening at the breech of a gun through which the powder is lighted. **6** A slit in a garment, especially one at the back of a coat. — *v.* **1** To let out at a vent. **2** To give expression to; as, to *vent* one's anger. **3** To furnish with a vent; as, a properly *vented* burner.

ven·ti·late \'vent-l-ˌāt\ *v.;* **ven·ti·lat·ed; ven·ti·lat·ing.** **1** To cause fresh air to circulate through; as, to open the windows long enough to *ventilate* a room. **2** To purify by oxygen breathed in from the air. The lungs *ventilate* the blood. **3** To give vent to; to discuss freely; as, to *ventilate* a complaint. **4** To provide with a vent, as for smoke.

ven·ti·la·tion \ˌvent-l-'āsh-n\ *n.* **1** The action or process of ventilating. **2** Circulation of fresh air; as, a schoolroom with good *ventilation.* **3** A system or means of providing fresh air.

ven·ti·la·tor \'vent-l-ˌāt-r\ *n.* One that ventilates; especially, a contrivance, as, a small shuttered opening, for supplying fresh air and permitting the escape of bad air.

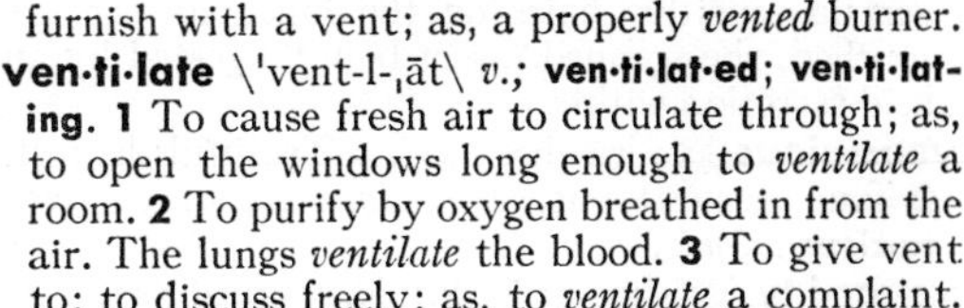

ventilator

ven·tral \'ven-trəl\ *adj.* **1** Of or relating to the belly; abdominal. **2** Of or relating to, on, or near that surface of the body which in man is the front but in most other animals is the lower surface; as, a fish's *ventral* fins.

ven·tri·cle \'ven-trik-l\ *n.* **1** A chamber of the heart that receives blood from the auricle of the same side and pumps it into the arteries. **2** One of the communicating cavities in the brain continuous with the central canal of the spinal cord.

ven·tric·u·lar \ven-'trik-yəl-r\ *adj.* **1** Of or relating to a ventricle. **2** Bulging out; bellied.

ven·tril·o·quism \ven-'tril-ə-ˌkwiz-m\ *n.* [From Latin *ventriloquus* meaning "ventriloquist", literally "belly-talker" + the English suffix *-ism.*] The art or practice of speaking in such a way that the voice seems to come from some source other than the mouth of the speaker, as from another person or a dummy. — **ven·tril·o·quist** \-kwəst\ *n.*

ven·tril·o·quy \ven-'tril-ə-kwē\ *n.* Ventriloquism.

ven·ture \'vench-r\ *n.* An undertaking in which there is risk or danger; especially, a speculative business undertaking. — **at a venture.** At random; by chance or on a chance. — *v.;* **ven·tured; ven·tur·ing** \-r(-)ing\. **1** To take the chances of; to have the courage to go, do, or undertake with no certainty of safety or success. **2** To expose to risk; as, to *venture* everything on a bet. **3** To dare or presume, as to speak or express something; as, to *venture* an opinion; to *venture* to disagree.

ven·ture·some \'vench-rs-m\ *adj.* **1** Inclined to venture; daring; bold; rash. **2** Risky; dangerous; uncertain. — For synonyms see *rash.*

ven·tur·ous \'vench-r(-)əs\ *adj.* Venturesome.

ven·ue \'ven-ˌyü\ *n.* **1** The place in which the subject of a legal action took place. **2** The place where the jury is impaneled and the trial held.

ven·ule \'ven-ˌyül\ *n.* A small vein; a small branch of a vein, as one in the wing of an insect.

Ve·nus's-fly·trap \'vē-nə-səz-'flī-ˌtrap\ *n.* A plant found growing wild on the coast of North and South Carolina and having the apex of the leaf modified into an insect trap which closes when certain sensitive hairs on the inner surface are touched, the trapped insect being digested by an acid secretion within.

ve·ra·cious \və-'rā-shəs\ *adj.* **1** Truthful; honest. **2** True; accurate; as, a *veracious* account. — **ve·ra·cious·ly**, *adv.*

ve·rac·i·ty \və-'ras-ət-ē\ *n.; pl.* **ve·rac·i·ties**. The quality of being veracious; truthfulness.

ve·ran·da or **ve·ran·dah** \və-'ran-də\ *n.* A porch; especially, a long roofed porch extending along one or more sides of a building.

verb \'vərb\ *n.* A word that expresses the occurrence of an action or the existence of a state or condition, as *ate* in the sentence "The boy ate the apple" and *is* in "This ball is red". — *adj.* Of a verb; playing the part of a verb; verbal; as, *verb* endings; a *verb* phrase.

ver·bal \'vərb-l\ *adj.* **1** Of or relating to words; in words; as, to make a few *verbal* changes in the speech. **2** Expressed in words, especially spoken words; spoken; oral; not written; as, a *verbal* answer. **3** Word for word; literal; as, a *verbal* translation. **4** Of, like, containing, or derived from a verb; as, a *verbal* adjective; a *verbal* noun. — For synonyms see *oral.* — *n.* An infinitive, gerund, or participle. — **ver·bal·ly** \-l-ē\ *adv.*

verbal noun. A noun formed from a verb by means of the ending *-ing* and meaning in general the act or process of doing something, as *stealing* in "Stealing is bad", or *skiing* in "Skiing is fun".

ver·ba·tim \(ˌ)vər-'bāt-m\ *adv.* In the same words as those used by another; word for word. — *adj.* Literal; verbal; as, a *verbatim* translation.

ver·be·na \(ˌ)vər-'bē-nə\ *n.* **1** Any of several American garden herbs with spikes or compact rounded clusters of five-petaled white, pink, red, blue, or purple flowers. **2** Any of a family of plants including these herbs and various other plants, as the **lemon verbena**, with white flowers and narrow lemon-scented leaves.

verbena

ver·bi·age \'vər-bē-ij\ *n.* Use of many unnecessary words or of words with little meaning; wordiness; verbosity.

ver·bose \(ˌ)vər-'bōs\ *adj.* Using more words than are needed; wordy. — **ver·bose·ly**, *adv.*

ver·bos·i·ty \(ˌ)vər-'bäs-ət-ē\ *n.; pl.* **ver·bos·i·ties**. The quality or state of being verbose; wordiness.

ver·dant \'vərd-nt\ *adj.* Green as fresh grass; covered with verdure. — **ver·dant·ly**, *adv.*

ver·dict \'vərd-(ˌ)ikt\ *n.* **1** The decision reached by a jury after hearing a case tried; as, a *verdict* of "not guilty". **2** A decision; a judgment.

ver·di·gris \'vərd-ə-ˌgrēs, -ˌgris\ *n.* A green or greenish blue poisonous pigment produced by the action of acetic acid on copper and common on brass surfaces exposed to the weather.

ver·dure \'vərj-r\ *n.* **1** Greenness, especially of vegetation. **2** Green vegetation; a green growth.

verge \'vərj\ *n.* **1** A staff carried as an emblem of authority or office. **2** In early England, the area within which certain high officials had special jurisdiction. **3** A border or boundary line; an edge, brink, or margin; as, on the *verge* of tears. — *v.;* **verged**; **verg·ing**. To border; as, conduct that *verges* on the absurd.

verge \'vərj\ *v.;* **verged**; **verg·ing**. **1** To tend; to incline; as, a hill *verging* to the north. **2** To be in transition from one state to another; as, evening *verging* into night.

verg·er \'vərj-r\ *n.* **1** A person who carries a verge, as before a bishop or a justice. **2** A sexton.

ver·i·fi·a·ble \'ver-ə-ˌfī-əb-l\ *adj.* Capable of being verified. — **ver·i·fi·a·bly** \-ə-blē\ *adv.*

ver·i·fi·ca·tion \ˌver-ə-fə-'kāsh-n\ *n.* The act or the result of verifying; confirmation.

ver·i·fy \'ver-ə-ˌfī\ *v.;* **ver·i·fied** \-ˌfīd\; **ver·i·fy·ing**. **1** To prove to be true or correct; to confirm. **2** To check or test the accuracy of. — **ver·i·fi·er** \-ˌfīr\ *n.*

ver·i·ly \'ver-ə-lē\ *adv.* In fact; truly.

ver·i·ta·ble \'ver-ət-əb-l\ *adj.* True; real; actual; genuine. — **ver·i·ta·bly** \-ə-blē\ *adv.*

ver·i·ty \'ver-ət-ē\ *n.; pl.* **ver·i·ties**. The quality or state of being true; truth; reality.

ver·mi·form appendix \'vər-mə-ˌfȯrm\. A worm-shaped, narrow tube about four inches long, closed at one end, and extending from the caecum in the lower right-hand part of the abdomen.

ver·mil·ion \vər-'mil-yən\ *n.* **1** Any of a number of bright red colors not quite as bright as scarlet. **2** Any pigment yielding one of these colors.

ver·min \'vər-mən\ *n. sing. and pl.* Insects such as fleas and cockroaches and small animals such as rats and mice that trouble people and animals.

ver·nac·u·lar \və(r)-'nak-yəl-r\ *adj.* **1** Of or relating to the ordinary spoken language; not literary or learned. **2** Written in or using a vernacular language. — *n.* **1** A vernacular language. **2** The common way of speaking or writing in a locality or in a trade or profession; as, in the *vernacular* of baseball. **3** A common name of a plant or animal, as distinguished from the Latinized scientific name.

ver·nal \'vərn-l\ *adj.* **1** Of, relating to, or occurring in the spring of the year; as, *vernal* flowers. **2** Characteristic of spring; youthful.

ver·ni·er \'vər-nē-ər\ *n.* Also **vernier scale.** A short scale made to slide along the divisions of a graduated instrument to indicate parts of divisions.

ve·ron·i·ca \və-'rän-ik-ə\ *n.* The speedwell.

ver·sa·tile \'vər-sət-l\ *adj.* Able to do many different kinds of things; as, a *versatile* person.

ver·sa·til·i·ty \ˌvər-sə-'til-ət-ē\ *n.; pl.* **ver·sa·til·i·ties**. The state of being versatile.

verse \'vərs\ *n.* **1** A single line of poetry. "My country, 'tis of thee" is the first *verse* of "America". **2** A stanza or group of lines of poetry. **3** Poetry; as, to write both *verse* and prose. **4** One of the short divisions of a chapter in the Bible.

versed \'vərst\ *adj.* Familiar from study or experience; skilled; as, *versed* in science.

ver·si·fi·ca·tion \ˌvər-sə-fə-'kāsh-n\ *n.* **1** The

making of verses; the action or practice of composing in meter. **2** The arrangement and relationship of syllables and words in meter; prosody.

ver·si·fy \'vər-sə-ˌfī\ *v.;* **ver·si·fied** \-ˌfīd\; **ver·si·fy·ing. 1** To write verse. **2** To turn into verse, especially from a prose form. — **ver·si·fi·er** \-ˌfīr\ *n.*

ver·sion \'vərzh-n\ *n.* **1** A translation; especially, a translation of the Bible; as, the Revised Standard *Version* of the Bible. **2** An account or description given by one person or group. The two boys gave very different *versions* of their fight. **3** A form or variation of another thing; as, an actor giving his *version* of a part in a play.

ver·sus \'vər-səs, -səz\ *prep.* Against; as, the case of John Doe *versus* Richard Roe.

ver·te·bra \'vərt-ə-brə\ *n.; pl.* **ver·te·brae** \-(ˌ)brē, -ˌbrā\ or **ver·te·bras** \-brəz\. One of the bony divisions of the spinal column.

ver·te·bral \'vərt-ə-brəl\ *adj.* Of or relating to a vertebra or vertebrae; spinal.

ver·te·brate \'vərt-ə-brət, -ˌbrāt\ *adj.* Having a backbone. — *n.* Any animal of a vertebrate division containing the mammals, birds, reptiles, amphibians, fishes, and elasmobranchs.

ver·tex \'vər-ˌteks\ *n.; pl.* **ver·tex·es** \-ˌteks-əz\ or **ver·ti·ces** \'vərt-ə-ˌsēz\. **1** The highest point; the top. **2** The point in the heavens directly overhead; the zenith. **3** In mathematics, the point opposite to and farthest from the base.

ver·ti·cal \'vərt-ik-l\ *adj.* Straight upward; rising perpendicularly from a level surface; as, a *vertical* line. — *n.* A vertical line, plane, or circle; especially, a perpendicular. — **ver·ti·cal·ly** \-ik-l(-)ē\ *adv.*

vertical
diagonal
horizontal

ver·ti·go \'vərt-i-ˌgō\ *n.; pl.* **ver·ti·goes** \-ˌgōz\ or **ver·tig·i·nes** \vər-'tij-ə-ˌnēz\. Dizziness; giddiness.

verve \'vərv\ *n.* Liveliness; enthusiasm; spirit; vigor, as in a dramatic performance.

very \'ver-ē\ *adj.;* **ver·i·er; ver·i·est. 1** Absolute; utter. The *veriest* fool knows that. **2** Exact; precise. It is the *very* truth. **3** Identical; same. That is the *very* man who was here before. **4** Even; even the; by way of example. The *very* dogs refused to eat the food. — *adv.* In a high degree; extremely.

very high frequency In radio and television, any frequency in the range from 30 to 300 megacycles.

ves·i·cle \'ves-ik-l\ *n.* A small cavity, cyst, or blister filled with fluid, gas, or air.

ves·per \'vesp-r\ *n.* **1** [with a capital letter] The evening star. **2** The evening. **3** An evening prayer, hymn, or service. **4** A bell sounded at evening. — *adj.* Of or relating to evening; especially, of or relating to a church service held in the late afternoon or evening; as, a *vesper* bell; a *vesper* hymn.

ves·pers \'vesp-rz\ *n. pl.* [often with a capital] A late afternoon or evening church service.

ves·sel \'ves-l\ *n.* **1** A hollow dish or receptacle; a utensil such as a bowl, pot, kettle, or barrel. **2** A boat; especially, a boat larger than a rowboat; a ship. **3** A tube or canal in the body of a person or animal through which blood or lymph flows.

vest \'vest\ *n.* **1** A sleeveless garment reaching just below the waist, worn by men over the shirt and under a coat; a waistcoat. **2** A similar garment worn by women. **3** A vestee. — *v.* **1** To clothe; to dress; especially, to dress in official robes; as, a *vested* clergyman. **2** To give certain powers or rights to; as, authority *vested* in the president. **3** To place in the possession or control of another. The estate is *vested* in the heirs.

vest

ves·tal \'vest-l\ *n.* **1** Also **vestal virgin.** In Roman religion, an unmarried woman who was consecrated to the goddess Vesta and kept the sacred fire burning in her temple. **2** A woman consecrated to virginity; a virgin. **3** A nun.

ves·ti·bule \'ves-tə-ˌbyül\ *n.* A passage, hall, or room between outer and inner doors, as of a building. — **ves·tib·u·lar** \ves-'tib-yəl-r\ *adj.*

ves·tige \'ves-tij\ *n.* **1** A visible trace or sign of something that once existed; a mark. Not a *vestige* remains. **2** In biology, a degenerate or imperfectly developed organ or part that was more fully developed in the ancestors. — **ves·tig·ial** \ves-'tij-l\ *adj.* — **ves·tig·ial·ly** \-'tij-l-ē\ *adv.*

vest·ment \'ves(t)-mənt\ *n.* A garment; clothing; garb; especially, a ceremonial garment worn by a person officiating at a religious service.

ves·try \'ves-trē\ *n.; pl.* **ves·tries. 1** A room in a church building for vestments. **2** Such a room used for chapel or Sunday School or for meetings. **3** In the Anglican Church, a group of persons who have charge of the business affairs of a parish.

ves·try·man \'ves-trē-mən\ *n.; pl.* **ves·try·men** \-mən\. A member of a vestry.

ves·ture \'ves-chər\ *n.* Clothing; dress.

vetch \'vech\ *n.* Any of several climbing plants related to the pea that are used for fodder.

vet·er·an \'vet-r-ən, 've-trən\ *n.* A person who has had long experience in something, especially in war. — *adj.* Grown old in experience; long practiced in something, especially in military life.

vet·er·i·nar·i·an \ˌvet-r-ə-'ner-ē-ən, ˌve-trə-, ˌvet-(r)n-'er-\ *n.* A veterinary.

vet·er·i·nary \'vet-r-ə-ˌner-ē, 've-trə-, 'vet-(r)n-ˌer-ē\ *n.; pl.* **vet·er·i·nar·ies.** A qualified veterinary practitioner. — *adj.* Of or relating to the medical care of animals; as, *veterinary* medicine.

ve·to \'vē-ˌtō\ *n.; pl.* **ve·toes.** [From Latin, meaning "I forbid".] **1** Authoritative refusal to approve or allow something. **2** The power (**veto power**) of one part of a government to forbid something attempted by another part; especially, the power of a chief executive, as a president or governor, to refuse to sign a bill passed by a legislative body and thereby to prevent its becoming a law. — *v.;* **ve·toed; ve·to·ing.** To use one's power of veto; as, to *veto* a suggestion. — **ve·to·er** \'vē-ˌtō-ər\ *n.*

vex \'veks\ *v.* **1** To toss about; to agitate; as, seas *vexed* by the wind. **2** To dispute about; to discuss — used chiefly in phrases such as *a vexed question.* **3** To annoy; to make cross or impatient; as, a *vexing* delay. **4** To trouble greatly; to afflict.

vex·a·tion \(')vek-'sāsh-n\ *n.* **1** The state of being vexed; a feeling of impatience; annoyance; irritation. **2** The action of vexing. **3** Something that vexes or may vex; a cause of worry.

vex·a·tious \(')vek-'sā-shəs\ *adj.* Causing vexation; irritating; annoying. — **vex·a·tious·ly**, *adv.*

VHF. Abbreviation for *very high frequency.*

via \'vī-ə, 'vē-ə\ *prep.* By way of; as, to go *via* the northern route; goods shipped *via* the canal.

vi·a·bil·i·ty \ˌvī-ə-'bil-ət-ē\ *n.* The quality or state of being viable; ability to live, grow, and develop.

vi·a·ble \'vī-əb-l\ *adj.* **1** Capable of living; as, *viable* offspring. **2** Capable of growing or developing; as, *viable* seeds.

vi·a·duct \'vī-ə-ˌdəkt\ *n.* A bridge with high supporting towers or piers, for carrying a road or railroad over something, as over a gorge or a highway.

viaduct

vi·al \'vī-əl, 'vīl\ *n.* A small glass bottle, as for medicines or chemicals.

vi·and \'vī-ənd\ *n.* An article of food; a food — used chiefly in the plural.

vi·at·i·cum \vī-'at-ik-m\ *n.; pl.* **vi·at·i·cums** \-ik-mz\ or **vi·at·i·ca** \-ik-ə\. **1** Provision, especially in money, for the needs and expenses of a journey. **2** Communion given to one dying.

vi·bran·cy \'vīb-rən-sē\ *n.; pl.* **vi·bran·cies.** The quality or state of being vibrant; resonance.

vi·brant \'vīb-rənt\ *adj.* **1** Vibrating; pulsing, as with life and energy; as, a *vibrant* personality. **2** Sounding as a result of vibration; deep or rich in sound; resonant. — **vi·brant·ly**, *adv.*

vi·bra·phone \'vīb-rə-ˌfōn\ *n.* A percussion instrument resembling a glockenspiel but having an electrically operated mechanism for sustaining its tones and creating a vibrato effect.

vi·brate \'vī-ˌbrāt\ *v.* **1** To swing or move back and forth, as a pendulum. **2** To set in vibration. **3** To produce a quivering effect or sound; to shake; to quiver. Mandolin strings *vibrate* when plucked. **4** To thrill; as, to feel one's heart *vibrate* with joy. **5** To waver; to fluctuate, as between two choices.

vi·bra·tion \vī-'brāsh-n\ *n.* **1** The action of vibrating or state of being vibrated; motion or a movement to and fro; oscillation; quiver. **2** In physics, a motion of the particles of an elastic body or medium rapidly to and fro, as when a stretched cord is pulled or struck and produces musical tones, or when particles of air transmit sounds to the ear. **3** A pulsing or throbbing appearance or effect, as of a living body.

vi·bra·to \vē-'brä-ˌtō\ *n.* A slight trembling or pulsating effect given to a musical tone through very small and rapid variations in the pitch.

vi·bra·tor \'vī-ˌbrāt-r\ *n.* One that vibrates or causes vibration, as a hammer in an electric bell.

vi·bra·to·ry \'vīb-rə-ˌtōr-ē, -ˌtȯr-ē\ *adj.* Vibrating; capable of, causing, or consisting of vibrations.

vi·bur·num \vī-'bər-nəm\ *n.* Any of several shrubs or small trees belonging to the same family as the honeysuckle, with small flowers in broad clusters.

vic·ar \'vik-r\ *n.* **1** A substitute in office; a deputy. **2** A clergyman of the Protestant Episcopal Church who is in charge of a single chapel as the deputy of another clergyman. **3** In the Roman Catholic Church, an ecclesiastic who acts as a substitute for or a representative of another.

vic·ar·age \'vik-r-ij\ *n.* A vicar's residence.

vi·car·i·ous \vī-'ker-ē-əs, -'kar-\ *adj.* **1** Acting for someone else; as, a *vicarious* agent. **2** Done or suffered for the benefit of someone else; as, a *vicarious* sacrifice. **3** Enjoyed by one person through his sympathetic sharing in the experience of another; as, *vicarious* pleasure. — **vi·car·i·ous·ly**, *adv.*

vice \'vīs\ *n.* **1** Evil conduct; wickedness; immorality; as, a life of *vice.* **2** A moral fault; an immoral practice or habit. **3** An undesirable habit; a fault or defect, as in a horse or dog.

vice \'vīs\. Variant of *vise.*

vice-. A prefix that can mean: **1** One who takes the place of another, deputy, substitute, as in *vice-president* or *viceroy.* **2** The office or state of such a person, as in *vice-presidency.* **3** Of or relating to such a person or his office, as in *vice-presidential* or *viceregal.*

vice admiral \'vīs\. A naval officer ranking above a rear admiral and below an admiral.

vi·cen·ni·al \vī-'sen-ē-əl\ *adj.* **1** Lasting twenty years. **2** Happening once in twenty years.

vice-pres·i·den·cy \'vīs-'prez-ə-dən-sē, -'prez-dən-, -ə-ˌden-sē\ *n.* The office or position of vice-president.

vice-pres·i·dent \'vīs-'prez-ə-dənt, -'prez-dənt, -ə-ˌdent\ *n.* An official, as of a government, whose rank is next below that of the president and who takes the place of the president when necessary.

vice·re·gal \'vīs-'rēg-l\ *adj.* Of or relating to a viceroy or viceroyalty. — **vice·re·gal·ly** \-'rēg-l-ē\ *adv.*

vice·roy \'vīs-ˌrȯi\ *n.* The governor of a country or province who represents a king or queen.

vice·roy·al·ty \'vīs-ˌrȯi-əl-tē, -ˌrȯil-tē\ *n.* The rank, office, or jurisdiction of a viceroy.

vi·ce ver·sa \'vī-sə 'vər-sə, 'vīs, 'vī-sē\. The relations being reversed; the other way round.

vic·i·nage \'vis-n(-)ij\ *n.* Vicinity; neighborhood.

vi·cin·i·ty \və-'sin-ət-ē\ *n.; pl.* **vi·cin·i·ties.** **1** Nearness; proximity; as, cities in close *vicinity* to each other. **2** Neighborhood; as, in the *vicinity* of Albany.

vi·cious \'vish-əs\ *adj.* **1** Addicted to vice; wicked; having immoral habits. **2** Incorrect; faulty; as, *vicious* reasoning. **3** Spiteful; as, *vicious* slander. **4** Savage; mean; as, a *vicious* dog.

vicious circle. A bad situation or condition that endlessly repeats itself, as when a cause produces an effect which in turn produces the original cause.

vi·cis·si·tude \və-'sis-ə-ˌtüd, vī-, -ˌtyüd\ *n.* A change or succession from one thing to another; especially, an irregular, unexpected, or surprising change; as, the *vicissitudes* of the weather.

vic·tim \'vikt-m\ *n.* **1** A living person or animal offered as a sacrifice in a religious rite. **2** A person or animal injured or killed, as by disease or accident. **3** A person who is cheated, fooled, insulted, or robbed, by someone else.

vic·tim·ize \'vikt-m-ˌīz\ *v.;* **vic·tim·ized**; **vic·tim·iz·ing.** To make a victim of, especially by deception; to cheat. — **vic·tim·iz·er** \-ˌīz-r\ *n.*

vic·tor \'vikt-r\ *n.* A winner; a conqueror.

vic·to·ria \vik-'tōr-ē-ə, -'tȯr-\ *n.* [Named after *Victoria* (1819–1901), queen of England.] A low-slung four-wheeled carriage with a folding top and a raised seat in front for the driver.

victoria

vic·to·ri·ous \vik-'tōr-ē-əs, -'tȯr-\ *adj.* Having won a victory; conquering; as, a *victorious* army; *victorious* strategy. — **vic·to·ri·ous·ly**, *adv.*

vic·to·ry \'vikt-r(-)ē\ *n.; pl.* **vic·to·ries.** The overcoming of an opponent; a conquest.

— The words *conquest* and *triumph* are synonyms of *victory: victory* usually suggests little more than the defeat of an opponent or opposing force in a struggle or contest, but may also suggest satisfaction felt by or praise given to the victor as a result; *conquest* refers to the overthrow and mastery of one's enemies or opponents; *triumph* nearly always indicates great acclaim, glory, and personal satisfaction that come as the result of brilliant victory or overwhelming conquest.

vict·ual \'vit-l\ *n.* Food for human beings — used chiefly in the plural. — *v.;* **vict·ualed** or **vict·ualled**; **vict·ual·ing** or **vict·ual·ling** \-l(-)ing\. To supply with provisions; to store with food, as a ship.

vict·ual·er or **vict·ual·ler** \'vit-l(-)ər\ *n.* One that furnishes provisions.

vi·cu·ña \vī-'k(y)ü-nə, vi-'kün-yə\ *n.; pl.* **vi·cu·ñas** or **vi·cu·ña.** **1** A cud-chewing, wool-bearing wild animal of the Andes related to the llama and the alpaca. **2** A fabric woven from the wool of the vicuña.

vicuña

vid·eo \'vid-ē-ˌō\ *adj.* Relating to or used in the transmission or reception of the image in television. — *n.* Television.

vie \'vī\ *v.;* **vied** \'vīd\; **vy·ing** \'vī-ing\. To strive for superiority; to contend.

Vi·et·nam·ese \vē-ˌet-nə-'mēz, -'mēs\ *adj.* Of or relating to Vietnam. — *n.* **1** *sing. and pl.* A native or inhabitant of Vietnam. **2** The Vietnamese language.

view \'vyü\ *n.* **1** The act or fact of seeing; inspection by the eye; a look; a sight; as, a good *view* of the ocean. **2** The act or fact of seeing or going over in the mind; mental perception or examination; as, a clear *view* of recent events. **3** The range of sight. The planes passed out of *view.* **4** Something seen; a scene; as, a beautiful *view.* **5** A picture of a scene; as, postcard *views* of Niagara Falls. **6** Opinion; judgment; as, to state one's *views* clearly and briefly. **7** An aim; intention; as, to put aside money with a *view* to taking a summer trip. — **in view of.** In consideration of. — **on view.** On exhibition; open to public inspection. — **with a view to.** With the purpose of. — *v.* **1** To see; to look at carefully; to examine. **2** To examine mentally; as, to *view* all sides of a question. — **view·er** \'vyü-ər, 'vyu̇r\ *n.*

view·point \'vyü-ˌpȯint\ *n.* Point of view; standpoint; a characteristic mental attitude.

vig·il \'vij-l\ *n.* **1** The day before a church feast; the eve of a holy day. **2** [in the plural] Prayers or devotional services held in the evening or at night. **3** The act of keeping awake or state of being awake; especially, wakeful attention; a watch; as, to keep *vigil.*

vig·i·lance \'vij-l-ən(t)s\ *n.* **1** Wakefulness. **2** The quality or state of being vigilant; caution.

vig·i·lant \'vij-l-ənt\ *adj.* Watchful, as one keeping vigil; alert to discover and avoid danger.

— The words *watchful* and *alert* are synonyms of *vigilant: watchful* is the most general of these terms and indicates being on the lookout, especially for dangers or opportunities; *vigilant* usually suggests extremely keen, wary, and suspicious watchfulness against danger, especially in the cause of right and justice; *alert* stresses the idea of readiness and promptness to meet some danger or emergency or to seize an opportunity.

vig·i·lan·te \ˌvij-l-'ant-ē\ *n.* A member of a local volunteer committee (**vigilance committee**) organized to suppress and punish crime.

vig·i·lant·ly \'vij-l-ənt-lē\ *adv.* In a vigilant manner; attentively; warily.

vi·gnette \vin-'yet\ *n.* **1** A small decorative design or illustration, as one on the title page of a book or at the beginning or end of a chapter. **2** A picture that shades off gradually into the surrounding ground. **3** A descriptive sketch in words.

vig·or \'vig-r\ *n.* **1** Active strength or energy of body or mind. **2** Intensity; force.

vig·or·ous \'vig-r(-)əs\ *adj.* **1** Having vigor; robust. **2** Done with vigor; carried out forcefully and energetically; as, a *vigorous* protest; *vigorous* exercise. — **vig·or·ous·ly**, *adv.*

vi·king \'vīk-ing\ *n.* One of the Norse pirates who plundered the coasts of Europe in the 8th to 10th centuries.

vile \'vīl\ *adj.;* **vil·er**; **vil·est.** **1** Filthy; unclean; nasty. **2** Morally impure; wicked; as, *vile* deeds. **3** Very bad; as, *vile* weather. — **vile·ly** \-lē\ *adv.*

vil·i·fy \'vil-ə-ˌfī\ *v.;* **vil·i·fied** \-ˌfīd\; **vil·i·fy·ing.** To blacken the character of with abusive language; to slander; to defame. — **vil·i·fi·ca·tion** \ˌvil-ə-fə-'kāsh-n\ *n.* — **vil·i·fi·er** \'vil-ə-ˌfīr\ *n.*

vil·la \'vil-ə\ *n.* A somewhat pretentious residence in the country or suburbs.

vil·lage \'vil-ij\ *n.* **1** A group of houses in the country, usually less in number than in a town and more than in a hamlet. **2** The people of a village.

vil·lag·er \'vil-ij-r\ *n.* One who lives in a village.

vil·lain \'vil-ən\ *n.* **1** A villein. **2** An evil person; a scoundrel; a rascal. **3** A character in a play or story drawn to represent such a person.

vil·lain·ous \'vil-ə-nəs\ *adj.* **1** Evil; wicked; befitting a villain. **2** Bad; detestable; as, *villainous* weather. — **vil·lain·ous·ly**, *adv.*

vil·lainy \'vil-ə-nē\ *n.; pl.* **vil·lain·ies. 1** Villainous conduct; a villainous act. **2** Villainous character or nature; wickedness.

vil·lein \'vil-ən, -ˌān, vi-'lān\ *n.* A member of a class of feudal serfs whose status gradually changed to that of free peasants.

vil·lous \'vil-əs\ *adj.* Covered with fine hairs.

vil·lus \'vil-əs\ *n.; pl.* **vil·li** \-ˌī\ or **vil·lus·es** \-ə-səz\. **1** One of the very small fingerlike projections of the mucous membrane of the small intestine that assist in absorbing nourishment. **2** Any of the fine, straight, soft hairs on plants.

vim \'vim\ *n.* Energy; force; vigor.

vin·di·cate \'vin-də-ˌkāt\ *v.;* **vin·di·cat·ed; vin·di·cat·ing. 1** To defend as true, correct, or honest; to sustain; to justify. Later discoveries *vindicated* the early explorers' claims. **2** To free from suspicion, as of wrongdoing. — **vin·di·ca·tor** \-ˌkāt-r\ *n.*

vin·di·ca·tion \ˌvin-də-'kāsh-n\ *n.* A vindicating or a being vindicated; defense; justification.

vin·dic·tive \vin-'dik-tiv\ *adj.* Tending to return evil for evil; revengeful; as, a *vindictive* attitude. — **vin·dic·tive·ly**, *adv.* — **vin·dic·tive·ness**, *n.*

vine \'vīn\ *n.* **1** A grapevine. **2** A plant whose stem requires support and which climbs or trails or creeps. **3** The stem of such a plant.

vin·e·gar \'vin-ig-r\ *n.* A sour liquid obtained by the fermentation of cider, wine, or malt, and used to flavor or preserve foods.

vinegar eel. A threadlike roundworm found in vinegar and other fermenting substances.

vin·e·gary \'vin-ig-r(-)ē\ *adj.* **1** Like vinegar. **2** Sour; cross; as, a *vinegary* remark.

vine·yard \'vin-yərd\ *n.* A field of grapevines.

vin·tage \'vint-ij\ *n.* **1** The grapes or wine produced during one season; as, the *vintage* of 1910. **2** The action or time of gathering grapes or making wine. **3** Wine; especially, a wine of a particular type or district in a stated year, especially one (**vintage wine**) of superior quality. **4** A type once popular; as, songs of the *vintage* of 1890.

vint·ner \'vint-nər\ *n.* A wine merchant; especially, a wholesaler of wine.

viny \'vī-nē\ *adj.;* **vin·i·er; vin·i·est.** Of or relating to vines; resembling vines; consisting of vines; full of vines.

vi·nyl resin \'vīn-l\ or **vi·nyl plastic.** Any of a group of elastic resins resistant to chemical agents, used for protective coatings and molded articles.

vi·ol \'vī-əl, 'vīl\ *n.* A medieval musical instrument resembling the violin.

vi·o·la \vē-'ō-lə\ *n.* A stringed musical instrument like a violin but slightly larger and lower in pitch.

vi·o·la \vī-'ō-lə, 'vī-ə-lə\ *n.* Any of numerous garden plants that are hybrids between garden pansies and a European violet and have flowers like but smaller than those of the pansies.

vi·o·late \'vī-ə-ˌlāt\ *v.;* **vi·o·lat·ed; vi·o·lat·ing. 1** To infringe on; as, to *violate* a person's rights. **2** To break or disregard, as a law, rule, or promise. **3** To rape. **4** To treat something sacred with disrespect or scorn. **5** To cross the boundary between two nations without the right to do so. **6** To interrupt; to disturb. The quiet of the night was *violated* by loud shouting. — **vi·o·la·tor** \-ˌlāt-r\ *n.*

vi·o·la·tion \ˌvī-ə-'lāsh-n\ *n.* **1** A breaking; as, a *violation* of the law. **2** An infringement; as, a *violation* of a person's rights. **3** A profaning, as of a church. **4** An interruption; a disturbance.

vi·o·lence \'vī-ə-lən(t)s\ *n.* **1** The use of force in a way that harms a person or thing; as, murder and other acts of *violence.* **2** Energy, especially destructive energy, in action; as, the *violence* of a storm. **3** Injury; damage; outrage. Receiving a public scolding would do *violence* to the child's pride. **4** Intensity, as of an emotion.

vi·o·lent \'vī-ə-lənt\ *adj.* **1** Moving, acting, or done by force; severe; as, a *violent* storm. **2** Great; extreme; intense; as, *violent* pain; colors in *violent* contrast. **3** Caused by force; not natural; as, a *violent* death. **4** Showing strong feelings, especially anger. A *violent* speech. — **vi·o·lent·ly**, *adv.*

vi·o·let \'vī-ə-lət\ *n.* **1** Any of numerous wild or garden plants related to the pansies and violas but having usually heart-shaped leaves and blue, violet, white, or yellow flowers. **2** The flower of a violet. **3** Any of various unrelated plants resembling violets. **4** The color of certain violets; purplish blue.

violets

vi·o·lin \ˌvī-ə-'lin\ *n.* **1** A musical instrument consisting of a hollow resonance box, with a slightly rounded front and back, a narrow neck, a low bridge, and four strings, played with a bow; a fiddle. **2** A violin player, especially in an orchestra.

vi·o·lin·ist \ˌvī-ə-'lin-əst\ *n.* A violin player.

vi·o·lon·cel·list \ˌvī-ə-lən-'chel-əst, ˌvē-\ *n.* A player on the violoncello.

vi·o·lon·cel·lo \ˌvī-ə-lən-'chel-ˌō, ˌvē-\ *n.; pl.* **vi·o·lon·cel·los.** A cello.

vi·per \'vīp-r\ *n.* A stout sluggish snake with broad, flat head and poison fangs in the upper jaw; especially, any poisonous snake (**pit viper**) having a hollow or pit between the eye and the nostril, including the rattlesnake, copperhead, and water moccasin.

vi·ra·go \və-'rā-ˌgō, -'räg-ˌō, -'ràg-ˌō\ *n.; pl.* **vi·ra·goes** or **vi·ra·gos.** A scolding, quarrelsome woman.

vir·eo \'vir-ē-ˌō\ *n.; pl.* **vir·e·os.** Any of a family of small, insect-eating songbirds, chiefly olive-green or grayish in color, with a musical song.

vir·gin \'vərj-n\ *n.* A maiden; a girl or woman who has not had sexual intercourse. — **The Virgin.** Mary, the mother of Jesus. — *adj.* **1** Being a virgin; chaste; modest. **2** Pure; clean; spotless; as, *virgin* snow. **3** Unused; undisturbed; as, a *virgin* forest. — **vir·gin·al** \'vərj-n-əl\ *adj.*

vir·gin·al \'vərj-n-əl\ *n.* A small rectangular spinet without legs.

Vir·gin·ia creeper \vər-'jin-yə\. A North American vine related to the grape, with tendrils having sucking disks and with five leaflets and bluish-black berries; the woodbine.

Virginia deer. The most widely distributed deer of the United States, with long tail, white on the under side, and forward-arching antlers — in its summer coat called also *red deer.*

Virginia reel. A country dance in which the partners have facing positions in two lines.

vir·gin·i·ty \vər-'jin-ət-ē\ *n.* A virgin condition; chastity.

vir·ile \'vir-əl\ *adj.* **1** Having the nature, powers, or qualities of a man. **2** Masterful; forceful; as, a *virile* personality.

vi·ril·i·ty \və-'ril-ət-ē\ *n.* **1** The quality or state of being virile. **2** Manhood. **3** Manly vigor, power, or force; as, *virility* of action.

vir·tu·al \'vər-chə-wəl, 'vərch-l\ *adj.* Being something in effect, though not commonly called by that name; as, the *virtual* ruler of a country. — **vir·tu·al·ly** \'vərch-l-ē, 'vər-chə-wə-lē\ *adv.*

vir·tue \'vər-(ˌ)chü\ *n.* **1** Moral action; moral excellence; morality; especially, chastity. **2** A particular moral excellence. Justice and patience are *virtues.* **3** Such qualities collectively. **4** The active power to accomplish a stated effect; as, a medicine that has *virtue* in this case. **5** Excellence; worth; merit; as, to enumerate the *virtues* of living in the country. — **by virtue of** or **in virtue of.** Through the force of; by authority of.

vir·tu·os·i·ty \ˌvər-chə-'wäs-ət-ē\ *n.; pl.* **vir·tu·os·i·ties.** Great technical skill in the practice of the fine arts, especially in music.

vir·tu·o·so \ˌvər-chə-'wō-ˌsō, -ˌzō\ *n.; pl.* **vir·tu·o·sos** \-ˌsōz, -ˌzōz\ or **vir·tu·o·si** \-ˌsē, -ˌzē\. **1** A person who is skilled in or has a taste for the fine arts; a collector, as of curios. **2** A person who excels in the technique of an art, as in playing the piano.

vir·tu·ous \'vər-chə-wəs\ *adj.* Having moral virtue; especially, chaste; pure. — **vir·tu·ous·ly,** *adv.*

vir·u·lent \'vir-yə-lənt, 'vir-ə-\ *adj.* **1** Extremely poisonous; deadly. **2** Bitterly hostile; as, *virulent* criticism. **3** Highly infectious — used of disease germs. **4** Developing rapidly, often with serious effects — used of diseases and infections. — **vir·u·lence** \-lən(t)s\ *n.* — **vir·u·lent·ly** \-lənt-lē\ *adv.*

vi·rus \'vī-rəs\ *n.* [From Latin, meaning "slime", "poison".] Any of several simple disease-causing agents smaller than bacteria; as, the polio *virus.*

vi·sa \'vē-zə\ *n.* Something written on a document, as a passport, to show that it has been approved by the proper authority. — *v.;* **vi·saed** \-zəd\; **vi·sa·ing.** To give a visa to.

vis·age \'viz-ij\ *n.* The face.

vis·cera \'vis-r-ə\ *n. pl.* The internal organs of the body, as the heart, liver, and intestines. — **vis·cer·al** \-r-əl\ *adj.*

vis·cid \'vis-əd\ *adj.* Viscous; gluey.

vis·cos·i·ty \vis-'käs-ət-ē\ *n.; pl.* **vis·cos·i·ties.** The quality of being viscous; especially, a tendency of a liquid to flow slowly resulting from friction of its molecules; as, the *viscosity* of oil.

vis·count \'vī-ˌkaunt\ *n.* A nobleman ranking just above a baron and below an earl or count.

vis·count·ess \'vī-ˌkaunt-əs\ *n.* **1** The wife or widow of a viscount. **2** A woman who has in her own right a rank equal to that of a viscount.

vis·cous \'vis-kəs\ *adj.* **1** Somewhat sticky; gluey; viscid. **2** Having or characterized by viscosity.

vise or **vice** \'vīs\ *n.* Any of various devices for holding or clamping, having two jaws operated by a screw or lever.

vise

vis·i·bil·i·ty \ˌviz-ə-'bil-ət-ē\ *n.* **1** The quality, condition, or degree of being visible. **2** The degree of clearness of the air; as, a thick fog with *visibility* zero.

vis·i·ble \'viz-əb-l\ *adj.* **1** Capable of being seen; apparent to the eye; as, stars *visible* to the naked eye. **2** Apparent; discoverable; as, no *visible* means of support.

vis·i·bly \'viz-ə-blē\ *adv.* In a way that can be seen; noticeably; plainly; as, *visibly* embarrassed.

vi·sion \'vizh-n\ *n.* **1** Something that is seen otherwise than by ordinary sight, as in a dream or a trance. **2** Something seen as an image in the mind as a result of thinking. **3** Any vivid picture created by the imagination; as, *visions* of wealth. **4** The power of calling up pictures by the imagination. **5** Unusual wisdom in foreseeing the course of future events; as, a statesman of *vision.* **6** The act or power of seeing; as, to have perfect *vision.* **7** The sense by which objects, light, and color are perceived. **8** That which is seen; especially, a lovely sight. — *v.;* **vi·sioned; vi·sion·ing** \-n(-)ing\. To see in or as if in a vision.

vi·sion·ary \'vizh-n-ˌer-ē\ *adj.* **1** Given to dreaming or imagining. **2** Of the nature of a vision; fanciful; not practical; as *visionary* schemes. — *n.; pl.* **vi·sion·ar·ies.** A person who sees visions; any person whose ideas or projects are impractical.

vis·it \'viz-ət\ *v.;* **vis·it·ed** \'viz-ət-əd, 'viz-təd\; **vis·it·ing** \'viz-ət-ing, 'viz-ting\. **1** To go or come to see in order to comfort or help; as, to *visit* the sick. **2** To call upon, either socially as a matter of respect or courtesy, or in a professional capacity. A doctor *visits* his patients. **3** To dwell with for a time as a guest; as, to *visit* a cousin for a week.

4 To come upon, especially as a punishment or affliction; as, to be *visited* by fears. 5 To inflict; to bring down; as, to *visit* one's wrath upon the guilty. 6 To make a visit, or regular visits. — *n.* An act of visiting; especially, a short stay.

vis·it·ant \'viz-ə-tənt, 'viz-tənt\ *n.* 1 A visitor, especially an important or extraordinary one. 2 A migratory animal, especially a bird, that appears at intervals for a limited period in a place.

vis·it·a·tion \ˌviz-ə-'tāsh-n\ *n.* 1 The act of visiting. 2 A visit; especially, an official visit, as one by a bishop to a church in his diocese. 3 Something considered to be a punishment, or, rarely, a reward, given by God; especially, a severe trial.

vis·it·ing card \'viz-ət-ing, 'viz-ting\. A small card bearing a person's name, sometimes left at a house at which a social call is made.

vis·i·tor \'viz-ət-r, 'viz-tər\ *n.* One that visits.

vi·sor or **vi·zor** \'vīz-r\ *n.* 1 The front piece of a helmet; especially, a movable upper piece that when raised shows the face and when lowered covers it. 2 The part of a cap that projects in front and shades the eyes.

visor

visor, 1

vis·ta \'vis-tə\ *n.* 1 A view, usually over some distance, as down an avenue or over a valley; the scene viewed. 2 A mental view over a period of time.

vi·su·al \'vizh-ə-wəl\ *adj.* 1 Of or relating to sight; used in seeing; as, the *visual* nerve. 2 Perceived, gained, or performed by means of vision; as, a *visual* impression; *visual* tests. 3 Capable of being seen; visible; as, *visual* objects.

visual aid. Any device that uses vision as the chief aid to instruction, as a chart, map, or model, but especially a moving picture or filmstrip.

vi·su·al·ize \'vizh-l-ˌīz, 'vizh-ə-wə-ˌlīz\ *v.;* **vi·su·al·ized; vi·su·al·iz·ing.** To form a mental image of something not before the eye.

vi·su·al·ly \'vizh-l-ē, 'vizh-ə-wə-lē\ *adv.* In a visual way; by or with respect to the sense of sight.

visual purple. A purple-red pigment in the retina in human eyes and those of most other animals, sensitive to dim light and functioning in night vision.

vi·tal \'vīt-l\ *adj.* 1 Of, relating to, or characteristic of life; showing the qualities of living things; as, *vital* force; *vital* statistics. 2 Necessary to the continuance of life; being some part which is essential to life; as, *vital* organs; wounded in a *vital* part. 3 Animated; full of vitality. 4 Fatal; mortal. 5 Fundamental; basic; of first importance.

vital capacity. The breathing capacity of the lungs, expressed by the number of cubic inches or cubic centimeters of air that can be forcibly exhaled after a full inspiration.

vi·tal·i·ty \vī-'tal-ət-ē\ *n.* 1 Life; vital force; the ability to keep on living. 2 The power of enduring or continuing; as, the *vitality* of old customs. 3 Liveliness; energy; vigor; animation.

vi·tal·ize \'vīt-l-ˌīz\ *v.;* **vi·tal·ized; vi·tal·iz·ing.** 1 To give life to; to make alive. 2 To give energy or vigor to; to animate; to increase the vitality of. — **vi·tal·i·za·tion** \ˌvīt-l-ə-'zāsh-n\ *n.*

vi·tal·ly \'vīt-l-ē\ *adv.* 1 In a manner or to a degree necessary to continued existence; essentially; indispensably; as, *vitally* important. 2 So as to affect or destroy life; in a vital part; fatally; mortally.

vi·tals \'vīt-lz\ *n. pl.* 1 The organs of the body necessary for life, as the heart, lungs, liver, and brain. 2 The essential parts of anything.

vital statistics. Statistics relating to births, deaths, marriages, health, and disease.

vi·ta·min or **vi·ta·mine** \'vīt-ə-mən\ *n.* Any of certain substances found in foods in their natural state, as in fresh fruits, vegetables, milk, cod-liver oil, and egg yolk, and necessary for the proper development and health of human beings and animals, including **vitamin A**, found especially in fish-liver oils, animal food products, and fresh-water fish, its lack resulting in hardening of certain tissues, as in the eye, and the failure of young animals to grow; the vitamin-B complex; **vitamin C** (ascorbic acid); **vitamin D**, of which various kinds, as D_2 and D_3, are known, found especially in fish-liver oils and egg yolk, and the lack of which results in rickets.

vitamin-B complex. A group of vitamins including **vitamin B_1** \'bē-'wən\ (thiamine); **vitamin B_2** \'bē-'tü\ (riboflavin); **vitamin B_6** \'bē-'siks\ (pyridoxine); **vitamin B_{12}** \'bē-'twelv\, extracted from liver and used in treating certain forms of anemia; niacin; pantothenic acid.

vi·ti·ate \'vish-ē-ˌāt\ *v.;* **vi·ti·at·ed; vi·ti·at·ing.** 1 To injure the quality of; to spoil; to weaken. 2 To destroy the validity of. Fraud *vitiates* a contract.

vit·re·ous \'vi-trē-əs\ *adj.* Of, relating to, or like glass; as, *vitreous* china; *vitreous* rocks.

vitreous humor. The clear, colorless jellylike substance at the back of the lens in the eyeball.

vit·ri·fy \'vi-trə-ˌfī\ *v.;* **vit·ri·fied** \-ˌfīd\; **vit·ri·fy·ing.** To change into glass or a glassy substance by heat and fusion, as some rocks. — **vit·ri·fi·ca·tion** \ˌvi-trə-fə-'kāsh-n\ or **vit·ri·fac·tion** \-'faksh-n\ *n.*

vit·ri·ol \'vi-trē-əl\ *n.* 1 A sulfate of any of various metals, as copper (**blue vitriol**\, iron (**green vitriol**), or zinc (**white vitriol**). 2 Sulfuric acid. 3 Anything likened to vitriol in being caustic or biting.

vit·ri·ol·ic \ˌvi-trē-'äl-ik\ *adj.* 1 Of or relating to vitriol. 2 Caustic; biting; as, a *vitriolic* speech.

vi·tu·per·ate \vī-'tüp-r-ˌāt, və-, -'tyüp-\ *v.;* **vi·tu·per·at·ed; vi·tu·per·at·ing.** To abuse in words, to scold. — **vi·tu·per·a·tion** \-ˌtüp-r-'āsh-n, -ˌtyüp-\ *n.*

vi·tu·per·a·tive \vī-'tüp-r-ˌāt-iv, və-, -'tyüp-, -r(-)ət-\ *adj.* Abusive; scolding. — **vi·tu·per·a·tive·ly,** *adv.*

vi·va·cious \vī-'vā-shəs, və-\ *adj.* Lively; active; animated; gay. — **vi·va·cious·ly,** *adv.*

vi·vac·i·ty \vī-'vas-ət-ē, və-\ *n.; pl.* **vi·vac·i·ties.** The quality or state of being vivacious.

vi·var·i·um \vī-'ver-ē-əm\ *n.; pl.* **vi·var·i·ums** \-ē-əmz\ or **vi·var·ia** \-ē-ə\. An enclosure for keeping or raising animals indoors.

viv·id \'viv-əd\ *adj.* **1** Having the appearance of vigorous life; as, a *vivid* portrait. **2** Very bright, lively, intense, or clear; as, *vivid* red; a *vivid* image. **3** Acting clearly and vigorously; as, a *vivid* imagination. **4** Calling forth lifelike mental images; as, a *vivid* description. — **viv·id·ly**, *adv.*

viv·i·fy \'viv-ə-ˌfī\ *v.;* **viv·i·fied** \-ˌfīd\; **viv·i·fy·ing.** **1** To put life into; to animate; to enliven. **2** To make vivid. — **viv·i·fi·ca·tion** \ˌviv-ə-fə-'kāsh-n\ *n.*

vi·vip·a·rous \vī-'vip-r(-)əs\ *adj.* Bringing forth living young from within the body rather than from eggs. Nearly all mammals are *viviparous.*

viv·i·sec·tion \ˌviv-ə-'seksh-n\ *n.* The cutting of, or operation on, a living animal, for purposes of scientific investigation. — **viv·i·sect** \'viv-ə-ˌsekt\ *v.* — **viv·i·sec·tor** \'viv-ə-ˌsekt-r\ *n.*

viv·i·sec·tion·ist \ˌviv-ə-'seksh-n(-)əst\ *n.* **1** A vivisector. **2** A supporter of vivisection.

vix·en \'viks-n\ *n.* **1** A female fox. **2** An ill-tempered, scolding, shrewish woman.

viz. \'nām-lē *or* 'viz\ *adv.* [An abbreviation of Latin *videlicet* meaning literally "it is easy to see".] Namely.

viz·ard \'viz-rd\ *n.* A mask; a visor.

vi·zier \və-'zir\ *n.* A minister or councilor of state in many Moslem countries, especially in the former Ottoman empire.

vizor. Variant of *visor.*

vo·cab·u·lary \vō-'kab-yə-ˌler-ē\ *n.; pl.* **vo·cab·u·lar·ies.** **1** A collection of words, usually alphabetically arranged and defined; a dictionary, as of a language, a book, an author, or a subject. **2** The stock of words used in a language or by a group or an individual; as, the *vocabulary* of school children.

vo·cal \'vōk-l\ *adj.* **1** Of or relating to the voice; as, *vocal* music; the *vocal* organs. **2** Having the power of speech. **3** Talkative; clamorous; as, to be very *vocal* in making a complaint.

vocal cords. Either of two pairs of membranous folds at the top of the windpipe that produce voice when drawn tight and vibrated by the outgoing breath.

vo·cal·ic \vō-'kal-ik\ *adj.* **1** Of, relating to, or containing, a vowel sound. **2** Like a vowel in sound.

vo·cal·ist \'vōk-l-əst\ *n.* A singer.

vo·cal·ize \'vōk-l-ˌīz\ *v.;* **vo·cal·ized; vo·cal·iz·ing.** **1** To give vocal expression to. **2** To sing.

vo·cal·ly \'vōk-l-ē\ *adv.* In a vocal manner; with the voice; by speaking or singing; orally.

vo·ca·tion \vō-'kāsh-n\ *n.* **1** A call or summons, as to a business, profession, or way of life. **2** The work to which one feels called or specially fitted. **3** Regular employment; occupation.

vo·ca·tion·al \vō-'kāsh-n(-)əl\ *adj.* Of or relating to vocation or vocations; carried on or done as a vocation; concerned with choice of vocations and training for them; as, *vocational* guidance; a *vocational* school. — **vo·ca·tion·al·ly** \-n(-)ə-lē\ *adv.*

vo·cif·er·ate \vō-'sif-r-ˌāt\ *v.;* **vo·cif·er·at·ed; vo·cif·er·at·ing.** To cry or call out loudly; to shout; to clamor. — **vo·cif·er·a·tion** \vō-ˌsif-r-'āsh-n\ *n.*

vo·cif·er·ous \vō-'sif-r(-)əs\ *adj.* Making a loud outcry; noisy; clamorous. — **vo·cif·er·ous·ly**, *adv.*

vod·ka \'väd-kə\ *n.* [From Russian, a diminutive of *voda* meaning "water".] A distilled alcoholic liquor made from grain, commonly rye.

vogue \'vōg\ *n.* **1** Popularity; a period of popularity; as, a year when horror stories had quite a *vogue.* **2** The fashion; something in fashion at a particular time. — **in vogue.** In fashion; popular.

voice \'vȯis\ *n.* **1** The sound uttered from the mouth of living beings, especially human beings, as in speaking, singing, or shouting. **2** The power of speaking; utterance; as, to lose one's *voice.* **3** Anything likened to human speech as a medium of expression. The ballot is the *voice* of the people. **4** Choice; vote; as, to have no *voice* in the matter. **5** Any sound likened to a vocal utterance; as, the *voice* of the sea. **6** Musical sound produced by the vocal cords; tones uttered in singing; as, the three male *voices*, tenor, baritone, and bass. **7** Also **voice part.** One of the parts in a vocal or instrumental composition. **8** The ability to sing; as, to have no *voice* at all. **9** The condition of the vocal cords with respect to the quality of tone produced; as, to be in good *voice.* **10** Grammatical difference in form taken by a verb to show the relation of the subject, whether as doer or object, by the action expressed by the verb; as, the active *voice.* In "the man was struck by a car", the verb "was struck" is in the passive *voice.* — *v.;* **voiced; voic·ing.** **1** To utter; as, to *voice* one's thanks. **2** To regulate the tone of, as organ pipes. **3** To vibrate the vocal cords in producing, as certain speech sounds.

voice box. The larynx.

voice·less \'vȯis-ləs\ *adj.* **1** Having no voice; silent; dumb. **2** Of a speech sound, not voiced. — **voice·less·ly**, *adv.*

void \'vȯid\ *adj.* **1** Empty; lacking; as, a remark *void* of sense. **2** Not producing any effect; useless; especially, having no legal force. The court declared the law *void.* — *n.* **1** An empty space; as, a vast *void.* **2** A feeling of emptiness. The father's departure left a *void* in the family. — *v.* **1** To make or leave void; evacuate. **2** To make of no effect; to nullify; as, to *void* a debt. — **void·a·ble**, *adj.*

voile \'vȯil\ *n.* A soft, sheer fabric of silk, cotton, rayon, or wool.

vol. Abbreviation for *volume.*

vol·a·tile \'väl-ət-l\ *adj.* **1** Evaporating quickly; readily becoming a vapor. **2** Lively; lighthearted. **3** Changeable; fickle; as, too *volatile* to be trustworthy. — **vol·a·til·i·ty** \ˌväl-ə-'til-ət-ē\ *n.*

vol·can·ic \väl-'kan-ik\ *adj.* **1** Of or relating to a volcano; as, a *volcanic* eruption. **2** Having volcanoes; as, a *volcanic* region. **3** Made of materials from volcanoes; as, *volcanic* rock.

vol·ca·no \väl-'kā-ˌnō\ *n.; pl.* **vol·ca·noes** or **vol·ca·nos.** **1** A hole in the earth from which molten rock, steam, and ashes are thrown up. **2** A hill or mountain composed of material thus thrown up.

vole \'vōl\ *n.* Any of several stout-bodied short-eared and short-tailed rodents with blunt snouts, harmful to crops.

vo·li·tion \vō-'lish-n\ *n.* **1** The act or power of making one's own choices or decisions; will. **2** The choice made or decision reached.

vol·ley \'väl-ē\ *n.; pl.* **vol·leys. 1** A shower of missiles, as arrows or bullets. **2** A discharge of a number of weapons at the same instant. **3** A bursting forth of a number of things at once; as, a *volley* of curses; a *volley* of laughter. **4** A volleying. — *v.* **1** To discharge in a volley. **2** To bat a ball back and forth, as over a net before it touches the ground, as in tennis.

vol·ley·ball \'väl-ē-ˌbȯl\ *n.* A game played by volleying by hand a large inflated ball over a net.

vol·plane \'väl-ˌplān\ *v.;* **vol·planed; vol·plan·ing.** To glide in an airplane. — *n.* A volplaning.

volt \'vōlt\ *n.* [Named after the Italian physicist Alessandro *Volta* (1745–1827).] The unit for measuring the force exerted to produce an electric current, being that force which when steadily applied to a conductor whose resistance is one ohm, will produce a current of one ampere.

volt·age \'vōl-tij\ *n.* Electric power measured in volts.

vol·ta·ic cell \väl-'tā-ik\. An apparatus for generating electricity through chemical action on two unlike metals in an electrolyte.

vol·tam·e·ter \väl-'tam-ət-r, vōlt-'am-\ *n.* An instrument for measuring the quantity of electricity passed through a conductor.

volt·me·ter \'vōlt-ˌmēt-r\ *n.* An instrument for measuring an electric current in volts.

vol·u·ble \'väl-yəb-l\ *adj.* Smooth and ready in talking; glib; talkative. — For synonyms see *talkative.* — **vol·u·bil·i·ty** \ˌväl-yə-'bil-ət-ē\ *n.*

vol·ume \'väl-yəm\ *n.* **1** A book; as, a dozen *volumes* on the shelf. **2** Any one of a series of books forming a complete work or collection; as, the fifth *volume* of an encyclopedia. **3** Space occupied; space included within certain limits, as measured in cubic units; as, the *volume* of a cylinder. **4** A mass; a bulk; a large amount; as, a *volume* of smoke. **5** In music, fullness or quantity of tone.

vol·u·met·ric \ˌväl-yə-'me-trik\ *adj.* Of or relating to the measurement of volume.

vo·lu·mi·nous \və-'lü-mə-nəs\ *adj.* **1** Consisting of many folds or windings; as, a *voluminous* garment. **2** Of great volume or bulk; large. **3** Enough to fill a large volume or several volumes; as, *voluminous* writings. — **vo·lu·mi·nous·ly,** *adv.*

vol·un·tar·i·ly \ˌväl-ən-'ter-ə-lē\ *adv.* Of one's own free will; by choice; willingly.

vol·un·tary \'väl-ən-ˌter-ē\ *adj.* **1** Done, given, or made in accordance with one's own free will or choice; as, *voluntary* contributions. **2** Not accidental; intentional; as, a *voluntary* slight; *voluntary* manslaughter. **3** Of or relating to the will; controlled by the will; as, *voluntary* muscles.
— The words *intentional* and *deliberate* are synonyms of *voluntary:* all three terms describe something that is done of one's own free will; *voluntary* usually suggests freedom from anything that might tend to restrict one's choice of action and often suggests spontaneousness, as in offering one's services; *intentional* generally indicates that the action is taken on purpose rather than accidentally or without previous thought; *deliberate* suggests full knowledge and awareness of the nature and probable consequences of one's action. — *n.; pl.* **vol·un·tar·ies. 1** Something done, made, or given voluntarily, as an offering in a church. **2** An organ solo played in a religious service.

vol·un·teer \ˌväl-ən-'tir\ *n.* **1** A person who of his own free will enters into, or offers himself for, any service or duty. **2** One who thus enters military or naval service. — *v.* **1** To offer or give voluntarily; as, to *volunteer* assistance. **2** To offer oneself as a volunteer. — \'väl-ən-ˌtir\ *adj.* **1** Composed of volunteers; as, a *volunteer* army. **2** Voluntary; as, *volunteer* aid.

vo·lup·tu·ary \və-'ləp-chə-ˌwer-ē\ *n.; pl.* **vo·lup·tu·ar·ies.** A person whose chief interest is in luxuries and sensual pleasures.

vo·lup·tu·ous \və-'ləp-chə-wəs, -chəs\ *adj.* **1** Giving pleasure to the senses; providing sensuous gratification. **2** Being a voluptuary. — **vo·lup·tu·ous·ly** \-chəs-lē, -chə-wəs-\ *adv.*

vom·it \'väm-ət\ *v.* **1** To throw up the contents of the stomach through the mouth. **2** To throw forth violently; to belch forth; as, a volcano *vomiting* lava. — *n.* Contents of the stomach vomited.

voo·doo \'vüd-ˌü\ *n.* **1** Voodooism. **2** One who practices voodooism.

voo·doo·ism \'vüd-ˌü-ˌiz-m\ *n.* **1** A religion, originally African and barbaric, consisting largely of magic and sorcery. **2** Belief in or practice of this religion. — **voo·doo·ist** \-əst\ *n.*

vo·ra·cious \və-'rā-shəs\ *adj.* **1** Greedy in eating; ravenous; as, a *voracious* animal; a *voracious* appetite. **2** Insatiable; as, a *voracious* reader. — **vo·ra·cious·ly,** *adv.* — **vo·rac·i·ty** \-'ras-ət-ē\ *n.*

vor·tex \'vȯr-ˌteks\ *n.; pl.* **vor·tex·es** \-ˌteks-əz\ or **vor·ti·ces** \'vȯrt-ə-ˌsēz\. **1** A mass of liquid in whirling motion, forming in the center a cavity toward which things are drawn; a whirlpool. **2** A whirling mass, as a whirlwind, tornado, or waterspout.

vo·ta·ry \'vōt-r-ē\ *n.; pl.* **vo·ta·ries.** A person bound or consecrated by a vow or solemn promise; a devoted adherent; as, *votaries* of science.

vote \'vōt\ *n.* **1** A wish or choice of a person or group, expressed in some regular or formal way, as by a ballot, spoken word, or raised hand. **2** The decision reached by voting. **3** A number of ballots considered together; votes, collectively; as, the *vote* for repeal. **4** The right to signify a wish or choice by use of a ballot; suffrage; as, to give women the *vote.* **5** The object or means by which a person registers his choice, as a ballot. **6** A voter. — *v.;* **vot·ed; vot·ing. 1** To express one's wish or choice by a vote; to cast a vote. **2** To make into law by a vote; as, to *vote* an income tax. **3** To elect;

as, to *vote* someone into office. **4** To declare by common consent. **5** To propose or suggest.

vot·er \'vōt-r\ *n.* **1** A person who votes. **2** A person who has the legal right to vote.

vot·ing machine \'vōt-ing\. A mechanical device for recording and counting votes.

vo·tive \'vōt-iv\ *adj.* Given in accordance with a vow or promise or from a feeling of reverence.

vouch \'vau̇ch\ *v.* To attest, as to truth or character; as, to *vouch* for the reliability of a friend.

vouch·er \'vau̇ch-r\ *n.* **1** One who vouches for another. **2** A document that serves to establish the truth of something; a receipt or other paper showing payment of a bill or debt.

vouch·safe \(')vau̇ch-'sāf\ *v.;* **vouch·safed; vouch·saf·ing.** To grant in the manner of one doing a favor; to condescend to give or grant.

vow \'vau̇\ *n.* **1** A solemn promise, especially one made to God. **2** Any pledge or promise; as, marriage *vows.* — *v.* To promise; to make a vow.

vow·el \'vau̇-əl, 'vau̇l\ *n.* **1** A speech sound produced when the outgoing breath meets less obstruction in the mouth than in the case of other sounds called *consonants.* **2** Any of the letters *a, e, i, o, u,* and sometimes *y* that stand for such sounds. — *adj.* Of a vowel.

voy·age \'vȯi-ij\ *n.* **1** A journey by water to a distant place or country. **2** A journey by air. — *v.;* **voy·aged; voy·ag·ing.** To take or make a voyage.

voy·ag·er \'vȯi-ij-r\ *n.* One that voyages.

vs. Abbreviation for *versus.*

v's. Pl. of *v.*

vul·can·ite \'vəlk-n-ˌīt\ *n.* A hard rubber used for making small articles, as buttons, and for insulating material in electric apparatus.

vul·can·ize \'vəlk-n-ˌīz\ *v.;* **vul·can·ized; vul·can·iz·ing.** To treat rubber chemically, as by heating it in combination with sulfur, to strengthen or to repair it. — **vul·can·iz·er** \'vəlk-n-ˌīz-r\ *n.*

vul·gar \'vəlg-r\ *adj.* **1** Of or relating to the common people; ordinary. **2** Vernacular; as, poems in the *vulgar* tongue. **3** Low and coarse; as, *vulgar* manners; a *vulgar* joke. — **vul·gar·ly,** *adv.*

vul·gar·ism \'vəlg-r-ˌiz-m\ *n.* Coarseness of manners or language; a coarse action or utterance.

vul·gar·i·ty \ˌvəl-'gar-ət-ē\ *n.; pl.* **vul·gar·i·ties. 1** The quality or state of being vulgar. **2** A vulgar utterance or action.

vul·gar·ize \'vəlg-r-ˌīz\ *v.;* **vul·gar·ized; vul·gar·iz·ing.** To make vulgar.

vul·ner·a·ble \'vəl-nər-əb-l, -nərb-l\ *adj.* **1** Exposed to easy attack; assailable. **2** Capable of being wounded; liable to suffer harm or injury if attacked; as, a child *vulnerable* to disease; a *vulnerable* reputation. — **vul·ner·a·bil·i·ty** \ˌvəl-nər-ə-'bil-ət-ē\ *n.* — **vul·ner·a·bly** \'vəl-nər-ə-blē\ *adv.*

vul·ture \'vəlch-r\ *n.* Any of certain large birds of prey related to hawks and eagles but having weaker claws and the head usually naked, living chiefly on carrion.

vying. Present part. of *vie.*

w \'dəb-l-(ˌ)yü, -yə; *in rapid speech, also* 'dəb-yə -yē\ *n.; pl.* **w's** \-(ˌ)yüz, -yəz, -yēz\. The twenty-third letter of the alphabet.

W. Abbreviation for: **1** *West.* **2** *Western.*

wabble. Variant of *wobble.*

wabbly. Variant of *wobbly.*

wad \'wäd\ *n.* **1** A little mass; a small lump; as, a *wad* of clay. **2** A soft plug or stopper to hold in a charge of powder, as in cannons or cartridges. **3** A soft mass of cotton, cloth, or fibers, used to plug up a hole or pad a garment. — *v.;* **wad·ded; wad·ding. 1** To form into a wad. **2** To push a wad into; as, to *wad* a gun. **3** To hold in by a wad; as, to *wad* a bullet in a gun. **4** To stuff or line with a wad or padding.

wad·dle \'wäd-l\ *v.;* **wad·dled; wad·dling** \-l(-)ing\. To walk with short steps, swaying from side to side like a duck. — *n.* A waddling walk.

wade \'wād\ *v.;* **wad·ed; wad·ing. 1** To walk or step through water, mud, sand, or any substance that offers more resistance than air. **2** To struggle slowly ahead; as, to *wade* through a dull book. — *n.* An act of wading.

wad·er \'wād-r\ *n.* **1** One that wades. **2** Any of many long-legged birds that wade in water. **3** [in the plural] High waterproof boots for wading.

wa·fer \'wāf-r\ *n.* **1** A thin, crisp cake or biscuit. **2** One of the thin round pieces of bread used by the Roman Catholic Church in the Eucharist. **3** A sticker for pasting display cards to windows.

waf·fle \'wäf-l\ *n.* A light griddlecake with a crisp indented crust, made by cooking batter in a hinged metal utensil (**waffle iron**).

waft \'wäft, 'waft\ *v.* To move, as by the action of waves or winds. — *n.* A puff of wind; a gust.

wag \'wag\ *v.;* **wagged; wag·ging.** To swing to and fro or from side to side. The dog *wagged* his tail. — *n.* **1** A wagging motion; a nod or shake. **2** A witty person. — **wag·gish** \'wag-ish\ *adj.*

wage \'wāj\ *v.;* **waged; wag·ing.** To engage in, as a struggle. He *waged* a long fight against poverty.

wage \'wāj\ *n.* [often in the plural] Payment for work or other services.

wa·ger \'wāj-r\ *n.* **1** A bet; as, to make a *wager* on a race. **2** The act of betting. — *v.;* **wa·gered; wa·ger·ing** \-r(-)ing\. To bet.

wag·gery \'wag-r-ē\ *n.; pl.* **wag·ger·ies. 1** Mischievous foolery; pleasantry. **2** A jest; a joke.

wag·gle \'wag-l\ *v.;* **wag·gled; wag·gling** \-l(-)ing\. To move backward and forward or from side to side; to wag. — *n.* A wagging or waggling.

wag·on \'wag-n\ *n.* **1** A four-wheeled vehicle, especially one drawn by animals, and used for carrying goods. **2** In full, **coaster wagon** or **express wagon.** A child's four-wheeled cart. **3** A station wagon. **4** A patrol wagon. — **on the wagon.** Abstaining from alcoholic liquors.

wag·on·er \'wag-n(-)ər\ *n.* A driver of a wagon.

waif \'wāf\ *n.* A stray person or animal, as a homeless child or a lost sheep; a wanderer; a castaway.

wail \'wāl\ *v.* **1** To grieve over; to lament for; to bewail. **2** To utter a mournful cry; to lament; to weep. — *n.* A loud lament; a cry, as of grief.

wain·scot \'wān-ˌskōt, -ˌskät, -skət\ *n.* **1** A wooden lining, often paneled, for a wall of a room. **2** The bottom three or four feet of an inside wall, especially when of a material different from the rest. — *v.;* **wain·scot·ed** or **wain·scot·ted**; **wain·scot·ing** or **wain·scot·ting**. To line a room with a wainscot.

wain·scot·ing \'wān-ˌskōt-ing, -ˌskät-, -skət-\ or **wain·scot·ting** \-ˌskät-, -skət-\ *n.* Wainscot.

waist \'wāst\ *n.* **1** The part of the human body that is between the bottom of the ribs and the hips. **2** The part of anything that is likened to the human waist; the central part of a thing; as, the *waist* of a ship; the *waist* of a violin. **3** A garment or the part of a garment that covers the body from the neck to the waist.

waist·band \'wās(t)-ˌband\ *n.* A band fitting around the waist, as on trousers or a skirt.

waist·coat \'wās(t)-ˌkōt, 'wes-kət\ *n.* A vest.

waist·line \'wāst-ˌlīn\ *n.* **1** A line thought of as surrounding the waist at its narrowest part. **2** The line at which the waist and skirt of a dress meet.

wait \'wāt\ *v.* **1** To be in expectation; as, to *wait* for sunrise. **2** To remain in readiness for some action. **3** To await; as, to *wait* orders. **4** To be a waiter or waitress at; to act as servant at; as, to *wait* table. **5** To postpone; as, to *wait* dinner. — **wait upon**. **1** To attend a person as a servant. **2** To visit, as on business or out of courtesy. A delegation *waited upon* the governor. — *n.* Time spent in waiting. — **lie in wait**. To wait in ambush.

wait·er \'wāt-r\ *n.* **1** A person who waits. **2** A man who waits on tables, as in a restaurant.

wait·ing room \'wāt-ing\. A room, as in a railroad station, for the use of persons waiting.

wait·ress \'wā-trəs\ *n.* A woman who waits table.

waive \'wāv\ *v.;* **waived**; **waiv·ing**. To give up claim to; as, to *waive* one's right to answer.

waiv·er \'wāv-r\ *n.* **1** A waiving. **2** A document containing a declaration of such waiving.

wake \'wāk\ *n.* **1** The track left by a vessel in the water. **2** Any track; as, in the *wake* of an army.

wake \'wāk\ *v.;* **waked** \'wākt\ or **woke** \'wōk\; **waked**; **wak·ing**. **1** To be awake; especially, to be watchful and alert; as, to *wake* to an opportunity. **2** To rouse or be roused from sleep or inactivity; to awake; to awaken. — *n.* The ritual of sitting up at night beside a dead body.

wake·ful \'wāk-fəl\ *adj.* Sleepless; watchful; alert.

wak·en \'wāk-n\ *v.;* **wak·ened**; **wak·en·ing** \-n(-)ing\. **1** To wake. **2** To rouse to action.

wake-rob·in \'wāk-ˌräb-n\ *n.* **1** A trillium. **2** A jack-in-the-pulpit.

wale \'wāl\ *n.* **1** A streak made on the skin by a rod or whip; a wheal. **2** Any narrow, raised surface or ridge, as on cloth. **3** [in the plural] The strakes on the sides of a vessel next above the water line.

walk \'wök\ *v.* [From Old English *wealcan* meaning "to move around", "turn", "revolve".] **1** To move along on foot; to advance by steps at a natural pace, not a run. **2** To cover or pass over at a walk; as, to *walk* the floor. **3** To cause to proceed at a walk; as, to *walk* a horse up a hill. **4** To give a base on balls to. — *n.* **1** A walking, especially for exercise or pleasure. **2** The manner of walking; gait. **3** Distance as measured by the time required to cover it while walking. **4** Usual place or range of action; as, people in that *walk* of life. **5** A place, path, or course for walking. **6** A base on balls. — **walk·er**, *n.*

walk·ie-talk·ie \'wök-ē-'tök-ē\ *n.* A small portable radio set for receiving and sending messages.

walk·ing stick \'wök-ing\. **1** A cane used in walking. **2** A sticklike insect with long, thin legs.

walk·out \'wök-ˌau̇t\ *n.* A labor strike.

walk·over \'wök-ˌōv-r\ *n.* An easy victory.

wall \'wöl\ *n.* **1** A structure, as of brick or stone, raised to some height and meant to enclose or shut off a space. **2** Something like a wall; especially, something that separates; a barrier. **3** The side or inner surface of a cavity or vessel; as, the *walls* of a boiler. — *v.* To build a wall in or around.

wal·la·by \'wäl-ə-bē\ *n.; pl.* **wal·la·bies** or **wal·la·by**. A small species of kangaroo.

wall·board \'wöl-ˌbōrd, -ˌbörd\ *n.* An artificial board of wood pulp, pressed sawdust, or cane fiber often used for inside walls or paneling.

wal·let \'wäl-ət\ *n.* **1** A bag or sack for carrying things on a journey. **2** A billfold.

wall·eye \'wöl-ˌī\ *n.* **1** An eye, as of a horse, with a whitish iris. **2** An eye which turns outward. **3** Any of certain fishes with large staring eyes. — **wall·eyed** \'wöl-ˌīd\ *adj.*

wall·flow·er \'wöl-ˌflau̇r\ *n.* **1** An herb of the mustard family, with sweet-scented yellow or orange flowers, common in Europe on old walls. **2** A person who remains by the wall at a dance, often because of not being chosen as a partner.

wal·lop \'wäl-əp\ *v.* **1** To beat soundly. **2** To hit very hard. — *n.* **1** A powerful blow. **2** The ability to deliver such a blow. The boy has quite a *wallop*.

wal·low \'wäl-ō\ *v.* **1** To roll oneself about in or as if in deep mud. The elephants *wallowed* in the river. **2** To live with excessive pleasure in some condition; as, to *wallow* in luxury. — *n.* A place where an animal wallows, or the depression it makes.

wall·pa·per \'wöl-ˌpāp-r\ *n.* Paper, usually with a printed decorative pattern, for walls of rooms.

wal·nut \'wöl-(ˌ)nət\ *n.* [From Old English *wealhhnutu* meaning literally "Celtic nut" or "Gallic nut".] **1** Any tree of a nut-bearing family with drooping catkins; especially, the **black walnut** or the **English walnut**. **2** The edible nut of any of these trees, especially the English walnut. **3** The wood of the walnut tree or the color of this wood.

wal·rus \'wöl-rəs, 'wäl-\ *n.; pl.* **wal·rus·es** or **wal·rus**. A large mammal of the Arctic region, somewhat like the seals but with large tusks in the male.

waltz \'wöl(t)s\ *n.* **1** A gliding dance done to

music in triple time. **2** Music for this dance. **—** *v.* To dance a waltz. — **waltz·er,** *n.*

wam·pum \'wämp-əm\ *n.* **1** Beads made of shells, formerly used for money or ornament by North American Indians. **2** *Slang.* Money.

wan \'wän\ *adj.* **1** Having a pale or sickly color; pale. **2** Sickly; languid; as, a *wan* smile.

wand \'wänd\ *n.* **1** A fairy's, diviner's, or magician's staff. **2** A light rod used in performing calisthenic exercises.

wan·der \'wänd-r\ *v.;* **wan·dered; wan·der·ing** \-r(-)ing\. **1** To move about aimlessly; to rove; to ramble; as, to *wander* about a city. He *wandered* home casually. **2** To stray; to go astray; as, to *wander* off the path. **3** To become delirious; to rave. — **wan·der·er** \-r-r\ *n.*

wan·der·lust \'wänd-r-ˌləst\ *n.* A strong wish or longing to travel.

wane \'wān\ *v.;* **waned; wan·ing. 1** To become smaller or less, as in strength or appearance; to diminish; to decrease. The moon *waned.* **2** To lose power, prosperity, or influence. **3** To draw near its end. Summer is *waning.* **—** *n.* The act, process, or fact of waning; the period of waning.

want \'wȯnt, 'wänt\ *v.* **1** To be without; to lack; as, to *want* even food. **2** To fall short by. He *wants* one year of being of full age. **3** To feel or suffer the need of. He cannot get the rest he *wants.* **4** To need; to require. Your house *wants* painting. **5** To desire, wish, or long for; as, to *want* to go to college. **—** *n.* **1** A lack; a shortage; as, a *want* of proper clothing. **2** Extreme poverty; destitution. The old man died in *want.* **3** A wish for something; a desire. **4** That which is wanted; a need.

want·ing \'wȯnt-ing, 'wänt-\ *adj.* **1** Absent; lacking. One oar is *wanting.* **2** Falling below a standard, a hope, or a need; as, an umpire *wanting* in experience. **3** Less; minus; as, a month *wanting* two days since he was here.

wan·ton \'wȯnt-n, 'wänt-n\ *adj.* **1** Not restrained; unruly; as, *wanton* boys. **2** Playful; as, *wanton* breezes. **3** Immoral. **4** Merciless; having no real or just cause; as, *wanton* slaughter. — **wan·ton·ly,** *adv.*

wap·i·ti \'wäp-ət-ē\ *n.; pl.* **wap·i·tis** or **wap·i·ti.** The American elk.

war \'wȯr\ *n.* **1** A contest by force between two or more nations; such a contest between a nation and a part of it in rebellion (**civil war**). **2** The action or attendant conditions of such a contest. **3** Military science; as, trained in *war.* **4** Strife; struggle; conflict; as, *war* between science and disease. **—** *v.;* **warred; war·ring.** To make war.

war·ble \'wȯrb-l\ *v.;* **war·bled; war·bling** \-l(-)ing\. **1** To sing with trills. The lark *warbled* overhead. **2** To express by warbling. **—** *n.* An act of warbling.

war·bler \'wȯrb-lər\ *n.* **1** A songster. **2** Any of a number of small, often bright-colored, songbirds.

war bonnet. An Indian ceremonial headdress, with a feathered extension down the back.

ward \'wȯrd\ *v.* **1** *Archaic.* To keep watch over; to guard; as, to *ward* someone from evil. **2** To turn aside; to repel; as, to *ward* off danger. **—** *n.* **1** The act of guarding. **2** A division of a hospital. **3** A district of a town or city for electoral or administrative purposes. **4** A person, as a child, under the protection of a guardian or of a law court.

-ward \wərd\ or **-wards** \wərdz\. A suffix that can mean: toward or in the direction of, as in *downward* and *homeward.*

ward·en \'wȯrd-n\ *n.* **1** A watchman, as at a gate. **2** Formerly, a governor, as of a town, district, or fortress. **3** A guard or keeper; as, a game *warden.* **4** A principal or chief keeper; as, the *warden* of a prison. **5** An official having the duty of protecting or warning against some danger or cause of destruction; as, a fire *warden.* **6** An officer in certain colleges, usually having the duties of a dean. **7** A churchwarden.

ward·er \'wȯrd-r\ *n.* A person who keeps guard; a watchman; a warden.

ward·robe \'wȯrd-ˌrōb\ *n.* **1** A room or closet, often a movable closet, where clothes are hung. **2** One's personal stock or supply of clothing.

-wards. Variant of *-ward.*

ware \'war, 'wer\ *n.* **1** [usually in the plural] Goods; merchandise. **2** Utensils of everyday use; as, plated *ware;* table *ware.* **3** Earthenware.

ware·house \'war-ˌhau̇s, 'wer-\ *n.; pl.* **ware·hous·es** \-ˌhau̇-zəz\. A building for storing goods and merchandise; a storehouse.

war·fare \'wȯr-ˌfar, -ˌfer\ *n.* **1** Military combat between enemies; war; as, international *warfare;* tribal *warfare.* **2** Violent or persistent conflict.

war·i·ly \'war-ə-lē, 'wer-\ *adv.* In a wary or cautious manner; as, to test the cold water *warily.*

war·like \'wȯr-ˌlīk\ *adj.* **1** Fond of war; as, *warlike* peoples. **2** Belonging to or having to do with war; military; martial. **3** Threatening war; hostile; as, *warlike* attitudes. — For synonyms see *martial.*

war·lock \'wȯr-ˌläk\ *n.* A sorcerer or wizard.

warm \'wȯrm\ *adj.* **1** Having a moderate degree of heat; as, *warm* milk; a *warm* climate. **2** Giving off heat; as, a *warm* sun. **3** Making one feel heat or suffer no loss of bodily heat; as, *warm* clothing. **4** Having a feeling of heat; as, to be *warm* from running. **5** Showing or marked by strong feeling, such as friendship or anger; as, a *warm* welcome. **6** Affecting or intended to affect a person disagreeably; as, to make things *warm* for the enemy. **7** Newly made; fresh; as, a *warm* scent or trail. **8** Near the object sought; as, evidence that one is getting *warm* in a search. **9** Giving a pleasant impression of warmth, cheerfulness, or friendliness; as, *warm* colors; a *warm* tone of voice. **—** *v.* **1** To make warm. The sun *warms* the earth. **2** To give an impression of warmth to; as, colors chosen to *warm* a room. **3** To show more interest or fervor than one first seemed to have; as, a speaker *warming* to his subject. — **warm up. 1** To exercise or practice, as before a contest, in order to limber up the muscles. **2** To run, as a motor, without a load before using it to full capacity. **3** To come to have increased liking; as, to *warm up* gradually to a new idea. — **warm·ly**, *adv.*

warm-blood·ed \'wȯrm-'bləd-əd\ *adj.* **1** Having the capacity to maintain a relatively high and constant body temperature, usually somewhat above that of the surroundings, as birds and mammals. **2** Warm in feeling; fervent.

warm front. The boundary between an advancing mass of warm air and a mass of colder air.

warm·heart·ed \'wȯrm-'härt-əd, -'hårt-\ *adj.* Having or indicating strong affection; cordial.

warm·ing pan \'wȯr-ming\. A long-handled covered pan into which live coals are put, formerly used for warming beds.

war·mon·ger \'wȯr-ˌməng-gr\ *n.* One who urges or attempts to stir up war.

warmth \'wȯrm(p)th\ *n.* **1** Gentle heat; as, the *warmth* of the sun. **2** Strong feeling, as of enthusiasm, anger, or affection. Her words held *warmth.*

warn \'wȯrn\ *v.* **1** To caution. **2** To notify, especially in advance. **3** To order to go or keep away; as, to *warn* trespassers off the grounds.

warn·ing \'wȯr-ning\ *n.* Something that warns; a sign or notice of something that may or will happen. — *adj.* That warns. — **warn·ing·ly**, *adv.*

warp \'wȯrp\ *n.* **1** In weaving, the threads that go lengthwise in the loom and are crossed by the woof. **2** A warping; a twist or curve that has come about in something originally flat or straight. — *v.* To curve or twist out of shape; to bias.

war·path \'wȯr-ˌpath\ *n.; pl.* **war·paths** \-ˌpathz\. **1** The course taken by a party of American Indians on a warlike expedition. **2** Any hostile course of action or frame of mind.

war·plane \'wȯr-ˌplān\ *n.* A military airplane.

war·rant \'wȯr-ənt, 'wär-\ *n.* **1** Authorization. **2** A document giving authorization. The police had a search *warrant.* **3** A certificate of appointment issued to a military officer of lower rank than a commissioned officer. **4** A person or thing that vouches for something; a guarantee. **5** Justification; right. What *warrant* did you have for this belief? — *v.* **1** To declare with positiveness. **2** To give power to do or keep from doing something; to authorize. **3** To justify; to be a reason for something. His need *warrants* the expenditure. **4** To guarantee; as, to *warrant* goods to be top grade.

warrant officer. An officer having a warrant.

war·ren \'wȯr-ən, 'wär-\ *n.* **1** A piece of ground kept for the breeding of rabbits or other small animals. **2** A crowded building or district.

war·rior \'wȯr-yər, 'wȯr-ē-ər, 'wär-ē-ər\ *n.* A soldier, especially one of long experience in war.

war·ship \'wȯr-ˌship\ *n.* A ship for use in war, especially one armed for attack.

wart \'wȯrt\ *n.* **1** A small, hard lump of thickened skin. **2** Any lump similar to a wart.

war·time \'wȯr-ˌtīm\ *n.* A time of war.

wary \'war-ē, 'wer-ē\ *adj.;* **war·i·er**; **war·i·est.** Very cautious; on guard against danger or deception. — For synonyms see *careful.*

was \(')wəz, (')wäz\. A form of the verb *be* showing past time, and used with *I, he, she,* or *it* or with words for which these stand.

wash \'wȯsh, 'wäsh\ *v.* **1** To cleanse with water; as, to *wash* clothes; to *wash* one's face. **2** To wet thoroughly with water or other liquid. **3** To flow along the border of. Waves *wash* the shore. **4** To pour or flow in a stream or current. The river *washes* against its banks. **5** To move or carry by the action of water; as, a man *washed* overboard. **6** To cover or daub lightly with a liquid, as whitewash or varnish. **7** To run water over in order to separate valuable matter from refuse; as, to *wash* sand for gold. **8** To bear washing without injury. **9** To stand a test or proof. That story won't *wash.* **10** To be worn away by washing. The heavy rain caused the bridge to *wash* out. — *n.* **1** The act of washing or process of being washed. **2** Articles, as of clothing, being or to be washed. **3** Swill fed to hogs. **4** That with which anything is washed, as a thin water color. **5** A liquid used for washing; as, a mouth *wash.* **6** The flow, sound, or action of water; as, the *wash* of waves on the shore. **7** A disturbance of water, as caused by the motion of a boat through it or by a storm. **8** The disturbance in the air caused by the passage of an airfoil. **9** A piece of ground washed by a sea or river, sometimes covered and sometimes left dry. **10** In the western United States, the bed of an intermittent stream, often at the bottom of a canyon; as, a dry *wash.* — *adj.* Washable; as, a *wash* dress.

wash·a·ble \'wȯsh-əb-l, 'wäsh-\ *adj.* Capable of being washed without damage; as, a *washable* silk. — **wash·a·bil·i·ty** \ˌwȯsh-ə-'bil-ət-ē, ˌwäsh-\ *n.*

wash·ba·sin \'wȯsh-ˌbās-n, 'wäsh-\ *n.* or **wash basin**. A basin to hold water for washing the hands and face.

wash·board \'wȯsh-ˌbōrd, 'wäsh-, -ˌbȯrd\ *n.* A grooved board to scrub clothes on.

wash·bowl \'wȯsh-ˌbōl, 'wäsh-\ *n.* **1** A washbasin. **2** A sink for washing the hands and face.

wash·er \'wȯsh-r, 'wäsh-r\ *n.* **1** One that washes. **2** A ring, as of metal or leather, used to make something fit tightly or to prevent rubbing.

wash·er·wom·an \'wȯsh-r-ˌwu̇m-ən, 'wäsh-\ *n.; pl.* **wash·er·wom·en** \-ˌwim-ən\. A woman who works at washing clothes.

wash·ing \'wȯsh-ing, 'wäsh-\ *n.* Articles, as of clothing, to be washed; a wash. — *adj.* Used for washing; as, *washing* powder; a *washing* machine.

washing soda. A form of sodium carbonate.

wash·out \'wȯsh-ˌau̇t, 'wäsh-\ *n.* **1** The washing away of earth by water, as on a railway. **2** A place so washed away. **3** *Slang.* A complete failure.

wash·stand \'wȯsh-ˌstand, 'wäsh-\ *n.* **1** A stand to hold articles, such as a pitcher of water, a basin, and soap, for use in washing. **2** A washbowl.

wash·tub \'wȯsh-ˌtəb, 'wäsh-\ *n.* A tub for washing clothes or for soaking them prior to washing.

wasn't \'wəz-nt, 'wäz-\ A contraction of *was not.*

wasp \'wäsp, 'wȯsp\ *n.* A winged insect, related

to the bees and ants, having a slender body with the abdomen attached by a narrow stalk, and, in females and workers, having a powerful sting.

wasp·ish \'wäs-pish, 'wȯs-\ *adj.* **1** Like a wasp in form; slender-waisted. **2** Spiteful; irritable.

was·sail \'wäs-l, 'wäs-ˌāl, wä-'sāl\ *interj.* [From medieval English *waes hail, wesseyl,* there borrowed from Old Norse *ves heill* meaning literally "be healthy!".] An anciently used exclamation expressing good wishes at a festivity, especially when drinking a health. — *n.* **1** The liquor used in drinking a health. **2** A drinking bout; a carouse. — *v.* To carouse. — **was·sail·er,** *n.*

wast \wəst, (')wäst\. An archaic form of *was,* used chiefly with *thou.*

wast·age \'wās-tij\ *n.* Loss, as by leakage; waste.

waste \'wāst\ *adj.* **1** Wild and uninhabited; desolate; barren. **2** Thrown away as worthless after being used. **3** Of no further use to a person, animal, or plant; as, means by which the body throws off *waste* matter. — *v.;* **wast·ed; wast·ing. 1** To lay waste. **2** To make or become enfeebled; as, *wasted* by fever. **3** To squander; as, to *waste* time and money. **4** To discard as waste. **5** To be gradually used up, worn away, or lost, as by evaporation; to dwindle. — *n.* **1** A waste place; desert; wilderness. **2** The action of wasting or an instance or example of wasting. **3** Something left over as waste; refuse; scrap. **4** Cotton or wool threads or other fiber left over from some industrial process, such as weaving, and used for wiping machinery and absorbing oil. **5** Material of no further use to a person, animal, or plant; as, organs for the ejection of *waste.* **6** Garbage; rubbish; sewage; as, disposal of city *waste.* — **lay waste.** To devastate; to ravage.

waste·bas·ket \'wās(t)-ˌbas-kət\ *n.* An open receptacle for wastepaper.

waste·ful \'wāst-fəl\ *adj.* **1** Wasting or causing waste; as, *wasteful* methods. **2** Spending needlessly or uselessly. — **waste·ful·ly** \-fə-lē\ *adv.*

waste·land \'wāst-ˌland\ *n.* Uncultivated, especially barren, land.

waste·pa·per \'wās(t)-'pāp-r\ *n.* Paper thrown away after being used or discarded as unfit for use.

wast·er \'wāst-r\ *n.* One that wastes or squanders.

wast·rel \'wās-trəl\ *n.* A waster; a spendthrift.

watch \'wäch\ *v.* **1** To stay awake intentionally, as at the bedside of a sick person or for purposes of religious devotion. **2** To be on the alert; to be on one's guard. **3** To be on the lookout. **4** To keep guard over; as, to *watch* outside the door. **5** To keep one's eyes on; to keep in view; as, to *watch* a game. **6** To keep in view so as to prevent harm or warn of danger; as, to *watch* a brush fire carefully. **7** To keep oneself informed about; as, to *watch* someone's career. **8** To be on the alert for the chance to make use of; as, to *watch* one's opportunity. — *n.* **1** A watching; especially, a long steady vigil. **2** A close lookout for guarding or for opportunity to learn or to carry out a purpose. **3** A sentry; a guard. **4** The period of time during which one of the divisions of a ship's crew is on duty. **5** The part of the crew on duty at one time. **6** A timepiece small enough to be carried or worn on the person. — **watch·er** \'wäch-r\ *n.*

watch·dog \'wäch-ˌdȯg\ *n.* **1** A dog kept to watch and guard property. **2** A watchful guardian.

watch·ful \'wäch-fəl\ *adj.* Attentive; vigilant. — For synonyms see *vigilant.* — **watch·ful·ly,** *adv.*

watch·man \'wäch-mən\ *n.; pl.* **watch·men** \-mən\. A person assigned to watch; a guard.

watch·tow·er \'wäch-ˌtau̇r\ *n.* A tower on which a sentinel or watchman may be placed.

watch·word \'wäch-ˌwərd\ *n.* **1** A secret word used as a signal or sign of recognition; a password. **2** A motto used as a slogan or rallying cry.

wa·ter \'wȯt-r, 'wät-r\ *n.* **1** The liquid that comes from the clouds as rain, and forms streams, ponds, lakes, and seas. **2** A body of water, as that which flows in a stream or is collected in a pond, lake, or sea — often used in the plural; as, the *waters* of Niagara. **3** A liquid that contains or resembles water; as, ammonia *water.* **4** Any of various bodily fluids, as urine, saliva, or serum. **5** The clearness and luster of a precious stone; as, a diamond of the purest *water.* **6** Degree of thoroughness or completeness; as, a scoundrel of the first *water.* **7** A wavy pattern such as is given to some silks, linens, and metals. — *v.* **1** To wet or supply with water; as, to *water* a garden. **2** To treat with water; especially, to treat cloth so as to give it a wavy pattern. **3** To add water to anything; to dilute; as, to *water* milk. **4** To fill with liquid; to secrete liquid, as saliva. The mouth *waters.* **5** To get or take on water. The ship *watered* at each port.

water beetle. Any of numerous beetles that swim swiftly with the fringed hind legs acting as oars.

wa·ter·buck \'wȯt-r-ˌbək, 'wät-\ *n.* A large reddish brown or grayish brown antelope of Africa which frequents rivers and swims easily.

water buffalo. An oxlike work animal of Asia.

water clock. A device or machine for measuring time by the fall or flow of water.

water closet. 1 A closet or room containing a toilet fitted with some device for flushing the bowl with water. **2** The toilet itself, with accessories.

water color. 1 A paint whose liquid part is water. **2** A picture painted with water color. **3** The art of painting with water color.

water clock

wa·ter·course \'wȯt-r-ˌkōrs, 'wät-, -ˌkōrs\ *n.* **1** A stream of water, such as a river or a brook. **2** The bed of a stream.

wa·ter·craft \'wȯt-r-ˌkraft, 'wät-\ *n.* **1** Skill in managing boats or in swimming and diving. **2** Any ship or boat; ships and boats, collectively.

water cress. 1 A plant with leaves that are crisp and rather peppery to the taste, growing usually in clear running water. **2** The leaves of this plant, used in salad or as a garnish.

wa·ter·fall \'wȯt-r-ˌfȯl, 'wät-\ *n.* A fall of water from a height; a cascade.

water flea. Any of various tiny freshwater crustaceans that are important as food for fish.

wa·ter·fowl \'wȯt-r-ˌfau̇l, 'wät-\ *n.; pl.* **wa·ter·fowl** or **wa·ter·fowls.** A bird that spends its time on or near water; especially, a swimming bird.

water front. Land, or a section of a town, that borders on a body of water.

water lily. A water plant with flat, roundish floating leaves and fragrant, many-petaled flowers.

water lily

wa·ter·logged \'wȯt-r-ˌlȯgd, 'wät-, -ˌlägd\ *adj.* So filled or soaked with water as to be heavy or hard to manage; as, a *waterlogged* boat.

wa·ter·mark \'wȯt-r-ˌmärk, 'wät-, -ˌmȧrk\ *n.* **1** A mark that indicates a line to which water has risen. **2** A mark, such as the maker's name or trademark, made in paper during manufacture and visible when the paper is held up to the light. — *v.* To mark with a watermark, as paper.

wa·ter·mel·on \'wȯt-r-ˌmel-ən, 'wät-\ *n.* The large edible fruit of a vine related to the cucumbers with a juicy pulp that is usually red in color.

water moccasin. A poisonous snake of the southern United States, closely related to the copperhead; a cottonmouth; a moccasin.

water polo. A game played in a swimming pool with a ball resembling a soccer ball.

water power. The power of moving water, used to run machinery, as for generating electricity.

wa·ter·proof \'wȯt-r-'prüf, 'wät-\ *adj.* Not letting water through. — *n.* An outer coat made of waterproof material. — *v.* To make waterproof.

wa·ter·shed \'wȯt-r-ˌshed, 'wät-\ *n.* **1** A dividing ridge, such as a mountain range, separating one drainage area from others. **2** The whole area that drains into a particular river or lake.

wa·ter·spout \'wȯt-r-ˌspau̇t, 'wät-\ *n.* **1** A pipe for carrying off water from a roof. **2** A slender, funnel-shaped cloud that extends down to a cloud of spray torn up from water by a whirlwind.

water table. The upper limit of the ground wholly saturated with water.

wa·ter·tight \'wȯt-r-'tīt, 'wät-\ *adj.* **1** So tight as to be waterproof. **2** So worded that the meaning is unmistakable; as, a *watertight* contract.

water vapor. The vapor of water, especially when below the boiling point and in diffused form, as in the atmosphere, as distinguished from steam.

wa·ter·way \'wȯt-r-ˌwā, 'wät-\ *n.* A channel by which ships can travel.

water wheel. Any wheel made to turn by a flow of water against it.

water wings. An air-filled device to give support to a person's body when swimming or learning to swim.

wa·ter·works \'wȯt-r-ˌwərks, 'wät-\ *n. pl.* A system of dams, reservoirs, pumps, and pipes for supplying water, as to a city — often used as a singular.

wa·tery \'wȯt-r-ē, 'wät-\ *adj.* **1** Of or having to do with water; as, a *watery* grave. **2** Containing, full of, or giving out water; as, *watery* clouds. **3** Like water; thin; weak; as, *watery* lemonade. **4** Soft and soggy; as, *watery* turnips.

watt \'wät\ *n.* [Named after the Scottish inventor James *Watt* (1736–1819).] A unit of electric power, equal to the power produced when a current of one ampere flows under a pressure of one volt.

watt·age \'wät-ij\ *n.* Amount of electric power expressed in watts.

watt-hour \'wät-'au̇r\ *n.* A unit for measuring energy, equal to work done by one watt in one hour.

wat·tle \'wät-l\ *n.* **1** A twig or flexible rod. **2** A framework made of such twigs or rods interlaced, used for roofs, walls, or fences. **3** A fleshy flap of skin that hangs from the throat of some birds and reptiles. — *v.;* **wat·tled**; **wat·tling** \-l(-)ing\. **1** To bind, fence, or cover with wattles. **2** To interweave, as twigs. **3** To form by interweaving twigs.

wave \'wāv\ *v.;* **waved**; **wav·ing.** **1** To flutter; as, flags *waving* in the breeze. **2** To move one way and the other; to brandish; as, to *wave* a sword. **3** To signal, as by moving the hand to and fro; as, to *wave* good-by. **4** To be or make wavy or curly, as hair. — *n.* **1** A moving swell or crest on the surface of water. **2** A wavelike formation or shape; as, a *wave* in the hair. **3** The action or process of making wavy or curly. **4** A waving motion, as of the hand or a flag. **5** A flow or gush. A *wave* of color swept the girl's face. **6** A surge or rapid increase; as, a *wave* of buying; a heat *wave.* **7** An effect that is like a wave in water and that goes out from a source, as of light or sound, or that is broadcast from a radio or television station; as, a light *wave.*

wave length. The distance in the line of travel of a wave from one point to the next similar point, as from crest to crest.

wave·let \'wāv-lət\ *n.* A little wave.

wa·ver \'wāv-r\ *v.;* **wa·vered**; **wa·ver·ing** \-r(-)ing\. **1** To sway one way and the other; to flicker or quiver, as a flame. **2** To be unsettled in opinion. **3** To show signs of giving way; to falter.

wavy \'wā-vē\ *adj.;* **wav·i·er**; **wav·i·est.** Having waves; moving in waves.

wax \'waks\ *v.* **1** To grow larger or stronger; especially, of the moon, to increase in apparent size and brightness. **2** To become; to grow; as, to *wax* merry.

wax \'waks\ *n.* **1** A dull-yellow sticky substance made by bees and used in building honeycomb; beeswax. **2** Any substance resembling beeswax; as, *wax* in the ear; sealing *wax.* — *adj.* Of or like wax; as, a *wax* doll. — *v.* To treat with wax.

wax bean. A string bean with tender yellow pods.

wax·en \'waks-n\ *adj.* Of or like wax.

wax myrtle. A shrub bearing small hard berries, called *bayberries*, used for making candles.

wax·wing \'waks-ˌwing\ *n.* A brownish smooth-feathered bird with red tips resembling sealing wax on some of the wing feathers; especially, the **cedar waxwing**, with yellowish under parts.

waxy \'waks-ē\ *adj.;* **wax·i·er; wax·i·est. 1** Resembling wax. **2** Made of or covered with wax.

way \'wā\ *n.* **1** A track for traveling along; a route. **2** Room to pass; as, to make *way* for an ambulance. **3** Travel or motion along some route or in some direction; as, to lead the *way;* one's *way* home. **4** Distance; as, a great *way* off. **5** Direction; as, uncertain which *way* to go. **6** Regular course; as, the *way* of the world. **7** [in the plural] Actions or conduct; as, to mend one's *ways.* **8** Means; method; as, a good *way* to do something. **9** Manner; style; fashion; as, one's *way* of combing one's hair; entertainment in a large *way.* **10** Feature; respect; point; as, good in every *way.* **11** State; condition; as, to be in a bad *way.* **12** [often in the plural] Behavior; habit; as, a person with odd *ways.* **13** Advance; progress; career; as, to have one's *way* to make. **14** Neighborhood; section of the country; as, down our *way.* **15** Motion; headway; as, a ship gathering *way.* **16** [in the plural] A sloping structure upon which a ship is built or launched. — **by the way.** Incidentally; in passing; by way of digression. — **by way of. 1** By a route through; as, to go *by way of* Chicago. **2** For the purpose of; as being of the nature of; as, to send flowers *by way of* apology. — **out of the way. 1** In such a place as not to obstruct or contact. **2** Away from the beaten track; far from routes of main travel. **3** Out of the proper course; improper; wrong. Nothing *out of the way* took place. — **under way.** In motion; making progress.

way·far·er \'wā-ˌfar-r, -ˌfer-r\ *n.* A traveler, especially on foot. — **way·far·ing** \-ˌfar-ing, -ˌfer-\ *adj.*

way·lay \wā-'lā, 'wā-ˌlā\ *v.;* **way·laid** \-'lād, -ˌlād\; **way·lay·ing. 1** To lie in wait for, especially in order to seize, rob, or kill. **2** To stop or attempt to stop so as to speak with.

way·side \'wā-ˌsīd\ *n.* The side of the way; the edge or border of a road.

way station. A station between main stations.

way·ward \'wā-wərd\ *adj.* **1** Taking one's own way; disobedient; as, *wayward* children. **2** Contrary; perverse; as, *wayward* weather. **3** Unsteady; irregular. — **way·ward·ly,** *adv.*

we \(')wē\ *pron.* **1** I and one or more others. **2** People in general, including myself. **3** I — as used by a sovereign or an editor or writer.

weak \'wēk\ *adj.* **1** Lacking physical strength; feeble; as, a *weak* body. **2** Not able to bear or exert a great weight or pressure; as, a *weak* bridge. **3** Easily overcome; as, a *weak* argument. **4** Lacking force; low; faint; as, a *weak* voice. **5** Not containing the usual amount or a large amount of the main ingredients; as, *weak* tea. **6** Lacking mental or moral strength; simple; foolish; as, a *weak* mind; *weak* character. **7** Coming from or showing lack of judgment or firmness; unwise; as, a *weak* policy. **8** Lacking experience or skill; as, a *weak* tennis player. **9** Of stress or accent, like that on the second syllable of the word *penetrate* \'pen-ə-ˌtrāt\. — The words *feeble* and *infirm* are synonyms of *weak: weak* suggests a lack of strength, vigor, power, or influence, or a temporary or permanent loss of any of these qualities; *feeble* generally suggests an extreme and pitiable weakness and is applied most frequently to persons or their actions; *infirm* is likely to stress the loss, especially permanent loss, of physical strength and soundness.

weak·en \'wēk-n\ *v.;* **weak·ened; weak·en·ing** \-n(-)ing\. To make or become weak or weaker.

weak·fish \'wēk-ˌfish\ *n.; pl.* **weak·fish** or **weak·fish·es.** A long-bodied spiny-finned food fish with a tender mouth, preyed upon by the bluefish.

weak·ling \'wēk-ling\ *n.* One lacking physical or moral strength.

weak·ly \'wēk-lē\ *adj.;* **weak·li·er; weak·li·est.** Not robust; feeble. — *adv.* In a weak manner.

weak·ness \'wēk-nəs\ *n.* **1** Lack of strength; feebleness. **2** A failing; a fault; a defect. **3** A liking or fondness which one indulges although feeling it should be resisted or restrained.

weal \'wēl\ *n. Archaic.* Well-being; prosperity.

weal \'wēl\ *n.* A wheal; a welt.

wealth \'welth\ *n.* **1** Large possessions; riches; property. **2** A great amount or number.

wealthy \'wel-thē\ *adj.;* **wealth·i·er; wealth·i·est.** Having wealth; rich.

wean \'wēn\ *v.* **1** To accustom a child or young animal to take food otherwise than by nursing. **2** To turn a person away from desiring something he has been fond of.

weap·on \'wep-n\ *n.* **1** An instrument that may be used to fight with, as a gun, knife, or club. **2** Any means by which one contends against another.

wear \'war, 'wer\ *v.;* **wore** \'wōr, 'wȯr\; **worn** \'wōrn, 'wȯrn\; **wear·ing. 1** To use as an article of clothing or decoration. **2** To carry on or as if on one's body; to bear. The cowboy *wore* a gun. **3** To show, as in one's expression or manner; as, to *wear* a smile. **4** To harm, waste, or lessen by use, or by scraping or rubbing; as, to *wear* down a pencil point. **5** To make tired; to weary; as, to be *worn* out by a trip. **6** To cause or make by rubbing; as, to *wear* a hole in the elbow of a coat. **7** To endure use; to stand up under use; to last; as, a cloth that *wears* well. — **wear out. 1** To use up the useful life of. **2** To tire. — *n.* **1** The act of wearing; the state of being worn; use; as, clothes for everyday *wear.* **2** Things worn or meant to be worn; as, women's *wear.* **3** Wearing quality; lasting quality; as, a coat with lots of *wear* in it. **4** The result of wearing or use; the signs of having been partially used up or worn out; as, a suit that shows *wear.* — **wear·a·ble** \'war-əb-l, 'wer-\ *adj.* — **wear·er** \-r\ *n.*

wea·ri·some \'wir-ēs-m\ *adj.* Tiresome.

wea·ry \'wir-ē\ *adj.;* **wea·ri·er; wea·ri·est. 1** Worn out; tired; fatigued; as, to be *weary* after a day's work. **2** Expressing or caused by fatigue; as, a *weary* sigh. **3** Having one's patience, pleasure, or interest worn out. **4** Causing fatigue; tiresome.

— *v.;* **wea·ried** \-ēd\; **wea·ry·ing**. To make or become weary. — **wea·ri·ly** \'wir-ə-lē\ *adv.*

wea·sel \'wēz-l\ *n.* **1** A small, slender, quick-moving animal that eats birds, mice, and rats. **2** The fur of this animal.

weath·er \'weth-r\ *n.* The state of the air and atmosphere with respect to warmth, cold, dryness, wetness, storminess, or clearness; as, good *weather;* cold *weather.* — *v.;* **weath·ered**; **weath·er·ing** \-r(-)ing\. **1** To expose to the air; to season, dry, discolor, or wear, by exposure to the air; as, wood *weathered* to a gray color; *weathered* rocks. **2** To bear up against and come safely through, as a storm. — *adj.* Windward; as, the *weather* side.

weath·er-beat·en \'weth-r-ˌbēt-n\ *adj.* **1** Worn or damaged by exposure to the weather. **2** Toughened or tanned by the weather.

weath·er·board \'weth-r-ˌbōrd, -ˌbȯrd\ *n.* A clapboard.

weath·er·cock \'weth-r-ˌkäk\ *n.* A weather vane, often having the shape of a cock.

weath·er·man \'weth-r-ˌman\ *n.;* *pl.* **weath·er·men** \-ˌmen\. One who records, issues reports on, and forecasts the state of the weather; a meteorologist.

weath·er·proof \'weth-r-'prüf\ *adj.* Able to withstand exposure to weather. — *v.* To make weatherproof.

weathercock

weather strip. A strip of material used to make a seal where a door or window joins the sill or casing.

weather vane. A plate or strip, as of metal, placed so as to be rotated by the wind and show the direction it is blowing from.

weave \'wēv\ *v.;* **wove** \'wōv\ or **weaved**; **wo·ven** \'wōv-n\ or **wove**; **weav·ing**. **1** To form by interlacing strands of material; especially, to make cloth on a loom by interlacing yarns; to interlace into a fabric, especially on a loom. **2** To spin, as spiders and other insects. The spider *weaves* its web. **3** To make by or as by interlacing; as, to *weave* a story. **4** To unite or entwine as if by weaving; as, to *weave* a moral into a story. **5** To move to and fro or up and down; as, to *weave* one's way through the crowd. — *n.* A particular method or pattern of weaving. — **weav·er** \'wēv-r\ *n.*

web \'web\ *n.* **1** A woven fabric, especially one on a loom or coming from a loom. **2** A cobweb. **3** A network; as, a *web* of railroads. **4** Something flimsy or entangling like a cobweb; as, a *web* of lies. **5** The skin that unites the toes of birds and some water animals. — *v.;* **webbed**; **web·bing**. To weave; to unite or envelop with a web; to entangle.

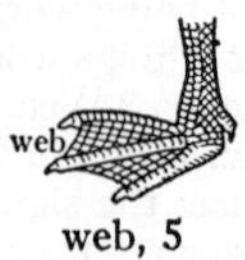

web, 5

webbed \'webd\ *adj.* **1** Formed like or with a web. **2** Having fingers or toes joined by webs; as, the *webbed* feet of a duck.

web·bing \'web-ing\ *n.* A stout, close-woven tape used for reins, straps, or belts.

web-foot·ed \'web-'fu̇t-əd\ *adj.* Having feet the toes of which are joined by webs, as ducks.

wed \'wed\ *v.;* **wed·ded**; **wed·ded** or **wed**; **wed·ding**. **1** To marry; to join or give in marriage. **2** To attach firmly; as, to be *wedded* to one's habits.

we'd \(')wēd\. A contraction of *we had* or *we would* or *we should.*

Wed. Abbreviation for *Wednesday.*

wed·ding \'wed-ing\ *n.* **1** A marriage ceremony; marriage. **2** An anniversary of the wedding day or a celebration of that anniversary, as in **silver wedding** (25th anniversary) or **golden wedding** (50th anniversary).

wedge \'wej\ *n.* **1** A piece of wood or metal tapered to a thin edge, used to split wood or rocks and in lifting heavy weights. **2** Anything shaped like a wedge, as a piece of pie, a piece of land, or wild geese flying. **3** A thing that serves to make a gradual opening or cause a change in something; as, to use every concession as an entering *wedge.* — *v.;* **wedged**; **wedg·ing**. **1** To separate or split by means of a wedge or wedges. **2** To fasten or tighten with a wedge; as, to *wedge* a rattling window. **3** To crowd in tightly; to push.

wedge, 1

wed·lock \'wed-ˌläk\ *n.* Marriage.

Wednes·day \'wenz-dē\ *n.* [From Old English *Wodnesdaeg* meaning literally "day of Woden" and named after *Woden* the chief Germanic god.] The fourth day of the week.

wee \'wē\ *adj.;* **we·er** \'wē-ər\; **we·est** \'wē-əst\. Very small; little; tiny.

weed \'wēd\ *n.* A plant growing wild that is useless, unpleasant in appearance, or harmful to cultivated plants. — *v.* To remove weeds; to remove something as if it were a weed. — **weed·er**, *n.*

weeds \'wēdz\ *n. pl.* Mourning clothes.

weedy \'wēd-ē\ *adj.;* **weed·i·er**; **weed·i·est**. **1** Having many weeds; as, a *weedy* garden. **2** Having to do with or like a weed; especially, growing rapidly and sturdily. **3** Thin; lanky; as, a *weedy* youth.

week \'wēk\ *n.* **1** Seven successive days. **2** A period of seven days beginning Sunday and ending Saturday. **3** The working days of the week.

week·day \'wēk-ˌdā\ *n.* Any day of the week except Sunday.

week·end \'wēk-ˌend\ *n.* or **week end**. The end of the week; especially, the time, often Saturday and Sunday, commonly devoted to recreation.

week·ly \'wēk-lē\ *adv.* Once a week. — *adj.* **1** Of or in a week; as, *weekly* production. **2** Coming, happening, or done every week. — *n.;* *pl.* **week·lies**. A paper or magazine issued every week.

ween \'wēn\ *v. Archaic.* To think; to believe.

weep \'wēp\ *v.;* **wept** \'wept\; **weep·ing**. **1** To shed tears; to cry, as on account of grief or, sometimes, other emotion; as, to *weep* for joy. **2** To lament; to bewail. **3** To shed, as tears; to pour forth. **4** To drop water or other liquid; to drip.

weep·ing \'wēp-ing\ *adj.* **1** That weeps. **2** Having slender, drooping branches; as, a *weeping* willow.

weer. Comparative of *wee*.

weest. Superlative of *wee*.

wee·vil \'wēv-l\ *n.* Any of various small, hard-shelled beetles with a long snout, many of which are pests injuring fruit, nuts, grain, or trees.

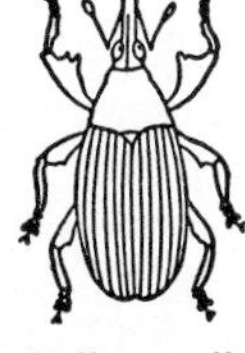
boll weevil

weft \'weft\ *n.* **1** In weaving, the threads, carried by a shuttle, that cross the warp; woof. **2** Yarn used for these threads. **3** A woven fabric: something woven.

weigh \'wā\ *v.* **1** To determine the weight of something. **2** To examine as if by weighing; to consider carefully; as, to *weigh* a question. **3** To measure out on or as if on scales. **4** To balance something in one's hands to determine, or as if to determine, its weight. **5** To heave up, as an anchor, before sailing. **6** To have weight; to have a certain weight; as, to *weigh* 100 pounds. **7** To be considered as important; to have influence; as, a fact that *weighs* against a person. **8** To bear heavily; to press hard. His worries *weigh* heavily on his mind. — **weigh·er** \'wā-ər\ *n.*

weight \'wāt\ *n.* **1** Heaviness; property of weighing or having mass. The *weight* of the stone prevented us from lifting it. **2** Heaviness as a measure or indication of amount or quantity. Sugar is sold by *weight.* **3** A unit for measuring heaviness. The pound is a standard *weight.* **4** A system of related units for measuring heaviness; as, avoirdupois *weight.* **5** A unit, piece, or mass of known heaviness used to balance and thus find out how heavy something else is; as, to add a pound *weight* to the scale. **6** Something heavy; something used to hold or press a thing down. **7** A burden; as, a *weight* on one's mind. **8** The amount that a person or thing weighs; the measure of the pull of gravity on a person or thing. **9** Importance; influence. His opinion has *weight.* — *v.* **1** To load with a weight; as, to *weight* a fishing line. **2** To burden; to weigh down.

weighty \'wāt-ē\ *adj.;* **weight·i·er**; **weight·i·est. 1** Having much weight; heavy. **2** Having importance or consequence; serious; momentous; as, *weighty* problems. **3** Expressing seriousness; as, a *weighty* manner. **4** Having authority or influence.

weir \'wir, 'war, 'wer\ *n.* **1** A river dam for such a purpose as leading water to a mill or making a pond. **2** A fence set across a stream to catch fish.

weird \'wird\ *adj.* Unnatural; ghostly; wild; strange; as, a *weird* noise. — **weird·ly**, *adv.*

wel·come \'welk-m\ *adj.* **1** Received gladly; as, a *welcome* visitor. **2** Giving pleasure; pleasing; as, *welcome* news. **3** Willingly permitted to do, have, or enjoy something. Anyone is *welcome* to use the swimming pool. — *n.* A cordial greeting or reception. — *v.;* **wel·comed**; **wel·com·ing. 1** To greet, as a visitor, cordially or courteously. **2** To receive or accept with pleasure.

weld \'weld\ *v.* **1** To join two pieces of metal by heating and allowing the edges to flow together, or by hammering or pressing together. **2** To join as if by welding; as, two persons *welded* together in friendship. **3** To be or be capable of being welded, as a metal. — *n.* **1** The joining of metals by welding. **2** A welded joint. — **weld·er**, *n.*

wel·fare \'wel-ˌfar, -ˌfer\ *n.* **1** Condition of health, happiness, and prosperity. **2** In full, **welfare work.** Organized effort for improving the conditions of life of a class or group; as, working in child *welfare.*

wel·kin \'welk-n\ *n.* The sky.

well \'wel\ *n.* **1** A spring with its pool; a fountain. **2** A hole made in the earth to reach a natural deposit, as of water, oil, or gas. **3** A source of supply. He is a *well* of information. **4** An open space extending vertically through floors, as for a staircase or elevator. **5** A vessel or container, as in *inkwell.* — *v.* To flow; to gush. Tears *welled* from her eyes.

well \'wel\ *adv.;* **bet·ter** \'bet-r\; **best** \'best\. **1** In a pleasing or desirable manner; satisfactorily; fortunately. The party turned out *well.* **2** In a good or proper manner; excellently; skillfully; as, to do one's work *well.* **3** Abundantly; fully; as, to eat *well.* **4** With reason or courtesy; properly. The girl could not very *well* refuse the invitation. **5** Completely; fully; as, *well* out of sight. **6** Intimately; closely; as, to know a person *well.* **7** Considerably; far; as, *well* ahead. **8** Easily; without trouble or difficulty. He could *well* have gone. **9** Exactly; definitely; as, to remember it *well.* — *adj.* **1** Fortunate. It is *well* that everyone is here. **2** Healthy; not sick; as, a *well* man. **3** In satisfactory condition or circumstances. **4** In a prosperous condition or style; as, to live *well.* — *interj.* An exclamation expressing satisfaction or surprise.

we'll \(')wēl\. A contraction of *we will* or *we shall.*

well-be·ing \'wel-'bē-ing\ *n.* The state or condition of being well, comfortable, or happy; welfare.

well·born \'wel-'bórn\ *adj.* **1** Coming from a good family; of gentle or noble birth. **2** Coming from healthy parents or a physically sound stock.

well-bred \'wel-'bred\ *adj.* Refined; polite.

well-nigh \'wel-ˌnī\ *adv.* Almost; nearly.

well-off \'wel-'óf\ *adj.* In a good condition or position; especially, prosperous; well-to-do.

well·spring \'wel-ˌspring\ *n.* **1** A spring; a fountainhead. **2** A source of continual supply.

well-to-do \'wel-tə-'dü\ *adj.* Prosperous; wealthy.

Welsh \'welsh, 'welch\ *adj.* Of or relating to Wales. — *n.* **1** The Welsh people — used as a plural with *the.* **2** The non-English language of Wales.

Welsh·man \'welsh-mən, 'welch-\ *n.; pl.* **Welsh·men** \-mən\. A native or citizen of Wales. — **Welsh·wom·an** \-ˌwům-ən\ *n.*

Welsh rabbit or **Welsh rarebit.** A dish made of melted cheese poured over toast or crackers.

welt \'welt\ *n.* **1** A ridge raised on the skin by a blow. **2** A heavy blow. **3** The narrow strip of leather between a shoe upper and sole, to which other parts are stitched.

wel·ter \'welt-r\ *v.;* **wel·tered**; **wel·ter·ing** \'welt-r-ing, 'wel-tring\. **1** To tumble about or wallow, as a hog in mire. **2** To roll or toss as if among waves. — *n.* A confused jumble or swirl; as, a *welter* of surging waves; a *welter* of books, papers.

wel·ter·weight \'welt-r-ˌwāt\ *n.* A boxer or wrestler whose weight is not over 147 pounds.

wen \'wen\ *n.* A painless and harmless skin tumor.

wench \'wench\ *n.* **1** A girl. **2** A female servant.

wend \'wend\ *v.* To go or go on; as, to *wend* one's way home.

went. Past tense of *go.*

wept. Past tense and past part. of *weep.*

were \(')wər\. The form of the verb *be* used with *you* (singular or plural) or with any plural to show past time and used also in a subordinate clause in a statement contrary to fact. *Were* you at the party? We *were* at the basketball game. If I *were* in Egypt, I would go to see the pyramids.

we're \(')wir, 'wē-ər, (')wər, (')wer\. A contraction of *we are.*

weren't \'wərnt, 'wər-ənt\. A contraction of *were not.*

were·wolf \'wir-ˌwu̇lf, 'wər-, 'wer-\ *n.; pl.* **were·wolves** \-ˌwu̇lvz\. [From Old English *werwulf,* compounded of *wer* meaning "man" and *wulf* meaning "wolf".] In folklore, a person changed into a wolf or able to take the form of a wolf.

wert \(')wərt\. An archaic form of *were,* used chiefly with *thou.*

west \'west\ *n.* **1** One of the four main points of the compass; the direction of the sunset. **2** Any country or region west of another. **3** [with a capital] The Western Hemisphere; the New World. **4** [with a capital] Europe and the Americas, as distinguished from Asia. **5** [with a capital] The western part of the United States. — *adj.* **1** Going or facing toward the west; situated at or in the west; as, the *west* side. **2** Coming from the west; as, a *west* wind. — *adv.* Westward; as, to travel *west.*

west·er·ly \'west-r-lē\ *adj.* **1** Situated, directed, or moving toward the west. **2** Coming from the west. — *adv.* Toward the west; westward. — *n.* A wind that blows from the west.

west·ern \'west-rn\ *adj.* **1** Of or relating to the west. **2** Going or facing toward the west. **3** Coming from the west. — *n.* A motion picture or radio or television program or a story dealing with life in the West, especially with life in pioneer days, or with cowboy life.

west·ern·er \'west-rn-r\ *n.* A person native to or living in the west; especially [with a capital], a person living in the western United States.

west·ern·ize \'west-r-ˌnīz\ *v.;* **west·ern·ized; west·ern·iz·ing.** To give western characteristics to.

west·ern·most \'west-rn-ˌmōst\ *adj.* Farthest west.

west·ward \'west-wərd\ or **west·wards** \-wərdz\ *adv.* Toward the west; as, to sail *westward.* — **west·ward·ly** \-wərd-lē\ *adj.* or *adv.*

west·ward \'west-wərd\ *adj.* Going or facing toward the west.

wet \'wet\ *adj.;* **wet·ter; wet·test. 1** Containing, covered with, or soaked with, water or other liquid; as, a *wet* cloth. **2** Rainy; as, *wet* weather. **3** Not yet dry; as, *wet* paint. — *n.* **1** Water or wetness; moisture. **2** Rainy weather; rain. — *v.;* **wet** or **wet·ted; wet·ting.** To make wet; to moisten or soak. — **wet·ness** \-nəs\ *n.*

weth·er \'weth-r\ *n.* A castrated ram.

we've \(')wēv\. A contraction of *we have.*

whack \'hwak\ *n.* **1** A sharp, noisy blow; as, to give someone a *whack* on the back. **2** The sound of such a blow; as, the loud *whack* of a bat on a ball. — *v.* To strike with a whack.

whale \'hwāl\ *n.* **1** A large air-breathing, warm-blooded fishlike mammal of the sea that suckles its young and is hunted for its oil. **2** Something impressive, as because of its size or excellence; as, a *whale* of a good job. — *v.;* **whaled; whal·ing.** To hunt for whales.

whale \'hwāl\ *v.;* **whaled; whal·ing.** To thrash.

whale·boat \'hwāl-ˌbōt\ *n.* A long narrow rowboat of a type originally used by whalers.

whale·bone \'hwāl-ˌbōn\ *n.* A horny substance from the upper jaw of some kinds of whales.

whal·er \'hwāl-r\ *n.* **1** A ship or person employed in whale fishing. **2** A whaleboat.

wharf \'hwȯrf\ *n.; pl.* **wharves** \'hwȯrvz\ or **wharfs** \'hwȯrfs\. A landing platform or structure built on the shore of a harbor, river, or canal for loading or unloading vessels; a pier or dock.

what \(')hwät, wät, (')hwət, wət\ *pron.* **1** Which thing or things? *What* did you say? **2** Which sort or kind of thing? *What* is this? **3** Which in name or kind? *What* is your trade? **4** That which; those things which. I have done *what* you asked. **5** Whatever. We'll get you *what* you want. — *adj.* **1** Which? *What* child was lost? **2** Of which kind, sort, or nature? *What* good will it do? **3** The sort of; as, to know *what* books one likes. **4** Any which. Ask *what* questions you please. **5** How great an amount of! *What* courage! — *adv.* **1** In what way? *What* does it matter? **2** In part. *What* with the cold and *what* with hunger, the man was nearly dead. — *conj.* That. Never fear but *what* he will return. — *interj.* An exclamation of surprise. *What!* Didn't you see him at school today?

what·ev·er \(h)wät-'ev-r, (h)wət-\ *pron.* **1** What surprising or unforeseeable thing? *Whatever* will he do now? **2** Anything or everything that. Take *whatever* is needed. **3** No matter what. Obey orders, *whatever* happens. — *adj.* Of any kind at all. Give him *whatever* food is there.

what·not \'hwät-ˌnät, 'hwət-\ *n.* A light open set of shelves for bric-a-brac.

what·so·ev·er \'hwät-sə-'wev-r, 'hwət-\ *pron.* or *adj.* Whatever.

wheal \'hwēl\ *n.* A wale; a welt.

wheat \'hwēt\ *n.* **1** A widely cultivated grass with long dense flower spikes containing white to dark-red kernels of grain. **2** The grain of this plant, used in making flour.

wheat·en \'hwēt-n\ *adj.* Made of wheat.

whee·dle \'hwēd-l\ *v.;* **whee·dled; whee·dling**

\-l(-)ing\. **1** To entice by gentle flattery; to coax. **2** To gain or get by coaxing or flattery; as, to *wheedle* money from one's parents.

wheel \'hwēl\ *n.* **1** A disk or circular frame capable of turning on a central axis. **2** Anything that is like a wheel, as in being round or in turning on an axis; as, a color *wheel.* **3** A device the main part of which is a wheel; as, a spinning *wheel.* **4** A bicycle. **5** A circular frame which when turned controls some apparatus; as, the steering *wheel* of an automobile. **6** [in the plural] The moving power or mechanism; as, the *wheels* of government. — *v.* **1** To carry or move on wheels or in a vehicle with wheels; as, to *wheel* a load into the barn. **2** To turn or cause to turn on an axis or in a circle; to revolve. The earth *wheels* about the sun. **3** To change direction as if revolving on an axis. — **wheeled** \'hwēld\ *adj.*

wheel·bar·row \'hwēl-ˌbar-ō\ *n.* A vehicle with two handles and usually one wheel, used to move small loads.

wheelbarrow

wheel·base \'hwēl-ˌbās\ *n.* The distance between the centers of the front and rear axles of an automobile.

wheel chair. A chair mounted on wheels, used especially by invalids.

wheel·house \'hwēl-ˌhaůs\ *n.; pl.* **wheel·hous·es** \-ˌhaů-zəz\. A pilothouse.

wheel·wright \'hwēl-ˌrīt\ *n.* One who makes or repairs wheels and wheeled vehicles such as wagons.

wheeze \'hwēz\ *v.;* **wheezed**; **wheez·ing**. **1** To breathe hard and noisily or with a whistling sound. **2** To make a sound like wheezing. — *n.* A wheezing sound. — **wheezy** \'hwē-zē\ *adj.*

whelk \'hwelk\ *n.* A large spiral-shelled sea snail, one kind of which is used in Europe for food.

whelm \'hwelm\ *v.* To overwhelm.

whelp \'hwelp\ *n.* One of the young of a dog or of a beast of prey; a puppy; a cub, as of a fox, wolf, bear, or lion. — *v.* To give birth to whelps.

when \(')hwen, wen, (h)wən\ *adv.* At what time? *When* are your classes over? — *conj.* **1** At or just after the time that. Come *when* you are ready. You may leave *when* you have finished. **2** Every time that; whenever. *When* she hears music, she cries. **3** During the time that; while. We stand *when* we sing the national anthem. **4** At which time; whereupon; and then; as, *when* he at once consented. We had just sat down *when* he came. **5** In spite of the fact that; although. Why do you tease, *when* no one likes it? — *pron.* **1** What time. Until *when* will you stay? **2** Which time. He left in April, since *when* I have not seen him.

whence \'hwen(t)s\ *adv.* **1** From what place; as, to tell *whence* he came. **2** From which place, person, or source; as, *whence* cometh help. **3** From which; as, the land *whence* he came.

when·ev·er \(h)wen-'ev-r, (h)wən-\ *conj.* At any or every time that. Stop *whenever* you wish. — *adv.* When? *Whenever* will he come?

when·so·ev·er \'hwen-sə-'wev-r\ *conj.* or *adv.* Whenever.

where \(')hwer, wer, (h)wər\ *adv.* **1** In, to, or at what place? *Where* are you going? **2** In or at which; as, the house *where* he was born. **3** At which part, stage, or passage — used interrogatively and relatively. *Where* do I come in? **4** To which; as, the place *where* I am going. **5** From what place or source; as, *where* did he get his suspicions? — *conj.* **1** At or in the place in which. Our friends work *where* we do. **2** In the situation or respect in which. *Where* others are weak, he is strong. **3** To the place at, in, or to which. Let me take you *where* you live. — *pron.* **1** What place or source? *Where* did that car come from? **2** The place in or at which; as, a mile from *where* we live. **3** The particular in which. That is *where* he is weak.

where·a·bouts \'hwer-ə-ˌbaůts\ *adv.* Where? At what place? Near what place? *Whereabouts* was the boy going? — *n. sing.* The place where a person or thing is. The boy's *wherabouts* is not known.

where·as \(h)wer-'az, (h)wər-\ *conj.* **1** Since it is true that; since it is the case that. *Whereas* February 22 is George Washington's birthday, it is fitting that the day be marked with special ceremonies. **2** While on the contrary. Water puts out fire, *whereas* alcohol burns.

where·at \(h)wer-'at, (h)wər-\ *adv.* **1** At which; as, the spot *whereat* he stood. **2** On which occasion; on which account; whereupon.

where·by \(h)wer-'bī, 'hwer-ˌbī, (h)wər-'bī\ *adv.* By or through which; by means of which; as, the organs *whereby* we see, hear, taste, smell, and feel.

where·fore \'hwer-ˌfōr, -ˌfȯr\ *adv.* **1** For what reason? Why? *Wherefore* did he do it? **2** Therefore; so. Our leader is experienced; *wherefore*, we should take his advice. — *n.* A reason; a cause; as, to ask the *wherefores* of his decision.

where·from \(h)wer-'frəm, (h)wər-, -'främ\ *adv.* From which.

where·in \(h)wer-'in, (h)wər-\ *adv.* **1** In what way? *Wherein* were you offended? **2** In which; as, the palace *wherein* the king lives.

where·of \(h)wer-'əv, (h)wər-, -'äv\ *adv.* Of which; about that of which; as, to know *whereof* one speaks.

where·on \(h)wer-'ȯn, (h)wər-, -'än\ *adv.* On which; as, the base *whereon* the statue rests.

where·so·ev·er \'hwer-sə-'wev-r\ *adv.* or *conj.* Wherever.

where·up·on \'hwer-ə-ˌpȯn, -ˌpän\ *adv.* **1** Upon which; whereon. **2** And then; at which time.

wher·ev·er \(h)wer-'ev-r, (h)wər-\ *adv.* At, to, or in any or every place in which.

where·with \(h)wer-'wiṯh, (h)wər-, -'with\ *adv.* With which; by means of which; as, the money *wherewith* to buy food.

where·with·al \ˌhwer-wi-'ṯhȯl, -'thȯl\ *adv.* Wherewith. — \'hwer-wi-ˌṯhȯl, -ˌthȯl\ *n.* That with which anything can be bought or done; as, the *wherewithal* for a good dinner.

wher·ry \'hwer-ē\ *n.; pl.* **wher·ries.** A long light rowboat pointed at both ends.

whet \'hwet\ *v.;* **whet·ted; whet·ting. 1** To sharpen, as a knife. **2** To make keen, as the appetite.

wheth·er \'hwet͟h-r, (h)wət͟h-r\ *conj.* **1** Whichever of a number of alternatives is the case; as, not knowing *whether* we are going or not. **2** If it be true, likely, or possible that; as, to ask *whether* one could come.

whet·stone \'hwet-ˌstōn\ *n.* A natural or artificial stone on which blades are sharpened.

whew, *interj.* An exclamation like a half-formed whistle, expressing surprise, relief, or admiration.

whey \'hwā\ *n.* The watery part of milk that separates after the milk sours and thickens.

which \(')hwich, wich\ *pron.* **1** What one (of two or more)? What ones (of three or more)? *Which* is your house? *Which* are your brothers? **2** That; as, books *which* are interesting. **3** Any one or ones that; whichever. Choose *which* you want. — *adj.* What (out of two or more)? *Which* house is yours?

which·ev·er \(h)wich-'ev-r\ *pron.* or *adj.* Any one that; no matter which; as, *whichever* way you go.

which·so·ev·er \'hwich-sə-'wev-r\ *pron.* or *adj.* Whichever.

whiff \'hwif\ *n.* **1** A slight gust; a puff; a breath; as, a *whiff* of fresh air. **2** An odor brought by or as by such a puff; as, a *whiff* of perfume. — *v.* To puff, blow out, or blow away, in whiffs.

whif·fle·tree \'hwif-l-(ˌ)trē\ *n.* A whippletree.

Whig \'hwig\ *n.* **1** A member of an English political party that started in the 17th century and defended the rights of parliament against the king. **2** A supporter of the American Revolution, as contrasted with a Tory. **3** A member of a 19th century political party formed to oppose the Democrats.

while \'hwīl, wīl\ *n.* **1** A space of time. Stay a *while.* **2** Time used in doing something; trouble; effort; as, something worth one's *while.* — *conj.* **1** During the time that; as long as; as, to repair a roof *while* the weather is good. **2** Although; in spite of the fact that. *While* the book is famous, it is seldom read. — *v.;* **whiled; whil·ing.** To spend; to pass; as, to *while* away time.

whi·lom \'hwī-ləm\ *adv. Archaic.* Formerly. — *adj.* Former; as, his *whilom* friends.

whilst \'hwīlst, wīlst\ *conj. Chiefly British.* While.

whim \'hwim\ *n.* A sudden wish or desire; a sudden change of mind; a sudden notion or fancy.

whim·per \'hwimp-r\ *v.;* **whim·pered; whim·per·ing** \-r(-)ing\. To cry in low, whining, broken tones; to whine. — *n.* A whimpering sound.

whim·si·cal \'hwim-zik-l\ *adj.* **1** Full of whims; capricious; as, a *whimsical* person. **2** Droll; fantastic; as, *whimsical* humor. — **whim·si·cal·ly** \-zik-l(-)ē\ *adv.*

whim·si·cal·i·ty \ˌhwim-zə-'kal-ət-ē\ *n.; pl.* **whim·si·cal·i·ties. 1** Quality or state of being whimsical. **2** Something whimsical.

whim·sy \'hwim-zē\ *n.; pl.* **whim·sies. 1** A whim. **2** Playful imaginative thinking; fantasy; imagination. **3** Something playfully imagined. **4** Something fanciful or fantastic in nature, form, or purpose. **5** Whimsicality.

whine \'hwīn\ *v.;* **whined; whin·ing. 1** To make a low, complaining cry. The dog *whined* at the door. **2** To make a sound like such a cry. The wind *whined* through the trees. **3** To beg or to complain in a childish way; as, to *whine* for candy. — *n.* Any whining sound. — **whin·er** \'hwīn-r\ *n.*

whin·ny \'hwin-ē\ *v.;* **whin·nied** \-ēd\; **whin·ny·ing.** To neigh, especially in a low, gentle fashion. — *n.; pl.* **whin·nies.** A low, gentle neigh.

whip \'hwip\ *v.;* **whipped** \'hwipt\ or **whipt** \'hwipt\; **whip·ping. 1** To move, snatch, or jerk quickly or forcibly; as, to *whip* out a gun. **2** To strike, as with a lash or whip; to beat or spank. **3** To beat to a froth; as, to *whip* cream. **4** To defeat; to conquer. **5** To thrash about; to swish; as, a flag *whipping* in the wind. — *n.* **1** An instrument used in whipping, as a lash. **2** A whipping motion. **3** A light dessert blended with whipped cream or whipped whites of eggs.

whip·cord \'hwip-ˌkȯrd\ *n.* **1** A braided cord, sometimes used in making whiplashes. **2** A hard-woven worsted fabric with fine close diagonal ridges.

whip·lash \'hwip-ˌlash\ *n.* The lash of a whip.

whip·per·snap·per \'hwip-r-ˌsnap-r\ *n.* **1** A diminutive or insignificant person. **2** A presumptuous or impertinent young person.

whip·pet \'hwip-ət\ *n.* A dog resembling the greyhound but somewhat smaller.

whip·ping post \'hwip-ing\. A post to which offenders are tied to be whipped.

whip·ple·tree \'hwip-l-(ˌ)trē\ *n.* The pivoted or swinging bar to which the traces of a harness are fastened; a singletree.

whippet

whip·poor·will \'hwip-r-ˌwil, -'wil\ *n.* [Imitative of the sound made by the bird.] A night-flying, insect-eating bird of eastern North America heard at nightfall and just before dawn.

whir or **whirr** \'hwər\ *v.;* **whirred; whir·ring.** To move or revolve rapidly with a buzzing, whizzing sound; to whiz. — *n.* A whirring sound.

whirl \'hwərl\ *v.* **1** To turn or move rapidly in circles; to revolve with great speed; as, to *whirl* a top; a dancer's *whirling* feet. **2** To feel giddiness; to reel. My head *whirls.* **3** To move or carry around or about very rapidly. The train *whirled* around the bend. — *n.* **1** A whirling movement; rapid rotation; as, the *whirl* of a top. **2** Anything that moves with a whirling motion; as, a *whirl* of dust. **3** Something caused by whirling; bustle; confusion. **4** Dizziness; a dizzy condition. My head is in a *whirl.*

whirl·i·gig \'hwər-lə-ˌgig\ *n.* **1** A child's toy with a whirling motion. **2** A dizzy rush or hurry.

whirl·pool \'hwərl-ˌpül\ *n.* A rapid swirl of water with a depression in the center into which floating objects are drawn; an eddy.

whirl·wind \'hwərl-ˌwind\ *n.* A violent windstorm

that whirls the air in a rapidly rising column.

whish \ˈhwish\ *v.* To move with a whizzing or swishing sound. — *n.* A whizzing sound.

whisk \ˈhwisk\ *n.* **1** A quick sweep or brush; as, to give one's coat a *whisk.* **2** A small short-handled brush made like a broom (**whisk broom**). **3** A kitchen utensil of wire, made for whipping, as eggs or cream. **4** A sudden quick motion; as, a *whisk* of the hand. — *v.* **1** To move suddenly and speedily; as, to *whisk* around the corner. **2** To beat into a froth; as, to *whisk* eggs. **3** To brush with a broom or whisk; as, to *whisk* dust off one's clothes.

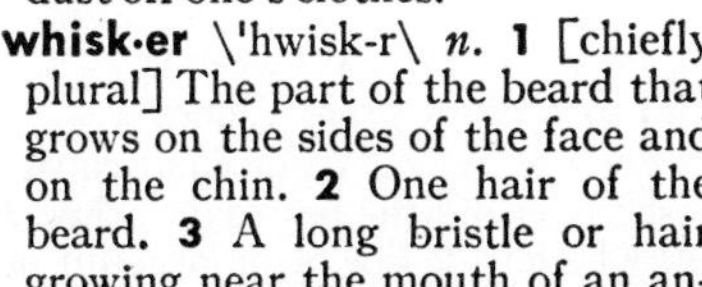

whisk, 2

whisk, 3

whisk·er \ˈhwisk-r\ *n.* **1** [chiefly plural] The part of the beard that grows on the sides of the face and on the chin. **2** One hair of the beard. **3** A long bristle or hair growing near the mouth of an animal, as a cat or a bird. — **whisk·ered** \-rd\ *adj.*

whis·key or **whis·ky** \ˈhwis-kē\ *n.; pl.* **whis·keys** or **whis·kies.** [From Irish Gaelic and Scottish Gaelic *uisge beatha* meaning literally "water of life".] A distilled alcoholic liquor made from any of various grains, as rye, barley, or corn.

whis·per \ˈhwisp-r\ *v.;* **whis·pered; whis·per·ing** \-r(-)ing\. **1** To speak very low or under the breath. **2** To tell by whispering; as, to *whisper* a secret. **3** To make a low rustling sound; as, the *whispering* leaves. — *n.* **1** A low, soft utterance that can be heard only by persons who are near. **2** The act of whispering; something that is said in a whisper. **3** A hint; a rumor; as, *whispers* of a scandal. **4** A low rustling sound; as, the *whisper* of leaves in the wind. — **whis·per·er** \-r-r\ *n.*

whist \ˈhwist\ *n.* A card game.

whis·tle \ˈhwis-l\ *v.;* **whis·tled; whis·tling** \-l(-)ing\. **1** To make a shrill sound by forcing the breath through the teeth or lips. **2** To make a sound like whistling. **3** To move, pass, or go with a sharp, shrill sound. Bullets *whistled* by. **4** To sound a whistle. **5** To utter by whistling; as, to *whistle* a tune. — *n.* **1** A device by which a shrill sound is produced; as, a tin *whistle;* a steam *whistle.* **2** A whistling sound. — **whis·tler** \-l(-)ər\ *n.*

whit \ˈhwit\ *n.* The least particle; a bit; as, to care not a *whit.*

white \ˈhwīt\ *adj.* **1** Of the color of pure snow. **2** Light in color; as, *white* wine. **3** Gray or silvery; as, *white* hair. **4** Pale; as, a face *white* with fear. **5** Blank; as, a *white* space in printed matter. **6** Snowy; as, a *white* Christmas. **7** Free from spot or blemish. **8** Innocent; pure. **9** Without evil purpose; with good intention; as, a *white* lie; *white* magic. **10** Of or relating to the Caucasian race; as, a *white* man. — *n.* **1** The color of pure snow. **2** The quality of being white; as, the *white* of snow. **3** The white part of anything. **4** [often in the plural] White clothes; as, tropical *whites.* **5** A white person. — *v.;* **whit·ed** \ˈhwīt-əd\; **whit·ing** \-ing\. To make white; to whiten; to bleach. — **white·ness** \-nəs\ *n.*

white ant. A termite.

white blood cell. One of the colorless cells of the blood of vertebrates, some kinds of which ingest germs and other foreign matter.

white·cap \ˈhwīt-ˌkap\ *n.* The top of a wave breaking into foam.

white elephant. [So called from the fact that in parts of Asia pale-colored elephants are held sacred and are maintained without being made to work.] Something requiring much care and expense and yielding little profit; any burdensome possession.

white·fish \ˈhwīt-ˌfish\ *n.; pl.* **white·fish** or **white·fish·es.** A freshwater food fish that is olive green above and silvery on the sides and below.

white flag. A white cloth that is raised as a request for a truce or as a sign of surrender.

white gold. A gold alloy resembling platinum.

white heat. **1** The temperature, higher than red heat, at which a body becomes brightly incandescent. **2** A state of intense strain or feeling. — **white-hot** \ˈhwīt-ˈhät\ *adj.*

white lead. A heavy, white, poisonous carbonate of lead, chiefly used as a pigment.

white matter. White nerve tissue, especially of the brain and spinal cord, consisting largely of sheathed nerve fibers.

whit·en \ˈhwīt-n\ *v.;* **whit·ened; whit·en·ing** \-n(-)ing\. To make or become white; to bleach.

white·wash \ˈhwīt-ˌwȯsh, -ˌwäsh\ *n.* **1** A white liquid used to whiten walls. **2** A clearing by whitewashing. — *v.* **1** To cover with whitewash. **2** To clear of a charge of wrongdoing by offering excuses, hiding facts, or conducting only a careless investigation. **3** To defeat an opponent without letting him score.

whith·er \ˈhwit͟h-r\ *adv.* **1** To what place? *Whither* does this road lead? **2** To which place or destination; as, success, *whither* only hard work leads.

whit·ing \ˈhwīt-ing\ *n.; pl.* **whit·ing** or **whit·ings.** Any of several edible fishes found mostly near seacoasts.

whit·ing \ˈhwīt-ing\ *n.* Pulverized chalk used especially for polishing metals or as a pigment.

whit·low \ˈhwit-ˌlō\ *n.* An inflammation of a finger or toe, especially near the nail, usually with pus.

Whit·sun·day \ˈhwit-ˌsən-dē; ˈhwits-n-ˌdā, -dē\ *n.* The seventh Sunday after Easter; Pentecost.

Whit·sun·tide \ˈhwits-n-ˌtīd\ *n.* The week beginning with Whitsunday, especially the first three days.

whit·tle \ˈhwit-l\ *v.;* **whit·tled; whit·tling** \-l(-)ing\. **1** To pare or cut off chips from wood. **2** To shape or form by such paring or cutting. **3** To reduce little by little; as, to *whittle* away the other team's lead. — **whit·tler** \-l(-)ər\ *n.*

whiz or **whizz** \ˈhwiz\ *v.;* **whizzed; whiz·zing.** To move, pass, or fly rapidly with a humming or whirring sound. — *n.* **1** A whizzing sound. **2** One highly skilled; an expert; as, a *whiz* at arithmetic.

who, *pron.* **1** \(')hü\ What person? Which person? *Who* is it? **2** \(')hü, ü\ That; as, the man *who* came in.

whoa \'wō, 'hō, 'hwō\ *interj.* Stop! Stand still! — used especially in addressing horses.

who·dun·it \hü-'dən-ət\ *n.* A detective story or play in which the identity of the criminal is discovered only near the end.

who·ev·er \hü-'ev-r\ *pron.* Whatever person; as, *whoever* he may be.

whole \'hōl\ *adj.* **1** Being in perfectly healthy or sound condition; uninjured; not broken or damaged. Every egg was *whole.* **2** Not cut up or ground; as, a *whole* pepper. **3** Containing all its essential elements in being made ready for the market; as, *whole* milk. **4** Containing all its parts; considered all at once; the total; as, the *whole* family; the *whole* sky. **5** Not scattered; not divided; as, one's *whole* attention. **6** All; each one of the; as, the *whole* ten days; the *whole* series. — *n.* **1** Something which is whole; as, the *whole* of an apple. **2** A sum of all the parts and elements; as, the *whole* of the country. — **on the whole. 1** Considering all things; in view of all the circumstances. **2** In general; with few or no exceptions.

whole·heart·ed \'hōl-'härt-əd, -'hȧrt-\ *adj.* Not holding back; sincere; devoted; earnest; as, *wholehearted* efforts. — **whole·heart·ed·ly**, *adv.*

whole number. A number which is not a fraction and does not have a fraction as a part of it; an integer. 3 is a *whole number* but ⅔ is not.

whole·sale \'hōl-ˌsāl\ *n.* The sale of goods in large quantities, especially to retail dealers; as, to buy at *wholesale.* — *adj.* **1** Selling at wholesale; as, a *wholesale* grocer. **2** Of or connected with a wholesale business; as, *wholesale* prices. **3** Extensive and general; as, *wholesale* slaughter. — *v.*; **whole·saled**; **whole·sal·ing.** To sell at wholesale.

whole·some \'hōls-m\ *adj.* **1** Promoting health; beneficial. **2** Healthy; sound in body, mind, and morals; as, a *wholesome* boy. **3** Indicating or suggesting health. — For synonyms see *healthy.*

whole-wheat \'hōl-'hwēt\ *adj.* Containing a considerable part of the bran; as, *whole-wheat* flour.

whol·ly \'hōl-(l)ē\ *adv.* **1** Entirely; totally; completely; fully. **2** Solely; exclusively.

whom \(')hüm, üm\ *pron.* The form of the word *who* that is used as the object of a preposition or of a verb.

whom·ev·er \hü-'mev-r\ *pron.* The form of the word *whoever* used as the object of a preposition or of a verb.

whom·so·ev·er \'hüm-sə-'wev-r\ *pron.* The form of the word *whosoever* used as the object of a preposition or of a verb.

whoop \'h(w)üp, 'h(w)u̇p\ *v.* **1** To shout loudly and vigorously; to cheer noisily and heartily. The boys *whooped* with joy. **2** To make the sound that follows an attack of coughing in the infectious disease called **whoop·ing cough.** — *n.* **1** The act of whooping. **2** A hoot, as of an owl or crane. — **whoop it up.** To raise a disturbance, as by loud roistering.

whop·per \'hwäp-r\ *n.* **1** Something huge of its kind. **2** A monstrous lie.

whop·ping \'hwäp-ing\ *adj.* That is a whopper; extremely large or great; enormous.

whore \'hōr, 'hȯr\ *n.* A prostitute.

whorl \'hwȯrl, 'hwərl\ *n.* **1** Something that whirls; as, the *whorl* of a rapid. **2** A coil; a spiral; as, embroidered *whorls* on a skirt; the *whorls* in one's fingerprints. **3** A row of leaves or flowers encircling a stem. **4** One of the turns of a univalve shell. — **whorled** \'hwȯrld, 'hwərld\ *adj.*

whose \(')hüz, üz\ *pron.* or *adj.* The possessive form of *who* and sometimes of *which. Whose* is it? *Whose* hat is that?

who·so \'hü-ˌsō\ *pron. Archaic.* Whosoever.

who·so·ev·er \'hü-sə-'wev-r\ *pron.* Whoever.

why \(')hwī, wī\ *adv.*; *pl.* **whys. 1** For what cause, reason, or purpose? *Why* did the boy leave school? No one knows *why* he left. **2** For or on account of which; as, the reason *why* the man went. — \'hwī\ *n.* The reason; the cause. Scientists seek the *why* of things. — \'wī, 'hwī\ *interj.* An exclamation expressing surprise or satisfaction. *Why!* This is the very book needed.

wick \'wik\ *n.* A cord, strip, or ring of loosely woven material through which a liquid, such as melted tallow, wax, or oil, is drawn to the top in a candle, lamp, or oil stove for burning.

wick·ed \'wik-əd\ *adj.* **1** Morally bad; evil in character, conduct, or principle; as, a *wicked* king; *wicked* deeds. **2** Harmful; dangerous; troublesome; as, *wicked* wounds. **3** Vile; unpleasant; as, a *wicked* odor; *wicked* weather. **4** Disposed to mischief; roguish. — **wick·ed·ly**, *adv.*

wick·er \'wik-r\ *n.* **1** A flexible twig, especially of willow, used in making baskets and chairs. **2** Wickerwork.

wick·er·work \'wik-r-ˌwərk\ *n.* **1** Plaited or woven wicker. **2** Articles made of wicker.

wick·et \'wik-ət\ *n.* **1** A small gate or door, especially one in or near a larger one. **2** A small window with a grille or grate, as at a ticket office. **3** In croquet, one of the curved wire frames through which the ball is driven; a hoop. **4** One of the two frames at which the ball is bowled in cricket, each consisting of three vertical sticks topped by two small horizontal sticks. **5** The playing surface between these two frames.

wide \'wīd\ *adj.*; **wid·er**; **wid·est. 1** Covering a vast area; far-spreading; as, the *wide* world. **2** Measured across or at right angles to length; as, cloth 54 inches *wide.* **3** Having a good measure across; broad. **4** Opened as far as possible; as, eyes *wide* with wonder. **5** Not limited; extensive; as, *wide* reading. **6** Far from the goal, mark, or truth; as, a *wide* guess. — *adv.* **1** Over a wide area;

to a wide extent; as, to travel far and *wide*. **2** So as to have or leave a wide space between; as, *wide* apart. **3** Far off; at a distance; as, to shoot *wide* of the mark. **4** Astray; afield. — **wide·ly**, *adv.*

wide-awake \'wīd-ə-'wāk\ *adj.* **1** Not sleepy, dull, or listless. **2** Alert; keen.

wide-eyed \'wīd-'īd\ *adj.* Having the eyes wide open; as, *wide-eyed* with wonder.

wide·mouthed \'wīd-'maůthd, -'maůtht\ *adj.* **1** Having a wide mouth; as, a *widemouthed* bottle. **2** Having one's mouth opened wide, as in awe.

wid·en \'wīd-n\ *v.;* **wid·ened**; **wid·en·ing** \-n(-)ing\. To make or become wide or wider.

wide·spread \'wīd-'spred\ *adj.* **1** Spread as far as possible; as, *widespread* wings. **2** Extending over a great area; as, *widespread* fields. **3** Widely scattered; widely distributed; widely effective.

widg·eon \'wij-n\ *n.; pl.* **widg·eon** or **widg·eons**. A freshwater duck having a white crown.

wid·ow \'wid-ō\ *n.* A woman who has lost her husband by death. — *v.* To make a widow of; as, *widowed* by war. — **wid·ow·hood** \-ˌhůd\ *n.*

wid·ow·er \'wid-ə-wər\ *n.* A man who has lost his wife by death.

width \'width\ *n.* **1** Measurement across; dimension at right angles to length. The *width* of the road is 30 feet. **2** Breadth; wideness. **3** A measured and cut piece of material; a breadth; as, to sew several *widths* together to make a skirt.

wield \'wēld\ *v.* **1** To use as an instrument, especially with skill or power; as, to *wield* a pen. **2** To exercise; as, to *wield* authority.

wie·ner \'wēn-r\ *n.* [From German *Wiener (würstchen)* meaning literally "Viennese sausage".] A sausage, usually of mixed beef and pork, shorter and slenderer than a frankfurter.

wife \'wīf\ *n.; pl.* **wives** \'wīvz\. **1** A woman — now chiefly in a few phrases; as, old *wives'* tales. **2** A woman united to a man in marriage.

wig \'wig\ *n.* A manufactured covering of hair for a person's head, often made of human hair.

wig·gle \'wig-l\ *v.;* **wig·gled**; **wig·gling** \-l(-)ing\. To wriggle; to squirm. — *n.* A wiggling motion.

wig·gler \'wig-l(-)ər\ *n.* **1** One that wiggles. **2** The larva or pupa of the mosquito.

wig·gly \'wig-l(-)ē\ *adj.* **1** That wiggles or wriggles; as, a *wiggly* worm. **2** Wavy; as, *wiggly* lines.

wight \'wīt\ *n. Archaic.* A creature; a human being.

wig·wag \'wig-ˌwag\ *v.;* **wig·wagged**; **wig·wag·ging**. **1** To move to and fro. **2** To signal by movements of a flag or light to left and right according to a code. — *n.* **1** The art or act of wigwagging. **2** A message sent by wigwag.

wig·wam \'wig-ˌwäm\ *n.* An Indian hut made of poles overlaid with bark, rush mats, or hides.

wild \'wīld\ *adj.* **1** Not tamed; not domesticated; as, *wild* animals. **2** Not cultivated; growing or produced naturally; as, *wild* carrots; *wild* honey. **3** Uninhabited and uncultivated; desolate; as, *wild* country. **4** Savage; not civilized; as, *wild* tribes. **5** Turbulent; violent; as, a *wild* storm. **6** Uncontrolled; as, *wild* rage. **7** Boisterous; rollicking; as, a *wild* party. **8** Fantastic; as, his *wild* garb. **9** Visionary; crazy; as, a *wild* project. **10** Wide of the mark; as, a *wild* guess. — *adv.* Wildly; without control or direction; as, children that run *wild*. — *n.* [often in the plural] A wilderness; a waste. — **wild·ly**, *adv.*

wild boar. A wild Old World hog from which most domestic swine have been derived.

wild·cat \'wīl(d)-ˌkat\ *n.* **1** Any small or medium-sized untamed cat, especially a lynx. **2** A savage, quick-tempered, hard-fighting person. **3** A locomotive running without cars. **4** A well drilled for oil or gas in a region not known to be productive. — *adj.* **1** Not sound or safe; as, *wildcat* schemes. **2** Running without control or contrary to orders; as, a *wildcat* train. **3** Considered to be outside the bounds of recognized or acceptable business practice; as, a *wildcat* brand of canned goods. **4** Not authorized by union officials; as, a *wildcat* strike. — *v.;* **wild·cat·ted**; **wild·cat·ting**. To drill wildcats. — **wild·cat·ter** \-ˌkat-r\ *n.*

wil·der·ness \'wild-r-nəs\ *n.* An uncultivated and uninhabited region; a wild; a waste.

wild·fire \'wīl(d)-ˌfīr\ *n.* An easily igniting and fast-spreading substance, very hard to put out, once used in war.

wild·flow·er \'wīl(d)-ˌflaůr\ *n.* **1** The flower of a wild or uncultivated plant. **2** A plant that bears such flowers.

wild·fowl \'wīl(d)-ˌfaůl\ *n.* Wild game and water birds, especially wild ducks and geese.

wild·life \'wīl-ˌ(d)līf\ *n.* The living creatures, as animals and birds, of the forest.

wild·wood \'wīl-ˌ(d)wůd\ *n.* A wild or unfrequented wood.

wile \'wīl\ *n.* A trick intended to deceive or tempt; an expression or look that lures; as, feminine *wiles*. — *v.;* **wiled**; **wil·ing**. To lure; to entice.

will \'wil\ *n.* **1** Wish or desire, often combined with determination; as, the *will* to win. **2** What is wished or decreed by another. Thy *will* be done. **3** The power to decide or control what one will do or how one will act. **4** A legal document in which a person states to whom his possessions are to be given after his death. — *v.* **1** To command; to order, sometimes in the form of a wish. The king so *wills* it. **2** To bring to a certain condition by the power of the will; as, to *will* oneself to sleep. **3** To leave or bequeath by will.

will \wəl, (ə)l, (')wil\ *v.;* **would** \wəd, (ə)d, (')wůd\. **1** Wish to. What *will* you have? **2** Am, is, or are willing to. I *will* go, if you ask me. **3** Am, is, or are determined to. He *will* go in spite of the storm. **4** Is or are going to. Everyone *will* be there. **5** Is or are commanded to. You *will* remain.

will·ful or **wil·ful** \'wilf-l\ *adj.* **1** Intentional; as, *willful* murder. **2** Governed by will without yielding to reason; obstinate; stubborn.
— The words *perverse* and *headstrong* are syno-

nyms of *willful: willful* generally suggests an obstinate determination to have one's own way and a refusal to be guided or bound by authority and wisdom; *headstrong* usually indicates completely stubborn, deliberate self-will and impatience at restraint, advice, or suggestion; *perverse* may suggest a deliberate intention to do the exact opposite of what other persons, social conventions, or sometimes even the law expects or demands of one.

will·ful·ly or **wil·ful·ly** \'wilf-l-ē\ *adv.* **1** Purposely; intentionally; deliberately; as, *willfully* to make a statement known to be false. **2** In a self-willed manner; obstinately; stubbornly. The child *willfully* refused to come to dinner.

will·ful·ness or **wil·ful·ness** \'wilf-l-nəs\ *n.* The state or quality of being willful.

will·ing \'wil-ing\ *adj.* **1** Favorably inclined or having no objection; as, *willing* to go. **2** Ambitious; not slow or lazy; as, a *willing* worker. **3** Made, done, or given of one's own choice; voluntary; as, a *willing* sacrifice. — **will·ing·ly**, *adv.*

will-o'-the-wisp \'wil-ə-thə-'wisp\ *n.* **1** A wandering light appearing at night over a marsh or swamp. **2** Something that lures and misleads.

wil·low \'wil-ō\ *n.* **1** A tree or shrub with narrow leaves, catkins for flowers, and tough pliable shoots used in basketry. **2** The wood of the willow tree, used in making baseball bats.

willow, leaves and catkin

wil·lowy \'wil-ə-wē\ *adj.* **1** Having many willows; edged, as a walk, with willow trees; as, the *willowy* drive. **2** Like a willow; pliant; flexible. **3** Tall and graceful — used of a person.

wil·ly-nil·ly \'wil-ē-'nil-ē\ *adv.* [An altered form of earlier *will I nill I* meaning "whether I want to or don't want to".] Whether one wants to or not. They rushed us along *willy-nilly.*

wilt \'wilt\ *v.* **1** To lose freshness and droop or become limp, as a cut flower. **2** To cause to wilt. **3** To grow weak. — *n.* Any of numerous plant diseases that cause the leaves to wilt and wither.

wilt \(')wilt\. An archaic form of *will*, used chiefly with *thou.*

wily \'wī-lē\ *adj.;* **wil·i·er**; **wil·i·est**. Full of wiles; cunning; crafty.

wim·ple \'wimp-l\ *n.* A cloth over the head and around the neck and chin, once common as a part of women's costume and still worn by some nuns.

win \'win\ *v.;* **won** \'wən\; **win·ning. 1** To gain the victory in a contest or competition. The local team *won.* **2** To get by effort or skill; to gain; as, to *win* praise. **3** To obtain by victory; as, to *win* a prize. **4** To be the victor in; as, to *win* a race. **5** To persuade; as, to try to *win* someone over. — *n.* The act or fact or an instance of winning.

wince \'win(t)s\ *v.;* **winced**; **winc·ing.** To draw back, as from a blow or pain; to flinch.

winch \'winch\ *n.* A machine having a roller or rollers on which rope is coiled for hauling or hoisting, operated by a crank or cranks.

winch

wind \'wīnd\ *v.;* **wound** \'waünd\; **wind·ing. 1** To twist or coil; as, to *wind* thread on a spool. **2** To cover with something coiled or twisted around; to wrap; as, to *wind* an arm with a bandage. **3** To wind up; as, to *wind* one's watch. **4** To curve; as, a road that *winds.* **5** To hoist or haul by a rope pulled by machinery; as, to *wind* a ship to the wharf. — **wind up. 1** To bring to a conclusion; to end. **2** In baseball, to swing the arm before pitching. **3** To tighten the spring of a clock or watch. **4** To make tense or tight. — *n.* A bend; a coil; a twist.

wind \'wind\ *n.* **1** A movement of the air; a breeze. There is quite a *wind* tonight. **2** A windstorm. **3** Power to breathe. The fall knocked the *wind* out of the boy. **4** Air carrying a scent, as of game. The hounds got *wind* of the fox. **5** Hint; limited advance knowledge. The girls got *wind* of the club's plans. **6** Mere breath or talk; idle words. **7** A wind instrument. **8** Air or gas in the stomach or bowels. — *v.* **1** To get a scent of. The dogs *winded* game. **2** To cause one to be out of breath. **3** To allow to rest, as a horse, so as to recover breath.

wind \'wīnd, 'wind\ *v.;* **wound** \'waünd\; **wind·ing.** To sound by blowing; as, to *wind* a horn.

wind·age \'win-dij\ *n.* **1** The influence of the wind in turning the course of a projectile. **2** The amount of deflection caused by the wind.

wind·break \'win(d)-ˌbrāk\ *n.* A shelter from the wind, such as a clump of trees.

wind·burn \'win(d)-ˌbərn\ *n.* Inflammation of skin from exposure to strong winds.

wind cone. A cone-shaped bag of cloth supported in the air, as at an airport or weather-observation station, that shows the direction of the wind.

wind·fall \'win(d)-ˌfȯl\ *n.* **1** Something blown down by the wind, as fruit from a tree. **2** An unexpected legacy, gift, or other gain.

wind·flow·er \'win(d)-ˌflaür\ *n.* An anemone.

wind·ing sheet \'wīn-ding\. A sheet used to wrap a corpse for burial; a shroud.

wind instrument. A musical instrument sounded by wind, especially by the breath, as a flute or a horn.

wind·jam·mer \'win(d)-ˌjam-r\ *n.* A sailing ship.

wind·lass \'win-dləs\ *n.* A winch used especially on ships for hauling and hoisting.

wind·mill \'win(d)-ˌmil\ *n.* A mill or a machine, as one for pumping water, worked by the wind turning sails or vanes at the top of a tower.

win·dow \'win-dō\ *n.* **1** An opening in a wall to admit light and air. **2** The glass and framework which fill this opening.

win·dow·pane \'win-dō-ˌpān\ *n.* A pane of glass in a window.

win·dow-shop \'win-dō-ˌshäp\ *v.;* **win·dow-shopped; win·dow-shop·ping.** To inspect articles on display in store windows without entering the stores or buying. — **win·dow-shop·per,** *n.*

win·dow·sill \'win-dō-ˌsil\ *n.* or **window sill.** The timber or stone on which a window rests.

wind·pipe \'win(d)-ˌpīp\ *n.* A firm tubular passage connecting the pharynx and lungs; the trachea.

wind·row \'win-ˌ(d)rō\ *n.* **1** A row of hay raked up to dry before being made into heaps. **2** Any similar row or line, as of dry leaves, dust, or sea foam, swept up by the wind.

wind·shield \'win(d)-ˌshēld\ *n.* A glass screen attached to the body of an automobile or other vehicle in front of the driver and passengers.

wind sleeve or **wind sock.** A wind cone.

wind·storm \'win(d)-ˌstȯrm\ *n.* A storm with strong wind and little or no rain.

wind tunnel. An enclosed passage through which wind is blown against structures, as airplanes, to test the effect of wind pressure on them.

wind·up \'wīn-ˌdəp\ *n.* **1** A conclusion; the end. **2** In baseball, the motion of a pitcher's arm as he prepares to throw the ball.

wind·ward \'win-(d)wərd, 'wind-rd\ *n.* The point or side from which the wind blows; as, to sail to *windward.* — *adv.* In the direction from which the wind blows. — *adj.* **1** Moving windward. **2** On the side toward the windward.

windy \'win-dē\ *adj.;* **wind·i·er; wind·i·est. 1** Having wind or winds; exposed to winds; as, a *windy* day; a *windy* site. **2** Indulging in or characterized by useless talk; as, a *windy* speaker.

wine \'wīn\ *n.* **1** The juice of grapes which has developed an alcoholic content through fermentation. **2** The juice of any fruit or plant that has undergone similar fermentation; as, blackberry *wine.* **3** A deep red or purplish color. — *v.* To supply with or drink wine; as, to *wine* and dine.

wing \'wing\ *n.* **1** One of the limblike parts by means of which certain animals including most birds, bats, and many insects are able to fly. **2** Something like a wing in appearance, use, or motion; as, the *wings* of an airplane. **3** The act of flying; flight; as, to shoot birds on the *wing.* **4** A faction; as, the conservative *wing* of a political party. **5** A part that projects from a main structure; as, a palace having several *wings.* **6** A division of an army or a fleet; as, the left and the right *wings* of an advancing body of troops. **7** In military aviation, a unit of aircraft, chiefly tactical, consisting of a varying number and combination of squadrons. **8** In a theater, a space or platform at either side of the stage proper. **9** In certain team games, a player playing on one side of the center. **10** [in the plural] Insignia having the appearance of a pair of bird's wings. — *v.;* **winged** \'wingd\; **wing·ing** \'wing-ing\. **1** To fly; to pass through in flight. **2** To wound in the wing; as, to *wing* a bird.

winged \'wingd, 'wing-əd\ *adj.* Having wings or parts like wings; as, *winged* insects.

wing·spread \'wing-ˌspred\ *n.* The distance between the tips of a pair of spread wings.

wink \'wingk\ *v.* **1** To close and open the eyes quickly; to blink. **2** To avoid seeing; to pretend not to see — followed by *at;* as, to *wink* at a violation of the law. **3** To flicker; to twinkle. The light *winked* and went out. **4** To close and open one eye quickly as a sign or hint. — *n.* **1** The act of winking. **2** A sign given by winking. **3** A short nap. **4** An instant; a moment; a flash.

win·ner \'win-r\ *n.* A person or thing that wins.

win·ning \'win-ing\ *adj.* **1** Being a winner; successful; as, the *winning* team. **2** Attractive; charming; pleasing; as, a *winning* manner. — *n.* **1** The act of a person or thing that wins. **2** [often in the plural] That which is won; especially, money won in gambling. — **win·ning·ly,** *adv.*

win·now \'win-ō\ *v.* **1** To blow or fan the chaff from threshed grain. **2** To sift or sort as if by winnowing; as, to *winnow* the truth from an account.

win·some \'win(t)s-m\ *adj.* Winning; pleasing; cheerful; as, a *winsome* girl; a *winsome* smile.

win·ter \'wint-r\ *n.* The season of the year between fall and spring; the coldest season of the year. — *adj.* **1** Of or relating to winter; suitable for winter; as, a *winter* coat. — *v.;* **win·tered; win·ter·ing** \'wint-r-ing, 'win-tring\. **1** To pass the winter; as, to *winter* in a warm climate. **2** To keep during winter; as, to *winter* cattle.

win·ter·green \'wint-r-ˌgrēn\ *n.* **1** A low-growing evergreen plant bearing white bell-shaped flowers followed by red berries and yielding an oil (**oil of wintergreen**) used in medicine and flavoring. **2** This oil or something flavored with it or with a synthetic substitute.

win·ter·time \'wint-r-ˌtīm\ *n.* The winter season.

win·tery \'wint-r-ē, 'win-trē\ *adj.* Wintry.

win·try \'win-trē\ *adj.;* **win·tri·er; win·tri·est. 1** Of or characteristic of winter; coming in winter; having to do with winter; as, *wintry* weather. **2** Chilling; cold; cheerless; as, a *wintry* welcome.

wipe \'wīp\ *v.;* **wiped; wip·ing. 1** To clean or dry by rubbing; as, to *wipe* dishes. **2** To remove by or as by rubbing; as, to *wipe* away tears. **3** To erase completely; to destroy. The regiment was *wiped* out. **4** To pass or draw something over a surface. — *n.* The act of wiping; a rub. — **wip·er** \'wīp-r\ *n.*

wire \'wīr\ *n.* **1** Metal drawn so as to resemble thread or cord; also, a piece of such metal. **2** Something made of wire; especially, a cable used in telegraph systems. **3** Telegraph; a telegram; as, to send a *wire.* — **pull wires.** To exert influence secretly; as, to *pull wires* to get oneself a promotion. — **under the wire.** Just in time; as, to get in *under the wire.* — *v.;* **wired; wir·ing. 1** To provide with wire; to use wire on or to bind with wire; as, to *wire* a house for electric lights. **2** To telegraph.

wire-haired \'wīr-'hard, -'herd\ *adj.* Having short, crisp, slightly curly hair.

wire·less \'wīr-ləs\ *adj.* Without a wire or wires, as in **wireless telegraphy.** — *n.* or *v. Chiefly British.* Radio.

wire recorder. A device that records sounds from a microphone magnetically on a fine wire.

wire·worm \'wīr-ˌwərm\ *n.* One of the wirelike larvae of certain kinds of beetles.

wiry \'wīr-ē\ *adj.;* **wir·i·er; wir·i·est. 1** Of or like wire. **2** Slender yet strong and sinewy.

wis·dom \'wizd-m\ *n.* **1** Quality of being wise; knowledge and the ability to utilize it to benefit oneself or others. **2** Wise sayings or acts.

wisdom tooth. The last, or back, tooth of the full set on each half of each jaw of an adult.

wise \'wīz\ *n.* Way; manner; fashion — used in such phrases as *in any wise, in no wise, in this wise.*

-wise \ˌwīz\. A suffix that can mean: **1** In the manner or way in question, as in *anywise, likewise, nowise, otherwise.* **2** In the manner, shape, or direction of, as in *crabwise, lengthwise, clockwise*

wise \'wīz\ *adj.* **1** Having or showing good sense or good judgment; sensible; sound. **2** Aware of what is going on; informed. — **wise·ly,** *adv.*

wise·acre \'wī-ˌzāk-r\ *n.* A person making claims to wisdom that he does not have.

wise·crack \'wīz-ˌkrak\ *n.* A jocular remark.

wish \'wish\ *v.* **1** To long for; to desire; to want; as, to *wish* to be rich. **2** To form or express a desire concerning; as, to *wish* someone a Merry Christmas. **3** To request. I *wish* you to go now. — *n.* The act or an instance of wishing; something wished.

wish·bone \'wish-ˌbōn\ *n.* The forked bone in front of the breastbone in most birds.

wish·ful \'wish-fəl\ *adj.* **1** Having a wish or wishes; desirous. **2** According with wishes rather than fact; as, *wishful* thinking.

wishy-washy \'wish-ē-ˌwȯsh-ē, -ˌwäsh-ē\ *adj.* Thin and pale; weak; spiritless.

wisp \'wisp\ *n.* **1** A small bunch of hay or straw. **2** A thin piece or strand; as, *wisps* of hair. **3** A thin, slight cloud or puff; as, *wisps* of smoke. **4** Anything or anyone small or slight; as, a mere *wisp* of a girl. — **wispy** \'wis-pē\ *adj.*

wis·tar·ia \wis-'tir-ē-ə, -'ter-\ or **wis·te·ria** \-'tir-ē-ə\ *n.* [Named after Caspar *Wistar* (1761–1818), American anatomist.] A strong vine with hanging clusters of usually purplish or lavender pealike flowers.

wistaria

wist·ful \'wist-fəl\ *adj.* Feeling or showing longing; as, a *wistful* expression. — **wist·ful·ly** \-fə-lē\ *adv.* — **wist·ful·ness** \-fəl-nəs\ *n.*

wit \'wit\ *v. Archaic.* To know; to learn. — **to wit.** That is to say; namely.

wit \'wit\ *n.* **1** [in the plural] The mental faculties, especially when sound; as, out of one's *wits;* to lose one's *wits.* **2** Practical good judgment; as, the *wit* to think of a quick way out of a difficulty. **3** The ability to be witty. **4** Witty remarks; as, a speech full of *wit.* **5** A witty person. — **at one's wit's end.** At a loss for a means of solving a perplexing problem.

witch \'wich\ *n.* **1** A person believed to have magic powers; a sorcerer or sorceress. **2** An ugly old woman; a hag. **3** A charming girl or woman.

witch·craft \'wich-ˌkraft\ *n.* The power or practices of a witch; sorcery.

witch doctor. A medicine man, especially among some African tribes; any practitioner of magic.

witch·ery \'wich-r(-)ē\ *n.; pl.* **witch·er·ies. 1** Witchcraft. **2** Power to charm or fascinate; as, the *witchery* of music.

witch ha·zel \'wich ˌhāz-l\. **1** A shrub with small yellow flowers that come out after the leaves have fallen. **2** An alcoholic solution made from the bark of this shrub and used as a remedy for bruises or sprains.

witch hazel flowers

witch·ing \'wich-ing\ *adj.* Bewitching; enchanting.

with \(')wit͟h, (')with\ *prep.* **1** Against; as, to fight *with* a neighbor. **2** In the employment of; as, now *with* another firm. **3** In possession of. Leave the box *with* me. **4** Between oneself and another; as, to make a trade *with* a friend. **5** Favorable to; for; not against; as, to vote *with* the majority. The tide was *with* them. **6** By means of; as, to walk *with* a crutch. The box was filled *with* sand. **7** As a result of; as, to dance *with* joy; eyes dim *with* tears. **8** In respect to likenesses, value, or skill; as, to be on equal terms *with* another. The red dress does not compare *with* the blue dress. **9** In respect to alliance or harmony; as, on friendly terms *with* all nations. **10** In the estimation, or opinion, or view of. Their arguments had weight *with* him. **11** Accompanying as a feature of; as, dismissed *with* thanks. **12** Having in one's care or in one's knowledge; bearing; as, to arrive *with* good news. **13** As well as; as, to play *with* the best of them. **14** At the same time as; as, to go to bed *with* the sun. **15** From the company, friendship, or possession of; as, to part *with* one's books; to break *with* a friend. **16** In the company of; as, to go *with* friends. **17** Using or showing; having; granted or given; as, to work *with* a will; *with* your permission. **18** Toward; as regards; as, to be pleased *with* someone; patient *with* children. **19** In spite of. *With* all his advantages, he never accomplished anything worthwhile.

with·al \wi-'t͟hȯl, -'thȯl\ *adv. Archaic.* Besides; in addition; for all that; still; as, pleasant but stubborn *withal.*

with·draw \wit͟h-'drȯ, with-\ *v.;* **with·drew** \-'drü\; **with·drawn** \-'drȯn\; **with·draw·ing. 1** To draw back; to take away from a person or place; to remove; as, to *withdraw* money from the bank. The allies *withdrew* their troops. **2** To take back, as something said or proposed; to recall; as, to *withdraw* a charge. **3** To leave; to go away; to retreat. The enemy *withdrew.* **4** To cease an activity; as, to *withdraw* from the charity campaign.

with·draw·al \with-'drȯ-əl, with-, -'drȯl\ *n.* A withdrawing; a removal; a retreat.

withe \'with\ *n.* An easily bent twig, especially one of willow, that can be used as a band or rope.

with·er \'with-r\ *v.;* **with·ered**; **with·er·ing** \'with-r(-)ing\. **1** To become or cause to become dry or shriveled; to fade; to cause to shrink. **2** To cause to feel as if shriveled or blighted.

with·ers \'with-rz\ *n. pl.* The ridge between the shoulder bones of a horse or other animal.

with·hold \with-'hōld, with-\ *v.;* **with·held** \-'held\; **with·hold·ing**. To hold back; to keep back; to refrain from giving or allowing.

with·in \wi-'thin, -'thin\ *adv.* **1** On the inner side; inside. **2** In or into the interior, as of the body or a building; as, the heart *within.* Inquire *within.* **3** Inwardly; as, to be raging *within.* — *prep.* **1** Inside of. Stay *within* the house. **2** Not beyond the bounds or limits of; as, to live *within* one's income.

with·out \wi-'thau̇t, -'thau̇t\ *adv.* **1** On the outer sides; outside. The house is shabby *without.* **2** Out of doors; as, the wind *without.* — *prep.* **1** On, at, or to the outside of; as, to stand *without* the gate. **2** Not having; lacking; as, to be *without* food. **3** With omission of; as, *without* breaking the yolk.

with·stand \with-'stand, with-\ *v.;* **with·stood** \-'stu̇d\; **with·stand·ing**. To stand against; to resist; to oppose successfully, as an attack.

wit·less \'wit-ləs\ *adj.* Lacking sense; foolish.

wit·ness \'wit-nəs\ *n.* **1** Testimony; as, to give false *witness.* **2** A proof; evidence. A deed bears *witness* of a person's ownership. **3** A person who sees or otherwise has direct knowledge of something; as, *witnesses* of an accident. **4** A person who gives testimony in court. **5** A person who is present at an action, such as the signing of a will, so that he can testify who performed the action. — *v.* **1** To give testimony to; to testify as a witness. **2** To be or give proof of. The man's actions *witness* his guilt. **3** To be a witness of. **4** To act as a witness to some action, as the signing of a will.

wit·ted \'wit-əd\ *adj.* Having wit or wits — used in combination, as quick-*witted;* slow-*witted.*

wit·ty \'wit-ē\ *adj.;* **wit·ti·er**; **wit·ti·est**. **1** Having wit, or power to make clever, amusing remarks. **2** Showing wit; as, a *witty* remark.

wives. Plural of *wife.*

wiz·ard \'wiz-rd\ *n.* **1** A magician; a sorcerer. **2** A very clever or skillful person; as, a *wizard* at chess.

wiz·ard·ry \'wiz-r-drē\ *n.* Magical skill; witchcraft; sorcery.

wiz·ened \'wiz-nd\ *adj.* Shriveled up; withered; as, a *wizened* face.

wk. Abbreviation for *week.*

wob·ble or **wab·ble** \'wäb-l\ *v.;* **wob·bled** or **wab·bled**; **wob·bling** or **wab·bling** \-l(-)ing\. **1** To move with an unsteady, side-to-side motion; to quiver; to tremble or shake. The wheel *wobbled* somewhat. **2** To waver; to be undecided. — *n.* A rocking motion from side to side. — **wob·bly** or **wab·bly** \'wäb-l(-)ē\ *adj.*

woe \'wō\ *n.* Sorrow; grief; misfortune; trouble; affliction; as, a tale of *woe;* the *woes* of age.

woe·be·gone \'wō-bē-ˌgȯn\ *adj.* Dismal or unhappy looking; miserable; wretched.

woe·ful or **wo·ful** \'wōf-l\ *adj.* **1** Full of grief or misery; as, a *woeful* heart. **2** Bringing woe or misery; as, a *woeful* day. **3** Deplorable; grievous; as, *woeful* grades in an examination. — **woe·ful·ly** or **wo·ful·ly** \-l(-)ē\ *adv.*

woke. A past tense of *wake.*

wold \'wōld\ *n.* An upland plain; a region without woods.

wolf \'wu̇lf\ *n.; pl.* **wolves** \'wu̇lvz\. **1** A large, doglike, flesh-eating wild animal, with erect ears and bushy tail, that is often destructive to game and domestic animals. **2** A person like a wolf in some respect. — *v.* To eat greedily; as, to *wolf* one's lunch.

wolf·hound \'wu̇lf-ˌhau̇nd, 'wu̇l-ˌfau̇nd\ *n.* A dog of a large-sized breed once used in hunting wolves, as the **Irish wolfhound** or the **Russian wolfhound**.

wolf·ish \'wu̇l-fish\ *adj.* **1** Like a wolf; savage. **2** Characteristic of a wolf; fierce and greedy.

wolf·ram \'wu̇l-frəm\ *n.* Tungsten.

wolfs·bane \'wu̇lfs-ˌbān\ *n.* A poisonous herb of the crowfoot family, having yellow flowers.

wol·ver·ine or **wol·ver·ene** \ˌwu̇lv-r-'ēn, 'wu̇lv-r-ˌēn\ *n.* A blackish, shaggy-furred, flesh-eating wild animal related to the martens and sables and found chiefly in northern North America.

wolves. Plural of *wolf.*

wom·an \'wu̇m-ən\ *n.; pl.* **wom·en** \'wim-ən\. [From Old English *wifmann,* compounded from *wif* meaning "woman" and *mann* meaning "human being".] **1** An adult female person. **2** A female attendant or servant; as, the queen and her *women.* **3** Womanhood.

wom·an·hood \'wu̇m-ən-ˌhu̇d\ *n.* **1** The state of being a woman. **2** Womanly qualities. **3** Women; as, the *womanhood* of a nation.

wom·an·ish \'wu̇m-ə-nish\ *adj.* **1** Like a woman. **2** Suitable to a woman rather than to a man.

wom·an·kind \'wu̇m-ən-ˌkīnd\ *n.* Women.

wom·an·like \'wu̇m-ən-ˌlīk\ *adj.* Womanly.

wom·an·ly \'wu̇m-ən-lē\ *adj.;* **wom·an·li·er**; **wom·an·li·est**. **1** Having the qualities considered proper or befitting a woman, as gentleness or modesty. **2** No longer girlish; as, a *womanly* figure.

womb \'wüm\ *n.* **1** An organ of female mammals, in which the young are formed and nourished before birth; the uterus. **2** Any cavity like a womb in containing and enveloping something.

wom·bat \'wäm-ˌbat\ *n.* A brownish gray burrowing animal of Australia, resembling a small bear in appearance, the female of which carries its young in a pouch.

wombat

women. Plural of *woman.*

wom·en·folk \'wim-ən-ˌfōk\ or **wom·en·folks** \-ˌfōks\ *n. pl.* Women, especially of a particular family or group.

won. Past tense and past part. of *win.*

won·der \ˈwənd-r\ *n.* **1** Something extraordinary; a marvel; as, the *wonders* of modern science. **2** The feeling aroused by something extraordinary; great astonishment. — *v.;* **won·dered; won·der·ing** \-r(-)ing\. **1** To feel surprise; as, to *wonder* at the might of a storm. **2** To feel doubt and curiosity; as, to *wonder* what will happen.

won·der·ful \ˈwənd-rf-l\ *adj.* Exciting wonder or awe; marvelous. — **won·der·ful·ly** \-rf-l(-)ē\ *adv.*

won·der·land \ˈwənd-r-ˌland, -lənd\ *n.* **1** A fairy-like imaginary realm. **2** A place of wonders.

won·der·ment \ˈwənd-r-mənt\ *n.* Surprise; wonder.

won·drous \ˈwən-drəs\ *adj.* Wonderful. — *adv.* Wonderfully. — **won·drous·ly,** *adv.*

wont \ˈwȯnt, ˈwōnt\ *adj.* Accustomed; in the habit of doing — used after a form of the verb *be.* The child slept longer than he was *wont.* — *n.* Custom; habit; usual practice.

won't \(ˈ)wōnt, ˈwənt\. A contraction of *will not.*

wont·ed \ˈwȯnt-əd, ˈwōnt-\ *adj.* Accustomed; usual; as, to take one's *wonted* rest.

woo \ˈwü\ *v.;* **wooed** \ˈwüd\; **woo·ing. 1** To try to gain the love of; to court. **2** To try to gain; as, to *woo* wealth and success; to *woo* the public favor.

wood \ˈwu̇d\ *n.* **1** [often in the plural] A thick growth of trees; a forest or grove. **2** The hard fibrous substance found under the bark of trees and shrubs. **3** The trunks or branches of trees cut or sawed for use; timber; lumber. **4** Firewood. **5** Something made of wood. **6** A woodwind. — *adj.* Of wood; made of wood; wooden. — *v.* **1** To cover with a growth of trees; to plant with trees. **2** To supply with wood, especially firewood.

wood·bine \ˈwu̇d-ˌbīn\ *n.* Any of several climbing vines of Europe and America, as honeysuckle and Virginia creeper.

woodbine

wood block. 1 A solid block of wood, as for paving. **2** A die for printing, cut in relief on wood; a woodcut. **3** A print from this kind of die.

wood·carv·er \ˈwu̇d-ˌkärv-r, -ˌkȧrv-r\ *n.* A person who carves ornamental objects of wood. — **wood·carv·ing** \-ˌkär-ving, -ˌkȧr-\ *n.*

wood·chuck \ˈwu̇d-ˌchək\ *n.* A reddish brown hibernating rodent; the ground hog; the marmot.

wood·cock \ˈwu̇d-ˌkäk\ *n.; pl.* **wood·cocks** or **wood·cock.** A long-billed brown game bird resembling the snipe.

wood·craft \ˈwu̇d-ˌkraft\ *n.* Knowledge about forests and how to take care of oneself in them.

wood·cut \ˈwu̇d-ˌkət\ *n.* **1** An engraving on wood. **2** A print from such an engraving.

wood·cut·ter \ˈwu̇d-ˌkət-r\ *n.* One who cuts wood, especially as an occupation.

wood·ed \ˈwu̇d-əd\ *adj.* Having woods.

wood·en \ˈwu̇d-n\ *adj.* **1** Made of wood; as, *wooden* dishes. **2** Stiff and awkward, as if made of wood. **3** Spiritless; dull. — **wood·en·ly,** *adv.*

wood·land \ˈwu̇d-lənd, -ˌland\ *n.* Land covered with trees; woods; timberland. — *adj.* **1** Having to do with woodland. **2** Growing in woodland.

wood·lot \ˈwu̇d-ˌlät\ *n.* A relatively small area bearing forest trees; as, a farm *woodlot.*

wood louse. A small grayish crustacean which lives especially under stones and bark.

wood·man \ˈwu̇d-mən\ *n.; pl.* **wood·men** \-mən\. A woodcutter.

wood·peck·er \ˈwu̇d-ˌpek-r\ *n.* A climbing bird with stiff spiny tail feathers that aid in climbing or resting on tree trunks, and a long bill used to drill into trees for insects.

wood·pile \ˈwu̇d-ˌpīl\ *n.* A pile of firewood.

wood·shed \ˈwu̇d-ˌshed\ *n.* A shed for storing wood, especially firewood.

woods·man \ˈwu̇dz-mən\ *n.; pl.* **woods·men** \-mən\. **1** A woodcutter. **2** One skilled in woodcraft.

wood sorrel. 1 A stemless spring-flowering herb with sour juice, leaves divided into three heart-shaped leaflets, and five-petaled white or rose flowers veined with purple. **2** Any of numerous closely related plants.

wood thrush. A large thrush of eastern North America, noted for its loud clear song.

wood·wind \ˈwu̇d-ˌwind\ *n.* or **woodwind instrument.** A flute, clarinet, oboe, or bassoon.

wood·work \ˈwu̇d-ˌwərk\ *n.* Work made of wood, especially fittings for house interiors.

wood·work·ing \ˈwu̇d-ˌwərk-ing\ *n.* Shaping or working things of wood.

woody \ˈwu̇d-ē\ *adj.;* **wood·i·er; wood·i·est. 1** Abounding with woods; as, a *woody* region. **2** Containing wood or wood fiber; as, *woody* parts of a bush. **3** Like wood; as, a plant with a *woody* stem.

woo·er \ˈwü-ər\ *n.* One that woos; a suitor.

woof \ˈwu̇f, ˈwüf\ *n.* **1** The threads that cross the warp in a woven fabric. **2** Texture; cloth.

wool \ˈwu̇l\ *n.* **1** The soft, curled coat of sheep and some other animals. **2** A material made from wool, as yarn, fabric, or clothing. **3** Short thick curly hair. **4** A substance light and fleecy like wool; as, glass *wool.* — *adj.* Made of wool.

wool·en or **wool·len** \ˈwu̇l-ən\ *adj.* **1** Made of wool. **2** Having to do with wool or with cloth made of wool; as, a *woolen* mill. — *n.* **1** Any fabric made of wool. **2** [in the plural] Garments made of wool.

wool·gath·er·ing \ˈwu̇l-ˌgath-r(-)ing\ *n.* The act of indulging in stray fancies without purpose.

wool·ly \ˈwu̇l-ē\ *adj.;* **wool·li·er; wool·li·est. 1** Consisting of wool, or like wool. **2** Bearing wool; as, a *woolly* sheep. **3** Confused; as, *woolly* thinking. **4** Characterized by the spirit of the West in frontier times; as, the wild and *woolly* West. — *n.; pl.* **wool·lies.** A woolen garment; especially [in the plural] underclothing.

woolly bear or **woolly bear caterpillar.** The hairy larva of any of several kinds of moths.

wooly \ˈwu̇l-ē\ *adj.* or *n.* Woolly.

word \ˈwərd\ *n.* **1** Something that is said; especially, a brief remark or conversation; as, a *word* of advice. I should like to have a *word* with you. **2** A password; a watchword. **3** A statement considered as implying the truthfulness or good faith of the person making it; promise; as, a man of his *word;* his *word* of honor. **4** News; as, to bring *word* of the victory. **5** The Christian gospel — used with *the;* as, to preach the *word.* **6** [often with a capital] The Bible — used with *the;* as, to read from the *Word.* **7** [in the plural] Talk; discourse; angry talk; dispute. They had *words* and separated. **8** A sound or a combination of sounds spoken by the human voice and standing for an idea; the smallest unit of speech that is used by itself with meaning. **9** The written or printed character or group of characters that expresses such a unit of speech. — *v.* To express in words; to phrase; as, a carefully *worded* message.

word·age \ˈwərd-ij\ *n.* Words collectively.

word·book \ˈwərd-ˌbu̇k\ *n.* A dictionary.

word·ing \ˈwərd-ing\ *n.* The way in which ideas are put into words; expression in words.

wordy \ˈwərd-ē\ *adj.;* **word·i·er**; **word·i·est.** Using more words than are needed; verbose; as, a *wordy* speech. — **word·i·ness** \ˈwərd-ē-nəs\ *n.*

wore. Past tense of *wear.*

work \ˈwərk\ *n.* **1** The use of a person's strength or ability in order to get something done or to achieve some desired result; labor; toil. **2** Employment; occupation; as, to be out of *work.* **3** Something that needs to be done; a task; a job; as, to have *work* to do. **4** A deed; an achievement; as, to honor a man for his good *works.* **5** The material on which effort is put in the process of making something. **6** Something produced by mental exertion or physical labor. **7** [usually in the plural] A place where industrial labor is carried on, such as the buildings, grounds, and machinery of a factory; as, a locomotive *works.* **8** [in the plural] The working or moving parts of a mechanical device; as, the *works* of a watch. **9** Manner of working; workmanship; as, a job spoiled by careless *work.* **10** A fortified structure of any kind. **11** In physics, the transference of energy, as when a force produces movement of a body. — *v.;* **worked** \ˈwərkt\ or **wrought** \ˈrȯt\; **work·ing. 1** To do work; especially, to do something for money or other gain or under necessity; to labor. **2** To cause to labor. The foreman *worked* his men hard. **3** To act or to cause to act as intended; to operate; as, a plan that *worked* well; to *work* a machine. **4** To move or cause to move slowly or with effort; to progress slowly; as, to *work* the liquid into the cloth. The screw *worked* loose. **5** To ferment. **6** To make; to shape; as, a vase that is beautifully *wrought.* **7** To bring to pass; to cause; to accomplish. The locusts *worked* great damage in the crops. **8** To treat or manipulate in the process of making or processing something; as, to *work* putty until it is soft. **9** To carry on one's occupation in, through, or along; to cover in one's operations; as, to *work* an entire city in a fund-raising drive. **10** To excite; as, to *work* oneself into a rage. **11** To find the solution of; to solve; as, to *work* a problem in arithmetic. **12** To influence in a subtle or tricky way for one's own ends; as, to *work* the management for free tickets. — **work in. 1** To mix into; to put in. **2** To find time for; to attend to between jobs. — **work it.** To manage so as to bring about a desired result; to contrive. — **work off.** To make or become less; to free oneself of. — **work on.** To try to influence or affect. — **work out. 1** To bring about by effort. **2** To solve, as a problem. **3** To develop; to arrange, as a plan. **4** In athletics, to have or take part in a workout. **5** To pay for something in work instead of money. **6** To prove to be practical, effective, or desirable; as, a plan that should *work out.* — **work over.** To do over again; to revise, as an essay. — **work up. 1** To excite; to stir up. **2** To create; to produce; to develop. **3** To make one's way from a lower to a higher position; as, to *work up* to the presidency.

— The words *labor* and *toil* are synonyms of *work: work* is a general term for mental or physical effort or exertion directed toward some specific end, whether the effort itself is enjoyable or is merely a means of achieving the end; *labor* suggests greater exertion, particularly hard or unpleasant physical effort, and more often suggests work that is necessary rather than enjoyable; *toil* is likely to indicate extremely hard, fatiguing, and prolonged work.

work·a·ble \ˈwərk-əb-l\ *adj.* Capable of being worked or done.

work·a·day \ˈwərk-ə-ˌdā\ *adj.* **1** Relating to or suited for working days; as, *workaday* clothes. **2** Ordinary; commonplace; as, a *workaday* world.

work·bench \ˈwərk-ˌbench\ *n.* A bench or table on which work is done, as by a carpenter, a potter, or a machinist.

work·book \ˈwərk-ˌbu̇k\ *n.* A student's exercise book made up of a series of problems or exercises intended as part of a course of study.

work·day \ˈwərk-ˌdā\ *n.* **1** A working day, as distinguished from Sunday and holidays. **2** The number of hours worked on such a day. — *adj.* Workaday.

work·er \ˈwərk-r\ *n.* **1** A person who works. **2** Among bees, ants, or termites, one of the sexually undeveloped individuals that perform all the building and food gathering and care for the young.

work·house \ˈwərk-ˌhau̇s\ *n.; pl.* **work·hous·es** \-ˌhau̇-zəz\. **1** *British.* A poorhouse. **2** A house of correction for petty offenders.

work·ing \ˈwərk-ing\ *adj.* **1** Doing work, especially for a living; as, a *working* girl. **2** Relating to work; taken up with work; used in, or fitted for use in, work. **3** Good enough to allow work to be done; as, a *working* majority; a *working* arrangement. — *n.* **1** The manner of work; operation; action; as, the *working* of a machine. **2** [usually in the plural] An excavation made in mining or tunneling.

work·ing·man \ˈwərk-ing-ˌman\ *n.; pl.* **work·ing·men** \-ˌmen\. A man who works, especially as a manual laborer or industrial worker.

work·man \'wərk-mən\ *n.; pl.* **work·men** \-mən\. A worker; often, a skilled worker.

work·man·like \'wərk-mən-ˌlīk\ *adj.* Befitting a good workman; skillful; well done.

work·man·ship \'wərk-mən-ˌship\ *n.* **1** The art or skill of a workman; the manner of making or doing anything. **2** The quality or character of a piece of work; as, the excellent *workmanship* of a chest of drawers.

work·out \'wərk-ˌau̇t\ *n.* An exercise or practice to test or improve ability or performance.

work·room \'wərk-ˌrüm, -ˌru̇m\ *n.* A room in which work is done.

work·shop \'wərk-ˌshäp\ *n.* A shop where work, especially skilled manual work, is carried on.

world \'wərld\ *n.* **1** The universe; creation. **2** The earth and its people. **3** Mankind; people in general; the public. **4** A state of existence; a scene of life and action; as, the *world* of the future. **5** A great number or quantity; as, a *world* of troubles. **6** A part or section of the earth or its inhabitants, regarded as apart by itself; as, the Old *World;* the musical *world.* **7** The affairs of men; as, to withdraw from the *world.* **8** Any heavenly body, especially when regarded as inhabited.

world·ling \'wərl-dling\ *n.* A worldly person.

world·ly \'wərl-(d)lē\ *adj.;* **world·li·er**; **world·li·est.** **1** Of or relating to this world, especially to the affairs of this present life as contrasted with those of any life to come; not heavenly or spiritual. **2** Worldly-wise; sophisticated.

world·ly-wise \'wərl-(d)lē-'wīz\ *adj.* Wise as to the things and ways of this world.

world war. A war involving all or most of the chief nations of the world; especially [with capitals] either of two such wars of the 20th century.

world·wide \'wərl-'dwīd\ *adj.* Extended throughout the world; as, *worldwide* fame.

worm \'wərm\ *n.* **1** Any of numerous small, long and slender creeping or crawling animals, usually with soft body and no limbs or practically none, as an earthworm or a fluke. **2** A person despised because of wretched condition or too humble manner. **3** [in the plural] A disease due to parasitic worms in the body. **4** Something spiral in shape or movement, as a screw thread. — *v.* **1** To move, go, or work slowly, in the manner of a worm; as, to *worm* one's way through a crowd. **2** To bring something about in such a manner; as, to *worm* the truth out of a witness. **3** To free of worms; as, to *worm* a dog.

worm cast. A tube-shaped mass of earth left on the ground by an earthworm.

worm gear. A gear consisting of a toothed wheel (**worm wheel**) meshing with a worm.

worm·wood \'wərm-ˌwu̇d\ *n.* **1** Any of several bitter-tasting herbs used as a tonic and in the manufacture of certain alcoholic liquors. **2** Anything very bitter; bitterness.

wormy \'wər-mē\ *adj.;* **worm·i·er**; **worm·i·est.** **1** Containing worms. **2** Worm-eaten. **3** Like a worm.

worn. Past part. of *wear.*

wor·ried \'wər-ēd, 'wə-rēd\ *adj.* Anxious; as, a *worried* glance at the gathering clouds.

wor·ri·some \'wər-ēs-m, 'wə-rēs-m\ *adj.* Inclined to worry; causing worry.

wor·ry \'wər-ē. 'wə-rē\ *v.;* **wor·ried** \'wər-ēd, 'wə-rēd\; **wor·ry·ing.** **1** To shake and tear or mangle with the teeth. A puppy likes to *worry* an old shoe. **2** To torment with anxiety; to fret; to trouble; as, to *worry* one's parents. **3** To feel or express great anxiety. — *n.; pl.* **wor·ries.** **1** Anxiety. **2** A cause of anxiety. — **wor·ri·er** \'wər-ē-ər, 'wə-rē-\ *n.*

worse \'wərs\ *adj.* Comparative of *bad* and of *ill.* **1** Bad or evil in a greater degree; poorer in quality or worth. **2** In poorer health; sicker. — *adv.* Comparative of *badly* and of *ill.* In a worse degree or manner; as, to play *worse* than before. — *n.* Something worse; as, to have *worse* to tell.

wors·en \'wərs-n\ *v.;* **wors·ened**; **wors·en·ing** \-n(-)ing\. To make or grow worse.

wor·ship \'wər-shəp\ *n.* **1** High honor or great respect. **2** A title of honor used in addressing certain officials and men of rank. **3** Reverence or adoration paid to God, a god, or a sacred object. — *v.;* **wor·shiped** or **wor·shipped**; **wor·ship·ing** or **wor·ship·ping.** **1** To pay divine honors to; to adore. **2** To idolize. The boy *worships* his father. **3** To perform acts of adoration; as, to *worship* at an altar. **4** To participate in a religious service of worship. — **wor·ship·er** or **wor·ship·per** \-r\ *n.*

wor·ship·ful \'wər-shəp-fəl\ *adj.* **1** Honorable; esteemed. **2** Worshiping.

worst \'wərst\ *adj.* Superlative of *bad* and of *ill.* Bad, ill, or evil in the highest degree; poorest. — *adv.* Superlative of *badly* and of *ill.* To the extreme degree of badness; as, the *worst*-lighted room in the building. — *n.* A person or a thing that is worst; as, to be prepared for the *worst.* — *v.* To get the better of; to defeat.

wor·sted \'wu̇s-təd, 'wərs-\ *n.* [Named after *Worsted* (now *Worstead*), village in Norfolk, England.] **1** A smooth yarn spun from pure wool. **2** The fabric woven from such yarn.

wort \'wərt, 'wȯrt\ *n.* Malt steeped in water, used especially in making beer.

worth \'wərth\ *prep.* **1** Deserving of; meriting; as, a souvenir *worth* keeping. **2** Equal in value to; of the value of; as, a coin *worth* fifty cents. **3** Having possessions equal to; as, a man *worth* a million dollars. — *n.* **1** The quality or sum of qualities of a thing making it valuable or useful; value. **2** Value in money; price. **3** Excellence; virtue; merit.

worth·less \'wərth-ləs\ *adj.* Having no worth.

worth·while \'wərth-'hwīl\ *adj.* Worth the time spent or effort put forth; as, a *worthwhile* project.

wor·thy \'wər-t͟hē\ *adj.;* **wor·thi·er**; **wor·thi·est.** **1** Having worth or excellence; deserving of praise; as, a *worthy* goal. **2** Meriting; deserving; as, *worthy* of promotion. — *n.; pl.* **wor·thies.** A person of great worth. — **wor·thi·ly** \'wər-t͟h-l-ē\ *adv.*

would \wəd, (ə)d, (')wu̇d\. Past tense of *will.*

1 Was or were going to. The boy promised that he *would* sing. **2** Was or were willing to. We knew that he *would* do us a favor. **3** Was or were determined to. She *would* not open the door. **4** Wish or wishes it were possible that. I *would* I were young again. **5** Was or were accustomed to. The dog *would* sleep for hours. **6** Can be expected to. That *would* cause gossip. **7** Should; should then. If I had tried harder, I *would* not have failed.

would-be \'wu̇d-ˌbē\ *adj.* Desiring or pretending to be; as, a *would-be* poet.

wouldn't \'wu̇d-nt\. A contraction of *would not.*

wouldst \wədst, (')wu̇dst\. An archaic form of *would* used chiefly with *thou.*

wound \'wünd\ *n.* **1** An injury cutting or breaking bodily tissue, as by violence, accident, or surgery. **2** An injury or hurt to feelings or reputation. — *v.* **1** To hurt by cutting or breaking tissue. **2** To hurt the feelings or pride of; to mortify, abash, or chagrin; as, *wounded* by being snubbed.

wound \'wau̇nd\. Past tense and past part. of *wind.*

wove. A past tense and past part. of *weave.*

woven. A past part. of *weave.*

wrack \'rak\ *n.* **1** Wreck — archaic except in the phrase *wrack and ruin.* **2** Any sea vegetation, as kelp or seaweed, cast up or growing on the shore.

wraith \'rāth\ *n.* **1** A ghostly appearance of a living person supposed to be seen just before his death. **2** A ghost; a specter.

wran·gle \'rang-gl\ *v.;* **wran·gled**; **wran·gling** \-gl(-)ing\. **1** To dispute angrily; to brawl. **2** To argue. **3** To herd or round up livestock, especially on the range. — *n.* An angry dispute; a noisy quarrel.

wran·gler \'rang-glər\ *n.* **1** One who wrangles or bickers. **2** A herdsman or cowboy, especially on the range.

wrap \'rap\ *v.;* **wrapped**; **wrap·ping. 1** To cover by winding or folding; to enfold in a garment; as, to *wrap* a baby in a blanket. **2** To enclose in a package; as, to *wrap* groceries. **3** To wind or roll together; to fold; as, to *wrap* up a bandage. **4** To surround or envelop; as, a city *wrapped* in darkness. **5** To engross; to absorb; as, to be *wrapped* up in one's hobby. — **wrap up. 1** To put on warm outer garments. **2** To make a package of. **3** To finish or complete, as a job or project. — *n.* A warm, loose outer garment, as a shawl, cape, coat, or jacket.

wrap·per \'rap-r\ *n.* **1** One that wraps. **2** That in which something is wrapped, as a paper cover for a book or an envelope. **3** A loose outer garment for wear indoors by women.

wrath \'rath\ *n.* Violent anger; rage. — **wrathy** \'rath-ē\ *adj.*

wrath·ful \'rath-fəl\ *adj.* **1** Filled with wrath; very angry; as, a *wrathful* man. **2** Showing wrath; as, a *wrathful* look. — **wrath·ful·ly** \-fə-lē\ *adv.*

wreak \'rēk\ *v.* **1** To exact as a punishment; to inflict; as, to *wreak* vengeance. **2** To give free scope or rein to, as anger.

wreath \'rēth\ *n.; pl.* **wreaths** \'rēthz, 'rēths\. **1** Something twisted or intertwined into a circular shape; as, a *wreath* of flowers; a *wreath* of smoke. **2** A garland, as of flowers or leaves, given or worn as a mark of honor, especially of victory.

wreath

wreathe \'rēth\ *v.;* **wreathed**; **wreath·ing. 1** To twist or become twisted so as to show folds or creases; as, a face *wreathed* in smiles. **2** To fold or coil around; to entwine. Vines *wreathed* the poles. **3** To form into wreaths. Smoke *wreathed* upward.

wreck \'rek\ *n.* **1** Goods cast upon the land by the sea after a shipwreck. **2** Broken remains, as of a ship or vehicle after heavy damage by storm, collision, or fire. **3** A person or beast broken in health or in strength. **4** Shipwreck. **5** The action of breaking up or destroying anything; a wrecking; as, to be injured in the *wreck* of a train. — *v.* **1** To destroy or disable; to break up or shatter; as, to *wreck* a building; to *wreck* a friendship. **2** To cause to suffer shipwreck.

wreck·age \'rek-ij\ *n.* **1** The act of wrecking or state of being wrecked. **2** The remains of a wreck.

wreck·er \'rek-r\ *n.* **1** One that wrecks. **2** A person who searches for or works upon wrecks of vessels. **3** A ship used in salvaging wrecks. **4** A truck equipped to remove wrecked or disabled cars.

wren \'ren\ *n.* **1** Any of a family of small brown singing birds with short rounded wings and short erect tail, as the **house wren**, which nests about houses. **2** Any of various small singing birds resembling the true wrens in size and habits.

wrench \'rench\ *n.* **1** A forcible twist to one side or out of shape. **2** An injury, as to an ankle, caused by twisting or straining; a sprain. **3** A tool used for exerting a twisting force, as in turning nuts or bolts. — *v.* **1** To pull or twist with or as if with a wrench; to wrest. **2** To injure by twisting; to strain; to sprain. **3** To distort, as the meaning of a word.

wrench, 3

wrest \'rest\ *v.* **1** To pull away by twisting or wringing; as, to *wrest* a gun from a burglar. **2** To snatch forcibly and hold for oneself; as, to *wrest* territory from another nation. **3** To obtain only by strenuous effort against great odds; as, to *wrest* a living from barren uplands. — *n.* A wrenching; a forcible twist.

wres·tle \'res-l\ *v.;* **wres·tled**; **wres·tling** \-l(-)ing\. **1** To grapple with an opponent in an attempt to trip him or throw him down. **2** To contend against in wrestling. **3** To struggle for mastery, as with something difficult; as, to *wrestle* with a problem. — *n.* **1** The action of wrestling; a bout of wrestling. **2** A struggle. — **wres·tler** \-l(-)ər\ *n.*

wres·tling \'res-l(-)ing\ *n.* The sport in which two opponents wrestle with one another.

wretch \'rech\ *n.* **1** A miserable, unhappy person. **2** A base, vile, degraded person.

wretch·ed \'rech-əd\ *adj.* **1** Very miserable or unhappy; deeply distressed. **2** Causing misery and distress; as, *wretched* poverty; a *wretched* accident. **3** Hateful; contemptible; as, a *wretched* trick. **4** Very poor; inferior; bad; as, a *wretched* piece of work. — **wretch·ed·ly**, *adv.*

wrier. Comparative of *wry*.

wriest. Superlative of *wry*.

wrig·gle \'rig-l\ *v.;* **wrig·gled**; **wrig·gling** \-l(-)ing\. **1** To twist or move like a worm; to twist about uneasily; to squirm; as, to *wriggle* in one's chair. **2** To proceed by twisting, dodging ways; as, to *wriggle* out of a difficulty. — *n.* The act of wriggling. — **wrig·gly** \-l(-)ē\ *adj.*

wrig·gler \'rig-l(-)ər\ *n.* **1** One that wriggles. **2** The larva or pupa of a mosquito.

wright \'rīt\ *n.* A builder or maker; one who constructs something — used chiefly in combination, as in *shipwright* or *wheelwright.*

wring \'ring\ *v.;* **wrung** \'rəng\; **wring·ing** \'ring-ing\. **1** To twist or press so as to squeeze out moisture; as, to *wring* clothes. **2** To twist; as, to kill a chicken by *wringing* its neck. **3** To get by or as if by twisting or pressing; as, to *wring* the truth out of someone. **4** To affect as if by wringing. Their distress *wrung* our hearts.

wring·er \'ring-r\ *n.* **1** One that wrings. **2** A machine for squeezing water out of wet clothes.

wrin·kle \'ringk-l\ *n.* **1** A crease or small fold on a surface, as in the skin or in cloth. **2** A clever notion or trick; a novelty; as, the latest *wrinkle* in beach hats. — *v.;* **wrin·kled**; **wrin·kling** \-l(-)ing\. To mark or become marked with wrinkles; to crease. — **wrin·kly** \-l(-)ē\ *adj.*

wrist \'rist\ *n.* The joint between the hand and arm or the region of this joint.

wrist·band \'ris(t)-ˌband\ *n.* A band that encircles the wrist, as a band or cuff on a sleeve or a leather strap worn to support the wrist.

wrist·bone \'ris(t)-ˌbōn\ *n.* Any bone of the wrist, or carpus; a carpal bone.

wrist·let \'ris(t)-lət\ *n.* **1** A band worn around the wrist, as for ornament. **2** A handcuff.

writ \'rit\ *n.* **1** That which is written — now chiefly in *Holy Writ.* **2** An order in writing signed by a court or judicial officer.

write \'rīt\ *v.;* **wrote** \'rōt\ or, archaic, **writ** \'rit\; **writ·ten** \'rit-n\ or, archaic, **writ** \'rit\; **writ·ing** \'rīt-ing\. [From Old English *writan* meaning literally "to scratch".] **1** To form letters or words with pen or pencil; as, to learn to read and *write.* **2** To form the letters or the words of, as on paper; as, to *write* one's name. **3** To put down on paper; to give expression to in writing; as, to *write* one's impressions of the circus. **4** To make up and set down for others to read, as a story or book. **5** To write or dictate a letter to; as, to *write* the president. **6** To communicate by letter; to correspond. **7** To be fitted for writing. This pen *writes* easily. — **write off. 1** To remove from an account; to cancel; as, to *write off* a bad debt. **2** To drop or eliminate, as from planning or consideration. — **write up. 1** To write an account of. **2** To write fully or in detail, as a set of notes.

writ·er \'rīt-r\ *n.* A person who writes, especially as a business or occupation; an author.

write-up \'rīt-ˌəp\ *n.* A written account or description, especially in a newspaper or magazine.

writhe \'rīth\ *v.;* **writhed**; **writh·ing. 1** To twist and turn this way and that; as, to *writhe* in pain. **2** To suffer with shame or confusion; to squirm.

writ·ing \'rīt-ing\ *n.* **1** The act of one who writes; the formation of letters to express words and ideas. **2** Something that is written, as a letter or book. **3** Handwriting. **4** The occupation of an author. **5** The practice of literary composition.

written. Past part. of *write.*

wrong \'ròng\ *adj.* **1** Not right morally; sinful. Cheating is *wrong.* **2** Not correct or true; false; as, a *wrong* answer. **3** Not the one wanted or intended; as, to take the *wrong* train. **4** Not as it should be; having something the matter; as, a dress that is somehow *wrong.* **5** Made so as to be placed down or under; as, the *wrong* side of a ribbon. **6** Not according to the rules; not proper; as, the *wrong* way to hold a fork. — *adv.* In a wrong direction, manner, position, or relation; incorrectly; as, to go *wrong;* to answer *wrong.* — *n.* **1** That which is wrong; wrong principles, practices, or acts; as, to know right from *wrong.* **2** An act of injustice; suffering unjustly caused; as, to suffer *wrongs.* **3** Error; mistake; as, to be in the *wrong.* **4** In law, a violation of the legal rights of another. — *v.;* **wronged** \'ròngd\; **wrong·ing** \'ròng-ing\. To do wrong to; to treat unjustly.

wrong·do·er \'ròng-'dü-ər\ *n.* A person who does wrong, especially moral wrong. — **wrong·do·ing** \-ing\ *n.*

wrong·ful \'ròng-fəl\ *adj.* Wrong; unjust; unlawful. — **wrong·ful·ly** \-fə-lē\ *adv.*

wrong·head·ed \'ròng-'hed-əd\ *adj.* Stubbornly wrong; not to be changed from a wrong opinion. — **wrong·head·ed·ly**, *adv.*

wrong·ly \'ròng-lē\ *adv.* In a wrong way; wrong; wrongfully; as, *wrongly* accused.

wrote. Past tense of *write.*

wroth \'ròth, 'rōth\ *adj.* Filled with wrath; angry.

wrought \'ròt\. A past tense and past part. of *work.* — *adj.* **1** Formed; fashioned. **2** Ornamented. **3** Of metals, beaten into shape; hammered.

wrought iron. A commercial form of iron that is tough but relatively soft and easy to work.

wrought-up \'ròt-'əp\ *adj.* Greatly excited.

wrung. Past tense and past part. of *wring.*

wry \'rī\ *adj.* **1** Twisted out of shape; crooked; as, a *wry* neck. **2** Made by twisting the features; as, a *wry* smile. — **wry·ly** \-lē\ *adv.*

wry·neck \'rī-ˌnek\ *n.* **1** A disease marked by a twisting of the neck and an unnatural position of the head. **2** A bird related to the woodpeckers, with a peculiar way of twisting its head and neck.

w's. Pl. of *w.*

wt. Abbreviation for *weight.*

x \'eks\ *n.; pl.* **x's** \'eks-əz\. **1** The 24th letter of the alphabet. **2** As a Roman numeral, 10.

X chromosome. One of the two kinds of chromosomes that in most animals are associated with the determination of sex.

xe·bec \'zē-ˌbek\ *n.* A ship, usually three-masted, of the Mediterranean, with long overhanging bow and stern.

xe·non \'zē-ˌnän\ *n.* A heavy, inert gaseous element, occurring in air in minute quantities.

xen·o·pho·bia \ˌzen-ə-'fō-bē-ə\ *n.* Fear or hatred of foreigners.

xe·ro·phyte \'zir-ə-ˌfīt\ *n.* A plant adapted for growth in drought or desert conditions, as agaves, cactuses, sagebrush, and yuccas.

Xmas \'kris-məs, 'eks-məs\. [*X* in this word is from the Greek letter *chi*, which is shaped like our *X* and is the first letter of and an abbreviation for Greek *Christos* meaning "Christ".] Abbreviation for *Christmas.*

X ray \'eks ˌrā\. **1** A ray of the same nature as light rays, but of very short wave length, that is generated by a stream of electrons striking against a metal surface in a vacuum tube and that is able to penetrate various thicknesses of solids and act on photographic film like light. **2** A photograph, especially of conditions inside the surface of a body, taken by the use of these rays. — **X-ray** \'eks-ˌrā\ *adj.*

X-ray \'eks-ˌrā\ *v.* To examine, treat, or photograph with X rays.

xy·lem \'zī-ləm, -ˌlem\ *n.* The innermost layer of woody tissue round the central pith of the stem of a plant, which carries water upwards from the roots and furnishes support for the plant.

xy·lo·phone \'zī-lə-ˌfōn\ *n.* A musical instrument consisting of a series of wooden bars varying in length and sounded by striking with two wooden hammers.

y \'wī\ *n.; pl.* **y's** \'wīz\. The 25th letter of the alphabet.

-y \ē\. A suffix that can mean: quality, activity, or state of, as in *jealousy* or *victory.*

-y \ē\. A suffix that can mean: one that is young or small or that is an object of affection, as in *Johnny, kitty,* or *sonny.*

-y \ē\. A suffix that can mean: **1** Characterized by, having, full of, or consisting of, as in *angry, icy, guilty,* or *stony.* **2** Tending or inclined to the action or state of, as in *chatty* or *sleepy.* **3** Somewhat, rather, as in *chilly, hoary,* or *lanky.* **4** Somewhat like, suggesting, as in *messy.*

☞ In a few words, such as *stilly* and *vasty,* no change of meaning results from the addition of *-y.*

-y \ē\. A suffix that can mean: the result of the action of, as in *augury* or *perjury.*

yacht \'yät\ *n.* [From Dutch *jacht,* short for *jachtschip* meaning "pursuit ship".] A boat, usually a sailboat, with a sharp prow and generally graceful lines, used as a pleasure boat.

yacht·ing \'yät-ing\ *n.* **1** The navigation of a yacht. **2** Traveling or cruising in a yacht.

yachts·man \'yäts-mən\ *n.; pl.* **yachts·men** \-mən\. A man who owns or sails a yacht.

yak \'yak\ *n.* A large blackish brown ox of Tibet, often domesticated and used as a beast of burden.

yam \'yam\ *n.* **1** A root vegetable resembling the sweet potato and grown mainly in tropical regions. **2** A sweet potato, usually one with a soft, moist texture when cooked.

yank \'yangk\ *v.* To pull sharply; to jerk.

Yan·kee \'yangk-ē\ *n.* **1** A native of New England. **2** A native of the northern United States as distinguished from a native of the southern states. **3** A citizen of the United States, especially as distinguished from a citizen of a foreign country. — *adj.* Of or relating to a Yankee or Yankees.

yap \'yap\ *n.* A quick, sharp bark; a yelp. — *v.;* **yapped; yap·ping.** To bark in yaps.

yard \'yärd, 'yȧrd\ *n.* **1** A measure of length equal to three feet, or 36 inches. **2** A long spar, tapering toward the ends, that supports a lugsail, a lateen sail, or any of the sails of a square-rigged vessel.

yard \'yärd, 'yȧrd\ *n.* **1** An area, often enclosed, around or by and belonging to a house, barn, or factory. **2** An enclosed place in which a certain kind of work is carried on; as, a navy *yard;* a lumber *yard.* **3** A place with a system of railroad tracks in which train cars and engines are connected, switched, or stored. — *v.* To enclose in a yard.

yard·age \'yärd-ij, 'yȧrd-\ *n.* **1** The total number of linear, square, or cubic yards. **2** The length of something measured in yards.

yard·arm \'yärd-ˌärm, 'yȧrd-ˌȧrm\ *n.* Either end of the yard of a square-rigged vessel.

yard·mas·ter \'yärd-ˌmast-r, 'yȧrd-\ *n.* The person who is in charge of a railroad yard.

yard·stick \'yärd-ˌstik, 'yȧrd-\ *n.* **1** A measuring stick a yard long. **2** A rule or standard by which something is measured; a criterion.

yarn \'yärn, 'yȧrn\ *n.* **1** Spun wool, cotton, flax, silk, or other fiber, as used in weaving, knitting, or the manufacture of thread. **2** An interesting or exciting story told without much regard for accuracy. — *v.* To tell yarns.

yar·row \'yar-ō\ *n.* A strong-scented herb with white or, rarely, pink flowers in flat clusters.

yaw \'yȯ\ *v.* To turn abruptly from a straight course, as a boat when struck by a heavy sea.

yawl \'yȯl\ *n.* **1** A small ship's boat, usually rowed by four or six oars. **2** A fore-and-aft rigged two-masted sailing vessel with the shorter mast aft of the point at which the stern rises from the water.

yawn \'yȯn, 'yän\ *v.* **1** To open the mouth wide, especially involuntarily, as from sleepiness. **2** To open or stand open in a way considered to resemble a mouth open in a yawn; as, the cave's entrance *yawned* before them. — *n.* The act of yawning or gaping; as, to stifle a *yawn.*

yaws \'yȯz\ *n. pl.* A contagious skin disease of certain tropical regions.

Y chromosome. One of the two kinds of chromosomes that in most animals are associated with the determination of sex.

y-clept or **y-cleped** \ē-'klept\ *adj.* [From the past part. of an obsolete verb *clepe* meaning "to call", "to summon", and derived from Old English *clipian, cleopian.*] *Archaic.* Named; called.

yd. Abbreviation for *yard.*

ye \(')yē\ *pron.* An archaic form of *you.*

yea \'yā\ *adv.* **1** Yes. **2** Indeed; truly — used to introduce a question or a statement. — *n.* **1** The answer "yes". **2** An affirmative vote.

year \'yir\ *n.* **1** The time of one apparent revolution of the sun around the ecliptic; the period of the earth's revolution around the sun, approximately 365¼ days. **2** A period of 365 days, or in leap year 366 days, beginning January 1. **3** The part of a year devoted to some certain kind of activity; as, the school *year.* **4** The time in which any planet completes a revolution around the sun; as, the *year* of Mars.

year·book \'yir-ˌbu̇k\ *n.* **1** A book published yearly; an annual. **2** A school publication recording the history and activities of a graduating class.

year·ling \'yir-ling, 'yər-\ *n.* One, usually an animal, that is a year old or in the second year of life.

year·ly \'yir-lē\ *adj.* **1** Of or for a year; annual; as, the company's *yearly* profits. **2** Occurring, made, done, or produced every year or once a year; as, a *yearly* crop. — *adv.* Once a year; annually.

yearn \'yərn\ *v.* **1** To be filled with longing; to desire eagerly. **2** To feel pity or sympathy.

yearn·ing \'yər-ning\ *n.* A tender longing.

yeast \'yēst\ *n.* **1** A minute fungus occurring as single cells or as small clusters budded from a parent cell and causing fermentation with the production of gas and alcohol in materials containing sugars. **2** A froth on or sediment in a body of fermenting material, as fruit juice, consisting largely of the bodies of yeast plants. **3** A small cake, as of meal, to which has been added some living yeast (**yeast·cake** \-ˌkāk\), used in making bread or beer. **4** Foam; froth. **5** Anything that is likened to yeast because of its stirring or leavening effect.

yell \'yel\ *v.* To cry out in loud, sharp tones; to shriek; to scream. — *n.* **1** The act or sound of yelling. **2** A shout or cheer, usually rhythmical, used especially by students; as, a school *yell.*

yel·low \'yel-ō\ *adj.* **1** Of the color yellow. **2** Having a yellow or yellowish complexion; as, the *yellow* races. **3** Cowardly or treacherous. — *n.* A color like that of butter or ripe lemons. — *v.* To make or become yellow, as from age.

yellow fever. An infectious, often fatal tropical disease carried by mosquitoes and characterized by yellowness of the skin, intestinal bleeding, and vomiting.

yel·low·ham·mer \'yel-ō-ˌham-r\ *n.* **1** A European finch, mostly bright yellow in the male. **2** A flicker.

yel·low·ish \'yel-ə-wish\ *adj.* Somewhat yellow.

yellow jack. **1** Yellow fever. **2** The flag raised on ships in quarantine.

yellow jacket. An American social wasp having the body partly bright yellow, noted for its irritable temper and painful sting.

yel·low·legs \'yel-ō-ˌlegz\ *n. sing. and pl.* Either of two American shore birds (**lesser yellowlegs** and **greater yellowlegs**) with long yellow legs.

yel·low·throat \'yel-ō-ˌthrōt\ *n.* Any of several American warblers with yellow breast and throat.

yellow warbler. A small North American warbler that is bright yellow with brown streaks on the underparts in the male.

yelp \'yelp\ *v.* To utter a sharp, quick cry; to bark or cry shrilly and, often, again and again, as in pain or fear. — *n.* A yelping cry or bark.

Yem·e·ni \'yem-ə-nē\ *adj.* Yemenite. — *n.; pl.* **Yem·e·nis** or **Yem·e·ni**. A Yemenite.

Yem·en·ite \'yem-ə-ˌnīt\ *adj.* Of or relating to Yemen. — *n.* A native or inhabitant of Yemen.

yen \'yen\ *n. sing. and pl.* Japanese monetary unit.

yen \'yen\ *n.* An intense desire; an urge; a longing; as, to have a *yen* to travel.

yeo·man \'yō-mən\ *n.; pl.* **yeo·men** \-mən\. **1** In former times, an attendant or retainer in a royal or noble household. **2** A small landowner. **3** A navy enlisted man who performs certain clerical duties.

yeo·man·ly \'yō-mən-lē\ *adj.* Becoming to a yeoman; sturdy; self-reliant.

yeo·man·ry \'yō-mən-rē\ *n.* A body of yeomen, especially one of small landowners.

yes \'yes\ *adv.* **1** It is so; it is right; it is permitted. **2** More than that. We are friends, *yes,* dear friends. — *n.* An affirmative reply.

yes man. A person who agrees with everything that is said to him; one who endorses without criticism every opinion of his employer or superior.

yes·ter·day \'yest-r-dē\ *n.* **1** The day next before this day. *Yesterday* was a holiday. **2** The time not far past; a recent time or period. — *adv.* **1** On the day next before this day. The letter arrived *yesterday.* **2** At a recent time or period.

yes·ter·night \'yest-r-'nīt\ *n.* Last night. — *adv.* During last night.

yes·ter·year \'yest-r-'yir\ *n.* The recent past; a period not long past.

yet \(')yet\ *adv.* **1** Up to now or then; before or at this or that time. The guests have not *yet* arrived. **2** For some time up to now; as, to be busy *yet.* **3** At some future time; as, a man who will be famous *yet.* **4** Still; even more; as, to go *yet* faster. **5** But in spite of that; nevertheless; as, strong, *yet* not strong enough.

yew \'yü\ *n.* **1** A tree or shrub with evergreen leaves and poisonous juice. **2** The heavy wood of the yew, used in making bows, hoops, and furniture.

yew

Yid·dish \'yid-ish\ *n.* A language which developed from a German dialect and borrowed many words from Hebrew and the Slavic languages, written in the Hebrew alphabet, and used by many Jews, especially in Russia, central Europe, and the United States. — *adj.* Belonging to, characteristic of, or written in Yiddish.

yield \'yēld\ *v.* **1** To produce, as fruit, profit, or other return. Fertile soil *yields* good crops. **2** To produce as payment or interest on what is spent or invested; as, a bond *yielding* three per cent. **3** To give or grant; to turn over; as, to *yield* the platform to the next speaker. **4** To give way, as to force, pressure, or influence; as, to *yield* to a friend's urgings. The door *yielded*. **5** To surrender; to give up; as, to *yield* the fort; to *yield* the right of way to an oncoming car. — *n.* Amount or quantity yielded or produced. There was a good *yield* of wheat this year.

yield·ing \'yēl-ding\ *adj.* Inclined to submit to others' wishes; compliant.

yip \'yip\ *v.;* **yipped; yip·ping.** To yelp — used especially of a dog. — *n.* A yelp.

yo·del \'yōd-l\ *v.;* **yo·deled** or **yo·delled; yo·del·ing** or **yo·del·ling** \-l(-)ing\. **1** To make sudden changes from a natural voice in singing to falsetto. **2** To call or shout in this manner. — *n.* A yodeled shout, call, or song. — **yo·del·er** or **yo·del·ler** \-l(-)ər\ *n.*

yo·ga or **Yo·ga** \'yō-gə\ *n.* **1** A system of mental self-discipline, practiced especially by followers of the Hindu religion, in which the attention is directed solely upon some object, which may be but is not necessarily the deity, with a view to the identification of consciousness with the object. **2** Any set of physical exercises and postures that constitute or are believed to constitute the proper preparatory steps to mental yoga.

yo·gi \'yō-gē\ *n.* One who practices yoga.

yo·gurt or **yo·ghurt** \'yōg-rt\ *n.* A semisolid preparation from milk partly evaporated and then fermented by a bacterium, used as a food.

yoke \'yōk\ *n.* **1** A bar or frame of wood fitting over the necks of two draft animals, as oxen, and holding them together for drawing a plow or a load. **2** Two animals joined together by a yoke; as, a *yoke* of oxen. **3** Something that joins together; a bond; a tie; as, the *yoke* of marriage. **4** A power that imposes bondage; rule; as, to throw off the *yoke* of oppression. **5** In a blouse or other garment, a shaped piece to fit the shoulders or hips, designed to support the weight of the hanging parts of the cloth. — *v.;* **yoked; yok·ing. 1** To put a yoke on; to join with a yoke; as, to *yoke* oxen. **2** To attach a draft animal to; as, to *yoke* a plow. **3** To join together; as, to *yoke* in matrimony.

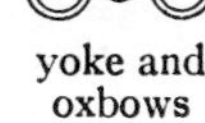

yoke and oxbows

yoke·fel·low \'yōk-ˌfel-ō\ *n.* A close companion; a mate.

yo·kel \'yōk-l\ *n.* A rustic; a bumpkin.

yolk \'yōk, 'yōlk\ *n.* **1** The yellow mass in the center of an egg. **2** The oily fat in sheep's wool.

Yom Kip·pur \yȯm 'kip-r, yəm; ˌyōm ki-'pu̇r\. An annual Jewish religious holiday in September or October, observed in fasting and prayer as a day of atonement.

yon \'yän\ *adj.* or *adv. Archaic* or *dial.* Yonder.

yond \'yänd\ *adj.* or *adv. Archaic* or *dial.* Yonder.

yon·der \'yänd-r\ *adv.* At or in that place; over there. — *adj.* **1** Farther away; more distant; as, on the *yonder* side of the stream. **2** Being within view but at some distance. *Yonder* trees are maples.

yore \'yōr, 'yȯr\ *n.* Time long past; as, men of *yore*.

you \(')yü, yə, yē\ *pron.* **1** The person or persons spoken or written to. I thank *you*. **2** Anyone. To increase speed, *you* press down.

you'd \(')yüd, yəd\. A contraction of *you had* or *you would*.

you'll \(')yül, (')yu̇l, yəl\. A contraction of *you will* or *you shall*.

young \'yəng\ *adj.;* **young·er** \'yəng-gr\; **young·est** \'yəng-gəst\. **1** Being in the early part of life; not old; youthful; as, *young* men. **2** Youthfully fresh or vigorous in body, mind, or feeling; as, *young* for her age. **3** Being or having the characteristics of a novice; immature, inexperienced, ignorant, or weak. **4** Of, relating to, or characteristic of youth or early life; as, a *young* spirit; *young* frailties. **5** Not having existed long; still in the early period of its existence. The night is *young*. **6** Representing a new tendency or movement; as, the *Young* Turks. **7** Not so old as another having the same name or title; junior; as, *young* Mr. Smith. **8** Having the typical characteristics except for being smaller, weaker, or less intense. We have a *young* hurricane outdoors. — *n.* **1** Those who are young; young people. The *young* enjoy this game more than their parents do. **2** Offspring of an animal. The *young* of the bear are playful. — **with young.** Pregnant.

young·ber·ry \'yəng-ˌber-ē\ *n.; pl.* **young·ber·ries.** The large sweet reddish black fruit of a hybrid between a trailing variety of blackberry and a southern dewberry, grown in the western and southern United States.

young·ish \'yəng-ish\ *adj.* Somewhat young.

young·ling \'yəng-ling\ *n.* A young person, animal, or plant. — *adj.* Young.

young·ster \'yəng(k)st-r\ *n.* A child; a young person.

youn·ker \'yəngk-r\ *n.* A youngster; a lad.

your \yər, (')yu̇r, (')yōr\ *adj.* **1** Of or belonging to you; received by or from you; affecting you; as, *your* book; *your* gifts; during *your* illness. **2** Used in front of a title of honor in addressing a person; as, *your* Majesty; *your* Honor.

you're \(')yůr, (')yōr, yər\. A contraction of *you are.*

yours \'yůrz, 'yōrz\ *pron.* The form of the word *you* used to show possession when no noun follows. The hat is *yours.*

your·self \yər-'self\ *pron.; pl.* **your·selves** \-'selvz\. **1** A form of the word *you* used to give emphasis or to show that the subject and object of a verb are the same person. **2** Your true or best self. You are not *yourself* today.

youth \'yüth\ *n.; pl.* **youths** \'yüt͟hz, 'yüths\. **1** Youthfulness. **2** The time of life that follows childhood and precedes maturity; the period usually from puberty to manhood or womanhood. **3** A young man. **4** Young people collectively; as, the *youth* of the community. **5** The early period of existence or growth of anything; as, during the *youth* of civilization.

youth·ful \'yüth-fəl\ *adj.* **1** Young. **2** Characteristic of or belonging to youth; as, *youthful* lightheartedness; *youthful* games. **3** Suitable for young persons; as, a *youthful* suit. **4** Youthfully fresh or vigorous. The old man remains *youthful* in spirit. — **youth·ful·ly** \-fə-lē\ *adv.* — **youth·ful·ness** \-fəl-nəs\ *n.*

you've \(')yüv, yəv\. A contraction of *you have.*

yowl \'yaůl\ *n.* A loud, long, mournful cry or howl, as of a dog or wildcat. — *v.* To utter, or utter with, a yowl.

yr. Abbreviation for *year.*

y's. Pl. of *y.*

yt·tri·um \'i-trē-əm\ *n.* A rare metallic chemical element.

yuc·ca \'yək-ə\ *n.* Any of several plants related to the lilies, growing in dry regions and having stiff, sharp-pointed leaves, mostly in a rosette at the base, and whitish flowers, mostly in erect clusters.

yucca

Yu·go·slav \'yü-gō-'släv, -'slav, -'slåv\ *n.* **1** A person belonging to one of the south Slavic peoples. **2** A native or inhabitant of Yugoslavia. — *adj.* **1** Of or relating to the south Slavic peoples; south Slavic. **2** Of or relating to Yugoslavia. — **Yu·go·slav·i·an** \ˌyü-gō-'släv-ē-ən, -'slav-, -'slåv-\ *adj.* or *n.* — **Yu·go·slav·ic** \-'slav-ik, -'släv-, -'slåv-\ *adj.*

yule \'yül\ *n.* Christmas; the Christmas season.

yule log. A large log formerly put on the hearth on Christmas Eve as a foundation for the fire.

yule·tide \'yül-ˌtīd\ *n.* The Christmas season.

yurt \'yůrt\ *n.* A light, round, movable tent consisting of skins or felt stretched over a lattice framework and used by various nomadic tribes in Siberia.

ywis \ī-'wis, ē-'wis\ *adv. Archaic.* Certainly; indeed.

z \'zē, *in Canada and Great Britain usually* 'zed\ *n.; pl.* **z's** \'zēz, 'zedz\. The 26th letter of the alphabet.

za·ny \'zā-nē\ *n.; pl.* **za·nies.** One who acts like a buffoon. — *adj.;* **za·ni·er; za·ni·est.** Being or characteristic of a zany.

zeal \'zēl\ *n.* Eagerness in pursuing any course or object; ardent and active interest; fervor.

zeal·ot \'zel-ət\ *n.* One who shows zeal, especially excessive zeal; a fanatic.

zeal·ous \'zel-əs\ *adj.* Full of or characterized by zeal; as, a *zealous* supporter of a cause. — **zeal·ous·ly,** *adv.*

ze·bra \'zēb-rə\ *n.; pl.* **ze·bras** or **ze·bra.** An African mammal related to the horse and ass, striped with black and white or black and buff.

ze·bu \'zēb-ˌyü, 'zē-ˌbü\ *n.; pl.* **ze·bus** or **ze·bu.** A bovine mammal with a large hump over the shoulders which is used as a domestic animal in Asia and eastern Africa.

ze·nith \'zē-nəth\ *n.* **1** The point in the heavens directly overhead. **2** The highest point; the apex; the summit; as, the *zenith* of a hero's glory.

zeph·yr \'zef-r\ *n.* **1** The west wind. **2** Any soft, gentle breeze. **3** A fine soft yarn or worsted, used for knitting and embroidery.

zep·pe·lin \'zep-l(-)ən\ *n.* [From German, there named after Count Ferdinand von *Zeppelin* (1838–1917), German army officer who designed it.] A huge dirigible balloon tapering at both ends that has a metal framework and is driven through the air by engines carried on its underside.

ze·ro \'zē-ˌrō, 'zir-ˌō\ *n.; pl.* **ze·ros** or **ze·roes. 1** Naught; the number 0. **2** The point on a scale, as of a thermometer, from which reckonings are made. **3** The temperature corresponding to zero on a thermometer. **4** The lowest point. The umpire's patience reached *zero.* — *adj.* No; not any. The pilot could not land the plane because of *zero* visibility.

zero hour. 1 The hour at which a previously planned military movement is scheduled to start. **2** The moment at which any ordeal is to begin; the moment of crisis.

zest \'zest\ *n.* Keen relish; great enjoyment; as, to eat with *zest.* — **zest·ful** \-fəl\ *adj.*

zesty \'zes-tē\ *adj.;* **zest·i·er; zest·i·est.** Characterized by or producing zest; exhilarating.

zig·zag \'zig-ˌzag\ *n.* A line or stripe or anything, as a path or road, like a line or stripe that has many sharp angles or turns at short intervals, often with each angle or turn taking the opposite direction from the preceding one. — *adj.* Shaped like a zigzag; as, *zigzag* lightning. — *adv.* In a zigzag; as, to move *zigzag.* — *v.;* **zig·zagged; zig·zag·ging.** To move or flow zigzag. The train *zigzagged* through the hills.

zigzags

zinc \'zingk\ *n.* A bluish white metallic element that tarnishes only slightly in moist air at ordinary temperatures, used especially as roofing, to make alloys, and to coat iron. — *v.;* **zincked** or **zinced** \'zing(k)t\; **zinck·ing** or **zinc·ing** \'zingk-ing\. To treat or coat with zinc; to galvanize.

zinc ointment. An ointment containing zinc oxide in a base, used in treating skin diseases.

zinc oxide. 1 A substance, in its typical form a light white powder, used as an ingredient in manufacturing various products, as paints, rubber, ointments, and cosmetics. **2** Zinc ointment.

zinc white. Zinc oxide used as a white pigment, especially in house paints and water colors.

zin·nia \'zin-ē-ə, 'zin-yə, 'zēn-\ *n.* An American herb of the aster family with leaves opposite each other on the stem and flower heads with yellow or brown disk flowers and ray flowers of various colors.

zinnias

zip \'zip\ *n.* **1** A sudden sharp hissing sound such as that made by a flying bullet. **2** Energy; vim; force; as, a person with a lot of *zip.* — *v.;* **zipped; zip·ping. 1** To move quickly or speedily, with or as if with zip; as, to *zip* over a racecourse. **2** To be full of energy or vim. **3** To open or close by pulling the tab of a slide fastener; as, to *zip* open a purse; to *zip* up one's jacket.

zip·per \'zip-r\ *n.* A slide fastener.

zir·con \'zər-ˌkän\ *n.* **1** A crystalline mineral, a silicate of zirconium, certain transparent varieties of which are used as material for gems. **2** A gem cut from this mineral.

zir·co·ni·um \(ˌ)zər-'kō-nē-əm\ *n.* A metallic element used especially in alloys and in nuclear reactors for producing atomic energy.

zith·er \'zith-r, 'zith-r\ *n.* A many-stringed musical instrument played with the fingers and a plectrum on the thumb.

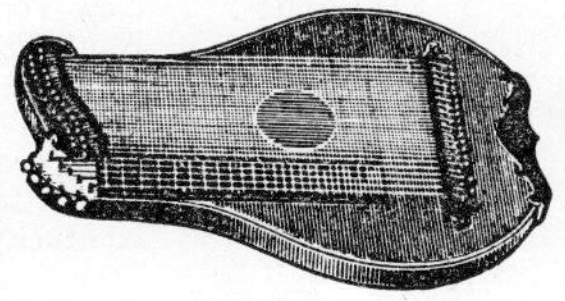

zither

zo·di·ac \'zōd-ē-ˌak\ *n.* An imaginary belt in the heavens that includes the paths of the moon and the principal planets and has for its middle line the apparent path of the sun, divided by early astronomers into twelve parts, or signs, named for twelve constellations.

zom·bi or **zom·bie** \'zäm-bē\ *n.; pl.* **zom·bis** or **zom·bies. 1** A corpse supposedly brought to life by supernatural power but lacking independence of will and capable of only automatic movement as if in a trance. **2** A very stupid person whose manner of action suggests that popularly supposed to characterize zombis.

zon·al \'zōn-l\ *adj.* **1** Of or having the form of a zone. **2** Arranged or living in zones.

zone \'zōn\ *n.* **1** An encircling band or belt; as, to climb beyond a mountain's tree *zone.* **2** One of the five divisions of the globe with respect to climate (two **Frigid Zones** around the poles, one **Torrid Zone** between the two tropics, and two **Temperate Zones** between the tropics and the polar circles). **3** A section set apart for some particular reason or standing out in some special way; as, a residential *zone;* a safety *zone.* **4** In the parcel-post system, any of the areas around a mailing point for which one rate of postage is charged for shipment from that point. **5** One of the numbered sections into which a large city is divided to help speed mail delivery. — *v.;* **zoned; zon·ing. 1** To divide or be divided into zones. **2** To divide into districts reserved for different purposes, as for residence, business, and industry; as, to *zone* a city.

zoo \'zü\ *n.; pl.* **zoos** \'züz\. A zoological garden.

zo·o·log·i·cal \ˌzō-ə-'läj-ik-l\ *adj.* Of or having to do with the study of animal life.— **zo·o·log·i·cal·ly** \-ik-l(-)ē\ *adv.*

zoological garden. A park or garden where wild animals are kept for exhibition.

zo·ol·o·gist \zō-'äl-ə-jəst\ *n.* A specialist in zoology.

zo·ol·o·gy \zō-'äl-ə-jē\ *n.* The science in which facts about animals are collected, studied, and explained.

zoom \'züm\ *v.* **1** To swoop upward at a sharp angle with a loud steady hum or buzz. The plane roared, *zoomed,* and vanished in the distance. **2** To speed along with a loud hum; to whiz. — *n.* A zooming.

zo·o·phyte \'zō-ə-ˌfīt\ *n.* Any of numerous invertebrate animals resembling plants in growth, as the corals and sponges.

Zo·ro·as·tri·an \ˌzōr-ə-'was-trē-ən, ˌzȯr-\ *adj.* Of or relating to the ancient Persian religious teacher Zoroaster or the religion (**Zo·ro·as·tri·an·ism** \-ə-ˌniz-m\) traditionally supposed to have been founded by him. — *n.* A believer in Zoroastrianism.

Zou·ave \zü-'äv, -'åv\ *n.* **1** A member of a French infantry unit wearing a brilliant oriental type of uniform. **2** A member of any body of soldiers using a uniform and a form of drill like that of the Zouaves.

zounds \'zaůn(d)z\ *interj.* [A shortened form of *God's wounds.*] *Archaic.* An exclamation expressing surprise or a mild degree of anger.

z's. Pl. of *z.*

zwie·back \'swē-ˌbak, 'swī-\ *n.* A kind of biscuit or rusk baked in a loaf and cut and toasted.

zy·gote \'zī-ˌgōt\ *n.* Any cell formed by the union of two sexual cells; a fertilized egg.

PRESIDENTS OF THE U.S.A.

Number	Name and Pronunciation of Surname	Life Dates	Birthplace	Term
1	George Washington \'wȯsh-ing-tən, 'wäsh-\	1732–1799	Virginia	1789–1797
2	John Adams \'ad-mz\	1735–1826	Massachusetts	1797–1801
3	Thomas Jefferson \'jef-rs-n\	1743–1826	Virginia	1801–1809
4	James Madison \'mad-əs-n\	1751–1836	Virginia	1809–1817
5	James Monroe \mən-'rō\	1758–1831	Virginia	1817–1825
6	John Quincy Adams \'ad-mz\	1767–1848	Massachusetts	1825–1829
7	Andrew Jackson \'jaks-n\	1767–1845	South Carolina	1829–1837
8	Martin Van Buren \van 'byu̇r-ən\	1782–1862	New York	1837–1841
9	William Henry Harrison \'har-əs-n\	1773–1841	Virginia	1841
10	John Tyler \'tīl-r\	1790–1862	Virginia	1841–1845
11	James Knox Polk \'pōk\	1795–1849	North Carolina	1845–1849
12	Zachary Taylor \'tāl-r\	1784–1850	Virginia	1849–1850
13	Millard Fillmore \'fil-ˌmōr, -ˌmȯr\	1800–1874	New York	1850–1853
14	Franklin Pierce \'pirs\	1804–1869	New Hampshire	1853–1857
15	James Buchanan \byü-'kan-ən, bə-\	1791–1868	Pennsylvania	1857–1861
16	Abraham Lincoln \'lingk-n\	1809–1865	Kentucky	1861–1865
17	Andrew Johnson \'jän(t)s-n\	1808–1875	North Carolina	1865–1869
18	Ulysses Simpson Grant \'grant\	1822–1885	Ohio	1869–1877
19	Rutherford Birchard Hayes \'hāz\	1822–1893	Ohio	1877–1881
20	James Abram Garfield \'gär-ˌfēld\	1831–1881	Ohio	1881
21	Chester Alan Arthur \'ärth-r\	1830–1886	Vermont	1881–1885
22	Grover Cleveland \'klēv-lənd\	1837–1908	New Jersey	1885–1889
23	Benjamin Harrison \'har-əs-n\	1833–1901	Ohio	1889–1893
24	Grover Cleveland \'klēv-lənd\	1837–1908	New Jersey	1893–1897
25	William McKinley \mə-'kin-lē\	1843–1901	Ohio	1897–1901
26	Theodore Roosevelt \'rō-zə-ˌvelt, -zəv-lt\	1858–1919	New York	1901–1909
27	William Howard Taft \'taft\	1857–1930	Ohio	1909–1913
28	Woodrow Wilson \'wils-n\	1856–1924	Virginia	1913–1921
29	Warren Gamaliel Harding \'härd-ing\	1865–1923	Ohio	1921–1923
30	Calvin Coolidge \'kü-lij\	1872–1933	Vermont	1923–1929
31	Herbert Clark Hoover \'hüv-r\	1874–1964	Iowa	1929–1933
32	Franklin Delano Roosevelt \'rō-zə-ˌvelt, -zəv-lt\	1882–1945	New York	1933–1945
33	Harry S Truman \'trü-mən\	1884–	Missouri	1945–1953
34	Dwight David Eisenhower \'īz-n-ˌhau̇r\	1890–	Texas	1953–1961
35	John Fitzgerald Kennedy \'ken-əd-ē\	1917–1963	Massachusetts	1961–1963
36	Lyndon Baines Johnson \'jän(t)s-n\	1908–	Texas	1963–

VICE-PRESIDENTS OF THE U.S.A.

Number	Name and Pronunciation of Surname	Life Dates	Birthplace	Term
1	John Adams \'ad-mz\	1735–1826	Massachusetts	1789–1797
2	Thomas Jefferson \'jef-rs-n\	1743–1826	Virginia	1797–1801
3	Aaron Burr \'bər\	1756–1836	New Jersey	1801–1805
4	George Clinton \'klint-n\	1739–1812	New York	1805–1812
5	Elbridge Gerry \'ger-ē\	1744–1814	Massachusetts	1813–1814
6	Daniel D. Tompkins \'täm(p)-kənz\	1774–1825	New York	1817–1825
7	John C. Calhoun \kal-'hün\	1782–1850	South Carolina	1825–1832
8	Martin Van Buren \van 'byu̇r-ən\	1782–1862	New York	1833–1837
9	Richard M. Johnson \'jän(t)s-n\	1780–1850	Kentucky	1837–1841
10	John Tyler \'tīl-r\	1790–1862	Virginia	1841
11	George M. Dallas \'dal-əs\	1792–1864	Pennsylvania	1845–1849
12	Millard Fillmore \'fil-ˌmōr, -ˌmȯr\	1800–1874	New York	1849–1850
13	William R. King \'king\	1786–1853	North Carolina	1853
14	John C. Breckinridge \'brek-n-ˌrij\	1821–1875	Kentucky	1857–1861
15	Hannibal Hamlin \'ham-lən\	1809–1891	Maine	1861–1865
16	Andrew Johnson \'jän(t)s-n\	1808–1875	North Carolina	1865
17	Schuyler Colfax \'kōl-ˌfaks\	1823–1885	New York	1869–1873
18	Henry Wilson \'wils-n\	1812–1875	New Hampshire	1873–1875
19	William A. Wheeler \'hwēl-r\	1819–1887	New York	1877–1881
20	Chester A. Arthur \'ärth-r\	1830–1886	Vermont	1881
21	Thomas A. Hendricks \'hen-driks\	1819–1885	Ohio	1885
22	Levi P. Morton \'mȯrt-n\	1824–1920	Vermont	1889–1893
23	Adlai E. Stevenson \'stēv-n-sən\	1835–1914	Kentucky	1893–1897
24	Garret A. Hobart \'hōb-rt, 'hō-ˌbärt\	1844–1899	New Jersey	1897–1899
25	Theodore Roosevelt \'rō-zə-ˌvelt, -zəv-lt\	1858–1919	New York	1901
26	Charles W. Fairbanks \'far-ˌbangks, 'fer-\	1852–1918	Ohio	1905–1909
27	James S. Sherman \'shər-mən\	1855–1912	New York	1909–1912
28	Thomas R. Marshall \'märsh-l\	1854–1925	Indiana	1913–1921
29	Calvin Coolidge \'kü-lij\	1872–1933	Vermont	1921–1923
30	Charles G. Dawes \'dȯz\	1865–1951	Ohio	1925–1929
31	Charles Curtis \'kərt-əs\	1860–1936	Kansas	1929–1933
32	John N. Garner \'gärn-r\	1868–	Texas	1933–1941
33	Henry A. Wallace \'wäl-əs\	1888–1965	Iowa	1941–1945
34	Harry S Truman \'trü-mən\	1884–	Missouri	1945
35	Alben W. Barkley \'bärk-lē\	1877–1956	Kentucky	1949–1953
36	Richard M. Nixon \'niks-n\	1913–	California	1953–1961
37	Lyndon B. Johnson \'jän(t)s-n\	1908–	Texas	1961–1963
38	Hubert H. Humphrey \'həm(p)-frē\	1911–	South Dakota	1965–

THE STATES OF THE U.S.A.

Name and Pronunciation	*State Capital and Pronunciation*
Alabama \ˌal-ə-'bam-ə\	Montgomery \mənt-'gəm-r(-)ē, mänt-\
Alaska \ə-'las-kə\	Juneau \'jü-ˌnō\
Arizona \ˌar-ə-'zō-nə\	Phoenix \'fē-niks\
Arkansas \'ärk-n-ˌsȯ\	Little Rock \'lit-l ˌräk\
California \ˌkal-ə-'fȯrn-yə\	Sacramento \ˌsak-rə-'ment-ˌō\
Colorado \ˌkäl-ə-'rad-ō, -'räd-\	Denver \'den-vər\
Connecticut \kə-'net-ik-ət\	Hartford \'härt-fərd\
Delaware \'del-ə-ˌwar, -ˌwer, -wər\	Dover \'dōv-r\
Florida \'flȯr-əd-ə, 'flär-\	Tallahassee \ˌtal-ə-'has-ē\
Georgia \'jȯr-jə\	Atlanta \ət-'lant-ə\
Hawaii \hə-'wī-(ˌ)ē, -'wä-(ˌ)ē, -'wȯ-yə\	Honolulu \ˌhän-l-'ü-ˌlü, ˌhōn-\
Idaho \'ī-də-ˌhō\	Boise \'bȯi-sē, -zē\
Illinois \ˌil-ə-'nȯi, -'nȯiz\	Springfield \'spring-ˌfēld\
Indiana \ˌin-dē-'an-ə\	Indianapolis \ˌin-dē-ə-'nap-l(-)əs\
Iowa \'ī-ə-wə\	Des Moines \dē 'mȯin\
Kansas \'kan-zəs\	Topeka \tə-'pēk-ə\
Kentucky \kən-'tək-ē\	Frankfort \'frangk-fərt\
Louisiana \lə-ˌwē-zē-'an-ə, ˌlü-ə-zē-\	Baton Rouge \ˌbat-n 'rüzh\
Maine \'mān\	Augusta \ȯ-'gəs-tə, ə-\
Maryland \'mer-ə-lənd\	Annapolis \ə-'nap-l(-)əs\
Massachusetts \ˌmas-ə-'chü-səts\	Boston \'bȯs-tən\
Michigan \'mish-ig-n\	Lansing \'lan(t)s-ing\
Minnesota \ˌmin-ə-'sōt-ə\	St. Paul \sānt 'pȯl\
Mississippi \ˌmis-ə-'sip-ē\	Jackson \'jaks-n\
Missouri \mə-'zu̇r-ē, -ə\	Jefferson City \'jef-rs-n\
Montana \män-'tan-ə\	Helena \'hel-ə-nə\
Nebraska \nə-'bras-kə\	Lincoln \'lingk-n\
Nevada \nə-'vad-ə, -'väd-\	Carson City \'kärs-n\
New Hampshire \'ham(p)sh-r, 'ham(p)-ˌshir\	Concord \'kängk-rd\
New Jersey \'jər-zē\	Trenton \'trent-n\
New Mexico \'meks-i-ˌkō\	Santa Fe \ˌsant-ə 'fā\
New York \'yȯrk\	Albany \'ȯlb-n-ē\
North Carolina \ˌkar-ə-'lī-nə\	Raleigh \'rȯl-ē, 'räl-ē\
North Dakota \də-'kōt-ə\	Bismarck \'biz-ˌmärk\
Ohio \ō-'hī-ō\	Columbus \kə-'ləm-bəs\
Oklahoma \ˌōk-lə-'hō-mə\	Oklahoma City
Oregon \'ȯr-ig-n, 'är-, -ə-ˌgän\	Salem \'sā-ləm\
Pennsylvania \ˌpen(t)s-l-'vān-yə\	Harrisburg \'har-əs-ˌbərg
Rhode Island \rō-'dī-lənd\	Providence \'präv-ə-dən(t)s, -ˌden(t)s\
South Carolina \ˌkar-ə-'lī-nə\	Columbia \kə-'ləm-bē-ə\
South Dakota \də-'kōt-ə\	Pierre \'pir\
Tennessee \ˌten-ə-'sē\	Nashville \'nash-ˌvil, -vəl
Texas \'teks-əs, -əz\	Austin \'ȯs-tən, 'äs-\
Utah \'yü-ˌtȯ, -ˌtä\	Salt Lake City \'sȯlt ˌlāk 'sit-ē\
Vermont \vər-'mänt\	Montpelier \mänt-'pēl-yə
Virginia \vər-'jin-yə\	Richmond \'rich-mənd\
Washington \'wȯsh-ing-tən, 'wäsh-\	Olympia \ō-'limp-ē-ə\
West Virginia \vər-'jin-yə\	Charleston \'chärl-stən\
Wisconsin \wis-'kän(t)s-n\	Madison \'mad-əs-n\
Wyoming \wī-'ō-ming\	Cheyenne \shī-'an, -'en\

THE PROVINCES OF CANADA

Name and Pronunciation	*Provincial Capital and Pronunciation*
Alberta \al-'bərt-ə\	Edmonton \'ed-mən-tən\
British Columbia \kə-'ləm-bē-ə\	Victoria \vik-'tōr-ē-ə, -'tȯr-\
Manitoba \ˌman-ə-'tō-bə\	Winnipeg \'win-ə-ˌpeg\
New Brunswick \'brənz-(ˌ)wik\	Fredericton \'fred-(ə-)rikt-n\
Newfoundland \'n(y)ü-fən(d)-lənd, n(y)ü-'fau̇n(d)-\	St. John's \sānt-'jänz\
Nova Scotia \ˌnō-və-'skō-shə\	Halifax \'hal-ə-ˌfaks\
Ontario \än-'ter-ē-ˌō\	Toronto \tə-'ränt-ō\
Prince Edward Island \'ed-wərd\	Charlottetown \'shär-lət-ˌtau̇n\
Quebec \kwē-'bek\	Quebec
Saskatchewan \sə-'skach-ə-wən, sa-'skach-ə-ˌwän\	Regina \rē-'jī-nə\

NATIONS OF THE WORLD

Name and Pronunciation	*Location*
Afghanistan \af-'gan-ə-ˌstan\	Asia
Albania \al-'bā-nē-ə, ȯl-\	Europe
Algeria \al-'jir-ē-ə\	Africa
Andorra \an-'dȯr-ə, -'där-ə\	Europe
Argentina \ˌärj-n-'tē-nə\	South America
Australia \ȯs-'trāl-yə, äs-\	Between Indian and Pacific Oceans
Austria \'ȯs-trē-ə, 'äs-\	Europe
Belgium \'belj-m\	Europe
Bhutan \bü-'tän, -'tan\	Asia
Bolivia \bə-'liv-ē-ə\	South America
Brazil \brə-'zil\	South America
Bulgaria \ˌbəl-'gar-ē-ə, bu̇l-, -'ger-\	Europe
Burma \'bər-mə\	Asia
Burundi \bu̇-'rün-dē\	Africa
Cambodia \kam-'bōd-ē-ə\	Asia
Cameroun \kam-'rün\	Africa
Canada \'kan-əd-ə\	North America
Central African Republic \'af-rik-n\	Africa
Ceylon \sē-'län, sā-\	Asia
Chad \'chad\	Africa
Chile \'chil-ē\	South America
China \'chī-nə\	Asia
Colombia \kə-'ləm-bē-ə, -'läm-\	South America
Congo (formerly Belgian Congo) \'käng-ˌgō\	Africa
Congo Republic (formerly Middle Congo)	Africa
Costa Rica \ˌkäs-tə 'rēk-ə, ˌkȯs-, ˌkōs-\	Central America
Cuba \'kyü-bə\	West Indies
Cyprus \'sīp-rəs\	Asia
Czechoslovakia \ˌchek-ə-slō-'väk-ē-ə\	Europe
Dahomey \də-'hō-mē\	Africa
Denmark \'den-ˌmärk\	Europe
Dominican Republic \də-'min-ik-n\	West Indies
Ecuador \'ek-wə-ˌdȯr\	South America
Ethiopia (Abyssinia) \ˌē-thē-'ōp-ē-ə (ˌab-ə-'sin-ē-ə, -'sin-yə)\	Africa
Finland \'fin-lənd\	Europe
France \'fran(t)s\	Europe
Gabon \ga-'bōn\	Africa
Germany \'jər-mə-nē\	Europe
Gambia \'gam-bē-ə\	Africa
Ghana \'gän-ə\	Africa
Greece \'grēs\	Europe
Guatemala \ˌgwät-m-'äl-ə\	Central America
Guinea \'gin-ē\	Africa
Guyana \gī-'an-ə\	South America
Haiti \'hāt-ē\	West Indies
Honduras \hän-'du̇r-əs, -'dyu̇r-\	Central America
Hungary \'həng-gr-ē\	Europe
Iceland \'īs-lənd, -ˌland\	North Atlantic Ocea
India \'in-dē-ə\	Asia
Indonesia \ˌin-də-'nē-zhə\	Asia
Iran (Persia) \i-'rän, -'ran ('pər-zhə)\	Asia
Iraq \i-'räk, -'rak\	Asia
Ireland, Republic of \'īr-lənd\	Europe

(*continued on next pag*

NATIONS OF THE WORLD

(continued from preceding page)

ame and Pronunciation	*Location*
rael \'iz-rē-əl\	Asia
aly \'it-l-ē\	Europe
vory Coast \'īv-r(-)ē\	Africa
amaica \jə-'mā-kə\	West Indies
apan \jə-'pan\	Asia
ordan \'jȯrd-n\	Asia
enya \'kēn-yə\	Africa
orea \kə-'rē-ə\	Asia
uwait \kə-'wāt\	Asia
aos \'lau̇s, 'lā-ˌäs\	Asia
ebanon \'leb-n-ən\	Asia
iberia \lī-'bir-ē-ə\	Africa
ibya \'lib-ē-ə\	Africa
iechtenstein \'lik-tən-ˌstīn\	Europe
uxembourg \'lu̇ks-m-ˌbu̇rg, 'ləks-m-ˌbərg\	Europe
alagasy Republic \ˌmal-ə-'gas-ē\	Africa
alawi \mə-'lä-wē\	Africa
alaysia \mə-'lā-zh(ē-)ə\	Asia
ali \'mäl-ē\	Africa
alta \'mȯl-tə\	Central Mediterranean
auritania \ˌmȯr-ə-'tā-nē-ə, -'tān-yə\	Africa
exico \'meks-i-ˌkō\	North America
onaco \'män-ə-ˌkō, mə-'näk-ˌō\	Europe
ongolian People's Republic \män(g)-'gōl-yən\	Asia
orocco \mə-'räk-ˌō\	Africa
uscat and Oman \'məs-ˌkat, ō-'män\	Asia
epal \nə-'pȯl\	Asia
etherlands \'net͟h-r-lən(d)z\	Europe
ew Zealand \'zē-lənd\	Southwest Pacific
icaragua \ˌnik-r-'äg-wə\	Central America
iger \'nīj-r\	Africa
igeria \nī-'jir-ē-ə\	Africa
orway \'nȯr-ˌwā\	Europe
akistan \'pak-ə-ˌstan, 'päk-ə-ˌstän\	Asia
anama \'pan-ə-ˌmȯ, -ˌmä\	Central America
araguay \'par-ə-ˌgwī, -ˌgwā\	South America
eru \pə-'rü\	South America
hilippines \'fil-ə-ˌpēnz\	Asia
oland \'pō-lənd\	Europe
ortugal \'pōrch-əg-l, 'pȯrch-\	Europe
omania \rō-'mā-nē-ə, rü-, -'mān-yə\	Europe

Name and Pronunciation	*Location*
Rwanda \ru̇-'än-də\	Africa
Salvador, El \el 'sal-və-ˌdȯr\	Central America
San Marino \ˌsan mə-'rē-ˌnō\	Europe
Saudi Arabia \'sau̇d-ē ə-'rā-bē-ə, sə-'üd-ē\	Asia
Senegal \ˌsen-ə-'gȯl, 'sen-ə-ˌgȯl\	Africa
Sierra Leone \sē-ˌer-ə lē-'ōn\	Africa
Singapore \'sing-(g)ə-ˌpōr, -ˌpȯr\	Asia
Somalia \sō-'mäl-ē-ə\	Africa
South Africa, Republic of	Africa
Spain \'spān\	Europe
Sudan \sü-'dan\	Africa
Sweden \'swēd-n\	Europe
Switzerland \'swits-r-lənd\	Europe
Syria \'sir-ē-ə\	Asia
Tanzania \ˌtan-zə-'nē-ə\	Africa
Thailand (Siam) \'tī-ˌland, -lənd (sī-'am)\	Asia
Togo \'tō-ˌgō\	Africa
Trinidad and Tobago \'trin-ə-ˌdad, tə-'bā-gō\	West Indies
Tunisia \tü-'nē-zhə, -'nizh-ə\	Africa
Turkey \'tərk-ē\	Asia and Europe
Uganda \(y)ü-'gan-də\	Africa
Union of Soviet Socialist Republics (U.S.S.R.) \'sō-vē-ˌet, -ət, 'säv-ē-(ˌ)yü-ˌes-ˌes-'är)\	Asia and Europe
United Arab Republic	Africa and Asia
United Kingdom of Great Britain and Northern Ireland \'brit-n, 'īr-lənd\	Europe
England \'ing-glənd\	
Northern Ireland	
Scotland \'skät-lənd\	
Wales \'wālz\	
United States of America \ə-'mer-ə-kə\	North America
Upper Volta \'väl-tə\	Africa
Uruguay \'yu̇r-ə-ˌgwī, -ˌgwā, 'u̇r-\	South America
Vatican City State \'vat-ik-n\	Europe
Venezuela \ˌven-ə-zə-'wā-lə, -'wē-\	South America
Vietnam \vē-'et-'näm, -'nam\	Asia
Western Samoa \sə-'mō-ə\	South Pacific
Yemen \'yem-ən\	Asia
Yugoslavia \ˌyü-gō-'släv-ē-ə, -'slav-\	Europe
Zambia \'zam-bē-ə\	Africa

LARGEST CITIES OF THE WORLD

(having over 150,000 inhabitants)

ame and Pronunciation	*Location*
achen \'äk-n\	Germany
badan \ˌä-bə-'dän\	Iran
berdeen \ˌab-r-'dēn\	Scotland
bidjan \ˌab-ə-'jän\	Ivory Coast
ccra \ə-'krä, 'ak-rə\	Ghana
dana \ˌäd-ə-'nä\	Turkey
ddis Ababa \'ad-əs 'ab-ə-bə\	Ethiopia
delaide \'ad-l-ˌād\	Australia
gra \'ä-grə\	India
hmadabad \'ä-məd-ə-ˌbäd\	India
jmer \ˌəj-'mir, -'mer\	India
kita \ä-'kēt-ə\	Japan
kron \'ak-rən\	Ohio
lbany \'ȯlb-n-ē\	New York
lbuquerque \'al-bə-ˌkərk-ē, ˌal-bə-'kərk-ē\	New Mexico
leppo \ə-'lep-ˌō\	United Arab Republic
lexandria \ˌal-ig-'zan-drē-ə, ˌel-\	United Arab Republic
lgiers \al-'jirz\	Algeria
ligarh \ˌal-i-'gär\	India
llahabad \'al-ə-hə-ˌbad\	India
lma-Ata \ˌal-mə-ə-'tä\	U.S.S.R.
magasaki \ˌam-ə-gə-'säk-ē\	Japan
mman \a-'man\	Jordan
moy \ə-'mȯi\	China
mritsar \ˌəm-'rits-r\	India
msterdam \'am-stər-ˌdam\	Netherlands
ngarsk \an-'gärsk\	U.S.S.R.

Name and Pronunciation	*Location*
Ankara \'angk-r-ə\	Turkey
Anshan \'än-ˌshän\	China
Antung \'än-'du̇ng\	China
Antwerp \'ant-(ˌ)wərp\	Belgium
Aomori \ˌä-ə-'mōr-ē\	Japan
Arkhangelsk \är-'kan-ˌgelsk\	U.S.S.R.
Asahikawa \'ä-sə-hi-'kä-wə\	Japan
Ashkhabad \'ash-kə-ˌbad\	U.S.S.R.
Astrakhan \'as-trə-ˌkan, -trək-n\	U.S.S.R.
Asunción \(ˌ)ä-ˌsün-sē-'ōn\	Paraguay
*Athens \'ath-ənz\	Greece
Atlanta \ət-'lant-ə\	Georgia
Auckland \'ȯk-lənd\	New Zealand
Augsburg \'au̇ks-ˌbu̇rg\	Germany
Austin \'ȯs-tən, 'äs-\	Texas
Avellaneda \ˌav-ə-zhə-'nā-t͟hə\	Argentina
Bacolod \bə-'kō-ˌlȯd\	Philippines
Baghdad \'bag-ˌdad\	Iraq
*Baku \bä-'kü\	U.S.S.R.
Baltimore \'bȯlt-m-ˌōr, -ˌȯr\	Maryland
Bamako \ˌbäm-ə-'kō\	Mali
Banaras \bə-'när-əs\	India
*Bandung \'bän-'du̇ng\	Indonesia
Bangalore \'bang-gə-ˌlōr, -ˌlȯr\	India
*Bangkok \'bang-ˌkäk, bang-'käk\	Thailand
*Barcelona \ˌbärs-l-'ō-nə\	Spain
Bareilly \bə-'rā-lē\	India
Bari \'bä-rē\	Italy
Barnaul \ˌbär-nə-'ül\	U.S.S.R.

(continued on next page)

*Having over 1,000,000 inhabitants

LARGEST CITIES OF THE WORLD

(continued from preceding page)

Name and Pronunciation	*Location*
Baroda \bə-'rō-də\	India
Barquisimeto \ˌbärk-ə-sə-'māt-ō\	Venezuela
Barranquilla \ˌbar-ən-'kē-ə\	Colombia
Basel \'bäz-l\	Switzerland
Basilan \bə-'sē-ˌlän\	Philippines
Basra \'bäs-rä, 'bəs-rə\	Iraq
Baton Rouge \ˌbat-n 'rüzh\	Louisiana
Beirut \bā-'rüt\	Lebanon
Belém \bə-'lem\	Brazil
Belfast \'bel-ˌfast, bel-'fast\	Northern Ireland
Belgrade \'bel-ˌgrād, bel-'grād\	Yugoslavia
Belo Horizonte \'bel-ō ˌhȯr-ə-'zänt-ē, ˌhär-\	Brazil
*Berlin \(ˌ)bər-'lin\	Germany
Bern \'bern, 'bərn\	Switzerland
Bhavnagar \bau̇-'nəg-r\	India
Bhopal \bō-'päl\	India
Bielefeld \'bē-lə-ˌfelt\	Germany
Bikaner \ˌbik-ə-'ner\	India
Bilbao \bil-'bä-ˌō\	Spain
Birmingham \'bər-ming-ˌham\	Alabama
*Birmingham \'bər-ming-m\	England
Bisk \'bisk\	U.S.S.R.
Blackpool \'blak-ˌpül\	England
Bochum \'bō-ˌku̇m\	Germany
*Bogotá \ˌbō-gə-'tȯ, -'tä\	Colombia
Bologna \bə-'lōn-yə\	Italy
Bolton \'bōlt-n\	England
*Bombay \(')bäm-'bā\	India
Bône \'bōn\	Algeria
Bonn \'bän\	Germany
Bordeaux \bȯr-'dō\	France
Boston \'bȯs-tən\	Massachusetts
Bradford \'brad-fərd\	England
Bratislava \ˌbrat-ə-'slä-və\	Czechoslovakia
Bremen \'brem-ən, 'brā-mən\	Germany
Brescia \'bresh-ə, 'brā-ˌshä\	Italy
Bridgeport \'brij-ˌpōrt, -ˌpȯrt\	Connecticut
Brighton \'brīt-n\	England
Brisbane \'briz-bən\	Australia
Bristol \'brist-l\	England
Brno \'bər-ˌnō\	Czechoslovakia
Brunswick \'brənz-(ˌ)wik\	Germany
*Brussels \'brəs-lz\	Belgium
Bryansk \brē-'än(t)sk\	U.S.S.R.
Bucaramanga \ˌbük-r-ə-'mäng-gə\	Colombia
*Bucharest \'bük-r-ˌest\	Romania
*Budapest \'büd-ə-ˌpest, -ˌpesht\	Hungary
*Buenos Aires \'bwā-nəs 'ar-ēz, 'bō-nəs, 'er-ēz, 'ī-rēz\	Argentina
Buffalo \'bəf-l-ˌō\	New York
Bulawayo \ˌbü-lə-'wā-ō\	Southern Rhodesia
Bursa \bu̇r-'sä\	Turkey
Bydgoszcz \'bid-ˌgȯshch\	Poland
Bytom \'bi-ˌtȯm\	Poland
Cagliari \'käl-yə-rē\	Italy
*Cairo \'kī-ˌrō\	United Arab Republic
*Calcutta \(')kal-'kət-ə\	India
Calgary \'kal-gər-ē\	Alberta
Cali \'kä-lē\	Colombia
Camagüey \ˌkä-mə-'gwā\	Cuba
*Canton \'kan-ˌtän\	China
Cape Town \'kāp ˌtau̇n\	South Africa
*Caracas \kə-'rak-əs, -'räk-\	Venezuela
Cardiff \'kärd-əf\	Wales
Cartagena \ˌkärt-ə-'gā-nə\	Colombia
Casablanca \ˌkas-ə-'blangk-ə\	Morocco
Catania \kə-'tān-yə\	Italy
Cebu \sā-'bü\	Philippines
Changchow \'chäng-'jō\	China
Changchun \'chäng-'chu̇n\	China
Changsha \'chäng-'shä\	China
Changteh \'chäng-'də\	China
Charlotte \'shär-lət\	North Carolina
Chelyabinsk \chel-'yä-bin(t)sk\	U.S.S.R.
Chengchow \'jəng-'jō\	China

*Having over 1,000,000 inhabitants

Name and Pronunciation	*Location*
Chengteh \'chəng-'də\	China
*Chengtu \'chəng-'dü\	China
Chernovtsy \cher-'nȯft-sē\	U.S.S.R.
Chiba \'chē-bə\	Japan
*Chicago \shə-'kȯg-ˌō, -'käg-\	Illinois
Chimkent \chim-'kent\	U.S.S.R.
Chinchow (Chinhsien) \'jin-'jō ('jin-shē-'en)\	China
Chinkiang \'jin-jē-'äng\	China
Chinwangtao \'chin-'hwäng-'dau̇\	China
Chita \chē-'tä\	U.S.S.R.
Chittagong \'chit-ə-ˌgäng\	Pakistan
Chkalov \chə-'kä-ləf\	U.S.S.R.
Cholon \'chō-'län\	Vietnam
Christchurch \'krīs(t)-ˌchərch\	New Zealand
*Chungking \'chu̇ng-'king\	China
Cincinnati \ˌsin(t)s-n-'at-ē, -'at-ə\	Ohio
Ciudad Juárez \sē-ˌü-'thä 'hwä-(ˌ)rās\	Mexico
Cleveland \'klēv-lənd\	Ohio
Cluj \'klüzh\	Romania
Coimbatore \ˌkȯim-bə-'tōr, -'tȯr\	India
Cologne \kə-'lōn\	Germany
Colombo \kə-'ləm-ˌbō\	Ceylon
Columbus \kə-'ləm-bəs\	Ohio
Concepción \kən-'sepsh-n\	Chile
Constantine \'kän(t)s-tən-ˌtēn\	Algeria
Copenhagen \ˌkōp-n-'hāg-n, -'häg-n\	Denmark
Córdoba \'kȯrd-ə-bə\	Argentina
Córdoba \'kȯrd-ə-bə\	Spain
Corpus Christi \ˌkȯrp-əs 'kris-tē\	Texas
Coventry \'käv-n-trē\	England
Croydon \'krȯid-n\	England
Curitiba \ˌku̇r-ə-'tē-bə\	Brazil
Czestochowa \ˌchen(t)s-tə-'kō-və\	Poland
Dacca \'dak-ə\	Pakistan
Dakar \dä-'kär\	Senegal
Dallas \'dal-əs\	Texas
Damascus \də-'mas-kəs\	Syria
Davao \'däv-ˌau̇\	Philippines
Dayton \'dāt-n\	Ohio
*Delhi \'del-ē\	India
Denver \'den-vər\	Colorado
Des Moines \dē 'mȯin\	Iowa
*Detroit \dē-'trȯit\	Michigan
*Djakarta \jə-'kärt-ə\	Indonesia
Djokjakarta \ˌjōk-yə-'kärt-ə\	Indonesia
Dneprodzerzhinsk \ˌnep-rō-dər-'zhin(t)sk\	U.S.S.R.
Dnepropetrovsk \ˌnep-rō-pə-'trȯfsk\	U.S.S.R.
Donetsk \də-'netsk\	U.S.S.R.
Dortmund \'dȯrt-ˌmu̇nt\	Germany
Dresden \'drez-dən\	Germany
Dublin \'dəb-lən\	Ireland
Duisburg \'düs-ˌbu̇rg\	Germany
Duluth \də-'lüth\	Minnesota
Dundee \ˌdən-'dē\	Scotland
Durban \'dər-bən\	South Africa
Düsseldorf \'dús-l-ˌdȯrf\	Germany
Dyushambe \dyü-'shäm-bə\	U.S.S.R.
Dzerzhinsk \dər-'zhin(t)sk\	U.S.S.R.
Ealing \'ē-ling\	England
Edinburgh \'ed-n-ˌbər-ə, -ˌbə-rə\	Scotland
Edmonton \'ed-mən-tən\	Alberta
Eindhoven \'īnt-ˌhōv-n\	Netherlands
Elisabethville \ə-'liz-ə-bəth-ˌvil\	Congo
Elizabeth \ə-'liz-ə-bəth\	New Jersey
El Mansûra \ˌel man-'su̇r-ə\	United Arab Republic
El Paso \el 'pas-ˌō\	Texas
Erfurt \'er-ˌfu̇rt\	Germany
Eskisehir \ˌes-ki-shə-'hir\	Turkey
Essen \'es-n\	Germany
Fatshan \'fät-'shän\	China
Ferrara \fə-'rär-ə\	Italy
Fez \'fez\	Morocco
Flint \'flint\	Michigan
Florence \'flȯr-ən(t)s, 'flär-\	Italy
Foochow \'fü-'jō\	China
Fortaleza \ˌfȯrt-l-'ā-zə\	Brazil

(continued on next page)

LARGEST CITIES OF THE WORLD

(continued from preceding page)

Name and Pronunciation	*Location*
Fort Wayne \fōrt 'wān, fȯrt\	Indiana
Fort Worth \fōrt 'wərth, fȯrt\	Texas
Frankfort \'frangk-fərt\	Germany
Frunze \'frün-zə\	U.S.S.R.
Fukuoka \ˌfü-ˌkü-'ōk-ə\	Japan
Fuse \'fü-zə\	Japan
Fushun \'fü-'shün\	China
Fusin \'fü-'shin\	China
Galati \gə-'läts\	Romania
Gary \'gar-ē, 'ger-ē\	Indiana
Gaya \gə-'yä\	India
Gdansk (Danzig) \gə-'dän(t)sk ('dän(t)s-ig)\	Poland
Gelsenkirchen \ˌgelz-n-'kirk-n\	Germany
General San Martín \ˌhā-nā-ˌräl ˌsan mär-'tēn\	Argentina
Geneva \jə-'nē-və\	Switzerland
Genoa \'jen-ə-wə\	Italy
Germiston \'jər-məs-tən\	South Africa
Ghent (Gent) \'gent ('kent)\	Belgium
Gifu \'gē-ˌfü\	Japan
Giza \'gē-zə\	United Arab Republic
Glasgow \'glas-ˌkō, -ˌgō\	Scotland
Gomel \'gōm-l\	U.S.S.R.
Gorakhpur \'gōr-ək-ˌpu̇r, 'gȯr-\	India
Gorki \'gȯrk-ē\	U.S.S.R.
Gorlovka \gər-'lȯf-kə\	U.S.S.R.
Göteborg \ˌyər-tə-'bȯr, ˌyā-tə-\	Sweden
Granada \grə-'näd-ə\	Spain
Grand Rapids \'gran-'(d)rap-ədz\	Michigan
Graz \'gräts\	Austria
Grenoble \grə-'nō-bəl\	France
Grozny \'grȯz-nē\	U.S.S.R.
Guadalajara \ˌgwäd-l-ə-'här-ə\	Mexico
Guatemala City \ˌgwät-m-ˌäl-ə 'sit-ē\	Guatemala
Guayaquil \ˌgwī-ə-ˌkēl\	Ecuador
Guntur \gu̇n-'tu̇r\	India
Gwalior \'gwäl-ē-ˌȯr\	India
Haarlem \'här-ləm\	Netherlands
Hagen \'häg-n\	Germany
Hague, The \t͟hə 'hāg\	Netherlands
Haifa \'hī-fə\	Israel
Haiphong \'hī-'fȯng\	Vietnam
Hakodate \ˌhäk-ō-'dät-ē\	Japan
Halifax \'hal-ə-ˌfaks\	Nova Scotia
Halle \'häl-ə\	Germany
Hama \'ham-ə\	Syria
Hamadan \'ham-ə-ˌdan\	Iran
Hamamatsu \ˌhä-mə-'mät-ˌsü\	Japan
Hamburg \'ham-ˌbərg, 'häm-ˌbu̇rg\	Germany
Hamilton \'ham-l-tən\	Ontario
Hangchow \'hang-'chau̇\	China
Hannover \'han-əv-r\	Germany
Hanoi \hä-'nȯi\	Vietnam
Harbin \'härb-n\	China
Harrow \'har-ō\	England
Hartford \'härt-fərd\	Connecticut
Havana \hə-'van-ə\	Cuba
Helsinki \'hel-ˌsingk-ē\	Finland
Hendon \'hen-dən\	England
Hengyang \'həng-'yäng\	China
Himeji \hi-'mej-ē\	Japan
Hiroshima \ˌhir-ə-'shē-mə, hi-'rō-shə-mə\	Japan
Hofei \'hə-'fā\	China
Holguín \ȯl-'gēn\	Cuba
Homs \'hȯm(p)s\	Syria
Hong Kong (see Victoria)	
Honolulu \ˌhän-l-'ü-ˌlü, ˌhōn-\	Hawaii
Houston \'hyüs-tən\	Texas
Howrah \'hau̇-rə\	India
Hubli \'hu̇b-lē\	India
Huhehot (Kweisui) \'hü-'hə-'hōt ('gwā-'swā)\	China
Hull \'həl\	England
Hwainan \'hwī-'nän\	China
Hyderabad \'hīd-r(-)ə-ˌbad\	India

*Having over 1,000,000 inhabitants

Name and Pronunciation	*Location*
Hyderabad \'hīd-r(-)ə-ˌbad\	Pakistan
Ibadan \ē-'bä-ˌdän\	Nigeria
Ilford \'il-frd\	England
Iloilo \ˌē-lō-'ē-lō\	Philippines
Inchon \'in-ˌchän\	Korea
Indianapolis \ˌin-dē-ə-'nap-l(-)əs\	Indiana
Indore \in-'dōr, -'dȯr\	India
Ipin \'ē-'pin\	China
Irkutsk \ir-'kütsk\	U.S.S.R.
Isfahan \ˌis-fə-ˌhan\	Iran
*Istanbul \ˌis-ˌtäm-'bül, -ˌtam-\	Turkey
Ivanovo \ē-'vä-nə-və\	U.S.S.R.
Izhevsk \'ē-ˌzhefsk\	U.S.S.R.
Izmir \iz-'mir\	Turkey
Jacksonville \'jaks-n-ˌvil\	Florida
Jaipur \'jī-ˌpu̇r\	India
Jamshedpur \'jäm-ˌshed-ˌpu̇r\	India
Jersey City \'jər-zē 'sit-ē\	New Jersey
Jerusalem \jə-'rüs-l(-)əm, -'rüz-l-əm\	Israel and Jordan
Jidda (Jedda) \'jid-ə ('jed-ə)\	Saudi Arabia
João Pessoa \ˌzhwau̇m pə-'sō-ə\	Brazil
Jodhpur \'jäd-pər\	India
Johannesburg \jō-'han-əs-ˌbərg\	South Africa
Jubbulpore (Jabalpur) \'jəb-l-ˌpōr, -ˌpȯr ('jəb-l-ˌpu̇r)\	India
Jullundur \'jəl-ənd-r\	India
Kabul \'käb-ˌül, kə-'bül\	Afghanistan
Kadiyevka \kə-'dyē-yəf-kə\	U.S.S.R.
Kagoshima \ˌkäg-ō-'shē-mə\	Japan
Kaifeng \'kī-'fəng\	China
Kalgan \'käl-'gän\	China
Kalinin \kə-'lē-nən\	U.S.S.R.
Kaliningrad \kə-'lē-nən-ˌgrad\	U.S.S.R.
Kaluga \kə-'lü-gə\	U.S.S.R.
Kamensk-Uralski \ˌkäm-ənsk-ü-'räl-skē\	U.S.S.R.
Kanazawa \ˌkan-ə-'zä-wə\	Japan
Kanpur (Cawnpore) \'kän-ˌpu̇r ('kȯn-ˌpōr, -ˌpȯr)\	India
Kansas City \'kan-zə(s) 'sit-ē\	Missouri
Kaohsiung \'kau̇-shē-'u̇ng\	Formosa
*Karachi \kə-'räch-ē\	Pakistan
Karaganda \ˌkar-ə-gən-'dä\	U.S.S.R.
Karl-Marx-Stadt (Chemnitz) \'kärl-'märks-ˌshtät ('kem-nits)\	Germany
Karlsruhe \'kärls-ˌrü-ə, 'kärlz-\	Germany
Kassel \'käs-l, 'kas-l\	Germany
Katmandu \ˌkat-ˌman-'dü\	Nepal
Katowice \ˌkät-ō-'vēt-sə\	Poland
Kaunas (Kovno) \'kau̇-ˌnäs ('kȯv-nə)\	U.S.S.R.
Kawasaki \ˌkä-wə-'säk-ē\	Japan
Kazan \kə-'zan\	U.S.S.R.
Keelung \'kē-'lu̇ng\	Formosa
Kemerovo \'kem-r-ˌō-və\	U.S.S.R.
Khabarovsk \kə-'bär-əfsk\	U.S.S.R.
Kharkov \'kär-ˌkȯf\	U.S.S.R.
Khartoum \kär-'tüm\	Sudan
Kherson \ker-'sȯn\	U.S.S.R.
Kiamusze \jē-ˌä-mü-'sü\	China
Kiel \'kēl\	Germany
*Kiev \'kē-ˌ(y)ef\	U.S.S.R.
Kingston \'king-stən\	Jamaica
Kirin \'kē-'rin\	China
Kirov \'kē-ˌrȯf\	U.S.S.R.
Kishinev \ˌkish-n-'yȯf\	U.S.S.R.
*Kita-Kyushu \kē-'tä-'kyü-shü\	Japan
Kitchener \'kich-ən-r\	Ontario
*Kobe \'kō-bē\	Japan
Kochi \'kō-chē\	Japan
Kofu \'kō-ˌfü\	Japan
Kokiu \'gō-jē-'ō\	China
Kolar Gold Fields \kō-'lär\	India
Kolhapur \'kō-lə-ˌpu̇r\	India
Komsomolsk \ˌkäm-sə-'mȯlsk\	U.S.S.R.
Kopeisk \kə-'pyāsk\	U.S.S.R.
Kostroma \ˌkäs-trə-'mä\	U.S.S.R.
Kowloon \'kau̇-'lün\	China
Kozhikode \'kō-zhə-ˌkōd\	India

(continued on next page)

(continued from preceding page)

Name and Pronunciation	*Location*
Krakow \\'krä-ˌküf\\	Poland
Krasnodar \\'kräs-nō-ˌdär\\	U.S.S.R.
Krasnoyarsk \\'kräs-nō-ˌyärsk\\	U.S.S.R
Krefeld \\'krā-ˌfelt\\	Germany
Krivoi Rog \\'kriv-ˌȯi 'rōg\\	U.S.S.R.
Kuala Lumpur \\ˌkwäl-ə 'lu̇m-ˌpu̇r\\	Malaysia
Kuibyshev \\'kwē-bə-ˌshef\\	U.S.S.R.
Kumamoto \\ˌkü-mə-'mō-ˌtō\\	Japan
Kumasi \\kü-'mäs-ē\\	Ghana
Kunming \\'ku̇n-'ming\\	China
Kure \\'ku̇r-ē\\	Japan
Kurgan \\ku̇r-'gan\\	U.S.S.R.
Kursk \\'ku̇rsk\\	U.S.S.R.
Kweilin \\'gwā-'lin\\	China
Kweiyang \\'gwā-'yäng\\	China
*Kyoto \\kē-'ō-ˌtō\\	Japan
La Coruña \\ˌlä kō-'rün-yə\\	Spain
Lagos \\'läg-əs\\	Nigeria
*Lahore \\lə-'hōr, -'hȯr\\	Pakistan
Lanchow \\'län-'jō\\	China
Lanús \\lä-'nüs\\	Argentina
La Paz \\lə 'paz, 'päs\\	Bolivia
La Plata \\lə 'plät-ə\\	Argentina
Las Palmas \\läs 'päl-məs\\	Spain (Canary Is.)
Leeds \\'lēdz\\	England
Leghorn \\'leg-ˌ(h)ȯrn\\	Italy
Le Havre \\lə-'häv-rə\\	France
Leicester \\'lest-r\\	England
Leipzig \\'līp-sig\\	Germany
*Leningrad \\'len-ən-ˌgrad\\	U.S.S.R.
León \\lā-'ōn\\	Mexico
Léopoldville \\'lā-ə-ˌpōld-ˌvil, 'lē-\\	Congo
Liège \\lē-'āzh, -'ezh\\	Belgium
Lille \\'lēl\\	France
*Lima \\'lē-mə\\	Peru
Linz \\'lints\\	Austria
Lipetsk \\'lē-ˌpetsk\\	U.S.S.R.
Lisbon \\'liz-bən\\	Portugal
Liuchow \\lē-'ü-'jō\\	China
Liverpool \\'liv-r-ˌpül\\	England
Ljubljana \\lē-'ü-blē-ə-ˌnä\\	Yugoslavia
Lodz \\'lüj\\	Poland
*London \\'lən-dən\\	England
London	Ontario
Long Beach \\'lȯng ˌbēch\\	California
*Los Angeles \\lȯs 'anj-l-əs, 'ang-gl(-)əs\\	California
Louisville \\'lü-ē-ˌvil, -ēv-l\\	Kentucky
Loyang \\'lō-'yäng\\	China
Lübeck \\'lü-ˌbek\\	Germany
Lublin \\'lü-blən\\	Poland
Luchow \\'lü-'jō\\	China
Lucknow \\'lək-ˌnau̇\\	India
Ludhiana \\ˌlüd-ē-'än-ə\\	India
Ludwigshafen \\ˌlüd-vigz-'häf-n\\	Germany
Lugansk \\lu̇-'gän(t)sk\\	U.S.S.R.
Lüta \\'lü-'dä\\	China
Lvov \\lə-'vȯf\\	U.S.S.R.
Lyallpur \\'lī-əl-ˌpu̇r\\	Pakistan
Lyons (Lyon) \\lē-'ōn, 'lī-ənz (lē-'ōn)\\	France
Maceió \\ˌmas-ā-'ō\\	Brazil
*Madras \\mə-'dras\\	India
*Madrid \\mə-'drid\\	Spain
Madurai \\ˌməd-ə-'rī\\	India
Magdeburg \\'mäg-də-ˌbu̇rg\\	Germany
Magnitogorsk \\mag-'nēt-ə-ˌgȯrsk\\	U.S.S.R.
Mahalla el Kubra \\mə-'hal-ə (ˌ)el 'kü-brə\\	United Arab Republic
Makassar \\mə-'kas-r\\	Indonesia
Makeevka \\mə-'kā-(y)əf-kə\\	U.S.S.R.
Málaga \\'mal-ə-gə\\	Spain
Malang \\mə-'läng\\	Indonesia
Malmö \\'mal-ˌmər, -ˌmō\\	Sweden
Managua \\mə-'näg-wə\\	Nicaragua
Manaus \\mə-'nau̇s\\	Brazil
Manchester \\'man-ˌchest-r\\	England
Mandalay \\ˌman-də-'lā\\	Burma

Name and Pronunciation	*Location*
*Manila \\mə-'nil-ə\\	Philippines
Manizales\\man-ə-' zäl-əs, -'zal-\\	Colombia
Mannheim \\'män-ˌhīm\\	Germany
Maracaibo \\ˌmar-ə-'kī-ˌbō\\	Venezuela
Marianao \\ˌmär-ē-ə-'nau̇\\	Cuba
Marrakesh \\mə-'räk-ish\\	Morocco
Marseilles \\mär-'sā, -'sālz\\	France
Matsuyama \\ˌmät-sü-'yäm-ə\\	Japan
Mecca \\'mek-ə\\	Saudi Arabia
Medan \\mā-'dän\\	Indonesia
Medellín \\ˌmā-t͟hə-'yēn, ˌmed-l-'ēn\\	Colombia
Meerut \\'mā-rət\\	India
Meknes \\mek-'nes\\	Morocco
*Melbourne \\'melb-rn\\	Australia
Memphis \\'mem(p)-fəs\\	Tennessee
Mérida \\'mer-əd-ə\\	Mexico
Meshed \\mə-'shed\\	Iran
Messina \\mə-'sē-nə\\	Italy
Mexicali \\'meks-i-'kal-ē\\	Mexico
*Mexico City \\'meks-i-ˌkō\\	Mexico
Miami \\mī-'am-ē, -'am-ə\\	Florida
Middlesbrough \\'mid-lz-brə\\	England
*Milan \\mə-'lan\\	Italy
Milwaukee \\mil-'wȯk-ē\\	Wisconsin
Minneapolis \\ˌmin-ē-'ap-l(-)əs\\	Minnesota
Minsk \\'min(t)sk\\	U.S.S.R.
Miskolc \\'mish-ˌkōlts\\	Hungary
Mobile \\mō-'bēl\\	Alabama
Mönchen-Gladbach \\ˌmen-kən-'glät-ˌbäk\\	Germany
Monterrey \\ˌmänt-r-'ā\\	Mexico
Montevideo \\ˌmänt-ə-və-'dā-ˌō, -ə-'vid-ē-ˌō\\	Uruguay
*Montreal \\ˌmän-trē-'ȯl\\	Quebec
Moradabad \\mə-'rad-ə-ˌbad\\	India
*Moscow \\'mäs-ˌkau̇, -ˌkō\\	U.S.S.R.
Mosul \\mō-'sül\\	Iraq
Mülheim \\'myül-ˌhīm\\	Germany
Multan \\mül-'tän\\	Pakistan
*Munich \\'myü-nik\\	Germany
Münster \\'myün(t)st-r, 'min(t)st-r\\	Germany
Murcia \\'mər-shē-ə\\	Spain
Murmansk \\mür-'män(t)sk\\	U.S.S.R.
Mutankiang \\'mü-'dän-jē-'äng\\	China
Mysore \\mī-'sōr, -'sȯr\\	India
Nagano \\nə-'gän-ō\\	Japan
Nagasaki \\ˌnäg-ə-'säk-ē\\	Japan
*Nagoya \\nə-'gȯi-ə\\	Japan
Nagpur \\'näg-ˌpu̇r\\	India
Nairobi \\nī-'rō-bē\\	Kenya
Nanchang \\'nän-'chäng\\	China
Nanchung \\'nän-'ju̇ng\\	China
*Nanking \\'nan-'king\\	China
Nanning \\'nän-'ning\\	China
Nantes \\'nan(t)s\\	France
Nantung \\'nän-'tu̇ng\\	China
*Naples \\'nāp-lz\\	Italy
Nashville \\'nash-ˌvil, -vəl\\	Tennessee
Neikiang \\'nā-jē-'äng\\	China
Newark \\'n(y)ü-ərk\\	New Jersey
Newcastle \\'n(y)ü-ˌkas-l\\	Australia
Newcastle upon Tyne \\'n(y)ü-ˌkas-l, 'tīn; n(y)ü-'kas-l\\	England
New Haven \\'hāv-n\\	Connecticut
New Orleans \\'ȯr-lē-ənz, 'ȯr-lənz\\	Louisiana
*New York \\'yȯrk\\	New York
Nice \\'nēs\\	France
Niigata \\nē-'gät-ə\\	Japan
Nikolaev \\ˌnik-l-'ī-əf\\	U.S.S.R.
Ningpo \\'ning-'pō\\	China
Nishinomiya \\ˌnish-n-ˌō-mē-'yä\\	Japan
Niterói \\ˌnēt-r-'ȯi\\	Brazil
Nizhni Tagil \\'nizh-nē tə-'gil\\	U.S.S.R.
Norfolk \\'nȯr-fək\\	Virginia
Nottingham \\'nät-ing-m\\	England
Novokuznetsk \\ˌnō-vō-ku̇z-'netsk\\	U.S.S.R.
Novosibirsk \\-sə-'birsk\\	U.S.S.R.

*Having over 1,000,000 inhabitants

(continued on next page)

LARGEST CITIES OF THE WORLD

(*continued from preceding page*)

ame and Pronunciation	*Location*
uremberg \'n(y)u̇r-əm-ˌbərg\	Germany
akland \'ōk-lənd\	California
berhausen \'ōb-r-ˌhau̇z-n\	Germany
dessa \ō-'des-ə\	U.S.S.R.
gbomosho \ˌäg-bə-'mō-ˌshō\	Nigeria
kayama \ˌōk-ə-'yäm-ə\	Japan
klahoma City \'ōk-lə-ˌhō-mə 'sit-ē\	Oklahoma
ldham \'ōld-m\	England
maha \'ō-mə-ˌhȯ, -ˌhä\	Nebraska
msk \'äm(p)sk\	U.S.S.R.
muta \'ō-mə-ˌtä\	Japan
porto (Porto) \ō-'pōrt-(ˌ)ō, -'pȯrt-\	Portugal
ran \ō-'rän\	Algeria
rdzhonikidze \ˌȯr-jän-ə-'kid-zə\	U.S.S.R.
rel \ō-'rel, ȯr-'yȯl\	U.S.S.R.
rsk \'ȯrsk\	U.S.S.R.
saka \ō-'säk-ə\	Japan
slo \'äz-ˌlō, 'ȯs-\	Norway
strava \'ȯs-trə-və\	Czechoslovakia
taru \ō-'tär-'ü\	Japan
ttawa \'ät-ə-wə, -ˌwä, -ˌwȯ\	Ontario
adua \'paj-ə-wə\	Italy
alembang \ˌpäl-əm-'bäng\	Indonesia
alermo \pə-'ler-ˌmō, -'lər-\	Italy
alma de Mallorca \'päl-mə (ˌ)thā mə-'yȯrk-ə\	Spain
anama City \'pan-ə-ˌmȯ 'sit-ē, -ˌmä\	Panama
aoting \'bau̇-'ding\	China
aotow \'bau̇-'tō\	China
araná \ˌpär-ə-'nä\	Argentina
aris \'par-əs\	France
atna \'pət-nə\	India
eking (Peiping) \'pē-'king ('bā-'ping)\	China
enang \pə-'nang\	Malaysia
engpu \'pəng-'pü\	China
enki \'bən-'chē\	China
enza \'pen-zə\	U.S.S.R.
eoria \pē-'ōr-ē-ə, -'ȯr-\	Illinois
erm \'pyerm\	U.S.S.R.
erth \'pərth\	Australia
eshawar \pə-'shau̇r\	Pakistan
hiladelphia \ˌfil-ə-'del-fē-ə\	Pennsylvania
hoenix \'fē-niks\	Arizona
iraeus \pi-'rē-əs\	Greece
ittsburgh \'pits-ˌbərg\	Pennsylvania
lovdiv \'plȯv-ˌdif\	Bulgaria
lymouth \'plim-əth\	England
nompenh \pə-'nȯm-'pen\	Cambodia
oltava \pəl-'täv-ə\	U.S.S.R.
oona \'pü-nə\	India
ort-au-Prince \ˌpōrt-ō-'prin(t)s, ˌpȯrt-\	Haiti
ort Elizabeth \ˌpōrt-l-'iz-ə-bəth, ˌpȯrt-\	South Africa
ortland \'pōrt-lənd, 'pȯrt-\	Oregon
ôrto Alegre \'pōrt-(ˌ)ō ə-'lā-grə, 'pȯrt-\	Brazil
ort Said \pōrt 'sīd, ˌpōrt sä-'ēd, (ˌ)pȯrt\	United Arab Republic
ortsmouth \'pōrts-məth, 'pȯrts-\	England
oznan \'pōz-ˌnän, 'pȯz-, -ˌnan\	Poland
rague \'präg\	Czechoslovakia
retoria \prē-'tōr-ē-ə, -'tȯr-\	South Africa
rokopevsk \prə-'kȯp-əfsk\	U.S.S.R.
rovidence \'präv-ə-dən(t)s, -ˌden(t)s\	Rhode Island
uebla \pü-'eb-lə, 'pweb-lə\	Mexico
usan \'pü-'sän\	Korea
yongyang \'pyȯng-'yäng\	Korea
uebec \kwē-'bek\	Quebec
uezon City \'kā-ˌsȯn\	Philippines
uito \'kē-ˌtō\	Ecuador
Rabat \rə-'bät\	Morocco
Rajkot \'räj-ˌkōt\	India
Rangoon \rang-'gün\	Burma
Rawalpindi \ˌrȯ-wəl-'pin-dē\	Pakistan
Recife \rə-'sē-fə\	Brazil
Reggio di Calabria \ˌrej-ō ˌdē kə-'läb-rē-ə, ˌrej-ē-ˌō\	Italy
Rennes \'ren\	France
Richmond \'rich-mənd\	Virginia

Name and Pronunciation	*Location*
Riga \'rē-gə\	U.S.S.R.
*Rio de Janeiro \'rē-ˌō ˌdāj-n-'er-(ˌ)ō, ˌdāzh-n-\	Brazil
Riyadh \rē-'yäd\	Saudi Arabia
Rochester \'räch-əst-r, -ˌest-r\	New York
*Rome \'rōm\	Italy
Rosario \rō-'sär-ē-ˌō, -'zär-\	Argentina
Rostock \'räs-ˌtäk\	Germany
Rostov \rə-'stȯf\	U.S.S.R.
Rotterdam \'rät-r-ˌdam\	Netherlands
Ryazan \ˌrē-ə-'zan\	U.S.S.R.
Rybinsk \'rib-ən(t)sk\	U.S.S.R.
Sacramento \ˌsak-rə-'ment-ˌō\	California
Saharanpur \sə-'här-ən-ˌpu̇r\	India
*Saigon, \sī-'gän, 'sī-ˌgän\	Vietnam
Saint-Etienne \ˌsant-ā-'tyen\	France
Saint Louis \sānt 'lü-əs\	Missouri
Saint Paul \sānt 'pȯl\	Minnesota
Saint Petersburg \sānt 'pēt-rz-ˌbərg\	Florida
Sakai \sä-'kī\	Japan
Salem \'sā-ləm\	India
Salford \'sȯlf-rd\	England
Salisbury \'sȯlz-ˌber-ē, -bə-rē\	Southern Rhodesia
Salt Lake City \'sȯlt ˌlāk 'sit-ē\	Utah
Salvador \'sal-və-ˌdȯr\	Brazil
Samarkand \'sam-r-ˌkand\	U.S.S.R.
San Antonio \ˌsan ən-'tō-nē-ˌō\	Texas
San Diego \ˌsan dē-'ā-ˌgō\	California
San Francisco \ˌsan frən-'sis-ˌkō\	California
San Jose \ˌsan (h)ō-'zā\	California
San José \ˌsan (h)ō-'zā, ˌsäng hō-'sā\	Costa Rica
San Juan \san 'wän\	Puerto Rico
San Luis Potosi \ˌsän lə-'wēs ˌpōt-ə-'sē\	Mexico
San Salvador \san 'sal-və-ˌdȯr\	El Salvador
Sante Fe \ˌsant-ə 'fā\	Argentina
Santander \ˌsän-ˌtän-'der\	Spain
*Santiago \ˌsant-ē-'äg-ˌō\	Chile
Santiago de Cuba \ˌsant-ē-'äg-ˌō də 'k(y)ü-bə\	Cuba
Santiago de los Caballeros \ˌlȯs ˌkäb-ə-'yer-ˌōs\	Dominican Republic
Santo Domingo \ˌsant-ə də-'ming-ˌgō\	Dominican Republic
Santos \'sant-əs\	Brazil
*São Paulo \(')sau̇m 'pau̇-ˌlü\	Brazil
Sapporo \sə-'pōr-ˌō, -'pȯr-\	Japan
Saragossa \ˌsar-ə-'gäs-ə\	Spain
Sarajevo \'sär-ə-ye-ˌvȯ\	Yugoslavia
Saratov \sə-'rät-əf\	U.S.S.R.
Sasebo \'sä-sə-ˌbō\	Japan
Seattle \sē-'at-l\	Washington
Semarang \sə-'mär-ˌäng\	Indonesia
Semipalatinsk \ˌsem-ē-pə-'lät-ˌin(t)sk\	U.S.S.R.
Sendai \(')sen-'dī\	Japan
*Seoul \'sōl\	Korea
Sevastopol \sə-'vas-tə-ˌpōl\	U.S.S.R.
Seville \sə-'vil\	Spain
Shakhty \'shäk-tē\	U.S.S.R.
*Shanghai \(')shang-'hī\	China
Shcherbakov \ˌshcher-bə-'kȯf\	U.S.S.R.
Sheffield \'shef-ˌēld\	England
*Shenyang \'shən-'yäng\	China
Shihkiachwang \'shir-jē-'ä-'jwäng\	China
Shimonoseki \ˌshim-ə-nō-'sek-ē\	Japan
Shiraz \shi-'räz\	Iran
Shizuoka \ˌshiz-(ˌ)ü-'ōk-ə\	Japan
Sholapur \'shō-lə-ˌpu̇r\	India
Shreveport \'shrēv-ˌpōrt, -ˌpȯrt\	Louisiana
Sialkot \sē-'äl-ˌkōt\	Pakistan
*Sian \'shē-'än\	China
Siangtan \shē-'äng-'tän\	China
Simferopol \ˌsim(p)f-r-'ȯp-l\	U.S.S.R.
*Singapore \'sing-(g)ə-ˌpōr, -ˌpȯr\	Malaysia
Sinhailien \'shin-'hī-lē-'en\	China
Sinsiang \'shin-shē-'äng\	China
Skopje (Skoplje) \'skäp-ˌyā ('skäp-l-ˌyā)\	Yugoslavia
Smolensk \smō-'len(t)sk\	U.S.S.R.
Sochi \'sō-chē\	U.S.S.R.

*Having over 1,000,000 inhabitants

(*continued on next page*)

LARGEST CITIES OF THE WORLD

(continued from preceding page)

Name and Pronunciation	*Location*
Sofia \'sō-fē-ə, sō-'fē-ə\	Bulgaria
Solingen \'zō-ling-ən\	Germany
Soochow \'sü-'jō\	China
Southampton \sau̇th-'(h)am(p)-tən\	England
Southend on Sea \(')sau̇-'thend, 'sē\	England
South Suburban \sə-'bərb-n\	India
Spokane \spō-'kan\	Washington
Springfield \'spring-ˌfēld\	Massachusetts
Srinagar \srē-'nəg-r\	Kashmir
Stavropol \stav-'rȯ-pəl\	U.S.S.R.
Stockholm \'stäk-ˌhōm\	Sweden
Stockport \'stäk-ˌpōrt, -ˌpȯrt\	England
Stoke on Trent \'stōk ˌȯn 'trent, ˌän\	England
Strasbourg \'sträs-ˌbu̇rg, 'sträz-\	France
Stuttgart \'s(h)tu̇t-ˌgärt\	Germany
Subotica \'sü-bə-ˌtēt-sə\	Yugoslavia
Suchow \'sü-'jō\	China
Suez \sü-'ez, 'sü-ˌez\	United Arab Republic
Sunderland \'sənd-r-lənd\	England
*Surabaja \ˌsu̇r-ə-'bä-yə, -'bī-ə\	Indonesia
Surakarta (Solo) \ˌsu̇r-ə-'kärt-ə ('sō-ˌlō)\	Indonesia
Surat \'su̇r-ət\	India
Sverdlovsk \sverd-'lȯfsk\	U.S.S.R.
Swansea \'swän-zē\	Wales
Swatow \'swä-ˌtau̇\	China
*Sydney \'sid-nē\	Australia
Syracuse \'sir-ə-ˌkyüs\	New York
Syzran \'siz-rən\	U.S.S.R.
Szczecin (Stettin) \'shchet-ˌsēn (shte-'tēn)\	Poland
Tabriz \tə-'brēz\	Iran
Taegu \ta-'gü\	Korea
Taganrog \ˌtag-n-'räg\	U.S.S.R.
Taichow \'tī-'jō\	China
Taichung \'tī-'chu̇ng\	Formosa
Tainan \'tī-'nän\	Formosa
Taipeh \'tī-'bā\	Formosa
*Taiyuan \'tī-yə-'wän\	China
Takamatsu \ˌtak-ə-'mät-sü\	Japan
Tallin \'tä-ˌlēn\	U.S.S.R.
Tambov \'täm-'bȯf\	U.S.S.R.
Tampa \'tamp-ə\	Florida
Tampere \'tamp-r-ə\	Finland
Tananarive \tə-ˌnän-r-'ēv\	Malagasy Republic
Tangier (')tan-'jir\	Morocco
Tangshan \'täng-'shän\	China
Tanta \'tänt-ə\	United Arab Republic
Taranto \'tar-ən-ˌtō, tə-'rant-ˌō\	Italy
*Tashkent \(')tash-'kent\	U.S.S.R.
Tatung \'dä-'tu̇ng\	China
*Tehran \ˌte-ə-'ran, -'rän, ˌtā-, ˌtē-\	Iran
Tel Aviv \ˌtel ə-'vēv\	Israel
Thessaloniki \ˌthes-l-ə-'nīk-ē\	Greece
*Tientsin \tē-'en-'(t)sin\	China
Tiflis (Tbilisi) \'tif-ləs (tə-'pē-lē-sē)\	U.S.S.R.
Tijuana \tē-'hwän-ə\	Mexico
Timiso[illegible]	Romania
Ti[illegible]	India

Name and Pronunciation	*Location*
*Tsingtao \'ching-'dau̇\	China
Tsitsihar \'(t)sēt-sē-ˌhär\	China
Tucson \tü-'sän, 'tü-ˌsän\	Arizona
Tucumán \ˌtük-ə-'män\	Argentina
Tula \'tü-lə\	U.S.S.R.
Tulsa \'təl-sə\	Oklahoma
Tunis \'tü-nəs, 'tyü-\	Tunisia
*Turin \'tu̇r-ən, 'tyu̇r-, t(y)ü-'rin\	Italy
Tyumen \tyə-'men\	U.S.S.R.
Tzekung \'dzə-'ku̇ng\	China
Tzepo \'dzə-'pō\	China
Ube \'ü-bā\	Japan
Ufa \ü-'fä\	U.S.S.R.
Ulan Bator (Urga) \'ü-ˌlän 'bä-ˌtȯr ('u̇r-gə)\	Mongolian People's Republic
Ulan-Ude \ˌü-lən-ˌü-'dā\	U.S.S.R.
Ulyanovsk \ül-'yän-əfsk\	U.S.S.R.
Ust Kamenogorsk \ˌüst kə-'men-ə-ˌgȯrsk\	U.S.S.R.
Utrecht \'yü-ˌtrekt\	Netherlands
Utsunomiya \ˌu̇t-sə-nə-'mē-yə\	Japan
Valencia \və-'lench-ə, -ē-ə\	Spain
Valladolid \ˌval-əd-ə-'lid, -'lē\	Spain
Valparaíso \ˌvalp-r-'ī-ˌzō\	Chile
Vancouver \van-'küv-r\	British Columbia
Venice \'ven-əs\	Italy
Verona \və-'rō-nə\	Italy
Victoria \vik-'tōr-ē-ə, -'tȯr-\	British Columbia
*Victoria (Hong Kong) \'häng ˌkäng\	Hong Kong Colony
*Vienna \vē-'en-ə\	Austria
Vigo \'vē-ˌgō\	Spain
Vijayavada \ˌvij-ə-yə-'vəd-ə\	India
Vilnyus (Vilna) \'vil-nē-əs ('vil-nə)\	U.S.S.R.
Visakhapatnam \vi-ˌsäk-ə-'pət-nəm\	India
Vitebsk \'vē-ˌtepsk\	U.S.S.R.
Vladimir \'vlad-m-ˌir\	U.S.S.R.
Vladivostok \ˌvlad-ə-və-'stäk, -'väs-ˌtäk\	U.S.S.R.
Volgograd \'väl-gə-ˌgrad\	U.S.S.R.
Voronezh \və-'rȯ-nish\	U.S.S.R.
Wakayama \ˌwäk-ə-'yäm-ə\	Japan
Warangal \'wər-əng-gəl, 'wə-rəng-\	India
*Warsaw \'wȯr-ˌsȯ\	Poland
Washington \'wosh-ing-tən, 'wäsh-\	District of Columbia
Wellington \'wel-ing-tən\	New Zealand
Wenchow \'wən-'jō\	China
West Ham \'west 'ham\	England
Wichita \'wich-ə-ˌtȯ\	Kansas
Wiesbaden \'vēs-ˌbäd-n, 'vis-\	Germany
Willesden \'wilz-dən\	England
Windsor \'winz-r\	Ontario
Winnipeg \'win-ə-ˌpeg\	Manitoba
Worcester \'wu̇st-r\	Massachusetts
Wroclaw \'vrȯts-ˌläf\	Poland
Wuchang \'wü-'chäng\	China
*Wuhan \'wü-'hän\	China
Wuhu \'wü-'hü\	China
Wuppertal \'vu̇p-r-ˌtäl\	Germany
Wusih \'wü-'shē\	China
Wutungkiao \'wü-'tu̇ng-chē-'au̇\	China
Yamagata \ˌyäm-ə-'gät-ə\	Japan
[illegible]chua[illegible] 'yäng-'jō\	China
[illegible]yl \ˌyär-[illegible]län\	China
[illegible]	U.S.S.[illegible]

PRONUNCIATION SYMBOLS

a ....mat, map

ā ....age, vein

ä ....cot, bother; most speakers have this vowel also in cart and father

ȧ ....cart, father when a speaker makes the *a* in these words different from the *o* in cot and bother

aů ...sound, now

b ....buy, rib

ch ...chin, itch [actually, this sound is t + sh]

d ....day, odd, ladder

e ....bet, bed

ē ....evenly, beat, sleepy [pronounce ē very lightly when it is in a syllable that does not have a stress mark before it — for example, the second ē in \'slēp-ē\]

f.....fig, cuff

g ....go, big

h ....hum, ahead

i .....tip, invent

ī.....side, buy [actually, this sound is ä + i, or ȧ + i]

j.....job, edge [actually, this sound is d + zh]

k ....kin, cook, ache

l.....lip, pill, vessels \'ves-lz\

m....me, dim, atoms \'at-mz\

n ....no, own, vacant \'vāk-nt\

ng ...sing, singer \'sing-r\, finger \'fing-gr\, ink \'ingk\ [actually, this is a single sound, not two]

ō ....bone, snow

ȯ ....corn, saw, all

ȯi....coin, boy

p ....pay, lip

r.....rid, tar, lizard \'liz-rd\

s.....so, less

sh ...shy, dish [actually, this is a single sound, not two]

t.....tie, bet, latter

th ...thin, ether [actually, this is a single sound, not two]

th ...then, either [actually, this is a single sound, not two]

ü ....rule, fool, few \'fyü\, union \'yün-yən\

u̇ ....pull, wood

v ....vote, give

w....we, away

y ....yard, cue \'kyü\, union \'yün-yən\

z ....zone, raise

zh ...vision \'vizh-n\ [actually, this is a single sound, not two]

ə					
banana	silent	capital	collect	suppose	perplex
bun	cut	putty	color	supper	pup
burn	curt	pert	curl	serpent	purple

In the words in the first line ə is spoken with very weak force. In the words in the second and third lines ə is spoken with stronger force.